# Sporting News BOOKS

# OFFICIAL NBA REGISTER

## 2005-2006 EDITION

D0775118

**Editors/Official NBA Register**
TRISH GARNER
ROB REHEUSER
ZACH BODENDIECK

**Contributing Editors/Official NBA Register**
JED TAI

Copyright © 2005 NBA Properties, Inc. All rights reserved.

Published by the Sporting News, a division of Vulcan Sports Media. 10176 Corporate Square Drive, Suite 200, St. Louis, MO 63132. Printed in the U.S.A.

ISBN: 0-89204-798-4

10 9 8 7 6 5 4 3 2 1

# CONTENTS

## EXPLANATION OF FOOTNOTES AND ABBREVIATIONS

\* Led league.
† Tied for league lead.
‡ College freshman or junior varsity statistics; not counted toward totals.
... Statistic unavailable, unofficial or mathematically impossible to calculate.
— Statistic inapplicable.

**POSITIONS: C:** center. **F:** forward. **G:** guard.

**STATISTICS: APG:** Assists per game. **Ast.:** Assists. **Blk.:** Blocked shots. **Def.:** Defensive rebounds. **Dq.:** Disqualifications. **FGA:** Field goals attempted. **FGM:** Field goals made. **FTA:** Free throws attempted. **FTM:** Free throws made. **G:** Games. **L:** Losses. **Min.:** Minutes. **Off.:** Offensive rebounds. **Pct.:** Percentage. **PF:** Personal fouls. **PPG:** Points per game. **Pts.:** Points. **Reb.:** Rebounds. **RPG:** Rebounds per game. **Stl.:** Steals. **TO:** Turnovers. **Tot.:** Total. **W:** Wins.

**LEAGUES/ORGANIZATIONS: AABA:** All-America Basketball Alliance. **ABA:** American Basketball Association. **ABL:** American Basketball League. **BAA:** Basketball Association of America. **CBA:** Continental Basketball Association. **EBL:** Eastern Basketball League. **IL:** Inter-State League. **MBL:** Metropolitan Basketball League. **NAIA:** National Association of Intercollegiate Athletics. **NBA:** National Basketball Association. **NBL:** National Basketball League or National League. **NCAA:** National Collegiate Athletic Association. **NIT:** National Invitation Tournament. **NYSL:** New York State League. **PBLA:** Professional Basketball League of America. **WBA:** Western Basketball Association.

**TEAMS: Ala.:** Alabama. **Al.:** Albany. **Amw. Zaragoza:** Amway Zaragoza. **And.:** Anderson. **Ark.:** Arkansas. **Atl.:** Atlanta. **Bakers.:** Bakersfield. **Balt.:** Baltimore. **Bay St.:** Bay State. **B., Bos.:** Boston. **Buck. Beer Bolo.:** Buckler Beer Bologna. **Buff.:** Buffalo. **Cha., Char.:** Charlotte. **Ch., Chi.:** Chicago. **Chip. Panionios:** Chipita Panionios. **Cin.:** Cincinnati. **Cl., Clev.:** Cleveland. **Col.:** Columbus. **Dal., Dall.:** Dallas. **Den.:** Denver. **Det.:** Detroit. **Fargo/Moor., F./M.:** Fargo-Moorhead. **Ft. Wayne, F.W.:** Fort Wayne. **Frank. & Marsh.:** Franklin & Marshall. **George Wash.:** George Washington. **Gold. St., G.S.:** Golden State. **G.R., Gr. Rap.:** Grand Rapids. **Grupo Ifa Espa.:** Grupo Ifa Espanol's. **Hfrd.:** Hartford. **Hou.:** Houston. **Ind.:** Indiana. **K.C.:** Kansas City. **K.C./O., K.C./Omaha:** Kansas City/Omaha. **L.A.:** Los Angeles. **L.A.C., LA Clip.:** Los Angeles Clippers. **La Cr.:** La Crosse. **L.A.L., LA Lak.:** Los Angeles Lakers. **Il Mess. Roma:** Il Messaggero Roma. **Mil.:** Milwaukee. **Min., Minn.:** Minnesota. **Neptunas Klaib.:** Neptunas Klaibeda. **N.J.:** New Jersey. **N.O.:** New Orleans. **N.Y.:** New York. **N.C.:** North Carolina. **Okla. C., O.C.:** Oklahoma City. **Or., Orl.:** Orlando. **Penn.:** Pennsylvania. **Pens.:** Pensacola. **Pfizer R. Calabria:** Pfizer Reggio Calabria. **Phi., Phil.:** Philadelphia. **Phoe.:** Phoenix. **Pitt.:** Pittsburgh. **Port.:** Portland. **Quad C., Q.C.:** Quad City. **Rancho San.:** Rancho Santiago. **Rap. C., R.C.:** Rapid City. **Roch.:** Rochester. **Rock.:** Rockford. **S.A., San Ant.:** San Antonio. **Sac.:** Sacramento. **S.F., San Fran.:** San Francisco. **Sav.:** Savannah. **Sea.:** Seattle. **Shamp. C. Cantu:** Shampoo Clear Cantu. **Shb.:** Sheboygan. **Sioux F.:** Sioux Falls. **St.L.:** St. Louis. **Syr., Syrac.:** Syracuse. **Team. Fabriano:** Teamsystem Fabriano. **Tele. Brescia:** Telemarket Brescia. **Teore. Milan:** Teorematur Milan. **Top.:** Topeka. **Tri C.:** Tri-Cities. **Tul.:** Tulsa. **Va.:** Virginia. **W.:** Warren. **Wash.:** Washington. **Wash. & Jeff.:** Washington & Jefferson. **Wis., Wisc.:** Wisconsin. **Yak.:** Yakima.

**BASEBALL STATISTICS: A.A.:** American Association. **A:** Assists. **AB:** At-bats. **A.L.:** American League. **Avg.:** Average. **BB:** Bases on balls. **E:** Errors. **East.:** Eastern League. **ER:** Earned runs. **ERA:** Earned-run average. **G:** Games. **H:** Hits. **HR:** Home runs. **Int'l.:** International. **IP:** Innings pitched. **L:** Losses. **N.L.:** National League. **NYP:** New York-Pennsylvania. **OF:** Outfield. **Pct.:** Winning percentage. **PO:** Putouts. **Pos.:** Position. **R:** Runs. **RBI:** Runs batted in. **SB:** Stolen bases. **SO:** Strikeouts. **South.:** Southern Association. **SS:** Shortstop. **Sv.:** Saves. **W:** Wins. **1B:** First base. **2B:** Doubles or second base. **3B:** Triples or third base.

**A**

## ABDUL-WAHAD, TARIQ          G/F          MAVERICKS

**PERSONAL:** Born November 3, 1974, in Maisons Alfort, France. ... 6-6/223. (1,98/101,2). ... Fomerly known as Olivier Saint-Jean.
**HIGH SCHOOL:** Lycee Aristide Briand (Evreux, France).
**COLLEGE:** Michigan, then San Jose State.
**TRANSACTIONS/CAREER NOTES:** Selected after junior season by Sacramento Kings in first round (11th pick overall) of 1997 NBA Draft. ... Traded by Kings with future first-round draft choice to Orlando Magic for G/F Nick Anderson (August 3, 1999). ... Traded by Magic with F/C Chris Gatling, a future first round draft choice and cash considerations to Denver Nuggets for G Chauncey Billups, G/F Ron Mercer, F Johnny Taylor and draft considerations (February 1, 2000). ... Traded by Nuggets with G Nick Van Exel, F/C Raef LaFrentz and G Avery Johnson to Dallas Mavericks for F Juwan Howard, G Tim Hardaway, F Donnell Harvey, cash considerations and first-round draft choice (February 21, 2002).

### FRENCH LEAGUE RECORD

| Season Team | G | Min. | FGM | FGA | Pct. | FTM | FTA | Pct. | Reb. | Ast. | Pts. | AVERAGES RPG | APG | PPG |
|---|---|---|---|---|---|---|---|---|---|---|---|---|---|---|
| 90-91—Evreux | 2 | 3 | 0 | 1 | .000 | 0 | 0 | ... | 0 | 0 | 0 | 0.0 | 0.0 | 0.0 |
| 91-92—Evreux | 8 | 40 | 7 | 16 | .438 | 1 | 3 | .333 | 5 | 1 | 15 | 0.6 | 0.1 | 1.9 |
| 92-93—Evreux | 17 | 238 | 40 | 80 | .500 | 13 | 25 | .520 | 64 | 8 | 93 | 3.8 | 0.5 | 5.5 |
| Totals | 27 | 281 | 47 | 97 | .485 | 14 | 28 | .500 | 69 | 9 | 108 | 2.6 | 0.3 | 4.0 |

### COLLEGIATE RECORD

**NOTES:** Injured knee (1994-95); granted extra year of eligibility.

| Season Team | G | Min. | FGM | FGA | Pct. | FTM | FTA | Pct. | Reb. | Ast. | Pts. | AVERAGES RPG | APG | PPG |
|---|---|---|---|---|---|---|---|---|---|---|---|---|---|---|
| 93-94—Michigan | 32 | 418 | 49 | 96 | .510 | 13 | 23 | .565 | 72 | 17 | 115 | 2.3 | 0.5 | 3.6 |
| 94-95—Michigan | 4 | 53 | 8 | 16 | .500 | 2 | 2 | 1.000 | 13 | 0 | 19 | 3.3 | 0.0 | 4.8 |
| 95-96—San Jose State | 25 | 698 | 148 | 332 | .446 | 117 | 158 | .741 | 157 | 64 | 431 | 6.3 | 2.6 | 17.2 |
| 96-97—San Jose State | 26 | 868 | 225 | 457 | .492 | 143 | 196 | .730 | 229 | 28 | 619 | 8.8 | 1.1 | 23.8 |
| Totals | 87 | 2037 | 430 | 901 | .477 | 275 | 379 | .726 | 471 | 109 | 1184 | 5.4 | 1.3 | 13.6 |

Three-point field goals: 1993-94, 4-for-14 (.286). 1994-95, 1-for-2 (.500). 1995-96, 18-for-65 (.277). 1996-97, 26-for-71 (.366). Totals, 49-for-152 (.322).

### NBA REGULAR-SEASON RECORD

| Season Team | G | Min. | FGM | FGA | Pct. | FTM | FTA | Pct. | REBOUNDS Off. | Def. | Tot. | Ast. | St. | Blk. | TO | Pts. | AVERAGES RPG | APG | PPG |
|---|---|---|---|---|---|---|---|---|---|---|---|---|---|---|---|---|---|---|---|
| 97-98—Sacramento | 59 | 959 | 144 | 357 | .403 | 84 | 125 | .672 | 44 | 72 | 116 | 51 | 35 | 13 | 65 | 376 | 2.0 | 0.9 | 6.4 |
| 98-99—Sacramento | 49 | 1205 | 177 | 407 | .435 | 94 | 136 | .691 | 72 | 114 | 186 | 50 | 50 | 16 | 70 | 454 | 3.8 | 1.0 | 9.3 |
| 99-00—Orl.-Den. | 61 | 1578 | 274 | 646 | .424 | 146 | 193 | .756 | 101 | 190 | 291 | 98 | 59 | 28 | 106 | 697 | 4.8 | 1.6 | 11.4 |
| 00-01—Denver | 29 | 420 | 43 | 111 | .387 | 21 | 36 | .583 | 14 | 45 | 59 | 22 | 14 | 13 | 34 | 111 | 2.0 | 0.8 | 3.8 |
| 01-02—Denver-Dallas | 24 | 441 | 55 | 147 | .374 | 24 | 33 | .727 | 41 | 43 | 84 | 24 | 20 | 10 | 27 | 135 | 3.5 | 1.0 | 5.6 |
| 02-03—Dallas | 14 | 204 | 27 | 58 | .466 | 3 | 6 | .500 | 14 | 26 | 40 | 21 | 6 | 3 | 7 | 57 | 2.9 | 1.5 | 4.1 |
| 03-04—Dallas | | | | | | | | Did not play—injured | | | | | | | | | | | |
| Totals | 236 | 4807 | 720 | 1726 | .417 | 372 | 529 | .703 | 286 | 490 | 776 | 266 | 184 | 83 | 309 | 1830 | 3.3 | 1.1 | 7.8 |

Three-point field goals: 1997-98, 4-for-19 (.211). 1998-99, 6-for-21 (.286). 1999-00, 3-for-23 (.130). 2000-01, 4-for-10 (.400). 2001-02, 1-for-2 (.500). 2002-03, 0-for-1. Totals, 18-for-76 (.237).
Personal fouls/disqualifications: 1997-98, 81/0. 1998-99, 121/0. 1999-00, 147/1. 2000-01, 54/0. 2001-02, 56/1. 2002-03, 26/0. Totals, 485/2.

### NBA PLAYOFF RECORD

| Season Team | G | Min. | FGM | FGA | Pct. | FTM | FTA | Pct. | REBOUNDS Off. | Def. | Tot. | Ast. | St. | Blk. | TO | Pts. | AVERAGES RPG | APG | PPG |
|---|---|---|---|---|---|---|---|---|---|---|---|---|---|---|---|---|---|---|---|
| 98-99—Sacramento | 5 | 99 | 15 | 33 | .455 | 13 | 16 | .813 | 6 | 13 | 19 | 4 | 4 | 4 | 3 | 43 | 3.8 | 0.8 | 8.6 |
| 02-03—Dallas | 8 | 79 | 9 | 30 | .300 | 7 | 8 | .875 | 11 | 11 | 22 | 7 | 0 | 0 | 1 | 25 | 2.8 | 0.9 | 3.1 |
| Totals | 13 | 178 | 24 | 63 | .381 | 20 | 24 | .833 | 17 | 24 | 41 | 11 | 4 | 4 | 4 | 68 | 3.2 | 0.8 | 5.2 |

Three-point field goals: 1998-99, 0-for-1. 2002-03, 0-for-2. Totals, 0-for-3 (.000).
Personal fouls/disqualifications: 1998-99, 8/0. 2002-03, 6/0. Totals, 14/0.

## ABDUR-RAHIM, SHAREEF          F          KINGS

**PERSONAL:** Born December 11, 1976, in Marietta, Ga. ... 6-9/230. (2.06/104.3). ... Name pronounced shah-REEF ab-DOOR-Rah-heem.
**HIGH SCHOOL:** Wheeler (Marietta, Ga.).
**COLLEGE:** California.
**TRANSACTIONS/CAREER NOTES:** Selected after freshman season by Vancouver Grizzlies in first round (third pick overall) of 1996 NBA Draft. ... Grizzlies franchise moved to Memphis for 2001-02 season. ... Traded by Grizzlies with draft rights to G Jamaal Tinsley to Atlanta Hawks for F/C Lorenzen Wright, G Brevin Knight and draft rights to F Pau Gasol (July 19, 2001). ... Traded by Hawks with C Theo Ratliff and G Dan Dickau to Portland Trail Blazers for F Rasheed Wallace and G Wesley Person (February 9, 2004). ... Traded by Trail Blazers to New Jersey Nets for 2006 first-round pick and Nets' trade exception (August 2, 2005). ... New Jersey rescinds trade with Portland (August 9, 2005). ... Signed as free agent by Sacramento Kings (August 12, 2005).
**MISCELLANEOUS:** Member of gold-medal-winning U.S. Olympic team (2000). ... Memphis Grizzlies franchise all-time scoring leader with 7,801 points, all-time leading rebounder with 3,070, all-time steals leader with 416 and all-time blocked shots leader with 374 (1996-97 through 2000-01).

### COLLEGIATE RECORD

| Season Team | G | Min. | FGM | FGA | Pct. | FTM | FTA | Pct. | Reb. | Ast. | Pts. | AVERAGES RPG | APG | PPG |
|---|---|---|---|---|---|---|---|---|---|---|---|---|---|---|
| 95-96—California | 28 | 972 | 206 | 398 | .518 | 170 | 249 | .683 | 236 | 29 | 590 | 8.4 | 1.0 | 21.1 |

Three-point field goals: 1995-96, 8-for-21 (.381). Totals, 8-for-21 (.381).

## NBA REGULAR-SEASON RECORD

**HONORS:** NBA All-Rookie first team (1997).

| Season Team | G | Min. | FGM | FGA | Pct. | FTM | FTA | Pct. | Off. | Def. | Tot. | Ast. | St. | Blk. | TO | Pts. | RPG | APG | PPG |
|---|---|---|---|---|---|---|---|---|---|---|---|---|---|---|---|---|---|---|---|
| 96-97—Vancouver...... | 80 | 2802 | 550 | 1214 | .453 | 387 | 519 | .746 | 216 | 339 | 555 | 175 | 79 | 79 | 225 | 1494 | 6.9 | 2.2 | 18.7 |
| 97-98—Vancouver...... | 82 | 2950 | 653 | 1347 | .485 | 502 | 640 | .784 | 227 | 354 | 581 | 213 | 89 | 76 | 257 | 1829 | 7.1 | 2.6 | 22.3 |
| 98-99—Vancouver...... | 50 | 2021 | 386 | 893 | .432 | 369 | 439 | .841 | 114 | 260 | 374 | 172 | 69 | 55 | *186 | 1152 | 7.5 | 3.4 | 23.0 |
| 99-00—Vancouver.... | 82 | 3223 | 594 | 1277 | .465 | 446 | 551 | .809 | 218 | 607 | 825 | 271 | 89 | 87 | 249 | 1663 | 10.1 | 3.3 | 20.3 |
| 00-01—Vancouver.... | 81 | 3241 | 604 | 1280 | .472 | 443 | 531 | .834 | 175 | 560 | 735 | 250 | 90 | 77 | 231 | 1663 | 9.1 | 3.1 | 20.5 |
| 01-02—Atlanta .......... | 77 | 2980 | 598 | 1297 | .461 | 419 | 523 | .801 | 198 | 498 | 696 | 239 | 98 | 81 | 250 | 1636 | 9.0 | 3.1 | 21.2 |
| 02-03—Atlanta .......... | 81 | 3087 | 566 | 1183 | .478 | 455 | 541 | .841 | 175 | 502 | 677 | 242 | 87 | 38 | 212 | 1608 | 8.4 | 3.0 | 19.9 |
| 03-04—Atl.-Portland ... | 85 | 2684 | 501 | 1054 | .475 | 373 | 429 | .869 | 189 | 450 | 639 | 174 | 68 | 37 | 184 | 1384 | 7.5 | 2.0 | 16.3 |
| 04-05—Portland......... | 54 | 1867 | 337 | 670 | .503 | 220 | 254 | .866 | 123 | 269 | 392 | 111 | 49 | 26 | 117 | 909 | 7.3 | 2.1 | 16.8 |
| **Totals** .................... | 672 | 24855 | 4789 | 10215 | .469 | 3614 | 4427 | .816 | 1635 | 3839 | 5474 | 1847 | 718 | 556 | 1911 | 13338 | 8.1 | 2.7 | 19.8 |

Three-point field goals: 1996-97, 7-for-27 (.259). 1997-98, 21-for-51 (.412). 1998-99, 11-for-36 (.306). 1999-00, 29-for-96 (.302). 2000-01, 12-for-64 (.188). 2001-02, 21-for-70 (.300). 2002-03, 21-for-60 (.350). 2003-04, 9-for-34 (.265). 2004-05, 15-for-39 (.385). Totals, 146-for-477 (.306).

Personal fouls/disqualifications: 1996-97, 199/0. 1997-98, 201/0. 1998-99, 137/1. 1999-00, 244/3. 2000-01, 238/1. 2001-02, 214/2. 2002-03, 240/2. 2003-04, 222/1. 2004-05, 150/3. Totals, 1845/13.

## NBA ALL-STAR GAME RECORD

| Season Team | Min. | FGM | FGA | Pct. | FTM | FTA | Pct. | Off. | Def. | Tot. | Ast. | PF | Dq. | St. | Blk. | TO | Pts. |
|---|---|---|---|---|---|---|---|---|---|---|---|---|---|---|---|---|---|
| 2002—Atlanta.................. | 21 | 4 | 4 | 1.000 | 0 | 0 | ... | 1 | 5 | 6 | 0 | 2 | 0 | 0 | 0 | 0 | 9 |

Three-point field goals: 2002, 1-for-1 (1.000). Totals, 1-for-1 (1.000).

## ALEXANDER, CORY          G          BOBCATS

**PERSONAL:** Born June 22, 1973, in Waynesboro, Va. ... 6-1/190. (1.85/86.2). ... Full name: Cory Lynn Alexander
**HIGH SCHOOL:** Oak Hill Academy (Mouth of Wilson, Va.).
**COLLEGE:** Virginia.
**TRANSACTIONS/CAREER NOTES:** Selected after junior season by San Antonio Spurs in first round (29th pick overall) of 1995 NBA Draft. ... Waived by Spurs (February 27, 1998). ... Signed as free agent by Denver Nuggets (March 4, 1998). ... Waived by Nuggets (October 30, 2000). ... Signed by Orlando Magic to the first of two consecutive 10-day contracts (January 29, 2001). ... Re-signed by Magic for remainder of season (February 23, 2001). ... Signed as free agent by Charlotte Bobcats (February 28, 2005).

## COLLEGIATE RECORD

**NOTES:** Broke ankle (1993-94); granted extra year of eligibility.

| Season Team | G | Min. | FGM | FGA | Pct. | FTM | FTA | Pct. | Reb. | Ast. | Pts. | RPG | APG | PPG |
|---|---|---|---|---|---|---|---|---|---|---|---|---|---|---|
| 91-92—Virginia.......................... | 33 | 1037 | 127 | 338 | .376 | 72 | 105 | .686 | 106 | 145 | 370 | 3.2 | 4.4 | 11.2 |
| 92-93—Virginia.......................... | 31 | 1118 | 213 | 470 | .453 | 93 | 132 | .705 | 107 | 144 | 583 | 3.5 | 4.6 | 18.8 |
| 93-94—Virginia.......................... | 1 | 11 | 0 | 4 | .000 | 0 | 2 | .000 | 1 | 2 | 0 | 1.0 | 2.0 | 0.0 |
| 94-95—Virginia.......................... | 20 | 692 | 119 | 263 | .452 | 61 | 87 | .701 | 84 | 110 | 333 | 4.2 | 5.5 | 16.7 |
| **Totals** ..................................... | 85 | 2858 | 459 | 1075 | .427 | 226 | 326 | .693 | 298 | 401 | 1286 | 3.5 | 4.7 | 15.1 |

Three-point field goals: 1991-92, 44-for-149 (.295). 1992-93, 64-for-174 (.368). 1993-94, 0-for-2. 1994-95, 34-for-97 (.351). Totals, 142-for-422 (.336).

## NBA REGULAR-SEASON RECORD

| Season Team | G | Min. | FGM | FGA | Pct. | FTM | FTA | Pct. | Off. | Def. | Tot. | Ast. | St. | Blk. | TO | Pts. | RPG | APG | PPG |
|---|---|---|---|---|---|---|---|---|---|---|---|---|---|---|---|---|---|---|---|
| 95-96—San Antonio.... | 60 | 560 | 63 | 155 | .406 | 16 | 25 | .640 | 9 | 33 | 42 | 121 | 27 | 2 | 68 | 168 | 0.7 | 2.0 | 2.8 |
| 96-97—San Antonio.... | 80 | 1454 | 194 | 490 | .396 | 95 | 129 | .736 | 29 | 94 | 123 | 254 | 82 | 16 | 146 | 577 | 1.5 | 3.2 | 7.2 |
| 97-98—S.A.-Denver.... | 60 | 1298 | 171 | 400 | .428 | 80 | 102 | .784 | 17 | 129 | 146 | 209 | 70 | 11 | 112 | 488 | 2.4 | 3.5 | 8.1 |
| 98-99—Denver.......... | 36 | 778 | 97 | 260 | .373 | 37 | 44 | .841 | 7 | 67 | 74 | 119 | 35 | 5 | 69 | 261 | 2.1 | 3.3 | 7.3 |
| 99-00—Denver.......... | 29 | 329 | 28 | 98 | .286 | 17 | 22 | .773 | 8 | 34 | 42 | 58 | 24 | 2 | 28 | 82 | 1.4 | 2.0 | 2.8 |
| 00-01—Orlando.......... | 26 | 227 | 18 | 56 | .321 | 12 | 18 | .667 | 0 | 25 | 25 | 36 | 16 | 0 | 25 | 52 | 1.0 | 1.4 | 2.0 |
| 04-05—Charlotte........ | 16 | 201 | 16 | 49 | .327 | 9 | 12 | .750 | 8 | 21 | 29 | 37 | 9 | 1 | 19 | 49 | 1.8 | 2.3 | 3.1 |
| **Totals** | 307 | 4847 | 587 | 1508 | .389 | 266 | 352 | .756 | 78 | 403 | 481 | 834 | 263 | 37 | 467 | 1677 | 1.6 | 2.7 | 5.5 |

Three-point field goals: 1995-96, 26-for-66 (.394). 1996-97, 94-for-252 (.373). 1997-98, 66-for-176 (.375). 1998-99, 30-for-105 (.286). 1999-00, 9-for-35 (.257). 2000-01, 4-for-16 (.250). 2004-05, 8-for-19 (.421). Totals, 237-for-669 (.354).

Personal fouls/disqualifications: 1995-96, 94/0. 1996-97, 148/0. 1997-98, 98/2. 1998-99, 77/0. 1999-00, 39/0. 2000-01, 29/0. 2004-05, 29/0. Totals, 514/2.

## NBA PLAYOFF RECORD

| Season Team | G | Min. | FGM | FGA | Pct. | FTM | FTA | Pct. | Off. | Def. | Tot. | Ast. | St. | Blk. | TO | Pts. | RPG | APG | PPG |
|---|---|---|---|---|---|---|---|---|---|---|---|---|---|---|---|---|---|---|---|
| 95-96—San Antonio.... | 9 | 70 | 10 | 24 | .417 | 5 | 7 | .714 | 4 | 5 | 9 | 9 | 2 | 0 | 6 | 26 | 1.0 | 1.0 | 2.9 |

Three-point field goals: 1995-96, 1-for-5 (.200). Totals, 1-for-5 (.200).
Personal fouls/disqualifications: 1995-96, 8/0. Totals, 8/0.

## NBDL RECORD

| Season Team | G | Min. | FGM | FGA | Pct. | FTM | FTA | Pct. | Reb. | Ast. | Pts. | RPG | APG | PPG |
|---|---|---|---|---|---|---|---|---|---|---|---|---|---|---|
| 02-03—Roanoke ........................ | 50 | 1794 | 288 | 693 | .416 | 186 | 230 | .809 | 206 | 306 | 827 | 4.1 | 6.1 | 16.5 |
| 04-05—Roanoke ........................ | 32 | 1107 | 174 | 405 | .430 | 154 | 186 | .828 | 114 | 267 | 525 | 3.6 | 8.3 | 16.4 |
| **Totals** ..................................... | 82 | 2901 | 462 | 1098 | .421 | 340 | 416 | .817 | 320 | 573 | 1352 | 3.9 | 7.0 | 16.5 |

Three-point field goals: 2002-03, 65-for-208 (.313). 2004-05, 23-for-60 (.383). Totals, 88-for-268 (.328).

## ITALIAN LEAGUE RECORD

| Season Team | G | Min. | FGM | FGA | Pct. | FTM | FTA | Pct. | Reb. | Ast. | Pts. | RPG | APG | PPG |
|---|---|---|---|---|---|---|---|---|---|---|---|---|---|---|
| 03-04—Lottomatica Roma.......... | 13 | 347 | 49 | 106 | .462 | 20 | 28 | .714 | 41 | 36 | 144 | 3.2 | 2.8 | 11.1 |

Three-point field goals: 2003-04, 26-for-55 (.473). Totals, 26-for-55 (.473).

## ALLEN, MALIK — F — BULLS

**PERSONAL:** Born June 27, 1978, in Willingboro, N.J. ... 6-10/255. (2.08/115.7).
**HIGH SCHOOL:** Shawnee (Medford, N.J.).
**COLLEGE:** Villanova.
**TRANSACTIONS/CAREER NOTES:** Not drafted by an NBA franchise. ... Played in American Basketball Association 2000 with San Diego Wild Fire (2000-01). ... Played in International Basketball Association with Trenton Stars (2000-01). ... Signed as free agent by Miami Heat (July 20, 2001). ... Traded by Heat to Charlotte Bobcats for G Steve Smith (February 24, 2005). Signed as free agent by Chicago Bulls (September 2, 2005).

### COLLEGIATE RECORD

| Season Team | G | Min. | FGM | FGA | Pct. | FTM | FTA | Pct. | Reb. | Ast. | Pts. | AVERAGES RPG | APG | PPG |
|---|---|---|---|---|---|---|---|---|---|---|---|---|---|---|
| 96-97—Villanova | 33 | 357 | 24 | 51 | .471 | 19 | 45 | .422 | 96 | 13 | 67 | 2.9 | 0.4 | 2.0 |
| 97-98—Villanova | 29 | 715 | 91 | 194 | .469 | 58 | 80 | .725 | 168 | 22 | 240 | 5.8 | 0.8 | 8.3 |
| 98-99—Villanova | 32 | 887 | 136 | 241 | .564 | 85 | 107 | .794 | 201 | 31 | 357 | 6.3 | 1.0 | 11.2 |
| 99-00—Villanova | 33 | 1103 | 184 | 360 | .511 | 99 | 143 | .692 | 243 | 32 | 467 | 7.4 | 1.0 | 14.2 |
| Totals | 127 | 3062 | 435 | 846 | .514 | 261 | 375 | .696 | 708 | 98 | 1131 | 5.6 | 0.8 | 8.9 |

### AMERICAN BASKETBALL ASSOCIATION RECORD

| Season Team | G | Min. | FGM | FGA | Pct. | FTM | FTA | Pct. | Reb. | Ast. | Pts. | AVERAGES RPG | APG | PPG |
|---|---|---|---|---|---|---|---|---|---|---|---|---|---|---|
| 00-01—San Diego | 31 | 1066 | 208 | 424 | .491 | 85 | 112 | .759 | 242 | 50 | 506 | 7.8 | 1.6 | 16.3 |

Three-point field goals: 2000-01, 4-for-8 (.500). Totals, 4-for-8 (.500).

### INTERNATIONAL BASKETBALL LEAGUE RECORD

| Season Team | G | Min. | FGM | FGA | Pct. | FTM | FTA | Pct. | Reb. | Ast. | Pts. | AVERAGES RPG | APG | PPG |
|---|---|---|---|---|---|---|---|---|---|---|---|---|---|---|
| 00-01—Trenton | 5 | 93 | 16 | 32 | .500 | 3 | 4 | .750 | 24 | 5 | 37 | 4.8 | 1.0 | 7.4 |

Three-point field goals: 2000-01, 16-for-42 (.381). Totals, 16-for-42 (.381).
Personal fouls/disqualifications: 2000-01, 17/0. Totals, 17/0.

### NBA REGULAR-SEASON RECORD

| Season Team | G | Min. | FGM | FGA | Pct. | FTM | FTA | Pct. | REBOUNDS Off. | Def. | Tot. | Ast. | St. | Blk. | TO | Pts. | AVERAGES RPG | APG | PPG |
|---|---|---|---|---|---|---|---|---|---|---|---|---|---|---|---|---|---|---|---|
| 01-02—Miami | 12 | 161 | 22 | 51 | .431 | 8 | 10 | .800 | 15 | 23 | 38 | 5 | 3 | 8 | 2 | 52 | 3.2 | 0.4 | 4.3 |
| 02-03—Miami | 80 | 2318 | 335 | 790 | .424 | 97 | 121 | .802 | 134 | 291 | 425 | 54 | 37 | 78 | 128 | 767 | 5.3 | 0.7 | 9.6 |
| 03-04—Miami | 45 | 616 | 83 | 198 | .419 | 25 | 33 | .758 | 42 | 77 | 119 | 16 | 12 | 28 | 27 | 191 | 2.6 | 0.4 | 4.2 |
| 04-05—Miami-Char. | 36 | 519 | 84 | 177 | .475 | 26 | 28 | .929 | 40 | 59 | 99 | 18 | 9 | 22 | 18 | 194 | 2.8 | 0.5 | 5.4 |
| Totals | 173 | 3614 | 524 | 1216 | .431 | 156 | 192 | .813 | 231 | 450 | 681 | 93 | 61 | 136 | 175 | 1204 | 3.9 | 0.5 | 7.0 |

Three-point field goals: 2001-02, 0-for-1. 2002-03, 0-for-4. Totals, 0-for-5 (.000).
Personal fouls/disqualifications: 2001-02, 16/0. 2002-03, 234/1. 2003-04, 81/0. 2004-05, 53/0. Totals, 384/1.

### NBA PLAYOFF RECORD

| Season Team | G | Min. | FGM | FGA | Pct. | FTM | FTA | Pct. | REBOUNDS Off. | Def. | Tot. | Ast. | St. | Blk. | TO | Pts. | AVERAGES RPG | APG | PPG |
|---|---|---|---|---|---|---|---|---|---|---|---|---|---|---|---|---|---|---|---|
| 03-04—Miami | 10 | 138 | 22 | 49 | .449 | 6 | 9 | .667 | 12 | 18 | 30 | 4 | 2 | 9 | 4 | 50 | 3.0 | 0.4 | 5.0 |

Personal fouls/disqualifications: 2003-04, 21/0. Totals, 21/0.

## ALLEN, RAY — G — SUPERSONICS

**PERSONAL:** Born July 20, 1975, in Merced, Calif. ... 6-5/205. (1.96/93.0). ... Full name: Walter Ray Allen
**HIGH SCHOOL:** Hillcrest (Dalzell, S.C.).
**COLLEGE:** Connecticut.
**TRANSACTIONS/CAREER NOTES:** Selected after junior season by Minnesota Timberwolves in first round (fifth pick overall) of 1996 NBA Draft. ... Draft rights traded by Timberwolves with future first-round draft choice to Milwaukee Bucks for draft rights to G Stephon Marbury (June 26, 1996). ... Traded by Bucks with G Kevin Ollie, G Ronald Murray and conditional first-round draft choice to Seattle SuperSonics for G Gary Payton and G Desmond Mason (February 20, 2003).
**MISCELLANEOUS:** Member of gold-medal-winning U.S. Olympic team (2000).

### COLLEGIATE RECORD

**NOTES:** THE SPORTING NEWS All-America first team (1996).

| Season Team | G | Min. | FGM | FGA | Pct. | FTM | FTA | Pct. | Reb. | Ast. | Pts. | AVERAGES RPG | APG | PPG |
|---|---|---|---|---|---|---|---|---|---|---|---|---|---|---|
| 93-94—Connecticut | 34 | 735 | 158 | 310 | .510 | 80 | 101 | .792 | 155 | 53 | 429 | 4.6 | 1.6 | 12.6 |
| 94-95—Connecticut | 32 | 1051 | 255 | 521 | .489 | 80 | 110 | .727 | 218 | 75 | 675 | 6.8 | 2.3 | 21.1 |
| 95-96—Connecticut | 35 | 1098 | 292 | 618 | .472 | 119 | 147 | .810 | 228 | 117 | 818 | 6.5 | 3.3 | 23.4 |
| Totals | 101 | 2884 | 705 | 1449 | .487 | 279 | 358 | .779 | 601 | 245 | 1922 | 6.0 | 2.4 | 19.0 |

Three-point field goals: 1993-94, 33-for-82 (.402). 1994-95, 85-for-191 (.445). 1995-96, 115-for-247 (.466). Totals, 233-for-520 (.448).

### NBA REGULAR-SEASON RECORD

**RECORDS:** Shares single-game record for most three-point field goals made in one half—8 (April 14, 2002, vs. Charlotte). ... Shares NBA record for most seasons leading league in three-point field goals made—2.
**HONORS:** All-NBA second team (2005). ... All-NBA third team (2001). ... NBA All-Rookie second team (1997). ... Long Distance Shootout winner (2001). ... NBA Sportsmanship Award (2003).
**NOTES:** Led NBA with 172 three-point field goals made and 407 three-point field goals attempted (2000). ... Led NBA with 202 three-point field goals made and 467 three-point field goals attempted (2001). ... Led NBA with 229 three-point field goals made and 528 three-point field goals attempted (2002). ... Led NBA with 201 three-point field goals made and 533 three-point field goals attempted (2003).

| Season Team | G | Min. | FGM | FGA | Pct. | FTM | FTA | Pct. | REBOUNDS Off. | Def. | Tot. | Ast. | St. | Blk. | TO | Pts. | AVERAGES RPG | APG | PPG |
|---|---|---|---|---|---|---|---|---|---|---|---|---|---|---|---|---|---|---|---|
| 96-97—Milwaukee | 82 | 2532 | 390 | 908 | .430 | 205 | 249 | .823 | 97 | 229 | 326 | 210 | 75 | 10 | 149 | 1102 | 4.0 | 2.6 | 13.4 |

| Season Team | G | Min. | FGM | FGA | Pct. | FTM | FTA | Pct. | REBOUNDS Off. | Def. | Tot. | Ast. | St. | Blk. | TO | Pts. | AVERAGES RPG | APG | PPG |
|---|---|---|---|---|---|---|---|---|---|---|---|---|---|---|---|---|---|---|---|
| 97-98—Milwaukee ...... | 82 | 3287 | 563 | 1315 | .428 | 342 | 391 | .875 | 127 | 278 | 405 | 356 | 111 | 12 | 263 | 1602 | 4.9 | 4.3 | 19.5 |
| 98-99—Milwaukee ...... | 50 | 1719 | 303 | 673 | .450 | 176 | 195 | .903 | 57 | 155 | 212 | 178 | 53 | 7 | 122 | 856 | 4.2 | 3.6 | 17.1 |
| 99-00—Milwaukee ...... | 82 | 3070 | 642 | 1411 | .455 | 353 | 398 | .887 | 83 | 276 | 359 | 308 | 110 | 19 | 183 | 1809 | 4.4 | 3.8 | 22.1 |
| 00-01—Milwaukee ...... | 82 | 3129 | 628 | 1309 | .480 | 348 | 392 | .888 | 101 | 327 | 428 | 374 | 124 | 20 | 204 | 1806 | 5.2 | 4.6 | 22.0 |
| 01-02—Milwaukee ...... | 69 | 2525 | 530 | 1148 | .462 | 214 | 245 | .873 | 81 | 231 | 312 | 271 | 88 | 18 | 159 | 1503 | 4.5 | 3.9 | 21.8 |
| 02-03—Milwaukee-Sea. | 76 | 2880 | 598 | 1363 | .439 | 316 | 345 | .916 | 94 | 287 | 381 | 334 | 103 | 14 | 198 | 1713 | 5.0 | 4.4 | 22.5 |
| 03-04—Seattle ........... | 56 | 2152 | 447 | 1017 | .440 | 245 | 271 | .904 | 69 | 217 | 286 | 268 | 71 | 11 | 156 | 1287 | 5.1 | 4.8 | 23.0 |
| 04-05—Seattle ........... | 78 | 3064 | 640 | 1494 | .428 | 378 | 428 | .883 | 79 | 268 | 347 | 289 | 84 | 5 | 171 | 1867 | 4.4 | 3.7 | 23.9 |
| Totals ................... | 657 | 24358 | 4741 | 10638 | .446 | 2577 | 2914 | .884 | 788 | 2268 | 3056 | 2588 | 819 | 116 | 1605 | 13545 | 4.7 | 3.9 | 20.6 |

Three-point field goals: 1996-97, 117-for-298 (.393). 1997-98, 134-for-368 (.364). 1998-99, 74-for-208 (.356). 1999-00, 172-for-407 (.423). 2000-01, 202-for-467 (.433). 2001-02, 229-for-528 (.434). 2002-03, 201-for-533 (.377). 2003-04, 148-for-378 (.392). 2004-05, 209-for-556 (.376). Totals, 1486-for-3743 (.397).

Personal fouls/disqualifications: 1996-97, 218/0. 1997-98, 244/2. 1998-99, 117/0. 1999-00, 187/1. 2000-01, 192/2. 2001-02, 157/0. 2002-03, 220/4. 2003-04, 132/2. 2004-05, 167/2. Totals, 1634/13.

### NBA PLAYOFF RECORD

| Season Team | G | Min. | FGM | FGA | Pct. | FTM | FTA | Pct. | REBOUNDS Off. | Def. | Tot. | Ast. | St. | Blk. | TO | Pts. | AVERAGES RPG | APG | PPG |
|---|---|---|---|---|---|---|---|---|---|---|---|---|---|---|---|---|---|---|---|
| 98-99—Milwaukee ...... | 3 | 120 | 25 | 47 | .532 | 8 | 13 | .615 | 8 | 14 | 22 | 13 | 3 | 1 | 11 | 67 | 7.3 | 4.3 | 22.3 |
| 99-00—Milwaukee ...... | 5 | 186 | 40 | 90 | .444 | 20 | 22 | .909 | 10 | 23 | 33 | 13 | 8 | 0 | 9 | 110 | 6.6 | 2.6 | 22.0 |
| 00-01—Milwaukee ...... | 18 | 768 | 158 | 331 | .477 | 79 | 86 | .919 | 14 | 55 | 74 | 108 | 24 | 10 | 43 | 452 | 4.1 | 6.0 | 25.1 |
| 04-05—Seattle ........... | 11 | 436 | 102 | 215 | .474 | 56 | 63 | .889 | 12 | 35 | 47 | 43 | 14 | 4 | 34 | 291 | 4.3 | 3.9 | 26.5 |
| Totals ................... | 37 | 1510 | 325 | 683 | .476 | 163 | 184 | .886 | 49 | 127 | 176 | 177 | 49 | 15 | 97 | 920 | 4.8 | 4.8 | 24.9 |

Three-point field goals: 1998-99, 9-for-19 (.474). 1999-00, 10-for-26 (.385). 2000-01, 57-for-119 (.479). 2004-05, 31-for-82 (.378). Totals, 107-for-246 (.435).

Personal fouls/disqualifications: 1998-99, 9/0. 1999-00, 10/0. 2000-01, 44/0. 2004-05, 22/0. Totals, 85/0.

### NBA ALL-STAR GAME RECORD

| Season Team | Min. | FGM | FGA | Pct. | FTM | FTA | Pct. | REBOUNDS Off. | Def. | Tot. | Ast. | PF | Dq. | St. | Blk. | TO | Pts. |
|---|---|---|---|---|---|---|---|---|---|---|---|---|---|---|---|---|---|
| 2000—Milwaukee ............ | 17 | 4 | 13 | .308 | 5 | 6 | .833 | 1 | 0 | 1 | 2 | 2 | 0 | 3 | 1 | 3 | 14 |
| 2001—Milwaukee ............ | 19 | 7 | 15 | .467 | 0 | 0 | ... | 1 | 2 | 3 | 2 | 0 | 0 | 1 | 1 | 1 | 15 |
| 2002—Milwaukee ............ | 25 | 6 | 17 | .353 | 0 | 0 | ... | 1 | 2 | 3 | 5 | 3 | 0 | 3 | 0 | 1 | 15 |
| 2004—Seattle ................. | 23 | 6 | 13 | .462 | 3 | 4 | .750 | 2 | 1 | 3 | 4 | 2 | 0 | 1 | 0 | 3 | 16 |
| 2005—Seattle ................. | 23 | 6 | 16 | .375 | 0 | 0 | ... | 0 | 4 | 4 | 1 | 2 | 0 | 0 | 0 | 1 | 17 |
| Totals ............................ | 107 | 29 | 74 | .392 | 8 | 10 | .800 | 5 | 9 | 14 | 14 | 9 | 0 | 8 | 2 | 9 | 77 |

Three-point field goals: 2000, 1-for-6 (.167). 2001, 1-for-7 (.143). 2002, 3-for-10 (.300). 2004, 1-for-4 (.250). 2005, 5-for-11 (.455). Totals, 11-for-38 (.289).

## ALLEN, TONY     G     CELTICS

**PERSONAL:** Born January 11, 1982, in Chicago. ... 6-4/213. (1.93/96.6).
**HIGH SCHOOL:** Crane (Chicago).
**JUNIOR COLLEGE:** Butler County Community (Kansas), then Wabash Valley.
**COLLEGE:** Oklahoma State.
**TRANSACTIONS/CAREER NOTES:** Selected by Boston Celtics in first round (25th pick overall) of 2004 NBA Draft.

### COLLEGIATE RECORD

| Season Team | G | Min. | FGM | FGA | Pct. | FTM | FTA | Pct. | Reb. | Ast. | Pts. | AVERAGES RPG | APG | PPG |
|---|---|---|---|---|---|---|---|---|---|---|---|---|---|---|
| 00-01—Butler County C.C......... | 32 | 967 | 207 | 406 | .510 | 101 | 166 | .608 | 194 | 105 | 527 | 6.1 | 3.3 | 16.5 |
| 01-02—Wabash Valley College ... | 38 | ... | 219 | 398 | .550 | 82 | 129 | .636 | 202 | 100 | 551 | 5.3 | 2.6 | 14.5 |
| 02-03—Oklahoma State ............. | 32 | 998 | 163 | 365 | .447 | 105 | 152 | .691 | 173 | 87 | 461 | 5.4 | 2.7 | 14.4 |
| 03-04—Oklahoma State ............. | 35 | 1107 | 204 | 405 | .504 | 236 | 346 | .682 | 193 | 109 | 561 | 5.5 | 3.1 | 16.0 |
| Junior College Totals............. | 70 | ... | 246 | 804 | .306 | 183 | 295 | .520 | 396 | 205 | 1078 | 5.7 | 2.9 | 15.4 |
| 4-Year-College Totals............. | 67 | 2074 | 367 | 770 | .477 | 341 | 498 | .585 | 366 | 196 | 1022 | 5.2 | 2.9 | 15.3 |

Three-point field goals: 2000-01, 12-for-32 (.375). 2001-02, 31-for-92 (.337). 2002-03, 30-for-76 (.395). 2003-04, 22-for-74 (.297). Totals, 95-for-274 (.347).

### NBA REGULAR-SEASON RECORD

| Season Team | G | Min. | FGM | FGA | Pct. | FTM | FTA | Pct. | REBOUNDS Off. | Def. | Tot. | Ast. | St. | Blk. | TO | Pts. | AVERAGES RPG | APG | PPG |
|---|---|---|---|---|---|---|---|---|---|---|---|---|---|---|---|---|---|---|---|
| 04-05—Boston ........... | 77 | 1262 | 184 | 387 | .475 | 112 | 152 | .737 | 85 | 136 | 221 | 64 | 76 | 24 | 77 | 492 | 2.9 | 0.8 | 6.4 |

Three-point field goals: 2004-05, 12-for-31 (.387). Totals, 12-for-31 (.387).
Personal fouls/disqualifications: 2004-05, 156/2. Totals, 156/2.

### NBA PLAYOFF RECORD

| Season Team | G | Min. | FGM | FGA | Pct. | FTM | FTA | Pct. | REBOUNDS Off. | Def. | Tot. | Ast. | St. | Blk. | TO | Pts. | AVERAGES RPG | APG | PPG |
|---|---|---|---|---|---|---|---|---|---|---|---|---|---|---|---|---|---|---|---|
| 04-05—Boston ........... | 7 | 90 | 8 | 18 | .444 | 3 | 7 | .429 | 4 | 8 | 12 | 2 | 3 | 2 | 5 | 19 | 1.7 | 0.3 | 2.7 |

Personal fouls/disqualifications: 2004-05, 17/1. Totals, 17/1.

## ALSTON, RAFER     G     RAPTORS

**PERSONAL:** Born July 24, 1976, in New York. ... 6-2/173. (1.88/78.5).
**HIGH SCHOOL:** Cardozo (Queens, N.Y.).
**JUNIOR COLLEGE:** Ventura College (Calif.), then Fresno (Calif.) Com.
**COLLEGE:** Fresno State.
**TRANSACTIONS/CAREER NOTES:** Selected after junior season by Milwaukee Bucks in second round (39th pick overall) of 1998 NBA Draft. ... Played in Continental Basketball Association with Idaho Stampede (1998-99). ... Signed as free agent by Golden State

Warriors (September 6, 2002). ... Waived by Warriors (October 23, 2002). ... Played in National Basketball Developmental League with Mobile Revelers (2002-03). ... Signed as free agent by Toronto Raptors (January 17, 2003). ... Signed as free agent by Miami Heat (September 4, 2003). ... Signed as free agent by Raptors (July 14, 2004).

**A**

## COLLEGIATE RECORD

| Season Team | G | Min. | FGM | FGA | Pct. | FTM | FTA | Pct. | Reb. | Ast. | Pts. | AVERAGES RPG | APG | PPG |
|---|---|---|---|---|---|---|---|---|---|---|---|---|---|---|
| 94-95—Ventura College | | | | | | Statistics unavailable. | | | | | | | | |
| 95-96—Fresno C.C. | | | | | | Did not play. | | | | | | | | |
| 96-97—Fresno C.C. | 32 | ... | 197 | 395 | .499 | 69 | 85 | .812 | 64 | 275 | 554 | 2.0 | 8.6 | 17.3 |
| 97-98—Fresno State | 33 | 1030 | 124 | 309 | .401 | 50 | 66 | .758 | 71 | 240 | 364 | 2.2 | 7.3 | 11.0 |
| Junior College Totals | 32 | ... | 197 | 395 | .499 | 69 | 85 | .812 | 64 | 275 | 554 | 2.0 | 8.6 | 17.3 |
| 4-Year-College Totals | 33 | 1030 | 124 | 309 | .401 | 50 | 66 | .758 | 71 | 240 | 364 | 2.2 | 7.3 | 11.0 |

Three-point field goals: 1996-97, 91-for-223 (.408). 1997-98, 66-for-196 (.337). Totals, 157-for-419 (.375).

## CBA RECORD

| Season Team | G | Min. | FGM | FGA | Pct. | FTM | FTA | Pct. | Reb. | Ast. | Pts. | AVERAGES RPG | APG | PPG |
|---|---|---|---|---|---|---|---|---|---|---|---|---|---|---|
| 98-99—Idaho | 17 | 427 | 45 | 116 | .388 | 13 | 19 | .684 | 33 | 106 | 111 | 1.9 | 6.2 | 6.5 |

Three-point field goals: 1998-99, 8-for-28 (.286). Totals, 8-for-28 (.286).
Personal fouls/disqualifications: 1998-99, 38/0. Totals, 38/0.

## NBA REGULAR-SEASON RECORD

| Season Team | G | Min. | FGM | FGA | Pct. | FTM | FTA | Pct. | REBOUNDS Off. | Def. | Tot. | Ast. | St. | Blk. | TO | Pts. | AVERAGES RPG | APG | PPG |
|---|---|---|---|---|---|---|---|---|---|---|---|---|---|---|---|---|---|---|---|
| 99-00—Milwaukee | 27 | 361 | 27 | 95 | .284 | 3 | 4 | .750 | 5 | 18 | 23 | 70 | 12 | 0 | 29 | 60 | 0.9 | 2.6 | 2.2 |
| 00-01—Milwaukee | 37 | 288 | 30 | 84 | .357 | 9 | 13 | .692 | 4 | 27 | 31 | 68 | 13 | 0 | 20 | 77 | 0.8 | 1.8 | 2.1 |
| 01-02—Milwaukee | 50 | 600 | 66 | 191 | .346 | 18 | 29 | .621 | 10 | 62 | 72 | 143 | 32 | 2 | 40 | 177 | 1.4 | 2.9 | 3.5 |
| 02-03—Toronto | 47 | 980 | 139 | 335 | .415 | 37 | 54 | .685 | 21 | 86 | 107 | 192 | 38 | 15 | 86 | 366 | 2.3 | 4.1 | 7.8 |
| 03-04—Miami | 82 | 2581 | 287 | 764 | .376 | 103 | 134 | .769 | 26 | 200 | 226 | 372 | 114 | 18 | 128 | 838 | 2.8 | 4.5 | 10.2 |
| 04-05—Toronto | 80 | 2717 | 403 | 974 | .414 | 191 | 258 | .740 | 42 | 237 | 279 | 514 | 118 | 7 | 170 | 1136 | 3.5 | 6.4 | 14.2 |
| Totals | 323 | 7527 | 952 | 2443 | .390 | 361 | 492 | .734 | 108 | 630 | 738 | 1359 | 327 | 42 | 473 | 2654 | 2.3 | 4.2 | 8.2 |

Three-point field goals: 1999-00, 3-for-14 (.214). 2000-01, 8-for-30 (.267). 2001-02, 27-for-71 (.380). 2002-03, 51-for-130 (.392). 2003-04, 161-for-434 (.371). 2004-05, 139-for-389 (.357). Totals, 389-for-1068 (.364).
Personal fouls/disqualifications: 1999-00, 29/0. 2000-01, 27/0. 2001-02, 42/0. 2002-03, 120/0. 2003-04, 212/1. 2004-05, 212/0. Totals, 642/1.

## NBA PLAYOFF RECORD

| Season Team | G | Min. | FGM | FGA | Pct. | FTM | FTA | Pct. | REBOUNDS Off. | Def. | Tot. | Ast. | St. | Blk. | TO | Pts. | AVERAGES RPG | APG | PPG |
|---|---|---|---|---|---|---|---|---|---|---|---|---|---|---|---|---|---|---|---|
| 99-00—Milwaukee | 4 | 16 | 0 | 3 | .000 | 0 | 2 | .000 | 0 | 0 | 0 | 1 | 0 | 0 | 1 | 0 | 0.0 | 0.3 | 0.0 |
| 00-01—Milwaukee | 5 | 8 | 0 | 1 | .000 | 0 | 0 | ... | 0 | 0 | 0 | 1 | 0 | 0 | 2 | 0 | 0.0 | 0.2 | 0.0 |
| 03-04—Miami | 13 | 295 | 29 | 91 | .319 | 21 | 25 | .840 | 4 | 25 | 29 | 22 | 5 | 1 | 10 | 91 | 2.2 | 1.7 | 7.0 |
| Totals | 22 | 319 | 29 | 95 | .305 | 21 | 27 | .778 | 4 | 25 | 29 | 24 | 5 | 1 | 13 | 91 | 1.3 | 1.1 | 4.1 |

Three-point field goals: 1999-00, 0-for-1. 2003-04, 12-for-52 (.231). Totals, 12-for-53 (.226).
Personal fouls/disqualifications: 2003-04, 22/0. Totals, 22/0.

## NBDL RECORD

| Season Team | G | Min. | FGM | FGA | Pct. | FTM | FTA | Pct. | Reb. | Ast. | Pts. | AVERAGES RPG | APG | PPG |
|---|---|---|---|---|---|---|---|---|---|---|---|---|---|---|
| 02-03—Mobile | 6 | 217 | 38 | 84 | .452 | 13 | 17 | .765 | 23 | 58 | 95 | 3.8 | 9.7 | 15.8 |

Three-point field goals: 2002-03, 6-for-13 (.462). Totals, 6-for-13 (.462).
Personal fouls/disqualifications: 2002-03, 17/0. Totals, 17/0.

# ANDERSEN, CHRIS      F/C      HORNETS

**PERSONAL:** Born July 7, 1978, in Iola, Texas. ... 6-10/230. (2.08/104.3).
**HIGH SCHOOL:** Iola (Texas).
**JUNIOR COLLEGE:** Blinn Community College (Texas).
**TRANSACTIONS/CAREER NOTES:** Not drafted by an NBA franchise. ... Played in China (1999-2000). ... Played in International Basketball League with New Mexico Slam (1999-2000). ... Played in International Basketball Association with Fargo-Moorhead Beez (2000-01). ... Played in National Basketball Development League with Fayetteville Patriots (2001-02). ... Signed as free agent by Denver Nuggets (November 21, 2001). ... Signed as free agent by New Orleans Hornets (July 19, 2004).

## COLLEGIATE RECORD

| Season Team | G | Min. | FGM | FGA | Pct. | FTM | FTA | Pct. | Reb. | Ast. | Pts. | AVERAGES RPG | APG | PPG |
|---|---|---|---|---|---|---|---|---|---|---|---|---|---|---|
| 97-98—Blinn C.C. | 29 | 618 | 108 | 214 | .505 | 70 | 133 | .526 | 224 | 20 | 292 | 7.7 | 0.7 | 10.1 |
| 98-99—Blinn C.C. | | | | | | | Did not play. | | | | | | | |
| Totals | 29 | 618 | 108 | 214 | .505 | 70 | 133 | .526 | 224 | 20 | 292 | 7.7 | 0.7 | 10.1 |

Three-point field goals: 1997-98, 6-for-25 (.240). Totals, 6-for-25 (.240).

## INTERNATIONAL BASKETBALL LEAGUE RECORD

| Season Team | G | Min. | FGM | FGA | Pct. | FTM | FTA | Pct. | Reb. | Ast. | Pts. | AVERAGES RPG | APG | PPG |
|---|---|---|---|---|---|---|---|---|---|---|---|---|---|---|
| 99-00—New Mexico | 10 | 55 | 4 | 15 | .267 | 3 | 4 | .750 | 16 | 1 | 11 | 1.6 | 0.1 | 1.1 |

## NBA REGULAR-SEASON RECORD

| Season Team | G | Min. | FGM | FGA | Pct. | FTM | FTA | Pct. | REBOUNDS Off. | Def. | Tot. | Ast. | St. | Blk. | TO | Pts. | AVERAGES RPG | APG | PPG |
|---|---|---|---|---|---|---|---|---|---|---|---|---|---|---|---|---|---|---|---|
| 01-02—Denver | 24 | 262 | 25 | 74 | .338 | 22 | 28 | .786 | 38 | 38 | 76 | 7 | 7 | 28 | 13 | 72 | 3.2 | 0.3 | 3.0 |
| 02-03—Denver | 59 | 907 | 114 | 285 | .400 | 77 | 140 | .550 | 109 | 165 | 274 | 32 | 30 | 60 | 60 | 305 | 4.6 | 0.5 | 5.2 |
| 03-04—Denver | 71 | 1029 | 90 | 203 | .443 | 63 | 107 | .589 | 89 | 209 | 298 | 35 | 34 | 114 | 48 | 243 | 4.2 | 0.5 | 3.4 |
| 04-05—New Orleans | 67 | 1430 | 191 | 358 | .534 | 131 | 190 | .689 | 137 | 273 | 410 | 71 | 14 | 100 | 64 | 513 | 6.1 | 1.1 | 7.7 |
| Totals | 221 | 3628 | 420 | 920 | .457 | 293 | 465 | .630 | 373 | 685 | 1058 | 145 | 85 | 302 | 185 | 1133 | 4.8 | 0.7 | 5.1 |

Three-point field goals: 2001-02, 0-for-4. 2002-03, 0-for-1. 2003-04, 0-for-1. 2004-05, 0-for-3. Totals, 0-for-9 (.000).
Personal fouls/disqualifications: 2001-02, 35/0. 2002-03, 90/1. 2003-04, 119/0. 2004-05, 144/0. Totals, 388/1.

## NBA PLAYOFF RECORD

| Season Team | G | Min. | FGM | FGA | Pct. | FTM | FTA | Pct. | REBOUNDS Off. | Def. | Tot. | Ast. | St. | Blk. | TO | Pts. | AVERAGES RPG | APG | PPG |
|---|---|---|---|---|---|---|---|---|---|---|---|---|---|---|---|---|---|---|---|
| 03-04—Denver | 5 | 34 | 3 | 9 | .333 | 0 | 0 | ... | 6 | 8 | 14 | 2 | 1 | 2 | 2 | 6 | 2.8 | 0.4 | 1.2 |

Personal fouls/disqualifications: 2003-04, 3/0. Totals, 3/0.

## NBDL RECORD

| Season Team | G | Min. | FGM | FGA | Pct. | FTM | FTA | Pct. | Reb. | Ast. | Pts. | AVERAGES RPG | APG | PPG |
|---|---|---|---|---|---|---|---|---|---|---|---|---|---|---|
| 01-02—Fayetteville | 3 | 42 | 4 | 9 | .444 | 6 | 8 | .750 | 11 | 1 | 14 | 3.7 | 0.3 | 4.7 |

Three-point field goals: 2001-02, 0-for-1. Totals, 0-for-1 (.000).
Personal fouls/disqualifications: 2001-02, 6/0. Totals, 6/0.

# ANDERSON, DEREK — G — ROCKETS

**PERSONAL:** Born July 18, 1974, in Louisville, Ky. ... 6-5/195. (1.96/88.5). ... Full name: Derek Lamont Anderson
**HIGH SCHOOL:** Doss (Louisville, Ky.).
**COLLEGE:** Ohio State, then Kentucky.
**TRANSACTIONS/CAREER NOTES:** Selected by Cleveland Cavaliers in first round (13th pick overall) of 1997 NBA Draft. ... Traded by Cavaliers with F Johnny Newman to Los Angeles Clippers for F Lamond Murray (August 4, 1999). ... Signed as free agent by San Antonio Spurs (August 4, 2000). ... Traded by Spurs with G Steve Kerr and 2003 second-round draft choice to Portland Trail Blazers for G Steve Smith (July 25, 2001). ... Waived by Trail Blazers (August 3, 2005). ... Signed as free agent by Houston Rockets (August 23, 2005).

## COLLEGIATE RECORD

**NOTES:** Member of NCAA Division I championship team (1996).

| Season Team | G | Min. | FGM | FGA | Pct. | FTM | FTA | Pct. | Reb. | Ast. | Pts. | AVERAGES RPG | APG | PPG |
|---|---|---|---|---|---|---|---|---|---|---|---|---|---|---|
| 92-93—Ohio State | 22 | 587 | 72 | 158 | .456 | 72 | 89 | .809 | 72 | 59 | 225 | 3.3 | 2.7 | 10.2 |
| 93-94—Ohio State | 22 | 695 | 108 | 232 | .466 | 92 | 113 | .814 | 108 | 107 | 329 | 4.9 | 4.9 | 15.0 |
| 94-95—Kentucky | | | | | | Did not play—transfer student. | | | | | | | | |
| 95-96—Kentucky | 36 | 700 | 117 | 230 | .509 | 80 | 102 | .784 | 122 | 88 | 337 | 3.4 | 2.4 | 9.4 |
| 96-97—Kentucky | 19 | 481 | 111 | 226 | .491 | 77 | 95 | .811 | 77 | 67 | 337 | 4.1 | 3.5 | 17.7 |
| Totals | 99 | 2463 | 408 | 846 | .482 | 321 | 399 | .805 | 379 | 321 | 1228 | 3.8 | 3.2 | 12.4 |

Three-point field goals: 1992-93, 9-for-35 (.257). 1993-94, 21-for-62 (.339). 1995-96, 23-for-59 (.390). 1996-97, 38-for-94 (.404). Totals, 91-for-250 (.364).
Personal fouls/disqualifications: 1995-96, 82/0. Totals, 82/0.

## NBA REGULAR-SEASON RECORD

**HONORS:** NBA All-Rookie second team (1998).

| Season Team | G | Min. | FGM | FGA | Pct. | FTM | FTA | Pct. | REBOUNDS Off. | Def. | Tot. | Ast. | St. | Blk. | TO | Pts. | AVERAGES RPG | APG | PPG |
|---|---|---|---|---|---|---|---|---|---|---|---|---|---|---|---|---|---|---|---|
| 97-98—Cleveland | 66 | 1839 | 239 | 586 | .408 | 275 | 315 | .873 | 55 | 132 | 187 | 227 | 86 | 13 | 128 | 770 | 2.8 | 3.4 | 11.7 |
| 98-99—Cleveland | 38 | 978 | 125 | 314 | .398 | 138 | 165 | .836 | 20 | 89 | 109 | 145 | 48 | 4 | 82 | 409 | 2.9 | 3.8 | 10.8 |
| 99-00—L.A. Clippers | 64 | 2201 | 377 | 860 | .438 | 271 | 309 | .877 | 80 | 178 | 258 | 220 | 90 | 11 | 167 | 1080 | 4.0 | 3.4 | 16.9 |
| 00-01—San Antonio | 82 | 2859 | 413 | 993 | .416 | 342 | 402 | .851 | 75 | 288 | 363 | 301 | 120 | 14 | 165 | 1269 | 4.4 | 3.7 | 15.5 |
| 01-02—Portland | 70 | 1860 | 247 | 612 | .404 | 178 | 208 | .856 | 47 | 142 | 189 | 216 | 68 | 8 | 87 | 757 | 2.7 | 3.1 | 10.8 |
| 02-03—Portland | 76 | 2556 | 355 | 832 | .427 | 231 | 269 | .859 | 53 | 211 | 264 | 325 | 90 | 16 | 128 | 1057 | 3.5 | 4.3 | 13.9 |
| 03-04—Portland | 51 | 1810 | 230 | 612 | .376 | 155 | 188 | .824 | 26 | 156 | 182 | 228 | 66 | 3 | 90 | 694 | 3.6 | 4.5 | 13.6 |
| 04-05—Portland | 47 | 1239 | 152 | 391 | .389 | 70 | 87 | .805 | 25 | 103 | 128 | 143 | 36 | 4 | 70 | 432 | 2.7 | 3.0 | 9.2 |
| Totals | 494 | 15342 | 2138 | 5200 | .411 | 1660 | 1943 | .854 | 381 | 1299 | 1680 | 1805 | 604 | 73 | 917 | 6468 | 3.4 | 3.7 | 13.1 |

Three-point field goals: 1997-98, 17-for-84 (.202). 1998-99, 21-for-69 (.304). 1999-00, 55-for-178 (.309). 2000-01, 101-for-253 (.399). 2001-02, 85-for-228 (.373). 2002-03, 116-for-331 (.350). 2003-04, 79-for-259 (.305). 2004-05, 58-for-151 (.384). Totals, 532-for-1553 (.343).
Personal fouls/disqualifications: 1997-98, 136/0. 1998-99, 73/0. 1999-00, 149/2. 2000-01, 188/1. 2001-02, 113/1. 2002-03, 141/1. 2003-04, 79/0. 2004-05, 89/0. Totals, 968/5.

## NBA PLAYOFF RECORD

| Season Team | G | Min. | FGM | FGA | Pct. | FTM | FTA | Pct. | REBOUNDS Off. | Def. | Tot. | Ast. | St. | Blk. | TO | Pts. | AVERAGES RPG | APG | PPG |
|---|---|---|---|---|---|---|---|---|---|---|---|---|---|---|---|---|---|---|---|
| 97-98—Cleveland | 4 | 103 | 10 | 22 | .455 | 23 | 26 | .885 | 0 | 9 | 9 | 11 | 5 | 1 | 12 | 43 | 2.3 | 2.8 | 10.8 |
| 00-01—San Antonio | 7 | 194 | 16 | 61 | .262 | 16 | 21 | .762 | 3 | 16 | 19 | 17 | 3 | 0 | 15 | 54 | 2.7 | 2.4 | 7.7 |
| 01-02—Portland | 3 | 76 | 13 | 30 | .433 | 16 | 18 | .889 | 3 | 4 | 7 | 7 | 2 | 0 | 6 | 44 | 2.3 | 2.3 | 14.7 |
| 02-03—Portland | 2 | 22 | 1 | 4 | .250 | 0 | 1 | .000 | 1 | 0 | 1 | 0 | 0 | 0 | 1 | 2 | 0.5 | 0.0 | 1.0 |
| Totals | 16 | 395 | 40 | 117 | .342 | 55 | 66 | .833 | 7 | 29 | 36 | 35 | 10 | 1 | 34 | 143 | 2.3 | 2.2 | 8.9 |

Three-point field goals: 2000-01, 6-for-22 (.273). 2001-02, 2-for-6 (.333). 2002-03, 0-for-1. Totals, 8-for-29 (.276).
Personal fouls/disqualifications: 1997-98, 10/0. 2000-01, 10/0. 2001-02, 1/0. 2002-03, 1/0. Totals, 22/0.

# ANDERSON, KENNY — G

**PERSONAL:** Born October 9, 1970, in Queens, N.Y. ... 6-1/168. (1.85/76.2).
**HIGH SCHOOL:** Archbishop Molloy (Queens, N.Y.).
**COLLEGE:** Georgia Tech.
**TRANSACTIONS/CAREER NOTES:** Selected after sophomore season by New Jersey Nets in first round (second pick overall) of 1991 NBA Draft. ... Traded by Nets with G/F Gerald Glass to Charlotte Hornets for G Kendall Gill and G Khalid Reeves (January 19, 1996). ... Signed as free agent by Portland Trail Blazers (July 23, 1996). ... Traded by Trail Blazers with G Alvin Williams, F Gary Trent and two first-round draft choices to Toronto Raptors for G Damon Stoudamire, F Walt Williams and F Carlos Rogers (February 13, 1998). ... Traded by Raptors with C Zan Tabak and F Popeye Jones to Boston Celtics for G Chauncey Billups, G Dee Brown, F John Thomas and F Roy

Rogers (February 18, 1998). ... Traded by Celtics with F/C Vitaly Potapenko and G Joseph Forte to Seattle SuperSonics for F Vin Baker and G Shammond Williams (July 22, 2002). ... Traded by SuperSonics to New Orleans Hornets for C Elden Campbell (February 20, 2003). ... Signed as free agent by Indiana Pacers (September 19, 2003). ... Signed as free agent by Atlanta Hawks (September 16, 2004). ... Waived by Hawks (February 24, 2005). ... Claimed on waivers by Los Angeles Clippers (February 28, 2005). ... Waived by Clippers (March 25, 2005).

**MISCELLANEOUS:** Member of bronze-medal-winning U.S. World Championship team (1990). ... New Jersey Nets franchise all-time assists leader with 2,363 (1991-92 through 1995-96).

## COLLEGIATE RECORD

**NOTES:** THE SPORTING NEWS All-America second team (1990, 1991).

| Season Team | G | Min. | FGM | FGA | Pct. | FTM | FTA | Pct. | Reb. | Ast. | Pts. | RPG | APG | PPG |
|---|---|---|---|---|---|---|---|---|---|---|---|---|---|---|
| 89-90—Georgia Tech | 35 | 1321 | 283 | 549 | .515 | 107 | 146 | .733 | 193 | 285 | 721 | 5.5 | 8.1 | 20.6 |
| 90-91—Georgia Tech | 30 | 1167 | 278 | 636 | .437 | 155 | 187 | .829 | 171 | 169 | 776 | 5.7 | 5.6 | 25.9 |
| Totals | 65 | 2488 | 561 | 1185 | .473 | 262 | 333 | .787 | 364 | 454 | 1497 | 5.6 | 7.0 | 23.0 |

Three-point field goals: 1989-90, 48-for-117 (.410). 1990-91, 65-for-185 (.351). Totals, 113-for-302 (.374).

## NBA REGULAR-SEASON RECORD

| Season Team | G | Min. | FGM | FGA | Pct. | FTM | FTA | Pct. | Off. | Def. | Tot. | Ast. | St. | Blk. | TO | Pts. | RPG | APG | PPG |
|---|---|---|---|---|---|---|---|---|---|---|---|---|---|---|---|---|---|---|---|
| 91-92—New Jersey | 64 | 1086 | 187 | 480 | .390 | 73 | 98 | .745 | 38 | 89 | 127 | 203 | 67 | 9 | 97 | 450 | 2.0 | 3.2 | 7.0 |
| 92-93—New Jersey | 55 | 2010 | 370 | 850 | .435 | 180 | 232 | .776 | 51 | 175 | 226 | 449 | 96 | 11 | 153 | 927 | 4.1 | 8.2 | 16.9 |
| 93-94—New Jersey | 82 | 3135 | 576 | 1381 | .417 | 346 | 423 | .818 | 89 | 233 | 322 | 784 | 158 | 15 | 266 | 1538 | 3.9 | 9.6 | 18.8 |
| 94-95—New Jersey | 72 | 2689 | 411 | 1031 | .399 | 348 | 414 | .841 | 73 | 177 | 250 | 680 | 103 | 14 | 225 | 1267 | 3.5 | 9.4 | 17.6 |
| 95-96—N.J.-Char. | 69 | 2344 | 349 | 834 | .418 | 260 | 338 | .769 | 63 | 140 | 203 | 575 | 111 | 14 | 146 | 1050 | 2.9 | 8.3 | 15.2 |
| 96-97—Portland | 82 | 3081 | 485 | 1137 | .427 | 334 | 435 | .768 | 91 | 272 | 363 | 584 | 162 | 15 | 193 | 1436 | 4.4 | 7.1 | 17.5 |
| 97-98—Port.-Boston | 61 | 1858 | 268 | 674 | .398 | 153 | 194 | .789 | 39 | 134 | 173 | 345 | 87 | 1 | 143 | 746 | 2.8 | 5.7 | 12.2 |
| 98-99—Boston | 34 | 1010 | 161 | 357 | .451 | 84 | 101 | .832 | 24 | 79 | 103 | 193 | 33 | 2 | 71 | 412 | 3.0 | 5.7 | 12.1 |
| 99-00—Boston | 82 | 2593 | 434 | 986 | .440 | 196 | 253 | .775 | 55 | 170 | 225 | 420 | 139 | 8 | 130 | 1149 | 2.7 | 5.1 | 14.0 |
| 00-01—Boston | 33 | 849 | 88 | 227 | .388 | 59 | 71 | .831 | 16 | 57 | 73 | 134 | 44 | 2 | 52 | 246 | 2.2 | 4.1 | 7.5 |
| 01-02—Boston | 76 | 2430 | 312 | 716 | .436 | 98 | 132 | .742 | 57 | 218 | 275 | 403 | 141 | 10 | 119 | 731 | 3.6 | 5.3 | 9.6 |
| 02-03—Seattle-N.O. | 61 | 1135 | 163 | 382 | .427 | 45 | 57 | .789 | 31 | 101 | 132 | 198 | 58 | 5 | 75 | 372 | 2.2 | 3.2 | 6.1 |
| 03-04—Indiana | 44 | 905 | 113 | 256 | .441 | 35 | 48 | .729 | 19 | 62 | 81 | 125 | 26 | 5 | 50 | 262 | 1.8 | 2.8 | 6.0 |
| 04-05—Atl.-L.A. Clippers | 43 | 743 | 85 | 201 | .423 | 27 | 37 | .730 | 24 | 64 | 88 | 103 | 33 | 0 | 49 | 203 | 2.0 | 2.4 | 4.7 |
| Totals | 858 | 25868 | 4002 | 9512 | .421 | 2238 | 2833 | .790 | 670 | 1971 | 2641 | 5196 | 1258 | 111 | 1769 | 10789 | 3.1 | 6.1 | 12.6 |

Three-point field goals: 1991-92, 3-for-13 (.231). 1992-93, 7-for-25 (.280). 1993-94, 40-for-132 (.303). 1994-95, 97-for-294 (.330). 1995-96, 92-for-256 (.359). 1996-97, 132-for-366 (.361). 1997-98, 57-for-160 (.356). 1998-99, 6-for-24 (.250). 1999-00, 85-for-220 (.386). 2000-01, 11-for-33 (.333). 2001-02, 9-for-33 (.273). 2002-03, 1-for-7 (.143). 2003-04, 1-for-4 (.250). 2004-05, 6-for-13 (.462). Totals, 547-for-1580 (.346).

Personal fouls/disqualifications: 1991-92, 68/0. 1992-93, 140/1. 1993-94, 201/0. 1994-95, 184/1. 1995-96, 178/1. 1996-97, 222/2. 1997-98, 135/1. 1998-99, 78/1. 1999-00, 230/4. 2000-01, 62/0. 2001-02, 210/4. 2002-03, 106/0. 2003-04, 73/0. 2004-05, 87/1. Totals, 1974/16.

## NBA PLAYOFF RECORD

| Season Team | G | Min. | FGM | FGA | Pct. | FTM | FTA | Pct. | Off. | Def. | Tot. | Ast. | St. | Blk. | TO | Pts. | RPG | APG | PPG |
|---|---|---|---|---|---|---|---|---|---|---|---|---|---|---|---|---|---|---|---|
| 91-92—New Jersey | 3 | 24 | 3 | 9 | .333 | 2 | 2 | 1.000 | 1 | 2 | 3 | 3 | 1 | 0 | 1 | 8 | 1.0 | 1.0 | 2.7 |
| 93-94—New Jersey | 4 | 181 | 19 | 54 | .352 | 22 | 33 | .667 | 2 | 10 | 12 | 27 | 9 | 0 | 9 | 63 | 3.0 | 6.8 | 15.8 |
| 96-97—Portland | 4 | 169 | 22 | 46 | .478 | 19 | 20 | .950 | 2 | 15 | 17 | 19 | 7 | 1 | 11 | 68 | 4.3 | 4.8 | 17.0 |
| 01-02—Boston | 16 | 560 | 82 | 197 | .416 | 28 | 35 | .800 | 13 | 37 | 50 | 76 | 21 | 0 | 28 | 192 | 3.1 | 4.8 | 12.0 |
| 02-03—New Orleans | 5 | 51 | 4 | 12 | .333 | 3 | 3 | 1.000 | 0 | 2 | 2 | 9 | 3 | 0 | 4 | 11 | 0.4 | 1.8 | 2.2 |
| 03-04—Indiana | 4 | 19 | 2 | 7 | .286 | 0 | 0 | ... | 0 | 1 | 1 | 1 | 1 | 0 | 5 | 4 | 0.3 | 0.3 | 1.0 |
| Totals | 36 | 1004 | 132 | 325 | .406 | 74 | 93 | .796 | 18 | 67 | 85 | 135 | 42 | 1 | 58 | 346 | 2.4 | 3.8 | 9.6 |

Three-point field goals: 1993-94, 3-for-10 (.300). 1996-97, 5-for-19 (.263). Totals, 8-for-29 (.276).

Personal fouls/disqualifications: 1991-92, 1/0. 1993-94, 11/0. 1996-97, 10/0. 2001-02, 58/1. 2002-03, 6/0. 2003-04, 3/0. Totals, 89/1.

## NBA ALL-STAR GAME RECORD

| Season Team | Min. | FGM | FGA | Pct. | FTM | FTA | Pct. | Off. | Def. | Tot. | Ast. | PF | Dq. | St. | Blk. | TO | Pts. |
|---|---|---|---|---|---|---|---|---|---|---|---|---|---|---|---|---|---|
| 1994—New Jersey | 16 | 3 | 10 | .300 | 0 | 0 | ... | 1 | 3 | 4 | 3 | 2 | 0 | 0 | 0 | 4 | 6 |

Three-point field goals: 1994, 0-for-1. Totals, 0-for-1 (.000).

# ANDERSON, SHANDON     F

**PERSONAL:** Born December 31, 1973, in Atlanta. ... 6-6/210. (1.98/95.3). ... Full name: Shandon Rodriguez Anderson ... Brother of Willie Anderson, guard/forward with San Antonio Spurs (1988-89 through 1994-95), Toronto Raptors (1995-96), New York Knicks (1995-96) and Miami Heat (1996-97).

**HIGH SCHOOL:** Crim (Atlanta).

**COLLEGE:** Georgia.

**TRANSACTIONS/CAREER NOTES:** Selected by Utah Jazz in second round (54th pick overall) of 1996 NBA Draft. ... Signed as free agent by Houston Rockets (September 29, 1999). ... Traded by Rockets to New York Knicks as part of three-team trade in which Knicks acquired G Howard Eisley from Mavericks, Mavericks acquired G Muggsy Bogues from Knicks and Rockets acquired F Glen Rice from Knicks and draft rights to G Kyle Hill from Mavericks (August 10, 2001). ... Waived by Knicks (November 9, 2004). ... Signed as free agent by Miami Heat (November 14, 2004).

## COLLEGIATE RECORD

| Season Team | G | Min. | FGM | FGA | Pct. | FTM | FTA | Pct. | Reb. | Ast. | Pts. | RPG | APG | PPG |
|---|---|---|---|---|---|---|---|---|---|---|---|---|---|---|
| 92-93—Georgia | 29 | 554 | 99 | 201 | .493 | 64 | 105 | .610 | 103 | 44 | 271 | 3.6 | 1.5 | 9.3 |
| 93-94—Georgia | 30 | 859 | 157 | 324 | .485 | 93 | 141 | .660 | 168 | 114 | 413 | 5.6 | 3.8 | 13.8 |
| 94-95—Georgia | 28 | 827 | 149 | 315 | .473 | 59 | 95 | .621 | 145 | 83 | 371 | 5.2 | 3.0 | 13.3 |
| 95-96—Georgia | 31 | 891 | 176 | 327 | .538 | 94 | 143 | .657 | 171 | 83 | 462 | 5.5 | 2.7 | 14.9 |
| Totals | 118 | 3131 | 581 | 1167 | .498 | 310 | 484 | .640 | 587 | 324 | 1517 | 5.0 | 2.7 | 12.9 |

Three-point field goals: 1992-93, 9-for-26 (.346). 1993-94, 6-for-34 (.176). 1994-95, 17-for-53 (.321). 1995-96, 16-for-52 (.308). Totals, 48-for-165 (.291).

### NBA REGULAR-SEASON RECORD

| Season Team | G | Min. | FGM | FGA | Pct. | FTM | FTA | Pct. | REBOUNDS Off. | Def. | Tot. | Ast. | St. | Blk. | TO | Pts. | AVERAGES RPG | APG | PPG |
|---|---|---|---|---|---|---|---|---|---|---|---|---|---|---|---|---|---|---|---|
| 96-97—Utah | 65 | 1066 | 147 | 318 | .462 | 68 | 99 | .687 | 52 | 127 | 179 | 49 | 27 | 8 | 73 | 386 | 2.8 | 0.8 | 5.9 |
| 97-98—Utah | 82 | 1602 | 269 | 500 | .538 | 136 | 185 | .735 | 86 | 141 | 227 | 89 | 66 | 18 | 92 | 681 | 2.8 | 1.1 | 8.3 |
| 98-99—Utah | 50 | 1072 | 162 | 363 | .446 | 89 | 125 | .712 | 49 | 83 | 132 | 56 | 39 | 10 | 66 | 427 | 2.6 | 1.1 | 8.5 |
| 99-00—Houston | 82 | 2700 | 368 | 778 | .473 | 194 | 253 | .767 | 91 | 293 | 384 | 239 | 96 | 32 | 194 | 1009 | 4.7 | 2.9 | 12.3 |
| 00-01—Houston | 82 | 2396 | 263 | 590 | .446 | 138 | 188 | .734 | 72 | 261 | 333 | 189 | 82 | 40 | 131 | 710 | 4.1 | 2.3 | 8.7 |
| 01-02—New York | 82 | 1596 | 149 | 373 | .399 | 74 | 107 | .692 | 57 | 192 | 249 | 76 | 48 | 15 | 97 | 411 | 3.0 | 0.9 | 5.0 |
| 02-03—New York | 82 | 1731 | 248 | 537 | .462 | 139 | 190 | .732 | 64 | 190 | 254 | 87 | 73 | 20 | 114 | 687 | 3.1 | 1.1 | 8.4 |
| 03-04—New York | 80 | 1974 | 238 | 564 | .422 | 123 | 161 | .764 | 53 | 169 | 222 | 122 | 68 | 17 | 118 | 635 | 2.8 | 1.5 | 7.9 |
| 04-05—N.Y.-Miami | 66 | 1171 | 98 | 217 | .452 | 54 | 66 | .818 | 41 | 150 | 191 | 70 | 40 | 14 | 50 | 255 | 2.9 | 1.1 | 3.9 |
| **Totals** | 671 | 15308 | 1942 | 4240 | .458 | 1015 | 1374 | .739 | 565 | 1606 | 2171 | 977 | 539 | 174 | 935 | 5201 | 3.2 | 1.5 | 7.8 |

Three-point field goals: 1996-97, 24-for-47 (.511). 1997-98, 7-for-32 (.219). 1998-99, 14-for-41 (.341). 1999-00, 79-for-225 (.351). 2000-01, 46-for-170 (.271). 2001-02, 39-for-141 (.277). 2002-03, 52-for-140 (.371). 2003-04, 36-for-128 (.281). 2004-05, 5-for-29 (.172). Totals, 302-for-953 (.317).
Personal fouls/disqualifications: 1996-97, 113/0. 1997-98, 145/0. 1998-99, 89/0. 1999-00, 182/0. 2000-01, 202/0. 2001-02, 134/1. 2002-03, 177/1. 2003-04, 182/1. 2004-05, 138/1. Totals, 1362/4.

### NBA PLAYOFF RECORD

| Season Team | G | Min. | FGM | FGA | Pct. | FTM | FTA | Pct. | REBOUNDS Off. | Def. | Tot. | Ast. | St. | Blk. | TO | Pts. | AVERAGES RPG | APG | PPG |
|---|---|---|---|---|---|---|---|---|---|---|---|---|---|---|---|---|---|---|---|
| 96-97—Utah | 18 | 296 | 29 | 66 | .439 | 20 | 28 | .714 | 20 | 28 | 48 | 13 | 11 | 1 | 13 | 83 | 2.7 | 0.7 | 4.6 |
| 97-98—Utah | 20 | 378 | 53 | 103 | .515 | 26 | 37 | .676 | 26 | 37 | 63 | 19 | 5 | 1 | 30 | 134 | 3.2 | 1.0 | 6.7 |
| 98-99—Utah | 11 | 297 | 37 | 77 | .481 | 24 | 34 | .706 | 8 | 33 | 41 | 13 | 6 | 3 | 14 | 104 | 3.7 | 1.2 | 9.5 |
| 03-04—New York | 4 | 117 | 7 | 27 | .259 | 1 | 2 | .500 | 5 | 4 | 9 | 11 | 4 | 1 | 8 | 17 | 2.3 | 2.8 | 4.3 |
| 04-05—Miami | 8 | 97 | 3 | 12 | .250 | 2 | 2 | 1.000 | 3 | 16 | 19 | 8 | 5 | 0 | 6 | 8 | 2.4 | 1.0 | 1.0 |
| **Totals** | 61 | 1185 | 129 | 285 | .453 | 72 | 103 | .699 | 62 | 118 | 180 | 64 | 31 | 6 | 71 | 346 | 3.0 | 1.0 | 5.7 |

Three-point field goals: 1996-97, 5-for-12 (.417). 1997-98, 3-for-11 (.273). 1998-99, 6-for-14 (.429). 2003-04, 2-for-7 (.286). 2004-05, 0-for-1. Totals, 16-for-45 (.356).
Personal fouls/disqualifications: 1996-97, 28/0. 1997-98, 30/0. 1998-99, 34/2. 2003-04, 19/0. 2004-05, 10/0. Totals, 121/2.

## ANTHONY, CARMELO     F     NUGGETS

**PERSONAL:** Born May 29, 1984, in New York, N.Y. ... 6-8/220. (2.03/99.8). ... Full name: Carmelo K. Anthony
**HIGH SCHOOL:** Towson Catholic (Towson, Md.), then Oak Hill Academy.
**COLLEGE:** Syracuse.
**TRANSACTIONS/CAREER NOTES:** Selected after freshman season by Denver Nuggets in first round (third pick overall) of 2003 NBA Draft.
**MISCELLANEOUS:** Member of bronze-medal-winning U.S. Olympic Team (2004).

### COLLEGIATE RECORD

**NOTES:** Member of NCAA Division I championship team (2003). ... The Sporting News All-America first team (2003). ... The Sporting News Freshman of the Year (2003). ... NCAA Division I Tournament Most Outstanding Player (2003).

| Season Team | G | Min. | FGM | FGA | Pct. | FTM | FTA | Pct. | Reb. | Ast. | Pts. | AVERAGES RPG | APG | PPG |
|---|---|---|---|---|---|---|---|---|---|---|---|---|---|---|
| 02-03—Syracuse | 35 | 1274 | 277 | 612 | .453 | 168 | 238 | .706 | 349 | 77 | 778 | 10.0 | 2.2 | 22.2 |

Three-point field goals: 2002-03, 56-for-166 (.337). Totals, 56-for-166 (.337).

### NBA REGULAR-SEASON RECORD

**HONORS:** NBA All-Rookie first team (2004).

| Season Team | G | Min. | FGM | FGA | Pct. | FTM | FTA | Pct. | REBOUNDS Off. | Def. | Tot. | Ast. | St. | Blk. | TO | Pts. | AVERAGES RPG | APG | PPG |
|---|---|---|---|---|---|---|---|---|---|---|---|---|---|---|---|---|---|---|---|
| 03-04—Denver | 82 | 2995 | 624 | 1465 | .426 | 408 | 525 | .777 | 183 | 315 | 498 | 227 | 97 | 41 | 247 | 1725 | 6.1 | 2.8 | 21.0 |
| 04-05—Denver | 75 | 2608 | 530 | 1230 | .431 | 456 | 573 | .796 | 141 | 285 | 426 | 194 | 68 | 30 | 224 | 1558 | 5.7 | 2.6 | 20.8 |
| **Totals** | 157 | 5603 | 1154 | 2695 | .428 | 864 | 1098 | .787 | 324 | 600 | 924 | 421 | 165 | 71 | 471 | 3283 | 5.9 | 2.7 | 20.9 |

Three-point field goals: 2003-04, 69-for-214 (.322). 2004-05, 42-for-158 (.266). Totals, 111-for-372 (.298).
Personal fouls/disqualifications: 2003-04, 225/1. 2004-05, 229/1. Totals, 454/2.

### NBA PLAYOFF RECORD

| Season Team | G | Min. | FGM | FGA | Pct. | FTM | FTA | Pct. | REBOUNDS Off. | Def. | Tot. | Ast. | St. | Blk. | TO | Pts. | AVERAGES RPG | APG | PPG |
|---|---|---|---|---|---|---|---|---|---|---|---|---|---|---|---|---|---|---|---|
| 03-04—Denver | 4 | 143 | 21 | 64 | .328 | 16 | 20 | .800 | 7 | 26 | 33 | 11 | 5 | 0 | 17 | 60 | 8.3 | 2.8 | 15.0 |
| 04-05—Denver | 5 | 180 | 35 | 83 | .422 | 26 | 32 | .813 | 14 | 13 | 27 | 10 | 3 | 1 | 13 | 96 | 5.4 | 2.0 | 19.2 |
| **Totals** | 9 | 323 | 56 | 147 | .381 | 42 | 52 | .808 | 21 | 39 | 60 | 21 | 8 | 1 | 30 | 156 | 6.7 | 2.3 | 17.3 |

Three-point field goals: 2003-04, 2-for-11 (.182). 2004-05, 0-for-1. Totals, 2-for-12 (.167).
Personal fouls/disqualifications: 2003-04, 11/1. 2004-05, 20/0. Totals, 31/1.

## ARAUJO, RAFAEL     C     RAPTORS

**PERSONAL:** Born August 12, 1980, in Curitiba, Brazil. ... 6-11/290. (2.11/131.5). ... Full name: Rafael Paulo Araujo
**HIGH SCHOOL:** Padre Anacleto (Sau Paulo, Brazil).
**JUNIOR COLLEGE:** Arizona Western.
**COLLEGE:** Brigham Young.
**TRANSACTIONS/CAREER NOTES:** Selected by Toronto Raptors in first round (eighth pick overall) of 2004 NBA Draft.

### COLLEGIATE RECORD

| Season Team | G | Min. | FGM | FGA | Pct. | FTM | FTA | Pct. | Reb. | Ast. | Pts. | AVERAGES RPG | APG | PPG |
|---|---|---|---|---|---|---|---|---|---|---|---|---|---|---|
| 00-01—Arizona Western College | 32 | 624 | 150 | 232 | .647 | 84 | 143 | .587 | 269 | 22 | 386 | 8.4 | 0.7 | 12.1 |
| 01-02—Arizona Western College | 31 | 697 | 220 | 386 | .570 | 101 | 149 | .678 | 331 | 29 | 555 | 10.7 | 0.9 | 17.9 |
| 02-03—Brigham Young | 32 | 802 | 155 | 278 | .558 | 70 | 109 | .642 | 286 | 38 | 383 | 8.9 | 1.2 | 12.0 |
| 03-04—Brigham Young | 30 | 895 | 211 | 368 | .573 | 122 | 169 | .722 | 303 | 37 | 552 | 10.1 | 1.2 | 18.4 |
| Junior College Totals | 63 | 1321 | 370 | 618 | .599 | 185 | 292 | .634 | 600 | 51 | 941 | 9.5 | 0.8 | 14.9 |
| 4-Year-College Totals | 62 | 1697 | 366 | 646 | .567 | 192 | 278 | .691 | 589 | 75 | 935 | 9.5 | 1.2 | 15.1 |

Three-point field goals: 2000-01, 2-for-5 (.400). 2001-02, 14-for-49 (.286). 2002-03, 3-for-11 (.273). 2003-04, 8-for-30 (.267). Totals, 27-for-95 (.284).

### NBA REGULAR-SEASON RECORD

| Season Team | G | Min. | FGM | FGA | Pct. | FTM | FTA | Pct. | REBOUNDS Off. | Def. | Tot. | Ast. | St. | Blk. | TO | Pts. | AVERAGES RPG | APG | PPG |
|---|---|---|---|---|---|---|---|---|---|---|---|---|---|---|---|---|---|---|---|
| 04-05—Toronto | 59 | 736 | 76 | 175 | .434 | 43 | 55 | .782 | 59 | 126 | 185 | 16 | 21 | 8 | 52 | 196 | 3.1 | 0.3 | 3.3 |

Three-point field goals: 2004-05, 1-for-3 (.333). Totals, 1-for-3 (.333).
Personal fouls/disqualifications: 2004-05, 157/0. Totals, 157/0.

## ARIZA, TREVOR     F     KNICKS

**PERSONAL:** Born June 30, 1985, in Miami, Fla. ... 6-7/194. (2.01/88.0). ... Full name: Trevor Anthony Ariza
**HIGH SCHOOL:** Westchester (Los Angeles).
**COLLEGE:** UCLA.
**TRANSACTIONS/CAREER NOTES:** Selected after freshman season by New York Knicks in second round (43rd pick overall) of 2004 NBA Draft.

### COLLEGIATE RECORD

| Season Team | G | Min. | FGM | FGA | Pct. | FTM | FTA | Pct. | Reb. | Ast. | Pts. | AVERAGES RPG | APG | PPG |
|---|---|---|---|---|---|---|---|---|---|---|---|---|---|---|
| 03-04—UCLA | 25 | 789 | 107 | 251 | .426 | 57 | 113 | .504 | 162 | 52 | 289 | 6.5 | 2.1 | 11.6 |

Three-point field goals: 2003-04, 18-for-76 (.237). Totals, 18-for-76 (.237).

### NBA REGULAR-SEASON RECORD

| Season Team | G | Min. | FGM | FGA | Pct. | FTM | FTA | Pct. | REBOUNDS Off. | Def. | Tot. | Ast. | St. | Blk. | TO | Pts. | AVERAGES RPG | APG | PPG |
|---|---|---|---|---|---|---|---|---|---|---|---|---|---|---|---|---|---|---|---|
| 04-05—New York | 80 | 1382 | 172 | 389 | .442 | 121 | 174 | .695 | 89 | 153 | 242 | 85 | 70 | 18 | 73 | 468 | 3.0 | 1.1 | 5.9 |

Three-point field goals: 2004-05, 3-for-13 (.231). Totals, 3-for-13 (.231).
Personal fouls/disqualifications: 2004-05, 150/0. Totals, 150/0.

## ARENAS, GILBERT     G     WIZARDS

**PERSONAL:** Born January 6, 1982, in Los Angeles. ... 6-3/191. (1.91/86.6). ... Full name: Gilbert Jay Arenas
**HIGH SCHOOL:** Grant (Van Nuys, Calif.).
**COLLEGE:** Arizona.
**TRANSACTIONS/CAREER NOTES:** Selected after sophomore season by Golden State Warriors in second round (31st pick overall) of 2001 NBA Draft. ... Signed as free agent by Washington Wizards (August 8, 2003).

### COLLEGIATE RECORD

| Season Team | G | Min. | FGM | FGA | Pct. | FTM | FTA | Pct. | Reb. | Ast. | Pts. | AVERAGES RPG | APG | PPG |
|---|---|---|---|---|---|---|---|---|---|---|---|---|---|---|
| 99-00—Arizona | 34 | 1093 | 187 | 413 | .453 | 111 | 148 | .750 | 138 | 71 | 523 | 4.1 | 2.1 | 15.4 |
| 00-01—Arizona | 36 | 1044 | 208 | 434 | .479 | 97 | 134 | .724 | 131 | 84 | 582 | 3.6 | 2.3 | 16.2 |
| Totals | 70 | 2137 | 395 | 847 | .466 | 208 | 282 | .738 | 269 | 155 | 1105 | 3.8 | 2.2 | 15.8 |

Three-point field goals: 1999-00, 38-for-130 (.292). 2000-01, 69-for-166 (.416). Totals, 107-for-296 (.361).
Personal fouls/disqualifications: 1999-00, 83/0. 2000-01, 82/0. Totals, 165/0.

**HONORS:** NBA Most Improved Player award (2003). ... All-NBA third team (2005).

### NBA REGULAR-SEASON RECORD

| Season Team | G | Min. | FGM | FGA | Pct. | FTM | FTA | Pct. | REBOUNDS Off. | Def. | Tot. | Ast. | St. | Blk. | TO | Pts. | AVERAGES RPG | APG | PPG |
|---|---|---|---|---|---|---|---|---|---|---|---|---|---|---|---|---|---|---|---|
| 01-02—Golden State | 47 | 1155 | 174 | 384 | .453 | 124 | 160 | .775 | 41 | 91 | 132 | 174 | 69 | 11 | 97 | 511 | 2.8 | 3.7 | 10.9 |
| 02-03—Golden State | 82 | 2866 | 509 | 1180 | .431 | 370 | 468 | .791 | 97 | 289 | 386 | 514 | 124 | 17 | 290 | 1497 | 4.7 | 6.3 | 18.3 |
| 03-04—Washington | 55 | 2066 | 358 | 914 | .392 | 237 | 317 | .748 | 55 | 199 | 254 | 275 | 103 | 12 | 226 | 1078 | 4.6 | 5.0 | 19.6 |
| 04-05—Washington | 80 | 3274 | 656 | 1523 | .431 | 521 | 640 | .814 | 83 | 295 | 378 | 411 | 139 | 23 | 242 | 2038 | 4.7 | 5.1 | 25.5 |
| Totals | 264 | 9361 | 1697 | 4001 | .424 | 1252 | 1585 | .790 | 276 | 874 | 1150 | 1374 | 435 | 63 | 855 | 5124 | 4.4 | 5.2 | 19.4 |

Three-point field goals: 2001-02, 39-for-113 (.345). 2002-03, 109-for-313 (.348). 2003-04, 125-for-333 (.375). 2004-05, 205-for-562 (.365). Totals, 478-for-1321 (.362).
Personal fouls/disqualifications: 2001-02, 115/3. 2002-03, 260/3. 2003-04, 176/2. 2004-05, 245/1. Totals, 796/9.

### NBA PLAYOFF RECORD

| Season Team | G | Min. | FGM | FGA | Pct. | FTM | FTA | Pct. | REBOUNDS Off. | Def. | Tot. | Ast. | St. | Blk. | TO | Pts. | AVERAGES RPG | APG | PPG |
|---|---|---|---|---|---|---|---|---|---|---|---|---|---|---|---|---|---|---|---|
| 04-05—Washington | 10 | 450 | 73 | 194 | .376 | 92 | 94 | .766 | 8 | 44 | 52 | 62 | 21 | 6 | 39 | 236 | 5.2 | 6.2 | 23.6 |

Three-point field goals: 2004-05, 18-for-77 (.234). Totals, 18-for-77 (.234).
Personal fouls/disqualifications: 2004-05, 34/1. Totals, 34/1.

### NBA ALL-STAR GAME RECORD

| Season Team | Min. | FGM | FGA | Pct. | FTM | FTA | Pct. | REBOUNDS Off. | Def. | Tot. | Ast. | PF | Dq. | St. | Blk. | TO | Pts. |
|---|---|---|---|---|---|---|---|---|---|---|---|---|---|---|---|---|---|
| 2005—Washington | 15 | 3 | 11 | .273 | 0 | 0 | ... | 1 | 1 | 2 | 2 | 1 | 0 | 0 | 0 | 0 | 7 |

Three-point field goals: 2005, 1-for-3 (.333). Totals, 1-for-3 (.333).

# ARMSTRONG, DARRELL　　　　　G　　　　　MAVERICKS

**PERSONAL:** Born June 22, 1968, in Gastonia, N.C. ... 6-1/180. (1.85/81.6).
**HIGH SCHOOL:** Ashbrook (Gastonia, N.C.).
**COLLEGE:** Fayetteville State.
**TRANSACTIONS/CAREER NOTES:** Not drafted by an NBA franchise. ... Played in Global Basketball Association with South Georgia (1991-93). ... Played in United States Basketball League with Atlanta Trojans (1992-94). ... Played in Continental Basketball Association with Capital Region Pontiacs (1992-93). ... Played in Cyprus (1993-94). ... Played in Spain (1994-95). ... Signed as free agent by Orlando Magic (April 8, 1995). ... Signed as free agent by New Orleans Hornets (July 29, 2003) ... Traded by Hornets to Dallas Mavericks for G Dan Dickau and a second-round draft choice (December 3, 2004).

## COLLEGIATE RECORD

| | | | | | | | | | | | | AVERAGES | | |
|---|---|---|---|---|---|---|---|---|---|---|---|---|---|---|
| Season Team | G | Min. | FGM | FGA | Pct. | FTM | FTA | Pct. | Reb. | Ast. | Pts. | RPG | APG | PPG |
| 87-88—Fayetteville State ........... | | | | | | | Did not play. | | | | | | | |
| 88-89—Fayetteville State ........... | 27 | 662 | 131 | 255 | .514 | 93 | 116 | .802 | 80 | 58 | 369 | 3.0 | 2.1 | 13.7 |
| 89-90—Fayetteville State ........... | 27 | 800 | 125 | 235 | .532 | 83 | 106 | .783 | 140 | 125 | 350 | 5.2 | 4.6 | 13.0 |
| 90-91—Fayetteville State ........... | 24 | 643 | 117 | 233 | .502 | 115 | 152 | .757 | 86 | 113 | 393 | 3.6 | 4.7 | 16.4 |
| Totals ..................................... | 78 | 2105 | 373 | 723 | .516 | 291 | 374 | .778 | 306 | 296 | 1112 | 3.9 | 3.8 | 14.3 |

Three-point field goals: 1988-89, 14-for-40 (.350). 1989-90, 17-for-40 (.425). 1990-91, 44-for-107 (.411). Totals, 75-for-187 (.401).

## CBA RECORD

| | | | | | | | | | | | | AVERAGES | | |
|---|---|---|---|---|---|---|---|---|---|---|---|---|---|---|
| Season Team | G | Min. | FGM | FGA | Pct. | FTM | FTA | Pct. | Reb. | Ast. | Pts. | RPG | APG | PPG |
| 92-93—Capital Region ................ | 2 | 13 | 1 | 3 | .333 | 0 | 0 | ... | 1 | 1 | 2 | 0.5 | 0.5 | 1.0 |

Three-point field goals: 1992-93, 0-for-2. Totals, 0-for-2 (.000).

## NBA REGULAR-SEASON RECORD

**HONORS:** NBA Sixth Man Award (1999). ... NBA Most Improved Player (1999).

| | | | | | | | | | REBOUNDS | | | | | | | | AVERAGES | | |
|---|---|---|---|---|---|---|---|---|---|---|---|---|---|---|---|---|---|---|---|---|
| Season Team | G | Min. | FGM | FGA | Pct. | FTM | FTA | Pct. | Off. | Def. | Tot. | Ast. | St. | Blk. | TO | Pts. | RPG | APG | PPG |
| 94-95—Orlando.......... | 3 | 8 | 3 | 8 | .375 | 2 | 2 | 1.000 | 1 | 0 | 1 | 3 | 1 | 0 | 1 | 10 | 0.3 | 1.0 | 3.3 |
| 95-96—Orlando.......... | 13 | 41 | 16 | 32 | .500 | 4 | 4 | 1.000 | 0 | 2 | 2 | 5 | 6 | 0 | 6 | 42 | 0.2 | 0.4 | 3.2 |
| 96-97—Orlando.......... | 67 | 1010 | 132 | 345 | .383 | 92 | 106 | .868 | 35 | 41 | 76 | 175 | 61 | 9 | 99 | 411 | 1.1 | 2.6 | 6.1 |
| 97-98—Orlando.......... | 48 | 1236 | 156 | 380 | .411 | 105 | 123 | .854 | 65 | 94 | 159 | 236 | 58 | 5 | 112 | 442 | 3.3 | 4.9 | 9.2 |
| 98-99—Orlando.......... | 50 | 1502 | 230 | 522 | .441 | 161 | 178 | .904 | 53 | 127 | 180 | 335 | 108 | 4 | 158 | 690 | 3.6 | 6.7 | 13.8 |
| 99-00—Orlando.......... | 82 | 2590 | 484 | 1119 | .433 | 225 | 247 | .911 | 65 | 205 | 270 | 501 | 169 | 9 | 248 | 1330 | 3.3 | 6.1 | 16.2 |
| 00-01—Orlando.......... | 75 | 2767 | 413 | 1002 | .412 | 220 | 249 | .884 | 94 | 249 | 343 | 524 | 135 | 13 | 200 | 1189 | 4.6 | 7.0 | 15.9 |
| 01-02—Orlando.......... | 82 | 2730 | 347 | 828 | .419 | 182 | 205 | .888 | 83 | 236 | 319 | 453 | 157 | 10 | 175 | 1015 | 3.9 | 5.5 | 12.4 |
| 02-03—Orlando.......... | 82 | 2350 | 263 | 643 | .409 | 165 | 188 | .878 | 91 | 204 | 295 | 323 | 135 | 13 | 160 | 769 | 3.6 | 3.9 | 9.4 |
| 03-04—New Orleans ... | 79 | 2247 | 291 | 736 | .395 | 123 | 144 | .854 | 63 | 163 | 226 | 311 | 133 | 16 | 155 | 840 | 2.9 | 3.9 | 10.6 |
| 04-05—N.O.-Dallas ... | 66 | 988 | 89 | 277 | .321 | 58 | 68 | .853 | 35 | 80 | 115 | 178 | 45 | 8 | 67 | 264 | 1.7 | 2.7 | 4.0 |
| Totals ................... | 647 | 17469 | 2424 | 5892 | .411 | 1337 | 1514 | .883 | 585 | 1401 | 1986 | 3044 | 1008 | 87 | 1381 | 7002 | 3.1 | 4.7 | 10.8 |

Three-point field goals: 1994-95, 2-for-6 (.333). 1995-96, 6-for-12 (.500). 1996-97, 55-for-181 (.304). 1997-98, 25-for-68 (.368). 1998-99, 69-for-189 (.365). 1999-00, 137-for-403 (.340). 2000-01, 143-for-403 (.355). 2001-02, 139-for-398 (.349). 2002-03, 78-for-232 (.336). 2003-04, 135-for-429 (.315). 2004-05, 28-for-111 (.252). Totals, 817-for-2432 (.336).

Personal fouls/disqualifications: 1994-95, 3/0. 1995-96, 4/0. 1996-97, 114/1. 1997-98, 96/1. 1998-99, 90/0. 1999-00, 137/0. 2000-01, 155/2. 2001-02, 166/2. 2002-03, 167/1. 2003-04, 148/1. 2004-05, 92/0. Totals, 1172/10.

## NBA PLAYOFF RECORD

| | | | | | | | | | REBOUNDS | | | | | | | | AVERAGES | | |
|---|---|---|---|---|---|---|---|---|---|---|---|---|---|---|---|---|---|---|---|---|
| Season Team | G | Min. | FGM | FGA | Pct. | FTM | FTA | Pct. | Off. | Def. | Tot. | Ast. | St. | Blk. | TO | Pts. | RPG | APG | PPG |
| 96-97—Orlando.......... | 5 | 143 | 20 | 42 | .476 | 11 | 13 | .846 | 3 | 18 | 21 | 17 | 8 | 1 | 7 | 57 | 4.2 | 3.4 | 11.4 |
| 98-99—Orlando.......... | 4 | 163 | 17 | 46 | .370 | 16 | 16 | 1.000 | 6 | 14 | 20 | 25 | 9 | 0 | 25 | 59 | 5.0 | 6.3 | 14.8 |
| 00-01—Orlando.......... | 4 | 167 | 17 | 45 | .378 | 12 | 13 | .923 | 5 | 17 | 22 | 19 | 8 | 2 | 11 | 53 | 5.5 | 4.8 | 13.3 |
| 01-02—Orlando.......... | 4 | 158 | 20 | 42 | .476 | 17 | 21 | .810 | 3 | 8 | 11 | 13 | 5 | 0 | 7 | 61 | 2.8 | 3.3 | 15.3 |
| 02-03—Orlando.......... | 7 | 226 | 20 | 44 | .455 | 20 | 22 | .909 | 7 | 10 | 17 | 26 | 6 | 0 | 17 | 66 | 2.4 | 3.7 | 9.4 |
| 03-04—New Orleans ... | 7 | 150 | 8 | 34 | .235 | 3 | 3 | 1.000 | 6 | 9 | 15 | 16 | 6 | 0 | 13 | 24 | 2.1 | 2.3 | 3.4 |
| 04-05—Dallas............. | 9 | 66 | 8 | 16 | .500 | 0 | 0 | ... | 3 | 1 | 4 | 9 | 3 | 2 | 2 | 18 | 0.4 | 1.0 | 2.0 |
| Totals ................... | 40 | 1073 | 110 | 269 | .409 | 79 | 88 | .898 | 33 | 77 | 110 | 125 | 45 | 5 | 82 | 338 | 2.8 | 3.1 | 8.5 |

Three-point field goals: 1996-97, 6-for-18 (.333). 1998-99, 9-for-24 (.375). 2000-01, 7-for-19 (.368). 2001-02, 4-for-17 (.235). 2002-03, 6-for-18 (.333). 2003-04, 5-for-25 (.200). 2004-05, 2-for-8 (.250). Totals, 39-for-129 (.302).

Personal fouls/disqualifications: 1996-97, 6/0. 1998-99, 16/1. 2000-01, 10/0. 2001-02, 14/0. 2002-03, 22/0. 2003-04, 10/0. 2004-05, 9/0. Totals, 87/1.

## SPANISH RECORD

| | | | | | | | | | | | | AVERAGES | | |
|---|---|---|---|---|---|---|---|---|---|---|---|---|---|---|
| Season Team | G | Min. | FGM | FGA | Pct. | FTM | FTA | Pct. | Reb. | Ast. | Pts. | RPG | APG | PPG |
| 94-95—Coren Orense ................ | 38 | 1481 | 309 | 631 | .490 | 176 | 293 | .601 | 170 | 94 | 936 | 4.5 | 2.5 | 24.6 |

Three-point field goals: 1994-95, 142-for-338 (.420). Totals, 142-for-338 (.420).
Personal fouls/disqualifications: 1994-95, 99/0. Totals, 99/0.

# ARROYO, CARLOS　　　　　G　　　　　PISTONS

**PERSONAL:** Born July 30, 1979, in Fajardo, Puerto Rico. ... 6-2/202. (1.88/91.6).
**HIGH SCHOOL:** Brookwood (Thomasville, Ga.), then Fajardo (Puerto.
**COLLEGE:** Florida International.
**TRANSACTIONS/CAREER NOTES:** Not drafted by an NBA franchise. ... Played in Spain (2001-02). ... Signed as free agent by Toronto Raptors (September 28, 2001). ... Waived by Raptors (January 8, 2002). ... Signed by Denver Nuggets to 10-

day contract (March 7, 2002). ... Signed by Nuggets for remainder of season (March 26, 2002). ... Signed as free agent by Utah Jazz (September 10, 2002). ... Traded by Jazz to Detroit Pistons for C Elden Campbell and a future first-round draft choice (January 21, 2005). **MISCELLANEOUS:** Member of Puerto Rican Olympic Team (2004).

A

### COLLEGIATE RECORD

| Season Team | G | Min. | FGM | FGA | Pct. | FTM | FTA | Pct. | Reb. | Ast. | Pts. | AVERAGES | | |
|---|---|---|---|---|---|---|---|---|---|---|---|---|---|---|
| | | | | | | | | | | | | RPG | APG | PPG |
| 97-98—Florida International ...... | 29 | 773 | 128 | 276 | .464 | 56 | 92 | .609 | 87 | 135 | 347 | 3.0 | 4.7 | 12.0 |
| 98-99—Florida International ...... | 20 | 596 | 83 | 190 | .437 | 50 | 72 | .694 | 57 | 93 | 249 | 2.9 | 4.7 | 12.5 |
| 99-00—Florida International .... | 22 | 792 | 136 | 299 | .455 | 63 | 87 | .724 | 57 | 114 | 389 | 2.6 | 5.2 | 17.7 |
| 00-01—Florida International ...... | 29 | 1113 | 215 | 499 | .431 | 134 | 180 | .744 | 100 | 117 | 616 | 3.4 | 4.0 | 21.2 |
| Totals .................................. | 100 | 3274 | 562 | 1264 | .445 | 303 | 431 | .703 | 301 | 459 | 1601 | 3.0 | 4.6 | 16.0 |

Three-point field goals: 1997-98, 35-for-94 (.372). 1998-99, 33-for-88 (.375). 1999-00, 63-for-87 (.724). 2000-01, 52-for-176 (.295). Totals, 183-for-445 (.411).

### NBA REGULAR-SEASON RECORD

| Season Team | G | Min. | FGM | FGA | Pct. | FTM | FTA | Pct. | REBOUNDS | | | Ast. | St. | Blk. | TO | Pts. | AVERAGES | | |
|---|---|---|---|---|---|---|---|---|---|---|---|---|---|---|---|---|---|---|---|
| | | | | | | | | | Off. | Def. | Tot. | | | | | | RPG | APG | PPG |
| 01-02—Toronto-Den. .. | 37 | 371 | 49 | 111 | .441 | 13 | 18 | .722 | 12 | 28 | 40 | 70 | 11 | 1 | 23 | 111 | 1.1 | 1.9 | 3.0 |
| 02-03—Utah .............. | 44 | 287 | 50 | 109 | .459 | 18 | 22 | .818 | 11 | 15 | 26 | 53 | 12 | 1 | 30 | 121 | 0.6 | 1.2 | 2.8 |
| 03-04—Utah .............. | 71 | 2008 | 339 | 768 | .441 | 181 | 225 | .804 | 41 | 144 | 185 | 355 | 63 | 5 | 156 | 897 | 2.6 | 5.0 | 12.6 |
| 04-05—Utah-Detroit.... | 70 | 1448 | 167 | 429 | .389 | 119 | 149 | .799 | 26 | 78 | 104 | 280 | 44 | 4 | 107 | 461 | 1.5 | 4.0 | 6.6 |
| Totals .................. | 222 | 4114 | 605 | 1417 | .427 | 331 | 414 | .800 | 90 | 265 | 355 | 758 | 130 | 11 | 316 | 1590 | 1.6 | 3.4 | 7.2 |

Three-point field goals: 2001-02, 0-for-2. 2002-03, 3-for-7 (.429). 2003-04, 38-for-117 (.325). 2004-05, 8-for-30 (.267). Totals, 49-for-156 (.314). Personal fouls/disqualifications: 2001-02, 30/0. 2002-03, 28/0. 2003-04, 165/0. 2004-05, 143/0. Totals, 366/0.

### NBA PLAYOFF RECORD

| Season Team | G | Min. | FGM | FGA | Pct. | FTM | FTA | Pct. | REBOUNDS | | | Ast. | St. | Blk. | TO | Pts. | AVERAGES | | |
|---|---|---|---|---|---|---|---|---|---|---|---|---|---|---|---|---|---|---|---|
| | | | | | | | | | Off. | Def. | Tot. | | | | | | RPG | APG | PPG |
| 02-03—Utah .............. | 3 | 27 | 3 | 9 | .333 | 3 | 4 | .750 | 2 | 0 | 2 | 5 | 0 | 0 | 0 | 9 | 0.7 | 1.7 | 3.0 |
| 04-05—Detroit .......... | 19 | 150 | 16 | 45 | .356 | 8 | 12 | .667 | 1 | 9 | 10 | 39 | 4 | 2 | 10 | 40 | 0.5 | 2.1 | 2.1 |
| Totals .................. | 22 | 177 | 19 | 54 | .352 | 11 | 16 | .688 | 3 | 9 | 12 | 44 | 4 | 2 | 10 | 49 | 0.5 | 2.0 | 2.2 |

Three-point field goals: 2004-05, 0-for-1. Totals, 0-for-1 (.000). Personal fouls/disqualifications: 2002-03, 2/0. 2004-05, 19/0. Totals, 21/0.

### SPANISH RECORD

| Season Team | G | Min. | FGM | FGA | Pct. | FTM | FTA | Pct. | Reb. | Ast. | Pts. | AVERAGES | | |
|---|---|---|---|---|---|---|---|---|---|---|---|---|---|---|
| | | | | | | | | | | | | RPG | APG | PPG |
| 01-02—Tau Ceramica................. | 4 | 32 | 3 | 9 | .333 | 10 | 11 | .909 | 2 | 4 | 17 | 0.5 | 1.0 | 4.3 |

Three-point field goals: 2001-02, 1-for-3 (.333). Totals, 1-for-3 (.333).

## ARTEST, RON     G/F     PACERS

**PERSONAL:** Born November 13, 1979, in Queensbridge, N.Y. ... 6-7/246. (2.01/111.6). ... Full name: Ronald William Artest **HIGH SCHOOL:** La Salle Academy (New York, N.Y.).
**COLLEGE:** St. John's.
**TRANSACTIONS/CAREER NOTES:** Selected after sophomore season by Chicago Bulls in first round (16th pick overall) of 1999 NBA Draft. ... Traded by Bulls with C Brad Miller, G Ron Mercer and G Kevin Ollie to Indiana Pacers for G Jalen Rose, G Travis Best, G Norman Richardson and conditional second-round draft choice (February 19, 2002).

### COLLEGIATE RECORD

| Season Team | G | Min. | FGM | FGA | Pct. | FTM | FTA | Pct. | Reb. | Ast. | Pts. | AVERAGES | | |
|---|---|---|---|---|---|---|---|---|---|---|---|---|---|---|
| | | | | | | | | | | | | RPG | APG | PPG |
| 97-98—St. John's ...................... | 32 | 870 | 139 | 335 | .415 | 60 | 114 | .526 | 201 | 62 | 372 | 6.3 | 1.9 | 11.6 |
| 98-99—St. John's ...................... | 37 | 1265 | 196 | 418 | .469 | 85 | 132 | .644 | 232 | 156 | 535 | 6.3 | 4.2 | 14.5 |
| Totals ...................................... | 69 | 2135 | 335 | 753 | .445 | 145 | 246 | .589 | 433 | 218 | 907 | 6.3 | 3.2 | 13.1 |

Three-point field goals: 1997-98, 34-for-104 (.327). 1998-99, 58-for-155 (.374). Totals, 92-for-259 (.355).

### NBA REGULAR-SEASON RECORD

**HONORS:** NBA Defensive Player of the Year (2004). ... All-NBA third team (2004). ... NBA All-Defensive first team (2004). ... NBA All-Defensive second team (2003). ... NBA All-Rookie second team (2000).

| Season Team | G | Min. | FGM | FGA | Pct. | FTM | FTA | Pct. | REBOUNDS | | | Ast. | St. | Blk. | TO | Pts. | AVERAGES | | |
|---|---|---|---|---|---|---|---|---|---|---|---|---|---|---|---|---|---|---|---|
| | | | | | | | | | Off. | Def. | Tot. | | | | | | RPG | APG | PPG |
| 99-00—Chicago ......... | 72 | 2238 | 309 | 759 | .407 | 188 | 279 | .674 | 62 | 246 | 308 | 202 | 119 | 39 | 166 | 866 | 4.3 | 2.8 | 12.0 |
| 00-01—Chicago ......... | 76 | 2363 | 327 | 815 | .401 | 210 | 280 | .750 | 59 | 235 | 294 | 228 | 152 | 45 | 159 | 907 | 3.9 | 3.0 | 11.9 |
| 01-02—Chi.-Indiana ... | 55 | 1642 | 269 | 636 | .423 | 136 | 204 | .667 | 73 | 198 | 271 | 127 | 141 | 39 | 118 | 727 | 4.9 | 2.3 | 13.2 |
| 02-03—Indiana.......... | 69 | 2317 | 362 | 846 | .428 | 273 | 371 | .736 | 101 | 261 | 362 | 198 | 159 | 50 | 145 | 1068 | 5.2 | 2.9 | 15.5 |
| 03-04—Indiana.......... | 73 | 2714 | 468 | 1112 | .421 | 322 | 439 | .733 | 100 | 285 | 385 | 272 | 152 | 50 | 202 | 1333 | 5.3 | 3.7 | 18.3 |
| 04-05—Indiana.......... | 7 | 291 | 59 | 119 | .496 | 47 | 51 | .922 | 8 | 37 | 45 | 22 | 12 | 6 | 17 | 172 | 6.4 | 3.1 | 24.6 |
| Totals .................. | 352 | 11565 | 1794 | 4287 | .418 | 1176 | 1624 | .724 | 403 | 1262 | 1665 | 1049 | 735 | 229 | 807 | 5073 | 4.7 | 3.0 | 14.4 |

Three-point field goals: 1999-00, 60-for-191 (.314). 2000-01, 43-for-148 (.291). 2001-02, 53-for-170 (.312). 2002-03, 71-for-211 (.336). 2003-04, 75-for-242 (.310). 2004-05, 7-for-17 (.412). Totals, 309-for-979 (.316).
Personal fouls/disqualifications: 1999-00, 159/0. 2000-01, 254/7. 2001-02, 217/10. 2002-03, 242/7. 2003-04, 194/2. 2004-05, 27/0. Totals, 1093/26.

### NBA PLAYOFF RECORD

| Season Team | G | Min. | FGM | FGA | Pct. | FTM | FTA | Pct. | REBOUNDS | | | Ast. | St. | Blk. | TO | Pts. | AVERAGES | | |
|---|---|---|---|---|---|---|---|---|---|---|---|---|---|---|---|---|---|---|---|
| | | | | | | | | | Off. | Def. | Tot. | | | | | | RPG | APG | PPG |
| 01-02—Indiana.......... | 5 | 167 | 22 | 54 | .407 | 9 | 13 | .692 | 6 | 24 | 30 | 16 | 13 | 3 | 9 | 59 | 6.0 | 3.2 | 11.8 |
| 02-03—Indiana.......... | 6 | 252 | 35 | 90 | .389 | 32 | 40 | .800 | 11 | 24 | 35 | 13 | 15 | 6 | 16 | 114 | 5.8 | 2.2 | 19.0 |
| 03-04—Indiana.......... | 15 | 584 | 98 | 259 | .378 | 61 | 85 | .718 | 24 | 74 | 98 | 48 | 21 | 16 | 37 | 276 | 6.5 | 3.2 | 18.4 |
| Totals .................. | 26 | 1003 | 155 | 403 | .385 | 102 | 138 | .739 | 41 | 122 | 163 | 77 | 49 | 25 | 62 | 449 | 6.3 | 3.0 | 17.3 |

Three-point field goals: 2001-02, 6-for-13 (.462). 2002-03, 12-for-31 (.387). 2003-04, 19-for-66 (.288). Totals, 37-for-110 (.336).

Personal fouls/disqualifications: 2001-02, 19/1. 2002-03, 25/2. 2003-04, 45/2. Totals, 89/5.

## NBA ALL-STAR GAME RECORD

| Season Team | Min. | FGM | FGA | Pct. | FTM | FTA | Pct. | REBOUNDS Off. | Def. | Tot. | Ast. | PF | Dq. | St. | Blk. | TO | Pts. |
|---|---|---|---|---|---|---|---|---|---|---|---|---|---|---|---|---|---|
| 2004—Indiana | 17 | 3 | 5 | .600 | 1 | 2 | .500 | 1 | 2 | 3 | 3 | 2 | 0 | 1 | 0 | 1 | 7 |

Three-point field goals: 2004, 0-for-1. Totals, 0-for-1 (.000).

A

# ATKINS, CHUCKY     G     WIZARDS

**PERSONAL:** Born August 14, 1974, in Orlando, Fla. ... 5-11/160. (1.80/72.6). ... Full name: Kenneth Lavon Atkins
**HIGH SCHOOL:** Evans (Orlando, Fla.).
**COLLEGE:** South Florida.
**TRANSACTIONS/CAREER NOTES:** Not drafted by an NBA franchise. ... Played in Continental Basketball Association with LaCrosse Catbirds (1996-97). ... Played in Croatia (1997-99). ... Signed as free agent by Orlando Magic (September 20, 1999). ... Traded by Magic with F Ben Wallace to Detroit Pistons for F Grant Hill (August 3, 2000). ... Traded by Pistons to Boston Celtics as part of three-team deal in which Celtics also received G Lindsey Hunter and a 2004 first-round draft choice from Pistons. Atlanta Hawks received F Zeljko Rebraca, G Bob Sura and a future first-round draft choice from Pistons and F Chris Mills from Celtics. Pistons received F/C Rasheed Wallace from Hawks and G Mike James from Celtics (February 19, 2004). ... Traded by Celtics with F/C Chris Mihm and F Jumaine Jones to Los Angeles Lakers for G Gary Payton, F Rick Fox and a first-round draft choice (August 6, 2004). ... Traded by Lakers with F Caron Butler to Washington Wizards for C Kwame Brown and F Laron Profit (August 2, 2005).

## COLLEGIATE RECORD

| Season Team | G | Min. | FGM | FGA | Pct. | FTM | FTA | Pct. | Reb. | Ast. | Pts. | AVERAGES RPG | APG | PPG |
|---|---|---|---|---|---|---|---|---|---|---|---|---|---|---|
| 92-93—South Florida | 27 | 867 | 94 | 221 | .425 | 46 | 72 | .639 | 93 | 108 | 275 | 3.4 | 4.0 | 10.2 |
| 93-94—South Florida | 26 | 787 | 96 | 269 | .357 | 70 | 94 | .745 | 62 | 105 | 299 | 2.4 | 4.0 | 11.5 |
| 94-95—South Florida | 30 | 1067 | 161 | 389 | .414 | 98 | 131 | .748 | 96 | 196 | 504 | 3.2 | 6.5 | 16.8 |
| 95-96—South Florida | 28 | 1064 | 175 | 405 | .432 | 109 | 141 | .773 | 85 | 111 | 541 | 3.0 | 4.0 | 19.3 |
| **Totals** | 111 | 3785 | 526 | 1284 | .410 | 323 | 438 | .737 | 336 | 520 | 1619 | 3.0 | 4.7 | 14.6 |

Three-point field goals: 1992-93, 41-for-101 (.406). 1993-94, 37-for-134 (.276). 1994-95, 84-for-219 (.384). 1995-96, 82-for-220 (.373). Totals, 244-for-674 (.362).

Personal fouls/disqualifications: 1992-93, 51/0. 1993-94, 48/0. 1994-95, 55/0. 1995-96, 54/0. Totals, 208/0.

## CBA RECORD

**NOTES:** CBA All-Rookie first team (1997).

| Season Team | G | Min. | FGM | FGA | Pct. | FTM | FTA | Pct. | Reb. | Ast. | Pts. | AVERAGES RPG | APG | PPG |
|---|---|---|---|---|---|---|---|---|---|---|---|---|---|---|
| 96-97—La Crosse | 50 | 1907 | 288 | 644 | .447 | 148 | 189 | .783 | 139 | 375 | 812 | 2.8 | 7.5 | 16.2 |

Three-point field goals: 1996-97, 88-for-240 (.367). Totals, 88-for-240 (.367).
Personal fouls/disqualifications: 1996-97, 128/0. Totals, 128/0.

## CROATION RECORD

| Season Team | G | Min. | FGM | FGA | Pct. | FTM | FTA | Pct. | Reb. | Ast. | Pts. | AVERAGES RPG | APG | PPG |
|---|---|---|---|---|---|---|---|---|---|---|---|---|---|---|
| 97-98—Cibona Zagreb | 26 | 603 | 108 | 190 | .568 | 76 | 98 | .776 | 98 | 97 | 318 | 3.8 | 3.7 | 12.2 |
| 98-99—Cibona Zagreb | 20 | 512 | 84 | 145 | .579 | 40 | 56 | .714 | 24 | 49 | 225 | 1.2 | 2.5 | 11.3 |
| **Totals** | 46 | 1115 | 192 | 335 | .573 | 116 | 154 | .753 | 122 | 146 | 543 | 2.7 | 3.2 | 11.8 |

Three-point field goals: 1997-98, 26-for-59 (.441). 1998-99, 17-for-48 (.354). Totals, 43-for-107 (.402).
Personal fouls/disqualifications: 1997-98, 24/0. 1998-99, 38/0. Totals, 62/0.

## NBA REGULAR-SEASON RECORD

**HONORS:** NBA All-Rookie second team (2000).

| Season Team | G | Min. | FGM | FGA | Pct. | FTM | FTA | Pct. | REBOUNDS Off. | Def. | Tot. | Ast. | St. | Blk. | TO | Pts. | AVERAGES RPG | APG | PPG |
|---|---|---|---|---|---|---|---|---|---|---|---|---|---|---|---|---|---|---|---|
| 99-00—Orlando | 82 | 1626 | 314 | 741 | .424 | 97 | 133 | .729 | 20 | 106 | 126 | 306 | 52 | 3 | 142 | 782 | 1.5 | 3.7 | 9.5 |
| 00-01—Detroit | 81 | 2363 | 380 | 952 | .399 | 90 | 130 | .692 | 28 | 145 | 173 | 330 | 67 | 5 | 149 | 971 | 2.1 | 4.1 | 12.0 |
| 01-02—Detroit | 79 | 2285 | 368 | 790 | .466 | 83 | 120 | .692 | 31 | 127 | 158 | 263 | 72 | 11 | 128 | 957 | 2.0 | 3.3 | 12.1 |
| 02-03—Detroit | 65 | 1398 | 168 | 465 | .361 | 40 | 49 | .816 | 21 | 75 | 96 | 175 | 27 | 4 | 77 | 462 | 1.5 | 2.7 | 7.1 |
| 03-04—Detroit-Boston | 64 | 1544 | 192 | 484 | .397 | 73 | 97 | .753 | 9 | 84 | 93 | 223 | 45 | 2 | 92 | 538 | 1.5 | 3.5 | 8.4 |
| 04-05—L.A. Lakers | 82 | 2903 | 388 | 910 | .426 | 163 | 203 | .803 | 31 | 166 | 197 | 358 | 73 | 2 | 151 | 1115 | 2.4 | 4.4 | 13.6 |
| **Totals** | 453 | 12119 | 1810 | 4342 | .417 | 546 | 732 | .746 | 140 | 703 | 843 | 1655 | 336 | 27 | 739 | 4825 | 1.9 | 3.7 | 10.7 |

Three-point field goals: 1999-00, 57-for-163 (.350). 2000-01, 121-for-339 (.357). 2001-02, 138-for-336 (.411). 2002-03, 86-for-242 (.355). 2003-04, 81-for-241 (.336). 2004-05, 176-for-455 (.387). Totals, 659-for-1776 (.371).
Personal fouls/disqualifications: 1999-00, 137/1. 2000-01, 184/2. 2001-02, 177/1. 2002-03, 108/0. 2003-04, 102/0. 2004-05, 181/0. Totals, 889/4.

## NBA PLAYOFF RECORD

| Season Team | G | Min. | FGM | FGA | Pct. | FTM | FTA | Pct. | REBOUNDS Off. | Def. | Tot. | Ast. | St. | Blk. | TO | Pts. | AVERAGES RPG | APG | PPG |
|---|---|---|---|---|---|---|---|---|---|---|---|---|---|---|---|---|---|---|---|
| 01-02—Detroit | 10 | 294 | 43 | 118 | .364 | 13 | 17 | .765 | 5 | 19 | 24 | 34 | 6 | 1 | 14 | 113 | 2.4 | 3.4 | 11.3 |
| 02-03—Detroit | 17 | 312 | 32 | 91 | .352 | 21 | 26 | .808 | 2 | 18 | 20 | 26 | 17 | 0 | 18 | 103 | 1.2 | 1.5 | 6.1 |
| 03-04—Boston | 4 | 133 | 17 | 39 | .436 | 17 | 19 | .895 | 3 | 11 | 14 | 15 | 3 | 0 | 10 | 54 | 3.5 | 3.8 | 13.5 |
| **Totals** | 31 | 739 | 92 | 248 | .371 | 51 | 62 | .823 | 10 | 48 | 58 | 75 | 26 | 1 | 42 | 270 | 1.9 | 2.4 | 8.7 |

Three-point field goals: 2001-02, 14-for-39 (.359). 2002-03, 18-for-49 (.367). 2003-04, 3-for-10 (.300). Totals, 35-for-98 (.357).
Personal fouls/disqualifications: 2001-02, 25/0. 2002-03, 39/0. 2003-04, 2/0. Totals, 66/0.

## AUGMON, STACEY — F — MAGIC

**PERSONAL:** Born August 1, 1968, in Pasadena, Calif. ... 6-8/213. (2.03/96.6). ... Full name: Stacey Orlando Augmon ... Name pronounced AWG-men.
**HIGH SCHOOL:** John Muir (Pasadena, Calif.).
**COLLEGE:** UNLV.
**TRANSACTIONS/CAREER NOTES:** Selected by Atlanta Hawks in first round (ninth pick overall) of 1991 NBA Draft. ... Traded by Hawks with F Grant Long to Detroit Pistons for three conditional draft choices (July 15, 1996). ... Traded by Pistons to Portland Trail Blazers for G Aaron McKie, G Randolph Childress and G Reggie Jordan (January 24, 1997). ... Traded by Trail Blazers with C Kelvin Cato, G/F Walt Williams, G Brian Shaw, G Ed Gray and F/C Carlos Rogers to Houston Rockets for F Scottie Pippen (October 2, 1999). ... Waived by Rockets (October 12, 1999). ... Signed as free agent by Trail Blazers (October 18, 1999). ... Signed as free agent by Charlotte Hornets (July 25, 2001). ... Hornets franchise moved to New Orleans for 2002-03 season. ... Signed as free agent by Orlando Magic (August 2, 2004).
**MISCELLANEOUS:** Member of bronze-medal-winning U.S. Olympic team (1988).

### COLLEGIATE RECORD

**NOTES:** THE SPORTING NEWS All-America first team (1991). ... Member of NCAA Division I championship team (1990).

| Season Team | G | Min. | FGM | FGA | Pct. | FTM | FTA | Pct. | Reb. | Ast. | Pts. | RPG | APG | PPG |
|---|---|---|---|---|---|---|---|---|---|---|---|---|---|---|
| 86-87—UNLV | | | | | | Did not play—ineligible. | | | | | | | | |
| 87-88—UNLV | 34 | 884 | 117 | 204 | .574 | 75 | 116 | .647 | 206 | 64 | 311 | 6.1 | 1.9 | 9.1 |
| 88-89—UNLV | 37 | 1091 | 210 | 405 | .519 | 106 | 160 | .663 | 274 | 101 | 567 | 7.4 | 2.7 | 15.3 |
| 89-90—UNLV | 39 | 1246 | 210 | 380 | .553 | 118 | 176 | .670 | 270 | 143 | 554 | 6.9 | 3.7 | 14.2 |
| 90-91—UNLV | 35 | 1062 | 220 | 375 | .587 | 101 | 139 | .727 | 255 | 125 | 579 | 7.3 | 3.6 | 16.5 |
| Totals | 145 | 4283 | 757 | 1364 | .555 | 400 | 591 | .677 | 1005 | 433 | 2011 | 6.9 | 3.0 | 13.9 |

Three-point field goals: 1987-88, 2-for-2 (1.000). 1988-89, 41-for-98 (.418). 1989-90, 16-for-50 (.320). 1990-91, 38-for-81 (.469). Totals, 97-for-231 (.420).

### NBA REGULAR-SEASON RECORD

**HONORS:** NBA All-Rookie first team (1992).

| Season Team | G | Min. | FGM | FGA | Pct. | FTM | FTA | Pct. | Off. | Def. | Tot. | Ast. | St. | Blk. | TO | Pts. | RPG | APG | PPG |
|---|---|---|---|---|---|---|---|---|---|---|---|---|---|---|---|---|---|---|---|
| 91-92—Atlanta | 82 | 2505 | 440 | 899 | .489 | 213 | 320 | .666 | 191 | 229 | 420 | 201 | 124 | 27 | 181 | 1094 | 5.1 | 2.5 | 13.3 |
| 92-93—Atlanta | 73 | 2112 | 397 | 792 | .501 | 227 | 307 | .739 | 141 | 146 | 287 | 170 | 91 | 18 | 157 | 1021 | 3.9 | 2.3 | 14.0 |
| 93-94—Atlanta | 82 | 2605 | 439 | 861 | .510 | 333 | 436 | .764 | 178 | 216 | 394 | 187 | 149 | 45 | 147 | 1212 | 4.8 | 2.3 | 14.8 |
| 94-95—Atlanta | 76 | 2362 | 397 | 876 | .453 | 252 | 346 | .728 | 157 | 211 | 368 | 197 | 100 | 47 | 152 | 1053 | 4.8 | 2.6 | 13.9 |
| 95-96—Atlanta | 77 | 2294 | 362 | 738 | .491 | 251 | 317 | .792 | 137 | 167 | 304 | 137 | 106 | 31 | 138 | 976 | 3.9 | 1.8 | 12.7 |
| 96-97—Portland | 60 | 942 | 105 | 220 | .477 | 69 | 97 | .711 | 47 | 91 | 138 | 56 | 42 | 17 | 64 | 279 | 2.3 | 0.9 | 4.7 |
| 97-98—Portland | 71 | 1445 | 154 | 372 | .414 | 94 | 156 | .603 | 104 | 131 | 235 | 88 | 57 | 32 | 81 | 403 | 3.3 | 1.2 | 5.7 |
| 98-99—Portland | 48 | 874 | 78 | 174 | .448 | 52 | 76 | .684 | 47 | 78 | 125 | 58 | 57 | 18 | 30 | 208 | 2.6 | 1.2 | 4.3 |
| 99-00—Portland | 59 | 692 | 83 | 175 | .474 | 37 | 55 | .673 | 42 | 74 | 116 | 53 | 27 | 11 | 38 | 203 | 2.0 | 0.9 | 3.4 |
| 00-01—Portland | 66 | 1182 | 127 | 266 | .477 | 57 | 87 | .655 | 60 | 99 | 159 | 98 | 48 | 21 | 48 | 311 | 2.4 | 1.5 | 4.7 |
| 01-02—Charlotte | 77 | 1319 | 140 | 328 | .427 | 77 | 101 | .762 | 59 | 166 | 225 | 103 | 56 | 12 | 54 | 357 | 2.9 | 1.3 | 4.6 |
| 02-03—New Orleans | 70 | 862 | 79 | 192 | .411 | 54 | 72 | .750 | 26 | 93 | 119 | 69 | 27 | 9 | 40 | 212 | 1.7 | 1.0 | 3.0 |
| 03-04—New Orleans | 69 | 1416 | 143 | 347 | .412 | 110 | 139 | .791 | 52 | 122 | 174 | 85 | 55 | 15 | 76 | 397 | 2.5 | 1.2 | 5.8 |
| 04-05—Orlando | 55 | 663 | 68 | 167 | .407 | 57 | 77 | .740 | 45 | 54 | 99 | 36 | 23 | 8 | 31 | 193 | 1.8 | 0.7 | 3.5 |
| Totals | 965 | 21273 | 3012 | 6407 | .470 | 1883 | 2586 | .728 | 1286 | 1877 | 3163 | 1538 | 962 | 311 | 1237 | 7919 | 3.3 | 1.6 | 8.2 |

Three-point field goals: 1991-92, 1-for-6 (.167). 1992-93, 0-for-4. 1993-94, 1-for-7 (.143). 1994-95, 7-for-26 (.269). 1995-96, 1-for-4 (.250). 1997-98, 1-for-7 (.143). 1998-99, 0-for-2. 1999-00, 0-for-2. 2000-01, 0-for-4. 2001-02, 0-for-3. 2002-03, 0-for-7. 2003-04, 1-for-7 (.143). Totals, 12-for-79 (.152).
Personal fouls/disqualifications: 1991-92, 161/0. 1992-93, 141/1. 1993-94, 179/0. 1994-95, 163/0. 1995-96, 188/1. 1996-97, 87/0. 1997-98, 144/0. 1998-99, 81/0. 1999-00, 69/0. 2000-01, 105/0. 2001-02, 115/0. 2002-03, 80/0. 2003-04, 114/2. 2004-05, 83/0. Totals, 1710/4.

### NBA PLAYOFF RECORD

| Season Team | G | Min. | FGM | FGA | Pct. | FTM | FTA | Pct. | Off. | Def. | Tot. | Ast. | St. | Blk. | TO | Pts. | RPG | APG | PPG |
|---|---|---|---|---|---|---|---|---|---|---|---|---|---|---|---|---|---|---|---|
| 92-93—Atlanta | 3 | 93 | 14 | 31 | .452 | 8 | 12 | .667 | 3 | 5 | 8 | 5 | 4 | 0 | 4 | 36 | 2.7 | 1.7 | 12.0 |
| 93-94—Atlanta | 11 | 324 | 46 | 89 | .517 | 27 | 38 | .711 | 13 | 16 | 29 | 28 | 7 | 2 | 15 | 119 | 2.6 | 2.5 | 10.8 |
| 94-95—Atlanta | 3 | 52 | 6 | 14 | .429 | 9 | 12 | .750 | 3 | 4 | 7 | 5 | 3 | 0 | 2 | 21 | 2.3 | 1.7 | 7.0 |
| 95-96—Atlanta | 10 | 314 | 35 | 72 | .486 | 33 | 40 | .825 | 9 | 27 | 36 | 27 | 11 | 6 | 17 | 103 | 3.6 | 2.7 | 10.3 |
| 96-97—Portland | 4 | 35 | 2 | 6 | .333 | 3 | 4 | .750 | 1 | 0 | 1 | 3 | 1 | 0 | 1 | 7 | 0.3 | 0.8 | 1.8 |
| 97-98—Portland | 4 | 28 | 2 | 4 | .500 | 1 | 2 | .500 | 1 | 2 | 3 | 1 | 2 | 1 | 2 | 5 | 0.8 | 0.3 | 1.3 |
| 98-99—Portland | 13 | 176 | 10 | 28 | .357 | 15 | 18 | .833 | 10 | 23 | 33 | 5 | 8 | 3 | 3 | 35 | 2.5 | 0.4 | 2.7 |
| 99-00—Portland | 7 | 34 | 4 | 12 | .333 | 1 | 2 | .500 | 0 | 2 | 2 | 0 | 0 | 0 | 0 | 9 | 0.3 | 0.0 | 1.3 |
| 00-01—Portland | 2 | 28 | 4 | 10 | .400 | 2 | 2 | 1.000 | 1 | 3 | 4 | 4 | 1 | 0 | 1 | 10 | 2.0 | 2.0 | 5.0 |
| 01-02—Charlotte | 9 | 152 | 16 | 41 | .390 | 16 | 21 | .762 | 7 | 20 | 27 | 13 | 10 | 1 | 12 | 48 | 3.0 | 1.4 | 5.3 |
| 02-03—New Orleans | 4 | 69 | 5 | 15 | .333 | 7 | 8 | .875 | 1 | 9 | 10 | 3 | 3 | 0 | 3 | 17 | 2.5 | 0.8 | 4.3 |
| 03-04—New Orleans | 7 | 168 | 18 | 48 | .375 | 16 | 18 | .889 | 4 | 15 | 19 | 7 | 6 | 1 | 13 | 52 | 2.7 | 1.0 | 7.4 |
| Totals | 77 | 1473 | 162 | 370 | .438 | 138 | 177 | .780 | 53 | 126 | 179 | 101 | 56 | 14 | 73 | 462 | 2.3 | 1.3 | 6.0 |

Three-point field goals: 1995-96, 0-for-1. 1998-99, 0-for-1. 2003-04, 0-for-1. Totals, 0-for-3 (.000).
Personal fouls/disqualifications: 1992-93, 7/0. 1993-94, 26/0. 1994-95, 8/0. 1995-96, 26/0. 1996-97, 6/0. 1997-98, 2/0. 1998-99, 15/0. 1999-00, 6/0. 2000-01, 3/0. 2001-02, 21/1. 2002-03, 8/0. 2003-04, 13/0. Totals, 141/1.

## BAKER, MAURICE — G — TRAIL BLAZERS

**PERSONAL:** Born July 28, 1979, in Madison, Ill. ... 6-2/200. (1.88/90.7).
**HIGH SCHOOL:** Madison (Ill.).
**JUNIOR COLLEGE:** Dixie (Utah).
**COLLEGE:** Oklahoma State.
**TRANSACTIONS/CAREER NOTES:** Not drafted by an NBA franchise. ... Signed by Los Angeles Clippers (February 22,

2005). ... Signed to 10-day contract by Portland Trail Blazers (March 12, 2005).

## COLLEGIATE RECORD

| Season Team | G | Min. | FGM | FGA | Pct. | FTM | FTA | Pct. | Reb. | Ast. | Pts. | AVERAGES RPG | APG | PPG |
|---|---|---|---|---|---|---|---|---|---|---|---|---|---|---|
| 98-99—Dixie JC | 36 | ... | 187 | 395 | .473 | 121 | 157 | .771 | 218 | 92 | 542 | 6.1 | 2.6 | 15.1 |
| 99-00—Dixie JC | 31 | 1107 | 185 | 401 | .461 | 159 | 193 | .824 | 213 | 142 | 583 | 6.9 | 4.6 | 18.8 |
| 00-01—Okla St | 30 | 1121 | 200 | 381 | .525 | 129 | 160 | .806 | 202 | 127 | 593 | 6.7 | 4.2 | 19.8 |
| 01-02—Okla St | 29 | 869 | 133 | 312 | .426 | 65 | 77 | .844 | 158 | 95 | 374 | 5.4 | 3.3 | 12.9 |
| Junior College Totals | 67 | ... | 372 | 796 | .467 | 280 | 350 | .800 | 431 | 234 | 1125 | 6.4 | 3.5 | 16.8 |
| 4-Year-College Totals | 59 | 1990 | 333 | 693 | .481 | 194 | 237 | .819 | 360 | 222 | 967 | 6.1 | 3.8 | 16.4 |

Three-point field goals: 1998-99, 47-for-137 (.343). 1999-00, 54-for-150 (.360). 2000-01, 64-for-157 (.408). 2001-02, 43-for-117 (.368). Totals, 208-for-561 (.371).

## CBA RECORD

| Season Team | G | Min. | FGM | FGA | Pct. | FTM | FTA | Pct. | Reb. | Ast. | Pts. | AVERAGES RPG | APG | PPG |
|---|---|---|---|---|---|---|---|---|---|---|---|---|---|---|
| 04-05—Dakota Wizards | 34 | 1184 | 212 | 427 | .496 | 137 | 167 | .820 | 184 | 237 | 591 | 5.4 | 7.0 | 17.4 |

Three-point field goals: 2004-05, 30-for-80 (.375). Totals, 30-for-80 (.375).

## NBA REGULAR-SEASON RECORD

| Season Team | G | Min. | FGM | FGA | Pct. | FTM | FTA | Pct. | REBOUNDS Off. | Def. | Tot. | Ast. | St. | Blk. | TO | Pts. | AVERAGES RPG | APG | PPG |
|---|---|---|---|---|---|---|---|---|---|---|---|---|---|---|---|---|---|---|---|
| 04-05—LAC-Port. | 5 | 19 | 0 | 1 | .000 | 0 | 0 | ... | 1 | 1 | 2 | 1 | 1 | 0 | 1 | 0 | 0.4 | 0.2 | 0.0 |

Personal fouls/disqualifications: 2004-05, 3/0. Totals, 3/0.

## BAKER, VIN     F     ROCKETS

**PERSONAL:** Born November 23, 1971, in Lake Wales, Fla. ... 6-11/250. (2.11/113.4). ... Full name: Vincent Lamont Baker.
**HIGH SCHOOL:** Old Saybrook (Conn.).
**COLLEGE:** Hartford.
**TRANSACTIONS/CAREER NOTES:** Selected by Milwaukee Bucks in first round (eighth pick overall) of 1993 NBA Draft. ... Traded by Bucks to Seattle SuperSonics in three-way deal in which SuperSonics sent F Shawn Kemp to Cavaliers and Bucks sent G Sherman Douglas to Cleveland Cavaliers for G Terrell Brandon and F Tyrone Hill (September 25, 1997); Bucks also received 1998 conditional first-round draft choice from Cavaliers. ... Traded by SuperSonics with G Shammond Williams to Boston Celtics for G Kenny Anderson, F/C Vitaly Potapenko and G Joseph Forte (July 22, 2002). ... Released by Celtics (February 18, 2004). ... Signed as free agent by New York Knicks (March 12, 2004). ... Traded by Knicks with G Moochie Norris and second-round pick in 2006 draft to Houston Rockets for F Maurice Taylor (February 24, 2005).
**MISCELLANEOUS:** Member of gold-medal-winning U.S. Olympic team (2000).

## COLLEGIATE RECORD

| Season Team | G | Min. | FGM | FGA | Pct. | FTM | FTA | Pct. | Reb. | Ast. | Pts. | AVERAGES RPG | APG | PPG |
|---|---|---|---|---|---|---|---|---|---|---|---|---|---|---|
| 89-90—Hartford | 28 | 374 | 58 | 94 | .617 | 16 | 41 | .390 | 82 | 7 | 132 | 2.9 | 0.3 | 4.7 |
| 90-91—Hartford | 29 | 899 | 216 | 440 | .491 | 137 | 202 | .678 | 302 | 18 | 569 | 10.4 | 0.6 | 19.6 |
| 91-92—Hartford | 27 | 997 | 281 | 638 | .440 | 142 | 216 | .657 | 267 | 36 | 745 | 9.9 | 1.3 | 27.6 |
| 92-93—Hartford | 28 | 1019 | 305 | 639 | .477 | 150 | 240 | .625 | 300 | 54 | 792 | 10.7 | 1.9 | 28.3 |
| Totals | 112 | 3289 | 860 | 1811 | .475 | 445 | 699 | .637 | 951 | 115 | 2238 | 8.5 | 1.0 | 20.0 |

Three-point field goals: 1991-92, 41-for-214 (.192). 1992-93, 32-for-119 (.269). Totals, 73-for-333 (.219).

## NBA REGULAR-SEASON RECORD

**HONORS:** All-NBA second team (1998). ... All-NBA third team (1997). ... NBA All-Rookie first team (1994).

| Season Team | G | Min. | FGM | FGA | Pct. | FTM | FTA | Pct. | REBOUNDS Off. | Def. | Tot. | Ast. | St. | Blk. | TO | Pts. | AVERAGES RPG | APG | PPG |
|---|---|---|---|---|---|---|---|---|---|---|---|---|---|---|---|---|---|---|---|
| 93-94—Milwaukee | 82 | 2560 | 435 | 869 | .501 | 234 | 411 | .569 | 277 | 344 | 621 | 163 | 60 | 114 | 162 | 1105 | 7.6 | 2.0 | 13.5 |
| 94-95—Milwaukee | 82 | *3361 | 594 | 1229 | .483 | 256 | 432 | .593 | 289 | 557 | 846 | 296 | 86 | 116 | 221 | 1451 | 10.3 | 3.6 | 17.7 |
| 95-96—Milwaukee | 82 | 3319 | 699 | 1429 | .489 | 321 | 479 | .670 | 263 | 545 | 808 | 212 | 68 | 91 | 216 | 1729 | 9.9 | 2.6 | 21.1 |
| 96-97—Milwaukee | 78 | 3159 | 632 | 1251 | .505 | 358 | 521 | .687 | 267 | 537 | 804 | 211 | 81 | 112 | 245 | 1637 | 10.3 | 2.7 | 21.0 |
| 97-98—Seattle | 82 | 2944 | 631 | 1164 | .542 | 311 | 526 | .591 | 286 | 370 | 656 | 152 | 91 | 86 | 174 | 1574 | 8.0 | 1.9 | 19.2 |
| 98-99—Seattle | 34 | 1162 | 198 | 437 | .453 | 72 | 160 | .450 | 86 | 125 | 211 | 56 | 32 | 34 | 76 | 468 | 6.2 | 1.6 | 13.8 |
| 99-00—Seattle | 79 | 2849 | 514 | 1129 | .455 | 281 | 412 | .682 | 227 | 378 | 605 | 148 | 47 | 66 | 213 | 1311 | 7.7 | 1.9 | 16.6 |
| 00-01—Seattle | 76 | 2129 | 347 | 822 | .422 | 232 | 321 | .723 | 179 | 251 | 430 | 90 | 38 | 73 | 158 | 927 | 5.7 | 1.2 | 12.2 |
| 01-02—Seattle | 55 | 1710 | 315 | 649 | .485 | 143 | 226 | .633 | 168 | 182 | 350 | 72 | 22 | 36 | 127 | 774 | 6.4 | 1.3 | 14.1 |
| 02-03—Boston | 52 | 942 | 99 | 207 | .478 | 72 | 107 | .673 | 90 | 108 | 198 | 29 | 22 | 30 | 61 | 270 | 3.8 | 0.6 | 5.2 |
| 03-04—Boston-N.Y. | 54 | 1313 | 208 | 432 | .481 | 114 | 157 | .726 | 112 | 168 | 280 | 66 | 29 | 32 | 77 | 531 | 5.2 | 1.2 | 9.8 |
| 04-05—N.Y.-Houston | 27 | 204 | 13 | 42 | .310 | 9 | 17 | .529 | 17 | 22 | 39 | 10 | 2 | 4 | 17 | 35 | 1.4 | 0.4 | 1.3 |
| Totals | 783 | 25652 | 4685 | 9660 | .485 | 2403 | 3769 | .638 | 2261 | 3587 | 5848 | 1505 | 578 | 794 | 1747 | 11812 | 7.5 | 1.9 | 15.1 |

Three-point field goals: 1993-94, 1-for-5 (.200). 1994-95, 7-for-24 (.292). 1995-96, 10-for-48 (.208). 1996-97, 15-for-54 (.278). 1997-98, 1-for-7 (.143). 1998-99, 0-for-3. 1999-00, 2-for-8 (.250). 2000-01, 1-for-16 (.063). 2001-02, 1-for-8 (.125). 2002-03, 0-for-4. 2003-04, 1-for-3 (.333). 2004-05, 0-for-1. Totals, 39-for-181 (.215).

Personal fouls/disqualifications: 1993-94, 231/3. 1994-95, 277/5. 1995-96, 272/3. 1996-97, 275/8. 1997-98, 278/7. 1998-99, 121/2. 1999-00, 288/6. 2000-01, 264/2. 2001-02, 197/4. 2002-03, 146/1. 2003-04, 160/3. 2004-05, 38/0. Totals, 2547/44.

## NBA PLAYOFF RECORD

| Season Team | G | Min. | FGM | FGA | Pct. | FTM | FTA | Pct. | REBOUNDS Off. | Def. | Tot. | Ast. | St. | Blk. | TO | Pts. | AVERAGES RPG | APG | PPG |
|---|---|---|---|---|---|---|---|---|---|---|---|---|---|---|---|---|---|---|---|
| 97-98—Seattle | 10 | 371 | 71 | 134 | .530 | 16 | 38 | .421 | 41 | 53 | 94 | 18 | 18 | 15 | 22 | 158 | 9.4 | 1.8 | 15.8 |

| Season Team | G | Min. | FGM | FGA | Pct. | FTM | FTA | Pct. | REBOUNDS Off. | Def. | Tot. | Ast. | St. | Blk. | TO | Pts. | AVERAGES RPG | APG | PPG |
|---|---|---|---|---|---|---|---|---|---|---|---|---|---|---|---|---|---|---|---|
| 99-00—Seattle ............ | 5 | 177 | 30 | 75 | .400 | 10 | 17 | .588 | 16 | 22 | 38 | 10 | 5 | 2 | 16 | 70 | 7.6 | 2.0 | 14.0 |
| 01-02—Seattle ........... | 5 | 144 | 29 | 58 | .500 | 7 | 9 | .778 | 11 | 14 | 25 | 4 | 3 | 6 | 4 | 66 | 5.0 | 0.8 | 13.2 |
| 03-04—New York ....... | 4 | 57 | 8 | 14 | .571 | 6 | 9 | .667 | 6 | 6 | 12 | 1 | 3 | 2 | 2 | 22 | 3.0 | 0.3 | 5.5 |
| Totals .................... | 24 | 749 | 138 | 281 | .491 | 39 | 73 | .534 | 74 | 95 | 169 | 33 | 29 | 25 | 44 | 316 | 7.0 | 1.4 | 13.2 |

Three-point field goals: 1999-00, 0-for-1. 2001-02, 1-for-1 (1.000). 2003-04, 1-for-2 (.500).
Personal fouls/disqualifications: 1997-98, 38/1. 1999-00, 19/0. 2001-02, 23/1. 2003-04, 8/1. Totals, 88/3.

### NBA ALL-STAR GAME RECORD

| Season Team | Min. | FGM | FGA | Pct. | FTM | FTA | Pct. | REBOUNDS Off. | Def. | Tot. | Ast. | PF | Dq. | St. | Blk. | TO | Pts. |
|---|---|---|---|---|---|---|---|---|---|---|---|---|---|---|---|---|---|
| 1995—Milwaukee ............ | 11 | 0 | 2 | .000 | 2 | 4 | .500 | 2 | 0 | 2 | 0 | 1 | 0 | 0 | 1 | 1 | 2 |
| 1996—Milwaukee ............ | 14 | 2 | 5 | .400 | 2 | 2 | 1.000 | 1 | 1 | 2 | 2 | 4 | 0 | 1 | 0 | 0 | 6 |
| 1997—Milwaukee ............ | 24 | 8 | 12 | .667 | 3 | 4 | .750 | 7 | 5 | 12 | 1 | 2 | 0 | 0 | 0 | 0 | 19 |
| 1998—Seattle ................. | 21 | 3 | 12 | .250 | 2 | 2 | 1.000 | 6 | 2 | 8 | 0 | 1 | 0 | 1 | 0 | 0 | 8 |
| Totals ........................... | 70 | 13 | 31 | .419 | 9 | 12 | .750 | 16 | 8 | 24 | 3 | 8 | 0 | 2 | 1 | 1 | 35 |

## B

## BANKS, MARCUS     G     CELTICS

**PERSONAL:** Born November 19, 1981, in in Las Vegas, Nev. ... 6-2/220. (1.88/99.8). ... Full name: Arthur Lemarcus Banks
**HIGH SCHOOL:** Cimarron-Memorial (Las Vegas, Nev.).
**COLLEGE:** Dixie College, then UNLV.
**TRANSACTIONS/CAREER NOTES:** Selected by Memphis Grizzlies in first round (13th pick overall) of 2003 NBA Draft. ... Draft rights traded by Grizzlies with draft rights to C Kendrick Perkins to Boston Celtics for draft rights to G Troy Bell and G/F Dahntay Jones (June 26, 2003).

### COLLEGIATE RECORD

| Season Team | G | Min. | FGM | FGA | Pct. | FTM | FTA | Pct. | Reb. | Ast. | Pts. | AVERAGES RPG | APG | PPG |
|---|---|---|---|---|---|---|---|---|---|---|---|---|---|---|
| 99-00—Dixie College ................. | 33 | ... | 234 | 471 | .497 | 87 | 140 | .621 | 120 | 111 | 592 | 3.6 | 3.4 | 17.9 |
| 00-01—Dixie College ................. | 37 | ... | 193 | 371 | .520 | 216 | 288 | .750 | 205 | 137 | 622 | 5.5 | 3.7 | 16.8 |
| 01-02—UNLV ............................ | 31 | 1006 | 158 | 336 | .470 | 150 | 213 | .704 | 103 | 94 | 490 | 3.3 | 3.0 | 15.8 |
| 02-03—UNLV ............................ | 32 | 1154 | 223 | 434 | .514 | 162 | 214 | .757 | 107 | 175 | 649 | 3.3 | 5.5 | 20.3 |
| Junior College Totals............. | 70 | ... | 427 | 842 | .507 | 303 | 428 | .708 | 325 | 248 | 1214 | 4.6 | 3.5 | 17.3 |
| 4-Year-College Totals ........... | 63 | 2160 | 381 | 770 | .495 | 312 | 427 | .731 | 210 | 269 | 1139 | 3.3 | 4.3 | 18.1 |

Three-point field goals: 2001-02, 24-for-75 (.320). 2002-03, 41-for-122 (.336). Totals, 65-for-197 (.330).

### NBA REGULAR-SEASON RECORD

| Season Team | G | Min. | FGM | FGA | Pct. | FTM | FTA | Pct. | REBOUNDS Off. | Def. | Tot. | Ast. | St. | Blk. | TO | Pts. | AVERAGES RPG | APG | PPG |
|---|---|---|---|---|---|---|---|---|---|---|---|---|---|---|---|---|---|---|---|
| 03-04—Boston ........... | 81 | 1385 | 177 | 442 | .400 | 99 | 131 | .756 | 30 | 103 | 133 | 175 | 88 | 13 | 125 | 480 | 1.6 | 2.2 | 5.9 |
| 04-05—Boston ........... | 81 | 1145 | 115 | 286 | .402 | 121 | 163 | .742 | 29 | 97 | 126 | 155 | 63 | 13 | 79 | 372 | 1.6 | 1.9 | 4.6 |
| Totals .................. | 162 | 2530 | 292 | 728 | .401 | 220 | 294 | .748 | 59 | 200 | 259 | 330 | 151 | 26 | 204 | 852 | 1.6 | 2.0 | 5.3 |

Three-point field goals: 2003-04, 27-for-86 (.314). 2004-05, 21-for-59 (.356). Totals, 48-for-145 (.331).
Personal fouls/disqualifications: 2003-04, 171/2. 2004-05, 146/2. Totals, 317/4.

### NBA PLAYOFF RECORD

| Season Team | G | Min. | FGM | FGA | Pct. | FTM | FTA | Pct. | REBOUNDS Off. | Def. | Tot. | Ast. | St. | Blk. | TO | Pts. | AVERAGES RPG | APG | PPG |
|---|---|---|---|---|---|---|---|---|---|---|---|---|---|---|---|---|---|---|---|
| 03-04—Boston ........... | 4 | 60 | 7 | 16 | .438 | 4 | 4 | 1.000 | 1 | 6 | 7 | 7 | 2 | 1 | 3 | 20 | 1.8 | 1.8 | 5.0 |
| 04-05—Boston ........... | 7 | 106 | 13 | 29 | .448 | 3 | 6 | .500 | 1 | 10 | 11 | 7 | 4 | 0 | 6 | 32 | 1.6 | 1.0 | 4.6 |
| Totals .................. | 11 | 166 | 20 | 45 | .444 | 7 | 10 | .700 | 2 | 16 | 18 | 14 | 6 | 1 | 9 | 52 | 1.6 | 1.3 | 4.7 |

Three-point field goals: 2003-04, 2-for-5 (.400). 2004-05, 3-for-6 (.500). Totals, 5-for-11 (.455).
Personal fouls/disqualifications: 2003-04, 9/0. 2004-05, 16/0. Totals, 25/0.

## BARBOSA, LEANDRO     G     SUNS

**PERSONAL:** Born November 28, 1982, in Sao Paulo, Brazil. ... 6-3/176. (1.91/79.8). ... Full name: Leandrinho Mateus Barbosa
**TRANSACTIONS/CAREER NOTES:** Played in Brazil (1999-2003). ... Selected by San Antonio Spurs in first round (28th pick overall) of 2003 NBA Draft. ... Draft rights traded by Spurs to Phoenix Suns for future first-round pick (June 26, 2003).

### BRAZILIAN LEAGUE RECORD

| Season Team | G | Min. | FGM | FGA | Pct. | FTM | FTA | Pct. | Reb. | Ast. | Pts. | AVERAGES RPG | APG | PPG |
|---|---|---|---|---|---|---|---|---|---|---|---|---|---|---|
| 01-02—Bauru Tilibra................. | 43 | ... | 253 | 464 | .545 | 103 | 142 | .725 | 155 | 275 | 678 | 3.6 | 6.4 | 15.8 |
| 02-03—Bauru Tilibra................. | 20 | ... | 190 | 378 | .503 | 100 | 120 | .833 | 80 | 140 | 564 | 4.0 | 7.0 | 28.2 |
| Totals ..................................... | 63 | ... | 443 | 842 | .526 | 203 | 262 | .775 | 235 | 415 | 1242 | 3.7 | 6.6 | 19.7 |

Three-point field goals: 2001-02, 64-for-150 (.427). 2002-03, 68-for-152 (.447). Totals, 132-for-302 (.437).

### NBA REGULAR-SEASON RECORD

| Season Team | G | Min. | FGM | FGA | Pct. | FTM | FTA | Pct. | REBOUNDS Off. | Def. | Tot. | Ast. | St. | Blk. | TO | Pts. | AVERAGES RPG | APG | PPG |
|---|---|---|---|---|---|---|---|---|---|---|---|---|---|---|---|---|---|---|---|
| 03-04—Phoenix ......... | 70 | 1500 | 210 | 470 | .447 | 47 | 61 | .770 | 23 | 100 | 123 | 165 | 93 | 7 | 120 | 550 | 1.8 | 2.4 | 7.9 |
| 04-05—Phoenix ......... | 63 | 1087 | 168 | 354 | .475 | 55 | 69 | .797 | 32 | 98 | 130 | 126 | 30 | 7 | 87 | 442 | 2.1 | 2.0 | 7.0 |
| Totals .................. | 133 | 2587 | 378 | 824 | .459 | 102 | 130 | .785 | 55 | 198 | 253 | 291 | 123 | 14 | 207 | 992 | 1.9 | 2.2 | 7.5 |

Three-point field goals: 2003-04, 83-for-210 (.395). 2004-05, 51-for-139 (.367). Totals, 134-for-349 (.384).
Personal fouls/disqualifications: 2003-04, 184/6. 2004-05, 127/0. Totals, 311/6.

### NBA PLAYOFF RECORD

| Season Team | G | Min. | FGM | FGA | Pct. | FTM | FTA | Pct. | REBOUNDS Off. | Def. | Tot. | Ast. | St. | Blk. | TO | Pts. | AVERAGES RPG | APG | PPG |
|---|---|---|---|---|---|---|---|---|---|---|---|---|---|---|---|---|---|---|---|
| 04-05—Phoenix ......... | 12 | 116 | 12 | 35 | .343 | 2 | 4 | .500 | 5 | 12 | 17 | 12 | 3 | 0 | 5 | 30 | 1.4 | 1.0 | 2.5 |

Three-point field goals: 2004-05, 4-for-10 (.400). Totals, 4-for-10 (.400).
Personal fouls/disqualifications: 2004-05, 8/0. Totals, 8/0.

# BARNES, MATT      F      76ERS

**PERSONAL:** Born March 9, 1980, in Santa Clara, Calif. ... 6-7/226. (2.01/102.5). ... Full name: Matt Kelly Barnes
**HIGH SCHOOL:** Del Campo (Sacramento).
**COLLEGE:** UCLA.
**TRANSACTIONS/CAREER NOTES:** Selected by Memphis Grizzlies in second round (46th pick overall) of NBA Draft. ... Draft rights traded by Grizzlies with G/F Nick Anderson to Cleveland Cavaliers for G/F Wesley Person (June 26, 2002). ... Waived by Cavaliers (October 18, 2002). ... Signed as free agent by Seattle SuperSonics (September 27, 2003). ... Waived by SuperSonics (October 13, 2003). ... Signed by Los Angeles Clippers to first of two consecutive 10-day contracts (January 18, 2004). ... Signed by Clippers for remainder of season (February 8, 2004). ... Traded by Kings to Philadelphia 76ers with Fs Michael Bradley and Chris Webber for Fs Kenny Thomas and Corliss Williamson and C Brian Skinner (February 23, 2005).

## COLLEGIATE RECORD

| | | | | | | | | | | | | AVERAGES | | |
| Season Team | G | Min. | FGM | FGA | Pct. | FTM | FTA | Pct. | Reb. | Ast. | Pts. | RPG | APG | PPG |
|---|---|---|---|---|---|---|---|---|---|---|---|---|---|---|
| 98-99—UCLA | 30 | 394 | 43 | 99 | .434 | 22 | 46 | .478 | 86 | 23 | 118 | 2.9 | 0.8 | 3.9 |
| 99-00—UCLA | 28 | 413 | 65 | 138 | .471 | 21 | 43 | .488 | 74 | 29 | 156 | 2.6 | 1.0 | 5.6 |
| 00-01—UCLA | 32 | 971 | 142 | 297 | .478 | 85 | 148 | .574 | 232 | 85 | 372 | 7.3 | 2.7 | 11.6 |
| 01-02—UCLA | 31 | 953 | 152 | 323 | .471 | 73 | 118 | .619 | 192 | 108 | 420 | 6.2 | 3.5 | 13.5 |
| Totals | 121 | 2731 | 402 | 857 | .469 | 201 | 355 | .566 | 584 | 245 | 1066 | 4.8 | 2.0 | 8.8 |

Three-point field goals: 1998-99, 10-for-34 (.294). 1999-00, 5-for-32 (.156). 2000-01, 3-for-25 (.120). 2001-02, 43-for-103 (.417). Totals, 61-for-194 (.314).

## NBDL RECORD

| | | | | | | | | | | | | AVERAGES | | |
| Season Team | G | Min. | FGM | FGA | Pct. | FTM | FTA | Pct. | Reb. | Ast. | Pts. | RPG | APG | PPG |
|---|---|---|---|---|---|---|---|---|---|---|---|---|---|---|
| 02-03—Fayetteville | 50 | 932 | 172 | 442 | .389 | 79 | 113 | .699 | 164 | 56 | 484 | 3.3 | 1.1 | 9.7 |

Three-point field goals: 2002-03, 61-for-175 (.349). Totals, 61-for-175 (.349).

## AMERICAN BASKETBALL ASSOCIATION RECORD

| | | | | | | | | | | | | AVERAGES | | |
| Season Team | G | Min. | FGM | FGA | Pct. | FTM | FTA | Pct. | Reb. | Ast. | Pts. | RPG | APG | PPG |
|---|---|---|---|---|---|---|---|---|---|---|---|---|---|---|
| 03-04—Long Beach | 17 | ... | 122 | 240 | .508 | 46 | 60 | .767 | 116 | 81 | 328 | 6.8 | 4.8 | 19.3 |

Three-point field goals: 2003-04, 38-for-104 (.365). Totals, 38-for-104 (.365).

## NBA REGULAR-SEASON RECORD

| | | | | | | | | REBOUNDS | | | | | | | | AVERAGES | | |
| Season Team | G | Min. | FGM | FGA | Pct. | FTM | FTA | Pct. | Off. | Def. | Tot. | Ast. | St. | Blk. | TO | Pts. | RPG | APG | PPG |
|---|---|---|---|---|---|---|---|---|---|---|---|---|---|---|---|---|---|---|---|
| 03-04—L.A. Clippers | 38 | 724 | 63 | 138 | .457 | 43 | 61 | .705 | 53 | 98 | 151 | 48 | 27 | 3 | 44 | 171 | 4.0 | 1.3 | 4.5 |
| 04-05—Sac.-Phila. | 43 | 715 | 62 | 151 | .411 | 35 | 58 | .603 | 49 | 84 | 133 | 57 | 30 | 7 | 45 | 164 | 3.1 | 1.3 | 3.8 |
| Totals | 81 | 1439 | 125 | 289 | .433 | 78 | 119 | .655 | 102 | 182 | 284 | 105 | 57 | 10 | 89 | 335 | 3.5 | 1.3 | 4.1 |

Three-point field goals: 2003-04, 2-for-13 (.154). 2004-05, 5-for-22 (.227). Totals, 7-for-35 (.200).
Personal fouls/disqualifications: 2003-04, 76/0. 2004-05, 80/0. Totals, 156/0.

---

# BARRETT, ANDRE      G

**PERSONAL:** Born February 21, 1982, in Bronx, N.Y. ... 5-10/173. (1.78/78.5). ... Full name: Andre Rashawd Barrett
**HIGH SCHOOL:** Rice (New York, N.Y.).
**COLLEGE:** Seton Hall.
**TRANSACTIONS:** Not drafted by an NBA franchise. ... Signed as free agent by Houston Rockets (October 28, 2004). ... Waived by Rockets (March 19, 2005). ... Signed to 10-day contract by Orlando Magic (March 31, 2005). ... Signed for remainder of season by Magic (April 10, 2005).

## COLLEGIATE RECORD

**NOTES:** The SPORTING NEWS All-America third team (2004).

| | | | | | | | | | | | | AVERAGES | | |
| Season Team | G | Min. | FGM | FGA | Pct. | FTM | FTA | Pct. | Reb. | Ast. | Pts. | RPG | APG | PPG |
|---|---|---|---|---|---|---|---|---|---|---|---|---|---|---|
| 00-01—Seton Hall | 31 | 1005 | 113 | 311 | .363 | 44 | 63 | .698 | 103 | 169 | 317 | 3.3 | 5.5 | 10.2 |
| 01-02—Seton Hall | 30 | 1035 | 164 | 414 | .396 | 110 | 146 | .753 | 108 | 151 | 506 | 3.6 | 5.0 | 16.9 |
| 02-03—Seton Hall | 30 | 1137 | 162 | 374 | .433 | 122 | 146 | .836 | 115 | 159 | 502 | 3.8 | 5.3 | 16.7 |
| 03-04—Seton Hall | 31 | 1119 | 187 | 411 | .455 | 89 | 117 | .761 | 120 | 183 | 536 | 3.9 | 5.9 | 17.3 |
| Totals | 122 | 4296 | 626 | 1510 | .415 | 365 | 472 | .773 | 446 | 662 | 1861 | 3.7 | 5.4 | 15.3 |

Three-point field goals: 2000-01, 47-for-156 (.301). 2001-02, 68-for-198 (.343). 2002-03, 56-for-152 (.368). 2003-04, 73-for-190 (.384). Totals, 244-for-696 (.351).

## NBA REGULAR-SEASON RECORD

| | | | | | | | | REBOUNDS | | | | | | | | AVERAGES | | |
| Season Team | G | Min. | FGM | FGA | Pct. | FTM | FTA | Pct. | Off. | Def. | Tot. | Ast. | St. | Blk. | TO | Pts. | RPG | APG | PPG |
|---|---|---|---|---|---|---|---|---|---|---|---|---|---|---|---|---|---|---|---|
| 04-05—Houston-Orl. | 38 | 483 | 45 | 124 | .363 | 14 | 19 | .737 | 11 | 29 | 40 | 69 | 19 | 1 | 27 | 118 | 1.1 | 1.8 | 3.1 |

Three-point field goals: 2004-05, 14-for-52 (.269). Totals, 14-for-52 (.269).
Personal fouls/disqualifications: 2004-05, 51/0. Totals, 51/0.

---

# BARRY, BRENT      G      SPURS

**PERSONAL:** Born December 31, 1971, in Hempstead, N.Y. ... 6-6/215. (1.98/97.5). ... Full name: Brent Robert Barry ... Son of Rick Barry, forward with San Francisco/Golden State Warriors (1965-66, 1966-67 and 1972-73 through 1977-78) and Houston Rockets of NBA (1978-79 and 1979-80) and three American Basketball Association teams (1968-69 through 1971-72) and member of Naismith Memorial Basketball Hall of Fame; brother of Jon Barry, guard, Houston Rockets; brother of Drew Barry, guard with Atlanta Hawks (1997-98 and 2000-01), Seattle SuperSonics (1998-99) and Golden State Warriors (2000-01).
**HIGH SCHOOL:** De La Salle Catholic (Concord, Calif.).

**COLLEGE:** Oregon State.

**TRANSACTIONS/CAREER NOTES:** Selected by Denver Nuggets in first round (15th pick overall) of 1995 NBA Draft. ... Draft rights traded by Nuggets with F Rodney Rogers to Los Angeles Clippers for G Randy Woods and draft rights to F Antonio McDyess (June 28, 1995). ... Traded by Clippers to Miami Heat for C Isaac Austin, G Charles Smith and 1998 first-round draft choice (February 19, 1998). ... Signed as free agent by Chicago Bulls (January 25, 1999). ... Traded by Bulls to Seattle SuperSonics for G Hersey Hawkins and G James Cotton (August 12, 1999). ... Signed as free agent by San Antonio Spurs (July 15, 2004).

**MISCELLANEOUS:** Member of NBA championship team (2005).

**COLLEGIATE RECORD**

| Season Team | G | Min. | FGM | FGA | Pct. | FTM | FTA | Pct. | Reb. | Ast. | Pts. | RPG | APG | PPG |
|---|---|---|---|---|---|---|---|---|---|---|---|---|---|---|
| 90-91—Oregon State ................ | | | | | | Did not play—redshirted. | | | | | | | | |
| 91-92—Oregon State ................ | 31 | 545 | 57 | 136 | .419 | 22 | 33 | .667 | 47 | 70 | 161 | 1.5 | 2.3 | 5.2 |
| 92-93—Oregon State ................ | 23 | 607 | 55 | 134 | .410 | 40 | 47 | .851 | 49 | 83 | 165 | 2.1 | 3.6 | 7.2 |
| 93-94—Oregon State ................ | 27 | 959 | 144 | 289 | .498 | 85 | 112 | .759 | 141 | 94 | 411 | 5.2 | 3.5 | 15.2 |
| 94-95—Oregon State ................ | 27 | 1012 | 181 | 352 | .514 | 153 | 186 | .823 | 159 | 104 | 567 | 5.9 | 3.9 | 21.0 |
| Totals ................................... | 108 | 3123 | 437 | 911 | .480 | 300 | 378 | .794 | 396 | 351 | 1304 | 3.7 | 3.3 | 12.1 |

Three-point field goals: 1991-92, 25-for-77 (.325). 1992-93, 15-for-64 (.234). 1993-94, 38-for-104 (.365). 1994-95, 52-for-132 (.394). Totals, 130-for-377 (.345).

**NBA REGULAR-SEASON RECORD**

**HONORS:** Slam Dunk championship winner (1996). ... NBA All-Rookie second team (1996).

**NOTES:** Led NBA with .476 three-point field goal percentage (2001).

| Season Team | G | Min. | FGM | FGA | Pct. | FTM | FTA | Pct. | REBOUNDS Off. | Def. | Tot. | Ast. | St. | Blk. | TO | Pts. | AVERAGES RPG | APG | PPG |
|---|---|---|---|---|---|---|---|---|---|---|---|---|---|---|---|---|---|---|---|
| 95-96—L.A. Clippers ... | 79 | 1898 | 283 | 597 | .474 | 111 | 137 | .810 | 38 | 130 | 168 | 230 | 95 | 22 | 120 | 800 | 2.1 | 2.9 | 10.1 |
| 96-97—L.A. Clippers ... | 59 | 1094 | 155 | 379 | .409 | 76 | 93 | .817 | 30 | 80 | 110 | 154 | 51 | 15 | 76 | 442 | 1.9 | 2.6 | 7.5 |
| 97-98—L.A.C.-Miami... | 58 | 1600 | 213 | 506 | .421 | 115 | 134 | .858 | 29 | 142 | 171 | 153 | 64 | 27 | 104 | 631 | 2.9 | 2.6 | 10.9 |
| 98-99—Chicago ......... | 37 | 1181 | 141 | 356 | .396 | 78 | 101 | .772 | 39 | 105 | 144 | 116 | 42 | 11 | 72 | 412 | 3.9 | 3.1 | 11.1 |
| 99-00—Seattle ........... | 80 | 2726 | 327 | 707 | .463 | 127 | 157 | .809 | 50 | 322 | 372 | 291 | 103 | 31 | 142 | 945 | 4.7 | 3.6 | 11.8 |
| 00-01—Seattle ........... | 67 | 1778 | 198 | 401 | .494 | 84 | 103 | .816 | 33 | 178 | 211 | 225 | 80 | 14 | 86 | 589 | 3.1 | 3.4 | 8.8 |
| 01-02—Seattle ........... | 81 | 3040 | 401 | 790 | .508 | 198 | 234 | .846 | 58 | 383 | 441 | 426 | 147 | 37 | 165 | 1164 | 5.4 | 5.3 | 14.4 |
| 02-03—Seattle ........... | 75 | 2480 | 264 | 577 | .458 | 128 | 161 | .795 | 48 | 253 | 301 | 384 | 113 | 15 | 142 | 774 | 4.0 | 5.1 | 10.3 |
| 03-04—Seattle ........... | 59 | 1803 | 215 | 427 | .504 | 91 | 110 | .827 | 21 | 183 | 204 | 342 | 85 | 16 | 139 | 635 | 3.5 | 5.8 | 10.8 |
| 04-05—San Antonio.... | 81 | 1742 | 194 | 459 | .423 | 113 | 135 | .837 | 29 | 161 | 190 | 178 | 39 | 20 | 64 | 601 | 2.3 | 2.2 | 7.4 |
| Totals ................... | 676 | 19342 | 2391 | 5199 | .460 | 1121 | 1365 | .821 | 375 | 1937 | 2312 | 2499 | 819 | 208 | 1110 | 6993 | 3.4 | 3.7 | 10.3 |

Three-point field goals: 1995-96, 123-for-296 (.416). 1996-97, 56-for-173 (.324). 1997-98, 90-for-229 (.393). 1998-99, 52-for-172 (.302). 1999-00, 164-for-399 (.411). 2000-01, 109-for-229 (.476). 2001-02, 164-for-387 (.424). 2002-03, 118-for-293 (.403). 2003-04, 114-for-252 (.452). 2004-05, 100-for-280 (.357). Totals, 1090-for-2710 (.402).

Personal fouls/disqualifications: 1995-96, 196/2. 1996-97, 88/1. 1997-98, 118/0. 1998-99, 98/2. 1999-00, 228/4. 2000-01, 126/1. 2001-02, 182/3. 2002-03, 199/1. 2003-04, 121/0. 2004-05, 123/0. Totals, 1479/14.

**NBA PLAYOFF RECORD**

| Season Team | G | Min. | FGM | FGA | Pct. | FTM | FTA | Pct. | REBOUNDS Off. | Def. | Tot. | Ast. | St. | Blk. | TO | Pts. | AVERAGES RPG | APG | PPG |
|---|---|---|---|---|---|---|---|---|---|---|---|---|---|---|---|---|---|---|---|
| 96-97—L.A. Clippers ... | 3 | 84 | 11 | 27 | .407 | 8 | 9 | .889 | 1 | 6 | 7 | 10 | 4 | 0 | 4 | 35 | 2.3 | 3.3 | 11.7 |
| 99-00—Seattle ........... | 5 | 155 | 12 | 33 | .364 | 10 | 14 | .714 | 3 | 10 | 13 | 15 | 3 | 3 | 7 | 42 | 2.6 | 3.0 | 8.4 |
| 01-02—Seattle ........... | 5 | 149 | 14 | 34 | .412 | 4 | 4 | 1.000 | 6 | 17 | 23 | 14 | 3 | 4 | 9 | 39 | 4.6 | 2.8 | 7.8 |
| 04-05—San Antonio.... | 23 | 555 | 48 | 105 | .457 | 17 | 21 | .810 | 13 | 43 | 56 | 44 | 15 | 4 | 27 | 141 | 2.4 | 1.9 | 6.1 |
| Totals ................... | 36 | 943 | 85 | 199 | .427 | 39 | 48 | .813 | 23 | 76 | 99 | 83 | 25 | 11 | 47 | 257 | 2.8 | 2.3 | 7.1 |

Three-point field goals: 1996-97, 5-for-11 (.455). 1999-00, 8-for-20 (.400). 2001-02, 7-for-16 (.438). 2004-05, 28-for-66 (.424). Totals, 48-for-113 (.425).
Personal fouls/disqualifications: 1996-97, 10/0. 1999-00, 20/2. 2001-02, 12/0. 2004-05, 44/1. Totals, 86/3.

## BARRY, JON     G     ROCKETS

**PERSONAL:** Born July 25, 1969, in Oakland. ... 6-5/210. (1.96/95.3). ... Full name: Jon Alan Barry ... Son of Rick Barry, forward with San Francisco/Golden State Warriors (1965-66, 1966-67 and 1972-73 through 1977-78) and Houston Rockets of NBA (1978-79 and 1979-80) and three American Basketball Association teams (1968-69 through 1971-72), and member of Naismith Memorial Basketball Hall of Fame; brother of Brent Barry, guard, San Antonio Spurs; and brother of Drew Barry, guard with Atlanta Hawks (1997-98 and 2000-01), Seattle SuperSonics (1998-99) and Golden State Warriors (2000-01).

**HIGH SCHOOL:** De La Salle Catholic (Concord, Calif.).

**JUNIOR COLLEGE:** Paris (Texas) Junior College.

**COLLEGE:** Pacific, then Georgia Tech.

**TRANSACTIONS/CAREER NOTES:** Selected by Boston Celtics in first round (21st pick overall) of 1992 NBA Draft. ... Traded by Celtics to Milwaukee Bucks for F Alaa Abdelnaby (December 4, 1992). ... Signed as unrestricted free agent by Golden State Warriors (October 4, 1995). ... Signed as free agent by Atlanta Hawks (August 13, 1996). ... Signed as free agent by Los Angeles Lakers (August 27, 1997). ... Signed as free agent by Sacramento Kings (January 22, 1999). ... Traded by Kings with future first-round draft choice to Detroit Pistons for G Mateen Cleaves (September 7, 2001). ... Signed as free agent by Denver Nuggets (August 19, 2003). ... Signed as free agent by Atlanta Hawks (September 16, 2004). ... Traded by Hawks to Houston Rockets for G Tyronn Lue (December 23, 2004).

**COLLEGIATE RECORD**

| Season Team | G | Min. | FGM | FGA | Pct. | FTM | FTA | Pct. | Reb. | Ast. | Pts. | RPG | APG | PPG |
|---|---|---|---|---|---|---|---|---|---|---|---|---|---|---|
| 87-88—Pacific .......................... | 29 | 809 | 100 | 269 | .372 | 53 | 71 | .746 | 74 | 108 | 275 | 2.6 | 3.7 | 9.5 |
| 88-89—Paris J.C. ..................... | | | | | | Did not play. | | | | | | | | |
| 89-90—Paris J.C. ..................... | 30 | ... | 204 | 358 | .570 | 58 | 73 | .795 | 108 | 90 | 513 | 3.6 | 3.0 | 17.1 |

**B**

| Season Team | G | Min. | FGM | FGA | Pct. | FTM | FTA | Pct. | Reb. | Ast. | Pts. | RPG | APG | PPG |
|---|---|---|---|---|---|---|---|---|---|---|---|---|---|---|
| 90-91—Georgia Tech | 30 | 1088 | 180 | 405 | .444 | 41 | 56 | .732 | 110 | 110 | 478 | 3.7 | 3.7 | 15.9 |
| 91-92—Georgia Tech | 35 | 1231 | 201 | 468 | .429 | 101 | 145 | .697 | 152 | 207 | 602 | 4.3 | 5.9 | 17.2 |
| Junior College Totals | 30 | ... | 204 | 358 | .570 | 58 | 73 | .795 | 108 | 90 | 513 | 3.6 | 3.0 | 17.1 |
| 4-Year-College Totals | 94 | 3128 | 481 | 1142 | .421 | 195 | 272 | .717 | 336 | 425 | 1355 | 3.6 | 4.5 | 14.4 |

Three-point field goals: 1987-88, 22-for-59 (.373). 1990-91, 77-for-209 (.368). 1991-92, 99-for-265 (.374). Totals, 245-for-533 (.460).

## NBA REGULAR-SEASON RECORD

| Season Team | G | Min. | FGM | FGA | Pct. | FTM | FTA | Pct. | Off. | Def. | Tot. | Ast. | St. | Blk. | TO | Pts. | RPG | APG | PPG |
|---|---|---|---|---|---|---|---|---|---|---|---|---|---|---|---|---|---|---|---|
| 92-93—Milwaukee | 47 | 552 | 76 | 206 | .369 | 33 | 49 | .673 | 10 | 33 | 43 | 68 | 35 | 3 | 42 | 206 | 0.9 | 1.4 | 4.4 |
| 93-94—Milwaukee | 72 | 1242 | 158 | 382 | .414 | 97 | 122 | .795 | 36 | 110 | 146 | 168 | 102 | 17 | 83 | 445 | 2.0 | 2.3 | 6.2 |
| 94-95—Milwaukee | 52 | 602 | 57 | 134 | .425 | 61 | 80 | .763 | 15 | 34 | 49 | 85 | 30 | 4 | 41 | 191 | 0.9 | 1.6 | 3.7 |
| 95-96—Golden State | 68 | 712 | 91 | 185 | .492 | 31 | 37 | .838 | 17 | 46 | 63 | 85 | 33 | 11 | 42 | 257 | 0.9 | 1.3 | 3.8 |
| 96-97—Atlanta | 58 | 965 | 100 | 246 | .407 | 37 | 46 | .804 | 26 | 73 | 99 | 115 | 55 | 3 | 59 | 285 | 1.7 | 2.0 | 4.9 |
| 97-98—L.A. Lakers | 49 | 374 | 38 | 104 | .365 | 27 | 29 | .931 | 8 | 29 | 37 | 51 | 24 | 3 | 22 | 121 | 0.8 | 1.0 | 2.5 |
| 98-99—Sacramento | 43 | 736 | 59 | 138 | .428 | 71 | 84 | .845 | 25 | 71 | 96 | 112 | 53 | 5 | 47 | 213 | 2.2 | 2.6 | 5.0 |
| 99-00—Sacramento | 62 | 1281 | 161 | 346 | .465 | 107 | 116 | .922 | 38 | 121 | 159 | 150 | 75 | 7 | 85 | 495 | 2.6 | 2.4 | 8.0 |
| 00-01—Sacramento | 62 | 1010 | 103 | 255 | .404 | 64 | 73 | .877 | 16 | 78 | 94 | 130 | 28 | 6 | 53 | 316 | 1.5 | 2.1 | 5.1 |
| 01-02—Detroit | 82 | 1985 | 255 | 522 | .489 | 108 | 116 | .931 | 42 | 192 | 234 | 274 | 94 | 20 | 111 | 739 | 2.9 | 3.3 | 9.0 |
| 02-03—Detroit | 80 | 1473 | 191 | 424 | .450 | 86 | 100 | .860 | 33 | 147 | 180 | 206 | 63 | 14 | 81 | 555 | 2.3 | 2.6 | 6.9 |
| 03-04—Denver | 57 | 1101 | 120 | 297 | .404 | 60 | 71 | .845 | 25 | 98 | 123 | 147 | 57 | 8 | 53 | 351 | 2.2 | 2.6 | 6.2 |
| 04-05—Atlanta-Hou. | 69 | 1505 | 161 | 368 | .438 | 62 | 71 | .873 | 26 | 133 | 159 | 167 | 60 | 9 | 67 | 455 | 2.3 | 2.4 | 6.6 |
| Totals | 801 | 13538 | 1570 | 3607 | .435 | 844 | 994 | .849 | 317 | 1165 | 1482 | 1758 | 709 | 110 | 786 | 4629 | 1.9 | 2.2 | 5.8 |

Three-point field goals: 1992-93, 21-for-63 (.333). 1993-94, 32-for-115 (.278). 1994-95, 16-for-48 (.333). 1995-96, 5-for-11 (.455). 1996-97, 48-for-124 (.387). 1997-98, 18-for-61 (.295). 1998-99, 24-for-79 (.304). 1999-00, 66-for-154 (.429). 2000-01, 46-for-132 (.348). 2001-02, 121-for-258 (.469). 2002-03, 87-for-214 (.407). 2003-04, 51-for-138 (.370). 2004-05, 71-for-165 (.430). Totals, 645-for-1644 (.392).

Personal fouls/disqualifications: 1992-93, 57/0. 1993-94, 110/0. 1994-95, 54/0. 1995-96, 51/1. 1996-97, 56/0. 1997-98, 33/0. 1998-99, 61/1. 1999-00, 104/1. 2000-01, 66/0. 2001-02, 134/0. 2002-03, 104/0. 2003-04, 66/0. 2004-05, 95/0. Totals, 991/3.

## NBA PLAYOFF RECORD

| Season Team | G | Min. | FGM | FGA | Pct. | FTM | FTA | Pct. | Off. | Def. | Tot. | Ast. | St. | Blk. | TO | Pts. | RPG | APG | PPG |
|---|---|---|---|---|---|---|---|---|---|---|---|---|---|---|---|---|---|---|---|
| 96-97—Atlanta | 2 | 9 | 0 | 3 | .000 | 0 | 0 | ... | 0 | 0 | 0 | 0 | 0 | 0 | 0 | 0 | 0.0 | 0.0 | 0.0 |
| 97-98—L.A. Lakers | 7 | 18 | 0 | 8 | .000 | 0 | 0 | ... | 0 | 2 | 2 | 0 | 1 | 0 | 0 | 0 | 0.3 | 0.0 | 0.0 |
| 98-99—Sacramento | 5 | 112 | 12 | 34 | .353 | 11 | 12 | .917 | 3 | 7 | 10 | 9 | 6 | 1 | 9 | 40 | 2.0 | 1.8 | 8.0 |
| 99-00—Sacramento | 5 | 102 | 9 | 21 | .429 | 14 | 16 | .875 | 2 | 10 | 12 | 12 | 3 | 0 | 4 | 39 | 2.4 | 2.4 | 7.8 |
| 00-01—Sacramento | 7 | 55 | 7 | 17 | .412 | 0 | 0 | ... | 3 | 0 | 3 | 4 | 1 | 0 | 3 | 16 | 0.4 | 0.6 | 2.3 |
| 01-02—Detroit | 10 | 177 | 29 | 61 | .475 | 5 | 8 | .625 | 4 | 16 | 20 | 21 | 5 | 1 | 19 | 80 | 2.0 | 2.1 | 8.0 |
| 02-03—Detroit | 14 | 172 | 23 | 54 | .426 | 9 | 9 | 1.000 | 5 | 19 | 24 | 20 | 8 | 1 | 7 | 70 | 1.7 | 1.4 | 5.0 |
| 03-04—Denver | 5 | 100 | 8 | 24 | .333 | 2 | 3 | .667 | 4 | 14 | 18 | 10 | 3 | 0 | 4 | 21 | 3.6 | 2.0 | 4.2 |
| 04-05—Houston | 7 | 183 | 21 | 48 | .438 | 7 | 8 | .875 | 1 | 28 | 29 | 9 | 5 | 0 | 6 | 60 | 4.1 | 1.3 | 8.6 |
| Totals | 62 | 928 | 109 | 270 | .404 | 48 | 56 | .857 | 22 | 96 | 118 | 85 | 32 | 3 | 52 | 326 | 1.9 | 1.4 | 5.3 |

Three-point field goals: 1997-98, 0-for-5. 1998-99, 5-for-19 (.263). 1999-00, 7-for-12 (.583). 2000-01, 2-for-7 (.286). 2001-02, 17-for-38 (.447). 2002-03, 15-for-33 (.455). 2003-04, 3-for-9 (.333). 2004-05, 11-for-23 (.478). Totals, 60-for-146 (.411).

Personal fouls/disqualifications: 1997-98, 1/0. 1998-99, 9/0. 1999-00, 7/0. 2000-01, 7/0. 2001-02, 14/0. 2002-03, 14/0. 2003-04, 4/0. 2004-05, 13/0. Totals, 69/0.

# BATTIE, TONY — F/C — MAGIC

**PERSONAL:** Born February 11, 1976, in Dallas. ... 6-11/240. (2.11/108.9). ... Full name: Demetrius Antonio Battie.
**HIGH SCHOOL:** South Oak Cliff (Dallas).
**COLLEGE:** Texas Tech.
**TRANSACTIONS/CAREER NOTES:** Selected after junior season by Denver Nuggets in first round (fifth pick overall) of 1997 NBA Draft. ... Traded by Nuggets with draft rights to G Tyronn Lue to Los Angeles Lakers for G Nick Van Exel (June 24, 1998). ... Traded by Lakers to Boston Celtics for C Travis Knight (January 21, 1999). ... Traded by Celtics to Cleveland Cavaliers for G Ricky Davis, F/C Chris Mihm, C Michael Stewart and a second-round draft choice (December 15, 2003). ... Traded by Cavaliers with two future second-round draft choices to Orlando Magic for F Drew Gooden, C Steven Hunter and the draft rights to F Anderson Varejao (July 23, 2004).

## COLLEGIATE RECORD

| Season Team | G | Min. | FGM | FGA | Pct. | FTM | FTA | Pct. | Reb. | Ast. | Pts. | RPG | APG | PPG |
|---|---|---|---|---|---|---|---|---|---|---|---|---|---|---|
| 94-95—Texas Tech | 29 | 368 | 47 | 96 | .490 | 18 | 27 | .667 | 129 | 17 | 112 | 4.4 | 0.6 | 3.9 |
| 95-96—Texas Tech | 30 | 806 | 114 | 221 | .516 | 60 | 95 | .632 | 266 | 32 | 292 | 8.9 | 1.1 | 9.7 |
| 96-97—Texas Tech | 28 | 978 | 206 | 356 | .579 | 107 | 163 | .656 | 329 | 23 | 525 | 11.8 | 0.8 | 18.8 |
| Totals | 87 | 2152 | 367 | 673 | .545 | 185 | 285 | .649 | 724 | 72 | 929 | 8.3 | 0.8 | 10.7 |

Three-point field goals: 1994-95, 0-for-6. 1995-96, 4-for-14 (.286). 1996-97, 6-for-16 (.375). Totals, 10-for-36 (.278).
Personal fouls/disqualifications: 1994-95, 50/1. 1995-96, 74/3. Totals, 138/4.

## NBA REGULAR-SEASON RECORD

| Season Team | G | Min. | FGM | FGA | Pct. | FTM | FTA | Pct. | Off. | Def. | Tot. | Ast. | St. | Blk. | TO | Pts. | RPG | APG | PPG |
|---|---|---|---|---|---|---|---|---|---|---|---|---|---|---|---|---|---|---|---|
| 97-98—Denver | 65 | 1506 | 234 | 525 | .446 | 73 | 104 | .702 | 138 | 213 | 351 | 60 | 54 | 69 | 98 | 544 | 5.4 | 0.9 | 8.4 |
| 98-99—Boston | 50 | 1121 | 147 | 283 | .519 | 41 | 61 | .672 | 96 | 204 | 300 | 53 | 29 | 71 | 45 | 335 | 6.0 | 1.1 | 6.7 |
| 99-00—Boston | 82 | 1505 | 219 | 459 | .477 | 102 | 151 | .675 | 152 | 258 | 410 | 63 | 47 | 70 | 67 | 541 | 5.0 | 0.8 | 6.6 |
| 00-01—Boston | 40 | 845 | 108 | 201 | .537 | 44 | 69 | .638 | 73 | 160 | 233 | 16 | 27 | 60 | 37 | 260 | 5.8 | 0.4 | 6.5 |
| 01-02—Boston | 74 | 1819 | 211 | 390 | .541 | 88 | 130 | .677 | 184 | 297 | 481 | 35 | 60 | 67 | 51 | 510 | 6.5 | 0.5 | 6.9 |
| 02-03—Boston | 77 | 1683 | 199 | 369 | .539 | 88 | 118 | .746 | 148 | 285 | 433 | 49 | 33 | 81 | 48 | 487 | 6.5 | 0.7 | 7.3 |
| 03-04—Boston-Cleve. | 73 | 1478 | 170 | 384 | .443 | 66 | 89 | .742 | 118 | 241 | 359 | 58 | 26 | 67 | 63 | 408 | 4.9 | 0.8 | 5.6 |
| 04-05—Orlando | 81 | 1894 | 163 | 354 | .460 | 68 | 94 | .723 | 109 | 343 | 452 | 42 | 30 | 81 | 81 | 394 | 5.6 | 0.5 | 4.9 |
| Totals | 532 | 11851 | 1451 | 2965 | .489 | 570 | 816 | .699 | 1018 | 2001 | 3019 | 376 | 306 | 566 | 490 | 3479 | 5.7 | 0.7 | 6.5 |

Three-point field goals: 1997-98, 3-for-14 (.214). 1998-99, 0-for-3. 1999-00, 1-for-8 (.125). 2000-01, 0-for-3. 2001-02, 0-for-2. 2002-03, 1-for-5 (.200). 2003-04, 2-for-9 (.222). 2004-05, 0-for-6. Totals, 7-for-50 (.140).
Personal fouls/disqualifications: 1997-98, 199/6. 1998-99, 159/1. 1999-00, 249/4. 2000-01, 126/3. 2001-02, 219/3. 2002-03, 197/2. 2003-04, 159/0. 2004-05, 244/3. Totals, 1552/22.

### NBA PLAYOFF RECORD

| Season Team | G | Min. | FGM | FGA | Pct. | FTM | FTA | Pct. | REBOUNDS Off. | Def. | Tot. | Ast. | St. | Blk. | TO | Pts. | AVERAGES RPG | APG | PPG |
|---|---|---|---|---|---|---|---|---|---|---|---|---|---|---|---|---|---|---|---|
| 01-02—Boston | 16 | 443 | 42 | 86 | .488 | 13 | 21 | .619 | 39 | 82 | 121 | 13 | 10 | 30 | 11 | 97 | 7.6 | 0.8 | 6.1 |
| 02-03—Boston | 10 | 213 | 31 | 55 | .564 | 4 | 8 | .500 | 13 | 36 | 49 | 5 | 4 | 14 | 7 | 66 | 4.9 | 0.5 | 6.6 |
| Totals | 26 | 656 | 73 | 141 | .518 | 17 | 29 | .586 | 52 | 118 | 170 | 18 | 14 | 44 | 18 | 163 | 6.5 | 0.7 | 6.3 |

Three-point field goals: 2002-03, 0-for-3. Totals, 0-for-3 (.000).
Personal fouls/disqualifications: 2001-02, 51/1. 2002-03, 42/1. Totals, 93/2.

## BATTIER, SHANE     F     GRIZZLIES

**B**

**PERSONAL:** Born September 9, 1978, in Birmingham, Mich. ... 6-8/220. (2.03/99.8). ... Full name: Shane Courtney Battier
**HIGH SCHOOL:** Detroit Country Day (Birmingham, Mich.).
**COLLEGE:** Duke.
**TRANSACTIONS/CAREER NOTES:** Selected by Vancouver Grizzlies in first round (sixth pick overall) of 2001 NBA Draft. ... Grizzlies franchise moved to Memphis for 2001-02 season.

### COLLEGIATE RECORD

**NOTES:** Member of NCAA Division I championship team (2001). ... The Sporting News All-America first team (2001). ... The Sporting News College Player of the Year (2001). ... Naismith Award winner (2001). ... Wooden Award winner (2001). ... NCAA Division I Tournament Most Outstanding Player (2001). ... The Sporting News All-America second team (2000).

| Season Team | G | Min. | FGM | FGA | Pct. | FTM | FTA | Pct. | Reb. | Ast. | Pts. | AVERAGES RPG | APG | PPG |
|---|---|---|---|---|---|---|---|---|---|---|---|---|---|---|
| 97-98—Duke | 36 | 887 | 96 | 178 | .539 | 79 | 108 | .731 | 230 | 40 | 275 | 6.4 | 1.1 | 7.6 |
| 98-99—Duke | 37 | 881 | 114 | 209 | .545 | 71 | 98 | .724 | 180 | 55 | 338 | 4.9 | 1.5 | 9.1 |
| 99-00—Duke | 34 | 1206 | 190 | 383 | .496 | 134 | 164 | .817 | 192 | 72 | 593 | 5.6 | 2.1 | 17.4 |
| 00-01—Duke | 39 | 1363 | 251 | 533 | .471 | 152 | 191 | .796 | 285 | 72 | 778 | 7.3 | 1.8 | 19.9 |
| Totals | 146 | 4337 | 651 | 1303 | .500 | 436 | 561 | .777 | 887 | 239 | 1984 | 6.1 | 1.6 | 13.6 |

Three-point field goals: 1997-98, 4-for-24 (.167). 1998-99, 39-for-94 (.415). 1999-00, 79-for-178 (.444). 2000-01, 124-for-296 (.419). Totals, 246-for-592 (.416).
Personal fouls/disqualifications: 1997-98, 67/0. 1998-99, 78/0. 1999-00, 71/0. 2000-01, 80/0. Totals, 296/0.

### NBA REGULAR-SEASON RECORD

**HONORS:** NBA All-Rookie first team (2002).

| Season Team | G | Min. | FGM | FGA | Pct. | FTM | FTA | Pct. | REBOUNDS Off. | Def. | Tot. | Ast. | St. | Blk. | TO | Pts. | AVERAGES RPG | APG | PPG |
|---|---|---|---|---|---|---|---|---|---|---|---|---|---|---|---|---|---|---|---|
| 01-02—Memphis | 78 | 3097 | 412 | 961 | .429 | 198 | 283 | .700 | 180 | 238 | 418 | 216 | 121 | 81 | 155 | 1125 | 5.4 | 2.8 | 14.4 |
| 02-03—Memphis | 78 | 2383 | 275 | 569 | .483 | 120 | 145 | .828 | 128 | 217 | 345 | 105 | 102 | 88 | 68 | 756 | 4.4 | 1.3 | 9.7 |
| 03-04—Memphis | 79 | 1947 | 242 | 543 | .446 | 120 | 164 | .732 | 102 | 201 | 303 | 101 | 101 | 58 | 56 | 669 | 3.8 | 1.3 | 8.5 |
| 04-05—Memphis | 80 | 2516 | 271 | 613 | .442 | 180 | 228 | .789 | 158 | 255 | 413 | 126 | 91 | 77 | 75 | 792 | 5.2 | 1.6 | 9.9 |
| Totals | 315 | 9943 | 1200 | 2686 | .447 | 618 | 820 | .754 | 568 | 911 | 1479 | 548 | 415 | 304 | 354 | 3342 | 4.7 | 1.7 | 10.6 |

Three-point field goals: 2001-02, 103-for-276 (.373). 2002-03, 86-for-216 (.398). 2003-04, 65-for-186 (.349). 2004-05, 70-for-177 (.395). Totals, 324-for-855 (.379).
Personal fouls/disqualifications: 2001-02, 215/2. 2002-03, 207/0. 2003-04, 187/1. 2004-05, 201/2. Totals, 810/5.

### NBA PLAYOFF RECORD

| Season Team | G | Min. | FGM | FGA | Pct. | FTM | FTA | Pct. | REBOUNDS Off. | Def. | Tot. | Ast. | St. | Blk. | TO | Pts. | AVERAGES RPG | APG | PPG |
|---|---|---|---|---|---|---|---|---|---|---|---|---|---|---|---|---|---|---|---|
| 03-04—Memphis | 4 | 69 | 6 | 15 | .400 | 4 | 6 | .667 | 6 | 6 | 12 | 1 | 0 | 1 | 4 | 19 | 3.0 | 0.3 | 4.8 |
| 04-05—Memphis | 4 | 119 | 13 | 31 | .419 | 2 | 5 | .400 | 10 | 17 | 27 | 6 | 2 | 4 | 4 | 29 | 6.8 | 1.5 | 7.3 |
| Totals | 8 | 188 | 19 | 46 | .413 | 6 | 11 | .545 | 16 | 23 | 39 | 7 | 2 | 5 | 8 | 48 | 4.9 | 0.9 | 6.0 |

Three-point field goals: 2003-04, 3-for-7 (.429). 2004-05, 1-for-7 (.143). Totals, 4-for-14 (.286).
Personal fouls/disqualifications: 2003-04, 17/0. 2004-05, 14/0. Totals, 31/0.

## BAXTER, LONNY     F

**PERSONAL:** Born July 27, 1979, in Silver Spring, Md. ... 6-8/264. (2.03/119.7). ... Full name: Lonny Leroy Baxter
**HIGH SCHOOL:** Richard Montgomery (Rockville, Md.), then Anacosti.
**COLLEGE:** Maryland.
**TRANSACTIONS/CAREER NOTES:** Selected by Chicago Bulls in second round (44th pick overall) of 2002 NBA Draft. ... Traded by Bulls with F Donyell Marshall and G Jalen Rose to Toronto Raptors for F/C Antonio Davis, F Chris Jefferies and F Jerome Williams (December 1, 2003). ... Waived by Raptors (February 29, 2004). ... Claimed off waivers by Washington Wizards (March 3, 2004). ... Selected by Charlotte Bobcats from Wizards in NBA Expansion Draft (June 22, 2004). ... Signed as free agent by Atlanta Hawks (October 4, 2004). ... Released by Hawks (October 28, 2004). ... Played in Continental Basketball Association (2004). ... Signed as free agent by New Orleans Hornets (December 12, 2004). ... Waived by Hornets (December 27, 2004).

### COLLEGIATE RECORD

**NOTES:** Member of NCAA Division I championship team (2002).

| Season Team | G | Min. | FGM | FGA | Pct. | FTM | FTA | Pct. | Reb. | Ast. | Pts. | AVERAGES RPG | APG | PPG |
|---|---|---|---|---|---|---|---|---|---|---|---|---|---|---|
| 98-99—Maryland | 32 | 463 | 82 | 137 | .599 | 51 | 89 | .573 | 116 | 18 | 217 | 3.6 | 0.6 | 6.8 |
| 99-00—Maryland | 35 | 970 | 218 | 409 | .533 | 111 | 187 | .594 | 308 | 31 | 547 | 8.8 | 0.9 | 15.6 |
| 00-01—Maryland | 36 | 935 | 219 | 387 | .566 | 122 | 206 | .592 | 286 | 19 | 561 | 7.9 | 0.5 | 15.6 |
| 01-02—Maryland | 35 | 1005 | 193 | 354 | .545 | 147 | 236 | .623 | 288 | 28 | 533 | 8.2 | 0.8 | 15.2 |
| Totals | 138 | 3373 | 712 | 1287 | .553 | 431 | 718 | .600 | 998 | 96 | 1858 | 7.2 | 0.7 | 13.5 |

Three-point field goals: 1998-99, 2-for-2 (1.000). 2000-01, 1-for-2 (.500). 2001-02, 0-for-1. Totals, 3-for-5 (.600).

## NBA REGULAR-SEASON RECORD

| Season Team | G | Min. | FGM | FGA | Pct. | FTM | FTA | Pct. | REBOUNDS Off. | Def. | Tot. | Ast. | St. | Blk. | TO | Pts. | AVERAGES RPG | APG | PPG |
|---|---|---|---|---|---|---|---|---|---|---|---|---|---|---|---|---|---|---|---|
| 02-03—Chicago ......... | 55 | 682 | 96 | 206 | .466 | 70 | 103 | .680 | 65 | 100 | 165 | 16 | 9 | 22 | 46 | 262 | 3.0 | 0.3 | 4.8 |
| 03-04—Chi.-Tor.-Wash.. | 62 | 766 | 103 | 209 | .493 | 44 | 76 | .579 | 64 | 123 | 187 | 20 | 17 | 29 | 38 | 251 | 3.0 | 0.3 | 4.0 |
| 04-05—New Orleans ... | 4 | 36 | 3 | 11 | .273 | 0 | 2 | .000 | 4 | 4 | 8 | 0 | 0 | 0 | 4 | 6 | 2.0 | 0.0 | 1.5 |
| Totals | 121 | 1484 | 202 | 426 | .474 | 114 | 181 | .630 | 133 | 227 | 360 | 36 | 26 | 51 | 88 | 519 | 3.0 | 0.3 | 4.3 |

Three-point field goals: 2002-03, 0-for-2. 2003-04, 1-for-3 (.333). Totals, 1-for-5 (.200).
Personal fouls/disqualifications: 2002-03, 135/1. 2003-04, 123/3. 2004-05, 10/0. Totals, 268/4.

## CBA RECORD

| Season Team | G | Min. | FGM | FGA | Pct. | FTM | FTA | Pct. | Reb. | Ast. | Pts. | AVERAGES RPG | APG | PPG |
|---|---|---|---|---|---|---|---|---|---|---|---|---|---|---|
| 04-05—Yakima ......................... | 6 | 180 | 38 | 85 | .447 | 22 | 33 | .667 | 222 | 45 | 98 | 37.0 | 7.5 | 16.3 |

## GREEK LEAGUE RECORD

| Season Team | G | Min. | FGM | FGA | Pct. | FTM | FTA | Pct. | Reb. | Ast. | Pts. | AVERAGES RPG | APG | PPG |
|---|---|---|---|---|---|---|---|---|---|---|---|---|---|---|
| 04-05—Panathinaikos................. | 12 | 174 | 37 | 57 | .649 | 12 | 60 | .200 | 59 | 2 | 86 | 4.9 | 0.2 | 7.2 |

# BELL, RAJA — G — SUNS

**PERSONAL:** Born September 19, 1976, in St. Croix, Virgin Islands. ... 6-5/215. (1.96/97.5).
**HIGH SCHOOL:** Killian (Miami).
**COLLEGE:** Boston University, then Florida International.
**TRANSACTIONS/CAREER NOTES:** Not drafted by an NBA franchise. ... Played in Continental Basketball Association with Yakima Sun Kings (1999-2001). ... Signed as free agent by San Antonio Spurs (August 2, 2000). ... Waived by Spurs (October 30, 2000). ... Signed by Philadelphia 76ers to 10-day contract (April 6, 2001). ... Re-signed by 76ers for remainder of season (April 16, 2001). ... Signed as free agent by Dallas Mavericks (October 1, 2002). ... Signed as free agent by Utah Jazz (September 26, 2003). ... Signed as free agent by Phoenix Suns (August 3, 2005).

## COLLEGIATE RECORD

| Season Team | G | Min. | FGM | FGA | Pct. | FTM | FTA | Pct. | Reb. | Ast. | Pts. | AVERAGES RPG | APG | PPG |
|---|---|---|---|---|---|---|---|---|---|---|---|---|---|---|
| 94-95—Boston University........... | 30 | 866 | 119 | 291 | .409 | 59 | 81 | .728 | 127 | 37 | 330 | 4.2 | 1.2 | 11.0 |
| 95-96—Boston University........... | 28 | 932 | 155 | 360 | .431 | 74 | 112 | .661 | 114 | 52 | 421 | 4.1 | 1.9 | 15.0 |
| 96-97—Florida International ....... | | | | | | Did not play—transfer student. | | | | | | | | |
| 97-98—Florida International ....... | 29 | 855 | 165 | 373 | .442 | 112 | 146 | .767 | 118 | 65 | 481 | 4.1 | 2.2 | 16.6 |
| 98-99—Florida International ....... | 29 | 1011 | 167 | 366 | .456 | 102 | 137 | .745 | 124 | 79 | 484 | 4.3 | 2.7 | 16.7 |
| Totals ..................................... | 116 | 3664 | 606 | 1390 | .436 | 347 | 476 | .729 | 483 | 233 | 1716 | 4.2 | 2.0 | 14.8 |

Three-point field goals: 1994-95, 33-for-77 (.429). 1995-96, 37-for-112 (.330). 1997-98, 39-for-121 (.322). 1998-99, 48-for-138 (.348). Totals, 157-for-448 (.350).
Personal fouls/disqualifications: 1994-95, 92/0. 1995-96, 73/0. 1997-98, 75/0. 1998-99, 87/0. Totals, 327/0.

## CBA RECORD

| Season Team | G | Min. | FGM | FGA | Pct. | FTM | FTA | Pct. | Reb. | Ast. | Pts. | AVERAGES RPG | APG | PPG |
|---|---|---|---|---|---|---|---|---|---|---|---|---|---|---|
| 99-00—Yakima ......................... | 52 | 1494 | 238 | 464 | .513 | 104 | 137 | .759 | 146 | 142 | 597 | 2.8 | 2.7 | 11.5 |
| 00-01—Yakima ......................... | 9 | 293 | 58 | 124 | .468 | 44 | 57 | .772 | 39 | 37 | 172 | 4.3 | 4.1 | 19.1 |
| Totals ..................................... | 61 | 1787 | 296 | 588 | .503 | 148 | 194 | .763 | 185 | 179 | 769 | 3.0 | 2.9 | 12.6 |

Three-point field goals: 1999-00, 17-for-46 (.370). 2000-01, 12-for-36 (.333). Totals, 29-for-82 (.354).
Personal fouls/disqualifications: 1999-00, 137/0. 2000-01, 22/0. Totals, 159/0.

## NBA REGULAR-SEASON RECORD

| Season Team | G | Min. | FGM | FGA | Pct. | FTM | FTA | Pct. | REBOUNDS Off. | Def. | Tot. | Ast. | St. | Blk. | TO | Pts. | AVERAGES RPG | APG | PPG |
|---|---|---|---|---|---|---|---|---|---|---|---|---|---|---|---|---|---|---|---|
| 00-01—Philadelphia .... | 5 | 30 | 2 | 7 | .286 | 0 | 0 | ... | 0 | 1 | 1 | 0 | 1 | 0 | 2 | 5 | 0.2 | 0.0 | 1.0 |
| 01-02—Philadelphia .... | 74 | 890 | 103 | 240 | .429 | 36 | 48 | .750 | 31 | 80 | 111 | 71 | 21 | 4 | 48 | 254 | 1.5 | 1.0 | 3.4 |
| 02-03—Dallas............. | 75 | 1173 | 93 | 211 | .441 | 23 | 34 | .676 | 47 | 98 | 145 | 57 | 52 | 8 | 43 | 230 | 1.9 | 0.8 | 3.1 |
| 03-04—Utah............... | 82 | 2020 | 329 | 805 | .409 | 195 | 248 | .786 | 60 | 181 | 241 | 107 | 63 | 13 | 111 | 915 | 2.9 | 1.3 | 11.2 |
| 04-05—Utah............... | 63 | 1790 | 303 | 667 | .454 | 112 | 150 | .747 | 48 | 153 | 201 | 91 | 44 | 8 | 79 | 772 | 3.2 | 1.4 | 12.3 |
| Totals ................... | 299 | 5903 | 830 | 1930 | .430 | 366 | 480 | .763 | 186 | 513 | 699 | 326 | 181 | 33 | 283 | 2176 | 2.3 | 1.1 | 7.3 |

Three-point field goals: 2000-01, 1-for-3 (.333). 2001-02, 12-for-44 (.273). 2002-03, 21-for-51 (.412). 2003-04, 62-for-166 (.373). 2004-05, 54-for-134 (.403). Totals, 150-for-398 (.377).
Personal fouls/disqualifications: 2000-01, 1/0. 2001-02, 109/0. 2002-03, 134/1. 2003-04, 262/6. 2004-05, 205/4. Totals, 711/11.

## NBA PLAYOFF RECORD

| Season Team | G | Min. | FGM | FGA | Pct. | FTM | FTA | Pct. | REBOUNDS Off. | Def. | Tot. | Ast. | St. | Blk. | TO | Pts. | AVERAGES RPG | APG | PPG |
|---|---|---|---|---|---|---|---|---|---|---|---|---|---|---|---|---|---|---|---|
| 00-01—Philadelphia .... | 15 | 124 | 12 | 27 | .444 | 8 | 14 | .571 | 4 | 9 | 13 | 7 | 15 | 0 | 5 | 34 | 0.9 | 0.5 | 2.3 |
| 01-02—Philadelphia .... | 3 | 8 | 1 | 3 | .333 | 0 | 0 | ... | 1 | 0 | 1 | 0 | 0 | 0 | 0 | 2 | 0.3 | 0.0 | 0.7 |
| 02-03—Dallas............. | 17 | 305 | 40 | 73 | .548 | 11 | 20 | .550 | 13 | 38 | 51 | 27 | 5 | 0 | 6 | 97 | 3.0 | 1.6 | 5.7 |
| Totals ................... | 35 | 437 | 53 | 103 | .515 | 19 | 34 | .559 | 18 | 47 | 65 | 34 | 20 | 0 | 11 | 133 | 1.9 | 1.0 | 3.8 |

Three-point field goals: 2000-01, 2-for-8 (.250). 2001-02, 0-for-2. 2002-03, 6-for-13 (.462). Totals, 8-for-23 (.348).
Personal fouls/disqualifications: 2000-01, 20/0. 2002-03, 41/0. Totals, 61/0.

## BENDER, JONATHAN — F — PACERS

**PERSONAL:** Born January 30, 1981, in Picayune, Miss. ... 6-11/220. (2.11/99.8). ... Full name: Jonathan Rene Bender
**HIGH SCHOOL:** Picayune (Miss.) Memorial.
**COLLEGE:** Did not attend college.
**TRANSACTIONS/CAREER NOTES:** Selected out of high school by Toronto Raptors in first round (fifth pick overall) of 1999 NBA Draft. ... Draft rights traded by Raptors to Indiana Pacers for F/C Antonio Davis (August 1, 1999).

### NBA REGULAR-SEASON RECORD

| Season Team | G | Min. | FGM | FGA | Pct. | FTM | FTA | Pct. | REBOUNDS Off. | Def. | Tot. | Ast. | St. | Blk. | TO | Pts. | RPG | APG | PPG |
|---|---|---|---|---|---|---|---|---|---|---|---|---|---|---|---|---|---|---|---|
| 99-00—Indiana | 24 | 130 | 23 | 70 | .329 | 16 | 24 | .667 | 4 | 17 | 21 | 3 | 1 | 5 | 7 | 64 | 0.9 | 0.1 | 2.7 |
| 00-01—Indiana | 59 | 574 | 66 | 186 | .355 | 50 | 68 | .735 | 14 | 60 | 74 | 32 | 7 | 28 | 42 | 193 | 1.3 | 0.5 | 3.3 |
| 01-02—Indiana | 78 | 1647 | 198 | 460 | .430 | 140 | 181 | .773 | 64 | 180 | 244 | 62 | 19 | 49 | 96 | 581 | 3.1 | 0.8 | 7.4 |
| 02-03—Indiana | 46 | 819 | 112 | 254 | .441 | 60 | 84 | .714 | 42 | 91 | 133 | 42 | 8 | 56 | 42 | 303 | 2.9 | 0.9 | 6.6 |
| 03-04—Indiana | 21 | 271 | 50 | 106 | .472 | 39 | 47 | .830 | 9 | 31 | 40 | 9 | 5 | 11 | 33 | 148 | 1.9 | 0.4 | 7.0 |
| 04-05—Indiana | 7 | 93 | 16 | 40 | .400 | 3 | 6 | .500 | 5 | 9 | 14 | 4 | 1 | 2 | 10 | 36 | 2.0 | 0.6 | 5.1 |
| Totals | 235 | 3534 | 465 | 1116 | .417 | 308 | 410 | .751 | 138 | 388 | 526 | 152 | 41 | 151 | 230 | 1325 | 2.2 | 0.6 | 5.6 |

Three-point field goals: 1999-00, 2-for-12 (.167). 2000-01, 11-for-41 (.268). 2001-02, 45-for-125 (.360). 2002-03, 19-for-53 (.358). 2003-04, 9-for-22 (.409). 2004-05, 1-for-5 (.200). Totals, 87-for-258 (.337).
Personal fouls/disqualifications: 1999-00, 18/0. 2000-01, 73/0. 2001-02, 147/1. 2002-03, 86/0. 2003-04, 23/0. 2004-05, 9/0. Totals, 356/1.

### NBA PLAYOFF RECORD

| Season Team | G | Min. | FGM | FGA | Pct. | FTM | FTA | Pct. | REBOUNDS Off. | Def. | Tot. | Ast. | St. | Blk. | TO | Pts. | RPG | APG | PPG |
|---|---|---|---|---|---|---|---|---|---|---|---|---|---|---|---|---|---|---|---|
| 99-00—Indiana | 9 | 21 | 4 | 6 | .667 | 3 | 6 | .500 | 0 | 3 | 3 | 0 | 1 | 0 | 0 | 12 | 0.3 | 0.0 | 1.3 |
| 00-01—Indiana | 1 | 4 | 0 | 1 | .000 | 0 | 0 | ... | 0 | 0 | 0 | 0 | 0 | 0 | 0 | 0 | 0.0 | 0.0 | 0.0 |
| 01-02—Indiana | 5 | 45 | 3 | 6 | .500 | 0 | 0 | ... | 0 | 4 | 4 | 2 | 2 | 3 | 5 | 6 | 0.8 | 0.4 | 1.2 |
| 02-03—Indiana | 3 | 34 | 5 | 15 | .333 | 4 | 6 | .667 | 3 | 4 | 7 | 0 | 0 | 2 | 0 | 17 | 2.3 | 0.0 | 5.7 |
| 03-04—Indiana | 16 | 200 | 28 | 69 | .406 | 12 | 16 | .750 | 10 | 18 | 28 | 7 | 2 | 14 | 12 | 77 | 1.8 | 0.4 | 4.8 |
| Totals | 34 | 304 | 40 | 97 | .412 | 19 | 28 | .679 | 13 | 29 | 42 | 9 | 5 | 19 | 17 | 112 | 1.2 | 0.3 | 3.3 |

Three-point field goals: 1999-00, 1-for-1 (1.000). 2001-02, 0-for-1. 2002-03, 3-for-9 (.333). 2003-04, 9-for-25 (.360). Totals, 13-for-36 (.361).
Personal fouls/disqualifications: 1999-00, 2/0. 2000-01, 1/0. 2001-02, 6/0. 2002-03, 2/0. 2003-04, 19/0. Totals, 30/0.

## BEST, TRAVIS — G

**PERSONAL:** Born July 12, 1972, in Springfield, Mass. ... 5-11/182. (1.80/82.6). ... Full name: Travis Eric Best
**HIGH SCHOOL:** Springfield (Mass.) Central.
**COLLEGE:** Georgia Tech.
**TRANSACTIONS/CAREER NOTES:** Selected by Indiana Pacers in first round (23rd pick overall) of 1995 NBA Draft. ... Traded by Pacers with G Jalen Rose, G Norman Richardson and conditional second-round draft choice to Chicago Bulls for C Brad Miller, G Ron Mercer, G/F Ron Artest and G Kevin Ollie (February 19, 2002). ... Signed as free agent by Miami Heat (September 5, 2002). ... Signed as free agent by Dallas Mavericks (August 22, 2003). ... Signed as free agent by New Jersey Nets (October 4, 2004).

### COLLEGIATE RECORD

| Season Team | G | Min. | FGM | FGA | Pct. | FTM | FTA | Pct. | Reb. | Ast. | Pts. | AVERAGES RPG | APG | PPG |
|---|---|---|---|---|---|---|---|---|---|---|---|---|---|---|
| 91-92—Georgia Tech | 35 | 1227 | 151 | 336 | .449 | 72 | 98 | .735 | 89 | 198 | 430 | 2.5 | 5.7 | 12.3 |
| 92-93—Georgia Tech | 30 | 1075 | 163 | 345 | .472 | 82 | 109 | .752 | 94 | 176 | 488 | 3.1 | 5.9 | 16.3 |
| 93-94—Georgia Tech | 29 | 1087 | 180 | 390 | .462 | 123 | 142 | .866 | 104 | 167 | 532 | 3.6 | 5.8 | 18.3 |
| 94-95—Georgia Tech | 30 | 1115 | 209 | 469 | .446 | 116 | 137 | .847 | 95 | 151 | 607 | 3.2 | 5.0 | 20.2 |
| Totals | 124 | 4504 | 703 | 1540 | .456 | 393 | 486 | .809 | 382 | 692 | 2057 | 3.1 | 5.6 | 16.6 |

Three-point field goals: 1991-92, 56-for-145 (.386). 1992-93, 80-for-175 (.457). 1993-94, 49-for-144 (.340). 1994-95, 73-for-192 (.380). Totals, 258-for-656 (.393).

### NBA REGULAR-SEASON RECORD

| Season Team | G | Min. | FGM | FGA | Pct. | FTM | FTA | Pct. | REBOUNDS Off. | Def. | Tot. | Ast. | St. | Blk. | TO | Pts. | RPG | APG | PPG |
|---|---|---|---|---|---|---|---|---|---|---|---|---|---|---|---|---|---|---|---|
| 95-96—Indiana | 59 | 571 | 69 | 163 | .423 | 75 | 90 | .833 | 11 | 33 | 44 | 97 | 20 | 3 | 63 | 221 | 0.7 | 1.6 | 3.7 |
| 96-97—Indiana | 76 | 2064 | 274 | 620 | .442 | 149 | 197 | .756 | 36 | 130 | 166 | 318 | 98 | 5 | 153 | 754 | 2.2 | 4.2 | 9.9 |
| 97-98—Indiana | 82 | 1547 | 201 | 480 | .419 | 112 | 131 | .855 | 28 | 94 | 122 | 281 | 85 | 5 | 111 | 535 | 1.5 | 3.4 | 6.5 |
| 98-99—Indiana | 49 | 1043 | 127 | 305 | .416 | 70 | 83 | .843 | 19 | 61 | 80 | 169 | 42 | 4 | 62 | 346 | 1.6 | 3.4 | 7.1 |
| 99-00—Indiana | 82 | 1691 | 271 | 561 | .483 | 156 | 190 | .821 | 16 | 126 | 142 | 272 | 76 | 5 | 107 | 733 | 1.7 | 3.3 | 8.9 |
| 00-01—Indiana | 77 | 2457 | 347 | 788 | .440 | 187 | 226 | .827 | 38 | 184 | 222 | 473 | 110 | 11 | 127 | 918 | 2.9 | 6.1 | 11.9 |
| 01-02—Ind.-Chicago | 74 | 1747 | 228 | 518 | .440 | 104 | 116 | .897 | 20 | 131 | 151 | 324 | 89 | 7 | 99 | 581 | 2.0 | 4.4 | 7.9 |
| 02-03—Miami | 72 | 1807 | 231 | 583 | .396 | 105 | 123 | .854 | 26 | 121 | 147 | 255 | 44 | 7 | 106 | 603 | 2.0 | 3.5 | 8.4 |
| 03-04—Dallas | 61 | 762 | 64 | 172 | .372 | 40 | 46 | .870 | 17 | 51 | 68 | 112 | 31 | 4 | 33 | 171 | 1.1 | 1.8 | 2.8 |
| 04-05—New Jersey | 76 | 1461 | 190 | 452 | .420 | 108 | 122 | .885 | 19 | 88 | 107 | 143 | 66 | 9 | 67 | 514 | 1.4 | 1.9 | 6.8 |
| Totals | 708 | 15150 | 2002 | 4642 | .431 | 1106 | 1324 | .835 | 230 | 1019 | 1249 | 2444 | 661 | 60 | 928 | 5376 | 1.8 | 3.5 | 7.6 |

Three-point field goals: 1995-96, 8-for-25 (.320). 1996-97, 57-for-155 (.368). 1997-98, 21-for-70 (.300). 1998-99, 22-for-59 (.373). 1999-00, 35-for-93 (.376). 2000-01, 37-for-97 (.381). 2001-02, 21-for-59 (.356). 2002-03, 36-for-109 (.330). 2003-04, 3-for-20 (.150). 2004-05, 26-for-85 (.306). Totals, 266-for-772 (.345).
Personal fouls/disqualifications: 1995-96, 80/0. 1996-97, 221/3. 1997-98, 193/3. 1998-99, 111/2. 1999-00, 204/1. 2000-01, 246/10. 2001-02, 173/6. 2002-03, 174/6. 2003-04, 66/0. 2004-05, 148/3. Totals, 1616/34.

### NBA PLAYOFF RECORD

| Season Team | G | Min. | FGM | FGA | Pct. | FTM | FTA | Pct. | REBOUNDS Off. | Def. | Tot. | Ast. | St. | Blk. | TO | Pts. | RPG | APG | PPG |
|---|---|---|---|---|---|---|---|---|---|---|---|---|---|---|---|---|---|---|---|
| 95-96—Indiana | 5 | 84 | 11 | 22 | .500 | 6 | 7 | .857 | 3 | 8 | 11 | 9 | 6 | 0 | 10 | 29 | 2.2 | 1.8 | 5.8 |
| 97-98—Indiana | 16 | 280 | 27 | 72 | .375 | 38 | 43 | .884 | 1 | 15 | 16 | 31 | 11 | 3 | 19 | 97 | 1.0 | 1.9 | 6.1 |

| Season Team | G | Min. | FGM | FGA | Pct. | FTM | FTA | Pct. | Off. | Def. | Tot. | Ast. | St. | Blk. | TO | Pts. | RPG | APG | PPG |
|---|---|---|---|---|---|---|---|---|---|---|---|---|---|---|---|---|---|---|---|
| 98-99—Indiana............ | 11 | 150 | 16 | 46 | .348 | 12 | 13 | .923 | 7 | 10 | 17 | 21 | 4 | 1 | 14 | 46 | 1.5 | 1.9 | 4.2 |
| 99-00—Indiana............ | 23 | 463 | 77 | 179 | .430 | 37 | 44 | .841 | 15 | 42 | 57 | 66 | 19 | 4 | 25 | 204 | 2.5 | 2.9 | 8.9 |
| 00-01—Indiana............ | 4 | 163 | 17 | 39 | .436 | 4 | 4 | 1.000 | 6 | 13 | 19 | 37 | 4 | 0 | 6 | 39 | 4.8 | 9.3 | 9.8 |
| 04-05—New Jersey..... | 4 | 82 | 9 | 22 | .409 | 8 | 9 | .889 | 2 | 4 | 6 | 9 | 1 | 0 | 3 | 27 | 1.5 | 2.3 | 6.8 |
| Totals .................... | 63 | 1222 | 157 | 380 | .413 | 105 | 120 | .875 | 34 | 92 | 126 | 173 | 45 | 8 | 77 | 442 | 2.0 | 2.7 | 7.0 |

Three-point field goals: 1995-96, 1-for-6 (.167). 1997-98, 5-for-18 (.278). 1998-99, 2-for-10 (.200). 1999-00, 13-for-30 (.433). 2000-01, 1-for-3 (.333). 2004-05, 1-for-9 (.111). Totals, 23-for-76 (.303).
Personal fouls/disqualifications: 1995-96, 10/0. 1997-98, 36/0. 1998-99, 34/1. 1999-00, 61/1. 2000-01, 15/1. 2004-05, 9/0. Totals, 165/3.

# BIBBY, MIKE       G        KINGS

**B**

**PERSONAL:** Born May 13, 1978, in Cherry Hill, N.J. ... 6-1/190. (1.85/86.2). ... Son of Henry Bibby, guard with New York Knicks (1972-73 through 1974-75), New Orleans Jazz (1974-75 and 1975-76), Philadelphia 76ers (1976-77 through 1979-80) and San Diego Clippers (1980-81); brother-in-law of Eddie House, guard, Sacramento Kings (2004-05).
**HIGH SCHOOL:** Shadow Mountain (Phoenix).
**COLLEGE:** Arizona.
**TRANSACTIONS/CAREER NOTES:** Selected after sophomore season by Vancouver Grizzlies in first round (second pick overall) of 1998 NBA Draft. ... Traded by Grizzlies with G Brent Price to Sacramento Kings for G Jason Williams and G/F Nick Anderson (June 27, 2001).
**MISCELLANEOUS:** Memphis Grizzlies franchise all-time assists leader with 1,675 (1998-99 through 2000-01).

### COLLEGIATE RECORD

**NOTES:** Member of NCAA Division I championship team (1997). ... The Sporting News All-America first team (1998).

| Season Team | G | Min. | FGM | FGA | Pct. | FTM | FTA | Pct. | Reb. | Ast. | Pts. | RPG | APG | PPG |
|---|---|---|---|---|---|---|---|---|---|---|---|---|---|---|
| 96-97—Arizona .......................... | 34 | 1110 | 151 | 339 | .445 | 89 | 127 | .701 | 109 | 176 | 458 | 3.2 | 5.2 | 13.5 |
| 97-98—Arizona .......................... | 35 | 1124 | 209 | 450 | .464 | 108 | 143 | .755 | 106 | 199 | 603 | 3.0 | 5.7 | 17.2 |
| Totals ..................................... | 69 | 2234 | 360 | 789 | .456 | 197 | 270 | .730 | 215 | 375 | 1061 | 3.1 | 5.4 | 15.4 |

Three-point field goals: 1996-97, 67-for-170 (.394). 1997-98, 77-for-199 (.387). Totals, 144-for-369 (.390).

### NBA REGULAR-SEASON RECORD

**HONORS:** NBA All-Rookie first team (1999).

| Season Team | G | Min. | FGM | FGA | Pct. | FTM | FTA | Pct. | Off. | Def. | Tot. | Ast. | St. | Blk. | TO | Pts. | RPG | APG | PPG |
|---|---|---|---|---|---|---|---|---|---|---|---|---|---|---|---|---|---|---|---|
| 98-99—Vancouver....... | 50 | 1758 | 260 | 605 | .430 | 127 | 169 | .751 | 30 | 106 | 136 | 325 | 78 | 5 | 146 | 662 | 2.7 | 6.5 | 13.2 |
| 99-00—Vancouver....... | 82 | 3155 | 459 | 1031 | .445 | 195 | 250 | .780 | 73 | 233 | 306 | 665 | 132 | 15 | 247 | 1190 | 3.7 | 8.1 | 14.5 |
| 00-01—Vancouver....... | 82 | 3190 | 525 | 1157 | .454 | 143 | 188 | .761 | 47 | 257 | 304 | 685 | 107 | 12 | 248 | 1301 | 3.7 | 8.4 | 15.9 |
| 01-02—Sacramento .... | 80 | 2659 | 446 | 985 | .453 | 155 | 193 | .803 | 37 | 185 | 222 | 403 | 87 | 15 | 134 | 1098 | 2.8 | 5.0 | 13.7 |
| 02-03—Sacramento .... | 55 | 1835 | 329 | 700 | .470 | 161 | 187 | .861 | 34 | 113 | 147 | 285 | 72 | 8 | 127 | 875 | 2.7 | 5.2 | 15.9 |
| 03-04—Sacramento .... | 82 | 2980 | 527 | 1170 | .450 | 304 | 373 | .815 | 67 | 210 | 277 | 444 | 112 | 18 | 175 | 1506 | 3.4 | 5.4 | 18.4 |
| 04-05—Sacramento .... | 80 | 3084 | 560 | 1264 | .443 | 320 | 413 | .775 | 77 | 255 | 332 | 541 | 124 | 30 | 203 | 1571 | 4.2 | 6.8 | 19.6 |
| Totals .................. | 511 | 18661 | 3106 | 6912 | .449 | 1405 | 1773 | .792 | 365 | 1359 | 1724 | 3348 | 712 | 103 | 1280 | 8203 | 3.4 | 6.6 | 16.1 |

Three-point field goals: 1998-99, 15-for-74 (.203). 1999-00, 77-for-212 (.363). 2000-01, 108-for-285 (.379). 2001-02, 51-for-138 (.370). 2002-03, 56-for-137 (.409). 2003-04, 148-for-378 (.392). 2004-05, 131-for-364 (.360). Totals, 586-for-1588 (.369).
Personal fouls/disqualifications: 1998-99, 122/0. 1999-00, 171/1. 2000-01, 148/1. 2001-02, 133/0. 2002-03, 93/0. 2003-04, 146/0. 2004-05, 191/0. Totals, 1004/2.

### NBA PLAYOFF RECORD

| Season Team | G | Min. | FGM | FGA | Pct. | FTM | FTA | Pct. | Off. | Def. | Tot. | Ast. | St. | Blk. | TO | Pts. | RPG | APG | PPG |
|---|---|---|---|---|---|---|---|---|---|---|---|---|---|---|---|---|---|---|---|
| 01-02—Sacramento .... | 16 | 661 | 114 | 257 | .444 | 71 | 86 | .826 | 14 | 46 | 60 | 80 | 23 | 3 | 37 | 324 | 3.8 | 5.0 | 20.3 |
| 02-03—Sacramento .... | 12 | 404 | 57 | 135 | .422 | 27 | 34 | .794 | 8 | 23 | 31 | 60 | 14 | 5 | 18 | 152 | 2.6 | 5.0 | 12.7 |
| 03-04—Sacramento .... | 12 | 497 | 84 | 196 | .429 | 48 | 55 | .873 | 9 | 41 | 50 | 84 | 23 | 5 | 35 | 240 | 4.2 | 7.0 | 20.0 |
| 04-05—Sacramento .... | 5 | 200 | 36 | 92 | .391 | 21 | 27 | .778 | 5 | 17 | 22 | 33 | 7 | 2 | 13 | 98 | 4.4 | 6.6 | 19.6 |
| Totals .................. | 45 | 1762 | 291 | 680 | .428 | 167 | 202 | .827 | 36 | 127 | 163 | 257 | 67 | 15 | 103 | 814 | 3.6 | 5.7 | 18.1 |

Three-point field goals: 2001-02, 25-for-59 (.424). 2002-03, 11-for-39 (.282). 2003-04, 24-for-55 (.436). 2004-05, 5-for-23 (.217). Totals, 65-for-176 (.369).
Personal fouls/disqualifications: 2001-02, 30/0. 2002-03, 31/1. 2003-04, 40/1. 2004-05, 11/0. Totals, 112/2.

# BIEDRINS, ANDRIS       F        WARRIORS

**PERSONAL:** Born April 2, 1986, in Riga, Latvia. ... 6-11/240. (2.11/108.9).
**HIGH SCHOOL:** Valters Basketball School (Latvia).
**TRANSACTIONS/CAREER NOTES:** Played in Latvia (2002-04). ... Selected by Golden State Warriors in first round (11th pick overall) of 2004 NBA Draft.

### LATVIAN BASKETBALL LEAGUE RECORD

| Season Team | G | Min. | FGM | FGA | Pct. | FTM | FTA | Pct. | Reb. | Ast. | Pts. | RPG | APG | PPG |
|---|---|---|---|---|---|---|---|---|---|---|---|---|---|---|
| 02-03—Skonto Riga................... | 41 | 541 | 55 | 92 | .598 | 14 | 43 | .326 | 190 | 22 | 124 | 4.6 | 0.5 | 3.0 |
| 03-04—Skonto Riga................... | 30 | 835 | 209 | 350 | .597 | 105 | 187 | .561 | 262 | 35 | 524 | 8.7 | 1.2 | 17.5 |
| Totals ..................................... | 71 | 1376 | 264 | 442 | .597 | 119 | 230 | .517 | 452 | 57 | 648 | 6.4 | 0.8 | 9.1 |

Three-point field goals: 2003-04, 1-for-2 (.500). Totals, 1-for-2 (.500).

### NBA REGULAR-SEASON RECORD

| Season Team | G | Min. | FGM | FGA | Pct. | FTM | FTA | Pct. | Off. | Def. | Tot. | Ast. | St. | Blk. | TO | Pts. | RPG | APG | PPG |
|---|---|---|---|---|---|---|---|---|---|---|---|---|---|---|---|---|---|---|---|
| 04-05—Golden State ... | 30 | 384 | 45 | 78 | .577 | 19 | 40 | .475 | 47 | 71 | 118 | 12 | 12 | 24 | 12 | 109 | 3.9 | 0.4 | 3.6 |

Three-point field goals: 2004-05, 0-for-1. Totals, 0-for-1 (.000).
Personal fouls/disqualifications: 2004-05, 87/2. Totals, 87/2.

# BILLUPS, CHAUNCEY                    G                    PISTONS

**PERSONAL:** Born September 25, 1976, in Denver. ... 6-3/202. (1.91/91.6). ... Full name: Chauncey Ray Billups
**HIGH SCHOOL:** George Washington (Denver).
**COLLEGE:** Colorado.
**TRANSACTIONS/CAREER NOTES:** Selected after sophomore season by Boston Celtics in first round (third pick overall) of 1997 NBA Draft. ... Traded by Celtics with G Dee Brown, F John Thomas and F Roy Rogers to Toronto Raptors for G Kenny Anderson, C Zan Tabak and F Popeye Jones (February 18, 1998). ... Traded by Raptors with draft rights to G Tyson Wheeler to Denver Nuggets in three-way deal in which Raptors received 1999 first-round draft choice from Nuggets and draft rights to F Zeljko Rebraca, G Micheal Williams and 1999 or 2000 first-round draft choice from Minnesota Timberwolves and Timberwolves received C Dean Garrett and G Bobby Jackson from Nuggets (January 21, 1999). ... Traded by Nuggets with G/F Ron Mercer, F Johnny Taylor and draft considerations to Orlando Magic for F/C Chris Gatling, F Tariq Abdul-Wahad, a future first-round draft pick and cash considerations (February 1, 2000). ... Signed as free agent by Timberwolves (August 8, 2000). ... Signed as free agent by Detroit Pistons (July 17, 2002).
**MISCELLANEOUS:** Member of NBA championship team (2004).

## COLLEGIATE RECORD
**NOTES:** THE SPORTING NEWS All-America second team (1997).

| Season Team | G | Min. | FGM | FGA | Pct. | FTM | FTA | Pct. | Reb. | Ast. | Pts. | RPG | APG | PPG |
|---|---|---|---|---|---|---|---|---|---|---|---|---|---|---|
| | | | | | | | | | | | | AVERAGES | | |
| 95-96—Colorado | 26 | 919 | 145 | 351 | .413 | 130 | 151 | .861 | 165 | 143 | 465 | 6.3 | 5.5 | 17.9 |
| 96-97—Colorado | 29 | 947 | 152 | 368 | .413 | 176 | 206 | .854 | 141 | 139 | 555 | 4.9 | 4.8 | 19.1 |
| Totals | 55 | 1866 | 297 | 719 | .413 | 306 | 357 | .857 | 306 | 282 | 1020 | 5.6 | 5.1 | 18.5 |

Three-point field goals: 1995-96, 45-for-127 (.354). 1996-97, 75-for-187 (.401). Totals, 120-for-314 (.382).
Personal fouls/disqualifications: 1995-96, 75/3. Totals, 75/3.

## NBA REGULAR-SEASON RECORD
**HONORS:** NBA All-Defensive second team (2005).

| Season Team | G | Min. | FGM | FGA | Pct. | FTM | FTA | Pct. | REBOUNDS Off. | Def. | Tot. | Ast. | St. | Blk. | TO | Pts. | AVERAGES RPG | APG | PPG |
|---|---|---|---|---|---|---|---|---|---|---|---|---|---|---|---|---|---|---|---|
| 97-98—Bos.-Tor. | 80 | 2216 | 280 | 749 | .374 | 226 | 266 | .850 | 62 | 128 | 190 | 314 | 107 | 4 | 174 | 893 | 2.4 | 3.9 | 11.2 |
| 98-99—Denver | 45 | 1488 | 191 | 495 | .386 | 157 | 172 | .913 | 24 | 72 | 96 | 173 | 58 | 14 | 98 | 624 | 2.1 | 3.8 | 13.9 |
| 99-00—Den.-Orl. | 13 | 305 | 34 | 101 | .337 | 37 | 44 | .841 | 8 | 26 | 34 | 39 | 10 | 2 | 24 | 112 | 2.6 | 3.0 | 8.6 |
| 00-01—Minnesota | 77 | 1790 | 248 | 587 | .422 | 144 | 171 | .842 | 32 | 126 | 158 | 260 | 51 | 11 | 111 | 713 | 2.1 | 3.4 | 9.3 |
| 01-02—Minnesota | 82 | 2355 | 348 | 823 | .423 | 207 | 234 | .885 | 35 | 191 | 226 | 450 | 66 | 17 | 138 | 1027 | 2.8 | 5.5 | 12.5 |
| 02-03—Detroit | 74 | 2327 | 366 | 870 | .421 | 318 | 362 | .878 | 38 | 235 | 273 | 287 | 63 | 15 | 134 | 1199 | 3.7 | 3.9 | 16.2 |
| 03-04—Detroit | 78 | 2758 | 392 | 996 | .394 | 404 | 460 | .878 | 35 | 241 | 276 | 446 | 84 | 8 | 189 | 1318 | 3.5 | 5.7 | 16.9 |
| 04-05—Detroit | 80 | 2866 | 404 | 913 | .442 | 343 | 382 | .898 | 48 | 223 | 271 | 464 | 81 | 9 | 180 | 1316 | 3.4 | 5.8 | 16.5 |
| Totals | 529 | 16105 | 2263 | 5534 | .409 | 1836 | 2091 | .878 | 282 | 1242 | 1524 | 2433 | 520 | 80 | 1048 | 7202 | 2.9 | 4.6 | 13.6 |

Three-point field goals: 1997-98, 107-for-325 (.329). 1998-99, 85-for-235 (.362). 1999-00, 7-for-41 (.171). 2000-01, 73-for-194 (.376). 2001-02, 124-for-315 (.394). 2002-03, 149-for-380 (.392). 2003-04, 130-for-335 (.388). 2004-05, 165-for-387 (.426). Totals, 840-for-2212 (.380).
Personal fouls/disqualifications: 1997-98, 172/2. 1998-99, 115/0. 1999-00, 27/0. 2000-01, 178/2. 2001-02, 169/1. 2002-03, 136/0. 2003-04, 177/2. 2004-05, 194/1. Totals, 1168/8.

## NBA PLAYOFF RECORD
**NOTES:** NBA Finals Most Valuable Player (2004).

| Season Team | G | Min. | FGM | FGA | Pct. | FTM | FTA | Pct. | REBOUNDS Off. | Def. | Tot. | Ast. | St. | Blk. | TO | Pts. | AVERAGES RPG | APG | PPG |
|---|---|---|---|---|---|---|---|---|---|---|---|---|---|---|---|---|---|---|---|
| 00-01—Minnesota | 3 | 26 | 1 | 6 | .167 | 1 | 1 | 1.000 | 1 | 4 | 5 | 2 | 0 | 0 | 1 | 3 | 1.7 | 0.7 | 1.0 |
| 01-02—Minnesota | 3 | 134 | 23 | 51 | .451 | 14 | 20 | .700 | 1 | 14 | 15 | 17 | 3 | 1 | 9 | 66 | 5.0 | 5.7 | 22.0 |
| 02-03—Detroit | 14 | 485 | 71 | 190 | .374 | 84 | 90 | .933 | 4 | 43 | 47 | 66 | 9 | 2 | 34 | 252 | 3.4 | 4.7 | 18.0 |
| 03-04—Detroit | 23 | 881 | 110 | 286 | .385 | 121 | 136 | .890 | 14 | 56 | 70 | 136 | 31 | 2 | 60 | 378 | 3.0 | 5.9 | 16.4 |
| 04-05—Detroit | 25 | 985 | 145 | 339 | .428 | 133 | 149 | .893 | 23 | 85 | 108 | 162 | 25 | 5 | 49 | 467 | 4.3 | 6.5 | 18.7 |
| Totals | 68 | 2511 | 350 | 872 | .401 | 353 | 396 | .891 | 43 | 202 | 245 | 383 | 68 | 10 | 153 | 1166 | 3.6 | 5.6 | 17.1 |

Three-point field goals: 2000-01, 0-for-1. 2001-02, 6-for-15 (.400). 2002-03, 26-for-84 (.310). 2003-04, 37-for-107 (.346). 2004-05, 44-for-126 (.349). Totals, 113-for-333 (.339).
Personal fouls/disqualifications: 2000-01, 5/0. 2001-02, 14/1. 2002-03, 38/0. 2003-04, 57/1. 2004-05, 71/1. Totals, 185/3.

# BLAKE, STEVE                    G                    WIZARDS

**PERSONAL:** Born February 26, 1980, in Hollywood, Fla. ... 6-3/172. (1.91/78.0). ... Full name: Steven Hanson Blake
**HIGH SCHOOL:** Miami Killian and Miami Senior (Miami, Fla.), then Oak Hill Academy (Mouth of Wilson, Va.).
**COLLEGE:** Maryland.
**TRANSACTIONS/CAREER NOTES:** Selected by Washington Wizards in second round (38th pick overall) of 2003 NBA Draft.

## COLLEGIATE RECORD
**NOTES:** Member of NCAA Division I championship team (2002).

| Season Team | G | Min. | FGM | FGA | Pct. | FTM | FTA | Pct. | Reb. | Ast. | Pts. | RPG | APG | PPG |
|---|---|---|---|---|---|---|---|---|---|---|---|---|---|---|
| | | | | | | | | | | | | AVERAGES | | |
| 99-00—Maryland | 35 | 1115 | 86 | 211 | .408 | 35 | 51 | .686 | 106 | 217 | 244 | 3.0 | 6.2 | 7.0 |
| 00-01—Maryland | 36 | 1036 | 83 | 208 | .399 | 45 | 63 | .714 | 108 | 248 | 248 | 3.0 | 6.9 | 6.9 |
| 01-02—Maryland | 36 | 1153 | 91 | 238 | .382 | 61 | 74 | .824 | 137 | 286 | 287 | 3.8 | 7.9 | 8.0 |
| 02-03—Maryland | 31 | 1009 | 114 | 275 | .415 | 68 | 83 | .819 | 114 | 221 | 360 | 3.7 | 7.1 | 11.6 |
| Totals | 138 | 4313 | 374 | 932 | .401 | 209 | 271 | .771 | 465 | 972 | 1139 | 3.4 | 7.0 | 8.3 |

Three-point field goals: 1999-00, 37-for-102 (.363). 2000-01, 37-for-94 (.394). 2001-02, 44-for-128 (.344). 2002-03, 64-for-154 (.416). Totals, 182-for-478 (.381).

## NBA REGULAR-SEASON RECORD

| | | | | | | | | REBOUNDS | | | | | | | | AVERAGES | | |
|---|---|---|---|---|---|---|---|---|---|---|---|---|---|---|---|---|---|---|
| Season Team | G | Min. | FGM | FGA | Pct. | FTM | FTA | Pct. | Off. | Def. | Tot. | Ast. | St. | Blk. | TO | Pts. | RPG APG PPG |
| 03-04—Washington .... | 75 | 1392 | 157 | 407 | .386 | 55 | 67 | .821 | 18 | 99 | 117 | 209 | 57 | 7 | 128 | 444 | 1.6 2.8 5.9 |
| 04-05—Washington .... | 44 | 648 | 61 | 186 | .328 | 33 | 41 | .805 | 18 | 53 | 71 | 69 | 13 | 0 | 39 | 191 | 1.6 1.6 4.3 |
| Totals .................. | 119 | 2040 | 218 | 593 | .368 | 88 | 108 | .815 | 36 | 152 | 188 | 278 | 70 | 7 | 167 | 635 | 1.6 2.3 5.3 |

Three-point field goals: 2003-04, 75-for-202 (.371). 2004-05, 36-for-93 (.387). Totals, 111-for-295 (.376).
Personal fouls/disqualifications: 2003-04, 100/0. 2004-05, 47/0. Totals, 147/0.

## NBA PLAYOFF RECORD

| | | | | | | | | REBOUNDS | | | | | | | | AVERAGES | | |
|---|---|---|---|---|---|---|---|---|---|---|---|---|---|---|---|---|---|---|
| Season Team | G | Min. | FGM | FGA | Pct. | FTM | FTA | Pct. | Off. | Def. | Tot. | Ast. | St. | Blk. | TO | Pts. | RPG APG PPG |
| 04-05—Washington .... | 4 | 17 | 1 | 4 | .250 | 0 | 0 | ... | 0 | 3 | 3 | 2 | 0 | 0 | 1 | 2 | 0.8 0.5 0.5 |

Three-point field goals: 2004-05, 0-for-1. Totals, 0-for-1 (.000).
Personal fouls/disqualifications: 2004-05, 3/0. Totals, 3/0.

**B**

# BLOUNT, MARK     C     CELTICS

**PERSONAL:** Born November 30, 1975, in Dobbs Ferry, N.Y. ... 7-0/230. (2.13/104.3). ... Full name: Mark D. Blount
**HIGH SCHOOL:** Oak Hill Academy (Mouth of Wilson, Va.), then Sacred Heart and Dobbs Ferry (N.Y.).
**COLLEGE:** Pittsburgh.
**TRANSACTIONS/CAREER NOTES:** Selected after sophomore season by Seattle SuperSonics in second round (55th pick overall) of 1997 NBA Draft. ... Waived by SuperSonics (October 7, 1997). ... Played in Continental Basketball Association with Yakima Sun Kings (1997-98). ... Signed as free agent by Los Angeles Clippers (January 22, 1999). ... Waived by Clippers (January 31, 1999). ... Played in International Basketball League with Baltimore Bayrunners (1999-2000). ... Signed as free agent by Boston Celtics (August 1, 2000). ... Signed as free agent by Denver Nuggets (August 8, 2002). ... Traded by Nuggets with F/C Mark Bryant to Celtics for G Shammond Williams, 2003 second-round draft choice and cash (February 20, 2003).

## COLLEGIATE RECORD

| | | | | | | | | | | | AVERAGES | | |
|---|---|---|---|---|---|---|---|---|---|---|---|---|---|
| Season Team | G | Min. | FGM | FGA | Pct. | FTM | FTA | Pct. | Reb. | Ast. | Pts. | RPG APG PPG |
| 95-96—Pittsburgh ................. | 27 | 389 | 35 | 85 | .412 | 26 | 48 | .542 | 80 | 9 | 96 | 3.0 0.3 3.6 |
| 96-97—Pittsburgh ................. | 29 | 760 | 101 | 207 | .488 | 61 | 120 | .508 | 198 | 30 | 264 | 6.8 1.0 9.1 |
| Totals ................. | 56 | 1149 | 136 | 292 | .466 | 87 | 168 | .518 | 278 | 39 | 360 | 5.0 0.7 6.4 |

Three-point field goals: 1996-97, 1-for-2 (.500). Totals, 1-for-2 (.500).
Personal fouls/disqualifications: 1995-96, 79/0. 1996-97, 94/0. Totals, 173/0.

## CBA RECORD

| | | | | | | | | | | | AVERAGES | | |
|---|---|---|---|---|---|---|---|---|---|---|---|---|---|
| Season Team | G | Min. | FGM | FGA | Pct. | FTM | FTA | Pct. | Reb. | Ast. | Pts. | RPG APG PPG |
| 97-98—Yakima ................. | 5 | 64 | 8 | 22 | .364 | 2 | 2 | 1.000 | 9 | 0 | 18 | 1.8 0.0 3.6 |

## INTERNATIONAL BASKETBALL LEAGUE RECORD

| | | | | | | | | | | | AVERAGES | | |
|---|---|---|---|---|---|---|---|---|---|---|---|---|---|
| Season Team | G | Min. | FGM | FGA | Pct. | FTM | FTA | Pct. | Reb. | Ast. | Pts. | RPG APG PPG |
| 99-00—Baltimore................. | 54 | 1077 | 189 | 352 | .537 | 98 | 152 | .645 | 274 | 44 | 471 | 5.1 0.8 8.7 |

Three-point field goals: 1999-00, 0-for-1. Totals, 0-for-1 (.000).
Personal fouls/disqualifications: 1999-00, 122/0. Totals, 122/0.

## NBA REGULAR-SEASON RECORD

| | | | | | | | | REBOUNDS | | | | | | | | AVERAGES | | |
|---|---|---|---|---|---|---|---|---|---|---|---|---|---|---|---|---|---|---|
| Season Team | G | Min. | FGM | FGA | Pct. | FTM | FTA | Pct. | Off. | Def. | Tot. | Ast. | St. | Blk. | TO | Pts. | RPG APG PPG |
| 00-01—Boston ............ | 64 | 1098 | 101 | 200 | .505 | 46 | 66 | .697 | 97 | 134 | 231 | 32 | 39 | 76 | 62 | 248 | 3.6 0.5 3.9 |
| 01-02—Boston ............ | 44 | 415 | 32 | 76 | .421 | 30 | 37 | .811 | 26 | 59 | 85 | 10 | 16 | 19 | 23 | 94 | 1.9 0.2 2.1 |
| 02-03—Den-Bos......... | 81 | 1403 | 150 | 347 | .432 | 101 | 139 | .727 | 111 | 197 | 308 | 56 | 42 | 68 | 103 | 401 | 3.8 0.7 5.0 |
| 03-04—Boston ............ | 82 | 2402 | 342 | 604 | .566 | 159 | 221 | .719 | 207 | 382 | 589 | 75 | 80 | 106 | 150 | 843 | 7.2 0.9 10.3 |
| 04-05—Boston ............ | 82 | 2130 | 327 | 618 | .529 | 117 | 164 | .713 | 143 | 254 | 397 | 129 | 33 | 64 | 158 | 771 | 4.8 1.6 9.4 |
| Totals ................. | 353 | 7448 | 952 | 1845 | .516 | 453 | 627 | .722 | 584 | 1026 | 1610 | 302 | 210 | 333 | 496 | 2357 | 4.6 0.9 6.7 |

Three-point field goals: 2004-05, 0-for-1. Totals, 0-for-1 (.000).
Personal fouls/disqualifications: 2000-01, 183/0. 2001-02, 59/0. 2002-03, 187/2. 2003-04, 253/4. 2004-05, 229/4. Totals, 911/10.

## NBA PLAYOFF RECORD

| | | | | | | | | REBOUNDS | | | | | | | | AVERAGES | | |
|---|---|---|---|---|---|---|---|---|---|---|---|---|---|---|---|---|---|---|
| Season Team | G | Min. | FGM | FGA | Pct. | FTM | FTA | Pct. | Off. | Def. | Tot. | Ast. | St. | Blk. | TO | Pts. | RPG APG PPG |
| 01-02—Boston ............ | 4 | 39 | 2 | 4 | .500 | 2 | 2 | 1.000 | 3 | 4 | 7 | 1 | 2 | 2 | 1 | 6 | 1.8 0.3 1.5 |
| 02-03—Boston ............ | 10 | 144 | 12 | 22 | .545 | 7 | 10 | .700 | 12 | 24 | 36 | 2 | 11 | 8 | 8 | 31 | 3.6 0.2 3.1 |
| 03-04—Boston ............ | 4 | 145 | 17 | 35 | .486 | 14 | 19 | .737 | 10 | 27 | 37 | 4 | 6 | 8 | 9 | 48 | 9.3 1.0 12.0 |
| 04-05—Boston ............ | 4 | 43 | 4 | 14 | .286 | 0 | 2 | .000 | 3 | 3 | 6 | 1 | 0 | 0 | 5 | 8 | 1.5 0.3 2.0 |
| Totals ................. | 22 | 371 | 35 | 75 | .467 | 23 | 33 | .697 | 28 | 58 | 86 | 8 | 19 | 18 | 23 | 93 | 3.9 0.4 4.2 |

Personal fouls/disqualifications: 2001-02, 7/0. 2002-03, 20/0. 2003-04, 17/0. 2004-05, 6/0. Totals, 50/0.

# BOBBITT, TONY     G     LAKERS

**PERSONAL:** Born October 22, 1979 ... 6-4/190. (1.93/86.2). ... Full name: Tony Rachuan Bobbitt.
**HIGH SCHOOL:** Mainland (Daytona Beach, Fla.).
**JUNIOR COLLEGE:** College of Southern Idaho.
**COLLEGE:** Cincinnati.
**TRANSACTIONS/CAREER NOTES:** Not drafted by an NBA franchise. ... Signed as free agent by Los Angeles Lakers (August 6, 2004).

## COLLEGIATE RECORD

| | | | | | | | | | | | AVERAGES | | |
|---|---|---|---|---|---|---|---|---|---|---|---|---|---|
| Season Team | G | Min. | FGM | FGA | Pct. | FTM | FTA | Pct. | Reb. | Ast. | Pts. | RPG APG PPG |
| 00-01—S Idaho......................... | 32 | 481 | 123 | 240 | .513 | 22 | 29 | .759 | 107 | 41 | 32 | 3.3 1.3 1.0 |
| 01-02—S Idaho......................... | 32 | 988 | 199 | 490 | .406 | 63 | 77 | .818 | 153 | 135 | 75 | 4.8 4.2 2.3 |

| Season Team | G | Min. | FGM | FGA | Pct. | FTM | FTA | Pct. | Reb. | Ast. | Pts. | AVERAGES | | |
|---|---|---|---|---|---|---|---|---|---|---|---|---|---|---|
| | | | | | | | | | | | | RPG | APG | PPG |
| 02-03—Cincinnati | 27 | 368 | 69 | 188 | .367 | 35 | 42 | .833 | 48 | 18 | 17 | 1.8 | 0.7 | 0.6 |
| 03-04—Cincinnati | 32 | 717 | 150 | 330 | .455 | 43 | 51 | .843 | 108 | 60 | 35 | 3.4 | 1.9 | 1.1 |
| Junior College Totals | 64 | 1469 | 322 | 730 | .441 | 85 | 106 | .802 | 260 | 176 | 107 | 4.1 | 2.8 | 1.7 |
| 4-Year-College Totals | 59 | 1085 | 219 | 518 | .423 | 78 | 93 | .839 | 156 | 78 | 52 | 2.6 | 1.3 | 0.9 |

Three-point field goals: 2000-01, 64-for-152 (.421). 2001-02, 110-for-279 (.394). 2002-03, 42-for-127 (.331). 2003-04, 85-for-212 (.401). Totals, 301-for-770 (.391).

### NBA REGULAR-SEASON RECORD

| Season Team | G | Min. | FGM | FGA | Pct. | FTM | FTA | Pct. | REBOUNDS | | | Ast. | St. | Blk. | TO | Pts. | AVERAGES | | |
|---|---|---|---|---|---|---|---|---|---|---|---|---|---|---|---|---|---|---|---|
| | | | | | | | | | Off. | Def. | Tot. | | | | | | RPG | APG | PPG |
| 04-05—L.A. Lakers | 2 | 12 | 2 | 5 | .400 | 0 | 0 | ... | 0 | 3 | 3 | 0 | 0 | 0 | 0 | 5 | 1.5 | 0.0 | 2.5 |

Three-point field goals: 2004-05, 1-for-2 (.500). Totals, 1-for-2 (.500).
Personal fouls/disqualifications: 2004-05, 1/0. Totals, 1/0.

## BOGANS, KEITH — G — BOBCATS

**PERSONAL:** Born May 12, 1980, in Washington, D.C. ... 6-5/215. (1.96/97.5). ... Full name: Keith Ramon Bogans
**HIGH SCHOOL:** DeMatha Catholic (Hyattsville, Md.).
**COLLEGE:** Kentucky.
**TRANSACTIONS/CAREER NOTES:** Selected by Milwaukee Bucks in second round (43rd pick overall) of 2003 NBA Draft. ... Draft rights traded to Orlando Magic for cash considerations (June 26, 2003). ... Traded by Magic to Charlotte Bobcats for F Brandon Hunter (November 1, 2004).

### COLLEGIATE RECORD

**NOTES:** The Sporting News All-America third team (2003).

| Season Team | G | Min. | FGM | FGA | Pct. | FTM | FTA | Pct. | Reb. | Ast. | Pts. | AVERAGES | | |
|---|---|---|---|---|---|---|---|---|---|---|---|---|---|---|
| | | | | | | | | | | | | RPG | APG | PPG |
| 99-00—Kentucky | 33 | 917 | 138 | 339 | .407 | 87 | 135 | .644 | 119 | 57 | 411 | 3.6 | 1.7 | 12.5 |
| 00-01—Kentucky | 34 | 1050 | 210 | 444 | .473 | 83 | 119 | .697 | 158 | 80 | 577 | 4.6 | 2.4 | 17.0 |

| Season Team | G | Min. | FGM | FGA | Pct. | FTM | FTA | Pct. | Reb. | Ast. | Pts. | AVERAGES | | |
|---|---|---|---|---|---|---|---|---|---|---|---|---|---|---|
| | | | | | | | | | | | | RPG | APG | PPG |
| 01-02—Kentucky | 32 | 878 | 129 | 327 | .394 | 61 | 91 | .670 | 137 | 79 | 371 | 4.3 | 2.5 | 11.6 |
| 02-03—Kentucky | 36 | 1068 | 194 | 425 | .456 | 96 | 130 | .738 | 138 | 98 | 564 | 3.8 | 2.7 | 15.7 |
| Totals | 135 | 3913 | 671 | 1535 | .437 | 327 | 475 | .688 | 552 | 314 | 1923 | 4.1 | 2.3 | 14.2 |

Three-point field goals: 1999-00, 48-for-164 (.293). 2000-01, 74-for-205 (.361). 2001-02, 52-for-165 (.315). 2002-03, 80-for-209 (.383). Totals, 254-for-743 (.342).

### NBA REGULAR-SEASON RECORD

| Season Team | G | Min. | FGM | FGA | Pct. | FTM | FTA | Pct. | REBOUNDS | | | Ast. | St. | Blk. | TO | Pts. | AVERAGES | | |
|---|---|---|---|---|---|---|---|---|---|---|---|---|---|---|---|---|---|---|---|
| | | | | | | | | | Off. | Def. | Tot. | | | | | | RPG | APG | PPG |
| 03-04—Orlando | 73 | 1787 | 183 | 454 | .403 | 65 | 103 | .631 | 106 | 211 | 317 | 98 | 46 | 10 | 75 | 498 | 4.3 | 1.3 | 6.8 |
| 04-05—Charlotte | 74 | 1791 | 262 | 688 | .381 | 133 | 183 | .727 | 76 | 150 | 226 | 135 | 68 | 8 | 122 | 714 | 3.1 | 1.8 | 9.6 |
| Totals | 147 | 3578 | 445 | 1142 | .390 | 198 | 286 | .692 | 182 | 361 | 543 | 233 | 114 | 18 | 197 | 1212 | 3.7 | 1.6 | 8.2 |

Three-point field goals: 2003-04, 67-for-187 (.358). 2004-05, 57-for-173 (.329). Totals, 124-for-360 (.344).
Personal fouls/disqualifications: 2003-04, 128/2. 2004-05, 167/1. Totals, 295/3.

## BONNER, MATT — F — RAPTORS

**PERSONAL:** Born April 5, 1980, in Concord, N.H. ... 6-10/240. (2.08/108.9). ... Full name: Matthew Robert Bonner
**HIGH SCHOOL:** Concord (N.H.).
**COLLEGE:** Florida.
**TRANSACTIONS/CAREER NOTES:** Selected by Chicago Bulls in second round (45th pick overall) of 2003 NBA Draft. ... Draft rights traded by Bulls to Toronto Raptors for future second-round draft pick (June 26, 2003).

### COLLEGIATE RECORD

| Season Team | G | Min. | FGM | FGA | Pct. | FTM | FTA | Pct. | Reb. | Ast. | Pts. | AVERAGES | | |
|---|---|---|---|---|---|---|---|---|---|---|---|---|---|---|
| | | | | | | | | | | | | RPG | APG | PPG |
| 99-00—Florida | 36 | 485 | 66 | 150 | .440 | 26 | 30 | .867 | 115 | 15 | 174 | 3.2 | 0.4 | 4.8 |
| 00-01—Florida | 31 | 883 | 150 | 292 | .514 | 71 | 107 | .664 | 238 | 46 | 411 | 7.7 | 1.5 | 13.3 |
| 01-02—Florida | 31 | 876 | 182 | 355 | .513 | 74 | 93 | .796 | 224 | 48 | 484 | 7.2 | 1.5 | 15.6 |
| 02-03—Florida | 33 | 1037 | 182 | 357 | .510 | 74 | 101 | .733 | 201 | 49 | 501 | 6.1 | 1.5 | 15.2 |
| Totals | 131 | 3281 | 580 | 1154 | .503 | 245 | 331 | .740 | 778 | 158 | 1570 | 5.9 | 1.2 | 12.0 |

Three-point field goals: 1999-00, 16-for-56 (.286). 2000-01, 40-for-105 (.381). 2001-02, 46-for-124 (.371). 2002-03, 63-for-133 (.474). Totals, 165-for-418 (.395).

### ITALIAN LEAGUE RECORD

| Season Team | G | Min. | FGM | FGA | Pct. | FTM | FTA | Pct. | Reb. | Ast. | Pts. | AVERAGES | | |
|---|---|---|---|---|---|---|---|---|---|---|---|---|---|---|
| | | | | | | | | | | | | RPG | APG | PPG |
| 03-04—Sicilia Messina | 33 | 1215 | 230 | 423 | .544 | 136 | 167 | .814 | 308 | 26 | 634 | 9.3 | 0.8 | 19.2 |

Three-point field goals: 2003-04, 38-for-105 (.362). Totals, 38-for-105 (.362).

### NBA REGULAR-SEASON RECORD

| Season Team | G | Min. | FGM | FGA | Pct. | FTM | FTA | Pct. | REBOUNDS | | | Ast. | St. | Blk. | TO | Pts. | AVERAGES | | |
|---|---|---|---|---|---|---|---|---|---|---|---|---|---|---|---|---|---|---|---|
| | | | | | | | | | Off. | Def. | Tot. | | | | | | RPG | APG | PPG |
| 04-05—Toronto | 82 | 1553 | 247 | 463 | .533 | 56 | 71 | .789 | 108 | 177 | 285 | 48 | 39 | 19 | 40 | 589 | 3.5 | 0.6 | 7.2 |

Three-point field goals: 2004-05, 39-for-92 (.424). Totals, 39-for-92 (.424).
Personal fouls/disqualifications: 2004-05, 220/1. Totals, 220/1.

## BOOTH, CALVIN      C

**PERSONAL:** Born May 7, 1976, in Reynoldsburg, Ohio. ... 6-11/241. (2.11/109.3). ... Full name: Calvin L. Booth
**HIGH SCHOOL:** Groveport Madison (Reynoldsburg, Ohio).
**COLLEGE:** Penn State.
**TRANSACTIONS/CAREER NOTES:** Selected by Washington Wizards in second round (35th pick overall) of 1999 NBA Draft. ... Traded by Wizards with F Juwan Howard and F Obinna Ekezie to Dallas Mavericks for F/C Christian Laettner, G Courtney Alexander, F Loy Vaught, G Hubert Davis, F/C Etan Thomas and cash considerations (February 22, 2001). ... Signed as free agent by Seattle SuperSonics (July 31, 2001). ... Traded by SuperSonics to Dallas Mavericks for F Danny Fortson (July 26, 2004). ... Traded by Mavericks with F Alan Henderson to Milwaukee Bucks for F Keith Van Horn (February 24, 2005). ... Waived by Bucks (August 15, 2005).

### COLLEGIATE RECORD

| Season Team | G | Min. | FGM | FGA | Pct. | FTM | FTA | Pct. | Reb. | Ast. | Pts. | RPG | APG | PPG |
|---|---|---|---|---|---|---|---|---|---|---|---|---|---|---|
| 94-95—Penn State | | | | | | Did not play—redshirted. | | | | | | | | |
| 95-96—Penn State | 28 | 670 | 100 | 182 | .549 | 61 | 96 | .635 | 150 | 35 | 261 | 5.4 | 1.3 | 9.3 |
| 96-97—Penn State | 27 | 706 | 87 | 204 | .426 | 61 | 84 | .726 | 134 | 15 | 236 | 5.0 | 0.6 | 8.7 |
| 97-98—Penn State | 32 | 955 | 156 | 294 | .531 | 65 | 97 | .670 | 208 | 8 | 377 | 6.5 | 0.3 | 11.8 |
| 98-99—Penn State | 27 | 942 | 157 | 306 | .513 | 100 | 129 | .775 | 236 | 24 | 414 | 8.7 | 0.9 | 15.3 |
| Totals | 114 | 3273 | 500 | 986 | .507 | 287 | 406 | .707 | 728 | 82 | 1288 | 6.4 | 0.7 | 11.3 |

Three-point field goals: 1996-97, 1-for-3 (.333). 1997-98, 0-for-1. 1998-99, 0-for-6. Totals, 1-for-10 (.100).

### NBA REGULAR-SEASON RECORD

| Season Team | G | Min. | FGM | FGA | Pct. | FTM | FTA | Pct. | Off. | Def. | Tot. | Ast. | St. | Blk. | TO | Pts. | RPG | APG | PPG |
|---|---|---|---|---|---|---|---|---|---|---|---|---|---|---|---|---|---|---|---|
| 99-00—Washington | 11 | 143 | 16 | 46 | .348 | 10 | 14 | .714 | 15 | 17 | 32 | 7 | 3 | 14 | 6 | 42 | 2.9 | 0.6 | 3.8 |
| 00-01—Wash.-Dallas | 55 | 933 | 120 | 252 | .476 | 53 | 78 | .679 | 77 | 169 | 246 | 42 | 29 | 111 | 53 | 293 | 4.5 | 0.8 | 5.3 |
| 01-02—Seattle | 15 | 279 | 35 | 82 | .427 | 23 | 24 | .958 | 20 | 34 | 54 | 16 | 6 | 13 | 16 | 93 | 3.6 | 1.1 | 6.2 |
| 02-03—Seattle | 47 | 575 | 52 | 119 | .437 | 34 | 47 | .723 | 32 | 77 | 109 | 12 | 11 | 33 | 22 | 138 | 2.3 | 0.3 | 2.9 |
| 03-04—Seattle | 71 | 1206 | 135 | 290 | .466 | 75 | 94 | .798 | 86 | 194 | 280 | 28 | 17 | 101 | 45 | 345 | 3.9 | 0.4 | 4.9 |
| 04-05—Dallas-Mil. | 51 | 451 | 49 | 108 | .454 | 26 | 32 | .813 | 29 | 78 | 107 | 8 | 15 | 28 | 16 | 124 | 2.1 | 0.2 | 2.4 |
| Totals | 250 | 3587 | 407 | 897 | .454 | 221 | 289 | .765 | 259 | 569 | 828 | 113 | 81 | 300 | 158 | 1035 | 3.3 | 0.5 | 4.1 |

Three-point field goals: 2002-03, 0-for-2. 2003-04, 0-for-2. 2004-05, 0-for-1. Totals, 0-for-5 (.000).
Personal fouls/disqualifications: 1999-00, 23/0. 2000-01, 146/1. 2001-02, 47/1. 2002-03, 74/0. 2003-04, 150/2. 2004-05, 78/0. Totals, 518/4.

### NBA PLAYOFF RECORD

| Season Team | G | Min. | FGM | FGA | Pct. | FTM | FTA | Pct. | Off. | Def. | Tot. | Ast. | St. | Blk. | TO | Pts. | RPG | APG | PPG |
|---|---|---|---|---|---|---|---|---|---|---|---|---|---|---|---|---|---|---|---|
| 00-01—Dallas | 10 | 137 | 15 | 37 | .405 | 8 | 9 | .889 | 16 | 12 | 28 | 2 | 7 | 6 | 4 | 38 | 2.8 | 0.2 | 3.8 |

Personal fouls/disqualifications: 2000-01, 29/0. Totals, 29/0.

## BOOZER, CARLOS      F/C      JAZZ

**PERSONAL:** Born November 20, 1981, in Juneau, Alaska. ... 6-8/258. (2.03/117.0).
**HIGH SCHOOL:** Juneau-Douglas (Juneau, Alaska).
**COLLEGE:** Duke.
**TRANSACTIONS/CAREER NOTES:** Selected after junior season by Cleveland Cavaliers in second round (35th pick overall) of 2002 NBA Draft. ... Signed as free agent by Utah Jazz (July 30, 2004).
**MISCELLANEOUS:** Member of bronze-medal-winning U.S. Olympic Team (2004).

### COLLEGIATE RECORD

**NOTES:** Member of NCAA Division I championship team (2001).

| Season Team | G | Min. | FGM | FGA | Pct. | FTM | FTA | Pct. | Reb. | Ast. | Pts. | RPG | APG | PPG |
|---|---|---|---|---|---|---|---|---|---|---|---|---|---|---|
| 99-00—Duke | 34 | 807 | 164 | 267 | .614 | 115 | 155 | .742 | 213 | 37 | 443 | 6.3 | 1.1 | 13.0 |
| 00-01—Duke | 32 | 820 | 160 | 265 | .604 | 105 | 146 | .719 | 208 | 40 | 425 | 6.5 | 1.3 | 13.3 |
| 01-02—Duke | 35 | 993 | 230 | 346 | .665 | 178 | 236 | .754 | 303 | 38 | 638 | 8.7 | 1.1 | 18.2 |
| Totals | 101 | 2620 | 554 | 878 | .631 | 398 | 537 | .741 | 724 | 115 | 1506 | 7.2 | 1.1 | 14.9 |

Three-point field goals: 2001-02, 0-for-1. Totals, 0-for-1 (.000).

### NBA REGULAR-SEASON RECORD

**HONORS:** NBA All-Rookie second team (2003).

| Season Team | G | Min. | FGM | FGA | Pct. | FTM | FTA | Pct. | Off. | Def. | Tot. | Ast. | St. | Blk. | TO | Pts. | RPG | APG | PPG |
|---|---|---|---|---|---|---|---|---|---|---|---|---|---|---|---|---|---|---|---|
| 02-03—Cleveland | 81 | 2049 | 331 | 618 | .536 | 148 | 192 | .771 | 202 | 407 | 609 | 106 | 59 | 50 | 103 | 810 | 7.5 | 1.3 | 10.0 |
| 03-04—Cleveland | 75 | 2592 | 471 | 900 | .523 | 219 | 285 | .768 | 230 | 627 | 857 | 148 | 74 | 55 | 134 | 1162 | 11.4 | 2.0 | 15.5 |
| 04-05—Utah | 51 | 1772 | 361 | 693 | .521 | 187 | 268 | .698 | 141 | 316 | 457 | 144 | 41 | 24 | 137 | 909 | 9.0 | 2.8 | 17.8 |
| Totals | 207 | 6413 | 1163 | 2211 | .526 | 554 | 745 | .744 | 573 | 1350 | 1923 | 398 | 174 | 129 | 374 | 2881 | 9.3 | 1.9 | 13.9 |

Three-point field goals: 2002-03, 0-for-1. 2003-04, 1-for-6 (.167). 2004-05, 0-for-1. Totals, 1-for-8 (.125).
Personal fouls/disqualifications: 2002-03, 224/2. 2003-04, 199/0. 2004-05, 179/3. Totals, 602/5.

## BORCHARDT, CURTIS      C      CELTICS

**PERSONAL:** Born September 13, 1980, in Buffalo. ... 7-0/240. (2.13/108.9). ... Full name: Curtis Alan Borchardt
**HIGH SCHOOL:** Eastlake (Redmond, Wash.).
**COLLEGE:** Stanford.
**TRANSACTIONS/CAREER NOTES:** Selected after junior season by Orlando Magic in first round (18th pick overall) of 2002 NBA Draft. ... Draft rights traded by Magic to Utah Jazz for draft rights to F Ryan Humphrey and draft rights to F/C Jamal

Sampson (June 26, 2002). ... Traded by Jazz to Boston Celtics in five-team deal (August 2, 2005).

## COLLEGIATE RECORD

| | | | | | | | | | | | | AVERAGES | | |
|---|---|---|---|---|---|---|---|---|---|---|---|---|---|---|
| Season Team | G | Min. | FGM | FGA | Pct. | FTM | FTA | Pct. | Reb. | Ast. | Pts. | RPG | APG | PPG |
| 99-00—Stanford | 20 | 250 | 31 | 81 | .383 | 9 | 13 | .692 | 74 | 11 | 72 | 3.7 | 0.6 | 3.6 |
| 00-01—Stanford | 17 | 280 | 31 | 58 | .534 | 43 | 56 | .768 | 72 | 12 | 108 | 4.2 | 0.7 | 6.4 |
| 01-02—Stanford | 29 | 896 | 171 | 297 | .576 | 138 | 206 | .670 | 332 | 59 | 491 | 11.4 | 2.0 | 16.9 |
| Totals | 66 | 1426 | 233 | 436 | .534 | 190 | 275 | .691 | 478 | 82 | 671 | 7.2 | 1.2 | 10.2 |

Three-point field goals: 1999-00, 1-for-6 (.167). 2000-01, 3-for-7 (.429). 2001-02, 11-for-27 (.407). Totals, 15-for-40 (.375).

## NBA REGULAR-SEASON RECORD

| | | | | | | | | | REBOUNDS | | | | | | | | AVERAGES | | |
|---|---|---|---|---|---|---|---|---|---|---|---|---|---|---|---|---|---|---|---|
| Season Team | G | Min. | FGM | FGA | Pct. | FTM | FTA | Pct. | Off. | Def. | Tot. | Ast. | St. | Blk. | TO | Pts. | RPG | APG | PPG |
| 02-03—Utah | | | | | | | Did not play—injured | | | | | | | | | | | | |
| 03-04—Utah | 16 | 258 | 22 | 56 | .393 | 14 | 18 | .778 | 13 | 41 | 54 | 15 | 4 | 14 | 18 | 58 | 3.4 | 0.9 | 3.6 |
| 04-05—Utah | 67 | 859 | 74 | 172 | .430 | 52 | 71 | .732 | 86 | 138 | 224 | 49 | 10 | 32 | 52 | 200 | 3.3 | 0.7 | 3.0 |
| Totals | 83 | 1117 | 96 | 228 | .421 | 66 | 89 | .742 | 99 | 179 | 278 | 64 | 14 | 46 | 70 | 258 | 3.3 | 0.8 | 3.1 |

Three-point field goals: 2003-04, 0-for-1. Totals, 0-for-1 (.000).
Personal fouls/disqualifications: 2003-04, 40/0. 2004-05, 160/1. Totals, 200/1.

# BOSH, CHRIS     F     RAPTORS

**PERSONAL:** Born March 2, 1984, in Dallas, Tex. ... 6-10/210. (2.08/95.3). ... Full name: Christopher Wesson Bosh
**HIGH SCHOOL:** Lincoln (Dallas, Tex.).
**COLLEGE:** Georgia Tech.
**TRANSACTIONS/CAREER NOTES:** Selected after freshman season by Toronto Raptors in first round (fourth pick overall) of 2003 NBA Draft.

## COLLEGIATE RECORD

| | | | | | | | | | | | | AVERAGES | | |
|---|---|---|---|---|---|---|---|---|---|---|---|---|---|---|
| Season Team | G | Min. | FGM | FGA | Pct. | FTM | FTA | Pct. | Reb. | Ast. | Pts. | RPG | APG | PPG |
| 02-03—Georgia Tech | 31 | 960 | 168 | 300 | .560 | 127 | 174 | .730 | 278 | 38 | 485 | 9.0 | 1.2 | 15.6 |

Three-point field goals: 2002-03, 22-for-46 (.478). Totals, 22-for-46 (.478).

## NBA REGULAR-SEASON RECORD

**HONORS:** NBA All-Rookie first team (2004).

| | | | | | | | | | REBOUNDS | | | | | | | | AVERAGES | | |
|---|---|---|---|---|---|---|---|---|---|---|---|---|---|---|---|---|---|---|---|
| Season Team | G | Min. | FGM | FGA | Pct. | FTM | FTA | Pct. | Off. | Def. | Tot. | Ast. | St. | Blk. | TO | Pts. | RPG | APG | PPG |
| 03-04—Toronto | 75 | 2510 | 327 | 712 | .459 | 202 | 288 | .701 | 191 | 366 | 557 | 78 | 59 | 106 | 107 | 861 | 7.4 | 1.0 | 11.5 |
| 04-05—Toronto | 81 | 3017 | 473 | 1005 | .471 | 412 | 542 | .760 | 194 | 524 | 718 | 153 | 76 | 113 | 187 | 1361 | 8.9 | 1.9 | 16.8 |
| Totals | 156 | 5527 | 800 | 1717 | .466 | 614 | 830 | .740 | 385 | 890 | 1275 | 231 | 135 | 219 | 294 | 2222 | 8.2 | 1.5 | 14.2 |

Three-point field goals: 2003-04, 5-for-14 (.357). 2004-05, 3-for-10 (.300). Totals, 8-for-24 (.333).
Personal fouls/disqualifications: 2003-04, 215/2. 2004-05, 226/3. Totals, 441/5.

# BOWEN, BRUCE     G     SPURS

**PERSONAL:** Born June 14, 1971, in Merced, Calif. ... 6-7/200. (2.01/90.7).
**HIGH SCHOOL:** Edison (Fresno, Calif.).
**COLLEGE:** Cal State Fullerton.
**TRANSACTIONS/CAREER NOTES:** Not drafted by an NBA franchise. ... Played in France (1994-97). ... Signed as free agent by Miami Heat (October 5, 1995). ... Waived by Heat (October 13, 1995). ... Played in Continental Basketball Association with Fort Wayne Fury (1995-96) and Rockford Lightning (1995-97). ... Signed by Heat to 10-day contract (March 15, 1997). ... Signed by Heat for remainder of season (March 25, 1997). ... Signed as free agent by Boston Celtics (July 28, 1997). ... Signed as free agent by Philadelphia 76ers (September 16, 1999). ... Traded by 76ers to Chicago Bulls for F Toni Kukoc in three-way deal in which 76ers sent G Larry Hughes and F/G Billy Owens to Golden State Warriors and Warriors sent G John Starks and future first-round draft choice to Bulls (February 16, 2000). ... Waived by Bulls (February 18, 2000). ... Signed as free agent by Heat (February 23, 2000). ... Signed as free agent by San Antonio Spurs (July 31, 2001).
**MISCELLANEOUS:** Member of NBA championship team (2003, 2005).

## COLLEGIATE RECORD

| | | | | | | | | | | | | AVERAGES | | |
|---|---|---|---|---|---|---|---|---|---|---|---|---|---|---|
| Season Team | G | Min. | FGM | FGA | Pct. | FTM | FTA | Pct. | Reb. | Ast. | Pts. | RPG | APG | PPG |
| 89-90—Cal State Fullerton | 18 | 98 | 9 | 22 | .409 | 10 | 13 | .769 | 18 | 4 | 31 | 1.0 | 0.2 | 1.7 |
| 90-91—Cal State Fullerton | 28 | 849 | 89 | 236 | .377 | 83 | 120 | .692 | 196 | 75 | 275 | 7.0 | 2.7 | 9.8 |
| 91-92—Cal State Fullerton | 28 | 969 | 138 | 311 | .444 | 120 | 161 | .745 | 196 | 75 | 408 | 7.0 | 2.7 | 14.6 |
| 92-93—Cal State Fullerton | 27 | 987 | 148 | 318 | .465 | 131 | 201 | .652 | 176 | 62 | 441 | 6.5 | 2.3 | 16.3 |
| Totals | 101 | 2903 | 384 | 887 | .433 | 344 | 495 | .695 | 586 | 216 | 1155 | 5.8 | 2.1 | 11.4 |

Three-point field goals: 1989-90, 3-for-5 (.600). 1990-91, 14-for-60 (.233). 1991-92, 12-for-44 (.273). 1992-93, 14-for-43 (.326). Totals, 43-for-152 (.283).

## FRENCH LEAGUE RECORD

| | | | | | | | | | | | | AVERAGES | | |
|---|---|---|---|---|---|---|---|---|---|---|---|---|---|---|
| Season Team | G | Min. | FGM | FGA | Pct. | FTM | FTA | Pct. | Reb. | Ast. | Pts. | RPG | APG | PPG |
| 94-95—Evreux | 21 | ... | ... | ... | ... | ... | ... | ... | 79 | 21 | 642 | 3.8 | 1.0 | 30.6 |
| 96-97—Bescanson | 20 | 768 | 173 | 333 | .520 | 97 | 142 | .683 | 70 | 55 | 509 | 3.5 | 2.8 | 25.5 |
| Totals | 41 | 768 | 173 | 333 | .520 | 97 | 142 | .683 | 149 | 76 | 1151 | 3.6 | 1.9 | 28.1 |

Three-point field goals: 1996-97, 25-for-67 (.373). Totals, 25-for-67 (.373).

B

## CBA RECORD

| | | | | | | | | | | | | AVERAGES | | |
|---|---|---|---|---|---|---|---|---|---|---|---|---|---|---|
| Season Team | G | Min. | FGM | FGA | Pct. | FTM | FTA | Pct. | Reb. | Ast. | Pts. | RPG | APG | PPG |
| 95-96—Fort Wayne-Rockford ..... | 46 | 1228 | 182 | 404 | .450 | 133 | 191 | .696 | 160 | 59 | 510 | 3.5 | 1.3 | 11.1 |
| 96-97—Rockford ....................... | 16 | 619 | 94 | 206 | .456 | 75 | 98 | .765 | 70 | 45 | 277 | 4.4 | 2.8 | 17.3 |
| Totals ............ | 62 | 1847 | 276 | 610 | .452 | 208 | 289 | .720 | 230 | 104 | 787 | 3.7 | 1.7 | 12.7 |

Three-point field goals: 1996-97, 14-for-43 (.326). Totals, 14-for-43 (.326).
Personal fouls/disqualifications: 1996-97, 46/0. Totals, 46/0.

## NBA REGULAR-SEASON RECORD

**HONORS:** NBA All-Defensive first team (2004, 2005). ... NBA All-Defensive second team (2001, 2002, 2003).

| | | | | | | | | | REBOUNDS | | | | | | | | AVERAGES | | |
|---|---|---|---|---|---|---|---|---|---|---|---|---|---|---|---|---|---|---|---|
| Season Team | G | Min. | FGM | FGA | Pct. | FTM | FTA | Pct. | Off. | Def. | Tot. | Ast. | St. | Blk. | TO | Pts. | RPG | APG | PPG |
| 96-97—Miami ............. | 1 | 1 | 0 | 0 | ... | 0 | 0 | ... | 0 | 0 | 0 | 0 | 0 | 1 | 0 | 0 | 0.0 | 0.0 | 0.0 |
| 97-98—Boston ........... | 61 | 1305 | 122 | 298 | .409 | 76 | 122 | .623 | 79 | 95 | 174 | 81 | 87 | 29 | 52 | 340 | 2.9 | 1.3 | 5.6 |
| 98-99—Boston ........... | 30 | 494 | 26 | 93 | .280 | 11 | 24 | .458 | 15 | 37 | 52 | 28 | 21 | 9 | 13 | 70 | 1.7 | 0.9 | 2.3 |
| 99-00—Phila.-Miami ... | 69 | 878 | 72 | 194 | .371 | 25 | 43 | .581 | 27 | 69 | 96 | 34 | 23 | 15 | 19 | 196 | 1.4 | 0.5 | 2.8 |
| 00-01—Miami ........... | 82 | 2685 | 211 | 581 | .363 | 98 | 161 | .609 | 45 | 200 | 245 | 132 | 83 | 53 | 74 | 623 | 3.0 | 1.6 | 7.6 |
| 01-02—San Antonio .... | 59 | 1699 | 155 | 398 | .389 | 46 | 96 | .479 | 42 | 120 | 162 | 88 | 62 | 25 | 66 | 412 | 2.7 | 1.5 | 7.0 |
| 02-03—San Antonio.... | 82 | 2566 | 223 | 479 | .466 | 36 | 89 | .404 | 59 | 180 | 239 | 113 | 66 | 42 | 72 | 583 | 2.9 | 1.4 | 7.1 |
| 03-04—San Antonio.... | 82 | 2624 | 211 | 502 | .420 | 66 | 114 | .579 | 45 | 208 | 253 | 113 | 84 | 33 | 90 | 565 | 3.1 | 1.4 | 6.9 |
| 04-05—San Antonio.... | 82 | 2627 | 251 | 598 | .420 | 71 | 112 | .634 | 50 | 235 | 285 | 126 | 55 | 39 | 57 | 675 | 3.5 | 1.5 | 8.2 |
| Totals ................... | 548 | 14879 | 1271 | 3143 | .404 | 429 | 761 | .564 | 362 | 1144 | 1506 | 715 | 481 | 246 | 443 | 3464 | 2.7 | 1.3 | 6.3 |

Three-point field goals: 1997-98, 20-for-59 (.339). 1998-99, 7-for-26 (.269). 1999-00, 27-for-58 (.466). 2000-01, 103-for-307 (.336). 2001-02, 56-for-148 (.378). 2002-03, 101-for-229 (.441). 2003-04, 77-for-212 (.363). 2004-05, 102-for-253 (.403). Totals, 493-for-1292 (.382).
Personal fouls/disqualifications: 1997-98, 174/0. 1998-99, 51/2. 1999-00, 118/0. 2000-01, 269/8. 2001-02, 116/0. 2002-03, 195/0. 2003-04, 166/1. 2004-05, 175/0. Totals, 1264/11.

## NBA PLAYOFF RECORD

| | | | | | | | | | REBOUNDS | | | | | | | | AVERAGES | | |
|---|---|---|---|---|---|---|---|---|---|---|---|---|---|---|---|---|---|---|---|
| Season Team | G | Min. | FGM | FGA | Pct. | FTM | FTA | Pct. | Off. | Def. | Tot. | Ast. | St. | Blk. | TO | Pts. | RPG | APG | PPG |
| 99-00—Miami ............. | 10 | 157 | 10 | 27 | .370 | 10 | 16 | .625 | 1 | 9 | 10 | 8 | 7 | 4 | 6 | 35 | 1.0 | 0.8 | 3.5 |
| 00-01—Miami ............. | 3 | 58 | 5 | 16 | .313 | 0 | 0 | ... | 1 | 1 | 2 | 2 | 2 | 2 | 2 | 12 | 0.7 | 0.7 | 4.0 |
| 01-02—San Antonio.... | 10 | 345 | 25 | 61 | .410 | 7 | 14 | .500 | 9 | 24 | 33 | 14 | 11 | 7 | 7 | 68 | 3.3 | 1.4 | 6.8 |
| 02-03—San Antonio.... | 24 | 750 | 54 | 145 | .372 | 23 | 42 | .548 | 14 | 55 | 69 | 39 | 20 | 17 | 15 | 166 | 2.9 | 1.6 | 6.9 |
| 03-04—San Antonio.... | 10 | 298 | 23 | 63 | .365 | 3 | 13 | .231 | 6 | 23 | 29 | 10 | 4 | 3 | 4 | 60 | 2.9 | 1.0 | 6.0 |
| 04-05—San Antonio.... | 23 | 814 | 46 | 128 | .359 | 11 | 17 | .647 | 9 | 57 | 66 | 36 | 11 | 13 | 15 | 132 | 2.9 | 1.6 | 5.7 |
| Totals ................... | 80 | 2422 | 163 | 440 | .370 | 54 | 102 | .529 | 40 | 169 | 209 | 109 | 55 | 46 | 49 | 473 | 2.6 | 1.4 | 5.9 |

Three-point field goals: 1999-00, 5-for-22 (.227). 2000-01, 2-for-8 (.250). 2001-02, 11-for-25 (.440). 2002-03, 35-for-80 (.438). 2003-04, 11-for-29 (.379). 2004-05, 29-for-67 (.433). Totals, 93-for-231 (.403).
Personal fouls/disqualifications: 1999-00, 27/1. 2000-01, 8/0. 2001-02, 28/0. 2002-03, 52/0. 2003-04, 24/0. 2004-05, 77/0. Totals, 216/1.

# BOWEN, RYAN — F — ROCKETS

**PERSONAL:** Born November 20, 1975, in Fort Madison, Iowa. ... 6-7/220. (2.01/99.8). ... Full name: Ryan Cleo Bowen
**HIGH SCHOOL:** Fort Madison (Iowa).
**COLLEGE:** Iowa.
**TRANSACTIONS/CAREER NOTES:** Selected by Denver Nuggets in second round (55th pick overall) of 1998 NBA Draft. ... Played in Turkey (1998-99). ... Signed as free agent by Houston Rockets (September 30, 2004).

## COLLEGIATE RECORD

| | | | | | | | | | | | | AVERAGES | | |
|---|---|---|---|---|---|---|---|---|---|---|---|---|---|---|---|
| Season Team | G | Min. | FGM | FGA | Pct. | FTM | FTA | Pct. | Reb. | Ast. | Pts. | RPG | APG | PPG |
| 94-95—Iowa .............................. | 33 | 647 | 58 | 110 | .527 | 35 | 59 | .593 | 148 | 16 | 151 | 4.5 | 0.5 | 4.6 |
| 95-96—Iowa .............................. | 27 | 554 | 55 | 91 | .604 | 39 | 58 | .672 | 121 | 16 | 149 | 4.5 | 0.6 | 5.5 |
| 96-97—Iowa .............................. | 29 | 827 | 120 | 217 | .553 | 93 | 135 | .689 | 264 | 35 | 343 | 9.1 | 1.2 | 11.8 |
| 97-98—Iowa .............................. | 31 | 852 | 164 | 272 | .603 | 111 | 161 | .689 | 271 | 48 | 447 | 8.7 | 1.5 | 14.4 |
| Totals .................................. | 120 | 2880 | 397 | 690 | .575 | 278 | 413 | .673 | 804 | 115 | 1090 | 6.7 | 1.0 | 9.1 |

Three-point field goals: 1994-95, 0-for-1. 1996-97, 10-for-32 (.313). 1997-98, 8-for-15 (.533). Totals, 18-for-48 (.375).

## TURKISH LEAGUE RECORD

| | | | | | | | | | | | | AVERAGES | | |
|---|---|---|---|---|---|---|---|---|---|---|---|---|---|---|
| Season Team | G | Min. | FGM | FGA | Pct. | FTM | FTA | Pct. | Reb. | Ast. | Pts. | RPG | APG | PPG |
| 98-99—Oyak Renau ................... | 23 | 873 | 139 | 271 | .513 | 64 | 80 | .800 | 189 | 39 | 370 | 8.2 | 1.7 | 16.1 |

Three-point field goals: 1998-99, 28-for-84 (.333). Totals, 28-for-84 (.333).

## NBA REGULAR-SEASON RECORD

| | | | | | | | | | REBOUNDS | | | | | | | | AVERAGES | | |
|---|---|---|---|---|---|---|---|---|---|---|---|---|---|---|---|---|---|---|---|
| Season Team | G | Min. | FGM | FGA | Pct. | FTM | FTA | Pct. | Off. | Def. | Tot. | Ast. | St. | Blk. | TO | Pts. | RPG | APG | PPG |
| 99-00—Denver ........... | 52 | 589 | 46 | 117 | .393 | 38 | 53 | .717 | 75 | 39 | 114 | 20 | 39 | 13 | 14 | 131 | 2.2 | 0.4 | 2.5 |
| 00-01—Denver ........... | 57 | 696 | 80 | 144 | .556 | 27 | 44 | .614 | 62 | 51 | 113 | 30 | 37 | 12 | 24 | 191 | 2.0 | 0.5 | 3.4 |
| 01-02—Denver ........... | 75 | 1686 | 147 | 307 | .479 | 69 | 92 | .750 | 134 | 165 | 299 | 52 | 75 | 41 | 41 | 364 | 4.0 | 0.7 | 4.9 |
| 02-03—Denver ........... | 62 | 996 | 97 | 197 | .492 | 27 | 41 | .659 | 78 | 79 | 157 | 54 | 65 | 29 | 43 | 223 | 2.5 | 0.9 | 3.6 |
| 03-04—Denver ........... | 52 | 392 | 18 | 53 | .340 | 10 | 12 | .833 | 39 | 48 | 87 | 18 | 18 | 16 | 6 | 46 | 1.7 | 0.3 | 0.9 |
| 04-05—Houston ......... | 66 | 604 | 47 | 111 | .423 | 14 | 21 | .667 | 21 | 55 | 76 | 18 | 23 | 5 | 7 | 111 | 1.2 | 0.3 | 1.7 |
| Totals ................... | 364 | 4963 | 435 | 929 | .468 | 185 | 263 | .703 | 409 | 437 | 846 | 192 | 257 | 116 | 135 | 1066 | 2.3 | 0.5 | 2.9 |

Three-point field goals: 1999-00, 1-for-9 (.111). 2000-01, 4-for-11 (.364). 2001-02, 1-for-12 (.083). 2002-03, 2-for-7 (.286). 2004-05, 3-for-6 (.500). Totals, 11-for-45 (.244).
Personal fouls/disqualifications: 1999-00, 95/0. 2000-01, 95/0. 2001-02, 171/1. 2002-03, 82/0. 2003-04, 47/0. 2004-05, 61/0. Totals, 551/1.

## NBA PLAYOFF RECORD

| Season Team | G | Min. | FGM | FGA | Pct. | FTM | FTA | Pct. | REBOUNDS Off. | Def. | Tot. | Ast. | St. | Blk. | TO | Pts. | AVERAGES RPG | APG | PPG |
|---|---|---|---|---|---|---|---|---|---|---|---|---|---|---|---|---|---|---|---|
| 03-04—Denver | 4 | 6 | 1 | 1 | 1.000 | 0 | 0 | ... | 0 | 0 | 0 | 0 | 0 | 0 | 0 | 2 | 0.0 | 0.0 | 0.5 |
| 04-05—Houston | 7 | 125 | 8 | 25 | .320 | 2 | 3 | .667 | 7 | 7 | 14 | 6 | 6 | 0 | 6 | 18 | 2.0 | 0.9 | 2.6 |
| Totals | 11 | 131 | 9 | 26 | .346 | 2 | 3 | .667 | 7 | 7 | 14 | 6 | 6 | 0 | 6 | 20 | 1.3 | 0.5 | 1.8 |

Personal fouls/disqualifications: 2004-05, 23/2. Totals, 23/2.

## BOYKINS, EARL    G    NUGGETS

**PERSONAL:** Born June 2, 1976, in Cleveland. ... 5-5/133. (1.65/60.3). ... Full name: Earl Antoine Boykins
**HIGH SCHOOL:** Central Catholic (Cleveland).
**COLLEGE:** Eastern Michigan.
**TRANSACTIONS/CAREER NOTES:** Not drafted by an NBA franchise. ... Played in Continental Basketball Association with Rockford Lightning (1998-2000). ... Signed as free agent by New Jersey Nets (January 21, 1999). ... Waived by Nets (February 19, 1999). ... Signed by Cleveland Cavaliers to 10-day contract (March 10, 1999). ... Waived by Cavaliers (March 19, 1999). ... Re-signed by Cavaliers to 10-day contract (March 23, 1999). ... Signed by Cavaliers for remainder of the season (April 2, 1999). ... Waived by Cavaliers (October 28, 1999). ... Signed as free agent by Orlando Magic (November 15, 1999). ... Waived by Magic (December 20, 1999). ... Signed by Cavaliers to first of two consecutive 10-day contracts (February 8, 2000). ... Re-signed by Cavaliers for remainder of season (February 28, 2000). ... Signed as free agent by Los Angeles Clippers (September 29, 2000). ... Waived by Clippers (June 28, 2002). ... Signed as free agent by Golden State Warriors (November 27, 2002). ... Signed as free agent by Denver Nuggets (August 18, 2003).

### COLLEGIATE RECORD

**NOTES:** Frances Pomeroy Naismith Award winner (1998).

| Season Team | G | Min. | FGM | FGA | Pct. | FTM | FTA | Pct. | Reb. | Ast. | Pts. | AVERAGES RPG | APG | PPG |
|---|---|---|---|---|---|---|---|---|---|---|---|---|---|---|
| 94-95—Eastern Michigan | 30 | 976 | 129 | 312 | .413 | 83 | 118 | .703 | 73 | 136 | 375 | 2.4 | 4.5 | 12.5 |
| 95-96—Eastern Michigan | 31 | 1029 | 156 | 361 | .432 | 144 | 179 | .804 | 71 | 181 | 479 | 2.3 | 5.8 | 15.5 |
| 96-97—Eastern Michigan | 32 | 1163 | 208 | 492 | .423 | 156 | 183 | .852 | 67 | 147 | 611 | 2.1 | 4.6 | 19.1 |
| 97-98—Eastern Michigan | 29 | 1070 | 266 | 563 | .472 | 129 | 158 | .816 | 66 | 160 | 746 | 2.3 | 5.5 | 25.7 |
| Totals | 122 | 4238 | 759 | 1728 | .439 | 512 | 638 | .803 | 277 | 624 | 2211 | 2.3 | 5.1 | 18.1 |

Three-point field goals: 1994-95, 34-for-99 (.343). 1995-96, 23-for-75 (.307). 1996-97, 39-for-130 (.300). 1997-98, 85-for-209 (.407). Totals, 181-for-513 (.353).

### CBA RECORD

| Season Team | G | Min. | FGM | FGA | Pct. | FTM | FTA | Pct. | Reb. | Ast. | Pts. | AVERAGES RPG | APG | PPG |
|---|---|---|---|---|---|---|---|---|---|---|---|---|---|---|
| 98-99—Rockford | 29 | 503 | 85 | 209 | .407 | 32 | 37 | .865 | 40 | 106 | 215 | 1.4 | 3.7 | 7.4 |
| 99-00—Rockford | 18 | 681 | 147 | 302 | .487 | 74 | 88 | .841 | 64 | 167 | 389 | 3.6 | 9.3 | 21.6 |
| Totals | 47 | 1184 | 232 | 511 | .454 | 106 | 125 | .848 | 104 | 273 | 604 | 2.2 | 5.8 | 12.9 |

Three-point field goals: 1998-99, 13-for-47 (.277). 1999-00, 21-for-59 (.356). Totals, 34-for-106 (.321).
Personal fouls/disqualifications: 1998-99, 36/0. 1999-00, 46/0. Totals, 82/0.

### NBA REGULAR-SEASON RECORD

| Season Team | G | Min. | FGM | FGA | Pct. | FTM | FTA | Pct. | REBOUNDS Off. | Def. | Tot. | Ast. | St. | Blk. | TO | Pts. | AVERAGES RPG | APG | PPG |
|---|---|---|---|---|---|---|---|---|---|---|---|---|---|---|---|---|---|---|---|
| 98-99—N.J.-Cleve. | 22 | 221 | 30 | 79 | .380 | 2 | 3 | .667 | 7 | 10 | 17 | 33 | 6 | 0 | 20 | 65 | 0.8 | 1.5 | 3.0 |
| 99-00—Orl.-Cleveland | 26 | 261 | 56 | 116 | .483 | 18 | 23 | .783 | 12 | 14 | 26 | 48 | 12 | 1 | 17 | 138 | 1.0 | 1.8 | 5.3 |
| 00-01—L.A. Clippers | 10 | 149 | 25 | 63 | .397 | 14 | 17 | .824 | 4 | 7 | 11 | 32 | 5 | 0 | 9 | 65 | 1.1 | 3.2 | 6.5 |
| 01-02—L.A. Clippers | 68 | 761 | 110 | 275 | .400 | 47 | 61 | .770 | 27 | 27 | 54 | 145 | 20 | 2 | 44 | 280 | 0.8 | 2.1 | 4.1 |
| 02-03—Golden State | 68 | 1321 | 199 | 464 | .429 | 173 | 200 | .865 | 35 | 53 | 88 | 221 | 38 | 4 | 73 | 600 | 1.3 | 3.3 | 8.8 |
| 03-04—Denver | 82 | 1849 | 321 | 766 | .419 | 142 | 162 | .877 | 42 | 101 | 143 | 295 | 51 | 3 | 100 | 839 | 1.7 | 3.6 | 10.2 |
| 04-05—Denver | 82 | 2162 | 340 | 824 | .413 | 279 | 303 | .921 | 37 | 106 | 143 | 372 | 78 | 12 | 121 | 1015 | 1.7 | 4.5 | 12.4 |
| Totals | 358 | 6724 | 1081 | 2587 | .418 | 675 | 769 | .878 | 164 | 318 | 482 | 1146 | 210 | 22 | 384 | 3002 | 1.3 | 3.2 | 8.4 |

Three-point field goals: 1998-99, 3-for-18 (.167). 1999-00, 8-for-20 (.400). 2000-01, 1-for-8 (.125). 2001-02, 13-for-42 (.310). 2002-03, 29-for-77 (.377). 2003-04, 55-for-171 (.322). 2004-05, 56-for-166 (.337). Totals, 165-for-502 (.329).
Personal fouls/disqualifications: 1998-99, 20/0. 1999-00, 23/0. 2000-01, 9/0. 2001-02, 44/0. 2002-03, 75/0. 2003-04, 84/0. 2004-05, 122/0. Totals, 377/0.

### NBA PLAYOFF RECORD

| Season Team | G | Min. | FGM | FGA | Pct. | FTM | FTA | Pct. | REBOUNDS Off. | Def. | Tot. | Ast. | St. | Blk. | TO | Pts. | AVERAGES RPG | APG | PPG |
|---|---|---|---|---|---|---|---|---|---|---|---|---|---|---|---|---|---|---|---|
| 03-04—Denver | 5 | 121 | 28 | 63 | .444 | 6 | 7 | .857 | 6 | 6 | 12 | 19 | 5 | 1 | 6 | 67 | 2.4 | 3.8 | 13.4 |
| 04-05—Denver | 5 | 152 | 27 | 68 | .397 | 17 | 19 | .895 | 2 | 3 | 5 | 19 | 4 | 1 | 9 | 71 | 1.0 | 3.8 | 14.2 |
| Totals | 10 | 273 | 55 | 131 | .420 | 23 | 26 | .885 | 8 | 9 | 17 | 38 | 9 | 2 | 15 | 138 | 1.7 | 3.8 | 13.8 |

Three-point field goals: 2003-04, 5-for-14 (.357). 2004-05, 0-for-7. Totals, 5-for-21 (.238).
Personal fouls/disqualifications: 2003-04, 6/0. 2004-05, 13/0. Totals, 19/0.

## BRADLEY, MICHAEL    F    76ERS

**PERSONAL:** Born April 18, 1979, in Worcester, Mass. ... 6-10/225. (2.08/102.1). ... Full name: Michael Thomas Bradley
**HIGH SCHOOL:** Burncoat (Worcester, Mass.).
**COLLEGE:** Kentucky, then Villanova.
**TRANSACTIONS/CAREER NOTES:** Selected after junior season by Toronto Raptors in first round (17th pick overall) of 2001 NBA Draft. ... Signed by Atlanta Hawks for remainder of season (March 18, 2004). ... Signed as free agent by Orlando Magic (July 29, 2004). ... Traded by Magic with G Cuttino Mobley to Sacramento Kings for G/F Doug Christie (January 10, 2005). ... Traded by Kings with Fs Chris Webber and Matt Barnes to Philadelphia 76ers for Fs Kenny Thomas and Corliss Williamson and C Brian Skinner (February 23, 2005).

### COLLEGIATE RECORD

**NOTES:** Member of NCAA Division I championship team (1998). ... The Sporting News All-America second team (2001).

| Season Team | G | Min. | FGM | FGA | Pct. | FTM | FTA | Pct. | Reb. | Ast. | Pts. | RPG | APG | PPG |
|---|---|---|---|---|---|---|---|---|---|---|---|---|---|---|
| 97-98—Kentucky | 32 | 221 | 30 | 45 | .667 | 18 | 35 | .514 | 55 | 15 | 78 | 1.7 | 0.5 | 2.4 |
| 98-99—Kentucky | 37 | 811 | 157 | 239 | .657 | 50 | 110 | .455 | 182 | 37 | 364 | 4.9 | 1.0 | 9.8 |
| 99-00—Villanova | | | | | | Did not play—transfer student. | | | | | | | | |
| 00-01—Villanova | 31 | 1053 | 254 | 367 | .692 | 125 | 212 | .590 | 303 | 81 | 645 | 9.8 | 2.6 | 20.8 |
| Totals | 100 | 2085 | 441 | 651 | .677 | 193 | 357 | .541 | 540 | 133 | 1087 | 5.4 | 1.3 | 10.9 |

Three-point field goals: 2000-01, 12-for-34 (.353). Totals, 12-for-34 (.353).
Personal fouls/disqualifications: 1997-98, 26/0. 1998-99, 72/0. 2000-01, 89/0. Totals, 187/0.

### NBA REGULAR-SEASON RECORD

| Season Team | G | Min. | FGM | FGA | Pct. | FTM | FTA | Pct. | REBOUNDS Off. | Def. | Tot. | Ast. | St. | Blk. | TO | Pts. | AVERAGES RPG | APG | PPG |
|---|---|---|---|---|---|---|---|---|---|---|---|---|---|---|---|---|---|---|---|
| 01-02—Toronto | 26 | 118 | 13 | 25 | .520 | 4 | 8 | .500 | 7 | 17 | 24 | 3 | 0 | 6 | 6 | 30 | 0.9 | 0.1 | 1.2 |
| 02-03—Toronto | 67 | 1314 | 151 | 314 | .481 | 35 | 67 | .522 | 162 | 247 | 409 | 67 | 16 | 32 | 76 | 338 | 6.1 | 1.0 | 5.0 |
| 03-04—Toronto-Atl. | 16 | 98 | 7 | 15 | .467 | 1 | 2 | .500 | 6 | 17 | 23 | 1 | 3 | 0 | 7 | 15 | 1.4 | 0.1 | 0.9 |
| 04-05—Orl.-Sac.-Phila. | 18 | 119 | 15 | 24 | .625 | 3 | 8 | .375 | 8 | 20 | 28 | 5 | 1 | 2 | 5 | 33 | 1.6 | 0.3 | 1.8 |
| Totals | 127 | 1649 | 186 | 378 | .492 | 43 | 85 | .506 | 183 | 301 | 484 | 76 | 20 | 40 | 94 | 416 | 3.8 | 0.6 | 3.3 |

Three-point field goals: 2001-02, 0-for-2. 2002-03, 1-for-6 (.167). 2004-05, 0-for-1. Totals, 1-for-9 (.111).
Personal fouls/disqualifications: 2001-02, 10/0. 2002-03, 125/0. 2003-04, 14/0. 2004-05, 12/0. Totals, 161/0.

### NBA PLAYOFF RECORD

| Season Team | G | Min. | FGM | FGA | Pct. | FTM | FTA | Pct. | REBOUNDS Off. | Def. | Tot. | Ast. | St. | Blk. | TO | Pts. | AVERAGES RPG | APG | PPG |
|---|---|---|---|---|---|---|---|---|---|---|---|---|---|---|---|---|---|---|---|
| 01-02—Toronto | 1 | 3 | 0 | 0 | ... | 0 | 0 | ... | 0 | 1 | 1 | 1 | 0 | 0 | 0 | 0 | 1.0 | 1.0 | 0.0 |

Personal fouls/disqualifications: 2001-02, 1/0. Totals, 1/0.

---

# BRADLEY, SHAWN                 C                 MAVERICKS

**PERSONAL:** Born March 22, 1972, in Landstuhl, West Germany. ... 7-6/265. (2.29/120.2). ... Full name: Shawn Paul Bradley.
**HIGH SCHOOL:** Emery County (Castle Dale, Utah).
**COLLEGE:** Brigham Young.
**TRANSACTIONS/CAREER NOTES:** Selected after freshman season by Philadelphia 76ers in first round (second pick overall) of 1993 NBA Draft. ... Traded by 76ers with F Tim Perry and G Greg Graham to New Jersey Nets for F Derrick Coleman, F Sean Higgins and G Rex Walters (November 30, 1995). ... Traded by Nets with F Ed O'Bannon, G Khalid Reeves and G Robert Pack to Dallas Mavericks for C Eric Montross, G Jim Jackson, F/C Chris Gatling, F/G George McCloud and G Sam Cassell (February 17, 1997).

### COLLEGIATE RECORD

**NOTES:** Shares NCAA Division I single-game record for most blocked shots—14 (December 7, 1990, vs. Eastern Kentucky). ... Led NCAA Division I with 5.2 blocked shots per game (1991).

| Season Team | G | Min. | FGM | FGA | Pct. | FTM | FTA | Pct. | Reb. | Ast. | Pts. | RPG | APG | PPG |
|---|---|---|---|---|---|---|---|---|---|---|---|---|---|---|
| 90-91—Brigham Young | 34 | 984 | 187 | 361 | .518 | 128 | 185 | .692 | 262 | 41 | 503 | 7.7 | 1.2 | 14.8 |
| 91-92—Brigham Young | | | | | | Did not play — church mission | | | | | | | | |
| 92-93—Brigham Young | | | | | | Did not play — church mission | | | | | | | | |
| Totals | 34 | 984 | 187 | 361 | .518 | 128 | 185 | .692 | 262 | 41 | 503 | 7.7 | 1.2 | 14.8 |

Three-point field goals: 1990-91, 1-for-1 (1.000). Totals, 1-for-1 (1.000).

### NBA REGULAR-SEASON RECORD

**HONORS:** NBA All-Rookie second team (1994).
**NOTES:** Led NBA with 338 personal fouls and 18 disqualifications (1995). ... Led NBA with 3.40 blocks per game (1997).

| Season Team | G | Min. | FGM | FGA | Pct. | FTM | FTA | Pct. | REBOUNDS Off. | Def. | Tot. | Ast. | St. | Blk. | TO | Pts. | AVERAGES RPG | APG | PPG |
|---|---|---|---|---|---|---|---|---|---|---|---|---|---|---|---|---|---|---|---|
| 93-94—Philadelphia | 49 | 1385 | 201 | 491 | .409 | 102 | 168 | .607 | 98 | 208 | 306 | 98 | 45 | 147 | 148 | 504 | 6.2 | 2.0 | 10.3 |
| 94-95—Philadelphia | 82 | 2365 | 315 | 693 | .455 | 148 | 232 | .638 | 243 | 416 | 659 | 53 | 54 | 274 | 142 | 778 | 8.0 | 0.6 | 9.5 |
| 95-96—Phila.-N.Y. | 79 | 2329 | 387 | 873 | .443 | 169 | 246 | .687 | 221 | 417 | 638 | 63 | 49 | 288 | 179 | 944 | 8.1 | 0.8 | 11.9 |
| 96-97—N.J.-Dal. | 73 | 2288 | 406 | 905 | .449 | 149 | 228 | .654 | 221 | 390 | 611 | 52 | 40 | 248 | 134 | 961 | 8.4 | 0.7 | 13.2 |
| 97-98—Dallas | 64 | 1822 | 300 | 711 | .422 | 130 | 180 | .722 | 164 | 354 | 518 | 60 | 51 | 214 | 96 | 731 | 8.1 | 0.9 | 11.4 |
| 98-99—Dallas | 49 | 1294 | 167 | 348 | .480 | 86 | 115 | .748 | 130 | 262 | 392 | 40 | 35 | 159 | 56 | 420 | 8.0 | 0.8 | 8.6 |
| 99-00—Dallas | 77 | 1901 | 266 | 555 | .479 | 114 | 149 | .765 | 160 | 337 | 497 | 60 | 71 | 190 | 74 | 647 | 6.5 | 0.8 | 8.4 |
| 00-01—Dallas | 82 | 2001 | 219 | 447 | .490 | 140 | 178 | .787 | 160 | 448 | 608 | 38 | 36 | /d228 | 88 | 579 | 7.4 | 0.5 | 7.1 |
| 01-02—Dallas | 53 | 757 | 78 | 163 | .479 | 59 | 64 | .922 | 53 | 123 | 176 | 20 | 28 | 64 | 25 | 215 | 3.3 | 0.4 | 4.1 |
| 02-03—Dallas | 81 | 1731 | 201 | 375 | .536 | 141 | 175 | .806 | 151 | 325 | 476 | 54 | 65 | 170 | 67 | 543 | 5.9 | 0.7 | 6.7 |
| 03-04—Dallas | 66 | 773 | 89 | 188 | .473 | 41 | 49 | .837 | 72 | 101 | 173 | 20 | 33 | 74 | 17 | 219 | 2.6 | 0.3 | 3.3 |
| 04-05—Dallas | 77 | 885 | 84 | 186 | .452 | 43 | 63 | .683 | 70 | 144 | 214 | 15 | 25 | 63 | 33 | 211 | 2.8 | 0.2 | 2.7 |
| Totals | 832 | 19531 | 2713 | 5935 | .457 | 1322 | 1847 | .716 | 1743 | 3525 | 5268 | 573 | 532 | 2119 | 1059 | 6752 | 6.3 | 0.7 | 8.1 |

Three-point field goals: 1993-94, 0-for-3. 1994-95, 0-for-3. 1995-96, 1-for-4 (.250). 1996-97, 0-for-8. 1997-98, 1-for-3 (.333). 1998-99, 0-for-4. 1999-00, 1-for-5 (.200). 2000-01, 1-for-6 (.167). 2001-02, 0-for-1. 2002-03, 0-for-1. 2003-04, 0-for-1. Totals, 4-for-39 (.103).
Personal fouls/disqualifications: 1993-94, 170/3. 1994-95, 338/18. 1995-96, 286/5. 1996-97, 237/7. 1997-98, 214/9. 1998-99, 153/2. 1999-00, 260/7. 2000-01, 256/6. 2001-02, 128/3. 2002-03, 242/5. 2003-04, 130/1. 2004-05, 153/1. Totals, 2567/67.

### NBA PLAYOFF RECORD

| Season Team | G | Min. | FGM | FGA | Pct. | FTM | FTA | Pct. | REBOUNDS Off. | Def. | Tot. | Ast. | St. | Blk. | TO | Pts. | AVERAGES RPG | APG | PPG |
|---|---|---|---|---|---|---|---|---|---|---|---|---|---|---|---|---|---|---|---|
| 00-01—Dallas | 10 | 256 | 27 | 51 | .529 | 10 | 13 | .769 | 24 | 47 | 71 | 5 | 4 | 30 | 10 | 64 | 7.1 | 0.5 | 6.4 |
| 01-02—Dallas | 7 | 25 | 3 | 6 | .500 | 0 | 0 | ... | 1 | 4 | 5 | 0 | 0 | 1 | 1 | 6 | 0.7 | 0.0 | 0.9 |
| 02-03—Dallas | 17 | 246 | 20 | 50 | .400 | 9 | 12 | .750 | 23 | 42 | 65 | 5 | 3 | 14 | 15 | 49 | 3.8 | 0.3 | 2.9 |
| 03-04—Dallas | 2 | 3 | 0 | 0 | ... | 0 | 0 | ... | 0 | 0 | 0 | 0 | 0 | 0 | 0 | 0 | 0.0 | 0.0 | 0.0 |
| 04-05—Dallas | 7 | 27 | 4 | 6 | .667 | 1 | 2 | .500 | 4 | 2 | 6 | 0 | 0 | 2 | 0 | 9 | 0.9 | 0.0 | 1.3 |
| Totals | 43 | 557 | 54 | 113 | .478 | 20 | 27 | .741 | 52 | 95 | 147 | 10 | 7 | 47 | 26 | 128 | 3.4 | 0.2 | 3.0 |

Three-point field goals: 2002-03, 0-for-1. Totals, 0-for-1 (.000).
Personal fouls/disqualifications: 2000-01, 37/1. 2001-02, 9/0. 2002-03, 48/2. 2003-04, 1/0. 2004-05, 7/0. Totals, 102/3.

## BRAGGS, TORRAYE        F

**PERSONAL:** Born May 15, 1976, in Fresno, Calif. ... 6-8/236. (2.03/107.0).
**HIGH SCHOOL:** Edison (Calif.).
**JUNIOR COLLEGE:** San Jose (Calif.) City College.
**COLLEGE:** Xavier.
**TRANSACTIONS/CAREER NOTES:** Selected by Utah Jazz in second round (57th pick overall) of 1998 NBA Draft. ... Played in Spain (1998-99). ... Waived by Jazz (October 27, 1999). ... Played in Continental Basketball Association with Rockford Lightning (1999-2000). ... Signed as free agent by Detroit Pistons (August 11, 2000). ... Waived by Pistons (November 20, 2000). ... Signed as free agent by Sacramento Kings (October 1, 2001). ... Waived by Kings (October 22, 2001). ... Played in Israel (2002-03). ... Signed as free agent by Houston Rockets (September 9, 2003). ... Waived by Rockets (November 23, 2003). ... Signed by Washington Wizards to first of two consecutive 10-day contracts (January 16, 2004). ... Signed as free agent by Rockets (March 19, 2005).

### COLLEGIATE RECORD

| Season Team | G | Min. | FGM | FGA | Pct. | FTM | FTA | Pct. | Reb. | Ast. | Pts. | RPG | APG | PPG |
|---|---|---|---|---|---|---|---|---|---|---|---|---|---|---|
| 94-95—San Jose City College..... | 34 | ... | 289 | 546 | .529 | 150 | 219 | .685 | 354 | 72 | 728 | 10.4 | 2.1 | 21.4 |
| 95-96—San Jose City College..... | 32 | ... | 263 | 477 | .551 | 118 | 175 | .674 | 360 | 120 | 645 | 11.3 | 3.8 | 20.2 |
| 96-97—Xavier ......................... | 29 | 896 | 148 | 265 | .558 | 107 | 148 | .723 | 214 | 74 | 403 | 7.4 | 2.6 | 13.9 |
| 97-98—Xavier ......................... | 30 | 892 | 132 | 244 | .541 | 125 | 171 | .731 | 246 | 72 | 389 | 8.2 | 2.4 | 13.0 |
| Junior College Totals............. | 66 | ... | 552 | 1023 | .540 | 268 | 394 | .680 | 714 | 192 | 1373 | 10.8 | 2.9 | 20.8 |
| 4-Year-College Totals ............ | 59 | 1788 | 280 | 509 | .550 | 232 | 319 | .727 | 460 | 146 | 792 | 7.8 | 2.5 | 13.4 |

Three-point field goals: 1994-95, 0-for-2. 1995-96, 1-for-1 (1.000). 1996-97, 0-for-1. Totals, 1-for-4 (.250).

### SPANISH RECORD

| Season Team | G | Min. | FGM | FGA | Pct. | FTM | FTA | Pct. | Reb. | Ast. | Pts. | RPG | APG | PPG |
|---|---|---|---|---|---|---|---|---|---|---|---|---|---|---|
| 98-99—C.B. Gran Cana.-Los Canja Cantabria | 20 | 601 | 127 | 267 | .476 | 82 | 113 | .726 | 149 | 31 | 336 | 7.5 | 1.6 | 16.8 |
| 99-00—TDK Manresa................. | 4 | 126 | 23 | 50 | .460 | 14 | 25 | .560 | 33 | 10 | 60 | 8.3 | 2.5 | 15.0 |
| Totals .................................... | 24 | 727 | 150 | 317 | .473 | 96 | 138 | .696 | 182 | 41 | 396 | 7.6 | 1.7 | 16.5 |

Three-point field goals: 1998-99, 0-for-6. 1999-00, 0-for-1. Totals, 0-for-7 (.000).
Personal fouls/disqualifications: 1998-99, 70/0. Totals, 70/0.

### CBA RECORD

| Season Team | G | Min. | FGM | FGA | Pct. | FTM | FTA | Pct. | Reb. | Ast. | Pts. | RPG | APG | PPG |
|---|---|---|---|---|---|---|---|---|---|---|---|---|---|---|
| 99-00—Rockford ...................... | 55 | 1689 | 327 | 643 | .509 | 228 | *337 | .677 | 533 | 166 | 882 | 9.7 | 3.0 | 16.0 |
| 03-04—Yakima-Sioux Falls ........ | 22 | 750 | 151 | 304 | .497 | 94 | 121 | .777 | 228 | 71 | 396 | 10.4 | 3.2 | 18.0 |
| Totals .................................... | 77 | 2439 | 478 | 947 | .505 | 322 | 458 | .703 | 761 | 237 | 1278 | 9.9 | 3.1 | 16.6 |

Three-point field goals: 1999-00, 0-for-2. Totals, 0-for-2 (.000).
Personal fouls/disqualifications: 1999-00, 244/0. Totals, 244/0.

### AMERICAN BASKETBALL ASSOCIATION RECORD

| Season Team | G | Min. | FGM | FGA | Pct. | FTM | FTA | Pct. | Reb. | Ast. | Pts. | RPG | APG | PPG |
|---|---|---|---|---|---|---|---|---|---|---|---|---|---|---|
| 00-01—Indiana ........................ | 6 | 203 | 38 | 80 | .475 | 33 | 37 | .892 | 52 | 25 | 109 | 8.7 | 4.2 | 18.2 |

### GREEK LEAGUE RECORD

| Season Team | G | Min. | FGM | FGA | Pct. | FTM | FTA | Pct. | Reb. | Ast. | Pts. | RPG | APG | PPG |
|---|---|---|---|---|---|---|---|---|---|---|---|---|---|---|
| 01-02—Aris............................. | 20 | 640 | 134 | 262 | .511 | 89 | 128 | .695 | 186 | 68 | 362 | 9.3 | 3.4 | 18.1 |
| 02-03—PAOK........................... | 5 | 159 | 26 | 54 | .481 | 16 | 23 | .696 | 50 | 22 | 68 | 10.0 | 4.4 | 13.6 |
| Totals .................................... | 25 | 799 | 160 | 316 | .506 | 105 | 151 | .695 | 236 | 90 | 430 | 9.4 | 3.6 | 17.2 |

Three-point field goals: 2001-02, 5-for-17 (.294). 2002-03, 0-for-2. Totals, 5-for-19 (.263).

### ISRAELI RECORD

| Season Team | G | Min. | FGM | FGA | Pct. | FTM | FTA | Pct. | Reb. | Ast. | Pts. | RPG | APG | PPG |
|---|---|---|---|---|---|---|---|---|---|---|---|---|---|---|
| 02-03—Hapoel Jerusalem........... | 14 | 422 | 90 | 155 | .581 | 51 | 74 | .689 | 96 | 27 | 233 | 6.9 | 1.9 | 16.6 |

Three-point field goals: 2002-03, 2-for-6 (.333). Totals, 2-for-6 (.333).

### NBA REGULAR-SEASON RECORD

| Season Team | G | Min. | FGM | FGA | Pct. | FTM | FTA | Pct. | Off. | Def. | Tot. | Ast. | St. | Blk. | TO | Pts. | RPG | APG | PPG |
|---|---|---|---|---|---|---|---|---|---|---|---|---|---|---|---|---|---|---|---|
| 03-04—Houston-Wash. | 15 | 154 | 16 | 33 | .485 | 8 | 12 | .667 | 18 | 21 | 39 | 7 | 4 | 2 | 13 | 40 | 2.6 | 0.5 | 2.7 |
| 04-05—Houston ......... | 7 | 24 | 3 | 7 | .429 | 0 | 0 | ... | 7 | 5 | 12 | 0 | 0 | 0 | 2 | 6 | 1.7 | 0.0 | 0.9 |
| Totals ................... | 22 | 178 | 19 | 40 | .475 | 8 | 12 | .667 | 25 | 26 | 51 | 7 | 4 | 2 | 15 | 46 | 2.3 | 0.3 | 2.1 |

Personal fouls/disqualifications: 2003-04, 29/0. 2004-05, 4/0. Totals, 33/0.

### RUSSIAN LEAGUE RECORD

| Season Team | G | Min. | FGM | FGA | Pct. | FTM | FTA | Pct. | Reb. | Ast. | Pts. | RPG | APG | PPG |
|---|---|---|---|---|---|---|---|---|---|---|---|---|---|---|
| 04-05—Spartak........................ | 22 | 635 | 148 | 278 | .532 | 102 | 151 | .675 | 163 | 67 | 398 | 7.4 | 3.0 | 18.1 |

Three-point field goals: 2004-05, 0-for-1. Totals, 0-for-1 (.000).

## BRAND, ELTON      F        CLIPPERS

**PERSONAL:** Born March 11, 1979, in Cortland, N.Y. ... 6-8/265. (2.03/120.2). ... Full name: Elton Tyron Brand
**HIGH SCHOOL:** Peekskill (N.Y.).
**COLLEGE:** Duke.
**TRANSACTIONS/CAREER NOTES:** Selected after sophomore season by Chicago Bulls in first round (first pick overall) of 1999 NBA Draft. ... Traded by Bulls to Los Angeles Clippers for F Brian Skinner and draft rights to C Tyson Chandler (June 27, 2001).

### COLLEGIATE RECORD

**NOTES:** The Sporting News College Player of the Year (1999). ... Wooden Award winner (1999). ... Naismith Award winner (1999). ... The Sporting News All-America first team (1999).

| Season Team | G | Min. | FGM | FGA | Pct. | FTM | FTA | Pct. | Reb. | Ast. | Pts. | RPG | APG | PPG |
|---|---|---|---|---|---|---|---|---|---|---|---|---|---|---|
| 97-98—Duke | 21 | 493 | 100 | 169 | .592 | 81 | 134 | .604 | 154 | 10 | 281 | 7.3 | 0.5 | 13.4 |
| 98-99—Duke | 39 | 1141 | 255 | 411 | .620 | 181 | 256 | .707 | 382 | 41 | 691 | 9.8 | 1.1 | 17.7 |
| Totals | 60 | 1634 | 355 | 580 | .612 | 262 | 390 | .672 | 536 | 51 | 972 | 8.9 | 0.9 | 16.2 |

### NBA REGULAR-SEASON RECORD

**HONORS:** NBA co-Rookie of the Year (2000). ... NBA All-Rookie first team (2000). ... MVP of Rookie Challenge (2000).

| Season Team | G | Min. | FGM | FGA | Pct. | FTM | FTA | Pct. | Off. | Def. | Tot. | Ast. | St. | Blk. | TO | Pts. | RPG | APG | PPG |
|---|---|---|---|---|---|---|---|---|---|---|---|---|---|---|---|---|---|---|---|
| 99-00—Chicago | 81 | 2999 | 630 | 1306 | .482 | 367 | 536 | .685 | 348 | 462 | *810 | 155 | 66 | 132 | 228 | 1627 | 10.0 | 1.9 | 20.1 |
| 00-01—Chicago | 74 | 2906 | 578 | 1215 | .476 | 334 | 472 | .708 | 285 | 461 | 746 | 240 | 71 | 118 | 219 | 1490 | 10.1 | 3.2 | 20.1 |
| 01-02—L.A. Clippers | 80 | 3020 | 532 | 1010 | .527 | 389 | 524 | .742 | 396 | 529 | *925 | 191 | 80 | 163 | 173 | 1453 | 11.6 | 2.4 | 18.2 |
| 02-03—L.A. Clippers | 62 | 2454 | 451 | 899 | .502 | 244 | 356 | .685 | 283 | 420 | 703 | 157 | 71 | 158 | 161 | 1146 | 11.3 | 2.5 | 18.5 |
| 03-04—L.A. Clippers | 69 | 2670 | 484 | 982 | .493 | 411 | 532 | .773 | 269 | 445 | 714 | 227 | 64 | 154 | 193 | 1379 | 10.3 | 3.3 | 20.0 |
| 04-05—L.A. Clippers | 81 | 3001 | 629 | 1251 | .503 | 364 | 484 | .752 | 296 | 474 | 770 | 208 | 62 | 169 | 183 | 1622 | 9.5 | 2.6 | 20.0 |
| Totals | 447 | 17050 | 3304 | 6663 | .496 | 2109 | 2904 | .726 | 1877 | 2791 | 4668 | 1178 | 414 | 894 | 1157 | 8717 | 10.4 | 2.6 | 19.5 |

Three-point field goals: 1999-00, 0-for-2. 2000-01, 0-for-2. 2002-03, 0-for-1. 2003-04, 0-for-1. 2004-05, 0-for-3. Totals, 0-for-9 (.000).
Personal fouls/disqualifications: 1999-00, 259/3. 2000-01, 243/4. 2001-02, 254/3. 2002-03, 204/3. 2003-04, 229/1. 2004-05, 240/2. Totals, 1429/16.

### NBA ALL-STAR GAME RECORD

| Season Team | Min. | FGM | FGA | Pct. | FTM | FTA | Pct. | Off. | Def. | Tot. | Ast. | PF | Dq. | St. | Blk. | TO | Pts. |
|---|---|---|---|---|---|---|---|---|---|---|---|---|---|---|---|---|---|
| 2002—L.A. Clippers | 19 | 3 | 5 | .600 | 0 | 0 | ... | 5 | 5 | 10 | 1 | 2 | 0 | 0 | 1 | 2 | 6 |

## BREWER, JAMISON     G

**PERSONAL:** Born November 19, 1980, in East Point, Ga. ... 6-4/180. (1.93/81.6). ... Full name: Jamison Rudy Van Brewer
**HIGH SCHOOL:** Tri-Cities (East Point, Ga.), then Newport School.
**COLLEGE:** Auburn.
**TRANSACTIONS/CAREER NOTES:** Selected after sophomore season by Indiana Pacers in second round (41st pick overall) of 2001 NBA Draft. ... Signed as free agent by New York Knicks (August 27, 2004). ... Traded by Knicks with F Nazr Mohammed to San Antonio Spurs for F Malik Rose and conditional first-round picks in 2005 and 2006 NBA drafts (February 24, 2005). ... Waived by Spurs (February 26, 2005).

### COLLEGIATE RECORD

| Season Team | G | Min. | FGM | FGA | Pct. | FTM | FTA | Pct. | Reb. | Ast. | Pts. | RPG | APG | PPG |
|---|---|---|---|---|---|---|---|---|---|---|---|---|---|---|
| 99-00—Auburn | 26 | 312 | 22 | 54 | .407 | 13 | 25 | .520 | 43 | 49 | 60 | 1.7 | 1.9 | 2.3 |
| 00-01—Auburn | 32 | 1035 | 97 | 207 | .469 | 64 | 121 | .529 | 230 | 187 | 268 | 7.2 | 5.8 | 8.4 |
| Totals | 58 | 1347 | 119 | 261 | .456 | 77 | 146 | .527 | 273 | 236 | 328 | 4.7 | 4.1 | 5.7 |

Three-point field goals: 1999-00, 3-for-15 (.200). 2000-01, 10-for-44 (.227). Totals, 13-for-59 (.220).
Personal fouls/disqualifications: 1999-00, 25/0. 2000-01, 49/0. Totals, 74/0.

### NBA REGULAR-SEASON RECORD

| Season Team | G | Min. | FGM | FGA | Pct. | FTM | FTA | Pct. | Off. | Def. | Tot. | Ast. | St. | Blk. | TO | Pts. | RPG | APG | PPG |
|---|---|---|---|---|---|---|---|---|---|---|---|---|---|---|---|---|---|---|---|
| 01-02—Indiana | 13 | 43 | 2 | 5 | .400 | 0 | 0 | ... | 2 | 6 | 8 | 9 | 2 | 0 | 3 | 4 | 0.6 | 0.7 | 0.3 |
| 02-03—Indiana | 10 | 80 | 9 | 17 | .529 | 4 | 9 | .444 | 5 | 4 | 9 | 18 | 2 | 1 | 6 | 22 | 0.9 | 1.8 | 2.2 |
| 03-04—Indiana | 13 | 160 | 13 | 35 | .371 | 1 | 6 | .167 | 2 | 9 | 11 | 17 | 7 | 0 | 10 | 32 | 0.8 | 1.3 | 2.5 |
| 04-05—New York | 18 | 185 | 11 | 37 | .297 | 6 | 13 | .462 | 6 | 16 | 22 | 12 | 8 | 1 | 13 | 31 | 1.2 | 0.7 | 1.7 |
| Totals | 54 | 468 | 35 | 94 | .372 | 11 | 28 | .393 | 15 | 35 | 50 | 56 | 19 | 2 | 32 | 89 | 0.9 | 1.0 | 1.6 |

Three-point field goals: 2001-02, 0-for-1. 2002-03, 0-for-2. 2003-04, 5-for-14 (.357). 2004-05, 3-for-15 (.200). Totals, 8-for-32 (.250).
Personal fouls/disqualifications: 2001-02, 3/0. 2002-03, 11/0. 2003-04, 9/0. 2004-05, 11/0. Totals, 34/0.

### NBA PLAYOFF RECORD

| Season Team | G | Min. | FGM | FGA | Pct. | FTM | FTA | Pct. | Off. | Def. | Tot. | Ast. | St. | Blk. | TO | Pts. | RPG | APG | PPG |
|---|---|---|---|---|---|---|---|---|---|---|---|---|---|---|---|---|---|---|---|
| 01-02—Indiana | 2 | 6 | 0 | 2 | .000 | 1 | 2 | .500 | 2 | 2 | 4 | 1 | 0 | 0 | 1 | 1 | 2.0 | 0.5 | 0.5 |

Personal fouls/disqualifications: 2001-02, 3/0. Totals, 3/0.

## BREZEC, PRIMOZ     F            BOBCATS

**PERSONAL:** Born October 2, 1979, in Postojna, Slovenia. ... 7-1/243. (2.16/110.2).
**TRANSACTIONS/CAREER NOTES:** Played in Slovenia (1997-2001). ... Selected by Indiana Pacers in first round (27th pick overall) of 2000 NBA Draft. ... Selected by Charlotte Bobcats from Pacers in NBA Expansion Draft (June 22, 2004).

### SLOVENIAN LEAGUE RECORD

| Season Team | G | Min. | FGM | FGA | Pct. | FTM | FTA | Pct. | Reb. | Ast. | Pts. | RPG | APG | PPG |
|---|---|---|---|---|---|---|---|---|---|---|---|---|---|---|
| 96-97—Kraski | 30 | ... | 164 | 283 | .580 | 201 | 258 | .779 | 207 | 12 | 577 | 6.9 | 0.4 | 19.2 |
| 97-98—Kraski | 12 | ... | 36 | 47 | .766 | 28 | 41 | .683 | 38 | 4 | 100 | 3.2 | 0.3 | 8.3 |
| 98-99—Olimpija Ljubljana | 23 | 203 | 40 | 52 | .769 | 31 | 45 | .689 | 40 | 4 | 111 | 1.7 | 0.2 | 4.8 |
| 99-00—Olimpija Ljubljana | 30 | 609 | 111 | 150 | .740 | 76 | 105 | .724 | 155 | 5 | 298 | 5.2 | 0.2 | 9.9 |
| 00-01—Olimpija Ljubljana | 30 | 618 | 132 | 190 | .695 | 78 | 122 | .639 | 127 | 19 | 342 | 4.2 | 0.6 | 11.4 |
| Totals | 125 | 1430 | 483 | 722 | .669 | 414 | 571 | .725 | 567 | 44 | 1428 | 4.5 | 0.4 | 11.4 |

Three-point field goals: 1996-97, 16-for-52 (.308). Totals, 16-for-52 (.308).
Personal fouls/disqualifications: 2000-01, 84/0. Totals, 84/0.

### NBA REGULAR-SEASON RECORD

| Season Team | G | Min. | FGM | FGA | Pct. | FTM | FTA | Pct. | Off. | Def. | Tot. | Ast. | St. | Blk. | TO | Pts. | RPG | APG | PPG |
|---|---|---|---|---|---|---|---|---|---|---|---|---|---|---|---|---|---|---|---|
| 01-02—Indiana | 22 | 160 | 14 | 29 | .483 | 15 | 25 | .600 | 16 | 12 | 28 | 6 | 0 | 7 | 6 | 43 | 1.3 | 0.3 | 2.0 |
| 02-03—Indiana | 22 | 111 | 15 | 38 | .395 | 12 | 20 | .600 | 13 | 10 | 23 | 4 | 2 | 4 | 7 | 42 | 1.0 | 0.2 | 1.9 |
| 03-04—Indiana | 18 | 72 | 12 | 26 | .462 | 4 | 6 | .667 | 5 | 10 | 15 | 3 | 0 | 3 | 6 | 28 | 0.8 | 0.2 | 1.6 |

| Season Team | G | Min. | FGM | FGA | Pct. | FTM | FTA | Pct. | REBOUNDS Off. | Def. | Tot. | Ast. | St. | Blk. | TO | Pts. | AVERAGES RPG | APG | PPG |
|---|---|---|---|---|---|---|---|---|---|---|---|---|---|---|---|---|---|---|---|
| 04-05—Charlotte ......... | 72 | 2276 | 387 | 756 | .512 | 164 | 220 | .745 | 226 | 305 | 531 | 86 | 33 | 55 | 106 | 938 | 7.4 | 1.2 | 13.0 |
| Totals ................... | 134 | 2619 | 428 | 849 | .504 | 195 | 271 | .720 | 260 | 337 | 597 | 99 | 35 | 69 | 125 | 1051 | 4.5 | 0.7 | 7.8 |

Three-point field goals: 2002-03, 0-for-1. Totals, 0-for-1 (.000).
Personal fouls/disqualifications: 2001-02, 28/0. 2002-03, 16/0. 2003-04, 13/0. 2004-05, 183/2. Totals, 240/2.

## BROWN, DAMONE — F

**PERSONAL:** Born June 28, 1979, in Buffalo. ... 6-8/202. (2.03/91.6). ... Full name: Damone Lamar Brown
**HIGH SCHOOL:** Seneca Vocational (Buffalo).
**COLLEGE:** Syracuse.
**TRANSACTIONS/CAREER NOTES:** Selected by Philadelphia 76ers in second round (37th pick overall) of 2001 NBA Draft. ... Waived by 76ers (October 23, 2002). ... Played in National Basketball Developmental League with Charleston Lowgators (2002-03). ... Signed as free agent by Toronto Raptors (January 13, 2003). ... Waived by Raptors (January 23, 2003). ... Signed as free agent by New Jersey Nets (September 30, 2003). ... Waived by Nets (December 22, 2003). ... Played in NBDL with Charleston Lowgators and Huntsville Flight (2003-04). ... Signed by Washington Wizards to first of two consecutive 10-day contracts (March 17, 2005). ... Signed by Wizards for remainder of season (April 10, 2005).

### COLLEGIATE RECORD

| Season Team | G | Min. | FGM | FGA | Pct. | FTM | FTA | Pct. | Reb. | Ast. | Pts. | AVERAGES RPG | APG | PPG |
|---|---|---|---|---|---|---|---|---|---|---|---|---|---|---|
| 97-98—Syracuse ...................... | 15 | 54 | 10 | 24 | .417 | 5 | 10 | .500 | 13 | 1 | 26 | 0.9 | 0.1 | 1.7 |
| 98-99—Syracuse ...................... | 33 | 815 | 128 | 256 | .500 | 45 | 60 | .750 | 180 | 42 | 314 | 5.5 | 1.3 | 9.5 |
| 99-00—Syracuse ...................... | 31 | 807 | 137 | 268 | .511 | 55 | 82 | .671 | 190 | 42 | 331 | 6.1 | 1.4 | 10.7 |
| 00-01—Syracuse ...................... | 34 | 1242 | 215 | 437 | .492 | 158 | 300 | .527 | 300 | 56 | 559 | 8.8 | 1.6 | 16.4 |
| Totals ..................................... | 113 | 2918 | 490 | 985 | .497 | 263 | 452 | .582 | 683 | 141 | 1230 | 6.0 | 1.2 | 10.9 |

Three-point field goals: 1997-98, 1-for-6 (.167). 1998-99, 13-for-57 (.228). 1999-00, 2-for-12 (.167). 2000-01, 4-for-14 (.286). Totals, 20-for-89 (.225).
Personal fouls/disqualifications: 1997-98, 9/0. 1998-99, 97/0. 1999-00, 86/0. 2000-01, 92/0. Totals, 284/0.

### NBA REGULAR-SEASON RECORD

| Season Team | G | Min. | FGM | FGA | Pct. | FTM | FTA | Pct. | REBOUNDS Off. | Def. | Tot. | Ast. | St. | Blk. | TO | Pts. | AVERAGES RPG | APG | PPG |
|---|---|---|---|---|---|---|---|---|---|---|---|---|---|---|---|---|---|---|---|
| 01-02—Philadelphia .... | 17 | 67 | 8 | 21 | .381 | 7 | 8 | .875 | 2 | 2 | 4 | 2 | 1 | 1 | 9 | 23 | 0.2 | 0.1 | 1.4 |
| 02-03—Toronto .......... | 5 | 115 | 11 | 35 | .314 | 6 | 8 | .750 | 3 | 12 | 15 | 3 | 1 | 0 | 6 | 28 | 3.0 | 0.6 | 5.6 |
| 03-04—New Jersey ..... | 3 | 17 | 1 | 10 | .100 | 1 | 2 | .500 | 3 | 2 | 5 | 0 | 2 | 0 | 1 | 3 | 1.7 | 0.0 | 1.0 |
| 04-05—Washington ... | 14 | 152 | 23 | 62 | .371 | 4 | 9 | .444 | 10 | 18 | 28 | 14 | 1 | 6 | 15 | 54 | 2.0 | 1.0 | 3.9 |
| Totals ..................... | 39 | 351 | 43 | 128 | .336 | 18 | 27 | .667 | 18 | 34 | 52 | 19 | 5 | 7 | 31 | 108 | 1.3 | 0.5 | 2.8 |

Three-point field goals: 2001-02, 0-for-1. 2002-03, 0-for-2. 2004-05, 4-for-11 (.364). Totals, 4-for-14 (.286).
Personal fouls/disqualifications: 2001-02, 11/0. 2002-03, 14/0. 2003-04, 2/0. 2004-05, 17/0. Totals, 44/0.

### NBDL RECORD

| Season Team | G | Min. | FGM | FGA | Pct. | FTM | FTA | Pct. | Reb. | Ast. | Pts. | AVERAGES RPG | APG | PPG |
|---|---|---|---|---|---|---|---|---|---|---|---|---|---|---|
| 02-03—North Charleston ........... | 42 | 1141 | 201 | 477 | .421 | 98 | 131 | .748 | 222 | 73 | 524 | 5.3 | 1.7 | 12.5 |
| 03-04—Charleston-Huntsville ..... | 26 | 718 | 118 | 279 | .423 | 82 | 101 | .812 | 123 | 46 | 342 | 4.7 | 1.8 | 13.2 |
| 04-05—Huntsville ...................... | 32 | 1091 | 196 | 465 | .422 | 112 | 151 | .742 | 183 | 71 | 510 | 5.7 | 2.2 | 15.9 |
| Totals ..................................... | 100 | 2950 | 515 | 1221 | .422 | 292 | 383 | .762 | 528 | 190 | 1376 | 5.3 | 1.9 | 13.8 |

Three-point field goals: 2002-03, 24-for-58 (.414). 2003-04, 24-for-62 (.387). 2004-05, 6-for-24 (.250). Totals, 54-for-144 (.375).

## BROWN, DEVIN — G — SPURS

**PERSONAL:** Born December 30, 1978, in Salt Lake City, Utah. ... 6-5/210. (1.96/95.3).
**HIGH SCHOOL:** South San West Campus (San Antonio, Tex.).
**COLLEGE:** University of Texas at San Antonio.
**TRANSACTIONS/CAREER NOTES:** Not drafted by an NBA franchise ... Played in National Basketball Developmental League with Fayetteville Patriots (2002-03). ... Signed by San Antonio Spurs (July 31, 2003).

### COLLEGIATE RECORD

| Season Team | G | Min. | FGM | FGA | Pct. | FTM | FTA | Pct. | Reb. | Ast. | Pts. | AVERAGES RPG | APG | PPG |
|---|---|---|---|---|---|---|---|---|---|---|---|---|---|---|
| 98-99—Texas-San Antonio ........ | 29 | 896 | 160 | 380 | .421 | 112 | 148 | .757 | 177 | 65 | 483 | 6.1 | 2.2 | 16.7 |
| 99-00—Texas-San Antonio ........ | 20 | 657 | 129 | 330 | .391 | 83 | 113 | .735 | 129 | 69 | 370 | 6.5 | 3.5 | 18.5 |
| 00-01—Texas-San Antonio ........ | 28 | 906 | 186 | 436 | .427 | 139 | 193 | .720 | 212 | 71 | 556 | 7.6 | 2.5 | 19.9 |
| 01-02—Texas-San Antonio ........ | 28 | 905 | 162 | 402 | .403 | 144 | 198 | .727 | 233 | 78 | 513 | 8.3 | 2.8 | 18.3 |
| Totals ..................................... | 105 | 3364 | 637 | 1548 | .411 | 478 | 652 | .733 | 751 | 283 | 1922 | 7.2 | 2.7 | 18.3 |

Three-point field goals: 1998-99, 51-for-156 (.327). 1999-00, 29-for-115 (.252). 2000-01, 45-for-157 (.287). 2001-02, 45-for-123 (.366). Totals, 170-for-551 (.309).

### NBA REGULAR-SEASON RECORD

| Season Team | G | Min. | FGM | FGA | Pct. | FTM | FTA | Pct. | REBOUNDS Off. | Def. | Tot. | Ast. | St. | Blk. | TO | Pts. | AVERAGES RPG | APG | PPG |
|---|---|---|---|---|---|---|---|---|---|---|---|---|---|---|---|---|---|---|---|
| 02-03—S.A.-Denver .... | 10 | 93 | 12 | 35 | .343 | 6 | 8 | .750 | 8 | 10 | 18 | 7 | 4 | 1 | 9 | 30 | 1.8 | 0.7 | 3.0 |
| 03-04—San Antonio.... | 58 | 627 | 85 | 196 | .434 | 60 | 74 | .811 | 38 | 92 | 130 | 33 | 15 | 4 | 38 | 234 | 2.2 | 0.6 | 4.0 |
| 04-05—San Antonio.... | 67 | 1238 | 173 | 409 | .423 | 103 | 130 | .792 | 37 | 139 | 176 | 92 | 39 | 12 | 53 | 494 | 2.6 | 1.4 | 7.4 |
| Totals ..................... | 135 | 1958 | 270 | 640 | .422 | 169 | 212 | .797 | 83 | 241 | 324 | 132 | 58 | 17 | 100 | 758 | 2.4 | 1.0 | 5.6 |

Three-point field goals: 2002-03, 0-for-1. 2003-04, 4-for-14 (.286). 2004-05, 45-for-121 (.372). Totals, 49-for-136 (.360).
Personal fouls/disqualifications: 2002-03, 14/0. 2003-04, 61/0. 2004-05, 83/0. Totals, 158/0.

| Season Team | G | Min. | FGM | FGA | Pct. | FTM | FTA | Pct. | REBOUNDS Off. | Def. | Tot. | Ast. | St. | Blk. | TO | Pts. | AVERAGES RPG | APG | PPG |
|---|---|---|---|---|---|---|---|---|---|---|---|---|---|---|---|---|---|---|---|
| 03-04—San Antonio.... | 9 | 130 | 18 | 37 | .486 | 10 | 17 | .588 | 4 | 14 | 18 | 9 | 3 | 1 | 7 | 52 | 2.0 | 1.0 | 5.8 |
| 04-05—San Antonio.... | 12 | 60 | 7 | 20 | .350 | 4 | 7 | .571 | 1 | 6 | 7 | 3 | 1 | 0 | 1 | 21 | 0.6 | 0.3 | 1.8 |
| Totals .................. | 21 | 190 | 25 | 57 | .439 | 14 | 24 | .583 | 5 | 20 | 25 | 12 | 4 | 1 | 8 | 73 | 1.2 | 0.6 | 3.5 |

Three-point field goals: 2003-04, 6-for-10 (.600). 2004-05, 3-for-7 (.429). Totals, 9-for-17 (.529).
Personal fouls/disqualifications: 2003-04, 18/1. 2004-05, 3/0. Totals, 21/1.

## NBDL RECORD

**HONORS:** All-NBDL first team (2002-03). ... Member of NBA championship team (2005).

| Season Team | G | Min. | FGM | FGA | Pct. | FTM | FTA | Pct. | Reb. | Ast. | Pts. | AVERAGES RPG | APG | PPG |
|---|---|---|---|---|---|---|---|---|---|---|---|---|---|---|
| 02-03—Fayetteville.................... | 44 | 1086 | 270 | 540 | .500 | 185 | 225 | .822 | 182 | 88 | 742 | 4.1 | 2.0 | 16.9 |

Three-point field goals: 2002-03, 17-for-46 (.370). Totals, 17-for-46 (.370).
Personal fouls/disqualifications: 2002-03, 108/0. Totals, 108/0.

# BROWN, KEDRICK                     F

**PERSONAL:** Born March 18, 1981, in Zachary, La. ... 6-7/222. (2.01/100.7). ... Full name: Albert Kedrick Brown
**HIGH SCHOOL:** Zachary (La.).
**JUNIOR COLLEGE:** Okaloosa-Walton Community College.
**TRANSACTIONS/CAREER NOTES:** Selected after sophomore season by Boston Celtics in first round (11th pick overall) of 2001 NBA Draft. ... Traded by Celtics with F/C Tony Battie and F Eric Williams to Cleveland Cavaliers for G Ricky Davis, F/C Chris Mihm, C Michael Stewart and a second-round draft choice (December 15, 2003). ... Traded by Cavaliers with G Kevin Ollie to Philadelphia 76ers for PG Eric Snow (July 20, 2004).

### COLLEGIATE RECORD

| Season Team | G | Min. | FGM | FGA | Pct. | FTM | FTA | Pct. | Reb. | Ast. | Pts. | AVERAGES RPG | APG | PPG |
|---|---|---|---|---|---|---|---|---|---|---|---|---|---|---|
| 99-00—Okaloosa-Walton J.C..... | 30 | ... | 187 | 332 | .563 | 87 | 110 | .791 | 317 | 111 | 499 | 10.6 | 3.7 | 16.6 |
| 00-01—Okaloosa-Walton J.C..... | 32 | ... | 266 | 504 | .528 | 124 | 169 | .734 | 280 | 97 | 732 | 8.8 | 3.0 | 22.9 |
| Totals .................. | 62 | ... | 453 | 836 | .542 | 211 | 279 | .756 | 597 | 208 | 1231 | 9.6 | 3.4 | 19.9 |

Three-point field goals: 1999-00, 38-for-106 (.358). 2000-01, 76-for-188 (.404). Totals, 114-for-294 (.388).

### NBA REGULAR-SEASON RECORD

| Season Team | G | Min. | FGM | FGA | Pct. | FTM | FTA | Pct. | REBOUNDS Off. | Def. | Tot. | Ast. | St. | Blk. | TO | Pts. | AVERAGES RPG | APG | PPG |
|---|---|---|---|---|---|---|---|---|---|---|---|---|---|---|---|---|---|---|---|
| 01-02—Boston ........... | 29 | 245 | 23 | 70 | .329 | 12 | 20 | .600 | 11 | 39 | 50 | 15 | 18 | 7 | 7 | 63 | 1.7 | 0.5 | 2.2 |
| 02-03—Boston ........... | 51 | 666 | 61 | 171 | .357 | 20 | 32 | .625 | 45 | 95 | 140 | 20 | 34 | 13 | 23 | 145 | 2.7 | 0.4 | 2.8 |
| 03-04—Boston-Cleve.... | 55 | 969 | 117 | 254 | .461 | 17 | 27 | .630 | 41 | 105 | 146 | 64 | 30 | 7 | 29 | 289 | 2.7 | 1.2 | 5.3 |
| 04-05—Philadelphia .... | 8 | 55 | 2 | 6 | .333 | 8 | 10 | .800 | 1 | 10 | 11 | 4 | 3 | 1 | 5 | 12 | 1.4 | 0.5 | 1.5 |
| Totals .................. | 143 | 1935 | 203 | 501 | .405 | 57 | 89 | .640 | 98 | 249 | 347 | 103 | 85 | 28 | 64 | 509 | 2.4 | 0.7 | 3.6 |

Three-point field goals: 2001-02, 5-for-27 (.185). 2002-03, 3-for-39 (.077). 2003-04, 38-for-99 (.384). 2004-05, 0-for-3. Totals, 46-for-168 (.274).
Personal fouls/disqualifications: 2001-02, 18/0. 2002-03, 68/0. 2003-04, 80/1. 2004-05, 4/0. Totals, 170/1.

### NBA PLAYOFF RECORD

| Season Team | G | Min. | FGM | FGA | Pct. | FTM | FTA | Pct. | REBOUNDS Off. | Def. | Tot. | Ast. | St. | Blk. | TO | Pts. | AVERAGES RPG | APG | PPG |
|---|---|---|---|---|---|---|---|---|---|---|---|---|---|---|---|---|---|---|---|
| 01-02—Boston ........... | 2 | 3 | 2 | 2 | 1.000 | 0 | 0 | ... | 0 | 0 | 0 | 0 | 0 | 1 | 0 | 5 | 0.0 | 0.0 | 2.5 |
| 02-03—Boston ........... | 3 | 11 | 1 | 4 | .250 | 1 | 2 | .500 | 2 | 0 | 2 | 0 | 1 | 0 | 0 | 3 | 0.7 | 0.0 | 1.0 |
| Totals .................. | 5 | 14 | 3 | 6 | .500 | 1 | 2 | .500 | 2 | 0 | 2 | 0 | 1 | 1 | 0 | 8 | 0.4 | 0.0 | 1.6 |

Three-point field goals: 2001-02, 1-for-1 (1.000). Totals, 1-for-1 (1.000).

# BROWN, KWAME                     C/F                     LAKERS

**PERSONAL:** Born March 10, 1982, in Charleston, S.C. ... 6-11/243. (2.11/110.2). ... Cousin of Jabari Smith, center, Sacramento Kings (2000-02) and Philadelphia 76ers (2001-02 and 2003-04).
**HIGH SCHOOL:** Glynn Academy (Brunswick, Ga.).
**COLLEGE:** Did not attend college.
**TRANSACTIONS/CAREER NOTES:** Selected out of high school by Washington Wizards in first round (first pick overall) of 2001 NBA Draft. ... Traded by Wizards with F Laron Profit to Los Angeles Lakers for F Caron Butler and G Chucky Atkins (August 2, 2005).

### NBA REGULAR-SEASON RECORD

| Season Team | G | Min. | FGM | FGA | Pct. | FTM | FTA | Pct. | REBOUNDS Off. | Def. | Tot. | Ast. | St. | Blk. | TO | Pts. | AVERAGES RPG | APG | PPG |
|---|---|---|---|---|---|---|---|---|---|---|---|---|---|---|---|---|---|---|---|
| 01-02—Washington .... | 57 | 817 | 94 | 243 | .387 | 70 | 99 | .707 | 63 | 135 | 198 | 43 | 16 | 26 | 43 | 258 | 3.5 | 0.8 | 4.5 |
| 02-03—Washington .... | 80 | 1773 | 224 | 502 | .446 | 145 | 217 | .668 | 128 | 298 | 426 | 58 | 50 | 80 | 110 | 593 | 5.3 | 0.7 | 7.4 |
| 03-04—Washington .... | 74 | 2239 | 288 | 589 | .489 | 228 | 334 | .683 | 178 | 372 | 550 | 112 | 66 | 52 | 140 | 805 | 7.4 | 1.5 | 10.9 |
| 04-05—Washington .... | 42 | 908 | 109 | 237 | .460 | 74 | 129 | .574 | 72 | 134 | 206 | 39 | 25 | 15 | 67 | 292 | 4.9 | 0.9 | 7.0 |
| Totals .................. | 253 | 5737 | 715 | 1571 | .455 | 517 | 779 | .664 | 441 | 939 | 1380 | 252 | 157 | 173 | 360 | 1948 | 5.5 | 1.0 | 7.7 |

Three-point field goals: 2001-02, 0-for-1. 2002-03, 0-for-3. 2003-04, 1-for-2 (.500). Totals, 1-for-6 (.167).
Personal fouls/disqualifications: 2001-02, 105/2. 2002-03, 159/1. 2003-04, 144/0. 2004-05, 112/0. Totals, 520/3.

### NBA PLAYOFF RECORD

| Season Team | G | Min. | FGM | FGA | Pct. | FTM | FTA | Pct. | REBOUNDS Off. | Def. | Tot. | Ast. | St. | Blk. | TO | Pts. | AVERAGES RPG | APG | PPG |
|---|---|---|---|---|---|---|---|---|---|---|---|---|---|---|---|---|---|---|---|
| 04-05—Washington .... | 3 | 60 | 5 | 13 | .385 | 5 | 9 | .556 | 4 | 11 | 15 | 3 | 0 | 2 | 2 | 15 | 5.0 | 1.0 | 5.0 |

Personal fouls/disqualifications: 2004-05, 5/0. Totals, 5/0.

## BROWN, P.J.  F  HORNETS

**PERSONAL:** Born October 14, 1969, in Detroit. ... 6-11/239. (2.11/108.4).
**HIGH SCHOOL:** Winnfield (La.) Senior.
**COLLEGE:** Louisiana Tech.
**TRANSACTIONS/CAREER NOTES:** Selected by New Jersey Nets in second round (29th pick overall) of 1992 NBA Draft. ... Played in Greece (1992-93). ... Signed as free agent by Miami Heat (July 18, 1996). ... Traded by Heat with F Jamal Mashburn, F/C Otis Thorpe, F Tim James and G/F Rodney Buford to Charlotte Hornets for G Eddie Jones, F Anthony Mason, G Ricky Davis and G/F Dale Ellis (August 1, 2000). ... Hornets franchise moved to New Orleans for 2002-03 season.

### COLLEGIATE RECORD

| Season Team | G | Min. | FGM | FGA | Pct. | FTM | FTA | Pct. | Reb. | Ast. | Pts. | AVERAGES RPG | APG | PPG |
|---|---|---|---|---|---|---|---|---|---|---|---|---|---|---|
| 88-89—Louisiana Tech | 32 | 569 | 61 | 147 | .415 | 25 | 44 | .568 | 178 | 36 | 149 | 5.6 | 1.1 | 4.7 |
| 89-90—Louisiana Tech | 27 | 672 | 94 | 204 | .461 | 48 | 81 | .593 | 230 | 29 | 239 | 8.5 | 1.1 | 8.9 |
| 90-91—Louisiana Tech | 31 | 936 | 170 | 315 | .540 | 98 | 150 | .653 | 301 | 58 | 445 | 9.7 | 1.9 | 14.4 |
| 91-92—Louisiana Tech | 31 | 931 | 151 | 309 | .489 | 84 | 115 | .730 | 308 | 53 | 395 | 9.9 | 1.7 | 12.7 |
| **Totals** | 121 | 3108 | 476 | 975 | .488 | 255 | 390 | .654 | 1017 | 176 | 1228 | 8.4 | 1.5 | 10.1 |

Three-point field goals: 1988-89, 2-for-3 (.667). 1989-90, 3-for-5 (.600). 1990-91, 7-for-20 (.350). 1991-92, 9-for-25 (.360). Totals, 21-for-53 (.396).
Personal fouls/disqualifications: 1988-89, 87/4. 1989-90, 80/3. 1990-91, 90/7. 1991-92, 97/4. Totals, 354/18.

### GREEK LEAGUE RECORD

| Season Team | G | Min. | FGM | FGA | Pct. | FTM | FTA | Pct. | Reb. | Ast. | Pts. | AVERAGES RPG | APG | PPG |
|---|---|---|---|---|---|---|---|---|---|---|---|---|---|---|
| 92-93—Panionios | 26 | ... | 164 | 299 | .548 | 107 | 151 | .709 | 357 | ... | 441 | 13.7 | ... | 17.0 |

### NBA REGULAR-SEASON RECORD

**HONORS:** NBA Sportsmanship Award (2004). ... J. Walter Kennedy Citizenship Award (1997). ... NBA All-Defensive second team (1997, 1999, 2001).

| Season Team | G | Min. | FGM | FGA | Pct. | FTM | FTA | Pct. | REBOUNDS Off. | Def. | Tot. | Ast. | St. | Blk. | TO | Pts. | AVERAGES RPG | APG | PPG |
|---|---|---|---|---|---|---|---|---|---|---|---|---|---|---|---|---|---|---|---|
| 93-94—New Jersey | 79 | 1950 | 167 | 402 | .415 | 115 | 152 | .757 | 188 | 305 | 493 | 93 | 71 | 93 | 72 | 450 | 6.2 | 1.2 | 5.7 |
| 94-95—New Jersey | 80 | 2466 | 254 | 570 | .446 | 139 | 207 | .671 | 178 | 309 | 487 | 135 | 69 | 135 | 80 | 651 | 6.1 | 1.7 | 8.1 |
| 95-96—New Jersey | 81 | 2942 | 354 | 798 | .444 | 204 | 265 | .770 | 215 | 345 | 560 | 165 | 79 | 100 | 133 | 915 | 6.9 | 2.0 | 11.3 |
| 96-97—Miami | 80 | 2592 | 300 | 656 | .457 | 161 | 220 | .732 | 239 | 431 | 670 | 92 | 85 | 98 | 113 | 761 | 8.4 | 1.2 | 9.5 |
| 97-98—Miami | 74 | 2362 | 278 | 590 | .471 | 151 | 197 | .766 | 235 | 400 | 635 | 103 | 66 | 98 | 97 | 707 | 8.6 | 1.4 | 9.6 |
| 98-99—Miami | 50 | 1611 | 229 | 477 | .480 | 113 | 146 | .774 | 115 | 231 | 346 | 66 | 46 | 48 | 69 | 571 | 6.9 | 1.3 | 11.4 |
| 99-00—Miami | 80 | 2302 | 322 | 671 | .480 | 120 | 159 | .755 | 216 | 384 | 600 | 145 | 65 | 61 | 100 | 764 | 7.5 | 1.8 | 9.6 |
| 00-01—Charlotte | 80 | 2811 | 249 | 561 | .444 | 178 | 209 | .852 | 257 | 485 | 742 | 127 | 78 | 92 | 108 | 676 | 9.3 | 1.6 | 8.5 |
| 01-02—Charlotte | 80 | 2563 | 250 | 527 | .474 | 169 | 197 | .858 | 273 | 513 | 786 | 107 | 59 | 78 | 85 | 669 | 9.8 | 1.3 | 8.4 |
| 02-03—New Orleans | 78 | 2609 | 319 | 601 | .531 | 194 | 232 | .836 | 243 | 458 | 701 | 147 | 67 | 80 | 98 | 832 | 9.0 | 1.9 | 10.7 |
| 03-04—New Orleans | 80 | 2753 | 339 | 712 | .476 | 158 | 185 | .854 | 237 | 453 | 690 | 155 | 78 | 73 | 101 | 836 | 8.6 | 1.9 | 10.5 |
| 04-05—New Orleans | 82 | 2817 | 338 | 758 | .446 | 210 | 243 | .864 | 266 | 471 | 737 | 178 | 74 | 50 | 101 | 886 | 9.0 | 2.2 | 10.8 |
| **Totals** | 924 | 29778 | 3399 | 7323 | .464 | 1912 | 2412 | .793 | 2662 | 4785 | 7447 | 1513 | 837 | 1006 | 1157 | 8718 | 8.1 | 1.6 | 9.4 |

Three-point field goals: 1993-94, 1-for-6 (.167). 1994-95, 4-for-24 (.167). 1995-96, 3-for-15 (.200). 1996-97, 0-for-2. 1999-00, 0-for-1. 2000-01, 0-for-4. 2002-03, 0-for-3. 2003-04, 0-for-1. Totals, 8-for-56 (.143).
Personal fouls/disqualifications: 1993-94, 177/1. 1994-95, 262/8. 1995-96, 249/5. 1996-97, 283/7. 1997-98, 264/9. 1998-99, 166/2. 1999-00, 264/4. 2000-01, 260/6. 2001-02, 222/1. 2002-03, 203/3. 2003-04, 203/2. 2004-05, 233/3. Totals, 2786/51.

### NBA PLAYOFF RECORD

| Season Team | G | Min. | FGM | FGA | Pct. | FTM | FTA | Pct. | REBOUNDS Off. | Def. | Tot. | Ast. | St. | Blk. | TO | Pts. | AVERAGES RPG | APG | PPG |
|---|---|---|---|---|---|---|---|---|---|---|---|---|---|---|---|---|---|---|---|
| 93-94—New Jersey | 4 | 56 | 2 | 9 | .222 | 8 | 8 | 1.000 | 4 | 4 | 8 | 3 | 0 | 2 | 3 | 12 | 2.0 | 0.8 | 3.0 |
| 96-97—Miami | 15 | 451 | 42 | 103 | .408 | 38 | 53 | .717 | 48 | 81 | 129 | 10 | 9 | 20 | 16 | 122 | 8.6 | 0.7 | 8.1 |
| 97-98—Miami | 5 | 190 | 19 | 37 | .514 | 8 | 22 | .364 | 15 | 29 | 44 | 4 | 7 | 3 | 6 | 46 | 8.8 | 0.8 | 9.2 |
| 98-99—Miami | 5 | 144 | 21 | 45 | .467 | 9 | 10 | .900 | 14 | 17 | 31 | 5 | 2 | 2 | 3 | 51 | 6.2 | 1.0 | 10.2 |
| 99-00—Miami | 10 | 308 | 35 | 82 | .427 | 5 | 6 | .833 | 26 | 56 | 82 | 11 | 8 | 4 | 11 | 75 | 8.2 | 1.1 | 7.5 |
| 00-01—Charlotte | 10 | 385 | 28 | 67 | .418 | 24 | 29 | .828 | 41 | 59 | 100 | 11 | 12 | 14 | 12 | 80 | 10.0 | 1.1 | 8.0 |
| 01-02—Charlotte | 9 | 331 | 32 | 75 | .427 | 28 | 37 | .757 | 29 | 57 | 86 | 14 | 6 | 12 | 8 | 92 | 9.6 | 1.6 | 10.2 |
| 02-03—New Orleans | 6 | 193 | 21 | 44 | .477 | 19 | 25 | .760 | 20 | 26 | 46 | 6 | 7 | 3 | 5 | 61 | 7.7 | 1.0 | 10.2 |
| 03-04—New Orleans | 7 | 256 | 26 | 71 | .366 | 10 | 11 | .909 | 29 | 39 | 68 | 15 | 3 | 11 | 13 | 62 | 9.7 | 2.1 | 8.9 |
| **Totals** | 71 | 2314 | 226 | 533 | .424 | 149 | 201 | .741 | 226 | 368 | 594 | 79 | 54 | 71 | 77 | 601 | 8.4 | 1.1 | 8.5 |

Three-point field goals: 1998-99, 0-for-1. Totals, 0-for-1 (.000).
Personal fouls/disqualifications: 1993-94, 13/0. 1996-97, 40/0. 1997-98, 22/1. 1998-99, 17/0. 1999-00, 42/3. 2000-01, 31/1. 2001-02, 37/3. 2002-03, 22/0. 2003-04, 16/0. Totals, 240/8.

---

## BROWN, TIERRE  G  LAKERS

**PERSONAL:** Born June 3, 1979, in Iowa, La. ... 6-2/189. (1.88/85.7).
**HIGH SCHOOL:** Iowa (La.).
**COLLEGE:** McNeese State.
**TRANSACTIONS/CAREER NOTES:** Not drafted by an NBA franchise. ... Signed as free agent by Houston Rockets (September 26, 2001). ... Played in the National Basketball Developmental League with the North Charleston Lowgators (2002-03). ... Signed to 10-day contract by Cleveland Cavaliers (March 3, 2003). ... Signed by Cavaliers for remainder of season (March 24, 2003). ... Signed as free agent by Golden State Warriors (October 20, 2003). ... Waived by Warriors (October 23, 2003). ... Played in NBDL with Charleston Lowgators (2003-04). ... Signed by New Orleans Hornets to 10-day contract (January 26, 2004).

### COLLEGIATE RECORD

| Season Team | G | Min. | FGM | FGA | Pct. | FTM | FTA | Pct. | Reb. | Ast. | Pts. | AVERAGES RPG | APG | PPG |
|---|---|---|---|---|---|---|---|---|---|---|---|---|---|---|
| 97-98—McNeese State | 26 | 738 | 135 | 261 | .517 | 54 | 80 | .675 | 92 | 75 | 22 | 3.5 | 2.9 | 0.8 |
| 98-99—McNeese State | 26 | 382 | 48 | 133 | .361 | 32 | 51 | .627 | 55 | 53 | 130 | 2.1 | 2.0 | 5.0 |
| 99-00—McNeese State | 27 | 962 | 217 | 469 | .463 | 129 | 177 | .729 | 135 | 121 | 593 | 5.0 | 4.5 | 22.0 |

| Season Team | G | Min. | FGM | FGA | Pct. | FTM | FTA | Pct. | Reb. | Ast. | Pts. | RPG | APG | PPG |
|---|---|---|---|---|---|---|---|---|---|---|---|---|---|---|
| 00-01—McNeese State ............... | 31 | 1064 | 213 | 518 | .411 | 146 | 184 | .793 | 177 | 111 | 623 | 5.7 | 3.6 | 20.1 |
| Totals ...................................... | 110 | 3146 | 613 | 1381 | .444 | 361 | 492 | .734 | 459 | 360 | 1368 | 4.2 | 3.3 | 12.4 |

Three-point field goals: 1998-99, 2-for-13 (.154). 1999-00, 30-for-94 (.319). 2000-01, 51-for-152 (.336). Totals, 136-for-259 (.525).

## NBA REGULAR-SEASON RECORD

| Season Team | G | Min. | FGM | FGA | Pct. | FTM | FTA | Pct. | Off. | Def. | Tot. | Ast. | St. | Blk. | TO | Pts. | RPG | APG | PPG |
|---|---|---|---|---|---|---|---|---|---|---|---|---|---|---|---|---|---|---|---|
| 01-02—Houston.......... | 40 | 403 | 49 | 115 | .426 | 21 | 28 | .750 | 12 | 30 | 42 | 70 | 19 | 3 | 40 | 123 | 1.1 | 1.8 | 3.1 |
| 02-03—Cleveland........ | 15 | 168 | 27 | 59 | .458 | 11 | 14 | .786 | 8 | 22 | 30 | 39 | 13 | 0 | 22 | 65 | 2.0 | 2.6 | 4.3 |
| 03-04—New Orleans ... | 3 | 17 | 2 | 4 | .500 | 2 | 4 | .500 | 0 | 1 | 1 | 2 | 0 | 0 | 7 | 6 | 0.3 | 0.7 | 2.0 |
| 04-05—L.A. Lakers ..... | 76 | 1066 | 124 | 348 | .356 | 59 | 75 | .787 | 21 | 72 | 93 | 155 | 32 | 1 | 74 | 333 | 1.2 | 2.0 | 4.4 |
| Totals ................... | 134 | 1654 | 202 | 526 | .384 | 93 | 121 | .769 | 41 | 125 | 166 | 266 | 64 | 4 | 143 | 527 | 1.2 | 2.0 | 3.9 |

Three-point field goals: 2001-02, 4-for-12 (.333). 2002-03, 0-for-1. 2004-05, 26-for-72 (.361). Totals, 30-for-85 (.353).

Personal fouls/disqualifications: 2001-02, 26/0. 2002-03, 9/0. 2003-04, 1/0. 2004-05, 59/0. Totals, 95/0.

## NBDL RECORD

**MISCELLANEOUS:** All-NBDL first team (2002-03).

| Season Team | G | Min. | FGM | FGA | Pct. | FTM | FTA | Pct. | Reb. | Ast. | Pts. | RPG | APG | PPG |
|---|---|---|---|---|---|---|---|---|---|---|---|---|---|---|
| 02-03—Charleston .................... | 44 | 1240 | 250 | 510 | .490 | 177 | 200 | .885 | 167 | 216 | 692 | 3.8 | 4.9 | 15.7 |
| 03-04—Charleston .................... | 41 | 1387 | 286 | 652 | .439 | 177 | 222 | .797 | 135 | 265 | 763 | 3.3 | 6.5 | 18.6 |
| Totals ...................................... | 85 | 2627 | 536 | 1162 | .461 | 354 | 422 | .839 | 302 | 481 | 1455 | 3.6 | 5.7 | 17.1 |

## BRUNSON, RICK     G     SUPERSONICS

**PERSONAL:** Born June 14, 1972, in Syracuse, N.Y. ... 6-4/190. (1.93/86.2). ... Full name: Rick Daniel Brunson
**HIGH SCHOOL:** Salem (Mass.).
**COLLEGE:** Temple.
**TRANSACTIONS/CAREER NOTES:** Not drafted by an NBA franchise. ... Played in Australia (1995-96). ... Played in Continental Basketball Association with Quad City Thunder (1996-97) and Connecticut Pride (1997-99). ... Signed as free agent by Orlando Magic (September 30, 1997). ... Waived by Magic (October 20, 1997). ... Signed as free agent by New York Knicks (October 23, 1997). ... Waived by Knicks (October 30, 1997). ... Signed as free agent by Portland Trail Blazers (December 2, 1997). ... Signed as free agent by Knicks (January 21, 1999). ... Signed as free agent by Miami Heat (September 28, 2000). ... Waived by Heat (October 20, 2000). ... Signed as free agent by Boston Celtics (November 6, 2000). ... Claimed on waivers by Knicks (November 27, 2000). ... Signed as free agent by Trail Blazers (September 21, 2002). ... Signed as free agent by Chicago Bulls (September 18, 2002). ... Signed as free agent by Toronto Raptors (August 13, 2003). ... Traded by Raptors to Chicago Bulls for G Roger Mason Jr. (December 16, 2003). ... Waived by Bulls (March 15, 2004). ... Signed as free agent by Los Angeles Clippers (September 30, 2004). ... Waived by Clippers (August 3, 2005). ... Signed as free agent by Seattle SuperSonics (August 5, 2005).

## COLLEGIATE RECORD

| Season Team | G | Min. | FGM | FGA | Pct. | FTM | FTA | Pct. | Reb. | Ast. | Pts. | RPG | APG | PPG |
|---|---|---|---|---|---|---|---|---|---|---|---|---|---|---|
| 91-92—Temple.......................... | 30 | 537 | 41 | 128 | .320 | 53 | 87 | .609 | 79 | 56 | 147 | 2.6 | 1.9 | 4.9 |
| 92-93—Temple.......................... | 33 | 1205 | 147 | 371 | .396 | 112 | 171 | .655 | 98 | 149 | 463 | 3.0 | 4.5 | 14.0 |
| 93-94—Temple.......................... | 31 | 1221 | 128 | 346 | .370 | 77 | 119 | .647 | 127 | 142 | 383 | 4.1 | 4.6 | 12.4 |
| 94-95—Temple.......................... | 30 | 1149 | 164 | 448 | .366 | 100 | 143 | .699 | 177 | 123 | 500 | 5.9 | 4.1 | 16.7 |
| Totals ...................................... | 124 | 4112 | 480 | 1293 | .371 | 342 | 520 | .658 | 481 | 470 | 1493 | 3.9 | 3.8 | 12.0 |

Three-point field goals: 1991-92, 12-for-53 (.226). 1992-93, 57-for-177 (.322). 1993-94, 50-for-167 (.299). 1994-95, 72-for-252 (.286). Totals, 191-for-649 (.294).

## CBA RECORD

| Season Team | G | Min. | FGM | FGA | Pct. | FTM | FTA | Pct. | Reb. | Ast. | Pts. | RPG | APG | PPG |
|---|---|---|---|---|---|---|---|---|---|---|---|---|---|---|
| 96-97—Quad City...................... | 56 | 1953 | 231 | 567 | .407 | 148 | 198 | .747 | 218 | 380 | 652 | 3.9 | 6.8 | 11.6 |
| 97-98—Connecticut ................... | 8 | 333 | 66 | 133 | .496 | 45 | 54 | .833 | 29 | 53 | 191 | 3.6 | 6.6 | 23.9 |
| 98-99—Connecticut ................... | 21 | 817 | 134 | 332 | .404 | 73 | 101 | .723 | 48 | 154 | 367 | 2.3 | 7.3 | 17.5 |
| Totals ...................................... | 85 | 3103 | 431 | 1032 | .418 | 266 | 353 | .754 | 295 | 587 | 1210 | 3.5 | 6.9 | 14.2 |

Three-point field goals: 1996-97, 42-for-154 (.273). 1997-98, 14-for-40 (.350). 1998-99, 26-for-82 (.317). Totals, 82-for-276 (.297).
Personal fouls/disqualifications: 1996-97, 134/0. 1997-98, 27/0. 1998-99, 50/0. Totals, 211/0.

## NBA REGULAR-SEASON RECORD

| Season Team | G | Min. | FGM | FGA | Pct. | FTM | FTA | Pct. | Off. | Def. | Tot. | Ast. | St. | Blk. | TO | Pts. | RPG | APG | PPG |
|---|---|---|---|---|---|---|---|---|---|---|---|---|---|---|---|---|---|---|---|
| 97-98—Portland.......... | 38 | 622 | 49 | 141 | .348 | 42 | 62 | .677 | 14 | 42 | 56 | 100 | 25 | 3 | 52 | 162 | 1.5 | 2.6 | 4.3 |
| 98-99—New York....... | 17 | 95 | 6 | 21 | .286 | 5 | 18 | .278 | 3 | 7 | 10 | 19 | 9 | 0 | 12 | 17 | 0.6 | 1.1 | 1.0 |
| 99-00—New York....... | 37 | 289 | 29 | 70 | .414 | 11 | 18 | .611 | 3 | 24 | 27 | 49 | 9 | 1 | 31 | 71 | 0.7 | 1.3 | 1.9 |
| 00-01—Boston-N.Y. .... | 22 | 208 | 18 | 54 | .333 | 8 | 15 | .533 | 5 | 16 | 21 | 31 | 8 | 1 | 17 | 46 | 1.0 | 1.4 | 2.1 |
| 01-02—Portland.......... | 59 | 520 | 45 | 113 | .398 | 29 | 41 | .707 | 23 | 45 | 68 | 114 | 25 | 2 | 47 | 125 | 1.2 | 1.9 | 2.1 |
| 02-03—Chicago.......... | 17 | 196 | 23 | 50 | .460 | 10 | 12 | .833 | 4 | 15 | 19 | 36 | 10 | 3 | 17 | 60 | 1.1 | 2.1 | 3.5 |
| 03-04—Tor.-Chi.......... | 40 | 412 | 40 | 105 | .381 | 27 | 31 | .871 | 9 | 28 | 37 | 82 | 25 | 3 | 33 | 118 | 0.9 | 2.1 | 3.0 |
| 04-05—L.A. Clippers ... | 80 | 1945 | 166 | 442 | .376 | 57 | 74 | .770 | 23 | 164 | 187 | 410 | 82 | 7 | 125 | 437 | 2.3 | 5.1 | 5.5 |
| Totals ................... | 310 | 4287 | 376 | 996 | .378 | 189 | 271 | .697 | 84 | 341 | 425 | 841 | 193 | 20 | 334 | 1036 | 1.4 | 2.7 | 3.3 |

Three-point field goals: 1997-98, 22-for-61 (.361). 1998-99, 0-for-5. 1999-00, 2-for-13 (.154). 2000-01, 2-for-14 (.143). 2001-02, 6-for-11 (.545). 2002-03, 4-for-6 (.667). 2003-04, 11-for-23 (.478). 2004-05, 48-for-130 (.369). Totals, 95-for-263 (.361).
Personal fouls/disqualifications: 1997-98, 55/0. 1998-99, 8/0. 1999-00, 35/0. 2000-01, 21/0. 2001-02, 51/0. 2002-03, 20/0. 2003-04, 44/0. 2004-05, 106/0. Totals, 340/0.

## NBA PLAYOFF RECORD

| Season Team | G | Min. | FGM | FGA | Pct. | FTM | FTA | Pct. | Off. | Def. | Tot. | Ast. | St. | Blk. | TO | Pts. | RPG | APG | PPG |
|---|---|---|---|---|---|---|---|---|---|---|---|---|---|---|---|---|---|---|---|
| 98-99—New York........ | 9 | 18 | 2 | 5 | .400 | 2 | 2 | 1.000 | 1 | 0 | 1 | 2 | 0 | 0 | 4 | 6 | 0.1 | 0.2 | 0.7 |

| Season Team | G | Min. | FGM | FGA | Pct. | FTM | FTA | Pct. | Off. | Def. | Tot. | Ast. | St. | Blk. | TO | Pts. | RPG | APG | PPG |
|---|---|---|---|---|---|---|---|---|---|---|---|---|---|---|---|---|---|---|---|
| 99-00—New York | 3 | 4 | 0 | 1 | .000 | 0 | 0 | ... | 0 | 0 | 0 | 1 | 1 | 0 | 0 | 0 | 0.0 | 0.3 | 0.0 |
| 00-01—New York | 2 | 4 | 0 | 1 | .000 | 3 | 4 | .750 | 0 | 0 | 0 | 0 | 0 | 0 | 1 | 3 | 0.0 | 0.0 | 1.5 |
| 01-02—Portland | 2 | 2 | 0 | 0 | ... | 0 | 0 | ... | 0 | 0 | 0 | 0 | 0 | 0 | 0 | 0 | 0.0 | 0.0 | 0.0 |
| **Totals** | 16 | 28 | 2 | 7 | .286 | 5 | 6 | .833 | 1 | 0 | 1 | 3 | 1 | 0 | 5 | 9 | 0.1 | 0.2 | 0.6 |

Personal fouls/disqualifications: 1998-99, 3/0. 1999-00, 2/0. Totals, 5/0.

# BRYANT, KOBE  G  LAKERS

**PERSONAL:** Born August 23, 1978, in Philadelphia. ... 6-7/210. (2.01/95.3). ... Full name: Kobe B. Bryant ... Son of Joe "Jelly Bean" Bryant, forward with Philadelphia 76ers (1975-76 through 1978-79), San Diego Clippers (1980-81 through 1981-82) and Houston Rockets (1982-83). ... Name pronounced Co-bee.
**HIGH SCHOOL:** Lower Merion (Pa.).
**COLLEGE:** Did not attend college.
**TRANSACTIONS/CAREER NOTES:** Selected out of high school by Charlotte Hornets in first round (13th pick overall) of 1996 NBA Draft. ... Draft rights traded by Hornets to Los Angeles Lakers for C Vlade Divac (July 11, 1996).
**MISCELLANEOUS:** Member of NBA championship team (2000, 2001, 2002).

## NBA REGULAR-SEASON RECORD

**RECORDS:** Holds NBA record for most three-point field goals made in one game—12 (January 7, 2003). ... Shares NBA record for most three-point field goals made in one half—8 (March 28, 2003).
**HONORS:** Slam Dunk championship winner (1997). ... All-NBA first team (2002, 2003). ... All-NBA second team (2000, 2001). ... All-NBA third team (1999, 2005). ... NBA All-Defensive first team (2000, 2003, 2004). ... NBA All-Defensive second team (2001, 2002). ... NBA All-Rookie second team (1997).
**NOTES:** Led NBA with 2,461 points scored (2003).

| Season Team | G | Min. | FGM | FGA | Pct. | FTM | FTA | Pct. | Off. | Def. | Tot. | Ast. | St. | Blk. | TO | Pts. | RPG | APG | PPG |
|---|---|---|---|---|---|---|---|---|---|---|---|---|---|---|---|---|---|---|---|
| 96-97—L.A. Lakers | 71 | 1103 | 176 | 422 | .417 | 136 | 166 | .819 | 47 | 85 | 132 | 91 | 49 | 23 | 112 | 539 | 1.9 | 1.3 | 7.6 |
| 97-98—L.A. Lakers | 79 | 2056 | 391 | 913 | .428 | 363 | 457 | .794 | 79 | 163 | 242 | 199 | 74 | 40 | 157 | 1220 | 3.1 | 2.5 | 15.4 |
| 98-99—L.A. Lakers | 50 | 1896 | 362 | 779 | .465 | 245 | 292 | .839 | 53 | 211 | 264 | 190 | 72 | 50 | 157 | 996 | 5.3 | 3.8 | 19.9 |
| 99-00—L.A. Lakers | 66 | 2524 | 554 | 1183 | .468 | 331 | 403 | .821 | 108 | 308 | 416 | 323 | 106 | 62 | 182 | 1485 | 6.3 | 4.9 | 22.5 |
| 00-01—L.A. Lakers | 68 | 2783 | 701 | 1510 | .464 | 475 | 557 | .853 | 104 | 295 | 399 | 338 | 114 | 43 | 220 | 1938 | 5.9 | 5.0 | 28.5 |
| 01-02—L.A. Lakers | 80 | 3063 | 749 | 1597 | .469 | 488 | 589 | .829 | 112 | 329 | 441 | 438 | 118 | 35 | 223 | 2019 | 5.5 | 5.5 | 25.2 |
| 02-03—L.A. Lakers | 82 | 3401 | 868 | 1924 | .451 | 601 | 713 | .843 | 106 | 458 | 564 | 481 | 181 | 67 | 288 | 2461 | 6.9 | 5.9 | 30.0 |
| 03-04—L.A. Lakers | 65 | 2447 | 516 | 1178 | .438 | 454 | 533 | .852 | 103 | 256 | 359 | 330 | 112 | 28 | 171 | 1557 | 5.5 | 5.1 | 24.0 |
| 04-05—L.A. Lakers | 66 | 2689 | 573 | 1324 | .433 | 542 | 664 | .816 | 95 | 297 | 392 | 398 | 86 | 53 | 270 | 1819 | 5.9 | 6.0 | 27.6 |
| **Totals** | 627 | 21962 | 4890 | 10830 | .452 | 3635 | 4374 | .831 | 807 | 2402 | 3209 | 2788 | 912 | 401 | 1780 | 14034 | 5.1 | 4.4 | 22.4 |

Three-point field goals: 1996-97, 51-for-136 (.375). 1997-98, 75-for-220 (.341). 1998-99, 27-for-101 (.267). 1999-00, 46-for-144 (.319). 2000-01, 61-for-200 (.305). 2001-02, 33-for-132 (.250). 2002-03, 124-for-324 (.383). 2003-04, 71-for-217 (.327). 2004-05, 131-for-387 (.339). Totals, 619-for-1861 (.333).
Personal fouls/disqualifications: 1996-97, 102/0. 1997-98, 180/1. 1998-99, 153/3. 1999-00, 220/4. 2000-01, 222/3. 2001-02, 228/1. 2002-03, 218/0. 2003-04, 176/0. 2004-05, 174/1. Totals, 1673/13.

## NBA PLAYOFF RECORD

**NOTES:** Shares single-game playoff record for most three-point field goal attempts in one half—11 (May 13, 2003).

| Season Team | G | Min. | FGM | FGA | Pct. | FTM | FTA | Pct. | Off. | Def. | Tot. | Ast. | St. | Blk. | TO | Pts. | RPG | APG | PPG |
|---|---|---|---|---|---|---|---|---|---|---|---|---|---|---|---|---|---|---|---|
| 96-97—L.A. Lakers | 9 | 133 | 21 | 55 | .382 | 26 | 30 | .867 | 1 | 10 | 11 | 11 | 3 | 2 | 14 | 74 | 1.2 | 1.2 | 8.2 |
| 97-98—L.A. Lakers | 11 | 220 | 31 | 76 | .408 | 31 | 45 | .689 | 7 | 14 | 21 | 16 | 3 | 8 | 11 | 96 | 1.9 | 1.5 | 8.7 |
| 98-99—L.A. Lakers | 8 | 315 | 61 | 142 | .430 | 28 | 35 | .800 | 13 | 42 | 55 | 37 | 15 | 10 | 31 | 158 | 6.9 | 4.6 | 19.8 |
| 99-00—L.A. Lakers | 22 | 857 | 174 | 394 | .442 | 95 | 126 | .754 | 26 | 72 | 98 | 97 | 32 | 32 | 55 | 465 | 4.5 | 4.4 | 21.1 |
| 00-01—L.A. Lakers | 16 | 694 | 168 | 358 | .469 | 124 | 151 | .821 | 29 | 87 | 116 | 97 | 25 | 12 | 51 | 471 | 7.3 | 6.1 | 29.4 |
| 01-02—L.A. Lakers | 19 | 833 | 187 | 431 | .434 | 110 | 145 | .759 | 28 | 83 | 111 | 87 | 27 | 17 | 54 | 506 | 5.8 | 4.6 | 26.6 |
| 02-03—L.A. Lakers | 12 | 531 | 137 | 317 | .432 | 86 | 104 | .827 | 16 | 45 | 61 | 62 | 14 | 1 | 42 | 385 | 5.1 | 5.2 | 32.1 |
| 03-04—L.A. Lakers | 22 | 973 | 190 | 460 | .413 | 135 | 166 | .813 | 18 | 86 | 104 | 121 | 42 | 7 | 61 | 539 | 4.7 | 5.5 | 24.5 |
| **Totals** | 119 | 4556 | 969 | 2233 | .434 | 635 | 802 | .792 | 138 | 439 | 577 | 528 | 161 | 89 | 319 | 2694 | 4.8 | 4.4 | 22.6 |

Three-point field goals: 1996-97, 6-for-23 (.261). 1997-98, 3-for-14 (.214). 1998-99, 8-for-23 (.348). 1999-00, 22-for-64 (.344). 2000-01, 11-for-34 (.324). 2001-02, 22-for-58 (.379). 2002-03, 25-for-62 (.403). 2003-04, 24-for-97 (.247). Totals, 121-for-375 (.323).
Personal fouls/disqualifications: 1996-97, 23/0. 1997-98, 28/0. 1998-99, 24/1. 1999-00, 89/1. 2000-01, 53/0. 2001-02, 65/1. 2002-03, 35/0. 2003-04, 59/0. Totals, 376/3.

## NBA ALL-STAR GAME RECORD

**NOTES:** NBA All-Star Game Most Valuable Player (2002).

| Season Team | Min. | FGM | FGA | Pct. | FTM | FTA | Pct. | Off. | Def. | Tot. | Ast. | PF | Dq. | St. | Blk. | TO | Pts. |
|---|---|---|---|---|---|---|---|---|---|---|---|---|---|---|---|---|---|
| 1998—L.A. Lakers | 22 | 7 | 16 | .438 | 2 | 2 | 1.000 | 2 | 4 | 6 | 1 | 1 | ... | 2 | 0 | 1 | 18 |
| 2000—L.A. Lakers | 28 | 7 | 16 | .438 | 0 | 0 | ... | 1 | 0 | 1 | 3 | 3 | 0 | 2 | 0 | 1 | 15 |
| 2001—L.A. Lakers | 30 | 9 | 17 | .529 | 0 | 0 | ... | 2 | 2 | 4 | 7 | 3 | 0 | 1 | 0 | 3 | 19 |
| 2002—L.A. Lakers | 30 | 12 | 25 | .480 | 7 | 7 | 1.000 | 2 | 3 | 5 | 5 | 2 | 0 | 1 | 0 | 0 | 31 |
| 2003—L.A. Lakers | 36 | 8 | 17 | .471 | 3 | 6 | .500 | 2 | 5 | 7 | 6 | 5 | 0 | 3 | 2 | 5 | 22 |
| 2004—L.A. Lakers | 36 | 9 | 12 | .750 | 0 | 1 | .000 | 1 | 3 | 4 | 4 | 3 | 0 | 5 | 1 | 6 | 20 |
| 2005—L.A. Lakers | 29 | 7 | 14 | .500 | 0 | 0 | ... | 3 | 3 | 6 | 7 | 5 | 0 | 3 | 1 | 4 | 16 |
| **Totals** | 211 | 59 | 117 | .504 | 12 | 16 | .750 | 13 | 20 | 33 | 33 | 22 | 0 | 17 | 4 | 20 | 141 |

Three-point field goals: 1998, 2-for-3 (.667). 2000, 1-for-4 (.250). 2001, 1-for-2 (.500). 2002, 0-for-4. 2003, 3-for-5 (.600). 2004, 2-for-3 (.667). 2005, 2-for-5 (.400). Totals, 11-for-26 (.423).

# BUCKNER, GREG　　　　　　　G　　　　　　　NUGGETS

**PERSONAL:** Born September 16, 1976, in Hopkinsville, Ky. ... 6-4/210. (1.93/95.3). ... Full name: Gregory Derayle Buckner
**HIGH SCHOOL:** University Heights Academy (Hopkinsville, Ky.).
**COLLEGE:** Clemson.
**TRANSACTIONS/CAREER NOTES:** Selected by Dallas Mavericks in second round (53rd pick overall) of 1998 NBA Draft. ... Played in Continental Basketball Association with Grand Rapids Hoops (1998-99). ... Waived by Mavericks (February 2, 1999). ... Re-signed as free agent by Mavericks (August 3, 1999). ... Waived by Mavericks (November 1, 1999). ... Signed by Mavericks to the first of two consecutive 10-day contracts (January 6, 2000). ... Re-signed by Mavericks for remainder of season (January 26, 2000). ... Signed as free agent by Philadelphia 76ers (July 25, 2002). ... Waived by 76ers (September 8, 2004). ... Signed as free agent by Denver Nuggets (October 4, 2004).

## COLLEGIATE RECORD

| | | | | | | | | | | | AVERAGES | | |
|---|---|---|---|---|---|---|---|---|---|---|---|---|---|
| Season Team | G | Min. | FGM | FGA | Pct. | FTM | FTA | Pct. | Reb. | Ast. | Pts. | RPG | APG | PPG |
| 94-95—Clemson | 28 | 911 | 141 | 268 | .526 | 41 | 80 | .513 | 165 | 58 | 336 | 5.9 | 2.1 | 12.0 |
| 95-96—Clemson | 29 | 950 | 144 | 305 | .472 | 92 | 137 | .672 | 147 | 48 | 381 | 5.1 | 1.7 | 13.1 |
| 96-97—Clemson | 33 | 1071 | 190 | 393 | .483 | 119 | 168 | .708 | 150 | 63 | 516 | 4.5 | 1.9 | 15.6 |
| 97-98—Clemson | 32 | 1022 | 204 | 380 | .537 | 94 | 135 | .696 | 130 | 83 | 521 | 4.1 | 2.6 | 16.3 |
| Totals | 122 | 3954 | 679 | 1346 | .504 | 346 | 520 | .665 | 592 | 252 | 1754 | 4.9 | 2.1 | 14.4 |

Three-point field goals: 1994-95, 13-for-44 (.295). 1995-96, 1-for-25 (.040). 1996-97, 17-for-54 (.315). 1997-98, 19-for-58 (.328). Totals, 50-for-181 (.276).

## CBA RECORD

| | | | | | | | | | | | AVERAGES | | |
|---|---|---|---|---|---|---|---|---|---|---|---|---|---|---|
| Season Team | G | Min. | FGM | FGA | Pct. | FTM | FTA | Pct. | Reb. | Ast. | Pts. | RPG | APG | PPG |
| 98-99—Grand Rapids | 47 | 1064 | 161 | 365 | .441 | 64 | 81 | .790 | 182 | 96 | 406 | 3.9 | 2.0 | 8.6 |

Three-point field goals: 1998-99, 20-for-87 (.230). Totals, 20-for-87 (.230).
Personal fouls/disqualifications: 1998-99, 144/0. Totals, 144/0.

## NBA REGULAR-SEASON RECORD

| | | | | | | | | REBOUNDS | | | | | | | | AVERAGES | | |
|---|---|---|---|---|---|---|---|---|---|---|---|---|---|---|---|---|---|---|
| Season Team | G | Min. | FGM | FGA | Pct. | FTM | FTA | Pct. | Off. | Def. | Tot. | Ast. | St. | Blk. | TO | Pts. | RPG | APG | PPG |
| 99-00—Dallas | 48 | 923 | 111 | 233 | .476 | 43 | 63 | .683 | 56 | 118 | 174 | 55 | 38 | 20 | 36 | 275 | 3.6 | 1.1 | 5.7 |
| 00-01—Dallas | 37 | 820 | 84 | 192 | .438 | 59 | 81 | .728 | 60 | 97 | 157 | 49 | 33 | 9 | 27 | 229 | 4.2 | 1.3 | 6.2 |
| 01-02—Dallas | 44 | 885 | 104 | 198 | .525 | 40 | 58 | .690 | 67 | 106 | 173 | 48 | 31 | 19 | 27 | 253 | 3.9 | 1.1 | 5.8 |
| 02-03—Philadelphia | 75 | 1514 | 185 | 398 | .465 | 65 | 81 | .802 | 72 | 144 | 216 | 96 | 72 | 16 | 62 | 450 | 2.9 | 1.3 | 6.0 |
| 03-04—Philadelphia | 53 | 703 | 66 | 175 | .377 | 20 | 27 | .741 | 28 | 75 | 103 | 45 | 21 | 4 | 34 | 164 | 1.9 | 0.8 | 3.1 |
| 04-05—Denver | 70 | 1522 | 160 | 303 | .528 | 63 | 81 | .778 | 66 | 142 | 208 | 133 | 75 | 6 | 49 | 432 | 3.0 | 1.9 | 6.2 |
| Totals | 327 | 6367 | 710 | 1499 | .474 | 290 | 391 | .742 | 349 | 682 | 1031 | 426 | 270 | 74 | 235 | 1803 | 3.2 | 1.3 | 5.5 |

Three-point field goals: 1999-00, 10-for-26 (.385). 2000-01, 2-for-7 (.286). 2001-02, 5-for-16 (.313). 2002-03, 15-for-55 (.273). 2003-04, 12-for-44 (.273). 2004-05, 49-for-121 (.405). Totals, 93-for-269 (.346).
Personal fouls/disqualifications: 1999-00, 148/1. 2000-01, 118/2. 2001-02, 124/1. 2002-03, 203/0. 2003-04, 77/0. 2004-05, 169/0. Totals, 839/4.

## NBA PLAYOFF RECORD

| | | | | | | | | REBOUNDS | | | | | | | | AVERAGES | | |
|---|---|---|---|---|---|---|---|---|---|---|---|---|---|---|---|---|---|---|
| Season Team | G | Min. | FGM | FGA | Pct. | FTM | FTA | Pct. | Off. | Def. | Tot. | Ast. | St. | Blk. | TO | Pts. | RPG | APG | PPG |
| 00-01—Dallas | 5 | 75 | 11 | 23 | .478 | 7 | 10 | .700 | 8 | 13 | 21 | 3 | 5 | 0 | 2 | 30 | 4.2 | 0.6 | 6.0 |
| 01-02—Dallas | 7 | 105 | 12 | 25 | .480 | 3 | 4 | .750 | 13 | 13 | 26 | 4 | 3 | 1 | 3 | 27 | 3.7 | 0.6 | 3.9 |
| 02-03—Philadelphia | 10 | 112 | 10 | 31 | .323 | 4 | 4 | 1.000 | 3 | 14 | 17 | 3 | 1 | 2 | 3 | 26 | 1.7 | 0.3 | 2.6 |
| 04-05—Denver | 5 | 100 | 4 | 18 | .222 | 0 | 0 | ... | 1 | 15 | 16 | 5 | 2 | 1 | 3 | 10 | 3.2 | 1.0 | 2.0 |
| Totals | 27 | 392 | 37 | 97 | .381 | 14 | 18 | .778 | 25 | 55 | 80 | 15 | 11 | 4 | 11 | 93 | 3.0 | 0.6 | 3.4 |

Three-point field goals: 2000-01, 1-for-3 (.333). 2001-02, 0-for-1. 2002-03, 2-for-9 (.222). 2004-05, 2-for-9 (.222). Totals, 5-for-22 (.227).
Personal fouls/disqualifications: 2000-01, 12/0. 2001-02, 15/0. 2002-03, 18/0. 2004-05, 14/0. Totals, 59/0.

# BUFORD, RODNEY　　　　　　　G/F

**PERSONAL:** Born November 2, 1977, in Milwaukee. ... 6-5/189. (1.96/85.7). ... Full name: Rodney Alan Buford
**HIGH SCHOOL:** Milwaukee (Wis.) Vincent.
**COLLEGE:** Creighton.
**TRANSACTIONS/CAREER NOTES:** Selected by Miami Heat in second round (53rd pick overall) of 1999 NBA Draft. ... Traded by Heat with F P.J. Brown, F Jamal Mashburn, F/C Otis Thorpe and F Tim James to Charlotte Hornets for G Eddie Jones, F Anthony Mason, G Ricky Davis and G/F Dale Ellis (August 1, 2000). ... Waived by Hornets (October 2, 2000). ... Played in Italy (2000-01). ... Signed as free agent by Philadelphia 76ers (December 22, 2000). ... Signed as free agent by Heat (September 24, 2001). ... Waived by Heat (October 25, 2001). ... Signed as free agent by Memphis Grizzlies (November 19, 2001). ... Played in Greece (2002-03). ... Signed as free agent by Sacramento Kings (August 29, 2003). ... Waived by Kings (December 8, 2003). ... Played in Continental Basketball Association (2003-04). ... Signed by Kings to first of two consecutive 10-day contracts (February 21, 2004). ... Signed by Kings for remainder of season (March 12, 2004). ... Signed as free agent by New Jersey Nets (July 29, 2004).

## COLLEGIATE RECORD

| | | | | | | | | | | | AVERAGES | | |
|---|---|---|---|---|---|---|---|---|---|---|---|---|---|---|
| Season Team | G | Min. | FGM | FGA | Pct. | FTM | FTA | Pct. | Reb. | Ast. | Pts. | RPG | APG | PPG |
| 95-96—Creighton | 29 | 752 | 158 | 342 | .462 | 59 | 81 | .728 | 122 | 41 | 421 | 4.2 | 1.4 | 14.5 |
| 96-97—Creighton | 30 | 947 | 225 | 512 | .439 | 81 | 110 | .736 | 168 | 48 | 589 | 5.6 | 1.6 | 19.6 |
| 97-98—Creighton | 28 | 864 | 189 | 446 | .424 | 99 | 138 | .717 | 204 | 58 | 530 | 7.3 | 2.1 | 18.9 |
| 98-99—Creighton | 31 | 1011 | 206 | 439 | .469 | 109 | 133 | .820 | 222 | 68 | 576 | 7.2 | 2.2 | 18.6 |
| Totals | 118 | 3574 | 778 | 1739 | .447 | 348 | 462 | .753 | 716 | 215 | 2116 | 6.1 | 1.8 | 17.9 |

Three-point field goals: 1995-96, 46-for-118 (.390). 1996-97, 58-for-153 (.379). 1997-98, 53-for-162 (.327). 1998-99, 55-for-125 (.440). Totals, 212-for-558 (.380).

## NBA REGULAR-SEASON RECORD

| Season Team | G | Min. | FGM | FGA | Pct. | FTM | FTA | Pct. | REBOUNDS Off. | REBOUNDS Def. | REBOUNDS Tot. | Ast. | St. | Blk. | TO | Pts. | AVERAGES RPG | AVERAGES APG | AVERAGES PPG |
|---|---|---|---|---|---|---|---|---|---|---|---|---|---|---|---|---|---|---|---|
| 99-00—Miami ............ | 34 | 386 | 62 | 151 | .411 | 16 | 22 | .727 | 10 | 38 | 48 | 21 | 10 | 8 | 9 | 147 | 1.4 | 0.6 | 4.3 |
| 00-01—Philadelphia .... | 47 | 573 | 104 | 241 | .432 | 24 | 29 | .828 | 16 | 58 | 74 | 17 | 17 | 6 | 29 | 248 | 1.6 | 0.4 | 5.3 |
| 01-02—Memphis ...... | 63 | 1769 | 258 | 593 | .435 | 58 | 80 | .725 | 52 | 220 | 272 | 71 | 42 | 12 | 63 | 591 | 4.3 | 1.1 | 9.4 |
| 03-04—Sacramento .... | 22 | 141 | 19 | 56 | .339 | 3 | 6 | .500 | 6 | 9 | 15 | 7 | 6 | 1 | 4 | 41 | 0.7 | 0.3 | 1.9 |
| 04-05—New Jersey ..... | 64 | 1313 | 187 | 489 | .382 | 37 | 45 | .822 | 33 | 156 | 189 | 63 | 40 | 4 | 35 | 445 | 3.0 | 1.0 | 7.0 |
| Totals ................... | 230 | 4182 | 630 | 1530 | .412 | 138 | 182 | .758 | 117 | 481 | 598 | 179 | 115 | 31 | 140 | 1472 | 2.6 | 0.8 | 6.4 |

Three-point field goals: 1999-00, 7-for-29 (.241). 2000-01, 16-for-38 (.421). 2001-02, 17-for-70 (.243). 2003-04, 0-for-2. 2004-05, 34-for-108 (.315). Totals, 74-for-247 (.300).

Personal fouls/disqualifications: 1999-00, 44/0. 2000-01, 68/0. 2001-02, 110/1. 2003-04, 9/0. 2004-05, 101/1. Totals, 332/2.

## NBA PLAYOFF RECORD

| Season Team | G | Min. | FGM | FGA | Pct. | FTM | FTA | Pct. | REBOUNDS Off. | REBOUNDS Def. | REBOUNDS Tot. | Ast. | St. | Blk. | TO | Pts. | AVERAGES RPG | AVERAGES APG | AVERAGES PPG |
|---|---|---|---|---|---|---|---|---|---|---|---|---|---|---|---|---|---|---|---|
| 99-00—Miami ............ | 1 | 16 | 4 | 8 | .500 | 2 | 2 | 1.000 | 0 | 1 | 1 | 1 | 0 | 0 | 0 | 11 | 1.0 | 1.0 | 11.0 |
| 00-01—Philadelphia .... | 15 | 72 | 8 | 24 | .333 | 2 | 2 | 1.000 | 5 | 7 | 12 | 3 | 4 | 1 | 4 | 21 | 0.8 | 0.2 | 1.4 |
| 03-04—Sacramento .... | 5 | 32 | 5 | 12 | .417 | 1 | 2 | .500 | 0 | 5 | 5 | 3 | 2 | 0 | 0 | 12 | 1.0 | 0.6 | 2.4 |
| 04-05—New Jersey ..... | 3 | 4 | 0 | 0 | ... | 0 | 0 | ... | 0 | 0 | 0 | 0 | 0 | 0 | 0 | 0 | 0.0 | 0.0 | 0.0 |
| Totals ................... | 24 | 124 | 17 | 44 | .386 | 5 | 6 | .833 | 5 | 13 | 18 | 7 | 6 | 1 | 4 | 44 | 0.8 | 0.3 | 1.8 |

Three-point field goals: 1999-00, 1-for-2 (.500). 2000-01, 3-for-6 (.500). 2003-04, 1-for-3 (.333). Totals, 5-for-11 (.455).

Personal fouls/disqualifications: 1999-00, 3/0. 2000-01, 15/0. 2003-04, 2/0. Totals, 20/0.

## ITALIAN LEAGUE RECORD

| Season Team | G | Min. | FGM | FGA | Pct. | FTM | FTA | Pct. | Reb. | Ast. | Pts. | AVERAGES RPG | AVERAGES APG | AVERAGES PPG |
|---|---|---|---|---|---|---|---|---|---|---|---|---|---|---|
| 00-01—Basket Rimini ................ | 10 | 364 | 87 | 179 | .486 | 40 | 50 | .800 | 52 | 21 | 241 | 5.2 | 2.1 | 24.1 |

Three-point field goals: 2000-01, 27-for-65 (.415). Totals, 27-for-65 (.415).

Personal fouls/disqualifications: 2000-01, 25/0. Totals, 25/0.

## GREEK LEAGUE RECORD

| Season Team | G | Min. | FGM | FGA | Pct. | FTM | FTA | Pct. | Reb. | Ast. | Pts. | AVERAGES RPG | AVERAGES APG | AVERAGES PPG |
|---|---|---|---|---|---|---|---|---|---|---|---|---|---|---|
| 02-03—Panathinaikos ................ | 22 | 575 | 98 | 202 | .485 | 37 | 42 | .881 | 108 | 23 | 258 | 4.9 | 1.0 | 11.7 |

Three-point field goals: 2002-03, 25-for-48 (.521). Totals, 25-for-48 (.521).

## CBA RECORD

| Season Team | G | Min. | FGM | FGA | Pct. | FTM | FTA | Pct. | Reb. | Ast. | Pts. | AVERAGES RPG | AVERAGES APG | AVERAGES PPG |
|---|---|---|---|---|---|---|---|---|---|---|---|---|---|---|
| 03-04—Dakota Wizards .............. | 4 | 148 | 42 | 79 | .532 | 15 | 16 | .938 | 29 | 12 | 105 | 7.3 | 3.0 | 26.3 |

Three-point field goals: 2003-04, 6-for-14 (.429). Totals, 6-for-14 (.429).

---

# BURKS, ANTONIO — G — GRIZZLIES

**PERSONAL:** Born February 25, 1980, in Memphis, Tenn. ... 6-0/195. (1.83/88.5). ... Full name: Antonio Cornell Burks
**HIGH SCHOOL:** Booker T. Washington (Memphis, Tenn.).
**JUNIOR COLLEGE:** Hiwassee College (Tenn.).
**COLLEGE:** Memphis.
**TRANSACTIONS/CAREER NOTES:** Selected by Orlando Magic in second round (36th pick overall) of 2004 NBA Draft. ... Draft rights traded by Magic to Memphis Grizzlies (June 24, 2004).

## COLLEGIATE RECORD

| Season Team | G | Min. | FGM | FGA | Pct. | FTM | FTA | Pct. | Reb. | Ast. | Pts. | AVERAGES RPG | AVERAGES APG | AVERAGES PPG |
|---|---|---|---|---|---|---|---|---|---|---|---|---|---|---|
| 99-00—Hiwassee College .......... | | | | | | | Statistics unavailable | | | | | | | |
| 00-01—Memphis ....................... | | | | | | | Did not play | | | | | | | |
| 01-02—Memphis ....................... | 36 | 1086 | 117 | 258 | .453 | 66 | 95 | .695 | 86 | 182 | 304 | 2.4 | 5.1 | 8.4 |
| 02-03—Memphis ....................... | 25 | 670 | 98 | 205 | .478 | 45 | 63 | .714 | 51 | 140 | 243 | 2.0 | 5.6 | 9.7 |
| 03-04—Memphis ....................... | 30 | 1030 | 176 | 371 | .474 | 72 | 114 | .632 | 96 | 165 | 481 | 3.2 | 5.5 | 16.0 |
| Totals ................................. | 91 | 2786 | 391 | 834 | .469 | 183 | 272 | .673 | 233 | 487 | 1028 | 2.6 | 5.4 | 11.3 |

Three-point field goals: 2001-02, 4-for-12 (.333). 2002-03, 2-for-7 (.286). 2003-04, 57-for-138 (.413). Totals, 63-for-157 (.401).

## NBA REGULAR-SEASON RECORD

| Season Team | G | Min. | FGM | FGA | Pct. | FTM | FTA | Pct. | REBOUNDS Off. | REBOUNDS Def. | REBOUNDS Tot. | Ast. | St. | Blk. | TO | Pts. | AVERAGES RPG | AVERAGES APG | AVERAGES PPG |
|---|---|---|---|---|---|---|---|---|---|---|---|---|---|---|---|---|---|---|---|
| 04-05—Memphis ........ | 24 | 219 | 28 | 60 | .467 | 14 | 19 | .737 | 1 | 11 | 12 | 28 | 13 | 1 | 12 | 73 | 0.5 | 1.2 | 3.0 |

Three-point field goals: 2004-05, 3-for-11 (.273). Totals, 3-for-11 (.273).

Personal fouls/disqualifications: 2004-05, 25/0. Totals, 25/0.

## NBA PLAYOFF RECORD

| Season Team | G | Min. | FGM | FGA | Pct. | FTM | FTA | Pct. | REBOUNDS Off. | REBOUNDS Def. | REBOUNDS Tot. | Ast. | St. | Blk. | TO | Pts. | AVERAGES RPG | AVERAGES APG | AVERAGES PPG |
|---|---|---|---|---|---|---|---|---|---|---|---|---|---|---|---|---|---|---|---|
| 04-05—Memphis ........ | 1 | 3 | 0 | 0 | ... | 0 | 0 | ... | 0 | 0 | 0 | 1 | 0 | 0 | 0 | 0 | 0.0 | 1.0 | 0.0 |

## BUTLER, CARON        F        WIZARDS

**PERSONAL:** Born March 13, 1980, in Racine, Wis. ... 6-7/235. (2.01/106.6). ... Full name: James Caron Butler
**HIGH SCHOOL:** Park (Racine, Wis.), then Maine Central Institute .
**COLLEGE:** Connecticut.
**TRANSACTIONS/CAREER NOTES:** Selected after sophomore season by Miami Heat in first round (10th pick overall) of 2002 NBA Draft. ... Traded by Heat with F Lamar Odom, F Brian Grant, a first-round draft choice and a second-round draft choice to Los Angeles Lakers for C Shaquille O'Neal (July 14, 2004). ... Traded by Lakers with G Chucky Atkins to Washington Wizards for C Kwame Brown and F Laron Profit (August 2, 2005).

### COLLEGIATE RECORD

**NOTES:** THE SPORTING NEWS All-America second team (2002).

| Season Team | G | Min. | FGM | FGA | Pct. | FTM | FTA | Pct. | Reb. | Ast. | Pts. | RPG | APG | PPG |
|---|---|---|---|---|---|---|---|---|---|---|---|---|---|---|
| 00-01—Connecticut | 29 | 950 | 151 | 347 | .435 | 129 | 171 | .754 | 221 | 89 | 445 | 7.6 | 3.1 | 15.3 |
| 01-02—Connecticut | 34 | 1223 | 253 | 521 | .486 | 155 | 199 | .779 | 256 | 101 | 691 | 7.5 | 3.0 | 20.3 |
| Totals | 63 | 2173 | 404 | 868 | .465 | 284 | 370 | .768 | 477 | 190 | 1136 | 7.6 | 3.0 | 18.0 |

Three-point field goals: 2000-01, 14-for-46 (.304). 2001-02, 30-for-75 (.400). Totals, 44-for-121 (.364).

### NBA REGULAR-SEASON RECORD

**HONORS:** NBA All-Rookie first team (2003).

| Season Team | G | Min. | FGM | FGA | Pct. | FTM | FTA | Pct. | Off. | Def. | Tot. | Ast. | St. | Blk. | TO | Pts. | RPG | APG | PPG |
|---|---|---|---|---|---|---|---|---|---|---|---|---|---|---|---|---|---|---|---|
| 02-03—Miami | 78 | 2858 | 429 | 1032 | .416 | 309 | 375 | .824 | 135 | 262 | 397 | 213 | 137 | 31 | 192 | 1201 | 5.1 | 2.7 | 15.4 |
| 03-04—Miami | 68 | 2030 | 240 | 631 | .380 | 133 | 176 | .756 | 92 | 234 | 326 | 126 | 75 | 13 | 91 | 623 | 4.8 | 1.9 | 9.2 |
| 04-05—L.A. Lakers | 77 | 2746 | 441 | 991 | .445 | 275 | 319 | .862 | 146 | 304 | 450 | 146 | 110 | 23 | 125 | 1195 | 5.8 | 1.9 | 15.5 |
| Totals | 223 | 7634 | 1110 | 2654 | .418 | 717 | 870 | .824 | 373 | 800 | 1173 | 485 | 322 | 67 | 408 | 3019 | 5.3 | 2.2 | 13.5 |

Three-point field goals: 2002-03, 34-for-107 (.318). 2003-04, 10-for-42 (.238). 2004-05, 38-for-125 (.304). Totals, 82-for-274 (.299).
Personal fouls/disqualifications: 2002-03, 230/3. 2003-04, 162/0. 2004-05, 213/2. Totals, 605/5.

### NBA PLAYOFF RECORD

| Season Team | G | Min. | FGM | FGA | Pct. | FTM | FTA | Pct. | Off. | Def. | Tot. | Ast. | St. | Blk. | TO | Pts. | RPG | APG | PPG |
|---|---|---|---|---|---|---|---|---|---|---|---|---|---|---|---|---|---|---|---|
| 03-04—Miami | 13 | 511 | 59 | 153 | .386 | 47 | 57 | .825 | 18 | 92 | 110 | 31 | 28 | 7 | 23 | 167 | 8.5 | 2.4 | 12.8 |

Three-point field goals: 2003-04, 2-for-11 (.182). Totals, 2-for-11 (.182).
Personal fouls/disqualifications: 2003-04, 45/0. Totals, 45/0.

## BUTLER, JACKIE        C        KNICKS

**PERSONAL:** Born March 10, 1985, in McComb, Miss. ... 6-10/250. (2.08/113.4).
**HIGH SCHOOL:** McComb (Miss.), then Laurinburg Institute (N.C.),.
**COLLEGE:** Did not attend college.
**TRANSACTIONS/CAREER NOTES:** Not drafted by an NBA franchise. ... Signed as free agent by New York Knicks (February 27, 2005).

### CBA RECORD

| Season Team | G | Min. | FGM | FGA | Pct. | FTM | FTA | Pct. | Reb. | Ast. | Pts. | RPG | APG | PPG |
|---|---|---|---|---|---|---|---|---|---|---|---|---|---|---|
| 04-05—Great Lakes | 41 | 1419 | 300 | 588 | .510 | 138 | 193 | .715 | 439 | 72 | 738 | 10.7 | 1.8 | 18.0 |

Three-point field goals: 2004-05, 0-for-6. Totals, 0-for-6 (.000).

### NBA REGULAR-SEASON RECORD

| Season Team | G | Min. | FGM | FGA | Pct. | FTM | FTA | Pct. | Off. | Def. | Tot. | Ast. | St. | Blk. | TO | Pts. | RPG | APG | PPG |
|---|---|---|---|---|---|---|---|---|---|---|---|---|---|---|---|---|---|---|---|
| 04-05—New York | 3 | 5 | 4 | 4 | 1.000 | 2 | 2 | 1.000 | 0 | 0 | 0 | 0 | 1 | 0 | 1 | 10 | 0.0 | 0.0 | 3.3 |

## BUTLER, RASUAL        F        HORNETS

**PERSONAL:** Born May 23, 1979, in Philadelphia. ... 6-7/205. (2.01/93.0).
**HIGH SCHOOL:** Roman Catholic (Philadelphia).
**COLLEGE:** La Salle.
**TRANSACTIONS/CAREER NOTES:** Selected by Miami Heat in second round (53rd pick overall) of 2002 NBA Draft. ... Traded by Heat to New Orleans Hornets in five-team trade (August 2, 2005).

### COLLEGIATE RECORD

| Season Team | G | Min. | FGM | FGA | Pct. | FTM | FTA | Pct. | Reb. | Ast. | Pts. | RPG | APG | PPG |
|---|---|---|---|---|---|---|---|---|---|---|---|---|---|---|
| 98-99—La Salle | 21 | 773 | 105 | 276 | .380 | 43 | 58 | .741 | 83 | 31 | 298 | 4.0 | 1.5 | 14.2 |
| 99-00—La Salle | 28 | 1072 | 183 | 450 | .407 | 67 | 82 | .817 | 148 | 45 | 516 | 5.3 | 1.6 | 18.4 |
| 00-01—La Salle | 29 | 1114 | 231 | 574 | .402 | 82 | 97 | .845 | 136 | 57 | 641 | 4.7 | 2.0 | 22.1 |
| 01-02—La Salle | 32 | 1252 | 233 | 537 | .434 | 147 | 172 | .855 | 283 | 44 | 670 | 8.8 | 1.4 | 20.9 |
| Totals | 110 | 4211 | 752 | 1837 | .409 | 339 | 409 | .829 | 650 | 177 | 2125 | 5.9 | 1.6 | 19.3 |

Three-point field goals: 1998-99, 45-for-137 (.328). 1999-00, 83-for-218 (.381). 2000-01, 91-for-272 (.335). 2001-02, 57-for-158 (.361). Totals, 276-for-785 (.352).

## NBA REGULAR-SEASON RECORD

| Season Team | G | Min. | FGM | FGA | Pct. | FTM | FTA | Pct. | Off. | Def. | Tot. | Ast. | St. | Blk. | TO | Pts. | RPG | APG | PPG |
|---|---|---|---|---|---|---|---|---|---|---|---|---|---|---|---|---|---|---|---|
| | | | | | | | | | REBOUNDS | | | | | | | | AVERAGES | | |
| 02-03—Miami ............ | 72 | 1514 | 207 | 572 | .362 | 76 | 104 | .731 | 29 | 157 | 186 | 93 | 21 | 43 | 77 | 540 | 2.6 | 1.3 | 7.5 |
| 03-04—Miami ............ | 45 | 675 | 119 | 250 | .476 | 16 | 21 | .762 | 4 | 57 | 61 | 23 | 10 | 13 | 28 | 304 | 1.4 | 0.5 | 6.8 |
| 04-05—Miami ............ | 65 | 1203 | 163 | 409 | .399 | 37 | 48 | .771 | 15 | 136 | 151 | 62 | 18 | 29 | 37 | 420 | 2.3 | 1.0 | 6.5 |
| Totals ................. | 182 | 3392 | 489 | 1231 | .397 | 129 | 173 | .746 | 48 | 350 | 398 | 178 | 49 | 85 | 142 | 1264 | 2.2 | 1.0 | 6.9 |

Three-point field goals: 2002-03, 50-for-171 (.292). 2003-04, 50-for-108 (.463). 2004-05, 57-for-153 (.373). Totals, 157-for-432 (.363).
Personal fouls/disqualifications: 2002-03, 105/0. 2003-04, 72/0. 2004-05, 104/0. Totals, 281/0.

## NBA PLAYOFF RECORD

| Season Team | G | Min. | FGM | FGA | Pct. | FTM | FTA | Pct. | Off. | Def. | Tot. | Ast. | St. | Blk. | TO | Pts. | RPG | APG | PPG |
|---|---|---|---|---|---|---|---|---|---|---|---|---|---|---|---|---|---|---|---|
| | | | | | | | | | REBOUNDS | | | | | | | | AVERAGES | | |
| 03-04—Miami ............ | 10 | 58 | 9 | 22 | .409 | 0 | 0 | ... | 0 | 11 | 11 | 2 | 1 | 0 | 1 | 21 | 1.1 | 0.2 | 2.1 |
| 04-05—Miami ............ | 12 | 182 | 22 | 59 | .373 | 1 | 3 | .333 | 1 | 17 | 18 | 7 | 1 | 1 | 2 | 56 | 1.5 | 0.6 | 4.7 |
| Totals ................... | 22 | 240 | 31 | 81 | .383 | 1 | 3 | .333 | 1 | 28 | 29 | 9 | 2 | 1 | 3 | 77 | 1.3 | 0.4 | 3.5 |

Three-point field goals: 2003-04, 3-for-9 (.333). 2004-05, 11-for-30 (.367). Totals, 14-for-39 (.359).
Personal fouls/disqualifications: 2003-04, 12/0. 2004-05, 21/0. Totals, 33/0.

# CABARKAPA, ZARKO　　　　F/C　　　　WARRIORS

**PERSONAL:** Born May 21, 1981, in Zrenjanin, Serbia & Montenegro. ... 6-11/235. (2.11/106.6).
**TRANSACTIONS/CAREER NOTES:** Selected by Phoenix Suns in first round (17th pick overall) of 2003 NBA Draft. ... Traded by Suns to Golden State Warriors for two future second-round draft choices (January 3, 2005).

## YUGOSLAVIAN LEAGUE RECORD

| Season Team | G | Min. | FGM | FGA | Pct. | FTM | FTA | Pct. | Reb. | Ast. | Pts. | RPG | APG | PPG |
|---|---|---|---|---|---|---|---|---|---|---|---|---|---|---|
| | | | | | | | | | | | | AVERAGES | | |
| 97-98—Beopetrol.................. | 9 | 47 | 4 | 12 | .333 | 0 | 1 | .000 | 3 | 3 | 8 | 0.3 | 0.3 | 0.9 |
| 98-99—Beopetrol.................. | 4 | 30 | 3 | 9 | .333 | 1 | 2 | .500 | 8 | 4 | 7 | 2.0 | 1.0 | 1.8 |
| 99-00—Beopetrol.................. | 21 | 445 | 55 | 107 | .514 | 33 | 51 | .647 | 56 | 13 | 152 | 2.7 | 0.6 | 7.2 |
| 00-01—Beopetrol.................. | 22 | 640 | 112 | 224 | .500 | 54 | 76 | .711 | 121 | 48 | 297 | 5.5 | 2.2 | 13.5 |
| 01-02—Buducnost ................. | 14 | 271 | 50 | 82 | .610 | 24 | 37 | .649 | 57 | 11 | 132 | 4.1 | 0.8 | 9.4 |
| 02-03—Buducnost ................. | 19 | 302 | 102 | 167 | .611 | 57 | 75 | .760 | 89 | 28 | 277 | 4.7 | 1.5 | 14.6 |
| Totals .................................. | 89 | 1735 | 326 | 601 | .542 | 169 | 242 | .698 | 334 | 107 | 873 | 3.8 | 1.2 | 9.8 |

Three-point field goals: 1997-98, 0-for-2. 1998-99, 0-for-2. 1999-00, 9-for-25 (.360). 2000-01, 19-for-54 (.352). 2001-02, 8-for-19 (.421). 2002-03, 16-for-41 (.390). Totals, 52-for-143 (.364).

## NBA REGULAR-SEASON RECORD

| Season Team | G | Min. | FGM | FGA | Pct. | FTM | FTA | Pct. | Off. | Def. | Tot. | Ast. | St. | Blk. | TO | Pts. | RPG | APG | PPG |
|---|---|---|---|---|---|---|---|---|---|---|---|---|---|---|---|---|---|---|---|
| | | | | | | | | | REBOUNDS | | | | | | | | AVERAGES | | |
| 03-04—Phoenix......... | 49 | 570 | 81 | 197 | .411 | 35 | 53 | .660 | 26 | 73 | 99 | 40 | 10 | 13 | 54 | 203 | 2.0 | 0.8 | 4.1 |
| 04-05—Pho.-Golden St.. | 40 | 475 | 86 | 177 | .486 | 53 | 65 | .815 | 35 | 67 | 102 | 25 | 10 | 5 | 30 | 238 | 2.6 | 0.6 | 6.0 |
| Totals ................. | 89 | 1045 | 167 | 374 | .447 | 88 | 118 | .746 | 61 | 140 | 201 | 65 | 20 | 18 | 84 | 441 | 2.3 | 0.7 | 5.0 |

Three-point field goals: 2003-04, 6-for-32 (.188). 2004-05, 13-for-36 (.361). Totals, 19-for-68 (.279).
Personal fouls/disqualifications: 2003-04, 75/0. 2004-05, 59/0. Totals, 134/0.

# CAMBY, MARCUS　　　　C　　　　NUGGETS

**PERSONAL:** Born March 22, 1974, in Hartford. ... 6-11/235. (2.11/106.6). ... Full name: Marcus D. Camby.
**HIGH SCHOOL:** Hartford Public (Conn.).
**COLLEGE:** Massachusetts.
**TRANSACTIONS/CAREER NOTES:** Selected after junior season by Toronto Raptors in first round (second pick overall) of 1996 NBA Draft. ... Traded by Raptors to New York Knicks for F Charles Oakley, draft rights to F/C Sean Marks and cash (June 25, 1998). ... Traded by Knicks with G Mark Jackson and draft rights to F/C Nene Hilario to Denver Nuggets for F Antonio McDyess, draft rights to G Frank Williams and 2003 second-round draft choice (June 26, 2002).
**MISCELLANEOUS:** Toronto Raptors all-time blocked shots leader with 360 (1996-97 and 1997-98).

## COLLEGIATE RECORD

**NOTES:** THE SPORTING NEWS College Player of the Year (1996). ... Naismith Award winner (1996). ... Wooden Award winner (1996). ... THE SPORTING NEWS All-America first team (1996).

| Season Team | G | Min. | FGM | FGA | Pct. | FTM | FTA | Pct. | Reb. | Ast. | Pts. | RPG | APG | PPG |
|---|---|---|---|---|---|---|---|---|---|---|---|---|---|---|
| | | | | | | | | | | | | AVERAGES | | |
| 93-94—Massachusetts ............... | 29 | 634 | 117 | 237 | .494 | 62 | 104 | .596 | 185 | 36 | 296 | 6.4 | 1.2 | 10.2 |
| 94-95—Massachusetts ............... | 30 | 679 | 166 | 302 | .550 | 83 | 129 | .643 | 186 | 37 | 416 | 6.2 | 1.2 | 13.9 |
| 95-96—Massachusetts ............... | 33 | 1011 | 256 | 537 | .477 | 163 | 233 | .700 | 271 | 58 | 675 | 8.2 | 1.8 | 20.5 |
| Totals ..................................... | 92 | 2324 | 539 | 1076 | .501 | 308 | 466 | .661 | 642 | 131 | 1387 | 7.0 | 1.4 | 15.1 |

Three-point field goals: 1993-94, 0-for-4. 1994-95, 1-for-1 (1.000). 1995-96, 0-for-13. Totals, 1-for-13 (.077).

## NBA REGULAR-SEASON RECORD

**HONORS:** NBA All-Rookie first team (1997). ... NBA All-Defensive second team (2005).
**NOTES:** Led NBA with 3.65 blocks per game (1998).

| Season Team | G | Min. | FGM | FGA | Pct. | FTM | FTA | Pct. | Off. | Def. | Tot. | Ast. | St. | Blk. | TO | Pts. | RPG | APG | PPG |
|---|---|---|---|---|---|---|---|---|---|---|---|---|---|---|---|---|---|---|---|
| | | | | | | | | | REBOUNDS | | | | | | | | AVERAGES | | |
| 96-97—Toronto .......... | 63 | 1897 | 375 | 778 | .482 | 183 | 264 | .693 | 131 | 263 | 394 | 97 | 66 | 130 | 134 | 935 | 6.3 | 1.5 | 14.8 |
| 97-98—Toronto .......... | 63 | 2002 | 308 | 747 | .412 | 149 | 244 | .611 | 203 | 263 | 466 | 111 | 68 | 230 | 134 | 765 | 7.4 | 1.8 | 12.1 |
| 98-99—New York ........ | 46 | 945 | 136 | 261 | .521 | 57 | 103 | .553 | 102 | 151 | 253 | 12 | 29 | 74 | 39 | 329 | 5.5 | 0.3 | 7.2 |
| 99-00—New York ........ | 59 | 1548 | 226 | 471 | .480 | 148 | 221 | .670 | 174 | 287 | 461 | 49 | 43 | 116 | 72 | 601 | 7.8 | 0.8 | 10.2 |

| Season Team | G | Min. | FGM | FGA | Pct. | FTM | FTA | Pct. | Off. | Def. | Tot. | Ast. | St. | Blk. | TO | Pts. | RPG | APG | PPG |
|---|---|---|---|---|---|---|---|---|---|---|---|---|---|---|---|---|---|---|---|
| 00-01—New York | 63 | 2127 | 304 | 580 | .524 | 150 | 225 | .667 | 196 | 527 | 723 | 52 | 66 | 136 | 63 | 759 | 11.5 | 0.8 | 12.0 |
| 01-02—New York | 29 | 1007 | 130 | 290 | .448 | 62 | 99 | .626 | 89 | 233 | 322 | 33 | 34 | 50 | 42 | 322 | 11.1 | 1.1 | 11.1 |
| 02-03—Denver | 29 | 616 | 93 | 227 | .410 | 33 | 50 | .660 | 75 | 133 | 208 | 47 | 20 | 40 | 27 | 221 | 7.2 | 1.6 | 7.6 |
| 03-04—Denver | 72 | 2162 | 262 | 549 | .477 | 98 | 136 | .721 | 211 | 516 | 727 | 132 | 86 | 187 | 98 | 622 | 10.1 | 1.8 | 8.6 |
| 04-05—Denver | 66 | 2015 | 279 | 600 | .465 | 125 | 173 | .723 | 131 | 530 | 661 | 152 | 61 | 199 | 103 | 683 | 10.0 | 2.3 | 10.3 |
| Totals | 490 | 14319 | 2113 | 4503 | .469 | 1005 | 1515 | .663 | 1312 | 2903 | 4215 | 685 | 473 | 1162 | 712 | 5237 | 8.6 | 1.4 | 10.7 |

Three-point field goals: 1996-97, 2-for-14 (.143). 1997-98, 0-for-2. 1999-00, 1-for-2 (.500). 2000-01, 1-for-8 (.125). 2001-02, 0-for-1. 2002-03, 2-for-5 (.400). 2003-04, 0-for-2. 2004-05, 0-for-4. Totals, 6-for-38 (.158).

Personal fouls/disqualifications: 1996-97, 214/7. 1997-98, 200/1. 1998-99, 131/2. 1999-00, 204/5. 2000-01, 205/4. 2001-02, 107/3. 2002-03, 69/1. 2003-04, 239/4. 2004-05, 177/0. Totals, 1546/27.

## NBA PLAYOFF RECORD

| Season Team | G | Min. | FGM | FGA | Pct. | FTM | FTA | Pct. | Off. | Def. | Tot. | Ast. | St. | Blk. | TO | Pts. | RPG | APG | PPG |
|---|---|---|---|---|---|---|---|---|---|---|---|---|---|---|---|---|---|---|---|
| 98-99—New York | 20 | 509 | 81 | 143 | .566 | 45 | 73 | .616 | 51 | 102 | 153 | 6 | 24 | 38 | 15 | 207 | 7.7 | 0.3 | 10.4 |
| 99-00—New York | 16 | 386 | 29 | 86 | .337 | 19 | 31 | .613 | 35 | 77 | 112 | 6 | 8 | 23 | 12 | 77 | 7.0 | 0.4 | 4.8 |
| 00-01—New York | 4 | 141 | 10 | 26 | .385 | 5 | 13 | .385 | 4 | 28 | 32 | 7 | 2 | 9 | 2 | 25 | 8.0 | 1.8 | 6.3 |
| 03-04—Denver | 5 | 194 | 27 | 55 | .491 | 8 | 14 | .571 | 14 | 43 | 57 | 12 | 4 | 7 | 6 | 63 | 11.4 | 2.4 | 12.6 |
| 04-05—Denver | 5 | 184 | 17 | 41 | .415 | 17 | 27 | .630 | 4 | 52 | 56 | 9 | 3 | 16 | 11 | 51 | 11.2 | 1.8 | 10.2 |
| Totals | 50 | 1414 | 164 | 351 | .467 | 94 | 158 | .595 | 108 | 302 | 410 | 40 | 41 | 93 | 46 | 423 | 8.2 | 0.8 | 8.5 |

Three-point field goals: 1998-99, 0-for-1. 1999-00, 0-for-1. 2003-04, 1-for-2 (.500). Totals, 1-for-4 (.250).
Personal fouls/disqualifications: 1998-99, 76/2. 1999-00, 51/1. 2000-01, 18/1. 2003-04, 21/0. 2004-05, 18/0. Totals, 184/4.

# CAMPBELL, ELDEN     C     PISTONS

**PERSONAL:** Born July 23, 1968, in Los Angeles. ... 7-0/279. (2.13/126.6). ... Full name: Elden Jerome Campbell.
**HIGH SCHOOL:** Morningside (Inglewood, Calif.).
**COLLEGE:** Clemson.
**TRANSACTIONS/CAREER NOTES:** Selected by Los Angeles Lakers in first round (27th pick overall) of 1990 NBA Draft. ... Traded by Lakers with G Eddie Jones to Charlotte Hornets for F Glen Rice, F/C J.R. Reid and G B.J. Armstrong (March 10, 1999). ... Hornets franchise moved to New Orleans for 2002-03 season. ... Traded by Hornets to Seattle SuperSonics for G Kenny Anderson (February 20, 2003). ... Signed as free agent by Detroit Pistons (July 26, 2003) ... Traded by Pistons with a future first-round draft choice to Utah Jazz for G Carlos Arroyo (January 21, 2005). ... Waived by Jazz (January 26, 2005). ... Claimed off waivers by New Jersey Nets (January 28, 2005). ... Waived by Nets (March 1, 2005). ... Signed by Detroit Pistons (March 4, 2005).
**MISCELLANEOUS:** Member of NBA championship team (2004).

## COLLEGIATE RECORD

| Season Team | G | Min. | FGM | FGA | Pct. | FTM | FTA | Pct. | Reb. | Ast. | Pts. | RPG | APG | PPG |
|---|---|---|---|---|---|---|---|---|---|---|---|---|---|---|
| 86-87—Clemson | 31 | 534 | 107 | 193 | .554 | 59 | 84 | .702 | 126 | 20 | 273 | 4.1 | 0.6 | 8.8 |
| 87-88—Clemson | 28 | 808 | 217 | 345 | .629 | 91 | 147 | .619 | 207 | 15 | 525 | 7.4 | 0.5 | 18.8 |
| 88-89—Clemson | 29 | 814 | 205 | 373 | .550 | 95 | 138 | .688 | 222 | 34 | 507 | 7.7 | 1.2 | 17.5 |
| 89-90—Clemson | 35 | 1038 | 225 | 431 | .522 | 124 | 207 | .599 | 281 | 44 | 575 | 8.0 | 1.3 | 16.4 |
| Totals | 123 | 3194 | 754 | 1342 | .562 | 369 | 576 | .641 | 836 | 113 | 1880 | 6.8 | 0.9 | 15.3 |

Three-point field goals: 1987-88, 0-for-4. 1988-89, 2-for-5 (.400). 1989-90, 1-for-1 (1.000). Totals, 3-for-10 (.300).

## NBA REGULAR-SEASON RECORD

**NOTES:** Tied for NBA lead with 300 personal fouls (1996).

| Season Team | G | Min. | FGM | FGA | Pct. | FTM | FTA | Pct. | Off. | Def. | Tot. | Ast. | St. | Blk. | TO | Pts. | RPG | APG | PPG |
|---|---|---|---|---|---|---|---|---|---|---|---|---|---|---|---|---|---|---|---|
| 90-91—L.A. Lakers | 52 | 380 | 56 | 123 | .455 | 32 | 49 | .653 | 40 | 56 | 96 | 10 | 11 | 38 | 16 | 144 | 1.8 | 0.2 | 2.8 |
| 91-92—L.A. Lakers | 81 | 1876 | 220 | 491 | .448 | 138 | 223 | .619 | 155 | 268 | 423 | 59 | 53 | 159 | 73 | 578 | 5.2 | 0.7 | 7.1 |
| 92-93—L.A. Lakers | 79 | 1551 | 238 | 520 | .458 | 130 | 204 | .637 | 127 | 205 | 332 | 48 | 59 | 100 | 69 | 606 | 4.2 | 0.6 | 7.7 |
| 93-94—L.A. Lakers | 76 | 2253 | 373 | 808 | .462 | 188 | 273 | .689 | 167 | 352 | 519 | 86 | 64 | 146 | 98 | 934 | 6.8 | 1.1 | 12.3 |
| 94-95—L.A. Lakers | 73 | 2076 | 360 | 785 | .459 | 193 | 290 | .666 | 168 | 277 | 445 | 92 | 69 | 132 | 98 | 913 | 6.1 | 1.3 | 12.5 |
| 95-96—L.A. Lakers | 82 | 2699 | 447 | 888 | .503 | 249 | 349 | .713 | 162 | 461 | 623 | 181 | 88 | 212 | 137 | 1143 | 7.6 | 2.2 | 13.9 |
| 96-97—L.A. Lakers | 77 | 2516 | 442 | 942 | .469 | 263 | 370 | .711 | 207 | 408 | 615 | 126 | 46 | 117 | 130 | 1148 | 8.0 | 1.6 | 14.9 |
| 97-98—L.A. Lakers | 81 | 1784 | 289 | 624 | .463 | 237 | 342 | .693 | 143 | 312 | 455 | 78 | 35 | 102 | 115 | 816 | 5.6 | 1.0 | 10.1 |
| 98-99—L.A.L.-Char. | 49 | 1459 | 222 | 465 | .477 | 172 | 269 | .639 | 126 | 271 | 397 | 69 | 39 | 73 | 80 | 616 | 8.1 | 1.4 | 12.6 |
| 99-00—Charlotte | 78 | 2538 | 370 | 829 | .446 | 247 | 358 | .690 | 168 | 422 | 590 | 129 | 56 | 150 | 127 | 987 | 7.6 | 1.7 | 12.7 |
| 00-01—Charlotte | 78 | 2337 | 367 | 834 | .440 | 288 | 406 | .709 | 157 | 451 | 608 | 104 | 60 | 140 | 144 | 1022 | 7.8 | 1.3 | 13.1 |
| 01-02—Charlotte | 77 | 2156 | 384 | 794 | .484 | 306 | 384 | .797 | 133 | 397 | 530 | 102 | 60 | 137 | 138 | 1074 | 6.9 | 1.3 | 13.9 |
| 02-03—NO-Sea | 56 | 869 | 117 | 295 | .397 | 109 | 136 | .801 | 47 | 134 | 181 | 51 | 33 | 39 | 50 | 343 | 3.2 | 0.9 | 6.1 |
| 03-04—Detroit | 65 | 892 | 138 | 314 | .439 | 85 | 124 | .685 | 52 | 157 | 209 | 45 | 21 | 50 | 63 | 361 | 3.2 | 0.7 | 5.6 |
| 04-05—N.J.-Detroit | 40 | 390 | 39 | 123 | .317 | 42 | 55 | .764 | 28 | 65 | 93 | 19 | 8 | 7 | 29 | 120 | 2.3 | 0.5 | 3.0 |
| Totals | 1044 | 25776 | 4062 | 8835 | .460 | 2679 | 3832 | .699 | 1880 | 4236 | 6116 | 1199 | 702 | 1602 | 1367 | 10805 | 5.9 | 1.1 | 10.3 |

Three-point field goals: 1991-92, 0-for-2. 1992-93, 0-for-3. 1993-94, 0-for-2. 1994-95, 0-for-1. 1995-96, 0-for-5. 1996-97, 1-for-4 (.250). 1997-98, 1-for-2 (.500). 1998-99, 0-for-1. 1999-00, 0-for-6. 2000-01, 0-for-6. 2001-02, 0-for-2. 2002-03, 0-for-1. 2004-05, 0-for-2. Totals, 2-for-37 (.054).
Personal fouls/disqualifications: 1990-91, 71/1. 1991-92, 203/1. 1992-93, 165/0. 1993-94, 241/2. 1994-95, 246/4. 1995-96, 300/4. 1996-97, 276/6. 1997-98, 209/1. 1998-99, 159/3. 1999-00, 269/6. 2000-01, 280/1. 2001-02, 264/4. 2002-03, 129/2. 2003-04, 137/0. 2004-05, 57/0. Totals, 3006/35.

## NBA PLAYOFF RECORD

| Season Team | G | Min. | FGM | FGA | Pct. | FTM | FTA | Pct. | Off. | Def. | Tot. | Ast. | St. | Blk. | TO | Pts. | RPG | APG | PPG |
|---|---|---|---|---|---|---|---|---|---|---|---|---|---|---|---|---|---|---|---|
| 90-91—L.A. Lakers | 14 | 138 | 25 | 38 | .658 | 7 | 15 | .467 | 8 | 21 | 29 | 3 | 6 | 8 | 6 | 57 | 2.1 | 0.2 | 4.1 |
| 91-92—L.A. Lakers | 4 | 117 | 14 | 37 | .378 | 12 | 18 | .667 | 9 | 16 | 25 | 6 | 3 | 6 | 4 | 40 | 6.3 | 1.5 | 10.0 |
| 92-93—L.A. Lakers | 5 | 178 | 29 | 69 | .420 | 12 | 24 | .500 | 17 | 25 | 42 | 7 | 6 | 12 | 12 | 70 | 8.4 | 1.4 | 14.0 |
| 94-95—L.A. Lakers | 10 | 376 | 64 | 132 | .485 | 29 | 44 | .659 | 26 | 47 | 73 | 16 | 4 | 30 | 15 | 157 | 7.3 | 1.6 | 15.7 |

| Season Team | G | Min. | FGM | FGA | Pct. | FTM | FTA | Pct. | REBOUNDS Off. | Def. | Tot. | Ast. | St. | Blk. | TO | Pts. | RPG | APG | PPG |
|---|---|---|---|---|---|---|---|---|---|---|---|---|---|---|---|---|---|---|---|
| 95-96—L.A. Lakers .... | 4 | 129 | 20 | 39 | .513 | 8 | 16 | .500 | 3 | 29 | 32 | 8 | 1 | 9 | 10 | 48 | 8.0 | 2.0 | 12.0 |
| 96-97—L.A. Lakers .... | 9 | 278 | 37 | 93 | .398 | 31 | 38 | .816 | 14 | 25 | 39 | 9 | 7 | 13 | 14 | 106 | 4.3 | 1.0 | 11.8 |
| 97-98—L.A. Lakers .... | 13 | 180 | 23 | 51 | .451 | 22 | 34 | .647 | 17 | 28 | 45 | 8 | 3 | 12 | 13 | 68 | 3.5 | 0.6 | 5.2 |
| 99-00—Charlotte........ | 4 | 150 | 22 | 47 | .468 | 13 | 14 | .929 | 9 | 24 | 33 | 4 | 2 | 4 | 8 | 57 | 8.3 | 1.0 | 14.3 |
| 00-01—Charlotte........ | 10 | 287 | 42 | 106 | .396 | 37 | 49 | .755 | 27 | 52 | 79 | 7 | 5 | 11 | 17 | 121 | 7.9 | 0.7 | 12.1 |
| 01-02—Charlotte........ | 9 | 254 | 49 | 110 | .445 | 24 | 34 | .706 | 14 | 46 | 60 | 16 | 6 | 23 | 17 | 122 | 6.7 | 1.8 | 13.6 |
| 03-04—Detroit ........... | 14 | 124 | 10 | 35 | .286 | 10 | 18 | .556 | 10 | 15 | 25 | 10 | 6 | 9 | 9 | 30 | 1.8 | 0.7 | 2.1 |
| 04-05—Detroit ........... | 10 | 57 | 4 | 13 | .308 | 4 | 8 | .500 | 3 | 15 | 18 | 5 | 2 | 0 | 4 | 12 | 1.8 | 0.5 | 1.2 |
| Totals ................... | 106 | 2268 | 339 | 770 | .440 | 209 | 312 | .670 | 157 | 343 | 500 | 99 | 51 | 137 | 129 | 888 | 4.7 | 0.9 | 8.4 |

Three-point field goals: 1995-96, 0-for-1. 1996-97, 1-for-1 (1.000). 1999-00, 0-for-1. 2001-02, 0-for-1. Totals, 1-for-4 (.250).

Personal fouls/disqualifications: 1990-91, 23/1. 1991-92, 14/0. 1992-93, 15/0. 1994-95, 44/2. 1995-96, 17/1. 1996-97, 30/0. 1997-98, 27/0. 1999-00, 16/0. 2000-01, 37/1. 2001-02, 34/0. 2003-04, 28/0. 2004-05, 13/0. Totals, 298/5.

## CARDINAL, BRIAN  F  GRIZZLIES

**PERSONAL:** Born May 2, 1977, in Tolono, Ill. ... 6-8/245. (2.03/111.1). ... Full name: Brian Lee Cardinal
**HIGH SCHOOL:** Unity (Tolono, Ill.).
**COLLEGE:** Purdue.
**TRANSACTIONS/CAREER NOTES:** Selected by Detroit Pistons in second round (44th pick overall) of 2000 NBA Draft. ... Traded by Pistons with G/F Jerry Stackhouse and C Ratko Varda to Washington Wizards for G/F Richard Hamilton, G/F Bobby Simmons and G Hubert Davis (September 11, 2002). ... Waived by Wizards (March 1, 2003). ... Played in Spain (2002-03). ... Signed as free agent by Memphis Grizzlies (July 14, 2004).

### COLLEGIATE RECORD

| Season Team | G | Min. | FGM | FGA | Pct. | FTM | FTA | Pct. | Reb. | Ast. | Pts. | RPG | APG | PPG |
|---|---|---|---|---|---|---|---|---|---|---|---|---|---|---|
| 95-96—Purdue ........................... | | | | | | Did not play—redshirted. | | | | | | | | |
| 96-97—Purdue ........................... | 30 | 865 | 100 | 220 | .455 | 98 | 139 | .705 | 182 | 58 | 319 | 6.1 | 1.9 | 10.6 |
| 97-98—Purdue ........................... | 36 | 925 | 140 | 275 | .509 | 122 | 155 | .787 | 178 | 66 | 432 | 4.9 | 1.8 | 12.0 |
| 98-99—Purdue ........................... | 34 | 960 | 118 | 246 | .480 | 114 | 147 | .776 | 186 | 82 | 387 | 5.5 | 2.4 | 11.4 |
| 99-00—Purdue ........................... | 32 | 943 | 137 | 333 | .411 | 130 | 169 | .769 | 203 | 71 | 446 | 6.3 | 2.2 | 13.9 |
| Totals ...................................... | 132 | 3693 | 495 | 1074 | .461 | 464 | 610 | .761 | 749 | 277 | 1584 | 5.7 | 2.1 | 12.0 |

Three-point field goals: 1996-97, 21-for-63 (.333). 1997-98, 30-for-70 (.429). 1998-99, 37-for-99 (.374). 1999-00, 42-for-124 (.339). Totals, 130-for-356 (.365).

### NBA REGULAR-SEASON RECORD

| Season Team | G | Min. | FGM | FGA | Pct. | FTM | FTA | Pct. | REBOUNDS Off. | Def. | Tot. | Ast. | St. | Blk. | TO | Pts. | RPG | APG | PPG |
|---|---|---|---|---|---|---|---|---|---|---|---|---|---|---|---|---|---|---|---|
| 00-01—Detroit ........... | 15 | 126 | 10 | 31 | .323 | 11 | 18 | .611 | 8 | 15 | 23 | 3 | 7 | 2 | 9 | 31 | 1.5 | 0.2 | 2.1 |
| 01-02—Detroit ........... | 8 | 43 | 6 | 13 | .462 | 2 | 2 | 1.000 | 2 | 4 | 6 | 2 | 1 | 0 | 0 | 17 | 0.8 | 0.3 | 2.1 |
| 02-03—Washington .... | 5 | 10 | 1 | 4 | .250 | 2 | 2 | 1.000 | 3 | 2 | 5 | 1 | 0 | 0 | 1 | 4 | 1.0 | 0.2 | 0.8 |
| 03-04—Golden State .. | 76 | 1634 | 220 | 466 | .472 | 238 | 271 | .878 | 100 | 217 | 317 | 103 | 66 | 20 | 84 | 733 | 4.2 | 1.4 | 9.6 |
| 04-05—Memphis ........ | 58 | 1433 | 160 | 432 | .370 | 158 | 181 | .873 | 63 | 162 | 225 | 114 | 88 | 19 | 83 | 522 | 3.9 | 2.0 | 9.0 |
| Totals .................... | 162 | 3251 | 397 | 946 | .420 | 411 | 474 | .867 | 176 | 400 | 576 | 223 | 162 | 41 | 177 | 1307 | 3.6 | 1.4 | 8.1 |

Three-point field goals: 2000-01, 0-for-5. 2001-02, 3-for-7 (.429). 2002-03, 0-for-1. 2003-04, 55-for-124 (.444). 2004-05, 44-for-125 (.352). Totals, 102-for-262 (.389).

Personal fouls/disqualifications: 2000-01, 27/0. 2001-02, 5/0. 2003-04, 206/0. 2004-05, 172/3. Totals, 410/3.

### NBA PLAYOFF RECORD

| Season Team | G | Min. | FGM | FGA | Pct. | FTM | FTA | Pct. | REBOUNDS Off. | Def. | Tot. | Ast. | St. | Blk. | TO | Pts. | RPG | APG | PPG |
|---|---|---|---|---|---|---|---|---|---|---|---|---|---|---|---|---|---|---|---|
| 04-05—Memphis ........ | 4 | 78 | 9 | 23 | .391 | 8 | 11 | .727 | 2 | 10 | 12 | 2 | 3 | 0 | 1 | 26 | 3.0 | 0.5 | 6.5 |

Three-point field goals: 2004-05, 0-for-4. Totals, 0-for-4 (.000).

Personal fouls/disqualifications: 2004-05, 11/0. Totals, 11/0.

### SPANISH RECORD

| Season Team | G | Min. | FGM | FGA | Pct. | FTM | FTA | Pct. | Reb. | Ast. | Pts. | RPG | APG | PPG |
|---|---|---|---|---|---|---|---|---|---|---|---|---|---|---|
| 02-03—Pamesa Valencia ............ | 4 | 80 | 8 | 25 | .320 | 2 | 4 | .500 | 16 | 3 | 22 | 4.0 | 0.8 | 5.5 |

Three-point field goals: 2002-03, 4-for-11 (.364). Totals, 4-for-11 (.364).

Personal fouls/disqualifications: 2002-03, 18/0. Totals, 18/0.

## CARLISLE, GENO  G

**PERSONAL:** Born August 13, 1976, in Grand Rapids, Mich. ... 6-3/200. (1.91/90.7). ... Full name: Geno Marcellus Carlisle
**HIGH SCHOOL:** Ottawa Hills (Grand Rapids, Mich.).
**COLLEGE:** Northwestern, then California.
**TRANSACTIONS/CAREER NOTES:** Played in Continental Basketball Association with Rockford Lightning (1999-2000). ... Signed as free agent by Miami Heat (October 1, 2001). ... Waived by Heat (October 9, 2001). ... Signed as free agent by Portland Trail Blazers (November 14, 2004). ... Waived by Trail Blazers (December 16, 2004).

### COLLEGIATE RECORD

| Season Team | G | Min. | FGM | FGA | Pct. | FTM | FTA | Pct. | Reb. | Ast. | Pts. | RPG | APG | PPG |
|---|---|---|---|---|---|---|---|---|---|---|---|---|---|---|
| 94-95—Northwestern ................ | 26 | 769 | 103 | 265 | .389 | 68 | 90 | .756 | 74 | 101 | 304 | 2.8 | 3.9 | 11.7 |
| 95-96—Northwestern ................ | 27 | 951 | 171 | 433 | .395 | 119 | 154 | .773 | 71 | 74 | 536 | 2.6 | 2.7 | 19.9 |
| 96-97—California........................ | | | | | | Did not play—transfer student. | | | | | | | | |
| 97-98—California........................ | 22 | 764 | 129 | 298 | .433 | 85 | 113 | .752 | 67 | 50 | 394 | 3.0 | 2.3 | 17.9 |
| 98-99—California........................ | 33 | 1111 | 171 | 452 | .378 | 143 | 185 | .773 | 81 | 129 | 526 | 2.5 | 3.9 | 15.9 |
| Totals ...................................... | 108 | 3595 | 574 | 1448 | .396 | 415 | 542 | .766 | 293 | 354 | 1760 | 2.7 | 3.3 | 16.3 |

Three-point field goals: 1994-95, 30-for-84 (.357). 1995-96, 75-for-201 (.373). 1997-98, 51-for-149 (.342). 1998-99, 41-for-134 (.306). Totals, 197-for-568 (.347).

Personal fouls/disqualifications: 1994-95, 48/3. 1995-96, 51/0. 1997-98, 33/0. Totals, 132/3.

## CBA RECORD

| Season Team | G | Min. | FGM | FGA | Pct. | FTM | FTA | Pct. | Reb. | Ast. | Pts. | AVERAGES | | |
| | | | | | | | | | | | | RPG | APG | PPG |
|---|---|---|---|---|---|---|---|---|---|---|---|---|---|---|
| 99-00—Rockford | 56 | 1309 | 218 | 503 | .433 | 149 | 177 | .842 | 91 | 141 | 593 | 1.6 | 2.5 | 10.6 |

Three-point field goals: 1999-00, 8-for-46 (.174). Totals, 8-for-46 (.174).
Personal fouls/disqualifications: 1999-00, 102/0. Totals, 102/0.

## AMERICAN BASKETBALL ASSOCIATION RECORD

| Season Team | G | Min. | FGM | FGA | Pct. | FTM | FTA | Pct. | Reb. | Ast. | Pts. | AVERAGES | | |
| | | | | | | | | | | | | RPG | APG | PPG |
|---|---|---|---|---|---|---|---|---|---|---|---|---|---|---|
| 00-01—San Diego | 26 | 869 | 201 | 450 | .447 | 95 | 133 | .714 | 82 | 82 | 593 | 3.2 | 3.2 | 22.8 |
| 03-04—Long Beach | 21 | ... | 152 | 300 | .507 | 55 | 74 | .743 | 60 | 51 | 430 | 2.9 | 2.4 | 20.5 |
| 04-05—Long Beach | 5 | 109 | 18 | 49 | .367 | 8 | 16 | .500 | 9 | 11 | 54 | 1.8 | 2.2 | 10.8 |
| Totals | 52 | ... | 371 | 799 | .464 | 158 | 223 | .709 | 151 | 144 | 1077 | 2.9 | 2.8 | 20.7 |

Three-point field goals: 2000-01, 96-for-222 (.432). 2003-04, 71-for-145 (.490). 2004-05, 10-for-21 (.476). Totals, 177-for-388 (.456).

## ITALIAN LEAGUE RECORD

| Season Team | G | Min. | FGM | FGA | Pct. | FTM | FTA | Pct. | Reb. | Ast. | Pts. | AVERAGES | | |
| | | | | | | | | | | | | RPG | APG | PPG |
|---|---|---|---|---|---|---|---|---|---|---|---|---|---|---|
| 00-01—Varese | 10 | 361 | 81 | 188 | .431 | 39 | 53 | .736 | 18 | 11 | 247 | 1.8 | 1.1 | 24.7 |
| 01-02—De Vizia Avellino | 6 | 210 | 38 | 92 | .413 | 21 | 24 | .875 | 16 | 17 | 106 | 2.7 | 2.8 | 17.7 |
| Totals | 16 | 571 | 119 | 280 | .425 | 60 | 77 | .779 | 34 | 28 | 353 | 2.1 | 1.8 | 22.1 |

Three-point field goals: 2000-01, 46-for-110 (.418). 2001-02, 9-for-29 (.310). Totals, 55-for-139 (.396).

## NBDL RECORD

| Season Team | G | Min. | FGM | FGA | Pct. | FTM | FTA | Pct. | Reb. | Ast. | Pts. | AVERAGES | | |
| | | | | | | | | | | | | RPG | APG | PPG |
|---|---|---|---|---|---|---|---|---|---|---|---|---|---|---|
| 02-03—Mobile | 2 | 53 | 5 | 12 | .417 | 2 | 2 | 1.000 | 5 | 7 | 12 | 2.5 | 3.5 | 6.0 |

Three-point field goals: 2002-03, 0-for-1. Totals, 0-for-1 (.000).

## NBA REGULAR-SEASON RECORD

| Season Team | G | Min. | FGM | FGA | Pct. | FTM | FTA | Pct. | REBOUNDS | | | Ast. | St. | Blk. | TO | Pts. | AVERAGES | | |
| | | | | | | | | | Off. | Def. | Tot. | | | | | | RPG | APG | PPG |
|---|---|---|---|---|---|---|---|---|---|---|---|---|---|---|---|---|---|---|---|
| 04-05—Portland | 6 | 16 | 2 | 3 | .667 | 4 | 6 | .667 | 1 | 0 | 1 | 1 | 0 | 0 | 1 | 8 | 0.2 | 0.2 | 1.3 |

Personal fouls/disqualifications: 2004-05, 1/0. Totals, 1/0.

## CARROLL, MATT — G — BOBCATS

**PERSONAL:** Born August 28, 1980, in Pittsburgh. ... 6-6/212. (1.98/96.2).
**HIGH SCHOOL:** Hatboro-Horsham (Horsham, Pa.).
**COLLEGE:** Notre Dame.
**TRANSACTIONS/CAREER NOTES:** Not drafted by an NBA franchise. ... Signed as free agent by New York Knicks (September 29, 2003). ... Waived by Knicks (October 27, 2003). ... Signed as free agent by Portland Trail Blazers (November 7, 2003). ... Waived by Trail Blazers (January 7, 2004). ... Played in NBDL with Roanoke Dazzle (2004). ... Signed by San Antonio Spurs (March 8, 2004). ... Signed as free agent by Golden State Warriors (October 4, 2004). ... Signed as free agent by Charlotte Bobcats (February 23, 2005).

### COLLEGIATE RECORD

| Season Team | G | Min. | FGM | FGA | Pct. | FTM | FTA | Pct. | Reb. | Ast. | Pts. | AVERAGES | | |
| | | | | | | | | | | | | RPG | APG | PPG |
|---|---|---|---|---|---|---|---|---|---|---|---|---|---|---|
| 99-00—Notre Dame | 37 | 968 | 125 | 310 | .403 | 50 | 65 | .769 | 98 | 78 | 364 | 2.6 | 2.1 | 9.8 |
| 00-01—Notre Dame | 30 | 991 | 128 | 274 | .467 | 51 | 61 | .836 | 150 | 114 | 372 | 5.0 | 3.8 | 12.4 |
| 01-02—Notre Dame | 32 | 1034 | 160 | 341 | .469 | 57 | 69 | .826 | 153 | 67 | 450 | 4.8 | 2.1 | 14.1 |
| 02-03—Notre Dame | 34 | 1154 | 215 | 487 | .441 | 135 | 160 | .844 | 169 | 55 | 664 | 5.0 | 1.6 | 19.5 |
| Totals | 133 | 4147 | 628 | 1412 | .445 | 293 | 355 | .825 | 570 | 314 | 1850 | 4.3 | 2.4 | 13.9 |

Three-point field goals: 1999-00, 64-for-183 (.350). 2000-01, 65-for-159 (.409). 2001-02, 73-for-177 (.412). 2002-03, 99-for-243 (.407). Totals, 301-for-762 (.395).

### NBA REGULAR-SEASON RECORD

| Season Team | G | Min. | FGM | FGA | Pct. | FTM | FTA | Pct. | REBOUNDS | | | Ast. | St. | Blk. | TO | Pts. | AVERAGES | | |
| | | | | | | | | | Off. | Def. | Tot. | | | | | | RPG | APG | PPG |
|---|---|---|---|---|---|---|---|---|---|---|---|---|---|---|---|---|---|---|---|
| 03-04—Portland-S.A. | 16 | 70 | 7 | 16 | .438 | 4 | 6 | .667 | 1 | 5 | 6 | 2 | 1 | 0 | 6 | 19 | 0.4 | 0.1 | 1.2 |
| 04-05—Charlotte | 25 | 430 | 70 | 180 | .389 | 71 | 83 | .855 | 13 | 47 | 60 | 17 | 17 | 2 | 25 | 224 | 2.4 | 0.7 | 9.0 |
| Totals | 41 | 500 | 77 | 196 | .393 | 75 | 89 | .843 | 14 | 52 | 66 | 19 | 18 | 2 | 31 | 243 | 1.6 | 0.5 | 5.9 |

Three-point field goals: 2003-04, 1-for-3 (.333). 2004-05, 13-for-39 (.333). Totals, 14-for-42 (.333).
Personal fouls/disqualifications: 2003-04, 8/0. 2004-05, 37/0. Totals, 45/0.

### NBDL RECORD

| Season Team | G | Min. | FGM | FGA | Pct. | FTM | FTA | Pct. | Reb. | Ast. | Pts. | AVERAGES | | |
| | | | | | | | | | | | | RPG | APG | PPG |
|---|---|---|---|---|---|---|---|---|---|---|---|---|---|---|
| 03-04—Roanoke | 11 | 956 | 62 | 146 | .425 | 35 | 39 | .897 | 31 | 25 | 171 | 2.8 | 2.3 | 15.5 |
| 04-05—Roanoke | 24 | 761 | 177 | 352 | .503 | 106 | 123 | .862 | 67 | 38 | 483 | 2.8 | 1.6 | 20.1 |
| Totals | 35 | 1717 | 239 | 498 | .480 | 141 | 162 | .870 | 98 | 63 | 654 | 2.8 | 1.8 | 18.7 |

Three-point field goals: 2003-04, 12-for-33 (.364). 2004-05, 23-for-38 (.605). Totals, 35-for-71 (.493).

# CARTER, ANTHONY      G      TIMBERWOLVES

**PERSONAL:** Born June 16, 1975, in Atlanta. ... 6-1/190. (1.85/86.2). ... Full name: Anthony Bernard Carter
**HIGH SCHOOL:** Alonzo A. Crim (Atlanta).
**JUNIOR COLLEGE:** Saddleback Community College (Calif.).
**COLLEGE:** Hawaii.
**TRANSACTIONS/CAREER NOTES:** Not drafted by an NBA franchise. ... Played in Continental Basketball Association with Yakima Sun Kings (1998-99). ... Signed as free agent by Miami Heat (August 6, 1999). ... Signed as free agent by San Antonio Spurs (July 30, 2003) ... Signed as free agent by Minnesota Timberwolves (October 4, 2004).

## COLLEGIATE RECORD

| Season Team | G | Min. | FGM | FGA | Pct. | FTM | FTA | Pct. | Reb. | Ast. | Pts. | AVERAGES RPG | APG | PPG |
|---|---|---|---|---|---|---|---|---|---|---|---|---|---|---|
| 94-95—Saddleback C.C. | 33 | ... | 261 | 508 | .514 | 100 | 146 | .685 | 203 | 116 | 641 | 6.2 | 3.5 | 19.4 |
| 95-96—Saddleback C.C. | 33 | ... | 324 | 668 | .485 | 209 | 278 | .752 | 216 | 178 | 889 | 6.5 | 5.4 | 26.9 |
| 96-97—Hawaii | 29 | 1005 | 211 | 426 | .495 | 89 | 138 | .645 | 107 | 191 | 543 | 3.7 | 6.6 | 18.7 |
| 97-98—Hawaii | 29 | 1041 | 191 | 422 | .453 | 111 | 142 | .782 | 152 | 212 | 527 | 5.2 | 7.3 | 18.2 |
| Junior College Totals | 66 | ... | 585 | 1176 | .497 | 309 | 424 | .729 | 419 | 294 | 1530 | 6.3 | 4.5 | 23.2 |
| 4-Year-College Totals | 58 | 2046 | 402 | 848 | .474 | 200 | 280 | .714 | 259 | 403 | 1070 | 4.5 | 6.9 | 18.4 |

Three-point field goals: 1994-95, 19-for-81 (.235). 1995-96, 32-for-110 (.291). 1996-97, 32-for-90 (.356). 1997-98, 34-for-110 (.309). Totals, 117-for-391 (.299).

Personal fouls/disqualifications: 1994-95, 77/0. 1995-96, 82/0. 1996-97, 86/0. 1997-98, 73/0. Totals, 318/0.

## CBA RECORD

| Season Team | G | Min. | FGM | FGA | Pct. | FTM | FTA | Pct. | Reb. | Ast. | Pts. | AVERAGES RPG | APG | PPG |
|---|---|---|---|---|---|---|---|---|---|---|---|---|---|---|
| 98-99—Yakima | 48 | 1202 | 220 | 502 | .438 | 101 | 141 | .716 | 130 | 209 | 555 | 2.7 | 4.4 | 11.6 |

Three-point field goals: 1998-99, 14-for-63 (.222). Totals, 14-for-63 (.222).
Personal fouls/disqualifications: 1998-99, 104/0. Totals, 104/0.

## NBA REGULAR-SEASON RECORD

| Season Team | G | Min. | FGM | FGA | Pct. | FTM | FTA | Pct. | REBOUNDS Off. | Def. | Tot. | Ast. | St. | Blk. | TO | Pts. | AVERAGES RPG | APG | PPG |
|---|---|---|---|---|---|---|---|---|---|---|---|---|---|---|---|---|---|---|---|
| 99-00—Miami | 79 | 1859 | 201 | 509 | .395 | 93 | 124 | .750 | 48 | 151 | 199 | 378 | 93 | 5 | 173 | 498 | 2.5 | 4.8 | 6.3 |
| 00-01—Miami | 72 | 1630 | 195 | 480 | .406 | 65 | 103 | .631 | 46 | 134 | 180 | 268 | 73 | 10 | 119 | 461 | 2.5 | 3.7 | 6.4 |
| 01-02—Miami | 46 | 1050 | 89 | 260 | .342 | 19 | 36 | .528 | 19 | 98 | 117 | 214 | 50 | 3 | 72 | 198 | 2.5 | 4.7 | 4.3 |
| 02-03—Miami | 49 | 912 | 83 | 233 | .356 | 33 | 50 | .660 | 12 | 71 | 83 | 203 | 45 | 5 | 81 | 199 | 1.7 | 4.1 | 4.1 |
| 03-04—San Antonio | 5 | 87 | 11 | 37 | .297 | 0 | 0 | ... | 2 | 9 | 11 | 12 | 4 | 0 | 12 | 22 | 2.2 | 2.4 | 4.4 |
| 04-05—Minnesota | 66 | 742 | 72 | 177 | .407 | 35 | 51 | .686 | 12 | 57 | 69 | 161 | 35 | 18 | 62 | 181 | 1.0 | 2.4 | 2.7 |
| Totals | 317 | 6280 | 651 | 1696 | .384 | 245 | 364 | .673 | 139 | 520 | 659 | 1236 | 300 | 41 | 519 | 1559 | 2.1 | 3.9 | 4.9 |

Three-point field goals: 1999-00, 3-for-23 (.130). 2000-01, 6-for-40 (.150). 2001-02, 1-for-19 (.053). 2002-03, 0-for-8. 2003-04, 0-for-3. 2004-05, 2-for-17 (.118). Totals, 12-for-110 (.109).

Personal fouls/disqualifications: 1999-00, 167/0. 2000-01, 154/1. 2001-02, 85/2. 2002-03, 70/0. 2003-04, 9/0. 2004-05, 88/2. Totals, 573/5.

## NBA PLAYOFF RECORD

| Season Team | G | Min. | FGM | FGA | Pct. | FTM | FTA | Pct. | REBOUNDS Off. | Def. | Tot. | Ast. | St. | Blk. | TO | Pts. | AVERAGES RPG | APG | PPG |
|---|---|---|---|---|---|---|---|---|---|---|---|---|---|---|---|---|---|---|---|
| 99-00—Miami | 10 | 275 | 32 | 77 | .416 | 12 | 16 | .750 | 8 | 32 | 40 | 56 | 12 | 2 | 23 | 77 | 4.0 | 5.6 | 7.7 |
| 00-01—Miami | 3 | 69 | 9 | 19 | .474 | 0 | 0 | ... | 0 | 6 | 6 | 11 | 2 | 1 | 10 | 18 | 2.0 | 3.7 | 6.0 |
| Totals | 13 | 344 | 41 | 96 | .427 | 12 | 16 | .750 | 8 | 38 | 46 | 67 | 14 | 3 | 33 | 95 | 3.5 | 5.2 | 7.3 |

Three-point field goals: 1999-00, 1-for-6 (.167). 2000-01, 0-for-1. Totals, 1-for-7 (.143).
Personal fouls/disqualifications: 1999-00, 22/0. 2000-01, 9/0. Totals, 31/0.

# CARTER, VINCE      G/F      NETS

**PERSONAL:** Born January 26, 1977, in Daytona Beach, Fla. ... 6-6/225. (1.98/102.1). ... Full name: Vincent Lamar Carter
**HIGH SCHOOL:** Daytona Beach (Fla.) Mainland.
**COLLEGE:** North Carolina.
**TRANSACTIONS/CAREER NOTES:** Selected after junior season by Golden State Warriors in first round (fifth pick overall) of 1998 NBA Draft. ... Draft rights traded by Warriors with cash to Toronto Raptors for draft rights to F Antawn Jamison (June 24, 1998). ... Traded by Raptors to New Jersey Nets for C Alonzo Mourning, F Aaron Williams, F Eric Williams and two first-round draft picks ( December 17, 2004).
**MISCELLANEOUS:** Member of gold-medal-winning U.S. Olympic team (2000). ... Toronto Raptors all-time points leader with 6,574 (1998-99 through 2001-02).

## COLLEGIATE RECORD

**NOTES:** The Sporting News All-America second team (1998).

| Season Team | G | Min. | FGM | FGA | Pct. | FTM | FTA | Pct. | Reb. | Ast. | Pts. | AVERAGES RPG | APG | PPG |
|---|---|---|---|---|---|---|---|---|---|---|---|---|---|---|
| 95-96—North Carolina | 31 | 555 | 91 | 185 | .492 | 31 | 45 | .689 | 119 | 40 | 232 | 3.8 | 1.3 | 7.5 |
| 96-97—North Carolina | 34 | 937 | 166 | 316 | .525 | 75 | 100 | .750 | 152 | 83 | 443 | 4.5 | 2.4 | 13.0 |
| 97-98—North Carolina | 38 | 1185 | 224 | 379 | .591 | 100 | 147 | .680 | 195 | 74 | 592 | 5.1 | 1.9 | 15.6 |
| Totals | 103 | 2677 | 481 | 880 | .547 | 206 | 292 | .705 | 466 | 197 | 1267 | 4.5 | 1.9 | 12.3 |

Three-point field goals: 1995-96, 19-for-55 (.345). 1996-97, 38-for-107 (.355). 1997-98, 44-for-107 (.411). Totals, 101-for-269 (.375).

## NBA REGULAR-SEASON RECORD

**HONORS:** NBA Rookie of the Year (1999). ... All-NBA second team (2001). ... All-NBA third team (2000). ... NBA All-Rookie first team (1999). ... Slam Dunk championship winner (2000).

| Season Team | G | Min. | FGM | FGA | Pct. | FTM | FTA | Pct. | Off. | Def. | Tot. | Ast. | St. | Blk. | TO | Pts. | RPG | APG | PPG |
|---|---|---|---|---|---|---|---|---|---|---|---|---|---|---|---|---|---|---|---|
| 98-99—Toronto | 50 | 1760 | 345 | 766 | .450 | 204 | 268 | .761 | 94 | 189 | 283 | 149 | 55 | 77 | 110 | 913 | 5.7 | 3.0 | 18.3 |
| 99-00—Toronto | 82 | 3126 | 788 | 1696 | .465 | 436 | 551 | .791 | 150 | 326 | 476 | 322 | 110 | 92 | 178 | 2107 | 5.8 | 3.9 | 25.7 |
| 00-01—Toronto | 75 | 2979 | 762 | 1656 | .460 | 384 | 502 | .765 | 176 | 240 | 416 | 291 | 114 | 82 | 167 | 2070 | 5.5 | 3.9 | 27.6 |
| 01-02—Toronto | 60 | 2385 | 559 | 1307 | .428 | 245 | 307 | .798 | 138 | 175 | 313 | 239 | 94 | 43 | 154 | 1484 | 5.2 | 4.0 | 24.7 |
| 02-03—Toronto | 43 | 1471 | 355 | 760 | .467 | 129 | 160 | .806 | 59 | 129 | 188 | 143 | 48 | 41 | 74 | 884 | 4.4 | 3.3 | 20.6 |
| 03-04—Toronto | 73 | 2785 | 608 | 1457 | .417 | 336 | 417 | .806 | 95 | 254 | 349 | 348 | 88 | 65 | 223 | 1645 | 4.8 | 4.8 | 22.5 |
| 04-05—Toronto-N.J. | 77 | 2828 | 696 | 1541 | .452 | 367 | 460 | .798 | 106 | 295 | 401 | 327 | 109 | 48 | 168 | 1886 | 5.2 | 4.2 | 24.5 |
| Totals | 460 | 17334 | 4113 | 9183 | .448 | 2101 | 2665 | .788 | 818 | 1608 | 2426 | 1819 | 618 | 448 | 1074 | 10989 | 5.3 | 4.0 | 23.9 |

Three-point field goals: 1998-99, 19-for-66 (.288). 1999-00, 95-for-236 (.403). 2000-01, 162-for-397 (.408). 2001-02, 121-for-313 (.387). 2002-03, 45-for-131 (.344). 2003-04, 93-for-243 (.383). 2004-05, 127-for-313 (.406). Totals, 662-for-1699 (.390).

Personal fouls/disqualifications: 1998-99, 140/2. 1999-00, 263/2. 2000-01, 205/1. 2001-02, 191/4. 2002-03, 121/2. 2003-04, 212/1. 2004-05, 243/3. Totals, 1375/15.

## NBA PLAYOFF RECORD

**NOTES:** Holds single-game record for most three-point field goals made in one half—8 (May 11, 2001, vs. Philadelphia).

| Season Team | G | Min. | FGM | FGA | Pct. | FTM | FTA | Pct. | Off. | Def. | Tot. | Ast. | St. | Blk. | TO | Pts. | RPG | APG | PPG |
|---|---|---|---|---|---|---|---|---|---|---|---|---|---|---|---|---|---|---|---|---|
| 99-00—Toronto | 3 | 119 | 15 | 50 | .300 | 27 | 31 | .871 | 9 | 9 | 18 | 19 | 3 | 4 | 8 | 58 | 6.0 | 6.3 | 19.3 |
| 00-01—Toronto | 12 | 539 | 122 | 280 | .436 | 58 | 74 | .784 | 37 | 41 | 78 | 56 | 20 | 20 | 27 | 327 | 6.5 | 4.7 | 27.3 |
| 04-05—New Jersey | 4 | 179 | 35 | 96 | .365 | 31 | 36 | .861 | 9 | 25 | 34 | 23 | 9 | 0 | 15 | 107 | 8.5 | 5.8 | 26.8 |
| Totals | 19 | 837 | 172 | 426 | .404 | 116 | 141 | .823 | 55 | 75 | 130 | 98 | 32 | 24 | 50 | 492 | 6.8 | 5.2 | 25.9 |

Three-point field goals: 1999-00, 1-for-10 (.100). 2000-01, 25-for-61 (.410). 2004-05, 6-for-19 (.316). Totals, 32-for-90 (.356).
Personal fouls/disqualifications: 1999-00, 12/0. 2000-01, 45/1. 2004-05, 17/0. Totals, 74/1.

## NBA ALL-STAR GAME RECORD

| Season Team | Min. | FGM | FGA | Pct. | FTM | FTA | Pct. | Off. | Def. | Tot. | Ast. | PF | Dq. | St. | Blk. | TO | Pts. |
|---|---|---|---|---|---|---|---|---|---|---|---|---|---|---|---|---|---|
| 2000—Toronto | 28 | 6 | 11 | .545 | 0 | 0 | ... | 2 | 2 | 4 | 2 | 0 | 0 | 2 | 0 | 2 | 12 |
| 2001—Toronto | 24 | 7 | 18 | .389 | 1 | 1 | 1.000 | 1 | 2 | 3 | 4 | 1 | 0 | 1 | 1 | 3 | 16 |
| 2002—Toronto | | | | | | | Selected, did not play—injured. | | | | | | | | | | |
| 2003—Toronto | 25 | 4 | 9 | .444 | 0 | 0 | ... | 1 | 0 | 1 | 2 | 1 | 0 | 0 | 0 | 1 | 9 |
| 2004—Toronto | 16 | 5 | 7 | .714 | 0 | 0 | ... | 1 | 1 | 2 | 0 | 1 | 0 | 2 | 0 | 2 | 11 |
| 2005—New Jersey | 18 | 4 | 8 | .500 | 0 | 0 | ... | 0 | 3 | 3 | 1 | 0 | 0 | 0 | 0 | 2 | 11 |
| Totals | 111 | 26 | 53 | .491 | 1 | 1 | 1.000 | 5 | 8 | 13 | 9 | 3 | 0 | 5 | 1 | 10 | 59 |

Three-point field goals: 2000, 0-for-2. 2001, 1-for-4 (.250). 2003, 1-for-1 (1.000). 2004, 1-for-3 (.333). 2005, 3-for-5 (.600). Totals, 6-for-15 (.400).

**C**

# CASSELL, SAM     G     CLIPPERS

**PERSONAL:** Born November 18, 1969, in Baltimore. ... 6-3/185. (1.91/83.9). ... Full name: Samuel James Cassell ... Name pronounced KUH-sell.
**HIGH SCHOOL:** Dunbar (Baltimore).
**JUNIOR COLLEGE:** San Jacinto College (Texas).
**COLLEGE:** Florida State.
**TRANSACTIONS/CAREER NOTES:** Selected by Houston Rockets in first round (24th pick overall) of 1993 NBA Draft. ... Traded by Rockets with F Chucky Brown, F Robert Horry and F Mark Bryant to Phoenix Suns for F Charles Barkley and 1999 second-round draft choice (August 19, 1996). ... Traded by Suns with F A.C. Green, F Michael Finley and 1997 or 1998 conditional second-round draft choice to Dallas Mavericks for G Jason Kidd, F Tony Dumas and C Loren Meyer (December 26, 1996). ... Traded by Mavericks with C Eric Montross, G Jim Jackson, F/C Chris Gatling and F/G George McCloud to New Jersey Nets for C Shawn Bradley, F Ed O'Bannon, G Khalid Reeves and G Robert Pack (February 17, 1997). ... Traded by Nets with F Chris Gatling to Milwaukee Bucks in three-way deal in which Bucks also received C Paul Grant from Minnesota Timberwolves, Timberwolves received F Brian Evans, 1999 first-round draft choice and an undisclosed draft choice from Nets, Bucks sent G Terrell Brandon to Timberwolves and Timberwolves sent G Stephon Marbury, G Chris Carr and F Bill Curley to Nets and Nets received G Elliot Perry from Bucks (March 11, 1999). ... Traded by Bucks with C Ervin Johnson to Minnesota Timberwolves for F Joe Smith and G Anthony Peeler (June 27, 2003). ... Traded by Timberwolves with first-round draft choice to Los Angeles Clippers for G Marko Jaric and G Lionel Chalmers (August 12, 2005).
**MISCELLANEOUS:** Member of NBA championship team (1994, 1995).

### COLLEGIATE RECORD

| Season Team | G | Min. | FGM | FGA | Pct. | FTM | FTA | Pct. | Reb. | Ast. | Pts. | RPG | APG | PPG |
|---|---|---|---|---|---|---|---|---|---|---|---|---|---|---|
| 89-90—San Jacinto College | 38 | 1061 | 296 | 597 | .496 | 136 | 170 | .800 | 208 | 200 | 810 | 5.5 | 5.3 | 21.3 |
| 90-91—San Jacinto College | 31 | 864 | 233 | 471 | .495 | 198 | 246 | .805 | 157 | 237 | 727 | 5.1 | 7.6 | 23.5 |
| 91-92—Florida State | 31 | 1046 | 206 | 454 | .454 | 100 | 142 | .704 | 141 | 119 | 570 | 4.5 | 3.8 | 18.4 |
| 92-93—Florida State | 35 | 1298 | 234 | 466 | .502 | 123 | 162 | .759 | 152 | 170 | 641 | 4.3 | 4.9 | 18.3 |
| Junior College Totals | 69 | 1925 | 529 | 1068 | .495 | 334 | 416 | .803 | 365 | 437 | 1537 | 5.3 | 6.3 | 22.3 |
| 4-Year-College Totals | 66 | 2344 | 440 | 920 | .478 | 223 | 304 | .734 | 293 | 289 | 1211 | 4.4 | 4.4 | 18.3 |

Three-point field goals: 1989-90, 82-for-184 (.446). 1990-91, 63-for-160 (.394). 1991-92, 58-for-164 (.354). 1992-93, 50-for-131 (.382). Totals, 253-for-639 (.396).

### NBA REGULAR-SEASON RECORD

**HONORS:** All-NBA second team (2004).

| Season Team | G | Min. | FGM | FGA | Pct. | FTM | FTA | Pct. | Off. | Def. | Tot. | Ast. | St. | Blk. | TO | Pts. | RPG | APG | PPG |
|---|---|---|---|---|---|---|---|---|---|---|---|---|---|---|---|---|---|---|---|---|
| 93-94—Houston | 66 | 1122 | 162 | 388 | .418 | 90 | 107 | .841 | 25 | 109 | 134 | 192 | 59 | 7 | 94 | 440 | 2.0 | 2.9 | 6.7 |
| 94-95—Houston | 82 | 1882 | 253 | 593 | .427 | 214 | 254 | .843 | 38 | 173 | 211 | 405 | 94 | 14 | 167 | 783 | 2.6 | 4.9 | 9.5 |
| 95-96—Houston | 61 | 1682 | 289 | 658 | .439 | 235 | 285 | .825 | 51 | 137 | 188 | 278 | 53 | 4 | 157 | 886 | 3.1 | 4.6 | 14.5 |
| 96-97—Pho.-Dal.-N.J. | 61 | 1714 | 337 | 783 | .430 | 212 | 251 | .845 | 47 | 135 | 182 | 305 | 77 | 19 | 168 | 967 | 3.0 | 5.0 | 15.9 |
| 97-98—New Jersey | 75 | 2606 | 510 | 1156 | .441 | 436 | 507 | .860 | 73 | 155 | 228 | 603 | 121 | 20 | 269 | 1471 | 3.0 | 8.0 | 19.6 |
| 98-99—N.J.-Mil. | 8 | 199 | 39 | 93 | .419 | 47 | 50 | .940 | 5 | 10 | 15 | 36 | 9 | 0 | 20 | 127 | 1.9 | 4.5 | 15.9 |
| 99-00—Milwaukee | 81 | 2899 | 545 | 1170 | .466 | 390 | 445 | .876 | 69 | 232 | 301 | 729 | 102 | 8 | 267 | 1506 | 3.7 | 9.0 | 18.6 |
| 00-01—Milwaukee | 76 | 2709 | 537 | 1132 | .474 | 277 | 323 | .858 | 46 | 244 | 290 | 580 | 88 | 8 | 220 | 1381 | 3.8 | 7.6 | 18.2 |
| 01-02—Milwaukee | 74 | 2605 | 554 | 1197 | .463 | 282 | 328 | .860 | 54 | 258 | 312 | 493 | 90 | 12 | 177 | 1461 | 4.2 | 6.7 | 19.7 |

| Season Team | G | Min. | FGM | FGA | Pct. | FTM | FTA | Pct. | REBOUNDS Off. | Def. | Tot. | Ast. | St. | Blk. | TO | Pts. | AVERAGES RPG | APG | PPG |
|---|---|---|---|---|---|---|---|---|---|---|---|---|---|---|---|---|---|---|---|
| 02-03—Milwaukee ...... | 78 | 2700 | 546 | 1162 | .470 | 385 | 447 | .861 | 57 | 285 | 342 | 450 | 88 | 14 | 177 | 1536 | 4.4 | 5.8 | 19.7 |
| 03-04—Minnesota...... | 81 | 2838 | 620 | 1270 | .488 | 289 | 331 | .873 | 44 | 227 | 271 | 592 | 102 | 18 | 220 | 1603 | 3.3 | 7.3 | 19.8 |
| 04-05—Minnesota...... | 59 | 1522 | 319 | 687 | .464 | 134 | 155 | .865 | 25 | 132 | 157 | 301 | 36 | 14 | 109 | 799 | 2.7 | 5.1 | 13.5 |
| Totals .................. | 802 | 24478 | 4711 | 10289 | .458 | 2991 | 3483 | .859 | 534 | 2097 | 2631 | 4964 | 919 | 138 | 2045 | 12960 | 3.3 | 6.2 | 16.2 |

Three-point field goals: 1993-94, 26-for-88 (.295). 1994-95, 63-for-191 (.330). 1995-96, 73-for-210 (.348). 1996-97, 81-for-231 (.351). 1997-98, 15-for-80 (.188). 1998-99, 2-for-10 (.200). 1999-00, 26-for-90 (.289). 2000-01, 30-for-98 (.306). 2001-02, 71-for-204 (.348). 2002-03, 59-for-163 (.362). 2003-04, 74-for-186 (.398). 2004-05, 27-for-103 (.262). Totals, 547-for-1654 (.331).

Personal fouls/disqualifications: 1993-94, 136/1. 1994-95, 209/3. 1995-96, 166/2. 1996-97, 200/9. 1997-98, 262/5. 1998-99, 22/1. 1999-00, 255/5. 2000-01, 214/5. 2001-02, 208/3. 2002-03, 216/1. 2003-04, 247/2. 2004-05, 160/2. Totals, 2295/39.

### NBA PLAYOFF RECORD

| Season Team | G | Min. | FGM | FGA | Pct. | FTM | FTA | Pct. | REBOUNDS Off. | Def. | Tot. | Ast. | St. | Blk. | TO | Pts. | AVERAGES RPG | APG | PPG |
|---|---|---|---|---|---|---|---|---|---|---|---|---|---|---|---|---|---|---|---|
| 93-94—Houston......... | 22 | 478 | 63 | 160 | .394 | 64 | 74 | .865 | 19 | 40 | 59 | 93 | 21 | 5 | 47 | 207 | 2.7 | 4.2 | 9.4 |
| 94-95—Houston......... | 22 | 485 | 74 | 169 | .438 | 71 | 85 | .835 | 8 | 34 | 42 | 89 | 21 | 2 | 33 | 243 | 1.9 | 4.0 | 11.0 |
| 95-96—Houston ...... | 8 | 206 | 26 | 81 | .321 | 23 | 29 | .793 | 1 | 16 | 17 | 34 | 6 | 1 | 18 | 83 | 2.1 | 4.3 | 10.4 |
| 97-98—New Jersey ..... | 3 | 26 | 3 | 9 | .333 | 0 | 0 | ... | 1 | 2 | 3 | 5 | 0 | 1 | 2 | 6 | 1.0 | 1.7 | 2.0 |
| 98-99—Milwaukee ....... | 3 | 102 | 16 | 32 | .500 | 14 | 16 | .875 | 0 | 6 | 6 | 26 | 3 | 0 | 7 | 46 | 2.0 | 8.7 | 15.3 |
| 99-00—Milwaukee ....... | 5 | 178 | 30 | 72 | .417 | 18 | 21 | .857 | 0 | 17 | 17 | 45 | 4 | 0 | 9 | 79 | 3.4 | 9.0 | 15.8 |
| 00-01—Milwaukee ....... | 18 | 682 | 110 | 278 | .396 | 84 | 97 | .866 | 12 | 71 | 83 | 120 | 19 | 3 | 52 | 314 | 4.6 | 6.7 | 17.4 |
| 02-03—Milwaukee ....... | 6 | 217 | 39 | 83 | .470 | 14 | 15 | .933 | 3 | 16 | 19 | 16 | 3 | 1 | 17 | 103 | 3.2 | 2.7 | 17.2 |
| 03-04—Minnesota ...... | 16 | 497 | 94 | 202 | .465 | 52 | 61 | .852 | 3 | 37 | 40 | 70 | 12 | 3 | 43 | 265 | 2.5 | 4.4 | 16.6 |
| Totals ................... | 103 | 2871 | 455 | 1086 | .419 | 340 | 398 | .854 | 47 | 239 | 286 | 498 | 89 | 16 | 228 | 1346 | 2.8 | 4.8 | 13.1 |

Three-point field goals: 1993-94, 17-for-45 (.378). 1994-95, 24-for-60 (.400). 1995-96, 8-for-29 (.276). 1998-99, 0-for-1. 1999-00, 1-for-5 (.200). 2000-01, 10-for-30 (.333). 2002-03, 11-for-21 (.524). 2003-04, 25-for-60 (.417). Totals, 96-for-251 (.382).

Personal fouls/disqualifications: 1993-94, 62/1. 1994-95, 66/1. 1995-96, 20/0. 1997-98, 7/0. 1998-99, 14/1. 1999-00, 19/1. 2000-01, 76/2. 2002-03, 20/0. 2003-04, 53/2. Totals, 337/8.

### NBA ALL-STAR GAME RECORD

| Season Team | Min. | FGM | FGA | Pct. | FTM | FTA | Pct. | REBOUNDS Off. | Def. | Tot. | Ast. | PF | Dq. | St. | Blk. | TO | Pts. |
|---|---|---|---|---|---|---|---|---|---|---|---|---|---|---|---|---|---|
| 2004—Minnesota ............. | 13 | 2 | 3 | .667 | 0 | 0 | ... | 0 | 1 | 1 | 7 | 0 | 0 | 1 | 0 | 1 | 4 |

## CATO, KELVIN      C      MAGIC

**PERSONAL:** Born August 26, 1974, in Atlanta. ... 6-11/275. (2.11/124.7). ... Full name: Kelvin T. Cato
**HIGH SCHOOL:** Lithonia (Decatur, Ga.).
**COLLEGE:** South Alabama, then Iowa State.
**TRANSACTIONS/CAREER NOTES:** Selected by Dallas Mavericks in first round (15th pick overall) of 1997 NBA Draft. ... Draft rights traded by Mavericks to Portland Trail Blazers for draft rights to C Chris Anstey and cash (June 25, 1997). ... Traded by Trail Blazers with F Stacy Augmon, G/F Walt Williams, G Brian Shaw, G Ed Gray and F/C Carlos Rogers to Houston Rockets for F Scottie Pippen (October 2, 1999). ... Traded by Rockets with G Steve Francis and G Cuttino Mobley to Orlando Magic for G Tracy McGrady, F Juwan Howard, G Tyronn Lue and G Reece Gaines (June 29, 2004).

### COLLEGIATE RECORD

| Season Team | G | Min. | FGM | FGA | Pct. | FTM | FTA | Pct. | Reb. | Ast. | Pts. | AVERAGES RPG | APG | PPG |
|---|---|---|---|---|---|---|---|---|---|---|---|---|---|---|
| 92-93—South Alabama.............. | | | | | | Did not play—ineligible. | | | | | | | | |
| 93-94—South Alabama.............. | 24 | 433 | 49 | 123 | .398 | 45 | 79 | .570 | 138 | 17 | 143 | 5.8 | 0.7 | 6.0 |
| 94-95—Iowa State ...................... | | | | | | Did not play—transfer student. | | | | | | | | |
| 95-96—Iowa State ...................... | 27 | 697 | 94 | 187 | .503 | 71 | 111 | .640 | 209 | 17 | 259 | 7.7 | 0.6 | 9.6 |
| 96-97—Iowa State ...................... | 28 | 801 | 128 | 234 | .547 | 61 | 113 | .540 | 235 | 15 | 317 | 8.4 | 0.5 | 11.3 |
| Totals ....................................... | 79 | 1931 | 271 | 544 | .498 | 177 | 303 | .584 | 582 | 49 | 719 | 7.4 | 0.6 | 9.1 |

Three-point field goals: 1996-97, 0-for-1. Totals, 0-for-1 (.000).
Personal fouls/disqualifications: 1993-94, 60/0. 1995-96, 87/4. Totals, 147/4.

### NBA REGULAR-SEASON RECORD

| Season Team | G | Min. | FGM | FGA | Pct. | FTM | FTA | Pct. | REBOUNDS Off. | Def. | Tot. | Ast. | St. | Blk. | TO | Pts. | AVERAGES RPG | APG | PPG |
|---|---|---|---|---|---|---|---|---|---|---|---|---|---|---|---|---|---|---|---|
| 97-98—Portland......... | 74 | 1007 | 98 | 229 | .428 | 86 | 125 | .688 | 91 | 161 | 252 | 23 | 29 | 94 | 44 | 282 | 3.4 | 0.3 | 3.8 |
| 98-99—Portland......... | 43 | 545 | 58 | 129 | .450 | 34 | 67 | .507 | 49 | 101 | 150 | 19 | 23 | 56 | 27 | 151 | 3.5 | 0.4 | 3.5 |
| 99-00—Houston......... | 65 | 1581 | 216 | 402 | .537 | 135 | 208 | .649 | 102 | 287 | 389 | 26 | 33 | 124 | 71 | 567 | 6.0 | 0.4 | 8.7 |
| 00-01—Houston......... | 35 | 624 | 64 | 111 | .577 | 37 | 57 | .649 | 47 | 94 | 141 | 11 | 13 | 31 | 25 | 165 | 4.0 | 0.3 | 4.7 |
| 01-02—Houston......... | 75 | 1917 | 190 | 326 | .583 | 113 | 194 | .582 | 176 | 349 | 525 | 29 | 40 | 95 | 53 | 493 | 7.0 | 0.4 | 6.6 |
| 02-03—Houston......... | 73 | 1247 | 133 | 256 | .520 | 66 | 124 | .532 | 132 | 296 | 428 | 20 | 38 | 85 | 56 | 332 | 5.9 | 0.3 | 4.5 |
| 03-04—Houston......... | 69 | 1743 | 161 | 360 | .447 | 96 | 142 | .676 | 153 | 319 | 472 | 72 | 52 | 96 | 84 | 418 | 6.8 | 1.0 | 6.1 |
| 04-05—Orlando.......... | 62 | 1525 | 160 | 297 | .539 | 112 | 143 | .783 | 102 | 314 | 416 | 40 | 55 | 82 | 64 | 432 | 6.7 | 0.6 | 7.0 |
| Totals ................... | 496 | 10189 | 1080 | 2110 | .512 | 679 | 1060 | .641 | 852 | 1921 | 2773 | 240 | 283 | 663 | 424 | 2840 | 5.6 | 0.5 | 5.7 |

Three-point field goals: 1997-98, 0-for-3. 1998-99, 1-for-1 (1.000). 1999-00, 0-for-4. 2001-02, 0-for-1. 2002-03, 0-for-4. Totals, 1-for-13 (.077).
Personal fouls/disqualifications: 1997-98, 164/3. 1998-99, 100/3. 1999-00, 175/1. 2000-01, 89/1. 2001-02, 208/5. 2002-03, 176/0. 2003-04, 203/0. 2004-05, 170/1. Totals, 1285/14.

### NBA PLAYOFF RECORD

| Season Team | G | Min. | FGM | FGA | Pct. | FTM | FTA | Pct. | REBOUNDS Off. | Def. | Tot. | Ast. | St. | Blk. | TO | Pts. | AVERAGES RPG | APG | PPG |
|---|---|---|---|---|---|---|---|---|---|---|---|---|---|---|---|---|---|---|---|
| 97-98—Portland......... | 4 | 58 | 9 | 17 | .529 | 8 | 11 | .727 | 3 | 9 | 12 | 1 | 1 | 7 | 4 | 26 | 3.0 | 0.3 | 6.5 |
| 98-99—Portland......... | 8 | 43 | 1 | 9 | .111 | 4 | 10 | .400 | 6 | 1 | 7 | 2 | 1 | 1 | 2 | 6 | 0.9 | 0.3 | 0.8 |
| 03-04—Houston......... | 5 | 148 | 13 | 22 | .591 | 3 | 7 | .429 | 14 | 20 | 34 | 2 | 5 | 4 | 5 | 29 | 6.8 | 0.4 | 5.8 |
| Totals ................. | 17 | 249 | 23 | 48 | .479 | 15 | 28 | .536 | 23 | 30 | 53 | 5 | 7 | 12 | 11 | 61 | 3.1 | 0.3 | 3.6 |

Three-point field goals: 1997-98, 0-for-1. Totals, 0-for-1 (.000).
Personal fouls/disqualifications: 1997-98, 12/0. 1998-99, 13/0. 2003-04, 18/1. Totals, 43/1.

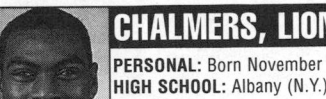

## CHALMERS, LIONEL — G — TIMBERWOLVES

**PERSONAL:** Born November 10, 1980, in Albany, N.Y. ... 6-0/180. (1.83/81.6).
**HIGH SCHOOL:** Albany (N.Y.).
**COLLEGE:** Xavier.
**TRANSACTIONS/CAREER NOTES:** Selected by Los Angeles Clippers in second round (33rd pick overall) of 2004 NBA Draft. ... Traded by Clippers with G Marko Jaric for G Sam Cassell and a first-round draft choice to Minnesota Timberwolves (August 12, 2005).

### COLLEGIATE RECORD

| Season Team | G | Min. | FGM | FGA | Pct. | FTM | FTA | Pct. | Reb. | Ast. | Pts. | RPG | APG | PPG |
|---|---|---|---|---|---|---|---|---|---|---|---|---|---|---|
| 00-01—Xavier | 29 | 735 | 85 | 233 | .365 | 51 | 76 | .671 | 63 | 55 | 259 | 2.2 | 1.9 | 8.9 |
| 01-02—Xavier | 32 | 1090 | 125 | 297 | .421 | 87 | 121 | .719 | 109 | 134 | 384 | 3.4 | 4.2 | 12.0 |
| 02-03—Xavier | 25 | 779 | 98 | 221 | .443 | 54 | 70 | .771 | 67 | 99 | 299 | 2.7 | 4.0 | 12.0 |
| 03-04—Xavier | 37 | 1293 | 204 | 454 | .449 | 105 | 148 | .709 | 122 | 117 | 614 | 3.3 | 3.2 | 16.6 |
| Totals | 123 | 3897 | 512 | 1205 | .425 | 297 | 415 | .716 | 361 | 405 | 1556 | 2.9 | 3.3 | 12.7 |

Three-point field goals: 2000-01, 38-for-126 (.302). 2001-02, 47-for-134 (.351). 2002-03, 49-for-125 (.392). 2003-04, 101-for-247 (.409). Totals, 235-for-632 (.372).

### NBA REGULAR-SEASON RECORD

| Season Team | G | Min. | FGM | FGA | Pct. | FTM | FTA | Pct. | Off. | Def. | Tot. | Ast. | St. | Blk. | TO | Pts. | RPG | APG | PPG |
|---|---|---|---|---|---|---|---|---|---|---|---|---|---|---|---|---|---|---|---|
| 04-05—L.A. Clippers | 36 | 433 | 42 | 125 | .336 | 15 | 24 | .625 | 4 | 27 | 31 | 51 | 13 | 0 | 24 | 111 | 0.9 | 1.4 | 3.1 |

Three-point field goals: 2004-05, 12-for-49 (.245). Totals, 12-for-49 (.245).
Personal fouls/disqualifications: 2004-05, 30/0. Totals, 30/0.

## CHANDLER, TYSON — F — BULLS

**PERSONAL:** Born October 2, 1982, in Hanford, Calif. ... 7-1/235. (2.16/106.6). ... Full name: Tyson Cleotis Chandler
**HIGH SCHOOL:** Dominguez (Compton, Calif.).
**COLLEGE:** Did not attend college.
**TRANSACTIONS/CAREER NOTES:** Selected out of high school by Los Angeles Clippers in first round (second pick overall) of 2001 NBA Draft. ... Draft rights traded by Clippers with F Brian Skinner to Chicago Bulls for F Elton Brand (June 27, 2001).

### NBA REGULAR-SEASON RECORD

| Season Team | G | Min. | FGM | FGA | Pct. | FTM | FTA | Pct. | Off. | Def. | Tot. | Ast. | St. | Blk. | TO | Pts. | RPG | APG | PPG |
|---|---|---|---|---|---|---|---|---|---|---|---|---|---|---|---|---|---|---|---|
| 01-02—Chicago | 71 | 1389 | 151 | 304 | .497 | 134 | 222 | .604 | 114 | 229 | 343 | 54 | 28 | 93 | 99 | 436 | 4.8 | 0.8 | 6.1 |
| 02-03—Chicago | 75 | 1827 | 257 | 484 | .531 | 177 | 291 | .608 | 169 | 345 | 514 | 76 | 37 | 106 | 135 | 691 | 6.9 | 1.0 | 9.2 |
| 03-04—Chicago | 35 | 782 | 67 | 158 | .424 | 79 | 118 | .669 | 82 | 188 | 270 | 23 | 17 | 43 | 38 | 213 | 7.7 | 0.7 | 6.1 |
| 04-05—Chicago | 80 | 2189 | 207 | 419 | .494 | 226 | 336 | .673 | 261 | 514 | 775 | 65 | 69 | 141 | 118 | 640 | 9.7 | 0.8 | 8.0 |
| Totals | 261 | 6187 | 682 | 1365 | .500 | 616 | 967 | .637 | 626 | 1276 | 1902 | 218 | 151 | 383 | 390 | 1980 | 7.3 | 0.8 | 7.6 |

Three-point field goals: 2003-04, 0-for-1. 2004-05, 0-for-2. Totals, 0-for-3 (.000).
Personal fouls/disqualifications: 2001-02, 179/1. 2002-03, 220/3. 2003-04, 87/2. 2004-05, 268/4. Totals, 754/10.

### NBA PLAYOFF RECORD

| Season Team | G | Min. | FGM | FGA | Pct. | FTM | FTA | Pct. | Off. | Def. | Tot. | Ast. | St. | Blk. | TO | Pts. | RPG | APG | PPG |
|---|---|---|---|---|---|---|---|---|---|---|---|---|---|---|---|---|---|---|---|
| 04-05—Chicago | 6 | 172 | 19 | 40 | .475 | 32 | 46 | .696 | 29 | 29 | 58 | 8 | 1 | 13 | 8 | 70 | 9.7 | 1.3 | 11.7 |

Personal fouls/disqualifications: 2004-05, 27/2. Totals, 27/2.

## CHEANEY, CALBERT — G/F — WARRIORS

**PERSONAL:** Born July 17, 1971, in Evansville, Ind. ... 6-7/217. (2.01/98.4). ... Full name: Calbert N. Cheaney ... Name pronounced CHAIN-ee.
**HIGH SCHOOL:** Harrison (Evansville, Ind.).
**COLLEGE:** Indiana.
**TRANSACTIONS/CAREER NOTES:** Selected by Washington Bullets in first round (sixth pick overall) of 1993 NBA Draft. ... Bullets franchise renamed Washington Wizards for 1997-98 season. ... Signed as free agent by Boston Celtics (August 5, 1999). ... Traded by Celtics with G Robert Pack to Denver Nuggets for G Chris Herren and G Bryant Stith (October 16, 2000). ... Signed as free agent by Utah Jazz (July 25, 2002). ... Signed as free agent by Golden State Warriors (August 27, 2003).

### COLLEGIATE RECORD

**NOTES:** THE SPORTING NEWS College Player of the Year (1993). ... Naismith Award winner (1993). ... Wooden Award winner (1993). ... THE SPORTING NEWS All-America first team (1993). ... THE SPORTING NEWS All-America third team (1991).

| Season Team | G | Min. | FGM | FGA | Pct. | FTM | FTA | Pct. | Reb. | Ast. | Pts. | RPG | APG | PPG |
|---|---|---|---|---|---|---|---|---|---|---|---|---|---|---|
| 89-90—Indiana | 29 | 928 | 199 | 348 | .572 | 72 | 96 | .750 | 133 | 48 | 495 | 4.6 | 1.7 | 17.1 |
| 90-91—Indiana | 34 | 1029 | 289 | 485 | .596 | 113 | 141 | .801 | 188 | 47 | 734 | 5.5 | 1.4 | 21.6 |
| 91-92—Indiana | 34 | 991 | 227 | 435 | .522 | 112 | 140 | .800 | 166 | 48 | 599 | 4.9 | 1.4 | 17.6 |
| 92-93—Indiana | 35 | 1181 | 303 | 552 | .549 | 132 | 166 | .795 | 223 | 84 | 785 | 6.4 | 2.4 | 22.4 |
| Totals | 132 | 4129 | 1018 | 1820 | .559 | 429 | 543 | .790 | 710 | 227 | 2613 | 5.4 | 1.7 | 19.8 |

Three-point field goals: 1989-90, 25-for-51 (.490). 1990-91, 43-for-91 (.473). 1991-92, 33-for-86 (.384). 1992-93, 47-for-110 (.427). Totals, 148-for-338 (.438).

**C**

## NBA REGULAR-SEASON RECORD

| Season Team | G | Min. | FGM | FGA | Pct. | FTM | FTA | Pct. | REBOUNDS Off. | Def. | Tot. | Ast. | St. | Blk. | TO | Pts. | RPG | APG | PPG |
|---|---|---|---|---|---|---|---|---|---|---|---|---|---|---|---|---|---|---|---|
| 93-94—Washington .... | 65 | 1604 | 327 | 696 | .470 | 124 | 161 | .770 | 88 | 102 | 190 | 126 | 63 | 10 | 108 | 779 | 2.9 | 1.9 | 12.0 |
| 94-95—Washington .... | 78 | 2651 | 512 | 1129 | .453 | 173 | 213 | .812 | 105 | 216 | 321 | 177 | 80 | 21 | 151 | 1293 | 4.1 | 2.3 | 16.6 |
| 95-96—Washington .... | 70 | 2324 | 426 | 905 | .471 | 151 | 214 | .706 | 67 | 172 | 239 | 154 | 67 | 18 | 129 | 1055 | 3.4 | 2.2 | 15.1 |
| 96-97—Washington .... | 79 | 2411 | 369 | 730 | .505 | 95 | 137 | .693 | 70 | 198 | 268 | 114 | 77 | 18 | 94 | 837 | 3.4 | 1.4 | 10.6 |
| 97-98—Washington .... | 82 | 2841 | 448 | 981 | .457 | 139 | 215 | .647 | 82 | 242 | 324 | 173 | 96 | 36 | 104 | 1050 | 4.0 | 2.1 | 12.8 |
| 98-99—Washington .... | 50 | 1266 | 172 | 415 | .414 | 33 | 67 | .493 | 33 | 108 | 141 | 73 | 39 | 16 | 42 | 385 | 2.8 | 1.5 | 7.7 |
| 99-00—Boston .......... | 67 | 1309 | 120 | 273 | .440 | 9 | 21 | .429 | 23 | 115 | 138 | 80 | 44 | 14 | 46 | 267 | 2.1 | 1.2 | 4.0 |
| 00-01—Denver .......... | 9 | 153 | 10 | 30 | .333 | 1 | 2 | .500 | 5 | 15 | 20 | 9 | 4 | 2 | 5 | 21 | 2.2 | 1.0 | 2.3 |
| 01-02—Denver .......... | 68 | 1631 | 224 | 466 | .481 | 46 | 67 | .687 | 57 | 183 | 240 | 110 | 34 | 21 | 70 | 494 | 3.5 | 1.6 | 7.3 |
| 02-03—Utah ............... | 81 | 2351 | 325 | 651 | .499 | 40 | 69 | .580 | 73 | 211 | 284 | 163 | 65 | 13 | 108 | 700 | 3.5 | 2.0 | 8.6 |
| 03-04—Golden State ... | 79 | 2067 | 278 | 578 | .481 | 47 | 77 | .610 | 77 | 183 | 260 | 136 | 60 | 12 | 85 | 603 | 3.3 | 1.7 | 7.6 |
| 04-05—Golden State ... | 55 | 951 | 113 | 265 | .426 | 24 | 37 | .649 | 32 | 92 | 124 | 64 | 17 | 15 | 35 | 250 | 2.3 | 1.2 | 4.5 |
| Totals ................... | 783 | 21559 | 3324 | 7119 | .467 | 882 | 1280 | .689 | 712 | 1837 | 2549 | 1379 | 646 | 196 | 977 | 7734 | 3.3 | 1.8 | 9.9 |

Three-point field goals: 1993-94, 1-for-23 (.043). 1994-95, 96-for-283 (.339). 1995-96, 52-for-154 (.338). 1996-97, 4-for-30 (.133). 1997-98, 15-for-53 (.283). 1998-99, 8-for-37 (.216). 1999-00, 18-for-54 (.333). 2001-02, 0-for-4. 2002-03, 10-for-25 (.400). 2003-04, 0-for-10. 2004-05, 0-for-3. Totals, 204-for-676 (.302).

Personal fouls/disqualifications: 1993-94, 148/0. 1994-95, 215/0. 1995-96, 205/1. 1996-97, 226/3. 1997-98, 264/4. 1998-99, 146/0. 1999-00, 158/3. 2000-01, 14/0. 2001-02, 156/1. 2002-03, 225/1. 2003-04, 184/1. 2004-05, 95/0. Totals, 2036/14.

## NBA PLAYOFF RECORD

| Season Team | G | Min. | FGM | FGA | Pct. | FTM | FTA | Pct. | REBOUNDS Off. | Def. | Tot. | Ast. | St. | Blk. | TO | Pts. | RPG | APG | PPG |
|---|---|---|---|---|---|---|---|---|---|---|---|---|---|---|---|---|---|---|---|
| 96-97—Washington .... | 3 | 120 | 18 | 41 | .439 | 9 | 12 | .750 | 6 | 5 | 11 | 4 | 3 | 2 | 5 | 45 | 3.7 | 1.3 | 15.0 |
| 02-03—Utah ............... | 5 | 122 | 10 | 27 | .370 | 2 | 4 | .500 | 3 | 4 | 7 | 8 | 2 | 1 | 7 | 22 | 1.4 | 1.6 | 4.4 |
| Totals ................... | 8 | 242 | 28 | 68 | .412 | 11 | 16 | .688 | 9 | 9 | 18 | 12 | 5 | 3 | 12 | 67 | 2.3 | 1.5 | 8.4 |

Three-point field goals: 1996-97, 0-for-2. Totals, 0-for-2 (.000).
Personal fouls/disqualifications: 1996-97, 10/0. 2002-03, 15/0. Totals, 25/0.

# CHILDRESS, JOSH    F    HAWKS

**PERSONAL:** Born June 20, 1983, in Harbor City, Calif. ... 6-8/210. (2.03/95.3). ... Full name: Joshua Malik Childress
**HIGH SCHOOL:** Mayfair (Lakewood, Calif.).
**COLLEGE:** Stanford.
**TRANSACTIONS/CAREER NOTES:** Selected after junior season by Atlanta Hawks in first round (sixth pick overall) of 2004 NBA Draft.

## COLLEGIATE RECORD

**NOTES:** The Sporting News All-America third team (2004).

| Season Team | G | Min. | FGM | FGA | Pct. | FTM | FTA | Pct. | Reb. | Ast. | Pts. | RPG | APG | PPG |
|---|---|---|---|---|---|---|---|---|---|---|---|---|---|---|
| 01-02—Stanford ....................... | 30 | 645 | 94 | 234 | .402 | 25 | 36 | .694 | 144 | 24 | 235 | 4.8 | 0.8 | 7.8 |
| 02-03—Stanford ....................... | 33 | 1128 | 168 | 393 | .427 | 82 | 114 | .719 | 266 | 70 | 466 | 8.1 | 2.1 | 14.1 |
| 03-04—Stanford ....................... | 23 | 685 | 124 | 254 | .488 | 78 | 95 | .821 | 173 | 61 | 360 | 7.5 | 2.7 | 15.7 |
| Totals ..................................... | 86 | 2458 | 386 | 881 | .438 | 185 | 245 | .755 | 583 | 155 | 1061 | 6.8 | 1.8 | 12.3 |

Three-point field goals: 2001-02, 22-for-80 (.275). 2002-03, 48-for-144 (.333). 2003-04, 34-for-86 (.395). Totals, 104-for-310 (.335).

## NBA REGULAR-SEASON RECORD

**HONORS:** NBA All-Rookie second team (2005).

| Season Team | G | Min. | FGM | FGA | Pct. | FTM | FTA | Pct. | REBOUNDS Off. | Def. | Tot. | Ast. | St. | Blk. | TO | Pts. | RPG | APG | PPG |
|---|---|---|---|---|---|---|---|---|---|---|---|---|---|---|---|---|---|---|---|
| 04-05—Atlanta ............ | 80 | 2376 | 302 | 642 | .470 | 190 | 231 | .823 | 195 | 287 | 482 | 151 | 74 | 35 | 106 | 807 | 6.0 | 1.9 | 10.1 |

Three-point field goals: 2004-05, 13-for-56 (.232). Totals, 13-for-56 (.232).
Personal fouls/disqualifications: 2004-05, 184/1. Totals, 184/1.

# CHRISTIE, DOUG    G/F    MAVERICKS

**PERSONAL:** Born May 9, 1970, in Seattle. ... 6-6/205. (1.98/93.0). ... Full name: Douglas Dale Christie ... Name pronounced CHRIS-tee.
**HIGH SCHOOL:** Rainier Beach (Seattle).
**COLLEGE:** Pepperdine.
**TRANSACTIONS/CAREER NOTES:** Selected by Seattle SuperSonics in first round (17th pick overall) of 1992 NBA Draft. ... Traded by SuperSonics with C Benoit Benjamin to Los Angeles Lakers for F/C Sam Perkins (February 22, 1993). ... Traded by Lakers to New York Knicks for two future second-round draft choices (October 13, 1994). ... Traded by Knicks with C/F Herb Williams and cash to Toronto Raptors for G Willie Anderson and F/C Victor Alexander (February 18, 1996). ... Traded by Raptors to Sacramento Kings for F Corliss Williamson (September 29, 2000). ... Traded by Kings to Orlando Magic for G Cuttino Mobley and F Michael Bradley (January 10, 2005). ... Waived by Magic (August 11, 2005). ... Signed as free agent by Dallas Mavericks (August 19, 2005).
**MISCELLANEOUS:** Toronto Raptors all-time steals leader with 664 (1995-96 through 1999-2000).

## COLLEGIATE RECORD

| Season Team | G | Min. | FGM | FGA | Pct. | FTM | FTA | Pct. | Reb. | Ast. | Pts. | RPG | APG | PPG |
|---|---|---|---|---|---|---|---|---|---|---|---|---|---|---|
| 88-89—Pepperdine ................... | | | | | | Did not play—ineligible. | | | | | | | | |
| 89-90—Pepperdine ................... | 28 | 687 | 84 | 167 | .503 | 70 | 98 | .714 | 115 | 112 | 250 | 4.1 | 4.0 | 8.9 |
| 90-91—Pepperdine ................... | 28 | 913 | 188 | 401 | .469 | 143 | 187 | .765 | 145 | 134 | 536 | 5.2 | 4.8 | 19.1 |
| 91-92—Pepperdine ................... | 31 | 1058 | 211 | 453 | .466 | 144 | 193 | .746 | 183 | 149 | 606 | 5.9 | 4.8 | 19.5 |
| Totals ..................................... | 87 | 2658 | 483 | 1021 | .473 | 357 | 478 | .747 | 443 | 395 | 1392 | 5.1 | 4.5 | 16.0 |

Three-point field goals: 1989-90, 12-for-47 (.255). 1990-91, 17-for-65 (.262). 1991-92, 40-for-120 (.333). Totals, 69-for-232 (.297).

**RECORDS:** Shares single-game record for most steals in one half—8 (April 2, 1997, at Philadelphia).
**HONORS:** NBA All-Defensive first team (2003). ... NBA All-Defensive second team (2001, 2002, 2004).

| Season Team | G | Min. | FGM | FGA | Pct. | FTM | FTA | Pct. | REBOUNDS Off. | Def. | Tot. | Ast. | St. | Blk. | TO | Pts. | AVERAGES RPG | APG | PPG |
|---|---|---|---|---|---|---|---|---|---|---|---|---|---|---|---|---|---|---|---|
| 92-93—L.A. Lakers ..... | 23 | 332 | 45 | 106 | .425 | 50 | 66 | .758 | 24 | 27 | 51 | 53 | 22 | 5 | 50 | 142 | 2.2 | 2.3 | 6.2 |
| 93-94—L.A. Lakers ..... | 65 | 1515 | 244 | 562 | .434 | 145 | 208 | .697 | 93 | 142 | 235 | 136 | 89 | 28 | 140 | 672 | 3.6 | 2.1 | 10.3 |
| 94-95—New York........ | 12 | 79 | 5 | 22 | .227 | 4 | 5 | .800 | 3 | 10 | 13 | 8 | 2 | 1 | 13 | 15 | 1.1 | 0.7 | 1.3 |
| 95-96—N.Y.-Tor........ | 55 | 1036 | 150 | 337 | .445 | 69 | 93 | .742 | 34 | 120 | 154 | 117 | 70 | 19 | 95 | 415 | 2.8 | 2.1 | 7.5 |
| 96-97—Toronto .......... | 81 | 3127 | 396 | 949 | .417 | 237 | 306 | .775 | 85 | 347 | 432 | 315 | 201 | 45 | 200 | 1176 | 5.3 | 3.9 | 14.5 |
| 97-98—Toronto .......... | 78 | 2939 | 458 | 1071 | .428 | 271 | 327 | .829 | 94 | 310 | 404 | 282 | 190 | 57 | 228 | 1287 | 5.2 | 3.6 | 16.5 |
| 98-99—Toronto .......... | 50 | 1768 | 252 | 650 | .388 | 207 | 246 | .841 | 59 | 148 | 207 | 187 | 113 | 26 | 119 | 760 | 4.1 | 3.7 | 15.2 |
| 99-00—Toronto .......... | 73 | 2264 | 311 | 764 | .407 | 182 | 216 | .843 | 63 | 222 | 285 | 321 | 102 | 43 | 144 | 903 | 3.9 | 4.4 | 12.4 |
| 00-01—Sacramento .... | 81 | 2939 | 311 | 788 | .395 | 280 | 312 | .897 | 95 | 260 | 355 | 289 | *183 | 45 | 154 | 996 | 4.4 | 3.6 | 12.3 |
| 01-02—Sacramento .... | 81 | 2798 | 338 | 735 | .460 | 206 | 242 | .851 | 74 | 300 | 374 | 340 | 160 | 25 | 164 | 972 | 4.6 | 4.2 | 12.0 |
| 02-03—Sacramento .... | 80 | 2710 | 267 | 557 | .479 | 141 | 174 | .810 | 61 | 281 | 342 | 376 | 180 | 37 | 144 | 748 | 4.3 | 4.7 | 9.4 |
| 03-04—Sacramento .... | 82 | 2780 | 317 | 688 | .461 | 148 | 172 | .860 | 69 | 260 | 329 | 347 | 151 | 41 | 155 | 831 | 4.0 | 4.2 | 10.1 |
| 04-05—Sac.-Orlando.. | 52 | 1525 | 130 | 332 | .392 | 70 | 78 | .897 | 38 | 139 | 177 | 199 | 80 | 18 | 104 | 345 | 3.4 | 3.8 | 6.6 |
| Totals ................... | 813 | 25812 | 3224 | 7561 | .426 | 2010 | 2445 | .822 | 792 | 2566 | 3358 | 2970 | 1543 | 390 | 1710 | 9262 | 4.1 | 3.7 | 11.4 |

Three-point field goals: 1992-93, 2-for-12 (.167). 1993-94, 39-for-119 (.328). 1994-95, 1-for-7 (.143). 1995-96, 46-for-106 (.434). 1996-97, 147-for-383 (.384). 1997-98, 100-for-307 (.326). 1998-99, 49-for-161 (.304). 1999-00, 99-for-275 (.360). 2000-01, 94-for-250 (.376). 2001-02, 90-for-256 (.352). 2002-03, 73-for-185 (.395). 2003-04, 49-for-142 (.345). 2004-05, 15-for-62 (.242). Totals, 804-for-2265 (.355).
Personal fouls/disqualifications: 1992-93, 53/0. 1993-94, 186/2. 1994-95, 18/1. 1995-96, 141/5. 1996-97, 245/6. 1997-98, 198/3. 1998-99, 111/1. 1999-00, 167/1. 2000-01, 224/2. 2001-02, 209/3. 2002-03, 186/1. 2003-04, 186/0. 2004-05, 106/0. Totals, 2030/25.

## NBA PLAYOFF RECORD

| Season Team | G | Min. | FGM | FGA | Pct. | FTM | FTA | Pct. | REBOUNDS Off. | Def. | Tot. | Ast. | St. | Blk. | TO | Pts. | AVERAGES RPG | APG | PPG |
|---|---|---|---|---|---|---|---|---|---|---|---|---|---|---|---|---|---|---|---|
| 92-93—L.A. Lakers ..... | 5 | 39 | 4 | 11 | .364 | 0 | 0 | ... | 1 | 3 | 4 | 6 | 2 | 2 | 4 | 9 | 0.8 | 1.2 | 1.8 |
| 94-95—New York........ | 2 | 6 | 0 | 4 | .000 | 0 | 0 | ... | 0 | 0 | 0 | 0 | 0 | 0 | 1 | 0 | 0.0 | 0.0 | 0.0 |
| 99-00—Toronto .......... | 3 | 61 | 3 | 13 | .231 | 3 | 6 | .500 | 1 | 4 | 5 | 6 | 4 | 1 | 4 | 12 | 1.7 | 2.0 | 4.0 |
| 00-01—Sacramento .... | 8 | 304 | 25 | 68 | .368 | 24 | 29 | .828 | 7 | 28 | 35 | 26 | 20 | 9 | 19 | 79 | 4.4 | 3.3 | 9.9 |
| 01-02—Sacramento .... | 16 | 644 | 54 | 132 | .409 | 52 | 65 | .800 | 19 | 73 | 92 | 79 | 33 | 9 | 44 | 177 | 5.8 | 4.9 | 11.1 |
| 02-03—Sacramento .... | 12 | 381 | 37 | 99 | .374 | 29 | 31 | .935 | 15 | 59 | 74 | 55 | 12 | 3 | 22 | 109 | 6.2 | 4.6 | 9.1 |
| 03-04—Sacramento .... | 12 | 461 | 56 | 141 | .397 | 41 | 48 | .854 | 17 | 57 | 74 | 47 | 22 | 5 | 22 | 166 | 6.2 | 3.9 | 13.8 |
| Totals ................... | 58 | 1896 | 179 | 468 | .382 | 149 | 179 | .832 | 60 | 224 | 284 | 219 | 93 | 29 | 116 | 552 | 4.9 | 3.8 | 9.5 |

Three-point field goals: 1992-93, 1-for-3 (.333). 1999-00, 3-for-8 (.375). 2000-01, 5-for-17 (.294). 2001-02, 17-for-64 (.266). 2002-03, 6-for-24 (.250). 2003-04, 13-for-33 (.394). Totals, 45-for-149 (.302).
Personal fouls/disqualifications: 1992-93, 5/0. 1994-95, 3/0. 1999-00, 10/0. 2000-01, 31/1. 2001-02, 64/3. 2002-03, 22/0. 2003-04, 35/0. Totals, 170/4.

# CLAXTON, SPEEDY     G     HORNETS

**PERSONAL:** Born May 8, 1978, in Hempstead, N.Y. ... 5-11/166. (1.80/75.3).
**HIGH SCHOOL:** Christ the King (Middle Village, N.Y.).
**COLLEGE:** Hofstra.
**TRANSACTIONS/CAREER NOTES:** Selected by Philadelphia 76ers in first round (20th pick overall) of 2000 NBA Draft. ... Traded by 76ers to San Antonio Spurs for F/C Mark Bryant, draft rights to G/F John Salmons and draft rights to F Randy Holcomb (June 26, 2002). ... Signed as free agent by Golden State Warriors (July 23, 2003) ... Traded by Warriors with F Dale Davis to New Orleans Hornets for G Baron Davis (February 24, 2005).
**MISCELLANEOUS:** Member of NBA championship team (2003).

## COLLEGIATE RECORD

| Season Team | G | Min. | FGM | FGA | Pct. | FTM | FTA | Pct. | Reb. | Ast. | Pts. | AVERAGES RPG | APG | PPG |
|---|---|---|---|---|---|---|---|---|---|---|---|---|---|---|
| 96-97—Hofstra ......................... | 27 | 916 | 134 | 310 | .432 | 132 | 187 | .706 | 123 | 91 | 406 | 4.6 | 3.4 | 15.0 |
| 97-98—Hofstra ......................... | 31 | 1081 | 182 | 375 | .485 | 138 | 189 | .730 | 144 | 224 | 504 | 4.6 | 7.2 | 16.3 |
| 98-99—Hofstra ......................... | 30 | 970 | 136 | 282 | .482 | 121 | 151 | .801 | 131 | 159 | 399 | 4.4 | 5.3 | 13.3 |
| 99-00—Hofstra ......................... | 31 | 1089 | 253 | 538 | .470 | 149 | 195 | .764 | 168 | 186 | 706 | 5.4 | 6.0 | 22.8 |
| Totals ....................................... | 119 | 4056 | 705 | 1505 | .468 | 540 | 722 | .748 | 566 | 660 | 2015 | 4.8 | 5.5 | 16.9 |

Three-point field goals: 1996-97, 6-for-38 (.158). 1997-98, 2-for-11 (.182). 1998-99, 6-for-19 (.316). 1999-00, 51-for-134 (.381). Totals, 65-for-202 (.322).

## NBA REGULAR-SEASON RECORD

| Season Team | G | Min. | FGM | FGA | Pct. | FTM | FTA | Pct. | REBOUNDS Off. | Def. | Tot. | Ast. | St. | Blk. | TO | Pts. | AVERAGES RPG | APG | PPG |
|---|---|---|---|---|---|---|---|---|---|---|---|---|---|---|---|---|---|---|---|
| 00-01—Philadelphia .... | | | | | | | | Did not play—injured. | | | | | | | | | | | |
| 01-02—Philadelphia .... | 67 | 1528 | 181 | 452 | .400 | 114 | 136 | .838 | 46 | 114 | 160 | 198 | 95 | 6 | 95 | 480 | 2.4 | 3.0 | 7.2 |
| 02-03—San Antonio.... | 30 | 471 | 67 | 145 | .462 | 39 | 57 | .684 | 22 | 34 | 56 | 75 | 22 | 7 | 35 | 173 | 1.9 | 2.5 | 5.8 |
| 03-04—Golden State... | 60 | 1595 | 224 | 524 | .427 | 182 | 224 | .813 | 38 | 118 | 156 | 267 | 97 | 9 | 102 | 634 | 2.6 | 4.5 | 10.6 |
| 04-05—Golden St.-N.O. | 62 | 1866 | 257 | 611 | .421 | 187 | 254 | .736 | 37 | 147 | 184 | 374 | 109 | 8 | 119 | 712 | 3.0 | 6.0 | 11.5 |
| Totals ................... | 219 | 5460 | 729 | 1732 | .421 | 522 | 671 | .778 | 143 | 413 | 556 | 914 | 323 | 30 | 351 | 1999 | 2.5 | 4.2 | 9.1 |

Three-point field goals: 2001-02, 4-for-33 (.121). 2002-03, 0-for-11. 2003-04, 4-for-22 (.182). 2004-05, 11-for-61 (.180). Totals, 19-for-127 (.150).
Personal fouls/disqualifications: 2001-02, 145/1. 2002-03, 43/0. 2003-04, 146/2. 2004-05, 184/7. Totals, 518/10.

## NBA PLAYOFF RECORD

| Season Team | G | Min. | FGM | FGA | Pct. | FTM | FTA | Pct. | REBOUNDS Off. | Def. | Tot. | Ast. | St. | Blk. | TO | Pts. | AVERAGES RPG | APG | PPG |
|---|---|---|---|---|---|---|---|---|---|---|---|---|---|---|---|---|---|---|---|
| 01-02—Philadelphia .... | 5 | 49 | 4 | 12 | .333 | 4 | 6 | .667 | 1 | 0 | 1 | 14 | 5 | 0 | 3 | 12 | 0.2 | 2.8 | 2.4 |
| 02-03—San Antonio.... | 24 | 326 | 46 | 105 | .438 | 33 | 44 | .750 | 7 | 38 | 45 | 45 | 16 | 5 | 24 | 125 | 1.9 | 1.9 | 5.2 |
| Totals ................... | 29 | 375 | 50 | 117 | .427 | 37 | 50 | .740 | 8 | 38 | 46 | 59 | 21 | 5 | 27 | 137 | 1.6 | 2.0 | 4.7 |

Three-point field goals: 2001-02, 0-for-1. Totals, 0-for-1 (.000).
Personal fouls/disqualifications: 2001-02, 8/0. 2002-03, 38/0. Totals, 46/0.

## CLEAVES, MATEEN            G            SUPERSONICS

**PERSONAL:** Born September 7, 1977, in Flint, Mich. ... 6-3/210. (1.91/95.3).
**HIGH SCHOOL:** Northern (Flint, Mich.).
**COLLEGE:** Michigan State.
**TRANSACTIONS/CAREER NOTES:** Selected by Detroit Pistons in first round (14th pick overall) of 2000 NBA Draft. ... Traded by Pistons to Sacramento Kings for G Jon Barry and future first-round draft choice (September 7, 2001). ... Traded by Kings to Cleveland Cavaliers for G Jumaine Jones (September 10, 2002); trade voided because Cleaves failed physical (September 17, 2002). ... Played in NBDL with Huntsville Flight (2003-04). ... Signed by Cavaliers to 10-day contract (March 29, 2004). ... Waived by Cavaliers (April 6, 2004).
**MISCELLANEOUS:** Member of bronze-medal-winning U.S. World Championship team (1998).

### COLLEGIATE RECORD

**NOTES:** Member of NCAA Division I championship team (2000). ... NCAA Division I Tournament Most Outstanding Player (2000). ... The Sporting News All-America first team (2000). ... The Sporting News All-America second team (1999).

| Season Team | G | Min. | FGM | FGA | Pct. | FTM | FTA | Pct. | Reb. | Ast. | Pts. | AVERAGES RPG | APG | PPG |
|---|---|---|---|---|---|---|---|---|---|---|---|---|---|---|
| 96-97—Michigan State .............. | 29 | 750 | 111 | 277 | .401 | 57 | 79 | .722 | 73 | 146 | 297 | 2.5 | 5.0 | 10.2 |
| 97-98—Michigan State .............. | 30 | 1005 | 161 | 403 | .400 | 111 | 158 | .703 | 75 | 217 | 484 | 2.5 | 7.2 | 16.1 |
| 98-99—Michigan State .............. | 38 | 1185 | 159 | 392 | .406 | 85 | 108 | .787 | 62 | 274 | 445 | 1.6 | 7.2 | 11.7 |
| 99-00—Michigan State .............. | 26 | 820 | 109 | 259 | .421 | 65 | 86 | .756 | 46 | 179 | 315 | 1.8 | 6.9 | 12.1 |
| **Totals** ...................................... | 123 | 3760 | 540 | 1331 | .406 | 318 | 431 | .738 | 256 | 816 | 1541 | 2.1 | 6.6 | 12.5 |

Three-point field goals: 1996-97, 18-for-76 (.237). 1997-98, 51-for-152 (.336). 1998-99, 42-for-144 (.292). 1999-00, 32-for-85 (.376). Totals, 143-for-457 (.313).

### NBA REGULAR-SEASON RECORD

| Season Team | G | Min. | FGM | FGA | Pct. | FTM | FTA | Pct. | REBOUNDS Off. | Def. | Tot. | Ast. | St. | Blk. | TO | Pts. | AVERAGES RPG | APG | PPG |
|---|---|---|---|---|---|---|---|---|---|---|---|---|---|---|---|---|---|---|---|
| 00-01—Detroit ........... | 78 | 1268 | 160 | 400 | .400 | 97 | 137 | .708 | 26 | 106 | 132 | 207 | 49 | 1 | 139 | 422 | 1.7 | 2.7 | 5.4 |
| 01-02—Sacramento .... | 32 | 153 | 30 | 68 | .441 | 8 | 9 | .889 | 1 | 7 | 8 | 25 | 7 | 0 | 27 | 70 | 0.3 | 0.8 | 2.2 |
| 02-03—Sacramento .... | 12 | 55 | 6 | 23 | .261 | 3 | 4 | .750 | 1 | 7 | 8 | 10 | 2 | 0 | 14 | 16 | 0.7 | 0.8 | 1.3 |
| 03-04—Cleveland ....... | 4 | 92 | 7 | 23 | .304 | 1 | 2 | .500 | 1 | 6 | 7 | 19 | 4 | 2 | 5 | 15 | 1.8 | 4.8 | 3.8 |
| 04-05—Seattle ........... | 14 | 65 | 5 | 14 | .357 | 3 | 4 | .750 | 2 | 4 | 6 | 7 | 2 | 0 | 2 | 13 | 0.4 | 0.5 | 0.9 |
| **Totals** ................... | 140 | 1633 | 208 | 528 | .394 | 112 | 156 | .718 | 31 | 130 | 161 | 268 | 64 | 3 | 187 | 536 | 1.2 | 1.9 | 3.8 |

Three-point field goals: 2000-01, 5-for-17 (.294). 2001-02, 2-for-8 (.250). 2002-03, 1-for-1 (1.000). 2003-04, 0-for-1. 2004-05, 0-for-2. Totals, 8-for-29 (.276).
Personal fouls/disqualifications: 2000-01, 153/1. 2001-02, 9/0. 2002-03, 6/0. 2003-04, 13/0. 2004-05, 2/0. Totals, 183/1.

### NBDL RECORD

| Season Team | G | Min. | FGM | FGA | Pct. | FTM | FTA | Pct. | Reb. | Ast. | Pts. | AVERAGES RPG | APG | PPG |
|---|---|---|---|---|---|---|---|---|---|---|---|---|---|---|
| 03-04—Huntsville ..................... | 42 | 1235 | 209 | 459 | .455 | 145 | 186 | .780 | 182 | 248 | 576 | 4.3 | 5.9 | 13.7 |

## COLEMAN, DERRICK            F

**PERSONAL:** Born June 21, 1967, in Mobile, Ala. ... 6-10/270. (2.08/122.5). ... Full name: Derrick D. Coleman
**HIGH SCHOOL:** Northern (Detroit).
**COLLEGE:** Syracuse.
**TRANSACTIONS/CAREER NOTES:** Selected by New Jersey Nets in first round (first pick overall) of 1990 NBA Draft. ... Traded by Nets with F Sean Higgins and G Rex Walters to Philadelphia 76ers for C Shawn Bradley, F Tim Perry and G Greg Graham (November 30, 1995). ... Signed as free agent by Charlotte Hornets (January 21, 1999). ... Traded by Hornets to 76ers as part of three-way deal in which Hornets received F George Lynch, F/C Robert Traylor and F Jerome Moiso from 76ers and F Chris Porter from Golden State Warriors, 76ers received G Vonteego Cummings and F Corie Blount from Warriors, and Warriors received F Cedric Henderson and conditional 2005 first-round draft choice from 76ers and cash considerations from Hornets (October 25, 2001). ... Traded by 76ers with F/C Amal McCaskill to Detroit Pistons for F Corliss Williamson (August 4, 2004). ... Waived by Pistons (January 5, 2005).
**MISCELLANEOUS:** Member of gold-medal-winning U.S. World Championship team (1994).

### COLLEGIATE RECORD

**NOTES:** THE SPORTING NEWS All-America first team (1990). ... 1986-87 minutes played total is missing one game.

| Season Team | G | Min. | FGM | FGA | Pct. | FTM | FTA | Pct. | Reb. | Ast. | Pts. | AVERAGES RPG | APG | PPG |
|---|---|---|---|---|---|---|---|---|---|---|---|---|---|---|
| 86-87—Syracuse ..................... | 38 | 1163 | 173 | 309 | .560 | 107 | 156 | .686 | 333 | 45 | 453 | 8.8 | 1.2 | 11.9 |
| 87-88—Syracuse ..................... | 35 | 1133 | 176 | 300 | .587 | 121 | 192 | .630 | 384 | 76 | 474 | 11.0 | 2.2 | 13.5 |
| 88-89—Syracuse ..................... | 37 | 1226 | 227 | 395 | .575 | 171 | 247 | .692 | 422 | 106 | 625 | 11.4 | 2.9 | 16.9 |
| 89-90—Syracuse ..................... | 33 | 1166 | 194 | 352 | .551 | 188 | 263 | .715 | 398 | 95 | 591 | 12.1 | 2.9 | 17.9 |
| **Totals** ...................................... | 143 | 4688 | 770 | 1356 | .568 | 587 | 858 | .684 | 1537 | 322 | 2143 | 10.7 | 2.3 | 15.0 |

Three-point field goals: 1987-88, 1-for-6 (.167). 1988-89, 0-for-8. 1989-90, 15-for-41 (.366). Totals, 16-for-55 (.291).

### NBA REGULAR-SEASON RECORD

**HONORS:** NBA Rookie of the Year (1991). ... All-NBA third team (1993, 1994). ... NBA All-Rookie first team (1991).

| Season Team | G | Min. | FGM | FGA | Pct. | FTM | FTA | Pct. | REBOUNDS Off. | Def. | Tot. | Ast. | St. | Blk. | TO | Pts. | AVERAGES RPG | APG | PPG |
|---|---|---|---|---|---|---|---|---|---|---|---|---|---|---|---|---|---|---|---|
| 90-91—New Jersey ..... | 74 | 2602 | 514 | 1100 | .467 | 323 | 442 | .731 | 269 | 490 | 759 | 163 | 71 | 99 | 217 | 1364 | 10.3 | 2.2 | 18.4 |
| 91-92—New Jersey ..... | 65 | 2207 | 483 | 958 | .504 | 300 | 393 | .763 | 203 | 415 | 618 | 205 | 54 | 98 | 248 | 1289 | 9.5 | 3.2 | 19.8 |
| 92-93—New Jersey ..... | 76 | 2759 | 564 | 1226 | .460 | 421 | 521 | .808 | 247 | 605 | 852 | 276 | 92 | 126 | 243 | 1572 | 11.2 | 3.6 | 20.7 |
| 93-94—New Jersey ..... | 77 | 2778 | 541 | 1209 | .447 | 439 | 567 | .774 | 262 | 608 | 870 | 262 | 68 | 142 | 208 | 1559 | 11.3 | 3.4 | 20.2 |
| 94-95—New Jersey ..... | 56 | 2103 | 371 | 875 | .424 | 376 | 490 | .767 | 167 | 424 | 591 | 187 | 35 | 94 | 172 | 1146 | 10.6 | 3.3 | 20.5 |
| 95-96—Philadelphia .... | 11 | 294 | 48 | 118 | .407 | 20 | 32 | .625 | 13 | 59 | 72 | 31 | 4 | 10 | 28 | 123 | 6.5 | 2.8 | 11.2 |
| 96-97—Philadelphia .... | 57 | 2102 | 364 | 836 | .435 | 272 | 365 | .745 | 157 | 416 | 573 | 193 | 50 | 75 | 184 | 1032 | 10.1 | 3.4 | 18.1 |
| 97-98—Philadelphia .... | 59 | 2135 | 356 | 867 | .411 | 302 | 391 | .772 | 149 | 438 | 587 | 145 | 46 | 68 | 157 | 1040 | 9.9 | 2.5 | 17.6 |

| Season Team | G | Min. | FGM | FGA | Pct. | FTM | FTA | Pct. | Off. | Def. | Tot. | Ast. | St. | Blk. | TO | Pts. | RPG | APG | PPG |
|---|---|---|---|---|---|---|---|---|---|---|---|---|---|---|---|---|---|---|---|
| | | | | | | | | | REBOUNDS | | | | | | | | AVERAGES | | |
| 98-99—Charlotte | 37 | 1178 | 168 | 406 | .414 | 143 | 190 | .753 | 76 | 252 | 328 | 78 | 24 | 42 | 90 | 486 | 8.9 | 2.1 | 13.1 |
| 99-00—Charlotte | 74 | 2347 | 446 | 979 | .456 | 296 | 377 | .785 | 124 | 508 | 632 | 175 | 34 | 130 | 173 | 1239 | 8.5 | 2.4 | 16.7 |
| 00-01—Charlotte | 34 | 683 | 97 | 255 | .380 | 63 | 92 | .685 | 46 | 138 | 184 | 39 | 10 | 21 | 42 | 277 | 5.4 | 1.1 | 8.1 |
| 01-02—Philadelphia | 58 | 2080 | 331 | 735 | .450 | 185 | 227 | .815 | 167 | 342 | 509 | 98 | 42 | 51 | 119 | 875 | 8.8 | 1.7 | 15.1 |
| 02-03—Philadelphia | 64 | 1742 | 223 | 498 | .448 | 134 | 171 | .784 | 151 | 299 | 450 | 87 | 53 | 69 | 96 | 602 | 7.0 | 1.4 | 9.4 |
| 03-04—Philadelphia | 34 | 843 | 107 | 259 | .413 | 49 | 65 | .754 | 45 | 147 | 192 | 46 | 23 | 26 | 57 | 271 | 5.6 | 1.4 | 8.0 |
| 04-05—Detroit | 5 | 50 | 3 | 14 | .214 | 3 | 3 | 1.000 | 3 | 12 | 15 | 0 | 0 | 0 | 2 | 9 | 3.0 | 0.0 | 1.8 |
| Totals | 781 | 25903 | 4616 | 10335 | .447 | 3326 | 4326 | .769 | 2079 | 5153 | 7232 | 1985 | 606 | 1051 | 2036 | 12884 | 9.3 | 2.5 | 16.5 |

Three-point field goals: 1990-91, 13-for-38 (.342). 1991-92, 23-for-75 (.303). 1992-93, 23-for-99 (.232). 1993-94, 38-for-121 (.314). 1994-95, 28-for-120 (.233). 1995-96, 7-for-21 (.333). 1996-97, 32-for-119 (.269). 1997-98, 26-for-98 (.265). 1998-99, 7-for-33 (.212). 1999-00, 51-for-141 (.362). 2000-01, 20-for-51 (.392). 2001-02, 28-for-83 (.337). 2002-03, 22-for-67 (.328). 2003-04, 8-for-36 (.222). 2004-05, 0-for-2. Totals, 326-for-1105 (.295).

Personal fouls/disqualifications: 1990-91, 217/3. 1991-92, 168/2. 1992-93, 210/1. 1993-94, 209/2. 1994-95, 162/2. 1995-96, 30/0. 1996-97, 164/1. 1997-98, 144/1. 1998-99, 96/1. 1999-00, 195/2. 2000-01, 53/1. 2001-02, 158/0. 2002-03, 171/2. 2003-04, 79/0. 2004-05, 6/0. Totals, 2062/18.

### NBA PLAYOFF RECORD

| Season Team | G | Min. | FGM | FGA | Pct. | FTM | FTA | Pct. | Off. | Def. | Tot. | Ast. | St. | Blk. | TO | Pts. | RPG | APG | PPG |
|---|---|---|---|---|---|---|---|---|---|---|---|---|---|---|---|---|---|---|---|
| 91-92—New Jersey | 4 | 162 | 36 | 74 | .486 | 16 | 21 | .762 | 13 | 32 | 45 | 21 | 7 | 4 | 11 | 89 | 11.3 | 5.3 | 22.3 |
| 92-93—New Jersey | 5 | 225 | 50 | 94 | .532 | 29 | 36 | .806 | 13 | 54 | 67 | 23 | 6 | 13 | 13 | 134 | 13.4 | 4.6 | 26.8 |
| 93-94—New Jersey | 4 | 173 | 27 | 68 | .397 | 39 | 50 | .780 | 19 | 38 | 57 | 10 | 2 | 5 | 18 | 98 | 14.3 | 2.5 | 24.5 |
| 99-00—Charlotte | 4 | 169 | 27 | 57 | .474 | 22 | 28 | .786 | 10 | 40 | 50 | 14 | 3 | 12 | 13 | 81 | 12.5 | 3.5 | 20.3 |
| 00-01—Charlotte | 5 | 88 | 9 | 34 | .265 | 7 | 9 | .778 | 9 | 16 | 25 | 6 | 4 | 2 | 5 | 27 | 5.0 | 1.2 | 5.4 |
| 01-02—Philadelphia | 5 | 191 | 22 | 42 | .524 | 16 | 20 | .800 | 15 | 31 | 46 | 10 | 1 | 7 | 5 | 64 | 9.2 | 2.0 | 12.8 |
| 02-03—Philadelphia | 12 | 449 | 59 | 118 | .500 | 41 | 47 | .872 | 29 | 67 | 96 | 24 | 7 | 16 | 17 | 163 | 8.0 | 2.0 | 13.6 |
| Totals | 39 | 1457 | 230 | 487 | .472 | 170 | 211 | .806 | 108 | 278 | 386 | 108 | 30 | 59 | 82 | 656 | 9.9 | 2.8 | 16.8 |

Three-point field goals: 1991-92, 1-for-6 (.167). 1992-93, 5-for-12 (.417). 1993-94, 5-for-9 (.556). 1999-00, 5-for-16 (.313). 2000-01, 2-for-8 (.250). 2001-02, 4-for-13 (.308). 2002-03, 4-for-10 (.400). Totals, 26-for-74 (.351).

Personal fouls/disqualifications: 1991-92, 12/0. 1992-93, 18/0. 1993-94, 12/0. 1999-00, 11/1. 2000-01, 12/0. 2001-02, 10/0. 2002-03, 36/0. Totals, 111/1.

### NBA ALL-STAR GAME RECORD

| Season Team | Min. | FGM | FGA | Pct. | FTM | FTA | Pct. | Off. | Def. | Tot. | Ast. | PF | Dq. | St. | Blk. | TO | Pts. |
|---|---|---|---|---|---|---|---|---|---|---|---|---|---|---|---|---|---|
| | | | | | | | | REBOUNDS | | | | | | | | | |
| 1994—New Jersey | 18 | 1 | 6 | .167 | 0 | 0 | ... | 1 | 2 | 3 | 1 | 3 | 0 | 1 | 1 | 0 | 2 |

Three-point field goals: 1994, 0-for-2. Totals, 0-for-2 (.000).

## COLLIER, JASON     F/C     HAWKS

**PERSONAL:** Born September 8, 1977, in Springfield, Ohio. ... 7-0/260. (2.13/117.9). ... Full name: Jason Jeffrey Collier
**HIGH SCHOOL:** Catholic Central (Springfield, Ohio).
**COLLEGE:** Indiana, then Georgia Tech.
**TRANSACTIONS/CAREER NOTES:** Selected by Milwaukee Bucks in first round (15th pick overall) of 2000 NBA Draft. ... Draft rights traded by Bucks with a future first-round draft choice to Houston Rockets for draft rights to C Joel Przybilla (June 28, 2000). ... Waived by Timberwolves (October 23, 2003). ... Played in NBDL with Fayetteville Patriots (2003-04). ... Signed by Atlanta Hawks to first of two consecutive 10-day contracts (March 8, 2004). ... Signed by Hawks for remainder for season (March 28, 2004).

### COLLEGIATE RECORD

| Season Team | G | Min. | FGM | FGA | Pct. | FTM | FTA | Pct. | Reb. | Ast. | Pts. | RPG | APG | PPG |
|---|---|---|---|---|---|---|---|---|---|---|---|---|---|---|
| 96-97—Indiana | 33 | 778 | 112 | 258 | .434 | 80 | 117 | .684 | 188 | 24 | 310 | 5.7 | 0.7 | 9.4 |
| 97-98—Indiana | 9 | 226 | 36 | 64 | .563 | 24 | 36 | .667 | 47 | 9 | 96 | 5.2 | 1.0 | 10.7 |
| 98-99—Georgia Tech | 25 | 849 | 153 | 347 | .441 | 92 | 128 | .719 | 182 | 36 | 430 | 7.3 | 1.4 | 17.2 |
| 99-00—Georgia Tech | 30 | 975 | 178 | 376 | .473 | 122 | 166 | .735 | 276 | 49 | 509 | 9.2 | 1.6 | 17.0 |
| Totals | 97 | 2828 | 479 | 1045 | .458 | 318 | 447 | .711 | 693 | 118 | 1345 | 7.1 | 1.2 | 13.9 |

Three-point field goals: 1996-97, 6-for-13 (.462). 1998-99, 32-for-90 (.356). 1999-00, 31-for-84 (.369). Totals, 69-for-187 (.369).

### NBA REGULAR-SEASON RECORD

| Season Team | G | Min. | FGM | FGA | Pct. | FTM | FTA | Pct. | Off. | Def. | Tot. | Ast. | St. | Blk. | TO | Pts. | RPG | APG | PPG |
|---|---|---|---|---|---|---|---|---|---|---|---|---|---|---|---|---|---|---|---|
| | | | | | | | | | REBOUNDS | | | | | | | | AVERAGES | | |
| 00-01—Houston | 23 | 222 | 27 | 71 | .380 | 17 | 24 | .708 | 12 | 25 | 37 | 6 | 2 | 3 | 11 | 71 | 1.6 | 0.3 | 3.1 |
| 01-02—Houston | 25 | 365 | 41 | 95 | .432 | 24 | 32 | .750 | 31 | 51 | 82 | 9 | 6 | 4 | 13 | 106 | 3.3 | 0.4 | 4.2 |
| 02-03—Houston | 13 | 104 | 17 | 36 | .472 | 2 | 2 | 1.000 | 12 | 17 | 29 | 1 | 2 | 1 | 2 | 36 | 2.2 | 0.1 | 2.8 |
| 03-04—Atlanta | 20 | 545 | 79 | 165 | .479 | 67 | 85 | .788 | 36 | 75 | 111 | 17 | 11 | 11 | 31 | 226 | 5.6 | 0.9 | 11.3 |
| 04-05—Atlanta | 70 | 942 | 174 | 376 | .463 | 48 | 71 | .676 | 84 | 100 | 184 | 18 | 15 | 13 | 63 | 402 | 2.6 | 0.3 | 5.7 |
| Totals | 151 | 2178 | 338 | 743 | .455 | 158 | 214 | .738 | 175 | 268 | 443 | 51 | 36 | 32 | 120 | 841 | 2.9 | 0.3 | 5.6 |

Three-point field goals: 2000-01, 0-for-1. 2001-02, 0-for-1. 2003-04, 1-for-4 (.250). 2004-05, 6-for-14 (.429). Totals, 7-for-20 (.350).

Personal fouls/disqualifications: 2000-01, 27/1. 2001-02, 40/0. 2002-03, 10/0. 2003-04, 71/3. 2004-05, 147/1. Totals, 295/5.

### NBDL RECORD

| Season Team | G | Min. | FGM | FGA | Pct. | FTM | FTA | Pct. | Reb. | Ast. | Pts. | RPG | APG | PPG |
|---|---|---|---|---|---|---|---|---|---|---|---|---|---|---|
| 03-04—Fayetteville | 30 | 845 | 159 | 348 | .457 | 142 | 175 | .811 | 216 | 24 | 462 | 7.2 | 0.8 | 15.4 |

## COLLINS, JARRON     F     JAZZ

**PERSONAL:** Born December 2, 1978, in Northridge, Calif. ... 6-11/255. (2.11/115.7). ... Full name: Jarron Thomas Collins ... Twin brother of Jason Collins, center, New Jersey Nets.
**HIGH SCHOOL:** Harvard-Westlake (North Hollywood, Calif.).
**COLLEGE:** Stanford.
**TRANSACTIONS/CAREER NOTES:** Selected by Utah Jazz in second round (53rd pick overall) of 2001 NBA Draft.

## COLLEGIATE RECORD

|  | | | | | | | | | | | | | AVERAGES | | |
|---|---|---|---|---|---|---|---|---|---|---|---|---|---|---|---|
| Season Team | G | Min. | FGM | FGA | Pct. | FTM | FTA | Pct. | Reb. | Ast. | Pts. | RPG | APG | PPG |
| 97-98—Stanford ....................... | 34 | 460 | 44 | 83 | .530 | 39 | 64 | .609 | 119 | 18 | 128 | 3.5 | 0.5 | 3.8 |
| 98-99—Stanford ....................... | 30 | 516 | 58 | 117 | .496 | 60 | 101 | .594 | 157 | 53 | 176 | 5.2 | 1.8 | 5.9 |
| 99-00—Stanford ....................... | 31 | 850 | 114 | 235 | .485 | 113 | 157 | .720 | 201 | 53 | 342 | 6.5 | 1.7 | 11.0 |
| 00-01—Stanford ....................... | 34 | 963 | 154 | 276 | .558 | 125 | 182 | .687 | 229 | 47 | 435 | 6.7 | 1.4 | 12.8 |
| Totals ...................................... | 129 | 2789 | 370 | 711 | .520 | 337 | 504 | .669 | 706 | 171 | 1081 | 5.5 | 1.3 | 8.4 |

Three-point field goals: 1997-98, 1-for-5 (.200). 1998-99, 0-for-1. 1999-00, 1-for-4 (.250). 2000-01, 2-for-6 (.333). Totals, 4-for-16 (.250).
Personal fouls/disqualifications: 1997-98, 69/0. 1998-99, 70/0. 1999-00, 76/0. 2000-01, 69/0. Totals, 284/0.

## NBA REGULAR-SEASON RECORD

|  | | | | | | | | | REBOUNDS | | | | | | | | AVERAGES | | |
|---|---|---|---|---|---|---|---|---|---|---|---|---|---|---|---|---|---|---|---|
| Season Team | G | Min. | FGM | FGA | Pct. | FTM | FTA | Pct. | Off. | Def. | Tot. | Ast. | St. | Blk. | TO | Pts. | RPG | APG | PPG |
| 01-02—Utah ............... | 70 | 1440 | 158 | 343 | .461 | 134 | 181 | .740 | 138 | 158 | 296 | 58 | 29 | 22 | 56 | 450 | 4.2 | 0.8 | 6.4 |
| 02-03—Utah ............... | 22 | 421 | 38 | 86 | .442 | 44 | 62 | .710 | 32 | 28 | 60 | 14 | 5 | 6 | 19 | 120 | 2.7 | 0.6 | 5.5 |
| 03-04—Utah ............... | 81 | 1732 | 147 | 295 | .498 | 188 | 262 | .718 | 117 | 199 | 316 | 77 | 26 | 18 | 79 | 482 | 3.9 | 1.0 | 6.0 |
| 04-05—Utah ............... | 50 | 961 | 65 | 157 | .414 | 83 | 119 | .697 | 57 | 107 | 164 | 61 | 11 | 6 | 34 | 213 | 3.3 | 1.2 | 4.3 |
| Totals ...................... | 223 | 4554 | 408 | 881 | .463 | 449 | 624 | .720 | 344 | 492 | 836 | 210 | 71 | 52 | 188 | 1265 | 3.7 | 0.9 | 5.7 |

Three-point field goals: 2001-02, 0-for-1. 2002-03, 0-for-1. 2003-04, 0-for-1. 2004-05, 0-for-1. Totals, 0-for-4 (.000).
Personal fouls/disqualifications: 2001-02, 234/4. 2002-03, 70/2. 2003-04, 255/3. 2004-05, 146/1. Totals, 705/10.

## NBA PLAYOFF RECORD

|  | | | | | | | | | REBOUNDS | | | | | | | | AVERAGES | | |
|---|---|---|---|---|---|---|---|---|---|---|---|---|---|---|---|---|---|---|---|
| Season Team | G | Min. | FGM | FGA | Pct. | FTM | FTA | Pct. | Off. | Def. | Tot. | Ast. | St. | Blk. | TO | Pts. | RPG | APG | PPG |
| 01-02—Utah ............... | 4 | 47 | 10 | 18 | .556 | 2 | 2 | 1.000 | 4 | 3 | 7 | 0 | 0 | 0 | 4 | 22 | 1.8 | 0.0 | 5.5 |

Personal fouls/disqualifications: 2001-02, 11/0. Totals, 11/0.

# COLLINS, JASON      C      NETS

**PERSONAL:** Born December 2, 1978, in Northridge, Calif. ... 7-0/260. (2.13/117.9). ... Full name: Jason Paul Collins ... Twin brother of Jarron Collins, forward, Utah Jazz.
**HIGH SCHOOL:** Harvard-Westlake (North Hollywood, Calif.).
**COLLEGE:** Stanford.
**TRANSACTIONS/CAREER NOTES:** Selected after sophomore season by Houston Rockets in first round (18th pick overall) of 2001 NBA Draft. ... Draft rights traded by Rockets with draft rights to F Richard Jefferson and G Brandon Armstrong to New Jersey Nets for draft rights to F Eddie Griffin (June 27, 2001).

## COLLEGIATE RECORD

**NOTES:** Granted medical redshirt (1997-98 and 1998-99).

|  | | | | | | | | | | | | | AVERAGES | | |
|---|---|---|---|---|---|---|---|---|---|---|---|---|---|---|---|---|
| Season Team | G | Min. | FGM | FGA | Pct. | FTM | FTA | Pct. | Reb. | Ast. | Pts. | RPG | APG | PPG |
| 97-98—Stanford ....................... | 1 | 15 | 1 | 4 | .250 | 5 | 7 | .714 | 6 | 0 | 7 | 6.0 | 0.0 | 7.0 |
| 98-99—Stanford ....................... | 7 | 89 | 9 | 18 | .500 | 11 | 23 | .478 | 23 | 2 | 29 | 3.3 | 0.3 | 4.1 |
| 99-00—Stanford ....................... | 31 | 607 | 84 | 135 | .622 | 88 | 133 | .662 | 190 | 20 | 256 | 6.1 | 0.6 | 8.3 |
| 00-01—Stanford ....................... | 34 | 895 | 168 | 271 | .620 | 145 | 185 | .784 | 265 | 51 | 493 | 7.8 | 1.5 | 14.5 |
| Totals ...................................... | 73 | 1606 | 262 | 428 | .612 | 249 | 348 | .716 | 484 | 73 | 785 | 6.6 | 1.0 | 10.8 |

Three-point field goals: 1999-00, 0-for-1. 2000-01, 12-for-26 (.462). Totals, 12-for-27 (.444).
Personal fouls/disqualifications: 1997-98, 4/0. 1998-99, 12/0. 1999-00, 71/0. 2000-01, 79/0. Totals, 166/0.

## NBA REGULAR-SEASON RECORD

|  | | | | | | | | | REBOUNDS | | | | | | | | AVERAGES | | |
|---|---|---|---|---|---|---|---|---|---|---|---|---|---|---|---|---|---|---|---|
| Season Team | G | Min. | FGM | FGA | Pct. | FTM | FTA | Pct. | Off. | Def. | Tot. | Ast. | St. | Blk. | TO | Pts. | RPG | APG | PPG |
| 01-02—New Jersey ..... | 77 | 1407 | 117 | 278 | .421 | 115 | 164 | .701 | 132 | 169 | 301 | 81 | 29 | 47 | 72 | 350 | 3.9 | 1.1 | 4.5 |
| 02-03—New Jersey ..... | 81 | 1900 | 140 | 338 | .414 | 180 | 236 | .763 | 136 | 232 | 368 | 87 | 47 | 44 | 85 | 460 | 4.5 | 1.1 | 5.7 |
| 03-04—New Jersey ..... | 78 | 2220 | 163 | 384 | .424 | 136 | 184 | .739 | 143 | 257 | 400 | 153 | 67 | 56 | 97 | 462 | 5.1 | 2.0 | 5.9 |
| 04-05—New Jersey ..... | 80 | 2542 | 186 | 451 | .412 | 137 | 209 | .656 | 153 | 335 | 488 | 105 | 71 | 71 | 91 | 511 | 6.1 | 1.3 | 6.4 |
| Totals ................... | 316 | 8069 | 606 | 1451 | .418 | 568 | 793 | .716 | 564 | 993 | 1557 | 426 | 214 | 218 | 345 | 1783 | 4.9 | 1.3 | 5.6 |

Three-point field goals: 2001-02, 1-for-2 (.500). 2002-03, 0-for-4. 2003-04, 0-for-2. 2004-05, 2-for-6 (.333). Totals, 3-for-14 (.214).
Personal fouls/disqualifications: 2001-02, 173/1. 2002-03, 252/4. 2003-04, 251/2. 2004-05, 322/14. Totals, 998/21.

## NBA PLAYOFF RECORD

|  | | | | | | | | | REBOUNDS | | | | | | | | AVERAGES | | |
|---|---|---|---|---|---|---|---|---|---|---|---|---|---|---|---|---|---|---|---|
| Season Team | G | Min. | FGM | FGA | Pct. | FTM | FTA | Pct. | Off. | Def. | Tot. | Ast. | St. | Blk. | TO | Pts. | RPG | APG | PPG |
| 01-02—New Jersey ..... | 17 | 227 | 12 | 33 | .364 | 25 | 38 | .658 | 24 | 17 | 41 | 7 | 5 | 6 | 12 | 49 | 2.4 | 0.4 | 2.9 |
| 02-03—New Jersey ..... | 20 | 529 | 33 | 91 | .363 | 51 | 61 | .836 | 51 | 74 | 125 | 17 | 13 | 12 | 18 | 117 | 6.3 | 0.9 | 5.9 |
| 03-04—New Jersey ..... | 11 | 266 | 14 | 38 | .368 | 12 | 16 | .750 | 18 | 26 | 44 | 17 | 3 | 10 | 15 | 40 | 4.0 | 1.5 | 3.6 |
| 04-05—New Jersey ..... | 4 | 128 | 4 | 17 | .235 | 8 | 8 | .375 | 9 | 17 | 26 | 1 | 2 | 0 | 5 | 11 | 6.5 | 0.3 | 2.8 |
| Totals ................... | 52 | 1150 | 63 | 179 | .352 | 91 | 123 | .740 | 102 | 134 | 236 | 42 | 23 | 28 | 50 | 217 | 4.5 | 0.8 | 4.2 |

Three-point field goals: 2002-03, 0-for-2. Totals, 0-for-2 (.000).
Personal fouls/disqualifications: 2001-02, 48/2. 2002-03, 74/2. 2003-04, 49/2. 2004-05, 19/0. Totals, 190/6.

# COLLISON, NICK      F      SUPERSONICS

**PERSONAL:** Born October 26, 1980, in Orange City, Iowa. ... 6-9/255. (2.06/115.7). ... Full name: Nicholas John Collison
**HIGH SCHOOL:** Iowa Falls (Iowa Falls, Iowa).
**COLLEGE:** Kansas.
**TRANSACTIONS/CAREER NOTES:** Selected by Seattle SuperSonics in first round (12th pick overall) of 2003 NBA Draft.

## COLLEGIATE RECORD

**NOTES:** The Sporting News All-America second team (2003).

| | | | | | | | | | | | | AVERAGES | | |
|---|---|---|---|---|---|---|---|---|---|---|---|---|---|---|
| Season Team | G | Min. | FGM | FGA | Pct. | FTM | FTA | Pct. | Reb. | Ast. | Pts. | RPG | APG | PPG |
| 99-00—Kansas | 34 | 774 | 145 | 292 | .497 | 62 | 92 | .674 | 234 | 38 | 357 | 6.9 | 1.1 | 10.5 |
| 00-01—Kansas | 33 | 892 | 187 | 313 | .597 | 85 | 136 | .625 | 222 | 71 | 461 | 6.7 | 2.2 | 14.0 |
| 01-02—Kansas | 37 | 990 | 245 | 414 | .592 | 84 | 146 | .575 | 307 | 64 | 577 | 8.3 | 1.7 | 15.6 |
| 02-03—Kansas | 38 | 1232 | 281 | 507 | .554 | 127 | 200 | .635 | 380 | 84 | 702 | 10.0 | 2.2 | 18.5 |
| **Totals** | 142 | 3888 | 858 | 1526 | .562 | 358 | 574 | .624 | 1143 | 257 | 2097 | 8.0 | 1.8 | 14.8 |

Three-point field goals: 1999-00, 5-for-13 (.385). 2000-01, 2-for-5 (.400). 2001-02, 3-for-8 (.375). 2002-03, 13-for-38 (.342). Totals, 23-for-64 (.359).

### NBA REGULAR-SEASON RECORD

| | | | | | | | | | REBOUNDS | | | | | | | | | AVERAGES | | |
|---|---|---|---|---|---|---|---|---|---|---|---|---|---|---|---|---|---|---|---|---|
| Season Team | G | Min. | FGM | FGA | Pct. | FTM | FTA | Pct. | Off. | Def. | Tot. | Ast. | St. | Blk. | TO | Pts. | RPG | APG | PPG |
| 03-04—Seattle | | | | | | | | | | | | | | | | | Did not play—injured | | |
| 04-05—Seattle | 82 | 1396 | 190 | 354 | .537 | 83 | 118 | .703 | 156 | 220 | 376 | 32 | 34 | 50 | 62 | 463 | 4.6 | 0.4 | 5.6 |
| **Totals** | 82 | 1396 | 190 | 354 | .537 | 83 | 118 | .703 | 156 | 220 | 376 | 32 | 34 | 50 | 62 | 463 | 4.6 | 0.4 | 5.6 |

Three-point field goals: 2004-05, 0-for-3. Totals, 0-for-3 (.000).
Personal fouls/disqualifications: 2004-05, 252/4. Totals, 252/4.

### NBA PLAYOFF RECORD

| | | | | | | | | | REBOUNDS | | | | | | | | | AVERAGES | | |
|---|---|---|---|---|---|---|---|---|---|---|---|---|---|---|---|---|---|---|---|---|
| Season Team | G | Min. | FGM | FGA | Pct. | FTM | FTA | Pct. | Off. | Def. | Tot. | Ast. | St. | Blk. | TO | Pts. | RPG | APG | PPG |
| 04-05—Seattle | 11 | 218 | 37 | 61 | .607 | 17 | 27 | .630 | 22 | 33 | 55 | 5 | 3 | 5 | 6 | 92 | 5.0 | 0.5 | 8.4 |

Three-point field goals: 2004-05, 1-for-1 (1.000). Totals, 1-for-1 (1.000).
Personal fouls/disqualifications: 2004-05, 40/0. Totals, 40/0.

**C**

# COOK, BRIAN          F          LAKERS

**PERSONAL:** Born December 4, 1980, in Lincoln, Ill. ... 6-10/240. (2.08/108.9). ... Full name: Brian Joshua Cook
**HIGH SCHOOL:** Lincoln (Lincoln, Ill.).
**COLLEGE:** Illinois.
**TRANSACTIONS/CAREER NOTES:** Selected by Los Angeles Lakers in first round (24th pick overall) of 2003 NBA Draft.

## COLLEGIATE RECORD

**NOTES:** The Sporting News All-America second team (2003).

| | | | | | | | | | | | | AVERAGES | | |
|---|---|---|---|---|---|---|---|---|---|---|---|---|---|---|---|
| Season Team | G | Min. | FGM | FGA | Pct. | FTM | FTA | Pct. | Reb. | Ast. | Pts. | RPG | APG | PPG |
| 99-00—Illinois | 32 | 595 | 112 | 213 | .526 | 51 | 83 | .614 | 143 | 24 | 287 | 4.5 | 0.8 | 9.0 |
| 00-01—Illinois | 35 | 846 | 147 | 269 | .546 | 69 | 86 | .802 | 212 | 43 | 391 | 6.1 | 1.2 | 11.2 |
| 01-02—Illinois | 35 | 1008 | 174 | 342 | .509 | 96 | 110 | .873 | 233 | 44 | 471 | 6.7 | 1.3 | 13.5 |
| 02-03—Illinois | 30 | 940 | 202 | 422 | .479 | 168 | 205 | .820 | 227 | 60 | 599 | 7.6 | 2.0 | 20.0 |
| **Totals** | 132 | 3389 | 635 | 1246 | .510 | 384 | 484 | .793 | 815 | 171 | 1748 | 6.2 | 1.3 | 13.2 |

Three-point field goals: 1999-00, 12-for-38 (.316). 2000-01, 28-for-76 (.368). 2001-02, 27-for-74 (.365). 2002-03, 27-for-89 (.303). Totals, 94-for-277 (.339).

### NBA REGULAR-SEASON RECORD

| | | | | | | | | | REBOUNDS | | | | | | | | | AVERAGES | | |
|---|---|---|---|---|---|---|---|---|---|---|---|---|---|---|---|---|---|---|---|---|
| Season Team | G | Min. | FGM | FGA | Pct. | FTM | FTA | Pct. | Off. | Def. | Tot. | Ast. | St. | Blk. | TO | Pts. | RPG | APG | PPG |
| 03-04—L.A. Lakers | 35 | 442 | 67 | 141 | .475 | 21 | 28 | .750 | 31 | 70 | 101 | 20 | 16 | 16 | 17 | 155 | 2.9 | 0.6 | 4.4 |
| 04-05—L.A. Lakers | 72 | 1087 | 176 | 422 | .417 | 28 | 37 | .757 | 63 | 153 | 216 | 35 | 23 | 26 | 29 | 458 | 3.0 | 0.5 | 6.4 |
| **Totals** | 107 | 1529 | 243 | 563 | .432 | 49 | 65 | .754 | 94 | 223 | 317 | 55 | 39 | 42 | 46 | 613 | 3.0 | 0.5 | 5.7 |

Three-point field goals: 2003-04, 0-for-5. 2004-05, 78-for-199 (.392). Totals, 78-for-204 (.382).
Personal fouls/disqualifications: 2003-04, 64/0. 2004-05, 139/3. Totals, 203/3.

### NBA PLAYOFF RECORD

| | | | | | | | | | REBOUNDS | | | | | | | | | AVERAGES | | |
|---|---|---|---|---|---|---|---|---|---|---|---|---|---|---|---|---|---|---|---|---|
| Season Team | G | Min. | FGM | FGA | Pct. | FTM | FTA | Pct. | Off. | Def. | Tot. | Ast. | St. | Blk. | TO | Pts. | RPG | APG | PPG |
| 03-04—L.A. Lakers | 13 | 46 | 5 | 15 | .333 | 2 | 2 | 1.000 | 3 | 9 | 12 | 1 | 1 | 0 | 3 | 12 | 0.9 | 0.1 | 0.9 |

Personal fouls/disqualifications: 2003-04, 7/0. Totals, 7/0.

# COOK, OMAR          G

**PERSONAL:** Born January 28, 1982, in Brooklyn, N.Y. ... 6-1/190. (1.85/86.2).
**HIGH SCHOOL:** Christ the King (Middle Village, N.Y.).
**COLLEGE:** St. John's.
**TRANSACTIONS/CAREER NOTES:** Selected after freshman season by Orlando Magic in second round (32nd pick overall) of 2001 NBA Draft. ... Draft rights traded by Magic to Denver Nuggets for future first-round draft choice (June 27, 2001). ... Waived by Nuggets (October 25, 2001). ... Signed as free agent by Dallas Mavericks (November 20, 2001). ... Waived by Mavericks (December 28, 2001). ... Played in National Basketball Development League with Fayetteville Patriots (2001-02). ... Signed as free agent by Boston Celtics (April 16, 2002). ... Signed as free agent by Magic (September 23, 2002). ... Waived by Magic (October 11, 2002). ... Played in NBDL with Fayetteville Patriots (2002-04). ... Signed by Portland Trail Blazers to first of two consecutive 10-day contracts (February 3, 2004). ... Signed as free agent by Charlotte Bobcats (August 3, 2004). ... Waived by Bobcats (October 25, 2004). ... Signed by Toronto Raptors to 10-day contract (April 9, 2005).

## COLLEGIATE RECORD

| | | | | | | | | | | | | AVERAGES | | |
|---|---|---|---|---|---|---|---|---|---|---|---|---|---|---|---|
| Season Team | G | Min. | FGM | FGA | Pct. | FTM | FTA | Pct. | Reb. | Ast. | Pts. | RPG | APG | PPG |
| 00-01—St. John's | 29 | 1107 | 141 | 392 | .360 | 95 | 128 | .742 | 88 | 252 | 445 | 3.0 | 8.7 | 15.3 |

Three-point field goals: 2000-01, 68-for-220 (.309). Totals, 68-for-220 (.309).
Personal fouls/disqualifications: 2000-01, 82/0. Totals, 82/0.

## NBDL RECORD

| Season Team | G | Min. | FGM | FGA | Pct. | FTM | FTA | Pct. | Reb. | Ast. | Pts. | AVERAGES | | |
|---|---|---|---|---|---|---|---|---|---|---|---|---|---|---|
| | | | | | | | | | | | | RPG | APG | PPG |
| 01-02—Fayetteville | 35 | 1105 | 139 | 366 | .380 | 109 | 142 | .768 | 103 | 272 | 428 | 2.9 | 7.8 | 12.2 |
| 02-03—Fayetteville | 50 | 1099 | 124 | 342 | .363 | 87 | 123 | .707 | 117 | 268 | 369 | 2.3 | 5.4 | 7.4 |
| 03-04—Fayetteville | 24 | 981 | 84 | 239 | .351 | 73 | 93 | .785 | 89 | 215 | 245 | 3.7 | 9.0 | 10.2 |
| 04-05—Fayetteville | 44 | 1677 | 205 | 508 | .404 | 87 | 121 | .719 | 159 | 380 | 508 | 3.6 | 8.6 | 11.5 |
| Totals | 153 | 4862 | 552 | 1455 | .379 | 356 | 479 | .743 | 468 | 1135 | 1550 | 3.1 | 7.4 | 10.1 |

Three-point field goals: 2001-02, 41-for-107 (.383). 2002-03, 34-for-107 (.318). 2003-04, 4-for-33 (.121). 2004-05, 11-for-31 (.355). Totals, 90-for-278 (.324).
Personal fouls/disqualifications: 2001-02, 109/0. Totals, 109/0.

## NBA REGULAR-SEASON RECORD

| Season Team | G | Min. | FGM | FGA | Pct. | FTM | FTA | Pct. | REBOUNDS | | | Ast. | St. | Blk. | TO | Pts. | AVERAGES | | |
|---|---|---|---|---|---|---|---|---|---|---|---|---|---|---|---|---|---|---|---|
| | | | | | | | | | Off. | Def. | Tot. | | | | | | RPG | APG | PPG |
| 03-04—Portland | 17 | 139 | 7 | 27 | .259 | 0 | 0 | ... | 3 | 3 | 6 | 24 | 10 | 0 | 10 | 14 | 0.4 | 1.4 | 0.8 |
| 04-05—Toronto | 5 | 74 | 10 | 24 | .417 | 3 | 6 | .500 | 2 | 5 | 7 | 22 | 6 | 1 | 6 | 23 | 1.4 | 4.4 | 4.6 |
| Totals | 22 | 213 | 17 | 51 | .333 | 3 | 6 | .500 | 5 | 8 | 13 | 46 | 16 | 1 | 16 | 37 | 0.6 | 2.1 | 1.7 |

Three-point field goals: 2003-04, 0-for-1. 2004-05, 0-for-4. Totals, 0-for-5 (.000).
Personal fouls/disqualifications: 2003-04, 14/0. 2004-05, 6/0. Totals, 20/0.

# CRAWFORD, JAMAL      G      KNICKS

**PERSONAL:** Born March 20, 1980, in Seattle. ... 6-5/175. (1.96/79.4).
**HIGH SCHOOL:** Rainier Beach (Seattle).
**COLLEGE:** Michigan.
**TRANSACTIONS/CAREER NOTES:** Selected after freshman season by Cleveland Cavaliers in first round (eighth pick overall) of 2000 NBA Draft. ... Draft rights traded by Cavaliers with cash to Chicago Bulls for draft rights to F/C Chris Mihm (June 28, 2000). ... Traded by Bulls with F Jerome Williams to New York Knicks for F Othella Harrington, C Dikembe Mutombo, C Cezary Trybanski and G Frank Williams (August 5, 2004).

## COLLEGIATE RECORD

| Season Team | G | Min. | FGM | FGA | Pct. | FTM | FTA | Pct. | Reb. | Ast. | Pts. | AVERAGES | | |
|---|---|---|---|---|---|---|---|---|---|---|---|---|---|---|
| | | | | | | | | | | | | RPG | APG | PPG |
| 99-00—Michigan | 17 | 577 | 105 | 255 | .412 | 40 | 51 | .784 | 47 | 76 | 283 | 2.8 | 4.5 | 16.6 |

Three-point field goals: 1999-00, 33-for-101 (.327). Totals, 33-for-101 (.327).

## NBA REGULAR-SEASON RECORD

| Season Team | G | Min. | FGM | FGA | Pct. | FTM | FTA | Pct. | REBOUNDS | | | Ast. | St. | Blk. | TO | Pts. | AVERAGES | | |
|---|---|---|---|---|---|---|---|---|---|---|---|---|---|---|---|---|---|---|---|
| | | | | | | | | | Off. | Def. | Tot. | | | | | | RPG | APG | PPG |
| 00-01—Chicago | 61 | 1050 | 107 | 304 | .352 | 27 | 34 | .794 | 9 | 80 | 89 | 141 | 43 | 14 | 85 | 282 | 1.5 | 2.3 | 4.6 |
| 01-02—Chicago | 23 | 481 | 89 | 187 | .476 | 10 | 13 | .769 | 5 | 29 | 34 | 55 | 18 | 5 | 32 | 214 | 1.5 | 2.4 | 9.3 |
| 02-03—Chicago | 80 | 1992 | 334 | 808 | .413 | 104 | 129 | .806 | 21 | 164 | 185 | 334 | 77 | 25 | 134 | 858 | 2.3 | 4.2 | 10.7 |
| 03-04—Chicago | 80 | 2811 | 509 | 1318 | .386 | 200 | 240 | .833 | 46 | 237 | 283 | 405 | 111 | 29 | 193 | 1383 | 3.5 | 5.1 | 17.3 |
| 04-05—New York | 70 | 2688 | 437 | 1097 | .398 | 182 | 216 | .843 | 33 | 170 | 203 | 302 | 92 | 19 | 148 | 1241 | 2.9 | 4.3 | 17.7 |
| Totals | 314 | 9022 | 1476 | 3714 | .397 | 523 | 632 | .828 | 114 | 680 | 794 | 1237 | 341 | 92 | 592 | 3978 | 2.5 | 3.9 | 12.7 |

Three-point field goals: 2000-01, 41-for-117 (.350). 2001-02, 26-for-58 (.448). 2002-03, 86-for-242 (.355). 2003-04, 165-for-521 (.317). 2004-05, 185-for-512 (.361). Totals, 503-for-1450 (.347).
Personal fouls/disqualifications: 2000-01, 68/0. 2001-02, 18/0. 2002-03, 126/0. 2003-04, 161/0. 2004-05, 135/0. Totals, 508/0.

# CROSHERE, AUSTIN      F      PACERS

**PERSONAL:** Born May 1, 1975, in Los Angeles. ... 6-9/242. (2.06/109.8). ... Full name: Austin Nathan Croshere
**HIGH SCHOOL:** Crossroads (Los Angeles).
**COLLEGE:** Providence.
**TRANSACTIONS/CAREER NOTES:** Selected by Indiana Pacers in first round (12th pick overall) of 1997 NBA Draft.

## COLLEGIATE RECORD

| Season Team | G | Min. | FGM | FGA | Pct. | FTM | FTA | Pct. | Reb. | Ast. | Pts. | AVERAGES | | |
|---|---|---|---|---|---|---|---|---|---|---|---|---|---|---|
| | | | | | | | | | | | | RPG | APG | PPG |
| 93-94—Providence | 25 | 233 | 38 | 95 | .400 | 29 | 40 | .725 | 55 | 3 | 115 | 2.2 | 0.1 | 4.6 |
| 94-95—Providence | 30 | 570 | 106 | 231 | .459 | 66 | 85 | .776 | 147 | 33 | 307 | 4.9 | 1.1 | 10.2 |
| 95-96—Providence | 30 | 863 | 151 | 359 | .421 | 109 | 128 | .852 | 173 | 33 | 458 | 5.8 | 1.1 | 15.3 |
| 96-97—Providence | 36 | 1192 | 200 | 440 | .455 | 182 | 205 | .888 | 270 | 54 | 643 | 7.5 | 1.5 | 17.9 |
| Totals | 121 | 2858 | 495 | 1125 | .440 | 386 | 458 | .843 | 645 | 123 | 1523 | 5.3 | 1.0 | 12.6 |

Three-point field goals: 1993-94, 10-for-31 (.323). 1994-95, 29-for-85 (.341). 1995-96, 47-for-141 (.333). 1996-97, 61-for-175 (.349). Totals, 147-for-432 (.340).

## NBA REGULAR-SEASON RECORD

| Season Team | G | Min. | FGM | FGA | Pct. | FTM | FTA | Pct. | REBOUNDS | | | Ast. | St. | Blk. | TO | Pts. | AVERAGES | | |
|---|---|---|---|---|---|---|---|---|---|---|---|---|---|---|---|---|---|---|---|
| | | | | | | | | | Off. | Def. | Tot. | | | | | | RPG | APG | PPG |
| 97-98—Indiana | 26 | 243 | 32 | 86 | .372 | 8 | 14 | .571 | 10 | 35 | 45 | 8 | 9 | 5 | 13 | 76 | 1.7 | 0.3 | 2.9 |

| | | | | | | | | | REBOUNDS | | | | | | | | AVERAGES | | |
| Season Team | G | Min. | FGM | FGA | Pct. | FTM | FTA | Pct. | Off. | Def. | Tot. | Ast. | St. | Blk. | TO | Pts. | RPG | APG | PPG |
|---|---|---|---|---|---|---|---|---|---|---|---|---|---|---|---|---|---|---|---|
| 98-99—Indiana | 27 | 249 | 32 | 75 | .427 | 20 | 23 | .870 | 16 | 29 | 45 | 10 | 7 | 8 | 23 | 92 | 1.7 | 0.4 | 3.4 |
| 99-00—Indiana | 81 | 1885 | 288 | 653 | .441 | 196 | 231 | .848 | 135 | 381 | 516 | 89 | 44 | 60 | 121 | 835 | 6.4 | 1.1 | 10.3 |
| 00-01—Indiana | 81 | 1874 | 276 | 701 | .394 | 200 | 231 | .866 | 123 | 264 | 387 | 92 | 36 | 50 | 136 | 822 | 4.8 | 1.1 | 10.1 |
| 01-02—Indiana | 76 | 1286 | 185 | 448 | .413 | 97 | 114 | .851 | 74 | 220 | 294 | 77 | 26 | 29 | 67 | 516 | 3.9 | 1.0 | 6.8 |
| 02-03—Indiana | 49 | 633 | 86 | 209 | .411 | 53 | 65 | .815 | 40 | 115 | 155 | 56 | 6 | 13 | 28 | 252 | 3.2 | 1.1 | 5.1 |
| 03-04—Indiana | 77 | 1051 | 119 | 307 | .388 | 93 | 104 | .894 | 60 | 183 | 243 | 52 | 24 | 14 | 55 | 387 | 3.2 | 0.7 | 5.0 |
| 04-05—Indiana | 73 | 1827 | 188 | 497 | .378 | 226 | 256 | .883 | 103 | 272 | 375 | 98 | 48 | 17 | 104 | 647 | 5.1 | 1.3 | 8.9 |
| Totals | 490 | 9048 | 1206 | 2976 | .405 | 893 | 1038 | .860 | 561 | 1499 | 2060 | 482 | 200 | 196 | 547 | 3627 | 4.2 | 1.0 | 7.4 |

Three-point field goals: 1997-98, 4-for-13 (.308). 1998-99, 8-for-29 (.276). 1999-00, 63-for-174 (.362). 2000-01, 70-for-207 (.338). 2001-02, 49-for-145 (.338). 2002-03, 27-for-69 (.391). 2003-04, 56-for-144 (.389). 2004-05, 45-for-174 (.259). Totals, 322-for-955 (.337).

Personal fouls/disqualifications: 1997-98, 32/1. 1998-99, 32/0. 1999-00, 203/2. 2000-01, 180/1. 2001-02, 106/0. 2002-03, 48/0. 2003-04, 101/0. 2004-05, 154/1. Totals, 856/5.

### NBA PLAYOFF RECORD

NOTES: Shares NBA Finals single-game record for most free throws made in one quarter—9 (June 16, 2000, vs. Los Angeles Lakers).

| | | | | | | | | | REBOUNDS | | | | | | | | AVERAGES | | |
| Season Team | G | Min. | FGM | FGA | Pct. | FTM | FTA | Pct. | Off. | Def. | Tot. | Ast. | St. | Blk. | TO | Pts. | RPG | APG | PPG |
|---|---|---|---|---|---|---|---|---|---|---|---|---|---|---|---|---|---|---|---|
| 98-99—Indiana | 1 | 1 | 0 | 1 | .000 | 2 | 2 | 1.000 | 1 | 0 | 1 | 0 | 0 | 0 | 0 | 2 | 1.0 | 0.0 | 2.0 |
| 99-00—Indiana | 23 | 490 | 64 | 153 | .418 | 73 | 87 | .839 | 31 | 78 | 109 | 19 | 9 | 16 | 25 | 216 | 4.7 | 0.8 | 9.4 |
| 00-01—Indiana | 4 | 129 | 14 | 35 | .400 | 13 | 15 | .867 | 5 | 15 | 20 | 6 | 4 | 2 | 9 | 43 | 5.0 | 1.5 | 10.8 |
| 01-02—Indiana | 4 | 59 | 8 | 20 | .400 | 6 | 8 | .750 | 4 | 10 | 14 | 2 | 1 | 1 | 6 | 24 | 3.5 | 0.5 | 6.0 |
| 02-03—Indiana | 4 | 46 | 5 | 19 | .263 | 6 | 7 | .857 | 8 | 9 | 17 | 3 | 0 | 1 | 3 | 16 | 4.3 | 0.8 | 4.0 |
| 03-04—Indiana | 13 | 214 | 19 | 55 | .345 | 17 | 21 | .810 | 13 | 27 | 40 | 12 | 4 | 3 | 6 | 63 | 3.1 | 0.9 | 4.8 |
| 04-05—Indiana | 10 | 88 | 4 | 10 | .400 | 15 | 18 | .833 | 7 | 10 | 17 | 0 | 4 | 1 | 6 | 25 | 1.7 | 0.0 | 2.5 |
| Totals | 59 | 1027 | 114 | 293 | .389 | 132 | 158 | .835 | 69 | 149 | 218 | 42 | 22 | 24 | 55 | 389 | 3.7 | 0.7 | 6.6 |

Three-point field goals: 1999-00, 15-for-37 (.405). 2000-01, 2-for-10 (.200). 2001-02, 2-for-6 (.333). 2002-03, 0-for-6. 2003-04, 8-for-24 (.333). 2004-05, 2-for-4 (.500). Totals, 29-for-87 (.333).

Personal fouls/disqualifications: 1999-00, 51/0. 2000-01, 15/1. 2001-02, 7/1. 2002-03, 5/0. 2003-04, 17/1. 2004-05, 10/0. Totals, 105/3.

## CURRY, EDDY     F/C     BULLS

**PERSONAL:** Born December 5, 1982, in Harvey, Ill. ... 6-11/285. (2.11/129.3).
**HIGH SCHOOL:** Thornwood (South Holland, Ill.).
**COLLEGE:** Did not attend college.
**TRANSACTIONS/CAREER NOTES:** Selected out of high school by Chicago Bulls in first round (fourth pick overall) of 2001 NBA Draft.

### NBA REGULAR-SEASON RECORD

| | | | | | | | | | REBOUNDS | | | | | | | | AVERAGES | | |
| Season Team | G | Min. | FGM | FGA | Pct. | FTM | FTA | Pct. | Off. | Def. | Tot. | Ast. | St. | Blk. | TO | Pts. | RPG | APG | PPG |
|---|---|---|---|---|---|---|---|---|---|---|---|---|---|---|---|---|---|---|---|
| 01-02—Chicago | 72 | 1150 | 189 | 377 | .501 | 105 | 160 | .656 | 111 | 161 | 272 | 25 | 16 | 53 | 69 | 483 | 3.8 | 0.3 | 6.7 |
| 02-03—Chicago | 81 | 1571 | 335 | 573 | .585 | 179 | 287 | .624 | 116 | 237 | 353 | 37 | 18 | 62 | 137 | 849 | 4.4 | 0.5 | 10.5 |
| 03-04—Chicago | 73 | 2154 | 417 | 840 | .496 | 235 | 350 | .671 | 143 | 308 | 451 | 68 | 24 | 83 | 177 | 1070 | 6.2 | 0.9 | 14.7 |
| 04-05—Chicago | 63 | 1808 | 393 | 730 | .538 | 226 | 314 | .720 | 116 | 222 | 338 | 37 | 21 | 58 | 163 | 1012 | 5.4 | 0.6 | 16.1 |
| Totals | 289 | 6683 | 1334 | 2520 | .529 | 745 | 1111 | .671 | 486 | 928 | 1414 | 167 | 79 | 256 | 546 | 3414 | 4.9 | 0.6 | 11.8 |

Three-point field goals: 2003-04, 1-for-1 (1.000). Totals, 1-for-1 (1.000).
Personal fouls/disqualifications: 2001-02, 173/0. 2002-03, 226/3. 2003-04, 258/11. 2004-05, 202/4. Totals, 859/18.

## CURRY, MICHAEL     G

**PERSONAL:** Born August 22, 1968, in Anniston, Ala. ... 6-5/227. (1.96/103.0).
**HIGH SCHOOL:** Glenn Hills (Augusta, Ga.).
**COLLEGE:** Georgia Southern.
**TRANSACTIONS/CAREER NOTES:** Not drafted by an NBA franchise. ... Played in Germany, Belgium and France (1990-92). ... Played in United States Basketball League with Long Island Surf (1992). ... Played in Continental Basketball Association with Capital Region Pontiacs (1992-93) and Omaha Racers (1995-96). ... Signed as free agent by Philadelphia 76ers (October 7, 1993). ... Waived by 76ers (December 29, 1993). ... Played in Italy (1993-94). ... Played in Spain (1994-95). ... Signed by Washington Bullets to 10-day contract (January 12, 1996). ... Signed by Detroit Pistons to first of two consecutive 10-day contracts (January 31, 1996). ... Re-signed by Pistons for remainder of season (February 22, 1996). ... Signed as free agent by Milwaukee Bucks (July 30, 1997). ... Signed as free agent by Pistons (August 2, 1999). ... Traded by Pistons to Toronto Raptors for G Lindsey Hunter (August 28, 2003). ... Signed as free agent by Indiana Pacers (December 13, 2004).

### COLLEGIATE RECORD

| | | | | | | | | | | | AVERAGES | | |
| Season Team | G | Min. | FGM | FGA | Pct. | FTM | FTA | Pct. | Reb. | Ast. | Pts. | RPG | APG | PPG |
|---|---|---|---|---|---|---|---|---|---|---|---|---|---|---|
| 86-87—Georgia Southern | 31 | 594 | 59 | 116 | .509 | 31 | 45 | .689 | 87 | 29 | 149 | 2.8 | 0.9 | 4.8 |
| 87-88—Georgia Southern | 31 | 836 | 82 | 151 | .543 | 33 | 51 | .647 | 154 | 44 | 198 | 5.0 | 1.4 | 6.4 |
| 88-89—Georgia Southern | 29 | 1014 | 117 | 219 | .534 | 75 | 108 | .694 | 211 | 89 | 309 | 7.3 | 3.1 | 10.7 |
| 89-90—Georgia Southern | 28 | 926 | 164 | 264 | .621 | 137 | 170 | .806 | 196 | 58 | 465 | 7.0 | 2.1 | 16.6 |
| Totals | 119 | 3370 | 422 | 750 | .563 | 276 | 374 | .738 | 648 | 220 | 1121 | 5.4 | 1.8 | 9.4 |

Three-point field goals: 1987-88, 1-for-6 (.167). 1988-89, 0-for-3. 1989-90, 0-for-3. Totals, 1-for-12 (.083).

## CBA RECORD

| Season Team | G | Min. | FGM | FGA | Pct. | FTM | FTA | Pct. | Reb. | Ast. | Pts. | RPG | APG | PPG |
|---|---|---|---|---|---|---|---|---|---|---|---|---|---|---|
| 92-93—Capital Region | 36 | 1391 | 268 | 482 | .556 | 161 | 200 | .805 | 179 | 75 | 698 | 5.0 | 2.1 | 19.4 |
| 95-96—Omaha | 11 | 404 | 84 | 153 | .549 | 46 | 61 | .754 | 37 | 44 | 237 | 3.4 | 4.0 | 21.5 |
| Totals | 47 | 1795 | 352 | 635 | .554 | 207 | 261 | .793 | 216 | 119 | 935 | 4.6 | 2.5 | 19.9 |

Three-point field goals: 1992-93, 1-for-7 (.143). 1995-96, 23-for-55 (.418). Totals, 24-for-62 (.387).
Personal fouls/disqualifications: 1992-93, 106/0. 1995-96, 42/0. Totals, 148/0.

## ITALIAN LEAGUE RECORD

| Season Team | G | Min. | FGM | FGA | Pct. | FTM | FTA | Pct. | Reb. | Ast. | Pts. | RPG | APG | PPG |
|---|---|---|---|---|---|---|---|---|---|---|---|---|---|---|
| 93-94—S. Clear | 25 | 966 | 208 | 387 | .537 | 166 | 192 | .865 | 127 | 33 | 637 | 5.1 | 1.3 | 25.5 |

Three-point field goals: 1993-94, 55-for-151 (.364). Totals, 55-for-151 (.364).

## NBA REGULAR-SEASON RECORD

| Season Team | G | Min. | FGM | FGA | Pct. | FTM | FTA | Pct. | Off. | Def. | Tot. | Ast. | St. | Blk. | TO | Pts. | RPG | APG | PPG |
|---|---|---|---|---|---|---|---|---|---|---|---|---|---|---|---|---|---|---|---|
| 93-94—Philadelphia | 10 | 43 | 3 | 14 | .214 | 3 | 4 | .750 | 0 | 1 | 1 | 1 | 1 | 0 | 3 | 9 | 0.1 | 0.1 | 0.9 |
| 95-96—Was.-Det. | 46 | 783 | 73 | 161 | .453 | 45 | 62 | .726 | 27 | 58 | 85 | 27 | 24 | 2 | 24 | 211 | 1.8 | 0.6 | 4.6 |
| 96-97—Detroit | 81 | 1217 | 99 | 221 | .448 | 97 | 108 | .898 | 23 | 96 | 119 | 43 | 31 | 12 | 28 | 318 | 1.5 | 0.5 | 3.9 |
| 97-98—Milwaukee | 82 | 1978 | 196 | 418 | .469 | 147 | 176 | .835 | 26 | 72 | 98 | 137 | 56 | 14 | 77 | 543 | 1.2 | 1.7 | 6.6 |
| 98-99—Milwaukee | 50 | 1146 | 90 | 206 | .437 | 63 | 79 | .797 | 19 | 89 | 108 | 78 | 42 | 7 | 37 | 244 | 2.2 | 1.6 | 4.9 |
| 99-00—Detroit | 82 | 1611 | 182 | 379 | .480 | 141 | 168 | .839 | 21 | 83 | 104 | 87 | 33 | 5 | 73 | 506 | 1.3 | 1.1 | 6.2 |
| 00-01—Detroit | 68 | 1485 | 145 | 319 | .455 | 62 | 73 | .849 | 21 | 100 | 121 | 132 | 27 | 3 | 61 | 356 | 1.8 | 1.9 | 5.2 |
| 01-02—Detroit | 82 | 1912 | 125 | 276 | .453 | 72 | 91 | .791 | 15 | 153 | 168 | 127 | 47 | 10 | 60 | 329 | 2.0 | 1.5 | 4.0 |
| 02-03—Detroit | 78 | 1555 | 92 | 229 | .402 | 36 | 45 | .800 | 16 | 111 | 127 | 104 | 44 | 4 | 43 | 236 | 1.6 | 1.3 | 3.0 |
| 03-04—Toronto | 70 | 1229 | 76 | 196 | .388 | 49 | 58 | .845 | 22 | 65 | 87 | 53 | 23 | 5 | 48 | 204 | 1.2 | 0.8 | 2.9 |
| 04-05—Indiana | 18 | 249 | 13 | 29 | .448 | 4 | 8 | .500 | 8 | 19 | 27 | 15 | 5 | 4 | 5 | 30 | 1.5 | 0.8 | 1.7 |
| Totals | 667 | 13208 | 1094 | 2448 | .447 | 719 | 872 | .825 | 198 | 847 | 1045 | 804 | 333 | 66 | 459 | 2986 | 1.6 | 1.2 | 4.5 |

Three-point field goals: 1993-94, 0-for-2. 1995-96, 20-for-53 (.377). 1996-97, 23-for-77 (.299). 1997-98, 4-for-9 (.444). 1998-99, 1-for-15 (.067). 1999-00, 1-for-5 (.200). 2000-01, 4-for-9 (.444). 2001-02, 7-for-26 (.269). 2002-03, 16-for-54 (.296). 2003-04, 3-for-15 (.200). Totals, 79-for-265 (.298).
Personal fouls/disqualifications: 1995-96, 92/1. 1996-97, 128/0. 1997-98, 218/1. 1998-99, 135/0. 1999-00, 209/3. 2000-01, 173/0. 2001-02, 207/1. 2002-03, 163/0. 2003-04, 153/1. 2004-05, 39/0. Totals, 1517/7.

## NBA PLAYOFF RECORD

| Season Team | G | Min. | FGM | FGA | Pct. | FTM | FTA | Pct. | Off. | Def. | Tot. | Ast. | St. | Blk. | TO | Pts. | RPG | APG | PPG |
|---|---|---|---|---|---|---|---|---|---|---|---|---|---|---|---|---|---|---|---|
| 95-96—Detroit | 3 | 43 | 3 | 7 | .429 | 0 | 0 | ... | 1 | 2 | 3 | 1 | 1 | 1 | 0 | 6 | 1.0 | 0.3 | 2.0 |
| 96-97—Detroit | 2 | 7 | 1 | 2 | .500 | 0 | 1 | .000 | 0 | 1 | 1 | 0 | 0 | 0 | 0 | 2 | 0.5 | 0.0 | 1.0 |
| 98-99—Milwaukee | 3 | 59 | 7 | 12 | .583 | 6 | 6 | 1.000 | 1 | 3 | 4 | 3 | 2 | 1 | 2 | 20 | 1.3 | 1.0 | 6.7 |
| 99-00—Detroit | 3 | 79 | 12 | 23 | .522 | 4 | 6 | .667 | 0 | 3 | 3 | 3 | 1 | 1 | 2 | 28 | 1.0 | 1.0 | 9.3 |
| 01-02—Detroit | 10 | 221 | 22 | 39 | .564 | 8 | 11 | .727 | 1 | 13 | 14 | 12 | 4 | 0 | 5 | 57 | 1.4 | 1.2 | 5.7 |
| 02-03—Detroit | 15 | 274 | 16 | 44 | .364 | 6 | 7 | .857 | 3 | 13 | 16 | 17 | 7 | 2 | 5 | 41 | 1.1 | 1.1 | 2.7 |
| Totals | 36 | 683 | 61 | 127 | .480 | 24 | 31 | .774 | 6 | 35 | 41 | 36 | 15 | 5 | 14 | 154 | 1.1 | 1.0 | 4.3 |

Three-point field goals: 1995-96, 0-for-1. 1998-99, 0-for-1. 2001-02, 5-for-13 (.385). 2002-03, 3-for-9 (.333). Totals, 8-for-24 (.333).
Personal fouls/disqualifications: 1995-96, 5/0. 1996-97, 1/0. 1998-99, 8/0. 1999-00, 5/0. 2001-02, 32/0. 2002-03, 35/0. Totals, 86/0.

## SPANISH RECORD

| Season Team | G | Min. | FGM | FGA | Pct. | FTM | FTA | Pct. | Reb. | Ast. | Pts. | RPG | APG | PPG |
|---|---|---|---|---|---|---|---|---|---|---|---|---|---|---|
| 94-95—Valvi Girona | 38 | 1371 | 216 | 456 | .474 | 171 | 214 | .799 | 128 | 60 | 672 | 3.4 | 1.6 | 17.7 |

Three-point field goals: 1994-95, 69-for-176 (.392). Totals, 69-for-176 (.392).
Personal fouls/disqualifications: 1994-95, 102/0. Totals, 102/0.

---

# DALEMBERT, SAMUEL　　　　C　　　　76ERS

**PERSONAL:** Born May 10, 1981, in Port-au-Prince, Haiti. ... 6-11/250. (2.11/113.4). ... Full name: Samuel Davis Dalembert
**HIGH SCHOOL:** Surenpagge (Montreal), then St. Patrick's (Elizabeth, N.J.).
**COLLEGE:** Seton Hall.
**TRANSACTIONS/CAREER NOTES:** Selected after sophomore season by Philadelphia 76ers in first round (26th pick overall) of 2001 NBA Draft.

## COLLEGIATE RECORD

| Season Team | G | Min. | FGM | FGA | Pct. | FTM | FTA | Pct. | Reb. | Ast. | Pts. | RPG | APG | PPG |
|---|---|---|---|---|---|---|---|---|---|---|---|---|---|---|
| 99-00—Seton Hall | 30 | 643 | 75 | 149 | .503 | 29 | 56 | .518 | 179 | 10 | 179 | 6.0 | 0.3 | 6.0 |
| 00-01—Seton Hall | 29 | 622 | 100 | 177 | .565 | 40 | 72 | .556 | 166 | 9 | 240 | 5.7 | 0.3 | 8.3 |
| Totals | 59 | 1265 | 175 | 326 | .537 | 69 | 128 | .539 | 345 | 19 | 419 | 5.8 | 0.3 | 7.1 |

Personal fouls/disqualifications: 1999-00, 92/0. 2000-01, 95/0. Totals, 187/0.

## NBA REGULAR-SEASON RECORD

| Season Team | G | Min. | FGM | FGA | Pct. | FTM | FTA | Pct. | Off. | Def. | Tot. | Ast. | St. | Blk. | TO | Pts. | RPG | APG | PPG |
|---|---|---|---|---|---|---|---|---|---|---|---|---|---|---|---|---|---|---|---|
| 01-02—Philadelphia | 34 | 177 | 22 | 50 | .440 | 7 | 18 | .389 | 25 | 43 | 68 | 5 | 6 | 13 | 14 | 51 | 2.0 | 0.1 | 1.5 |

| Season Team | G | Min. | FGM | FGA | Pct. | FTM | FTA | Pct. | REBOUNDS Off. | Def. | Tot. | Ast. | St. | Blk. | TO | Pts. | AVERAGES RPG | APG | PPG |
|---|---|---|---|---|---|---|---|---|---|---|---|---|---|---|---|---|---|---|---|
| 02-03—Philadelphia... | | | | | | Did not play—injured | | | | | | | | | | | | | |
| 03-04—Philadelphia .. | 82 | 2198 | 270 | 499 | .541 | 112 | 174 | .644 | 194 | 432 | 626 | 21 | 44 | 189 | 86 | 652 | 7.6 | 0.3 | 8.0 |
| 04-05—Philadelphia .. | 72 | 1785 | 250 | 477 | .524 | 89 | 148 | .601 | 187 | 355 | 542 | 35 | 46 | 121 | 114 | 589 | 7.5 | 0.5 | 8.2 |
| Totals ................. | 188 | 4160 | 542 | 1026 | .528 | 208 | 340 | .612 | 406 | 830 | 1236 | 61 | 96 | 323 | 214 | 1292 | 6.6 | 0.3 | 6.9 |

Three-point field goals: 2003-04, 0-for-1. Totals, 0-for-1 (.000).
Personal fouls/disqualifications: 2001-02, 30/0. 2003-04, 273/4. 2004-05, 241/4. Totals, 544/8.

### NBA PLAYOFF RECORD

| Season Team | G | Min. | FGM | FGA | Pct. | FTM | FTA | Pct. | REBOUNDS Off. | Def. | Tot. | Ast. | St. | Blk. | TO | Pts. | AVERAGES RPG | APG | PPG |
|---|---|---|---|---|---|---|---|---|---|---|---|---|---|---|---|---|---|---|---|
| 04-05—Philadelphia .. | 5 | 192 | 26 | 47 | .553 | 6 | 15 | .400 | 18 | 46 | 64 | 2 | 2 | 7 | 9 | 58 | 12.8 | 0.4 | 11.6 |

Personal fouls/disqualifications: 2004-05, 19/0. Totals, 19/0.

## DAMPIER, ERICK　　　　C　　　　MAVERICKS

**PERSONAL:** Born July 14, 1974, in Jackson, Miss. ... 6-11/265. (2.11/120.2). ... Full name: Erick Trevez Dampier
**HIGH SCHOOL:** Lawrence County (Monticello, Miss.).
**COLLEGE:** Mississippi State.
**TRANSACTIONS/CAREER NOTES:** Selected after junior season by Indiana Pacers in first round (10th pick overall) of 1996 NBA Draft. ... Traded by Pacers with F Duane Ferrell to Golden State Warriors for F Chris Mullin (August 12, 1997). ... Traded by Warriors with G Dan Dickau, C Evan Eschmeyer and draft rights to G Steve Logan to Dallas Mavericks for F/C Christian Laettner, F Eduardo Najera, draft rights to G Luis Flores and G/F Mladen Sekularac, two future first-round draft choices and cash (August 24, 2004).

### COLLEGIATE RECORD

| Season Team | G | Min. | FGM | FGA | Pct. | FTM | FTA | Pct. | Reb. | Ast. | Pts. | AVERAGES RPG | APG | PPG |
|---|---|---|---|---|---|---|---|---|---|---|---|---|---|---|
| 93-94—Mississippi State............ | 29 | 678 | 133 | 226 | .588 | 78 | 159 | .491 | 251 | 23 | 344 | 8.7 | 0.8 | 11.9 |
| 94-95—Mississippi State............ | 30 | 853 | 153 | 239 | .640 | 87 | 146 | .596 | 291 | 28 | 393 | 9.7 | 0.9 | 13.1 |
| 95-96—Mississippi State............ | 34 | 1112 | 195 | 354 | .551 | 104 | 170 | .612 | 317 | 77 | 494 | 9.3 | 2.3 | 14.5 |
| Totals ..................................... | 93 | 2643 | 481 | 819 | .587 | 269 | 475 | .566 | 859 | 128 | 1231 | 9.2 | 1.4 | 13.2 |

### NBA REGULAR-SEASON RECORD

| Season Team | G | Min. | FGM | FGA | Pct. | FTM | FTA | Pct. | REBOUNDS Off. | Def. | Tot. | Ast. | St. | Blk. | TO | Pts. | AVERAGES RPG | APG | PPG |
|---|---|---|---|---|---|---|---|---|---|---|---|---|---|---|---|---|---|---|---|
| 96-97—Indiana............ | 72 | 1052 | 131 | 336 | .390 | 107 | 168 | .637 | 96 | 198 | 294 | 43 | 19 | 73 | 84 | 370 | 4.1 | 0.6 | 5.1 |
| 97-98—Golden State ... | 82 | 2656 | 352 | 791 | .445 | 267 | 399 | .669 | 272 | 443 | 715 | 94 | 39 | 139 | 175 | 971 | 8.7 | 1.1 | 11.8 |
| 98-99—Golden State ... | 50 | 1414 | 161 | 414 | .389 | 120 | 204 | .588 | 164 | 218 | 382 | 54 | 26 | 58 | 92 | 442 | 7.6 | 1.1 | 8.8 |
| 99-00—Golden State ... | 21 | 495 | 70 | 173 | .405 | 27 | 51 | .529 | 48 | 86 | 134 | 19 | 8 | 15 | 29 | 167 | 6.4 | 0.9 | 8.0 |
| 00-01—Golden State ... | 43 | 1038 | 126 | 314 | .401 | 67 | 126 | .532 | 97 | 153 | 250 | 59 | 17 | 58 | 82 | 319 | 5.8 | 1.4 | 7.4 |
| 01-02—Golden State ... | 73 | 1740 | 209 | 480 | .435 | 136 | 211 | .645 | 167 | 220 | 387 | 87 | 17 | 167 | 156 | 554 | 5.3 | 1.2 | 7.6 |
| 02-03—Golden State ... | 82 | 1978 | 259 | 522 | .496 | 155 | 222 | .698 | 248 | 295 | 543 | 58 | 27 | 154 | 112 | 673 | 6.6 | 0.7 | 8.2 |
| 03-04—Golden State ... | 74 | 2403 | 348 | 650 | .535 | 217 | 332 | .654 | 344 | 543 | 887 | 60 | 33 | 137 | 131 | 913 | 12.0 | 0.8 | 12.3 |
| 04-05—Dallas.............. | 59 | 1609 | 202 | 367 | .550 | 138 | 228 | .605 | 183 | 318 | 501 | 51 | 15 | 80 | 102 | 542 | 8.5 | 0.9 | 9.2 |
| Totals ................... | 556 | 14385 | 1858 | 4047 | .459 | 1234 | 1941 | .636 | 1619 | 2474 | 4093 | 525 | 201 | 881 | 963 | 4951 | 7.4 | 0.9 | 8.9 |

Three-point field goals: 1996-97, 1-for-1 (1.000). 1997-98, 0-for-2. 2000-01, 0-for-2. 2002-03, 0-for-2. 2003-04, 0-for-2. 2004-05, 0-for-3. Totals, 1-for-12 (.083).
Personal fouls/disqualifications: 1996-97, 153/1. 1997-98, 281/6. 1998-99, 165/2. 1999-00, 75/1. 2000-01, 123/3. 2001-02, 235/4. 2002-03, 242/3. 2003-04, 227/3. 2004-05, 205/2. Totals, 1706/25.

### NBA PLAYOFF RECORD

| Season Team | G | Min. | FGM | FGA | Pct. | FTM | FTA | Pct. | REBOUNDS Off. | Def. | Tot. | Ast. | St. | Blk. | TO | Pts. | AVERAGES RPG | APG | PPG |
|---|---|---|---|---|---|---|---|---|---|---|---|---|---|---|---|---|---|---|---|
| 04-05—Dallas.............. | 13 | 308 | 40 | 67 | .597 | 11 | 28 | .393 | 51 | 46 | 97 | 7 | 7 | 18 | 12 | 91 | 7.5 | 0.5 | 7.0 |

Three-point field goals: 2004-05, 0-for-1. Totals, 0-for-1 (.000).
Personal fouls/disqualifications: 2004-05, 54/2. Totals, 54/2.

## DANIELS, ANTONIO　　　　G　　　　WIZARDS

**PERSONAL:** Born March 19, 1975, in Columbus, Ohio. ... 6-4/205. (1.93/93.0). ... Full name: Antonio Robert Daniels
**HIGH SCHOOL:** St. Francis DeSales (Columbus, Ohio).
**COLLEGE:** Bowling Green.
**TRANSACTIONS/CAREER NOTES:** Selected by Vancouver Grizzlies in first round (fourth pick overall) of 1997 NBA Draft. ... Traded by Grizzlies to San Antonio Spurs for F Carl Herrera and draft rights to G Felipe Lopez (June 24, 1998). ... Traded by Spurs with G Charles Smith and F/C Amal McCaskill to Portland Trail Blazers for G Erick Barkley and G Steve Kerr (August 5, 2002). ... Signed as free agent by Seattle SuperSonics (July 19, 2003). ... Signed as free agent by Washington Wizards (August 2, 2005).
**MISCELLANEOUS:** Member of NBA championship team (1999).

### COLLEGIATE RECORD

| Season Team | G | Min. | FGM | FGA | Pct. | FTM | FTA | Pct. | Reb. | Ast. | Pts. | AVERAGES RPG | APG | PPG |
|---|---|---|---|---|---|---|---|---|---|---|---|---|---|---|
| 93-94—Bowling Green State....... | 28 | 864 | 132 | 258 | .512 | 84 | 103 | .816 | 81 | 110 | 354 | 2.9 | 3.9 | 12.6 |
| 94-95—Bowling Green State....... | 26 | 753 | 97 | 196 | .495 | 58 | 83 | .699 | 73 | 100 | 268 | 2.8 | 3.8 | 10.3 |
| 95-96—Bowling Green State....... | 25 | 922 | 142 | 297 | .478 | 99 | 137 | .723 | 77 | 147 | 400 | 3.1 | 5.9 | 16.0 |

**D**

| Season Team | G | Min. | FGM | FGA | Pct. | FTM | FTA | Pct. | Reb. | Ast. | Pts. | RPG | APG | PPG |
|---|---|---|---|---|---|---|---|---|---|---|---|---|---|---|
| | | | | | | | | | | | | AVERAGES | | |
| 96-97—Bowling Green State....... | 32 | 1161 | 279 | 510 | .547 | 164 | 211 | .777 | 90 | 216 | 767 | 2.8 | 6.8 | 24.0 |
| Totals ..................................... | 111 | 3700 | 650 | 1261 | .515 | 405 | 534 | .758 | 321 | 573 | 1789 | 2.9 | 5.2 | 16.1 |

Three-point field goals: 1993-94, 4-for-17 (.235). 1994-95, 16-for-38 (.421). 1995-96, 17-for-37 (.459). 1996-97, 45-for-104 (.433). Totals, 82-for-196 (.418).

### NBA REGULAR-SEASON RECORD

| Season Team | G | Min. | FGM | FGA | Pct. | FTM | FTA | Pct. | REBOUNDS Off. | Def. | Tot. | Ast. | St. | Blk. | TO | Pts. | AVERAGES RPG | APG | PPG |
|---|---|---|---|---|---|---|---|---|---|---|---|---|---|---|---|---|---|---|---|
| 97-98—Vancouver....... | 74 | 1956 | 228 | 548 | .416 | 112 | 170 | .659 | 22 | 121 | 143 | 334 | 55 | 10 | 164 | 579 | 1.9 | 4.5 | 7.8 |
| 98-99—San Antonio.... | 47 | 614 | 83 | 183 | .454 | 49 | 65 | .754 | 13 | 41 | 54 | 106 | 30 | 6 | 44 | 220 | 1.1 | 2.3 | 4.7 |
| 99-00—San Antonio.... | 68 | 1195 | 163 | 344 | .474 | 72 | 101 | .713 | 16 | 70 | 86 | 177 | 55 | 5 | 58 | 420 | 1.3 | 2.6 | 6.2 |
| 00-01—San Antonio.... | 79 | 2060 | 275 | 588 | .468 | 121 | 156 | .776 | 26 | 137 | 163 | 304 | 61 | 14 | 109 | 745 | 2.1 | 3.8 | 9.4 |
| 01-02—San Antonio.... | 82 | 2175 | 269 | 612 | .440 | 158 | 210 | .752 | 23 | 153 | 176 | 228 | 48 | 12 | 70 | 753 | 2.1 | 2.8 | 9.2 |
| 02-03—Portland.......... | 67 | 872 | 84 | 186 | .452 | 65 | 76 | .855 | 11 | 61 | 72 | 85 | 33 | 9 | 32 | 251 | 1.1 | 1.3 | 3.7 |
| 03-04—Seattle ........... | 71 | 1512 | 187 | 398 | .470 | 155 | 184 | .842 | 23 | 119 | 142 | 298 | 45 | 6 | 61 | 571 | 2.0 | 4.2 | 8.0 |
| 04-05—Seattle ........... | 75 | 2026 | 273 | 623 | .438 | 248 | 304 | .816 | 20 | 149 | 169 | 309 | 51 | 3 | 78 | 843 | 2.3 | 4.1 | 11.2 |
| Totals ................... | 563 | 12410 | 1562 | 3482 | .449 | 980 | 1266 | .774 | 154 | 851 | 1005 | 1841 | 378 | 65 | 616 | 4382 | 1.8 | 3.3 | 7.8 |

Three-point field goals: 1997-98, 11-for-52 (.212). 1998-99, 5-for-17 (.294). 1999-00, 22-for-66 (.333). 2000-01, 74-for-183 (.404). 2001-02, 57-for-196 (.291). 2002-03, 18-for-59 (.305). 2003-04, 42-for-116 (.362). 2004-05, 49-for-165 (.297). Totals, 278-for-854 (.326).

Personal fouls/disqualifications: 1997-98, 88/0. 1998-99, 39/0. 1999-00, 73/0. 2000-01, 120/0. 2001-02, 104/0. 2002-03, 43/0. 2003-04, 64/0. 2004-05, 78/0. Totals, 609/0.

### NBA PLAYOFF RECORD

| Season Team | G | Min. | FGM | FGA | Pct. | FTM | FTA | Pct. | REBOUNDS Off. | Def. | Tot. | Ast. | St. | Blk. | TO | Pts. | AVERAGES RPG | APG | PPG |
|---|---|---|---|---|---|---|---|---|---|---|---|---|---|---|---|---|---|---|---|
| 98-99—San Antonio.... | 15 | 106 | 9 | 21 | .429 | 5 | 6 | .833 | 1 | 9 | 10 | 16 | 4 | 0 | 10 | 27 | 0.7 | 1.1 | 1.8 |
| 99-00—San Antonio.... | 4 | 82 | 9 | 23 | .391 | 9 | 13 | .692 | 2 | 8 | 10 | 6 | 7 | 0 | 6 | 29 | 2.5 | 1.5 | 7.3 |
| 00-01—San Antonio.... | 13 | 406 | 63 | 131 | .481 | 33 | 35 | .943 | 4 | 22 | 26 | 38 | 7 | 1 | 13 | 176 | 2.0 | 2.9 | 13.5 |
| 01-02—San Antonio.... | 10 | 224 | 35 | 77 | .455 | 19 | 22 | .864 | 3 | 24 | 27 | 15 | 7 | 3 | 5 | 95 | 2.7 | 1.5 | 9.5 |
| 02-03—Portland.......... | 6 | 98 | 9 | 19 | .474 | 1 | 2 | .500 | 3 | 5 | 8 | 12 | 1 | 1 | 2 | 22 | 1.3 | 2.0 | 3.7 |
| 04-05—Seattle ........... | 11 | 331 | 44 | 94 | .468 | 60 | 70 | .857 | 4 | 27 | 31 | 49 | 11 | 0 | 11 | 152 | 2.8 | 4.5 | 13.8 |
| Totals ................... | 59 | 1247 | 169 | 365 | .463 | 127 | 148 | .858 | 17 | 95 | 112 | 136 | 37 | 5 | 47 | 501 | 1.9 | 2.3 | 8.5 |

Three-point field goals: 1998-99, 4-for-6 (.667). 1999-00, 2-for-8 (.250). 2000-01, 17-for-46 (.370). 2001-02, 6-for-16 (.375). 2002-03, 3-for-5 (.600). 2004-05, 4-for-14 (.286). Totals, 36-for-95 (.379).

Personal fouls/disqualifications: 1998-99, 7/0. 1999-00, 5/0. 2000-01, 22/0. 2001-02, 13/0. 2002-03, 5/0. 2004-05, 13/0. Totals, 65/0.

## DANIELS, ERIK     F     KINGS

**PERSONAL:** Born April 1, 1982, in Cincinnati, Ohio. ... 6-8/214. (2.03/97.1). ... Full name: Erik Christopher Daniels.
**HIGH SCHOOL:** Princeton (Cincinnati, Ohio).
**COLLEGE:** Kentucky.
**TRANSACTIONS/CAREER NOTES:** Not drafted by an NBA franchise. ... Signed as free agent by Sacramento Kings (October 1, 2004).

### COLLEGIATE RECORD

| Season Team | G | Min. | FGM | FGA | Pct. | FTM | FTA | Pct. | Reb. | Ast. | Pts. | AVERAGES RPG | APG | PPG |
|---|---|---|---|---|---|---|---|---|---|---|---|---|---|---|
| 00-01—Kentucky ........................ | 33 | 427 | 64 | 113 | .566 | 38 | 63 | .603 | 85 | 26 | 171 | 2.6 | 0.8 | 5.2 |
| 01-02—Kentucky ........................ | 30 | 392 | 46 | 100 | .460 | 17 | 31 | .548 | 86 | 36 | 112 | 2.9 | 1.2 | 3.7 |
| 02-03—Kentucky ........................ | 32 | 821 | 136 | 240 | .567 | 29 | 46 | .630 | 156 | 71 | 305 | 4.9 | 2.2 | 9.5 |
| 03-04—Kentucky ........................ | 32 | 959 | 201 | 346 | .581 | 56 | 89 | .629 | 195 | 90 | 465 | 6.1 | 2.8 | 14.5 |
| Totals ..................................... | 127 | 2599 | 447 | 799 | .559 | 140 | 229 | .611 | 522 | 223 | 1053 | 4.1 | 1.8 | 8.3 |

Three-point field goals: 2000-01, 5-for-18 (.278). 2001-02, 3-for-19 (.158). 2002-03, 4-for-13 (.308). 2003-04, 7-for-23 (.304). Totals, 19-for-73 (.260).

### NBA REGULAR-SEASON RECORD

| Season Team | G | Min. | FGM | FGA | Pct. | FTM | FTA | Pct. | REBOUNDS Off. | Def. | Tot. | Ast. | St. | Blk. | TO | Pts. | AVERAGES RPG | APG | PPG |
|---|---|---|---|---|---|---|---|---|---|---|---|---|---|---|---|---|---|---|---|
| 04-05—Sacramento .... | 21 | 72 | 6 | 18 | .333 | 0 | 0 | ... | 7 | 11 | 18 | 4 | 2 | 0 | 6 | 13 | 0.9 | 0.2 | 0.6 |

Three-point field goals: 2004-05, 1-for-2 (.500). Totals, 1-for-2 (.500).
Personal fouls/disqualifications: 2004-05, 7/0. Totals, 7/0.

## DANIELS, MARQUIS     F     MAVERICKS

**PERSONAL:** Born January 7, 1981, in Orlando, Fla. ... 6-6/200. (1.98/90.7). ... Full name: Marquis Antwane Daniels.
**HIGH SCHOOL:** Mount Zion Christian Academy (Durham, N.C.).
**COLLEGE:** Auburn.
**TRANSACTIONS/CAREER NOTES:** Not drafted by an NBA franchise. ... Signed as free agent by Dallas Mavericks (July 29, 2003).

### COLLEGIATE RECORD

| Season Team | G | Min. | FGM | FGA | Pct. | FTM | FTA | Pct. | Reb. | Ast. | Pts. | AVERAGES RPG | APG | PPG |
|---|---|---|---|---|---|---|---|---|---|---|---|---|---|---|
| 99-00—Auburn ......................... | 17 | 216 | 32 | 72 | .444 | 10 | 20 | .500 | 45 | 8 | 77 | 2.6 | 0.5 | 4.5 |
| 00-01—Auburn ......................... | 32 | 974 | 206 | 395 | .522 | 80 | 124 | .645 | 223 | 50 | 503 | 7.0 | 1.6 | 15.7 |
| 01-02—Auburn ......................... | 28 | 807 | 115 | 260 | .442 | 73 | 115 | .635 | 148 | 116 | 325 | 5.3 | 4.1 | 11.6 |
| 02-03—Auburn ......................... | 34 | 1187 | 244 | 476 | .513 | 107 | 159 | .673 | 210 | 113 | 625 | 6.2 | 3.3 | 18.4 |
| Totals ..................................... | 111 | 3184 | 597 | 1203 | .496 | 270 | 418 | .646 | 626 | 287 | 1530 | 5.6 | 2.6 | 13.8 |

Three-point field goals: 1999-00, 3-for-15 (.200). 2000-01, 11-for-48 (.229). 2001-02, 22-for-62 (.355). 2002-03, 30-for-98 (.306). Totals, 66-for-223 (.296).

**HONORS:** NBA All-Rookie second team (2004).

| Season Team | G | Min. | FGM | FGA | Pct. | FTM | FTA | Pct. | Off. | Def. | Tot. | Ast. | St. | Blk. | TO | Pts. | RPG | APG | PPG |
|---|---|---|---|---|---|---|---|---|---|---|---|---|---|---|---|---|---|---|---|
| | | | | | | | | | REBOUNDS | | | | | | | | AVERAGES | | |
| 03-04—Dallas............. | 56 | 1039 | 203 | 411 | .494 | 60 | 78 | .769 | 66 | 80 | 146 | 116 | 53 | 12 | 44 | 477 | 2.6 | 2.1 | 8.5 |
| 04-05—Dallas............. | 60 | 1412 | 220 | 504 | .437 | 98 | 133 | .737 | 87 | 129 | 216 | 128 | 83 | 14 | 86 | 545 | 3.6 | 2.1 | 9.1 |
| Totals .................. | 116 | 2451 | 423 | 915 | .462 | 158 | 211 | .749 | 153 | 209 | 362 | 244 | 136 | 26 | 130 | 1022 | 3.1 | 2.1 | 8.8 |

Three-point field goals: 2003-04, 11-for-36 (.306). 2004-05, 7-for-35 (.200). Totals, 18-for-71 (.254).
Personal fouls/disqualifications: 2003-04, 51/0. 2004-05, 124/0. Totals, 175/0.

### NBA PLAYOFF RECORD

| Season Team | G | Min. | FGM | FGA | Pct. | FTM | FTA | Pct. | Off. | Def. | Tot. | Ast. | St. | Blk. | TO | Pts. | RPG | APG | PPG |
|---|---|---|---|---|---|---|---|---|---|---|---|---|---|---|---|---|---|---|---|
| | | | | | | | | | REBOUNDS | | | | | | | | AVERAGES | | |
| 03-04—Dallas............. | 5 | 184 | 32 | 75 | .427 | 14 | 22 | .636 | 10 | 21 | 31 | 15 | 10 | 3 | 15 | 79 | 6.2 | 3.0 | 15.8 |
| 04-05—Dallas............. | 11 | 165 | 26 | 60 | .433 | 19 | 27 | .704 | 15 | 19 | 34 | 14 | 6 | 3 | 13 | 72 | 3.1 | 1.3 | 6.5 |
| Totals .................. | 16 | 349 | 58 | 135 | .430 | 33 | 49 | .673 | 25 | 40 | 65 | 29 | 16 | 6 | 28 | 151 | 4.1 | 1.8 | 9.4 |

Three-point field goals: 2003-04, 1-for-7 (.143). 2004-05, 1-for-6 (.167). Totals, 2-for-13 (.154).
Personal fouls/disqualifications: 2003-04, 14/0. 2004-05, 15/0. Totals, 29/0.

# DAVIS, ANTONIO     F/C     BULLS

**PERSONAL:** Born October 31, 1968, in Oakland. ... 6-9/230. (2.06/104.3). ... Full name: Antonio Lee Davis
**HIGH SCHOOL:** McClymonds (Oakland).
**COLLEGE:** Texas-El Paso.
**TRANSACTIONS/CAREER NOTES:** Selected by Indiana Pacers in second round (45th pick overall) of 1990 NBA Draft. ... Played in Greece (1990-92). ... Played in Italy (1992-93). ... Traded by Pacers to Toronto Raptors for draft rights to F Jonathan Bender (August 1, 1999). ... Traded by Raptors with F Chris Jefferies and F Jerome Williams to Chicago Bulls for F Lonny Baxter, F Donyell Marshall and G Jalen Rose (December 1, 2003).
**MISCELLANEOUS:** Toronto Raptors all-time leading rebounder with 2,223 (1999-2000 through 2001-02).

### COLLEGIATE RECORD

| Season Team | G | Min. | FGM | FGA | Pct. | FTM | FTA | Pct. | Reb. | Ast. | Pts. | RPG | APG | PPG |
|---|---|---|---|---|---|---|---|---|---|---|---|---|---|---|
| | | | | | | | | | | | | AVERAGES | | |
| 86-87—Texas-El Paso ................ | 28 | 240 | 11 | 32 | .344 | 13 | 30 | .433 | 51 | 4 | 35 | 1.8 | 0.1 | 1.3 |
| 87-88—Texas-El Paso ................ | 30 | 907 | 108 | 183 | .590 | 63 | 115 | .548 | 195 | 20 | 279 | 6.5 | 0.7 | 9.3 |
| 88-89—Texas-El Paso ................ | 32 | 1014 | 162 | 298 | .544 | 135 | 218 | .619 | 255 | 14 | 459 | 8.0 | 0.4 | 14.3 |
| 89-90—Texas-El Paso ................ | 32 | 991 | 119 | 228 | .522 | 106 | 165 | .642 | 243 | 21 | 344 | 7.6 | 0.7 | 10.8 |
| Totals ...................... | 122 | 3152 | 400 | 741 | .540 | 317 | 528 | .600 | 744 | 59 | 1117 | 6.1 | 0.5 | 9.2 |

Three-point field goals: 1988-89, 0-for-1. 1989-90, 0-for-1. Totals, 0-for-2 (.000).

### ITALIAN LEAGUE RECORD

| Season Team | G | Min. | FGM | FGA | Pct. | FTM | FTA | Pct. | Reb. | Ast. | Pts. | RPG | APG | PPG |
|---|---|---|---|---|---|---|---|---|---|---|---|---|---|---|
| | | | | | | | | | | | | AVERAGES | | |
| 92-93—Philips Milano ............... | 29 | 892 | 121 | 195 | .621 | 81 | 130 | .623 | 286 | 5 | 323 | 9.9 | 0.2 | 11.1 |

Three-point field goals: 1992-93, 0-for-1. Totals, 0-for-1 (.000).
Personal fouls/disqualifications: 1992-93, 0/7. Totals, 0/7.

### NBA REGULAR-SEASON RECORD

| Season Team | G | Min. | FGM | FGA | Pct. | FTM | FTA | Pct. | Off. | Def. | Tot. | Ast. | St. | Blk. | TO | Pts. | RPG | APG | PPG |
|---|---|---|---|---|---|---|---|---|---|---|---|---|---|---|---|---|---|---|---|
| | | | | | | | | | REBOUNDS | | | | | | | | AVERAGES | | |
| 93-94—Indiana........... | 81 | 1732 | 216 | 425 | .508 | 194 | 302 | .642 | 190 | 315 | 505 | 55 | 45 | 84 | 107 | 626 | 6.2 | 0.7 | 7.7 |
| 94-95—Indiana........... | 44 | 1030 | 109 | 245 | .445 | 117 | 174 | .672 | 105 | 175 | 280 | 25 | 19 | 29 | 64 | 335 | 6.4 | 0.6 | 7.6 |
| 95-96—Indiana........... | 82 | 2092 | 236 | 482 | .490 | 246 | 345 | .713 | 188 | 313 | 501 | 43 | 33 | 66 | 87 | 719 | 6.1 | 0.5 | 8.8 |
| 96-97—Indiana........... | 82 | 2335 | 308 | 641 | .480 | 241 | 362 | .666 | 190 | 408 | 598 | 65 | 42 | 84 | 141 | 858 | 7.3 | 0.8 | 10.5 |
| 97-98—Indiana........... | 82 | 2191 | 254 | 528 | .481 | 277 | 398 | .696 | 192 | 368 | 560 | 61 | 45 | 72 | 103 | 785 | 6.8 | 0.7 | 9.6 |
| 98-99—Indiana........... | 49 | 1271 | 164 | 348 | .471 | 135 | 192 | .703 | 116 | 228 | 344 | 33 | 22 | 42 | 50 | 463 | 7.0 | 0.7 | 9.4 |
| 99-00—Toronto .......... | 79 | 2479 | 313 | 712 | .440 | 284 | 371 | .765 | 235 | 461 | 696 | 105 | 38 | 100 | 121 | 910 | 8.8 | 1.3 | 11.5 |
| 00-01—Toronto .......... | 78 | 2729 | 375 | 866 | .433 | 319 | 423 | .754 | 274 | 513 | 787 | 106 | 22 | 151 | 135 | 1069 | 10.1 | 1.4 | 13.7 |
| 01-02—Toronto .......... | 77 | 2978 | 410 | 963 | .426 | 293 | 358 | .818 | 254 | 486 | 740 | 155 | 54 | 83 | 159 | 1113 | 9.6 | 2.0 | 14.5 |
| 02-03—Toronto .......... | 53 | 1894 | 261 | 641 | .407 | 216 | 280 | .771 | 130 | 307 | 437 | 131 | 23 | 62 | 118 | 738 | 8.2 | 2.5 | 13.9 |
| 03-04—Tor.-Chi. ........ | 80 | 2570 | 266 | 660 | .403 | 176 | 230 | .765 | 207 | 464 | 671 | 137 | 37 | 65 | 114 | 708 | 8.4 | 1.7 | 8.9 |
| 04-05—Chicago ......... | 72 | 1843 | 193 | 419 | .461 | 115 | 152 | .757 | 152 | 276 | 428 | 80 | 27 | 41 | 96 | 501 | 5.9 | 1.1 | 7.0 |
| Totals ................... | 859 | 25144 | 3105 | 6930 | .448 | 2613 | 3587 | .728 | 2233 | 4314 | 6547 | 996 | 407 | 879 | 1295 | 8825 | 7.6 | 1.2 | 10.3 |

Three-point field goals: 1993-94, 0-for-1. 1995-96, 1-for-2 (.500). 1996-97, 1-for-14 (.071). 1997-98, 0-for-3. 2000-01, 0-for-1. 2001-02, 0-for-1. Totals, 2-for-22 (.091).
Personal fouls/disqualifications: 1993-94, 189/1. 1994-95, 134/2. 1995-96, 248/6. 1996-97, 260/4. 1997-98, 234/6. 1998-99, 136/3. 1999-00, 267/2. 2000-01, 230/4. 2001-02, 225/3. 2002-03, 150/0. 2003-04, 206/1. 2004-05, 147/0. Totals, 2426/32.

### NBA PLAYOFF RECORD

| Season Team | G | Min. | FGM | FGA | Pct. | FTM | FTA | Pct. | Off. | Def. | Tot. | Ast. | St. | Blk. | TO | Pts. | RPG | APG | PPG |
|---|---|---|---|---|---|---|---|---|---|---|---|---|---|---|---|---|---|---|---|
| | | | | | | | | | REBOUNDS | | | | | | | | AVERAGES | | |
| 93-94—Indiana........... | 16 | 401 | 48 | 89 | .539 | 37 | 66 | .561 | 37 | 69 | 106 | 7 | 11 | 18 | 22 | 134 | 6.6 | 0.4 | 8.4 |
| 94-95—Indiana........... | 17 | 367 | 32 | 71 | .451 | 37 | 59 | .627 | 38 | 59 | 97 | 7 | 9 | 11 | 23 | 101 | 5.7 | 0.4 | 5.9 |
| 95-96—Indiana........... | 5 | 127 | 13 | 25 | .520 | 13 | 15 | .867 | 12 | 19 | 31 | 3 | 3 | 6 | 10 | 39 | 6.2 | 0.6 | 7.8 |
| 97-98—Indiana........... | 16 | 459 | 42 | 91 | .462 | 63 | 94 | .670 | 37 | 71 | 108 | 14 | 12 | 18 | 25 | 147 | 6.8 | 0.9 | 9.2 |
| 98-99—Indiana........... | 13 | 326 | 31 | 75 | .413 | 41 | 62 | .661 | 23 | 69 | 92 | 8 | 5 | 14 | 20 | 103 | 7.1 | 0.6 | 7.9 |
| 99-00—Toronto .......... | 3 | 105 | 14 | 24 | .583 | 11 | 14 | .786 | 7 | 18 | 25 | 3 | 1 | 4 | 4 | 39 | 8.3 | 1.0 | 13.0 |
| 00-01—Toronto .......... | 12 | 485 | 77 | 154 | .500 | 43 | 53 | .811 | 41 | 92 | 133 | 23 | 10 | 22 | 21 | 197 | 11.1 | 1.9 | 16.4 |
| 01-02—Toronto .......... | 5 | 202 | 34 | 75 | .453 | 17 | 28 | .607 | 16 | 37 | 53 | 7 | 2 | 5 | 10 | 85 | 10.6 | 1.4 | 17.0 |

**D**

| Season Team | G | Min. | FGM | FGA | Pct. | FTM | FTA | Pct. | REBOUNDS Off. | Def. | Tot. | Ast. | St. | Blk. | TO | Pts. | AVERAGES RPG | APG | PPG |
|---|---|---|---|---|---|---|---|---|---|---|---|---|---|---|---|---|---|---|---|
| 04-05—Chicago .......... | 6 | 175 | 20 | 46 | .435 | 17 | 23 | .739 | 17 | 24 | 41 | 11 | 4 | 4 | 9 | 57 | 6.8 | 1.8 | 9.5 |
| Totals ................... | 93 | 2647 | 311 | 650 | .478 | 279 | 414 | .674 | 228 | 458 | 686 | 83 | 57 | 102 | 144 | 902 | 7.4 | 0.9 | 9.7 |

Three-point field goals: 1993-94, 1-for-1 (1.000). Totals, 1-for-1 (1.000).

Personal fouls/disqualifications: 1993-94, 47/0. 1994-95, 61/0. 1995-96, 12/0. 1997-98, 65/5. 1998-99, 39/0. 1999-00, 9/0. 2000-01, 35/0. 2001-02, 17/0. 2004-05, 25/1. Totals, 310/6.

## NBA ALL-STAR GAME RECORD

| Season Team | Min. | FGM | FGA | Pct. | FTM | FTA | Pct. | REBOUNDS Off. | Def. | Tot. | Ast. | PF | Dq. | St. | Blk. | TO | Pts. |
|---|---|---|---|---|---|---|---|---|---|---|---|---|---|---|---|---|---|
| 2001—Toronto ................ | 20 | 4 | 11 | .364 | 0 | 0 | ... | 7 | 2 | 9 | 0 | 0 | 0 | 1 | 1 | 0 | 8 |

# DAVIS, BARON       G       WARRIORS

**PERSONAL:** Born April 13, 1979, in Los Angeles. ... 6-3/223. (1.91/101.2).
**HIGH SCHOOL:** Crossroads (Santa Monica, Calif.).
**COLLEGE:** UCLA.
**TRANSACTIONS/CAREER NOTES:** Selected after sophomore season by Charlotte Hornets in first round (third pick overall) of 1999 NBA Draft. ... Hornets franchise moved to New Orleans for 2002-03 season. ... Traded by Hornets to Golden State Warriors for G Speedy Claxton and F Dale Davis (February 24, 2005).

## COLLEGIATE RECORD

| Season Team | G | Min. | FGM | FGA | Pct. | FTM | FTA | Pct. | Reb. | Ast. | Pts. | AVERAGES RPG | APG | PPG |
|---|---|---|---|---|---|---|---|---|---|---|---|---|---|---|
| 97-98—UCLA............................ | 32 | 1003 | 137 | 259 | .529 | 75 | 111 | .676 | 129 | 161 | 373 | 4.0 | 5.0 | 11.7 |
| 98-99—UCLA.......................... | 27 | 828 | 150 | 312 | .481 | 94 | 157 | .599 | 97 | 97 | 429 | 3.6 | 3.6 | 15.9 |
| Totals ...................................... | 59 | 1831 | 287 | 571 | .503 | 169 | 268 | .631 | 226 | 258 | 802 | 3.8 | 4.4 | 13.6 |

Three-point field goals: 1997-98, 24-for-78 (.308). 1998-99, 59-for-180 (.328). Totals, 83-for-258 (.322).

Personal fouls/disqualifications: 1997-98, 111/9. Totals, 111/9.

## NBA REGULAR-SEASON RECORD

**HONORS:** All-NBA third team (2004).

| Season Team | G | Min. | FGM | FGA | Pct. | FTM | FTA | Pct. | REBOUNDS Off. | Def. | Tot. | Ast. | St. | Blk. | TO | Pts. | AVERAGES RPG | APG | PPG |
|---|---|---|---|---|---|---|---|---|---|---|---|---|---|---|---|---|---|---|---|
| 99-00—Charlotte ........ | 82 | 1523 | 182 | 433 | .420 | 97 | 153 | .634 | 48 | 117 | 165 | 309 | 97 | 19 | 140 | 486 | 2.0 | 3.8 | 5.9 |
| 00-01—Charlotte ........ | 82 | 3192 | 409 | 957 | .427 | 228 | 337 | .677 | 129 | 279 | 408 | 598 | 170 | 36 | 226 | 1131 | 5.0 | 7.3 | 13.8 |
| 01-02—Charlotte ........ | 82 | 3318 | 559 | 1341 | .417 | 196 | 338 | .580 | 93 | 256 | 349 | 698 | 172 | 47 | 246 | 1484 | 4.3 | 8.5 | 18.1 |
| 02-03—New Orleans ... | 50 | 1889 | 332 | 798 | .416 | 93 | 131 | .710 | 56 | 130 | 186 | 320 | 91 | 22 | 140 | 856 | 3.7 | 6.4 | 17.1 |
| 03-04—New Orleans ... | 67 | 2686 | 554 | 1402 | .395 | 237 | 352 | .673 | 66 | 221 | 287 | 501 | 158 | 27 | 215 | 1532 | 4.3 | 7.5 | 22.9 |
| 04-05—N.O.-Golden St. | 46 | 1581 | 291 | 752 | .387 | 185 | 243 | .761 | 32 | 143 | 175 | 362 | 81 | 14 | 131 | 885 | 3.8 | 7.9 | 19.2 |
| Totals ................... | 409 | 14189 | 2327 | 5683 | .409 | 1036 | 1554 | .667 | 424 | 1146 | 1570 | 2788 | 769 | 165 | 1098 | 6374 | 3.8 | 6.8 | 15.6 |

Three-point field goals: 1999-00, 25-for-111 (.225). 2000-01, 85-for-274 (.310). 2001-02, 170-for-478 (.356). 2002-03, 99-for-283 (.350). 2003-04, 187-for-582 (.321). 2004-05, 118-for-354 (.333). Totals, 684-for-2082 (.329).

Personal fouls/disqualifications: 1999-00, 201/1. 2000-01, 267/1. 2001-02, 241/0. 2002-03, 148/3. 2003-04, 178/2. 2004-05, 126/1. Totals, 1161/8.

## NBA PLAYOFF RECORD

| Season Team | G | Min. | FGM | FGA | Pct. | FTM | FTA | Pct. | REBOUNDS Off. | Def. | Tot. | Ast. | St. | Blk. | TO | Pts. | AVERAGES RPG | APG | PPG |
|---|---|---|---|---|---|---|---|---|---|---|---|---|---|---|---|---|---|---|---|
| 99-00—Charlotte ........ | 4 | 57 | 10 | 23 | .435 | 2 | 4 | .500 | 3 | 3 | 6 | 6 | 4 | 0 | 3 | 23 | 1.5 | 1.5 | 5.8 |
| 00-01—Charlotte ........ | 10 | 397 | 59 | 123 | .480 | 40 | 56 | .714 | 9 | 35 | 44 | 58 | 28 | 5 | 22 | 178 | 4.4 | 5.8 | 17.8 |
| 01-02—Charlotte ........ | 9 | 401 | 71 | 188 | .378 | 40 | 67 | .597 | 16 | 47 | 63 | 71 | 32 | 5 | 27 | 203 | 7.0 | 7.9 | 22.6 |
| 02-03—New Orleans ... | 5 | 194 | 37 | 83 | .446 | 16 | 22 | .727 | 4 | 14 | 18 | 42 | 7 | 2 | 15 | 102 | 3.6 | 8.4 | 20.4 |
| 03-04—New Orleans ... | 7 | 260 | 43 | 114 | .377 | 25 | 33 | .758 | 6 | 23 | 29 | 49 | 11 | 5 | 19 | 127 | 4.1 | 7.0 | 18.1 |
| Totals ................... | 35 | 1309 | 220 | 531 | .414 | 123 | 182 | .676 | 38 | 122 | 160 | 226 | 82 | 17 | 86 | 633 | 4.6 | 6.5 | 18.1 |

Three-point field goals: 1999-00, 1-for-6 (.167). 2000-01, 20-for-50 (.400). 2001-02, 21-for-62 (.339). 2002-03, 12-for-35 (.343). 2003-04, 16-for-49 (.327). Totals, 70-for-202 (.347).

Personal fouls/disqualifications: 1999-00, 6/0. 2000-01, 33/0. 2001-02, 36/2. 2002-03, 20/0. 2003-04, 21/0. Totals, 116/2.

## NBA ALL-STAR GAME RECORD

**NOTES:** Won NBA All-Star Sports Skills Challenge (2004).

| Season Team | Min. | FGM | FGA | Pct. | FTM | FTA | Pct. | REBOUNDS Off. | Def. | Tot. | Ast. | PF | Dq. | St. | Blk. | TO | Pts. |
|---|---|---|---|---|---|---|---|---|---|---|---|---|---|---|---|---|---|---|
| 2002—Charlotte ............... | 13 | 1 | 5 | .200 | 0 | 0 | ... | 0 | 1 | 1 | 5 | 1 | 0 | 0 | 0 | 3 | 2 |
| 2004—New Orleans.......... | 16 | 3 | 9 | .333 | 0 | 0 | ... | 0 | 0 | 0 | 7 | 0 | 0 | 1 | 0 | 1 | 7 |
| Totals........................... | 29 | 4 | 14 | .286 | 0 | 0 | ... | 0 | 1 | 1 | 12 | 1 | 0 | 1 | 0 | 4 | 9 |

Three-point field goals: 2002, 0-for-3. 2004, 1-for-6 (.167). Totals, 1-for-9 (.111).

# DAVIS, DALE       F       PISTONS

**PERSONAL:** Born March 25, 1969, in Toccoa, Ga. ... 6-11/252. (2.11/114.3). ... Full name: Elliott Lydell Davis
**HIGH SCHOOL:** Stephens County (Toccoa, Ga.).
**COLLEGE:** Clemson.
**TRANSACTIONS/CAREER NOTES:** Selected by Indiana Pacers in first round (13th pick overall) of 1991 NBA Draft. ... Traded by Pacers to Portland Trail Blazers for F Jermaine O'Neal and C Joe Kleine (August 31, 2000). ... Traded by Trail Blazers

with G Dan Dickau to Golden State Warriors for G Nick Van Exel (July 20, 2004). ... Traded by Warriors with G Speedy Claxton to New Orleans Hornets for G Baron Davis (February 24, 2005). ... Waived by Hornets (March 1, 2005). ... Signed as free agent by Detroit Pistons (August 26, 2005).

### COLLEGIATE RECORD

| Season Team | G | Min. | FGM | FGA | Pct. | FTM | FTA | Pct. | Reb. | Ast. | Pts. | AVERAGES RPG | APG | PPG |
|---|---|---|---|---|---|---|---|---|---|---|---|---|---|---|
| 87-88—Clemson | 29 | 714 | 91 | 171 | .532 | 45 | 89 | .506 | 223 | 10 | 227 | 7.7 | 0.3 | 7.8 |
| 88-89—Clemson | 29 | 736 | 146 | 218 | .670 | 93 | 144 | .646 | 258 | 16 | 385 | 8.9 | 0.6 | 13.3 |
| 89-90—Clemson | 35 | 1077 | 205 | 328 | .625 | 127 | 213 | .596 | 395 | 21 | 537 | 11.3 | 0.6 | 15.3 |
| 90-91—Clemson | 28 | 971 | 191 | 359 | .532 | 119 | 205 | .580 | 340 | 37 | 501 | 12.1 | 1.3 | 17.9 |
| Totals | 121 | 3498 | 633 | 1076 | .588 | 384 | 651 | .590 | 1216 | 84 | 1650 | 10.0 | 0.7 | 13.6 |

Three-point field goals: 1989-90, 0-for-1. 1990-91, 0-for-2. Totals, 0-for-3 (.000).

### NBA REGULAR-SEASON RECORD

| Season Team | G | Min. | FGM | FGA | Pct. | FTM | FTA | Pct. | REBOUNDS Off. | Def. | Tot. | Ast. | St. | Blk. | TO | Pts. | AVERAGES RPG | APG | PPG |
|---|---|---|---|---|---|---|---|---|---|---|---|---|---|---|---|---|---|---|---|
| 91-92—Indiana | 64 | 1301 | 154 | 279 | .552 | 87 | 152 | .572 | 158 | 252 | 410 | 30 | 27 | 74 | 49 | 395 | 6.4 | 0.5 | 6.2 |
| 92-93—Indiana | 82 | 2264 | 304 | 535 | .568 | 119 | 225 | .529 | 291 | 432 | 723 | 69 | 63 | 148 | 79 | 727 | 8.8 | 0.8 | 8.9 |
| 93-94—Indiana | 66 | 2292 | 308 | 582 | .529 | 155 | 294 | .527 | 280 | 438 | 718 | 100 | 48 | 106 | 102 | 771 | 10.9 | 1.5 | 11.7 |
| 94-95—Indiana | 74 | 2346 | 324 | 576 | .563 | 138 | 259 | .533 | 259 | 437 | 696 | 58 | 72 | 116 | 124 | 786 | 9.4 | 0.8 | 10.6 |
| 95-96—Indiana | 78 | 2617 | 334 | 599 | .558 | 135 | 289 | .467 | 252 | 457 | 709 | 76 | 56 | 112 | 119 | 803 | 9.1 | 1.0 | 10.3 |
| 96-97—Indiana | 80 | 2589 | 370 | 688 | .538 | 92 | 215 | .428 | 301 | 471 | 772 | 59 | 60 | 77 | 108 | 832 | 9.7 | 0.7 | 10.4 |
| 97-98—Indiana | 78 | 2174 | 273 | 498 | .548 | 80 | 172 | .465 | 233 | 378 | 611 | 70 | 51 | 87 | 73 | 626 | 7.8 | 0.9 | 8.0 |
| 98-99—Indiana | 50 | 1374 | 161 | 302 | .533 | 76 | 123 | .618 | 155 | 261 | 416 | 22 | 20 | 57 | 43 | 398 | 8.3 | 0.4 | 8.0 |
| 99-00—Indiana | 74 | 2127 | 302 | 602 | .502 | 139 | 203 | .685 | 256 | 473 | 729 | 64 | 52 | 94 | 91 | 743 | 9.9 | 0.9 | 10.0 |
| 00-01—Portland | 81 | 2162 | 242 | 487 | .497 | 96 | 152 | .632 | 233 | 373 | 606 | 103 | 44 | 76 | 67 | 580 | 7.5 | 1.3 | 7.2 |
| 01-02—Portland | 78 | 2447 | 296 | 580 | .510 | 150 | 212 | .708 | 262 | 426 | 688 | 96 | 62 | 83 | 62 | 742 | 8.8 | 1.2 | 9.5 |
| 02-03—Portland | 78 | 2282 | 237 | 438 | .541 | 105 | 166 | .633 | 233 | 331 | 564 | 94 | 51 | 70 | 71 | 579 | 7.2 | 1.2 | 7.4 |
| 03-04—Portland | 76 | 1682 | 133 | 281 | .473 | 65 | 106 | .613 | 158 | 240 | 398 | 72 | 43 | 62 | 40 | 331 | 5.2 | 0.9 | 4.4 |
| 04-05—G.S.-N.O.Ind.... | 61 | 1307 | 112 | 234 | .479 | 60 | 99 | .606 | 152 | 223 | 375 | 47 | 32 | 65 | 43 | 284 | 6.1 | 0.8 | 4.7 |
| Totals | 1020 | 28964 | 3550 | 6681 | .531 | 1497 | 2667 | .561 | 3223 | 5192 | 8415 | 960 | 681 | 1227 | 1071 | 8597 | 8.3 | 0.9 | 8.4 |

Three-point field goals: 1991-92, 0-for-1. 1993-94, 0-for-1. 1994-95, 0-for-1. 2000-01, 0-for-4. Totals, 0-for-7 (.000).
Personal fouls/disqualifications: 1991-92, 191/2. 1992-93, 274/5. 1993-94, 214/1. 1994-95, 222/2. 1995-96, 238/0. 1996-97, 233/3. 1997-98, 209/1. 1998-99, 115/0. 1999-00, 203/1. 2000-01, 199/0. 2001-02, 193/1. 2002-03, 189/1. 2003-04, 154/1. 2004-05, 162/1. Totals, 2796/19.

### NBA PLAYOFF RECORD

| Season Team | G | Min. | FGM | FGA | Pct. | FTM | FTA | Pct. | REBOUNDS Off. | Def. | Tot. | Ast. | St. | Blk. | TO | Pts. | AVERAGES RPG | APG | PPG |
|---|---|---|---|---|---|---|---|---|---|---|---|---|---|---|---|---|---|---|---|
| 91-92—Indiana | 3 | 69 | 4 | 10 | .400 | 0 | 0 | ... | 5 | 14 | 19 | 2 | 0 | 5 | 1 | 8 | 6.3 | 0.7 | 2.7 |
| 92-93—Indiana | 4 | 117 | 8 | 12 | .667 | 1 | 4 | .250 | 4 | 28 | 32 | 4 | 4 | 4 | 3 | 17 | 8.0 | 1.0 | 4.3 |
| 93-94—Indiana | 16 | 578 | 56 | 106 | .528 | 11 | 36 | .306 | 63 | 96 | 159 | 11 | 18 | 17 | 30 | 123 | 9.9 | 0.7 | 7.7 |
| 94-95—Indiana | 17 | 490 | 56 | 105 | .533 | 23 | 47 | .489 | 53 | 83 | 136 | 6 | 7 | 14 | 22 | 135 | 8.0 | 0.4 | 7.9 |
| 95-96—Indiana | 5 | 184 | 16 | 31 | .516 | 4 | 11 | .364 | 20 | 36 | 56 | 4 | 3 | 6 | 10 | 36 | 11.2 | 0.8 | 7.2 |
| 97-98—Indiana | 16 | 466 | 56 | 86 | .651 | 29 | 64 | .453 | 44 | 76 | 120 | 12 | 5 | 18 | 21 | 141 | 7.5 | 0.8 | 8.8 |
| 98-99—Indiana | 13 | 394 | 45 | 77 | .584 | 28 | 50 | .560 | 45 | 87 | 132 | 11 | 10 | 18 | 21 | 118 | 10.2 | 0.8 | 9.1 |
| 99-00—Indiana | 23 | 714 | 79 | 151 | .523 | 32 | 59 | .542 | 83 | 180 | 263 | 17 | 11 | 31 | 18 | 190 | 11.4 | 0.7 | 8.3 |
| 00-01—Portland | 2 | 20 | 0 | 2 | .000 | 1 | 2 | .500 | 3 | 1 | 4 | 0 | 1 | 0 | 1 | 1 | 2.0 | 0.0 | 0.5 |
| 01-02—Portland | 3 | 70 | 3 | 11 | .273 | 1 | 2 | .500 | 6 | 14 | 20 | 4 | 4 | 3 | 2 | 7 | 6.7 | 1.3 | 2.3 |
| 02-03—Portland | 6 | 162 | 14 | 24 | .583 | 17 | 26 | .654 | 20 | 28 | 48 | 9 | 5 | 2 | 10 | 45 | 8.0 | 1.5 | 7.5 |
| 04-05—Indiana | 13 | 311 | 26 | 58 | .448 | 17 | 25 | .680 | 37 | 44 | 81 | 5 | 9 | 6 | 9 | 69 | 6.2 | 0.4 | 5.3 |
| Totals | 121 | 3575 | 363 | 673 | .539 | 164 | 326 | .503 | 383 | 687 | 1070 | 85 | 77 | 124 | 148 | 890 | 8.8 | 0.7 | 7.4 |

Three-point field goals: 1993-94, 0-for-1. 2000-01, 0-for-1. Totals, 0-for-2 (.000).
Personal fouls/disqualifications: 1991-92, 8/0. 1992-93, 15/0. 1993-94, 52/0. 1994-95, 56/0. 1995-96, 16/0. 1997-98, 42/0. 1998-99, 42/0. 1999-00, 83/4. 2000-01, 7/1. 2001-02, 16/2. 2002-03, 11/0. 2004-05, 35/0. Totals, 383/7.

### NBA ALL-STAR GAME RECORD

| Season Team | Min. | FGM | FGA | Pct. | FTM | FTA | Pct. | REBOUNDS Off. | Def. | Tot. | Ast. | PF | Dq. | St. | Blk. | TO | Pts. |
|---|---|---|---|---|---|---|---|---|---|---|---|---|---|---|---|---|---|
| 2001—Indiana | 14 | 2 | 3 | .667 | 0 | 0 | ... | 3 | 5 | 8 | 1 | 0 | ... | 0 | 0 | 0 | 4 |

# DAVIS, JOSH     F

**PERSONAL:** Born August 10, 1980 ... 6-8/240. (2.03/108.9).
**HIGH SCHOOL:** Salem Academy (Oregon).
**COLLEGE:** Wyoming.
**TRANSACTIONS/CAREER NOTES:** Not drafted by an NBA franchise. ... Played in Italy (2002-03). ... Signed as free agent by Chicago Bulls (September 29, 2003). ... Waived by Bulls (October 20, 2003). ... Played in Continental Basketball Association (2003-04). ... Signed by Atlanta Hawks to 10-day contract (March 9, 2004).

### COLLEGIATE RECORD

| Season Team | G | Min. | FGM | FGA | Pct. | FTM | FTA | Pct. | Reb. | Ast. | Pts. | AVERAGES RPG | APG | PPG |
|---|---|---|---|---|---|---|---|---|---|---|---|---|---|---|
| 98-99—Wyoming | 27 | 590 | 93 | 198 | .470 | 30 | 53 | .566 | 161 | 28 | 231 | 6.0 | 1.0 | 8.6 |
| 99-00—Wyoming | 31 | 842 | 175 | 351 | .499 | 67 | 104 | .644 | 270 | 39 | 442 | 8.7 | 1.3 | 14.3 |
| 00-01—Wyoming | 30 | 851 | 150 | 309 | .485 | 88 | 120 | .733 | 281 | 53 | 404 | 9.4 | 1.8 | 13.5 |
| 01-02—Wyoming | 31 | 848 | 142 | 268 | .530 | 70 | 120 | .583 | 244 | 47 | 362 | 7.9 | 1.5 | 11.7 |
| Totals | 119 | 3131 | 560 | 1126 | .497 | 255 | 397 | .642 | 956 | 167 | 1439 | 8.0 | 1.4 | 12.1 |

Three-point field goals: 1998-99, 15-for-53 (.283). 1999-00, 25-for-55 (.455). 2000-01, 16-for-79 (.203). 2001-02, 8-for-43 (.186). Totals, 64-for-230 (.278).

| Season Team | G | Min. | FGM | FGA | Pct. | FTM | FTA | Pct. | Reb. | Ast. | Pts. | AVERAGES | | |
|---|---|---|---|---|---|---|---|---|---|---|---|---|---|---|
| | | | | | | | | | | | | RPG | APG | PPG |
| 02-03—Sicc Cucine Jesi ............. | 20 | 449 | 78 | 142 | .549 | 30 | 45 | .667 | 145 | 10 | 200 | 7.3 | 0.5 | 10.0 |

Three-point field goals: 2002-03, 14-for-31 (.452). Totals, 14-for-31 (.452).

## CBA RECORD

| Season Team | G | Min. | FGM | FGA | Pct. | FTM | FTA | Pct. | Reb. | Ast. | Pts. | AVERAGES | | |
|---|---|---|---|---|---|---|---|---|---|---|---|---|---|---|
| | | | | | | | | | | | | RPG | APG | PPG |
| 03-04—Idaho ............................. | 40 | 1340 | 299 | 507 | .590 | 89 | 108 | .824 | 385 | 96 | 747 | 9.6 | 2.4 | 18.7 |

Three-point field goals: 2003-04, 60-for-146 (.411). Totals, 60-for-146 (.411).

## NBA REGULAR-SEASON RECORD

| Season Team | G | Min. | FGM | FGA | Pct. | FTM | FTA | Pct. | REBOUNDS | | | Ast. | St. | Blk. | TO | Pts. | AVERAGES | | |
|---|---|---|---|---|---|---|---|---|---|---|---|---|---|---|---|---|---|---|---|
| | | | | | | | | | Off. | Def. | Tot. | | | | | | RPG | APG | PPG |
| 03-04—Atlanta ............ | 4 | 23 | 2 | 5 | .400 | 1 | 1 | 1.000 | 1 | 4 | 5 | 0 | 0 | 0 | 2 | 5 | 1.3 | 0.0 | 1.3 |
| 04-05—Philadelphia .... | 42 | 328 | 42 | 111 | .378 | 14 | 17 | .824 | 29 | 50 | 79 | 12 | 8 | 4 | 15 | 117 | 1.9 | 0.3 | 2.8 |
| Totals ................... | 46 | 351 | 44 | 116 | .379 | 15 | 18 | .833 | 30 | 54 | 84 | 12 | 8 | 4 | 17 | 122 | 1.8 | 0.3 | 2.7 |

Three-point field goals: 2003-04, 0-for-2. 2004-05, 19-for-53 (.358). Totals, 19-for-55 (.345).
Personal fouls/disqualifications: 2003-04, 3/0. 2004-05, 45/0. Totals, 48/0.

## NBA PLAYOFF RECORD

| Season Team | G | Min. | FGM | FGA | Pct. | FTM | FTA | Pct. | REBOUNDS | | | Ast. | St. | Blk. | TO | Pts. | AVERAGES | | |
|---|---|---|---|---|---|---|---|---|---|---|---|---|---|---|---|---|---|---|---|
| | | | | | | | | | Off. | Def. | Tot. | | | | | | RPG | APG | PPG |
| 04-05—Philadelphia .... | 2 | 4 | 0 | 1 | .000 | 0 | 0 | ... | 0 | 1 | 1 | 0 | 0 | 0 | 0 | 0 | 0.5 | 0.0 | 0.0 |

Three-point field goals: 2004-05, 0-for-1. Totals, 0-for-1 (.000).
Personal fouls/disqualifications: 2004-05, 1/0. Totals, 1/0.

# DAVIS, RICKY          G          CELTICS

**PERSONAL:** Born September 23, 1979, in Las Vegas. ... 6-7/197. (2.01/89.4). ... Full name: Tyree Ricardo Davis
**HIGH SCHOOL:** North (Davenport, Iowa).
**COLLEGE:** Iowa.
**TRANSACTIONS/CAREER NOTES:** Selected after freshman season by Charlotte Hornets in first round (21st pick overall) of 1998 NBA Draft. ... Traded by Hornets with G Eddie Jones, F Anthony Mason and G/F Dale Ellis to Miami Heat for F P.J. Brown, F Jamal Mashburn, F/C Otis Thorpe, F Tim James and G/F Rodney Buford (August 1, 2000). ... Traded by Heat to Cleveland Cavaliers as part of three-way deal in which Toronto Raptors sent F/C Brian Skinner to Cavaliers, Cavaliers sent F/C Chris Gatling to Cavaliers and Heat sent F Don MacLean and cash considerations to Raptors (October 26, 2001). ... Traded by Cavaliers with F/C Chris Mihm, C Michael Stewart and a second-round draft choice to Boston Celtics for F/C Tony Battie, F Kedrick Brown and F Eric Williams (December 15, 2003).

## COLLEGIATE RECORD

| Season Team | G | Min. | FGM | FGA | Pct. | FTM | FTA | Pct. | Reb. | Ast. | Pts. | AVERAGES | | |
|---|---|---|---|---|---|---|---|---|---|---|---|---|---|---|
| | | | | | | | | | | | | RPG | APG | PPG |
| 97-98—Iowa .............................. | 31 | 825 | 173 | 371 | .466 | 90 | 129 | .698 | 148 | 74 | 464 | 4.8 | 2.4 | 15.0 |

Three-point field goals: 1997-98, 28-for-91 (.308). Totals, 28-for-91 (.308).

## NBA REGULAR-SEASON RECORD

| Season Team | G | Min. | FGM | FGA | Pct. | FTM | FTA | Pct. | REBOUNDS | | | Ast. | St. | Blk. | TO | Pts. | AVERAGES | | |
|---|---|---|---|---|---|---|---|---|---|---|---|---|---|---|---|---|---|---|---|
| | | | | | | | | | Off. | Def. | Tot. | | | | | | RPG | APG | PPG |
| 98-99—Charlotte ......... | 46 | 557 | 81 | 200 | .405 | 45 | 59 | .763 | 40 | 44 | 84 | 58 | 30 | 7 | 54 | 209 | 1.8 | 1.3 | 4.5 |
| 99-00—Charlotte ......... | 48 | 570 | 94 | 187 | .503 | 39 | 51 | .765 | 29 | 54 | 83 | 62 | 30 | 8 | 46 | 227 | 1.7 | 1.3 | 4.7 |
| 00-01—Miami ............. | 7 | 70 | 12 | 29 | .414 | 7 | 8 | .875 | 1 | 6 | 7 | 11 | 5 | 2 | 5 | 32 | 1.0 | 1.6 | 4.6 |
| 01-02—Cleveland ........ | 82 | 1954 | 376 | 781 | .481 | 196 | 248 | .790 | 63 | 180 | 243 | 178 | 69 | 23 | 148 | 959 | 3.0 | 2.2 | 11.7 |
| 02-03—Cleveland ........ | 79 | 3131 | 602 | 1470 | .410 | 348 | 465 | .748 | 97 | 293 | 390 | 436 | 125 | 36 | 277 | 1626 | 4.9 | 5.5 | 20.6 |
| 03-04—Cleve.-Bos. ..... | 79 | 2474 | 446 | 950 | .469 | 196 | 273 | .718 | 77 | 281 | 358 | 259 | 96 | 22 | 189 | 1140 | 4.5 | 3.3 | 14.4 |
| 04-05—Boston ........... | 82 | 2696 | 481 | 1041 | .462 | 286 | 351 | .815 | 66 | 183 | 249 | 246 | 89 | 27 | 205 | 1309 | 3.0 | 3.0 | 16.0 |
| Totals ................... | 423 | 11452 | 2092 | 4658 | .449 | 1117 | 1455 | .768 | 373 | 1041 | 1414 | 1250 | 444 | 125 | 924 | 5502 | 3.3 | 3.0 | 13.0 |

Three-point field goals: 1998-99, 2-for-12 (.167). 1999-00, 0-for-4. 2000-01, 1-for-1 (1.000). 2001-02, 11-for-35 (.314). 2002-03, 74-for-204 (.363). 2003-04, 52-for-140 (.371). 2004-05, 61-for-180 (.339). Totals, 201-for-576 (.349).
Personal fouls/disqualifications: 1998-99, 46/0. 1999-00, 39/0. 2000-01, 7/0. 2001-02, 145/0. 2002-03, 180/0. 2003-04, 171/1. 2004-05, 174/1. Totals, 762/2.

## NBA PLAYOFF RECORD

| Season Team | G | Min. | FGM | FGA | Pct. | FTM | FTA | Pct. | REBOUNDS | | | Ast. | St. | Blk. | TO | Pts. | AVERAGES | | |
|---|---|---|---|---|---|---|---|---|---|---|---|---|---|---|---|---|---|---|---|
| | | | | | | | | | Off. | Def. | Tot. | | | | | | RPG | APG | PPG |
| 03-04—Boston ............ | 4 | 123 | 16 | 40 | .400 | 11 | 16 | .688 | 3 | 9 | 12 | 14 | 2 | 0 | 12 | 47 | 3.0 | 3.5 | 11.8 |
| 04-05—Boston ............ | 7 | 240 | 32 | 74 | .432 | 20 | 26 | .769 | 5 | 20 | 25 | 14 | 9 | 2 | 21 | 87 | 3.6 | 2.0 | 12.4 |
| Totals ................... | 11 | 363 | 48 | 114 | .421 | 31 | 42 | .738 | 8 | 29 | 37 | 28 | 11 | 2 | 33 | 134 | 3.4 | 2.5 | 12.2 |

Three-point field goals: 2003-04, 4-for-10 (.400). 2004-05, 3-for-9 (.333). Totals, 7-for-19 (.368).
Personal fouls/disqualifications: 2003-04, 7/0. 2004-05, 23/1. Totals, 30/1.

# DECLERCQ, ANDREW          F/C          MAGIC

**PERSONAL:** Born February 1, 1973, in Detroit. ... 6-10/255. (2.08/115.7). ... Name pronounced Dah-CLAIR-k.
**HIGH SCHOOL:** Countryside (Clearwater, Fla.).
**COLLEGE:** Florida.
**TRANSACTIONS/CAREER NOTES:** Selected by Golden State Warriors in second round (34th pick overall) of 1995 NBA Draft. ... Signed as free agent by Boston Celtics (July 28, 1997). ... Traded by Celtics with 1999 first-round draft choice to Cleveland Cavaliers for C/F Vitaly Potapenko (March 11, 1999). ... Traded by Cavaliers to Orlando Magic for F Matt Harpring (August 3, 2000).

## COLLEGIATE RECORD

| Season Team | G | Min. | FGM | FGA | Pct. | FTM | FTA | Pct. | Reb. | Ast. | Pts. | RPG | APG | PPG |
|---|---|---|---|---|---|---|---|---|---|---|---|---|---|---|
| | | | | | | | | | | | | AVERAGES | | |
| 91-92—Florida | 33 | 825 | 117 | 231 | .506 | 57 | 87 | .655 | 203 | 26 | 291 | 6.2 | 0.8 | 8.8 |
| 92-93—Florida | 28 | 715 | 118 | 208 | .567 | 59 | 101 | .584 | 198 | 15 | 295 | 7.1 | 0.5 | 10.5 |
| 93-94—Florida | 37 | 998 | 129 | 237 | .544 | 68 | 104 | .654 | 292 | 54 | 327 | 7.9 | 1.5 | 8.8 |
| 94-95—Florida | 30 | 966 | 138 | 270 | .511 | 115 | 159 | .723 | 265 | 42 | 396 | 8.8 | 1.4 | 13.2 |
| Totals | 128 | 3504 | 502 | 946 | .531 | 299 | 451 | .663 | 958 | 137 | 1309 | 7.5 | 1.1 | 10.2 |

Three-point field goals: 1993-94, 1-for-3 (.333). 1994-95, 5-for-15 (.333). Totals, 6-for-18 (.333).

## NBA REGULAR-SEASON RECORD

| Season Team | G | Min. | FGM | FGA | Pct. | FTM | FTA | Pct. | Off. | Def. | Tot. | Ast. | St. | Blk. | TO | Pts. | RPG | APG | PPG |
|---|---|---|---|---|---|---|---|---|---|---|---|---|---|---|---|---|---|---|---|
| | | | | | | | | | REBOUNDS | | | | | | | | AVERAGES | | |
| 95-96—Golden State | 22 | 203 | 24 | 50 | .480 | 11 | 19 | .579 | 18 | 21 | 39 | 9 | 7 | 5 | 4 | 59 | 1.8 | 0.4 | 2.7 |
| 96-97—Golden State | 71 | 1065 | 142 | 273 | .520 | 91 | 151 | .603 | 122 | 176 | 298 | 32 | 33 | 27 | 76 | 375 | 4.2 | 0.5 | 5.3 |
| 97-98—Boston | 81 | 1523 | 169 | 340 | .497 | 101 | 168 | .601 | 180 | 212 | 392 | 59 | 85 | 49 | 84 | 439 | 4.8 | 0.7 | 5.4 |
| 98-99—Boston-Cleve. | 47 | 1102 | 138 | 276 | .500 | 95 | 141 | .674 | 104 | 151 | 255 | 31 | 50 | 29 | 54 | 371 | 5.4 | 0.7 | 7.9 |
| 99-00—Cleveland | 82 | 1831 | 225 | 443 | .508 | 94 | 160 | .588 | 156 | 283 | 439 | 58 | 63 | 66 | 108 | 544 | 5.4 | 0.7 | 6.6 |
| 00-01—Orlando | 67 | 903 | 107 | 193 | .554 | 47 | 82 | .573 | 91 | 145 | 236 | 32 | 41 | 33 | 51 | 261 | 3.5 | 0.5 | 3.9 |
| 01-02—Orlando | 61 | 633 | 67 | 149 | .450 | 28 | 50 | .560 | 74 | 89 | 163 | 22 | 23 | 24 | 34 | 162 | 2.7 | 0.4 | 2.7 |
| 02-03—Orlando | 77 | 1327 | 149 | 279 | .534 | 67 | 104 | .644 | 142 | 197 | 339 | 52 | 39 | 36 | 84 | 365 | 4.4 | 0.7 | 4.7 |
| 03-04—Orlando | 71 | 1211 | 93 | 195 | .477 | 44 | 54 | .815 | 131 | 186 | 317 | 44 | 47 | 32 | 54 | 230 | 4.5 | 0.6 | 3.2 |
| 04-05—Orlando | 8 | 49 | 4 | 9 | .444 | 1 | 3 | .333 | 7 | 3 | 10 | 0 | 2 | 0 | 1 | 9 | 1.3 | 0.0 | 1.1 |
| Totals | 587 | 9847 | 1118 | 2207 | .507 | 579 | 932 | .621 | 1025 | 1463 | 2488 | 339 | 390 | 301 | 550 | 2815 | 4.2 | 0.6 | 4.8 |

Three-point field goals: 1995-96, 0-for-1. 1997-98, 0-for-1. Totals, 0-for-2 (.000).
Personal fouls/disqualifications: 1995-96, 30/0. 1996-97, 229/3. 1997-98, 277/3. 1998-99, 161/3. 1999-00, 275/6. 2000-01, 198/2. 2001-02, 130/0. 2002-03, 258/5. 2003-04, 217/7. 2004-05, 14/0. Totals, 1789/29.

## NBA PLAYOFF RECORD

| Season Team | G | Min. | FGM | FGA | Pct. | FTM | FTA | Pct. | Off. | Def. | Tot. | Ast. | St. | Blk. | TO | Pts. | RPG | APG | PPG |
|---|---|---|---|---|---|---|---|---|---|---|---|---|---|---|---|---|---|---|---|
| | | | | | | | | | REBOUNDS | | | | | | | | AVERAGES | | |
| 00-01—Orlando | 4 | 54 | 8 | 14 | .571 | 4 | 8 | .500 | 7 | 9 | 16 | 1 | 2 | 2 | 2 | 20 | 4.0 | 0.3 | 5.0 |
| 01-02—Orlando | 2 | 9 | 0 | 0 | ... | 0 | 2 | .000 | 0 | 0 | 0 | 0 | 0 | 0 | 1 | 0 | 0.0 | 0.0 | 0.0 |
| 02-03—Orlando | 7 | 104 | 12 | 20 | .600 | 4 | 5 | .800 | 8 | 15 | 23 | 2 | 2 | 5 | 9 | 28 | 3.3 | 0.3 | 4.0 |
| Totals | 13 | 167 | 20 | 34 | .588 | 8 | 15 | .533 | 15 | 24 | 39 | 3 | 4 | 7 | 12 | 48 | 3.0 | 0.2 | 3.7 |

Personal fouls/disqualifications: 2000-01, 17/1. 2001-02, 3/0. 2002-03, 25/1. Totals, 45/2.

# DELFINO, CARLOS    G/F    PISTONS

**PERSONAL:** Born August 29, 1982, in Santa Fe, Argentina. ... 6-6/230. (1.98/104.3). ... Full name: Carlos Francisco Delfino

**TRANSACTIONS/CAREER NOTES:** Played in Argentina (1998-2000). ... Played in Italy (2000-03). ... Selected by Detroit Pistons in first round (25th pick overall) of 2003 NBA Draft.

**MISCELLANEOUS:** Member of gold-medal-winning Argentian Olympic Team (2004).

## ITALIAN LEAGUE RECORD

| Season Team | G | Min. | FGM | FGA | Pct. | FTM | FTA | Pct. | Reb. | Ast. | Pts. | RPG | APG | PPG |
|---|---|---|---|---|---|---|---|---|---|---|---|---|---|---|
| | | | | | | | | | | | | AVERAGES | | |
| 00-01—Reggio Calabria | 24 | 495 | 71 | 154 | .461 | 36 | 56 | .643 | 61 | 23 | 211 | 2.5 | 1.0 | 8.8 |
| 01-02—Reggio Calabria | 31 | 955 | 143 | 315 | .454 | 94 | 119 | .790 | 157 | 52 | 420 | 5.1 | 1.7 | 13.5 |
| 02-03—Skipper Bologna | 26 | 670 | 92 | 213 | .432 | 40 | 54 | .741 | 145 | 27 | 255 | 5.6 | 1.0 | 9.8 |
| 03-04—Skipper Bologna | 34 | 861 | 124 | 295 | .420 | 54 | 76 | .711 | 161 | 41 | 343 | 4.7 | 1.2 | 10.1 |
| Totals | 115 | 2981 | 430 | 977 | .440 | 224 | 305 | .734 | 524 | 143 | 1229 | 4.6 | 1.2 | 10.7 |

Three-point field goals: 2000-01, 33-for-95 (.347). 2001-02, 40-for-139 (.288). 2002-03, 31-for-89 (.348). 2003-04, 42-for128 (.320). Totals, 145-for-451 (.322).

## NBA REGULAR-SEASON RECORD

| Season Team | G | Min. | FGM | FGA | Pct. | FTM | FTA | Pct. | Off. | Def. | Tot. | Ast. | St. | Blk. | TO | Pts. | RPG | APG | PPG |
|---|---|---|---|---|---|---|---|---|---|---|---|---|---|---|---|---|---|---|---|
| | | | | | | | | | REBOUNDS | | | | | | | | AVERAGES | | |
| 04-05—Detroit | 30 | 459 | 42 | 117 | .359 | 23 | 40 | .575 | 13 | 42 | 55 | 38 | 22 | 6 | 23 | 116 | 1.8 | 1.3 | 3.9 |

Three-point field goals: 2004-05, 9-for-35 (.257). Totals, 9-for-35 (.257).
Personal fouls/disqualifications: 2004-05, 44/0. Totals, 44/0.

# DELK, TONY    G    HAWKS

**PERSONAL:** Born January 28, 1974, in Covington, Tenn. ... 6-2/189. (1.88/85.7). ... Full name: Tony Lorenzo Delk

**HIGH SCHOOL:** Haywood (Brownsville, Tenn.).

**COLLEGE:** Kentucky.

**TRANSACTIONS/CAREER NOTES:** Selected by Charlotte Hornets in first round (16th pick overall) of 1996 NBA Draft. ... Traded by Hornets with G Muggsy Bogues to Golden State Warriors for G B.J. Armstrong (November 7, 1997). ... Signed as free agent by Sacramento Kings (August 16, 1999). ... Signed as free agent by Phoenix Suns (August 1, 2000). ... Traded by Suns with F Rodney Rogers to Boston Celtics for G/F Joe Johnson, G Milt Palacio, G Randy Brown and 2002 first-round draft choice (February 20, 2002). ... Traded by Celtics with F Antoine Walker to Dallas Mavericks for F/C Raef LaFrentz, F Chris Mills, G Jiri Welsch and 2004 first-round draft choice (October 20, 2003). ... Traded by Mavericks with F Antoine Walker to Atlanta Hawks for G Jason Terry, F Alan Henderson and a future first-round draft choice (August 4, 2004).

## COLLEGIATE RECORD

**NOTES:** Member of NCAA Division I championship team (1996). ... THE SPORTING NEWS All-America second team (1996). ... NCAA Division I Tournament Most Outstanding Player (1996).

| Season Team | G | Min. | FGM | FGA | Pct. | FTM | FTA | Pct. | Reb. | Ast. | Pts. | RPG | APG | PPG |
|---|---|---|---|---|---|---|---|---|---|---|---|---|---|---|
| | | | | | | | | | | | | **AVERAGES** | | |
| 92-93—Kentucky | 30 | 287 | 47 | 104 | .452 | 24 | 33 | .727 | 57 | 22 | 136 | 1.9 | 0.7 | 4.5 |
| 93-94—Kentucky | 34 | 957 | 200 | 440 | .455 | 69 | 108 | .639 | 153 | 59 | 564 | 4.5 | 1.7 | 16.6 |
| 94-95—Kentucky | 33 | 960 | 207 | 433 | .478 | 60 | 89 | .674 | 110 | 65 | 551 | 3.3 | 2.0 | 16.7 |
| 95-96—Kentucky | 36 | 947 | 229 | 464 | .494 | 88 | 110 | .800 | 150 | 64 | 639 | 4.2 | 1.8 | 17.8 |
| Totals | 133 | 3151 | 683 | 1441 | .474 | 241 | 340 | .709 | 470 | 210 | 1890 | 3.5 | 1.6 | 14.2 |

Three-point field goals: 1992-93, 18-for-51 (.353). 1993-94, 95-for-254 (.374). 1994-95, 77-for-197 (.391). 1995-96, 93-for-210 (.443). Totals, 283-for-712 (.397).

## NBA REGULAR-SEASON RECORD

| Season Team | G | Min. | FGM | FGA | Pct. | FTM | FTA | Pct. | Off. | Def. | Tot. | Ast. | St. | Blk. | TO | Pts. | RPG | APG | PPG |
|---|---|---|---|---|---|---|---|---|---|---|---|---|---|---|---|---|---|---|---|
| | | | | | | | | | **REBOUNDS** | | | | | | | | **AVERAGES** | | |
| 96-97—Charlotte | 61 | 867 | 119 | 256 | .465 | 42 | 51 | .824 | 31 | 68 | 99 | 99 | 36 | 6 | 68 | 332 | 1.6 | 1.6 | 5.4 |
| 97-98—Char.-G.S. | 77 | 1681 | 314 | 798 | .393 | 111 | 151 | .735 | 38 | 134 | 172 | 172 | 73 | 12 | 109 | 781 | 2.2 | 2.2 | 10.1 |
| 98-99—Golden State | 36 | 630 | 92 | 253 | .364 | 46 | 71 | .648 | 11 | 43 | 54 | 95 | 16 | 6 | 45 | 246 | 1.5 | 2.6 | 6.8 |
| 99-00—Sacramento | 46 | 682 | 120 | 279 | .430 | 47 | 59 | .797 | 36 | 52 | 88 | 55 | 35 | 5 | 32 | 296 | 1.9 | 1.2 | 6.4 |
| 00-01—Phoenix | 82 | 2288 | 383 | 923 | .415 | 185 | 235 | .787 | 76 | 185 | 261 | 160 | 75 | 17 | 101 | 1005 | 3.2 | 2.0 | 12.3 |
| 01-02—Pho.-Boston | 63 | 1447 | 226 | 588 | .384 | 78 | 97 | .804 | 58 | 145 | 203 | 132 | 53 | 10 | 59 | 597 | 3.2 | 2.1 | 9.5 |
| 02-03—Boston | 67 | 1873 | 233 | 560 | .416 | 68 | 87 | .782 | 41 | 191 | 232 | 146 | 72 | 10 | 69 | 654 | 3.5 | 2.2 | 9.8 |
| 03-04—Dallas | 33 | 509 | 70 | 184 | .380 | 37 | 44 | .841 | 16 | 43 | 59 | 28 | 27 | 7 | 17 | 197 | 1.8 | 0.8 | 6.0 |
| 04-05—Atlanta | 56 | 1340 | 246 | 591 | .416 | 103 | 136 | .757 | 28 | 102 | 130 | 104 | 47 | 3 | 54 | 667 | 2.3 | 1.9 | 11.9 |
| Totals | 521 | 11317 | 1803 | 4432 | .407 | 717 | 931 | .770 | 335 | 963 | 1298 | 991 | 434 | 76 | 554 | 4775 | 2.5 | 1.9 | 9.2 |

Three-point field goals: 1996-97, 52-for-112 (.464). 1997-98, 42-for-157 (.268). 1998-99, 16-for-66 (.242). 1999-00, 9-for-40 (.225). 2000-01, 54-for-168 (.321). 2001-02, 67-for-214 (.313). 2002-03, 120-for-304 (.395). 2003-04, 20-for-66 (.303). 2004-05, 72-for-202 (.356). Totals, 452-for-1329 (.340).
Personal fouls/disqualifications: 1996-97, 71/1. 1997-98, 96/0. 1998-99, 47/0. 1999-00, 58/0. 2000-01, 171/1. 2001-02, 98/0. 2002-03, 124/0. 2003-04, 46/0. 2004-05, 123/3. Totals, 834/5.

## NBA PLAYOFF RECORD

| Season Team | G | Min. | FGM | FGA | Pct. | FTM | FTA | Pct. | Off. | Def. | Tot. | Ast. | St. | Blk. | TO | Pts. | RPG | APG | PPG |
|---|---|---|---|---|---|---|---|---|---|---|---|---|---|---|---|---|---|---|---|
| | | | | | | | | | **REBOUNDS** | | | | | | | | **AVERAGES** | | |
| 96-97—Charlotte | 3 | 85 | 13 | 31 | .419 | 0 | 0 | | 5 | 5 | 10 | 6 | 2 | 0 | 2 | 31 | 3.3 | 2.0 | 10.3 |
| 99-00—Sacramento | 5 | 101 | 18 | 41 | .439 | 17 | 23 | .739 | 11 | 7 | 18 | 7 | 3 | 0 | 8 | 56 | 3.6 | 1.4 | 11.2 |
| 00-01—Phoenix | 4 | 114 | 18 | 43 | .419 | 7 | 11 | .636 | 5 | 11 | 16 | 4 | 3 | 0 | 5 | 47 | 4.0 | 1.0 | 11.8 |
| 01-02—Boston | 14 | 227 | 23 | 65 | .354 | 7 | 12 | .583 | 8 | 26 | 34 | 16 | 8 | 5 | 15 | 66 | 2.4 | 1.1 | 4.7 |
| 02-03—Boston | 10 | 368 | 54 | 114 | .474 | 28 | 32 | .875 | 5 | 42 | 47 | 36 | 12 | 4 | 13 | 158 | 4.7 | 3.6 | 15.8 |
| 03-04—Dallas | 1 | 5 | 0 | 0 | | 0 | 0 | | 0 | 1 | 1 | 2 | 1 | 0 | 0 | 0 | 1.0 | 2.0 | 0.0 |
| Totals | 37 | 900 | 126 | 294 | .429 | 59 | 78 | .756 | 34 | 92 | 126 | 71 | 29 | 9 | 43 | 358 | 3.4 | 1.9 | 9.7 |

Three-point field goals: 1996-97, 5-for-13 (.385). 1999-00, 3-for-5 (.600). 2000-01, 4-for-10 (.400). 2001-02, 13-for-33 (.394). 2002-03, 22-for-49 (.449). Totals, 47-for-110 (.427).
Personal fouls/disqualifications: 1996-97, 10/0. 1999-00, 11/0. 2000-01, 7/0. 2001-02, 13/0. 2002-03, 24/0. Totals, 65/0.

# DENG, LUOL      F      BULLS

**PERSONAL:** Born April 16, 1985, in The Sudan. ... 6-8/220. (2.03/99.8).
**HIGH SCHOOL:** Blair Academy (Blairstown, N.J.).
**COLLEGE:** Duke.
**TRANSACTIONS/CAREER NOTES:** Selected after freshman season by Phoenix Suns in first round (seventh pick overall) of 2004 NBA Draft. ... Draft rights traded by Suns to Chicago Bulls for draft rights to F/C Jackson Vroman and future first-round draft choice (June 24, 2004).

## COLLEGIATE RECORD

| Season Team | G | Min. | FGM | FGA | Pct. | FTM | FTA | Pct. | Reb. | Ast. | Pts. | RPG | APG | PPG |
|---|---|---|---|---|---|---|---|---|---|---|---|---|---|---|
| | | | | | | | | | | | | **AVERAGES** | | |
| 03-04—Duke | 37 | 1149 | 210 | 442 | .475 | 98 | 138 | .710 | 255 | 68 | 558 | 6.9 | 1.8 | 15.1 |

Three-point field goals: 2003-04, 40-for-111 (.360). Totals, 40-for-111 (.360).

**HONORS:** NBA All-Rookie first team (2005).

## NBA REGULAR-SEASON RECORD

| Season Team | G | Min. | FGM | FGA | Pct. | FTM | FTA | Pct. | Off. | Def. | Tot. | Ast. | St. | Blk. | TO | Pts. | RPG | APG | PPG |
|---|---|---|---|---|---|---|---|---|---|---|---|---|---|---|---|---|---|---|---|
| | | | | | | | | | **REBOUNDS** | | | | | | | | **AVERAGES** | | |
| 04-05—Chicago | 61 | 1663 | 280 | 645 | .434 | 120 | 162 | .741 | 92 | 230 | 322 | 135 | 48 | 27 | 118 | 711 | 5.3 | 2.2 | 11.7 |

Three-point field goals: 2004-05, 31-for-117 (.265). Totals, 31-for-117 (.265).
Personal fouls/disqualifications: 2004-05, 98/0. Totals, 98/0.

# DIAW, BORIS      G/F      SUNS

**PERSONAL:** Born April 16, 1982, in Cormeille-en-Parisis, France. ... 6-8/203. (2.03/92.1).
**TRANSACTIONS/CAREER NOTES:** Played in France (1998-2003). ... Selected by Atlanta Hawks in first round (21st pick overall) of 2003 NBA Draft. ... Traded by Hawks with two future first-round draft picks to Phoenix Suns for G Joe Johnson (August 19, 2005).

## FRENCH LEAGUE RECORD

| Season Team | G | Min. | FGM | FGA | Pct. | FTM | FTA | Pct. | Reb. | Ast. | Pts. | RPG | APG | PPG |
|---|---|---|---|---|---|---|---|---|---|---|---|---|---|---|
| | | | | | | | | | | | | **AVERAGES** | | |
| 98-99—Centre Federal | 25 | ... | 70 | 130 | .538 | 25 | 43 | .581 | 90 | 63 | 178 | 3.6 | 2.5 | 7.1 |
| 99-00—Centre Federal | 25 | 884 | 163 | 296 | .551 | 66 | 109 | .606 | 231 | 126 | 420 | 9.2 | 5.0 | 16.8 |
| 00-01—Pau Orthez | 27 | 390 | 39 | 69 | .565 | 20 | 27 | .741 | 72 | 42 | 107 | 2.7 | 1.6 | 4.0 |
| 01-02—Pau Orthez | 29 | 610 | 89 | 155 | .574 | 41 | 63 | .651 | 135 | 57 | 226 | 4.7 | 2.0 | 7.8 |
| 02-03—Pau Orthez | 27 | 677 | 77 | 142 | .542 | 24 | 43 | .558 | 140 | 110 | 194 | 5.2 | 4.1 | 7.2 |
| Totals | 133 | 2561 | 438 | 792 | .553 | 176 | 285 | .618 | 668 | 398 | 1125 | 5.0 | 3.0 | 8.5 |

Three-point field goals: 1998-99, 13-for-39 (.333). 1999-00, 28-for-80 (.350). 2000-01, 9-for-22 (.409). 2001-02, 7-for-30 (.233). 2002-03, 16-for-38 (.421). Totals, 73-for-209 (.349).

## NBA REGULAR-SEASON RECORD

| Season Team | G | Min. | FGM | FGA | Pct. | FTM | FTA | Pct. | REBOUNDS Off. | Def. | Tot. | Ast. | St. | Blk. | TO | Pts. | AVERAGES RPG | APG | PPG |
|---|---|---|---|---|---|---|---|---|---|---|---|---|---|---|---|---|---|---|---|
| 03-04—Atlanta ........... | 76 | 1919 | 140 | 313 | .447 | 56 | 93 | .602 | 111 | 231 | 342 | 182 | 59 | 37 | 126 | 342 | 4.5 | 2.4 | 4.5 |
| 04-05—Atlanta ........... | 66 | 1201 | 124 | 294 | .422 | 57 | 77 | .740 | 54 | 116 | 170 | 149 | 37 | 18 | 87 | 314 | 2.6 | 2.3 | 4.8 |
| Totals ................... | 142 | 3120 | 264 | 607 | .435 | 113 | 170 | .665 | 165 | 347 | 512 | 331 | 96 | 55 | 213 | 656 | 3.6 | 2.3 | 4.6 |

Three-point field goals: 2003-04, 6-for-26 (.231). 2004-05, 9-for-50 (.180). Totals, 15-for-76 (.197).
Personal fouls/disqualifications: 2003-04, 191/2. 2004-05, 123/0. Totals, 314/2.

# DICKAU, DAN      G      HORNETS

**PERSONAL:** Born September 16, 1978, in Portland. ... 6-0/190. (1.83/86.2). ... Full name: Daniel David Dickau.
**HIGH SCHOOL:** Prairie (Vancouver, Wash.).
**COLLEGE:** Washington, then Gonzaga.
**TRANSACTIONS/CAREER NOTES:** Selected by Sacramento Kings in first round (28th pick overall) of 2002 NBA Draft. ... Draft rights traded by Kings to Atlanta Hawks for future first-round draft choice (June 26, 2002). ... Traded by Hawks with F Shareef Abdur-Rahim and C Theo Ratliff to Portland Trail Blazers for F Rasheed Wallace and G Wesley Person (February 9, 2004). ... Traded by Trail Blazers with F Dale Davis to Golden State Warriors for G Nick Van Exel (July 20, 2004). ... Traded by Warriors with C Erick Dampier, C Evan Eschmeyer and draft rights to G Steve Logan to Dallas Mavericks for F/C Christian Laettner, F Eduardo Najera, draft rights to G Luis Flores and G/F Mladen Sekularac, two future first-round draft choices and cash (August 24, 2004). ... Traded by Mavericks with a second-round draft choice to New Orleans Hornets for G Darrell Armstrong (December 3, 2004).

## COLLEGIATE RECORD

**NOTES:** THE SPORTING NEWS All-America first team (2002).

| Season Team | G | Min. | FGM | FGA | Pct. | FTM | FTA | Pct. | Reb. | Ast. | Pts. | AVERAGES RPG | APG | PPG |
|---|---|---|---|---|---|---|---|---|---|---|---|---|---|---|
| 97-98—Washington .................. | 28 | 262 | 26 | 69 | .377 | 31 | 39 | .795 | 24 | 29 | 105 | 0.9 | 1.0 | 3.8 |
| 98-99—Washington .................. | 13 | 296 | 22 | 56 | .393 | 5 | 7 | .714 | 38 | 34 | 60 | 2.9 | 2.6 | 4.6 |
| 99-00—Gonzaga ......................... | | | | | | Did not play—transfer student. | | | | | | | | |
| 00-01—Gonzaga ......................... | 24 | 809 | 133 | 274 | .485 | 116 | 134 | .866 | 79 | 150 | 453 | 3.3 | 6.3 | 18.9 |
| 01-02—Gonzaga ......................... | 32 | 1110 | 195 | 442 | .441 | 165 | 191 | .864 | 95 | 149 | 672 | 3.0 | 4.7 | 21.0 |
| Totals ....................................... | 97 | 2477 | 376 | 841 | .447 | 317 | 371 | .854 | 236 | 362 | 1290 | 2.4 | 3.7 | 13.3 |

Three-point field goals: 1997-98, 16-for-30 (.533). 1998-99, 11-for-31 (.355). 2000-01, 71-for-148 (.480). 2001-02, 117-for-256 (.457). Totals, 215-for-465 (.462).

## NBA REGULAR-SEASON RECORD

| Season Team | G | Min. | FGM | FGA | Pct. | FTM | FTA | Pct. | REBOUNDS Off. | Def. | Tot. | Ast. | St. | Blk. | TO | Pts. | AVERAGES RPG | APG | PPG |
|---|---|---|---|---|---|---|---|---|---|---|---|---|---|---|---|---|---|---|---|
| 02-03—Atlanta ........... | 50 | 515 | 70 | 170 | .412 | 21 | 26 | .808 | 9 | 34 | 43 | 85 | 14 | 2 | 53 | 183 | 0.9 | 1.7 | 3.7 |
| 03-04—Atlanta-Port. ... | 43 | 294 | 37 | 98 | .378 | 11 | 14 | .786 | 7 | 19 | 26 | 38 | 17 | 0 | 26 | 95 | 0.6 | 0.9 | 2.2 |
| 04-05—Dallas-N.O. .712090 | 306 | 756 | .405 | 190 | 228 | .833 | 34 | 146 | 180 | 347 | 76 | 4 | 145 | 887 | 2.5 | 4.9 | 12.5 | |
| Totals ................... | 164 | 2899 | 413 | 1024 | .403 | 222 | 268 | .828 | 50 | 199 | 249 | 470 | 107 | 6 | 224 | 1165 | 1.5 | 2.9 | 7.1 |

Three-point field goals: 2002-03, 22-for-61 (.361). 2003-04, 10-for-30 (.333). 2004-05, 85-for-245 (.347). Totals, 117-for-336 (.348).
Personal fouls/disqualifications: 2002-03, 66/0. 2003-04, 44/0. 2004-05, 201/3. Totals, 311/3.

# DICKENS, KANIEL      F

**PERSONAL:** Born July 21, 1978, in Denver. ... 6-8/235. (2.03/106.6).
**HIGH SCHOOL:** East (Denver).
**JUNIOR COLLEGE:** Butler County Community College (Kan.), then Tyler.
**COLLEGE:** Idaho.
**TRANSACTIONS/CAREER NOTES:** Selected after junior season by Utah Jazz in second round (50th pick overall) of 2000 NBA Draft. ... Played in Russia (2000-01). ... Played in NBDL with Dakota Wizards (2001-02). ... Played in China (2002-03). ... Played in Continental Basketball Association (2003-04). ... Signed as free agent by Portland Trail Blazers (December 19, 2003). ... Waived by Trail Blazers (January 7, 2004). ... Played in Spain (2004). ... Signed as free agent by Los Angeles Clippers (October 4, 2004). ... Waived by Clippers (October 28, 2004). ... Signed as free agent by New Jersey Nets (December 8, 2004). ... Waived by Nets (January 5, 2005). ... Signed by New Jersey Nets to 10-day contract (January 10, 2005).

## COLLEGIATE RECORD

| Season Team | G | Min. | FGM | FGA | Pct. | FTM | FTA | Pct. | Reb. | Ast. | Pts. | AVERAGES RPG | APG | PPG |
|---|---|---|---|---|---|---|---|---|---|---|---|---|---|---|
| 96-97—Butler County C.C........... | | | | | | | Did not play. | | | | | | | |
| 97-98—Tyler Junior College........ | 17 | ... | 44 | 108 | .407 | 22 | 40 | .550 | 73 | 2 | 114 | 4.3 | 0.1 | 6.7 |
| 98-99—Idaho............................. | 26 | 427 | 66 | 138 | .478 | 31 | 51 | .608 | 124 | 7 | 163 | 4.8 | 0.3 | 6.3 |
| 99-00—Idaho............................. | 29 | 796 | 118 | 243 | .486 | 102 | 160 | .638 | 192 | 27 | 351 | 6.6 | 0.9 | 12.1 |
| Junior College totals........... | 17 | ... | 44 | 108 | .407 | 22 | 40 | .550 | 73 | 2 | 114 | 4.3 | 0.1 | 6.7 |
| 4-Year-College totals............. | 55 | 1223 | 184 | 381 | .483 | 133 | 211 | .630 | 316 | 34 | 514 | 5.8 | 0.6 | 9.4 |

Three-point field goals: 1997-98, 4-for-14 (.286). 1998-99, 0-for-3. 1999-00, 13-for-34 (.382). Totals, 17-for-51 (.333).

## RUSSIAN LEAGUE RECORD

| Season Team | G | Min. | FGM | FGA | Pct. | FTM | FTA | Pct. | Reb. | Ast. | Pts. | AVERAGES RPG | APG | PPG |
|---|---|---|---|---|---|---|---|---|---|---|---|---|---|---|
| 00-01—Ural ................................ | 7 | 81 | 12 | 32 | .375 | 11 | 12 | .917 | 13 | 4 | 35 | 1.9 | 0.6 | 5.0 |

Three-point field goals: 2000-01, 0-for-4. Totals, 0-for-4 (.000).

### NBDL RECORD

| Season Team | G | Min. | FGM | FGA | Pct. | FTM | FTA | Pct. | Reb. | Ast. | Pts. | AVERAGES RPG | APG | PPG |
|---|---|---|---|---|---|---|---|---|---|---|---|---|---|---|
| 01-02—Fayetteville-Mobile......... | 27 | 376 | 42 | 109 | .385 | 50 | 76 | .658 | 66 | 3 | 139 | 2.4 | 0.1 | 5.1 |

Three-point field goals: 2001-02, 5-for-20 (.250). Totals, 5-for-20 (.250).

### CBA RECORD

| Season Team | G | Min. | FGM | FGA | Pct. | FTM | FTA | Pct. | Reb. | Ast. | Pts. | AVERAGES RPG | APG | PPG |
|---|---|---|---|---|---|---|---|---|---|---|---|---|---|---|
| 03-04—Dakota Wizards ............. | 29 | 376 | 189 | 372 | .508 | 115 | 137 | .839 | 175 | 54 | 550 | 6.0 | 1.9 | 19.0 |
| 04-05—Idaho ............................ | 25 | 858 | 160 | 336 | .476 | 94 | 116 | .810 | 180 | 35 | 470 | 7.2 | 1.4 | 18.8 |
| Totals ..................................... | 54 | 1234 | 349 | 708 | .493 | 209 | 253 | .826 | 355 | 89 | 1020 | 6.6 | 1.6 | 18.9 |

Three-point field goals: 2003-04, 57-for-131 (.435). 2004-05, 56-for-152 (.368). Totals, 113-for-283 (.399).

### NBA REGULAR-SEASON RECORD

| Season Team | G | Min. | FGM | FGA | Pct. | FTM | FTA | Pct. | REBOUNDS Off. | Def. | Tot. | Ast. | St. | Blk. | TO | Pts. | AVERAGES RPG | APG | PPG |
|---|---|---|---|---|---|---|---|---|---|---|---|---|---|---|---|---|---|---|---|
| 03-04—Portland.......... | 3 | 12 | 3 | 3 | 1.000 | 1 | 2 | .500 | 2 | 0 | 2 | 0 | 0 | 0 | 1 | 7 | 0.7 | 0.0 | 2.3 |
| 04-05—New Jersey..... | 11 | 61 | 4 | 14 | .286 | 2 | 2 | 1.000 | 3 | 6 | 9 | 1 | 2 | 1 | 2 | 13 | 0.8 | 0.1 | 1.2 |
| Totals ................... | 14 | 73 | 7 | 17 | .412 | 3 | 4 | .750 | 5 | 6 | 11 | 1 | 2 | 1 | 3 | 20 | 0.8 | 0.1 | 1.4 |

Three-point field goals: 2004-05, 3-for-9 (.333). Totals, 3-for-9 (.333).
Personal fouls/disqualifications: 2003-04, 3/0. 2004-05, 5/0. Totals, 8/0.

### SPANISH RECORD

| Season Team | G | Min. | FGM | FGA | Pct. | FTM | FTA | Pct. | Reb. | Ast. | Pts. | AVERAGES RPG | APG | PPG |
|---|---|---|---|---|---|---|---|---|---|---|---|---|---|---|
| 03-04—DKV Joventut ................ | 5 | 58 | 11 | 26 | .423 | 2 | 5 | .400 | 10 | 0 | 27 | 2.0 | 0.0 | 5.4 |

Three-point field goals: 2003-04, 3-for-11 (.273). Totals, 3-for-11 (.273).

## DIOP, DESAGANA                C                MAVERICKS

**PERSONAL:** Born January 30, 1982, in Dakar, Senegal. ... 7-0/300. (2.13/136.1). ... Full name: DeSagana Ngagne Diop
**HIGH SCHOOL:** Oak Hill Academy (Mouth of Wilson, Va.).
**COLLEGE:** Did not attend college.
**TRANSACTIONS/CAREER NOTES:** Selected out of high school by Cleveland Cavaliers in first round (eighth pick overall) of 2001 NBA Draft. ... Signed as free agent by Dallas Mavericks (August 19, 2005).

### NBA REGULAR-SEASON RECORD

| Season Team | G | Min. | FGM | FGA | Pct. | FTM | FTA | Pct. | REBOUNDS Off. | Def. | Tot. | Ast. | St. | Blk. | TO | Pts. | AVERAGES RPG | APG | PPG |
|---|---|---|---|---|---|---|---|---|---|---|---|---|---|---|---|---|---|---|---|
| 01-02—Cleveland ....... | 18 | 109 | 12 | 29 | .414 | 1 | 5 | .200 | 5 | 12 | 17 | 5 | 1 | 10 | 12 | 25 | 0.9 | 0.3 | 1.4 |
| 02-03—Cleveland ....... | 80 | 943 | 54 | 154 | .351 | 11 | 30 | .367 | 63 | 152 | 215 | 43 | 33 | 81 | 56 | 119 | 2.7 | 0.5 | 1.5 |
| 03-04—Cleveland ....... | 56 | 730 | 57 | 147 | .388 | 12 | 20 | .600 | 72 | 127 | 199 | 34 | 26 | 51 | 29 | 126 | 3.6 | 0.6 | 2.3 |
| 04-05—Cleveland ....... | 39 | 306 | 20 | 69 | .290 | 0 | 5 | .000 | 30 | 40 | 70 | 15 | 8 | 27 | 12 | 40 | 1.8 | 0.4 | 1.0 |
| Totals ................... | 193 | 2088 | 143 | 399 | .358 | 24 | 60 | .400 | 170 | 331 | 501 | 97 | 68 | 169 | 109 | 310 | 2.6 | 0.5 | 1.6 |

Three-point field goals: 2004-05, 0-for-2. Totals, 0-for-2 (.000).
Personal fouls/disqualifications: 2001-02, 19/0. 2002-03, 148/4. 2003-04, 116/1. 2004-05, 53/0. Totals, 336/5.

## DIVAC, VLADE                C                LAKERS

**PERSONAL:** Born February 3, 1968, in Prijepolje, Yugoslavia. ... 7-1/260. (2.16/117.9). ... Name pronounced Vlah-day De-vats.
**HIGH SCHOOL:** Belgrade (Yugoslavia).
**COLLEGE:** Did not attend college.
**TRANSACTIONS/CAREER NOTES:** Selected by Los Angeles Lakers in first round (26th pick overall) of 1989 NBA Draft. ... Traded by Lakers to Charlotte Hornets for draft rights to G Kobe Bryant (July 11, 1996). ... Signed as free agent by Sacramento Kings (January 22, 1999). ... Signed as free agent by Lakers (July 20, 2004).
**MISCELLANEOUS:** Member of silver-medal-winning Yugoslavian Olympic teams (1988, 1996).

### NBA REGULAR-SEASON RECORD

**HONORS:** J. Walter Kennedy Citizenship Award (2000). ... NBA All-Rookie first team (1990).

| Season Team | G | Min. | FGM | FGA | Pct. | FTM | FTA | Pct. | REBOUNDS Off. | Def. | Tot. | Ast. | St. | Blk. | TO | Pts. | AVERAGES RPG | APG | PPG |
|---|---|---|---|---|---|---|---|---|---|---|---|---|---|---|---|---|---|---|---|
| 89-90—L.A. Lakers ..... | 82 | 1611 | 274 | 549 | .499 | 153 | 216 | .708 | 167 | 345 | 512 | 75 | 79 | 114 | 110 | 701 | 6.2 | 0.9 | 8.5 |
| 90-91—L.A. Lakers ..... | 82 | 2310 | 360 | 637 | .565 | 196 | 279 | .703 | 205 | 461 | 666 | 92 | 106 | 127 | 146 | 921 | 8.1 | 1.1 | 11.2 |
| 91-92—L.A. Lakers ..... | 36 | 979 | 157 | 317 | .495 | 86 | 112 | .768 | 87 | 160 | 247 | 60 | 55 | 35 | 88 | 405 | 6.9 | 1.7 | 11.3 |
| 92-93—L.A. Lakers ..... | 82 | 2525 | 397 | 819 | .485 | 235 | 341 | .689 | 220 | 509 | 729 | 232 | 128 | 140 | 214 | 1050 | 8.9 | 2.8 | 12.8 |
| 93-94—L.A. Lakers ..... | 79 | 2685 | 453 | 895 | .506 | 208 | 303 | .686 | 282 | 569 | 851 | 307 | 92 | 112 | 191 | 1123 | 10.8 | 3.9 | 14.2 |
| 94-95—L.A. Lakers ..... | 80 | 2807 | 485 | 957 | .507 | 297 | 382 | .777 | 261 | 568 | 829 | 329 | 109 | 174 | 205 | 1277 | 10.4 | 4.1 | 16.0 |
| 95-96—L.A. Lakers ..... | 79 | 2470 | 414 | 807 | .513 | 189 | 295 | .641 | 198 | 481 | 679 | 261 | 76 | 131 | 199 | 1020 | 8.6 | 3.3 | 12.9 |
| 96-97—Charlotte......... | 81 | 2840 | 418 | 847 | .494 | 177 | 259 | .683 | 241 | 484 | 725 | 301 | 103 | 180 | 193 | 1024 | 9.0 | 3.7 | 12.6 |
| 97-98—Charlotte......... | 64 | 1805 | 267 | 536 | .498 | 130 | 188 | .691 | 183 | 335 | 518 | 172 | 83 | 94 | 114 | 667 | 8.1 | 2.7 | 10.4 |
| 98-99—Sacramento .... | 50 | 1761 | 262 | 557 | .470 | 179 | 255 | .702 | 140 | 361 | 501 | 215 | 44 | 51 | 131 | 714 | 10.0 | 4.3 | 14.3 |
| 99-00—Sacramento .... | 82 | 2374 | 384 | 764 | .503 | 230 | 333 | .691 | 174 | 482 | 656 | 244 | 103 | 103 | 190 | 1005 | 8.0 | 3.0 | 12.3 |
| 00-01—Sacramento .... | 81 | 2420 | 364 | 755 | .482 | 242 | 350 | .691 | 207 | 466 | 673 | 231 | 87 | 93 | 192 | 974 | 8.3 | 2.9 | 12.0 |
| 01-02—Sacramento .... | 80 | 2420 | 338 | 716 | .472 | 209 | 340 | .615 | 205 | 466 | 671 | 297 | 79 | 94 | 158 | 888 | 8.4 | 3.7 | 11.1 |
| 02-03—Sacramento .... | 80 | 2384 | 305 | 655 | .466 | 179 | 251 | .713 | 157 | 417 | 574 | 274 | 83 | 105 | 152 | 795 | 7.2 | 3.4 | 9.9 |
| 03-04—Sacramento .... | 81 | 2317 | 314 | 668 | .470 | 170 | 260 | .654 | 136 | 327 | 463 | 432 | 57 | 77 | 173 | 800 | 5.7 | 5.3 | 9.9 |
| 04-05—L.A. Lakers ..... | 15 | 130 | 13 | 31 | .419 | 8 | 12 | .667 | 18 | 14 | 32 | 19 | 4 | 1 | 14 | 34 | 2.1 | 1.3 | 2.3 |
| Totals ................... | 1134 | 33838 | 5205 | 10510 | .495 | 2888 | 4176 | .692 | 2881 | 6445 | 9326 | 3541 | 1288 | 1631 | 2470 | 13398 | 8.2 | 3.1 | 11.8 |

D

Three-point field goals: 1989-90, 0-for-5. 1990-91, 5-for-14 (.357). 1991-92, 5-for-19 (.263). 1992-93, 21-for-75 (.280). 1993-94, 9-for-47 (.191). 1994-95, 10-for-53 (.189). 1995-96, 3-for-18 (.167). 1996-97, 11-for-47 (.234). 1997-98, 3-for-14 (.214). 1998-99, 11-for-43 (.256). 1999-00, 7-for-26 (.269). 2000-01, 4-for-14 (.286). 2001-02, 3-for-13 (.231). 2002-03, 6-for-25 (.240). 2003-04, 2-for-13 (.154). Totals, 100-for-426 (.235).

Personal fouls/disqualifications: 1989-90, 240/2. 1990-91, 247/3. 1991-92, 114/3. 1992-93, 311/7. 1993-94, 288/5. 1994-95, 305/8. 1995-96, 274/5. 1996-97, 277/6. 1997-98, 179/1. 1998-99, 166/2. 1999-00, 251/2. 2000-01, 242/5. 2001-02, 229/1. 2002-03, 239/3. 2003-04, 222/2. 2004-05, 25/0. Totals, 3609/55.

## NBA PLAYOFF RECORD

| Season Team | G | Min. | FGM | FGA | Pct. | FTM | FTA | Pct. | REBOUNDS Off. | Def. | Tot. | Ast. | St. | Blk. | TO | Pts. | AVERAGES RPG | APG | PPG |
|---|---|---|---|---|---|---|---|---|---|---|---|---|---|---|---|---|---|---|---|
| 89-90—L.A. Lakers ..... | 9 | 175 | 32 | 44 | .727 | 17 | 19 | .895 | 16 | 32 | 48 | 10 | 8 | 15 | 13 | 82 | 5.3 | 1.1 | 9.1 |
| 90-91—L.A. Lakers ..... | 19 | 609 | 97 | 172 | .564 | 57 | 71 | .803 | 49 | 78 | 127 | 21 | 27 | 41 | 41 | 252 | 6.7 | 1.1 | 13.3 |
| 91-92—L.A. Lakers ..... | 4 | 143 | 15 | 43 | .349 | 9 | 10 | .900 | 6 | 16 | 22 | 15 | 5 | 3 | 18 | 39 | 5.5 | 3.8 | 9.8 |
| 92-93—L.A. Lakers ..... | 5 | 167 | 37 | 74 | .500 | 12 | 22 | .545 | 17 | 30 | 47 | 28 | 6 | 12 | 11 | 90 | 9.4 | 5.6 | 18.0 |
| 94-95—L.A. Lakers ..... | 10 | 388 | 57 | 122 | .467 | 40 | 62 | .645 | 34 | 51 | 85 | 31 | 8 | 13 | 28 | 156 | 8.5 | 3.1 | 15.6 |
| 95-96—L.A. Lakers ..... | 4 | 115 | 15 | 35 | .429 | 5 | 8 | .625 | 11 | 19 | 30 | 8 | 0 | 5 | 8 | 36 | 7.5 | 2.0 | 9.0 |
| 96-97—Charlotte ........ | 3 | 116 | 21 | 46 | .457 | 12 | 15 | .800 | 13 | 13 | 26 | 10 | 3 | 6 | 6 | 54 | 8.7 | 3.3 | 18.0 |
| 97-98—Charlotte ........ | 9 | 345 | 42 | 87 | .483 | 20 | 33 | .606 | 25 | 73 | 98 | 31 | 7 | 14 | 22 | 104 | 10.9 | 3.4 | 11.6 |
| 98-99—Sacramento .... | 5 | 198 | 25 | 56 | .446 | 30 | 36 | .833 | 9 | 41 | 50 | 23 | 8 | 4 | 19 | 81 | 10.0 | 4.6 | 16.2 |
| 99-00—Sacramento .... | 5 | 160 | 20 | 56 | .357 | 16 | 23 | .696 | 9 | 27 | 36 | 14 | 7 | 4 | 9 | 56 | 7.2 | 2.8 | 11.2 |
| 00-01—Sacramento .... | 8 | 225 | 28 | 80 | .350 | 29 | 38 | .763 | 20 | 47 | 67 | 19 | 8 | 12 | 18 | 86 | 8.4 | 2.4 | 10.8 |
| 01-02—Sacramento .... | 16 | 535 | 70 | 151 | .464 | 74 | 98 | .755 | 46 | 103 | 149 | 27 | 18 | 20 | 37 | 216 | 9.3 | 1.7 | 13.5 |
| 02-03—Sacramento .... | 12 | 317 | 51 | 91 | .560 | 35 | 52 | .673 | 30 | 39 | 69 | 27 | 8 | 11 | 16 | 137 | 5.8 | 2.3 | 11.4 |
| 03-04—Sacramento .... | 12 | 235 | 31 | 71 | .437 | 17 | 23 | .739 | 22 | 37 | 59 | 22 | 4 | 5 | 14 | 79 | 4.9 | 1.8 | 6.6 |
| Totals ................... | 121 | 3728 | 541 | 1128 | .480 | 373 | 510 | .731 | 307 | 606 | 913 | 286 | 117 | 165 | 260 | 1468 | 7.5 | 2.4 | 12.1 |

Three-point field goals: 1989-90, 1-for-2 (.500). 1990-91, 1-for-6 (.167). 1991-92, 0-for-2. 1992-93, 4-for-9 (.444). 1994-95, 2-for-9 (.222). 1995-96, 1-for-5 (.200). 1996-97, 0-for-3. 1997-98, 0-for-1. 1998-99, 1-for-5 (.200). 1999-00, 0-for-2. 2000-01, 1-for-3 (.333). 2001-02, 2-for-7 (.286). Totals, 13-for-54 (.241).

Personal fouls/disqualifications: 1989-90, 27/1. 1990-91, 65/2. 1991-92, 17/1. 1992-93, 22/0. 1994-95, 44/2. 1995-96, 10/0. 1996-97, 11/0. 1997-98, 34/1. 1998-99, 17/0. 1999-00, 22/0. 2000-01, 25/1. 2001-02, 26/6. 2002-03, 38/0. 2003-04, 31/0. Totals, 439/14.

## NBA ALL-STAR GAME RECORD

| Season Team | Min. | FGM | FGA | Pct. | FTM | FTA | Pct. | REBOUNDS Off. | Def. | Tot. | Ast. | PF | Dq. | St. | Blk. | TO | Pts. |
|---|---|---|---|---|---|---|---|---|---|---|---|---|---|---|---|---|---|
| 2001—Sacramento.......... | 9 | 4 | 6 | .667 | 0 | 0 | ... | 1 | 2 | 3 | 1 | 0 | 0 | 2 | 0 | 1 | 8 |

# DIXON, JUAN     G     TRAIL BLAZERS    D

**PERSONAL:** Born October 9, 1978, in Baltimore. ... 6-3/164. (1.91/74.4).
**HIGH SCHOOL:** Calvert Hall (Baltimore).
**COLLEGE:** Maryland.
**TRANSACTIONS/CAREER NOTES:** Selected by Washington Wizards in first round (17th pick overall) of 2002 NBA Draft. ... Signed as free agent by Portland Trail Blazers (August 4, 2005).

## COLLEGIATE RECORD

**NOTES:** THE SPORTING NEWS All-America first team (2002). ... Member of NCAA Tournament championship team (2002). ... NCAA Division I Tournament Most Outstanding Player (2002).

| Season Team | G | Min. | FGM | FGA | Pct. | FTM | FTA | Pct. | Reb. | Ast. | Pts. | AVERAGES RPG | APG | PPG |
|---|---|---|---|---|---|---|---|---|---|---|---|---|---|---|
| 97-98—Maryland ...................... | | | | | | Did not play—redshirted. | | | | | | | | |
| 98-99—Maryland ...................... | 34 | 505 | 85 | 192 | .443 | 44 | 53 | .830 | 88 | 47 | 250 | 2.6 | 1.4 | 7.4 |
| 99-00—Maryland ...................... | 35 | 1190 | 234 | 506 | .462 | 113 | 143 | .790 | 192 | 127 | 630 | 5.5 | 3.6 | 18.0 |
| 00-01—Maryland ...................... | 36 | 1098 | 232 | 480 | .483 | 128 | 148 | .865 | 153 | 93 | 654 | 4.3 | 2.6 | 18.2 |
| 01-02—Maryland ...................... | 36 | 1209 | 251 | 535 | .469 | 141 | 157 | .898 | 166 | 104 | 735 | 4.6 | 2.9 | 20.4 |
| Totals ..................................... | 141 | 4002 | 802 | 1713 | .468 | 426 | 501 | .850 | 599 | 371 | 2269 | 4.2 | 2.6 | 16.1 |

Three-point field goals: 1998-99, 36-for-97 (.371). 1999-00, 49-for-135 (.363). 2000-01, 62-for-151 (.411). 2001-02, 92-for-232 (.397). Totals, 239-for-615 (.389).

## NBA REGULAR-SEASON RECORD

| Season Team | G | Min. | FGM | FGA | Pct. | FTM | FTA | Pct. | REBOUNDS Off. | Def. | Tot. | Ast. | St. | Blk. | TO | Pts. | AVERAGES RPG | APG | PPG |
|---|---|---|---|---|---|---|---|---|---|---|---|---|---|---|---|---|---|---|---|
| 02-03—Washington .... | 42 | 647 | 104 | 271 | .384 | 37 | 46 | .804 | 13 | 59 | 72 | 40 | 26 | 3 | 42 | 270 | 1.7 | 1.0 | 6.4 |
| 03-04—Washington .... | 71 | 1478 | 247 | 637 | .388 | 111 | 139 | .799 | 30 | 118 | 148 | 137 | 82 | 4 | 104 | 664 | 2.1 | 1.9 | 9.4 |
| 04-05—Washington .... | 63 | 1054 | 186 | 447 | .416 | 87 | 97 | .897 | 32 | 87 | 119 | 111 | 43 | 4 | 68 | 507 | 1.9 | 1.8 | 8.0 |
| Totals ................... | 176 | 3179 | 537 | 1355 | .396 | 235 | 282 | .833 | 75 | 264 | 339 | 288 | 151 | 11 | 214 | 1441 | 1.9 | 1.6 | 8.2 |

Three-point field goals: 2002-03, 25-for-84 (.298). 2003-04, 59-for-198 (.298). 2004-05, 48-for-147 (.327). Totals, 132-for-429 (.308).
Personal fouls/disqualifications: 2002-03, 54/0. 2003-04, 111/1. 2004-05, 98/0. Totals, 263/1.

## NBA PLAYOFF RECORD

| Season Team | G | Min. | FGM | FGA | Pct. | FTM | FTA | Pct. | REBOUNDS Off. | Def. | Tot. | Ast. | St. | Blk. | TO | Pts. | AVERAGES RPG | APG | PPG |
|---|---|---|---|---|---|---|---|---|---|---|---|---|---|---|---|---|---|---|---|
| 04-05—Washington .... | 10 | 219 | 41 | 101 | .406 | 21 | 25 | .840 | 3 | 23 | 26 | 13 | 7 | 0 | 12 | 114 | 2.6 | 1.3 | 11.4 |

Three-point field goals: 2004-05, 11-for-34 (.324). Totals, 11-for-34 (.324).
Personal fouls/disqualifications: 2004-05, 19/0. Totals, 19/0.

# DOLEAC, MICHAEL     C     HEAT

**PERSONAL:** Born June 15, 1977, in San Antonio. ... 6-11/262. (2.11/118.8). ... Full name: Michael Scott Doleac
**HIGH SCHOOL:** Central Catholic (Portland, Ore.).
**COLLEGE:** Utah.
**TRANSACTIONS/CAREER NOTES:** Selected by Orlando Magic in first round (12th pick overall) of 1998 NBA Draft. ... Traded by Magic to Cleveland Cavaliers for draft rights to C Brendan Haywood (June 27, 2001). ... Signed as free agent by New

York Knicks (August 7, 2002). ... Traded by Knicks to Atlanta Hawks in three-team deal in which Knicks also traded 2005 second-round draft choice to Hawks and F Keith Van Horn to Milwaukee Bucks. Hawks also acquired C Joel Przybilla from Bucks. Knicks acquired F Nazr Mohammed from Hawks and F Tim Thomas from Bucks (February 15, 2004). ... Waived by Hawks (February 18, 2004). ... Signed as free agent by Denver Nuggets (February 20, 2004). ... Signed as free agent by Miami Heat (July 15, 2004).

## COLLEGIATE RECORD

| Season Team | G | Min. | FGM | FGA | Pct. | FTM | FTA | Pct. | Reb. | Ast. | Pts. | AVERAGES RPG | APG | PPG |
|---|---|---|---|---|---|---|---|---|---|---|---|---|---|---|
| 94-95—Utah | 32 | 547 | 81 | 179 | .453 | 72 | 97 | .742 | 144 | 6 | 234 | 4.5 | 0.2 | 7.3 |
| 95-96—Utah | 34 | 819 | 101 | 218 | .463 | 92 | 116 | .793 | 261 | 26 | 294 | 7.7 | 0.8 | 8.6 |
| 96-97—Utah | 33 | 876 | 166 | 309 | .537 | 135 | 174 | .776 | 253 | 25 | 475 | 7.7 | 0.8 | 14.4 |
| 97-98—Utah | 32 | 876 | 165 | 338 | .488 | 173 | 215 | .805 | 228 | 17 | 516 | 7.1 | 0.5 | 16.1 |
| Totals | 131 | 3118 | 513 | 1044 | .491 | 472 | 602 | .784 | 886 | 74 | 1519 | 6.8 | 0.6 | 11.6 |

Three-point field goals: 1994-95, 0-for-1. 1995-96, 0-for-1. 1996-97, 8-for-18 (.444). 1997-98, 13-for-32 (.406). Totals, 21-for-52 (.404).

### NBA REGULAR-SEASON RECORD

HONORS: NBA All-Rookie second team (1999).

| Season Team | G | Min. | FGM | FGA | Pct. | FTM | FTA | Pct. | REBOUNDS Off. | Def. | Tot. | Ast. | St. | Blk. | TO | Pts. | AVERAGES RPG | APG | PPG |
|---|---|---|---|---|---|---|---|---|---|---|---|---|---|---|---|---|---|---|---|
| 98-99—Orlando | 49 | 780 | 125 | 267 | .468 | 54 | 80 | .675 | 66 | 82 | 148 | 20 | 19 | 17 | 26 | 304 | 3.0 | 0.4 | 6.2 |
| 99-00—Orlando | 81 | 1335 | 242 | 535 | .452 | 80 | 95 | .842 | 89 | 245 | 334 | 63 | 29 | 34 | 65 | 565 | 4.1 | 0.8 | 7.0 |
| 00-01—Orlando | 77 | 1398 | 220 | 527 | .417 | 50 | 59 | .847 | 70 | 203 | 273 | 65 | 37 | 41 | 59 | 490 | 3.5 | 0.8 | 6.4 |
| 01-02—Cleveland | 42 | 705 | 78 | 187 | .417 | 38 | 46 | .826 | 47 | 121 | 168 | 25 | 15 | 11 | 37 | 194 | 4.0 | 0.6 | 4.6 |
| 02-03—New York | 75 | 1041 | 146 | 343 | .426 | 36 | 46 | .783 | 65 | 154 | 219 | 42 | 16 | 16 | 49 | 328 | 2.9 | 0.6 | 4.4 |
| 04-05—Miami | 80 | 1175 | 148 | 331 | .447 | 25 | 41 | .610 | 74 | 185 | 259 | 47 | 23 | 22 | 36 | 321 | 3.2 | 0.6 | 4.0 |
| Totals | 404 | 6434 | 959 | 2190 | .438 | 283 | 367 | .771 | 411 | 990 | 1401 | 262 | 139 | 141 | 272 | 2202 | 3.5 | 0.6 | 5.5 |

Three-point field goals: 1999-00, 1-for-2 (.500). 2000-01, 0-for-3. 2004-05, 0-for-2. Totals, 1-for-7 (.143).
Personal fouls/disqualifications: 1998-99, 117/1. 1999-00, 224/3. 2000-01, 239/10. 2001-02, 98/4. 2002-03, 150/1. 2004-05, 160/0. Totals, 988/19.

### NBA PLAYOFF RECORD

| Season Team | G | Min. | FGM | FGA | Pct. | FTM | FTA | Pct. | REBOUNDS Off. | Def. | Tot. | Ast. | St. | Blk. | TO | Pts. | AVERAGES RPG | APG | PPG |
|---|---|---|---|---|---|---|---|---|---|---|---|---|---|---|---|---|---|---|---|
| 98-99—Orlando | 4 | 43 | 5 | 18 | .278 | 7 | 9 | .778 | 5 | 7 | 12 | 0 | 0 | 1 | 3 | 17 | 3.0 | 0.0 | 4.3 |
| 00-01—Orlando | 4 | 45 | 6 | 16 | .375 | 0 | 0 | ... | 4 | 10 | 14 | 1 | 3 | 0 | 2 | 12 | 3.5 | 0.3 | 3.0 |
| 03-04—Denver | 5 | 49 | 5 | 10 | .500 | 0 | 0 | ... | 2 | 5 | 7 | 3 | 0 | 0 | 1 | 10 | 1.4 | 0.6 | 2.0 |
| 04-05—Miami | 9 | 65 | 7 | 16 | .438 | 2 | 2 | 1.000 | 2 | 12 | 14 | 0 | 1 | 1 | 3 | 16 | 1.6 | 0.0 | 1.8 |
| Totals | 22 | 202 | 23 | 60 | .383 | 9 | 11 | .818 | 13 | 34 | 47 | 4 | 4 | 2 | 9 | 55 | 2.1 | 0.2 | 2.5 |

Three-point field goals: 1998-99, 0-for-1. Totals, 0-for-1 (.000).
Personal fouls/disqualifications: 1998-99, 6/0. 2000-01, 10/0. 2003-04, 8/0. 2004-05, 13/0. Totals, 37/0.

## DOOLING, KEYON     G     MAGIC

PERSONAL: Born May 8, 1980, in Fort Lauderdale, Fla. ... 6-3/196. (1.91/88.9). ... Full name: Keyon Latwae Dooling
HIGH SCHOOL: Dillard (Fort Lauderdale, Fla.).
COLLEGE: Missouri.
TRANSACTIONS/CAREER NOTES: Selected after sophomore season by Orlando Magic in first round (10th pick overall) of 2000 NBA Draft. ... Draft rights traded by Magic with F Corey Maggette and F Derek Strong to Los Angeles Clippers for a future first-round draft choice (June 28, 2000). ... Signed as free agent by Miami Heat (July 22, 2004). ... Signed as free agent by Orlando Magic (August 3, 2005).

### COLLEGIATE RECORD

| Season Team | G | Min. | FGM | FGA | Pct. | FTM | FTA | Pct. | Reb. | Ast. | Pts. | AVERAGES RPG | APG | PPG |
|---|---|---|---|---|---|---|---|---|---|---|---|---|---|---|
| 98-99—Missouri | 28 | 676 | 78 | 170 | .459 | 79 | 110 | .718 | 58 | 85 | 243 | 2.1 | 3.0 | 8.7 |
| 99-00—Missouri | 31 | 983 | 145 | 373 | .389 | 124 | 167 | .743 | 84 | 113 | 473 | 2.7 | 3.6 | 15.3 |
| Totals | 59 | 1659 | 223 | 543 | .411 | 203 | 277 | .733 | 142 | 198 | 716 | 2.4 | 3.4 | 12.1 |

Three-point field goals: 1998-99, 8-for-28 (.286). 1999-00, 59-for-170 (.347). Totals, 67-for-198 (.338).

### NBA REGULAR-SEASON RECORD

| Season Team | G | Min. | FGM | FGA | Pct. | FTM | FTA | Pct. | REBOUNDS Off. | Def. | Tot. | Ast. | St. | Blk. | TO | Pts. | AVERAGES RPG | APG | PPG |
|---|---|---|---|---|---|---|---|---|---|---|---|---|---|---|---|---|---|---|---|
| 00-01—L.A. Clippers | 76 | 1237 | 148 | 362 | .409 | 125 | 179 | .698 | 8 | 81 | 89 | 177 | 41 | 11 | 94 | 449 | 1.2 | 2.3 | 5.9 |
| 01-02—L.A. Clippers | 14 | 155 | 22 | 57 | .386 | 10 | 12 | .833 | 0 | 3 | 3 | 12 | 4 | 3 | 10 | 58 | 0.2 | 0.9 | 4.1 |
| 02-03—L.A. Clippers | 55 | 969 | 128 | 329 | .389 | 44 | 57 | .772 | 9 | 63 | 72 | 89 | 24 | 6 | 60 | 350 | 1.3 | 1.6 | 6.4 |
| 03-04—L.A. Clippers | 58 | 1137 | 137 | 352 | .389 | 78 | 94 | .830 | 17 | 62 | 79 | 130 | 45 | 6 | 65 | 360 | 1.4 | 2.2 | 6.2 |
| 04-05—Miami | 74 | 1184 | 139 | 345 | .403 | 85 | 109 | .780 | 11 | 79 | 90 | 132 | 39 | 11 | 65 | 382 | 1.2 | 1.8 | 5.2 |
| Totals | 277 | 4682 | 574 | 1445 | .397 | 342 | 451 | .758 | 45 | 288 | 333 | 540 | 153 | 37 | 294 | 1599 | 1.2 | 1.9 | 5.8 |

Three-point field goals: 2000-01, 28-for-80 (.350). 2001-02, 4-for-14 (.286). 2002-03, 50-for-139 (.360). 2003-04, 8-for-46 (.174). 2004-05, 19-for-75 (.253). Totals, 109-for-354 (.308).
Personal fouls/disqualifications: 2000-01, 107/0. 2001-02, 20/0. 2002-03, 93/0. 2003-04, 108/2. 2004-05, 120/0. Totals, 448/2.

### NBA PLAYOFF RECORD

| Season Team | G | Min. | FGM | FGA | Pct. | FTM | FTA | Pct. | REBOUNDS Off. | Def. | Tot. | Ast. | St. | Blk. | TO | Pts. | AVERAGES RPG | APG | PPG |
|---|---|---|---|---|---|---|---|---|---|---|---|---|---|---|---|---|---|---|---|
| 04-05—Miami | 15 | 264 | 43 | 87 | .494 | 17 | 21 | .810 | 1 | 15 | 16 | 25 | 6 | 1 | 14 | 110 | 1.1 | 1.7 | 7.3 |

Three-point field goals: 2004-05, 7-for-19 (.368). Totals, 7-for-19 (.368).
Personal fouls/disqualifications: 2004-05, 34/0. Totals, 34/0.

# DROBNJAK, PREDRAG      C

**PERSONAL:** Born October 27, 1975, in Bijelo Polje, Yugoslavia. ... 6-11/270. (2.11/122.5).
**TRANSACTIONS/CAREER NOTES:** Played in Yugoslavia (1996-98). ... Selected by Washington Wizards in second round (49th pick overall) of 1997 NBA Draft. ... Played in Turkey (1998-2001). ... Draft rights traded by Wizards to Seattle SuperSonics for draft rights to F Bobby Simmons (June 27, 2001). ... Traded by SuperSonics to Los Angeles Clippers for future second-round draft choice (September 28, 2003). ... Selected by Charlotte Bobcats from Clippers in NBA Expansion Draft (June 22, 2004). ... Traded by Bobcats to Atlanta Hawks for a 2005 second-round draft choice (August 16, 2004).
**MISCELLANEOUS:** Member of Yugoslavian Olympic team (2000).

## YUGOSLAVIAN LEAGUE RECORD

| Season Team | G | Min. | FGM | FGA | Pct. | FTM | FTA | Pct. | Reb. | Ast. | Pts. | RPG | APG | PPG |
|---|---|---|---|---|---|---|---|---|---|---|---|---|---|---|
| 96-97—Partizan Belgrade | 25 | 600 | 117 | 181 | .646 | 80 | 108 | .741 | 150 | 16 | 314 | 6.0 | 0.6 | 12.6 |
| 97-98—Partizan Belgrade | 24 | 735 | 155 | 251 | .618 | 88 | 114 | .772 | 177 | 16 | 410 | 7.4 | 0.7 | 17.1 |
| Totals | 49 | 1335 | 272 | 432 | .630 | 168 | 222 | .757 | 327 | 32 | 724 | 6.7 | 0.7 | 14.8 |

Three-point field goals: 1997-98, 12-for-36 (.333). Totals, 12-for-36 (.333).

## TURKISH LEAGUE RECORD

| Season Team | G | Min. | FGM | FGA | Pct. | FTM | FTA | Pct. | Reb. | Ast. | Pts. | RPG | APG | PPG |
|---|---|---|---|---|---|---|---|---|---|---|---|---|---|---|
| 98-99—Efes Pilsen | 36 | 924 | 169 | 312 | .542 | 73 | 102 | .716 | 188 | 48 | 415 | 5.2 | 1.3 | 11.5 |
| 99-00—Efes Pilsen | 35 | 979 | 154 | 256 | .602 | 82 | 102 | .804 | 199 | 26 | 401 | 5.7 | 0.7 | 11.5 |
| 00-01—Efes Pilsen | 25 | 652 | 122 | 234 | .521 | 57 | 73 | .781 | 149 | 28 | 309 | 6.0 | 1.1 | 12.4 |
| Totals | 96 | 2555 | 445 | 802 | .555 | 212 | 277 | .765 | 536 | 102 | 1125 | 5.6 | 1.1 | 11.7 |

Three-point field goals: 1998-99, 4-for-18 (.222). 1999-00, 11-for-31 (.355). 2000-01, 8-for-40 (.200). Totals, 23-for-89 (.258).

## NBA REGULAR-SEASON RECORD

| Season Team | G | Min. | FGM | FGA | Pct. | FTM | FTA | Pct. | Off. | Def. | Tot. | Ast. | St. | Blk. | TO | Pts. | RPG | APG | PPG |
|---|---|---|---|---|---|---|---|---|---|---|---|---|---|---|---|---|---|---|---|
| 01-02—Seattle | 64 | 1174 | 191 | 414 | .461 | 55 | 73 | .753 | 75 | 144 | 219 | 51 | 20 | 31 | 51 | 437 | 3.4 | 0.8 | 6.8 |
| 02-03—Seattle | 82 | 1984 | 325 | 789 | .412 | 91 | 115 | .791 | 111 | 209 | 320 | 86 | 48 | 38 | 65 | 771 | 3.9 | 1.0 | 9.4 |
| 03-04—L.A. Clippers | 61 | 949 | 149 | 379 | .393 | 73 | 86 | .849 | 54 | 142 | 196 | 39 | 22 | 24 | 48 | 382 | 3.2 | 0.6 | 6.3 |
| 04-05—Atlanta | 71 | 1435 | 238 | 543 | .438 | 96 | 120 | .800 | 73 | 165 | 238 | 49 | 42 | 24 | 78 | 597 | 3.4 | 0.7 | 8.4 |
| Totals | 278 | 5542 | 903 | 2125 | .425 | 315 | 394 | .799 | 313 | 660 | 973 | 225 | 132 | 117 | 242 | 2187 | 3.5 | 0.8 | 7.9 |

Three-point field goals: 2001-02, 0-for-2. 2002-03, 30-for-85 (.353). 2003-04, 11-for-36 (.306). 2004-05, 25-for-71 (.352). Totals, 66-for-194 (.340).
Personal fouls/disqualifications: 2001-02, 109/0. 2002-03, 180/0. 2003-04, 85/1. 2004-05, 138/0. Totals, 512/1.

## NBA PLAYOFF RECORD

| Season Team | G | Min. | FGM | FGA | Pct. | FTM | FTA | Pct. | Off. | Def. | Tot. | Ast. | St. | Blk. | TO | Pts. | RPG | APG | PPG |
|---|---|---|---|---|---|---|---|---|---|---|---|---|---|---|---|---|---|---|---|
| 01-02—Seattle | 3 | 38 | 4 | 12 | .333 | 2 | 4 | .500 | 3 | 5 | 8 | 2 | 1 | 0 | 1 | 10 | 2.7 | 0.7 | 3.3 |

Personal fouls/disqualifications: 2001-02, 2/0. Totals, 2/0.

# DUHON, CHRIS      G      BULLS

**PERSONAL:** Born August 31, 1982, in Mamou, La. ... 6-1/185. (1.85/83.9). ... Full name: Chris Nicholas Duhon
**HIGH SCHOOL:** Salmen (Slidell, La.).
**COLLEGE:** Duke.
**TRANSACTIONS/CAREER NOTES:** Selected by Chicago Bulls in second round (38th pick overall) of 2004 NBA Draft.

## COLLEGIATE RECORD

**NOTES:** Member of NCAA Division I championship team (2001).

| Season Team | G | Min. | FGM | FGA | Pct. | FTM | FTA | Pct. | Reb. | Ast. | Pts. | RPG | APG | PPG |
|---|---|---|---|---|---|---|---|---|---|---|---|---|---|---|
| 00-01—Duke | 39 | 1085 | 92 | 217 | .424 | 52 | 80 | .650 | 124 | 174 | 280 | 3.2 | 4.5 | 7.2 |
| 01-02—Duke | 35 | 1229 | 100 | 244 | .410 | 59 | 83 | .711 | 109 | 208 | 313 | 3.1 | 5.9 | 8.9 |
| 02-03—Duke | 33 | 1188 | 102 | 264 | .386 | 66 | 96 | .688 | 106 | 212 | 305 | 3.2 | 6.4 | 9.2 |
| 03-04—Duke | 37 | 1311 | 138 | 308 | .448 | 65 | 90 | .722 | 150 | 225 | 370 | 4.1 | 6.1 | 10.0 |
| Totals | 144 | 4813 | 432 | 1033 | .418 | 242 | 349 | .693 | 489 | 819 | 1268 | 3.4 | 5.7 | 8.8 |

## NBA REGULAR-SEASON RECORD

| Season Team | G | Min. | FGM | FGA | Pct. | FTM | FTA | Pct. | Off. | Def. | Tot. | Ast. | St. | Blk. | TO | Pts. | RPG | APG | PPG |
|---|---|---|---|---|---|---|---|---|---|---|---|---|---|---|---|---|---|---|---|
| 04-05—Chicago | 82 | 2177 | 172 | 488 | .352 | 49 | 67 | .731 | 23 | 190 | 213 | 398 | 82 | 3 | 119 | 487 | 2.6 | 4.9 | 5.9 |

Three-point field goals: 2004-05, 94-for-265 (.355). Totals, 94-for-265 (.355).
Personal fouls/disqualifications: 2004-05, 205/1. Totals, 205/1.

## NBA PLAYOFF RECORD

| Season Team | G | Min. | FGM | FGA | Pct. | FTM | FTA | Pct. | Off. | Def. | Tot. | Ast. | St. | Blk. | TO | Pts. | RPG | APG | PPG |
|---|---|---|---|---|---|---|---|---|---|---|---|---|---|---|---|---|---|---|---|
| 04-05—Chicago | 6 | 159 | 11 | 37 | .297 | 9 | 11 | .818 | 6 | 20 | 26 | 21 | 2 | 0 | 12 | 37 | 4.3 | 3.5 | 6.2 |

Three-point field goals: 2004-05, 6-for-22 (.273). Totals, 6-for-22 (.273).
Personal fouls/disqualifications: 2004-05, 6/0. Totals, 6/0.

# DUNCAN, TIM　　　　　F/C　　　　　SPURS

**PERSONAL:** Born April 25, 1976, in St. Croix, Virgin Islands. ... 7-0/260. (2.13/117.9). ... Full name: Timothy Theodore Duncan
**HIGH SCHOOL:** St. Dunstan's Episcopal High (Virgin Islands).
**COLLEGE:** Wake Forest.
**TRANSACTIONS/CAREER NOTES:** Selected by San Antonio Spurs in first round (first pick overall) of 1997 NBA Draft.
**MISCELLANEOUS:** Member of NBA championship team (1999, 2003, 2005). ... Member of bronze-medal-winning U.S. Olympic Team (2004).

## COLLEGIATE RECORD

**NOTES:** The Sporting News College Player of the Year (1997). ... Naismith Award winner (1997). ... Wooden Award winner (1997). ... The Sporting News All-America first team (1996 and 1997). ... Holds NCAA Division I career record for most rebounds in four-year career (since 1973)—1,570. ... Led NCAA Division I with 14.7 rebounds per game (1997).

| Season Team | G | Min. | FGM | FGA | Pct. | FTM | FTA | Pct. | Reb. | Ast. | Pts. | AVERAGES RPG | APG | PPG |
|---|---|---|---|---|---|---|---|---|---|---|---|---|---|---|
| 93-94—Wake Forest | 33 | 997 | 120 | 220 | .545 | 82 | 110 | .745 | 317 | 30 | 323 | 9.6 | 0.9 | 9.8 |
| 94-95—Wake Forest | 32 | 1168 | 208 | 352 | .591 | 118 | 159 | .742 | 401 | 67 | 537 | 12.5 | 2.1 | 16.8 |
| 95-96—Wake Forest | 32 | 1190 | 228 | 411 | .555 | 149 | 217 | .687 | 395 | 93 | 612 | 12.3 | 2.9 | 19.1 |
| 96-97—Wake Forest | 31 | 1137 | 234 | 385 | .608 | 171 | 269 | .636 | 457 | 98 | 645 | 14.7 | 3.2 | 20.8 |
| Totals | 128 | 4492 | 790 | 1368 | .577 | 520 | 755 | .689 | 1570 | 288 | 2117 | 12.3 | 2.3 | 16.5 |

Three-point field goals: 1993-94, 1-for-1 (1.000). 1994-95, 3-for-7 (.429). 1995-96, 7-for-23 (.304). 1996-97, 6-for-22 (.273). Totals, 17-for-53 (.321).
Personal fouls/disqualifications: 1993-94, 82/2. 1994-95, 79/3. 1995-96, 74/0. Totals, 235/5.

## NBA REGULAR-SEASON RECORD

**HONORS:** NBA Most Valuable Player (2002, 2003). ... NBA Rookie of the Year (1998). ... IBM Award, for all-around contributions to team's success (2002). ... All-NBA first team (1998, 1999, 2000, 2001, 2002, 2003, 2004, 2005). ... NBA All-Defensive first team (1999, 2000, 2001, 2002, 2003, 2005). ... NBA All-Defensive second team (1998, 2004). ... NBA All-Rookie first team (1998).

| Season Team | G | Min. | FGM | FGA | Pct. | FTM | FTA | Pct. | REBOUNDS Off. | Def. | Tot. | Ast. | St. | Blk. | TO | Pts. | AVERAGES RPG | APG | PPG |
|---|---|---|---|---|---|---|---|---|---|---|---|---|---|---|---|---|---|---|---|
| 97-98—San Antonio | 82 | 3204 | 706 | 1287 | .549 | 319 | 482 | .662 | 274 | 703 | 977 | 224 | 55 | 206 | 279 | 1731 | 11.9 | 2.7 | 21.1 |
| 98-99—San Antonio | 50 | 1963 | 418 | 845 | .495 | 247 | 358 | .690 | 159 | 412 | 571 | 121 | 45 | 126 | 146 | 1084 | 11.4 | 2.4 | 21.7 |
| 99-00—San Antonio | 74 | 2875 | 628 | 1281 | .490 | 459 | 603 | .761 | 262 | 656 | 918 | 234 | 66 | 165 | 242 | 1716 | 12.4 | 3.2 | 23.2 |
| 00-01—San Antonio | 82 | 3174 | 702 | 1406 | .499 | 409 | 662 | .618 | 259 | 738 | 997 | 245 | 70 | 192 | 242 | 1820 | 12.2 | 3.0 | 22.2 |
| 01-02—San Antonio | 82 | 3329 | *764 | *1504 | .508 | *560 | 701 | .799 | *268 | *774 | 1042 | 307 | 61 | 203 | 263 | 2089 | 12.7 | 3.7 | 25.5 |
| 02-03—San Antonio | 81 | 3181 | 714 | 1392 | .513 | 450 | 634 | .710 | 259 | 784 | 1043 | 316 | 55 | 237 | 248 | 1884 | 12.9 | 3.9 | 23.3 |
| 03-04—San Antonio | 69 | 2527 | 592 | 1181 | .501 | 352 | 588 | .599 | 227 | 632 | 859 | 213 | 62 | 185 | 183 | 1538 | 12.4 | 3.1 | 22.3 |
| 04-05—San Antonio | 66 | 2203 | 517 | 1042 | .496 | 305 | 455 | .670 | 202 | 530 | 732 | 179 | 45 | 174 | 127 | 1342 | 11.1 | 2.7 | 20.3 |
| Totals | 586 | 22456 | 5041 | 9938 | .507 | 3101 | 4483 | .692 | 1910 | 5229 | 7139 | 1839 | 459 | 1488 | 1730 | 13204 | 12.2 | 3.1 | 22.5 |

Three-point field goals: 1997-98, 0-for-10. 1998-99, 1-for-7 (.143). 1999-00, 1-for-11 (.091). 2000-01, 7-for-27 (.259). 2001-02, 1-for-10 (.100). 2002-03, 6-for-22 (.273). 2003-04, 2-for-12 (.167). 2004-05, 3-for-9 (.333). Totals, 21-for-108 (.194).
Personal fouls/disqualifications: 1997-98, 254/1. 1998-99, 147/2. 1999-00, 210/1. 2000-01, 247/0. 2001-02, 217/2. 2002-03, 231/2. 2003-04, 164/1. 2004-05, 144/0. Totals, 1614/9.

## NBA PLAYOFF RECORD

**NOTES:** NBA Finals Most Valuable Player (1999, 2003, 2005). ... Holds NBA Finals record for most blocked shots—32 (2003). ... Shares NBA Finals single-game record for blocked shots—8 (June 15, 2003, vs. New Jersey).

| Season Team | G | Min. | FGM | FGA | Pct. | FTM | FTA | Pct. | REBOUNDS Off. | Def. | Tot. | Ast. | St. | Blk. | TO | Pts. | AVERAGES RPG | APG | PPG |
|---|---|---|---|---|---|---|---|---|---|---|---|---|---|---|---|---|---|---|---|
| 97-98—San Antonio | 9 | 374 | 73 | 140 | .521 | 40 | 60 | .667 | 20 | 61 | 81 | 17 | 5 | 23 | 25 | 186 | 9.0 | 1.9 | 20.7 |
| 98-99—San Antonio | 17 | 733 | 144 | 282 | .511 | 107 | 143 | .748 | 55 | 140 | 195 | 48 | 13 | 45 | 52 | 395 | 11.5 | 2.8 | 23.2 |
| 00-01—San Antonio | 13 | 526 | 120 | 246 | .488 | 76 | 119 | .639 | 54 | 134 | 188 | 49 | 14 | 35 | 50 | 317 | 14.5 | 3.8 | 24.4 |
| 01-02—San Antonio | 9 | 380 | 82 | 181 | .453 | 83 | 101 | .822 | 28 | 102 | 130 | 45 | 6 | 39 | 37 | 248 | 14.4 | 5.0 | 27.6 |
| 02-03—San Antonio | 24 | 1021 | 218 | 412 | .529 | 157 | 232 | .677 | 96 | 273 | 369 | 127 | 15 | 79 | 76 | 593 | 15.4 | 5.3 | 24.7 |
| 03-04—San Antonio | 10 | 405 | 83 | 159 | .522 | 55 | 87 | .632 | 33 | 80 | 113 | 32 | 8 | 20 | 42 | 221 | 11.3 | 3.2 | 22.1 |
| 04-05—San Antonio | 23 | 869 | 197 | 425 | .464 | 147 | 205 | .717 | 87 | 199 | 286 | 63 | 8 | 52 | 62 | 542 | 12.4 | 2.7 | 23.6 |
| Totals | 105 | 4308 | 917 | 1845 | .497 | 665 | 947 | .702 | 373 | 989 | 1362 | 381 | 69 | 293 | 344 | 2502 | 13.0 | 3.6 | 23.8 |

Three-point field goals: 1997-98, 0-for-1. 1998-99, 0-for-3. 2000-01, 1-for-1 (1.000). 2001-02, 1-for-3 (.333). 2002-03, 0-for-7. 2003-04, 0-for-1. 2004-05, 1-for-5 (.200). Totals, 3-for-21 (.143).
Personal fouls/disqualifications: 1997-98, 24/1. 1998-99, 50/1. 2000-01, 43/0. 2001-02, 22/0. 2002-03, 78/0. 2003-04, 34/0. 2004-05, 66/1. Totals, 317/3.

## NBA ALL-STAR GAME RECORD

**NOTES:** NBA All-Star Game co-Most Valuable Player (2000).

| Season Team | Min. | FGM | FGA | Pct. | FTM | FTA | Pct. | REBOUNDS Off. | Def. | Tot. | Ast. | PF | Dq. | St. | Blk. | TO | Pts. |
|---|---|---|---|---|---|---|---|---|---|---|---|---|---|---|---|---|---|
| 1998—San Antonio | 14 | 1 | 4 | .250 | 0 | 0 | ... | 1 | 10 | 11 | 1 | 0 | 0 | 0 | 0 | 2 | 2 |
| 2000—San Antonio | 33 | 12 | 14 | .857 | 0 | 0 | ... | 7 | 7 | 14 | 4 | 3 | 0 | 1 | 1 | 2 | 24 |
| 2001—San Antonio | 28 | 5 | 11 | .455 | 4 | 4 | 1.000 | 4 | 10 | 14 | 1 | 1 | 0 | 2 | 1 | 2 | 14 |
| 2002—San Antonio | 29 | 7 | 11 | .636 | 0 | 0 | ... | 3 | 11 | 14 | 2 | 1 | 0 | 0 | 2 | 3 | 14 |
| 2003—San Antonio | 40 | 8 | 18 | .444 | 3 | 3 | 1.000 | 5 | 10 | 15 | 4 | 2 | 0 | 1 | 0 | 3 | 19 |
| 2004—San Antonio | 26 | 6 | 11 | .545 | 2 | 4 | .500 | 2 | 11 | 13 | 5 | 2 | 0 | 1 | 0 | 2 | 14 |
| 2005—San Antonio | 16 | 7 | 10 | .700 | 0 | 1 | .000 | 2 | 7 | 9 | 2 | 0 | 0 | 0 | 0 | 2 | 15 |
| Totals | 186 | 46 | 79 | .582 | 9 | 12 | .750 | 24 | 66 | 90 | 19 | 9 | 0 | 5 | 4 | 16 | 102 |

Three-point field goals: 1998, 0-for-1. 2005, 1-for-1 (1.000). Totals, 1-for-2 (.500).

## DUNLEAVY, MIKE      G/F      WARRIORS

**PERSONAL:** Born September 15, 1980, in Fort Worth, Texas. ... 6-9/221. (2.06/100.2). ... Full name: Michael Joseph Dunleavy ... Son of Mike Dunleavy, guard with four NBA teams (1976-77 through 1983-84, 1988-89 and 1989-90) and head coach with Los Angeles Lakers (1990-91 through 1995-96), Portland Trail Blazers (1997-98 through 2000-01) and Los Angeles Clippers (2003-04).
**HIGH SCHOOL:** Jesuit (Portland).
**COLLEGE:** Duke.
**TRANSACTIONS/CAREER NOTES:** Selected after junior season by Golden State Warriors in first round (third pick overall) of 2002 NBA Draft.

### COLLEGIATE RECORD

**NOTES:** THE SPORTING NEWS All-America second team (2002). ... Member of NCAA Division I championship team (2001).

| | | | | | | | | | | | AVERAGES | | |
|---|---|---|---|---|---|---|---|---|---|---|---|---|---|
| Season Team | G | Min. | FGM | FGA | Pct. | FTM | FTA | Pct. | Reb. | Ast. | Pts. | RPG | APG | PPG |
| 99-00—Duke | 30 | 724 | 97 | 211 | .460 | 45 | 61 | .738 | 128 | 50 | 273 | 4.3 | 1.7 | 9.1 |
| 00-01—Duke | 39 | 1137 | 184 | 388 | .474 | 68 | 98 | .694 | 222 | 103 | 493 | 5.7 | 2.6 | 12.6 |
| 01-02—Duke | 35 | 1133 | 218 | 451 | .483 | 81 | 119 | .681 | 251 | 72 | 605 | 7.2 | 2.1 | 17.3 |
| Totals | 104 | 2994 | 499 | 1050 | .475 | 194 | 278 | .698 | 601 | 225 | 1371 | 5.8 | 2.2 | 13.2 |

Three-point field goals: 1999-00, 34-for-97 (.351). 2000-01, 57-for-153 (.373). 2001-02, 88-for-233 (.378). Totals, 179-for-483 (.371).

### NBA REGULAR-SEASON RECORD

| | | | | | | | | | REBOUNDS | | | | | | | AVERAGES | | |
|---|---|---|---|---|---|---|---|---|---|---|---|---|---|---|---|---|---|---|
| Season Team | G | Min. | FGM | FGA | Pct. | FTM | FTA | Pct. | Off. | Def. | Tot. | Ast. | St. | Blk. | TO | Pts. | RPG | APG | PPG |
| 02-03—Golden State | 82 | 1305 | 168 | 417 | .403 | 78 | 100 | .780 | 66 | 148 | 214 | 106 | 53 | 19 | 86 | 466 | 2.6 | 1.3 | 5.7 |
| 03-04—Golden State | 75 | 2336 | 323 | 720 | .449 | 137 | 185 | .741 | 87 | 355 | 442 | 220 | 68 | 13 | 143 | 877 | 5.9 | 2.9 | 11.7 |
| 04-05—Golden State | 79 | 2570 | 408 | 905 | .451 | 134 | 172 | .779 | 97 | 338 | 435 | 203 | 79 | 26 | 132 | 1057 | 5.5 | 2.6 | 13.4 |
| Totals | 236 | 6211 | 899 | 2042 | .440 | 349 | 457 | .764 | 250 | 841 | 1091 | 529 | 200 | 58 | 361 | 2400 | 4.6 | 2.2 | 10.2 |

Three-point field goals: 2002-03, 52-for-150 (.347). 2003-04, 94-for-254 (.370). 2004-05, 107-for-276 (.388). Totals, 253-for-680 (.372).
Personal fouls/disqualifications: 2002-03, 120/0. 2003-04, 169/2. 2004-05, 198/3. Totals, 487/5.

---

## DUPREE, RONALD      F      PISTONS

**PERSONAL:** Born January 26, 1981, in Biloxi, Miss. ... 6-7/209. (2.01/94.8). ... Full name: Ronald Edmund Dupree
**HIGH SCHOOL:** Biloxi (Miss.).
**COLLEGE:** Louisiana State.
**TRANSACTIONS/CAREER NOTES:** Not drafted by an NBA franchise. ... Signed as free agent by Detroit Pistons (September 29, 2003). ... Waived by Pistons (October 23, 2003). ... Played in NBDL with Huntsville Flight (2003-04). ... Signed by Chicago Bulls to 10-day contract (January 7, 2004). ... Signed by Bulls for remainder of season (January 28, 2004). ... Signed as free agent by Detroit Pistons (July 2004).

### COLLEGIATE RECORD

| | | | | | | | | | | | AVERAGES | | |
|---|---|---|---|---|---|---|---|---|---|---|---|---|---|---|
| Season Team | G | Min. | FGM | FGA | Pct. | FTM | FTA | Pct. | Reb. | Ast. | Pts. | RPG | APG | PPG |
| 99-00—Louisiana State | 34 | 433 | 63 | 136 | .463 | 39 | 68 | .574 | 112 | 14 | 167 | 3.3 | 0.4 | 4.9 |
| 00-01—Louisiana State | 29 | 1012 | 183 | 377 | .485 | 116 | 166 | .699 | 256 | 41 | 503 | 8.8 | 1.4 | 17.3 |
| 01-02—Louisiana State | 34 | 1203 | 220 | 487 | .452 | 81 | 145 | .559 | 290 | 73 | 552 | 8.5 | 2.1 | 16.2 |
| 02-03—Louisiana State | 32 | 1063 | 199 | 376 | .529 | 93 | 137 | .679 | 249 | 77 | 504 | 7.8 | 2.4 | 15.8 |
| Totals | 129 | 3711 | 665 | 1376 | .483 | 329 | 516 | .638 | 907 | 205 | 1726 | 7.0 | 1.6 | 13.4 |

Three-point field goals: 1999-00, 2-for-14 (.143). 2000-01, 21-for-64 (.328). 2001-02, 31-for-108 (.287). 2002-03, 13-for-37 (.351). Totals, 67-for-223 (.300).

### NBA REGULAR-SEASON RECORD

| | | | | | | | | | REBOUNDS | | | | | | | AVERAGES | | |
|---|---|---|---|---|---|---|---|---|---|---|---|---|---|---|---|---|---|---|
| Season Team | G | Min. | FGM | FGA | Pct. | FTM | FTA | Pct. | Off. | Def. | Tot. | Ast. | St. | Blk. | TO | Pts. | RPG | APG | PPG |
| 03-04—Chicago | 47 | 893 | 111 | 282 | .394 | 66 | 105 | .629 | 55 | 112 | 167 | 55 | 32 | 18 | 51 | 292 | 3.6 | 1.2 | 6.2 |
| 04-05—Detroit | 47 | 472 | 61 | 127 | .480 | 29 | 47 | .617 | 34 | 61 | 95 | 24 | 7 | 10 | 22 | 152 | 2.0 | 0.5 | 3.2 |
| Totals | 94 | 1365 | 172 | 409 | .421 | 95 | 152 | .625 | 89 | 173 | 262 | 79 | 39 | 28 | 73 | 444 | 2.8 | 0.8 | 4.7 |

Three-point field goals: 2003-04, 4-for-9 (.444). 2004-05, 1-for-2 (.500). Totals, 5-for-11 (.455).
Personal fouls/disqualifications: 2003-04, 134/4. 2004-05, 60/0. Totals, 194/4.

### NBA PLAYOFF RECORD

| | | | | | | | | | REBOUNDS | | | | | | | AVERAGES | | |
|---|---|---|---|---|---|---|---|---|---|---|---|---|---|---|---|---|---|---|
| Season Team | G | Min. | FGM | FGA | Pct. | FTM | FTA | Pct. | Off. | Def. | Tot. | Ast. | St. | Blk. | TO | Pts. | RPG | APG | PPG |
| 04-05—Detroit | 14 | 38 | 2 | 7 | .286 | 0 | 0 | ... | 2 | 4 | 6 | 0 | 0 | 0 | 1 | 4 | 0.4 | 0.0 | 0.3 |

Personal fouls/disqualifications: 2004-05, 6/0. Totals, 6/0.

### NBDL RECORD

| | | | | | | | | | | | AVERAGES | | |
|---|---|---|---|---|---|---|---|---|---|---|---|---|---|---|
| Season Team | G | Min. | FGM | FGA | Pct. | FTM | FTA | Pct. | Reb. | Ast. | Pts. | RPG | APG | PPG |
| 03-04—Huntsville | 15 | 483 | 104 | 187 | .556 | 45 | 59 | .763 | 69 | 22 | 254 | 4.6 | 1.5 | 16.9 |

---

## EBI, NDUDI      F      TIMBERWOLVES

**PERSONAL:** Born June 18, 1984, in London, England. ... 6-9/195. (2.06/88.5).
**HIGH SCHOOL:** Westbury Christian (Houston, Tex.).
**COLLEGE:** Did not attend college.
**TRANSACTIONS/CAREER NOTES:** Selected by Minnesota Timberwolves in first round (26th pick overall) of 2003 NBA Draft.

## NBA REGULAR-SEASON RECORD

| Season Team | G | Min. | FGM | FGA | Pct. | FTM | FTA | Pct. | REBOUNDS Off. | REBOUNDS Def. | REBOUNDS Tot. | Ast. | St. | Blk. | TO | Pts. | AVERAGES RPG | AVERAGES APG | AVERAGES PPG |
|---|---|---|---|---|---|---|---|---|---|---|---|---|---|---|---|---|---|---|---|
| 03-04—Minnesota ..... | 17 | 32 | 6 | 14 | .429 | 1 | 4 | .250 | 2 | 1 | 3 | 3 | 0 | 4 | 3 | 13 | 0.2 | 0.2 | 0.8 |
| 04-05—Minnesota ..... | 2 | 54 | 11 | 21 | .524 | 5 | 9 | .556 | 6 | 10 | 16 | 1 | 1 | 1 | 3 | 27 | 8.0 | 0.5 | 13.5 |
| Totals ................. | 19 | 86 | 17 | 35 | .486 | 6 | 13 | .462 | 8 | 11 | 19 | 4 | 1 | 5 | 6 | 40 | 1.0 | 0.2 | 2.1 |

Three-point field goals: 2004-05, 0-for-1. Totals, 0-for-1 (.000).
Personal fouls/disqualifications: 2003-04, 6/0. 2004-05, 7/0. Totals, 13/0.

# EDWARDS, CORSLEY     F     HORNETS

**PERSONAL:** Born March 5, 1979, in Baltimore. ... 6-9/275. (2.06/124.7).
**HIGH SCHOOL:** Lake Clifton (Md.).
**COLLEGE:** Central Connecticut State.
**TRANSACTIONS/CAREER NOTES:** Selected by Sacramento Kings in second round (58th pick overall) of 2002 NBA Draft. ... Signed as free agent by Orlando Magic (October 4, 2004). ... Signed as free agent by New Orleans Hornets (December 4, 2004). ... Waived by Hornets (January 3, 2005). ... Signed as free agent by Hornets (January 5, 2005).

## COLLEGIATE RECORD

| Season Team | G | Min. | FGM | FGA | Pct. | FTM | FTA | Pct. | Reb. | Ast. | Pts. | AVERAGES RPG | AVERAGES APG | AVERAGES PPG |
|---|---|---|---|---|---|---|---|---|---|---|---|---|---|---|
| 97-98—Central Conn. State ........ | | | | | | Did not play—ineligible. | | | | | | | | |
| 98-99—Central Conn. State ........ | 32 | 759 | 160 | 315 | .508 | 85 | 131 | .649 | 237 | 16 | 405 | 7.4 | 0.5 | 12.7 |
| 99-00—Central Conn. State ........ | 31 | 813 | 153 | 305 | .502 | 76 | 129 | .589 | 231 | 21 | 379 | 7.5 | 0.7 | 12.2 |
| 00-01—Central Conn. State ........ | 28 | 834 | 161 | 307 | .524 | 132 | 181 | .729 | 221 | 23 | 454 | 7.9 | 0.8 | 16.2 |
| 01-02—Central Conn. State ........ | 32 | 992 | 178 | 353 | .504 | 137 | 180 | .761 | 278 | 33 | 493 | 8.7 | 1.0 | 15.4 |
| Totals ..................... | 123 | 3398 | 652 | 1280 | .509 | 430 | 621 | .692 | 967 | 93 | 1731 | 7.9 | 0.8 | 14.1 |

Three-point field goals: 1999-00, 0-for-1. 2000-01, 0-for-1. Totals, 0-for-2 (.000).

## CBA RECORD

| Season Team | G | Min. | FGM | FGA | Pct. | FTM | FTA | Pct. | Reb. | Ast. | Pts. | AVERAGES RPG | AVERAGES APG | AVERAGES PPG |
|---|---|---|---|---|---|---|---|---|---|---|---|---|---|---|
| 02-03—Yakima-Sioux Falls ........ | 43 | 1070 | 228 | 487 | .468 | 144 | 199 | .724 | 284 | 44 | 600 | 6.6 | 1.0 | 14.0 |
| 04-05—Sioux Falls ..................... | 16 | 425 | 95 | 171 | .556 | 97 | 124 | .782 | 158 | 18 | 287 | 9.9 | 1.1 | 17.9 |
| Totals ..................... | 59 | 1495 | 323 | 658 | .491 | 241 | 323 | .746 | 442 | 62 | 887 | 7.5 | 1.1 | 15.0 |

Three-point field goals: 2002-03, 0-for-12. Totals, 0-for-12 (.000).

## ITALIAN LEAGUE RECORD

| Season Team | G | Min. | FGM | FGA | Pct. | FTM | FTA | Pct. | Reb. | Ast. | Pts. | AVERAGES RPG | AVERAGES APG | AVERAGES PPG |
|---|---|---|---|---|---|---|---|---|---|---|---|---|---|---|
| 02-03—Carife Ferrara .................. | 5 | 150 | 29 | 54 | .537 | 19 | 29 | .655 | 42 | 4 | 77 | 8.4 | 0.8 | 15.4 |
| 03-04—Agricola Gloria M.T. ........ | 32 | 972 | 210 | 384 | .547 | 99 | 134 | .739 | 305 | 11 | 520 | 9.5 | 0.3 | 16.3 |
| Totals ..................... | 37 | 1122 | 239 | 438 | .546 | 118 | 163 | .724 | 347 | 15 | 597 | 9.4 | 0.4 | 16.1 |

Three-point field goals: 2003-04, 1-for-4 (.250). Totals, 1-for-4 (.250).

## NBA REGULAR-SEASON RECORD

| Season Team | G | Min. | FGM | FGA | Pct. | FTM | FTA | Pct. | REBOUNDS Off. | REBOUNDS Def. | REBOUNDS Tot. | Ast. | St. | Blk. | TO | Pts. | AVERAGES RPG | AVERAGES APG | AVERAGES PPG |
|---|---|---|---|---|---|---|---|---|---|---|---|---|---|---|---|---|---|---|---|
| 04-05—New Orleans ... | 10 | 110 | 10 | 31 | .323 | 7 | 12 | .583 | 12 | 13 | 25 | 3 | 3 | 4 | 2 | 27 | 2.5 | 0.3 | 2.7 |

Personal fouls/disqualifications: 2004-05, 19/1. Totals, 19/1.

# EDWARDS, JOHN     C     HAWKS

**PERSONAL:** Born July 31, 1981 ... 7-0/275. (2.13/124.7).
**HIGH SCHOOL:** Hudson (Ohio).
**COLLEGE:** Kent State.
**TRANSACTIONS/CAREER NOTES:** Not drafted by an NBA franchise. ... Signed as free agent by Indiana Pacers (September 14, 2004). Signed as free agent by Atlanta Hawks (August 30, 2005).

## COLLEGIATE RECORD

| Season Team | G | Min. | FGM | FGA | Pct. | FTM | FTA | Pct. | Reb. | Ast. | Pts. | AVERAGES RPG | AVERAGES APG | AVERAGES PPG |
|---|---|---|---|---|---|---|---|---|---|---|---|---|---|---|
| 99-00—Kent St ........................... | | | | | | Did Not Play - Redshirted | | | | | | | | |
| 00-01—Kent St ........................... | 32 | 218 | 25 | 58 | .431 | 14 | 30 | .467 | 54 | 3 | 64 | 1.7 | 0.1 | 2.0 |
| 01-02—Kent St ........................... | 35 | 422 | 49 | 81 | .605 | 24 | 37 | .649 | 72 | 2 | 122 | 2.1 | 0.1 | 3.5 |
| 02-03—Kent St ........................... | 31 | 521 | 93 | 147 | .633 | 37 | 52 | .712 | 106 | 10 | 223 | 3.4 | 0.3 | 7.2 |
| 03-04—Kent St ........................... | 30 | 775 | 157 | 297 | .529 | 81 | 120 | .675 | 197 | 12 | 395 | 6.6 | 0.4 | 13.2 |
| Totals ..................... | 128 | 1936 | 324 | 583 | .556 | 156 | 239 | .653 | 429 | 27 | 804 | 3.4 | 0.2 | 6.3 |

## NBA REGULAR-SEASON RECORD

| Season Team | G | Min. | FGM | FGA | Pct. | FTM | FTA | Pct. | REBOUNDS Off. | REBOUNDS Def. | REBOUNDS Tot. | Ast. | St. | Blk. | TO | Pts. | AVERAGES RPG | AVERAGES APG | AVERAGES PPG |
|---|---|---|---|---|---|---|---|---|---|---|---|---|---|---|---|---|---|---|---|
| 04-05—Indiana ........... | 25 | 139 | 11 | 30 | .367 | 7 | 14 | .500 | 8 | 11 | 19 | 3 | 3 | 4 | 8 | 29 | 0.8 | 0.1 | 1.2 |

Personal fouls/disqualifications: 2004-05, 12/0. Totals, 12/0.

E

# EISLEY, HOWARD　　　　　　　　G

**PERSONAL:** Born December 4, 1972, in Detroit. ... 6-2/180. (1.88/81.6). ... Full name: Howard Jonathan Eisley
**HIGH SCHOOL:** Southwestern (Detroit).
**COLLEGE:** Boston College.
**TRANSACTIONS/CAREER NOTES:** Selected by Minnesota Timberwolves in second round (30th pick overall) of 1994 NBA Draft. ... Waived by Timberwolves (February 13, 1995). ... Signed by San Antonio Spurs to first of two consecutive 10-day contracts (February 26, 1995). ... Signed by Spurs for remainder of season (March 18, 1995). ... Waived by Spurs (April 17, 1995). ... Signed as free agent by Utah Jazz (October 5, 1995). ... Waived by Jazz (October 30, 1995). ... Played in Continental Basketball Association with Rockford Lightning (1995-96). ... Signed as free agent by Jazz (December 7, 1995). ... Traded by Jazz to Dallas Mavericks as part of four-team deal in which Boston Celtics received G Robert Pack, C John Williams and cash considerations from Mavericks and a conditional first-round draft choice from Jazz, Mavericks received G Dana Barros from Celtics, F Bill Curley from Golden State Warriors, Jazz received F Donyell Marshall from Warriors and C Bruno Sundov from Mavericks and Warriors received F Danny Fortson from Celtics and F Adam Keefe from Jazz (August 16, 2000). ... Traded by Mavericks to New York Knicks as part of three-team trade in which Knicks acquired F Shandon Anderson from Houston Rockets, Mavericks acquired G Muggsy Bogues from Knicks and Rockets acquired F Glen Rice from Knicks and draft rights to G Kyle Hill from Mavericks (August 10, 2001). ... Traded by Knicks with F Maciej Lampe, F Antonio McDyess, G Charlie Ward, draft rights to G Milos Vujanic, 2004 first-round draft choice and future first-round draft choice to Phoenix Suns for G Stephon Marbury, F/G Anfernee Hardaway and C Cezary Trybanski (January 5, 2004). ... Waived by Suns (October 29, 2004).

## COLLEGIATE RECORD

| Season Team | G | Min. | FGM | FGA | Pct. | FTM | FTA | Pct. | Reb. | Ast. | Pts. | AVERAGES RPG | APG | PPG |
|---|---|---|---|---|---|---|---|---|---|---|---|---|---|---|
| 90-91—Boston College | 30 | 1011 | 95 | 264 | .360 | 81 | 108 | .750 | 79 | 100 | 297 | 2.6 | 3.3 | 9.9 |
| 91-92—Boston College | 31 | 1071 | 118 | 242 | .488 | 88 | 118 | .746 | 111 | 135 | 361 | 3.6 | 4.4 | 11.6 |
| 92-93—Boston College | 31 | 1162 | 131 | 296 | .443 | 121 | 145 | .834 | 107 | 153 | 426 | 3.5 | 4.9 | 13.7 |
| 93-94—Boston College | 34 | 1203 | 529 | 1191 | .444 | 373 | 476 | .784 | 116 | 156 | 544 | 3.4 | 4.6 | 16.0 |
| **Totals** | 126 | 4447 | 873 | 1993 | .438 | 663 | 847 | .783 | 413 | 544 | 1628 | 3.3 | 4.3 | 12.9 |

Three-point field goals: 1990-91, 26-for-74 (.351). 1991-92, 37-for-75 (.493). 1992-93, 43-for-104 (.413). 1993-94, 91-for-188 (.484). Totals, 197-for-441 (.447).

## NBA REGULAR-SEASON RECORD

| Season Team | G | Min. | FGM | FGA | Pct. | FTM | FTA | Pct. | REBOUNDS Off. | Def. | Tot. | Ast. | St. | Blk. | TO | Pts. | AVERAGES RPG | APG | PPG |
|---|---|---|---|---|---|---|---|---|---|---|---|---|---|---|---|---|---|---|---|
| 94-95—Minn.-San Ant. | 49 | 552 | 40 | 122 | .328 | 31 | 40 | .775 | 12 | 36 | 48 | 95 | 18 | 6 | 50 | 120 | 1.0 | 1.9 | 2.4 |
| 95-96—Utah | 65 | 961 | 104 | 242 | .430 | 65 | 77 | .844 | 22 | 56 | 78 | 146 | 29 | 3 | 77 | 287 | 1.2 | 2.2 | 4.4 |
| 96-97—Utah | 82 | 1083 | 139 | 308 | .451 | 70 | 89 | .787 | 20 | 64 | 84 | 198 | 44 | 10 | 110 | 368 | 1.0 | 2.4 | 4.5 |
| 97-98—Utah | 82 | 1726 | 229 | 519 | .441 | 127 | 149 | .852 | 25 | 141 | 166 | 346 | 54 | 13 | 160 | 633 | 2.0 | 4.2 | 7.7 |
| 98-99—Utah | 50 | 1038 | 140 | 314 | .446 | 67 | 80 | .838 | 12 | 82 | 94 | 185 | 30 | 2 | 109 | 368 | 1.9 | 3.7 | 7.4 |
| 99-00—Utah | 82 | 2096 | 282 | 675 | .418 | 84 | 102 | .824 | 23 | 147 | 170 | 347 | 59 | 9 | 132 | 708 | 2.1 | 4.2 | 8.6 |
| 00-01—Dallas | 82 | 2426 | 265 | 675 | .393 | 104 | 126 | .825 | 23 | 174 | 197 | 295 | 99 | 12 | 102 | 741 | 2.4 | 3.6 | 9.0 |
| 01-02—New York | 39 | 609 | 59 | 175 | .337 | 39 | 49 | .796 | 9 | 40 | 49 | 100 | 24 | 3 | 53 | 171 | 1.3 | 2.6 | 4.4 |
| 02-03—New York | 82 | 2243 | 262 | 628 | .417 | 89 | 105 | .848 | 24 | 162 | 186 | 444 | 71 | 9 | 149 | 744 | 2.3 | 5.4 | 9.1 |
| 03-04—N.Y.-Phoenix | 67 | 1457 | 166 | 451 | .368 | 76 | 89 | .854 | 20 | 109 | 129 | 273 | 56 | 5 | 98 | 460 | 1.9 | 4.1 | 6.9 |
| 04-05—Phoenix | 74 | 1428 | 161 | 405 | .398 | 66 | 83 | .795 | 15 | 75 | 90 | 250 | 45 | 9 | 111 | 415 | 1.2 | 3.4 | 5.6 |
| **Totals** | 754 | 15619 | 1847 | 4514 | .409 | 818 | 989 | .827 | 205 | 1086 | 1291 | 2679 | 529 | 81 | 1151 | 5015 | 1.7 | 3.6 | 6.7 |

Three-point field goals: 1994-95, 9-for-37 (.243). 1995-96, 14-for-62 (.226). 1996-97, 20-for-72 (.278). 1997-98, 48-for-118 (.407). 1998-99, 21-for-50 (.420). 1999-00, 60-for-163 (.368). 2000-01, 107-for-269 (.398). 2001-02, 14-for-58 (.241). 2002-03, 131-for-337 (.389). 2003-04, 52-for-163 (.319). 2004-05, 27-for-103 (.262). Totals, 503-for-1432 (.351).
Personal fouls/disqualifications: 1994-95, 81/0. 1995-96, 130/0. 1996-97, 141/0. 1997-98, 182/3. 1998-99, 122/0. 1999-00, 223/2. 2000-01, 218/3. 2001-02, 55/0. 2002-03, 222/1. 2003-04, 137/1. 2004-05, 156/1. Totals, 1667/11.

## NBA PLAYOFF RECORD

| Season Team | G | Min. | FGM | FGA | Pct. | FTM | FTA | Pct. | REBOUNDS Off. | Def. | Tot. | Ast. | St. | Blk. | TO | Pts. | AVERAGES RPG | APG | PPG |
|---|---|---|---|---|---|---|---|---|---|---|---|---|---|---|---|---|---|---|---|
| 95-96—Utah | 18 | 202 | 16 | 42 | .381 | 18 | 22 | .818 | 4 | 18 | 22 | 44 | 3 | 2 | 11 | 53 | 1.2 | 2.4 | 2.9 |
| 96-97—Utah | 20 | 217 | 38 | 76 | .500 | 27 | 28 | .964 | 4 | 14 | 18 | 40 | 3 | 0 | 17 | 112 | 0.9 | 2.0 | 5.6 |
| 97-98—Utah | 20 | 366 | 46 | 125 | .368 | 12 | 13 | .923 | 4 | 36 | 40 | 81 | 12 | 5 | 31 | 112 | 2.0 | 4.1 | 5.6 |
| 98-99—Utah | 11 | 241 | 26 | 71 | .366 | 24 | 29 | .828 | 3 | 17 | 20 | 32 | 7 | 3 | 20 | 81 | 1.8 | 2.9 | 7.4 |
| 99-00—Utah | 10 | 200 | 17 | 55 | .309 | 8 | 9 | .889 | 1 | 17 | 18 | 19 | 6 | 1 | 13 | 51 | 1.8 | 1.9 | 5.1 |
| 00-01—Dallas | 9 | 194 | 19 | 53 | .358 | 4 | 4 | 1.000 | 1 | 11 | 12 | 17 | 5 | 1 | 13 | 52 | 1.3 | 1.9 | 5.8 |
| **Totals** | 88 | 1420 | 162 | 422 | .384 | 93 | 105 | .886 | 17 | 113 | 130 | 233 | 36 | 12 | 105 | 461 | 1.5 | 2.6 | 5.2 |

Three-point field goals: 1995-96, 3-for-9 (.333). 1996-97, 9-for-19 (.474). 1997-98, 8-for-27 (.296). 1998-99, 5-for-24 (.208). 1999-00, 9-for-19 (.474). 2000-01, 10-for-26 (.385). Totals, 44-for-124 (.355).
Personal fouls/disqualifications: 1995-96, 29/0. 1996-97, 27/1. 1997-98, 42/0. 1998-99, 27/0. 1999-00, 24/0. 2000-01, 18/0. Totals, 167/1.

## CBA RECORD

| Season Team | G | Min. | FGM | FGA | Pct. | FTM | FTA | Pct. | Reb. | Ast. | Pts. | AVERAGES RPG | APG | PPG |
|---|---|---|---|---|---|---|---|---|---|---|---|---|---|---|
| 95-96—Rockford | 7 | 168 | 32 | 58 | .552 | 17 | 17 | 1.000 | 16 | 23 | 87 | 2.3 | 3.3 | 12.4 |

Three-point field goals: 1995-96, 6-for-15 (.400). Totals, 6-for-15 (.400).
Personal fouls/disqualifications: 1995-96, 21/0. Totals, 21/0.

# EKEZIE, OBINNA　　　　　　　　F

**PERSONAL:** Born August 22, 1975, in Port Harcourt, Nigeria. ... 6-9/270. (2.06/122.5). ... Full name: Obinna Ralph Ekezie
**HIGH SCHOOL:** Worcester (Mass.) Academy.
**COLLEGE:** Maryland.
**TRANSACTIONS/CAREER NOTES:** Selected by Vancouver Grizzlies in second round (37th pick overall) of 1999 NBA Draft. ... Traded by Grizzlies with G/F Dennis Scott, F/C Cherokee Parks and G Felipe Lopez to Washington Wizards for C Ike Austin

E

(August 22, 2000). ... Traded by Wizards with F/C Cherokee Parks to Los Angeles Clippers for F Tyrone Nesby (November 28, 2000). ... Claimed on waivers by Wizards (December 1, 2000). ... Traded by Wizards with F Juwan Howard and C Calvin Booth to Dallas Mavericks for F/C Christian Laettner, G Courtney Alexander, F Loy Vaught, G Hubert Davis, F/C Etan Thomas and cash considerations (February 22, 2001). ... Signed as free agent by Los Angeles Clippers (September 28, 2001). ... Waived by Clippers (July 19, 2002). ... Signed as free agent by Orlando Magic (September 23, 2002). ... Played in NBDL (2004-05). ... Signed by Atlanta Hawks to first of two consecutive 10-day contracts (January 10, 2005). ... Signed by Hawks for remainder of season (January 31, 2005). ... Waived by Hawks (July 5, 2005).

### COLLEGIATE RECORD

| Season Team | G | Min. | FGM | FGA | Pct. | FTM | FTA | Pct. | Reb. | Ast. | Pts. | AVERAGES RPG | APG | PPG |
|---|---|---|---|---|---|---|---|---|---|---|---|---|---|---|
| 95-96—Maryland | 30 | 463 | 51 | 108 | .472 | 33 | 60 | .550 | 111 | 10 | 135 | 3.7 | 0.3 | 4.5 |
| 96-97—Maryland | 32 | 858 | 115 | 209 | .550 | 92 | 144 | .639 | 212 | 22 | 322 | 6.6 | 0.7 | 10.1 |
| 97-98—Maryland | 32 | 895 | 138 | 285 | .484 | 134 | 200 | .670 | 207 | 51 | 410 | 6.5 | 1.6 | 12.8 |
| 98-99—Maryland | 24 | 614 | 104 | 213 | .488 | 97 | 140 | .693 | 141 | 21 | 305 | 5.9 | 0.9 | 12.7 |
| **Totals** | 118 | 2830 | 408 | 815 | .501 | 356 | 544 | .654 | 671 | 104 | 1172 | 5.7 | 0.9 | 9.9 |

Three-point field goals: 1998-99, 0-for-2. Totals, 0-for-2 (.000).

### NBA REGULAR-SEASON RECORD

| Season Team | G | Min. | FGM | FGA | Pct. | FTM | FTA | Pct. | REBOUNDS Off. | Def. | Tot. | Ast. | St. | Blk. | TO | Pts. | AVERAGES RPG | APG | PPG |
|---|---|---|---|---|---|---|---|---|---|---|---|---|---|---|---|---|---|---|---|
| 99-00—Vancouver | 39 | 351 | 41 | 88 | .466 | 43 | 64 | .672 | 34 | 58 | 92 | 8 | 9 | 4 | 26 | 125 | 2.4 | 0.2 | 3.2 |
| 00-01—Wash.-Dallas | 33 | 281 | 32 | 81 | .395 | 37 | 53 | .698 | 31 | 47 | 78 | 9 | 5 | 5 | 14 | 101 | 2.4 | 0.3 | 3.1 |
| 01-02—L.A. Clippers | 29 | 152 | 13 | 39 | .333 | 28 | 40 | .700 | 12 | 22 | 34 | 3 | 2 | 6 | 10 | 54 | 1.2 | 0.1 | 1.9 |
| 04-05—Atlanta | 42 | 732 | 79 | 182 | .434 | 72 | 93 | .774 | 69 | 110 | 179 | 11 | 22 | 12 | 45 | 230 | 4.3 | 0.3 | 5.5 |
| **Totals** | 143 | 1516 | 165 | 390 | .423 | 180 | 250 | .720 | 146 | 237 | 383 | 31 | 38 | 27 | 95 | 510 | 2.7 | 0.2 | 3.6 |

Three-point field goals: 2004-05, 0-for-1. Totals, 0-for-1 (.000).
Personal fouls/disqualifications: 1999-00, 61/0. 2000-01, 48/0. 2001-02, 16/0. 2004-05, 129/2. Totals, 254/2.

### ADRIATIC LEAGUE RECORD

| Season Team | G | Min. | FGM | FGA | Pct. | FTM | FTA | Pct. | Reb. | Ast. | Pts. | AVERAGES RPG | APG | PPG |
|---|---|---|---|---|---|---|---|---|---|---|---|---|---|---|
| 02-03—Crvena Zvezda | 11 | 246 | 61 | 82 | .744 | 50 | 60 | .833 | 85 | 14 | 172 | 7.7 | 1.3 | 15.6 |

### NBDL RECORD

| Season Team | G | Min. | FGM | FGA | Pct. | FTM | FTA | Pct. | Reb. | Ast. | Pts. | AVERAGES RPG | APG | PPG |
|---|---|---|---|---|---|---|---|---|---|---|---|---|---|---|
| 04-05—Columbus | 11 | 278 | 47 | 105 | .448 | 45 | 67 | .672 | 74 | 19 | 139 | 6.7 | 1.7 | 12.6 |

Three-point field goals: 2004-05, 0-for-1. Totals, 0-for-1 (.000).

---

## ELSON, FRANCISCO — C — NUGGETS

**PERSONAL:** Born February 28, 1976, in Rotterdam, the Netherlands. ... 6-11/230. (2.11/104.3). ... Full name: Francisco Marinho Robby Elson
**HIGH SCHOOL:** Maria Regina M.A.V.O. (Rotterdam, the Netherlands).
**JUNIOR COLLEGE:** Kilgore Junior College (Texas).
**COLLEGE:** California.
**TRANSACTIONS/CAREER NOTES:** Selected by Denver Nuggets in second round (41st pick overall) of 1999 NBA Draft. ... Played in Spain (1999-2004).

### COLLEGIATE RECORD

| Season Team | G | Min. | FGM | FGA | Pct. | FTM | FTA | Pct. | Reb. | Ast. | Pts. | AVERAGES RPG | APG | PPG |
|---|---|---|---|---|---|---|---|---|---|---|---|---|---|---|
| 95-96—Kilgore College | 18 | ... | ... | ... | ... | ... | ... | ... | 68 | ... | 52 | 3.8 | ... | 2.9 |
| 96-97—Kilgore College | 22 | ... | 145 | 285 | .509 | 88 | 127 | .693 | 257 | 31 | 378 | 11.7 | 1.4 | 17.2 |
| 97-98—California | 27 | 497 | 53 | 123 | .431 | 30 | 49 | .612 | 126 | 14 | 136 | 4.7 | 0.5 | 5.0 |
| 98-99—California | 32 | 632 | 80 | 156 | .513 | 21 | 51 | .412 | 162 | 16 | 181 | 5.1 | 0.5 | 5.7 |
| **Junior College totals** | 40 | ... | ... | ... | ... | ... | ... | ... | 325 | ... | 430 | 8.0 | ... | 10.8 |
| **4-Year-College totals** | 59 | 1129 | 133 | 279 | .477 | 51 | 100 | .510 | 288 | 30 | 317 | 4.9 | 0.5 | 5.4 |

Three-point field goals: 1996-97, 0-for-3. Totals, 0-for-3 (.000).
Personal fouls/disqualifications: 1997-98, 83/5. Totals, 83/5.

### SPANISH RECORD

| Season Team | G | Min. | FGM | FGA | Pct. | FTM | FTA | Pct. | Reb. | Ast. | Pts. | AVERAGES RPG | APG | PPG |
|---|---|---|---|---|---|---|---|---|---|---|---|---|---|---|
| 99-00—FC Barcelona | 32 | 473 | 47 | 73 | .644 | 14 | 27 | .519 | 124 | 6 | 109 | 3.9 | 0.2 | 3.4 |
| 00-01—FC Barcelona | 34 | 703 | 98 | 152 | .645 | 37 | 63 | .587 | 152 | 13 | 233 | 4.5 | 0.4 | 6.9 |
| 01-02—Pamesa Valencia | 34 | 542 | 140 | 235 | .596 | 26 | 50 | .520 | 148 | 18 | 140 | 4.4 | 0.5 | 4.1 |
| 02-03—Caja San Fernando | 34 | 932 | 140 | 235 | .596 | 50 | 91 | .549 | 281 | 33 | 330 | 8.3 | 1.0 | 9.7 |
| **Totals** | 134 | 2650 | 425 | 695 | .612 | 127 | 231 | .550 | 705 | 70 | 812 | 5.3 | 0.5 | 6.1 |

Three-point field goals: 1999-00, 1-for-1 (1.000). 2000-01, 0-for-1. 2001-02, 0-for-2. 2002-03, 0-for-1. Totals, 1-for-5 (.200).

### NBA REGULAR-SEASON RECORD

| Season Team | G | Min. | FGM | FGA | Pct. | FTM | FTA | Pct. | REBOUNDS Off. | Def. | Tot. | Ast. | St. | Blk. | TO | Pts. | AVERAGES RPG | APG | PPG |
|---|---|---|---|---|---|---|---|---|---|---|---|---|---|---|---|---|---|---|---|
| 03-04—Denver | 62 | 875 | 94 | 199 | .472 | 30 | 45 | .667 | 65 | 138 | 203 | 32 | 35 | 39 | 35 | 218 | 3.3 | 0.5 | 3.5 |
| 04-05—Denver | 67 | 939 | 101 | 216 | .468 | 45 | 79 | .570 | 61 | 140 | 201 | 34 | 34 | 41 | 40 | 248 | 3.0 | 0.5 | 3.7 |
| **Totals** | 129 | 1814 | 195 | 415 | .470 | 75 | 124 | .605 | 126 | 278 | 404 | 66 | 69 | 80 | 75 | 466 | 3.1 | 0.5 | 3.6 |

Three-point field goals: 2003-04, 0-for-1. 2004-05, 1-for-3 (.333). Totals, 1-for-4 (.250).
Personal fouls/disqualifications: 2003-04, 145/2. 2004-05, 129/1. Totals, 274/3.

| Season Team | G | Min. | FGM | FGA | Pct. | FTM | FTA | Pct. | Off. | Def. | Tot. | Ast. | St. | Blk. | TO | Pts. | RPG | APG | PPG |
|---|---|---|---|---|---|---|---|---|---|---|---|---|---|---|---|---|---|---|---|
| | | | | | | | | | | REBOUNDS | | | | | | | | AVERAGES | |
| 03-04—Denver............ | 4 | 60 | 7 | 12 | .583 | 1 | 2 | .500 | 1 | 8 | 9 | 2 | 2 | 1 | 3 | 15 | 2.3 | 0.5 | 3.8 |
| 04-05—Denver............ | 1 | 6 | 0 | 1 | .000 | 0 | 0 | ... | 0 | 3 | 3 | 0 | 0 | 0 | 0 | 0 | 3.0 | 0.0 | 0.0 |
| Totals ................... | 5 | 66 | 7 | 13 | .538 | 1 | 2 | .500 | 1 | 11 | 12 | 2 | 2 | 1 | 3 | 15 | 2.4 | 0.4 | 3.0 |

Personal fouls/disqualifications: 2003-04, 14/0. Totals, 14/0.

## ELY, MELVIN  F/C  BOBCATS

**PERSONAL:** Born May 2, 1978, in Harvey, Ill. ... 6-10/260. (2.08/117.9).
**HIGH SCHOOL:** Thornton Township (Harvey, Ill.).
**COLLEGE:** Fresno State.
**TRANSACTIONS/CAREER NOTES:** Selected by Los Angeles Clippers in first round (12th pick overall) of 2002 NBA Draft. ... Traded by Clippers with G Eddie House to Charlotte Bobcats for second-round draft choices in 2005 and 2006 (July 14, 2004).

### COLLEGIATE RECORD

| Season Team | G | Min. | FGM | FGA | Pct. | FTM | FTA | Pct. | Reb. | Ast. | Pts. | RPG | APG | PPG |
|---|---|---|---|---|---|---|---|---|---|---|---|---|---|---|
| | | | | | | | | | | | | | AVERAGES | |
| 97-98—Fresno State .................. | | | | | Did not play—ineligible. | | | | | | | | | |
| 98-99—Fresno State .................. | 32 | 988 | 155 | 276 | .562 | 48 | 111 | .432 | 207 | 17 | 359 | 6.5 | 0.5 | 11.2 |
| 99-00—Fresno State .................. | 31 | 1035 | 180 | 297 | .606 | 51 | 77 | .662 | 216 | 27 | 411 | 7.0 | 0.9 | 13.3 |
| 00-01—Fresno State .................. | 33 | 1009 | 208 | 357 | .583 | 112 | 167 | .671 | 247 | 45 | 528 | 7.5 | 1.4 | 16.0 |
| 01-02—Fresno State .................. | 28 | 999 | 246 | 437 | .563 | 161 | 219 | .735 | 254 | 50 | 653 | 9.1 | 1.8 | 23.3 |
| Totals ..................................... | 124 | 4031 | 789 | 1367 | .577 | 372 | 574 | .648 | 924 | 139 | 1951 | 7.5 | 1.1 | 15.7 |

Three-point field goals: 1998-99, 1-for-2 (.500). 2001-02, 1-for-2 (.500). Totals, 2-for-4 (.500).

### NBA REGULAR-SEASON RECORD

| Season Team | G | Min. | FGM | FGA | Pct. | FTM | FTA | Pct. | Off. | Def. | Tot. | Ast. | St. | Blk. | TO | Pts. | RPG | APG | PPG |
|---|---|---|---|---|---|---|---|---|---|---|---|---|---|---|---|---|---|---|---|
| | | | | | | | | | | REBOUNDS | | | | | | | | AVERAGES | |
| 02-03—L.A. Clippers... | 52 | 802 | 92 | 186 | .495 | 52 | 74 | .703 | 64 | 110 | 174 | 15 | 10 | 32 | 50 | 236 | 3.3 | 0.3 | 4.5 |
| 03-04—L.A. Clippers... | 42 | 510 | 66 | 153 | .431 | 25 | 42 | .595 | 48 | 53 | 101 | 22 | 9 | 17 | 20 | 157 | 2.4 | 0.5 | 3.7 |
| 04-05—Charlotte......... | 79 | 1649 | 227 | 526 | .432 | 122 | 212 | .575 | 142 | 184 | 326 | 76 | 32 | 69 | 115 | 576 | 4.1 | 1.0 | 7.3 |
| Totals ................... | 173 | 2961 | 385 | 865 | .445 | 199 | 328 | .607 | 254 | 347 | 601 | 113 | 51 | 118 | 185 | 969 | 3.5 | 0.7 | 5.6 |

Three-point field goals: 2003-04, 0-for-1. Totals, 0-for-1 (.000).
Personal fouls/disqualifications: 2002-03, 95/0. 2003-04, 68/0. 2004-05, 199/1. Totals, 362/1.

## EMMETT, ANDRE  G  HEAT

**PERSONAL:** Born August 27, 1982, in Dallas. ... 6-5/230. (1.96/104.3).
**HIGH SCHOOL:** David W. Carter (Dallas).
**COLLEGE:** Texas Tech.
**TRANSACTIONS/CAREER NOTES:** Selected by Seattle SuperSonics in second round (35th pick overall) of 2004 NBA Draft. ... Draft rights traded by SuperSonics to Memphis Grizzlies for future second-round draft choice (June 24, 2004). ... Traded by Grizzlies with F James Posey and G Jason Williams to Miami Heat in five-team trade (August 2, 2005).

**NOTES:** The Sporting News All-America third team (2004).

### COLLEGIATE RECORD

| Season Team | G | Min. | FGM | FGA | Pct. | FTM | FTA | Pct. | Reb. | Ast. | Pts. | RPG | APG | PPG |
|---|---|---|---|---|---|---|---|---|---|---|---|---|---|---|
| | | | | | | | | | | | | | AVERAGES | |
| 00-01—Texas Tech..................... | 28 | 575 | 83 | 210 | .395 | 31 | 49 | .633 | 102 | 28 | 215 | 3.6 | 1.0 | 7.7 |
| 01-02—Texas Tech..................... | 32 | 1048 | 242 | 466 | .519 | 106 | 157 | .675 | 212 | 48 | 599 | 6.6 | 1.5 | 18.7 |
| 02-03—Texas Tech..................... | 34 | 1258 | 297 | 595 | .499 | 136 | 191 | .712 | 226 | 63 | 741 | 6.6 | 1.9 | 21.8 |
| 03-04—Texas Tech..................... | 34 | 1259 | 260 | 494 | .526 | 165 | 226 | .730 | 225 | 62 | 701 | 6.6 | 1.8 | 20.6 |
| Totals ..................................... | 128 | 4140 | 882 | 1765 | .500 | 438 | 623 | .703 | 765 | 201 | 2256 | 6.0 | 1.6 | 17.6 |

Three-point field goals: 2000-01, 18-for-62 (.290). 2001-02, 9-for-28 (.321). 2002-03, 11-for-38 (.289). 2003-04, 16-for-45 (.356). Totals, 54-for-173 (.312).

### NBA REGULAR-SEASON RECORD

| Season Team | G | Min. | FGM | FGA | Pct. | FTM | FTA | Pct. | Off. | Def. | Tot. | Ast. | St. | Blk. | TO | Pts. | RPG | APG | PPG |
|---|---|---|---|---|---|---|---|---|---|---|---|---|---|---|---|---|---|---|---|
| | | | | | | | | | | REBOUNDS | | | | | | | | AVERAGES | |
| 04-05—Memphis ........ | 8 | 28 | 2 | 6 | .333 | 3 | 5 | .600 | 0 | 2 | 2 | 0 | 0 | 0 | 1 | 7 | 0.3 | 0.0 | 0.9 |

Personal fouls/disqualifications: 2004-05, 4/0. Totals, 4/0.

## EVANS, MAURICE  G  PISTONS

**PERSONAL:** Born November 8, 1978, in Wichita, Kan. ... 6-5/220. (1.96/99.8). ... Full name: Maurice Eugene Evans
**HIGH SCHOOL:** Wichita Collegiate (Wichita, Kan.).
**COLLEGE:** Wichita State, then Texas.
**TRANSACTIONS/CAREER NOTES:** Not drafted by an NBA franchise. ... Signed as free agent by Minnesota Timberwolves (July 23, 2001). ... Waived by Timberwolves (October 24, 2002). ... Signed as free agent by Sacramento Kings (2004). ... Signed as free agent by Detroit Pistons (August 24, 2005).

### COLLEGIATE RECORD

| Season Team | G | Min. | FGM | FGA | Pct. | FTM | FTA | Pct. | Reb. | Ast. | Pts. | RPG | APG | PPG |
|---|---|---|---|---|---|---|---|---|---|---|---|---|---|---|
| | | | | | | | | | | | | | AVERAGES | |
| 97-98—Wichita State ................. | 31 | 761 | 130 | 339 | .383 | 66 | 98 | .673 | 141 | 27 | 375 | 4.5 | 0.9 | 12.1 |

**E**

| Season Team | G | Min. | FGM | FGA | Pct. | FTM | FTA | Pct. | Reb. | Ast. | Pts. | AVERAGES RPG | APG | PPG |
|---|---|---|---|---|---|---|---|---|---|---|---|---|---|---|
| 98-99—Wichita State | 28 | 903 | 211 | 458 | .461 | 141 | 178 | .792 | 130 | 57 | 632 | 4.6 | 2.0 | 22.6 |
| 99-00—Texas | | | | | | Did not play—transfer student | | | | | | | | |
| 00-01—Texas | 34 | 1122 | 181 | 411 | .440 | 84 | 111 | .757 | 179 | 56 | 532 | 5.3 | 1.6 | 15.6 |
| Totals | 93 | 2786 | 522 | 1208 | .432 | 291 | 387 | .752 | 450 | 140 | 1539 | 4.8 | 1.5 | 16.5 |

Three-point field goals: 1997-98, 49-for-149 (.329). 1998-99, 69-for-164 (.421). 2000-01, 86-for-221 (.389). Totals, 204-for-534 (.382).
Personal fouls/disqualifications: 1997-98, 88/0. 1998-99, 81/0. 2000-01, 101/0. Totals, 270/0.

### NBA REGULAR-SEASON RECORD

| Season Team | G | Min. | FGM | FGA | Pct. | FTM | FTA | Pct. | REBOUNDS Off. | Def. | Tot. | Ast. | St. | Blk. | TO | Pts. | AVERAGES RPG | APG | PPG |
|---|---|---|---|---|---|---|---|---|---|---|---|---|---|---|---|---|---|---|---|
| 01-02—Minnesota | 10 | 45 | 9 | 19 | .474 | 3 | 4 | .750 | 3 | 1 | 4 | 4 | 0 | 0 | 2 | 21 | 0.4 | 0.4 | 2.1 |
| 04-05—Sacramento | 65 | 1233 | 165 | 373 | .442 | 59 | 78 | .756 | 88 | 113 | 201 | 45 | 37 | 8 | 34 | 416 | 3.1 | 0.7 | 6.4 |
| Totals | 75 | 1278 | 174 | 392 | .444 | 62 | 82 | .756 | 91 | 114 | 205 | 49 | 37 | 8 | 36 | 437 | 2.7 | 0.7 | 5.8 |

Three-point field goals: 2001-02, 0-for-3. 2004-05, 27-for-82 (.329). Totals, 27-for-85 (.318).
Personal fouls/disqualifications: 2001-02, 9/0. 2004-05, 104/1. Totals, 113/1.

### NBA PLAYOFF RECORD

| Season Team | G | Min. | FGM | FGA | Pct. | FTM | FTA | Pct. | REBOUNDS Off. | Def. | Tot. | Ast. | St. | Blk. | TO | Pts. | AVERAGES RPG | APG | PPG |
|---|---|---|---|---|---|---|---|---|---|---|---|---|---|---|---|---|---|---|---|
| 04-05—Sacramento | 3 | 56 | 6 | 10 | .600 | 4 | 5 | .800 | 2 | 5 | 7 | 3 | 2 | 0 | 0 | 18 | 2.3 | 1.0 | 6.0 |

Three-point field goals: 2004-05, 2-for-4 (.500). Totals, 2-for-4 (.500).
Personal fouls/disqualifications: 2004-05, 6/0. Totals, 6/0.

### ITALIAN LEAGUE RECORD

| Season Team | G | Min. | FGM | FGA | Pct. | FTM | FTA | Pct. | Reb. | Ast. | Pts. | AVERAGES RPG | APG | PPG |
|---|---|---|---|---|---|---|---|---|---|---|---|---|---|---|
| 03-04—Benetton Treviso | 27 | 854 | 191 | 358 | .534 | 69 | 90 | .767 | 123 | 39 | 520 | 4.6 | 1.4 | 19.3 |

Three-point field goals: 2003-04, 69-for-143 (.483). Totals, 69-for-143 (.483).

## EVANS, REGGIE          F          SUPERSONICS

**PERSONAL:** Born May 18, 1980, in Pensacola, Fla. ... 6-8/245. (2.03/111.1).
**HIGH SCHOOL:** Woodham (Pensacola, Fla.).
**COLLEGE:** Iowa.
**TRANSACTIONS/CAREER NOTES:** Not drafted by an NBA franchise ... Signed as free agent with Seattle SuperSonics (September 30, 2002).

### COLLEGIATE RECORD

| Season Team | G | Min. | FGM | FGA | Pct. | FTM | FTA | Pct. | Reb. | Ast. | Pts. | AVERAGES RPG | APG | PPG |
|---|---|---|---|---|---|---|---|---|---|---|---|---|---|---|
| 98-99—Coffeyville | 27 | ... | 140 | 277 | .505 | 146 | 250 | .584 | 285 | 37 | 426 | 10.6 | 1.4 | 15.8 |
| 99-00—Coffeyville | 26 | 900 | 186 | 361 | .515 | 204 | 332 | .614 | 310 | 48 | 584 | 11.9 | 1.8 | 22.5 |
| 00-01—Iowa | 35 | 1220 | 155 | 326 | .475 | 218 | 346 | .630 | 416 | 55 | 529 | 11.9 | 1.6 | 15.1 |
| 01-02—Iowa | 34 | 1156 | 169 | 341 | .496 | 187 | 302 | .619 | 378 | 44 | 525 | 11.1 | 1.3 | 15.4 |
| Junior College Totals | 53 | 900 | 326 | 638 | .511 | 350 | 582 | .601 | 595 | 85 | 1010 | 11.2 | 1.6 | 19.1 |
| 4-Year-College Totals | 69 | 2376 | 324 | 667 | .486 | 405 | 648 | .625 | 794 | 99 | 1054 | 11.5 | 1.4 | 15.3 |

Three-point field goals: 1998-99, 0-for-2. 1999-00, 8-for-20 (.400). 2000-01, 1-for-1 (1.000). 2001-02, 0-for-1. Totals, 9-for-24 (.375).

### NBA REGULAR-SEASON RECORD

| Season Team | G | Min. | FGM | FGA | Pct. | FTM | FTA | Pct. | REBOUNDS Off. | Def. | Tot. | Ast. | St. | Blk. | TO | Pts. | AVERAGES RPG | APG | PPG |
|---|---|---|---|---|---|---|---|---|---|---|---|---|---|---|---|---|---|---|---|
| 02-03—Seattle | 67 | 1365 | 66 | 140 | .471 | 80 | 154 | .519 | 167 | 278 | 445 | 34 | 38 | 11 | 52 | 212 | 6.6 | 0.5 | 3.2 |
| 03-04—Seattle | 75 | 1280 | 67 | 165 | .406 | 83 | 148 | .561 | 156 | 252 | 408 | 33 | 54 | 10 | 65 | 217 | 5.4 | 0.4 | 2.9 |
| 04-05—Seattle | 79 | 1881 | 131 | 275 | .476 | 125 | 234 | .534 | 254 | 482 | 736 | 58 | 58 | 15 | 104 | 387 | 9.3 | 0.7 | 4.9 |
| Totals | 221 | 4526 | 264 | 580 | .455 | 288 | 536 | .537 | 577 | 1012 | 1589 | 125 | 150 | 36 | 221 | 816 | 7.2 | 0.6 | 3.7 |

Three-point field goals: 2003-04, 0-for-3. 2004-05, 0-for-2. Totals, 0-for-5 (.000).
Personal fouls/disqualifications: 2002-03, 173/2. 2003-04, 176/0. 2004-05, 202/0. Totals, 551/2.

### NBA PLAYOFF RECORD

| Season Team | G | Min. | FGM | FGA | Pct. | FTM | FTA | Pct. | REBOUNDS Off. | Def. | Tot. | Ast. | St. | Blk. | TO | Pts. | AVERAGES RPG | APG | PPG |
|---|---|---|---|---|---|---|---|---|---|---|---|---|---|---|---|---|---|---|---|
| 04-05—Seattle | 11 | 208 | 15 | 37 | .405 | 11 | 21 | .524 | 27 | 54 | 81 | 5 | 5 | 3 | 11 | 41 | 7.4 | 0.5 | 3.7 |

Personal fouls/disqualifications: 2004-05, 32/0. Totals, 32/0.

## FINLEY, MICHAEL          G/F          SPURS

**PERSONAL:** Born March 6, 1973, in Melrose Park, Ill. ... 6-7/215. (2.01/97.5). ... Full name: Michael H. Finley
**HIGH SCHOOL:** Proviso East (Maywood, Ill.).
**COLLEGE:** Wisconsin.
**TRANSACTIONS/CAREER NOTES:** Selected by Phoenix Suns in first round (21st pick overall) of 1995 NBA Draft. ... Traded by Suns with G Sam Cassell, F A.C. Green and 1997 or 1998 conditional second-round draft choice to Dallas Mavericks for G Jason Kidd, F Tony Dumas and C Loren Meyer (December 26, 1996). ... Waived by Mavericks (August 15, 2005). Signed as free agent by San Antonio Spurs (September 2, 2005).

### COLLEGIATE RECORD

| Season Team | G | Min. | FGM | FGA | Pct. | FTM | FTA | Pct. | Reb. | Ast. | Pts. | AVERAGES RPG | APG | PPG |
|---|---|---|---|---|---|---|---|---|---|---|---|---|---|---|
| 91-92—Wisconsin | 31 | 920 | 130 | 287 | .453 | 95 | 128 | .742 | 152 | 85 | 381 | 4.9 | 2.7 | 12.3 |

| Season Team | G | Min. | FGM | FGA | Pct. | FTM | FTA | Pct. | Reb. | Ast. | Pts. | AVERAGES | | |
|---|---|---|---|---|---|---|---|---|---|---|---|---|---|---|
| | | | | | | | | | | | | RPG | APG | PPG |
| 91-92—Wisconsin | 31 | 920 | 130 | 287 | .453 | 95 | 128 | .742 | | | | 5.8 | 3.1 | 22.1 |
| 92-93—Wisconsin | 28 | 979 | 223 | 478 | .467 | 111 | 144 | .771 | 161 | 86 | 620 | 5.8 | 3.1 | 22.1 |
| 93-94—Wisconsin | 29 | 1046 | 208 | 446 | .466 | 110 | 140 | .786 | 194 | 92 | 592 | 6.7 | 3.2 | 20.4 |
| 94-95—Wisconsin | 27 | 1000 | 178 | 470 | .379 | 140 | 181 | .773 | 141 | 108 | 554 | 5.2 | 4.0 | 20.5 |
| Totals | 115 | 3945 | 739 | 1681 | .440 | 456 | 593 | .769 | 648 | 371 | 2147 | 5.6 | 3.2 | 18.7 |

Three-point field goals: 1991-92, 26-for-72 (.361). 1992-93, 63-for-173 (.364). 1993-94, 66-for-182 (.363). 1994-95, 58-for-204 (.284). Totals, 213-for-631 (.338).

## NBA REGULAR-SEASON RECORD

**HONORS:** NBA All-Rookie first team (1996).

| Season Team | G | Min. | FGM | FGA | Pct. | FTM | FTA | Pct. | REBOUNDS | | | Ast. | St. | Blk. | TO | Pts. | AVERAGES | | |
|---|---|---|---|---|---|---|---|---|---|---|---|---|---|---|---|---|---|---|---|
| | | | | | | | | | Off. | Def. | Tot. | | | | | | RPG | APG | PPG |
| 95-96—Phoenix | 82 | 3212 | 465 | 976 | .476 | 242 | 323 | .749 | 139 | 235 | 374 | 289 | 85 | 31 | 133 | 1233 | 4.6 | 3.5 | 15.0 |
| 96-97—Pho.-Dal. | 83 | 2790 | 475 | 1071 | .444 | 198 | 245 | .808 | 88 | 284 | 372 | 224 | 68 | 24 | 164 | 1249 | 4.5 | 2.7 | 15.0 |
| 97-98—Dallas | 82 | *3394 | 675 | 1505 | .449 | 326 | 416 | .784 | 149 | 289 | 438 | 405 | 132 | 30 | 219 | 1763 | 5.3 | 4.9 | 21.5 |
| 98-99—Dallas | 50 | 2051 | 389 | 876 | .444 | 186 | 226 | .823 | 69 | 194 | 263 | 218 | 66 | 15 | 107 | 1009 | 5.3 | 4.4 | 20.2 |
| 99-00—Dallas | 82 | 3464 | 748 | 1636 | .457 | 260 | 317 | .820 | 122 | 396 | 518 | 438 | 109 | 32 | 196 | 1855 | 6.3 | 5.3 | 22.6 |
| 00-01—Dallas | 82 | *3443 | 711 | 1552 | .458 | 252 | 325 | .775 | 109 | 316 | 425 | 360 | 118 | 32 | 190 | 1765 | 5.2 | 4.4 | 21.5 |
| 01-02—Dallas | 69 | 2754 | 569 | 1228 | .463 | 210 | 251 | .837 | 90 | 270 | 360 | 230 | 65 | 25 | 117 | 1424 | 5.2 | 3.3 | 20.6 |
| 02-03—Dallas | 69 | 2642 | 507 | 1193 | .425 | 198 | 230 | .861 | 107 | 295 | 402 | 205 | 76 | 21 | 114 | 1331 | 5.8 | 3.0 | 19.3 |
| 03-04—Dallas | 72 | 2778 | 514 | 1159 | .443 | 164 | 193 | .850 | 78 | 247 | 325 | 212 | 84 | 39 | 83 | 1342 | 4.5 | 2.9 | 18.6 |
| 04-05—Dallas | 64 | 2358 | 387 | 907 | .427 | 113 | 136 | .831 | 45 | 217 | 262 | 169 | 48 | 18 | 60 | 1003 | 4.1 | 2.6 | 15.7 |
| Totals | 735 | 28886 | 5440 | 12103 | .449 | 2149 | 2662 | .807 | 996 | 2743 | 3739 | 2750 | 851 | 267 | 1383 | 13974 | 5.1 | 3.7 | 19.0 |

Three-point field goals: 1995-96, 61-for-186 (.328). 1996-97, 101-for-280 (.361). 1997-98, 87-for-244 (.357). 1998-99, 45-for-136 (.331). 1999-00, 99-for-247 (.401). 2000-01, 91-for-263 (.346). 2001-02, 76-for-224 (.339). 2002-03, 119-for-322 (.370). 2003-04, 150-for-370 (.405). 2004-05, 116-for-285 (.407). Totals, 945-for-2557 (.370).

Personal fouls/disqualifications: 1995-96, 199/1. 1996-97, 138/0. 1997-98, 163/0. 1998-99, 96/1. 1999-00, 171/1. 2000-01, 174/2. 2001-02, 144/1. 2002-03, 105/0. 2003-04, 118/0. 2004-05, 123/0. Totals, 1431/6.

## NBA PLAYOFF RECORD

| Season Team | G | Min. | FGM | FGA | Pct. | FTM | FTA | Pct. | REBOUNDS | | | Ast. | St. | Blk. | TO | Pts. | AVERAGES | | |
|---|---|---|---|---|---|---|---|---|---|---|---|---|---|---|---|---|---|---|---|
| | | | | | | | | | Off. | Def. | Tot. | | | | | | RPG | APG | PPG |
| 00-01—Dallas | 10 | 434 | 72 | 200 | .360 | 36 | 44 | .818 | 13 | 40 | 53 | 44 | 12 | 2 | 24 | 197 | 5.3 | 4.4 | 19.7 |
| 01-02—Dallas | 8 | 373 | 69 | 148 | .466 | 45 | 50 | .900 | 13 | 37 | 50 | 18 | 12 | 4 | 15 | 197 | 6.3 | 2.3 | 24.6 |
| 02-03—Dallas | 20 | 822 | 131 | 301 | .435 | 57 | 66 | .864 | 25 | 90 | 115 | 60 | 26 | 12 | 31 | 366 | 5.8 | 3.0 | 18.3 |
| 03-04—Dallas | 5 | 196 | 26 | 68 | .382 | 6 | 10 | .600 | 6 | 10 | 16 | 13 | 4 | 3 | 9 | 65 | 3.2 | 2.6 | 13.0 |
| 04-05—Dallas | 13 | 491 | 65 | 153 | .425 | 16 | 18 | .889 | 13 | 43 | 56 | 28 | 17 | 0 | 13 | 170 | 4.3 | 2.2 | 13.1 |
| Totals | 56 | 2316 | 363 | 870 | .417 | 160 | 188 | .851 | 70 | 220 | 290 | 163 | 71 | 21 | 92 | 995 | 5.2 | 2.9 | 17.8 |

Three-point field goals: 2000-01, 17-for-47 (.362). 2001-02, 14-for-37 (.378). 2002-03, 47-for-114 (.412). 2003-04, 7-for-26 (.269). 2004-05, 24-for-61 (.393). Totals, 109-for-285 (.382).

Personal fouls/disqualifications: 2000-01, 23/0. 2001-02, 24/0. 2002-03, 46/0. 2003-04, 8/0. 2004-05, 32/0. Totals, 133/0.

## NBA ALL-STAR GAME RECORD

| Season Team | Min. | FGM | FGA | Pct. | FTM | FTA | Pct. | REBOUNDS | | | Ast. | PF | Dq. | St. | Blk. | TO | Pts. |
|---|---|---|---|---|---|---|---|---|---|---|---|---|---|---|---|---|---|
| | | | | | | | | Off. | Def. | Tot. | | | | | | | |
| 2000—Dallas | 10 | 5 | 6 | .833 | 0 | 0 | | 0 | 1 | 1 | 0 | 0 | 0 | 0 | 0 | 1 | 11 |
| 2001—Dallas | 19 | 5 | 15 | .333 | 2 | 2 | 1.000 | 2 | 1 | 3 | 5 | 0 | 0 | 0 | 0 | 1 | 12 |
| Totals | 29 | 10 | 21 | .476 | 2 | 2 | 1.000 | 2 | 2 | 4 | 5 | 0 | 0 | 0 | 0 | 2 | 23 |

Three-point field goals: 2000, 1-for-2 (.500). 2001, 0-for-2. Totals, 1-for-4 (.250).

# FISHER, DEREK        G        WARRIORS

**PERSONAL:** Born August 9, 1974, in Little Rock, Ark. ... 6-1/200. (1.85/90.7). ... Brother of Duane Washington, guard with New Jersey Nets (1987-88) and Los Angeles Clippers (1992-93).
**HIGH SCHOOL:** Parkview (Little Rock, Ark.).
**COLLEGE:** Arkansas-Little Rock.
**TRANSACTIONS/CAREER NOTES:** Selected by Los Angeles Lakers in first round (24th pick overall) of 1996 NBA Draft. ... Signed as free agent by Golden State Warriors (July 16, 2004).
**MISCELLANEOUS:** Member of NBA championship team (2000, 2001, 2002).

F

## COLLEGIATE RECORD

| Season Team | G | Min. | FGM | FGA | Pct. | FTM | FTA | Pct. | Reb. | Ast. | Pts. | AVERAGES | | |
|---|---|---|---|---|---|---|---|---|---|---|---|---|---|---|
| | | | | | | | | | | | | RPG | APG | PPG |
| 92-93—Arkansas-Little Rock | 27 | 749 | 57 | 138 | .413 | 71 | 92 | .772 | 89 | 92 | 194 | 3.3 | 3.4 | 7.2 |
| 93-94—Arkansas-Little Rock | 28 | 888 | 94 | 212 | .443 | 72 | 93 | .774 | 109 | 102 | 283 | 3.9 | 3.6 | 10.1 |
| 94-95—Arkansas-Little Rock | 27 | 938 | 153 | 386 | .396 | 130 | 180 | .722 | 135 | 124 | 479 | 5.0 | 4.6 | 17.7 |
| 95-96—Arkansas-Little Rock | 30 | 1041 | 128 | 313 | .409 | 126 | 169 | .746 | 155 | 154 | 437 | 5.2 | 5.1 | 14.6 |
| Totals | 112 | 3616 | 432 | 1049 | .412 | 399 | 534 | .747 | 488 | 472 | 1393 | 4.4 | 4.2 | 12.4 |

Three-point field goals: 1992-93, 9-for-31 (.290). 1993-94, 23-for-55 (.418). 1994-95, 43-for-113 (.381). 1995-96, 50-for-130 (.385). Totals, 125-for-329 (.380).

## NBA REGULAR-SEASON RECORD

| Season Team | G | Min. | FGM | FGA | Pct. | FTM | FTA | Pct. | REBOUNDS | | | Ast. | St. | Blk. | TO | Pts. | AVERAGES | | |
|---|---|---|---|---|---|---|---|---|---|---|---|---|---|---|---|---|---|---|---|
| | | | | | | | | | Off. | Def. | Tot. | | | | | | RPG | APG | PPG |
| 96-97—L.A. Lakers | 80 | 921 | 104 | 262 | .397 | 79 | 120 | .658 | 25 | 72 | 97 | 119 | 41 | 5 | 71 | 309 | 1.2 | 1.5 | 3.9 |
| 97-98—L.A. Lakers | 82 | 1760 | 164 | 378 | .434 | 115 | 152 | .757 | 38 | 155 | 193 | 333 | 75 | 5 | 119 | 474 | 2.4 | 4.1 | 5.8 |
| 98-99—L.A. Lakers | 50 | 1131 | 99 | 263 | .376 | 60 | 79 | .759 | 21 | 70 | 91 | 197 | 61 | 1 | 77 | 296 | 1.8 | 3.9 | 5.9 |
| 99-00—L.A. Lakers | 78 | 1803 | 167 | 483 | .346 | 105 | 145 | .724 | 22 | 121 | 143 | 216 | 80 | 3 | 75 | 491 | 1.8 | 2.8 | 6.3 |
| 00-01—L.A. Lakers | 20 | 709 | 77 | 187 | .412 | 50 | 62 | .806 | 5 | 54 | 59 | 87 | 39 | 2 | 29 | 229 | 3.0 | 4.4 | 11.5 |
| 01-02—L.A. Lakers | 70 | 1974 | 274 | 666 | .411 | 94 | 111 | .847 | 15 | 131 | 146 | 181 | 66 | 9 | 62 | 786 | 2.1 | 2.6 | 11.2 |
| 02-03—L.A. Lakers | 82 | 2829 | 339 | 775 | .437 | 100 | 125 | .800 | 40 | 199 | 239 | 298 | 93 | 15 | 94 | 863 | 2.9 | 3.6 | 10.5 |
| 03-04—L.A. Lakers | 82 | 1769 | 203 | 576 | .352 | 122 | 153 | .797 | 30 | 122 | 152 | 187 | 103 | 4 | 79 | 580 | 1.9 | 2.3 | 7.1 |
| 04-05—Golden State | 74 | 2222 | 297 | 755 | .393 | 175 | 203 | .862 | 38 | 180 | 218 | 301 | 76 | 4 | 129 | 877 | 2.9 | 4.1 | 11.9 |
| Totals | 618 | 15118 | 1724 | 4345 | .397 | 900 | 1150 | .783 | 234 | 1104 | 1338 | 1919 | 634 | 48 | 735 | 4905 | 2.2 | 3.1 | 7.9 |

Three-point field goals: 1996-97, 22-for-73 (.301). 1997-98, 31-for-81 (.383). 1998-99, 38-for-97 (.392). 1999-00, 52-for-166 (.313). 2000-01, 25-for-63 (.397). 2001-02, 144-for-349 (.413). 2002-03, 85-for-212 (.401). 2003-04, 52-for-179 (.291). 2004-05, 108-for-291 (.371). Totals, 557-for-1511 (.369).

### NBA PLAYOFF RECORD

| Season Team | G | Min. | FGM | FGA | Pct. | FTM | FTA | Pct. | REBOUNDS Off. | Def. | Tot. | Ast. | St. | Blk. | TO | Pts. | AVERAGES RPG | APG | PPG |
|---|---|---|---|---|---|---|---|---|---|---|---|---|---|---|---|---|---|---|---|
| 96-97—L.A. Lakers ..... | 6 | 34 | 3 | 11 | .273 | 2 | 3 | .667 | 0 | 3 | 3 | 6 | 1 | 0 | 6 | 8 | 0.5 | 1.0 | 1.3 |
| 97-98—L.A. Lakers ..... | 13 | 278 | 27 | 68 | .397 | 18 | 29 | .621 | 2 | 23 | 25 | 49 | 17 | 0 | 15 | 78 | 1.9 | 3.8 | 6.0 |
| 98-99—L.A. Lakers ..... | 8 | 238 | 28 | 67 | .418 | 12 | 15 | .800 | 6 | 23 | 29 | 39 | 8 | 0 | 11 | 78 | 3.6 | 4.9 | 9.8 |
| 99-00—L.A. Lakers ..... | 21 | 322 | 34 | 79 | .430 | 19 | 25 | .760 | 4 | 18 | 22 | 41 | 11 | 1 | 9 | 99 | 1.0 | 2.0 | 4.7 |
| 00-01—L.A. Lakers ..... | 16 | 576 | 77 | 159 | .484 | 26 | 34 | .765 | 5 | 56 | 61 | 48 | 21 | 1 | 12 | 215 | 3.8 | 3.0 | 13.4 |
| 01-02—L.A. Lakers ..... | 19 | 649 | 60 | 168 | .357 | 44 | 56 | .786 | 10 | 52 | 62 | 52 | 19 | 1 | 20 | 193 | 3.3 | 2.7 | 10.2 |
| 02-03—L.A. Lakers ..... | 12 | 424 | 53 | 102 | .520 | 18 | 22 | .818 | 5 | 31 | 36 | 22 | 18 | 1 | 18 | 153 | 3.0 | 1.8 | 12.8 |
| 03-04—L.A. Lakers ..... | 22 | 507 | 60 | 148 | .405 | 23 | 35 | .657 | 10 | 46 | 56 | 49 | 18 | 0 | 19 | 166 | 2.5 | 2.2 | 7.5 |
| **Totals** ................... | 117 | 3028 | 342 | 802 | .426 | 162 | 219 | .740 | 42 | 252 | 294 | 306 | 113 | 4 | 110 | 990 | 2.5 | 2.6 | 8.5 |

Three-point field goals: 1996-97, 0-for-5. 1997-98, 6-for-20 (.300). 1998-99, 10-for-29 (.345). 1999-00, 12-for-29 (.414). 2000-01, 35-for-68 (.515). 2001-02, 29-for-81 (.358). 2002-03, 29-for-47 (.617). 2003-04, 23-for-55 (.418). Totals, 144-for-334 (.431).

Personal fouls/disqualifications: 1996-97, 4/0. 1997-98, 33/0. 1998-99, 20/1. 1999-00, 30/0. 2000-01, 44/1. 2001-02, 49/0. 2002-03, 39/1. 2003-04, 47/0. Totals, 266/3.

## FIZER, MARCUS F

**PERSONAL:** Born August 10, 1978, in Detroit. ... 6-8/260. (2.03/117.9). ... Full name: Darnell Marcus Lamar Fizer
**HIGH SCHOOL:** Arcadia (La.).
**COLLEGE:** Iowa State.
**TRANSACTIONS/CAREER NOTES:** Selected after junior season by Chicago Bulls in first round (fourth pick overall) of 2000 NBA Draft. ... Selected by Charlotte Bobcats from Bulls in NBA Expansion Draft (June 22, 2004). ... Signed as free agent by Milwaukee Bucks (November 4, 2005).

### COLLEGIATE RECORD

**NOTES:** The Sporting News All-America second team (2000).

| Season Team | G | Min. | FGM | FGA | Pct. | FTM | FTA | Pct. | Reb. | Ast. | Pts. | AVERAGES RPG | APG | PPG |
|---|---|---|---|---|---|---|---|---|---|---|---|---|---|---|
| 97-98—Iowa State ................... | 30 | 784 | 173 | 365 | .474 | 101 | 164 | .616 | 202 | 19 | 447 | 6.7 | 0.6 | 14.9 |
| 98-99—Iowa State ................... | 30 | 961 | 190 | 422 | .450 | 153 | 208 | .736 | 229 | 34 | 539 | 7.6 | 1.1 | 18.0 |
| 99-00—Iowa State ................... | 37 | 1243 | 327 | 562 | .582 | 175 | 239 | .732 | 285 | 41 | 844 | 7.7 | 1.1 | 22.8 |
| **Totals** ................... | 97 | 2988 | 690 | 1349 | .511 | 429 | 611 | .702 | 716 | 94 | 1830 | 7.4 | 1.0 | 18.9 |

Three-point field goals: 1997-98, 0-for-2. 1998-99, 6-for-28 (.214). 1999-00, 15-for-42 (.357). Totals, 21-for-72 (.292).

### NBA REGULAR-SEASON RECORD

**HONORS:** NBA All-Rookie second team (2001).

| Season Team | G | Min. | FGM | FGA | Pct. | FTM | FTA | Pct. | REBOUNDS Off. | Def. | Tot. | Ast. | St. | Blk. | TO | Pts. | AVERAGES RPG | APG | PPG |
|---|---|---|---|---|---|---|---|---|---|---|---|---|---|---|---|---|---|---|---|
| 00-01—Chicago ......... | 72 | 1580 | 278 | 646 | .430 | 117 | 161 | .727 | 76 | 237 | 313 | 76 | 30 | 19 | 124 | 683 | 4.3 | 1.1 | 9.5 |
| 01-02—Chicago ......... | 76 | 1963 | 371 | 848 | .438 | 189 | 283 | .668 | 128 | 299 | 427 | 120 | 49 | 24 | 131 | 938 | 5.6 | 1.6 | 12.3 |
| 02-03—Chicago ......... | 38 | 809 | 178 | 383 | .465 | 88 | 134 | .657 | 80 | 136 | 216 | 48 | 14 | 17 | 57 | 445 | 5.7 | 1.3 | 11.7 |
| 03-04—Chicago ......... | 46 | 738 | 134 | 350 | .383 | 90 | 120 | .750 | 61 | 141 | 202 | 43 | 16 | 8 | 51 | 360 | 4.4 | 0.9 | 7.8 |
| 04-05—Milwaukee ...... | 54 | 903 | 133 | 292 | .455 | 70 | 103 | .680 | 29 | 146 | 175 | 64 | 25 | 13 | 63 | 336 | 3.2 | 1.2 | 6.2 |
| **Totals** ................... | 286 | 5993 | 1094 | 2519 | .434 | 554 | 801 | .692 | 374 | 959 | 1333 | 351 | 134 | 81 | 426 | 2762 | 4.7 | 1.2 | 9.7 |

Three-point field goals: 2000-01, 10-for-39 (.256). 2001-02, 7-for-41 (.171). 2002-03, 1-for-6 (.167). 2003-04, 2-for-17 (.118). 2004-05, 0-for-6. Totals, 20-for-109 (.183).

Personal fouls/disqualifications: 2000-01, 175/0. 2001-02, 186/1. 2002-03, 89/0. 2003-04, 97/0. 2004-05, 96/0. Totals, 643/1.

## FLORES, LUIS G

**PERSONAL:** Born April 11, 1981, in Dominican Republic. ... 6-2/195. (1.88/88.5). ... Full name: Luis Alberto Flores
**HIGH SCHOOL:** Norman Thomas (New York, N.Y.).
**COLLEGE:** Rutgers, then Manhattan.
**TRANSACTIONS/CAREER NOTES:** Selected by Houston Rockets in second round (55th pick overall) of 2004 NBA Draft. ... Draft rights traded by Rockets to Dallas Mavericks for draft rights to G Vassilis Spanoulis (June 24, 2004). ... Draft rights traded by Mavericks with F Eduardo Najera, F/C Christian Laettner, draft rights to G Mladen Sekularac, two future first-round draft choices and cash to Golden State Warriors for C Erick Dampier, C Evan Eschmeyer, G Dan Dickau and draft rights to G Steve Logan (August 24, 2004). ... Traded by Warriors with F Eduardo Najera and future first-round pick to Denver Nuggets for F Nikoloz Tskitishvili and F Rodney White (February 24, 2005). ... Waived by Nuggets (August 31, 2005).

### COLLEGIATE RECORD

| Season Team | G | Min. | FGM | FGA | Pct. | FTM | FTA | Pct. | Reb. | Ast. | Pts. | AVERAGES RPG | APG | PPG |
|---|---|---|---|---|---|---|---|---|---|---|---|---|---|---|
| 99-00—Rutgers ........................ | 29 | 312 | 38 | 82 | .463 | 35 | 48 | .729 | 41 | 23 | 114 | 1.4 | 0.8 | 3.9 |
| 00-01—Manhattan ..................... | | | | | | Did not play—transfer student. | | | | | | | | |
| 01-02—Manhattan ..................... | 29 | 1055 | 180 | 395 | .456 | 164 | 188 | .872 | 114 | 69 | 563 | 3.9 | 2.4 | 19.4 |
| 02-03—Manhattan ..................... | 30 | 1166 | 231 | 508 | .455 | 221 | 245 | .902 | 169 | 87 | 739 | 5.6 | 2.9 | 24.6 |
| 03-04—Manhattan ..................... | 31 | 1121 | 234 | 529 | .442 | 208 | 241 | .863 | 122 | 50 | 744 | 3.9 | 1.6 | 24.0 |
| **Totals** ................................... | 119 | 3654 | 683 | 1514 | .451 | 628 | 722 | .870 | 446 | 229 | 2160 | 3.7 | 1.9 | 18.2 |

Three-point field goals: 1999-00, 3-for-16 (.188). 2001-02, 39-for-95 (.411). 2002-03, 56-for-145 (.386). 2003-04, 68-for-182 (.374). Totals, 166-for-438 (.379).

### NBA REGULAR-SEASON RECORD

| Season Team | G | Min. | FGM | FGA | Pct. | FTM | FTA | Pct. | REBOUNDS Off. | Def. | Tot. | Ast. | St. | Blk. | TO | Pts. | AVERAGES RPG | APG | PPG |
|---|---|---|---|---|---|---|---|---|---|---|---|---|---|---|---|---|---|---|---|
| 04-05—Golden St.-Den. | 16 | 77 | 14 | 29 | .483 | 2 | 2 | 1.000 | 1 | 2 | 3 | 11 | 2 | 0 | 11 | 35 | 0.2 | 0.7 | 2.2 |

Three-point field goals: 2004-05, 5-for-10 (.500). Totals, 5-for-10 (.500).
Personal fouls/disqualifications: 2004-05, 9/0. Totals, 9/0.

# FORTSON, DANNY            F            SUPERSONICS

**PERSONAL:** Born March 27, 1976, in Philadelphia. ... 6-8/260. (2.03/117.9). ... Full name: Daniel Anthony Fortson
**HIGH SCHOOL:** Altoona (Pa.), then Shaler (Pittsburgh).
**COLLEGE:** Cincinnati.
**TRANSACTIONS/CAREER NOTES:** Selected after junior season by Milwaukee Bucks in first round (10th pick overall) of 1997 NBA Draft. ... Draft rights traded by Bucks with F Johnny Newman and F/C Joe Wolf to Denver Nuggets for C Ervin Johnson (June 25, 1997). ... Traded by Nuggets with F Eric Williams, G Eric Washington and first-round draft choice within the next three years to Boston Celtics for G/F Ron Mercer, F Popeye Jones and C Dwayne Schintzius (August 3, 1999). ... Traded by Celtics with a future draft choice to Toronto Raptors for G Alvin Williams, F/C Sean Marks and cash considerations (February 9, 2000); trade later voided because Williams failed physical. ... Traded by Celtics to Golden State Warriors as part of four-team deal in which Celtics received F Robert Pack, C John Williams and cash considerations from Dallas Mavericks and a conditional first-round draft choice from Utah Jazz, Mavericks received G Dana Barros from Celtics, F Bill Curley from Warriors and G Howard Eisley from Jazz, Jazz received F Donyell Marshall from Warriors and C Bruno Sundov from Mavericks and Warriors received F Adam Keefe from Jazz (August 16, 2000). ... Traded by Warriors with F Antawn Jamison, F Chris Mills and G Jiri Welsch to Dallas Mavericks for G Nick Van Exel, G Avery Johnson, F Popeye Jones, F Antoine Rigaudeau and C Evan Eschmeyer (August 18, 2003). ... Traded by Mavericks to Seattle SuperSonics for C Calvin Booth (July 26, 2004).

## COLLEGIATE RECORD
**NOTES:** THE SPORTING NEWS All-America second team (1996). ... THE SPORTING NEWS All-America first team (1997).

| | | | | | | | | | | | | AVERAGES | | |
| Season Team | G | Min. | FGM | FGA | Pct. | FTM | FTA | Pct. | Reb. | Ast. | Pts. | RPG | APG | PPG |
|---|---|---|---|---|---|---|---|---|---|---|---|---|---|---|
| 94-95—Cincinnati | 34 | 797 | 190 | 355 | .535 | 134 | 196 | .684 | 258 | 38 | 514 | 7.6 | 1.1 | 15.1 |
| 95-96—Cincinnati | 33 | 909 | 222 | 413 | .538 | 220 | 292 | .753 | 316 | 45 | 664 | 9.6 | 1.4 | 20.1 |
| 96-97—Cincinnati | 33 | 986 | 243 | 392 | .620 | 217 | 281 | .772 | 299 | 36 | 703 | 9.1 | 1.1 | 21.3 |
| Totals | 100 | 2692 | 655 | 1160 | .565 | 571 | 769 | .743 | 873 | 119 | 1881 | 8.7 | 1.2 | 18.8 |

Three-point field goals: 1994-95, 0-for-1. 1995-96, 0-for-1. 1996-97, 0-for-1. Totals, 0-for-3 (.000).
Personal fouls/disqualifications: 1994-95, 119/5. 1995-96, 118/4. Totals, 237/9.

## NBA REGULAR-SEASON RECORD
**NOTES:** Led NBA with 212 personal fouls (1999) and tied for NBA lead with nine disqualifications (1999).

| | | | | | | | | | REBOUNDS | | | | | | | | AVERAGES | | |
| Season Team | G | Min. | FGM | FGA | Pct. | FTM | FTA | Pct. | Off. | Def. | Tot. | Ast. | St. | Blk. | TO | Pts. | RPG | APG | PPG |
|---|---|---|---|---|---|---|---|---|---|---|---|---|---|---|---|---|---|---|---|
| 97-98—Denver | 80 | 1811 | 276 | 611 | .452 | 263 | 339 | .776 | 182 | 266 | 448 | 76 | 44 | 30 | 157 | 816 | 5.6 | 1.0 | 10.2 |
| 98-99—Denver | 50 | 1417 | 191 | 386 | .495 | 168 | 231 | .727 | 210 | 371 | *581 | 32 | 31 | 22 | 77 | 550 | 11.6 | 0.6 | 11.0 |
| 99-00—Boston | 55 | 856 | 140 | 265 | .528 | 139 | 189 | .735 | 141 | 225 | 366 | 29 | 20 | 5 | 67 | 419 | 6.7 | 0.5 | 7.6 |
| 00-01—Golden State | 6 | 203 | 29 | 50 | .580 | 42 | 54 | .778 | 29 | 69 | 98 | 5 | 2 | 0 | 10 | 100 | 16.3 | 0.8 | 16.7 |
| 01-02—Golden State | 77 | 2216 | 309 | 722 | .428 | 245 | 308 | .795 | 290 | 609 | 899 | 127 | 44 | 17 | 160 | 864 | 11.7 | 1.6 | 11.2 |
| 02-03—Golden State | 17 | 223 | 20 | 54 | .370 | 19 | 29 | .655 | 28 | 45 | 73 | 12 | 9 | 0 | 15 | 59 | 4.3 | 0.7 | 3.5 |
| 03-04—Dallas | 56 | 625 | 71 | 139 | .511 | 75 | 92 | .815 | 114 | 136 | 250 | 9 | 12 | 11 | 37 | 217 | 4.5 | 0.2 | 3.9 |
| 04-05—Seattle | 62 | 1047 | 118 | 226 | .522 | 227 | 258 | .880 | 157 | 191 | 348 | 8 | 15 | 7 | 91 | 463 | 5.6 | 0.1 | 7.5 |
| Totals | 403 | 8398 | 1154 | 2453 | .470 | 1178 | 1500 | .785 | 1151 | 1912 | 3063 | 298 | 177 | 92 | 614 | 3488 | 7.6 | 0.7 | 8.7 |

Three-point field goals: 1997-98, 1-for-3 (.333). 1998-99, 0-for-3. 2001-02, 1-for-4 (.250). 2002-03, 0-for-1. Totals, 2-for-11 (.182).
Personal fouls/disqualifications: 1997-98, 314/7. 1998-99, 212/9. 1999-00, 180/4. 2000-01, 22/1. 2001-02, 255/5. 2002-03, 43/0. 2003-04, 148/0. 2004-05, 265/12. Totals, 1439/38.

## NBA PLAYOFF RECORD

| | | | | | | | | | REBOUNDS | | | | | | | | AVERAGES | | |
| Season Team | G | Min. | FGM | FGA | Pct. | FTM | FTA | Pct. | Off. | Def. | Tot. | Ast. | St. | Blk. | TO | Pts. | RPG | APG | PPG |
|---|---|---|---|---|---|---|---|---|---|---|---|---|---|---|---|---|---|---|---|
| 04-05—Seattle | 11 | 105 | 12 | 21 | .571 | 12 | 15 | .800 | 5 | 21 | 26 | 0 | 3 | 1 | 13 | 36 | 2.4 | 0.0 | 3.3 |

Personal fouls/disqualifications: 2004-05, 42/0. Totals, 42/0.


# FOSTER, JEFF            F            PACERS

**PERSONAL:** Born January 16, 1977, in San Antonio. ... 6-11/242. (2.11/109.8). ... Full name: Jeffrey Douglas Foster
**HIGH SCHOOL:** James Madison (San Antonio).
**COLLEGE:** Southwest Texas State.
**TRANSACTIONS/CAREER NOTES:** Selected by Golden State Warriors in first round (21st pick overall) of 1999 NBA Draft. ... Draft rights traded by Warriors to Indiana Pacers for draft rights to G Vonteego Cummings and future first-round draft choice (June 30, 1999).

## COLLEGIATE RECORD

| | | | | | | | | | | | | AVERAGES | | |
| Season Team | G | Min. | FGM | FGA | Pct. | FTM | FTA | Pct. | Reb. | Ast. | Pts. | RPG | APG | PPG |
|---|---|---|---|---|---|---|---|---|---|---|---|---|---|---|
| 95-96—Southwest Texas State | 26 | 340 | 31 | 70 | .443 | 19 | 39 | .487 | 108 | 19 | 82 | 4.2 | 0.7 | 3.2 |
| 96-97—Southwest Texas State | 29 | 637 | 87 | 170 | .512 | 71 | 110 | .645 | 222 | 25 | 248 | 7.7 | 0.9 | 8.6 |
| 97-98—Southwest Texas State | 28 | 816 | 140 | 263 | .532 | 77 | 126 | .611 | 285 | 44 | 357 | 10.2 | 1.6 | 12.8 |
| 98-99—Southwest Texas State | 28 | 787 | 142 | 285 | .498 | 113 | 163 | .693 | 316 | 43 | 397 | 11.3 | 1.5 | 14.2 |
| Totals | 111 | 2580 | 400 | 788 | .508 | 280 | 438 | .639 | 931 | 131 | 1084 | 8.4 | 1.2 | 9.8 |

Three-point field goals: 1995-96, 1-for-1 (1.000). 1996-97, 3-for-3 (1.000). Totals, 4-for-4 (1.000).

## NBA REGULAR-SEASON RECORD

| | | | | | | | | | REBOUNDS | | | | | | | | AVERAGES | | |
| Season Team | G | Min. | FGM | FGA | Pct. | FTM | FTA | Pct. | Off. | Def. | Tot. | Ast. | St. | Blk. | TO | Pts. | RPG | APG | PPG |
|---|---|---|---|---|---|---|---|---|---|---|---|---|---|---|---|---|---|---|---|
| 99-00—Indiana | 19 | 86 | 13 | 23 | .565 | 17 | 25 | .680 | 12 | 20 | 32 | 5 | 5 | 1 | 2 | 43 | 1.7 | 0.3 | 2.3 |
| 00-01—Indiana | 71 | 1152 | 100 | 213 | .469 | 47 | 91 | .516 | 144 | 245 | 389 | 33 | 39 | 28 | 52 | 249 | 5.5 | 0.5 | 3.5 |
| 01-02—Indiana | 82 | 1786 | 177 | 394 | .449 | 111 | 182 | .610 | 206 | 350 | 556 | 70 | 71 | 38 | 79 | 467 | 6.8 | 0.9 | 5.7 |
| 02-03—Indiana | 77 | 802 | 64 | 178 | .360 | 34 | 63 | .540 | 118 | 161 | 279 | 51 | 28 | 21 | 34 | 162 | 3.6 | 0.7 | 2.1 |
| 03-04—Indiana | 82 | 1961 | 197 | 362 | .544 | 103 | 154 | .669 | 248 | 362 | 610 | 64 | 71 | 27 | 60 | 497 | 7.4 | 0.8 | 6.1 |
| 04-05—Indiana | 61 | 1594 | 168 | 324 | .519 | 90 | 142 | .634 | 205 | 345 | 550 | 43 | 46 | 12 | 55 | 426 | 9.0 | 0.7 | 7.0 |
| Totals | 392 | 7381 | 719 | 1494 | .481 | 402 | 657 | .612 | 933 | 1483 | 2416 | 266 | 260 | 127 | 282 | 1844 | 6.2 | 0.7 | 4.7 |

Three-point field goals: 1999-00, 0-for-1. 2000-01, 2-for-7 (.286). 2001-02, 2-for-15 (.133). 2002-03, 0-for-2. 2003-04, 0-for-4. 2004-05, 0-for-5. Totals, 4-for-34 (.118).
Personal fouls/disqualifications: 1999-00, 18/0. 2000-01, 152/3. 2001-02, 232/4. 2002-03, 103/0. 2003-04, 189/1. 2004-05, 186/3. Totals, 880/11.

| Season Team | G | Min. | FGM | FGA | Pct. | FTM | FTA | Pct. | Off. | Def. | Tot. | Ast. | St. | Blk. | TO | Pts. | RPG | APG | PPG |
|---|---|---|---|---|---|---|---|---|---|---|---|---|---|---|---|---|---|---|---|
| 00-01—Indiana........... | 4 | 52 | 4 | 9 | .444 | 2 | 2 | 1.000 | 3 | 9 | 12 | 2 | 0 | 3 | 4 | 10 | 3.0 | 0.5 | 2.5 |
| 01-02—Indiana........... | 5 | 78 | 7 | 13 | .538 | 4 | 9 | .444 | 5 | 19 | 24 | 7 | 3 | 1 | 9 | 20 | 4.8 | 1.4 | 4.0 |
| 02-03—Indiana........... | 6 | 38 | 6 | 11 | .545 | 2 | 2 | 1.000 | 4 | 4 | 8 | 2 | 0 | 3 | 0 | 14 | 1.3 | 0.3 | 2.3 |
| 03-04—Indiana........... | 16 | 307 | 25 | 43 | .581 | 8 | 10 | .800 | 44 | 61 | 105 | 12 | 13 | 5 | 13 | 58 | 6.6 | 0.8 | 3.6 |
| 04-05—Indiana........... | 13 | 245 | 31 | 52 | .596 | 15 | 21 | .714 | 46 | 50 | 96 | 5 | 6 | 12 | 8 | 77 | 7.4 | 0.4 | 5.9 |
| Totals ................... | 44 | 720 | 73 | 128 | .570 | 31 | 44 | .705 | 102 | 143 | 245 | 28 | 22 | 24 | 34 | 179 | 5.6 | 0.6 | 4.1 |

Three-point field goals: 2001-02, 2-for-4 (.500). 2003-04, 0-for-1. Totals, 2-for-5 (.400).
Personal fouls/disqualifications: 2000-01, 8/0. 2001-02, 13/0. 2002-03, 3/0. 2003-04, 37/0. 2004-05, 27/0. Totals, 88/0.

## FOWLKES, TREMAINE                    F

**PERSONAL:** Born April 11, 1976, in Los Angeles. ... 6-7/208. (2.01/94.3).
**HIGH SCHOOL:** Crenshaw (Los Angeles).
**COLLEGE:** California, then Fresno State.
**TRANSACTIONS/CAREER NOTES:** Selected after junior season by Denver Nuggets in second round (54th pick overall) of 1998 NBA Draft. ... Played in Continental Basketball Association with Yakima Sun Kings (1998-99). ... Played in International Basketball League with Cincinnati Stuff (1999-2000). ... Played in Venezuela (2000-01). ... Played in National Basketball Development League with Columbus Riverdragons (2001-02). ... Signed by Los Angeles Clippers to first of two consecutive 10-day contracts (February 23, 2002). ... Signed by Clippers for remainder of season (March 15, 2002). ... Waived by Clippers (October 22, 2003). ... Signed as free agent by Detroit Pistons (October 28, 2003). ... Signed as free agent by New Orleans Hornets (September 29, 2004). ... Waived by Hornets (October 28, 2004). ... Signed as free agent by Indiana Pacers (November 25, 2004). ... Waived by Pacers (December 13, 2004).

### COLLEGIATE RECORD

| Season Team | G | Min. | FGM | FGA | Pct. | FTM | FTA | Pct. | Reb. | Ast. | Pts. | RPG | APG | PPG |
|---|---|---|---|---|---|---|---|---|---|---|---|---|---|---|
| 94-95—California...................... | 27 | 699 | 125 | 275 | .455 | 94 | 147 | .639 | 180 | 27 | 361 | 6.7 | 1.0 | 13.4 |
| 95-96—California...................... | 13 | 351 | 49 | 123 | .398 | 47 | 68 | .691 | 80 | 7 | 157 | 6.2 | 0.5 | 12.1 |
| 96-97—Fresno State.................. | | | | | | Did not play—transfer student. | | | | | | | | |
| 97-98—Fresno State.................. | 32 | 904 | 161 | 328 | .491 | 117 | 184 | .636 | 359 | 31 | 445 | 11.2 | 1.0 | 13.9 |
| Totals ...................................... | 72 | 1954 | 335 | 726 | .461 | 258 | 399 | .647 | 619 | 65 | 963 | 8.6 | 0.9 | 13.4 |

Three-point field goals: 1994-95, 17-for-56 (.304). 1995-96, 12-for-40 (.300). 1997-98, 6-for-37 (.162). Totals, 35-for-133 (.263).

### CBA RECORD

| Season Team | G | Min. | FGM | FGA | Pct. | FTM | FTA | Pct. | Reb. | Ast. | Pts. | RPG | APG | PPG |
|---|---|---|---|---|---|---|---|---|---|---|---|---|---|---|
| 98-99—Yakima ........................ | 10 | 163 | 28 | 63 | .444 | 13 | 29 | .448 | 38 | 5 | 69 | 3.8 | 0.5 | 6.9 |

Three-point field goals: 1998-99, 0-for-6. Totals, 0-for-6 (.000).
Personal fouls/disqualifications: 1998-99, 27/0. Totals, 27/0.

### INTERNATIONAL BASKETBALL LEAGUE RECORD

| Season Team | G | Min. | FGM | FGA | Pct. | FTM | FTA | Pct. | Reb. | Ast. | Pts. | RPG | APG | PPG |
|---|---|---|---|---|---|---|---|---|---|---|---|---|---|---|
| 99-00—Cincinnati ...................... | 61 | 2245 | 408 | 862 | .473 | 299 | 417 | .717 | 556 | 108 | 1178 | 9.1 | 1.8 | 19.3 |

Three-point field goals: 1999-00, 63-for-197 (.320). Totals, 63-for-197 (.320).

### VENEZUELAN LEAGUE RECORD

| Season Team | G | Min. | FGM | FGA | Pct. | FTM | FTA | Pct. | Reb. | Ast. | Pts. | RPG | APG | PPG |
|---|---|---|---|---|---|---|---|---|---|---|---|---|---|---|
| 00-01—Zulia ............................. | 6 | 133 | 28 | 67 | .418 | 7 | 14 | .500 | 35 | 10 | 71 | 5.8 | 1.7 | 11.8 |

Three-point field goals: 2000-01, 8-for-19 (.421). Totals, 8-for-19 (.421).

### NBA REGULAR-SEASON RECORD

| Season Team | G | Min. | FGM | FGA | Pct. | FTM | FTA | Pct. | Off. | Def. | Tot. | Ast. | St. | Blk. | TO | Pts. | RPG | APG | PPG |
|---|---|---|---|---|---|---|---|---|---|---|---|---|---|---|---|---|---|---|---|
| 01-02—L.A. Clippers ... | 22 | 343 | 25 | 64 | .391 | 24 | 31 | .774 | 32 | 32 | 64 | 17 | 11 | 1 | 13 | 74 | 2.9 | 0.8 | 3.4 |
| 02-03—L.A. Clippers ... | 37 | 573 | 56 | 128 | .438 | 50 | 59 | .847 | 41 | 62 | 103 | 23 | 25 | 2 | 20 | 164 | 2.8 | 0.6 | 4.4 |
| 03-04—Detroit ............ | 36 | 261 | 15 | 48 | .313 | 13 | 18 | .722 | 18 | 35 | 53 | 14 | 9 | 3 | 12 | 44 | 1.5 | 0.4 | 1.2 |
| 04-05—Indiana............ | 8 | 56 | 9 | 17 | .529 | 0 | 2 | .000 | 3 | 5 | 8 | 0 | 2 | 0 | 5 | 19 | 1.0 | 0.0 | 2.4 |
| Totals ................... | 103 | 1233 | 105 | 257 | .409 | 87 | 110 | .791 | 94 | 134 | 228 | 54 | 47 | 6 | 50 | 301 | 2.2 | 0.5 | 2.9 |

Three-point field goals: 2002-03, 2-for-9 (.222). 2003-04, 1-for-8 (.125). 2004-05, 1-for-3 (.333). Totals, 4-for-20 (.200).
Personal fouls/disqualifications: 2001-02, 39/0. 2002-03, 63/0. 2003-04, 37/0. 2004-05, 7/0. Totals, 146/0.

### NBDL RECORD

**MISCELLANEOUS:** All-NBDL first team (2002).

| Season Team | G | Min. | FGM | FGA | Pct. | FTM | FTA | Pct. | Reb. | Ast. | Pts. | RPG | APG | PPG |
|---|---|---|---|---|---|---|---|---|---|---|---|---|---|---|
| 01-02—Columbus...................... | 42 | 1338 | 212 | 513 | .413 | 269 | 364 | .739 | 242 | 62 | 701 | 5.8 | 1.5 | 16.7 |
| 04-05—Florida .......................... | 10 | 248 | 28 | 80 | .350 | 35 | 58 | .603 | 41 | 12 | 92 | 4.1 | 1.2 | 9.2 |
| Totals ...................................... | 52 | 1586 | 240 | 593 | .405 | 304 | 422 | .720 | 283 | 74 | 793 | 5.4 | 1.4 | 15.3 |

Three-point field goals: 2001-02, 8-for-39 (.205). 2004-05, 1-for-6 (.167). Totals, 9-for-45 (.200).
Personal fouls/disqualifications: 2001-02, 131/0. Totals, 131/0.

# FOYLE, ADONAL                    C                    WARRIORS

**PERSONAL:** Born March 9, 1975, in Island of Canouan, Grenadines. ... 6-10/250. (2.08/113.4). ... Full name: Adonal David Foyle
**HIGH SCHOOL:** Hamilton (N.Y.).
**COLLEGE:** Colgate.
**TRANSACTIONS/CAREER NOTES:** Selected after junior season by Golden State Warriors in first round (eighth pick overall) of 1997 NBA Draft.

## COLLEGIATE RECORD

**NOTES:** Holds NCAA Division I career record for most blocked shots—492. ... Holds NCAA Division I single-season record for highest blocked-shots-per-game average-6.4 (1997). ... Led NCAA Division I with 6.4 blocked shots per game (1997).

| | | | | | | | | | | | AVERAGES | | |
| Season Team | G | Min. | FGM | FGA | Pct. | FTM | FTA | Pct. | Reb. | Ast. | Pts. | RPG | APG | PPG |
|---|---|---|---|---|---|---|---|---|---|---|---|---|---|---|
| 94-95—Colgate | 30 | 1063 | 207 | 370 | .559 | 95 | 190 | .500 | 371 | 36 | 682 | 12.4 | 1.2 | 22.7 |
| 95-96—Colgate | 29 | 1060 | 228 | 441 | .517 | 129 | 264 | .489 | 364 | 44 | 585 | 12.6 | 1.5 | 20.2 |
| 96-97—Colgate | 28 | 1055 | 277 | 490 | .565 | 127 | 261 | .487 | 368 | 54 | 682 | 13.1 | 1.9 | 24.4 |
| Totals | 87 | 3178 | 712 | 1301 | .547 | 351 | 715 | .491 | 1103 | 134 | 1949 | 12.7 | 1.5 | 22.4 |

Three-point field goals: 1995-96, 0-for-3. 1996-97, 1-for-10 (.100). Totals, 1-for-13 (.077).

## NBA REGULAR-SEASON RECORD

| | | | | | | | | | REBOUNDS | | | | | | | | AVERAGES | | |
| Season Team | G | Min. | FGM | FGA | Pct. | FTM | FTA | Pct. | Off. | Def. | Tot. | Ast. | St. | Blk. | TO | Pts. | RPG | APG | PPG |
|---|---|---|---|---|---|---|---|---|---|---|---|---|---|---|---|---|---|---|---|
| 97-98—Golden State | 55 | 656 | 69 | 170 | .406 | 27 | 62 | .435 | 73 | 111 | 184 | 14 | 13 | 52 | 50 | 165 | 3.3 | 0.3 | 3.0 |
| 98-99—Golden State | 44 | 614 | 52 | 121 | .430 | 25 | 51 | .490 | 79 | 115 | 194 | 18 | 15 | 43 | 31 | 129 | 4.4 | 0.4 | 2.9 |
| 99-00—Golden State | 76 | 1654 | 193 | 380 | .508 | 34 | 90 | .378 | 174 | 250 | 424 | 42 | 26 | 136 | 71 | 420 | 5.6 | 0.6 | 5.5 |
| 00-01—Golden State | 58 | 1457 | 156 | 375 | .416 | 30 | 68 | .441 | 156 | 249 | 405 | 48 | 31 | 156 | 79 | 342 | 7.0 | 0.8 | 5.9 |
| 01-02—Golden State | 79 | 1485 | 171 | 385 | .444 | 37 | 93 | .398 | 150 | 234 | 384 | 41 | 36 | 168 | 76 | 379 | 4.9 | 0.5 | 4.8 |
| 02-03—Golden State | 82 | 1787 | 185 | 345 | .536 | 70 | 104 | .673 | 176 | 314 | 490 | 37 | 40 | 205 | 73 | 440 | 6.0 | 0.5 | 5.4 |
| 03-04—Golden State | 44 | 572 | 59 | 130 | .454 | 19 | 35 | .543 | 54 | 113 | 167 | 17 | 6 | 46 | 21 | 137 | 3.8 | 0.4 | 3.1 |
| 04-05—Golden State | 78 | 1700 | 156 | 311 | .502 | 40 | 72 | .556 | 165 | 264 | 429 | 56 | 26 | 159 | 58 | 352 | 5.5 | 0.7 | 4.5 |
| Totals | 516 | 9925 | 1041 | 2217 | .470 | 282 | 575 | .490 | 1027 | 1650 | 2677 | 273 | 193 | 965 | 459 | 2364 | 5.2 | 0.5 | 4.6 |

Three-point field goals: 1997-98, 0-for-1. 2002-03, 0-for-1. Totals, 0-for-2 (.000).
Personal fouls/disqualifications: 1997-98, 94/0. 1998-99, 90/0. 1999-00, 218/2. 2000-01, 136/0. 2001-02, 179/2. 2002-03, 214/3. 2003-04, 68/1. 2004-05, 201/5. Totals, 1200/13.

# FRAHM, RICHIE                    G

**PERSONAL:** Born August 14, 1977 ... 6-5/210. (1.96/95.3).
**HIGH SCHOOL:** Battle Ground (Wash.).
**COLLEGE:** Gonzaga.
**TRANSACTIONS/CAREER NOTES:** Not drafted by an NBA franchise. ... Played in Philippines (2001-02). ... Played in American Basketball Association (2001-02). ... Played in Turkey (2002-03). ... Signed as free agent by Seattle SuperSonics (September 27, 2003). ... Selected by Charlotte Bobcats from SuperSonics in NBA Expansion Draft (June 22, 2004). ... Signed as free agent by Portland Trail Blazers (July 15, 2004).

## COLLEGIATE RECORD

| | | | | | | | | | | | | AVERAGES | | |
| Season Team | G | Min. | FGM | FGA | Pct. | FTM | FTA | Pct. | Reb. | Ast. | Pts. | RPG | APG | PPG |
|---|---|---|---|---|---|---|---|---|---|---|---|---|---|---|
| 96-97—Gonzaga | 27 | 381 | 44 | 107 | .411 | 17 | 23 | .739 | 57 | 25 | 125 | 2.1 | 0.9 | 4.6 |
| 97-98—Gonzaga | 33 | 899 | 132 | 292 | .452 | 58 | 70 | .829 | 127 | 60 | 399 | 3.8 | 1.8 | 12.1 |
| 98-99—Gonzaga | 35 | 980 | 165 | 378 | .437 | 81 | 100 | .810 | 149 | 70 | 504 | 4.3 | 2.0 | 14.4 |
| 99-00—Gonzaga | 35 | 1165 | 194 | 414 | .469 | 115 | 146 | .788 | 153 | 88 | 593 | 4.4 | 2.5 | 16.9 |
| Totals | 130 | 3425 | 535 | 1191 | .449 | 271 | 339 | .799 | 486 | 243 | 1621 | 3.7 | 1.9 | 12.5 |

Three-point field goals: 1996-97, 20-for-48 (.417). 1997-98, 77-for-173 (.445). 1998-99, 93-for-217 (.429). 1999-00, 90-for-224 (.402). Totals, 280-for-662 (.423).

## NBA REGULAR-SEASON RECORD

| | | | | | | | | | REBOUNDS | | | | | | | | AVERAGES | | |
| Season Team | G | Min. | FGM | FGA | Pct. | FTM | FTA | Pct. | Off. | Def. | Tot. | Ast. | St. | Blk. | TO | Pts. | RPG | APG | PPG |
|---|---|---|---|---|---|---|---|---|---|---|---|---|---|---|---|---|---|---|---|
| 03-04—Seattle | 54 | 469 | 63 | 139 | .453 | 23 | 26 | .885 | 12 | 44 | 56 | 24 | 16 | 4 | 7 | 183 | 1.0 | 0.4 | 3.4 |
| 04-05—Portland | 43 | 499 | 56 | 140 | .400 | 21 | 25 | .840 | 17 | 44 | 61 | 30 | 15 | 4 | 14 | 164 | 1.4 | 0.7 | 3.8 |
| Totals | 97 | 968 | 119 | 279 | .427 | 44 | 51 | .863 | 29 | 88 | 117 | 54 | 31 | 8 | 21 | 347 | 1.2 | 0.6 | 3.6 |

Three-point field goals: 2003-04, 34-for-92 (.370). 2004-05, 31-for-80 (.388). Totals, 65-for-172 (.378).
Personal fouls/disqualifications: 2003-04, 50/0. 2004-05, 35/0. Totals, 85/0.

# FRANCIS, STEVE                    G                    MAGIC

**PERSONAL:** Born February 21, 1977, in Silver Spring, Md. ... 6-3/195. (1.91/88.5). ... Full name: Steve D'Shawn Francis
**HIGH SCHOOL:** Montgomery Blair (Silver Spring, Md.).
**JUNIOR COLLEGE:** San Jacinto College (Texas), then Allegany (Md.) C.
**COLLEGE:** Maryland.
**TRANSACTIONS/CAREER NOTES:** Selected after junior season by Vancouver Grizzlies in first round (second pick overall)

F

of 1999 NBA Draft. ... Draft rights traded by Grizzlies with F Tony Massenburg to Houston Rockets as part of three-way deal in which Grizzlies received G Michael Dickerson, F/C Othella Harrington, G Brent Price, F/C Antoine Carr and future first-round draft choice from Rockets, Rockets received F Don MacLean and future first-round draft choice from Orlando Magic, and Magic received G Michael Smith, G/F Rodrick Rhodes, G Lee Mayberry and F Makhtar Ndiaye from Grizzles (August 27, 1999). ... Traded by Rockets with G Cuttino Mobley and C Kelvin Cato to Orlando Magic for G Tracy McGrady, F Juwan Howard, G Tyronn Lue and G Reece Gaines (June 29, 2004).

## COLLEGIATE RECORD

**NOTES:** The Sporting News All-America second team (1999).

| Season Team | G | Min. | FGM | FGA | Pct. | FTM | FTA | Pct. | Reb. | Ast. | Pts. | RPG | APG | PPG |
|---|---|---|---|---|---|---|---|---|---|---|---|---|---|---|
| 96-97—San Jacinto College....... | 35 | 971 | 138 | 248 | .556 | 146 | 184 | .793 | 263 | 264 | 437 | 7.5 | 7.5 | 12.5 |
| 97-98—Allegany C.C. ................. | 35 | ... | 295 | 561 | .526 | 204 | 248 | .823 | 248 | 304 | 885 | 7.1 | 8.7 | 25.3 |
| 98-99—Maryland ...................... | 34 | 1044 | 205 | 392 | .523 | 124 | 157 | .790 | 154 | 152 | 579 | 4.5 | 4.5 | 17.0 |
| **Junior College Totals**............. | 70 | 971 | 433 | 809 | .535 | 350 | 432 | .810 | 511 | 568 | 1322 | 7.3 | 8.1 | 18.9 |
| **4-Year-College Totals**............. | 34 | 1044 | 205 | 392 | .523 | 124 | 157 | .790 | 154 | 152 | 579 | 4.5 | 4.5 | 17.0 |

Three-point field goals: 1996-97, 15-for-39 (.385). 1997-98, 91-for-241 (.378). 1998-99, 45-for-116 (.388). Totals, 151-for-396 (.381).

## NBA REGULAR-SEASON RECORD

**HONORS:** NBA Co-Rookie of the Year (2000). ... NBA All-Rookie first team (2000).

| Season Team | G | Min. | FGM | FGA | Pct. | FTM | FTA | Pct. | Off. | Def. | Tot. | Ast. | St. | Blk. | TO | Pts. | RPG | APG | PPG |
|---|---|---|---|---|---|---|---|---|---|---|---|---|---|---|---|---|---|---|---|
| 99-00—Houston......... | 77 | 2776 | 497 | 1117 | .445 | 287 | 365 | .786 | 152 | 257 | 409 | 507 | 118 | 29 | 306 | 1388 | 5.3 | 6.6 | 18.0 |
| 00-01—Houston......... | 80 | 3194 | 550 | 1219 | .451 | 358 | 438 | .817 | 190 | 363 | 553 | 517 | 141 | 31 | 265 | 1591 | 6.9 | 6.5 | 19.9 |
| 01-02—Houston......... | 57 | 2343 | 420 | 1007 | .417 | 326 | 422 | .773 | 102 | 299 | 401 | 362 | 71 | 25 | 221 | 1234 | 7.0 | 6.4 | 21.6 |
| 02-03—Houston......... | 81 | 3318 | 571 | 1312 | .435 | 476 | 595 | .800 | 159 | 340 | 499 | 502 | 141 | 41 | 299 | 1703 | 6.2 | 6.2 | 21.0 |
| 03-04—Houston......... | 79 | 3194 | 450 | 1117 | .403 | 337 | 435 | .775 | 116 | 317 | 433 | 493 | 139 | 35 | 294 | 1310 | 5.5 | 6.2 | 16.6 |
| 04-05—Orlando........... | 78 | 2978 | 563 | 1330 | .423 | 499 | 606 | .823 | 126 | 324 | 450 | 547 | 112 | 28 | 317 | 1663 | 5.8 | 7.0 | 21.3 |
| **Totals** ................... | 452 | 17803 | 3051 | 7102 | .430 | 2283 | 2861 | .798 | 845 | 1900 | 2745 | 2928 | 722 | 189 | 1702 | 8889 | 6.1 | 6.5 | 19.7 |

Three-point field goals: 1999-00, 107-for-310 (.345). 2000-01, 133-for-336 (.396). 2001-02, 68-for-210 (.324). 2002-03, 85-for-240 (.354). 2003-04, 73-for-250 (.292). 2004-05, 38-for-127 (.299). Totals, 504-for-1473 (.342).

Personal fouls/disqualifications: 1999-00, 231/2. 2000-01, 274/7. 2001-02, 172/2. 2002-03, 251/2. 2003-04, 257/3. 2004-05, 273/5. Totals, 1458/21.

## NBA PLAYOFF RECORD

| Season Team | G | Min. | FGM | FGA | Pct. | FTM | FTA | Pct. | Off. | Def. | Tot. | Ast. | St. | Blk. | TO | Pts. | RPG | APG | PPG |
|---|---|---|---|---|---|---|---|---|---|---|---|---|---|---|---|---|---|---|---|
| 03-04—Houston......... | 5 | 222 | 30 | 70 | .429 | 29 | 40 | .725 | 6 | 36 | 42 | 38 | 7 | 1 | 21 | 96 | 8.4 | 7.6 | 19.2 |

Three-point field goals: 2003-04, 7-for-17 (.412). Totals, 7-for-17 (.412).

Personal fouls/disqualifications: 2003-04, 18/1. Totals, 18/1.

## NBA ALL-STAR GAME RECORD

| Season Team | Min. | FGM | FGA | Pct. | FTM | FTA | Pct. | Off. | Def. | Tot. | Ast. | PF | Dq. | St. | Blk. | TO | Pts. |
|---|---|---|---|---|---|---|---|---|---|---|---|---|---|---|---|---|---|
| 2002—Houston ............... | 18 | 1 | 8 | .125 | 1 | 2 | .500 | 1 | 1 | 2 | 3 | 1 | 0 | 2 | 0 | 2 | 3 |
| 2003—Houston ............... | 32 | 9 | 12 | .750 | 0 | 0 | ... | 1 | 1 | 2 | 9 | 1 | 0 | 0 | 0 | 3 | 20 |
| 2004—Houston ............... | 23 | 6 | 9 | .667 | 0 | 0 | ... | 1 | 3 | 4 | 4 | 1 | 0 | 0 | 0 | 1 | 13 |
| **Totals**........................... | 73 | 16 | 29 | .552 | 1 | 2 | .500 | 3 | 5 | 8 | 16 | 3 | 0 | 2 | 0 | 6 | 36 |

Three-point field goals: 2002, 0-for-1. 2003, 2-for-3 (.667). 2004, 1-for-2 (.500). Totals, 3-for-6 (.500).

# FREIJE, MATT        F

**PERSONAL:** Born October 2, 1981, in Overland Park, Kan. ... 6-10/249. (2.08/112.9). ... Full name: Matthew Wayne Freije.
**HIGH SCHOOL:** Shawnee Mission West (Overland Park, Kan.).
**COLLEGE:** Vanderbilt.
**TRANSACTIONS/CAREER NOTES:** Selected by Miami Heat in second round (53rd pick overall) of 2004 NBA Draft. ... Waived by Heat (November 14, 2005). ... Signed as free agent by New Orleans Hornets (November 19, 2005). ... Waived by Hornets (January 21, 2005).

## COLLEGIATE RECORD

**NOTES:** The Sporting News All-America third team (2004).

| Season Team | G | Min. | FGM | FGA | Pct. | FTM | FTA | Pct. | Reb. | Ast. | Pts. | RPG | APG | PPG |
|---|---|---|---|---|---|---|---|---|---|---|---|---|---|---|
| 00-01—Vanderbilt...................... | 27 | 645 | 98 | 197 | .497 | 61 | 77 | .792 | 120 | 16 | 280 | 4.4 | 0.6 | 10.4 |
| 01-02—Vanderbilt...................... | 32 | 939 | 171 | 367 | .466 | 109 | 142 | .768 | 164 | 35 | 484 | 5.1 | 1.1 | 15.1 |
| 02-03—Vanderbilt...................... | 29 | 903 | 178 | 402 | .443 | 99 | 124 | .798 | 129 | 33 | 520 | 4.4 | 1.1 | 17.9 |
| 03-04—Vanderbilt...................... | 33 | 985 | 185 | 446 | .415 | 175 | 222 | .788 | 178 | 30 | 607 | 5.4 | 0.9 | 18.4 |
| **Totals** ...................................... | 121 | 3472 | 632 | 1412 | .448 | 444 | 565 | .786 | 591 | 114 | 1891 | 4.9 | 0.9 | 15.6 |

Three-point field goals: 2000-01, 23-for-59 (.390). 2001-02, 33-for-97 (.340). 2002-03, 65-for-185 (.351). 2003-04, 62-for-174 (.356). Totals, 183-for-515 (.355).

## NBA REGULAR-SEASON RECORD

| Season Team | G | Min. | FGM | FGA | Pct. | FTM | FTA | Pct. | Off. | Def. | Tot. | Ast. | St. | Blk. | TO | Pts. | RPG | APG | PPG |
|---|---|---|---|---|---|---|---|---|---|---|---|---|---|---|---|---|---|---|---|
| 04-05—New Orleans ... | 23 | 441 | 37 | 127 | .291 | 5 | 8 | .625 | 16 | 45 | 61 | 20 | 13 | 2 | 17 | 93 | 2.7 | 0.9 | 4.0 |

Three-point field goals: 2004-05, 14-for-54 (.259). Totals, 14-for-54 (.259).

Personal fouls/disqualifications: 2004-05, 40/1. Totals, 40/1.

# FUNDERBURKE, LAWRENCE          F

**PERSONAL:** Born December 15, 1970, in Columbus, Ohio. ... 6-9/230. (2.06/104.3).
**HIGH SCHOOL:** Worthington (Ohio) Christian, then Wehrle (Columbu.
**JUNIOR COLLEGE:** St. Catharine College (Ky.).
**COLLEGE:** Indiana, then Ohio State.
**TRANSACTIONS/CAREER NOTES:** Selected by Sacramento Kings in second round (51st pick overall) of 1994 NBA Draft. ... Played in Greece (1994-96). ... Played in France (1996-97). ... Waived by Kings (February 23, 2004). ... Signed as free agent by Chicago Bulls (April 18, 2005).

### COLLEGIATE RECORD

| Season Team | G | Min. | FGM | FGA | Pct. | FTM | FTA | Pct. | Reb. | Ast. | Pts. | RPG | APG | PPG |
|---|---|---|---|---|---|---|---|---|---|---|---|---|---|---|
| 89-90—Indiana | 6 | 144 | 28 | 57 | .491 | 14 | 27 | .519 | 40 | 8 | 70 | 6.7 | 1.3 | 11.7 |
| 89-90—St. Catharine | | | | | | | | Did not play. | | | | | | |
| 90-91—Ohio State | | | | | | | Did not play—transfer student. | | | | | | | |
| 91-92—Ohio State | 23 | 668 | 115 | 210 | .548 | 51 | 78 | .654 | 149 | 18 | 281 | 6.5 | 0.8 | 12.2 |
| 92-93—Ohio State | 28 | 878 | 186 | 349 | .533 | 84 | 135 | .622 | 190 | 34 | 457 | 6.8 | 1.2 | 16.3 |
| 93-94—Ohio State | 29 | 847 | 188 | 345 | .545 | 63 | 106 | .594 | 190 | 28 | 441 | 6.6 | 1.0 | 15.2 |
| **Totals** | 86 | 2537 | 517 | 961 | .538 | 212 | 346 | .613 | 569 | 88 | 1249 | 6.6 | 1.0 | 14.5 |

Three-point field goals: 1992-93, 1-for-3 (.333). 1993-94, 2-for-7 (.286). Totals, 3-for-10 (.300).

### GREEK LEAGUE RECORD

| Season Team | G | Min. | FGM | FGA | Pct. | FTM | FTA | Pct. | Reb. | Ast. | Pts. | RPG | APG | PPG |
|---|---|---|---|---|---|---|---|---|---|---|---|---|---|---|
| 94-95—Ampelokipi Afisorama | 25 | 971 | 236 | 473 | .499 | 141 | 192 | .734 | 189 | 26 | 627 | 7.6 | 1.0 | 25.1 |
| 95-96—PAOK | 14 | ... | ... | ... | ... | ... | ... | ... | 121 | 20 | 244 | 8.6 | 1.4 | 17.4 |
| **Totals** | 39 | 971 | 236 | 473 | .499 | 141 | 192 | .734 | 310 | 46 | 871 | 7.9 | 1.2 | 22.3 |

Three-point field goals: 1994-95, 14-for-55 (.255). Totals, 14-for-55 (.255).
Personal fouls/disqualifications: 1994-95, 146/0. Totals, 146/0.

### FRENCH LEAGUE RECORD

| Season Team | G | Min. | FGM | FGA | Pct. | FTM | FTA | Pct. | Reb. | Ast. | Pts. | RPG | APG | PPG |
|---|---|---|---|---|---|---|---|---|---|---|---|---|---|---|
| 96-97—Pau Orthez | 20 | 889 | 181 | 283 | .640 | 59 | 82 | .720 | 155 | 37 | 444 | 7.8 | 1.9 | 22.2 |

### NBA REGULAR-SEASON RECORD

| Season Team | G | Min. | FGM | FGA | Pct. | FTM | FTA | Pct. | Off. | Def. | Tot. | Ast. | St. | Blk. | TO | Pts. | RPG | APG | PPG |
|---|---|---|---|---|---|---|---|---|---|---|---|---|---|---|---|---|---|---|---|
| 97-98—Sacramento | 52 | 1094 | 191 | 390 | .490 | 110 | 162 | .679 | 80 | 154 | 234 | 63 | 19 | 15 | 62 | 493 | 4.5 | 1.2 | 9.5 |
| 98-99—Sacramento | 47 | 936 | 167 | 299 | .559 | 85 | 120 | .708 | 101 | 121 | 222 | 30 | 22 | 23 | 52 | 420 | 4.7 | 0.6 | 8.9 |
| 99-00—Sacramento | 75 | 1026 | 184 | 352 | .523 | 115 | 163 | .706 | 98 | 136 | 234 | 33 | 32 | 20 | 40 | 483 | 3.1 | 0.4 | 6.4 |
| 00-01—Sacramento | 59 | 698 | 120 | 242 | .496 | 48 | 77 | .623 | 74 | 122 | 196 | 17 | 9 | 13 | 32 | 288 | 3.3 | 0.3 | 4.9 |
| 01-02—Sacramento | 56 | 722 | 115 | 245 | .469 | 34 | 56 | .607 | 76 | 122 | 198 | 32 | 11 | 18 | 33 | 264 | 3.5 | 0.6 | 4.7 |
| 02-03—Sacramento | 27 | 229 | 32 | 72 | .444 | 10 | 17 | .588 | 17 | 38 | 55 | 8 | 1 | 11 | 6 | 74 | 2.0 | 0.3 | 2.7 |
| 04-05—Chicago | 2 | 21 | 3 | 6 | .500 | 3 | 5 | .600 | 1 | 2 | 3 | 0 | 0 | 0 | 0 | 9 | 1.5 | 0.0 | 4.5 |
| **Totals** | 318 | 4726 | 812 | 1606 | .506 | 405 | 600 | .675 | 447 | 695 | 1142 | 183 | 94 | 100 | 225 | 2031 | 3.6 | 0.6 | 6.4 |

Three-point field goals: 1997-98, 1-for-7 (.143). 1998-99, 1-for-5 (.200). 1999-00, 0-for-2. 2001-02, 0-for-3. Totals, 2-for-17 (.118).
Personal fouls/disqualifications: 1997-98, 56/0. 1998-99, 77/0. 1999-00, 91/0. 2000-01, 44/0. 2001-02, 65/0. 2002-03, 25/0. 2004-05, 2/0. Totals, 360/0.

### NBA PLAYOFF RECORD

| Season Team | G | Min. | FGM | FGA | Pct. | FTM | FTA | Pct. | Off. | Def. | Tot. | Ast. | St. | Blk. | TO | Pts. | RPG | APG | PPG |
|---|---|---|---|---|---|---|---|---|---|---|---|---|---|---|---|---|---|---|---|
| 98-99—Sacramento | 3 | 31 | 5 | 12 | .417 | 0 | 0 | ... | 2 | 2 | 4 | 1 | 3 | 0 | 3 | 10 | 1.3 | 0.3 | 3.3 |
| 99-00—Sacramento | 4 | 34 | 4 | 9 | .444 | 2 | 4 | .500 | 4 | 7 | 11 | 0 | 1 | 0 | 0 | 10 | 2.8 | 0.0 | 2.5 |
| 00-01—Sacramento | 3 | 17 | 3 | 8 | .375 | 1 | 1 | 1.000 | 4 | 2 | 6 | 0 | 2 | 2 | 1 | 7 | 2.0 | 0.0 | 2.3 |
| 01-02—Sacramento | 5 | 20 | 2 | 3 | .667 | 2 | 2 | 1.000 | 1 | 1 | 2 | 0 | 0 | 0 | 0 | 6 | 0.4 | 0.0 | 1.2 |
| 02-03—Sacramento | 6 | 15 | 3 | 8 | .375 | 3 | 4 | .750 | 3 | 5 | 8 | 0 | 0 | 0 | 1 | 9 | 1.3 | 0.0 | 1.5 |
| 04-05—Chicago | 5 | 28 | 1 | 2 | .500 | 1 | 2 | .500 | 0 | 3 | 3 | 1 | 0 | 0 | 0 | 3 | 0.6 | 0.2 | 0.6 |
| **Totals** | 26 | 145 | 18 | 42 | .429 | 9 | 13 | .692 | 14 | 20 | 34 | 2 | 6 | 2 | 5 | 45 | 1.3 | 0.1 | 1.7 |

Personal fouls/disqualifications: 1998-99, 3/0. 2000-01, 4/0. 2001-02, 5/0. 2002-03, 2/0. 2004-05, 8/0. Totals, 22/0.

# GADZURIC, DAN          C          BUCKS

**PERSONAL:** Born August 2, 1978, in Den Haag, Holland. ... 6-11/240. (2.11/108.9).
**HIGH SCHOOL:** Gov. Drummer Academy (Byfield, Mass.).
**COLLEGE:** UCLA.
**TRANSACTIONS/CAREER NOTES:** Selected by Milwaukee Bucks in second round (34th pick overall) of 2002 NBA Draft.

### COLLEGIATE RECORD

| Season Team | G | Min. | FGM | FGA | Pct. | FTM | FTA | Pct. | Reb. | Ast. | Pts. | RPG | APG | PPG |
|---|---|---|---|---|---|---|---|---|---|---|---|---|---|---|
| 98-99—UCLA | 24 | 480 | 88 | 163 | .540 | 31 | 62 | .500 | 136 | 17 | 207 | 5.7 | 0.7 | 8.6 |
| 99-00—UCLA | 33 | 740 | 140 | 248 | .565 | 39 | 101 | .386 | 136 | 17 | 319 | 4.1 | 0.5 | 9.7 |

**G**

| Season Team | G | Min. | FGM | FGA | Pct. | FTM | FTA | Pct. | Reb. | Ast. | Pts. | AVERAGES RPG | APG | PPG |
|---|---|---|---|---|---|---|---|---|---|---|---|---|---|---|
| 00-01—UCLA | 32 | 861 | 156 | 292 | .534 | 63 | 139 | .453 | 275 | 18 | 375 | 8.6 | 0.6 | 11.7 |
| 01-02—UCLA | 33 | 865 | 164 | 296 | .554 | 58 | 123 | .472 | 255 | 23 | 386 | 7.7 | 0.7 | 11.7 |
| Totals | 122 | 2946 | 548 | 999 | .549 | 191 | 425 | .449 | 802 | 75 | 1287 | 6.6 | 0.6 | 10.5 |

Three-point field goals: 2001-02, 0-for-1. Totals, 0-for-1 (.000).

### NBA REGULAR-SEASON RECORD

| Season Team | G | Min. | FGM | FGA | Pct. | FTM | FTA | Pct. | REBOUNDS Off. | Def. | Tot. | Ast. | St. | Blk. | TO | Pts. | AVERAGES RPG | APG | PPG |
|---|---|---|---|---|---|---|---|---|---|---|---|---|---|---|---|---|---|---|---|
| 02-03—Milwaukee | 49 | 760 | 70 | 145 | .483 | 29 | 56 | .518 | 66 | 131 | 197 | 9 | 22 | 52 | 27 | 169 | 4.0 | 0.2 | 3.4 |
| 03-04—Milwaukee | 75 | 1260 | 183 | 349 | .524 | 58 | 118 | .492 | 126 | 220 | 346 | 28 | 51 | 105 | 45 | 424 | 4.6 | 0.4 | 5.7 |
| 04-05—Milwaukee | 81 | 1783 | 243 | 451 | .539 | 107 | 199 | .538 | 261 | 413 | 674 | 30 | 47 | 106 | 81 | 593 | 8.3 | 0.4 | 7.3 |
| Totals | 205 | 3803 | 496 | 945 | .525 | 194 | 373 | .520 | 453 | 764 | 1217 | 67 | 120 | 263 | 153 | 1186 | 5.9 | 0.3 | 5.8 |

Three-point field goals: 2002-03, 0-for-1. 2003-04, 0-for-1. Totals, 0-for-2 (.000).
Personal fouls/disqualifications: 2002-03, 125/3. 2003-04, 186/0. 2004-05, 224/1. Totals, 535/4.

### NBA PLAYOFF RECORD

| Season Team | G | Min. | FGM | FGA | Pct. | FTM | FTA | Pct. | REBOUNDS Off. | Def. | Tot. | Ast. | St. | Blk. | TO | Pts. | AVERAGES RPG | APG | PPG |
|---|---|---|---|---|---|---|---|---|---|---|---|---|---|---|---|---|---|---|---|
| 03-04—Milwaukee | 1 | 9 | 2 | 4 | .500 | 0 | 1 | .000 | 0 | 1 | 1 | 2 | 1 | 0 | 0 | 4 | 1.0 | 2.0 | 4.0 |

Personal fouls/disqualifications: 2003-04, 1/0. Totals, 1/0.

# GAINES, REECE     G     BUCKS

**PERSONAL:** Born January 7, 1981, in Madison, Wis. ... 6-6/205. (1.98/93.0). ... Full name: Clifton Reece Gaines
**HIGH SCHOOL:** Madison West (Madison, Wis.).
**COLLEGE:** Louisville.
**TRANSACTIONS/CAREER NOTES:** Selected by Orlando Magic in first round (15th overall pick) of 2003 NBA Draft. ... Traded by Magic with G Tracy McGrady, F Juwan Howard and G Tyronn Lue to Houston Rockets for G Steve Francis, G Cuttino Mobley and C Kelvin Cato (June 29, 2004). ... Traded by Rockets with second-round picks in 2006 and 2007 NBA drafts to Milwaukee Bucks for G Mike James and C Zendon Hamilton (February 24, 2005).

### COLLEGIATE RECORD

**NOTES:** The Sporting News All-America third team (2003).

| Season Team | G | Min. | FGM | FGA | Pct. | FTM | FTA | Pct. | Reb. | Ast. | Pts. | AVERAGES RPG | APG | PPG |
|---|---|---|---|---|---|---|---|---|---|---|---|---|---|---|
| 99-00—Louisville | 31 | 921 | 98 | 220 | .445 | 66 | 86 | .767 | 101 | 104 | 281 | 3.3 | 3.4 | 9.1 |
| 00-01—Louisville | 30 | 946 | 148 | 337 | .439 | 81 | 120 | .675 | 105 | 98 | 417 | 3.5 | 3.3 | 13.9 |
| 01-02—Louisville | 32 | 1049 | 209 | 458 | .456 | 164 | 205 | .800 | 124 | 114 | 673 | 3.9 | 3.6 | 21.0 |
| 02-03—Louisville | 32 | 1030 | 177 | 383 | .462 | 145 | 197 | .736 | 94 | 159 | 574 | 2.9 | 5.0 | 17.9 |
| Totals | 125 | 3946 | 632 | 1398 | .452 | 456 | 608 | .750 | 424 | 475 | 1945 | 3.4 | 3.8 | 15.6 |

Three-point field goals: 1999-00, 19-for-61 (.311). 2000-01, 40-for-94 (.426). 2001-02, 91-for-241 (.378). 2002-03, 75-for-192 (.391). Totals, 225-for-588 (.383).

### NBA REGULAR-SEASON RECORD

| Season Team | G | Min. | FGM | FGA | Pct. | FTM | FTA | Pct. | REBOUNDS Off. | Def. | Tot. | Ast. | St. | Blk. | TO | Pts. | AVERAGES RPG | APG | PPG |
|---|---|---|---|---|---|---|---|---|---|---|---|---|---|---|---|---|---|---|---|
| 03-04—Orlando | 38 | 364 | 25 | 86 | .291 | 16 | 25 | .640 | 8 | 31 | 39 | 40 | 11 | 2 | 18 | 69 | 1.0 | 1.1 | 1.8 |
| 04-05—Houston-Mil. | 21 | 187 | 17 | 50 | .340 | 3 | 4 | .750 | 1 | 13 | 14 | 7 | 5 | 1 | 7 | 41 | 0.7 | 0.3 | 2.0 |
| Totals | 59 | 551 | 42 | 136 | .309 | 19 | 29 | .655 | 9 | 44 | 53 | 47 | 16 | 3 | 25 | 110 | 0.9 | 0.8 | 1.9 |

Three-point field goals: 2003-04, 3-for-10 (.300). 2004-05, 4-for-14 (.286). Totals, 7-for-24 (.292).
Personal fouls/disqualifications: 2003-04, 22/0. 2004-05, 17/0. Totals, 39/0.

# GARCIA, ALEX     G/F

**PERSONAL:** Born March 4, 1980 ... 6-3/195. (1.91/88.5).
**TRANSACTIONS/CAREER NOTES:** Not drafted by an NBA franchise. ... Played in Brazil (1999-2003).

### NBA REGULAR-SEASON RECORD

| Season Team | G | Min. | FGM | FGA | Pct. | FTM | FTA | Pct. | REBOUNDS Off. | Def. | Tot. | Ast. | St. | Blk. | TO | Pts. | AVERAGES RPG | APG | PPG |
|---|---|---|---|---|---|---|---|---|---|---|---|---|---|---|---|---|---|---|---|
| 03-04—San Antonio | 2 | 13 | 1 | 7 | .143 | 1 | 2 | .500 | 0 | 0 | 0 | 2 | 0 | 1 | 3 | 3 | 0.0 | 0.0 | 1.5 |
| 04-05—New Orleans | 8 | 146 | 18 | 52 | .346 | 3 | 4 | .750 | 7 | 8 | 15 | 18 | 4 | 1 | 8 | 44 | 1.9 | 2.3 | 5.5 |
| Totals | 10 | 159 | 19 | 59 | .322 | 4 | 6 | .667 | 7 | 8 | 15 | 18 | 6 | 1 | 9 | 47 | 1.5 | 1.8 | 4.7 |

Three-point field goals: 2004-05, 5-for-18 (.278). Totals, 5-for-18 (.278).
Personal fouls/disqualifications: 2004-05, 15/0. Totals, 15/0.

**G**

# GARNETT, KEVIN     F     TIMBERWOLVES

**PERSONAL:** Born May 19, 1976, in Mauldin, S.C. ... 6-11/220. (2.11/99.8).
**HIGH SCHOOL:** Mauldin (S.C.), then Farragut Academy (Chicago).
**COLLEGE:** Did not attend college.
**TRANSACTIONS/CAREER NOTES:** Selected out of high school by Minnesota Timberwolves in first round (fifth pick overall) of 1995 NBA Draft.
**MISCELLANEOUS:** Member of gold-medal-winning U.S. Olympic team (2000). ... Minnesota Timberwolves all-time points leader with 15,681, all-time steals leader with 1,089, all-time leading rebounder with 8,601, all-time assists leader with 3,525 and all-time blocked shots leader with 1,343 (1995-96 through 2004-05).

## NBA REGULAR-SEASON RECORD

**HONORS:** NBA Most Valuable Player (2004). ... All-NBA first team (2000, 2003, 2004). ... All-NBA second team (2001, 2002, 2005). ... All-NBA third team (1999). ... NBA All-Defensive first team (2000, 2001, 2002, 2003, 2004, 2005). ... NBA All-Rookie second team (1996).

| Season Team | G | Min. | FGM | FGA | Pct. | FTM | FTA | Pct. | REBOUNDS Off. | Def. | Tot. | Ast. | St. | Blk. | TO | Pts. | AVERAGES RPG | APG | PPG |
|---|---|---|---|---|---|---|---|---|---|---|---|---|---|---|---|---|---|---|---|
| 95-96—Minnesota | 80 | 2293 | 361 | 735 | .491 | 105 | 149 | .705 | 175 | 326 | 501 | 145 | 86 | 131 | 110 | 835 | 6.3 | 1.8 | 10.4 |
| 96-97—Minnesota | 77 | 2995 | 549 | 1100 | .499 | 205 | 272 | .754 | 190 | 428 | 618 | 236 | 105 | 163 | 175 | 1309 | 8.0 | 3.1 | 17.0 |
| 97-98—Minnesota | 82 | 3222 | 635 | 1293 | .491 | 245 | 332 | .738 | 222 | 564 | 786 | 348 | 139 | 150 | 192 | 1518 | 9.6 | 4.2 | 18.5 |
| 98-99—Minnesota | 47 | 1780 | 414 | 900 | .460 | 145 | 206 | .704 | 166 | 323 | 489 | 202 | 78 | 83 | 135 | 977 | 10.4 | 4.3 | 20.8 |
| 99-00—Minnesota | 81 | 3243 | 759 | 1526 | .497 | 309 | 404 | .765 | 223 | 733 | 956 | 401 | 120 | 126 | 268 | 1857 | 11.8 | 5.0 | 22.9 |
| 00-01—Minnesota | 81 | 3202 | 704 | 1475 | .477 | 357 | 467 | .764 | 219 | 702 | 921 | 401 | 111 | 145 | 230 | 1784 | 11.4 | 5.0 | 22.0 |
| 01-02—Minnesota | 81 | 3175 | 659 | 1401 | .470 | 359 | 448 | .801 | 243 | 738 | 981 | 422 | 96 | 126 | 229 | 1714 | 12.1 | 5.2 | 21.2 |
| 02-03—Minnesota | 82 | 3321 | 743 | 1481 | .502 | 377 | 502 | .751 | 244 | 858 | 1102 | 495 | 113 | 129 | 229 | 1883 | 13.4 | 6.0 | 23.0 |
| 03-04—Minnesota | 82 | 3231 | 804 | 1611 | .499 | 368 | 465 | .791 | 245 | 894 | 1139 | 409 | 120 | 178 | 212 | 1987 | 13.9 | 5.0 | 24.2 |
| 04-05—Minnesota | 82 | 3121 | 683 | 1360 | .502 | 445 | 549 | .811 | 247 | 861 | 1108 | 466 | 121 | 112 | 222 | 1817 | 13.5 | 5.7 | 22.2 |
| Totals | 775 | 29583 | 6311 | 12882 | .490 | 2915 | 3794 | .768 | 2174 | 6427 | 8601 | 3525 | 1089 | 1343 | 2002 | 15681 | 11.1 | 4.5 | 20.2 |

Three-point field goals: 1995-96, 8-for-28 (.286). 1996-97, 6-for-21 (.286). 1997-98, 3-for-16 (.188). 1998-99, 4-for-14 (.286). 1999-00, 30-for-81 (.370). 2000-01, 19-for-66 (.288). 2001-02, 37-for-116 (.319). 2002-03, 20-for-71 (.282). 2003-04, 11-for-43 (.256). 2004-05, 6-for-25 (.240). Totals, 144-for-481 (.299).

Personal fouls/disqualifications: 1995-96, 189/2. 1996-97, 199/2. 1997-98, 224/1. 1998-99, 152/5. 1999-00, 205/1. 2000-01, 204/0. 2001-02, 184/0. 2002-03, 199/0. 2003-04, 202/1. 2004-05, 207/0. Totals, 1965/12.

## NBA PLAYOFF RECORD

| Season Team | G | Min. | FGM | FGA | Pct. | FTM | FTA | Pct. | REBOUNDS Off. | Def. | Tot. | Ast. | St. | Blk. | TO | Pts. | AVERAGES RPG | APG | PPG |
|---|---|---|---|---|---|---|---|---|---|---|---|---|---|---|---|---|---|---|---|
| 96-97—Minnesota | 3 | 125 | 24 | 51 | .471 | 3 | 3 | 1.000 | 14 | 14 | 28 | 11 | 4 | 3 | 4 | 52 | 9.3 | 3.7 | 17.3 |
| 97-98—Minnesota | 5 | 194 | 36 | 75 | .480 | 7 | 9 | .778 | 17 | 31 | 48 | 20 | 4 | 12 | 22 | 79 | 9.6 | 4.0 | 15.8 |
| 98-99—Minnesota | 4 | 170 | 35 | 79 | .443 | 17 | 23 | .739 | 16 | 32 | 48 | 15 | 7 | 8 | 13 | 87 | 12.0 | 3.8 | 21.8 |
| 99-00—Minnesota | 4 | 171 | 30 | 78 | .385 | 13 | 16 | .813 | 13 | 30 | 43 | 35 | 5 | 3 | 11 | 75 | 10.8 | 8.8 | 18.8 |
| 00-01—Minnesota | 4 | 165 | 27 | 58 | .466 | 30 | 36 | .833 | 10 | 38 | 48 | 17 | 4 | 6 | 6 | 84 | 12.0 | 4.3 | 21.0 |
| 01-02—Minnesota | 3 | 130 | 24 | 56 | .429 | 23 | 32 | .719 | 16 | 40 | 56 | 15 | 5 | 5 | 12 | 72 | 18.7 | 5.0 | 24.0 |
| 02-03—Minnesota | 6 | 265 | 71 | 138 | .514 | 17 | 28 | .607 | 11 | 83 | 94 | 31 | 10 | 10 | 18 | 162 | 15.7 | 5.2 | 27.0 |
| 03-04—Minnesota | 18 | 783 | 168 | 372 | .452 | 97 | 125 | .776 | 39 | 224 | 263 | 92 | 24 | 41 | 75 | 438 | 14.6 | 5.1 | 24.3 |
| Totals | 47 | 2003 | 415 | 907 | .458 | 207 | 272 | .761 | 136 | 492 | 628 | 236 | 63 | 88 | 161 | 1049 | 13.4 | 5.0 | 22.3 |

Three-point field goals: 1996-97, 1-for-1 (1.000). 1998-99, 0-for-2. 1999-00, 2-for-3 (.667). 2000-01, 0-for-3. 2001-02, 1-for-2 (.500). 2002-03, 3-for-9 (.333). 2003-04, 5-for-16 (.313). Totals, 12-for-36 (.333).

Personal fouls/disqualifications: 1996-97, 6/0. 1997-98, 17/0. 1998-99, 10/0. 1999-00, 12/0. 2000-01, 13/0. 2001-02, 11/0. 2002-03, 23/1. 2003-04, 57/2. Totals, 149/3.

## NBA ALL-STAR GAME RECORD

**NOTES:** Shares record for most field goals in one game—17 (2003). ... NBA All-Star Game Most Valuable Player (2003).

| Season Team | Min. | FGM | FGA | Pct. | FTM | FTA | Pct. | REBOUNDS Off. | Def. | Tot. | Ast. | PF | Dq. | St. | Blk. | TO | Pts. |
|---|---|---|---|---|---|---|---|---|---|---|---|---|---|---|---|---|---|
| 1997—Minnesota | 18 | 1 | 7 | .143 | 4 | 4 | 1.000 | 1 | 8 | 9 | 1 | 2 | 0 | 0 | 1 | 0 | 6 |
| 1998—Minnesota | 21 | 6 | 11 | .545 | 0 | 0 | ... | 1 | 3 | 4 | 2 | 0 | ... | 2 | 1 | 3 | 12 |
| 2000—Minnesota | 35 | 10 | 19 | .526 | 4 | 4 | 1.000 | 3 | 7 | 10 | 5 | 1 | 0 | 1 | 1 | 0 | 24 |
| 2001—Minnesota | 27 | 7 | 12 | .583 | 0 | 0 | ... | 1 | 3 | 4 | 4 | 0 | 0 | 1 | 3 | 2 | 14 |
| 2002—Minnesota | 24 | 7 | 15 | .467 | 0 | 0 | ... | 6 | 6 | 12 | 2 | 1 | 0 | 2 | 0 | 0 | 14 |
| 2003—Minnesota | 41 | 17 | 24 | .708 | 3 | 3 | 1.000 | 1 | 8 | 9 | 3 | 3 | 0 | 5 | 1 | 4 | 37 |
| 2004—Minnesota | 29 | 6 | 14 | .429 | 0 | 0 | ... | 3 | 4 | 7 | 6 | 0 | 0 | 2 | 1 | 1 | 12 |
| 2005—Minnesota | 16 | 5 | 8 | .625 | 0 | 1 | .000 | 0 | 3 | 3 | 2 | 2 | 0 | 0 | 0 | 2 | 10 |
| Totals | 211 | 59 | 110 | .536 | 11 | 12 | .917 | 16 | 42 | 58 | 25 | 9 | 0 | 13 | 8 | 12 | 129 |

Three-point field goals: 1998, 0-for-1. 2000, 0-for-1. 2002, 0-for-1. 2004, 0-for-1. Totals, 0-for-4 (.000).

# GARRITY, PAT      F      MAGIC

**PERSONAL:** Born August 23, 1976, in Las Vegas. ... 6-9/238. (2.06/108.0). ... Full name: Patrick Joseph Garrity.
**HIGH SCHOOL:** Lewis Palmer (Monument, Colo.).
**COLLEGE:** Notre Dame.
**TRANSACTIONS/CAREER NOTES:** Selected by Milwaukee Bucks in first round (19th pick overall) of 1998 NBA Draft. ... Draft rights traded by Bucks with draft rights to C Dirk Nowitzki to Dallas Mavericks for draft rights to F Robert Traylor (June 24, 1998). ... Draft rights traded by Mavericks with F Martin Muursepp, G/F Bubba Wells and 1999 first-round draft choice to Phoenix Suns for G Steve Nash (June 24, 1998). ... Traded by Suns with F/C Danny Manning and two future first-round draft choices to Orlando Magic for G Anfernee Hardaway (August 5, 1999).

## COLLEGIATE RECORD

**NOTES:** The Sporting News All-America second team (1998).

| Season Team | G | Min. | FGM | FGA | Pct. | FTM | FTA | Pct. | Reb. | Ast. | Pts. | AVERAGES RPG | APG | PPG |
|---|---|---|---|---|---|---|---|---|---|---|---|---|---|---|
| 94-95—Notre Dame | 27 | 744 | 136 | 260 | .523 | 82 | 107 | .766 | 137 | 34 | 361 | 5.1 | 1.3 | 13.4 |
| 95-96—Notre Dame | 27 | 893 | 177 | 372 | .476 | 96 | 140 | .686 | 193 | 38 | 464 | 7.1 | 1.4 | 17.2 |
| 96-97—Notre Dame | 30 | 1056 | 221 | 457 | .484 | 152 | 196 | .776 | 221 | 84 | 633 | 7.4 | 2.8 | 21.1 |
| 97-98—Notre Dame | 27 | 956 | 214 | 445 | .481 | 159 | 212 | .750 | 225 | 66 | 627 | 8.3 | 2.4 | 23.2 |
| Totals | 111 | 3649 | 748 | 1534 | .488 | 489 | 655 | .747 | 776 | 222 | 2085 | 7.0 | 2.0 | 18.8 |

Three-point field goals: 1994-95, 7-for-18 (.389). 1995-96, 14-for-51 (.275). 1996-97, 39-for-102 (.382). 1997-98, 40-for-108 (.370). Totals, 100-for-279 (.358).

## NBA REGULAR-SEASON RECORD

| Season Team | G | Min. | FGM | FGA | Pct. | FTM | FTA | Pct. | REBOUNDS Off. | Def. | Tot. | Ast. | St. | Blk. | TO | Pts. | AVERAGES RPG | APG | PPG |
|---|---|---|---|---|---|---|---|---|---|---|---|---|---|---|---|---|---|---|---|
| 98-99—Phoenix | 39 | 538 | 85 | 170 | .500 | 40 | 56 | .714 | 26 | 49 | 75 | 18 | 8 | 3 | 20 | 217 | 1.9 | 0.5 | 5.6 |
| 99-00—Orlando | 82 | 1479 | 258 | 585 | .441 | 80 | 111 | .721 | 44 | 166 | 210 | 58 | 31 | 19 | 85 | 675 | 2.6 | 0.7 | 8.2 |

G

| Season Team | G | Min. | FGM | FGA | Pct. | FTM | FTA | Pct. | REBOUNDS Off. | Def. | Tot. | Ast. | St. | Blk. | TO | Pts. | AVERAGES RPG | APG | PPG |
|---|---|---|---|---|---|---|---|---|---|---|---|---|---|---|---|---|---|---|---|
| 00-01—Orlando.......... | 76 | 1579 | 223 | 576 | .387 | 85 | 98 | .867 | 51 | 159 | 210 | 51 | 40 | 15 | 68 | 628 | 2.8 | 0.7 | 8.3 |
| 01-02—Orlando.......... | 80 | 2406 | 327 | 767 | .426 | 61 | 73 | .836 | 77 | 261 | 338 | 99 | 61 | 28 | 68 | 884 | 4.2 | 1.2 | 11.1 |
| 02-03—Orlando.......... | 81 | 2584 | 312 | 744 | .419 | 83 | 100 | .830 | 72 | 234 | 306 | 121 | 62 | 20 | 77 | 868 | 3.8 | 1.5 | 10.7 |
| 03-04—Orlando.......... | 2 | 22 | 1 | 3 | .333 | 0 | 0 | ... | 0 | 0 | 0 | 1 | 0 | 0 | 0 | 2 | 0.0 | 0.5 | 1.0 |
| 04-05—Orlando.......... | 71 | 955 | 123 | 306 | .402 | 29 | 33 | .879 | 21 | 103 | 124 | 30 | 19 | 9 | 30 | 324 | 1.7 | 0.4 | 4.6 |
| Totals ................... | 431 | 9563 | 1329 | 3151 | .422 | 378 | 471 | .803 | 291 | 972 | 1263 | 378 | 221 | 94 | 348 | 3598 | 2.9 | 0.9 | 8.3 |

Three-point field goals: 1998-99, 7-for-18 (.389). 1999-00, 79-for-197 (.401). 2000-01, 97-for-224 (.433). 2001-02, 169-for-396 (.427). 2002-03, 161-for-407 (.396). 2004-05, 49-for-147 (.333). Totals, 562-for-1389 (.405).

Personal fouls/disqualifications: 1998-99, 62/0. 1999-00, 197/1. 2000-01, 241/3. 2001-02, 230/1. 2002-03, 255/1. 2003-04, 2/0. 2004-05, 107/0. Totals, 1094/6.

### NBA PLAYOFF RECORD

| Season Team | G | Min. | FGM | FGA | Pct. | FTM | FTA | Pct. | REBOUNDS Off. | Def. | Tot. | Ast. | St. | Blk. | TO | Pts. | AVERAGES RPG | APG | PPG |
|---|---|---|---|---|---|---|---|---|---|---|---|---|---|---|---|---|---|---|---|
| 98-99—Phoenix ......... | 3 | 52 | 9 | 17 | .529 | 6 | 6 | 1.000 | 6 | 3 | 9 | 1 | 1 | 1 | 3 | 27 | 3.0 | 0.3 | 9.0 |
| 00-01—Orlando.......... | 4 | 117 | 17 | 36 | .472 | 4 | 5 | .800 | 1 | 4 | 5 | 2 | 0 | 1 | 2 | 48 | 1.3 | 0.5 | 12.0 |
| 01-02—Orlando.......... | 4 | 147 | 12 | 32 | .375 | 3 | 4 | .750 | 4 | 26 | 30 | 9 | 2 | 1 | 3 | 34 | 7.5 | 2.3 | 8.5 |
| 02-03—Orlando.......... | 7 | 163 | 10 | 35 | .286 | 4 | 4 | 1.000 | 4 | 14 | 18 | 5 | 2 | 3 | 5 | 28 | 2.6 | 0.7 | 4.0 |
| Totals ................... | 18 | 479 | 48 | 120 | .400 | 17 | 19 | .895 | 15 | 47 | 62 | 17 | 5 | 6 | 13 | 137 | 3.4 | 0.9 | 7.6 |

Three-point field goals: 1998-99, 3-for-3 (1.000). 2000-01, 10-for-20 (.500). 2001-02, 7-for-18 (.389). 2002-03, 4-for-17 (.235). Totals, 24-for-58 (.414).

Personal fouls/disqualifications: 1998-99, 9/0. 2000-01, 11/0. 2001-02, 18/0. 2002-03, 24/0. Totals, 62/0.

## GASOL, PAU     F     GRIZZLIES

**PERSONAL:** Born July 6, 1980, in Barcelona, Spain. ... 7-0/227. (2.13/103.0).
**COLLEGE:** Did not attend college.
**TRANSACTIONS/CAREER NOTES:** Played in Spain (1998-2001). ... Selected by Atlanta Hawks in first round (third pick overall) of 2001 NBA Draft. ... Draft rights traded by Hawks with F/C Lorenzen Wright and G Brevin Knight to Memphis Grizzlies for F Shareef Abdur-Rahim and draft rights to G Jamaal Tinsley (July 19, 2001).
**MISCELLANEOUS:** Member of Spanish Olympic Team (2004).

### SPANISH RECORD

| Season Team | G | Min. | FGM | FGA | Pct. | FTM | FTA | Pct. | Reb. | Ast. | Pts. | AVERAGES RPG | APG | PPG |
|---|---|---|---|---|---|---|---|---|---|---|---|---|---|---|
| 98-99—FC Barcelona ................. | 2 | 11 | 2 | 4 | .500 | 1 | 3 | .333 | 2 | 1 | 6 | 1.0 | 0.5 | 3.0 |
| 99-00—FC Barcelona ................. | 26 | 385 | 40 | 79 | .506 | 23 | 44 | .523 | 68 | 12 | 109 | 2.6 | 0.5 | 4.2 |
| 00-01—FC Barcelona ................. | 30 | 716 | 129 | 235 | .549 | 70 | 119 | .588 | 156 | 23 | 328 | 5.2 | 0.8 | 10.9 |
| Totals ................................... | 58 | 1112 | 171 | 318 | .538 | 94 | 166 | .566 | 226 | 36 | 443 | 3.9 | 0.6 | 7.6 |

Three-point field goals: 1998-99, 1-for-3 (.333). 1999-00, 6-for-20 (.300). 2000-01, 15-for-43 (.349). Totals, 22-for-66 (.333).

Personal fouls/disqualifications: 1998-99, 1/0. 1999-00, 27/0. 2000-01, 58/0. Totals, 86/0.

### NBA REGULAR-SEASON RECORD

**HONORS:** NBA Rookie of the Year (2002). ... NBA All-Rookie first team (2002).

| Season Team | G | Min. | FGM | FGA | Pct. | FTM | FTA | Pct. | REBOUNDS Off. | Def. | Tot. | Ast. | St. | Blk. | TO | Pts. | AVERAGES RPG | APG | PPG |
|---|---|---|---|---|---|---|---|---|---|---|---|---|---|---|---|---|---|---|---|
| 01-02—Memphis ........ | 82 | 3007 | 551 | 1064 | .518 | 338 | 477 | .709 | 238 | 492 | 730 | 223 | 41 | 169 | 224 | 1441 | 8.9 | 2.7 | 17.6 |
| 02-03—Memphis ........ | 82 | 2948 | 569 | 1116 | .510 | 416 | 565 | .736 | 192 | 528 | 720 | 229 | 34 | 148 | 213 | 1555 | 8.8 | 2.8 | 19.0 |
| 03-04—Memphis ........ | 78 | 2458 | 506 | 1049 | .482 | 365 | 511 | .714 | 206 | 394 | 600 | 198 | 44 | 132 | 187 | 1381 | 7.7 | 2.5 | 17.7 |
| 04-05—Memphis ........ | 56 | 1790 | 357 | 695 | .514 | 282 | 367 | .768 | 130 | 280 | 410 | 135 | 37 | 93 | 137 | 997 | 7.3 | 2.4 | 17.8 |
| Totals ................... | 298 | 10203 | 1983 | 3924 | .505 | 1401 | 1920 | .730 | 766 | 1694 | 2460 | 785 | 156 | 542 | 761 | 5374 | 8.3 | 2.6 | 18.0 |

Three-point field goals: 2001-02, 1-for-5 (.200). 2002-03, 1-for-10 (.100). 2003-04, 4-for-15 (.267). 2004-05, 1-for-6 (.167). Totals, 7-for-36 (.194).

Personal fouls/disqualifications: 2001-02, 195/2. 2002-03, 220/3. 2003-04, 185/1. 2004-05, 146/1. Totals, 746/7.

### NBA PLAYOFF RECORD

| Season Team | G | Min. | FGM | FGA | Pct. | FTM | FTA | Pct. | REBOUNDS Off. | Def. | Tot. | Ast. | St. | Blk. | TO | Pts. | AVERAGES RPG | APG | PPG |
|---|---|---|---|---|---|---|---|---|---|---|---|---|---|---|---|---|---|---|---|
| 03-04—Memphis ........ | 4 | 134 | 28 | 49 | .571 | 18 | 20 | .900 | 4 | 16 | 20 | 10 | 4 | 6 | 5 | 74 | 5.0 | 2.5 | 18.5 |
| 04-05—Memphis ........ | 4 | 133 | 39 | 80 | .488 | 6 | 12 | .500 | 15 | 15 | 30 | 10 | 2 | 7 | 7 | 85 | 7.5 | 2.5 | 21.3 |
| Totals ................... | 8 | 267 | 67 | 129 | .519 | 24 | 32 | .750 | 19 | 31 | 50 | 20 | 6 | 13 | 12 | 159 | 6.3 | 2.5 | 19.9 |

Three-point field goals: 2004-05, 1-for-1 (1.000). Totals, 1-for-1 (1.000).

Personal fouls/disqualifications: 2003-04, 10/0. 2004-05, 12/0. Totals, 22/0.

## G

## GEORGE, DEVEAN     G/F     LAKERS

**PERSONAL:** Born August 29, 1977, in Minneapolis. ... 6-8/220. (2.03/99.8). ... Full name: Devean Jamar George
**HIGH SCHOOL:** Benilde-St. Margaret (St. Louis Park, Minn.).
**COLLEGE:** Augsburg (Minn.).
**TRANSACTIONS/CAREER NOTES:** Selected by Los Angeles Lakers in first round (23rd pick overall) of 1999 NBA Draft.
**MISCELLANEOUS:** Member of NBA championship team (2000, 2001, 2002).

### COLLEGIATE RECORD

| Season Team | G | Min. | FGM | FGA | Pct. | FTM | FTA | Pct. | Reb. | Ast. | Pts. | AVERAGES RPG | APG | PPG |
|---|---|---|---|---|---|---|---|---|---|---|---|---|---|---|
| 95-96—Augsburg (Minn.).......... | 17 | 500 | 93 | 185 | .503 | 55 | 78 | .705 | 111 | 28 | 258 | 6.5 | 1.6 | 15.2 |
| 96-97—Augsburg (Minn.).......... | 25 | 766 | 207 | 419 | .494 | 109 | 152 | .717 | 178 | 39 | 566 | 7.1 | 1.6 | 22.6 |
| 97-98—Augsburg (Minn.).......... | 26 | 751 | 218 | 433 | .503 | 185 | 246 | .752 | 262 | 31 | 664 | 10.1 | 1.2 | 25.5 |

| Season Team | G | Min. | FGM | FGA | Pct. | FTM | FTA | Pct. | Reb. | Ast. | Pts. | AVERAGES RPG | APG | PPG |
|---|---|---|---|---|---|---|---|---|---|---|---|---|---|---|
| 98-99—Augsburg (Minn.)........... | 28 | 969 | 281 | 542 | .518 | 163 | 213 | .765 | 317 | 58 | 770 | 11.3 | 2.1 | 27.5 |
| Totals ...................................... | 96 | 2986 | 799 | 1579 | .506 | 512 | 689 | .743 | 868 | 156 | 2258 | 9.0 | 1.6 | 23.5 |

Three-point field goals: 1995-96, 17-for-40 (.425). 1996-97, 43-for-129 (.333). 1997-98, 43-for-134 (.321). 1998-99, 45-for-138 (.326). Totals, 148-for-441 (.336).

## NBA REGULAR-SEASON RECORD

| Season Team | G | Min. | FGM | FGA | Pct. | FTM | FTA | Pct. | REBOUNDS Off. | Def. | Tot. | Ast. | St. | Blk. | TO | Pts. | AVERAGES RPG | APG | PPG |
|---|---|---|---|---|---|---|---|---|---|---|---|---|---|---|---|---|---|---|---|
| 99-00—L.A. Lakers ..... | 49 | 345 | 56 | 144 | .389 | 27 | 41 | .659 | 29 | 46 | 75 | 12 | 10 | 4 | 21 | 155 | 1.5 | 0.2 | 3.2 |
| 00-01—L.A. Lakers ..... | 59 | 593 | 64 | 207 | .309 | 39 | 55 | .709 | 35 | 75 | 110 | 19 | 15 | 15 | 34 | 182 | 1.9 | 0.3 | 3.1 |
| 01-02—L.A. Lakers ..... | 82 | 1759 | 215 | 523 | .411 | 85 | 126 | .675 | 78 | 225 | 303 | 111 | 71 | 42 | 66 | 581 | 3.7 | 1.4 | 7.1 |
| 02-03—L.A. Lakers ..... | 71 | 1613 | 180 | 461 | .390 | 83 | 105 | .790 | 91 | 195 | 286 | 92 | 56 | 38 | 65 | 492 | 4.0 | 1.3 | 6.9 |
| 03-04—L.A. Lakers ..... | 82 | 1951 | 233 | 571 | .408 | 73 | 96 | .760 | 87 | 245 | 332 | 112 | 81 | 38 | 88 | 604 | 4.0 | 1.4 | 7.4 |
| 04-05—L.A. Lakers ..... | 15 | 306 | 37 | 104 | .356 | 15 | 20 | .750 | 13 | 40 | 53 | 14 | 8 | 2 | 12 | 110 | 3.5 | 0.9 | 7.3 |
| Totals ................... | 358 | 6567 | 785 | 2010 | .391 | 322 | 443 | .727 | 333 | 826 | 1159 | 360 | 241 | 139 | 286 | 2124 | 3.2 | 1.0 | 5.9 |

Three-point field goals: 1999-00, 16-for-47 (.340). 2000-01, 15-for-68 (.221). 2001-02, 66-for-178 (.371). 2002-03, 49-for-132 (.371). 2003-04, 65-for-186 (.349). 2004-05, 21-for-58 (.362). Totals, 232-for-669 (.347).

Personal fouls/disqualifications: 1999-00, 54/0. 2000-01, 87/1. 2001-02, 190/3. 2002-03, 180/2. 2003-04, 189/4. 2004-05, 32/1. Totals, 732/11.

## NBA PLAYOFF RECORD

| Season Team | G | Min. | FGM | FGA | Pct. | FTM | FTA | Pct. | REBOUNDS Off. | Def. | Tot. | Ast. | St. | Blk. | TO | Pts. | AVERAGES RPG | APG | PPG |
|---|---|---|---|---|---|---|---|---|---|---|---|---|---|---|---|---|---|---|---|
| 99-00—L.A. Lakers ..... | 9 | 45 | 7 | 19 | .368 | 6 | 11 | .545 | 4 | 6 | 10 | 2 | 1 | 0 | 3 | 22 | 1.1 | 0.2 | 2.4 |
| 00-01—L.A. Lakers ..... | 7 | 27 | 6 | 12 | .500 | 1 | 2 | .500 | 3 | 2 | 5 | 1 | 0 | 0 | 3 | 14 | 0.7 | 0.1 | 2.0 |
| 01-02—L.A. Lakers ..... | 19 | 327 | 38 | 104 | .365 | 11 | 15 | .733 | 24 | 44 | 68 | 11 | 11 | 10 | 12 | 95 | 3.6 | 0.6 | 5.0 |
| 02-03—L.A. Lakers ..... | 11 | 318 | 35 | 78 | .449 | 8 | 9 | .889 | 11 | 38 | 49 | 24 | 11 | 4 | 12 | 88 | 4.5 | 2.2 | 8.0 |
| 03-04—L.A. Lakers ..... | 22 | 470 | 43 | 100 | .430 | 13 | 20 | .650 | 11 | 39 | 50 | 11 | 21 | 8 | 11 | 121 | 2.3 | 0.5 | 5.5 |
| Totals ................... | 68 | 1187 | 129 | 313 | .412 | 39 | 57 | .684 | 53 | 129 | 182 | 49 | 44 | 22 | 41 | 340 | 2.7 | 0.7 | 5.0 |

Three-point field goals: 1999-00, 2-for-10 (.200). 2000-01, 1-for-2 (.500). 2001-02, 8-for-35 (.229). 2002-03, 10-for-30 (.333). 2003-04, 22-for-59 (.373). Totals, 43-for-136 (.316).

Personal fouls/disqualifications: 1999-00, 5/0. 2000-01, 6/0. 2001-02, 51/0. 2002-03, 29/0. 2003-04, 45/0. Totals, 136/0.

## GILL, EDDIE     G     PACERS

**PERSONAL:** Born August 16, 1978, in Aurora, Colo. ... 6-0/190. (1.83/86.2).
**HIGH SCHOOL:** Overland (Colo.).
**JUNIOR COLLEGE:** Eastern Utah, then Salt Lake Community College.
**COLLEGE:** Weber State.
**TRANSACTIONS/CAREER NOTES:** Not drafted by an NBA franchise. ... Played in Italy (2000-01). ... Played in International Basketball League with Las Vegas Bandits (2000-01). ... Played in American Basketball Association 2000 with Kansas City Knights (2000-02). ... Signed by New Jersey Nets to the first of two consecutive 10-day contracts (March 29, 2001). ... Signed to 10-day contract by Memphis Grizzlies (February 23, 2002). ... Signed by Grizzlies for remainder of season (March 4, 2002). ... Waived by Grizzlies (October 24, 2002). ... Played in Continental Basketball Association (2003-04). ... Signed as free agent by Portland Trail Blazers (February 5, 2004). ... Traded by Trail Blazers to New Jersey Nets for draft rights to F Viktor Khryapa (June 24, 2004). ... Waived by Nets (July 6, 2004). ... Signed as free agent by Indiana Pacers (July 28, 2004).

### COLLEGIATE RECORD

| Season Team | G | Min. | FGM | FGA | Pct. | FTM | FTA | Pct. | Reb. | Ast. | Pts. | AVERAGES RPG | APG | PPG |
|---|---|---|---|---|---|---|---|---|---|---|---|---|---|---|
| 96-97—College of Eastern Utah.. | 33 | ... | 70 | 165 | .424 | 32 | 55 | .582 | 62 | 79 | 200 | 1.9 | 2.4 | 6.1 |
| 97-98—Salt Lake C.C. ................ | 31 | ... | 148 | 325 | .455 | 144 | 184 | .783 | 131 | 197 | 507 | 4.2 | 6.4 | 16.4 |
| 98-99—Weber State.................. | 33 | 1145 | 141 | 331 | .426 | 97 | 111 | .874 | 129 | 150 | 462 | 3.9 | 4.5 | 14.0 |
| 99-00—Weber State.................. | 28 | 1009 | 128 | 325 | .394 | 149 | 173 | .861 | 179 | 194 | 457 | 6.4 | 6.9 | 16.3 |
| Junior College Totals............. | 64 | ... | 218 | 490 | .445 | 176 | 239 | .736 | 193 | 276 | 707 | 3.0 | 4.3 | 11.0 |
| 4-Year-College Totals............. | 61 | 2154 | 269 | 656 | .410 | 246 | 284 | .866 | 308 | 344 | 919 | 5.0 | 5.6 | 15.1 |

Three-point field goals: 1996-97, 28-for-73 (.384). 1997-98, 67-for-159 (.421). 1998-99, 83-for-203 (.409). 1999-00, 52-for-142 (.366). Totals, 230-for-577 (.399).

Personal fouls/disqualifications: 1998-99, 73/0. 1999-00, 74/0. Totals, 147/0.

### AMERICAN BASKETBALL ASSOCIATION 2000 RECORD

| Season Team | G | Min. | FGM | FGA | Pct. | FTM | FTA | Pct. | Reb. | Ast. | Pts. | AVERAGES RPG | APG | PPG |
|---|---|---|---|---|---|---|---|---|---|---|---|---|---|---|
| 00-01—Kansas City ................... | 1 | 28 | 4 | 8 | .500 | 1 | 2 | .500 | 1 | 9 | 10 | 1.0 | 9.0 | 10.0 |
| 01-02—Kansas City ................... | 18 | 606 | 67 | 173 | .387 | 50 | 57 | .877 | 88 | 120 | 214 | 4.9 | 6.7 | 11.9 |
| Totals ...................................... | 19 | 634 | 71 | 181 | .392 | 51 | 59 | .864 | 89 | 129 | 224 | 4.7 | 6.8 | 11.8 |

Three-point field goals: 2000-01, 1-for-3 (.333). 2001-02, 30-for-82 (.366). Totals, 31-for-85 (.365).

### ITALIAN LEAGUE RECORD

| Season Team | G | Min. | FGM | FGA | Pct. | FTM | FTA | Pct. | Reb. | Ast. | Pts. | AVERAGES RPG | APG | PPG |
|---|---|---|---|---|---|---|---|---|---|---|---|---|---|---|
| 00-01—Fortitudo Bologna........... | 1 | 29 | 2 | 8 | .250 | 7 | 8 | .875 | 4 | 4 | 12 | 4.0 | 4.0 | 12.0 |

Three-point field goals: 2000-01, 1-for-5 (.200). Totals, 1-for-5 (.200).
Personal fouls/disqualifications: 2000-01, 1/0. Totals, 1/0.

### INTERNATIONAL BASKETBALL LEAGUE RECORD

| Season Team | G | Min. | FGM | FGA | Pct. | FTM | FTA | Pct. | Reb. | Ast. | Pts. | AVERAGES RPG | APG | PPG |
|---|---|---|---|---|---|---|---|---|---|---|---|---|---|---|
| 00-01—Las Vegas...................... | 31 | 1169 | 134 | 324 | .414 | 113 | 156 | .724 | 129 | 213 | 436 | 4.2 | 6.9 | 14.1 |

Three-point field goals: 2000-01, 55-for-139 (.396). Totals, 55-for-139 (.396).
Personal fouls/disqualifications: 2000-01, 104/0. Totals, 104/0.

**G**

## NBA REGULAR-SEASON RECORD

| | | | | | | | | REBOUNDS | | | | | | | | AVERAGES | | |
|---|---|---|---|---|---|---|---|---|---|---|---|---|---|---|---|---|---|---|
| Season Team | G | Min. | FGM | FGA | Pct. | FTM | FTA | Pct. | Off. | Def. | Tot. | Ast. | St. | Blk. | TO | Pts. | RPG | APG | PPG |
| 00-01—New Jersey ..... | 8 | 152 | 16 | 41 | .390 | 4 | 5 | .800 | 0 | 9 | 9 | 24 | 4 | 1 | 10 | 39 | 1.1 | 3.0 | 4.9 |
| 01-02—Memphis ........ | 23 | 384 | 39 | 92 | .424 | 31 | 39 | .795 | 7 | 21 | 28 | 49 | 11 | 3 | 34 | 116 | 1.2 | 2.1 | 5.0 |
| 03-04—Portland ......... | 22 | 157 | 15 | 36 | .417 | 17 | 20 | .850 | 4 | 13 | 17 | 16 | 9 | 1 | 12 | 50 | 0.8 | 0.7 | 2.3 |
| 04-05—Indiana ........... | 73 | 1021 | 81 | 242 | .335 | 71 | 81 | .877 | 16 | 96 | 112 | 83 | 59 | 5 | 60 | 269 | 1.5 | 1.1 | 3.7 |
| Totals ................... | 126 | 1714 | 151 | 411 | .367 | 123 | 145 | .848 | 27 | 139 | 166 | 172 | 83 | 10 | 116 | 474 | 1.3 | 1.4 | 3.8 |

Three-point field goals: 2000-01, 3-for-9 (.333). 2001-02, 7-for-22 (.318). 2003-04, 3-for-8 (.375). 2004-05, 36-for-117 (.308). Totals, 49-for-156 (.314).
Personal fouls/disqualifications: 2000-01, 9/0. 2001-02, 38/0. 2003-04, 16/0. 2004-05, 105/0. Totals, 168/0.

## NBA PLAYOFF RECORD

| | | | | | | | | REBOUNDS | | | | | | | | AVERAGES | | |
|---|---|---|---|---|---|---|---|---|---|---|---|---|---|---|---|---|---|---|
| Season Team | G | Min. | FGM | FGA | Pct. | FTM | FTA | Pct. | Off. | Def. | Tot. | Ast. | St. | Blk. | TO | Pts. | RPG | APG | PPG |
| 04-05—Indiana ........... | 7 | 45 | 5 | 16 | .313 | 13 | 15 | .867 | 0 | 4 | 4 | 5 | 1 | 0 | 3 | 24 | 0.6 | 0.7 | 3.4 |

Three-point field goals: 2004-05, 1-for-6 (.167). Totals, 1-for-6 (.167).

## CBA RECORD

| | | | | | | | | | | | | AVERAGES | | |
|---|---|---|---|---|---|---|---|---|---|---|---|---|---|---|
| Season Team | G | Min. | FGM | FGA | Pct. | FTM | FTA | Pct. | Reb. | Ast. | Pts. | RPG | APG | PPG |
| 03-04—Dakota Wizards .............. | 25 | 913 | 136 | 307 | .443 | 152 | 171 | .889 | 121 | 200 | 452 | 4.8 | 8.0 | 18.1 |

Three-point field goals: 2003-04, 28-for-73 (.384). Totals, 28-for-73 (.384).

# GILL, KENDALL                    G/F

**PERSONAL:** Born May 25, 1968, in Chicago. ... 6-5/216. (1.96/98.0). ... Full name: Kendall Cedric Gill
**HIGH SCHOOL:** Rich Central (Olympia Fields, Ill.).
**COLLEGE:** Illinois.
**TRANSACTIONS/CAREER NOTES:** Selected by Charlotte Hornets in first round (fifth pick overall) of 1990 NBA Draft. ... Traded by Hornets to Seattle SuperSonics for F Eddie Johnson, G Dana Barros and option to switch 1994 first-round draft choices (September 1, 1993). ... Traded by SuperSonics to Hornets for G Hersey Hawkins and G/F David Wingate (June 27, 1995). ... Traded by Hornets with G Khalid Reeves to New Jersey Nets for G Kenny Anderson and G/F Gerald Glass (January 19, 1996). ... Signed as free agent by Miami Heat (August 5, 2001). ... Signed as free agent by Minnesota Timberwolves (September 25, 2002). ... Signed as free agent by Chicago Bulls (August 20, 2003). ... Signed as free agent by Milwaukee Bucks (December 6, 2004). ... Waived by Bucks (January 5, 2005).

## COLLEGIATE RECORD

**NOTES:** THE SPORTING NEWS All-America third team (1990).

| | | | | | | | | | | | | AVERAGES | | |
|---|---|---|---|---|---|---|---|---|---|---|---|---|---|---|
| Season Team | G | Min. | FGM | FGA | Pct. | FTM | FTA | Pct. | Reb. | Ast. | Pts. | RPG | APG | PPG |
| 86-87—Illinois ......................... | 31 | 345 | 40 | 83 | .482 | 34 | 53 | .642 | 42 | 27 | 114 | 1.4 | 0.9 | 3.7 |
| 87-88—Illinois ......................... | 33 | 946 | 128 | 272 | .471 | 67 | 89 | .753 | 73 | 138 | 344 | 2.2 | 4.2 | 10.4 |
| 88-89—Illinois ......................... | 24 | 681 | 143 | 264 | .542 | 46 | 58 | .793 | 70 | 91 | 370 | 2.9 | 3.8 | 15.4 |
| 89-90—Illinois ......................... | 29 | 1000 | 211 | 422 | .500 | 136 | 175 | .777 | 143 | 96 | 581 | 4.9 | 3.3 | 20.0 |
| Totals ..................................... | 117 | 2972 | 522 | 1041 | .501 | 283 | 375 | .755 | 328 | 352 | 1409 | 2.8 | 3.0 | 12.0 |

Three-point field goals: 1986-87, 0-for-1. 1987-88, 21-for-69 (.304). 1988-89, 38-for-83 (.458). 1989-90, 23-for-66 (.348). Totals, 82-for-219 (.374).

## NBA REGULAR-SEASON RECORD

**RECORDS:** Shares single-game record for most steals—11 (April 3, 1999, vs. Miami).
**HONORS:** NBA All-Rookie first team (1991).
**NOTES:** Led NBA with 2.68 steals per game (1999).

| | | | | | | | | REBOUNDS | | | | | | | | AVERAGES | | |
|---|---|---|---|---|---|---|---|---|---|---|---|---|---|---|---|---|---|---|
| Season Team | G | Min. | FGM | FGA | Pct. | FTM | FTA | Pct. | Off. | Def. | Tot. | Ast. | St. | Blk. | TO | Pts. | RPG | APG | PPG |
| 90-91—Charlotte ...... | 82 | 1944 | 376 | 836 | .450 | 152 | 182 | .835 | 105 | 158 | 263 | 303 | 104 | 39 | 163 | 906 | 3.2 | 3.7 | 11.0 |
| 91-92—Charlotte ......... | 79 | 2906 | 666 | 1427 | .467 | 284 | 381 | .745 | 165 | 237 | 402 | 329 | 154 | 46 | 180 | 1622 | 5.1 | 4.2 | 20.5 |
| 92-93—Charlotte ......... | 69 | 2430 | 463 | 1032 | .449 | 224 | 290 | .772 | 120 | 220 | 340 | 268 | 98 | 36 | 174 | 1167 | 4.9 | 3.9 | 16.9 |
| 93-94—Seattle ............ | 79 | 2435 | 429 | 969 | .443 | 215 | 275 | .782 | 91 | 177 | 268 | 275 | 151 | 32 | 143 | 1111 | 3.4 | 3.5 | 14.1 |
| 94-95—Seattle ............ | 73 | 2125 | 392 | 858 | .457 | 155 | 209 | .742 | 99 | 191 | 290 | 192 | 117 | 28 | 138 | 1002 | 4.0 | 2.6 | 13.7 |
| 95-96—Char.-N.J........ | 47 | 1683 | 246 | 524 | .469 | 138 | 176 | .784 | 72 | 160 | 232 | 260 | 64 | 24 | 131 | 656 | 4.9 | 5.5 | 14.0 |
| 96-97—New Jersey ..... | 82 | 3199 | 644 | 1453 | .443 | 427 | 536 | .797 | 183 | 316 | 499 | 326 | 154 | 46 | 218 | 1789 | 6.1 | 4.0 | 21.8 |
| 97-98—New Jersey ..... | 81 | 2733 | 418 | 974 | .429 | 225 | 327 | .688 | 112 | 279 | 391 | 200 | 156 | 64 | 124 | 1087 | 4.8 | 2.5 | 13.4 |
| 98-99—New Jersey ..... | 50 | 1606 | 236 | 593 | .398 | 114 | 167 | .683 | 61 | 183 | 244 | 123 | *134 | 26 | 71 | 588 | 4.9 | 2.5 | 11.8 |
| 99-00—New Jersey ..... | 76 | 2355 | 396 | 956 | .414 | 181 | 255 | .710 | 82 | 201 | 283 | 210 | 139 | 41 | 89 | 993 | 3.7 | 2.8 | 13.1 |
| 00-01—New Jersey ..... | 31 | 892 | 107 | 323 | .331 | 65 | 90 | .722 | 32 | 99 | 131 | 87 | 47 | 7 | 48 | 283 | 4.2 | 2.8 | 9.1 |
| 01-02—Miami .............. | 65 | 1410 | 162 | 422 | .384 | 42 | 62 | .677 | 29 | 155 | 184 | 100 | 44 | 8 | 55 | 372 | 2.8 | 1.5 | 5.7 |
| 02-03—Minnesota ...... | 82 | 2068 | 286 | 677 | .422 | 123 | 161 | .764 | 51 | 197 | 248 | 156 | 78 | 15 | 108 | 714 | 3.0 | 1.9 | 8.7 |
| 03-04—Chicago .......... | 56 | 1411 | 215 | 548 | .392 | 100 | 136 | .735 | 61 | 129 | 190 | 89 | 65 | 16 | 83 | 539 | 3.4 | 1.6 | 9.6 |
| 04-05—Milwaukee ...... | 14 | 284 | 32 | 80 | .400 | 18 | 20 | .900 | 11 | 26 | 37 | 27 | 14 | 4 | 9 | 85 | 2.6 | 1.9 | 6.1 |
| Totals ................... | 966 | 29481 | 5068 | 11672 | .434 | 2463 | 3267 | .754 | 1274 | 2728 | 4002 | 2945 | 1519 | 432 | 1734 | 12914 | 4.1 | 3.0 | 13.4 |

Three-point field goals: 1990-91, 2-for-14 (.143). 1991-92, 6-for-25 (.240). 1992-93, 17-for-62 (.274). 1993-94, 38-for-120 (.317). 1994-95, 63-for-171 (.368). 1995-96, 26-for-79 (.329). 1996-97, 74-for-220 (.336). 1997-98, 26-for-101 (.257). 1998-99, 2-for-17 (.118). 1999-00, 20-for-78 (.256). 2000-01, 4-for-14 (.286). 2001-02, 6-for-44 (.136). 2002-03, 19-for-59 (.322). 2003-04, 9-for-38 (.237). 2004-05, 3-for-9 (.333). Totals, 315-for-1051 (.300).
Personal fouls/disqualifications: 1990-91, 186/0. 1991-92, 237/1. 1992-93, 191/2. 1993-94, 194/1. 1994-95, 186/0. 1995-96, 131/2. 1996-97, 225/2. 1997-98, 268/4. 1998-99, 162/4. 1999-00, 211/3. 2000-01, 64/0. 2001-02, 140/0. 2002-03, 176/2. 2003-04, 107/0. 2004-05, 37/0. Totals, 2515/21.

## NBA PLAYOFF RECORD

| | | | | | | | | REBOUNDS | | | | | | | | AVERAGES | | |
|---|---|---|---|---|---|---|---|---|---|---|---|---|---|---|---|---|---|---|
| Season Team | G | Min. | FGM | FGA | Pct. | FTM | FTA | Pct. | Off. | Def. | Tot. | Ast. | St. | Blk. | TO | Pts. | RPG | APG | PPG |
| 92-93—Charlotte ......... | 9 | 353 | 65 | 162 | .401 | 25 | 35 | .714 | 26 | 20 | 46 | 26 | 21 | 6 | 19 | 156 | 5.1 | 2.9 | 17.3 |

**G**

| Season Team | G | Min. | FGM | FGA | Pct. | FTM | FTA | Pct. | Off. | Def. | Tot. | Ast. | St. | Blk. | TO | Pts. | RPG | APG | PPG |
|---|---|---|---|---|---|---|---|---|---|---|---|---|---|---|---|---|---|---|---|
| | | | | | | | | | | REBOUNDS | | | | | | | AVERAGES | | |
| 93-94—Seattle ........... | 5 | 153 | 26 | 60 | .433 | 13 | 21 | .619 | 7 | 17 | 24 | 10 | 6 | 1 | 6 | 67 | 4.8 | 2.0 | 13.4 |
| 94-95—Seattle ........... | 4 | 72 | 9 | 25 | .360 | 5 | 8 | .625 | 1 | 3 | 4 | 10 | 4 | 1 | 4 | 25 | 1.0 | 2.5 | 6.3 |
| 97-98—New Jersey ..... | 3 | 100 | 18 | 40 | .450 | 7 | 8 | .875 | 3 | 10 | 13 | 3 | 4 | 1 | 4 | 43 | 4.3 | 1.0 | 14.3 |
| 02-03—Minnesota....... | 6 | 118 | 10 | 27 | .370 | 9 | 14 | .643 | 6 | 7 | 13 | 7 | 4 | 1 | 4 | 31 | 2.2 | 1.2 | 5.2 |
| Totals ................... | 27 | 796 | 128 | 314 | .408 | 59 | 86 | .686 | 43 | 57 | 100 | 56 | 39 | 10 | 37 | 322 | 3.7 | 2.1 | 11.9 |

Three-point field goals: 1992-93, 1-for-6 (.167). 1993-94, 2-for-9 (.222). 1994-95, 2-for-8 (.250). 2002-03, 2-for-4 (.500). Totals, 7-for-27 (.259).
Personal fouls/disqualifications: 1992-93, 29/0. 1993-94, 12/0. 1994-95, 6/0. 1997-98, 15/1. 2002-03, 12/0. Totals, 74/1.

## GINOBILI, MANU · G · SPURS

**PERSONAL:** Born July 28, 1977 ... 6-6/210. (1.98/95.3).
**TRANSACTIONS/CAREER NOTES:** Played in Argentina (1997-98). ... Played in Italy (1998-2002). ... Selected by San Antonio Spurs in second round (57th pick overall) of 1999 NBA Draft.
**MISCELLANEOUS:** Member of NBA championship team (2003, 2005). ... Member of gold-medal-winning Argentian Olympic Team (2004).

### ARGENTINIAN LEAGUE RECORD

| Season Team | G | Min. | FGM | FGA | Pct. | FTM | FTA | Pct. | Reb. | Ast. | Pts. | RPG | APG | PPG |
|---|---|---|---|---|---|---|---|---|---|---|---|---|---|---|
| | | | | | | | | | | | | | AVERAGES | |
| 97-98—Estudiante ..................... | 49 | 1666 | 370 | 807 | .458 | 303 | 428 | .708 | 195 | 114 | 1155 | 4.0 | 2.3 | 23.6 |

Three-point field goals: 1997-98, 111-for-371 (.299). Totals, 111-for-371 (.299).

### ITALIAN LEAGUE RECORD

| Season Team | G | Min. | FGM | FGA | Pct. | FTM | FTA | Pct. | Reb. | Ast. | Pts. | RPG | APG | PPG |
|---|---|---|---|---|---|---|---|---|---|---|---|---|---|---|
| | | | | | | | | | | | | | AVERAGES | |
| 98-99—Reggio Calabria.............. | 29 | 802 | 159 | 329 | .483 | 122 | 161 | .758 | 81 | 44 | 490 | 2.8 | 1.5 | 16.9 |
| 99-00—Reggio Calabria.............. | 30 | 917 | 168 | 362 | .464 | 115 | 163 | .706 | 93 | 73 | 509 | 3.1 | 2.4 | 17.0 |
| 00-01—Kinder Bologna.............. | 34 | 981 | 199 | 387 | .514 | 116 | 155 | .748 | 150 | 86 | 580 | 4.4 | 2.5 | 17.1 |
| 01-02—Kinder Bologna.............. | 36 | 1163 | 236 | 445 | .530 | 175 | 250 | .700 | 158 | 79 | 715 | 4.4 | 2.2 | 19.9 |
| Totals ..................................... | 129 | 3863 | 762 | 1523 | .500 | 528 | 729 | .724 | 482 | 282 | 2294 | 3.7 | 2.2 | 17.8 |

Three-point field goals: 1998-99, 49-for-146 (.336). 1999-00, 58-for-164 (.354). 2000-01, 66-for-173 (.382). 2001-02, 68-for-171 (.398). Totals, 241-for-654 (.369).

### NBA REGULAR-SEASON RECORD

**HONORS:** NBA All-Rookie second team (2003)

| Season Team | G | Min. | FGM | FGA | Pct. | FTM | FTA | Pct. | Off. | Def. | Tot. | Ast. | St. | Blk. | TO | Pts. | RPG | APG | PPG |
|---|---|---|---|---|---|---|---|---|---|---|---|---|---|---|---|---|---|---|---|
| | | | | | | | | | | REBOUNDS | | | | | | | AVERAGES | | |
| 02-03—San Antonio.... | 69 | 1431 | 174 | 397 | .438 | 126 | 171 | .737 | 47 | 114 | 161 | 138 | 96 | 17 | 100 | 525 | 2.3 | 2.0 | 7.6 |
| 03-04—San Antonio.... | 77 | 2260 | 330 | 789 | .418 | 239 | 298 | .802 | 86 | 258 | 344 | 291 | 136 | 16 | 161 | 987 | 4.5 | 3.8 | 12.8 |
| 04-05—San Antonio.... | 74 | 2193 | 367 | 780 | .471 | 355 | 442 | .803 | 75 | 254 | 329 | 288 | 119 | 27 | 172 | 1186 | 4.4 | 3.9 | 16.0 |
| Totals ................... | 220 | 5884 | 871 | 1966 | .443 | 720 | 911 | .790 | 208 | 626 | 834 | 717 | 351 | 60 | 433 | 2698 | 3.8 | 3.3 | 12.3 |

Three-point field goals: 2002-03, 51-for-148 (.345). 2003-04, 88-for-245 (.359). 2004-05, 97-for-258 (.376). Totals, 236-for-651 (.363).
Personal fouls/disqualifications: 2002-03, 170/3. 2003-04, 181/0. 2004-05, 190/1. Totals, 541/4.

### NBA PLAYOFF RECORD

| Season Team | G | Min. | FGM | FGA | Pct. | FTM | FTA | Pct. | Off. | Def. | Tot. | Ast. | St. | Blk. | TO | Pts. | RPG | APG | PPG |
|---|---|---|---|---|---|---|---|---|---|---|---|---|---|---|---|---|---|---|---|
| | | | | | | | | | | REBOUNDS | | | | | | | AVERAGES | | |
| 02-03—San Antonio.... | 24 | 660 | 71 | 184 | .386 | 56 | 74 | .757 | 29 | 63 | 92 | 70 | 41 | 9 | 36 | 226 | 3.8 | 2.9 | 9.4 |
| 03-04—San Antonio.... | 10 | 280 | 42 | 94 | .447 | 36 | 44 | .818 | 15 | 38 | 53 | 31 | 17 | 1 | 21 | 130 | 5.3 | 3.1 | 13.0 |
| 04-05—San Antonio.... | 23 | 772 | 145 | 286 | .507 | 147 | 185 | .795 | 19 | 114 | 133 | 97 | 28 | 6 | 66 | 479 | 5.8 | 4.2 | 20.8 |
| Totals ................... | 57 | 1712 | 258 | 564 | .457 | 239 | 303 | .789 | 63 | 215 | 278 | 198 | 86 | 16 | 123 | 835 | 4.9 | 3.5 | 14.6 |

Three-point field goals: 2002-03, 28-for-73 (.384). 2003-04, 10-for-35 (.286). 2004-05, 42-for-96 (.438). Totals, 80-for-204 (.392).
Personal fouls/disqualifications: 2002-03, 62/1. 2003-04, 30/0. 2004-05, 69/0. Totals, 161/1.

### NBA ALL-STAR GAME RECORD

| Season Team | Min. | FGM | FGA | Pct. | FTM | FTA | Pct. | Off. | Def. | Tot. | Ast. | PF | Dq. | St. | Blk. | TO | Pts. |
|---|---|---|---|---|---|---|---|---|---|---|---|---|---|---|---|---|---|
| | | | | | | | | | REBOUNDS | | | | | | | | |
| 2005—San Antonio ......... | 22 | 3 | 6 | .500 | 2 | 2 | 1.000 | 2 | 1 | 3 | 1 | 3 | 0 | 1 | 1 | 3 | 8 |

Three-point field goals: 2005, 0-for-2. Totals, 0-for-2 (.000).

## GIRICEK, GORDAN · F · JAZZ

**PERSONAL:** Born June 20, 1977, in Zagreb, Croatia. ... 6-5/210. (1.96/95.3).
**TRANSACTIONS/CAREER NOTES:** Played in Croatia (1996-2001). ... Played in Russia (2001-02). ... Selected by Dallas Mavericks in second round (40th pick overall) of 1999 NBA Draft. ... Draft rights traded by Mavericks with future second-round draft choice to San Antonio Spurs for draft rights to F Leon Smith (June 30, 1999). ... Draft rights traded by Spurs to Memphis Grizzlies for cash (June 28, 2002). ... Traded by Grizzlies with F Drew Gooden to Orlando Magic for F Mike Miller, F Ryan Humphrey, 2003 first-round draft choice and 2004 second-round draft choice (February 19, 2003). ... Traded by Magic to Utah Jazz for G DeShawn Stevenson and conditional second-round draft choice (February 19, 2004).

### CROATION RECORD

| Season Team | G | Min. | FGM | FGA | Pct. | FTM | FTA | Pct. | Reb. | Ast. | Pts. | RPG | APG | PPG |
|---|---|---|---|---|---|---|---|---|---|---|---|---|---|---|
| | | | | | | | | | | | | | AVERAGES | |
| 96-97—Cibona Zagreb ................ | 12 | ... | 22 | 42 | .524 | 10 | 16 | .625 | 15 | 6 | 59 | 1.3 | 0.5 | 4.9 |
| 97-98—Cibona.......................... | 22 | 480 | 105 | 173 | .607 | 53 | 60 | .883 | 48 | 24 | 290 | 2.2 | 1.1 | 13.2 |
| 98-99—Cibona.......................... | 20 | 542 | 112 | 187 | .599 | 69 | 91 | .758 | 64 | 34 | 324 | 3.2 | 1.7 | 16.2 |
| 99-00—Cibona Zagreb ................ | 21 | 588 | 156 | 265 | .589 | 79 | 104 | .760 | 82 | 55 | 428 | 3.9 | 2.6 | 20.4 |

G

| Season Team | G | Min. | FGM | FGA | Pct. | FTM | FTA | Pct. | Reb. | Ast. | Pts. | AVERAGES RPG | APG | PPG |
|---|---|---|---|---|---|---|---|---|---|---|---|---|---|---|
| 00-01—Cibona Zagreb | 16 | 475 | 103 | 222 | .464 | 34 | 43 | .791 | 62 | 22 | 268 | 3.9 | 1.4 | 16.8 |
| Totals | 91 | 2085 | 498 | 889 | .560 | 245 | 314 | .780 | 271 | 141 | 1369 | 3.0 | 1.5 | 15.0 |

Three-point field goals: 1996-97, 5-for-15 (.333). 1997-98, 27-for-65 (.415). 1998-99, 31-for-64 (.484). 1999-00, 38-for-81 (.469). 2000-01, 28-for-76 (.368). Totals, 129-for-301 (.429).

## RUSSIAN LEAGUE RECORD

| Season Team | G | Min. | FGM | FGA | Pct. | FTM | FTA | Pct. | Reb. | Ast. | Pts. | AVERAGES RPG | APG | PPG |
|---|---|---|---|---|---|---|---|---|---|---|---|---|---|---|
| 01-02—CSKA | 33 | 865 | 224 | 402 | .557 | 147 | 178 | .826 | 102 | 56 | 646 | 3.1 | 1.7 | 19.6 |

Three-point field goals: 2001-02, 51-for-115 (.443). Totals, 51-for-115 (.443).

## NBA REGULAR-SEASON RECORD

**HONORS:** NBA All-Rookie second team (2003).

| Season Team | G | Min. | FGM | FGA | Pct. | FTM | FTA | Pct. | REBOUNDS Off. | Def. | Tot. | Ast. | St. | Blk. | TO | Pts. | AVERAGES RPG | APG | PPG |
|---|---|---|---|---|---|---|---|---|---|---|---|---|---|---|---|---|---|---|---|
| 02-03—Mem-Orl | 76 | 2148 | 350 | 803 | .436 | 150 | 183 | .820 | 36 | 202 | 238 | 137 | 52 | 8 | 145 | 935 | 3.1 | 1.8 | 12.3 |
| 03-04—Orlando-Utah | 73 | 2041 | 316 | 724 | .436 | 135 | 158 | .854 | 51 | 175 | 226 | 122 | 56 | 15 | 103 | 827 | 3.1 | 1.7 | 11.3 |
| 04-05—Utah | 81 | 1660 | 283 | 632 | .448 | 111 | 137 | .810 | 25 | 157 | 182 | 137 | 46 | 11 | 90 | 715 | 2.2 | 1.7 | 8.8 |
| Totals | 230 | 5849 | 949 | 2159 | .440 | 396 | 478 | .828 | 112 | 534 | 646 | 396 | 154 | 34 | 338 | 2477 | 2.8 | 1.7 | 10.8 |

Three-point field goals: 2002-03, 85-for-249 (.341). 2003-04, 60-for-152 (.395). 2004-05, 38-for-105 (.362). Totals, 183-for-506 (.362).
Personal fouls/disqualifications: 2002-03, 159/0. 2003-04, 144/0. 2004-05, 155/1. Totals, 458/1.

## NBA PLAYOFF RECORD

| Season Team | G | Min. | FGM | FGA | Pct. | FTM | FTA | Pct. | REBOUNDS Off. | Def. | Tot. | Ast. | St. | Blk. | TO | Pts. | AVERAGES RPG | APG | PPG |
|---|---|---|---|---|---|---|---|---|---|---|---|---|---|---|---|---|---|---|---|
| 02-03—Orlando | 7 | 223 | 26 | 56 | .464 | 9 | 11 | .818 | 4 | 18 | 22 | 7 | 2 | 1 | 13 | 66 | 3.1 | 1.0 | 9.4 |

Three-point field goals: 2002-03, 5-for-15 (.333). Totals, 5-for-15 (.333).
Personal fouls/disqualifications: 2002-03, 27/0. Totals, 27/0.

---

# GLOVER, DION     G

**PERSONAL:** Born October 22, 1978, in Marietta, Ga. ... 6-5/228. (1.96/103.4). ... Full name: Micaiah Diondae Glover
**HIGH SCHOOL:** Cedar Grove (Decatur, Ga.).
**COLLEGE:** Georgia Tech.
**TRANSACTIONS/CAREER NOTES:** Selected after redshirt sophomore season by Atlanta Hawks in first round (20th pick overall) of 1999 NBA Draft. ... Waived by Hawks (February 25, 2004). ... Signed for remainder of season by Toronto Raptors (February 28, 2004). ... Signed by San Antonio Spurs to first of two consecutive 10-day contracts (March 17, 2005). ... Waived by Spurs (April 4, 2005).

## COLLEGIATE RECORD

| Season Team | G | Min. | FGM | FGA | Pct. | FTM | FTA | Pct. | Reb. | Ast. | Pts. | AVERAGES RPG | APG | PPG |
|---|---|---|---|---|---|---|---|---|---|---|---|---|---|---|
| 97-98—Georgia Tech | 33 | 1163 | 222 | 503 | .441 | 119 | 186 | .640 | 166 | 86 | 608 | 5.0 | 2.6 | 18.4 |
| 98-99—Georgia Tech | | | | | | | Did not play—injured. | | | | | | | |
| Totals | 33 | 1163 | 222 | 503 | .441 | 119 | 186 | .640 | 166 | 86 | 608 | 5.0 | 2.6 | 18.4 |

Three-point field goals: 1997-98, 45-for-166 (.271). Totals, 45-for-166 (.271).

## NBA REGULAR-SEASON RECORD

| Season Team | G | Min. | FGM | FGA | Pct. | FTM | FTA | Pct. | REBOUNDS Off. | Def. | Tot. | Ast. | St. | Blk. | TO | Pts. | AVERAGES RPG | APG | PPG |
|---|---|---|---|---|---|---|---|---|---|---|---|---|---|---|---|---|---|---|---|
| 99-00—Atlanta | 30 | 446 | 66 | 171 | .386 | 51 | 70 | .729 | 15 | 23 | 38 | 27 | 15 | 4 | 28 | 195 | 1.3 | 0.9 | 6.5 |
| 00-01—Atlanta | 57 | 929 | 141 | 336 | .420 | 47 | 69 | .681 | 39 | 92 | 131 | 69 | 49 | 10 | 54 | 338 | 2.3 | 1.2 | 5.9 |
| 01-02—Atlanta | 55 | 1156 | 192 | 456 | .421 | 78 | 103 | .757 | 36 | 133 | 169 | 84 | 45 | 14 | 76 | 492 | 3.1 | 1.5 | 8.9 |
| 02-03—Atlanta | 76 | 1890 | 277 | 648 | .427 | 127 | 162 | .784 | 62 | 220 | 282 | 141 | 71 | 15 | 108 | 737 | 3.7 | 1.9 | 9.7 |
| 03-04—Atlanta-Tor. | 69 | 1643 | 230 | 589 | .390 | 120 | 156 | .769 | 58 | 208 | 266 | 130 | 50 | 19 | 102 | 620 | 3.9 | 1.9 | 9.0 |
| 04-05—San Antonio | 7 | 68 | 8 | 22 | .364 | 8 | 10 | .800 | 3 | 8 | 11 | 4 | 3 | 3 | 2 | 25 | 1.6 | 0.6 | 3.6 |
| Totals | 294 | 6132 | 914 | 2222 | .411 | 431 | 570 | .756 | 213 | 684 | 897 | 455 | 233 | 65 | 370 | 2407 | 3.1 | 1.5 | 8.2 |

Three-point field goals: 1999-00, 12-for-45 (.267). 2000-01, 9-for-46 (.196). 2001-02, 30-for-91 (.330). 2002-03, 56-for-158 (.354). 2003-04, 40-for-119 (.336). 2004-05, 1-for-8 (.125). Totals, 148-for-467 (.317).
Personal fouls/disqualifications: 1999-00, 28/0. 2000-01, 92/1. 2001-02, 89/1. 2002-03, 146/0. 2003-04, 123/0. 2004-05, 9/0. Totals, 487/2.

## TURKISH LEAGUE RECORD

| Season Team | G | Min. | FGM | FGA | Pct. | FTM | FTA | Pct. | Reb. | Ast. | Pts. | AVERAGES RPG | APG | PPG |
|---|---|---|---|---|---|---|---|---|---|---|---|---|---|---|
| 04-05—Ulker | 16 | 382 | 66 | 159 | .415 | 33 | 47 | .702 | 58 | 34 | 179 | 3.6 | 2.1 | 11.2 |

Three-point field goals: 2004-05, 14-for-40 (.350). Totals, 14-for-40 (.350).

**G**

---

# GOLDWIRE, ANTHONY     G*

**PERSONAL:** Born September 6, 1971, in West Palm Beach, Fla. ... 6-2/182. (1.88/82.6).
**HIGH SCHOOL:** Suncoast (Riviera Beach, Fla.).
**JUNIOR COLLEGE:** Pensacola Junior College (Fla.).
**COLLEGE:** Houston.
**TRANSACTIONS/CAREER NOTES:** Selected by Phoenix Suns in second round (52nd pick overall) of 1994 NBA Draft. ... Waived by Suns (November 1, 1994). ... Played in Continental Basketball Association with Yakima Sun Kings (1994-96). ... Signed by Charlotte Hornets to 10-day contract (January 22, 1996). ... Re-signed by Hornets for remainder of season (January 31, 1996). ... Traded by Hornets with C George Zidek to Denver Nuggets for G Ricky Pierce (February 20, 1997). ... Played in Greece (1998-99). ... Played in Spain (1999-2000). ... Signed as free agent by Nuggets (October 2, 2000). ... Waived by Nuggets (October 25, 2000). ... Played in American Basketball Association 2000 with Kansas City Knights (2000-01). ... Signed by Nuggets to first of two consecutive 10-day contracts (January 29, 2001). ... Signed by Nuggets for remainder of season (February 18, 2001). ... Signed as free agent by Cleveland Cavaliers (October 1, 2001). ...

Waived by Cavaliers (October 23, 2001). ... Signed as free agent by Suns (September 30, 2002). ... Waived by Suns (October 23, 2002). ... Played in Italy (2001-02) ... Signed as free agent by San Antonio Spurs (November 20, 2002). ... Waived by Spurs (December 28, 2002). ... Signed by Washington Wizards to first of two consecutive 10-day contracts (March 1, 2003). ... Waived by Wizards (March 13, 2003). ... Played in CBA (2003-04). ... Signed by Minnesota Timberwolves to 10-day contract (January 7, 2004). ... Released by Timberwolves (January 27, 2004). ... Signed by Milwaukee Bucks to 10-day contract (February 28, 2004). ... Released by Bucks (March 5, 2004). ... Signed by New Jersey Nets to first of two consecutive 10-day contracts (March 22, 2004). ... Waived by Nets (April 6, 2004). ... Signed as free agent by Minnesota Timberwolves (October 4, 2004). ... Waived by Timberwolves (October 28, 2004). ... Signed by Milwaukee Bucks for remainder of season (March 7, 2005).

## COLLEGIATE RECORD

| Season Team | G | Min. | FGM | FGA | Pct. | FTM | FTA | Pct. | Reb. | Ast. | Pts. | RPG | APG | PPG |
|---|---|---|---|---|---|---|---|---|---|---|---|---|---|---|
| 90-91—Pensacola J.C. | 30 | ... | 105 | 234 | .449 | 84 | 104 | .808 | 91 | 169 | 305 | 3.0 | 5.6 | 10.2 |
| 91-92—Pensacola J.C. | 31 | 939 | 155 | 360 | .431 | 128 | 168 | .762 | 128 | 241 | 477 | 4.1 | 7.8 | 15.4 |
| 92-93—Houston | 30 | 1110 | 139 | 313 | .444 | 124 | 158 | .785 | 92 | 170 | 427 | 3.1 | 5.7 | 14.2 |
| 93-94—Houston | 27 | 995 | 144 | 366 | .393 | 138 | 171 | .807 | 100 | 164 | 463 | 3.7 | 6.1 | 17.1 |
| Junior College Totals | 61 | 939 | 260 | 594 | .438 | 212 | 272 | .779 | 219 | 410 | 782 | 3.6 | 6.7 | 12.8 |
| 4-Year-College Totals | 57 | 2105 | 283 | 679 | .417 | 262 | 329 | .796 | 192 | 334 | 890 | 3.4 | 5.9 | 15.6 |

Three-point field goals: 1990-91, 11-for-39 (.282). 1991-92, 39-for-95 (.411). 1992-93, 25-for-88 (.284). 1993-94, 37-for-123 (.301). Totals, 112-for-345 (.325).

## CBA RECORD

**NOTES:** Member of CBA championship team (1995). ... CBA All-Rookie second team (1995).

| Season Team | G | Min. | FGM | FGA | Pct. | FTM | FTA | Pct. | Reb. | Ast. | Pts. | RPG | APG | PPG |
|---|---|---|---|---|---|---|---|---|---|---|---|---|---|---|
| 94-95—Yakima | 55 | 1121 | 150 | 312 | .481 | 119 | 160 | .744 | 83 | 217 | 439 | 1.5 | 3.9 | 8.0 |
| 95-96—Yakima | 27 | 977 | 171 | 373 | .458 | 139 | 163 | .853 | 96 | 189 | 519 | 3.6 | 7.0 | 19.2 |
| 02-03—Yakima | 17 | 523 | 108 | 212 | .509 | 62 | 72 | .861 | 42 | 81 | 307 | 2.5 | 4.8 | 18.1 |
| 03-04—Yakima | 37 | 1600 | 277 | 619 | .447 | 219 | 252 | .869 | 114 | 221 | 861 | 3.1 | 6.0 | 23.3 |
| Totals | 136 | 4221 | 706 | 1516 | .466 | 539 | 647 | .833 | 335 | 708 | 2126 | 2.5 | 5.2 | 15.6 |

Three-point field goals: 1994-95, 20-for-60 (.333). 1995-96, 38-for-99 (.384). 2002-03, 29-for-58 (.500). Totals, 87-for-217 (.401).
Personal fouls/disqualifications: 1994-95, 107/0. 1995-96, 72/0. 2002-03, 19/0. Totals, 198/0.

## NBA REGULAR-SEASON RECORD

| Season Team | G | Min. | FGM | FGA | Pct. | FTM | FTA | Pct. | Off. | Def. | Tot. | Ast. | St. | Blk. | TO | Pts. | RPG | APG | PPG |
|---|---|---|---|---|---|---|---|---|---|---|---|---|---|---|---|---|---|---|---|
| 95-96—Charlotte | 42 | 621 | 76 | 189 | .402 | 46 | 60 | .767 | 8 | 35 | 43 | 112 | 16 | 0 | 63 | 231 | 1.0 | 2.7 | 5.5 |
| 96-97—Charlotte-Den. | 60 | 1188 | 131 | 330 | .397 | 61 | 78 | .782 | 12 | 72 | 84 | 219 | 33 | 2 | 76 | 387 | 1.4 | 3.7 | 6.5 |
| 97-98—Denver | 82 | 2212 | 269 | 636 | .423 | 150 | 186 | .806 | 40 | 107 | 147 | 277 | 86 | 7 | 85 | 751 | 1.8 | 3.4 | 9.2 |
| 00-01—Denver | 20 | 201 | 30 | 80 | .375 | 13 | 17 | .765 | 1 | 11 | 12 | 34 | 9 | 0 | 15 | 82 | 0.6 | 1.7 | 4.1 |
| 02-03—S.A.-Wash. | 15 | 85 | 9 | 25 | .360 | 4 | 7 | .571 | 0 | 6 | 6 | 4 | 3 | 0 | 6 | 25 | 0.4 | 0.3 | 1.7 |
| 03-04—Minn.-Mil.-N.Y. | 11 | 85 | 7 | 22 | .318 | 1 | 1 | 1.000 | 1 | 6 | 7 | 11 | 5 | 0 | 3 | 17 | 0.6 | 1.0 | 1.5 |
| 04-05—Detroit-Mil. | 33 | 537 | 57 | 136 | .419 | 26 | 31 | .839 | 10 | 49 | 59 | 78 | 15 | 0 | 15 | 172 | 1.8 | 2.4 | 5.2 |
| Totals | 263 | 4929 | 579 | 1418 | .408 | 301 | 380 | .792 | 72 | 286 | 358 | 735 | 167 | 9 | 263 | 1665 | 1.4 | 2.8 | 6.3 |

Three-point field goals: 1995-96, 33-for-83 (.398). 1996-97, 64-for-153 (.418). 1997-98, 63-for-164 (.384). 2000-01, 9-for-34 (.265). 2002-03, 3-for-9 (.333). 2003-04, 2-for-8 (.250). 2004-05, 32-for-80 (.400). Totals, 206-for-531 (.388).
Personal fouls/disqualifications: 1995-96, 79/0. 1996-97, 104/1. 1997-98, 149/0. 2000-01, 13/0. 2002-03, 6/0. 2003-04, 5/0. 2004-05, 32/0. Totals, 388/1.

## GREEK LEAGUE RECORD

| Season Team | G | Min. | FGM | FGA | Pct. | FTM | FTA | Pct. | Reb. | Ast. | Pts. | RPG | APG | PPG |
|---|---|---|---|---|---|---|---|---|---|---|---|---|---|---|
| 98-99—Olympiakos S.F.P. | 25 | 784 | 95 | 227 | .419 | 58 | 80 | .725 | 38 | 60 | 295 | 1.5 | 2.4 | 11.8 |

Three-point field goals: 1998-99, 47-for-108 (.435). Totals, 47-for-108 (.435).

## SPANISH RECORD

| Season Team | G | Min. | FGM | FGA | Pct. | FTM | FTA | Pct. | Reb. | Ast. | Pts. | RPG | APG | PPG |
|---|---|---|---|---|---|---|---|---|---|---|---|---|---|---|
| 99-00—FC Barcelona | 33 | 750 | 114 | 266 | .429 | 80 | 97 | .825 | 56 | 60 | 363 | 1.7 | 1.8 | 11.0 |

Three-point field goals: 1999-00, 55-for-144 (.382). Totals, 55-for-144 (.382).
Personal fouls/disqualifications: 1999-00, 59/0. Totals, 59/0.

## AMERICAN BASKETBALL ASSOCIATION 2000 RECORD

| Season Team | G | Min. | FGM | FGA | Pct. | FTM | FTA | Pct. | Reb. | Ast. | Pts. | RPG | APG | PPG |
|---|---|---|---|---|---|---|---|---|---|---|---|---|---|---|
| 00-01—Kansas City | 14 | 504 | 98 | 216 | .454 | 47 | 49 | .959 | 44 | 68 | 290 | 3.1 | 4.9 | 20.7 |

Three-point field goals: 2000-01, 41-for-98 (.418). Totals, 41-for-98 (.418).

## ITALIAN LEAGUE RECORD

| Season Team | G | Min. | FGM | FGA | Pct. | FTM | FTA | Pct. | Reb. | Ast. | Pts. | RPG | APG | PPG |
|---|---|---|---|---|---|---|---|---|---|---|---|---|---|---|
| 01-02—Skipper Bologna | 23 | 236 | 73 | 194 | .376 | 53 | 63 | .841 | 58 | 47 | 236 | 2.5 | 2.0 | 10.3 |

Three-point field goals: 2001-02, 37-for-104 (.356). Totals, 37-for-104 (.356).
Personal fouls/disqualifications: 2001-02, 54/0. Totals, 54/0.

**G**

# GOODEN, DREW      F      CAVALIERS

**PERSONAL:** Born September 24, 1981, in Oakland. ... 6-10/230. (2.08/104.3). ... Full name: Andrew Melvin Gooden
**HIGH SCHOOL:** El Cerrito (Calif.).
**COLLEGE:** Kansas.
**TRANSACTIONS/CAREER NOTES:** Selected after junior season by Memphis Grizzlies in first round (fourth pick overall) of 2002 NBA Draft. ... Traded by Grizzlies with F Gordan Giricek to Orlando Magic for F Mike Miller, F Ryan Humphrey, 2003

first-round draft choice and 2004 second-round draft choice (February 19, 2003). ... Traded by Magic with C Steven Hunter and the draft rights to F Anderson Varejao to Cleveland Cavaliers for F/C Tony Battie and two future second-round draft choices (July 23, 2004).

### COLLEGIATE RECORD

**NOTES:** THE SPORTING NEWS All-America first team (2002).

| Season Team | G | Min. | FGM | FGA | Pct. | FTM | FTA | Pct. | Reb. | Ast. | Pts. | AVERAGES RPG | APG | PPG |
|---|---|---|---|---|---|---|---|---|---|---|---|---|---|---|
| 99-00—Kansas | 33 | 686 | 143 | 317 | .451 | 60 | 91 | .659 | 248 | 36 | 351 | 7.5 | 1.1 | 10.6 |
| 00-01—Kansas | 28 | 761 | 166 | 322 | .516 | 105 | 162 | .648 | 234 | 47 | 441 | 8.4 | 1.7 | 15.8 |
| 01-02—Kansas | 37 | 1119 | 285 | 566 | .504 | 154 | 204 | .755 | 423 | 73 | 734 | 11.4 | 2.0 | 19.8 |
| Totals | 98 | 2566 | 594 | 1205 | .493 | 319 | 457 | .698 | 905 | 156 | 1526 | 9.2 | 1.6 | 15.6 |

Three-point field goals: 1999-00, 5-for-16 (.313). 2000-01, 4-for-10 (.400). 2001-02, 10-for-36 (.278). Totals, 19-for-62 (.306).

### NBA REGULAR-SEASON RECORD

**HONORS:** NBA All-Rookie first team (2003).

| Season Team | G | Min. | FGM | FGA | Pct. | FTM | FTA | Pct. | REBOUNDS Off. | Def. | Tot. | Ast. | St. | Blk. | TO | Pts. | AVERAGES RPG | APG | PPG |
|---|---|---|---|---|---|---|---|---|---|---|---|---|---|---|---|---|---|---|---|
| 02-03—Mem-Orl | 70 | 1873 | 355 | 777 | .457 | 151 | 212 | .712 | 163 | 292 | 455 | 83 | 53 | 35 | 150 | 875 | 6.5 | 1.2 | 12.5 |
| 03-04—Orlando | 79 | 2134 | 369 | 829 | .445 | 167 | 262 | .637 | 160 | 356 | 516 | 89 | 62 | 72 | 126 | 914 | 6.5 | 1.1 | 11.6 |
| 04-05—Cleveland | 82 | 2523 | 464 | 943 | .492 | 251 | 310 | .810 | 207 | 546 | 753 | 130 | 77 | 76 | 133 | 1184 | 9.2 | 1.6 | 14.4 |
| Totals | 231 | 6530 | 1188 | 2549 | .466 | 569 | 784 | .726 | 530 | 1194 | 1724 | 302 | 192 | 183 | 409 | 2973 | 7.5 | 1.3 | 12.9 |

Three-point field goals: 2002-03, 14-for-48 (.292). 2003-04, 9-for-42 (.214). 2004-05, 5-for-28 (.179). Totals, 28-for-118 (.237).
Personal fouls/disqualifications: 2002-03, 172/2. 2003-04, 196/2. 2004-05, 233/2. Totals, 601/6.

### NBA PLAYOFF RECORD

| Season Team | G | Min. | FGM | FGA | Pct. | FTM | FTA | Pct. | REBOUNDS Off. | Def. | Tot. | Ast. | St. | Blk. | TO | Pts. | AVERAGES RPG | APG | PPG |
|---|---|---|---|---|---|---|---|---|---|---|---|---|---|---|---|---|---|---|---|
| 02-03—Orlando | 7 | 234 | 36 | 90 | .400 | 26 | 36 | .722 | 28 | 61 | 89 | 4 | 3 | 6 | 12 | 98 | 12.7 | 0.6 | 14.0 |

Three-point field goals: 2002-03, 0-for-3. Totals, 0-for-3 (.000).
Personal fouls/disqualifications: 2002-03, 23/1. Totals, 23/1.

## GORDON, BEN — G — BULLS

**PERSONAL:** Born April 4, 1983, in London, England. ... 6-3/200. (1.91/90.7).
**HIGH SCHOOL:** Mount Vernon (N.Y.).
**COLLEGE:** Connecticut.
**TRANSACTIONS/CAREER NOTES:** Selected after junior season by Chicago Bulls in first round (third pick overall) of 2004 NBA Draft.

### COLLEGIATE RECORD

**NOTES:** Member of NCAA Division I championship team (2004).

| Season Team | G | Min. | FGM | FGA | Pct. | FTM | FTA | Pct. | Reb. | Ast. | Pts. | AVERAGES RPG | APG | PPG |
|---|---|---|---|---|---|---|---|---|---|---|---|---|---|---|
| 01-02—Connecticut | 34 | 844 | 140 | 315 | .444 | 85 | 117 | .726 | 93 | 105 | 427 | 2.7 | 3.1 | 12.6 |
| 02-03—Connecticut | 33 | 1101 | 211 | 476 | .443 | 143 | 177 | .808 | 138 | 156 | 645 | 4.2 | 4.7 | 19.5 |
| 03-04—Connecticut | 39 | 1346 | 239 | 551 | .434 | 141 | 170 | .829 | 184 | 176 | 723 | 4.7 | 4.5 | 18.5 |
| Totals | 106 | 3291 | 590 | 1342 | .440 | 369 | 464 | .795 | 415 | 437 | 1795 | 3.9 | 4.1 | 16.9 |

Three-point field goals: 2001-02, 62-for-150 (.413). 2002-03, 80-for-191 (.419). 2003-04, 104-for-240 (.433). Totals, 246-for-581 (.423).

### NBA REGULAR-SEASON RECORD

**HONORS:** NBA Sixth Man Award (2005). ... NBA All-Rookie first team (2005).

| Season Team | G | Min. | FGM | FGA | Pct. | FTM | FTA | Pct. | REBOUNDS Off. | Def. | Tot. | Ast. | St. | Blk. | TO | Pts. | AVERAGES RPG | APG | PPG |
|---|---|---|---|---|---|---|---|---|---|---|---|---|---|---|---|---|---|---|---|
| 04-05—Chicago | 82 | 2002 | 434 | 1056 | .411 | 233 | 270 | .863 | 55 | 160 | 215 | 164 | 53 | 10 | 186 | 1235 | 2.6 | 2.0 | 15.1 |

Three-point field goals: 2004-05, 134-for-331 (.405). Totals, 134-for-331 (.405).
Personal fouls/disqualifications: 2004-05, 224/1. Totals, 224/1.

### NBA PLAYOFF RECORD

| Season Team | G | Min. | FGM | FGA | Pct. | FTM | FTA | Pct. | REBOUNDS Off. | Def. | Tot. | Ast. | St. | Blk. | TO | Pts. | AVERAGES RPG | APG | PPG |
|---|---|---|---|---|---|---|---|---|---|---|---|---|---|---|---|---|---|---|---|
| 04-05—Chicago | 6 | 153 | 30 | 74 | .405 | 20 | 25 | .800 | 6 | 10 | 16 | 15 | 5 | 2 | 13 | 87 | 2.7 | 2.5 | 14.5 |

Three-point field goals: 2004-05, 7-for-22 (.318). Totals, 7-for-22 (.318).
Personal fouls/disqualifications: 2004-05, 18/0. Totals, 18/0.

**G**

## GRANT, BRIAN — F — SUNS

**PERSONAL:** Born March 5, 1972, in Columbus, Ohio. ... 6-9/254. (2.06/115.2). ... Full name: Brian Wade Grant
**HIGH SCHOOL:** Georgetown (Ohio).
**COLLEGE:** Xavier.
**TRANSACTIONS/CAREER NOTES:** Selected by Sacramento Kings in first round (eighth pick overall) of 1994 NBA Draft. ... Signed as free agent by Portland Trail Blazers (August 23, 1997). ... Traded by Trail Blazers to Miami Heat as part of three-way deal in which Heat sent F/C Chris Gatling, F Clarence Weatherspoon, future first-round draft choice and cash to Cleveland Cavaliers, Cavaliers sent F Shawn Kemp to Trail Blazers and Trail Blazers sent G Gary Grant to Cavaliers (August 30, 2000). ... Traded by Heat with F Lamar Odom, F Caron Butler, a first-round draft choice and a second-round draft choice to Los Angeles Lakers for C Shaquille O'Neal (July 14, 2004). ... Waived by Lakers (August 10, 2005). ... Signed as free agent by Phoenix Suns (August 18, 2005).

## COLLEGIATE RECORD

| Season Team | G | Min. | FGM | FGA | Pct. | FTM | FTA | Pct. | Reb. | Ast. | Pts. | RPG | APG | PPG |
|---|---|---|---|---|---|---|---|---|---|---|---|---|---|---|
| 90-91—Xavier | 32 | 932 | 135 | 236 | .572 | 100 | 144 | .694 | 273 | 20 | 370 | 8.5 | 0.6 | 11.6 |
| 91-92—Xavier | 26 | 729 | 117 | 203 | .576 | 74 | 127 | .583 | 237 | 23 | 308 | 9.1 | 0.9 | 11.8 |
| 92-93—Xavier | 30 | 944 | 223 | 341 | .654 | 110 | 159 | .692 | 283 | 46 | 556 | 9.4 | 1.5 | 18.5 |
| 93-94—Xavier | 29 | 894 | 181 | 324 | .559 | 122 | 171 | .713 | 287 | 47 | 485 | 9.9 | 1.6 | 16.7 |
| **Totals** | 117 | 3499 | 656 | 1104 | .594 | 406 | 601 | .676 | 1080 | 136 | 1719 | 9.2 | 1.2 | 14.7 |

Three-point field goals: 1993-94, 1-for-3 (.333). Totals, 1-for-3 (.333).

## NBA REGULAR-SEASON RECORD

**HONORS:** J. Walter Kennedy Citizenship Award (1999). ... NBA All-Rookie first team (1995).

| | | | | | | | | | REBOUNDS | | | | | | | | AVERAGES | | |
|---|---|---|---|---|---|---|---|---|---|---|---|---|---|---|---|---|---|---|---|
| Season Team | G | Min. | FGM | FGA | Pct. | FTM | FTA | Pct. | Off. | Def. | Tot. | Ast. | St. | Blk. | TO | Pts. | RPG | APG | PPG |
| 94-95—Sacramento | 80 | 2289 | 413 | 809 | .511 | 231 | 363 | .636 | 207 | 391 | 598 | 99 | 49 | 116 | 163 | 1058 | 7.5 | 1.2 | 13.2 |
| 95-96—Sacramento | 78 | 2398 | 427 | 842 | .507 | 262 | 358 | .732 | 175 | 370 | 545 | 127 | 40 | 103 | 185 | 1120 | 7.0 | 1.6 | 14.4 |
| 96-97—Sacramento | 24 | 607 | 91 | 207 | .440 | 70 | 90 | .778 | 49 | 93 | 142 | 28 | 19 | 25 | 44 | 252 | 5.9 | 1.2 | 10.5 |
| 97-98—Portland | 61 | 1921 | 283 | 557 | .508 | 171 | 228 | .750 | 197 | 358 | 555 | 86 | 44 | 45 | 110 | 737 | 9.1 | 1.4 | 12.1 |
| 98-99—Portland | 48 | 1525 | 183 | 382 | .479 | 184 | 226 | .814 | 173 | 297 | 470 | 67 | 21 | 34 | 96 | 550 | 9.8 | 1.4 | 11.5 |
| 99-00—Portland | 63 | 1322 | 173 | 352 | .491 | 112 | 166 | .675 | 121 | 223 | 344 | 64 | 32 | 28 | 84 | 459 | 5.5 | 1.0 | 7.3 |
| 00-01—Miami | 82 | 2771 | 484 | 1010 | .479 | 282 | 354 | .797 | 217 | 501 | 718 | 101 | 60 | 71 | 170 | 1250 | 8.8 | 1.2 | 15.2 |
| 01-02—Miami | 72 | 2256 | 286 | 610 | .469 | 101 | 119 | .849 | 168 | 407 | 575 | 137 | 48 | 31 | 122 | 673 | 8.0 | 1.9 | 9.3 |
| 02-03—Miami | 82 | 2641 | 344 | 676 | .509 | 158 | 205 | .771 | 241 | 596 | 837 | 104 | 63 | 47 | 129 | 846 | 10.2 | 1.3 | 10.3 |
| 03-04—Miami | 76 | 2303 | 289 | 613 | .471 | 86 | 110 | .782 | 174 | 350 | 524 | 69 | 51 | 35 | 82 | 664 | 6.9 | 0.9 | 8.7 |
| 04-05—L.A. Lakers | 69 | 1136 | 103 | 209 | .493 | 57 | 79 | .722 | 101 | 156 | 257 | 34 | 23 | 23 | 43 | 263 | 3.7 | 0.5 | 3.8 |
| **Totals** | 735 | 21169 | 3076 | 6267 | .491 | 1714 | 2298 | .746 | 1823 | 3742 | 5565 | 916 | 450 | 558 | 1228 | 7872 | 7.6 | 1.2 | 10.7 |

Three-point field goals: 1994-95, 1-for-4 (.250). 1995-96, 4-for-17 (.235). 1997-98, 0-for-1. 1999-00, 1-for-2 (.500). 2000-01, 0-for-1. 2001-02, 0-for-2. 2003-04, 0-for-1. Totals, 6-for-28 (.214).

Personal fouls/disqualifications: 1994-95, 276/4. 1995-96, 269/9. 1996-97, 75/0. 1997-98, 184/3. 1998-99, 136/1. 1999-00, 166/2. 2000-01, 293/5. 2001-02, 236/6. 2002-03, 300/8. 2003-04, 254/4. 2004-05, 175/2. Totals, 2364/44.

## NBA PLAYOFF RECORD

| | | | | | | | | | REBOUNDS | | | | | | | | AVERAGES | | |
|---|---|---|---|---|---|---|---|---|---|---|---|---|---|---|---|---|---|---|---|
| Season Team | G | Min. | FGM | FGA | Pct. | FTM | FTA | Pct. | Off. | Def. | Tot. | Ast. | St. | Blk. | TO | Pts. | RPG | APG | PPG |
| 95-96—Sacramento | 4 | 124 | 16 | 42 | .381 | 7 | 14 | .500 | 7 | 13 | 20 | 4 | 2 | 7 | 13 | 39 | 5.0 | 1.0 | 9.8 |
| 97-98—Portland | 4 | 135 | 19 | 36 | .528 | 15 | 18 | .833 | 18 | 25 | 43 | 6 | 4 | 3 | 5 | 53 | 10.8 | 1.5 | 13.3 |
| 98-99—Portland | 13 | 482 | 63 | 119 | .529 | 45 | 72 | .625 | 34 | 85 | 119 | 14 | 10 | 16 | 21 | 171 | 9.2 | 1.1 | 13.2 |
| 99-00—Portland | 16 | 320 | 29 | 65 | .446 | 29 | 39 | .744 | 37 | 55 | 92 | 8 | 6 | 6 | 17 | 87 | 5.8 | 0.5 | 5.4 |
| 00-01—Miami | 3 | 84 | 10 | 24 | .417 | 10 | 14 | .714 | 6 | 18 | 24 | 1 | 0 | 5 | 6 | 30 | 8.0 | 0.3 | 10.0 |
| 03-04—Miami | 13 | 399 | 42 | 98 | .429 | 8 | 14 | .571 | 45 | 67 | 112 | 10 | 7 | 8 | 18 | 92 | 8.6 | 0.8 | 7.1 |
| **Totals** | 53 | 1544 | 179 | 384 | .466 | 114 | 171 | .667 | 147 | 263 | 410 | 43 | 29 | 45 | 80 | 472 | 7.7 | 0.8 | 8.9 |

Three-point field goals: 2003-04, 0-for-1. Totals, 0-for-1 (.000).

Personal fouls/disqualifications: 1995-96, 14/1. 1997-98, 20/0. 1998-99, 48/1. 1999-00, 53/1. 2000-01, 9/0. 2003-04, 52/1. Totals, 196/4.

---

# GREEN, WILLIE     G     76ERS

**PERSONAL:** Born July 28, 1981, in Detroit, Mich. ... 6-4/200. (1.93/90.7). ... Full name: Willie J. Green.
**HIGH SCHOOL:** Cooley (Detroit, Mich.).
**COLLEGE:** Detroit Mercy.
**TRANSACTIONS/CAREER NOTES:** Selected by Seattle SuperSonics in second round (41st pick overall) of 2003 NBA Draft. ... Draft rights traded by SuperSonics to Philadelphia 76ers for draft rights to G Paccelis Morlende (June 26, 2003).

## COLLEGIATE RECORD

| Season Team | G | Min. | FGM | FGA | Pct. | FTM | FTA | Pct. | Reb. | Ast. | Pts. | RPG | APG | PPG |
|---|---|---|---|---|---|---|---|---|---|---|---|---|---|---|
| 99-00—Detroit Mercy | 32 | 800 | 91 | 218 | .417 | 61 | 75 | .813 | 83 | 60 | 269 | 2.6 | 1.9 | 8.4 |
| 00-01—Detroit Mercy | 33 | 1012 | 167 | 352 | .474 | 70 | 97 | .722 | 166 | 80 | 436 | 5.0 | 2.4 | 13.2 |
| 01-02—Detroit Mercy | 29 | 888 | 147 | 341 | .431 | 77 | 115 | .670 | 122 | 55 | 396 | 4.2 | 1.9 | 13.7 |
| 02-03—Detroit Mercy | 30 | 1021 | 244 | 498 | .490 | 153 | 190 | .805 | 148 | 75 | 678 | 4.9 | 2.5 | 22.6 |
| **Totals** | 124 | 3721 | 649 | 1409 | .461 | 361 | 477 | .757 | 519 | 270 | 1779 | 4.2 | 2.2 | 14.3 |

Three-point field goals: 1999-00, 26-for-68 (.382). 2000-01, 32-for-89 (.372). 2001-02, 25-for-88 (.284). 2002-03, 37-for-99 (.374). Totals, 120-for-341 (.352).

## NBA REGULAR-SEASON RECORD

| | | | | | | | | | REBOUNDS | | | | | | | | AVERAGES | | |
|---|---|---|---|---|---|---|---|---|---|---|---|---|---|---|---|---|---|---|---|
| Season Team | G | Min. | FGM | FGA | Pct. | FTM | FTA | Pct. | Off. | Def. | Tot. | Ast. | St. | Blk. | TO | Pts. | RPG | APG | PPG |
| 03-04—Philadelphia | 53 | 767 | 143 | 357 | .401 | 59 | 81 | .728 | 16 | 49 | 65 | 53 | 26 | 5 | 59 | 364 | 1.2 | 1.0 | 6.9 |
| 04-05—Philadelphia | 57 | 1066 | 155 | 423 | .366 | 97 | 125 | .776 | 22 | 111 | 133 | 100 | 34 | 6 | 75 | 437 | 2.3 | 1.8 | 7.7 |
| **Totals** | 110 | 1833 | 298 | 780 | .382 | 156 | 206 | .757 | 38 | 160 | 198 | 153 | 60 | 11 | 134 | 801 | 1.8 | 1.4 | 7.3 |

Three-point field goals: 2003-04, 19-for-61 (.311). 2004-05, 30-for-105 (.286). Totals, 49-for-166 (.295).

Personal fouls/disqualifications: 2003-04, 83/0. 2004-05, 121/0. Totals, 204/0.

## NBA PLAYOFF RECORD

| | | | | | | | | | REBOUNDS | | | | | | | | AVERAGES | | |
|---|---|---|---|---|---|---|---|---|---|---|---|---|---|---|---|---|---|---|---|
| Season Team | G | Min. | FGM | FGA | Pct. | FTM | FTA | Pct. | Off. | Def. | Tot. | Ast. | St. | Blk. | TO | Pts. | RPG | APG | PPG |
| 04-05—Philadelphia | 5 | 63 | 8 | 18 | .444 | 9 | 10 | .900 | 3 | 6 | 9 | 3 | 1 | 0 | 2 | 27 | 1.8 | 0.6 | 5.4 |

Three-point field goals: 2004-05, 2-for-9 (.222). Totals, 2-for-9 (.222).

Personal fouls/disqualifications: 2004-05, 5/0. Totals, 5/0.

G

# GRIFFIN, ADRIAN  G/F  BULLS

**PERSONAL:** Born July 4, 1974, in Wichita, Kan. ... 6-5/215. (1.96/97.5).
**HIGH SCHOOL:** Wichita East (Kansas).
**COLLEGE:** Seton Hall.
**TRANSACTIONS/CAREER NOTES:** Not drafted by an NBA franchise. ... Played in Continental Basketball Association with Connecticut Pride (1996-99). ... Played in Italy (1998-99). ... Signed by Miami Heat (January 21, 1999). ... Waived by Heat (February 1, 1999). ... Signed as free agent by Boston Celtics (August 1, 1999). ... Signed as free agent by Dallas Mavericks (July 27, 2001). ... Signed as free agent by Houston Rockets (August 7, 2003) ... Traded by Rockets with G Mike Wilks and G/F Eric Piatkowski to Chicago Bulls for C Dikembe Mutombo (September 8, 2004).

## COLLEGIATE RECORD

| Season Team | G | Min. | FGM | FGA | Pct. | FTM | FTA | Pct. | Reb. | Ast. | Pts. | RPG | APG | PPG |
|---|---|---|---|---|---|---|---|---|---|---|---|---|---|---|
| | | | | | | | | | | | | AVERAGES | | |
| 92-93—Seton Hall | 35 | 465 | 44 | 87 | .506 | 31 | 53 | .585 | 123 | 29 | 29 | 3.5 | 0.8 | 0.8 |
| 93-94—Seton Hall | 30 | 893 | 106 | 224 | .473 | 76 | 126 | .603 | 233 | 66 | 290 | 7.8 | 2.2 | 9.7 |
| 94-95—Seton Hall | 30 | 949 | 184 | 332 | .554 | 86 | 119 | .723 | 216 | 85 | 460 | 7.2 | 2.8 | 15.3 |
| 95-96—Seton Hall | 28 | 983 | 213 | 438 | .486 | 107 | 161 | .665 | 231 | 86 | 454 | 8.3 | 3.1 | 16.2 |
| Totals | 123 | 3290 | 547 | 1081 | .506 | 300 | 459 | .654 | 803 | 266 | 1233 | 6.5 | 2.2 | 10.0 |

Three-point field goals: 1992-93, 0-for-2. 1993-94, 2-for-6 (.333). 1994-95, 6-for-20 (.300). 1995-96, 12-for-44 (.273). Totals, 20-for-72 (.278).
Personal fouls/disqualifications: 1992-93, 41/0. 1993-94, 75/0. 1994-95, 77/0. 1995-96, 82/0. Totals, 275/0.

## CBA RECORD

**NOTES:** Member of CBA championship team (1999). ... CBA Most Valuable Player (1999). ... CBA Finals MVP (1999). ... CBA All-League first team (1998, 1999). ... CBA All-Defensive team (1998, 1999). ... CBA All-Rookie first team (1997).

| Season Team | G | Min. | FGM | FGA | Pct. | FTM | FTA | Pct. | Reb. | Ast. | Pts. | RPG | APG | PPG |
|---|---|---|---|---|---|---|---|---|---|---|---|---|---|---|
| | | | | | | | | | | | | AVERAGES | | |
| 96-97—Connecticut | 54 | 1894 | 312 | 621 | .502 | 127 | 169 | .751 | 361 | 116 | 751 | 6.7 | 2.1 | 13.9 |
| 97-98—Connecticut | 56 | 2157 | 391 | 798 | .490 | 165 | 213 | .775 | 376 | 188 | 961 | 6.7 | 3.4 | 17.2 |
| 98-99—Connecticut | 47 | 1758 | 319 | 699 | .456 | *222 | 261 | .851 | 358 | 159 | 888 | 7.6 | 3.4 | 18.9 |
| Totals | 157 | 5809 | 1022 | 2118 | .483 | 514 | 643 | .799 | 1095 | 463 | 2600 | 7.0 | 2.9 | 16.6 |

Three-point field goals: 1996-97, 0-for-9. 1997-98, 14-for-52 (.269). 1998-99, 28-for-84 (.333). Totals, 42-for-145 (.290).
Personal fouls/disqualifications: 1996-97, 178/0. 1997-98, 186/0. 1998-99, 138/0. Totals, 502/0.

## ITALIAN LEAGUE RECORD

| Season Team | G | Min. | FGM | FGA | Pct. | FTM | FTA | Pct. | Reb. | Ast. | Pts. | RPG | APG | PPG |
|---|---|---|---|---|---|---|---|---|---|---|---|---|---|---|
| | | | | | | | | | | | | AVERAGES | | |
| 98-99—Cordivari | 8 | 226 | 41 | 71 | .577 | 19 | 30 | .633 | 48 | 7 | 103 | 6.0 | 0.9 | 12.9 |

Three-point field goals: 1998-99, 2-for-6 (.333). Totals, 2-for-6 (.333).
Personal fouls/disqualifications: 1998-99, 26/0. Totals, 26/0.

## NBA REGULAR-SEASON RECORD

| Season Team | G | Min. | FGM | FGA | Pct. | FTM | FTA | Pct. | Off. | Def. | Tot. | Ast. | St. | Blk. | TO | Pts. | RPG | APG | PPG |
|---|---|---|---|---|---|---|---|---|---|---|---|---|---|---|---|---|---|---|---|
| | | | | | | | | | REBOUNDS | | | | | | | | AVERAGES | | |
| 99-00—Boston | 72 | 1927 | 175 | 413 | .424 | 119 | 158 | .753 | 128 | 244 | 372 | 177 | 116 | 15 | 93 | 485 | 5.2 | 2.5 | 6.7 |
| 00-01—Boston | 44 | 377 | 33 | 97 | .340 | 18 | 24 | .750 | 27 | 60 | 87 | 27 | 18 | 5 | 18 | 93 | 2.0 | 0.6 | 2.1 |
| 01-02—Dallas | 58 | 1383 | 179 | 359 | .499 | 41 | 49 | .837 | 68 | 161 | 229 | 106 | 75 | 12 | 42 | 415 | 3.9 | 1.8 | 7.2 |
| 02-03—Dallas | 74 | 1373 | 146 | 337 | .433 | 27 | 32 | .844 | 88 | 176 | 264 | 105 | 77 | 6 | 47 | 325 | 3.6 | 1.4 | 4.4 |
| 03-04—Houston | 19 | 133 | 5 | 18 | .278 | 0 | 4 | .000 | 1 | 18 | 19 | 10 | 7 | 2 | 11 | 11 | 1.0 | 0.5 | 0.6 |
| 04-05—Chicago | 69 | 667 | 58 | 161 | .360 | 33 | 44 | .750 | 52 | 94 | 146 | 53 | 43 | 4 | 30 | 151 | 2.1 | 0.8 | 2.2 |
| Totals | 336 | 5860 | 596 | 1385 | .430 | 238 | 311 | .765 | 364 | 753 | 1117 | 478 | 336 | 44 | 233 | 1480 | 3.3 | 1.4 | 4.4 |

Three-point field goals: 1999-00, 16-for-57 (.281). 2000-01, 9-for-26 (.346). 2001-02, 16-for-54 (.296). 2002-03, 6-for-24 (.250). 2003-04, 1-for-2 (.500). 2004-05, 2-for-9 (.222). Totals, 50-for-172 (.291).
Personal fouls/disqualifications: 1999-00, 222/3. 2000-01, 45/0. 2001-02, 142/2. 2002-03, 157/0. 2003-04, 17/0. 2004-05, 78/0. Totals, 661/5.

## NBA PLAYOFF RECORD

| Season Team | G | Min. | FGM | FGA | Pct. | FTM | FTA | Pct. | Off. | Def. | Tot. | Ast. | St. | Blk. | TO | Pts. | RPG | APG | PPG |
|---|---|---|---|---|---|---|---|---|---|---|---|---|---|---|---|---|---|---|---|
| | | | | | | | | | REBOUNDS | | | | | | | | AVERAGES | | |
| 01-02—Dallas | 4 | 57 | 10 | 17 | .588 | 0 | 2 | .000 | 2 | 7 | 9 | 4 | 2 | 1 | 3 | 20 | 2.3 | 1.0 | 5.0 |
| 02-03—Dallas | 15 | 131 | 17 | 41 | .415 | 2 | 2 | 1.000 | 17 | 27 | 44 | 8 | 4 | 0 | 9 | 37 | 2.9 | 0.5 | 2.5 |
| 04-05—Chicago | 5 | 86 | 15 | 29 | .517 | 4 | 5 | .800 | 5 | 15 | 20 | 9 | 5 | 0 | 3 | 34 | 4.0 | 1.8 | 6.8 |
| Totals | 24 | 274 | 42 | 87 | .483 | 6 | 9 | .667 | 24 | 49 | 73 | 21 | 11 | 1 | 15 | 91 | 3.0 | 0.9 | 3.8 |

Three-point field goals: 2001-02, 0-for-2. 2002-03, 1-for-3 (.333). Totals, 1-for-5 (.200).
Personal fouls/disqualifications: 2001-02, 6/0. 2002-03, 24/0. 2004-05, 14/1. Totals, 44/1.

# GRIFFIN, EDDIE  F  TIMBERWOLVES

**PERSONAL:** Born May 30, 1982, in Philadelphia. ... 6-10/222. (2.08/100.7). ... Full name: Eddie J. Griffin
**HIGH SCHOOL:** Roman Catholic (Philadelphia).
**COLLEGE:** Seton Hall.
**TRANSACTIONS/CAREER NOTES:** Selected after freshman season by New Jersey Nets in first round (seventh pick overall) of 2001 NBA Draft. ... Draft rights traded by Nets to Houston Rockets for draft rights to F Richard Jefferson, C Jason Collins and G Brandon Armstrong (June 27, 2001). ... Released by Rockets (December 19, 2003). ... Signed as free agent by Nets (January 8, 2004). ... Waived by Nets (February 27, 2004). ... Signed as free agent by Minnesota Timberwolves (October 4, 2004).

## COLLEGIATE RECORD

**NOTES:** The Sporting News Freshman of the Year (2001).

| Season Team | G | Min. | FGM | FGA | Pct. | FTM | FTA | Pct. | Reb. | Ast. | Pts. | RPG | APG | PPG |
|---|---|---|---|---|---|---|---|---|---|---|---|---|---|---|
| | | | | | | | | | | | | AVERAGES | | |
| 00-01—Seton Hall | 30 | 979 | 206 | 480 | .429 | 80 | 109 | .734 | 323 | 49 | 533 | 10.8 | 1.6 | 17.8 |

Three-point field goals: 2000-01, 41-for-128 (.320). Totals, 41-for-128 (.320).
Personal fouls/disqualifications: 2000-01, 71/0. Totals, 71/0.

**NBA REGULAR-SEASON RECORD**

HONORS: NBA All-Rookie second team (2002).

| | | | | | | | | REBOUNDS | | | | | | | | AVERAGES | | |
|---|---|---|---|---|---|---|---|---|---|---|---|---|---|---|---|---|---|---|
| Season Team | G | Min. | FGM | FGA | Pct. | FTM | FTA | Pct. | Off. | Def. | Tot. | Ast. | St. | Blk. | TO | Pts. | RPG | APG | PPG |
| 01-02—Houston | 73 | 1896 | 244 | 666 | .366 | 64 | 86 | .744 | 117 | 299 | 416 | 53 | 17 | 134 | 47 | 642 | 5.7 | 0.7 | 8.8 |
| 02-03—Houston | 77 | 1890 | 271 | 678 | .400 | 58 | 94 | .617 | 138 | 323 | 461 | 86 | 52 | 111 | 76 | 664 | 6.0 | 1.1 | 8.6 |
| 04-05—Minnesota | 70 | 1492 | 202 | 522 | .387 | 56 | 78 | .718 | 128 | 325 | 453 | 53 | 23 | 118 | 55 | 527 | 6.5 | 0.8 | 7.5 |
| Totals | 220 | 5278 | 717 | 1866 | .384 | 178 | 258 | .690 | 383 | 947 | 1330 | 192 | 92 | 363 | 178 | 1833 | 6.0 | 0.9 | 8.3 |

Three-point field goals: 2001-02, 90-for-273 (.330). 2002-03, 64-for-192 (.333). 2004-05, 67-for-204 (.328). Totals, 221-for-669 (.330).
Personal fouls/disqualifications: 2001-02, 117/1. 2002-03, 136/1. 2004-05, 120/1. Totals, 373/3.

# GUGLIOTTA, TOM    F

**PERSONAL:** Born December 19, 1969, in Huntington Station, N.Y. ... 6-10/240. (2.08/108.9). ... Full name: Thomas James Gugliotta ... Name pronounced GOOG-lee-ah-tah.
**HIGH SCHOOL:** Walt Whitman (Huntington Station, N.Y.).
**COLLEGE:** North Carolina State.
**TRANSACTIONS/CAREER NOTES:** Selected by Washington Bullets in first round (sixth pick overall) of 1992 NBA Draft. ... Traded by Bullets with 1996, 1998 and 2000 first-round draft choices to Golden State Warriors for F Chris Webber (November 17, 1994). ... Traded by Warriors to Minnesota Timberwolves for F Donyell Marshall (February 18, 1995). ... Signed as free agent by Phoenix Suns (January 23, 1999). ... Traded by Suns with two conditional first-round draft choices and a 2005 second-round draft choice to Utah Jazz for F Keon Clark and C Ben Handlogten (February 19, 2004). ... Signed as free agent by Boston Celtics (August 16, 2004). ... Traded by Celtics with G Gary Payton, C Michael Stewart and 2005 or future first-round draft pick to Atlanta Hawks for F Antoine Walker (February 24, 2005).

**COLLEGIATE RECORD**

| | | | | | | | | | | | AVERAGES | | |
|---|---|---|---|---|---|---|---|---|---|---|---|---|---|
| Season Team | G | Min. | FGM | FGA | Pct. | FTM | FTA | Pct. | Reb. | Ast. | Pts. | RPG | APG | PPG |
| 88-89—North Carolina State | 21 | 171 | 18 | 42 | .429 | 19 | 29 | .655 | 35 | 5 | 56 | 1.7 | 0.2 | 2.7 |
| 89-90—North Carolina State | 30 | 886 | 135 | 268 | .504 | 41 | 61 | .672 | 211 | 47 | 334 | 7.0 | 1.6 | 11.1 |
| 90-91—North Carolina State | 31 | 1123 | 170 | 340 | .500 | 65 | 101 | .644 | 281 | 87 | 471 | 9.1 | 2.8 | 15.2 |
| 91-92—North Carolina State | 30 | 1107 | 240 | 534 | .449 | 102 | 149 | .685 | 293 | 92 | 675 | 9.8 | 3.1 | 22.5 |
| Totals | 112 | 3287 | 563 | 1184 | .476 | 227 | 340 | .668 | 820 | 231 | 1536 | 7.3 | 2.1 | 13.7 |

Three-point field goals: 1988-89, 1-for-2 (.500). 1989-90, 34-for-47 (.489). 1990-91, 66-for-166 (.398). 1991-92, 93-for-233 (.399). Totals, 183-for-448 (.408).

**NBA REGULAR-SEASON RECORD**

HONORS: NBA All-Rookie first team (1993).

| | | | | | | | | REBOUNDS | | | | | | | | AVERAGES | | |
|---|---|---|---|---|---|---|---|---|---|---|---|---|---|---|---|---|---|---|
| Season Team | G | Min. | FGM | FGA | Pct. | FTM | FTA | Pct. | Off. | Def. | Tot. | Ast. | St. | Blk. | TO | Pts. | RPG | APG | PPG |
| 92-93—Washington | 81 | 2795 | 484 | 1135 | .426 | 181 | 281 | .644 | 219 | 562 | 781 | 306 | 134 | 35 | 230 | 1187 | 9.6 | 3.8 | 14.7 |
| 93-94—Washington | 78 | 2795 | 540 | 1159 | .466 | 213 | 311 | .685 | 189 | 539 | 728 | 276 | 172 | 51 | 247 | 1333 | 9.3 | 3.5 | 17.1 |
| 94-95—Was.-G.S.-Min. | 77 | 2568 | 371 | 837 | .443 | 174 | 252 | .690 | 165 | 407 | 572 | 279 | 132 | 62 | 189 | 976 | 7.4 | 3.6 | 12.7 |
| 95-96—Minnesota | 78 | 2835 | 473 | 1004 | .471 | 289 | 374 | .773 | 176 | 514 | 690 | 238 | 139 | 96 | 234 | 1261 | 8.8 | 3.1 | 16.2 |
| 96-97—Minnesota | 81 | 3131 | 592 | 1339 | .442 | 464 | 566 | .820 | 187 | 515 | 702 | 335 | 130 | 89 | 293 | 1672 | 8.7 | 4.1 | 20.6 |
| 97-98—Minnesota | 41 | 1582 | 319 | 635 | .502 | 183 | 223 | .821 | 106 | 250 | 356 | 167 | 61 | 22 | 109 | 823 | 8.7 | 4.1 | 20.1 |
| 98-99—Phoenix | 43 | 1563 | 277 | 573 | .483 | 173 | 218 | .794 | 131 | 250 | 381 | 121 | 96 | 21 | 88 | 729 | 8.9 | 2.8 | 17.0 |
| 99-00—Phoenix | 54 | 1767 | 310 | 645 | .481 | 117 | 151 | .775 | 141 | 284 | 425 | 124 | 80 | 31 | 106 | 738 | 7.9 | 2.3 | 13.7 |
| 00-01—Phoenix | 57 | 1159 | 149 | 380 | .392 | 61 | 77 | .792 | 76 | 179 | 255 | 55 | 47 | 21 | 51 | 362 | 4.5 | 1.0 | 6.4 |
| 01-02—Phoenix | 44 | 1129 | 127 | 301 | .422 | 28 | 37 | .757 | 59 | 162 | 221 | 77 | 39 | 30 | 61 | 285 | 5.0 | 1.8 | 6.5 |
| 02-03—Phoenix | 27 | 447 | 60 | 132 | .455 | 9 | 9 | 1.000 | 25 | 75 | 100 | 31 | 14 | 5 | 31 | 129 | 3.7 | 1.1 | 4.8 |
| 03-04—Phoenix-Utah | 55 | 819 | 70 | 203 | .345 | 20 | 28 | .714 | 65 | 122 | 187 | 63 | 31 | 12 | 39 | 161 | 3.4 | 1.1 | 2.9 |
| 04-05—Bos-Atl | 47 | 966 | 99 | 241 | .411 | 33 | 43 | .767 | 56 | 135 | 191 | 68 | 41 | 17 | 57 | 239 | 4.1 | 1.4 | 5.1 |
| Totals | 763 | 23556 | 3871 | 8584 | .451 | 1945 | 2570 | .757 | 1595 | 3994 | 5589 | 2140 | 1079 | 492 | 1735 | 9895 | 7.3 | 2.8 | 13.0 |

Three-point field goals: 1992-93, 38-for-135 (.281). 1993-94, 40-for-148 (.270). 1994-95, 60-for-186 (.323). 1995-96, 26-for-86 (.302). 1996-97, 24-for-93 (.258). 1997-98, 2-for-17 (.118). 1998-99, 2-for-7 (.286). 1999-00, 1-for-8 (.125). 2000-01, 3-for-12 (.250). 2001-02, 3-for-9 (.333). 2002-03, 0-for-1. 2003-04, 1-for-4 (.250). 2004-05, 8-for-26 (.308). Totals, 208-for-732 (.284).
Personal fouls/disqualifications: 1992-93, 195/0. 1993-94, 174/0. 1994-95, 203/2. 1995-96, 265/1. 1996-97, 237/3. 1997-98, 102/0. 1998-99, 110/0. 1999-00, 152/2. 2000-01, 110/0. 2001-02, 116/1. 2002-03, 35/0. 2003-04, 81/0. 2004-05, 104/0. Totals, 1884/9.

**NBA PLAYOFF RECORD**

| | | | | | | | | REBOUNDS | | | | | | | | AVERAGES | | |
|---|---|---|---|---|---|---|---|---|---|---|---|---|---|---|---|---|---|---|
| Season Team | G | Min. | FGM | FGA | Pct. | FTM | FTA | Pct. | Off. | Def. | Tot. | Ast. | St. | Blk. | TO | Pts. | RPG | APG | PPG |
| 96-97—Minnesota | 3 | 121 | 23 | 52 | .442 | 6 | 10 | .600 | 2 | 14 | 16 | 13 | 7 | 2 | 6 | 55 | 5.3 | 4.3 | 18.3 |
| 98-99—Phoenix | 3 | 118 | 13 | 35 | .371 | 6 | 8 | .750 | 6 | 19 | 25 | 10 | 4 | 3 | 8 | 32 | 8.3 | 3.3 | 10.7 |
| 00-01—Phoenix | 4 | 86 | 8 | 26 | .308 | 7 | 9 | .778 | 4 | 11 | 15 | 3 | 8 | 1 | 5 | 23 | 3.8 | 0.8 | 5.8 |
| 02-03—Phoenix | 2 | 10 | 2 | 4 | .500 | 1 | 2 | .500 | 0 | 2 | 2 | 0 | 0 | 0 | 0 | 5 | 1.0 | 0.0 | 2.5 |
| Totals | 12 | 335 | 46 | 117 | .393 | 20 | 29 | .690 | 12 | 46 | 58 | 26 | 19 | 6 | 19 | 115 | 4.8 | 2.2 | 9.6 |

Three-point field goals: 1996-97, 3-for-4 (.750). Totals, 3-for-4 (.750).
Personal fouls/disqualifications: 1996-97, 13/0. 1998-99, 10/0. 2000-01, 9/0. 2002-03, 2/0. Totals, 34/0.

**NBA ALL-STAR GAME RECORD**

| | | | | | | | | REBOUNDS | | | | | | | | |
|---|---|---|---|---|---|---|---|---|---|---|---|---|---|---|---|---|
| Season Team | Min. | FGM | FGA | Pct. | FTM | FTA | Pct. | Off. | Def. | Tot. | Ast. | PF | Dq. | St. | Blk. | TO | Pts. |
| 1997—Minnesota | 19 | 3 | 7 | .429 | 3 | 4 | .750 | 1 | 7 | 8 | 3 | 3 | 0 | 2 | 0 | 3 | 9 |

Three-point field goals: 1997, 0-for-1. Totals, 0-for-1 (.000).

G

– 99 –

## HA, SEUNG-JIN   C   TRAIL BLAZERS

**PERSONAL:** Born August 4, 1985, in Seoul, Korea. ... 7-3/305. (2.21/138.3).
**HIGH SCHOOL:** Samil Commercial (Korea).
**COLLEGE:** Yonsei University (Korea).
**TRANSACTIONS/CAREER NOTES:** Selected by Portland Trail Blazers in second round (46th pick overall) of 2004 NBA Draft.

### AMERICAN BASKETBALL ASSOCIATION RECORD

| Season Team | G | Min. | FGM | FGA | Pct. | FTM | FTA | Pct. | Reb. | Ast. | Pts. | RPG | APG | PPG |
|---|---|---|---|---|---|---|---|---|---|---|---|---|---|---|
| 04-05—Portland | 6 | ... | 10 | 14 | .714 | 8 | 19 | .421 | 43 | 7 | 28 | 7.2 | 1.2 | 4.7 |

### NBA REGULAR-SEASON RECORD

| Season Team | G | Min. | FGM | FGA | Pct. | FTM | FTA | Pct. | Off. | Def. | Tot. | Ast. | St. | Blk. | TO | Pts. | RPG | APG | PPG |
|---|---|---|---|---|---|---|---|---|---|---|---|---|---|---|---|---|---|---|---|
| 04-05—Portland | 19 | 104 | 10 | 23 | .435 | 6 | 11 | .545 | 6 | 12 | 18 | 2 | 1 | 5 | 12 | 26 | 0.9 | 0.1 | 1.4 |

Personal fouls/disqualifications: 2004-05, 21/0. Totals, 21/0.

## HAISLIP, MARCUS   F

**PERSONAL:** Born December 22, 1980, in Lewisburg, Tenn. ... 6-10/230. (2.08/104.3). ... Full name: Marcus Deshon Haislip
**HIGH SCHOOL:** Marshall County (Lewisburg, Tenn.).
**COLLEGE:** Tennessee.
**TRANSACTIONS/CAREER NOTES:** Selected after junior season by Milwaukee Bucks in first round (13th pick overall) of 2002 NBA Draft. ... Signed as free agent by Indiana Pacers (December 1, 2004). ... Waived by Pacers (December 24, 2004).

### COLLEGIATE RECORD

| Season Team | G | Min. | FGM | FGA | Pct. | FTM | FTA | Pct. | Reb. | Ast. | Pts. | RPG | APG | PPG |
|---|---|---|---|---|---|---|---|---|---|---|---|---|---|---|
| 99-00—Tennessee | 31 | 251 | 52 | 88 | .591 | 22 | 39 | .564 | 57 | 0 | 135 | 1.8 | 0.0 | 4.4 |
| 00-01—Tennessee | 33 | 435 | 63 | 122 | .516 | 53 | 70 | .757 | 83 | 17 | 193 | 2.5 | 0.5 | 5.8 |
| 01-02—Tennessee | 25 | 839 | 161 | 311 | .518 | 80 | 111 | .721 | 167 | 24 | 417 | 6.7 | 1.0 | 16.7 |
| Totals | 89 | 1525 | 276 | 521 | .530 | 155 | 220 | .705 | 307 | 41 | 745 | 3.4 | 0.5 | 8.4 |

Three-point field goals: 1999-00, 9-for-17 (.529). 2000-01, 14-for-39 (.359). 2001-02, 15-for-46 (.326). Totals, 38-for-102 (.373).

### NBA REGULAR-SEASON RECORD

| Season Team | G | Min. | FGM | FGA | Pct. | FTM | FTA | Pct. | Off. | Def. | Tot. | Ast. | St. | Blk. | TO | Pts. | RPG | APG | PPG |
|---|---|---|---|---|---|---|---|---|---|---|---|---|---|---|---|---|---|---|---|
| 02-03—Milwaukee | 39 | 441 | 66 | 153 | .431 | 26 | 38 | .684 | 21 | 32 | 53 | 9 | 7 | 18 | 21 | 161 | 1.4 | 0.2 | 4.1 |
| 03-04—Milwaukee | 31 | 263 | 36 | 74 | .486 | 20 | 28 | .714 | 21 | 32 | 53 | 4 | 6 | 12 | 9 | 93 | 1.7 | 0.1 | 3.0 |
| 04-05—Milwaukee-Ind. | 9 | 106 | 13 | 38 | .342 | 6 | 11 | .545 | 5 | 10 | 15 | 3 | 2 | 2 | 6 | 32 | 1.7 | 0.3 | 3.6 |
| Totals | 79 | 810 | 115 | 265 | .434 | 52 | 77 | .675 | 47 | 74 | 121 | 16 | 15 | 32 | 36 | 286 | 1.5 | 0.2 | 3.6 |

Three-point field goals: 2002-03, 3-for-12 (.250). 2003-04, 1-for-2 (.500). 2004-05, 0-for-1. Totals, 4-for-15 (.267).
Personal fouls/disqualifications: 2002-03, 55/1. 2003-04, 25/0. 2004-05, 15/0. Totals, 95/1.

### NBA PLAYOFF RECORD

| Season Team | G | Min. | FGM | FGA | Pct. | FTM | FTA | Pct. | Off. | Def. | Tot. | Ast. | St. | Blk. | TO | Pts. | RPG | APG | PPG |
|---|---|---|---|---|---|---|---|---|---|---|---|---|---|---|---|---|---|---|---|
| 02-03—Milwaukee | 2 | 24 | 4 | 6 | .667 | 2 | 4 | .500 | 2 | 4 | 6 | 2 | 2 | 1 | 1 | 10 | 2.0 | 1.0 | 5.0 |
| 03-04—Milwaukee | 1 | 3 | 1 | 1 | 1.000 | 0 | 0 | ... | 1 | 0 | 1 | 0 | 0 | 0 | 0 | 2 | 1.0 | 0.0 | 2.0 |
| Totals | 3 | 27 | 5 | 7 | .714 | 2 | 4 | .500 | 3 | 2 | 5 | 2 | 2 | 1 | 1 | 12 | 1.7 | 0.7 | 4.0 |

Personal fouls/disqualifications: 2002-03, 5/0. Totals, 5/0.

## HAM, DARVIN   F   PISTONS

**PERSONAL:** Born July 23, 1973, in Saginaw, Mich. ... 6-7/240. (2.01/108.9).
**HIGH SCHOOL:** Saginaw (Mich.).
**JUNIOR COLLEGE:** Otero Junior College (Colo.).
**COLLEGE:** Texas Tech.
**TRANSACTIONS/CAREER NOTES:** Not drafted by an NBA franchise. ... Played in United States Basketball League with Florida Sharks (1996). ... Signed as free agent by Denver Nuggets (October 1, 1996). ... Traded by Nuggets to Indiana Pacers for G Jerome Allen (February 20, 1997). ... Signed as free agent by Washington Wizards (September 30, 1997). ... Played in Spain (1998-99). ... Signed as free agent by Milwaukee Bucks (September 22, 1999). ... Signed as free agent by Atlanta Hawks (September 17, 2002). ... Signed as free agent by Detroit Pistons (September 23, 2003).
**MISCELLANEOUS:** Member of NBA championship team (2004).

### COLLEGIATE RECORD

| Season Team | G | Min. | FGM | FGA | Pct. | FTM | FTA | Pct. | Reb. | Ast. | Pts. | RPG | APG | PPG |
|---|---|---|---|---|---|---|---|---|---|---|---|---|---|---|
| 91-92—Otero J.C. | ... | ... | ... | ... | ... | ... | ... | ... | ... | ... | ... | ... | ... | 1.4 |
| 92-93—Otero J.C. | | | | | | Did not play—redshirted. | | | | | | | | |
| 93-94—Texas Tech | 28 | 668 | 97 | 157 | .618 | 36 | 72 | .500 | 152 | 34 | 230 | 5.4 | 1.2 | 8.2 |
| 94-95—Texas Tech | 30 | 638 | 78 | 131 | .595 | 50 | 85 | .588 | 129 | 26 | 206 | 4.3 | 0.9 | 6.9 |
| 95-96—Texas Tech | 32 | 752 | 115 | 198 | .581 | 61 | 138 | .442 | 181 | 31 | 291 | 5.7 | 1.0 | 9.1 |
| Junior College Totals | ... | ... | ... | ... | ... | ... | ... | ... | ... | ... | ... | ... | ... | ... |
| 4-Year-College Totals | 90 | 2058 | 290 | 486 | .597 | 147 | 295 | .498 | 462 | 91 | 727 | 5.1 | 1.0 | 8.1 |

H

Three-point field goals: 1995-96, 0-for-1. Totals, 0-for-1 (.000).
Personal fouls/disqualifications: 1993-94, 94/0. 1994-95, 76/0. 1995-96, 74/0. Totals, 244/0.

### NBA REGULAR-SEASON RECORD

| | | | | | | | | REBOUNDS | | | | | | | | AVERAGES | | |
|---|---|---|---|---|---|---|---|---|---|---|---|---|---|---|---|---|---|---|
| Season Team | G | Min. | FGM | FGA | Pct. | FTM | FTA | Pct. | Off. | Def. | Tot. | Ast. | St. | Blk. | TO | Pts. | RPG | APG | PPG |
| 96-97—Den.-Indiana ... | 36 | 318 | 33 | 62 | .532 | 17 | 35 | .486 | 29 | 27 | 56 | 14 | 9 | 8 | 22 | 83 | 1.6 | 0.4 | 2.3 |
| 97-98—Washington .... | 71 | 635 | 55 | 104 | .529 | 35 | 74 | .473 | 72 | 59 | 131 | 16 | 21 | 25 | 37 | 145 | 1.8 | 0.2 | 2.0 |
| 99-00—Milwaukee ...... | 35 | 792 | 71 | 128 | .555 | 35 | 78 | .449 | 85 | 87 | 172 | 42 | 29 | 29 | 29 | 177 | 4.9 | 1.2 | 5.1 |
| 00-01—Milwaukee ...... | 29 | 540 | 39 | 80 | .488 | 29 | 49 | .592 | 56 | 65 | 121 | 25 | 17 | 21 | 33 | 109 | 4.2 | 0.9 | 3.8 |
| 01-02—Milwaukee ...... | 70 | 1208 | 120 | 211 | .569 | 62 | 123 | .504 | 91 | 111 | 202 | 73 | 25 | 37 | 83 | 303 | 2.9 | 1.0 | 4.3 |
| 02-03—Atlanta ............ | 75 | 926 | 71 | 159 | .447 | 38 | 79 | .481 | 73 | 80 | 153 | 38 | 16 | 19 | 65 | 180 | 2.0 | 0.5 | 2.4 |
| 03-04—Detroit ............ | 54 | 484 | 37 | 75 | .493 | 21 | 35 | .600 | 47 | 46 | 93 | 16 | 13 | 8 | 31 | 96 | 1.7 | 0.3 | 1.8 |
| 04-05—Detroit ............ | 47 | 275 | 17 | 37 | .459 | 12 | 31 | .387 | 19 | 16 | 35 | 5 | 6 | 7 | 8 | 46 | 0.7 | 0.1 | 1.0 |
| Totals ................... | 417 | 5178 | 443 | 856 | .518 | 249 | 504 | .494 | 472 | 491 | 963 | 229 | 136 | 154 | 308 | 1139 | 2.3 | 0.5 | 2.7 |

Three-point field goals: 1999-00, 0-for-1. 2000-01, 2-for-3 (.667). 2001-02, 1-for-7 (.143). 2002-03, 0-for-3. 2003-04, 1-for-2 (.500). Totals, 4-for-16 (.250).
Personal fouls/disqualifications: 1996-97, 57/3. 1997-98, 118/1. 1999-00, 102/1. 2000-01, 85/0. 2001-02, 175/0. 2002-03, 127/0. 2003-04, 63/0. 2004-05, 39/1. Totals, 766/6.

### NBA PLAYOFF RECORD

| | | | | | | | | REBOUNDS | | | | | | | | AVERAGES | | |
|---|---|---|---|---|---|---|---|---|---|---|---|---|---|---|---|---|---|---|
| Season Team | G | Min. | FGM | FGA | Pct. | FTM | FTA | Pct. | Off. | Def. | Tot. | Ast. | St. | Blk. | TO | Pts. | RPG | APG | PPG |
| 99-00—Milwaukee ...... | 5 | 144 | 11 | 17 | .647 | 3 | 9 | .333 | 17 | 12 | 29 | 7 | 1 | 8 | 7 | 25 | 5.8 | 1.4 | 5.0 |
| 00-01—Milwaukee ...... | 14 | 132 | 9 | 15 | .600 | 11 | 20 | .550 | 10 | 9 | 19 | 5 | 4 | 7 | 6 | 29 | 1.4 | 0.4 | 2.1 |
| 03-04—Detroit ............ | 21 | 107 | 8 | 16 | .500 | 0 | 0 | ... | 8 | 6 | 14 | 1 | 3 | 4 | 8 | 16 | 0.7 | 0.0 | 0.8 |
| 04-05—Detroit ............ | 14 | 24 | 1 | 3 | .333 | 2 | 2 | 1.000 | 3 | 0 | 3 | 0 | 0 | 0 | 0 | 4 | 0.2 | 0.0 | 0.3 |
| Totals ................... | 54 | 407 | 29 | 51 | .569 | 16 | 31 | .516 | 38 | 27 | 65 | 13 | 8 | 19 | 21 | 74 | 1.2 | 0.2 | 1.4 |

Three-point field goals: 1999-00, 0-for-1. 2003-04, 0-for-1. Totals, 0-for-2 (.000).
Personal fouls/disqualifications: 1999-00, 22/0. 2000-01, 31/1. 2003-04, 19/0. 2004-05, 2/0. Totals, 74/1.

### SPANISH RECORD

| | | | | | | | | | | | AVERAGES | | |
|---|---|---|---|---|---|---|---|---|---|---|---|---|---|
| Season Team | G | Min. | FGM | FGA | Pct. | FTM | FTA | Pct. | Reb. | Ast. | Pts. | RPG | APG | PPG |
| 98-99—Coviran-C.Alhambra ....... | 12 | 398 | 58 | 100 | .580 | 24 | 54 | .444 | 84 | 15 | 140 | 7.0 | 1.3 | 11.7 |

Three-point field goals: 1998-99, 0-for-1. Totals, 0-for-1 (.000).
Personal fouls/disqualifications: 1998-99, 31/0. Totals, 31/0.

## HAMILTON, RICHARD          G/F          PISTONS

**PERSONAL:** Born February 14, 1978, in Coatesville, Pa. ... 6-6/185. (1.98/83.9). ... Full name: Richard Clay Hamilton
**HIGH SCHOOL:** Coatesville (Pa.) Area.
**COLLEGE:** Connecticut.
**TRANSACTIONS/CAREER NOTES:** Selected after junior season by Washington Wizards in first round (seventh pick overall) of 1999 NBA Draft. ... Traded by Wizards with G/F Bobby Simmons and G Hubert Davis to Detroit Pistons for G/F Jerry Stackhouse, F Brian Cardinal and G Hubert Davis (September 11, 2002).
**MISCELLANEOUS:** Member of NBA championship team (2004).

### COLLEGIATE RECORD

**NOTES:** Member of NCAA Division I championship team (1999). ... NCAA Division I Tournament Most Outstanding Player (1999). ... The Sporting News All-America first team (1999). ... The Sporting News All-America second team (1998).

| | | | | | | | | | | | AVERAGES | | |
|---|---|---|---|---|---|---|---|---|---|---|---|---|---|
| Season Team | G | Min. | FGM | FGA | Pct. | FTM | FTA | Pct. | Reb. | Ast. | Pts. | RPG | APG | PPG |
| 96-97—Connecticut ................... | 32 | 980 | 174 | 451 | .386 | 91 | 116 | .784 | 138 | 88 | 509 | 4.3 | 2.8 | 15.9 |
| 97-98—Connecticut ................... | 37 | 1203 | 270 | 614 | .440 | 156 | 185 | .843 | 163 | 87 | 795 | 4.4 | 2.4 | 21.5 |
| 98-99—Connecticut ................... | 34 | 1091 | 247 | 557 | .443 | 170 | 204 | .833 | 163 | 91 | 732 | 4.8 | 2.7 | 21.5 |
| Totals ..................................... | 103 | 3274 | 691 | 1622 | .426 | 417 | 505 | .826 | 464 | 266 | 2036 | 4.5 | 2.6 | 19.8 |

Three-point field goals: 1996-97, 70-for-186 (.376). 1997-98, 99-for-245 (.404). 1998-99, 68-for-196 (.347). Totals, 237-for-627 (.378).

### NBA REGULAR-SEASON RECORD

| | | | | | | | | REBOUNDS | | | | | | | | AVERAGES | | |
|---|---|---|---|---|---|---|---|---|---|---|---|---|---|---|---|---|---|---|
| Season Team | G | Min. | FGM | FGA | Pct. | FTM | FTA | Pct. | Off. | Def. | Tot. | Ast. | St. | Blk. | TO | Pts. | RPG | APG | PPG |
| 99-00—Washington .... | 71 | 1373 | 254 | 605 | .420 | 103 | 133 | .774 | 38 | 91 | 129 | 108 | 28 | 6 | 84 | 639 | 1.8 | 1.5 | 9.0 |
| 00-01—Washington .... | 78 | 2519 | 547 | 1249 | .438 | 277 | 319 | .868 | 75 | 163 | 238 | 224 | 75 | 10 | 201 | 1411 | 3.1 | 2.9 | 18.1 |
| 01-02—Washington .... | 63 | 2203 | 472 | 1084 | .435 | 300 | 337 | .890 | 73 | 143 | 216 | 171 | 38 | 14 | 132 | 1260 | 3.4 | 2.7 | 20.0 |
| 02-03—Detroit ............ | 82 | 2640 | 570 | 1286 | .443 | 440 | 528 | .833 | 88 | 230 | 318 | 208 | 64 | 13 | 200 | 1612 | 3.9 | 2.5 | 19.7 |
| 03-04—Detroit ............ | 78 | 2772 | 530 | 1166 | .455 | 297 | 342 | .868 | 78 | 201 | 279 | 310 | 103 | 17 | 210 | 1375 | 3.6 | 4.0 | 17.6 |
| 04-05—Detroit ............ | 76 | 2926 | 510 | 1160 | .440 | 368 | 429 | .858 | 74 | 221 | 295 | 372 | 77 | 13 | 217 | 1424 | 3.9 | 4.9 | 18.7 |
| Totals ................... | 448 | 14433 | 2883 | 6550 | .440 | 1785 | 2088 | .855 | 426 | 1049 | 1475 | 1393 | 385 | 73 | 1044 | 7721 | 3.3 | 3.1 | 17.2 |

Three-point field goals: 1999-00, 28-for-77 (.364). 2000-01, 40-for-146 (.274). 2001-02, 16-for-42 (.381). 2002-03, 32-for-119 (.269). 2003-04, 18-for-68 (.265). 2004-05, 36-for-118 (.305). Totals, 170-for-570 (.298).
Personal fouls/disqualifications: 1999-00, 142/2. 2000-01, 203/2. 2001-02, 136/0. 2002-03, 249/2. 2003-04, 222/3. 2004-05, 232/8. Totals, 1184/17.

### NBA PLAYOFF RECORD

| | | | | | | | | REBOUNDS | | | | | | | | AVERAGES | | |
|---|---|---|---|---|---|---|---|---|---|---|---|---|---|---|---|---|---|---|
| Season Team | G | Min. | FGM | FGA | Pct. | FTM | FTA | Pct. | Off. | Def. | Tot. | Ast. | St. | Blk. | TO | Pts. | RPG | APG | PPG |
| 02-03—Detroit ............ | 17 | 659 | 134 | 303 | .442 | 106 | 117 | .906 | 18 | 48 | 66 | 45 | 13 | 1 | 57 | 383 | 3.9 | 2.6 | 22.5 |
| 03-04—Detroit ............ | 23 | 924 | 181 | 405 | .447 | 117 | 138 | .848 | 32 | 74 | 106 | 97 | 27 | 1 | 72 | 494 | 4.6 | 4.2 | 21.5 |
| 04-05—Detroit ............ | 25 | 1079 | 198 | 437 | .453 | 95 | 119 | .798 | 30 | 78 | 108 | 107 | 21 | 3 | 78 | 501 | 4.3 | 4.3 | 20.0 |
| Totals ................... | 65 | 2662 | 513 | 1145 | .448 | 318 | 374 | .850 | 80 | 200 | 280 | 249 | 61 | 5 | 207 | 1378 | 4.3 | 3.8 | 21.2 |

Three-point field goals: 2002-03, 9-for-27 (.333). 2003-04, 15-for-39 (.385). 2004-05, 10-for-34 (.294). Totals, 34-for-100 (.340).
Personal fouls/disqualifications: 2002-03, 51/0. 2003-04, 72/2. 2004-05, 79/1. Totals, 202/3.

H

## HAMILTON, ZENDON        C        ROCKETS

**PERSONAL:** Born April 29, 1975, in Queens, N.Y. ... 6-11/240. (2.11/108.9).
**HIGH SCHOOL:** Sewanhaka (Floral Park, N.Y.).
**COLLEGE:** St. John's.
**TRANSACTIONS/CAREER NOTES:** Not drafted by an NBA franchise. ... Played in Spain (1998-99). ... Signed as free agent by Dallas Mavericks (October 4, 1999). ... Waived by Mavericks (October 15, 1999). ... Played in Greece (1999-2000). ... Signed as free agent by Los Angeles Clippers (September 29, 2000). ... Signed by Toronto Raptors to 10-day contract (January 27, 2003). ... Waived by Raptors (February 10, 2003). ... Waived by Warriors (October 27, 2003). ... Waived by 76ers (January 6, 2004). ... Played in Continental Basketball Association (2003-04). ... Signed by Philadelphia 76ers to first of two consecutive 10-day contracts (January 9, 2004). ... Signed by 76ers for remainder of season (January 30, 2004). ... Signed as free agent by Milwaukee Bucks (August 5, 2004). ... Traded by Bucks with G Mike James to Houston Rockets for Reece Gaines and second-round picks in 2006 and 2007 NBA drafts (February 24, 2005).

### COLLEGIATE RECORD

| Season Team | G | Min. | FGM | FGA | Pct. | FTM | FTA | Pct. | Reb. | Ast. | Pts. | RPG | APG | PPG |
|---|---|---|---|---|---|---|---|---|---|---|---|---|---|---|
| 94-95—St. John's | 28 | 693 | 112 | 214 | .523 | 95 | 154 | .617 | 141 | 18 | 319 | 5.0 | 0.6 | 11.4 |
| 95-96—St. John's | 27 | 958 | 179 | 368 | .486 | 204 | 256 | .797 | 277 | 21 | 542 | 10.3 | 0.8 | 20.1 |
| 96-97—St. John's | 27 | 882 | 132 | 306 | .431 | 173 | 242 | .715 | 254 | 11 | 437 | 9.4 | 0.4 | 16.2 |
| 97-98—St. John's | 32 | 1038 | 161 | 341 | .472 | 170 | 260 | .654 | 277 | 12 | 492 | 8.7 | 0.4 | 15.4 |
| **Totals** | 114 | 3571 | 584 | 1229 | .475 | 642 | 912 | .704 | 949 | 62 | 1790 | 8.3 | 0.5 | 15.7 |

Three-point field goals: 1994-95, 0-for-1. 1995-96, 0-for-4. 1996-97, 0-for-1. Totals, 0-for-6 (.000).

### SPANISH RECORD

| Season Team | G | Min. | FGM | FGA | Pct. | FTM | FTA | Pct. | Reb. | Ast. | Pts. | RPG | APG | PPG |
|---|---|---|---|---|---|---|---|---|---|---|---|---|---|---|
| 98-99—Forum Valladolid | 18 | 443 | 84 | 175 | .480 | 67 | 100 | .670 | 111 | 6 | 235 | 6.2 | 0.3 | 13.1 |

Three-point field goals: 1998-99, 0-for-2. Totals, 0-for-2 (.000).
Personal fouls/disqualifications: 1998-99, 35/0. Totals, 35/0.

### GREEK LEAGUE RECORD

| Season Team | G | Min. | FGM | FGA | Pct. | FTM | FTA | Pct. | Reb. | Ast. | Pts. | RPG | APG | PPG |
|---|---|---|---|---|---|---|---|---|---|---|---|---|---|---|
| 99-00—Dafni | 21 | 620 | 109 | 245 | .445 | 88 | 119 | .739 | 143 | 13 | 310 | 6.8 | 0.6 | 14.8 |

Three-point field goals: 1999-00, 4-for-15 (.267). Totals, 4-for-15 (.267).

### NBA REGULAR-SEASON RECORD

| Season Team | G | Min. | FGM | FGA | Pct. | FTM | FTA | Pct. | Off. | Def. | Tot. | Ast. | St. | Blk. | TO | Pts. | RPG | APG | PPG |
|---|---|---|---|---|---|---|---|---|---|---|---|---|---|---|---|---|---|---|---|
| 00-01—L.A. Clippers | 3 | 19 | 2 | 9 | .222 | 5 | 8 | .625 | 3 | 5 | 8 | 0 | 0 | 0 | 2 | 9 | 2.7 | 0.0 | 3.0 |
| 01-02—Denver | 54 | 848 | 103 | 245 | .420 | 118 | 181 | .652 | 110 | 143 | 253 | 14 | 21 | 18 | 60 | 324 | 4.7 | 0.3 | 6.0 |
| 02-03—Toronto | 3 | 12 | 2 | 5 | .400 | 2 | 2 | 1.000 | 1 | 3 | 4 | 0 | 1 | 0 | 1 | 6 | 1.3 | 0.0 | 2.0 |
| 03-04—Philadelphia | 45 | 472 | 51 | 95 | .537 | 67 | 96 | .698 | 49 | 97 | 146 | 13 | 8 | 8 | 27 | 169 | 3.2 | 0.3 | 3.8 |
| 04-05—Milwaukee-Hou. | 16 | 159 | 11 | 32 | .344 | 29 | 48 | .604 | 18 | 24 | 42 | 6 | 5 | 2 | 12 | 51 | 2.6 | 0.4 | 3.2 |
| **Totals** | 121 | 1510 | 169 | 386 | .438 | 221 | 335 | .660 | 181 | 272 | 453 | 33 | 35 | 28 | 102 | 559 | 3.7 | 0.3 | 4.6 |

Personal fouls/disqualifications: 2000-01, 4/0. 2001-02, 104/0. 2002-03, 2/0. 2003-04, 74/0. 2004-05, 26/0. Totals, 210/0.

### CBA RECORD

| Season Team | G | Min. | FGM | FGA | Pct. | FTM | FTA | Pct. | Reb. | Ast. | Pts. | RPG | APG | PPG |
|---|---|---|---|---|---|---|---|---|---|---|---|---|---|---|
| 03-04—Yakima | 11 | 371 | 63 | 116 | .543 | 94 | 118 | .797 | 154 | 26 | 220 | 14.0 | 2.4 | 20.0 |

## HANDLOGTEN, BEN        C        JAZZ

**PERSONAL:** Born November 16, 1973, in Grand Rapids, Mich. ... 6-10/240. (2.08/108.9).
**HIGH SCHOOL:** South Christian (Grand Rapids, Mich.).
**COLLEGE:** Western Michigan.
**TRANSACTIONS/CAREER NOTES:** Not drafted by an NBA franchise. ... Played in Continental Basketball Association (1996-97). ... Played in Turkey (1997-98; 1999-2001). ... Played in Italy (2001-02). ... Signed as free agent by Utah Jazz (September 30, 2003). ... Traded by Jazz with F Keon Clark to Phoenix Suns for F Tom Gugliotta, two conditional first-round draft choices and a 2005 second-round draft choice (February 19, 2004). ... Waived by Suns (February 20, 2004). ... Signed by Utah Jazz for remainder of season (March 29, 2005).

### COLLEGIATE RECORD

| Season Team | G | Min. | FGM | FGA | Pct. | FTM | FTA | Pct. | Reb. | Ast. | Pts. | RPG | APG | PPG |
|---|---|---|---|---|---|---|---|---|---|---|---|---|---|---|
| 92-93—Western Michigan | 27 | 512 | 66 | 118 | .559 | 27 | 50 | .540 | 153 | 19 | 159 | 5.7 | 0.7 | 5.9 |
| 93-94—Western Michigan | 28 | 687 | 98 | 219 | .447 | 51 | 74 | .689 | 198 | 21 | 248 | 7.1 | 0.8 | 8.9 |
| 94-95—Western Michigan | 27 | 571 | 53 | 125 | .424 | 22 | 42 | .524 | 83 | 3 | 128 | 3.1 | 0.1 | 4.7 |
| 95-96—Western Michigan | 27 | 845 | 154 | 257 | .599 | 116 | 173 | .671 | 238 | 43 | 425 | 8.8 | 1.6 | 15.7 |
| **Totals** | 109 | 2615 | 371 | 719 | .516 | 216 | 339 | .637 | 672 | 86 | 960 | 6.2 | 0.8 | 8.8 |

Three-point field goals: 1993-94, 1-for-1 (1.000). 1995-96, 1-for-1 (1.000). Totals, 2-for-2 (1.000).

### CBA RECORD

| Season Team | G | Min. | FGM | FGA | Pct. | FTM | FTA | Pct. | Reb. | Ast. | Pts. | RPG | APG | PPG |
|---|---|---|---|---|---|---|---|---|---|---|---|---|---|---|
| 96-97—Grand Rapids | 49 | 640 | 81 | 169 | .479 | 45 | 75 | .600 | 196 | 10 | 207 | 4.0 | 0.2 | 4.2 |

Three-point field goals: 1996-97, 0-for-1. Totals, 0-for-1 (.000).

### TURKISH LEAGUE RECORD

| Season Team | G | Min. | FGM | FGA | Pct. | FTM | FTA | Pct. | Reb. | Ast. | Pts. | RPG | APG | PPG |
|---|---|---|---|---|---|---|---|---|---|---|---|---|---|---|
| 97-98—Oyak | 28 | ... | 183 | 325 | .563 | 111 | 171 | .649 | 267 | 57 | 477 | 9.5 | 2.0 | 17.0 |
| 99-00—Galatasaray | 22 | 719 | 176 | 322 | .547 | 76 | 115 | .661 | 209 | 25 | 428 | 9.5 | 1.1 | 19.5 |
| 00-01—Ulker | 26 | 773 | 181 | 297 | .609 | 91 | 127 | .717 | 227 | 32 | 453 | 8.7 | 1.2 | 17.4 |
| **Totals** | 76 | 1492 | 540 | 944 | .572 | 278 | 413 | .673 | 703 | 114 | 1358 | 9.3 | 1.5 | 17.9 |

Three-point field goals: 1997-98, 0-for-5. 1999-00, 0-for-9. 2000-01, 0-for-1. Totals, 0-for-15 (.000).

**H**

## ITALIAN LEAGUE RECORD

| Season Team | G | Min. | FGM | FGA | Pct. | FTM | FTA | Pct. | Reb. | Ast. | Pts. | RPG | APG | PPG |
|---|---|---|---|---|---|---|---|---|---|---|---|---|---|---|
| | | | | | | | | | | | | AVERAGES | | |
| 01-02—Wurth Roma.................. | 29 | 799 | 156 | 261 | .598 | 115 | 257 | .447 | 257 | 20 | 381 | 8.9 | 0.7 | 13.1 |

Three-point field goals: 2001-02, 1-for-1 (1.000). Totals, 1-for-1 (1.000).

## GREEK LEAGUE RECORD

| Season Team | G | Min. | FGM | FGA | Pct. | FTM | FTA | Pct. | Reb. | Ast. | Pts. | RPG | APG | PPG |
|---|---|---|---|---|---|---|---|---|---|---|---|---|---|---|
| | | | | | | | | | | | | AVERAGES | | |
| 02-03—Makedonikos................. | 25 | 865 | 160 | 282 | .567 | 96 | 136 | .706 | 321 | 35 | 420 | 12.8 | 1.4 | 16.8 |

Three-point field goals: 2002-03, 4-for-15 (.267). Totals, 4-for-15 (.267).

## NBA REGULAR-SEASON RECORD

| | | | | | | | | | REBOUNDS | | | | | | | | AVERAGES | | |
|---|---|---|---|---|---|---|---|---|---|---|---|---|---|---|---|---|---|---|---|
| Season Team | G | Min. | FGM | FGA | Pct. | FTM | FTA | Pct. | Off. | Def. | Tot. | Ast. | St. | Blk. | TO | Pts. | RPG | APG | PPG |
| 03-04—Utah............... | 17 | 172 | 25 | 47 | .532 | 18 | 27 | .667 | 22 | 33 | 55 | 6 | 3 | 4 | 10 | 68 | 3.2 | 0.4 | 4.0 |
| 04-05—Utah............... | 21 | 297 | 43 | 83 | .518 | 9 | 17 | .529 | 23 | 42 | 65 | 13 | 7 | 5 | 18 | 95 | 3.1 | 0.6 | 4.5 |
| Totals ................... | 38 | 469 | 68 | 130 | .523 | 27 | 44 | .614 | 45 | 75 | 120 | 19 | 10 | 9 | 28 | 163 | 3.2 | 0.5 | 4.3 |

Three-point field goals: 2004-05, 0-for-1. Totals, 0-for-1 (.000).
Personal fouls/disqualifications: 2003-04, 32/0. 2004-05, 55/2. Totals, 87/2.

# HARDAWAY, ANFERNEE     G/F     KNICKS

**PERSONAL:** Born July 18, 1971, in Memphis. ... 6-7/215. (2.01/97.5). ... Full name: Anfernee Deon Hardaway ... Nickname: Penny. ... Name pronounced ANN-fur-nee.
**HIGH SCHOOL:** Treadwell (Memphis).
**COLLEGE:** Memphis.
**TRANSACTIONS/CAREER NOTES:** Selected after junior season by Golden State Warriors in first round (third pick overall) of 1993 NBA Draft. ... Draft rights traded by Warriors with 1996, 1998 and 2000 first-round draft choices to Orlando Magic for draft rights F/C Chris Webber (June 30, 1993). ... Traded by Magic to Phoenix Suns for F/C Danny Manning, F Pat Garrity and two future first-round draft choices (August 5, 1999). ... Traded by Suns with G Stephon Marbury and C Cezary Trybanski to New York Knicks for G Howard Eisley, F Maciej Lampe, F Antonio McDyess, G Charlie Ward, draft rights to G Milos Vujanic, 2004 first-round draft choice and future first-round draft choice (January 5, 2004).
**MISCELLANEOUS:** Member of gold-medal-winning U.S. Olympic team (1996).

## COLLEGIATE RECORD

**NOTES:** THE SPORTING NEWS All-America first team (1993).

| Season Team | G | Min. | FGM | FGA | Pct. | FTM | FTA | Pct. | Reb. | Ast. | Pts. | RPG | APG | PPG |
|---|---|---|---|---|---|---|---|---|---|---|---|---|---|---|
| | | | | | | | | | | | | AVERAGES | | |
| 90-91—Memphis ...................... | | | | | | Did not play—ineligible. | | | | | | | | |
| 91-92—Memphis ...................... | 34 | 1224 | 209 | 483 | .433 | 103 | 158 | .652 | 237 | 188 | 590 | 7.0 | 5.5 | 17.4 |
| 92-93—Memphis ...................... | 32 | 1196 | 249 | 522 | .477 | 158 | 206 | .767 | 273 | 204 | 729 | 8.5 | 6.4 | 22.8 |
| Totals ..................................... | 66 | 2420 | 458 | 1005 | .456 | 261 | 364 | .717 | 510 | 392 | 1319 | 7.7 | 5.9 | 20.0 |

Three-point field goals: 1991-92, 69-for-190 (.363). 1992-93, 73-for-220 (.332). Totals, 142-for-410 (.346).

## NBA REGULAR-SEASON RECORD

**HONORS:** All-NBA first team (1995, 1996). ... All-NBA third team (1997). ... NBA All-Rookie first team (1994). ... MVP of Rookie Game (1994).

| | | | | | | | | | REBOUNDS | | | | | | | | AVERAGES | | |
|---|---|---|---|---|---|---|---|---|---|---|---|---|---|---|---|---|---|---|---|
| Season Team | G | Min. | FGM | FGA | Pct. | FTM | FTA | Pct. | Off. | Def. | Tot. | Ast. | St. | Blk. | TO | Pts. | RPG | APG | PPG |
| 93-94—Orlando.......... | 82 | 3015 | 509 | 1092 | .466 | 245 | 330 | .742 | 192 | 247 | 439 | 544 | 190 | 51 | 292 | 1313 | 5.4 | 6.6 | 16.0 |
| 94-95—Orlando.......... | 77 | 2901 | 585 | 1142 | .512 | 356 | 463 | .769 | 139 | 197 | 336 | 551 | 130 | 26 | 258 | 1613 | 4.4 | 7.2 | 20.9 |
| 95-96—Orlando.......... | 82 | 3015 | 623 | 1215 | .513 | 445 | 580 | .767 | 129 | 225 | 354 | 582 | 166 | 41 | 229 | 1780 | 4.3 | 7.1 | 21.7 |
| 96-97—Orlando.......... | 59 | 2221 | 421 | 941 | .447 | 283 | 345 | .820 | 82 | 181 | 263 | 332 | 93 | 35 | 145 | 1210 | 4.5 | 5.6 | 20.5 |
| 97-98—Orlando.......... | 19 | 625 | 100 | 273 | .377 | 90 | 118 | .763 | 8 | 68 | 76 | 68 | 28 | 15 | 46 | 311 | 4.0 | 3.6 | 16.4 |
| 98-99—Orlando.......... | 50 | 1944 | 301 | 717 | .420 | 149 | 211 | .706 | 74 | 210 | 284 | 266 | 111 | 23 | 150 | 791 | 5.7 | 5.3 | 15.8 |
| 99-00—Phoenix ......... | 60 | 2253 | 378 | 798 | .474 | 226 | 286 | .790 | 91 | 256 | 347 | 315 | 94 | 38 | 153 | 1015 | 5.8 | 5.3 | 16.9 |
| 00-01—Phoenix ......... | 4 | 112 | 15 | 36 | .417 | 7 | 11 | .636 | 5 | 13 | 18 | 15 | 6 | 1 | 3 | 39 | 4.5 | 3.8 | 9.8 |
| 01-02—Phoenix ......... | 80 | 2462 | 389 | 931 | .418 | 158 | 195 | .810 | 98 | 252 | 350 | 324 | 122 | 32 | 189 | 959 | 4.4 | 4.1 | 12.0 |
| 02-03—Phoenix ......... | 58 | 1777 | 256 | 573 | .447 | 77 | 97 | .794 | 66 | 192 | 258 | 235 | 66 | 26 | 145 | 615 | 4.4 | 4.1 | 10.6 |
| 03-04—Phoenix-N.Y.... | 76 | 2095 | 279 | 679 | .411 | 111 | 138 | .804 | 69 | 218 | 287 | 176 | 70 | 20 | 107 | 699 | 3.8 | 2.3 | 9.2 |
| 04-05—New York....... | 37 | 894 | 110 | 260 | .423 | 34 | 46 | .739 | 19 | 70 | 89 | 74 | 28 | 3 | 50 | 269 | 2.4 | 2.0 | 7.3 |
| Totals ................... | 684 | 23314 | 3969 | 8657 | .458 | 2181 | 2820 | .773 | 972 | 2129 | 3101 | 3482 | 1104 | 311 | 1767 | 10614 | 4.5 | 5.1 | 15.5 |

Three-point field goals: 1993-94, 50-for-187 (.267). 1994-95, 87-for-249 (.349). 1995-96, 89-for-283 (.314). 1996-97, 85-for-267 (.318). 1997-98, 15-for-50 (.300). 1998-99, 40-for-140 (.286). 1999-00, 33-for-102 (.324). 2000-01, 2-for-8 (.250). 2001-02, 23-for-83 (.277). 2002-03, 26-for-73 (.356). 2003-04, 30-for-79 (.380). 2004-05, 15-for-50 (.300). Totals, 495-for-1571 (.315).
Personal fouls/disqualifications: 1993-94, 205/2. 1994-95, 158/1. 1995-96, 160/0. 1996-97, 123/1. 1997-98, 45/0. 1998-99, 111/0. 1999-00, 164/1. 2000-01, 6/0. 2001-02, 184/0. 2002-03, 150/1. 2003-04, 146/1. 2004-05, 79/0. Totals, 1531/7.

## NBA PLAYOFF RECORD

| | | | | | | | | | REBOUNDS | | | | | | | | AVERAGES | | |
|---|---|---|---|---|---|---|---|---|---|---|---|---|---|---|---|---|---|---|---|
| Season Team | G | Min. | FGM | FGA | Pct. | FTM | FTA | Pct. | Off. | Def. | Tot. | Ast. | St. | Blk. | TO | Pts. | RPG | APG | PPG |
| 93-94—Orlando.......... | 3 | 133 | 22 | 50 | .440 | 7 | 10 | .700 | 8 | 12 | 20 | 21 | 5 | 6 | 20 | 56 | 6.7 | 7.0 | 18.7 |
| 94-95—Orlando.......... | 21 | 849 | 144 | 305 | .472 | 84 | 111 | .757 | 30 | 49 | 79 | 162 | 40 | 15 | 73 | 412 | 3.8 | 7.7 | 19.6 |
| 95-96—Orlando.......... | 12 | 473 | 101 | 217 | .465 | 58 | 78 | .744 | 20 | 36 | 56 | 72 | 20 | 4 | 26 | 280 | 4.7 | 6.0 | 23.3 |
| 96-97—Orlando.......... | 5 | 220 | 52 | 111 | .468 | 40 | 54 | .741 | 7 | 23 | 30 | 17 | 12 | 7 | 9 | 155 | 6.0 | 3.4 | 31.0 |
| 98-99—Orlando.......... | 4 | 167 | 20 | 57 | .351 | 30 | 39 | .769 | 9 | 11 | 20 | 22 | 9 | 1 | 12 | 76 | 5.0 | 5.5 | 19.0 |
| 99-00—Phoenix ......... | 9 | 386 | 67 | 145 | .462 | 44 | 62 | .710 | 14 | 30 | 44 | 51 | 14 | 9 | 25 | 183 | 4.9 | 5.7 | 20.3 |
| 02-03—Phoenix ......... | 6 | 244 | 27 | 70 | .386 | 13 | 18 | .722 | 9 | 27 | 36 | 26 | 13 | 5 | 13 | 76 | 6.0 | 4.3 | 12.7 |
| 03-04—New York....... | 4 | 168 | 23 | 63 | .365 | 15 | 18 | .833 | 4 | 14 | 18 | 23 | 6 | 1 | 10 | 66 | 4.5 | 5.8 | 16.5 |
| Totals ................... | 64 | 2640 | 456 | 1018 | .448 | 291 | 390 | .746 | 101 | 202 | 303 | 394 | 119 | 48 | 188 | 1304 | 4.7 | 6.2 | 20.4 |

Three-point field goals: 1993-94, 5-for-11 (.455). 1994-95, 40-for-99 (.404). 1995-96, 20-for-55 (.364). 1996-97, 11-for-30 (.367). 1998-99, 6-for-13 (.462). 1999-00, 5-for-19 (.263). 2002-03, 9-for-25 (.360). 2003-04, 5-for-14 (.357). Totals, 101-for-266 (.380).
Personal fouls/disqualifications: 1993-94, 10/0. 1994-95, 70/0. 1995-96, 27/1. 1996-97, 14/0. 1998-99, 13/0. 1999-00, 29/0. 2002-03, 26/2. 2003-04, 8/0. Totals, 197/3.

**H**

### NBA ALL-STAR GAME RECORD

| Season Team | Min. | FGM | FGA | Pct. | FTM | FTA | Pct. | REBOUNDS Off. | Def. | Tot. | Ast. | PF | Dq. | St. | Blk. | TO | Pts. |
|---|---|---|---|---|---|---|---|---|---|---|---|---|---|---|---|---|---|
| 1995—Orlando | 31 | 4 | 9 | .444 | 4 | 6 | .667 | 4 | 1 | 5 | 11 | 1 | 0 | 0 | 0 | 3 | 12 |
| 1996—Orlando | 31 | 6 | 8 | .750 | 4 | 4 | 1.000 | 0 | 3 | 3 | 7 | 0 | 0 | 2 | 0 | 3 | 18 |
| 1997—Orlando | 24 | 7 | 10 | .700 | 2 | 2 | 1.000 | 4 | 3 | 7 | 3 | 2 | 0 | 2 | 0 | 1 | 19 |
| 1998—Orlando | 12 | 3 | 5 | .600 | 0 | 0 | ... | 0 | 0 | 0 | 3 | 0 | 0 | 0 | 0 | 1 | 6 |
| **Totals** | 98 | 20 | 32 | .625 | 10 | 12 | .833 | 8 | 4 | 15 | 24 | 3 | 0 | 4 | 0 | 8 | 55 |

Three-point field goals: 1995, 0-for-2. 1996, 2-for-4 (.500). 1997, 3-for-5 (.600). 1998, 0-for-1. Totals, 5-for-12 (.417).

---

# HARPRING, MATT      F      JAZZ

**PERSONAL:** Born May 31, 1976, in Cincinnati. ... 6-7/231. (2.01/104.8). ... Full name: Matthew Joseph Harpring
**HIGH SCHOOL:** Marist (Atlanta).
**COLLEGE:** Georgia Tech.
**TRANSACTIONS/CAREER NOTES:** Selected by Orlando Magic in first round (15th pick overall) of 1998 NBA Draft. ... Traded by Magic to Cleveland Cavaliers for F/C Andrew DeClercq (August 3, 2000). ... Traded by Cavaliers with F Cedric Henderson and F/C Robert Traylor to Philadelphia 76ers for F Tyrone Hill and F Jumaine Jones (August 3, 2001). ... Signed as free agent by Utah Jazz (August 15, 2003).

### COLLEGIATE RECORD

| Season Team | G | Min. | FGM | FGA | Pct. | FTM | FTA | Pct. | Reb. | Ast. | Pts. | RPG | AVERAGES APG | PPG |
|---|---|---|---|---|---|---|---|---|---|---|---|---|---|---|
| 94-95—Georgia Tech | 29 | 966 | 121 | 250 | .484 | 81 | 110 | .736 | 180 | 68 | 351 | 6.2 | 2.3 | 12.1 |
| 95-96—Georgia Tech | 36 | 1328 | 233 | 457 | .510 | 138 | 181 | .762 | 293 | 79 | 670 | 8.1 | 2.2 | 18.6 |
| 96-97—Georgia Tech | 27 | 1015 | 169 | 410 | .412 | 110 | 163 | .675 | 222 | 60 | 513 | 8.2 | 2.2 | 19.0 |
| 97-98—Georgia Tech | 32 | 1163 | 230 | 504 | .456 | 179 | 221 | .810 | 302 | 82 | 691 | 9.4 | 2.6 | 21.6 |
| **Totals** | 124 | 4472 | 753 | 1621 | .465 | 508 | 675 | .753 | 997 | 289 | 2225 | 8.0 | 2.3 | 17.9 |

Three-point field goals: 1994-95, 28-for-73 (.384). 1995-96, 66-for-154 (.429). 1996-97, 65-for-190 (.342). 1997-98, 52-for-168 (.310). Totals, 211-for-585 (.361).

### NBA REGULAR-SEASON RECORD

**HONORS:** NBA All-Rookie first team (1999).

| Season Team | G | Min. | FGM | FGA | Pct. | FTM | FTA | Pct. | REBOUNDS Off. | Def. | Tot. | Ast. | St. | Blk. | TO | Pts. | RPG | AVERAGES APG | PPG |
|---|---|---|---|---|---|---|---|---|---|---|---|---|---|---|---|---|---|---|---|
| 98-99—Orlando | 50 | 1114 | 148 | 320 | .463 | 102 | 143 | .713 | 88 | 126 | 214 | 45 | 30 | 6 | 73 | 408 | 4.3 | 0.9 | 8.2 |
| 99-00—Orlando | 4 | 63 | 4 | 17 | .235 | 6 | 7 | .857 | 5 | 7 | 12 | 8 | 5 | 1 | 1 | 16 | 3.0 | 2.0 | 4.0 |
| 00-01—Cleveland | 56 | 1615 | 238 | 524 | .454 | 134 | 165 | .812 | 90 | 152 | 242 | 102 | 42 | 17 | 90 | 623 | 4.3 | 1.8 | 11.1 |
| 01-02—Philadelphia | 81 | 2541 | 386 | 838 | .461 | 165 | 222 | .743 | 203 | 370 | 573 | 107 | 70 | 5 | 127 | 958 | 7.1 | 1.3 | 11.8 |
| 02-03—Utah | 78 | 2557 | 521 | 1020 | .511 | 262 | 331 | .792 | 190 | 324 | 514 | 133 | 73 | 17 | 160 | 1370 | 6.6 | 1.7 | 17.6 |
| 03-04—Utah | 31 | 1134 | 193 | 410 | .471 | 108 | 157 | .688 | 91 | 156 | 247 | 63 | 22 | 2 | 65 | 502 | 8.0 | 2.0 | 16.2 |
| 04-05—Utah | 78 | 2584 | 418 | 855 | .489 | 245 | 315 | .778 | 196 | 284 | 480 | 142 | 70 | 16 | 133 | 1090 | 6.2 | 1.8 | 14.0 |
| **Totals** | 378 | 11608 | 1908 | 3984 | .479 | 1022 | 1340 | .763 | 863 | 1419 | 2282 | 600 | 312 | 64 | 649 | 4967 | 6.0 | 1.6 | 13.1 |

Three-point field goals: 1998-99, 10-for-25 (.400). 1999-00, 2-for-2 (1.000). 2000-01, 13-for-52 (.250). 2001-02, 21-for-69 (.304). 2002-03, 66-for-160 (.413). 2003-04, 8-for-33 (.242). 2004-05, 9-for-43 (.209). Totals, 129-for-384 (.336).
Personal fouls/disqualifications: 1998-99, 112/0. 1999-00, 7/0. 2000-01, 161/1. 2001-02, 201/1. 2002-03, 217/4. 2003-04, 102/1. 2004-05, 250/2. Totals, 1050/9.

### NBA PLAYOFF RECORD

| Season Team | G | Min. | FGM | FGA | Pct. | FTM | FTA | Pct. | REBOUNDS Off. | Def. | Tot. | Ast. | St. | Blk. | TO | Pts. | RPG | AVERAGES APG | PPG |
|---|---|---|---|---|---|---|---|---|---|---|---|---|---|---|---|---|---|---|---|
| 98-99—Orlando | 4 | 82 | 12 | 26 | .462 | 8 | 11 | .727 | 7 | 13 | 20 | 7 | 1 | 0 | 5 | 33 | 5.0 | 1.8 | 8.3 |
| 01-02—Philadelphia | 5 | 119 | 22 | 44 | .500 | 7 | 9 | .778 | 13 | 13 | 26 | 7 | 5 | 0 | 5 | 51 | 5.2 | 1.4 | 10.2 |
| 02-03—Utah | 5 | 156 | 30 | 62 | .484 | 13 | 16 | .813 | 9 | 18 | 27 | 5 | 5 | 1 | 8 | 74 | 5.4 | 1.0 | 14.8 |
| **Totals** | 14 | 357 | 64 | 132 | .485 | 28 | 36 | .778 | 29 | 44 | 73 | 19 | 11 | 1 | 18 | 158 | 5.2 | 1.4 | 11.3 |

Three-point field goals: 1998-99, 1-for-5 (.200). 2002-03, 1-for-7 (.143). Totals, 2-for-12 (.167).
Personal fouls/disqualifications: 1998-99, 9/0. 2001-02, 12/0. 2002-03, 23/1. Totals, 44/1.

---

# HARRINGTON, AL      F      HAWKS

**PERSONAL:** Born February 17, 1980, in Los Angeles. ... 6-9/250. (2.06/113.4).
**HIGH SCHOOL:** Roselle (N.J.), then St. Patrick's (Elizabeth, N.J.).
**COLLEGE:** Did not attend college.
**TRANSACTIONS/CAREER NOTES:** Selected out of high school by Indiana Pacers in first round (25th pick overall) of 1998 NBA Draft. ... Traded by Pacers to Atlanta Hawks for G Stephen Jackson (July 15, 2004).

### NBA REGULAR-SEASON RECORD

| Season Team | G | Min. | FGM | FGA | Pct. | FTM | FTA | Pct. | REBOUNDS Off. | Def. | Tot. | Ast. | St. | Blk. | TO | Pts. | RPG | AVERAGES APG | PPG |
|---|---|---|---|---|---|---|---|---|---|---|---|---|---|---|---|---|---|---|---|
| 98-99—Indiana | 21 | 160 | 18 | 56 | .321 | 9 | 15 | .600 | 20 | 19 | 39 | 5 | 4 | 2 | 11 | 45 | 1.9 | 0.2 | 2.1 |
| 99-00—Indiana | 50 | 854 | 121 | 264 | .458 | 78 | 111 | .703 | 47 | 112 | 159 | 38 | 25 | 9 | 65 | 328 | 3.2 | 0.8 | 6.6 |
| 00-01—Indiana | 78 | 1892 | 241 | 543 | .444 | 103 | 157 | .656 | 119 | 262 | 381 | 130 | 63 | 18 | 148 | 586 | 4.9 | 1.7 | 7.5 |
| 01-02—Indiana | 44 | 1313 | 230 | 484 | .475 | 115 | 144 | .799 | 96 | 180 | 276 | 54 | 41 | 21 | 78 | 576 | 6.3 | 1.2 | 13.1 |
| 02-03—Indiana | 82 | 2467 | 389 | 896 | .434 | 211 | 274 | .770 | 159 | 352 | 511 | 125 | 71 | 33 | 163 | 1002 | 6.2 | 1.5 | 12.2 |
| 03-04—Indiana | 79 | 2441 | 421 | 909 | .463 | 185 | 252 | .734 | 163 | 345 | 508 | 131 | 80 | 22 | 163 | 1048 | 6.4 | 1.7 | 13.3 |
| 04-05—Atlanta | 66 | 2550 | 453 | 986 | .459 | 236 | 351 | .672 | 145 | 316 | 461 | 208 | 85 | 16 | 204 | 1158 | 7.0 | 3.2 | 17.5 |
| **Totals** | 420 | 11677 | 1873 | 4138 | .453 | 937 | 1304 | .719 | 749 | 1586 | 2335 | 691 | 369 | 121 | 832 | 4743 | 5.6 | 1.6 | 11.3 |

Three-point field goals: 1998-99, 0-for-5. 1999-00, 8-for-34 (.235). 2000-01, 1-for-7 (.143). 2001-02, 1-for-3 (.333). 2002-03, 13-for-46 (.283). 2003-04, 21-for-77 (.273). 2004-05, 16-for-74 (.216). Totals, 60-for-246 (.244).
Personal fouls/disqualifications: 1998-99, 26/0. 1999-00, 130/0. 2000-01, 223/2. 2001-02, 166/4. 2002-03, 280/3. 2003-04, 250/1. 2004-05, 249/2. Totals, 1324/12.

**H**

## NBA PLAYOFF RECORD

| | | | | | | | | REBOUNDS | | | | | | | AVERAGES | | |
|---|---|---|---|---|---|---|---|---|---|---|---|---|---|---|---|---|---|
| Season Team | G | Min. | FGM | FGA | Pct. | FTM | FTA | Pct. | Off. | Def. | Tot. | Ast. | St. | Blk. | TO | Pts. | RPG APG PPG |
| 00-01—Indiana.......... | 3 | 40 | 2 | 13 | .154 | 1 | 2 | .500 | 3 | 1 | 4 | 3 | 0 | 0 | 1 | 5 | 1.3 1.0 1.7 |
| 02-03—Indiana.......... | 6 | 103 | 7 | 33 | .212 | 4 | 6 | .667 | 7 | 15 | 22 | 5 | 6 | 3 | 10 | 18 | 3.7 0.8 3.0 |
| 03-04—Indiana.......... | 16 | 427 | 60 | 140 | .429 | 30 | 55 | .545 | 33 | 69 | 102 | 12 | 23 | 9 | 28 | 152 | 6.4 0.8 9.5 |
| Totals ................. | 25 | 570 | 69 | 186 | .371 | 35 | 63 | .556 | 43 | 85 | 128 | 20 | 29 | 12 | 39 | 175 | 5.1 0.8 7.0 |

Three-point field goals: 2000-01, 0-for-2. 2002-03, 0-for-4. 2003-04, 2-for-5 (.400). Totals, 2-for-11 (.182).
Personal fouls/disqualifications: 2000-01, 8/0. 2002-03, 21/0. 2003-04, 56/1. Totals, 85/1.

# HARRINGTON, LORINZA          G

**PERSONAL:** Born October 2, 1980, in Wagram, N.C. ... 6-4/180. (1.93/81.6).
**HIGH SCHOOL:** Scotland County (Wagram, N.C.).
**COLLEGE:** Wingate.
**TRANSACTIONS/CAREER NOTES:** Not drafted by an NBA team. ... Signed as a free agent by Denver Nuggets (July 18, 2002). ... Waived by Nuggets (October 27, 2003). ... Signed as free agent by New Orleans Hornets (September 30, 2004). ... Waived by Hornets (January 21, 2005). ... Signed by Hornets to 10-day contract (January 28, 2005).

## COLLEGIATE RECORD

| | | | | | | | | | | | | AVERAGES | | |
|---|---|---|---|---|---|---|---|---|---|---|---|---|---|---|
| Season Team | G | Min. | FGM | FGA | Pct. | FTM | FTA | Pct. | Reb. | Ast. | Pts. | RPG | APG | PPG |
| 98-99—Wingate ................... | 29 | 669 | 33 | 84 | .393 | 46 | 73 | .630 | 81 | 84 | 113 | 2.8 | 2.9 | 3.9 |
| 99-00—Wingate ................... | 30 | 818 | 69 | 130 | .531 | 56 | 84 | .667 | 115 | 103 | 196 | 3.8 | 3.4 | 6.5 |
| 00-01—Wingate ................... | 30 | 920 | 100 | 207 | .483 | 93 | 133 | .699 | 132 | 193 | 304 | 4.4 | 6.4 | 10.1 |
| 01-02—Wingate ................... | 32 | 1037 | 164 | 318 | .516 | 128 | 171 | .749 | 189 | 204 | 472 | 5.9 | 6.4 | 14.8 |
| Totals ..................................... | 121 | 3444 | 366 | 739 | .495 | 323 | 461 | .701 | 517 | 584 | 1085 | 4.3 | 4.8 | 9.0 |

Three-point field goals: 1998-99, 1-for-9 (.111). 1999-00, 2-for-13 (.154). 2000-01, 11-for-31 (.355). 2001-02, 16-for-46 (.348). Totals, 30-for-99 (.303).

## NBA REGULAR-SEASON RECORD

| | | | | | | | | REBOUNDS | | | | | | | AVERAGES | | |
|---|---|---|---|---|---|---|---|---|---|---|---|---|---|---|---|---|---|
| Season Team | G | Min. | FGM | FGA | Pct. | FTM | FTA | Pct. | Off. | Def. | Tot. | Ast. | St. | Blk. | TO | Pts. | RPG APG PPG |
| 02-03—Denver ........... | 82 | 2003 | 169 | 467 | .362 | 73 | 112 | .652 | 44 | 206 | 250 | 277 | 80 | 15 | 157 | 418 | 3.0 3.4 5.1 |
| 04-05—New Orleans ... | 29 | 550 | 64 | 178 | .360 | 29 | 35 | .829 | 13 | 50 | 63 | 62 | 25 | 5 | 41 | 163 | 2.2 2.1 5.6 |
| Totals ................... | 111 | 2553 | 233 | 645 | .361 | 102 | 147 | .694 | 57 | 256 | 313 | 339 | 105 | 20 | 198 | 581 | 2.8 3.1 5.2 |

Three-point field goals: 2002-03, 7-for-28 (.250). 2004-05, 6-for-19 (.316). Totals, 13-for-47 (.277).
Personal fouls/disqualifications: 2002-03, 250/6. 2004-05, 72/1. Totals, 322/7.

## CBA RECORD

| | | | | | | | | | | | | AVERAGES | | |
|---|---|---|---|---|---|---|---|---|---|---|---|---|---|---|
| Season Team | G | Min. | FGM | FGA | Pct. | FTM | FTA | Pct. | Reb. | Ast. | Pts. | RPG | APG | PPG |
| 03-04—Dakota Wizards .............. | 1 | 21 | 4 | 6 | .667 | 1 | 3 | .333 | 2 | 3 | 9 | 2.0 | 3.0 | 9.0 |

# HARRINGTON, OTHELLA          F          BULLS

**PERSONAL:** Born January 31, 1974, in Jackson, Miss. ... 6-9/235. (2.06/106.6).
**HIGH SCHOOL:** Murrah (Jackson, Miss.).
**COLLEGE:** Georgetown.
**TRANSACTIONS/CAREER NOTES:** Selected by Houston Rockets in second round (30th pick overall) of 1996 NBA Draft. ... Traded by Rockets with G Michael Dickerson, G Brent Price, F/C Antoine Carr and future first-round draft choice to Vancouver Grizzlies as part of three-way deal in which Rockets received draft rights to G Steve Francis and F Tony Massenburg from Grizzlies and F Don MacLean and future first-round draft choice from Orlando Magic, and Magic received F Michael Smith, G/F Rodrick Rhodes, G Lee Mayberry and F Makhtar Ndiaye from Grizzles (August 27, 1999). ... Traded by Grizzlies to New York Knicks for G Erick Strickland, 2001 first-round draft choice and 2001 second-round draft choice (January 30, 2001). ... Traded by Knicks with C Dikembe Mutombo, C Cezary Trybanski and G Frank Williams to Chicago Bulls for G Jamal Crawford and F Jerome Williams (August 5, 2004).

## COLLEGIATE RECORD

| | | | | | | | | | | | | AVERAGES | | |
|---|---|---|---|---|---|---|---|---|---|---|---|---|---|---|
| Season Team | G | Min. | FGM | FGA | Pct. | FTM | FTA | Pct. | Reb. | Ast. | Pts. | RPG | APG | PPG |
| 92-93—Georgetown.................. | 33 | 1075 | 205 | 358 | .573 | 144 | 193 | .746 | 291 | 32 | 554 | 8.8 | 1.0 | 16.8 |
| 93-94—Georgetown.................. | 31 | 897 | 152 | 276 | .551 | 151 | 206 | .733 | 248 | 36 | 455 | 8.0 | 1.2 | 14.7 |
| 94-95—Georgetown.................. | 31 | 767 | 132 | 236 | .559 | 115 | 163 | .706 | 187 | 25 | 379 | 6.0 | 0.8 | 12.2 |
| 95-96—Georgetown.................. | 37 | 983 | 161 | 288 | .559 | 129 | 174 | .741 | 257 | 44 | 451 | 6.9 | 1.2 | 12.2 |
| Totals ..................................... | 132 | 3722 | 650 | 1158 | .561 | 539 | 736 | .732 | 983 | 137 | 1839 | 7.4 | 1.0 | 13.9 |

## NBA REGULAR-SEASON RECORD

| | | | | | | | | REBOUNDS | | | | | | | AVERAGES | | |
|---|---|---|---|---|---|---|---|---|---|---|---|---|---|---|---|---|---|
| Season Team | G | Min. | FGM | FGA | Pct. | FTM | FTA | Pct. | Off. | Def. | Tot. | Ast. | St. | Blk. | TO | Pts. | RPG APG PPG |
| 96-97—Houston......... | 57 | 860 | 112 | 204 | .549 | 49 | 81 | .605 | 75 | 123 | 198 | 18 | 12 | 22 | 57 | 273 | 3.5 0.3 4.8 |
| 97-98—Houston......... | 58 | 903 | 129 | 266 | .485 | 92 | 122 | .754 | 73 | 134 | 207 | 24 | 10 | 27 | 47 | 350 | 3.6 0.4 6.0 |
| 98-99—Houston......... | 41 | 903 | 156 | 304 | .513 | 88 | 122 | .721 | 72 | 174 | 246 | 15 | 6 | 25 | 61 | 400 | 6.0 0.4 9.8 |
| 99-00—Vancouver....... | 82 | 2677 | 420 | 830 | .506 | 236 | 298 | .792 | 196 | 367 | 563 | 97 | 36 | 58 | 217 | 1076 | 6.9 1.2 13.1 |
| 00-01—Van.-New York | 74 | 1815 | 247 | 507 | .487 | 171 | 224 | .763 | 139 | 249 | 388 | 56 | 34 | 45 | 145 | 665 | 5.2 0.8 9.0 |
| 01-02—New York ...... | 77 | 1563 | 237 | 450 | .527 | 122 | 172 | .709 | 125 | 224 | 349 | 37 | 30 | 36 | 95 | 596 | 4.5 0.5 7.7 |
| 02-03—New York ...... | 74 | 1850 | 225 | 443 | .508 | 123 | 150 | .820 | 165 | 311 | 476 | 62 | 12 | 23 | 90 | 573 | 6.4 0.8 7.7 |
| 03-04—New York ...... | 56 | 872 | 100 | 202 | .495 | 58 | 78 | .744 | 58 | 119 | 177 | 29 | 12 | 14 | 65 | 258 | 3.2 0.5 4.6 |
| 04-05—Chicago ......... | 70 | 1271 | 217 | 424 | .512 | 127 | 177 | .718 | 106 | 186 | 292 | 56 | 24 | 18 | 84 | 561 | 4.2 0.8 8.0 |
| Totals ................... | 589 | 12714 | 1843 | 3630 | .508 | 1066 | 1424 | .749 | 1009 | 1887 | 2896 | 394 | 176 | 268 | 861 | 4752 | 4.9 0.7 8.1 |

Three-point field goals: 1996-97, 0-for-3. 1997-98, 0-for-1. 1999-00, 0-for-2. 2000-01, 0-for-3. 2001-02, 0-for-2. Totals, 0-for-11 (.000).

**H**

Personal fouls/disqualifications: 1996-97, 112/2. 1997-98, 112/1. 1998-99, 103/0. 1999-00, 287/3. 2000-01, 237/4. 2001-02, 250/5. 2002-03, 231/2. 2003-04, 134/3. 2004-05, 188/2. Totals, 1654/22.

## NBA PLAYOFF RECORD

| Season Team | G | Min. | FGM | FGA | Pct. | FTM | FTA | Pct. | Off. | Def. | Tot. | Ast. | St. | Blk. | TO | Pts. | RPG | APG | PPG |
|---|---|---|---|---|---|---|---|---|---|---|---|---|---|---|---|---|---|---|---|
| | | | | | | | | | REBOUNDS | | | | | | | | AVERAGES | | |
| 96-97—Houston.......... | 7 | 15 | 1 | 2 | .500 | 7 | 10 | .700 | 1 | 3 | 4 | 0 | 0 | 0 | 2 | 9 | 0.6 | 0.0 | 1.3 |
| 97-98—Houston.......... | 3 | 23 | 6 | 12 | .500 | 4 | 5 | .800 | 3 | 4 | 7 | 0 | 0 | 1 | 0 | 16 | 2.3 | 0.0 | 5.3 |
| 98-99—Houston.......... | 4 | 42 | 9 | 14 | .643 | 4 | 6 | .667 | 5 | 9 | 14 | 1 | 0 | 1 | 3 | 22 | 3.5 | 0.3 | 5.5 |
| 00-01—New York........ | 5 | 77 | 7 | 14 | .500 | 4 | 5 | .800 | 7 | 8 | 15 | 2 | 4 | 2 | 3 | 18 | 3.0 | 0.4 | 3.6 |
| 04-05—Chicago ......... | 6 | 103 | 21 | 42 | .500 | 6 | 11 | .545 | 6 | 9 | 15 | 3 | 1 | 0 | 8 | 48 | 2.5 | 0.5 | 8.0 |
| Totals .................. | 25 | 260 | 44 | 84 | .524 | 25 | 37 | .676 | 22 | 33 | 55 | 6 | 5 | 4 | 16 | 113 | 2.2 | 0.2 | 4.5 |

Three-point field goals: 1997-98, 0-for-1. Totals, 0-for-1 (.000).
Personal fouls/disqualifications: 1996-97, 1/0. 1997-98, 1/0. 1998-99, 2/0. 2000-01, 16/1. 2004-05, 19/0. Totals, 39/1.

---

## HARRIS, DEVIN                    G                    MAVERICKS

**PERSONAL:** Born February 27, 1983, in Milwaukee. ... 6-3/185. (1.91/83.9). ... Full name: Devin Lamar Harris
**HIGH SCHOOL:** Wauwatosa East (Milwaukee).
**COLLEGE:** Wisconsin.
**TRANSACTIONS/CAREER NOTES:** Selected after junior season by Washington Wizards in first round (fifth pick overall) of 2004 NBA Draft. ... Draft rights traded by Wizards with G Jerry Stackhouse and F/C Christian Laettner to Dallas Mavericks for F Antawn Jamison (June 24, 2004).

## COLLEGIATE RECORD
**NOTES:** The Sporting News All-America second team (2004).

| Season Team | G | Min. | FGM | FGA | Pct. | FTM | FTA | Pct. | Reb. | Ast. | Pts. | RPG | APG | PPG |
|---|---|---|---|---|---|---|---|---|---|---|---|---|---|---|
| | | | | | | | | | | | | | AVERAGES | |
| 01-02—Wisconsin................... | 32 | 1094 | 117 | 283 | .413 | 101 | 130 | .777 | 105 | 56 | 394 | 3.3 | 1.8 | 12.3 |
| 02-03—Wisconsin................... | 32 | 1100 | 132 | 285 | .463 | 90 | 119 | .756 | 147 | 98 | 407 | 4.6 | 3.1 | 12.7 |
| 03-04—Wisconsin................... | 32 | 1162 | 189 | 412 | .459 | 171 | 216 | .792 | 139 | 141 | 624 | 4.3 | 4.4 | 19.5 |
| Totals ................................. | 96 | 3356 | 438 | 980 | .447 | 362 | 465 | .778 | 391 | 295 | 1425 | 4.1 | 3.1 | 14.8 |

Three-point field goals: 2001-02, 59-for-161 (.366). 2002-03, 80-for-191 (.419). 2003-04, 104-for-240 (.433). Totals, 243-for-592 (.410).

## NBA REGULAR-SEASON RECORD

| Season Team | G | Min. | FGM | FGA | Pct. | FTM | FTA | Pct. | Off. | Def. | Tot. | Ast. | St. | Blk. | TO | Pts. | RPG | APG | PPG |
|---|---|---|---|---|---|---|---|---|---|---|---|---|---|---|---|---|---|---|---|
| | | | | | | | | | REBOUNDS | | | | | | | | AVERAGES | | |
| 04-05—Dallas............ | 76 | 1173 | 157 | 366 | .429 | 78 | 103 | .757 | 28 | 74 | 102 | 169 | 77 | 19 | 82 | 436 | 1.3 | 2.2 | 5.7 |

Three-point field goals: 2004-05, 44-for-131 (.336). Totals, 44-for-131 (.336).
Personal fouls/disqualifications: 2004-05, 139/0. Totals, 139/0.

## NBA PLAYOFF RECORD

| Season Team | G | Min. | FGM | FGA | Pct. | FTM | FTA | Pct. | Off. | Def. | Tot. | Ast. | St. | Blk. | TO | Pts. | RPG | APG | PPG |
|---|---|---|---|---|---|---|---|---|---|---|---|---|---|---|---|---|---|---|---|
| | | | | | | | | | REBOUNDS | | | | | | | | AVERAGES | | |
| 04-05—Dallas............ | 9 | 80 | 7 | 16 | .438 | 6 | 9 | .667 | 0 | 11 | 11 | 11 | 4 | 1 | 10 | 22 | 1.2 | 1.2 | 2.4 |

Three-point field goals: 2004-05, 2-for-6 (.333). Totals, 2-for-6 (.333).
Personal fouls/disqualifications: 2004-05, 5/0. Totals, 5/0.

---

## HARRIS, LUCIOUS                    G                    CAVALIERS

**PERSONAL:** Born December 18, 1970, in Los Angeles. ... 6-5/205. (1.96/93.0). ... Full name: Lucious H. Harris ... Name pronounced LOO-shus.
**HIGH SCHOOL:** Cleveland (Los Angeles).
**COLLEGE:** Long Beach State.
**TRANSACTIONS/CAREER NOTES:** Selected by Dallas Mavericks in second round (28th pick overall) of 1993 NBA Draft. ... Signed as free agent by Philadelphia 76ers (July 23, 1996). ... Traded by 76ers with C Michael Cage, F Don MacLean and draft rights to F Keith Van Horn to New Jersey Nets for draft rights to F Tim Thomas, draft rights to G Anthony Parker, G Jim Jackson and C Eric Montross (June 27, 1997). ... Waived by Nets (September 15, 2004). ... Signed as free agent by Cleveland Cavaliers (October 1, 2004).

## COLLEGIATE RECORD

| Season Team | G | Min. | FGM | FGA | Pct. | FTM | FTA | Pct. | Reb. | Ast. | Pts. | RPG | APG | PPG |
|---|---|---|---|---|---|---|---|---|---|---|---|---|---|---|
| | | | | | | | | | | | | | AVERAGES | |
| 89-90—Long Beach State .......... | 32 | 945 | 147 | 342 | .430 | 118 | 170 | .694 | 152 | 52 | 457 | 4.8 | 1.6 | 14.3 |
| 90-91—Long Beach State .......... | 28 | 940 | 181 | 457 | .396 | 140 | 200 | .700 | 131 | 69 | 552 | 4.7 | 2.5 | 19.7 |
| 91-92—Long Beach State .......... | 30 | 1132 | 197 | 418 | .471 | 127 | 173 | .734 | 129 | 97 | 564 | 4.3 | 3.2 | 18.8 |
| 92-93—Long Beach State .......... | 32 | 1166 | 251 | 478 | .525 | 164 | 212 | .774 | 169 | 79 | 739 | 5.3 | 2.5 | 23.1 |
| Totals ................................. | 122 | 4183 | 776 | 1695 | .458 | 549 | 755 | .727 | 581 | 297 | 2312 | 4.8 | 2.4 | 19.0 |

Three-point field goals: 1989-90, 45-for-136 (.331). 1990-91, 50-for-153 (.327). 1991-92, 43-for-117 (.368). 1992-93, 73-for-177 (.412). Totals, 211-for-583 (.362).

## NBA REGULAR-SEASON RECORD

| Season Team | G | Min. | FGM | FGA | Pct. | FTM | FTA | Pct. | Off. | Def. | Tot. | Ast. | St. | Blk. | TO | Pts. | RPG | APG | PPG |
|---|---|---|---|---|---|---|---|---|---|---|---|---|---|---|---|---|---|---|---|
| | | | | | | | | | REBOUNDS | | | | | | | | AVERAGES | | |
| 93-94—Dallas............ | 77 | 1165 | 162 | 385 | .421 | 87 | 119 | .731 | 45 | 112 | 157 | 106 | 49 | 10 | 78 | 418 | 2.0 | 1.4 | 5.4 |
| 94-95—Dallas............ | 79 | 1695 | 280 | 610 | .459 | 136 | 170 | .800 | 85 | 135 | 220 | 132 | 58 | 14 | 77 | 751 | 2.8 | 1.7 | 9.5 |
| 95-96—Dallas............ | 61 | 1016 | 183 | 397 | .461 | 68 | 87 | .782 | 41 | 81 | 122 | 79 | 35 | 3 | 46 | 481 | 2.0 | 1.3 | 7.9 |
| 96-97—Philadelphia .... | 54 | 813 | 112 | 294 | .381 | 33 | 47 | .702 | 27 | 44 | 71 | 50 | 41 | 3 | 34 | 293 | 1.3 | 0.9 | 5.4 |
| 97-98—New Jersey ..... | 50 | 671 | 69 | 177 | .390 | 41 | 55 | .745 | 21 | 31 | 52 | 42 | 42 | 5 | 21 | 191 | 1.0 | 0.8 | 3.8 |
| 98-99—New Jersey ..... | 36 | 602 | 73 | 181 | .403 | 36 | 48 | .750 | 21 | 46 | 67 | 31 | 18 | 7 | 18 | 193 | 1.9 | 0.9 | 5.4 |
| 99-00—New Jersey ..... | 77 | 1510 | 198 | 463 | .428 | 79 | 99 | .798 | 53 | 134 | 187 | 100 | 65 | 6 | 42 | 513 | 2.4 | 1.3 | 6.7 |
| 00-01—New Jersey ..... | 73 | 2071 | 265 | 624 | .425 | 107 | 139 | .770 | 71 | 217 | 288 | 135 | 74 | 16 | 64 | 683 | 3.9 | 1.8 | 9.4 |

H

| Season Team | G | Min. | FGM | FGA | Pct. | FTM | FTA | Pct. | Off. | Def. | Tot. | Ast. | St. | Blk. | TO | Pts. | RPG | APG | PPG |
|---|---|---|---|---|---|---|---|---|---|---|---|---|---|---|---|---|---|---|---|
| | | | | | | | | | REBOUNDS | | | | | | | | AVERAGES | | |
| 01-02—New Jersey..... | 74 | 1553 | 249 | 537 | .464 | 133 | 158 | .842 | 49 | 158 | 207 | 116 | 53 | 6 | 61 | 675 | 2.8 | 1.6 | 9.1 |
| 02-03—New Jersey..... | 77 | 1973 | 298 | 721 | .413 | 152 | 189 | .804 | 63 | 169 | 232 | 155 | 53 | 8 | 71 | 795 | 3.0 | 2.0 | 10.3 |
| 03-04—New Jersey..... | 69 | 1504 | 187 | 463 | .404 | 66 | 78 | .846 | 39 | 101 | 140 | 135 | 41 | 2 | 53 | 478 | 2.0 | 2.0 | 6.9 |
| 04-05—Cleveland ....... | 73 | 1128 | 118 | 299 | .395 | 56 | 69 | .812 | 39 | 82 | 121 | 49 | 27 | 6 | 29 | 313 | 1.7 | 0.7 | 4.3 |
| Totals ................... | 800 | 15701 | 2194 | 5151 | .426 | 994 | 1258 | .790 | 554 | 1310 | 1864 | 1130 | 556 | 86 | 594 | 5784 | 2.3 | 1.4 | 7.2 |

Three-point field goals: 1993-94, 7-for-33 (.212). 1994-95, 55-for-142 (.387). 1995-96, 47-for-125 (.376). 1996-97, 36-for-99 (.364). 1997-98, 12-for-39 (.308). 1998-99, 11-for-50 (.220). 1999-00, 38-for-115 (.330). 2000-01, 46-for-132 (.348). 2001-02, 44-for-118 (.373). 2002-03, 47-for-136 (.346). 2003-04, 38-for-101 (.376). 2004-05, 21-for-65 (.323). Totals, 402-for-1155 (.348).

Personal fouls/disqualifications: 1993-94, 117/0. 1994-95, 105/0. 1995-96, 56/0. 1996-97, 45/0. 1997-98, 77/0. 1998-99, 52/1. 1999-00, 98/0. 2000-01, 127/1. 2001-02, 99/1. 2002-03, 95/0. 2003-04, 74/0. 2004-05, 68/0. Totals, 1013/3.

### NBA PLAYOFF RECORD

| Season Team | G | Min. | FGM | FGA | Pct. | FTM | FTA | Pct. | Off. | Def. | Tot. | Ast. | St. | Blk. | TO | Pts. | RPG | APG | PPG |
|---|---|---|---|---|---|---|---|---|---|---|---|---|---|---|---|---|---|---|---|
| | | | | | | | | | REBOUNDS | | | | | | | | AVERAGES | | |
| 97-98—New Jersey..... | 3 | 52 | 2 | 6 | .333 | 5 | 6 | .833 | 1 | 7 | 8 | 1 | 2 | 0 | 2 | 9 | 2.7 | 0.3 | 3.0 |
| 01-02—New Jersey..... | 20 | 418 | 65 | 133 | .489 | 39 | 47 | .830 | 13 | 41 | 54 | 18 | 13 | 0 | 16 | 177 | 2.7 | 0.9 | 8.9 |
| 02-03—New Jersey..... | 20 | 435 | 54 | 138 | .391 | 36 | 46 | .783 | 19 | 33 | 52 | 32 | 9 | 0 | 22 | 155 | 2.6 | 1.6 | 7.8 |
| 03-04—New Jersey..... | 11 | 182 | 19 | 49 | .388 | 14 | 18 | .778 | 10 | 12 | 22 | 10 | 7 | 1 | 5 | 55 | 2.0 | 0.9 | 5.0 |
| Totals ................... | 54 | 1087 | 140 | 326 | .429 | 94 | 117 | .803 | 43 | 93 | 136 | 61 | 31 | 1 | 45 | 396 | 2.5 | 1.1 | 7.3 |

Three-point field goals: 1997-98, 0-for-2. 2001-02, 8-for-22 (.364). 2002-03, 11-for-33 (.333). 2003-04, 3-for-12 (.250). Totals, 22-for-69 (.319).
Personal fouls/disqualifications: 1997-98, 11/0. 2001-02, 29/0. 2002-03, 39/0. 2003-04, 16/0. Totals, 95/0.

## HARRISON, DAVID  C  PACERS

**PERSONAL:** Born August 15, 1982, in Nashville, Tenn. ... 7-0/250. (2.13/113.4). ... Full name: David Joshua Harrison
**HIGH SCHOOL:** Brentwood Academy (Nashville, Tenn.).
**COLLEGE:** Colorado.
**TRANSACTIONS/CAREER NOTES:** Selected after junior season by Indiana Pacers in first round (29th pick overall) of 2004 NBA Draft.

### COLLEGIATE RECORD

| Season Team | G | Min. | FGM | FGA | Pct. | FTM | FTA | Pct. | Reb. | Ast. | Pts. | RPG | APG | PPG |
|---|---|---|---|---|---|---|---|---|---|---|---|---|---|---|
| | | | | | | | | | | | | AVERAGES | | |
| 01-02—Colorado....................... | 27 | 656 | 139 | 218 | .638 | 97 | 173 | .561 | 188 | 11 | 375 | 7.0 | 0.4 | 13.9 |
| 02-03—Colorado....................... | 32 | 908 | 164 | 300 | .547 | 117 | 208 | .563 | 265 | 16 | 445 | 8.3 | 0.5 | 13.9 |
| 03-04—Colorado....................... | 29 | 916 | 186 | 295 | .631 | 125 | 232 | .539 | 254 | 25 | 497 | 8.8 | 0.9 | 17.1 |
| Totals ..................................... | 88 | 2480 | 489 | 813 | .601 | 339 | 613 | .553 | 707 | 52 | 1317 | 8.0 | 0.6 | 15.0 |

Three-point field goals: 2003-04, 0-for-1. Totals, 0-for-1 (.000).

### NBA REGULAR-SEASON RECORD

| Season Team | G | Min. | FGM | FGA | Pct. | FTM | FTA | Pct. | Off. | Def. | Tot. | Ast. | St. | Blk. | TO | Pts. | RPG | APG | PPG |
|---|---|---|---|---|---|---|---|---|---|---|---|---|---|---|---|---|---|---|---|
| | | | | | | | | | REBOUNDS | | | | | | | | AVERAGES | | |
| 04-05—Indiana............ | 43 | 760 | 106 | 184 | .576 | 52 | 91 | .571 | 48 | 87 | 135 | 13 | 16 | 55 | 53 | 264 | 3.1 | 0.3 | 6.1 |

Personal fouls/disqualifications: 2004-05, 134/6. Totals, 134/6.

## HART, JASON  G  KINGS

**PERSONAL:** Born April 29, 1978, in Los Angeles. ... 6-3/185. (1.91/83.9). ... Full name: Jason Keema Hart
**HIGH SCHOOL:** Inglewood (Calif.).
**COLLEGE:** Syracuse.
**TRANSACTIONS/CAREER NOTES:** Selected by Milwaukee Bucks in second round (49th pick overall) of 2000 NBA Draft. ... Waived by Bucks (October 29, 2001). ... Played in National Basketball Development League with Asheville Altitude (2001-02). ... Signed as free agent by San Antonio Spurs (December 19, 2001). ... Played in Greece (2002-03). ... Signed as free agent by Seattle SuperSonics (September 27, 2003). ... Waived by SuperSonics (October 23, 2003). ... Signed as free agent by Spurs (October 31, 2003). ... Signed as free agent by Charlotte Bobcats (July 14, 2004). ... Traded by Bobcats to Sacramento Kings for future second-round draft pick (August 2, 2005).

### COLLEGIATE RECORD

| Season Team | G | Min. | FGM | FGA | Pct. | FTM | FTA | Pct. | Reb. | Ast. | Pts. | RPG | APG | PPG |
|---|---|---|---|---|---|---|---|---|---|---|---|---|---|---|
| | | | | | | | | | | | | AVERAGES | | |
| 96-97—Syracuse ...................... | 32 | 1142 | 113 | 298 | .379 | 58 | 84 | .690 | 113 | 184 | 307 | 3.5 | 5.8 | 9.6 |
| 97-98—Syracuse ...................... | 35 | 1198 | 120 | 328 | .366 | 91 | 133 | .684 | 126 | 174 | 356 | 3.6 | 5.0 | 10.2 |
| 98-99—Syracuse ...................... | 33 | 1068 | 167 | 407 | .410 | 71 | 96 | .740 | 98 | 143 | 458 | 3.0 | 4.3 | 13.9 |
| 99-00—Syracuse ...................... | 32 | 1083 | 125 | 304 | .411 | 94 | 128 | .734 | 96 | 208 | 382 | 3.0 | 6.5 | 11.9 |
| Totals ..................................... | 132 | 4491 | 525 | 1337 | .393 | 314 | 441 | .712 | 433 | 709 | 1503 | 3.3 | 5.4 | 11.4 |

Three-point field goals: 1996-97, 23-for-70 (.329). 1997-98, 25-for-96 (.260). 1998-99, 53-for-145 (.366). Totals, 101-for-311 (.325).

### NBA REGULAR-SEASON RECORD

| Season Team | G | Min. | FGM | FGA | Pct. | FTM | FTA | Pct. | Off. | Def. | Tot. | Ast. | St. | Blk. | TO | Pts. | RPG | APG | PPG |
|---|---|---|---|---|---|---|---|---|---|---|---|---|---|---|---|---|---|---|---|
| | | | | | | | | | REBOUNDS | | | | | | | | AVERAGES | | |
| 00-01—Milwaukee ...... | 1 | 10 | 1 | 1 | 1.000 | 0 | 0 | ... | 0 | 0 | 0 | 1 | 0 | 0 | 2 | 2 | 0.0 | 1.0 | 2.0 |
| 01-02—San Antonio .... | 10 | 92 | 10 | 19 | .526 | 6 | 6 | 1.000 | 4 | 9 | 13 | 12 | 7 | 1 | 8 | 26 | 1.3 | 1.2 | 2.6 |
| 03-04—San Antonio .... | 53 | 660 | 71 | 159 | .447 | 33 | 43 | .767 | 10 | 69 | 79 | 81 | 28 | 5 | 29 | 177 | 1.5 | 1.5 | 3.3 |
| 04-05—Charlotte ........ | 74 | 1887 | 257 | 573 | .449 | 157 | 200 | .785 | 18 | 185 | 203 | 367 | 99 | 14 | 102 | 706 | 2.7 | 5.0 | 9.5 |
| Totals ................... | 138 | 2649 | 339 | 752 | .451 | 196 | 249 | .787 | 32 | 263 | 295 | 461 | 134 | 20 | 141 | 911 | 2.1 | 3.3 | 6.6 |

Three-point field goals: 2001-02, 0-for-2. 2003-04, 2-for-9 (.222). 2004-05, 35-for-95 (.368). Totals, 37-for-106 (.349).
Personal fouls/disqualifications: 2001-02, 16/0. 2003-04, 59/0. 2004-05, 167/1. Totals, 242/1.

**H**

## NBA PLAYOFF RECORD

| Season Team | G | Min. | FGM | FGA | Pct. | FTM | FTA | Pct. | REBOUNDS Off. | Def. | Tot. | Ast. | St. | Blk. | TO | Pts. | AVERAGES RPG | APG | PPG |
|---|---|---|---|---|---|---|---|---|---|---|---|---|---|---|---|---|---|---|---|
| 03-04—San Antonio.... | 7 | 62 | 11 | 20 | .550 | 0 | 0 | ... | 0 | 3 | 3 | 1 | 5 | 0 | 1 | 22 | 0.4 | 0.1 | 3.1 |

Personal fouls/disqualifications: 2003-04, 5/0. Totals, 5/0.

## NBDL RECORD

| Season Team | G | Min. | FGM | FGA | Pct. | FTM | FTA | Pct. | Reb. | Ast. | Pts. | AVERAGES RPG | APG | PPG |
|---|---|---|---|---|---|---|---|---|---|---|---|---|---|---|
| 01-02—Asheville.......................... | 12 | 304 | 58 | 130 | .446 | 31 | 39 | .795 | 52 | 47 | 152 | 4.3 | 3.9 | 12.7 |

Three-point field goals: 2001-02, 5-for-14 (.357). Totals, 5-for-14 (.357).
Personal fouls/disqualifications: 2001-02, 32/0. Totals, 32/0.

## GREEK LEAGUE RECORD

| Season Team | G | Min. | FGM | FGA | Pct. | FTM | FTA | Pct. | Reb. | Ast. | Pts. | AVERAGES RPG | APG | PPG |
|---|---|---|---|---|---|---|---|---|---|---|---|---|---|---|
| 02-03—Makedonikos................. | 23 | 745 | 113 | 250 | .452 | 86 | 109 | .789 | 72 | 101 | 344 | 3.1 | 4.4 | 15.0 |

Three-point field goals: 2002-03, 32-for-74 (.432). Totals, 32-for-74 (.432).

# HARVEY, DONNELL          F

**PERSONAL:** Born August 26, 1980, in Shellman, Ga. ... 6-8/216. (2.03/98.0). ... Full name: Donnell Eugene Harvey
**HIGH SCHOOL:** Randolph Clay (Cuthbert, Ga.).
**COLLEGE:** Florida.
**TRANSACTIONS/CAREER NOTES:** Selected after freshman season by New York Knicks in first round (22nd pick overall) of 2000 NBA Draft. ... Draft rights traded by Knicks with F John Wallace to Dallas Mavericks for G Erick Strickland and draft rights to F Pete Mickeal (June 28, 2000). ... Traded by Mavericks with F Juwan Howard, G Tim Hardaway, cash considerations and first-round draft choice to Denver Nuggets for G Nick Van Exel, F/C Raef LaFrentz, G Avery Johnson and G/F Tariq Abdul-Wahad (February 21, 2002). ... Signed as free agent by Orlando Magic (September 23, 2003). ... Traded by Magic to Phoenix Suns for 2004 second-round draft choice (December 23, 2003). ... Signed as free agent by Atlanta Hawks (October 22, 2004). ... Released by Hawks (October 28, 2004). ... Signed by New Jersey Nets to first of two consecutive 10-day contracts (February 1, 2005). ... Waived by Nets (February 14, 2005).

## COLLEGIATE RECORD

| Season Team | G | Min. | FGM | FGA | Pct. | FTM | FTA | Pct. | Reb. | Ast. | Pts. | AVERAGES RPG | APG | PPG |
|---|---|---|---|---|---|---|---|---|---|---|---|---|---|---|
| 99-00—Florida .......................... | 37 | 746 | 144 | 284 | .507 | 86 | 141 | .610 | 258 | 37 | 374 | 7.0 | 1.0 | 10.1 |

## NBA REGULAR-SEASON RECORD

| Season Team | G | Min. | FGM | FGA | Pct. | FTM | FTA | Pct. | REBOUNDS Off. | Def. | Tot. | Ast. | St. | Blk. | TO | Pts. | AVERAGES RPG | APG | PPG |
|---|---|---|---|---|---|---|---|---|---|---|---|---|---|---|---|---|---|---|---|
| 00-01—Dallas.............. | 18 | 65 | 8 | 14 | .571 | 6 | 16 | .375 | 6 | 14 | 20 | 2 | 3 | 1 | 7 | 22 | 1.1 | 0.1 | 1.2 |
| 01-02—Dallas-Denver . | 47 | 841 | 108 | 217 | .498 | 54 | 90 | .600 | 80 | 147 | 227 | 37 | 21 | 24 | 33 | 270 | 4.8 | 0.8 | 5.7 |
| 02-03—Denver ........... | 77 | 1613 | 246 | 551 | .446 | 118 | 176 | .670 | 125 | 284 | 409 | 100 | 48 | 27 | 123 | 611 | 5.3 | 1.3 | 7.9 |
| 03-04—Orl.-Phoenix ... | 60 | 783 | 89 | 201 | .443 | 61 | 83 | .735 | 48 | 116 | 164 | 21 | 24 | 27 | 45 | 239 | 2.7 | 0.4 | 4.0 |
| 04-05—New Jersey ..... | 3 | 16 | 2 | 2 | 1.000 | 4 | 4 | 1.000 | 2 | 5 | 7 | 1 | 1 | 1 | 1 | 8 | 2.3 | 0.3 | 2.7 |
| Totals .................. | 205 | 3318 | 453 | 985 | .460 | 243 | 369 | .659 | 261 | 566 | 827 | 161 | 97 | 80 | 209 | 1150 | 4.0 | 0.8 | 5.6 |

Three-point field goals: 2002-03, 1-for-7 (.143). 2003-04, 0-for-3. Totals, 1-for-10 (.100).
Personal fouls/disqualifications: 2000-01, 15/0. 2001-02, 115/1. 2002-03, 203/2. 2003-04, 129/0. 2004-05, 2/0. Totals, 464/3.

## CBA RECORD

| Season Team | G | Min. | FGM | FGA | Pct. | FTM | FTA | Pct. | Reb. | Ast. | Pts. | AVERAGES RPG | APG | PPG |
|---|---|---|---|---|---|---|---|---|---|---|---|---|---|---|
| 04-05—Sioux Falls.................... | 13 | 406 | 63 | 134 | .470 | 51 | 71 | .718 | 129 | 14 | 177 | 9.9 | 1.1 | 13.6 |

# HASLEM, UDONIS          C          HEAT

**PERSONAL:** Born June 9, 1980, in Miami, Fla. ... 6-9/246. (2.06/111.6).
**HIGH SCHOOL:** Miami Senior (Miami, Fla.).
**COLLEGE:** Florida.
**TRANSACTIONS/CAREER NOTES:** Not drafted by an NBA franchise ... Signed by Miami Heat (August 6, 2003).

## COLLEGIATE RECORD

| Season Team | G | Min. | FGM | FGA | Pct. | FTM | FTA | Pct. | Reb. | Ast. | Pts. | AVERAGES RPG | APG | PPG |
|---|---|---|---|---|---|---|---|---|---|---|---|---|---|---|
| 98-99—Florida .......................... | 31 | 660 | 117 | 194 | .603 | 93 | 157 | .592 | 154 | 24 | 327 | 5.0 | 0.8 | 10.5 |
| 99-00—Florida .......................... | 37 | 830 | 169 | 292 | .579 | 99 | 155 | .639 | 189 | 33 | 437 | 5.1 | 0.9 | 11.8 |
| 00-01—Florida .......................... | 31 | 870 | 188 | 315 | .597 | 146 | 206 | .709 | 232 | 31 | 522 | 7.5 | 1.0 | 16.8 |
| 01-02—Florida .......................... | 31 | 876 | 159 | 283 | .562 | 177 | 255 | .694 | 256 | 51 | 495 | 8.3 | 1.6 | 16.0 |
| Totals ..................................... | 130 | 3236 | 633 | 1084 | .584 | 515 | 773 | .666 | 831 | 139 | 1781 | 6.4 | 1.1 | 13.7 |

Three-point field goals: 1998-99, 0-for-2. 2001-02, 0-for-1. Totals, 0-for-3 (.000).

## FRENCH LEAGUE RECORD

| Season Team | G | Min. | FGM | FGA | Pct. | FTM | FTA | Pct. | Reb. | Ast. | Pts. | AVERAGES RPG | APG | PPG |
|---|---|---|---|---|---|---|---|---|---|---|---|---|---|---|
| 02-03—Chalon.......................... | 30 | 924 | 181 | 315 | .575 | 120 | 167 | .719 | 282 | 43 | 482 | 9.4 | 1.4 | 16.1 |

Three-point field goals: 2002-03, 0-for-3. Totals, 0-for-3 (.000).

## NBA REGULAR-SEASON RECORD

**HONORS:** NBA All-Rookie second team (2004).

| Season Team | G | Min. | FGM | FGA | Pct. | FTM | FTA | Pct. | Off. | Def. | Tot. | Ast. | St. | Blk. | TO | Pts. | RPG | APG | PPG |
|---|---|---|---|---|---|---|---|---|---|---|---|---|---|---|---|---|---|---|---|
| 03-04—Miami | 75 | 1795 | 205 | 447 | .459 | 140 | 183 | .765 | 189 | 284 | 473 | 51 | 33 | 24 | 74 | 550 | 6.3 | 0.7 | 7.3 |
| 04-05—Miami | 80 | 2675 | 346 | 641 | .540 | 178 | 225 | .791 | 239 | 487 | 726 | 108 | 63 | 41 | 113 | 870 | 9.1 | 1.4 | 10.9 |
| Totals | 155 | 4470 | 551 | 1088 | .506 | 318 | 408 | .779 | 428 | 771 | 1199 | 159 | 96 | 65 | 187 | 1420 | 7.7 | 1.0 | 9.2 |

Three-point field goals: 2003-04, 0-for-3. 2004-05, 0-for-4. Totals, 0-for-7 (.000).
Personal fouls/disqualifications: 2003-04, 197/2. 2004-05, 260/5. Totals, 457/7.

### NBA PLAYOFF RECORD

| Season Team | G | Min. | FGM | FGA | Pct. | FTM | FTA | Pct. | Off. | Def. | Tot. | Ast. | St. | Blk. | TO | Pts. | RPG | APG | PPG |
|---|---|---|---|---|---|---|---|---|---|---|---|---|---|---|---|---|---|---|---|
| 03-04—Miami | 13 | 199 | 13 | 33 | .394 | 21 | 31 | .677 | 18 | 26 | 44 | 3 | 5 | 3 | 3 | 47 | 3.4 | 0.2 | 3.6 |
| 04-05—Miami | 15 | 543 | 52 | 106 | .491 | 34 | 46 | .739 | 38 | 112 | 150 | 15 | 8 | 6 | 18 | 138 | 10.0 | 1.0 | 9.2 |
| Totals | 28 | 742 | 65 | 139 | .468 | 55 | 77 | .714 | 56 | 138 | 194 | 18 | 13 | 9 | 21 | 185 | 6.9 | 0.6 | 6.6 |

Personal fouls/disqualifications: 2003-04, 22/0. 2004-05, 48/0. Totals, 70/0.

## HASSELL, TRENTON     G     TIMBERWOLVES

**PERSONAL:** Born March 4, 1979, in Clarksville, Tenn. ... 6-5/200. (1.96/90.7). ... Full name: Trenton Lavar Hassell
**HIGH SCHOOL:** Clarksville (Tenn.).
**COLLEGE:** Austin Peay.
**TRANSACTIONS/CAREER NOTES:** Selected after junior season by Chicago Bulls in second round (30th pick overall) of 2001 NBA Draft. ... Waived by Bulls (October 23, 2003). ... Signed as free agent by Minnesota Timberwolves (October 29, 2003).

### COLLEGIATE RECORD

| Season Team | G | Min. | FGM | FGA | Pct. | FTM | FTA | Pct. | Reb. | Ast. | Pts. | RPG | APG | PPG |
|---|---|---|---|---|---|---|---|---|---|---|---|---|---|---|
| 97-98—Austin Peay | | | | | | Did not play—ineligible. | | | | | | | | |
| 98-99—Austin Peay | 25 | 963 | 166 | 369 | .450 | 107 | 140 | .764 | 251 | 102 | 481 | 10.0 | 4.1 | 19.2 |
| 99-00—Austin Peay | 25 | 868 | 167 | 352 | .474 | 91 | 118 | .771 | 185 | 129 | 452 | 7.4 | 5.2 | 18.1 |
| 00-01—Austin Peay | 32 | 1213 | 246 | 507 | .485 | 148 | 186 | .796 | 249 | 144 | 693 | 7.8 | 4.5 | 21.7 |
| Totals | 82 | 3044 | 579 | 1228 | .471 | 346 | 444 | .779 | 685 | 375 | 1626 | 8.4 | 4.6 | 19.8 |

Three-point field goals: 1998-99, 42-for-136 (.309). 1999-00, 27-for-82 (.329). 2000-01, 53-for-136 (.390). Totals, 122-for-354 (.345).
Personal fouls/disqualifications: 1998-99, 53/0. 1999-00, 34/0. 2000-01, 67/0. Totals, 154/0.

### NBA REGULAR-SEASON RECORD

| Season Team | G | Min. | FGM | FGA | Pct. | FTM | FTA | Pct. | Off. | Def. | Tot. | Ast. | St. | Blk. | TO | Pts. | RPG | APG | PPG |
|---|---|---|---|---|---|---|---|---|---|---|---|---|---|---|---|---|---|---|---|
| 01-02—Chicago | 78 | 2237 | 267 | 628 | .425 | 87 | 114 | .763 | 65 | 190 | 255 | 172 | 55 | 44 | 101 | 681 | 3.3 | 2.2 | 8.7 |
| 02-03—Chicago | 82 | 1999 | 144 | 392 | .367 | 41 | 55 | .745 | 37 | 218 | 255 | 151 | 45 | 61 | 83 | 342 | 3.1 | 1.8 | 4.2 |
| 03-04—Minnesota | 81 | 2264 | 177 | 381 | .465 | 48 | 61 | .787 | 68 | 189 | 257 | 133 | 36 | 54 | 46 | 406 | 3.2 | 1.6 | 5.0 |
| 04-05—Minnesota | 82 | 2068 | 225 | 475 | .474 | 90 | 114 | .789 | 80 | 139 | 219 | 128 | 30 | 30 | 64 | 541 | 2.7 | 1.6 | 6.6 |
| Totals | 323 | 8568 | 813 | 1876 | .433 | 266 | 344 | .773 | 250 | 736 | 986 | 584 | 166 | 189 | 294 | 1970 | 3.1 | 1.8 | 6.1 |

Three-point field goals: 2001-02, 60-for-165 (.364). 2002-03, 13-for-40 (.325). 2003-04, 4-for-13 (.308). 2004-05, 1-for-11 (.091). Totals, 78-for-229 (.341).
Personal fouls/disqualifications: 2001-02, 184/2. 2002-03, 197/2. 2003-04, 200/1. 2004-05, 200/1. Totals, 781/6.

### NBA PLAYOFF RECORD

| Season Team | G | Min. | FGM | FGA | Pct. | FTM | FTA | Pct. | Off. | Def. | Tot. | Ast. | St. | Blk. | TO | Pts. | RPG | APG | PPG |
|---|---|---|---|---|---|---|---|---|---|---|---|---|---|---|---|---|---|---|---|
| 03-04—Minnesota | 18 | 472 | 52 | 119 | .521 | 13 | 16 | .813 | 21 | 23 | 44 | 27 | 10 | 7 | 16 | 138 | 2.4 | 1.5 | 7.7 |

Three-point field goals: 2003-04, 1-for-2 (.500). Totals, 1-for-2 (.500).
Personal fouls/disqualifications: 2003-04, 42/0. Totals, 42/0.

## HAYES, JARVIS     G/F     WIZARDS

**PERSONAL:** Born August 9, 1981, in Atlanta, Ga. ... 6-7/220. (2.01/99.8). ... Full name: Jarvis James Hayes
**HIGH SCHOOL:** Frederick Douglass (Atlanta, Ga.).
**COLLEGE:** Western Carolina, then Georgia.
**TRANSACTIONS/CAREER NOTES:** Selected after junior season by Washington Wizards (10th pick overall) in 2003 NBA Draft.

### COLLEGIATE RECORD

| Season Team | G | Min. | FGM | FGA | Pct. | FTM | FTA | Pct. | Reb. | Ast. | Pts. | RPG | APG | PPG |
|---|---|---|---|---|---|---|---|---|---|---|---|---|---|---|
| 99-00—Western Carolina | 28 | 784 | 178 | 420 | .424 | 69 | 90 | .767 | 151 | 28 | 479 | 5.4 | 1.0 | 17.1 |
| 00-01—Georgia | | | | | | Did not play—transfer student | | | | | | | | |
| 01-02—Georgia | 29 | 980 | 212 | 470 | .451 | 65 | 85 | .765 | 152 | 45 | 538 | 5.2 | 1.6 | 18.6 |
| 02-03—Georgia | 27 | 872 | 185 | 368 | .503 | 69 | 88 | .784 | 119 | 54 | 493 | 4.4 | 2.0 | 18.3 |
| Totals | 84 | 2636 | 575 | 1258 | .457 | 203 | 263 | .772 | 422 | 127 | 1510 | 5.0 | 1.5 | 18.0 |

Three-point field goals: 1999-00, 54-for-149 (.362). 2001-02, 49-for-150 (.327). 2002-03, 54-for-127 (.425). Totals, 157-for-426 (.369).

### NBA REGULAR-SEASON RECORD

**HONORS:** NBA All-Rookie second team (2004).

| Season Team | G | Min. | FGM | FGA | Pct. | FTM | FTA | Pct. | Off. | Def. | Tot. | Ast. | St. | Blk. | TO | Pts. | RPG | APG | PPG |
|---|---|---|---|---|---|---|---|---|---|---|---|---|---|---|---|---|---|---|---|
| 03-04—Washington | 70 | 2044 | 278 | 695 | .400 | 77 | 98 | .786 | 71 | 193 | 264 | 106 | 71 | 11 | 110 | 673 | 3.8 | 1.5 | 9.6 |
| 04-05—Washington | 54 | 1560 | 206 | 530 | .389 | 99 | 118 | .839 | 41 | 186 | 227 | 90 | 49 | 9 | 62 | 553 | 4.2 | 1.7 | 10.2 |
| Totals | 124 | 3604 | 484 | 1225 | .395 | 176 | 216 | .815 | 112 | 379 | 491 | 196 | 120 | 20 | 172 | 1226 | 4.0 | 1.6 | 9.9 |

**H**

Three-point field goals: 2003-04, 40-for-131 (.305). 2004-05, 42-for-123 (.341). Totals, 82-for-254 (.323).
Personal fouls/disqualifications: 2003-04, 157/1. 2004-05, 107/1. Totals, 264/2.

## HAYWOOD, BRENDAN　　　　C　　　　WIZARDS

**PERSONAL:** Born November 11, 1979, in New York. ... 7-0/268. (2.13/121.6). ... Full name: Brendan Todd Haywood
**HIGH SCHOOL:** Dudley (Greensboro, N.C.).
**COLLEGE:** North Carolina.
**TRANSACTIONS/CAREER NOTES:** Selected by Cleveland Cavaliers in first round (20th pick overall) of 2001 NBA Draft. ... Draft rights traded by Cavaliers to Orlando Magic for C Michael Doleac (June 27, 2001). ... Draft rights traded by Magic to Washington Wizards for G/F Laron Profit and future first-round draft choice (August 1, 2001).

### COLLEGIATE RECORD

**NOTES:** The Sporting News All-America second team (2001).

| Season Team | G | Min. | FGM | FGA | Pct. | FTM | FTA | Pct. | Reb. | Ast. | Pts. | RPG | APG | PPG |
|---|---|---|---|---|---|---|---|---|---|---|---|---|---|---|
| 97-98—North Carolina | 38 | 308 | 35 | 66 | .530 | 40 | 63 | .635 | 91 | 6 | 110 | 2.4 | 0.2 | 2.9 |
| 98-99—North Carolina | 34 | 1035 | 160 | 247 | .648 | 88 | 131 | .672 | 235 | 33 | 408 | 6.9 | 1.0 | 12.0 |
| 99-00—North Carolina | 36 | 1071 | 191 | 274 | .697 | 106 | 179 | .592 | 271 | 37 | 488 | 7.5 | 1.0 | 13.6 |
| 00-01—North Carolina | 33 | 901 | 155 | 262 | .592 | 95 | 184 | .516 | 242 | 42 | 405 | 7.3 | 1.3 | 12.3 |
| **Totals** | 141 | 3315 | 541 | 849 | .637 | 329 | 557 | .591 | 839 | 118 | 1411 | 6.0 | 0.8 | 10.0 |

Personal fouls/disqualifications: 1997-98, 44/0. 1998-99, 96/0. 1999-00, 108/0. 2000-01, 97/0. Totals, 345/0.

### NBA REGULAR-SEASON RECORD

| Season Team | G | Min. | FGM | FGA | Pct. | FTM | FTA | Pct. | Off. | Def. | Tot. | Ast. | St. | Blk. | TO | Pts. | RPG | APG | PPG |
|---|---|---|---|---|---|---|---|---|---|---|---|---|---|---|---|---|---|---|---|
| 01-02—Washington | 62 | 1266 | 109 | 221 | .493 | 97 | 160 | .606 | 143 | 179 | 322 | 29 | 21 | 91 | 50 | 315 | 5.2 | 0.5 | 5.1 |
| 02-03—Washington | 81 | 1930 | 173 | 339 | .510 | 155 | 245 | .633 | 192 | 212 | 404 | 29 | 32 | 119 | 65 | 501 | 5.0 | 0.4 | 6.2 |
| 03-04—Washington | 77 | 1484 | 200 | 388 | .515 | 137 | 234 | .585 | 186 | 201 | 387 | 43 | 32 | 100 | 80 | 537 | 5.0 | 0.6 | 7.0 |
| 04-05—Washington | 68 | 1865 | 239 | 427 | .560 | 159 | 261 | .609 | 202 | 262 | 464 | 57 | 52 | 114 | 96 | 637 | 6.8 | 0.8 | 9.4 |
| **Totals** | 288 | 6545 | 721 | 1375 | .524 | 548 | 900 | .609 | 723 | 854 | 1577 | 158 | 137 | 424 | 291 | 1990 | 5.5 | 0.5 | 6.9 |

Three-point field goals: 2003-04, 0-for-1. Totals, 0-for-1 (.000).
Personal fouls/disqualifications: 2001-02, 158/1. 2002-03, 225/3. 2003-04, 154/0. 2004-05, 218/6. Totals, 755/10.

### NBA PLAYOFF RECORD

| Season Team | G | Min. | FGM | FGA | Pct. | FTM | FTA | Pct. | Off. | Def. | Tot. | Ast. | St. | Blk. | TO | Pts. | RPG | APG | PPG |
|---|---|---|---|---|---|---|---|---|---|---|---|---|---|---|---|---|---|---|---|
| 04-05—Washington | 10 | 296 | 39 | 72 | .542 | 28 | 44 | .636 | 35 | 41 | 76 | 10 | 14 | 20 | 10 | 106 | 7.6 | 1.0 | 10.6 |

Personal fouls/disqualifications: 2004-05, 40/1. Totals, 40/1.

## HENDERSON, ALAN　　　　F　　　　MAVERICKS

**PERSONAL:** Born December 2, 1972, in Indianapolis. ... 6-9/240. (2.06/108.9). ... Full name: Alan Lybrooks Henderson
**HIGH SCHOOL:** Brebeuf Prep (Indianapolis).
**COLLEGE:** Indiana.
**TRANSACTIONS/CAREER NOTES:** Selected by Atlanta Hawks in first round (16th pick overall) of 1995 NBA Draft. ... Traded by Hawks with G Jason Terry and a future first-round draft choice to Dallas Mavericks for F Antoine Walker and G Tony Delk (August 4, 2004). ... Traded by Mavericks with C Calvin Booth to Milwaukee Bucks for F Keith Van Horn (February 24, 2005). ... Waived by Bucks (February 25, 2005). ... Signed as free agent by Dallas Mavericks (March 1, 2005).

### COLLEGIATE RECORD

| Season Team | G | Min. | FGM | FGA | Pct. | FTM | FTA | Pct. | Reb. | Ast. | Pts. | RPG | APG | PPG |
|---|---|---|---|---|---|---|---|---|---|---|---|---|---|---|
| 91-92—Indiana | 33 | 783 | 151 | 297 | .508 | 80 | 121 | .661 | 238 | 17 | 383 | 7.2 | 0.5 | 11.6 |
| 92-93—Indiana | 30 | 737 | 130 | 267 | .487 | 72 | 113 | .637 | 243 | 27 | 333 | 8.1 | 0.9 | 11.1 |
| 93-94—Indiana | 30 | 983 | 198 | 373 | .531 | 136 | 207 | .657 | 308 | 36 | 534 | 10.3 | 1.2 | 17.8 |
| 94-95—Indiana | 31 | 1093 | 284 | 476 | .597 | 159 | 251 | .633 | 302 | 54 | 729 | 9.7 | 1.7 | 23.5 |
| **Totals** | 124 | 3596 | 763 | 1413 | .540 | 447 | 692 | .646 | 1091 | 134 | 1979 | 8.8 | 1.1 | 16.0 |

Three-point field goals: 1991-92, 1-for-4 (.250). 1992-93, 1-for-6 (.167). 1993-94, 2-for-6 (.333). 1994-95, 2-for-10 (.200). Totals, 6-for-26 (.231).

### NBA REGULAR-SEASON RECORD

**HONORS:** NBA Most Improved Player (1998).

| Season Team | G | Min. | FGM | FGA | Pct. | FTM | FTA | Pct. | Off. | Def. | Tot. | Ast. | St. | Blk. | TO | Pts. | RPG | APG | PPG |
|---|---|---|---|---|---|---|---|---|---|---|---|---|---|---|---|---|---|---|---|
| 95-96—Atlanta | 79 | 1416 | 192 | 434 | .442 | 119 | 200 | .595 | 164 | 192 | 356 | 51 | 44 | 43 | 87 | 503 | 4.5 | 0.6 | 6.4 |
| 96-97—Atlanta | 30 | 501 | 77 | 162 | .475 | 45 | 75 | .600 | 47 | 69 | 116 | 23 | 21 | 6 | 29 | 199 | 3.9 | 0.8 | 6.6 |
| 97-98—Atlanta | 69 | 2000 | 365 | 753 | .485 | 253 | 388 | .652 | 199 | 243 | 442 | 73 | 42 | 36 | 110 | 986 | 6.4 | 1.1 | 14.3 |
| 98-99—Atlanta | 38 | 1142 | 187 | 423 | .442 | 100 | 149 | .671 | 100 | 150 | 250 | 28 | 33 | 19 | 58 | 474 | 6.6 | 0.7 | 12.5 |
| 99-00—Atlanta | 82 | 2775 | 429 | 930 | .461 | 224 | 334 | .671 | 265 | 306 | 571 | 77 | 81 | 54 | 139 | 1083 | 7.0 | 0.9 | 13.2 |
| 00-01—Atlanta | 73 | 1810 | 298 | 671 | .444 | 173 | 271 | .638 | 180 | 226 | 406 | 50 | 51 | 29 | 126 | 769 | 5.6 | 0.7 | 10.5 |
| 01-02—Atlanta | 26 | 422 | 59 | 116 | .509 | 24 | 45 | .533 | 31 | 66 | 97 | 11 | 11 | 15 | 21 | 143 | 3.7 | 0.4 | 5.5 |
| 02-03—Atlanta | 82 | 1494 | 153 | 327 | .468 | 88 | 138 | .638 | 156 | 242 | 398 | 41 | 33 | 32 | 61 | 394 | 4.9 | 0.5 | 4.8 |
| 03-04—Atlanta | 6 | 10 | 21 | .476 | 4 | 6 | .667 | 11 | 10 | 21 | 2 | 1 | 2 | 3 | 24 | 3.5 | 0.3 | 4.0 |
| 04-05—Dallas | 78 | 1203 | 116 | 220 | .527 | 41 | 76 | .539 | 164 | 184 | 348 | 21 | 29 | 37 | 49 | 273 | 4.5 | 0.3 | 3.5 |
| **Totals** | 563 | 12831 | 1886 | 4057 | .465 | 1071 | 1682 | .637 | 1317 | 1688 | 3005 | 377 | 346 | 273 | 683 | 4848 | 5.3 | 0.7 | 8.6 |

Three-point field goals: 1995-96, 0-for-3. 1997-98, 3-for-6 (.500). 1998-99, 0-for-1. 1999-00, 1-for-10 (.100). 2000-01, 0-for-1. 2001-02, 1-for-1 (1.000).

H

2002-03, 0-for-2. 2004-05, 0-for-2. Totals, 5-for-26 (.192).
  Personal fouls/disqualifications: 1995-96, 217/5. 1996-97, 73/1. 1997-98, 175/1. 1998-99, 96/1. 1999-00, 233/3. 2000-01, 164/2. 2001-02, 40/0. 2002-03, 168/1. 2003-04, 1/0. 2004-05, 149/1. Totals, 1316/15.

### NBA PLAYOFF RECORD

| Season Team | G | Min. | FGM | FGA | Pct. | FTM | FTA | Pct. | Off. | Def. | Tot. | Ast. | St. | Blk. | TO | Pts. | RPG | APG | PPG |
|---|---|---|---|---|---|---|---|---|---|---|---|---|---|---|---|---|---|---|---|
| 95-96—Atlanta | 10 | 145 | 23 | 40 | .575 | 7 | 10 | .700 | 17 | 10 | 27 | 7 | 1 | 4 | 9 | 53 | 2.7 | 0.7 | 5.3 |
| 96-97—Atlanta | 10 | 136 | 19 | 34 | .559 | 20 | 26 | .769 | 11 | 22 | 33 | 0 | 1 | 3 | 7 | 58 | 3.3 | 0.0 | 5.8 |
| 97-98—Atlanta | 4 | 126 | 20 | 38 | .526 | 11 | 18 | .611 | 10 | 12 | 22 | 4 | 3 | 1 | 6 | 51 | 5.5 | 1.0 | 12.8 |
| 98-99—Atlanta | 1 | 4 | 0 | 0 | ... | 0 | 0 | ... | 0 | 0 | 0 | 0 | 0 | 0 | 0 | 0 | 0.0 | 0.0 | 0.0 |
| 04-05—Dallas | 9 | 92 | 8 | 14 | .571 | 2 | 2 | 1.000 | 11 | 6 | 17 | 0 | 2 | 2 | 2 | 18 | 1.9 | 0.0 | 2.0 |
| Totals | 34 | 503 | 70 | 126 | .556 | 40 | 56 | .714 | 49 | 50 | 99 | 11 | 7 | 10 | 24 | 180 | 2.9 | 0.3 | 5.3 |

  Three-point field goals: 1997-98, 0-for-1. Totals, 0-for-1 (.000).
  Personal fouls/disqualifications: 1995-96, 20/0. 1996-97, 26/0. 1997-98, 13/0. 1998-99, 1/0. 2004-05, 15/0. Totals, 75/0.

## HILL, GRANT     F     MAGIC

**PERSONAL:** Born October 5, 1972, in Dallas. ... 6-8/225. (2.03/102.1). ... Full name: Grant Henry Hill ... Son of Calvin Hill, running back with three NFL teams (1969-74 and 1976-81) and the Hawaii Hawaiians of the World Football League (1975). **HIGH SCHOOL:** South Lakes (Reston, Va.).
**COLLEGE:** Duke.
**TRANSACTIONS/CAREER NOTES:** Selected by Detroit Pistons in first round (third pick overall) of 1994 NBA Draft. ... Traded by Pistons to Orlando Magic for G Chucky Atkins and F Ben Wallace (August 3, 2000).
**MISCELLANEOUS:** Member of gold-medal-winning U.S. Olympic team (1996).

### COLLEGIATE RECORD

**NOTES:** THE SPORTING NEWS All-America first team (1994). ... Member of NCAA Division I championship team (1991, 1992).

| Season Team | G | Min. | FGM | FGA | Pct. | FTM | FTA | Pct. | Reb. | Ast. | Pts. | RPG | APG | PPG |
|---|---|---|---|---|---|---|---|---|---|---|---|---|---|---|
| 90-91—Duke | 36 | 887 | 160 | 310 | .516 | 81 | 133 | .609 | 185 | 79 | 402 | 5.1 | 2.2 | 11.2 |
| 91-92—Duke | 33 | 1000 | 182 | 298 | .611 | 99 | 135 | .733 | 187 | 134 | 463 | 5.7 | 4.1 | 14.0 |
| 92-93—Duke | 26 | 822 | 185 | 320 | .578 | 94 | 126 | .746 | 166 | 72 | 468 | 6.4 | 2.8 | 18.0 |
| 93-94—Duke | 34 | 1213 | 218 | 472 | .462 | 116 | 165 | .703 | 233 | 176 | 591 | 6.9 | 5.2 | 17.4 |
| Totals | 129 | 3922 | 745 | 1400 | .532 | 390 | 559 | .698 | 771 | 461 | 1924 | 6.0 | 3.6 | 14.9 |

  Three-point field goals: 1990-91, 1-for-2 (.500). 1991-92, 0-for-1. 1992-93, 4-for-14 (.286). 1993-94, 39-for-100 (.390). Totals, 44-for-117 (.376).

### NBA REGULAR-SEASON RECORD

**HONORS:** NBA Co-Rookie of the Year (1995). ... IBM Award, for all-around contributions to team's success (1997). ... All-NBA first team (1997). ... All-NBA second team (1996, 1998, 1999, 2000). ... NBA All-Rookie first team (1995).

| Season Team | G | Min. | FGM | FGA | Pct. | FTM | FTA | Pct. | Off. | Def. | Tot. | Ast. | St. | Blk. | TO | Pts. | RPG | APG | PPG |
|---|---|---|---|---|---|---|---|---|---|---|---|---|---|---|---|---|---|---|---|
| 94-95—Detroit | 70 | 2678 | 508 | 1064 | .477 | 374 | 511 | .732 | 125 | 320 | 445 | 353 | 124 | 62 | 202 | 1394 | 6.4 | 5.0 | 19.9 |
| 95-96—Detroit | 80 | 3260 | 564 | 1221 | .462 | 485 | 646 | .751 | 127 | 656 | 783 | 548 | 100 | 48 | 263 | 1618 | 9.8 | 6.9 | 20.2 |
| 96-97—Detroit | 80 | 3147 | 625 | 1259 | .496 | 450 | 633 | .711 | 123 | 598 | 721 | 583 | 144 | 48 | 259 | 1710 | 9.0 | 7.3 | 21.4 |
| 97-98—Detroit | 81 | 3294 | 615 | 1361 | .452 | 479 | 647 | .740 | 93 | 530 | 623 | 551 | 143 | 53 | 285 | 1712 | 7.7 | 6.8 | 21.1 |
| 98-99—Detroit | 50 | 1852 | 384 | 802 | .479 | 285 | 379 | .752 | 65 | 290 | 355 | 300 | 80 | 27 | 184 | 1053 | 7.1 | 6.0 | 21.1 |
| 99-00—Detroit | 74 | 2776 | 696 | 1422 | .489 | 480 | 604 | .795 | 97 | 393 | 490 | 385 | 103 | 43 | 240 | 1906 | 6.6 | 5.2 | 25.8 |
| 00-01—Orlando | 4 | 133 | 19 | 43 | .442 | 16 | 26 | .615 | 8 | 17 | 25 | 25 | 5 | 2 | 11 | 55 | 6.3 | 6.3 | 13.8 |
| 01-02—Orlando | 14 | 512 | 83 | 195 | .426 | 69 | 80 | .863 | 29 | 96 | 125 | 64 | 8 | 4 | 37 | 235 | 8.9 | 4.6 | 16.8 |
| 02-03—Orlando | 29 | 843 | 151 | 307 | .492 | 118 | 144 | .819 | 40 | 166 | 206 | 122 | 28 | 13 | 84 | 421 | 7.1 | 4.2 | 14.5 |
| 03-04—Orlando | | | | | | | | Did not play—injured | | | | | | | | | | | |
| 04-05—Orlando | 67 | 2338 | 517 | 1015 | .509 | 280 | 341 | .821 | 77 | 241 | 318 | 220 | 97 | 28 | 161 | 1317 | 4.7 | 3.3 | 19.7 |
| Totals | 549 | 20833 | 4162 | 8689 | .479 | 3036 | 4011 | .757 | 784 | 3307 | 4091 | 3151 | 832 | 328 | 1726 | 11421 | 7.5 | 5.7 | 20.8 |

  Three-point field goals: 1994-95, 4-for-27 (.148). 1995-96, 5-for-26 (.192). 1996-97, 10-for-33 (.303). 1997-98, 3-for-21 (.143). 1998-99, 0-for-14. 1999-00, 34-for-98 (.347). 2000-01, 1-for-1 (1.000). 2001-02, 0-for-2. 2002-03, 1-for-4 (.250). 2004-05, 3-for-13 (.231). Totals, 61-for-239 (.255).
  Personal fouls/disqualifications: 1994-95, 203/1. 1995-96, 242/1. 1996-97, 186/0. 1997-98, 196/1. 1998-99, 114/0. 1999-00, 190/0. 2000-01, 9/0. 2001-02, 40/2. 2002-03, 46/0. 2004-05, 144/1. Totals, 1370/6.

### NBA PLAYOFF RECORD

| Season Team | G | Min. | FGM | FGA | Pct. | FTM | FTA | Pct. | Off. | Def. | Tot. | Ast. | St. | Blk. | TO | Pts. | RPG | APG | PPG |
|---|---|---|---|---|---|---|---|---|---|---|---|---|---|---|---|---|---|---|---|
| 95-96—Detroit | 3 | 115 | 22 | 39 | .564 | 12 | 14 | .857 | 4 | 18 | 22 | 11 | 3 | 0 | 8 | 57 | 7.3 | 3.7 | 19.0 |
| 96-97—Detroit | 5 | 203 | 45 | 103 | .437 | 28 | 39 | .718 | 13 | 21 | 34 | 27 | 4 | 5 | 19 | 118 | 6.8 | 5.4 | 23.6 |
| 98-99—Detroit | 5 | 176 | 42 | 92 | .457 | 13 | 16 | .813 | 7 | 29 | 36 | 37 | 10 | 2 | 12 | 97 | 7.2 | 7.4 | 19.4 |
| 99-00—Detroit | 2 | 55 | 6 | 16 | .375 | 9 | 10 | .900 | 0 | 11 | 11 | 9 | 1 | 0 | 10 | 22 | 5.5 | 4.5 | 11.0 |
| Totals | 15 | 549 | 115 | 250 | .460 | 62 | 79 | .785 | 24 | 79 | 103 | 84 | 18 | 7 | 49 | 294 | 6.9 | 5.6 | 19.6 |

  Three-point field goals: 1995-96, 1-for-2 (.500). 1998-99, 0-for-1. 1999-00, 1-for-2 (.500). Totals, 2-for-5 (.400).
  Personal fouls/disqualifications: 1995-96, 13/0. 1996-97, 14/0. 1998-99, 12/0. 1999-00, 7/0. Totals, 46/0.

### NBA ALL-STAR GAME RECORD

| Season Team | Min. | FGM | FGA | Pct. | FTM | FTA | Pct. | Off. | Def. | Tot. | Ast. | PF | Dq. | St. | Blk. | TO | Pts. |
|---|---|---|---|---|---|---|---|---|---|---|---|---|---|---|---|---|---|
| 1995—Detroit | 20 | 5 | 8 | .625 | 0 | 4 | .000 | 0 | 0 | 0 | 3 | 2 | 0 | 2 | 0 | 1 | 10 |
| 1996—Detroit | 26 | 6 | 10 | .600 | 2 | 2 | 1.000 | 1 | 2 | 3 | 2 | 1 | 0 | 1 | 0 | 2 | 14 |
| 1997—Detroit | 22 | 4 | 7 | .571 | 3 | 4 | .750 | 2 | 1 | 3 | 2 | 2 | 0 | 1 | 1 | 3 | 11 |
| 1998—Detroit | 28 | 7 | 11 | .636 | 0 | 0 | ... | 0 | 3 | 3 | 5 | 1 | 0 | 1 | 0 | 0 | 15 |
| 2000—Detroit | 19 | 3 | 7 | .429 | 1 | 1 | 1.000 | 0 | 3 | 3 | 5 | 0 | 0 | 1 | 0 | 3 | 7 |
| 2001—Orlando | | | | | | | Selected, did not play—injured | | | | | | | | | | |
| 2005—Orlando | 18 | 3 | 6 | .500 | 0 | 0 | ... | 1 | 2 | 3 | 2 | 1 | 0 | 1 | 0 | 1 | 6 |
| Totals | 133 | 28 | 49 | .571 | 6 | 11 | .545 | 4 | 11 | 15 | 19 | 7 | 0 | 7 | 1 | 10 | 63 |

  Three-point field goals: 1998, 1-for-1 (1.000). 2000, 0-for-1. Totals, 1-for-2 (.500).

**H**

# HINRICH, KIRK G

**PERSONAL:** Born January 2, 1981, in Sioux City, Iowa. ... 6-3/190. (1.91/86.2). ... Full name: Kirk James Hinrich
**HIGH SCHOOL:** Sioux City West (Sioux City, Iowa).
**COLLEGE:** Kansas.
**TRANSACTIONS/CAREER NOTES:** Selected by Chicago Bulls in first round (seventh pick overall) of 2003 NBA Draft.

### COLLEGIATE RECORD

**NOTES:** The Sporting News All-America third team (2002, 2003).

| Season Team | G | Min. | FGM | FGA | Pct. | FTM | FTA | Pct. | Reb. | Ast. | Pts. | RPG | APG | PPG |
|---|---|---|---|---|---|---|---|---|---|---|---|---|---|---|
| 99-00—Kansas | 34 | 726 | 69 | 161 | .429 | 25 | 34 | .735 | 82 | 123 | 188 | 2.4 | 3.6 | 5.5 |
| 00-01—Kansas | 33 | 1079 | 116 | 232 | .500 | 91 | 108 | .843 | 134 | 229 | 378 | 4.1 | 6.9 | 11.5 |
| 01-02—Kansas | 37 | 1142 | 198 | 366 | .541 | 84 | 104 | .808 | 177 | 186 | 546 | 4.8 | 5.0 | 14.8 |
| 02-03—Kansas | 37 | 1241 | 232 | 488 | .475 | 88 | 125 | .704 | 139 | 130 | 641 | 3.8 | 3.5 | 17.3 |
| Totals | 141 | 4188 | 615 | 1247 | .493 | 288 | 371 | .776 | 532 | 668 | 1753 | 3.8 | 4.7 | 12.4 |

Three-point field goals: 1999-00, 25-for-80 (.313). 2000-01, 55-for-109 (.505). 2001-02, 66-for-138 (.478). 2002-03, 89-for-219 (.406). Totals, 235-for-546 (.430).

### NBA REGULAR-SEASON RECORD

**HONORS:** NBA All-Rookie first team (2004).

| Season Team | G | Min. | FGM | FGA | Pct. | FTM | FTA | Pct. | REBOUNDS Off. | Def. | Tot. | Ast. | St. | Blk. | TO | Pts. | RPG | APG | PPG |
|---|---|---|---|---|---|---|---|---|---|---|---|---|---|---|---|---|---|---|---|
| 03-04—Chicago | 76 | 2706 | 318 | 823 | .386 | 135 | 168 | .804 | 42 | 217 | 259 | 517 | 101 | 21 | 204 | 915 | 3.4 | 6.8 | 12.0 |
| 04-05—Chicago | 77 | 2800 | 445 | 1122 | .397 | 171 | 216 | .792 | 32 | 272 | 304 | 494 | 122 | 21 | 176 | 1206 | 3.9 | 6.4 | 15.7 |
| Totals | 153 | 5506 | 763 | 1945 | .392 | 306 | 384 | .797 | 74 | 489 | 563 | 1011 | 223 | 42 | 380 | 2121 | 3.7 | 6.6 | 13.9 |

Three-point field goals: 2003-04, 144-for-369 (.390). 2004-05, 145-for-408 (.355). Totals, 289-for-777 (.372).
Personal fouls/disqualifications: 2003-04, 276/9. 2004-05, 244/9. Totals, 520/18.

### NBA PLAYOFF RECORD

| Season Team | G | Min. | FGM | FGA | Pct. | FTM | FTA | Pct. | REBOUNDS Off. | Def. | Tot. | Ast. | St. | Blk. | TO | Pts. | RPG | APG | PPG |
|---|---|---|---|---|---|---|---|---|---|---|---|---|---|---|---|---|---|---|---|
| 04-05—Chicago | 6 | 213 | 45 | 100 | .450 | 20 | 29 | .690 | 4 | 18 | 22 | 35 | 12 | 4 | 14 | 127 | 3.7 | 5.8 | 21.2 |

Three-point field goals: 2004-05, 17-for-33 (.515). Totals, 17-for-33 (.515).
Personal fouls/disqualifications: 2004-05, 18/0. Totals, 18/0.

# HOIBERG, FRED G

**PERSONAL:** Born October 15, 1972, in Lincoln, Neb. ... 6-5/210. (1.96/95.3). ... Full name: Fredrick Kristian Hoiberg ... Nickname: The Mayor. ... Name pronounced HOY-berg.
**HIGH SCHOOL:** Ames (Iowa).
**COLLEGE:** Iowa State.
**TRANSACTIONS/CAREER NOTES:** Selected by Indiana Pacers in second round (52nd pick overall) of 1995 NBA Draft. ... Signed as free agent by Chicago Bulls (September 14, 1999). ... Signed as free agent by Minnesota Timberwolves (July 28, 2003). ... Waived by Timberwolves (August 15, 2005).

### COLLEGIATE RECORD

| Season Team | G | Min. | FGM | FGA | Pct. | FTM | FTA | Pct. | Reb. | Ast. | Pts. | RPG | APG | PPG |
|---|---|---|---|---|---|---|---|---|---|---|---|---|---|---|
| 91-92—Iowa State | 34 | 1037 | 161 | 281 | .573 | 75 | 93 | .806 | 181 | 85 | 410 | 5.3 | 2.5 | 12.1 |
| 92-93—Iowa State | 31 | 1018 | 127 | 231 | .550 | 84 | 103 | .816 | 194 | 93 | 360 | 6.3 | 3.0 | 11.6 |
| 93-94—Iowa State | 27 | 971 | 177 | 331 | .535 | 133 | 154 | .864 | 181 | 97 | 546 | 6.7 | 3.6 | 20.2 |
| 94-95—Iowa State | 34 | 1252 | 207 | 473 | .438 | 174 | 202 | .861 | 192 | 75 | 677 | 5.6 | 2.2 | 19.9 |
| Totals | 126 | 4278 | 672 | 1316 | .511 | 466 | 552 | .844 | 748 | 350 | 1993 | 5.9 | 2.8 | 15.8 |

Three-point field goals: 1991-92, 13-for-50 (.260). 1992-93, 22-for-60 (.367). 1993-94, 59-for-131 (.450). 1994-95, 89-for-216 (.412). Totals, 183-for-457 (.400).

### NBA REGULAR-SEASON RECORD

| Season Team | G | Min. | FGM | FGA | Pct. | FTM | FTA | Pct. | REBOUNDS Off. | Def. | Tot. | Ast. | St. | Blk. | TO | Pts. | RPG | APG | PPG |
|---|---|---|---|---|---|---|---|---|---|---|---|---|---|---|---|---|---|---|---|
| 95-96—Indiana | 15 | 85 | 8 | 19 | .421 | 15 | 18 | .833 | 4 | 5 | 9 | 8 | 6 | 1 | 7 | 32 | 0.6 | 0.5 | 2.1 |
| 96-97—Indiana | 47 | 572 | 67 | 156 | .429 | 61 | 77 | .792 | 13 | 68 | 81 | 41 | 27 | 6 | 22 | 224 | 1.7 | 0.9 | 4.8 |
| 97-98—Indiana | 65 | 874 | 85 | 222 | .383 | 59 | 69 | .855 | 14 | 109 | 123 | 45 | 40 | 3 | 22 | 261 | 1.9 | 0.7 | 4.0 |
| 98-99—Indiana | 12 | 87 | 6 | 21 | .286 | 6 | 6 | 1.000 | 2 | 9 | 11 | 4 | 0 | 0 | 3 | 19 | 0.9 | 0.3 | 1.6 |
| 99-00—Chicago | 31 | 845 | 89 | 230 | .387 | 69 | 76 | .908 | 7 | 103 | 110 | 85 | 40 | 2 | 43 | 279 | 3.5 | 2.7 | 9.0 |
| 00-01—Chicago | 74 | 2247 | 217 | 495 | .438 | 136 | 157 | .866 | 21 | 287 | 308 | 263 | 98 | 12 | 74 | 673 | 4.2 | 3.6 | 9.1 |
| 01-02—Chicago | 79 | 1408 | 121 | 291 | .416 | 79 | 94 | .840 | 18 | 192 | 210 | 136 | 61 | 5 | 32 | 345 | 2.7 | 1.7 | 4.4 |
| 02-03—Chicago | 63 | 784 | 49 | 126 | .389 | 41 | 50 | .820 | 11 | 126 | 137 | 70 | 40 | 5 | 25 | 144 | 2.2 | 1.1 | 2.3 |
| 03-04—Minnesota | 79 | 1804 | 178 | 383 | .465 | 98 | 116 | .845 | 21 | 247 | 268 | 109 | 66 | 10 | 44 | 530 | 3.4 | 1.4 | 6.7 |
| 04-05—Minnesota | 76 | 1272 | 139 | 284 | .489 | 89 | 102 | .873 | 32 | 149 | 181 | 85 | 50 | 15 | 20 | 437 | 2.4 | 1.1 | 5.8 |
| Totals | 541 | 9978 | 959 | 2227 | .431 | 653 | 765 | .854 | 143 | 1295 | 1438 | 846 | 428 | 59 | 292 | 2944 | 2.7 | 1.6 | 5.4 |

Three-point field goals: 1995-96, 1-for-3 (.333). 1996-97, 29-for-70 (.414). 1997-98, 32-for-85 (.376). 1998-99, 1-for-9 (.111). 1999-00, 32-for-94 (.340). 2000-01, 103-for-250 (.412). 2001-02, 24-for-92 (.261). 2002-03, 5-for-21 (.238). 2003-04, 76-for-172 (.442). 2004-05, 70-for-145 (.483). Totals, 373-for-941 (.396).

Personal fouls/disqualifications: 1995-96, 12/0. 1996-97, 51/0. 1997-98, 101/0. 1998-99, 11/0. 1999-00, 66/0. 2000-01, 155/0. 2001-02, 87/2. 2002-03, 59/0. 2003-04, 136/0. 2004-05, 105/0. Totals, 783/2.

**H**

## NBA PLAYOFF RECORD

| | | | | | | | | | REBOUNDS | | | | | | | AVERAGES | | |
|---|---|---|---|---|---|---|---|---|---|---|---|---|---|---|---|---|---|---|
| Season Team | G | Min. | FGM | FGA | Pct. | FTM | FTA | Pct. | Off. | Def. | Tot. | Ast. | St. | Blk. | TO | Pts. | RPG | APG | PPG |
| 97-98—Indiana............ | 2 | 20 | 3 | 8 | .375 | 2 | 2 | 1.000 | 1 | 3 | 4 | 1 | 1 | 0 | 0 | 9 | 2.0 | 0.5 | 4.5 |
| 98-99—Indiana............ | 4 | 20 | 2 | 4 | .500 | 0 | 0 | ... | 0 | 3 | 3 | 2 | 3 | 0 | 0 | 4 | 0.8 | 0.5 | 1.0 |
| 03-04—Minnesota...... | 18 | 438 | 39 | 86 | .453 | 15 | 16 | .938 | 9 | 57 | 66 | 23 | 16 | 0 | 8 | 115 | 3.7 | 1.3 | 6.4 |
| Totals ................... | 24 | 478 | 44 | 98 | .449 | 17 | 18 | .944 | 10 | 63 | 73 | 26 | 20 | 0 | 8 | 128 | 3.0 | 1.1 | 5.3 |

Three-point field goals: 1997-98, 1-for-2 (.500). 2003-04, 22-for-48 (.458). Totals, 23-for-50 (.460).
Personal fouls/disqualifications: 1997-98, 2/0. 1998-99, 1/0. 2003-04, 29/0. Totals, 32/0.

# HORRY, ROBERT        F        SPURS

**PERSONAL:** Born August 25, 1970, in Hartford, Md. ... 6-10/235. (2.08/106.6). ... Full name: Robert Keith Horry ... Name pronounced OR-ee.
**HIGH SCHOOL:** Andalusia (Ala.).
**COLLEGE:** Alabama.
**TRANSACTIONS/CAREER NOTES:** Selected by Houston Rockets in first round (11th pick overall) of 1992 NBA Draft. ... Traded by Rockets with F Matt Bullard and two future second-round draft choices to Detroit Pistons for F Sean Elliott (February 4, 1994); trade voided when Elliott failed physical (February 7, 1994). ... Traded by Rockets with G Sam Cassell, F Chucky Brown and F Mark Bryant to Phoenix Suns for F Charles Barkley and 1999 second-round draft choice (August 19, 1996). ... Traded by Suns with C Joe Kleine to Los Angeles Lakers for F Cedric Ceballos and G Rumeal Robinson (January 10, 1997). ... Signed as free agent by San Antonio Spurs (July 24, 2003).
**MISCELLANEOUS:** Member of NBA championship team (1994, 1995, 2000, 2001, 2002, 2005).

## COLLEGIATE RECORD

| | | | | | | | | | | | AVERAGES | | |
|---|---|---|---|---|---|---|---|---|---|---|---|---|---|
| Season Team | G | Min. | FGM | FGA | Pct. | FTM | FTA | Pct. | Reb. | Ast. | Pts. | RPG | APG | PPG |
| 88-89—Alabama ..................... | 31 | 590 | 79 | 185 | .427 | 38 | 59 | .644 | 156 | 35 | 200 | 5.0 | 1.1 | 6.5 |
| 89-90—Alabama ..................... | 35 | 1022 | 164 | 351 | .467 | 79 | 104 | .760 | 217 | 9 | 457 | 6.2 | 0.3 | 13.1 |
| 90-91—Alabama ..................... | 32 | 959 | 133 | 296 | .449 | 82 | 102 | .804 | 260 | 56 | 381 | 8.1 | 1.8 | 11.9 |
| 91-92—Alabama ..................... | 35 | 1185 | 196 | 417 | .470 | 120 | 165 | .727 | 296 | 88 | 554 | 8.5 | 2.5 | 15.8 |
| Totals ..................................... | 133 | 3756 | 572 | 1249 | .458 | 319 | 430 | .742 | 929 | 188 | 1592 | 7.0 | 1.4 | 12.0 |

Three-point field goals: 1988-89, 4-for-13 (.308). 1989-90, 50-for-117 (.427). 1990-91, 33-for-98 (.337). 1991-92, 42-for-120 (.350). Totals, 129-for-348 (.371).

## NBA REGULAR-SEASON RECORD

**HONORS:** NBA All-Rookie second team (1993).

| | | | | | | | | | REBOUNDS | | | | | | | | AVERAGES | | |
|---|---|---|---|---|---|---|---|---|---|---|---|---|---|---|---|---|---|---|---|
| Season Team | G | Min. | FGM | FGA | Pct. | FTM | FTA | Pct. | Off. | Def. | Tot. | Ast. | St. | Blk. | TO | Pts. | RPG | APG | PPG |
| 92-93—Houston .......... | 79 | 2330 | 323 | 682 | .474 | 143 | 200 | .715 | 113 | 279 | 392 | 191 | 80 | 83 | 156 | 801 | 5.0 | 2.4 | 10.1 |
| 93-94—Houston .......... | 81 | 2370 | 322 | 702 | .459 | 115 | 157 | .732 | 128 | 312 | 440 | 231 | 119 | 75 | 137 | 803 | 5.4 | 2.9 | 9.9 |
| 94-95—Houston .......... | 64 | 2074 | 240 | 537 | .447 | 86 | 113 | .761 | 81 | 243 | 324 | 216 | 94 | 76 | 122 | 652 | 5.1 | 3.4 | 10.2 |
| 95-96—Houston .......... | 71 | 2634 | 300 | 732 | .410 | 111 | 143 | .776 | 97 | 315 | 412 | 281 | 116 | 109 | 160 | 853 | 5.8 | 4.0 | 12.0 |
| 96-97—Phoe.-L.A.L. .... | 54 | 1395 | 157 | 360 | .436 | 60 | 90 | .667 | 68 | 169 | 237 | 110 | 66 | 55 | 72 | 423 | 4.4 | 2.0 | 7.8 |
| 97-98—L.A. Lakers .... | 72 | 2192 | 200 | 420 | .476 | 117 | 169 | .692 | 186 | 356 | 542 | 163 | 112 | 94 | 99 | 536 | 7.5 | 2.3 | 7.4 |
| 98-99—L.A. Lakers .... | 38 | 744 | 67 | 146 | .459 | 34 | 46 | .739 | 56 | 96 | 152 | 56 | 36 | 39 | 49 | 188 | 4.0 | 1.5 | 4.9 |
| 99-00—L.A. Lakers .... | 76 | 1685 | 159 | 363 | .438 | 89 | 113 | .788 | 133 | 228 | 361 | 118 | 84 | 80 | 73 | 436 | 4.8 | 1.6 | 5.7 |
| 00-01—L.A. Lakers .... | 79 | 1587 | 147 | 380 | .387 | 59 | 83 | .711 | 93 | 203 | 296 | 128 | 54 | 54 | 79 | 407 | 3.7 | 1.6 | 5.2 |
| 01-02—L.A. Lakers .... | 81 | 2140 | 183 | 460 | .398 | 108 | 138 | .783 | 130 | 349 | 479 | 232 | 77 | 89 | 88 | 550 | 5.9 | 2.9 | 6.8 |
| 02-03—L.A. Lakers .... | 80 | 2343 | 184 | 476 | .387 | 103 | 134 | .769 | 181 | 333 | 514 | 233 | 96 | 61 | 112 | 522 | 6.4 | 2.9 | 6.5 |
| 03-04—San Antonio .... | 81 | 1290 | 141 | 348 | .405 | 69 | 107 | .645 | 108 | 164 | 272 | 101 | 48 | 49 | 55 | 392 | 3.4 | 1.2 | 4.8 |
| 04-05—San Antonio .... | 75 | 1396 | 157 | 375 | .419 | 86 | 109 | .789 | 91 | 177 | 268 | 80 | 67 | 60 | 69 | 451 | 3.6 | 1.1 | 6.0 |
| Totals ................... | 931 | 24180 | 2580 | 5981 | .431 | 1180 | 1602 | .737 | 1465 | 3224 | 4689 | 2140 | 1049 | 924 | 1271 | 7014 | 5.0 | 2.3 | 7.5 |

Three-point field goals: 1992-93, 12-for-47 (.255). 1993-94, 44-for-136 (.324). 1994-95, 86-for-227 (.379). 1995-96, 142-for-388 (.366). 1996-97, 49-for-154 (.318). 1997-98, 19-for-93 (.204). 1998-99, 20-for-45 (.444). 1999-00, 29-for-94 (.309). 2000-01, 54-for-156 (.346). 2001-02, 76-for-203 (.374). 2002-03, 51-for-177 (.288). 2003-04, 41-for-108 (.380). 2004-05, 51-for-138 (.370). Totals, 674-for-1966 (.343).
Personal fouls/disqualifications: 1992-93, 210/1. 1993-94, 186/0. 1994-95, 161/0. 1995-96, 197/3. 1996-97, 153/2. 1997-98, 238/5. 1998-99, 103/2. 1999-00, 189/0. 2000-01, 210/3. 2001-02, 208/1. 2002-03, 247/2. 2003-04, 165/0. 2004-05, 138/1. Totals, 2405/20.

## NBA PLAYOFF RECORD

**NOTES:** Holds NBA Finals single-game record for most steals—7 (June 9, 1995, at Orlando). ... Holds single-game playoff records for most three-point field goals, none missed—7 (May 6, 1997, vs. Utah).

| | | | | | | | | | REBOUNDS | | | | | | | | AVERAGES | | |
|---|---|---|---|---|---|---|---|---|---|---|---|---|---|---|---|---|---|---|---|
| Season Team | G | Min. | FGM | FGA | Pct. | FTM | FTA | Pct. | Off. | Def. | Tot. | Ast. | St. | Blk. | TO | Pts. | RPG | APG | PPG |
| 92-93—Houston .......... | 12 | 374 | 47 | 101 | .465 | 20 | 27 | .741 | 14 | 48 | 62 | 38 | 18 | 16 | 28 | 123 | 5.2 | 3.2 | 10.3 |
| 93-94—Houston .......... | 23 | 778 | 98 | 226 | .434 | 39 | 51 | .765 | 40 | 101 | 141 | 82 | 35 | 20 | 27 | 269 | 6.1 | 3.6 | 11.7 |
| 94-95—Houston .......... | 22 | 841 | 93 | 209 | .445 | 58 | 78 | .744 | 40 | 115 | 155 | 76 | 32 | 26 | 25 | 288 | 7.0 | 3.5 | 13.1 |
| 95-96—Houston .......... | 8 | 308 | 37 | 91 | .407 | 10 | 23 | .435 | 15 | 42 | 57 | 24 | 21 | 13 | 15 | 105 | 7.1 | 3.0 | 13.1 |
| 96-97—L.A. Lakers .... | 9 | 279 | 17 | 38 | .447 | 14 | 18 | .778 | 12 | 36 | 48 | 13 | 10 | 7 | 11 | 60 | 5.3 | 1.4 | 6.7 |
| 97-98—L.A. Lakers .... | 13 | 422 | 39 | 70 | .557 | 28 | 41 | .683 | 34 | 50 | 84 | 40 | 14 | 14 | 18 | 112 | 6.5 | 3.1 | 8.6 |
| 98-99—L.A. Lakers .... | 8 | 177 | 12 | 26 | .462 | 11 | 14 | .786 | 10 | 26 | 36 | 11 | 6 | 6 | 7 | 40 | 4.5 | 1.4 | 5.0 |
| 99-00—L.A. Lakers .... | 23 | 618 | 59 | 145 | .407 | 40 | 57 | .702 | 38 | 85 | 123 | 58 | 20 | 19 | 30 | 175 | 5.3 | 2.5 | 7.6 |
| 00-01—L.A. Lakers .... | 16 | 382 | 32 | 87 | .368 | 13 | 22 | .591 | 30 | 53 | 83 | 31 | 22 | 16 | 18 | 94 | 5.2 | 1.9 | 5.9 |
| 01-02—L.A. Lakers .... | 19 | 703 | 61 | 136 | .449 | 30 | 38 | .789 | 36 | 118 | 154 | 61 | 33 | 16 | 30 | 176 | 8.1 | 3.2 | 9.3 |
| 02-03—L.A. Lakers .... | 12 | 373 | 30 | 94 | .319 | 5 | 9 | .556 | 23 | 57 | 80 | 37 | 15 | 12 | 17 | 67 | 6.7 | 3.1 | 5.6 |
| 03-04—San Antonio .... | 10 | 211 | 20 | 43 | .465 | 13 | 14 | .929 | 25 | 38 | 63 | 9 | 8 | 2 | 10 | 61 | 6.3 | 0.9 | 6.1 |
| 04-05—San Antonio .... | 23 | 618 | 73 | 163 | .448 | 30 | 41 | .732 | 46 | 79 | 125 | 47 | 21 | 20 | 20 | 214 | 5.4 | 2.0 | 9.3 |
| Totals ................... | 198 | 6084 | 618 | 1429 | .432 | 311 | 433 | .718 | 363 | 848 | 1211 | 527 | 255 | 187 | 256 | 1784 | 6.1 | 2.7 | 9.0 |

Three-point field goals: 1992-93, 9-for-30 (.300). 1993-94, 34-for-89 (.382). 1994-95, 44-for-110 (.400). 1995-96, 21-for-53 (.396). 1996-97, 12-for-28

**H**

(.429). 1997-98, 6-for-17 (.353). 1998-99, 5-for-12 (.417). 1999-00, 17-for-59 (.288). 2000-01, 17-for-47 (.362). 2001-02, 24-for-62 (.387). 2002-03, 2-for-38 (.053). 2003-04, 8-for-22 (.364). 2004-05, 38-for-85 (.447). Totals, 237-for-652 (.363).

Personal fouls/disqualifications: 1992-93, 30/1. 1993-94, 68/0. 1994-95, 69/2. 1995-96, 29/1. 1996-97, 27/0. 1997-98, 45/0. 1998-99, 29/1. 1999-00, 88/3. 2000-01, 50/0. 2001-02, 66/1. 2002-03, 37/0. 2003-04, 31/0. 2004-05, 53/0. Totals, 622/9.

## HOUSE, EDDIE — G

**PERSONAL:** Born May 14, 1978, in Berkeley, Calif. ... 6-0/176. (1.83/79.8). ... Full name: Edward L. House ... Son-in-law of Henry Bibby, guard with New York Knicks (1972-73 through 1974-75), New Orleans Jazz (1974-75 and 1975-76), Philadelphia 76ers (1976-77 through 1979-80) and San Diego Clippers (1980-81); brother-in-law of Mike Bibby, guard, Sacramento Kings.
**HIGH SCHOOL:** Hayward (Union City, Calif.).
**COLLEGE:** Arizona State.
**TRANSACTIONS/CAREER NOTES:** Selected by Miami Heat in second round (37th pick overall) of 2000 NBA Draft. ... Signed as free agent by Los Angeles Clippers (August 13, 2003). ... Traded by Clippers with F/C Melvin Ely to Charlotte Bobcats for second-round draft choices in 2005 and 2006 (July 14, 2004). ... Waived by Bobcats (December 4, 2004). ... Signed as free agent by Milwaukee Bucks (December 18, 2004). ... Waived by Bucks (January 5, 2005). ... Claimed off waivers by Sacramento Kings (January 7, 2005).

### COLLEGIATE RECORD

| Season Team | G | Min. | FGM | FGA | Pct. | FTM | FTA | Pct. | Reb. | Ast. | Pts. | RPG | APG | PPG |
|---|---|---|---|---|---|---|---|---|---|---|---|---|---|---|
| 96-97—Arizona State | 30 | 886 | 151 | 363 | .416 | 18 | 28 | .643 | 84 | 108 | 377 | 2.8 | 3.6 | 12.6 |
| 97-98—Arizona State | 32 | 983 | 143 | 331 | .432 | 22 | 29 | .759 | 96 | 93 | 363 | 3.0 | 2.9 | 11.3 |
| 98-99—Arizona State | 30 | 1106 | 206 | 477 | .432 | 91 | 115 | .791 | 147 | 93 | 568 | 4.9 | 3.1 | 18.9 |
| 99-00—Arizona State | 32 | 1189 | 263 | 623 | .422 | 137 | 164 | .835 | 175 | 111 | 736 | 5.5 | 3.5 | 23.0 |
| **Totals** | 124 | 4164 | 763 | 1794 | .425 | 268 | 336 | .798 | 502 | 405 | 2044 | 4.0 | 3.3 | 16.5 |

Three-point field goals: 1996-97, 57-for-179 (.318). 1997-98, 55-for-137 (.401). 1998-99, 65-for-167 (.389). 1999-00, 73-for-200 (.365). Totals, 250-for-683 (.366).

### NBA REGULAR-SEASON RECORD

| Season Team | G | Min. | FGM | FGA | Pct. | FTM | FTA | Pct. | Off. | Def. | Tot. | Ast. | St. | Blk. | TO | Pts. | RPG | APG | PPG |
|---|---|---|---|---|---|---|---|---|---|---|---|---|---|---|---|---|---|---|---|
| 00-01—Miami | 50 | 550 | 104 | 247 | .421 | 24 | 35 | .686 | 5 | 37 | 42 | 52 | 13 | 0 | 35 | 251 | 0.8 | 1.0 | 5.0 |
| 01-02—Miami | 64 | 1230 | 209 | 524 | .399 | 42 | 49 | .857 | 17 | 93 | 110 | 123 | 43 | 5 | 80 | 514 | 1.7 | 1.9 | 8.0 |
| 02-03—Miami | 55 | 1025 | 172 | 444 | .387 | 31 | 36 | .861 | 17 | 84 | 101 | 87 | 44 | 1 | 46 | 411 | 1.8 | 1.6 | 7.5 |
| 03-04—L.A. Clippers | 60 | 1188 | 161 | 449 | .359 | 36 | 45 | .800 | 28 | 110 | 138 | 148 | 65 | 4 | 63 | 409 | 2.3 | 2.5 | 6.8 |
| 04-05—Char.Mil.-Sac. | 68 | 891 | 165 | 366 | .451 | 23 | 27 | .852 | 16 | 67 | 83 | 96 | 44 | 6 | 35 | 397 | 1.2 | 1.4 | 5.8 |
| **Totals** | 297 | 4884 | 811 | 2030 | .400 | 156 | 192 | .813 | 83 | 391 | 474 | 506 | 209 | 16 | 259 | 1982 | 1.6 | 1.7 | 6.7 |

Three-point field goals: 2000-01, 19-for-55 (.345). 2001-02, 54-for-157 (.344). 2002-03, 36-for-120 (.300). 2003-04, 51-for-136 (.375). 2004-05, 44-for-97 (.454). Totals, 204-for-565 (.361).

Personal fouls/disqualifications: 2000-01, 58/0. 2001-02, 98/1. 2002-03, 73/0. 2003-04, 92/1. 2004-05, 65/0. Totals, 386/2.

### NBA PLAYOFF RECORD

| Season Team | G | Min. | FGM | FGA | Pct. | FTM | FTA | Pct. | Off. | Def. | Tot. | Ast. | St. | Blk. | TO | Pts. | RPG | APG | PPG |
|---|---|---|---|---|---|---|---|---|---|---|---|---|---|---|---|---|---|---|---|
| 00-01—Miami | 3 | 64 | 16 | 40 | .400 | 4 | 5 | .800 | 1 | 4 | 5 | 5 | 3 | 1 | 5 | 38 | 1.7 | 1.7 | 12.7 |
| 04-05—Sacramento | 3 | 23 | 3 | 8 | .375 | 2 | 2 | 1.000 | 1 | 1 | 2 | 4 | 0 | 0 | 1 | 9 | 0.7 | 1.3 | 3.0 |
| **Totals** | 6 | 87 | 19 | 48 | .396 | 6 | 7 | .857 | 2 | 5 | 7 | 9 | 3 | 1 | 6 | 47 | 1.2 | 1.5 | 7.8 |

Three-point field goals: 2000-01, 2-for-7 (.286). 2004-05, 1-for-1 (1.000). Totals, 3-for-8 (.375).
Personal fouls/disqualifications: 2000-01, 7/0. 2004-05, 2/0. Totals, 9/0.

## HOUSTON, ALLAN — G — KNICKS

**PERSONAL:** Born April 20, 1971, in Louisville, Ky. ... 6-6/200. (1.98/90.7). ... Full name: Allan Wade Houston
**HIGH SCHOOL:** Ballard (Louisville, Ky.).
**COLLEGE:** Tennessee.
**TRANSACTIONS/CAREER NOTES:** Selected by Detroit Pistons in first round (11th pick overall) of 1993 NBA Draft. ... Signed as free agent by New York Knicks (July 14, 1996).
**MISCELLANEOUS:** Member of gold-medal-winning U.S. Olympic team (2000).

### COLLEGIATE RECORD

**NOTES:** THE SPORTING NEWS All-America second team (1993).

| Season Team | G | Min. | FGM | FGA | Pct. | FTM | FTA | Pct. | Reb. | Ast. | Pts. | RPG | APG | PPG |
|---|---|---|---|---|---|---|---|---|---|---|---|---|---|---|
| 89-90—Tennessee | 30 | 1083 | 203 | 465 | .437 | 120 | 149 | .805 | 88 | 127 | 609 | 2.9 | 4.2 | 20.3 |
| 90-91—Tennessee | 34 | 1212 | 265 | 550 | .482 | 177 | 205 | .863 | 104 | 131 | 806 | 3.1 | 3.9 | 23.7 |
| 91-92—Tennessee | 34 | 1236 | 223 | 492 | .453 | 189 | 225 | .840 | 180 | 110 | 717 | 5.3 | 3.2 | 21.1 |
| 92-93—Tennessee | 30 | 1075 | 211 | 454 | .465 | 165 | 188 | .878 | 145 | 92 | 669 | 4.8 | 3.1 | 22.3 |
| **Totals** | 128 | 4606 | 902 | 1961 | .460 | 651 | 767 | .849 | 517 | 460 | 2801 | 4.0 | 3.6 | 21.9 |

Three-point field goals: 1989-90, 83-for-192 (.432). 1990-91, 99-for-231 (.429). 1991-92, 82-for-196 (.418). 1992-93, 82-for-198 (.414). Totals, 346-for-817 (.424).

### NBA REGULAR-SEASON RECORD

| Season Team | G | Min. | FGM | FGA | Pct. | FTM | FTA | Pct. | Off. | Def. | Tot. | Ast. | St. | Blk. | TO | Pts. | RPG | APG | PPG |
|---|---|---|---|---|---|---|---|---|---|---|---|---|---|---|---|---|---|---|---|
| 93-94—Detroit | 79 | 1519 | 272 | 671 | .405 | 89 | 108 | .824 | 19 | 101 | 120 | 100 | 34 | 13 | 99 | 668 | 1.5 | 1.3 | 8.5 |
| 94-95—Detroit | 76 | 1996 | 398 | 859 | .463 | 147 | 171 | .860 | 29 | 138 | 167 | 164 | 61 | 14 | 113 | 1101 | 2.2 | 2.2 | 14.5 |
| 95-96—Detroit | 82 | 3072 | 564 | 1244 | .453 | 298 | 362 | .823 | 54 | 246 | 300 | 250 | 61 | 16 | 233 | 1617 | 3.7 | 3.0 | 19.7 |

H

| Season Team | G | Min. | FGM | FGA | Pct. | FTM | FTA | Pct. | REBOUNDS Off. | Def. | Tot. | Ast. | St. | Blk. | TO | Pts. | AVERAGES RPG | APG | PPG |
|---|---|---|---|---|---|---|---|---|---|---|---|---|---|---|---|---|---|---|---|
| 96-97—New York........ | 81 | 2681 | 437 | 1032 | .423 | 175 | 218 | .803 | 43 | 197 | 240 | 179 | 41 | 18 | 167 | 1197 | 3.0 | 2.2 | 14.8 |
| 97-98—New York........ | 82 | 2848 | 571 | 1277 | .447 | 285 | 335 | .851 | 43 | 231 | 274 | 212 | 63 | 24 | 200 | 1509 | 3.3 | 2.6 | 18.4 |
| 98-99—New York........ | 50 | 1815 | 294 | 703 | .418 | 168 | 195 | .862 | 20 | 132 | 152 | 137 | 35 | 9 | 130 | 813 | 3.0 | 2.7 | 16.3 |
| 99-00—New York........ | 82 | 3169 | 614 | 1271 | .483 | 280 | 334 | .838 | 38 | 233 | 271 | 224 | 65 | 14 | 186 | 1614 | 3.3 | 2.7 | 19.7 |
| 00-01—New York........ | 78 | 2858 | 542 | 1208 | .449 | 279 | 307 | .909 | 20 | 263 | 283 | 173 | 52 | 10 | 161 | 1459 | 3.6 | 2.2 | 18.7 |
| 01-02—New York........ | 77 | 2914 | 568 | 1301 | .437 | 295 | 339 | .870 | 37 | 215 | 252 | 190 | 54 | 10 | 170 | 1567 | 3.3 | 2.5 | 20.4 |
| 02-03—New York........ | 82 | 3108 | 652 | 1465 | .445 | 363 | 395 | .919 | 26 | 205 | 231 | 220 | 54 | 7 | 178 | 1845 | 2.8 | 2.7 | 22.5 |
| 03-04—New York........ | 50 | 1799 | 340 | 781 | .435 | 157 | 172 | .913 | 20 | 101 | 121 | 99 | 38 | 2 | 102 | 924 | 2.4 | 2.0 | 18.5 |
| 04-05—New York........ | 20 | 532 | 85 | 205 | .415 | 36 | 43 | .837 | 4 | 19 | 23 | 42 | 8 | 2 | 21 | 237 | 1.2 | 2.1 | 11.9 |
| Totals.................. | 839 | 28311 | 5337 | 12017 | .444 | 2572 | 2979 | .863 | 353 | 2081 | 2434 | 1990 | 566 | 139 | 1760 | 14551 | 2.9 | 2.4 | 17.3 |

Three-point field goals: 1993-94, 35-for-117 (.299). 1994-95, 158-for-373 (.424). 1995-96, 191-for-447 (.427). 1996-97, 148-for-384 (.385). 1997-98, 82-for-213 (.385). 1998-99, 57-for-140 (.407). 1999-00, 106-for-243 (.436). 2000-01, 96-for-252 (.381). 2001-02, 136-for-346 (.393). 2002-03, 178-for-450 (.396). 2003-04, 87-for-202 (.431). 2004-05, 31-for-80 (.388). Totals, 1305-for-3247 (.402).

Personal fouls/disqualifications: 1993-94, 165/2. 1994-95, 182/0. 1995-96, 233/1. 1996-97, 233/6. 1997-98, 207/2. 1998-99, 115/1. 1999-00, 219/1. 2000-01, 190/5. 2001-02, 182/0. 2002-03, 191/2. 2003-04, 105/1. 2004-05, 40/0. Totals, 2062/21.

### NBA PLAYOFF RECORD

| Season Team | G | Min. | FGM | FGA | Pct. | FTM | FTA | Pct. | REBOUNDS Off. | Def. | Tot. | Ast. | St. | Blk. | TO | Pts. | AVERAGES RPG | APG | PPG |
|---|---|---|---|---|---|---|---|---|---|---|---|---|---|---|---|---|---|---|---|
| 95-96—Detroit ............ | 3 | 136 | 25 | 58 | .431 | 18 | 20 | .900 | 1 | 7 | 8 | 6 | 0 | 1 | 11 | 75 | 2.7 | 2.0 | 25.0 |
| 96-97—New York........ | 9 | 360 | 58 | 133 | .436 | 31 | 35 | .886 | 3 | 20 | 23 | 21 | 6 | 3 | 24 | 173 | 2.6 | 2.3 | 19.2 |
| 97-98—New York........ | 10 | 403 | 76 | 175 | .434 | 50 | 58 | .862 | 6 | 32 | 38 | 28 | 5 | 1 | 32 | 211 | 3.8 | 2.8 | 21.1 |
| 98-99—New York........ | 20 | 783 | 135 | 305 | .443 | 91 | 103 | .883 | 6 | 48 | 54 | 51 | 8 | 1 | 50 | 370 | 2.7 | 2.6 | 18.5 |
| 99-00—New York........ | 16 | 654 | 103 | 235 | .438 | 56 | 65 | .862 | 3 | 49 | 52 | 26 | 19 | 3 | 36 | 281 | 3.3 | 1.6 | 17.6 |
| 00-01—New York........ | 5 | 189 | 38 | 64 | .594 | 22 | 22 | 1.000 | 0 | 9 | 9 | 7 | 5 | 1 | 10 | 104 | 1.8 | 1.4 | 20.8 |
| Totals ................... | 63 | 2525 | 435 | 970 | .448 | 268 | 303 | .884 | 19 | 165 | 184 | 139 | 43 | 10 | 163 | 1214 | 2.9 | 2.2 | 19.3 |

Three-point field goals: 1995-96, 7-for-21 (.333). 1996-97, 26-for-52 (.500). 1997-98, 9-for-23 (.391). 1998-99, 9-for-36 (.250). 1999-00, 19-for-38 (.500). 2000-01, 6-for-11 (.545). Totals, 76-for-181 (.420).

Personal fouls/disqualifications: 1995-96, 11/0. 1996-97, 14/0. 1997-98, 27/0. 1998-99, 40/0. 1999-00, 42/0. 2000-01, 17/0. Totals, 151/0.

### NBA ALL-STAR GAME RECORD

| Season Team | Min. | FGM | FGA | Pct. | FTM | FTA | Pct. | REBOUNDS Off. | Def. | Tot. | Ast. | PF | Dq. | St. | Blk. | TO | Pts. |
|---|---|---|---|---|---|---|---|---|---|---|---|---|---|---|---|---|---|
| 2000—New York ............. | 18 | 3 | 10 | .300 | 4 | 4 | 1.000 | 0 | 0 | 0 | 2 | 1 | 0 | 1 | 0 | 1 | 11 |
| 2001—New York ............. | 15 | 2 | 5 | .400 | 0 | 0 | ... | 0 | 3 | 3 | 3 | 0 | 0 | 0 | 0 | 1 | 5 |
| Totals ........................... | 33 | 5 | 15 | .333 | 4 | 4 | 1.000 | 0 | 3 | 3 | 5 | 1 | 0 | 1 | 0 | 2 | 16 |

Three-point field goals: 2000, 1-for-3 (.333). 2001, 1-for-2 (.500). Totals, 2-for-5 (.400).

# HOWARD, DWIGHT     F     MAGIC

**PERSONAL:** Born December 8, 1985, in Atlanta. ... 6-11/240. (2.11/108.9). ... Full name: Dwight David Howard
**HIGH SCHOOL:** Southwest Atlanta Christian Academy (Atlanta).
**COLLEGE:** Did not attend college.
**TRANSACTIONS/CAREER NOTES:** Selected out of high school by Orlando Magic in first round (first pick overall) of 2004 NBA Draft.

### NBA REGULAR-SEASON RECORD

**HONORS:** NBA All-Rookie first team (2005).

| Season Team | G | Min. | FGM | FGA | Pct. | FTM | FTA | Pct. | REBOUNDS Off. | Def. | Tot. | Ast. | St. | Blk. | TO | Pts. | AVERAGES RPG | APG | PPG |
|---|---|---|---|---|---|---|---|---|---|---|---|---|---|---|---|---|---|---|---|
| 04-05—Orlando........... | 82 | 2670 | 352 | 677 | .520 | 277 | 413 | .671 | 287 | 536 | 823 | 75 | 77 | 136 | 165 | 981 | 10.0 | 0.9 | 12.0 |

Three-point field goals: 2004-05, 0-for-2. Totals, 0-for-2 (.000).
Personal fouls/disqualifications: 2004-05, 232/3. Totals, 232/3.

# HOWARD, JOSH     F     MAVERICKS

**PERSONAL:** Born January 2, 1981, in Winston-Salem, N.C. ... 6-6/203. (1.98/92.1). ... Full name: Joshua Jay Howard
**HIGH SCHOOL:** Glenn (Winston-Salem, N.C.), then Hargrave Academy.
**COLLEGE:** Wake Forest.
**TRANSACTIONS/CAREER NOTES:** Selected by Dallas Mavericks in first round (29th pick overall) of 2003 NBA Draft.

### COLLEGIATE RECORD

**NOTES:** The Sporting News All-America first team (2003).

| Season Team | G | Min. | FGM | FGA | Pct. | FTM | FTA | Pct. | Reb. | Ast. | Pts. | AVERAGES RPG | APG | PPG |
|---|---|---|---|---|---|---|---|---|---|---|---|---|---|---|
| 99-00—Wake Forest ................. | 36 | 896 | 128 | 278 | .460 | 63 | 108 | .583 | 168 | 64 | 331 | 4.7 | 1.8 | 9.2 |
| 00-01—Wake Forest ................. | 29 | 790 | 143 | 292 | .490 | 89 | 130 | .685 | 171 | 52 | 393 | 5.9 | 1.8 | 13.6 |
| 01-02—Wake Forest ................. | 31 | 848 | 170 | 337 | .504 | 65 | 99 | .657 | 240 | 64 | 431 | 7.7 | 2.1 | 13.9 |
| 02-03—Wake Forest ................. | 31 | 1002 | 204 | 428 | .477 | 145 | 174 | .833 | 257 | 59 | 606 | 8.3 | 1.9 | 19.5 |
| Totals ..................................... | 127 | 3536 | 645 | 1335 | .483 | 362 | 511 | .708 | 836 | 239 | 1761 | 6.6 | 1.9 | 13.9 |

Three-point field goals: 1999-00, 12-for-42 (.286). 2000-01, 18-for-46 (.391). 2001-02, 26-for-79 (.329). 2002-03, 53-for-142 (.373). Totals, 109-for-309 (.353).

### NBA REGULAR-SEASON RECORD

**HONORS:** NBA All-Rookie second team (2004).

**H**

| Season Team | G | Min. | FGM | FGA | Pct. | FTM | FTA | Pct. | Off. | Def. | Tot. | Ast. | St. | Blk. | TO | Pts. | RPG | APG | PPG |
|---|---|---|---|---|---|---|---|---|---|---|---|---|---|---|---|---|---|---|---|
| | | | | | | | | | REBOUNDS | | | | | | | | AVERAGES | | |
| 03-04—Dallas............. | 67 | 1589 | 229 | 532 | .430 | 97 | 138 | .703 | 149 | 219 | 368 | 97 | 69 | 54 | 67 | 575 | 5.5 | 1.4 | 8.6 |
| 04-05—Dallas............. | 76 | 2446 | 377 | 793 | .475 | 170 | 232 | .733 | 169 | 315 | 484 | 109 | 116 | 49 | 122 | 958 | 6.4 | 1.4 | 12.6 |
| Totals .................. | 143 | 4035 | 606 | 1325 | .457 | 267 | 370 | .722 | 318 | 534 | 852 | 206 | 185 | 103 | 189 | 1533 | 6.0 | 1.4 | 10.7 |

Three-point field goals: 2003-04, 20-for-66 (.303). 2004-05, 34-for-115 (.296). Totals, 54-for-181 (.298).
Personal fouls/disqualifications: 2003-04, 168/6. 2004-05, 211/3. Totals, 379/9.

### NBA PLAYOFF RECORD

| Season Team | G | Min. | FGM | FGA | Pct. | FTM | FTA | Pct. | Off. | Def. | Tot. | Ast. | St. | Blk. | TO | Pts. | RPG | APG | PPG |
|---|---|---|---|---|---|---|---|---|---|---|---|---|---|---|---|---|---|---|---|
| | | | | | | | | | REBOUNDS | | | | | | | | AVERAGES | | |
| 03-04—Dallas............. | 5 | 86 | 8 | 36 | .222 | 10 | 11 | .909 | 17 | 15 | 32 | 4 | 6 | 6 | 7 | 27 | 6.4 | 0.8 | 5.4 |
| 04-05—Dallas............. | 13 | 428 | 78 | 155 | .503 | 41 | 55 | .745 | 33 | 63 | 96 | 24 | 11 | 7 | 28 | 201 | 7.4 | 1.8 | 15.5 |
| Totals .................. | 18 | 514 | 86 | 191 | .450 | 51 | 66 | .773 | 50 | 78 | 128 | 28 | 17 | 13 | 35 | 228 | 7.1 | 1.6 | 12.7 |

Three-point field goals: 2003-04, 1-for-5 (.200). 2004-05, 4-for-16 (.250). Totals, 5-for-21 (.238).
Personal fouls/disqualifications: 2003-04, 12/0. 2004-05, 60/3. Totals, 72/3.

# HOWARD, JUWAN     F     ROCKETS

**PERSONAL:** Born February 7, 1973, in Chicago. ... 6-9/250. (2.06/113.4). ... Full name: Juwan Antonio Howard
**HIGH SCHOOL:** Vocational (Chicago).
**COLLEGE:** Michigan.
**TRANSACTIONS/CAREER NOTES:** Selected after junior season by Washington Bullets in first round (fifth pick overall) of 1994 NBA Draft. ... Signed as free agent by Miami Heat (July 15, 1996). ... Contract disallowed by NBA (July 31, 1996). ... Re-signed as free agent by Bullets (August 5, 1996). ... Bullets franchise renamed Washington Wizards for 1997-98 season. ... Traded by Wizards with C Calvin Booth and F Obinna Ekezie to Dallas Mavericks for F/C Christian Laettner, G Courtney Alexander, F Loy Vaught, G Hubert Davis, F/C Etan Thomas and cash considerations (February 22, 2001). ... Traded by Mavericks with G Tim Hardaway, F Donnell Harvey, cash considerations and first-round draft choice to Denver Nuggets for G Nick Van Exel, F/C Raef LaFrentz, G Avery Johnson and G/F Tariq Abdul-Wahad (February 21, 2002). ... Signed as free agent by Orlando Magic (July 16, 2003) ... Traded by Magic with G Tracy McGrady, G Tyronn Lue and G Reece Gaines to Houston Rockets for G Steve Francis, G Cuttino Mobley and C Kelvin Cato (June 29, 2004).

### COLLEGIATE RECORD

| Season Team | G | Min. | FGM | FGA | Pct. | FTM | FTA | Pct. | Reb. | Ast. | Pts. | RPG | APG | PPG |
|---|---|---|---|---|---|---|---|---|---|---|---|---|---|---|
| | | | | | | | | | | | | AVERAGES | | |
| 91-92—Michigan ...................... | 34 | 956 | 150 | 333 | .450 | 77 | 112 | .688 | 212 | 62 | 377 | 6.2 | 1.8 | 11.1 |
| 92-93—Michigan ...................... | 36 | 1095 | 206 | 407 | .506 | 112 | 160 | .700 | 267 | 69 | 524 | 7.4 | 1.9 | 14.6 |
| 93-94—Michigan ...................... | 30 | 1020 | 261 | 469 | .557 | 102 | 151 | .675 | 266 | 71 | 625 | 8.9 | 2.4 | 20.8 |
| Totals .................. | 100 | 3071 | 617 | 1209 | .510 | 291 | 423 | .688 | 745 | 202 | 1526 | 7.5 | 2.0 | 15.3 |

Three-point field goals: 1991-92, 0-for-2. 1992-93, 0-for-2. 1993-94, 1-for-7 (.143). Totals, 1-for-11 (.091).

### NBA REGULAR-SEASON RECORD

**HONORS:** All-NBA third team (1996). ... NBA All-Rookie second team (1995).

| Season Team | G | Min. | FGM | FGA | Pct. | FTM | FTA | Pct. | Off. | Def. | Tot. | Ast. | St. | Blk. | TO | Pts. | RPG | APG | PPG |
|---|---|---|---|---|---|---|---|---|---|---|---|---|---|---|---|---|---|---|---|
| | | | | | | | | | REBOUNDS | | | | | | | | AVERAGES | | |
| 94-95—Washington .... | 65 | 2348 | 455 | 931 | .489 | 194 | 292 | .664 | 184 | 361 | 545 | 165 | 52 | 15 | 166 | 1104 | 8.4 | 2.5 | 17.0 |
| 95-96—Washington .... | 81 | 3294 | 733 | 1500 | .489 | 319 | 426 | .749 | 188 | 472 | 660 | 360 | 67 | 39 | 303 | 1789 | 8.1 | 4.4 | 22.1 |
| 96-97—Washington .... | 82 | 3324 | 638 | 1313 | .486 | 294 | 389 | .756 | 202 | 450 | 652 | 311 | 93 | 23 | 246 | 1570 | 8.0 | 3.8 | 19.1 |
| 97-98—Washington .... | 64 | 2559 | 463 | 991 | .467 | 258 | 358 | .721 | 161 | 288 | 449 | 208 | 82 | 23 | 185 | 1184 | 7.0 | 3.3 | 18.5 |
| 98-99—Washington .... | 36 | 1430 | 286 | 604 | .474 | 110 | 146 | .753 | 90 | 203 | 293 | 107 | 42 | 14 | 95 | 682 | 8.1 | 3.0 | 18.9 |
| 99-00—Washington .... | 82 | 2909 | 509 | 1108 | .459 | 202 | 275 | .735 | 132 | 338 | 470 | 247 | 67 | 21 | 225 | 1220 | 5.7 | 3.0 | 14.9 |
| 00-01—Wash.-Dallas .. | 81 | 2974 | 583 | 1218 | .479 | 296 | 383 | .773 | 171 | 401 | 572 | 224 | 75 | 37 | 242 | 1462 | 7.1 | 2.8 | 18.0 |
| 01-02—Dallas-Denver . | 81 | 2635 | 462 | 1005 | .460 | 261 | 343 | .761 | 223 | 389 | 612 | 169 | 46 | 47 | 152 | 1185 | 7.6 | 2.1 | 14.6 |
| 02-03—Denver ........... | 77 | 2730 | 567 | 1261 | .450 | 282 | 351 | .803 | 181 | 404 | 585 | 234 | 77 | 27 | 189 | 1418 | 7.6 | 3.0 | 18.4 |
| 03-04—Orlando .......... | 81 | 2877 | 529 | 1169 | .453 | 318 | 393 | .809 | 171 | 399 | 570 | 158 | 54 | 22 | 178 | 1376 | 7.0 | 2.0 | 17.0 |
| 04-05—Houston ......... | 61 | 1624 | 244 | 541 | .451 | 97 | 115 | .843 | 126 | 220 | 346 | 94 | 32 | 5 | 79 | 585 | 5.7 | 1.5 | 9.6 |
| Totals .................. | 791 | 28704 | 5469 | 11641 | .470 | 2631 | 3471 | .758 | 1829 | 3925 | 5754 | 2277 | 687 | 273 | 2060 | 13575 | 7.3 | 2.9 | 17.2 |

Three-point field goals: 1994-95, 0-for-7. 1995-96, 4-for-13 (.308). 1996-97, 0-for-2. 1997-98, 0-for-2. 1998-99, 0-for-3. 1999-00, 0-for-7. 2000-01, 0-for-3. 2001-02, 0-for-2. 2002-03, 2-for-4 (.500). 2003-04, 0-for-1. 2004-05, 0-for-1. Totals, 6-for-45 (.133).
Personal fouls/disqualifications: 1994-95, 236/2. 1995-96, 269/3. 1996-97, 259/3. 1997-98, 225/3. 1998-99, 130/1. 1999-00, 299/2. 2000-01, 292/2. 2001-02, 265/4. 2002-03, 239/2. 2003-04, 284/1. 2004-05, 143/0. Totals, 2641/23.

### NBA PLAYOFF RECORD

| Season Team | G | Min. | FGM | FGA | Pct. | FTM | FTA | Pct. | Off. | Def. | Tot. | Ast. | St. | Blk. | TO | Pts. | RPG | APG | PPG |
|---|---|---|---|---|---|---|---|---|---|---|---|---|---|---|---|---|---|---|---|
| | | | | | | | | | REBOUNDS | | | | | | | | AVERAGES | | |
| 96-97—Washington .... | 3 | 129 | 20 | 43 | .465 | 16 | 18 | .889 | 10 | 8 | 18 | 5 | 2 | 2 | 3 | 56 | 6.0 | 1.7 | 18.7 |
| 00-01—Dallas............. | 10 | 391 | 49 | 136 | .360 | 36 | 45 | .800 | 29 | 54 | 83 | 14 | 6 | 5 | 14 | 134 | 8.3 | 1.4 | 13.4 |
| Totals .................. | 13 | 520 | 69 | 179 | .385 | 52 | 63 | .825 | 39 | 62 | 101 | 19 | 8 | 7 | 17 | 190 | 7.8 | 1.5 | 14.6 |

Personal fouls/disqualifications: 1996-97, 9/0. 2000-01, 38/0. Totals, 47/0.

### NBA ALL-STAR GAME RECORD

| Season Team | Min. | FGM | FGA | Pct. | FTM | FTA | Pct. | Off. | Def. | Tot. | Ast. | PF | Dq. | St. | Blk. | TO | Pts. |
|---|---|---|---|---|---|---|---|---|---|---|---|---|---|---|---|---|---|
| | | | | | | | | REBOUNDS | | | | | | | | | |
| 1996—Washington.......... | 16 | 1 | 5 | .200 | 0 | 0 | ... | 4 | 2 | 6 | 2 | 3 | 0 | 1 | 0 | 0 | 2 |

# HUDSON, TROY     G     TIMBERWOLVES

**PERSONAL:** Born March 13, 1976, in Carbondale, Ill. ... 6-1/170. (1.85/77.1).
**HIGH SCHOOL:** Carbondale (Ill.).
**COLLEGE:** Missouri, then Southern Illinois.
**TRANSACTIONS/CAREER NOTES:** Not drafted by an NBA franchise. ... Signed as free agent by Utah Jazz (October 3, 1997). ... Waived by Jazz (December 28, 1997). ... Played in Continental Basketball Association with Yakima Sun Kings (1997-98) and Sioux Falls Skyforce (1997-98 and 1998-99). ... Signed as free agent by Minnesota Timberwolves (January 22, 1999). ... Waived by

**H**

Timberwolves (February 3, 1999). ... Signed by Los Angeles Clippers to first of two consecutive 10-day contracts (March 23, 1999). ... Re-signed by Clippers for remainder of season (April 13, 1999). ... Waived by Clippers (March 27, 2000). ... Signed as free agent by Orlando Magic (August 10, 2000). ... Signed as free agent by Timberwolves (August 26, 2002).

## COLLEGIATE RECORD

| Season Team | G | Min. | FGM | FGA | Pct. | FTM | FTA | Pct. | Reb. | Ast. | Pts. | RPG | APG | PPG |
|---|---|---|---|---|---|---|---|---|---|---|---|---|---|---|
| | | | | | | | | | | | | AVERAGES | | |
| 94-95—Missouri | 2 | 20 | 4 | 10 | .400 | 1 | 2 | .500 | 2 | 4 | 10 | 1.0 | 2.0 | 5.0 |
| 95-96—Southern Illinois | 25 | 812 | 179 | 459 | .390 | 82 | 103 | .796 | 110 | 38 | 533 | 4.4 | 1.5 | 21.3 |
| 96-97—Southern Illinois | 30 | 1075 | 209 | 534 | .391 | 79 | 96 | .823 | 107 | 83 | 631 | 3.6 | 2.8 | 21.0 |
| Totals | 57 | 1907 | 392 | 1003 | .391 | 162 | 201 | .806 | 219 | 125 | 1174 | 3.8 | 2.2 | 20.6 |

Three-point field goals: 1994-95, 1-for-6 (.167). 1995-96, 82-for-103 (.796). 1996-97, 134-for-362 (.370). Totals, 217-for-471 (.461).
Personal fouls/disqualifications: 1994-95, 1/0. 1995-96, 39/0. 1996-97, 50/0. Totals, 90/0.

## CBA RECORD

| Season Team | G | Min. | FGM | FGA | Pct. | FTM | FTA | Pct. | Reb. | Ast. | Pts. | RPG | APG | PPG |
|---|---|---|---|---|---|---|---|---|---|---|---|---|---|---|
| | | | | | | | | | | | | AVERAGES | | |
| 97-98—Yakima-Sioux Falls | 22 | 399 | 71 | 163 | .436 | 25 | 31 | .806 | 46 | 38 | 199 | 2.1 | 1.7 | 9.0 |
| 98-99—Sioux Falls | 37 | 1213 | 173 | 449 | .385 | 52 | 60 | .867 | 113 | 170 | 461 | 3.1 | 4.6 | 12.5 |
| Totals | 59 | 1612 | 244 | 612 | .399 | 77 | 91 | .846 | 159 | 208 | 660 | 2.7 | 3.5 | 11.2 |

Three-point field goals: 1997-98, 32-for-78 (.410). 1998-99, 63-for-205 (.307). Totals, 95-for-283 (.336).
Personal fouls/disqualifications: 1998-99, 48/0. Totals, 48/0.

## NBA REGULAR-SEASON RECORD

| Season Team | G | Min. | FGM | FGA | Pct. | FTM | FTA | Pct. | Off. | Def. | Tot. | Ast. | St. | Blk. | TO | Pts. | RPG | APG | PPG |
|---|---|---|---|---|---|---|---|---|---|---|---|---|---|---|---|---|---|---|---|
| | | | | | | | | | REBOUNDS | | | | | | | | AVERAGES | | |
| 97-98—Utah | 8 | 23 | 6 | 14 | .429 | 0 | 0 | ... | 1 | 1 | 2 | 4 | 2 | 0 | 1 | 12 | 0.3 | 0.5 | 1.5 |
| 98-99—L.A. Clippers | 25 | 524 | 60 | 150 | .400 | 34 | 38 | .895 | 15 | 40 | 55 | 92 | 11 | 2 | 38 | 169 | 2.2 | 3.7 | 6.8 |
| 99-00—L.A. Clippers | 62 | 1592 | 204 | 541 | .377 | 77 | 95 | .811 | 28 | 120 | 148 | 242 | 43 | 0 | 108 | 545 | 2.4 | 3.9 | 8.8 |
| 00-01—Orlando | 75 | 1008 | 125 | 372 | .336 | 85 | 104 | .817 | 38 | 67 | 105 | 162 | 37 | 3 | 92 | 357 | 1.4 | 2.2 | 4.8 |
| 01-02—Orlando | 81 | 1354 | 354 | 815 | .434 | 176 | 201 | .876 | 30 | 115 | 145 | 255 | 57 | 6 | 163 | 950 | 1.8 | 3.1 | 11.7 |
| 02-03—Minnesota | 79 | 2600 | 409 | 956 | .428 | 208 | 231 | .900 | 42 | 141 | 183 | 452 | 60 | 7 | 182 | 1123 | 2.3 | 5.7 | 14.2 |
| 03-04—Minnesota | 29 | 503 | 80 | 207 | .386 | 27 | 33 | .818 | 4 | 31 | 35 | 70 | 7 | 0 | 34 | 218 | 1.2 | 2.4 | 7.5 |
| 04-05—Minnesota | 79 | 1729 | 266 | 664 | .401 | 70 | 90 | .778 | 19 | 86 | 105 | 283 | 27 | 6 | 113 | 691 | 1.3 | 3.6 | 8.7 |
| Totals | 438 | 9833 | 1504 | 3719 | .404 | 677 | 792 | .855 | 177 | 601 | 778 | 1560 | 244 | 24 | 731 | 4065 | 1.8 | 3.6 | 9.3 |

Three-point field goals: 1997-98, 0-for-3. 1998-99, 15-for-47 (.319). 1999-00, 60-for-193 (.311). 2000-01, 22-for-109 (.202). 2001-02, 66-for-187 (.353). 2002-03, 97-for-266 (.365). 2003-04, 31-for-77 (.403). 2004-05, 89-for-258 (.345). Totals, 380-for-1140 (.333).
Personal fouls/disqualifications: 1997-98, 1/0. 1998-99, 28/1. 1999-00, 65/0. 2000-01, 82/0. 2001-02, 119/0. 2002-03, 160/1. 2003-04, 32/0. 2004-05, 121/0. Totals, 608/2.

## NBA PLAYOFF RECORD

| Season Team | G | Min. | FGM | FGA | Pct. | FTM | FTA | Pct. | Off. | Def. | Tot. | Ast. | St. | Blk. | TO | Pts. | RPG | APG | PPG |
|---|---|---|---|---|---|---|---|---|---|---|---|---|---|---|---|---|---|---|---|
| | | | | | | | | | REBOUNDS | | | | | | | | AVERAGES | | |
| 00-01—Orlando | 4 | 56 | 6 | 21 | .286 | 5 | 6 | .833 | 5 | 4 | 9 | 9 | 1 | 0 | 3 | 17 | 2.3 | 2.3 | 4.3 |
| 01-02—Orlando | 4 | 106 | 18 | 48 | .375 | 15 | 16 | .938 | 0 | 4 | 4 | 6 | 0 | 0 | 8 | 51 | 1.0 | 1.5 | 12.8 |
| 02-03—Minnesota | 6 | 221 | 44 | 106 | .415 | 36 | 38 | .947 | 1 | 11 | 12 | 33 | 8 | 0 | 16 | 141 | 2.0 | 5.5 | 23.5 |
| Totals | 14 | 383 | 68 | 175 | .389 | 56 | 60 | .933 | 6 | 19 | 25 | 48 | 9 | 0 | 27 | 209 | 1.8 | 3.4 | 14.9 |

Three-point field goals: 2000-01, 0-for-3. 2001-02, 0-for-5. 2002-03, 17-for-39 (.436). Totals, 17-for-47 (.362).
Personal fouls/disqualifications: 2000-01, 3/0. 2001-02, 4/0. 2002-03, 5/0. Totals, 12/0.

# HUGHES, LARRY     G     CAVALIERS

**PERSONAL:** Born January 23, 1979, in St. Louis. ... 6-5/184. (1.96/83.5). ... Full name: Larry Darnell Hughes
**HIGH SCHOOL:** Christian Brothers (St. Louis).
**COLLEGE:** Saint Louis.
**TRANSACTIONS/CAREER NOTES:** Selected after freshman season by Philadelphia 76ers in first round (eighth pick overall) of 1998 NBA Draft. ... Traded by 76ers with F/G Billy Owens to Golden State Warriors in three-way deal in which Warriors sent G John Starks and a future first-round draft choice to Chicago Bulls and 76ers sent F Bruce Bowen to Bulls for F Toni Kukoc (February 16, 2000). ... Signed as free agent by Washington Wizards (July 18, 2002). ... Signed as free agent by Cleveland Cavaliers (August 2, 2005).

## COLLEGIATE RECORD

**NOTES:** The Sporting News Freshman of the Year (1998).

| Season Team | G | Min. | FGM | FGA | Pct. | FTM | FTA | Pct. | Reb. | Ast. | Pts. | RPG | APG | PPG |
|---|---|---|---|---|---|---|---|---|---|---|---|---|---|---|
| | | | | | | | | | | | | AVERAGES | | |
| 97-98—St. Louis | 32 | 1038 | 224 | 540 | .415 | 180 | 260 | .692 | 162 | 77 | 670 | 5.1 | 2.4 | 20.9 |

Three-point field goals: 1997-98, 42-for-145 (.290). Totals, 42-for-145 (.290).

## NBA REGULAR-SEASON RECORD

**HONORS:** NBA All-Defensive first team (2005).

| Season Team | G | Min. | FGM | FGA | Pct. | FTM | FTA | Pct. | Off. | Def. | Tot. | Ast. | St. | Blk. | TO | Pts. | RPG | APG | PPG |
|---|---|---|---|---|---|---|---|---|---|---|---|---|---|---|---|---|---|---|---|
| | | | | | | | | | REBOUNDS | | | | | | | | AVERAGES | | |
| 98-99—Philadelphia | 50 | 988 | 170 | 414 | .411 | 107 | 151 | .709 | 83 | 106 | 189 | 77 | 44 | 14 | 68 | 455 | 3.8 | 1.5 | 9.1 |
| 99-00—Phila.-G.S. | 82 | 2324 | 459 | 1147 | .400 | 279 | 377 | .740 | 113 | 236 | 349 | 205 | 115 | 28 | 195 | 1226 | 4.3 | 2.5 | 15.0 |
| 00-01—Golden State | 50 | 1846 | 308 | 805 | .383 | 193 | 252 | .766 | 76 | 200 | 276 | 223 | 96 | 29 | 152 | 823 | 5.5 | 4.5 | 16.5 |
| 01-02—Golden State | 73 | 2049 | 343 | 810 | .423 | 191 | 259 | .737 | 83 | 162 | 245 | 316 | 113 | 23 | 171 | 895 | 3.4 | 4.3 | 12.3 |
| 02-03—Washington | 67 | 2137 | 346 | 741 | .467 | 136 | 186 | .731 | 67 | 241 | 308 | 205 | 86 | 24 | 136 | 857 | 4.6 | 3.1 | 12.8 |
| 03-04—Washington | 61 | 2061 | 401 | 1009 | .397 | 267 | 335 | .797 | 96 | 230 | 326 | 148 | 95 | 26 | 152 | 1148 | 5.3 | 2.4 | 18.8 |
| 04-05—Washington | 61 | 2358 | 467 | 1086 | .430 | 352 | 453 | .777 | 74 | 308 | 382 | 285 | 176 | 18 | 153 | 1345 | 6.3 | 4.7 | 22.0 |
| Totals | 444 | 13763 | 2494 | 6012 | .415 | 1525 | 2013 | .758 | 592 | 1483 | 2075 | 1459 | 725 | 162 | 1027 | 6749 | 4.7 | 3.3 | 15.2 |

Three-point field goals: 1998-99, 8-for-52 (.154). 1999-00, 29-for-125 (.232). 2000-01, 14-for-75 (.187). 2001-02, 18-for-93 (.194). 2002-03, 29-for-79 (.367). 2003-04, 79-for-232 (.341). 2004-05, 59-for-209 (.282). Totals, 236-for-865 (.273).
Personal fouls/disqualifications: 1998-99, 97/0. 1999-00, 191/2. 2000-01, 147/2. 2001-02, 150/0. 2002-03, 149/1. 2003-04, 147/2. 2004-05, 168/0. Totals, 1049/7.

H

| Season Team | G | Min. | FGM | FGA | Pct. | FTM | FTA | Pct. | REBOUNDS Off. | Def. | Tot. | Ast. | St. | Blk. | TO | Pts. | AVERAGES RPG | APG | PPG |
|---|---|---|---|---|---|---|---|---|---|---|---|---|---|---|---|---|---|---|---|
| 98-99—Philadelphia .... | 8 | 198 | 31 | 77 | .403 | 20 | 24 | .833 | 17 | 20 | 37 | 16 | 15 | 9 | 12 | 82 | 4.6 | 2.0 | 10.3 |
| 04-05—Washington ... | 10 | 401 | 68 | 181 | .376 | 64 | 77 | .831 | 17 | 54 | 71 | 37 | 20 | 7 | 25 | 207 | 7.1 | 3.7 | 20.7 |
| **Totals** | 18 | 599 | 99 | 258 | .384 | 84 | 101 | .832 | 34 | 74 | 108 | 53 | 35 | 16 | 37 | 289 | 6.0 | 2.9 | 16.1 |

Three-point field goals: 1998-99, 0-for-7. 2004-05, 7-for-33 (.212). Totals, 7-for-40 (.175).
Personal fouls/disqualifications: 1998-99, 21/0. 2004-05, 35/1. Totals, 56/1.

## HUMPHREY, RYAN     F     GRIZZLIES

**PERSONAL:** Born July 24, 1979, in Tulsa, Okla. ... 6-8/235. (2.03/106.6). ... Full name: Ryan Ashley Humphrey
**HIGH SCHOOL:** Booker T. Washington (Tulsa, Okla.).
**COLLEGE:** Oklahoma, then Notre Dame.
**TRANSACTIONS/CAREER NOTES:** Selected by Utah Jazz in first round (19th pick overall) of 2002 NBA Draft. ... Draft rights traded by Jazz with draft rights to F/C Jamal Sampson to Orlando Magic for draft rights to C Curtis Borchardt (June 26, 2002). ... Traded by Magic with F Mike Miller, 2003 first-round draft choice and 2004 second-round draft choice to Memphis Grizzlies for F Drew Gooden and F Gordan Giricek (February 19, 2003).

### COLLEGIATE RECORD

| Season Team | G | Min. | FGM | FGA | Pct. | FTM | FTA | Pct. | Reb. | Ast. | Pts. | AVERAGES RPG | APG | PPG |
|---|---|---|---|---|---|---|---|---|---|---|---|---|---|---|
| 97-98—Oklahoma ..................... | 32 | 744 | 110 | 228 | .482 | 73 | 133 | .549 | 211 | 18 | 293 | 6.6 | 0.6 | 9.2 |
| 98-99—Oklahoma ..................... | 31 | 831 | 140 | 279 | .502 | 63 | 141 | .447 | 232 | 19 | 343 | 7.5 | 0.6 | 11.1 |
| 99-00—Notre Dame ................... | | | | | | Did not play—transfer student. | | | | | | | | |
| 00-01—Notre Dame ................... | 29 | 863 | 166 | 329 | .505 | 73 | 140 | .521 | 260 | 41 | 410 | 9.0 | 1.4 | 14.1 |
| 01-02—Notre Dame ................... | 31 | 1103 | 231 | 472 | .489 | 122 | 204 | .598 | 337 | 80 | 587 | 10.9 | 2.6 | 18.9 |
| **Totals** ..................................... | 123 | 3541 | 647 | 1308 | .495 | 331 | 618 | .536 | 1040 | 158 | 1633 | 8.5 | 1.3 | 13.3 |

Three-point field goals: 1997-98, 0-for-1. 2000-01, 5-for-15 (.333). 2001-02, 3-for-6 (.500). Totals, 8-for-22 (.364).

### NBA REGULAR-SEASON RECORD

| Season Team | G | Min. | FGM | FGA | Pct. | FTM | FTA | Pct. | REBOUNDS Off. | Def. | Tot. | Ast. | St. | Blk. | TO | Pts. | AVERAGES RPG | APG | PPG |
|---|---|---|---|---|---|---|---|---|---|---|---|---|---|---|---|---|---|---|---|
| 02-03—Orl-Mem ......... | 48 | 444 | 35 | 120 | .292 | 23 | 39 | .590 | 34 | 65 | 99 | 11 | 9 | 18 | 23 | 93 | 2.1 | 0.2 | 1.9 |
| 03-04—Memphis ........ | 2 | 11 | 1 | 4 | .250 | 0 | 0 | ... | 2 | 1 | 3 | 1 | 1 | 0 | 2 | 2 | 1.5 | 0.5 | 1.0 |
| 04-05—Memphis ........ | 35 | 317 | 42 | 103 | .408 | 18 | 37 | .486 | 50 | 37 | 87 | 6 | 10 | 1 | 23 | 102 | 2.5 | 0.2 | 2.9 |
| **Totals** ................... | 85 | 772 | 78 | 227 | .344 | 41 | 76 | .539 | 86 | 103 | 189 | 18 | 20 | 19 | 48 | 197 | 2.2 | 0.2 | 2.3 |

Three-point field goals: 2003-04, 0-for-1. 2004-05, 0-for-2. Totals, 0-for-3 (.000).
Personal fouls/disqualifications: 2002-03, 75/1. 2003-04, 3/0. 2004-05, 35/0. Totals, 113/1.

### NBA PLAYOFF RECORD

| Season Team | G | Min. | FGM | FGA | Pct. | FTM | FTA | Pct. | REBOUNDS Off. | Def. | Tot. | Ast. | St. | Blk. | TO | Pts. | AVERAGES RPG | APG | PPG |
|---|---|---|---|---|---|---|---|---|---|---|---|---|---|---|---|---|---|---|---|
| 03-04—Memphis ........ | 3 | 5 | 1 | 1 | 1.000 | 0 | 0 | ... | 1 | 1 | 2 | 0 | 0 | 0 | 0 | 2 | 0.7 | 0.0 | 0.7 |

## HUMPHRIES, KRIS     F     JAZZ

**PERSONAL:** Born February 6, 1985, in Minneapolis. ... 6-9/235. (2.06/106.6). ... Full name: Kris Nathan Humphries
**HIGH SCHOOL:** Hopkins (Minneapolis).
**COLLEGE:** Minnesota.
**TRANSACTIONS/CAREER NOTES:** Selected after freshman season by Utah Jazz in first round (14th pick overall) of 2004 NBA Draft.

### COLLEGIATE RECORD

| Season Team | G | Min. | FGM | FGA | Pct. | FTM | FTA | Pct. | Reb. | Ast. | Pts. | AVERAGES RPG | APG | PPG |
|---|---|---|---|---|---|---|---|---|---|---|---|---|---|---|
| 03-04—Minnesota ..................... | 29 | 990 | 221 | 498 | .444 | 170 | 229 | .742 | 293 | 20 | 629 | 10.1 | 0.7 | 21.7 |

Three-point field goals: 2003-04, 17-for-50 (.340). Totals, 17-for-50 (.340).

### NBA REGULAR-SEASON RECORD

| Season Team | G | Min. | FGM | FGA | Pct. | FTM | FTA | Pct. | REBOUNDS Off. | Def. | Tot. | Ast. | St. | Blk. | TO | Pts. | AVERAGES RPG | APG | PPG |
|---|---|---|---|---|---|---|---|---|---|---|---|---|---|---|---|---|---|---|---|
| 04-05—Utah ............... | 67 | 873 | 116 | 287 | .404 | 44 | 101 | .436 | 73 | 124 | 197 | 43 | 25 | 18 | 52 | 278 | 2.9 | 0.6 | 4.1 |

Three-point field goals: 2004-05, 2-for-6 (.333). Totals, 2-for-6 (.333).
Personal fouls/disqualifications: 2004-05, 96/0. Totals, 96/0.

## HUNTER, BRANDON     F     MAGIC

**PERSONAL:** Born November 24, 1980, in Cincinnati, Ohio. ... 6-7/260. (2.01/117.9).
**HIGH SCHOOL:** Withrow (Cincinnati, Ohio).
**COLLEGE:** Ohio University.
**TRANSACTIONS/CAREER NOTES:** Selected by Boston Celtics in second round (56th pick overall) of 2003 NBA Draft. ... Selected by Charlotte Bobcats from Celtics in NBA Expansion Draft (June 22, 2004). ... Traded by Bobcats to Orlando Magic for G Keith Bogans (November 1, 2004).

**H**

| Season Team | G | Min. | FGM | FGA | Pct. | FTM | FTA | Pct. | Reb. | Ast. | Pts. | AVERAGES | | |
|---|---|---|---|---|---|---|---|---|---|---|---|---|---|---|
| | | | | | | | | | | | | RPG | APG | PPG |
| 99-00—Ohio University.............. | 33 | 905 | 149 | 290 | .514 | 76 | 138 | .551 | 206 | 35 | 374 | 6.2 | 1.1 | 11.3 |
| 00-01—Ohio University.............. | 30 | 988 | 181 | 355 | .510 | 178 | 271 | .657 | 282 | 80 | 543 | 9.4 | 2.7 | 18.1 |
| 01-02—Ohio University.............. | 26 | 842 | 159 | 325 | .489 | 108 | 179 | .603 | 237 | 59 | 451 | 9.1 | 2.3 | 17.3 |
| 02-03—Ohio University.............. | 30 | 1146 | 217 | 415 | .523 | 199 | 335 | .594 | 378 | 78 | 644 | 12.6 | 2.6 | 21.5 |
| Totals ..................................... | 119 | 3881 | 706 | 1385 | .510 | 561 | 923 | .608 | 1103 | 252 | 2012 | 9.3 | 2.1 | 16.9 |

Three-point field goals: 1999-00, 0-for-2. 2000-01, 3-for-9 (.333). 2001-02, 25-for-67 (.373). 2002-03, 11-for-37 (.297). Totals, 39-for-115 (.339).

### NBA REGULAR-SEASON RECORD

| Season Team | G | Min. | FGM | FGA | Pct. | FTM | FTA | Pct. | REBOUNDS | | | Ast. | St. | Blk. | TO | Pts. | AVERAGES | | |
|---|---|---|---|---|---|---|---|---|---|---|---|---|---|---|---|---|---|---|---|
| | | | | | | | | | Off. | Def. | Tot. | | | | | | RPG | APG | PPG |
| 03-04—Boston ........... | 36 | 406 | 53 | 116 | .457 | 19 | 43 | .442 | 12 | 68 | 118 | 19 | 13 | 1 | 22 | 125 | 3.3 | 0.5 | 3.5 |
| 04-05—Orlando .......... | 31 | 224 | 37 | 73 | .507 | 21 | 39 | .538 | 25 | 44 | 69 | 3 | 4 | 7 | 22 | 95 | 2.2 | 0.1 | 3.1 |
| Totals .................... | 67 | 630 | 90 | 189 | .476 | 40 | 82 | .488 | 75 | 112 | 187 | 22 | 17 | 8 | 44 | 220 | 2.8 | 0.3 | 3.3 |

Three-point field goals: 2003-04, 0-for-3. Totals, 0-for-3 (.000).
Personal fouls/disqualifications: 2003-04, 40/0. 2004-05, 42/0. Totals, 82/0.

### NBA PLAYOFF RECORD

| Season Team | G | Min. | FGM | FGA | Pct. | FTM | FTA | Pct. | REBOUNDS | | | Ast. | St. | Blk. | TO | Pts. | AVERAGES | | |
|---|---|---|---|---|---|---|---|---|---|---|---|---|---|---|---|---|---|---|---|
| | | | | | | | | | Off. | Def. | Tot. | | | | | | RPG | APG | PPG |
| 03-04—Boston ........... | 3 | 10 | 1 | 1 | 1.000 | 0 | 0 | ... | 2 | 1 | 3 | 1 | 0 | 1 | 1 | 2 | 1.0 | 0.3 | 0.7 |

Personal fouls/disqualifications: 2003-04, 2/0. Totals, 2/0.

# HUNTER, LINDSEY      G      PISTONS

**PERSONAL:** Born December 3, 1970, in Utica, Miss. ... 6-2/195. (1.88/88.5). ... Full name: Lindsey Benson Hunter
**HIGH SCHOOL:** Murrah (Jackson, Miss.).
**COLLEGE:** Alcorn State, then Jackson State.
**TRANSACTIONS/CAREER NOTES:** Selected by Detroit Pistons in first round (10th pick overall) of 1993 NBA Draft. ... Traded by Pistons to Milwaukee Bucks for F Billy Owens (August 22, 2000). ... Traded by Bucks to Los Angeles Lakers for C Greg Foster (June 28, 2001). ... Traded by Lakers with draft rights to F Chris Jeffries to Toronto Raptors for F Tracy Murray and draft rights to G Kareem Rush (June 26, 2002). ... Traded by Raptors to Detroit Pistons for G Michael Curry (August 28, 2003). ... Traded by Pistons to Boston Celtics as part of three-team trade in which Celtics also received G Chucky Atkins and a 2004 first-round draft choice from Pistons. Atlanta Hawks received F Zeljko Rebraca, G Bob Sura and a first-round draft choice from Pistons and F Chris Mills from Celtics. Pistons received F/C Rasheed Wallace from Hawks and G Mike James from Celtics (February 19, 2004). ... Waived by Celtics (February 25, 2004). ... Signed as free agent by Pistons (February 26, 2004).
**MISCELLANEOUS:** Member of NBA championship team (2002, 2004).

### COLLEGIATE RECORD

**NOTES:** Holds NCAA Division I single-game record for most three-point field goals attempted—26 (December 27, 1992, vs. Kansas, 11 made).

| Season Team | G | Min. | FGM | FGA | Pct. | FTM | FTA | Pct. | Reb. | Ast. | Pts. | AVERAGES | | |
|---|---|---|---|---|---|---|---|---|---|---|---|---|---|---|
| | | | | | | | | | | | | RPG | APG | PPG |
| 88-89—Alcorn State................... | 27 | 624 | 70 | 178 | .393 | 23 | 32 | .719 | 67 | 99 | 167 | 2.5 | 3.7 | 6.2 |
| 89-90—Jackson State................. | | | | | Did not play—transfer student. | | | | | | | | | |
| 90-91—Jackson State............... | 30 | 1042 | 229 | 560 | .409 | 82 | 118 | .695 | 100 | 105 | 626 | 3.3 | 3.5 | 20.9 |
| 91-92—Jackson State............... | 28 | 960 | 249 | 605 | .412 | 100 | 157 | .637 | 96 | 121 | 693 | 3.4 | 4.3 | 24.8 |
| 92-93—Jackson State............... | 34 | 1152 | 320 | 777 | .412 | 155 | 201 | .771 | 115 | 115 | 907 | 3.4 | 3.4 | 26.7 |
| Totals .................................... | 119 | 3778 | 868 | 2120 | .409 | 360 | 508 | .709 | 378 | 440 | 2393 | 3.2 | 3.7 | 20.1 |

Three-point field goals: 1988-89, 4-for-21 (.190). 1990-91, 86-for-235 (.366). 1991-92, 95-for-257 (.370). 1992-93, 112-for-328 (.341). Totals, 297-for-841 (.353).

### NBA REGULAR-SEASON RECORD

**HONORS:** NBA All-Rookie second team (1994).

| Season Team | G | Min. | FGM | FGA | Pct. | FTM | FTA | Pct. | REBOUNDS | | | Ast. | St. | Blk. | TO | Pts. | AVERAGES | | |
|---|---|---|---|---|---|---|---|---|---|---|---|---|---|---|---|---|---|---|---|
| | | | | | | | | | Off. | Def. | Tot. | | | | | | RPG | APG | PPG |
| 93-94—Detroit ........... | 82 | 2172 | 335 | 893 | .375 | 104 | 142 | .732 | 47 | 142 | 189 | 390 | 121 | 10 | 184 | 843 | 2.3 | 4.8 | 10.3 |
| 94-95—Detroit ........... | 42 | 944 | 119 | 318 | .374 | 40 | 55 | .727 | 24 | 51 | 75 | 159 | 51 | 7 | 79 | 314 | 1.8 | 3.8 | 7.5 |
| 95-96—Detroit ........... | 80 | 2138 | 239 | 628 | .381 | 84 | 120 | .700 | 44 | 150 | 194 | 188 | 84 | 18 | 80 | 679 | 2.4 | 2.4 | 8.5 |
| 96-97—Detroit ........... | 82 | 3023 | 421 | 1042 | .404 | 158 | 203 | .778 | 59 | 174 | 233 | 154 | 129 | 24 | 96 | 1166 | 2.8 | 1.9 | 14.2 |
| 97-98—Detroit ........... | 71 | 2505 | 316 | 826 | .383 | 145 | 196 | .740 | 61 | 186 | 247 | 224 | 123 | 10 | 110 | 862 | 3.5 | 3.2 | 12.1 |
| 98-99—Detroit ........... | 49 | 1755 | 228 | 524 | .435 | 67 | 89 | .753 | 26 | 142 | 168 | 193 | 86 | 9 | 92 | 582 | 3.4 | 3.9 | 11.9 |
| 99-00—Detroit ........... | 82 | 2919 | 379 | 892 | .425 | 117 | 154 | .760 | 35 | 215 | 250 | 327 | 129 | 22 | 145 | 1043 | 3.0 | 4.0 | 12.7 |
| 00-01—Milwaukee ..... | 82 | 2002 | 298 | 783 | .381 | 77 | 96 | .802 | 32 | 137 | 169 | 222 | 102 | 12 | 68 | 825 | 2.1 | 2.7 | 10.1 |
| 01-02—L.A. Lakers ..... | 82 | 1616 | 187 | 490 | .382 | 20 | 40 | .500 | 18 | 103 | 121 | 129 | 66 | 19 | 55 | 473 | 1.5 | 1.6 | 5.8 |
| 02-03—Toronto .......... | 29 | 673 | 106 | 302 | .351 | 34 | 47 | .723 | 15 | 44 | 59 | 71 | 35 | 5 | 57 | 280 | 2.0 | 2.4 | 9.7 |
| 03-04—Detroit ........... | 33 | 661 | 49 | 143 | .343 | 5 | 8 | .625 | 13 | 54 | 67 | 85 | 39 | 6 | 34 | 117 | 2.0 | 2.6 | 3.5 |
| 04-05—Detroit ........... | 76 | 1144 | 108 | 302 | .358 | 46 | 58 | .793 | 38 | 85 | 123 | 130 | 68 | 13 | 68 | 285 | 1.6 | 1.7 | 3.8 |
| Totals .................... | 790 | 21552 | 2785 | 7143 | .390 | 897 | 1208 | .743 | 412 | 1483 | 1895 | 2272 | 1033 | 154 | 1068 | 7469 | 2.4 | 2.9 | 9.5 |

Three-point field goals: 1993-94, 69-for-207 (.333). 1994-95, 36-for-108 (.333). 1995-96, 117-for-289 (.405). 1996-97, 166-for-468 (.355). 1997-98, 85-for-265 (.321). 1998-99, 59-for-153 (.386). 1999-00, 168-for-389 (.432). 2000-01, 152-for-407 (.373). 2001-02, 79-for-208 (.380). 2002-03, 34-for-107 (.318). 2003-04, 14-for-50 (.280). 2004-05, 23-for-84 (.274). Totals, 1002-for-2735 (.366).
Personal fouls/disqualifications: 1993-94, 174/1. 1994-95, 94/1. 1995-96, 185/0. 1996-97, 206/1. 1997-98, 174/3. 1998-99, 126/2. 1999-00, 216/2. 2000-01, 172/1. 2001-02, 120/0. 2002-03, 50/1. 2003-04, 45/0. 2004-05, 125/0. Totals, 1687/12.

### NBA PLAYOFF RECORD

| Season Team | G | Min. | FGM | FGA | Pct. | FTM | FTA | Pct. | REBOUNDS | | | Ast. | St. | Blk. | TO | Pts. | AVERAGES | | |
|---|---|---|---|---|---|---|---|---|---|---|---|---|---|---|---|---|---|---|---|
| | | | | | | | | | Off. | Def. | Tot. | | | | | | RPG | APG | PPG |
| 95-96—Detroit ........... | 2 | 36 | 2 | 8 | .250 | 1 | 2 | .500 | 1 | 1 | 2 | 1 | 1 | 0 | 0 | 6 | 1.0 | 0.5 | 3.0 |

**H**

| Season Team | G | Min. | FGM | FGA | Pct. | FTM | FTA | Pct. | Off. | Def. | Tot. | Ast. | St. | Blk. | TO | Pts. | RPG | APG | PPG |
|---|---|---|---|---|---|---|---|---|---|---|---|---|---|---|---|---|---|---|---|
| 96-97—Detroit ........... | 5 | 201 | 29 | 66 | .439 | 5 | 7 | .714 | 4 | 14 | 18 | 6 | 6 | 1 | 1 | 75 | 3.6 | 1.2 | 15.0 |
| 98-99—Detroit ........... | 5 | 180 | 14 | 53 | .264 | 5 | 5 | 1.000 | 5 | 10 | 15 | 12 | 7 | 0 | 7 | 36 | 3.0 | 2.4 | 7.2 |
| 99-00—Detroit ........... | 3 | 93 | 10 | 32 | .313 | 4 | 6 | .667 | 0 | 7 | 7 | 5 | 5 | 1 | 5 | 25 | 2.3 | 1.7 | 8.3 |
| 00-01—Milwaukee ...... | 18 | 289 | 24 | 99 | .242 | 8 | 11 | .727 | 2 | 29 | 31 | 34 | 14 | 3 | 13 | 64 | 1.7 | 1.9 | 3.6 |
| 01-02—L.A. Lakers ..... | 18 | 132 | 14 | 45 | .311 | 0 | 0 | ... | 2 | 5 | 7 | 10 | 2 | 0 | 5 | 36 | 0.4 | 0.6 | 2.0 |
| 03-04—Detroit ........... | 23 | 273 | 19 | 65 | .292 | 11 | 12 | .917 | 5 | 28 | 33 | 21 | 18 | 4 | 13 | 56 | 1.4 | 0.9 | 2.4 |
| 04-05—Detroit ........... | 25 | 374 | 36 | 113 | .319 | 16 | 22 | .727 | 10 | 30 | 40 | 39 | 22 | 7 | 15 | 96 | 1.6 | 1.6 | 3.8 |
| Totals ................... | 99 | 1578 | 148 | 481 | .308 | 50 | 65 | .769 | 29 | 124 | 153 | 128 | 75 | 16 | 59 | 394 | 1.5 | 1.3 | 4.0 |

Three-point field goals: 1995-96, 1-for-4 (.250). 1996-97, 12-for-29 (.414). 1998-99, 3-for-11 (.273). 1999-00, 1-for-9 (.111). 2000-01, 8-for-53 (.151). 2001-02, 8-for-29 (.276). 2003-04, 7-for-30 (.233). 2004-05, 8-for-36 (.222). Totals, 48-for-201 (.239).

Personal fouls/disqualifications: 1995-96, 2/0. 1996-97, 9/0. 1998-99, 11/0. 1999-00, 4/0. 2000-01, 24/0. 2001-02, 19/0. 2003-04, 42/0. 2004-05, 45/0. Totals, 156/0.

## HUNTER, STEVEN      C      76ERS

**PERSONAL:** Born October 31, 1981, in Chicago. ... 7-0/220. (2.13/99.8). ... Full name: Steven D. Hunter
**HIGH SCHOOL:** Proviso East (Maywood, Ill.).
**COLLEGE:** DePaul.
**TRANSACTIONS/CAREER NOTES:** Selected after sophomore season by Orlando Magic in first round (15th pick overall) of 2001 NBA Draft. ... Traded by Magic with F Drew Gooden and the draft rights to F Anderson Varejao to Cleveland Cavaliers for F/C Tony Battie and two future second-round draft choices (July 23, 2004). ... Waived by Cavaliers (August 10, 2004). ... Signed as free agent by Phoenix Suns (August 20, 2004). ... Signed as free agent by Philadelphia 76ers (August 11, 2005).

### COLLEGIATE RECORD

| Season Team | G | Min. | FGM | FGA | Pct. | FTM | FTA | Pct. | Reb. | Ast. | Pts. | RPG | APG | PPG |
|---|---|---|---|---|---|---|---|---|---|---|---|---|---|---|
| 99-00—DePaul........................... | 33 | 744 | 114 | 197 | .579 | 53 | 75 | .707 | 128 | 9 | 281 | 3.9 | 0.3 | 8.5 |
| 00-01—DePaul........................... | 30 | 808 | 138 | 233 | .592 | 67 | 125 | .536 | 169 | 15 | 343 | 5.6 | 0.5 | 11.4 |
| Totals ....................................... | 63 | 1552 | 252 | 430 | .586 | 120 | 200 | .600 | 297 | 24 | 624 | 4.7 | 0.4 | 9.9 |

Three-point field goals: 1999-00, 0-for-2. Totals, 0-for-2 (.000).
Personal fouls/disqualifications: 1999-00, 71/0. 2000-01, 70/0. Totals, 141/0.

### NBA REGULAR-SEASON RECORD

| Season Team | G | Min. | FGM | FGA | Pct. | FTM | FTA | Pct. | Off. | Def. | Tot. | Ast. | St. | Blk. | TO | Pts. | RPG | APG | PPG |
|---|---|---|---|---|---|---|---|---|---|---|---|---|---|---|---|---|---|---|---|
| 01-02—Orlando........... | 53 | 516 | 67 | 147 | .456 | 55 | 94 | .585 | 40 | 57 | 97 | 5 | 5 | 43 | 16 | 189 | 1.8 | 0.1 | 3.6 |
| 02-03—Orlando........... | 33 | 447 | 56 | 103 | .544 | 18 | 44 | .409 | 38 | 55 | 93 | 6 | 9 | 36 | 15 | 130 | 2.8 | 0.2 | 3.9 |
| 03-04—Orlando........... | 59 | 789 | 82 | 155 | .529 | 23 | 69 | .333 | 54 | 116 | 170 | 12 | 5 | 73 | 29 | 187 | 2.9 | 0.2 | 3.2 |
| 04-05—Phoenix ......... | 76 | 1046 | 135 | 220 | .614 | 78 | 163 | .479 | 98 | 129 | 227 | 13 | 4 | 102 | 44 | 348 | 3.0 | 0.2 | 4.6 |
| Totals ................... | 221 | 2798 | 340 | 625 | .544 | 174 | 370 | .470 | 230 | 357 | 587 | 36 | 23 | 254 | 104 | 854 | 2.7 | 0.2 | 3.9 |

Three-point field goals: 2004-05, 0-for-1. Totals, 0-for-1 (.000).
Personal fouls/disqualifications: 2001-02, 81/0. 2002-03, 56/0. 2003-04, 101/0. 2004-05, 131/1. Totals, 369/1.

### NBA PLAYOFF RECORD

| Season Team | G | Min. | FGM | FGA | Pct. | FTM | FTA | Pct. | Off. | Def. | Tot. | Ast. | St. | Blk. | TO | Pts. | RPG | APG | PPG |
|---|---|---|---|---|---|---|---|---|---|---|---|---|---|---|---|---|---|---|---|
| 02-03—Orlando.......... | 7 | 40 | 3 | 10 | .300 | 0 | 3 | .000 | 1 | 2 | 3 | 1 | 0 | 3 | 1 | 6 | 0.4 | 0.1 | 0.9 |
| 04-05—Phoenix ......... | 15 | 213 | 24 | 43 | .558 | 12 | 20 | .600 | 17 | 21 | 38 | 3 | 1 | 18 | 8 | 60 | 2.5 | 0.2 | 4.0 |
| Totals ................... | 22 | 253 | 27 | 53 | .509 | 12 | 23 | .522 | 18 | 23 | 41 | 4 | 1 | 21 | 9 | 66 | 1.9 | 0.2 | 3.0 |

Personal fouls/disqualifications: 2002-03, 10/0. 2004-05, 25/0. Totals, 35/0.

## IGUODALA, ANDRE      F      76ERS

**PERSONAL:** Born January 28, 1984, in Springfield, Ill. ... 6-6/207. (1.98/93.9). ... Full name: Andre Tyler Iguodala
**HIGH SCHOOL:** Lanphier (Springfield, Ill.).
**COLLEGE:** Arizona.
**TRANSACTIONS/CAREER NOTES:** Selected after sophomore season by Philadelphia 76ers in first round (ninth pick overall) of 2004 NBA Draft.

### COLLEGIATE RECORD

| Season Team | G | Min. | FGM | FGA | Pct. | FTM | FTA | Pct. | Reb. | Ast. | Pts. | RPG | APG | PPG |
|---|---|---|---|---|---|---|---|---|---|---|---|---|---|---|
| 02-03—Arizona ...................... | 32 | 614 | 69 | 181 | .381 | 59 | 88 | .670 | 156 | 66 | 206 | 4.9 | 2.1 | 6.4 |
| 03-04—Arizona ...................... | 30 | 962 | 136 | 302 | .450 | 93 | 118 | .788 | 253 | 147 | 388 | 8.4 | 4.9 | 12.9 |
| Totals .................................... | 62 | 1576 | 205 | 483 | .424 | 152 | 206 | .738 | 409 | 213 | 594 | 6.6 | 3.4 | 9.6 |

Three-point field goals: 2002-03, 9-for-44 (.205). 2003-04, 23-for-73 (.315). Totals, 32-for-117 (.274).

**HONORS:** NBA All-Rookie first team (2005).

### NBA REGULAR-SEASON RECORD

| Season Team | G | Min. | FGM | FGA | Pct. | FTM | FTA | Pct. | Off. | Def. | Tot. | Ast. | St. | Blk. | TO | Pts. | RPG | APG | PPG |
|---|---|---|---|---|---|---|---|---|---|---|---|---|---|---|---|---|---|---|---|
| 04-05—Philadelphia .. | 82 | 2686 | 269 | 546 | .493 | 156 | 210 | .743 | 89 | 375 | 464 | 246 | 138 | 48 | 139 | 741 | 5.7 | 3.0 | 9.0 |

Three-point field goals: 2004-05, 47-for-142 (.331). Totals, 47-for-142 (.331).
Personal fouls/disqualifications: 2004-05, 204/2. Totals, 204/2.

| Season Team | G | Min. | FGM | FGA | Pct. | FTM | FTA | Pct. | REBOUNDS Off. | Def. | Tot. | Ast. | St. | Blk. | TO | Pts. | AVERAGES RPG | APG | PPG |
|---|---|---|---|---|---|---|---|---|---|---|---|---|---|---|---|---|---|---|---|
| 04-05—Philadelphia .. | 5 | 192 | 20 | 43 | .465 | 6 | 12 | .500 | 8 | 15 | 23 | 15 | 14 | 5 | 5 | 49 | 4.6 | 3.0 | 9.8 |

Three-point field goals: 2004-05, 3-for-9 (.333). Totals, 3-for-9 (.333).
Personal fouls/disqualifications: 2004-05, 12/0. Totals, 12/0.

# ILGAUSKAS, ZYDRUNAS                    C                    CAVALIERS

**PERSONAL:** Born June 5, 1975, in Kaunas, Lithuania. ... 7-3/260. (2.21/117.9). ... Name pronounced ZHEE-drew-nus ill-GAUS-kus.
**TRANSACTIONS/CAREER NOTES:** Played in Lithuania (1994-96). ... Selected by Cleveland Cavaliers in first round (20th pick overall) of 1996 NBA Draft.

## LITHUANIAN LEAGUE RECORDS RECORD

| Season Team | G | Min. | FGM | FGA | Pct. | FTM | FTA | Pct. | Reb. | Ast. | Pts. | AVERAGES RPG | APG | PPG |
|---|---|---|---|---|---|---|---|---|---|---|---|---|---|---|
| 94-95—Atletas | 36 | 1091 | 303 | 504 | .601 | 123 | 180 | .683 | 460 | 26 | 731 | 12.8 | 0.7 | 20.3 |
| 95-96—Atletas | | | | | | | Did not play—injured. | | | | | | |
| Totals | 36 | 1091 | 303 | 504 | .601 | 123 | 180 | .683 | 460 | 26 | 731 | 12.8 | 0.7 | 20.3 |

Three-point field goals: 1994-95, 2-for-9 (.222). Totals, 2-for-9 (.222).

## NBA REGULAR-SEASON RECORD

**HONORS:** NBA All-Rookie first team (1998). ... MVP of Rookie game (1998).

| Season Team | G | Min. | FGM | FGA | Pct. | FTM | FTA | Pct. | REBOUNDS Off. | Def. | Tot. | Ast. | St. | Blk. | TO | Pts. | AVERAGES RPG | APG | PPG |
|---|---|---|---|---|---|---|---|---|---|---|---|---|---|---|---|---|---|---|---|
| 96-97—Cleveland | | | | | | | | Did not play—injured. | | | | | | | | | | | |
| 97-98—Cleveland | 82 | 2379 | 454 | 876 | .518 | 230 | 302 | .762 | 279 | 444 | 723 | 71 | 52 | 135 | 146 | 1139 | 8.8 | 0.9 | 13.9 |
| 98-99—Cleveland | 5 | 171 | 29 | 57 | .509 | 18 | 30 | .600 | 17 | 27 | 44 | 4 | 4 | 7 | 9 | 76 | 8.8 | 0.8 | 15.2 |
| 99-00—Cleveland | | | | | | | | Did not play—injured. | | | | | | | | | | | |
| 00-01—Cleveland | 24 | 616 | 114 | 234 | .487 | 53 | 78 | .679 | 65 | 95 | 160 | 18 | 15 | 37 | 60 | 281 | 6.7 | 0.8 | 11.7 |
| 01-02—Cleveland | 62 | 1329 | 241 | 567 | .425 | 208 | 276 | .754 | 136 | 198 | 334 | 70 | 17 | 84 | 94 | 690 | 5.4 | 1.1 | 11.1 |
| 02-03—Cleveland | 81 | 2432 | 495 | 1122 | .441 | 400 | 512 | .781 | 240 | 371 | 611 | 127 | 56 | 152 | 210 | 1390 | 7.5 | 1.6 | 17.2 |
| 03-04—Cleveland | 81 | 2539 | 466 | 965 | .483 | 303 | 406 | .746 | 279 | 374 | 653 | 109 | 39 | 201 | 163 | 1237 | 8.1 | 1.3 | 15.3 |
| 04-05—Cleveland | 78 | 2615 | 458 | 979 | .468 | 402 | 503 | .799 | 299 | 373 | 672 | 100 | 53 | 165 | 191 | 1320 | 8.6 | 1.3 | 16.9 |
| Totals | 413 | 12081 | 2257 | 4800 | .470 | 1614 | 2107 | .766 | 1315 | 1882 | 3197 | 499 | 236 | 781 | 873 | 6133 | 7.7 | 1.2 | 14.8 |

Three-point field goals: 1997-98, 1-for-4 (.250). 2000-01, 0-for-2. 2001-02, 0-for-5. 2002-03, 0-for-5. 2003-04, 2-for-7 (.286). 2004-05, 2-for-7 (.286). Totals, 5-for-30 (.167).
Personal fouls/disqualifications: 1997-98, 288/4. 1998-99, 24/1. 2000-01, 78/0. 2001-02, 187/4. 2002-03, 274/4. 2003-04, 277/2. 2004-05, 313/7. Totals, 1441/22.

## NBA PLAYOFF RECORD

| Season Team | G | Min. | FGM | FGA | Pct. | FTM | FTA | Pct. | REBOUNDS Off. | Def. | Tot. | Ast. | St. | Blk. | TO | Pts. | AVERAGES RPG | APG | PPG |
|---|---|---|---|---|---|---|---|---|---|---|---|---|---|---|---|---|---|---|---|
| 97-98—Cleveland | 4 | 147 | 28 | 49 | .571 | 13 | 25 | .520 | 14 | 16 | 30 | 2 | 2 | 5 | 10 | 69 | 7.5 | 0.5 | 17.3 |

Personal fouls/disqualifications: 1997-98, 22/2. Totals, 22/2.

## NBA ALL-STAR GAME RECORD

| Season Team | Min. | FGM | FGA | Pct. | FTM | FTA | Pct. | REBOUNDS Off. | Def. | Tot. | Ast. | PF | Dq. | St. | Blk. | TO | Pts. |
|---|---|---|---|---|---|---|---|---|---|---|---|---|---|---|---|---|---|
| 2003—Cleveland | 4 | 0 | 1 | .000 | 0 | 0 | ... | 0 | 0 | 0 | 0 | 1 | 0 | 0 | 0 | 1 | 0 |
| 2005—Cleveland | 17 | 5 | 8 | .625 | 2 | 2 | 1.000 | 3 | 4 | 7 | 1 | 2 | 0 | 0 | 2 | 1 | 12 |
| Totals | 21 | 5 | 9 | .556 | 2 | 2 | 1.000 | 3 | 4 | 7 | 1 | 3 | 0 | 0 | 2 | 2 | 12 |

# IVERSON, ALLEN                    G                    76ERS

**PERSONAL:** Born June 7, 1975, in Hampton, Va. ... 6-0/165. (1.83/74.8).
**HIGH SCHOOL:** Bethel (Hampton, Va.).
**COLLEGE:** Georgetown.
**TRANSACTIONS/CAREER NOTES:** Selected after sophomore season by Philadelphia 76ers in first round (first pick overall) of 1996 NBA Draft.
**MISCELLANEOUS:** Member of bronze-medal-winning U.S. Olympic Team (2004).

## COLLEGIATE RECORD

**NOTES:** The Sporting News All-America first team (1996).

| Season Team | G | Min. | FGM | FGA | Pct. | FTM | FTA | Pct. | Reb. | Ast. | Pts. | AVERAGES RPG | APG | PPG |
|---|---|---|---|---|---|---|---|---|---|---|---|---|---|---|
| 94-95—Georgetown | 30 | 966 | 203 | 520 | .390 | 172 | 250 | .688 | 99 | 134 | 613 | 3.3 | 4.5 | 20.4 |
| 95-96—Georgetown | 37 | 1213 | 312 | 650 | .480 | 215 | 317 | .678 | 141 | 173 | 926 | 3.8 | 4.7 | 25.0 |
| Totals | 67 | 2179 | 515 | 1170 | .440 | 387 | 567 | .683 | 240 | 307 | 1539 | 3.6 | 4.6 | 23.0 |

Three-point field goals: 1994-95, 35-for-151 (.232). 1995-96, 87-for-238 (.366). Totals, 122-for-389 (.314).

## NBA REGULAR-SEASON RECORD

**RECORDS:** Shares NBA record for most seasons leading league in steals—3 (2001, 2002, 2003). ... Holds career record for most consecutive seasons leading league in steals—3 (2000-01 through 2002-03).
**HONORS:** NBA Most Valuable Player (2001). ... NBA Rookie of the Year (1997). ... All-NBA first team (1999, 2001, 2005). ... All-NBA second team (2000, 2002, 2003). ... NBA All-Rookie first team (1997). ... MVP of Rookie Game (1997).
**NOTES:** Led NBA with 2.51 steals per game (2001), 2.80 steals per game (2002) and 2.74 steals per game (2003).

| Season Team | G | Min. | FGM | FGA | Pct. | FTM | FTA | Pct. | Off. | Def. | Tot. | Ast. | St. | Blk. | TO | Pts. | RPG | APG | PPG |
|---|---|---|---|---|---|---|---|---|---|---|---|---|---|---|---|---|---|---|---|
| 96-97—Philadelphia .... | 76 | 3045 | 625 | 1504 | .416 | 382 | 544 | .702 | 115 | 197 | 312 | 567 | 157 | 24 | *337 | 1787 | 4.1 | 7.5 | 23.5 |
| 97-98—Philadelphia .... | 80 | 3150 | 649 | 1407 | .461 | 390 | 535 | .729 | 86 | 210 | 296 | 494 | 176 | 25 | 244 | 1758 | 3.7 | 6.2 | 22.0 |
| 98-99—Philadelphia .... | 48 | 1990 | 435 | *1056 | .412 | 356 | 474 | .751 | 66 | 170 | 236 | 223 | 110 | 7 | 167 | 1284 | 4.9 | 4.6 | *26.8 |
| 99-00—Philadelphia .... | 70 | 2853 | 729 | 1733 | .421 | 442 | 620 | .713 | 71 | 196 | 267 | 328 | 144 | 5 | 230 | 1989 | 3.8 | 4.7 | 28.4 |
| 00-01—Philadelphia .... | 71 | 2979 | 762 | 1813 | .420 | 585 | 719 | .814 | 50 | 223 | 273 | 325 | 178 | 20 | 237 | 2207 | 3.8 | 4.6 | *31.1 |
| 01-02—Philadelphia .... | 60 | 2622 | 665 | 1669 | .398 | 475 | 585 | .812 | 44 | 225 | 269 | 331 | 168 | 13 | 237 | 1883 | 4.5 | 5.5 | *31.4 |
| 02-03—Philadelphia .... | 82 | 3485 | 804 | 1940 | .414 | 570 | 736 | .774 | 68 | 276 | 344 | 454 | 225 | 13 | 286 | 2262 | 4.2 | 5.5 | 27.6 |
| 03-04—Philadelphia .... | 48 | 2040 | 435 | 1125 | .387 | 339 | 455 | .745 | 34 | 144 | 178 | 324 | 115 | 5 | 209 | 1266 | 3.7 | 6.8 | 26.4 |
| 04-05—Philadelphia .... | 75 | 3174 | 771 | 1818 | .424 | 656 | 786 | .835 | 51 | 248 | 299 | 596 | 180 | 9 | 344 | 2302 | 4.0 | 7.9 | 30.7 |
| Totals .................. | 610 | 25338 | 5875 | 14065 | .418 | 4195 | 5454 | .769 | 585 | 1889 | 2474 | 3642 | 1453 | 121 | 2291 | 16738 | 4.1 | 6.0 | 27.4 |

Three-point field goals: 1996-97, 155-for-455 (.341). 1997-98, 70-for-235 (.298). 1998-99, 58-for-199 (.291). 1999-00, 89-for-261 (.341). 2000-01, 98-for-306 (.320). 2001-02, 78-for-268 (.291). 2002-03, 84-for-303 (.277). 2003-04, 57-for-199 (.286). 2004-05, 104-for-338 (.308). Totals, 793-for-2564 (.309).

Personal fouls/disqualifications: 1996-97, 233/5. 1997-98, 200/2. 1998-99, 98/0. 1999-00, 162/1. 2000-01, 147/0. 2001-02, 102/0. 2002-03, 149/2. 2003-04, 87/0. 2004-05, 140/1. Totals, 1318/11.

## NBA PLAYOFF RECORD

**NOTES:** Holds single-game playoff record for most steals—10 (May 13, 1999, vs. Orlando). ... Shares NBA Finals single-game record for most free throws made in one quarter—9 (June 10, 2001, vs. Los Angeles Lakers).

| Season Team | G | Min. | FGM | FGA | Pct. | FTM | FTA | Pct. | Off. | Def. | Tot. | Ast. | St. | Blk. | TO | Pts. | RPG | APG | PPG |
|---|---|---|---|---|---|---|---|---|---|---|---|---|---|---|---|---|---|---|---|
| 98-99—Philadelphia .... | 8 | 358 | 88 | 214 | .411 | 37 | 52 | .712 | 14 | 19 | 33 | 39 | 20 | 2 | 24 | 228 | 4.1 | 4.9 | 28.5 |
| 99-00—Philadelphia .... | 10 | 444 | 91 | 237 | .384 | 68 | 92 | .739 | 14 | 26 | 40 | 45 | 12 | 1 | 32 | 262 | 4.0 | 4.5 | 26.2 |
| 00-01—Philadelphia .... | 22 | 1016 | 257 | 661 | .389 | 161 | 208 | .774 | 15 | 89 | 104 | 134 | 52 | 7 | 63 | 723 | 4.7 | 6.1 | 32.9 |
| 01-02—Philadelphia .... | 5 | 209 | 45 | 118 | .381 | 51 | 63 | .810 | 1 | 17 | 18 | 21 | 13 | 0 | 12 | 150 | 3.6 | 4.2 | 30.0 |
| 02-03—Philadelphia .... | 12 | 557 | 137 | 329 | .416 | 87 | 118 | .737 | 11 | 41 | 52 | 89 | 29 | 1 | 47 | 380 | 4.3 | 7.4 | 31.7 |
| 04-05—Philadelphia .... | 5 | 238 | 59 | 126 | .468 | 26 | 29 | .897 | 0 | 11 | 11 | 50 | 10 | 2 | 21 | 156 | 2.2 | 10.0 | 31.2 |
| Totals .................. | 62 | 2822 | 677 | 1685 | .402 | 430 | 562 | .765 | 55 | 203 | 258 | 378 | 136 | 13 | 199 | 1899 | 4.2 | 6.1 | 30.6 |

Three-point field goals: 1998-99, 15-for-53 (.283). 1999-00, 12-for-39 (.308). 2000-01, 48-for-142 (.338). 2001-02, 9-for-27 (.333). 2002-03, 19-for-55 (.345). 2004-05, 12-for-29 (.414). Totals, 115-for-345 (.333).

Personal fouls/disqualifications: 1998-99, 19/0. 1999-00, 24/0. 2000-01, 55/0. 2001-02, 8/0. 2002-03, 25/0. 2004-05, 12/0. Totals, 143/0.

## NBA ALL-STAR GAME RECORD

**NOTES:** NBA All-Star Game Most Valuable Player (2001). ... Holds career record for highest points per game average—22.8.

| Season Team | Min. | FGM | FGA | Pct. | FTM | FTA | Pct. | Off. | Def. | Tot. | Ast. | PF | Dq. | St. | Blk. | TO | Pts. |
|---|---|---|---|---|---|---|---|---|---|---|---|---|---|---|---|---|---|
| 2000—Philadelphia ......... | 28 | 10 | 18 | .556 | 4 | 5 | .800 | 2 | 0 | 2 | 9 | 0 | 0 | 2 | 0 | 5 | 26 |
| 2001—Philadelphia ......... | 27 | 9 | 21 | .429 | 6 | 6 | 1.000 | 0 | 2 | 2 | 5 | 0 | 0 | 4 | 0 | 4 | 25 |
| 2002—Philadelphia ......... | 25 | 2 | 9 | .222 | 1 | 2 | .500 | 1 | 3 | 4 | 3 | 0 | 0 | 0 | 0 | 2 | 5 |
| 2003—Philadelphia ......... | 41 | 13 | 23 | .565 | 8 | 9 | .889 | 3 | 2 | 5 | 7 | 2 | 0 | 5 | 0 | 6 | 35 |
| 2004—Philadelphia ......... | 23 | 1 | 6 | .167 | 1 | 4 | .250 | 0 | 1 | 1 | 11 | 3 | 0 | 0 | 0 | 4 | 3 |
| 2005—Philadelphia ......... | 32 | 4 | 14 | .286 | 7 | 7 | 1.000 | 0 | 4 | 4 | 10 | 0 | 0 | 5 | 0 | 7 | 15 |
| Totals........................... | 176 | 39 | 91 | .429 | 27 | 33 | .818 | 6 | 12 | 18 | 45 | 5 | 0 | 16 | 0 | 28 | 109 |

Three-point field goals: 2000, 2-for-2 (1.000). 2001, 1-for-1 (1.000). 2003, 1-for-3 (.333). Totals, 4-for-6 (.667).

# JACKSON, BOBBY     G     GRIZZLIES

**PERSONAL:** Born March 13, 1973, in East Spencer, N.C. ... 6-1/185. (1.85/83.9).
**HIGH SCHOOL:** Salisbury (N.C.).
**JUNIOR COLLEGE:** Western Nebraska Community College.
**COLLEGE:** Minnesota.
**TRANSACTIONS/CAREER NOTES:** Selected by Seattle SuperSonics in first round (23rd pick overall) of 1997 NBA Draft. ... Draft rights traded by SuperSonics to Denver Nuggets for draft rights to G James Cotton and 1998 second-round draft choice (June 25, 1997). ... Traded by Nuggets with C Dean Garrett to Minnesota Timberwolves in three-way deal in which Nuggets received G Chauncey Billups and draft rights to G Tyson Wheeler from Toronto Raptors and Raptors received 1999 first-round draft choice from Nuggets and draft rights to F Zeljko Rebraca, G Michael Williams and 1999 or 2000 first-round draft choice from Timberwolves (January 21, 1999). ... Signed as free agent by Sacramento Kings (August 1, 2000). ... Traded by Kings with C Greg Ostertag to Memphis Grizzlies for F Bonzi Wells (August 2, 2005).

## COLLEGIATE RECORD

| Season Team | G | Min. | FGM | FGA | Pct. | FTM | FTA | Pct. | Reb. | Ast. | Pts. | RPG | APG | PPG |
|---|---|---|---|---|---|---|---|---|---|---|---|---|---|---|
| 93-94—Western Nebraska C.C. | 39 | ... | 155 | 298 | .520 | 98 | 136 | .721 | 158 | 105 | 413 | 4.1 | 2.7 | 10.6 |
| 94-95—Western Nebraska C.C. | 32 | ... | 166 | 302 | .550 | 52 | 79 | .658 | 161 | 143 | 406 | 5.0 | 4.5 | 12.7 |
| 95-96—Minnesota.................. | 25 | 683 | 115 | 283 | .406 | 74 | 94 | .787 | 119 | 68 | 332 | 4.8 | 2.7 | 13.3 |
| 96-97—Minnesota.................. | 35 | 1101 | 191 | 433 | .441 | 121 | 154 | .786 | 213 | 139 | 534 | 6.1 | 4.0 | 15.3 |
| Junior College Totals .......... | 71 | ... | 321 | 600 | .535 | 150 | 215 | .698 | 319 | 248 | 819 | 4.5 | 3.5 | 11.5 |
| 4-Year-College Totals .......... | 60 | 1784 | 306 | 716 | .427 | 195 | 248 | .786 | 332 | 207 | 866 | 5.5 | 3.5 | 14.4 |

Three-point field goals: 1993-94, 5-for-28 (.179). 1994-95, 22-for-67 (.328). 1995-96, 28-for-95 (.295). 1996-97, 31-for-97 (.320). Totals, 86-for-287 (.300).

Personal fouls/disqualifications: 1995-96, 63/1. Totals, 63/1.

## NBA REGULAR-SEASON RECORD

**HONORS:** NBA All-Rookie second team (1998). ... NBA Sixth Man Award (2003).

| Season Team | G | Min. | FGM | FGA | Pct. | FTM | FTA | Pct. | Off. | Def. | Tot. | Ast. | St. | Blk. | TO | Pts. | RPG | APG | PPG |
|---|---|---|---|---|---|---|---|---|---|---|---|---|---|---|---|---|---|---|---|
| 97-98—Denver .......... | 68 | 2042 | 310 | 791 | .392 | 149 | 183 | .814 | 78 | 224 | 302 | 317 | 105 | 11 | 184 | 790 | 4.4 | 4.7 | 11.6 |
| 98-99—Minnesota ..... | 50 | 941 | 141 | 348 | .405 | 61 | 79 | .772 | 43 | 92 | 135 | 167 | 39 | 3 | 75 | 353 | 2.7 | 3.3 | 7.1 |
| 99-00—Minnesota ..... | 73 | 1034 | 140 | 346 | .405 | 76 | 98 | .776 | 50 | 103 | 153 | 172 | 48 | 7 | 58 | 369 | 2.1 | 2.4 | 5.1 |

| Season Team | G | Min. | FGM | FGA | Pct. | FTM | FTA | Pct. | Off. | Def. | Tot. | Ast. | St. | Blk. | TO | Pts. | RPG | APG | PPG |
|---|---|---|---|---|---|---|---|---|---|---|---|---|---|---|---|---|---|---|---|
| 00-01—Sacramento... | 79 | 1648 | 231 | 526 | .439 | 65 | 88 | .739 | 74 | 172 | 246 | 161 | 87 | 7 | 103 | 566 | 3.1 | 2.0 | 7.2 |
| 01-02—Sacramento... | 81 | 1750 | 334 | 754 | .443 | 149 | 184 | .810 | 82 | 169 | 251 | 162 | 73 | 11 | 93 | 896 | 3.1 | 2.0 | 11.1 |
| 02-03—Sacramento... | 59 | 1676 | 340 | 732 | .464 | 126 | 149 | .846 | 57 | 162 | 219 | 182 | 71 | 3 | 106 | 895 | 3.7 | 3.1 | 15.2 |
| 03-04—Sacramento... | 50 | 1185 | 263 | 592 | .444 | 82 | 109 | .752 | 55 | 119 | 174 | 105 | 49 | 8 | 63 | 689 | 3.5 | 2.1 | 13.8 |
| 04-05—Sacramento... | 25 | 536 | 109 | 255 | .427 | 50 | 58 | .862 | 23 | 62 | 85 | 59 | 14 | 2 | 28 | 301 | 3.4 | 2.4 | 12.0 |
| Totals ................ | 485 | 10812 | 1868 | 4344 | .430 | 758 | 948 | .800 | 462 | 1103 | 1565 | 1327 | 486 | 52 | 710 | 4859 | 3.2 | 2.7 | 10.0 |

Three-point field goals: 1997-98, 21-for-81 (.259). 1998-99, 10-for-27 (.370). 1999-00, 13-for-46 (.283). 2000-01, 39-for-104 (.375). 2001-02, 79-for-219 (.361). 2002-03, 89-for-235 (.379). 2003-04, 81-for-219 (.370). 2004-05, 33-for-96 (.344). Totals, 365-for-1027 (.355).

Personal fouls/disqualifications: 1997-98, 160/0. 1998-99, 75/1. 1999-00, 114/0. 2000-01, 139/0. 2001-02, 145/1. 2002-03, 126/0. 2003-04, 106/1. 2004-05, 58/1. Totals, 923/4.

## NBA PLAYOFF RECORD

| Season Team | G | Min. | FGM | FGA | Pct. | FTM | FTA | Pct. | Off. | Def. | Tot. | Ast. | St. | Blk. | TO | Pts. | RPG | APG | PPG |
|---|---|---|---|---|---|---|---|---|---|---|---|---|---|---|---|---|---|---|---|
| 98-99—Minnesota ..... | 4 | 27 | 2 | 10 | .200 | 0 | 0 | ... | 1 | 3 | 4 | 2 | 0 | 0 | 1 | 4 | 1.0 | 0.5 | 1.0 |
| 99-00—Minnesota ..... | 3 | 30 | 4 | 8 | .500 | 6 | 6 | 1.000 | 0 | 5 | 5 | 4 | 2 | 1 | 2 | 15 | 1.7 | 1.3 | 5.0 |
| 00-01—Sacramento ... | 8 | 182 | 21 | 48 | .438 | 10 | 14 | .714 | 6 | 20 | 26 | 18 | 8 | 0 | 7 | 56 | 3.3 | 2.3 | 7.0 |
| 01-02—Sacramento ... | 16 | 374 | 65 | 146 | .445 | 34 | 43 | .791 | 15 | 37 | 52 | 32 | 14 | 3 | 18 | 175 | 3.3 | 2.0 | 10.9 |
| 02-03—Sacramento ... | 12 | 331 | 63 | 138 | .457 | 31 | 35 | .886 | 11 | 43 | 54 | 40 | 12 | 1 | 17 | 172 | 4.5 | 3.3 | 14.3 |
| 04-05—Sacramento ... | 5 | 79 | 10 | 37 | .270 | 3 | 3 | 1.000 | 2 | 4 | 6 | 9 | 1 | 1 | 3 | 26 | 1.2 | 1.8 | 5.2 |
| Totals ................ | 48 | 1023 | 165 | 387 | .426 | 84 | 101 | .832 | 35 | 112 | 147 | 105 | 37 | 6 | 48 | 448 | 3.1 | 2.2 | 9.3 |

Three-point field goals: 1998-99, 0-for-3. 1999-00, 1-for-3 (.333). 2000-01, 4-for-14 (.286). 2001-02, 11-for-43 (.256). 2002-03, 15-for-43 (.349). 2004-05, 3-for-18 (.167). Totals, 34-for-124 (.274).

Personal fouls/disqualifications: 1998-99, 3/0. 1999-00, 4/0. 2000-01, 18/0. 2001-02, 31/0. 2002-03, 22/1. 2004-05, 5/0. Totals, 83/1.

# JACKSON, JIM     G     SUNS

**PERSONAL:** Born October 14, 1970, in Toledo, Ohio. ... 6-6/220. (1.98/99.8). ... Full name: James Arthur Jackson
**HIGH SCHOOL:** Macomber-Whitney (Toledo, Ohio).
**COLLEGE:** Ohio State.
**TRANSACTIONS/CAREER NOTES:** Selected after junior season by Dallas Mavericks in first round (fourth pick overall) of 1992 NBA Draft. ... Traded by Mavericks with C Eric Montross, F/C Chris Gatling, F/G George McCloud and G Sam Cassell to New Jersey Nets for C Shawn Bradley, F Ed O'Bannon, G Khalid Reeves and G Robert Pack (February 17, 1997). ... Traded by Nets with draft rights to F Tim Thomas, draft rights to G Anthony Parker and C Eric Montross to Philadelphia 76ers for C Michael Cage, G Lucious Harris, F Don MacLean and draft rights to F Keith Van Horn (June 27, 1997). ... Traded by 76ers with F Clarence Weatherspoon to Golden State Warriors for F Joe Smith and G Brian Shaw (February 17, 1998). ... Signed as free agent by Portland Trail Blazers (February 2, 1999). ... Traded by Trail Blazers with G Isaiah Rider to Atlanta Hawks for G Steve Smith and G Ed Gray (August 2, 1999). ... Traded by Hawks with G Anthony Johnson and F/G Larry Robinson to Cleveland Cavaliers for G Brevin Knight (January 2, 2001). ... Signed as free agent by Miami Heat (December 2, 2001). ... Signed as free agent by Sacramento Kings (November 30, 2002). ... Signed as free agent by Houston Rockets (September 30, 2003). ... Traded with F Bostjan Nachbar to New Orleans Hornets for G David Wesley (December 27, 2004). ... Traded by Hornets with a 2005 second-round draft choice to Phoenix Suns for G/F Casey Jacobsen, F Maciej Lampe and F/C Jackson Vroman (January 21, 2005).

## COLLEGIATE RECORD

**NOTES:** THE SPORTING NEWS All-America first team (1992). ... THE SPORTING NEWS All-America third team (1991).

| Season Team | G | Min. | FGM | FGA | Pct. | FTM | FTA | Pct. | Reb. | Ast. | Pts. | RPG | APG | PPG |
|---|---|---|---|---|---|---|---|---|---|---|---|---|---|---|
| 89-90—Ohio State .................. | 30 | 1035 | 194 | 389 | .499 | 73 | 93 | .785 | 166 | 110 | 482 | 5.5 | 3.7 | 16.1 |
| 90-91—Ohio State .................. | 31 | 997 | 228 | 441 | .517 | 112 | 149 | .752 | 169 | 133 | 585 | 5.5 | 4.3 | 18.9 |
| 91-92—Ohio State .................. | 32 | 1133 | 264 | 535 | .493 | 146 | 180 | .811 | 217 | 129 | 718 | 6.8 | 4.0 | 22.4 |
| Totals ..................................... | 93 | 3165 | 686 | 1365 | .503 | 331 | 422 | .784 | 552 | 372 | 1785 | 5.9 | 4.0 | 19.2 |

Three-point field goals: 1989-90, 21-for-59 (.356). 1990-91, 17-for-51 (.333). 1991-92, 44-for-108 (.407). Totals, 82-for-218 (.376).

## NBA REGULAR-SEASON RECORD

| Season Team | G | Min. | FGM | FGA | Pct. | FTM | FTA | Pct. | Off. | Def. | Tot. | Ast. | St. | Blk. | TO | Pts. | RPG | APG | PPG |
|---|---|---|---|---|---|---|---|---|---|---|---|---|---|---|---|---|---|---|---|
| 92-93—Dallas............. | 28 | 938 | 184 | 466 | .395 | 68 | 92 | .739 | 42 | 80 | 122 | 131 | 40 | 11 | 115 | 457 | 4.4 | 4.7 | 16.3 |
| 93-94—Dallas............. | 82 | 3066 | 637 | 1432 | .445 | 285 | 347 | .821 | 169 | 219 | 388 | 374 | 87 | 25 | *334 | 1576 | 4.7 | 4.6 | 19.2 |
| 94-95—Dallas............. | 51 | 1982 | 484 | 1026 | .472 | 306 | 380 | .805 | 120 | 140 | 260 | 191 | 28 | 12 | 160 | 1309 | 5.1 | 3.7 | 25.7 |
| 95-96—Dallas............. | 82 | 2820 | 569 | 1308 | .435 | 345 | 418 | .825 | 173 | 237 | 410 | 235 | 47 | 22 | 191 | 1604 | 5.0 | 2.9 | 19.6 |
| 96-97—Dal.-N.J.......... | 77 | 2831 | 444 | 1029 | .431 | 252 | 310 | .813 | 132 | 279 | 411 | 316 | 86 | 32 | 208 | 1226 | 5.3 | 4.1 | 15.9 |
| 97-98—Phila.-G.S....... | 79 | 3046 | 476 | 1107 | .430 | 229 | 282 | .812 | 130 | 270 | 400 | 381 | 79 | 8 | 263 | 1242 | 5.1 | 4.8 | 15.7 |
| 98-99—Portland.......... | 49 | 1175 | 152 | 370 | .411 | 85 | 101 | .842 | 36 | 123 | 159 | 128 | 43 | 6 | 82 | 414 | 3.2 | 2.6 | 8.4 |
| 99-00—Atlanta ........... | 79 | 2767 | 507 | 1235 | .411 | 186 | 212 | .877 | 101 | 293 | 394 | 230 | 57 | 10 | 185 | 1317 | 5.0 | 2.9 | 16.7 |
| 00-01—Atl.-Cleve........ | 56 | 1690 | 239 | 632 | .378 | 139 | 169 | .822 | 53 | 171 | 224 | 163 | 53 | 10 | 130 | 643 | 4.0 | 2.9 | 11.5 |
| 01-02—Miami ............. | 55 | 1825 | 238 | 538 | .442 | 75 | 87 | .862 | 54 | 236 | 290 | 140 | 42 | 14 | 106 | 589 | 5.3 | 2.5 | 10.7 |
| 02-03—Sacramento ... | 63 | 1309 | 204 | 462 | .442 | 47 | 55 | .855 | 84 | 178 | 262 | 118 | 31 | 4 | 80 | 487 | 4.2 | 1.9 | 7.7 |
| 03-04—Houston......... | 80 | 3119 | 382 | 900 | .424 | 107 | 127 | .843 | 52 | 435 | 487 | 226 | 86 | 23 | 175 | 1033 | 6.1 | 2.8 | 12.9 |
| 04-05—Hou.-N.O.-Pho. | 64 | 1987 | 248 | 582 | .426 | 54 | 58 | .931 | 33 | 236 | 269 | 183 | 35 | 5 | 115 | 672 | 4.2 | 2.9 | 10.5 |
| Totals ................... | 845 | 28555 | 4764 | 11087 | .430 | 2178 | 2638 | .826 | 1179 | 2897 | 4076 | 2816 | 714 | 182 | 2144 | 12569 | 4.8 | 3.3 | 14.9 |

Three-point field goals: 1992-93, 21-for-73 (.288). 1993-94, 17-for-50 (.283). 1994-95, 35-for-110 (.318). 1995-96, 121-for-333 (.363). 1996-97, 86-for-247 (.348). 1997-98, 61-for-191 (.319). 1998-99, 25-for-90 (.278). 1999-00, 117-for-303 (.386). 2000-01, 26-for-80 (.325). 2001-02, 38-for-81 (.469). 2002-03, 32-for-71 (.451). 2003-04, 162-for-405 (.400). 2004-05, 122-for-295 (.414). Totals, 863-for-2339 (.369).

Personal fouls/disqualifications: 1992-93, 80/0. 1993-94, 161/0. 1994-95, 92/0. 1995-96, 165/0. 1996-97, 194/0. 1997-98, 186/0. 1998-99, 80/0. 1999-00, 167/0. 2000-01, 139/0. 2001-02, 145/0. 2002-03, 132/0. 2003-04, 153/1. 2004-05, 153/1. Totals, 1921/2.

## NBA PLAYOFF RECORD

| Season Team | G | Min. | FGM | FGA | Pct. | FTM | FTA | Pct. | Off. | Def. | Tot. | Ast. | St. | Blk. | TO | Pts. | RPG | APG | PPG |
|---|---|---|---|---|---|---|---|---|---|---|---|---|---|---|---|---|---|---|---|
| 98-99—Portland.......... | 13 | 265 | 26 | 72 | .361 | 38 | 42 | .905 | 8 | 22 | 30 | 19 | 7 | 1 | 18 | 95 | 2.3 | 1.5 | 7.3 |

| Season Team | G | Min. | FGM | FGA | Pct. | FTM | FTA | Pct. | REBOUNDS Off. | Def. | Tot. | Ast. | St. | Blk. | TO | Pts. | AVERAGES RPG | APG | PPG |
|---|---|---|---|---|---|---|---|---|---|---|---|---|---|---|---|---|---|---|---|
| 02-03—Sacramento .... | 12 | 296 | 49 | 98 | .500 | 24 | 31 | .774 | 16 | 31 | 47 | 14 | 8 | 3 | 17 | 135 | 3.9 | 1.2 | 11.3 |
| 03-04—Houston ......... | 5 | 221 | 29 | 73 | .397 | 8 | 12 | .667 | 3 | 49 | 52 | 10 | 5 | 1 | 9 | 74 | 10.4 | 2.0 | 14.8 |
| 04-05—Phoenix ......... | 15 | 474 | 63 | 129 | .488 | 7 | 8 | .875 | 13 | 48 | 61 | 22 | 10 | 8 | 10 | 165 | 4.1 | 1.5 | 11.0 |
| **Totals** ................... | 45 | 1256 | 167 | 372 | .449 | 77 | 93 | .828 | 40 | 150 | 190 | 65 | 30 | 13 | 54 | 469 | 4.2 | 1.4 | 10.4 |

Three-point field goals: 1998-99, 5-for-18 (.278). 2002-03, 13-for-28 (.464). 2003-04, 8-for-29 (.276). 2004-05, 32-for-62 (.516). Totals, 58-for-137 (.423).

Personal fouls/disqualifications: 1998-99, 26/0. 2002-03, 34/1. 2003-04, 9/0. 2004-05, 42/1. Totals, 111/2.

## JACKSON, LUKE　　　　　F　　　　　CAVALIERS

**PERSONAL:** Born November 6, 1981, in Eugene, Ore. ... 6-7/215. (2.01/97.5). ... Full name: Luke Ryan Jackson
**HIGH SCHOOL:** Creswell (Ore.).
**COLLEGE:** Oregon.
**TRANSACTIONS/CAREER NOTES:** Selected by Cleveland Cavaliers in first round (10th pick overall) of 2004 NBA Draft.

### COLLEGIATE RECORD

**NOTES:** The Sporting News All-America first team (2004).

| Season Team | G | Min. | FGM | FGA | Pct. | FTM | FTA | Pct. | Reb. | Ast. | Pts. | AVERAGES RPG | APG | PPG |
|---|---|---|---|---|---|---|---|---|---|---|---|---|---|---|
| 00-01—Oregon ....................... | 28 | 506 | 73 | 172 | .424 | 54 | 73 | .740 | 114 | 55 | 218 | 4.1 | 2.0 | 7.8 |
| 01-02—Oregon ....................... | 35 | 1069 | 189 | 413 | .458 | 159 | 184 | .864 | 188 | 115 | 583 | 5.4 | 3.3 | 16.7 |
| 02-03—Oregon ....................... | 32 | 1018 | 173 | 383 | .452 | 130 | 150 | .867 | 221 | 115 | 513 | 6.9 | 3.6 | 16.0 |
| 03-04—Oregon ....................... | 31 | 1072 | 210 | 430 | .488 | 163 | 189 | .862 | 223 | 139 | 656 | 7.2 | 4.5 | 21.2 |
| **Totals** ...................................... | 126 | 3665 | 645 | 1398 | .461 | 506 | 596 | .849 | 746 | 424 | 1970 | 5.9 | 3.4 | 15.6 |

Three-point field goals: 2000-01, 18-for-50 (.360). 2001-02, 46-for-115 (.400). 2002-03, 37-for-102 (.363). 2003-04, 73-for-166 (.440). Totals, 174-for-433 (.402).

### NBA REGULAR-SEASON RECORD

| Season Team | G | Min. | FGM | FGA | Pct. | FTM | FTA | Pct. | REBOUNDS Off. | Def. | Tot. | Ast. | St. | Blk. | TO | Pts. | AVERAGES RPG | APG | PPG |
|---|---|---|---|---|---|---|---|---|---|---|---|---|---|---|---|---|---|---|---|
| 04-05—Cleveland ........ | 10 | 43 | 10 | 27 | .370 | 5 | 6 | .833 | 2 | 4 | 6 | 3 | 0 | 0 | 2 | 29 | 0.6 | 0.3 | 2.9 |

Three-point field goals: 2004-05, 4-for-6 (.667). Totals, 4-for-6 (.667).
Personal fouls/disqualifications: 2004-05, 4/0. Totals, 4/0.

## JACKSON, MARC　　　　　F/C　　　　　NETS

**PERSONAL:** Born January 16, 1975, in Philadelphia. ... 6-10/270. (2.08/122.5). ... Full name: Marc Anthony Jackson
**HIGH SCHOOL:** Roman Catholic (Philadelphia).
**COLLEGE:** Virginia Commonwealth, then Temple.
**TRANSACTIONS/CAREER NOTES:** Selected after junior season by Golden State Warriors in second round (38th pick overall) of 1997 NBA Draft. ... Played in Turkey (1997-98). ... Played in Spain (1998-2000). ... Traded by Warriors to Minnesota Timberwolves for C Dean Garrett and 2007 second-round draft choice (February 21, 2002). ... Traded by Timberwolves to Philadelphia 76ers in three-team deal in which Timberwolves also dealt G Terrell Brandon to Atlanta Hawks and acquired G Latrell Sprewell from New York Knicks. Knicks acquired F Keith Van Horn from 76ers, Hawks acquired F Randy Holcomb, a first-round draft pick and cash considerations from 76ers and 76ers acquired F Glenn Robinson and 2006 second-round pick from Hawks (July 23, 2003) ... Traded by 76ers to New Jersey Nets for a conditional second-round draft pick (August 9, 2005).

### COLLEGIATE RECORD

| Season Team | G | Min. | FGM | FGA | Pct. | FTM | FTA | Pct. | Reb. | Ast. | Pts. | AVERAGES RPG | APG | PPG |
|---|---|---|---|---|---|---|---|---|---|---|---|---|---|---|
| 93-94—Virginia Commonwealth . | 22 | 277 | 23 | 52 | .442 | 12 | 21 | .571 | 67 | 9 | 58 | 3.0 | 0.4 | 2.6 |
| 94-95—Temple........................... | | | | | | Did not play—transfer student. | | | | | | | | |
| 95-96—Temple........................... | 32 | 1117 | 183 | 384 | .477 | 133 | 199 | .668 | 287 | 24 | 501 | 9.0 | 0.8 | 15.7 |
| 96-97—Temple........................... | 31 | 1201 | 175 | 366 | .478 | 148 | 193 | .767 | 278 | 38 | 500 | 9.0 | 1.2 | 16.1 |
| **Totals** ...................................... | 85 | 2595 | 381 | 802 | .475 | 293 | 413 | .709 | 632 | 71 | 1059 | 7.4 | 0.8 | 12.5 |

Three-point field goals: 1995-96, 2-for-4 (.500). 1996-97, 2-for-6 (.333). Totals, 4-for-10 (.400).
Personal fouls/disqualifications: 1993-94, 35/0. 1995-96, 50/0. 1996-97, 62/0. Totals, 97/0.

### TURKISH LEAGUE RECORD

| Season Team | G | Min. | FGM | FGA | Pct. | FTM | FTA | Pct. | Reb. | Ast. | Pts. | AVERAGES RPG | APG | PPG |
|---|---|---|---|---|---|---|---|---|---|---|---|---|---|---|
| 97-98—Tofas Bursa ................... | 27 | ... | 179 | 316 | .566 | 155 | 206 | .752 | 293 | 39 | 518 | 10.9 | 1.4 | 19.2 |

Three-point field goals: 1997-98, 7-for-15 (.467). Totals, 7-for-15 (.467).

### SPANISH RECORD

| Season Team | G | Min. | FGM | FGA | Pct. | FTM | FTA | Pct. | Reb. | Ast. | Pts. | AVERAGES RPG | APG | PPG |
|---|---|---|---|---|---|---|---|---|---|---|---|---|---|---|
| 98-99—Lobos Caja Cantabria ..... | 14 | 505 | 119 | 254 | .469 | 60 | 79 | .759 | 130 | 27 | 298 | 9.3 | 1.9 | 21.3 |
| 99-00—Cantabria Lobos ............ | 23 | 852 | 156 | 315 | .495 | 108 | 168 | .643 | 192 | 27 | 427 | 8.3 | 1.2 | 18.6 |
| **Totals** ...................................... | 37 | 1357 | 275 | 569 | .483 | 168 | 247 | .680 | 322 | 54 | 725 | 8.7 | 1.5 | 19.6 |

Three-point field goals: 1998-99, 0-for-9 (.000). 1999-00, 7-for-17 (.412). Totals, 7-for-26 (.269).
Personal fouls/disqualifications: 1998-99, 34/0. 1999-00, 66/0. Totals, 100/0.

### NBA REGULAR-SEASON RECORD

**HONORS:** NBA All-Rookie first team (2001).

| Season Team | G | Min. | FGM | FGA | Pct. | FTM | FTA | Pct. | REBOUNDS Off. | Def. | Tot. | Ast. | St. | Blk. | TO | Pts. | AVERAGES RPG | APG | PPG |
|---|---|---|---|---|---|---|---|---|---|---|---|---|---|---|---|---|---|---|---|
| 00-01—Golden State ... | 48 | 1410 | 237 | 508 | .467 | 154 | 192 | .802 | 119 | 242 | 361 | 59 | 34 | 27 | 93 | 633 | 7.5 | 1.2 | 13.2 |
| 01-02—G.S.-Minn. ...... | 39 | 495 | 60 | 164 | .366 | 66 | 80 | .825 | 48 | 80 | 128 | 14 | 11 | 6 | 30 | 186 | 3.3 | 0.4 | 4.8 |

| Season Team | G | Min. | FGM | FGA | Pct. | FTM | FTA | Pct. | REBOUNDS Off. | Def. | Tot. | Ast. | St. | Blk. | TO | Pts. | AVERAGES RPG | APG | PPG |
|---|---|---|---|---|---|---|---|---|---|---|---|---|---|---|---|---|---|---|---|
| 02-03—Minnesota...... | 77 | 1041 | 153 | 349 | .438 | 114 | 149 | .765 | 86 | 139 | 225 | 37 | 24 | 30 | 59 | 421 | 2.9 | 0.5 | 5.5 |
| 03-04—Philadelphia.... | 22 | 598 | 71 | 171 | .415 | 64 | 81 | .790 | 45 | 81 | 126 | 18 | 12 | 6 | 24 | 206 | 5.7 | 0.8 | 9.4 |
| 04-05—Philadelphia.... | 81 | 1976 | 340 | 731 | .465 | 289 | 349 | .828 | 184 | 222 | 406 | 81 | 32 | 18 | 131 | 969 | 5.0 | 1.0 | 12.0 |
| Totals ................. | 267 | 5520 | 861 | 1923 | .448 | 687 | 851 | .807 | 482 | 764 | 1246 | 209 | 113 | 87 | 337 | 2415 | 4.7 | 0.8 | 9.0 |

Three-point field goals: 2000-01, 5-for-23 (.217). 2001-02, 0-for-1. 2002-03, 1-for-1 (1.000). 2003-04, 0-for-1. 2004-05, 0-for-2. Totals, 6-for-28 (.214).
Personal fouls/disqualifications: 2000-01, 138/1. 2001-02, 69/0. 2002-03, 137/0. 2003-04, 45/0. 2004-05, 171/0. Totals, 560/1.

### NBA PLAYOFF RECORD

| Season Team | G | Min. | FGM | FGA | Pct. | FTM | FTA | Pct. | REBOUNDS Off. | Def. | Tot. | Ast. | St. | Blk. | TO | Pts. | AVERAGES RPG | APG | PPG |
|---|---|---|---|---|---|---|---|---|---|---|---|---|---|---|---|---|---|---|---|
| 01-02—Minnesota...... | 1 | 1 | 0 | 0 | ... | 0 | 0 | ... | 0 | 0 | 0 | 0 | 0 | 0 | 0 | 0 | 0.0 | 0.0 | 0.0 |
| 02-03—Minnesota...... | 6 | 110 | 17 | 32 | .531 | 16 | 19 | .842 | 10 | 23 | 33 | 8 | 2 | 1 | 9 | 50 | 5.5 | 1.3 | 8.3 |
| 04-05—Philadelphia.... | 5 | 65 | 5 | 20 | .250 | 7 | 11 | .636 | 3 | 5 | 8 | 0 | 2 | 2 | 6 | 17 | 1.6 | 0.0 | 3.4 |
| Totals ................. | 12 | 176 | 22 | 52 | .423 | 23 | 30 | .767 | 13 | 28 | 41 | 8 | 4 | 3 | 15 | 67 | 3.4 | 0.7 | 5.6 |

Three-point field goals: 2002-03, 0-for-1. Totals, 0-for-1 (.000).
Personal fouls/disqualifications: 2001-02, 1/0. 2002-03, 19/0. 2004-05, 9/0. Totals, 29/0.

## JACKSON, STEPHEN     G/F     PACERS

**PERSONAL:** Born April 5, 1978, in Houston. ... 6-8/218. (2.03/98.9). ... Full name: Stephen Jesse Jackson
**HIGH SCHOOL:** Lincoln (Port Arthur, Texas), then Oak Hill Academ.
**JUNIOR COLLEGE:** Butler County Community College, Kan. (did not pla.
**TRANSACTIONS/CAREER NOTES:** Selected after freshman season by Phoenix Suns in second round (43rd pick overall) of 1997 NBA Draft. ... Waived by Suns (October 30, 1997). ... Played in Continental Basketball Association with La Crosse Bobcats (1997-98) and Fort Wayne Fury (1999-2000). ... Played in Venezuela (1999-2000). ... Signed as free agent by Vancouver Grizzlies (October 4, 1999). ... Waived by Grizzlies (October 28, 1999). ... Signed as free agent by New Jersey Nets (October 2, 2000). ... Signed as free agent by San Antonio Spurs (August 2, 2001). ... Signed as free agent by Atlanta Hawks (October 3, 2003). ... Traded by Hawks to Indiana Pacers for F Al Harrington (July 15, 2004).
**MISCELLANEOUS:** Member of NBA championship team (2003).

### CBA RECORD

| Season Team | G | Min. | FGM | FGA | Pct. | FTM | FTA | Pct. | Reb. | Ast. | Pts. | AVERAGES RPG | APG | PPG |
|---|---|---|---|---|---|---|---|---|---|---|---|---|---|---|
| 97-98—La Crosse ..................... | 6 | 76 | 8 | 20 | .400 | 0 | 0 | ... | 2 | 4 | 16 | 0.3 | 0.7 | 2.7 |
| 99-00—Fort Wayne ................... | 5 | 84 | 12 | 31 | .387 | 2 | 3 | .667 | 8 | 5 | 26 | 1.6 | 1.0 | 5.2 |
| Totals ................. | 11 | 160 | 20 | 51 | .392 | 2 | 3 | .667 | 10 | 9 | 42 | 0.9 | 0.8 | 3.8 |

Three-point field goals: 1997-98, 0-for-1. 1999-00, 0-for-2. Totals, 0-for-3 (.000).
Personal fouls/disqualifications: 1999-00, 16/0. Totals, 16/0.

### VENEZUELAN LEAGUE RECORD

| Season Team | G | Min. | FGM | FGA | Pct. | FTM | FTA | Pct. | Reb. | Ast. | Pts. | AVERAGES RPG | APG | PPG |
|---|---|---|---|---|---|---|---|---|---|---|---|---|---|---|
| 99-00—Marinos ........................ | 50 | 1776 | 437 | 756 | .578 | 191 | 265 | .721 | 143 | 197 | 1153 | 2.9 | 3.9 | 23.1 |

Three-point field goals: 1999-00, 88-for-199 (.442). Totals, 88-for-199 (.442).
Personal fouls/disqualifications: 1999-00, 136/0. Totals, 136/0.

### NBA REGULAR-SEASON RECORD

| Season Team | G | Min. | FGM | FGA | Pct. | FTM | FTA | Pct. | REBOUNDS Off. | Def. | Tot. | Ast. | St. | Blk. | TO | Pts. | AVERAGES RPG | APG | PPG |
|---|---|---|---|---|---|---|---|---|---|---|---|---|---|---|---|---|---|---|---|
| 00-01—New Jersey ..... | 77 | 1660 | 243 | 572 | .425 | 97 | 135 | .719 | 41 | 167 | 208 | 140 | 86 | 14 | 130 | 635 | 2.7 | 1.8 | 8.2 |
| 01-02—San Antonio.... | 23 | 227 | 34 | 91 | .374 | 12 | 17 | .706 | 3 | 23 | 26 | 11 | 15 | 3 | 23 | 89 | 1.1 | 0.5 | 3.9 |
| 02-03—San Antonio.... | 80 | 2254 | 356 | 818 | .435 | 139 | 183 | .760 | 66 | 220 | 286 | 183 | 125 | 30 | 176 | 946 | 3.6 | 2.3 | 11.8 |
| 03-04—Atlanta ........... | 80 | 2940 | 536 | 1261 | .425 | 233 | 297 | .785 | 97 | 273 | 370 | 244 | 142 | 20 | 223 | 1450 | 4.6 | 3.1 | 18.1 |
| 04-05—Indiana........... | 51 | 1806 | 330 | 819 | .403 | 190 | 229 | .830 | 44 | 206 | 250 | 119 | 64 | 14 | 123 | 953 | 4.9 | 2.3 | 18.7 |
| Totals ................. | 311 | 8887 | 1499 | 3561 | .421 | 671 | 861 | .779 | 251 | 889 | 1140 | 697 | 432 | 81 | 675 | 4073 | 3.7 | 2.2 | 13.1 |

Three-point field goals: 2000-01, 52-for-155 (.335). 2001-02, 9-for-36 (.250). 2002-03, 95-for-297 (.320). 2003-04, 145-for-427 (.340). 2004-05, 103-for-286 (.360). Totals, 404-for-1201 (.336).
Personal fouls/disqualifications: 2000-01, 166/2. 2001-02, 29/0. 2002-03, 202/1. 2003-04, 216/3. 2004-05, 154/4. Totals, 767/10.

### NBA PLAYOFF RECORD

| Season Team | G | Min. | FGM | FGA | Pct. | FTM | FTA | Pct. | REBOUNDS Off. | Def. | Tot. | Ast. | St. | Blk. | TO | Pts. | AVERAGES RPG | APG | PPG |
|---|---|---|---|---|---|---|---|---|---|---|---|---|---|---|---|---|---|---|---|
| 02-03—San Antonio.... | 24 | 811 | 108 | 261 | .414 | 53 | 66 | .803 | 19 | 79 | 98 | 65 | 33 | 9 | 68 | 307 | 4.1 | 2.7 | 12.8 |
| 04-05—Indiana........... | 13 | 472 | 70 | 178 | .393 | 49 | 60 | .817 | 7 | 43 | 50 | 29 | 25 | 6 | 34 | 209 | 3.8 | 2.2 | 16.1 |
| Totals ................. | 37 | 1283 | 178 | 439 | .405 | 102 | 126 | .810 | 26 | 122 | 148 | 94 | 58 | 15 | 102 | 516 | 4.0 | 2.5 | 13.9 |

Three-point field goals: 2002-03, 38-for-113 (.336). 2004-05, 20-for-63 (.317). Totals, 58-for-176 (.330).
Personal fouls/disqualifications: 2002-03, 53/0. 2004-05, 39/0. Totals, 92/0.

## JACOBSEN, CASEY     G/F     HORNETS

**PERSONAL:** Born March 19, 1981, in Glendora, Calif. ... 6-6/215. (1.98/97.5). ... Full name: Casey Gardner Jacobsen
**HIGH SCHOOL:** Glendora (Calif.).
**COLLEGE:** Stanford.
**TRANSACTIONS/CAREER NOTES:** Selected after junior season by Phoenix Suns in first round (22nd pick overall) of 2002 NBA Draft. ... Traded by Suns with F Maciej Lampe and F/C Jackson Vroman to New Orleans Hornets for G Jim Jackson and a 2005 second-round draft choice (January 21, 2005).

J

## COLLEGIATE RECORD

**NOTES:** The Sporting News All-America first team (2001). ... The Sporting News Freshman of the Year (2000).

| Season Team | G | Min. | FGM | FGA | Pct. | FTM | FTA | Pct. | Reb. | Ast. | Pts. | AVERAGES RPG | APG | PPG |
|---|---|---|---|---|---|---|---|---|---|---|---|---|---|---|
| 99-00—Stanford | 31 | 883 | 139 | 298 | .466 | 97 | 136 | .713 | 93 | 70 | 449 | 3.0 | 2.3 | 14.5 |
| 00-01—Stanford | 34 | 1079 | 203 | 400 | .508 | 126 | 155 | .813 | 136 | 78 | 616 | 4.0 | 2.3 | 18.1 |
| 01-02—Stanford | 30 | 1058 | 205 | 465 | .441 | 184 | 237 | .776 | 135 | 106 | 658 | 4.5 | 3.5 | 21.9 |
| Totals | 95 | 3020 | 547 | 1163 | .470 | 407 | 528 | .771 | 364 | 254 | 1723 | 3.8 | 2.7 | 18.1 |

Three-point field goals: 1999-00, 74-for-170 (.435). 2000-01, 84-for-178 (.472). 2001-02, 64-for-172 (.372). Totals, 222-for-520 (.427).

## NBA REGULAR-SEASON RECORD

| Season Team | G | Min. | FGM | FGA | Pct. | FTM | FTA | Pct. | REBOUNDS Off. | Def. | Tot. | Ast. | St. | Blk. | TO | Pts. | AVERAGES RPG | APG | PPG |
|---|---|---|---|---|---|---|---|---|---|---|---|---|---|---|---|---|---|---|---|
| 02-03—Phoenix | 72 | 1147 | 122 | 327 | .373 | 72 | 105 | .686 | 29 | 54 | 83 | 73 | 35 | 6 | 55 | 368 | 1.2 | 1.0 | 5.1 |
| 03-04—Phoenix | 78 | 1828 | 150 | 360 | .417 | 91 | 111 | .820 | 42 | 159 | 201 | 98 | 48 | 9 | 68 | 466 | 2.6 | 1.3 | 6.0 |
| 04-05—Phoenix-N.O. | 84 | 1798 | 165 | 408 | .404 | 151 | 192 | .786 | 35 | 132 | 167 | 113 | 33 | 8 | 71 | 547 | 2.0 | 1.3 | 6.5 |
| Totals | 234 | 4773 | 437 | 1095 | .399 | 314 | 408 | .770 | 106 | 345 | 451 | 284 | 116 | 23 | 194 | 1381 | 1.9 | 1.2 | 5.9 |

Three-point field goals: 2002-03, 52-for-165 (.315). 2003-04, 75-for-180 (.417). 2004-05, 66-for-177 (.373). Totals, 193-for-522 (.370).
Personal fouls/disqualifications: 2002-03, 90/0. 2003-04, 144/0. 2004-05, 104/0. Totals, 338/0.

## NBA PLAYOFF RECORD

| Season Team | G | Min. | FGM | FGA | Pct. | FTM | FTA | Pct. | REBOUNDS Off. | Def. | Tot. | Ast. | St. | Blk. | TO | Pts. | AVERAGES RPG | APG | PPG |
|---|---|---|---|---|---|---|---|---|---|---|---|---|---|---|---|---|---|---|---|
| 02-03—Phoenix | 6 | 39 | 2 | 10 | .200 | 0 | 2 | .000 | 1 | 2 | 3 | 2 | 3 | 0 | 1 | 6 | 0.5 | 0.3 | 1.0 |

Three-point field goals: 2002-03, 2-for-5 (.400). Totals, 2-for-5 (.400).
Personal fouls/disqualifications: 2002-03, 4/0. Totals, 4/0.

# JAMES, JEROME          C          SUPERSONICS

**PERSONAL:** Born November 17, 1975, in Tampa. ... 7-1/300. (2.16/136.1). ... Full name: Jerome Keith James
**HIGH SCHOOL:** Pentacostal Christian Academy (Tampa).
**COLLEGE:** Florida A&M.
**TRANSACTIONS/CAREER NOTES:** Selected by Sacramento Kings in second round (36th pick overall) of 1998 NBA Draft. ... Waived by Kings (October 20, 2000). ... Played in Yugoslavia (2000-01). ... Signed as free agent by Seattle SuperSonics (September 5, 2001). ... Signed as free agent by New York Knicks (August 2, 2005).

## COLLEGIATE RECORD

**NOTES:** Led NCAA Division I with 4.6 blocked shots per game (1998).

| Season Team | G | Min. | FGM | FGA | Pct. | FTM | FTA | Pct. | Reb. | Ast. | Pts. | AVERAGES RPG | APG | PPG |
|---|---|---|---|---|---|---|---|---|---|---|---|---|---|---|
| 94-95—Florida A&M | | | | | | Did not play—ineligible. | | | | | | | | |
| 95-96—Florida A&M | 27 | 685 | 129 | 288 | .448 | 62 | 137 | .453 | 219 | 8 | 320 | 8.1 | 0.3 | 11.9 |
| 96-97—Florida A&M | 27 | 706 | 177 | 334 | .530 | 82 | 147 | .558 | 242 | 16 | 436 | 9.0 | 0.6 | 16.1 |
| 97-98—Florida A&M | 27 | 799 | 208 | 416 | .500 | 120 | 217 | .553 | 282 | 30 | 536 | 10.4 | 1.1 | 19.9 |
| Totals | 81 | 2190 | 514 | 1038 | .495 | 264 | 501 | .527 | 743 | 54 | 1292 | 9.2 | 0.7 | 16.0 |

Three-point field goals: 1995-96, 0-for-1. 1996-97, 0-for-1. Totals, 0-for-2 (.000).

## NBA REGULAR-SEASON RECORD

| Season Team | G | Min. | FGM | FGA | Pct. | FTM | FTA | Pct. | REBOUNDS Off. | Def. | Tot. | Ast. | St. | Blk. | TO | Pts. | AVERAGES RPG | APG | PPG |
|---|---|---|---|---|---|---|---|---|---|---|---|---|---|---|---|---|---|---|---|
| 98-99—Sacramento | 16 | 42 | 9 | 24 | .375 | 6 | 12 | .500 | 6 | 11 | 17 | 1 | 2 | 6 | 9 | 24 | 1.1 | 0.1 | 1.5 |
| 99-00—Sacramento | | | | | | Did not play—injured. | | | | | | | | | | | | | |
| 01-02—Seattle | 56 | 949 | 134 | 273 | .491 | 30 | 60 | .500 | 89 | 143 | 232 | 24 | 25 | 86 | 74 | 298 | 4.1 | 0.4 | 5.3 |
| 02-03—Seattle | 51 | 766 | 111 | 232 | .478 | 54 | 92 | .587 | 78 | 138 | 216 | 27 | 12 | 82 | 75 | 276 | 4.2 | 0.5 | 5.4 |
| 03-04—Seattle | 65 | 990 | 129 | 259 | .498 | 66 | 100 | .660 | 78 | 152 | 230 | 32 | 20 | 60 | 82 | 324 | 3.5 | 0.5 | 5.0 |
| 04-05—Seattle | 80 | 1330 | 174 | 342 | .509 | 47 | 65 | .723 | 81 | 160 | 241 | 19 | 23 | 111 | 88 | 395 | 3.0 | 0.2 | 4.9 |
| Totals | 268 | 4077 | 557 | 1130 | .493 | 203 | 329 | .617 | 332 | 604 | 936 | 103 | 82 | 345 | 328 | 1317 | 3.5 | 0.4 | 4.9 |

Three-point field goals: 2004-05, 0-for-2. Totals, 0-for-2 (.000).
Personal fouls/disqualifications: 1998-99, 11/0. 2001-02, 64/0. 2002-03, 166/3. 2003-04, 180/1. 2004-05, 279/5. Totals, 810/9.

## NBA PLAYOFF RECORD

| Season Team | G | Min. | FGM | FGA | Pct. | FTM | FTA | Pct. | REBOUNDS Off. | Def. | Tot. | Ast. | St. | Blk. | TO | Pts. | AVERAGES RPG | APG | PPG |
|---|---|---|---|---|---|---|---|---|---|---|---|---|---|---|---|---|---|---|---|
| 98-99—Sacramento | 1 | 4 | 1 | 2 | .500 | 3 | 4 | .750 | 1 | 1 | 2 | 0 | 0 | 0 | 1 | 5 | 2.0 | 0.0 | 5.0 |
| 01-02—Seattle | 5 | 70 | 9 | 23 | .391 | 0 | 2 | .000 | 4 | 8 | 12 | 4 | 0 | 5 | 4 | 18 | 2.4 | 0.8 | 3.6 |
| 04-05—Seattle | 11 | 295 | 57 | 111 | .514 | 23 | 30 | .767 | 33 | 42 | 75 | 5 | 6 | 20 | 14 | 137 | 6.8 | 0.5 | 12.5 |
| Totals | 17 | 369 | 67 | 136 | .493 | 26 | 36 | .722 | 38 | 51 | 89 | 9 | 6 | 25 | 19 | 160 | 5.2 | 0.5 | 9.4 |

Personal fouls/disqualifications: 1998-99, 1/0. 2001-02, 18/1. 2004-05, 48/3. Totals, 67/4.

## YUGOSLAVIAN LEAGUE RECORD

| Season Team | G | Min. | FGM | FGA | Pct. | FTM | FTA | Pct. | Reb. | Ast. | Pts. | AVERAGES RPG | APG | PPG |
|---|---|---|---|---|---|---|---|---|---|---|---|---|---|---|
| 00-01—Buducnost | 10 | 154 | 47 | 76 | .618 | 27 | 42 | .643 | 67 | 6 | 121 | 6.7 | 0.6 | 12.1 |

Three-point field goals: 2000-01, 0-for-1. Totals, 0-for-1 (.000).

# JAMES, LEBRON          F          CAVALIERS

**PERSONAL:** Born December 30, 1984, in Akron, Ohio. ... 6-8/240. (2.03/108.9).
**HIGH SCHOOL:** St. Vincent-St. Mary (Akron, Ohio).
**COLLEGE:** Did not attend college.
**TRANSACTIONS/CAREER NOTES:** Selected out of high school by Cleveland Cavaliers in first round (first pick overall) of 2003 NBA Draft.

**MISCELLANEOUS:** Member of bronze-medal-winning U.S. Olympic Team (2004).

### NBA REGULAR-SEASON RECORD
**HONORS:** NBA Rookie of the Year (2004). ... NBA All-Rookie first team (2004). ... All-NBA second team (2005).

| | | | | | | | | REBOUNDS | | | | | | | AVERAGES | | |
|---|---|---|---|---|---|---|---|---|---|---|---|---|---|---|---|---|---|
| Season Team | G | Min. | FGM | FGA | Pct. | FTM | FTA | Pct. | Off. | Def. | Tot. | Ast. | St. | Blk. | TO | Pts. | RPG | APG | PPG |
| 03-04—Cleveland | 79 | 3122 | 622 | 1492 | .417 | 347 | 460 | .754 | 99 | 333 | 432 | 465 | 130 | 58 | 273 | 1654 | 5.5 | 5.9 | 20.9 |
| 04-05—Cleveland | 80 | 3388 | 795 | 1684 | .472 | 477 | 636 | .750 | 111 | 477 | 588 | 577 | 177 | 52 | 262 | 2175 | 7.4 | 7.2 | 27.2 |
| Totals | 159 | 6510 | 1417 | 3176 | .446 | 824 | 1096 | .752 | 210 | 810 | 1020 | 1042 | 307 | 110 | 535 | 3829 | 6.4 | 6.6 | 24.1 |

Three-point field goals: 2003-04, 63-for-217 (.290). 2004-05, 108-for-308 (.351). Totals, 171-for-525 (.326).
Personal fouls/disqualifications: 2003-04, 149/0. 2004-05, 146/1. Totals, 295/1.

### NBA ALL-STAR GAME RECORD

| | | | | | | | REBOUNDS | | | | | | | | |
|---|---|---|---|---|---|---|---|---|---|---|---|---|---|---|---|
| Season Team | Min. | FGM | FGA | Pct. | FTM | FTA | Pct. | Off. | Def. | Tot. | Ast. | PF | Dq. | St. | Blk. | TO | Pts. |
| 2005—Cleveland | 31 | 6 | 13 | .462 | 0 | 1 | .000 | 1 | 7 | 8 | 6 | 0 | 0 | 2 | 0 | 3 | 13 |

Three-point field goals: 2005, 1-for-4 (.250). Totals, 1-for-4 (.250).

## JAMES, MIKE — G — ROCKETS

**PERSONAL:** Born June 23, 1975, in Amityville, N.Y. ... 6-2/188. (1.88/85.3). ... Full name: Michael Lamont James
**HIGH SCHOOL:** Amityville (N.Y.).
**COLLEGE:** Duquesne.
**TRANSACTIONS/CAREER NOTES:** Not drafted by an NBA franchise. ... Played in Austria (1998-99). ... Played in France (1999-2001). ... Signed as free agent by Miami Heat (July 20, 2001). ... Waived by Heat (October 25, 2001). ... Played in Continental Basketball Association with Rockford Lightning (2001-02). ... Re-signed as free agent by Heat (December 18, 2001). ... Signed as free agent by Boston Celtics (July 25, 2003). ... Traded by Celtics to Detroit Pistons in three-team deal in which Pistons also received F/C Rasheed Wallace from Atlanta Hawks. Celtics received G Chucky Atkins, G Lindsey Hunter and a 2004 first-round draft choice from Pistons. Hawks received F Zeljko Rebraca, G Bob Sura and a future first-round draft choice from Pistons and F Chris Mills from Celtics (February 19, 2004). ... Signed as free agent by Milwaukee Bucks (August 5, 2004). ... Traded by Bucks with C Zendon Hamilton to Houston Rockets for Reece Gaines and second-round picks in 2006 and 2007 NBA drafts (February 24, 2005).
**MISCELLANEOUS:** Member of NBA championship team (2004).

### COLLEGIATE RECORD

| | | | | | | | | | | | AVERAGES | | |
|---|---|---|---|---|---|---|---|---|---|---|---|---|---|
| Season Team | G | Min. | FGM | FGA | Pct. | FTM | FTA | Pct. | Reb. | Ast. | Pts. | RPG | APG | PPG |
| 94-95—Duquesne | 27 | 381 | 55 | 123 | .447 | 24 | 35 | .686 | 36 | 27 | 135 | 1.3 | 1.0 | 5.0 |
| 95-96—Duquesne | 27 | 843 | 151 | 318 | .475 | 79 | 108 | .731 | 94 | 106 | 384 | 3.5 | 3.9 | 14.2 |
| 96-97—Duquesne | 27 | 862 | 141 | 325 | .434 | 60 | 84 | .714 | 93 | 76 | 366 | 3.4 | 2.8 | 13.6 |
| 97-98—Duquesne | 30 | 1029 | 190 | 443 | .429 | 81 | 109 | .743 | 106 | 104 | 526 | 3.5 | 3.5 | 17.5 |
| Totals | 111 | 3115 | 537 | 1209 | .444 | 244 | 336 | .726 | 329 | 313 | 1411 | 3.0 | 2.8 | 12.7 |

Three-point field goals: 1994-95, 1-for-13 (.077). 1995-96, 3-for-19 (.158). 1996-97, 24-for-67 (.358). 1997-98, 65-for-184 (.353). Totals, 93-for-283 (.329).

### AUSTRIAN RECORD

| | | | | | | | | | | | AVERAGES | | |
|---|---|---|---|---|---|---|---|---|---|---|---|---|---|
| Season Team | G | Min. | FGM | FGA | Pct. | FTM | FTA | Pct. | Reb. | Ast. | Pts. | RPG | APG | PPG |
| 98-99—St. Polten | 15 | 556 | 103 | 217 | .475 | 61 | 80 | .763 | 83 | 110 | 282 | 5.5 | 7.3 | 18.8 |

Three-point field goals: 1998-99, 15-for-56 (.268). Totals, 15-for-56 (.268).

### FRENCH LEAGUE RECORD

| | | | | | | | | | | | AVERAGES | | |
|---|---|---|---|---|---|---|---|---|---|---|---|---|---|
| Season Team | G | Min. | FGM | FGA | Pct. | FTM | FTA | Pct. | Reb. | Ast. | Pts. | RPG | APG | PPG |
| 99-00—ESPE | 30 | 1061 | 196 | 422 | .464 | 104 | 124 | .839 | 91 | 144 | 536 | 3.0 | 4.8 | 17.9 |
| 00-01—SLUC | 30 | 1028 | 169 | 360 | .469 | 67 | 90 | .744 | 109 | 154 | 451 | 3.6 | 5.1 | 15.0 |
| Totals | 60 | 2089 | 365 | 782 | .467 | 171 | 214 | .799 | 200 | 298 | 987 | 3.3 | 5.0 | 16.5 |

Three-point field goals: 1999-00, 40-for-99 (.404). 2000-01, 46-for-125 (.368). Totals, 86-for-224 (.384).

### CBA RECORD

| | | | | | | | | | | | AVERAGES | | |
|---|---|---|---|---|---|---|---|---|---|---|---|---|---|
| Season Team | G | Min. | FGM | FGA | Pct. | FTM | FTA | Pct. | Reb. | Ast. | Pts. | RPG | APG | PPG |
| 01-02—Rockford | 14 | 620 | 124 | 259 | .479 | 40 | 49 | .816 | 92 | 88 | 326 | 6.6 | 6.3 | 23.3 |

Three-point field goals: 2001-02, 38-for-91 (.418). Totals, 38-for-91 (.418).

### NBA REGULAR-SEASON RECORD

| | | | | | | | | REBOUNDS | | | | | | | AVERAGES | | |
|---|---|---|---|---|---|---|---|---|---|---|---|---|---|---|---|---|---|
| Season Team | G | Min. | FGM | FGA | Pct. | FTM | FTA | Pct. | Off. | Def. | Tot. | Ast. | St. | Blk. | TO | Pts. | RPG | APG | PPG |
| 01-02—Miami | 15 | 119 | 15 | 43 | .349 | 4 | 7 | .571 | 2 | 12 | 14 | 19 | 6 | 1 | 13 | 42 | 0.9 | 1.3 | 2.8 |
| 02-03—Miami | 78 | 1722 | 218 | 585 | .373 | 104 | 142 | .732 | 26 | 123 | 149 | 246 | 64 | 5 | 108 | 607 | 1.9 | 3.2 | 7.8 |
| 03-04—Boston-Detroit | 81 | 2196 | 272 | 657 | .414 | 103 | 127 | .811 | 28 | 206 | 234 | 339 | 96 | 3 | 124 | 753 | 2.9 | 4.2 | 9.3 |
| 04-05—Milwaukee-Hou. | 74 | 1859 | 331 | 751 | .441 | 109 | 145 | .752 | 35 | 173 | 208 | 263 | 65 | 6 | 106 | 871 | 2.8 | 3.6 | 11.8 |
| Totals | 248 | 5896 | 836 | 2036 | .411 | 320 | 421 | .760 | 91 | 514 | 605 | 867 | 231 | 15 | 351 | 2273 | 2.4 | 3.5 | 9.2 |

Three-point field goals: 2001-02, 8-for-21 (.381). 2002-03, 67-for-228 (.294). 2003-04, 106-for-281 (.377). 2004-05, 100-for-259 (.386). Totals, 281-for-789 (.356).
Personal fouls/disqualifications: 2001-02, 17/0. 2002-03, 176/1. 2003-04, 156/0. 2004-05, 174/2. Totals, 523/3.

### NBA PLAYOFF RECORD

| | | | | | | | | REBOUNDS | | | | | | | AVERAGES | | |
|---|---|---|---|---|---|---|---|---|---|---|---|---|---|---|---|---|---|
| Season Team | G | Min. | FGM | FGA | Pct. | FTM | FTA | Pct. | Off. | Def. | Tot. | Ast. | St. | Blk. | TO | Pts. | RPG | APG | PPG |
| 03-04—Detroit | 22 | 195 | 21 | 53 | .396 | 9 | 16 | .563 | 7 | 19 | 26 | 24 | 5 | 0 | 15 | 57 | 1.2 | 1.1 | 2.6 |

| Season Team | G | Min. | FGM | FGA | Pct. | FTM | FTA | Pct. | Off. | Def. | Tot. | Ast. | St. | Blk. | TO | Pts. | RPG | APG | PPG |
|---|---|---|---|---|---|---|---|---|---|---|---|---|---|---|---|---|---|---|---|
| 04-05—Houston.......... | 7 | 171 | 29 | 62 | .468 | 23 | 24 | .958 | 2 | 11 | 13 | 16 | 6 | 2 | 10 | 81 | 1.9 | 2.3 | 11.6 |
| Totals ................... | 29 | 366 | 50 | 115 | .435 | 32 | 40 | .800 | 9 | 30 | 39 | 40 | 11 | 2 | 25 | 138 | 1.3 | 1.4 | 4.8 |

Three-point field goals: 2003-04, 6-for-14 (.429). 2004-05, 0-for-9. Totals, 6-for-23 (.261).
Personal fouls/disqualifications: 2003-04, 23/0. 2004-05, 17/0. Totals, 40/0.

# JAMISON, ANTAWN     F     WIZARDS

**PERSONAL:** Born June 12, 1976, in Shreveport, La. ... 6-9/223. (2.06/101.2). ... Full name: Antawn Cortez Jamison
**HIGH SCHOOL:** Providence (Charlotte).
**COLLEGE:** North Carolina.
**TRANSACTIONS/CAREER NOTES:** Selected after junior season by Toronto Raptors in first round (fourth pick overall) of 1998 NBA Draft. ... Draft rights traded by Raptors to Golden State Warriors for draft rights to G Vince Carter and cash (June 24, 1998). ... Traded by Warriors with F Danny Fortson, F Chris Mills and G Jiri Welsch to Dallas Mavericks for G Nick Van Exel, G Avery Johnson, F Popeye Jones, F Antoine Rigaudeau and C Evan Eschmeyer (August 18, 2003). ... Traded by Mavericks to Washington Wizards for G Jerry Stackhouse, F/C Christian Laettner and draft rights to G Devin Harris (June 24, 2004).

## COLLEGIATE RECORD

**NOTES:** The Sporting News College Player of the Year (1998). ... Naismith Award winner (1998). ... Wooden Award winner (1998). ... The Sporting News All-America first team (1998). ... The Sporting News All-America second team (1997).

| Season Team | G | Min. | FGM | FGA | Pct. | FTM | FTA | Pct. | Reb. | Ast. | Pts. | RPG | APG | PPG |
|---|---|---|---|---|---|---|---|---|---|---|---|---|---|---|
| 95-96—North Carolina ............... | 32 | 1052 | 201 | 322 | .624 | 82 | 156 | .526 | 309 | 33 | 484 | 9.7 | 1.0 | 15.1 |
| 96-97—North Carolina ............... | 35 | 1199 | 270 | 496 | .544 | 126 | 203 | .621 | 329 | 30 | 668 | 9.4 | 0.9 | 19.1 |
| 97-98—North Carolina ............... | 37 | 1227 | 316 | 546 | .579 | 184 | 276 | .667 | 389 | 30 | 822 | 10.5 | 0.8 | 22.2 |
| Totals ...................................... | 104 | 3478 | 787 | 1364 | .577 | 392 | 635 | .617 | 1027 | 93 | 1974 | 9.9 | 0.9 | 19.0 |

Three-point field goals: 1995-96, 0-for-1. 1996-97, 2-for-11 (.182). 1997-98, 6-for-15 (.400). Totals, 8-for-27 (.296).

## NBA REGULAR-SEASON RECORD

**HONORS:** NBA Sixth Man Award (2004). ... NBA All-Rookie second team (1999).

| Season Team | G | Min. | FGM | FGA | Pct. | FTM | FTA | Pct. | Off. | Def. | Tot. | Ast. | St. | Blk. | TO | Pts. | RPG | APG | PPG |
|---|---|---|---|---|---|---|---|---|---|---|---|---|---|---|---|---|---|---|---|
| 98-99—Golden State ... | 47 | 1058 | 178 | 394 | .452 | 90 | 153 | .588 | 131 | 170 | 301 | 34 | 38 | 16 | 68 | 449 | 6.4 | 0.7 | 9.6 |
| 99-00—Golden State ... | 43 | 1556 | 356 | 756 | .471 | 127 | 208 | .611 | 172 | 187 | 359 | 90 | 30 | 15 | 113 | 841 | 8.3 | 2.1 | 19.6 |
| 00-01—Golden State ... | 82 | 3394 | 800 | 1812 | .442 | 382 | 534 | .715 | 280 | 435 | 715 | 164 | 114 | 28 | 199 | 2044 | 8.7 | 2.0 | 24.9 |
| 01-02—Golden State ... | 82 | 3033 | 614 | 1375 | .447 | 323 | 440 | .734 | 211 | 345 | 556 | 161 | 70 | 45 | 161 | 1619 | 6.8 | 2.0 | 19.7 |
| 02-03—Golden State ... | 82 | 3226 | 691 | 1471 | .470 | 375 | 475 | .789 | 195 | 383 | 578 | 156 | 76 | 45 | 177 | 1822 | 7.0 | 1.9 | 22.2 |
| 03-04—Dallas.............. | 82 | 2376 | 488 | 913 | .535 | 220 | 294 | .748 | 233 | 287 | 520 | 70 | 83 | 30 | 81 | 1212 | 6.3 | 0.9 | 14.8 |
| 04-05—Washington .... | 68 | 2605 | 519 | 1189 | .437 | 225 | 296 | .760 | 160 | 359 | 519 | 154 | 55 | 16 | 118 | 1334 | 7.6 | 2.3 | 19.6 |
| Totals ................... | 486 | 17248 | 3646 | 7910 | .461 | 1742 | 2400 | .726 | 1382 | 2166 | 3548 | 829 | 466 | 195 | 917 | 9321 | 7.3 | 1.7 | 19.2 |

Three-point field goals: 1998-99, 3-for-10 (.300). 1999-00, 2-for-7 (.286). 2000-01, 62-for-205 (.302). 2001-02, 68-for-210 (.324). 2002-03, 65-for-209 (.311). 2003-04, 16-for-40 (.400). 2004-05, 71-for-208 (.341). Totals, 287-for-889 (.323).
Personal fouls/disqualifications: 1998-99, 102/1. 1999-00, 115/0. 2000-01, 225/2. 2001-02, 187/0. 2002-03, 197/1. 2003-04, 174/2. 2004-05, 151/1. Totals, 1151/7.

## NBA PLAYOFF RECORD

| Season Team | G | Min. | FGM | FGA | Pct. | FTM | FTA | Pct. | Off. | Def. | Tot. | Ast. | St. | Blk. | TO | Pts. | RPG | APG | PPG |
|---|---|---|---|---|---|---|---|---|---|---|---|---|---|---|---|---|---|---|---|
| 03-04—Dallas.............. | 5 | 109 | 26 | 57 | .456 | 11 | 15 | .733 | 15 | 10 | 25 | 2 | 5 | 2 | 5 | 65 | 5.0 | 0.4 | 13.0 |
| 04-05—Washington .... | 10 | 380 | 73 | 162 | .451 | 22 | 32 | .688 | 16 | 47 | 63 | 12 | 7 | 4 | 16 | 185 | 6.3 | 1.2 | 18.5 |
| Totals ................... | 15 | 489 | 99 | 219 | .452 | 33 | 47 | .702 | 31 | 57 | 88 | 14 | 12 | 6 | 21 | 250 | 5.9 | 0.9 | 16.7 |

Three-point field goals: 2003-04, 2-for-8 (.250). 2004-05, 17-for-34 (.500). Totals, 19-for-42 (.452).
Personal fouls/disqualifications: 2003-04, 15/0. 2004-05, 24/0. Totals, 39/0.

## NBA ALL-STAR GAME RECORD

| Season Team | Min. | FGM | FGA | Pct. | FTM | FTA | Pct. | Off. | Def. | Tot. | Ast. | PF | Dq. | St. | Blk. | TO | Pts. |
|---|---|---|---|---|---|---|---|---|---|---|---|---|---|---|---|---|---|
| 2005—Washington........... | 13 | 2 | 5 | .400 | 0 | 0 | ... | 1 | 3 | 4 | 1 | 0 | 0 | 0 | 0 | 0 | 5 |

Three-point field goals: 2005, 1-for-1 (1.000). Totals, 1-for-1 (1.000).

# JARIC, MARKO     G     TIMBERWOLVES

**PERSONAL:** Born December 10, 1978, in Belgrade, Yugoslavia. ... 6-8/210. (2.03/95.3).
**TRANSACTIONS/CAREER NOTES:** Played in Greece (1996-98). ... Played in Italy (1998-2002). ... Selected by Los Angeles Clippers in second round (30th pick overall) of 2000 NBA Draft. ... Traded by Clippers with G Lionel Chalmers to Minnesota Timberwolves for G Sam Cassell and a conditional first-round draft choice (August 12, 2005).

## GREEK LEAGUE RECORD

| Season Team | G | Min. | FGM | FGA | Pct. | FTM | FTA | Pct. | Reb. | Ast. | Pts. | RPG | APG | PPG |
|---|---|---|---|---|---|---|---|---|---|---|---|---|---|---|
| 96-97—Peristeri Nikas ............... | 30 | 247 | 27 | 52 | .519 | 22 | 33 | .667 | 36 | 15 | 76 | 1.2 | 0.5 | 2.5 |
| 97-98—Peristeri Nikas ............... | 29 | 554 | 50 | 98 | .510 | 38 | 49 | .776 | 73 | 35 | 165 | 2.5 | 1.2 | 5.7 |
| Totals ...................................... | 59 | 801 | 77 | 150 | .513 | 60 | 82 | .732 | 109 | 50 | 241 | 1.8 | 0.8 | 4.1 |

Three-point field goals: 1996-97, 0-for-3. 1997-98, 9-for-24 (.375). Totals, 9-for-27 (.333).

| Season Team | G | Min. | FGM | FGA | Pct. | FTM | FTA | Pct. | Reb. | Ast. | Pts. | AVERAGES RPG | APG | PPG |
|---|---|---|---|---|---|---|---|---|---|---|---|---|---|---|
| 98-99—Fortitudo Bologna.......... | 25 | 587 | 42 | 73 | .575 | 43 | 49 | .878 | 73 | 34 | 196 | 2.9 | 1.4 | 7.8 |
| 99-00—Fortitudo Bologna.......... | 26 | 627 | 72 | 126 | .571 | 57 | 77 | .740 | 74 | 36 | 258 | 2.8 | 1.4 | 9.9 |
| 00-01—Virtus Kinder Bologna .... | 33 | 971 | 152 | 327 | .465 | 71 | 104 | .683 | 127 | 81 | 406 | 3.8 | 2.5 | 12.3 |
| 01-02—Virtus Kinder Bologna .... | 33 | 987 | 171 | 374 | .457 | 107 | 142 | .754 | 162 | 87 | 503 | 4.9 | 2.6 | 15.2 |
| Totals ...................................... | 117 | 3172 | 437 | 900 | .486 | 278 | 372 | .747 | 436 | 238 | 1363 | 3.7 | 2.0 | 11.6 |

Three-point field goals: 1998-99, 23-for-59 (.390). 1999-00, 42-for-117 (.359). 2000-01, 31-for-98 (.316). 2001-02, 54-for-139 (.388). Totals, 150-for-413 (.363).

### NBA REGULAR-SEASON RECORD

| Season Team | G | Min. | FGM | FGA | Pct. | FTM | FTA | Pct. | REBOUNDS Off. | Def. | Tot. | Ast. | St. | Blk. | TO | Pts. | AVERAGES RPG | APG | PPG |
|---|---|---|---|---|---|---|---|---|---|---|---|---|---|---|---|---|---|---|---|
| 02-03—L.A. Clippers ... | 66 | 1379 | 179 | 446 | .401 | 79 | 105 | .752 | 35 | 125 | 160 | 193 | 97 | 11 | 103 | 490 | 2.4 | 2.9 | 7.4 |
| 03-04—L.A. Clippers ... | 58 | 1760 | 185 | 477 | .388 | 74 | 101 | .733 | 44 | 131 | 175 | 281 | 93 | 20 | 115 | 495 | 3.0 | 4.8 | 8.5 |
| 04-05—L.A. Clippers ... | 50 | 1656 | 189 | 457 | .414 | 59 | 82 | .720 | 20 | 141 | 161 | 303 | 84 | 17 | 98 | 493 | 3.2 | 6.1 | 9.9 |
| Totals ...................................... | 174 | 4795 | 553 | 1380 | .401 | 212 | 288 | .736 | 99 | 397 | 496 | 777 | 274 | 48 | 316 | 1478 | 2.9 | 4.5 | 8.5 |

Three-point field goals: 2002-03, 53-for-166 (.319). 2003-04, 51-for-150 (.340). 2004-05, 56-for-151 (.371). Totals, 160-for-467 (.343).
Personal fouls/disqualifications: 2002-03, 125/0. 2003-04, 132/1. 2004-05, 107/0. Totals, 364/1.

# JEFFERSON, AL    F    CELTICS

**PERSONAL:** Born January 4, 1985, in Monticello, Miss. ... 6-10/265. (2.08/120.2).
**HIGH SCHOOL:** Prentiss (Miss.).
**COLLEGE:** Did not attend college.
**TRANSACTIONS/CAREER NOTES:** Selected out of high school by Boston Celtics in first round (15th pick overall) of 2004 NBA Draft.

**HONORS:** NBA All-Rookie second team (2005).

### NBA REGULAR-SEASON RECORD

| Season Team | G | Min. | FGM | FGA | Pct. | FTM | FTA | Pct. | REBOUNDS Off. | Def. | Tot. | Ast. | St. | Blk. | TO | Pts. | AVERAGES RPG | APG | PPG |
|---|---|---|---|---|---|---|---|---|---|---|---|---|---|---|---|---|---|---|---|
| 04-05—Boston ............ | 71 | 1051 | 195 | 369 | .528 | 85 | 135 | .630 | 119 | 193 | 312 | 24 | 22 | 55 | 66 | 475 | 4.4 | 0.3 | 6.7 |

Three-point field goals: 2004-05, 0-for-3. Totals, 0-for-3 (.000).
Personal fouls/disqualifications: 2004-05, 195/4. Totals, 195/4.

### NBA PLAYOFF RECORD

| Season Team | G | Min. | FGM | FGA | Pct. | FTM | FTA | Pct. | REBOUNDS Off. | Def. | Tot. | Ast. | St. | Blk. | TO | Pts. | AVERAGES RPG | APG | PPG |
|---|---|---|---|---|---|---|---|---|---|---|---|---|---|---|---|---|---|---|---|
| 04-05—Boston ............ | 7 | 136 | 17 | 41 | .415 | 9 | 12 | .750 | 17 | 28 | 45 | 2 | 4 | 8 | 4 | 43 | 6.4 | 0.3 | 6.1 |

Personal fouls/disqualifications: 2004-05, 16/0. Totals, 16/0.

# JEFFERSON, RICHARD    F    NETS

**PERSONAL:** Born June 21, 1980, in Los Angeles. ... 6-7/222. (2.01/100.7). ... Full name: Richard Allen Jefferson
**HIGH SCHOOL:** Moon Valley (Phoenix).
**COLLEGE:** Arizona.
**TRANSACTIONS/CAREER NOTES:** Selected after junior season by Houston Rockets in first round (13th pick overall) of 2001 NBA Draft. ... Draft rights traded by Rockets with draft rights to C Jason Collins and G Brandon Armstrong to New Jersey Nets for draft rights to F Eddie Griffin (June 27, 2001).
**MISCELLANEOUS:** Member of bronze-medal-winning U.S. Olympic Team (2004).

### COLLEGIATE RECORD

| Season Team | G | Min. | FGM | FGA | Pct. | FTM | FTA | Pct. | Reb. | Ast. | Pts. | AVERAGES RPG | APG | PPG |
|---|---|---|---|---|---|---|---|---|---|---|---|---|---|---|
| 98-99—Arizona ......................... | 28 | 755 | 104 | 210 | .495 | 97 | 125 | .776 | 134 | 80 | 317 | 4.8 | 2.9 | 11.3 |
| 99-00—Arizona ......................... | 21 | 495 | 84 | 167 | .503 | 45 | 63 | .714 | 92 | 58 | 230 | 4.4 | 2.8 | 11.0 |
| 00-01—Arizona ......................... | 35 | 961 | 147 | 307 | .479 | 72 | 110 | .655 | 190 | 94 | 397 | 5.4 | 2.7 | 11.3 |
| Totals ...................................... | 84 | 2211 | 335 | 684 | .490 | 214 | 298 | .718 | 416 | 232 | 944 | 5.0 | 2.8 | 11.2 |

Three-point field goals: 1998-99, 12-for-33 (.364). 1999-00, 17-for-40 (.425). 2000-01, 31-for-90 (.344). Totals, 60-for-163 (.368).
Personal fouls/disqualifications: 1998-99, 68/0. 1999-00, 53/0. 2000-01, 98/0. Totals, 219/0.

**HONORS:** NBA All-Rookie second team (2002).

### NBA REGULAR-SEASON RECORD

| Season Team | G | Min. | FGM | FGA | Pct. | FTM | FTA | Pct. | REBOUNDS Off. | Def. | Tot. | Ast. | St. | Blk. | TO | Pts. | AVERAGES RPG | APG | PPG |
|---|---|---|---|---|---|---|---|---|---|---|---|---|---|---|---|---|---|---|---|
| 01-02—New Jersey ..... | 79 | 1917 | 270 | 591 | .457 | 189 | 265 | .713 | 85 | 208 | 293 | 140 | 64 | 48 | 107 | 742 | 3.7 | 1.8 | 9.4 |
| 02-03—New Jersey ..... | 80 | 2879 | 456 | 911 | .501 | 324 | 436 | .743 | 150 | 364 | 514 | 201 | 80 | 44 | 156 | 1242 | 6.4 | 2.5 | 15.5 |
| 03-04—New Jersey ..... | 82 | 3133 | 555 | 1115 | .498 | 357 | 468 | .763 | 109 | 355 | 464 | 315 | 92 | 28 | 198 | 1515 | 5.7 | 3.8 | 18.5 |
| 04-05—New Jersey ..... | 33 | 1355 | 238 | 564 | .422 | 227 | 269 | .844 | 49 | 191 | 240 | 133 | 33 | 17 | 132 | 733 | 7.3 | 4.0 | 22.2 |
| Totals ...................... | 274 | 9284 | 1519 | 3181 | .478 | 1097 | 1438 | .763 | 393 | 1118 | 1511 | 789 | 269 | 137 | 593 | 4232 | 5.5 | 2.9 | 15.4 |

Three-point field goals: 2001-02, 13-for-56 (.232). 2002-03, 6-for-24 (.250). 2003-04, 48-for-132 (.364). 2004-05, 30-for-89 (.337). Totals, 97-for-301 (.322).
Personal fouls/disqualifications: 2001-02, 211/5. 2002-03, 216/1. 2003-04, 224/1. 2004-05, 109/1. Totals, 760/8.

### NBA PLAYOFF RECORD

| Season Team | G | Min. | FGM | FGA | Pct. | FTM | FTA | Pct. | REBOUNDS Off. | Def. | Tot. | Ast. | St. | Blk. | TO | Pts. | AVERAGES RPG | APG | PPG |
|---|---|---|---|---|---|---|---|---|---|---|---|---|---|---|---|---|---|---|---|
| 01-02—New Jersey ..... | 20 | 441 | 53 | 114 | .465 | 33 | 60 | .550 | 16 | 76 | 92 | 25 | 11 | 9 | 26 | 139 | 4.6 | 1.3 | 7.0 |

| Season Team | G | Min. | FGM | FGA | Pct. | FTM | FTA | Pct. | REBOUNDS Off. | Def. | Tot. | Ast. | St. | Blk. | TO | Pts. | AVERAGES RPG | APG | PPG |
|---|---|---|---|---|---|---|---|---|---|---|---|---|---|---|---|---|---|---|---|
| 02-03—New Jersey..... | 20 | 711 | 110 | 231 | .476 | 61 | 85 | .718 | 29 | 98 | 127 | 47 | 16 | 4 | 46 | 281 | 6.4 | 2.4 | 14.1 |
| 03-04—New Jersey..... | 11 | 460 | 66 | 158 | .418 | 77 | 108 | .713 | 14 | 55 | 69 | 42 | 14 | 8 | 43 | 218 | 6.3 | 3.8 | 19.8 |
| 04-05—New Jersey..... | 4 | 140 | 20 | 50 | .400 | 21 | 31 | .677 | 8 | 14 | 22 | 9 | 3 | 0 | 8 | 63 | 5.5 | 2.3 | 15.8 |
| Totals ................... | 55 | 1752 | 249 | 553 | .450 | 192 | 284 | .676 | 67 | 243 | 310 | 123 | 44 | 21 | 123 | 701 | 5.6 | 2.2 | 12.7 |

Three-point field goals: 2001-02, 0-for-2. 2002-03, 0-for-3. 2003-04, 9-for-33 (.273). 2004-05, 2-for-10 (.200). Totals, 11-for-48 (.229).
Personal fouls/disqualifications: 2001-02, 40/0. 2002-03, 67/0. 2003-04, 35/0. 2004-05, 14/0. Totals, 156/0.

# JEFFRIES, JARED  F  WIZARDS

**PERSONAL:** Born November 25, 1981, in Bloomington, Ind. ... 6-10/215. (2.08/97.5). ... Full name: Jared Scott Carter Jeffries
**HIGH SCHOOL:** Bloomington North (Bloomington, Ind.).
**COLLEGE:** Indiana.
**TRANSACTIONS/CAREER NOTES:** Selected after sophomore season by Washington Wizards in first round (11th pick overall) of 2002 NBA Draft.

### COLLEGIATE RECORD

**NOTES:** The Sporting News All-America third team (2002).

| Season Team | G | Min. | FGM | FGA | Pct. | FTM | FTA | Pct. | Reb. | Ast. | Pts. | AVERAGES RPG | APG | PPG |
|---|---|---|---|---|---|---|---|---|---|---|---|---|---|---|
| 00-01—Indiana .......................... | 34 | 1108 | 164 | 971 | .169 | 129 | 208 | .620 | 234 | 82 | 469 | 6.9 | 2.4 | 13.8 |
| 01-02—Indiana .......................... | 36 | 1175 | 189 | 414 | .457 | 134 | 201 | .667 | 273 | 74 | 539 | 7.6 | 2.1 | 15.0 |
| Totals ...................................... | 70 | 2283 | 353 | 1385 | .255 | 263 | 409 | .643 | 507 | 156 | 1008 | 7.2 | 2.2 | 14.4 |

Three-point field goals: 2000-01, 12-for-49 (.245). 2001-02, 27-for-71 (.380). Totals, 39-for-120 (.325).

### NBA REGULAR-SEASON RECORD

| Season Team | G | Min. | FGM | FGA | Pct. | FTM | FTA | Pct. | REBOUNDS Off. | Def. | Tot. | Ast. | St. | Blk. | TO | Pts. | AVERAGES RPG | APG | PPG |
|---|---|---|---|---|---|---|---|---|---|---|---|---|---|---|---|---|---|---|---|
| 02-03—Washington .... | 20 | 292 | 30 | 63 | .476 | 16 | 29 | .552 | 26 | 32 | 58 | 16 | 8 | 5 | 21 | 79 | 2.9 | 0.8 | 4.0 |
| 03-04—Washington .... | 82 | 1913 | 177 | 469 | .377 | 105 | 171 | .614 | 180 | 244 | 424 | 93 | 48 | 28 | 107 | 464 | 5.2 | 1.1 | 5.7 |
| 04-05—Washington .... | 77 | 2007 | 203 | 434 | .468 | 101 | 173 | .584 | 152 | 222 | 374 | 151 | 66 | 35 | 114 | 523 | 4.9 | 2.0 | 6.8 |
| Totals ................... | 179 | 4212 | 410 | 966 | .424 | 222 | 373 | .595 | 358 | 498 | 856 | 260 | 122 | 68 | 242 | 1066 | 4.8 | 1.5 | 6.0 |

Three-point field goals: 2002-03, 3-for-6 (.500). 2003-04, 5-for-30 (.167). 2004-05, 16-for-51 (.314). Totals, 24-for-87 (.276).
Personal fouls/disqualifications: 2002-03, 28/0. 2003-04, 212/3. 2004-05, 206/1. Totals, 446/4.

### NBA PLAYOFF RECORD

| Season Team | G | Min. | FGM | FGA | Pct. | FTM | FTA | Pct. | REBOUNDS Off. | Def. | Tot. | Ast. | St. | Blk. | TO | Pts. | AVERAGES RPG | APG | PPG |
|---|---|---|---|---|---|---|---|---|---|---|---|---|---|---|---|---|---|---|---|
| 04-05—Washington .... | 10 | 247 | 24 | 49 | .490 | 13 | 17 | .765 | 19 | 22 | 41 | 18 | 9 | 9 | 13 | 64 | 4.1 | 1.8 | 6.4 |

Three-point field goals: 2004-05, 3-for-6 (.500). Totals, 3-for-6 (.500).
Personal fouls/disqualifications: 2004-05, 34/0. Totals, 34/0.

# JENKINS, HORACE  G

**PERSONAL:** Born October 14, 1974, in Elizabeth, N.J. ... 6-1/180. (1.85/81.6).
**HIGH SCHOOL:** Elizabeth (N.J.).
**JUNIOR COLLEGE:** Union County (N.J.).
**COLLEGE:** William Patterson.
**TRANSACTIONS/CAREER NOTES:** Not drafted by an NBA franchise. ... Signed as a free agent by Detroit Pistons (August 4, 2004).

### COLLEGIATE RECORD

| Season Team | G | Min. | FGM | FGA | Pct. | FTM | FTA | Pct. | Reb. | Ast. | Pts. | AVERAGES RPG | APG | PPG |
|---|---|---|---|---|---|---|---|---|---|---|---|---|---|---|
| 93-94—Union County Junior College | 16 | ... | 101 | 275 | .367 | 53 | 76 | .697 | 63 | 57 | 295 | 3.9 | 3.6 | 18.4 |
| 98-99—WPU.............................. | 23 | 837 | 175 | 376 | .465 | 101 | 138 | .732 | 142 | 97 | 503 | 6.2 | 4.2 | 21.9 |
| 99-00—WPU.............................. | 28 | 998 | 199 | 475 | .419 | 141 | 192 | .734 | 198 | 111 | 596 | 7.1 | 4.0 | 21.3 |
| 00-01—WPU.............................. | 31 | 1134 | 255 | 568 | .449 | 257 | 312 | .824 | 173 | 104 | 841 | 5.6 | 3.4 | 27.1 |
| Junior College Totals............. | 16 | ... | 101 | 275 | .367 | 53 | 76 | .697 | 63 | 57 | 295 | 3.9 | 3.6 | 18.4 |
| 4-Year-College Totals........... | 82 | 2969 | 629 | 1419 | .443 | 499 | 642 | .777 | 513 | 312 | 1940 | 6.3 | 3.8 | 23.7 |

Three-point field goals: 1993-94, 40-for-134 (.299). 1998-99, 52-for-139 (.374). 1999-00, 57-for-166 (.343). 2000-01, 74-for-224 (.330). Totals, 223-for-663 (.336).

### ITALIAN LEAGUE RECORD

| Season Team | G | Min. | FGM | FGA | Pct. | FTM | FTA | Pct. | Reb. | Ast. | Pts. | AVERAGES RPG | APG | PPG |
|---|---|---|---|---|---|---|---|---|---|---|---|---|---|---|
| 01-02—Cimberio Borgomanero-A2 | 36 | 1319 | 360 | 701 | .514 | 280 | 347 | .807 | 170 | 100 | 1096 | 4.7 | 2.8 | 30.4 |
| 02-03—Lottomatica RM-A1 ........ | 34 | 1047 | 171 | 379 | .451 | 117 | 146 | .801 | 147 | 70 | 517 | 4.3 | 2.1 | 15.2 |
| Totals ...................................... | 70 | 2366 | 531 | 1080 | .492 | 397 | 493 | .805 | 317 | 170 | 1613 | 4.5 | 2.4 | 23.0 |

Three-point field goals: 2001-02, 96-for-254 (.378). 2002-03, 58-for-160 (.363). Totals, 154-for-414 (.372).

### GREEK LEAGUE RECORD

| Season Team | G | Min. | FGM | FGA | Pct. | FTM | FTA | Pct. | Reb. | Ast. | Pts. | AVERAGES RPG | APG | PPG |
|---|---|---|---|---|---|---|---|---|---|---|---|---|---|---|
| 03-04—AEK ................................ | 22 | 676 | 111 | 252 | .440 | 78 | 94 | .830 | 54 | 64 | 333 | 2.5 | 2.9 | 15.1 |

Three-point field goals: 2003-04, 33-for-111 (.297). Totals, 33-for-111 (.297).

## NBA REGULAR-SEASON RECORD

| Season Team | G | Min. | FGM | FGA | Pct. | FTM | FTA | Pct. | REBOUNDS Off. | Def. | Tot. | Ast. | St. | Blk. | TO | Pts. | RPG | APG | PPG |
|---|---|---|---|---|---|---|---|---|---|---|---|---|---|---|---|---|---|---|---|
| 04-05—Detroit ........... | 15 | 104 | 15 | 45 | .333 | 12 | 13 | .923 | 3 | 6 | 9 | 9 | 5 | 1 | 7 | 42 | 0.6 | 0.6 | 2.8 |

Three-point field goals: 2004-05, 0-for-9. Totals, 0-for-9 (.000).
Personal fouls/disqualifications: 2004-05, 6/0. Totals, 6/0.

## JOHNSEN, BRITTON      F

**PERSONAL:** Born July 8, 1979, in Salt Lake City. ... 6-10/210. (2.08/95.3). ... Full name: Britton Weaver Johnsen
**HIGH SCHOOL:** Murray (Utah).
**COLLEGE:** Utah.
**TRANSACTIONS/CAREER NOTES:** Not drafted by an NBA franchise. ... Signed as free agent by Orlando Magic (September 11, 2004). ... Waived by Magic (November 16, 2003). ... Played in NBDL with Fayetteville Patriots (2003-04). ... Signed by Magic to 10-day contract (March 10, 2004). ... Signed by Magic for remainder of season (March 30, 2004). ... Signed as free agent by New Orleans Hornets (September 29, 2004). ... Waived by Hornets (October 31, 2004). ... Signed as free agent by Indiana Pacers (November 25, 2004). ... Waived by Pacers (December 7, 2004).

### COLLEGIATE RECORD

| Season Team | G | Min. | FGM | FGA | Pct. | FTM | FTA | Pct. | Reb. | Ast. | Pts. | RPG | APG | PPG |
|---|---|---|---|---|---|---|---|---|---|---|---|---|---|---|
| 97-98—Utah ............................ | 21 | 234 | 26 | 57 | .456 | 17 | 33 | .515 | 34 | 10 | 73 | 1.6 | 0.5 | 3.5 |
| 98-99—Utah ............................ | | | | | | Did not play—church mission. | | | | | | | | |
| 99-00—Utah ............................ | | | | | | Did not play—church mission. | | | | | | | | |
| 00-01—Utah ............................ | 31 | 684 | 100 | 220 | .455 | 65 | 100 | .650 | 166 | 10 | 285 | 5.4 | 0.3 | 9.2 |
| 01-02—Utah ............................ | 30 | 836 | 131 | 264 | .496 | 86 | 143 | .601 | 189 | 46 | 379 | 6.3 | 1.5 | 12.6 |
| 02-03—Utah ............................ | 27 | 789 | 123 | 258 | .477 | 51 | 96 | .531 | 181 | 54 | 314 | 6.7 | 2.0 | 11.6 |
| Totals .................................... | 109 | 2543 | 380 | 799 | .476 | 219 | 372 | .589 | 570 | 120 | 1051 | 5.2 | 1.1 | 9.6 |

Three-point field goals: 1997-98, 4-for-13 (.308). 2000-01, 20-for-47 (.426). 2001-02, 31-for-87 (.356). 2002-03, 17-for-66 (.258). Totals, 72-for-213 (.338).

### NBA REGULAR-SEASON RECORD

| Season Team | G | Min. | FGM | FGA | Pct. | FTM | FTA | Pct. | REBOUNDS Off. | Def. | Tot. | Ast. | St. | Blk. | TO | Pts. | RPG | APG | PPG |
|---|---|---|---|---|---|---|---|---|---|---|---|---|---|---|---|---|---|---|---|
| 03-04—Orlando.......... | 20 | 290 | 17 | 59 | .288 | 7 | 16 | .438 | 15 | 30 | 45 | 12 | 7 | 1 | 14 | 42 | 2.3 | 0.6 | 2.1 |
| 04-05—Indiana............ | 6 | 87 | 6 | 22 | .273 | 0 | 0 | ... | 5 | 5 | 10 | 4 | 1 | 0 | 3 | 12 | 1.7 | 0.7 | 2.0 |
| Totals ................... | 26 | 377 | 23 | 81 | .284 | 7 | 16 | .438 | 20 | 35 | 55 | 16 | 8 | 1 | 17 | 54 | 2.1 | 0.6 | 2.1 |

Three-point field goals: 2003-04, 1-for-12 (.083). 2004-05, 0-for-4. Totals, 1-for-16 (.063).
Personal fouls/disqualifications: 2003-04, 28/0. 2004-05, 10/0. Totals, 38/0.

### NBDL RECORD

| Season Team | G | Min. | FGM | FGA | Pct. | FTM | FTA | Pct. | Reb. | Ast. | Pts. | RPG | APG | PPG |
|---|---|---|---|---|---|---|---|---|---|---|---|---|---|---|
| 03-04—Fayetteville..................... | 34 | 1057 | 176 | 372 | .473 | 125 | 170 | .735 | 202 | 62 | 495 | 5.9 | 1.8 | 14.6 |

### CBA RECORD

| Season Team | G | Min. | FGM | FGA | Pct. | FTM | FTA | Pct. | Reb. | Ast. | Pts. | RPG | APG | PPG |
|---|---|---|---|---|---|---|---|---|---|---|---|---|---|---|
| 04-05—Idaho ............................ | 40 | 1288 | 262 | 532 | .492 | 162 | 201 | .806 | 237 | 104 | 728 | 5.9 | 2.6 | 18.2 |

Three-point field goals: 2004-05, 42-for-127 (.331). Totals, 42-for-127 (.331).

## JOHNSON, ANTHONY      G      PACERS

**PERSONAL:** Born October 10, 1974, in Charleston, S.C. ... 6-3/190. (1.91/86.2). ... Full name: Anthony Mark Johnson
**HIGH SCHOOL:** Stall (Charleston, S.C.).
**COLLEGE:** College of Charleston.
**TRANSACTIONS/CAREER NOTES:** Selected by Sacramento Kings in second round (40th pick overall) of 1997 NBA Draft. ... Signed as free agent by Atlanta Hawks (January 21, 1999). ... Traded by Hawks to Orlando Magic for condidtional second-round draft choice (February 24, 2000). ... Signed as free agent by Hawks (August 21, 2000). ... Traded by Hawks with G Jim Jackson and F/G Larry Robinson to Cleveland Cavaliers for G Brevin Knight (January 2, 2001). ... Played in National Basketball Development League with Mobile Revelers (2001-02). ... Signed by New Jersey Nets to first ot two consecutive 10-day contracts (January 7, 2002). ... Re-signed by Nets for remainder of season (January 28, 2002). ... Signed as free agent by Cleveland Cavaliers (September 30, 2002). ... Waived by Cavaliers (October 23, 2002). ... Signed as free agent by Nets (October 25, 2002). ... Signed as free agent by Indiana Pacers (July 24, 2003)

### COLLEGIATE RECORD

| Season Team | G | Min. | FGM | FGA | Pct. | FTM | FTA | Pct. | Reb. | Ast. | Pts. | RPG | APG | PPG |
|---|---|---|---|---|---|---|---|---|---|---|---|---|---|---|
| 92-93—College of Charleston ..... | 27 | 273 | 23 | 58 | .397 | 37 | 52 | .712 | 44 | 30 | 84 | 1.6 | 1.1 | 3.1 |
| 93-94—College of Charleston ..... | | | | | | Did not play—redshirted. | | | | | | | | |
| 94-95—College of Charleston ..... | 29 | 490 | 34 | 87 | .391 | 22 | 34 | .647 | 53 | 68 | 100 | 1.8 | 2.3 | 3.4 |
| 95-96—College of Charleston ..... | 29 | 946 | 119 | 259 | .459 | 65 | 97 | .670 | 92 | 193 | 329 | 3.2 | 6.7 | 11.3 |
| 96-97—College of Charleston ..... | 32 | 1138 | 158 | 313 | .505 | 100 | 126 | .794 | 113 | 229 | 446 | 3.5 | 7.2 | 13.9 |
| Totals .................................... | 117 | 2847 | 334 | 717 | .466 | 224 | 309 | .725 | 302 | 520 | 959 | 2.6 | 4.4 | 8.2 |

Three-point field goals: 1992-93, 1-for-3 (.333). 1994-95, 10-for-25 (.400). 1995-96, 26-for-64 (.406). 1996-97, 30-for-74 (.405). Totals, 67-for-166 (.404).

## NBA REGULAR-SEASON RECORD

| Season Team | G | Min. | FGM | FGA | Pct. | FTM | FTA | Pct. | REBOUNDS Off. | Def. | Tot. | Ast. | St. | Blk. | TO | Pts. | AVERAGES RPG | APG | PPG |
|---|---|---|---|---|---|---|---|---|---|---|---|---|---|---|---|---|---|---|---|
| 97-98—Sacramento .... | 77 | 2266 | 226 | 609 | .371 | 80 | 110 | .727 | 51 | 120 | 171 | 329 | 64 | 6 | 120 | 574 | 2.2 | 4.3 | 7.5 |
| 98-99—Atlanta ........... | 49 | 885 | 91 | 225 | .404 | 57 | 82 | .695 | 16 | 59 | 75 | 107 | 35 | 7 | 65 | 244 | 1.5 | 2.2 | 5.0 |
| 99-00—Atlanta-Orl. ...... | 56 | 637 | 62 | 164 | .378 | 28 | 39 | .718 | 21 | 30 | 51 | 72 | 33 | 4 | 32 | 154 | 0.9 | 1.3 | 2.8 |
| 00-01—Atl.-Cleve. ....... | 53 | 511 | 53 | 152 | .349 | 23 | 33 | .697 | 10 | 34 | 44 | 78 | 23 | 6 | 34 | 130 | 0.8 | 1.5 | 2.5 |
| 01-02—New Jersey..... | 34 | 366 | 37 | 90 | .411 | 16 | 25 | .640 | 10 | 19 | 29 | 48 | 31 | 1 | 20 | 94 | 0.9 | 1.4 | 2.8 |
| 02-03—New Jersey..... | 66 | 842 | 103 | 231 | .446 | 51 | 74 | .689 | 13 | 65 | 78 | 86 | 37 | 5 | 41 | 270 | 1.2 | 1.3 | 4.1 |
| 03-04—Indiana........... | 73 | 1598 | 167 | 411 | .406 | 75 | 94 | .798 | 28 | 102 | 130 | 202 | 64 | 8 | 75 | 450 | 1.8 | 2.8 | 6.2 |
| 04-05—Indiana........... | 63 | 1747 | 203 | 456 | .445 | 85 | 113 | .752 | 32 | 147 | 179 | 302 | 59 | 15 | 96 | 532 | 2.8 | 4.8 | 8.4 |
| **Totals** ................... | 471 | 8852 | 942 | 2338 | .403 | 415 | 570 | .728 | 181 | 576 | 757 | 1224 | 346 | 52 | 483 | 2448 | 1.6 | 2.6 | 5.2 |

Three-point field goals: 1997-98, 42-for-128 (.328). 1998-99, 5-for-19 (.263). 1999-00, 2-for-11 (.182). 2000-01, 1-for-5 (.200). 2001-02, 4-for-12 (.333). 2002-03, 13-for-35 (.371). 2003-04, 41-for-122 (.336). 2004-05, 41-for-108 (.380). Totals, 149-for-440 (.339).

Personal fouls/disqualifications: 1997-98, 188/1. 1998-99, 67/0. 1999-00, 58/0. 2000-01, 62/0. 2001-02, 30/0. 2002-03, 93/1. 2003-04, 138/0. 2004-05, 144/0. Totals, 780/2.

## NBA PLAYOFF RECORD

| Season Team | G | Min. | FGM | FGA | Pct. | FTM | FTA | Pct. | REBOUNDS Off. | Def. | Tot. | Ast. | St. | Blk. | TO | Pts. | AVERAGES RPG | APG | PPG |
|---|---|---|---|---|---|---|---|---|---|---|---|---|---|---|---|---|---|---|---|
| 98-99—Atlanta ........... | 9 | 111 | 8 | 29 | .276 | 7 | 10 | .700 | 3 | 6 | 9 | 10 | 1 | 1 | 5 | 24 | 1.0 | 1.1 | 2.7 |
| 01-02—New Jersey..... | 19 | 161 | 20 | 53 | .377 | 9 | 11 | .818 | 2 | 12 | 14 | 21 | 6 | 0 | 8 | 50 | 0.7 | 1.1 | 2.6 |
| 02-03—New Jersey..... | 17 | 122 | 17 | 31 | .548 | 5 | 6 | .833 | 3 | 9 | 12 | 19 | 2 | 0 | 8 | 42 | 0.7 | 1.1 | 2.5 |
| 03-04—Indiana........... | 16 | 332 | 25 | 69 | .362 | 17 | 22 | .773 | 7 | 27 | 34 | 34 | 13 | 4 | 11 | 73 | 2.1 | 2.1 | 4.6 |
| 04-05—Indiana........... | 13 | 316 | 27 | 77 | .351 | 29 | 36 | .806 | 4 | 34 | 38 | 66 | 13 | 5 | 25 | 91 | 2.9 | 5.1 | 7.0 |
| **Totals** ................... | 74 | 1042 | 97 | 259 | .375 | 67 | 85 | .788 | 19 | 88 | 107 | 150 | 35 | 10 | 57 | 280 | 1.4 | 2.0 | 3.8 |

Three-point field goals: 1998-99, 1-for-2 (.500). 2001-02, 1-for-10 (.100). 2002-03, 3-for-6 (.500). 2003-04, 6-for-20 (.300). 2004-05, 8-for-23 (.348). Totals, 19-for-61 (.311).

Personal fouls/disqualifications: 1998-99, 9/0. 2001-02, 24/0. 2002-03, 15/0. 2003-04, 34/0. 2004-05, 28/0. Totals, 110/0.

## NBDL RECORD

| Season Team | G | Min. | FGM | FGA | Pct. | FTM | FTA | Pct. | Reb. | Ast. | Pts. | AVERAGES RPG | APG | PPG |
|---|---|---|---|---|---|---|---|---|---|---|---|---|---|---|
| 01-02—Mobile ........................ | 15 | 394 | 72 | 156 | .462 | 32 | 43 | .744 | 46 | 44 | 179 | 3.1 | 2.9 | 11.9 |

Three-point field goals: 2001-02, 3-for-12 (.250). Totals, 3-for-12 (.250).

Personal fouls/disqualifications: 2001-02, 40/0. Totals, 40/0.

# JOHNSON, DERMARR     G

**PERSONAL:** Born May 5, 1980, in Washington, D.C. ... 6-9/201. (2.06/91.2). ... Full name: DerMarr Miles Johnson.
**HIGH SCHOOL:** Bladensburg (Md.), then Parkdale (Riverdale, Md.).
**COLLEGE:** Cincinnati.
**TRANSACTIONS/CAREER NOTES:** Selected after freshman season by Atlanta Hawks in first round (sixth pick overall) of 2000 NBA Draft. ... Signed as free agent by Phoenix Suns (October 1, 2003). ... Waived by Suns (October 16, 2003). ... Signed as free agent by Denver Nuggets (October 18, 2004).

## COLLEGIATE RECORD

| Season Team | G | Min. | FGM | FGA | Pct. | FTM | FTA | Pct. | Reb. | Ast. | Pts. | AVERAGES RPG | APG | PPG |
|---|---|---|---|---|---|---|---|---|---|---|---|---|---|---|
| 99-00—Cincinnati ...................... | 32 | 879 | 140 | 293 | .478 | 70 | 95 | .737 | 123 | 45 | 402 | 3.8 | 1.4 | 12.6 |

Three-point field goals: 1999-00, 52-for-140 (.371). Totals, 52-for-140 (.371).

## NBA REGULAR-SEASON RECORD

| Season Team | G | Min. | FGM | FGA | Pct. | FTM | FTA | Pct. | REBOUNDS Off. | Def. | Tot. | Ast. | St. | Blk. | TO | Pts. | AVERAGES RPG | APG | PPG |
|---|---|---|---|---|---|---|---|---|---|---|---|---|---|---|---|---|---|---|---|
| 00-01—Atlanta ............ | 78 | 1313 | 146 | 390 | .374 | 64 | 87 | .736 | 56 | 122 | 178 | 64 | 43 | 30 | 93 | 397 | 2.3 | 0.8 | 5.1 |
| 01-02—Atlanta ............ | 72 | 1727 | 214 | 540 | .396 | 105 | 130 | .810 | 59 | 188 | 247 | 81 | 62 | 56 | 102 | 602 | 3.4 | 1.1 | 8.4 |
| 02-03—Atlanta............. | | | | | | | | Did not play—injured | | | | | | | | | | | |
| 03-04—New York........ | 21 | 287 | 36 | 97 | .371 | 28 | 31 | .903 | 5 | 34 | 39 | 11 | 8 | 7 | 16 | 113 | 1.9 | 0.5 | 5.4 |
| 04-05—Denver ........... | 71 | 1232 | 185 | 371 | .499 | 80 | 101 | .792 | 43 | 108 | 151 | 75 | 43 | 18 | 65 | 503 | 2.1 | 1.1 | 7.1 |
| **Totals** ................... | 242 | 4559 | 581 | 1398 | .416 | 257 | 324 | .793 | 163 | 452 | 615 | 231 | 156 | 111 | 276 | 1615 | 2.5 | 1.0 | 6.7 |

Three-point field goals: 2000-01, 41-for-127 (.323). 2001-02, 89-for-247 (.360). 2003-04, 13-for-36 (.361). 2004-05, 53-for-148 (.358). Totals, 196-for-558 (.351).

Personal fouls/disqualifications: 2000-01, 134/0. 2001-02, 163/1. 2003-04, 32/0. 2004-05, 140/0. Totals, 469/1.

## NBA PLAYOFF RECORD

| Season Team | G | Min. | FGM | FGA | Pct. | FTM | FTA | Pct. | REBOUNDS Off. | Def. | Tot. | Ast. | St. | Blk. | TO | Pts. | AVERAGES RPG | APG | PPG |
|---|---|---|---|---|---|---|---|---|---|---|---|---|---|---|---|---|---|---|---|
| 03-04—New York ........ | 3 | 17 | 0 | 5 | .000 | 0 | 0 | ... | 0 | 2 | 2 | 2 | 0 | 1 | 0 | 0 | 0.7 | 0.7 | 0.0 |
| 04-05—Denver ........... | 4 | 78 | 11 | 20 | .550 | 3 | 3 | 1.000 | 3 | 5 | 8 | 3 | 2 | 2 | 0 | 29 | 2.0 | 0.8 | 7.3 |
| **Totals** ................... | 7 | 95 | 11 | 25 | .440 | 3 | 3 | 1.000 | 3 | 7 | 10 | 5 | 2 | 3 | 0 | 29 | 1.4 | 0.7 | 4.1 |

Three-point field goals: 2003-04, 0-for-3. 2004-05, 4-for-11 (.364). Totals, 4-for-14 (.286).

Personal fouls/disqualifications: 2003-04, 2/0. 2004-05, 9/0. Totals, 11/0.

## AMERICAN BASKETBALL ASSOCIATION RECORD

| Season Team | G | Min. | FGM | FGA | Pct. | FTM | FTA | Pct. | Reb. | Ast. | Pts. | AVERAGES RPG | APG | PPG |
|---|---|---|---|---|---|---|---|---|---|---|---|---|---|---|
| 03-04—Long Beach .................. | 20 | ... | 152 | 321 | .474 | 87 | 102 | .853 | 135 | 63 | 441 | 6.8 | 3.2 | 22.1 |

Three-point field goals: 2003-04, 50-for-132 (.379). Totals, 50-for-132 (.379).

**PERSONAL:** Born December 21, 1967, in New Orleans. ... 6-11/255. (2.11/115.7).
**HIGH SCHOOL:** Block (Jonesville, La.).
**COLLEGE:** New Orleans.
**TRANSACTIONS/CAREER NOTES:** Selected by Seattle SuperSonics in first round (23rd pick overall) of 1993 NBA Draft. ... Signed as free agent by Denver Nuggets (July 17, 1996). ... Traded by Nuggets to Milwaukee Bucks for F Johnny Newman, F/C Joe Wolf and draft rights to F Danny Fortson (June 25, 1997). ... Traded by Bucks with G Sam Cassell to Minnesota Timberwolves for F Joe Smith and G Anthony Peeler (June 27, 2003). ... Signed as free agent by Milwaukee Bucks (August 30, 2005).

J

## COLLEGIATE RECORD

| Season Team | G | Min. | FGM | FGA | Pct. | FTM | FTA | Pct. | Reb. | Ast. | Pts. | RPG | APG | PPG |
|---|---|---|---|---|---|---|---|---|---|---|---|---|---|---|
| 88-89—New Orleans | | | | | | Did not play—redshirted. | | | | | | | | |
| 89-90—New Orleans | 32 | 757 | 84 | 145 | .579 | 32 | 57 | .561 | 218 | 29 | 200 | 6.8 | 0.9 | 6.3 |
| 90-91—New Orleans | 30 | 899 | 162 | 283 | .572 | 58 | 108 | .537 | 367 | 34 | 382 | 12.2 | 1.1 | 12.7 |
| 91-92—New Orleans | 32 | 1073 | 185 | 317 | .584 | 122 | 171 | .713 | 356 | 56 | 492 | 11.1 | 1.8 | 15.4 |
| 92-93—New Orleans | 29 | 965 | 208 | 336 | .619 | 118 | 175 | .674 | 346 | 16 | 534 | 11.9 | 0.6 | 18.4 |
| Totals | 123 | 3694 | 639 | 1081 | .591 | 330 | 511 | .646 | 1287 | 135 | 1608 | 10.5 | 1.1 | 13.1 |

### NBA REGULAR-SEASON RECORD

**NOTES:** Led NBA with 321 personal fouls (1998).

| Season Team | G | Min. | FGM | FGA | Pct. | FTM | FTA | Pct. | Off. | Def. | Tot. | Ast. | St. | Blk. | TO | Pts. | RPG | APG | PPG |
|---|---|---|---|---|---|---|---|---|---|---|---|---|---|---|---|---|---|---|---|
| 93-94—Seattle | 45 | 280 | 44 | 106 | .415 | 29 | 46 | .630 | 48 | 70 | 118 | 7 | 10 | 22 | 24 | 117 | 2.6 | 0.2 | 2.6 |
| 94-95—Seattle | 64 | 907 | 85 | 192 | .443 | 29 | 46 | .630 | 101 | 188 | 289 | 16 | 17 | 67 | 54 | 199 | 4.5 | 0.3 | 3.1 |
| 95-96—Seattle | 81 | 1519 | 180 | 352 | .511 | 85 | 127 | .669 | 129 | 304 | 433 | 48 | 40 | 129 | 98 | 446 | 5.3 | 0.6 | 5.5 |
| 96-97—Denver | 82 | 2599 | 243 | 467 | .520 | 96 | 156 | .615 | *231 | 682 | 913 | 71 | 65 | 227 | 118 | 582 | 11.1 | 0.9 | 7.1 |
| 97-98—Milwaukee | 81 | 2261 | 253 | 471 | .537 | 143 | 238 | .601 | 242 | 443 | 685 | 59 | 79 | 158 | 117 | 649 | 8.5 | 0.7 | 8.0 |
| 98-99—Milwaukee | 50 | 1027 | 96 | 189 | .508 | 64 | 105 | .610 | 120 | 200 | 320 | 19 | 29 | 57 | 47 | 256 | 6.4 | 0.4 | 5.1 |
| 99-00—Milwaukee | 80 | 2129 | 144 | 279 | .516 | 95 | 157 | .605 | 233 | 415 | 648 | 44 | 81 | 127 | 80 | 383 | 8.1 | 0.6 | 4.8 |
| 00-01—Milwaukee | 82 | 1981 | 108 | 198 | .545 | 50 | 93 | .538 | 205 | 408 | 613 | 40 | 44 | 97 | 47 | 266 | 7.5 | 0.5 | 3.2 |
| 01-02—Milwaukee | 81 | 1660 | 89 | 193 | .461 | 30 | 66 | .455 | 142 | 324 | 466 | 27 | 37 | 82 | 52 | 208 | 5.8 | 0.3 | 2.6 |
| 02-03—Milwaukee | 69 | 1170 | 61 | 135 | .452 | 30 | 44 | .682 | 117 | 177 | 294 | 24 | 34 | 63 | 34 | 152 | 4.3 | 0.3 | 2.2 |
| 03-04—Minnesota | 66 | 965 | 55 | 103 | .534 | 17 | 28 | .607 | 61 | 171 | 232 | 24 | 27 | 43 | 30 | 127 | 3.5 | 0.4 | 1.9 |
| 04-05—Minnesota | 46 | 410 | 28 | 54 | .519 | 16 | 25 | .640 | 43 | 70 | 113 | 6 | 7 | 13 | 18 | 73 | 2.5 | 0.1 | 1.6 |
| Totals | 827 | 16908 | 1386 | 2739 | .506 | 684 | 1131 | .605 | 1672 | 3452 | 5124 | 385 | 470 | 1085 | 719 | 3458 | 6.2 | 0.5 | 4.2 |

Three-point field goals: 1994-95, 0-for-1. 1995-96, 1-for-3 (.333). 1996-97, 0-for-2. 1999-00, 0-for-1. 2001-02, 0-for-1. 2003-04, 0-for-1. 2004-05, 1-for-1 (1.000). Totals, 2-for-10 (.200).
Personal fouls/disqualifications: 1993-94, 45/0. 1994-95, 243/1. 1995-96, 245/3. 1996-97, 288/5. 1997-98, 321/7. 1998-99, 151/1. 1999-00, 298/6. 2000-01, 257/4. 2001-02, 219/4. 2002-03, 178/3. 2003-04, 156/1. 2004-05, 86/0. Totals, 2407/35.

### NBA PLAYOFF RECORD

| Season Team | G | Min. | FGM | FGA | Pct. | FTM | FTA | Pct. | Off. | Def. | Tot. | Ast. | St. | Blk. | TO | Pts. | RPG | APG | PPG |
|---|---|---|---|---|---|---|---|---|---|---|---|---|---|---|---|---|---|---|---|
| 93-94—Seattle | 2 | 8 | 0 | 1 | .000 | 0 | 0 | | 0 | 4 | 4 | 0 | 0 | 0 | 1 | 0 | 2.0 | 0.0 | 0.0 |
| 94-95—Seattle | 4 | 54 | 4 | 14 | .286 | 6 | 6 | 1.000 | 8 | 13 | 21 | 0 | 1 | 4 | 1 | 14 | 5.3 | 0.0 | 3.5 |
| 95-96—Seattle | 18 | 253 | 23 | 62 | .371 | 9 | 11 | .818 | 28 | 42 | 70 | 7 | 6 | 15 | 14 | 55 | 3.9 | 0.4 | 3.1 |
| 98-99—Milwaukee | 3 | 92 | 6 | 13 | .462 | 1 | 2 | .500 | 8 | 10 | 18 | 1 | 2 | 5 | 0 | 13 | 6.0 | 0.3 | 4.3 |
| 99-00—Milwaukee | 5 | 155 | 10 | 20 | .500 | 11 | 18 | .611 | 14 | 35 | 49 | 2 | 6 | 6 | 3 | 31 | 9.8 | 0.4 | 6.2 |
| 00-01—Milwaukee | 18 | 577 | 39 | 68 | .574 | 20 | 32 | .625 | 59 | 135 | 194 | 10 | 9 | 37 | 12 | 98 | 10.8 | 0.6 | 5.4 |
| 02-03—Milwaukee | 6 | 76 | 3 | 8 | .375 | 0 | 0 | | 6 | 18 | 24 | 3 | 3 | 5 | 3 | 6 | 4.0 | 0.5 | 1.0 |
| 03-04—Minnesota | 18 | 356 | 19 | 38 | .500 | 10 | 16 | .625 | 27 | 57 | 84 | 13 | 11 | 10 | 6 | 48 | 4.7 | 0.7 | 2.7 |
| Totals | 74 | 1571 | 104 | 224 | .464 | 57 | 85 | .671 | 150 | 314 | 464 | 36 | 38 | 82 | 40 | 265 | 6.3 | 0.5 | 3.6 |

Personal fouls/disqualifications: 1993-94, 1/0. 1994-95, 16/0. 1995-96, 45/0. 1998-99, 9/0. 1999-00, 19/0. 2000-01, 52/1. 2002-03, 20/0. 2003-04, 56/0. Totals, 218/1.

**PERSONAL:** Born July 29, 1981, in Little Rock, Ark. ... 6-7/225. (2.01/102.1). ... Full name: Joe Marcus Johnson
**HIGH SCHOOL:** Little Rock Central (Little Rock, Ark.).
**COLLEGE:** Arkansas.
**TRANSACTIONS/CAREER NOTES:** Selected after sophomore season by Boston Celtics in first round (10th pick overall) of 2001 NBA Draft. ... Traded by Celtics with G Milt Palacio, G Randy Brown and 2002 first-round draft choice to Phoenix Suns for G Tony Delk and F Rodney Rogers (February 20, 2002). ... Traded by Suns to Atlanta Hawks for G Boris Diaw and two conditional first-round draft choices (August 19, 2005).

## COLLEGIATE RECORD

| Season Team | G | Min. | FGM | FGA | Pct. | FTM | FTA | Pct. | Reb. | Ast. | Pts. | RPG | APG | PPG |
|---|---|---|---|---|---|---|---|---|---|---|---|---|---|---|
| 99-00—Arkansas | 23 | 732 | 140 | 302 | .464 | 60 | 79 | .759 | 132 | 50 | 368 | 5.7 | 2.2 | 16.0 |
| 00-01—Arkansas | 30 | 873 | 162 | 346 | .468 | 68 | 91 | .747 | 193 | 77 | 427 | 6.4 | 2.6 | 14.2 |
| Totals | 53 | 1605 | 302 | 648 | .466 | 128 | 170 | .753 | 325 | 127 | 795 | 6.1 | 2.4 | 15.0 |

Three-point field goals: 1999-00, 28-for-76 (.368). 2000-01, 35-for-79 (.443). Totals, 63-for-155 (.406).
Personal fouls/disqualifications: 1999-00, 44/0. 2000-01, 46/0. Totals, 90/0.

### NBA REGULAR-SEASON RECORD

**HONORS:** NBA All-Rookie second team (2002).

| Season Team | G | Min. | FGM | FGA | Pct. | FTM | FTA | Pct. | REBOUNDS Off. | Def. | Tot. | Ast. | St. | Blk. | TO | Pts. | AVERAGES RPG | APG | PPG |
|---|---|---|---|---|---|---|---|---|---|---|---|---|---|---|---|---|---|---|---|
| 01-02—Bos.-Phoenix .. | 77 | 1916 | 251 | 584 | .430 | 41 | 53 | .774 | 75 | 182 | 257 | 179 | 59 | 20 | 71 | 581 | 3.3 | 2.3 | 7.5 |
| 02-03—Phoenix ......... | 82 | 2255 | 316 | 796 | .397 | 96 | 124 | .774 | 57 | 207 | 264 | 210 | 62 | 19 | 108 | 803 | 3.2 | 2.6 | 9.8 |
| 03-04—Phoenix ......... | 82 | 3331 | 555 | 1291 | .430 | 174 | 232 | .750 | 80 | 305 | 385 | 362 | 93 | 26 | 199 | 1367 | 4.7 | 4.4 | 16.7 |
| 04-05—Phoenix ......... | 82 | 3240 | 544 | 1179 | .461 | 135 | 180 | .750 | 120 | 302 | 422 | 291 | 79 | 24 | 148 | 1400 | 5.1 | 3.5 | 17.1 |
| Totals ................... | 323 | 10742 | 1666 | 3850 | .433 | 446 | 589 | .757 | 332 | 996 | 1328 | 1042 | 293 | 89 | 526 | 4151 | 4.1 | 3.2 | 12.9 |

Three-point field goals: 2001-02, 38-for-130 (.292). 2002-03, 75-for-205 (.366). 2003-04, 83-for-272 (.305). 2004-05, 177-for-370 (.478). Totals, 373-for-977 (.382).

Personal fouls/disqualifications: 2001-02, 114/0. 2002-03, 143/0. 2003-04, 177/1. 2004-05, 167/0. Totals, 601/1.

### NBA PLAYOFF RECORD

| Season Team | G | Min. | FGM | FGA | Pct. | FTM | FTA | Pct. | REBOUNDS Off. | Def. | Tot. | Ast. | St. | Blk. | TO | Pts. | AVERAGES RPG | APG | PPG |
|---|---|---|---|---|---|---|---|---|---|---|---|---|---|---|---|---|---|---|---|
| 02-03—Phoenix ......... | 6 | 164 | 14 | 51 | .275 | 2 | 5 | .400 | 6 | 20 | 26 | 8 | 4 | 2 | 12 | 32 | 4.3 | 1.3 | 5.3 |
| 04-05—Phoenix ......... | 9 | 355 | 63 | 125 | .504 | 23 | 33 | .697 | 7 | 32 | 39 | 30 | 10 | 4 | 10 | 169 | 4.3 | 3.3 | 18.8 |
| Totals ................... | 15 | 519 | 77 | 176 | .438 | 25 | 38 | .658 | 13 | 52 | 65 | 38 | 14 | 6 | 22 | 201 | 4.3 | 2.5 | 13.4 |

Three-point field goals: 2002-03, 2-for-13 (.154). 2004-05, 20-for-36 (.556). Totals, 22-for-49 (.449).
Personal fouls/disqualifications: 2002-03, 15/0. 2004-05, 18/0. Totals, 33/0.

## JOHNSON, LINTON     F     SPURS

**PERSONAL:** Born June 13, 1980, in Chicago. ... 6-8/205. (2.03/93.0).
**HIGH SCHOOL:** Providence St. Mel (Chicago).
**COLLEGE:** Tulane.
**TRANSACTIONS/CAREER NOTES:** Not drafted by an NBA franchise. ... Signed as free agent by Chicago Bulls (September 29, 2003). ... Waived by Bulls (January 6, 2004). ... Played in Continental Basketball Association (2004). ... Signed by Bulls to first of two consecutive 10-day contracts (February 28, 2004). ... Signed by Bulls for remainder of season (March 19, 2004). ... Signed as free agent by San Antonio Spurs (August 25, 2004).

### COLLEGIATE RECORD

| Season Team | G | Min. | FGM | FGA | Pct. | FTM | FTA | Pct. | Reb. | Ast. | Pts. | AVERAGES RPG | APG | PPG |
|---|---|---|---|---|---|---|---|---|---|---|---|---|---|---|
| 98-99—Tulane........................... | 25 | 205 | 16 | 46 | .348 | 9 | 20 | .450 | 47 | 8 | 42 | 1.9 | 0.3 | 1.7 |
| 99-00—Tulane........................... | 31 | 350 | 33 | 68 | .485 | 20 | 31 | .645 | 98 | 13 | 87 | 3.2 | 0.4 | 2.8 |
| 00-01—Tulane........................... | 30 | 1018 | 153 | 300 | .510 | 59 | 87 | .678 | 242 | 73 | 394 | 8.1 | 2.4 | 13.1 |
| 01-02—Tulane........................... | 21 | 500 | 77 | 179 | .430 | 19 | 25 | .760 | 136 | 24 | 189 | 6.5 | 1.1 | 9.0 |
| Totals ..................................... | 107 | 2073 | 279 | 593 | .470 | 107 | 163 | .656 | 523 | 118 | 712 | 4.9 | 1.1 | 6.7 |

Three-point field goals: 1998-99, 1-for-8 (.125). 1999-00, 1-for-5 (.200). 2000-01, 29-for-80 (.363). 2001-02, 16-for-56 (.286). Totals, 47-for-149 (.315).

### CBA RECORD

| Season Team | G | Min. | FGM | FGA | Pct. | FTM | FTA | Pct. | Reb. | Ast. | Pts. | AVERAGES RPG | APG | PPG |
|---|---|---|---|---|---|---|---|---|---|---|---|---|---|---|
| 03-04—Rockford ....................... | 22 | 715 | 136 | 285 | .477 | 39 | 55 | .709 | 183 | 39 | 332 | 8.3 | 1.8 | 15.1 |

Three-point field goals: 2003-04, 21-for-57 (.368). Totals, 21-for-57 (.368).

### NBA REGULAR-SEASON RECORD

| Season Team | G | Min. | FGM | FGA | Pct. | FTM | FTA | Pct. | REBOUNDS Off. | Def. | Tot. | Ast. | St. | Blk. | TO | Pts. | AVERAGES RPG | APG | PPG |
|---|---|---|---|---|---|---|---|---|---|---|---|---|---|---|---|---|---|---|---|
| 03-04—Chicago ......... | 41 | 734 | 72 | 203 | .355 | 22 | 37 | .595 | 59 | 124 | 183 | 27 | 37 | 32 | 37 | 173 | 4.5 | 0.7 | 4.2 |
| 04-05—San Antonio.... | 2 | 15 | 0 | 2 | .000 | 0 | 0 | ... | 0 | 3 | 3 | 0 | 1 | 0 | 1 | 0 | 1.5 | 0.0 | 0.0 |
| Totals ................... | 43 | 749 | 72 | 205 | .351 | 22 | 37 | .595 | 59 | 127 | 186 | 27 | 38 | 32 | 38 | 173 | 4.3 | 0.6 | 4.0 |

Three-point field goals: 2003-04, 7-for-33 (.212). 2004-05, 0-for-1. Totals, 7-for-34 (.206).
Personal fouls/disqualifications: 2003-04, 90/2. 2004-05, 1/0. Totals, 91/2.

## JONES, DAHNTAY     G/F     GRIZZLIES

**PERSONAL:** Born December 27, 1980, in Trenton, N.J. ... 6-6/210. (1.98/95.3). ... Full name: Dahntay Lavall Jones
**HIGH SCHOOL:** Steinert (Hamilton, N.J.).
**COLLEGE:** Rutgers, then Duke.
**TRANSACTIONS/CAREER NOTES:** Selected by Boston Celtics in first round (20th pick overall) of 2003 NBA Draft. ... Draft rights traded by Celtics with draft rights to G Troy Bell to Memphis Grizzlies for draft rights to G Marcus Banks and C Kendrick Perkins (June 26, 2003).

### COLLEGIATE RECORD

| Season Team | G | Min. | FGM | FGA | Pct. | FTM | FTA | Pct. | Reb. | Ast. | Pts. | AVERAGES RPG | APG | PPG |
|---|---|---|---|---|---|---|---|---|---|---|---|---|---|---|
| 98-99—Rutgers ......................... | 32 | 841 | 119 | 281 | .423 | 92 | 113 | .814 | 130 | 49 | 341 | 4.1 | 1.5 | 10.7 |
| 99-00—Rutgers ......................... | 31 | 1041 | 166 | 401 | .414 | 124 | 175 | .709 | 142 | 63 | 495 | 4.6 | 2.0 | 16.0 |
| 00-01—Duke............................. | | | | | | Did not play—transfer student. | | | | | | | | |
| 01-02—Duke............................. | 35 | 1011 | 153 | 303 | .505 | 74 | 102 | .725 | 146 | 40 | 392 | 4.2 | 1.1 | 11.2 |
| 02-03—Duke............................. | 33 | 1014 | 198 | 421 | .470 | 140 | 187 | .749 | 180 | 29 | 583 | 5.5 | 0.9 | 17.7 |
| Totals ..................................... | 131 | 3907 | 636 | 1406 | .452 | 430 | 577 | .745 | 598 | 181 | 1811 | 4.6 | 1.4 | 13.8 |

Three-point field goals: 1998-99, 11-for-34 (.324). 1999-00, 39-for-113 (.345). 2001-02, 12-for-52 (.231). 2002-03, 47-for-118 (.398). Totals, 109-for-317 (.344).

### NBA REGULAR-SEASON RECORD

| Season Team | G | Min. | FGM | FGA | Pct. | FTM | FTA | Pct. | REBOUNDS Off. | Def. | Tot. | Ast. | St. | Blk. | TO | Pts. | AVERAGES RPG | APG | PPG |
|---|---|---|---|---|---|---|---|---|---|---|---|---|---|---|---|---|---|---|---|
| 03-04—Memphis ........ | 20 | 154 | 15 | 53 | .283 | 5 | 11 | .455 | 7 | 16 | 23 | 12 | 5 | 6 | 12 | 36 | 1.2 | 0.6 | 1.8 |

| Season Team | G | Min. | FGM | FGA | Pct. | FTM | FTA | Pct. | Off. | Def. | Tot. | Ast. | St. | Blk. | TO | Pts. | RPG | APG | PPG |
|---|---|---|---|---|---|---|---|---|---|---|---|---|---|---|---|---|---|---|---|
| 04-05—Memphis ........ | 52 | 649 | 83 | 190 | .437 | 44 | 64 | .688 | 11 | 58 | 69 | 21 | 13 | 11 | 29 | 233 | 1.3 | 0.4 | 4.5 |
| Totals .................. | 72 | 803 | 98 | 243 | .403 | 49 | 75 | .653 | 18 | 74 | 92 | 33 | 18 | 17 | 41 | 269 | 1.3 | 0.5 | 3.7 |

Three-point field goals: 2003-04, 1-for-4 (.250). 2004-05, 23-for-60 (.383). Totals, 24-for-64 (.375).
Personal fouls/disqualifications: 2003-04, 23/0. 2004-05, 81/0. Totals, 104/0.

## NBA PLAYOFF RECORD

| Season Team | G | Min. | FGM | FGA | Pct. | FTM | FTA | Pct. | Off. | Def. | Tot. | Ast. | St. | Blk. | TO | Pts. | RPG | APG | PPG |
|---|---|---|---|---|---|---|---|---|---|---|---|---|---|---|---|---|---|---|---|
| 04-05—Memphis ........ | 3 | 71 | 8 | 21 | .381 | 3 | 4 | .750 | 2 | 7 | 9 | 1 | 1 | 0 | 2 | 22 | 3.0 | 0.3 | 7.3 |

Three-point field goals: 2004-05, 3-for-5 (.600). Totals, 3-for-5 (.600).
Personal fouls/disqualifications: 2004-05, 8/0. Totals, 8/0.

# JONES, DAMON      G      HEAT

**J**

**PERSONAL:** Born August 25, 1976, in Galveston, Texas. ... 6-3/185. (1.91/83.9).
**HIGH SCHOOL:** Ball (Galveston, Texas).
**COLLEGE:** Houston.
**TRANSACTIONS/CAREER NOTES:** Not drafted by an NBA franchise. ... Played in International Basketball Association with Black Hills Posse (1997-98). ... Played in Continental Basketball Association with Idaho Stampede (1998-99). ... Signed as free agent by Orlando Magic (January 21, 1999). ... Waived by Magic (February 2, 1999). ... Signed as free agent by New Jersey Nets (February 16, 1999). ... Waived by Nets (March 8, 1999). ... Signed by Boston Celtics to first of two consecutive 10-day contracts (April 14, 1999). ... Re-signed by Celtics for remainder of season (May 4, 1999). ... Signed as free agent by Golden State Warriors (October 4, 1999). ... Waived by Warriors (November 30, 1999). ... Signed as free agent by Dallas Mavericks (December 2, 1999). ... Waived by Mavericks (January 5, 2000). ... Signed by Mavericks to first of two consecutive 10-day contracts (January 8, 2000). ... Re-signed by Mavericks for remainder of season (January 28, 2000). ... Signed as free agent by Vancouver Grizzlies (August 8, 2000). ... Signed as free agent by Houston Rockets (October 1, 2001). ... Waived by Rockets (October 25, 2001). ... Signed as free agent by Detroit Pistons (October 29, 2001). ... Signed as free agent by Sacramento Kings (October 18, 2002). ... Signed as free agent by Milwaukee Bucks (July 23, 2003). ... Signed as free agent by Miami Heat (August 6, 2004).

## COLLEGIATE RECORD

| Season Team | G | Min. | FGM | FGA | Pct. | FTM | FTA | Pct. | Reb. | Ast. | Pts. | RPG | APG | PPG |
|---|---|---|---|---|---|---|---|---|---|---|---|---|---|---|
| 94-95—Houston ............... | 27 | 781 | 91 | 262 | .347 | 40 | 64 | .625 | 92 | 77 | 277 | 3.4 | 2.9 | 10.3 |
| 95-96—Houston ............... | 27 | 857 | 115 | 266 | .432 | 34 | 51 | .667 | 111 | 105 | 321 | 4.1 | 3.9 | 11.9 |
| 96-97—Houston ............... | 27 | 968 | 159 | 341 | .466 | 55 | 78 | .705 | 120 | 132 | 443 | 4.4 | 4.9 | 16.4 |
| Totals ............................ | 81 | 2606 | 365 | 869 | .420 | 129 | 193 | .668 | 323 | 314 | 1041 | 4.0 | 3.9 | 12.9 |

Three-point field goals: 1994-95, 55-for-168 (.327). 1995-96, 57-for-167 (.341). 1996-97, 70-for-186 (.376). Totals, 182-for-521 (.349).
Personal fouls/disqualifications: 1994-95, 40/0. 1995-96, 37/0. 1996-97, 49/0. Totals, 126/0.

## IBA RECORD

| Season Team | G | Min. | FGM | FGA | Pct. | FTM | FTA | Pct. | Reb. | Ast. | Pts. | RPG | APG | PPG |
|---|---|---|---|---|---|---|---|---|---|---|---|---|---|---|
| 97-98—Black Hills ..................... | 34 | 726 | 148 | 330 | .448 | 53 | 75 | .707 | 84 | 115 | 423 | 2.5 | 3.4 | 12.4 |

Three-point field goals: 1997-98, 74-for-200 (.370). Totals, 74-for-200 (.370).

## CBA RECORD

**NOTES:** CBA Newcomer of the Year (1999). ... CBA All-League first team (1999). ... Led CBA with 120 three-point field goals made and 336 three-point field goals attempted (1999).

| Season Team | G | Min. | FGM | FGA | Pct. | FTM | FTA | Pct. | Reb. | Ast. | Pts. | RPG | APG | PPG |
|---|---|---|---|---|---|---|---|---|---|---|---|---|---|---|
| 98-99—Idaho ............................. | 35 | 1400 | 269 | 645 | .417 | 100 | 130 | .769 | 137 | 222 | 758 | 3.9 | 6.3 | *21.7 |

Three-point field goals: 1998-99, 120-for-336 (.357). Totals, 120-for-336 (.357).
Personal fouls/disqualifications: 1998-99, 68/0. Totals, 68/0.

## NBA REGULAR-SEASON RECORD

| Season Team | G | Min. | FGM | FGA | Pct. | FTM | FTA | Pct. | Off. | Def. | Tot. | Ast. | St. | Blk. | TO | Pts. | RPG | APG | PPG |
|---|---|---|---|---|---|---|---|---|---|---|---|---|---|---|---|---|---|---|---|
| 98-99—N.J.-Boston .... | 24 | 344 | 43 | 119 | .361 | 14 | 17 | .824 | 6 | 38 | 44 | 42 | 13 | 0 | 17 | 125 | 1.8 | 1.8 | 5.2 |
| 99-00—Golden State-Dal. | 55 | 612 | 80 | 208 | .385 | 32 | 48 | .667 | 12 | 43 | 55 | 96 | 18 | 1 | 40 | 233 | 1.0 | 1.7 | 4.2 |
| 00-01—Vancouver....... | 71 | 1415 | 170 | 416 | .409 | 37 | 52 | .712 | 16 | 108 | 124 | 224 | 36 | 1 | 76 | 461 | 1.7 | 3.2 | 6.5 |
| 01-02—Detroit .......... | 67 | 1083 | 114 | 284 | .401 | 43 | 59 | .729 | 13 | 90 | 103 | 140 | 23 | 1 | 61 | 340 | 1.5 | 2.1 | 5.1 |
| 02-03—Sacramento .... | 49 | 709 | 80 | 210 | .381 | 20 | 27 | .741 | 11 | 59 | 70 | 80 | 18 | 4 | 23 | 224 | 1.4 | 1.6 | 4.6 |
| 03-04—Milwaukee ...... | 82 | 2016 | 210 | 524 | .401 | 55 | 72 | .764 | 15 | 155 | 170 | 478 | 30 | 4 | 103 | 573 | 2.1 | 5.8 | 7.0 |
| 04-05—Miami ............. | 82 | 2576 | 331 | 726 | .456 | 68 | 86 | .791 | 14 | 217 | 231 | 350 | 44 | 5 | 98 | 955 | 2.8 | 4.3 | 11.6 |
| Totals ................... | 430 | 8755 | 1028 | 2487 | .413 | 269 | 361 | .745 | 87 | 710 | 797 | 1410 | 182 | 16 | 418 | 2911 | 1.9 | 3.3 | 6.8 |

Three-point field goals: 1998-99, 25-for-62 (.403). 1999-00, 41-for-114 (.360). 2000-01, 84-for-231 (.364). 2001-02, 69-for-186 (.371). 2002-03, 44-for-121 (.364). 2003-04, 98-for-273 (.359). 2004-05, 225-for-521 (.432). Totals, 586-for-1508 (.389).
Personal fouls/disqualifications: 1998-99, 23/0. 1999-00, 34/0. 2000-01, 58/0. 2001-02, 83/0. 2002-03, 42/0. 2003-04, 92/0. 2004-05, 121/0. Totals, 453/0.

## NBA PLAYOFF RECORD

| Season Team | G | Min. | FGM | FGA | Pct. | FTM | FTA | Pct. | Off. | Def. | Tot. | Ast. | St. | Blk. | TO | Pts. | RPG | APG | PPG |
|---|---|---|---|---|---|---|---|---|---|---|---|---|---|---|---|---|---|---|---|
| 01-02—Detroit ........... | 10 | 181 | 16 | 42 | .381 | 3 | 4 | .750 | 1 | 20 | 21 | 25 | 5 | 0 | 6 | 43 | 2.1 | 2.5 | 4.3 |
| 03-04—Milwaukee ...... | 5 | 144 | 18 | 34 | .529 | 4 | 6 | .667 | 2 | 18 | 20 | 37 | 5 | 0 | 9 | 50 | 4.0 | 7.4 | 10.0 |
| 04-05—Miami ............. | 15 | 498 | 62 | 129 | .481 | 18 | 30 | .600 | 3 | 38 | 41 | 60 | 7 | 0 | 17 | 181 | 2.7 | 4.0 | 12.1 |
| Totals ................... | 30 | 823 | 96 | 205 | .468 | 25 | 40 | .625 | 6 | 76 | 82 | 122 | 17 | 0 | 32 | 274 | 2.7 | 4.1 | 9.1 |

Three-point field goals: 2001-02, 8-for-27 (.296). 2003-04, 10-for-21 (.476). 2004-05, 39-for-91 (.429). Totals, 57-for-139 (.410).
Personal fouls/disqualifications: 2001-02, 14/0. 2003-04, 14/0. 2004-05, 24/0. Totals, 52/0.

## JONES, EDDIE       G       GRIZZLIES

**PERSONAL:** Born October 20, 1971, in Pompano Beach, Fla. ... 6-7/194. (2.01/88.0). ... Full name: Eddie Charles Jones
**HIGH SCHOOL:** Ely (Pompano Beach, Fla.).
**COLLEGE:** Temple.
**TRANSACTIONS/CAREER NOTES:** Selected by Los Angeles Lakers in first round (10th pick overall) of 1994 NBA Draft. ... Traded by Lakers with F/C Elden Campbell to Charlotte Hornets for F Glen Rice, F/C J.R. Reid and G B.J. Armstrong (March 10, 1999). ... Traded by Hornets with F Anthony Mason, G Ricky Davis and G/F Dale Ellis to Miami Heat for F P.J. Brown, F Jamal Mashburn, F/C Otis Thorpe, F Tim James and G/F Rodney Buford (August 1, 2000). ... Traded by Heat to Memphis Grizzlies in five-team trade (August 2, 2005).

### COLLEGIATE RECORD

| Season Team | G | Min. | FGM | FGA | Pct. | FTM | FTA | Pct. | Reb. | Ast. | Pts. | RPG | APG | PPG |
|---|---|---|---|---|---|---|---|---|---|---|---|---|---|---|
| 90-91—Temple.................... | | | | | | Did not play—ineligible. | | | | | | | | |
| 91-92—Temple.................... | 29 | 764 | 122 | 279 | .437 | 41 | 75 | .547 | 122 | 30 | 332 | 4.2 | 1.0 | 11.4 |
| 92-93—Temple.................... | 32 | 1169 | 212 | 463 | .458 | 70 | 116 | .603 | 225 | 56 | 543 | 7.0 | 1.8 | 17.0 |
| 93-94—Temple.................... | 31 | 1184 | 231 | 491 | .470 | 88 | 133 | .662 | 210 | 58 | 595 | 6.8 | 1.9 | 19.2 |
| Totals ..................... | 92 | 3117 | 565 | 1233 | .458 | 199 | 324 | .614 | 557 | 144 | 1470 | 6.1 | 1.6 | 16.0 |

Three-point field goals: 1991-92, 47-for-134 (.351). 1992-93, 49-for-141 (.348). 1993-94, 45-for-128 (.352). Totals, 141-for-403 (.350).

### NBA REGULAR-SEASON RECORD

**HONORS:** All-NBA third team (2000). ... NBA All-Defensive second team (1998, 1999, 2000). ... NBA All-Rookie first team (1995). ... MVP of Rookie Game (1995).
**NOTES:** Led NBA with 2.7 steals per game (2000).

| Season Team | G | Min. | FGM | FGA | Pct. | FTM | FTA | Pct. | Off. | Def. | Tot. | Ast. | St. | Blk. | TO | Pts. | RPG | APG | PPG |
|---|---|---|---|---|---|---|---|---|---|---|---|---|---|---|---|---|---|---|---|
| 94-95—L.A. Lakers ..... | 64 | 1981 | 342 | 744 | .460 | 122 | 169 | .722 | 79 | 170 | 249 | 128 | 131 | 41 | 75 | 897 | 3.9 | 2.0 | 14.0 |
| 95-96—L.A. Lakers ..... | 70 | 2184 | 337 | 685 | .492 | 136 | 184 | .739 | 45 | 188 | 233 | 246 | 129 | 45 | 99 | 893 | 3.3 | 3.5 | 12.8 |
| 96-97—L.A. Lakers ..... | 80 | 2998 | 473 | 1081 | .438 | 276 | 337 | .819 | 90 | 236 | 326 | 270 | 189 | 49 | 169 | 1374 | 4.1 | 3.4 | 17.2 |
| 97-98—L.A. Lakers ..... | 80 | 2910 | 486 | 1005 | .484 | 234 | 306 | .765 | 85 | 217 | 302 | 246 | 160 | 55 | 146 | 1349 | 3.8 | 3.1 | 16.9 |
| 98-99—L.A.L.-Char. ..... | 50 | 1881 | 260 | 595 | .437 | 212 | 271 | .782 | 50 | 144 | 194 | 186 | 125 | 58 | 93 | 780 | 3.9 | 3.7 | 15.6 |
| 99-00—Charlotte ......... | 72 | 2807 | 478 | 1119 | .427 | 362 | 419 | .864 | 81 | 262 | 343 | 305 | *192 | 49 | 160 | 1446 | 4.8 | 4.2 | 20.1 |
| 00-01—Miami ........... | 63 | 2282 | 388 | 871 | .445 | 228 | 270 | .844 | 75 | 217 | 292 | 171 | 110 | 58 | 135 | 1094 | 4.6 | 2.7 | 17.4 |
| 01-02—Miami ........... | 81 | 3156 | 517 | 1198 | .432 | 297 | 355 | .837 | 61 | 317 | 378 | 262 | 117 | 77 | 148 | 1480 | 4.7 | 3.2 | 18.3 |
| 02-03—Miami ........... | 47 | 1789 | 291 | 688 | .423 | 189 | 230 | .822 | 35 | 191 | 226 | 173 | 64 | 31 | 85 | 869 | 4.8 | 3.7 | 18.5 |
| 03-04—Miami ........... | 81 | 2998 | 473 | 1156 | .409 | 278 | 333 | .835 | 38 | 270 | 308 | 258 | 92 | 34 | 129 | 1401 | 3.8 | 3.2 | 17.3 |
| 04-05—Miami ........... | 80 | 2839 | 351 | 820 | .428 | 174 | 216 | .806 | 38 | 367 | 405 | 212 | 86 | 38 | 99 | 1018 | 5.1 | 2.7 | 12.7 |
| Totals ................... | 768 | 27825 | 4396 | 9962 | .441 | 2508 | 3090 | .812 | 677 | 2579 | 3256 | 2457 | 1395 | 535 | 1338 | 12601 | 4.2 | 3.2 | 16.4 |

Three-point field goals: 1994-95, 91-for-246 (.370). 1995-96, 83-for-227 (.366). 1996-97, 152-for-389 (.391). 1997-98, 143-for-368 (.389). 1998-99, 48-for-142 (.338). 1999-00, 128-for-341 (.375). 2000-01, 90-for-238 (.378). 2001-02, 149-for-382 (.390). 2002-03, 98-for-241 (.407). 2003-04, 177-for-479 (.370). 2004-05, 142-for-382 (.372). Totals, 1301-for-3435 (.379).

Personal fouls/disqualifications: 1994-95, 175/1. 1995-96, 162/0. 1996-97, 226/3. 1997-98, 164/0. 1998-99, 128/1. 1999-00, 176/1. 2000-01, 183/5. 2001-02, 258/2. 2002-03, 137/1. 2003-04, 226/2. 2004-05, 251/4. Totals, 2086/20.

### NBA PLAYOFF RECORD

| Season Team | G | Min. | FGM | FGA | Pct. | FTM | FTA | Pct. | Off. | Def. | Tot. | Ast. | St. | Blk. | TO | Pts. | RPG | APG | PPG |
|---|---|---|---|---|---|---|---|---|---|---|---|---|---|---|---|---|---|---|---|
| 94-95—L.A. Lakers ..... | 10 | 286 | 30 | 80 | .375 | 15 | 21 | .714 | 7 | 25 | 32 | 20 | 8 | 9 | 17 | 87 | 3.2 | 2.0 | 8.7 |
| 95-96—L.A. Lakers ..... | 4 | 155 | 27 | 49 | .551 | 5 | 8 | .625 | 7 | 14 | 21 | 6 | 8 | 1 | 4 | 69 | 5.3 | 1.5 | 17.3 |
| 96-97—L.A. Lakers ..... | 9 | 283 | 33 | 72 | .458 | 26 | 35 | .743 | 8 | 23 | 31 | 29 | 9 | 4 | 13 | 101 | 3.4 | 3.2 | 11.2 |
| 97-98—L.A. Lakers ..... | 13 | 476 | 69 | 148 | .466 | 63 | 76 | .829 | 12 | 39 | 51 | 32 | 26 | 21 | 17 | 221 | 3.9 | 2.5 | 17.0 |
| 99-00—Charlotte ......... | 4 | 171 | 22 | 58 | .379 | 15 | 16 | .938 | 4 | 16 | 20 | 19 | 10 | 3 | 5 | 68 | 5.0 | 4.8 | 17.0 |
| 00-01—Miami ........... | 3 | 108 | 22 | 44 | .500 | 6 | 7 | .857 | 2 | 16 | 18 | 7 | 3 | 1 | 7 | 57 | 6.0 | 2.3 | 19.0 |
| 03-04—Miami ........... | 13 | 478 | 56 | 153 | .366 | 40 | 50 | .800 | 3 | 44 | 47 | 29 | 18 | 11 | 19 | 172 | 3.6 | 2.2 | 13.2 |
| 04-05—Miami ........... | 15 | 601 | 71 | 156 | .455 | 31 | 42 | .738 | 10 | 77 | 87 | 39 | 18 | 9 | 22 | 205 | 5.8 | 2.6 | 13.7 |
| Totals ................... | 71 | 2558 | 330 | 760 | .434 | 201 | 255 | .788 | 53 | 254 | 307 | 181 | 100 | 59 | 104 | 980 | 4.3 | 2.5 | 13.8 |

Three-point field goals: 1994-95, 12-for-27 (.444). 1995-96, 10-for-19 (.526). 1996-97, 9-for-24 (.375). 1997-98, 20-for-48 (.417). 1999-00, 9-for-26 (.346). 2000-01, 7-for-16 (.438). 2003-04, 20-for-67 (.299). 2004-05, 32-for-80 (.400). Totals, 119-for-307 (.388).

Personal fouls/disqualifications: 1994-95, 27/0. 1995-96, 16/0. 1996-97, 24/0. 1997-98, 37/0. 1999-00, 12/0. 2000-01, 9/0. 2003-04, 37/0. 2004-05, 57/1. Totals, 219/1.

### NBA ALL-STAR GAME RECORD

| Season Team | Min. | FGM | FGA | Pct. | FTM | FTA | Pct. | Off. | Def. | Tot. | Ast. | PF | Dq. | St. | Blk. | TO | Pts. |
|---|---|---|---|---|---|---|---|---|---|---|---|---|---|---|---|---|---|
| 1997—L.A. Lakers........... | 17 | 3 | 4 | .750 | 4 | 7 | .571 | 1 | 0 | 1 | 1 | 1 | 0 | 1 | 2 | 3 | 10 |
| 1998—L.A. Lakers........... | 25 | 7 | 19 | .368 | 1 | 2 | .500 | 7 | 4 | 11 | 1 | 1 | 0 | 2 | 0 | 0 | 15 |
| 2000—Charlotte .............. | 21 | 4 | 7 | .571 | 0 | 0 | ... | 1 | 3 | 4 | 3 | 1 | 0 | 1 | 0 | 1 | 10 |
| Totals........................ | 63 | 14 | 30 | .467 | 5 | 9 | .556 | 9 | 7 | 16 | 5 | 3 | 0 | 4 | 2 | 4 | 35 |

Three-point field goals: 1997, 0-for-1. 1998, 0-for-7. 2000, 2-for-3 (.667). Totals, 2-for-11 (.182).

## JONES, FRED       G       PACERS

**PERSONAL:** Born March 11, 1979, in Malvern, Ark. ... 6-4/210. (1.93/95.3). ... Full name: Frederick Terrell Jones
**HIGH SCHOOL:** Barlow (Gresham, Ore.).
**COLLEGE:** Oregon.
**TRANSACTIONS/CAREER NOTES:** Selected by Indiana Pacers in first round (14th pick overall) of 2002 NBA Draft.

## COLLEGIATE RECORD

| Season Team | G | Min. | FGM | FGA | Pct. | FTM | FTA | Pct. | Reb. | Ast. | Pts. | RPG | APG | PPG |
|---|---|---|---|---|---|---|---|---|---|---|---|---|---|---|
| 98-99—Oregon | 32 | 675 | 103 | 201 | .512 | 50 | 74 | .676 | 108 | 62 | 290 | 3.4 | 1.9 | 9.1 |
| 99-00—Oregon | 30 | 857 | 100 | 249 | .402 | 62 | 81 | .765 | 177 | 99 | 291 | 5.9 | 3.3 | 9.7 |
| 00-01—Oregon | 28 | 892 | 136 | 288 | .472 | 108 | 134 | .806 | 157 | 95 | 413 | 5.6 | 3.4 | 14.8 |
| 01-02—Oregon | 35 | 1103 | 215 | 413 | .521 | 169 | 194 | .871 | 189 | 111 | 650 | 5.4 | 3.2 | 18.6 |
| **Totals** | 125 | 3527 | 554 | 1151 | .481 | 389 | 483 | .805 | 631 | 367 | 1644 | 5.0 | 2.9 | 13.2 |

Three-point field goals: 1998-99, 34-for-83 (.410). 1999-00, 29-for-107 (.271). 2000-01, 33-for-108 (.306). 2001-02, 51-for-137 (.372). Totals, 147-for-435 (.338).

## NBA REGULAR-SEASON RECORD

| Season Team | G | Min. | FGM | FGA | Pct. | FTM | FTA | Pct. | Off. | Def. | Tot. | Ast. | St. | Blk. | TO | Pts. | RPG | APG | PPG |
|---|---|---|---|---|---|---|---|---|---|---|---|---|---|---|---|---|---|---|---|
| 02-03—Indiana | 19 | 115 | 9 | 24 | .375 | 3 | 4 | .750 | 4 | 5 | 9 | 5 | 6 | 1 | 6 | 23 | 0.5 | 0.3 | 1.2 |
| 03-04—Indiana | 81 | 1508 | 123 | 311 | .395 | 124 | 149 | .832 | 25 | 101 | 126 | 173 | 65 | 18 | 73 | 397 | 1.6 | 2.1 | 4.9 |
| 04-05—Indiana | 77 | 2268 | 275 | 647 | .425 | 176 | 207 | .850 | 34 | 208 | 242 | 196 | 61 | 31 | 114 | 813 | 3.1 | 2.5 | 10.6 |
| **Totals** | 177 | 3891 | 407 | 982 | .414 | 303 | 360 | .842 | 63 | 314 | 377 | 374 | 132 | 50 | 193 | 1233 | 2.1 | 2.1 | 7.0 |

Three-point field goals: 2002-03, 2-for-7 (.286). 2003-04, 27-for-89 (.303). 2004-05, 87-for-229 (.380). Totals, 116-for-325 (.357).
Personal fouls/disqualifications: 2002-03, 13/0. 2003-04, 132/0. 2004-05, 171/1. Totals, 316/1.

## NBA PLAYOFF RECORD

| Season Team | G | Min. | FGM | FGA | Pct. | FTM | FTA | Pct. | Off. | Def. | Tot. | Ast. | St. | Blk. | TO | Pts. | RPG | APG | PPG |
|---|---|---|---|---|---|---|---|---|---|---|---|---|---|---|---|---|---|---|---|
| 03-04—Indiana | 14 | 263 | 25 | 51 | .490 | 5 | 7 | .714 | 3 | 30 | 33 | 16 | 7 | 7 | 9 | 66 | 2.4 | 1.1 | 4.7 |
| 04-05—Indiana | 13 | 234 | 16 | 54 | .296 | 12 | 13 | .923 | 1 | 22 | 23 | 13 | 8 | 2 | 15 | 53 | 1.8 | 1.0 | 4.1 |
| **Totals** | 27 | 497 | 41 | 105 | .390 | 17 | 20 | .850 | 4 | 52 | 56 | 29 | 15 | 9 | 24 | 119 | 2.1 | 1.1 | 4.4 |

Three-point field goals: 2003-04, 11-for-22 (.500). 2004-05, 9-for-23 (.391). Totals, 20-for-45 (.444).
Personal fouls/disqualifications: 2003-04, 31/0. 2004-05, 13/0. Totals, 44/0.

# JONES, JAMES     F     SUNS

**PERSONAL:** Born October 4, 1980, in Miami, Fla. ... 6-8/215. (2.03/97.5). ... Full name: James Andrew Jones
**HIGH SCHOOL:** American Senior (Miami, Fla.).
**COLLEGE:** Miami (Fla.).
**TRANSACTIONS/CAREER NOTES:** Selected by Indiana Pacers in second round (49th pick overall) of 2003 NBA Draft. ... Traded by Pacers to Suns for a future second-round draft choice (August 25, 2005).

## COLLEGIATE RECORD

| Season Team | G | Min. | FGM | FGA | Pct. | FTM | FTA | Pct. | Reb. | Ast. | Pts. | RPG | APG | PPG |
|---|---|---|---|---|---|---|---|---|---|---|---|---|---|---|
| 99-00—Miami (Fla.) | 33 | 424 | 52 | 122 | .426 | 15 | 18 | .833 | 64 | 11 | 129 | 1.9 | 0.3 | 3.9 |
| 00-01—Miami (Fla.) | 29 | 922 | 122 | 285 | .428 | 60 | 74 | .811 | 170 | 34 | 345 | 5.9 | 1.2 | 11.9 |
| 01-02—Miami (Fla.) | 32 | 1048 | 133 | 332 | .401 | 111 | 132 | .841 | 203 | 48 | 410 | 6.3 | 1.5 | 12.8 |
| 02-03—Miami (Fla.) | 28 | 957 | 157 | 351 | .447 | 118 | 142 | .831 | 169 | 49 | 472 | 6.0 | 1.8 | 16.9 |
| **Totals** | 122 | 3351 | 464 | 1090 | .426 | 304 | 366 | .831 | 606 | 142 | 1356 | 5.0 | 1.2 | 11.1 |

Three-point field goals: 1999-00, 10-for-32 (.313). 2000-01, 41-for-87 (.471). 2001-02, 33-for-105 (.314). 2002-03, 40-for-100 (.400). Totals, 124-for-324 (.383).

## NBA REGULAR-SEASON RECORD

| Season Team | G | Min. | FGM | FGA | Pct. | FTM | FTA | Pct. | Off. | Def. | Tot. | Ast. | St. | Blk. | TO | Pts. | RPG | APG | PPG |
|---|---|---|---|---|---|---|---|---|---|---|---|---|---|---|---|---|---|---|---|
| 03-04—Indiana | 6 | 26 | 2 | 9 | .222 | 2 | 2 | 1.000 | 0 | 2 | 2 | 0 | 1 | 0 | 0 | 7 | 0.3 | 0.0 | 1.2 |
| 04-05—Indiana | 75 | 1330 | 126 | 318 | .396 | 53 | 62 | .855 | 39 | 135 | 174 | 57 | 31 | 28 | 43 | 371 | 2.3 | 0.8 | 4.9 |
| **Totals** | 81 | 1356 | 128 | 327 | .391 | 55 | 64 | .859 | 39 | 137 | 176 | 57 | 32 | 28 | 43 | 378 | 2.2 | 0.7 | 4.7 |

Three-point field goals: 2003-04, 1-for-4 (.250). 2004-05, 66-for-166 (.398). Totals, 67-for-170 (.394).
Personal fouls/disqualifications: 2003-04, 1/0. 2004-05, 123/1. Totals, 124/1.

## NBA PLAYOFF RECORD

| Season Team | G | Min. | FGM | FGA | Pct. | FTM | FTA | Pct. | Off. | Def. | Tot. | Ast. | St. | Blk. | TO | Pts. | RPG | APG | PPG |
|---|---|---|---|---|---|---|---|---|---|---|---|---|---|---|---|---|---|---|---|
| 04-05—Indiana | 13 | 214 | 19 | 46 | .413 | 4 | 9 | .444 | 5 | 22 | 27 | 10 | 7 | 7 | 4 | 52 | 2.1 | 0.8 | 4.0 |

Three-point field goals: 2004-05, 10-for-25 (.400). Totals, 10-for-25 (.400).
Personal fouls/disqualifications: 2004-05, 18/0. Totals, 18/0.

# JONES, JUMAINE     F     LAKERS

**PERSONAL:** Born February 10, 1979, in Cocoa, Fla. ... 6-8/218. (2.03/98.9). ... Full name: Jumaine Lanard Jones
**HIGH SCHOOL:** Mitchell-Baker (Camilla, Ga.).
**COLLEGE:** Georgia.
**TRANSACTIONS/CAREER NOTES:** Selected after sophomore season by Atlanta Hawks in first round (27th pick overall) of 1999 NBA Draft. ... Draft rights traded by Hawks to Philadelphia 76ers for future first-round draft choice (June 30, 1999). ... Traded by 76ers with F Tyrone Hill to Cleveland Cavaliers for F Matt Harpring, F Cedric Henderson and F/C Robert Traylor (August 3, 2001). ... Traded by Cavaliers to Sacramento Kings for G Mateen Cleaves (September 10, 2002); trade voided because Cleaves failed physical (September 17, 2002). ... Traded by Cavaliers to Boston Celtics for G J.R. Bremer, C Bruno Sundov and conditional second-round draft pick (July 29, 2003) ... Traded by Celtics with F/C Chris Mihm and G Chucky Atkins to Los Angeles Lakers for G Gary Payton, F Rick Fox and a first-round draft choice (August 13, 2004).

## COLLEGIATE RECORD

| Season Team | G | Min. | FGM | FGA | Pct. | FTM | FTA | Pct. | Reb. | Ast. | Pts. | RPG | APG | PPG |
|---|---|---|---|---|---|---|---|---|---|---|---|---|---|---|
| 97-98—Georgia | 35 | 1031 | 188 | 415 | .453 | 95 | 121 | .785 | 299 | 30 | 515 | 8.5 | 0.9 | 14.7 |

| Season Team | G | Min. | FGM | FGA | Pct. | FTM | FTA | Pct. | Reb. | Ast. | Pts. | RPG | APG | PPG |
|---|---|---|---|---|---|---|---|---|---|---|---|---|---|---|
| | | | | | | | | | | | | AVERAGES | | |
| 98-99—Georgia | 30 | 1032 | 197 | 443 | .445 | 122 | 168 | .726 | 284 | 30 | 564 | 9.5 | 1.0 | 18.8 |
| Totals | 65 | 2063 | 385 | 858 | .449 | 217 | 289 | .751 | 583 | 60 | 1079 | 9.0 | 0.9 | 16.6 |

Three-point field goals: 1997-98, 44-for-124 (.355). 1998-99, 48-for-138 (.348). Totals, 92-for-262 (.351).

### NBA REGULAR-SEASON RECORD

| Season Team | G | Min. | FGM | FGA | Pct. | FTM | FTA | Pct. | REBOUNDS Off. | Def. | Tot. | Ast. | St. | Blk. | TO | Pts. | AVERAGES RPG | APG | PPG |
|---|---|---|---|---|---|---|---|---|---|---|---|---|---|---|---|---|---|---|---|
| 99-00—Philadelphia | 33 | 138 | 22 | 58 | .379 | 11 | 18 | .611 | 16 | 22 | 38 | 5 | 6 | 5 | 14 | 57 | 1.2 | 0.2 | 1.7 |
| 00-01—Philadelphia | 65 | 866 | 122 | 275 | .444 | 40 | 53 | .755 | 63 | 126 | 189 | 32 | 30 | 15 | 39 | 304 | 2.9 | 0.5 | 4.7 |
| 01-02—Cleveland | 81 | 2142 | 287 | 640 | .448 | 45 | 68 | .662 | 125 | 365 | 490 | 116 | 75 | 46 | 79 | 671 | 6.0 | 1.4 | 8.3 |
| 02-03—Cleveland | 80 | 2204 | 308 | 710 | .434 | 57 | 83 | .687 | 106 | 299 | 405 | 112 | 67 | 22 | 107 | 784 | 5.1 | 1.4 | 9.8 |
| 03-04—Boston | 42 | 373 | 33 | 96 | .344 | 14 | 23 | .609 | 24 | 44 | 68 | 14 | 12 | 9 | 19 | 93 | 1.6 | 0.3 | 2.2 |
| 04-05—L.A. Lakers | 76 | 1830 | 210 | 486 | .432 | 55 | 75 | .733 | 107 | 291 | 398 | 65 | 44 | 24 | 49 | 577 | 5.2 | 0.9 | 7.6 |
| Totals | 377 | 7553 | 982 | 2265 | .434 | 222 | 320 | .694 | 441 | 1147 | 1588 | 344 | 234 | 121 | 307 | 2486 | 4.2 | 0.9 | 6.6 |

Three-point field goals: 1999-00, 2-for-4 (.500). 2000-01, 20-for-60 (.333). 2001-02, 52-for-168 (.310). 2002-03, 111-for-314 (.354). 2003-04, 13-for-44 (.295). 2004-05, 102-for-261 (.391). Totals, 300-for-851 (.353).

Personal fouls/disqualifications: 1999-00, 10/0. 2000-01, 68/0. 2001-02, 184/3. 2002-03, 176/1. 2003-04, 48/0. 2004-05, 165/1. Totals, 651/5.

### NBA PLAYOFF RECORD

| Season Team | G | Min. | FGM | FGA | Pct. | FTM | FTA | Pct. | REBOUNDS Off. | Def. | Tot. | Ast. | St. | Blk. | TO | Pts. | AVERAGES RPG | APG | PPG |
|---|---|---|---|---|---|---|---|---|---|---|---|---|---|---|---|---|---|---|---|
| 99-00—Philadelphia | 4 | 8 | 1 | 3 | .333 | 0 | 0 | ... | 0 | 0 | 0 | 0 | 0 | 0 | 0 | 2 | 0.0 | 0.0 | 0.5 |
| 00-01—Philadelphia | 23 | 447 | 52 | 125 | .416 | 15 | 21 | .714 | 35 | 49 | 84 | 17 | 10 | 11 | 14 | 127 | 3.7 | 0.7 | 5.5 |
| 03-04—Boston | 2 | 28 | 2 | 6 | .333 | 0 | 0 | ... | 1 | 4 | 5 | 2 | 0 | 0 | 0 | 4 | 2.5 | 1.0 | 2.0 |
| Totals | 29 | 483 | 55 | 134 | .410 | 15 | 21 | .714 | 36 | 53 | 89 | 19 | 10 | 11 | 14 | 133 | 3.1 | 0.7 | 4.6 |

Three-point field goals: 1999-00, 0-for-2. 2000-01, 8-for-32 (.250). 2003-04, 0-for-2. Totals, 8-for-36 (.222).
Personal fouls/disqualifications: 2000-01, 33/0. 2003-04, 4/0. Totals, 37/0.

# JONES, MARK  G  MAGIC

**PERSONAL:** Born May 25, 1975 ... 6-6/215. (1.98/97.5).
**COLLEGE:** Central Florida.
**TRANSACTIONS/CAREER NOTES:** Was not drafted by an NBA franchise. ... Signed as free agent to 10-day contract by Orlando Magic (March 23, 2005). ... Released from 10-day contract (March 30, 2005). ... Signed for remainder of season by Magic (April 8, 2005).

### COLLEGIATE RECORD

| Season Team | G | Min. | FGM | FGA | Pct. | FTM | FTA | Pct. | Reb. | Ast. | Pts. | AVERAGES RPG | APG | PPG |
|---|---|---|---|---|---|---|---|---|---|---|---|---|---|---|
| 93-94—Anderson | | | | | | Statistics unavailable. | | | | | | | | |
| 94-95—Anderson | | | | | | Statistics unavailable. | | | | | | | | |
| 95-96—Minnesota | 32 | 592 | 104 | 229 | .454 | 33 | 60 | .550 | 102 | 38 | 256 | 3.2 | 1.2 | 8.0 |
| 96-97—C Florida | | | | | | Did not play—transfer student. | | | | | | | | |
| 97-98—C Florida | 28 | 914 | 220 | 446 | .493 | 111 | 165 | .673 | 201 | 62 | 581 | 7.2 | 2.2 | 20.8 |
| Totals | 60 | 1506 | 324 | 675 | .480 | 144 | 225 | .640 | 303 | 100 | 837 | 5.1 | 1.7 | 14.0 |

Three-point field goals: 1995-96, 15-for-51 (.294). 1997-98, 30-for-85 (.353). Totals, 45-for-136 (.331).

### CBA RECORD

| Season Team | G | Min. | FGM | FGA | Pct. | FTM | FTA | Pct. | Reb. | Ast. | Pts. | AVERAGES RPG | APG | PPG |
|---|---|---|---|---|---|---|---|---|---|---|---|---|---|---|
| 98-99—Fort Wayne | 8 | 147 | 16 | 45 | .356 | 2 | 6 | .333 | 22 | 8 | 43 | 2.8 | 1.0 | 5.4 |
| 04-05—Great Lakes | 41 | 1603 | 311 | 657 | .473 | 203 | 253 | .802 | 220 | 107 | 852 | 5.4 | 2.6 | 20.8 |
| Totals | 49 | 1750 | 327 | 702 | .466 | 205 | 259 | .792 | 242 | 115 | 895 | 4.9 | 2.3 | 18.3 |

Three-point field goals: 1998-99, 9-for-13 (.692). 2004-05, 27-for-85 (.318). Totals, 36-for-98 (.367).

### SWITZERLAND RECORD

| Season Team | G | Min. | FGM | FGA | Pct. | FTM | FTA | Pct. | Reb. | Ast. | Pts. | AVERAGES RPG | APG | PPG |
|---|---|---|---|---|---|---|---|---|---|---|---|---|---|---|
| 99-00—Morges | 10 | 390 | 116 | 232 | .500 | 50 | 60 | .833 | 68 | 34 | 299 | 6.8 | 3.4 | 29.9 |

Three-point field goals: 1999-00, 17-for-49 (.347). Totals, 17-for-49 (.347).

### FRENCH LEAGUE RECORD

| Season Team | G | Min. | FGM | FGA | Pct. | FTM | FTA | Pct. | Reb. | Ast. | Pts. | AVERAGES RPG | APG | PPG |
|---|---|---|---|---|---|---|---|---|---|---|---|---|---|---|
| 00-01—Bourg-en-Bresse | 10 | 322 | 79 | 171 | .462 | 17 | 31 | .548 | 62 | 29 | 196 | 6.2 | 2.9 | 19.6 |
| 01-02—Chalon | 2 | 18 | 2 | 6 | .333 | 0 | 0 | ... | 1 | 0 | 4 | 0.5 | 0.0 | 2.0 |
| Totals | 12 | 340 | 81 | 177 | .458 | 17 | 31 | .548 | 63 | 29 | 200 | 5.3 | 2.4 | 16.7 |

Three-point field goals: 2000-01, 21-for-58 (.362). 2001-02, 0-for-2. Totals, 21-for-60 (.350).

### VENEZUELAN LEAGUE RECORD

| Season Team | G | Min. | FGM | FGA | Pct. | FTM | FTA | Pct. | Reb. | Ast. | Pts. | AVERAGES RPG | APG | PPG |
|---|---|---|---|---|---|---|---|---|---|---|---|---|---|---|
| 03-04—Cocodrilos | 3 | ... | ... | ... | ... | ... | ... | ... | 7 | 6 | 77 | 2.3 | 2.0 | 25.7 |

### NBA REGULAR-SEASON RECORD

| Season Team | G | Min. | FGM | FGA | Pct. | FTM | FTA | Pct. | REBOUNDS Off. | Def. | Tot. | Ast. | St. | Blk. | TO | Pts. | AVERAGES RPG | APG | PPG |
|---|---|---|---|---|---|---|---|---|---|---|---|---|---|---|---|---|---|---|---|
| 04-05—Orlando | 10 | 116 | 9 | 31 | .290 | 5 | 10 | .500 | 6 | 7 | 13 | 6 | 5 | 2 | 3 | 23 | 1.3 | 0.6 | 2.3 |

Three-point field goals: 2004-05, 0-for-4. Totals, 0-for-4 (.000).
Personal fouls/disqualifications: 2004-05, 16/0. Totals, 16/0.

# KAMAN, CHRIS      C      CLIPPERS

**PERSONAL:** Born April 28, 1982, in Grand Rapids, Mich. ... 7-0/255. (2.13/115.7). ... Full name: Christopher Zane Kaman
**HIGH SCHOOL:** Tri-unity Christian (Wyoming, Mich.).
**COLLEGE:** Central Michigan.
**TRANSACTIONS/CAREER NOTES:** Selected after junior season by Los Angeles Clippers in first round (sixth overall pick) of 2003 NBA Draft.

### COLLEGIATE RECORD

| Season Team | G | Min. | FGM | FGA | Pct. | FTM | FTA | Pct. | Reb. | Ast. | Pts. | AVERAGES RPG | APG | PPG |
|---|---|---|---|---|---|---|---|---|---|---|---|---|---|---|
| 00-01—Central Michigan | 28 | 520 | 105 | 183 | .574 | 63 | 90 | .700 | 135 | 6 | 273 | 4.8 | 0.2 | 9.8 |
| 01-02—Central Michigan | 24 | 604 | 97 | 158 | .614 | 89 | 137 | .650 | 199 | 22 | 283 | 8.3 | 0.9 | 11.8 |
| 02-03—Central Michigan | 31 | 1055 | 244 | 392 | .622 | 206 | 275 | .749 | 373 | 37 | 694 | 12.0 | 1.2 | 22.4 |
| Totals | 83 | 2179 | 446 | 733 | .608 | 358 | 502 | .713 | 707 | 65 | 1250 | 8.5 | 0.8 | 15.1 |

### NBA REGULAR-SEASON RECORD

| Season Team | G | Min. | FGM | FGA | Pct. | FTM | FTA | Pct. | REBOUNDS Off. | Def. | Tot. | Ast. | St. | Blk. | TO | Pts. | AVERAGES RPG | APG | PPG |
|---|---|---|---|---|---|---|---|---|---|---|---|---|---|---|---|---|---|---|---|
| 03-04—L.A. Clippers | 82 | 1843 | 200 | 435 | .460 | 99 | 142 | .697 | 126 | 335 | 461 | 85 | 23 | 73 | 155 | 499 | 5.6 | 1.0 | 6.1 |
| 04-05—L.A. Clippers | 63 | 1632 | 246 | 495 | .497 | 80 | 121 | .661 | 135 | 288 | 423 | 73 | 26 | 68 | 115 | 572 | 6.7 | 1.2 | 9.1 |
| Totals | 145 | 3475 | 446 | 930 | .480 | 179 | 263 | .681 | 261 | 623 | 884 | 158 | 49 | 141 | 270 | 1071 | 6.1 | 1.1 | 7.4 |

Three-point field goals: 2003-04, 0-for-2. 2004-05, 0-for-1. Totals, 0-for-3 (.000).
Personal fouls/disqualifications: 2003-04, 211/1. 2004-05, 182/2. Totals, 393/3.

# KAPONO, JASON      F      BOBCATS

**PERSONAL:** Born February 2, 1981, in Long Beach, Calif. ... 6-8/213. (2.03/96.6). ... Full name: Jason Alan Kapono
**HIGH SCHOOL:** Artesia (Los Angeles, Calif.).
**COLLEGE:** UCLA.
**TRANSACTIONS/CAREER NOTES:** Selected by Cleveland Cavaliers in second round (31st pick overall) of 2003 NBA Draft. ... Selected by Charlotte Bobcats from Cavaliers in NBA Expansion Draft (June 22, 2004).

### COLLEGIATE RECORD

| Season Team | G | Min. | FGM | FGA | Pct. | FTM | FTA | Pct. | Reb. | Ast. | Pts. | AVERAGES RPG | APG | PPG |
|---|---|---|---|---|---|---|---|---|---|---|---|---|---|---|
| 99-00—UCLA | 33 | 1080 | 191 | 368 | .519 | 65 | 95 | .684 | 144 | 64 | 529 | 4.4 | 1.9 | 16.0 |
| 00-01—UCLA | 32 | 1122 | 167 | 379 | .441 | 133 | 153 | .869 | 183 | 72 | 551 | 5.7 | 2.3 | 17.2 |
| 01-02—UCLA | 33 | 1142 | 170 | 370 | .459 | 101 | 118 | .856 | 169 | 70 | 528 | 5.1 | 2.1 | 16.0 |
| 02-03—UCLA | 29 | 969 | 171 | 374 | .457 | 81 | 92 | .880 | 151 | 59 | 487 | 5.2 | 2.0 | 16.8 |
| Totals | 127 | 4313 | 699 | 1491 | .469 | 380 | 458 | .830 | 647 | 265 | 2095 | 5.1 | 2.1 | 16.5 |

Three-point field goals: 1999-00, 82-for-173 (.474). 2000-01, 84-for-184 (.457). 2001-02, 87-for-192 (.453). 2002-03, 64-for-161 (.398). Totals, 317-for-710 (.446).

### NBA REGULAR-SEASON RECORD

| Season Team | G | Min. | FGM | FGA | Pct. | FTM | FTA | Pct. | REBOUNDS Off. | Def. | Tot. | Ast. | St. | Blk. | TO | Pts. | AVERAGES RPG | APG | PPG |
|---|---|---|---|---|---|---|---|---|---|---|---|---|---|---|---|---|---|---|---|
| 03-04—Cleveland | 41 | 427 | 52 | 129 | .403 | 20 | 24 | .833 | 19 | 36 | 55 | 14 | 13 | 2 | 21 | 145 | 1.3 | 0.3 | 3.5 |
| 04-05—Charlotte | 81 | 1491 | 269 | 671 | .401 | 70 | 85 | .824 | 32 | 132 | 164 | 61 | 40 | 6 | 46 | 688 | 2.0 | 0.8 | 8.5 |
| Totals | 122 | 1918 | 321 | 800 | .401 | 90 | 109 | .826 | 51 | 168 | 219 | 75 | 53 | 8 | 67 | 833 | 1.8 | 0.6 | 6.8 |

Three-point field goals: 2003-04, 21-for-44 (.477). 2004-05, 80-for-194 (.412). Totals, 101-for-238 (.424).
Personal fouls/disqualifications: 2003-04, 41/0. 2004-05, 132/1. Totals, 173/1.

# KASUN, MARIO      C      MAGIC

**PERSONAL:** Born April 5, 1980, in Croatia. ... 7-1/260. (2.16/117.9).
**TRANSACTIONS/CAREER NOTES:** Played in Croatia (1998-99 and 1999-2000). ... Played in Germany (2001-03). ... Selected by Los Angeles Clippers in second round (41st pick overall) of 2002 NBA Draft. ... Draft rights traded by Clippers to Orlando Magic for future considerations (June 26, 2002). ... Signed as free agent by Orlando Magic (August 16, 2004).

### CROATION RECORD

| Season Team | G | Min. | FGM | FGA | Pct. | FTM | FTA | Pct. | Reb. | Ast. | Pts. | AVERAGES RPG | APG | PPG |
|---|---|---|---|---|---|---|---|---|---|---|---|---|---|---|
| 98-99—KK Zagreb | 11 | 94 | 14 | 19 | .737 | 10 | 16 | .625 | 19 | 3 | 38 | 1.7 | 0.3 | 3.5 |
| 98-99—Zagreb | 11 | 94 | 14 | 19 | .737 | 10 | 16 | .625 | 19 | 3 | 38 | 1.7 | 0.3 | 3.5 |
| 99-00—KK Zagreb | 19 | 266 | 43 | 85 | .506 | 18 | 31 | .581 | 55 | 4 | 104 | 2.9 | 0.2 | 5.5 |
| 99-00—Zagreb | 19 | 266 | 43 | 85 | .506 | 18 | 31 | .581 | 55 | 4 | 104 | 2.9 | 0.2 | 5.5 |
| Totals | 60 | 720 | 114 | 208 | .548 | 56 | 94 | .596 | 148 | 14 | 284 | 2.5 | 0.2 | 4.7 |

Three-point field goals: 1999-00, 0-for-1. 1999-00, 0-for-1. Totals, 0-for-2 (.000).

### COLLEGIATE RECORD

| Season Team | G | Min. | FGM | FGA | Pct. | FTM | FTA | Pct. | Reb. | Ast. | Pts. | AVERAGES RPG | APG | PPG |
|---|---|---|---|---|---|---|---|---|---|---|---|---|---|---|
| 00-01—Gonzaga | | | | | | | Did not play. | | | | | | | |

K

## NBA REGULAR-SEASON RECORD

| Season Team | G | Min. | FGM | FGA | Pct. | FTM | FTA | Pct. | REBOUNDS Off. | Def. | Tot. | Ast. | St. | Blk. | TO | Pts. | AVERAGES RPG | APG | PPG |
|---|---|---|---|---|---|---|---|---|---|---|---|---|---|---|---|---|---|---|---|
| 04-05—Orlando.......... | 45 | 356 | 47 | 98 | .480 | 24 | 43 | .558 | 52 | 76 | 128 | 8 | 8 | 13 | 26 | 118 | 2.8 | 0.2 | 2.6 |
| Totals .................... | 45 | 356 | 47 | 98 | .480 | 24 | 43 | .558 | 52 | 76 | 128 | 8 | 8 | 13 | 26 | 118 | 2.8 | 0.2 | 2.6 |

Three-point field goals: 2004-05, 0-for-1. Totals, 0-for-1 (.000).
Personal fouls/disqualifications: 2004-05, 86/1. Totals, 86/1.

## GERMAN LEAGUE RECORD

| Season Team | G | Min. | FGM | FGA | Pct. | FTM | FTA | Pct. | Reb. | Ast. | Pts. | AVERAGES RPG | APG | PPG |
|---|---|---|---|---|---|---|---|---|---|---|---|---|---|---|
| 01-02—Cologne ........................ | 1 | 1 | 0 | 0 | ... | 0 | 0 | ... | 0 | 0 | 0 | 0.0 | 0.0 | 0.0 |
| 02-03—Frankfurt..................... | 20 | 383 | 74 | 136 | .544 | 58 | 96 | .604 | 109 | 12 | 206 | 5.5 | 0.6 | 10.3 |
| 03-04—Frankfurt..................... | 27 | 553 | 105 | 185 | .568 | 42 | 85 | .494 | 193 | 15 | 252 | 7.1 | 0.6 | 9.3 |
| Totals ................................. | 48 | 937 | 179 | 321 | .558 | 100 | 181 | .552 | 302 | 27 | 458 | 6.3 | 0.6 | 9.5 |

Three-point field goals: 2003-04, 0-for-1. Totals, 0-for-1 (.000).

# KHRYAPA, VIKTOR — F — TRAIL BLAZERS

**PERSONAL:** Born August 3, 1982, in Kiev, Ukraine. ... 6-9/210. (2.06/95.3).
**TRANSACTIONS/CAREER NOTES:** Played in Russia (2000-04). ... Selected by New Jersey Nets in first round (22nd pick overall) of 2004 NBA Draft. ... Draft rights traded by Nets to Portland Trail Blazers for G Eddie Gill (June 24, 2004).

## RUSSIAN LEAGUE RECORD

| Season Team | G | Min. | FGM | FGA | Pct. | FTM | FTA | Pct. | Reb. | Ast. | Pts. | AVERAGES RPG | APG | PPG |
|---|---|---|---|---|---|---|---|---|---|---|---|---|---|---|
| 99-00—Avtodor Saratov ............ | 13 | 137 | 17 | 32 | .531 | 10 | 13 | .769 | 33 | 12 | 46 | 2.5 | 0.9 | 3.5 |
| 00-01—Avtodor Saratov ............ | 34 | 445 | 157 | 310 | .506 | 116 | 192 | .604 | 193 | 87 | 445 | 5.7 | 2.6 | 13.1 |
| 01-02—Avtodor Saratov ............ | 32 | 1036 | 150 | 262 | .573 | 104 | 139 | .748 | 234 | 155 | 419 | 7.3 | 4.8 | 13.1 |
| 02-03—CSKA........................... | 30 | 652 | 107 | 189 | .566 | 62 | 73 | .849 | 178 | 75 | 312 | 5.9 | 2.5 | 10.4 |
| 03-04—CSKA........................... | 32 | 584 | 69 | 129 | .535 | 62 | 73 | .849 | 126 | 56 | 219 | 3.9 | 1.8 | 6.8 |
| Totals ................................. | 141 | 2854 | 500 | 922 | .542 | 354 | 490 | .722 | 764 | 385 | 1441 | 5.4 | 2.7 | 10.2 |

Three-point field goals: 1999-00, 2-for-7 (.286). 2000-01, 15-for-55 (.273). 2001-02, 15-for-49 (.306). 2002-03, 36-for-58 (.621). 2003-04, 26-for-57 (.456). Totals, 94-for-226 (.416).

## NBA REGULAR-SEASON RECORD

| Season Team | G | Min. | FGM | FGA | Pct. | FTM | FTA | Pct. | REBOUNDS Off. | Def. | Tot. | Ast. | St. | Blk. | TO | Pts. | AVERAGES RPG | APG | PPG |
|---|---|---|---|---|---|---|---|---|---|---|---|---|---|---|---|---|---|---|---|
| 04-05—Portland.......... | 32 | 523 | 54 | 124 | .435 | 23 | 42 | .548 | 28 | 80 | 108 | 25 | 20 | 18 | 33 | 135 | 3.4 | 0.8 | 4.2 |

Three-point field goals: 2004-05, 4-for-11 (.364). Totals, 4-for-11 (.364).
Personal fouls/disqualifications: 2004-05, 80/0. Totals, 80/0.

# KIDD, JASON — G — NETS

**PERSONAL:** Born March 23, 1973, in San Francisco. ... 6-4/212. (1.93/96.2). ... Full name: Jason Frederick Kidd
**HIGH SCHOOL:** St. Joseph of Notre Dame (Alameda, Calif.).
**COLLEGE:** California.
**TRANSACTIONS/CAREER NOTES:** Selected after sophomore season by Dallas Mavericks in first round (second pick overall) of 1994 NBA Draft. ... Traded by Mavericks with G Tony Dumas and C Loren Meyer to Phoenix Suns for G Sam Cassell, F A.C. Green, F Michael Finley and 1997 or 1998 conditional second-round draft choice (December 26, 1996). ... Traded by Suns with C Chris Dudley to New Jersey Nets for G Stephon Marbury, F Johnny Newman and C Soumaila Samake (July 18, 2001).
**MISCELLANEOUS:** Member of gold-medal-winning U.S. Olympic team (2000).

## COLLEGIATE RECORD

**NOTES:** THE SPORTING NEWS All-America first team (1994). ... Led NCAA Division I with 3.8 steals per game (1993). ... Led NCAA Division I with 9.1 assists per game (1994).

| Season Team | G | Min. | FGM | FGA | Pct. | FTM | FTA | Pct. | Reb. | Ast. | Pts. | AVERAGES RPG | APG | PPG |
|---|---|---|---|---|---|---|---|---|---|---|---|---|---|---|
| 92-93—California ...................... | 29 | 922 | 133 | 287 | .463 | 88 | 134 | .657 | 142 | 222 | 378 | 4.9 | 7.7 | 13.0 |
| 93-94—California ...................... | 30 | 1053 | 166 | 352 | .472 | 117 | 169 | .692 | 207 | 272 | 500 | 6.9 | 9.1 | 16.7 |
| Totals ................................. | 59 | 1975 | 299 | 639 | .468 | 205 | 303 | .677 | 349 | 494 | 878 | 5.9 | 8.4 | 14.9 |

Three-point field goals: 1992-93, 24-for-84 (.286). 1993-94, 51-for-141 (.362). Totals, 75-for-225 (.333).

## NBA REGULAR-SEASON RECORD

**RECORDS:** Shares single-game record for most turnovers—14 (November 17, 2000, vs. New York).
**HONORS:** NBA Co-Rookie of the Year (1995). ... All-NBA first team (1999, 2000, 2001, 2002, 2004). ... All-NBA second team (2003). ... NBA All-Defensive first team (1999, 2001, 2002). ... NBA All-Defensive second team (2000, 2003, 2004, 2005). ... NBA All-Rookie first team (1995).
**NOTES:** Led NBA with 8.9 assists per game (2003).

| Season Team | G | Min. | FGM | FGA | Pct. | FTM | FTA | Pct. | REBOUNDS Off. | Def. | Tot. | Ast. | St. | Blk. | TO | Pts. | AVERAGES RPG | APG | PPG |
|---|---|---|---|---|---|---|---|---|---|---|---|---|---|---|---|---|---|---|---|
| 94-95—Dallas.............. | 79 | 2668 | 330 | 857 | .385 | 192 | 275 | .698 | 152 | 278 | 430 | 607 | 151 | 24 | 250 | 922 | 5.4 | 7.7 | 11.7 |
| 95-96—Dallas.............. | 81 | 3034 | 493 | 1293 | .381 | 229 | 331 | .692 | 203 | 350 | 553 | 783 | 175 | 26 | *328 | 1348 | 6.8 | 9.7 | 16.6 |
| 96-97—Dal.-Pho.......... | 55 | 1964 | 213 | 529 | .403 | 112 | 165 | .679 | 64 | 185 | 249 | 496 | 124 | 20 | 142 | 599 | 4.5 | 9.0 | 10.9 |
| 97-98—Phoenix .......... | 82 | 3118 | 357 | 859 | .416 | 167 | 209 | .799 | 108 | 402 | 510 | 745 | 162 | 26 | 261 | 954 | 6.2 | 9.1 | 11.6 |
| 98-99—Phoenix .......... | 50 | *2060 | 310 | 698 | .444 | 181 | 239 | .757 | 87 | 252 | 339 | *539 | 114 | 19 | 150 | 846 | 6.8 | *10.8 | 16.9 |

| Season Team | G | Min. | FGM | FGA | Pct. | FTM | FTA | Pct. | REBOUNDS Off. | Def. | Tot. | Ast. | St. | Blk. | TO | Pts. | AVERAGES RPG | APG | PPG |
|---|---|---|---|---|---|---|---|---|---|---|---|---|---|---|---|---|---|---|---|
| 99-00—Phoenix | 67 | 2616 | 350 | 855 | .409 | 203 | 245 | .829 | 96 | 387 | 483 | 678 | 134 | 28 | 226 | 959 | 7.2 | *10.1 | 14.3 |
| 00-01—Phoenix | 77 | 3065 | 451 | 1097 | .411 | 328 | 403 | .814 | 91 | 403 | 494 | *753 | 166 | 23 | 286 | 1299 | 6.4 | *9.8 | 16.9 |
| 01-02—New Jersey | 82 | 3056 | 445 | 1138 | .391 | 201 | 247 | .814 | 130 | 465 | 595 | 808 | *175 | 20 | *286 | 1208 | 7.3 | 9.9 | 14.7 |
| 02-03—New Jersey | 80 | 2989 | 515 | 1244 | .414 | 339 | 403 | .841 | 110 | 394 | 504 | 711 | 179 | 25 | 296 | 1495 | 6.3 | 8.9 | 18.7 |
| 03-04—New Jersey | 67 | 2450 | 368 | 959 | .384 | 206 | 249 | .827 | 85 | 343 | 428 | 618 | 122 | 14 | 214 | 1036 | 6.4 | 9.2 | 15.5 |
| 04-05—New Jersey | 66 | 2435 | 340 | 855 | .398 | 142 | 192 | .740 | 94 | 394 | 488 | 545 | 123 | 9 | 167 | 951 | 7.4 | 8.3 | 14.4 |
| Totals | 786 | 29455 | 4172 | 10384 | .402 | 2300 | 2958 | .778 | 1220 | 3853 | 5073 | 7283 | 1625 | 234 | 2606 | 11617 | 6.5 | 9.3 | 14.8 |

Three-point field goals: 1994-95, 70-for-257 (.272). 1995-96, 133-for-396 (.336). 1996-97, 61-for-165 (.370). 1997-98, 73-for-233 (.313). 1998-99, 45-for-123 (.366). 1999-00, 56-for-166 (.337). 2000-01, 69-for-232 (.297). 2001-02, 117-for-364 (.321). 2002-03, 126-for-370 (.341). 2003-04, 94-for-293 (.321). 2004-05, 129-for-358 (.360). Totals, 973-for-2957 (.329).

Personal fouls/disqualifications: 1994-95, 146/0. 1995-96, 155/0. 1996-97, 114/0. 1997-98, 142/0. 1998-99, 108/1. 1999-00, 148/2. 2000-01, 171/1. 2001-02, 136/0. 2002-03, 127/0. 2003-04, 110/0. 2004-05, 110/0. Totals, 1467/4.

### NBA PLAYOFF RECORD

| Season Team | G | Min. | FGM | FGA | Pct. | FTM | FTA | Pct. | REBOUNDS Off. | Def. | Tot. | Ast. | St. | Blk. | TO | Pts. | AVERAGES RPG | APG | PPG |
|---|---|---|---|---|---|---|---|---|---|---|---|---|---|---|---|---|---|---|---|
| 96-97—Phoenix | 5 | 207 | 21 | 53 | .396 | 10 | 19 | .526 | 4 | 26 | 30 | 49 | 11 | 2 | 13 | 60 | 6.0 | 9.8 | 12.0 |
| 97-98—Phoenix | 4 | 171 | 22 | 58 | .379 | 13 | 16 | .813 | 5 | 18 | 23 | 31 | 16 | 2 | 12 | 57 | 5.8 | 7.8 | 14.3 |
| 98-99—Phoenix | 3 | 126 | 18 | 43 | .419 | 5 | 7 | .714 | 1 | 6 | 7 | 31 | 5 | 1 | 9 | 45 | 2.3 | 10.3 | 15.0 |
| 99-00—Phoenix | 6 | 229 | 22 | 55 | .400 | 7 | 9 | .778 | 8 | 32 | 40 | 53 | 11 | 1 | 23 | 59 | 6.7 | 8.8 | 9.8 |
| 00-01—Phoenix | 4 | 166 | 22 | 69 | .319 | 9 | 12 | .750 | 9 | 15 | 24 | 53 | 8 | 0 | 12 | 57 | 6.0 | 13.3 | 14.3 |
| 01-02—New Jersey | 20 | 803 | 147 | 354 | .415 | 80 | 99 | .808 | 42 | 122 | 164 | 182 | 34 | 8 | 67 | 391 | 8.2 | 9.1 | 19.6 |
| 02-03—New Jersey | 20 | 852 | 137 | 341 | .402 | 94 | 114 | .825 | 36 | 118 | 154 | 163 | 36 | 4 | 79 | 402 | 7.7 | 8.2 | 20.1 |
| 03-04—New Jersey | 11 | 474 | 43 | 129 | .333 | 43 | 53 | .811 | 16 | 57 | 73 | 99 | 25 | 6 | 43 | 139 | 6.6 | 9.0 | 12.6 |
| 04-05—New Jersey | 4 | 182 | 26 | 67 | .388 | 6 | 11 | .545 | 10 | 26 | 36 | 29 | 10 | 0 | 9 | 69 | 9.0 | 7.3 | 17.3 |
| Totals | 77 | 3210 | 458 | 1169 | .392 | 267 | 340 | .785 | 131 | 420 | 551 | 690 | 156 | 24 | 267 | 1279 | 7.2 | 9.0 | 16.6 |

Three-point field goals: 1996-97, 8-for-22 (.364). 1997-98, 0-for-7. 1998-99, 4-for-16 (.250). 1999-00, 8-for-22 (.364). 2000-01, 4-for-17 (.235). 2001-02, 17-for-90 (.189). 2002-03, 34-for-104 (.327). 2003-04, 10-for-48 (.208). 2004-05, 11-for-30 (.367). Totals, 96-for-356 (.270).

Personal fouls/disqualifications: 1996-97, 11/0. 1997-98, 13/0. 1998-99, 12/0. 1999-00, 14/0. 2000-01, 13/0. 2001-02, 40/0. 2002-03, 46/0. 2003-04, 15/0. 2004-05, 16/0. Totals, 180/0.

### NBA ALL-STAR GAME RECORD

| Season Team | Min. | FGM | FGA | Pct. | FTM | FTA | Pct. | REBOUNDS Off. | Def. | Tot. | Ast. | PF | Dq. | St. | Blk. | TO | Pts. |
|---|---|---|---|---|---|---|---|---|---|---|---|---|---|---|---|---|---|
| 1996—Dallas | 22 | 3 | 4 | .750 | 0 | 0 | ... | 2 | 4 | 6 | 10 | 1 | 0 | 2 | 0 | 2 | 7 |
| 1998—Phoenix | 19 | 0 | 1 | .000 | 0 | 0 | ... | 0 | 1 | 1 | 9 | 2 | 0 | 0 | 0 | 2 | 0 |
| 2000—Phoenix | 34 | 4 | 9 | .444 | 0 | 0 | ... | 0 | 5 | 5 | 14 | 0 | 0 | 4 | 0 | 6 | 11 |
| 2001—Phoenix | 30 | 4 | 6 | .667 | 0 | 0 | ... | 0 | 4 | 4 | 2 | 3 | 0 | 1 | 0 | 5 | 11 |
| 2002—New Jersey | 18 | 1 | 2 | .500 | 0 | 0 | ... | 0 | 1 | 1 | 3 | 0 | 0 | 1 | 0 | 1 | 2 |
| 2003—New Jersey | 33 | 4 | 9 | .444 | 2 | 2 | 1.000 | 1 | 4 | 5 | 10 | 0 | 0 | 5 | 0 | 2 | 11 |
| 2004—New Jersey | 22 | 4 | 6 | .667 | 3 | 4 | .750 | 0 | 3 | 3 | 10 | 1 | 0 | 2 | 0 | 3 | 14 |
| Totals | 178 | 20 | 37 | .541 | 5 | 6 | .833 | 3 | 22 | 25 | 58 | 7 | 0 | 15 | 0 | 21 | 56 |

Three-point field goals: 1996, 1-for-2 (.500). 2000, 3-for-6 (.500). 2001, 3-for-4 (.750). 2002, 0-for-1. 2003, 1-for-4 (.250). 2004, 3-for-4 (.750). Totals, 11-for-21 (.524).

# KIRILENKO, ANDREI     F     JAZZ

**PERSONAL:** Born February 18, 1981, in Russia. ... 6-9/210. (2.06/95.3).
**TRANSACTIONS/CAREER NOTES:** Played in Russia (1996-2001). ... Selected by Utah Jazz in first round (24th pick overall) of 1999 NBA Draft.
**MISCELLANEOUS:** Member of Russian Olympic team (2000).

### RUSSIAN LEAGUE RECORD

| Season Team | G | Min. | FGM | FGA | Pct. | FTM | FTA | Pct. | Reb. | Ast. | Pts. | AVERAGES RPG | APG | PPG |
|---|---|---|---|---|---|---|---|---|---|---|---|---|---|---|
| 96-97—Spartak | 3 | 16 | 2 | 5 | .400 | 2 | 4 | .500 | 4 | 1 | 6 | 1.3 | 0.3 | 2.0 |
| 97-98—Spartak | 41 | 993 | 164 | 315 | .521 | 143 | 223 | .641 | 188 | 58 | 486 | 4.6 | 1.4 | 11.9 |
| 98-99—CSKA | 26 | 495 | 116 | 178 | .652 | 86 | 125 | .688 | 110 | 54 | 323 | 4.2 | 2.1 | 12.4 |
| 99-00—CSKA | 37 | 841 | 173 | 235 | .736 | 131 | 185 | .708 | 227 | 94 | 488 | 6.1 | 2.5 | 13.2 |
| 00-01—CSKA | 26 | 376 | 128 | 214 | .598 | 106 | 162 | .654 | 141 | 59 | 376 | 5.4 | 2.3 | 14.5 |
| Totals | 133 | 2721 | 583 | 947 | .616 | 468 | 699 | .670 | 670 | 266 | 1679 | 5.0 | 2.0 | 12.6 |

Three-point field goals: 1996-97, 0-for-1. 1997-98, 15-for-48 (.313). 1998-99, 5-for-11 (.455). 1999-00, 11-for-24 (.458). 2000-01, 14-for-42 (.333). Totals, 45-for-126 (.357).

### NBA REGULAR-SEASON RECORD

**HONORS:** NBA All-Defensive second team (2004, 2005). ... NBA All-Rookie first team (2002).

| Season Team | G | Min. | FGM | FGA | Pct. | FTM | FTA | Pct. | REBOUNDS Off. | Def. | Tot. | Ast. | St. | Blk. | TO | Pts. | AVERAGES RPG | APG | PPG |
|---|---|---|---|---|---|---|---|---|---|---|---|---|---|---|---|---|---|---|---|
| 01-02—Utah | 82 | 2151 | 285 | 633 | .450 | 285 | 371 | .768 | 149 | 253 | 402 | 94 | 116 | 159 | 108 | 880 | 4.9 | 1.1 | 10.7 |
| 02-03—Utah | 80 | 2213 | 315 | 642 | .491 | 296 | 370 | .800 | 147 | 273 | 420 | 138 | 118 | 175 | 136 | 963 | 5.3 | 1.7 | 12.0 |
| 03-04—Utah | 78 | 2895 | 412 | 931 | .443 | 392 | 496 | .790 | 226 | 403 | 629 | 244 | 150 | 215 | 215 | 1284 | 8.1 | 3.1 | 16.5 |
| 04-05—Utah | 41 | 1349 | 207 | 420 | .493 | 203 | 259 | .784 | 89 | 166 | 255 | 132 | 67 | 136 | 90 | 640 | 6.2 | 3.2 | 15.6 |
| Totals | 281 | 8608 | 1219 | 2626 | .464 | 1176 | 1496 | .786 | 611 | 1095 | 1706 | 608 | 451 | 685 | 549 | 3767 | 6.1 | 2.2 | 13.4 |

Three-point field goals: 2001-02, 25-for-100 (.250). 2002-03, 37-for-114 (.325). 2003-04, 68-for-201 (.338). 2004-05, 23-for-77 (.299). Totals, 153-for-492 (.311).

Personal fouls/disqualifications: 2001-02, 156/2. 2002-03, 185/0. 2003-04, 174/0. 2004-05, 101/1. Totals, 616/3.

## NBA PLAYOFF RECORD

| Season Team | G | Min. | FGM | FGA | Pct. | FTM | FTA | Pct. | REBOUNDS Off. | Def. | Tot. | Ast. | St. | Blk. | TO | Pts. | AVERAGES RPG | APG | PPG |
|---|---|---|---|---|---|---|---|---|---|---|---|---|---|---|---|---|---|---|---|
| 01-02—Utah............... | 4 | 122 | 11 | 28 | .393 | 13 | 16 | .813 | 4 | 11 | 15 | 4 | 7 | 10 | 6 | 35 | 3.8 | 1.0 | 8.8 |
| 02-03—Utah............... | 5 | 145 | 18 | 43 | .419 | 21 | 24 | .875 | 8 | 16 | 24 | 7 | 3 | 10 | 6 | 58 | 4.8 | 1.4 | 11.6 |
| **Totals** ................. | 9 | 267 | 29 | 71 | .408 | 34 | 40 | .850 | 12 | 27 | 39 | 11 | 10 | 20 | 12 | 93 | 4.3 | 1.2 | 10.3 |

Three-point field goals: 2001-02, 0-for-4. 2002-03, 1-for-7 (.143). Totals, 1-for-11 (.091).
Personal fouls/disqualifications: 2001-02, 10/0. 2002-03, 6/0. Totals, 16/0.

## NBA ALL-STAR GAME RECORD

| Season Team | Min. | FGM | FGA | Pct. | FTM | FTA | Pct. | REBOUNDS Off. | Def. | Tot. | Ast. | PF | Dq. | St. | Blk. | TO | Pts. |
|---|---|---|---|---|---|---|---|---|---|---|---|---|---|---|---|---|---|
| 2004—Utah ..................... | 12 | 1 | 3 | .333 | 0 | 0 | ... | 0 | 1 | 1 | 0 | 0 | 0 | 0 | 1 | 0 | 2 |

Three-point field goals: 2004, 0-for-1. Totals, 0-for-1 (.000).

# KITTLES, KERRY　　　　　　　　　　G

**PERSONAL:** Born June 12, 1974, in Dayton, Ohio. ... 6-5/180. (1.96/81.6).
**HIGH SCHOOL:** St. Augustine (New Orleans).
**COLLEGE:** Villanova.
**TRANSACTIONS/CAREER NOTES:** Selected by New Jersey Nets in first round (eighth pick overall) of 1996 NBA Draft. ... Traded by Nets to Los Angeles Clippers for second-round draft choice (July 29, 2004). ... Waived by Clippers (August 3, 2005).

## COLLEGIATE RECORD

**NOTES:** The Sporting News All-America first team (1996).

| Season Team | G | Min. | FGM | FGA | Pct. | FTM | FTA | Pct. | Reb. | Ast. | Pts. | AVERAGES RPG | APG | PPG |
|---|---|---|---|---|---|---|---|---|---|---|---|---|---|---|
| 92-93—Villanova...................... | 27 | 875 | 108 | 224 | .482 | 37 | 55 | .673 | 94 | 79 | 294 | 3.5 | 2.9 | 10.9 |
| 93-94—Villanova...................... | 32 | 1258 | 233 | 516 | .452 | 91 | 129 | .705 | 207 | 109 | 630 | 6.5 | 3.4 | 19.7 |
| 94-95—Villanova...................... | 33 | 1218 | 264 | 504 | .524 | 92 | 120 | .767 | 201 | 115 | 706 | 6.1 | 3.5 | 21.4 |
| 95-96—Villanova...................... | 30 | 1059 | 216 | 475 | .455 | 103 | 145 | .710 | 213 | 105 | 613 | 7.1 | 3.5 | 20.4 |
| **Totals** ...................................... | 122 | 4410 | 821 | 1719 | .478 | 323 | 449 | .719 | 715 | 408 | 2243 | 5.9 | 3.3 | 18.4 |

Three-point field goals: 1992-93, 41-for-95 (.432). 1993-94, 73-for-209 (.349). 1994-95, 86-for-209 (.411). 1995-96, 78-for-193 (.404). Totals, 278-for-706 (.394).

## NBA REGULAR-SEASON RECORD

**RECORDS:** Holds single-season record for most three-point field goals made by a rookie—158 (1997).
**HONORS:** NBA All-Rookie second team (1997).

| Season Team | G | Min. | FGM | FGA | Pct. | FTM | FTA | Pct. | REBOUNDS Off. | Def. | Tot. | Ast. | St. | Blk. | TO | Pts. | AVERAGES RPG | APG | PPG |
|---|---|---|---|---|---|---|---|---|---|---|---|---|---|---|---|---|---|---|---|
| 96-97—New Jersey ..... | 82 | 3012 | 507 | 1189 | .426 | 175 | 227 | .771 | 106 | 213 | 319 | 249 | 157 | 35 | 127 | 1347 | 3.9 | 3.0 | 16.4 |
| 97-98—New Jersey ..... | 77 | 2814 | 508 | 1154 | .440 | 202 | 250 | .808 | 132 | 230 | 362 | 176 | 132 | 37 | 106 | 1328 | 4.7 | 2.3 | 17.2 |
| 98-99—New Jersey ..... | 46 | 1570 | 227 | 613 | .370 | 88 | 114 | .772 | 52 | 139 | 191 | 116 | 79 | 26 | 66 | 592 | 4.2 | 2.5 | 12.9 |
| 99-00—New Jersey ..... | 62 | 1896 | 305 | 698 | .437 | 101 | 127 | .795 | 46 | 179 | 225 | 142 | 79 | 19 | 56 | 807 | 3.6 | 2.3 | 13.0 |
| 00-01—New Jersey ..... |  |  |  |  |  | Did not play—injured. |  |  |  |  |  |  |  |  |  |  |  |  |  |
| 01-02—New Jersey ..... | 82 | 2601 | 438 | 940 | .466 | 128 | 172 | .744 | 68 | 207 | 275 | 216 | 130 | 31 | 109 | 1102 | 3.4 | 2.6 | 13.4 |
| 02-03—New Jersey ..... | 65 | 1951 | 332 | 711 | .467 | 106 | 135 | .785 | 52 | 200 | 252 | 170 | 101 | 30 | 55 | 848 | 3.9 | 2.6 | 13.0 |
| 03-04—New Jersey ..... | 82 | 2842 | 434 | 959 | .453 | 107 | 136 | .787 | 56 | 271 | 327 | 206 | 125 | 40 | 95 | 1072 | 4.0 | 2.5 | 13.1 |
| 04-05—L.A. Clippers ... | 11 | 243 | 28 | 73 | .384 | 6 | 10 | .600 | 1 | 31 | 32 | 20 | 8 | 3 | 7 | 69 | 2.9 | 1.8 | 6.3 |
| **Totals** ................... | 507 | 16929 | 2779 | 6337 | .439 | 913 | 1171 | .780 | 513 | 1470 | 1983 | 1295 | 811 | 221 | 621 | 7165 | 3.9 | 2.6 | 14.1 |

Three-point field goals: 1996-97, 158-for-419 (.377). 1997-98, 110-for-263 (.418). 1998-99, 50-for-158 (.316). 1999-00, 96-for-240 (.400). 2001-02, 98-for-242 (.405). 2002-03, 78-for-219 (.356). 2003-04, 97-for-276 (.351). 2004-05, 7-for-21 (.333). Totals, 694-for-1838 (.378).
Personal fouls/disqualifications: 1996-97, 165/1. 1997-98, 152/0. 1998-99, 82/0. 1999-00, 120/0. 2001-02, 108/0. 2002-03, 110/1. 2003-04, 144/0. 2004-05, 12/0. Totals, 893/2.

## NBA PLAYOFF RECORD

| Season Team | G | Min. | FGM | FGA | Pct. | FTM | FTA | Pct. | REBOUNDS Off. | Def. | Tot. | Ast. | St. | Blk. | TO | Pts. | AVERAGES RPG | APG | PPG |
|---|---|---|---|---|---|---|---|---|---|---|---|---|---|---|---|---|---|---|---|
| 97-98—New Jersey ..... | 3 | 126 | 17 | 40 | .425 | 10 | 11 | .909 | 0 | 15 | 15 | 8 | 4 | 2 | 7 | 49 | 5.0 | 2.7 | 16.3 |
| 01-02—New Jersey ..... | 20 | 580 | 94 | 216 | .435 | 35 | 45 | .778 | 19 | 44 | 63 | 45 | 32 | 9 | 17 | 241 | 3.2 | 2.3 | 12.1 |
| 02-03—New Jersey ..... | 20 | 613 | 79 | 200 | .395 | 32 | 42 | .762 | 19 | 51 | 70 | 40 | 29 | 5 | 17 | 216 | 3.5 | 2.0 | 10.8 |
| 03-04—New Jersey ..... | 11 | 415 | 60 | 134 | .448 | 21 | 34 | .618 | 10 | 37 | 47 | 23 | 22 | 10 | 11 | 158 | 4.3 | 2.1 | 14.4 |
| **Totals** ................... | 54 | 1734 | 250 | 590 | .424 | 98 | 132 | .742 | 48 | 147 | 195 | 116 | 87 | 26 | 52 | 664 | 3.6 | 2.1 | 12.3 |

Three-point field goals: 1997-98, 5-for-13 (.385). 2001-02, 18-for-68 (.265). 2002-03, 26-for-63 (.413). 2003-04, 17-for-52 (.327). Totals, 66-for-196 (.337).
Personal fouls/disqualifications: 1997-98, 12/1. 2001-02, 37/0. 2002-03, 39/0. 2003-04, 28/0. Totals, 116/1.

# KNIGHT, BRANDIN　　　　　　　　G

**PERSONAL:** Born December 16, 1981, in Livingston, N.J. ... 6-0, 190. ... Full name: Brandin Adar Knight. ... Brother of Brevin Knight, guard, Bobcats.
**HIGH SCHOOL:** Seton Hall Prep (East Orange, N.J.).
**COLLEGE:** Pittsburgh.
**TRANSACTIONS/CAREER NOTES:** Not drafted by an NBA franchise. ... Signed to 10-day contract by Houston Rockets (January 15, 2005). ... Waived by Rockets (January 19, 2005).

## COLLEGIATE RECORD

| Season Team | G | Min. | FGM | FGA | Pct. | FTM | FTA | Pct. | Reb. | Ast. | Pts. | AVERAGES RPG | APG | PPG |
|---|---|---|---|---|---|---|---|---|---|---|---|---|---|---|
| 99-00—Pittsburgh ..................... | 28 | 937 | 85 | 212 | .401 | 43 | 78 | .551 | 106 | 154 | 239 | 3.8 | 5.5 | 8.5 |

**K**

| Season Team | G | Min. | FGM | FGA | Pct. | FTM | FTA | Pct. | Reb. | Ast. | Pts. | RPG | APG | PPG |
|---|---|---|---|---|---|---|---|---|---|---|---|---|---|---|
| 00-01—Pittsburgh | 31 | 999 | 91 | 235 | .387 | 70 | 115 | .609 | 102 | 171 | 285 | 3.3 | 5.5 | 9.2 |
| 01-02—Pittsburgh | 35 | 1284 | 194 | 454 | .427 | 65 | 147 | .442 | 167 | 251 | 546 | 4.8 | 7.2 | 15.6 |
| 02-03—Pittsburgh | 33 | 1087 | 122 | 332 | .367 | 69 | 120 | .575 | 117 | 209 | 370 | 3.5 | 6.3 | 11.2 |
| Totals | 127 | 4307 | 492 | 1233 | .399 | 247 | 460 | .537 | 492 | 785 | 1440 | 3.9 | 6.2 | 11.3 |

Three-point field goals: 1999-00, 26-for-80 (.325). 2000-01, 33-for-128 (.258). 2001-02, 93-for-261 (.356). 2002-03, 57-for-185 (.308). Totals, 209-for-654 (.320).

## NBDL RECORD

| Season Team | G | Min. | FGM | FGA | Pct. | FTM | FTA | Pct. | Reb. | Ast. | Pts. | RPG | APG | PPG |
|---|---|---|---|---|---|---|---|---|---|---|---|---|---|---|
| 03-04—Asheville | 38 | 907 | 128 | 273 | .469 | 41 | 61 | .672 | 89 | 186 | 302 | 2.3 | 4.9 | 7.9 |
| 04-05—Asheville | 22 | 625 | 90 | 209 | .431 | 46 | 72 | .639 | 79 | 111 | 232 | 3.6 | 5.0 | 10.5 |
| Totals | 60 | 1532 | 218 | 482 | .452 | 87 | 133 | .654 | 168 | 297 | 534 | 2.8 | 5.0 | 8.9 |

Three-point field goals: 2003-04, 5-for-25 (.200). 2004-05, 6-for-16 (.375). Totals, 11-for-41 (.268).

## NBA REGULAR-SEASON RECORD

| Season Team | G | Min. | FGM | FGA | Pct. | FTM | FTA | Pct. | Off. | Def. | Tot. | Ast. | St. | Blk. | TO | Pts. | RPG | APG | PPG |
|---|---|---|---|---|---|---|---|---|---|---|---|---|---|---|---|---|---|---|---|
| 04-05—Houston | 1 | 3 | 0 | 1 | .000 | 0 | 0 | ... | 0 | 0 | 0 | 1 | 0 | 0 | 0 | 0 | 0.0 | 1.0 | 0.0 |

# KNIGHT, BREVIN     G     BOBCATS

**PERSONAL:** Born November 8, 1975, in Livingston, N.J. ... 5-10/170. (1.78/77.1). ... Brother of Brandin Knight, guard, Rockets (2004-05).
**HIGH SCHOOL:** Seton Hall Prep (East Orange, N.J.).
**COLLEGE:** Stanford.
**TRANSACTIONS/CAREER NOTES:** Selected by Cleveland Cavaliers in first round (16th pick overall) of 1997 NBA Draft. ... Traded by Cavaliers to Atlanta Hawks for G Jim Jackson, G Anthony Johnson and F/G Larry Robinson (January 2, 2001). ... Traded by Hawks with F/C Lorenzen Wright and draft rights to Pau Gasol to Memphis Grizzlies for F Shareef Abdur-Rahim and draft rights to G Jamaal Tinsley (July 19, 2001). ... Traded by Grizzlies with C Cezary Trybanski and F Robert Archibald to Phoenix Suns for F Bo Outlaw and C Jake Tsakalidis (September 30, 2003). ... Traded by Suns to Washington Wizards for C Jahidi White (November 5, 2003). ... Released by Wizards (March 2, 2004). ... Signed as free agent by Milwaukee Bucks (March 5, 2004). ... Signed as free agent by Charlotte Bobcats (August 31, 2004).

### COLLEGIATE RECORD

**NOTES:** Frances Pomeroy Naismith Award winner (1997). ... THE SPORTING NEWS All-America first team (1997).

| Season Team | G | Min. | FGM | FGA | Pct. | FTM | FTA | Pct. | Reb. | Ast. | Pts. | RPG | APG | PPG |
|---|---|---|---|---|---|---|---|---|---|---|---|---|---|---|
| 93-94—Stanford | 28 | 916 | 90 | 254 | .354 | 121 | 160 | .756 | 108 | 150 | 312 | 3.9 | 5.4 | 11.1 |
| 94-95—Stanford | 28 | 912 | 146 | 321 | .455 | 153 | 204 | .750 | 109 | 184 | 464 | 3.9 | 6.6 | 16.6 |
| 95-96—Stanford | 29 | 915 | 140 | 323 | .433 | 151 | 178 | .848 | 110 | 212 | 449 | 3.8 | 7.3 | 15.5 |
| 96-97—Stanford | 30 | 960 | 139 | 341 | .408 | 166 | 199 | .834 | 111 | 234 | 489 | 3.7 | 7.8 | 16.3 |
| Totals | 115 | 3703 | 515 | 1239 | .416 | 591 | 741 | .798 | 438 | 780 | 1714 | 3.8 | 6.8 | 14.9 |

Three-point field goals: 1993-94, 11-for-55 (.200). 1994-95, 19-for-51 (.373). 1995-96, 18-for-61 (.295). 1996-97, 45-for-110 (.409). Totals, 93-for-277 (.336).

### NBA REGULAR-SEASON RECORD

**HONORS:** NBA All-Rookie first team (1998).

| Season Team | G | Min. | FGM | FGA | Pct. | FTM | FTA | Pct. | Off. | Def. | Tot. | Ast. | St. | Blk. | TO | Pts. | RPG | APG | PPG |
|---|---|---|---|---|---|---|---|---|---|---|---|---|---|---|---|---|---|---|---|
| 97-98—Cleveland | 80 | 2483 | 261 | 592 | .441 | 201 | 251 | .801 | 67 | 186 | 253 | 656 | *196 | 18 | 194 | 723 | 3.2 | 8.2 | 9.0 |
| 98-99—Cleveland | 39 | 1186 | 134 | 315 | .425 | 105 | 141 | .745 | 16 | 115 | 131 | 302 | 70 | 7 | 105 | 373 | 3.4 | 7.7 | 9.6 |
| 99-00—Cleveland | 65 | 1754 | 230 | 558 | .412 | 140 | 184 | .761 | 38 | 155 | 193 | 458 | 107 | 21 | 157 | 602 | 3.0 | 7.0 | 9.3 |
| 00-01—Clev.-Atla. | 53 | 1457 | 139 | 371 | .375 | 54 | 66 | .818 | 23 | 145 | 168 | 311 | 101 | 4 | 91 | 333 | 3.2 | 5.9 | 6.3 |
| 01-02—Memphis | 53 | 1151 | 141 | 334 | .422 | 87 | 115 | .757 | 11 | 98 | 109 | 302 | 79 | 7 | 111 | 371 | 2.1 | 5.7 | 7.0 |
| 02-03—Memphis | 55 | 928 | 97 | 228 | .425 | 20 | 37 | .541 | 15 | 66 | 81 | 233 | 69 | 2 | 94 | 216 | 1.5 | 4.2 | 3.9 |
| 03-04—Pho.-Wash.Miami | 56 | 1037 | 105 | 246 | .427 | 49 | 65 | .754 | 14 | 98 | 112 | 204 | 84 | 1 | 72 | 261 | 2.0 | 3.6 | 4.7 |
| 04-05—Charlotte | 66 | 1944 | 248 | 587 | .422 | 167 | 196 | .852 | 21 | 149 | 170 | 591 | 131 | 5 | 147 | 666 | 2.6 | 9.0 | 10.1 |
| Totals | 467 | 11940 | 1355 | 3231 | .419 | 823 | 1055 | .780 | 205 | 1012 | 1217 | 3057 | 837 | 65 | 971 | 3545 | 2.6 | 6.5 | 7.6 |

Three-point field goals: 1997-98, 0-for-7. 1998-99, 0-for-5. 1999-00, 2-for-10 (.200). 2000-01, 1-for-10 (.100). 2001-02, 2-for-8 (.250). 2002-03, 2-for-8 (.250). 2003-04, 2-for-8 (.250). 2004-05, 3-for-20 (.150). Totals, 12-for-76 (.158).
Personal fouls/disqualifications: 1997-98, 271/5. 1998-99, 115/1. 1999-00, 185/2. 2000-01, 155/2. 2001-02, 135/1. 2002-03, 123/0. 2003-04, 107/1. 2004-05, 192/1. Totals, 1283/13.

### NBA PLAYOFF RECORD

| Season Team | G | Min. | FGM | FGA | Pct. | FTM | FTA | Pct. | Off. | Def. | Tot. | Ast. | St. | Blk. | TO | Pts. | RPG | APG | PPG |
|---|---|---|---|---|---|---|---|---|---|---|---|---|---|---|---|---|---|---|---|
| 97-98—Cleveland | 4 | 132 | 6 | 21 | .286 | 6 | 10 | .600 | 0 | 16 | 16 | 23 | 10 | 1 | 8 | 18 | 4.0 | 5.8 | 4.5 |
| 03-04—Milwaukee | 5 | 101 | 6 | 23 | .261 | 9 | 11 | .818 | 3 | 8 | 11 | 17 | 14 | 1 | 7 | 21 | 2.2 | 3.4 | 4.2 |
| Totals | 9 | 233 | 12 | 44 | .273 | 15 | 21 | .714 | 3 | 24 | 27 | 40 | 24 | 2 | 15 | 39 | 3.0 | 4.4 | 4.3 |

Personal fouls/disqualifications: 1997-98, 16/1. 2003-04, 12/1. Totals, 28/2.

# KORVER, KYLE     F     76ERS

**PERSONAL:** Born March 17, 1981, in Lakewood, Calif. ... 6-7/210. (2.01/95.3). ... Full name: Kyle Elliot Korver.
**HIGH SCHOOL:** Pella (Pella, Iowa).
**COLLEGE:** Creighton.
**TRANSACTIONS/CAREER NOTES:** Selected by New Jersey Nets in second round (51st overall pick) of 2003 NBA Draft. ... Draft rights traded by Nets to Philadelphia 76ers for cash considerations (June 26, 2003).

**NOTES:** The Sporting News All-America second team (2003).

| Season Team | G | Min. | FGM | FGA | Pct. | FTM | FTA | Pct. | Reb. | Ast. | Pts. | AVERAGES | | |
|---|---|---|---|---|---|---|---|---|---|---|---|---|---|---|
| | | | | | | | | | | | | RPG | APG | PPG |
| 99-00—Creighton | 33 | 601 | 97 | 204 | .475 | 34 | 38 | .895 | 101 | 32 | 291 | 3.1 | 1.0 | 8.8 |
| 00-01—Creighton | 32 | 941 | 148 | 315 | .470 | 72 | 83 | .867 | 186 | 63 | 468 | 5.8 | 2.0 | 14.6 |
| 01-02—Creighton | 29 | 916 | 131 | 274 | .478 | 97 | 109 | .890 | 160 | 95 | 438 | 5.5 | 3.3 | 15.1 |
| 02-03—Creighton | 34 | 1082 | 183 | 391 | .468 | 109 | 120 | .908 | 217 | 104 | 604 | 6.4 | 3.1 | 17.8 |
| Totals | 128 | 3540 | 559 | 1184 | .472 | 312 | 350 | .891 | 664 | 294 | 1801 | 5.2 | 2.3 | 14.1 |

Three-point field goals: 1999-00, 63-for-145 (.434). 2000-01, 100-for-221 (.452). 2001-02, 79-for-184 (.429). 2002-03, 129-for-269 (.480). Totals, 371-for-819 (.453).

### NBA REGULAR-SEASON RECORD

| Season Team | G | Min. | FGM | FGA | Pct. | FTM | FTA | Pct. | REBOUNDS | | | Ast. | St. | Blk. | TO | Pts. | AVERAGES | | |
|---|---|---|---|---|---|---|---|---|---|---|---|---|---|---|---|---|---|---|---|
| | | | | | | | | | Off. | Def. | Tot. | | | | | | RPG | APG | PPG |
| 03-04—Philadelphia | 74 | 882 | 115 | 327 | .352 | 19 | 24 | .792 | 30 | 81 | 111 | 40 | 25 | 8 | 41 | 330 | 1.5 | 0.5 | 4.5 |
| 04-05—Philadelphia | 82 | 2667 | 317 | 759 | .418 | 82 | 96 | .854 | 40 | 339 | 379 | 182 | 103 | 33 | 106 | 942 | 4.6 | 2.2 | 11.5 |
| Totals | 156 | 3549 | 432 | 1086 | .398 | 101 | 120 | .842 | 70 | 420 | 490 | 222 | 128 | 41 | 147 | 1272 | 3.1 | 1.4 | 8.2 |

Three-point field goals: 2003-04, 81-for-207 (.391). 2004-05, 226-for-558 (.405). Totals, 307-for-765 (.401).
Personal fouls/disqualifications: 2003-04, 102/2. 2004-05, 265/2. Totals, 367/4.

### NBA PLAYOFF RECORD

| Season Team | G | Min. | FGM | FGA | Pct. | FTM | FTA | Pct. | REBOUNDS | | | Ast. | St. | Blk. | TO | Pts. | AVERAGES | | |
|---|---|---|---|---|---|---|---|---|---|---|---|---|---|---|---|---|---|---|---|
| | | | | | | | | | Off. | Def. | Tot. | | | | | | RPG | APG | PPG |
| 04-05—Philadelphia | 5 | 147 | 8 | 28 | .286 | 2 | 2 | 1.000 | 3 | 10 | 13 | 8 | 4 | 1 | 8 | 25 | 2.6 | 1.6 | 5.0 |

Three-point field goals: 2004-05, 7-for-24 (.292). Totals, 7-for-24 (.292).
Personal fouls/disqualifications: 2004-05, 18/0. Totals, 18/0.

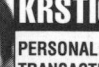

# KRSTIC, NENAD     F/C     NETS

**PERSONAL:** Born July 25, 1983, in Kraljevo, Yugoslavia. ... 6-11/210. (2.11/95.3).
**TRANSACTIONS/CAREER NOTES:** Played in Yugoslavia (2000-04). ... Selected by New Jersey Nets in first round (24th pick overall) of 2002 NBA Draft.
**MISCELLANEOUS:** Member of Serbia-Montenegro Olympic Team (2004).

### YUGOSLAVIAN LEAGUE RECORD

| Season Team | G | Min. | FGM | FGA | Pct. | FTM | FTA | Pct. | Reb. | Ast. | Pts. | AVERAGES | | |
|---|---|---|---|---|---|---|---|---|---|---|---|---|---|---|
| | | | | | | | | | | | | RPG | APG | PPG |
| 00-01—Partizan | 8 | 24 | 1 | 3 | .333 | 6 | 8 | .750 | 4 | 0 | 8 | 0.5 | 0.0 | 1.0 |
| 01-02—Partizan | 21 | 396 | 60 | 110 | .545 | 50 | 64 | .781 | 120 | 6 | 170 | 5.7 | 0.3 | 8.1 |
| 02-03—Partizan | 19 | 522 | 92 | 152 | .605 | 99 | 123 | .805 | 119 | 14 | 285 | 6.3 | 0.7 | 15.0 |
| 03-04—Partizan | 10 | 263 | 55 | 90 | .611 | 39 | 52 | .750 | 61 | 10 | 149 | 6.1 | 1.0 | 14.9 |
| Totals | 58 | 1205 | 208 | 355 | .586 | 194 | 247 | .785 | 304 | 30 | 612 | 5.2 | 0.5 | 10.6 |

Three-point field goals: 2000-01, 0-for-1. 2001-02, 0-for-2. 2002-03, 2-for-2 (1.000). 2003-04, 0-for-3. Totals, 2-for-8 (.250).

**HONORS:** NBA All-Rookie second team (2005).

### NBA REGULAR-SEASON RECORD

| Season Team | G | Min. | FGM | FGA | Pct. | FTM | FTA | Pct. | REBOUNDS | | | Ast. | St. | Blk. | TO | Pts. | AVERAGES | | |
|---|---|---|---|---|---|---|---|---|---|---|---|---|---|---|---|---|---|---|---|
| | | | | | | | | | Off. | Def. | Tot. | | | | | | RPG | APG | PPG |
| 04-05—New Jersey | 75 | 1965 | 281 | 570 | .493 | 185 | 255 | .725 | 161 | 240 | 401 | 77 | 32 | 63 | 112 | 747 | 5.3 | 1.0 | 10.0 |

Three-point field goals: 2004-05, 0-for-2. Totals, 0-for-2 (.000).
Personal fouls/disqualifications: 2004-05, 280/7. Totals, 280/7.

### NBA PLAYOFF RECORD

| Season Team | G | Min. | FGM | FGA | Pct. | FTM | FTA | Pct. | REBOUNDS | | | Ast. | St. | Blk. | TO | Pts. | AVERAGES | | |
|---|---|---|---|---|---|---|---|---|---|---|---|---|---|---|---|---|---|---|---|
| | | | | | | | | | Off. | Def. | Tot. | | | | | | RPG | APG | PPG |
| 04-05—New Jersey | 4 | 154 | 27 | 48 | .563 | 19 | 24 | .792 | 10 | 20 | 30 | 7 | 1 | 2 | 6 | 73 | 7.5 | 1.8 | 18.3 |

Personal fouls/disqualifications: 2004-05, 20/1. Totals, 20/1.

# KUKOC, TONI     F     BUCKS

**PERSONAL:** Born September 18, 1968, in Split, Croatia. ... 6-11/235. (2.11/106.6). ... Name pronounced COO-coach.
**TRANSACTIONS/CAREER NOTES:** Played in Yugoslavia (1989-91). ... Selected by Chicago Bulls in second round (29th pick overall) of 1990 NBA Draft. ... Played in Italy (1991-93). ... Traded by Bulls to Philadelphia 76ers for F Bruce Bowen in three-way deal in which 76ers sent G Larry Hughes and F/G Billy Owens to Golden State Warriors and Warriors sent G John Starks and future first-round draft choice to Bulls (February 16, 2000). ... Traded by 76ers with F/C Theo Ratliff, C Nazr Mohammed and G Pepe Sanchez to Atlanta Hawks for C Dikembe Mutombo and F Roshown McLeod (February 22, 2001). ... Traded by Hawks with F Leon Smith and 2003 first-round draft choice to Milwaukee Bucks for F Glenn Robinson (August 2, 2002).
**MISCELLANEOUS:** Member of NBA championship team (1996, 1997, 1998). ... Member of silver-medal-winning Yugoslavian Olympic team (1988). ... Member of silver-medal-winning Croatian Olympic team (1992). ... Member of Croatian Olympic team (1996).

### ITALIAN LEAGUE RECORD

| Season Team | G | Min. | FGM | FGA | Pct. | FTM | FTA | Pct. | Reb. | Ast. | Pts. | AVERAGES | | |
|---|---|---|---|---|---|---|---|---|---|---|---|---|---|---|
| | | | | | | | | | | | | RPG | APG | PPG |
| 91-92—Benetton Treviso | 22 | 826 | 173 | 313 | .553 | 59 | 89 | .663 | 118 | 121 | 464 | 5.4 | 5.5 | 21.1 |
| 92-93—Benetton Treviso | 29 | 1084 | 191 | 363 | .526 | 117 | 150 | .780 | 187 | 152 | 551 | 6.4 | 5.2 | 19.0 |
| Totals | 51 | 1910 | 364 | 676 | .538 | 176 | 239 | .736 | 305 | 273 | 1015 | 6.0 | 5.4 | 19.9 |

Three-point field goals: 1991-92, 59-for-130 (.454). 1992-93, 52-for-130 (.400). Totals, 111-for-260 (.427).
Personal fouls/disqualifications: 1991-92, 0/2. 1992-93, 0/1. Totals, 0/3.

K

**HONORS:** NBA Sixth Man Award (1996). ... NBA All-Rookie second team (1994).

| | | | | | | | REBOUNDS | | | | | | | | AVERAGES | | |
|---|---|---|---|---|---|---|---|---|---|---|---|---|---|---|---|---|---|
| Season Team | G | Min. | FGM | FGA | Pct. | FTM | FTA | Pct. | Off. | Def. | Tot. | Ast. | St. | Blk. | TO | Pts. | RPG | APG | PPG |
| 93-94—Chicago | 75 | 1808 | 313 | 726 | .431 | 156 | 210 | .743 | 98 | 199 | 297 | 252 | 81 | 33 | 167 | 814 | 4.0 | 3.4 | 10.9 |
| 94-95—Chicago | 81 | 2584 | 487 | 967 | .504 | 235 | 314 | .748 | 155 | 285 | 440 | 372 | 102 | 16 | 165 | 1271 | 5.4 | 4.6 | 15.7 |
| 95-96—Chicago | 81 | 2103 | 386 | 787 | .490 | 206 | 267 | .772 | 115 | 208 | 323 | 287 | 64 | 28 | 114 | 1065 | 4.0 | 3.5 | 13.1 |
| 96-97—Chicago | 57 | 1610 | 285 | 605 | .471 | 134 | 174 | .770 | 94 | 167 | 261 | 256 | 60 | 29 | 91 | 754 | 4.6 | 4.5 | 13.2 |
| 97-98—Chicago | 74 | 2235 | 383 | 841 | .455 | 155 | 219 | .708 | 121 | 206 | 327 | 314 | 76 | 37 | 154 | 984 | 4.4 | 4.2 | 13.3 |
| 98-99—Chicago | 44 | 1654 | 315 | 750 | .420 | 159 | 215 | .740 | 65 | 245 | 310 | 235 | 49 | 11 | 121 | 828 | 7.0 | 5.3 | 18.8 |
| 99-00—Chi.-Phil. | 56 | 1784 | 297 | 728 | .408 | 192 | 265 | .725 | 75 | 198 | 273 | 265 | 77 | 28 | 146 | 830 | 4.9 | 4.7 | 14.8 |
| 00-01—Phila.-Atlanta.. | 65 | 1597 | 275 | 582 | .473 | 101 | 160 | .631 | 66 | 193 | 259 | 199 | 48 | 11 | 111 | 721 | 4.0 | 3.1 | 11.1 |
| 01-02—Atlanta | 59 | 1494 | 211 | 504 | .419 | 109 | 153 | .712 | 43 | 175 | 218 | 210 | 48 | 17 | 113 | 584 | 3.7 | 3.6 | 9.9 |
| 02-03—Milwaukee | 63 | 1704 | 249 | 577 | .432 | 137 | 194 | .706 | 67 | 199 | 266 | 230 | 81 | 29 | 122 | 730 | 4.2 | 3.7 | 11.6 |
| 03-04—Milwaukee | 73 | 1522 | 211 | 506 | .417 | 145 | 199 | .729 | 60 | 211 | 271 | 200 | 59 | 21 | 110 | 616 | 3.7 | 2.7 | 8.4 |
| 04-05—Milwaukee | 53 | 1099 | 105 | 256 | .410 | 44 | 61 | .721 | 31 | 129 | 160 | 160 | 39 | 13 | 64 | 296 | 3.0 | 3.0 | 5.6 |
| Totals | 781 | 21194 | 3517 | 7829 | .449 | 1773 | 2431 | .729 | 990 | 2415 | 3405 | 2984 | 784 | 273 | 1478 | 9493 | 4.4 | 3.8 | 12.2 |

Three-point field goals: 1993-94, 32-for-118 (.271). 1994-95, 62-for-198 (.313). 1995-96, 87-for-216 (.403). 1996-97, 50-for-151 (.331). 1997-98, 63-for-174 (.362). 1998-99, 39-for-137 (.285). 1999-00, 44-for-168 (.262). 2000-01, 70-for-157 (.446). 2001-02, 53-for-171 (.310). 2002-03, 95-for-263 (.361). 2003-04, 49-for-168 (.292). 2004-05, 42-for-116 (.362). Totals, 686-for-2037 (.337).

Personal fouls/disqualifications: 1993-94, 122/0. 1994-95, 163/1. 1995-96, 150/0. 1996-97, 97/1. 1997-98, 149/0. 1998-99, 82/0. 1999-00, 112/0. 2000-01, 98/0. 2001-02, 91/0. 2002-03, 134/0. 2003-04, 110/0. 2004-05, 70/0. Totals, 1378/2.

## NBA PLAYOFF RECORD

| | | | | | | | REBOUNDS | | | | | | | | AVERAGES | | |
|---|---|---|---|---|---|---|---|---|---|---|---|---|---|---|---|---|---|
| Season Team | G | Min. | FGM | FGA | Pct. | FTM | FTA | Pct. | Off. | Def. | Tot. | Ast. | St. | Blk. | TO | Pts. | RPG | APG | PPG |
| 93-94—Chicago | 10 | 194 | 30 | 67 | .448 | 25 | 34 | .735 | 11 | 29 | 40 | 36 | 5 | 3 | 17 | 93 | 4.0 | 3.6 | 9.3 |
| 94-95—Chicago | 10 | 372 | 53 | 111 | .477 | 18 | 26 | .692 | 20 | 48 | 68 | 57 | 10 | 2 | 19 | 138 | 6.8 | 5.7 | 13.8 |
| 95-96—Chicago | 15 | 439 | 59 | 151 | .391 | 31 | 37 | .838 | 19 | 44 | 63 | 58 | 14 | 4 | 26 | 162 | 4.2 | 3.9 | 10.8 |
| 96-97—Chicago | 19 | 423 | 45 | 125 | .360 | 41 | 58 | .707 | 13 | 41 | 54 | 54 | 13 | 4 | 17 | 150 | 2.8 | 2.8 | 7.9 |
| 97-98—Chicago | 21 | 637 | 106 | 218 | .486 | 40 | 62 | .645 | 24 | 57 | 81 | 60 | 26 | 10 | 27 | 275 | 3.9 | 2.9 | 13.1 |
| 99-00—Philadelphia | 10 | 257 | 36 | 93 | .387 | 10 | 17 | .588 | 7 | 30 | 37 | 17 | 10 | 3 | 15 | 93 | 3.7 | 1.7 | 9.3 |
| 02-03—Milwaukee | 6 | 184 | 32 | 65 | .492 | 14 | 20 | .700 | 6 | 19 | 25 | 22 | 13 | 1 | 11 | 89 | 4.2 | 3.7 | 14.8 |
| 03-04—Milwaukee | 5 | 105 | 17 | 34 | .500 | 4 | 8 | .500 | 4 | 10 | 14 | 4 | 3 | 2 | 6 | 42 | 2.8 | 0.8 | 8.4 |
| Totals | 96 | 2611 | 378 | 864 | .438 | 183 | 262 | .698 | 104 | 278 | 382 | 308 | 94 | 29 | 138 | 1042 | 4.0 | 3.2 | 10.9 |

Three-point field goals: 1993-94, 8-for-19 (.421). 1994-95, 14-for-32 (.438). 1995-96, 13-for-68 (.191). 1996-97, 19-for-53 (.358). 1997-98, 23-for-61 (.377). 1999-00, 11-for-34 (.324). 2002-03, 11-for-29 (.379). 2003-04, 4-for-12 (.333). Totals, 103-for-308 (.334).

Personal fouls/disqualifications: 1993-94, 15/0. 1994-95, 23/0. 1995-96, 33/0. 1996-97, 30/0. 1997-98, 57/1. 1999-00, 26/0. 2002-03, 12/0. 2003-04, 11/0. Totals, 207/1.

# KUTLUAY, IBRAHIM    G

**PERSONAL:** Born July 1, 1974, in Istanbul. ... 6-6, 200.
**TRANSACTIONS/CAREER NOTES:** Not drafted by an NBA franchise. ... Signed as free agent by Seattle SuperSonics (September 22, 2004).

## TURKISH LEAGUE RECORD

| | | | | | | | | | | | AVERAGES | | |
|---|---|---|---|---|---|---|---|---|---|---|---|---|---|
| Season Team | G | Min. | FGM | FGA | Pct. | FTM | FTA | Pct. | Reb. | Ast. | Pts. | RPG | APG | PPG |
| 93-94—Fenerbahce | 24 | ... | 66 | 120 | .550 | 41 | 55 | .745 | 52 | 14 | 185 | 2.2 | 0.6 | 7.7 |
| 94-95—Fenerbahce | 42 | ... | 219 | 446 | .491 | 89 | 118 | .754 | 140 | 82 | 586 | 3.3 | 2.0 | 14.0 |
| 95-96—Fenerbahce | 30 | ... | 210 | 404 | .520 | 117 | 156 | .750 | 89 | 43 | 601 | 3.0 | 1.4 | 20.0 |
| 96-97—Fenerbahce | 32 | ... | 220 | 449 | .490 | 119 | 142 | .838 | 85 | 47 | 638 | 2.7 | 1.5 | 19.9 |
| 97-98—Fenerbahce | 30 | ... | 201 | 409 | .491 | 124 | 167 | .743 | 55 | 44 | 580 | 1.8 | 1.5 | 19.3 |
| 98-99—Fenerbahce | 26 | 1014 | 208 | 446 | .466 | 138 | 176 | .784 | 73 | 42 | 620 | 2.8 | 1.6 | 23.8 |
| 99-00—Efes Pilsen | 26 | 859 | 129 | 253 | .510 | 70 | 99 | .707 | 48 | 56 | 380 | 1.8 | 2.2 | 14.6 |
| 03-04—Ulker | 28 | 829 | 119 | 288 | .413 | 70 | 102 | .686 | 70 | 55 | 361 | 2.5 | 2.0 | 12.9 |
| Totals | 238 | ... | 1372 | 2815 | .487 | 768 | 1015 | .757 | 612 | 383 | 3951 | 2.6 | 1.6 | 16.6 |

Three-point field goals: 1993-94, 12-for-21 (.571). 1994-95, 59-for-155 (.381). 1995-96, 64-for-162 (.395). 1996-97, 79-for-215 (.367). 1997-98, 54-for-147 (.367). 1998-99, 66-for-195 (.338). 1999-00, 52-for-115 (.452). 2003-04, 53-for-159 (.333). Totals, 439-for-1169 (.376).

## GREEK LEAGUE RECORD

| | | | | | | | | | | | AVERAGES | | |
|---|---|---|---|---|---|---|---|---|---|---|---|---|---|
| Season Team | G | Min. | FGM | FGA | Pct. | FTM | FTA | Pct. | Reb. | Ast. | Pts. | RPG | APG | PPG |
| 00-01—AEK | 19 | 573 | 105 | 244 | .430 | 78 | 99 | .788 | 44 | 31 | 347 | 2.3 | 1.6 | 18.3 |
| 01-02—Panathinaikos | 21 | 606 | 92 | 201 | .458 | 48 | 62 | .774 | 55 | 32 | 267 | 2.6 | 1.5 | 12.7 |
| 02-03—Panathinaikos | 25 | 642 | 120 | 227 | .529 | 78 | 101 | .772 | 58 | 30 | 360 | 2.3 | 1.2 | 14.4 |
| 04-05—Panathinaikos | 9 | 161 | 25 | 46 | .543 | 11 | 11 | 1.000 | 14 | 4 | 70 | 1.6 | 0.4 | 7.8 |
| Totals | 74 | 1982 | 342 | 718 | .476 | 215 | 273 | .788 | 171 | 97 | 1044 | 2.3 | 1.3 | 14.1 |

Three-point field goals: 2000-01, 59-for-151 (.391). 2001-02, 35-for-98 (.357). 2002-03, 42-for-97 (.433). 2003-04, 9-for-24 (.375). Totals, 145-for-370 (.392).

## NBA REGULAR-SEASON RECORD

| | | | | | | | REBOUNDS | | | | | | | | AVERAGES | | |
|---|---|---|---|---|---|---|---|---|---|---|---|---|---|---|---|---|---|
| Season Team | G | Min. | FGM | FGA | Pct. | FTM | FTA | Pct. | Off. | Def. | Tot. | Ast. | St. | Blk. | TO | Pts. | RPG | APG | PPG |
| 04-05—Seattle | 5 | 12 | 0 | 1 | .000 | 0 | 0 | ... | 0 | 1 | 1 | 0 | 0 | 0 | 2 | 0 | 0.2 | 0.0 | 0.0 |

Personal fouls/disqualifications: 2004-05, 1/0. Totals, 1/0.

# LAETTNER, CHRISTIAN      F/C      HEAT

**PERSONAL:** Born August 17, 1969, in Angola, N.Y. ... 6-11/245. (2.11/111.1). ... Full name: Christian Donald Laettner ... Name pronounced LATE-ner.
**HIGH SCHOOL:** Nichols School (Buffalo).
**COLLEGE:** Duke.
**TRANSACTIONS/CAREER NOTES:** Selected by Minnesota Timberwolves in first round (third pick overall) of 1992 NBA Draft. ... Traded by Timberwolves with C Sean Rooks to Atlanta Hawks for G Spud Webb and C Andrew Lang (February 22, 1996). ... Traded by Hawks to Detroit Pistons for C Scot Pollard and 1999 first-round draft choice (January 22, 1999). ... Traded by Pistons with F Terry Mills to Dallas Mavericks for F Cedric Ceballos, F John Wallace and G Eric Murdock (August 29, 2000). ... Traded by Mavericks with G Courtney Alexander, F Loy Vaught, G Hubert Davis, F/C Etan Thomas and cash considerations to Washington Wizards for F Juwan Howard, C Calvin Booth and F Obinna Ekezie (February 22, 2001). ... Traded by Wizards with G Jerry Stackhouse and draft rights to G Devin Harris to Dallas Mavericks for F Antawn Jamison (June 24, 2004). ... Traded by Mavericks with F Eduardo Najera, draft rights to G Luis Flores and G/F Mladen Sekularac, two future first-round draft choices and cash to Golden State Warriors for C Erick Dampier, G Dan Dickau, C Evan Eschmeyer and draft rights to G Steve Logan (August 24, 2004). ... Waived by Warriors (September 9, 2004). ... Signed as free agent by Miami Heat (September 15, 2004).
**MISCELLANEOUS:** Member of gold-medal-winning U.S. Olympic team (1992). ... Member of bronze-medal-winning U.S. World Championship team (1990).

## COLLEGIATE RECORD

**NOTES:** THE SPORTING NEWS College Player of the Year (1992). ... Naismith Award winner (1992). ... Wooden Award winner (1992). ... THE SPORTING NEWS All-America first team (1992). ... THE SPORTING NEWS All-America second team (1991). ... THE SPORTING NEWS All-America third team (1990). ... NCAA Division I Tournament Most Outstanding Player (1991). ... Member of NCAA Division I championship team (1991, 1992).

| Season Team | G | Min. | FGM | FGA | Pct. | FTM | FTA | Pct. | Reb. | Ast. | Pts. | RPG | APG | PPG |
|---|---|---|---|---|---|---|---|---|---|---|---|---|---|---|
| 88-89—Duke | 36 | 607 | 115 | 159 | .723 | 88 | 121 | .727 | 170 | 44 | 319 | 4.7 | 1.2 | 8.9 |
| 89-90—Duke | 38 | 1135 | 194 | 380 | .511 | 225 | 269 | .836 | 364 | 84 | 619 | 9.6 | 2.2 | 16.3 |
| 90-91—Duke | 39 | 1178 | 271 | 471 | .575 | 211 | 263 | .802 | 340 | 76 | 771 | 8.7 | 1.9 | 19.8 |
| 91-92—Duke | 35 | 1128 | 254 | 442 | .575 | 189 | 232 | .815 | 275 | 69 | 751 | 7.9 | 2.0 | 21.5 |
| Totals | 148 | 4048 | 834 | 1452 | .574 | 713 | 885 | .806 | 1149 | 273 | 2460 | 7.8 | 1.8 | 16.6 |

Three-point field goals: 1988-89, 1-for-1 (1.000). 1989-90, 6-for-12 (.500). 1990-91, 18-for-53 (.340). 1991-92, 54-for-97 (.557). Totals, 79-for-163 (.485).

## NBA REGULAR-SEASON RECORD

**HONORS:** NBA All-Rookie first team (1993).

| Season Team | G | Min. | FGM | FGA | Pct. | FTM | FTA | Pct. | Off. | Def. | Tot. | Ast. | St. | Blk. | TO | Pts. | RPG | APG | PPG |
|---|---|---|---|---|---|---|---|---|---|---|---|---|---|---|---|---|---|---|---|
| 92-93—Minnesota | 81 | 2823 | 503 | 1061 | .474 | 462 | 553 | .835 | 171 | 537 | 708 | 223 | 105 | 83 | 275 | 1472 | 8.7 | 2.8 | 18.2 |
| 93-94—Minnesota | 70 | 2428 | 396 | 883 | .448 | 375 | 479 | .783 | 160 | 442 | 602 | 307 | 87 | 86 | 259 | 1173 | 8.6 | 4.4 | 16.8 |
| 94-95—Minnesota | 81 | 2770 | 450 | 920 | .489 | 409 | 500 | .818 | 164 | 449 | 613 | 234 | 101 | 87 | 225 | 1322 | 7.6 | 2.9 | 16.3 |
| 95-96—Minn.-Atl. | 74 | 2495 | 442 | 907 | .487 | 324 | 396 | .818 | 184 | 354 | 538 | 197 | 71 | 71 | 187 | 1217 | 7.3 | 2.7 | 16.4 |
| 96-97—Atlanta | 82 | 3140 | 548 | 1128 | .486 | 359 | 440 | .816 | 212 | 508 | 720 | 223 | 102 | 64 | 218 | 1486 | 8.8 | 2.7 | 18.1 |
| 97-98—Atlanta | 74 | 2282 | 354 | 730 | .485 | 306 | 354 | .864 | 142 | 345 | 487 | 190 | 71 | 73 | 183 | 1020 | 6.6 | 2.6 | 13.8 |
| 98-99—Detroit | 16 | 337 | 38 | 106 | .358 | 44 | 57 | .772 | 21 | 33 | 54 | 24 | 15 | 12 | 19 | 121 | 3.4 | 1.5 | 7.6 |
| 99-00—Detroit | 82 | 2443 | 379 | 801 | .473 | 237 | 292 | .812 | 175 | 378 | 553 | 186 | 83 | 45 | 186 | 1002 | 6.7 | 2.3 | 12.2 |
| 00-01—Dallas-Wash. | 78 | 1663 | 277 | 551 | .503 | 170 | 204 | .833 | 118 | 247 | 365 | 124 | 71 | 46 | 137 | 728 | 4.7 | 1.6 | 9.3 |
| 01-02—Washington | 57 | 1441 | 168 | 362 | .464 | 66 | 76 | .868 | 74 | 227 | 301 | 151 | 60 | 25 | 85 | 404 | 5.3 | 2.6 | 7.1 |
| 02-03—Washington | 76 | 2215 | 255 | 516 | .494 | 120 | 144 | .833 | 114 | 388 | 502 | 235 | 82 | 40 | 87 | 632 | 6.6 | 3.1 | 8.3 |
| 03-04—Washington | 48 | 984 | 119 | 256 | .465 | 40 | 50 | .800 | 50 | 182 | 232 | 89 | 37 | 28 | 42 | 284 | 4.8 | 1.9 | 5.9 |
| 04-05—Miami | 49 | 739 | 107 | 184 | .582 | 45 | 59 | .763 | 36 | 95 | 131 | 41 | 32 | 15 | 29 | 260 | 2.7 | 0.8 | 5.3 |
| Totals | 868 | 25760 | 4036 | 8405 | .480 | 2957 | 3604 | .820 | 1621 | 4185 | 5806 | 2224 | 917 | 675 | 1932 | 11121 | 6.7 | 2.6 | 12.8 |

Three-point field goals: 1992-93, 4-for-40 (.100). 1993-94, 6-for-25 (.240). 1994-95, 13-for-40 (.325). 1995-96, 9-for-39 (.231). 1996-97, 31-for-88 (.352). 1997-98, 6-for-27 (.222). 1998-99, 1-for-3 (.333). 1999-00, 7-for-24 (.292). 2000-01, 4-for-13 (.308). 2001-02, 2-for-10 (.200). 2002-03, 2-for-16 (.125). 2003-04, 6-for-21 (.286). 2004-05, 1-for-7 (.143). Totals, 92-for-353 (.261).

Personal fouls/disqualifications: 1992-93, 290/4. 1993-94, 264/6. 1994-95, 302/4. 1995-96, 276/7. 1996-97, 277/8. 1997-98, 246/6. 1998-99, 30/0. 1999-00, 326/10. 2000-01, 242/1. 2001-02, 129/1. 2002-03, 206/0. 2003-04, 102/1. 2004-05, 78/0. Totals, 2768/48.

## NBA PLAYOFF RECORD

| Season Team | G | Min. | FGM | FGA | Pct. | FTM | FTA | Pct. | Off. | Def. | Tot. | Ast. | St. | Blk. | TO | Pts. | RPG | APG | PPG |
|---|---|---|---|---|---|---|---|---|---|---|---|---|---|---|---|---|---|---|---|
| 95-96—Atlanta | 10 | 334 | 59 | 122 | .484 | 38 | 54 | .704 | 27 | 42 | 69 | 15 | 12 | 10 | 21 | 157 | 6.9 | 1.5 | 15.7 |
| 96-97—Atlanta | 10 | 403 | 62 | 153 | .405 | 48 | 56 | .857 | 19 | 53 | 72 | 26 | 10 | 8 | 31 | 176 | 7.2 | 2.6 | 17.6 |
| 97-98—Atlanta | 4 | 87 | 12 | 35 | .343 | 15 | 17 | .882 | 3 | 14 | 17 | 4 | 6 | 1 | 8 | 39 | 4.3 | 1.0 | 9.8 |
| 98-99—Detroit | 5 | 123 | 20 | 47 | .426 | 11 | 14 | .786 | 6 | 8 | 14 | 11 | 4 | 1 | 3 | 51 | 2.8 | 2.2 | 10.2 |
| 99-00—Detroit | 3 | 75 | 7 | 17 | .412 | 6 | 8 | .750 | 2 | 13 | 15 | 6 | 0 | 1 | 3 | 20 | 5.0 | 2.0 | 6.7 |
| 04-05—Miami | 13 | 136 | 12 | 24 | .500 | 5 | 6 | .833 | 3 | 22 | 25 | 7 | 4 | 0 | 6 | 29 | 1.9 | 0.5 | 2.2 |
| Totals | 45 | 1158 | 172 | 398 | .432 | 123 | 155 | .794 | 60 | 152 | 212 | 69 | 36 | 21 | 72 | 472 | 4.7 | 1.5 | 10.5 |

Three-point field goals: 1995-96, 1-for-3 (.333). 1996-97, 4-for-21 (.190). 1997-98, 0-for-3. 2004-05, 0-for-1. Totals, 5-for-28 (.179).
Personal fouls/disqualifications: 1995-96, 41/1. 1996-97, 32/0. 1997-98, 16/1. 1998-99, 14/0. 1999-00, 14/0. 2004-05, 17/0. Totals, 134/2.

## NBA ALL-STAR GAME RECORD

| Season Team | Min. | FGM | FGA | Pct. | FTM | FTA | Pct. | Off. | Def. | Tot. | Ast. | PF | Dq. | St. | Blk. | TO | Pts. |
|---|---|---|---|---|---|---|---|---|---|---|---|---|---|---|---|---|---|
| 1997—Atlanta | 24 | 3 | 5 | .600 | 1 | 1 | 1.000 | 4 | 7 | 11 | 2 | 4 | 0 | 1 | 1 | 2 | 7 |

# LAFRENTZ, RAEF  F/C  CELTICS

**PERSONAL:** Born May 29, 1976, in Hampton, Iowa. ... 6-11/240. (2.11/108.9). ... Full name: Raef Andrew LaFrentz
**HIGH SCHOOL:** Mar-Mac (Monona, Iowa).
**COLLEGE:** Kansas.
**TRANSACTIONS/CAREER NOTES:** Selected by Denver Nuggets in first round (third pick overall) of 1998 NBA Draft. ... Traded by Nuggets with G Nick Van Exel, G Avery Johnson and G/F Tariq Abdul-Wahad to Dallas Mavericks for F Juwan Howard, G Tim Hardaway, F Donnell Harvey, cash considerations and first-round draft choice (February 21, 2002). ... Traded by Mavericks with F Chris Mills, G Jiri Welsch and 2004 first-round draft choice to Boston Celtics for G Tony Delk and F Antoine Walker (October 20, 2003).

## COLLEGIATE RECORD

**NOTES:** The Sporting News All-America first team (1998). ... The Sporting News All-America second team (1997).

| Season Team | G | Min. | FGM | FGA | Pct. | FTM | FTA | Pct. | Reb. | Ast. | Pts. | AVERAGES RPG | APG | PPG |
|---|---|---|---|---|---|---|---|---|---|---|---|---|---|---|
| 94-95—Kansas | 31 | 732 | 143 | 268 | .534 | 65 | 102 | .637 | 231 | 17 | 353 | 7.5 | 0.5 | 11.4 |
| 95-96—Kansas | 34 | 917 | 189 | 348 | .543 | 74 | 112 | .661 | 278 | 14 | 454 | 8.2 | 0.4 | 13.4 |
| 96-97—Kansas | 36 | 1041 | 261 | 447 | .584 | 143 | 188 | .761 | 335 | 25 | 666 | 9.3 | 0.7 | 18.5 |
| 97-98—Kansas | 30 | 906 | 232 | 423 | .548 | 121 | 164 | .738 | 342 | 30 | 593 | 11.4 | 1.0 | 19.8 |
| Totals | 131 | 3596 | 825 | 1486 | .555 | 403 | 566 | .712 | 1186 | 86 | 2066 | 9.1 | 0.7 | 15.8 |

Three-point field goals: 1994-95, 2-for-5 (.400). 1995-96, 1-for-5 (.200). 1996-97, 1-for-3 (.333). 1997-98, 8-for-17 (.471). Totals, 12-for-30 (.400).

## NBA REGULAR-SEASON RECORD

**NOTES:** Led NBA with 11 disqualifications (2002).

| Season Team | G | Min. | FGM | FGA | Pct. | FTM | FTA | Pct. | REBOUNDS Off. | Def. | Tot. | Ast. | St. | Blk. | TO | Pts. | AVERAGES RPG | APG | PPG |
|---|---|---|---|---|---|---|---|---|---|---|---|---|---|---|---|---|---|---|---|
| 98-99—Denver | 12 | 387 | 59 | 129 | .457 | 36 | 48 | .750 | 33 | 58 | 91 | 8 | 9 | 17 | 9 | 166 | 7.6 | 0.7 | 13.8 |
| 99-00—Denver | 81 | 2435 | 392 | 879 | .446 | 162 | 236 | .686 | 170 | 471 | 641 | 97 | 42 | 180 | 96 | 1006 | 7.9 | 1.2 | 12.4 |
| 00-01—Denver | 78 | 2457 | 387 | 812 | .477 | 183 | 262 | .698 | 173 | 434 | 607 | 107 | 37 | 206 | 97 | 1008 | 7.8 | 1.4 | 12.9 |
| 01-02—Denver-Dallas | 78 | 2455 | 421 | 920 | .458 | 105 | 151 | .695 | 176 | 403 | 579 | 89 | 55 | 213 | 94 | 1051 | 7.4 | 1.1 | 13.5 |
| 02-03—Dallas | 69 | 1611 | 266 | 514 | .518 | 60 | 88 | .682 | 125 | 205 | 330 | 54 | 35 | 91 | 46 | 639 | 4.8 | 0.8 | 9.3 |
| 03-04—Boston | 17 | 328 | 57 | 124 | .460 | 10 | 13 | .769 | 30 | 49 | 79 | 24 | 8 | 13 | 11 | 132 | 4.6 | 1.4 | 7.8 |
| 04-05—Boston | 80 | 2196 | 341 | 688 | .496 | 120 | 148 | .811 | 154 | 399 | 553 | 98 | 42 | 99 | 70 | 884 | 6.9 | 1.2 | 11.1 |
| Totals | 415 | 11869 | 1923 | 4066 | .473 | 676 | 946 | .715 | 861 | 2019 | 2880 | 477 | 228 | 819 | 423 | 4886 | 6.9 | 1.1 | 11.8 |

Three-point field goals: 1998-99, 12-for-31 (.387). 1999-00, 60-for-183 (.328). 2000-01, 51-for-139 (.367). 2001-02, 104-for-268 (.388). 2002-03, 47-for-116 (.405). 2003-04, 8-for-40 (.200). 2004-05, 82-for-225 (.364). Totals, 364-for-1002 (.363).
Personal fouls/disqualifications: 1998-99, 38/2. 1999-00, 292/6. 2000-01, 290/9. 2001-02, 281/11. 2002-03, 264/8. 2003-04, 47/1. 2004-05, 262/2. Totals, 1474/39.

## NBA PLAYOFF RECORD

| Season Team | G | Min. | FGM | FGA | Pct. | FTM | FTA | Pct. | REBOUNDS Off. | Def. | Tot. | Ast. | St. | Blk. | TO | Pts. | AVERAGES RPG | APG | PPG |
|---|---|---|---|---|---|---|---|---|---|---|---|---|---|---|---|---|---|---|---|
| 01-02—Dallas | 8 | 245 | 39 | 78 | .500 | 6 | 11 | .545 | 18 | 43 | 61 | 5 | 2 | 22 | 6 | 90 | 7.6 | 0.6 | 11.3 |
| 02-03—Dallas | 20 | 491 | 68 | 157 | .433 | 16 | 19 | .842 | 36 | 52 | 88 | 5 | 11 | 43 | 14 | 160 | 4.4 | 0.3 | 8.0 |
| 04-05—Boston | 7 | 185 | 16 | 41 | .390 | 8 | 10 | .800 | 6 | 28 | 34 | 8 | 6 | 12 | 7 | 48 | 4.9 | 1.1 | 6.9 |
| Totals | 35 | 921 | 123 | 276 | .446 | 30 | 40 | .750 | 60 | 123 | 183 | 18 | 19 | 77 | 27 | 298 | 5.2 | 0.5 | 8.5 |

Three-point field goals: 2001-02, 6-for-18 (.333). 2002-03, 8-for-40 (.200). 2004-05, 8-for-16 (.500). Totals, 22-for-74 (.297).
Personal fouls/disqualifications: 2001-02, 39/2. 2002-03, 86/3. 2004-05, 27/1. Totals, 152/6.

# LAMPE, MACIEJ  F  HORNETS

**PERSONAL:** Born February 5, 1985, in Lodz, Poland. ... 6-11/240. (2.11/108.9). ... Full name: Maciej Boleslaw Lampe
**TRANSACTIONS/CAREER NOTES:** Played in Spain (2001-02 through 2002-03). ... Selected by New York Knicks in second round (30th pick overall) of 2003 NBA Draft. ... Traded by Knicks with G Howard Eisley, F Antonio McDyess, G Charlie Ward, draft rights to G Milos Vujanic, 2004 first-round draft choice and future first-round draft choice to Phoenix Suns for G Stephon Marbury, F/G Anfernee Hardaway and C Cezary Trybanski (January 5, 2004). ... Traded by Suns with G/F Casey Jacobsen and F/C Jackson Vroman to New Orleans Hornets for G Jim Jackson and a 2005 second-round draft choice (January 21, 2005).

## SPANISH RECORD

| Season Team | G | Min. | FGM | FGA | Pct. | FTM | FTA | Pct. | Reb. | Ast. | Pts. | AVERAGES RPG | APG | PPG |
|---|---|---|---|---|---|---|---|---|---|---|---|---|---|---|
| 01-02—Real Madrid II | 15 | 460 | 105 | 258 | .407 | 34 | 47 | .723 | 130 | 16 | 261 | 8.7 | 1.1 | 17.4 |
| 02-03—Universidad Complutense | 22 | 725 | 159 | 305 | .521 | 70 | 88 | .795 | 168 | 26 | 421 | 7.6 | 1.2 | 19.1 |
| Totals | 37 | 1185 | 264 | 563 | .469 | 104 | 135 | .770 | 298 | 42 | 682 | 8.1 | 1.1 | 18.4 |

Three-point field goals: 2001-02, 17-for-88 (.193). 2002-03, 33-for-73 (.452). Totals, 50-for-161 (.311).

## NBA REGULAR-SEASON RECORD

| Season Team | G | Min. | FGM | FGA | Pct. | FTM | FTA | Pct. | REBOUNDS Off. | Def. | Tot. | Ast. | St. | Blk. | TO | Pts. | AVERAGES RPG | APG | PPG |
|---|---|---|---|---|---|---|---|---|---|---|---|---|---|---|---|---|---|---|---|
| 03-04—Phoenix | 21 | 224 | 43 | 88 | .489 | 10 | 13 | .769 | 9 | 35 | 44 | 9 | 3 | 3 | 15 | 96 | 2.1 | 0.4 | 4.6 |
| 04-05—Phoenix-N.O. | 37 | 380 | 49 | 132 | .371 | 15 | 22 | .682 | 24 | 65 | 89 | 11 | 5 | 7 | 17 | 115 | 2.4 | 0.3 | 3.1 |
| Totals | 58 | 604 | 92 | 220 | .418 | 25 | 35 | .714 | 33 | 100 | 133 | 20 | 8 | 10 | 32 | 211 | 2.3 | 0.3 | 3.6 |

Three-point field goals: 2003-04, 0-for-4. 2004-05, 2-for-4 (.500). Totals, 2-for-8 (.250).
Personal fouls/disqualifications: 2003-04, 28/0. 2004-05, 51/0. Totals, 79/0.

# LENARD, VOSHON  G  NUGGETS

**PERSONAL:** Born May 14, 1973, in Detroit. ... 6-4/205. (1.93/93.0). ... Full name: Voshon Kelan Lenard ... Name pronounced Va-SHON.
**HIGH SCHOOL:** Southwestern (Detroit).
**COLLEGE:** Minnesota.
**TRANSACTIONS/CAREER NOTES:** Selected after junior season by Milwaukee Bucks in second round (46th pick overall) of

L

1994 NBA Draft. ... Returned to college for senior season (1994-95). ... Waived by Bucks (October 25, 1995). ... Played in Continental Basketball Association with Oklahoma City Cavalry (1995-96). ... Signed as free agent by Miami Heat for remainder of season (December 29, 1995). ... Traded by Heat with F Mark Strickland to Denver Nuggets for F/C Chris Gatling and a 2000 second-round draft choice (June 27, 2000). ... Signed as free agent by Toronto Raptors (October 23, 2002). ... Signed as free agent by Denver Nuggets (September 12, 2003).

### COLLEGIATE RECORD

| Season Team | G | Min. | FGM | FGA | Pct. | FTM | FTA | Pct. | Reb. | Ast. | Pts. | AVERAGES RPG | APG | PPG |
|---|---|---|---|---|---|---|---|---|---|---|---|---|---|---|
| 91-92—Minnesota | 32 | 868 | 139 | 330 | .421 | 82 | 101 | .812 | 118 | 86 | 411 | 3.7 | 2.7 | 12.8 |
| 92-93—Minnesota | 31 | 883 | 192 | 399 | .481 | 89 | 111 | .802 | 113 | 82 | 531 | 3.6 | 2.6 | 17.1 |
| 93-94—Minnesota | 33 | 1029 | 218 | 462 | .472 | 103 | 122 | .844 | 123 | 74 | 625 | 3.7 | 2.2 | 18.9 |
| 94-95—Minnesota | 31 | 992 | 174 | 422 | .412 | 107 | 141 | .759 | 134 | 80 | 536 | 4.3 | 2.6 | 17.3 |
| Totals | 127 | 3772 | 723 | 1613 | .448 | 381 | 475 | .802 | 488 | 322 | 2103 | 3.8 | 2.5 | 16.6 |

Three-point field goals: 1991-92, 51-for-144 (.354). 1992-93, 58-for-158 (.367). 1993-94, 86-for-209 (.411). 1994-95, 81-for-244 (.332). Totals, 276-for-755 (.366).

### CBA RECORD

| Season Team | G | Min. | FGM | FGA | Pct. | FTM | FTA | Pct. | Reb. | Ast. | Pts. | AVERAGES RPG | APG | PPG |
|---|---|---|---|---|---|---|---|---|---|---|---|---|---|---|
| 95-96—Oklahoma City | 18 | 711 | 189 | 387 | | 75 | 100 | .750 | 60 | 70 | 541 | 3.3 | 3.9 | 30.1 |

Three-point field goals: 1995-96, 88-for-203 (.433). Totals, 88-for-203 (.433).
Personal fouls/disqualifications: 1995-96, 66/0. Totals, 66/0.

### NBA REGULAR-SEASON RECORD

| Season Team | G | Min. | FGM | FGA | Pct. | FTM | FTA | Pct. | REBOUNDS Off. | Def. | Tot. | Ast. | St. | Blk. | TO | Pts. | AVERAGES RPG | APG | PPG |
|---|---|---|---|---|---|---|---|---|---|---|---|---|---|---|---|---|---|---|---|
| 95-96—Miami | 30 | 323 | 53 | 141 | .376 | 34 | 43 | .791 | 12 | 40 | 52 | 31 | 6 | 1 | 23 | 176 | 1.7 | 1.0 | 5.9 |
| 96-97—Miami | 73 | 2111 | 314 | 684 | .459 | 86 | 105 | .819 | 38 | 179 | 217 | 161 | 50 | 18 | 109 | 897 | 3.0 | 2.2 | 12.3 |
| 97-98—Miami | 81 | 2621 | 363 | 854 | .425 | 141 | 179 | .788 | 72 | 220 | 292 | 180 | 58 | 16 | 99 | 1020 | 3.6 | 2.2 | 12.6 |
| 98-99—Miami | 12 | 190 | 31 | 79 | .392 | 8 | 11 | .727 | 4 | 12 | 16 | 10 | 3 | 1 | 7 | 82 | 1.3 | 0.8 | 6.8 |
| 99-00—Miami | 53 | 1434 | 228 | 560 | .407 | 84 | 106 | .792 | 37 | 116 | 153 | 136 | 41 | 15 | 80 | 629 | 2.9 | 2.6 | 11.9 |
| 00-01—Denver | 80 | 2331 | 336 | 846 | .397 | 153 | 192 | .797 | 47 | 184 | 231 | 190 | 65 | 18 | 102 | 972 | 2.9 | 2.4 | 12.2 |
| 01-02—Denver | 71 | 1665 | 315 | 769 | .410 | 94 | 120 | .783 | 38 | 145 | 183 | 130 | 59 | 25 | 91 | 813 | 2.6 | 1.8 | 11.5 |
| 02-03—Toronto | 63 | 1929 | 325 | 809 | .402 | 156 | 194 | .804 | 48 | 164 | 212 | 144 | 59 | 21 | 103 | 898 | 3.4 | 2.3 | 14.3 |
| 03-04—Denver | 73 | 2233 | 394 | 933 | .422 | 144 | 182 | .791 | 46 | 154 | 200 | 151 | 61 | 12 | 101 | 1038 | 2.7 | 2.1 | 14.2 |
| 04-05—Denver | 3 | 54 | 10 | 26 | .385 | 5 | 8 | .625 | 0 | 6 | 6 | 6 | 1 | 0 | 2 | 29 | 2.0 | 2.0 | 9.7 |
| Totals | 539 | 14891 | 2369 | 5701 | .416 | 905 | 1140 | .794 | 342 | 1220 | 1562 | 1139 | 403 | 127 | 717 | 6554 | 2.9 | 2.1 | 12.2 |

Three-point field goals: 1995-96, 36-for-101 (.356). 1996-97, 183-for-442 (.414). 1997-98, 153-for-378 (.405). 1998-99, 12-for-35 (.343). 1999-00, 89-for-228 (.390). 2000-01, 147-for-382 (.385). 2001-02, 89-for-240 (.371). 2002-03, 92-for-252 (.365). 2003-04, 106-for-289 (.367). 2004-05, 4-for-12 (.333). Totals, 911-for-2359 (.386).

Personal fouls/disqualifications: 1995-96, 31/0. 1996-97, 168/1. 1997-98, 219/0. 1998-99, 18/0. 1999-00, 127/2. 2000-01, 170/1. 2001-02, 105/0. 2002-03, 156/1. 2003-04, 177/1. 2004-05, 2/0. Totals, 1173/6.

### NBA PLAYOFF RECORD

| Season Team | G | Min. | FGM | FGA | Pct. | FTM | FTA | Pct. | REBOUNDS Off. | Def. | Tot. | Ast. | St. | Blk. | TO | Pts. | AVERAGES RPG | APG | PPG |
|---|---|---|---|---|---|---|---|---|---|---|---|---|---|---|---|---|---|---|---|
| 96-97—Miami | 17 | 548 | 63 | 155 | .406 | 32 | 37 | .865 | 12 | 38 | 50 | 36 | 11 | 3 | 30 | 194 | 2.9 | 2.1 | 11.4 |
| 97-98—Miami | 5 | 186 | 24 | 52 | .462 | 15 | 20 | .750 | 1 | 18 | 19 | 7 | 1 | 2 | 11 | 72 | 3.8 | 1.4 | 14.4 |
| 98-99—Miami | 4 | 57 | 12 | 22 | .545 | 4 | 4 | 1.000 | 0 | 1 | 1 | 3 | 0 | 1 | 1 | 37 | 0.3 | 0.8 | 9.3 |
| 03-04—Denver | 5 | 161 | 32 | 75 | .427 | 10 | 14 | .714 | 4 | 9 | 13 | 12 | 4 | 0 | 9 | 85 | 2.6 | 2.4 | 17.0 |
| Totals | 31 | 952 | 131 | 304 | .431 | 61 | 75 | .813 | 17 | 66 | 83 | 58 | 16 | 6 | 51 | 388 | 2.7 | 1.9 | 12.5 |

Three-point field goals: 1996-97, 36-for-91 (.396). 1997-98, 9-for-26 (.346). 1998-99, 9-for-14 (.643). 2003-04, 11-for-24 (.458). Totals, 65-for-155 (.419).

Personal fouls/disqualifications: 1996-97, 49/0. 1997-98, 20/0. 1998-99, 4/0. 2003-04, 13/0. Totals, 86/0.

## LEWIS, RASHARD      F      SUPERSONICS

**PERSONAL:** Born August 8, 1979, in Pineville, La. ... 6-10/215. (2.08/97.5). ... Full name: Rashard Quovon Lewis
**HIGH SCHOOL:** Alief (Texas) Elsik.
**COLLEGE:** Did not attend college.
**TRANSACTIONS/CAREER NOTES:** Selected out of high school by Seattle SuperSonics in second round (32nd pick overall) of 1998 NBA Draft.

### NBA REGULAR-SEASON RECORD

| Season Team | G | Min. | FGM | FGA | Pct. | FTM | FTA | Pct. | REBOUNDS Off. | Def. | Tot. | Ast. | St. | Blk. | TO | Pts. | AVERAGES RPG | APG | PPG |
|---|---|---|---|---|---|---|---|---|---|---|---|---|---|---|---|---|---|---|---|
| 98-99—Seattle | 20 | 145 | 19 | 52 | .365 | 8 | 14 | .571 | 13 | 12 | 25 | 4 | 8 | 1 | 20 | 47 | 1.3 | 0.2 | 2.4 |
| 99-00—Seattle | 82 | 1575 | 275 | 566 | .486 | 84 | 123 | .683 | 127 | 209 | 336 | 70 | 62 | 36 | 78 | 674 | 4.1 | 0.9 | 8.2 |
| 00-01—Seattle | 78 | 2720 | 426 | 887 | .480 | 176 | 213 | .826 | 143 | 398 | 541 | 125 | 91 | 45 | 129 | 1151 | 6.9 | 1.6 | 14.8 |
| 01-02—Seattle | 71 | 2585 | 455 | 972 | .468 | 162 | 200 | .810 | 139 | 359 | 498 | 123 | 104 | 40 | 97 | 1195 | 7.0 | 1.7 | 16.8 |
| 02-03—Seattle | 77 | 3044 | 519 | 1149 | .452 | 283 | 345 | .820 | 152 | 351 | 503 | 133 | 99 | 35 | 143 | 1396 | 6.5 | 1.7 | 18.1 |
| 03-04—Seattle | 80 | 2931 | 535 | 1229 | .435 | 206 | 270 | .763 | 133 | 385 | 518 | 175 | 99 | 54 | 135 | 1421 | 6.5 | 2.2 | 17.8 |

| Season Team | G | Min. | FGM | FGA | Pct. | FTM | FTA | Pct. | Off. | Def. | Tot. | Ast. | St. | Blk. | TO | Pts. | RPG | APG | PPG |
|---|---|---|---|---|---|---|---|---|---|---|---|---|---|---|---|---|---|---|---|
| 04-05—Seattle | 71 | 2697 | 532 | 1151 | .462 | 220 | 283 | .777 | 110 | 278 | 388 | 94 | 75 | 62 | 123 | 1457 | 5.5 | 1.3 | 20.5 |
| Totals | 479 | 15697 | 2761 | 6006 | .460 | 1139 | 1448 | .787 | 817 | 1992 | 2809 | 724 | 538 | 273 | 725 | 7341 | 5.9 | 1.5 | 15.3 |

Three-point field goals: 1998-99, 1-for-6 (.167). 1999-00, 40-for-120 (.333). 2000-01, 123-for-285 (.432). 2001-02, 123-for-316 (.389). 2002-03, 75-for-217 (.346). 2003-04, 145-for-386 (.376). 2004-05, 173-for-432 (.400). Totals, 680-for-1762 (.386).

Personal fouls/disqualifications: 1998-99, 19/0. 1999-00, 163/0. 2000-01, 191/2. 2001-02, 174/3. 2002-03, 205/1. 2003-04, 233/3. 2004-05, 158/1. Totals, 1143/10.

## NBA PLAYOFF RECORD

| Season Team | G | Min. | FGM | FGA | Pct. | FTM | FTA | Pct. | Off. | Def. | Tot. | Ast. | St. | Blk. | TO | Pts. | RPG | APG | PPG |
|---|---|---|---|---|---|---|---|---|---|---|---|---|---|---|---|---|---|---|---|
| 99-00—Seattle | 5 | 157 | 26 | 59 | .441 | 16 | 20 | .800 | 12 | 19 | 31 | 3 | 5 | 3 | 10 | 77 | 6.2 | 0.6 | 15.4 |
| 01-02—Seattle | 3 | 79 | 12 | 32 | .375 | 13 | 13 | 1.000 | 4 | 7 | 11 | 2 | 1 | 0 | 2 | 38 | 3.7 | 0.7 | 12.7 |
| 04-05—Seattle | 8 | 312 | 43 | 106 | .406 | 44 | 50 | .880 | 11 | 32 | 43 | 13 | 3 | 6 | 16 | 135 | 5.4 | 1.6 | 16.9 |
| Totals | 16 | 548 | 81 | 197 | .411 | 73 | 83 | .880 | 27 | 58 | 85 | 18 | 9 | 6 | 28 | 250 | 5.3 | 1.1 | 15.6 |

Three-point field goals: 1999-00, 9-for-19 (.474). 2001-02, 1-for-6 (.167). 2004-05, 5-for-25 (.200). Totals, 15-for-50 (.300).
Personal fouls/disqualifications: 1999-00, 11/0. 2001-02, 10/0. 2004-05, 25/0. Totals, 46/0.

## NBA ALL-STAR GAME RECORD

| Season Team | Min. | FGM | FGA | Pct. | FTM | FTA | Pct. | Off. | Def. | Tot. | Ast. | PF | Dq. | St. | Blk. | TO | Pts. |
|---|---|---|---|---|---|---|---|---|---|---|---|---|---|---|---|---|---|
| 2005—Seattle | 14 | 1 | 7 | .143 | 0 | 0 | ... | 1 | 3 | 4 | 1 | 2 | 0 | 1 | 0 | 1 | 2 |

Three-point field goals: 2005, 0-for-2. Totals, 0-for-2 (.000).

# LIVINGSTON, RANDY     G

**PERSONAL:** Born April 2, 1975, in New Orleans. ... 6-4/209. (1.93/94.8). ... Full name: Randy Anthony Livingston
**HIGH SCHOOL:** Newman (New Orleans).
**COLLEGE:** Louisiana State.
**TRANSACTIONS/CAREER NOTES:** Selected after sophomore season by Houston Rockets in second round (42nd pick overall) of 1996 NBA Draft. ... Waived by Rockets (October 30, 1997). ... Signed as free agent by Atlanta Hawks (November 7, 1997). ... Waived by Hawks (November 20, 1997). ... Played in Continental Basketball Association with Sioux Falls Skyforce (1997-98, 1998-99 and 2001-02), Idaho Stampede (2000-01, 2003-04) and Gary Steelheads (2001-02). ... Re-signed as free agent by Hawks (December 9, 1997). ... Waived by Hawks (December 19, 1997). ... Re-signed by Hawks to 10-day contract (January 10, 1998). ... Signed as free agent by Miami Heat (January 21, 1999). ... Waived by Heat (January 30, 1999). ... Signed as free agent by Phoenix Suns for remainder of season (May 4, 1999). ... Waived by Suns (August 31, 2000). ... Signed as free agent by Seattle SuperSonics (October 2, 2000). ... Claimed on waivers by Orlando Magic (October 13, 2000). ... Waived by Magic (October 30, 2000). ... Signed as free agent by Golden State Warriors (November 15, 2000). ... Waived by Warriors (November 21, 2000). ... Played in International Basketball League with Sioux Falls Skyforce (2000-01). ... Signed as free agent by Utah Jazz (October 2, 2001). ... Waived by Jazz (October 25, 2001). ... Signed by Seattle SuperSonics to 10-day contract (March 8, 2002). ... Signed by SuperSonics for remainder of season (March 27, 2002). ... Signed as free agent by Minnesota Timberwolves (October 1, 2002). ... Waived by Timberwolves (October 28, 2002). ... Signed by New Orleans Hornets to 10-day contract (January 27, 2003). ... Waived by Hornets (February 5, 2003). ... Signed by Los Angeles Clippers to 10-day contract (March 28, 2004). ... Signed by Utah Jazz to 10-day contract (March 2, 2005).

## COLLEGIATE RECORD

| Season Team | G | Min. | FGM | FGA | Pct. | FTM | FTA | Pct. | Reb. | Ast. | Pts. | RPG | APG | PPG |
|---|---|---|---|---|---|---|---|---|---|---|---|---|---|---|
| 93-94—Louisiana State | | | | | | Did not play—redshirted. | | | | | | | | |
| 94-95—Louisiana State | 16 | 550 | 81 | 185 | .438 | 42 | 62 | .677 | 64 | 151 | 224 | 4.0 | 9.4 | 14.0 |
| 95-96—Louisiana State | 13 | 318 | 24 | 83 | .289 | 30 | 38 | .789 | 30 | 69 | 79 | 2.3 | 5.3 | 6.1 |
| Totals | 29 | 868 | 105 | 268 | .392 | 72 | 100 | .720 | 94 | 220 | 303 | 3.2 | 7.6 | 10.4 |

Three-point field goals: 1994-95, 20-for-65 (.308). 1995-96, 1-for-20 (.050). Totals, 21-for-85 (.247).

## NBA REGULAR-SEASON RECORD

| Season Team | G | Min. | FGM | FGA | Pct. | FTM | FTA | Pct. | Off. | Def. | Tot. | Ast. | St. | Blk. | TO | Pts. | RPG | APG | PPG |
|---|---|---|---|---|---|---|---|---|---|---|---|---|---|---|---|---|---|---|---|
| 96-97—Houston | 64 | 981 | 100 | 229 | .437 | 42 | 65 | .646 | 32 | 62 | 94 | 155 | 39 | 12 | 102 | 251 | 1.5 | 2.4 | 3.9 |
| 97-98—Atlanta | 12 | 82 | 3 | 12 | .250 | 4 | 5 | .800 | 1 | 5 | 6 | 5 | 7 | 2 | 6 | 10 | 0.5 | 0.4 | 0.8 |
| 98-99—Phoenix | 1 | 22 | 5 | 8 | .625 | 2 | 2 | 1.000 | 0 | 2 | 2 | 3 | 2 | 0 | 1 | 12 | 2.0 | 3.0 | 12.0 |
| 99-00—Phoenix | 79 | 1081 | 155 | 373 | .416 | 52 | 62 | .839 | 25 | 105 | 130 | 170 | 49 | 13 | 92 | 381 | 1.6 | 2.2 | 4.8 |
| 00-01—Golden State | 2 | 7 | 0 | 2 | .000 | 0 | 0 | ... | 0 | 1 | 1 | 1 | 0 | 0 | 0 | 0 | 0.5 | 0.5 | 0.0 |
| 01-02—Seattle | 13 | 176 | 15 | 54 | .278 | 10 | 11 | .909 | 9 | 16 | 25 | 26 | 9 | 2 | 2 | 41 | 1.9 | 2.0 | 3.2 |
| 02-03—New Orleans | 2 | 12 | 2 | 4 | .500 | 2 | 2 | 1.000 | 0 | 0 | 0 | 1 | 0 | 0 | 0 | 6 | 0.0 | 0.5 | 3.0 |
| 03-04—L.A. Clippers | 2 | 48 | 2 | 10 | .200 | 4 | 6 | .667 | 2 | 5 | 7 | 4 | 2 | 0 | 4 | 8 | 1.8 | 1.0 | 2.0 |
| 04-05—Utah | 17 | 227 | 22 | 52 | .423 | 15 | 17 | .882 | 3 | 9 | 12 | 45 | 12 | 2 | 14 | 64 | 0.7 | 2.6 | 3.8 |
| Totals | 194 | 2636 | 304 | 744 | .409 | 131 | 170 | .771 | 72 | 205 | 277 | 410 | 120 | 31 | 221 | 773 | 1.4 | 2.1 | 4.0 |

Three-point field goals: 1996-97, 9-for-22 (.409). 1999-00, 19-for-55 (.345). 2000-01, 0-for-1. 2001-02, 1-for-8 (.125). 2003-04, 0-for-3. 2004-05, 5-for-8 (.625). Totals, 34-for-97 (.351).
Personal fouls/disqualifications: 1996-97, 107/0. 1997-98, 6/0. 1998-99, 1/0. 1999-00, 129/1. 2001-02, 11/0. 2003-04, 7/0. 2004-05, 28/0. Totals, 289/1.

## NBA PLAYOFF RECORD

| Season Team | G | Min. | FGM | FGA | Pct. | FTM | FTA | Pct. | Off. | Def. | Tot. | Ast. | St. | Blk. | TO | Pts. | RPG | APG | PPG |
|---|---|---|---|---|---|---|---|---|---|---|---|---|---|---|---|---|---|---|---|
| 96-97—Houston | 2 | 15 | 1 | 4 | .250 | 0 | 0 | ... | 0 | 0 | 0 | 4 | 1 | 0 | 1 | 3 | 0.0 | 2.0 | 1.5 |
| 98-99—Phoenix | 3 | 24 | 6 | 15 | .400 | 4 | 4 | 1.000 | 5 | 2 | 7 | 2 | 1 | 0 | 2 | 16 | 2.3 | 0.7 | 5.3 |
| 99-00—Phoenix | 7 | 63 | 6 | 27 | .222 | 0 | 0 | ... | 2 | 5 | 7 | 4 | 4 | 1 | 4 | 14 | 1.0 | 0.6 | 2.0 |
| 01-02—Seattle | 5 | 80 | 7 | 17 | .412 | 5 | 5 | 1.000 | 1 | 5 | 6 | 10 | 2 | 0 | 1 | 20 | 1.2 | 2.0 | 4.0 |
| Totals | 17 | 182 | 20 | 63 | .317 | 9 | 9 | 1.000 | 8 | 12 | 20 | 20 | 8 | 1 | 8 | 53 | 1.2 | 1.2 | 3.1 |

Three-point field goals: 1996-97, 1-for-1 (1.000). 1998-99, 0-for-1. 1999-00, 2-for-6 (.333). 2001-02, 1-for-3 (.333). Totals, 4-for-11 (.364).
Personal fouls/disqualifications: 1996-97, 1/0. 1998-99, 6/0. 1999-00, 6/0. 2001-02, 7/0. Totals, 20/0.

**NOTES:** CBA All-League second team (1999).

| Season Team | G | Min. | FGM | FGA | Pct. | FTM | FTA | Pct. | Reb. | Ast. | Pts. | RPG | APG | PPG |
|---|---|---|---|---|---|---|---|---|---|---|---|---|---|---|
| 97-98—Sioux Falls | 28 | 1049 | 160 | 387 | .413 | 91 | 128 | .711 | 151 | 187 | 424 | 5.4 | 6.7 | 15.1 |
| 98-99—Sioux Falls | 40 | 1321 | 196 | 483 | .406 | 128 | 159 | .805 | 168 | 259 | 546 | 4.2 | 6.5 | 13.7 |
| 00-01—Idaho | 24 | 892 | 128 | 328 | .390 | 56 | 65 | .862 | 87 | 174 | 339 | 3.6 | 7.3 | 14.1 |
| 01-02—Gary-Sioux Falls | 36 | 1195 | 128 | 361 | .355 | 101 | 114 | .886 | 151 | 259 | 401 | 4.2 | 7.2 | 11.1 |
| 02-03—Sioux Falls | 12 | 494 | 57 | 149 | .383 | 42 | 48 | .875 | 64 | 98 | 168 | 5.3 | 8.2 | 14.0 |
| 03-04—Idaho | 32 | 1185 | 139 | 367 | .379 | 96 | 109 | .881 | 147 | 303 | 410 | 4.6 | 9.5 | 12.8 |
| 04-05—Sioux Falls | 40 | 1464 | 167 | 408 | .409 | 156 | 187 | .834 | 202 | 336 | 527 | 5.1 | 8.4 | 13.2 |
| Totals | 212 | 7600 | 975 | 2483 | .393 | 670 | 810 | .827 | 970 | 1616 | 2815 | 4.6 | 7.6 | 13.3 |

Three-point field goals: 1997-98, 13-for-57 (.228). 1998-99, 26-for-101 (.257). 2000-01, 27-for-105 (.257). 2001-02, 44-for-168 (.262). 2002-03, 12-for-34 (.353). 2003-04, 36-for-114 (.316). 2004-05, 37-for-123 (.301). Totals, 195-for-702 (.278).
Personal fouls/disqualifications: 1998-99, 132/0. 2000-01, 77/0. 2002-03, 43/0. Totals, 252/0.

## INTERNATIONAL BASKETBALL LEAGUE RECORD

| Season Team | G | Min. | FGM | FGA | Pct. | FTM | FTA | Pct. | Reb. | Ast. | Pts. | RPG | APG | PPG |
|---|---|---|---|---|---|---|---|---|---|---|---|---|---|---|
| 00-01—Sioux Falls | 26 | 885 | 138 | 335 | .412 | 74 | 88 | .841 | 100 | 164 | 400 | 3.8 | 6.3 | 15.4 |

Three-point field goals: 2000-01, 50-for-126 (.397). Totals, 50-for-126 (.397).

# LIVINGSTON, SHAUN  G  CLIPPERS

**PERSONAL:** Born September 11, 1985, in Peoria, Ill. ... 6-7/175. (2.01/79.4).
**HIGH SCHOOL:** Peoria Richwoods (Ill.), then Peoria Central (Ill.
**COLLEGE:** Did not attend college.
**TRANSACTIONS/CAREER NOTES:** Selected out of high school by Los Angeles Clippers in first round (fourth pick overall) of 2004 NBA Draft.

## NBA REGULAR-SEASON RECORD

| Season Team | G | Min. | FGM | FGA | Pct. | FTM | FTA | Pct. | REBOUNDS Off. | Def. | Tot. | Ast. | St. | Blk. | TO | Pts. | RPG | APG | PPG |
|---|---|---|---|---|---|---|---|---|---|---|---|---|---|---|---|---|---|---|---|
| 04-05—L.A. Clippers | 30 | 814 | 89 | 215 | .414 | 44 | 59 | .746 | 22 | 67 | 89 | 151 | 32 | 11 | 75 | 222 | 3.0 | 5.0 | 7.4 |

Three-point field goals: 2004-05, 0-for-2. Totals, 0-for-2 (.000).
Personal fouls/disqualifications: 2004-05, 82/1. Totals, 82/1.

# LOPEZ, RAUL  G

**PERSONAL:** Born April 15, 1980, in Vic, Spain. ... 6-0/180. (1.83/81.6).
**COLLEGE:** Did not attend college.
**TRANSACTIONS/CAREER NOTES:** Played in Spain (1997-2002). ... Selected by Utah Jazz in first round (24th pick overall) of 2001 NBA Draft. ... Signed by Jazz (September 26, 2002). ... Traded by Jazz to Memphis Grizzlies in five-team trade (August 2, 2005). ... Waived by Grizzlies (August 16, 2005).
**MISCELLANEOUS:** Member of Spanish Olympic team (2000).

## SPANISH RECORD

| Season Team | G | Min. | FGM | FGA | Pct. | FTM | FTA | Pct. | Reb. | Ast. | Pts. | RPG | APG | PPG |
|---|---|---|---|---|---|---|---|---|---|---|---|---|---|---|
| 97-98—Festina Andorra | 1 | 18 | 3 | 6 | .500 | 1 | 2 | .500 | 2 | 4 | 10 | 2.0 | 4.0 | 10.0 |
| 98-99—Pinturas Bruguer Badalona | 34 | 500 | 44 | 113 | .389 | 49 | 65 | .754 | 42 | 54 | 149 | 1.2 | 1.6 | 4.4 |
| 99-00—Pinturas Bruguer Badalona | 32 | 757 | 116 | 246 | .472 | 61 | 73 | .836 | 50 | 90 | 323 | 1.6 | 2.8 | 10.1 |
| 00-01—Real Madrid | 32 | 654 | 73 | 157 | .465 | 48 | 65 | .738 | 48 | 79 | 225 | 1.5 | 2.5 | 7.0 |
| 01-02—Real Madrid | 9 | 181 | 22 | 77 | .286 | 13 | 16 | .813 | 25 | 26 | 62 | 2.8 | 2.9 | 6.9 |
| Totals | 108 | 2110 | 258 | 599 | .431 | 172 | 221 | .778 | 167 | 253 | 769 | 1.5 | 2.3 | 7.1 |

Three-point field goals: 1997-98, 3-for-3 (1.000). 1998-99, 12-for-30 (.400). 1999-00, 30-for-79 (.380). 2000-01, 31-for-79 (.392). 2001-02, 5-for-22 (.227). Totals, 81-for-213 (.380).
Personal fouls/disqualifications: 1997-98, 2/0. 1998-99, 61/0. 1999-00, 77/0. 2000-01, 75/0. Totals, 215/0.

## NBA REGULAR-SEASON RECORD

| Season Team | G | Min. | FGM | FGA | Pct. | FTM | FTA | Pct. | REBOUNDS Off. | Def. | Tot. | Ast. | St. | Blk. | TO | Pts. | RPG | APG | PPG |
|---|---|---|---|---|---|---|---|---|---|---|---|---|---|---|---|---|---|---|---|
| 02-03—Utah | | | | | | | Did not play; injured. | | | | | | | | | | | | |
| 03-04—Utah | 82 | 1617 | 223 | 517 | .431 | 101 | 117 | .863 | 24 | 131 | 155 | 305 | 62 | 2 | 174 | 572 | 1.9 | 3.7 | 7.0 |
| 04-05—Utah | 31 | 518 | 57 | 135 | .422 | 27 | 33 | .818 | 7 | 32 | 39 | 123 | 22 | 3 | 47 | 161 | 1.3 | 4.0 | 5.2 |
| Totals | 113 | 2135 | 280 | 652 | .429 | 128 | 150 | .853 | 31 | 163 | 194 | 428 | 84 | 5 | 221 | 733 | 1.7 | 3.8 | 6.5 |

Three-point field goals: 2003-04, 25-for-85 (.294). 2004-05, 20-for-45 (.444). Totals, 45-for-130 (.346).
Personal fouls/disqualifications: 2003-04, 200/2. 2004-05, 78/0. Totals, 278/2.

# LUE, TYRONN  G  HAWKS

**PERSONAL:** Born May 3, 1977, in Mexico, Mo. ... 6-0/178. (1.83/80.7). ... Full name: Tyronn Jamar Lue
**HIGH SCHOOL:** Raytown (Kansas City, Mo.).
**COLLEGE:** Nebraska.
**TRANSACTIONS/CAREER NOTES:** Selected after junior season by Denver Nuggets in first round (23rd pick overall) of 1998 NBA Draft. ... Draft rights traded by Nuggets with F Tony Battie to Los Angeles Lakers for G Nick Van Exel (June 24, 1998). ... Signed as free agent by Washington Wizards (July 18, 2001). ... Signed as free agent by Orlando Magic (July 23, 2003) ... Traded by Magic

L

with G Tracy McGrady, F Juwan Howard and G Reece Gaines to Houston Rockets for G Steve Francis, G Cuttino Mobley and C Kelvin Cato (June 29, 2004). ... Traded by Rockets to Atlanta Hawks for G Jon Barry (December 23, 2004).
**MISCELLANEOUS:** Member of NBA championship team (2000, 2001).

## COLLEGIATE RECORD

| Season Team | G | Min. | FGM | FGA | Pct. | FTM | FTA | Pct. | Reb. | Ast. | Pts. | AVERAGES RPG | APG | PPG |
|---|---|---|---|---|---|---|---|---|---|---|---|---|---|---|
| 95-96—Nebraska ...... | 35 | 1033 | 105 | 232 | .453 | 66 | 96 | .688 | 106 | 144 | 296 | 3.0 | 4.1 | 8.5 |
| 96-97—Nebraska ...... | 32 | 1150 | 215 | 476 | .452 | 126 | 155 | .813 | 93 | 136 | 603 | 2.9 | 4.3 | 18.8 |
| 97-98—Nebraska ...... | 32 | 1149 | 240 | 547 | .439 | 120 | 145 | .828 | 137 | 152 | 678 | 4.3 | 4.8 | 21.2 |
| Totals ...................... | 99 | 3332 | 560 | 1255 | .446 | 312 | 396 | .788 | 336 | 432 | 1577 | 3.4 | 4.4 | 15.9 |

Three-point field goals: 1995-96, 20-for-61 (.328). 1996-97, 47-for-137 (.343). 1997-98, 78-for-209 (.373). Totals, 145-for-407 (.356).

## NBA REGULAR-SEASON RECORD

| Season Team | G | Min. | FGM | FGA | Pct. | FTM | FTA | Pct. | REBOUNDS Off. | Def. | Tot. | Ast. | St. | Blk. | TO | Pts. | AVERAGES RPG | APG | PPG |
|---|---|---|---|---|---|---|---|---|---|---|---|---|---|---|---|---|---|---|---|
| 98-99—L.A. Lakers .... | 15 | 188 | 28 | 65 | .431 | 12 | 21 | .571 | 2 | 4 | 6 | 25 | 5 | 0 | 11 | 75 | 0.4 | 1.7 | 5.0 |
| 99-00—L.A. Lakers .... | 8 | 146 | 19 | 39 | .487 | 6 | 8 | .750 | 2 | 10 | 12 | 17 | 3 | 0 | 9 | 48 | 1.5 | 2.1 | 6.0 |
| 00-01—L.A. Lakers .... | 38 | 468 | 50 | 117 | .427 | 19 | 24 | .792 | 5 | 27 | 32 | 45 | 19 | 0 | 27 | 130 | 0.8 | 1.2 | 3.4 |
| 01-02—Washington ... | 71 | 1458 | 222 | 520 | .427 | 48 | 63 | .762 | 14 | 108 | 122 | 246 | 49 | 0 | 96 | 555 | 1.7 | 3.5 | 7.8 |
| 02-03—Washington ... | 75 | 1986 | 248 | 573 | .433 | 91 | 104 | .875 | 22 | 127 | 149 | 263 | 47 | 1 | 77 | 647 | 2.0 | 3.5 | 8.6 |
| 03-04—Orlando.......... | 76 | 2332 | 309 | 714 | .433 | 101 | 131 | .771 | 26 | 161 | 187 | 317 | 61 | 5 | 124 | 799 | 2.5 | 4.2 | 10.5 |
| 04-05—Houston-Atl. ... | 70 | 2007 | 295 | 654 | .451 | 142 | 165 | .861 | 14 | 135 | 149 | 322 | 33 | 0 | 105 | 787 | 2.1 | 4.6 | 11.2 |
| Totals ................... | 353 | 8585 | 1171 | 2682 | .437 | 419 | 516 | .812 | 85 | 572 | 657 | 1235 | 217 | 6 | 449 | 3041 | 1.9 | 3.5 | 8.6 |

Three-point field goals: 1998-99, 7-for-16 (.438). 1999-00, 4-for-8 (.500). 2000-01, 11-for-34 (.324). 2001-02, 63-for-141 (.447). 2002-03, 60-for-176 (.341). 2003-04, 80-for-209 (.383). 2004-05, 55-for-155 (.355). Totals, 280-for-739 (.379).
Personal fouls/disqualifications: 1998-99, 28/0. 1999-00, 17/0. 2000-01, 54/1. 2001-02, 120/2. 2002-03, 151/0. 2003-04, 185/0. 2004-05, 168/2. Totals, 723/5.

## NBA PLAYOFF RECORD

| Season Team | G | Min. | FGM | FGA | Pct. | FTM | FTA | Pct. | REBOUNDS Off. | Def. | Tot. | Ast. | St. | Blk. | TO | Pts. | AVERAGES RPG | APG | PPG |
|---|---|---|---|---|---|---|---|---|---|---|---|---|---|---|---|---|---|---|---|
| 98-99—L.A. Lakers ..... | 3 | 33 | 7 | 17 | .412 | 0 | 0 | ... | 0 | 2 | 2 | 6 | 2 | 0 | 4 | 14 | 0.7 | 2.0 | 4.7 |
| 00-01—L.A. Lakers ..... | 15 | 131 | 10 | 29 | .345 | 4 | 5 | .800 | 1 | 9 | 10 | 10 | 12 | 1 | 8 | 29 | 0.7 | 0.7 | 1.9 |
| Totals ................... | 18 | 164 | 17 | 46 | .370 | 4 | 5 | .800 | 1 | 11 | 12 | 16 | 14 | 1 | 12 | 43 | 0.7 | 0.9 | 2.4 |

Three-point field goals: 1998-99, 0-for-2. 2000-01, 5-for-13 (.385). Totals, 5-for-15 (.333).
Personal fouls/disqualifications: 1998-99, 4/0. 2000-01, 11/0. Totals, 15/0.

---

# LYNCH, GEORGE   F   HORNETS

**PERSONAL:** Born September 3, 1970, in Roanoke, Va. ... 6-8/235. (2.03/106.6). ... Full name: George DeWitt Lynch.
**HIGH SCHOOL:** Patrick Henry (Roanoke, Va.), then Flint Hill Prep.
**COLLEGE:** North Carolina.
**TRANSACTIONS/CAREER NOTES:** Selected by Los Angeles Lakers in first round (12th pick overall) of 1993 NBA Draft. ... Traded by Lakers with G Anthony Peeler and 1997 and 1998 second-round draft choices to Vancouver Grizzlies for 1997 and 1998 second-round draft choices (July 16, 1996). ... Signed as free agent by Philadelphia 76ers (January 21, 1999). ... Traded by 76ers to Charlotte Hornets as part of three-way deal in which Hornets received F/C Robert Traylor and F Jerome Moiso from 76ers and F Chris Porter from Golden State Warriors, 76ers received F Derrick Coleman from Hornets and G Vonteego Cummings and F Corie Blount from Warriors, and Warriors received F Cedric Henderson and conditional 2005 first-round draft choice from 76ers and cash considerations from Hornets (October 25, 2001). ... Hornets franchise moved to New Orleans for 2002-03 season.

## COLLEGIATE RECORD

**NOTES:** Member of NCAA Division I championship team (1993).

| Season Team | G | Min. | FGM | FGA | Pct. | FTM | FTA | Pct. | Reb. | Ast. | Pts. | AVERAGES RPG | APG | PPG |
|---|---|---|---|---|---|---|---|---|---|---|---|---|---|---|
| 89-90—North Carolina.............. | 34 | 663 | 112 | 215 | .521 | 67 | 101 | .663 | 183 | 34 | 292 | 5.4 | 1.0 | 8.6 |
| 90-91—North Carolina.............. | 35 | 912 | 172 | 329 | .523 | 85 | 135 | .630 | 258 | 41 | 436 | 7.4 | 1.2 | 12.5 |
| 91-92—North Carolina.............. | 33 | 982 | 192 | 356 | .539 | 74 | 114 | .649 | 291 | 86 | 459 | 8.8 | 2.6 | 13.9 |
| 92-93—North Carolina.............. | 38 | 1148 | 235 | 469 | .501 | 88 | 132 | .667 | 365 | 72 | 560 | 9.6 | 1.9 | 14.7 |
| Totals ..................................... | 140 | 3705 | 711 | 1369 | .519 | 314 | 482 | .651 | 1097 | 233 | 1747 | 7.8 | 1.7 | 12.5 |

Three-point field goals: 1989-90, 1-for-3 (.333). 1990-91, 7-for-10 (.700). 1991-92, 1-for-8 (.125). 1992-93, 2-for-11 (.182). Totals, 11-for-32 (.344).

## NBA REGULAR-SEASON RECORD

| Season Team | G | Min. | FGM | FGA | Pct. | FTM | FTA | Pct. | REBOUNDS Off. | Def. | Tot. | Ast. | St. | Blk. | TO | Pts. | AVERAGES RPG | APG | PPG |
|---|---|---|---|---|---|---|---|---|---|---|---|---|---|---|---|---|---|---|---|
| 93-94—L.A. Lakers ..... | 71 | 1762 | 291 | 573 | .508 | 99 | 166 | .596 | 220 | 190 | 410 | 96 | 102 | 27 | 87 | 681 | 5.8 | 1.4 | 9.6 |
| 94-95—L.A. Lakers ..... | 56 | 953 | 138 | 295 | .468 | 62 | 86 | .721 | 75 | 109 | 184 | 62 | 51 | 10 | 73 | 341 | 3.3 | 1.1 | 6.1 |
| 95-96—L.A. Lakers ..... | 76 | 1012 | 117 | 272 | .430 | 53 | 80 | .663 | 82 | 127 | 209 | 51 | 47 | 10 | 40 | 291 | 2.8 | 0.7 | 3.8 |
| 96-97—Vancouver...... | 41 | 1059 | 137 | 291 | .471 | 60 | 97 | .619 | 98 | 163 | 261 | 76 | 63 | 17 | 64 | 342 | 6.4 | 1.9 | 8.3 |
| 97-98—Vancouver....... | 82 | 1493 | 248 | 516 | .481 | 111 | 158 | .703 | 147 | 215 | 362 | 122 | 65 | 41 | 104 | 616 | 4.4 | 1.5 | 7.5 |
| 98-99—Philadelphia ... | 43 | 1315 | 147 | 349 | .421 | 53 | 84 | .631 | 110 | 169 | 279 | 76 | 85 | 22 | 79 | 356 | 6.5 | 1.8 | 8.3 |
| 99-00—Philadelphia ... | 75 | 2416 | 297 | 644 | .461 | 113 | 183 | .617 | 216 | 366 | 582 | 136 | 119 | 38 | 120 | 722 | 7.8 | 1.8 | 9.6 |
| 00-01—Philadelphia ... | 82 | 2649 | 274 | 616 | .445 | 123 | 171 | .719 | 200 | 390 | 590 | 139 | 99 | 30 | 109 | 686 | 7.2 | 1.7 | 8.4 |
| 01-02—Charlotte ....... | 45 | 893 | 73 | 198 | .369 | 25 | 40 | .625 | 70 | 116 | 186 | 54 | 40 | 14 | 41 | 172 | 4.1 | 1.2 | 3.8 |
| 02-03—New Orleans ... | 81 | 1497 | 147 | 359 | .409 | 41 | 74 | .554 | 139 | 214 | 353 | 104 | 66 | 19 | 52 | 363 | 4.4 | 1.3 | 4.5 |
| 03-04—New Orleans ... | 78 | 1701 | 149 | 375 | .397 | 34 | 51 | .667 | 96 | 216 | 312 | 117 | 48 | 18 | 64 | 375 | 4.0 | 1.5 | 4.8 |
| 04-05—New Orleans ... | 44 | 933 | 68 | 189 | .360 | 17 | 23 | .739 | 55 | 119 | 174 | 88 | 32 | 12 | 57 | 164 | 4.0 | 2.0 | 3.7 |
| Totals ................... | 774 | 17683 | 2086 | 4677 | .446 | 791 | 1213 | .652 | 1508 | 2394 | 3902 | 1121 | 817 | 258 | 890 | 5109 | 5.0 | 1.4 | 6.6 |

Three-point field goals: 1993-94, 0-for-5. 1994-95, 3-for-21 (.143). 1995-96, 4-for-13 (.308). 1996-97, 8-for-31 (.258). 1997-98, 9-for-30 (.300). 1998-99, 9-for-23 (.391). 1999-00, 15-for-36 (.417). 2000-01, 15-for-57 (.263). 2001-02, 1-for-6 (.167). 2002-03, 28-for-79 (.354). 2003-04, 43-for-139 (.309).

2004-05, 11-for-37 (.297). Totals, 146-for-477 (.306).

Personal fouls/disqualifications: 1993-94, 177/1. 1994-95, 86/0. 1995-96, 106/0. 1996-97, 97/1. 1997-98, 161/0. 1998-99, 142/2. 1999-00, 231/2. 2000-01, 222/2. 2001-02, 75/1. 2002-03, 136/1. 2003-04, 159/1. 2004-05, 83/0. Totals, 1675/11.

## NBA PLAYOFF RECORD

| Season Team | G | Min. | FGM | FGA | Pct. | FTM | FTA | Pct. | REBOUNDS Off. | Def. | Tot. | Ast. | St. | Blk. | TO | Pts. | AVERAGES RPG | APG | PPG |
|---|---|---|---|---|---|---|---|---|---|---|---|---|---|---|---|---|---|---|---|
| 94-95—L.A. Lakers ..... | 10 | 136 | 15 | 32 | .469 | 13 | 20 | .650 | 13 | 17 | 30 | 7 | 8 | 0 | 9 | 44 | 3.0 | 0.7 | 4.4 |
| 95-96—L.A. Lakers ..... | 2 | 15 | 2 | 4 | .500 | 0 | 0 | ... | 0 | 3 | 3 | 1 | 0 | 0 | 2 | 4 | 1.5 | 0.5 | 2.0 |
| 98-99—Philadelphia .... | 8 | 249 | 29 | 65 | .446 | 12 | 17 | .706 | 28 | 25 | 53 | 16 | 18 | 2 | 13 | 72 | 6.6 | 2.0 | 9.0 |
| 99-00—Philadelphia .... | 10 | 293 | 22 | 65 | .338 | 14 | 18 | .778 | 26 | 45 | 71 | 14 | 9 | 5 | 8 | 59 | 7.1 | 1.4 | 5.9 |
| 00-01—Philadelphia .... | 10 | 222 | 24 | 50 | .480 | 9 | 14 | .643 | 20 | 31 | 51 | 12 | 13 | 2 | 13 | 57 | 5.1 | 1.2 | 5.7 |
| 01-02—Charlotte ........ | 9 | 286 | 29 | 59 | .492 | 9 | 13 | .692 | 32 | 44 | 76 | 14 | 10 | 6 | 10 | 69 | 8.4 | 1.6 | 7.7 |
| 02-03—New Orleans ... | 6 | 163 | 18 | 42 | .429 | 1 | 4 | .250 | 10 | 27 | 37 | 10 | 6 | 5 | 8 | 42 | 6.2 | 1.7 | 7.0 |
| 03-04—New Orleans ... | 7 | 147 | 25 | 57 | .439 | 5 | 8 | .625 | 13 | 24 | 37 | 12 | 3 | 3 | 7 | 58 | 5.3 | 1.7 | 8.3 |
| Totals .................. | 62 | 1511 | 164 | 374 | .439 | 63 | 94 | .670 | 142 | 216 | 358 | 86 | 67 | 23 | 70 | 405 | 5.8 | 1.4 | 6.5 |

Three-point field goals: 1994-95, 1-for-5 (.200). 1995-96, 0-for-6 (.333). 1999-00, 2-for-6 (.333). 1999-00, 1-for-7 (.143). 2000-01, 0-for-1. 2001-02, 2-for-6 (.333). 2002-03, 5-for-18 (.278). 2003-04, 3-for-12 (.250). Totals, 14-for-56 (.250).

Personal fouls/disqualifications: 1994-95, 22/0. 1995-96, 4/0. 1998-99, 30/1. 1999-00, 33/1. 2000-01, 30/0. 2001-02, 26/0. 2002-03, 14/0. 2003-04, 15/0. Totals, 174/2.

---

# MADSEN, MARK     F     TIMBERWOLVES

**PERSONAL:** Born January 28, 1976, in Walnut Creek, Calif. ... 6-9/236. (2.06/107.0). ... Full name: Mark Ellsworth Madsen
**HIGH SCHOOL:** San Ramon Valley (Danville, Calif.).
**COLLEGE:** Stanford.
**TRANSACTIONS/CAREER NOTES:** Selected by Los Angeles Lakers in first round (29th pick overall) of 2000 NBA Draft. ... Signed as free agent by Minnesota Timberwolves (July 28, 2003).
**MISCELLANEOUS:** Member of NBA championship team (2001, 2002).

## COLLEGIATE RECORD

| Season Team | G | Min. | FGM | FGA | Pct. | FTM | FTA | Pct. | Reb. | Ast. | Pts. | AVERAGES RPG | APG | PPG |
|---|---|---|---|---|---|---|---|---|---|---|---|---|---|---|
| 96-97—Stanford ...................... | 25 | 410 | 51 | 95 | .537 | 45 | 74 | .608 | 126 | 8 | 147 | 5.0 | 0.3 | 5.9 |
| 97-98—Stanford ...................... | 27 | 706 | 116 | 197 | .589 | 83 | 132 | .629 | 220 | 20 | 315 | 8.1 | 0.7 | 11.7 |
| 98-99—Stanford ...................... | 33 | 969 | 153 | 253 | .605 | 127 | 218 | .583 | 297 | 16 | 433 | 9.0 | 0.5 | 13.1 |
| 99-00—Stanford ...................... | 23 | 628 | 108 | 184 | .587 | 65 | 113 | .575 | 214 | 25 | 281 | 9.3 | 1.1 | 12.2 |
| Totals ............................... | 108 | 2713 | 428 | 729 | .587 | 320 | 537 | .596 | 857 | 69 | 1176 | 7.9 | 0.6 | 10.9 |

Three-point field goals: 1997-98, 0-for-1. 1998-99, 0-for-1. Totals, 0-for-2 (.000).

## NBA REGULAR-SEASON RECORD

| Season Team | G | Min. | FGM | FGA | Pct. | FTM | FTA | Pct. | REBOUNDS Off. | Def. | Tot. | Ast. | St. | Blk. | TO | Pts. | AVERAGES RPG | APG | PPG |
|---|---|---|---|---|---|---|---|---|---|---|---|---|---|---|---|---|---|---|---|
| 00-01—L.A. Lakers.... | 70 | 641 | 55 | 113 | .487 | 26 | 37 | .703 | 74 | 78 | 152 | 24 | 8 | 8 | 27 | 137 | 2.2 | 0.3 | 2.0 |
| 01-02—L.A. Lakers.... | 59 | 650 | 66 | 146 | .452 | 35 | 54 | .648 | 89 | 73 | 162 | 44 | 16 | 13 | 22 | 167 | 2.7 | 0.7 | 2.8 |
| 02-03—L.A. Lakers.... | 54 | 781 | 69 | 163 | .423 | 36 | 61 | .590 | 86 | 73 | 159 | 38 | 15 | 19 | 27 | 174 | 2.9 | 0.7 | 3.2 |
| 03-04—Minnesota ..... | 72 | 1246 | 101 | 204 | .495 | 57 | 118 | .483 | 134 | 138 | 272 | 28 | 33 | 18 | 47 | 259 | 3.8 | 0.4 | 3.6 |
| 04-05—Minnesota ..... | 41 | 601 | 34 | 66 | .515 | 20 | 40 | .500 | 63 | 65 | 128 | 18 | 7 | 14 | 24 | 88 | 3.1 | 0.4 | 2.1 |
| Totals ................. | 296 | 3919 | 325 | 692 | .470 | 174 | 310 | .561 | 446 | 427 | 873 | 152 | 79 | 72 | 147 | 825 | 2.9 | 0.5 | 2.8 |

Three-point field goals: 2000-01, 1-for-1 (1.000). 2001-02, 0-for-2. 2003-04, 0-for-6. Totals, 1-for-9 (.111).

Personal fouls/disqualifications: 2000-01, 111/2. 2001-02, 104/0. 2002-03, 116/0. 2003-04, 175/2. 2004-05, 103/1. Totals, 609/5.

## NBA PLAYOFF RECORD

| Season Team | G | Min. | FGM | FGA | Pct. | FTM | FTA | Pct. | REBOUNDS Off. | Def. | Tot. | Ast. | St. | Blk. | TO | Pts. | AVERAGES RPG | APG | PPG |
|---|---|---|---|---|---|---|---|---|---|---|---|---|---|---|---|---|---|---|---|
| 00-01—L.A. Lakers.... | 13 | 48 | 1 | 13 | .077 | 3 | 5 | .600 | 6 | 4 | 10 | 4 | 0 | 2 | 2 | 5 | 0.8 | 0.3 | 0.4 |
| 01-02—L.A. Lakers.... | 7 | 10 | 0 | 1 | .000 | 0 | 0 | ... | 0 | 2 | 2 | 0 | 0 | 0 | 1 | 0 | 0.3 | 0.0 | 0.0 |
| 02-03—L.A. Lakers.... | 12 | 169 | 13 | 31 | .419 | 7 | 16 | .438 | 14 | 14 | 28 | 12 | 3 | 2 | 8 | 33 | 2.3 | 1.0 | 2.8 |
| 03-04—Minnesota ..... | 17 | 222 | 17 | 32 | .531 | 13 | 29 | .448 | 28 | 30 | 58 | 2 | 5 | 4 | 7 | 47 | 3.4 | 0.1 | 2.8 |
| Totals ................. | 49 | 449 | 31 | 77 | .403 | 23 | 50 | .460 | 48 | 50 | 98 | 18 | 8 | 8 | 18 | 85 | 2.0 | 0.4 | 1.7 |

Three-point field goals: 2001-02, 0-for-1. 2002-03, 0-for-1. Totals, 0-for-2 (.000).

Personal fouls/disqualifications: 2000-01, 4/0. 2001-02, 1/0. 2002-03, 32/0. 2003-04, 43/0. Totals, 80/0.

---

# MAGGETTE, COREY     F     CLIPPERS

**PERSONAL:** Born November 12, 1979, in Melrose Park, Ill. ... 6-6/228. (1.98/103.4). ... Full name: Corey Antoine Maggette
**HIGH SCHOOL:** Fenwick (Oak Park, Ill.).
**COLLEGE:** Duke.
**TRANSACTIONS/CAREER NOTES:** Selected after freshman season by Seattle SuperSonics in first round (13th pick overall) of 1999 NBA Draft. ... Draft rights traded by SuperSonics with F/G Billy Owens, G/F Dale Ellis and F Don MacLean to Orlando Magic for F Horace Grant and 2001 and 2002 second-round draft choices (June 30, 1999). ... Traded by Magic with F Derek Strong and draft rights to G Keyon Dooling to Los Angeles Clippers for a future first-round draft choice (June 28, 2000).

## COLLEGIATE RECORD

| Season Team | G | Min. | FGM | FGA | Pct. | FTM | FTA | Pct. | Reb. | Ast. | Pts. | AVERAGES RPG | APG | PPG |
|---|---|---|---|---|---|---|---|---|---|---|---|---|---|---|
| 98-99—Duke............................. | 39 | 691 | 137 | 261 | .525 | 111 | 155 | .716 | 151 | 59 | 414 | 3.9 | 1.5 | 10.6 |

Three-point field goals: 1998-99, 29-for-84 (.345). Totals, 29-for-84 (.345).

## NBA REGULAR-SEASON RECORD

| Season Team | G | Min. | FGM | FGA | Pct. | FTM | FTA | Pct. | REBOUNDS Off. | Def. | Tot. | Ast. | St. | Blk. | TO | Pts. | AVERAGES RPG | APG | PPG |
|---|---|---|---|---|---|---|---|---|---|---|---|---|---|---|---|---|---|---|---|
| 99-00—Orlando.......... | 77 | 1370 | 224 | 469 | .478 | 196 | 261 | .751 | 123 | 180 | 303 | 61 | 24 | 26 | 138 | 646 | 3.9 | 0.8 | 8.4 |
| 00-01—L.A. Clippers... | 69 | 1359 | 225 | 487 | .462 | 223 | 288 | .774 | 88 | 203 | 291 | 82 | 35 | 9 | 106 | 690 | 4.2 | 1.2 | 10.0 |
| 01-02—L.A. Clippers... | 63 | 1615 | 235 | 530 | .443 | 201 | 251 | .801 | 54 | 177 | 231 | 112 | 41 | 19 | 116 | 717 | 3.7 | 1.8 | 11.4 |
| 02-03—L.A. Clippers... | 64 | 2006 | 343 | 773 | .444 | 325 | 405 | .802 | 77 | 245 | 322 | 123 | 55 | 16 | 147 | 1073 | 5.0 | 1.9 | 16.8 |
| 03-04—L.A. Clippers... | 73 | 2628 | 453 | 1013 | .447 | 526 | 620 | .848 | 96 | 334 | 430 | 224 | 65 | 16 | 207 | 1508 | 5.9 | 3.1 | 20.7 |
| 04-05—L.A. Clippers... | 66 | 2436 | 425 | 986 | .431 | 563 | 657 | .857 | 70 | 324 | 394 | 225 | 70 | 8 | 195 | 1464 | 6.0 | 3.4 | 22.2 |
| Totals .................. | 412 | 11414 | 1905 | 4258 | .447 | 2034 | 2482 | .820 | 508 | 1463 | 1971 | 827 | 290 | 94 | 909 | 6098 | 4.8 | 2.0 | 14.8 |

Three-point field goals: 1999-00, 2-for-11 (.182). 2000-01, 17-for-56 (.304). 2001-02, 46-for-139 (.331). 2002-03, 62-for-177 (.350). 2003-04, 76-for-231 (.329). 2004-05, 51-for-168 (.304). Totals, 254-for-782 (.325).
Personal fouls/disqualifications: 1999-00, 169/1. 2000-01, 140/1. 2001-02, 155/0. 2002-03, 194/6. 2003-04, 217/2. 2004-05, 191/1. Totals, 1066/11.

# MAGLOIRE, JAMAAL                    F/C                    HORNETS

**PERSONAL:** Born May 21, 1978, in Toronto. ... 6-11/259. (2.11/117.5). ... Full name: Jamaal Dane Magloire
**HIGH SCHOOL:** Eastern School of Commerce (Toronto).
**COLLEGE:** Kentucky.
**TRANSACTIONS/CAREER NOTES:** Selected by Charlotte Hornets in first round (19th pick overall) of 2000 NBA Draft. ... Hornets franchise moved to New Orleans for 2002-03 season.

## COLLEGIATE RECORD

**NOTES:** Member of NCAA Division I championship team (1998).

| Season Team | G | Min. | FGM | FGA | Pct. | FTM | FTA | Pct. | Reb. | Ast. | Pts. | AVERAGES RPG | APG | PPG |
|---|---|---|---|---|---|---|---|---|---|---|---|---|---|---|
| 96-97—Kentucky ...................... | 40 | 626 | 75 | 153 | .490 | 45 | 82 | .549 | 177 | 15 | 195 | 4.4 | 0.4 | 4.9 |
| 97-98—Kentucky ...................... | 38 | 526 | 77 | 158 | .487 | 43 | 64 | .672 | 161 | 11 | 197 | 4.2 | 0.3 | 5.2 |
| 98-99—Kentucky ...................... | 34 | 668 | 94 | 177 | .531 | 49 | 85 | .576 | 151 | 18 | 237 | 4.4 | 0.5 | 7.0 |
| 99-00—Kentucky ...................... | 33 | 978 | 148 | 296 | .500 | 139 | 203 | .685 | 300 | 18 | 435 | 9.1 | 0.5 | 13.2 |
| Totals ..................................... | 145 | 2798 | 394 | 784 | .503 | 276 | 434 | .636 | 789 | 62 | 1064 | 5.4 | 0.4 | 7.3 |

## NBA REGULAR-SEASON RECORD

| Season Team | G | Min. | FGM | FGA | Pct. | FTM | FTA | Pct. | REBOUNDS Off. | Def. | Tot. | Ast. | St. | Blk. | TO | Pts. | AVERAGES RPG | APG | PPG |
|---|---|---|---|---|---|---|---|---|---|---|---|---|---|---|---|---|---|---|---|
| 00-01—Charlotte......... | 74 | 1095 | 122 | 271 | .450 | 95 | 145 | .655 | 103 | 192 | 295 | 27 | 18 | 78 | 61 | 339 | 4.0 | 0.4 | 4.6 |
| 01-02—Charlotte......... | 82 | 1549 | 228 | 414 | .551 | 243 | 333 | .730 | 153 | 308 | 461 | 31 | 27 | 86 | 118 | 699 | 5.6 | 0.4 | 8.5 |
| 02-03—New Orleans ... | 82 | 2443 | 305 | 635 | .480 | 231 | 322 | .717 | 260 | 464 | 724 | 88 | 49 | 111 | 158 | 841 | 8.8 | 1.1 | 10.3 |
| 03-04—New Orleans ... | 82 | 2777 | 383 | 809 | .473 | 353 | 470 | .751 | 268 | 579 | 847 | 86 | 43 | 101 | 201 | 1119 | 10.3 | 1.0 | 13.6 |
| 04-05—New Orleans ... | 23 | 703 | 98 | 227 | .432 | 74 | 123 | .602 | 79 | 126 | 205 | 29 | 8 | 23 | 59 | 270 | 8.9 | 1.3 | 11.7 |
| Totals .................. | 343 | 8567 | 1136 | 2356 | .482 | 996 | 1393 | .715 | 863 | 1669 | 2532 | 261 | 145 | 399 | 597 | 3268 | 7.4 | 0.8 | 9.5 |

Three-point field goals: 2000-01, 0-for-2. 2001-02, 0-for-1. 2002-03, 0-for-3. 2003-04, 0-for-1. Totals, 0-for-7 (.000).
Personal fouls/disqualifications: 2000-01, 139/0. 2001-02, 201/0. 2002-03, 276/4. 2003-04, 278/6. 2004-05, 74/0. Totals, 968/10.

## NBA PLAYOFF RECORD

| Season Team | G | Min. | FGM | FGA | Pct. | FTM | FTA | Pct. | REBOUNDS Off. | Def. | Tot. | Ast. | St. | Blk. | TO | Pts. | AVERAGES RPG | APG | PPG |
|---|---|---|---|---|---|---|---|---|---|---|---|---|---|---|---|---|---|---|---|
| 00-01—Charlotte......... | 10 | 110 | 16 | 28 | .571 | 7 | 23 | .304 | 8 | 20 | 28 | 3 | 0 | 6 | 4 | 39 | 2.8 | 0.3 | 3.9 |
| 01-02—Charlotte......... | 8 | 168 | 22 | 40 | .550 | 54 | 71 | .761 | 17 | 28 | 45 | 5 | 0 | 15 | 17 | 98 | 5.6 | 0.6 | 12.3 |
| 02-03—New Orleans ... | 6 | 188 | 22 | 49 | .449 | 25 | 33 | .758 | 17 | 33 | 50 | 2 | 4 | 6 | 9 | 69 | 8.3 | 0.3 | 11.5 |
| 03-04—New Orleans ... | 7 | 239 | 28 | 67 | .418 | 21 | 28 | .750 | 16 | 48 | 64 | 5 | 3 | 7 | 11 | 77 | 9.1 | 0.7 | 11.0 |
| Totals .................. | 31 | 705 | 88 | 184 | .478 | 107 | 155 | .690 | 58 | 129 | 187 | 15 | 7 | 34 | 41 | 283 | 6.0 | 0.5 | 9.1 |

Three-point field goals: 2003-04, 0-for-1. Totals, 0-for-1 (.000).
Personal fouls/disqualifications: 2000-01, 20/0. 2001-02, 30/1. 2002-03, 15/0. 2003-04, 22/1. Totals, 87/2.

## NBA ALL-STAR GAME RECORD

| Season Team | Min. | FGM | FGA | Pct. | FTM | FTA | Pct. | REBOUNDS Off. | Def. | Tot. | Ast. | PF | Dq. | St. | Blk. | TO | Pts. |
|---|---|---|---|---|---|---|---|---|---|---|---|---|---|---|---|---|---|
| 2004—New Orleans......... | 21 | 9 | 16 | .563 | 1 | 2 | .500 | 3 | 5 | 8 | 0 | 2 | 0 | 1 | 1 | 1 | 19 |

# MARBURY, STEPHON                    G                    KNICKS

**PERSONAL:** Born February 20, 1977, in Brooklyn, N.Y. ... 6-2/180. (1.88/81.6). ... Cousin of Jamel Thomas, forward with Boston Celtics (1999-2000), Golden State Warriors (1999-2000), Portland Trail Blazers (1999-2000) and New Jersey Nets (2000-01); cousin of Sebastian Telfair, guard, Portland Trail Blazers.
**HIGH SCHOOL:** Abraham Lincoln (Brooklyn, N.Y.).
**COLLEGE:** Georgia Tech.
**TRANSACTIONS/CAREER NOTES:** Selected after freshman season by Milwaukee Bucks in first round (fourth pick overall) of 1996 NBA Draft. ... Draft rights traded by Bucks to Minnesota Timberwolves for draft rights to G Ray Allen and a first-round draft choice (June 26, 1996). ... Traded by Timberwolves with F Bill Curley and G Chris Carr to New Jersey Nets in three-way deal in which Nets also received G Elliot Perry from Milwaukee Bucks, Timberwolves received F Brian Evans, 1999 first-round draft choice and an undisclosed draft choice from Nets, Bucks sent G Terrell Brandon to Timberwolves, Timberwolves sent C Paul Grant to Bucks and Nets sent G Sam Cassell and F/C Chris Gatling to Bucks (March 11, 1999). ... Traded by Nets with F Johnny Newman and C Soumaila Samake to Phoenix Suns for G Jason Kidd and C Chris Dudley (July 18, 2001). ... Traded by Suns with F/G Anfernee Hardaway and C Cezary Trybanski to New York Knicks for G Howard Eisley, F Maciej Lampe, F Antonio McDyess, G Charlie Ward, draft rights to G Milos Vujanic, 2004 first-round draft choice and future first-round draft choice (January 5, 2004).
**MISCELLANEOUS:** Member of bronze-medal-winning U.S. Olympic Team (2004).

M

## COLLEGIATE RECORD

| Season Team | G | Min. | FGM | FGA | Pct. | FTM | FTA | Pct. | Reb. | Ast. | Pts. | RPG | APG | PPG |
|---|---|---|---|---|---|---|---|---|---|---|---|---|---|---|
| | | | | | | | | | | | | AVERAGES | | |
| 95-96—Georgia Tech ................ | 36 | 1345 | 235 | 514 | .457 | 121 | 164 | .738 | 113 | 161 | 679 | 3.1 | 4.5 | 18.9 |

Three-point field goals: 1995-96, 88-for-238 (.370). Totals, 88-for-238 (.370).

## NBA REGULAR-SEASON RECORD

**HONORS:** All-NBA third team (2000, 2003). ... NBA All-Rookie first team (1997).

| Season Team | G | Min. | FGM | FGA | Pct. | FTM | FTA | Pct. | Off. | Def. | Tot. | Ast. | St. | Blk. | TO | Pts. | RPG | APG | PPG |
|---|---|---|---|---|---|---|---|---|---|---|---|---|---|---|---|---|---|---|---|
| | | | | | | | | | REBOUNDS | | | | | | | | AVERAGES | | |
| 96-97—Minnesota...... | 67 | 2324 | 355 | 871 | .408 | 245 | 337 | .727 | 54 | 130 | 184 | 522 | 67 | 19 | 210 | 1057 | 2.7 | 7.8 | 15.8 |
| 97-98—Minnesota...... | 82 | 3112 | 513 | 1237 | .415 | 329 | 450 | .731 | 58 | 172 | 230 | 704 | 104 | 7 | 256 | 1450 | 2.8 | 8.6 | 17.7 |
| 98-99—Minn.-N.J....... | 49 | 1895 | 378 | 883 | .428 | 222 | 278 | .799 | 37 | 105 | 142 | 437 | 59 | 8 | 164 | 1044 | 2.9 | 8.9 | 21.3 |
| 99-00—New Jersey ..... | 74 | 2881 | 569 | 1317 | .432 | 436 | 536 | .813 | 61 | 179 | 240 | 622 | 112 | 15 | 270 | 1640 | 3.2 | 8.4 | 22.2 |
| 00-01—New Jersey .... | 67 | 2557 | 563 | 1277 | .441 | 362 | 458 | .790 | 53 | 152 | 205 | 506 | 79 | 5 | 197 | 1598 | 3.1 | 7.6 | 23.9 |
| 01-02—Phoenix ......... | 82 | 3187 | 625 | 1413 | .442 | 353 | 452 | .781 | 75 | 191 | 266 | 666 | 77 | 13 | 284 | 1674 | 3.2 | 8.1 | 20.4 |
| 02-03—Phoenix ......... | 81 | 3240 | 671 | 1530 | .439 | 375 | 467 | .803 | 53 | 210 | 263 | 654 | 108 | 20 | 263 | 1806 | 3.2 | 8.1 | 22.3 |
| 03-04—Phoenix-N.Y.... | 81 | 3254 | 598 | 1386 | .431 | 356 | 436 | .817 | 58 | 205 | 263 | 719 | 129 | 9 | 249 | 1639 | 3.2 | 8.9 | 20.2 |
| 04-05—New York ....... | 82 | 3281 | 604 | 1308 | .462 | 458 | 549 | .834 | 50 | 198 | 248 | 668 | 122 | 6 | 233 | 1781 | 3.0 | 8.1 | 21.7 |
| **Totals ..............** | **665** | **25731** | **4876** | **11222** | **.435** | **3136** | **3963** | **.791** | **499** | **1542** | **2041** | **5498** | **857** | **102** | **2126** | **13689** | **3.1** | **8.3** | **20.6** |

Three-point field goals: 1996-97, 102-for-288 (.354). 1997-98, 95-for-304 (.313). 1998-99, 66-for-197 (.335). 1999-00, 66-for-233 (.283). 2000-01, 110-for-335 (.328). 2001-02, 71-for-248 (.286). 2002-03, 89-for-296 (.301). 2003-04, 87-for-274 (.318). 2004-05, 115-for-325 (.354). Totals, 801-for-2500 (.320).

Personal fouls/disqualifications: 1996-97, 159/2. 1997-98, 222/0. 1998-99, 125/0. 1999-00, 195/4. 2000-01, 150/1. 2001-02, 186/0. 2002-03, 200/1. 2003-04, 172/0. 2004-05, 186/1. Totals, 1595/9.

## NBA PLAYOFF RECORD

| Season Team | G | Min. | FGM | FGA | Pct. | FTM | FTA | Pct. | Off. | Def. | Tot. | Ast. | St. | Blk. | TO | Pts. | RPG | APG | PPG |
|---|---|---|---|---|---|---|---|---|---|---|---|---|---|---|---|---|---|---|---|
| | | | | | | | | | REBOUNDS | | | | | | | | AVERAGES | | |
| 96-97—Minnesota...... | 3 | 117 | 26 | 65 | .400 | 6 | 10 | .600 | 2 | 10 | 12 | 23 | 2 | 0 | 9 | 64 | 4.0 | 7.7 | 21.3 |
| 97-98—Minnesota...... | 5 | 209 | 22 | 72 | .306 | 18 | 23 | .783 | 5 | 11 | 16 | 38 | 12 | 0 | 18 | 69 | 3.2 | 7.6 | 13.8 |
| 02-03—Phoenix ......... | 6 | 272 | 51 | 136 | .375 | 25 | 33 | .758 | 6 | 18 | 24 | 34 | 7 | 0 | 23 | 132 | 4.0 | 5.7 | 22.0 |
| 03-04—New York ....... | 4 | 174 | 31 | 83 | .373 | 17 | 25 | .680 | 5 | 12 | 17 | 26 | 7 | 0 | 14 | 85 | 4.3 | 6.5 | 21.3 |
| **Totals ...............** | **18** | **772** | **130** | **356** | **.365** | **66** | **91** | **.725** | **18** | **51** | **69** | **121** | **28** | **0** | **64** | **350** | **3.8** | **6.7** | **19.4** |

Three-point field goals: 1996-97, 6-for-20 (.300). 1997-98, 7-for-25 (.280). 2002-03, 5-for-22 (.227). 2003-04, 6-for-20 (.300). Totals, 24-for-87 (.276).
Personal fouls/disqualifications: 1996-97, 9/0. 1997-98, 16/0. 2002-03, 26/1. 2003-04, 9/0. Totals, 60/1.

## NBA ALL-STAR GAME RECORD

| Season Team | Min. | FGM | FGA | Pct. | FTM | FTA | Pct. | Off. | Def. | Tot. | Ast. | PF | Dq. | St. | Blk. | TO | Pts. |
|---|---|---|---|---|---|---|---|---|---|---|---|---|---|---|---|---|---|
| | | | | | | | | REBOUNDS | | | | | | | | | |
| 2001—New Jersey .......... | 18 | 5 | 9 | .556 | 0 | 2 | .000 | 0 | 0 | 0 | 4 | 2 | 0 | 0 | 0 | 3 | 12 |
| 2003—Phoenix................ | 15 | 1 | 3 | .333 | 2 | 2 | 1.000 | 0 | 1 | 1 | 6 | 0 | 0 | 0 | 0 | 2 | 4 |
| **Totals..........................** | **33** | **6** | **12** | **.500** | **2** | **4** | **.500** | **0** | **1** | **1** | **10** | **2** | **0** | **0** | **0** | **5** | **16** |

Three-point field goals: 2001, 2-for-3 (.667). 2003, 0-for-2. Totals, 2-for-5 (.400).

# M

# MARION, SHAWN     F     SUNS

**PERSONAL:** Born May 7, 1978, in Chicago. ... 6-7/215. (2.01/97.5). ... Full name: Shawn Dwayne Marion
**HIGH SCHOOL:** Clarksville (Tenn.).
**JUNIOR COLLEGE:** Vincennes (Ind.) University.
**COLLEGE:** UNLV.
**TRANSACTIONS/CAREER NOTES:** Selected after junior season by Phoenix Suns in first round (ninth pick overall) of 1999 NBA Draft.
**MISCELLANEOUS:** Member of bronze-medal-winning U.S. Olympic Team (2004).

## COLLEGIATE RECORD

| Season Team | G | Min. | FGM | FGA | Pct. | FTM | FTA | Pct. | Reb. | Ast. | Pts. | RPG | APG | PPG |
|---|---|---|---|---|---|---|---|---|---|---|---|---|---|---|
| | | | | | | | | | | | | AVERAGES | | |
| 96-97—Vincennes..................... | 36 | ... | 346 | 581 | .596 | 124 | 178 | .697 | 462 | 124 | 838 | 12.8 | 3.4 | 23.3 |
| 97-98—Vincennes..................... | 36 | ... | 352 | 605 | .582 | 122 | 163 | .748 | 471 | 99 | 847 | 13.1 | 2.8 | 23.5 |
| 98-99—UNLV............................. | 29 | 954 | 221 | 418 | .529 | 81 | 111 | .730 | 269 | 36 | 543 | 9.3 | 1.2 | 18.7 |
| **Junior College Totals.............** | **72** | | **698** | **1186** | **.589** | **246** | **341** | **.721** | **933** | **223** | **1685** | **13.0** | **3.1** | **23.4** |
| **4-Year-College Totals .............** | **29** | **954** | **221** | **418** | **.529** | **81** | **111** | **.730** | **269** | **36** | **543** | **9.3** | **1.2** | **18.7** |

Three-point field goals: 1996-97, 22-for-65 (.338). 1997-98, 21-for-56 (.375). 1998-99, 20-for-67 (.299). Totals, 63-for-188 (.335).

## NBA REGULAR-SEASON RECORD

**HONORS:** NBA All-Rookie second team (2000). ... All-NBA third team (2005).

| Season Team | G | Min. | FGM | FGA | Pct. | FTM | FTA | Pct. | Off. | Def. | Tot. | Ast. | St. | Blk. | TO | Pts. | RPG | APG | PPG |
|---|---|---|---|---|---|---|---|---|---|---|---|---|---|---|---|---|---|---|---|
| | | | | | | | | | REBOUNDS | | | | | | | | AVERAGES | | |
| 99-00—Phoenix .......... | 51 | 1260 | 222 | 471 | .471 | 72 | 85 | .847 | 105 | 227 | 332 | 69 | 38 | 53 | 51 | 520 | 6.5 | 1.4 | 10.2 |
| 00-01—Phoenix .......... | 79 | 2857 | 557 | 1160 | .480 | 234 | 289 | .810 | 220 | 628 | 848 | 160 | 132 | 108 | 129 | 1369 | 10.7 | 2.0 | 17.3 |
| 01-02—Phoenix .......... | 81 | 3109 | 654 | 1395 | .469 | 191 | 226 | .845 | 211 | 592 | 803 | 162 | 149 | 86 | 144 | 1547 | 9.9 | 2.0 | 19.1 |
| 02-03—Phoenix .......... | 81 | 3373 | 662 | 1466 | .452 | 251 | 295 | .851 | 199 | 574 | 773 | 198 | 185 | 95 | 157 | 1716 | 9.5 | 2.4 | 21.2 |
| 03-04—Phoenix .......... | 79 | 3217 | 590 | 1341 | .440 | 228 | 268 | .851 | 212 | 525 | 737 | 214 | 167 | 104 | 156 | 1498 | 9.3 | 2.7 | 19.0 |
| 04-05—Phoenix .......... | 81 | 3146 | 613 | 1289 | .476 | 229 | 275 | .833 | 235 | 680 | 915 | 154 | 163 | 119 | 125 | 1569 | 11.3 | 1.9 | 19.4 |
| **Totals .................** | **452** | **16962** | **3298** | **7122** | **.463** | **1205** | **1438** | **.838** | **1182** | **3226** | **4408** | **957** | **834** | **565** | **762** | **8219** | **9.8** | **2.1** | **18.2** |

Three-point field goals: 1999-00, 4-for-22 (.182). 2000-01, 21-for-82 (.256). 2001-02, 48-for-122 (.393). 2002-03, 141-for-364 (.387). 2003-04, 90-for-265 (.340). 2004-05, 114-for-341 (.334). Totals, 418-for-1196 (.349).

Personal fouls/disqualifications: 1999-00, 113/0. 2000-01, 211/2. 2001-02, 214/0. 2002-03, 208/0. 2003-04, 203/1. 2004-05, 199/0. Totals, 1148/3.

## NBA PLAYOFF RECORD

| Season Team | G | Min. | FGM | FGA | Pct. | FTM | FTA | Pct. | Off. | Def. | Tot. | Ast. | St. | Blk. | TO | Pts. | RPG | APG | PPG |
|---|---|---|---|---|---|---|---|---|---|---|---|---|---|---|---|---|---|---|---|
| | | | | | | | | | REBOUNDS | | | | | | | | AVERAGES | | |
| 99-00—Phoenix ......... | 9 | 281 | 36 | 86 | .419 | 9 | 11 | .818 | 21 | 58 | 79 | 7 | 6 | 14 | 7 | 82 | 8.8 | 0.8 | 9.1 |
| 00-01—Phoenix ......... | 4 | 139 | 23 | 62 | .371 | 12 | 14 | .857 | 10 | 23 | 33 | 3 | 6 | 6 | 6 | 59 | 8.3 | 0.8 | 14.8 |
| 02-03—Phoenix ......... | 6 | 282 | 40 | 107 | .374 | 22 | 26 | .846 | 21 | 49 | 70 | 12 | 11 | 11 | 13 | 111 | 11.7 | 2.0 | 18.5 |
| 04-05—Phoenix ......... | 15 | 635 | 108 | 223 | .484 | 30 | 39 | .769 | 46 | 131 | 177 | 23 | 21 | 26 | 21 | 264 | 11.8 | 1.5 | 17.6 |
| Totals ................... | 34 | 1337 | 207 | 478 | .433 | 73 | 90 | .811 | 98 | 261 | 359 | 45 | 44 | 57 | 47 | 516 | 10.6 | 1.3 | 15.2 |

Three-point field goals: 1999-00, 1-for-6 (.167). 2000-01, 1-for-1 (1.000). 2002-03, 9-for-28 (.321). 2004-05, 18-for-43 (.419). Totals, 29-for-78 (.372).

Personal fouls/disqualifications: 1999-00, 17/0. 2000-01, 13/0. 2002-03, 17/0. 2004-05, 47/0. Totals, 94/0.

## NBA ALL-STAR GAME RECORD

| Season Team | Min. | FGM | FGA | Pct. | FTM | FTA | Pct. | Off. | Def. | Tot. | Ast. | PF | Dq. | St. | Blk. | TO | Pts. |
|---|---|---|---|---|---|---|---|---|---|---|---|---|---|---|---|---|---|
| | | | | | | | | REBOUNDS | | | | | | | | | |
| 2003—Phoenix................ | 23 | 4 | 9 | .444 | 0 | 0 | | 5 | 2 | 7 | 4 | 1 | 0 | 3 | 1 | 0 | 8 |
| 2005—Phoenix................ | 16 | 5 | 7 | .714 | 0 | 1 | .000 | 3 | 0 | 3 | 4 | 0 | 0 | 0 | 0 | 1 | 10 |
| Totals.......................... | 39 | 9 | 16 | .563 | 0 | 1 | .000 | 8 | 2 | 10 | 8 | 1 | 0 | 3 | 1 | 1 | 18 |

Three-point field goals: 2003, 0-for-1. Totals, 0-for-1 (.000).

# MARSHALL, DONYELL   F   CAVALIERS

**PERSONAL:** Born May 18, 1973, in Reading, Pa. ... 6-9/230. (2.06/104.3). ... Full name: Donyell Lamar Marshall ... Name pronounced Don-YELL.
**HIGH SCHOOL:** Reading (Pa.).
**COLLEGE:** Connecticut.
**TRANSACTIONS/CAREER NOTES:** Selected after junior season by Minnesota Timberwolves in first round (fourth pick overall) of 1994 NBA Draft. ... Traded by Timberwolves to Golden State Warriors for F Tom Gugliotta (February 18, 1995). ... Traded by Warriors to Utah Jazz as part of four-team deal in which Boston Celtics received G Robert Pack, C John Williams and cash considerations from Dallas Mavericks and a conditional first-round draft choice from Jazz, Mavericks received G Dana Barros from Celtics, F Bill Curley from Warriors and G Howard Eisley from Jazz, Jazz received C Bruno Sundov from Mavericks and Warriors received F Danny Fortson from Celtics and F Adam Keefe from Jazz (August 16, 2000). ... Signed as free agent by Chicago Bulls (August 16, 2002). ... Traded by Bulls with F Lonny Baxter and G Jalen Rose to Toronto Raptors for F/C Antonio Davis, F Chris Jefferies and F Jerome Williams (December 1, 2003). ... Signed as free agent by Cleveland Cavaliers (August 2, 2005).

## COLLEGIATE RECORD

**NOTES:** THE SPORTING NEWS All-America first team (1994).

| Season Team | G | Min. | FGM | FGA | Pct. | FTM | FTA | Pct. | Reb. | Ast. | Pts. | RPG | APG | PPG |
|---|---|---|---|---|---|---|---|---|---|---|---|---|---|---|
| | | | | | | | | | | | | AVERAGES | | |
| 91-92—Connecticut ................... | 30 | 806 | 125 | 295 | .424 | 69 | 93 | .742 | 183 | 45 | 334 | 6.1 | 1.5 | 11.1 |
| 92-93—Connecticut ................... | 27 | 854 | 166 | 332 | .500 | 107 | 129 | .829 | 210 | 30 | 459 | 7.8 | 1.1 | 17.0 |
| 93-94—Connecticut ................... | 34 | 1157 | 306 | 599 | .511 | 200 | 266 | .752 | 302 | 56 | 853 | 8.9 | 1.6 | 25.1 |
| Totals ..................................... | 91 | 2817 | 597 | 1226 | .487 | 376 | 488 | .770 | 695 | 131 | 1646 | 7.6 | 1.4 | 18.1 |

Three-point field goals: 1991-92, 15-for-62 (.242). 1992-93, 20-for-54 (.370). 1993-94, 41-for-132 (.311). Totals, 76-for-248 (.306).

## NBA REGULAR-SEASON RECORD

**HONORS:** NBA All-Rookie second team (1995).

| Season Team | G | Min. | FGM | FGA | Pct. | FTM | FTA | Pct. | Off. | Def. | Tot. | Ast. | St. | Blk. | TO | Pts. | RPG | APG | PPG |
|---|---|---|---|---|---|---|---|---|---|---|---|---|---|---|---|---|---|---|---|
| | | | | | | | | | REBOUNDS | | | | | | | | AVERAGES | | |
| 94-95—Minn.-G.S. ...... | 72 | 2086 | 345 | 876 | .394 | 147 | 222 | .662 | 137 | 268 | 405 | 105 | 45 | 88 | 115 | 906 | 5.6 | 1.5 | 12.6 |
| 95-96—Golden State ... | 62 | 934 | 125 | 314 | .398 | 64 | 83 | .771 | 65 | 148 | 213 | 49 | 22 | 31 | 48 | 342 | 3.4 | 0.8 | 5.5 |
| 96-97—Golden State ... | 61 | 1022 | 174 | 421 | .413 | 61 | 98 | .622 | 92 | 184 | 276 | 54 | 25 | 46 | 55 | 444 | 4.5 | 0.9 | 7.3 |
| 97-98—Golden State ... | 73 | 2611 | 451 | 1091 | .413 | 158 | 216 | .731 | 210 | 418 | 628 | 159 | 95 | 73 | 147 | 1123 | 8.6 | 2.2 | 15.4 |
| 98-99—Golden State ... | 48 | 1250 | 208 | 494 | .421 | 88 | 121 | .727 | 115 | 227 | 342 | 66 | 47 | 37 | 80 | 530 | 7.1 | 1.4 | 11.0 |
| 99-00—Golden State ... | 64 | 2071 | 331 | 840 | .394 | 199 | 255 | .780 | 189 | 448 | 637 | 167 | 68 | 68 | 123 | 910 | 10.0 | 2.6 | 14.2 |
| 00-01—Utah................ | 81 | 2326 | 427 | 849 | .503 | 205 | 273 | .751 | 172 | 394 | 566 | 133 | 85 | 78 | 128 | 1100 | 7.0 | 1.6 | 13.6 |
| 01-02—Utah................ | 58 | 1750 | 343 | 661 | .519 | 160 | 226 | .708 | 158 | 285 | 443 | 101 | 50 | 67 | 124 | 859 | 7.6 | 1.7 | 14.8 |
| 02-03—Chicago .......... | 78 | 2378 | 421 | 918 | .459 | 167 | 221 | .756 | 234 | 465 | 699 | 137 | 95 | 85 | 135 | 1042 | 9.0 | 1.8 | 13.4 |
| 03-04—Chicago-Tor. ... | 82 | 2988 | 470 | 1020 | .461 | 134 | 182 | .736 | 210 | 598 | 808 | 122 | 93 | 124 | 117 | 1205 | 9.9 | 1.5 | 14.7 |
| 04-05—Toronto .......... | 65 | 1645 | 262 | 592 | .443 | 72 | 91 | .791 | 95 | 333 | 428 | 81 | 57 | 46 | 42 | 747 | 6.6 | 1.2 | 11.5 |
| Totals ................... | 744 | 21061 | 3557 | 8076 | .440 | 1455 | 1988 | .732 | 1677 | 3768 | 5445 | 1174 | 682 | 743 | 1114 | 9208 | 7.3 | 1.6 | 12.4 |

Three-point field goals: 1994-95, 69-for-243 (.284). 1995-96, 28-for-94 (.298). 1996-97, 35-for-111 (.315). 1997-98, 63-for-201 (.313). 1998-99, 26-for-72 (.361). 1999-00, 49-for-138 (.355). 2000-01, 41-for-128 (.320). 2001-02, 13-for-42 (.310). 2002-03, 33-for-87 (.379). 2003-04, 131-for-325 (.403). 2004-05, 151-for-363 (.416). Totals, 639-for-1804 (.354).

Personal fouls/disqualifications: 1994-95, 157/1. 1995-96, 83/0. 1996-97, 96/0. 1997-98, 226/1. 1998-99, 123/1. 1999-00, 180/1. 2000-01, 196/0. 2001-02, 150/1. 2002-03, 234/3. 2003-04, 247/1. 2004-05, 136/0. Totals, 1828/9.

## NBA PLAYOFF RECORD

| Season Team | G | Min. | FGM | FGA | Pct. | FTM | FTA | Pct. | Off. | Def. | Tot. | Ast. | St. | Blk. | TO | Pts. | RPG | APG | PPG |
|---|---|---|---|---|---|---|---|---|---|---|---|---|---|---|---|---|---|---|---|
| | | | | | | | | | REBOUNDS | | | | | | | | AVERAGES | | |
| 00-01—Utah................ | 5 | 160 | 22 | 54 | .407 | 7 | 9 | .778 | 13 | 25 | 38 | 8 | 2 | 5 | 9 | 52 | 7.6 | 1.6 | 10.4 |
| 01-02—Utah................ | 4 | 124 | 21 | 50 | .420 | 12 | 16 | .750 | 14 | 17 | 31 | 11 | 3 | 6 | 5 | 57 | 7.8 | 2.8 | 14.3 |
| Totals ................... | 9 | 284 | 43 | 104 | .413 | 19 | 25 | .760 | 27 | 42 | 69 | 19 | 5 | 11 | 14 | 109 | 7.7 | 2.1 | 12.1 |

Three-point field goals: 2000-01, 1-for-8 (.125). 2001-02, 3-for-6 (.500). Totals, 4-for-14 (.286).

Personal fouls/disqualifications: 2000-01, 19/1. 2001-02, 5/0. Totals, 24/1.

## MARTIN, DARRICK       G

**PERSONAL:** Born March 6, 1971, in Denver. ... 5-11/170. (1.80/77.1).
**HIGH SCHOOL:** St. Anthony (Long Beach, Calif.).
**COLLEGE:** UCLA.
**TRANSACTIONS/CAREER NOTES:** Not drafted by an NBA franchise. ... Played with Magic Johnson All-Stars (1992-93 and 1993-94). ... Played in Continental Basketball Association with Sioux Falls Skyforce (1994-95). ... Signed by Minnesota Timberwolves to first of two consecutive 10-day contracts (February 13, 1995). ... Re-signed by Timberwolves for remainder of season (March 7, 1995). ... Signed as free agent by Vancouver Grizzlies (November 3, 1995). ... Traded by Grizzlies to Timberwolves for 1996 second-round draft choice (January 12, 1996). ... Signed as free agent by Los Angeles Clippers (September 19, 1996). ... Signed as free agent by Sacramento Kings (August 4, 1999). ... Signed as free agent by Dallas Mavericks (August 2, 2001). ... Waived by Mavericks (November 20, 2001). ... Played in American Basketball Association 2000 with Las Vegas Slam (2001-02). ... Waived by Nuggets (October 18, 2002). ... Played in Continental Basketball Association (2002-04). ... Played in Russia and Italy (2002-03). ... Signed by Minnesota Timberwolves to first of two consecutive 10-day contracts (January 30, 2004). ... Signed by Timberwolves for remainder of season (March 31, 2004). ... Signed by Los Angeles Clippers to 10-day contract (January 5, 2005).

### COLLEGIATE RECORD

| Season Team | G | Min. | FGM | FGA | Pct. | FTM | FTA | Pct. | Reb. | Ast. | Pts. | AVERAGES RPG | APG | PPG |
|---|---|---|---|---|---|---|---|---|---|---|---|---|---|---|
| 88-89—UCLA | 31 | 929 | 92 | 203 | .453 | 68 | 91 | .747 | 59 | 90 | 265 | 1.9 | 2.9 | 8.5 |
| 89-90—UCLA | 33 | 1069 | 132 | 283 | .466 | 90 | 126 | .714 | 71 | 199 | 374 | 2.2 | 6.0 | 11.3 |
| 90-91—UCLA | 32 | 1030 | 129 | 278 | .464 | 90 | 120 | .750 | 77 | 217 | 371 | 2.4 | 6.8 | 11.6 |
| 91-92—UCLA | 33 | 642 | 52 | 120 | .433 | 68 | 82 | .829 | 43 | 130 | 185 | 1.3 | 3.9 | 5.6 |
| **Totals** | 129 | 3670 | 405 | 884 | .458 | 316 | 419 | .754 | 250 | 636 | 1195 | 1.9 | 4.9 | 9.3 |

Three-point field goals: 1988-89, 13-for-37 (.351). 1989-90, 20-for-63 (.317). 1990-91, 23-for-79 (.291). 1991-92, 13-for-35 (.371). Totals, 69-for-214 (.322).

### CBA RECORD

**NOTES:** CBA All-League second team (1995).

| Season Team | G | Min. | FGM | FGA | Pct. | FTM | FTA | Pct. | Reb. | Ast. | Pts. | AVERAGES RPG | APG | PPG |
|---|---|---|---|---|---|---|---|---|---|---|---|---|---|---|
| 94-95—Sioux Falls | 37 | 1422 | 285 | 518 | .550 | 196 | 226 | .867 | 96 | 289 | 777 | 2.6 | 7.8 | 21.0 |
| 02-03—Yakima | 20 | 635 | 118 | 266 | .444 | 93 | 100 | .930 | 53 | 138 | 366 | 2.7 | 6.9 | 18.3 |
| 03-04—Yakima-Sioux Falls | 27 | 1028 | 155 | 371 | .418 | 109 | 121 | .901 | 82 | 199 | 470 | 3.0 | 7.4 | 17.4 |
| 04-05—Michigan | 30 | 1171 | 163 | 446 | .365 | 100 | 109 | .917 | 80 | 214 | 475 | 2.7 | 7.1 | 15.8 |
| **Totals** | 114 | 4256 | 721 | 1601 | .450 | 498 | 556 | .896 | 311 | 840 | 2088 | 2.7 | 7.4 | 18.3 |

Three-point field goals: 1994-95, 11-for-39 (.282). 2002-03, 37-for-93 (.398). 2003-04, 51-for-137 (.372). 2004-05, 49-for-137 (.358). Totals, 148-for-406 (.365).

Personal fouls/disqualifications: 1994-95, 124/0. Totals, 124/0.

### NBA REGULAR-SEASON RECORD

| Season Team | G | Min. | FGM | FGA | Pct. | FTM | FTA | Pct. | REBOUNDS Off. | Def. | Tot. | Ast. | St. | Blk. | TO | Pts. | AVERAGES RPG | APG | PPG |
|---|---|---|---|---|---|---|---|---|---|---|---|---|---|---|---|---|---|---|---|
| 94-95—Minnesota | 34 | 803 | 95 | 233 | .408 | 57 | 65 | .877 | 14 | 50 | 64 | 133 | 34 | 0 | 62 | 254 | 1.9 | 3.9 | 7.5 |
| 95-96—Van.-Minn. | 59 | 1149 | 147 | 362 | .406 | 101 | 120 | .842 | 16 | 66 | 82 | 217 | 53 | 3 | 107 | 415 | 1.4 | 3.7 | 7.0 |
| 96-97—L.A. Clippers | 82 | 1820 | 292 | 718 | .407 | 218 | 250 | .872 | 26 | 87 | 113 | 339 | 57 | 2 | 127 | 893 | 1.4 | 4.1 | 10.9 |
| 97-98—L.A. Clippers | 82 | 2299 | 275 | 730 | .377 | 184 | 217 | .848 | 19 | 145 | 164 | 331 | 82 | 10 | 154 | 841 | 2.0 | 4.0 | 10.3 |
| 98-99—L.A. Clippers | 37 | 941 | 102 | 278 | .367 | 61 | 76 | .803 | 5 | 43 | 48 | 144 | 43 | 4 | 67 | 296 | 1.3 | 3.9 | 8.0 |
| 99-00—Sacramento | 71 | 893 | 133 | 350 | .380 | 98 | 119 | .824 | 7 | 37 | 44 | 122 | 28 | 2 | 62 | 402 | 0.6 | 1.7 | 5.7 |
| 00-01—Sacramento | 31 | 176 | 29 | 76 | .382 | 31 | 35 | .886 | 2 | 14 | 16 | 14 | 7 | 0 | 10 | 103 | 0.5 | 0.5 | 3.3 |
| 01-02—Dallas | 3 | 22 | 0 | 10 | .000 | 1 | 2 | .500 | 0 | 1 | 1 | 3 | 2 | 0 | 1 | 1 | 0.3 | 1.0 | 0.3 |
| 03-04—Minnesota | 16 | 172 | 20 | 67 | .299 | 9 | 9 | 1.000 | 2 | 5 | 7 | 23 | 2 | 1 | 7 | 55 | 0.4 | 1.4 | 3.4 |
| 04-05—L.A. Clippers | 11 | 190 | 16 | 50 | .320 | 5 | 8 | .625 | 3 | 7 | 10 | 28 | 6 | 0 | 6 | 42 | 0.9 | 2.5 | 3.8 |
| **Totals** | 426 | 8465 | 1109 | 2874 | .386 | 765 | 901 | .849 | 94 | 455 | 549 | 1354 | 314 | 22 | 603 | 3302 | 1.3 | 3.2 | 7.8 |

Three-point field goals: 1994-95, 7-for-38 (.184). 1995-96, 20-for-69 (.290). 1996-97, 91-for-234 (.389). 1997-98, 107-for-293 (.365). 1998-99, 31-for-106 (.292). 1999-00, 38-for-124 (.306). 2000-01, 14-for-27 (.519). 2001-02, 0-for-2. 2003-04, 6-for-26 (.231). 2004-05, 5-for-18 (.278). Totals, 319-for-937 (.340).

Personal fouls/disqualifications: 1994-95, 88/0. 1995-96, 123/0. 1996-97, 165/1. 1997-98, 198/2. 1998-99, 82/1. 1999-00, 89/0. 2000-01, 27/0. 2001-02, 4/0. 2003-04, 23/0. 2004-05, 19/0. Totals, 818/4.

### NBA PLAYOFF RECORD

| Season Team | G | Min. | FGM | FGA | Pct. | FTM | FTA | Pct. | REBOUNDS Off. | Def. | Tot. | Ast. | St. | Blk. | TO | Pts. | AVERAGES RPG | APG | PPG |
|---|---|---|---|---|---|---|---|---|---|---|---|---|---|---|---|---|---|---|---|
| 96-97—L.A. Clippers | 3 | 77 | 11 | 25 | .440 | 6 | 9 | .667 | 1 | 1 | 2 | 13 | 0 | 0 | 2 | 33 | 0.7 | 4.3 | 11.0 |
| 99-00—Sacramento | 2 | 21 | 3 | 9 | .333 | 3 | 4 | .750 | 1 | 2 | 3 | 2 | 1 | 0 | 3 | 10 | 1.5 | 1.0 | 5.0 |
| 00-01—Sacramento | 2 | 9 | 0 | 6 | .000 | 0 | 0 | ... | 0 | 0 | 0 | 3 | 0 | 0 | 1 | 0 | 0.0 | 1.5 | 0.0 |
| 03-04—Minnesota | 16 | 182 | 14 | 51 | .275 | 16 | 20 | .800 | 5 | 9 | 14 | 23 | 4 | 0 | 8 | 50 | 0.9 | 1.4 | 3.1 |
| **Totals** | 23 | 289 | 28 | 91 | .308 | 25 | 33 | .758 | 7 | 12 | 19 | 41 | 5 | 0 | 14 | 93 | 0.8 | 1.8 | 4.0 |

Three-point field goals: 1996-97, 5-for-9 (.556). 1999-00, 1-for-3 (.333). 2000-01, 0-for-2. 2003-04, 6-for-20 (.300). Totals, 12-for-34 (.353).
Personal fouls/disqualifications: 1996-97, 9/0. 1999-00, 4/0. 2000-01, 1/0. 2003-04, 17/0. Totals, 31/0.

### AMERICAN BASKETBALL ASSOCIATION 2000 RECORD

| Season Team | G | Min. | FGM | FGA | Pct. | FTM | FTA | Pct. | Reb. | Ast. | Pts. | AVERAGES RPG | APG | PPG |
|---|---|---|---|---|---|---|---|---|---|---|---|---|---|---|
| 01-02—Las Vegas | 16 | 505 | 89 | 224 | .397 | 46 | 55 | .836 | 45 | 77 | 265 | 2.8 | 4.8 | 16.6 |

Three-point field goals: 2001-02, 41-for-108 (.380). Totals, 41-for-108 (.380).

### ITALIAN LEAGUE RECORD

| Season Team | G | Min. | FGM | FGA | Pct. | FTM | FTA | Pct. | Reb. | Ast. | Pts. | AVERAGES RPG | APG | PPG |
|---|---|---|---|---|---|---|---|---|---|---|---|---|---|---|
| 02-03—Rida Scafati | 3 | 97 | 12 | 35 | .343 | 9 | 12 | .750 | 8 | 9 | 40 | 2.7 | 3.0 | 13.3 |

Three-point field goals: 2002-03, 7-for-18 (.389). Totals, 7-for-18 (.389).

| Season Team | G | Min. | FGM | FGA | Pct. | FTM | FTA | Pct. | Reb. | Ast. | Pts. | RPG | APG | PPG |
|---|---|---|---|---|---|---|---|---|---|---|---|---|---|---|
| | | | | | | | | | | | | AVERAGES | | |
| 02-03—Avtodor Saratov ............ | 4 | 106 | 17 | 38 | .447 | 12 | 14 | .857 | 8 | 11 | 51 | 2.0 | 2.8 | 12.8 |

Three-point field goals: 2002-03, 5-for-14 (.357). Totals, 5-for-14 (.357).

# MARTIN, KENYON  F  NUGGETS

**PERSONAL:** Born December 30, 1977, in Saginaw, Mich. ... 6-9/230. (2.06/104.3). ... Full name: Kenyon Lee Martin
**HIGH SCHOOL:** Bryan Adams (Dallas).
**COLLEGE:** Cincinnati.
**TRANSACTIONS/CAREER NOTES:** Selected by New Jersey Nets in first round (first pick overall) of 2000 NBA Draft. ... Traded by Nets to Denver Nuggets for three future first-round draft choices (July 15, 2004).

## COLLEGIATE RECORD

**NOTES:** The Sporting News College Player of the Year (2000). ... Wooden Award winner (2000). ... Naismith Award winner (2000). ... The Sporting News All-America first team (2000).

| Season Team | G | Min. | FGM | FGA | Pct. | FTM | FTA | Pct. | Reb. | Ast. | Pts. | RPG | APG | PPG |
|---|---|---|---|---|---|---|---|---|---|---|---|---|---|---|
| | | | | | | | | | | | | AVERAGES | | |
| 96-97—Cincinnati ...................... | 22 | 233 | 26 | 40 | .650 | 10 | 32 | .313 | 74 | 10 | 62 | 3.4 | 0.5 | 2.8 |
| 97-98—Cincinnati ...................... | 30 | 858 | 124 | 198 | .626 | 50 | 105 | .476 | 267 | 41 | 298 | 8.9 | 1.4 | 9.9 |
| 98-99—Cincinnati ...................... | 33 | 900 | 142 | 248 | .573 | 50 | 89 | .562 | 228 | 49 | 334 | 6.9 | 1.5 | 10.1 |
| 99-00—Cincinnati ...................... | 31 | 909 | 221 | 389 | .568 | 141 | 206 | .684 | 300 | 42 | 585 | 9.7 | 1.4 | 18.9 |
| **Totals** .................................. | 116 | 2900 | 513 | 875 | .586 | 251 | 432 | .581 | 869 | 142 | 1279 | 7.5 | 1.2 | 11.0 |

Three-point field goals: 1997-98, 0-for-1. 1998-99, 0-for-1. 1999-00, 2-for-7 (.286). Totals, 2-for-9 (.222).

## NBA REGULAR-SEASON RECORD

**HONORS:** NBA All-Rookie first team (2001).

| Season Team | G | Min. | FGM | FGA | Pct. | FTM | FTA | Pct. | Off. | Def. | Tot. | Ast. | St. | Blk. | TO | Pts. | RPG | APG | PPG |
|---|---|---|---|---|---|---|---|---|---|---|---|---|---|---|---|---|---|---|---|
| | | | | | | | | | REBOUNDS | | | | | | | | AVERAGES | | |
| 00-01—New Jersey ..... | 68 | 2272 | 346 | 777 | .445 | 121 | 192 | .630 | 137 | 365 | 502 | 131 | 78 | 113 | 138 | 814 | 7.4 | 1.9 | 12.0 |
| 01-02—New Jersey ..... | 73 | 2504 | 445 | 962 | .463 | 181 | 267 | .678 | 113 | 275 | 388 | 192 | 90 | 121 | 172 | 1086 | 5.3 | 2.6 | 14.9 |
| 02-03—New Jersey ..... | 77 | 2628 | 509 | 1082 | .470 | 256 | 392 | .653 | 164 | 476 | 640 | 185 | 98 | 70 | 192 | 1283 | 8.3 | 2.4 | 16.7 |
| 03-04—New Jersey ..... | 65 | 2252 | 439 | 900 | .488 | 201 | 294 | .684 | 133 | 484 | 617 | 160 | 95 | 82 | 168 | 1086 | 9.5 | 2.5 | 16.7 |
| 04-05—Denver ........... | 70 | 2272 | 444 | 907 | .490 | 199 | 308 | .646 | 146 | 365 | 511 | 170 | 100 | 78 | 149 | 1087 | 7.3 | 2.4 | 15.5 |
| **Totals** ................... | 353 | 11928 | 2183 | 4628 | .472 | 958 | 1453 | .659 | 693 | 1965 | 2658 | 838 | 461 | 464 | 819 | 5356 | 7.5 | 2.4 | 15.2 |

Three-point field goals: 2000-01, 1-for-11 (.091). 2001-02, 15-for-67 (.224). 2002-03, 9-for-43 (.209). 2003-04, 7-for-25 (.280). 2004-05, 0-for-12. Totals, 32-for-158 (.203).
Personal fouls/disqualifications: 2000-01, 281/10. 2001-02, 261/8. 2002-03, 294/6. 2003-04, 230/5. 2004-05, 228/4. Totals, 1294/33.

## NBA PLAYOFF RECORD

| Season Team | G | Min. | FGM | FGA | Pct. | FTM | FTA | Pct. | Off. | Def. | Tot. | Ast. | St. | Blk. | TO | Pts. | RPG | APG | PPG |
|---|---|---|---|---|---|---|---|---|---|---|---|---|---|---|---|---|---|---|---|
| | | | | | | | | | REBOUNDS | | | | | | | | AVERAGES | | |
| 01-02—New Jersey ..... | 20 | 749 | 129 | 304 | .424 | 76 | 110 | .691 | 30 | 86 | 116 | 57 | 24 | 25 | 52 | 336 | 5.8 | 2.9 | 16.8 |
| 02-03—New Jersey ..... | 20 | 777 | 149 | 329 | .453 | 79 | 114 | .693 | 50 | 137 | 187 | 57 | 29 | 31 | 58 | 378 | 9.4 | 2.9 | 18.9 |
| 03-04—New Jersey ..... | 11 | 409 | 81 | 152 | .533 | 48 | 64 | .750 | 25 | 96 | 121 | 12 | 13 | 14 | 32 | 210 | 11.0 | 1.1 | 19.1 |
| 04-05—Denver ........... | 5 | 164 | 27 | 58 | .466 | 8 | 13 | .615 | 7 | 21 | 28 | 6 | 5 | 5 | 7 | 62 | 5.6 | 1.2 | 12.4 |
| **Totals** ................... | 56 | 2099 | 386 | 843 | .458 | 211 | 301 | .701 | 112 | 340 | 452 | 132 | 71 | 75 | 149 | 986 | 8.1 | 2.4 | 17.6 |

Three-point field goals: 2001-02, 2-for-9 (.222). 2002-03, 1-for-11 (.091). 2003-04, 0-for-4. 2004-05, 0-for-1. Totals, 3-for-25 (.120).
Personal fouls/disqualifications: 2001-02, 86/3. 2002-03, 92/2. 2003-04, 50/3. 2004-05, 22/1. Totals, 250/9.

## NBA ALL-STAR GAME RECORD

| Season  Team | Min. | FGM | FGA | Pct. | FTM | FTA | Pct. | Off. | Def. | Tot. | Ast. | PF | Dq. | St. | Blk. | TO | Pts. |
|---|---|---|---|---|---|---|---|---|---|---|---|---|---|---|---|---|---|
| | | | | | | | | REBOUNDS | | | | | | | | | |
| 2004—New Jersey .......... | 23 | 8 | 10 | .800 | 1 | 2 | .500 | 4 | 3 | 7 | 3 | 1 | 0 | 0 | 0 | 3 | 17 |

**M**

# MARTIN, KEVIN  G  KINGS

**PERSONAL:** Born February 1, 1983, in Zanesville, Ohio. ... 6-7/185. (2.01/83.9). ... Full name: Kevin Dallas Martin
**HIGH SCHOOL:** Zanesville (Ohio).
**COLLEGE:** Western Carolina.
**TRANSACTIONS/CAREER NOTES:** Selected after junior season by Sacramento Kings in first round (26th pick overall) of 2004 NBA Draft.

## COLLEGIATE RECORD

| Season Team | G | Min. | FGM | FGA | Pct. | FTM | FTA | Pct. | Reb. | Ast. | Pts. | RPG | APG | PPG |
|---|---|---|---|---|---|---|---|---|---|---|---|---|---|---|
| | | | | | | | | | | | | AVERAGES | | |
| 01-02—Western Carolina ........ | 28 | 913 | 196 | 405 | .484 | 154 | 186 | .828 | 133 | 43 | 619 | 4.8 | 1.5 | 22.1 |
| 02-03—Western Carolina ........ | 24 | 759 | 161 | 380 | .424 | 174 | 197 | .883 | 91 | 43 | 546 | 3.8 | 1.8 | 22.8 |
| 03-04—Western Carolina ........ | 27 | 843 | 208 | 439 | .474 | 206 | 252 | .817 | 130 | 47 | 673 | 4.8 | 1.7 | 24.9 |
| **Totals** .................................. | 79 | 2515 | 565 | 1224 | .462 | 534 | 635 | .841 | 354 | 133 | 1838 | 4.5 | 1.7 | 23.3 |

Three-point field goals: 2001-02, 73-for-191 (.382). 2002-03, 50-for-160 (.313). 2003-04, 51-for-152 (.336). Totals, 174-for-503 (.346).

## NBA REGULAR-SEASON RECORD

| Season Team | G | Min. | FGM | FGA | Pct. | FTM | FTA | Pct. | Off. | Def. | Tot. | Ast. | St. | Blk. | TO | Pts. | RPG | APG | PPG |
|---|---|---|---|---|---|---|---|---|---|---|---|---|---|---|---|---|---|---|---|
| | | | | | | | | | REBOUNDS | | | | | | | | AVERAGES | | |
| 04-05—Sacramento... | 45 | 455 | 45 | 117 | .385 | 36 | 55 | .655 | 29 | 29 | 58 | 22 | 16 | 3 | 24 | 131 | 1.3 | 0.5 | 2.9 |

Three-point field goals: 2004-05, 5-for-25 (.200). Totals, 5-for-25 (.200).
Personal foul

## MASHBURN, JAMAL  G/F  76ERS

**PERSONAL:** Born November 29, 1972, in New York. ... 6-8/247. (2.03/112.0).
**HIGH SCHOOL:** Cardinal Hayes (Bronx, N.Y.).
**COLLEGE:** Kentucky.
**TRANSACTIONS/CAREER NOTES:** Selected after junior season by Dallas Mavericks in first round (fourth pick overall) of 1993 NBA Draft. ... Traded by Mavericks to Miami Heat for G Sasha Danilovic, F Kurt Thomas and F Martin Muursepp (February 14, 1997). ... Traded by Heat with F P.J. Brown, F/C Otis Thorpe, F Tim James and G/F Rodney Buford to Charlotte Hornets for G Eddie Jones, F Anthony Mason, G Ricky Davis and G/F Dale Ellis (August 1, 2000). ... Hornets franchise moved to New Orleans for 2002-03 season. ... Traded by Hornets with F Rodney Rogers to Philadelphia 76ers for F Glenn Robinson (February 24, 2005).

### COLLEGIATE RECORD

**NOTES:** THE SPORTING NEWS All-America first team (1993).

| | | | | | | | | | | | | AVERAGES | | |
|---|---|---|---|---|---|---|---|---|---|---|---|---|---|---|
| Season Team | G | Min. | FGM | FGA | Pct. | FTM | FTA | Pct. | Reb. | Ast. | Pts. | RPG | APG | PPG |
| 90-91—Kentucky | 28 | 677 | 137 | 289 | .474 | 64 | 88 | .727 | 195 | 42 | 362 | 7.0 | 1.5 | 12.9 |
| 91-92—Kentucky | 36 | 1176 | 279 | 492 | .567 | 151 | 213 | .709 | 281 | 52 | 767 | 7.8 | 1.4 | 21.3 |
| 92-93—Kentucky | 34 | 1109 | 259 | 526 | .492 | 130 | 194 | .670 | 284 | 124 | 714 | 8.4 | 3.6 | 21.0 |
| Totals | 98 | 2962 | 675 | 1307 | .516 | 345 | 495 | .697 | 760 | 218 | 1843 | 7.8 | 2.2 | 18.8 |

Three-point field goals: 1990-91, 23-for-82 (.280). 1991-92, 58-for-132 (.439). 1992-93, 66-for-180 (.367). Totals, 147-for-394 (.373).

### NBA REGULAR-SEASON RECORD

**HONORS:** NBA All-Rookie first team (1994). ... All-NBA third team (2003).

| | | | | | | | | | REBOUNDS | | | | | | | | AVERAGES | | |
|---|---|---|---|---|---|---|---|---|---|---|---|---|---|---|---|---|---|---|---|
| Season Team | G | Min. | FGM | FGA | Pct. | FTM | FTA | Pct. | Off. | Def. | Tot. | Ast. | St. | Blk. | TO | Pts. | RPG | APG | PPG |
| 93-94—Dallas | 79 | 2896 | 561 | 1382 | .406 | 306 | 438 | .699 | 107 | 246 | 353 | 266 | 89 | 14 | 245 | 1513 | 4.5 | 3.4 | 19.2 |
| 94-95—Dallas | 80 | 2980 | 683 | 1566 | .436 | 447 | 605 | .739 | 116 | 215 | 331 | 298 | 82 | 8 | 235 | 1926 | 4.1 | 3.7 | 24.1 |
| 95-96—Dallas | 18 | 669 | 145 | 383 | .379 | 97 | 133 | .729 | 37 | 60 | 97 | 50 | 14 | 3 | 55 | 422 | 5.4 | 2.8 | 23.4 |
| 96-97—Dallas-Miami.. | 69 | 2164 | 286 | 743 | .385 | 160 | 228 | .702 | 69 | 225 | 294 | 204 | 78 | 12 | 114 | 822 | 4.3 | 3.0 | 11.9 |
| 97-98—Miami | 48 | 1729 | 251 | 577 | .435 | 184 | 231 | .797 | 72 | 164 | 236 | 132 | 43 | 14 | 108 | 723 | 4.9 | 2.8 | 15.1 |
| 98-99—Miami | 24 | 855 | 134 | 297 | .451 | 75 | 104 | .721 | 24 | 122 | 146 | 75 | 20 | 3 | 60 | 356 | 6.1 | 3.1 | 14.8 |
| 99-00—Miami | 76 | 2828 | 515 | 1158 | .445 | 186 | 239 | .778 | 64 | 317 | 381 | 298 | 79 | 14 | 180 | 1328 | 5.0 | 3.9 | 17.5 |
| 00-01—Charlotte | 76 | 2989 | 573 | 1388 | .413 | 279 | 364 | .766 | 92 | 484 | 576 | 411 | 85 | 13 | 211 | 1528 | 7.6 | 5.4 | 20.1 |
| 01-02—Charlotte | 40 | 1601 | 303 | 744 | .407 | 211 | 241 | .876 | 31 | 211 | 242 | 171 | 45 | 6 | 110 | 858 | 6.1 | 4.3 | 21.5 |
| 02-03—New Orleans .. | 82 | 3321 | 670 | 1586 | .422 | 313 | 369 | .848 | 66 | 432 | 498 | 462 | 83 | 17 | 230 | 1772 | 6.1 | 5.6 | 21.6 |
| 03-04—New Orleans .. | 19 | 730 | 156 | 398 | .392 | 65 | 80 | .813 | 19 | 98 | 117 | 47 | 14 | 5 | 37 | 396 | 6.2 | 2.5 | 20.8 |
| Totals | 611 | 22762 | 4277 | 10222 | .418 | 2323 | 3032 | .766 | 697 | 2574 | 3271 | 2414 | 632 | 109 | 1585 | 11644 | 5.4 | 4.0 | 19.1 |

Three-point field goals: 1993-94, 85-for-299 (.284). 1994-95, 113-for-344 (.328). 1995-96, 35-for-102 (.343). 1996-97, 90-for-277 (.325). 1997-98, 37-for-122 (.303). 1998-99, 13-for-30 (.433). 1999-00, 112-for-278 (.403). 2000-01, 103-for-289 (.356). 2001-02, 41-for-112 (.366). 2002-03, 119-for-306 (.389). 2003-04, 19-for-67 (.284). Totals, 767-for-2226 (.345).

Personal fouls/disqualifications: 1993-94, 205/0. 1994-95, 190/0. 1995-96, 39/0. 1996-97, 186/4. 1997-98, 137/1. 1998-99, 58/0. 1999-00, 215/3. 2000-01, 185/1. 2001-02, 80/0. 2002-03, 196/0. 2003-04, 42/0. Totals, 1533/9.

### NBA PLAYOFF RECORD

| | | | | | | | | | REBOUNDS | | | | | | | | AVERAGES | | |
|---|---|---|---|---|---|---|---|---|---|---|---|---|---|---|---|---|---|---|---|
| Season Team | G | Min. | FGM | FGA | Pct. | FTM | FTA | Pct. | Off. | Def. | Tot. | Ast. | St. | Blk. | TO | Pts. | RPG | APG | PPG |
| 96-97—Miami | 17 | 554 | 65 | 168 | .387 | 26 | 40 | .650 | 22 | 62 | 84 | 35 | 17 | 2 | 30 | 178 | 4.9 | 2.1 | 10.5 |
| 97-98—Miami | 5 | 129 | 12 | 45 | .267 | 3 | 4 | .750 | 4 | 18 | 22 | 9 | 3 | 1 | 9 | 31 | 4.4 | 1.8 | 6.2 |
| 98-99—Miami | 5 | 152 | 19 | 49 | .388 | 6 | 9 | .667 | 4 | 9 | 13 | 10 | 2 | 0 | 10 | 50 | 2.6 | 2.0 | 10.0 |
| 99-00—Miami | 10 | 423 | 63 | 157 | .401 | 36 | 42 | .857 | 9 | 37 | 46 | 32 | 11 | 2 | 24 | 175 | 4.6 | 3.2 | 17.5 |
| 00-01—Charlotte | 10 | 419 | 84 | 208 | .404 | 74 | 88 | .841 | 18 | 44 | 62 | 57 | 12 | 3 | 30 | 249 | 6.2 | 5.7 | 24.9 |
| 01-02—Charlotte | 1 | 10 | 0 | 6 | .000 | 0 | 0 | ... | 0 | 1 | 1 | 1 | 0 | 0 | 0 | 0 | 1.0 | 1.0 | 0.0 |
| 02-03—New Orleans .. | 4 | 162 | 34 | 79 | .430 | 25 | 35 | .714 | 0 | 14 | 14 | 21 | 4 | 1 | 10 | 99 | 3.5 | 5.3 | 24.8 |
| Totals | 52 | 1849 | 277 | 712 | .389 | 170 | 218 | .780 | 57 | 185 | 242 | 165 | 49 | 9 | 113 | 782 | 4.7 | 3.2 | 15.0 |

Three-point field goals: 1996-97, 22-for-62 (.355). 1997-98, 4-for-11 (.364). 1998-99, 6-for-14 (.429). 1999-00, 13-for-33 (.394). 2000-01, 7-for-21 (.333). 2001-02, 0-for-1. 2002-03, 6-for-15 (.400). Totals, 58-for-157 (.369).

Personal fouls/disqualifications: 1996-97, 58/2. 1997-98, 21/2. 1998-99, 11/0. 1999-00, 30/0. 2000-01, 24/0. 2002-03, 4/0. Totals, 148/4.

### NBA ALL-STAR GAME RECORD

| | | | | | | | REBOUNDS | | | | | | | | |
|---|---|---|---|---|---|---|---|---|---|---|---|---|---|---|---|
| Season Team | Min. | FGM | FGA | Pct. | FTM | FTA | Pct. | Off. | Def. | Tot. | Ast. | PF | Dq. | St. | Blk. | TO | Pts. |
| 2003—New Orleans | 14 | 4 | 7 | .571 | 0 | 0 | ... | 0 | 4 | 4 | 2 | 0 | 0 | 2 | 0 | 0 | 10 |

Three-point field goals: 2003, 2-for-2 (1.000). Totals, 2-for-2 (1.000).

## MASON, DESMOND  G  BUCKS

**PERSONAL:** Born October 11, 1977, in Waxahachie, Texas. ... 6-5/222. (1.96/100.7). ... Full name: Desmond Tremaine Mason
**HIGH SCHOOL:** Waxahachie (Texas).
**COLLEGE:** Oklahoma State.
**TRANSACTIONS/CAREER NOTES:** Selected by Seattle SuperSonics in first round (17th pick overall) of 2000 NBA Draft. ... Traded by SuperSonics with G Gary Payton to Milwaukee Bucks for G Ray Allen, G Kevin Ollie, G Ronald Murray and conditional first-round draft choice (February 20, 2003).

### COLLEGIATE RECORD

| | | | | | | | | | | | | AVERAGES | | |
|---|---|---|---|---|---|---|---|---|---|---|---|---|---|---|
| Season Team | G | Min. | FGM | FGA | Pct. | FTM | FTA | Pct. | Reb. | Ast. | Pts. | RPG | APG | PPG |
| 96-97—Oklahoma State | 32 | 539 | 52 | 138 | .377 | 23 | 37 | .622 | 80 | 22 | 144 | 2.5 | 0.7 | 4.5 |
| 97-98—Oklahoma State | 29 | 947 | 157 | 299 | .525 | 86 | 126 | .683 | 223 | 45 | 422 | 7.7 | 1.6 | 14.6 |
| 98-99—Oklahoma State | 34 | 1180 | 196 | 408 | .480 | 106 | 142 | .746 | 267 | 28 | 525 | 7.9 | 0.8 | 15.4 |

| Season Team | G | Min. | FGM | FGA | Pct. | FTM | FTA | Pct. | Reb. | Ast. | Pts. | RPG | APG | PPG |
|---|---|---|---|---|---|---|---|---|---|---|---|---|---|---|
| 99-00—Oklahoma State | 34 | 1202 | 211 | 423 | .499 | 125 | 163 | .767 | 225 | 52 | 611 | 6.6 | 1.5 | 18.0 |
| Totals | 129 | 3868 | 616 | 1268 | .486 | 340 | 468 | .726 | 795 | 147 | 1702 | 6.2 | 1.1 | 13.2 |

Three-point field goals: 1996-97, 17-for-52 (.327). 1997-98, 22-for-69 (.319). 1998-99, 27-for-79 (.342). 1999-00, 64-for-149 (.430). Totals, 130-for-349 (.372).

## NBA REGULAR-SEASON RECORD

**HONORS:** Slam Dunk championship winner (2001). ... NBA All-Rookie second team (2001).

| Season Team | G | Min. | FGM | FGA | Pct. | FTM | FTA | Pct. | Off. | Def. | Tot. | Ast. | St. | Blk. | TO | Pts. | RPG | APG | PPG |
|---|---|---|---|---|---|---|---|---|---|---|---|---|---|---|---|---|---|---|---|
| 00-01—Seattle | 78 | 1522 | 189 | 439 | .431 | 67 | 91 | .736 | 72 | 177 | 249 | 63 | 39 | 20 | 53 | 463 | 3.2 | 0.8 | 5.9 |
| 01-02—Seattle | 75 | 2420 | 357 | 769 | .464 | 201 | 237 | .848 | 92 | 259 | 351 | 104 | 67 | 27 | 104 | 931 | 4.7 | 1.4 | 12.4 |
| 02-03—Seattle-Mil. | 80 | 2763 | 457 | 1017 | .449 | 212 | 283 | .749 | 154 | 369 | 523 | 163 | 67 | 32 | 115 | 1147 | 6.5 | 2.0 | 14.3 |
| 03-04—Milwaukee | 82 | 2534 | 409 | 867 | .472 | 356 | 463 | .769 | 93 | 266 | 359 | 152 | 60 | 24 | 148 | 1183 | 4.4 | 1.9 | 14.4 |
| 04-05—Milwaukee | 80 | 2893 | 478 | 1079 | .443 | 420 | 524 | .802 | 85 | 227 | 312 | 217 | 58 | 27 | 164 | 1377 | 3.9 | 2.7 | 17.2 |
| Totals | 395 | 12132 | 1890 | 4171 | .453 | 1256 | 1598 | .786 | 496 | 1298 | 1794 | 699 | 291 | 130 | 584 | 5101 | 4.5 | 1.8 | 12.9 |

Three-point field goals: 2000-01, 18-for-67 (.269). 2001-02, 16-for-59 (.271). 2002-03, 21-for-72 (.292). 2003-04, 9-for-39 (.231). 2004-05, 1-for-8 (.125). Totals, 65-for-245 (.265).
Personal fouls/disqualifications: 2000-01, 146/0. 2001-02, 170/0. 2002-03, 210/1. 2003-04, 191/2. 2004-05, 198/1. Totals, 915/4.

## NBA PLAYOFF RECORD

| Season Team | G | Min. | FGM | FGA | Pct. | FTM | FTA | Pct. | Off. | Def. | Tot. | Ast. | St. | Blk. | TO | Pts. | RPG | APG | PPG |
|---|---|---|---|---|---|---|---|---|---|---|---|---|---|---|---|---|---|---|---|
| 01-02—Seattle | 5 | 205 | 24 | 57 | .421 | 10 | 17 | .588 | 5 | 26 | 31 | 9 | 4 | 2 | 5 | 59 | 6.2 | 1.8 | 11.8 |
| 02-03—Milwaukee | 6 | 204 | 28 | 55 | .509 | 22 | 31 | .710 | 6 | 36 | 42 | 5 | 6 | 4 | 7 | 78 | 7.0 | 0.8 | 13.0 |
| 03-04—Milwaukee | 5 | 198 | 25 | 74 | .338 | 22 | 26 | .846 | 4 | 20 | 24 | 12 | 4 | 2 | 12 | 72 | 4.8 | 2.4 | 14.4 |
| Totals | 16 | 607 | 77 | 186 | .414 | 54 | 74 | .730 | 15 | 82 | 97 | 26 | 14 | 8 | 24 | 209 | 6.1 | 1.6 | 13.1 |

Three-point field goals: 2001-02, 1-for-3 (.333). 2002-03, 0-for-4. 2003-04, 0-for-2. Totals, 1-for-9 (.111).
Personal fouls/disqualifications: 2001-02, 11/0. 2002-03, 19/1. 2003-04, 16/0. Totals, 46/1.

# MASSENBURG, TONY   F   SPURS

**PERSONAL:** Born July 31, 1967, in Sussex, Va. ... 6-9/250. (2.06/113.4). ... Full name: Tony Arnel Massenburg
**HIGH SCHOOL:** Sussex (Va.) Central.
**COLLEGE:** Maryland.
**TRANSACTIONS/CAREER NOTES:** Selected by San Antonio Spurs in second round (43rd pick overall) of 1990 NBA Draft. ... Waived by Spurs (December 2, 1991). ... Played in Italy (1991-92). ... Signed as free agent by Charlotte Hornets (December 11, 1991). ... Waived by Hornets (January 7, 1992). ... Signed by Boston Celtics to first of two consecutive 10-day contracts (January 10, 1992). ... Signed by Golden State Warriors to first of two consecutive 10-day contracts (February 13, 1992). ... Played in Spain (1992-94). ... Signed as free agent by Los Angeles Clippers (June 27, 1994). ... Selected by Toronto Raptors from Clippers in NBA Expansion Draft (June 24, 1995). ... Traded by Raptors with F Ed Pinckney and right to swap 1996 or 1997 first-round draft choices to Philadelphia 76ers for F Sharone Wright (February 22, 1996). ... Signed as free agent by New Jersey Nets (September 10, 1996). ... Signed as free agent by Celtics (July 28, 1997). ... Traded by Celtics with future second-round draft choice to Vancouver Grizzlies for F Roy Rogers (October 28, 1997). ... Traded by Grizzlies with draft rights to G Steve Francis as part of three-way deal in which Grizzlies received G Michael Dickerson, F/C Othella Harrington, G Brent Price, F/C Antoine Carr and future first-round draft choice from Rockets, Rockets received F Don MacLean and future first-round draft choice from Orlando Magic, and Magic received G Michael Smith, G/F Rodrick Rhodes, G Lee Mayberry and F Makhtar Ndiaye from Grizzlies (August 27, 1999). ... Signed as free agent by Grizzlies (August 8, 2000). ... Grizzlies franchise moved to Memphis for 2001-02 season. ... Waived by Grizzlies (October 30, 2002). ... Signed as free agent by Sacramento Kings (August 22, 2003). ... Signed as free agent by San Antonio Spurs (August 4, 2004).
**MISCELLANEOUS:** Member of NBA championship team (2005).

M

## COLLEGIATE RECORD

| Season Team | G | Min. | FGM | FGA | Pct. | FTM | FTA | Pct. | Reb. | Ast. | Pts. | RPG | APG | PPG |
|---|---|---|---|---|---|---|---|---|---|---|---|---|---|---|
| 85-86—Maryland | 29 | 349 | 28 | 56 | .500 | 27 | 48 | .563 | 60 | 0 | 83 | 2.1 | 0.0 | 2.9 |
| 86-87—Maryland | | | | | | | | Did not play. | | | | | | |
| 87-88—Maryland | 23 | 616 | 93 | 179 | .520 | 47 | 82 | .573 | 122 | 10 | 233 | 5.3 | 0.4 | 10.1 |
| 88-89—Maryland | 29 | 1001 | 197 | 358 | .550 | 87 | 145 | .600 | 226 | 21 | 481 | 7.8 | 0.7 | 16.6 |
| 89-90—Maryland | 31 | 973 | 206 | 408 | .505 | 145 | 201 | .721 | 314 | 20 | 557 | 10.1 | 0.6 | 18.0 |
| Totals | 112 | 2939 | 524 | 1001 | .523 | 306 | 476 | .643 | 722 | 51 | 1354 | 6.4 | 0.5 | 12.1 |

Three-point field goals: 1988-89, 0-for-1. 1989-90, 0-for-2. Totals, 0-for-3 (.000).

## NBA REGULAR-SEASON RECORD

| Season Team | G | Min. | FGM | FGA | Pct. | FTM | FTA | Pct. | Off. | Def. | Tot. | Ast. | St. | Blk. | TO | Pts. | RPG | APG | PPG |
|---|---|---|---|---|---|---|---|---|---|---|---|---|---|---|---|---|---|---|---|
| 90-91—San Antonio | 35 | 161 | 27 | 60 | .450 | 28 | 45 | .622 | 23 | 35 | 58 | 4 | 4 | 9 | 13 | 82 | 1.7 | 0.1 | 2.3 |
| 91-92—SA-Char.-Bos.-GS | 18 | 90 | 10 | 25 | .400 | 9 | 15 | .600 | 7 | 18 | 25 | 0 | 1 | 1 | 9 | 29 | 1.4 | 0.0 | 1.6 |
| 94-95—L.A. Clippers | 80 | 2127 | 282 | 601 | .469 | 177 | 235 | .753 | 160 | 295 | 455 | 67 | 48 | 58 | 118 | 741 | 5.7 | 0.8 | 9.3 |
| 95-96—Tor.-Phil. | 54 | 1463 | 214 | 432 | .495 | 111 | 157 | .707 | 127 | 225 | 352 | 30 | 28 | 20 | 73 | 539 | 6.5 | 0.6 | 10.0 |
| 96-97—New Jersey | 79 | 1954 | 219 | 452 | .485 | 130 | 206 | .631 | 222 | 295 | 517 | 23 | 38 | 50 | 91 | 568 | 6.5 | 0.3 | 7.2 |
| 97-98—Vancouver | 61 | 894 | 148 | 309 | .479 | 100 | 137 | .730 | 80 | 152 | 232 | 21 | 25 | 24 | 60 | 396 | 3.8 | 0.3 | 6.5 |
| 98-99—Vancouver | 43 | 1143 | 189 | 388 | .487 | 103 | 155 | .665 | 83 | 174 | 257 | 23 | 26 | 39 | 64 | 481 | 6.0 | 0.5 | 11.2 |
| 99-00—Houston | 10 | 109 | 16 | 36 | .444 | 14 | 16 | .875 | 7 | 20 | 27 | 3 | 2 | 5 | 9 | 46 | 2.7 | 0.3 | 4.6 |
| 00-01—Vancouver | 52 | 823 | 92 | 199 | .462 | 49 | 70 | .700 | 75 | 135 | 210 | 9 | 10 | 28 | 48 | 233 | 4.0 | 0.2 | 4.5 |
| 01-02—Memphis | 73 | 1247 | 159 | 349 | .456 | 84 | 117 | .718 | 100 | 224 | 324 | 26 | 30 | 31 | 65 | 403 | 4.4 | 0.4 | 5.5 |
| 02-03—Utah | 58 | 792 | 104 | 232 | .448 | 65 | 84 | .774 | 59 | 97 | 156 | 17 | 17 | 19 | 50 | 273 | 2.7 | 0.3 | 4.7 |
| 03-04—Sacramento | 59 | 789 | 104 | 219 | .475 | 43 | 63 | .683 | 57 | 131 | 188 | 29 | 14 | 18 | 45 | 251 | 3.2 | 0.5 | 4.3 |
| 04-05—San Antonio | 61 | 699 | 74 | 182 | .407 | 48 | 63 | .762 | 54 | 109 | 163 | 14 | 18 | 20 | 40 | 196 | 2.7 | 0.2 | 3.2 |
| Totals | 683 | 12291 | 1638 | 3484 | .470 | 961 | 1363 | .705 | 1054 | 1910 | 2964 | 266 | 261 | 322 | 685 | 4238 | 4.3 | 0.4 | 6.2 |

Three-point field goals: 1994-95, 0-for-3. 1995-96, 0-for-3. 1996-97, 1-for-1. 1998-99, 0-for-2. 2001-02, 1-for-1 (1.000). 2003-04, 0-for-1. Totals, 1-for-11 (.091).

Personal fouls/disqualifications: 1990-91, 26/0. 1991-92, 21/0. 1994-95, 253/2. 1995-96, 140/0. 1996-97, 217/2. 1997-98, 123/0. 1998-99, 108/0. 1999-00, 13/0. 2000-01, 122/0. 2001-02, 174/2. 2002-03, 144/1. 2003-04, 144/0. 2004-05, 122/1. Totals, 1607/8.

## NBA PLAYOFF RECORD

| Season Team | G | Min. | FGM | FGA | Pct. | FTM | FTA | Pct. | REBOUNDS Off. | Def. | Tot. | Ast. | St. | Blk. | TO | Pts. | AVERAGES RPG | APG | PPG |
|---|---|---|---|---|---|---|---|---|---|---|---|---|---|---|---|---|---|---|---|
| 90-91—San Antonio.... | 1 | 1 | 0 | 0 | ... | 0 | 0 | ... | 0 | 0 | 0 | 0 | 0 | 0 | 0 | 0 | 0.0 | 0.0 | 0.0 |
| 02-03—Utah ............. | 5 | 70 | 10 | 21 | .476 | 5 | 9 | .556 | 7 | 14 | 21 | 2 | 0 | 4 | 5 | 25 | 4.2 | 0.4 | 5.0 |
| 04-05—San Antonio.... | 9 | 28 | 1 | 6 | .167 | 1 | 2 | .500 | 4 | 7 | 11 | 0 | 0 | 0 | 0 | 3 | 1.2 | 0.0 | 0.3 |
| Totals .................. | 15 | 99 | 11 | 27 | .407 | 6 | 11 | .545 | 11 | 21 | 32 | 2 | 0 | 4 | 5 | 28 | 2.1 | 0.1 | 1.9 |

Personal fouls/disqualifications: 2002-03, 9/0. 2004-05, 2/0. Totals, 11/0.

## ITALIAN LEAGUE RECORD

| Season Team | G | Min. | FGM | FGA | Pct. | FTM | FTA | Pct. | Reb. | Ast. | Pts. | AVERAGES RPG | APG | PPG |
|---|---|---|---|---|---|---|---|---|---|---|---|---|---|---|
| 91-92—Sidis Reggio Emilia ....... | 4 | 133 | 35 | 60 | .583 | 21 | 33 | .636 | 40 | 0 | 91 | 10.0 | 0.0 | 22.8 |

Personal fouls/disqualifications: 1991-92, 15/0. Totals, 15/0.

## SPANISH RECORD

| Season Team | G | Min. | FGM | FGA | Pct. | FTM | FTA | Pct. | Reb. | Ast. | Pts. | AVERAGES RPG | APG | PPG |
|---|---|---|---|---|---|---|---|---|---|---|---|---|---|---|
| 92-93—Unicaja-Mayoral ............ | 30 | 1008 | 195 | 351 | .556 | 72 | 106 | .679 | 293 | 10 | 462 | 9.8 | 0.3 | 15.4 |
| 93-94—Barcelona ...................... | 25 | 759 | 150 | 264 | .568 | 88 | 127 | .693 | 199 | 12 | 388 | 8.0 | 0.5 | 15.5 |
| Totals ...................................... | 55 | 1767 | 345 | 615 | .561 | 160 | 233 | .687 | 492 | 22 | 850 | 8.9 | 0.4 | 15.5 |

# MBENGA, D.J.                        C                    MAVERICKS

**PERSONAL:** Born December 30, 1980, in Kinshasa, Congo. ... 7-0/245. (2.13/111.1). ... Full name: Didier Ilunga-Mbenga.
**TRANSACTIONS/CAREER NOTES:** Signed as free agent by Dallas Mavericks (September 14, 2004).

## BELGIAN LEAGUE RECORD

| Season Team | G | Min. | FGM | FGA | Pct. | FTM | FTA | Pct. | Reb. | Ast. | Pts. | AVERAGES RPG | APG | PPG |
|---|---|---|---|---|---|---|---|---|---|---|---|---|---|---|
| 02-03—Spirou Charleroi ............ | 21 | ... | 77 | 157 | .490 | 16 | 33 | .485 | 171 | 12 | 170 | 8.1 | 0.6 | 8.1 |
| 03-04—Spirou Charleroi ............ | 34 | 490 | 88 | 161 | .547 | 35 | 50 | .700 | 149 | 14 | 211 | 4.4 | 0.4 | 6.2 |
| Totals ...................................... | 55 | 490 | 165 | 318 | .519 | 51 | 83 | .614 | 320 | 26 | 381 | 5.8 | 0.5 | 6.9 |

## NBA REGULAR-SEASON RECORD

| Season Team | G | Min. | FGM | FGA | Pct. | FTM | FTA | Pct. | REBOUNDS Off. | Def. | Tot. | Ast. | St. | Blk. | TO | Pts. | AVERAGES RPG | APG | PPG |
|---|---|---|---|---|---|---|---|---|---|---|---|---|---|---|---|---|---|---|---|
| 04-05—Dallas.............. | 15 | 58 | 6 | 14 | .429 | 3 | 4 | .750 | 3 | 5 | 8 | 0 | 0 | 5 | 5 | 15 | 0.5 | 0.0 | 1.0 |

Personal fouls/disqualifications: 2004-05, 13/0. Totals, 13/0.

# MCCARTY, WALTER                    F

**PERSONAL:** Born February 1, 1974, in Evansville, Ind. ... 6-10/230. (2.08/104.3). ... Full name: Walter Lee McCarty
**HIGH SCHOOL:** Harrison (Evansville, Ind.).
**COLLEGE:** Kentucky.
**TRANSACTIONS/CAREER NOTES:** Selected by New York Knicks in first round (19th pick overall) of 1996 NBA Draft. ... Traded by Knicks with F Dontae' Jones, F John Thomas, G Scott Brooks and two future second-round draft choices to Boston Celtics for F Chris Mills (October 22, 1997). ... Traded by Celtics to Phoenix Suns for 2005 second-round draft choice (February 8, 2005).

## COLLEGIATE RECORD

**NOTES:** Member of NCAA Division I championship team (1996).

| Season Team | G | Min. | FGM | FGA | Pct. | FTM | FTA | Pct. | Reb. | Ast. | Pts. | AVERAGES RPG | APG | PPG |
|---|---|---|---|---|---|---|---|---|---|---|---|---|---|---|
| 92-93—Kentucky ........................ | | | | | | Did not play—ineligible. | | | | | | | | |
| 93-94—Kentucky ........................ | 34 | 484 | 72 | 153 | .471 | 31 | 56 | .554 | 131 | 39 | 194 | 3.9 | 1.1 | 5.7 |
| 94-95—Kentucky ........................ | 33 | 744 | 128 | 251 | .510 | 61 | 84 | .726 | 185 | 50 | 345 | 5.6 | 1.5 | 10.5 |
| 95-96—Kentucky ........................ | 36 | 888 | 152 | 280 | .543 | 75 | 104 | .721 | 206 | 92 | 407 | 5.7 | 2.6 | 11.3 |
| Totals ...................................... | 103 | 2116 | 352 | 684 | .515 | 167 | 244 | .684 | 522 | 181 | 946 | 5.1 | 1.8 | 9.2 |

Three-point field goals: 1993-94, 19-for-50 (.380). 1994-95, 28-for-77 (.364). 1995-96, 28-for-60 (.467). Totals, 75-for-187 (.401).

## NBA REGULAR-SEASON RECORD

| Season Team | G | Min. | FGM | FGA | Pct. | FTM | FTA | Pct. | REBOUNDS Off. | Def. | Tot. | Ast. | St. | Blk. | TO | Pts. | AVERAGES RPG | APG | PPG |
|---|---|---|---|---|---|---|---|---|---|---|---|---|---|---|---|---|---|---|---|
| 96-97—New York ........ | 35 | 192 | 26 | 68 | .382 | 8 | 14 | .571 | 8 | 15 | 23 | 13 | 7 | 9 | 17 | 64 | 0.7 | 0.4 | 1.8 |
| 97-98—Boston ............ | 82 | 2340 | 295 | 730 | .404 | 144 | 194 | .742 | 141 | 223 | 364 | 171 | 110 | 44 | 141 | 788 | 4.4 | 2.2 | 9.6 |
| 98-99—Boston ............ | 32 | 659 | 64 | 177 | .362 | 40 | 57 | .702 | 36 | 79 | 115 | 40 | 24 | 13 | 40 | 181 | 3.6 | 1.3 | 5.7 |
| 99-00—Boston ............ | 61 | 879 | 78 | 230 | .339 | 39 | 54 | .722 | 33 | 77 | 110 | 70 | 24 | 23 | 67 | 229 | 1.8 | 1.1 | 3.8 |
| 00-01—Boston ............ | 60 | 478 | 45 | 126 | .357 | 22 | 28 | .786 | 24 | 57 | 81 | 39 | 14 | 7 | 20 | 131 | 1.4 | 0.7 | 2.2 |
| 01-02—Boston ............ | 56 | 718 | 80 | 180 | .444 | 13 | 19 | .684 | 32 | 96 | 128 | 41 | 18 | 7 | 22 | 212 | 2.3 | 0.7 | 3.8 |
| 02-03—Boston ............ | 82 | 1949 | 173 | 418 | .414 | 61 | 98 | .622 | 64 | 224 | 288 | 106 | 78 | 28 | 67 | 498 | 3.5 | 1.3 | 6.1 |
| 03-04—Boston ............ | 77 | 1900 | 203 | 523 | .388 | 62 | 82 | .756 | 28 | 211 | 239 | 124 | 72 | 22 | 91 | 605 | 3.1 | 1.6 | 7.9 |
| 04-05—Bos.-Phoenix .. | 72 | 906 | 95 | 235 | .404 | 15 | 29 | .517 | 29 | 109 | 138 | 37 | 25 | 15 | 36 | 260 | 1.9 | 0.5 | 3.6 |
| Totals ................... | 557 | 10021 | 1059 | 2687 | .394 | 404 | 575 | .703 | 395 | 1091 | 1486 | 647 | 372 | 168 | 501 | 2968 | 2.7 | 1.2 | 5.3 |

Three-point field goals: 1996-97, 4-for-14 (.286). 1997-98, 54-for-175 (.309). 1998-99, 13-for-50 (.260). 1999-00, 34-for-110 (.309). 2000-01, 19-for-56 (.339). 2001-02, 39-for-99 (.394). 2002-03, 91-for-248 (.367). 2003-04, 137-for-366 (.374). 2004-05, 55-for-155 (.355). Totals, 446-for-1273 (.350).

Personal fouls/disqualifications: 1996-97, 38/0. 1997-98, 274/6. 1998-99, 88/0. 1999-00, 83/1. 2000-01, 82/0. 2001-02, 83/0. 2002-03, 188/1. 2003-04, 179/1. 2004-05, 144/1. Totals, 1159/10.

## NBA PLAYOFF RECORD

| | | | | | | | | REBOUNDS | | | | | | | AVERAGES | | |
|---|---|---|---|---|---|---|---|---|---|---|---|---|---|---|---|---|---|
| Season Team | G | Min. | FGM | FGA | Pct. | FTM | FTA | Pct. | Off. | Def. | Tot. | Ast. | St. | Blk. | TO | Pts. | RPG | APG | PPG |
| 96-97—New York | 2 | 4 | 2 | 2 | 1.000 | 0 | 0 | ... | 0 | 0 | 0 | 0 | 1 | 0 | 0 | 4 | 0.0 | 0.0 | 2.0 |
| 01-02—Boston | 14 | 194 | 17 | 38 | .447 | 7 | 9 | .778 | 8 | 26 | 34 | 4 | 4 | 0 | 4 | 44 | 2.4 | 0.3 | 3.1 |
| 02-03—Boston | 10 | 352 | 36 | 75 | .480 | 6 | 7 | .857 | 10 | 33 | 43 | 22 | 8 | 5 | 11 | 99 | 4.3 | 2.2 | 9.9 |
| 03-04—Boston | 4 | 127 | 11 | 23 | .478 | 0 | 0 | ... | 3 | 18 | 21 | 8 | 2 | 2 | 4 | 28 | 5.3 | 2.0 | 7.0 |
| 04-05—Phoenix | 8 | 55 | 2 | 9 | .222 | 0 | 2 | .000 | 0 | 6 | 6 | 3 | 2 | 2 | 1 | 6 | 0.8 | 0.4 | 0.8 |
| Totals | 38 | 732 | 68 | 147 | .463 | 13 | 18 | .722 | 21 | 83 | 104 | 37 | 17 | 9 | 20 | 181 | 2.7 | 1.0 | 4.8 |

Three-point field goals: 2001-02, 3-for-18 (.167). 2002-03, 21-for-52 (.404). 2003-04, 6-for-15 (.400). 2004-05, 2-for-6 (.333). Totals, 32-for-91 (.352). Personal fouls/disqualifications: 2001-02, 19/0. 2002-03, 35/0. 2003-04, 7/0. 2004-05, 13/0. Totals, 74/0.

## MCCOY, JELANI                    F/C

**PERSONAL:** Born December 6, 1977, in Oakland. ... 6-10/245. (2.08/111.1). ... Full name: Jelani Marwan McCoy
**HIGH SCHOOL:** St. Augustine (San Diego).
**COLLEGE:** UCLA.
**TRANSACTIONS/CAREER NOTES:** Selected after junior season by Seattle SuperSonics in second round (33rd pick overall) of 1998 NBA Draft. ... Signed as free agent by Los Angeles Lakers (September 21, 2001). ... Signed as free agent by Toronto Raptors (September 27, 2002). ... Signed as free agent by Cleveland Cavaliers (October 2, 2003). ... Waived by Cavaliers (November 6, 2003). ... Signed as free agent by Milwaukee Bucks (September 23, 2004). ... Waived by Bucks (October 28, 2004). ... Signed as free agent by Atlanta Hawks (November 8, 2004). ... Waived by Hawks (December 14, 2004).
**MISCELLANEOUS:** Member of NBA championship team (2002).

### COLLEGIATE RECORD

| | | | | | | | | | | | | AVERAGES | | |
|---|---|---|---|---|---|---|---|---|---|---|---|---|---|---|
| Season Team | G | Min. | FGM | FGA | Pct. | FTM | FTA | Pct. | Reb. | Ast. | Pts. | RPG | APG | PPG |
| 95-96—UCLA | 31 | 921 | 138 | 204 | .676 | 40 | 92 | .435 | 214 | 28 | 316 | 6.9 | 0.9 | 10.2 |
| 96-97—UCLA | 32 | 846 | 152 | 201 | .756 | 45 | 101 | .446 | 207 | 48 | 349 | 6.5 | 1.5 | 10.9 |
| 97-98—UCLA | 15 | 319 | 57 | 95 | .600 | 35 | 67 | .522 | 107 | 13 | 149 | 7.1 | 0.9 | 9.9 |
| Totals | 78 | 2086 | 347 | 500 | .694 | 120 | 260 | .462 | 528 | 89 | 814 | 6.8 | 1.1 | 10.4 |

### NBA REGULAR-SEASON RECORD

| | | | | | | | | REBOUNDS | | | | | | | AVERAGES | | |
|---|---|---|---|---|---|---|---|---|---|---|---|---|---|---|---|---|---|
| Season Team | G | Min. | FGM | FGA | Pct. | FTM | FTA | Pct. | Off. | Def. | Tot. | Ast. | St. | Blk. | TO | Pts. | RPG | APG | PPG |
| 98-99—Seattle | 26 | 331 | 56 | 76 | .737 | 21 | 42 | .500 | 27 | 52 | 79 | 4 | 11 | 20 | 10 | 133 | 3.0 | 0.2 | 5.1 |
| 99-00—Seattle | 58 | 746 | 102 | 177 | .576 | 45 | 91 | .495 | 54 | 125 | 179 | 24 | 15 | 46 | 45 | 249 | 3.1 | 0.4 | 4.3 |
| 00-01—Seattle | 70 | 1143 | 138 | 264 | .523 | 41 | 93 | .441 | 92 | 159 | 251 | 57 | 18 | 49 | 75 | 317 | 3.6 | 0.8 | 4.5 |
| 01-02—L.A. Lakers | 21 | 104 | 12 | 21 | .571 | 2 | 8 | .250 | 8 | 17 | 25 | 7 | 0 | 5 | 8 | 26 | 1.2 | 0.3 | 1.2 |
| 02-03—Toronto | 67 | 1367 | 194 | 395 | .491 | 69 | 126 | .548 | 95 | 260 | 355 | 43 | 28 | 60 | 96 | 457 | 5.3 | 0.6 | 6.8 |
| 03-04—Cleveland | 2 | 12 | 0 | 0 | ... | 0 | 0 | ... | 1 | 3 | 4 | 0 | 0 | 0 | 1 | 0 | 2.0 | 0.0 | 0.0 |
| 04-05—Atlanta | 10 | 88 | 7 | 13 | .538 | 1 | 5 | .200 | 7 | 14 | 21 | 0 | 3 | 8 | 6 | 15 | 2.1 | 0.0 | 1.5 |
| Totals | 254 | 3791 | 509 | 946 | .538 | 179 | 365 | .490 | 284 | 630 | 914 | 135 | 75 | 188 | 241 | 1197 | 3.6 | 0.5 | 4.7 |

Personal fouls/disqualifications: 1998-99, 42/0. 1999-00, 127/0. 2000-01, 141/0. 2001-02, 14/0. 2002-03, 162/2. 2003-04, 4/0. 2004-05, 24/0. Totals, 514/2.

### NBA PLAYOFF RECORD

| | | | | | | | | REBOUNDS | | | | | | | AVERAGES | | |
|---|---|---|---|---|---|---|---|---|---|---|---|---|---|---|---|---|---|
| Season Team | G | Min. | FGM | FGA | Pct. | FTM | FTA | Pct. | Off. | Def. | Tot. | Ast. | St. | Blk. | TO | Pts. | RPG | APG | PPG |
| 99-00—Seattle | 3 | 26 | 2 | 5 | .400 | 0 | 3 | .000 | 0 | 6 | 6 | 2 | 0 | 0 | 2 | 4 | 2.0 | 0.7 | 1.3 |

Personal fouls/disqualifications: 1999-00, 6/0. Totals, 6/0.

### AMERICAN BASKETBALL ASSOCIATION RECORD

| | | | | | | | | | | | | AVERAGES | | |
|---|---|---|---|---|---|---|---|---|---|---|---|---|---|---|
| Season Team | G | Min. | FGM | FGA | Pct. | FTM | FTA | Pct. | Reb. | Ast. | Pts. | RPG | APG | PPG |
| 04-05—Long Beach | 3 | ... | 15 | 27 | .556 | 12 | 21 | .571 | 18 | 5 | 42 | 6.0 | 1.7 | 14.0 |

## MCDYESS, ANTONIO              F              PISTONS

**PERSONAL:** Born September 7, 1974, in Quitman, Miss. ... 6-9/245. (2.06/111.1). ... Full name: Antonio Keithflen McDyess ... Name pronounced mick-DICE.
**HIGH SCHOOL:** Quitman (Miss.).
**COLLEGE:** Alabama.
**TRANSACTIONS/CAREER NOTES:** Selected after sophomore season by Los Angeles Clippers in first round (second pick overall) of 1995 NBA Draft. ... Draft rights traded by Clippers with G Randy Woods to Denver Nuggets for F Rodney Rogers and draft rights to G Brent Barry (June 28, 1995). ... Traded by Nuggets to Phoenix Suns for a minimum of three first-round draft choices and two second-round draft choices (October 1, 1997). ... Signed as free agent by Nuggets (January 22, 1999). ... Traded by Nuggets with draft rights to G Frank Williams and 2003 second-round draft choice to New York Knicks for F/C Marcus Camby, G Mark Jackson and draft rights to F/C Nene Hilario (June 26, 2002). ... Traded by Knicks with G Howard Eisley, F Maciej Lampe, G Charlie Ward, draft rights to G Milos Vujanic, 2004 first-round draft choice and future first-round draft choice to Phoenix Suns for G Stephon Marbury, F/G Anfernee Hardaway and C Cezary Trybanski (January 5, 2004). ... Signed as free agent by Detroit Pistons (July 16, 2004).
**MISCELLANEOUS:** Member of gold-medal-winning U.S. Olympic team (2000).

### COLLEGIATE RECORD

| | | | | | | | | | | | | AVERAGES | | |
|---|---|---|---|---|---|---|---|---|---|---|---|---|---|---|
| Season Team | G | Min. | FGM | FGA | Pct. | FTM | FTA | Pct. | Reb. | Ast. | Pts. | RPG | APG | PPG |
| 93-94—Alabama | 26 | 618 | 132 | 234 | .564 | 32 | 60 | .533 | 210 | 11 | 296 | 8.1 | 0.4 | 11.4 |

M

| Season Team | G | Min. | FGM | FGA | Pct. | FTM | FTA | Pct. | Reb. | Ast. | Pts. | RPG | APG | PPG |
|---|---|---|---|---|---|---|---|---|---|---|---|---|---|---|
| 94-95—Alabama ...................... | 33 | 861 | 185 | 361 | .512 | 88 | 132 | .667 | 337 | 21 | 458 | 10.2 | 0.6 | 13.9 |
| Totals ............... | 59 | 1479 | 317 | 595 | .533 | 120 | 192 | .625 | 547 | 32 | 754 | 9.3 | 0.5 | 12.8 |

Three-point field goals: 1994-95, 0-for-1. Totals, 0-for-1 (.000).

## NBA REGULAR-SEASON RECORD

**HONORS:** All-NBA Third Team (1999). ... NBA All-Rookie first team (1996).

| Season Team | G | Min. | FGM | FGA | Pct. | FTM | FTA | Pct. | REBOUNDS | | | Ast. | St. | Blk. | TO | Pts. | AVERAGES | | |
|---|---|---|---|---|---|---|---|---|---|---|---|---|---|---|---|---|---|---|---|
| | | | | | | | | | Off. | Def. | Tot. | | | | | | RPG | APG | PPG |
| 95-96—Denver ............ | 76 | 2280 | 427 | 881 | .485 | 166 | 243 | .683 | 229 | 343 | 572 | 75 | 54 | 114 | 154 | 1020 | 7.5 | 1.0 | 13.4 |
| 96-97—Denver ............ | 74 | 2565 | 536 | 1157 | .463 | 274 | 387 | .708 | 155 | 382 | 537 | 106 | 62 | 126 | 199 | 1352 | 7.3 | 1.4 | 18.3 |
| 97-98—Phoenix ......... | 81 | 2441 | 497 | 927 | .536 | 231 | 329 | .702 | 206 | 407 | 613 | 106 | 100 | 135 | 142 | 1225 | 7.6 | 1.3 | 15.1 |
| 98-99—Denver ............ | 50 | 1937 | 415 | 882 | .471 | 230 | 338 | .680 | 168 | 369 | 537 | 82 | 73 | 115 | 138 | 1061 | 10.7 | 1.6 | 21.2 |
| 99-00—Denver ............ | 81 | 2698 | 614 | 1211 | .507 | 323 | 516 | .626 | 234 | 451 | 685 | 159 | 69 | 139 | 230 | 1551 | 8.5 | 2.0 | 19.1 |
| 00-01—Denver ............ | 70 | 2555 | 577 | 1165 | .495 | 304 | 434 | .700 | 240 | 605 | 845 | 146 | 43 | 102 | 162 | 1458 | 12.1 | 2.1 | 20.8 |
| 01-02—Denver ............ | 10 | 236 | 43 | 75 | .573 | 27 | 33 | .818 | 18 | 37 | 55 | 18 | 10 | 8 | 20 | 113 | 5.5 | 1.8 | 11.3 |
| 02-03—New York ........ | | | | | | | | Did not play—injured | | | | | | | | | | |
| 03-04—N.Y.Phoenix ... | 42 | 927 | 126 | 268 | .470 | 38 | 69 | .551 | 70 | 187 | 257 | 36 | 37 | 24 | 57 | 290 | 6.1 | 0.9 | 6.9 |
| 04-05—Detroit ........... | 77 | 1797 | 307 | 598 | .513 | 126 | 192 | .656 | 177 | 305 | 482 | 71 | 46 | 52 | 93 | 740 | 6.3 | 0.9 | 9.6 |
| Totals ................... | 561 | 17436 | 3542 | 7164 | .494 | 1719 | 2541 | .677 | 1497 | 3086 | 4583 | 799 | 494 | 815 | 1195 | 8810 | 8.2 | 1.4 | 15.7 |

Three-point field goals: 1995-96, 0-for-4. 1996-97, 6-for-35 (.171). 1997-98, 0-for-2. 1998-99, 1-for-9 (.111). 1999-00, 0-for-2. 2004-05, 0-for-1. Totals, 7-for-53 (.132).

Personal fouls/disqualifications: 1995-96, 250/4. 1996-97, 276/9. 1997-98, 292/6. 1998-99, 175/5. 1999-00, 316/12. 2000-01, 220/2. 2001-02, 20/0. 2003-04, 117/5. 2004-05, 204/3. Totals, 1870/46.

## NBA PLAYOFF RECORD

| Season Team | G | Min. | FGM | FGA | Pct. | FTM | FTA | Pct. | REBOUNDS | | | Ast. | St. | Blk. | TO | Pts. | AVERAGES | | |
|---|---|---|---|---|---|---|---|---|---|---|---|---|---|---|---|---|---|---|---|
| | | | | | | | | | Off. | Def. | Tot. | | | | | | RPG | APG | PPG |
| 97-98—Phoenix .......... | 4 | 147 | 31 | 65 | .477 | 9 | 14 | .643 | 18 | 35 | 53 | 4 | 2 | 6 | 5 | 71 | 13.3 | 1.0 | 17.8 |
| 04-05—Detroit ............ | 25 | 494 | 88 | 181 | .486 | 25 | 36 | .694 | 46 | 101 | 147 | 19 | 14 | 23 | 25 | 201 | 5.9 | 0.8 | 8.0 |
| Totals ................... | 29 | 641 | 119 | 246 | .484 | 34 | 50 | .680 | 64 | 136 | 200 | 23 | 16 | 29 | 30 | 272 | 6.9 | 0.8 | 9.4 |

Personal fouls/disqualifications: 1997-98, 12/0. 2004-05, 78/0. Totals, 90/0.

## NBA ALL-STAR GAME RECORD

| Season Team | Min. | FGM | FGA | Pct. | FTM | FTA | Pct. | REBOUNDS | | | Ast. | PF | Dq. | St. | Blk. | TO | Pts. |
|---|---|---|---|---|---|---|---|---|---|---|---|---|---|---|---|---|---|
| | | | | | | | | Off. | Def. | Tot. | | | | | | | |
| 2001—Denver ................. | 15 | 4 | 9 | .444 | 0 | 0 | ... | 3 | 5 | 8 | 2 | 2 | 0 | 1 | 0 | 0 | 8 |

---

# MCGRADY, TRACY      G      ROCKETS

**M**

**PERSONAL:** Born May 24, 1979, in Bartow, Fla. ... 6-8/210. (2.03/95.3). ... Full name: Tracy Lamar McGrady
**HIGH SCHOOL:** Auburndale (Tampa, Fla.), then Mount Zion Christia.
**COLLEGE:** Did not attend college.
**TRANSACTIONS/CAREER NOTES:** Selected out of high school by Toronto Raptors in first round (ninth pick overall) of 1997 NBA Draft. ... Traded by Raptors to Orlando Magic for future first-round draft choice (August 3, 2000). ... Traded by Magic with F Juwan Howard, G Tyronn Lue and G Reece Gaines to Houston Rockets for G Steve Francis, G Cuttino Mobley and C Kelvin Cato (June 29, 2004).

## NBA REGULAR-SEASON RECORD

**HONORS:** NBA Most Improved Player award (2001). ... All-NBA first team (2002, 2003). ... All-NBA second team (2001, 2004). ... All-NBA third team (2005).

| Season Team | G | Min. | FGM | FGA | Pct. | FTM | FTA | Pct. | REBOUNDS | | | Ast. | St. | Blk. | TO | Pts. | AVERAGES | | |
|---|---|---|---|---|---|---|---|---|---|---|---|---|---|---|---|---|---|---|---|
| | | | | | | | | | Off. | Def. | Tot. | | | | | | RPG | APG | PPG |
| 97-98—Toronto .......... | 64 | 1179 | 179 | 398 | .450 | 79 | 111 | .712 | 105 | 164 | 269 | 98 | 49 | 61 | 66 | 451 | 4.2 | 1.5 | 7.0 |
| 98-99—Toronto .......... | 49 | 1106 | 168 | 385 | .436 | 114 | 157 | .726 | 120 | 158 | 278 | 113 | 52 | 66 | 80 | 458 | 5.7 | 2.3 | 9.3 |
| 99-00—Toronto .......... | 79 | 2462 | 459 | 1018 | .451 | 277 | 392 | .707 | 188 | 313 | 501 | 263 | 90 | 151 | 160 | 1213 | 6.3 | 3.3 | 15.4 |
| 00-01—Orlando .......... | 77 | 3087 | 788 | 1724 | .457 | 430 | 587 | .733 | 192 | 388 | 580 | 352 | 116 | 118 | 198 | 2065 | 7.5 | 4.6 | 26.8 |
| 01-02—Orlando .......... | 76 | 2912 | 715 | 1586 | .451 | 415 | 555 | .748 | 150 | 447 | 597 | 400 | 119 | 73 | 189 | 1948 | 7.9 | 5.3 | 25.6 |
| 02-03—Orlando .......... | 75 | 2954 | 829 | 1813 | .457 | 576 | 726 | .793 | 121 | 367 | 488 | 411 | 124 | 59 | 195 | 2407 | 6.5 | 5.5 | 32.1 |
| 03-04—Orlando .......... | 67 | 2675 | 653 | 1566 | .417 | 398 | 500 | .796 | 95 | 307 | 402 | 370 | 93 | 42 | 179 | 1878 | 6.0 | 5.5 | 28.0 |
| 04-05—Houston .......... | 78 | 3182 | 715 | 1660 | .431 | 431 | 557 | .774 | 71 | 413 | 484 | 448 | 135 | 52 | 201 | 2003 | 6.2 | 5.7 | 25.7 |
| Totals ................... | 565 | 19557 | 4506 | 10150 | .444 | 2720 | 3585 | .759 | 1042 | 2557 | 3599 | 2455 | 778 | 622 | 1268 | 12423 | 6.4 | 4.3 | 22.0 |

Three-point field goals: 1997-98, 14-for-41 (.341). 1998-99, 8-for-35 (.229). 1999-00, 18-for-65 (.277). 2000-01, 59-for-166 (.355). 2001-02, 103-for-283 (.364). 2002-03, 173-for-448 (.386). 2003-04, 174-for-513 (.339). 2004-05, 142-for-435 (.326). Totals, 691-for-1986 (.348).

Personal fouls/disqualifications: 1997-98, 86/0. 1998-99, 94/1. 1999-00, 201/2. 2000-01, 160/0. 2001-02, 139/1. 2002-03, 156/0. 2003-04, 129/1. 2004-05, 167/0. Totals, 1132/5.

## NBA PLAYOFF RECORD

| Season Team | G | Min. | FGM | FGA | Pct. | FTM | FTA | Pct. | REBOUNDS | | | Ast. | St. | Blk. | TO | Pts. | AVERAGES | | |
|---|---|---|---|---|---|---|---|---|---|---|---|---|---|---|---|---|---|---|---|
| | | | | | | | | | Off. | Def. | Tot. | | | | | | RPG | APG | PPG |
| 99-00—Toronto .......... | 3 | 111 | 17 | 44 | .386 | 14 | 16 | .875 | 10 | 11 | 21 | 9 | 3 | 3 | 10 | 50 | 7.0 | 3.0 | 16.7 |
| 00-01—Orlando .......... | 4 | 178 | 51 | 123 | .415 | 31 | 38 | .816 | 6 | 20 | 26 | 33 | 7 | 5 | 8 | 135 | 6.5 | 8.3 | 33.8 |
| 01-02—Orlando .......... | 4 | 178 | 42 | 91 | .462 | 34 | 46 | .739 | 6 | 19 | 25 | 22 | 2 | 7 | 13 | 123 | 6.3 | 5.5 | 30.8 |
| 02-03—Orlando .......... | 7 | 308 | 74 | 165 | .448 | 58 | 75 | .773 | 10 | 37 | 47 | 33 | 14 | 6 | 26 | 222 | 6.7 | 4.7 | 31.7 |
| 04-05—Houston .......... | 7 | 301 | 78 | 171 | .456 | 42 | 51 | .824 | 12 | 40 | 52 | 47 | 11 | 10 | 26 | 215 | 7.4 | 6.7 | 30.7 |
| Totals ................... | 25 | 1076 | 262 | 594 | .441 | 179 | 226 | .792 | 44 | 127 | 171 | 144 | 37 | 31 | 83 | 745 | 6.8 | 5.8 | 29.8 |

Three-point field goals: 1999-00, 2-for-7 (.286). 2000-01, 2-for-10 (.200). 2001-02, 5-for-16 (.313). 2002-03, 16-for-47 (.340). 2004-05, 17-for-46 (.370). Totals, 42-for-126 (.333).

Personal fouls/disqualifications: 1999-00, 10/0. 2000-01, 11/0. 2001-02, 11/0. 2002-03, 16/0. 2004-05, 20/0. Totals, 68/0.

## NBA ALL-STAR GAME RECORD

| Season Team | Min. | FGM | FGA | Pct. | FTM | FTA | Pct. | Off. | Def. | Tot. | Ast. | PF | Dq. | St. | Blk. | TO | Pts. |
|---|---|---|---|---|---|---|---|---|---|---|---|---|---|---|---|---|---|
| 2001—Orlando ............... | 21 | 1 | 4 | .250 | 0 | 0 | ... | 1 | 0 | 1 | 0 | 0 | 0 | 2 | 1 | 4 | 2 |
| 2002—Orlando ............... | 23 | 9 | 15 | .600 | 4 | 4 | 1.000 | 2 | 1 | 3 | 4 | 1 | 0 | 3 | 0 | 1 | 24 |
| 2003—Orlando ............... | 36 | 10 | 17 | .588 | 5 | 6 | .833 | 1 | 4 | 5 | 2 | 3 | 0 | 0 | 0 | 1 | 29 |
| 2004—Orlando ............... | 23 | 5 | 11 | .455 | 2 | 4 | .500 | 1 | 3 | 4 | 3 | 0 | 0 | 0 | 0 | 1 | 13 |
| 2005—Houston ............... | 24 | 4 | 13 | .308 | 0 | 0 | ... | 1 | 4 | 5 | 5 | 1 | 0 | 3 | 2 | 3 | 8 |
| Totals........................... | 127 | 29 | 60 | .483 | 11 | 14 | .786 | 6 | 12 | 18 | 14 | 5 | 0 | 8 | 3 | 10 | 76 |

Three-point field goals: 2001, 0-for-1. 2002, 2-for-4 (.500). 2003, 4-for-7 (.571). 2004, 1-for-6 (.167). 2005, 0-for-4. Totals, 7-for-22 (.318).

# MCINNIS, JEFF   G   NETS

**PERSONAL:** Born October 22, 1974, in Charlotte. ... 6-4/190. (1.93/86.2). ... Full name: Jeff Lemans McInnis.
**HIGH SCHOOL:** West Charlotte (Charlotte), then Oak Hill Academy .
**COLLEGE:** North Carolina.
**TRANSACTIONS/CAREER NOTES:** Selected after junior season by Denver Nuggets in second round (37th pick overall) of 1996 NBA Draft. ... Waived by Nuggets (December 12, 1996). ... Played in Greece (1996-97). ... Played in Continental Basketball Association with Quad City Thunder (1997-98 through 1999-2000). ... Signed as free agent by Washington Wizards (January 21, 1999). ... Traded by Wizards with F/C Terry Davis, F Ben Wallace and G Tim Legler to Orlando Magic for C Isaac Austin (August 11, 1999). ... Waived by Magic (September 16, 1999). ... Signed by Los Angeles Clippers to first of two consecutive 10-day contracts (February 26, 2000). ... Re-signed by Clippers for remainder of season (March 16, 2000). ... Signed as free agent by Portland Trail Blazers (August 12, 2002). ... Traded by Trail Blazers with C Ruben Boumtje-Boumtje to Cleveland Cavaliers for F Darius Miles (January 21, 2004). ... Signed as free agent by New Jersey Nets (August 11, 2005).

## COLLEGIATE RECORD

| Season Team | G | Min. | FGM | FGA | Pct. | FTM | FTA | Pct. | Reb. | Ast. | Pts. | RPG | APG | PPG |
|---|---|---|---|---|---|---|---|---|---|---|---|---|---|---|
| 93-94—North Carolina ............... | 35 | 512 | 70 | 153 | .458 | 30 | 47 | .638 | 58 | 85 | 197 | 1.7 | 2.4 | 5.6 |
| 94-95—North Carolina ............... | 34 | 981 | 155 | 316 | .491 | 66 | 99 | .667 | 138 | 180 | 420 | 4.1 | 5.3 | 12.4 |
| 95-96—North Carolina ............... | 31 | 1067 | 178 | 409 | .435 | 88 | 110 | .800 | 81 | 170 | 511 | 2.6 | 5.5 | 16.5 |
| Totals ..................................... | 100 | 2560 | 403 | 878 | .459 | 184 | 256 | .719 | 277 | 435 | 1128 | 2.8 | 4.4 | 11.3 |

Three-point field goals: 1993-94, 27-for-65 (.415). 1994-95, 44-for-112 (.393). 1995-96, 67-for-171 (.392). Totals, 138-for-348 (.397).

## GREEK LEAGUE RECORD

| Season Team | G | Min. | FGM | FGA | Pct. | FTM | FTA | Pct. | Reb. | Ast. | Pts. | RPG | APG | PPG |
|---|---|---|---|---|---|---|---|---|---|---|---|---|---|---|
| 96-97—Panionios ...................... | 6 | 227 | 46 | 121 | .380 | 19 | 25 | .760 | 19 | 22 | 123 | 3.2 | 3.7 | 20.5 |

Three-point field goals: 1996-97, 12-for-44 (.273). Totals, 12-for-44 (.273).

## NBA REGULAR-SEASON RECORD

| Season Team | G | Min. | FGM | FGA | Pct. | FTM | FTA | Pct. | Off. | Def. | Tot. | Ast. | St. | Blk. | TO | Pts. | RPG | APG | PPG |
|---|---|---|---|---|---|---|---|---|---|---|---|---|---|---|---|---|---|---|---|
| 96-97—Denver ............ | 13 | 117 | 23 | 49 | .469 | 7 | 10 | .700 | 2 | 4 | 6 | 18 | 2 | 1 | 13 | 65 | 0.5 | 1.4 | 5.0 |
| 98-99—Washington ... | 35 | 427 | 50 | 134 | .373 | 21 | 28 | .750 | 9 | 12 | 21 | 73 | 19 | 1 | 30 | 130 | 0.6 | 2.1 | 3.7 |
| 99-00—L.A. Clippers ... | 25 | 597 | 80 | 186 | .430 | 13 | 17 | .765 | 18 | 54 | 72 | 89 | 15 | 2 | 27 | 180 | 2.9 | 3.6 | 7.2 |
| 00-01—L.A. Clippers ... | 81 | 2831 | 432 | 933 | .463 | 130 | 161 | .807 | 41 | 179 | 220 | 447 | 75 | 7 | 113 | 1046 | 2.7 | 5.5 | 12.9 |
| 01-02—L.A. Clippers ... | 81 | 3030 | 463 | 1121 | .413 | 183 | 219 | .836 | 45 | 168 | 213 | 500 | 63 | 6 | 147 | 1184 | 2.6 | 6.2 | 14.6 |
| 02-03—Portland ......... | 75 | 1311 | 188 | 423 | .444 | 50 | 67 | .746 | 22 | 75 | 97 | 170 | 21 | 2 | 75 | 432 | 1.3 | 2.3 | 5.8 |
| 03-04—Port.-Cleve. ... | 70 | 2365 | 334 | 747 | .447 | 114 | 143 | .797 | 33 | 143 | 176 | 430 | 72 | 6 | 120 | 828 | 2.5 | 6.1 | 11.8 |
| 04-05—Cleveland ........ | 76 | 2651 | 377 | 915 | .412 | 130 | 160 | .813 | 32 | 125 | 157 | 391 | 56 | 1 | 117 | 975 | 2.1 | 5.1 | 12.8 |
| Totals ................... | 456 | 13329 | 1947 | 4508 | .432 | 648 | 805 | .805 | 202 | 760 | 962 | 2118 | 323 | 26 | 642 | 4840 | 2.1 | 4.6 | 10.6 |

Three-point field goals: 1996-97, 12-for-26 (.462). 1998-99, 9-for-35 (.257). 1999-00, 7-for-21 (.333). 2000-01, 52-for-144 (.361). 2001-02, 75-for-234 (.321). 2002-03, 6-for-35 (.171). 2003-04, 46-for-127 (.362). 2004-05, 91-for-264 (.345). Totals, 298-for-886 (.336).

Personal fouls/disqualifications: 1996-97, 16/0. 1998-99, 36/0. 1999-00, 55/0. 2000-01, 199/2. 2001-02, 202/2. 2002-03, 117/1. 2003-04, 163/4. 2004-05, 177/1. Totals, 965/10.

## NBA PLAYOFF RECORD

| Season Team | G | Min. | FGM | FGA | Pct. | FTM | FTA | Pct. | Off. | Def. | Tot. | Ast. | St. | Blk. | TO | Pts. | RPG | APG | PPG |
|---|---|---|---|---|---|---|---|---|---|---|---|---|---|---|---|---|---|---|---|
| 02-03—Portland .......... | 7 | 99 | 9 | 26 | .346 | 3 | 4 | .750 | 5 | 7 | 12 | 19 | 2 | 1 | 6 | 21 | 1.7 | 2.7 | 3.0 |

Three-point field goals: 2002-03, 0-for-3. Totals, 0-for-3 (.000).

Personal fouls/disqualifications: 2002-03, 11/0. Totals, 11/0.

## CBA RECORD

**NOTES:** Member of CBA championship team (1998). ... CBA Newcomer of the Year (1998). ... CBA All-League second team (1998). ... CBA All-Defensive team (1998). ... CBA Most Valuable Player (2000). ... CBA All-League first team (2000).

| Season Team | G | Min. | FGM | FGA | Pct. | FTM | FTA | Pct. | Reb. | Ast. | Pts. | RPG | APG | PPG |
|---|---|---|---|---|---|---|---|---|---|---|---|---|---|---|
| 97-98—Quad City...................... | 56 | 1734 | 315 | 705 | .447 | 168 | 206 | .816 | 135 | 316 | 834 | 2.4 | 5.6 | 14.9 |
| 98-99—Quad City...................... | 21 | 825 | 175 | 348 | .503 | 65 | 88 | .739 | 54 | 119 | 442 | 2.6 | 5.7 | 21.0 |
| 99-00—Quad City...................... | 41 | 1629 | 316 | 719 | .439 | 123 | 149 | .826 | 136 | *319 | 807 | 3.3 | 7.8 | 19.7 |
| Totals ..................................... | 118 | 4188 | 806 | 1772 | .455 | 356 | 443 | .804 | 325 | 754 | 2083 | 2.8 | 6.4 | 17.7 |

Three-point field goals: 1997-98, 36-for-119 (.303). 1998-99, 27-for-77 (.351). 1999-00, 52-for-167 (.311). Totals, 115-for-363 (.317).

Personal fouls/disqualifications: 1997-98, 121/0. 1998-99, 57/0. 1999-00, 95/0. Totals, 273/0.

# MCKIE, AARON　　　　　　　　G　　　　　　　　LAKERS

**PERSONAL:** Born October 2, 1972, in Philadelphia. ... 6-5/209. (1.96/94.8). ... Full name: Aaron Fitzgerald McKie ... Name pronounced mik-KEY.
**HIGH SCHOOL:** Simon Gratz (Philadelphia).
**COLLEGE:** Temple.
**TRANSACTIONS/CAREER NOTES:** Selected by Portland Trail Blazers in first round (17th pick overall) of 1994 NBA Draft. ... Traded by Trail Blazers with G Randolph Childress and G Reggie Jordan to Detroit Pistons for F Stacey Augmon (January 24, 1997). ... Traded by Pistons with C Theo Ratliff and conditional first-round draft choice to Philadelphia 76ers for G Jerry Stackhouse and C Eric Montross (December 18, 1997). ... Waived by 76ers (August 12, 2005). ... Signed as free agent by Los Angeles Lakers (August 22, 2005).

## COLLEGIATE RECORD

| Season Team | G | Min. | FGM | FGA | Pct. | FTM | FTA | Pct. | Reb. | Ast. | Pts. | RPG | APG | PPG |
|---|---|---|---|---|---|---|---|---|---|---|---|---|---|---|
| 90-91—Temple | | | | | | Did not play—ineligible. | | | | | | | | |
| 91-92—Temple | 28 | 1011 | 130 | 300 | .433 | 86 | 114 | .754 | 167 | 94 | 388 | 6.0 | 3.4 | 13.9 |
| 92-93—Temple | 33 | 1272 | 240 | 555 | .432 | 123 | 156 | .788 | 195 | 109 | 680 | 5.9 | 3.3 | 20.6 |
| 93-94—Temple | 31 | 1214 | 193 | 481 | .401 | 137 | 168 | .815 | 224 | 98 | 582 | 7.2 | 3.2 | 18.8 |
| **Totals** | 92 | 3497 | 563 | 1336 | .421 | 346 | 438 | .790 | 586 | 301 | 1650 | 6.4 | 3.3 | 17.9 |

Three-point field goals: 1991-92, 42-for-131 (.321). 1992-93, 77-for-196 (.393). 1993-94, 59-for-159 (.371). Totals, 178-for-486 (.366).

## NBA REGULAR-SEASON RECORD

**HONORS:** NBA Sixth Man Award (2001).

| Season Team | G | Min. | FGM | FGA | Pct. | FTM | FTA | Pct. | REBOUNDS Off. | Def. | Tot. | Ast. | St. | Blk. | TO | Pts. | RPG | APG | PPG |
|---|---|---|---|---|---|---|---|---|---|---|---|---|---|---|---|---|---|---|---|
| 94-95—Portland | 45 | 827 | 116 | 261 | .444 | 50 | 73 | .685 | 35 | 94 | 129 | 89 | 36 | 16 | 39 | 293 | 2.9 | 2.0 | 6.5 |
| 95-96—Portland | 81 | 2259 | 337 | 722 | .467 | 152 | 199 | .764 | 86 | 218 | 304 | 205 | 92 | 21 | 135 | 864 | 3.8 | 2.5 | 10.7 |
| 96-97—Port.-Detroit | 83 | 1625 | 150 | 365 | .411 | 92 | 110 | .836 | 40 | 181 | 221 | 161 | 77 | 22 | 90 | 433 | 2.7 | 1.9 | 5.2 |
| 97-98—Det.-Phila. | 81 | 1813 | 139 | 381 | .365 | 42 | 55 | .764 | 58 | 173 | 231 | 175 | 101 | 13 | 76 | 332 | 2.9 | 2.2 | 4.1 |
| 98-99—Philadelphia | 50 | 959 | 95 | 237 | .401 | 44 | 62 | .710 | 27 | 113 | 140 | 100 | 63 | 3 | 57 | 240 | 2.8 | 2.0 | 4.8 |
| 99-00—Philadelphia | 82 | 1952 | 244 | 593 | .411 | 121 | 146 | .829 | 47 | 199 | 246 | 204 | 108 | 18 | 113 | 653 | 3.0 | 2.9 | 8.0 |
| 00-01—Philadelphia | 76 | 2394 | 338 | 714 | .473 | 149 | 194 | .768 | 33 | 278 | 311 | 377 | 106 | 8 | 203 | 878 | 4.1 | 5.0 | 11.6 |
| 01-02—Philadelphia | 48 | 1471 | 220 | 490 | .449 | 96 | 122 | .787 | 26 | 166 | 192 | 179 | 56 | 14 | 93 | 587 | 4.0 | 3.7 | 12.2 |
| 02-03—Philadelphia | 80 | 2374 | 286 | 666 | .429 | 112 | 134 | .836 | 61 | 289 | 350 | 278 | 131 | 9 | 109 | 721 | 4.4 | 3.5 | 9.0 |
| 03-04—Philadelphia | 75 | 2112 | 265 | 577 | .459 | 84 | 111 | .757 | 45 | 208 | 253 | 195 | 85 | 23 | 103 | 689 | 3.4 | 2.6 | 9.2 |
| 04-05—Philadelphia | 68 | 1118 | 61 | 142 | .430 | 10 | 16 | .625 | 20 | 152 | 172 | 103 | 48 | 17 | 31 | 152 | 2.5 | 1.5 | 2.2 |
| **Totals** | 769 | 18904 | 2251 | 5148 | .437 | 952 | 1222 | .779 | 478 | 2071 | 2549 | 2102 | 903 | 164 | 1049 | 5842 | 3.3 | 2.7 | 7.6 |

Three-point field goals: 1994-95, 11-for-28 (.393). 1995-96, 38-for-117 (.325). 1996-97, 41-for-103 (.398). 1997-98, 12-for-63 (.190). 1998-99, 6-for-31 (.194). 1999-00, 44-for-121 (.364). 2000-01, 53-for-170 (.312). 2001-02, 51-for-128 (.398). 2002-03, 37-for-112 (.330). 2003-04, 75-for-172 (.436). 2004-05, 20-for-62 (.323). Totals, 388-for-1107 (.350).
Personal fouls/disqualifications: 1994-95, 97/1. 1995-96, 205/5. 1996-97, 130/1. 1997-98, 164/0. 1998-99, 90/1. 1999-00, 194/3. 2000-01, 178/3. 2001-02, 74/0. 2002-03, 177/2. 2003-04, 142/1. 2004-05, 116/2. Totals, 1567/19.

## NBA PLAYOFF RECORD

| Season Team | G | Min. | FGM | FGA | Pct. | FTM | FTA | Pct. | REBOUNDS Off. | Def. | Tot. | Ast. | St. | Blk. | TO | Pts. | RPG | APG | PPG |
|---|---|---|---|---|---|---|---|---|---|---|---|---|---|---|---|---|---|---|---|
| 94-95—Portland | 3 | 34 | 8 | 14 | .571 | 0 | 0 | ... | 0 | 2 | 2 | 1 | 3 | 0 | 0 | 17 | 0.7 | 0.3 | 5.7 |
| 95-96—Portland | 5 | 134 | 11 | 30 | .367 | 7 | 9 | .778 | 4 | 14 | 18 | 9 | 6 | 2 | 9 | 31 | 3.6 | 1.8 | 6.2 |
| 96-97—Detroit | 5 | 97 | 7 | 20 | .350 | 0 | 0 | ... | 1 | 9 | 10 | 10 | 6 | 2 | 3 | 15 | 2.0 | 2.0 | 3.0 |
| 98-99—Philadelphia | 6 | 97 | 7 | 23 | .304 | 6 | 7 | .857 | 4 | 11 | 15 | 11 | 4 | 0 | 1 | 20 | 2.5 | 1.8 | 3.3 |
| 99-00—Philadelphia | 10 | 331 | 50 | 103 | .485 | 26 | 31 | .839 | 4 | 32 | 36 | 46 | 4 | 2 | 16 | 138 | 3.6 | 4.6 | 13.8 |
| 00-01—Philadelphia | 23 | 892 | 125 | 301 | .415 | 59 | 75 | .787 | 24 | 95 | 119 | 121 | 34 | 3 | 46 | 336 | 5.2 | 5.3 | 14.6 |
| 01-02—Philadelphia | 5 | 146 | 20 | 46 | .435 | 7 | 10 | .700 | 2 | 16 | 18 | 12 | 10 | 0 | 10 | 53 | 3.6 | 2.4 | 10.6 |
| 02-03—Philadelphia | 12 | 315 | 38 | 71 | .535 | 12 | 14 | .857 | 5 | 38 | 43 | 22 | 10 | 2 | 15 | 93 | 3.6 | 1.8 | 7.8 |
| 04-05—Philadelphia | 5 | 85 | 3 | 7 | .429 | 0 | 0 | ... | 1 | 11 | 12 | 5 | 4 | 0 | 1 | 7 | 2.4 | 1.0 | 1.4 |
| **Totals** | 74 | 2131 | 269 | 615 | .437 | 117 | 146 | .801 | 45 | 228 | 273 | 237 | 81 | 11 | 101 | 710 | 3.7 | 3.2 | 9.6 |

Three-point field goals: 1994-95, 1-for-2 (.500). 1995-96, 2-for-8 (.250). 1996-97, 1-for-5 (.200). 1998-99, 0-for-1. 1999-00, 12-for-35 (.343). 2000-01, 27-for-64 (.422). 2001-02, 6-for-16 (.375). 2002-03, 5-for-9 (.556). 2004-05, 1-for-3 (.333). Totals, 55-for-143 (.385).
Personal fouls/disqualifications: 1994-95, 4/0. 1995-96, 13/0. 1996-97, 12/0. 1998-99, 17/0. 1999-00, 26/0. 2000-01, 67/0. 2001-02, 12/0. 2002-03, 31/0. 2004-05, 9/0. Totals, 191/0.

# MCLEOD, KEITH　　　　　　　　G　　　　　　　　JAZZ

**PERSONAL:** Born November 5, 1979, in Canton, Ohio. ... 6-2/190. (1.88/86.2).
**HIGH SCHOOL:** Canton McKinley (Canton, Ohio).
**COLLEGE:** Bowling Green.
**TRANSACTIONS/CAREER NOTES:** Not drafted by an NBA franchise. ... Played in Italy (2002-04). ... Signed as free agent by Minnesota Timberwolves (September 30, 2003). ... Waived by Timberwolves (October 21, 2003). ... Signed by Timberwolves (October 25, 2003). ... Waived by Timberwolves (January 7, 2004). ... Signed as free agent by Utah Jazz (September 30, 2004).

## COLLEGIATE RECORD

| Season Team | G | Min. | FGM | FGA | Pct. | FTM | FTA | Pct. | Reb. | Ast. | Pts. | RPG | APG | PPG |
|---|---|---|---|---|---|---|---|---|---|---|---|---|---|---|
| 98-99—Bowling Green State | 20 | 596 | 84 | 213 | .394 | 55 | 70 | .786 | 57 | 47 | 247 | 2.9 | 2.4 | 12.4 |
| 99-00—Bowling Green State | 30 | 927 | 115 | 269 | .428 | 105 | 144 | .729 | 65 | 77 | 386 | 2.2 | 2.6 | 12.9 |
| 00-01—Bowling Green State | 28 | 936 | 149 | 365 | .408 | 174 | 214 | .813 | 96 | 82 | 507 | 3.4 | 2.9 | 18.1 |
| 01-02—Bowling Green State | 33 | 1109 | 224 | 496 | .452 | 218 | 270 | .807 | 137 | 90 | 755 | 4.2 | 2.7 | 22.9 |
| **Totals** | 111 | 3568 | 572 | 1343 | .426 | 552 | 698 | .791 | 355 | 296 | 1895 | 3.2 | 2.7 | 17.1 |

Three-point field goals: 1998-99, 24-for-77 (.312). 1999-00, 51-for-107 (.477). 2000-01, 35-for-99 (.354). 2001-02, 89-for-216 (.412). Totals, 199-for-499 (.399).

M

## ITALIAN LEAGUE RECORD

| Season Team | G | Min. | FGM | FGA | Pct. | FTM | FTA | Pct. | Reb. | Ast. | Pts. | AVERAGES | | |
|---|---|---|---|---|---|---|---|---|---|---|---|---|---|---|
| | | | | | | | | | | | | RPG | APG | PPG |
| 02-03—Mabo | 31 | 876 | 126 | 296 | .426 | 99 | 124 | .798 | 61 | 57 | 389 | 2.0 | 1.8 | 12.5 |
| 03-04—Lottomatica RM | 11 | 332 | 56 | 126 | .444 | 28 | 41 | .683 | 35 | 35 | 154 | 3.2 | 3.2 | 14.0 |
| Totals | 42 | 1208 | 182 | 422 | .431 | 127 | 165 | .770 | 96 | 92 | 543 | 2.3 | 2.2 | 12.9 |

Three-point field goals: 2002-03, 38-for-113 (.336). 2003-04, 14-for-54 (.259). Totals, 52-for-167 (.311).

## NBA REGULAR-SEASON RECORD

| Season Team | G | Min. | FGM | FGA | Pct. | FTM | FTA | Pct. | REBOUNDS | | | Ast. | St. | Blk. | TO | Pts. | AVERAGES | | |
|---|---|---|---|---|---|---|---|---|---|---|---|---|---|---|---|---|---|---|---|
| | | | | | | | | | Off. | Def. | Tot. | | | | | | RPG | APG | PPG |
| 03-04—Minnesota | 33 | 391 | 27 | 82 | .329 | 33 | 43 | .767 | 5 | 29 | 34 | 59 | 16 | 1 | 29 | 88 | 1.0 | 1.8 | 2.7 |
| 04-05—Utah | 53 | 1382 | 143 | 408 | .350 | 112 | 146 | .767 | 20 | 93 | 113 | 236 | 63 | 12 | 99 | 416 | 2.1 | 4.5 | 7.8 |
| Totals | 86 | 1773 | 170 | 490 | .347 | 145 | 189 | .767 | 25 | 122 | 147 | 295 | 79 | 13 | 128 | 504 | 1.7 | 3.4 | 5.9 |

Three-point field goals: 2003-04, 1-for-10 (.100). 2004-05, 18-for-72 (.250). Totals, 19-for-82 (.232).
Personal fouls/disqualifications: 2003-04, 39/0. 2004-05, 138/0. Totals, 177/0.

# MEDVEDENKO, SLAVA     F     LAKERS

**PERSONAL:** Born April 4, 1979, in Ukraine. ... 6-10/250. (2.08/113.4).
**TRANSACTIONS/CAREER NOTES:** Not drafted by an NBA franchise. ... Played in Lithuania (1998-99). ... Played in Ukraine (1999-2000). ... Signed as free agent by Los Angeles Lakers (August 15, 2000).
**MISCELLANEOUS:** Member of NBA championship team (2001, 2002).

## LITHUANIAN LEAGUE RECORD

| Season Team | G | Min. | FGM | FGA | Pct. | FTM | FTA | Pct. | Reb. | Ast. | Pts. | AVERAGES | | |
|---|---|---|---|---|---|---|---|---|---|---|---|---|---|---|
| | | | | | | | | | | | | RPG | APG | PPG |
| 98-99—Alytus Alita | 24 | 698 | 166 | 300 | .553 | 75 | 97 | .773 | 180 | 25 | 410 | 7.5 | 1.0 | 17.1 |

Three-point field goals: 1998-99, 3-for-8 (.375). Totals, 3-for-8 (.375).

## UKRANIAN RECORD

| Season Team | G | Min. | FGM | FGA | Pct. | FTM | FTA | Pct. | Reb. | Ast. | Pts. | AVERAGES | | |
|---|---|---|---|---|---|---|---|---|---|---|---|---|---|---|
| | | | | | | | | | | | | RPG | APG | PPG |
| 99-00—Kyiv Kiev | 19 | 554 | 169 | 337 | .501 | 64 | 95 | .674 | 143 | 21 | 405 | 7.5 | 1.1 | 21.3 |

Three-point field goals: 1999-00, 3-for-18 (.167). Totals, 3-for-18 (.167).

## NBA REGULAR-SEASON RECORD

| Season Team | G | Min. | FGM | FGA | Pct. | FTM | FTA | Pct. | REBOUNDS | | | Ast. | St. | Blk. | TO | Pts. | AVERAGES | | |
|---|---|---|---|---|---|---|---|---|---|---|---|---|---|---|---|---|---|---|---|
| | | | | | | | | | Off. | Def. | Tot. | | | | | | RPG | APG | PPG |
| 00-01—L.A. Lakers | 7 | 39 | 12 | 25 | .480 | 7 | 12 | .583 | 1 | 8 | 9 | 2 | 1 | 1 | 3 | 32 | 1.3 | 0.3 | 4.6 |
| 01-02—L.A. Lakers | 71 | 729 | 145 | 304 | .477 | 41 | 62 | .661 | 85 | 73 | 158 | 43 | 29 | 11 | 42 | 331 | 2.2 | 0.6 | 4.7 |
| 02-03—L.A. Lakers | 58 | 620 | 112 | 258 | .434 | 31 | 43 | .721 | 66 | 75 | 141 | 18 | 11 | 8 | 37 | 255 | 2.4 | 0.3 | 4.4 |
| 03-04—L.A. Lakerš | 68 | 1442 | 237 | 537 | .441 | 89 | 116 | .767 | 148 | 195 | 343 | 57 | 38 | 18 | 59 | 563 | 5.0 | 0.8 | 8.3 |
| 04-05—L.A. Lakers | 43 | 423 | 71 | 156 | .455 | 23 | 28 | .821 | 31 | 48 | 79 | 13 | 9 | 2 | 13 | 165 | 1.8 | 0.3 | 3.8 |
| Totals | 247 | 3253 | 577 | 1280 | .451 | 191 | 261 | .732 | 331 | 399 | 730 | 133 | 88 | 40 | 154 | 1346 | 3.0 | 0.5 | 5.4 |

Three-point field goals: 2000-01, 1-for-1 (1.000). 2001-02, 0-for-4. 2002-03, 0-for-2. 2003-04, 0-for-3. 2004-05, 0-for-1. Totals, 1-for-11 (.091).
Personal fouls/disqualifications: 2000-01, 9/0. 2001-02, 119/0. 2002-03, 118/0. 2003-04, 191/1. 2004-05, 64/0. Totals, 501/1.

## NBA PLAYOFF RECORD

| Season Team | G | Min. | FGM | FGA | Pct. | FTM | FTA | Pct. | REBOUNDS | | | Ast. | St. | Blk. | TO | Pts. | AVERAGES | | |
|---|---|---|---|---|---|---|---|---|---|---|---|---|---|---|---|---|---|---|---|
| | | | | | | | | | Off. | Def. | Tot. | | | | | | RPG | APG | PPG |
| 01-02—L.A. Lakers | 7 | 21 | 3 | 5 | .600 | 0 | 0 | ... | 1 | 3 | 4 | 0 | 0 | 0 | 1 | 6 | 0.6 | 0.0 | 0.9 |
| 02-03—L.A. Lakers | 9 | 73 | 15 | 27 | .556 | 4 | 6 | .667 | 4 | 14 | 18 | 1 | 1 | 1 | 3 | 34 | 2.0 | 0.1 | 3.8 |
| 03-04—L.A. Lakers | 21 | 237 | 33 | 75 | .440 | 17 | 21 | .810 | 23 | 30 | 53 | 10 | 4 | 4 | 5 | 83 | 2.5 | 0.5 | 4.0 |
| Totals | 37 | 331 | 51 | 107 | .477 | 21 | 27 | .778 | 28 | 47 | 75 | 11 | 5 | 5 | 9 | 123 | 2.0 | 0.3 | 3.3 |

Personal fouls/disqualifications: 2001-02, 8/0. 2002-03, 14/0. 2003-04, 50/0. Totals, 72/0.

# MERCER, RON     G/F

**PERSONAL:** Born May 18, 1976, in Nashville. ... 6-7/210. (2.01/95.3). ... Full name: Ronald Eugene Mercer
**HIGH SCHOOL:** Goodpasture (Nashville), then Oak Hill Academy (Mo.
**COLLEGE:** Kentucky.
**TRANSACTIONS/CAREER NOTES:** Selected after sophomore season by Boston Celtics in first round (sixth pick overall) of 1997 NBA Draft. ... Traded by Celtics with F Popeye Jones and C Dwayne Schintzius to Denver Nuggets for F Danny Fortson, F Eric Williams, G Eric Washington and first-round draft choice within the next three years (August 3, 1999). ... Traded by Nuggets with G Chauncey Billups, F Johnny Taylor and draft considerations to Orlando Magic for F/C Chris Gatling, F Tariq Abdul-Wahad, a future first-round draft pick and cash considerations (February 1, 2000). ... Signed as free agent by Chicago Bulls (August 1, 2000). ... Traded by Bulls with C Brad Miller, G/F Ron Artest and G Kevin Ollie to Indiana Pacers for G Jalen Rose, G Travis Best, G Norman Richardson and second-round draft choice (February 19, 2002). ... Traded by Pacers to San Antonio Spurs in three-team deal in which Pacers also traded F/C Brad Miller to Sacramento Kings and acquired F Scot Pollard from Kings and F Danny Ferry from San Antonio Spurs. Spurs also acquired F/G Hedo Turkoglu from Kings (July 24, 2003) ... Waived by Spurs (February 27, 2004). ... Signed as free agent by New Jersey Nets (August 12, 2004). ... Waived by Nets (August 15, 2005).

## COLLEGIATE RECORD

**NOTES:** Member of NCAA Division I championship team (1996). ... THE SPORTING NEWS All-America second team (1997).

| Season Team | G | Min. | FGM | FGA | Pct. | FTM | FTA | Pct. | Reb. | Ast. | Pts. | AVERAGES | | |
|---|---|---|---|---|---|---|---|---|---|---|---|---|---|---|
| | | | | | | | | | | | | RPG | APG | PPG |
| 95-96—Kentucky | 36 | 677 | 107 | 234 | .457 | 51 | 65 | .785 | 104 | 50 | 288 | 2.9 | 1.4 | 8.0 |

M

| Season Team | G | Min. | FGM | FGA | Pct. | FTM | FTA | Pct. | Reb. | Ast. | Pts. | AVERAGES | | |
|---|---|---|---|---|---|---|---|---|---|---|---|---|---|---|
| | | | | | | | | | | | | RPG | APG | PPG |
| 96-97—Kentucky | 40 | 1299 | 297 | 603 | .493 | 82 | 105 | .781 | 210 | 97 | 725 | 5.3 | 2.4 | 18.1 |
| Totals | 76 | 1976 | 404 | 837 | .483 | 133 | 170 | .782 | 314 | 147 | 1013 | 4.1 | 1.9 | 13.3 |

Three-point field goals: 1995-96, 23-for-68 (.338). 1996-97, 49-for-141 (.348). Totals, 72-for-209 (.344).

Personal fouls/disqualifications: 1995-96, 51/0. Totals, 51/0.

### NBA REGULAR-SEASON RECORD

**HONORS:** NBA All-Rookie first team (1998).

| Season Team | G | Min. | FGM | FGA | Pct. | FTM | FTA | Pct. | REBOUNDS | | | Ast. | St. | Blk. | TO | Pts. | AVERAGES | | |
|---|---|---|---|---|---|---|---|---|---|---|---|---|---|---|---|---|---|---|---|
| | | | | | | | | | Off. | Def. | Tot. | | | | | | RPG | APG | PPG |
| 97-98—Boston | 80 | 2662 | 515 | 1145 | .450 | 188 | 224 | .839 | 109 | 171 | 280 | 176 | 125 | 17 | 132 | 1221 | 3.5 | 2.2 | 15.3 |
| 98-99—Boston | 41 | 1551 | 305 | 707 | .431 | 83 | 105 | .790 | 37 | 118 | 155 | 104 | 67 | 12 | 89 | 698 | 3.8 | 2.5 | 17.0 |
| 99-00—Den.-Orl. | 68 | 2377 | 460 | 1080 | .426 | 213 | 270 | .789 | 64 | 186 | 250 | 158 | 75 | 23 | 151 | 1148 | 3.7 | 2.3 | 16.9 |
| 00-01—Chicago | 61 | 2535 | 500 | 1121 | .446 | 188 | 228 | .825 | 72 | 164 | 236 | 201 | 78 | 27 | 129 | 1202 | 3.9 | 3.3 | 19.7 |
| 01-02—Chi.-Indiana | 53 | 1716 | 311 | 784 | .397 | 95 | 119 | .798 | 50 | 128 | 178 | 128 | 32 | 13 | 88 | 735 | 3.4 | 2.4 | 13.9 |
| 02-03—Indiana | 72 | 1671 | 244 | 597 | .409 | 65 | 81 | .802 | 32 | 122 | 154 | 112 | 49 | 14 | 54 | 556 | 2.1 | 1.6 | 7.7 |
| 03-04—San Antonio | 39 | 516 | 90 | 211 | .427 | 13 | 17 | .765 | 10 | 39 | 49 | 22 | 14 | 5 | 26 | 195 | 1.3 | 0.6 | 5.0 |
| 04-05—New Jersey | 18 | 390 | 65 | 158 | .411 | 7 | 10 | .700 | 9 | 31 | 40 | 20 | 16 | 2 | 14 | 137 | 2.2 | 1.1 | 7.6 |
| Totals | 432 | 13418 | 2490 | 5803 | .429 | 852 | 1054 | .808 | 383 | 959 | 1342 | 921 | 456 | 113 | 683 | 5892 | 3.1 | 2.1 | 13.6 |

Three-point field goals: 1997-98, 3-for-28 (.107). 1998-99, 5-for-30 (.167). 1999-00, 15-for-48 (.313). 2000-01, 14-for-46 (.304). 2001-02, 18-for-62 (.290). 2002-03, 3-for-16 (.188). 2003-04, 2-for-7 (.286). 2004-05, 0-for-3. Totals, 60-for-240 (.250).

Personal fouls/disqualifications: 1997-98, 213/2. 1998-99, 81/1. 2000-01, 148/3. 2001-02, 108/1. 2002-03, 123/1. 2003-04, 37/0. 2004-05, 20/0. Totals, 881/10.

### NBA PLAYOFF RECORD

| Season Team | G | Min. | FGM | FGA | Pct. | FTM | FTA | Pct. | REBOUNDS | | | Ast. | St. | Blk. | TO | Pts. | AVERAGES | | |
|---|---|---|---|---|---|---|---|---|---|---|---|---|---|---|---|---|---|---|---|
| | | | | | | | | | Off. | Def. | Tot. | | | | | | RPG | APG | PPG |
| 01-02—Indiana | 5 | 117 | 18 | 36 | .500 | 3 | 4 | .750 | 0 | 10 | 10 | 4 | 1 | 1 | 3 | 39 | 2.0 | 0.8 | 7.8 |
| 02-03—Indiana | 6 | 135 | 16 | 49 | .327 | 7 | 8 | .875 | 2 | 11 | 13 | 7 | 6 | 1 | 5 | 39 | 2.2 | 1.2 | 6.5 |
| Totals | 11 | 252 | 34 | 85 | .400 | 10 | 12 | .833 | 2 | 21 | 23 | 11 | 7 | 2 | 8 | 78 | 2.1 | 1.0 | 7.1 |

Personal fouls/disqualifications: 2001-02, 9/0. 2002-03, 11/0. Totals, 20/0.

## MIHM, CHRIS          F/C          LAKERS

**PERSONAL:** Born July 16, 1979, in Milwaukee. ... 7-0/265. (2.13/120.2). ... Full name: Christopher Steven Mihm
**HIGH SCHOOL:** Westlake (Austin, Texas).
**COLLEGE:** Texas.
**TRANSACTIONS/CAREER NOTES:** Selected after junior season by Chicago Bulls in first round (seventh pick overall) of 2000 NBA Draft. ... Draft rights traded by Bulls to Cleveland Cavaliers for draft rights to G Jamal Crawford and cash (June 28, 2000). ... Traded by Cavaliers with G Ricky Davis, C Michael Stewart and a second-round draft choice to Boston Celtics for F/C Tony Battie, F Kedrick Brown and F Eric Williams (December 15, 2003). ... Traded by Celtics with G Chucky Atkins and F Jumaine Jones to Los Angeles Lakers for G Gary Payton, F Rick Fox and a first-round draft choice (August 6, 2004).

### COLLEGIATE RECORD

**NOTES:** The Sporting News All-America second team (2000).

| Season Team | G | Min. | FGM | FGA | Pct. | FTM | FTA | Pct. | Reb. | Ast. | Pts. | AVERAGES | | |
|---|---|---|---|---|---|---|---|---|---|---|---|---|---|---|
| | | | | | | | | | | | | RPG | APG | PPG |
| 97-98—Texas | 31 | 769 | 148 | 288 | .514 | 86 | 133 | .647 | 248 | 14 | 384 | 8.0 | 0.5 | 12.4 |
| 98-99—Texas | 32 | 1027 | 144 | 321 | .449 | 149 | 218 | .683 | 351 | 19 | 437 | 11.0 | 0.6 | 13.7 |
| 99-00—Texas | 33 | 1014 | 206 | 394 | .523 | 164 | 232 | .707 | 346 | 22 | 583 | 10.5 | 0.7 | 17.7 |
| Totals | 96 | 2810 | 498 | 1003 | .497 | 399 | 583 | .684 | 945 | 55 | 1404 | 9.8 | 0.6 | 14.6 |

Three-point field goals: 1997-98, 2-for-11 (.182). 1998-99, 0-for-4. 1999-00, 7-for-15 (.467). Totals, 9-for-30 (.300).

### NBA REGULAR-SEASON RECORD

**HONORS:** NBA All-Rookie second team (2001).

| Season Team | G | Min. | FGM | FGA | Pct. | FTM | FTA | Pct. | REBOUNDS | | | Ast. | St. | Blk. | TO | Pts. | AVERAGES | | |
|---|---|---|---|---|---|---|---|---|---|---|---|---|---|---|---|---|---|---|---|
| | | | | | | | | | Off. | Def. | Tot. | | | | | | RPG | APG | PPG |
| 00-01—Cleveland | 59 | 1166 | 173 | 391 | .442 | 100 | 126 | .794 | 106 | 174 | 280 | 16 | 20 | 53 | 80 | 446 | 4.7 | 0.3 | 7.6 |
| 01-02—Cleveland | 74 | 1659 | 221 | 526 | .420 | 124 | 179 | .693 | 133 | 259 | 392 | 24 | 18 | 89 | 97 | 569 | 5.3 | 0.3 | 7.7 |
| 02-03—Cleveland | 52 | 809 | 116 | 287 | .404 | 76 | 105 | .724 | 93 | 138 | 231 | 28 | 18 | 38 | 48 | 308 | 4.4 | 0.5 | 5.9 |
| 03-04—Cleve.-Bos. | 76 | 1330 | 186 | 381 | .488 | 110 | 166 | .663 | 156 | 257 | 413 | 21 | 37 | 63 | 90 | 482 | 5.4 | 0.3 | 6.3 |
| 04-05—L.A. Lakers | 75 | 1870 | 280 | 552 | .507 | 175 | 258 | .678 | 197 | 305 | 502 | 50 | 14 | 108 | 110 | 735 | 6.7 | 0.7 | 9.8 |
| Totals | 336 | 6834 | 976 | 2137 | .457 | 585 | 834 | .701 | 685 | 1133 | 1818 | 139 | 107 | 351 | 425 | 2540 | 5.4 | 0.4 | 7.6 |

Three-point field goals: 2000-01, 0-for-1. 2001-02, 3-for-7 (.429). 2002-03, 0-for-3. 2004-05, 0-for-2. Totals, 3-for-13 (.231).

Personal fouls/disqualifications: 2000-01, 156/2. 2001-02, 260/7. 2002-03, 124/0. 2003-04, 208/3. 2004-05, 237/1. Totals, 985/13.

### NBA PLAYOFF RECORD

| Season Team | G | Min. | FGM | FGA | Pct. | FTM | FTA | Pct. | REBOUNDS | | | Ast. | St. | Blk. | TO | Pts. | AVERAGES | | |
|---|---|---|---|---|---|---|---|---|---|---|---|---|---|---|---|---|---|---|---|
| | | | | | | | | | Off. | Def. | Tot. | | | | | | RPG | APG | PPG |
| 03-04—Boston | 4 | 65 | 7 | 22 | .318 | 6 | 10 | .600 | 8 | 10 | 18 | 0 | 4 | 4 | 3 | 20 | 4.5 | 0.0 | 5.0 |

Personal fouls/disqualifications: 2003-04, 12/1. Totals, 12/1.

## MILES, DARIUS          F          TRAIL BLAZERS

**PERSONAL:** Born October 9, 1981, in Belleville, Ill. ... 6-9/210. (2.06/95.3). ... Full name: Darius LaVar Miles
**HIGH SCHOOL:** East St. Louis (Ill.).
**COLLEGE:** Did not attend college.
**TRANSACTIONS/CAREER NOTES:** Selected out of high school by Los Angeles Clippers in first round (third pick overall) of 2000 NBA Draft. ... Traded by Clippers with F Harold Jamison to Cleveland Cavaliers for G Andre Miller and G Bryant Stith (July 30, 2002). ... Traded by Cavaliers to Portland Trail Blazers for G Jeff McInnis and C Ruben Boumtje-Boumtje (January 21, 2004).

**HONORS:** NBA All-Rookie first team (2001).

| | | | | | | | | | REBOUNDS | | | | | | | | AVERAGES | | |
|---|---|---|---|---|---|---|---|---|---|---|---|---|---|---|---|---|---|---|---|
| Season Team | G | Min. | FGM | FGA | Pct. | FTM | FTA | Pct. | Off. | Def. | Tot. | Ast. | St. | Blk. | TO | Pts. | RPG | APG | PPG |
| 00-01—L.A. Clippers | 81 | 2133 | 318 | 630 | .505 | 124 | 238 | .521 | 127 | 350 | 477 | 99 | 51 | 125 | 147 | 761 | 5.9 | 1.2 | 9.4 |
| 01-02—L.A. Clippers | 82 | 2227 | 309 | 642 | .481 | 158 | 255 | .620 | 109 | 344 | 453 | 184 | 71 | 103 | 160 | 779 | 5.5 | 2.2 | 9.5 |
| 02-03—Cleveland | 67 | 2008 | 263 | 642 | .410 | 92 | 155 | .594 | 113 | 250 | 363 | 176 | 67 | 69 | 178 | 618 | 5.4 | 2.6 | 9.2 |
| 03-04—Cleve.-Port. | 79 | 2079 | 365 | 753 | .485 | 124 | 193 | .642 | 112 | 247 | 359 | 162 | 67 | 61 | 130 | 861 | 4.5 | 2.1 | 10.9 |
| 04-05—Portland | 63 | 1699 | 336 | 697 | .482 | 129 | 215 | .600 | 71 | 228 | 299 | 129 | 75 | 78 | 157 | 809 | 4.7 | 2.0 | 12.8 |
| Totals | 372 | 10146 | 1591 | 3364 | .473 | 627 | 1056 | .594 | 532 | 1419 | 1951 | 750 | 331 | 436 | 772 | 3828 | 5.2 | 2.0 | 10.3 |

Three-point field goals: 2000-01, 1-for-19 (.053). 2001-02, 3-for-19 (.158). 2002-03, 0-for-14. 2003-04, 7-for-40 (.175). 2004-05, 8-for-23 (.348). Totals, 19-for-115 (.165).

Personal fouls/disqualifications: 2000-01, 191/1. 2001-02, 184/2. 2002-03, 159/3. 2003-04, 168/0. 2004-05, 189/0. Totals, 891/6.

---

# MILICIC, DARKO     F/C     PISTONS

**PERSONAL:** Born June 20, 1985, in Novi Sad, Montenegro. ... 7-0/245. (2.13/111.1).
**HIGH SCHOOL:** Hemiska (Montenegro).
**TRANSACTIONS/CAREER NOTES:** Played in Yugoslavia (2001-03). ... Played in North European Basketball League in 2002-03. ... Selected by Detroit Pistons in first round (second pick overall) of 2003 NBA Draft.
**MISCELLANEOUS:** Member of NBA championship team (2004).

## YUGOSLAVIAN LEAGUE RECORD

| | | | | | | | | | | | | AVERAGES | | |
|---|---|---|---|---|---|---|---|---|---|---|---|---|---|---|
| Season Team | G | Min. | FGM | FGA | Pct. | FTM | FTA | Pct. | Reb. | Ast. | Pts. | RPG | APG | PPG |
| 01-02—Hemofarm | 18 | 338 | 38 | 81 | .469 | 20 | 31 | .645 | 55 | 8 | 97 | 3.1 | 0.4 | 5.4 |
| 02-03—Hemofarm | 20 | 395 | 59 | 124 | .476 | 71 | 105 | .676 | 92 | 15 | 190 | 4.6 | 0.8 | 9.5 |
| Totals | 38 | 733 | 97 | 205 | .473 | 91 | 136 | .669 | 147 | 23 | 287 | 3.9 | 0.6 | 7.6 |

Three-point field goals: 2001-02, 1-for-5 (.200). 2002-03, 1-for-5 (.200). Totals, 2-for-10 (.200).

## NBA REGULAR-SEASON RECORD

| | | | | | | | | | REBOUNDS | | | | | | | | AVERAGES | | |
|---|---|---|---|---|---|---|---|---|---|---|---|---|---|---|---|---|---|---|---|
| Season Team | G | Min. | FGM | FGA | Pct. | FTM | FTA | Pct. | Off. | Def. | Tot. | Ast. | St. | Blk. | TO | Pts. | RPG | APG | PPG |
| 03-04—Detroit | 34 | 159 | 17 | 65 | .262 | 14 | 24 | .583 | 11 | 32 | 43 | 7 | 7 | 15 | 13 | 48 | 1.3 | 0.2 | 1.4 |
| 04-05—Detroit | 37 | 254 | 25 | 76 | .329 | 17 | 24 | .708 | 3 | 40 | 43 | 7 | 2 | 17 | 16 | 67 | 1.2 | 0.2 | 1.8 |
| Totals | 71 | 413 | 42 | 141 | .298 | 31 | 48 | .646 | 14 | 72 | 86 | 14 | 9 | 32 | 29 | 115 | 1.2 | 0.2 | 1.6 |

Three-point field goals: 2003-04, 0-for-1. Totals, 0-for-1 (.000).
Personal fouls/disqualifications: 2003-04, 33/0. 2004-05, 31/0. Totals, 64/0.

## NBA PLAYOFF RECORD

| | | | | | | | | | REBOUNDS | | | | | | | | AVERAGES | | |
|---|---|---|---|---|---|---|---|---|---|---|---|---|---|---|---|---|---|---|---|
| Season Team | G | Min. | FGM | FGA | Pct. | FTM | FTA | Pct. | Off. | Def. | Tot. | Ast. | St. | Blk. | TO | Pts. | RPG | APG | PPG |
| 03-04—Detroit | 8 | 14 | 0 | 4 | .000 | 1 | 4 | .250 | 1 | 2 | 3 | 1 | 1 | 0 | 3 | 1 | 0.4 | 0.1 | 0.1 |
| 04-05—Detroit | 9 | 21 | 2 | 7 | .286 | 1 | 1 | 1.000 | 1 | 3 | 4 | 1 | 0 | 1 | 1 | 5 | 0.4 | 0.1 | 0.6 |
| Totals | 17 | 35 | 2 | 11 | .182 | 2 | 5 | .400 | 2 | 5 | 7 | 2 | 1 | 1 | 4 | 6 | 0.4 | 0.1 | 0.4 |

Personal fouls/disqualifications: 2003-04, 1/0. 2004-05, 3/0. Totals, 4/0.

**M**

---

# MILLER, ANDRE     G     NUGGETS

**PERSONAL:** Born March 19, 1976, in Los Angeles. ... 6-2/200. (1.88/90.7). ... Full name: Andre Lloyd Miller.
**HIGH SCHOOL:** Verbum Dei (Los Angeles).
**COLLEGE:** Utah.
**TRANSACTIONS/CAREER NOTES:** Selected by Cleveland Cavaliers in first round (eighth pick overall) of 1999 NBA Draft. ... Traded by Cavaliers with G Bryant Stith to Los Angeles Clippers for F Darius Miles and F Harold Jamison (July 30, 2002). ... Signed by Denver Nuggets (August 1, 2003).

## COLLEGIATE RECORD

**NOTES:** The Sporting News All-America first team (1999).

| | | | | | | | | | | | | AVERAGES | | |
|---|---|---|---|---|---|---|---|---|---|---|---|---|---|---|
| Season Team | G | Min. | FGM | FGA | Pct. | FTM | FTA | Pct. | Reb. | Ast. | Pts. | RPG | APG | PPG |
| 94-95—Utah | | | | | | Did not play—ineligible. | | | | | | | | |
| 95-96—Utah | 34 | 872 | 104 | 195 | .533 | 78 | 113 | .690 | 126 | 157 | 292 | 3.7 | 4.6 | 8.6 |
| 96-97—Utah | 33 | 974 | 121 | 249 | .486 | 71 | 122 | .582 | 154 | 201 | 323 | 4.7 | 6.1 | 9.8 |
| 97-98—Utah | 34 | 1076 | 173 | 315 | .549 | 117 | 162 | .722 | 185 | 177 | 483 | 5.4 | 5.2 | 14.2 |
| 98-99—Utah | 33 | 1092 | 190 | 387 | .491 | 118 | 171 | .690 | 178 | 186 | 520 | 5.4 | 5.6 | 15.8 |
| Totals | 134 | 4014 | 588 | 1146 | .513 | 384 | 568 | .676 | 643 | 721 | 1618 | 4.8 | 5.4 | 12.1 |

Three-point field goals: 1995-96, 6-for-19 (.316). 1996-97, 10-for-35 (.286). 1997-98, 20-for-60 (.333). 1998-99, 22-for-83 (.265). Totals, 58-for-197 (.294).

Personal fouls/disqualifications: 1995-96, 67/1. 1996-97, 62/1. 1997-98, 72/1. Totals, 201/3.

## NBA REGULAR-SEASON RECORD

**HONORS:** NBA All-Rookie first team (2000).

| | | | | | | | | | REBOUNDS | | | | | | | | AVERAGES | | |
|---|---|---|---|---|---|---|---|---|---|---|---|---|---|---|---|---|---|---|---|
| Season Team | G | Min. | FGM | FGA | Pct. | FTM | FTA | Pct. | Off. | Def. | Tot. | Ast. | St. | Blk. | TO | Pts. | RPG | APG | PPG |
| 99-00—Cleveland | 82 | 2093 | 339 | 755 | .449 | 226 | 292 | .774 | 85 | 195 | 280 | 476 | 84 | 17 | 166 | 914 | 3.4 | 5.8 | 11.1 |
| 00-01—Cleveland | 82 | 2848 | 452 | 999 | .452 | 375 | 450 | .833 | 94 | 266 | 360 | 657 | 119 | 28 | 265 | 1296 | 4.4 | 8.0 | 15.8 |
| 01-02—Cleveland | 81 | 3023 | 474 | 1045 | .454 | 365 | 447 | .817 | 108 | 271 | 379 | *882 | 126 | 34 | 245 | 1335 | 4.7 | *10.9 | 16.5 |
| 02-03—L.A. Clippers | 80 | 2913 | 377 | 928 | .406 | 311 | 391 | .795 | 84 | 232 | 316 | 537 | 99 | 11 | 206 | 1088 | 4.0 | 6.7 | 13.6 |

| Season Team | G | Min. | FGM | FGA | Pct. | FTM | FTA | Pct. | REBOUNDS Off. | Def. | Tot. | Ast. | St. | Blk. | TO | Pts. | AVERAGES RPG | APG | PPG |
|---|---|---|---|---|---|---|---|---|---|---|---|---|---|---|---|---|---|---|---|
| 03-04—Denver | 82 | 2838 | 430 | 941 | .457 | 342 | 411 | .832 | 127 | 239 | 366 | 501 | 142 | 25 | 215 | 1214 | 4.5 | 6.1 | 14.8 |
| 04-05—Denver | 82 | 2852 | 427 | 895 | .477 | 253 | 302 | .838 | 100 | 238 | 338 | 569 | 121 | 8 | 220 | 1113 | 4.1 | 6.9 | 13.6 |
| **Totals** | 489 | 16567 | 2499 | 5563 | .449 | 1872 | 2293 | .816 | 598 | 1441 | 2039 | 3622 | 691 | 123 | 1317 | 6960 | 4.2 | 7.4 | 14.2 |

Three-point field goals: 1999-00, 10-for-49 (.204). 2000-01, 17-for-64 (.266). 2001-02, 22-for-87 (.253). 2002-03, 23-for-108 (.213). 2003-04, 12-for-65 (.185). 2004-05, 6-for-39 (.154). Totals, 90-for-412 (.218).

Personal fouls/disqualifications: 1999-00, 194/1. 2000-01, 229/0. 2001-02, 228/1. 2002-03, 203/3. 2003-04, 194/2. 2004-05, 204/1. Totals, 1252/8.

### NBA PLAYOFF RECORD

| Season Team | G | Min. | FGM | FGA | Pct. | FTM | FTA | Pct. | REBOUNDS Off. | Def. | Tot. | Ast. | St. | Blk. | TO | Pts. | AVERAGES RPG | APG | PPG |
|---|---|---|---|---|---|---|---|---|---|---|---|---|---|---|---|---|---|---|---|
| 03-04—Denver | 5 | 174 | 34 | 72 | .472 | 9 | 11 | .818 | 15 | 8 | 23 | 16 | 8 | 0 | 10 | 77 | 4.6 | 3.2 | 15.4 |
| 04-05—Denver | 5 | 184 | 28 | 66 | .424 | 23 | 32 | .719 | 9 | 17 | 26 | 26 | 10 | 1 | 12 | 81 | 5.2 | 5.2 | 16.2 |
| **Totals** | 10 | 358 | 62 | 138 | .449 | 32 | 43 | .744 | 24 | 25 | 49 | 42 | 18 | 1 | 22 | 158 | 4.9 | 4.2 | 15.8 |

Three-point field goals: 2003-04, 0-for-2. 2004-05, 2-for-4 (.500). Totals, 2-for-6 (.333).

Personal fouls/disqualifications: 2003-04, 16/1. 2004-05, 22/2. Totals, 38/3.

## MILLER, ANTHONY          F          HAWKS

**PERSONAL:** Born October 27, 1971, in Benton Harbor, Mich. ... 6-9/255. (2.06/115.7). ... Nickname: Pig.
**HIGH SCHOOL:** Benton Harbor (Mich.).
**COLLEGE:** Michigan State.
**TRANSACTIONS/CAREER NOTES:** Selected by Golden State Warriors in second round (39th pick overall) of 1994 NBA Draft. ... Draft rights traded by Warriors to Los Angeles Lakers for 1995 second-round draft choice (July 1, 1994). ... Signed as free agent by Seattle SuperSonics (September 30, 1996). ... Waived by SuperSonics (October 26, 1996). ... Signed as free agent by Atlanta Hawks (November 14, 1996). ... Waived by Hawks (November 18, 1996). ... Played in Continental Basketball Association with Florida Beachdogs (1996-97). ... Signed as free agent by Hawks (September 26, 1997). ... Signed as free agent by Houston Rockets (January 21, 1999). ... Signed as free agent by Minnesota Timberwolves (October 18, 1999). ... Waived by Timberwolves (October 21, 1999). ... Signed by Houston Rockets to the first of two consecutive 10-day contracts (January 6, 2000). ... Re-signed by Rockets for remainder of season (January 26, 2000). ... Signed as free agent by Hawks (October 3, 2000). ... Waived by Hawks (November 8, 2000). ... Signed as free agent by Rockets (December 8, 2000). ... Waived by Rockets (December 28, 2000). ... Signed as free agent by Philadelphia 76ers (March 7, 2001). ... Waived by 76ers (March 15, 2001). ... Signed as free agent by Warriors (September 30, 2002). ... Waived by Warriors (October 23, 2002). ... Signed as free agent by Rockets (October 16, 2003). ... Waived by Rockets (October 23, 2003). ... Signed as free agent by Atlanta Hawks (October 5, 2004).

### COLLEGIATE RECORD

| Season Team | G | Min. | FGM | FGA | Pct. | FTM | FTA | Pct. | Reb. | Ast. | Pts. | AVERAGES RPG | APG | PPG |
|---|---|---|---|---|---|---|---|---|---|---|---|---|---|---|
| 90-91—Michigan State | | | | | | | Did not play—ineligible. | | | | | | | |
| 91-92—Michigan State | 30 | 555 | 83 | 154 | .539 | 50 | 80 | .625 | 156 | 24 | 216 | 5.2 | 0.8 | 7.2 |
| 92-93—Michigan State | 27 | 474 | 76 | 124 | .613 | 26 | 48 | .542 | 139 | 12 | 179 | 5.1 | 0.4 | 6.6 |
| 93-94—Michigan State | 32 | 910 | 162 | 249 | .651 | 78 | 136 | .574 | 287 | 30 | 402 | 9.0 | 0.9 | 12.6 |
| **Totals** | 89 | 1939 | 321 | 527 | .609 | 154 | 264 | .583 | 582 | 66 | 797 | 6.5 | 0.7 | 9.0 |

Three-point field goals: 1992-93, 1-for-1 (1.000). 1993-94, 0-for-1. Totals, 1-for-2 (.500).

### NBA REGULAR-SEASON RECORD

| Season Team | G | Min. | FGM | FGA | Pct. | FTM | FTA | Pct. | REBOUNDS Off. | Def. | Tot. | Ast. | St. | Blk. | TO | Pts. | AVERAGES RPG | APG | PPG |
|---|---|---|---|---|---|---|---|---|---|---|---|---|---|---|---|---|---|---|---|
| 94-95—L.A. Lakers | 46 | 527 | 70 | 132 | .530 | 47 | 76 | .618 | 67 | 85 | 152 | 35 | 20 | 7 | 38 | 189 | 3.3 | 0.8 | 4.1 |
| 95-96—L.A. Lakers | 27 | 123 | 15 | 35 | .429 | 6 | 10 | .600 | 11 | 14 | 25 | 4 | 4 | 1 | 8 | 36 | 0.9 | 0.1 | 1.3 |
| 96-97—Atlanta | 1 | 14 | 0 | 5 | .000 | 0 | 0 | ... | 2 | 5 | 7 | 0 | 0 | 0 | 0 | 0 | 7.0 | 0.0 | 0.0 |
| 97-98—Atlanta | 37 | 228 | 29 | 52 | .558 | 21 | 39 | .538 | 30 | 40 | 70 | 3 | 15 | 3 | 14 | 79 | 1.9 | 0.1 | 2.1 |
| 98-99—Houston | 29 | 249 | 28 | 60 | .467 | 14 | 22 | .636 | 26 | 41 | 67 | 7 | 7 | 5 | 9 | 70 | 2.3 | 0.2 | 2.4 |
| 99-00—Houston | 35 | 476 | 52 | 97 | .536 | 26 | 51 | .510 | 49 | 115 | 164 | 16 | 11 | 10 | 19 | 130 | 4.7 | 0.5 | 3.7 |
| 00-01—Atl.-Hou.-Phila. | 4 | 11 | 1 | 2 | .500 | 0 | 0 | ... | 0 | 2 | 2 | 0 | 0 | 0 | 1 | 2 | 0.5 | 0.0 | 0.5 |
| 04-05—Atlanta | 2 | 9 | 2 | 3 | .667 | 0 | 0 | ... | 0 | 1 | 1 | 1 | 1 | 0 | 1 | 4 | 0.5 | 0.5 | 2.0 |
| **Totals** | 181 | 1637 | 197 | 386 | .510 | 114 | 198 | .576 | 185 | 303 | 488 | 66 | 58 | 26 | 90 | 510 | 2.7 | 0.4 | 2.8 |

Three-point field goals: 1994-95, 2-for-5 (.400). 1995-96, 0-for-2. 1998-99, 0-for-1. Totals, 2-for-8 (.250).

Personal fouls/disqualifications: 1994-95, 77/2. 1995-96, 19/0. 1996-97, 2/0. 1997-98, 41/0. 1998-99, 34/0. 1999-00, 68/1. 2000-01, 1/0. 2004-05, 2/0. Totals, 244/3.

### NBA PLAYOFF RECORD

| Season Team | G | Min. | FGM | FGA | Pct. | FTM | FTA | Pct. | REBOUNDS Off. | Def. | Tot. | Ast. | St. | Blk. | TO | Pts. | AVERAGES RPG | APG | PPG |
|---|---|---|---|---|---|---|---|---|---|---|---|---|---|---|---|---|---|---|---|
| 94-95—L.A. Lakers | 4 | 15 | 0 | 2 | .000 | 0 | 0 | ... | 2 | 4 | 6 | 1 | 1 | 0 | 1 | 0 | 1.5 | 0.3 | 0.0 |
| 97-98—Atlanta | 4 | 33 | 3 | 8 | .375 | 2 | 2 | 1.000 | 5 | 4 | 9 | 1 | 2 | 1 | 3 | 8 | 2.3 | 0.3 | 2.0 |
| **Totals** | 8 | 48 | 3 | 10 | .300 | 2 | 2 | 1.000 | 7 | 8 | 15 | 2 | 3 | 1 | 4 | 8 | 1.9 | 0.3 | 1.0 |

Personal fouls/disqualifications: 1994-95, 2/0. 1997-98, 5/0. Totals, 7/0.

### CBA RECORD

| Season Team | G | Min. | FGM | FGA | Pct. | FTM | FTA | Pct. | Reb. | Ast. | Pts. | AVERAGES RPG | APG | PPG |
|---|---|---|---|---|---|---|---|---|---|---|---|---|---|---|
| 96-97—Florida | 16 | 334 | 51 | 102 | .500 | 27 | 40 | .675 | 135 | 3 | 129 | 8.4 | 0.2 | 8.1 |
| 02-03—Yakima | 20 | 570 | 100 | 220 | .455 | 51 | 84 | .607 | 196 | 44 | 252 | 9.8 | 2.2 | 12.6 |
| 03-04—Yakima | 34 | 1176 | 179 | 330 | .542 | 83 | 126 | .659 | 398 | 63 | 441 | 11.7 | 1.9 | 13.0 |
| **Totals** | 70 | 2080 | 330 | 652 | .506 | 161 | 250 | .644 | 729 | 110 | 822 | 10.4 | 1.6 | 11.7 |

Three-point field goals: 1996-97, 0-for-1. 2002-03, 1-for-3 (.333). Totals, 1-for-4 (.250).

### AMERICAN BASKETBALL ASSOCIATION RECORD

| Season Team | G | Min. | FGM | FGA | Pct. | FTM | FTA | Pct. | Reb. | Ast. | Pts. | AVERAGES RPG | APG | PPG |
|---|---|---|---|---|---|---|---|---|---|---|---|---|---|---|
| 04-05—Atlanta | 5 | ... | 35 | 63 | .556 | 27 | 32 | .844 | 63 | 15 | 100 | 12.6 | 3.0 | 20.0 |

Three-point field goals: 2004-05, 3-for-5 (.600). Totals, 3-for-5 (.600).

M

# MILLER, BRAD      C      KINGS

**PERSONAL:** Born April 12, 1976, in Fort Wayne, Ind. ... 7-0/261. (2.13/118.4). ... Full name: Bradley Alan Miller
**HIGH SCHOOL:** East Noble (Berwick, Maine), Maine Central Institu.
**COLLEGE:** Purdue.
**TRANSACTIONS/CAREER NOTES:** Not drafted by an NBA franchise. ... Played in Italy (1998-99). ... Signed as free agent by Charlotte Hornets (January 21, 1999). ... Signed as free agent by Chicago Bulls (September 7, 2000). ... Traded by Bulls with G Ron Mercer, G/F Ron Artest and G Kevin Ollie to Indiana Pacers for G Jalen Rose, G Travis Best, G Norman Richardson and conditional second-round draft choice (February 19, 2002). ... Traded by Pacers to Sacramento Kings in three-team deal in which Pacers also traded G Ron Mercer to San Antonio Spurs and acquired F Scot Pollard from Kings and F Danny Ferry from Spurs. Spurs also acquired F/G Hedo Turkoglu from Kings (July 24, 2003).
**MISCELLANEOUS:** Member of bronze-medal-winning U.S. World Championship team (1998).

## COLLEGIATE RECORD

| Season Team | G | Min. | FGM | FGA | Pct. | FTM | FTA | Pct. | Reb. | Ast. | Pts. | RPG | APG | PPG |
|---|---|---|---|---|---|---|---|---|---|---|---|---|---|---|
| 94-95—Purdue | 32 | 574 | 71 | 122 | .582 | 66 | 100 | .660 | 153 | 39 | 208 | 4.8 | 1.2 | 6.5 |
| 95-96—Purdue | 32 | 682 | 100 | 193 | .518 | 107 | 145 | .738 | 158 | 46 | 308 | 4.9 | 1.4 | 9.6 |
| 96-97—Purdue | 30 | 929 | 128 | 239 | .536 | 171 | 220 | .777 | 249 | 86 | 430 | 8.3 | 2.9 | 14.3 |
| 97-98—Purdue | 33 | 964 | 186 | 291 | .639 | 196 | 251 | .781 | 291 | 84 | 571 | 8.8 | 2.5 | 17.3 |
| Totals | 127 | 3149 | 485 | 845 | .574 | 540 | 716 | .754 | 851 | 255 | 1517 | 6.7 | 2.0 | 11.9 |

Three-point field goals: 1995-96, 1-for-6 (.167). 1996-97, 3-for-11 (.273). 1997-98, 3-for-9 (.333). Totals, 7-for-26 (.269).

## ITALIAN LEAGUE RECORD

| Season Team | G | Min. | FGM | FGA | Pct. | FTM | FTA | Pct. | Reb. | Ast. | Pts. | RPG | APG | PPG |
|---|---|---|---|---|---|---|---|---|---|---|---|---|---|---|
| 98-99—Bini Viaggi | 16 | 484 | 95 | 170 | .559 | 61 | 73 | .836 | 140 | 17 | 253 | 8.8 | 1.1 | 15.8 |

Three-point field goals: 1998-99, 2-for-6 (.333). Totals, 2-for-6 (.333).

## NBA REGULAR-SEASON RECORD

| Season Team | G | Min. | FGM | FGA | Pct. | FTM | FTA | Pct. | Off. | Def. | Tot. | Ast. | St. | Blk. | TO | Pts. | RPG | APG | PPG |
|---|---|---|---|---|---|---|---|---|---|---|---|---|---|---|---|---|---|---|---|
| 98-99—Charlotte | 38 | 469 | 78 | 138 | .565 | 81 | 102 | .794 | 35 | 82 | 117 | 22 | 9 | 18 | 32 | 238 | 3.1 | 0.6 | 6.3 |
| 99-00—Charlotte | 55 | 961 | 135 | 293 | .461 | 153 | 195 | .785 | 113 | 180 | 293 | 45 | 23 | 35 | 48 | 423 | 5.3 | 0.8 | 7.7 |
| 00-01—Chicago | 57 | 1434 | 168 | 386 | .435 | 168 | 226 | .743 | 144 | 275 | 419 | 107 | 33 | 38 | 73 | 505 | 7.4 | 1.9 | 8.9 |
| 01-02—Chi.-Indiana | 76 | 2263 | 366 | 733 | .499 | 297 | 383 | .775 | 252 | 369 | 621 | 152 | 76 | 41 | 115 | 1032 | 8.2 | 2.0 | 13.6 |
| 02-03—Indiana | 73 | 2270 | 329 | 667 | .493 | 292 | 357 | .818 | 185 | 418 | 603 | 193 | 65 | 43 | 118 | 955 | 8.3 | 2.6 | 13.1 |
| 03-04—Sacramento | 72 | 2621 | 373 | 731 | .510 | 256 | 329 | .778 | 191 | 552 | 743 | 312 | 68 | 86 | 144 | 1014 | 10.3 | 4.3 | 14.1 |
| 04-05—Sacramento | 56 | 2089 | 319 | 609 | .524 | 233 | 287 | .812 | 139 | 382 | 521 | 220 | 69 | 68 | 82 | 876 | 9.3 | 3.9 | 15.6 |
| Totals | 427 | 12107 | 1768 | 3557 | .497 | 1480 | 1879 | .788 | 1059 | 2258 | 3317 | 1051 | 343 | 329 | 612 | 5043 | 7.8 | 2.5 | 11.8 |

Three-point field goals: 1998-99, 1-for-2 (.500). 1999-00, 0-for-2. 2000-01, 1-for-5 (.200). 2001-02, 3-for-7 (.429). 2002-03, 5-for-16 (.313). 2003-04, 12-for-38 (.316). 2004-05, 5-for-19 (.263). Totals, 27-for-89 (.303).
Personal fouls/disqualifications: 1998-99, 65/0. 1999-00, 111/1. 2000-01, 176/5. 2001-02, 244/3. 2002-03, 203/0. 2003-04, 247/7. 2004-05, 181/4. Totals, 1227/20.

## NBA PLAYOFF RECORD

| Season Team | G | Min. | FGM | FGA | Pct. | FTM | FTA | Pct. | Off. | Def. | Tot. | Ast. | St. | Blk. | TO | Pts. | RPG | APG | PPG |
|---|---|---|---|---|---|---|---|---|---|---|---|---|---|---|---|---|---|---|---|
| 99-00—Charlotte | 4 | 62 | 9 | 17 | .529 | 12 | 15 | .800 | 8 | 5 | 13 | 3 | 0 | 9 | 9 | 30 | 3.3 | 0.8 | 7.5 |
| 01-02—Indiana | 5 | 180 | 20 | 44 | .455 | 16 | 20 | .800 | 17 | 32 | 49 | 7 | 4 | 2 | 7 | 56 | 9.8 | 1.4 | 11.2 |
| 02-03—Indiana | 6 | 135 | 18 | 40 | .450 | 16 | 22 | .727 | 10 | 23 | 33 | 15 | 5 | 0 | 9 | 52 | 5.5 | 2.5 | 8.7 |
| 03-04—Sacramento | 12 | 366 | 48 | 91 | .527 | 29 | 48 | .604 | 30 | 74 | 104 | 38 | 9 | 11 | 20 | 126 | 8.7 | 3.2 | 10.5 |
| 04-05—Sacramento | 5 | 139 | 23 | 40 | .575 | 10 | 14 | .714 | 8 | 11 | 19 | 16 | 1 | 3 | 9 | 56 | 3.8 | 3.2 | 11.2 |
| Totals | 32 | 882 | 118 | 232 | .509 | 83 | 119 | .697 | 73 | 145 | 218 | 79 | 19 | 19 | 54 | 320 | 6.8 | 2.5 | 10.0 |

Three-point field goals: 2003-04, 1-for-7 (.143). 2004-05, 0-for-2. Totals, 1-for-9 (.111).
Personal fouls/disqualifications: 1999-00, 11/0. 2001-02, 16/0. 2002-03, 17/1. 2003-04, 46/0. 2004-05, 21/0. Totals, 111/1.

## NBA ALL-STAR GAME RECORD

| Season Team | Min. | FGM | FGA | Pct. | FTM | FTA | Pct. | Off. | Def. | Tot. | Ast. | PF | Dq. | St. | Blk. | TO | Pts. |
|---|---|---|---|---|---|---|---|---|---|---|---|---|---|---|---|---|---|
| 2003—Indiana | 17 | 2 | 4 | .500 | 1 | 2 | .500 | 3 | 3 | 6 | 3 | 2 | 0 | 0 | 0 | 2 | 5 |
| 2004—Sacramento | 10 | 4 | 5 | .800 | 0 | 0 | ... | 1 | 2 | 3 | 0 | 0 | 0 | 0 | 0 | 2 | 8 |
| Totals | 27 | 6 | 9 | .667 | 1 | 2 | .500 | 4 | 5 | 9 | 3 | 2 | 0 | 0 | 0 | 4 | 13 |

# MILLER, MIKE      F      GRIZZLIES

**PERSONAL:** Born February 19, 1980, in Mitchell, S.D. ... 6-9/218. (2.06/98.9). ... Full name: Michael Lloyd Miller
**HIGH SCHOOL:** Mitchell (S.D.).
**COLLEGE:** Florida.
**TRANSACTIONS/CAREER NOTES:** Selected after sophomore season by Orlando Magic in first round (fifth pick overall) of 2000 NBA Draft. ... Traded by Magic with F Ryan Humphrey, 2003 first-round draft choice and 2004 second-round draft choice to Memphis Grizzlies for F Drew Gooden and F Gordan Giricek (February 19, 2003).

## COLLEGIATE RECORD

| Season Team | G | Min. | FGM | FGA | Pct. | FTM | FTA | Pct. | Reb. | Ast. | Pts. | RPG | APG | PPG |
|---|---|---|---|---|---|---|---|---|---|---|---|---|---|---|
| 98-99—Florida | 28 | 677 | 115 | 233 | .494 | 80 | 114 | .702 | 146 | 58 | 341 | 5.2 | 2.1 | 12.2 |
| 99-00—Florida | 37 | 1058 | 175 | 368 | .476 | 124 | 170 | .729 | 243 | 91 | 521 | 6.6 | 2.5 | 14.1 |
| Totals | 65 | 1735 | 290 | 601 | .483 | 204 | 284 | .718 | 389 | 149 | 862 | 6.0 | 2.3 | 13.3 |

Three-point field goals: 1998-99, 31-for-87 (.356). 1999-00, 47-for-139 (.338). Totals, 78-for-226 (.345).

**HONORS:** NBA Rookie of the Year (2001). ... NBA All-Rookie first team (2001).

| Season Team | G | Min. | FGM | FGA | Pct. | FTM | FTA | Pct. | Off. | Def. | Tot. | Ast. | St. | Blk. | TO | Pts. | RPG | APG | PPG |
|---|---|---|---|---|---|---|---|---|---|---|---|---|---|---|---|---|---|---|---|
| 00-01—Orlando | 82 | 2390 | 368 | 845 | .436 | 91 | 128 | .711 | 66 | 261 | 327 | 140 | 51 | 19 | 97 | 975 | 4.0 | 1.7 | 11.9 |
| 01-02—Orlando | 63 | 2123 | 351 | 802 | .438 | 138 | 181 | .762 | 49 | 224 | 273 | 198 | 47 | 23 | 108 | 956 | 4.3 | 3.1 | 15.2 |
| 02-03—Orl-Mem | 65 | 2186 | 373 | 859 | .434 | 156 | 186 | .839 | 46 | 295 | 341 | 170 | 42 | 21 | 125 | 1011 | 5.2 | 2.6 | 15.6 |
| 03-04—Memphis | 65 | 1770 | 270 | 616 | .438 | 102 | 141 | .723 | 42 | 174 | 216 | 232 | 59 | 14 | 107 | 722 | 3.3 | 3.6 | 11.1 |
| 04-05—Memphis | 76 | 2278 | 387 | 766 | .505 | 108 | 150 | .720 | 36 | 264 | 300 | 220 | 54 | 23 | 127 | 1022 | 3.9 | 2.9 | 13.4 |
| **Totals** | 351 | 10747 | 1749 | 3888 | .450 | 595 | 786 | .757 | 239 | 1218 | 1457 | 960 | 253 | 100 | 564 | 4686 | 4.2 | 2.7 | 13.4 |

Three-point field goals: 2000-01, 148-for-364 (.407). 2001-02, 116-for-303 (.383). 2002-03, 109-for-300 (.363). 2003-04, 80-for-215 (.372). 2004-05, 140-for-323 (.433). Totals, 593-for-1505 (.394).

Personal fouls/disqualifications: 2000-01, 200/2. 2001-02, 145/0. 2002-03, 173/2. 2003-04, 162/3. 2004-05, 197/2. Totals, 877/9.

**NBA PLAYOFF RECORD**

| Season Team | G | Min. | FGM | FGA | Pct. | FTM | FTA | Pct. | Off. | Def. | Tot. | Ast. | St. | Blk. | TO | Pts. | RPG | APG | PPG |
|---|---|---|---|---|---|---|---|---|---|---|---|---|---|---|---|---|---|---|---|
| 00-01—Orlando | 4 | 112 | 19 | 48 | .396 | 3 | 4 | .750 | 5 | 13 | 18 | 7 | 0 | 3 | 3 | 48 | 4.5 | 1.8 | 12.0 |
| 01-02—Orlando | 4 | 72 | 7 | 21 | .333 | 4 | 4 | 1.000 | 0 | 5 | 5 | 5 | 4 | 0 | 4 | 19 | 1.3 | 1.3 | 4.8 |
| 03-04—Memphis | 4 | 98 | 12 | 34 | .353 | 1 | 3 | .333 | 0 | 12 | 12 | 3 | 5 | 0 | 5 | 30 | 3.0 | 0.8 | 7.5 |
| 04-05—Memphis | 4 | 110 | 18 | 37 | .486 | 4 | 4 | 1.000 | 0 | 10 | 10 | 11 | 0 | 3 | 5 | 48 | 2.5 | 2.8 | 12.0 |
| **Totals** | 16 | 392 | 56 | 140 | .400 | 12 | 15 | .800 | 5 | 40 | 45 | 26 | 9 | 6 | 17 | 145 | 2.8 | 1.6 | 9.1 |

Three-point field goals: 2000-01, 7-for-18 (.389). 2001-02, 1-for-8 (.125). 2003-04, 5-for-13 (.385). 2004-05, 8-for-17 (.471). Totals, 21-for-56 (.375).

Personal fouls/disqualifications: 2000-01, 13/0. 2001-02, 8/0. 2003-04, 4/0. 2004-05, 7/0. Totals, 32/0.

## MILLER, REGGIE — G — PACERS

**PERSONAL:** Born August 24, 1965, in Riverside, Calif. ... 6-7/190. (2.01/86.2). ... Full name: Reginald Wayne Miller ... Brother of Darrell Miller, outfielder/catcher with California Angels (1984-88); and brother of Cheryl Miller, member of gold-medal-winning U.S. Olympic women's basketball team (1984), and head coach and general manager, Phoenix Mercury of the WNBA (1997-2000). **HIGH SCHOOL:** Riverside (Calif.) Polytechnic.

**COLLEGE:** UCLA.

**TRANSACTIONS/CAREER NOTES:** Selected by Indiana Pacers in first round (11th pick overall) of 1987 NBA Draft. ... Waived by Pacers (August 15, 2005).

**MISCELLANEOUS:** Member of gold-medal-winning U.S. Olympic team (1996). ... Member of gold-medal-winning U.S. World Championship team (1994). ... Indiana Pacers franchise all-time leading scorer with 25,279 points and all-time steals leader with 1,505 (1987-88 through 2004-05).

**COLLEGIATE RECORD**

| Season Team | G | Min. | FGM | FGA | Pct. | FTM | FTA | Pct. | Reb. | Ast. | Pts. | RPG | APG | PPG |
|---|---|---|---|---|---|---|---|---|---|---|---|---|---|---|
| 83-84—UCLA | 28 | 384 | 56 | 110 | .509 | 18 | 28 | .643 | 42 | 21 | 130 | 1.5 | 0.8 | 4.6 |
| 84-85—UCLA | 33 | 1174 | 192 | 347 | .553 | 119 | 148 | .804 | 141 | 86 | 503 | 4.3 | 2.6 | 15.2 |
| 85-86—UCLA | 29 | 1112 | 274 | 493 | .556 | 202 | 229 | .882 | 153 | 69 | 750 | 5.3 | 2.4 | 25.9 |
| 86-87—UCLA | 32 | 1166 | 247 | 455 | .543 | 149 | 179 | .832 | 173 | 71 | 712 | 5.4 | 2.2 | 22.3 |
| **Totals** | 122 | 3836 | 769 | 1405 | .547 | 488 | 584 | .836 | 509 | 247 | 2095 | 4.2 | 2.0 | 17.2 |

Three-point field goals: 1986-87, 69-for-157 (.439). Totals, 69-for-157 (.439).

**NBA REGULAR-SEASON RECORD**

**RECORDS:** Holds career record for most three-point field goals made—2,560; and most three-point field goals attempted—6,486. ... Shares NBA record for most seasons leading league in three-point field goals made—2.

**HONORS:** J. Walter Kennedy Citizenship Award (2004). ... All-NBA Third Team (1995, 1996, 1998).

**NOTES:** Led NBA with 167 three-point field goals made (1993) and 229 three-point field goals made (1997).

| Season Team | G | Min. | FGM | FGA | Pct. | FTM | FTA | Pct. | Off. | Def. | Tot. | Ast. | St. | Blk. | TO | Pts. | RPG | APG | PPG |
|---|---|---|---|---|---|---|---|---|---|---|---|---|---|---|---|---|---|---|---|
| 87-88—Indiana | 82 | 1840 | 306 | 627 | .488 | 149 | 186 | .801 | 95 | 95 | 190 | 132 | 53 | 19 | 101 | 822 | 2.3 | 1.6 | 10.0 |
| 88-89—Indiana | 74 | 2536 | 398 | 831 | .479 | 287 | 340 | .844 | 73 | 219 | 292 | 227 | 93 | 29 | 143 | 1181 | 3.9 | 3.1 | 16.0 |
| 89-90—Indiana | 82 | 3192 | 661 | 1287 | .514 | 544 | 627 | .868 | 95 | 200 | 295 | 311 | 110 | 18 | 222 | 2016 | 3.6 | 3.8 | 24.6 |
| 90-91—Indiana | 82 | 2972 | 596 | 1164 | .512 | 551 | 600 | *.918 | 81 | 200 | 281 | 331 | 109 | 13 | 163 | 1855 | 3.4 | 4.0 | 22.6 |
| 91-92—Indiana | 82 | 3120 | 562 | 1121 | .501 | 442 | 515 | .858 | 82 | 236 | 318 | 314 | 105 | 26 | 157 | 1695 | 3.9 | 3.8 | 20.7 |
| 92-93—Indiana | 82 | 2954 | 571 | 1193 | .479 | 427 | 485 | .880 | 67 | 191 | 258 | 262 | 120 | 26 | 145 | 1736 | 3.1 | 3.2 | 21.2 |
| 93-94—Indiana | 79 | 2638 | 524 | 1042 | .503 | 403 | 444 | .908 | 30 | 182 | 212 | 248 | 119 | 24 | 175 | 1574 | 2.7 | 3.1 | 19.9 |
| 94-95—Indiana | 81 | 2665 | 505 | 1092 | .462 | 383 | 427 | .897 | 30 | 180 | 210 | 242 | 98 | 16 | 151 | 1588 | 2.6 | 3.0 | 19.6 |
| 95-96—Indiana | 76 | 2621 | 504 | 1066 | .473 | 430 | 498 | .863 | 38 | 176 | 214 | 253 | 77 | 13 | 189 | 1606 | 2.8 | 3.3 | 21.1 |
| 96-97—Indiana | 81 | 2966 | 552 | 1244 | .444 | 418 | 475 | .880 | 53 | 233 | 286 | 273 | 75 | 25 | 166 | 1751 | 3.5 | 3.4 | 21.6 |
| 97-98—Indiana | 81 | 2795 | 516 | 1081 | .477 | 382 | 440 | .868 | 46 | 186 | 232 | 171 | 78 | 11 | 128 | 1578 | 2.9 | 2.1 | 19.5 |
| 98-99—Indiana | 50 | 1787 | 294 | 671 | .438 | 226 | 247 | *.915 | 25 | 110 | 135 | 112 | 37 | 9 | 76 | 920 | 2.7 | 2.2 | 18.4 |
| 99-00—Indiana | 81 | 2987 | 466 | 1041 | .448 | 373 | 406 | .919 | 50 | 189 | 239 | 187 | 85 | 25 | 129 | 1470 | 3.0 | 2.3 | 18.1 |
| 00-01—Indiana | 81 | 3181 | 517 | 1176 | .440 | 323 | 348 | *.928 | 38 | 247 | 285 | 260 | 81 | 15 | 133 | 1527 | 3.5 | 3.2 | 18.9 |
| 01-02—Indiana | 79 | 2889 | 414 | 913 | .453 | 296 | 325 | *.911 | 23 | 196 | 219 | 253 | 88 | 10 | 120 | 1304 | 2.8 | 3.2 | 16.5 |
| 02-03—Indiana | 70 | 2117 | 281 | 637 | .441 | 207 | 230 | .900 | 21 | 151 | 172 | 170 | 62 | 4 | 66 | 882 | 2.5 | 2.4 | 12.6 |
| 03-04—Indiana | 80 | 2254 | 260 | 594 | .438 | 146 | 165 | .885 | 18 | 170 | 188 | 249 | 65 | 11 | 68 | 800 | 2.4 | 3.1 | 10.0 |
| 04-05—Indiana | 66 | 2105 | 314 | 719 | .437 | 250 | 268 | .933 | 18 | 138 | 156 | 146 | 50 | 5 | 77 | 974 | 2.4 | 2.2 | 14.8 |
| **Totals** | 1389 | 47619 | 8241 | 17499 | .471 | 6237 | 7026 | .888 | 883 | 3299 | 4182 | 4141 | 1505 | 299 | 2409 | 25279 | 3.0 | 3.0 | 18.2 |

Three-point field goals: 1987-88, 61-for-172 (.355). 1988-89, 98-for-244 (.402). 1989-90, 150-for-362 (.414). 1990-91, 112-for-322 (.348). 1991-92, 129-for-341 (.378). 1992-93, 167-for-419 (.399). 1993-94, 123-for-242 (.421). 1994-95, 195-for-470 (.415). 1995-96, 168-for-410 (.410). 1996-97, 229-for-536 (.427). 1997-98, 164-for-382 (.429). 1998-99, 106-for-275 (.385). 1999-00, 165-for-404 (.408). 2000-01, 170-for-464 (.366). 2001-02, 180-for-439 (.406). 2002-03, 113-for-318 (.355). 2003-04, 134-for-334 (.401). 2004-05, 96-for-298 (.322). Totals, 2560-for-6486 (.395).

Personal fouls/disqualifications: 1987-88, 157/0. 1988-89, 170/2. 1989-90, 175/1. 1990-91, 165/1. 1991-92, 210/1. 1992-93, 182/0. 1993-94, 193/2.

M

1994-95, 157/0. 1995-96, 175/0. 1996-97, 172/1. 1997-98, 148/2. 1998-99, 101/1. 1999-00, 126/0. 2000-01, 162/0. 2001-02, 143/0. 2002-03, 89/0. 2003-04, 96/0. 2004-05, 109/0. Totals, 2730/11.

## NBA PLAYOFF RECORD

| | | | | | | | | | REBOUNDS | | | | | | | | AVERAGES | | |
|---|---|---|---|---|---|---|---|---|---|---|---|---|---|---|---|---|---|---|---|
| Season Team | G | Min. | FGM | FGA | Pct. | FTM | FTA | Pct. | Off. | Def. | Tot. | Ast. | St. | Blk. | TO | Pts. | RPG | APG | PPG |
| 89-90—Indiana | 3 | 125 | 20 | 35 | .571 | 19 | 21 | .905 | 1 | 11 | 12 | 6 | 3 | 0 | 3 | 62 | 4.0 | 2.0 | 20.7 |
| 90-91—Indiana | 5 | 193 | 34 | 70 | .486 | 32 | 37 | .865 | 5 | 11 | 16 | 14 | 8 | 2 | 12 | 108 | 3.2 | 2.8 | 21.6 |
| 91-92—Indiana | 3 | 130 | 25 | 43 | .581 | 24 | 30 | .800 | 4 | 3 | 7 | 14 | 4 | 0 | 4 | 81 | 2.3 | 4.7 | 27.0 |
| 92-93—Indiana | 4 | 175 | 40 | 75 | .533 | 36 | 38 | .947 | 4 | 8 | 12 | 11 | 3 | 0 | 10 | 126 | 3.0 | 2.8 | 31.5 |
| 93-94—Indiana | 16 | 576 | 121 | 270 | .448 | 94 | 112 | .839 | 11 | 37 | 48 | 46 | 21 | 4 | 32 | 371 | 3.0 | 2.9 | 23.2 |
| 94-95—Indiana | 17 | 641 | 138 | 290 | .476 | 104 | 121 | .860 | 9 | 52 | 61 | 36 | 15 | 4 | 39 | 434 | 3.6 | 2.1 | 25.5 |
| 95-96—Indiana | 1 | 31 | 7 | 17 | .412 | 13 | 15 | .867 | 1 | 0 | 1 | 1 | 1 | 0 | 0 | 29 | 1.0 | 1.0 | 29.0 |
| 97-98—Indiana | 16 | 628 | 98 | 230 | .426 | 85 | 94 | .904 | 5 | 23 | 28 | 32 | 19 | 3 | 27 | 319 | 1.8 | 2.0 | 19.9 |
| 98-99—Indiana | 13 | 481 | 79 | 199 | .397 | 77 | 86 | .895 | 13 | 38 | 51 | 34 | 9 | 3 | 21 | 263 | 3.9 | 2.6 | 20.2 |
| 99-00—Indiana | 22 | 892 | 174 | 385 | .452 | 121 | 129 | .938 | 9 | 44 | 53 | 60 | 23 | 10 | 28 | 527 | 2.4 | 2.7 | 24.0 |
| 00-01—Indiana | 4 | 177 | 41 | 90 | .456 | 28 | 30 | .933 | 7 | 13 | 20 | 10 | 3 | 2 | 11 | 125 | 5.0 | 2.5 | 31.3 |
| 01-02—Indiana | 5 | 198 | 42 | 83 | .506 | 21 | 24 | .875 | 0 | 16 | 16 | 14 | 8 | 1 | 14 | 118 | 3.2 | 2.8 | 23.6 |
| 02-03—Indiana | 6 | 176 | 15 | 53 | .283 | 21 | 23 | .913 | 1 | 13 | 14 | 14 | 1 | 1 | 7 | 55 | 2.3 | 2.3 | 9.2 |
| 03-04—Indiana | 16 | 455 | 45 | 112 | .402 | 47 | 51 | .922 | 3 | 34 | 37 | 45 | 18 | 3 | 28 | 161 | 2.3 | 2.8 | 10.1 |
| 04-05—Indiana | 13 | 430 | 62 | 143 | .434 | 48 | 51 | .941 | 4 | 36 | 40 | 20 | 10 | 1 | 21 | 193 | 3.1 | 1.5 | 14.8 |
| **Totals** | 144 | 5308 | 941 | 2095 | .449 | 770 | 862 | .893 | 77 | 339 | 416 | 357 | 146 | 34 | 257 | 2972 | 2.9 | 2.5 | 20.6 |

Three-point field goals: 1989-90, 3-for-7 (.429). 1990-91, 8-for-19 (.421). 1991-92, 7-for-11 (.636). 1992-93, 10-for-19 (.526). 1993-94, 35-for-83 (.422). 1994-95, 54-for-128 (.422). 1995-96, 2-for-6 (.333). 1997-98, 38-for-95 (.400). 1998-99, 28-for-84 (.333). 1999-00, 58-for-147 (.395). 2000-01, 15-for-35 (.429). 2001-02, 13-for-31 (.419). 2002-03, 4-for-25 (.160). 2003-04, 24-for-64 (.375). 2004-05, 21-for-66 (.318). Totals, 320-for-820 (.390).

Personal fouls/disqualifications: 1989-90, 6/0. 1990-91, 14/0. 1991-92, 12/1. 1992-93, 11/0. 1993-94, 34/0. 1994-95, 35/0. 1995-96, 1/0. 1997-98, 26/0. 1998-99, 26/0. 1999-00, 37/0. 2000-01, 3/0. 2001-02, 10/0. 2002-03, 9/0. 2003-04, 23/0. 2004-05, 28/0. Totals, 275/1.

## NBA ALL-STAR GAME RECORD

| | | | | | | | | REBOUNDS | | | | | | | | |
|---|---|---|---|---|---|---|---|---|---|---|---|---|---|---|---|---|
| Season Team | Min. | FGM | FGA | Pct. | FTM | FTA | Pct. | Off. | Def. | Tot. | Ast. | PF | Dq. | St. | Blk. | TO | Pts. |
| 1990—Indiana | 14 | 2 | 3 | .667 | 0 | 0 | ... | 0 | 1 | 1 | 3 | 1 | 0 | 1 | 0 | 0 | 4 |
| 1995—Indiana | 23 | 3 | 9 | .333 | 0 | 0 | ... | 0 | 0 | 0 | 2 | 0 | 0 | 1 | 1 | 1 | 9 |
| 1996—Indiana | 18 | 4 | 8 | .500 | 0 | 0 | ... | 0 | 0 | 2 | 2 | 2 | 0 | 1 | 0 | 1 | 8 |
| 1998—Indiana | 20 | 6 | 8 | .750 | 1 | 2 | .500 | 0 | 0 | 0 | 0 | 2 | ... | 1 | 0 | 0 | 14 |
| 2000—Indiana | 21 | 1 | 7 | .143 | 2 | 2 | 1.000 | 0 | 2 | 2 | 3 | 1 | 0 | 1 | 0 | 1 | 5 |
| **Totals** | 96 | 16 | 35 | .457 | 3 | 4 | .750 | 0 | 3 | 5 | 10 | 6 | 0 | 5 | 1 | 3 | 40 |

Three-point field goals: 1990, 0-for-1. 1995, 3-for-6 (.500). 1996, 0-for-4. 1998, 1-for-2 (.500). 2000, 1-for-6 (.167). Totals, 5-for-19 (.263).

---

# MOBLEY, CUTTINO           G           CLIPPERS

**PERSONAL:** Born September 1, 1975, in Philadelphia. ... 6-4/210. (1.93/95.3). ... Full name: Cuttino Rashawn Mobley **HIGH SCHOOL:** Cardinal Dougherty (Philadelphia), then Maine Central Institute (Pittsfield, Maine).
**COLLEGE:** Rhode Island.
**TRANSACTIONS/CAREER NOTES:** Selected by Houston Rockets in second round (41st pick overall) of 1998 NBA Draft. ... Traded by Rockets with G Steve Francis and C Kelvin Cato to Orlando Magic for G Tracy McGrady, F Juwan Howard, G Tyronn Lue and G Reece Gaines (June 29, 2004). ... Traded by Magic with F Michael Bradley to Sacramento Kings for G/F Doug Christie (January 10, 2005). ... Signed as free agent by Los Angeles Clippers (August 3, 2005).

M

## COLLEGIATE RECORD

**NOTES:** Granted medical redshirt (1995-96).

| | | | | | | | | | | | | AVERAGES | | |
|---|---|---|---|---|---|---|---|---|---|---|---|---|---|---|
| Season Team | G | Min. | FGM | FGA | Pct. | FTM | FTA | Pct. | Reb. | Ast. | Pts. | RPG | APG | PPG |
| 93-94—Rhode Island | | | | | | Did not play—ineligible. | | | | | | | | |
| 94-95—Rhode Island | 27 | 864 | 126 | 334 | .377 | 63 | 81 | .778 | 129 | 39 | 358 | 4.8 | 1.4 | 13.3 |
| 95-96—Rhode Island | 2 | 35 | 9 | 14 | .643 | 1 | 2 | .500 | 0 | 5 | 24 | 0.0 | 2.5 | 12.0 |
| 96-97—Rhode Island | 30 | 730 | 138 | 315 | .438 | 61 | 76 | .803 | 117 | 44 | 366 | 3.9 | 1.5 | 12.2 |
| 97-98—Rhode Island | 34 | 1133 | 193 | 402 | .480 | 131 | 153 | .856 | 147 | 88 | 586 | 4.3 | 2.6 | 17.2 |
| **Totals** | 93 | 2762 | 466 | 1065 | .438 | 256 | 312 | .821 | 393 | 176 | 1334 | 4.2 | 1.9 | 14.3 |

Three-point field goals: 1994-95, 43-for-142 (.303). 1995-96, 5-for-7 (.714). 1996-97, 29-for-97 (.299). 1997-98, 69-for-166 (.416). Totals, 146-for-412 (.354).

## NBA REGULAR-SEASON RECORD

**HONORS:** NBA All-Rookie second team (1999).

| | | | | | | | | | REBOUNDS | | | | | | | | AVERAGES | | |
|---|---|---|---|---|---|---|---|---|---|---|---|---|---|---|---|---|---|---|---|
| Season Team | G | Min. | FGM | FGA | Pct. | FTM | FTA | Pct. | Off. | Def. | Tot. | Ast. | St. | Blk. | TO | Pts. | RPG | APG | PPG |
| 98-99—Houston | 49 | 1456 | 172 | 405 | .425 | 90 | 110 | .818 | 22 | 89 | 111 | 121 | 44 | 23 | 79 | 487 | 2.3 | 2.5 | 9.9 |
| 99-00—Houston | 81 | 2496 | 437 | 1016 | .430 | 299 | 353 | .847 | 59 | 229 | 288 | 208 | 87 | 32 | 186 | 1277 | 3.6 | 2.6 | 15.8 |
| 00-01—Houston | 79 | 3002 | 527 | 1214 | .434 | 394 | 474 | .831 | 83 | 314 | 397 | 195 | 84 | 26 | 165 | 1538 | 5.0 | 2.5 | 19.5 |
| 01-02—Houston | 74 | 3116 | 595 | 1358 | .438 | 267 | 314 | .850 | 63 | 237 | 300 | 187 | 109 | 37 | 180 | 1606 | 4.1 | 2.5 | 21.7 |
| 02-03—Houston | 73 | 3044 | 463 | 1067 | .434 | 242 | 282 | .858 | 70 | 233 | 303 | 208 | 95 | 36 | 166 | 1280 | 4.2 | 2.8 | 17.5 |
| 03-04—Houston | 80 | 3229 | 460 | 1081 | .426 | 176 | 217 | .811 | 40 | 322 | 362 | 258 | 107 | 33 | 180 | 1260 | 4.5 | 3.2 | 15.8 |
| 04-05—Orlando-Sac.... | 66 | 2388 | 408 | 932 | .438 | 168 | 205 | .820 | 45 | 184 | 229 | 188 | 74 | 30 | 133 | 1134 | 3.5 | 2.8 | 17.2 |
| **Totals** | 502 | 18731 | 3062 | 7073 | .433 | 1636 | 1955 | .837 | 382 | 1608 | 1990 | 1365 | 600 | 217 | 1089 | 8582 | 4.0 | 2.7 | 17.1 |

Three-point field goals: 1998-99, 53-for-148 (.358). 1999-00, 104-for-292 (.356). 2000-01, 90-for-252 (.357). 2001-02, 149-for-377 (.395). 2002-03, 112-for-318 (.352). 2003-04, 164-for-420 (.390). 2004-05, 150-for-342 (.439). Totals, 822-for-2149 (.383).

Personal fouls/disqualifications: 1998-99, 98/0. 1999-00, 171/0. 2000-01, 169/1. 2001-02, 189/3. 2002-03, 185/0. 2003-04, 179/0. 2004-05, 152/1. Totals, 1143/5.

## NBA PLAYOFF RECORD

| | | | | | | | | | REBOUNDS | | | | | | | | AVERAGES | | |
|---|---|---|---|---|---|---|---|---|---|---|---|---|---|---|---|---|---|---|---|
| Season Team | G | Min. | FGM | FGA | Pct. | FTM | FTA | Pct. | Off. | Def. | Tot. | Ast. | St. | Blk. | TO | Pts. | RPG | APG | PPG |
| 98-99—Houston | 4 | 94 | 7 | 15 | .467 | 10 | 11 | .909 | 0 | 4 | 4 | 11 | 2 | 0 | 5 | 28 | 1.0 | 2.8 | 7.0 |

| Season Team | G | Min. | FGM | FGA | Pct. | FTM | FTA | Pct. | REBOUNDS Off. | Def. | Tot. | Ast. | St. | Blk. | TO | Pts. | AVERAGES RPG | APG | PPG |
|---|---|---|---|---|---|---|---|---|---|---|---|---|---|---|---|---|---|---|---|
| 03-04—Houston | 5 | 210 | 29 | 75 | .387 | 8 | 10 | .800 | 5 | 19 | 24 | 14 | 3 | 3 | 18 | 72 | 4.8 | 2.8 | 14.4 |
| 04-05—Sacramento | 5 | 159 | 31 | 70 | .443 | 5 | 7 | .714 | 4 | 10 | 14 | 9 | 6 | 2 | 6 | 74 | 2.8 | 1.8 | 14.8 |
| Totals | 14 | 463 | 67 | 160 | .419 | 23 | 28 | .821 | 9 | 33 | 42 | 34 | 11 | 5 | 29 | 174 | 3.0 | 2.4 | 12.4 |

Three-point field goals: 1998-99, 4-for-7 (.571). 2003-04, 6-for-21 (.286). 2004-05, 7-for-25 (.280). Totals, 17-for-53 (.321).
Personal fouls/disqualifications: 1998-99, 11/0. 2003-04, 14/0. 2004-05, 13/0. Totals, 38/0.

## MOHAMMED, NAZR          C          SPURS

**PERSONAL:** Born September 5, 1977, in Chicago. ... 6-10/250. (2.08/113.4). ... Full name: Nazr Tahiru Mohammed ... Name pronounced NAH-zee.
**HIGH SCHOOL:** Kenwood (Chicago).
**COLLEGE:** Kentucky.
**TRANSACTIONS/CAREER NOTES:** Selected after junior season by Utah Jazz in first round (29th pick overall) of 1998 NBA Draft. ... Draft rights traded by Jazz to Philadelphia 76ers for future first-round draft choice (June 24, 1998). ... Traded by 76ers with F/C Theo Ratliff, F/G Toni Kukoc and G Pepe Sanchez to Atlanta Hawks for C Dikembe Mutombo and F Roshown McLeod (February 22, 2001). ... Traded by Hawks to New York Knicks in three-team trade in which Hawks acquired C Joel Przybilla from Milwaukee Bucks and C Michael Doleac and 2005 second-round draft choice from New York Knicks. Knicks acquired F Tim Thomas from Bucks and traded F Keith Van Horn to Bucks (February 15, 2004). ... Traded by Knicks with G Jamison Brewer to San Antonio Spurs for F Malik Rose and conditional first-round picks in 2005 and 2006 NBA drafts (February 24, 2005).
**MISCELLANEOUS:** Member of NBA championship team (2005).

### COLLEGIATE RECORD
**NOTES:** Member of NCAA Division I championship team (1996, 1998).

| Season Team | G | Min. | FGM | FGA | Pct. | FTM | FTA | Pct. | Reb. | Ast. | Pts. | AVERAGES RPG | APG | PPG |
|---|---|---|---|---|---|---|---|---|---|---|---|---|---|---|
| 95-96—Kentucky | 16 | 88 | 13 | 29 | .448 | 11 | 24 | .458 | 24 | 3 | 37 | 1.5 | 0.2 | 2.3 |
| 96-97—Kentucky | 39 | 617 | 132 | 259 | .510 | 45 | 89 | .506 | 226 | 12 | 309 | 5.8 | 0.3 | 7.9 |
| 97-98—Kentucky | 39 | 819 | 190 | 318 | .597 | 88 | 135 | .652 | 282 | 28 | 468 | 7.2 | 0.7 | 12.0 |
| Totals | 94 | 1524 | 335 | 606 | .553 | 144 | 248 | .581 | 532 | 43 | 814 | 5.7 | 0.5 | 8.7 |

Three-point field goals: 1996-97, 0-for-2. Totals, 0-for-2 (.000).

### NBA REGULAR-SEASON RECORD

| Season Team | G | Min. | FGM | FGA | Pct. | FTM | FTA | Pct. | REBOUNDS Off. | Def. | Tot. | Ast. | St. | Blk. | TO | Pts. | AVERAGES RPG | APG | PPG |
|---|---|---|---|---|---|---|---|---|---|---|---|---|---|---|---|---|---|---|---|
| 98-99—Philadelphia | 26 | 121 | 15 | 42 | .357 | 12 | 21 | .571 | 18 | 19 | 37 | 2 | 5 | 4 | 12 | 42 | 1.4 | 0.1 | 1.6 |
| 99-00—Philadelphia | 28 | 190 | 21 | 54 | .389 | 12 | 22 | .545 | 16 | 34 | 50 | 2 | 4 | 12 | 18 | 54 | 1.8 | 0.1 | 1.9 |
| 00-01—Phila.-Atlanta | 58 | 912 | 176 | 369 | .477 | 89 | 126 | .706 | 115 | 192 | 307 | 19 | 29 | 35 | 64 | 441 | 5.3 | 0.3 | 7.6 |
| 01-02—Atlanta | 82 | 2168 | 329 | 713 | .461 | 137 | 222 | .617 | 242 | 409 | 651 | 33 | 63 | 61 | 118 | 795 | 7.9 | 0.4 | 9.7 |
| 02-03—Atlanta | 35 | 445 | 67 | 159 | .421 | 26 | 41 | .634 | 47 | 82 | 129 | 6 | 16 | 21 | 25 | 160 | 3.7 | 0.2 | 4.6 |
| 03-04—Atlanta-N.Y. | 80 | 1611 | 246 | 472 | .521 | 100 | 169 | .592 | 178 | 296 | 474 | 36 | 55 | 52 | 96 | 592 | 5.9 | 0.5 | 7.4 |
| 04-05—N.Y.-San Antonio | 77 | 1933 | 289 | 602 | .480 | 153 | 227 | .674 | 247 | 339 | 586 | 34 | 58 | 86 | 108 | 731 | 7.6 | 0.4 | 9.5 |
| Totals | 386 | 7380 | 1143 | 2411 | .474 | 529 | 828 | .639 | 863 | 1371 | 2234 | 132 | 230 | 271 | 441 | 2815 | 5.8 | 0.3 | 7.3 |

Three-point field goals: 2000-01, 0-for-1. 2001-02, 0-for-1. 2004-05, 0-for-1. Totals, 0-for-3 (.000).
Personal fouls/disqualifications: 1998-99, 22/0. 1999-00, 29/0. 2000-01, 113/0. 2001-02, 252/2. 2002-03, 79/0. 2003-04, 195/1. 2004-05, 236/3. Totals, 926/6.

### NBA PLAYOFF RECORD

| Season Team | G | Min. | FGM | FGA | Pct. | FTM | FTA | Pct. | REBOUNDS Off. | Def. | Tot. | Ast. | St. | Blk. | TO | Pts. | AVERAGES RPG | APG | PPG |
|---|---|---|---|---|---|---|---|---|---|---|---|---|---|---|---|---|---|---|---|
| 98-99—Philadelphia | 3 | 3 | 0 | 0 | ... | 0 | 0 | ... | 0 | 0 | 0 | 0 | 0 | 0 | 0 | 0 | 0.0 | 0.0 | 0.0 |
| 03-04—New York | 4 | 97 | 15 | 30 | .500 | 11 | 16 | .688 | 10 | 13 | 23 | 1 | 6 | 3 | 7 | 41 | 5.8 | 0.3 | 10.3 |
| 04-05—San Antonio | 23 | 528 | 66 | 125 | .528 | 30 | 47 | .638 | 75 | 79 | 154 | 8 | 14 | 23 | 24 | 163 | 6.7 | 0.3 | 7.1 |
| Totals | 30 | 628 | 81 | 155 | .523 | 41 | 63 | .651 | 85 | 92 | 177 | 9 | 20 | 26 | 31 | 204 | 5.9 | 0.3 | 6.8 |

Three-point field goals: 2004-05, 1-for-1 (1.000). Totals, 1-for-1 (1.000).
Personal fouls/disqualifications: 2003-04, 18/1. 2004-05, 65/0. Totals, 83/1.

## MOISO, JEROME          F

**PERSONAL:** Born June 15, 1978, in Paris, France. ... 6-10/232. (2.08/105.2).
**HIGH SCHOOL:** INSEP (Paris, France), then Milford (Conn.) Academy.
**COLLEGE:** UCLA.
**TRANSACTIONS/CAREER NOTES:** Played in France (1994-97). ... Selected after sophomore season by Boston Celtics in first round (11th pick overall) of 2000 NBA Draft. ... Traded by Celtics to Philadelphia 76ers for F Roshown McLeod and conditional first-round draft choice (August 3, 2001). ... Traded by 76ers to Charlotte Hornets as part of three-way deal in which Hornets received F George Lynch and F/C Maurice Traylor from 76ers and F Chris Porter from Golden State Warriors, 76ers received F Derrick Coleman from Hornets and G Vonteego Cummings and F Corie Blount from Warriors, and Warriors received F Cedric Henderson and conditional 2005 first-round draft choice from 76ers and cash considerations from Hornets (October 25, 2001). ... Hornets franchise moved to New Orleans for 2002-03 season. ... Signed as free agent by Toronto Raptors (July 16, 2003) ... Signed as free agent by New Jersey Nets (December 28, 2004). ... Waived by Nets (January 3, 2005). ... Signed by Nets to first of two consecutive 10-day contracts (January 5, 2005). ... Signed by Cleveland Cavaliers to first of two consecutive 10-day contracts (February 1, 2005).

### FRENCH LEAGUE RECORD

| Season Team | G | Min. | FGM | FGA | Pct. | FTM | FTA | Pct. | Reb. | Ast. | Pts. | AVERAGES RPG | APG | PPG |
|---|---|---|---|---|---|---|---|---|---|---|---|---|---|---|
| 94-95—INSEP | 25 | ... | 101 | 179 | .564 | 33 | 61 | .541 | 175 | 22 | 235 | 7.0 | 0.9 | 9.4 |

M

| Season Team | G | Min. | FGM | FGA | Pct. | FTM | FTA | Pct. | Reb. | Ast. | Pts. | RPG | APG | PPG |
|---|---|---|---|---|---|---|---|---|---|---|---|---|---|---|
| | | | | | | | | | | | | **AVERAGES** | | |
| 95-96—INSEP | 27 | ... | 160 | 272 | .588 | 42 | 65 | .646 | 230 | 44 | 366 | 8.5 | 1.6 | 13.6 |
| 96-97—INSEP | 28 | ... | 198 | 371 | .534 | 94 | 130 | .723 | 286 | 65 | 493 | 10.2 | 2.3 | 17.6 |
| Totals | 80 | ... | 459 | 822 | .558 | 169 | 256 | .660 | 691 | 131 | 1094 | 8.6 | 1.6 | 13.7 |

Three-point field goals: 1994-95, 0-for-2. 1995-96, 4-for-6 (.667). 1996-97, 3-for-14 (.214). Totals, 7-for-22 (.318).

## COLLEGIATE RECORD

| Season Team | G | Min. | FGM | FGA | Pct. | FTM | FTA | Pct. | Reb. | Ast. | Pts. | RPG | APG | PPG |
|---|---|---|---|---|---|---|---|---|---|---|---|---|---|---|
| | | | | | | | | | | | | **AVERAGES** | | |
| 98-99—UCLA | 29 | 689 | 131 | 269 | .487 | 48 | 78 | .615 | 169 | 26 | 314 | 5.8 | 0.9 | 10.8 |
| 99-00—UCLA | 33 | 972 | 170 | 339 | .501 | 87 | 142 | .613 | 252 | 40 | 428 | 7.6 | 1.2 | 13.0 |
| Totals | 62 | 1661 | 301 | 608 | .495 | 135 | 220 | .614 | 421 | 66 | 742 | 6.8 | 1.1 | 12.0 |

Three-point field goals: 1998-99, 4-for-16 (.250). 1999-00, 1-for-6 (.167). Totals, 5-for-22 (.227).

## NBA REGULAR-SEASON RECORD

| Season Team | G | Min. | FGM | FGA | Pct. | FTM | FTA | Pct. | Off. | Def. | Tot. | Ast. | St. | Blk. | TO | Pts. | RPG | APG | PPG |
|---|---|---|---|---|---|---|---|---|---|---|---|---|---|---|---|---|---|---|---|
| | | | | | | | | | **REBOUNDS** | | | | | | | | **AVERAGES** | | |
| 00-01—Boston | 24 | 135 | 12 | 30 | .400 | 11 | 26 | .423 | 12 | 30 | 42 | 3 | 3 | 4 | 18 | 35 | 1.8 | 0.1 | 1.5 |
| 01-02—Charlotte | 15 | 76 | 8 | 20 | .400 | 0 | 0 | ... | 4 | 21 | 25 | 4 | 3 | 2 | 8 | 16 | 1.7 | 0.3 | 1.1 |
| 02-03—New Orleans | 51 | 644 | 89 | 171 | .520 | 27 | 41 | .659 | 59 | 119 | 178 | 22 | 19 | 44 | 46 | 205 | 3.5 | 0.4 | 4.0 |
| 03-04—Toronto | 35 | 417 | 40 | 84 | .476 | 22 | 38 | .579 | 41 | 72 | 113 | 8 | 17 | 12 | 25 | 102 | 3.2 | 0.2 | 2.9 |
| 04-05—Tor.-N.Y.-Cleve. | 20 | 120 | 9 | 18 | .500 | 10 | 13 | .769 | 10 | 27 | 37 | 1 | 3 | 6 | 7 | 28 | 1.9 | 0.1 | 1.4 |
| Totals | 145 | 1392 | 158 | 323 | .489 | 70 | 118 | .593 | 126 | 269 | 395 | 38 | 45 | 68 | 104 | 386 | 2.7 | 0.3 | 2.7 |

Three-point field goals: 2000-01, 0-for-1. 2003-04, 0-for-1. 2004-05, 0-for-1. Totals, 0-for-3 (.000).
Personal fouls/disqualifications: 2000-01, 29/0. 2001-02, 12/0. 2002-03, 87/1. 2003-04, 42/0. 2004-05, 13/0. Totals, 183/1.

## NBA PLAYOFF RECORD

| Season Team | G | Min. | FGM | FGA | Pct. | FTM | FTA | Pct. | Off. | Def. | Tot. | Ast. | St. | Blk. | TO | Pts. | RPG | APG | PPG |
|---|---|---|---|---|---|---|---|---|---|---|---|---|---|---|---|---|---|---|---|
| | | | | | | | | | **REBOUNDS** | | | | | | | | **AVERAGES** | | |
| 02-03—New Orleans | 4 | 60 | 10 | 16 | .625 | 3 | 4 | .750 | 8 | 8 | 16 | 5 | 0 | 7 | 4 | 23 | 4.0 | 1.3 | 5.8 |

Personal fouls/disqualifications: 2002-03, 9/0. Totals, 9/0.

---

# MOORE, MIKKI     C     SUPERSONICS

**PERSONAL:** Born November 4, 1975, in Orangeburg, S.C. ... 7-0/225. (2.13/102.1).
**HIGH SCHOOL:** Blackburg (Gaffney, S.C.).
**COLLEGE:** Nebraska.
**TRANSACTIONS/CAREER NOTES:** Not drafted by an NBA franchise. ... Signed as free agent by Minnesota Timberwolves (September 30, 1997). ... Waived by Timberwolves (October 28, 1997). ... Played in Continental Basketball Association with Fort Wayne Fury (1997-99). ... Played in Greece (1998-99). ... Signed as free agent by Minnesota Timberwolves (January 21, 1999). ... Waived by Timberwolves (January 27, 1999). ... Signed as free agent by Detroit Pistons (January 29, 1999). ... Waived by Pistons (February 18, 1999). ... Signed as free agent by Pistons (October 5, 1999). ... Waived by Pistons (August 5, 2002). ... Waived by Spurs (October 24, 2002). ... Played in NBDL with Roanoke Dazzle (2002-03). ... Signed by Boston Celtics to 10-day contract (January 6, 2003). ... Signed by Atlanta Hawks for remainder of season (April 14, 2003). ... Signed as free agent by Seattle SuperSonics (September 27, 2003). ... Waived by SuperSonics (October 21, 2003). ... Played in NBDL with Roanoke Dazzle (2003-04). ... Signed as free agent by New Jersey Nets (December 22, 2003). ... Waived by Nets (January 7, 2004). ... Signed by Utah Jazz to first of two consecutive 10-day contracts (January 28, 2004). ... Signed by Jazz for remainder of season (March 4, 2004). ... Signed as free agent by Los Angeles Clippers (August 20, 2004). ... Signed as free agent by Seattle SuperSonics (August 31, 2005).

## COLLEGIATE RECORD

| Season Team | G | Min. | FGM | FGA | Pct. | FTM | FTA | Pct. | Reb. | Ast. | Pts. | RPG | APG | PPG |
|---|---|---|---|---|---|---|---|---|---|---|---|---|---|---|
| | | | | | | | | | | | | **AVERAGES** | | |
| 93-94—Nebraska | 14 | 87 | 10 | 22 | .455 | 11 | 18 | .611 | 13 | 1 | 31 | 0.9 | 0.1 | 2.2 |
| 94-95—Nebraska | 32 | 788 | 102 | 205 | .498 | 49 | 89 | .551 | 198 | 25 | 255 | 6.2 | 0.8 | 8.0 |
| 95-96—Nebraska | 35 | 968 | 118 | 202 | .584 | 79 | 115 | .687 | 205 | 36 | 315 | 5.9 | 1.0 | 9.0 |
| 96-97—Nebraska | 33 | 1011 | 144 | 247 | .583 | 96 | 137 | .701 | 245 | 43 | 385 | 7.4 | 1.3 | 11.7 |
| Totals | 114 | 2854 | 374 | 676 | .553 | 235 | 359 | .655 | 661 | 105 | 986 | 5.8 | 0.9 | 8.6 |

Three-point field goals: 1993-94, 0-for-2. 1994-95, 2-for-8 (.250). 1996-97, 1-for-2 (.500). Totals, 3-for-12 (.250).
Personal fouls/disqualifications: 1993-94, 13/0. 1994-95, 94/0. 1995-96, 112/0. 1996-97, 105/0. Totals, 324/0.

## CBA RECORD

**NOTES:** CBA All-League first team (1999). ... CBA All-Defensive team (1999). ... CBA All-Rookie team (1998).

| Season Team | G | Min. | FGM | FGA | Pct. | FTM | FTA | Pct. | Reb. | Ast. | Pts. | RPG | APG | PPG |
|---|---|---|---|---|---|---|---|---|---|---|---|---|---|---|
| | | | | | | | | | | | | **AVERAGES** | | |
| 97-98—Fort Wayne | 55 | 1478 | 262 | 450 | .582 | 122 | 174 | .701 | 346 | 60 | 647 | 6.3 | 1.1 | 11.8 |
| 98-99—Fort Wayne | 29 | 1026 | 156 | 277 | *.563 | 143 | 195 | .733 | 219 | 41 | 455 | 7.6 | 1.4 | 15.7 |
| Totals | 84 | 2504 | 418 | 727 | .575 | 265 | 369 | .718 | 565 | 101 | 1102 | 6.7 | 1.2 | 13.1 |

Three-point field goals: 1997-98, 1-for-9 (.111). Totals, 1-for-9 (.111).
Personal fouls/disqualifications: 1997-98, 190/0. 1998-99, 98/0. Totals, 288/0.

## GREEK LEAGUE RECORD

| Season Team | G | Min. | FGM | FGA | Pct. | FTM | FTA | Pct. | Reb. | Ast. | Pts. | RPG | APG | PPG |
|---|---|---|---|---|---|---|---|---|---|---|---|---|---|---|
| | | | | | | | | | | | | **AVERAGES** | | |
| 98-99—Papagou | 9 | 283 | 39 | 71 | .549 | 22 | 29 | .759 | 78 | 8 | 106 | 8.7 | 0.9 | 11.8 |

Three-point field goals: 1998-99, 6-for-12 (.500). Totals, 6-for-12 (.500).

## NBA REGULAR-SEASON RECORD

| Season Team | G | Min. | FGM | FGA | Pct. | FTM | FTA | Pct. | Off. | Def. | Tot. | Ast. | St. | Blk. | TO | Pts. | RPG | APG | PPG |
|---|---|---|---|---|---|---|---|---|---|---|---|---|---|---|---|---|---|---|---|
| | | | | | | | | | **REBOUNDS** | | | | | | | | **AVERAGES** | | |

| 98-99—Detroit ........... | 2 | 6 | 1 | 1 | 1.000 | 2 | 2 | 1.000 | 0 | 1 | 1 | 0 | 0 | 0 | 0 | 4 | 0.5 | 0.0 | 2.0 |

| | | | | | | | | | | REBOUNDS | | | | | | | | AVERAGES | |
| Season Team | G | Min. | FGM | FGA | Pct. | FTM | FTA | Pct. | Off. | Def. | Tot. | Ast. | St. | Blk. | TO | Pts. | RPG | APG | PPG |
|---|---|---|---|---|---|---|---|---|---|---|---|---|---|---|---|---|---|---|---|
| 99-00—Detroit ........... | 29 | 488 | 87 | 140 | .621 | 54 | 68 | .794 | 44 | 68 | 112 | 17 | 9 | 31 | 23 | 228 | 3.9 | 0.6 | 7.9 |
| 00-01—Detroit ........... | 81 | 1154 | 132 | 268 | .493 | 95 | 130 | .731 | 121 | 195 | 316 | 33 | 24 | 61 | 74 | 359 | 3.9 | 0.4 | 4.4 |
| 01-02—Detroit ........... | 30 | 217 | 29 | 61 | .475 | 20 | 26 | .769 | 22 | 31 | 53 | 11 | 7 | 9 | 14 | 79 | 1.8 | 0.4 | 2.6 |
| 02-03—Bos-Atl .......... | 8 | 43 | 5 | 13 | .385 | 8 | 10 | .800 | 6 | 2 | 8 | 3 | 0 | 4 | 2 | 18 | 1.0 | 0.4 | 2.3 |
| 03-04—N.J.-Utah ....... | 32 | 395 | 50 | 99 | .505 | 30 | 35 | .857 | 29 | 55 | 84 | 19 | 7 | 13 | 22 | 130 | 2.6 | 0.6 | 4.1 |
| 04-05—L.A. Clippers... | 74 | 1178 | 144 | 287 | .502 | 107 | 136 | .787 | 97 | 149 | 246 | 47 | 19 | 32 | 63 | 396 | 3.3 | 0.6 | 5.4 |
| Totals .................... | 256 | 3481 | 448 | 869 | .516 | 316 | 407 | .776 | 319 | 501 | 820 | 130 | 66 | 150 | 198 | 1214 | 3.2 | 0.5 | 4.7 |

Three-point field goals: 2000-01, 0-for-1. 2001-02, 1-for-2 (.500). 2004-05, 1-for-5 (.200). Totals, 2-for-8 (.250).

Personal fouls/disqualifications: 1999-00, 104/5. 2000-01, 35/0. 2001-02, 7/0. 2002-03, 65/1. 2004-05, 173/1. Totals, 586/9.

## NBA PLAYOFF RECORD

| | | | | | | | | | | REBOUNDS | | | | | | | AVERAGES | | |
| Season Team | G | Min. | FGM | FGA | Pct. | FTM | FTA | Pct. | Off. | Def. | Tot. | Ast. | St. | Blk. | TO | Pts. | RPG | APG | PPG |
|---|---|---|---|---|---|---|---|---|---|---|---|---|---|---|---|---|---|---|---|
| 99-00—Detroit ........... | 3 | 42 | 5 | 12 | .417 | 8 | 8 | 1.000 | 7 | 5 | 12 | 3 | 1 | 0 | 4 | 18 | 4.0 | 1.0 | 6.0 |

Personal fouls/disqualifications: 1999-00, 9/0. Totals, 9/0.

## NBDL RECORD

| | | | | | | | | | | | | AVERAGES | | |
| Season Team | G | Min. | FGM | FGA | Pct. | FTM | FTA | Pct. | Reb. | Ast. | Pts. | RPG | APG | PPG |
|---|---|---|---|---|---|---|---|---|---|---|---|---|---|---|
| 02-03—Roanoke ........................ | 42 | 1409 | 252 | 477 | .528 | 164 | 218 | .752 | 352 | 104 | 674 | 8.4 | 2.5 | 16.0 |
| 03-04—Roanoke ........................ | 17 | 687 | 122 | 226 | .540 | 101 | 132 | .765 | 152 | 48 | 347 | 8.9 | 2.8 | 20.4 |
| Totals ..................................... | 59 | 2096 | 374 | 703 | .532 | 265 | 350 | .757 | 504 | 152 | 1021 | 8.5 | 2.6 | 17.3 |

Three-point field goals: 2002-03, 6-for-24 (.250). Totals, 6-for-24 (.250).

Personal fouls/disqualifications: 2002-03, 162/0. Totals, 162/0.

# MOURNING, ALONZO      C      HEAT

**PERSONAL:** Born February 8, 1970, in Chesapeake, Va. ... 6-10/261. (2.08/118.4).

**HIGH SCHOOL:** Indian River (Chesapeake, Va.).

**COLLEGE:** Georgetown.

**TRANSACTIONS/CAREER NOTES:** Selected by Charlotte Hornets in first round (second pick overall) of 1992 NBA Draft. ... Traded by Hornets with C LeRon Ellis and G Pete Myers to Miami Heat for G/F Glen Rice, G Khalid Reeves, C Matt Geiger and 1996 first-round draft choice (November 3, 1995). ... Signed as free agent by New Jersey Nets (July 16, 2003). ... Traded by Nets with F Eric Williams and F Aaron Williams and two first-round picks in the 2005 draft to Toronto Raptors for Vince Carter (December 17, 2004). ... Waived by Raptors (February 11, 2005). ... Signed as free agent by Miami Heat (March 1, 2005).

**MISCELLANEOUS:** Member of gold-medal-winning U.S. Olympic team (2000). ... Member of bronze-medal-winning U.S. World Championship team (1990) and gold-medal-winning U.S. World Championship team (1994). ... Charlotte Hornets all-time blocked shots leader with 684 (1992-93 through 1994-95). ... Miami Heat all-time blocked shots leader with 1,199 (1995-96 through 2001-02).

## COLLEGIATE RECORD

**NOTES:** THE SPORTING NEWS All-America second team (1990, 1992). ... Led NCAA Division I with 4.97 blocked shots per game (1989). ... Led NCAA Division I in blocked shots with 169 (1989) and 160 (1992).

| | | | | | | | | | | | | AVERAGES | | |
| Season Team | G | Min. | FGM | FGA | Pct. | FTM | FTA | Pct. | Reb. | Ast. | Pts. | RPG | APG | PPG |
|---|---|---|---|---|---|---|---|---|---|---|---|---|---|---|
| 88-89—Georgetown................... | 34 | 962 | 158 | 262 | .603 | 130 | 195 | .667 | 248 | 24 | 447 | 7.3 | 0.7 | 13.1 |
| 89-90—Georgetown................... | 31 | 937 | 145 | 276 | .525 | 220 | 281 | .783 | 265 | 36 | 510 | 8.5 | 1.2 | 16.5 |
| 90-91—Georgetown................... | 23 | 682 | 105 | 201 | .522 | 149 | 188 | .793 | 176 | 25 | 363 | 7.7 | 1.1 | 15.8 |
| 91-92—Georgetown................... | 32 | 1051 | 204 | 343 | .595 | 272 | 359 | .758 | 343 | 53 | 681 | 10.7 | 1.7 | 21.3 |
| Totals ..................................... | 120 | 3632 | 612 | 1082 | .566 | 771 | 1023 | .754 | 1032 | 138 | 2001 | 8.6 | 1.2 | 16.7 |

Three-point field goals: 1988-89, 1-for-4 (.250). 1989-90, 0-for-2. 1990-91, 4-for-13 (.308). 1991-92, 6-for-23 (.261). Totals, 11-for-42 (.262).

## NBA REGULAR-SEASON RECORD

**HONORS:** J. Walter Kennedy Citizenship Award (2002). ... NBA Defensive Player of the Year (1999, 2000). ... All-NBA first team (1999). ... All-NBA second team (2000). ... NBA All-Defensive first team (1999, 2000). ... NBA All-Rookie first team (1993).

**NOTES:** Led NBA with 3.91 blocked shots per game (1999) and 3.7 blocks per game (2000).

| | | | | | | | | | | REBOUNDS | | | | | | | AVERAGES | | |
| Season Team | G | Min. | FGM | FGA | Pct. | FTM | FTA | Pct. | Off. | Def. | Tot. | Ast. | St. | Blk. | TO | Pts. | RPG | APG | PPG |
|---|---|---|---|---|---|---|---|---|---|---|---|---|---|---|---|---|---|---|---|
| 92-93—Charlotte ........ | 78 | 2644 | 572 | 1119 | .511 | 495 | 634 | .781 | 263 | 542 | 805 | 76 | 27 | 271 | 236 | 1639 | 10.3 | 1.0 | 21.0 |
| 93-94—Charlotte ........ | 60 | 2018 | 427 | 845 | .505 | 433 | 568 | .762 | 177 | 433 | 610 | 86 | 27 | 188 | 199 | 1287 | 10.2 | 1.4 | 21.5 |
| 94-95—Charlotte ........ | 77 | 2941 | 571 | 1101 | .519 | 490 | 644 | .761 | 200 | 561 | 761 | 111 | 49 | 225 | 241 | 1643 | 9.9 | 1.4 | 21.3 |
| 95-96—Miami ............ | 70 | 2671 | 563 | 1076 | .523 | 488 | 712 | .685 | 218 | 509 | 727 | 159 | 70 | 189 | 262 | 1623 | 10.4 | 2.3 | 23.2 |
| 96-97—Miami ............ | 66 | 2320 | 473 | 885 | .534 | 363 | 565 | .642 | 189 | 467 | 656 | 104 | 56 | 189 | 226 | 1310 | 9.9 | 1.6 | 19.8 |
| 97-98—Miami ............ | 58 | 1939 | 403 | 732 | .551 | 309 | 465 | .665 | 193 | 365 | 558 | 52 | 40 | 130 | 179 | 1115 | 9.6 | 0.9 | 19.2 |
| 98-99—Miami ............ | 46 | 1753 | 324 | 634 | .511 | 276 | 423 | .652 | 166 | 341 | 507 | 74 | 34 | *180 | 139 | 924 | 11.0 | 1.6 | 20.1 |
| 99-00—Miami ............ | 79 | 2748 | 652 | 1184 | .551 | 414 | 582 | .711 | 215 | 538 | 753 | 123 | 40 | *294 | 217 | 1718 | 9.5 | 1.6 | 21.7 |
| 00-01—Miami ............ | 13 | 306 | 73 | 141 | .518 | 31 | 55 | .564 | 15 | 66 | 101 | 12 | 4 | 31 | 28 | 177 | 7.8 | 0.9 | 13.6 |
| 01-02—Miami ............ | 75 | 2455 | 447 | 866 | .516 | 283 | 431 | .657 | 182 | 450 | 632 | 87 | 27 | 186 | 182 | 1178 | 8.4 | 1.2 | 15.7 |
| 02-03—Miami............. | | | | | | Did not play—injured | | | | | | | | | | | | | |
| 03-04—New Jersey ..... | 12 | 215 | 33 | 71 | .465 | 30 | 34 | .882 | 8 | 19 | 27 | 8 | 2 | 6 | 10 | 96 | 2.3 | 0.7 | 8.0 |
| 04-05—N.J.-Tor.-Miami | 37 | 702 | 100 | 212 | .472 | 82 | 141 | .582 | 53 | 145 | 198 | 18 | 8 | 74 | 57 | 282 | 5.4 | 0.5 | 7.6 |
| Totals ...... | 671 | 22712 | 4638 | 8866 | .523 | 3694 | 5254 | .703 | 1899 | 4436 | 6335 | 910 | 384 | 1963 | 1976 | 12992 | 9.4 | 1.4 | 19.4 |

Three-point field goals: 1992-93, 0-for-3. 1993-94, 0-for-2. 1994-95, 1-for-34 (.324). 1995-96, 9-for-30 (.300). 1996-97, 1-for-9 (.111). 1998-99, 0-for-2. 1999-00, 0-for-4. 2000-01, 0-for-1. 2001-02, 1-for-3 (.333). Totals, 22-for-88 (.250).

Personal fouls/disqualifications: 1992-93, 286/6. 1993-94, 207/3. 1994-95, 275/5. 1995-96, 245/5. 1996-97, 272/9. 1997-98, 208/4. 1998-99, 161/1. 1999-00, 308/8. 2000-01, 24/0. 2001-02, 258/7. 2003-04, 32/0. 2004-05, 82/1. Totals, 2358/49.

## NBA PLAYOFF RECORD

| Season Team | G | Min. | FGM | FGA | Pct. | FTM | FTA | Pct. | Off. | Def. | Tot. | Ast. | St. | Blk. | TO | Pts. | RPG | APG | PPG |
|---|---|---|---|---|---|---|---|---|---|---|---|---|---|---|---|---|---|---|---|
| | | | | | | | | | | REBOUNDS | | | | | | | | AVERAGES | |
| 92-93—Charlotte | 9 | 367 | 71 | 148 | .480 | 72 | 93 | .774 | 28 | 61 | 89 | 13 | 6 | 31 | 37 | 214 | 9.9 | 1.4 | 23.8 |
| 94-95—Charlotte | 4 | 174 | 24 | 57 | .421 | 36 | 43 | .837 | 14 | 39 | 53 | 11 | 3 | 13 | 14 | 88 | 13.3 | 2.8 | 22.0 |
| 95-96—Miami | 3 | 92 | 17 | 35 | .486 | 20 | 28 | .714 | 3 | 15 | 18 | 4 | 2 | 3 | 16 | 54 | 6.0 | 1.3 | 18.0 |
| 96-97—Miami | 17 | 630 | 107 | 218 | .491 | 86 | 155 | .555 | 44 | 129 | 173 | 18 | 11 | 46 | 70 | 303 | 10.2 | 1.1 | 17.8 |
| 97-98—Miami | 4 | 138 | 29 | 56 | .518 | 19 | 29 | .655 | 10 | 24 | 34 | 5 | 3 | 10 | 8 | 77 | 8.5 | 1.3 | 19.3 |
| 98-99—Miami | 5 | 194 | 38 | 73 | .521 | 32 | 49 | .653 | 7 | 34 | 41 | 4 | 8 | 14 | 12 | 108 | 8.2 | 0.8 | 21.6 |
| 99-00—Miami | 10 | 376 | 76 | 157 | .484 | 64 | 96 | .667 | 31 | 69 | 100 | 14 | 2 | 33 | 24 | 216 | 10.0 | 1.4 | 21.6 |
| 00-01—Miami | 3 | 91 | 12 | 25 | .480 | 11 | 19 | .579 | 3 | 13 | 16 | 3 | 0 | 5 | 5 | 35 | 5.3 | 1.0 | 11.7 |
| 04-05—Miami | 15 | 254 | 31 | 44 | .705 | 29 | 52 | .558 | 21 | 51 | 72 | 5 | 5 | 33 | 22 | 91 | 4.8 | 0.3 | 6.1 |
| Totals | 70 | 2316 | 405 | 813 | .498 | 369 | 564 | .654 | 161 | 435 | 596 | 77 | 40 | 188 | 208 | 1186 | 8.5 | 1.1 | 16.9 |

Three-point field goals: 1992-93, 0-for-2. 1994-95, 4-for-8 (.500). 1996-97, 3-for-8 (.375). 1999-00, 0-for-1. Totals, 7-for-19 (.368).
Personal fouls/disqualifications: 1992-93, 37/1. 1994-95, 17/0. 1995-96, 13/1. 1996-97, 73/2. 1997-98, 18/0. 1998-99, 19/0. 1999-00, 40/1. 2000-01, 9/0. 2004-05, 49/2. Totals, 275/7.

## NBA ALL-STAR GAME RECORD

| Season Team | Min. | FGM | FGA | Pct. | FTM | FTA | Pct. | Off. | Def. | Tot. | Ast. | PF | Dq. | St. | Blk. | TO | Pts. |
|---|---|---|---|---|---|---|---|---|---|---|---|---|---|---|---|---|---|
| | | | | | | | | | REBOUNDS | | | | | | | | |
| 1994—Charlotte | | | | | | | Selected, did not play—injured. | | | | | | | | | | |
| 1995—Charlotte | 19 | 4 | 9 | .444 | 2 | 3 | .667 | 0 | 8 | 8 | 1 | 5 | 0 | 0 | 1 | 1 | 10 |
| 1996—Miami | 13 | 1 | 6 | .167 | 0 | 0 | ... | 0 | 1 | 1 | 0 | 2 | 0 | 0 | 1 | 2 | 2 |
| 1997—Miami | | | | | | | Selected, did not play—injured. | | | | | | | | | | |
| 2000—Miami | 27 | 7 | 11 | .636 | 1 | 2 | .500 | 2 | 5 | 7 | 1 | 4 | 0 | 3 | 4 | 1 | 15 |
| 2001—Miami | | | | | | | Selected, did not play—injured. | | | | | | | | | | |
| 2002—Miami | 16 | 6 | 7 | .857 | 1 | 1 | 1.000 | 1 | 2 | 3 | 2 | 1 | 0 | 0 | 2 | 1 | 13 |
| Totals | 75 | 18 | 33 | .545 | 4 | 6 | .667 | 3 | 16 | 19 | 4 | 12 | 0 | 3 | 8 | 5 | 40 |

Three-point field goals: 1995, 0-for-1. Totals, 0-for-1 (.000).

# MURPHY, TROY    F    WARRIORS

**PERSONAL:** Born May 2, 1980, in Sparta, N.J. ... 6-11/245. (2.11/111.1). ... Full name: Troy Brandon Murphy
**HIGH SCHOOL:** Delbarton (Morristown, N.J.).
**COLLEGE:** Notre Dame.
**TRANSACTIONS/CAREER NOTES:** Selected after junior season by Golden State Warriors in first round (14th pick overall) of 2001 NBA Draft.

## COLLEGIATE RECORD

**NOTES:** The Sporting News All-America first team (2001). ... The Sporting News All-America second team (2000).

| Season Team | G | Min. | FGM | FGA | Pct. | FTM | FTA | Pct. | Reb. | Ast. | Pts. | RPG | APG | PPG |
|---|---|---|---|---|---|---|---|---|---|---|---|---|---|---|
| | | | | | | | | | | | | | AVERAGES | |
| 98-99—Notre Dame | 27 | 890 | 180 | 340 | .529 | 149 | 201 | .741 | 267 | 38 | 519 | 9.9 | 1.4 | 19.2 |
| 99-00—Notre Dame | 37 | 1318 | 274 | 557 | .492 | 261 | 323 | .808 | 380 | 58 | 839 | 10.3 | 1.6 | 22.7 |
| 00-01—Notre Dame | 30 | 1090 | 223 | 473 | .471 | 177 | 231 | .766 | 277 | 62 | 653 | 9.2 | 2.1 | 21.8 |
| Totals | 94 | 3298 | 677 | 1370 | .494 | 587 | 755 | .777 | 924 | 158 | 2011 | 9.8 | 1.7 | 21.4 |

Three-point field goals: 1998-99, 4-for-13 (.308). 1999-00, 30-for-92 (.326). 2000-01, 30-for-86 (.349). Totals, 64-for-191 (.335).
Personal fouls/disqualifications: 1998-99, 77/0. 1999-00, 101/0. 2000-01, 96/0. Totals, 274/0.

## NBA REGULAR-SEASON RECORD

| Season Team | G | Min. | FGM | FGA | Pct. | FTM | FTA | Pct. | Off. | Def. | Tot. | Ast. | St. | Blk. | TO | Pts. | RPG | APG | PPG |
|---|---|---|---|---|---|---|---|---|---|---|---|---|---|---|---|---|---|---|---|
| | | | | | | | | | | REBOUNDS | | | | | | | | AVERAGES | |
| 01-02—Golden State | 82 | 1448 | 178 | 423 | .421 | 121 | 156 | .776 | 99 | 223 | 322 | 70 | 36 | 21 | 84 | 480 | 3.9 | 0.9 | 5.9 |
| 02-03—Golden State | 79 | 2510 | 338 | 749 | .451 | 244 | 290 | .841 | 228 | 578 | 806 | 106 | 65 | 30 | 111 | 923 | 10.2 | 1.3 | 11.7 |
| 03-04—Golden State | 28 | 610 | 107 | 243 | .440 | 60 | 80 | .750 | 48 | 125 | 173 | 20 | 12 | 17 | 34 | 279 | 6.2 | 0.7 | 10.0 |
| 04-05—Golden State | 70 | 2375 | 392 | 947 | .414 | 233 | 319 | .730 | 251 | 505 | 756 | 97 | 53 | 33 | 108 | 1076 | 10.8 | 1.4 | 15.4 |
| Totals | 259 | 6943 | 1015 | 2362 | .430 | 658 | 845 | .779 | 626 | 1431 | 2057 | 293 | 166 | 101 | 337 | 2758 | 7.9 | 1.1 | 10.6 |

Three-point field goals: 2001-02, 3-for-9 (.333). 2002-03, 3-for-14 (.214). 2003-04, 5-for-17 (.294). 2004-05, 59-for-148 (.399). Totals, 70-for-188 (.372).
Personal fouls/disqualifications: 2001-02, 217/2. 2002-03, 246/1. 2003-04, 58/1. 2004-05, 190/2. Totals, 711/6.

# MURRAY, LAMOND    F

**PERSONAL:** Born April 20, 1973, in Pasadena, Calif. ... 6-7/236. (2.01/107.0). ... Full name: Lamond Maurice Murray ... Cousin of Tracy Murray, forward, Los Angeles Lakers.
**HIGH SCHOOL:** John Kennedy (Fremont, Calif.).
**COLLEGE:** California.
**TRANSACTIONS/CAREER NOTES:** Selected after junior season by Los Angeles Clippers in first round (seventh pick overall) of 1994 NBA Draft. ... Traded by Clippers to Cleveland Cavaliers for G Derek Anderson and F Johnny Newman (August 4, 1999). ... Traded by Cavaliers with future second-round draft choice to Toronto Raptors for C Michael Stewart and future first-round draft choice (September 25, 2002).

## COLLEGIATE RECORD

| Season Team | G | Min. | FGM | FGA | Pct. | FTM | FTA | Pct. | Reb. | Ast. | Pts. | RPG | APG | PPG |
|---|---|---|---|---|---|---|---|---|---|---|---|---|---|---|
| | | | | | | | | | | | | | AVERAGES | |
| 91-92—California | 28 | 745 | 152 | 321 | .474 | 66 | 93 | .710 | 171 | 56 | 387 | 6.1 | 2.0 | 13.8 |
| 92-93—California | 30 | 897 | 230 | 445 | .517 | 76 | 121 | .628 | 189 | 41 | 572 | 6.3 | 1.4 | 19.1 |
| 93-94—California | 30 | 1047 | 262 | 550 | .476 | 159 | 208 | .764 | 236 | 63 | 729 | 7.9 | 2.1 | 24.3 |
| Totals | 88 | 2689 | 644 | 1316 | .489 | 301 | 422 | .713 | 596 | 160 | 1688 | 6.8 | 1.8 | 19.2 |

Three-point field goals: 1991-92, 17-for-56 (.304). 1992-93, 36-for-99 (.364). 1993-94, 46-for-139 (.331). Totals, 99-for-294 (.337).

| Season Team | G | Min. | FGM | FGA | Pct. | FTM | FTA | Pct. | Off. | Def. | Tot. | Ast. | St. | Blk. | TO | Pts. | RPG | APG | PPG |
|---|---|---|---|---|---|---|---|---|---|---|---|---|---|---|---|---|---|---|---|
| 94-95—L.A. Clippers... | 81 | 2556 | 439 | 1093 | .402 | 199 | 264 | .754 | 132 | 222 | 354 | 133 | 72 | 55 | 163 | 1142 | 4.4 | 1.6 | 14.1 |
| 95-96—L.A. Clippers... | 77 | 1816 | 257 | 575 | .447 | 99 | 132 | .750 | 89 | 157 | 246 | 84 | 61 | 25 | 108 | 650 | 3.2 | 1.1 | 8.4 |
| 96-97—L.A. Clippers... | 74 | 1295 | 181 | 435 | .416 | 156 | 211 | .739 | 85 | 148 | 233 | 57 | 53 | 29 | 86 | 549 | 3.1 | 0.8 | 7.4 |
| 97-98—L.A. Clippers... | 79 | 2579 | 473 | 984 | .481 | 220 | 294 | .748 | 172 | 312 | 484 | 142 | 118 | 54 | 171 | 1220 | 6.1 | 1.8 | 15.4 |
| 98-99—L.A. Clippers... | 50 | 1317 | 226 | 578 | .391 | 126 | 157 | .803 | 59 | 136 | 195 | 61 | 58 | 20 | 99 | 612 | 3.9 | 1.2 | 12.2 |
| 99-00—Cleveland....... | 74 | 2365 | 460 | 1019 | .451 | 204 | 268 | .761 | 127 | 296 | 423 | 132 | 105 | 36 | 184 | 1175 | 5.7 | 1.8 | 15.9 |
| 00-01—Cleveland....... | 78 | 2225 | 391 | 925 | .423 | 155 | 211 | .735 | 104 | 236 | 340 | 124 | 83 | 27 | 141 | 998 | 4.4 | 1.6 | 12.8 |
| 01-02—Cleveland....... | 71 | 2312 | 430 | 986 | .436 | 215 | 263 | .817 | 81 | 291 | 372 | 157 | 70 | 43 | 141 | 1176 | 5.2 | 2.2 | 16.6 |
| 02-03—Toronto ......... | | | | | | | Did not play—injured | | | | | | | | | | | | |
| 03-04—Toronto ......... | 33 | 518 | 76 | 215 | .353 | 24 | 35 | .686 | 14 | 76 | 90 | 28 | 15 | 7 | 38 | 197 | 2.7 | 0.8 | 6.0 |
| 04-05—Toronto ......... | 62 | 918 | 132 | 310 | .426 | 61 | 80 | .763 | 44 | 120 | 164 | 47 | 32 | 16 | 54 | 371 | 2.6 | 0.8 | 6.0 |
| **Totals** ................ | 679 | 17901 | 3065 | 7120 | .430 | 1459 | 1915 | .762 | 907 | 1994 | 2901 | 965 | 667 | 312 | 1185 | 8090 | 4.3 | 1.4 | 11.9 |

Three-point field goals: 1994-95, 65-for-218 (.298). 1995-96, 37-for-116 (.319). 1996-97, 31-for-91 (.341). 1997-98, 54-for-153 (.353). 1998-99, 34-for-103 (.330). 1999-00, 51-for-139 (.367). 2000-01, 61-for-165 (.370). 2001-02, 101-for-238 (.424). 2003-04, 21-for-60 (.350). 2004-05, 46-for-105 (.438). Totals, 501-for-1388 (.361).

Personal fouls/disqualifications: 1994-95, 180/3. 1995-96, 151/0. 1996-97, 113/3. 1997-98, 193/3. 1998-99, 107/1. 1999-00, 208/2. 2000-01, 173/0. 2001-02, 148/1. 2003-04, 47/0. 2004-05, 85/0. Totals, 1405/13.

### NBA PLAYOFF RECORD

| Season Team | G | Min. | FGM | FGA | Pct. | FTM | FTA | Pct. | Off. | Def. | Tot. | Ast. | St. | Blk. | TO | Pts. | RPG | APG | PPG |
|---|---|---|---|---|---|---|---|---|---|---|---|---|---|---|---|---|---|---|---|
| 96-97—L.A. Clippers... | 3 | 65 | 6 | 20 | .300 | 7 | 7 | 1.000 | 2 | 9 | 11 | 3 | 2 | 3 | 4 | 21 | 3.7 | 1.0 | 7.0 |

Three-point field goals: 1996-97, 2-for-8 (.250). Totals, 2-for-8 (.250).
Personal fouls/disqualifications: 1996-97, 7/0. Totals, 7/0.

# MURRAY, RONALD      G      SUPERSONICS

**PERSONAL:** Born July 29, 1979, in Philadelphia. ... 6-4/190. (1.93/86.2).
**HIGH SCHOOL:** Strawberry Mansion (Philadelphia).
**JUNIOR COLLEGE:** Meridian (Miss.) Community College, then Philadelphia Community College.
**COLLEGE:** Shaw (N.C.).
**TRANSACTIONS/CAREER NOTES:** Selected by Milwaukee Bucks in second round (42nd pick overall) of 2002 NBA Draft. ... Traded by Bucks with G Ray Allen, G Kevin Ollie and conditional first-round draft choice to Seattle SuperSonics for G Gary Payton and G Desmond Mason (February 20, 2003).

### COLLEGIATE RECORD

| Season Team | G | Min. | FGM | FGA | Pct. | FTM | FTA | Pct. | Reb. | Ast. | Pts. | RPG | APG | PPG |
|---|---|---|---|---|---|---|---|---|---|---|---|---|---|---|
| 97-98—Meridian C.C.................. | ... | ... | ... | ... | ... | ... | ... | ... | ... | ... | ... | 3.5 | 2.0 | 1.8 |
| 98-99—Meridian C.C.................. | 34 | ... | 255 | 506 | .504 | 123 | 177 | .695 | 169 | 56 | 681 | 5.0 | 1.6 | 20.0 |
| 99-00—Philadelphia C.C. ........... | | | | | | Did not play. | | | | | | | | |
| 00-01—Shaw .............................. | 23 | 876 | 173 | 382 | .453 | 139 | 192 | .724 | 129 | 109 | 510 | 5.6 | 4.7 | 22.2 |
| 01-02—Shaw .............................. | 33 | 1202 | 256 | 526 | .487 | 220 | 285 | .772 | 209 | 205 | 777 | 6.3 | 6.2 | 23.5 |
| **Junior College Totals**............. | 34 | ... | 255 | 506 | .504 | 123 | 177 | .695 | 169 | 56 | 681 | 5.0 | 1.6 | 20.0 |
| **4-Year-College Totals** ........... | 56 | 2078 | 429 | 908 | .472 | 359 | 477 | .753 | 338 | 314 | 1287 | 6.0 | 5.6 | 23.0 |

Three-point field goals: 1998-99, 48-for-145 (.331). 2000-01, 25-for-71 (.352). 2001-02, 45-for-129 (.349). Totals, 118-for-345 (.342).

### NBA REGULAR-SEASON RECORD

| Season Team | G | Min. | FGM | FGA | Pct. | FTM | FTA | Pct. | Off. | Def. | Tot. | Ast. | St. | Blk. | TO | Pts. | RPG | APG | PPG |
|---|---|---|---|---|---|---|---|---|---|---|---|---|---|---|---|---|---|---|---|
| 02-03—Mil.-Sea. ......... | 14 | 62 | 11 | 31 | .355 | 5 | 8 | .625 | 0 | 4 | 4 | 5 | 4 | 0 | 8 | 27 | 0.3 | 0.4 | 1.9 |
| 03-04—Seattle ........... | 82 | 2021 | 389 | 915 | .425 | 168 | 235 | .715 | 45 | 159 | 204 | 205 | 81 | 28 | 149 | 1013 | 2.5 | 2.5 | 12.4 |
| 04-05—Seattle ........... | 49 | 883 | 131 | 363 | .361 | 59 | 80 | .738 | 15 | 83 | 98 | 65 | 30 | 11 | 57 | 345 | 2.0 | 1.3 | 7.0 |
| **Totals** ................... | 145 | 2966 | 531 | 1309 | .406 | 232 | 323 | .718 | 60 | 246 | 306 | 275 | 115 | 39 | 214 | 1385 | 2.1 | 1.9 | 9.6 |

Three-point field goals: 2002-03, 0-for-5. 2003-04, 67-for-229 (.293). 2004-05, 24-for-95 (.253). Totals, 91-for-329 (.277).
Personal fouls/disqualifications: 2003-04, 158/0. 2004-05, 59/0. Totals, 217/0.

### NBA PLAYOFF RECORD

| Season Team | G | Min. | FGM | FGA | Pct. | FTM | FTA | Pct. | Off. | Def. | Tot. | Ast. | St. | Blk. | TO | Pts. | RPG | APG | PPG |
|---|---|---|---|---|---|---|---|---|---|---|---|---|---|---|---|---|---|---|---|
| 04-05—Seattle ........... | 4 | 62 | 4 | 19 | .211 | 4 | 7 | .571 | 2 | 4 | 6 | 5 | 0 | 2 | 12 | 12 | 1.5 | 1.3 | 3.0 |

Three-point field goals: 2004-05, 0-for-2. Totals, 0-for-2 (.000).
Personal fouls/disqualifications: 2004-05, 8/0. Totals, 8/0.

# MUTOMBO, DIKEMBE      C      ROCKETS

**PERSONAL:** Born June 25, 1966, in Kinshasa, Zaire. ... 7-2/261. (2.18/118.4). ... Name pronounced di-KEM-bay moo-TUM-bow.
**HIGH SCHOOL:** Institute Boboto (Kinshasa, Zaire).
**COLLEGE:** Georgetown.
**TRANSACTIONS/CAREER NOTES:** Selected by Denver Nuggets in first round (fourth pick overall) of 1991 NBA Draft. ... Signed as free agent by Atlanta Hawks (July 15, 1996). ... Traded by Hawks with F Roshown McLeod to Philadelphia 76ers for F/C Theo Ratliff, F/G Toni Kukoc, C Nazr Mohammed and G Pepe Sanchez (February 22, 2001). ... Traded by 76ers to New Jersey Nets for F Keith Van Horn and C Todd MacCulloch (August 6, 2002). ... Waived by Nets (October 7, 2003). ... Signed as free agent by New York Knicks (October 9, 2003). ... Traded by Knicks with F Othella Harrington, C Cezary Trybanski and G Frank Williams to Chicago Bulls for G Jamal Crawford and F Jerome

M

Williams (August 5, 2004). ... Traded by Bulls to Houston Rockets for G Mike Wilks, G/F Eric Piatkowski and G/F Adrian Griffin (September 8, 2004).

**MISCELLANEOUS:** Denver Nuggets franchise all-time blocked shots leader with 1,486 (1991-92 through 1995-96).

## COLLEGIATE RECORD

**NOTES:** THE SPORTING NEWS All-America third team (1991).

| Season Team | G | Min. | FGM | FGA | Pct. | FTM | FTA | Pct. | Reb. | Ast. | Pts. | RPG | APG | PPG |
|---|---|---|---|---|---|---|---|---|---|---|---|---|---|---|
| 87-88—Georgetown.............. | | | | | | | Did not play. | | | | | | | |
| 88-89—Georgetown.............. | 33 | 374 | 53 | 75 | .707 | 23 | 48 | .479 | 109 | 5 | 129 | 3.3 | 0.2 | 3.9 |
| 89-90—Georgetown.............. | 31 | 797 | 129 | 182 | .709 | 73 | 122 | .598 | 325 | 18 | 331 | 10.5 | 0.6 | 10.7 |
| 90-91—Georgetown.............. | 32 | 1090 | 170 | 290 | .586 | 147 | 209 | .703 | 389 | 52 | 487 | 12.2 | 1.6 | 15.2 |
| Totals ................................. | 96 | 2261 | 352 | 547 | .644 | 243 | 379 | .641 | 823 | 75 | 947 | 8.6 | 0.8 | 9.9 |

## NBA REGULAR-SEASON RECORD

**RECORDS:** Holds career record for most consecutive seasons leading league in blocked shots per game—3 (1993-94 through 1995-96).
**HONORS:** J. Walter Kennedy Citizenship Award (2001). ... NBA Defensive Player of the Year (1995, 1997, 1998, 2001). ... IBM Award, for all-around contributions to team's success (1999). ... All-NBA second team (2001). ... All-NBA Third Team (1998, 2002). ... NBA All-Defensive first team (1997, 1998, 2001). ... NBA All-Defensive second team (1995, 1999, 2002). ... NBA All-Rookie first team (1992).
**NOTES:** Led NBA with 4.10 blocked shots per game (1994), 3.91 blocked shots per game (1995) and 4.49 blocked shots per game (1996).

| Season Team | G | Min. | FGM | FGA | Pct. | FTM | FTA | Pct. | Off. | Def. | Tot. | Ast. | St. | Blk. | TO | Pts. | RPG | APG | PPG |
|---|---|---|---|---|---|---|---|---|---|---|---|---|---|---|---|---|---|---|---|
| 91-92—Denver .......... | 71 | 2716 | 428 | 869 | .493 | 321 | 500 | .642 | 316 | 554 | 870 | 156 | 43 | 210 | 252 | 1177 | 12.3 | 2.2 | 16.6 |
| 92-93—Denver .......... | 82 | 3029 | 398 | 781 | .510 | 335 | 492 | .681 | 344 | 726 | 1070 | 147 | 43 | 287 | 216 | 1131 | 13.0 | 1.8 | 13.8 |
| 93-94—Denver .......... | 82 | 2853 | 365 | 642 | .569 | 256 | 439 | .583 | 286 | 685 | 971 | 127 | 59 | *336 | 206 | 986 | 11.8 | 1.5 | 12.0 |
| 94-95—Denver .......... | 82 | 3100 | 349 | 628 | .556 | 248 | 379 | .654 | 319 | *710 | 1029 | 113 | 40 | *321 | 192 | 946 | 12.5 | 1.4 | 11.5 |
| 95-96—Denver .......... | 74 | 2713 | 284 | 569 | .499 | 246 | 354 | .695 | 249 | 622 | 871 | 108 | 38 | *332 | 150 | 814 | 11.8 | 1.5 | 11.0 |
| 96-97—Atlanta .......... | 80 | 2973 | 380 | 721 | .527 | 306 | 434 | .705 | 268 | 661 | 929 | 110 | 49 | *264 | 186 | 1066 | 11.6 | 1.4 | 13.3 |
| 97-98—Atlanta .......... | 82 | 2917 | 399 | 743 | .537 | 303 | 452 | .670 | 276 | 656 | 932 | 82 | 34 | 277 | 168 | 1101 | 11.4 | 1.0 | 13.4 |
| 98-99—Atlanta .......... | 50 | 1829 | 173 | 338 | .512 | 195 | 285 | .684 | *192 | *418 | 610 | 57 | 16 | 147 | 94 | 541 | 12.2 | 1.1 | 10.8 |
| 99-00—Atlanta .......... | 82 | 2984 | 322 | 573 | .562 | 298 | 421 | .708 | *304 | *853 | 1157 | 105 | 27 | 269 | 174 | 942 | *14.1 | 1.3 | 11.5 |
| 00-01—Atlanta-Phila... | 75 | 2591 | 269 | 556 | .484 | 211 | 291 | .725 | 307 | 708 | *1015 | 76 | 29 | 203 | 144 | 749 | *13.5 | 1.0 | 10.0 |
| 01-02—Philadelphia ... | 80 | 2907 | 321 | 641 | .501 | 278 | 364 | .764 | 254 | 609 | 863 | 83 | 29 | 190 | 156 | 920 | 10.8 | 1.0 | 11.5 |
| 02-03—New Jersey .... | 24 | 514 | 49 | 131 | .374 | 40 | 55 | .727 | 54 | 99 | 153 | 19 | 4 | 37 | 34 | 138 | 6.4 | 0.8 | 5.8 |
| 03-04—New York ...... | 65 | 1494 | 141 | 295 | .478 | 81 | 119 | .681 | 145 | 292 | 437 | 25 | 17 | 123 | 54 | 363 | 6.7 | 0.4 | 5.6 |
| 04-05—Houston ........ | 80 | 1212 | 108 | 217 | .498 | 106 | 143 | .741 | 150 | 276 | 426 | 10 | 16 | 101 | 51 | 322 | 5.3 | 0.1 | 4.0 |
| Totals .................. | 1009 | 33832 | 3986 | 7704 | .517 | 3224 | 4728 | .682 | 3464 | 7869 | 11333 | 1218 | 444 | 3097 | 2077 | 11196 | 11.2 | 1.2 | 11.1 |

Three-point field goals: 1993-94, 0-for-1. 1995-96, 0-for-1. Totals, 0-for-2 (.000).
Personal fouls/disqualifications: 1991-92, 273/1. 1992-93, 284/5. 1993-94, 262/2. 1994-95, 284/2. 1995-96, 258/4. 1996-97, 249/3. 1997-98, 254/1. 1998-99, 145/2. 1999-00, 248/3. 2000-01, 204/2. 2001-02, 200/3. 2002-03, 54/0. 2003-04, 141/0. 2004-05, 135/1. Totals, 3033/28.

## NBA PLAYOFF RECORD

| Season Team | G | Min. | FGM | FGA | Pct. | FTM | FTA | Pct. | Off. | Def. | Tot. | Ast. | St. | Blk. | TO | Pts. | RPG | APG | PPG |
|---|---|---|---|---|---|---|---|---|---|---|---|---|---|---|---|---|---|---|---|
| 93-94—Denver .......... | 12 | 511 | 50 | 108 | .463 | 59 | 98 | .602 | 40 | 104 | 144 | 21 | 8 | 69 | 30 | 159 | 12.0 | 1.8 | 13.3 |
| 94-95—Denver .......... | 3 | 84 | 6 | 10 | .600 | 6 | 9 | .667 | 4 | 15 | 19 | 1 | 0 | 7 | 7 | 18 | 6.3 | 0.3 | 6.0 |
| 96-97—Atlanta .......... | 10 | 415 | 54 | 86 | .628 | 46 | 64 | .719 | 37 | 86 | 123 | 13 | 1 | 26 | 20 | 154 | 12.3 | 1.3 | 15.4 |
| 97-98—Atlanta .......... | 4 | 136 | 11 | 24 | .458 | 10 | 16 | .625 | 13 | 38 | 51 | 1 | 1 | 9 | 8 | 32 | 12.8 | 0.3 | 8.0 |
| 98-99—Atlanta .......... | 9 | 380 | 40 | 71 | .563 | 33 | 47 | .702 | 36 | 89 | 125 | 11 | 5 | 23 | 18 | 113 | 13.9 | 1.2 | 12.6 |
| 00-01—Philadelphia ... | 23 | 981 | 102 | 208 | .490 | 115 | 148 | .777 | 113 | 203 | 316 | 17 | 15 | 72 | 36 | 319 | 13.7 | 0.7 | 13.9 |
| 01-02—Philadelphia ... | 5 | 173 | 14 | 31 | .452 | 16 | 26 | .615 | 14 | 39 | 53 | 3 | 2 | 9 | 11 | 44 | 10.6 | 0.6 | 8.8 |
| 02-03—New Jersey .... | 10 | 115 | 7 | 15 | .467 | 4 | 4 | 1.000 | 8 | 19 | 27 | 6 | 3 | 9 | 8 | 18 | 2.7 | 0.6 | 1.8 |
| 03-04—New York ...... | 3 | 38 | 2 | 6 | .333 | 3 | 3 | 1.000 | 4 | 6 | 10 | 0 | 1 | 4 | 3 | 7 | 3.3 | 0.0 | 2.3 |
| 04-05—Houston ........ | 7 | 101 | 6 | 11 | .545 | 10 | 13 | .769 | 11 | 24 | 35 | 2 | 2 | 7 | 7 | 22 | 5.0 | 0.3 | 3.1 |
| Totals .................. | 86 | 2934 | 292 | 570 | .512 | 302 | 428 | .706 | 280 | 623 | 903 | 75 | 38 | 235 | 148 | 886 | 10.5 | 0.9 | 10.3 |

Three-point field goals: 2000-01, 0-for-1. Totals, 0-for-1 (.000).
Personal fouls/disqualifications: 1993-94, 42/0. 1994-95, 15/1. 1996-97, 30/0. 1997-98, 10/0. 1998-99, 28/0. 2000-01, 56/1. 2001-02, 16/0. 2002-03, 21/0. 2003-04, 6/0. 2004-05, 15/0. Totals, 239/2.

## NBA ALL-STAR GAME RECORD

| Season Team | Min. | FGM | FGA | Pct. | FTM | FTA | Pct. | Off. | Def. | Tot. | Ast. | PF | Dq. | St. | Blk. | TO | Pts. |
|---|---|---|---|---|---|---|---|---|---|---|---|---|---|---|---|---|---|
| 1992—Denver ................. | 10 | 2 | 4 | .500 | 0 | 0 | ... | 1 | 1 | 2 | 1 | 0 | 0 | 1 | 0 | 2 | 4 |
| 1995—Denver ................. | 20 | 6 | 8 | .750 | 0 | 0 | ... | 3 | 5 | 8 | 1 | 3 | 0 | 4 | 0 | 12 | 12 |
| 1996—Denver ................. | 11 | 2 | 4 | .500 | 0 | 0 | ... | 6 | 3 | 9 | 0 | 3 | 0 | 0 | 0 | 3 | 4 |
| 1997—Atlanta................. | 15 | 1 | 5 | .200 | 1 | 2 | .500 | 2 | 6 | 8 | 0 | 0 | 0 | 0 | 1 | 1 | 3 |
| 1998—Atlanta................. | 19 | 4 | 5 | .800 | 1 | 2 | .500 | 1 | 6 | 7 | 0 | 3 | ... | 0 | 1 | 0 | 9 |
| 2000—Atlanta................. | 16 | 2 | 4 | .500 | 0 | 0 | ... | 2 | 6 | 8 | 0 | 0 | 0 | 0 | 0 | 2 | 4 |
| 2001—Atlanta................. | 28 | 2 | 2 | 1.000 | 2 | 2 | 1.000 | 3 | 19 | 22 | 0 | 5 | 0 | 2 | 3 | 2 | 6 |
| 2002—Philadelphia .......... | 21 | 3 | 5 | .600 | 2 | 2 | 1.000 | 6 | 4 | 10 | 0 | 0 | 0 | 0 | 1 | 2 | 8 |
| Totals............................. | 140 | 22 | 37 | .595 | 6 | 8 | .750 | 24 | 50 | 74 | 2 | 14 | 0 | 3 | 10 | 12 | 50 |

M

## N'DIAYE, MAMADOU      C

**PERSONAL:** Born June 16, 1975, in Dakar, Senegal. ... 7-0/255. (2.13/115.7).
**HIGH SCHOOL:** Delafosse (Dakar, Senegal), then Maine Central Institute (Pittsfield, Maine).
**COLLEGE:** Auburn.
**TRANSACTIONS/CAREER NOTES:** Selected by Denver Nuggets in first round (26th pick overall) of 2000 NBA Draft. ... Traded by Nuggets with F Tracy Murray, F/C Keon Clark to Toronto Raptors for F/C Kevin Willis, C Aleksandar Radojevic, C Garth Joseph and 2001 or 2002 second-round draft choice (January 12, 2001). ... Played in NBDL with Asheville Altitude (2003-04). ... Signed by Dallas Mavericks to first of two consecutive 10-day contracts (January 6, 2004). ... Signed by Atlanta Hawks to first of two consecutive 10-day contracts (February 18, 2004). ... Signed by Hawks for remainder of season (March 15, 2004). ... Signed as free agent by Los Angeles Clippers (August 16, 2004). ... Waived by Clippers (June 29, 2005).

### COLLEGIATE RECORD

| Season Team | G | Min. | FGM | FGA | Pct. | FTM | FTA | Pct. | Reb. | Ast. | Pts. | RPG | APG | PPG |
|---|---|---|---|---|---|---|---|---|---|---|---|---|---|---|
| 96-97—Auburn | 31 | 350 | 42 | 86 | .488 | 10 | 19 | .526 | 76 | 7 | 94 | 2.5 | 0.2 | 3.0 |
| 97-98—Auburn | 30 | 747 | 89 | 177 | .503 | 61 | 99 | .616 | 208 | 22 | 239 | 6.9 | 0.7 | 8.0 |
| 98-99—Auburn | 33 | 785 | 88 | 180 | .489 | 63 | 97 | .649 | 247 | 29 | 239 | 7.5 | 0.9 | 7.2 |
| 99-00—Auburn | 34 | 903 | 100 | 187 | .535 | 103 | 155 | .665 | 267 | 18 | 303 | 7.9 | 0.5 | 8.9 |
| Totals | 128 | 2785 | 319 | 630 | .506 | 237 | 370 | .641 | 798 | 76 | 875 | 6.2 | 0.6 | 6.8 |

Three-point field goals: 1996-97, 0-for-1. 1998-99, 0-for-1. Totals, 0-for-2 (.000).

### NBA REGULAR-SEASON RECORD

| Season Team | G | Min. | FGM | FGA | Pct. | FTM | FTA | Pct. | Off. | Def. | Tot. | Ast. | St. | Blk. | TO | Pts. | RPG | APG | PPG |
|---|---|---|---|---|---|---|---|---|---|---|---|---|---|---|---|---|---|---|---|
| 00-01—Toronto | 3 | 10 | 1 | 4 | .250 | 2 | 2 | 1.000 | 1 | 1 | 2 | 0 | 0 | 0 | 0 | 4 | 0.7 | 0.0 | 1.3 |
| 01-02—Toronto | 5 | 46 | 6 | 10 | .600 | 8 | 10 | .800 | 6 | 5 | 11 | 0 | 0 | 2 | 1 | 20 | 2.2 | 0.0 | 4.0 |
| 02-03—Toronto | 22 | 364 | 43 | 96 | .448 | 34 | 47 | .723 | 29 | 53 | 82 | 7 | 8 | 32 | 21 | 120 | 3.7 | 0.3 | 5.5 |
| 03-04—Dallas-Atlanta | 28 | 366 | 27 | 69 | .391 | 44 | 59 | .746 | 43 | 69 | 112 | 0 | 8 | 25 | 18 | 98 | 4.0 | 0.0 | 3.5 |
| 04-05—L.A. Clippers | 11 | 72 | 8 | 20 | .400 | 4 | 7 | .571 | 9 | 9 | 18 | 1 | 1 | 5 | 0 | 20 | 1.6 | 0.1 | 1.8 |
| Totals | 69 | 858 | 85 | 199 | .427 | 92 | 125 | .736 | 88 | 137 | 225 | 8 | 17 | 64 | 40 | 262 | 3.3 | 0.1 | 3.8 |

Three-point field goals: 2004-05, 0-for-1. Totals, 0-for-1 (.000).
Personal fouls/disqualifications: 2000-01, 3/0. 2001-02, 6/0. 2002-03, 58/0. 2003-04, 59/1. 2004-05, 20/0. Totals, 146/1.

### NBDL RECORD

| Season Team | G | Min. | FGM | FGA | Pct. | FTM | FTA | Pct. | Reb. | Ast. | Pts. | RPG | APG | PPG |
|---|---|---|---|---|---|---|---|---|---|---|---|---|---|---|
| 03-04—Asheville | 6 | 126 | 16 | 34 | .471 | 21 | 30 | .700 | 38 | 1 | 53 | 6.3 | 0.2 | 8.8 |

## NACHBAR, BOSTJAN      F      HORNETS

**PERSONAL:** Born July 3, 1980, in Slovenj Gradec, Slovenia. ... 6-9/221. (2.06/100.2).
**TRANSACTIONS/CAREER NOTES:** Played in Slovenia (1996-2000). ... Played in Italy (2000-02). ... Selected by Houston Rockets in first round (15th pick overall) of 2002 NBA Draft. ... Traded with G Jim Jackson to New Orleans Hornets for G David Wesley (December 27, 2004).

### SLOVENIAN LEAGUE RECORD

| Season Team | G | Min. | FGM | FGA | Pct. | FTM | FTA | Pct. | Reb. | Ast. | Pts. | RPG | APG | PPG |
|---|---|---|---|---|---|---|---|---|---|---|---|---|---|---|
| 96-97—KK Maribor | 8 | 107 | 18 | 35 | .514 | 12 | 21 | .571 | 14 | 3 | 52 | 1.8 | 0.4 | 6.5 |
| 97-98—Olimpija Ljubljana | 24 | 475 | 67 | 123 | .545 | 38 | 50 | .760 | 58 | 19 | 178 | 2.4 | 0.8 | 7.4 |
| 98-99—KK Maribor | 26 | 633 | 106 | 217 | .488 | 101 | 131 | .771 | 84 | 19 | 321 | 3.2 | 0.7 | 12.3 |
| 99-00—KK Pivovarna Lasko | 32 | 1002 | 95 | 186 | .511 | 81 | 117 | .692 | 84 | 37 | 288 | 2.6 | 1.2 | 9.0 |
| Totals | 90 | 2217 | 286 | 561 | .510 | 232 | 319 | .727 | 240 | 78 | 839 | 2.7 | 0.9 | 9.3 |

Three-point field goals: 1996-97, 4-for-11 (.364). 1997-98, 6-for-28 (.214). 1998-99, 8-for-44 (.182). 1999-00, 17-for-40 (.425). Totals, 35-for-123 (.285).

### ITALIAN LEAGUE RECORD

| Season Team | G | Min. | FGM | FGA | Pct. | FTM | FTA | Pct. | Reb. | Ast. | Pts. | RPG | APG | PPG |
|---|---|---|---|---|---|---|---|---|---|---|---|---|---|---|
| 00-01—Benetton Treviso | 30 | 329 | 42 | 109 | .385 | 37 | 48 | .771 | 51 | 11 | 128 | 1.7 | 0.4 | 4.3 |
| 01-02—Benetton Treviso | 35 | 863 | 169 | 326 | .518 | 109 | 139 | .784 | 146 | 49 | 491 | 4.2 | 1.4 | 14.0 |
| Totals | 65 | 1192 | 211 | 435 | .485 | 146 | 187 | .781 | 197 | 60 | 619 | 3.0 | 0.9 | 9.5 |

Three-point field goals: 2000-01, 7-for-29 (.241). 2001-02, 44-for-119 (.370). Totals, 51-for-148 (.345).

### NBA REGULAR-SEASON RECORD

| Season Team | G | Min. | FGM | FGA | Pct. | FTM | FTA | Pct. | Off. | Def. | Tot. | Ast. | St. | Blk. | TO | Pts. | RPG | APG | PPG |
|---|---|---|---|---|---|---|---|---|---|---|---|---|---|---|---|---|---|---|---|
| 02-03—Houston | 14 | 77 | 11 | 31 | .355 | 5 | 10 | .500 | 3 | 8 | 11 | 3 | 2 | 2 | 6 | 29 | 0.8 | 0.2 | 2.1 |
| 03-04—Houston | 45 | 516 | 47 | 132 | .356 | 21 | 29 | .724 | 8 | 62 | 70 | 30 | 14 | 14 | 23 | 138 | 1.6 | 0.7 | 3.1 |
| 04-05—Houston-N.O. | 71 | 1341 | 161 | 411 | .392 | 97 | 117 | .829 | 24 | 158 | 182 | 74 | 29 | 16 | 73 | 494 | 2.6 | 1.0 | 7.0 |
| Totals | 130 | 1934 | 219 | 574 | .382 | 123 | 156 | .788 | 35 | 228 | 263 | 107 | 45 | 32 | 102 | 661 | 2.0 | 0.8 | 5.1 |

Three-point field goals: 2002-03, 2-for-10 (.200). 2003-04, 23-for-63 (.365). 2004-05, 75-for-196 (.383). Totals, 100-for-269 (.372).
Personal fouls/disqualifications: 2002-03, 13/0. 2003-04, 72/1. 2004-05, 183/1. Totals, 268/2.

### NBA PLAYOFF RECORD

| Season Team | G | Min. | FGM | FGA | Pct. | FTM | FTA | Pct. | Off. | Def. | Tot. | Ast. | St. | Blk. | TO | Pts. | RPG | APG | PPG |
|---|---|---|---|---|---|---|---|---|---|---|---|---|---|---|---|---|---|---|---|
| 03-04—Houston | 5 | 41 | 4 | 9 | .444 | 5 | 5 | 1.000 | 1 | 5 | 6 | 2 | 1 | 0 | 2 | 14 | 1.2 | 0.4 | 2.8 |

Three-point field goals: 2003-04, 1-for-3 (.333). Totals, 1-for-3 (.333).
Personal fouls/disqualifications: 2003-04, 9/0. Totals, 9/0.

**N**

**PERSONAL:** Born February 22, 1975, in South Bend, Ind. ... 6-8/241. (2.03/109.3).
**HIGH SCHOOL:** Clay (South Bend, Ind.).
**JUNIOR COLLEGE:** Southeastern Community (Iowa),then Butler County (Kansas).
**COLLEGE:** Texas Christian.
**TRANSACTIONS/CAREER NOTES:** Selected by Charlotte Hornets in second round (43rd pick overall) of 1999 NBA Draft. ... Played in Italy (1999-2000). ... Waived by Hornets (October 23, 2002). ... Signed as free agent by New York Knicks (October 30, 2002). ... Signed as free agent by Atlanta Hawks (September 30, 2003). ... Waived by Hawks (December 29, 2003). ... Played in Continental Basketball Association (2003-04). ... Signed by Orlando Magic to first of two consecutive 10-day contracts (January 5, 2004). ... Signed by Cleveland Cavaliers to first of two consecutive 10-day contracts (March 3, 2004). ... Signed by Cavaliers for remainder of season (March 23, 2004). ... Signed as free agent by New Orleans Hornets (September 30, 2004).

## COLLEGIATE RECORD

| Season Team | G | Min. | FGM | FGA | Pct. | FTM | FTA | Pct. | Reb. | Ast. | Pts. | RPG | APG | PPG |
|---|---|---|---|---|---|---|---|---|---|---|---|---|---|---|
| 95-96—Southeastern C.C. | 31 | 892 | 311 | 500 | .622 | 112 | 155 | .723 | 252 | 83 | 735 | 8.1 | 2.7 | 23.7 |
| 96-97—Butler County C.C. | 34 | 887 | 292 | 443 | .659 | 101 | 154 | .656 | 250 | 117 | 686 | 7.4 | 3.4 | 20.2 |
| 97-98—Texas Christian | 32 | 1066 | 329 | 594 | .554 | 137 | 184 | .745 | 285 | 61 | 796 | 8.9 | 1.9 | 24.9 |
| 98-99—Texas Christian | 31 | 990 | 266 | 524 | .508 | 171 | 239 | .715 | 288 | 79 | 707 | 9.3 | 2.5 | 22.8 |
| Junior College Totals | 65 | 1779 | 603 | 943 | .639 | 213 | 309 | .689 | 502 | 200 | 1421 | 7.7 | 3.1 | 21.9 |
| 4-Year-College Totals | 63 | 2056 | 595 | 1118 | .532 | 308 | 423 | .728 | 573 | 140 | 1503 | 9.1 | 2.2 | 23.9 |

Three-point field goals: 1995-96, 1-for-13 (.077). 1996-97, 0-for-1. 1997-98, 1-for-2 (.500). 1998-99, 4-for-15 (.267). Totals, 6-for-31 (.194).
Personal fouls/disqualifications: 1997-98, 110/0. Totals, 110/0.

## ITALIAN LEAGUE RECORD

| Season Team | G | Min. | FGM | FGA | Pct. | FTM | FTA | Pct. | Reb. | Ast. | Pts. | RPG | APG | PPG |
|---|---|---|---|---|---|---|---|---|---|---|---|---|---|---|
| 99-00—Milano | 18 | 584 | 139 | 260 | .535 | 45 | 61 | .738 | 79 | 20 | 327 | 4.4 | 1.1 | 18.2 |

Three-point field goals: 1999-00, 4-for-10 (.400). Totals, 4-for-10 (.400).

## NBA REGULAR-SEASON RECORD

| Season Team | G | Min. | FGM | FGA | Pct. | FTM | FTA | Pct. | Off. | Def. | Tot. | Ast. | St. | Blk. | TO | Pts. | RPG | APG | PPG |
|---|---|---|---|---|---|---|---|---|---|---|---|---|---|---|---|---|---|---|---|
| 00-01—Charlotte | 42 | 469 | 66 | 136 | .485 | 32 | 43 | .744 | 29 | 63 | 92 | 24 | 9 | 5 | 27 | 164 | 2.2 | 0.6 | 3.9 |
| 01-02—Charlotte | 79 | 1912 | 369 | 764 | .483 | 112 | 150 | .747 | 103 | 188 | 291 | 94 | 59 | 17 | 96 | 851 | 3.7 | 1.2 | 10.8 |
| 02-03—New York | 38 | 405 | 84 | 190 | .442 | 42 | 51 | .824 | 32 | 38 | 70 | 26 | 6 | 3 | 32 | 210 | 1.8 | 0.7 | 5.5 |
| 03-04—Atl.-Orl.-Cleve. | 57 | 780 | 147 | 327 | .450 | 47 | 58 | .810 | 64 | 79 | 143 | 38 | 15 | 8 | 45 | 341 | 2.5 | 0.7 | 6.0 |
| 04-05—New Orleans | 68 | 2017 | 415 | 869 | .478 | 133 | 165 | .806 | 128 | 170 | 298 | 109 | 36 | 16 | 110 | 963 | 4.4 | 1.6 | 14.2 |
| Totals | 284 | 5583 | 1081 | 2286 | .473 | 366 | 467 | .784 | 356 | 538 | 894 | 291 | 125 | 49 | 310 | 2529 | 3.1 | 1.0 | 8.9 |

Three-point field goals: 2000-01, 0-for-1. 2001-02, 1-for-2 (.500). 2002-03, 0-for-1. 2003-04, 0-for-3. 2004-05, 0-for-2. Totals, 1-for-9 (.111).
Personal fouls/disqualifications: 2000-01, 60/0. 2001-02, 175/1. 2002-03, 46/0. 2003-04, 93/0. 2004-05, 190/1. Totals, 564/2.

## NBA PLAYOFF RECORD

| Season Team | G | Min. | FGM | FGA | Pct. | FTM | FTA | Pct. | Off. | Def. | Tot. | Ast. | St. | Blk. | TO | Pts. | RPG | APG | PPG |
|---|---|---|---|---|---|---|---|---|---|---|---|---|---|---|---|---|---|---|---|
| 01-02—Charlotte | 9 | 160 | 27 | 59 | .458 | 15 | 19 | .789 | 10 | 14 | 24 | 6 | 3 | 0 | 7 | 69 | 2.7 | 0.7 | 7.7 |

Three-point field goals: 2001-02, 0-for-1. Totals, 0-for-1 (.000).
Personal fouls/disqualifications: 2001-02, 17/0. Totals, 17/0.

## CBA RECORD

| Season Team | G | Min. | FGM | FGA | Pct. | FTM | FTA | Pct. | Reb. | Ast. | Pts. | RPG | APG | PPG |
|---|---|---|---|---|---|---|---|---|---|---|---|---|---|---|
| 03-04—Gary | 3 | 81 | 29 | 58 | .500 | 9 | 9 | 1.000 | 30 | 3 | 67 | 10.0 | 1.0 | 22.3 |

**N**

# NAJERA, EDUARDO      F      NUGGETS

**PERSONAL:** Born July 11, 1976, in Meoqui, Chihuahua, Mexico. ... 6-8/240. (2.03/108.9). ... Full name: Eduardo Alonso Najera
**HIGH SCHOOL:** Cornerstone Christian Academy (San Antonio).
**COLLEGE:** Oklahoma.
**TRANSACTIONS/CAREER NOTES:** Selected by Houston Rockets in second round (38th pick overall) of 2000 NBA Draft. ... Draft rights traded by Rockets with a future second-round draft pick to Dallas Mavericks for draft rights to F Dan Langhi (June 28, 2000). ... Traded by Mavericks with F/C Christian Laettner, draft rights to G Luis Flores and G Mladen Sekularac, two future first-round draft choices and cash to Golden State Warriors for C Erick Dampier, G Dan Dickau and draft rights to G Steve Logan (August 24, 2004). ... Traded by Warriors with G Luis Flores and future first-round pick to Denver Nuggets for F Nikoloz Tskitishvili and F Rodney White (February 24, 2005).

## COLLEGIATE RECORD

| Season Team | G | Min. | FGM | FGA | Pct. | FTM | FTA | Pct. | Reb. | Ast. | Pts. | RPG | APG | PPG |
|---|---|---|---|---|---|---|---|---|---|---|---|---|---|---|
| 96-97—Oklahoma | 30 | 739 | 72 | 178 | .404 | 64 | 92 | .696 | 167 | 32 | 211 | 5.6 | 1.1 | 7.0 |
| 97-98—Oklahoma | 30 | 855 | 119 | 280 | .425 | 64 | 101 | .634 | 163 | 42 | 315 | 5.4 | 1.4 | 10.5 |
| 98-99—Oklahoma | 32 | 1100 | 187 | 451 | .415 | 70 | 109 | .642 | 266 | 69 | 495 | 8.3 | 2.2 | 15.5 |
| 99-00—Oklahoma | 34 | 1162 | 234 | 514 | .455 | 139 | 202 | .688 | 314 | 72 | 625 | 9.2 | 2.1 | 18.4 |
| Totals | 126 | 3856 | 612 | 1423 | .430 | 337 | 504 | .669 | 910 | 215 | 1646 | 7.2 | 1.7 | 13.1 |

Three-point field goals: 1996-97, 3-for-15 (.200). 1997-98, 13-for-49 (.265). 1998-99, 51-for-149 (.342). 1999-00, 18-for-82 (.220). Totals, 85-for-295 (.288).

| Season Team | G | Min. | FGM | FGA | Pct. | FTM | FTA | Pct. | Off. | Def. | Tot. | Ast. | St. | Blk. | TO | Pts. | RPG | APG | PPG |
|---|---|---|---|---|---|---|---|---|---|---|---|---|---|---|---|---|---|---|---|
| 00-01—Dallas............ | 40 | 431 | 58 | 111 | .523 | 14 | 33 | .424 | 41 | 54 | 95 | 27 | 13 | 8 | 17 | 131 | 2.4 | 0.7 | 3.3 |
| 01-02—Dallas............ | 62 | 1357 | 150 | 300 | .500 | 100 | 148 | .676 | 149 | 193 | 342 | 38 | 56 | 30 | 40 | 400 | 5.5 | 0.6 | 6.5 |
| 02-03—Dallas............ | 48 | 1103 | 129 | 231 | .558 | 62 | 91 | .681 | 90 | 133 | 223 | 47 | 40 | 22 | 23 | 320 | 4.6 | 1.0 | 6.7 |
| 03-04—Dallas............ | 58 | 720 | 72 | 162 | .444 | 30 | 46 | .652 | 67 | 89 | 156 | 25 | 35 | 19 | 29 | 176 | 2.7 | 0.4 | 3.0 |
| 04-05—Golden St.-Den. | 68 | 1185 | 145 | 322 | .450 | 58 | 91 | .637 | 102 | 141 | 243 | 65 | 41 | 24 | 61 | 354 | 3.6 | 1.0 | 5.2 |
| **Totals** | 276 | 4796 | 554 | 1126 | .492 | 264 | 409 | .645 | 449 | 610 | 1059 | 202 | 185 | 103 | 170 | 1381 | 3.8 | 0.7 | 5.0 |

Three-point field goals: 2000-01, 1-for-3 (.333). 2001-02, 0-for-2. 2002-03, 0-for-1. 2003-04, 2-for-4 (.500). 2004-05, 6-for-21 (.286). Totals, 9-for-31 (.290).

Personal fouls/disqualifications: 2000-01, 48/0. 2001-02, 156/2. 2002-03, 129/1. 2003-04, 90/1. 2004-05, 148/0. Totals, 571/4.

### NBA PLAYOFF RECORD

| Season Team | G | Min. | FGM | FGA | Pct. | FTM | FTA | Pct. | Off. | Def. | Tot. | Ast. | St. | Blk. | TO | Pts. | RPG | APG | PPG |
|---|---|---|---|---|---|---|---|---|---|---|---|---|---|---|---|---|---|---|---|
| 00-01—Dallas............ | 7 | 44 | 9 | 17 | .529 | 0 | 0 | ... | 7 | 8 | 15 | 1 | 1 | 1 | 1 | 21 | 2.1 | 0.1 | 3.0 |
| 01-02—Dallas............ | 8 | 122 | 16 | 23 | .696 | 5 | 8 | .625 | 3 | 10 | 13 | 1 | 3 | 0 | 2 | 37 | 1.6 | 0.1 | 4.6 |
| 02-03—Dallas............ | 19 | 394 | 39 | 86 | .453 | 38 | 48 | .792 | 36 | 38 | 74 | 15 | 14 | 4 | 16 | 116 | 3.9 | 0.8 | 6.1 |
| 03-04—Dallas............ | 5 | 57 | 5 | 11 | .455 | 2 | 2 | 1.000 | 10 | 7 | 17 | 3 | 3 | 2 | 2 | 12 | 3.4 | 0.6 | 2.4 |
| 04-05—Denver ........... | 2 | 13 | 0 | 2 | .000 | 0 | 0 | ... | 1 | 1 | 2 | 1 | 0 | 0 | 1 | 0 | 1.0 | 0.5 | 0.0 |
| **Totals** | 41 | 630 | 69 | 139 | .496 | 45 | 58 | .776 | 57 | 64 | 121 | 21 | 21 | 7 | 22 | 186 | 3.0 | 0.5 | 4.5 |

Three-point field goals: 2000-01, 3-for-4 (.750). Totals, 3-for-4 (.750).

Personal fouls/disqualifications: 2000-01, 8/0. 2001-02, 22/0. 2002-03, 53/1. 2003-04, 12/0. 2004-05, 1/0. Totals, 96/1.

# NASH, STEVE     G     SUNS

**PERSONAL:** Born February 7, 1974, in Johannesburg, South Africa. ... 6-3/195. (1.91/88.5). ... Full name: Stephen John Nash
**HIGH SCHOOL:** St. Michael's Victoria (British Columbia).
**COLLEGE:** Santa Clara.
**TRANSACTIONS/CAREER NOTES:** Selected by Phoenix Suns in first round (15th pick overall) of 1996 NBA Draft. ... Traded by Suns to Dallas Mavericks for F Martin Muursepp, G/F Bubba Wells, draft rights to F Pat Garrity and 1999 first-round draft choice (June 24, 1998). ... Signed as free agent by Suns (July 14, 2004).
**MISCELLANEOUS:** Member of Canadian Olympic team (2000).

## COLLEGIATE RECORD

| Season Team | G | Min. | FGM | FGA | Pct. | FTM | FTA | Pct. | Reb. | Ast. | Pts. | RPG | APG | PPG |
|---|---|---|---|---|---|---|---|---|---|---|---|---|---|---|
| 92-93—Santa Clara.................... | 31 | 743 | 78 | 184 | .424 | 47 | 57 | .825 | 79 | 67 | 252 | 2.5 | 2.2 | 8.1 |
| 93-94—Santa Clara.................... | 26 | 778 | 122 | 295 | .414 | 69 | 83 | .831 | 65 | 95 | 380 | 2.5 | 3.7 | 14.6 |
| 94-95—Santa Clara.................... | 27 | 902 | 164 | 369 | .444 | 153 | 174 | .879 | 102 | 174 | 565 | 3.8 | 6.4 | 20.9 |
| 95-96—Santa Clara.................... | 29 | 979 | 164 | 381 | .430 | 101 | 113 | .894 | 102 | 174 | 492 | 3.5 | 6.0 | 17.0 |
| **Totals** | 113 | 3402 | 528 | 1229 | .430 | 370 | 427 | .867 | 348 | 510 | 1689 | 3.1 | 4.5 | 14.9 |

Three-point field goals: 1992-93, 49-for-120 (.408). 1993-94, 67-for-168 (.399). 1994-95, 84-for-185 (.454). 1995-96, 63-for-183 (.344). Totals, 263-for-656 (.401).

### NBA REGULAR-SEASON RECORD

**HONORS:** All-NBA third team (2002, 2003). ... NBA Most Valuable Player (2005). ... All-NBA first team (2005).

| Season Team | G | Min. | FGM | FGA | Pct. | FTM | FTA | Pct. | Off. | Def. | Tot. | Ast. | St. | Blk. | TO | Pts. | RPG | APG | PPG |
|---|---|---|---|---|---|---|---|---|---|---|---|---|---|---|---|---|---|---|---|
| 96-97—Phoenix ......... | 65 | 684 | 74 | 175 | .423 | 42 | 51 | .824 | 16 | 47 | 63 | 138 | 20 | 0 | 63 | 213 | 1.0 | 2.1 | 3.3 |
| 97-98—Phoenix ......... | 76 | 1664 | 268 | 584 | .459 | 74 | 86 | .860 | 32 | 128 | 160 | 262 | 63 | 4 | 98 | 691 | 2.1 | 3.4 | 9.1 |
| 98-99—Dallas ............ | 40 | 1269 | 114 | 314 | .363 | 38 | 46 | .826 | 32 | 82 | 114 | 219 | 37 | 2 | 83 | 315 | 2.9 | 5.5 | 7.9 |
| 99-00—Dallas ............ | 56 | 1532 | 173 | 363 | .477 | 75 | 85 | .882 | 34 | 87 | 121 | 272 | 37 | 3 | 102 | 481 | 2.2 | 4.9 | 8.6 |
| 00-01—Dallas ............ | 70 | 2387 | 386 | 792 | .487 | 231 | 258 | .895 | 46 | 177 | 223 | 509 | 72 | 5 | 205 | 1092 | 3.2 | 7.3 | 15.6 |
| 01-02—Dallas ............ | 82 | 2837 | 525 | 1088 | .483 | 260 | 293 | .887 | 50 | 204 | 254 | 634 | 53 | 4 | 229 | 1466 | 3.1 | 7.7 | 17.9 |
| 02-03—Dallas ............ | 82 | 2711 | 518 | 1114 | .465 | 308 | 339 | .909 | 63 | 171 | 234 | 598 | 85 | 6 | 192 | 1455 | 2.9 | 7.3 | 17.7 |
| 03-04—Dallas ............ | 78 | 2612 | 397 | 845 | .470 | 230 | 251 | .916 | 59 | 173 | 232 | 687 | 67 | 8 | 209 | 1128 | 3.0 | 8.8 | 14.5 |
| 04-05—Phoenix ......... | 75 | 2573 | 430 | 857 | .502 | 211 | 238 | .887 | 57 | 192 | 249 | 861 | 74 | 6 | 245 | 1165 | 3.3 | 11.5 | 15.5 |
| **Totals** | 624 | 18269 | 2885 | 6132 | .470 | 1469 | 1647 | .892 | 389 | 1261 | 1650 | 4180 | 508 | 38 | 1426 | 8006 | 2.6 | 6.7 | 12.8 |

Three-point field goals: 1996-97, 23-for-55 (.418). 1997-98, 81-for-195 (.415). 1998-99, 49-for-131 (.374). 1999-00, 60-for-149 (.403). 2000-01, 89-for-219 (.406). 2001-02, 156-for-343 (.455). 2002-03, 111-for-269 (.413). 2003-04, 104-for-257 (.405). 2004-05, 94-for-218 (.431). Totals, 767-for-1836 (.418).

Personal fouls/disqualifications: 1996-97, 92/1. 1997-98, 145/1. 1998-99, 98/2. 1999-00, 122/1. 2000-01, 158/0. 2001-02, 164/0. 2002-03, 134/0. 2003-04, 139/0. 2004-05, 136/0. Totals, 1188/5.

### NBA PLAYOFF RECORD

| Season Team | G | Min. | FGM | FGA | Pct. | FTM | FTA | Pct. | Off. | Def. | Tot. | Ast. | St. | Blk. | TO | Pts. | RPG | APG | PPG |
|---|---|---|---|---|---|---|---|---|---|---|---|---|---|---|---|---|---|---|---|
| 96-97—Phoenix ......... | 4 | 15 | 2 | 9 | .222 | 0 | 0 | ... | 1 | 0 | 1 | 1 | 1 | 1 | 2 | 5 | 0.3 | 0.3 | 1.3 |
| 97-98—Phoenix ......... | 4 | 51 | 8 | 18 | .444 | 5 | 8 | .625 | 2 | 8 | 10 | 7 | 2 | 0 | 3 | 22 | 2.5 | 1.8 | 5.5 |
| 00-01—Dallas ............ | 10 | 370 | 45 | 108 | .417 | 30 | 34 | .882 | 6 | 26 | 32 | 64 | 6 | 1 | 25 | 136 | 3.2 | 6.4 | 13.6 |
| 01-02—Dallas ............ | 8 | 323 | 51 | 118 | .432 | 34 | 35 | .971 | 7 | 25 | 32 | 70 | 4 | 0 | 30 | 156 | 4.0 | 8.8 | 19.5 |
| 02-03—Dallas ............ | 20 | 729 | 115 | 257 | .447 | 55 | 63 | .873 | 15 | 55 | 70 | 145 | 17 | 1 | 51 | 322 | 3.5 | 7.3 | 16.1 |
| 03-04—Dallas ............ | 5 | 197 | 27 | 70 | .386 | 8 | 9 | .889 | 6 | 20 | 26 | 45 | 4 | 0 | 12 | 68 | 5.2 | 9.0 | 13.6 |
| 04-05—Phoenix ......... | 15 | 610 | 140 | 269 | .520 | 57 | 62 | .919 | 9 | 63 | 72 | 170 | 14 | 3 | 70 | 358 | 4.8 | 11.3 | 23.9 |
| **Totals** | 66 | 2295 | 388 | 849 | .457 | 189 | 211 | .896 | 46 | 197 | 243 | 502 | 48 | 6 | 193 | 1067 | 3.7 | 7.6 | 16.2 |

Three-point field goals: 1996-97, 1-for-4 (.250). 1997-98, 1-for-5 (.200). 2000-01, 16-for-39 (.410). 2001-02, 20-for-45 (.444). 2002-03, 37-for-76 (.487). 2003-04, 6-for-16 (.375). 2004-05, 21-for-54 (.389). Totals, 102-for-239 (.427).

Personal fouls/disqualifications: 1996-97, 5/0. 1997-98, 7/0. 2000-01, 19/0. 2001-02, 20/0. 2002-03, 47/0. 2003-04, 14/0. 2004-05, 36/0. Totals, 148/0.

**N**

**NOTES:** Won NBA All-Star Skills competition (2005).

| Season Team | Min. | FGM | FGA | Pct. | FTM | FTA | Pct. | REBOUNDS Off. | Def. | Tot. | Ast. | PF | Dq. | St. | Blk. | TO | Pts. |
|---|---|---|---|---|---|---|---|---|---|---|---|---|---|---|---|---|---|
| 2002—Dallas.................. | 24 | 3 | 9 | .333 | 0 | 0 | ... | 2 | 1 | 3 | 9 | 1 | 0 | 1 | 0 | 0 | 8 |
| 2003—Dallas.................. | 16 | 1 | 3 | .333 | 0 | 1 | .000 | 2 | 3 | 5 | 3 | 1 | 0 | 1 | 0 | 4 | 2 |
| 2005—Phoenix............... | 17 | 1 | 2 | .500 | 0 | 0 | ... | 0 | 0 | 0 | 6 | 0 | 0 | 0 | 0 | 3 | 2 |
| Totals........................... | 57 | 5 | 14 | .357 | 0 | 1 | .000 | 4 | 4 | 8 | 18 | 2 | 0 | 2 | 0 | 7 | 12 |

Three-point field goals: 2002, 2-for-4 (.500). 2003, 0-for-2. 2005, 0-for-1. Totals, 2-for-7 (.286).

# NELSON, JAMEER  G  MAGIC

**PERSONAL:** Born February 9, 1982, in Chester, Pa. ... 6-0/190. (1.83/86.2).
**HIGH SCHOOL:** Chester (Pa.).
**COLLEGE:** Saint Joseph's.
**TRANSACTIONS/CAREER NOTES:** Selected by Denver Nuggets in first round (20th pick overall) of 2004 NBA Draft. ... Draft rights traded by Nuggets to Orlando Magic for future first-round draft choice (June 24, 2004).

## COLLEGIATE RECORD

**NOTES:** The Sporting News Player of the Year (2004). ... The Sporting News All-America first team (2004). ... Naismith Award winner (2004). ... Wooden Award winner (2004).

| Season Team | G | Min. | FGM | FGA | Pct. | FTM | FTA | Pct. | Reb. | Ast. | Pts. | AVERAGES RPG | APG | PPG |
|---|---|---|---|---|---|---|---|---|---|---|---|---|---|---|
| 00-01—St. Joseph's................ | 33 | 1114 | 131 | 284 | .461 | 109 | 133 | .820 | 133 | 213 | 412 | 4.0 | 6.5 | 12.5 |
| 01-02—St. Joseph's................ | 30 | 1064 | 144 | 329 | .438 | 93 | 122 | .762 | 144 | 188 | 432 | 4.8 | 6.3 | 14.4 |
| 02-03—St. Joseph's................ | 30 | 1048 | 194 | 444 | .437 | 139 | 180 | .772 | 154 | 142 | 591 | 5.1 | 4.7 | 19.7 |
| 03-04—St. Joseph's................ | 32 | 1085 | 234 | 493 | .475 | 118 | 149 | .792 | 150 | 170 | 659 | 4.7 | 5.3 | 20.6 |
| Totals............................ | 125 | 4311 | 703 | 1550 | .454 | 459 | 584 | .786 | 581 | 713 | 2094 | 4.6 | 5.7 | 16.8 |

Three-point field goals: 2000-01, 41-for-110 (.373). 2001-02, 51-for-142 (.359). 2002-03, 64-for-189 (.339). 2003-04, 73-for-187 (.390). Totals, 229-for-628 (.365).

## NBA REGULAR-SEASON RECORD

**HONORS:** NBA All-Rookie second team (2005).

| Season Team | G | Min. | FGM | FGA | Pct. | FTM | FTA | Pct. | REBOUNDS Off. | Def. | Tot. | Ast. | St. | Blk. | TO | Pts. | AVERAGES RPG | APG | PPG |
|---|---|---|---|---|---|---|---|---|---|---|---|---|---|---|---|---|---|---|---|
| 04-05—Orlando......... | 79 | 1612 | 286 | 628 | .455 | 73 | 107 | .682 | 52 | 141 | 193 | 237 | 78 | 3 | 117 | 689 | 2.4 | 3.0 | 8.7 |

Three-point field goals: 2004-05, 44-for-141 (.312). Totals, 44-for-141 (.312).
Personal fouls/disqualifications: 2004-05, 199/4. Totals, 199/4.

# NENE  F/C  NUGGETS

**PERSONAL:** Born September 13, 1982, in Sao Carlos, Brazil. ... 6-11/260. (2.11/117.9). ... Formerly known as Maybyner Rodney Hilario.
**HIGH SCHOOL:** Instituto Alvaro Guiao (Sao Carlos, Brazil).
**TRANSACTIONS/CAREER NOTES:** Played in Brazil (2000-02). ... Selected by New York Knicks in first round (seventh pick overall) of 2002 NBA Draft. ... Draft rights traded by Knicks with F/C Marcus Camby and G Mark Jackson to Denver Nuggets for F Antonio McDyess, draft rights to G Frank Williams and 2003 second-round draft choice (June 26, 2002).

## BRAZILIAN LEAGUE RECORD

| Season Team | G | Min. | FGM | FGA | Pct. | FTM | FTA | Pct. | Reb. | Ast. | Pts. | AVERAGES RPG | APG | PPG |
|---|---|---|---|---|---|---|---|---|---|---|---|---|---|---|
| 00-01—Vasco da Gama ............. | 38 | ... | 118 | 171 | .690 | 68 | 117 | .581 | 224 | 27 | 304 | 5.9 | 0.7 | 8.0 |
| 01-02—Vasco da Gama ............. | 15 | 450 | 78 | 117 | .667 | 41 | 60 | .683 | 151 | 25 | 198 | 10.1 | 1.7 | 13.2 |
| Totals ..................................... | 53 | 450 | 196 | 288 | .681 | 109 | 177 | .616 | 375 | 52 | 502 | 7.1 | 1.0 | 9.5 |

**HONORS:** NBA All-Rookie first team (2003).

## NBA REGULAR-SEASON RECORD

| Season Team | G | Min. | FGM | FGA | Pct. | FTM | FTA | Pct. | REBOUNDS Off. | Def. | Tot. | Ast. | St. | Blk. | TO | Pts. | AVERAGES RPG | APG | PPG |
|---|---|---|---|---|---|---|---|---|---|---|---|---|---|---|---|---|---|---|---|
| 02-03—Denver ........... | 80 | 2258 | 321 | 619 | .519 | 197 | 341 | .578 | 208 | 283 | 491 | 149 | 127 | 65 | 181 | 839 | 6.1 | 1.9 | 10.5 |
| 03-04—Denver ........... | 77 | 2504 | 334 | 630 | .530 | 240 | 352 | .682 | 154 | 349 | 503 | 168 | 116 | 41 | 183 | 908 | 6.5 | 2.2 | 11.8 |
| 04-05—Denver ........... | 55 | 1317 | 194 | 386 | .503 | 140 | 212 | .660 | 104 | 221 | 325 | 84 | 50 | 48 | 94 | 528 | 5.9 | 1.5 | 9.6 |
| Totals ................... | 212 | 6079 | 849 | 1635 | .519 | 577 | 905 | .638 | 466 | 853 | 1319 | 401 | 293 | 154 | 458 | 2275 | 6.2 | 1.9 | 10.7 |

Three-point field goals: 2002-03, 0-for-3. 2003-04, 0-for-2. 2004-05, 0-for-2. Totals, 0-for-7 (.000).
Personal fouls/disqualifications: 2002-03, 295/4. 2003-04, 280/3. 2004-05, 167/0. Totals, 742/7.

## NBA PLAYOFF RECORD

| Season Team | G | Min. | FGM | FGA | Pct. | FTM | FTA | Pct. | REBOUNDS Off. | Def. | Tot. | Ast. | St. | Blk. | TO | Pts. | AVERAGES RPG | APG | PPG |
|---|---|---|---|---|---|---|---|---|---|---|---|---|---|---|---|---|---|---|---|
| 03-04—Denver ........... | 5 | 132 | 16 | 36 | .444 | 7 | 13 | .538 | 12 | 13 | 25 | 15 | 5 | 3 | 9 | 39 | 5.0 | 3.0 | 7.8 |
| 04-05—Denver ........... | 5 | 101 | 9 | 21 | .429 | 15 | 23 | .652 | 9 | 16 | 25 | 2 | 2 | 2 | 5 | 33 | 5.0 | 0.4 | 6.6 |
| Totals ................... | 10 | 233 | 25 | 57 | .439 | 22 | 36 | .611 | 21 | 29 | 50 | 17 | 7 | 5 | 14 | 72 | 5.0 | 1.7 | 7.2 |

Personal fouls/disqualifications: 2003-04, 22/0. 2004-05, 16/0. Totals, 38/0.

# NESTEROVIC, RASHO  C  SPURS

**PERSONAL:** Born May 30, 1976, in Ljubljana, Slovenia. ... 7-0/250. (2.13/113.4).
**HIGH SCHOOL:** Gymnasium (Sremski Karlovci, Slovenia).
**TRANSACTIONS/CAREER NOTES:** Played in Slovenia (1996-97). ... Played in Italy (1997-99). ... Selected by Minnesota Timberwolves in first round (17th pick overall) of 1998 NBA Draft. ... Signed as free agent by San Antonio Spurs (July 16, 2003).

**N**

**MISCELLANEOUS:** Member of NBA championship team (2005).

## ITALIAN LEAGUE RECORD

| | | | | | | | | | | | | AVERAGES | | |
|---|---|---|---|---|---|---|---|---|---|---|---|---|---|---|
| Season Team | G | Min. | FGM | FGA | Pct. | FTM | FTA | Pct. | Reb. | Ast. | Pts. | RPG | APG | PPG |
| 97-98—Virtus Kinder Bologna .... | 26 | 587 | 84 | 124 | .677 | 13 | 30 | .433 | 139 | 3 | 181 | 5.3 | 0.1 | 7.0 |
| 98-99—Virtus Roma ................. | 26 | 852 | 152 | 233 | .652 | 47 | 79 | .595 | 162 | 11 | 351 | 6.2 | 0.4 | 13.5 |
| Totals ......................... | 52 | 1439 | 236 | 357 | .661 | 60 | 109 | .550 | 301 | 14 | 532 | 5.8 | 0.3 | 10.2 |

Three-point field goals: 1997-98, 0-for-1. Totals, 0-for-1 (.000).

## NBA REGULAR-SEASON RECORD

| | | | | | | | | | REBOUNDS | | | | | | | | AVERAGES | | |
|---|---|---|---|---|---|---|---|---|---|---|---|---|---|---|---|---|---|---|---|
| Season Team | G | Min. | FGM | FGA | Pct. | FTM | FTA | Pct. | Off. | Def. | Tot. | Ast. | St. | Blk. | TO | Pts. | RPG | APG | PPG |
| 98-99—Minnesota....... | 2 | 30 | 3 | 12 | .250 | 2 | 2 | 1.000 | 3 | 5 | 8 | 1 | 0 | 0 | 1 | 8 | 4.0 | 0.5 | 4.0 |
| 99-00—Minnesota....... | 82 | 1723 | 206 | 433 | .476 | 59 | 103 | .573 | 135 | 244 | 379 | 93 | 21 | 85 | 71 | 471 | 4.6 | 1.1 | 5.7 |
| 00-01—Minnesota....... | 73 | 1233 | 147 | 319 | .461 | 34 | 65 | .523 | 99 | 187 | 286 | 45 | 25 | 63 | 55 | 328 | 3.9 | 0.6 | 4.5 |
| 01-02—Minnesota....... | 82 | 2218 | 324 | 657 | .493 | 39 | 71 | .549 | 200 | 334 | 534 | 75 | 45 | 109 | 94 | 687 | 6.5 | 0.9 | 8.4 |
| 02-03—Minnesota....... | 77 | 2337 | 400 | 762 | .525 | 61 | 95 | .642 | 146 | 358 | 504 | 114 | 39 | 116 | 99 | 861 | 6.5 | 1.5 | 11.2 |
| 03-04—San Antonio .... | 82 | 2353 | 328 | 700 | .469 | 54 | 114 | .474 | 257 | 376 | 633 | 114 | 51 | 165 | 107 | 710 | 7.7 | 1.4 | 8.7 |
| 04-05—San Antonio .... | 70 | 1785 | 198 | 430 | .460 | 14 | 30 | .467 | 184 | 275 | 459 | 71 | 31 | 117 | 73 | 410 | 6.6 | 1.0 | 5.9 |
| Totals ................. | 468 | 11679 | 1606 | 3313 | .485 | 263 | 480 | .548 | 1024 | 1779 | 2803 | 513 | 212 | 655 | 500 | 3475 | 6.0 | 1.1 | 7.4 |

Three-point field goals: 1999-00, 0-for-2. 2000-01, 0-for-1. 2001-02, 0-for-1. 2002-03, 0-for-2. Totals, 0-for-6 (.000).
Personal fouls/disqualifications: 1998-99, 5/0. 1999-00, 262/9. 2000-01, 189/3. 2001-02, 262/3. 2002-03, 256/9. 2003-04, 247/5. 2004-05, 207/1. Totals, 1428/30.

## NBA PLAYOFF RECORD

| | | | | | | | | | REBOUNDS | | | | | | | | AVERAGES | | |
|---|---|---|---|---|---|---|---|---|---|---|---|---|---|---|---|---|---|---|---|
| Season Team | G | Min. | FGM | FGA | Pct. | FTM | FTA | Pct. | Off. | Def. | Tot. | Ast. | St. | Blk. | TO | Pts. | RPG | APG | PPG |
| 98-99—Minnesota....... | 3 | 29 | 4 | 8 | .500 | 0 | 0 | ... | 4 | 3 | 7 | 3 | 0 | 0 | 1 | 8 | 2.3 | 1.0 | 2.7 |
| 99-00—Minnesota....... | 4 | 126 | 11 | 25 | .440 | 3 | 6 | .500 | 5 | 8 | 13 | 6 | 3 | 7 | 4 | 25 | 3.3 | 1.5 | 6.3 |
| 00-01—Minnesota....... | 4 | 49 | 5 | 13 | .385 | 0 | 0 | ... | 5 | 7 | 12 | 3 | 1 | 3 | 3 | 10 | 3.0 | 0.8 | 2.5 |
| 01-02—Minnesota....... | 3 | 92 | 15 | 31 | .484 | 4 | 9 | .444 | 6 | 14 | 20 | 3 | 1 | 0 | 4 | 34 | 6.7 | 1.0 | 11.3 |
| 02-03—Minnesota....... | 6 | 169 | 19 | 38 | .500 | 4 | 6 | .667 | 9 | 21 | 30 | 4 | 1 | 4 | 5 | 42 | 5.0 | 0.7 | 7.0 |
| 03-04—San Antonio .... | 10 | 261 | 29 | 67 | .433 | 1 | 6 | .167 | 21 | 34 | 55 | 10 | 3 | 11 | 8 | 59 | 5.5 | 1.0 | 5.9 |
| 04-05—San Antonio .... | 15 | 114 | 5 | 12 | .417 | 0 | 2 | .000 | 11 | 15 | 26 | 2 | 1 | 5 | 4 | 10 | 1.7 | 0.1 | 0.7 |
| Totals ................. | 45 | 840 | 88 | 194 | .454 | 12 | 29 | .414 | 61 | 102 | 163 | 31 | 10 | 30 | 29 | 188 | 3.6 | 0.7 | 4.2 |

Three-point field goals: 2003-04, 0-for-1. Totals, 0-for-1 (.000).
Personal fouls/disqualifications: 1998-99, 4/0. 1999-00, 20/1. 2000-01, 9/0. 2001-02, 10/0. 2002-03, 28/1. 2003-04, 38/0. 2004-05, 16/0. Totals, 125/2.

# NEWBLE, IRA                    F                    CAVALIERS

**PERSONAL:** Born January 20, 1975, in Detroit. ... 6-7/220. (2.01/99.8).
**HIGH SCHOOL:** Southfield (Mich.).
**JUNIOR COLLEGE:** Mississippi Gulf Coast Junior College.
**COLLEGE:** Miami of Ohio.
**TRANSACTIONS/CAREER NOTES:** Not drafted by an NBA franchise. ... Played in International Basketball Association with Wisconsin Blast (1997-98). ... Played in Continental Basketball Association with Idaho Stampede (1997-98 through 1999-2000) and Flint Fuze (2001-02). ... Signed as free agent by San Antonio Spurs (September 25, 1999). ... Waived by Spurs (October 27, 1999). ... Played in Cyprus (1999-2000). ... Re-signed by Spurs (August 12, 2000). ... Signed as free agent by Atlanta Hawks (October 1, 2001). ... Waived by Hawks (October 24, 2001). ... Re-signed by Hawks to 10-day contract (January 23, 2002). ... Signed by Hawks for remainder of season (February 12, 2002). ... Signed as free agent by Cleveland Cavaliers (July 22, 2003).

## COLLEGIATE RECORD

| | | | | | | | | | | | | AVERAGES | | |
|---|---|---|---|---|---|---|---|---|---|---|---|---|---|---|
| Season Team | G | Min. | FGM | FGA | Pct. | FTM | FTA | Pct. | Reb. | Ast. | Pts. | RPG | APG | PPG |
| 93-94—Mississippi Gulf Coast.... | | | | | | Statistics unavailable. | | | | | | | | |
| 94-95—Mississippi Gulf Coast.... | | | | | | Statistics unavailable. | | | | | | | | |
| 95-96—Miami of Ohio ............... | 29 | 452 | 86 | 178 | .483 | 14 | 24 | .583 | 152 | 12 | 186 | 5.2 | 0.4 | 6.4 |
| 96-97—Miami of Ohio ............... | 29 | 756 | 138 | 231 | .597 | 49 | 74 | .662 | 218 | 35 | 329 | 7.5 | 1.2 | 11.3 |
| Totals ......................... | 58 | 1208 | 224 | 409 | .548 | 63 | 98 | .643 | 370 | 47 | 515 | 6.4 | 0.8 | 8.9 |

Three-point field goals: 1995-96, 0-for-7. 1996-97, 4-for-10 (.400). Totals, 4-for-17 (.235).
Personal fouls/disqualifications: 1995-96, 51/0. 1996-97, 93/0. Totals, 144/0.

## CBA RECORD

| | | | | | | | | | | | | AVERAGES | | |
|---|---|---|---|---|---|---|---|---|---|---|---|---|---|---|
| Season Team | G | Min. | FGM | FGA | Pct. | FTM | FTA | Pct. | Reb. | Ast. | Pts. | RPG | APG | PPG |
| 97-98—Idaho.................... | 16 | 260 | 50 | 87 | .575 | 20 | 29 | .690 | 66 | 10 | 123 | 4.1 | 0.6 | 7.7 |
| 98-99—Idaho.................... | 31 | 838 | 148 | 267 | .554 | 57 | 85 | .671 | 141 | 37 | 359 | 4.5 | 1.2 | 11.6 |
| 99-00—Idaho.................... | 53 | 2026 | 330 | 622 | .531 | 133 | 174 | .764 | 369 | 149 | 818 | 7.0 | 2.8 | 15.4 |
| 01-02—Flint.................... | 15 | 584 | 123 | 249 | .494 | 70 | 82 | .854 | 108 | 43 | 321 | 7.2 | 2.9 | 21.4 |
| Totals ......................... | 115 | 3708 | 651 | 1225 | .531 | 280 | 370 | .757 | 684 | 239 | 1621 | 5.9 | 2.1 | 14.1 |

Three-point field goals: 1997-98, 3-for-6 (.500). 1998-99, 6-for-25 (.240). 1999-00, 25-for-67 (.373). 2001-02, 5-for-25 (.200). Totals, 39-for-123 (.317).
Personal fouls/disqualifications: 1997-98, 40/0. 1998-99, 74/0. 1999-00, 173/0. Totals, 287/0.

## IBA RECORD

| | | | | | | | | | | | | AVERAGES | | |
|---|---|---|---|---|---|---|---|---|---|---|---|---|---|---|
| Season Team | G | Min. | FGM | FGA | Pct. | FTM | FTA | Pct. | Reb. | Ast. | Pts. | RPG | APG | PPG |
| 97-98—Wisconsin ..................... | 13 | 369 | 92 | 165 | .558 | 26 | 41 | .634 | 98 | 20 | 214 | 7.5 | 1.5 | 16.5 |

Three-point field goals: 1997-98, 4-for-4 (1.000). Totals, 4-for-4 (1.000).

## CYPRUS RECORD

| Season Team | G | Min. | FGM | FGA | Pct. | FTM | FTA | Pct. | Reb. | Ast. | Pts. | AVERAGES RPG | APG | PPG |
|---|---|---|---|---|---|---|---|---|---|---|---|---|---|---|
| 99-00—Keravnos Keo Nicosia .... | 44 | 1649 | 259 | 499 | .519 | 108 | 141 | .766 | 312 | 126 | 642 | 7.1 | 2.9 | 14.6 |

Three-point field goals: 1999-00, 16-for-46 (.348). Totals, 16-for-46 (.348).

## NBA REGULAR-SEASON RECORD

| Season Team | G | Min. | FGM | FGA | Pct. | FTM | FTA | Pct. | REBOUNDS Off. | Def. | Tot. | Ast. | St. | Blk. | TO | Pts. | AVERAGES RPG | APG | PPG |
|---|---|---|---|---|---|---|---|---|---|---|---|---|---|---|---|---|---|---|---|
| 00-01—San Antonio.... | 27 | 184 | 21 | 55 | .382 | 8 | 16 | .500 | 13 | 22 | 35 | 6 | 2 | 4 | 7 | 54 | 1.3 | 0.2 | 2.0 |
| 01-02—Atlanta ........... | 42 | 1273 | 131 | 263 | .498 | 75 | 88 | .852 | 80 | 142 | 222 | 45 | 38 | 20 | 49 | 338 | 5.3 | 1.1 | 8.0 |
| 02-03—Atlanta ........... | 73 | 1931 | 231 | 467 | .495 | 70 | 90 | .778 | 86 | 185 | 271 | 99 | 50 | 26 | 69 | 564 | 3.7 | 1.4 | 7.7 |
| 03-04—Cleveland ....... | 64 | 1245 | 108 | 276 | .391 | 36 | 46 | .783 | 65 | 90 | 155 | 72 | 25 | 19 | 54 | 254 | 2.4 | 1.1 | 4.0 |
| 04-05—Cleveland ....... | 74 | 1832 | 182 | 424 | .429 | 55 | 69 | .797 | 78 | 142 | 220 | 91 | 50 | 18 | 61 | 438 | 3.0 | 1.2 | 5.9 |
| Totals ................... | 280 | 6465 | 673 | 1485 | .453 | 244 | 309 | .790 | 322 | 581 | 903 | 313 | 165 | 87 | 240 | 1648 | 3.2 | 1.1 | 5.9 |

Three-point field goals: 2000-01, 4-for-9 (.444). 2001-02, 1-for-7 (.143). 2002-03, 32-for-84 (.381). 2003-04, 2-for-19 (.105). 2004-05, 19-for-53 (.358). Totals, 58-for-172 (.337).
Personal fouls/disqualifications: 2000-01, 18/0. 2001-02, 117/2. 2002-03, 174/1. 2003-04, 109/1. 2004-05, 144/1. Totals, 562/5.

# NOCIONI, ANDRES  F  BULLS

**PERSONAL:** Born November 30, 1979, in Santa Fe, Argentina. ... 6-7/225. (2.01/102.1).
**TRANSACTIONS/CAREER NOTES:** Not drafted by an NBA franchise. ... Played in Argentina (1995-99). ... Played in Spain (1999-2004). ... Signed as free agent by Chicago Bulls (August 11, 2004).
**MISCELLANEOUS:** Member of gold-medal-winning Argentian Olympic Team (2004).

## ARGENTINIAN LEAGUE RECORD

| Season Team | G | Min. | FGM | FGA | Pct. | FTM | FTA | Pct. | Reb. | Ast. | Pts. | AVERAGES RPG | APG | PPG |
|---|---|---|---|---|---|---|---|---|---|---|---|---|---|---|
| 95-96—Racing Club Avellaneda.. | 31 | ... | 76 | 130 | .585 | 24 | 43 | .558 | 47 | 10 | 185 | 1.5 | 0.3 | 6.0 |
| 96-97—Olympia Venada Tuerto .. | 34 | ... | 68 | 135 | .504 | 57 | 84 | .679 | 63 | 4 | 205 | 1.9 | 0.1 | 6.0 |
| 97-98—Independiente General Pico | 50 | ... | 168 | 292 | .575 | 112 | 169 | .663 | 187 | 14 | 453 | 3.7 | 0.3 | 9.1 |
| 98-99—Independiente General Pico | 60 | ... | 274 | 478 | .573 | 145 | 217 | .668 | 265 | 31 | 717 | 4.4 | 0.5 | 12.0 |
| Totals ..................................... | 175 | ... | 586 | 1035 | .566 | 338 | 513 | .659 | 562 | 59 | 1560 | 3.2 | 0.3 | 8.9 |

Three-point field goals: 1995-96, 9-for-16 (.563). 1996-97, 12-for-29 (.414). 1997-98, 5-for-19 (.263). 1998-99, 24-for-53 (.453). Totals, 50-for-117 (.427).

## SPANISH RECORD

| Season Team | G | Min. | FGM | FGA | Pct. | FTM | FTA | Pct. | Reb. | Ast. | Pts. | AVERAGES RPG | APG | PPG |
|---|---|---|---|---|---|---|---|---|---|---|---|---|---|---|
| 99-00—Tau Ceramica.................. | 8 | 84 | 11 | 21 | .524 | 9 | 15 | .600 | 16 | 1 | 33 | 2.0 | 0.1 | 4.1 |
| 00-01—Tau Ceramica.................. | 33 | 768 | 137 | 292 | .469 | 78 | 106 | .736 | 176 | 28 | 395 | 5.3 | 0.8 | 12.0 |
| 02-03—Tau Ceramica.................. | 34 | 1036 | 209 | 451 | .463 | 122 | 158 | .772 | 232 | 52 | 590 | 6.8 | 1.5 | 17.4 |
| 03-04—Tau Ceramica.................. | 29 | 880 | 170 | 364 | .467 | 79 | 110 | .718 | 222 | 52 | 465 | 7.7 | 1.8 | 16.0 |
| Totals ..................................... | 104 | 2768 | 527 | 1128 | .467 | 288 | 389 | .740 | 646 | 133 | 1483 | 6.2 | 1.3 | 14.3 |

Three-point field goals: 1999-00, 2-for-3 (.667). 2000-01, 43-for-127 (.339). 2002-03, 50-for-139 (.360). 2003-04, 46-for-119 (.387). Totals, 141-for-388 (.363).

## NBA REGULAR-SEASON RECORD

| Season Team | G | Min. | FGM | FGA | Pct. | FTM | FTA | Pct. | REBOUNDS Off. | Def. | Tot. | Ast. | St. | Blk. | TO | Pts. | AVERAGES RPG | APG | PPG |
|---|---|---|---|---|---|---|---|---|---|---|---|---|---|---|---|---|---|---|---|
| 04-05—Chicago .......... | 81 | 1892 | 241 | 601 | .401 | 170 | 222 | .766 | 69 | 317 | 386 | 122 | 37 | 34 | 135 | 677 | 4.8 | 1.5 | 8.4 |

Three-point field goals: 2004-05, 25-for-97 (.258). Totals, 25-for-97 (.258).
Personal fouls/disqualifications: 2004-05, 208/3. Totals, 208/3.

## NBA PLAYOFF RECORD

| Season Team | G | Min. | FGM | FGA | Pct. | FTM | FTA | Pct. | REBOUNDS Off. | Def. | Tot. | Ast. | St. | Blk. | TO | Pts. | AVERAGES RPG | APG | PPG |
|---|---|---|---|---|---|---|---|---|---|---|---|---|---|---|---|---|---|---|---|
| 04-05—Chicago .......... | 6 | 202 | 27 | 67 | .403 | 17 | 23 | .739 | 8 | 41 | 49 | 14 | 1 | 6 | 11 | 77 | 8.2 | 2.3 | 12.8 |

Three-point field goals: 2004-05, 6-for-17 (.353). Totals, 6-for-17 (.353).
Personal fouls/disqualifications: 2004-05, 20/0. Totals, 20/0.

**N**

# NORRIS, MOOCHIE  G  ROCKETS

**PERSONAL:** Born July 27, 1973, in Washington, D.C. ... 6-1/175. (1.85/79.4).
**HIGH SCHOOL:** Cardoza (Washington, D.C.).
**JUNIOR COLLEGE:** Odessa (Texas) Junior College.
**COLLEGE:** Auburn, then West Florida.
**TRANSACTIONS/CAREER NOTES:** Selected by Milwaukee Bucks in second round (33rd pick overall) of 1996 NBA Draft. ... Waived by Bucks (November 22, 1996). ... Played in Continental Basketball Association with Florida Beachdogs (1996-97) and Fort Wayne Fury (1996-97 through 1999-2000). ... Signed as free agent by Vancouver Grizzlies (December 12, 1996). ... Waived by Grizzlies (December 30, 1996). ... Played in France (1997-98). ... Signed as free agent by Seattle SuperSonics (January 21, 1999). ... Waived by SuperSonics (March 23, 1999). ... Signed by Houston Rockets to first of two consecutive 10-day contracts (February 8, 2000). ... Re-signed by Rockets for remainder of season (February 28, 2000). ... Traded by Rockets with F/C John Amaechi to New York Knicks for F Clarence Weatherspoon (December 30, 2003). ... Traded by Knicks with F Vin Baker and second-round pick in 2006 draft to Houston Rockets for F Maurice Taylor (February 24, 2005).

## COLLEGIATE RECORD

| Season Team | G | Min. | FGM | FGA | Pct. | FTM | FTA | Pct. | Reb. | Ast. | Pts. | AVERAGES RPG | APG | PPG |
|---|---|---|---|---|---|---|---|---|---|---|---|---|---|---|
| 92-93—Odessa J.C. ................... | 32 | ... | 160 | 290 | .552 | 121 | 171 | .708 | 91 | 225 | 459 | 2.8 | 7.0 | 14.3 |

| Season Team | G | Min. | FGM | FGA | Pct. | FTM | FTA | Pct. | Reb. | Ast. | Pts. | RPG | APG | PPG |
|---|---|---|---|---|---|---|---|---|---|---|---|---|---|---|
| 93-94—Odessa J.C. ............ | 27 | ... | 147 | 264 | .557 | 83 | 120 | .692 | 104 | 214 | 401 | 3.9 | 7.9 | 14.9 |
| 94-95—Auburn ............ | 29 | 1009 | 124 | 312 | .397 | 58 | 83 | .699 | 116 | 143 | 363 | 4.0 | 4.9 | 12.5 |
| 95-96—West Florida ............ | 16 | 615 | 121 | 265 | .457 | 86 | 113 | .761 | 92 | 143 | 378 | 5.8 | 8.9 | 23.6 |
| Junior College Totals............ | 75 | 615 | 428 | 819 | .523 | 290 | 404 | .718 | 287 | 582 | 1238 | 3.8 | 7.8 | 16.5 |
| 4-Year-College Totals............ | 29 | 1009 | 124 | 312 | .397 | 58 | 83 | .699 | 116 | 143 | 363 | 4.0 | 4.9 | 12.5 |

Three-point field goals: 1992-93, 18-for-43 (.419). 1993-94, 24-for-60 (.400). 1994-95, 57-for-161 (.354). 1995-96, 50-for-118 (.424). Totals, 149-for-382 (.390).

## CBA RECORD

**NOTES:** CBA All-League second team (1998). ... CBA All-Rookie second team (1997). ... CBA All-League first team (2000).

| Season Team | G | Min. | FGM | FGA | Pct. | FTM | FTA | Pct. | Reb. | Ast. | Pts. | RPG | APG | PPG |
|---|---|---|---|---|---|---|---|---|---|---|---|---|---|---|
| 96-97—Florida-Fort Wayne........ | 31 | 745 | 97 | 226 | .429 | 58 | 81 | .716 | 82 | 94 | 273 | 2.6 | 3.0 | 8.8 |
| 97-98—Fort Wayne.................. | 46 | 1413 | 208 | 404 | .515 | 126 | 167 | .754 | 226 | 244 | 552 | 4.9 | 5.3 | 12.0 |
| 98-99—Fort Wayne.................. | 18 | 669 | 95 | 189 | .503 | 80 | 97 | .825 | 105 | 144 | 278 | 5.8 | 8.0 | 15.4 |
| 99-00—Fort Wayne.................. | 33 | 1372 | 239 | 488 | .490 | 165 | 202 | .817 | 166 | 200 | 664 | 5.0 | 6.1 | 20.1 |
| Totals ........................ | 128 | 4199 | 639 | 1307 | .489 | 429 | 547 | .784 | 579 | 682 | 1767 | 4.5 | 5.3 | 13.8 |

Three-point field goals: 1996-97, 21-for-76 (.276). 1997-98, 10-for-39 (.256). 1998-99, 8-for-16 (.500). 1999-00, 21-for-61 (.344). Totals, 60-for-192 (.313).

Personal fouls/disqualifications: 1996-97, 54/0. 1997-98, 93/0. 1998-99, 29/0. 1999-00, 76/0. Totals, 252/0.

## NBA REGULAR-SEASON RECORD

| Season Team | G | Min. | FGM | FGA | Pct. | FTM | FTA | Pct. | REBOUNDS | | | Ast. | St. | Blk. | TO | Pts. | AVERAGES | | |
|---|---|---|---|---|---|---|---|---|---|---|---|---|---|---|---|---|---|---|---|
| | | | | | | | | | Off. | Def. | Tot. | | | | | | RPG | APG | PPG |
| 96-97—Vancouver....... | 8 | 89 | 4 | 22 | .182 | 2 | 5 | .400 | 3 | 9 | 12 | 23 | 4 | 0 | 5 | 12 | 1.5 | 2.9 | 1.5 |
| 98-99—Seattle ............ | 12 | 140 | 13 | 40 | .325 | 6 | 16 | .375 | 4 | 16 | 20 | 24 | 7 | 0 | 16 | 38 | 1.7 | 2.0 | 3.2 |
| 99-00—Houston......... | 30 | 502 | 69 | 159 | .434 | 57 | 73 | .781 | 16 | 52 | 68 | 94 | 23 | 1 | 30 | 207 | 2.3 | 3.1 | 6.9 |
| 00-01—Houston......... | 82 | 1654 | 184 | 413 | .446 | 151 | 194 | .778 | 44 | 154 | 198 | 283 | 69 | 2 | 107 | 544 | 2.4 | 3.5 | 6.6 |
| 01-02—Houston......... | 82 | 2249 | 251 | 631 | .398 | 127 | 169 | .751 | 73 | 173 | 246 | 403 | 81 | 4 | 156 | 665 | 3.0 | 4.9 | 8.1 |
| 02-03—Houston......... | 82 | 1375 | 134 | 330 | .406 | 78 | 114 | .684 | 37 | 122 | 159 | 196 | 55 | 4 | 86 | 357 | 1.9 | 2.4 | 4.4 |
| 03-04—Houston-N.Y. .. | 66 | 847 | 80 | 217 | .369 | 54 | 71 | .761 | 10 | 55 | 65 | 121 | 44 | 5 | 64 | 234 | 1.0 | 1.8 | 3.5 |
| 04-05—N.Y.-Houston .. | 38 | 360 | 35 | 109 | .321 | 20 | 24 | .833 | 10 | 36 | 46 | 39 | 18 | 2 | 27 | 90 | 1.2 | 1.0 | 2.4 |
| Totals ................... | 400 | 7216 | 770 | 1921 | .401 | 495 | 666 | .743 | 197 | 617 | 814 | 1183 | 301 | 18 | 491 | 2147 | 2.0 | 3.0 | 5.4 |

Three-point field goals: 1996-97, 2-for-10 (.200). 1998-99, 6-for-15 (.400). 1999-00, 12-for-29 (.414). 2000-01, 25-for-89 (.281). 2001-02, 36-for-134 (.269). 2002-03, 11-for-45 (.244). 2003-04, 20-for-58 (.345). 2004-05, 0-for-12. Totals, 112-for-392 (.286).

Personal fouls/disqualifications: 1996-97, 5/0. 1998-99, 17/0. 1999-00, 32/0. 2000-01, 84/0. 2001-02, 130/0. 2002-03, 72/0. 2003-04, 51/0. 2004-05, 44/0. Totals, 435/0.

## NBA PLAYOFF RECORD

| Season Team | G | Min. | FGM | FGA | Pct. | FTM | FTA | Pct. | REBOUNDS | | | Ast. | St. | Blk. | TO | Pts. | AVERAGES | | |
|---|---|---|---|---|---|---|---|---|---|---|---|---|---|---|---|---|---|---|---|
| | | | | | | | | | Off. | Def. | Tot. | | | | | | RPG | APG | PPG |
| 04-05—Houston.......... | 2 | 7 | 0 | 1 | .000 | 0 | 0 | ... | 0 | 0 | 0 | 0 | 0 | 0 | 0 | 0 | 0.0 | 0.0 | 0.0 |

## FRENCH LEAGUE RECORD

| Season Team | G | Min. | FGM | FGA | Pct. | FTM | FTA | Pct. | Reb. | Ast. | Pts. | RPG | APG | PPG |
|---|---|---|---|---|---|---|---|---|---|---|---|---|---|---|
| 97-98—Pau Orthez.................... | 8 | 177 | 26 | 45 | .578 | 24 | 33 | .727 | 33 | 21 | 79 | 4.1 | 2.6 | 9.9 |

## VENEZUELAN LEAGUE RECORD

| Season Team | G | Min. | FGM | FGA | Pct. | FTM | FTA | Pct. | Reb. | Ast. | Pts. | RPG | APG | PPG |
|---|---|---|---|---|---|---|---|---|---|---|---|---|---|---|
| 99-00—Gaiteros........................ | 6 | 217 | 44 | 86 | .512 | 37 | 64 | .578 | 17 | 48 | 136 | 2.8 | 8.0 | 22.7 |

Three-point field goals: 1999-00, 7-for-22 (.318). Totals, 7-for-22 (.318).
Personal fouls/disqualifications: 1999-00, 18/0. Totals, 18/0.

# NOWITZKI, DIRK          F          MAVERICKS

**PERSONAL:** Born June 19, 1978, in Wurzburg, Germany. ... 7-0/250. (2.13/113.4).
**HIGH SCHOOL:** Rontgen Gymnasium (Wurzburg, Germany).
**TRANSACTIONS/CAREER NOTES:** Played in Germany (1997-99). ... Selected by Milwaukee Bucks in first round (ninth pick overall) of 1998 NBA Draft. ... Draft rights traded by Bucks with draft rights to F Pat Garrity to Dallas Mavericks for draft rights to F Robert Traylor (June 24, 1998).

## GERMAN LEAGUE RECORD

| Season Team | G | Min. | FGM | FGA | Pct. | FTM | FTA | Pct. | Reb. | Ast. | Pts. | RPG | APG | PPG |
|---|---|---|---|---|---|---|---|---|---|---|---|---|---|---|
| 97-98—DJK Wurzburg............... | 20 | 699 | 206 | 367 | .561 | 135 | 177 | .763 | 198 | 20 | 565 | 9.9 | 1.0 | 28.3 |
| 98-99—DJK Wurzburg............... | 16 | 599 | 123 | 275 | .447 | 100 | 128 | .781 | 135 | 50 | 366 | 8.4 | 3.1 | 22.9 |
| Totals ..................................... | 36 | 1298 | 329 | 642 | .512 | 235 | 305 | .770 | 333 | 70 | 931 | 9.3 | 1.9 | 25.9 |

Three-point field goals: 1997-98, 18-for-54 (.333). 1998-99, 20-for-76 (.263). Totals, 38-for-130 (.292).

## NBA REGULAR-SEASON RECORD

**HONORS:** All-NBA second team (2002, 2003). ... All-NBA third team (2001, 2004). ... All-NBA first team (2005).

| Season Team | G | Min. | FGM | FGA | Pct. | FTM | FTA | Pct. | REBOUNDS | | | Ast. | St. | Blk. | TO | Pts. | AVERAGES | | |
|---|---|---|---|---|---|---|---|---|---|---|---|---|---|---|---|---|---|---|---|
| | | | | | | | | | Off. | Def. | Tot. | | | | | | RPG | APG | PPG |
| 98-99—Dallas.............. | 47 | 958 | 136 | 336 | .405 | 99 | 128 | .773 | 41 | 121 | 162 | 47 | 29 | 27 | 73 | 385 | 3.4 | 1.0 | 8.2 |
| 99-00—Dallas.............. | 82 | 2938 | 515 | 1118 | .461 | 289 | 348 | .830 | 102 | 430 | 532 | 203 | 63 | 68 | 141 | 1435 | 6.5 | 2.5 | 17.5 |
| 00-01—Dallas.............. | 82 | 3125 | 591 | 1247 | .474 | 451 | 538 | .838 | 119 | 635 | 754 | 173 | 79 | 101 | 156 | 1784 | 9.2 | 2.1 | 21.8 |

| Season Team | G | Min. | FGM | FGA | Pct. | FTM | FTA | Pct. | REBOUNDS Off. | Def. | Tot. | Ast. | St. | Blk. | TO | Pts. | AVERAGES RPG | APG | PPG |
|---|---|---|---|---|---|---|---|---|---|---|---|---|---|---|---|---|---|---|---|
| 01-02—Dallas | 76 | 2891 | 600 | 1258 | .477 | 440 | 516 | .853 | 120 | 635 | 755 | 186 | 83 | 77 | 145 | 1779 | 9.9 | 2.4 | 23.4 |
| 02-03—Dallas | 80 | 3117 | 690 | 1489 | .463 | 483 | 548 | .881 | 81 | 710 | 791 | 239 | 111 | 82 | 152 | 2011 | 9.9 | 3.0 | 25.1 |
| 03-04—Dallas | 77 | 2915 | 605 | 1310 | .462 | 371 | 423 | .877 | 90 | 580 | 670 | 207 | 92 | 104 | 135 | 1680 | 8.7 | 2.7 | 21.8 |
| 04-05—Dallas | 78 | 3020 | 663 | 1445 | .459 | 615 | 708 | .869 | 96 | 661 | 757 | 240 | 97 | 119 | 176 | 2032 | 9.7 | 3.1 | 26.1 |
| **Totals** | 522 | 18964 | 3800 | 8203 | .463 | 2748 | 3209 | .856 | 649 | 3772 | 4421 | 1295 | 554 | 578 | 978 | 11106 | 8.5 | 2.5 | 21.3 |

Three-point field goals: 1998-99, 14-for-68 (.206). 1999-00, 116-for-306 (.379). 2000-01, 151-for-390 (.387). 2001-02, 139-for-350 (.397). 2002-03, 148-for-390 (.379). 2003-04, 99-for-290 (.341). 2004-05, 91-for-228 (.399). Totals, 758-for-2022 (.375).

Personal fouls/disqualifications: 1998-99, 105/5. 1999-00, 256/4. 2000-01, 245/1. 2001-02, 222/2. 2002-03, 206/2. 2003-04, 216/3. 2004-05, 219/1. Totals, 1469/18.

## NBA PLAYOFF RECORD

| Season Team | G | Min. | FGM | FGA | Pct. | FTM | FTA | Pct. | REBOUNDS Off. | Def. | Tot. | Ast. | St. | Blk. | TO | Pts. | AVERAGES RPG | APG | PPG |
|---|---|---|---|---|---|---|---|---|---|---|---|---|---|---|---|---|---|---|---|
| 00-01—Dallas | 10 | 399 | 69 | 163 | .423 | 83 | 94 | .883 | 14 | 67 | 81 | 14 | 11 | 8 | 14 | 234 | 8.1 | 1.4 | 23.4 |
| 01-02—Dallas | 8 | 357 | 73 | 164 | .445 | 65 | 74 | .878 | 17 | 88 | 105 | 18 | 16 | 6 | 22 | 227 | 13.1 | 2.3 | 28.4 |
| 02-03—Dallas | 17 | 722 | 150 | 313 | .479 | 103 | 113 | .912 | 15 | 181 | 196 | 37 | 21 | 16 | 40 | 430 | 11.5 | 2.2 | 25.3 |
| 03-04—Dallas | 5 | 212 | 45 | 100 | .450 | 36 | 42 | .857 | 13 | 46 | 59 | 7 | 7 | 13 | 6 | 133 | 11.8 | 1.4 | 26.6 |
| 04-05—Dallas | 13 | 551 | 103 | 256 | .402 | 92 | 111 | .829 | 25 | 106 | 131 | 43 | 18 | 21 | 33 | 308 | 10.1 | 3.3 | 23.7 |
| **Totals** | 53 | 2241 | 440 | 996 | .442 | 379 | 434 | .873 | 84 | 488 | 572 | 119 | 73 | 64 | 115 | 1332 | 10.8 | 2.2 | 25.1 |

Three-point field goals: 2000-01, 13-for-46 (.283). 2001-02, 16-for-28 (.571). 2002-03, 27-for-61 (.443). 2003-04, 7-for-15 (.467). 2004-05, 10-for-30 (.333). Totals, 73-for-180 (.406).

Personal fouls/disqualifications: 2000-01, 37/1. 2001-02, 27/1. 2002-03, 52/0. 2003-04, 16/0. 2004-05, 42/0. Totals, 174/2.

## NBA ALL-STAR GAME RECORD

| Season Team | Min. | FGM | FGA | Pct. | FTM | FTA | Pct. | REBOUNDS Off. | Def. | Tot. | Ast. | PF | Dq. | St. | Blk. | TO | Pts. |
|---|---|---|---|---|---|---|---|---|---|---|---|---|---|---|---|---|---|
| 2002—Dallas | 24 | 5 | 11 | .455 | 1 | 1 | 1.000 | 2 | 6 | 8 | 3 | 1 | 0 | 0 | 0 | 2 | 12 |
| 2003—Dallas | 16 | 4 | 8 | .500 | 0 | 0 | ... | 0 | 1 | 1 | 1 | 1 | 0 | 0 | 0 | 2 | 9 |
| 2004—Dallas | 13 | 1 | 3 | .333 | 0 | 0 | ... | 0 | 0 | 0 | 1 | 0 | 0 | 2 | 0 | 2 | 2 |
| 2005—Dallas | 21 | 4 | 10 | .400 | 1 | 2 | .500 | 3 | 5 | 8 | 2 | 1 | 0 | 4 | 4 | 3 | 10 |
| **Totals** | 74 | 14 | 32 | .438 | 2 | 3 | .667 | 5 | 12 | 17 | 7 | 3 | 0 | 6 | 4 | 9 | 33 |

Three-point field goals: 2002, 1-for-4 (.250). 2003, 1-for-4 (.250). 2004, 0-for-1. 2005, 1-for-3 (.333). Totals, 3-for-12 (.250).

# O'NEAL, JERMAINE          F/C          PACERS

**PERSONAL:** Born October 13, 1978, in Columbia, S.C. ... 6-11/230. (2.11/104.3).
**HIGH SCHOOL:** Eau Claire (Columbia, S.C.).
**COLLEGE:** Did not attend college.
**TRANSACTIONS/CAREER NOTES:** Selected out of high school by Portland Trail Blazers in first round (17th pick overall) of 1996 NBA Draft. ... Traded by Trail Blazers with C Joe Kleine to Indiana Pacers for F Dale Davis (August 31, 2000).

## NBA REGULAR-SEASON RECORD

**HONORS:** NBA Most Improved Player Award (2002). ... All-NBA second team (2004). ... All-NBA third team (2002, 2003).

| Season Team | G | Min. | FGM | FGA | Pct. | FTM | FTA | Pct. | REBOUNDS Off. | Def. | Tot. | Ast. | St. | Blk. | TO | Pts. | AVERAGES RPG | APG | PPG |
|---|---|---|---|---|---|---|---|---|---|---|---|---|---|---|---|---|---|---|---|
| 96-97—Portland | 45 | 458 | 69 | 153 | .451 | 47 | 78 | .603 | 39 | 85 | 124 | 8 | 2 | 26 | 27 | 185 | 2.8 | 0.2 | 4.1 |
| 97-98—Portland | 60 | 808 | 112 | 231 | .485 | 45 | 89 | .506 | 80 | 121 | 201 | 17 | 15 | 58 | 55 | 269 | 3.4 | 0.3 | 4.5 |
| 98-99—Portland | 36 | 311 | 36 | 83 | .434 | 18 | 35 | .514 | 42 | 55 | 97 | 13 | 4 | 14 | 14 | 90 | 2.7 | 0.4 | 2.5 |
| 99-00—Portland | 70 | 859 | 108 | 222 | .486 | 57 | 98 | .582 | 97 | 132 | 229 | 18 | 11 | 55 | 47 | 273 | 3.3 | 0.3 | 3.9 |
| 00-01—Indiana | 81 | 2641 | 404 | 868 | .465 | 233 | 388 | .601 | 249 | 545 | 794 | 98 | 49/d228 | 161 | 1041 | 9.8 | 1.2 | 12.9 |
| 01-02—Indiana | 72 | 2707 | 543 | 1133 | .479 | 284 | 413 | .688 | 188 | 569 | 757 | 118 | 45 | 166 | 174 | 1371 | 10.5 | 1.6 | 19.0 |
| 02-03—Indiana | 77 | 2864 | 610 | 1260 | .484 | 373 | 510 | .731 | 202 | 594 | 796 | 155 | 66 | 178 | 180 | 1600 | 10.3 | 2.0 | 20.8 |
| 03-04—Indiana | 78 | 2788 | 608 | 1400 | .434 | 348 | 460 | .757 | 193 | 585 | 778 | 164 | 59 | 199 | 181 | 1566 | 10.0 | 2.1 | 20.1 |
| 04-05—Indiana | 44 | 1530 | 386 | 854 | .452 | 295 | 391 | .754 | 85 | 303 | 388 | 82 | 25 | 88 | 131 | 1068 | 8.8 | 1.9 | 24.3 |
| **Totals** | 563 | 14966 | 2876 | 6204 | .464 | 1700 | 2462 | .690 | 1175 | 2989 | 4164 | 673 | 276 | 1012 | 970 | 7463 | 7.4 | 1.2 | 13.3 |

Three-point field goals: 1996-97, 0-for-1. 1997-98, 0-for-2. 1998-99, 0-for-1. 1999-00, 0-for-1. 2000-01, 0-for-5. 2001-02, 1-for-14 (.071). 2002-03, 7-for-21 (.333). 2003-04, 2-for-18 (.111). 2004-05, 1-for-6 (.167). Totals, 11-for-69 (.159).

Personal fouls/disqualifications: 1996-97, 46/0. 1997-98, 101/0. 1998-99, 41/0. 1999-00, 127/1. 2000-01, 280/5. 2001-02, 269/4. 2002-03, 277/5. 2003-04, 248/2. 2004-05, 173/4. Totals, 1562/21.

## NBA PLAYOFF RECORD

| Season Team | G | Min. | FGM | FGA | Pct. | FTM | FTA | Pct. | REBOUNDS Off. | Def. | Tot. | Ast. | St. | Blk. | TO | Pts. | AVERAGES RPG | APG | PPG |
|---|---|---|---|---|---|---|---|---|---|---|---|---|---|---|---|---|---|---|---|
| 96-97—Portland | 2 | 4 | 0 | 2 | .000 | 0 | 2 | .000 | 0 | 1 | 1 | 0 | 0 | 1 | 0 | 0 | 0.5 | 0.0 | 0.0 |
| 97-98—Portland | 1 | 3 | 0 | 3 | .000 | 0 | 0 | ... | 1 | 0 | 1 | 0 | 0 | 2 | 0 | 0 | 1.0 | 0.0 | 0.0 |
| 98-99—Portland | 9 | 55 | 4 | 10 | .400 | 6 | 12 | .500 | 8 | 9 | 17 | 1 | 0 | 3 | 2 | 14 | 1.9 | 0.1 | 1.6 |
| 99-00—Portland | 8 | 38 | 3 | 11 | .273 | 6 | 9 | .667 | 2 | 5 | 7 | 1 | 0 | 3 | 0 | 12 | 0.9 | 0.1 | 1.5 |
| 00-01—Indiana | 4 | 157 | 17 | 39 | .436 | 5 | 10 | .500 | 12 | 38 | 50 | 7 | 0 | 10 | 7 | 39 | 12.5 | 1.8 | 9.8 |
| 01-02—Indiana | 5 | 192 | 34 | 76 | .447 | 18 | 24 | .750 | 6 | 32 | 38 | 5 | 4 | 8 | 14 | 86 | 7.6 | 1.0 | 17.2 |
| 02-03—Indiana | 6 | 272 | 43 | 92 | .467 | 51 | 65 | .785 | 24 | 81 | 105 | 4 | 3 | 18 | 18 | 137 | 17.5 | 0.7 | 22.8 |
| 03-04—Indiana | 16 | 604 | 115 | 272 | .423 | 77 | 110 | .700 | 29 | 117 | 146 | 19 | 8 | 36 | 29 | 307 | 9.1 | 1.2 | 19.2 |
| 04-05—Indiana | 13 | 476 | 77 | 211 | .365 | 54 | 72 | .750 | 21 | 83 | 104 | 29 | 7 | 34 | 36 | 208 | 8.0 | 2.2 | 16.0 |
| **Totals** | 64 | 1801 | 293 | 716 | .409 | 217 | 304 | .714 | 103 | 366 | 469 | 66 | 22 | 115 | 106 | 803 | 7.3 | 1.0 | 12.5 |

Three-point field goals: 1996-97, 0-for-1. 1997-98, 0-for-1. 2000-01, 0-for-1. 2001-02, 0-for-2. 2002-03, 0-for-3. 2003-04, 0-for-4. 2004-05, 0-for-3. Totals, 0-for-14 (.000).

Personal fouls/disqualifications: 1997-98, 1/0. 1998-99, 11/0. 1999-00, 9/0. 2000-01, 13/0. 2001-02, 24/1. 2002-03, 22/0. 2003-04, 53/0. 2004-05, 48/1. Totals, 181/2.

## NBA ALL-STAR GAME RECORD

| Season Team | Min. | FGM | FGA | Pct. | FTM | FTA | Pct. | REBOUNDS | | | Ast. | PF | Dq. | St. | Blk. | TO | Pts. |
|---|---|---|---|---|---|---|---|---|---|---|---|---|---|---|---|---|---|
| | | | | | | | | Off. | Def. | Tot. | | | | | | | |
| 2002—Indiana | 17 | 2 | 5 | .400 | 3 | 4 | .750 | 0 | 7 | 7 | 0 | 1 | 0 | 0 | 0 | 1 | 7 |
| 2003—Indiana | 33 | 3 | 10 | .300 | 4 | 6 | .667 | 4 | 6 | 10 | 0 | 2 | 0 | 2 | 4 | 2 | 10 |
| 2004—Indiana | 28 | 7 | 13 | .538 | 2 | 4 | .500 | 2 | 7 | 9 | 2 | 0 | 0 | 1 | 0 | 2 | 16 |
| 2005—Indiana | 19 | 6 | 10 | .600 | 3 | 4 | .750 | 1 | 4 | 5 | 1 | 1 | 0 | 1 | 1 | 1 | 15 |
| Totals | 97 | 18 | 38 | .474 | 12 | 18 | .667 | 7 | 24 | 31 | 3 | 4 | 0 | 4 | 5 | 6 | 48 |

## O'NEAL, SHAQUILLE     C     HEAT

**PERSONAL:** Born March 6, 1972, in Newark, N.J. ... 7-1/315. (2.16/142.9). ... Full name: Shaquille Rashaun O'Neal ... Nickname: Shaq. ... Name pronounced shuh-KEEL.
**HIGH SCHOOL:** Cole (San Antonio).
**COLLEGE:** Louisiana State.
**TRANSACTIONS/CAREER NOTES:** Selected after junior season by Orlando Magic in first round (first pick overall) of 1992 NBA Draft. ... Signed as free agent by Los Angeles Lakers (July 18, 1996). ... Traded by Lakers to Miami Heat for F Lamar Odom, F Caron Butler, F Brian Grant, a first-round draft choice and a second-round draft choice (July 14, 2004).
**CAREER HONORS:** NBA 50th Anniversary All-Time Team (1996).
**MISCELLANEOUS:** Member of NBA championship team (2000, 2001, 2002). ... Member of gold-medal-winning U.S. Olympic team (1996). ... Member of gold-medal-winning U.S. World Championship team (1994). ... Orlando Magic all-time leading rebounder with 3,691 and all-time blocked shots leader with 824 (1992-93 through 1995-96).

### COLLEGIATE RECORD

**NOTES:** THE SPORTING NEWS All-America first team (1991, 1992). ... Led NCAA Division I with 14.7 rebounds per game (1991). ... Led NCAA Division I with 5.2 blocked shots per game (1992).

| Season Team | G | Min. | FGM | FGA | Pct. | FTM | FTA | Pct. | Reb. | Ast. | Pts. | AVERAGES | | |
|---|---|---|---|---|---|---|---|---|---|---|---|---|---|---|
| | | | | | | | | | | | | RPG | APG | PPG |
| 89-90—Louisiana State | 32 | 901 | 180 | 314 | .573 | 85 | 153 | .556 | 385 | 61 | 445 | 12.0 | 1.9 | 13.9 |
| 90-91—Louisiana State | 28 | 881 | 312 | 497 | .628 | 150 | 235 | .638 | 411 | 45 | 774 | 14.7 | 1.6 | 27.6 |
| 91-92—Louisiana State | 30 | 959 | 294 | 478 | .615 | 134 | 254 | .528 | 421 | 46 | 722 | 14.0 | 1.5 | 24.1 |
| Totals | 90 | 2741 | 786 | 1289 | .610 | 369 | 642 | .575 | 1217 | 152 | 1941 | 13.5 | 1.7 | 21.6 |

### NBA REGULAR-SEASON RECORD

**RECORDS:** Holds single-game record for most free throws attempted, none made—11 (December 8, 2000, vs. Seattle).
**HONORS:** NBA Most Valuable Player (2000). ... NBA Rookie of the Year (1993). ... IBM Award, for all-around contributions to team's success (2000, 2001). ... All-NBA first team (1998, 2000, 2001, 2002, 2003, 2004, 2005). ... All-NBA second team (1995, 1999). ... All-NBA third team (1994, 1996, 1997). ... NBA All-Defensive second team (2000, 2001, 2003). ... NBA All-Rookie first team (1993).

| Season Team | G | Min. | FGM | FGA | Pct. | FTM | FTA | Pct. | REBOUNDS | | | Ast. | St. | Blk. | TO | Pts. | AVERAGES | | |
|---|---|---|---|---|---|---|---|---|---|---|---|---|---|---|---|---|---|---|---|
| | | | | | | | | | Off. | Def. | Tot. | | | | | | RPG | APG | PPG |
| 92-93—Orlando | 81 | 3071 | 733 | 1304 | .562 | 427 | 721 | .592 | 342 | 780 | 1122 | 152 | 60 | 286 | *307 | 1893 | 13.9 | 1.9 | 23.4 |
| 93-94—Orlando | 81 | 3224 | *953 | 1591 | *.599 | 471 | 850 | .554 | 384 | 688 | 1072 | 195 | 76 | 231 | 222 | 2377 | 13.2 | 2.4 | 29.3 |
| 94-95—Orlando | 79 | 2923 | *930 | *1594 | .583 | 455 | *854 | .533 | 328 | 573 | 901 | 214 | 73 | 192 | 204 | *2315 | 11.4 | 2.7 | *29.3 |
| 95-96—Orlando | 54 | 1946 | 592 | 1033 | .573 | 249 | 511 | .487 | 182 | 414 | 596 | 155 | 34 | 115 | 155 | 1434 | 11.0 | 2.9 | 26.6 |
| 96-97—L.A. Lakers | 51 | 1941 | 552 | 991 | .557 | 232 | 479 | .484 | 195 | 445 | 640 | 159 | 46 | 147 | 146 | 1336 | 12.5 | 3.1 | 26.2 |
| 97-98—L.A. Lakers | 60 | 2175 | 670 | 1147 | *.584 | 359 | 681 | .527 | 208 | 473 | 681 | 142 | 39 | 144 | 175 | 1699 | 11.4 | 2.4 | 28.3 |
| 98-99—L.A. Lakers | 49 | 1705 | *510 | 885 | *.576 | 269 | *498 | .540 | 187 | 338 | 525 | 114 | 36 | 82 | 122 | *1289 | 10.7 | 2.3 | 26.3 |
| 99-00—L.A. Lakers | 79 | 3163 | *956 | *1665 | *.574 | *432 | *824 | .524 | 336 | 742 | 1078 | 299 | 36 | 239 | 223 | *2344 | 13.6 | 3.8 | *29.7 |
| 00-01—L.A. Lakers | 74 | 2924 | *813 | 1422 | *.572 | 499 | *972 | .513 | 291 | 649 | 940 | 277 | 47 | 204 | 218 | 2125 | 12.7 | 3.7 | 28.7 |
| 01-02—L.A. Lakers | 67 | 2422 | 712 | 1229 | *.579 | 398 | *717 | .555 | 235 | 480 | 715 | 200 | 41 | 137 | 171 | 1822 | 10.7 | 3.0 | 27.2 |
| 02-03—L.A. Lakers | 67 | 2535 | 695 | 1211 | .574 | 451 | 725 | .622 | 259 | 483 | 742 | 206 | 38 | 159 | 196 | 1841 | 11.1 | 3.1 | 27.5 |
| 03-04—L.A. Lakers | 67 | 2464 | 554 | 948 | .584 | 331 | 676 | .490 | 246 | 523 | 769 | 196 | 34 | 166 | 195 | 1439 | 11.5 | 2.9 | 21.5 |
| 04-05—Miami | 73 | 2492 | 658 | 1095 | .601 | 353 | 765 | .461 | 253 | 507 | 760 | 200 | 36 | 171 | 203 | 1669 | 10.4 | 2.7 | 22.9 |
| Totals | 882 | 32985 | 9328 | 16115 | .579 | 4926 | 9273 | .531 | 3446 | 7095 | 10541 | 2509 | 596 | 2273 | 2537 | 23583 | 12.0 | 2.8 | 26.7 |

Three-point field goals: 1992-93, 0-for-2. 1993-94, 0-for-2. 1994-95, 0-for-5. 1995-96, 1-for-2 (.500). 1996-97, 0-for-4. 1998-99, 0-for-1. 1999-00, 0-for-1. 2000-01, 0-for-2. 2001-02, 0-for-1. Totals, 1-for-20 (.050).

Personal fouls/disqualifications: 1992-93, 321/8. 1993-94, 281/3. 1994-95, 258/1. 1995-96, 193/1. 1996-97, 180/2. 1997-98, 193/1. 1998-99, 155/4. 1999-00, 255/2. 2000-01, 256/6. 2001-02, 199/2. 2002-03, 229/4. 2003-04, 225/3. 2004-05, 262/4. Totals, 3007/41.

### NBA PLAYOFF RECORD

**NOTES:** NBA Finals Most Valuable Player (2000, 2001). ... Holds NBA Finals records for most points in a four game series—145, most free throw attempts—68; and most free throws made—45 (2002, vs. New Jersey). ... Holds NBA Finals single-game record for most free throws attempted in one quarter—16 (June 9, 2000, vs. Indiana; June 5, 2002, vs. New Jersey; most free throws made in one half—13; and most free throws attempted in one game—39 (June 9, 2000, vs. Indiana). ... Shares NBA Finals single-game records for most free throws made in one quarter—9 (June 9, 2000, vs. Indiana); and most blocked shots—8 (June 8, 2001, vs. Philadelphia). ... Holds single-game playoff record for most free throws attempted—39 (June 9, 2000, vs. Indiana); most free throws attempted in one half—27; and most free throws attempted in one quarter—25 (May 20, 2000, vs. Portland).

| Season Team | G | Min. | FGM | FGA | Pct. | FTM | FTA | Pct. | REBOUNDS | | | Ast. | St. | Blk. | TO | Pts. | AVERAGES | | |
|---|---|---|---|---|---|---|---|---|---|---|---|---|---|---|---|---|---|---|---|
| | | | | | | | | | Off. | Def. | Tot. | | | | | | RPG | APG | PPG |
| 93-94—Orlando | 3 | 126 | 23 | 45 | .511 | 16 | 34 | .471 | 17 | 23 | 40 | 7 | 2 | 9 | 10 | 62 | 13.3 | 2.3 | 20.7 |
| 94-95—Orlando | 21 | 805 | 195 | 338 | .577 | 149 | 261 | .571 | 95 | 155 | 250 | 70 | 18 | 40 | 73 | 539 | 11.9 | 3.3 | 25.7 |
| 95-96—Orlando | 12 | 459 | 131 | 216 | .606 | 48 | 122 | .393 | 49 | 71 | 120 | 55 | 9 | 15 | 44 | 310 | 10.0 | 4.6 | 25.8 |
| 96-97—L.A. Lakers | 9 | 326 | 89 | 173 | .514 | 64 | 105 | .610 | 38 | 57 | 95 | 29 | 5 | 17 | 22 | 242 | 10.6 | 3.2 | 26.9 |
| 97-98—L.A. Lakers | 13 | 501 | 158 | 258 | .612 | 80 | 159 | .503 | 48 | 84 | 132 | 38 | 7 | 34 | 43 | 396 | 10.2 | 2.9 | 30.5 |
| 98-99—L.A. Lakers | 8 | 315 | 79 | 155 | .510 | 55 | 118 | .466 | 44 | 49 | 93 | 18 | 7 | 23 | 18 | 213 | 11.6 | 2.3 | 26.6 |
| 99-00—L.A. Lakers | 23 | 1000 | 286 | 505 | .566 | 135 | 296 | .456 | 119 | 236 | 355 | 71 | 13 | 55 | 56 | 707 | 15.4 | 3.1 | 30.7 |
| 00-01—L.A. Lakers | 16 | 676 | 191 | 344 | .555 | 105 | 200 | .525 | 91 | 156 | 247 | 51 | 7 | 38 | 57 | 487 | 15.4 | 3.2 | 30.4 |
| 01-02—L.A. Lakers | 19 | 776 | 203 | 384 | .529 | 135 | 208 | .649 | 67 | 172 | 239 | 54 | 10 | 48 | 62 | 541 | 12.6 | 2.8 | 28.5 |
| 02-03—L.A. Lakers | 12 | 481 | 121 | 226 | .535 | 82 | 132 | .621 | 63 | 115 | 178 | 44 | 7 | 34 | 35 | 324 | 14.8 | 3.7 | 27.0 |
| 03-04—L.A. Lakers | 22 | 917 | 182 | 307 | .593 | 109 | 254 | .429 | 91 | 200 | 291 | 55 | 7 | 61 | 55 | 473 | 13.2 | 2.5 | 21.5 |
| 04-05—Miami | 13 | 431 | 101 | 181 | .558 | 50 | 106 | .472 | 19 | 83 | 102 | 25 | 5 | 19 | 42 | 252 | 7.8 | 1.9 | 19.4 |
| Totals | 171 | 6813 | 1759 | 3132 | .562 | 1028 | 1995 | .515 | 741 | 1401 | 2142 | 517 | 97 | 393 | 517 | 4546 | 12.5 | 3.0 | 26.6 |

O

Personal fouls/disqualifications: 1993-94, 13/0. 1994-95, 84/1. 1995-96, 40/0. 1996-97, 37/1. 1997-98, 41/1. 1998-99, 29/0. 1999-00, 67/1. 2000-01, 55/2. 2001-02, 62/1. 2002-03, 34/1. 2003-04, 90/1. 2004-05, 52/1. Totals, 604/10.

### NBA ALL-STAR GAME RECORD

**NOTES:** NBA All-Star Game Most Valuable Player (2004). ... NBA All-Star Game co-Most Valuable Player (2000).

| | | | | | | | | | REBOUNDS | | | | | | | | |
|---|---|---|---|---|---|---|---|---|---|---|---|---|---|---|---|---|---|
| Season Team | Min. | FGM | FGA | Pct. | FTM | FTA | Pct. | Off. | Def. | Tot. | Ast. | PF | Dq. | St. | Blk. | TO | Pts. |
| 1993—Orlando | 25 | 4 | 9 | .444 | 6 | 9 | .667 | 3 | 4 | 7 | 0 | 3 | 0 | 0 | 0 | 0 | 14 |
| 1994—Orlando | 26 | 2 | 12 | .167 | 4 | 11 | .364 | 4 | 6 | 10 | 0 | 2 | 0 | 1 | 4 | 1 | 8 |
| 1995—Orlando | 26 | 9 | 16 | .563 | 4 | 7 | .571 | 4 | 3 | 7 | 1 | 2 | 0 | 3 | 2 | 2 | 22 |
| 1996—Orlando | 28 | 10 | 16 | .625 | 5 | 11 | .455 | 3 | 7 | 10 | 1 | 3 | 0 | 1 | 2 | 2 | 25 |
| 1997—L.A. Lakers | | | | | | | Selected, did not play—injured. | | | | | | | | | | |
| 1998—L.A. Lakers | 18 | 5 | 10 | .500 | 2 | 4 | .500 | 2 | 2 | 4 | 1 | 2 | ... | 0 | 0 | 2 | 12 |
| 2000—L.A. Lakers | 25 | 11 | 20 | .550 | 0 | 2 | .000 | 4 | 5 | 9 | 3 | 2 | 0 | 0 | 3 | 4 | 22 |
| 2001—L.A. Lakers | | | | | | | Selected, did not play—injured. | | | | | | | | | | |
| 2002—L.A. Lakers | | | | | | | Selected, did not play—injured. | | | | | | | | | | |
| 2003—L.A. Lakers | 26 | 8 | 14 | .571 | 3 | 5 | .600 | 3 | 10 | 13 | 1 | 3 | 0 | 2 | 1 | 3 | 19 |
| 2004—L.A. Lakers | 24 | 12 | 19 | .632 | 0 | 1 | .000 | 5 | 6 | 11 | 1 | 3 | 0 | 2 | 2 | 4 | 24 |
| 2005—Miami | 25 | 6 | 11 | .545 | 0 | 3 | .000 | 0 | 6 | 6 | 1 | 2 | 0 | 3 | 3 | 0 | 12 |
| **Totals** | 223 | 67 | 127 | .528 | 24 | 53 | .453 | 28 | 49 | 77 | 9 | 22 | 0 | 12 | 17 | 18 | 158 |

Three-point field goals: 1995, 0-for-1. 2005, 0-for-1. Totals, 0-for-2 (.000).

---

# ODOM, LAMAR  F  LAKERS

**PERSONAL:** Born November 6, 1979, in Jamaica, N.Y. ... 6-10/221. (2.08/100.2). ... Full name: Lamar Joseph Odom
**HIGH SCHOOL:** Christian Redemption Academy (Troy, N.Y.), then Ch.
**COLLEGE:** UNLV, then Rhode Island.
**TRANSACTIONS/CAREER NOTES:** Selected after sophomore season by Los Angeles Clippers in first round (fourth pick overall) of 1999 NBA Draft. ... Signed as free agent by Miami Heat (August 26, 2003). ... Traded by Heat with F Caron Butler, F Brian Grant, a first-round draft choice and a second-round draft choice to Los Angeles Lakers for C Shaquille O'Neal (July 14, 2004).
**MISCELLANEOUS:** Member of bronze-medal-winning U.S. Olympic Team (2004).

### COLLEGIATE RECORD

| | | | | | | | | | | | | AVERAGES | | |
|---|---|---|---|---|---|---|---|---|---|---|---|---|---|---|
| Season Team | G | Min. | FGM | FGA | Pct. | FTM | FTA | Pct. | Reb. | Ast. | Pts. | RPG | APG | PPG |
| 97-98—Rhode Island | | | | | | | Did not play. | | | | | | | | |
| 98-99—Rhode Island | 32 | 1116 | 203 | 421 | .482 | 125 | 182 | .687 | 302 | 122 | 564 | 9.4 | 3.8 | 17.6 |
| **Totals** | 32 | 1116 | 203 | 421 | .482 | 125 | 182 | .687 | 302 | 122 | 564 | 9.4 | 3.8 | 17.6 |

Three-point field goals: 1998-99, 33-for-100 (.330). Totals, 33-for-100 (.330).

### NBA REGULAR-SEASON RECORD

**HONORS:** NBA All-Rookie first team (2000).
**NOTES:** Tied for NBA lead with 13 disqualifications (2000).

| | | | | | | | | | REBOUNDS | | | | | | | | AVERAGES | | |
|---|---|---|---|---|---|---|---|---|---|---|---|---|---|---|---|---|---|---|---|
| Season Team | G | Min. | FGM | FGA | Pct. | FTM | FTA | Pct. | Off. | Def. | Tot. | Ast. | St. | Blk. | TO | Pts. | RPG | APG | PPG |
| 99-00—L.A. Clippers | 76 | 2767 | 449 | 1024 | .438 | 302 | 420 | .719 | 159 | 436 | 595 | 317 | 91 | 95 | 258 | 1259 | 7.8 | 4.2 | 16.6 |
| 00-01—L.A. Clippers | 76 | 2836 | 481 | 1046 | .460 | 262 | 386 | .679 | 110 | 482 | 592 | 392 | 74 | 122 | 264 | 1304 | 7.8 | 5.2 | 17.2 |
| 01-02—L.A. Clippers | 29 | 999 | 151 | 360 | .419 | 61 | 93 | .656 | 31 | 145 | 176 | 171 | 23 | 36 | 97 | 379 | 6.1 | 5.9 | 13.1 |
| 02-03—L.A. Clippers | 49 | 1679 | 268 | 611 | .439 | 136 | 175 | .777 | 59 | 267 | 326 | 178 | 42 | 41 | 140 | 714 | 6.7 | 3.6 | 14.6 |
| 03-04—Miami | 80 | 3003 | 485 | 1127 | .430 | 340 | 458 | .742 | 160 | 616 | 776 | 327 | 85 | 71 | 236 | 1371 | 9.7 | 4.1 | 17.1 |
| 04-05—L.A. Lakers | 64 | 2320 | 366 | 774 | .473 | 207 | 298 | .695 | 134 | 519 | 653 | 238 | 42 | 65 | 161 | 975 | 10.2 | 3.7 | 15.2 |
| **Totals** | 374 | 13604 | 2200 | 4942 | .445 | 1308 | 1830 | .715 | 653 | 2465 | 3118 | 1623 | 357 | 430 | 1156 | 6002 | 8.3 | 4.3 | 16.0 |

Three-point field goals: 1999-00, 59-for-164 (.360). 2000-01, 80-for-253 (.316). 2001-02, 16-for-84 (.190). 2002-03, 42-for-129 (.326). 2003-04, 61-for-205 (.298). 2004-05, 36-for-117 (.308). Totals, 294-for-952 (.309).
Personal fouls/disqualifications: 1999-00, 291/13. 2000-01, 236/4. 2001-02, 91/3. 2002-03, 181/6. 2003-04, 273/5. 2004-05, 211/3. Totals, 1283/34.

### NBA PLAYOFF RECORD

| | | | | | | | | | REBOUNDS | | | | | | | | AVERAGES | | |
|---|---|---|---|---|---|---|---|---|---|---|---|---|---|---|---|---|---|---|---|
| Season Team | G | Min. | FGM | FGA | Pct. | FTM | FTA | Pct. | Off. | Def. | Tot. | Ast. | St. | Blk. | TO | Pts. | RPG | APG | PPG |
| 03-04—Miami | 13 | 512 | 81 | 182 | .445 | 49 | 72 | .681 | 32 | 76 | 108 | 37 | 15 | 10 | 42 | 219 | 8.3 | 2.8 | 16.8 |

Three-point field goals: 2003-04, 8-for-26 (.308). Totals, 8-for-26 (.308).
Personal fouls/disqualifications: 2003-04, 58/2. Totals, 58/2.

---

# OKAFOR, EMEKA  F/C  BOBCATS

**PERSONAL:** Born September 28, 1982, in Houston. ... 6-10/252. (2.08/114.3). ... Full name: Chukwuemeka Noubuisi Okafor
**HIGH SCHOOL:** Bellaire (Houston).
**COLLEGE:** Connecticut.
**TRANSACTIONS/CAREER NOTES:** Selected after junior season by Charlotte Bobcats in first round (second pick overall) of 2004 NBA Draft.
**MISCELLANEOUS:** Member of bronze-medal-winning U.S. Olympic Team (2004).

**O**

### COLLEGIATE RECORD

**NOTES:** Member of NCAA Division I championship team (2004). ... The Sporting News All-America first team (2004). ... NCAA Tournament Division I Most Outstanding Player (2004).

| | | | | | | | | | | | | AVERAGES | | |
|---|---|---|---|---|---|---|---|---|---|---|---|---|---|---|
| Season Team | G | Min. | FGM | FGA | Pct. | FTM | FTA | Pct. | Reb. | Ast. | Pts. | RPG | APG | PPG |
| 01-02—Connecticut | 34 | 1021 | 105 | 178 | .590 | 57 | 92 | .620 | 306 | 27 | 267 | 9.0 | 0.8 | 7.9 |
| 02-03—Connecticut | 33 | 1087 | 221 | 381 | .580 | 82 | 137 | .599 | 370 | 18 | 524 | 11.2 | 0.5 | 15.9 |
| 03-04—Connecticut | 36 | 1166 | 261 | 436 | .599 | 113 | 218 | .518 | 415 | 36 | 635 | 11.5 | 1.0 | 17.6 |
| **Totals** | 103 | 3274 | 587 | 995 | .590 | 252 | 447 | .564 | 1091 | 81 | 1426 | 10.6 | 0.8 | 13.8 |

## NBA REGULAR-SEASON RECORD

**HONORS:** NBA Rookie of the Year (2005). ... NBA All-Rookie first team (2005).

| | | | | | | | | REBOUNDS | | | | | | | | AVERAGES | | |
|---|---|---|---|---|---|---|---|---|---|---|---|---|---|---|---|---|---|---|
| Season Team | G | Min. | FGM | FGA | Pct. | FTM | FTA | Pct. | Off. | Def. | Tot. | Ast. | St. | Blk. | TO | Pts. | RPG | APG | PPG |
| 04-05—Charlotte ....... | 73 | 2600 | 448 | 1003 | .447 | 209 | 343 | .609 | 275 | 520 | 795 | 64 | 62 | 125 | 125 | 1105 | 10.9 | 0.9 | 15.1 |

Three-point field goals: 2004-05, 0-for-1. Totals, 0-for-1 (.000).
Personal fouls/disqualifications: 2004-05, 214/0. Totals, 214/0.

---

# OKUR, MEHMET       F/C       JAZZ

**PERSONAL:** Born May 26, 1979, in Yalova, Turkey. ... 6-11/249. (2.11/112.9).
**HIGH SCHOOL:** Cem Sultan (Gazcilar Bursa).
**COLLEGE:** Did not attend college.
**TRANSACTIONS/CAREER NOTES:** Played in Turkey (1997-2002). ... Selected by Detroit Pistons in second round (38th pick overall) of 2001 NBA Draft. ... Signed as free agent by Utah Jazz (July 27, 2004).
**MISCELLANEOUS:** Member of NBA championship team (2004).

## TURKISH LEAGUE RECORD

| | | | | | | | | | | | | AVERAGES | | |
|---|---|---|---|---|---|---|---|---|---|---|---|---|---|---|
| Season Team | G | Min. | FGM | FGA | Pct. | FTM | FTA | Pct. | Reb. | Ast. | Pts. | RPG | APG | PPG |
| 97-98—Oyak Renau .............. | 25 | 332 | 47 | 108 | .435 | 17 | 26 | .654 | 81 | 18 | 111 | 3.2 | 0.7 | 4.4 |
| 98-99—Tofas Bursa .............. | 33 | 440 | 55 | 112 | .491 | 29 | 42 | .690 | 142 | 12 | 155 | 4.3 | 0.4 | 4.7 |
| 99-00—Tofas Bursa .............. | 37 | 731 | 94 | 212 | .443 | 35 | 50 | .700 | 210 | 32 | 243 | 5.7 | 0.9 | 6.6 |
| 00-01—Efes Pilsen.............. | 26 | 477 | 91 | 163 | .558 | 35 | 42 | .833 | 161 | 12 | 231 | 6.2 | 0.5 | 8.9 |
| 01-02—Efes Pilsen.............. | 22 | 602 | 112 | 211 | .531 | 62 | 77 | .805 | 186 | 30 | 298 | 8.5 | 1.4 | 13.5 |
| Totals .................. | 143 | 2582 | 399 | 806 | .495 | 178 | 237 | .751 | 780 | 104 | 1038 | 5.5 | 0.7 | 7.3 |

Three-point field goals: 1998-99, 16-for-31 (.516). 1999-00, 20-for-60 (.333). 2000-01, 14-for-27 (.519). 2001-02, 12-for-28 (.429). Totals, 62-for-146 (.425).
Personal fouls/disqualifications: 2000-01, 45/0. Totals, 45/0.

## NBA REGULAR-SEASON RECORD

| | | | | | | | | REBOUNDS | | | | | | | | AVERAGES | | |
|---|---|---|---|---|---|---|---|---|---|---|---|---|---|---|---|---|---|---|
| Season Team | G | Min. | FGM | FGA | Pct. | FTM | FTA | Pct. | Off. | Def. | Tot. | Ast. | St. | Blk. | TO | Pts. | RPG | APG | PPG |
| 02-03—Detroit ............ | 72 | 1366 | 180 | 423 | .426 | 96 | 131 | .733 | 117 | 218 | 335 | 71 | 25 | 39 | 66 | 494 | 4.7 | 1.0 | 6.9 |
| 03-04—Detroit .............. | 71 | 1580 | 251 | 542 | .463 | 162 | 209 | .775 | 160 | 261 | 421 | 69 | 36 | 63 | 101 | 682 | 5.9 | 1.0 | 9.6 |
| 04-05—Utah .............. | 82 | 2304 | 354 | 756 | .468 | 329 | 387 | .850 | 194 | 422 | 616 | 166 | 32 | 68 | 141 | 1054 | 7.5 | 2.0 | 12.9 |
| Totals ................... | 225 | 5250 | 785 | 1721 | .456 | 587 | 727 | .807 | 471 | 901 | 1372 | 306 | 93 | 170 | 308 | 2230 | 6.1 | 1.4 | 9.9 |

Three-point field goals: 2002-03, 38-for-112 (.339). 2003-04, 18-for-48 (.375). 2004-05, 17-for-63 (.270). Totals, 73-for-223 (.327).
Personal fouls/disqualifications: 2002-03, 167/0. 2003-04, 138/0. 2004-05, 227/2. Totals, 532/2.

## NBA PLAYOFF RECORD

| | | | | | | | | REBOUNDS | | | | | | | | AVERAGES | | |
|---|---|---|---|---|---|---|---|---|---|---|---|---|---|---|---|---|---|---|
| Season Team | G | Min. | FGM | FGA | Pct. | FTM | FTA | Pct. | Off. | Def. | Tot. | Ast. | St. | Blk. | TO | Pts. | RPG | APG | PPG |
| 02-03—Detroit ............ | 17 | 323 | 35 | 80 | .438 | 17 | 32 | .531 | 24 | 46 | 70 | 13 | 12 | 12 | 14 | 94 | 4.1 | 0.8 | 5.5 |
| 03-04—Detroit ............ | 22 | 252 | 31 | 66 | .470 | 18 | 26 | .692 | 16 | 45 | 61 | 8 | 5 | 9 | 15 | 82 | 2.8 | 0.4 | 3.7 |
| Totals .................. | 39 | 575 | 66 | 146 | .452 | 35 | 58 | .603 | 40 | 91 | 131 | 21 | 17 | 21 | 29 | 176 | 3.4 | 0.5 | 4.5 |

Three-point field goals: 2002-03, 7-for-13 (.538). 2003-04, 2-for-5 (.400). Totals, 9-for-18 (.500).
Personal fouls/disqualifications: 2002-03, 39/0. 2003-04, 20/0. Totals, 59/0.

---

# OLLIE, KEVIN       G       76ERS

**PERSONAL:** Born December 27, 1972, in Dallas. ... 6-4/195. (1.93/88.5). ... Full name: Kevin Jermaine Ollie ... Cousin of Arnaz Battle, wide receiver, San Francisco 49ers.
**HIGH SCHOOL:** Crenshaw (Los Angeles).
**COLLEGE:** Connecticut.
**TRANSACTIONS/CAREER NOTES:** Not drafted by an NBA franchise. ... Signed as free agent by Golden State Warriors (October 4, 1995). ... Waived by Warriors (October 11, 1995). ... Played in Continental Basketball Association with Connecticut Pride (1995-96 through 1997-98 and 1999-2000). ... Signed as free agent by Dallas Mavericks (October 7, 1997). ... Waived by Mavericks (December 17, 1997). ... Signed by Orlando Magic to first of two consecutive 10-day contracts (March 2, 1998). ... Signed by Magic for remainder of season (March 22, 1998). ... Signed as free agent by Sacramento Kings (January 21, 1999). ... Waived by Kings (February 19, 1999). ... Re-signed by Magic to 10-day contract (March 8, 1999). ... Waived by Magic (March 14, 1999). ... Signed as free agent by Mavericks (October 6, 1999). ... Waived by Mavericks (October 29, 1999). ... Signed as free agent by Philadelphia 76ers (November 24, 1999). ... Signed as free agent by New Jersey Nets (October 3, 2000). ... Waived by Nets (December 15, 2000). ... Signed as free agent by 76ers (December 22, 2000). ... Signed as free agent by Chicago Bulls (September 24, 2001). ... Traded by Bulls with C Brad Miller, G Ron Mercer and G/F Ron Artest to Indiana Pacers for G Jalen Rose, G Travis Best, G Norman Richardson and conditional second-round draft choice (February 19, 2002). ... Signed as free agent by Milwaukee Bucks (September 6, 2002). ... Traded by Bucks with G Ray Allen, G Ronald Murray and conditional first-round draft choice to Seattle SuperSonics for G Gary Payton and G Desmond Mason (February 20, 2003). ... Signed as free agent by Cleveland Cavaliers (July 17, 2003) ... Traded by Cavaliers with F Kedrick Brown to Philadelphia 76ers for G Eric Snow (July 20, 2004).

## COLLEGIATE RECORD

| | | | | | | | | | | | | AVERAGES | | |
|---|---|---|---|---|---|---|---|---|---|---|---|---|---|---|
| Season Team | G | Min. | FGM | FGA | Pct. | FTM | FTA | Pct. | Reb. | Ast. | Pts. | RPG | APG | PPG |
| 91-92—Connecticut .................. | 29 | 294 | 17 | 45 | .378 | 28 | 39 | .718 | 23 | 40 | 62 | 0.8 | 1.4 | 2.1 |
| 92-93—Connecticut .................. | 28 | 864 | 69 | 176 | .392 | 81 | 109 | .743 | 64 | 158 | 220 | 2.3 | 5.6 | 7.9 |
| 93-94—Connecticut .................. | 34 | 973 | 73 | 155 | .471 | 71 | 97 | .732 | 83 | 209 | 219 | 2.4 | 6.1 | 6.4 |
| 94-95—Connecticut .................. | 33 | 1025 | 112 | 222 | .505 | 87 | 108 | .806 | 82 | 212 | 324 | 2.5 | 6.4 | 9.8 |
| Totals ....................................... | 124 | 3156 | 271 | 598 | .453 | 267 | 353 | .756 | 252 | 619 | 825 | 2.0 | 5.0 | 6.7 |

Three-point field goals: 1992-93, 1-for-9 (.111). 1993-94, 2-for-10 (.200). 1994-95, 13-for-42 (.310). Totals, 16-for-61 (.262).

O

## CBA RECORD

NOTES: Member of CBA championship team (1999).

| Season Team | G | Min. | FGM | FGA | Pct. | FTM | FTA | Pct. | Reb. | Ast. | Pts. | AVERAGES | | |
|---|---|---|---|---|---|---|---|---|---|---|---|---|---|---|
| | | | | | | | | | | | | RPG | APG | PPG |
| 95-96—Connecticut | 56 | 1448 | 161 | 378 | .426 | 134 | 178 | .753 | 154 | 226 | 459 | 2.8 | 4.0 | 8.2 |
| 96-97—Connecticut | 52 | 2226 | 277 | 565 | .490 | 204 | 251 | .813 | 202 | 300 | 763 | 3.9 | 5.8 | 14.7 |
| 97-98—Connecticut | 24 | 886 | 177 | 379 | .467 | 108 | 136 | .794 | 77 | 118 | 474 | 3.2 | 4.9 | 19.8 |
| 99-00—Connecticut | 2 | 81 | 12 | 24 | .500 | 15 | 16 | .938 | 7 | 15 | 40 | 3.5 | 7.5 | 20.0 |
| Totals | 134 | 4641 | 627 | 1346 | .466 | 461 | 581 | .793 | 440 | 659 | 1736 | 3.3 | 4.9 | 13.0 |

Three-point field goals: 1995-96, 3-for-18 (.167). 1996-97, 5-for-14 (.357). 1997-98, 12-for-34 (.353). 1999-00, 1-for-2 (.500). Totals, 21-for-68 (.309).
Personal fouls/disqualifications: 1995-96, 84/0. 1996-97, 126/0. 1997-98, 55/0. 1999-00, 6/0. Totals, 281/0.

## NBA REGULAR-SEASON RECORD

| Season Team | G | Min. | FGM | FGA | Pct. | FTM | FTA | Pct. | REBOUNDS | | | Ast. | St. | Blk. | TO | Pts. | AVERAGES | | |
|---|---|---|---|---|---|---|---|---|---|---|---|---|---|---|---|---|---|---|---|
| | | | | | | | | | Off. | Def. | Tot. | | | | | | RPG | APG | PPG |
| 97-98—Dallas-Orlando | 35 | 430 | 37 | 98 | .378 | 49 | 70 | .700 | 9 | 30 | 39 | 65 | 13 | 0 | 44 | 123 | 1.1 | 1.9 | 3.5 |
| 98-99—Sac.-Orlando | 8 | 72 | 4 | 14 | .286 | 5 | 7 | .714 | 0 | 7 | 7 | 3 | 3 | 1 | 3 | 13 | 0.9 | 0.4 | 1.6 |
| 99-00—Philadelphia | 40 | 290 | 22 | 49 | .449 | 28 | 37 | .757 | 4 | 27 | 31 | 46 | 10 | 0 | 10 | 72 | 0.8 | 1.2 | 1.8 |
| 00-01—N.J.-Phila. | 70 | 925 | 76 | 192 | .396 | 63 | 89 | .708 | 16 | 79 | 95 | 146 | 30 | 1 | 49 | 216 | 1.4 | 2.1 | 3.1 |
| 01-02—Chi.-Indiana | 81 | 1723 | 137 | 353 | .388 | 187 | 227 | .824 | 25 | 159 | 184 | 291 | 62 | 2 | 106 | 462 | 2.3 | 3.6 | 5.7 |
| 02-03—Mil.-Sea. | 82 | 1897 | 199 | 441 | .451 | 134 | 178 | .753 | 25 | 157 | 182 | 291 | 69 | 5 | 72 | 534 | 2.2 | 3.5 | 6.5 |
| 03-04—Cleveland | 82 | 1401 | 95 | 257 | .370 | 147 | 176 | .835 | 23 | 147 | 170 | 234 | 51 | 8 | 81 | 341 | 2.1 | 2.9 | 4.2 |
| 04-05—Philadelphia | 26 | 158 | 11 | 31 | .355 | 6 | 9 | .667 | 3 | 16 | 19 | 19 | 5 | 0 | 6 | 28 | 0.7 | 0.7 | 1.1 |
| Totals | 424 | 6896 | 581 | 1435 | .405 | 619 | 793 | .781 | 105 | 622 | 727 | 1095 | 243 | 17 | 371 | 1789 | 1.7 | 2.6 | 4.2 |

Three-point field goals: 1997-98, 0-for-1. 1998-99, 5-for-7 (.714). 2000-01, 1-for-3 (.333). 2001-02, 1-for-2 (.500). 2002-03, 2-for-6 (.333). 2003-04, 4-for-9 (.444). Totals, 13-for-28 (.464).
Personal fouls/disqualifications: 1997-98, 31/0. 1998-99, 9/0. 1999-00, 27/0. 2000-01, 84/0. 2001-02, 97/1. 2002-03, 122/0. 2003-04, 119/0. 2004-05, 16/0. Totals, 505/1.

## NBA PLAYOFF RECORD

| Season Team | G | Min. | FGM | FGA | Pct. | FTM | FTA | Pct. | REBOUNDS | | | Ast. | St. | Blk. | TO | Pts. | AVERAGES | | |
|---|---|---|---|---|---|---|---|---|---|---|---|---|---|---|---|---|---|---|---|
| | | | | | | | | | Off. | Def. | Tot. | | | | | | RPG | APG | PPG |
| 99-00—Philadelphia | 10 | 65 | 6 | 12 | .500 | 8 | 9 | .889 | 0 | 5 | 5 | 12 | 2 | 0 | 3 | 20 | 0.5 | 1.2 | 2.0 |
| 00-01—Philadelphia | 23 | 123 | 10 | 27 | .370 | 13 | 14 | .929 | 2 | 7 | 9 | 23 | 0 | 0 | 8 | 33 | 0.4 | 1.0 | 1.4 |
| 01-02—Indiana | 5 | 118 | 11 | 26 | .423 | 6 | 6 | 1.000 | 0 | 12 | 12 | 23 | 3 | 0 | 5 | 29 | 2.4 | 4.6 | 5.8 |
| Totals | 38 | 306 | 27 | 65 | .415 | 27 | 29 | .931 | 2 | 24 | 26 | 58 | 5 | 0 | 16 | 82 | 0.7 | 1.5 | 2.2 |

Three-point field goals: 2001-02, 1-for-2 (.500). Totals, 1-for-2 (.500).
Personal fouls/disqualifications: 1999-00, 5/0. 2000-01, 12/0. 2001-02, 6/0. Totals, 23/0.

# OLOWOKANDI, MICHAEL     C     TIMBERWOLVES

**PERSONAL:** Born April 3, 1975, in Lagos, Nigeria. ... 7-0/269. (2.13/122.0).
**HIGH SCHOOL:** Newlands Manor School (East Sussex, England).
**COLLEGE:** Brunel (Middlesex, England); did not play basketba.
**TRANSACTIONS/CAREER NOTES:** Selected by Los Angeles Clippers in first round (first pick overall) of 1998 NBA Draft. ... Played in Italy (1998-99). ... Signed as free agent by Minnesota Timberwolves (July 16, 2003).

## COLLEGIATE RECORD

| Season Team | G | Min. | FGM | FGA | Pct. | FTM | FTA | Pct. | Reb. | Ast. | Pts. | AVERAGES | | |
|---|---|---|---|---|---|---|---|---|---|---|---|---|---|---|
| | | | | | | | | | | | | RPG | APG | PPG |
| 95-96—Pacific | 25 | 257 | 40 | 76 | .526 | 20 | 36 | .556 | 84 | 4 | 100 | 3.4 | 0.2 | 4.0 |
| 96-97—Pacific | 19 | 433 | 94 | 165 | .570 | 19 | 57 | .333 | 126 | 8 | 207 | 6.6 | 0.4 | 10.9 |
| 97-98—Pacific | 33 | 1046 | 309 | 508 | .608 | 114 | 235 | .485 | 369 | 26 | 732 | 11.2 | 0.8 | 22.2 |
| Totals | 77 | 1736 | 443 | 749 | .591 | 153 | 328 | .466 | 579 | 38 | 1039 | 7.5 | 0.5 | 13.5 |

## ITALIAN LEAGUE RECORD

| Season Team | G | Min. | FGM | FGA | Pct. | FTM | FTA | Pct. | Reb. | Ast. | Pts. | AVERAGES | | |
|---|---|---|---|---|---|---|---|---|---|---|---|---|---|---|
| | | | | | | | | | | | | RPG | APG | PPG |
| 98-99—Bologna Arimo | 3 | 52 | 6 | 14 | .429 | 2 | 4 | .500 | 17 | 1 | 14 | 5.7 | 0.3 | 4.7 |

Personal fouls/disqualifications: 1998-99, 6/0. Totals, 6/0.

## NBA REGULAR-SEASON RECORD

HONORS: NBA All-Rookie second team (1999).

| Season Team | G | Min. | FGM | FGA | Pct. | FTM | FTA | Pct. | REBOUNDS | | | Ast. | St. | Blk. | TO | Pts. | AVERAGES | | |
|---|---|---|---|---|---|---|---|---|---|---|---|---|---|---|---|---|---|---|---|
| | | | | | | | | | Off. | Def. | Tot. | | | | | | RPG | APG | PPG |
| 98-99—L.A. Clippers | 45 | 1279 | 172 | 399 | .431 | 57 | 118 | .483 | 120 | 237 | 357 | 25 | 27 | 55 | 85 | 401 | 7.9 | 0.6 | 8.9 |
| 99-00—L.A. Clippers | 80 | 2493 | 330 | 756 | .437 | 123 | 189 | .651 | 194 | 462 | 656 | 38 | 35 | 140 | 177 | 783 | 8.2 | 0.5 | 9.8 |
| 00-01—L.A. Clippers | 82 | 2127 | 308 | 708 | .435 | 85 | 156 | .545 | 168 | 357 | 525 | 46 | 30 | 108 | 169 | 701 | 6.4 | 0.6 | 8.5 |
| 01-02—L.A. Clippers | 80 | 2568 | 384 | 886 | .433 | 117 | 188 | .622 | 164 | 547 | 711 | 90 | 55 | 145 | 175 | 885 | 8.9 | 1.1 | 11.1 |
| 02-03—L.A. Clippers | 36 | 1369 | 186 | 436 | .427 | 69 | 105 | .657 | 57 | 271 | 328 | 47 | 18 | 79 | 98 | 441 | 9.1 | 1.3 | 12.3 |
| 03-04—Minnesota | 43 | 925 | 121 | 285 | .425 | 36 | 61 | .590 | 78 | 167 | 245 | 24 | 16 | 68 | 54 | 278 | 5.7 | 0.6 | 6.5 |
| 04-05—Minnesota | 62 | 1215 | 161 | 353 | .456 | 46 | 69 | .667 | 106 | 218 | 324 | 29 | 15 | 56 | 68 | 368 | 5.2 | 0.5 | 5.9 |
| Totals | 428 | 11976 | 1662 | 3823 | .435 | 533 | 886 | .602 | 887 | 2259 | 3146 | 299 | 196 | 651 | 826 | 3857 | 7.4 | 0.7 | 9.0 |

Personal fouls/disqualifications: 1998-99, 137/2. 1999-00, 304/10. 2000-01, 250/4. 2001-02, 217/1. 2002-03, 110/5. 2003-04, 137/3. 2004-05, 193/3. Totals, 1348/28.

## NBA PLAYOFF RECORD

| Season Team | G | Min. | FGM | FGA | Pct. | FTM | FTA | Pct. | REBOUNDS | | | Ast. | St. | Blk. | TO | Pts. | AVERAGES | | |
|---|---|---|---|---|---|---|---|---|---|---|---|---|---|---|---|---|---|---|---|
| | | | | | | | | | Off. | Def. | Tot. | | | | | | RPG | APG | PPG |
| 03-04—Minnesota | 15 | 224 | 12 | 37 | .324 | 7 | 8 | .875 | 16 | 36 | 52 | 2 | 2 | 11 | 17 | 31 | 3.5 | 0.1 | 2.1 |

Three-point field goals: 2003-04, 0-for-1. Totals, 0-for-1 (.000).
Personal fouls/disqualifications: 2003-04, 50/0. Totals, 50/0.

## OSTERTAG, GREG　　　　　　　　　　　C　　　　　　　　　　　JAZZ

**PERSONAL:** Born March 6, 1973, in Dallas. ... 7-2/280. (2.18/127.0). ... Full name: Gregory Donovan Ostertag ... Name pronounced OH-stir-tag.
**HIGH SCHOOL:** Duncanville (Texas).
**COLLEGE:** Kansas.
**TRANSACTIONS/CAREER NOTES:** Selected by Utah Jazz in first round (28th pick overall) of 1995 NBA Draft. ... Signed as free agent by Sacramento Kings (July 20, 2004). ... Traded by Kings with G Bobby Jackson to Memphis Grizzlies for G Bonzi Wells (August 2, 2005). ... Traded by Grizzlies to Utah Jazz in five-team trade (August 2, 2005).

### COLLEGIATE RECORD

| Season Team | G | Min. | FGM | FGA | Pct. | FTM | FTA | Pct. | Reb. | Ast. | Pts. | RPG | APG | PPG |
|---|---|---|---|---|---|---|---|---|---|---|---|---|---|---|
| 91-92—Kansas | 32 | 311 | 61 | 112 | .545 | 32 | 49 | .653 | 112 | 5 | 154 | 3.5 | 0.2 | 4.8 |
| 92-93—Kansas | 29 | 389 | 61 | 118 | .517 | 33 | 55 | .600 | 118 | 11 | 155 | 4.1 | 0.4 | 5.3 |
| 93-94—Kansas | 35 | 739 | 145 | 272 | .533 | 70 | 111 | .631 | 307 | 12 | 360 | 8.8 | 0.3 | 10.3 |
| 94-95—Kansas | 31 | 603 | 121 | 203 | .596 | 57 | 103 | .553 | 233 | 13 | 299 | 7.5 | 0.4 | 9.6 |
| **Totals** | 127 | 2042 | 388 | 705 | .550 | 192 | 318 | .604 | 770 | 41 | 968 | 6.1 | 0.3 | 7.6 |

Three-point field goals: 1991-92, 0-for-1. 1993-94, 0-for-2. Totals, 0-for-3 (.000).

### NBA REGULAR-SEASON RECORD

| Season Team | G | Min. | FGM | FGA | Pct. | FTM | FTA | Pct. | Off. | Def. | Tot. | Ast. | St. | Blk. | TO | Pts. | RPG | APG | PPG |
|---|---|---|---|---|---|---|---|---|---|---|---|---|---|---|---|---|---|---|---|
| 95-96—Utah | 57 | 661 | 86 | 182 | .473 | 36 | 54 | .667 | 57 | 118 | 175 | 5 | 5 | 63 | 25 | 208 | 3.1 | 0.1 | 3.6 |
| 96-97—Utah | 77 | 1818 | 210 | 408 | .515 | 139 | 205 | .678 | 180 | 385 | 565 | 27 | 24 | 152 | 74 | 559 | 7.3 | 0.4 | 7.3 |
| 97-98—Utah | 63 | 1288 | 115 | 239 | .481 | 67 | 140 | .479 | 134 | 240 | 374 | 25 | 28 | 132 | 74 | 297 | 5.9 | 0.4 | 4.7 |
| 98-99—Utah | 48 | 1340 | 99 | 208 | .476 | 75 | 121 | .620 | 105 | 243 | 348 | 23 | 12 | 131 | 45 | 273 | 7.3 | 0.5 | 5.7 |
| 99-00—Utah | 81 | 1606 | 124 | 267 | .464 | 119 | 187 | .636 | 172 | 310 | 482 | 18 | 20 | 172 | 79 | 367 | 6.0 | 0.2 | 4.5 |
| 00-01—Utah | 81 | 1491 | 139 | 281 | .495 | 84 | 151 | .556 | 164 | 251 | 415 | 22 | 22 | 142 | 63 | 363 | 5.1 | 0.3 | 4.5 |
| 01-02—Utah | 74 | 1107 | 91 | 201 | .453 | 63 | 130 | .485 | 125 | 188 | 313 | 50 | 15 | 109 | 51 | 245 | 4.2 | 0.7 | 3.3 |
| 02-03—Utah | 81 | 1926 | 169 | 326 | .518 | 100 | 196 | .510 | 180 | 323 | 503 | 55 | 20 | 147 | 104 | 438 | 6.2 | 0.7 | 5.4 |
| 03-04—Utah | 78 | 2153 | 208 | 437 | .476 | 113 | 195 | .579 | 221 | 357 | 578 | 123 | 30 | 139 | 99 | 529 | 7.4 | 1.6 | 6.8 |
| 04-05—Sacramento | 56 | 556 | 37 | 84 | .440 | 13 | 38 | .342 | 55 | 112 | 167 | 7 | 7 | 40 | 24 | 87 | 3.0 | 0.7 | 1.6 |
| **Totals** | 696 | 13946 | 1278 | 2633 | .485 | 809 | 1417 | .571 | 1393 | 2527 | 3920 | 385 | 183 | 1227 | 638 | 3366 | 5.6 | 0.6 | 4.8 |

Three-point field goals: 1996-97, 0-for-4. 1999-00, 0-for-1. 2000-01, 1-for-2 (.500). 2003-04, 0-for-1. 2004-05, 0-for-2. Totals, 1-for-10 (.100).
Personal fouls/disqualifications: 1995-96, 91/1. 1996-97, 233/2. 1997-98, 166/1. 1998-99, 140/2. 1999-00, 196/2. 2000-01, 215/3. 2001-02, 152/1. 2002-03, 235/4. 2003-04, 228/1. 2004-05, 88/1. Totals, 1744/18.

### NBA PLAYOFF RECORD

| Season Team | G | Min. | FGM | FGA | Pct. | FTM | FTA | Pct. | Off. | Def. | Tot. | Ast. | St. | Blk. | TO | Pts. | RPG | APG | PPG |
|---|---|---|---|---|---|---|---|---|---|---|---|---|---|---|---|---|---|---|---|
| 95-96—Utah | 15 | 212 | 20 | 45 | .444 | 13 | 21 | .619 | 18 | 32 | 50 | 1 | 2 | 21 | 4 | 53 | 3.3 | 0.1 | 3.5 |
| 96-97—Utah | 20 | 459 | 34 | 83 | .410 | 26 | 35 | .743 | 52 | 85 | 137 | 6 | 10 | 47 | 18 | 94 | 6.9 | 0.3 | 4.7 |
| 97-98—Utah | 19 | 336 | 26 | 46 | .565 | 12 | 25 | .480 | 25 | 56 | 81 | 5 | 7 | 37 | 12 | 64 | 4.3 | 0.3 | 3.4 |
| 98-99—Utah | 11 | 261 | 13 | 35 | .371 | 18 | 28 | .643 | 18 | 47 | 65 | 6 | 2 | 24 | 8 | 44 | 5.9 | 0.5 | 4.0 |
| 99-00—Utah | 8 | 172 | 10 | 19 | .526 | 10 | 22 | .455 | 19 | 26 | 45 | 2 | 2 | 17 | 8 | 30 | 5.6 | 0.3 | 3.8 |
| 00-01—Utah | 5 | 64 | 4 | 11 | .364 | 0 | 4 | .000 | 6 | 12 | 18 | 1 | 0 | 2 | 2 | 8 | 3.6 | 0.2 | 1.6 |
| 01-02—Utah | 4 | 87 | 13 | 21 | .619 | 1 | 10 | .100 | 19 | 15 | 34 | 2 | 2 | 6 | 6 | 27 | 8.5 | 0.5 | 6.8 |
| 02-03—Utah | 5 | 151 | 16 | 36 | .444 | 14 | 19 | .737 | 19 | 24 | 43 | 8 | 3 | 9 | 8 | 46 | 8.6 | 1.6 | 9.2 |
| 04-05—Sacramento | 2 | 26 | 3 | 3 | 1.000 | 0 | 0 | ... | 4 | 5 | 9 | 0 | 1 | 2 | 2 | 6 | 4.5 | 0.0 | 3.0 |
| **Totals** | 89 | 1768 | 139 | 299 | .465 | 94 | 164 | .573 | 180 | 302 | 482 | 31 | 29 | 165 | 68 | 372 | 5.4 | 0.3 | 4.2 |

Personal fouls/disqualifications: 1995-96, 28/0. 1996-97, 76/3. 1997-98, 51/0. 1998-99, 27/0. 1999-00, 20/0. 2000-01, 10/1. 2001-02, 14/1. 2002-03, 17/0. 2004-05, 4/0. Totals, 247/5.

---

## OUTLAW, BO　　　　　　　　　　　F　　　　　　　　　　　SUNS

**PERSONAL:** Born April 13, 1971, in San Antonio. ... 6-8/210. (2.03/95.3). ... Nickname: Bo.
**HIGH SCHOOL:** John Jay (San Antonio).
**JUNIOR COLLEGE:** South Plains College (Texas).
**COLLEGE:** Houston.
**TRANSACTIONS/CAREER NOTES:** Not drafted by an NBA franchise. ... Played in Spain (1993-94). ... Played in Continental Basketball Association with Grand Rapids Hoops (1993-94). ... Signed by Los Angeles Clippers to first of two consecutive 10-day contracts (February 14, 1994). ... Re-signed by Clippers for remainder of season (March 8, 1994). ... Signed as free agent by Orlando Magic (September 5, 1997). ... Traded by Magic to Phoenix Suns as part of three-way deal in which Suns traded G/F Jud Buechler to Magic, Suns acquired first-round draft choice and cash considerations from Magic and Los Angeles Clippers acquired G Vinny Del Negro from Suns and cash considerations and right to swap 2005 second-round draft choice from Magic (November 16, 2001). ... Traded by Suns with C Jake Tsakalidis to Memphis Grizzlies for G Brevin Knight, C Cezary Trybanski and F Robert Archibald (September 30, 2003). ... Released by Grizzlies (November 1, 2004). ... Signed as free agent by Phoenix Suns (November 8, 2004).

### COLLEGIATE RECORD

**NOTES:** Led NCAA Division I with .684 field goal percentage (1992) and .658 field goal percentage (1993).

| Season Team | G | Min. | FGM | FGA | Pct. | FTM | FTA | Pct. | Reb. | Ast. | Pts. | RPG | APG | PPG |
|---|---|---|---|---|---|---|---|---|---|---|---|---|---|---|
| 89-90—South Plains College | 30 | ... | 147 | 261 | .563 | 69 | 136 | .507 | 289 | 54 | 364 | 9.6 | 1.8 | 12.1 |
| 90-91—South Plains College | 30 | ... | 160 | 242 | .661 | 70 | 122 | .574 | 326 | 87 | 395 | 10.9 | 2.9 | 13.2 |
| 91-92—Houston | 31 | 970 | 156 | 228 | .684 | 57 | 129 | .442 | 254 | 81 | 369 | 8.2 | 2.6 | 11.9 |
| 92-93—Houston | 30 | 1055 | 196 | 298 | .658 | 95 | 192 | .495 | 301 | 99 | 487 | 10.0 | 3.3 | 16.2 |
| **Junior College Totals** | 60 | | 307 | 503 | .610 | 139 | 258 | .539 | 615 | 141 | 759 | 10.3 | 2.4 | 12.7 |
| **4-Year-College Totals** | 61 | 2025 | 352 | 526 | .669 | 152 | 321 | .474 | 555 | 180 | 856 | 9.1 | 3.0 | 14.0 |

Three-point field goals: 1989-90, 0-for-1. 1990-91, 5-for-10 (.500). Totals, 5-for-11 (.455).

**NOTES:** Led CBA with 3.8 blocked shots per game (1994). ... CBA All-League second team (1994). ... CBA All-Defensive team (1994). ... CBA All-Rookie first team (1994).

| Season Team | G | Min. | FGM | FGA | Pct. | FTM | FTA | Pct. | Reb. | Ast. | Pts. | AVERAGES | | |
|---|---|---|---|---|---|---|---|---|---|---|---|---|---|---|
| | | | | | | | | | | | | RPG | APG | PPG |
| 93-94—Grand Rapids ................ | 32 | 1211 | 167 | 243 | *.687 | 83 | 160 | .519 | 349 | 56 | 417 | 10.9 | 1.8 | 13.0 |

Three-point field goals: 1993-94, 0-for-1. Totals, 0-for-1 (.000).
Personal fouls/disqualifications: 1993-94, 114/0. Totals, 114/0.

### NBA REGULAR-SEASON RECORD

| Season Team | G | Min. | FGM | FGA | Pct. | FTM | FTA | Pct. | REBOUNDS | | | Ast. | St. | Blk. | TO | Pts. | AVERAGES | | |
|---|---|---|---|---|---|---|---|---|---|---|---|---|---|---|---|---|---|---|---|
| | | | | | | | | | Off. | Def. | Tot. | | | | | | RPG | APG | PPG |
| 93-94—L.A. Clippers ... | 37 | 871 | 98 | 167 | .587 | 61 | 103 | .592 | 81 | 131 | 212 | 36 | 36 | 37 | 31 | 257 | 5.7 | 1.0 | 6.9 |
| 94-95—L.A. Clippers ... | 81 | 1655 | 170 | 325 | .523 | 82 | 186 | .441 | 121 | 192 | 313 | 84 | 90 | 151 | 78 | 422 | 3.9 | 1.0 | 5.2 |
| 95-96—L.A. Clippers ... | 80 | 985 | 107 | 186 | .575 | 72 | 162 | .444 | 87 | 113 | 200 | 50 | 44 | 91 | 45 | 286 | 2.5 | 0.6 | 3.6 |
| 96-97—L.A. Clippers ... | 82 | 2195 | 254 | 417 | .609 | 117 | 232 | .504 | 174 | 280 | 454 | 157 | 94 | 142 | 107 | 625 | 5.5 | 1.9 | 7.6 |
| 97-98—Orlando .......... | 82 | 2953 | 301 | 543 | .554 | 180 | 313 | .575 | 255 | 382 | 637 | 216 | 107 | 181 | 175 | 783 | 7.8 | 2.6 | 9.5 |
| 98-99—Orlando .......... | 31 | 851 | 84 | 154 | .545 | 35 | 81 | .432 | 54 | 113 | 167 | 56 | 40 | 43 | 58 | 203 | 5.4 | 1.8 | 6.5 |
| 99-00—Orlando .......... | 82 | 2326 | 204 | 339 | .602 | 82 | 162 | .506 | 202 | 323 | 525 | 245 | 113 | 148 | 133 | 490 | 6.4 | 3.0 | 6.0 |
| 00-01—Orlando .......... | 80 | 2534 | 226 | 368 | .614 | 129 | 225 | .573 | 211 | 408 | 619 | 225 | 105 | 137 | 141 | 582 | 7.7 | 2.8 | 7.3 |
| 01-02—Orl.-Phoenix .. | 83 | 1928 | 166 | 299 | .555 | 43 | 102 | .422 | 147 | 217 | 364 | 127 | 70 | 92 | 96 | 376 | 4.4 | 1.5 | 4.5 |
| 02-03—Phoenix .......... | 80 | 1800 | 153 | 278 | .550 | 72 | 116 | .621 | 134 | 234 | 368 | 112 | 50 | 71 | 76 | 378 | 4.6 | 1.4 | 4.7 |
| 03-04—Memphis ........ | 82 | 1606 | 159 | 312 | .510 | 61 | 116 | .526 | 125 | 217 | 342 | 90 | 73 | 70 | 69 | 379 | 4.2 | 1.1 | 4.6 |
| 04-05—Phoenix .......... | 39 | 214 | 12 | 34 | .353 | 5 | 9 | .556 | 16 | 37 | 53 | 13 | 6 | 12 | 8 | 29 | 1.4 | 0.3 | 0.7 |
| **Totals** .................. | 839 | 19918 | 1934 | 3422 | .565 | 939 | 1807 | .520 | 1607 | 2647 | 4254 | 1411 | 828 | 1175 | 1017 | 4810 | 5.1 | 1.7 | 5.7 |

Three-point field goals: 1993-94, 0-for-2. 1994-95, 0-for-5. 1995-96, 0-for-3. 1996-97, 0-for-8. 1997-98, 1-for-4 (.250). 1998-99, 0-for-3. 1999-00, 0-for-3. 2000-01, 1-for-2 (.500). 2001-02, 0-for-4. 2002-03, 0-for-4. 2003-04, 0-for-4. Totals, 3-for-38 (.079).
Personal fouls/disqualifications: 1993-94, 94/1. 1994-95, 227/4. 1995-96, 127/0. 1996-97, 227/5. 1997-98, 260/1. 1998-99, 79/1. 1999-00, 203/0. 2000-01, 241/4. 2001-02, 205/1. 2002-03, 194/1. 2003-04, 170/0. 2004-05, 29/0. Totals, 2056/18.

### NBA PLAYOFF RECORD

| Season Team | G | Min. | FGM | FGA | Pct. | FTM | FTA | Pct. | REBOUNDS | | | Ast. | St. | Blk. | TO | Pts. | AVERAGES | | |
|---|---|---|---|---|---|---|---|---|---|---|---|---|---|---|---|---|---|---|---|
| | | | | | | | | | Off. | Def. | Tot. | | | | | | RPG | APG | PPG |
| 96-97—L.A. Clippers .. | 3 | 66 | 6 | 11 | .545 | 3 | 10 | .300 | 6 | 8 | 14 | 4 | 1 | 2 | 3 | 15 | 4.7 | 1.3 | 5.0 |
| 98-99—Orlando .......... | 4 | 83 | 6 | 10 | .600 | 6 | 13 | .462 | 3 | 12 | 15 | 2 | 1 | 8 | 6 | 18 | 3.8 | 0.5 | 4.5 |
| 00-01—Orlando .......... | 4 | 134 | 16 | 26 | .615 | 2 | 11 | .182 | 11 | 31 | 42 | 9 | 5 | 6 | 9 | 34 | 10.5 | 2.3 | 8.5 |
| 02-03—Phoenix .......... | 6 | 70 | 1 | 10 | .100 | 2 | 4 | .500 | 6 | 7 | 13 | 5 | 1 | 1 | 6 | 4 | 2.2 | 0.8 | 0.7 |
| 03-04—Memphis ........ | 4 | 61 | 0 | 7 | .000 | 2 | 4 | .500 | 1 | 3 | 4 | 6 | 2 | 2 | 3 | 2 | 1.0 | 1.5 | 0.5 |
| 04-05—Phoenix .......... | 1 | 2 | 0 | 1 | .000 | 0 | 0 | ... | 0 | 0 | 0 | 1 | 1 | 0 | 0 | 0 | 0.0 | 1.0 | 0.0 |
| **Totals** .................. | 22 | 416 | 29 | 65 | .446 | 15 | 42 | .357 | 27 | 61 | 88 | 27 | 11 | 19 | 27 | 73 | 4.0 | 1.2 | 3.3 |

Three-point field goals: 1996-97, 0-for-1. Totals, 0-for-1 (.000).
Personal fouls/disqualifications: 1996-97, 5/0. 1998-99, 9/0. 2000-01, 15/0. 2002-03, 19/1. 2003-04, 9/0. Totals, 57/1.

### SPANISH RECORD

| Season Team | G | Min. | FGM | FGA | Pct. | FTM | FTA | Pct. | Reb. | Ast. | Pts. | AVERAGES | | |
|---|---|---|---|---|---|---|---|---|---|---|---|---|---|---|
| | | | | | | | | | | | | RPG | APG | PPG |
| 93-94—Estudiante Caja Postal.... | 2 | 10 | 0 | 3 | .000 | 0 | 2 | .000 | 2 | 0 | 0 | 1.0 | 0.0 | 0.0 |

## OUTLAW, TRAVIS — F — TRAIL BLAZERS

**PERSONAL:** Born September 18, 1984, in Starkville, Miss. ... 6-9/210. (2.06/95.3). ... Full name: Travis Marquez Outlaw
**HIGH SCHOOL:** Starkville (Starkville, Miss.).
**COLLEGE:** Did not attend college.
**TRANSACTIONS/CAREER NOTES:** Selected out of high school by Portland Trail Blazers in first round (23rd pick overall) of 2003 NBA Draft.

### NBA REGULAR-SEASON RECORD

| Season Team | G | Min. | FGM | FGA | Pct. | FTM | FTA | Pct. | REBOUNDS | | | Ast. | St. | Blk. | TO | Pts. | AVERAGES | | |
|---|---|---|---|---|---|---|---|---|---|---|---|---|---|---|---|---|---|---|---|
| | | | | | | | | | Off. | Def. | Tot. | | | | | | RPG | APG | PPG |
| 03-04—Portland.......... | 8 | 19 | 3 | 7 | .429 | 2 | 4 | .500 | 2 | 2 | 4 | 1 | 1 | 0 | 1 | 8 | 0.5 | 0.1 | 1.0 |
| 04-05—Portland.......... | 59 | 793 | 133 | 267 | .498 | 49 | 75 | .653 | 40 | 81 | 121 | 35 | 30 | 40 | 39 | 319 | 2.1 | 0.6 | 5.4 |
| **Totals** .................. | 67 | 812 | 136 | 274 | .496 | 51 | 79 | .646 | 42 | 83 | 125 | 36 | 31 | 40 | 40 | 327 | 1.9 | 0.5 | 4.9 |

Three-point field goals: 2004-05, 4-for-10 (.400). Totals, 4-for-10 (.400).
Personal fouls/disqualifications: 2003-04, 1/0. 2004-05, 77/0. Totals, 78/0.

## PACHULIA, ZAZA — F/C — HAWKS

**PERSONAL:** Born February 10, 1984, in Tbilisi, Georgia. ... 6-11/240. (2.11/108.9). ... Full name: Zaur Pachulia.
**TRANSACTIONS/CAREER NOTES:** Played in Turkey (1999-2003). ... Selected by Orlando Magic in second round (42nd pick overall) of 2003 NBA Draft. ... Selected by Charlotte Bobcats from Magic in NBA Expansion Draft (June 22, 2004). ... Traded by Bobcats to Milwaukee Bucks for 2004 second-round draft choice (June 23, 2004). ... Signed as free agent by Atlanta Hawks (August 11, 2005).

### TURKISH LEAGUE RECORD

| Season Team | G | Min. | FGM | FGA | Pct. | FTM | FTA | Pct. | Reb. | Ast. | Pts. | AVERAGES | | |
|---|---|---|---|---|---|---|---|---|---|---|---|---|---|---|
| | | | | | | | | | | | | RPG | APG | PPG |
| 99-00—Ulker .......................... | 10 | ... | 11 | 22 | .500 | 9 | 13 | .692 | 24 | 5 | 31 | 2.4 | 0.5 | 3.1 |
| 00-01—Ulker .......................... | 17 | ... | 25 | 48 | .521 | 9 | 18 | .500 | 39 | 6 | 59 | 2.3 | 0.4 | 3.5 |
| 01-02—Ulker .......................... | 25 | ... | 52 | 95 | .547 | 41 | 64 | .641 | 101 | 10 | 145 | 4.0 | 0.4 | 5.8 |
| 02-03—Ulker .......................... | 21 | ... | 69 | 120 | .575 | 62 | 79 | .785 | 115 | 17 | 200 | 5.5 | 0.8 | 9.5 |
| **Totals** .................. | 73 | ... | 157 | 285 | .551 | 121 | 174 | .695 | 279 | 38 | 435 | 3.8 | 0.5 | 6.0 |

P

## NBA REGULAR-SEASON RECORD

| Season Team | G | Min. | FGM | FGA | Pct. | FTM | FTA | Pct. | Off. | Def. | Tot. | Ast. | St. | Blk. | TO | Pts. | RPG | APG | PPG |
|---|---|---|---|---|---|---|---|---|---|---|---|---|---|---|---|---|---|---|---|
| 03-04—Orlando......... | 59 | 664 | 68 | 175 | .389 | 58 | 90 | .644 | 69 | 105 | 174 | 13 | 21 | 12 | 34 | 194 | 2.9 | 0.2 | 3.3 |
| 04-05—Milwaukee..... | 74 | 1397 | 160 | 354 | .452 | 138 | 185 | .746 | 131 | 247 | 378 | 60 | 44 | 34 | 70 | 458 | 5.1 | 0.6 | 6.2 |
| Totals ................ | 133 | 2061 | 228 | 529 | .431 | 196 | 275 | .713 | 200 | 352 | 552 | 73 | 65 | 46 | 104 | 652 | 4.2 | 0.5 | 4.9 |

Three-point field goals: 2004-05, 0-for-1. Totals, 0-for-1 (.000).
Personal fouls/disqualifications: 2003-04, 87/0. 2004-05, 166/0. Totals, 253/0.

# PADGETT, SCOTT       F

**PERSONAL:** Born April 19, 1976, in Louisville, Ky. ... 6-9/240. (2.06/108.9). ... Full name: Scott Anthony Padgett.
**HIGH SCHOOL:** St. Xavier (Louisville, Ky.).
**COLLEGE:** Kentucky.
**TRANSACTIONS/CAREER NOTES:** Selected by Utah Jazz in first round (28th pick overall) of 1999 NBA Draft. ... Signed as free agent by Houston Rockets (October 28, 2003).

## COLLEGIATE RECORD

**NOTES:** Member of NCAA Division I championship team (1998).

| Season Team | G | Min. | FGM | FGA | Pct. | FTM | FTA | Pct. | Reb. | Ast. | Pts. | RPG | APG | PPG |
|---|---|---|---|---|---|---|---|---|---|---|---|---|---|---|
| 94-95—Kentucky ...................... | 14 | 57 | 7 | 27 | .259 | 10 | 12 | .833 | 17 | 4 | 28 | 1.2 | 0.3 | 2.0 |
| 95-96—Kentucky ...................... | | | | | | Did not play—ineligible. | | | | | | | | |
| 96-97—Kentucky ...................... | 32 | 759 | 100 | 244 | .410 | 61 | 80 | .763 | 162 | 56 | 308 | 5.1 | 1.8 | 9.6 |
| 97-98—Kentucky ...................... | 39 | 1089 | 161 | 338 | .476 | 87 | 102 | .853 | 255 | 82 | 449 | 6.5 | 2.1 | 11.5 |
| 98-99—Kentucky ...................... | 37 | 1075 | 156 | 335 | .466 | 94 | 138 | .681 | 217 | 96 | 467 | 5.9 | 2.6 | 12.6 |
| Totals ...................................... | 122 | 2980 | 424 | 944 | .449 | 252 | 332 | .759 | 651 | 238 | 1252 | 5.3 | 2.0 | 10.3 |

Three-point field goals: 1994-95, 4-for-13 (.308). 1996-97, 47-for-138 (.341). 1997-98, 40-for-107 (.374). 1998-99, 61-for-160 (.381). Totals, 152-for-418 (.364).
Personal fouls/disqualifications: 1994-95, 12/0. 1996-97, 91/6. 1997-98, 93/1. Totals, 196/7.

## NBA REGULAR-SEASON RECORD

| Season Team | G | Min. | FGM | FGA | Pct. | FTM | FTA | Pct. | Off. | Def. | Tot. | Ast. | St. | Blk. | TO | Pts. | RPG | APG | PPG |
|---|---|---|---|---|---|---|---|---|---|---|---|---|---|---|---|---|---|---|---|
| 99-00—Utah............... | 47 | 432 | 44 | 140 | .314 | 19 | 27 | .704 | 24 | 64 | 88 | 25 | 14 | 8 | 22 | 120 | 1.9 | 0.5 | 2.6 |
| 00-01—Utah............... | 27 | 127 | 18 | 43 | .419 | 15 | 20 | .750 | 19 | 20 | 39 | 5 | 6 | 3 | 10 | 56 | 1.4 | 0.2 | 2.1 |
| 01-02—Utah............... | 75 | 1295 | 188 | 395 | .476 | 75 | 102 | .735 | 111 | 174 | 285 | 82 | 43 | 13 | 69 | 500 | 3.8 | 1.1 | 6.7 |
| 02-03—Utah............... | 82 | 1321 | 170 | 423 | .402 | 81 | 107 | .757 | 83 | 189 | 272 | 86 | 41 | 24 | 70 | 466 | 3.3 | 1.0 | 5.7 |
| 03-04—Houston......... | 58 | 547 | 74 | 167 | .443 | 24 | 32 | .750 | 46 | 93 | 139 | 23 | 12 | 13 | 22 | 200 | 2.4 | 0.4 | 3.4 |
| 04-05—Houston......... | 66 | 942 | 98 | 233 | .421 | 29 | 40 | .725 | 47 | 138 | 185 | 55 | 33 | 10 | 30 | 275 | 2.8 | 0.8 | 4.2 |
| Totals ................... | 355 | 4664 | 592 | 1401 | .423 | 243 | 328 | .741 | 330 | 678 | 1008 | 276 | 149 | 71 | 223 | 1617 | 2.8 | 0.8 | 4.6 |

Three-point field goals: 1999-00, 13-for-44 (.295). 2000-01, 5-for-9 (.556). 2001-02, 49-for-113 (.434). 2002-03, 45-for-133 (.338). 2003-04, 28-for-65 (.431). 2004-05, 50-for-126 (.397). Totals, 190-for-490 (.388).
Personal fouls/disqualifications: 1999-00, 55/1. 2000-01, 21/0. 2001-02, 140/0. 2002-03, 148/1. 2003-04, 73/0. 2004-05, 119/0. Totals, 556/2.

## NBA PLAYOFF RECORD

| Season Team | G | Min. | FGM | FGA | Pct. | FTM | FTA | Pct. | Off. | Def. | Tot. | Ast. | St. | Blk. | TO | Pts. | RPG | APG | PPG |
|---|---|---|---|---|---|---|---|---|---|---|---|---|---|---|---|---|---|---|---|
| 99-00—Utah............... | 8 | 59 | 6 | 16 | .375 | 0 | 0 | ... | 3 | 14 | 17 | 5 | 1 | 2 | 4 | 15 | 2.1 | 0.6 | 1.9 |
| 01-02—Utah............... | 4 | 47 | 6 | 13 | .462 | 4 | 5 | .800 | 7 | 7 | 14 | 2 | 1 | 1 | 5 | 16 | 3.5 | 0.5 | 4.0 |
| 02-03—Utah............... | 4 | 53 | 8 | 19 | .421 | 1 | 2 | .500 | 6 | 3 | 9 | 4 | 3 | 0 | 5 | 19 | 2.3 | 1.0 | 4.8 |
| 03-04—Houston......... | 4 | 14 | 2 | 5 | .400 | 0 | 0 | ... | 1 | 2 | 3 | 0 | 1 | 1 | 1 | 5 | 0.8 | 0.0 | 1.3 |
| 04-05—Houston......... | 7 | 109 | 9 | 24 | .375 | 2 | 2 | 1.000 | 9 | 10 | 19 | 4 | 3 | 2 | 3 | 25 | 2.7 | 0.6 | 3.6 |
| Totals ................... | 27 | 282 | 31 | 77 | .403 | 7 | 9 | .778 | 26 | 36 | 62 | 15 | 9 | 6 | 18 | 80 | 2.3 | 0.6 | 3.0 |

Three-point field goals: 1999-00, 3-for-9 (.333). 2001-02, 0-for-3. 2002-03, 2-for-7 (.286). 2003-04, 1-for-3 (.333). 2004-05, 5-for-12 (.417). Totals, 11-for-34 (.324).
Personal fouls/disqualifications: 1999-00, 10/0. 2001-02, 6/0. 2002-03, 6/0. 2003-04, 1/0. 2004-05, 18/0. Totals, 41/0.

# PALACIO, MILT       G

**PERSONAL:** Born February 7, 1978, in Los Angeles. ... 6-3/195. (1.91/88.5). ... Full name: Milton S. Palacio
**HIGH SCHOOL:** Gardena (Los Angeles).
**JUNIOR COLLEGE:** Midland (Texas) College.
**COLLEGE:** Colorado State.
**TRANSACTIONS/CAREER NOTES:** Not drafted by an NBA franchise. ... Signed as free agent by Vancouver Grizzlies (September 29, 1999). ... Signed as free agent by Washington Wizards (October 2, 2000). ... Waived by Wizards (October 16, 2000). ... Signed as free agent by Boston Celtics (December 7, 2000). ... Waived by Celtics (January 5, 2001). ... Re-signed by Celtics to the first of two consecutive 10-day contracts (January 10, 2001). ... Signed by Celtics for remainder of season (January 29, 2001). ... Traded by Celtics with G/F Joe Johnson, G Randy Brown and 2002 first-round draft choice to Phoenix Suns for G Tony Delk and F Rodney Rogers (February 20, 2002). ... Traded by Suns to Cleveland Cavaliers for future second-round draft choice (September 17, 2002). ... Signed as free agent by Toronto Raptors (July 16, 2003).

## COLLEGIATE RECORD

| Season Team | G | Min. | FGM | FGA | Pct. | FTM | FTA | Pct. | Reb. | Ast. | Pts. | RPG | APG | PPG |
|---|---|---|---|---|---|---|---|---|---|---|---|---|---|---|
| 95-96—Midland .......................... | 29 | ... | 83 | 167 | .497 | 65 | 84 | .774 | 114 | 142 | 254 | 3.9 | 4.9 | 8.8 |
| 96-97—Colorado State............... | 29 | 898 | 75 | 151 | .497 | 62 | 89 | .697 | 111 | 147 | 230 | 3.8 | 5.1 | 7.9 |
| 97-98—Colorado State............... | 29 | 957 | 98 | 205 | .478 | 64 | 97 | .660 | 103 | 148 | 283 | 3.6 | 5.1 | 9.8 |
| 98-99—Colorado State............... | 30 | 1073 | 188 | 418 | .450 | 135 | 179 | .754 | 154 | 130 | 552 | 5.1 | 4.3 | 18.4 |
| Junior College Totals............. | 29 | ... | 83 | 167 | .497 | 65 | 84 | .774 | 114 | 142 | 254 | 3.9 | 4.9 | 8.8 |
| 4-Year-College Totals............. | 88 | 2928 | 361 | 774 | .466 | 261 | 365 | .715 | 368 | 425 | 1065 | 4.2 | 4.8 | 12.1 |

**P**

Three-point field goals: 1995-96, 23-for-57 (.404). 1996-97, 18-for-47 (.383). 1997-98, 23-for-61 (.377). 1998-99, 41-for-119 (.345). Totals, 105-for-284 (.370).
Personal fouls/disqualifications: 1995-96, 69/0. 1996-97, 62/0. 1997-98, 67/0. 1998-99, 72/0. Totals, 270/0.

## NBA REGULAR-SEASON RECORD

| | | | | | | | | | REBOUNDS | | | | | | | | AVERAGES | | |
|---|---|---|---|---|---|---|---|---|---|---|---|---|---|---|---|---|---|---|---|
| Season Team | G | Min. | FGM | FGA | Pct. | FTM | FTA | Pct. | Off. | Def. | Tot. | Ast. | St. | Blk. | TO | Pts. | RPG | APG | PPG |
| 99-00—Vancouver | 53 | 394 | 43 | 98 | .439 | 22 | 37 | .595 | 17 | 34 | 51 | 48 | 20 | 0 | 44 | 108 | 1.0 | 0.9 | 2.0 |
| 00-01—Boston | 58 | 1141 | 126 | 267 | .472 | 78 | 92 | .848 | 25 | 77 | 102 | 151 | 48 | 0 | 80 | 342 | 1.8 | 2.6 | 5.9 |
| 01-02—Bos.-Phoenix | 69 | 790 | 82 | 214 | .383 | 54 | 74 | .730 | 11 | 62 | 73 | 83 | 30 | 4 | 40 | 231 | 1.1 | 1.2 | 3.3 |
| 02-03—Cleveland | 80 | 1976 | 162 | 388 | .418 | 65 | 87 | .747 | 48 | 187 | 235 | 259 | 68 | 16 | 131 | 397 | 2.9 | 3.2 | 5.0 |
| 03-04—Toronto | 59 | 1211 | 104 | 298 | .349 | 45 | 68 | .662 | 15 | 87 | 102 | 184 | 41 | 11 | 87 | 257 | 1.7 | 3.1 | 4.4 |
| 04-05—Toronto | 80 | 1533 | 175 | 392 | .446 | 115 | 155 | .742 | 26 | 108 | 134 | 279 | 48 | 13 | 104 | 467 | 1.7 | 3.5 | 5.8 |
| Totals | 399 | 7045 | 692 | 1657 | .418 | 379 | 513 | .739 | 142 | 555 | 697 | 1004 | 255 | 44 | 486 | 1802 | 1.7 | 2.5 | 4.5 |

Three-point field goals: 1999-00, 0-for-2. 2000-01, 12-for-36 (.333). 2001-02, 13-for-41 (.317). 2002-03, 8-for-37 (.216). 2003-04, 4-for-26 (.154). 2004-05, 2-for-12 (.167). Totals, 39-for-154 (.253).
Personal fouls/disqualifications: 1999-00, 32/0. 2000-01, 83/0. 2001-02, 61/0. 2002-03, 168/2. 2003-04, 90/0. 2004-05, 126/0. Totals, 560/2.

# PARGO, JANNERO          G          BULLS

**PERSONAL:** Born September 22, 1979, in Chicago. ... 6-2/170. (1.88/77.1).
**HIGH SCHOOL:** Robeson (Chicago).
**JUNIOR COLLEGE:** Neosho County Community College (Kan.).
**COLLEGE:** Arkansas.
**TRANSACTIONS/CAREER NOTES:** Not drafted by an NBA franchise. ... Signed as free agent by Los Angeles Lakers (July 26, 2002). ... Waived by Lakers (January 7, 2004). ... Signed by Toronto Raptors for remainder of season (February 24, 2004). ... Released by Raptors (March 5, 2004). ... Signed by Chicago Bulls to 10-day contract (March 15, 2004). ... Signed by Bulls for remainder of season (March 25, 2004).

## COLLEGIATE RECORD

| | | | | | | | | | | | | AVERAGES | | |
|---|---|---|---|---|---|---|---|---|---|---|---|---|---|---|
| Season Team | G | Min. | FGM | FGA | Pct. | FTM | FTA | Pct. | Reb. | Ast. | Pts. | RPG | APG | PPG |
| 98-99—Neosho County C.C. | 26 | ... | 112 | 257 | .436 | 64 | 78 | .821 | 84 | 140 | 356 | 3.2 | 5.4 | 13.7 |
| 99-00—Neosho County C.C. | 32 | ... | 226 | 499 | .453 | 107 | 131 | .817 | 148 | 200 | 708 | 4.6 | 6.3 | 22.1 |
| 00-01—Arkansas | 31 | 742 | 132 | 294 | .449 | 43 | 49 | .878 | 64 | 72 | 380 | 2.1 | 2.3 | 12.3 |
| 01-02—Arkansas | 29 | 789 | 165 | 359 | .460 | 57 | 73 | .781 | 69 | 96 | 482 | 2.4 | 3.3 | 16.6 |
| Junior College Totals | 58 | ... | 338 | 756 | .447 | 171 | 209 | .818 | 232 | 340 | 1064 | 4.0 | 5.9 | 18.3 |
| 4-Year-College Totals | 60 | 1531 | 297 | 653 | .455 | 100 | 122 | .820 | 133 | 168 | 862 | 2.2 | 2.8 | 14.4 |

Three-point field goals: 1998-99, 68-for-154 (.442). 1999-00, 149-for-348 (.428). 2000-01, 73-for-175 (.417). 2001-02, 95-for-220 (.432). Totals, 385-for-897 (.429).

## NBA REGULAR-SEASON RECORD

| | | | | | | | | | REBOUNDS | | | | | | | | AVERAGES | | |
|---|---|---|---|---|---|---|---|---|---|---|---|---|---|---|---|---|---|---|---|
| Season Team | G | Min. | FGM | FGA | Pct. | FTM | FTA | Pct. | Off. | Def. | Tot. | Ast. | St. | Blk. | TO | Pts. | RPG | APG | PPG |
| 02-03—L.A. Lakers | 34 | 342 | 37 | 93 | .398 | 4 | 4 | 1.000 | 9 | 28 | 37 | 39 | 13 | 2 | 23 | 85 | 1.1 | 1.1 | 2.5 |
| 04-05—Chicago | 32 | 453 | 82 | 213 | .385 | 17 | 23 | .739 | 12 | 35 | 47 | 76 | 16 | 1 | 45 | 204 | 1.5 | 2.4 | 6.4 |
| Totals | 66 | 795 | 119 | 306 | .389 | 21 | 27 | .778 | 21 | 63 | 84 | 115 | 29 | 3 | 68 | 289 | 1.3 | 1.7 | 4.4 |

Three-point field goals: 2002-03, 7-for-24 (.292). 2004-05, 23-for-66 (.348). Totals, 30-for-90 (.333).
Personal fouls/disqualifications: 2002-03, 45/0. 2004-05, 53/0. Totals, 98/0.

## NBA PLAYOFF RECORD

| | | | | | | | | | REBOUNDS | | | | | | | | AVERAGES | | |
|---|---|---|---|---|---|---|---|---|---|---|---|---|---|---|---|---|---|---|---|
| Season Team | G | Min. | FGM | FGA | Pct. | FTM | FTA | Pct. | Off. | Def. | Tot. | Ast. | St. | Blk. | TO | Pts. | RPG | APG | PPG |
| 02-03—L.A. Lakers | 11 | 129 | 8 | 24 | .333 | 3 | 4 | .750 | 3 | 6 | 9 | 14 | 8 | 1 | 7 | 23 | 0.8 | 1.3 | 2.1 |
| 04-05—Chicago | 5 | 76 | 18 | 51 | .353 | 3 | 5 | .600 | 1 | 4 | 5 | 10 | 3 | 0 | 8 | 52 | 1.0 | 2.0 | 10.4 |
| Totals | 16 | 205 | 26 | 75 | .347 | 6 | 9 | .667 | 4 | 10 | 14 | 24 | 11 | 1 | 15 | 75 | 0.9 | 1.5 | 4.7 |

Three-point field goals: 2002-03, 4-for-15 (.267). 2004-05, 13-for-32 (.406). Totals, 17-for-47 (.362).
Personal fouls/disqualifications: 2002-03, 22/0. 2004-05, 14/0. Totals, 36/0.

## AMERICAN BASKETBALL ASSOCIATION RECORD

| | | | | | | | | | | | | AVERAGES | | |
|---|---|---|---|---|---|---|---|---|---|---|---|---|---|---|
| Season Team | G | Min. | FGM | FGA | Pct. | FTM | FTA | Pct. | Reb. | Ast. | Pts. | RPG | APG | PPG |
| 03-04—Long Beach | 3 | ... | 15 | 30 | .500 | 3 | 4 | .750 | 5 | 7 | 42 | 1.7 | 2.3 | 14.0 |

Three-point field goals: 2003-04, 9-for-19 (.474). Totals, 9-for-19 (.474).

# PARKER, TONY          G          SPURS

**PERSONAL:** Born May 17, 1982, in Bruges, Belgium. ... 6-2/177. (1.88/80.3). ... Full name: William Anthony Parker
**HIGH SCHOOL:** INSEP (Paris, France).
**COLLEGE:** Did not attend college.
**TRANSACTIONS/CAREER NOTES:** Played in France (1997-2001). ... Selected by San Antonio Spurs in first round (28th pick overall) of 2001 NBA Draft.
**MISCELLANEOUS:** Member of NBA championship team (2003, 2005).

## FRENCH LEAGUE RECORD

| | | | | | | | | | | | | AVERAGES | | |
|---|---|---|---|---|---|---|---|---|---|---|---|---|---|---|
| Season Team | G | Min. | FGM | FGA | Pct. | FTM | FTA | Pct. | Reb. | Ast. | Pts. | RPG | APG | PPG |
| 97-98—Centre Federal | 29 | ... | 146 | 292 | .500 | 97 | 145 | .669 | 78 | 162 | 426 | 2.7 | 5.6 | 14.7 |
| 98-99—Centre Federal | 30 | ... | 252 | 488 | .516 | 113 | 173 | .653 | 120 | 195 | 663 | 4.0 | 6.5 | 22.1 |
| 99-00—Paris Racing | 23 | 231 | 33 | 76 | .434 | 13 | 26 | .500 | 20 | 40 | 90 | 0.9 | 1.7 | 3.9 |
| 00-01—Paris Racing | 30 | 992 | 163 | 333 | .489 | 80 | 107 | .748 | 82 | 168 | 440 | 2.7 | 5.6 | 14.7 |
| Totals | 112 | 1223 | 594 | 1189 | .500 | 303 | 451 | .672 | 300 | 565 | 1619 | 2.7 | 5.0 | 14.5 |

P

Three-point field goals: 1997-98, 37-for-108 (.343). 1998-99, 46-for-156 (.295). 1999-00, 11-for-34 (.324). 2000-01, 34-for-112 (.304). Totals, 128-for-410 (.312).

Personal fouls/disqualifications: 2000-01, 89/0. Totals, 89/0.

### NBA REGULAR-SEASON RECORD

**HONORS:** NBA All-Rookie first team (2002).

| Season Team | G | Min. | FGM | FGA | Pct. | FTM | FTA | Pct. | Off. | Def. | Tot. | Ast. | St. | Blk. | TO | Pts. | RPG | APG | PPG |
|---|---|---|---|---|---|---|---|---|---|---|---|---|---|---|---|---|---|---|---|
| 01-02—San Antonio.... | 77 | 2267 | 268 | 639 | .419 | 108 | 160 | .675 | 33 | 164 | 197 | 334 | 89 | 7 | 151 | 705 | 2.6 | 4.3 | 9.2 |
| 02-03—San Antonio.... | 82 | 2774 | 484 | 1043 | .464 | 219 | 290 | .755 | 33 | 183 | 216 | 432 | 71 | 4 | 198 | 1269 | 2.6 | 5.3 | 15.5 |
| 03-04—San Antonio.... | 75 | 2577 | 423 | 946 | .447 | 191 | 272 | .702 | 43 | 194 | 237 | 411 | 61 | 7 | 179 | 1099 | 3.2 | 5.5 | 14.7 |
| 04-05—San Antonio.... | 80 | 2735 | 539 | 1118 | .482 | 210 | 323 | .650 | 47 | 251 | 298 | 491 | 98 | 4 | 215 | 1331 | 3.7 | 6.1 | 16.6 |
| Totals .................. | 314 | 10353 | 1714 | 3746 | .458 | 728 | 1045 | .697 | 156 | 792 | 948 | 1668 | 319 | 22 | 743 | 4404 | 3.0 | 5.3 | 14.0 |

Three-point field goals: 2001-02, 61-for-189 (.323). 2002-03, 82-for-243 (.337). 2003-04, 62-for-199 (.312). 2004-05, 43-for-156 (.276). Totals, 248-for-787 (.315).

Personal fouls/disqualifications: 2001-02, 166/1. 2002-03, 174/2. 2003-04, 148/0. 2004-05, 167/0. Totals, 655/3.

### NBA PLAYOFF RECORD

| Season Team | G | Min. | FGM | FGA | Pct. | FTM | FTA | Pct. | Off. | Def. | Tot. | Ast. | St. | Blk. | TO | Pts. | RPG | APG | PPG |
|---|---|---|---|---|---|---|---|---|---|---|---|---|---|---|---|---|---|---|---|
| 01-02—San Antonio.... | 10 | 341 | 62 | 136 | .456 | 21 | 28 | .750 | 5 | 24 | 29 | 40 | 9 | 1 | 22 | 155 | 2.9 | 4.0 | 15.5 |
| 02-03—San Antonio.... | 24 | 814 | 135 | 335 | .403 | 67 | 94 | .713 | 8 | 58 | 66 | 85 | 22 | 3 | 47 | 352 | 2.8 | 3.5 | 14.7 |
| 03-04—San Antonio.... | 10 | 386 | 72 | 168 | .429 | 23 | 35 | .657 | 5 | 16 | 21 | 70 | 13 | 1 | 31 | 184 | 2.1 | 7.0 | 18.4 |
| 04-05—San Antonio.... | 23 | 858 | 166 | 366 | .454 | 55 | 87 | .632 | 13 | 53 | 66 | 100 | 17 | 2 | 71 | 396 | 2.9 | 4.3 | 17.2 |
| Totals .................. | 67 | 2399 | 435 | 1005 | .433 | 166 | 244 | .680 | 31 | 151 | 182 | 295 | 61 | 7 | 171 | 1087 | 2.7 | 4.4 | 16.2 |

Three-point field goals: 2001-02, 10-for-27 (.370). 2002-03, 15-for-56 (.268). 2003-04, 17-for-43 (.395). 2004-05, 9-for-48 (.188). Totals, 51-for-174 (.293).

Personal fouls/disqualifications: 2001-02, 22/0. 2002-03, 51/0. 2003-04, 15/0. 2004-05, 69/0. Totals, 157/0.

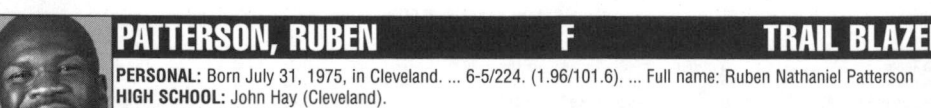

# PARKER, WILLIAM     G     LAKERS

**PERSONAL:** Born June 1, 1981, in Newark, N.J. ... 6-4/180. (1.93/81.6). ... Nickname: Smush.
**HIGH SCHOOL:** Newtown (N.Y.).
**COLLEGE:** Fordham.
**TRANSACTIONS/CAREER NOTES:** Not drafted by an NBA franchise. ... Signed as free agent by Cleveland Cavaliers (September 26, 2002). ... Signed as free agent by Detroit Pistons (October 1, 2004). ... Waived by Pistons (January 4, 2005). ... Signed by Phoenix Suns to 10-day contract (January 19, 2005). ... Waived by Suns (February 8, 2005). ... Signed as free agent by Los Angeles Lakers (August 2, 2005).

### COLLEGIATE RECORD

| Season Team | G | Min. | FGM | FGA | Pct. | FTM | FTA | Pct. | Reb. | Ast. | Pts. | RPG | APG | PPG |
|---|---|---|---|---|---|---|---|---|---|---|---|---|---|---|
| 99-00—Southern Idaho .............. | 21 | 473 | 88 | 184 | .478 | 51 | 63 | .810 | 60 | 126 | 245 | 2.9 | 6.0 | 11.7 |
| 00-01—Fordham ........................ | | | | | | | Did not play. | | | | | | | |
| 01-02—Fordham ........................ | 28 | 980 | 153 | 353 | .433 | 100 | 137 | .730 | 122 | 125 | 463 | 4.4 | 4.5 | 16.5 |
| Junior College Totals.............. | 21 | 473 | 88 | 184 | .478 | 51 | 63 | .810 | 60 | 126 | 245 | 2.9 | 6.0 | 11.7 |
| 4-Year-College Totals............. | 28 | 980 | 153 | 353 | .433 | 100 | 137 | .730 | 122 | 125 | 463 | 4.4 | 4.5 | 16.5 |

Three-point field goals: 1999-00, 18-for-70 (.257). 2001-02, 57-for-174 (.328). Totals, 75-for-244 (.307).

### NBA REGULAR-SEASON RECORD

| Season Team | G | Min. | FGM | FGA | Pct. | FTM | FTA | Pct. | Off. | Def. | Tot. | Ast. | St. | Blk. | TO | Pts. | RPG | APG | PPG |
|---|---|---|---|---|---|---|---|---|---|---|---|---|---|---|---|---|---|---|---|
| 02-03—Cleveland ....... | 66 | 1103 | 136 | 338 | .402 | 98 | 118 | .831 | 29 | 90 | 119 | 162 | 48 | 12 | 133 | 408 | 1.8 | 2.5 | 6.2 |
| 04-05—Detroit-Pho.... | 16 | 144 | 18 | 43 | .419 | 9 | 13 | .692 | 4 | 8 | 12 | 15 | 5 | 0 | 19 | 48 | 0.8 | 0.9 | 3.0 |
| Totals .................. | 82 | 1247 | 154 | 381 | .404 | 107 | 131 | .817 | 33 | 98 | 131 | 177 | 53 | 12 | 152 | 456 | 1.6 | 2.2 | 5.6 |

Three-point field goals: 2002-03, 38-for-118 (.322). 2004-05, 3-for-13 (.231). Totals, 41-for-131 (.313).
Personal fouls/disqualifications: 2002-03, 106/1. 2004-05, 16/0. Totals, 122/1.

### CBA RECORD

| Season Team | G | Min. | FGM | FGA | Pct. | FTM | FTA | Pct. | Reb. | Ast. | Pts. | RPG | APG | PPG |
|---|---|---|---|---|---|---|---|---|---|---|---|---|---|---|
| 03-04—Idaho .............. | 9 | 353 | 61 | 112 | .545 | 55 | 77 | .714 | 41 | 44 | 189 | 4.6 | 4.9 | 21.0 |

Three-point field goals: 2003-04, 12-for-35 (.343). Totals, 12-for-35 (.343).

### GREEK LEAGUE RECORD

| Season Team | G | Min. | FGM | FGA | Pct. | FTM | FTA | Pct. | Reb. | Ast. | Pts. | RPG | APG | PPG |
|---|---|---|---|---|---|---|---|---|---|---|---|---|---|---|
| 03-04—Aris.............. | 15 | 450 | 69 | 155 | .445 | 60 | 78 | .769 | 44 | 83 | 217 | 2.9 | 5.5 | 14.5 |

Three-point field goals: 2003-04, 19-for-62 (.306). Totals, 19-for-62 (.306).

### NBDL RECORD

| Season Team | G | Min. | FGM | FGA | Pct. | FTM | FTA | Pct. | Reb. | Ast. | Pts. | RPG | APG | PPG |
|---|---|---|---|---|---|---|---|---|---|---|---|---|---|---|
| 04-05—Florida .......................... | 23 | 833 | 166 | 348 | .477 | 94 | 129 | .729 | 109 | 209 | 440 | 4.7 | 9.1 | 19.1 |

Three-point field goals: 2004-05, 14-for-32 (.438). Totals, 14-for-32 (.438).

# PATTERSON, RUBEN     F     TRAIL BLAZERS

**PERSONAL:** Born July 31, 1975, in Cleveland. ... 6-5/224. (1.96/101.6). ... Full name: Ruben Nathaniel Patterson
**HIGH SCHOOL:** John Hay (Cleveland).
**JUNIOR COLLEGE:** Independence (Kan.) Community College.
**COLLEGE:** Cincinnati.
**TRANSACTIONS/CAREER NOTES:** Selected by Los Angeles Lakers in second round (31st pick overall) of 1998 NBA Draft.

P

... Played in Greece (1998-99). ... Signed as free agent by Seattle SuperSonics (August 10, 1999). ... Signed as free agent by Portland Trail Blazers (July 30, 2001).

## COLLEGIATE RECORD

| Season Team | G | Min. | FGM | FGA | Pct. | FTM | FTA | Pct. | Reb. | Ast. | Pts. | RPG | APG | PPG |
|---|---|---|---|---|---|---|---|---|---|---|---|---|---|---|
| 94-95—Independence C.C. | 33 | ... | 274 | 417 | .657 | 132 | 220 | .600 | 210 | 48 | 690 | 6.4 | 1.5 | 20.9 |
| 95-96—Independence C.C. | 32 | ... | 296 | 464 | .638 | 260 | 382 | .681 | 298 | 79 | 868 | 9.3 | 2.5 | 27.1 |
| 96-97—Cincinnati | 31 | 723 | 164 | 299 | .548 | 87 | 144 | .604 | 174 | 44 | 426 | 5.6 | 1.4 | 13.7 |
| 97-98—Cincinnati | 19 | 530 | 109 | 231 | .472 | 77 | 126 | .611 | 119 | 41 | 313 | 6.3 | 2.2 | 16.5 |
| Junior College Totals | 65 | ... | 570 | 881 | .647 | 392 | 602 | .651 | 508 | 127 | 1558 | 7.8 | 2.0 | 24.0 |
| 4-Year-College Totals | 50 | 1253 | 273 | 530 | .515 | 164 | 270 | .607 | 293 | 85 | 739 | 5.9 | 1.7 | 14.8 |

Three-point field goals: 1994-95, 10-for-18 (.556). 1995-96, 16-for-39 (.410). 1996-97, 11-for-39 (.282). 1997-98, 18-for-67 (.269). Totals, 55-for-163 (.337).

Personal fouls/disqualifications: 1994-95, 76/0. Totals, 76/0.

## BRAZILIAN LEAGUE RECORD

| Season Team | G | Min. | FGM | FGA | Pct. | FTM | FTA | Pct. | Reb. | Ast. | Pts. | RPG | APG | PPG |
|---|---|---|---|---|---|---|---|---|---|---|---|---|---|---|
| 98-99—Franca | 10 | 275 | 45 | 93 | .484 | 28 | 42 | .667 | 34 | 20 | 124 | 3.4 | 2.0 | 12.4 |

Three-point field goals: 1998-99, 6-for-23 (.261). Totals, 6-for-23 (.261).

## NBA REGULAR-SEASON RECORD

| Season Team | G | Min. | FGM | FGA | Pct. | FTM | FTA | Pct. | Off. | Def. | Tot. | Ast. | St. | Blk. | TO | Pts. | RPG | APG | PPG |
|---|---|---|---|---|---|---|---|---|---|---|---|---|---|---|---|---|---|---|---|
| 98-99—L.A. Lakers | 24 | 144 | 21 | 51 | .412 | 22 | 31 | .710 | 17 | 13 | 30 | 2 | 5 | 3 | 12 | 65 | 1.3 | 0.1 | 2.7 |
| 99-00—Seattle | 81 | 2097 | 354 | 661 | .536 | 222 | 321 | .692 | 218 | 216 | 434 | 126 | 94 | 40 | 144 | 942 | 5.4 | 1.6 | 11.6 |
| 00-01—Seattle | 76 | 2059 | 370 | 749 | .494 | 246 | 361 | .681 | 183 | 199 | 382 | 161 | 103 | 45 | 155 | 988 | 5.0 | 2.1 | 13.0 |
| 01-02—Portland | 75 | 1765 | 319 | 619 | .515 | 192 | 274 | .701 | 155 | 143 | 298 | 107 | 79 | 37 | 114 | 839 | 4.0 | 1.4 | 11.2 |
| 02-03—Portland | 78 | 1655 | 254 | 516 | .492 | 138 | 220 | .627 | 120 | 144 | 264 | 101 | 73 | 29 | 117 | 649 | 3.4 | 1.3 | 8.3 |
| 03-04—Portland | 73 | 1651 | 200 | 395 | .506 | 105 | 190 | .553 | 129 | 139 | 268 | 139 | 84 | 21 | 105 | 507 | 3.7 | 1.9 | 6.9 |
| 04-05—Portland | 70 | 1957 | 319 | 601 | .531 | 169 | 282 | .599 | 126 | 147 | 273 | 138 | 106 | 21 | 143 | 809 | 3.9 | 2.0 | 11.6 |
| Totals | 477 | 11328 | 1837 | 3592 | .511 | 1094 | 1679 | .652 | 948 | 1001 | 1949 | 774 | 544 | 196 | 790 | 4799 | 4.1 | 1.6 | 10.1 |

Three-point field goals: 1998-99, 1-for-6 (.167). 1999-00, 12-for-27 (.444). 2000-01, 2-for-36 (.056). 2001-02, 9-for-36 (.250). 2002-03, 3-for-20 (.150). 2003-04, 2-for-12 (.167). 2004-05, 2-for-25 (.080). Totals, 31-for-162 (.191).

Personal fouls/disqualifications: 1998-99, 16/0. 1999-00, 190/0. 2000-01, 176/1. 2001-02, 140/1. 2002-03, 161/0. 2003-04, 152/0. 2004-05, 164/0. Totals, 999/2.

## NBA PLAYOFF RECORD

| Season Team | G | Min. | FGM | FGA | Pct. | FTM | FTA | Pct. | Off. | Def. | Tot. | Ast. | St. | Blk. | TO | Pts. | RPG | APG | PPG |
|---|---|---|---|---|---|---|---|---|---|---|---|---|---|---|---|---|---|---|---|
| 98-99—L.A. Lakers | 3 | 5 | 0 | 1 | .000 | 0 | 0 | ... | 0 | 0 | 0 | 0 | 0 | 0 | 1 | 0 | 0.0 | 0.0 | 0.0 |
| 99-00—Seattle | 5 | 84 | 14 | 26 | .538 | 13 | 15 | .867 | 9 | 6 | 15 | 2 | 3 | 2 | 8 | 41 | 3.0 | 0.4 | 8.2 |
| 01-02—Portland | 3 | 65 | 5 | 15 | .333 | 6 | 8 | .750 | 2 | 5 | 7 | 1 | 3 | 1 | 3 | 16 | 2.3 | 0.3 | 5.3 |
| 02-03—Portland | 7 | 155 | 25 | 52 | .481 | 20 | 29 | .690 | 14 | 12 | 26 | 11 | 4 | 1 | 10 | 70 | 3.7 | 1.6 | 10.0 |
| Totals | 18 | 309 | 44 | 94 | .468 | 39 | 52 | .750 | 25 | 23 | 48 | 14 | 10 | 4 | 22 | 127 | 2.7 | 0.8 | 7.1 |

Three-point field goals: 1999-00, 0-for-2. 2001-02, 0-for-1. 2002-03, 0-for-4. Totals, 0-for-7 (.000).
Personal fouls/disqualifications: 1999-00, 6/0. 2001-02, 7/0. 2002-03, 10/0. Totals, 23/0.

# PAVLOVIC, SASHA     F     CAVALIERS

**PERSONAL:** Born November 15, 1983, in Bar, Serbia & Montenegro. ... 6-7/210. (2.01/95.3).
**TRANSACTIONS/CAREER NOTES:** Played in Yugoslavia (2000-03). ... Selected by Utah Jazz in first round (19th pick overall) of 2003 NBA Draft. ... Selected by Charlotte Bobcats from Jazz in NBA Expansion Draft (June 22, 2004). ... Traded by Bobcats to Cleveland Cavaliers for future first-round draft choice (June 23, 2004).
**MISCELLANEOUS:** Member of Serbia-Montenegro Olympic Team (2004).

## YUGOSLAVIAN LEAGUE RECORD

| Season Team | G | Min. | FGM | FGA | Pct. | FTM | FTA | Pct. | Reb. | Ast. | Pts. | RPG | APG | PPG |
|---|---|---|---|---|---|---|---|---|---|---|---|---|---|---|
| 00-01—Buducnost | 14 | 68 | 7 | 19 | .368 | 2 | 2 | 1.000 | 6 | 1 | 18 | 0.4 | 0.1 | 1.3 |
| 01-02—Buducnost | 3 | 45 | 7 | 10 | .700 | 3 | 4 | .750 | 1 | 1 | 20 | 0.3 | 0.3 | 6.7 |
| 02-03—Buducnost | 20 | 394 | 76 | 155 | .490 | 34 | 48 | .708 | 48 | 16 | 201 | 2.4 | 0.8 | 10.1 |
| Totals | 37 | 507 | 90 | 184 | .489 | 39 | 54 | .722 | 55 | 18 | 239 | 1.5 | 0.5 | 6.5 |

Three-point field goals: 2000-01, 2-for-9 (.222). 2001-02, 3-for-4 (.750). 2002-03, 15-for-54 (.278). Totals, 20-for-67 (.299).

## NBA REGULAR-SEASON RECORD

| Season Team | G | Min. | FGM | FGA | Pct. | FTM | FTA | Pct. | Off. | Def. | Tot. | Ast. | St. | Blk. | TO | Pts. | RPG | APG | PPG |
|---|---|---|---|---|---|---|---|---|---|---|---|---|---|---|---|---|---|---|---|
| 03-04—Utah | 79 | 1144 | 149 | 376 | .396 | 65 | 84 | .774 | 44 | 115 | 159 | 60 | 41 | 16 | 67 | 382 | 2.0 | 0.8 | 4.8 |
| 04-05—Cleveland | 65 | 862 | 120 | 276 | .435 | 44 | 64 | .688 | 15 | 56 | 71 | 49 | 29 | 4 | 47 | 314 | 1.1 | 0.8 | 4.8 |
| Totals | 144 | 2006 | 269 | 652 | .413 | 109 | 148 | .736 | 59 | 171 | 230 | 109 | 70 | 20 | 114 | 696 | 1.6 | 0.8 | 4.8 |

Three-point field goals: 2003-04, 19-for-70 (.271). 2004-05, 30-for-78 (.385). Totals, 49-for-148 (.331).
Personal fouls/disqualifications: 2003-04, 187/3. 2004-05, 121/0. Totals, 308/3.

# PAYTON, GARY     G

**PERSONAL:** Born July 23, 1968, in Oakland. ... 6-4/180. (1.93/81.6). ... Full name: Gary Dwayne Payton
**HIGH SCHOOL:** Skyline (Oakland).
**COLLEGE:** Oregon State.
**TRANSACTIONS/CAREER NOTES:** Selected by Seattle SuperSonics in first round (second pick overall) of 1990 NBA Draft. ... Traded by SuperSonics with G Desmond Mason to Milwaukee Bucks for G Ray Allen, G Kevin Ollie, G Ronald Murray

P

and conditional first-round draft choice (February 20, 2003). ... Signed as free agent by Los Angeles Lakers (July 16, 2003) ... Traded by Lakers with F Rick Fox and a first-round draft choice to Boston Celtics for F/C Chris Mihm, G Chucky Atkins and F Jumaine Jones (August 6, 2004). ... Traded by Celtics with F Tom Gugliotta, C Michael Stewart and 2005 or future first-round pick to Atlanta Hawks for F Antoine Walker (February 24, 2005). ... Waived by Hawks (March 1, 2005). ... Signed by Boston Celtics (March 4, 2005).

**MISCELLANEOUS:** Member of gold-medal-winning U.S. Olympic team (2000). ... Member of gold-medal-winning U.S. Olympic team (1996). ... Seattle SuperSonics franchise all-time points leader with 17,123, all-time assists leader with 6,927 and all-time steals leader with 2,014 (1990-91 through 2001-02).

## COLLEGIATE RECORD

**NOTES:** THE SPORTING NEWS All-America first team (1990).

| Season Team | G | Min. | FGM | FGA | Pct. | FTM | FTA | Pct. | Reb. | Ast. | Pts. | RPG | APG | PPG |
|---|---|---|---|---|---|---|---|---|---|---|---|---|---|---|
| 86-87—Oregon State | 30 | 1115 | 153 | 333 | .459 | 55 | 82 | .671 | 120 | 229 | 374 | 4.0 | 7.6 | 12.5 |
| 87-88—Oregon State | 31 | 1178 | 180 | 368 | .489 | 58 | 83 | .699 | 103 | 230 | 449 | 3.3 | 7.4 | 14.5 |
| 88-89—Oregon State | 30 | 1140 | 208 | 438 | .475 | 105 | 155 | .677 | 122 | 244 | 603 | 4.1 | 8.1 | 20.1 |
| 89-90—Oregon State | 29 | 1095 | 288 | 571 | .504 | 118 | 171 | .690 | 135 | 235 | 746 | 4.7 | 8.1 | 25.7 |
| **Totals** | 120 | 4528 | 829 | 1710 | .485 | 336 | 491 | .684 | 480 | 938 | 2172 | 4.0 | 7.8 | 18.1 |

Three-point field goals: 1986-87, 13-for-35 (.371). 1987-88, 31-for-78 (.397). 1988-89, 82-for-213 (.385). 1989-90, 52-for-156 (.333). Totals, 178-for-482 (.369).

## NBA REGULAR-SEASON RECORD

**HONORS:** NBA Defensive Player of the Year (1996). ... All-NBA first team (1998, 2000). ... All-NBA second team (1995, 1996, 1997, 1999, 2002). ... All-NBA third team (1994, 2001). ... NBA All-Defensive first team (1994, 1995, 1996, 1997, 1998, 1999, 2000, 2001, 2002). ... NBA All-Rookie second team (1991).

**NOTES:** Led NBA with 2.85 steals per game (1996).

| | | | | | | | | | REBOUNDS | | | | | | | | AVERAGES | | |
|---|---|---|---|---|---|---|---|---|---|---|---|---|---|---|---|---|---|---|---|
| Season Team | G | Min. | FGM | FGA | Pct. | FTM | FTA | Pct. | Off. | Def. | Tot. | Ast. | St. | Blk. | TO | Pts. | RPG | APG | PPG |
| 90-91—Seattle | 82 | 2244 | 259 | 575 | .450 | 69 | 97 | .711 | 108 | 135 | 243 | 528 | 165 | 15 | 180 | 588 | 3.0 | 6.4 | 7.2 |
| 91-92—Seattle | 81 | 2549 | 331 | 734 | .451 | 99 | 148 | .669 | 123 | 172 | 295 | 506 | 147 | 21 | 174 | 764 | 3.6 | 6.2 | 9.4 |
| 92-93—Seattle | 82 | 2548 | 476 | 963 | .494 | 151 | 196 | .770 | 95 | 186 | 281 | 399 | 177 | 21 | 148 | 1110 | 3.4 | 4.9 | 13.5 |
| 93-94—Seattle | 82 | 2881 | 584 | 1159 | .504 | 166 | 279 | .595 | 105 | 164 | 269 | 494 | 188 | 19 | 173 | 1349 | 3.3 | 6.0 | 16.5 |
| 94-95—Seattle | 82 | 3015 | 685 | 1345 | .509 | 249 | 348 | .716 | 108 | 173 | 281 | 583 | 204 | 13 | 201 | 1689 | 3.4 | 7.1 | 20.6 |
| 95-96—Seattle | 81 | 3162 | 618 | 1276 | .484 | 229 | 306 | .748 | 104 | 235 | 339 | 608 | *231 | 19 | 260 | 1563 | 4.2 | 7.5 | 19.3 |
| 96-97—Seattle | 82 | 3213 | 706 | 1482 | .476 | 254 | 355 | .715 | 106 | 272 | 378 | 583 | 197 | 18 | 215 | 1785 | 4.6 | 7.1 | 21.8 |
| 97-98—Seattle | 82 | 3145 | 579 | 1278 | .453 | 279 | 375 | .744 | 77 | 299 | 376 | 679 | 185 | 18 | 229 | 1571 | 4.6 | 8.3 | 19.2 |
| 98-99—Seattle | 50 | 2008 | 401 | 923 | .434 | 199 | 276 | .721 | 62 | 182 | 244 | 436 | 109 | 12 | 154 | 1084 | 4.9 | 8.7 | 21.7 |
| 99-00—Seattle | 82 | 3425 | 747 | 1666 | .448 | 311 | 423 | .735 | 100 | 429 | 529 | *732 | 153 | 18 | 224 | 1982 | 6.5 | 8.9 | 24.2 |
| 00-01—Seattle | 79 | 3244 | 725 | 1591 | .456 | 271 | 354 | .766 | 73 | 288 | 361 | 642 | 127 | 26 | 209 | 1823 | 4.6 | 8.1 | 23.1 |
| 01-02—Seattle | 82 | 3301 | 737 | 1578 | .467 | 267 | 335 | .797 | 80 | 316 | 396 | 737 | 131 | 26 | 209 | 1815 | 4.8 | 9.0 | 22.1 |
| 02-03—Seattle-Mil. | 80 | 3208 | 665 | 1466 | .454 | 250 | 352 | .710 | 79 | 255 | 334 | 663 | 133 | 20 | 187 | 1634 | 4.2 | 8.3 | 20.4 |
| 03-04—L.A. Lakers | 82 | 2825 | 482 | 1024 | .471 | 180 | 252 | .714 | 72 | 270 | 342 | 449 | 96 | 19 | 151 | 1199 | 4.2 | 5.5 | 14.6 |
| 04-05—Atlanta-Boston | 77 | 2541 | 339 | 725 | .468 | 153 | 201 | .761 | 48 | 188 | 236 | 469 | 88 | 12 | 148 | 873 | 3.1 | 6.1 | 11.3 |
| **Totals** | 1186 | 43309 | 8334 | 17785 | .469 | 3127 | 4297 | .728 | 1340 | 3564 | 4904 | 8508 | 2331 | 272 | 2862 | 20829 | 4.1 | 7.2 | 17.6 |

Three-point field goals: 1990-91, 1-for-13 (.077). 1991-92, 3-for-23 (.130). 1992-93, 7-for-34 (.206). 1993-94, 15-for-54 (.278). 1994-95, 70-for-232 (.302). 1995-96, 98-for-299 (.328). 1996-97, 119-for-380 (.313). 1997-98, 134-for-397 (.338). 1998-99, 83-for-281 (.295). 1999-00, 177-for-520 (.340). 2000-01, 102-for-272 (.375). 2001-02, 74-for-236 (.314). 2002-03, 54-for-182 (.297). 2003-04, 55-for-165 (.333). 2004-05, 42-for-129 (.326). Totals, 1034-for-3217 (.321).

Personal fouls/disqualifications: 1990-91, 249/3. 1991-92, 248/0. 1992-93, 250/1. 1993-94, 227/0. 1994-95, 206/1. 1995-96, 221/1. 1996-97, 208/1. 1997-98, 195/0. 1998-99, 115/0. 1999-00, 178/0. 2000-01, 184/0. 2001-02, 179/0. 2002-03, 181/0. 2003-04, 169/0. 2004-05, 121/0. Totals, 2931/7.

## NBA PLAYOFF RECORD

**NOTES:** Shares single-game playoff record for most three-point field goal attempts in one half—11 (May 4, 1996, vs. Houston).

| | | | | | | | | | REBOUNDS | | | | | | | | AVERAGES | | |
|---|---|---|---|---|---|---|---|---|---|---|---|---|---|---|---|---|---|---|---|
| Season Team | G | Min. | FGM | FGA | Pct. | FTM | FTA | Pct. | Off. | Def. | Tot. | Ast. | St. | Blk. | TO | Pts. | RPG | APG | PPG |
| 90-91—Seattle | 5 | 135 | 11 | 27 | .407 | 2 | 2 | 1.000 | 5 | 8 | 13 | 32 | 8 | 1 | 9 | 24 | 2.6 | 6.4 | 4.8 |
| 91-92—Seattle | 8 | 221 | 27 | 58 | .466 | 7 | 12 | .583 | 6 | 15 | 21 | 38 | 8 | 2 | 10 | 61 | 2.6 | 4.8 | 7.6 |
| 92-93—Seattle | 19 | 605 | 104 | 235 | .443 | 25 | 37 | .676 | 22 | 41 | 63 | 70 | 34 | 3 | 34 | 234 | 3.3 | 3.7 | 12.3 |
| 93-94—Seattle | 5 | 181 | 34 | 69 | .493 | 8 | 19 | .421 | 6 | 11 | 17 | 28 | 8 | 2 | 8 | 79 | 3.4 | 5.6 | 15.8 |
| 94-95—Seattle | 4 | 172 | 32 | 67 | .478 | 5 | 12 | .417 | 6 | 4 | 10 | 21 | 5 | 0 | 8 | 71 | 2.5 | 5.3 | 17.8 |
| 95-96—Seattle | 21 | 911 | 162 | 334 | .485 | 69 | 109 | .633 | 19 | 89 | 108 | 143 | 37 | 7 | 62 | 434 | 5.1 | 6.8 | 20.7 |
| 96-97—Seattle | 12 | 546 | 105 | 255 | .412 | 50 | 61 | .820 | 20 | 45 | 65 | 104 | 26 | 4 | 35 | 285 | 5.4 | 8.7 | 23.8 |
| 97-98—Seattle | 10 | 428 | 87 | 183 | .475 | 47 | 50 | .940 | 9 | 25 | 34 | 70 | 18 | 1 | 26 | 240 | 3.4 | 7.0 | 24.0 |
| 99-00—Seattle | 5 | 221 | 50 | 113 | .442 | 20 | 26 | .769 | 8 | 30 | 38 | 37 | 9 | 1 | 18 | 129 | 7.6 | 7.4 | 25.8 |
| 01-02—Seattle | 5 | 207 | 45 | 106 | .425 | 17 | 29 | .586 | 10 | 33 | 43 | 29 | 3 | 2 | 13 | 111 | 8.6 | 5.8 | 22.2 |
| 02-03—Milwaukee | 6 | 251 | 48 | 112 | .429 | 14 | 20 | .700 | 4 | 14 | 18 | 52 | 8 | 1 | 13 | 111 | 3.0 | 8.7 | 18.5 |
| 03-04—L.A. Lakers | 22 | 772 | 68 | 186 | .366 | 21 | 28 | .750 | 19 | 53 | 72 | 116 | 23 | 4 | 28 | 171 | 3.3 | 5.3 | 7.8 |
| 04-05—Boston | 7 | 239 | 33 | 74 | .446 | 5 | 6 | .833 | 8 | 21 | 29 | 32 | 6 | 1 | 11 | 72 | 4.1 | 4.6 | 10.3 |
| **Totals** | 129 | 4889 | 806 | 1819 | .443 | 290 | 411 | .706 | 142 | 389 | 531 | 772 | 193 | 29 | 275 | 2022 | 4.1 | 6.0 | 15.7 |

Three-point field goals: 1990-91, 0-for-1. 1991-92, 0-for-2. 1992-93, 1-for-6 (.167). 1993-94, 3-for-9 (.333). 1994-95, 2-for-10 (.200). 1995-96, 41-for-100 (.410). 1996-97, 25-for-75 (.333). 1997-98, 19-for-50 (.380). 1999-00, 9-for-23 (.391). 2001-02, 4-for-15 (.267). 2002-03, 1-for-15 (.067). 2003-04, 14-for-52 (.250). 2004-05, 1-for-14 (.071). Totals, 120-for-376 (.319).

Personal fouls/disqualifications: 1990-91, 16/0. 1991-92, 26/1. 1992-93, 64/1. 1993-94, 15/0. 1994-95, 13/0. 1995-96, 69/0. 1996-97, 26/0. 1997-98, 31/1. 1999-00, 16/0. 2001-02, 12/0. 2002-03, 18/0. 2003-04, 60/0. 2004-05, 10/0. Totals, 376/3.

## NBA ALL-STAR GAME RECORD

**NOTES:** Shares career record for most three-point field goal attempts—23.

| | | | | | | | | REBOUNDS | | | | | | | | |
|---|---|---|---|---|---|---|---|---|---|---|---|---|---|---|---|---|
| Season Team | Min. | FGM | FGA | Pct. | FTM | FTA | Pct. | Off. | Def. | Tot. | Ast. | PF | Dq. | St. | Blk. | TO | Pts. |
| 1994—Seattle | 17 | 3 | 4 | .750 | 0 | 0 | ... | 2 | 4 | 6 | 9 | 2 | 0 | 0 | 0 | 0 | 6 |
| 1995—Seattle | 23 | 3 | 10 | .300 | 0 | 0 | ... | 3 | 2 | 5 | 15 | 1 | 0 | 3 | 0 | 3 | 6 |
| 1996—Seattle | 28 | 6 | 10 | .600 | 6 | 6 | 1.000 | 3 | 2 | 5 | 5 | 1 | 0 | 5 | 0 | 6 | 18 |
| 1997—Seattle | 28 | 7 | 15 | .467 | 2 | 2 | 1.000 | 0 | 1 | 1 | 10 | 2 | 0 | 2 | 0 | 4 | 17 |

P

| Season Team | Min. | FGM | FGA | Pct. | FTM | FTA | Pct. | REBOUNDS Off. | Def. | Tot. | Ast. | PF | Dq. | St. | Blk. | TO | Pts. |
|---|---|---|---|---|---|---|---|---|---|---|---|---|---|---|---|---|---|
| 1998—Seattle | 24 | 3 | 7 | .429 | 0 | 0 | ... | 2 | 1 | 3 | 13 | 0 | 0 | 2 | 0 | 4 | 7 |
| 2000—Seattle | 20 | 1 | 8 | .125 | 3 | 3 | 1.000 | 0 | 4 | 4 | 8 | 1 | 0 | 2 | 0 | 2 | 5 |
| 2001—Seattle | 18 | 0 | 5 | .000 | 0 | 0 | ... | 2 | 2 | 4 | 5 | 2 | 0 | 2 | 0 | 1 | 0 |
| 2002—Seattle | 22 | 7 | 13 | .538 | 0 | 0 | ... | 0 | 1 | 1 | 6 | 1 | 0 | 3 | 0 | 3 | 18 |
| 2003—Seattle | 15 | 4 | 6 | .667 | 0 | 0 | ... | 1 | 0 | 1 | 2 | 3 | 0 | 0 | 0 | 3 | 8 |
| Totals | 195 | 34 | 78 | .436 | 11 | 11 | 1.000 | 13 | 17 | 30 | 73 | 13 | 0 | 19 | 0 | 26 | 85 |

Three-point field goals: 1995, 0-for-3. 1996, 0-for-1. 1997, 1-for-5 (.200). 1998, 1-for-3 (.333). 2000, 0-for-4. 2002, 4-for-6 (.667). 2003, 0-for-1. Totals, 6-for-23 (.261).

## PEELER, ANTHONY G

**PERSONAL:** Born November 25, 1969, in Kansas City, Mo. ... 6-4/208. (1.93/94.3). ... Full name: Anthony Eugene Peeler
**HIGH SCHOOL:** Paseo (Kansas City, Mo.).
**COLLEGE:** Missouri.
**TRANSACTIONS/CAREER NOTES:** Selected by Los Angeles Lakers in first round (15th pick overall) of 1992 NBA Draft. ... Traded by Lakers with F George Lynch and 1997 and 1998 second-round draft choices to Vancouver Grizzlies for 1997 and 1998 second-round draft choices (July 16, 1996). ... Traded by Grizzlies to Minnesota Timberwolves for G Doug West (February 18, 1998). ... Traded by Timberwolves with F Joe Smith to Milwaukee Bucks for G Sam Cassell and C Ervin Johnson (June 27, 2003) ... Waived by Bucks (July 7, 2003) ... Signed as free agent by Sacramento Kings (August 15, 2003). ... Signed as free agent by Washington Wizards (July 29, 2004).
**MISCELLANEOUS:** Selected by Texas Rangers organization in 41st round of free-agent draft (June 1, 1988); did not sign.

### COLLEGIATE RECORD

| Season Team | G | Min. | FGM | FGA | Pct. | FTM | FTA | Pct. | Reb. | Ast. | Pts. | AVERAGES RPG | APG | PPG |
|---|---|---|---|---|---|---|---|---|---|---|---|---|---|---|
| 88-89—Missouri | 36 | 801 | 130 | 258 | .504 | 89 | 118 | .754 | 134 | 102 | 362 | 3.7 | 2.8 | 10.1 |
| 89-90—Missouri | 31 | 1031 | 184 | 413 | .446 | 130 | 169 | .769 | 168 | 179 | 522 | 5.4 | 5.8 | 16.8 |
| 90-91—Missouri | 21 | 725 | 134 | 282 | .475 | 116 | 151 | .768 | 131 | 104 | 408 | 6.2 | 5.0 | 19.4 |
| 91-92—Missouri | 29 | 1026 | 218 | 475 | .459 | 187 | 232 | .806 | 160 | 112 | 678 | 5.5 | 3.9 | 23.4 |
| Totals | 117 | 3583 | 666 | 1428 | .466 | 522 | 670 | .779 | 593 | 497 | 1970 | 5.1 | 4.2 | 16.8 |

Three-point field goals: 1988-89, 13-for-37 (.351). 1989-90, 24-for-68 (.353). 1990-91, 24-for-58 (.414). 1991-92, 55-for-132 (.417). Totals, 116-for-295 (.393).

### NBA REGULAR-SEASON RECORD

| Season Team | G | Min. | FGM | FGA | Pct. | FTM | FTA | Pct. | REBOUNDS Off. | Def. | Tot. | Ast. | St. | Blk. | TO | Pts. | AVERAGES RPG | APG | PPG |
|---|---|---|---|---|---|---|---|---|---|---|---|---|---|---|---|---|---|---|---|
| 92-93—L.A. Lakers | 77 | 1656 | 297 | 634 | .468 | 162 | 206 | .786 | 64 | 115 | 179 | 166 | 60 | 14 | 123 | 802 | 2.3 | 2.2 | 10.4 |
| 93-94—L.A. Lakers | 30 | 923 | 176 | 409 | .430 | 57 | 71 | .803 | 48 | 61 | 109 | 94 | 43 | 8 | 59 | 423 | 3.6 | 3.1 | 14.1 |
| 94-95—L.A. Lakers | 73 | 1559 | 285 | 659 | .432 | 102 | 128 | .797 | 62 | 106 | 168 | 122 | 52 | 13 | 82 | 756 | 2.3 | 1.7 | 10.4 |
| 95-96—L.A. Lakers | 73 | 1608 | 272 | 602 | .452 | 61 | 86 | .709 | 45 | 92 | 137 | 118 | 59 | 10 | 56 | 710 | 1.9 | 1.6 | 9.7 |
| 96-97—Vancouver | 72 | 2291 | 402 | 1011 | .398 | 109 | 133 | .820 | 54 | 193 | 247 | 256 | 105 | 17 | 157 | 1041 | 3.4 | 3.6 | 14.5 |
| 97-98—Van.-Minn. | 38 | 1193 | 190 | 420 | .452 | 36 | 47 | .766 | 37 | 86 | 123 | 137 | 61 | 6 | 51 | 469 | 3.2 | 3.6 | 12.3 |
| 98-99—Minnesota | 28 | 810 | 103 | 272 | .379 | 30 | 41 | .732 | 30 | 54 | 84 | 78 | 35 | 6 | 38 | 270 | 3.0 | 2.8 | 9.6 |
| 99-00—Minnesota | 82 | 2073 | 316 | 725 | .436 | 87 | 109 | .798 | 58 | 174 | 232 | 195 | 62 | 10 | 85 | 804 | 2.8 | 2.4 | 9.8 |
| 00-01—Minnesota | 75 | 2126 | 308 | 732 | .421 | 75 | 87 | .862 | 44 | 148 | 192 | 192 | 91 | 18 | 105 | 791 | 2.6 | 2.6 | 10.5 |
| 01-02—Minnesota | 82 | 2060 | 288 | 684 | .421 | 50 | 58 | .862 | 37 | 169 | 206 | 177 | 61 | 11 | 76 | 737 | 2.5 | 2.2 | 9.0 |
| 02-03—Minnesota | 82 | 2245 | 252 | 609 | .414 | 39 | 50 | .780 | 40 | 201 | 241 | 244 | 72 | 13 | 82 | 630 | 2.9 | 3.0 | 7.7 |
| 03-04—Sacramento | 75 | 1391 | 156 | 348 | .448 | 51 | 61 | .836 | 31 | 122 | 153 | 120 | 56 | 10 | 77 | 431 | 2.0 | 1.6 | 5.7 |
| 04-05—Washington | 40 | 529 | 56 | 150 | .373 | 16 | 18 | .889 | 14 | 51 | 65 | 57 | 18 | 2 | 28 | 153 | 1.6 | 1.4 | 3.8 |
| Totals | 827 | 20464 | 3101 | 7255 | .427 | 875 | 1095 | .799 | 564 | 1572 | 2136 | 1956 | 775 | 138 | 1019 | 8017 | 2.6 | 2.4 | 9.7 |

Three-point field goals: 1992-93, 46-for-118 (.390). 1993-94, 14-for-63 (.222). 1994-95, 84-for-216 (.389). 1995-96, 105-for-254 (.413). 1996-97, 128-for-343 (.373). 1997-98, 53-for-125 (.424). 1998-99, 34-for-114 (.298). 1999-00, 85-for-255 (.333). 2000-01, 100-for-256 (.391). 2001-02, 111-for-283 (.392). 2002-03, 87-for-212 (.410). 2003-04, 68-for-141 (.482). 2004-05, 25-for-65 (.385). Totals, 940-for-2445 (.384).

Personal fouls/disqualifications: 1992-93, 193/0. 1993-94, 93/0. 1994-95, 143/1. 1995-96, 139/0. 1996-97, 168/0. 1997-98, 97/0. 1998-99, 60/0. 1999-00, 171/1. 2000-01, 166/1. 2001-02, 137/0. 2002-03, 161/0. 2003-04, 103/0. 2004-05, 39/0. Totals, 1670/3.

### NBA PLAYOFF RECORD

| Season Team | G | Min. | FGM | FGA | Pct. | FTM | FTA | Pct. | REBOUNDS Off. | Def. | Tot. | Ast. | St. | Blk. | TO | Pts. | AVERAGES RPG | APG | PPG |
|---|---|---|---|---|---|---|---|---|---|---|---|---|---|---|---|---|---|---|---|
| 94-95—L.A. Lakers | 10 | 268 | 32 | 79 | .405 | 17 | 22 | .773 | 8 | 20 | 28 | 25 | 10 | 2 | 12 | 89 | 2.8 | 2.5 | 8.9 |
| 95-96—L.A. Lakers | 3 | 72 | 9 | 27 | .333 | 4 | 4 | 1.000 | 2 | 6 | 8 | 3 | 6 | 0 | 3 | 28 | 2.7 | 1.0 | 9.3 |
| 97-98—Minnesota | 5 | 213 | 31 | 77 | .403 | 4 | 4 | 1.000 | 16 | 22 | 38 | 18 | 10 | 3 | 8 | 81 | 7.6 | 3.6 | 16.2 |
| 98-99—Minnesota | 4 | 125 | 11 | 35 | .314 | 0 | 0 | ... | 7 | 9 | 16 | 6 | 4 | 0 | 4 | 27 | 4.0 | 1.5 | 6.8 |
| 99-00—Minnesota | 4 | 90 | 11 | 24 | .458 | 6 | 8 | .750 | 2 | 7 | 9 | 5 | 3 | 1 | 1 | 30 | 2.3 | 1.3 | 7.5 |
| 00-01—Minnesota | 4 | 137 | 14 | 53 | .264 | 0 | 0 | ... | 3 | 11 | 14 | 7 | 7 | 1 | 6 | 34 | 3.5 | 1.8 | 8.5 |
| 01-02—Minnesota | 3 | 67 | 9 | 20 | .450 | 4 | 6 | .667 | 1 | 12 | 13 | 2 | 4 | 0 | 6 | 27 | 4.3 | 0.7 | 9.0 |
| 02-03—Minnesota | 6 | 166 | 13 | 38 | .342 | 1 | 2 | .500 | 5 | 16 | 21 | 18 | 4 | 1 | 4 | 29 | 3.5 | 3.0 | 4.8 |
| 03-04—Sacramento | 11 | 236 | 19 | 63 | .302 | 5 | 6 | .833 | 7 | 28 | 35 | 15 | 14 | 2 | 14 | 50 | 3.2 | 1.4 | 4.5 |
| 04-05—Washington | 7 | 43 | 1 | 9 | .111 | 2 | 2 | 1.000 | 0 | 7 | 7 | 3 | 1 | 0 | 3 | 4 | 1.0 | 0.4 | 0.6 |
| Totals | 57 | 1417 | 150 | 425 | .353 | 43 | 54 | .796 | 51 | 138 | 189 | 102 | 63 | 10 | 61 | 399 | 3.3 | 1.8 | 7.0 |

Three-point field goals: 1994-95, 8-for-31 (.258). 1995-96, 6-for-14 (.429). 1997-98, 15-for-31 (.484). 1998-99, 5-for-13 (.385). 1999-00, 2-for-10 (.200). 2000-01, 6-for-17 (.353). 2001-02, 5-for-9 (.556). 2002-03, 2-for-16 (.125). 2003-04, 7-for-26 (.269). 2004-05, 0-for-3. Totals, 56-for-170 (.329).

Personal fouls/disqualifications: 1994-95, 23/0. 1995-96, 6/0. 1997-98, 15/0. 1998-99, 12/1. 1999-00, 9/0. 2000-01, 10/0. 2001-02, 5/0. 2002-03, 14/0. 2003-04, 19/0. 2004-05, 4/0. Totals, 117/1.

P

# PENNEY, KIRK                                      G

**PERSONAL:** Born November 23, 1980, in Auckland, New Zealand. ... 6-5/220. (1.96/99.8).
**HIGH SCHOOL:** Westlake Boys (Auckland, New Zealand).
**COLLEGE:** Wisconsin.
**TRANSACTIONS/CAREER NOTES:** Not drafted by an NBA franchise. ... Signed as free agent by Miami Heat (November 3, 2003). ... Waived by Heat (November 7, 2003). ... Played in Spain (2003-04). ... Played in NBDL (2004). ... Signed as free agent by Los Angeles Clippers (December 26, 2004). ... Waived by Clippers (January 3, 2005).
**MISCELLANEOUS:** Member of New Zealand Olympic Team (2004).

## COLLEGIATE RECORD

| Season Team | G | Min. | FGM | FGA | Pct. | FTM | FTA | Pct. | Reb. | Ast. | Pts. | AVERAGES RPG | APG | PPG |
|---|---|---|---|---|---|---|---|---|---|---|---|---|---|---|
| 99-00—Wisconsin | 34 | 433 | 45 | 135 | .333 | 14 | 19 | .737 | 48 | 27 | 127 | 1.4 | 0.8 | 3.7 |
| 00-01—Wisconsin | 29 | 824 | 70 | 162 | .432 | 40 | 56 | .714 | 88 | 32 | 326 | 3.0 | 1.1 | 11.2 |
| 01-02—Wisconsin | 32 | 1040 | 167 | 368 | .454 | 86 | 112 | .768 | 157 | 55 | 482 | 4.9 | 1.7 | 15.1 |
| 02-03—Wisconsin | 32 | 1119 | 183 | 410 | .446 | 91 | 121 | .752 | 191 | 100 | 519 | 6.0 | 3.1 | 16.2 |
| Totals | 127 | 3416 | 465 | 1075 | .433 | 231 | 308 | .750 | 484 | 214 | 1454 | 3.8 | 1.7 | 11.4 |

Three-point field goals: 1999-00, 23-for-77 (.299). 2000-01, 70-for-162 (.432). 2001-02, 62-for-161 (.385). 2002-03, 62-for-161 (.385). Totals, 217-for-561 (.387).

## NBA REGULAR-SEASON RECORD

| Season Team | G | Min. | FGM | FGA | Pct. | FTM | FTA | Pct. | REBOUNDS Off. | Def. | Tot. | Ast. | St. | Blk. | TO | Pts. | AVERAGES RPG | APG | PPG |
|---|---|---|---|---|---|---|---|---|---|---|---|---|---|---|---|---|---|---|---|
| 03-04—Miami | 2 | 18 | 1 | 6 | .167 | 0 | 0 | ... | 0 | 1 | 1 | 1 | 1 | 0 | 3 | 3 | 0.5 | 0.5 | 1.5 |
| 04-05—L.A. Clippers | 4 | 12 | 1 | 3 | .333 | 0 | 0 | ... | 0 | 1 | 1 | 1 | 0 | 0 | 2 | 2 | 0.3 | 0.3 | 0.5 |
| Totals | 6 | 30 | 2 | 9 | .222 | 0 | 0 | ... | 0 | 2 | 2 | 2 | 1 | 0 | 5 | 5 | 0.3 | 0.3 | 0.8 |

Three-point field goals: 2003-04, 1-for-3 (.333). 2004-05, 0-for-1. Totals, 1-for-4 (.250).
Personal fouls/disqualifications: 2003-04, 1/0. Totals, 1/0.

## SPANISH RECORD

| Season Team | G | Min. | FGM | FGA | Pct. | FTM | FTA | Pct. | Reb. | Ast. | Pts. | AVERAGES RPG | APG | PPG |
|---|---|---|---|---|---|---|---|---|---|---|---|---|---|---|
| 03-04—Auna Gran Canaria | 24 | 549 | 81 | 199 | .407 | 43 | 54 | .796 | 52 | 14 | 256 | 2.2 | 0.6 | 10.7 |

Three-point field goals: 2003-04, 51-for-125 (.408). Totals, 51-for-125 (.408).

## NBDL RECORD

| Season Team | G | Min. | FGM | FGA | Pct. | FTM | FTA | Pct. | Reb. | Ast. | Pts. | AVERAGES RPG | APG | PPG |
|---|---|---|---|---|---|---|---|---|---|---|---|---|---|---|
| 04-05—Asheville | 46 | 1288 | 212 | 445 | .476 | 119 | 137 | .869 | 149 | 66 | 554 | 3.2 | 1.4 | 12.0 |

Three-point field goals: 2004-05, 11-for-31 (.355). Totals, 11-for-31 (.355).

# PERKINS, KENDRICK                         C                    CELTICS

**PERSONAL:** Born November 10, 1984, in Nederland, Tex. ... 6-10/280. (2.08/127.0).
**HIGH SCHOOL:** Clifton J. Ozen (Beaumont, Texas).
**COLLEGE:** Did not attend college.
**TRANSACTIONS/CAREER NOTES:** Selected by Memphis Grizzlies in first round (27th pick overall) of 2003 NBA Draft. ... Draft rights traded by Grizzlies with draft rights to G Marcus Banks to Boston Celtics for draft rights to G Troy Bell and G/F Dahntay Jones (June 26, 2003).

## NBA REGULAR-SEASON RECORD

| Season Team | G | Min. | FGM | FGA | Pct. | FTM | FTA | Pct. | REBOUNDS Off. | Def. | Tot. | Ast. | St. | Blk. | TO | Pts. | AVERAGES RPG | APG | PPG |
|---|---|---|---|---|---|---|---|---|---|---|---|---|---|---|---|---|---|---|---|
| 03-04—Boston | 10 | 35 | 8 | 15 | .533 | 6 | 9 | .667 | 5 | 9 | 14 | 3 | 0 | 2 | 5 | 22 | 1.4 | 0.3 | 2.2 |
| 04-05—Boston | 60 | 548 | 56 | 119 | .471 | 37 | 58 | .638 | 53 | 123 | 176 | 21 | 9 | 37 | 43 | 149 | 2.9 | 0.4 | 2.5 |
| Totals | 70 | 583 | 64 | 134 | .478 | 43 | 67 | .642 | 58 | 132 | 190 | 24 | 9 | 39 | 48 | 171 | 2.7 | 0.3 | 2.4 |

Personal fouls/disqualifications: 2003-04, 6/0. 2004-05, 98/1. Totals, 104/1.

## NBA PLAYOFF RECORD

| Season Team | G | Min. | FGM | FGA | Pct. | FTM | FTA | Pct. | REBOUNDS Off. | Def. | Tot. | Ast. | St. | Blk. | TO | Pts. | AVERAGES RPG | APG | PPG |
|---|---|---|---|---|---|---|---|---|---|---|---|---|---|---|---|---|---|---|---|
| 04-05—Boston | 6 | 28 | 4 | 5 | .800 | 1 | 3 | .333 | 3 | 3 | 6 | 0 | 0 | 3 | 3 | 9 | 1.0 | 0.0 | 1.5 |

Personal fouls/disqualifications: 2004-05, 7/0. Totals, 7/0.

# PERSON, WESLEY                            G/F

**PERSONAL:** Born March 28, 1971, in Crenshaw, Ala. ... 6-6/200. (1.98/90.7). ... Full name: Wesley Lavon Person ... Brother of Chuck Person, forward with Indiana Pacers (1986-87 through 1991-92), Minnesota Timberwolves (1992-93 and 1993-94), San Antonio Spurs (1994-95 through 1997-98) and Charlotte Hornets (1998-99).
**HIGH SCHOOL:** Brantley (Ala.).
**COLLEGE:** Auburn.
**TRANSACTIONS/CAREER NOTES:** Selected by Phoenix Suns in first round (23rd pick overall) of 1994 NBA Draft. ... Traded by Suns with G Tony Dumas to Cleveland Cavaliers for first-round draft choice no earlier than 2000 (October 1, 1997). ... Traded by Cavaliers to Memphis Grizzlies for G\F Nick Anderson and draft rights to F Matt Barnes (June 26, 2002). ... Traded by Grizzlies with 2004 first-round draft choice to Portland Trail Blazers for F/G Bonzi Wells (December 3, 2003). ... Traded by Trail Blazers with F Rasheed Wallace to Atlanta Hawks for F Shareef Abdur-Rahim, C Theo Ratliff and G Dan Dickau (February 9, 2004). ... Signed as free agent by Miami Heat (August 11, 2004). ... Waived by Heat (March 1, 2005). ... Signed as free agent by Denver Nuggets (March 3, 2005).

P

## COLLEGIATE RECORD

| | | | | | | | | | | | AVERAGES | | |
|---|---|---|---|---|---|---|---|---|---|---|---|---|---|
| Season Team | G | Min. | FGM | FGA | Pct. | FTM | FTA | Pct. | Reb. | Ast. | Pts. | RPG | APG | PPG |
| 90-91—Auburn ......... | 26 | 857 | 153 | 325 | .471 | 52 | 68 | .765 | 147 | 48 | 400 | 5.7 | 1.8 | 15.4 |
| 91-92—Auburn ......... | 27 | 955 | 208 | 411 | .506 | 53 | 73 | .726 | 183 | 55 | 538 | 6.8 | 2.0 | 19.9 |
| 92-93—Auburn ......... | 27 | 957 | 194 | 349 | .556 | 61 | 79 | .772 | 192 | 102 | 507 | 7.1 | 3.8 | 18.8 |
| 93-94—Auburn ......... | 28 | 1006 | 217 | 448 | .484 | 94 | 128 | .734 | 179 | 79 | 621 | 6.4 | 2.8 | 22.2 |
| Totals ..................... | 108 | 3775 | 772 | 1533 | .504 | 260 | 348 | .747 | 701 | 284 | 2066 | 6.5 | 2.6 | 19.1 |

Three-point field goals: 1990-91, 42-for-118 (.356). 1991-92, 69-for-141 (.489). 1992-93, 58-for-125 (.464). 1993-94, 93-for-210 (.443). Totals, 262-for-594 (.441).

## NBA REGULAR-SEASON RECORD

**HONORS:** NBA All-Rookie second team (1995).
**NOTES:** Led NBA with 192 three-point field goals made (1998).

| | | | | | | | | | REBOUNDS | | | | | | | | AVERAGES | | |
|---|---|---|---|---|---|---|---|---|---|---|---|---|---|---|---|---|---|---|---|
| Season Team | G | Min. | FGM | FGA | Pct. | FTM | FTA | Pct. | Off. | Def. | Tot. | Ast. | St. | Blk. | TO | Pts. | RPG | APG | PPG |
| 94-95—Phoenix ......... | 78 | 1800 | 309 | 638 | .484 | 80 | 101 | .792 | 67 | 134 | 201 | 105 | 48 | 24 | 79 | 814 | 2.6 | 1.3 | 10.4 |
| 95-96—Phoenix ......... | 82 | 2609 | 390 | 877 | .445 | 148 | 192 | .771 | 56 | 265 | 321 | 138 | 55 | 22 | 89 | 1045 | 3.9 | 1.7 | 12.7 |
| 96-97—Phoenix ......... | 80 | 2326 | 409 | 903 | .453 | 91 | 114 | .798 | 68 | 224 | 292 | 123 | 86 | 20 | 76 | 1080 | 3.7 | 1.5 | 13.5 |
| 97-98—Cleveland ....... | 82 | 3198 | 440 | 957 | .460 | 132 | 170 | .776 | 65 | 298 | 363 | 188 | 129 | 49 | 110 | 1204 | 4.4 | 2.3 | 14.7 |
| 98-99—Cleveland ....... | 45 | 1342 | 198 | 437 | .453 | 32 | 53 | .604 | 19 | 123 | 142 | 80 | 37 | 16 | 41 | 503 | 3.2 | 1.8 | 11.2 |
| 99-00—Cleveland ....... | 79 | 2056 | 280 | 654 | .428 | 61 | 77 | .792 | 44 | 223 | 267 | 146 | 40 | 19 | 60 | 727 | 3.4 | 1.8 | 9.2 |
| 00-01—Cleveland ....... | 44 | 958 | 128 | 292 | .438 | 24 | 30 | .800 | 11 | 119 | 130 | 64 | 27 | 11 | 40 | 314 | 3.0 | 1.5 | 7.1 |
| 01-02—Cleveland ....... | 78 | 2793 | 467 | 944 | .495 | 99 | 124 | .798 | 50 | 244 | 294 | 173 | 77 | 37 | 74 | 1176 | 3.8 | 2.2 | 15.1 |
| 02-03—Memphis ......... | 66 | 1941 | 274 | 601 | .456 | 79 | 97 | .814 | 24 | 168 | 192 | 112 | 42 | 19 | 56 | 727 | 2.9 | 1.7 | 11.0 |
| 03-04—Mem.-Port.-Atl. | 58 | 1037 | 126 | 314 | .401 | 31 | 39 | .795 | 16 | 101 | 117 | 66 | 19 | 9 | 38 | 338 | 2.0 | 1.1 | 5.8 |
| 04-05—Miami-Denver ... | 41 | 667 | 107 | 226 | .473 | 9 | 13 | .692 | 3 | 80 | 83 | 39 | 19 | 4 | 17 | 264 | 2.0 | 1.0 | 6.4 |
| Totals ..................... | 733 | 20727 | 3128 | 6843 | .457 | 786 | 1010 | .778 | 423 | 1979 | 2402 | 1234 | 579 | 230 | 680 | 8192 | 3.3 | 1.7 | 11.2 |

Three-point field goals: 1994-95, 116-for-266 (.436). 1995-96, 117-for-313 (.374). 1996-97, 171-for-414 (.413). 1997-98, 192-for-447 (.430). 1998-99, 75-for-200 (.375). 1999-00, 106-for-250 (.424). 2000-01, 34-for-84 (.405). 2001-02, 143-for-322 (.444). 2002-03, 100-for-231 (.433). 2003-04, 55-for-138 (.399). 2004-05, 41-for-89 (.461). Totals, 1150-for-2754 (.418).

Personal fouls/disqualifications: 1994-95, 149/0. 1995-96, 148/0. 1996-97, 102/0. 1997-98, 108/0. 1998-99, 52/0. 1999-00, 119/1. 2000-01, 62/0. 2001-02, 93/0. 2002-03, 64/0. 2003-04, 38/0. 2004-05, 30/0. Totals, 965/1.

## NBA PLAYOFF RECORD

| | | | | | | | | | REBOUNDS | | | | | | | | AVERAGES | | |
|---|---|---|---|---|---|---|---|---|---|---|---|---|---|---|---|---|---|---|---|
| Season Team | G | Min. | FGM | FGA | Pct. | FTM | FTA | Pct. | Off. | Def. | Tot. | Ast. | St. | Blk. | TO | Pts. | RPG | APG | PPG |
| 94-95—Phoenix ......... | 10 | 247 | 34 | 83 | .410 | 11 | 12 | .917 | 9 | 12 | 21 | 11 | 3 | 2 | 9 | 96 | 2.1 | 1.1 | 9.6 |
| 95-96—Phoenix ......... | 4 | 183 | 22 | 56 | .393 | 4 | 5 | .800 | 8 | 15 | 23 | 3 | 3 | 1 | 5 | 57 | 5.8 | 0.8 | 14.3 |
| 96-97—Phoenix ......... | 5 | 163 | 25 | 53 | .472 | 14 | 18 | .778 | 5 | 28 | 33 | 6 | 4 | 3 | 4 | 78 | 6.6 | 1.2 | 15.6 |
| 97-98—Cleveland ....... | 4 | 136 | 11 | 29 | .379 | 3 | 4 | .750 | 2 | 7 | 9 | 10 | 3 | 0 | 1 | 32 | 2.3 | 2.5 | 8.0 |
| 04-05—Denver ........... | 4 | 54 | 6 | 14 | .429 | 0 | 0 | ... | 1 | 0 | 1 | 1 | 1 | 0 | 1 | 15 | 0.3 | 0.3 | 3.8 |
| Totals ................. | 27 | 783 | 98 | 235 | .417 | 32 | 39 | .821 | 25 | 62 | 87 | 31 | 14 | 6 | 20 | 278 | 3.2 | 1.1 | 10.3 |

Three-point field goals: 1994-95, 17-for-45 (.378). 1995-96, 9-for-29 (.310). 1996-97, 14-for-33 (.424). 1997-98, 7-for-19 (.368). 2004-05, 3-for-8 (.375). Totals, 50-for-134 (.373).

Personal fouls/disqualifications: 1994-95, 19/0. 1995-96, 7/0. 1996-97, 5/0. 1997-98, 5/0. Totals, 36/0.

---

# PETERSON, MORRIS       F       RAPTORS

**PERSONAL:** Born August 26, 1977, in Flint, Mich. ... 6-7/215. (2.01/97.5).
**HIGH SCHOOL:** Northwestern (Flint, Mich.).
**COLLEGE:** Michigan State.
**TRANSACTIONS/CAREER NOTES:** Selected by Toronto Raptors in first round (21st pick overall) of 2000 NBA Draft.

## COLLEGIATE RECORD

**NOTES:** Granted medical redshirt (1995-96). ... Member of NCAA Division I championship team (2000). ... The Sporting News All-America first team (2000).

| | | | | | | | | | | | | AVERAGES | | |
|---|---|---|---|---|---|---|---|---|---|---|---|---|---|---|
| Season Team | G | Min. | FGM | FGA | Pct. | FTM | FTA | Pct. | Reb. | Ast. | Pts. | RPG | APG | PPG |
| 95-96—Michigan State .............. | 4 | 12 | 1 | 1 | 1.000 | 0 | 1 | .000 | 3 | 2 | 2 | 0.8 | 0.5 | 0.5 |
| 96-97—Michigan State .............. | 29 | 518 | 72 | 166 | .434 | 36 | 51 | .706 | 97 | 18 | 196 | 3.3 | 0.6 | 6.8 |
| 97-98—Michigan State .............. | 27 | 503 | 81 | 182 | .445 | 32 | 58 | .552 | 94 | 24 | 217 | 3.5 | 0.9 | 8.0 |
| 98-99—Michigan State .............. | 38 | 907 | 190 | 343 | .554 | 114 | 140 | .814 | 216 | 36 | 516 | 5.7 | 0.9 | 13.6 |
| 99-00—Michigan State .............. | 39 | 1136 | 218 | 469 | .465 | 136 | 176 | .773 | 235 | 49 | 657 | 6.0 | 1.3 | 16.8 |
| Totals .................. | 137 | 3076 | 562 | 1161 | .484 | 318 | 426 | .746 | 645 | 129 | 1588 | 4.7 | 0.9 | 11.6 |

Three-point field goals: 1996-97, 16-for-59 (.271). 1997-98, 23-for-69 (.333). 1998-99, 22-for-59 (.373). 1999-00, 85-for-200 (.425). Totals, 146-for-387 (.377).

## NBA REGULAR-SEASON RECORD

**HONORS:** NBA All-Rookie first team (2001).

| | | | | | | | | | REBOUNDS | | | | | | | | AVERAGES | | |
|---|---|---|---|---|---|---|---|---|---|---|---|---|---|---|---|---|---|---|---|
| Season Team | G | Min. | FGM | FGA | Pct. | FTM | FTA | Pct. | Off. | Def. | Tot. | Ast. | St. | Blk. | TO | Pts. | RPG | APG | PPG |
| 00-01—Toronto ......... | 80 | 1809 | 290 | 673 | .431 | 104 | 145 | .717 | 112 | 147 | 259 | 105 | 63 | 20 | 78 | 747 | 3.2 | 1.3 | 9.3 |
| 01-02—Toronto ......... | 63 | 1988 | 336 | 768 | .438 | 127 | 169 | .751 | 91 | 132 | 223 | 153 | 73 | 11 | 86 | 883 | 3.5 | 2.4 | 14.0 |
| 02-03—Toronto ......... | 82 | 2949 | 421 | 1073 | .392 | 195 | 247 | .789 | 97 | 266 | 363 | 188 | 88 | 32 | 128 | 1153 | 4.4 | 2.3 | 14.1 |
| 03-04—Toronto ......... | 82 | 2148 | 238 | 587 | .405 | 76 | 94 | .809 | 35 | 226 | 261 | 113 | 88 | 14 | 69 | 678 | 3.2 | 1.4 | 8.3 |
| 04-05—Toronto ......... | 82 | 2510 | 356 | 848 | .420 | 188 | 226 | .832 | 71 | 269 | 340 | 169 | 91 | 18 | 93 | 1029 | 4.1 | 2.1 | 12.5 |
| Totals .................. | 389 | 11404 | 1641 | 3949 | .416 | 690 | 881 | .783 | 406 | 1040 | 1446 | 728 | 403 | 95 | 454 | 4490 | 3.7 | 1.9 | 11.5 |

Three-point field goals: 2000-01, 63-for-165 (.382). 2001-02, 84-for-231 (.364). 2002-03, 116-for-344 (.337). 2003-04, 126-for-340 (.371). 2004-05, 129-for-335 (.385). Totals, 518-for-1415 (.366).

Personal fouls/disqualifications: 2000-01, 164/0. 2001-02, 174/2. 2002-03, 232/1. 2003-04, 206/0. 2004-05, 219/2. Totals, 995/5.

**P**

| Season Team | G | Min. | FGM | FGA | Pct. | FTM | FTA | Pct. | Off. | Def. | Tot. | Ast. | St. | Blk. | TO | Pts. | RPG | APG | PPG |
|---|---|---|---|---|---|---|---|---|---|---|---|---|---|---|---|---|---|---|---|
| | | | | | | | | | REBOUNDS | | | | | | | | AVERAGES | | |
| 00-01—Toronto .......... | 8 | 110 | 18 | 35 | .514 | 3 | 4 | .750 | 2 | 10 | 12 | 15 | 6 | 0 | 6 | 43 | 1.5 | 1.9 | 5.4 |
| 01-02—Toronto .......... | 5 | 154 | 18 | 49 | .367 | 8 | 10 | .800 | 3 | 11 | 14 | 11 | 5 | 3 | 7 | 46 | 2.8 | 2.2 | 9.2 |
| Totals ................... | 13 | 264 | 36 | 84 | .429 | 11 | 14 | .786 | 5 | 21 | 26 | 26 | 11 | 3 | 13 | 89 | 2.0 | 2.0 | 6.8 |

Three-point field goals: 2000-01, 4-for-9 (.444). 2001-02, 2-for-17 (.118). Totals, 6-for-26 (.231).
Personal fouls/disqualifications: 2000-01, 10/0. 2001-02, 17/0. Totals, 27/0.

# PIATKOWSKI, ERIC          G/F                    BULLS

**PERSONAL:** Born September 30, 1970, in Steubenville, Ohio. ... 6-6/215. (1.98/97.5). ... Full name: Eric Todd Piatkowski ... Son of Walt Piatkowski, forward with Denver Rockets and Miami Floridians of American Basketball Association (1968-69 through 1971-1972). ... Name pronounced pie-it-COW-ski.
**HIGH SCHOOL:** Stevens (Rapid City, S.D.).
**COLLEGE:** Nebraska.
**TRANSACTIONS/CAREER NOTES:** Selected by Indiana Pacers in first round (15th pick overall) of 1994 NBA Draft. ... Draft rights traded by Pacers with F Malik Sealy and G Pooh Richardson to Los Angeles Clippers for G Mark Jackson and draft rights to G Greg Minor (June 30, 1994). ... Signed as free agent by Houston Rockets (July 26, 2003) ... Traded by Rockets with G Mike Wilks and G/F Adrian Griffin to Chicago Bulls for C Dikembe Mutombo (September 8, 2004).

## COLLEGIATE RECORD

| Season Team | G | Min. | FGM | FGA | Pct. | FTM | FTA | Pct. | Reb. | Ast. | Pts. | RPG | APG | PPG |
|---|---|---|---|---|---|---|---|---|---|---|---|---|---|---|
| | | | | | | | | | | | | AVERAGES | | |
| 89-90—Nebraska ..................... | | | | | | Did not play—redshirted. | | | | | | | | |
| 90-91—Nebraska ..................... | 34 | 679 | 128 | 275 | .465 | 72 | 86 | .837 | 125 | 68 | 372 | 3.7 | 2.0 | 10.9 |
| 91-92—Nebraska ..................... | 29 | 873 | 144 | 338 | .426 | 79 | 109 | .725 | 184 | 97 | 414 | 6.3 | 3.3 | 14.3 |
| 92-93—Nebraska ..................... | 30 | 894 | 178 | 367 | .485 | 98 | 129 | .760 | 171 | 75 | 502 | 5.7 | 2.5 | 16.7 |
| 93-94—Nebraska ..................... | 30 | 972 | 226 | 456 | .496 | 131 | 165 | .794 | 189 | 82 | 646 | 6.3 | 2.7 | 21.5 |
| Totals .................................... | 123 | 3418 | 676 | 1436 | .471 | 380 | 489 | .777 | 669 | 322 | 1934 | 5.4 | 2.6 | 15.7 |

Three-point field goals: 1990-91, 44-for-127 (.346). 1991-92, 47-for-136 (.346). 1992-93, 48-for-129 (.372). 1993-94, 63-for-172 (.366). Totals, 202-for-564 (.358).

## NBA REGULAR-SEASON RECORD

| Season Team | G | Min. | FGM | FGA | Pct. | FTM | FTA | Pct. | Off. | Def. | Tot. | Ast. | St. | Blk. | TO | Pts. | RPG | APG | PPG |
|---|---|---|---|---|---|---|---|---|---|---|---|---|---|---|---|---|---|---|---|
| | | | | | | | | | REBOUNDS | | | | | | | | AVERAGES | | |
| 94-95—L.A. Clippers ... | 81 | 1208 | 201 | 456 | .441 | 90 | 115 | .783 | 63 | 70 | 133 | 77 | 37 | 15 | 63 | 566 | 1.6 | 1.0 | 7.0 |
| 95-96—L.A. Clippers ... | 65 | 784 | 98 | 242 | .405 | 67 | 82 | .817 | 40 | 63 | 103 | 48 | 24 | 10 | 45 | 301 | 1.6 | 0.7 | 4.6 |
| 96-97—L.A. Clippers ... | 65 | 747 | 134 | 298 | .450 | 69 | 84 | .821 | 49 | 56 | 105 | 52 | 33 | 10 | 46 | 388 | 1.6 | 0.8 | 6.0 |
| 97-98—L.A. Clippers ... | 67 | 1740 | 257 | 568 | .452 | 140 | 170 | .824 | 70 | 166 | 236 | 85 | 51 | 12 | 80 | 760 | 3.5 | 1.3 | 11.3 |
| 98-99—L.A. Clippers ... | 49 | 1242 | 180 | 417 | .432 | 88 | 102 | .863 | 39 | 101 | 140 | 53 | 44 | 6 | 53 | 513 | 2.9 | 1.1 | 10.5 |
| 99-00—L.A. Clippers ... | 75 | 1712 | 238 | 573 | .415 | 85 | 100 | .850 | 74 | 148 | 222 | 81 | 44 | 13 | 57 | 654 | 3.0 | 1.1 | 8.7 |
| 00-01—L.A. Clippers ... | 81 | 2144 | 291 | 672 | .433 | 158 | 181 | .873 | 54 | 187 | 241 | 96 | 46 | 19 | 76 | 860 | 3.0 | 1.2 | 10.6 |
| 01-02—L.A. Clippers ... | 71 | 1718 | 207 | 471 | .439 | 101 | 113 | .894 | 43 | 141 | 184 | 112 | 41 | 12 | 64 | 626 | 2.6 | 1.6 | 8.8 |
| 02-03—L.A. Clippers ... | 62 | 1360 | 210 | 446 | .471 | 101 | 122 | .828 | 44 | 112 | 156 | 70 | 33 | 9 | 56 | 601 | 2.5 | 1.1 | 9.7 |
| 03-04—Houston .......... | 49 | 703 | 72 | 191 | .377 | 14 | 16 | .875 | 10 | 63 | 73 | 26 | 16 | 5 | 29 | 201 | 1.5 | 0.5 | 4.1 |
| 04-05—Chicago .......... | 68 | 841 | 111 | 258 | .430 | 45 | 56 | .804 | 15 | 64 | 79 | 51 | 29 | 1 | 37 | 324 | 1.2 | 0.8 | 4.8 |
| Totals .................... | 733 | 14199 | 1999 | 4592 | .435 | 958 | 1141 | .840 | 501 | 1171 | 1672 | 751 | 398 | 112 | 606 | 5794 | 2.3 | 1.0 | 7.9 |

Three-point field goals: 1994-95, 74-for-198 (.374). 1995-96, 38-for-114 (.333). 1996-97, 51-for-120 (.425). 1997-98, 106-for-259 (.409). 1998-99, 65-for-165 (.394). 1999-00, 93-for-243 (.383). 2000-01, 120-for-297 (.404). 2001-02, 111-for-238 (.466). 2002-03, 80-for-201 (.398). 2003-04, 43-for-122 (.352). 2004-05, 57-for-134 (.425). Totals, 838-for-2091 (.401).
Personal fouls/disqualifications: 1994-95, 150/1. 1995-96, 83/0. 1996-97, 85/0. 1997-98, 137/0. 1998-99, 86/0. 1999-00, 140/0. 2000-01, 123/0. 2001-02, 110/0. 2002-03, 92/0. 2003-04, 42/0. 2004-05, 67/0. Totals, 1115/1.

## NBA PLAYOFF RECORD

| Season Team | G | Min. | FGM | FGA | Pct. | FTM | FTA | Pct. | Off. | Def. | Tot. | Ast. | St. | Blk. | TO | Pts. | RPG | APG | PPG |
|---|---|---|---|---|---|---|---|---|---|---|---|---|---|---|---|---|---|---|---|
| | | | | | | | | | REBOUNDS | | | | | | | | AVERAGES | | |
| 96-97—L.A. Clippers ... | 3 | 38 | 4 | 11 | .364 | 6 | 7 | .857 | 1 | 1 | 2 | 0 | 1 | 0 | 0 | 16 | 0.7 | 0.0 | 5.3 |
| 03-04—Houston .......... | 1 | 4 | 0 | 1 | .000 | 0 | 0 | ... | 0 | 1 | 1 | 0 | 0 | 0 | 0 | 0 | 1.0 | 0.0 | 0.0 |
| 04-05—Chicago .......... | 5 | 66 | 6 | 19 | .316 | 6 | 7 | .857 | 1 | 8 | 9 | 3 | 4 | 1 | 1 | 23 | 1.8 | 0.6 | 4.6 |
| Totals ................... | 9 | 108 | 10 | 31 | .323 | 12 | 14 | .857 | 2 | 10 | 12 | 3 | 5 | 1 | 1 | 39 | 1.3 | 0.3 | 4.3 |

Three-point field goals: 1996-97, 2-for-5 (.400). 2004-05, 5-for-13 (.385). Totals, 7-for-18 (.389).
Personal fouls/disqualifications: 1996-97, 5/0. 2003-04, 1/0. 2004-05, 3/0. Totals, 9/0.

# PIERCE, PAUL              F                    CELTICS

**PERSONAL:** Born October 13, 1977, in Oakland. ... 6-6/230. (1.98/104.3). ... Full name: Paul Anthony Pierce
**HIGH SCHOOL:** Inglewood (Calif.).
**COLLEGE:** Kansas.
**TRANSACTIONS/CAREER NOTES:** Selected after junior season by Boston Celtics in first round (10th pick overall) of 1998 NBA Draft.

## COLLEGIATE RECORD

**NOTES:** The Sporting News All-America first team (1998).

**P**

| Season Team | G | Min. | FGM | FGA | Pct. | FTM | FTA | Pct. | Reb. | Ast. | Pts. | RPG | APG | PPG |
|---|---|---|---|---|---|---|---|---|---|---|---|---|---|---|
| | | | | | | | | | | | | AVERAGES | | |
| 95-96—Kansas ........................ | 34 | 862 | 143 | 341 | .419 | 83 | 137 | .606 | 180 | 61 | 404 | 5.3 | 1.8 | 11.9 |
| 96-97—Kansas ........................ | 36 | 1013 | 215 | 441 | .488 | 124 | 173 | .717 | 243 | 77 | 587 | 6.8 | 2.1 | 16.3 |
| 97-98—Kansas ........................ | 38 | 1155 | 287 | 559 | .513 | 163 | 221 | .738 | 253 | 98 | 777 | 6.7 | 2.6 | 20.4 |
| Totals .................................... | 108 | 3030 | 645 | 1341 | .481 | 370 | 531 | .697 | 676 | 236 | 1768 | 6.3 | 2.2 | 16.4 |

Three-point field goals: 1995-96, 35-for-115 (.304). 1996-97, 33-for-71 (.465). 1997-98, 40-for-116 (.345). Totals, 108-for-302 (.358).

## NBA REGULAR-SEASON RECORD

**HONORS:** All-NBA third team (2002, 2003). ... NBA All-Rookie first team (1999).

| | | | | | | | | REBOUNDS | | | | | | | | AVERAGES | | |
|---|---|---|---|---|---|---|---|---|---|---|---|---|---|---|---|---|---|---|
| Season Team | G | Min. | FGM | FGA | Pct. | FTM | FTA | Pct. | Off. | Def. | Tot. | Ast. | St. | Blk. | TO | Pts. | RPG | APG | PPG |
| 98-99—Boston | 48 | 1632 | 284 | 647 | .439 | 139 | 195 | .713 | 117 | 192 | 309 | 115 | 82 | 50 | 113 | 791 | 6.4 | 2.4 | 16.5 |
| 99-00—Boston | 73 | 2583 | 486 | 1099 | .442 | 359 | 450 | .798 | 83 | 313 | 396 | 221 | 152 | 62 | 178 | 1427 | 5.4 | 3.0 | 19.5 |
| 00-01—Boston | 82 | 3120 | 687 | 1513 | .454 | 550 | 738 | .745 | 94 | 428 | 522 | 253 | 138 | 69 | 262 | 2071 | 6.4 | 3.1 | 25.3 |
| 01-02—Boston | 82 | 3302 | 707 | 1598 | .442 | 520 | 643 | .809 | 81 | 485 | 566 | 261 | 154 | 86 | 241 | *2144 | 6.9 | 3.2 | 26.1 |
| 02-03—Boston | 79 | 3096 | 663 | 1592 | .416 | 604 | 753 | .802 | 106 | 472 | 578 | 349 | 139 | 62 | 288 | 2048 | 7.3 | 4.4 | 25.9 |
| 03-04—Boston | 80 | 3099 | 602 | 1497 | .402 | 517 | 631 | .819 | 69 | 453 | 522 | 410 | 131 | 52 | 303 | 1836 | 6.5 | 5.1 | 23.0 |
| 04-05—Boston | 82 | 2960 | 556 | 1223 | .455 | 549 | 668 | .822 | 78 | 461 | 539 | 348 | 133 | 39 | 230 | 1769 | 6.6 | 4.2 | 21.6 |
| Totals | 526 | 19792 | 3985 | 9169 | .435 | 3238 | 4078 | .794 | 628 | 2804 | 3432 | 1957 | 929 | 420 | 1615 | 12086 | 6.5 | 3.7 | 23.0 |

Three-point field goals: 1998-99, 84-for-204 (.412). 1999-00, 96-for-280 (.343). 2000-01, 147-for-384 (.383). 2001-02, 210-for-520 (.404). 2002-03, 118-for-391 (.302). 2003-04, 115-for-384 (.299). 2004-05, 108-for-292 (.370). Totals, 878-for-2455 (.358).
Personal fouls/disqualifications: 1998-99, 139/1. 1999-00, 237/5. 2000-01, 251/3. 2001-02, 237/1. 2002-03, 227/2. 2003-04, 234/3. 2004-05, 255/1. Totals, 1580/16.

## NBA PLAYOFF RECORD

**NOTES:** Holds single-game record for most free throws made, none missed—21 (April 19, 2003).

| | | | | | | | | REBOUNDS | | | | | | | | AVERAGES | | |
|---|---|---|---|---|---|---|---|---|---|---|---|---|---|---|---|---|---|---|
| Season Team | G | Min. | FGM | FGA | Pct. | FTM | FTA | Pct. | Off. | Def. | Tot. | Ast. | St. | Blk. | TO | Pts. | RPG | APG | PPG |
| 01-02—Boston | 16 | 672 | 122 | 303 | .403 | 120 | 157 | .764 | 27 | 110 | 137 | 66 | 27 | 20 | 61 | 394 | 8.6 | 4.1 | 24.6 |
| 02-03—Boston | 10 | 445 | 77 | 193 | .399 | 101 | 117 | .863 | 11 | 79 | 90 | 67 | 21 | 8 | 44 | 271 | 9.0 | 6.7 | 27.1 |
| 03-04—Boston | 4 | 162 | 26 | 76 | .342 | 26 | 31 | .839 | 6 | 29 | 35 | 10 | 5 | 4 | 25 | 83 | 8.8 | 2.5 | 20.8 |
| 04-05—Boston | 7 | 277 | 47 | 93 | .505 | 59 | 68 | .868 | 7 | 47 | 54 | 32 | 13 | 10 | 19 | 160 | 7.7 | 4.6 | 22.9 |
| Totals | 37 | 1556 | 272 | 665 | .409 | 306 | 373 | .820 | 51 | 265 | 316 | 175 | 66 | 42 | 149 | 908 | 8.5 | 4.7 | 24.5 |

Three-point field goals: 2001-02, 30-for-104 (.288). 2002-03, 16-for-45 (.356). 2003-04, 5-for-17 (.294). 2004-05, 7-for-27 (.259). Totals, 58-for-193 (.301).
Personal fouls/disqualifications: 2001-02, 52/0. 2002-03, 38/0. 2003-04, 12/0. 2004-05, 18/0. Totals, 120/0.

## NBA ALL-STAR GAME RECORD

| | | | | | | | | REBOUNDS | | | | | | | | |
|---|---|---|---|---|---|---|---|---|---|---|---|---|---|---|---|---|
| Season Team | Min. | FGM | FGA | Pct. | FTM | FTA | Pct. | Off. | Def. | Tot. | Ast. | PF | Dq. | St. | Blk. | TO | Pts. |
| 2002—Boston | 23 | 9 | 18 | .500 | 0 | 0 | ... | 3 | 4 | 7 | 3 | 1 | 0 | 1 | 0 | 0 | 19 |
| 2003—Boston | 18 | 4 | 11 | .364 | 0 | 0 | ... | 0 | 2 | 2 | 1 | 0 | 4 | 0 | 2 | 8 | 8 |
| 2004—Boston | 13 | 4 | 8 | .500 | 0 | 0 | ... | 0 | 1 | 1 | 2 | 2 | 0 | 1 | 0 | 1 | 8 |
| 2005—Boston | 14 | 4 | 7 | .571 | 1 | 1 | 1.000 | 0 | 3 | 3 | 3 | 2 | 0 | 2 | 0 | 0 | 9 |
| Totals | 68 | 21 | 44 | .477 | 1 | 1 | 1.000 | 3 | 10 | 13 | 11 | 6 | 0 | 8 | 0 | 3 | 44 |

Three-point field goals: 2002, 1-for-6 (.167). 2003, 0-for-5. 2004, 0-for-1. 2005, 0-for-2. Totals, 1-for-14 (.071).

# PIETRUS, MICKAEL          G/F          WARRIORS

**PERSONAL:** Born February 7, 1982, in Les Abymes, Guadeloupe, France. ... 6-6/200. (1.98/90.7).
**TRANSACTIONS/CAREER NOTES:** Played in France (1999-2003). ... Selected by Golden State Warriors in first round (11th pick overall) of 2003 NBA Draft.

## FRENCH LEAGUE RECORD

| | | | | | | | | | | | AVERAGES | | |
|---|---|---|---|---|---|---|---|---|---|---|---|---|---|
| Season Team | G | Min. | FGM | FGA | Pct. | FTM | FTA | Pct. | Reb. | Ast. | Pts. | RPG | APG | PPG |
| 99-00—Pau Orthez | 7 | 65 | 8 | 21 | .381 | 4 | 8 | .500 | 7 | 0 | 24 | 1.0 | 0.0 | 3.4 |
| 00-01—Pau Orthez | 29 | 448 | 86 | 171 | .503 | 34 | 47 | .723 | 63 | 34 | 230 | 2.2 | 1.2 | 7.9 |
| 01-02—Pau Orthez | 30 | 527 | 79 | 192 | .411 | 62 | 92 | .674 | 74 | 33 | 255 | 2.5 | 1.1 | 8.5 |
| 02-03—Pau Orthez | 28 | 608 | 110 | 226 | .487 | 75 | 100 | .750 | 101 | 47 | 340 | 3.6 | 1.7 | 12.1 |
| Totals | 94 | 1648 | 283 | 610 | .464 | 175 | 247 | .709 | 245 | 114 | 849 | 2.6 | 1.2 | 9.0 |

Three-point field goals: 1999-00, 4-for-12 (.333). 2000-01, 24-for-62 (.387). 2001-02, 35-for-100 (.350). 2002-03, 45-for-112 (.402). Totals, 108-for-286 (.378).

## NBA REGULAR-SEASON RECORD

| | | | | | | | | REBOUNDS | | | | | | | | AVERAGES | | |
|---|---|---|---|---|---|---|---|---|---|---|---|---|---|---|---|---|---|---|
| Season Team | G | Min. | FGM | FGA | Pct. | FTM | FTA | Pct. | Off. | Def. | Tot. | Ast. | St. | Blk. | TO | Pts. | RPG | APG | PPG |
| 03-04—Golden State | 53 | 748 | 96 | 231 | .416 | 52 | 75 | .693 | 48 | 71 | 119 | 27 | 32 | 12 | 40 | 279 | 2.2 | 0.5 | 5.3 |
| 04-05—Golden State | 67 | 1340 | 214 | 501 | .427 | 141 | 202 | .698 | 65 | 124 | 189 | 82 | 46 | 18 | 92 | 636 | 2.8 | 1.2 | 9.5 |
| Totals | 120 | 2088 | 310 | 732 | .423 | 193 | 277 | .697 | 113 | 195 | 308 | 109 | 78 | 30 | 132 | 915 | 2.6 | 0.9 | 7.6 |

Three-point field goals: 2003-04, 35-for-105 (.333). 2004-05, 67-for-195 (.344). Totals, 102-for-300 (.340).
Personal fouls/disqualifications: 2003-04, 100/1. 2004-05, 139/2. Totals, 239/3.

# PLANINIC, ZORAN          G/F          NETS

**PERSONAL:** Born September 12, 1982, in Mostar, Bosnia-Herzegovina. ... 6-7/195. (2.01/88.5).
**TRANSACTIONS/CAREER NOTES:** Played in Croatia (1999-2003). ... Selected by New Jersey Nets in first round (22nd pick overall) of 2003 NBA Draft.

## CROATION RECORD

| | | | | | | | | | | | AVERAGES | | |
|---|---|---|---|---|---|---|---|---|---|---|---|---|---|---|
| Season Team | G | Min. | FGM | FGA | Pct. | FTM | FTA | Pct. | Reb. | Ast. | Pts. | RPG | APG | PPG |
| 99-00—Benston Zagreb | 22 | 574 | 72 | 162 | .444 | 37 | 58 | .638 | 48 | 37 | 189 | 2.2 | 1.7 | 8.6 |
| 00-01—Cibona | 20 | 328 | 59 | 115 | .513 | 19 | 32 | .594 | 46 | 38 | 145 | 2.3 | 1.9 | 7.3 |
| 01-02—Cibona | 7 | 196 | 25 | 56 | .446 | 21 | 35 | .600 | 18 | 24 | 75 | 2.6 | 3.4 | 10.7 |
| 02-03—Cibona | 21 | 381 | 56 | 118 | .475 | 30 | 54 | .556 | 38 | 47 | 154 | 1.8 | 2.2 | 7.3 |
| Totals | 70 | 1479 | 212 | 451 | .470 | 107 | 179 | .598 | 150 | 146 | 563 | 2.1 | 2.1 | 8.0 |

Three-point field goals: 1999-00, 8-for-38 (.211). 2000-01, 8-for-30 (.267). 2001-02, 4-for-9 (.444). 2002-03, 12-for-34 (.353). Totals, 32-for-111 (.288).

**P**

## NBA REGULAR-SEASON RECORD

| Season Team | G | Min. | FGM | FGA | Pct. | FTM | FTA | Pct. | REBOUNDS Off. | Def. | Tot. | Ast. | St. | Blk. | TO | Pts. | RPG | APG | PPG |
|---|---|---|---|---|---|---|---|---|---|---|---|---|---|---|---|---|---|---|---|
| 03-04—New Jersey ..... | 49 | 473 | 53 | 129 | .411 | 38 | 60 | .633 | 14 | 41 | 55 | 68 | 13 | 3 | 36 | 153 | 1.1 | 1.4 | 3.1 |
| 04-05—New Jersey ..... | 43 | 515 | 78 | 174 | .448 | 46 | 66 | .697 | 19 | 50 | 69 | 44 | 25 | 0 | 41 | 217 | 1.6 | 1.0 | 5.0 |
| Totals ................. | 92 | 988 | 131 | 303 | .432 | 84 | 126 | .667 | 33 | 91 | 124 | 112 | 38 | 3 | 77 | 370 | 1.3 | 1.2 | 4.0 |

Three-point field goals: 2003-04, 9-for-32 (.281). 2004-05, 15-for-40 (.375). Totals, 24-for-72 (.333).
Personal fouls/disqualifications: 2003-04, 70/1. 2004-05, 76/2. Totals, 146/3.

## NBA PLAYOFF RECORD

| Season Team | G | Min. | FGM | FGA | Pct. | FTM | FTA | Pct. | REBOUNDS Off. | Def. | Tot. | Ast. | St. | Blk. | TO | Pts. | RPG | APG | PPG |
|---|---|---|---|---|---|---|---|---|---|---|---|---|---|---|---|---|---|---|---|
| 03-04—New Jersey ..... | 6 | 15 | 0 | 2 | .000 | 1 | 2 | .500 | 0 | 1 | 1 | 2 | 0 | 0 | 2 | 1 | 0.2 | 0.3 | 0.2 |
| 04-05—New Jersey ..... | 3 | 3 | 0 | 0 | ... | 0 | 0 | ... | 0 | 0 | 0 | 0 | 0 | 0 | 0 | 0 | 0.0 | 0.0 | 0.0 |
| Totals ................. | 9 | 18 | 0 | 2 | .000 | 1 | 2 | .500 | 0 | 1 | 1 | 2 | 0 | 0 | 2 | 1 | 0.1 | 0.2 | 0.1 |

Three-point field goals: 2003-04, 0-for-1. Totals, 0-for-1 (.000).
Personal fouls/disqualifications: 2003-04, 2/0. Totals, 2/0.

# PODKOLZIN, PAVEL      C      MAVERICKS

**PERSONAL:** Born January 15, 1985, in Novosibirsk, Russia. ... 7-5/260. (2.26/117.9).
**TRANSACTIONS/CAREER NOTES:** Played in Italy (2001-04). ... Selected by Utah Jazz in first round (21st pick overall) of 2004 NBA Draft. ... Draft rights traded by Jazz to Dallas Mavericks for 2005 first-round draft choice (June 24, 2004).

## ITALIAN LEAGUE RECORD

| Season Team | G | Min. | FGM | FGA | Pct. | FTM | FTA | Pct. | Reb. | Ast. | Pts. | RPG | APG | PPG |
|---|---|---|---|---|---|---|---|---|---|---|---|---|---|---|
| 02-03—Varese ......................... | 11 | 62 | 10 | 16 | .625 | 4 | 7 | .571 | 20 | 1 | 24 | 1.8 | 0.1 | 2.2 |
| 03-04—Varese ......................... | 28 | 248 | 17 | 37 | .459 | 23 | 33 | .697 | 50 | 4 | 57 | 1.8 | 0.1 | 2.0 |
| Totals ..................................... | 39 | 310 | 27 | 53 | .509 | 27 | 40 | .675 | 70 | 5 | 81 | 1.8 | 0.1 | 2.1 |

Three-point field goals: 2003-04, 0-for-1. Totals, 0-for-1 (.000).

## NBA REGULAR-SEASON RECORD

| Season Team | G | Min. | FGM | FGA | Pct. | FTM | FTA | Pct. | REBOUNDS Off. | Def. | Tot. | Ast. | St. | Blk. | TO | Pts. | RPG | APG | PPG |
|---|---|---|---|---|---|---|---|---|---|---|---|---|---|---|---|---|---|---|---|
| 04-05—Dallas.............. | 5 | 10 | 0 | 0 | ... | 1 | 2 | .500 | 0 | 2 | 2 | 0 | 0 | 0 | 2 | 1 | 0.4 | 0.0 | 0.2 |

Personal fouls/disqualifications: 2004-05, 4/0. Totals, 4/0.

# POLLARD, SCOT      F/C      PACERS

**PERSONAL:** Born February 12, 1975, in Murray, Utah. ... 6-11/265. (2.11/120.2).
**HIGH SCHOOL:** Torrey Pines (San Diego).
**COLLEGE:** Kansas.
**TRANSACTIONS/CAREER NOTES:** Selected by Detroit Pistons in first round (19th pick overall) of 1997 NBA Draft. ... Traded by Pistons with 1999 first-round draft choice to Atlanta Hawks for F/C Christian Laettner (January 22, 1999). ... Waived by Hawks (February 19, 1999). ... Signed as free agent by Sacramento Kings (February 24, 1999). ... Traded by Kings to Indiana Pacers in three-team deal in which Kings also acquired F/C Brad Miller from Pacers and traded F/G Hedo Turkoglu to San Antonio Spurs. Spurs also acquired G Ron Mercer from Pacers and traded F Danny Ferry to Pacers (July 24, 2003)

## COLLEGIATE RECORD

| Season Team | G | Min. | FGM | FGA | Pct. | FTM | FTA | Pct. | Reb. | Ast. | Pts. | RPG | APG | PPG |
|---|---|---|---|---|---|---|---|---|---|---|---|---|---|---|
| 93-94—Kansas ......................... | 35 | 597 | 95 | 175 | .543 | 74 | 108 | .685 | 173 | 13 | 264 | 4.9 | 0.4 | 7.5 |
| 94-95—Kansas ......................... | 31 | 620 | 113 | 203 | .557 | 89 | 136 | .654 | 192 | 17 | 315 | 6.2 | 0.5 | 10.2 |
| 95-96—Kansas ......................... | 34 | 835 | 123 | 218 | .564 | 96 | 151 | .636 | 253 | 10 | 342 | 7.4 | 0.3 | 10.1 |
| 96-97—Kansas ......................... | 28 | 702 | 94 | 178 | .528 | 99 | 140 | .707 | 232 | 19 | 288 | 8.3 | 0.7 | 10.3 |
| Totals ..................................... | 128 | 2754 | 425 | 774 | .549 | 358 | 535 | .669 | 850 | 59 | 1209 | 6.6 | 0.5 | 9.4 |

Three-point field goals: 1996-97, 1-for-1 (1.000). Totals, 1-for-1 (1.000).

## NBA REGULAR-SEASON RECORD

| Season Team | G | Min. | FGM | FGA | Pct. | FTM | FTA | Pct. | REBOUNDS Off. | Def. | Tot. | Ast. | St. | Blk. | TO | Pts. | RPG | APG | PPG |
|---|---|---|---|---|---|---|---|---|---|---|---|---|---|---|---|---|---|---|---|
| 97-98—Detroit ........... | 33 | 317 | 35 | 70 | .500 | 19 | 23 | .826 | 34 | 40 | 74 | 9 | 8 | 10 | 12 | 89 | 2.2 | 0.3 | 2.7 |
| 98-99—Sacramento .... | 16 | 259 | 33 | 61 | .541 | 16 | 23 | .696 | 38 | 44 | 82 | 4 | 18 | 5 | 8 | 82 | 5.1 | 0.3 | 5.1 |
| 99-00—Sacramento .... | 76 | 1336 | 149 | 283 | .527 | 114 | 159 | .717 | 168 | 236 | 404 | 43 | 55 | 59 | 50 | 412 | 5.3 | 0.6 | 5.4 |
| 00-01—Sacramento .... | 77 | 1658 | 185 | 395 | .468 | 128 | 171 | .749 | 173 | 292 | 465 | 47 | 48 | 97 | 66 | 498 | 6.0 | 0.6 | 6.5 |
| 01-02—Sacramento .... | 80 | 1881 | 197 | 358 | .550 | 115 | 166 | .693 | 188 | 377 | 565 | 53 | 70 | 76 | 68 | 509 | 7.1 | 0.7 | 6.4 |
| 02-03—Sacramento .... | 23 | 325 | 40 | 87 | .460 | 23 | 38 | .605 | 46 | 60 | 106 | 6 | 13 | 15 | 15 | 103 | 4.6 | 0.3 | 4.5 |
| 03-04—Indiana........... | 61 | 678 | 47 | 114 | .412 | 12 | 21 | .571 | 67 | 97 | 164 | 10 | 23 | 26 | 22 | 106 | 2.7 | 0.2 | 1.7 |
| 04-05—Indiana........... | 49 | 865 | 79 | 167 | .473 | 33 | 49 | .673 | 85 | 120 | 205 | 18 | 30 | 24 | 31 | 191 | 4.2 | 0.4 | 3.9 |
| Totals .................. | 415 | 7319 | 765 | 1535 | .498 | 460 | 650 | .708 | 799 | 1266 | 2065 | 190 | 255 | 325 | 269 | 1990 | 5.0 | 0.5 | 4.8 |

Three-point field goals: 2000-01, 0-for-2. Totals, 0-for-2 (.000).
Personal fouls/disqualifications: 1997-98, 48/0. 1998-99, 41/0. 1999-00, 213/3. 2000-01, 206/4. 2001-02, 202/1. 2002-03, 50/0. 2003-04, 110/0. 2004-05, 123/1. Totals, 993/9.

## NBA PLAYOFF RECORD

| Season Team | G | Min. | FGM | FGA | Pct. | FTM | FTA | Pct. | REBOUNDS Off. | Def. | Tot. | Ast. | St. | Blk. | TO | Pts. | RPG | APG | PPG |
|---|---|---|---|---|---|---|---|---|---|---|---|---|---|---|---|---|---|---|---|
| 98-99—Sacramento .... | 5 | 74 | 6 | 9 | .667 | 3 | 5 | .600 | 5 | 6 | 11 | 1 | 4 | 6 | 2 | 15 | 2.2 | 0.2 | 3.0 |

| Season Team | G | Min. | FGM | FGA | Pct. | FTM | FTA | Pct. | Off. | Def. | Tot. | Ast. | St. | Blk. | TO | Pts. | RPG | APG | PPG |
|---|---|---|---|---|---|---|---|---|---|---|---|---|---|---|---|---|---|---|---|
| 99-00—Sacramento .... | 5 | 70 | 9 | 16 | .563 | 2 | 6 | .333 | 6 | 10 | 16 | 1 | 2 | 1 | 3 | 20 | 3.2 | 0.2 | 4.0 |
| 00-01—Sacramento .... | 8 | 141 | 19 | 30 | .633 | 10 | 17 | .588 | 23 | 32 | 55 | 2 | 1 | 7 | 6 | 48 | 6.9 | 0.3 | 6.0 |
| 01-02—Sacramento .... | 15 | 193 | 21 | 40 | .525 | 8 | 12 | .667 | 29 | 24 | 53 | 3 | 7 | 5 | 3 | 50 | 3.5 | 0.2 | 3.3 |
| 02-03—Sacramento .... | 8 | 91 | 7 | 24 | .292 | 10 | 13 | .769 | 17 | 13 | 30 | 2 | 1 | 7 | 7 | 24 | 3.8 | 0.3 | 3.0 |
| 03-04—Indiana........... | 3 | 13 | 0 | 2 | .000 | 2 | 4 | .500 | 1 | 3 | 4 | 0 | 1 | 0 | 0 | 2 | 1.3 | 0.0 | 0.7 |
| 04-05—Indiana........... | 9 | 67 | 6 | 15 | .400 | 1 | 2 | .500 | 4 | 7 | 11 | 1 | 1 | 0 | 4 | 13 | 1.2 | 0.1 | 1.4 |
| Totals ................... | 53 | 649 | 68 | 136 | .500 | 36 | 59 | .610 | 85 | 95 | 180 | 10 | 17 | 26 | 25 | 172 | 3.4 | 0.2 | 3.2 |

Personal fouls/disqualifications: 1998-99, 13/0. 1999-00, 18/1. 2000-01, 30/0. 2001-02, 36/1. 2002-03, 15/1. 2003-04, 2/0. 2004-05, 9/0. Totals, 123/3.

## POPE, MARK   F

**PERSONAL:** Born September 11, 1972, in Omaha, Neb. ... 6-10/235. (2.08/106.6). ... Full name: Mark Edward Pope
**HIGH SCHOOL:** Newport (Bellevue, Wash.).
**COLLEGE:** Washington, then Kentucky.
**TRANSACTIONS/CAREER NOTES:** Selected by Indiana Pacers in second round (52nd pick overall) of 1996 NBA Draft. ... Played in Turkey (1996-97 and 1999-2000). ... Waived by Pacers (October 30, 1999). ... Played in Continental Basketball Association with LaCrosse Bobcats (1999-2000). ... Signed as free agent by Milwaukee Bucks (September 27, 2000). ... Signed as free agent by New York Knicks (September 30, 2002). ... Signed as free agent by Denver Nuggets (September 29, 2003). ... Signed by Denver Nuggets to first of two consecutive 10-day contracts (February 15, 2005). ... Signed by Nuggets for remainder of season (March 7, 2005).

### COLLEGIATE RECORD

**NOTES:** Member of NCAA Division I championship team (1996).

| Season Team | G | Min. | FGM | FGA | Pct. | FTM | FTA | Pct. | Reb. | Ast. | Pts. | RPG | APG | PPG |
|---|---|---|---|---|---|---|---|---|---|---|---|---|---|---|
| 91-92—Washington .................. | 29 | 872 | 110 | 190 | .579 | 74 | 92 | .804 | 234 | 58 | 300 | 8.1 | 2.0 | 10.3 |
| 92-93—Washington .................. | 27 | 868 | 106 | 201 | .527 | 112 | 130 | .862 | 217 | 34 | 329 | 8.0 | 1.3 | 12.2 |
| 94-95—Kentucky ...................... | 33 | 728 | 89 | 173 | .514 | 72 | 99 | .727 | 207 | 29 | 271 | 6.3 | 0.9 | 8.2 |
| 95-96—Kentucky ...................... | 36 | 716 | 94 | 195 | .482 | 71 | 104 | .683 | 187 | 37 | 275 | 5.2 | 1.0 | 7.6 |
| Totals ..................................... | 125 | 3184 | 399 | 759 | .526 | 329 | 425 | .774 | 845 | 158 | 1175 | 6.8 | 1.3 | 9.4 |

Three-point field goals: 1991-92, 21-for-44 (.477). 1992-93, 5-for-20 (.250). 1994-95, 21-for-44 (.477). 1995-96, 16-for-45 (.356). Totals, 63-for-153 (.412).

### TURKISH LEAGUE RECORD

| Season Team | G | Min. | FGM | FGA | Pct. | FTM | FTA | Pct. | Reb. | Ast. | Pts. | RPG | APG | PPG |
|---|---|---|---|---|---|---|---|---|---|---|---|---|---|---|
| 96-97—Efes Pilsen..................... | 9 | 182 | 17 | 42 | .405 | 10 | 11 | .909 | 30 | · 6 | 51 | 3.3 | 0.7 | 5.7 |
| 99-00—Ulker.............................. | 15 | 493 | 71 | 146 | .486 | 27 | 46 | .587 | 113 | 17 | 188 | 7.5 | 1.1 | 12.5 |
| Totals ................... | 24 | 675 | 88 | 188 | .468 | 37 | 57 | .649 | 143 | 23 | 239 | 6.0 | 1.0 | 10.0 |

Three-point field goals: 1996-97, 7-for-19 (.368). 1999-00, 19-for-50 (.380). Totals, 26-for-69 (.377).

### NBA REGULAR-SEASON RECORD

| Season Team | G | Min. | FGM | FGA | Pct. | FTM | FTA | Pct. | Off. | Def. | Tot. | Ast. | St. | Blk. | TO | Pts. | RPG | APG | PPG |
|---|---|---|---|---|---|---|---|---|---|---|---|---|---|---|---|---|---|---|---|
| 97-98—Indiana........... | 28 | 193 | 14 | 41 | .341 | 10 | 17 | .588 | 9 | 17 | 26 | 7 | 3 | 6 | 10 | 39 | 0.9 | 0.3 | 1.4 |
| 98-99—Indiana........... | 4 | 26 | 1 | 7 | .143 | 0 | 1 | .000 | 2 | 2 | 4 | 0 | 0 | 0 | 1 | 2 | 1.0 | 0.0 | 0.5 |
| 00-01—Milwaukee ...... | 63 | 942 | 62 | 142 | .437 | 22 | 35 | .629 | 56 | 91 | 147 | 38 | 16 | 26 | 17 | 151 | 2.3 | 0.6 | 2.4 |
| 01-02—Milwaukee ...... | 45 | 426 | 36 | 91 | .396 | 11 | 21 | .524 | 20 | 53 | 73 | 17 | 11 | 11 | 15 | 87 | 1.6 | 0.4 | 1.9 |
| 02-03—New York ........ | | | | | | | | Did not play—injured | | | | | | | | | | | |
| 03-04—Denver ........... | 4 | 20 | 1 | 2 | .500 | 0 | 0 | 1 .000 | 0 | 3 | 3 | 0 | 1 | 0 | 3 | 2 | 0.8 | 0.0 | 0.5 |
| 04-05—Denver ........... | 9 | 27 | 2 | 6 | .333 | 0 | 0 | ... | 5 | 3 | 8 | 1 | 1 | 2 | 1 | 4 | 0.9 | 0.1 | 0.4 |
| Totals ................... | 153 | 1634 | 116 | 289 | .401 | 43 | 75 | .573 | 92 | 169 | 261 | 63 | 32 | 45 | 47 | 285 | 1.7 | 0.4 | 1.9 |

Three-point field goals: 1997-98, 1-for-3 (.333). 1998-99, 0-for-4. 2000-01, 5-for-24 (.208). 2001-02, 4-for-25 (.160). Totals, 10-for-56 (.179).
Personal fouls/disqualifications: 1997-98, 36/0. 1998-99, 6/0. 2000-01, 140/2. 2001-02, 47/0. 2003-04, 8/0. 2004-05, 5/0. Totals, 242/2.

### NBA PLAYOFF RECORD

| Season Team | G | Min. | FGM | FGA | Pct. | FTM | FTA | Pct. | Off. | Def. | Tot. | Ast. | St. | Blk. | TO | Pts. | RPG | APG | PPG |
|---|---|---|---|---|---|---|---|---|---|---|---|---|---|---|---|---|---|---|---|
| 97-98—Indiana........... | 7 | 42 | 4 | 6 | .667 | 1 | 1 | 1.000 | 2 | 3 | 5 | 1 | 1 | 0 | 1 | 9 | 0.7 | 0.1 | 1.3 |
| 00-01—Milwaukee ...... | 6 | 46 | 5 | 10 | .500 | 0 | 0 | ... | 5 | 7 | 12 | 2 | 2 | 0 | 0 | 10 | 2.0 | 0.3 | 1.7 |
| Totals ................... | 13 | 88 | 9 | 16 | .563 | 1 | 1 | 1.000 | 7 | 10 | 17 | 3 | 3 | 0 | 1 | 19 | 1.3 | 0.2 | 1.5 |

Three-point field goals: 1997-98, 0-for-1. 2000-01, 0-for-1. Totals, 0-for-2 (.000).
Personal fouls/disqualifications: 1997-98, 8/0. 2000-01, 6/0. Totals, 14/0.

### CBA RECORD

| Season Team | G | Min. | FGM | FGA | Pct. | FTM | FTA | Pct. | Reb. | Ast. | Pts. | RPG | APG | PPG |
|---|---|---|---|---|---|---|---|---|---|---|---|---|---|---|
| 99-00—La Crosse ..................... | 9 | 305 | 38 | 83 | .458 | 11 | 16 | .688 | 79 | 18 | 89 | 8.8 | 2.0 | 9.9 |

Three-point field goals: 1999-00, 2-for-8 (.250). Totals, 2-for-8 (.250).
Personal fouls/disqualifications: 1999-00, 32/0. Totals, 32/0.

## POSEY, JAMES   G/F   HEAT

**PERSONAL:** Born January 13, 1977, in Cleveland. ... 6-8/215. (2.03/97.5). ... Full name: James Mikley Mantell Posey
**HIGH SCHOOL:** R.B. Chamberlain (Twinsburg, Ohio).
**COLLEGE:** Xavier.
**TRANSACTIONS/CAREER NOTES:** Selected by Denver Nuggets in first round (18th pick overall) of 1999 NBA Draft. ... Traded by Nuggets to Houston Rockets in three-way deal in which Rockets sent F Kenny Thomas to Philadelphia 76ers, 76ers sent F/C Mark Bryant, F Art Long and future first-round draft choice to Nuggets and Rockets sent future second-round draft choice to

P

Nuggets (December 18, 2002). ... Signed by Memphis Grizzlies when Rockets elected not to match offer sheet (August 9, 2003) ... Traded by Grizzlies with Gs Jason Williams and Andre Emmett to Miami Heat in five-team trade (August 2, 2005).

## COLLEGIATE RECORD

| Season Team | G | Min. | FGM | FGA | Pct. | FTM | FTA | Pct. | Reb. | Ast. | Pts. | RPG | APG | PPG |
|---|---|---|---|---|---|---|---|---|---|---|---|---|---|---|
| 95-96—Xavier | | | | | | Did not play—ineligible. | | | | | | | | |
| 96-97—Xavier | 29 | 780 | 130 | 232 | .560 | 121 | 155 | .781 | 226 | 40 | 387 | 7.8 | 1.4 | 13.3 |
| 97-98—Xavier | 30 | 864 | 145 | 261 | .556 | 150 | 182 | .824 | 253 | 39 | 459 | 8.4 | 1.3 | 15.3 |
| 98-99—Xavier | 36 | 1268 | 191 | 391 | .488 | 179 | 220 | .814 | 322 | 84 | 609 | 8.9 | 2.3 | 16.9 |
| Totals | 95 | 2912 | 466 | 884 | .527 | 450 | 557 | .808 | 801 | 163 | 1455 | 8.4 | 1.7 | 15.3 |

Three-point field goals: 1996-97, 6-for-32 (.188). 1997-98, 19-for-59 (.322). 1998-99, 48-for-131 (.366). Totals, 73-for-222 (.329).

**HONORS:** NBA All-Rookie second team (2000).

## NBA REGULAR-SEASON RECORD

| Season Team | G | Min. | FGM | FGA | Pct. | FTM | FTA | Pct. | REBOUNDS Off. | Def. | Tot. | Ast. | St. | Blk. | TO | Pts. | RPG | APG | PPG |
|---|---|---|---|---|---|---|---|---|---|---|---|---|---|---|---|---|---|---|---|
| 99-00—Denver | 81 | 2052 | 230 | 536 | .429 | 120 | 150 | .800 | 85 | 232 | 317 | 146 | 98 | 33 | 95 | 662 | 3.9 | 1.8 | 8.2 |
| 00-01—Denver | 82 | 2255 | 243 | 590 | .412 | 115 | 141 | .816 | 125 | 306 | 431 | 163 | 93 | 40 | 102 | 666 | 5.3 | 2.0 | 8.1 |
| 01-02—Denver | 73 | 2238 | 277 | 736 | .376 | 161 | 203 | .793 | 109 | 320 | 429 | 180 | 114 | 39 | 127 | 782 | 5.9 | 2.5 | 10.7 |
| 02-03—Den-Hou | 83 | 2518 | 309 | 752 | .411 | 205 | 246 | .833 | 90 | 336 | 426 | 184 | 106 | 15 | 144 | 893 | 5.1 | 2.2 | 10.8 |
| 03-04—Memphis | 82 | 2451 | 368 | 770 | .478 | 278 | 335 | .830 | 92 | 311 | 403 | 122 | 137 | 40 | 112 | 1126 | 4.9 | 1.5 | 13.7 |
| 04-05—Memphis | 50 | 1382 | 127 | 356 | .357 | 96 | 111 | .865 | 45 | 174 | 219 | 88 | 48 | 23 | 69 | 405 | 4.4 | 1.8 | 8.1 |
| Totals | 451 | 12896 | 1554 | 3740 | .416 | 975 | 1186 | .822 | 546 | 1679 | 2225 | 883 | 596 | 190 | 649 | 4534 | 4.9 | 2.0 | 10.1 |

Three-point field goals: 1999-00, 82-for-220 (.373). 2000-01, 65-for-217 (.300). 2001-02, 67-for-237 (.283). 2002-03, 70-for-229 (.306). 2003-04, 112-for-290 (.386). 2004-05, 55-for-178 (.309). Totals, 451-for-1371 (.329).

Personal fouls/disqualifications: 1999-00, 207/1. 2000-01, 226/2. 2001-02, 224/3. 2002-03, 197/1. 2003-04, 248/5. 2004-05, 134/0. Totals, 1236/12.

## NBA PLAYOFF RECORD

| Season Team | G | Min. | FGM | FGA | Pct. | FTM | FTA | Pct. | REBOUNDS Off. | Def. | Tot. | Ast. | St. | Blk. | TO | Pts. | RPG | APG | PPG |
|---|---|---|---|---|---|---|---|---|---|---|---|---|---|---|---|---|---|---|---|
| 03-04—Memphis | 4 | 130 | 15 | 37 | .405 | 19 | 21 | .905 | 8 | 14 | 22 | 4 | 9 | 2 | 6 | 50 | 5.5 | 1.0 | 12.5 |
| 04-05—Memphis | 4 | 100 | 11 | 25 | .440 | 10 | 13 | .769 | 1 | 12 | 13 | 4 | 2 | 1 | 5 | 39 | 3.3 | 1.0 | 9.8 |
| Totals | 8 | 230 | 26 | 62 | .419 | 29 | 34 | .853 | 9 | 26 | 35 | 8 | 11 | 3 | 11 | 89 | 4.4 | 1.0 | 11.1 |

Three-point field goals: 2003-04, 1-for-6 (.167). 2004-05, 7-for-15 (.467). Totals, 8-for-21 (.381).
Personal fouls/disqualifications: 2003-04, 13/0. 2004-05, 14/0. Totals, 27/0.

# POTAPENKO, VITALY     F/C     SUPERSONICS

**PERSONAL:** Born March 21, 1975, in Kiev, Ukraine. ... 6-10/285. (2.08/129.3). ... Full name: Vitaly Nikolaevich Potapenko ... Name pronounced VEE-tal-lee poe-TAH-pen-koe.
**COLLEGE:** Wright State.
**TRANSACTIONS/CAREER NOTES:** Selected after junior season by Cleveland Cavaliers in first round (12th pick overall) of 1996 NBA Draft. ... Traded by Cavaliers to Boston Celtics for F/C Andrew DeClercq and a 1999 first-round draft choice (March 11, 1999). ... Traded by Celtics with G Kenny Anderson and G Joseph Forte to Seattle SuperSonics for F Vin Baker and G Shammond Williams (July 22, 2002).

## COLLEGIATE RECORD

| Season Team | G | Min. | FGM | FGA | Pct. | FTM | FTA | Pct. | Reb. | Ast. | Pts. | RPG | APG | PPG |
|---|---|---|---|---|---|---|---|---|---|---|---|---|---|---|
| 94-95—Wright State | 30 | 900 | 212 | 352 | .602 | 151 | 206 | .733 | 193 | 41 | 575 | 6.4 | 1.4 | 19.2 |
| 95-96—Wright State | 25 | 807 | 197 | 322 | .612 | 139 | 195 | .713 | 182 | 36 | 534 | 7.3 | 1.4 | 21.4 |
| Totals | 55 | 1707 | 409 | 674 | .607 | 290 | 401 | .723 | 375 | 77 | 1109 | 6.8 | 1.4 | 20.2 |

Three-point field goals: 1995-96, 1-for-6 (.167). Totals, 1-for-6 (.167).

## NBA REGULAR-SEASON RECORD

| Season Team | G | Min. | FGM | FGA | Pct. | FTM | FTA | Pct. | REBOUNDS Off. | Def. | Tot. | Ast. | St. | Blk. | TO | Pts. | RPG | APG | PPG |
|---|---|---|---|---|---|---|---|---|---|---|---|---|---|---|---|---|---|---|---|
| 96-97—Cleveland | 80 | 1238 | 186 | 423 | .440 | 92 | 125 | .736 | 105 | 112 | 217 | 40 | 26 | 34 | 109 | 465 | 2.7 | 0.5 | 5.8 |
| 97-98—Cleveland | 80 | 1412 | 234 | 488 | .480 | 102 | 144 | .708 | 110 | 203 | 313 | 57 | 27 | 28 | 132 | 570 | 3.9 | 0.7 | 7.1 |
| 98-99—Cleve.-Bos. | 50 | 1394 | 204 | 412 | .495 | 91 | 155 | .587 | 114 | 218 | 332 | 75 | 35 | 36 | 100 | 499 | 6.6 | 1.5 | 10.0 |
| 99-00—Boston | 79 | 1797 | 307 | 615 | .499 | 109 | 160 | .681 | 182 | 317 | 499 | 77 | 41 | 29 | 145 | 723 | 6.3 | 1.0 | 9.2 |
| 00-01—Boston | 82 | 1901 | 248 | 521 | .476 | 115 | 158 | .728 | 206 | 289 | 495 | 64 | 52 | 23 | 105 | 611 | 6.0 | 0.8 | 7.5 |
| 01-02—Boston | 79 | 1343 | 137 | 301 | .455 | 89 | 120 | .742 | 167 | 180 | 347 | 30 | 37 | 18 | 63 | 363 | 4.4 | 0.4 | 4.6 |
| 02-03—Seattle | 26 | 403 | 41 | 93 | .441 | 22 | 29 | .759 | 25 | 64 | 89 | 4 | 9 | 8 | 25 | 104 | 3.4 | 0.2 | 4.0 |
| 03-04—Seattle | 65 | 1419 | 200 | 409 | .489 | 59 | 92 | .641 | 101 | 188 | 289 | 53 | 22 | 28 | 77 | 459 | 4.4 | 0.8 | 7.1 |
| 04-05—Seattle | 33 | 335 | 45 | 87 | .517 | 27 | 31 | .871 | 30 | 48 | 78 | 9 | 7 | 3 | 12 | 117 | 2.4 | 0.3 | 3.5 |
| Totals | 574 | 11242 | 1602 | 3349 | .478 | 706 | 1014 | .696 | 1040 | 1619 | 2659 | 409 | 256 | 207 | 768 | 3911 | 4.6 | 0.7 | 6.8 |

Three-point field goals: 1996-97, 1-for-2 (.500). 1997-98, 0-for-1. 1998-99, 0-for-1. 1999-00, 0-for-1. 2004-05, 0-for-1. Totals, 1-for-6 (.167).
Personal fouls/disqualifications: 1996-97, 216/3. 1997-98, 198/2. 1998-99, 169/4. 1999-00, 239/4. 2000-01, 228/2. 2001-02, 174/0. 2002-03, 46/0. 2003-04, 161/2. 2004-05, 53/0. Totals, 1484/17.

## NBA PLAYOFF RECORD

| Season Team | G | Min. | FGM | FGA | Pct. | FTM | FTA | Pct. | REBOUNDS Off. | Def. | Tot. | Ast. | St. | Blk. | TO | Pts. | RPG | APG | PPG |
|---|---|---|---|---|---|---|---|---|---|---|---|---|---|---|---|---|---|---|---|
| 97-98—Cleveland | 4 | 70 | 6 | 15 | .400 | 5 | 10 | .500 | 3 | 8 | 11 | 3 | 2 | 0 | 6 | 17 | 2.8 | 0.8 | 4.3 |
| 04-05—Seattle | 5 | 37 | 5 | 10 | .500 | 0 | 0 | ... | 3 | 4 | 7 | 0 | 0 | 0 | 0 | 10 | 1.4 | 0.0 | 2.0 |
| Totals | 9 | 107 | 11 | 25 | .440 | 5 | 10 | .500 | 6 | 12 | 18 | 3 | 2 | 0 | 6 | 27 | 2.0 | 0.3 | 3.0 |

Personal fouls/disqualifications: 1997-98, 8/0. 2004-05, 8/0. Totals, 16/0.

**P**

## PRINCE, TAYSHAUN　　　　　　　　F　　　　　　　　PISTONS

**PERSONAL:** Born February 28, 1980, in Compton, Calif. ... 6-9/215. (2.06/97.5). ... Full name: Tayshaun Durell Prince
**HIGH SCHOOL:** Dominguez (Compton, Calif.).
**COLLEGE:** Kentucky.
**TRANSACTIONS/CAREER NOTES:** Selected by Detroit Pistons in first round (23rd pick overall) of 2002 NBA Draft.
**MISCELLANEOUS:** Member of NBA championship team (2004).

### COLLEGIATE RECORD

**NOTES:** The Sporting News All-America second team (2003).

| Season Team | G | Min. | FGM | FGA | Pct. | FTM | FTA | Pct. | Reb. | Ast. | Pts. | RPG | APG | PPG |
|---|---|---|---|---|---|---|---|---|---|---|---|---|---|---|
| | | | | | | | | | | | | AVERAGES | | |
| 98-99—Kentucky | 37 | 747 | 82 | 198 | .414 | 21 | 32 | .656 | 142 | 45 | 214 | 3.8 | 1.2 | 5.8 |
| 99-00—Kentucky | 32 | 1087 | 153 | 362 | .423 | 74 | 105 | .705 | 192 | 58 | 426 | 6.0 | 1.8 | 13.3 |
| 00-01—Kentucky | 34 | 1117 | 207 | 418 | .495 | 97 | 115 | .843 | 221 | 99 | 575 | 6.5 | 2.9 | 16.9 |
| 01-02—Kentucky | 32 | 1067 | 206 | 441 | .467 | 83 | 118 | .703 | 202 | 52 | 560 | 6.3 | 1.6 | 17.5 |
| Totals | 135 | 4018 | 648 | 1419 | .457 | 275 | 370 | .743 | 757 | 254 | 1775 | 5.6 | 1.9 | 13.1 |

Three-point field goals: 1998-99, 29-for-101 (.287). 1999-00, 46-for-150 (.307). 2000-01, 64-for-179 (.358). 2001-02, 65-for-191 (.340). Totals, 204-for-621 (.329).

### NBA REGULAR-SEASON RECORD

**HONORS:** NBA All-Defensive second team (2005).

| | | | | | | | | | REBOUNDS | | | | | | | AVERAGES | | |
| Season Team | G | Min. | FGM | FGA | Pct. | FTM | FTA | Pct. | Off. | Def. | Tot. | Ast. | St. | Blk. | TO | Pts. | RPG | APG | PPG |
|---|---|---|---|---|---|---|---|---|---|---|---|---|---|---|---|---|---|---|---|
| 02-03—Detroit | 42 | 435 | 53 | 118 | .449 | 11 | 17 | .647 | 5 | 40 | 45 | 24 | 10 | 14 | 21 | 137 | 1.1 | 0.6 | 3.3 |
| 03-04—Detroit | 82 | 2701 | 338 | 723 | .467 | 108 | 141 | .766 | 93 | 297 | 390 | 191 | 63 | 69 | 119 | 841 | 4.8 | 2.3 | 10.3 |
| 04-05—Detroit | 82 | 3039 | 469 | 963 | .487 | 221 | 274 | .807 | 133 | 302 | 435 | 247 | 56 | 71 | 135 | 1206 | 5.3 | 3.0 | 14.7 |
| Totals | 206 | 6175 | 860 | 1804 | .477 | 340 | 432 | .787 | 231 | 639 | 870 | 462 | 129 | 154 | 275 | 2184 | 4.2 | 2.2 | 10.6 |

Three-point field goals: 2002-03, 20-for-47 (.426). 2003-04, 57-for-157 (.363). 2004-05, 47-for-138 (.341). Totals, 124-for-342 (.363).
Personal fouls/disqualifications: 2002-03, 25/0. 2003-04, 149/0. 2004-05, 161/1. Totals, 335/1.

### NBA PLAYOFF RECORD

| | | | | | | | | | REBOUNDS | | | | | | | AVERAGES | | |
| Season Team | G | Min. | FGM | FGA | Pct. | FTM | FTA | Pct. | Off. | Def. | Tot. | Ast. | St. | Blk. | TO | Pts. | RPG | APG | PPG |
|---|---|---|---|---|---|---|---|---|---|---|---|---|---|---|---|---|---|---|---|
| 02-03—Detroit | 15 | 382 | 49 | 115 | .426 | 29 | 38 | .763 | 11 | 46 | 57 | 23 | 8 | 13 | 16 | 141 | 3.8 | 1.5 | 9.4 |
| 03-04—Detroit | 23 | 795 | 87 | 212 | .410 | 41 | 55 | .745 | 41 | 96 | 137 | 53 | 25 | 31 | 19 | 228 | 6.0 | 2.3 | 9.9 |
| 04-05—Detroit | 25 | 1023 | 133 | 307 | .433 | 48 | 60 | .800 | 56 | 102 | 158 | 83 | 26 | 9 | 37 | 336 | 6.3 | 3.3 | 13.4 |
| Totals | 63 | 2200 | 269 | 634 | .424 | 118 | 153 | .771 | 108 | 244 | 352 | 159 | 59 | 53 | 72 | 705 | 5.6 | 2.5 | 11.2 |

Three-point field goals: 2002-03, 14-for-48 (.292). 2003-04, 13-for-49 (.265). 2004-05, 22-for-60 (.367). Totals, 49-for-157 (.312).
Personal fouls/disqualifications: 2002-03, 20/0. 2003-04, 61/1. 2004-05, 50/0. Totals, 131/1.

## PROFIT, LARON　　　　　　　　G/F　　　　　　　　LAKERS

**PERSONAL:** Born August 5, 1977, in Charleston, S.C. ... 6-5/204. (1.96/92.5). ... Full name: Bronta Laron Profit
**HIGH SCHOOL:** Caesar Rodney (Dover, Del.).
**COLLEGE:** Maryland.
**TRANSACTIONS/CAREER NOTES:** Selected by Orlando Magic in second round (38th pick overall) of 1999 NBA Draft. ... Draft rights traded by Magic to Washington Wizards for conditional 2001 second-round draft choice (September 22, 1999). ... Traded by Wizards with future first-round draft choice to Magic for draft rights to C Brendan Haywood (August 1, 2001). ... Signed as free agent by Milwaukee Bucks (September 25, 2002). ... Waived by Bucks (October 24, 2002). ... Signed as free agent by Washington Wizards (October 1, 2004). ... Traded by Wizards with C Kwame Brown to Los Angeles Lakers for F Caron Butler and G Chucky Atkins (August 2, 2005).

### COLLEGIATE RECORD

| | | | | | | | | | | | | AVERAGES | | |
| Season Team | G | Min. | FGM | FGA | Pct. | FTM | FTA | Pct. | Reb. | Ast. | Pts. | RPG | APG | PPG |
|---|---|---|---|---|---|---|---|---|---|---|---|---|---|---|
| 95-96—Maryland | 27 | 366 | 54 | 112 | .482 | 34 | 45 | .756 | 74 | 32 | 154 | 2.7 | 1.2 | 5.7 |
| 96-97—Maryland | 32 | 1033 | 160 | 337 | .475 | 57 | 91 | .626 | 171 | 78 | 412 | 5.3 | 2.4 | 12.9 |
| 97-98—Maryland | 32 | 1008 | 184 | 412 | .447 | 104 | 147 | .707 | 165 | 104 | 506 | 5.2 | 3.3 | 15.8 |
| 98-99—Maryland | 34 | 982 | 185 | 368 | .503 | 100 | 148 | .676 | 162 | 73 | 494 | 4.8 | 2.1 | 14.5 |
| Totals | 125 | 3389 | 583 | 1229 | .474 | 295 | 431 | .684 | 572 | 287 | 1566 | 4.6 | 2.3 | 12.5 |

Three-point field goals: 1995-96, 12-for-33 (.364). 1996-97, 35-for-99 (.354). 1997-98, 34-for-117 (.291). 1998-99, 24-for-77 (.312). Totals, 105-for-326 (.322).

### NBA REGULAR-SEASON RECORD

| | | | | | | | | | REBOUNDS | | | | | | | AVERAGES | | |
| Season Team | G | Min. | FGM | FGA | Pct. | FTM | FTA | Pct. | Off. | Def. | Tot. | Ast. | St. | Blk. | TO | Pts. | RPG | APG | PPG |
|---|---|---|---|---|---|---|---|---|---|---|---|---|---|---|---|---|---|---|---|
| 99-00—Washington | 33 | 225 | 21 | 59 | .356 | 4 | 10 | .400 | 2 | 24 | 26 | 25 | 7 | 4 | 19 | 49 | 0.8 | 0.8 | 1.5 |
| 00-01—Washington | 35 | 605 | 56 | 142 | .394 | 33 | 45 | .733 | 18 | 46 | 64 | 89 | 36 | 11 | 46 | 152 | 1.8 | 2.5 | 4.3 |
| 04-05—Washington | 42 | 428 | 56 | 128 | .438 | 16 | 25 | .640 | 24 | 52 | 76 | 37 | 16 | 5 | 27 | 136 | 1.8 | 0.9 | 3.2 |
| Totals | 110 | 1258 | 133 | 329 | .404 | 53 | 80 | .663 | 44 | 122 | 166 | 151 | 59 | 20 | 92 | 337 | 1.5 | 1.4 | 3.1 |

Three-point field goals: 1999-00, 3-for-17 (.176). 2000-01, 7-for-26 (.269). 2004-05, 8-for-28 (.286). Totals, 18-for-71 (.254).
Personal fouls/disqualifications: 1999-00, 26/0. 2000-01, 43/0. 2004-05, 44/0. Totals, 113/0.

### NBA PLAYOFF RECORD

| | | | | | | | | | REBOUNDS | | | | | | | AVERAGES | | |
| Season Team | G | Min. | FGM | FGA | Pct. | FTM | FTA | Pct. | Off. | Def. | Tot. | Ast. | St. | Blk. | TO | Pts. | RPG | APG | PPG |
|---|---|---|---|---|---|---|---|---|---|---|---|---|---|---|---|---|---|---|---|
| 04-05—Washington | 3 | 5 | 0 | 2 | .000 | 0 | 0 | ... | 0 | 1 | 1 | 1 | 0 | 0 | 0 | 0 | 0.3 | 0.3 | 0.0 |

### ITALIAN LEAGUE RECORD

| | | | | | | | | | | | | AVERAGES | | |
| Season Team | G | Min. | FGM | FGA | Pct. | FTM | FTA | Pct. | Reb. | Ast. | Pts. | RPG | APG | PPG |
|---|---|---|---|---|---|---|---|---|---|---|---|---|---|---|
| 01-02—Premiata Montegranaro.. | 6 | 151 | 28 | 77 | .364 | 17 | 21 | .810 | 17 | 7 | 82 | 2.8 | 1.2 | 13.7 |

Three-point field goals: 2001-02, 9-for-25 (.360). Totals, 9-for-25 (.360).

**P**

## PRZYBILLA, JOEL      C      TRAIL BLAZERS

**PERSONAL:** Born October 10, 1979, in Monticello, Minn. ... 7-1/255. (2.16/115.7). ... Full name: Joel Anthony Przybilla
**HIGH SCHOOL:** Monticello (Minn.).
**COLLEGE:** Minnesota.
**TRANSACTIONS/CAREER NOTES:** Selected after sophomore season by Houston Rockets in first round (ninth pick overall) of 2000 NBA Draft. ... Draft rights traded by Rockets to Milwaukee Bucks for draft rights to C Jason Collier and a future first-round draft choice (June 28, 2000). ... Traded by Bucks to Atlanta Hawks as part of three-team trade in which Bucks also traded F Tim Thomas to New York Knicks. Hawks also acquired C Michael Doleac and 2005 second-round draft choice from Knicks and traded C Nazr Mohammed to Knicks. Bucks acquired F Keith Van Horn from Knicks (February 15, 2004). ... Signed as free agent by Portland Trail Blazers (August 25, 2004).

### COLLEGIATE RECORD

| Season Team | G | Min. | FGM | FGA | Pct. | FTM | FTA | Pct. | Reb. | Ast. | Pts. | RPG | APG | PPG |
|---|---|---|---|---|---|---|---|---|---|---|---|---|---|---|
| 98-99—Minnesota | 28 | 713 | 79 | 141 | .560 | 30 | 52 | .577 | 163 | 41 | 188 | 5.8 | 1.5 | 6.7 |
| 99-00—Minnesota | 21 | 638 | 122 | 199 | .613 | 55 | 111 | .495 | 176 | 50 | 299 | 8.4 | 2.4 | 14.2 |
| Totals | 49 | 1351 | 201 | 340 | .591 | 85 | 163 | .521 | 339 | 91 | 487 | 6.9 | 1.9 | 9.9 |

### NBA REGULAR-SEASON RECORD

| Season Team | G | Min. | FGM | FGA | Pct. | FTM | FTA | Pct. | Off. | Def. | Tot. | Ast. | St. | Blk. | TO | Pts. | RPG | APG | PPG |
|---|---|---|---|---|---|---|---|---|---|---|---|---|---|---|---|---|---|---|---|
| 00-01—Milwaukee | 33 | 270 | 12 | 35 | .343 | 3 | 11 | .273 | 29 | 42 | 71 | 2 | 3 | 30 | 13 | 27 | 2.2 | 0.1 | 0.8 |
| 01-02—Milwaukee | 71 | 1128 | 76 | 142 | .535 | 38 | 90 | .422 | 78 | 205 | 283 | 21 | 20 | 118 | 43 | 190 | 4.0 | 0.3 | 2.7 |
| 02-03—Milwaukee | 32 | 546 | 18 | 46 | .391 | 12 | 24 | .500 | 48 | 97 | 145 | 12 | 10 | 45 | 19 | 48 | 4.5 | 0.4 | 1.5 |
| 03-04—Milwaukee-Atl. | 17 | 347 | 18 | 50 | .360 | 13 | 31 | .419 | 32 | 79 | 111 | 7 | 5 | 17 | 18 | 49 | 6.5 | 0.4 | 2.9 |
| 04-05—Portland | 76 | 1858 | 199 | 333 | .598 | 90 | 174 | .517 | 178 | 410 | 588 | 74 | 24 | 163 | 98 | 488 | 7.7 | 1.0 | 6.4 |
| Totals | 229 | 4149 | 323 | 606 | .533 | 156 | 330 | .473 | 365 | 833 | 1198 | 116 | 62 | 373 | 191 | 802 | 5.2 | 0.5 | 3.5 |

Three-point field goals: 2001-02, 0-for-1. Totals, 0-for-1 (.000).
Personal fouls/disqualifications: 2000-01, 56/0. 2001-02, 199/3. 2002-03, 85/1. 2003-04, 53/1. 2004-05, 239/1. Totals, 632/6.

### NBA PLAYOFF RECORD

| Season Team | G | Min. | FGM | FGA | Pct. | FTM | FTA | Pct. | Off. | Def. | Tot. | Ast. | St. | Blk. | TO | Pts. | RPG | APG | PPG |
|---|---|---|---|---|---|---|---|---|---|---|---|---|---|---|---|---|---|---|---|
| 00-01—Milwaukee | 1 | 2 | 0 | 0 | ... | 0 | 0 | ... | 0 | 0 | 0 | 0 | 0 | 0 | 0 | 0 | 0.0 | 0.0 | 0.0 |
| 02-03—Milwaukee | 4 | 33 | 1 | 1 | 1.000 | 0 | 0 | ... | 2 | 8 | 10 | 1 | 0 | 2 | 1 | 2 | 2.5 | 0.3 | 0.5 |
| Totals | 5 | 35 | 1 | 1 | 1.000 | 0 | 0 | ... | 2 | 8 | 10 | 1 | 0 | 2 | 1 | 2 | 2.0 | 0.2 | 0.4 |

Personal fouls/disqualifications: 2002-03, 11/0. Totals, 11/0.

---

## RADMANOVIC, VLADIMIR      F      SUPERSONICS

**PERSONAL:** Born November 19, 1980, in Trebinje, Yugoslavia. ... 6-9/206. (2.06/93.4).
**COLLEGE:** Did not attend college.
**TRANSACTIONS/CAREER NOTES:** Played in Yugoslavia (1998-2001). ... Selected by Seattle SuperSonics in first round (12th pick overall) of 2001 NBA Draft.
**MISCELLANEOUS:** Member of Serbia-Montenegro Olympic Team (2004).

### YUGOSLAVIAN LEAGUE RECORD

| Season Team | G | Min. | FGM | FGA | Pct. | FTM | FTA | Pct. | Reb. | Ast. | Pts. | RPG | APG | PPG |
|---|---|---|---|---|---|---|---|---|---|---|---|---|---|---|
| 98-99—Crvena Zveda Belgrade | 10 | 150 | 23 | 35 | .657 | 6 | 8 | .750 | 28 | 8 | 59 | 2.8 | 0.8 | 5.9 |
| 99-00—Crvena Zveda Belgrade | 21 | 539 | 54 | 113 | .478 | 33 | 45 | .733 | 115 | 31 | 152 | 5.5 | 1.5 | 7.2 |
| 00-01—FMP Zeleznik | 19 | 623 | 119 | 216 | .551 | 56 | 71 | .789 | 139 | 51 | 327 | 7.3 | 2.7 | 17.2 |
| Totals | 50 | 1312 | 196 | 364 | .538 | 95 | 124 | .766 | 282 | 90 | 538 | 5.6 | 1.8 | 10.8 |

Three-point field goals: 1998-99, 7-for-10 (.700). 1999-00, 11-for-44 (.250). 2000-01, 33-for-85 (.388). Totals, 51-for-139 (.367).

**HONORS:** NBA All-Rookie second team (2002).

### NBA REGULAR-SEASON RECORD

| Season Team | G | Min. | FGM | FGA | Pct. | FTM | FTA | Pct. | Off. | Def. | Tot. | Ast. | St. | Blk. | TO | Pts. | RPG | APG | PPG |
|---|---|---|---|---|---|---|---|---|---|---|---|---|---|---|---|---|---|---|---|
| 01-02—Seattle | 61 | 1230 | 146 | 354 | .412 | 49 | 72 | .681 | 45 | 185 | 230 | 81 | 56 | 24 | 72 | 407 | 3.8 | 1.3 | 6.7 |
| 02-03—Seattle | 72 | 1910 | 274 | 668 | .410 | 72 | 102 | .706 | 76 | 247 | 323 | 97 | 64 | 22 | 100 | 724 | 4.5 | 1.3 | 10.1 |
| 03-04—Seattle | 77 | 2321 | 345 | 812 | .425 | 95 | 127 | .748 | 104 | 302 | 406 | 142 | 90 | 45 | 109 | 925 | 5.3 | 1.8 | 12.0 |
| 04-05—Seattle | 63 | 1856 | 266 | 650 | .409 | 81 | 103 | .786 | 52 | 237 | 289 | 86 | 57 | 31 | 80 | 741 | 4.6 | 1.4 | 11.8 |
| Totals | 273 | 7317 | 1031 | 2484 | .415 | 297 | 404 | .735 | 277 | 971 | 1248 | 406 | 257 | 119 | 361 | 2797 | 4.6 | 1.5 | 10.2 |

Three-point field goals: 2001-02, 66-for-157 (.420). 2002-03, 104-for-293 (.355). 2003-04, 140-for-377 (.371). 2004-05, 128-for-329 (.389). Totals, 438-for-1156 (.379).
Personal fouls/disqualifications: 2001-02, 119/0. 2002-03, 136/0. 2003-04, 187/1. 2004-05, 172/2. Totals, 614/3.

### NBA PLAYOFF RECORD

| Season Team | G | Min. | FGM | FGA | Pct. | FTM | FTA | Pct. | Off. | Def. | Tot. | Ast. | St. | Blk. | TO | Pts. | RPG | APG | PPG |
|---|---|---|---|---|---|---|---|---|---|---|---|---|---|---|---|---|---|---|---|
| 01-02—Seattle | 5 | 113 | 14 | 32 | .438 | 3 | 3 | 1.000 | 6 | 12 | 18 | 5 | 1 | 1 | 5 | 38 | 3.6 | 1.0 | 7.6 |
| 04-05—Seattle | 6 | 122 | 13 | 35 | .371 | 1 | 2 | .500 | 1 | 17 | 18 | 3 | 4 | 3 | 6 | 32 | 3.0 | 0.5 | 5.3 |
| Totals | 11 | 235 | 27 | 67 | .403 | 4 | 5 | .800 | 7 | 29 | 36 | 8 | 5 | 4 | 11 | 70 | 3.3 | 0.7 | 6.4 |

Three-point field goals: 2001-02, 7-for-13 (.538). 2004-05, 5-for-21 (.238). Totals, 12-for-34 (.353).
Personal fouls/disqualifications: 2001-02, 11/0. 2004-05, 9/0. Totals, 20/0.

## RADOJEVIC, ALEK      C

**PERSONAL:** Born August 8, 1976, in Hercg-Novi, Yugoslavia. ... 7-3/250. (2.21/113.4).
**HIGH SCHOOL:** Maldost-Bajela (Montenegro).
**JUNIOR COLLEGE:** Barton County Community College (Kan.).
**TRANSACTIONS/CAREER NOTES:** Selected after sophomore season by Toronto Raptors in first round (12th pick overall) of 1999 NBA Draft. ... Traded by Raptors with F/C Kevin Willis, C Garth Joseph and 2001 or 2002 second-round draft choice to Denver Nuggets for F Tracy Murray, F/C Keon Clark and C Mamadou N'diaye (January 12, 2001). ... Traded by Nuggets with F/C Kevin Willis to Milwaukee Bucks for C/F Scott Williams and future first-round draft choice (October 22, 2001). ... Waived by Bucks (October 29, 2001). ... Signed as free agent by Utah Jazz (August 2004). ... Waived by Jazz (January 4, 2005).

### COLLEGIATE RECORD

| Season Team | G | Min. | FGM | FGA | Pct. | FTM | FTA | Pct. | Reb. | Ast. | Pts. | RPG | APG | PPG |
|---|---|---|---|---|---|---|---|---|---|---|---|---|---|---|
| 97-98—Barton County C.C. | 33 | ... | 140 | 241 | .581 | 60 | 102 | .588 | 198 | 23 | 340 | 6.0 | 0.7 | 10.3 |
| 98-99—Barton County C.C. | 38 | 1072 | 231 | 381 | .606 | 121 | 191 | .634 | 342 | 49 | 585 | 9.0 | 1.3 | 15.4 |
| Totals | 71 | 1072 | 371 | 622 | .596 | 181 | 293 | .618 | 540 | 72 | 925 | 7.6 | 1.0 | 13.0 |

Three-point field goals: 1997-98, 0-for-1. 1998-99, 2-for-3 (.667). Totals, 2-for-4 (.500).

### NBA REGULAR-SEASON RECORD

| Season Team | G | Min. | FGM | FGA | Pct. | FTM | FTA | Pct. | Off. | Def. | Tot. | Ast. | St. | Blk. | TO | Pts. | RPG | APG | PPG |
|---|---|---|---|---|---|---|---|---|---|---|---|---|---|---|---|---|---|---|---|
| 99-00—Toronto | 3 | 24 | 2 | 7 | .286 | 3 | 6 | .500 | 2 | 6 | 8 | 1 | 2 | 1 | 5 | 7 | 2.7 | 0.3 | 2.3 |
| 00-01—Toronto-Denver | | | | | | | | Did not play—injured. | | | | | | | | | | | |
| 04-05—Utah | 12 | 128 | 6 | 19 | .316 | 7 | 10 | .700 | 9 | 19 | 28 | 6 | 0 | 2 | 15 | 19 | 2.3 | 0.5 | 1.6 |
| Totals | 15 | 152 | 8 | 26 | .308 | 10 | 16 | .625 | 11 | 25 | 36 | 7 | 2 | 3 | 20 | 26 | 2.4 | 0.5 | 1.7 |

Personal fouls/disqualifications: 1999-00, 5/0. 2004-05, 32/1. Totals, 37/1.

### ADRIATIC LEAGUE RECORD

| Season Team | G | Min. | FGM | FGA | Pct. | FTM | FTA | Pct. | Reb. | Ast. | Pts. | RPG | APG | PPG |
|---|---|---|---|---|---|---|---|---|---|---|---|---|---|---|
| 01-02—Union Olimpija | 9 | 105 | 15 | 23 | .652 | 13 | 19 | .684 | 26 | 4 | 43 | 2.9 | 0.4 | 4.8 |

### ITALIAN LEAGUE RECORD

| Season Team | G | Min. | FGM | FGA | Pct. | FTM | FTA | Pct. | Reb. | Ast. | Pts. | RPG | APG | PPG |
|---|---|---|---|---|---|---|---|---|---|---|---|---|---|---|
| 01-02—Livorno | 9 | 90 | 9 | 19 | .474 | 11 | 17 | .647 | 18 | 3 | 29 | 2.0 | 0.3 | 3.2 |

### GERMAN LEAGUE RECORD

| Season Team | G | Min. | FGM | FGA | Pct. | FTM | FTA | Pct. | Reb. | Ast. | Pts. | RPG | APG | PPG |
|---|---|---|---|---|---|---|---|---|---|---|---|---|---|---|
| 02-03—Bonn | 35 | 810 | 106 | 177 | .599 | 106 | 180 | .589 | 262 | 31 | 318 | 7.5 | 0.9 | 9.1 |

Three-point field goals: 2002-03, 0-for-3. Totals, 0-for-3 (.000).

### GREEK LEAGUE RECORD

| Season Team | G | Min. | FGM | FGA | Pct. | FTM | FTA | Pct. | Reb. | Ast. | Pts. | RPG | APG | PPG |
|---|---|---|---|---|---|---|---|---|---|---|---|---|---|---|
| 03-04—PAOK | 26 | 429 | 62 | 118 | .525 | 31 | 55 | .564 | 146 | 14 | 155 | 5.6 | 0.5 | 6.0 |

### POLISH LEAGUE RECORD

| Season Team | G | Min. | FGM | FGA | Pct. | FTM | FTA | Pct. | Reb. | Ast. | Pts. | RPG | APG | PPG |
|---|---|---|---|---|---|---|---|---|---|---|---|---|---|---|
| 04-05—Prokom Trefl Sopot | 20 | 230 | 30 | 54 | .556 | 31 | 51 | .608 | 56 | 6 | 91 | 2.8 | 0.3 | 4.6 |

## RAMOS, PETER JOHN      C      WIZARDS

**PERSONAL:** Born May 23, 1985, in Fajardo, Puerto Rico. ... 7-3/275. (2.21/124.7).
**TRANSACTIONS/CAREER NOTES:** Played in Puerto Rico (2000-04). ... Selected by Washington Wizards in second round (32nd pick overall) of 2004 NBA Draft.
**MISCELLANEOUS:** Member of Puerto Rican Olympic Team (2004).

### PUERTO RICAN RECORD

| Season Team | G | Min. | FGM | FGA | Pct. | FTM | FTA | Pct. | Reb. | Ast. | Pts. | RPG | APG | PPG |
|---|---|---|---|---|---|---|---|---|---|---|---|---|---|---|
| 00-01—Criollos de Caguas | 5 | 40 | 3 | 13 | .231 | 0 | 2 | .000 | 9 | 2 | 6 | 1.8 | 0.4 | 1.2 |
| 01-02—Criollos de Caguas | 23 | 249 | 26 | 64 | .406 | 4 | 10 | .400 | 59 | 8 | 56 | 2.6 | 0.3 | 2.4 |
| 02-03—Criollos de Caguas | 30 | 924 | 164 | 309 | .531 | 40 | 67 | .597 | 257 | 29 | 368 | 8.6 | 1.0 | 12.3 |
| 03-04—Criollos de Caguas | 24 | 978 | 218 | 424 | .514 | 62 | 108 | .574 | 229 | 75 | 498 | 9.5 | 3.1 | 20.8 |
| Totals | 82 | 2191 | 411 | 810 | .507 | 106 | 187 | .567 | 554 | 114 | 928 | 6.8 | 1.4 | 11.3 |

### NBA REGULAR-SEASON RECORD

| Season Team | G | Min. | FGM | FGA | Pct. | FTM | FTA | Pct. | Off. | Def. | Tot. | Ast. | St. | Blk. | TO | Pts. | RPG | APG | PPG |
|---|---|---|---|---|---|---|---|---|---|---|---|---|---|---|---|---|---|---|---|
| 04-05—Washington | 6 | 20 | 5 | 10 | .500 | 1 | 2 | .500 | 1 | 3 | 4 | 0 | 0 | 1 | 3 | 11 | 0.7 | 0.0 | 1.8 |

Personal fouls/disqualifications: 2004-05, 4/0. Totals, 4/0.

## RANDOLPH, ZACH      F      TRAIL BLAZERS

**PERSONAL:** Born July 16, 1981, in Marion, Ind. ... 6-9/270. (2.06/122.5).
**HIGH SCHOOL:** Marion (Ind.).
**COLLEGE:** Michigan State.
**TRANSACTIONS/CAREER NOTES:** Selected after freshman season by Portland Trail Blazers in first round (19th pick overall) of 2001 NBA Draft.

## COLLEGIATE RECORD

| Season Team | G | Min. | FGM | FGA | Pct. | FTM | FTA | Pct. | Reb. | Ast. | Pts. | AVERAGES | | |
|---|---|---|---|---|---|---|---|---|---|---|---|---|---|---|
| | | | | | | | | | | | | RPG | APG | PPG |
| 00-01—Michigan State ............... | 33 | 654 | 138 | 235 | .587 | 80 | 126 | .635 | 221 | 34 | 356 | 6.7 | 1.0 | 10.8 |

Three-point field goals: 2000-01, 0-for-1. Totals, 0-for-1 (.000).
Personal fouls/disqualifications: 2000-01, 60/0. Totals, 60/0.

## NBA REGULAR-SEASON RECORD

**HONORS:** NBA Most Improved Player (2004).

| Season Team | G | Min. | FGM | FGA | Pct. | FTM | FTA | Pct. | REBOUNDS | | | Ast. | St. | Blk. | TO | Pts. | AVERAGES | | |
|---|---|---|---|---|---|---|---|---|---|---|---|---|---|---|---|---|---|---|---|
| | | | | | | | | | Off. | Def. | Tot. | | | | | | RPG | APG | PPG |
| 01-02—Portland .......... | 41 | 238 | 48 | 107 | .449 | 18 | 27 | .667 | 31 | 38 | 69 | 13 | 7 | 4 | 15 | 114 | 1.7 | 0.3 | 2.8 |
| 02-03—Portland .......... | 77 | 1301 | 264 | 515 | .513 | 122 | 161 | .758 | 139 | 204 | 343 | 41 | 42 | 14 | 62 | 650 | 4.5 | 0.5 | 8.4 |
| 03-04—Portland .......... | 81 | 3067 | 663 | 1368 | .485 | 299 | 393 | .761 | 242 | 609 | 851 | 163 | 68 | 41 | 247 | 1626 | 10.5 | 2.0 | 20.1 |
| 04-05—Portland .......... | 46 | 1603 | 332 | 741 | .448 | 207 | 254 | .815 | 142 | 300 | 442 | 86 | 34 | 17 | 112 | 871 | 9.6 | 1.9 | 18.9 |
| **Totals ...................** | 245 | 6209 | 1307 | 2731 | .479 | 646 | 835 | .774 | 554 | 1151 | 1705 | 303 | 151 | 76 | 436 | 3261 | 7.0 | 1.2 | 13.3 |

Three-point field goals: 2002-03, 0-for-5. 2003-04, 1-for-5 (.200). 2004-05, 0-for-6. Totals, 1-for-16 (.063).
Personal fouls/disqualifications: 2001-02, 29/0. 2002-03, 141/0. 2003-04, 227/0. 2004-05, 112/3. Totals, 509/3.

## NBA PLAYOFF RECORD

| Season Team | G | Min. | FGM | FGA | Pct. | FTM | FTA | Pct. | REBOUNDS | | | Ast. | St. | Blk. | TO | Pts. | AVERAGES | | |
|---|---|---|---|---|---|---|---|---|---|---|---|---|---|---|---|---|---|---|---|
| | | | | | | | | | Off. | Def. | Tot. | | | | | | RPG | APG | PPG |
| 01-02—Portland .......... | 1 | 1 | 0 | 0 | ... | 0 | 0 | ... | 0 | 0 | 0 | 0 | 0 | 0 | 0 | 0 | 0.0 | 0.0 | 0.0 |
| 02-03—Portland .......... | 7 | 205 | 32 | 61 | .525 | 33 | 37 | .892 | 22 | 39 | 61 | 11 | 3 | 2 | 13 | 97 | 8.7 | 1.6 | 13.9 |
| **Totals ...................** | 8 | 206 | 32 | 61 | .525 | 33 | 37 | .892 | 22 | 39 | 61 | 11 | 3 | 2 | 13 | 97 | 7.6 | 1.4 | 12.1 |

Personal fouls/disqualifications: 2002-03, 17/0. Totals, 17/0.

# RATLIFF, THEO                F/C                TRAIL BLAZERS

**PERSONAL:** Born April 17, 1973, in Demopolis, Ala. ... 6-10/230. (2.08/104.3). ... Full name: Theo Curtis Ratliff
**HIGH SCHOOL:** Demopolis (Ala.).
**COLLEGE:** Wyoming.
**TRANSACTIONS/CAREER NOTES:** Selected by Detroit Pistons in first round (18th pick overall) of 1995 NBA Draft. ... Traded by Pistons with G Aaron McKie and conditional first-round draft choice to Philadelphia 76ers for G Jerry Stackhouse and C Eric Montross (December 18, 1997). ... Traded by 76ers with F/G Toni Kukoc, C Nazr Mohammed and G Pepe Sanchez to Atlanta Hawks for C Dikembe Mutombo and F Roshown McLeod (February 22, 2001). ... Traded by Hawks with F Shareef Abdur-Rahim and G Dan Dickau to Portland Trail Blazers for F Rasheed Wallace and G Wesley Person (February 9, 2004).

## COLLEGIATE RECORD

**NOTES:** Led NCAA Division I with 4.4 blocked shots per game (1993).

| Season Team | G | Min. | FGM | FGA | Pct. | FTM | FTA | Pct. | Reb. | Ast. | Pts. | AVERAGES | | |
|---|---|---|---|---|---|---|---|---|---|---|---|---|---|---|
| | | | | | | | | | | | | RPG | APG | PPG |
| 91-92—Wyoming ...................... | 27 | 298 | 14 | 32 | .438 | 21 | 36 | .583 | 54 | 8 | 49 | 2.0 | 0.3 | 1.8 |
| 92-93—Wyoming ...................... | 28 | 824 | 99 | 184 | .538 | 60 | 116 | .517 | 173 | 8 | 258 | 6.2 | 0.3 | 9.2 |
| 93-94—Wyoming ...................... | 28 | 892 | 160 | 281 | .569 | 111 | 171 | .649 | 217 | 27 | 431 | 7.8 | 1.0 | 15.4 |
| 94-95—Wyoming ...................... | 28 | 912 | 148 | 272 | .544 | 107 | 169 | .633 | 211 | 31 | 404 | 7.5 | 1.1 | 14.4 |
| **Totals .....................................** | 111 | 2926 | 421 | 769 | .547 | 299 | 492 | .608 | 655 | 74 | 1142 | 5.9 | 0.7 | 10.3 |

Three-point field goals: 1992-93, 0-for-1. 1993-94, 0-for-1. 1994-95, 1-for-5 (.200). Totals, 1-for-7 (.143).

## NBA REGULAR-SEASON RECORD

**HONORS:** NBA All-Defensive second team (1999, 2004).
**NOTES:** Led NBA with 3.74 blocks per game (2001) and 3.23 blocks per game (2003).

| Season Team | G | Min. | FGM | FGA | Pct. | FTM | FTA | Pct. | REBOUNDS | | | Ast. | St. | Blk. | TO | Pts. | AVERAGES | | |
|---|---|---|---|---|---|---|---|---|---|---|---|---|---|---|---|---|---|---|---|
| | | | | | | | | | Off. | Def. | Tot. | | | | | | RPG | APG | PPG |
| 95-96—Detroit ........... | 75 | 1305 | 128 | 230 | .557 | 85 | 120 | .708 | 110 | 187 | 297 | 13 | 16 | 116 | 56 | 341 | 4.0 | 0.2 | 4.5 |
| 96-97—Detroit ........... | 76 | 1292 | 179 | 337 | .531 | 81 | 116 | .698 | 109 | 147 | 256 | 13 | 29 | 111 | 56 | 439 | 3.4 | 0.2 | 5.8 |
| 97-98—Det.-Phila........ | 82 | 2447 | 306 | 597 | .513 | 197 | 281 | .701 | 221 | 326 | 547 | 57 | 50 | 258 | 116 | 809 | 6.7 | 0.7 | 9.9 |
| 98-99—Philadelphia .... | 50 | 1627 | 197 | 419 | .470 | 166 | 229 | .725 | 139 | 268 | 407 | 30 | 45 | 149 | 92 | 560 | 8.1 | 0.6 | 11.2 |
| 99-00—Philadelphia .... | 57 | 1795 | 247 | 491 | .503 | 182 | 236 | .771 | 140 | 295 | 435 | 36 | 32 | 171 | 108 | 676 | 7.6 | 0.6 | 11.9 |
| 00-01—Phila.-Atlanta .. | 50 | 1800 | 228 | 457 | .499 | 165 | 217 | .760 | 125 | 288 | 413 | 58 | 30 | 187 | 126 | 621 | 8.3 | 1.2 | 12.4 |
| 01-02—Atlanta ........... | 3 | 82 | 10 | 20 | .500 | 6 | 11 | .545 | 5 | 11 | 16 | 1 | 1 | 8 | 7 | 26 | 5.3 | 0.3 | 8.7 |
| 02-03—Atlanta ........... | 81 | 2518 | 276 | 595 | .464 | 154 | 214 | .720 | 154 | 453 | 607 | 73 | 56 | 262 | 137 | 706 | 7.5 | 0.9 | 8.7 |
| 03-04—Atl-Portland .... | 85 | 2664 | 266 | 549 | .485 | 140 | 217 | .645 | 195 | 419 | 614 | 71 | 54 | 307 | 120 | 672 | 7.2 | 0.8 | 7.9 |
| 04-05—Portland ......... | 63 | 1731 | 115 | 257 | .447 | 74 | 107 | .692 | 111 | 220 | 331 | 34 | 23 | 158 | 56 | 304 | 5.3 | 0.5 | 4.8 |
| **Totals ...................** | 622 | 17261 | 1952 | 3952 | .494 | 1250 | 1748 | .715 | 1309 | 2614 | 3923 | 386 | 336 | 1727 | 874 | 5154 | 6.3 | 0.6 | 8.3 |

Three-point field goals: 1995-96, 0-for-1. Totals, 0-for-1 (.000).
Personal fouls/disqualifications: 1995-96, 144/1. 1996-97, 181/2. 1997-98, 292/8. 1998-99, 180/8. 1999-00, 185/4. 2000-01, 165/3. 2001-02, 8/0. 2002-03, 271/3. 2003-04, 300/3. 2004-05, 183/4. Totals, 1909/36.

## NBA PLAYOFF RECORD

| Season Team | G | Min. | FGM | FGA | Pct. | FTM | FTA | Pct. | REBOUNDS | | | Ast. | St. | Blk. | TO | Pts. | AVERAGES | | |
|---|---|---|---|---|---|---|---|---|---|---|---|---|---|---|---|---|---|---|---|
| | | | | | | | | | Off. | Def. | Tot. | | | | | | RPG | APG | PPG |
| 95-96—Detroit ........... | 1 | 4 | 0 | 0 | ... | 0 | 0 | ... | 0 | 0 | 0 | 0 | 0 | 0 | 0 | 0 | 0.0 | 0.0 | 0.0 |
| 96-97—Detroit ........... | 3 | 18 | 3 | 4 | .750 | 2 | 4 | .500 | 2 | 2 | 4 | 1 | 1 | 4 | 3 | 8 | 1.3 | 0.3 | 2.7 |
| 98-99—Philadelphia .... | 7 | 204 | 20 | 43 | .465 | 11 | 19 | .579 | 23 | 28 | 51 | 6 | 5 | 18 | 7 | 51 | 7.3 | 0.9 | 7.3 |
| 99-00—Philadelphia .... | 10 | 374 | 48 | 101 | .475 | 34 | 47 | .723 | 28 | 51 | 79 | 9 | 10 | 30 | 17 | 130 | 7.9 | 0.9 | 13.0 |
| **Totals ....:............** | 21 | 600 | 71 | 148 | .480 | 47 | 70 | .671 | 53 | 81 | 134 | 16 | 16 | 52 | 27 | 189 | 6.4 | 0.8 | 9.0 |

Personal fouls/disqualifications: 1996-97, 5/0. 1998-99, 19/0. 1999-00, 35/1. Totals, 59/1.

## NBA ALL-STAR GAME RECORD

| Season Team | Min. | FGM | FGA | Pct. | FTM | FTA | Pct. | REBOUNDS | | | Ast. | PF | Dq. | St. | Blk. | TO | Pts. |
|---|---|---|---|---|---|---|---|---|---|---|---|---|---|---|---|---|---|
| | | | | | | | | Off. | Def. | Tot. | | | | | | | |
| 2001—Philadelphia .......... | | | | | | | Selected, did not play—injured | | | | | | | | | | |

# REBRACA, ZELJKO F CLIPPERS

**PERSONAL:** Born April 9, 1972, in Prigrevica, Yugoslavia. ... 6-11/240. (2.11/108.9). ... Name pronounced Reh-bhra-tcha.
**TRANSACTIONS/CAREER NOTES:** Played in Yugoslavia (1993-95). ... Selected by Seattle SuperSonics in second round (54th pick overall) of 1994 NBA Draft. ... Draft rights traded by SuperSonics to Minnesota Timberwolves for 1996 second-round draft choice (June 30, 1994). ... Played in Italy (1995-99). ... Played in Greece (1999-2001). ... Traded by Timberwolves with G Micheal Williams and 1999 or 2000 first-round draft choice to Toronto Raptors in three-way deal in which Raptors also received 1999 first-round draft choice from Denver Nuggets, Timberwolves received C Dean Garrett and G Bobby Jackson from Nuggets and Nuggets received G Chauncey Billups and draft rights to G Tyson Wheeler from Raptors (January 21, 1999). ... Traded by Raptors to Detroit Pistons for 2002 second-round draft choice (July 18, 2001). ... Traded by Pistons to Atlanta Hawks as part of three-team deal in which Hawks also received G Bob Sura and a future first-round draft choice from Pistons and F Chris Mills from Boston Celtics. Pistons received F/C Rasheed Wallace from Hawks and G Mike James from Celtics. Celtics received G Chucky Atkins, G Lindsey Hunter and a 2004 first-round draft choice from Pistons (February 19, 2004). ... Signed as free agent by Los Angeles Clippers (August 12, 2004).
**MISCELLANEOUS:** Member of silver-medal winning Yugoslavian Olympic team (1996). ... Member of Yugoslavian Olympic team (2000).

## YUGOSLAVIAN LEAGUE RECORD

| Season Team | G | Min. | FGM | FGA | Pct. | FTM | FTA | Pct. | Reb. | Ast. | Pts. | AVERAGES RPG | APG | PPG |
|---|---|---|---|---|---|---|---|---|---|---|---|---|---|---|
| 93-94—Belgrade Partizan .......... | 20 | ... | 114 | 251 | .454 | 60 | 82 | .732 | 131 | 8 | 288 | 6.6 | 0.4 | 14.4 |
| 94-95—Belgrade Partizan .......... | 20 | ... | ... | ... | ... | ... | ... | ... | 136 | ... | 518 | 6.8 | ... | 25.9 |
| **Totals** | 40 | ... | 114 | 251 | .454 | 60 | 82 | .732 | 267 | 8 | 806 | 6.7 | 0.2 | 20.2 |

Three-point field goals: 1993-94, 0-for-1. Totals, 0-for-1 (.000).

## ITALIAN LEAGUE RECORD

| Season Team | G | Min. | FGM | FGA | Pct. | FTM | FTA | Pct. | Reb. | Ast. | Pts. | AVERAGES RPG | APG | PPG |
|---|---|---|---|---|---|---|---|---|---|---|---|---|---|---|
| 95-96—Benetton ........................ | 40 | 1149 | 241 | 362 | .666 | 106 | 137 | .774 | 262 | 15 | 588 | 6.6 | 0.4 | 14.7 |
| 96-97—Benetton ........................ | 38 | 1057 | 202 | 335 | .603 | 120 | 156 | .769 | 255 | 17 | 526 | 6.7 | 0.4 | 13.8 |
| 97-98—Benetton ........................ | 30 | 931 | 201 | 320 | .628 | 107 | 136 | .787 | 217 | 23 | 509 | 7.2 | 0.8 | 17.0 |
| 98-99—Benetton ........................ | 34 | 880 | 145 | 237 | .612 | 116 | 147 | .789 | 184 | 26 | 406 | 5.4 | 0.8 | 11.9 |
| **Totals** ...................................... | 142 | 4017 | 789 | 1254 | .629 | 449 | 576 | .780 | 918 | 81 | 2029 | 6.5 | 0.6 | 14.3 |

Three-point field goals: 1995-96, 0-for-1. 1996-97, 2-for-3 (.667). 1997-98, 0-for-1. Totals, 2-for-5 (.400).

## GREEK LEAGUE RECORD

| Season Team | G | Min. | FGM | FGA | Pct. | FTM | FTA | Pct. | Reb. | Ast. | Pts. | AVERAGES RPG | APG | PPG |
|---|---|---|---|---|---|---|---|---|---|---|---|---|---|---|
| 99-00—Panathinaikos................. | 24 | 666 | 116 | 191 | .607 | 54 | 74 | .730 | 156 | 20 | 287 | 6.5 | 0.8 | 12.0 |
| 00-01—Panathinaikos................. | 21 | 414 | 79 | 121 | .653 | 47 | 63 | .746 | 148 | 19 | 205 | 7.0 | 0.9 | 9.8 |
| **Totals** ...................................... | 45 | 1080 | 195 | 312 | .625 | 101 | 137 | .737 | 304 | 39 | 492 | 6.8 | 0.9 | 10.9 |

Three-point field goals: 1999-00, 1-for-1 (1.000). Totals, 1-for-1 (1.000).

## NBA REGULAR-SEASON RECORD

**HONORS:** NBA All-Rookie second team (2002).

| Season Team | G | Min. | FGM | FGA | Pct. | FTM | FTA | Pct. | REBOUNDS Off. | Def. | Tot. | Ast. | St. | Blk. | TO | Pts. | AVERAGES RPG | APG | PPG |
|---|---|---|---|---|---|---|---|---|---|---|---|---|---|---|---|---|---|---|---|
| 01-02—Detroit ............ | 74 | 1179 | 189 | 374 | .505 | 135 | 175 | .771 | 84 | 206 | 290 | 38 | 28 | 73 | 84 | 513 | 3.9 | 0.5 | 6.9 |
| 02-03—Detroit ............ | 30 | 488 | 80 | 145 | .552 | 38 | 48 | .792 | 27 | 65 | 92 | 9 | 6 | 17 | 29 | 198 | 3.1 | 0.3 | 6.6 |
| 03-04—Detroit-Atlanta | 24 | 273 | 34 | 77 | .442 | 23 | 30 | .767 | 23 | 35 | 58 | 6 | 5 | 11 | 17 | 91 | 2.4 | 0.3 | 3.8 |
| 04-05—L.A. Clippers... | 58 | 928 | 133 | 234 | .568 | 73 | 85 | .859 | 49 | 135 | 184 | 26 | 13 | 40 | 49 | 339 | 3.2 | 0.4 | 5.8 |
| **Totals** ................... | 186 | 2868 | 436 | 830 | .525 | 269 | 338 | .796 | 183 | 441 | 624 | 79 | 52 | 141 | 179 | 1141 | 3.4 | 0.4 | 6.1 |

Personal fouls/disqualifications: 2001-02, 192/0. 2002-03, 79/1. 2003-04, 52/1. 2004-05, 130/3. Totals, 453/5.

## NBA PLAYOFF RECORD

| Season Team | G | Min. | FGM | FGA | Pct. | FTM | FTA | Pct. | REBOUNDS Off. | Def. | Tot. | Ast. | St. | Blk. | TO | Pts. | AVERAGES RPG | APG | PPG |
|---|---|---|---|---|---|---|---|---|---|---|---|---|---|---|---|---|---|---|---|
| 01-02—Detroit ............ | 5 | 69 | 5 | 11 | .455 | 11 | 14 | .786 | 4 | 6 | 10 | 0 | 1 | 1 | 4 | 21 | 2.0 | 0.0 | 4.2 |
| 02-03—Detroit ............ | 4 | 29 | 6 | 17 | .353 | 5 | 7 | .714 | 2 | 3 | 5 | 0 | 0 | 0 | 1 | 17 | 1.3 | 0.0 | 4.3 |
| **Totals** ................... | 9 | 98 | 11 | 28 | .393 | 16 | 21 | .762 | 6 | 9 | 15 | 0 | 1 | 1 | 5 | 38 | 1.7 | 0.0 | 4.2 |

Personal fouls/disqualifications: 2001-02, 14/0. 2002-03, 9/1. Totals, 23/1.

# REDD, MICHAEL G BUCKS

**PERSONAL:** Born August 24, 1979, in Columbus, Ohio. ... 6-6/214. (1.98/97.1). ... Full name: Michael Wesley Redd
**HIGH SCHOOL:** West (Columbus).
**COLLEGE:** Ohio State.
**TRANSACTIONS/CAREER NOTES:** Selected after junior season by Milwaukee Bucks in second round (43rd pick overall) of 2000 NBA Draft.

## COLLEGIATE RECORD

| Season Team | G | Min. | FGM | FGA | Pct. | FTM | FTA | Pct. | Reb. | Ast. | Pts. | AVERAGES RPG | APG | PPG |
|---|---|---|---|---|---|---|---|---|---|---|---|---|---|---|
| 97-98—Ohio State ..................... | 30 | 1137 | 241 | 550 | .438 | 130 | 211 | .616 | 194 | 91 | 658 | 6.5 | 3.0 | 21.9 |
| 98-99—Ohio State ..................... | 36 | 1183 | 261 | 560 | .466 | 135 | 220 | .614 | 203 | 85 | 703 | 5.6 | 2.4 | 19.5 |
| 99-00—Ohio State ..................... | 30 | 1004 | 197 | 452 | .436 | 90 | 116 | .776 | 196 | 62 | 518 | 6.5 | 2.1 | 17.3 |
| **Totals** ...................................... | 96 | 3324 | 699 | 1562 | .448 | 355 | 547 | .649 | 593 | 238 | 1879 | 6.2 | 2.5 | 19.6 |

Three-point field goals: 1997-98, 46-for-152 (.303). 1998-99, 46-for-135 (.341). 1999-00, 31-for-99 (.313). Totals, 123-for-386 (.319).

## NBA REGULAR-SEASON RECORD

**RECORDS:** Holds single-game record for most three-point field goals made in one quarter—8 (February 20, 2002, vs. Houston). ... Shares single-game record for most three-point field goals made in one half—8 (February 20, 2002, vs. Houston).
**HONORS:** All-NBA third team (2004).

**R**

| Season Team | G | Min. | FGM | FGA | Pct. | FTM | FTA | Pct. | Off. | Def. | Tot. | Ast. | St. | Blk. | TO | Pts. | RPG | APG | PPG |
|---|---|---|---|---|---|---|---|---|---|---|---|---|---|---|---|---|---|---|---|
| 00-01—Milwaukee ...... | 6 | 35 | 5 | 19 | .263 | 3 | 6 | .500 | 3 | 1 | 4 | 1 | 1 | 0 | 1 | 13 | 0.7 | 0.2 | 2.2 |
| 01-02—Milwaukee ...... | 67 | 1417 | 294 | 609 | .483 | 91 | 115 | .791 | 77 | 147 | 224 | 91 | 42 | 7 | 57 | 767 | 3.3 | 1.4 | 11.4 |
| 02-03—Milwaukee ...... | 82 | 2316 | 455 | 971 | .469 | 149 | 185 | .805 | 98 | 273 | 371 | 117 | 100 | 13 | 74 | 1241 | 4.5 | 1.4 | 15.1 |
| 03-04—Milwaukee ...... | 82 | 3021 | 633 | 1439 | .440 | 383 | 441 | .868 | 118 | 289 | 407 | 185 | 81 | 6 | 116 | 1776 | 5.0 | 2.3 | 21.7 |
| 04-05—Milwaukee ...... | 75 | 2848 | 625 | 1418 | .441 | 369 | 432 | .854 | 72 | 240 | 312 | 172 | 63 | 8 | 133 | 1723 | 4.2 | 2.3 | 23.0 |
| Totals ................. | 312 | 9637 | 2012 | 4456 | .452 | 995 | 1179 | .844 | 368 | 950 | 1318 | 566 | 287 | 34 | 381 | 5520 | 4.2 | 1.8 | 17.7 |

Three-point field goals: 2000-01, 0-for-3. 2001-02, 88-for-198 (.444). 2002-03, 182-for-416 (.438). 2003-04, 127-for-363 (.350). 2004-05, 104-for-293 (.355). Totals, 501-for-1273 (.394).

Personal fouls/disqualifications: 2000-01, 2/0. 2001-02, 96/0. 2002-03, 143/0. 2003-04, 152/0. 2004-05, 152/0. Totals, 545/0.

### NBA PLAYOFF RECORD

| Season Team | G | Min. | FGM | FGA | Pct. | FTM | FTA | Pct. | Off. | Def. | Tot. | Ast. | St. | Blk. | TO | Pts. | RPG | APG | PPG |
|---|---|---|---|---|---|---|---|---|---|---|---|---|---|---|---|---|---|---|---|
| 02-03—Milwaukee ...... | 6 | 128 | 21 | 52 | .404 | 13 | 14 | .929 | 9 | 12 | 21 | 11 | 2 | 1 | 7 | 58 | 3.5 | 1.8 | 9.7 |
| 03-04—Milwaukee ...... | 5 | 192 | 34 | 83 | .410 | 16 | 21 | .762 | 6 | 19 | 25 | 13 | 0 | 0 | 19 | 90 | 5.0 | 2.6 | 18.0 |
| Totals ................... | 11 | 320 | 55 | 135 | .407 | 29 | 35 | .829 | 15 | 31 | 46 | 24 | 2 | 1 | 26 | 148 | 4.2 | 2.2 | 13.5 |

Three-point field goals: 2002-03, 3-for-12 (.250). 2003-04, 6-for-20 (.300). Totals, 9-for-32 (.281).
Personal fouls/disqualifications: 2002-03, 15/0. 2003-04, 16/0. Totals, 31/0.

### NBA ALL-STAR GAME RECORD

| Season Team | Min. | FGM | FGA | Pct. | FTM | FTA | Pct. | Off. | Def. | Tot. | Ast. | PF | Dq. | St. | Blk. | TO | Pts. |
|---|---|---|---|---|---|---|---|---|---|---|---|---|---|---|---|---|---|
| 2004—Milwaukee............ | 15 | 5 | 12 | .417 | 0 | 0 | ... | 2 | 1 | 3 | 2 | 0 | 0 | 3 | 0 | 1 | 13 |

Three-point field goals: 2004, 3-for-6 (.500). Totals, 3-for-6 (.500).

## REED, JUSTIN      F      CELTICS

**PERSONAL:** Born January 16, 1982, in Jackson, Miss. ... 6-8/240. (2.03/108.9). ... Full name: Justin Michael Reed.
**HIGH SCHOOL:** Provine (Jackson, Miss.).
**COLLEGE:** Mississippi.
**TRANSACTIONS/CAREER NOTES:** Selected by Boston Celtics in second round (40th pick overall) of 2004 NBA Draft.

### COLLEGIATE RECORD

| Season Team | G | Min. | FGM | FGA | Pct. | FTM | FTA | Pct. | Reb. | Ast. | Pts. | RPG | APG | PPG |
|---|---|---|---|---|---|---|---|---|---|---|---|---|---|---|
| 00-01—Mississippi .................. | 35 | 862 | 160 | 335 | .478 | 62 | 113 | .549 | 205 | 27 | 385 | 5.9 | 0.8 | 11.0 |
| 01-02—Mississippi .................. | 31 | 870 | 167 | 348 | .480 | 111 | 141 | .787 | 205 | 34 | 453 | 6.6 | 1.1 | 14.6 |
| 02-03—Mississippi .................. | 28 | 825 | 159 | 326 | .488 | 92 | 126 | .730 | 147 | 30 | 430 | 5.3 | 1.1 | 15.4 |
| 03-04—Mississippi .................. | 28 | 939 | 193 | 416 | .464 | 117 | 160 | .731 | 209 | 41 | 517 | 7.5 | 1.5 | 18.5 |
| Totals ..................................... | 122 | 3496 | 679 | 1425 | .476 | 382 | 540 | .707 | 766 | 132 | 1785 | 6.3 | 1.1 | 14.6 |

Three-point field goals: 2000-01, 3-for-23 (.130). 2001-02, 8-for-29 (.276). 2002-03, 20-for-47 (.426). 2003-04, 14-for-59 (.237). Totals, 45-for-158 (.285).

### NBA REGULAR-SEASON RECORD

| Season Team | G | Min. | FGM | FGA | Pct. | FTM | FTA | Pct. | Off. | Def. | Tot. | Ast. | St. | Blk. | TO | Pts. | RPG | APG | PPG |
|---|---|---|---|---|---|---|---|---|---|---|---|---|---|---|---|---|---|---|---|
| 04-05—Boston ............ | 23 | 121 | 15 | 29 | .517 | 11 | 15 | .733 | 8 | 8 | 16 | 10 | 3 | 1 | 5 | 41 | 0.7 | 0.4 | 1.8 |

Three-point field goals: 2004-05, 0-for-3. Totals, 0-for-3 (.000).
Personal fouls/disqualifications: 2004-05, 12/0. Totals, 12/0.

### NBA PLAYOFF RECORD

| Season Team | G | Min. | FGM | FGA | Pct. | FTM | FTA | Pct. | Off. | Def. | Tot. | Ast. | St. | Blk. | TO | Pts. | RPG | APG | PPG |
|---|---|---|---|---|---|---|---|---|---|---|---|---|---|---|---|---|---|---|---|
| 04-05—Boston ............ | 6 | 22 | 2 | 6 | .333 | 3 | 4 | .750 | 0 | 1 | 1 | 0 | 0 | 0 | 2 | 7 | 0.2 | 0.0 | 1.2 |

Three-point field goals: 2004-05, 0-for-2. Totals, 0-for-2 (.000).
Personal fouls/disqualifications: 2004-05, 2/0. Totals, 2/0.

## REINER, JARED      C      BULLS

**PERSONAL:** Born April 8, 1982, in Tripp, S.D. ... 6-11/255. (2.11/115.7).
**HIGH SCHOOL:** Tripp-Delmont (Tripp, S.D.).
**COLLEGE:** Iowa.
**TRANSACTIONS/CAREER NOTES:** Not drafted by an NBA franchise. ... Signed as free agent by Chicago Bulls (October 29, 2004).

### COLLEGIATE RECORD

| Season Team | G | Min. | FGM | FGA | Pct. | FTM | FTA | Pct. | Reb. | Ast. | Pts. | RPG | APG | PPG |
|---|---|---|---|---|---|---|---|---|---|---|---|---|---|---|
| 00-01—Iowa ............................. | 35 | 464 | 37 | 90 | .411 | 33 | 49 | .673 | 100 | 18 | 107 | 2.9 | 0.5 | 3.1 |
| 01-02—Iowa ............................. | 33 | 463 | 42 | 79 | .532 | 19 | 28 | .679 | 83 | 24 | 103 | 2.5 | 0.7 | 3.1 |
| 02-03—Iowa ............................. | 28 | 760 | 92 | 170 | .541 | 87 | 117 | .744 | 231 | 38 | 271 | 8.3 | 1.4 | 9.7 |
| 03-04—Iowa ............................. | 13 | 306 | 43 | 96 | .448 | 51 | 76 | .671 | 93 | 20 | 137 | 7.2 | 1.5 | 10.5 |
| Totals ..................................... | 109 | 1993 | 214 | 435 | .492 | 190 | 270 | .704 | 507 | 100 | 618 | 4.7 | 0.9 | 5.7 |

### NBA REGULAR-SEASON RECORD

| Season Team | G | Min. | FGM | FGA | Pct. | FTM | FTA | Pct. | Off. | Def. | Tot. | Ast. | St. | Blk. | TO | Pts. | RPG | APG | PPG |
|---|---|---|---|---|---|---|---|---|---|---|---|---|---|---|---|---|---|---|---|
| 04-05—Chicago ......... | 19 | 132 | 10 | 30 | .333 | 1 | 4 | .250 | 13 | 25 | 38 | 1 | 3 | 7 | 9 | 21 | 2.0 | 0.1 | 1.1 |

Personal fouls/disqualifications: 2004-05, 35/0. Totals, 35/0.

| Season Team | G | Min. | FGM | FGA | Pct. | FTM | FTA | Pct. | Off. | Def. | Tot. | Ast. | St. | Blk. | TO | Pts. | RPG | APG | PPG |
|---|---|---|---|---|---|---|---|---|---|---|---|---|---|---|---|---|---|---|---|
| 04-05—Chicago ......... | 3 | 7 | 0 | 1 | .000 | 0 | 0 | ... | 2 | 1 | 3 | 0 | 0 | 0 | 1 | 0 | 1.0 | 0.0 | 0.0 |

Personal fouls/disqualifications: 2004-05, 3/0. Totals, 3/0.

## RICHARDSON, JASON    G    WARRIORS

**PERSONAL:** Born January 20, 1981, in Saginaw, Mich. ... 6-6/220. (1.98/99.8). ... Full name: Jason Anthony Richardson
**HIGH SCHOOL:** Arthur Hill (Saginaw, Mich.).
**COLLEGE:** Michigan State.
**TRANSACTIONS/CAREER NOTES:** Selected after sophomore season by Golden State Warriors in first round (fifth pick overall) of 2001 NBA Draft.

### COLLEGIATE RECORD

**NOTES:** The Sporting News All-America second team (2001). ... Member of NCAA Division I championship team (2000).

| Season Team | G | Min. | FGM | FGA | Pct. | FTM | FTA | Pct. | Reb. | Ast. | Pts. | RPG | APG | PPG |
|---|---|---|---|---|---|---|---|---|---|---|---|---|---|---|
| 99-00—Michigan State .............. | 37 | 582 | 79 | 157 | .503 | 23 | 42 | .548 | 153 | 23 | 189 | 4.1 | 0.6 | 5.1 |
| 00-01—Michigan State .............. | 33 | 940 | 182 | 362 | .503 | 73 | 106 | .689 | 195 | 73 | 486 | 5.9 | 2.2 | 14.7 |
| Totals ..................................... | 70 | 1522 | 261 | 519 | .503 | 96 | 148 | .649 | 348 | 96 | 675 | 5.0 | 1.4 | 9.6 |

Three-point field goals: 1999-00, 8-for-27 (.296). 2000-01, 49-for-122 (.402). Totals, 57-for-149 (.383).
Personal fouls/disqualifications: 1999-00, 56/0. 2000-01, 74/0. Totals, 130/0.

### NBA REGULAR-SEASON RECORD

**HONORS:** Slam Dunk championship winner (2002, 2003). ... NBA All-Rookie first team (2002). ... MVP of Rookie Challenge (2002).

| Season Team | G | Min. | FGM | FGA | Pct. | FTM | FTA | Pct. | Off. | Def. | Tot. | Ast. | St. | Blk. | TO | Pts. | RPG | APG | PPG |
|---|---|---|---|---|---|---|---|---|---|---|---|---|---|---|---|---|---|---|---|
| 01-02—Golden State ... | 80 | 2629 | 454 | 1090 | .417 | 141 | 210 | .671 | 124 | 216 | 340 | 236 | 106 | 31 | 160 | 1151 | 4.3 | 3.0 | 14.4 |
| 02-03—Golden State ... | 82 | 2698 | 476 | 1161 | .410 | 207 | 271 | .764 | 111 | 267 | 378 | 247 | 90 | 23 | 179 | 1282 | 4.6 | 3.0 | 15.6 |
| 03-04—Golden State ... | 78 | 2936 | 563 | 1284 | .438 | 258 | 377 | .684 | 124 | 400 | 524 | 226 | 86 | 41 | 196 | 1461 | 6.7 | 2.9 | 18.7 |
| 04-05—Golden State ... | 72 | 2724 | 610 | 1368 | .446 | 214 | 309 | .693 | 125 | 299 | 424 | 281 | 105 | 32 | 169 | 1559 | 5.9 | 3.9 | 21.7 |
| Totals ................... | 312 | 10987 | 2103 | 4903 | .429 | 820 | 1167 | .703 | 484 | 1182 | 1666 | 990 | 387 | 127 | 704 | 5453 | 5.3 | 3.2 | 17.5 |

Three-point field goals: 2001-02, 82-for-246 (.333). 2002-03, 123-for-334 (.368). 2003-04, 77-for-273 (.282). 2004-05, 125-for-370 (.338). Totals, 407-for-1223 (.333).
Personal fouls/disqualifications: 2001-02, 195/2. 2002-03, 201/1. 2003-04, 182/1. 2004-05, 156/0. Totals, 734/4.

## RICHARDSON, QUENTIN    G    KNICKS

**PERSONAL:** Born April 13, 1980, in Chicago. ... 6-6/236. (1.98/107.0). ... Full name: Quentin L. Richardson
**HIGH SCHOOL:** Whitney Young (Chicago).
**COLLEGE:** DePaul.
**TRANSACTIONS/CAREER NOTES:** Selected after sophomore season by Los Angeles Clippers in first round (18th pick overall) of 2000 NBA Draft. ... Signed as free agent by Phoenix Suns (July 29, 2004). ... Traded by Suns with draft rights to G Nate Robinson and future considerations to New York Knicks for F Kurt Thomas and draft rights to F Dijon Thompson (June 28, 2005).

### COLLEGIATE RECORD

**NOTES:** The Sporting News Freshman of the Year (1999).

| Season Team | G | Min. | FGM | FGA | Pct. | FTM | FTA | Pct. | Reb. | Ast. | Pts. | RPG | APG | PPG |
|---|---|---|---|---|---|---|---|---|---|---|---|---|---|---|
| 98-99—DePaul .......................... | 31 | 1040 | 203 | 425 | .478 | 136 | 183 | .743 | 327 | 32 | 586 | 10.5 | 1.0 | 18.9 |
| 99-00—DePaul .......................... | 33 | 1150 | 202 | 468 | .432 | 84 | 119 | .706 | 325 | 72 | 561 | 9.8 | 2.2 | 17.0 |
| Totals ..................................... | 64 | 2190 | 405 | 893 | .454 | 220 | 302 | .728 | 652 | 104 | 1147 | 10.2 | 1.6 | 17.9 |

Three-point field goals: 1998-99, 44-for-127 (.346). 1999-00, 73-for-190 (.384). Totals, 117-for-317 (.369).

### NBA REGULAR-SEASON RECORD

| Season Team | G | Min. | FGM | FGA | Pct. | FTM | FTA | Pct. | Off. | Def. | Tot. | Ast. | St. | Blk. | TO | Pts. | RPG | APG | PPG |
|---|---|---|---|---|---|---|---|---|---|---|---|---|---|---|---|---|---|---|---|
| 00-01—L.A. Clippers ... | 76 | 1358 | 232 | 525 | .442 | 99 | 158 | .627 | 105 | 152 | 257 | 62 | 42 | 7 | 64 | 613 | 3.4 | 0.8 | 8.1 |
| 01-02—L.A. Clippers ... | 81 | 2152 | 400 | 926 | .432 | 143 | 187 | .765 | 113 | 221 | 334 | 128 | 78 | 21 | 102 | 1076 | 4.1 | 1.6 | 13.3 |
| 02-03—L.A. Clippers ... | 59 | 1368 | 203 | 546 | .372 | 85 | 124 | .685 | 98 | 183 | 281 | 52 | 35 | 10 | 64 | 552 | 4.8 | 0.9 | 9.4 |
| 03-04—L.A. Clippers ... | 65 | 2338 | 425 | 1068 | .398 | 151 | 204 | .740 | 146 | 268 | 414 | 139 | 67 | 19 | 141 | 1121 | 6.4 | 2.1 | 17.2 |
| 04-05—Phoenix ......... | 79 | 2839 | 407 | 1045 | .389 | 136 | 184 | .739 | 91 | 388 | 479 | 158 | 96 | 27 | 102 | 1176 | 6.1 | 2.0 | 14.9 |
| Totals ................... | 360 | 10055 | 1667 | 4110 | .406 | 614 | 857 | .716 | 553 | 1212 | 1765 | 539 | 318 | 84 | 473 | 4538 | 4.9 | 1.5 | 12.6 |

Three-point field goals: 2000-01, 50-for-151 (.331). 2001-02, 133-for-349 (.381). 2002-03, 61-for-198 (.308). 2003-04, 120-for-341 (.352). 2004-05, 226-for-631 (.358). Totals, 590-for-1670 (.353).
Personal fouls/disqualifications: 2000-01, 98/0. 2001-02, 142/0. 2002-03, 92/0. 2003-04, 130/0. 2004-05, 197/4. Totals, 659/6.

### NBA PLAYOFF RECORD

| Season Team | G | Min. | FGM | FGA | Pct. | FTM | FTA | Pct. | Off. | Def. | Tot. | Ast. | St. | Blk. | TO | Pts. | RPG | APG | PPG |
|---|---|---|---|---|---|---|---|---|---|---|---|---|---|---|---|---|---|---|---|
| 04-05—Phoenix ......... | 15 | 564 | 62 | 154 | .403 | 23 | 36 | .639 | 24 | 53 | 77 | 25 | 19 | 3 | 15 | 179 | 5.1 | 1.7 | 11.9 |

Three-point field goals: 2004-05, 32-for-82 (.390). Totals, 32-for-82 (.390).
Personal fouls/disqualifications: 2004-05, 53/0. Totals, 53/0.

# RIDNOUR, LUKE — G — SUPERSONICS

**PERSONAL:** Born February 13, 1981, in Coeur d' Alene, Idaho. ... 6-2/175. (1.88/79.4). ... Full name: Lukas Robin Ridnour **HIGH SCHOOL:** Blaine (Wash.).
**COLLEGE:** Oregon.
**TRANSACTIONS/CAREER NOTES:** Selected after junior season by Seattle SuperSonics in first round (14th pick overall) of 2003 NBA Draft.

## COLLEGIATE RECORD

**NOTES:** The Sporting News All-America third team (2003).

| Season Team | G | Min. | FGM | FGA | Pct. | FTM | FTA | Pct. | Reb. | Ast. | Pts. | AVERAGES RPG | APG | PPG |
|---|---|---|---|---|---|---|---|---|---|---|---|---|---|---|
| 00-01—Oregon | 28 | 848 | 59 | 174 | .339 | 61 | 77 | .792 | 70 | 106 | 208 | 2.5 | 3.8 | 7.4 |
| 01-02—Oregon | 35 | 1209 | 169 | 361 | .468 | 111 | 128 | .867 | 103 | 176 | 542 | 2.9 | 5.0 | 15.5 |
| 02-03—Oregon | 33 | 1169 | 203 | 470 | .432 | 162 | 184 | .880 | 112 | 218 | 649 | 3.4 | 6.6 | 19.7 |
| Totals | 96 | 3226 | 431 | 1005 | .429 | 334 | 389 | .859 | 285 | 500 | 1399 | 3.0 | 5.2 | 14.6 |

Three-point field goals: 2000-01, 29-for-99 (.293). 2001-02, 93-for-211 (.441). 2002-03, 81-for-212 (.382). Totals, 203-for-522 (.389).

## NBA REGULAR-SEASON RECORD

| Season Team | G | Min. | FGM | FGA | Pct. | FTM | FTA | Pct. | REBOUNDS Off. | Def. | Tot. | Ast. | St. | Blk. | TO | Pts. | AVERAGES RPG | APG | PPG |
|---|---|---|---|---|---|---|---|---|---|---|---|---|---|---|---|---|---|---|---|
| 03-04—Seattle | 69 | 1114 | 145 | 350 | .414 | 65 | 79 | .823 | 35 | 73 | 108 | 163 | 52 | 7 | 80 | 382 | 1.6 | 2.4 | 5.5 |
| 04-05—Seattle | 82 | 2571 | 299 | 739 | .405 | 159 | 180 | .883 | 55 | 149 | 204 | 483 | 94 | 23 | 149 | 824 | 2.5 | 5.9 | 10.0 |
| Totals | 151 | 3685 | 444 | 1089 | .408 | 224 | 259 | .865 | 90 | 222 | 312 | 646 | 146 | 30 | 229 | 1206 | 2.1 | 4.3 | 8.0 |

Three-point field goals: 2003-04, 27-for-80 (.338). 2004-05, 67-for-178 (.376). Totals, 94-for-258 (.364).
Personal fouls/disqualifications: 2003-04, 105/0. 2004-05, 185/0. Totals, 290/0.

## NBA PLAYOFF RECORD

| Season Team | G | Min. | FGM | FGA | Pct. | FTM | FTA | Pct. | REBOUNDS Off. | Def. | Tot. | Ast. | St. | Blk. | TO | Pts. | AVERAGES RPG | APG | PPG |
|---|---|---|---|---|---|---|---|---|---|---|---|---|---|---|---|---|---|---|---|
| 04-05—Seattle | 11 | 378 | 42 | 107 | .393 | 19 | 20 | .950 | 10 | 26 | 36 | 47 | 13 | 8 | 18 | 107 | 3.3 | 4.3 | 9.7 |

Three-point field goals: 2004-05, 4-for-17 (.235). Totals, 4-for-17 (.235).
Personal fouls/disqualifications: 2004-05, 23/0. Totals, 23/0.

# ROBINSON, BERNARD — G/F — BOBCATS

**PERSONAL:** Born December 26, 1980, in Washington, D.C. ... 6-6/210. (1.98/95.3). ... Full name: Bernard Gregory Robinson
**HIGH SCHOOL:** Dunbar (Washington, D.C.).
**COLLEGE:** Michigan.
**TRANSACTIONS/CAREER NOTES:** Selected by Charlotte Bobcats in second round (45th pick overall) of 2004 NBA Draft.

## COLLEGIATE RECORD

| Season Team | G | Min. | FGM | FGA | Pct. | FTM | FTA | Pct. | Reb. | Ast. | Pts. | AVERAGES RPG | APG | PPG |
|---|---|---|---|---|---|---|---|---|---|---|---|---|---|---|
| 00-01—Michigan | 28 | 813 | 142 | 304 | .467 | 93 | 116 | .802 | 136 | 63 | 404 | 4.9 | 2.3 | 14.4 |
| 01-02—Michigan | 29 | 825 | 134 | 328 | .409 | 71 | 83 | .855 | 132 | 71 | 351 | 4.6 | 2.4 | 12.1 |
| 02-03—Michigan | 29 | 933 | 124 | 272 | .456 | 78 | 92 | .848 | 178 | 100 | 339 | 6.1 | 3.4 | 11.7 |
| 03-04—Michigan | 34 | 1095 | 150 | 347 | .432 | 94 | 122 | .770 | 194 | 130 | 411 | 5.7 | 3.8 | 12.1 |
| Totals | 120 | 3666 | 550 | 1251 | .440 | 336 | 413 | .814 | 640 | 364 | 1505 | 5.3 | 3.0 | 12.5 |

Three-point field goals: 2000-01, 27-for-78 (.346). 2001-02, 12-for-49 (.245). 2002-03, 13-for-37 (.351). 2003-04, 17-for-68 (.250). Totals, 69-for-232 (.297).

## NBA REGULAR-SEASON RECORD

| Season Team | G | Min. | FGM | FGA | Pct. | FTM | FTA | Pct. | REBOUNDS Off. | Def. | Tot. | Ast. | St. | Blk. | TO | Pts. | AVERAGES RPG | APG | PPG |
|---|---|---|---|---|---|---|---|---|---|---|---|---|---|---|---|---|---|---|---|
| 04-05—Charlotte | 31 | 328 | 36 | 81 | .444 | 18 | 26 | .692 | 14 | 34 | 48 | 30 | 11 | 4 | 20 | 93 | 1.5 | 1.0 | 3.0 |

Three-point field goals: 2004-05, 3-for-8 (.375). Totals, 3-for-8 (.375).
Personal fouls/disqualifications: 2004-05, 42/1. Totals, 42/1.

# ROBINSON, CLIFFORD — F — NETS

**PERSONAL:** Born December 16, 1966, in Buffalo. ... 6-10/225. (2.08/102.1). ... Full name: Clifford Ralph Robinson
**HIGH SCHOOL:** Riverside (Buffalo).
**COLLEGE:** Connecticut.
**TRANSACTIONS/CAREER NOTES:** Selected by Portland Trail Blazers in second round (36th pick overall) of 1989 NBA Draft. ... Signed as free agent by Phoenix Suns (August 25, 1997). ... Traded by Suns to Detroit Pistons for G/F Jud Buechler and F John Wallace (July 18, 2001). ... Traded by Pistons with G Pepe Sanchez to Golden State Warriors for G Bob Sura (August 21, 2003). ... Traded by Warriors to New Jersey Nets for second-round picks in 2005 and 2007 NBA drafts.

## COLLEGIATE RECORD

| Season Team | G | Min. | FGM | FGA | Pct. | FTM | FTA | Pct. | Reb. | Ast. | Pts. | AVERAGES RPG | APG | PPG |
|---|---|---|---|---|---|---|---|---|---|---|---|---|---|---|
| 85-86—Connecticut | 28 | 442 | 60 | 164 | .366 | 36 | 59 | .610 | 88 | 14 | 156 | 3.1 | 0.5 | 5.6 |
| 86-87—Connecticut | 16 | 556 | 107 | 255 | .420 | 69 | 121 | .570 | 119 | 32 | 289 | 7.4 | 2.0 | 18.1 |
| 87-88—Connecticut | 34 | 1079 | 222 | 463 | .479 | 156 | 238 | .655 | 233 | 44 | 600 | 6.9 | 1.3 | 17.6 |
| 88-89—Connecticut | 31 | 974 | 235 | 500 | .470 | 145 | 212 | .684 | 228 | 46 | 619 | 7.4 | 1.5 | 20.0 |
| Totals | 109 | 3051 | 624 | 1382 | .452 | 406 | 630 | .644 | 668 | 136 | 1664 | 6.1 | 1.2 | 15.3 |

Three-point field goals: 1986-87, 6-for-18 (.333). 1988-89, 4-for-12 (.333). Totals, 10-for-30 (.333).

## NBA REGULAR-SEASON RECORD

**HONORS:** NBA Sixth Man Award (1993). ... NBA All-Defensive second team (2000, 2002).

| Season Team | G | Min. | FGM | FGA | Pct. | FTM | FTA | Pct. | REBOUNDS Off. | Def. | Tot. | Ast. | St. | Blk. | TO | Pts. | RPG | APG | PPG |
|---|---|---|---|---|---|---|---|---|---|---|---|---|---|---|---|---|---|---|---|
| 89-90—Portland | 82 | 1565 | 298 | 751 | .397 | 138 | 251 | .550 | 110 | 198 | 308 | 72 | 53 | 53 | 129 | 746 | 3.8 | 0.9 | 9.1 |
| 90-91—Portland | 82 | 1940 | 373 | 806 | .463 | 205 | 314 | .653 | 123 | 226 | 349 | 151 | 78 | 76 | 133 | 957 | 4.3 | 1.8 | 11.7 |
| 91-92—Portland | 82 | 2124 | 398 | 854 | .466 | 219 | 330 | .664 | 140 | 276 | 416 | 137 | 85 | 107 | 154 | 1016 | 5.1 | 1.7 | 12.4 |
| 92-93—Portland | 82 | 2575 | 632 | 1336 | .473 | 287 | 416 | .690 | 165 | 377 | 542 | 182 | 98 | 163 | 173 | 1570 | 6.6 | 2.2 | 19.1 |
| 93-94—Portland | 82 | 2853 | 641 | 1404 | .457 | 352 | 460 | .765 | 164 | 386 | 550 | 159 | 118 | 111 | 169 | 1647 | 6.7 | 1.9 | 20.1 |
| 94-95—Portland | 75 | 2725 | 597 | 1320 | .452 | 265 | 382 | .694 | 152 | 271 | 423 | 198 | 79 | 82 | 158 | 1601 | 5.6 | 2.6 | 21.3 |
| 95-96—Portland | 78 | 2980 | 553 | 1306 | .423 | 360 | 542 | .664 | 123 | 320 | 443 | 190 | 86 | 68 | 194 | 1644 | 5.7 | 2.4 | 21.1 |
| 96-97—Portland | 81 | 3077 | 444 | 1043 | .426 | 215 | 309 | .696 | 90 | 231 | 321 | 261 | 99 | 66 | 172 | 1224 | 4.0 | 3.2 | 15.1 |
| 97-98—Phoenix | 80 | 2359 | 429 | 895 | .479 | 248 | 360 | .689 | 152 | 258 | 410 | 170 | 92 | 90 | 140 | 1133 | 5.1 | 2.1 | 14.2 |
| 98-99—Phoenix | 50 | 1740 | 299 | 629 | .475 | 163 | 234 | .697 | 69 | 158 | 227 | 128 | 75 | 59 | 88 | 819 | 4.5 | 2.6 | 16.4 |
| 99-00—Phoenix | 80 | 2839 | 530 | 1142 | .464 | 298 | 381 | .782 | 105 | 254 | 359 | 224 | 90 | 61 | 166 | 1478 | 4.5 | 2.8 | 18.5 |
| 00-01—Phoenix | 82 | 2751 | 501 | 1186 | .422 | 253 | 357 | .709 | 105 | 229 | 334 | 237 | 87 | 82 | 186 | 1345 | 4.1 | 2.9 | 16.4 |
| 01-02—Detroit | 80 | 2855 | 454 | 1069 | .425 | 143 | 206 | .694 | 79 | 307 | 386 | 202 | 89 | 95 | 151 | 1166 | 4.8 | 2.5 | 14.6 |
| 02-03—Detroit | 81 | 2825 | 372 | 935 | .398 | 161 | 238 | .676 | 81 | 237 | 318 | 268 | 87 | 88 | 158 | 992 | 3.9 | 3.3 | 12.2 |
| 03-04—Golden State | 82 | 2846 | 366 | 945 | .387 | 123 | 173 | .711 | 54 | 268 | 322 | 271 | 68 | 73 | 173 | 967 | 3.9 | 3.3 | 11.8 |
| 04-05—Golden St.-N.J. | 71 | 1689 | 202 | 523 | .386 | 62 | 97 | .639 | 54 | 155 | 209 | 104 | 62 | 53 | 66 | 533 | 2.9 | 1.5 | 7.5 |
| **Totals** | 1250 | 39743 | 7089 | 16144 | .439 | 3492 | 5050 | .691 | 1766 | 4151 | 5917 | 2954 | 1346 | 1327 | 2410 | 18838 | 4.7 | 2.4 | 15.1 |

Three-point field goals: 1989-90, 12-for-44 (.273). 1990-91, 6-for-19 (.316). 1991-92, 1-for-11 (.091). 1992-93, 19-for-77 (.247). 1993-94, 13-for-53 (.245). 1994-95, 142-for-383 (.371). 1995-96, 178-for-471 (.378). 1996-97, 121-for-350 (.346). 1997-98, 27-for-84 (.321). 1998-99, 58-for-139 (.417). 1999-00, 120-for-324 (.370). 2000-01, 90-for-249 (.361). 2001-02, 115-for-304 (.378). 2002-03, 87-for-259 (.336). 2003-04, 112-for-314 (.357). 2004-05, 67-for-193 (.347). Totals, 1168-for-3274 (.357).

Personal fouls/disqualifications: 1989-90, 226/4. 1990-91, 263/2. 1991-92, 274/11. 1992-93, 287/8. 1993-94, 263/0. 1994-95, 240/3. 1995-96, 248/3. 1996-97, 251/6. 1997-98, 249/5. 1998-99, 153/2. 1999-00, 239/3. 2000-01, 258/6. 2001-02, 243/4. 2002-03, 259/5. 2003-04, 237/2. 2004-05, 181/3. Totals, 3871/67.

## NBA PLAYOFF RECORD

| Season Team | G | Min. | FGM | FGA | Pct. | FTM | FTA | Pct. | REBOUNDS Off. | Def. | Tot. | Ast. | St. | Blk. | TO | Pts. | RPG | APG | PPG |
|---|---|---|---|---|---|---|---|---|---|---|---|---|---|---|---|---|---|---|---|
| 89-90—Portland | 21 | 391 | 54 | 151 | .358 | 29 | 52 | .558 | 32 | 55 | 87 | 23 | 19 | 24 | 25 | 137 | 4.1 | 1.1 | 6.5 |
| 90-91—Portland | 16 | 354 | 63 | 117 | .538 | 38 | 69 | .551 | 24 | 39 | 63 | 18 | 7 | 16 | 25 | 165 | 3.9 | 1.1 | 10.3 |
| 91-92—Portland | 21 | 522 | 91 | 197 | .462 | 44 | 77 | .571 | 25 | 63 | 88 | 43 | 22 | 21 | 28 | 227 | 4.2 | 2.0 | 10.8 |
| 92-93—Portland | 4 | 131 | 16 | 61 | .262 | 9 | 22 | .409 | 10 | 7 | 17 | 6 | 6 | 7 | 8 | 41 | 4.3 | 1.5 | 10.3 |
| 93-94—Portland | 4 | 149 | 28 | 68 | .412 | 7 | 8 | .875 | 11 | 14 | 25 | 10 | 3 | 6 | 11 | 65 | 6.3 | 2.5 | 16.3 |
| 94-95—Portland | 3 | 119 | 17 | 47 | .362 | 9 | 16 | .563 | 7 | 12 | 19 | 8 | 2 | 1 | 8 | 47 | 6.3 | 2.7 | 15.7 |
| 95-96—Portland | 5 | 181 | 21 | 61 | .344 | 28 | 37 | .757 | 4 | 14 | 18 | 8 | 7 | 5 | 16 | 76 | 3.6 | 1.6 | 15.2 |
| 96-97—Portland | 4 | 161 | 17 | 47 | .362 | 11 | 16 | .688 | 12 | 15 | 27 | 12 | 2 | 4 | 10 | 48 | 6.8 | 3.0 | 12.0 |
| 97-98—Phoenix | 4 | 92 | 9 | 33 | .273 | 7 | 9 | .778 | 6 | 6 | 12 | 3 | 3 | 2 | 5 | 25 | 3.0 | 0.8 | 6.3 |
| 98-99—Phoenix | 3 | 117 | 19 | 40 | .475 | 7 | 11 | .636 | 7 | 9 | 16 | 8 | 6 | 1 | 7 | 47 | 5.3 | 2.7 | 15.7 |
| 99-00—Phoenix | 9 | 333 | 56 | 145 | .386 | 33 | 45 | .733 | 18 | 36 | 54 | 19 | 11 | 7 | 18 | 158 | 6.0 | 2.1 | 17.6 |
| 00-01—Phoenix | 4 | 114 | 21 | 50 | .420 | 14 | 22 | .636 | 6 | 10 | 16 | 4 | 6 | 2 | 9 | 60 | 4.0 | 1.0 | 15.0 |
| 01-02—Detroit | 10 | 409 | 45 | 124 | .363 | 24 | 30 | .800 | 5 | 25 | 30 | 29 | 18 | 19 | 21 | 132 | 3.0 | 2.9 | 13.2 |
| 02-03—Detroit | 17 | 525 | 57 | 159 | .358 | 22 | 37 | .595 | 14 | 32 | 46 | 49 | 16 | 13 | 28 | 158 | 2.7 | 2.9 | 9.3 |
| 04-05—New Jersey | 4 | 71 | 11 | 27 | .407 | 2 | 2 | 1.000 | 2 | 8 | 10 | 5 | 3 | 1 | 0 | 28 | 2.5 | 1.3 | 7.0 |
| **Totals** | 129 | 3669 | 525 | 1327 | .396 | 284 | 453 | .627 | 183 | 345 | 528 | 245 | 131 | 129 | 219 | 1414 | 4.1 | 1.9 | 11.0 |

Three-point field goals: 1989-90, 0-for-4. 1990-91, 1-for-3 (.333). 1991-92, 1-for-6 (.167). 1992-93, 0-for-1. 1993-94, 2-for-9 (.222). 1994-95, 4-for-17 (.235). 1995-96, 6-for-23 (.261). 1996-97, 3-for-16 (.188). 1997-98, 0-for-1. 1998-99, 2-for-9 (.222). 1999-00, 13-for-40 (.325). 2000-01, 4-for-16 (.250). 2001-02, 18-for-53 (.340). 2002-03, 22-for-59 (.373). 2004-05, 4-for-14 (.286). Totals, 80-for-271 (.295).

Personal fouls/disqualifications: 1989-90, 71/1. 1990-91, 47/1. 1991-92, 84/3. 1992-93, 17/1. 1993-94, 13/0. 1994-95, 13/0. 1995-96, 19/0. 1996-97, 13/0. 1997-98, 19/1. 1998-99, 12/1. 1999-00, 35/0. 2000-01, 14/0. 2001-02, 28/0. 2002-03, 62/1. 2004-05, 20/1. Totals, 467/10.

## NBA ALL-STAR GAME RECORD

| Season Team | Min. | FGM | FGA | Pct. | FTM | FTA | Pct. | REBOUNDS Off. | Def. | Tot. | Ast. | PF | Dq. | St. | Blk. | TO | Pts. |
|---|---|---|---|---|---|---|---|---|---|---|---|---|---|---|---|---|---|
| 1994—Portland | 18 | 5 | 8 | .625 | 0 | 0 | ... | 1 | 1 | 2 | 5 | 0 | 0 | 1 | 0 | 0 | 10 |

Three-point field goals: 1994, 0-for-1. Totals, 0-for-1 (.000).

## ROBINSON, GLENN  F

**PERSONAL:** Born January 10, 1973, in Gary, Ind. ... 6-7/230. (2.01/104.3). ... Full name: Glenn A. Robinson ... Nickname: Big Dog.
**HIGH SCHOOL:** Roosevelt (Gary, Ind.).
**COLLEGE:** Purdue.
**TRANSACTIONS/CAREER NOTES:** Selected after junior season by Milwaukee Bucks in first round (first pick overall) of 1994 NBA Draft. ... Traded by Bucks to Atlanta Hawks for F Toni Kukoc, F Leon Smith and 2003 first-round draft choice (August 2, 2002). ... Traded by Hawks with a 2006 second-round pick to Philadelphia 76ers in three-team deal in which Hawks acquired F Randy Holcomb, a first-round pick and cash considerations from 76ers and G Terrell Brandon from Minnesota Timberwolves; 76ers also traded F Keith Van Horn to the New York Knicks and acquired F/C Marc Jackson from Timberwolves;Timberwolves acquired G Latrell Sprewell from Knicks (July 23, 2003). ... Traded by 76ers to New Orleans Hornets for F Rodney Rogers and G/F Jamal Mashburn (February 24, 2005). ... Waived by Hornets (March 1, 2005). ... Signed as free agent by San Antonio Spurs (April 4, 2005).
**MISCELLANEOUS:** Member of NBA championship team (2005).

### COLLEGIATE RECORD

**NOTES:** THE SPORTING NEWS College Player of the Year (1994). ... Naismith Award winner (1994). ... Wooden Award winner (1994). ... THE SPORTING NEWS All-America first team (1994). ... THE SPORTING NEWS All-America second team (1993). ... Led NCAA Division I with 30.3 points per game (1994).

| Season Team | G | Min. | FGM | FGA | Pct. | FTM | FTA | Pct. | Reb. | Ast. | Pts. | RPG | APG | PPG |
|---|---|---|---|---|---|---|---|---|---|---|---|---|---|---|
| 91-92—Purdue | | | | | | Did not play—ineligible. | | | | | | | | |
| 92-93—Purdue | 28 | 1010 | 246 | 519 | .474 | 152 | 205 | .741 | 258 | 49 | 676 | 9.2 | 1.8 | 24.1 |

| Season Team | G | Min. | FGM | FGA | Pct. | FTM | FTA | Pct. | Reb. | Ast. | Pts. | RPG | APG | PPG |
|---|---|---|---|---|---|---|---|---|---|---|---|---|---|---|
| 93-94—Purdue ............ | 34 | 1166 | 368 | 762 | .483 | 215 | 270 | .796 | 344 | 66 | 1030 | 10.1 | 1.9 | 30.3 |
| Totals ................... | 62 | 2176 | 614 | 1281 | .479 | 367 | 475 | .773 | 602 | 115 | 1706 | 9.7 | 1.9 | 27.5 |

Three-point field goals: 1992-93, 32-for-80 (.400). 1993-94, 79-for-208 (.380). Totals, 111-for-288 (.385).

## NBA REGULAR-SEASON RECORD

**HONORS:** NBA All-Rookie first team (1995).

| Season Team | G | Min. | FGM | FGA | Pct. | FTM | FTA | Pct. | REBOUNDS Off. | Def. | Tot. | Ast. | St. | Blk. | TO | Pts. | RPG | APG | PPG |
|---|---|---|---|---|---|---|---|---|---|---|---|---|---|---|---|---|---|---|---|
| 94-95—Milwaukee ...... | 80 | 2958 | 636 | 1410 | .451 | 397 | 499 | .796 | 169 | 344 | 513 | 197 | 115 | 22 | *313 | 1755 | 6.4 | 2.5 | 21.9 |
| 95-96—Milwaukee ...... | 82 | 3249 | 627 | 1382 | .454 | 316 | 389 | .812 | 136 | 368 | 504 | 293 | 95 | 42 | 282 | 1660 | 6.1 | 3.6 | 20.2 |
| 96-97—Milwaukee ...... | 80 | 3114 | 669 | 1438 | .465 | 288 | 364 | .791 | 130 | 372 | 502 | 248 | 103 | 68 | 269 | 1689 | 6.3 | 3.1 | 21.1 |
| 97-98—Milwaukee ...... | 56 | 2294 | 534 | 1136 | .470 | 215 | 266 | .808 | 82 | 225 | 307 | 158 | 69 | 34 | 200 | 1308 | 5.5 | 2.8 | 23.4 |
| 98-99—Milwaukee ...... | 47 | 1579 | 347 | 756 | .459 | 140 | 161 | .870 | 73 | 203 | 276 | 100 | 46 | 41 | 106 | 865 | 5.9 | 2.1 | 18.4 |
| 99-00—Milwaukee ...... | 81 | 2909 | 690 | 1461 | .472 | 227 | 283 | .802 | 107 | 378 | 485 | 193 | 78 | 41 | 223 | 1693 | 6.0 | 2.4 | 20.9 |
| 00-01—Milwaukee ...... | 76 | 2813 | 684 | 1460 | .468 | 251 | 306 | .820 | 124 | 402 | 526 | 252 | 86 | 62 | 219 | 1674 | 6.9 | 3.3 | 22.0 |
| 01-02—Milwaukee ...... | 66 | 2346 | 536 | 1147 | .467 | 236 | 282 | .837 | 70 | 336 | 406 | 168 | 97 | 41 | 174 | 1366 | 6.2 | 2.5 | 20.7 |
| 02-03—Atlanta ......... | 69 | 2591 | 539 | 1248 | .432 | 268 | 306 | .876 | 86 | 371 | 457 | 205 | 91 | 26 | 248 | 1436 | 6.6 | 3.0 | 20.8 |
| 03-04—Philadelphia ... | 42 | 1336 | 275 | 614 | .448 | 114 | 137 | .832 | 46 | 143 | 189 | 57 | 42 | 9 | 106 | 698 | 4.5 | 1.4 | 16.6 |
| 04-05—San Antonio .... | 9 | 157 | 34 | 77 | .442 | 20 | 23 | .870 | 4 | 20 | 24 | 8 | 4 | 3 | 7 | 90 | 2.7 | 0.9 | 10.0 |
| Totals ................ | 688 | 25346 | 5571 | 12129 | .459 | 2472 | 3016 | .820 | 1027 | 3162 | 4189 | 1879 | 826 | 389 | 2147 | 14234 | 6.1 | 2.7 | 20.7 |

Three-point field goals: 1994-95, 86-for-268 (.321). 1995-96, 90-for-263 (.342). 1996-97, 63-for-180 (.350). 1997-98, 25-for-65 (.385). 1998-99, 31-for-79 (.392). 1999-00, 86-for-237 (.363). 2000-01, 55-for-184 (.299). 2001-02, 58-for-178 (.326). 2002-03, 90-for-263 (.342). 2003-04, 34-for-100 (.340). 2004-05, 2-for-6 (.333). Totals, 620-for-1823 (.340).

Personal fouls/disqualifications: 1994-95, 234/2. 1995-96, 236/2. 1996-97, 225/5. 1997-98, 164/2. 1998-99, 114/1. 1999-00, 212/3. 2000-01, 191/2. 2001-02, 173/1. 2002-03, 183/0. 2003-04, 96/1. 2004-05, 19/0. Totals, 1847/19.

## NBA PLAYOFF RECORD

| Season Team | G | Min. | FGM | FGA | Pct. | FTM | FTA | Pct. | REBOUNDS Off. | Def. | Tot. | Ast. | St. | Blk. | TO | Pts. | RPG | APG | PPG |
|---|---|---|---|---|---|---|---|---|---|---|---|---|---|---|---|---|---|---|---|
| 98-99—Milwaukee ...... | 3 | 118 | 21 | 51 | .412 | 16 | 18 | .889 | 4 | 21 | 25 | 5 | 3 | 2 | 10 | 62 | 8.3 | 1.7 | 20.7 |
| 99-00—Milwaukee ...... | 5 | 174 | 32 | 79 | .405 | 11 | 13 | .846 | 0 | 21 | 21 | 13 | 8 | 4 | 15 | 77 | 4.2 | 2.6 | 15.4 |
| 00-01—Milwaukee ...... | 18 | 687 | 138 | 322 | .429 | 50 | 56 | .893 | 26 | 90 | 116 | 60 | 11 | 24 | 46 | 350 | 6.4 | 3.3 | 19.4 |
| 04-05—San Antonio .... | 13 | 113 | 16 | 45 | .356 | 15 | 17 | .882 | 2 | 19 | 21 | 1 | 3 | 7 | 6 | 50 | 1.6 | 0.1 | 3.8 |
| Totals ................. | 39 | 1092 | 207 | 497 | .416 | 92 | 104 | .885 | 32 | 151 | 183 | 79 | 25 | 37 | 77 | 539 | 4.7 | 2.0 | 13.8 |

Three-point field goals: 1998-99, 4-for-8 (.500). 1999-00, 2-for-7 (.286). 2000-01, 24-for-62 (.387). 2004-05, 3-for-10 (.300). Totals, 33-for-87 (.379).

Personal fouls/disqualifications: 1998-99, 5/0. 1999-00, 18/0. 2000-01, 43/1. 2004-05, 20/1. Totals, 86/2.

## NBA ALL-STAR GAME RECORD

| Season Team | Min. | FGM | FGA | Pct. | FTM | FTA | Pct. | REBOUNDS Off. | Def. | Tot. | Ast. | PF | Dq. | St. | Blk. | TO | Pts. |
|---|---|---|---|---|---|---|---|---|---|---|---|---|---|---|---|---|---|
| 2000—Milwaukee ............ | 17 | 5 | 10 | .500 | 0 | 0 | ... | 2 | 4 | 6 | 0 | 0 | 0 | 0 | 0 | 0 | 10 |
| 2001—Milwaukee ............ | 18 | 4 | 7 | .571 | 0 | 0 | ... | 1 | 3 | 4 | 1 | 0 | 0 | 1 | 1 | 0 | 8 |
| Totals ......................... | 35 | 9 | 17 | .529 | 0 | 0 | ... | 3 | 7 | 10 | 1 | 0 | 0 | 1 | 1 | 0 | 18 |

# ROGERS, RODNEY　　　　　　　　F　　　　　　　76ERS

**PERSONAL:** Born June 20, 1971, in Durham, N.C. ... 6-7/255. (2.01/115.7). ... Full name: Rodney Ray Rogers
**HIGH SCHOOL:** Hillside (Durham, N.C.).
**COLLEGE:** Wake Forest.
**TRANSACTIONS/CAREER NOTES:** Selected after junior season by Denver Nuggets in first round (ninth pick overall) of 1993 NBA Draft. ... Traded by Nuggets with draft rights to G Brent Barry to Los Angeles Clippers for G Randy Woods and draft rights to F Antonio McDyess (June 28, 1995). ... Signed as free agent by Phoenix Suns (August 3, 1999). ... Traded by Suns with G Tony Delk to Boston Celtics for G/F Joe Johnson, G Milt Palacio, G Randy Brown and 2002 first-round draft choice (February 20, 2002). ... Signed as free agent by New Jersey Nets (August 14, 2002). ... Signed as free agent by New Orleans Hornets (August 3, 2004). ... Traded by Hornets with G/F Jamal Mashburn to Philadelphia 76ers for F Glenn Robinson (February 24, 2005).

## COLLEGIATE RECORD

**NOTES:** THE SPORTING NEWS All-America second team (1993).

| Season Team | G | Min. | FGM | FGA | Pct. | FTM | FTA | Pct. | Reb. | Ast. | Pts. | RPG | APG | PPG |
|---|---|---|---|---|---|---|---|---|---|---|---|---|---|---|
| 90-91—Wake Forest ................. | 30 | 895 | 199 | 349 | .570 | 81 | 121 | .669 | 237 | 46 | 489 | 7.9 | 1.5 | 16.3 |
| 91-92—Wake Forest ................. | 29 | 945 | 245 | 399 | .614 | 86 | 126 | .683 | 247 | 81 | 595 | 8.5 | 2.8 | 20.5 |
| 92-93—Wake Forest ................. | 30 | 981 | 239 | 431 | .555 | 134 | 187 | .717 | 221 | 68 | 636 | 7.4 | 2.3 | 21.2 |
| Totals ..................................... | 89 | 2821 | 683 | 1179 | .579 | 301 | 434 | .694 | 705 | 195 | 1720 | 7.9 | 2.2 | 19.3 |

Three-point field goals: 1990-91, 10-for-35 (.286). 1991-92, 19-for-50 (.380). 1992-93, 24-for-67 (.358). Totals, 53-for-152 (.349).

## NBA REGULAR-SEASON RECORD

**HONORS:** NBA Sixth Man Award (2000).

| Season Team | G | Min. | FGM | FGA | Pct. | FTM | FTA | Pct. | REBOUNDS Off. | Def. | Tot. | Ast. | St. | Blk. | TO | Pts. | RPG | APG | PPG |
|---|---|---|---|---|---|---|---|---|---|---|---|---|---|---|---|---|---|---|---|
| 93-94—Denver ............ | 79 | 1406 | 239 | 545 | .439 | 127 | 189 | .672 | 90 | 136 | 226 | 101 | 63 | 48 | 131 | 640 | 2.9 | 1.3 | 8.1 |
| 94-95—Denver ............ | 80 | 2142 | 375 | 769 | .488 | 179 | 275 | .651 | 132 | 253 | 385 | 161 | 95 | 46 | 173 | 979 | 4.8 | 2.0 | 12.2 |
| 95-96—L.A. Clippers ... | 67 | 1950 | 306 | 641 | .477 | 113 | 180 | .628 | 113 | 173 | 286 | 167 | 75 | 35 | 144 | 774 | 4.3 | 2.5 | 11.6 |
| 96-97—L.A. Clippers ... | 81 | 2480 | 408 | 884 | .462 | 191 | 288 | .663 | 137 | 274 | 411 | 222 | 88 | 61 | 221 | 1072 | 5.1 | 2.7 | 13.2 |
| 97-98—L.A. Clippers ... | 76 | 2499 | 426 | 935 | .456 | 225 | 328 | .686 | 155 | 269 | 424 | 202 | 93 | 38 | 193 | 1149 | 5.6 | 2.7 | 15.1 |
| 98-99—L.A. Clippers ... | 47 | 968 | 131 | 297 | .441 | 68 | 101 | .673 | 65 | 114 | 179 | 77 | 47 | 22 | 66 | 348 | 3.8 | 1.6 | 7.4 |
| 99-00—Phoenix ........... | 82 | 2286 | 428 | 881 | .486 | 159 | 249 | .639 | 138 | 309 | 447 | 170 | 94 | 47 | 163 | 1130 | 5.5 | 2.1 | 13.8 |
| 00-01—Phoenix ......... | 82 | 2183 | 377 | 876 | .430 | 188 | 247 | .761 | 94 | 265 | 359 | 180 | 97 | 47 | 157 | 1130 | 4.4 | 2.2 | 12.2 |
| 01-02—Phoenix-Bos. .. | 77 | 1880 | 356 | 756 | .471 | 117 | 149 | .785 | 129 | 219 | 348 | 112 | 66 | 29 | 108 | 917 | 4.5 | 1.5 | 11.9 |

| Season Team | G | Min. | FGM | FGA | Pct. | FTM | FTA | Pct. | Off. | Def. | Tot. | Ast. | St. | Blk. | TO | Pts. | RPG | APG | PPG |
|---|---|---|---|---|---|---|---|---|---|---|---|---|---|---|---|---|---|---|---|
| 02-03—New Jersey | 68 | 1303 | 183 | 455 | .402 | 68 | 90 | .756 | 61 | 202 | 263 | 107 | 50 | 31 | 91 | 478 | 3.9 | 1.6 | 7.0 |
| 03-04—New Jersey | 69 | 1409 | 207 | 505 | .410 | 75 | 98 | .765 | 100 | 207 | 307 | 137 | 59 | 27 | 98 | 539 | 4.4 | 2.0 | 7.8 |
| 04-05—N.O.-Phila. | 58 | 1367 | 172 | 450 | .382 | 52 | 70 | .743 | 61 | 185 | 246 | 86 | 41 | 20 | 86 | 444 | 4.2 | 1.5 | 7.7 |
| Totals | 866 | 21873 | 3608 | 7994 | .451 | 1562 | 2264 | .690 | 1275 | 2606 | 3881 | 1722 | 868 | 451 | 1631 | 9468 | 4.5 | 2.0 | 10.9 |

Three-point field goals: 1993-94, 35-for-92 (.380). 1994-95, 50-for-148 (.338). 1995-96, 49-for-153 (.320). 1996-97, 65-for-180 (.361). 1997-98, 72-for-212 (.340). 1998-99, 18-for-63 (.286). 1999-00, 115-for-262 (.439). 2000-01, 56-for-189 (.296). 2001-02, 88-for-235 (.374). 2002-03, 44-for-132 (.333). 2003-04, 50-for-152 (.329). 2004-05, 48-for-168 (.286). Totals, 690-for-1986 (.347).

Personal fouls/disqualifications: 1993-94, 195/3. 1994-95, 281/7. 1995-96, 216/2. 1996-97, 272/5. 1997-98, 242/5. 1998-99, 140/2. 1999-00, 290/5. 2000-01, 269/5. 2001-02, 226/3. 2002-03, 192/2. 2003-04, 183/2. 2004-05, 172/1. Totals, 2678/42.

### NBA PLAYOFF RECORD

| Season Team | G | Min. | FGM | FGA | Pct. | FTM | FTA | Pct. | Off. | Def. | Tot. | Ast. | St. | Blk. | TO | Pts. | RPG | APG | PPG |
|---|---|---|---|---|---|---|---|---|---|---|---|---|---|---|---|---|---|---|---|
| 93-94—Denver | 12 | 190 | 19 | 49 | .388 | 17 | 27 | .630 | 8 | 13 | 21 | 16 | 7 | 6 | 8 | 61 | 1.8 | 1.3 | 5.1 |
| 94-95—Denver | 3 | 76 | 12 | 22 | .545 | 1 | 4 | .250 | 1 | 11 | 12 | 5 | 3 | 4 | 5 | 26 | 4.0 | 1.7 | 8.7 |
| 96-97—L.A. Clippers | 3 | 85 | 12 | 29 | .414 | 6 | 8 | .750 | 3 | 4 | 7 | 6 | 4 | 3 | 7 | 32 | 2.3 | 2.0 | 10.7 |
| 99-00—Phoenix | 9 | 263 | 48 | 115 | .417 | 23 | 31 | .742 | 16 | 45 | 61 | 14 | 10 | 10 | 15 | 127 | 6.8 | 1.6 | 14.1 |
| 00-01—Phoenix | 4 | 82 | 12 | 40 | .300 | 9 | 14 | .643 | 3 | 11 | 14 | 2 | 2 | 3 | 5 | 35 | 3.5 | 0.5 | 8.8 |
| 01-02—Boston | 16 | 394 | 46 | 108 | .426 | 31 | 35 | .886 | 28 | 60 | 88 | 34 | 16 | 7 | 22 | 142 | 5.5 | 2.1 | 8.9 |
| 02-03—New Jersey | 20 | 350 | 45 | 121 | .372 | 27 | 38 | .711 | 22 | 34 | 56 | 27 | 6 | 3 | 25 | 134 | 2.8 | 1.4 | 6.7 |
| 03-04—New Jersey | 11 | 228 | 23 | 72 | .319 | 16 | 20 | .800 | 9 | 46 | 55 | 12 | 6 | 3 | 17 | 67 | 5.0 | 1.1 | 6.1 |
| 04-05—Philadelphia | 4 | 49 | 6 | 13 | .462 | 5 | 7 | .714 | 0 | 4 | 4 | 1 | 0 | 2 | 1 | 20 | 1.0 | 0.3 | 5.0 |
| Totals | 82 | 1717 | 223 | 569 | .392 | 135 | 184 | .734 | 90 | 228 | 318 | 117 | 54 | 41 | 105 | 644 | 3.9 | 1.4 | 7.9 |

Three-point field goals: 1993-94, 6-for-19 (.316). 1994-95, 1-for-4 (.250). 1996-97, 2-for-10 (.200). 1999-00, 8-for-36 (.222). 2000-01, 2-for-10 (.200). 2001-02, 19-for-52 (.365). 2002-03, 17-for-42 (.405). 2003-04, 5-for-22 (.227). 2004-05, 3-for-8 (.375). Totals, 63-for-203 (.310).

Personal fouls/disqualifications: 1993-94, 25/0. 1994-95, 13/1. 1996-97, 13/0. 1999-00, 31/1. 2000-01, 16/0. 2001-02, 42/1. 2002-03, 51/0. 2003-04, 31/1. 2004-05, 4/0. Totals, 226/4.

# ROSE, JALEN  G  RAPTORS

**PERSONAL:** Born January 30, 1973, in Detroit. ... 6-8/210. (2.03/95.3). ... Son of Jimmy Walker, guard with Detroit Pistons (1967-68 through 1971-72), Houston Rockets (1972-73 and 1973-74), Kansas City/Omaha Kings (1973-74 and 1974-75) and Kansas City Kings (1975-76). ... Name pronounced JAY-lin.
**HIGH SCHOOL:** Southwestern (Detroit).
**COLLEGE:** Michigan.
**TRANSACTIONS/CAREER NOTES:** Selected after junior season by Denver Nuggets in first round (13th pick overall) of 1994 NBA Draft. ... Traded by Nuggets with F Reggie Williams and 1996 first-round draft choice to Indiana Pacers for G Mark Jackson, G Ricky Pierce and 1996 first-round draft choice (June 13, 1996). ... Traded by Pacers with G Travis Best, G Norman Richardson and conditional second-round draft choice to Chicago Bulls for C Brad Miller, G Ron Mercer, G/F Ron Artest and G Kevin Ollie (February 19, 2002). ... Traded by Bulls with F Lonny Baxter and F Donyell Marshall to Toronto Raptors for F/C Antonio Davis, F Chris Jefferies and F Jerome Williams (December 1, 2003).

### COLLEGIATE RECORD

**NOTES:** THE SPORTING NEWS All-America first team (1994).

| Season Team | G | Min. | FGM | FGA | Pct. | FTM | FTA | Pct. | Reb. | Ast. | Pts. | RPG | APG | PPG |
|---|---|---|---|---|---|---|---|---|---|---|---|---|---|---|
| 91-92—Michigan | 34 | 1126 | 206 | 424 | .486 | 149 | 197 | .756 | 146 | 135 | 597 | 4.3 | 4.0 | 17.6 |
| 92-93—Michigan | 36 | 1232 | 203 | 455 | .446 | 116 | 161 | .720 | 150 | 140 | 555 | 4.2 | 3.9 | 15.4 |
| 93-94—Michigan | 32 | 1152 | 220 | 477 | .461 | 141 | 192 | .734 | 181 | 126 | 636 | 5.7 | 3.9 | 19.9 |
| Totals | 102 | 3510 | 629 | 1356 | .464 | 406 | 550 | .738 | 477 | 401 | 1788 | 4.7 | 3.9 | 17.5 |

Three-point field goals: 1991-92, 36-for-111 (.324). 1992-93, 33-for-103 (.320). 1993-94, 55-for-155 (.355). Totals, 124-for-369 (.336).

### NBA REGULAR-SEASON RECORD

**HONORS:** NBA Most Improved Player (2000). ... NBA All-Rookie second team (1995).

| Season Team | G | Min. | FGM | FGA | Pct. | FTM | FTA | Pct. | Off. | Def. | Tot. | Ast. | St. | Blk. | TO | Pts. | RPG | APG | PPG |
|---|---|---|---|---|---|---|---|---|---|---|---|---|---|---|---|---|---|---|---|
| 94-95—Denver | 81 | 1798 | 227 | 500 | .454 | 173 | 234 | .739 | 57 | 160 | 217 | 389 | 65 | 22 | 160 | 663 | 2.7 | 4.8 | 8.2 |
| 95-96—Denver | 80 | 2134 | 290 | 604 | .480 | 191 | 277 | .690 | 46 | 214 | 260 | 495 | 53 | 39 | 234 | 803 | 3.3 | 6.2 | 10.0 |
| 96-97—Indiana | 66 | 1188 | 172 | 377 | .456 | 117 | 156 | .750 | 27 | 94 | 121 | 155 | 57 | 18 | 107 | 482 | 1.8 | 2.3 | 7.3 |
| 97-98—Indiana | 82 | 1706 | 290 | 607 | .478 | 166 | 228 | .728 | 28 | 167 | 195 | 155 | 56 | 14 | 132 | 771 | 2.4 | 1.9 | 9.4 |
| 98-99—Indiana | 49 | 1238 | 200 | 496 | .403 | 125 | 158 | .791 | 34 | 120 | 154 | 93 | 50 | 15 | 72 | 542 | 3.1 | 1.9 | 11.1 |
| 99-00—Indiana | 80 | 2978 | 563 | 1196 | .470 | 471 | 254 | .307 | 42 | 345 | 387 | 320 | 84 | 49 | 188 | 1457 | 4.8 | 4.0 | 18.2 |
| 00-01—Indiana | 72 | 2943 | 567 | 1242 | .457 | 285 | 344 | .828 | 37 | 322 | 359 | 435 | 65 | 43 | 211 | 1478 | 5.0 | 6.0 | 20.5 |
| 01-02—Indiana-Chic. | 83 | 3153 | 663 | 1458 | .455 | 281 | 335 | .839 | 43 | 330 | 373 | 355 | 78 | 45 | 201 | 1696 | 4.5 | 4.3 | 20.4 |
| 02-03—Chicago | 82 | 3351 | 642 | 1583 | .406 | 399 | 467 | .854 | 68 | 283 | 351 | 395 | 72 | 23 | 285 | 1816 | 4.3 | 4.8 | 22.1 |
| 03-04—Chicago-Tor. | 66 | 2497 | 383 | 952 | .402 | 187 | 231 | .810 | 34 | 232 | 266 | 329 | 51 | 22 | 208 | 1022 | 4.0 | 5.0 | 15.5 |
| 04-05—Toronto | 81 | 2710 | 527 | 1159 | .455 | 333 | 390 | .854 | 44 | 232 | 276 | 209 | 63 | 10 | 180 | 1495 | 3.4 | 2.6 | 18.5 |
| Totals | 822 | 25696 | 4524 | 10174 | .445 | 2511 | 3127 | .803 | 460 | 2499 | 2959 | 3330 | 694 | 300 | 1978 | 12225 | 3.6 | 4.1 | 14.9 |

Three-point field goals: 1994-95, 36-for-114 (.316). 1995-96, 32-for-108 (.296). 1996-97, 21-for-72 (.292). 1997-98, 25-for-73 (.342). 1998-99, 17-for-65 (.262). 1999-00, 77-for-196 (.393). 2000-01, 59-for-174 (.339). 2001-02, 89-for-246 (.362). 2002-03, 133-for-359 (.370). 2003-04, 69-for-202 (.342). 2004-05, 108-for-274 (.394). Totals, 666-for-1883 (.354).

Personal fouls/disqualifications: 1994-95, 206/0. 1995-96, 229/3. 1996-97, 136/1. 1997-98, 171/0. 1998-99, 128/0. 1999-00, 234/1. 2000-01, 230/2. 2001-02, 251/2. 2002-03, 271/2. 2003-04, 184/2. 2004-05, 190/0. Totals, 2230/13.

### NBA PLAYOFF RECORD

| Season Team | G | Min. | FGM | FGA | Pct. | FTM | FTA | Pct. | Off. | Def. | Tot. | Ast. | St. | Blk. | TO | Pts. | RPG | APG | PPG |
|---|---|---|---|---|---|---|---|---|---|---|---|---|---|---|---|---|---|---|---|
| 94-95—Denver | 3 | 99 | 13 | 28 | .464 | 3 | 5 | .600 | 4 | 7 | 11 | 18 | 3 | 2 | 9 | 30 | 3.7 | 6.0 | 10.0 |
| 97-98—Indiana | 15 | 293 | 48 | 100 | .480 | 20 | 27 | .741 | 1 | 26 | 27 | 28 | 11 | 6 | 25 | 122 | 1.8 | 1.9 | 8.1 |
| 98-99—Indiana | 13 | 355 | 61 | 138 | .442 | 28 | 34 | .824 | 11 | 20 | 31 | 32 | 13 | 5 | 25 | 158 | 2.4 | 2.5 | 12.2 |

| Season Team | G | Min. | FGM | FGA | Pct. | FTM | FTA | Pct. | REBOUNDS Off. | Def. | Tot. | Ast. | St. | Blk. | TO | Pts. | AVERAGES RPG | APG | PPG |
|---|---|---|---|---|---|---|---|---|---|---|---|---|---|---|---|---|---|---|---|
| 99-00—Indiana............ | 23 | 964 | 171 | 391 | .437 | 107 | 133 | .805 | 10 | 91 | 101 | 78 | 16 | 11 | 50 | 479 | 4.4 | 3.4 | 20.8 |
| 00-01—Indiana............ | 4 | 164 | 30 | 79 | .380 | 7 | 7 | 1.000 | 3 | 15 | 18 | 11 | 6 | 1 | 9 | 72 | 4.5 | 2.8 | 18.0 |
| Totals ................... | 58 | 1875 | 323 | 736 | .439 | 165 | 206 | .801 | 29 | 159 | 188 | 167 | 49 | 25 | 118 | 861 | 3.2 | 2.9 | 14.8 |

Three-point field goals: 1994-95, 1-for-4 (.250). 1997-98, 6-for-16 (.375). 1998-99, 8-for-23 (.348). 1999-00, 30-for-70 (.429). 2000-01, 5-for-16 (.313). Totals, 50-for-129 (.388).

Personal fouls/disqualifications: 1994-95, 9/0. 1997-98, 37/0. 1998-99, 39/0. 1999-00, 71/0. 2000-01, 18/0. Totals, 174/0.

# ROSE, MALIK — F — KNICKS

**PERSONAL:** Born November 23, 1974, in Philadelphia. ... 6-7/255. (2.01/115.7). ... Full name: Malik Jabari Rose ... Name pronounced Ma-leek.
**HIGH SCHOOL:** Overbrook (Philadelphia).
**COLLEGE:** Drexel.
**TRANSACTIONS/CAREER NOTES:** Selected by Charlotte Hornets in second round (44th pick overall) of 1996 NBA Draft. ... Signed as free agent by San Antonio Spurs (September 29, 1997). ... Traded by Spurs with conditional first-round picks in 2005 and 2006 NBA drafts to New York Knicks for F Nazr Mohammed and G Jamison Brewer (February 24, 2005).
**MISCELLANEOUS:** Member of NBA championship team (1999, 2003).

## COLLEGIATE RECORD

| Season Team | G | Min. | FGM | FGA | Pct. | FTM | FTA | Pct. | Reb. | Ast. | Pts. | AVERAGES RPG | APG | PPG |
|---|---|---|---|---|---|---|---|---|---|---|---|---|---|---|
| 92-93—Drexel.......................... | 29 | 820 | 144 | 287 | .502 | 107 | 190 | .563 | 330 | 10 | 395 | 11.4 | 0.3 | 13.6 |
| 93-94—Drexel.......................... | 30 | 875 | 154 | 296 | .520 | 110 | 202 | .545 | 371 | 20 | 418 | 12.4 | 0.7 | 13.9 |
| 94-95—Drexel.......................... | 30 | 984 | 216 | 384 | .563 | 152 | 213 | .714 | 404 | 36 | 584 | 13.5 | 1.2 | 19.5 |
| 95-96—Drexel.......................... | 31 | 972 | 219 | 368 | .595 | 182 | 255 | .714 | 409 | 53 | 627 | 13.2 | 1.7 | 20.2 |
| Totals ..................................... | 120 | 3651 | 733 | 1335 | .549 | 551 | 860 | .641 | 1514 | 119 | 2024 | 12.6 | 1.0 | 16.9 |

Three-point field goals: 1994-95, 0-for-3. 1995-96, 7-for-21 (.333). Totals, 7-for-24 (.292).

## NBA REGULAR-SEASON RECORD

| Season Team | G | Min. | FGM | FGA | Pct. | FTM | FTA | Pct. | REBOUNDS Off. | Def. | Tot. | Ast. | St. | Blk. | TO | Pts. | AVERAGES RPG | APG | PPG |
|---|---|---|---|---|---|---|---|---|---|---|---|---|---|---|---|---|---|---|---|
| 96-97—Charlotte ......... | 54 | 525 | 61 | 128 | .477 | 38 | 62 | .613 | 70 | 94 | 164 | 32 | 28 | 17 | 41 | 160 | 3.0 | 0.6 | 3.0 |
| 97-98—San Antonio .... | 53 | 429 | 59 | 136 | .434 | 39 | 61 | .639 | 40 | 50 | 90 | 19 | 21 | 7 | 44 | 158 | 1.7 | 0.4 | 3.0 |
| 98-99—San Antonio .... | 47 | 608 | 93 | 201 | .463 | 98 | 146 | .671 | 90 | 92 | 182 | 29 | 40 | 22 | 56 | 284 | 3.9 | 0.6 | 6.0 |
| 99-00—San Antonio .... | 74 | 1341 | 176 | 385 | .457 | 143 | 198 | .722 | 133 | 202 | 335 | 47 | 35 | 52 | 99 | 496 | 4.5 | 0.6 | 6.7 |
| 00-01—San Antonio .... | 57 | 1219 | 160 | 368 | .435 | 114 | 160 | .713 | 95 | 213 | 308 | 48 | 58 | 40 | 74 | 437 | 5.4 | 0.8 | 7.7 |
| 01-02—San Antonio .... | 82 | 1725 | 293 | 633 | .463 | 185 | 257 | .720 | 172 | 320 | 492 | 61 | 70 | 42 | 140 | 772 | 6.0 | 0.7 | 9.4 |
| 02-03—San Antonio .... | 79 | 1933 | 289 | 630 | .459 | 242 | 306 | .791 | 148 | 358 | 506 | 124 | 57 | 40 | 170 | 822 | 6.4 | 1.6 | 10.4 |
| 03-04—San Antonio .... | 67 | 1256 | 173 | 404 | .428 | 183 | 225 | .813 | 110 | 210 | 320 | 69 | 36 | 24 | 112 | 529 | 4.8 | 1.0 | 7.9 |
| 04-05—S.A.-N.Y. ......... | 76 | 1475 | 198 | 441 | .449 | 137 | 186 | .737 | 129 | 212 | 341 | 59 | 46 | 16 | 102 | 534 | 4.5 | 0.8 | 7.0 |
| Totals ................... | 589 | 10511 | 1502 | 3326 | .452 | 1179 | 1601 | .736 | 987 | 1751 | 2738 | 488 | 392 | 260 | 838 | 4192 | 4.6 | 0.8 | 7.1 |

Three-point field goals: 1996-97, 0-for-2. 1997-98, 1-for-3 (.333). 1998-99, 0-for-3 (.333). 2000-01, 3-for-17 (.176). 2001-02, 1-for-12 (.083). 2002-03, 2-for-5 (.400). 2003-04, 0-for-3. 2004-05, 1-for-10 (.100). Totals, 9-for-56 (.161).

Personal fouls/disqualifications: 1996-97, 114/3. 1997-98, 79/1. 1998-99, 120/0. 1999-00, 232/2. 2000-01, 148/1. 2001-02, 208/2. 2002-03, 206/2. 2003-04, 164/1. 2004-05, 208/2. Totals, 1479/14.

## NBA PLAYOFF RECORD

| Season Team | G | Min. | FGM | FGA | Pct. | FTM | FTA | Pct. | REBOUNDS Off. | Def. | Tot. | Ast. | St. | Blk. | TO | Pts. | AVERAGES RPG | APG | PPG |
|---|---|---|---|---|---|---|---|---|---|---|---|---|---|---|---|---|---|---|---|
| 96-97—Charlotte ......... | 2 | 12 | 2 | 4 | .500 | 0 | 0 | ... | 4 | 1 | 5 | 1 | 0 | 0 | 2 | 4 | 2.5 | 0.5 | 2.0 |
| 97-98—San Antonio .... | 5 | 18 | 4 | 6 | .667 | 2 | 4 | .500 | 3 | 4 | 7 | 1 | 1 | 0 | 4 | 10 | 1.4 | 0.2 | 2.0 |
| 98-99—San Antonio .... | 17 | 194 | 14 | 38 | .368 | 18 | 26 | .692 | 17 | 22 | 39 | 3 | 7 | 4 | 10 | 46 | 2.3 | 0.2 | 2.7 |
| 99-00—San Antonio .... | 4 | 83 | 8 | 18 | .444 | 5 | 9 | .556 | 5 | 14 | 19 | 1 | 2 | 3 | 7 | 21 | 4.8 | 0.3 | 5.3 |
| 00-01—San Antonio .... | 13 | 215 | 23 | 55 | .418 | 17 | 20 | .850 | 16 | 33 | 49 | 4 | 3 | 1 | 10 | 64 | 3.8 | 0.3 | 4.9 |
| 01-02—San Antonio .... | 10 | 292 | 46 | 96 | .479 | 37 | 50 | .740 | 27 | 52 | 79 | 14 | 10 | 5 | 12 | 129 | 7.9 | 1.4 | 12.9 |
| 02-03—San Antonio .... | 24 | 560 | 75 | 179 | .419 | 72 | 94 | .766 | 49 | 89 | 138 | 24 | 16 | 11 | 43 | 222 | 5.8 | 1.0 | 9.3 |
| 03-04—San Antonio .... | 7 | 58 | 4 | 16 | .250 | 2 | 4 | .500 | 12 | 5 | 17 | 6 | 4 | 2 | 8 | 10 | 2.4 | 0.9 | 1.4 |
| Totals ................... | 82 | 1432 | 176 | 412 | .427 | 153 | 207 | .739 | 133 | 220 | 353 | 54 | 43 | 26 | 96 | 506 | 4.3 | 0.7 | 6.2 |

Three-point field goals: 2000-01, 1-for-3 (.333). 2001-02, 0-for-1. 2002-03, 0-for-3. 2003-04, 0-for-2. Totals, 1-for-9 (.111).

Personal fouls/disqualifications: 1996-97, 2/0. 1997-98, 2/0. 1998-99, 52/0. 1999-00, 12/0. 2000-01, 38/0. 2001-02, 31/0. 2002-03, 72/0. 2003-04, 6/0. Totals, 215/0.

# ROSS, QUINTON — G — CLIPPERS

**PERSONAL:** Born April 30, 1981, in Dallas ... 6-6/193. (1.98/87.5). ... Full name: Quinton Lenord Ross.
**HIGH SCHOOL:** Justin F Kimball (Dallas).
**COLLEGE:** Southern Methodist.
**TRANSACTIONS/CAREER NOTES:** Not drafted by an NBA franchise. ... Signed as free agent by Los Angeles Clippers (August 16, 2004).

## COLLEGIATE RECORD

| Season Team | G | Min. | FGM | FGA | Pct. | FTM | FTA | Pct. | Reb. | Ast. | Pts. | AVERAGES RPG | APG | PPG |
|---|---|---|---|---|---|---|---|---|---|---|---|---|---|---|
| 99-00—SMU.............................. | 30 | 585 | 76 | 175 | .434 | 50 | 78 | .641 | 120 | 40 | 224 | 4.0 | 1.3 | 7.5 |
| 00-01—SMU.............................. | 30 | 970 | 146 | 307 | .476 | 86 | 116 | .741 | 152 | 59 | 426 | 5.1 | 2.0 | 14.2 |
| 01-02—SMU.............................. | 29 | 1004 | 162 | 386 | .420 | 123 | 160 | .769 | 188 | 60 | 505 | 6.5 | 2.1 | 17.4 |
| 02-03—SMU.............................. | 30 | 1056 | 191 | 422 | .453 | 184 | 232 | .793 | 191 | 63 | 608 | 6.4 | 2.1 | 20.3 |
| Totals ..................................... | 119 | 3615 | 575 | 1290 | .446 | 443 | 586 | .756 | 651 | 222 | 1763 | 5.5 | 1.9 | 14.8 |

Three-point field goals: 1999-00, 22-for-61 (.361). 2000-01, 48-for-129 (.372). 2001-02, 58-for-182 (.319). 2002-03, 42-for-141 (.298). Totals, 170-for-513 (.331).

## BELGIAN LEAGUE RECORD

| Season Team | G | Min. | FGM | FGA | Pct. | FTM | FTA | Pct. | Reb. | Ast. | Pts. | AVERAGES | | |
|---|---|---|---|---|---|---|---|---|---|---|---|---|---|---|
| | | | | | | | | | | | | RPG | APG | PPG |
| 03-04—Telindus Oostende | 31 | ... | 186 | 365 | .510 | 77 | 109 | .706 | 150 | 56 | 517 | 4.8 | 1.8 | 16.7 |

Three-point field goals: 2003-04, 68-for-153 (.444). Totals, 68-for-153 (.444).

## NBA REGULAR-SEASON RECORD

| Season Team | G | Min. | FGM | FGA | Pct. | FTM | FTA | Pct. | REBOUNDS | | | Ast. | St. | Blk. | TO | Pts. | AVERAGES | | |
|---|---|---|---|---|---|---|---|---|---|---|---|---|---|---|---|---|---|---|---|
| | | | | | | | | | Off. | Def. | Tot. | | | | | | RPG | APG | PPG |
| 04-05—L.A. Clippers | 78 | 1659 | 161 | 373 | .432 | 74 | 110 | .673 | 59 | 151 | 210 | 109 | 51 | 22 | 54 | 397 | 2.7 | 1.4 | 5.1 |

Three-point field goals: 2004-05, 1-for-4 (.250). Totals, 1-for-4 (.250).
Personal fouls/disqualifications: 2004-05, 165/0. Totals, 165/0.

# RUFFIN, MICHAEL — F — WIZARDS

**PERSONAL:** Born January 21, 1977, in Denver. ... 6-8/248. (2.03/112.5). ... Full name: Michael David Ruffin
**HIGH SCHOOL:** Cherry Creek (Englewood, Colo.).
**COLLEGE:** Tulsa.
**TRANSACTIONS/CAREER NOTES:** Selected by Chicago Bulls in second round (32nd overall) of 1999 NBA Draft. ... Waived by Bulls (October 25, 2001). ... Signed as free agent by Philadelphia 76ers (November 22, 2001). ... Waived by 76ers (December 28, 2001). ... Played in Spain (2001-03). ... Signed as free agent by Utah Jazz (August 6, 2003) ... Signed as free agent by Washington Wizards (August 3, 2004).

## COLLEGIATE RECORD

| Season Team | G | Min. | FGM | FGA | Pct. | FTM | FTA | Pct. | Reb. | Ast. | Pts. | AVERAGES | | |
|---|---|---|---|---|---|---|---|---|---|---|---|---|---|---|
| | | | | | | | | | | | | RPG | APG | PPG |
| 95-96—Tulsa | 30 | 689 | 78 | 146 | .534 | 57 | 123 | .463 | 232 | 22 | 213 | 7.7 | 0.7 | 7.1 |
| 96-97—Tulsa | 34 | 965 | 98 | 174 | .563 | 95 | 150 | .633 | 341 | 37 | 291 | 10.0 | 1.1 | 8.6 |
| 97-98—Tulsa | 31 | 1030 | 109 | 217 | .502 | 104 | 154 | .675 | 296 | 46 | 322 | 9.5 | 1.5 | 10.4 |
| 98-99—Tulsa | 33 | 1063 | 117 | 222 | .527 | 149 | 247 | .603 | 342 | 45 | 383 | 10.4 | 1.4 | 11.6 |
| Totals | 128 | 3747 | 402 | 759 | .530 | 405 | 674 | .601 | 1211 | 150 | 1209 | 9.5 | 1.2 | 9.4 |

Three-point field goals: 1995-96, 0-for-1. 1996-97, 0-for-1. 1997-98, 0-for-4. 1998-99, 0-for-4. Totals, 0-for-10 (.000).

## NBA REGULAR-SEASON RECORD

| Season Team | G | Min. | FGM | FGA | Pct. | FTM | FTA | Pct. | REBOUNDS | | | Ast. | St. | Blk. | TO | Pts. | AVERAGES | | |
|---|---|---|---|---|---|---|---|---|---|---|---|---|---|---|---|---|---|---|---|
| | | | | | | | | | Off. | Def. | Tot. | | | | | | RPG | APG | PPG |
| 99-00—Chicago | 71 | 975 | 58 | 138 | .420 | 43 | 88 | .489 | 117 | 133 | 250 | 44 | 26 | 26 | 59 | 159 | 3.5 | 0.6 | 2.2 |
| 00-01—Chicago | 45 | 879 | 40 | 90 | .444 | 39 | 77 | .506 | 101 | 161 | 262 | 39 | 30 | 38 | 46 | 119 | 5.8 | 0.9 | 2.6 |
| 01-02—Philadelphia | 15 | 169 | 7 | 26 | .269 | 2 | 8 | .250 | 23 | 28 | 51 | 5 | 5 | 8 | 11 | 16 | 3.4 | 0.3 | 1.1 |
| 03-04—Utah | 41 | 733 | 38 | 117 | .325 | 16 | 38 | .421 | 78 | 129 | 207 | 41 | 22 | 21 | 42 | 92 | 5.0 | 1.0 | 2.2 |
| 04-05—Washington | 79 | 1262 | 41 | 99 | .414 | 29 | 67 | .433 | 157 | 175 | 332 | 64 | 43 | 41 | 44 | 111 | 4.2 | 0.8 | 1.4 |
| Totals | 251 | 4018 | 184 | 470 | .391 | 129 | 278 | .464 | 476 | 626 | 1102 | 193 | 126 | 134 | 202 | 497 | 4.4 | 0.8 | 2.0 |

Three-point field goals: 2004-05, 0-for-1. Totals, 0-for-1 (.000).
Personal fouls/disqualifications: 1999-00, 170/1. 2000-01, 131/2. 2001-02, 23/0. 2003-04, 103/1. 2004-05, 193/4. Totals, 620/8.

## NBA PLAYOFF RECORD

| Season Team | G | Min. | FGM | FGA | Pct. | FTM | FTA | Pct. | REBOUNDS | | | Ast. | St. | Blk. | TO | Pts. | AVERAGES | | |
|---|---|---|---|---|---|---|---|---|---|---|---|---|---|---|---|---|---|---|---|
| | | | | | | | | | Off. | Def. | Tot. | | | | | | RPG | APG | PPG |
| 04-05—Washington | 9 | 156 | 7 | 10 | .700 | 9 | 16 | .563 | 15 | 22 | 37 | 9 | 3 | 3 | 4 | 23 | 4.1 | 1.0 | 2.6 |

Personal fouls/disqualifications: 2004-05, 33/2. Totals, 33/2.

## SPANISH RECORD

| Season Team | G | Min. | FGM | FGA | Pct. | FTM | FTA | Pct. | Reb. | Ast. | Pts. | AVERAGES | | |
|---|---|---|---|---|---|---|---|---|---|---|---|---|---|---|
| | | | | | | | | | | | | RPG | APG | PPG |
| 01-02—Caprabo Lleida | 20 | 577 | 47 | 95 | .495 | 24 | 50 | .480 | 163 | 14 | 118 | 8.2 | 0.7 | 5.9 |
| 02-03—Caprabo Lleida | 34 | 855 | 81 | 165 | .491 | 53 | 116 | .457 | 251 | 31 | 215 | 7.4 | 0.9 | 6.3 |
| Totals | 54 | 1432 | 128 | 260 | .492 | 77 | 166 | .464 | 414 | 45 | 333 | 7.7 | 0.8 | 6.2 |

Three-point field goals: 2001-02, 0-for-2. Totals, 0-for-2 (.000).
Personal fouls/disqualifications: 2002-03, 106/0. Totals, 106/0.

# RUSH, KAREEM — G — BOBCATS

**PERSONAL:** Born October 30, 1980, in Kansas City, Mo. ... 6-6/215. (1.98/97.5). ... Full name: Kareem Lamar Rush
**HIGH SCHOOL:** Pembroke Hill (Kansas City, Mo.).
**COLLEGE:** Missouri.
**TRANSACTIONS/CAREER NOTES:** Selected after junior season by Toronto Raptors in first round (20th pick overall) of 2002 NBA Draft. ... Draft rights traded by Raptors with F Tracy Murray to Los Angeles Lakers for G Lindsey Hunter and draft rights to F Chris Jeffries (June 26, 2002). ... Traded by Lakers to Charlotte Bobcats for second-round draft choices in 2005 and 2008 (December 6, 2004).

## COLLEGIATE RECORD

| Season Team | G | Min. | FGM | FGA | Pct. | FTM | FTA | Pct. | Reb. | Ast. | Pts. | AVERAGES | | |
|---|---|---|---|---|---|---|---|---|---|---|---|---|---|---|
| | | | | | | | | | | | | RPG | APG | PPG |
| 99-00—Missouri | 22 | 591 | 109 | 216 | .505 | 59 | 78 | .756 | 94 | 34 | 323 | 4.3 | 1.5 | 14.7 |
| 00-01—Missouri | 26 | 796 | 192 | 434 | .442 | 96 | 120 | .800 | 174 | 51 | 549 | 6.7 | 2.0 | 21.1 |
| 01-02—Missouri | 36 | 1149 | 249 | 585 | .426 | 103 | 134 | .769 | 188 | 89 | 712 | 5.2 | 2.5 | 19.8 |
| Totals | 84 | 2536 | 550 | 1235 | .445 | 258 | 332 | .777 | 456 | 174 | 1584 | 5.4 | 2.1 | 18.9 |

Three-point field goals: 1999-00, 46-for-108 (.426). 2000-01, 69-for-154 (.448). 2001-02, 111-for-274 (.405). Totals, 226-for-536 (.422).

## NBA REGULAR-SEASON RECORD

| Season Team | G | Min. | FGM | FGA | Pct. | FTM | FTA | Pct. | REBOUNDS Off. | Def. | Tot. | Ast. | St. | Blk. | TO | Pts. | AVERAGES RPG | APG | PPG |
|---|---|---|---|---|---|---|---|---|---|---|---|---|---|---|---|---|---|---|---|
| 02-03—L.A. Lakers ..... | 76 | 872 | 96 | 244 | .393 | 16 | 23 | .696 | 26 | 68 | 94 | 68 | 10 | 11 | 63 | 227 | 1.2 | 0.9 | 3.0 |
| 03-04—L.A. Lakers ..... | 72 | 1244 | 190 | 432 | .440 | 31 | 52 | .596 | 20 | 77 | 97 | 59 | 33 | 20 | 48 | 459 | 1.3 | 0.8 | 6.4 |
| 04-05—L.A.L.-Char..... | 48 | 968 | 157 | 406 | .387 | 37 | 48 | .771 | 20 | 69 | 89 | 68 | 20 | 7 | 47 | 402 | 1.9 | 1.4 | 8.4 |
| **Totals** ................... | 196 | 3084 | 443 | 1082 | .409 | 84 | 123 | .683 | 66 | 214 | 280 | 195 | 63 | 38 | 158 | 1088 | 1.4 | 1.0 | 5.6 |

Three-point field goals: 2002-03, 19-for-68 (.279). 2003-04, 48-for-138 (.348). 2004-05, 51-for-137 (.372). Totals, 118-for-343 (.344).
Personal fouls/disqualifications: 2002-03, 71/0. 2003-04, 109/0. 2004-05, 74/0. Totals, 254/0.

## NBA PLAYOFF RECORD

| Season Team | G | Min. | FGM | FGA | Pct. | FTM | FTA | Pct. | REBOUNDS Off. | Def. | Tot. | Ast. | St. | Blk. | TO | Pts. | AVERAGES RPG | APG | PPG |
|---|---|---|---|---|---|---|---|---|---|---|---|---|---|---|---|---|---|---|---|
| 02-03—L.A. Lakers ..... | 9 | 64 | 11 | 29 | .379 | 4 | 4 | 1.000 | 2 | 1 | 3 | 2 | 1 | 0 | 3 | 30 | 0.3 | 0.2 | 3.3 |
| 03-04—L.A. Lakers ..... | 22 | 315 | 30 | 78 | .385 | 2 | 3 | .667 | 0 | 16 | 16 | 17 | 10 | 3 | 14 | 82 | 0.7 | 0.8 | 3.7 |
| **Totals** ................... | 31 | 379 | 41 | 107 | .383 | 6 | 7 | .857 | 2 | 17 | 19 | 19 | 11 | 3 | 17 | 112 | 0.6 | 0.6 | 3.6 |

Three-point field goals: 2002-03, 4-for-11 (.364). 2003-04, 20-for-50 (.400). Totals, 24-for-61 (.393).
Personal fouls/disqualifications: 2002-03, 2/0. 2003-04, 33/0. Totals, 35/0.

# RUSSELL, BRYON      F

**PERSONAL:** Born December 31, 1970, in San Bernardino, Calif. ... 6-7/225. (2.01/102.1). ... Full name: Bryon Demetrise Russell
**HIGH SCHOOL:** San Bernardino (Calif.).
**COLLEGE:** Long Beach State.
**TRANSACTIONS/CAREER NOTES:** Selected by Utah Jazz in second round (45th pick overall) of 1993 NBA Draft. ... Signed as free agent by Washington Wizards (September 10, 2002). ... Signed as free agent by Los Angeles Lakers (October 1, 2003). ... Signed as free agent by Denver Nuggets (October 6, 2004).

## COLLEGIATE RECORD

| Season Team | G | Min. | FGM | FGA | Pct. | FTM | FTA | Pct. | Reb. | Ast. | Pts. | AVERAGES RPG | APG | PPG |
|---|---|---|---|---|---|---|---|---|---|---|---|---|---|---|
| 89-90—Long Beach State ........... | | | | | | Did not play—ineligible. | | | | | | | | |
| 90-91—Long Beach State .......... | 28 | 552 | 83 | 193 | .430 | 45 | 69 | .652 | 162 | 41 | 220 | 5.8 | 1.5 | 7.9 |
| 91-92—Long Beach State .......... | 26 | 776 | 126 | 227 | .555 | 99 | 151 | .656 | 192 | 30 | 362 | 7.4 | 1.2 | 13.9 |
| 92-93—Long Beach State .......... | 32 | 1006 | 153 | 285 | .537 | 104 | 143 | .727 | 213 | 66 | 421 | 6.7 | 2.1 | 13.2 |
| **Totals** ...................................... | 86 | 2334 | 362 | 705 | .513 | 248 | 363 | .683 | 567 | 137 | 1003 | 6.6 | 1.6 | 11.7 |

Three-point field goals: 1990-91, 9-for-28 (.321). 1991-92, 11-for-28 (.393). 1992-93, 11-for-34 (.324). Totals, 31-for-90 (.344).

## NBA REGULAR-SEASON RECORD

| Season Team | G | Min. | FGM | FGA | Pct. | FTM | FTA | Pct. | REBOUNDS Off. | Def. | Tot. | Ast. | St. | Blk. | TO | Pts. | AVERAGES RPG | APG | PPG |
|---|---|---|---|---|---|---|---|---|---|---|---|---|---|---|---|---|---|---|---|
| 93-94—Utah ............... | 67 | 1121 | 135 | 279 | .484 | 62 | 101 | .614 | 61 | 120 | 181 | 54 | 68 | 19 | 55 | 334 | 2.7 | 0.8 | 5.0 |
| 94-95—Utah ............... | 63 | 860 | 104 | 238 | .437 | 62 | 93 | .667 | 44 | 97 | 141 | 34 | 48 | 11 | 42 | 283 | 2.2 | 0.5 | 4.5 |
| 95-96—Utah ............... | 59 | 577 | 56 | 142 | .394 | 48 | 67 | .716 | 28 | 62 | 90 | 29 | 29 | 8 | 36 | 174 | 1.5 | 0.5 | 2.9 |
| 96-97—Utah ............... | 81 | 2525 | 297 | 620 | .479 | 171 | 244 | .701 | 79 | 252 | 331 | 123 | 129 | 27 | 94 | 873 | 4.1 | 1.5 | 10.8 |
| 97-98—Utah ............... | 82 | 2219 | 226 | 525 | .430 | 213 | 278 | .766 | 78 | 248 | 326 | 101 | 90 | 31 | 81 | 738 | 4.0 | 1.2 | 9.0 |
| 98-99—Utah ............... | 50 | 1770 | 217 | 468 | .464 | 136 | 171 | .795 | 65 | 201 | 266 | 74 | 76 | 15 | 76 | 622 | 5.3 | 1.5 | 12.4 |
| 99-00—Utah ............... | 82 | 2900 | 408 | 914 | .446 | 237 | 316 | .750 | 99 | 328 | 427 | 158 | 128 | 23 | 101 | 1159 | 5.2 | 1.9 | 14.1 |
| 00-01—Utah ............... | 78 | 2473 | 308 | 700 | .440 | 222 | 285 | .779 | 94 | 236 | 330 | 160 | 96 | 20 | 113 | 933 | 4.2 | 2.1 | 12.0 |
| 01-02—Utah ............... | 66 | 1998 | 222 | 584 | .380 | 115 | 140 | .821 | 79 | 216 | 295 | 136 | 64 | 19 | 110 | 636 | 4.5 | 2.1 | 9.6 |
| 02-03—Washington .... | 70 | 1388 | 108 | 306 | .353 | 53 | 69 | .768 | 43 | 165 | 208 | 72 | 70 | 7 | 55 | 315 | 3.0 | 1.0 | 4.5 |
| 03-04—L.A. Lakers .... | 72 | 945 | 98 | 244 | .402 | 50 | 65 | .769 | 32 | 114 | 146 | 71 | 32 | 12 | 37 | 289 | 2.0 | 1.0 | 4.0 |
| 04-05—Denver .......... | 70 | 1026 | 95 | 252 | .377 | 61 | 77 | .792 | 50 | 122 | 172 | 72 | 44 | 11 | 35 | 307 | 2.5 | 1.0 | 4.4 |
| **Totals** | 840 | 19802 | 2274 | 5272 | .431 | 1430 | 1906 | .750 | 752 | 2161 | 2913 | 1084 | 874 | 203 | 835 | 6663 | 3.5 | 1.3 | 7.9 |

Three-point field goals: 1993-94, 2-for-22 (.091). 1994-95, 13-for-44 (.295). 1995-96, 14-for-40 (.350). 1996-97, 108-for-264 (.409). 1997-98, 73-for-214 (.341). 1998-99, 52-for-147 (.354). 1999-00, 106-for-268 (.396). 2000-01, 95-for-230 (.413). 2001-02, 77-for-226 (.341). 2002-03, 46-for-140 (.329). 2003-04, 43-for-112 (.384). 2004-05, 56-for-149 (.376). Totals, 685-for-1856 (.369).
Personal fouls/disqualifications: 1993-94, 138/0. 1994-95, 101/0. 1995-96, 66/0. 1996-97, 237/2. 1997-98, 229/2. 1998-99, 154/3. 1999-00, 255/3. 2000-01, 229/1. 2001-02, 205/1. 2002-03, 130/1. 2003-04, 110/0. 2004-05, 130/0. Totals, 1984/13.

## NBA PLAYOFF RECORD

| Season Team | G | Min. | FGM | FGA | Pct. | FTM | FTA | Pct. | REBOUNDS Off. | Def. | Tot. | Ast. | St. | Blk. | TO | Pts. | AVERAGES RPG | APG | PPG |
|---|---|---|---|---|---|---|---|---|---|---|---|---|---|---|---|---|---|---|---|
| 93-94—Utah ............... | 6 | 36 | 4 | 10 | .400 | 6 | 6 | 1.000 | 4 | 5 | 9 | 3 | 0 | 0 | 1 | 16 | 1.5 | 0.5 | 2.7 |
| 94-95—Utah ............... | 2 | 13 | 4 | 7 | .571 | 1 | 2 | .500 | 1 | 1 | 2 | 3 | 1 | 0 | 0 | 11 | 1.0 | 1.5 | 5.5 |
| 95-96—Utah ............... | 18 | 459 | 58 | 124 | .468 | 31 | 38 | .816 | 17 | 58 | 75 | 22 | 23 | 9 | 10 | 172 | 4.2 | 1.2 | 9.6 |
| 96-97—Utah ............... | 20 | 758 | 89 | 193 | .461 | 31 | 43 | .721 | 18 | 74 | 92 | 27 | 21 | 6 | 20 | 245 | 4.6 | 1.4 | 12.3 |
| 97-98—Utah ............... | 20 | 698 | 69 | 147 | .469 | 58 | 81 | .716 | 12 | 81 | 93 | 22 | 21 | 5 | 17 | 219 | 4.7 | 1.1 | 11.0 |
| 98-99—Utah ............... | 11 | 387 | 49 | 115 | .426 | 26 | 36 | .722 | 17 | 50 | 67 | 13 | 20 | 2 | 11 | 133 | 6.1 | 1.2 | 12.1 |
| 99-00—Utah ............... | 10 | 371 | 48 | 114 | .421 | 31 | 41 | .756 | 9 | 43 | 52 | 21 | 16 | 5 | 15 | 140 | 5.2 | 2.1 | 14.0 |
| 00-01—Utah ............... | 5 | 214 | 25 | 56 | .446 | 11 | 12 | .917 | 4 | 32 | 36 | 15 | 3 | 1 | 2 | 71 | 7.2 | 3.0 | 14.2 |
| 01-02—Utah ............... | 4 | 120 | 9 | 36 | .250 | 4 | 4 | 1.000 | 6 | 11 | 17 | 7 | 4 | 0 | 9 | 28 | 4.3 | 1.8 | 7.0 |
| 03-04—L.A. Lakers .... | 6 | 16 | 0 | 3 | .000 | 0 | 0 | ... | 1 | 0 | 1 | 2 | 1 | 0 | 0 | 0 | 0.2 | 0.3 | 0.0 |
| 04-05—Denver .......... | 3 | 9 | 0 | 1 | .000 | 3 | 3 | 1.000 | 0 | 0 | 0 | 0 | 0 | 0 | 0 | 3 | 0.0 | 0.0 | 1.0 |
| **Totals** | 105 | 3081 | 355 | 806 | .440 | 202 | 266 | .759 | 89 | 355 | 444 | 135 | 110 | 28 | 85 | 1038 | 4.2 | 1.3 | 9.9 |

Three-point field goals: 1993-94, 2-for-3 (.667). 1994-95, 2-for-4 (.500). 1995-96, 25-for-53 (.472). 1996-97, 36-for-101 (.356). 1997-98, 23-for-63 (.365). 1998-99, 9-for-36 (.250). 1999-00, 13-for-45 (.289). 2000-01, 10-for-22 (.455). 2001-02, 6-for-15 (.400). 2003-04, 0-for-2. 2004-05, 0-for-1. Totals, 126-for-345 (.365).
Personal fouls/disqualifications: 1993-94, 3/0. 1994-95, 2/0. 1995-96, 42/0. 1996-97, 59/1. 1997-98, 49/0. 1998-99, 37/0. 1999-00, 27/0. 2000-01, 13/0. 2001-02, 15/1. 2003-04, 2/0. Totals, 249/2.

## SALMONS, JOHN G/F 76ERS

**PERSONAL:** Born December 12, 1979, in Philadelphia. ... 6-7/210. (2.01/95.3). ... Full name: John Rashall Salmons
**HIGH SCHOOL:** Plymouth Whitemarsh (Plymouth Meeting, Pa.).
**COLLEGE:** Miami.
**TRANSACTIONS/CAREER NOTES:** Selected by San Antonio Spurs in first round (26th pick overall) of 2002 NBA Draft. ... Draft rights traded by Spurs with F/C Mark Bryant and draft rights to F Randy Holcomb to Philadelphia 76ers for G Craig Claxton (June 26, 2002).

### COLLEGIATE RECORD

| | | | | | | | | | | | | AVERAGES | | |
|---|---|---|---|---|---|---|---|---|---|---|---|---|---|---|
| Season Team | G | Min. | FGM | FGA | Pct. | FTM | FTA | Pct. | Reb. | Ast. | Pts. | RPG | APG | PPG |
| 98-99—Miami (Fla.) | 29 | 705 | 61 | 127 | .480 | 29 | 40 | .725 | 141 | 57 | 161 | 4.9 | 2.0 | 5.6 |
| 99-00—Miami (Fla.) | 34 | 1104 | 109 | 240 | .454 | 73 | 92 | .793 | 182 | 66 | 320 | 5.4 | 1.9 | 9.4 |
| 00-01—Miami (Fla.) | 29 | 928 | 137 | 289 | .474 | 88 | 111 | .793 | 173 | 115 | 387 | 6.0 | 4.0 | 13.3 |
| 01-02—Miami (Fla.) | 32 | 1077 | 137 | 297 | .461 | 123 | 146 | .842 | 191 | 195 | 419 | 6.0 | 6.1 | 13.1 |
| Totals | 124 | 3814 | 444 | 953 | .466 | 313 | 389 | .805 | 687 | 433 | 1287 | 5.5 | 3.5 | 10.4 |

Three-point field goals: 1998-99, 10-for-41 (.244). 1999-00, 29-for-85 (.341). 2000-01, 25-for-71 (.352). 2001-02, 22-for-71 (.310). Totals, 86-for-268 (.321).

### NBA REGULAR-SEASON RECORD

| | | | | | | | | | REBOUNDS | | | | | | | | AVERAGES | | |
|---|---|---|---|---|---|---|---|---|---|---|---|---|---|---|---|---|---|---|---|
| Season Team | G | Min. | FGM | FGA | Pct. | FTM | FTA | Pct. | Off. | Def. | Tot. | Ast. | St. | Blk. | TO | Pts. | RPG | APG | PPG |
| 02-03—Philadelphia | 64 | 504 | 48 | 116 | .414 | 26 | 35 | .743 | 16 | 43 | 59 | 47 | 17 | 6 | 29 | 132 | 0.9 | 0.7 | 2.1 |
| 03-04—Philadelphia | 77 | 1603 | 161 | 416 | .387 | 71 | 92 | .772 | 38 | 158 | 196 | 134 | 62 | 16 | 77 | 443 | 2.5 | 1.7 | 5.8 |
| 04-05—Philadelphia | 58 | 993 | 85 | 210 | .405 | 35 | 48 | .729 | 12 | 109 | 121 | 114 | 40 | 13 | 51 | 236 | 2.1 | 2.0 | 4.1 |
| Totals | 199 | 3100 | 294 | 742 | .396 | 132 | 175 | .754 | 66 | 310 | 376 | 295 | 119 | 35 | 157 | 811 | 1.9 | 1.5 | 4.1 |

Three-point field goals: 2002-03, 10-for-31 (.323). 2003-04, 50-for-147 (.340). 2004-05, 31-for-91 (.341). Totals, 91-for-269 (.338).
Personal fouls/disqualifications: 2002-03, 53/1. 2003-04, 122/0. 2004-05, 92/1. Totals, 267/2.

### NBA PLAYOFF RECORD

| | | | | | | | | | REBOUNDS | | | | | | | | AVERAGES | | |
|---|---|---|---|---|---|---|---|---|---|---|---|---|---|---|---|---|---|---|---|
| Season Team | G | Min. | FGM | FGA | Pct. | FTM | FTA | Pct. | Off. | Def. | Tot. | Ast. | St. | Blk. | TO | Pts. | RPG | APG | PPG |
| 02-03—Philadelphia | 6 | 16 | 0 | 1 | .000 | 0 | 2 | .000 | 0 | 3 | 3 | 0 | 0 | 0 | 2 | 0 | 0.5 | 0.0 | 0.0 |
| 04-05—Philadelphia | 2 | 4 | 0 | 0 | ... | 0 | 0 | ... | 0 | 0 | 0 | 1 | 0 | 0 | 0 | 0 | 0.0 | 0.5 | 0.0 |
| Totals | 8 | 20 | 0 | 1 | .000 | 0 | 2 | .000 | 0 | 3 | 3 | 1 | 0 | 0 | 2 | 0 | 0.4 | 0.1 | 0.0 |

Three-point field goals: 2002-03, 0-for-1. Totals, 0-for-1 (.000).

## SAMPSON, JAMAL F/C KINGS

**PERSONAL:** Born May 15, 1983, in Inglewood, Calif. ... 6-11/235. (2.11/106.6). ... Full name: Jamal Wesley Sampson
**HIGH SCHOOL:** Mater Dei (Santa Ana, Calif.).
**COLLEGE:** California.
**TRANSACTIONS/CAREER NOTES:** Selected after freshman season by Utah Jazz in second round (47th pick overall) of 2002 NBA Draft. ... Draft rights traded by Jazz with draft rights to F Ryan Humphrey to Orlando Magic for draft rights to C Curtis Borchardt (June 26, 2002). ... Draft rights traded by Magic to Milwaukee Bucks for C Rashard Griffith (June 26, 2002). ... Signed as free agent by Los Angeles Lakers (July 24, 2003). ... Selected by Charlotte Bobcats from Lakers in NBA Expansion Draft (June 22, 2004). ... Waived by Bobcats (February 8, 2005). ... Signed as free agent by Sacramento Kings (August 10, 2005).

### COLLEGIATE RECORD

| | | | | | | | | | | | | AVERAGES | | |
|---|---|---|---|---|---|---|---|---|---|---|---|---|---|---|
| Season Team | G | Min. | FGM | FGA | Pct. | FTM | FTA | Pct. | Reb. | Ast. | Pts. | RPG | APG | PPG |
| 01-02—California | 32 | 797 | 78 | 183 | .426 | 50 | 95 | .526 | 209 | 38 | 206 | 6.5 | 1.2 | 6.4 |

### NBA REGULAR-SEASON RECORD

| | | | | | | | | | REBOUNDS | | | | | | | | AVERAGES | | |
|---|---|---|---|---|---|---|---|---|---|---|---|---|---|---|---|---|---|---|---|
| Season Team | G | Min. | FGM | FGA | Pct. | FTM | FTA | Pct. | Off. | Def. | Tot. | Ast. | St. | Blk. | TO | Pts. | RPG | APG | PPG |
| 02-03—Milwaukee | 5 | 8 | 0 | 2 | .000 | 0 | 0 | ... | 1 | 1 | 2 | 1 | 1 | 0 | 0 | 0 | 0.4 | 0.2 | 0.0 |
| 03-04—L.A. Lakers | 10 | 130 | 11 | 23 | .478 | 7 | 12 | .583 | 23 | 29 | 52 | 7 | 2 | 4 | 6 | 29 | 5.2 | 0.7 | 2.9 |
| 04-05—Charlotte | 23 | 329 | 28 | 62 | .452 | 23 | 39 | .590 | 36 | 86 | 122 | 8 | 4 | 17 | 17 | 79 | 5.3 | 0.3 | 3.4 |
| Totals | 38 | 467 | 39 | 87 | .448 | 30 | 51 | .588 | 60 | 116 | 176 | 16 | 7 | 21 | 23 | 108 | 4.6 | 0.4 | 2.8 |

Personal fouls/disqualifications: 2003-04, 16/0. 2004-05, 53/0. Totals, 69/0.

## SANTIAGO, DANIEL C BUCKS

**PERSONAL:** Born June 24, 1976, in Lubbock, Texas. ... 7-1/250. (2.16/113.4). ... Full name: Daniel Gregg Santiago
**HIGH SCHOOL:** Del Norte (Albuquerque, N.M.).
**JUNIOR COLLEGE:** New Mexico Military Institute.
**COLLEGE:** New Mexico, then St. Vincent College (Pa.).
**TRANSACTIONS/CAREER NOTES:** Not drafted by an NBA franchise. ... Played in Italy (1998-2000). ... Signed as free agent by Phoenix Suns (August 2, 2000). ... Waived by Suns (January 7, 2002). ... Played in Puerto Rico (2001-02). ... Signed as free agent by Milwaukee Bucks (July 17, 2003).
**MISCELLANEOUS:** Member of Puerto Rican Olympic Team (2004).

### COLLEGIATE RECORD

| | | | | | | | | | | | | AVERAGES | | |
|---|---|---|---|---|---|---|---|---|---|---|---|---|---|---|
| Season Team | G | Min. | FGM | FGA | Pct. | FTM | FTA | Pct. | Reb. | Ast. | Pts. | RPG | APG | PPG |
| 94-95—New Mexico Mil. Inst. | 31 | ... | 198 | 319 | .621 | 98 | 151 | .649 | 256 | 47 | 494 | 8.3 | 1.5 | 15.9 |

| Season Team | G | Min. | FGM | FGA | Pct. | FTM | FTA | Pct. | Reb. | Ast. | Pts. | AVERAGES RPG | APG | PPG |
|---|---|---|---|---|---|---|---|---|---|---|---|---|---|---|
| 95-96—New Mexico | 33 | 224 | 36 | 51 | .706 | 35 | 48 | .729 | 51 | 4 | 107 | 1.5 | 0.1 | 3.2 |
| 96-97—New Mexico | 23 | 173 | 29 | 40 | .725 | 29 | 37 | .784 | 35 | 9 | 87 | 1.5 | 0.4 | 3.8 |
| Junior College Totals | 31 | ... | 198 | 319 | .621 | 98 | 151 | .649 | 256 | 47 | 494 | 8.3 | 1.5 | 15.9 |
| 4-Year-College Totals | 56 | 397 | 65 | 91 | .714 | 64 | 85 | .753 | 86 | 13 | 194 | 1.5 | 0.2 | 3.5 |

Three-point field goals: 1996-97, 0-for-1. Totals, 0-for-1 (.000).
Personal fouls/disqualifications: 1994-95, 107/0. 1995-96, 37/0. 1996-97, 20/0. Totals, 164/0.

## NAIA DIVISION II RECORD

| Season Team | G | Min. | FGM | FGA | Pct. | FTM | FTA | Pct. | Reb. | Ast. | Pts. | AVERAGES RPG | APG | PPG |
|---|---|---|---|---|---|---|---|---|---|---|---|---|---|---|
| 97-98—St. Vincent | 33 | 833 | 239 | 355 | .673 | 117 | 174 | .672 | 301 | 48 | 595 | 9.1 | 1.5 | 18.0 |

Personal fouls/disqualifications: 1997-98, 96/0. Totals, 96/0.

## ITALIAN LEAGUE RECORD

| Season Team | G | Min. | FGM | FGA | Pct. | FTM | FTA | Pct. | Reb. | Ast. | Pts. | AVERAGES RPG | APG | PPG |
|---|---|---|---|---|---|---|---|---|---|---|---|---|---|---|
| 98-99—Pall. Varese | 25 | 460 | 49 | 82 | .598 | 54 | 79 | .684 | 89 | 4 | 152 | 3.6 | 0.2 | 6.1 |
| 99-00—Pall. Varese | 24 | 717 | 118 | 210 | .562 | 72 | 112 | .643 | 177 | 16 | 309 | 7.4 | 0.7 | 12.9 |
| 02-03—Virtus Roma | 33 | 978 | 171 | 304 | .563 | 80 | 125 | .640 | 276 | 32 | 423 | 8.4 | 1.0 | 12.8 |
| Totals | 82 | 2155 | 338 | 596 | .567 | 206 | 316 | .652 | 542 | 52 | 884 | 6.6 | 0.6 | 10.8 |

Three-point field goals: 1999-00, 1-for-3 (.333). 2002-03, 1-for-3 (.333). Totals, 2-for-6 (.333).

## NBA REGULAR-SEASON RECORD

| Season Team | G | Min. | FGM | FGA | Pct. | FTM | FTA | Pct. | REBOUNDS Off. | Def. | Tot. | Ast. | St. | Blk. | TO | Pts. | AVERAGES RPG | APG | PPG |
|---|---|---|---|---|---|---|---|---|---|---|---|---|---|---|---|---|---|---|---|
| 00-01—Phoenix | 54 | 581 | 64 | 134 | .478 | 42 | 61 | .689 | 35 | 67 | 102 | 11 | 17 | 21 | 47 | 170 | 1.9 | 0.2 | 3.1 |
| 01-02—Phoenix | 3 | 24 | 4 | 8 | .500 | 0 | 0 | ... | 0 | 7 | 7 | 2 | 0 | 1 | 2 | 8 | 2.3 | 0.7 | 2.7 |
| 03-04—Milwaukee | 54 | 708 | 78 | 163 | .479 | 61 | 90 | .678 | 35 | 97 | 132 | 24 | 19 | 21 | 32 | 217 | 2.4 | 0.4 | 4.0 |
| 04-05—Milwaukee | 11 | 105 | 7 | 21 | .333 | 8 | 11 | .727 | 6 | 13 | 19 | 1 | 3 | 4 | 4 | 22 | 1.7 | 0.1 | 2.0 |
| Totals | 122 | 1418 | 153 | 326 | .469 | 111 | 162 | .685 | 76 | 184 | 260 | 38 | 39 | 47 | 85 | 417 | 2.1 | 0.3 | 3.4 |

Personal fouls/disqualifications: 2000-01, 101/1. 2001-02, 4/0. 2003-04, 98/0. 2004-05, 28/1. Totals, 231/2.

## NBA PLAYOFF RECORD

| Season Team | G | Min. | FGM | FGA | Pct. | FTM | FTA | Pct. | REBOUNDS Off. | Def. | Tot. | Ast. | St. | Blk. | TO | Pts. | AVERAGES RPG | APG | PPG |
|---|---|---|---|---|---|---|---|---|---|---|---|---|---|---|---|---|---|---|---|
| 00-01—Phoenix | 1 | 12 | 1 | 2 | .500 | 0 | 0 | ... | 1 | 4 | 5 | 0 | 0 | 2 | 1 | 2 | 5.0 | 0.0 | 2.0 |
| 03-04—Milwaukee | 1 | 1 | 0 | 0 | ... | 0 | 0 | ... | 0 | 0 | 0 | 0 | 0 | 0 | 0 | 0 | 0.0 | 0.0 | 0.0 |
| Totals | 2 | 13 | 1 | 2 | .500 | 0 | 0 | ... | 1 | 4 | 5 | 0 | 0 | 2 | 1 | 2 | 2.5 | 0.0 | 1.0 |

Personal fouls/disqualifications: 2000-01, 2/0. 2003-04, 1/0. Totals, 3/0.

## PUERTO RICAN RECORD

| Season Team | G | Min. | FGM | FGA | Pct. | FTM | FTA | Pct. | Reb. | Ast. | Pts. | AVERAGES RPG | APG | PPG |
|---|---|---|---|---|---|---|---|---|---|---|---|---|---|---|
| 01-02—Bayamon | 27 | 698 | 168 | 279 | .602 | 69 | 90 | .767 | 187 | 29 | 405 | 6.9 | 1.0 | 1.5 |

Three-point field goals: 2001-02, 0-for-4. Totals, 0-for-4 (.000).

# SCALABRINE, BRIAN                F                CELTICS

**PERSONAL:** Born March 18, 1978, in Long Beach, Calif. ... 6-9/240. (2.06/108.9). ... Full name: Brian David Scalabrine
**HIGH SCHOOL:** Enumclaw (Wash.).
**JUNIOR COLLEGE:** Highline (Wash.).
**COLLEGE:** Southern California.
**TRANSACTIONS/CAREER NOTES:** Selected by New Jersey Nets in second round (35th pick overall) of 2000 NBA Draft. ... Signed as free agent by Boston Celtics (August 2, 2005).

## COLLEGIATE RECORD

| Season Team | G | Min. | FGM | FGA | Pct. | FTM | FTA | Pct. | Reb. | Ast. | Pts. | AVERAGES RPG | APG | PPG |
|---|---|---|---|---|---|---|---|---|---|---|---|---|---|---|
| 96-97—Highline C.C. | 32 | 932 | 207 | 350 | .591 | 108 | 144 | .750 | 308 | 94 | 522 | 9.6 | 2.9 | 16.3 |
| 97-98—Highline C.C. | | | | | Did not play—redshirted. | | | | | | | | | |
| 98-99—Southern California | 28 | 869 | 152 | 286 | .531 | 103 | 130 | .792 | 178 | 68 | 408 | 6.4 | 2.4 | 14.6 |
| 99-00—Southern California | 30 | 1052 | 203 | 382 | .531 | 103 | 144 | .715 | 180 | 85 | 534 | 6.0 | 2.8 | 17.8 |
| 00-01—Southern California | 34 | 1116 | 173 | 362 | .478 | 133 | 166 | .801 | 202 | 96 | 499 | 5.9 | 2.8 | 14.7 |
| Junior College Totals | 32 | 932 | 207 | 350 | .591 | 108 | 144 | .750 | 308 | 94 | 522 | 9.6 | 2.9 | 16.3 |
| 4-Year-College Totals | 92 | 3037 | 528 | 1030 | .513 | 339 | 440 | .770 | 560 | 249 | 1441 | 6.1 | 2.7 | 15.7 |

Three-point field goals: 1996-97, 0-for-6. 1998-99, 1-for-6 (.167). 1999-00, 25-for-62 (.403). 2000-01, 20-for-66 (.303). Totals, 46-for-140 (.329).
Personal fouls/disqualifications: 1996-97, 83/0. 1998-99, 81/0. 1999-00, 87/0. 2000-01, 89/0. Totals, 340/0.

## NBA REGULAR-SEASON RECORD

| Season Team | G | Min. | FGM | FGA | Pct. | FTM | FTA | Pct. | REBOUNDS Off. | Def. | Tot. | Ast. | St. | Blk. | TO | Pts. | AVERAGES RPG | APG | PPG |
|---|---|---|---|---|---|---|---|---|---|---|---|---|---|---|---|---|---|---|---|
| 01-02—New Jersey | 28 | 290 | 23 | 67 | .343 | 11 | 15 | .733 | 12 | 39 | 51 | 21 | 9 | 2 | 24 | 60 | 1.8 | 0.8 | 2.1 |
| 02-03—New Jersey | 59 | 724 | 68 | 169 | .402 | 30 | 36 | .833 | 40 | 101 | 141 | 46 | 16 | 18 | 46 | 180 | 2.4 | 0.8 | 3.1 |
| 03-04—New Jersey | 69 | 928 | 86 | 218 | .394 | 58 | 70 | .829 | 42 | 131 | 173 | 65 | 21 | 14 | 42 | 240 | 2.5 | 0.9 | 3.5 |
| 04-05—New Jersey | 54 | 1167 | 132 | 332 | .398 | 53 | 69 | .768 | 83 | 161 | 244 | 88 | 34 | 18 | 66 | 339 | 4.5 | 1.6 | 6.3 |
| Totals | 210 | 3109 | 309 | 786 | .393 | 152 | 190 | .800 | 177 | 432 | 609 | 220 | 80 | 52 | 178 | 819 | 2.9 | 1.0 | 3.9 |

Three-point field goals: 2001-02, 3-for-10 (.300). 2002-03, 14-for-39 (.359). 2003-04, 10-for-41 (.244). 2004-05, 22-for-68 (.324). Totals, 49-for-158 (.310).
Personal fouls/disqualifications: 2001-02, 39/0. 2002-03, 77/0. 2003-04, 113/0. 2004-05, 111/3. Totals, 340/3.

## NBA PLAYOFF RECORD

| | | | | | | | | REBOUNDS | | | | | | | AVERAGES | | |
|---|---|---|---|---|---|---|---|---|---|---|---|---|---|---|---|---|---|
| Season Team | G | Min. | FGM | FGA | Pct. | FTM | FTA | Pct. | Off. | Def. | Tot. | Ast. | St. | Blk. | TO | Pts. | RPG | APG | PPG |
| 01-02—New Jersey..... | 6 | 14 | 1 | 3 | .333 | 0 | 0 | ... | 1 | 2 | 3 | 0 | 0 | 1 | 1 | 2 | 0.5 | 0.0 | 0.3 |
| 02-03—New Jersey..... | 7 | 20 | 2 | 4 | .500 | 0 | 0 | ... | 1 | 3 | 4 | 0 | 0 | 0 | 1 | 4 | 0.6 | 0.0 | 0.6 |
| 03-04—New Jersey..... | 9 | 73 | 11 | 17 | .647 | 3 | 6 | .500 | 7 | 5 | 12 | 1 | 3 | 0 | 4 | 30 | 1.3 | 0.1 | 3.3 |
| 04-05—New Jersey..... | 4 | 61 | 2 | 11 | .182 | 4 | 4 | 1.000 | 2 | 5 | 7 | 2 | 1 | 2 | 4 | 9 | 1.8 | 0.5 | 2.3 |
| Totals ................. | 26 | 168 | 16 | 35 | .457 | 7 | 10 | .700 | 11 | 15 | 26 | 3 | 4 | 3 | 10 | 45 | 1.0 | 0.1 | 1.7 |

Three-point field goals: 2001-02, 0-for-1. 2002-03, 0-for-1. 2003-04, 5-for-6 (.833). 2004-05, 1-for-4 (.250). Totals, 6-for-12 (.500).
Personal fouls/disqualifications: 2002-03, 3/0. 2003-04, 15/0. 2004-05, 6/0. Totals, 24/0.

---

## SESAY, ANSU      F

**PERSONAL:** Born July 29, 1976, in Greensboro, N.C. ... 6-8/223. (2.03/101.2). ... Full name: Ansu Martin Sesay
**HIGH SCHOOL:** Willowridge (Houston).
**COLLEGE:** Mississippi.
**TRANSACTIONS/CAREER NOTES:** Selected by Dallas Mavericks in second round (30th pick overall) of 1998 NBA Draft. ... Played in Continental Basketball Association with Rockford Lightning (1999-2000) and Quad City Thunder (2000-01). ... Traded by Mavericks with G Dana Barros to Detroit Pistons for F Loy Vaught (October 17, 2000). ... Waived by Pistons (October 18, 2000). ... Signed as free agent by Los Angeles Clippers (September 28, 2001). ... Waived by Clippers (October 12, 2001). ... Played in National Basketball Development League with Greenville Groove (2001-02). ... Signed by Seattle SuperSonics to 10-day contract (March 29, 2002). ... Signed by SuperSonics for remainder of season (April 8, 2002). ... Signed as free agent by Golden State Warriors (October 4, 2004). ... Waived by Warriors (January 3, 2005).
**MISCELLANEOUS:** All-NBDL first team (2002). ... NBDL Most Valuable Player (2002).

### COLLEGIATE RECORD

| | | | | | | | | | | | | AVERAGES | | |
|---|---|---|---|---|---|---|---|---|---|---|---|---|---|---|
| Season Team | G | Min. | FGM | FGA | Pct. | FTM | FTA | Pct. | Reb. | Ast. | Pts. | RPG | APG | PPG |
| 94-95—Mississippi .................... | 27 | 586 | 63 | 178 | .354 | 52 | 76 | .684 | 103 | 32 | 195 | 3.8 | 1.2 | 7.2 |
| 95-96—Mississippi .................... | 25 | 664 | 93 | 235 | .396 | 70 | 99 | .707 | 146 | 44 | 264 | 5.8 | 1.8 | 10.6 |
| 96-97—Mississippi .................... | 29 | 987 | 150 | 329 | .456 | 114 | 152 | .750 | 229 | 71 | 429 | 7.9 | 2.4 | 14.8 |
| 97-98—Mississippi .................... | 29 | 961 | 181 | 397 | .456 | 157 | 216 | .727 | 221 | 80 | 540 | 7.6 | 2.8 | 18.6 |
| Totals ................................ | 110 | 3198 | 487 | 1139 | .428 | 393 | 543 | .724 | 699 | 227 | 1428 | 6.4 | 2.1 | 13.0 |

Three-point field goals: 1994-95, 17-for-72 (.236). 1995-96, 8-for-42 (.190). 1996-97, 15-for-54 (.278). 1997-98, 21-for-60 (.350). Totals, 61-for-228 (.268).

### NBA REGULAR-SEASON RECORD

| | | | | | | | | REBOUNDS | | | | | | | AVERAGES | | |
|---|---|---|---|---|---|---|---|---|---|---|---|---|---|---|---|---|---|
| Season Team | G | Min. | FGM | FGA | Pct. | FTM | FTA | Pct. | Off. | Def. | Tot. | Ast. | St. | Blk. | TO | Pts. | RPG | APG | PPG |
| 98-99—Dallas .............. | | | | | | | Did not play—injured. | | | | | | | | | | | | |
| 01-02—Seattle ........... | 9 | 142 | 22 | 44 | .500 | 14 | 20 | .700 | 7 | 13 | 20 | 8 | 3 | 2 | 2 | 58 | 2.2 | 0.9 | 6.4 |
| 02-03—Seattle ........... | 45 | 448 | 41 | 107 | .383 | 12 | 21 | .571 | 34 | 39 | 73 | 23 | 14 | 5 | 25 | 94 | 1.6 | 0.5 | 2.1 |
| 03-04—Seattle ........... | 57 | 583 | 81 | 178 | .455 | 32 | 46 | .696 | 43 | 49 | 92 | 19 | 19 | 20 | 23 | 200 | 1.6 | 0.3 | 3.5 |
| 04-05—Golden State ... | 16 | 128 | 17 | 42 | .405 | 13 | 24 | .542 | 18 | 20 | 38 | 12 | 2 | 3 | 8 | 49 | 2.4 | 0.8 | 3.1 |
| Totals | 127 | 1301 | 161 | 371 | .434 | 71 | 111 | .640 | 102 | 121 | 223 | 62 | 38 | 30 | 58 | 401 | 1.8 | 0.5 | 3.2 |

Three-point field goals: 2003-04, 6-for-21 (.286). 2004-05, 2-for-8 (.250). Totals, 8-for-29 (.276).
Personal fouls/disqualifications: 2001-02, 18/0. 2002-03, 62/1. 2003-04, 66/0. 2004-05, 16/0. Totals, 162/1.

### NBA PLAYOFF RECORD

| | | | | | | | | REBOUNDS | | | | | | | AVERAGES | | |
|---|---|---|---|---|---|---|---|---|---|---|---|---|---|---|---|---|---|
| Season Team | G | Min. | FGM | FGA | Pct. | FTM | FTA | Pct. | Off. | Def. | Tot. | Ast. | St. | Blk. | TO | Pts. | RPG | APG | PPG |
| 01-02—Seattle ........... | 4 | 60 | 3 | 8 | .375 | 1 | 1 | 1.000 | 2 | 12 | 14 | 4 | 0 | 4 | 2 | 7 | 3.5 | 1.0 | 1.8 |

Personal fouls/disqualifications: 2001-02, 8/0. Totals, 8/0.

### CBA RECORD

| | | | | | | | | | | | | AVERAGES | | |
|---|---|---|---|---|---|---|---|---|---|---|---|---|---|---|
| Season Team | G | Min. | FGM | FGA | Pct. | FTM | FTA | Pct. | Reb. | Ast. | Pts. | RPG | APG | PPG |
| 99-00—Rockford ...................... | 54 | 1564 | 235 | 503 | .467 | 161 | 216 | .745 | 253 | 109 | 634 | 4.7 | 2.0 | 11.7 |
| 00-01—Quad City...................... | 13 | 442 | 51 | 132 | .386 | 35 | 46 | .761 | 73 | 32 | 137 | 5.6 | 2.5 | 10.5 |
| Totals .................................... | 67 | 2006 | 286 | 635 | .450 | 196 | 262 | .748 | 326 | 141 | 771 | 4.9 | 2.1 | 11.5 |

Three-point field goals: 1999-00, 3-for-14 (.214). 2000-01, 0-for-2. Totals, 3-for-16 (.188).
Personal fouls/disqualifications: 1999-00, 168/0. 2000-01, 55/0. Totals, 223/0.

### NBDL RECORD

| | | | | | | | | | | | | AVERAGES | | |
|---|---|---|---|---|---|---|---|---|---|---|---|---|---|---|
| Season Team | G | Min. | FGM | FGA | Pct. | FTM | FTA | Pct. | Reb. | Ast. | Pts. | RPG | APG | PPG |
| 01-02—Greenville ...................... | 45 | 1376 | 230 | 522 | .441 | 163 | 220 | .741 | 205 | 112 | 626 | 4.6 | 2.5 | 13.9 |

Three-point field goals: 2001-02, 3-for-21 (.143). Totals, 3-for-21 (.143).
Personal fouls/disqualifications: 2001-02, 117/0. Totals, 117/0.

### ITALIAN LEAGUE RECORD

| | | | | | | | | | | | | AVERAGES | | |
|---|---|---|---|---|---|---|---|---|---|---|---|---|---|---|
| Season Team | G | Min. | FGM | FGA | Pct. | FTM | FTA | Pct. | Reb. | Ast. | Pts. | RPG | APG | PPG |
| 04-05—Sedima Roseto.............. | 15 | 502 | 96 | 186 | .516 | 34 | 50 | .680 | 101 | 28 | 260 | 6.7 | 1.9 | 17.3 |

Three-point field goals: 2004-05, 34-for-73 (.466). Totals, 34-for-73 (.466).

---

## SHIRLEY, PAUL      F      **SUNS**

**PERSONAL:** Born December 23, 1977, in Redwood City, Calif. ... 6-10/210. (2.08/95.3).
**HIGH SCHOOL:** Jefferson West (Meriden, Kan.).
**COLLEGE:** Iowa State.
**TRANSACTIONS/CAREER NOTES:** Not drafted by an NBA franchise. ... Played in Greece (2001-02). ... Waived by Hornets (October 23, 2003). ... Signed by Chicago Bulls to first of two consecutive 10-day contracts (March 4, 2004). ... Signed by

Bulls for remainder of season (March 25, 2004). ... Waived by Bulls (August 20, 2004). ... Signed as free agent by Phoenix Suns (January 23, 2005).

## COLLEGIATE RECORD

| Season Team | G | Min. | FGM | FGA | Pct. | FTM | FTA | Pct. | Reb. | Ast. | Pts. | AVERAGES RPG | APG | PPG |
|---|---|---|---|---|---|---|---|---|---|---|---|---|---|---|
| 96-97—Iowa State | 19 | 180 | 12 | 25 | .480 | 20 | 30 | .667 | 29 | 9 | 44 | 1.5 | 0.5 | 2.3 |
| 97-98—Iowa State | 29 | 653 | 75 | 127 | .591 | 82 | 115 | .713 | 169 | 17 | 232 | 5.8 | 0.6 | 8.0 |
| 98-99—Iowa State | | | | | | Did not play—redshirted | | | | | | | | |
| 99-00—Iowa State | 29 | 512 | 77 | 129 | .597 | 69 | 104 | .663 | 129 | 14 | 223 | 4.4 | 0.5 | 7.7 |
| 00-01—Iowa State | 31 | 838 | 116 | 223 | .520 | 78 | 116 | .672 | 215 | 29 | 311 | 6.9 | 0.9 | 10.0 |
| **Totals** | 108 | 2183 | 280 | 504 | .556 | 249 | 365 | .682 | 542 | 69 | 810 | 5.0 | 0.6 | 7.5 |

Three-point field goals: 2000-01, 1-for-2 (.500). Totals, 1-for-2 (.500).

## GREEK LEAGUE RECORD

| Season Team | G | Min. | FGM | FGA | Pct. | FTM | FTA | Pct. | Reb. | Ast. | Pts. | AVERAGES RPG | APG | PPG |
|---|---|---|---|---|---|---|---|---|---|---|---|---|---|---|
| 01-02—Panionios | 20 | 403 | 64 | 113 | .566 | 30 | 51 | .588 | 104 | 13 | 158 | 5.2 | 0.7 | 7.9 |

Three-point field goals: 2001-02, 0-for-1. Totals, 0-for-1 (.000).
Personal fouls/disqualifications: 2001-02, 51/0. Totals, 51/0.

## CBA RECORD

| Season Team | G | Min. | FGM | FGA | Pct. | FTM | FTA | Pct. | Reb. | Ast. | Pts. | AVERAGES RPG | APG | PPG |
|---|---|---|---|---|---|---|---|---|---|---|---|---|---|---|
| 02-03—Yakima | 19 | 594 | 112 | 206 | .544 | 61 | 86 | .709 | 125 | 34 | 286 | 6.6 | 1.8 | 15.1 |

Three-point field goals: 2002-03, 1-for-2 (.500). Totals, 1-for-2 (.500).
Personal fouls/disqualifications: 2002-03, 67/0. Totals, 67/0.

## NBA REGULAR-SEASON RECORD

| Season Team | G | Min. | FGM | FGA | Pct. | FTM | FTA | Pct. | REBOUNDS Off. | Def. | Tot. | Ast. | St. | Blk. | TO | Pts. | AVERAGES RPG | APG | PPG |
|---|---|---|---|---|---|---|---|---|---|---|---|---|---|---|---|---|---|---|---|
| 02-03—Atlanta | 2 | 5 | 0 | 4 | .000 | 0 | 0 | — | 0 | 1 | 1 | 0 | 0 | 0 | 0 | 0 | 0.5 | 0.0 | 0.0 |
| 03-04—Chicago | 7 | 86 | 10 | 23 | .435 | 1 | 3 | .333 | 8 | 8 | 16 | 4 | 1 | 1 | 9 | 21 | 2.3 | 0.6 | 3.0 |
| 04-05—Phoenix | 9 | 30 | 5 | 11 | .455 | 2 | 4 | .500 | 1 | 1 | 2 | 3 | 0 | 0 | 1 | 12 | 0.2 | 0.3 | 1.3 |
| **Totals** | 18 | 121 | 15 | 38 | .395 | 3 | 7 | .429 | 9 | 10 | 19 | 7 | 1 | 1 | 10 | 33 | 1.1 | 0.4 | 1.8 |

Three-point field goals: 2003-04, 0-for-1. Totals, 0-for-1 (.000).
Personal fouls/disqualifications: 2003-04, 9/0. 2004-05, 3/0. Totals, 12/0.

## RUSSIAN LEAGUE RECORD

| Season Team | G | Min. | FGM | FGA | Pct. | FTM | FTA | Pct. | Reb. | Ast. | Pts. | AVERAGES RPG | APG | PPG |
|---|---|---|---|---|---|---|---|---|---|---|---|---|---|---|
| 04-05—Unics Kazan | 6 | 113 | 13 | 33 | .394 | 2 | 7 | .286 | 24 | 28 | 28 | 4.0 | 4.7 | 4.7 |

# SIMMONS, BOBBY                    G/F                    BUCKS

**PERSONAL:** Born June 2, 1980, in Chicago. ... 6-7/210. (2.01/95.3).
**HIGH SCHOOL:** Simeon (Chicago).
**COLLEGE:** DePaul.
**TRANSACTIONS/CAREER NOTES:** Selected after junior season by Seattle SuperSonics in second round (42nd pick overall) of 2001 NBA Draft. ... Draft rights traded by SuperSonics to Washington Wizards for draft rights to C Predrag Drobnjak (June 27, 2001). ... Traded by Wizards with G/F Richard Hamilton and G Hubert Davis to Detroit Pistons for G/F Jerry Stackhouse, F Brian Cardinal and G Hubert Davis (September 11, 2002). ... Waived by Pistons (September 24, 2002). ... Signed as free agent by Wizards (October 1, 2002). ... Signed as free agent by Los Angeles Clippers (September 27, 2003). ... Signed as free agent by Milwaukee Bucks (August 8, 2005).

## COLLEGIATE RECORD

| Season Team | G | Min. | FGM | FGA | Pct. | FTM | FTA | Pct. | Reb. | Ast. | Pts. | AVERAGES RPG | APG | PPG |
|---|---|---|---|---|---|---|---|---|---|---|---|---|---|---|
| 98-99—DePaul | 31 | 949 | 112 | 300 | .373 | 92 | 116 | .793 | 190 | 82 | 347 | 6.1 | 2.6 | 11.2 |
| 99-00—DePaul | 33 | 1009 | 142 | 308 | .461 | 120 | 158 | .759 | 262 | 53 | 433 | 7.9 | 1.6 | 13.1 |
| 00-01—DePaul | 29 | 981 | 149 | 333 | .447 | 124 | 155 | .800 | 248 | 72 | 483 | 8.6 | 2.5 | 16.7 |
| **Totals** | 93 | 2939 | 403 | 941 | .428 | 336 | 429 | .783 | 700 | 207 | 1263 | 7.5 | 2.2 | 13.6 |

Three-point field goals: 1998-99, 31-for-112 (.277). 1999-00, 29-for-89 (.326). 2000-01, 61-for-165 (.370). Totals, 121-for-366 (.331).
Personal fouls/disqualifications: 1998-99, 77/0. 1999-00, 97/0. 2000-01, 97/0. Totals, 271/0.

**HONORS:** NBA Most Improved Player (2005).

## NBA REGULAR-SEASON RECORD

| Season Team | G | Min. | FGM | FGA | Pct. | FTM | FTA | Pct. | REBOUNDS Off. | Def. | Tot. | Ast. | St. | Blk. | TO | Pts. | AVERAGES RPG | APG | PPG |
|---|---|---|---|---|---|---|---|---|---|---|---|---|---|---|---|---|---|---|---|
| 01-02—Washington | 30 | 343 | 43 | 95 | .453 | 22 | 30 | .733 | 25 | 27 | 52 | 17 | 13 | 5 | 14 | 112 | 1.7 | 0.6 | 3.7 |
| 02-03—Washington | 36 | 378 | 44 | 112 | .393 | 32 | 35 | .914 | 33 | 44 | 77 | 20 | 10 | 3 | 8 | 120 | 2.1 | 0.6 | 3.3 |
| 03-04—L.A. Clippers | 56 | 1376 | 147 | 373 | .394 | 141 | 169 | .834 | 115 | 147 | 262 | 96 | 51 | 17 | 73 | 437 | 4.7 | 1.7 | 7.8 |
| 04-05—L.A. Clippers | 75 | 2799 | 474 | 1017 | .466 | 231 | 273 | .846 | 128 | 318 | 446 | 205 | 106 | 16 | 135 | 1229 | 5.9 | 2.7 | 16.4 |
| **Totals** | 197 | 4896 | 708 | 1597 | .443 | 426 | 507 | .840 | 301 | 536 | 837 | 338 | 180 | 41 | 230 | 1898 | 4.2 | 1.7 | 9.6 |

Three-point field goals: 2001-02, 4-for-14 (.286). 2002-03, 0-for-5. 2003-04, 2-for-12 (.167). 2004-05, 50-for-115 (.435). Totals, 56-for-146 (.384).
Personal fouls/disqualifications: 2001-02, 31/1. 2002-03, 51/0. 2003-04, 169/2. 2004-05, 227/4. Totals, 478/7.

## NBDL RECORD

| Season Team | G | Min. | FGM | FGA | Pct. | FTM | FTA | Pct. | Reb. | Ast. | Pts. | AVERAGES RPG | APG | PPG |
|---|---|---|---|---|---|---|---|---|---|---|---|---|---|---|
| 02-03—Mobile | 14 | 423 | 76 | 180 | .422 | 86 | 103 | .835 | 73 | 22 | 240 | 5.2 | 1.6 | 17.1 |

Three-point field goals: 2002-03, 2-for-10 (.200). Totals, 2-for-10 (.200).
Personal fouls/disqualifications: 2002-03, 47/0. Totals, 47/0.

# SKINNER, BRIAN         F/C         KINGS

**PERSONAL:** Born May 19, 1976, in Temple, Texas. ... 6-9/255. (2.06/115.7).
**HIGH SCHOOL:** Temple (Texas).
**COLLEGE:** Baylor.
**TRANSACTIONS/CAREER NOTES:** Selected by Los Angeles Clippers in first round (22nd pick overall) of 1998 NBA Draft. ... Traded by Clippers with rights to C Tyson Chandler to Chicago Bulls for F Elton Brand (June 27, 2001). ... Traded by Bulls to Toronto Raptors for F Charles Oakley and 2002 second-round draft choice (July 18, 2001). ... Traded by Raptors to Cleveland Cavaliers as part of three-way deal in which Cavaliers sent F/C Chris Gatling to Cavaliers, Heat sent G Ricky Davis to Cavaliers and Heat sent F Don MacLean and cash considerations to Raptors (October 26, 2001). ... Signed as free agent by Philadelphia 76ers (August 27, 2002). ... Signed as free agent by Milwaukee Bucks (July 17, 2003). ... Signed as free agent by 76ers (July 14, 2004). ... Traded by 76ers with Fs Kenny Thomas and Corliss Williamson to Sacramento Kings for Fs Chris Webber, Michael Bradley and Matt Barnes (February 23, 2005).

## COLLEGIATE RECORD

| Season Team | G | Min. | FGM | FGA | Pct. | FTM | FTA | Pct. | Reb. | Ast. | Pts. | RPG | APG | PPG |
|---|---|---|---|---|---|---|---|---|---|---|---|---|---|---|
| 94-95—Baylor | 18 | 501 | 98 | 164 | .598 | 40 | 95 | .421 | 147 | 9 | 236 | 8.2 | 0.5 | 13.1 |
| 95-96—Baylor | 27 | 900 | 187 | 311 | .601 | 101 | 163 | .620 | 250 | 16 | 475 | 9.3 | 0.6 | 17.6 |
| 96-97—Baylor | 30 | 973 | 196 | 349 | .562 | 92 | 172 | .535 | 253 | 26 | 484 | 8.4 | 0.9 | 16.1 |
| 97-98—Baylor | 28 | 908 | 192 | 347 | .553 | 123 | 208 | .591 | 265 | 15 | 507 | 9.5 | 0.5 | 18.1 |
| Totals | 103 | 3282 | 673 | 1171 | .575 | 356 | 638 | .558 | 915 | 66 | 1702 | 8.9 | 0.6 | 16.5 |

## NBA REGULAR-SEASON RECORD

| Season Team | G | Min. | FGM | FGA | Pct. | FTM | FTA | Pct. | Off. | Def. | Tot. | Ast. | St. | Blk. | TO | Pts. | RPG | APG | PPG |
|---|---|---|---|---|---|---|---|---|---|---|---|---|---|---|---|---|---|---|---|
| 98-99—L.A. Clippers | 21 | 258 | 33 | 71 | .465 | 20 | 33 | .606 | 20 | 33 | 53 | 1 | 10 | 13 | 19 | 86 | 2.5 | 0.0 | 4.1 |
| 99-00—L.A. Clippers | 33 | 775 | 68 | 134 | .507 | 43 | 65 | .662 | 63 | 138 | 201 | 11 | 16 | 44 | 37 | 179 | 6.1 | 0.3 | 5.4 |
| 00-01—L.A. Clippers | 39 | 584 | 64 | 161 | .398 | 32 | 59 | .542 | 55 | 113 | 168 | 18 | 14 | 11 | 32 | 160 | 4.3 | 0.5 | 4.1 |
| 01-02—Cleveland | 65 | 1107 | 88 | 162 | .543 | 48 | 79 | .608 | 93 | 188 | 281 | 17 | 24 | 61 | 42 | 224 | 4.3 | 0.3 | 3.4 |
| 02-03—Philadelphia | 77 | 1381 | 182 | 331 | .550 | 97 | 161 | .602 | 136 | 230 | 366 | 19 | 47 | 53 | 62 | 461 | 4.8 | 0.2 | 6.0 |
| 03-04—Milwaukee | 56 | 1577 | 255 | 513 | .497 | 79 | 138 | .572 | 119 | 292 | 411 | 49 | 30 | 61 | 78 | 589 | 7.3 | 0.9 | 10.5 |
| 04-05—Phila.-Sac. | 49 | 941 | 104 | 205 | .507 | 25 | 70 | .357 | 107 | 173 | 280 | 43 | 31 | 49 | 40 | 233 | 5.7 | 0.9 | 4.8 |
| Totals | 340 | 6623 | 794 | 1577 | .503 | 344 | 605 | .569 | 593 | 1167 | 1760 | 158 | 172 | 292 | 310 | 1932 | 5.2 | 0.5 | 5.7 |

Three-point field goals: 2004-05, 0-for-1. Totals, 0-for-1 (.000).
Personal fouls/disqualifications: 1998-99, 20/0. 1999-00, 75/0. 2000-01, 61/0. 2001-02, 130/1. 2002-03, 176/1. 2003-04, 165/3. 2004-05, 102/0. Totals, 729/5.

## NBA PLAYOFF RECORD

| Season Team | G | Min. | FGM | FGA | Pct. | FTM | FTA | Pct. | Off. | Def. | Tot. | Ast. | St. | Blk. | TO | Pts. | RPG | APG | PPG |
|---|---|---|---|---|---|---|---|---|---|---|---|---|---|---|---|---|---|---|---|
| 02-03—Philadelphia | 8 | 38 | 1 | 6 | .167 | 4 | 4 | 1.000 | 3 | 3 | 6 | 0 | 0 | 1 | 2 | 6 | 0.8 | 0.0 | 0.8 |
| 03-04—Milwaukee | 5 | 94 | 11 | 21 | .524 | 5 | 12 | .417 | 8 | 14 | 22 | 0 | 1 | 3 | 7 | 27 | 4.4 | 0.0 | 5.4 |
| 04-05—Sacramento | 4 | 47 | 4 | 8 | .500 | 0 | 0 | ... | 6 | 5 | 11 | 2 | 2 | 4 | 5 | 8 | 2.8 | 0.5 | 2.0 |
| Totals | 17 | 179 | 16 | 35 | .457 | 9 | 16 | .563 | 17 | 22 | 39 | 2 | 3 | 8 | 14 | 41 | 2.3 | 0.1 | 2.4 |

Three-point field goals: 2002-03, 0-for-1. Totals, 0-for-1 (.000).
Personal fouls/disqualifications: 2002-03, 6/0. 2003-04, 8/0. 2004-05, 5/0. Totals, 19/0.

# SLAY, TAMAR         G

**PERSONAL:** Born April 2, 1980, in Beckley, W.Va. ... 6-9/215. (2.06/97.5). ... Full name: Tamar Ulysses Slay
**HIGH SCHOOL:** Woodrow Wilson (Beckley, W.Va.).
**COLLEGE:** Marshall.
**TRANSACTIONS/CAREER NOTES:** Selected by New Jersey Nets in second round (54th pick overall) of 2002 NBA Draft. ... Selected by Charlotte Bobcats from Nets in NBA Expansion Draft (June 22, 2004).

## COLLEGIATE RECORD

| Season Team | G | Min. | FGM | FGA | Pct. | FTM | FTA | Pct. | Reb. | Ast. | Pts. | RPG | APG | PPG |
|---|---|---|---|---|---|---|---|---|---|---|---|---|---|---|
| 98-99—Marshall | 27 | 401 | 60 | 161 | .373 | 20 | 29 | .690 | 68 | 36 | 162 | 2.5 | 1.3 | 6.0 |
| 99-00—Marshall | 30 | 921 | 216 | 434 | .498 | 72 | 102 | .706 | 132 | 69 | 597 | 4.4 | 2.3 | 19.9 |
| 00-01—Marshall | 27 | 926 | 154 | 380 | .405 | 102 | 125 | .816 | 146 | 72 | 466 | 5.4 | 2.7 | 17.3 |
| 01-02—Marshall | 30 | 1031 | 196 | 439 | .446 | 95 | 130 | .731 | 161 | 72 | 567 | 5.4 | 2.4 | 18.9 |
| Totals | 114 | 3279 | 626 | 1414 | .443 | 289 | 386 | .749 | 507 | 249 | 1792 | 4.4 | 2.2 | 15.7 |

Three-point field goals: 1998-99, 22-for-73 (.301). 1999-00, 93-for-215 (.433). 2000-01, 56-for-171 (.327). 2001-02, 80-for-191 (.419). Totals, 251-for-650 (.386).

## NBA REGULAR-SEASON RECORD

| Season Team | G | Min. | FGM | FGA | Pct. | FTM | FTA | Pct. | Off. | Def. | Tot. | Ast. | St. | Blk. | TO | Pts. | RPG | APG | PPG |
|---|---|---|---|---|---|---|---|---|---|---|---|---|---|---|---|---|---|---|---|
| 02-03—New Jersey | 36 | 274 | 39 | 103 | .379 | 7 | 10 | .700 | 8 | 23 | 31 | 14 | 14 | 3 | 20 | 92 | 0.9 | 0.4 | 2.6 |
| 03-04—New Jersey | 22 | 165 | 21 | 60 | .350 | 7 | 14 | .500 | 10 | 15 | 25 | 14 | 7 | 1 | 11 | 53 | 1.1 | 0.6 | 2.4 |
| 04-05—Charlotte | 8 | 78 | 13 | 39 | .333 | 0 | 2 | .000 | 6 | 8 | 14 | 3 | 5 | 0 | 8 | 28 | 1.8 | 0.4 | 3.5 |
| Totals | 66 | 517 | 73 | 202 | .361 | 14 | 26 | .538 | 24 | 46 | 70 | 31 | 26 | 4 | 39 | 173 | 1.1 | 0.5 | 2.6 |

Three-point field goals: 2002-03, 7-for-25 (.280). 2003-04, 4-for-12 (.333). 2004-05, 2-for-12 (.167). Totals, 13-for-49 (.265).
Personal fouls/disqualifications: 2002-03, 31/0. 2003-04, 20/0. 2004-05, 20/0. Totals, 71/0.

## NBA PLAYOFF RECORD

| Season Team | G | Min. | FGM | FGA | Pct. | FTM | FTA | Pct. | Off. | Def. | Tot. | Ast. | St. | Blk. | TO | Pts. | RPG | APG | PPG |
|---|---|---|---|---|---|---|---|---|---|---|---|---|---|---|---|---|---|---|---|
| 02-03—New Jersey | 6 | 11 | 1 | 4 | .250 | 0 | 0 | ... | 0 | 0 | 0 | 0 | 0 | 0 | 2 | 3 | 0.0 | 0.0 | 0.5 |
| 03-04—New Jersey | 6 | 12 | 1 | 5 | .200 | 2 | 2 | 1.000 | 0 | 2 | 2 | 0 | 1 | 0 | 0 | 4 | 0.3 | 0.0 | 0.7 |
| Totals | 12 | 23 | 2 | 9 | .222 | 2 | 2 | 1.000 | 0 | 2 | 2 | 0 | 1 | 0 | 2 | 7 | 0.2 | 0.0 | 0.6 |

Three-point field goals: 2002-03, 1-for-1 (1.000). 2003-04, 0-for-1. Totals, 1-for-2 (.500).
Personal fouls/disqualifications: 2002-03, 1/0. Totals, 1/0.

## SMITH, DONTA  G  HAWKS

**PERSONAL:** Born November 27, 1983, in Louisville, Ky. ... 6-7/215. (2.01/97.5). ... Full name: Donta Lamont Smith
**HIGH SCHOOL:** Oldham County (LaGrange, Ky.).
**JUNIOR COLLEGE:** Southeastern Illinois.
**TRANSACTIONS/CAREER NOTES:** Selected after sophomore season by Atlanta Hawks in second round (34th pick overall) of 2004 NBA Draft.

### COLLEGIATE RECORD

| Season Team | G | Min. | FGM | FGA | Pct. | FTM | FTA | Pct. | Reb. | Ast. | Pts. | RPG | APG | PPG |
|---|---|---|---|---|---|---|---|---|---|---|---|---|---|---|
| 02-03—S.E. Illinois College ........ | 36 | ... | 219 | 376 | .582 | 97 | 136 | .713 | 199 | 107 | 582 | 5.5 | 3.0 | 16.2 |
| 03-04—S.E. Illinois College ........ | 33 | ... | 278 | 515 | .540 | 231 | 284 | .813 | 236 | 113 | 851 | 7.2 | 3.4 | 25.8 |
| Totals ................................. | 69 | | 497 | 891 | .558 | 328 | 420 | .781 | 435 | 220 | 1433 | 6.3 | 3.2 | 20.8 |

Three-point field goals: 2002-03, 47-for-101 (.465). 2003-04, 64-for-165 (.388). Totals, 111-for-266 (.417).

### NBA REGULAR-SEASON RECORD

| Season Team | G | Min. | FGM | FGA | Pct. | FTM | FTA | Pct. | Off. | Def. | Tot. | Ast. | St. | Blk. | TO | Pts. | RPG | APG | PPG |
|---|---|---|---|---|---|---|---|---|---|---|---|---|---|---|---|---|---|---|---|
| 04-05—Atlanta ............ | 38 | 433 | 44 | 113 | .389 | 33 | 48 | .688 | 19 | 33 | 52 | 39 | 23 | 5 | 25 | 127 | 1.4 | 1.0 | 3.3 |

Three-point field goals: 2004-05, 6-for-22 (.273). Totals, 6-for-22 (.273).
Personal fouls/disqualifications: 2004-05, 50/0. Totals, 50/0.

## SMITH, J.R.  G  HORNETS

**PERSONAL:** Born September 9, 1985, in Freehold,N.J. ... 6-6/220. (1.98/99.8).
**HIGH SCHOOL:** Lakewood (N.J.), then St. Benedict's Prep (Newark, N.J.).
**COLLEGE:** Did not attend college.
**TRANSACTIONS/CAREER NOTES:** Selected out of high school by New Orleans Hornets in first round (18th pick overall) in 2004 NBA Draft.

### NBA REGULAR-SEASON RECORD

| Season Team | G | Min. | FGM | FGA | Pct. | FTM | FTA | Pct. | Off. | Def. | Tot. | Ast. | St. | Blk. | TO | Pts. | RPG | APG | PPG |
|---|---|---|---|---|---|---|---|---|---|---|---|---|---|---|---|---|---|---|---|
| 04-05—New Orleans ... | 76 | 1859 | 295 | 748 | .394 | 111 | 161 | .689 | 39 | 113 | 152 | 142 | 55 | 11 | 109 | 782 | 2.0 | 1.9 | 10.3 |

Three-point field goals: 2004-05, 81-for-281 (.288). Totals, 81-for-281 (.288).
Personal fouls/disqualifications: 2004-05, 135/0. Totals, 135/0.

## SMITH, JABARI  C

**PERSONAL:** Born February 12, 1977, in Atlanta. ... 6-11/240. (2.11/108.9). ... Full name: Jabari Montsho Smith ... Cousin of Kwame Brown, forward/center, Los Angeles Lakers.
**HIGH SCHOOL:** Booker T. Washington (Atlanta).
**JUNIOR COLLEGE:** Atlanta Metropolitan College.
**COLLEGE:** Louisiana State.
**TRANSACTIONS/CAREER NOTES:** Selected by Sacramento Kings in second round (45th pick overall) of 2000 NBA Draft. ... Waived by Kings (December 18, 2001). ... Signed as free agent by Philadelphia 76ers (December 29, 2001). ... Signed as free agent by Orlando Magic (September 12, 2002). ... Waived by Magic (October 7, 2002). ... Played in Spain (2002-03). ... Signed as free agent by 76ers (December 10, 2003). ... Waived by 76ers (January 6, 2004). ... Signed by 76ers to the first of two consecutive 10-day contracts (January 10, 2004). ... Signed by 76ers for remainder of season (January 30, 2004). ... Signed as free agent by New Jersey Nets (October 4, 2004).

### COLLEGIATE RECORD

| Season Team | G | Min. | FGM | FGA | Pct. | FTM | FTA | Pct. | Reb. | Ast. | Pts. | RPG | APG | PPG |
|---|---|---|---|---|---|---|---|---|---|---|---|---|---|---|
| 95-96—Atlanta College .............. | 32 | ... | 182 | 314 | .580 | 142 | 179 | .793 | 380 | 100 | 506 | 11.9 | 3.1 | 15.8 |
| 96-97—Atlanta College .............. | 24 | ... | ... | ... | ... | 158 | 213 | .742 | 312 | 73 | 467 | 13.0 | 3.0 | 19.5 |
| 97-98—Atlanta College .............. | | | | | | | Did not play. | | | | | | | |
| 98-99—Louisiana State.............. | 27 | 808 | 115 | 227 | .507 | 100 | 145 | .690 | 262 | 51 | 342 | 9.7 | 1.9 | 12.7 |
| 99-00—Louisiana State.............. | 34 | 969 | 156 | 282 | .553 | 100 | 168 | .595 | 239 | 75 | 425 | 7.0 | 2.2 | 12.5 |
| Junior College Totals............ | 56 | | 182 | 314 | .580 | 300 | 392 | .765 | 692 | 173 | 973 | 12.4 | 3.1 | 17.4 |
| 4-Year-College Totals ............ | 61 | 1777 | 271 | 509 | .532 | 200 | 313 | .639 | 501 | 126 | 767 | 8.2 | 2.1 | 12.6 |

Three-point field goals: 1998-99, 12-for-49 (.245). 1999-00, 13-for-35 (.371). Totals, 25-for-84 (.298).

### NBA REGULAR-SEASON RECORD

| Season Team | G | Min. | FGM | FGA | Pct. | FTM | FTA | Pct. | Off. | Def. | Tot. | Ast. | St. | Blk. | TO | Pts. | RPG | APG | PPG |
|---|---|---|---|---|---|---|---|---|---|---|---|---|---|---|---|---|---|---|---|
| 00-01—Sacramento .... | 9 | 66 | 11 | 22 | .500 | 4 | 6 | .667 | 1 | 7 | 8 | 6 | 4 | 0 | 3 | 26 | 0.9 | 0.7 | 2.9 |
| 01-02—Sac.-Phila. ...... | 23 | 181 | 26 | 63 | .413 | 21 | 32 | .656 | 8 | 20 | 28 | 11 | 6 | 6 | 5 | 73 | 1.2 | 0.5 | 3.2 |
| 03-04—Sacramento .... | 31 | 168 | 26 | 70 | .371 | 12 | 20 | .600 | 11 | 20 | 31 | 11 | 2 | 6 | 7 | 64 | 1.0 | 0.4 | 2.1 |
| 04-05—New Jersey ..... | 45 | 648 | 62 | 148 | .419 | 41 | 55 | .745 | 29 | 82 | 111 | 38 | 25 | 14 | 39 | 166 | 2.5 | 0.8 | 3.7 |
| Totals ................... | 108 | 1063 | 125 | 303 | .413 | 78 | 113 | .690 | 49 | 129 | 178 | 66 | 37 | 26 | 54 | 329 | 1.6 | 0.6 | 3.0 |

Three-point field goals: 2001-02, 0-for-3. 2003-04, 0-for-3. 2004-05, 1-for-2 (.500). Totals, 1-for-8 (.125).
Personal fouls/disqualifications: 2000-01, 7/0. 2001-02, 31/1. 2003-04, 25/0. 2004-05, 103/0. Totals, 166/1.

## NBA PLAYOFF RECORD

| Season Team | G | Min. | FGM | FGA | Pct. | FTM | FTA | Pct. | REBOUNDS Off. | Def. | Tot. | Ast. | St. | Blk. | TO | Pts. | AVERAGES RPG | APG | PPG |
|---|---|---|---|---|---|---|---|---|---|---|---|---|---|---|---|---|---|---|---|
| 03-04—Sacramento .... | 4 | 10 | 1 | 2 | .500 | 3 | 4 | .750 | 1 | 2 | 3 | 0 | 0 | 1 | 0 | 5 | 0.8 | 0.0 | 1.3 |
| 04-05—New Jersey ..... | 3 | 4 | 0 | 0 | ... | 0 | 0 | ... | 0 | 0 | 0 | 0 | 0 | 0 | 0 | 0 | 0.0 | 0.0 | 0.0 |
| Totals ................. | 7 | 14 | 1 | 2 | .500 | 3 | 4 | .750 | 1 | 2 | 3 | 0 | 0 | 1 | 0 | 5 | 0.4 | 0.0 | 0.7 |

Personal fouls/disqualifications: 2003-04, 2/0. 2004-05, 2/0. Totals, 4/0.

## SPANISH RECORD

| Season Team | G | Min. | FGM | FGA | Pct. | FTM | FTA | Pct. | Reb. | Ast. | Pts. | AVERAGES RPG | APG | PPG |
|---|---|---|---|---|---|---|---|---|---|---|---|---|---|---|
| 02-03—C.B. Granada ................. | 7 | 161 | 20 | 58 | .345 | 17 | 23 | .739 | 29 | 6 | 58 | 4.1 | 0.9 | 8.3 |

Three-point field goals: 2002-03, 1-for-14 (.071). Totals, 1-for-14 (.071).

# SMITH, JOE          F          BUCKS

**PERSONAL:** Born July 26, 1975, in Norfolk, Va. ... 6-10/225. (2.08/102.1). ... Full name: Joseph Leynard Smith
**HIGH SCHOOL:** Maury (Norfolk, Va.).
**COLLEGE:** Maryland.
**TRANSACTIONS/CAREER NOTES:** Selected after sophomore season by Golden State Warriors in first round (first pick overall) of 1995 NBA Draft. ... Traded by Warriors with G Brian Shaw to Philadelphia 76ers for F Clarence Weatherspoon and G Jim Jackson (February 17, 1998). ... Signed as free agent by Minnesota Timberwolves (January 22, 1999). ... Contract voided by NBA (October 25, 2000). ... Signed as free agent by Detroit Pistons (November 20, 2000). ... Signed as free agent by Timberwolves (July 30, 2001). ... Traded by Timberwolves with G Anthony Peeler to Milwaukee Bucks for G Sam Cassell and C Ervin Johnson (June 27, 2003)

### COLLEGIATE RECORD

**NOTES:** Naismith Award winner (1995). ... THE SPORTING NEWS All-America second team (1995).

| Season Team | G | Min. | FGM | FGA | Pct. | FTM | FTA | Pct. | Reb. | Ast. | Pts. | AVERAGES RPG | APG | PPG |
|---|---|---|---|---|---|---|---|---|---|---|---|---|---|---|
| 93-94—Maryland ...................... | 30 | 988 | 206 | 395 | .522 | 168 | 229 | .734 | 321 | 25 | 582 | 10.7 | 0.8 | 19.4 |
| 94-95—Maryland ...................... | 34 | 1110 | 245 | 424 | .578 | 209 | 282 | .741 | 362 | 40 | 708 | 10.6 | 1.2 | 20.8 |
| Totals ...................................... | 64 | 2098 | 451 | 819 | .551 | 377 | 511 | .738 | 683 | 65 | 1290 | 10.7 | 1.0 | 20.2 |

Three-point field goals: 1993-94, 2-for-5 (.400). 1994-95, 9-for-21 (.429). Totals, 11-for-26 (.423).

### NBA REGULAR-SEASON RECORD

**HONORS:** NBA All-Rookie first team (1996).

| Season Team | G | Min. | FGM | FGA | Pct. | FTM | FTA | Pct. | REBOUNDS Off. | Def. | Tot. | Ast. | St. | Blk. | TO | Pts. | AVERAGES RPG | APG | PPG |
|---|---|---|---|---|---|---|---|---|---|---|---|---|---|---|---|---|---|---|---|
| 95-96—Golden State ... | 82 | 2821 | 469 | 1024 | .458 | 303 | 392 | .773 | 300 | 417 | 717 | 79 | 85 | 134 | 138 | 1251 | 8.7 | 1.0 | 15.3 |
| 96-97—Golden State ... | 80 | 3086 | 587 | 1293 | .454 | 307 | 377 | .814 | 261 | 418 | 679 | 125 | 74 | 86 | 192 | 1493 | 8.5 | 1.6 | 18.7 |
| 97-98—G.S.-Phila. ...... | 79 | 2344 | 464 | 1070 | .434 | 227 | 293 | .775 | 199 | 272 | 471 | 94 | 62 | 51 | 158 | 1155 | 6.0 | 1.2 | 14.6 |
| 98-99—Minnesota ....... | 43 | 1418 | 223 | 522 | .427 | 142 | 188 | .755 | 154 | 200 | 354 | 68 | 32 | 66 | 66 | 588 | 8.2 | 1.6 | 13.7 |
| 99-00—Minnesota ....... | 78 | 1975 | 289 | 623 | .464 | 195 | 258 | .756 | 186 | 298 | 484 | 88 | 45 | 85 | 119 | 774 | 6.2 | 1.1 | 9.9 |
| 00-01—Detroit ............ | 69 | 1941 | 308 | 765 | .403 | 231 | 287 | .805 | 160 | 331 | 491 | 79 | 47 | 50 | 88 | 847 | 7.1 | 1.1 | 12.3 |
| 01-02—Minnesota ....... | 72 | 1922 | 297 | 581 | .511 | 171 | 206 | .830 | 152 | 301 | 453 | 82 | 39 | 59 | 86 | 767 | 6.3 | 1.1 | 10.7 |
| 02-03—Minnesota ....... | 54 | 1117 | 151 | 328 | .460 | 102 | 131 | .779 | 111 | 159 | 270 | 38 | 14 | 55 | 43 | 404 | 5.0 | 0.7 | 7.5 |
| 03-04—Milwaukee ..... | 76 | 2254 | 311 | 708 | .439 | 207 | 241 | .859 | 230 | 413 | 643 | 78 | 47 | 94 | 82 | 830 | 8.5 | 1.0 | 10.9 |
| 04-05—Milwaukee ..... | 74 | 2265 | 319 | 621 | .514 | 175 | 228 | .768 | 179 | 362 | 541 | 67 | 43 | 38 | 79 | 813 | 7.3 | 0.9 | 11.0 |
| Totals .................. | 707 | 21143 | 3418 | 7535 | .454 | 2060 | 2601 | .792 | 1932 | 3171 | 5103 | 798 | 488 | 718 | 1051 | 8922 | 7.2 | 1.1 | 12.6 |

Three-point field goals: 1995-96, 10-for-28 (.357). 1996-97, 12-for-46 (.261). 1997-98, 0-for-8. 1998-99, 0-for-3. 1999-00, 1-for-1 (1.000). 2000-01, 0-for-5. 2001-02, 2-for-3 (.667). 2002-03, 0-for-2. 2003-04, 1-for-5 (.200). 2004-05, 0-for-1. Totals, 26-for-102 (.255).
Personal fouls/disqualifications: 1995-96, 224/5. 1996-97, 244/3. 1997-98, 263/2. 1998-99, 147/3. 1999-00, 302/8. 2000-01, 258/5. 2001-02, 250/2. 2002-03, 171/2. 2003-04, 209/1. 2004-05, 222/5. Totals, 2290/36.

### NBA PLAYOFF RECORD

| Season Team | G | Min. | FGM | FGA | Pct. | FTM | FTA | Pct. | REBOUNDS Off. | Def. | Tot. | Ast. | St. | Blk. | TO | Pts. | AVERAGES RPG | APG | PPG |
|---|---|---|---|---|---|---|---|---|---|---|---|---|---|---|---|---|---|---|---|
| 98-99—Minnesota ....... | 4 | 120 | 11 | 37 | .297 | 8 | 11 | .727 | 10 | 16 | 26 | 5 | 2 | 8 | 5 | 30 | 6.5 | 1.3 | 7.5 |
| 99-00—Minnesota ....... | 4 | 79 | 8 | 17 | .471 | 2 | 2 | 1.000 | 7 | 5 | 12 | 1 | 3 | 1 | 4 | 18 | 3.0 | 0.3 | 4.5 |
| 01-02—Minnesota ....... | 3 | 43 | 3 | 7 | .429 | 7 | 8 | .875 | 4 | 7 | 11 | 0 | 0 | 1 | 1 | 13 | 3.7 | 0.0 | 4.3 |
| 02-03—Minnesota ....... | 5 | 40 | 4 | 6 | .667 | 6 | 6 | 1.000 | 0 | 6 | 6 | 0 | 1 | 1 | 3 | 14 | 1.2 | 0.0 | 2.8 |
| 03-04—Milwaukee ..... | 5 | 175 | 27 | 55 | .491 | 12 | 13 | .923 | 23 | 27 | 50 | 2 | 4 | 10 | 6 | 66 | 10.0 | 0.4 | 13.2 |
| Totals .................. | 21 | 457 | 53 | 122 | .434 | 35 | 40 | .875 | 44 | 61 | 105 | 8 | 10 | 21 | 19 | 141 | 5.0 | 0.4 | 6.7 |

Three-point field goals: 1999-00, 0-for-1. 2003-04, 0-for-1. Totals, 0-for-2 (.000).
Personal fouls/disqualifications: 1998-99, 15/0. 1999-00, 15/0. 2001-02, 8/0. 2002-03, 14/0. 2003-04, 15/0. Totals, 67/0.

# SMITH, JOSH          F          HAWKS

**PERSONAL:** Born December 5, 1985, in College Park, Ga. ... 6-9/210. (2.06/95.3).
**HIGH SCHOOL:** McEachern (Powder Springs, Ga.), then Oak Hill Aca.
**COLLEGE:** Did not attend college.
**TRANSACTIONS/CAREER NOTES:** Selected out of high school by Atlanta Hawks in first round (17th overall pick) of 2004 NBA Draft.

### NBA REGULAR-SEASON RECORD

**HONORS:** NBA All-Rookie second team (2005).

| Season Team | G | Min. | FGM | FGA | Pct. | FTM | FTA | Pct. | REBOUNDS Off. | Def. | Tot. | Ast. | St. | Blk. | TO | Pts. | AVERAGES RPG | APG | PPG |
|---|---|---|---|---|---|---|---|---|---|---|---|---|---|---|---|---|---|---|---|
| 04-05—Atlanta ............ | 74 | 2050 | 274 | 602 | .455 | 163 | 237 | .688 | 147 | 310 | 457 | 127 | 59 | 144 | 135 | 715 | 6.2 | 1.7 | 9.7 |

Three-point field goals: 2004-05, 4-for-23 (.174). Totals, 4-for-23 (.174).
Personal fouls/disqualifications: 2004-05, 157/1. Totals, 157/1.

# SMITH, STEVE  G

**PERSONAL:** Born March 31, 1969, in Highland Park, Mich. ... 6-8/221. (2.03/100.2). ... Full name: Steven Delano Smith.
**HIGH SCHOOL:** Pershing (Detroit).
**COLLEGE:** Michigan State.
**TRANSACTIONS/CAREER NOTES:** Selected by Miami Heat in first round (fifth pick overall) of 1991 NBA Draft. ... Traded by Heat with F Grant Long and conditional second-round draft choice to Atlanta Hawks for F Kevin Willis and conditional first-round draft choice (November 7, 1994). ... Traded by Hawks with G Ed Gray to Portland Trail Blazers for G Isaiah Rider and G Jim Jackson (August 2, 1999). ... Traded by Trail Blazers to San Antonio Spurs for G Derek Anderson, G Steve Kerr and 2003 second-round draft choice (July 25, 2001). ... Signed as free agent by New Orleans Hornets (October 29, 2003). ... Signed as free agent by Charlotte Bobcats (September 16, 2004). ... Traded by Bobcats to Miami Heat for F Malik Allen (February 24, 2005).
**MISCELLANEOUS:** Member of gold-medal-winning U.S. Olympic team (2000). ... Member of gold-medal winning U.S. World Championship team (1994). ... Member of NBA championship team (2003).

## COLLEGIATE RECORD

**NOTES:** THE SPORTING NEWS All-America first team (1990, 1991).

| Season Team | G | Min. | FGM | FGA | Pct. | FTM | FTA | Pct. | Reb. | Ast. | Pts. | RPG | APG | PPG |
|---|---|---|---|---|---|---|---|---|---|---|---|---|---|---|
| 87-88—Michigan State ............... | 28 | 812 | 108 | 232 | .466 | 69 | 91 | .758 | 112 | 82 | 299 | 4.0 | 2.9 | 10.7 |
| 88-89—Michigan State ............... | 33 | 1168 | 217 | 454 | .478 | 129 | 169 | .763 | 229 | 112 | 585 | 6.9 | 3.4 | 17.7 |
| 89-90—Michigan State ............... | 31 | 1081 | 233 | 443 | .526 | 116 | 167 | .695 | 216 | 150 | 627 | 7.0 | 4.8 | 20.2 |
| 90-91—Michigan State ............... | 30 | 1134 | 268 | 566 | .473 | 150 | 187 | .802 | 183 | 109 | 752 | 6.1 | 3.6 | 25.1 |
| **Totals** ............................. | 122 | 4195 | 826 | 1695 | .487 | 464 | 614 | .756 | 740 | 453 | 2263 | 6.1 | 3.7 | 18.5 |

Three-point field goals: 1987-88, 14-for-30 (.467). 1988-89, 22-for-63 (.349). 1989-90, 45-for-98 (.459). 1990-91, 66-for-162 (.407). Totals, 147-for-353 (.416).

## NBA REGULAR-SEASON RECORD

**HONORS:** J. Walter Kennedy Citizenship Award (1998). ... NBA Sportsmanship Award (2002). ... NBA All-Rookie first team (1992).
**NOTES:** Led NBA with .472 three-point field goal percentage (2002).

| Season Team | G | Min. | FGM | FGA | Pct. | FTM | FTA | Pct. | REBOUNDS Off. | Def. | Tot. | Ast. | St. | Blk. | TO | Pts. | AVERAGES RPG | APG | PPG |
|---|---|---|---|---|---|---|---|---|---|---|---|---|---|---|---|---|---|---|---|
| 91-92—Miami ............ | 61 | 1806 | 297 | 654 | .454 | 95 | 127 | .748 | 81 | 107 | 188 | 278 | 59 | 19 | 152 | 729 | 3.1 | 4.6 | 12.0 |
| 92-93—Miami ............ | 48 | 1610 | 279 | 619 | .451 | 155 | 197 | .787 | 56 | 141 | 197 | 267 | 50 | 16 | 129 | 766 | 4.1 | 5.6 | 16.0 |
| 93-94—Miami ............ | 78 | 2776 | 491 | 1076 | .456 | 273 | 327 | .835 | 156 | 196 | 352 | 394 | 84 | 35 | 202 | 1346 | 4.5 | 5.1 | 17.3 |
| 94-95—Miami-Atlanta . | 80 | 2665 | 428 | 1005 | .426 | 312 | 371 | .841 | 104 | 172 | 276 | 274 | 62 | 33 | 155 | 1305 | 3.5 | 3.4 | 16.3 |
| 95-96—Atlanta .......... | 80 | 2856 | 494 | 1143 | .432 | 318 | 385 | .826 | 124 | 202 | 326 | 224 | 68 | 17 | 151 | 1446 | 4.1 | 2.8 | 18.1 |
| 96-97—Atlanta .......... | 72 | 2818 | 491 | 1145 | .429 | 333 | 393 | .847 | 90 | 148 | 238 | 305 | 62 | 23 | 176 | 1445 | 3.3 | 4.2 | 20.1 |
| 97-98—Atlanta .......... | 73 | 2857 | 489 | 1101 | .444 | 389 | 455 | .855 | 133 | 176 | 309 | 292 | 75 | 29 | 176 | 1464 | 4.2 | 4.0 | 20.1 |
| 98-99—Atlanta .......... | 36 | 1314 | 217 | 540 | .402 | 191 | 225 | .849 | 50 | 101 | 151 | 118 | 36 | 11 | 99 | 672 | 4.2 | 3.3 | 18.7 |
| 99-00—Portland ......... | 82 | 2689 | 420 | 900 | .467 | 289 | 340 | .850 | 123 | 190 | 313 | 209 | 71 | 31 | 117 | 1225 | 3.8 | 2.5 | 14.9 |
| 00-01—Portland ......... | 81 | 2542 | 359 | 788 | .456 | 309 | 347 | .890 | 87 | 185 | 272 | 213 | 48 | 24 | 137 | 1105 | 3.4 | 2.6 | 13.6 |
| 01-02—San Antonio .... | 77 | 2211 | 310 | 682 | .455 | 159 | 181 | .878 | 45 | 148 | 193 | 151 | 54 | 15 | 108 | 895 | 2.5 | 2.0 | 11.6 |
| 02-03—San Antonio .... | 53 | 1032 | 113 | 291 | .388 | 95 | 114 | .833 | 21 | 78 | 99 | 70 | 28 | 9 | 43 | 360 | 1.9 | 1.3 | 6.8 |
| 03-04—New Orleans ... | 71 | 929 | 119 | 293 | .406 | 77 | 83 | .928 | 27 | 54 | 81 | 56 | 15 | 6 | 42 | 358 | 1.1 | 0.8 | 5.0 |
| 04-05—Char.Miami .... | 50 | 750 | 102 | 248 | .411 | 69 | 80 | .863 | 15 | 50 | 65 | 71 | 14 | 7 | 27 | 314 | 1.3 | 1.4 | 6.3 |
| **Totals** ................... | 942 | 28855 | 4609 | 10485 | .440 | 3064 | 3625 | .845 | 1112 | 1948 | 3060 | 2922 | 726 | 275 | 1714 | 13430 | 3.2 | 3.1 | 14.3 |

Three-point field goals: 1991-92, 40-for-125 (.320). 1992-93, 53-for-132 (.402). 1993-94, 91-for-262 (.347). 1994-95, 137-for-416 (.329). 1995-96, 140-for-423 (.331). 1996-97, 130-for-388 (.335). 1997-98, 97-for-276 (.351). 1998-99, 47-for-139 (.338). 1999-00, 96-for-241 (.398). 2000-01, 78-for-230 (.339). 2001-02, 116-for-246 (.472). 2002-03, 39-for-118 (.331). 2003-04, 43-for-107 (.402). 2004-05, 41-for-105 (.390). Totals, 1148-for-3208 (.358).
Personal fouls/disqualifications: 1991-92, 162/1. 1992-93, 148/3. 1993-94, 217/6. 1994-95, 225/2. 1995-96, 207/1. 1996-97, 173/2. 1997-98, 219/4. 1998-99, 100/2. 1999-00, 214/0. 2000-01, 203/0. 2001-02, 158/0. 2002-03, 79/0. 2003-04, 91/0. 2004-05, 82/2. Totals, 2278/23.

## NBA PLAYOFF RECORD

| Season Team | G | Min. | FGM | FGA | Pct. | FTM | FTA | Pct. | REBOUNDS Off. | Def. | Tot. | Ast. | St. | Blk. | TO | Pts. | AVERAGES RPG | APG | PPG |
|---|---|---|---|---|---|---|---|---|---|---|---|---|---|---|---|---|---|---|---|
| 91-92—Miami ............ | 3 | 100 | 18 | 34 | .529 | 5 | 6 | .833 | 3 | 3 | 6 | 15 | 4 | 1 | 3 | 48 | 2.0 | 5.0 | 16.0 |
| 93-94—Miami ............ | 5 | 192 | 33 | 80 | .413 | 21 | 25 | .840 | 17 | 13 | 30 | 11 | 4 | 2 | 10 | 96 | 6.0 | 2.2 | 19.2 |
| 94-95—Atlanta .......... | 3 | 108 | 17 | 43 | .395 | 16 | 19 | .842 | 1 | 7 | 8 | 6 | 6 | 1 | 3 | 57 | 2.7 | 2.0 | 19.0 |
| 95-96—Atlanta .......... | 10 | 421 | 75 | 171 | .439 | 42 | 52 | .808 | 15 | 26 | 41 | 32 | 13 | 13 | 16 | 217 | 4.1 | 3.2 | 21.7 |
| 96-97—Atlanta .......... | 10 | 421 | 55 | 139 | .396 | 61 | 74 | .824 | 12 | 27 | 39 | 17 | 4 | 1 | 28 | 189 | 3.9 | 1.7 | 18.9 |
| 97-98—Atlanta .......... | 4 | 160 | 39 | 68 | .574 | 11 | 16 | .688 | 2 | 9 | 11 | 9 | 2 | 3 | 5 | 99 | 2.8 | 2.3 | 24.8 |
| 98-99—Atlanta .......... | 9 | 356 | 54 | 153 | .353 | 39 | 43 | .907 | 14 | 17 | 31 | 30 | 14 | 2 | 21 | 156 | 3.4 | 3.3 | 17.3 |
| 99-00—Portland ......... | 16 | 604 | 88 | 181 | .486 | 69 | 78 | .885 | 13 | 27 | 40 | 44 | 19 | 4 | 27 | 274 | 2.5 | 2.8 | 17.1 |
| 00-01—Portland ......... | 3 | 122 | 16 | 34 | .471 | 15 | 16 | .938 | 5 | 8 | 13 | 7 | 2 | 1 | 10 | 51 | 4.3 | 2.3 | 17.0 |
| 01-02—San Antonio .... | 10 | 298 | 32 | 87 | .368 | 29 | 30 | .967 | 14 | 20 | 34 | 17 | 8 | 1 | 7 | 103 | 3.4 | 1.7 | 10.3 |
| 02-03—San Antonio .... | 9 | 66 | 5 | 24 | .208 | 4 | 4 | 1.000 | 1 | 6 | 7 | 6 | 1 | 0 | 2 | 16 | 0.8 | 0.7 | 1.8 |
| 03-04—New Orleans ... | 5 | 46 | 12 | 26 | .462 | 2 | 3 | .667 | 2 | 6 | 8 | 1 | 0 | 0 | 3 | 32 | 1.6 | 0.2 | 6.4 |
| 04-05—Miami ............ | 3 | 8 | 0 | 2 | .000 | 0 | 0 | ... | 0 | 0 | 0 | 0 | 0 | 0 | 0 | 0 | 0.0 | 0.0 | 0.0 |
| **Totals** ................... | 90 | 2902 | 444 | 1042 | .426 | 314 | 366 | .858 | 99 | 169 | 268 | 195 | 77 | 29 | 135 | 1338 | 3.0 | 2.2 | 14.9 |

Three-point field goals: 1991-92, 7-for-11 (.636). 1993-94, 9-for-22 (.409). 1994-95, 7-for-18 (.389). 1995-96, 25-for-61 (.410). 1996-97, 18-for-55 (.327). 1997-98, 10-for-20 (.500). 1998-99, 9-for-33 (.273). 1999-00, 29-for-53 (.547). 2000-01, 4-for-11 (.364). 2001-02, 10-for-38 (.263). 2002-03, 2-for-12 (.167). 2003-04, 6-for-11 (.545). Totals, 136-for-345 (.394).
Personal fouls/disqualifications: 1991-92, 2/0. 1993-94, 12/0. 1994-95, 14/0. 1995-96, 31/0. 1996-97, 38/0. 1997-98, 17/1. 1998-99, 32/0. 1999-00, 44/0. 2000-01, 3/0. 2001-02, 20/0. 2002-03, 3/0. 2003-04, 5/0. Totals, 221/1.

## NBA ALL-STAR GAME RECORD

| Season Team | Min. | FGM | FGA | Pct. | FTM | FTA | Pct. | REBOUNDS Off. | Def. | Tot. | Ast. | PF | Dq. | St. | Blk. | TO | Pts. |
|---|---|---|---|---|---|---|---|---|---|---|---|---|---|---|---|---|---|
| 1998—Atlanta.................. | 16 | 6 | 12 | .500 | 0 | 0 | ... | 2 | 1 | 3 | 0 | 0 | ... | 0 | 0 | 0 | 14 |

Three-point field goals: 1998, 2-for-5 (.400). Totals, 2-for-5 (.400).

# SMITH, THERON                    F

**PERSONAL:** Born October 3, 1980, in Winter Haven, Fla. ... 6-8/225. (2.03/102.1). ... Full name: Theron Augustus Smith
**HIGH SCHOOL:** Aburndale (Winter Haven, Fla.).
**COLLEGE:** Ball State.
**TRANSACTIONS/CAREER NOTES:** Not drafted by an NBA franchise. ... Signed as free agent by Memphis Grizzlies (July 16, 2003). ... Selected by Charlotte Bobcats from Grizzlies in NBA Expansion Draft (June 22, 2004).

## COLLEGIATE RECORD

| | | | | | | | | | | | | AVERAGES | | |
|---|---|---|---|---|---|---|---|---|---|---|---|---|---|---|
| Season Team | G | Min. | FGM | FGA | Pct. | FTM | FTA | Pct. | Reb. | Ast. | Pts. | RPG | APG | PPG |
| 99-00—Ball State | 31 | 994 | 134 | 289 | .464 | 79 | 111 | .712 | 237 | 47 | 377 | 7.6 | 1.5 | 12.2 |
| 00-01—Ball State | 30 | 1004 | 176 | 381 | .462 | 96 | 137 | .701 | 244 | 48 | 489 | 8.1 | 1.6 | 16.3 |
| 01-02—Ball State | 35 | 1156 | 233 | 454 | .513 | 176 | 237 | .743 | 381 | 48 | 687 | 10.9 | 1.4 | 19.6 |
| 02-03—Ball State | 3 | 100 | 13 | 36 | .361 | 18 | 24 | .750 | 20 | 5 | 46 | 6.7 | 1.7 | 15.3 |
| Totals | 99 | 3254 | 556 | 1160 | .479 | 369 | 509 | .725 | 882 | 148 | 1599 | 8.9 | 1.5 | 16.2 |

Three-point field goals: 1999-00, 30-for-75 (.400). 2000-01, 41-for-114 (.360). 2001-02, 45-for-119 (.378). 2002-03, 2-for-11 (.182). Totals, 118-for-319 (.370).

## NBA REGULAR-SEASON RECORD

| | | | | | | | | | REBOUNDS | | | | | | | | AVERAGES | | |
|---|---|---|---|---|---|---|---|---|---|---|---|---|---|---|---|---|---|---|---|
| Season Team | G | Min. | FGM | FGA | Pct. | FTM | FTA | Pct. | Off. | Def. | Tot. | Ast. | St. | Blk. | TO | Pts. | RPG | APG | PPG |
| 03-04—Memphis | 20 | 178 | 16 | 43 | .372 | 6 | 8 | .750 | 13 | 28 | 41 | 7 | 5 | 5 | 14 | 44 | 2.1 | 0.4 | 2.2 |
| 04-05—Charlotte | 33 | 510 | 44 | 136 | .324 | 14 | 16 | .875 | 39 | 77 | 116 | 28 | 6 | 4 | 27 | 105 | 3.5 | 0.8 | 3.2 |
| Totals | 53 | 688 | 60 | 179 | .335 | 20 | 24 | .833 | 52 | 105 | 157 | 35 | 11 | 9 | 41 | 149 | 3.0 | 0.7 | 2.8 |

Three-point field goals: 2003-04, 6-for-12 (.500). 2004-05, 3-for-12 (.250). Totals, 9-for-24 (.375).
Personal fouls/disqualifications: 2003-04, 18/0. 2004-05, 58/0. Totals, 76/0.

# SNOW, ERIC              G              CAVALIERS

**PERSONAL:** Born April 24, 1973, in Canton, Ohio. ... 6-3/204. (1.91/92.5). ... Brother of Percy Snow, linebacker with Kansas City Chiefs (1990 through 1992), Chicago Bears (1993) and Rhein Fire of World League (1996).
**HIGH SCHOOL:** McKinley (Canton, Ohio).
**COLLEGE:** Michigan State.
**TRANSACTIONS/CAREER NOTES:** Selected by Milwaukee Bucks in second round (43rd pick overall) of 1995 NBA Draft. ... Draft rights traded by Bucks to Seattle SuperSonics for draft rights to C Aurelijius Zukauskas and 1996 second-round draft choice (June 28, 1995). ... Traded by SuperSonics to Philadelphia 76ers for 1998 second-round draft choice (January 18, 1998). ... Traded by 76ers to Cleveland Cavaliers for F Kedrick Brown and G Kevin Ollie (July 20, 2004).

## COLLEGIATE RECORD

| | | | | | | | | | | | | AVERAGES | | |
|---|---|---|---|---|---|---|---|---|---|---|---|---|---|---|
| Season Team | G | Min. | FGM | FGA | Pct. | FTM | FTA | Pct. | Reb. | Ast. | Pts. | RPG | APG | PPG |
| 91-92—Michigan State | 25 | 144 | 12 | 25 | .480 | 3 | 15 | .200 | 15 | 24 | 27 | 0.6 | 1.0 | 1.1 |
| 92-93—Michigan State | 28 | 798 | 53 | 97 | .546 | 15 | 56 | .268 | 73 | 145 | 121 | 2.6 | 5.2 | 4.3 |
| 93-94—Michigan State | 32 | 992 | 91 | 177 | .514 | 22 | 49 | .449 | 111 | 213 | 217 | 3.5 | 6.7 | 6.8 |
| 94-95—Michigan State | 28 | 916 | 117 | 225 | .520 | 62 | 102 | .608 | 92 | 217 | 303 | 3.3 | 7.8 | 10.8 |
| Totals | 113 | 2850 | 273 | 524 | .521 | 102 | 222 | .459 | 291 | 599 | 668 | 2.6 | 5.3 | 5.9 |

Three-point field goals: 1991-92, 0-for-2. 1992-93, 0-for-5. 1993-94, 13-for-45 (.289). 1994-95, 7-for-24 (.292). Totals, 20-for-76 (.263).

## NBA REGULAR-SEASON RECORD

**HONORS:** NBA Sportsmanship Award (2000). ... NBA All-Defensive second team (2003).

| | | | | | | | | | REBOUNDS | | | | | | | | AVERAGES | | |
|---|---|---|---|---|---|---|---|---|---|---|---|---|---|---|---|---|---|---|---|
| Season Team | G | Min. | FGM | FGA | Pct. | FTM | FTA | Pct. | Off. | Def. | Tot. | Ast. | St. | Blk. | TO | Pts. | RPG | APG | PPG |
| 95-96—Seattle | 43 | 389 | 42 | 100 | .420 | 29 | 49 | .592 | 9 | 34 | 43 | 73 | 28 | 0 | 38 | 115 | 1.0 | 1.7 | 2.7 |
| 96-97—Seattle | 67 | 775 | 74 | 164 | .451 | 47 | 66 | .712 | 17 | 53 | 70 | 159 | 37 | 3 | 48 | 199 | 1.0 | 2.4 | 3.0 |
| 97-98—Seattle-Phila. | 64 | 918 | 79 | 184 | .429 | 49 | 71 | .690 | 19 | 62 | 81 | 177 | 60 | 5 | 63 | 209 | 1.3 | 2.8 | 3.3 |
| 98-99—Philadelphia | 48 | 1716 | 149 | 348 | .428 | 110 | 150 | .733 | 25 | 137 | 162 | 301 | 100 | 1 | 111 | 413 | 3.4 | 6.3 | 8.6 |
| 99-00—Philadelphia | 82 | 2866 | 257 | 597 | .430 | 126 | 177 | .712 | 42 | 219 | 261 | 624 | 140 | 8 | 162 | 651 | 3.2 | 7.6 | 7.9 |
| 00-01—Philadelphia | 50 | 1740 | 182 | 435 | .418 | 122 | 154 | .792 | 27 | 139 | 166 | 369 | 77 | 7 | 124 | 491 | 3.3 | 7.4 | 9.8 |
| 01-02—Philadelphia | 61 | 2225 | 276 | 624 | .442 | 183 | 227 | .806 | 33 | 182 | 215 | 400 | 95 | 9 | 138 | 738 | 3.5 | 6.6 | 12.1 |
| 02-03—Philadelphia | 82 | 3108 | 361 | 799 | .452 | 325 | 379 | .858 | 71 | 230 | 301 | 544 | 133 | 11 | 194 | 1054 | 3.7 | 6.6 | 12.9 |
| 03-04—Philadelphia | 82 | 2966 | 295 | 715 | .413 | 252 | 316 | .797 | 62 | 219 | 281 | 563 | 97 | 6 | 187 | 844 | 3.4 | 6.9 | 10.3 |
| 04-05—Cleveland | 81 | 1844 | 125 | 327 | .382 | 59 | 80 | .738 | 37 | 118 | 155 | 317 | 67 | 16 | 89 | 322 | 1.9 | 3.9 | 4.0 |
| Totals | 660 | 18547 | 1840 | 4293 | .429 | 1302 | 1669 | .780 | 342 | 1393 | 1735 | 3527 | 834 | 66 | 1154 | 5036 | 2.6 | 5.3 | 7.6 |

Three-point field goals: 1995-96, 2-for-10 (.200). 1996-97, 4-for-15 (.267). 1997-98, 2-for-17 (.118). 1998-99, 5-for-21 (.238). 1999-00, 11-for-45 (.244). 2000-01, 5-for-19 (.263). 2001-02, 3-for-27 (.111). 2002-03, 7-for-32 (.219). 2003-04, 2-for-18 (.111). 2004-05, 13-for-45 (.289). Totals, 54-for-249 (.217).
Personal fouls/disqualifications: 1995-96, 53/0. 1996-97, 94/0. 1997-98, 114/0. 1998-99, 149/2. 1999-00, 243/2. 2000-01, 123/1. 2001-02, 167/1. 2002-03, 235/2. 2003-04, 213/1. 2004-05, 189/0. Totals, 1580/9.

## NBA PLAYOFF RECORD

| | | | | | | | | | REBOUNDS | | | | | | | | AVERAGES | | |
|---|---|---|---|---|---|---|---|---|---|---|---|---|---|---|---|---|---|---|---|
| Season Team | G | Min. | FGM | FGA | Pct. | FTM | FTA | Pct. | Off. | Def. | Tot. | Ast. | St. | Blk. | TO | Pts. | RPG | APG | PPG |
| 95-96—Seattle | 10 | 24 | 1 | 7 | .143 | 0 | 0 | ... | 0 | 4 | 4 | 6 | 2 | 0 | 4 | 2 | 0.4 | 0.6 | 0.2 |
| 96-97—Seattle | 8 | 48 | 5 | 11 | .455 | 1 | 2 | .500 | 0 | 2 | 2 | 12 | 4 | 0 | 13 | 13 | 0.3 | 1.5 | 1.6 |
| 98-99—Philadelphia | 8 | 306 | 37 | 88 | .420 | 22 | 27 | .815 | 3 | 30 | 33 | 57 | 8 | 1 | 25 | 99 | 4.1 | 7.1 | 12.4 |
| 99-00—Philadelphia | 5 | 138 | 15 | 31 | .484 | 4 | 4 | 1.000 | 0 | 10 | 10 | 35 | 4 | 1 | 7 | 37 | 2.0 | 7.0 | 7.4 |
| 00-01—Philadelphia | 23 | 717 | 87 | 210 | .414 | 40 | 55 | .727 | 26 | 60 | 86 | 104 | 27 | 2 | 45 | 214 | 3.7 | 4.5 | 9.3 |
| 01-02—Philadelphia | 5 | 171 | 18 | 56 | .321 | 17 | 22 | .773 | 3 | 19 | 22 | 27 | 6 | 0 | 15 | 54 | 4.4 | 5.4 | 10.8 |
| 02-03—Philadelphia | 12 | 415 | 43 | 102 | .422 | 51 | 58 | .879 | 9 | 31 | 40 | 67 | 18 | 0 | 30 | 138 | 3.3 | 5.6 | 11.5 |
| Totals | 71 | 1819 | 206 | 505 | .408 | 135 | 168 | .804 | 41 | 156 | 197 | 308 | 69 | 4 | 126 | 557 | 2.8 | 4.3 | 7.8 |

Three-point field goals: 1995-96, 0-for-2. 1996-97, 2-for-4 (.500). 1998-99, 3-for-13 (.231). 1999-00, 3-for-4 (.750). 2000-01, 0-for-7. 2001-02, 1-for-6 (.167). 2002-03, 1-for-10 (.100). Totals, 10-for-46 (.217).
Personal fouls/disqualifications: 1995-96, 3/0. 1996-97, 7/0. 1998-99, 26/0. 1999-00, 14/0. 2000-01, 63/0. 2001-02, 13/0. 2002-03, 47/1. Totals, 173/1.

## SNYDER, KIRK     G     HORNETS

**PERSONAL:** Born June 5, 1983, in Los Angeles. ... 6-6/225. (1.98/102.1). ... Full name: Kirk Patrick Snyder
**HIGH SCHOOL:** Upland (Calif.).
**COLLEGE:** Nevada.
**TRANSACTIONS/CAREER NOTES:** Selected after junior season by Utah Jazz in first round (16th pick overall) of 2004 NBA Draft. ... Traded by Jazz to New Orleans Hornets in five-team trade (August 2, 2005).

### COLLEGIATE RECORD

| Season Team | G | Min. | FGM | FGA | Pct. | FTM | FTA | Pct. | Reb. | Ast. | Pts. | AVERAGES RPG | APG | PPG |
|---|---|---|---|---|---|---|---|---|---|---|---|---|---|---|
| 01-02—Nevada-Reno | 18 | 494 | 81 | 215 | .377 | 65 | 104 | .625 | 83 | 26 | 246 | 4.6 | 1.4 | 13.7 |
| 02-03—Nevada-Reno | 32 | 1013 | 187 | 420 | .445 | 113 | 177 | .638 | 259 | 81 | 520 | 8.1 | 2.5 | 16.3 |
| 03-04—Nevada-Reno | 34 | 1079 | 209 | 485 | .431 | 166 | 227 | .731 | 195 | 117 | 638 | 5.7 | 3.4 | 18.8 |
| Totals | 84 | 2586 | 477 | 1120 | .426 | 344 | 508 | .677 | 537 | 224 | 1404 | 6.4 | 2.7 | 16.7 |

Three-point field goals: 2001-02, 19-for-64 (.297). 2002-03, 33-for-123 (.268). 2003-04, 54-for-155 (.348). Totals, 106-for-342 (.310).

### NBA REGULAR-SEASON RECORD

| Season Team | G | Min. | FGM | FGA | Pct. | FTM | FTA | Pct. | REBOUNDS Off. | Def. | Tot. | Ast. | St. | Blk. | TO | Pts. | AVERAGES RPG | APG | PPG |
|---|---|---|---|---|---|---|---|---|---|---|---|---|---|---|---|---|---|---|---|
| 04-05—Utah | 68 | 906 | 122 | 328 | .372 | 64 | 96 | .667 | 50 | 71 | 121 | 36 | 26 | 19 | 58 | 338 | 1.8 | 0.5 | 5.0 |

Three-point field goals: 2004-05, 30-for-85 (.353). Totals, 30-for-85 (.353).
Personal fouls/disqualifications: 2004-05, 116/0. Totals, 116/0.

## SONGAILA, DARIUS     F     KINGS

**PERSONAL:** Born February 14, 1978, in Marijampole, Lithuania. ... 6-9/248. (2.06/112.5).
**HIGH SCHOOL:** New Hampton Prep (New Hampton, N.H.).
**COLLEGE:** Wake Forest.
**TRANSACTIONS/CAREER NOTES:** Selected by Boston Celtics in second round (50th pick overall) of 2002 NBA Draft. ... Traded by Celtics to Sacramento Kings for 2003 and 2005 second-round picks. ... Played in Russia (2002-03). ... Signed by Kings (June 25, 2003).
**MISCELLANEOUS:** Member of bronze-medal-winning Lithuanian Olympic team (2000). ... Member of Lithuanian Olympic Team (2004).

### COLLEGIATE RECORD

| Season Team | G | Min. | FGM | FGA | Pct. | FTM | FTA | Pct. | Reb. | Ast. | Pts. | AVERAGES RPG | APG | PPG |
|---|---|---|---|---|---|---|---|---|---|---|---|---|---|---|
| 98-99—Wake Forest | 31 | 757 | 125 | 248 | .504 | 123 | 153 | .804 | 165 | 48 | 375 | 5.3 | 1.5 | 12.1 |
| 99-00—Wake Forest | 35 | 842 | 162 | 317 | .511 | 157 | 188 | .835 | 191 | 41 | 481 | 5.5 | 1.2 | 13.7 |
| 00-01—Wake Forest | 30 | 766 | 145 | 290 | .500 | 102 | 125 | .816 | 181 | 51 | 396 | 6.0 | 1.7 | 13.2 |
| 01-02—Wake Forest | 34 | 1036 | 204 | 390 | .523 | 193 | 226 | .854 | 276 | 89 | 607 | 8.1 | 2.6 | 17.9 |
| Totals | 130 | 3401 | 636 | 1245 | .511 | 575 | 692 | .831 | 813 | 229 | 1859 | 6.3 | 1.8 | 14.3 |

Three-point field goals: 1998-99, 2-for-8 (.250). 1999-00, 0-for-2. 2000-01, 4-for-9 (.444). 2001-02, 6-for-16 (.375). Totals, 12-for-35 (.343).

### RUSSIAN LEAGUE RECORD

| Season Team | G | Min. | FGM | FGA | Pct. | FTM | FTA | Pct. | Reb. | Ast. | Pts. | AVERAGES RPG | APG | PPG |
|---|---|---|---|---|---|---|---|---|---|---|---|---|---|---|
| 02-03—CSKA | 27 | 584 | 127 | 256 | .496 | 128 | 153 | .837 | 149 | 43 | 392 | 5.5 | 1.6 | 14.5 |

Three-point field goals: 2002-03, 10-for-22 (.455). Totals, 10-for-22 (.455).

### NBA REGULAR-SEASON RECORD

| Season Team | G | Min. | FGM | FGA | Pct. | FTM | FTA | Pct. | REBOUNDS Off. | Def. | Tot. | Ast. | St. | Blk. | TO | Pts. | AVERAGES RPG | APG | PPG |
|---|---|---|---|---|---|---|---|---|---|---|---|---|---|---|---|---|---|---|---|
| 03-04—Sacramento | 73 | 976 | 133 | 273 | .487 | 71 | 88 | .807 | 91 | 134 | 225 | 48 | 42 | 12 | 43 | 337 | 3.1 | 0.7 | 4.6 |
| 04-05—Sacramento | 81 | 1668 | 257 | 488 | .527 | 94 | 111 | .847 | 125 | 219 | 344 | 114 | 51 | 18 | 70 | 608 | 4.2 | 1.4 | 7.5 |
| Totals | 154 | 2644 | 390 | 761 | .512 | 165 | 199 | .829 | 216 | 353 | 569 | 162 | 93 | 30 | 113 | 945 | 3.7 | 1.1 | 6.1 |

Three-point field goals: 2004-05, 0-for-3. Totals, 0-for-3 (.000).
Personal fouls/disqualifications: 2003-04, 126/1. 2004-05, 206/2. Totals, 332/3.

### NBA PLAYOFF RECORD

| Season Team | G | Min. | FGM | FGA | Pct. | FTM | FTA | Pct. | REBOUNDS Off. | Def. | Tot. | Ast. | St. | Blk. | TO | Pts. | AVERAGES RPG | APG | PPG |
|---|---|---|---|---|---|---|---|---|---|---|---|---|---|---|---|---|---|---|---|
| 03-04—Sacramento | 7 | 85 | 10 | 16 | .625 | 6 | 6 | 1.000 | 6 | 7 | 13 | 2 | 0 | 1 | 5 | 26 | 1.9 | 0.3 | 3.7 |
| 04-05—Sacramento | 5 | 75 | 8 | 19 | .421 | 4 | 5 | .800 | 6 | 8 | 14 | 3 | 2 | 1 | 2 | 20 | 2.8 | 0.6 | 4.0 |
| Totals | 12 | 160 | 18 | 35 | .514 | 10 | 11 | .909 | 12 | 15 | 27 | 5 | 2 | 2 | 7 | 46 | 2.3 | 0.4 | 3.8 |

Personal fouls/disqualifications: 2003-04, 14/1. 2004-05, 14/0. Totals, 28/1.

## SOW, PAPE     F     RAPTORS

**PERSONAL:** Born November 22, 1981, in Dakar, Senegal. ... 6-10/250. (2.08/113.4).
**HIGH SCHOOL:** Jean Di La Fontaine (Dakar, Senegal).
**JUNIOR COLLEGE:** Chaffey (Rancho Cucamonga, Calif.).
**COLLEGE:** Cal State Fullerton.
**TRANSACTIONS/CAREER NOTES:** Selected by Miami Heat in second round (47th pick overall) of 2004 NBA Draft. ... Draft

rights traded by Heat to Toronto Raptors for F Albert Miralles and a future second-round draft choice (June 24, 2004).

## COLLEGIATE RECORD

| Season Team | G | Min. | FGM | FGA | Pct. | FTM | FTA | Pct. | Reb. | Ast. | Pts. | AVERAGES RPG | APG | PPG |
|---|---|---|---|---|---|---|---|---|---|---|---|---|---|---|
| 00-01—Chaffey | | | | | | | Statistics unavailable. | | | | | | | |
| 01-02—Cal State Fullerton | 26 | 867 | 139 | 330 | .421 | 118 | 182 | .648 | 223 | 18 | 402 | 8.6 | 0.7 | 15.5 |
| 02-03—Cal State Fullerton | 18 | 566 | 82 | 160 | .513 | 79 | 116 | .681 | 159 | 13 | 249 | 8.8 | 0.7 | 13.8 |
| 03-04—Cal State Fullerton | 28 | 901 | 160 | 324 | .494 | 156 | 231 | .675 | 272 | 25 | 484 | 9.7 | 0.9 | 17.3 |
| Totals | 72 | 2334 | 381 | 814 | .468 | 353 | 529 | .667 | 654 | 56 | 1135 | 9.1 | 0.8 | 15.8 |

Three-point field goals: 2001-02, 6-for-32 (.188). 2002-03, 6-for-12 (.500). 2003-04, 8-for-24 (.333). Totals, 20-for-68 (.294).

## NBA REGULAR-SEASON RECORD

| Season Team | G | Min. | FGM | FGA | Pct. | FTM | FTA | Pct. | REBOUNDS Off. | Def. | Tot. | Ast. | St. | Blk. | TO | Pts. | AVERAGES RPG | APG | PPG |
|---|---|---|---|---|---|---|---|---|---|---|---|---|---|---|---|---|---|---|---|
| 04-05—Toronto | 27 | 255 | 23 | 58 | .397 | 16 | 27 | .593 | 18 | 39 | 57 | 2 | 12 | 4 | 10 | 62 | 2.1 | 0.1 | 2.3 |

Personal fouls/disqualifications: 2004-05, 46/0. Totals, 46/0.

# SPREWELL, LATRELL          G/F

**PERSONAL:** Born September 8, 1970, in Milwaukee. ... 6-5/190. (1.96/86.2). ... Full name: Latrell Fontaine Sprewell ... Name pronounced Lah-TRELL SPREE-well.
**HIGH SCHOOL:** Washington (Milwaukee).
**JUNIOR COLLEGE:** Three Rivers Community College (Mo.).
**COLLEGE:** Alabama.

**TRANSACTIONS/CAREER NOTES:** Selected by Golden State Warriors in first round (24th pick overall) of 1992 NBA Draft. ... Contract terminated (December 3, 1997). ... Contract reinstated by arbitrator (March 4, 1998). ... Suspended for remainder of 1997-98 season. ... Traded by Warriors to New York Knicks for G John Starks, F Chris Mills and F Terry Cummings (January 21, 1999). ... Traded by Knicks to Minnesota Timberwolves in three-team deal in which Knicks acquired F Keith Van Horn from Philadelphia 76ers. Atlanta Hawks acquired F Randy Holcomb, a first-round draft pick and cash considerations from 76ers and G Terrell Brandon from Timberwolves. 76ers acquired F Glenn Robinson and 2006 second-round pick from Hawks and F/C Marc Jackson from Timberwolves (July 23, 2003).

## COLLEGIATE RECORD

| Season Team | G | Min. | FGM | FGA | Pct. | FTM | FTA | Pct. | Reb. | Ast. | Pts. | AVERAGES RPG | APG | PPG |
|---|---|---|---|---|---|---|---|---|---|---|---|---|---|---|
| 88-89—Three Rivers C.C. | 26 | ... | 169 | 327 | .517 | 88 | 133 | .662 | 218 | 45 | 429 | 8.4 | 1.7 | 16.5 |
| 89-90—Three Rivers C.C. | 40 | ... | 421 | 827 | .509 | 217 | 281 | .772 | 365 | 81 | 1064 | 9.1 | 2.0 | 26.6 |
| 90-91—Alabama | 33 | 865 | 116 | 217 | .535 | 58 | 84 | .690 | 165 | 62 | 295 | 5.0 | 1.9 | 8.9 |
| 91-92—Alabama | 35 | 1266 | 227 | 460 | .493 | 101 | 131 | .771 | 183 | 74 | 623 | 5.2 | 2.1 | 17.8 |
| Junior College Totals | 66 | ... | 590 | 1154 | .511 | 305 | 414 | .737 | 583 | 126 | 1493 | 8.8 | 1.9 | 22.6 |
| 4-Year-College Totals | 68 | 2131 | 343 | 677 | .507 | 159 | 215 | .740 | 348 | 136 | 918 | 5.1 | 2.0 | 13.5 |

Three-point field goals: 1988-89, 3-for-4 (.750). 1989-90, 5-for-17 (.294). 1990-91, 5-for-12 (.417). 1991-92, 68-for-171 (.398). Totals, 81-for-204 (.397).

## NBA REGULAR-SEASON RECORD

**RECORDS:** Holds NBA single-game record for most three-point field goals, none missed—9 (Feb. 4, 2003).
**HONORS:** All-NBA First Team (1994). ... NBA All-Defensive second team (1994). ... NBA All-Rookie second team (1993).

| Season Team | G | Min. | FGM | FGA | Pct. | FTM | FTA | Pct. | REBOUNDS Off. | Def. | Tot. | Ast. | St. | Blk. | TO | Pts. | AVERAGES RPG | APG | PPG |
|---|---|---|---|---|---|---|---|---|---|---|---|---|---|---|---|---|---|---|---|
| 92-93—Golden State | 77 | 2741 | 449 | 968 | .464 | 211 | 283 | .746 | 79 | 192 | 271 | 295 | 126 | 52 | 203 | 1182 | 3.5 | 3.8 | 15.4 |
| 93-94—Golden State | 82 | *3533 | 613 | 1417 | .433 | 353 | 456 | .774 | 80 | 321 | 401 | 385 | 180 | 76 | 226 | 1720 | 4.9 | 4.7 | 21.0 |
| 94-95—Golden State | 69 | 2771 | 490 | 1171 | .418 | 350 | 448 | .781 | 58 | 198 | 256 | 279 | 112 | 46 | 230 | 1420 | 3.7 | 4.0 | 20.6 |
| 95-96—Golden State | 78 | 3064 | 515 | 1202 | .428 | 352 | 446 | .789 | 124 | 256 | 380 | 328 | 127 | 45 | 222 | 1473 | 4.9 | 4.2 | 18.9 |
| 96-97—Golden State | 80 | 3353 | 649 | 1444 | .449 | 493 | 585 | .843 | 58 | 308 | 366 | 507 | 132 | 45 | 322 | 1938 | 4.6 | 6.3 | 24.2 |
| 97-98—Golden State | 14 | 547 | 110 | 277 | .397 | 70 | 94 | .745 | 7 | 44 | 51 | 68 | 19 | 5 | 44 | 299 | 3.6 | 4.9 | 21.4 |
| 98-99—New York | 37 | 1233 | 215 | 518 | .415 | 155 | 191 | .812 | 41 | 115 | 156 | 91 | 46 | 2 | 79 | 606 | 4.2 | 2.5 | 16.4 |
| 99-00—New York | 82 | 3276 | 568 | 1305 | .435 | 344 | 397 | .866 | 49 | 300 | 349 | 332 | 109 | 22 | 226 | 1524 | 4.3 | 4.0 | 18.6 |
| 00-01—New York | 77 | 3017 | 524 | 1219 | .430 | 275 | 351 | .783 | 49 | 298 | 347 | 269 | 106 | 28 | 218 | 1364 | 4.5 | 3.5 | 17.7 |
| 01-02—New York | 81 | 3326 | 573 | 1419 | .404 | 284 | 346 | .821 | 59 | 239 | 298 | 313 | 94 | 14 | 223 | 1575 | 3.7 | 3.9 | 19.4 |
| 02-03—New York | 74 | 2859 | 454 | 1127 | .403 | 173 | 218 | .794 | 45 | 240 | 285 | 332 | 102 | 22 | 172 | 1215 | 3.9 | 4.5 | 16.4 |
| 03-04—Minnesota | 82 | 3100 | 518 | 1266 | .409 | 240 | 295 | .814 | 56 | 254 | 310 | 286 | 88 | 21 | 158 | 1375 | 3.8 | 3.5 | 16.8 |
| 04-05—Minnesota | 80 | 2450 | 398 | 961 | .414 | 156 | 188 | .830 | 65 | 189 | 254 | 179 | 53 | 21 | 127 | 1021 | 3.2 | 2.2 | 12.8 |
| Totals | 913 | 35270 | 6076 | 14294 | .425 | 3456 | 4298 | .804 | 770 | 2954 | 3724 | 3664 | 1294 | 399 | 2450 | 16712 | 4.1 | 4.0 | 18.3 |

Three-point field goals: 1992-93, 73-for-198 (.369). 1993-94, 141-for-391 (.361). 1994-95, 90-for-326 (.276). 1995-96, 91-for-282 (.323). 1996-97, 147-for-415 (.354). 1997-98, 9-for-48 (.188). 1998-99, 21-for-77 (.273). 1999-00, 44-for-127 (.346). 2000-01, 41-for-135 (.304). 2001-02, 145-for-403 (.360). 2002-03, 134-for-360 (.372). 2003-04, 99-for-299 (.331). 2004-05, 69-for-211 (.327). Totals, 1104-for-3272 (.337).

Personal fouls/disqualifications: 1992-93, 166/2. 1993-94, 158/0. 1994-95, 108/0. 1995-96, 150/1. 1996-97, 153/0. 1997-98, 26/0. 1998-99, 65/0. 1999-00, 184/0. 2000-01, 159/1. 2001-02, 161/0. 2002-03, 134/2. 2003-04, 101/0. 2004-05, 124/0. Totals, 1689/6.

## NBA PLAYOFF RECORD

| Season Team | G | Min. | FGM | FGA | Pct. | FTM | FTA | Pct. | REBOUNDS Off. | Def. | Tot. | Ast. | St. | Blk. | TO | Pts. | AVERAGES RPG | APG | PPG |
|---|---|---|---|---|---|---|---|---|---|---|---|---|---|---|---|---|---|---|---|
| 93-94—Golden State | 3 | 122 | 26 | 60 | .433 | 8 | 12 | .667 | 1 | 8 | 9 | 21 | 2 | 3 | 9 | 68 | 3.0 | 7.0 | 22.7 |
| 98-99—New York | 20 | 743 | 145 | 346 | .419 | 113 | 133 | .850 | 24 | 72 | 96 | 43 | 19 | 6 | 58 | 407 | 4.8 | 2.2 | 20.4 |
| 99-00—New York | 16 | 700 | 110 | 266 | .414 | 69 | 88 | .784 | 12 | 58 | 70 | 58 | 18 | 5 | 37 | 299 | 4.4 | 3.6 | 18.7 |
| 00-01—New York | 5 | 212 | 35 | 86 | .407 | 19 | 25 | .760 | 3 | 12 | 15 | 17 | 5 | 1 | 20 | 92 | 3.0 | 3.4 | 18.4 |
| 03-04—Minnesota | 18 | 771 | 130 | 309 | .421 | 60 | 77 | .779 | 11 | 68 | 79 | 72 | 29 | 12 | 47 | 357 | 4.4 | 4.0 | 19.8 |
| Totals | 62 | 2548 | 446 | 1067 | .418 | 269 | 335 | .803 | 51 | 218 | 269 | 211 | 73 | 27 | 171 | 1223 | 4.3 | 3.4 | 19.7 |

Three-point field goals: 1993-94, 8-for-23 (.348). 1998-99, 4-for-25 (.160). 1999-00, 10-for-30 (.333). 2000-01, 3-for-14 (.214). 2003-04, 37-for-96 (.385). Totals, 62-for-188 (.330).

Personal fouls/disqualifications: 1993-94, 15/0. 1998-99, 40/1. 1999-00, 28/0. 2000-01, 17/0. 2003-04, 35/0. Totals, 135/1.

## NBA ALL-STAR GAME RECORD

| Season Team | Min. | FGM | FGA | Pct. | FTM | FTA | Pct. | REBOUNDS Off. | Def. | Tot. | Ast. | PF | Dq. | St. | Blk. | TO | Pts. |
|---|---|---|---|---|---|---|---|---|---|---|---|---|---|---|---|---|---|
| 1994—Golden State ........ | 15 | 3 | 8 | .375 | 3 | 7 | .429 | 4 | 3 | 7 | 1 | 1 | 0 | 0 | 0 | 2 | 9 |
| 1995—Golden State ........ | 22 | 4 | 9 | .444 | 1 | 1 | 1.000 | 2 | 2 | 4 | 4 | 0 | 0 | 3 | 0 | 1 | 9 |
| 1997—Golden State ........ | 25 | 7 | 12 | .583 | 4 | 6 | .667 | 1 | 2 | 3 | 1 | 2 | 0 | 2 | 0 | 1 | 19 |
| 2001—New York ............. | 15 | 3 | 6 | .500 | 1 | 3 | .333 | 1 | 0 | 1 | 4 | 1 | 0 | 0 | 0 | 1 | 7 |
| **Totals**........................... | 77 | 17 | 35 | .486 | 9 | 17 | .529 | 8 | 7 | 15 | 10 | 4 | 0 | 5 | 0 | 5 | 44 |

Three-point field goals: 1994, 0-for-2. 1995, 0-for-2. 1997, 1-for-3 (.333). 2001, 0-for-1. Totals, 1-for-8 (.125).

# STACKHOUSE, JERRY     G/F     MAVERICKS

**PERSONAL:** Born November 5, 1974, in Kinston, N.C. ... 6-6/218. (1.98/98.9). ... Full name: Jerry Darnell Stackhouse ... Brother of Tony Dawson, forward with Sacramento Kings (1990-91) and Boston Celtics (1994-95).
**HIGH SCHOOL:** Kinston (N.C.), then Oak Hill Academy (Mouth of Wilson, Va.).
**COLLEGE:** North Carolina.
**TRANSACTIONS/CAREER NOTES:** Selected after sophomore season by Philadelphia 76ers in first round (third pick overall) of 1995 NBA Draft. ... Traded by 76ers with C Eric Montross to Detroit Pistons for C Theo Ratliff, G Aaron McKie and conditional first-round draft choice (December 18, 1997). ... Traded by Pistons with F Brian Cardinal and C Ratko Varda to Washington Wizards for G/F Richard Hamilton, G/F Bobby Simmons and G Hubert Davis (September 11, 2002). ... Traded by Wizards with F/C Christian Laettner and draft rights to G Devin Harris to Dallas Mavericks for F Antawn Jamison (June 24, 2004).

## COLLEGIATE RECORD

**NOTES:** THE SPORTING NEWS All-America second team (1995).

| Season Team | G | Min. | FGM | FGA | Pct. | FTM | FTA | Pct. | Reb. | Ast. | Pts. | AVERAGES RPG | APG | PPG |
|---|---|---|---|---|---|---|---|---|---|---|---|---|---|---|
| 93-94—North Carolina............... | 35 | 734 | 138 | 296 | .466 | 150 | 205 | .732 | 176 | 69 | 428 | 5.0 | 2.0 | 12.2 |
| 94-95—North Carolina............... | 34 | 1170 | 215 | 416 | .517 | 185 | 260 | .712 | 280 | 93 | 652 | 8.2 | 2.7 | 19.2 |
| **Totals** ...................................... | 69 | 1904 | 353 | 712 | .496 | 335 | 465 | .720 | 456 | 162 | 1080 | 6.6 | 2.3 | 15.7 |

Three-point field goals: 1993-94, 2-for-20 (.100). 1994-95, 37-for-90 (.411). Totals, 39-for-110 (.355).

## NBA REGULAR-SEASON RECORD

**HONORS:** NBA All-Rookie first team (1996).

| Season Team | G | Min. | FGM | FGA | Pct. | FTM | FTA | Pct. | REBOUNDS Off. | Def. | Tot. | Ast. | St. | Blk. | TO | Pts. | AVERAGES RPG | APG | PPG |
|---|---|---|---|---|---|---|---|---|---|---|---|---|---|---|---|---|---|---|---|
| 95-96—Philadelphia .... | 72 | 2701 | 452 | 1091 | .414 | 387 | 518 | .747 | 90 | 175 | 265 | 278 | 76 | 79 | 252 | 1384 | 3.7 | 3.9 | 19.2 |
| 96-97—Philadelphia .... | 81 | 3166 | 533 | 1308 | .407 | 511 | 667 | .766 | 156 | 182 | 338 | 253 | 93 | 63 | 316 | 1679 | 4.2 | 3.1 | 20.7 |
| 97-98—Phila.-Det......... | 79 | 2545 | 424 | 975 | .435 | 354 | 450 | .787 | 105 | 161 | 266 | 241 | 89 | 59 | 224 | 1249 | 3.4 | 3.1 | 15.8 |
| 98-99—Detroit ............ | 42 | 1188 | 181 | 488 | .371 | 210 | 247 | .850 | 26 | 81 | 107 | 118 | 34 | 19 | 121 | 607 | 2.5 | 2.8 | 14.5 |
| 99-00—Detroit ............ | 82 | 3148 | 619 | 1447 | .428 | 618 | 758 | .815 | 118 | 197 | 315 | 365 | 103 | 36 | *311 | 1939 | 3.8 | 4.5 | 23.6 |
| 00-01—Detroit ............ | 80 | 3215 | 774 | *1927 | .402 | *666 | 810 | .822 | 99 | 216 | 315 | 410 | 97 | 54 | *326 | *2380 | 3.9 | 5.1 | 29.8 |
| 01-02—Detroit ............ | 76 | 2685 | 524 | 1319 | .397 | 495 | 577 | .858 | 77 | 238 | 315 | 403 | 77 | 37 | 266 | 1629 | 4.1 | 5.3 | 21.4 |
| 02-03—Washington .... | 70 | 2747 | 491 | 1201 | .409 | 455 | 518 | .878 | 61 | 197 | 258 | 316 | 65 | 28 | 193 | 1508 | 3.7 | 4.5 | 21.5 |
| 03-04—Washington .... | 26 | 774 | 128 | 321 | .399 | 83 | 103 | .806 | 16 | 78 | 94 | 103 | 24 | 3 | 88 | 362 | 3.6 | 4.0 | 13.9 |
| 04-05—Dallas.............. | 56 | 1617 | 274 | 662 | .414 | 253 | 298 | .849 | 38 | 145 | 183 | 127 | 53 | 10 | 106 | 833 | 3.3 | 2.3 | 14.9 |
| **Totals** .................... | 664 | 23786 | 4400 | 10739 | .410 | 4032 | 4946 | .815 | 786 | 1670 | 2456 | 2614 | 711 | 388 | 2203 | 13570 | 3.7 | 3.9 | 20.4 |

Three-point field goals: 1995-96, 93-for-292 (.318). 1996-97, 102-for-342 (.298). 1997-98, 47-for-195 (.241). 1998-99, 35-for-126 (.278). 1999-00, 83-for-288 (.288). 2000-01, 166-for-473 (.351). 2001-02, 86-for-300 (.287). 2002-03, 71-for-245 (.290). 2003-04, 23-for-65 (.354). 2004-05, 32-for-120 (.267). Totals, 738-for-2446 (.302).
Personal fouls/disqualifications: 1995-96, 179/0. 1996-97, 219/2. 1997-98, 175/2. 1998-99, 79/0. 1999-00, 188/1. 2000-01, 160/1. 2001-02, 163/0. 2002-03, 130/1. 2003-04, 49/0. 2004-05, 104/0. Totals, 1446/7.

## NBA PLAYOFF RECORD

| Season Team | G | Min. | FGM | FGA | Pct. | FTM | FTA | Pct. | REBOUNDS Off. | Def. | Tot. | Ast. | St. | Blk. | TO | Pts. | AVERAGES RPG | APG | PPG |
|---|---|---|---|---|---|---|---|---|---|---|---|---|---|---|---|---|---|---|---|
| 98-99—Detroit ............ | 5 | 124 | 18 | 46 | .391 | 14 | 14 | .857 | 3 | 5 | 8 | 6 | 2 | 1 | 10 | 50 | 1.6 | 1.2 | 10.0 |
| 99-00—Detroit ............ | 3 | 120 | 24 | 59 | .407 | 23 | 31 | .742 | 1 | 11 | 12 | 10 | 2 | 0 | 14 | 74 | 4.0 | 3.3 | 24.7 |
| 01-02—Detroit ............ | 10 | 361 | 53 | 165 | .321 | 52 | 63 | .825 | 9 | 34 | 43 | 43 | 6 | 6 | 27 | 176 | 4.3 | 4.3 | 17.6 |
| 04-05—Dallas.............. | 13 | 403 | 68 | 176 | .386 | 57 | 66 | .864 | 20 | 33 | 53 | 30 | 8 | 3 | 21 | 209 | 4.1 | 2.3 | 16.1 |
| **Totals** .................... | 31 | 1008 | 163 | 446 | .365 | 144 | 174 | .828 | 33 | 83 | 116 | 89 | 18 | 10 | 72 | 509 | 3.7 | 2.9 | 16.4 |

Three-point field goals: 1998-99, 2-for-8 (.250). 1999-00, 3-for-7 (.429). 2001-02, 18-for-53 (.340). 2004-05, 16-for-40 (.400). Totals, 39-for-108 (.361).
Personal fouls/disqualifications: 1998-99, 11/0. 1999-00, 4/0. 2001-02, 26/0. 2004-05, 22/0. Totals, 63/0.

## NBA ALL-STAR GAME RECORD

| Season Team | Min. | FGM | FGA | Pct. | FTM | FTA | Pct. | REBOUNDS Off. | Def. | Tot. | Ast. | PF | Dq. | St. | Blk. | TO | Pts. |
|---|---|---|---|---|---|---|---|---|---|---|---|---|---|---|---|---|---|
| 2000—Detroit................... | 14 | 4 | 7 | .571 | 0 | 0 | ... | 0 | 1 | 1 | 2 | 2 | 0 | 0 | 0 | 1 | 8 |
| 2001—Detroit................... | 15 | 3 | 8 | .375 | 0 | 2 | .000 | 2 | 0 | 2 | 2 | 1 | 0 | 0 | 0 | 0 | 7 |
| **Totals**........................... | 29 | 7 | 15 | .467 | 0 | 2 | .000 | 2 | 1 | 3 | 4 | 3 | 0 | 0 | 0 | 1 | 15 |

Three-point field goals: 2001, 1-for-1 (1.000). Totals, 1-for-1 (1.000).

# STEVENSON, DESHAWN     G     MAGIC

**PERSONAL:** Born April 3, 1981, in Fresno, Calif. ... 6-5/210. (1.96/95.3).
**HIGH SCHOOL:** Washington Union (Fresno, Calif.).
**COLLEGE:** Did not attend college.
**TRANSACTIONS/CAREER NOTES:** Selected out of high school by Utah Jazz in first round (23rd pick overall) of 2000 NBA Draft. ... Traded by Jazz with conditional second-round draft choice to Orlando Magic for F Gordan Giricek (February 19, 2004).

## NBA REGULAR-SEASON RECORD

| Season Team | G | Min. | FGM | FGA | Pct. | FTM | FTA | Pct. | Off. | Def. | Tot. | Ast. | St. | Blk. | TO | Pts. | RPG | APG | PPG |
|---|---|---|---|---|---|---|---|---|---|---|---|---|---|---|---|---|---|---|---|
| | | | | | | | | | REBOUNDS | | | | | | | | AVERAGES | | |
| 00-01—Utah | 40 | 293 | 31 | 91 | .341 | 26 | 38 | .684 | 9 | 19 | 28 | 18 | 10 | 2 | 28 | 89 | 0.7 | 0.5 | 2.2 |
| 01-02—Utah | 67 | 1134 | 143 | 371 | .385 | 37 | 53 | .698 | 44 | 87 | 131 | 116 | 29 | 24 | 68 | 325 | 2.0 | 1.7 | 4.9 |
| 02-03—Utah | 61 | 760 | 114 | 284 | .401 | 47 | 68 | .691 | 22 | 63 | 85 | 40 | 22 | 8 | 49 | 279 | 1.4 | 0.7 | 4.6 |
| 03-04—Utah-Orlando.. | 80 | 2444 | 376 | 871 | .432 | 138 | 204 | .676 | 79 | 219 | 298 | 158 | 52 | 17 | 120 | 909 | 3.7 | 2.0 | 11.4 |
| 04-05—Orlando | 55 | 1089 | 174 | 426 | .408 | 56 | 101 | .554 | 38 | 64 | 102 | 69 | 16 | 9 | 57 | 429 | 1.9 | 1.3 | 7.8 |
| Totals | 303 | 5720 | 838 | 2043 | .410 | 304 | 464 | .655 | 192 | 452 | 644 | 401 | 129 | 60 | 322 | 2031 | 2.1 | 1.3 | 6.7 |

Three-point field goals: 2000-01, 1-for-12 (.083). 2001-02, 2-for-25 (.080). 2002-03, 4-for-12 (.333). 2003-04, 19-for-71 (.268). 2004-05, 25-for-67 (.373). Totals, 51-for-187 (.273).
Personal fouls/disqualifications: 2000-01, 29/0. 2001-02, 82/0. 2002-03, 57/0. 2003-04, 140/0. 2004-05, 73/0. Totals, 381/0.

## NBA PLAYOFF RECORD

| Season Team | G | Min. | FGM | FGA | Pct. | FTM | FTA | Pct. | Off. | Def. | Tot. | Ast. | St. | Blk. | TO | Pts. | RPG | APG | PPG |
|---|---|---|---|---|---|---|---|---|---|---|---|---|---|---|---|---|---|---|---|
| | | | | | | | | | REBOUNDS | | | | | | | | AVERAGES | | |
| 00-01—Utah | 1 | 8 | 1 | 2 | .500 | 0 | 0 | ... | 0 | 1 | 1 | 0 | 0 | 0 | 1 | 2 | 1.0 | 0.0 | 2.0 |
| 02-03—Utah | 4 | 37 | 6 | 15 | .400 | 6 | 6 | 1.000 | 2 | 5 | 7 | 4 | 1 | 0 | 0 | 18 | 1.8 | 1.0 | 4.5 |
| Totals | 5 | 45 | 7 | 17 | .412 | 6 | 6 | 1.000 | 2 | 6 | 8 | 4 | 1 | 0 | 1 | 20 | 1.6 | 0.8 | 4.0 |

Three-point field goals: 2002-03, 0-for-2. Totals, 0-for-2 (.000).
Personal fouls/disqualifications: 2002-03, 3/0. Totals, 3/0.

# STEWART, MICHAEL　　　　C　　　　HAWKS

**PERSONAL:** Born April 24, 1975, in Cutq Trepied Stella Plage, France. ... 6-10/230. (2.08/104.3). ... Full name: Michael Curtis Stewart
**HIGH SCHOOL:** Kennedy (Sacramento).
**COLLEGE:** California.
**TRANSACTIONS/CAREER NOTES:** Not drafted by an NBA franchise. ... Signed as free agent by Sacramento Kings (September 11, 1997). ... Signed as free agent by Toronto Raptors (January 21, 1999). ... Traded by Raptors with future first-round draft choice to Cleveland Cavaliers for F Lamond Murray and future second-round draft choice (September 25, 2002). ... Traded by Cavaliers with G Ricky Davis, F/C Chris Mihm and a second-round draft choice to Boston Celtics for F/C Tony Battie, F Kedrick Brown and F Eric Williams (December 15, 2003). ... Traded by Celtics with F Tom Gugliotta, G Gary Payton and 2005 draft or future first-round pick to Atlanta Hawks for F Antoine Walker (February 24, 2005).

## COLLEGIATE RECORD

| Season Team | G | Min. | FGM | FGA | Pct. | FTM | FTA | Pct. | Reb. | Ast. | Pts. | RPG | APG | PPG |
|---|---|---|---|---|---|---|---|---|---|---|---|---|---|---|
| | | | | | | | | | | | | AVERAGES | | |
| 93-94—California | 30 | 696 | 40 | 85 | .471 | 31 | 65 | .477 | 152 | 9 | 111 | 5.1 | 0.3 | 3.7 |
| 94-95—California | 27 | 470 | 43 | 85 | .506 | 18 | 39 | .462 | 116 | 7 | 104 | 4.3 | 0.3 | 3.9 |
| 95-96—California | 28 | 440 | 35 | 65 | .538 | 12 | 27 | .444 | 121 | 8 | 82 | 4.3 | 0.3 | 2.9 |
| 96-97—California | 32 | 659 | 83 | 159 | .522 | 36 | 68 | .529 | 160 | 8 | 202 | 5.0 | 0.3 | 6.3 |
| Totals | 117 | 2265 | 201 | 394 | .510 | 97 | 199 | .487 | 549 | 32 | 499 | 4.7 | 0.3 | 4.3 |

Personal fouls/disqualifications: 1993-94, 86/0. 1994-95, 73/0. 1995-96, 73/0. 1996-97, 82/0. Totals, 314/0.

## NBA REGULAR-SEASON RECORD

| Season Team | G | Min. | FGM | FGA | Pct. | FTM | FTA | Pct. | Off. | Def. | Tot. | Ast. | St. | Blk. | TO | Pts. | RPG | APG | PPG |
|---|---|---|---|---|---|---|---|---|---|---|---|---|---|---|---|---|---|---|---|
| | | | | | | | | | REBOUNDS | | | | | | | | AVERAGES | | |
| 97-98—Sacramento | 81 | 1761 | 155 | 323 | .480 | 65 | 142 | .458 | 197 | 339 | 536 | 61 | 29 | 195 | 85 | 375 | 6.6 | 0.8 | 4.6 |
| 98-99—Toronto | 42 | 394 | 22 | 53 | .415 | 17 | 25 | .680 | 43 | 56 | 99 | 5 | 4 | 28 | 12 | 61 | 2.4 | 0.1 | 1.5 |
| 99-00—Toronto | 42 | 389 | 20 | 53 | .377 | 18 | 32 | .563 | 33 | 61 | 94 | 6 | 5 | 19 | 17 | 58 | 2.2 | 0.1 | 1.4 |
| 00-01—Toronto | 26 | 123 | 11 | 34 | .324 | 11 | 18 | .611 | 16 | 13 | 29 | 2 | 4 | 3 | 5 | 33 | 1.1 | 0.1 | 1.3 |
| 01-02—Toronto | 11 | 93 | 8 | 23 | .348 | 6 | 11 | .545 | 12 | 13 | 25 | 3 | 4 | 3 | 4 | 22 | 2.3 | 0.3 | 2.0 |
| 02-03—Cleveland | 47 | 251 | 14 | 37 | .378 | 8 | 12 | .667 | 19 | 36 | 55 | 6 | 2 | 15 | 10 | 36 | 1.2 | 0.1 | 0.8 |
| 03-04—Cleve.-Bos. | 25 | 147 | 5 | 12 | .417 | 3 | 4 | .750 | 8 | 21 | 29 | 0 | 2 | 10 | 3 | 13 | 1.2 | 0.0 | 0.5 |
| 04-05—Bos-Atl | 12 | 145 | 11 | 21 | .524 | 3 | 7 | .429 | 21 | 19 | 40 | 5 | 6 | 5 | 6 | 25 | 3.3 | 0.4 | 2.1 |
| Totals | 286 | 3303 | 246 | 556 | .442 | 131 | 251 | .522 | 349 | 558 | 907 | 88 | 56 | 278 | 142 | 623 | 3.2 | 0.3 | 2.2 |

Personal fouls/disqualifications: 1997-98, 251/6. 1998-99, 76/0. 1999-00, 81/3. 2000-01, 19/0. 2001-02, 22/0. 2002-03, 42/0. 2003-04, 34/0. 2004-05, 32/1. Totals, 557/10.

## NBA PLAYOFF RECORD

| Season Team | G | Min. | FGM | FGA | Pct. | FTM | FTA | Pct. | Off. | Def. | Tot. | Ast. | St. | Blk. | TO | Pts. | RPG | APG | PPG |
|---|---|---|---|---|---|---|---|---|---|---|---|---|---|---|---|---|---|---|---|
| | | | | | | | | | REBOUNDS | | | | | | | | AVERAGES | | |
| 00-01—Toronto | 2 | 4 | 0 | 1 | .000 | 0 | 0 | ... | 1 | 0 | 1 | 0 | 0 | 0 | 0 | 0 | 0.5 | 0.0 | 0.0 |
| 01-02—Toronto | 1 | 8 | 2 | 2 | 1.000 | 0 | 0 | ... | 0 | 3 | 3 | 0 | 0 | 1 | 1 | 4 | 3.0 | 0.0 | 4.0 |
| 03-04—Boston | 1 | 2 | 0 | 0 | ... | 0 | 0 | ... | 0 | 0 | 0 | 0 | 0 | 0 | 0 | 0 | 0.0 | 0.0 | 0.0 |
| Totals | 4 | 14 | 2 | 3 | .667 | 0 | 0 | ... | 1 | 3 | 4 | 0 | 0 | 1 | 1 | 4 | 1.0 | 0.0 | 1.0 |

Personal fouls/disqualifications: 2001-02, 2/0. 2003-04, 2/0. Totals, 4/0.

# STOJAKOVIC, PEJA　　　　F　　　　KINGS

**PERSONAL:** Born June 9, 1977, in Belgrade, Yugoslavia. ... 6-9/229. (2.06/103.9).
**COLLEGE:** PAOK (Greece).
**TRANSACTIONS/CAREER NOTES:** Played in Greece (1995-98). ... Selected by Sacramento Kings in first round (14th pick overall) of 1996 NBA Draft.
**MISCELLANEOUS:** Member of Yugoslavia Olympic team (2000).

## GREEK LEAGUE RECORD

| Season Team | G | Min. | FGM | FGA | Pct. | FTM | FTA | Pct. | Reb. | Ast. | Pts. | RPG | APG | PPG |
|---|---|---|---|---|---|---|---|---|---|---|---|---|---|---|
| | | | | | | | | | | | | AVERAGES | | |
| 95-96—PAOK | 31 | ... | 185 | 343 | .539 | 115 | 145 | .793 | 159 | 47 | 523 | 5.1 | 1.5 | 16.9 |

| Season Team | G | Min. | FGM | FGA | Pct. | FTM | FTA | Pct. | Reb. | Ast. | Pts. | RPG | APG | PPG |
|---|---|---|---|---|---|---|---|---|---|---|---|---|---|---|
| 96-97—PAOK | 16 | 554 | 110 | 218 | .505 | 71 | 82 | .866 | 74 | 17 | 324 | 4.6 | 1.1 | 20.3 |
| 97-98—PAOK | 24 | 884 | 187 | 405 | .462 | 131 | 147 | .891 | 118 | 59 | 574 | 4.9 | 2.5 | 23.9 |
| Totals | 71 | 1438 | 482 | 966 | .499 | 317 | 374 | .848 | 351 | 123 | 1421 | 4.9 | 1.7 | 20.0 |

Three-point field goals: 1995-96, 38-for-98 (.388). 1996-97, 33-for-86 (.384). 1997-98, 69-for-170 (.406). Totals, 140-for-354 (.395).

**HONORS:** All-NBA second team (2004).

### NBA REGULAR-SEASON RECORD

| Season Team | G | Min. | FGM | FGA | Pct. | FTM | FTA | Pct. | Off. | Def. | Tot. | Ast. | St. | Blk. | TO | Pts. | RPG | APG | PPG |
|---|---|---|---|---|---|---|---|---|---|---|---|---|---|---|---|---|---|---|---|
| 98-99—Sacramento | 48 | 1025 | 141 | 373 | .378 | 63 | 74 | .851 | 43 | 100 | 143 | 72 | 41 | 7 | 53 | 402 | 3.0 | 1.5 | 8.4 |
| 99-00—Sacramento | 74 | 1749 | 321 | 717 | .448 | 135 | 153 | .882 | 74 | 202 | 276 | 106 | 52 | 7 | 88 | 877 | 3.7 | 1.4 | 11.9 |
| 00-01—Sacramento | 75 | 2905 | 559 | 1189 | .470 | 267 | 312 | .856 | 93 | 341 | 434 | 164 | 91 | 13 | 146 | 1529 | 5.8 | 2.2 | 20.4 |
| 01-02—Sacramento | 71 | 2649 | 547 | 1130 | .484 | 283 | 323 | .876 | 72 | 301 | 373 | 175 | 81 | 14 | 140 | 1506 | 5.3 | 2.5 | 21.2 |
| 02-03—Sacramento | 72 | 2450 | 497 | 1034 | .481 | 231 | 264 | .875 | 61 | 336 | 397 | 141 | 72 | 5 | 101 | 1380 | 5.5 | 2.0 | 19.2 |
| 03-04—Sacramento | 81 | 3264 | 665 | 1386 | .480 | 394 | 425 | .927 | 91 | 417 | 508 | 173 | 108 | 14 | 153 | 1964 | 6.3 | 2.1 | 24.2 |
| 04-05—Sacramento | 66 | 2534 | 451 | 1016 | .444 | 253 | 275 | .920 | 62 | 223 | 285 | 138 | 79 | 12 | 102 | 1329 | 4.3 | 2.1 | 20.1 |
| Totals | 487 | 16576 | 3181 | 6845 | .465 | 1626 | 1826 | .890 | 496 | 1920 | 2416 | 969 | 524 | 72 | 783 | 8987 | 5.0 | 2.0 | 18.5 |

Three-point field goals: 1998-99, 57-for-178 (.320). 1999-00, 100-for-267 (.375). 2000-01, 144-for-360 (.400). 2001-02, 129-for-310 (.416). 2002-03, 155-for-406 (.382). 2003-04, 240-for-554 (.433). 2004-05, 174-for-433 (.402). Totals, 999-for-2508 (.398).

Personal fouls/disqualifications: 1998-99, 43/0. 1999-00, 97/0. 2000-01, 144/0. 2001-02, 120/0. 2002-03, 143/1. 2003-04, 159/0. 2004-05, 157/0. Totals, 863/1.

### NBA PLAYOFF RECORD

| Season Team | G | Min. | FGM | FGA | Pct. | FTM | FTA | Pct. | Off. | Def. | Tot. | Ast. | St. | Blk. | TO | Pts. | RPG | APG | PPG |
|---|---|---|---|---|---|---|---|---|---|---|---|---|---|---|---|---|---|---|---|
| 98-99—Sacramento | 5 | 108 | 9 | 26 | .346 | 3 | 3 | 1.000 | 12 | 7 | 19 | 2 | 3 | 0 | 6 | 24 | 3.8 | 0.4 | 4.8 |
| 99-00—Sacramento | 5 | 129 | 16 | 40 | .400 | 6 | 9 | .667 | 2 | 15 | 17 | 3 | 4 | 0 | 5 | 44 | 3.4 | 0.6 | 8.8 |
| 00-01—Sacramento | 8 | 307 | 52 | 128 | .406 | 60 | 62 | .968 | 17 | 34 | 51 | 3 | 5 | 3 | 18 | 173 | 6.4 | 0.4 | 21.6 |
| 01-02—Sacramento | 10 | 338 | 50 | 133 | .376 | 35 | 39 | .897 | 16 | 47 | 63 | 10 | 5 | 0 | 19 | 148 | 6.3 | 1.0 | 14.8 |
| 02-03—Sacramento | 12 | 486 | 97 | 202 | .480 | 51 | 60 | .850 | 17 | 66 | 83 | 30 | 10 | 5 | 12 | 277 | 6.9 | 2.5 | 23.1 |
| 03-04—Sacramento | 12 | 517 | 76 | 198 | .384 | 35 | 39 | .897 | 15 | 69 | 84 | 18 | 22 | 3 | 14 | 210 | 7.0 | 1.5 | 17.5 |
| 04-05—Sacramento | 5 | 203 | 39 | 83 | .470 | 21 | 22 | .955 | 6 | 20 | 26 | 7 | 4 | 1 | 2 | 110 | 5.2 | 1.4 | 22.0 |
| Totals | 57 | 2088 | 339 | 810 | .419 | 211 | 234 | .902 | 85 | 258 | 343 | 73 | 53 | 12 | 76 | 986 | 6.0 | 1.3 | 17.3 |

Three-point field goals: 1998-99, 3-for-14 (.214). 1999-00, 6-for-13 (.462). 2000-01, 9-for-26 (.346). 2001-02, 13-for-48 (.271). 2002-03, 32-for-70 (.457). 2003-04, 23-for-73 (.315). 2004-05, 11-for-30 (.367). Totals, 97-for-274 (.354).

Personal fouls/disqualifications: 1998-99, 7/0. 1999-00, 7/0. 2000-01, 17/0. 2001-02, 22/0. 2002-03, 34/0. 2003-04, 26/0. 2004-05, 15/0. Totals, 128/0.

### NBA ALL-STAR GAME RECORD

| Season Team | Min. | FGM | FGA | Pct. | FTM | FTA | Pct. | Off. | Def. | Tot. | Ast. | PF | Dq. | St. | Blk. | TO | Pts. |
|---|---|---|---|---|---|---|---|---|---|---|---|---|---|---|---|---|---|
| 2002—Sacramento | 18 | 4 | 10 | .400 | 0 | 0 | ... | 2 | 0 | 2 | 1 | 0 | 0 | 0 | 0 | 0 | 11 |
| 2003—Sacramento | 13 | 2 | 7 | .286 | 0 | 0 | ... | 0 | 3 | 3 | 1 | 0 | 0 | 1 | 0 | 1 | 5 |
| 2004—Sacramento | 12 | 2 | 5 | .400 | 0 | 0 | ... | 0 | 1 | 1 | 1 | 0 | 0 | 0 | 0 | 2 | 5 |
| Totals | 43 | 8 | 22 | .364 | 0 | 0 | ... | 2 | 4 | 6 | 3 | 0 | 0 | 1 | 0 | 3 | 21 |

Three-point field goals: 2002, 3-for-5 (.600). 2003, 1-for-4 (.250). 2004, 1-for-4 (.250). Totals, 5-for-13 (.385).

# STOREY, AWVEE                                F

**PERSONAL:** Born April 18, 1977, in Chicago. ... 6-6/225. (1.98/102.1).
**HIGH SCHOOL:** Proviso West (Maywood, Ill.), then New Hampton Prep (N.H.).
**COLLEGE:** Illinois, then Arizona State.
**TRANSACTIONS/CAREER NOTES:** Not drafted by an NBA franchise. ... Signed as free agent by New Jersey Nets (October, 2004). ... Waived by Nets (December 9, 2004).

### COLLEGIATE RECORD

| Season Team | G | Min. | FGM | FGA | Pct. | FTM | FTA | Pct. | Reb. | Ast. | Pts. | RPG | APG | PPG |
|---|---|---|---|---|---|---|---|---|---|---|---|---|---|---|
| 97-98—Illinois | 27 | 153 | 24 | 57 | .421 | 6 | 16 | .375 | 32 | 6 | 54 | 1.2 | 0.2 | 2.0 |
| 98-99—Illinois | | | | | | Did Not Play - Transfer Student | | | | | | | | |
| 99-00—Arizona St. | 32 | 794 | 115 | 274 | .420 | 66 | 106 | .623 | 243 | 110 | 296 | 7.6 | 3.4 | 9.3 |
| 00-01—Arizona St. | 29 | 769 | 163 | 327 | .498 | 53 | 88 | .602 | 263 | 81 | 381 | 9.1 | 2.8 | 13.1 |
| 01-02—Arizona St. | 24 | 388 | 76 | 165 | .461 | 30 | 43 | .698 | 96 | 59 | 182 | 4.0 | 2.5 | 7.6 |
| Totals | 112 | 2104 | 378 | 823 | .459 | 155 | 253 | .613 | 634 | 256 | 913 | 5.7 | 2.3 | 8.2 |

Three-point field goals: 1997-98, 0-for-1. 1999-00, 0-for-3. 2000-01, 2-for-4 (.500). 2001-02, 0-for-2. Totals, 2-for-10 (.200).

### CBA RECORD

| Season Team | G | Min. | FGM | FGA | Pct. | FTM | FTA | Pct. | Reb. | Ast. | Pts. | RPG | APG | PPG |
|---|---|---|---|---|---|---|---|---|---|---|---|---|---|---|
| 04-05—Idaho | 7 | 212 | 34 | 74 | .459 | 16 | 24 | .667 | 34 | 19 | 97 | 4.9 | 2.7 | 13.9 |

Three-point field goals: 2004-05, 13-for-25 (.520). Totals, 13-for-25 (.520).

### NBA REGULAR-SEASON RECORD

| Season Team | G | Min. | FGM | FGA | Pct. | FTM | FTA | Pct. | Off. | Def. | Tot. | Ast. | St. | Blk. | TO | Pts. | RPG | APG | PPG |
|---|---|---|---|---|---|---|---|---|---|---|---|---|---|---|---|---|---|---|---|
| 04-05—New Jersey | 9 | 32 | 3 | 10 | .300 | 1 | 2 | .500 | 4 | 1 | 5 | 1 | 0 | 0 | 0 | 8 | 0.6 | 0.1 | 0.9 |

Three-point field goals: 2004-05, 1-for-2 (.500). Totals, 1-for-2 (.500).
Personal fouls/disqualifications: 2004-05, 3/0. Totals, 3/0.

# STOUDAMIRE, DAMON       G       GRIZZLIES

**PERSONAL:** Born September 3, 1973, in Portland, Ore. ... 5-10/171. (1.78/77.6). ... Full name: Damon Lamon Stoudamire ... Name pronounced DAY-min STOD-a-mire.
**HIGH SCHOOL:** Woodrow Wilson (Portland, Ore.).
**COLLEGE:** Arizona.
**TRANSACTIONS/CAREER NOTES:** Selected by Toronto Raptors in first round (seventh pick overall) of 1995 NBA Draft. ... Traded by Raptors with F Walt Williams and F Carlos Rogers to Portland Trail Blazers for G Kenny Anderson, G Alvin Williams, F Gary Trent and two first-round draft choices (February 13, 1998). ... Signed as free agent by Memphis Grizzlies (August 5, 2005).

## COLLEGIATE RECORD

**NOTES:** THE SPORTING NEWS All-America first team (1995).

| Season Team | G | Min. | FGM | FGA | Pct. | FTM | FTA | Pct. | Reb. | Ast. | Pts. | AVERAGES RPG | APG | PPG |
|---|---|---|---|---|---|---|---|---|---|---|---|---|---|---|
| 91-92—Arizona | 30 | 540 | 76 | 167 | .455 | 37 | 48 | .771 | 65 | 76 | 217 | 2.2 | 2.5 | 7.2 |
| 92-93—Arizona | 28 | 870 | 99 | 226 | .438 | 72 | 91 | .791 | 116 | 159 | 309 | 4.1 | 5.7 | 11.0 |
| 93-94—Arizona | 35 | 1164 | 217 | 484 | .448 | 112 | 140 | .800 | 157 | 208 | 639 | 4.5 | 5.9 | 18.3 |
| 94-95—Arizona | 30 | 1092 | 222 | 466 | .476 | 128 | 155 | .826 | 128 | 220 | 684 | 4.3 | 7.3 | 22.8 |
| Totals | 123 | 3666 | 614 | 1343 | .457 | 349 | 434 | .804 | 466 | 663 | 1849 | 3.8 | 5.4 | 15.0 |

Three-point field goals: 1991-92, 28-for-69 (.406). 1992-93, 39-for-102 (.382). 1993-94, 93-for-265 (.351). 1994-95, 112-for-241 (.465). Totals, 272-for-677 (.402).

## NBA REGULAR-SEASON RECORD

**HONORS:** NBA Rookie of the Year (1996). ... NBA All-Rookie first team (1996).

| Season Team | G | Min. | FGM | FGA | Pct. | FTM | FTA | Pct. | REBOUNDS Off. | Def. | Tot. | Ast. | St. | Blk. | TO | Pts. | AVERAGES RPG | APG | PPG |
|---|---|---|---|---|---|---|---|---|---|---|---|---|---|---|---|---|---|---|---|
| 95-96—Toronto | 70 | 2865 | 481 | 1129 | .426 | 236 | 296 | .797 | 59 | 222 | 281 | 653 | 98 | 19 | 267 | 1331 | 4.0 | 9.3 | 19.0 |
| 96-97—Toronto | 81 | 3311 | 564 | 1407 | .401 | 330 | 401 | .823 | 86 | 244 | 330 | 709 | 123 | 13 | 288 | 1634 | 4.1 | 8.8 | 20.2 |
| 97-98—Tor.-Port. | 71 | 2839 | 448 | 1091 | .411 | 238 | 287 | .829 | 87 | 211 | 298 | 580 | 113 | 7 | 223 | 1225 | 4.2 | 8.2 | 17.3 |
| 98-99—Portland | 50 | 1673 | 249 | 629 | .396 | 89 | 122 | .730 | 41 | 126 | 167 | 312 | 49 | 4 | 110 | 631 | 3.3 | 6.2 | 12.6 |
| 99-00—Portland | 78 | 2372 | 386 | 894 | .432 | 122 | 145 | .841 | 61 | 182 | 243 | 405 | 77 | 1 | 149 | 974 | 3.1 | 5.2 | 12.5 |
| 00-01—Portland | 82 | 2655 | 406 | 935 | .434 | 172 | 207 | .831 | 69 | 234 | 303 | 468 | 106 | 8 | 191 | 1066 | 3.7 | 5.7 | 13.0 |
| 01-02—Portland | 75 | 2796 | 369 | 918 | .402 | 174 | 196 | .888 | 78 | 214 | 292 | 490 | 67 | 7 | 149 | 1016 | 3.9 | 6.5 | 13.5 |
| 02-03—Portland | 59 | 1315 | 156 | 415 | .376 | 53 | 67 | .791 | 40 | 115 | 155 | 204 | 39 | 6 | 82 | 409 | 2.6 | 3.5 | 6.9 |
| 03-04—Portland | 82 | 3118 | 408 | 1018 | .401 | 127 | 145 | .876 | 52 | 256 | 308 | 500 | 99 | 9 | 180 | 1099 | 3.8 | 6.1 | 13.4 |
| 04-05—Portland | 81 | 2762 | 457 | 1165 | .392 | 182 | 199 | .915 | 56 | 254 | 310 | 458 | 86 | 2 | 164 | 1277 | 3.8 | 5.7 | 15.8 |
| Totals | 729 | 25706 | 3924 | 9601 | .409 | 1723 | 2065 | .834 | 629 | 2058 | 2687 | 4779 | 857 | 76 | 1803 | 10662 | 3.7 | 6.6 | 14.6 |

Three-point field goals: 1995-96, 133-for-337 (.395). 1996-97, 176-for-496 (.355). 1997-98, 91-for-304 (.299). 1998-99, 44-for-142 (.310). 1999-00, 80-for-212 (.377). 2000-01, 82-for-219 (.374). 2001-02, 104-for-295 (.353). 2002-03, 44-for-114 (.386). 2003-04, 156-for-427 (.365). 2004-05, 181-for-490 (.369). Totals, 1091-for-3036 (.359).
Personal fouls/disqualifications: 1995-96, 166/0. 1996-97, 162/1. 1997-98, 150/0. 1998-99, 81/0. 1999-00, 173/0. 2000-01, 202/1. 2001-02, 153/0. 2002-03, 67/0. 2003-04, 173/2. 2004-05, 158/0. Totals, 1485/4.

## NBA PLAYOFF RECORD

| Season Team | G | Min. | FGM | FGA | Pct. | FTM | FTA | Pct. | REBOUNDS Off. | Def. | Tot. | Ast. | St. | Blk. | TO | Pts. | AVERAGES RPG | APG | PPG |
|---|---|---|---|---|---|---|---|---|---|---|---|---|---|---|---|---|---|---|---|
| 97-98—Portland | 4 | 166 | 25 | 63 | .397 | 13 | 13 | 1.000 | 6 | 11 | 17 | 38 | 5 | 1 | 16 | 71 | 4.3 | 9.5 | 17.8 |
| 98-99—Portland | 13 | 403 | 49 | 129 | .380 | 24 | 34 | .706 | 7 | 34 | 41 | 73 | 8 | 1 | 38 | 132 | 3.2 | 5.6 | 10.2 |
| 99-00—Portland | 16 | 447 | 56 | 135 | .415 | 20 | 24 | .833 | 8 | 34 | 42 | 58 | 8 | 4 | 19 | 142 | 2.6 | 3.6 | 8.9 |
| 00-01—Portland | 3 | 114 | 19 | 46 | .413 | 13 | 13 | 1.000 | 1 | 8 | 9 | 13 | 2 | 1 | 9 | 53 | 3.0 | 4.3 | 17.7 |
| 01-02—Portland | 3 | 99 | 5 | 22 | .227 | 2 | 3 | .667 | 1 | 6 | 7 | 10 | 2 | 0 | 4 | 15 | 2.3 | 3.3 | 5.0 |
| 02-03—Portland | 7 | 232 | 36 | 79 | .456 | 20 | 21 | .952 | 7 | 29 | 36 | 39 | 6 | 2 | 12 | 107 | 5.1 | 5.6 | 15.3 |
| Totals | 46 | 1461 | 190 | 474 | .401 | 92 | 108 | .852 | 30 | 122 | 152 | 231 | 31 | 9 | 98 | 520 | 3.3 | 5.0 | 11.3 |

Three-point field goals: 1997-98, 8-for-22 (.364). 1998-99, 10-for-22 (.455). 1999-00, 10-for-30 (.333). 2000-01, 2-for-13 (.154). 2001-02, 3-for-4 (.750). 2002-03, 15-for-31 (.484). Totals, 48-for-122 (.393).
Personal fouls/disqualifications: 1997-98, 13/0. 1998-99, 31/0. 1999-00, 43/1. 2000-01, 6/0. 2001-02, 5/0. 2002-03, 22/0. Totals, 120/1.

# STOUDEMIRE, AMARE       F/C       SUNS

**PERSONAL:** Born November 16, 1982, in Lake Wales, Fla. ... 6-10/245. (2.08/111.1).
**HIGH SCHOOL:** Cypress Creek (Orlando).
**COLLEGE:** Did not attend college.
**TRANSACTIONS/CAREER NOTES:** Selected out of high school by Phoenix Suns in first round (ninth pick overall) of 2002 NBA Draft.
**MISCELLANEOUS:** Member of bronze-medal-winning U.S. Olympic Team (2004).

## NBA REGULAR-SEASON RECORD

**HONORS:** NBA Rookie of the Year (2003). ... NBA All-Rookie first team (2003). ... All-NBA second team (2005).

| Season Team | G | Min. | FGM | FGA | Pct. | FTM | FTA | Pct. | REBOUNDS Off. | Def. | Tot. | Ast. | St. | Blk. | TO | Pts. | AVERAGES RPG | APG | PPG |
|---|---|---|---|---|---|---|---|---|---|---|---|---|---|---|---|---|---|---|---|
| 02-03—Phoenix | 82 | 2570 | 392 | 830 | .472 | 320 | 484 | .661 | 250 | 471 | 721 | 78 | 62 | 87 | 189 | 1106 | 8.8 | 1.0 | 13.5 |
| 03-04—Phoenix | 55 | 2025 | 411 | 865 | .475 | 310 | 435 | .713 | 157 | 339 | 496 | 78 | 64 | 89 | 177 | 1133 | 9.0 | 1.4 | 20.6 |
| 04-05—Phoenix | 80 | 2889 | 747 | 1336 | .559 | 583 | 795 | .733 | 219 | 494 | 713 | 131 | 77 | 130 | 189 | 2080 | 8.9 | 1.6 | 26.0 |
| Totals | 217 | 7484 | 1550 | 3031 | .511 | 1213 | 1714 | .708 | 626 | 1304 | 1930 | 287 | 203 | 306 | 555 | 4319 | 8.9 | 1.3 | 19.9 |

Three-point field goals: 2002-03, 2-for-10 (.200). 2003-04, 1-for-5 (.200). 2004-05, 3-for-16 (.188). Totals, 6-for-31 (.194).
Personal fouls/disqualifications: 2002-03, 269/3. 2003-04, 188/5. 2004-05, 278/5. Totals, 735/13.

### NBA PLAYOFF RECORD

| | | | | | | | | REBOUNDS | | | | | | | | AVERAGES | | |
|---|---|---|---|---|---|---|---|---|---|---|---|---|---|---|---|---|---|---|
| Season Team | G | Min. | FGM | FGA | Pct. | FTM | FTA | Pct. | Off. | Def. | Tot. | Ast. | St. | Blk. | TO | Pts. | RPG | APG | PPG |
| 02-03—Phoenix | 6 | 203 | 34 | 65 | .523 | 16 | 28 | .571 | 16 | 31 | 47 | 7 | 10 | 9 | 19 | 85 | 7.8 | 1.2 | 14.2 |
| 04-05—Phoenix | 15 | 601 | 153 | 284 | .539 | 143 | 183 | .781 | 60 | 100 | 160 | 18 | 10 | 30 | 47 | 449 | 10.7 | 1.2 | 29.9 |
| Totals | 21 | 804 | 187 | 349 | .536 | 159 | 211 | .754 | 76 | 131 | 207 | 25 | 20 | 39 | 66 | 534 | 9.9 | 1.2 | 25.4 |

Three-point field goals: 2002-03, 1-for-1 (1.000). 2004-05, 0-for-3. Totals, 1-for-4 (.250).
Personal fouls/disqualifications: 2002-03, 28/1. 2004-05, 59/1. Totals, 87/2.

### NBA ALL-STAR GAME RECORD

**NOTES:** MVP of Rookie Challenge (2004).

| | | | | | | | REBOUNDS | | | | | | | | |
|---|---|---|---|---|---|---|---|---|---|---|---|---|---|---|---|
| Season Team | Min. | FGM | FGA | Pct. | FTM | FTA | Pct. | Off. | Def. | Tot. | Ast. | PF | Dq. | St. | Blk. | TO | Pts. |
| 2005—Phoenix | 20 | 3 | 11 | .273 | 0 | 2 | .000 | 4 | 5 | 9 | 2 | 2 | 0 | 1 | 0 | 1 | 6 |

## STRICKLAND, ERICK     G

**PERSONAL:** Born November 25, 1973, in Opelika, Ala. ... 6-3/210. (1.91/95.3). ... Full name: Demerick Montae Strickland.
**HIGH SCHOOL:** West (Bellevue, Neb.).
**COLLEGE:** Nebraska.
**TRANSACTIONS/CAREER NOTES:** Not drafted by an NBA franchise. ... Signed as free agent by Dallas Mavericks (October 1, 1996). ... Waived by Mavericks (January 7, 1997). ... Played in Continental Basketball Association with Oklahoma City Cavalry (1996-97) and Quad City Thunder (1996-97). ... Signed by Mavericks to 10-day contract (February 17, 1997). ... Signed by Mavericks for remainder of season (February 25, 1997). ... Traded by Mavericks with draft rights to F Pete Mickeal to New York Knicks for F John Wallace and draft rights to F Donnell Harvey (June 28, 2000). ... Traded by Knicks with 2001 first-round draft choice and 2001 second-round draft choice to Vancouver Grizzlies for F Othella Harrington (January 30, 2001). ... Signed as free agent by Boston Celtics (November 1, 2001). ... Signed as free agent by Indiana Pacers (September 11, 2002). ... Signed as free agent by Milwaukee Bucks (July 17, 2003).

### COLLEGIATE RECORD

| | | | | | | | | | | | | AVERAGES | | |
|---|---|---|---|---|---|---|---|---|---|---|---|---|---|---|
| Season Team | G | Min. | FGM | FGA | Pct. | FTM | FTA | Pct. | Reb. | Ast. | Pts. | RPG | APG | PPG |
| 92-93—Nebraska | 31 | 534 | 84 | 185 | .454 | 43 | 59 | .729 | 63 | 66 | 243 | 2.0 | 2.1 | 7.8 |
| 93-94—Nebraska | 30 | 672 | 102 | 241 | .423 | 77 | 95 | .811 | 103 | 96 | 322 | 3.4 | 3.2 | 10.7 |
| 94-95—Nebraska | 31 | 942 | 175 | 394 | .444 | 101 | 139 | .727 | 167 | 133 | 505 | 5.4 | 4.3 | 16.3 |
| 95-96—Nebraska | 35 | 1087 | 174 | 399 | .436 | 116 | 141 | .823 | 170 | 119 | 516 | 4.9 | 3.4 | 14.7 |
| Totals | 127 | 3235 | 535 | 1219 | .439 | 337 | 434 | .776 | 503 | 414 | 1586 | 4.0 | 3.3 | 12.5 |

Three-point field goals: 1992-93, 32-for-88 (.364). 1993-94, 41-for-117 (.350). 1994-95, 54-for-160 (.338). 1995-96, 52-for-148 (.351). Totals, 179-for-513 (.349).

### CBA RECORD

| | | | | | | | | | | | | AVERAGES | | |
|---|---|---|---|---|---|---|---|---|---|---|---|---|---|---|
| Season Team | G | Min. | FGM | FGA | Pct. | FTM | FTA | Pct. | Reb. | Ast. | Pts. | RPG | APG | PPG |
| 96-97—Okla.City-Quad City | 16 | 303 | 59 | 118 | .500 | 42 | 49 | .857 | 53 | 51 | 187 | 3.3 | 3.2 | 11.7 |

Three-point field goals: 1996-97, 27-for-61 (.443). Totals, 27-for-61 (.443).
Personal fouls/disqualifications: 1996-97, 48/0. Totals, 48/0.

### NBA REGULAR-SEASON RECORD

| | | | | | | | | REBOUNDS | | | | | | | | AVERAGES | | |
|---|---|---|---|---|---|---|---|---|---|---|---|---|---|---|---|---|---|---|
| Season Team | G | Min. | FGM | FGA | Pct. | FTM | FTA | Pct. | Off. | Def. | Tot. | Ast. | St. | Blk. | TO | Pts. | RPG | APG | PPG |
| 96-97—Dallas | 28 | 759 | 102 | 256 | .398 | 65 | 80 | .813 | 21 | 69 | 90 | 68 | 27 | 5 | 66 | 297 | 3.2 | 2.4 | 10.6 |
| 97-98—Dallas | 67 | 1505 | 199 | 558 | .357 | 65 | 84 | .774 | 35 | 126 | 161 | 167 | 56 | 8 | 106 | 511 | 2.4 | 2.5 | 7.6 |
| 98-99—Dallas | 33 | 567 | 89 | 221 | .403 | 53 | 65 | .815 | 12 | 71 | 83 | 64 | 40 | 2 | 36 | 249 | 2.5 | 1.9 | 7.5 |
| 99-00—Dallas | 68 | 2025 | 316 | 730 | .433 | 162 | 195 | .831 | 69 | 254 | 323 | 211 | 105 | 13 | 102 | 867 | 4.8 | 3.1 | 12.8 |
| 00-01—New York-Van. | 50 | 830 | 81 | 267 | .303 | 68 | 79 | .861 | 18 | 110 | 128 | 95 | 44 | 2 | 48 | 260 | 2.6 | 1.9 | 5.2 |
| 01-02—Boston | 79 | 1643 | 190 | 488 | .389 | 131 | 155 | .845 | 22 | 191 | 213 | 184 | 56 | 1 | 94 | 606 | 2.7 | 2.3 | 7.7 |
| 02-03—Indiana | 71 | 1275 | 163 | 380 | .429 | 70 | 87 | .805 | 23 | 122 | 145 | 209 | 38 | 7 | 98 | 458 | 2.0 | 2.9 | 6.5 |
| 03-04—Milwaukee | 43 | 571 | 79 | 196 | .403 | 44 | 51 | .863 | 13 | 58 | 71 | 90 | 26 | 2 | 54 | 231 | 1.7 | 2.1 | 5.4 |
| 04-05—Milwaukee | 62 | 1014 | 114 | 304 | .375 | 52 | 64 | .813 | 11 | 92 | 103 | 115 | 30 | 1 | 64 | 301 | 1.7 | 1.9 | 4.9 |
| Totals | 501 | 10189 | 1333 | 3400 | .392 | 710 | 860 | .826 | 224 | 1093 | 1317 | 1203 | 422 | 41 | 668 | 3780 | 2.6 | 2.4 | 7.5 |

Three-point field goals: 1996-97, 28-for-92 (.304). 1997-98, 48-for-163 (.294). 1998-99, 18-for-59 (.305). 1999-00, 73-for-186 (.392). 2000-01, 30-for-95 (.316). 2001-02, 95-for-247 (.385). 2002-03, 62-for-160 (.388). 2003-04, 29-for-66 (.439). 2004-05, 21-for-83 (.253). Totals, 404-for-1151 (.351).
Personal fouls/disqualifications: 1996-97, 75/3. 1997-98, 140/1. 1998-99, 44/0. 1999-00, 190/3. 2000-01, 88/0. 2001-02, 145/1. 2002-03, 111/0. 2003-04, 63/0. 2004-05, 103/1. Totals, 959/9.

### NBA PLAYOFF RECORD

| | | | | | | | | REBOUNDS | | | | | | | | AVERAGES | | |
|---|---|---|---|---|---|---|---|---|---|---|---|---|---|---|---|---|---|---|
| Season Team | G | Min. | FGM | FGA | Pct. | FTM | FTA | Pct. | Off. | Def. | Tot. | Ast. | St. | Blk. | TO | Pts. | RPG | APG | PPG |
| 01-02—Boston | 12 | 118 | 11 | 39 | .282 | 9 | 9 | 1.000 | 2 | 11 | 13 | 17 | 5 | 1 | 9 | 35 | 1.1 | 1.4 | 2.9 |
| 02-03—Indiana | 5 | 42 | 6 | 14 | .429 | 8 | 10 | .800 | 3 | 4 | 7 | 8 | 1 | 0 | 1 | 21 | 1.4 | 1.6 | 4.2 |
| 03-04—Milwaukee | 3 | 41 | 5 | 12 | .417 | 4 | 4 | 1.000 | 0 | 5 | 5 | 9 | 2 | 0 | 3 | 14 | 1.7 | 3.0 | 4.7 |
| Totals | 20 | 201 | 22 | 65 | .338 | 21 | 23 | .913 | 5 | 20 | 25 | 34 | 8 | 1 | 13 | 70 | 1.3 | 1.7 | 3.5 |

Three-point field goals: 2001-02, 4-for-20 (.200). 2002-03, 1-for-5 (.200). 2003-04, 0-for-5. Totals, 5-for-30 (.167).
Personal fouls/disqualifications: 2001-02, 15/0. 2002-03, 4/0. 2003-04, 3/0. Totals, 22/0.

## STRICKLAND, ROD     G

**PERSONAL:** Born July 11, 1966, in Bronx, N.Y. ... 6-3/185. (1.91/83.9).
**HIGH SCHOOL:** Harry S. Truman (Bronx, N.Y.), then Oak Hill Academy (Mouth of Wilson, Va.).
**COLLEGE:** DePaul.
**TRANSACTIONS/CAREER NOTES:** Selected after junior season by New York Knicks in first round (19th pick overall) of 1988 NBA Draft. ... Traded by Knicks to San Antonio Spurs for G Maurice Cheeks (February 21, 1990). ... Signed as free agent

by Portland Trail Blazers (July 3, 1992). ... Traded by Trail Blazers with F Harvey Grant to Washington Bullets for F Rasheed Wallace and G Mitchell Butler (July 15, 1996). ... Bullets franchise renamed Washington Wizards for 1997-98 season. ... Waived by Wizards (March 1, 2001). ... Signed as free agent by Trail Blazers (March 5, 2001). ... Signed as free agent by Miami Heat (October 22, 2001). ... Signed as free agent by Minnesota Timberwolves (October 27, 2002). ... Signed as free agent by Orlando Magic (November 25, 2003). ... Waived by Magic (March 1, 2004). ... Signed by Toronto Raptors for remainder of season (March 5, 2004). ... Signed as free agent by Houston Rockets (January 19, 2005).

## COLLEGIATE RECORD

NOTES: THE SPORTING NEWS All-America first team (1988).

| Season Team | G | Min. | FGM | FGA | Pct. | FTM | FTA | Pct. | Reb. | Ast. | Pts. | AVERAGES RPG | APG | PPG |
|---|---|---|---|---|---|---|---|---|---|---|---|---|---|---|
| 85-86—DePaul | 31 | 1063 | 176 | 354 | .497 | 85 | 126 | .675 | 84 | 159 | 437 | 2.7 | 5.1 | 14.1 |
| 86-87—DePaul | 30 | 980 | 188 | 323 | .582 | 106 | 175 | .606 | 113 | 196 | 490 | 3.8 | 6.5 | 16.3 |
| 87-88—DePaul | 26 | 837 | 207 | 392 | .528 | 83 | 137 | .606 | 98 | 202 | 521 | 3.8 | 7.8 | 20.0 |
| Totals | 87 | 2880 | 571 | 1069 | .534 | 274 | 438 | .626 | 295 | 557 | 1448 | 3.4 | 6.4 | 16.6 |

Three-point field goals: 1986-87, 8-for-15 (.533). 1987-88, 24-for-54 (.444). Totals, 32-for-69 (.464).

## NBA REGULAR-SEASON RECORD

HONORS: All-NBA Second Team (1998). ... NBA All-Rookie second team (1989).

| Season Team | G | Min. | FGM | FGA | Pct. | FTM | FTA | Pct. | REBOUNDS Off. | Def. | Tot. | Ast. | St. | Blk. | TO | Pts. | AVERAGES RPG | APG | PPG |
|---|---|---|---|---|---|---|---|---|---|---|---|---|---|---|---|---|---|---|---|
| 88-89—New York | 81 | 1358 | 265 | 567 | .467 | 172 | 231 | .745 | 51 | 109 | 160 | 319 | 98 | 3 | 148 | 721 | 2.0 | 3.9 | 8.9 |
| 89-90—N.Y.-San Antonio | 82 | 2140 | 343 | 756 | .454 | 174 | 278 | .626 | 90 | 169 | 259 | 468 | 127 | 14 | 170 | 868 | 3.2 | 5.7 | 10.6 |
| 90-91—San Antonio | 58 | 2076 | 314 | 651 | .482 | 161 | 211 | .763 | 57 | 162 | 219 | 463 | 117 | 11 | 156 | 800 | 3.8 | 8.0 | 13.8 |
| 91-92—San Antonio | 57 | 2053 | 300 | 659 | .455 | 182 | 265 | .687 | 92 | 173 | 265 | 491 | 118 | 17 | 160 | 787 | 4.6 | 8.6 | 13.8 |
| 92-93—Portland | 78 | 2474 | 396 | 816 | .485 | 273 | 381 | .717 | 120 | 217 | 337 | 559 | 131 | 24 | 199 | 1069 | 4.3 | 7.2 | 13.7 |
| 93-94—Portland | 82 | 2889 | 528 | 1093 | .483 | 353 | 471 | .749 | 122 | 248 | 370 | 740 | 147 | 24 | 257 | 1411 | 4.5 | 9.0 | 17.2 |
| 94-95—Portland | 64 | 2267 | 441 | 946 | .466 | 283 | 380 | .745 | 73 | 244 | 317 | 562 | 123 | 9 | 209 | 1211 | 5.0 | 8.8 | 18.9 |
| 95-96—Portland | 67 | 2526 | 471 | 1023 | .460 | 276 | 423 | .652 | 89 | 208 | 297 | 640 | 97 | 16 | 255 | 1256 | 4.4 | 9.6 | 18.7 |
| 96-97—Washington | 82 | 2997 | 515 | 1105 | .466 | 367 | 497 | .738 | 95 | 240 | 335 | 727 | 143 | 14 | 270 | 1410 | 4.1 | 8.9 | 17.2 |
| 97-98—Washington | 76 | 3020 | 490 | 1130 | .434 | 357 | 492 | .726 | 112 | 293 | *801 | 405 | 126 | 25 | 266 | 1349 | 5.3 | *10.5 | 17.8 |
| 98-99—Washington | 44 | 1632 | 251 | 603 | .416 | 176 | 236 | .746 | 56 | 156 | 212 | 434 | 76 | 5 | 142 | 690 | 4.8 | 9.9 | 15.7 |
| 99-00—Washington | 69 | 2188 | 327 | 762 | .429 | 214 | 305 | .702 | 73 | 186 | 259 | 519 | 94 | 18 | 187 | 869 | 3.8 | 7.5 | 12.6 |
| 00-01—Wash.-Port. | 54 | 1371 | 182 | 429 | .424 | 130 | 173 | .751 | 36 | 104 | 140 | 303 | 53 | 5 | 107 | 498 | 2.6 | 5.6 | 9.2 |
| 01-02—Miami | 76 | 2294 | 316 | 714 | .443 | 154 | 201 | .766 | 49 | 183 | 232 | 463 | 82 | 11 | 159 | 794 | 3.1 | 6.1 | 10.4 |
| 02-03—Minnesota | 47 | 956 | 120 | 278 | .432 | 79 | 107 | .738 | 20 | 75 | 95 | 215 | 46 | 6 | 76 | 320 | 2.0 | 4.6 | 6.8 |
| 03-04—Orlando-Tor. | 61 | 1197 | 150 | 353 | .425 | 72 | 98 | .735 | 34 | 121 | 155 | 244 | 35 | 11 | 85 | 382 | 2.5 | 4.0 | 6.3 |
| 04-05—Houston | 16 | 196 | 9 | 43 | .209 | 9 | 10 | .900 | 3 | 24 | 27 | 39 | 3 | 2 | 16 | 28 | 1.7 | 2.4 | 1.8 |
| Totals | 1094 | 33634 | 5418 | 11928 | .454 | 3432 | 4759 | .721 | 1172 | 2912 | 4084 | 7987 | 1616 | 215 | 2862 | 14463 | 3.7 | 7.3 | 13.2 |

Three-point field goals: 1988-89, 19-for-59 (.322). 1989-90, 8-for-30 (.267). 1990-91, 11-for-33 (.333). 1991-92, 5-for-15 (.333). 1992-93, 4-for-30 (.133). 1993-94, 2-for-10 (.200). 1994-95, 46-for-123 (.374). 1995-96, 38-for-111 (.342). 1996-97, 13-for-77 (.169). 1997-98, 12-for-48 (.250). 1998-99, 12-for-42 (.286). 1999-00, 1-for-21 (.048). 2000-01, 4-for-17 (.235). 2001-02, 8-for-26 (.308). 2002-03, 1-for-11 (.091). 2003-04, 10-for-36 (.278). 2004-05, 1-for-2 (.500). Totals, 195-for-691 (.282).

Personal fouls/disqualifications: 1988-89, 142/2. 1989-90, 160/3. 1990-91, 125/0. 1991-92, 122/0. 1992-93, 153/1. 1993-94, 171/0. 1994-95, 118/0. 1995-96, 135/2. 1996-97, 166/2. 1997-98, 182/2. 1998-99, 91/0. 1999-00, 147/1. 2000-01, 76/0. 2001-02, 114/0. 2002-03, 55/0. 2003-04, 76/0. 2004-05, 15/0. Totals, 2048/13.

## NBA PLAYOFF RECORD

| Season Team | G | Min. | FGM | FGA | Pct. | FTM | FTA | Pct. | REBOUNDS Off. | Def. | Tot. | Ast. | St. | Blk. | TO | Pts. | AVERAGES RPG | APG | PPG |
|---|---|---|---|---|---|---|---|---|---|---|---|---|---|---|---|---|---|---|---|
| 88-89—New York | 9 | 111 | 22 | 49 | .449 | 9 | 17 | .529 | 6 | 7 | 13 | 25 | 4 | 1 | 13 | 54 | 1.4 | 2.8 | 6.0 |
| 89-90—San Antonio | 10 | 384 | 54 | 127 | .425 | 15 | 27 | .556 | 22 | 31 | 53 | 112 | 14 | 0 | 34 | 123 | 5.3 | 11.2 | 12.3 |
| 90-91—San Antonio | 4 | 168 | 29 | 67 | .433 | 17 | 21 | .810 | 5 | 16 | 21 | 35 | 9 | 0 | 13 | 75 | 5.3 | 8.8 | 18.8 |
| 91-92—San Antonio | 2 | 80 | 13 | 22 | .591 | 5 | 8 | .625 | 0 | 7 | 7 | 19 | 3 | 2 | 6 | 31 | 3.5 | 9.5 | 15.5 |
| 92-93—Portland | 4 | 156 | 22 | 52 | .423 | 10 | 12 | .833 | 9 | 17 | 26 | 37 | 5 | 2 | 7 | 54 | 6.5 | 9.3 | 13.5 |
| 93-94—Portland | 4 | 154 | 36 | 72 | .500 | 22 | 27 | .815 | 3 | 13 | 16 | 39 | 4 | 2 | 10 | 94 | 4.0 | 9.8 | 23.5 |
| 94-95—Portland | 3 | 126 | 27 | 65 | .415 | 14 | 18 | .778 | 1 | 11 | 12 | 37 | 3 | 2 | 10 | 70 | 4.0 | 12.3 | 23.3 |
| 95-96—Portland | 5 | 202 | 37 | 84 | .440 | 23 | 36 | .639 | 12 | 19 | 31 | 42 | 5 | 0 | 12 | 103 | 6.2 | 8.4 | 20.6 |
| 96-97—Washington | 3 | 124 | 22 | 52 | .423 | 14 | 19 | .737 | 5 | 13 | 18 | 25 | 3 | 0 | 11 | 59 | 6.0 | 8.3 | 19.7 |
| 00-01—Portland | 2 | 19 | 2 | 6 | .333 | 4 | 6 | .667 | 2 | 2 | 4 | 2 | 2 | 0 | 1 | 8 | 2.0 | 1.0 | 4.0 |
| 02-03—Minnesota | 6 | 73 | 11 | 21 | .524 | 6 | 6 | 1.000 | 0 | 6 | 6 | 17 | 4 | 2 | 8 | 28 | 1.0 | 2.8 | 4.7 |
| Totals | 52 | 1597 | 275 | 617 | .446 | 139 | 197 | .706 | 65 | 142 | 207 | 390 | 56 | 11 | 125 | 699 | 4.0 | 7.5 | 13.4 |

Three-point field goals: 1988-89, 1-for-1 (1.000). 1989-90, 0-for-7. 1990-91, 0-for-6. 1992-93, 0-for-1. 1993-94, 0-for-1. 1994-95, 2-for-5 (.400). 1995-96, 6-for-12 (.500). 1996-97, 1-for-2 (.500). Totals, 10-for-35 (.286).

Personal fouls/disqualifications: 1988-89, 21/0. 1989-90, 30/2. 1990-91, 14/0. 1991-92, 8/0. 1992-93, 10/0. 1993-94, 13/0. 1994-95, 11/0. 1995-96, 14/0. 1996-97, 8/0. 2000-01, 1/0. 2002-03, 5/0. Totals, 135/2.

## SUNDOV, BRUNO — C

PERSONAL: Born February 10, 1980, in Split, Croatia. ... 7-2/239. (2.18/108.4).
HIGH SCHOOL: Winchendon Prep School (Mass.).
TRANSACTIONS/CAREER NOTES: Selected by Dallas Mavericks in second round (35th pick overall) of 1998 NBA Draft. ... Traded by Mavericks to Utah Jazz as part of four-team deal in which Boston Celtics received G Robert Pack, C John Williams and cash considerations from Mavericks and a conditional first-round draft choice from Jazz, Mavericks received G Dana Barros from Celtics, F Bill Curley from Golden State Warriors and G Howard Eisley from Jazz, Jazz received F Donyell Marshall from Warriors and Warriors received F Danny Fortson from Celtics and F Adam Keefe from Jazz (August 16, 2000). ... Waived by Jazz (September 26, 2000). ... Signed as free agent by Indiana Pacers (October 3, 2000). ... Signed as free agent by Boston Celtics (July 19, 2002). ... Traded by Celtics with G J.R. Bremer and conditional second-round draft pick to Cleveland Cavaliers for F Jumaine Jones (July 29, 2003) ... Waived by Cavaliers (January 15, 2004). ... Signed by New York Knicks to 10-day contract (January 21, 2004). ... Played in Continental Basketball Association (2004). ... Signed as free agent by Knicks (September 8, 2004).

## NBA REGULAR-SEASON RECORD

| Season Team | G | Min. | FGM | FGA | Pct. | FTM | FTA | Pct. | REBOUNDS Off. | Def. | Tot. | Ast. | St. | Blk. | TO | Pts. | AVERAGES RPG | APG | PPG |
|---|---|---|---|---|---|---|---|---|---|---|---|---|---|---|---|---|---|---|---|
| 98-99—Dallas............ | 3 | 11 | 2 | 7 | .286 | 0 | 0 | ... | 0 | 0 | 0 | 1 | 0 | 0 | 1 | 4 | 0.0 | 0.3 | 1.3 |
| 99-00—Dallas............ | 14 | 61 | 12 | 31 | .387 | 2 | 2 | 1.000 | 5 | 7 | 12 | 2 | 2 | 2 | 4 | 26 | 0.9 | 0.1 | 1.9 |
| 00-01—Indiana.......... | 11 | 120 | 20 | 41 | .488 | 3 | 5 | .600 | 4 | 19 | 23 | 2 | 2 | 4 | 3 | 43 | 2.1 | 0.2 | 3.9 |
| 01-02—Indiana.......... | 22 | 88 | 16 | 40 | .400 | 0 | 2 | .000 | 7 | 14 | 21 | 3 | 3 | 3 | 4 | 32 | 1.0 | 0.1 | 1.5 |
| 02-03—Boston........... | 26 | 138 | 14 | 56 | .250 | 0 | 2 | .000 | 8 | 20 | 28 | 7 | 6 | 3 | 9 | 32 | 1.1 | 0.3 | 1.2 |
| 03-04—Cleveland-N.Y. | 5 | 33 | 4 | 10 | .400 | 3 | 6 | .500 | 2 | 8 | 10 | 1 | 0 | 0 | 3 | 11 | 2.0 | 0.2 | 2.2 |
| 04-05—New York ....... | 21 | 73 | 11 | 37 | .297 | 2 | 2 | 1.000 | 6 | 7 | 13 | 2 | 2 | 2 | 6 | 25 | 0.6 | 0.1 | 1.2 |
| **Totals** .................. | 102 | 524 | 79 | 222 | .356 | 10 | 19 | .526 | 32 | 75 | 107 | 18 | 15 | 14 | 30 | 173 | 1.0 | 0.2 | 1.7 |

Three-point field goals: 2000-01, 0-for-4. 2001-02, 0-for-1. 2002-03, 4-for-16 (.250). 2004-05, 1-for-3 (.333). Totals, 5-for-24 (.208).
Personal fouls/disqualifications: 1998-99, 4/0. 1999-00, 16/0. 2000-01, 21/1. 2001-02, 16/0. 2002-03, 24/0. 2003-04, 9/0. 2004-05, 16/0. Totals, 106/1.

## NBA PLAYOFF RECORD

| Season Team | G | Min. | FGM | FGA | Pct. | FTM | FTA | Pct. | REBOUNDS Off. | Def. | Tot. | Ast. | St. | Blk. | TO | Pts. | AVERAGES RPG | APG | PPG |
|---|---|---|---|---|---|---|---|---|---|---|---|---|---|---|---|---|---|---|---|
| 01-02—Indiana............ | 1 | 2 | 1 | 1 | 1.000 | 0 | 0 | ... | 0 | 0 | 0 | 0 | 0 | 0 | 0 | 2 | 0.0 | 0.0 | 2.0 |

## CBA RECORD

| Season Team | G | Min. | FGM | FGA | Pct. | FTM | FTA | Pct. | Reb. | Ast. | Pts. | AVERAGES RPG | APG | PPG |
|---|---|---|---|---|---|---|---|---|---|---|---|---|---|---|
| 03-04—Gary ............................. | 2 | 26 | 2 | 13 | .154 | 0 | 0 | ... | 6 | 0 | 4 | 3.0 | 0.0 | 2.0 |

# SURA, BOB　　　　　　　　　　G　　　　　　　　　　ROCKETS

**PERSONAL:** Born March 25, 1973, in Wilkes-Barre, Pa. ... 6-5/200. (1.96/90.7).
**HIGH SCHOOL:** G.A.R. Memorial (Wilkes-Barre, Pa.).
**COLLEGE:** Florida State.
**TRANSACTIONS/CAREER NOTES:** Selected by Cleveland Cavaliers in first round (17th pick overall) of 1995 NBA Draft. ... Traded by Cavaliers to Golden State Warriors as part of three-way deal in which Warriors received G Vinny Del Negro from Milwaukee Bucks, Bucks traded F/C J.R. Reid and F Robert Traylor to Cavaliers and Warriors traded F Jason Caffey and F/G Billy Owens to Bucks (June 27, 2000). ... Traded by Warriors to Detroit Pistons for F Clifford Robinson and G Pepe Sanchez (August 21, 2003). ... Traded by Pistons to Atlanta Hawks as part of three-team deal in which Hawks also received F Zeljko Rebraca and a future first-round draft choice from Pistons and F Chris Mills from Boston Celtics. Pistons received F/C Rasheed Wallace from Hawks and G Mike James from Celtics and Celtics received G Chucky Atkins, G Lindsey Hunter and a 2004 first-round draft choice from Pistons (February 19, 2004). ... Signed as free agent by Houston Rockets (August 9, 2004).

## COLLEGIATE RECORD

| Season Team | G | Min. | FGM | FGA | Pct. | FTM | FTA | Pct. | Reb. | Ast. | Pts. | AVERAGES RPG | APG | PPG |
|---|---|---|---|---|---|---|---|---|---|---|---|---|---|---|
| 91-92—Florida State .................. | 31 | 872 | 124 | 269 | .461 | 94 | 150 | .627 | 107 | 76 | 380 | 3.5 | 2.5 | 12.3 |
| 92-93—Florida State .................. | 34 | 1213 | 241 | 533 | .452 | 120 | 188 | .638 | 209 | 92 | 675 | 6.1 | 2.7 | 19.9 |
| 93-94—Florida State .................. | 27 | 932 | 202 | 431 | .469 | 117 | 179 | .654 | 213 | 121 | 573 | 7.9 | 4.5 | 21.2 |
| 94-95—Florida State .................. | 27 | 981 | 164 | 393 | .417 | 123 | 179 | .687 | 185 | 146 | 502 | 6.9 | 5.4 | 18.6 |
| **Totals** .................. | 119 | 3998 | 731 | 1626 | .450 | 454 | 696 | .652 | 714 | 435 | 2130 | 6.0 | 3.7 | 17.9 |

Three-point field goals: 1991-92, 38-for-98 (.388). 1992-93, 73-for-220 (.332). 1993-94, 52-for-164 (.317). 1994-95, 51-for-158 (.323). Totals, 214-for-640 (.334).

## NBA REGULAR-SEASON RECORD

| Season Team | G | Min. | FGM | FGA | Pct. | FTM | FTA | Pct. | REBOUNDS Off. | Def. | Tot. | Ast. | St. | Blk. | TO | Pts. | AVERAGES RPG | APG | PPG |
|---|---|---|---|---|---|---|---|---|---|---|---|---|---|---|---|---|---|---|---|
| 95-96—Cleveland ........ | 79 | 1150 | 148 | 360 | .411 | 99 | 141 | .702 | 34 | 101 | 135 | 233 | 56 | 21 | 115 | 422 | 1.7 | 2.9 | 5.3 |
| 96-97—Cleveland ........ | 82 | 2269 | 253 | 587 | .431 | 196 | 319 | .614 | 76 | 232 | 308 | 390 | 90 | 33 | 181 | 755 | 3.8 | 4.8 | 9.2 |
| 97-98—Cleveland ........ | 46 | 942 | 87 | 231 | .377 | 74 | 131 | .565 | 25 | 69 | 94 | 171 | 44 | 7 | 93 | 267 | 2.0 | 3.7 | 5.8 |
| 98-99—Cleveland ........ | 50 | 841 | 70 | 210 | .333 | 65 | 103 | .631 | 21 | 81 | 102 | 152 | 46 | 14 | 67 | 214 | 2.0 | 3.0 | 4.3 |
| 99-00—Cleveland ........ | 73 | 2216 | 356 | 815 | .437 | 175 | 251 | .697 | 50 | 238 | 288 | 284 | 91 | 19 | 148 | 1009 | 3.9 | 3.9 | 13.8 |
| 00-01—Golden State ... | 53 | 1684 | 202 | 518 | .390 | 135 | 189 | .714 | 54 | 173 | 227 | 242 | 54 | 8 | 160 | 586 | 4.3 | 4.6 | 11.1 |
| 01-02—Golden State ... | 78 | 1780 | 250 | 590 | .424 | 236 | 328 | .720 | 89 | 167 | 256 | 275 | 88 | 17 | 133 | 778 | 3.3 | 3.5 | 10.0 |
| 02-03—Golden State ... | 55 | 1130 | 135 | 328 | .412 | 103 | 148 | .696 | 58 | 109 | 167 | 177 | 45 | 2 | 82 | 401 | 3.0 | 3.2 | 7.3 |
| 03-04—Detroit-Atlanta | 80 | 1663 | 202 | 485 | .416 | 171 | 226 | .757 | 100 | 226 | 326 | 233 | 62 | 14 | 105 | 596 | 4.1 | 2.9 | 7.5 |
| 04-05—Houston.......... | 61 | 1922 | 215 | 504 | .427 | 141 | 188 | .750 | 79 | 258 | 337 | 317 | 65 | 7 | 147 | 626 | 5.5 | 5.2 | 10.3 |
| **Totals** .................. | 657 | 15597 | 1918 | 4628 | .414 | 1395 | 2024 | .689 | 586 | 1654 | 2240 | 2474 | 641 | 142 | 1231 | 5654 | 3.4 | 3.8 | 8.6 |

Three-point field goals: 1995-96, 27-for-78 (.346). 1996-97, 53-for-164 (.323). 1997-98, 19-for-60 (.317). 1998-99, 9-for-45 (.200). 1999-00, 122-for-332 (.367). 2000-01, 47-for-172 (.273). 2001-02, 42-for-133 (.316). 2002-03, 28-for-85 (.329). 2003-04, 21-for-79 (.266). 2004-05, 55-for-155 (.355). Totals, 423-for-1303 (.325).
Personal fouls/disqualifications: 1995-96, 126/1. 1996-97, 218/3. 1997-98, 113/0. 1998-99, 98/1. 1999-00, 201/0. 2000-01, 127/0. 2001-02, 160/1. 2002-03, 108/0. 2003-04, 158/0. 2004-05, 168/2. Totals, 1477/8.

## NBA PLAYOFF RECORD

| Season Team | G | Min. | FGM | FGA | Pct. | FTM | FTA | Pct. | REBOUNDS Off. | Def. | Tot. | Ast. | St. | Blk. | TO | Pts. | AVERAGES RPG | APG | PPG |
|---|---|---|---|---|---|---|---|---|---|---|---|---|---|---|---|---|---|---|---|
| 95-96—Cleveland ........ | 3 | 18 | 2 | 3 | .667 | 0 | 0 | ... | 0 | 1 | 1 | 3 | 1 | 0 | 4 | 4 | 0.3 | 1.0 | 1.3 |
| 97-98—Cleveland ........ | 3 | 31 | 1 | 5 | .200 | 2 | 3 | .667 | 0 | 3 | 3 | 4 | 1 | 0 | 2 | 4 | 1.0 | 1.3 | 1.3 |
| 04-05—Houston.......... | 7 | 182 | 20 | 46 | .435 | 8 | 12 | .667 | 6 | 21 | 27 | 14 | 7 | 0 | 11 | 55 | 3.9 | 2.0 | 7.9 |
| **Totals** .................. | 13 | 231 | 23 | 54 | .426 | 10 | 15 | .667 | 6 | 25 | 31 | 21 | 9 | 0 | 17 | 63 | 2.4 | 1.6 | 4.8 |

Three-point field goals: 1997-98, 0-for-2. 2004-05, 7-for-13 (.538). Totals, 7-for-15 (.467).
Personal fouls/disqualifications: 1995-96, 4/0. 1997-98, 4/0. 2004-05, 15/0. Totals, 23/0.

## SWEETNEY, MIKE F KNICKS

**PERSONAL:** Born October 25, 1982, in Washington, D.C. ... 6-8/260. (2.03/117.9). ... Full name: Michael Damien Sweetney
**HIGH SCHOOL:** Oxon Hill (Oxon Hill, Md.).
**COLLEGE:** Georgetown.
**TRANSACTIONS/CAREER NOTES:** Selected after junior season by New York Knicks in first round (ninth overall pick) of 2003 NBA Draft.

### COLLEGIATE RECORD

**NOTES:** The Sporting News All-America third team (2003).

| Season Team | G | Min. | FGM | FGA | Pct. | FTM | FTA | Pct. | Reb. | Ast. | Pts. | RPG | APG | PPG |
|---|---|---|---|---|---|---|---|---|---|---|---|---|---|---|
| | | | | | | | | | | | | AVERAGES | | |
| 00-01—Georgetown | 33 | 798 | 159 | 308 | .516 | 104 | 168 | .619 | 245 | 59 | 422 | 7.4 | 1.8 | 12.8 |
| 01-02—Georgetown | 29 | 883 | 185 | 326 | .567 | 182 | 231 | .788 | 290 | 49 | 552 | 10.0 | 1.7 | 19.0 |
| 02-03—Georgetown | 34 | 1100 | 264 | 483 | .547 | 248 | 336 | .738 | 352 | 66 | 776 | 10.4 | 1.9 | 22.8 |
| Totals | 96 | 2781 | 608 | 1117 | .544 | 534 | 735 | .727 | 887 | 174 | 1750 | 9.2 | 1.8 | 18.2 |

Three-point field goals: 2001-02, 0-for-1. 2002-03, 0-for-3. Totals, 0-for-4 (.000).

### NBA REGULAR-SEASON RECORD

| Season Team | G | Min. | FGM | FGA | Pct. | FTM | FTA | Pct. | Off. | Def. | Tot. | Ast. | St. | Blk. | TO | Pts. | RPG | APG | PPG |
|---|---|---|---|---|---|---|---|---|---|---|---|---|---|---|---|---|---|---|---|
| | | | | | | | | | REBOUNDS | | | | | | | | AVERAGES | | |
| 03-04—New York | 42 | 494 | 69 | 140 | .493 | 42 | 58 | .724 | 68 | 89 | 157 | 14 | 18 | 12 | 32 | 180 | 3.7 | 0.3 | 4.3 |
| 04-05—New York | 77 | 1509 | 237 | 446 | .531 | 176 | 235 | .749 | 169 | 249 | 418 | 44 | 27 | 28 | 108 | 650 | 5.4 | 0.6 | 8.4 |
| Totals | 119 | 2003 | 306 | 586 | .522 | 218 | 293 | .744 | 237 | 338 | 575 | 58 | 45 | 40 | 140 | 830 | 4.8 | 0.5 | 7.0 |

Three-point field goals: 2003-04, 0-for-1. 2004-05, 0-for-1. Totals, 0-for-2 (.000).
Personal fouls/disqualifications: 2003-04, 57/0. 2004-05, 224/5. Totals, 281/5.

### NBA PLAYOFF RECORD

| Season Team | G | Min. | FGM | FGA | Pct. | FTM | FTA | Pct. | Off. | Def. | Tot. | Ast. | St. | Blk. | TO | Pts. | RPG | APG | PPG |
|---|---|---|---|---|---|---|---|---|---|---|---|---|---|---|---|---|---|---|---|
| | | | | | | | | | REBOUNDS | | | | | | | | AVERAGES | | |
| 03-04—New York | 4 | 57 | 6 | 11 | .545 | 4 | 6 | .667 | 4 | 6 | 10 | 0 | 0 | 1 | 0 | 16 | 2.5 | 0.0 | 4.0 |

Personal fouls/disqualifications: 2003-04, 7/0. Totals, 7/0.

## SWIFT, ROBERT C SUPERSONICS

**PERSONAL:** Born December 3, 1985, in Bakersfield, Calif. ... 7-0/245. (2.13/111.1).
**HIGH SCHOOL:** Garces Memorial (Bakersfield, Calif.), then Bakersfield (Calif.).
**COLLEGE:** Did not attend college.
**TRANSACTIONS/CAREER NOTES:** Selected out of high school by Seattle SuperSonics in first round (12th pick overall) of 2004 NBA Draft.

### NBA REGULAR-SEASON RECORD

| Season Team | G | Min. | FGM | FGA | Pct. | FTM | FTA | Pct. | Off. | Def. | Tot. | Ast. | St. | Blk. | TO | Pts. | RPG | APG | PPG |
|---|---|---|---|---|---|---|---|---|---|---|---|---|---|---|---|---|---|---|---|
| | | | | | | | | | REBOUNDS | | | | | | | | AVERAGES | | |
| 04-05—Seattle | 16 | 72 | 5 | 11 | .455 | 5 | 9 | .556 | 1 | 4 | 5 | 2 | 1 | 7 | 4 | 15 | 0.3 | 0.1 | 0.9 |

Personal fouls/disqualifications: 2004-05, 16/0. Totals, 16/0.

## SWIFT, STROMILE F ROCKETS

**PERSONAL:** Born November 21, 1979, in Shreveport, La. ... 6-10/220. (2.08/99.8).
**HIGH SCHOOL:** Fair Park (Shreveport, La.).
**COLLEGE:** Louisiana State.
**TRANSACTIONS/CAREER NOTES:** Selected after sophomore season by Vancouver Grizzlies in first round (second pick overall) of 2000 NBA Draft. ... Grizzlies franchise moved to Memphis for 2001-02 season. ... Signed as free agent by Houston Rockets (August 2, 2005).

### COLLEGIATE RECORD

| Season Team | G | Min. | FGM | FGA | Pct. | FTM | FTA | Pct. | Reb. | Ast. | Pts. | RPG | APG | PPG |
|---|---|---|---|---|---|---|---|---|---|---|---|---|---|---|
| | | | | | | | | | | | | AVERAGES | | |
| 98-99—Louisiana State | 16 | 319 | 45 | 110 | .409 | 30 | 50 | .600 | 69 | 5 | 121 | 4.3 | 0.3 | 7.6 |
| 99-00—Louisiana State | 34 | 1013 | 208 | 342 | .608 | 127 | 206 | .617 | 279 | 32 | 550 | 8.2 | 0.9 | 16.2 |
| Totals | 50 | 1332 | 253 | 452 | .560 | 157 | 256 | .613 | 348 | 37 | 671 | 7.0 | 0.7 | 13.4 |

Three-point field goals: 1998-99, 1-for-8 (.125). 1999-00, 7-for-25 (.280). Totals, 8-for-33 (.242).

### NBA REGULAR-SEASON RECORD

| Season Team | G | Min. | FGM | FGA | Pct. | FTM | FTA | Pct. | Off. | Def. | Tot. | Ast. | St. | Blk. | TO | Pts. | RPG | APG | PPG |
|---|---|---|---|---|---|---|---|---|---|---|---|---|---|---|---|---|---|---|---|
| | | | | | | | | | REBOUNDS | | | | | | | | AVERAGES | | |
| 00-01—Vancouver | 80 | 1312 | 153 | 339 | .451 | 85 | 141 | .603 | 109 | 175 | 284 | 28 | 62 | 82 | 64 | 391 | 3.6 | 0.4 | 4.9 |
| 01-02—Memphis | 68 | 1805 | 293 | 611 | .480 | 217 | 305 | .711 | 161 | 269 | 430 | 50 | 53 | 113 | 122 | 803 | 6.3 | 0.7 | 11.8 |
| 02-03—Memphis | 67 | 1478 | 235 | 489 | .481 | 177 | 245 | .722 | 114 | 270 | 384 | 45 | 55 | 104 | 99 | 647 | 5.7 | 0.7 | 9.7 |
| 03-04—Memphis | 77 | 1528 | 268 | 571 | .469 | 190 | 262 | .725 | 141 | 237 | 378 | 38 | 56 | 118 | 88 | 727 | 4.9 | 0.5 | 9.4 |
| 04-05—Memphis | 60 | 1279 | 219 | 488 | .449 | 166 | 219 | .758 | 92 | 181 | 273 | 43 | 41 | 92 | 90 | 604 | 4.6 | 0.7 | 10.1 |
| Totals | 352 | 7402 | 1168 | 2498 | .468 | 835 | 1172 | .712 | 617 | 1132 | 1749 | 204 | 267 | 509 | 463 | 3172 | 5.0 | 0.6 | 9.0 |

Three-point field goals: 2000-01, 0-for-4. 2001-02, 0-for-3. 2002-03, 0-for-2. 2003-04, 1-for-4 (.250). 2004-05, 0-for-4. Totals, 1-for-17 (.059).
Personal fouls/disqualifications: 2000-01, 160/0. 2001-02, 178/3. 2002-03, 152/3. 2003-04, 188/4. 2004-05, 182/0. Totals, 860/10.

## NBA PLAYOFF RECORD

| Season Team | G | Min. | FGM | FGA | Pct. | FTM | FTA | Pct. | REBOUNDS Off. | Def. | Tot. | Ast. | St. | Blk. | TO | Pts. | AVERAGES RPG | APG | PPG |
|---|---|---|---|---|---|---|---|---|---|---|---|---|---|---|---|---|---|---|---|
| 03-04—Memphis ........ | 4 | 74 | 9 | 26 | .346 | 6 | 8 | .750 | 6 | 13 | 19 | 3 | 3 | 6 | 3 | 24 | 4.8 | 0.8 | 6.0 |
| 04-05—Memphis ........ | 3 | 48 | 12 | 20 | .600 | 4 | 7 | .571 | 7 | 7 | 14 | 1 | 1 | 0 | 2 | 28 | 4.7 | 0.3 | 9.3 |
| Totals ................... | 7 | 122 | 21 | 46 | .457 | 10 | 15 | .667 | 13 | 20 | 33 | 4 | 4 | 6 | 5 | 52 | 4.7 | 0.6 | 7.4 |

Personal fouls/disqualifications: 2003-04, 6/0. 2004-05, 3/0. Totals, 9/0.

# SZCZERBIAK, WALLY      F      TIMBERWOLVES

S

**PERSONAL:** Born March 5, 1977, in Madrid, Spain. ... 6-7/244. (2.01/110.7). ... Full name: Walter Robert Szczerbiak ... Son of Walter Szczerbiak, forward with Pittsburgh Condors of American Basketball Association (1971-72) and Real Madrid of Spanish League.
**HIGH SCHOOL:** Cold Spring Harbor (N.Y.).
**COLLEGE:** Miami (Ohio).
**TRANSACTIONS/CAREER NOTES:** Selected by Minnesota Timberwolves in first round (sixth pick overall) of 1999 NBA Draft.

## COLLEGIATE RECORD

**NOTES:** The Sporting News All-America first team (1999).

| Season Team | G | Min. | FGM | FGA | Pct. | FTM | FTA | Pct. | Reb. | Ast. | Pts. | AVERAGES RPG | APG | PPG |
|---|---|---|---|---|---|---|---|---|---|---|---|---|---|---|
| 95-96—Miami of Ohio ............... | 22 | 382 | 66 | 127 | .520 | 22 | 28 | .786 | 72 | 23 | 176 | 3.3 | 1.0 | 8.0 |
| 96-97—Miami of Ohio ............... | 30 | 927 | 150 | 316 | .475 | 28 | 39 | .718 | 162 | 63 | 384 | 5.4 | 2.1 | 12.8 |
| 97-98—Miami of Ohio ............... | 21 | 803 | 185 | 350 | .529 | 79 | 98 | .806 | 160 | 52 | 512 | 7.6 | 2.5 | 24.4 |
| 98-99—Miami of Ohio ............... | 32 | 1081 | 270 | 517 | .522 | 172 | 207 | .831 | 272 | 93 | 775 | 8.5 | 2.9 | 24.2 |
| Totals ...................................... | 105 | 3193 | 671 | 1310 | .512 | 301 | 372 | .809 | 666 | 231 | 1847 | 6.3 | 2.2 | 17.6 |

Three-point field goals: 1995-96, 22-for-47 (.468). 1996-97, 56-for-121 (.463). 1997-98, 63-for-128 (.492). 1998-99, 63-for-177 (.356). Totals, 204-for-473 (.431).

## NBA REGULAR-SEASON RECORD

**HONORS:** NBA All-Rookie first team (2000). ... MVP of Rookie Challenge (2001).

| Season Team | G | Min. | FGM | FGA | Pct. | FTM | FTA | Pct. | REBOUNDS Off. | Def. | Tot. | Ast. | St. | Blk. | TO | Pts. | AVERAGES RPG | APG | PPG |
|---|---|---|---|---|---|---|---|---|---|---|---|---|---|---|---|---|---|---|---|
| 99-00—Minnesota....... | 73 | 2171 | 342 | 669 | .511 | 133 | 161 | .826 | 89 | 183 | 272 | 201 | 58 | 23 | 83 | 845 | 3.7 | 2.8 | 11.6 |
| 00-01—Minnesota....... | 82 | 2856 | 469 | 920 | .510 | 181 | 208 | .870 | 133 | 314 | 447 | 260 | 59 | 33 | 138 | 1145 | 5.5 | 3.2 | 14.0 |
| 01-02—Minnesota....... | 82 | 3117 | 609 | 1200 | .508 | 226 | 272 | .831 | 120 | 271 | 391 | 257 | 66 | 21 | 181 | 1531 | 4.8 | 3.1 | 18.7 |
| 02-03—Minnesota....... | 52 | 1836 | 351 | 729 | .481 | 150 | 173 | .867 | 53 | 188 | 241 | 136 | 44 | 22 | 87 | 913 | 4.6 | 2.6 | 17.6 |
| 03-04—Minnesota....... | 28 | 622 | 106 | 236 | .449 | 53 | 64 | .828 | 24 | 64 | 88 | 33 | 12 | 1 | 28 | 285 | 3.1 | 1.2 | 10.2 |
| 04-05—Minnesota....... | 81 | 2558 | 465 | 919 | .506 | 260 | 304 | .855 | 82 | 221 | 303 | 191 | 40 | 16 | 132 | 1253 | 3.7 | 2.4 | 15.5 |
| Totals ................... | 398 | 13160 | 2342 | 4673 | .501 | 1003 | 1182 | .849 | 501 | 1241 | 1742 | 1078 | 279 | 116 | 649 | 5972 | 4.4 | 2.7 | 15.0 |

Three-point field goals: 1999-00, 28-for-78 (.359). 2000-01, 26-for-77 (.338). 2001-02, 87-for-191 (.455). 2002-03, 61-for-145 (.421). 2003-04, 20-for-46 (.435). 2004-05, 63-for-169 (.373). Totals, 285-for-706 (.404).
Personal fouls/disqualifications: 1999-00, 175/3. 2000-01, 226/4. 2001-02, 188/1. 2002-03, 123/0. 2003-04, 42/0. 2004-05, 178/0. Totals, 932/8.

## NBA PLAYOFF RECORD

| Season Team | G | Min. | FGM | FGA | Pct. | FTM | FTA | Pct. | REBOUNDS Off. | Def. | Tot. | Ast. | St. | Blk. | TO | Pts. | AVERAGES RPG | APG | PPG |
|---|---|---|---|---|---|---|---|---|---|---|---|---|---|---|---|---|---|---|---|
| 99-00—Minnesota....... | 4 | 94 | 12 | 30 | .400 | 0 | 0 | ... | 2 | 6 | 8 | 2 | 3 | 1 | 1 | 24 | 2.0 | 0.5 | 6.0 |
| 00-01—Minnesota....... | 4 | 143 | 18 | 37 | .486 | 20 | 25 | .800 | 4 | 14 | 18 | 10 | 5 | 3 | 12 | 56 | 4.5 | 2.5 | 14.0 |
| 01-02—Minnesota....... | 3 | 131 | 21 | 44 | .477 | 16 | 18 | .889 | 9 | 12 | 21 | 6 | 2 | 0 | 8 | 60 | 7.0 | 2.0 | 20.0 |
| 02-03—Minnesota....... | 6 | 252 | 29 | 61 | .475 | 26 | 30 | .867 | 6 | 24 | 30 | 13 | 6 | 1 | 18 | 87 | 5.0 | 2.2 | 14.5 |
| 03-04—Minnesota....... | 12 | 298 | 47 | 112 | .420 | 38 | 41 | .927 | 9 | 30 | 39 | 20 | 6 | 2 | 24 | 142 | 3.3 | 1.7 | 11.8 |
| Totals ................... | 29 | 918 | 127 | 284 | .447 | 100 | 114 | .877 | 30 | 86 | 116 | 51 | 22 | 7 | 63 | 369 | 4.0 | 1.8 | 12.7 |

Three-point field goals: 1999-00, 0-for-3. 2000-01, 0-for-1. 2001-02, 2-for-9 (.222). 2002-03, 3-for-14 (.214). 2003-04, 10-for-29 (.345). Totals, 15-for-56 (.268).
Personal fouls/disqualifications: 1999-00, 7/0. 2000-01, 6/0. 2001-02, 8/0. 2002-03, 19/0. 2003-04, 31/0. Totals, 71/0.

## NBA ALL-STAR GAME RECORD

| Season Team | Min. | FGM | FGA | Pct. | FTM | FTA | Pct. | REBOUNDS Off. | Def. | Tot. | Ast. | PF | Dq. | St. | Blk. | TO | Pts. |
|---|---|---|---|---|---|---|---|---|---|---|---|---|---|---|---|---|---|
| 2002—Minnesota ............. | 12 | 4 | 6 | .667 | 0 | 0 | ... | 1 | 2 | 3 | 3 | 0 | 0 | 1 | 0 | 0 | 10 |

Three-point field goals: 2002, 2-for-3 (.667). Totals, 2-for-3 (.667).

# TABUSE, YUTA      G

**PERSONAL:** Born October 5, 1980, in Yokohama, Japan. ... 5-9/165. (1.75/74.8).
**HIGH SCHOOL:** Noshiro Kogyo (Yokohama, Japan).
**COLLEGE:** BYU-Hawaii.
**TRANSACTIONS/CAREER NOTES:** Not drafted by an NBA franchise. ... Signed as free agent by Phoenix Suns (September 7, 2004).

## COLLEGIATE RECORD

| Season Team | G | Min. | FGM | FGA | Pct. | FTM | FTA | Pct. | Reb. | Ast. | Pts. | AVERAGES RPG | APG | PPG |
|---|---|---|---|---|---|---|---|---|---|---|---|---|---|---|
| 01-02—BYU-Hawaii ................. | 28 | 801 | 69 | 160 | .431 | 62 | 80 | .775 | 52 | 184 | 214 | 1.9 | 6.6 | 7.6 |

Three-point field goals: 2001-02, 14-for-49 (.286). Totals, 14-for-49 (.286).

## AMERICAN BASKETBALL ASSOCIATION RECORD

| Season Team | G | Min. | FGM | FGA | Pct. | FTM | FTA | Pct. | Reb. | Ast. | Pts. | AVERAGES RPG | APG | PPG |
|---|---|---|---|---|---|---|---|---|---|---|---|---|---|---|
| 03-04—Long Beach ................ | 18 | ... | 37 | 83 | .446 | 19 | 22 | .864 | 43 | 113 | 96 | 2.4 | 6.3 | 5.3 |
| 04-05—Long Beach ................ | 14 | 363 | 50 | 107 | .467 | 19 | 27 | .704 | 56 | 99 | 123 | 4.0 | 7.1 | 8.8 |
| Totals ...................................... | 32 | 363 | 87 | 190 | .458 | 38 | 49 | .776 | 99 | 212 | 219 | 3.1 | 6.6 | 6.8 |

Three-point field goals: 2003-04, 3-for-19 (.158). 2004-05, 4-for-17 (.235). Totals, 7-for-36 (.194).

## NBA REGULAR-SEASON RECORD

| | | | | | | | | REBOUNDS | | | | | | | | AVERAGES | | |
|---|---|---|---|---|---|---|---|---|---|---|---|---|---|---|---|---|---|---|
| Season Team | G | Min. | FGM | FGA | Pct. | FTM | FTA | Pct. | Off. | Def. | Tot. | Ast. | St. | Blk. | TO | Pts. | RPG | APG | PPG |
| 04-05—Phoenix......... | 4 | 17 | 1 | 6 | .167 | 4 | 4 | 1.000 | 2 | 2 | 4 | 3 | 0 | 0 | 1 | 7 | 1.0 | 0.8 | 1.8 |

Three-point field goals: 2004-05, 1-for-1 (1.000). Totals, 1-for-1 (1.000).
Personal fouls/disqualifications: 2004-05, 1/0. Totals, 1/0.

# TAYLOR, MAURICE   F   KNICKS

**PERSONAL:** Born October 30, 1976, in Detroit. ... 6-9/260. (2.06/117.9). ... Full name: Maurice De Shawn Taylor
**HIGH SCHOOL:** Henry Ford (Detroit).
**COLLEGE:** Michigan.
**TRANSACTIONS/CAREER NOTES:** Selected after junior season by Los Angeles Clippers in first round (14th pick overall) of 1997 NBA Draft. ... Signed as free agent by Houston Rockets (August 25, 2000). ... Traded by Rockets to New York Knicks for G Moochie Norris, F Vin Baker and second-round pick in 2006 NBA draft (February 24, 2005).

## COLLEGIATE RECORD

| | | | | | | | | | | | AVERAGES | | |
|---|---|---|---|---|---|---|---|---|---|---|---|---|---|
| Season Team | G | Min. | FGM | FGA | Pct. | FTM | FTA | Pct. | Reb. | Ast. | Pts. | RPG | APG | PPG |
| 94-95—Michigan ...................... | 30 | 830 | 157 | 332 | .473 | 59 | 98 | .602 | 151 | 31 | 376 | 5.0 | 1.0 | 12.5 |
| 95-96—Michigan ...................... | 32 | 908 | 194 | 380 | .511 | 58 | 98 | .592 | 223 | 42 | 447 | 7.0 | 1.3 | 14.0 |
| 96-97—Michigan ...................... | 35 | 1055 | 173 | 341 | .507 | 84 | 117 | .718 | 218 | 40 | 431 | 6.2 | 1.1 | 12.3 |
| Totals ..................................... | 97 | 2793 | 524 | 1053 | .498 | 201 | 313 | .642 | 592 | 113 | 1254 | 6.1 | 1.2 | 12.9 |

Three-point field goals: 1994-95, 3-for-7 (.429). 1995-96, 1-for-4 (.250). 1996-97, 1-for-5 (.200). Totals, 5-for-16 (.313).
Personal fouls/disqualifications: 1994-95, 98/5. 1995-96, 92/1. Totals, 190/6.

**HONORS:** NBA All-Rookie second team (1998).

## NBA REGULAR-SEASON RECORD

| | | | | | | | | REBOUNDS | | | | | | | | AVERAGES | | |
|---|---|---|---|---|---|---|---|---|---|---|---|---|---|---|---|---|---|---|
| Season Team | G | Min. | FGM | FGA | Pct. | FTM | FTA | Pct. | Off. | Def. | Tot. | Ast. | St. | Blk. | TO | Pts. | RPG | APG | PPG |
| 97-98—L.A. Clippers... | 71 | 1513 | 321 | 675 | .476 | 173 | 244 | .709 | 118 | 178 | 296 | 53 | 34 | 40 | 107 | 815 | 4.2 | 0.7 | 11.5 |
| 98-99—L.A. Clippers... | 46 | 1505 | 311 | 675 | .461 | 150 | 206 | .728 | 100 | 142 | 242 | 67 | 16 | 29 | 120 | 773 | 5.3 | 1.5 | 16.8 |
| 99-00—L.A. Clippers... | 62 | 2227 | 458 | 988 | .464 | 143 | 201 | .711 | 96 | 304 | 400 | 101 | 51 | 48 | 169 | 1060 | 6.5 | 1.6 | 17.1 |
| 00-01—Houston.......... | 69 | 1972 | 390 | 797 | .489 | 119 | 162 | .735 | 109 | 269 | 378 | 104 | 28 | 38 | 125 | 899 | 5.5 | 1.5 | 13.0 |
| 01-02—Houston.......... | | | | | | | | Did not play—injured. | | | | | | | | | | | |
| 02-03—Houston.......... | 67 | 1377 | 231 | 535 | .432 | 100 | 138 | .725 | 95 | 143 | 238 | 66 | 22 | 22 | 100 | 562 | 3.6 | 1.0 | 8.4 |
| 03-04—Houston.......... | 75 | 2081 | 367 | 765 | .480 | 128 | 174 | .736 | 131 | 253 | 384 | 107 | 43 | 47 | 149 | 862 | 5.1 | 1.4 | 11.5 |
| 04-05—Houston-N.Y... | 65 | 1336 | 203 | 446 | .455 | 63 | 103 | .612 | 67 | 190 | 257 | 67 | 27 | 20 | 94 | 472 | 4.0 | 1.0 | 7.3 |
| Totals ................... | 455 | 12011 | 2281 | 4881 | .467 | 876 | 1228 | .713 | 716 | 1479 | 2195 | 565 | 221 | 244 | 864 | 5443 | 4.8 | 1.2 | 12.0 |

Three-point field goals: 1997-98, 0-for-1. 1998-99, 1-for-6 (.167). 1999-00, 1-for-8 (.125). 2000-01, 0-for-4. 2002-03, 0-for-2. 2003-04, 0-for-2. 2004-05, 3-for-9 (.333). Totals, 5-for-32 (.156).
Personal fouls/disqualifications: 1997-98, 222/7. 1998-99, 179/5. 1999-00, 217/4. 2000-01, 208/3. 2002-03, 151/0. 2003-04, 253/5. 2004-05, 180/3. Totals, 1410/27.

## NBA PLAYOFF RECORD

| | | | | | | | | REBOUNDS | | | | | | | | AVERAGES | | |
|---|---|---|---|---|---|---|---|---|---|---|---|---|---|---|---|---|---|---|
| Season Team | G | Min. | FGM | FGA | Pct. | FTM | FTA | Pct. | Off. | Def. | Tot. | Ast. | St. | Blk. | TO | Pts. | RPG | APG | PPG |
| 03-04—Houston.......... | 5 | 115 | 18 | 38 | .474 | 13 | 17 | .765 | 5 | 11 | 16 | 5 | 0 | 1 | 7 | 49 | 3.2 | 1.0 | 9.8 |

Personal fouls/disqualifications: 2003-04, 20/0. Totals, 20/0.

# TELFAIR, SEBASTIAN   G   TRAIL BLAZERS

**PERSONAL:** Born June 9, 1985, in Brooklyn, N.Y. ... 6-0/165. (1.83/74.8).... Cousin of Stephon Marbury, guard, New York Knicks.
**HIGH SCHOOL:** Abraham Lincoln (Brooklyn, N.Y.).
**COLLEGE:** Did not attend college.
**TRANSACTIONS/CAREER NOTES:** Selected out of high school by Portland Trail Blazers in first round (13th overall pick) of 2004 NBA Draft.

## NBA REGULAR-SEASON RECORD

| | | | | | | | | REBOUNDS | | | | | | | | AVERAGES | | |
|---|---|---|---|---|---|---|---|---|---|---|---|---|---|---|---|---|---|---|
| Season Team | G | Min. | FGM | FGA | Pct. | FTM | FTA | Pct. | Off. | Def. | Tot. | Ast. | St. | Blk. | TO | Pts. | RPG | APG | PPG |
| 04-05—Portland.......... | 68 | 1330 | 169 | 430 | .393 | 105 | 133 | .789 | 10 | 94 | 104 | 224 | 35 | 4 | 125 | 460 | 1.5 | 3.3 | 6.8 |

Three-point field goals: 2004-05, 17-for-69 (.246). Totals, 17-for-69 (.246).
Personal fouls/disqualifications: 2004-05, 120/0. Totals, 120/0.

# TERRY, JASON   G   MAVERICKS

**PERSONAL:** Born September 15, 1977, in Seattle. ... 6-2/180. (1.88/81.6). ... Full name: Jason Eugene Terry
**HIGH SCHOOL:** Franklin (Seattle).
**COLLEGE:** Arizona.
**TRANSACTIONS/CAREER NOTES:** Selected by Atlanta Hawks in first round (10th pick overall) of 1999 NBA Draft. ... Traded by Hawks with F Alan Henderson and a future first-round draft choice to Dallas Mavericks for F Antoine Walker and G Tony Delk (August 4, 2004).

## COLLEGIATE RECORD

**NOTES:** Member of NCAA Division I championship team (1997). ... The Sporting News All-America first team (1999).

| Season Team | G | Min. | FGM | FGA | Pct. | FTM | FTA | Pct. | Reb. | Ast. | Pts. | AVERAGES RPG | APG | PPG |
|---|---|---|---|---|---|---|---|---|---|---|---|---|---|---|
| 95-96—Arizona | 31 | 303 | 32 | 59 | .542 | 16 | 27 | .593 | 23 | 35 | 95 | 0.7 | 1.1 | 3.1 |
| 96-97—Arizona | 34 | 1037 | 124 | 280 | .443 | 72 | 101 | .713 | 91 | 150 | 360 | 2.7 | 4.4 | 10.6 |
| 97-98—Arizona | 35 | 797 | 124 | 294 | .422 | 62 | 75 | .827 | 84 | 149 | 371 | 2.4 | 4.3 | 10.6 |
| 98-99—Arizona | 29 | 1107 | 209 | 472 | .443 | 141 | 168 | .839 | 97 | 159 | 635 | 3.3 | 5.5 | 21.9 |
| Totals | 129 | 3244 | 489 | 1105 | .443 | 291 | 371 | .784 | 295 | 493 | 1461 | 2.3 | 3.8 | 11.3 |

Three-point field goals: 1995-96, 15-for-26 (.577). 1996-97, 40-for-121 (.331). 1997-98, 61-for-176 (.347). 1998-99, 76-for-191 (.398). Totals, 192-for-514 (.374).

Personal fouls/disqualifications: 1995-96, 28/0. 1996-97, 66/1. 1997-98, 55/0. Totals, 149/1.

### NBA REGULAR-SEASON RECORD

**HONORS:** NBA All-Rookie second team (2000).

| Season Team | G | Min. | FGM | FGA | Pct. | FTM | FTA | Pct. | REBOUNDS Off. | Def. | Tot. | Ast. | St. | Blk. | TO | Pts. | AVERAGES RPG | APG | PPG |
|---|---|---|---|---|---|---|---|---|---|---|---|---|---|---|---|---|---|---|---|
| 99-00—Atlanta | 81 | 1888 | 249 | 600 | .415 | 113 | 140 | .807 | 24 | 142 | 166 | 346 | 90 | 10 | 156 | 657 | 2.0 | 4.3 | 8.1 |
| 00-01—Atlanta | 82 | 3089 | 596 | 1367 | .436 | 303 | 358 | .846 | 42 | 227 | 269 | 403 | 104 | 12 | 239 | 1619 | 3.3 | 4.9 | 19.7 |
| 01-02—Atlanta | 78 | 2967 | 524 | 1219 | .430 | 284 | 340 | .835 | 40 | 230 | 270 | 444 | 144 | 13 | 181 | 1504 | 3.5 | 5.7 | 19.3 |
| 02-03—Atlanta | 81 | 3081 | 488 | 1141 | .428 | 259 | 292 | .887 | 37 | 242 | 279 | 600 | 126 | 14 | 249 | 1395 | 3.4 | 7.4 | 17.2 |
| 03-04—Atlanta | 81 | 3018 | 499 | 1196 | .417 | 215 | 260 | .827 | 49 | 287 | 336 | 437 | 124 | 16 | 229 | 1359 | 4.1 | 5.4 | 16.8 |
| 04-05—Dallas | 80 | 2401 | 372 | 743 | .501 | 146 | 173 | .844 | 38 | 150 | 188 | 429 | 109 | 15 | 147 | 993 | 2.4 | 5.4 | 12.4 |
| Totals | 483 | 16444 | 2728 | 6266 | .435 | 1320 | 1563 | .845 | 230 | 1278 | 1508 | 2659 | 697 | 80 | 1201 | 7527 | 3.1 | 5.5 | 15.6 |

Three-point field goals: 1999-00, 46-for-157 (.293). 2000-01, 124-for-314 (.395). 2001-02, 172-for-444 (.387). 2002-03, 160-for-431 (.371). 2003-04, 146-for-421 (.347). 2004-05, 103-for-245 (.420). Totals, 751-for-2012 (.373).

Personal fouls/disqualifications: 1999-00, 133/0. 2000-01, 204/2. 2001-02, 156/0. 2002-03, 175/2. 2003-04, 192/2. 2004-05, 177/0. Totals, 1037/6.

### NBA PLAYOFF RECORD

| Season Team | G | Min. | FGM | FGA | Pct. | FTM | FTA | Pct. | REBOUNDS Off. | Def. | Tot. | Ast. | St. | Blk. | TO | Pts. | AVERAGES RPG | APG | PPG |
|---|---|---|---|---|---|---|---|---|---|---|---|---|---|---|---|---|---|---|---|
| 04-05—Dallas | 13 | 501 | 81 | 160 | .506 | 38 | 43 | .884 | 9 | 45 | 54 | 60 | 17 | 7 | 30 | 227 | 4.2 | 4.6 | 17.5 |

Three-point field goals: 2004-05, 27-for-55 (.491). Totals, 27-for-55 (.491).
Personal fouls/disqualifications: 2004-05, 28/0. Totals, 28/0.

## THOMAS, BILLY — G

**PERSONAL:** Born December 23, 1975, in Shreveport, La. ... 6-5/218. (1.96/98.9).
**HIGH SCHOOL:** Loyola College Prep (Shreveport, La.).
**COLLEGE:** Kansas.
**TRANSACTIONS/CAREER NOTES:** Not drafted by an NBA franchise. ... Signed as free agent by Washington Wizards (October 1, 2004). ... Signed as free agent by New Jersey Nets (February 10, 2005).

### COLLEGIATE RECORD

| Season Team | G | Min. | FGM | FGA | Pct. | FTM | FTA | Pct. | Reb. | Ast. | Pts. | AVERAGES RPG | APG | PPG |
|---|---|---|---|---|---|---|---|---|---|---|---|---|---|---|
| 94-95—Kansas | 31 | 472 | 77 | 177 | .435 | 22 | 29 | .759 | 67 | 20 | 225 | 2.2 | 0.6 | 7.3 |
| 95-96—Kansas | 34 | 358 | 54 | 151 | .358 | 10 | 14 | .714 | 51 | 21 | 160 | 1.5 | 0.6 | 4.7 |
| 96-97—Kansas | 36 | 573 | 97 | 242 | .401 | 11 | 15 | .733 | 64 | 27 | 278 | 1.8 | 0.8 | 7.7 |
| 97-98—Kansas | 36 | 962 | 181 | 387 | .468 | 22 | 32 | .688 | 108 | 101 | 489 | 3.0 | 2.8 | 13.6 |
| Totals | 137 | 2365 | 409 | 957 | .427 | 65 | 90 | .722 | 290 | 169 | 1152 | 2.1 | 1.2 | 8.4 |

Three-point field goals: 1994-95, 49-for-126 (.389). 1995-96, 42-for-125 (.336). 1996-97, 73-for-178 (.410). 1997-98, 105-for-262 (.401). Totals, 269-for-691 (.389).

### INTERNATIONAL BASKETBALL LEAGUE RECORD

| Season Team | G | Min. | FGM | FGA | Pct. | FTM | FTA | Pct. | Reb. | Ast. | Pts. | AVERAGES RPG | APG | PPG |
|---|---|---|---|---|---|---|---|---|---|---|---|---|---|---|
| 00-01—Cincinnati | 51 | 1799 | 291 | 678 | .429 | 89 | 111 | .802 | 195 | 165 | 833 | 3.8 | 3.2 | 16.3 |

Three-point field goals: 2000-01, 162-for-411 (.394). Totals, 162-for-411 (.394).

### NBDL RECORD

| Season Team | G | Min. | FGM | FGA | Pct. | FTM | FTA | Pct. | Reb. | Ast. | Pts. | AVERAGES RPG | APG | PPG |
|---|---|---|---|---|---|---|---|---|---|---|---|---|---|---|
| 01-02—Greenville | 45 | 1373 | 220 | 529 | .416 | 105 | 121 | .868 | 124 | 89 | 629 | 2.8 | 2.0 | 14.0 |
| 02-03—Greenville | 49 | 1551 | 288 | 662 | .435 | 125 | 162 | .772 | 161 | 99 | 785 | 3.3 | 2.0 | 16.0 |
| Totals | 94 | 2924 | 508 | 1191 | .427 | 230 | 283 | .813 | 285 | 188 | 1414 | 3.0 | 2.0 | 15.0 |

Three-point field goals: 2001-02, 84-for-228 (.368). 2002-03, 84-for-241 (.349). Totals, 168-for-469 (.358).

### ITALIAN LEAGUE RECORD

| Season Team | G | Min. | FGM | FGA | Pct. | FTM | FTA | Pct. | Reb. | Ast. | Pts. | AVERAGES RPG | APG | PPG |
|---|---|---|---|---|---|---|---|---|---|---|---|---|---|---|
| 03-04—Coop Nordest Trieste | 26 | 773 | 126 | 279 | .452 | 17 | 23 | .739 | 73 | 32 | 330 | 2.8 | 1.2 | 12.7 |

Three-point field goals: 2003-04, 61-for-167 (.365). Totals, 61-for-167 (.365).

### CBA RECORD

| Season Team | G | Min. | FGM | FGA | Pct. | FTM | FTA | Pct. | Reb. | Ast. | Pts. | AVERAGES RPG | APG | PPG |
|---|---|---|---|---|---|---|---|---|---|---|---|---|---|---|
| 04-05—Dakota Wizards | 24 | 1002 | 183 | 357 | .513 | 64 | 79 | .810 | 100 | 108 | 500 | 4.2 | 4.5 | 20.8 |

Three-point field goals: 2004-05, 70-for-157 (.446). Totals, 70-for-157 (.446).

## NBA REGULAR-SEASON RECORD

| | | | | | | | | REBOUNDS | | | | | | | AVERAGES | | |
|---|---|---|---|---|---|---|---|---|---|---|---|---|---|---|---|---|---|
| Season Team | G | Min. | FGM | FGA | Pct. | FTM | FTA | Pct. | Off. | Def. | Tot. | Ast. | St. | Blk. | TO | Pts. | RPG APG PPG |
| 04-05—New Jersey ..... | 25 | 356 | 34 | 94 | .362 | 7 | 9 | .778 | 7 | 29 | 36 | 17 | 14 | 1 | 9 | 92 | 1.4 0.7 3.7 |

Three-point field goals: 2004-05, 17-for-56 (.304). Totals, 17-for-56 (.304).
Personal fouls/disqualifications: 2004-05, 29/0. Totals, 29/0.

## NBA PLAYOFF RECORD

| | | | | | | | | REBOUNDS | | | | | | | AVERAGES | | |
|---|---|---|---|---|---|---|---|---|---|---|---|---|---|---|---|---|---|
| Season Team | G | Min. | FGM | FGA | Pct. | FTM | FTA | Pct. | Off. | Def. | Tot. | Ast. | St. | Blk. | TO | Pts. | RPG APG PPG |
| 04-05—New Jersey ..... | 2 | 2 | 0 | 1 | .000 | 0 | 0 | ... | 0 | 0 | 0 | 0 | 0 | 0 | 0 | 0 | 0.0 0.0 0.0 |

# THOMAS, ETAN          F/C          WIZARDS

**PERSONAL:** Born April 1, 1978, in Harlem, N.Y. ... 6-9/256. (2.06/116.1). ... Full name: Dedreck Etan Thomas
**HIGH SCHOOL:** Booker T. Washington (Tulsa, Okla.).
**COLLEGE:** Syracuse.
**TRANSACTIONS/CAREER NOTES:** Selected by Dallas Mavericks in first round (12th pick overall) of 2000 NBA Draft. ... Traded by Mavericks with F/C Christian Laettner, G Courtney Alexander, F Loy Vaught, G Hubert Davis and cash considerations to Washington Wizards for F Juwan Howard, C Calvin Booth and F Obinna Ekezie (February 22, 2001).

## COLLEGIATE RECORD

| | | | | | | | | | | | | AVERAGES | | |
|---|---|---|---|---|---|---|---|---|---|---|---|---|---|---|
| Season Team | G | Min. | FGM | FGA | Pct. | FTM | FTA | Pct. | Reb. | Ast. | Pts. | RPG | APG | PPG |
| 96-97—Syracuse ...................... | 25 | 408 | 55 | 103 | .534 | 33 | 71 | .465 | 105 | 3 | 143 | 4.2 | 0.1 | 5.7 |
| 97-98—Syracuse ...................... | 35 | 1009 | 144 | 236 | .610 | 109 | 178 | .612 | 230 | 15 | 397 | 6.6 | 0.4 | 11.3 |
| 98-99—Syracuse ...................... | 33 | 913 | 148 | 240 | .617 | 109 | 190 | .574 | 243 | 17 | 405 | 7.4 | 0.5 | 12.3 |
| 99-00—Syracuse ...................... | 29 | 940 | 148 | 246 | .602 | 99 | 146 | .678 | 269 | 16 | 395 | 9.3 | 0.6 | 13.6 |
| Totals ...................................... | 122 | 3270 | 495 | 825 | .600 | 350 | 585 | .598 | 847 | 51 | 1340 | 6.9 | 0.4 | 11.0 |

## NBA REGULAR-SEASON RECORD

| | | | | | | | | REBOUNDS | | | | | | | AVERAGES | | |
|---|---|---|---|---|---|---|---|---|---|---|---|---|---|---|---|---|---|
| Season Team | G | Min. | FGM | FGA | Pct. | FTM | FTA | Pct. | Off. | Def. | Tot. | Ast. | St. | Blk. | TO | Pts. | RPG APG PPG |
| 00-01—Dallas-Wash.... | | | | | | | Did not play—injured. | | | | | | | | | | |
| 01-02—Washington .... | 47 | 618 | 81 | 151 | .536 | 41 | 74 | .554 | 55 | 126 | 181 | 6 | 17 | 35 | 26 | 203 | 3.9 0.1 4.3 |
| 02-03—Washington .... | 38 | 513 | 61 | 124 | .492 | 60 | 94 | .638 | 70 | 95 | 165 | 3 | 8 | 23 | 33 | 182 | 4.3 0.1 4.8 |
| 03-04—Washington .... | 79 | 1901 | 257 | 526 | .489 | 191 | 295 | .647 | 183 | 345 | 528 | 68 | 36 | 123 | 113 | 705 | 6.7 0.9 8.9 |
| 04-05—Washington .... | 47 | 976 | 128 | 255 | .502 | 76 | 144 | .528 | 85 | 159 | 244 | 20 | 17 | 51 | 50 | 332 | 5.2 0.4 7.1 |
| Totals ................... | 211 | 4008 | 527 | 1056 | .499 | 368 | 607 | .606 | 393 | 725 | 1118 | 97 | 78 | 232 | 222 | 1422 | 5.3 0.5 6.7 |

Personal fouls/disqualifications: 2001-02, 76/0. 2002-03, 66/0. 2003-04, 219/1. 2004-05, 133/2. Totals, 494/3.

## NBA PLAYOFF RECORD

| | | | | | | | | REBOUNDS | | | | | | | AVERAGES | | |
|---|---|---|---|---|---|---|---|---|---|---|---|---|---|---|---|---|---|
| Season Team | G | Min. | FGM | FGA | Pct. | FTM | FTA | Pct. | Off. | Def. | Tot. | Ast. | St. | Blk. | TO | Pts. | RPG APG PPG |
| 04-05—Washington .... | 8 | 126 | 19 | 29 | .655 | 10 | 22 | .455 | 12 | 24 | 36 | 2 | 0 | 7 | 9 | 48 | 4.5 0.3 6.0 |

Personal fouls/disqualifications: 2004-05, 23/0. Totals, 23/0.

# THOMAS, JAMES          F

**PERSONAL:** Born November 22, 1980, in Schenectady, N.Y. ... 6-8/235. (2.03/106.6).
**HIGH SCHOOL:** Hargrave Academy (Chatham, Va.).
**COLLEGE:** Texas.
**TRANSACTIONS/CAREER NOTES:** Signed to 10-day contract by Portland Trail Blazers (January 9, 2005). ... Waived by Trail Blazers (January 31, 2005). ... Signed to 10-day contract by Cleveland Cavaliers (February 22, 2005). ... Signed for rest of season by Hawks (April 9, 2005). ... Waived by Atlanta Hawks (July 5, 2005).

## COLLEGIATE RECORD

| | | | | | | | | | | | | AVERAGES | | |
|---|---|---|---|---|---|---|---|---|---|---|---|---|---|---|
| Season Team | G | Min. | FGM | FGA | Pct. | FTM | FTA | Pct. | Reb. | Ast. | Pts. | RPG | APG | PPG |
| 00-01—Texas ............................ | 34 | 0 | 90 | 186 | .484 | 58 | 127 | .457 | 221 | 13 | 238 | 6.5 | 0.4 | 7.0 |
| 01-02—Texas ............................ | 34 | 0 | 128 | 235 | .545 | 107 | 169 | .633 | 302 | 14 | 363 | 8.9 | 0.4 | 10.7 |
| 02-03—Texas ............................ | 33 | 806 | 125 | 243 | .514 | 117 | 178 | .657 | 363 | 15 | 367 | 11.0 | 0.5 | 11.1 |
| 03-04—Texas ............................ | 33 | 516 | 62 | 134 | .463 | 57 | 88 | .648 | 191 | 11 | 181 | 5.8 | 0.3 | 5.5 |
| Totals ...................................... | 134 | 1322 | 405 | 798 | .508 | 339 | 562 | .603 | 1077 | 53 | 1149 | 8.0 | 0.4 | 8.6 |

## NBA REGULAR-SEASON RECORD

| | | | | | | | | REBOUNDS | | | | | | | AVERAGES | | |
|---|---|---|---|---|---|---|---|---|---|---|---|---|---|---|---|---|---|
| Season Team | G | Min. | FGM | FGA | Pct. | FTM | FTA | Pct. | Off. | Def. | Tot. | Ast. | St. | Blk. | TO | Pts. | RPG APG PPG |
| 04-05—Port.-Cleve.-Atl. | 11 | 117 | 12 | 20 | .600 | 2 | 6 | .333 | 17 | 20 | 37 | 4 | 4 | 4 | 7 | 26 | 3.4 0.4 2.4 |

Personal fouls/disqualifications: 2004-05, 13/0. Totals, 13/0.

## NBDL RECORD

| | | | | | | | | | | | | AVERAGES | | |
|---|---|---|---|---|---|---|---|---|---|---|---|---|---|---|
| Season Team | G | Min. | FGM | FGA | Pct. | FTM | FTA | Pct. | Reb. | Ast. | Pts. | RPG | APG | PPG |
| 04-05—Roanoke ........................ | 36 | 1276 | 165 | 312 | .529 | 118 | 172 | .686 | 480 | 24 | 448 | 13.3 | 0.7 | 12.4 |

Three-point field goals: 2004-05, 0-for-1. Totals, 0-for-1 (.000).

## THOMAS, KENNY — F — KINGS

**PERSONAL:** Born July 25, 1977, in Atlanta. ... 6-7/245. (2.01/111.1). ... Full name: Kenneth Cornelius Thomas
**HIGH SCHOOL:** El Paso (Texas), then Albuquerque (N.M.).
**COLLEGE:** New Mexico.
**TRANSACTIONS/CAREER NOTES:** Selected by Houston Rockets in first round (22nd pick overall) of 1999 NBA Draft. ... Traded by Rockets to Philadelphia 76ers in three-way deal in which 76ers sent F/C Mark Bryant, F Art Long and future first-round draft choice to Denver Nuggets, Nuggets sent G/F James Posey to Rockets and Rockets sent future second-round draft choice to Nuggets (December 18, 2002). ... Traded by 76ers with F Corliss Williamson and C Brian Skinner to Sacramento Kings for Fs Chris Webber, Michael Bradley and Matt Barnes (February 23, 2005).

### COLLEGIATE RECORD

**NOTES:** The Sporting News All-America second team (1998).

| Season Team | G | Min. | FGM | FGA | Pct. | FTM | FTA | Pct. | Reb. | Ast. | Pts. | RPG | APG | PPG |
|---|---|---|---|---|---|---|---|---|---|---|---|---|---|---|
| 95-96—New Mexico | 33 | 981 | 170 | 294 | .578 | 144 | 203 | .709 | 256 | 53 | 484 | 7.8 | 1.6 | 14.7 |
| 96-97—New Mexico | 32 | 1000 | 139 | 264 | .527 | 155 | 206 | .752 | 220 | 63 | 444 | 6.9 | 2.0 | 13.9 |
| 97-98—New Mexico | 32 | 1047 | 195 | 385 | .506 | 122 | 159 | .767 | 297 | 95 | 539 | 9.3 | 3.0 | 16.8 |
| 98-99—New Mexico | 26 | 903 | 162 | 297 | .545 | 113 | 154 | .734 | 259 | 51 | 464 | 10.0 | 2.0 | 17.8 |
| Totals | 123 | 3931 | 666 | 1240 | .537 | 534 | 722 | .740 | 1032 | 262 | 1931 | 8.4 | 2.1 | 15.7 |

Three-point field goals: 1995-96, 0-for-3. 1996-97, 11-for-36 (.306). 1997-98, 27-for-72 (.375). 1998-99, 27-for-73 (.370). Totals, 65-for-184 (.353).

### NBA REGULAR-SEASON RECORD

| Season Team | G | Min. | FGM | FGA | Pct. | FTM | FTA | Pct. | Off. | Def. | Tot. | Ast. | St. | Blk. | TO | Pts. | RPG | APG | PPG |
|---|---|---|---|---|---|---|---|---|---|---|---|---|---|---|---|---|---|---|---|
| 99-00—Houston | 72 | 1797 | 212 | 531 | .399 | 138 | 209 | .660 | 147 | 290 | 437 | 113 | 54 | 22 | 112 | 594 | 6.1 | 1.6 | 8.3 |
| 00-01—Houston | 74 | 1820 | 206 | 465 | .443 | 91 | 126 | .722 | 122 | 295 | 417 | 77 | 40 | 43 | 116 | 528 | 5.6 | 1.0 | 7.1 |
| 01-02—Houston | 72 | 2484 | 396 | 829 | .478 | 223 | 336 | .664 | 158 | 358 | 516 | 137 | 85 | 66 | 143 | 1015 | 7.2 | 1.9 | 14.1 |
| 02-03—Hou-Phil | 66 | 1978 | 260 | 559 | .465 | 147 | 197 | .746 | 185 | 344 | 529 | 112 | 62 | 28 | 116 | 667 | 8.0 | 1.7 | 10.1 |
| 03-04—Philadelphia | 74 | 2699 | 381 | 813 | .469 | 243 | 323 | .752 | 261 | 489 | 750 | 111 | 82 | 33 | 172 | 1006 | 10.1 | 1.5 | 13.6 |
| 04-05—Phila.-Sac. | 73 | 2167 | 367 | 781 | .470 | 173 | 227 | .762 | 184 | 351 | 535 | 152 | 67 | 17 | 131 | 908 | 7.3 | 2.1 | 12.4 |
| Totals | 431 | 12945 | 1822 | 3978 | .458 | 1015 | 1418 | .716 | 1057 | 2127 | 3184 | 702 | 390 | 209 | 790 | 4718 | 7.4 | 1.6 | 10.9 |

Three-point field goals: 1999-00, 32-for-122 (.262). 2000-01, 25-for-92 (.272). 2001-02, 0-for-16. 2003-04, 1-for-5 (.200). 2004-05, 1-for-5 (.200). Totals, 59-for-240 (.246).

Personal fouls/disqualifications: 1999-00, 167/0. 2000-01, 178/4. 2001-02, 195/5. 2002-03, 169/2. 2003-04, 219/2. 2004-05, 227/3. Totals, 1155/16.

### NBA PLAYOFF RECORD

| Season Team | G | Min. | FGM | FGA | Pct. | FTM | FTA | Pct. | Off. | Def. | Tot. | Ast. | St. | Blk. | TO | Pts. | RPG | APG | PPG |
|---|---|---|---|---|---|---|---|---|---|---|---|---|---|---|---|---|---|---|---|
| 02-03—Philadelphia | 12 | 389 | 54 | 101 | .535 | 19 | 29 | .655 | 42 | 70 | 112 | 11 | 8 | 5 | 19 | 127 | 9.3 | 0.9 | 10.6 |
| 04-05—Sacramento | 5 | 153 | 23 | 45 | .511 | 14 | 20 | .700 | 17 | 27 | 44 | 12 | 4 | 2 | 8 | 60 | 8.8 | 2.4 | 12.0 |
| Totals | 17 | 542 | 77 | 146 | .527 | 33 | 49 | .673 | 59 | 97 | 156 | 23 | 12 | 7 | 27 | 187 | 9.2 | 1.4 | 11.0 |

Personal fouls/disqualifications: 2002-03, 42/1. 2004-05, 22/1. Totals, 64/2.

## THOMAS, KURT — F — SUNS

**PERSONAL:** Born October 4, 1972, in Dallas. ... 6-9/230. (2.06/104.3). ... Full name: Kurt Vincent Thomas
**HIGH SCHOOL:** Hillcrest (Dallas).
**COLLEGE:** Texas Christian.
**TRANSACTIONS/CAREER NOTES:** Selected by Miami Heat in first round (10th pick overall) of 1995 NBA Draft. ... Traded by Heat with G Sasha Danilovic and F Martin Muursepp to Dallas Mavericks for F Jamal Mashburn (February 14, 1997). ... Signed as free agent by New York Knicks (January 22, 1999). ... Traded by Knicks with draft rights to F Dijon Thompson to Phoenix Suns for G Quentin Richardson, draft rights to G Nate Robinson and future considerations (June 28, 2005).

### COLLEGIATE RECORD

**NOTES:** Led NCAA Division I with 28.9 points per game and 14.6 rebounds per game (1995). ... One of only three players in NCAA history to lead nation in both scoring and rebounding in same season (1995).

| Season Team | G | Min. | FGM | FGA | Pct. | FTM | FTA | Pct. | Reb. | Ast. | Pts. | RPG | APG | PPG |
|---|---|---|---|---|---|---|---|---|---|---|---|---|---|---|
| 90-91—Texas Christian | 28 | 42 | 8 | 18 | .444 | 7 | 14 | .500 | 13 | 2 | 23 | 0.5 | 0.1 | 0.8 |
| 91-92—Texas Christian | 21 | 347 | 58 | 119 | .487 | 34 | 51 | .667 | 114 | 24 | 150 | 5.4 | 1.1 | 7.1 |
| 92-93—Texas Christian | | | | | Did not play—leg injury. | | | | | | | | | |
| 93-94—Texas Christian | 27 | 805 | 224 | 440 | .509 | 98 | 152 | .645 | 262 | 50 | 558 | 9.7 | 1.9 | 20.7 |
| 94-95—Texas Christian | 27 | 872 | 288 | 526 | .548 | 202 | 283 | .714 | 393 | 32 | 781 | 14.6 | 1.2 | 28.9 |
| Totals | 103 | 2066 | 578 | 1103 | .524 | 341 | 500 | .682 | 782 | 108 | 1512 | 7.6 | 1.0 | 14.7 |

Three-point field goals: 1990-91, 0-for-2. 1993-94, 12-for-46 (.261). 1994-95, 3-for-12 (.250). Totals, 15-for-60 (.250).

### NBA REGULAR-SEASON RECORD

**NOTES:** Led NBA with 341 personal fouls (2002), with 344 personal fouls (2003).

| Season Team | G | Min. | FGM | FGA | Pct. | FTM | FTA | Pct. | Off. | Def. | Tot. | Ast. | St. | Blk. | TO | Pts. | RPG | APG | PPG |
|---|---|---|---|---|---|---|---|---|---|---|---|---|---|---|---|---|---|---|---|
| 95-96—Miami | 74 | 1655 | 274 | 547 | .501 | 118 | 178 | .663 | 122 | 317 | 439 | 46 | 47 | 36 | 98 | 666 | 5.9 | 0.6 | 9.0 |
| 96-97—Miami | 18 | 374 | 39 | 105 | .371 | 35 | 46 | .761 | 31 | 76 | 107 | 9 | 12 | 9 | 25 | 113 | 5.9 | 0.5 | 6.3 |
| 97-98—Dallas | 5 | 73 | 17 | 45 | .378 | 3 | 3 | 1.000 | 8 | 16 | 24 | 3 | 1 | 0 | 10 | 37 | 4.8 | 0.6 | 7.4 |
| 98-99—New York | 50 | 1182 | 170 | 368 | .462 | 66 | 108 | .611 | 82 | 204 | 286 | 55 | 45 | 17 | 73 | 406 | 5.7 | 1.1 | 8.1 |
| 99-00—New York | 80 | 1971 | 270 | 535 | .505 | 100 | 128 | .781 | 144 | 361 | 505 | 82 | 51 | 42 | 105 | 641 | 6.3 | 1.0 | 8.0 |
| 00-01—New York | 77 | 2125 | 314 | 614 | .511 | 171 | 210 | .814 | 172 | 343 | 515 | 63 | 61 | 69 | 99 | 800 | 6.7 | 0.8 | 10.4 |
| 01-02—New York | 82 | 2771 | 463 | 938 | .494 | 216 | 265 | .815 | 214 | 533 | 747 | 87 | 71 | 79 | 153 | 1143 | 9.1 | 1.1 | 13.9 |
| 02-03—New York | 81 | 2577 | 497 | 1028 | .483 | 138 | 184 | .750 | 160 | 477 | 637 | 162 | 81 | 97 | 138 | 1134 | 7.9 | 2.0 | 14.0 |

T

| Season Team | G | Min. | FGM | FGA | Pct. | FTM | FTA | Pct. | Off. | Def. | Tot. | Ast. | St. | Blk. | TO | Pts. | RPG | APG | PPG |
|---|---|---|---|---|---|---|---|---|---|---|---|---|---|---|---|---|---|---|---|
| 03-04—New York | 80 | 2548 | 392 | 829 | .473 | 106 | 127 | .835 | 145 | 517 | 662 | 149 | 56 | 80 | 132 | 890 | 8.3 | 1.9 | 11.1 |
| 04-05—New York | 80 | 2855 | 424 | 901 | .471 | 66 | 84 | .786 | 170 | 661 | 831 | 160 | 70 | 79 | 99 | 916 | 10.4 | 2.0 | 11.5 |
| Totals | 627 | 18131 | 2860 | 5910 | .484 | 1019 | 1333 | .764 | 1248 | 3505 | 4753 | 816 | 495 | 508 | 932 | 6746 | 7.6 | 1.3 | 10.8 |

Three-point field goals: 1995-96, 0-for-2. 1996-97, 0-for-1. 1998-99, 0-for-1. 1999-00, 1-for-3 (.333). 2000-01, 1-for-3 (.333). 2001-02, 1-for-6 (.167). 2002-03, 2-for-3 (.667). 2003-04, 0-for-3. 2004-05, 2-for-4 (.500). Totals, 7-for-26 (.269).

Personal fouls/disqualifications: 1995-96, 271/7. 1996-97, 67/3. 1997-98, 19/1. 1998-99, 159/3. 1999-00, 278/6. 2000-01, 287/6. 2001-02, 341/8. 2002-03, 344/12. 2003-04, 298/4. 2004-05, 310/6. Totals, 2374/56.

## NBA PLAYOFF RECORD

| Season Team | G | Min. | FGM | FGA | Pct. | FTM | FTA | Pct. | Off. | Def. | Tot. | Ast. | St. | Blk. | TO | Pts. | RPG | APG | PPG |
|---|---|---|---|---|---|---|---|---|---|---|---|---|---|---|---|---|---|---|---|
| 95-96—Miami | 3 | 60 | 4 | 10 | .400 | 4 | 4 | 1.000 | 4 | 12 | 16 | 3 | 2 | 1 | 5 | 12 | 5.3 | 1.0 | 4.0 |
| 98-99—New York | 20 | 419 | 45 | 118 | .381 | 16 | 23 | .696 | 38 | 72 | 110 | 7 | 15 | 12 | 19 | 106 | 5.5 | 0.4 | 5.3 |
| 99-00—New York | 16 | 251 | 31 | 61 | .508 | 7 | 10 | .700 | 18 | 32 | 50 | 5 | 3 | 6 | 14 | 69 | 3.1 | 0.3 | 4.3 |
| 00-01—New York | 5 | 186 | 25 | 47 | .532 | 22 | 31 | .710 | 17 | 39 | 56 | 9 | 2 | 5 | 9 | 72 | 11.2 | 1.8 | 14.4 |
| 03-04—New York | 4 | 139 | 21 | 49 | .429 | 9 | 12 | .750 | 9 | 37 | 46 | 6 | 7 | 3 | 10 | 51 | 11.5 | 1.5 | 12.8 |
| Totals | 48 | 1055 | 126 | 285 | .442 | 58 | 80 | .725 | 86 | 192 | 278 | 30 | 29 | 27 | 57 | 310 | 5.8 | 0.6 | 6.5 |

Personal fouls/disqualifications: 1995-96, 13/1. 1998-99, 76/0. 1999-00, 44/1. 2000-01, 26/1. 2003-04, 17/0. Totals, 176/3.

# THOMAS, TIM     F     KNICKS

**PERSONAL:** Born February 26, 1977, in Paterson, N.J. ... 6-10/230. (2.08/104.3). ... Full name: Timothy Mark Thomas
**HIGH SCHOOL:** Paterson Catholic (Paterson, N.J.).
**COLLEGE:** Villanova.
**TRANSACTIONS/CAREER NOTES:** Selected after freshman season by New Jersey Nets in first round (seventh pick overall) of 1997 NBA Draft. ... Draft rights traded by Nets with draft rights to G Anthony Parker, G Jim Jackson and C Eric Montross to Philadelphia 76ers for C Michael Cage, G Lucious Harris, F Don MacLean and draft rights to F Keith Van Horn (June 27, 1997). ... Traded by 76ers with C/F Scott Williams to Milwaukee Bucks for F Tyrone Hill and F/G Jerald Honeycutt (March 11, 1999). ... Traded by Bucks to New York Knicks as part of three-team trade in which Bucks also traded C Joel Przybilla to Atlanta Hawks. Knicks also acquired C Nazr Mohammed from Hawks and traded F Keith Van Horn to Bucks and C Michael Doleac and 2005 second-round draft choice to Hawks (February 15, 2004).

## COLLEGIATE RECORD

**NOTES:** The Sporting News Freshman of the Year (1997).

| Season Team | G | Min. | FGM | FGA | Pct. | FTM | FTA | Pct. | Reb. | Ast. | Pts. | RPG | APG | PPG |
|---|---|---|---|---|---|---|---|---|---|---|---|---|---|---|
| 96-97—Villanova | 32 | 1005 | 187 | 416 | .450 | 121 | 152 | .796 | 193 | 66 | 542 | 6.0 | 2.1 | 16.9 |

Three-point field goals: 1996-97, 47-for-140 (.336). Totals, 47-for-140 (.336).

## NBA REGULAR-SEASON RECORD

**RECORDS:** Shares single-game record for most three-point field goals made in one half—8 (January 5, 2001, vs. Portland).
**HONORS:** NBA All-Rookie second team (1998).

| Season Team | G | Min. | FGM | FGA | Pct. | FTM | FTA | Pct. | Off. | Def. | Tot. | Ast. | St. | Blk. | TO | Pts. | RPG | APG | PPG |
|---|---|---|---|---|---|---|---|---|---|---|---|---|---|---|---|---|---|---|---|
| 97-98—Philadelphia | 77 | 1779 | 306 | 684 | .447 | 171 | 231 | .740 | 107 | 181 | 288 | 90 | 54 | 17 | 118 | 845 | 3.7 | 1.2 | 11.0 |
| 98-99—Phila.-Mil. | 50 | 812 | 132 | 279 | .473 | 73 | 112 | .652 | 49 | 77 | 126 | 46 | 26 | 12 | 46 | 358 | 2.5 | 0.9 | 7.2 |
| 99-00—Milwaukee | 80 | 2093 | 347 | 753 | .461 | 188 | 243 | .774 | 100 | 232 | 332 | 113 | 59 | 31 | 129 | 945 | 4.2 | 1.4 | 11.8 |
| 00-01—Milwaukee | 76 | 2086 | 326 | 758 | .430 | 195 | 253 | .771 | 79 | 234 | 313 | 138 | 78 | 45 | 114 | 954 | 4.1 | 1.8 | 12.6 |
| 01-02—Milwaukee | 74 | 1987 | 316 | 753 | .420 | 142 | 179 | .793 | 64 | 236 | 300 | 105 | 65 | 32 | 127 | 869 | 4.1 | 1.4 | 11.7 |
| 02-03—Milwaukee | 80 | 2358 | 412 | 930 | .443 | 145 | 186 | .780 | 97 | 292 | 389 | 102 | 70 | 49 | 133 | 1066 | 4.9 | 1.3 | 13.3 |
| 03-04—Mil.-New York | 66 | 2089 | 363 | 813 | .446 | 171 | 218 | .784 | 64 | 256 | 320 | 124 | 64 | 20 | 116 | 970 | 4.8 | 1.9 | 14.7 |
| 04-05—New York | 71 | 1940 | 315 | 718 | .439 | 136 | 173 | .786 | 45 | 192 | 237 | 110 | 41 | 17 | 113 | 851 | 3.3 | 1.5 | 12.0 |
| Totals | 574 | 15144 | 2517 | 5688 | .443 | 1221 | 1595 | .766 | 605 | 1700 | 2305 | 828 | 457 | 223 | 896 | 6858 | 4.0 | 1.4 | 11.9 |

Three-point field goals: 1997-98, 62-for-171 (.363). 1998-99, 21-for-68 (.309). 1999-00, 63-for-182 (.346). 2000-01, 107-for-260 (.412). 2001-02, 95-for-291 (.326). 2002-03, 97-for-265 (.366). 2003-04, 73-for-194 (.376). 2004-05, 85-for-208 (.409). Totals, 603-for-1639 (.368).

Personal fouls/disqualifications: 1997-98, 185/2. 1998-99, 107/2. 1999-00, 227/3. 2000-01, 194/5. 2001-02, 200/3. 2002-03, 257/5. 2003-04, 196/4. 2004-05, 222/3. Totals, 1588/27.

## NBA PLAYOFF RECORD

| Season Team | G | Min. | FGM | FGA | Pct. | FTM | FTA | Pct. | Off. | Def. | Tot. | Ast. | St. | Blk. | TO | Pts. | RPG | APG | PPG |
|---|---|---|---|---|---|---|---|---|---|---|---|---|---|---|---|---|---|---|---|
| 98-99—Milwaukee | 3 | 60 | 8 | 18 | .444 | 7 | 12 | .583 | 4 | 8 | 12 | 1 | 1 | 1 | 5 | 23 | 4.0 | 0.3 | 7.7 |
| 99-00—Milwaukee | 5 | 142 | 29 | 59 | .492 | 14 | 17 | .824 | 6 | 18 | 24 | 10 | 1 | 4 | 1 | 77 | 4.8 | 2.0 | 15.4 |
| 00-01—Milwaukee | 18 | 479 | 64 | 143 | .448 | 53 | 65 | .815 | 22 | 59 | 81 | 29 | 9 | 10 | 21 | 203 | 4.5 | 1.6 | 11.3 |
| 02-03—Milwaukee | 6 | 191 | 36 | 78 | .462 | 23 | 32 | .719 | 8 | 21 | 29 | 8 | 3 | 6 | 8 | 107 | 4.8 | 1.3 | 17.8 |
| 03-04—New York | 1 | 22 | 4 | 10 | .400 | 4 | 5 | .800 | 1 | 4 | 5 | 3 | 0 | 0 | 2 | 12 | 5.0 | 3.0 | 12.0 |
| Totals | 33 | 894 | 141 | 308 | .458 | 101 | 131 | .771 | 41 | 110 | 151 | 51 | 14 | 21 | 37 | 422 | 4.6 | 1.5 | 12.8 |

Three-point field goals: 1998-99, 0-for-2. 1999-00, 5-for-15 (.333). 2000-01, 22-for-51 (.431). 2002-03, 12-for-21 (.571). 2003-04, 0-for-1. Totals, 39-for-90 (.433).

Personal fouls/disqualifications: 1998-99, 11/0. 1999-00, 14/0. 2000-01, 52/1. 2002-03, 27/2. 2003-04, 5/0. Totals, 109/3.

# TINSLEY, JAMAAL     G     PACERS

**PERSONAL:** Born February 28, 1978, in Brooklyn, N.Y. ... 6-3/195. (1.91/88.5).
**HIGH SCHOOL:** Samuel J. Tilden (Brooklyn, N.Y.), did not play basketball.
**JUNIOR COLLEGE:** Mount San Jacinto (Calif.).
**COLLEGE:** Iowa State.
**TRANSACTIONS/CAREER NOTES:** Selected by Vancouver Grizzlies in first round (27th pick overall) of 2001 NBA Draft. ...

Draft rights traded by Grizzlies with F Shareef Abdur-Rahim to Atlanta Hawks for F/C Lorenzen Wright, G Brevin Knight and draft rights to F Pau Gasol (June 27, 2001). ... Draft rights traded by Hawks to Indiana Pacers for future first-round draft choice (July 19, 2001).

## COLLEGIATE RECORD

**NOTES:** The Sporting News All-America second team (2001).

| Season Team | G | Min. | FGM | FGA | Pct. | FTM | FTA | Pct. | Reb. | Ast. | Pts. | AVERAGES RPG | APG | PPG |
|---|---|---|---|---|---|---|---|---|---|---|---|---|---|---|
| 97-98—Mount San Jacinto | 36 | ... | 194 | 403 | .481 | 94 | 159 | .591 | 153 | 341 | 509 | 4.3 | 9.5 | 14.1 |
| 98-99—Mount San Jacinto | 37 | ... | 281 | 502 | .560 | 201 | 287 | .700 | 160 | 362 | 814 | 4.3 | 9.8 | 22.0 |
| 99-00—Iowa State | 37 | 1212 | 145 | 382 | .378 | 102 | 151 | .675 | 189 | 244 | 407 | 5.1 | 6.6 | 11.0 |
| 00-01—Iowa State | 31 | 999 | 139 | 348 | .399 | 128 | 185 | .692 | 117 | 187 | 443 | 3.8 | 6.0 | 14.3 |
| **Junior College Totals** | 73 | ... | 475 | 905 | .525 | 295 | 446 | .661 | 313 | 703 | 1323 | 4.3 | 9.6 | 18.1 |
| **4-Year-College Totals** | 68 | 2211 | 284 | 732 | .388 | 230 | 336 | .685 | 306 | 431 | 850 | 4.5 | 6.3 | 12.5 |

Three-point field goals: 1997-98, 27-for-100 (.270). 1998-99, 51-for-139 (.367). 1999-00, 15-for-62 (.242). 2000-01, 37-for-97 (.381). Totals, 130-for-398 (.327).

## NBA REGULAR-SEASON RECORD

**HONORS:** NBA All-Rookie second team (2002).

| Season Team | G | Min. | FGM | FGA | Pct. | FTM | FTA | Pct. | REBOUNDS Off. | Def. | Tot. | Ast. | St. | Blk. | TO | Pts. | AVERAGES RPG | APG | PPG |
|---|---|---|---|---|---|---|---|---|---|---|---|---|---|---|---|---|---|---|---|
| 01-02—Indiana | 80 | 2442 | 289 | 760 | .380 | 131 | 186 | .704 | 78 | 220 | 298 | 647 | 138 | 40 | 270 | 751 | 3.7 | 8.1 | 9.4 |
| 02-03—Indiana | 73 | 2237 | 220 | 556 | .396 | 80 | 112 | .714 | 58 | 202 | 260 | 548 | 125 | 18 | 192 | 566 | 3.6 | 7.5 | 7.8 |
| 03-04—Indiana | 52 | 1378 | 153 | 370 | .414 | 49 | 67 | .731 | 28 | 108 | 136 | 303 | 84 | 17 | 110 | 432 | 2.6 | 5.8 | 8.3 |
| 04-05—Indiana | 40 | 1301 | 218 | 522 | .418 | 122 | 164 | .744 | 26 | 134 | 160 | 257 | 81 | 12 | 134 | 616 | 4.0 | 6.4 | 15.4 |
| **Totals** | 245 | 7358 | 880 | 2208 | .399 | 382 | 529 | .722 | 190 | 664 | 854 | 1755 | 428 | 87 | 706 | 2365 | 3.5 | 7.2 | 9.7 |

Three-point field goals: 2001-02, 42-for-175 (.240). 2002-03, 46-for-166 (.277). 2003-04, 77-for-207 (.372). 2004-05, 58-for-156 (.372). Totals, 223-for-704 (.317).

Personal fouls/disqualifications: 2001-02, 248/9. 2002-03, 201/2. 2003-04, 132/2. 2004-05, 112/3. Totals, 693/16.

## NBA PLAYOFF RECORD

| Season Team | G | Min. | FGM | FGA | Pct. | FTM | FTA | Pct. | REBOUNDS Off. | Def. | Tot. | Ast. | St. | Blk. | TO | Pts. | AVERAGES RPG | APG | PPG |
|---|---|---|---|---|---|---|---|---|---|---|---|---|---|---|---|---|---|---|---|
| 01-02—Indiana | 5 | 88 | 8 | 19 | .421 | 2 | 3 | .667 | 2 | 8 | 10 | 25 | 2 | 0 | 12 | 18 | 2.0 | 5.0 | 3.6 |
| 02-03—Indiana | 6 | 185 | 20 | 35 | .571 | 3 | 6 | .500 | 6 | 12 | 18 | 39 | 4 | 0 | 8 | 51 | 3.0 | 6.5 | 8.5 |
| 03-04—Indiana | 16 | 422 | 49 | 123 | .398 | 15 | 16 | .938 | 6 | 40 | 46 | 80 | 28 | 3 | 31 | 129 | 2.9 | 5.0 | 8.1 |
| 04-05—Indiana | 9 | 247 | 32 | 89 | .360 | 12 | 21 | .571 | 6 | 24 | 30 | 51 | 14 | 3 | 27 | 78 | 3.3 | 5.7 | 8.7 |
| **Totals** | 36 | 942 | 109 | 266 | .410 | 32 | 46 | .696 | 20 | 84 | 104 | 195 | 48 | 6 | 78 | 276 | 2.9 | 5.4 | 7.7 |

Three-point field goals: 2001-02, 0-for-1. 2002-03, 8-for-13 (.615). 2003-04, 16-for-54 (.296). 2004-05, 2-for-13 (.111). Totals, 26-for-86 (.302).
Personal fouls/disqualifications: 2001-02, 12/0. 2002-03, 20/0. 2003-04, 56/2. 2004-05, 31/0. Totals, 119/2.

# TRAYLOR, ROBERT     F

**PERSONAL:** Born February 1, 1977, in Detroit. ... 6-8/284. (2.03/128.8). ... Full name: Robert DeShaun Traylor.
**HIGH SCHOOL:** Murray-Wright (Detroit).
**COLLEGE:** Michigan.
**TRANSACTIONS/CAREER NOTES:** Selected after junior season by Dallas Mavericks in first round (sixth pick overall) of 1998 NBA Draft. ... Draft rights traded by Mavericks to Milwaukee Bucks for draft rights to C Dirk Nowitzki and F Pat Garrity (June 24, 1998). ... Traded by Bucks with F/C J.R. Reid to Cleveland Cavaliers as part of three-way deal in which Cavaliers traded G Bob Sura to Golden State Warriors, Warriors traded F Jason Caffey and F/G Billy Owens to Bucks and Bucks traded G Vinny Del Negro to Warriors (June 27, 2000). ... Traded by Cavaliers with F Matt Harpring and F Cedric Henderson to Philadelphia 76ers for F Tyrone Hill and F Jumaine Jones (August 3, 2001). ... Traded by 76ers to Charlotte Hornets as part of three-way deal in which Hornets received F George Lynch and F Jerome Moiso from 76ers and F Chris Porter from Golden State Warriors, 76ers received F Derrick Coleman from Hornets and G Vonteego Cummings and F Corie Blount from Warriors, and Warriors received F Cedric Henderson and conditional 2005 first-round draft choice from 76ers and cash considerations from Hornets (October 25, 2001). ... Signed as free agent by Cavaliers (August 5, 2004).

## COLLEGIATE RECORD

| Season Team | G | Min. | FGM | FGA | Pct. | FTM | FTA | Pct. | Reb. | Ast. | Pts. | AVERAGES RPG | APG | PPG |
|---|---|---|---|---|---|---|---|---|---|---|---|---|---|---|
| 95-96—Michigan | 22 | 438 | 82 | 148 | .554 | 34 | 62 | .548 | 130 | 12 | 198 | 5.9 | 0.5 | 9.0 |
| 96-97—Michigan | 35 | 955 | 190 | 342 | .556 | 80 | 176 | .455 | 271 | 33 | 460 | 7.7 | 0.9 | 13.1 |
| 97-98—Michigan | 34 | 1090 | 224 | 387 | .579 | 104 | 162 | .642 | 344 | 88 | 552 | 10.1 | 2.6 | 16.2 |
| **Totals** | 91 | 2483 | 496 | 877 | .566 | 218 | 400 | .545 | 745 | 133 | 1210 | 8.2 | 1.5 | 13.3 |

Three-point field goals: 1997-98, 0-for-1. Totals, 0-for-1 (.000).

## NBA REGULAR-SEASON RECORD

| Season Team | G | Min. | FGM | FGA | Pct. | FTM | FTA | Pct. | REBOUNDS Off. | Def. | Tot. | Ast. | St. | Blk. | TO | Pts. | AVERAGES RPG | APG | PPG |
|---|---|---|---|---|---|---|---|---|---|---|---|---|---|---|---|---|---|---|---|
| 98-99—Milwaukee | 49 | 786 | 108 | 201 | .537 | 43 | 80 | .538 | 80 | 102 | 182 | 38 | 44 | 44 | 42 | 259 | 3.7 | 0.8 | 5.3 |
| 99-00—Milwaukee | 44 | 447 | 58 | 122 | .475 | 41 | 68 | .603 | 50 | 65 | 115 | 20 | 25 | 25 | 27 | 157 | 2.6 | 0.5 | 3.6 |
| 00-01—Cleveland | 70 | 1212 | 161 | 324 | .497 | 80 | 141 | .567 | 124 | 176 | 300 | 63 | 49 | 76 | 98 | 402 | 4.3 | 0.9 | 5.7 |
| 01-02—Charlotte | 61 | 678 | 87 | 204 | .426 | 53 | 84 | .631 | 67 | 120 | 187 | 37 | 24 | 37 | 45 | 228 | 3.1 | 0.6 | 3.7 |
| 02-03—New Orleans | 69 | 851 | 105 | 237 | .443 | 57 | 98 | .648 | 108 | 154 | 262 | 50 | 45 | 37 | 53 | 268 | 3.8 | 0.7 | 3.9 |
| 03-04—New Orleans | 71 | 942 | 145 | 287 | .505 | 70 | 128 | .547 | 106 | 156 | 262 | 43 | 39 | 37 | 62 | 362 | 3.7 | 0.6 | 5.1 |
| 04-05—Cleveland | 74 | 1327 | 177 | 399 | .444 | 55 | 102 | .539 | 136 | 196 | 332 | 61 | 54 | 50 | 73 | 409 | 4.5 | 0.8 | 5.5 |
| **Totals** | 438 | 6243 | 841 | 1774 | .474 | 399 | 691 | .577 | 671 | 969 | 1640 | 312 | 280 | 306 | 400 | 2085 | 3.7 | 0.7 | 4.8 |

Three-point field goals: 1998-99, 0-for-1. 1999-00, 0-for-4. 2000-01, 0-for-2. 2001-02, 1-for-1 (1.000). 2002-03, 1-for-3 (.333). 2003-04, 2-for-5 (.400). 2004-05, 0-for-8. Totals, 4-for-24 (.167).

Personal fouls/disqualifications: 1998-99, 140/4. 1999-00, 79/0. 2000-01, 24/3. 2001-02, 127/1. 2002-03, 153/1. 2003-04, 161/3. 2004-05, 215/2. Totals, 1079/14.

## NBA PLAYOFF RECORD

| Season Team | G | Min. | FGM | FGA | Pct. | FTM | FTA | Pct. | REBOUNDS Off. | Def. | Tot. | Ast. | St. | Blk. | TO | Pts. | AVERAGES RPG | APG | PPG |
|---|---|---|---|---|---|---|---|---|---|---|---|---|---|---|---|---|---|---|---|
| 98-99—Milwaukee | 3 | 45 | 7 | 9 | .778 | 2 | 4 | .500 | 6 | 6 | 12 | 2 | 2 | 4 | 4 | 16 | 4.0 | 0.7 | 5.3 |

| Season Team | G | Min. | FGM | FGA | Pct. | FTM | FTA | Pct. | REBOUNDS Off. | Def. | Tot. | Ast. | St. | Blk. | TO | Pts. | AVERAGES RPG | APG | PPG |
|---|---|---|---|---|---|---|---|---|---|---|---|---|---|---|---|---|---|---|---|
| 99-00—Milwaukee ...... | 1 | 4 | 0 | 1 | .000 | 0 | 0 | ... | 1 | 1 | 2 | 1 | 0 | 1 | 0 | 0 | 2.0 | 1.0 | 0.0 |
| 01-02—Charlotte ........ | 8 | 62 | 7 | 20 | .350 | 4 | 6 | .667 | 4 | 12 | 16 | 3 | 2 | 2 | 4 | 18 | 2.0 | 0.4 | 2.3 |
| 02-03—New Orleans ... | 6 | 94 | 10 | 22 | .455 | 1 | 4 | .250 | 11 | 19 | 30 | 4 | 3 | 5 | 6 | 21 | 5.0 | 0.7 | 3.5 |
| 03-04—New Orleans ... | 4 | 40 | 4 | 9 | .444 | 2 | 3 | .667 | 1 | 9 | 10 | 1 | 3 | 1 | 2 | 10 | 2.5 | 0.3 | 2.5 |
| Totals ................... | 22 | 245 | 28 | 61 | .459 | 9 | 17 | .529 | 23 | 47 | 70 | 11 | 10 | 13 | 16 | 65 | 3.2 | 0.5 | 3.0 |

Three-point field goals: 2001-02, 0-for-1. Totals, 0-for-1 (.000).
Personal fouls/disqualifications: 1998-99, 15/1. 1999-00, 2/0. 2001-02, 15/0. 2002-03, 17/0. 2003-04, 8/0. Totals, 57/1.

## TSAKALIDIS, JAKE     C     GRIZZLIES

**PERSONAL:** Born June 10, 1979, in Rustavi, Republic of Georgia. ... 7-2/285. (2.18/129.3).
**TRANSACTIONS/CAREER NOTES:** Played in Greece (1996-2000). ... Selected by Phoenix Suns in first round (25th overall) of 2000 NBA Draft. ... Traded by Suns with F Bo Outlaw to Memphis Grizzlies for G Brevin Knight, F Robert Archibald and C Cezary Trybanski (September 30, 2003).

### GREEK LEAGUE RECORD

| Season Team | G | Min. | FGM | FGA | Pct. | FTM | FTA | Pct. | Reb. | Ast. | Pts. | AVERAGES RPG | APG | PPG |
|---|---|---|---|---|---|---|---|---|---|---|---|---|---|---|
| 96-97—AEK ............... | 1 | 13 | 1 | 2 | .500 | 2 | 2 | 1.000 | 4 | 0 | 4 | 4.0 | 0.0 | 4.0 |
| 97-98—AEK ............... | 18 | 336 | 35 | 63 | .556 | 24 | 43 | .558 | 101 | 4 | 94 | 5.6 | 0.2 | 5.2 |
| 98-99—AEK ............... | 25 | 515 | 63 | 121 | .521 | 35 | 55 | .636 | 149 | 5 | 161 | 6.0 | 0.2 | 6.4 |
| 99-00—AEK ............... | 22 | 563 | 73 | 123 | .593 | 57 | 103 | .553 | 153 | 14 | 203 | 7.0 | 0.6 | 9.2 |
| Totals ..................... | 66 | 1427 | 172 | 309 | .557 | 118 | 203 | .581 | 407 | 23 | 462 | 6.2 | 0.3 | 7.0 |

### NBA REGULAR-SEASON RECORD

| Season Team | G | Min. | FGM | FGA | Pct. | FTM | FTA | Pct. | REBOUNDS Off. | Def. | Tot. | Ast. | St. | Blk. | TO | Pts. | AVERAGES RPG | APG | PPG |
|---|---|---|---|---|---|---|---|---|---|---|---|---|---|---|---|---|---|---|---|
| 00-01—Phoenix ......... | 57 | 947 | 101 | 215 | .470 | 54 | 91 | .593 | 83 | 159 | 242 | 19 | 10 | 55 | 66 | 256 | 4.2 | 0.3 | 4.5 |
| 01-02—Phoenix ......... | 67 | 1582 | 190 | 400 | .475 | 111 | 159 | .698 | 130 | 244 | 374 | 23 | 23 | 69 | 78 | 491 | 5.6 | 0.3 | 7.3 |
| 02-03—Phoenix ......... | 33 | 543 | 61 | 135 | .452 | 39 | 58 | .672 | 45 | 77 | 122 | 13 | 6 | 17 | 26 | 161 | 3.7 | 0.4 | 4.9 |
| 03-04—Memphis ....... | 40 | 533 | 67 | 133 | .504 | 36 | 61 | .590 | 37 | 91 | 128 | 18 | 9 | 22 | 23 | 170 | 3.2 | 0.5 | 4.3 |
| 04-05—Memphis ....... | 31 | 278 | 32 | 64 | .500 | 14 | 18 | .778 | 21 | 35 | 56 | 10 | 3 | 16 | 12 | 78 | 1.8 | 0.3 | 2.5 |
| Totals ................... | 228 | 3883 | 451 | 947 | .476 | 254 | 387 | .656 | 316 | 606 | 922 | 83 | 51 | 179 | 205 | 1156 | 4.0 | 0.4 | 5.1 |

Three-point field goals: 2001-02, 0-for-1. Totals, 0-for-1 (.000).
Personal fouls/disqualifications: 2000-01, 137/1. 2001-02, 193/4. 2002-03, 80/1. 2003-04, 79/1. 2004-05, 42/0. Totals, 531/7.

### NBA PLAYOFF RECORD

| Season Team | G | Min. | FGM | FGA | Pct. | FTM | FTA | Pct. | REBOUNDS Off. | Def. | Tot. | Ast. | St. | Blk. | TO | Pts. | AVERAGES RPG | APG | PPG |
|---|---|---|---|---|---|---|---|---|---|---|---|---|---|---|---|---|---|---|---|
| 00-01—Phoenix ......... | 4 | 75 | 6 | 16 | .375 | 0 | 0 | ... | 10 | 18 | 28 | 0 | 0 | 7 | 1 | 12 | 7.0 | 0.0 | 3.0 |
| 03-04—Memphis ........ | 1 | 3 | 0 | 0 | ... | 2 | 2 | 1.000 | 0 | 0 | 0 | 0 | 0 | 0 | 3 | 2 | 0.0 | 0.0 | 2.0 |
| Totals ................... | 5 | 78 | 6 | 16 | .375 | 2 | 2 | 1.000 | 10 | 18 | 28 | 0 | 0 | 7 | 4 | 14 | 5.6 | 0.0 | 2.8 |

Personal fouls/disqualifications: 2000-01, 11/0. Totals, 11/0.

## TSKITISHVILI, NIKOLOZ     F     TIMBERWOLVES

**PERSONAL:** Born April 14, 1983, in Tbilisi, U.S.S.R. ... 7-0/225. (2.13/102.1).
**HIGH SCHOOL:** 58 Sports School (Tbilisi, U.S.S.R.).
**TRANSACTIONS/CAREER NOTES:** Played in Slovenia (1999-2000 and 2000-01). ... Played in Italy (2001-02). ... Selected by Denver Nuggets in first round (fifth pick overall) of 2002 NBA Draft. ... Traded by Nuggets with F Rodney White to Golden State Warriors for F Eduardo Najera, G Luis Flores and future first-round draft pick (February 24, 2005). ... Signed as free agent by Minnesota Timberwolves (August 9, 2005).

### SLOVENIAN LEAGUE RECORD

| Season Team | G | Min. | FGM | FGA | Pct. | FTM | FTA | Pct. | Reb. | Ast. | Pts. | AVERAGES RPG | APG | PPG |
|---|---|---|---|---|---|---|---|---|---|---|---|---|---|---|
| 99-00—KK Slovan..................... | 31 | 253 | 33 | 68 | .485 | 15 | 29 | .517 | 49 | 5 | 81 | 1.6 | 0.2 | 2.6 |
| 00-01—KK Slovan..................... | 31 | ... | 91 | 180 | .506 | 55 | 80 | .688 | 113 | 6 | 250 | 3.6 | 0.2 | 8.1 |
| Totals ..................................... | 62 | 253 | 124 | 248 | .500 | 70 | 109 | .642 | 162 | 11 | 331 | 2.6 | 0.2 | 5.3 |

Three-point field goals: 1999-00, 0-for-3. 2000-01, 13-for-45 (.289). Totals, 13-for-48 (.271).

### ITALIAN LEAGUE RECORD

| Season Team | G | Min. | FGM | FGA | Pct. | FTM | FTA | Pct. | Reb. | Ast. | Pts. | AVERAGES RPG | APG | PPG |
|---|---|---|---|---|---|---|---|---|---|---|---|---|---|---|
| 01-02—Benetton Treviso ........... | 11 | 140 | 30 | 50 | .600 | 5 | 6 | .833 | 20 | 4 | 73 | 1.8 | 0.4 | 6.6 |

Three-point field goals: 2001-02, 8-for-20 (.400). Totals, 8-for-20 (.400).

### NBA REGULAR-SEASON RECORD

| Season Team | G | Min. | FGM | FGA | Pct. | FTM | FTA | Pct. | REBOUNDS Off. | Def. | Tot. | Ast. | St. | Blk. | TO | Pts. | AVERAGES RPG | APG | PPG |
|---|---|---|---|---|---|---|---|---|---|---|---|---|---|---|---|---|---|---|---|
| 02-03—Denver ........... | 81 | 1320 | 115 | 393 | .293 | 48 | 65 | .738 | 64 | 117 | 181 | 91 | 31 | 29 | 84 | 315 | 2.2 | 1.1 | 3.9 |
| 03-04—Denver ........... | 39 | 307 | 40 | 122 | .328 | 23 | 29 | .793 | 24 | 39 | 63 | 10 | 6 | 8 | 17 | 106 | 1.6 | 0.3 | 2.7 |
| 04-05—Den.-Golden St. | 35 | 220 | 22 | 74 | .297 | 4 | 7 | .571 | 12 | 29 | 41 | 10 | 8 | 11 | 19 | 50 | 1.2 | 0.3 | 1.4 |
| Totals ................... | 155 | 1847 | 177 | 589 | .301 | 75 | 101 | .743 | 100 | 185 | 285 | 111 | 45 | 48 | 120 | 471 | 1.8 | 0.7 | 3.0 |

Three-point field goals: 2002-03, 37-for-152 (.243). 2003-04, 3-for-11 (.273). 2004-05, 2-for-17 (.118). Totals, 42-for-180 (.233).
Personal fouls/disqualifications: 2002-03, 136/1. 2003-04, 50/0. 2004-05, 33/0. Totals, 219/1.

## TURKOGLU, HEDO　　　　　　　　F　　　　　　　　MAGIC

**PERSONAL:** Born March 19, 1979, in Istanbul, Turkey. ... 6-8/220. (2.03/99.8). ... Full name: Hidayet Turkoglu
**TRANSACTIONS/CAREER NOTES:** Played in Turkey (1996-2000). ... Selected by Sacramento Kings in first round (16th pick overall) of 2000 NBA Draft. ... Traded by Kings to San Antonio Spurs in three-team trade in which Kings also traded F Scot Pollard to Indiana Pacers and acquired F/C Brad Miller from Pacers. Spurs also picked up G Ron Mercer from Pacers and traded F Danny Ferry to Pacers (July 24, 2003) ... Signed as free agent by Orlando Magic (July 14, 2004).

### TURKISH LEAGUE RECORD

| | | | | | | | | | | | | AVERAGES | | |
|---|---|---|---|---|---|---|---|---|---|---|---|---|---|---|
| Season Team | G | Min. | FGM | FGA | Pct. | FTM | FTA | Pct. | Reb. | Ast. | Pts. | RPG | APG | PPG |
| 96-97—Efes Pilsen.................... | 11 | ... | 27 | 38 | .711 | 8 | 16 | .500 | 30 | 17 | 83 | 2.7 | 1.5 | 7.5 |
| 97-98—Efes Pilsen.................... | 29 | 386 | 45 | 93 | .484 | 25 | 38 | .658 | 87 | 35 | 121 | 3.0 | 1.2 | 4.2 |
| 98-99—Efes Pilsen.................... | 23 | 575 | 69 | 146 | .473 | 33 | 42 | .786 | 95 | 37 | 192 | 4.1 | 1.6 | 8.3 |
| 99-00—Efes Pilsen.................... | 24 | 812 | 110 | 211 | .521 | 66 | 88 | .750 | 129 | 53 | 328 | 5.4 | 2.2 | 13.7 |
| **Totals** ..................................... | 87 | 1773 | 251 | 488 | .514 | 132 | 184 | .717 | 341 | 142 | 724 | 3.9 | 1.6 | 8.3 |

Three-point field goals: 1996-97, 7-for-17 (.412). 1997-98, 6-for-22 (.273). 1998-99, 21-for-65 (.323). 1999-00, 42-for-81 (.519). Totals, 76-for-185 (.411).

### NBA REGULAR-SEASON RECORD

**HONORS:** NBA All-Rookie second team (2001).

| | | | | | | | | | REBOUNDS | | | | | | | | AVERAGES | | |
|---|---|---|---|---|---|---|---|---|---|---|---|---|---|---|---|---|---|---|---|
| Season Team | G | Min. | FGM | FGA | Pct. | FTM | FTA | Pct. | Off. | Def. | Tot. | Ast. | St. | Blk. | TO | Pts. | RPG | APG | PPG |
| 00-01—Sacramento .... | 74 | 1245 | 138 | 335 | .412 | 87 | 112 | .777 | 49 | 161 | 210 | 69 | 52 | 24 | 55 | 391 | 2.8 | 0.9 | 5.3 |
| 01-02—Sacramento .... | 80 | 1970 | 290 | 687 | .422 | 167 | 230 | .726 | 63 | 300 | 363 | 163 | 57 | 31 | 81 | 810 | 4.5 | 2.0 | 10.1 |
| 02-03—Sacramento .... | 67 | 1175 | 165 | 391 | .422 | 88 | 110 | .800 | 35 | 153 | 188 | 87 | 25 | 12 | 50 | 447 | 2.8 | 1.3 | 6.7 |
| 03-04—San Antonio .... | 80 | 2073 | 262 | 645 | .406 | 114 | 161 | .708 | 52 | 306 | 358 | 154 | 80 | 32 | 94 | 739 | 4.5 | 1.9 | 9.2 |
| 04-05—Orlando.......... | 67 | 1757 | 328 | 782 | .419 | 188 | 225 | .836 | 62 | 171 | 233 | 153 | 41 | 18 | 119 | 937 | 3.5 | 2.3 | 14.0 |
| **Totals** ................... | 368 | 8220 | 1183 | 2840 | .417 | 644 | 838 | .768 | 261 | 1091 | 1352 | 626 | 255 | 117 | 399 | 3324 | 3.7 | 1.7 | 9.0 |

Three-point field goals: 2000-01, 28-for-86 (.326). 2001-02, 63-for-171 (.368). 2002-03, 29-for-78 (.372). 2003-04, 101-for-241 (.419). 2004-05, 93-for-245 (.380). Totals, 314-for-821 (.382).
Personal fouls/disqualifications: 2000-01, 139/1. 2001-02, 184/0. 2002-03, 125/0. 2003-04, 165/0. 2004-05, 140/0. Totals, 753/1.

### NBA PLAYOFF RECORD

| | | | | | | | | | REBOUNDS | | | | | | | | AVERAGES | | |
|---|---|---|---|---|---|---|---|---|---|---|---|---|---|---|---|---|---|---|---|
| Season Team | G | Min. | FGM | FGA | Pct. | FTM | FTA | Pct. | Off. | Def. | Tot. | Ast. | St. | Blk. | TO | Pts. | RPG | APG | PPG |
| 00-01—Sacramento .... | 8 | 141 | 20 | 46 | .435 | 12 | 12 | 1.000 | 7 | 21 | 28 | 11 | 3 | 1 | 6 | 60 | 3.5 | 1.4 | 7.5 |
| 01-02—Sacramento .... | 16 | 443 | 55 | 137 | .401 | 16 | 31 | .516 | 17 | 66 | 83 | 23 | 6 | 9 | 23 | 138 | 5.2 | 1.4 | 8.6 |
| 02-03—Sacramento .... | 10 | 174 | 18 | 50 | .360 | 13 | 18 | .722 | 5 | 24 | 29 | 14 | 12 | 5 | 5 | 53 | 2.9 | 1.4 | 5.3 |
| 03-04—San Antonio .... | 10 | 271 | 26 | 81 | .321 | 11 | 18 | .611 | 5 | 40 | 45 | 15 | 9 | 1 | 16 | 77 | 4.5 | 1.5 | 7.7 |
| **Totals** ................... | 44 | 1029 | 119 | 314 | .379 | 52 | 79 | .658 | 34 | 151 | 185 | 63 | 30 | 16 | 50 | 328 | 4.2 | 1.4 | 7.5 |

Three-point field goals: 2000-01, 8-for-14 (.571). 2001-02, 12-for-34 (.353). 2002-03, 4-for-14 (.286). 2003-04, 14-for-42 (.333). Totals, 38-for-104 (.365).
Personal fouls/disqualifications: 2000-01, 18/0. 2001-02, 49/0. 2002-03, 19/0. 2003-04, 20/0. Totals, 106/0.

## UDRIH, BENO　　　　　　　　G　　　　　　　　SPURS

**PERSONAL:** Born July 5, 1982, in Celje, Slovenia. ... 6-3/203. (1.91/92.1).
**TRANSACTIONS/CAREER NOTES:** Played in Slovenia (1999-2001). ... Played in Adriatic League (2001-03). ... Played in Russia and Italy (2003-04). ... Selected by San Antonio Spurs in first round (28th pick overall) of 2004 NBA Draft.
**MISCELLANEOUS:** Member of NBA championship team (2005).

### ADRIATIC LEAGUE RECORD

| | | | | | | | | | | | | AVERAGES | | |
|---|---|---|---|---|---|---|---|---|---|---|---|---|---|---|---|
| Season Team | G | Min. | FGM | FGA | Pct. | FTM | FTA | Pct. | Reb. | Ast. | Pts. | RPG | APG | PPG |
| 01-02—Olimpija Ljubljana........ | 18 | 431 | 67 | 124 | .540 | 21 | 33 | .636 | 34 | 39 | 172 | 1.9 | 2.2 | 9.6 |
| 02-03—Maccabi Tel-Aviv......... | 21 | 550 | 84 | 158 | .532 | 42 | 49 | .857 | 52 | 69 | 224 | 2.5 | 3.3 | 10.7 |
| **Totals** ..................................... | 39 | 981 | 151 | 282 | .535 | 63 | 82 | .768 | 86 | 108 | 396 | 2.2 | 2.8 | 10.2 |

Three-point field goals: 2001-02, 17-for-36 (.472). 2002-03, 14-for-35 (.400).Totals, 31-for-71 (.437).

### SLOVENIAN LEAGUE RECORD

| | | | | | | | | | | | | AVERAGES | | |
|---|---|---|---|---|---|---|---|---|---|---|---|---|---|---|---|
| Season Team | G | Min. | FGM | FGA | Pct. | FTM | FTA | Pct. | Reb. | Ast. | Pts. | RPG | APG | PPG |
| 98-99—Savinjski..................... | 8 | 17 | 0 | 2 | .000 | 0 | 0 | ... | 0 | 1 | 0 | 0.0 | 0.1 | 0.0 |
| 99-00—Savinjski..................... | 29 | 608 | 111 | 189 | .587 | 64 | 91 | .703 | 60 | 22 | 300 | 2.1 | 0.8 | 10.3 |
| 00-01—Olimpija Ljubljana........ | 21 | 533 | 69 | 117 | .590 | 38 | 51 | .745 | 54 | 56 | 182 | 2.6 | 2.7 | 8.7 |
| **Totals** ..................................... | 58 | 1158 | 180 | 308 | .584 | 102 | 142 | .718 | 114 | 79 | 482 | 2.0 | 1.4 | 8.3 |

Three-point field goals: 1999-00, 14-for-38 (.368). 2000-01, 6-for-19 (.316). Totals, 20-for-57 (.351).

### ISRAELI RECORD

| | | | | | | | | | | | | AVERAGES | | |
|---|---|---|---|---|---|---|---|---|---|---|---|---|---|---|---|
| Season Team | G | Min. | FGM | FGA | Pct. | FTM | FTA | Pct. | Reb. | Ast. | Pts. | RPG | APG | PPG |
| 02-03—Maccabi Tel-Aviv.......... | 25 | 467 | 51 | 110 | .464 | 8 | 13 | .615 | 43 | 67 | 122 | 1.7 | 2.7 | 4.9 |

Three-point field goals: 2002-03, 12-for-37 (.324).

### ITALIAN LEAGUE RECORD

| | | | | | | | | | | | | AVERAGES | | |
|---|---|---|---|---|---|---|---|---|---|---|---|---|---|---|---|
| Season Team | G | Min. | FGM | FGA | Pct. | FTM | FTA | Pct. | Reb. | Ast. | Pts. | RPG | APG | PPG |
| 03-04—Breil Milano ................. | 16 | 413 | 67 | 126 | .532 | 25 | 27 | .926 | 29 | 36 | 173 | 1.8 | 2.3 | 10.8 |

Three-point field goals: 2003-04, 14-for-33 (.424).

## RUSSIAN LEAGUE RECORD

| Season Team | G | Min. | FGM | FGA | Pct. | FTM | FTA | Pct. | Reb. | Ast. | Pts. | AVERAGES RPG | APG | PPG |
|---|---|---|---|---|---|---|---|---|---|---|---|---|---|---|
| 03-04—Avtodor Saratov.......... | 5 | 170 | 37 | 68 | .544 | 21 | 29 | .724 | 17 | 21 | 98 | 3.4 | 4.2 | 19.6 |

Three-point field goals: 2003-04, 3-for-8 (.375). Totals, 3-for-8 (.375).

## NBA REGULAR-SEASON RECORD

| Season Team | G | Min. | FGM | FGA | Pct. | FTM | FTA | Pct. | REBOUNDS Off. | Def. | Tot. | Ast. | St. | Blk. | TO | Pts. | AVERAGES RPG | APG | PPG |
|---|---|---|---|---|---|---|---|---|---|---|---|---|---|---|---|---|---|---|---|
| 04-05—San Antonio .. | 80 | 1149 | 173 | 390 | .444 | 67 | 89 | .753 | 16 | 67 | 83 | 150 | 41 | 10 | 77 | 471 | 1.0 | 1.9 | 5.9 |

Three-point field goals: 2004-05, 58-for-142 (.408). Totals, 58-for-142 (.408).
Personal fouls/disqualifications: 2004-05, 96/0. Totals, 96/0.

## NBA PLAYOFF RECORD

| Season Team | G | Min. | FGM | FGA | Pct. | FTM | FTA | Pct. | REBOUNDS Off. | Def. | Tot. | Ast. | St. | Blk. | TO | Pts. | AVERAGES RPG | APG | PPG |
|---|---|---|---|---|---|---|---|---|---|---|---|---|---|---|---|---|---|---|---|
| 04-05—San Antonio .. | 21 | 241 | 28 | 78 | .359 | 12 | 14 | .857 | 4 | 13 | 17 | 22 | 9 | 1 | 20 | 78 | 0.8 | 1.0 | 3.7 |

Three-point field goals: 2004-05, 10-for-37 (.270). Totals, 10-for-37 (.270).
Personal fouls/disqualifications: 2004-05, 20/0. Totals, 20/0.

# VAN EXEL, NICK          G          SPURS

**PERSONAL:** Born November 27, 1971, in Kenosha, Wis. ... 6-1/190. (1.85/86.2). ... Full name: Nickey Maxwell Van Exel ... Name pronounced van EX-el.
**HIGH SCHOOL:** St. Joseph's (Kenosha, Wis.).
**JUNIOR COLLEGE:** Trinity Valley Community College (Texas).
**COLLEGE:** Cincinnati.
**TRANSACTIONS/CAREER NOTES:** Selected by Los Angeles Lakers in second round (37th pick overall) of 1993 NBA Draft. ... Traded by Lakers to Denver Nuggets for F Tony Battie and draft rights to G Tyronn Lue (June 24, 1998). ... Traded by Nuggets with F/C Raef LaFrentz, G Avery Johnson and G/F Tariq Abdul-Wahad to Dallas Mavericks for F Juwan Howard, G Tim Hardaway, F Donnell Harvey, cash considerations and first-round draft choice (February 21, 2002). ... Traded by Mavericks with G Avery Johnson, F Popeye Jones, F Antoine Rigaudeau and C Evan Eschmeyer to Golden State Warriors for F Antawn Jamison, F Chris Mills, F Danny Fortson and G Jiri Welsch (August 18, 2003). ... Traded by Warriors to Portland Trail Blazers for F Dale Davis and G Dan Dickau (July 20, 2004). ... Waived by Trail Blazers (August 3, 2005). ... Signed as free agent by San Antonio Spurs (August 29, 2005).

## COLLEGIATE RECORD

| Season Team | G | Min. | FGM | FGA | Pct. | FTM | FTA | Pct. | Reb. | Ast. | Pts. | AVERAGES RPG | APG | PPG |
|---|---|---|---|---|---|---|---|---|---|---|---|---|---|---|
| 89-90—Trinity Valley C.C.......... | 31 | ... | 200 | 415 | .482 | 88 | 128 | .688 | 101 | 166 | 542 | 3.3 | 5.4 | 17.5 |
| 90-91—Trinity Valley C.C.......... | 27 | ... | 190 | 441 | .431 | 105 | 147 | .714 | 110 | 185 | 551 | 4.1 | 6.9 | 20.4 |
| 91-92—Cincinnati ................... | 34 | 834 | 144 | 323 | .446 | 68 | 101 | .673 | 87 | 99 | 418 | 2.6 | 2.9 | 12.3 |
| 92-93—Cincinnati ................... | 31 | 1049 | 198 | 513 | .386 | 87 | 120 | .725 | 75 | 138 | 568 | 2.4 | 4.5 | 18.3 |
| Junior College Totals .......... | 58 | ... | 390 | 856 | .456 | 193 | 275 | .702 | 211 | 351 | 1093 | 3.6 | 6.1 | 18.8 |
| 4-Year-College Totals ......... | 65 | 1883 | 342 | 836 | .409 | 155 | 221 | .701 | 162 | 237 | 986 | 2.5 | 3.6 | 15.2 |

Three-point field goals: 1989-90, 71-for-186 (.382). 1990-91, 66-for-186 (.355). 1991-92, 62-for-163 (.380). 1992-93, 85-for-248 (.343). Totals, 284-for-783 (.363).

## NBA REGULAR-SEASON RECORD

**HONORS:** NBA All-Rookie second team (1994).

| Season Team | G | Min. | FGM | FGA | Pct. | FTM | FTA | Pct. | REBOUNDS Off. | Def. | Tot. | Ast. | St. | Blk. | TO | Pts. | AVERAGES RPG | APG | PPG |
|---|---|---|---|---|---|---|---|---|---|---|---|---|---|---|---|---|---|---|---|
| 93-94—L.A. Lakers.... | 81 | 2700 | 413 | 1049 | .394 | 150 | 192 | .781 | 47 | 191 | 238 | 466 | 85 | 8 | 145 | 1099 | 2.9 | 5.8 | 13.6 |
| 94-95—L.A. Lakers.... | 80 | 2944 | 465 | 1107 | .420 | 235 | 300 | .783 | 27 | 196 | 223 | 660 | 97 | 6 | 220 | 1348 | 2.8 | 8.3 | 16.9 |
| 95-96—L.A. Lakers.... | 74 | 2513 | 396 | 950 | .417 | 163 | 204 | .799 | 29 | 152 | 181 | 509 | 70 | 10 | 156 | 1099 | 2.4 | 6.9 | 14.9 |
| 96-97—L.A. Lakers.... | 79 | 2937 | 432 | 1075 | .402 | 165 | 200 | .825 | 44 | 182 | 226 | 672 | 75 | 10 | 212 | 1206 | 2.9 | 8.5 | 15.3 |
| 97-98—L.A. Lakers.... | 64 | 2053 | 311 | 743 | .419 | 136 | 172 | .791 | 31 | 163 | 194 | 442 | 64 | 6 | 104 | 881 | 3.0 | 6.9 | 13.8 |
| 98-99—Denver ......... | 50 | 1802 | 306 | 769 | .398 | 142 | 175 | .811 | 14 | 99 | 113 | 368 | 40 | 3 | 121 | 826 | 2.3 | 7.4 | 16.5 |
| 99-00—Denver ......... | 79 | 2950 | 473 | 1213 | .390 | 196 | 240 | .817 | 34 | 277 | 311 | 714 | 68 | 11 | 221 | 1275 | 3.9 | 9.0 | 16.1 |
| 00-01—Denver ......... | 71 | 2688 | 460 | 1112 | .414 | 204 | 249 | .819 | 44 | 197 | 241 | 600 | 61 | 18 | 165 | 1259 | 3.4 | 8.5 | 17.7 |
| 01-02—Denver-Dallas | 72 | 2496 | 501 | 1226 | .409 | 201 | 251 | .801 | 28 | 226 | 254 | 478 | 44 | 11 | 156 | 1322 | 3.5 | 6.6 | 18.4 |
| 02-03—Dallas........... | 73 | 2026 | 342 | 831 | .412 | 110 | 144 | .764 | 35 | 173 | 208 | 312 | 42 | 4 | 123 | 912 | 2.8 | 4.3 | 12.5 |
| 03-04—Golden State . | 39 | 1255 | 187 | 479 | .390 | 70 | 99 | .707 | 16 | 88 | 104 | 206 | 20 | 2 | 78 | 490 | 2.7 | 5.3 | 12.6 |
| 04-05—Portland ........ | 53 | 1619 | 214 | 561 | .381 | 58 | 74 | .784 | 20 | 141 | 161 | 227 | 44 | 0 | 92 | 586 | 3.0 | 4.3 | 11.1 |
| Totals ................. | 815 | 27983 | 4500 | 11115 | .405 | 1830 | 2300 | .796 | 369 | 2085 | 2454 | 5654 | 710 | 89 | 1793 | 12303 | 3.0 | 6.9 | 15.1 |

Three-point field goals: 1993-94, 123-for-364 (.338). 1994-95, 183-for-511 (.358). 1995-96, 144-for-403 (.357). 1996-97, 177-for-468 (.378). 1997-98, 123-for-316 (.389). 1998-99, 72-for-234 (.308). 1999-00, 133-for-401 (.332). 2000-01, 135-for-358 (.377). 2001-02, 119-for-350 (.340). 2002-03, 118-for-312 (.378). 2003-04, 46-for-150 (.307). 2004-05, 100-for-257 (.389). Totals, 1473-for-4124 (.357).
Personal fouls/disqualifications: 1993-94, 154/1. 1994-95, 157/0. 1995-96, 115/0. 1996-97, 110/0. 1997-98, 120/0. 1998-99, 90/0. 1999-00, 148/0. 2000-01, 109/1. 2001-02, 104/0. 2002-03, 86/1. 2003-04, 57/0. 2004-05, 70/0. Totals, 1320/3.

## NBA PLAYOFF RECORD

| Season Team | G | Min. | FGM | FGA | Pct. | FTM | FTA | Pct. | REBOUNDS Off. | Def. | Tot. | Ast. | St. | Blk. | TO | Pts. | AVERAGES RPG | APG | PPG |
|---|---|---|---|---|---|---|---|---|---|---|---|---|---|---|---|---|---|---|---|
| 94-95—L.A. Lakers.... | 10 | 464 | 67 | 162 | .414 | 45 | 59 | .763 | 9 | 29 | 38 | 73 | 21 | 3 | 22 | 200 | 3.8 | 7.3 | 20.0 |
| 95-96—L.A. Lakers.... | 4 | 137 | 16 | 54 | .296 | 10 | 13 | .769 | 4 | 12 | 16 | 27 | 2 | 0 | 11 | 47 | 4.0 | 6.8 | 11.8 |
| 96-97—L.A. Lakers.... | 9 | 353 | 45 | 119 | .378 | 28 | 34 | .824 | 6 | 25 | 31 | 58 | 10 | 0 | 18 | 130 | 3.4 | 6.4 | 14.4 |
| 97-98—L.A. Lakers.... | 13 | 367 | 50 | 151 | .331 | 29 | 40 | .725 | 9 | 23 | 32 | 54 | 8 | 1 | 22 | 151 | 2.5 | 4.2 | 11.6 |
| 01-02—Dallas........... | 8 | 264 | 37 | 101 | .366 | 8 | 12 | .667 | 7 | 17 | 24 | 31 | 8 | 0 | 12 | 89 | 3.0 | 3.9 | 11.1 |

| Season Team | G | Min. | FGM | FGA | Pct. | FTM | FTA | Pct. | REBOUNDS Off. | Def. | Tot. | Ast. | St. | Blk. | TO | Pts. | AVERAGES RPG | APG | PPG |
|---|---|---|---|---|---|---|---|---|---|---|---|---|---|---|---|---|---|---|---|
| 02-03—Dallas............ | 20 | 672 | 150 | 326 | .460 | 45 | 64 | .703 | 18 | 50 | 68 | 82 | 12 | 0 | 39 | 389 | 3.4 | 4.1 | 19.5 |
| Totals ................. | 64 | 2257 | 365 | 913 | .400 | 165 | 222 | .743 | 53 | 156 | 209 | 325 | 61 | 4 | 124 | 1006 | 3.3 | 5.1 | 15.7 |

Three-point field goals: 1994-95, 21-for-66 (.318). 1995-96, 5-for-16 (.313). 1996-97, 12-for-44 (.273). 1997-98, 22-for-70 (.314). 2001-02, 7-for-34 (.206). 2002-03, 44-for-112 (.393). Totals, 111-for-342 (.325).

Personal fouls/disqualifications: 1994-95, 33/0. 1995-96, 10/0. 1996-97, 19/0. 1997-98, 30/0. 2001-02, 26/0. 2002-03, 47/0. Totals, 165/0.

### NBA ALL-STAR GAME RECORD

| Season Team | Min. | FGM | FGA | Pct. | FTM | FTA | Pct. | REBOUNDS Off. | Def. | Tot. | Ast. | PF | Dq. | St. | Blk. | TO | Pts. |
|---|---|---|---|---|---|---|---|---|---|---|---|---|---|---|---|---|---|
| 1998—L.A. Lakers......... | 20 | 5 | 14 | .357 | 2 | 2 | 1.000 | 1 | 2 | 3 | 2 | 0 | ... | 0 | 0 | 2 | 13 |

Three-point field goals: 1998, 1-for-6 (.167). Totals, 1-for-6 (.167).

## VAN HORN, KEITH — F — MAVERICKS

**PERSONAL:** Born October 23, 1975, in Fullerton, Calif. ... 6-10/240. (2.08/108.9). ... Full name: Keith Adam Van Horn
**HIGH SCHOOL:** Diamond Bar (Calif.).
**COLLEGE:** Utah.
**TRANSACTIONS/CAREER NOTES:** Selected by Philadelphia 76ers in first round (second pick overall) of 1997 NBA Draft. ... Draft rights traded by 76ers with C Michael Cage, G Lucious Harris and F Don MacLean to New Jersey Nets for draft rights to F Tim Thomas, draft rights to G Anthony Parker, G Jim Jackson and C Eric Montross (June 27, 1997). ... Traded by Nets with C Todd MacCulloch to 76ers for C Dikembe Mutombo (August 6, 2002). ... Traded by 76ers to New York Knicks in a three-team deal in which 76ers also traded F Randy Holcomb, a first-round draft pick and cash considerations to Atlanta Hawks and acquired F Glenn Robinson and a 2006 second-round pick from Atlanta Hawks and F/C Marc Jackson from Minnesota Timberwolves. Knicks traded G Latrell Sprewell to Timberwolves and Timberwolves traded G Terrell Brandon to Hawks (July 23, 2003) ... Traded by Knicks to Milwaukee Bucks in a three-team deal in which Knicks also traded C Michael Doleac and 2005 second-round draft choice to Atlanta Hawks. Bucks also traded F Tim Thomas to Knicks and C Joel Przybilla to Hawks (February 15, 2004). ... Traded by Bucks to Dallas Mavericks for F Alan Henderson and C Calvin Booth (February 24, 2005).

### COLLEGIATE RECORD

**NOTES:** THE SPORTING NEWS All-America first team (1997). ... THE SPORTING NEWS All-America second team (1996).

| Season Team | G | Min. | FGM | FGA | Pct. | FTM | FTA | Pct. | Reb. | Ast. | Pts. | AVERAGES RPG | APG | PPG |
|---|---|---|---|---|---|---|---|---|---|---|---|---|---|---|
| 93-94—Utah ..................... | 25 | 740 | 161 | 312 | .516 | 100 | 129 | .775 | 208 | 21 | 457 | 8.3 | 0.8 | 18.3 |
| 94-95—Utah ..................... | 33 | 994 | 246 | 451 | .545 | 143 | 167 | .856 | 280 | 45 | 694 | 8.5 | 1.4 | 21.0 |
| 95-96—Utah ..................... | 32 | 990 | 236 | 439 | .538 | 160 | 188 | .851 | 283 | 31 | 686 | 8.8 | 1.0 | 21.4 |
| 96-97—Utah ..................... | 32 | 1008 | 248 | 504 | .492 | 151 | 167 | .904 | 303 | 45 | 705 | 9.5 | 1.4 | 22.0 |
| Totals ..................... | 122 | 3732 | 891 | 1706 | .522 | 554 | 651 | .851 | 1074 | 142 | 2542 | 8.8 | 1.2 | 20.8 |

Three-point field goals: 1993-94, 35-for-79 (.443). 1994-95, 59-for-153 (.386). 1995-96, 54-for-132 (.409). 1996-97, 58-for-150 (.387). Totals, 206-for-514 (.401).

Personal fouls/disqualifications: 1993-94, 60/2. 1994-95, 69/1. 1995-96, 63/1. Totals, 192/4.

### NBA REGULAR-SEASON RECORD

**HONORS:** NBA All-Rookie first team (1998).

| Season Team | G | Min. | FGM | FGA | Pct. | FTM | FTA | Pct. | REBOUNDS Off. | Def. | Tot. | Ast. | St. | Blk. | TO | Pts. | AVERAGES RPG | APG | PPG |
|---|---|---|---|---|---|---|---|---|---|---|---|---|---|---|---|---|---|---|---|
| 97-98—New Jersey ..... | 62 | 2325 | 446 | 1047 | .426 | 258 | 305 | .846 | 142 | 266 | 408 | 106 | 64 | 25 | 164 | 1219 | 6.6 | 1.7 | 19.7 |
| 98-99—New Jersey ..... | 42 | 1576 | 322 | 752 | .428 | 256 | 298 | .859 | 114 | 244 | 358 | 65 | 43 | 53 | 133 | 916 | 8.5 | 1.5 | 21.8 |
| 99-00—New Jersey ..... | 80 | 2782 | 559 | 1257 | .445 | 333 | 393 | .847 | 200 | 476 | 676 | 158 | 64 | 60 | 245 | 1535 | 8.5 | 2.0 | 19.2 |
| 00-01—New Jersey ..... | 49 | 1733 | 308 | 708 | .435 | 150 | 186 | .806 | 78 | 269 | 347 | 82 | 40 | 20 | 103 | 831 | 7.1 | 1.7 | 17.0 |
| 01-02—New Jersey ..... | 81 | 2465 | 471 | 1089 | .433 | 156 | 195 | .800 | 137 | 472 | 609 | 164 | 63 | 42 | 146 | 1199 | 7.5 | 2.0 | 14.8 |
| 02-03—Philadelphia ... | 74 | 2337 | 459 | 952 | .482 | 193 | 240 | .804 | 159 | 365 | 524 | 93 | 63 | 33 | 150 | 1176 | 7.1 | 1.3 | 15.9 |
| 03-04—N.Y.-Mil. ......... | 72 | 2340 | 410 | 903 | .454 | 249 | 290 | .859 | 149 | 352 | 501 | 120 | 68 | 33 | 169 | 1162 | 7.0 | 1.7 | 16.1 |
| 04-05—Mil.-Dallas ...... | 62 | 1502 | 257 | 564 | .456 | 128 | 157 | .815 | 89 | 205 | 294 | 75 | 36 | 21 | 81 | 696 | 4.7 | 1.2 | 11.2 |
| Totals ................... | 522 | 17060 | 3232 | 7272 | .444 | 1723 | 2064 | .835 | 1068 | 2649 | 3717 | 863 | 441 | 284 | 1191 | 8734 | 7.1 | 1.7 | 16.7 |

Three-point field goals: 1997-98, 69-for-224 (.308). 1998-99, 16-for-53 (.302). 1999-00, 84-for-228 (.368). 2000-01, 65-for-170 (.382). 2001-02, 101-for-293 (.345). 2002-03, 65-for-176 (.369). 2003-04, 93-for-233 (.399). 2004-05, 54-for-142 (.380). Totals, 547-for-1519 (.360).

Personal fouls/disqualifications: 1997-98, 216/0. 1998-99, 134/2. 1999-00, 258/5. 2000-01, 150/4. 2001-02, 221/1. 2002-03, 251/7. 2003-04, 215/6. 2004-05, 170/2. Totals, 1615/27.

### NBA PLAYOFF RECORD

| Season Team | G | Min. | FGM | FGA | Pct. | FTM | FTA | Pct. | REBOUNDS Off. | Def. | Tot. | Ast. | St. | Blk. | TO | Pts. | AVERAGES RPG | APG | PPG |
|---|---|---|---|---|---|---|---|---|---|---|---|---|---|---|---|---|---|---|---|
| 97-98—New Jersey ..... | 3 | 77 | 13 | 29 | .448 | 12 | 15 | .800 | 2 | 7 | 9 | 1 | 0 | 0 | 2 | 38 | 3.0 | 0.3 | 12.7 |
| 01-02—New Jersey ..... | 20 | 643 | 97 | 241 | .402 | 35 | 49 | .714 | 32 | 101 | 133 | 41 | 19 | 9 | 35 | 266 | 6.7 | 2.1 | 13.3 |
| 02-03—Philadelphia .... | 12 | 402 | 42 | 110 | .382 | 27 | 30 | .900 | 24 | 66 | 90 | 9 | 10 | 2 | 26 | 125 | 7.5 | 0.8 | 10.4 |
| 03-04—Milwaukee ...... | 5 | 137 | 16 | 48 | .333 | 4 | 6 | .667 | 5 | 18 | 23 | 7 | 7 | 3 | 10 | 40 | 4.6 | 1.4 | 8.0 |
| 04-05—Dallas.............. | 3 | 33 | 7 | 15 | .467 | 8 | 9 | .889 | 3 | 3 | 6 | 1 | 1 | 0 | 1 | 22 | 2.0 | 0.3 | 7.3 |
| Totals ................... | 43 | 1292 | 175 | 443 | .395 | 86 | 109 | .789 | 66 | 195 | 261 | 59 | 37 | 14 | 74 | 491 | 6.1 | 1.4 | 11.4 |

Three-point field goals: 1997-98, 0-for-2. 2001-02, 37-for-84 (.440). 2002-03, 14-for-32 (.438). 2003-04, 4-for-11 (.364). 2004-05, 0-for-4. Totals, 55-for-133 (.414).

Personal fouls/disqualifications: 1997-98, 7/0. 2001-02, 56/2. 2002-03, 41/1. 2003-04, 15/0. 2004-05, 6/0. Totals, 125/3.

## VAREJAO, ANDERSON — F — CAVALIERS

**PERSONAL:** Born September 28, 1982, in Santa Teresa, Brazil. ... 6-10/230. (2.08/104.3). ... Full name: Anderson Franca Varejao
**TRANSACTIONS/CAREER NOTES:** Played in Brazil (2001-04). ... Selected by Orlando Magic in second round (30th pick overall) of 2004 NBA Draft. ... Draft rights traded by Magic with F Drew Gooden and C Steven Hunter to Cleveland Cavaliers for F/C Tony Battie and two future second-round draft choices (July 23, 2004).

### BRAZILIAN LEAGUE RECORD

| Season Team | G | Min. | FGM | FGA | Pct. | FTM | FTA | Pct. | Reb. | Ast. | Pts. | AVERAGES | | |
|---|---|---|---|---|---|---|---|---|---|---|---|---|---|---|
| | | | | | | | | | | | | RPG | APG | PPG |
| 00-01—Franca ........................ | 37 | 394 | 51 | 96 | .531 | 25 | 51 | .490 | 88 | 11 | 127 | 2.4 | 0.3 | 3.4 |

### SPANISH RECORD

| Season Team | G | Min. | FGM | FGA | Pct. | FTM | FTA | Pct. | Reb. | Ast. | Pts. | AVERAGES | | |
|---|---|---|---|---|---|---|---|---|---|---|---|---|---|---|
| | | | | | | | | | | | | RPG | APG | PPG |
| 01-02—FC Barcelona............... | 2 | 28 | 3 | 8 | .375 | 2 | 2 | 1.000 | 11 | 1 | 8 | 5.5 | 0.5 | 4.0 |
| 02-03—FC Barcelona............... | 4 | 92 | 13 | 21 | .619 | 6 | 13 | .462 | 24 | 1 | 33 | 6.0 | 0.3 | 8.3 |
| 03-04—FC Barcelona............... | 27 | 542 | 79 | 161 | .491 | 37 | 61 | .607 | 119 | 28 | 203 | 4.4 | 1.0 | 7.5 |
| Totals .................................. | 33 | 662 | 95 | 190 | .500 | 45 | 76 | .592 | 154 | 30 | 244 | 4.7 | 0.9 | 7.4 |

Three-point field goals: 2002-03, 1-for-3 (.333). 2003-04, 8-for-29 (.276). Totals, 9-for-32 (.281).

### NBA REGULAR-SEASON RECORD

| Season Team | G | Min. | FGM | FGA | Pct. | FTM | FTA | Pct. | REBOUNDS | | | Ast. | St. | Blk. | TO | Pts. | AVERAGES | | |
|---|---|---|---|---|---|---|---|---|---|---|---|---|---|---|---|---|---|---|---|
| | | | | | | | | | Off. | Def. | Tot. | | | | | | RPG | APG | PPG |
| 04-05—Cleveland ...... | 54 | 863 | 99 | 193 | .513 | 68 | 127 | .535 | 109 | 148 | 257 | 27 | 41 | 38 | 26 | 266 | 4.8 | 0.5 | 4.9 |

Three-point field goals: 2004-05, 0-for-2. Totals, 0-for-2 (.000).
Personal fouls/disqualifications: 2004-05, 122/0. Totals, 122/0.

## VAUGHN, JACQUE  G  NETS

**PERSONAL:** Born February 11, 1975, in Los Angeles. ... 6-1/190. (1.85/86.2).
**HIGH SCHOOL:** John Muir (Pasadena, Calif.).
**COLLEGE:** Kansas.
**TRANSACTIONS/CAREER NOTES:** Selected by Utah Jazz in first round (27th pick overall) of 1997 NBA Draft. ... Signed as free agent by Atlanta Hawks (July 30, 2001). ... Signed as free agent by Orlando Magic (July 17, 2002). ... Signed as free agent by Atlanta Hawks (September 4, 2003). ... Signed as free agent by New Jersey Nets (July 29, 2004).

### COLLEGIATE RECORD

**NOTES:** THE SPORTING NEWS All-America first team (1997). ... THE SPORTING NEWS All-America second team (1996).

| Season Team | G | Min. | FGM | FGA | Pct. | FTM | FTA | Pct. | Reb. | Ast. | Pts. | AVERAGES | | |
|---|---|---|---|---|---|---|---|---|---|---|---|---|---|---|
| | | | | | | | | | | | | RPG | APG | PPG |
| 93-94—Kansas ........................ | 35 | 896 | 91 | 195 | .467 | 63 | 94 | .670 | 89 | 181 | 273 | 2.5 | 5.2 | 7.8 |
| 94-95—Kansas ........................ | 31 | 1046 | 94 | 208 | .452 | 92 | 134 | .687 | 116 | 238 | 300 | 3.7 | 7.7 | 9.7 |
| 95-96—Kansas ........................ | 34 | 1045 | 120 | 249 | .482 | 91 | 131 | .695 | 106 | 223 | 370 | 3.1 | 6.6 | 10.9 |
| 96-97—Kansas ........................ | 26 | 820 | 79 | 185 | .427 | 88 | 113 | .779 | 62 | 162 | 264 | 2.4 | 6.2 | 10.2 |
| Totals .................................. | 126 | 3807 | 384 | 837 | .459 | 334 | 472 | .708 | 373 | 804 | 1207 | 3.0 | 6.4 | 9.6 |

Three-point field goals: 1993-94, 28-for-70 (.400). 1994-95, 20-for-58 (.345). 1995-96, 39-for-92 (.424). 1996-97, 18-for-54 (.333). Totals, 105-for-274 (.383).

### NBA REGULAR-SEASON RECORD

| Season Team | G | Min. | FGM | FGA | Pct. | FTM | FTA | Pct. | REBOUNDS | | | Ast. | St. | Blk. | TO | Pts. | AVERAGES | | |
|---|---|---|---|---|---|---|---|---|---|---|---|---|---|---|---|---|---|---|---|
| | | | | | | | | | Off. | Def. | Tot. | | | | | | RPG | APG | PPG |
| 97-98—Utah............... | 45 | 419 | 44 | 122 | .361 | 48 | 68 | .706 | 4 | 34 | 38 | 84 | 9 | 1 | 56 | 139 | 0.8 | 1.9 | 3.1 |
| 98-99—Utah............... | 19 | 87 | 11 | 30 | .367 | 20 | 24 | .833 | 1 | 10 | 11 | 12 | 5 | 0 | 14 | 44 | 0.6 | 0.6 | 2.3 |
| 99-00—Utah............... | 78 | 884 | 109 | 262 | .416 | 57 | 76 | .750 | 11 | 54 | 65 | 121 | 32 | 0 | 77 | 289 | 0.8 | 1.6 | 3.7 |
| 00-01—Utah............... | 82 | 1620 | 170 | 393 | .433 | 128 | 164 | .780 | 18 | 132 | 150 | 323 | 48 | 3 | 129 | 498 | 1.8 | 3.9 | 6.1 |
| 01-02—Atlanta ........... | 82 | 1856 | 206 | 438 | .470 | 104 | 126 | .825 | 18 | 150 | 168 | 349 | 65 | 2 | 112 | 540 | 2.0 | 4.3 | 6.6 |
| 02-03—Orlando........... | 80 | 1686 | 184 | 411 | .448 | 97 | 125 | .776 | 26 | 92 | 118 | 232 | 64 | 2 | 97 | 473 | 1.5 | 2.9 | 5.9 |
| 03-04—Atlanta ......... | 71 | 1271 | 107 | 277 | .386 | 53 | 68 | .779 | 12 | 104 | 116 | 195 | 44 | 2 | 84 | 270 | 1.6 | 2.7 | 3.8 |
| 04-05—New Jersey ..... | 71 | 1410 | 146 | 325 | .449 | 76 | 91 | .835 | 17 | 90 | 107 | 135 | 41 | 1 | 62 | 373 | 1.5 | 1.9 | 5.3 |
| Totals .................... | 528 | 9233 | 977 | 2258 | .433 | 583 | 742 | .786 | 107 | 666 | 773 | 1451 | 308 | 11 | 631 | 2626 | 1.5 | 2.7 | 5.0 |

Three-point field goals: 1997-98, 3-for-8 (.375). 1998-99, 2-for-8 (.250). 1999-00, 14-for-34 (.412). 2000-01, 30-for-78 (.385). 2001-02, 24-for-54 (.444). 2002-03, 8-for-34 (.235). 2003-04, 3-for-20 (.150). 2004-05, 5-for-15 (.333). Totals, 89-for-251 (.355).
Personal fouls/disqualifications: 1997-98, 63/1. 1998-99, 14/0. 1999-00, 92/0. 2000-01, 145/0. 2001-02, 183/0. 2002-03, 169/1. 2003-04, 126/0. 2004-05, 138/1. Totals, 930/3.

### NBA PLAYOFF RECORD

| Season Team | G | Min. | FGM | FGA | Pct. | FTM | FTA | Pct. | REBOUNDS | | | Ast. | St. | Blk. | TO | Pts. | AVERAGES | | |
|---|---|---|---|---|---|---|---|---|---|---|---|---|---|---|---|---|---|---|---|
| | | | | | | | | | Off. | Def. | Tot. | | | | | | RPG | APG | PPG |
| 97-98—Utah............... | 7 | 24 | 2 | 10 | .200 | 2 | 2 | 1.000 | 0 | 3 | 3 | 4 | 0 | 0 | 4 | 7 | 0.4 | 0.6 | 1.0 |
| 98-99—Utah............... | 2 | 6 | 1 | 2 | .500 | 0 | 0 | ... | 0 | 0 | 0 | 2 | 0 | 0 | 0 | 3 | 0.0 | 1.0 | 1.5 |
| 99-00—Utah............... | 7 | 67 | 10 | 28 | .357 | 7 | 8 | .875 | 4 | 8 | 12 | 11 | 4 | 1 | 9 | 28 | 1.7 | 1.6 | 4.0 |
| 00-01—Utah............... | 5 | 57 | 1 | 10 | .100 | 0 | 0 | ... | 0 | 2 | 2 | 8 | 0 | 1 | 1 | 3 | 0.4 | 1.6 | 0.6 |
| 02-03—Orlando........... | 7 | 131 | 12 | 33 | .364 | 10 | 13 | .769 | 1 | 5 | 6 | 25 | 4 | 1 | 9 | 34 | 0.9 | 3.6 | 4.9 |
| Totals .................... | 28 | 285 | 26 | 83 | .313 | 19 | 23 | .826 | 5 | 18 | 23 | 50 | 8 | 3 | 23 | 75 | 0.8 | 1.8 | 2.7 |

Three-point field goals: 1997-98, 1-for-2 (.500). 1998-99, 1-for-1 (1.000). 1999-00, 1-for-2 (.500). 2000-01, 1-for-2 (.500). 2002-03, 0-for-1. Totals, 4-for-8 (.500).
Personal fouls/disqualifications: 1998-99, 2/0. 1999-00, 5/0. 2000-01, 13/0. 2002-03, 18/0. Totals, 38/0.

V

## VOSKUHL, JAKE — C — BOBCATS

**PERSONAL:** Born November 1, 1977, in Tulsa, Okla. ... 6-11/245. (2.11/111.1). ... Full name: Robert Jake Voskuhl
**HIGH SCHOOL:** Strake Jesuit College Prep (Houston).
**COLLEGE:** Connecticut.
**TRANSACTIONS/CAREER NOTES:** Selected by Chicago Bulls in second round (33rd pick overall) of 2000 NBA Draft. ... Traded by Bulls to Phoenix Suns for C Soumaila Samake and 2003 second-round draft choice (October 29, 2001). ... Traded by Suns to Charlotte Bobcats for conditional 2007 second-round draft pick.

### COLLEGIATE RECORD

**NOTES:** Member of NCAA Division I championship team (1999).

| Season Team | G | Min. | FGM | FGA | Pct. | FTM | FTA | Pct. | Reb. | Ast. | Pts. | RPG | APG | PPG |
|---|---|---|---|---|---|---|---|---|---|---|---|---|---|---|
| 96-97—Connecticut | 33 | 678 | 48 | 99 | .485 | 36 | 57 | .632 | 181 | 20 | 132 | 5.5 | 0.6 | 4.0 |
| 97-98—Connecticut | 37 | 877 | 100 | 177 | .565 | 56 | 83 | .675 | 262 | 27 | 256 | 7.1 | 0.7 | 6.9 |
| 98-99—Connecticut | 34 | 728 | 66 | 129 | .512 | 54 | 87 | .621 | 218 | 38 | 186 | 6.4 | 1.1 | 5.5 |
| 99-00—Connecticut | 34 | 778 | 109 | 191 | .571 | 71 | 104 | .683 | 219 | 39 | 289 | 6.4 | 1.1 | 8.5 |
| Totals | 138 | 3061 | 323 | 596 | .542 | 217 | 331 | .656 | 880 | 124 | 863 | 6.4 | 0.9 | 6.3 |

### NBA REGULAR-SEASON RECORD

| Season Team | G | Min. | FGM | FGA | Pct. | FTM | FTA | Pct. | Off. | Def. | Tot. | Ast. | St. | Blk. | TO | Pts. | RPG | APG | PPG |
|---|---|---|---|---|---|---|---|---|---|---|---|---|---|---|---|---|---|---|---|
| 00-01—Chicago | 16 | 143 | 11 | 25 | .440 | 8 | 14 | .571 | 12 | 22 | 34 | 5 | 5 | 6 | 12 | 30 | 2.1 | 0.3 | 1.9 |
| 01-02—Phoenix | 59 | 900 | 107 | 193 | .554 | 82 | 109 | .752 | 103 | 147 | 250 | 18 | 11 | 23 | 48 | 296 | 4.2 | 0.3 | 5.0 |
| 02-03—Phoenix | 65 | 947 | 92 | 163 | .564 | 64 | 96 | .667 | 97 | 128 | 225 | 36 | 18 | 29 | 48 | 248 | 3.5 | 0.6 | 3.8 |
| 03-04—Phoenix | 66 | 1606 | 152 | 300 | .507 | 134 | 181 | .740 | 120 | 123 | 220 | 343 | 57 | 42 | 25 | 77 | 438 | 5.2 | 0.9 | 6.6 |
| 04-05—Phoenix | 38 | 360 | 27 | 59 | .458 | 26 | 38 | .684 | 30 | 62 | 92 | 17 | 4 | 11 | 20 | 80 | 2.4 | 0.4 | 2.1 |
| Totals | 244 | 3956 | 389 | 740 | .526 | 314 | 438 | .717 | 365 | 579 | 944 | 133 | 80 | 94 | 205 | 1092 | 3.9 | 0.5 | 4.5 |

Personal fouls/disqualifications: 2000-01, 38/0. 2001-02, 139/1. 2002-03, 172/0. 2003-04, 258/8. 2004-05, 60/0. Totals, 667/9.

### NBA PLAYOFF RECORD

| Season Team | G | Min. | FGM | FGA | Pct. | FTM | FTA | Pct. | Off. | Def. | Tot. | Ast. | St. | Blk. | TO | Pts. | RPG | APG | PPG |
|---|---|---|---|---|---|---|---|---|---|---|---|---|---|---|---|---|---|---|---|
| 02-03—Phoenix | 6 | 98 | 12 | 17 | .706 | 12 | 13 | .923 | 9 | 13 | 22 | 2 | 4 | 4 | 6 | 36 | 3.7 | 0.3 | 6.0 |

Personal fouls/disqualifications: 2002-03, 21/0. Totals, 21/0.

## VROMAN, JACKSON — F/C — HORNETS

**PERSONAL:** Born January 6, 1981, in Laguna, Calif. ... 6-10/220. (2.08/99.8).
**HIGH SCHOOL:** Viewmont (Bountiful, Utah).
**JUNIOR COLLEGE:** Snow (Utah).
**COLLEGE:** Iowa State.
**TRANSACTIONS/CAREER NOTES:** Selected by Chicago Bulls in second round (31st pick overall) of 2004 NBA Draft. ... Draft rights traded by Bulls with future first-round draft choice to Phoenix Suns for draft rights to F Luol Deng (June 24, 2004). ... Traded by Suns with G/F Casey Jacobsen and F Maciej Lampe to New Orleans Hornets for G Jim Jackson and a 2005 second-round draft choice (January 21, 2005).

### COLLEGIATE RECORD

| Season Team | G | Min. | FGM | FGA | Pct. | FTM | FTA | Pct. | Reb. | Ast. | Pts. | RPG | APG | PPG |
|---|---|---|---|---|---|---|---|---|---|---|---|---|---|---|
| 00-01—Snow College | 32 | ... | 132 | 243 | .543 | 194 | 290 | .669 | 179 | 58 | 346 | 5.6 | 1.8 | 10.8 |
| 01-02—Snow College | 33 | ... | 295 | 474 | .622 | 194 | 290 | .669 | 316 | 82 | 788 | 9.6 | 2.5 | 23.9 |
| 02-03—Iowa State | 31 | 947 | 155 | 281 | .552 | 79 | 153 | .516 | 291 | 56 | 389 | 9.4 | 1.8 | 12.5 |
| 03-04—Iowa State | 32 | 983 | 186 | 330 | .564 | 72 | 142 | .507 | 307 | 75 | 445 | 9.6 | 2.3 | 13.9 |
| Junior College Totals | 65 | ... | 427 | 717 | .596 | 388 | 580 | .669 | 495 | 140 | 1134 | 7.6 | 2.2 | 17.4 |
| 4-Year-College Totals | 63 | 1930 | 341 | 611 | .558 | 151 | 295 | .512 | 598 | 131 | 834 | 9.5 | 2.1 | 13.2 |

Three-point field goals: 2000-01, 0-for-6. 2001-02, 4-for-16 (.250). 2002-03, 0-for-6. 2003-04, 1-for-7 (.143). Totals, 5-for-35 (.143).

### NBA REGULAR-SEASON RECORD

| Season Team | G | Min. | FGM | FGA | Pct. | FTM | FTA | Pct. | Off. | Def. | Tot. | Ast. | St. | Blk. | TO | Pts. | RPG | APG | PPG |
|---|---|---|---|---|---|---|---|---|---|---|---|---|---|---|---|---|---|---|---|
| 04-05—Phoenix-N.O. | 46 | 705 | 82 | 199 | .412 | 48 | 75 | .640 | 64 | 111 | 175 | 40 | 25 | 19 | 64 | 212 | 3.8 | 0.9 | 4.6 |

Three-point field goals: 2004-05, 0-for-3. Totals, 0-for-3 (.000).
Personal fouls/disqualifications: 2004-05, 105/3. Totals, 105/3.

## VUJACIC, SASHA — G — LAKERS

**PERSONAL:** Born March 8, 1984, in Maribor, Slovenia. ... 6-7/193. (2.01/87.5).
**TRANSACTIONS/CAREER NOTES:** Played in Italy (2001-04). ... Selected by Los Angeles Lakers in first round (27th pick overall) of 2004 NBA Draft.

### ITALIAN LEAGUE RECORD

| Season Team | G | Min. | FGM | FGA | Pct. | FTM | FTA | Pct. | Reb. | Ast. | Pts. | RPG | APG | PPG |
|---|---|---|---|---|---|---|---|---|---|---|---|---|---|---|
| 01-02—Snaidero UD | 24 | 162 | 12 | 39 | .308 | 3 | 4 | .750 | 21 | 8 | 30 | 0.9 | 0.3 | 1.3 |

W

| Season Team | G | Min. | FGM | FGA | Pct. | FTM | FTA | Pct. | Reb. | Ast. | Pts. | RPG | APG | PPG |
|---|---|---|---|---|---|---|---|---|---|---|---|---|---|---|
| 02-03—Snaidero UD | 28 | 748 | 96 | 213 | .451 | 76 | 93 | .817 | 86 | 55 | 311 | 3.1 | 2.0 | 11.1 |
| 03-04—Snaidero UD | 33 | 908 | 137 | 331 | .414 | 143 | 173 | .827 | 123 | 72 | 475 | 3.7 | 2.2 | 14.4 |
| Totals | 85 | 1818 | 245 | 583 | .420 | 222 | 270 | .822 | 230 | 135 | 816 | 2.7 | 1.6 | 9.6 |

Three-point field goals: 2001-02, 3-for-19 (.158). 2002-03, 43-for-123 (.350). 2003-04, 58-for-178 (.326). Totals, 104-for-320 (.325).

### NBA REGULAR-SEASON RECORD

| Season Team | G | Min. | FGM | FGA | Pct. | FTM | FTA | Pct. | Off. | Def. | Tot. | Ast. | St. | Blk. | TO | Pts. | RPG | APG | PPG |
|---|---|---|---|---|---|---|---|---|---|---|---|---|---|---|---|---|---|---|---|
| 04-05—L.A. Lakers | 35 | 403 | 33 | 117 | .282 | 18 | 19 | .947 | 13 | 49 | 62 | 51 | 12 | 2 | 15 | 101 | 1.8 | 1.5 | 2.9 |

Three-point field goals: 2004-05, 17-for-63 (.270). Totals, 17-for-63 (.270).
Personal fouls/disqualifications: 2004-05, 41/1. Totals, 41/1.

# WADE, DWYANE       G       HEAT

**PERSONAL:** Born January 17, 1982, in Chicago, Ill. ... 6-4/210. (1.93/95.3). ... Full name: Dwyane Tyrone Wade
**HIGH SCHOOL:** Richards (Oak Lawn, Ill.).
**COLLEGE:** Marquette.
**TRANSACTIONS/CAREER NOTES:** Selected after junior season by Miami Heat in first round (fifth overall pick) of 2003 NBA Draft.
**MISCELLANEOUS:** Member of bronze-medal-winning U.S. Olympic Team (2004).

### COLLEGIATE RECORD

**NOTES:** The Sporting News All-America first team (2003). ... The Sporting News All-America third team (2002).

| Season Team | G | Min. | FGM | FGA | Pct. | FTM | FTA | Pct. | Reb. | Ast. | Pts. | RPG | APG | PPG |
|---|---|---|---|---|---|---|---|---|---|---|---|---|---|---|
| 00-01—Marquette | | | | | | Did not play—ineligible | | | | | | | | |
| 01-02—Marquette | 32 | 935 | 223 | 458 | .487 | 107 | 155 | .690 | 211 | 110 | 571 | 6.6 | 3.4 | 17.8 |
| 02-03—Marquette | 33 | 1058 | 251 | 501 | .501 | 194 | 249 | .779 | 209 | 145 | 710 | 6.3 | 4.4 | 21.5 |
| Totals | 65 | 1993 | 474 | 959 | .494 | 301 | 404 | .745 | 420 | 255 | 1281 | 6.5 | 3.9 | 19.7 |

Three-point field goals: 2001-02, 18-for-52 (.346). 2002-03, 14-for-44 (.318). Totals, 32-for-96 (.333).

### NBA REGULAR-SEASON RECORD

**HONORS:** All-NBA second team (2005). ... NBA All-Defensive second team (2005). ... NBA All-Rookie first team (2004).

| Season Team | G | Min. | FGM | FGA | Pct. | FTM | FTA | Pct. | Off. | Def. | Tot. | Ast. | St. | Blk. | TO | Pts. | RPG | APG | PPG |
|---|---|---|---|---|---|---|---|---|---|---|---|---|---|---|---|---|---|---|---|
| 03-04—Miami | 61 | 2126 | 371 | 798 | .465 | 233 | 312 | .747 | 85 | 162 | 247 | 275 | 86 | 34 | 196 | 991 | 4.0 | 4.5 | 16.2 |
| 04-05—Miami | 77 | 2974 | 630 | 1318 | .478 | 581 | 762 | .762 | 110 | 287 | 397 | 520 | 121 | 82 | 321 | 1854 | 5.2 | 6.8 | 24.1 |
| Totals | 138 | 5100 | 1001 | 2116 | .473 | 814 | 1074 | .758 | 195 | 449 | 644 | 795 | 207 | 116 | 517 | 2845 | 4.7 | 5.8 | 20.6 |

Three-point field goals: 2003-04, 16-for-53 (.302). 2004-05, 13-for-45 (.289). Totals, 29-for-98 (.296).
Personal fouls/disqualifications: 2003-04, 140/0. 2004-05, 230/4. Totals, 370/4.

### NBA PLAYOFF RECORD

| Season Team | G | Min. | FGM | FGA | Pct. | FTM | FTA | Pct. | Off. | Def. | Tot. | Ast. | St. | Blk. | TO | Pts. | RPG | APG | PPG |
|---|---|---|---|---|---|---|---|---|---|---|---|---|---|---|---|---|---|---|---|
| 03-04—Miami | 13 | 510 | 86 | 189 | .455 | 59 | 75 | .787 | 16 | 36 | 52 | 73 | 17 | 4 | 54 | 234 | 4.0 | 5.6 | 18.0 |
| 04-05—Miami | 14 | 571 | 136 | 281 | .484 | 111 | 139 | .799 | 23 | 57 | 80 | 93 | 22 | 16 | 62 | 384 | 5.7 | 6.6 | 27.4 |
| Totals | 27 | 1081 | 222 | 470 | .472 | 170 | 214 | .794 | 39 | 93 | 132 | 166 | 39 | 20 | 116 | 618 | 4.9 | 6.1 | 22.9 |

Three-point field goals: 2003-04, 3-for-8 (.375). 2004-05, 1-for-10 (.100). Totals, 4-for-18 (.222).
Personal fouls/disqualifications: 2003-04, 45/0. 2004-05, 43/0. Totals, 88/0.

### NBA ALL-STAR GAME RECORD

| Season Team | Min. | FGM | FGA | Pct. | FTM | FTA | Pct. | Off. | Def. | Tot. | Ast. | PF | Dq. | St. | Blk. | TO | Pts. |
|---|---|---|---|---|---|---|---|---|---|---|---|---|---|---|---|---|---|
| 2005—Miami | 23 | 6 | 13 | .462 | 2 | 2 | 1.000 | 2 | 1 | 3 | 1 | 2 | 0 | 2 | 1 | 1 | 14 |

Three-point field goals: 2005, 0-for-1. Totals, 0-for-1 (.000).

**W**

# WAGNER, DAJUAN       G       CAVALIERS

**PERSONAL:** Born February 4, 1983, in Camden, N.J. ... 6-3/200. (1.91/90.7). ... Full name: Dajuan Marquett Wagner ... Son of Milt Wagner, guard with Los Angeles Lakers (1987-88) and Miami Heat (1990-91).
**HIGH SCHOOL:** Camden (N.J.).
**COLLEGE:** Memphis.
**TRANSACTIONS/CAREER NOTES:** Selected freshman season by Cleveland Cavaliers in first round (sixth pick overall) of 2002 NBA Draft.

### COLLEGIATE RECORD

| Season Team | G | Min. | FGM | FGA | Pct. | FTM | FTA | Pct. | Reb. | Ast. | Pts. | RPG | APG | PPG |
|---|---|---|---|---|---|---|---|---|---|---|---|---|---|---|
| 01-02—Memphis | 36 | 1146 | 265 | 647 | .410 | 166 | 230 | .722 | 89 | 128 | 762 | 2.5 | 3.6 | 21.2 |

Three-point field goals: 2001-02, 66-for-208 (.317). Totals, 66-for-208 (.317).

### NBA REGULAR-SEASON RECORD

| Season Team | G | Min. | FGM | FGA | Pct. | FTM | FTA | Pct. | Off. | Def. | Tot. | Ast. | St. | Blk. | TO | Pts. | RPG | APG | PPG |
|---|---|---|---|---|---|---|---|---|---|---|---|---|---|---|---|---|---|---|---|
| 02-03—Cleveland | 47 | 1385 | 223 | 605 | .369 | 128 | 160 | .800 | 20 | 62 | 82 | 130 | 38 | 7 | 85 | 629 | 1.7 | 2.8 | 13.4 |
| 03-04—Cleveland | 44 | 708 | 112 | 306 | .366 | 32 | 47 | .681 | 9 | 49 | 58 | 51 | 26 | 7 | 41 | 287 | 1.3 | 1.2 | 6.5 |
| 04-05—Cleveland | 11 | 102 | 18 | 55 | .327 | 3 | 4 | .750 | 0 | 2 | 2 | 13 | 5 | 0 | 9 | 44 | 0.2 | 1.2 | 4.0 |
| Totals | 102 | 2195 | 353 | 966 | .365 | 163 | 211 | .773 | 29 | 113 | 142 | 194 | 69 | 14 | 135 | 960 | 1.4 | 1.9 | 9.4 |

Three-point field goals: 2002-03, 55-for-174 (.316). 2003-04, 31-for-86 (.360). 2004-05, 5-for-26 (.192). Totals, 91-for-286 (.318).
Personal fouls/disqualifications: 2002-03, 107/2. 2003-04, 89/0. 2004-05, 15/0. Totals, 211/2.

## WALKER, ANTOINE　　　　　　F　　　　　　HEAT

**PERSONAL:** Born August 12, 1976, in Chicago. ... 6-9/245. (2.06/111.1). ... Full name: Antoine Devon Walker
**HIGH SCHOOL:** Mt. Carmel (Chicago).
**COLLEGE:** Kentucky.
**TRANSACTIONS/CAREER NOTES:** Selected after sophomore season by Boston Celtics in first round (sixth pick overall) of 1996 NBA Draft. ... Traded by Celtics with G Tony Delk to Dallas Mavericks for F/C Raef LaFrentz, F Chris Mills, G Jiri Welsch and 2004 first-round draft choice (October 20, 2003). ... Traded by Mavericks with G Tony Delk to Atlanta Hawks for G Jason Terry, F Alan Henderson and a future first-round draft choice (August 4, 2004). ... Traded by Hawks to Boston Celtics for G Gary Payton, F Tom Gugliotta, C Michael Stewart and 2005 draft or future first-round pick (February 24, 2005). ... Traded by Celtics to Miami Heat in five-team trade (August 2, 2005).

### COLLEGIATE RECORD

**NOTES:** Member of NCAA Division I championship team (1996).

| Season Team | G | Min. | FGM | FGA | Pct. | FTM | FTA | Pct. | Reb. | Ast. | Pts. | RPG | APG | PPG |
|---|---|---|---|---|---|---|---|---|---|---|---|---|---|---|
| 94-95—Kentucky | 33 | 479 | 95 | 227 | .419 | 52 | 73 | .712 | 148 | 47 | 259 | 4.5 | 1.4 | 7.8 |
| 95-96—Kentucky | 36 | 971 | 228 | 492 | .463 | 82 | 130 | .631 | 302 | 104 | 547 | 8.4 | 2.9 | 15.2 |
| **Totals** | 69 | 1450 | 323 | 719 | .449 | 134 | 203 | .660 | 450 | 151 | 806 | 6.5 | 2.2 | 11.7 |

Three-point field goals: 1994-95, 17-for-55 (.309). 1995-96, 9-for-48 (.188). Totals, 26-for-103 (.252).

### NBA REGULAR-SEASON RECORD

**RECORDS:** Holds single-game record for most three-point field goals attempted, none made—11 (December 17, 2001, vs. Philadelphia).
**HONORS:** NBA All-Rookie first team (1997).
**NOTES:** Led NBA with 221 three-point field goals made and 603 three-point field goals attempted (2001).

| Season Team | G | Min. | FGM | FGA | Pct. | FTM | FTA | Pct. | REBOUNDS Off. | Def. | Tot. | Ast. | St. | Blk. | TO | Pts. | RPG | APG | PPG |
|---|---|---|---|---|---|---|---|---|---|---|---|---|---|---|---|---|---|---|---|
| 96-97—Boston | 82 | 2970 | 576 | 1354 | .425 | 231 | 366 | .631 | 288 | 453 | 741 | 262 | 105 | 53 | 230 | 1435 | 9.0 | 3.2 | 17.5 |
| 97-98—Boston | 82 | 3268 | 722 | 1705 | .423 | 305 | 473 | .645 | 270 | 566 | 836 | 273 | 142 | 60 | *292 | 1840 | 10.2 | 3.3 | 22.4 |
| 98-99—Boston | 42 | 1549 | 303 | 735 | .412 | 113 | 202 | .559 | 106 | 253 | 359 | 130 | 63 | 28 | 119 | 784 | 8.5 | 3.1 | 18.7 |
| 99-00—Boston | 82 | 3003 | 648 | 1506 | .430 | 311 | 445 | .699 | 199 | 453 | 652 | 305 | 117 | 32 | 259 | 1680 | 8.0 | 3.7 | 20.5 |
| 00-01—Boston | 81 | 3396 | 711 | 1720 | .413 | 249 | 348 | .716 | 151 | 568 | 719 | 445 | 138 | 49 | 301 | 1892 | 8.9 | 5.5 | 23.4 |
| 01-02—Boston | 81 | *3406 | 666 | 1689 | .394 | 240 | 324 | .741 | 150 | 564 | 714 | 407 | 122 | 38 | 251 | 1794 | 8.8 | 5.0 | 22.1 |
| 02-03—Boston | 78 | 3235 | 603 | 1554 | .388 | 176 | 286 | .615 | 99 | 464 | 563 | 373 | 116 | 31 | 260 | 1570 | 7.2 | 4.8 | 20.1 |
| 03-04—Dallas | 82 | 2840 | 483 | 1129 | .428 | 103 | 186 | .554 | 198 | 486 | 684 | 369 | 65 | 65 | 202 | 1151 | 8.3 | 4.5 | 14.0 |
| 04-05—Atlanta-Boston | 77 | 2955 | 581 | 1377 | .422 | 201 | 373 | .539 | 182 | 513 | 695 | 265 | 89 | 58 | 253 | 1473 | 9.0 | 3.4 | 19.1 |
| **Totals** | 687 | 26622 | 5293 | 12769 | .415 | 1929 | 3003 | .642 | 1643 | 4320 | 5963 | 2829 | 957 | 414 | 2167 | 13619 | 8.7 | 4.1 | 19.8 |

Three-point field goals: 1996-97, 52-for-159 (.327). 1997-98, 91-for-292 (.312). 1998-99, 65-for-176 (.369). 1999-00, 73-for-285 (.256). 2000-01, 221-for-603 (.367). 2001-02, 222-for-645 (.344). 2002-03, 188-for-582 (.323). 2003-04, 82-for-305 (.269). 2004-05, 110-for-341 (.323). Totals, 1104-for-3388 (.326).

Personal fouls/disqualifications: 1996-97, 271/1. 1997-98, 262/2. 1998-99, 142/2. 1999-00, 263/4. 2000-01, 251/2. 2001-02, 237/2. 2002-03, 221/4. 2003-04, 212/3. 2004-05, 217/0. Totals, 2076/20.

### NBA PLAYOFF RECORD

**NOTES:** Holds single-game playoff record most three-point field goals made in one quarter—6 (April 28, 2002, at Philadelphia).

| Season Team | G | Min. | FGM | FGA | Pct. | FTM | FTA | Pct. | REBOUNDS Off. | Def. | Tot. | Ast. | St. | Blk. | TO | Pts. | RPG | APG | PPG |
|---|---|---|---|---|---|---|---|---|---|---|---|---|---|---|---|---|---|---|---|
| 01-02—Boston | 16 | 703 | 131 | 319 | .411 | 50 | 64 | .781 | 23 | 115 | 138 | 52 | 24 | 6 | 55 | 354 | 8.6 | 3.3 | 22.1 |
| 02-03—Boston | 10 | 440 | 73 | 176 | .415 | 11 | 22 | .500 | 20 | 67 | 87 | 43 | 17 | 4 | 37 | 173 | 8.7 | 4.3 | 17.3 |
| 03-04—Dallas | 5 | 140 | 22 | 61 | .361 | 4 | 7 | .571 | 23 | 27 | 50 | 12 | 6 | 3 | 9 | 49 | 10.0 | 2.4 | 9.8 |
| 04-05—Boston | 6 | 224 | 43 | 104 | .413 | 7 | 11 | .636 | 16 | 28 | 44 | 14 | 7 | 6 | 18 | 100 | 7.3 | 2.3 | 16.7 |
| **Totals** | 37 | 1507 | 269 | 660 | .408 | 72 | 104 | .692 | 82 | 237 | 319 | 121 | 54 | 19 | 119 | 676 | 8.6 | 3.3 | 18.3 |

Three-point field goals: 2001-02, 42-for-109 (.385). 2002-03, 16-for-45 (.356). 2003-04, 1-for-10 (.100). 2004-05, 7-for-19 (.368). Totals, 66-for-183 (.361).
Personal fouls/disqualifications: 2001-02, 56/2. 2002-03, 44/3. 2003-04, 13/0. 2004-05, 19/0. Totals, 132/5.

### NBA ALL-STAR GAME RECORD

| Season Team | Min. | FGM | FGA | Pct. | FTM | FTA | Pct. | REBOUNDS Off. | Def. | Tot. | Ast. | PF | Dq. | St. | Blk. | TO | Pts. |
|---|---|---|---|---|---|---|---|---|---|---|---|---|---|---|---|---|---|
| 1998—Boston | 15 | 2 | 8 | .250 | 0 | 0 | ... | 1 | 2 | 3 | 3 | 0 | 0 | 1 | 0 | 1 | 4 |
| 2002—Boston | 16 | 3 | 8 | .375 | 0 | 0 | ... | 0 | 2 | 2 | 1 | 1 | 0 | 1 | 0 | 2 | 8 |
| 2003—Boston | 9 | 2 | 4 | .500 | 1 | 2 | .500 | 0 | 1 | 1 | 0 | 0 | 0 | 0 | 0 | 1 | 6 |
| **Totals** | 40 | 7 | 20 | .350 | 1 | 2 | .500 | 1 | 5 | 6 | 4 | 1 | 0 | 2 | 0 | 4 | 18 |

Three-point field goals: 1998, 0-for-3. 2002, 2-for-4 (.500). 2003, 1-for-3 (.333). Totals, 3-for-10 (.300).

## WALKER, SAMAKI　　　　　　F

**PERSONAL:** Born February 25, 1976, in Columbus, Ohio. ... 6-9/260. (2.06/117.9). ... Full name: Samaki Ijuma Walker ... Name pronounced Suh-MAH-kee.
**HIGH SCHOOL:** Whitehall (Columbus, Ohio).
**COLLEGE:** Louisville.
**TRANSACTIONS/CAREER NOTES:** Selected after sophomore season by Dallas Mavericks in first round (ninth pick overall) of 1996 NBA Draft. ... Signed as free agent by San Antonio Spurs (August 26, 1999). ... Waived by Spurs (June 29, 2001). ... Signed as free agent by Los Angeles Lakers (July 20, 2001). ... Signed as free agent by Miami Heat (August 2, 2003) ... Signed as free agent by Washington Wizards (August 4, 2004). ... Released by Wizards (March 18, 2005).
**MISCELLANEOUS:** Member of NBA championship team (2002).

### COLLEGIATE RECORD

| Season Team | G | Min. | FGM | FGA | Pct. | FTM | FTA | Pct. | Reb. | Ast. | Pts. | RPG | APG | PPG |
|---|---|---|---|---|---|---|---|---|---|---|---|---|---|---|
| 94-95—Louisville | 29 | 841 | 153 | 279 | .548 | 88 | 164 | .537 | 210 | 37 | 396 | 7.2 | 1.3 | 13.7 |
| 95-96—Louisville | 21 | 634 | 124 | 207 | .599 | 70 | 114 | .614 | 157 | 23 | 318 | 7.5 | 1.1 | 15.1 |
| **Totals** | 50 | 1475 | 277 | 486 | .570 | 158 | 278 | .568 | 367 | 60 | 714 | 7.3 | 1.2 | 14.3 |

Three-point field goals: 1994-95, 2-for-6 (.333). 1995-96, 0-for-1. Totals, 2-for-7 (.286).

## NBA REGULAR-SEASON RECORD

| Season Team | G | Min. | FGM | FGA | Pct. | FTM | FTA | Pct. | REBOUNDS Off. | Def. | Tot. | Ast. | St. | Blk. | TO | Pts. | AVERAGES RPG | APG | PPG |
|---|---|---|---|---|---|---|---|---|---|---|---|---|---|---|---|---|---|---|---|
| 96-97—Dallas............. | 43 | 602 | 83 | 187 | .444 | 48 | 74 | .649 | 47 | 100 | 147 | 17 | 15 | 22 | 39 | 214 | 3.4 | 0.4 | 5.0 |
| 97-98—Dallas............. | 41 | 1027 | 156 | 321 | .486 | 53 | 97 | .546 | 96 | 206 | 302 | 24 | 30 | 40 | 61 | 365 | 7.4 | 0.6 | 8.9 |
| 98-99—Dallas............. | 39 | 568 | 88 | 190 | .463 | 53 | 98 | .541 | 46 | 97 | 143 | 6 | 9 | 16 | 37 | 229 | 3.7 | 0.2 | 5.9 |
| 99-00—San Antonio.... | 71 | 980 | 137 | 305 | .449 | 86 | 126 | .683 | 77 | 195 | 272 | 38 | 10 | 35 | 64 | 360 | 3.8 | 0.5 | 5.1 |
| 00-01—San Antonio.... | 61 | 963 | 121 | 252 | .480 | 78 | 124 | .629 | 67 | 176 | 243 | 29 | 10 | 41 | 68 | 321 | 4.0 | 0.5 | 5.3 |
| 01-02—L.A. Lakers ..... | 69 | 1655 | 187 | 365 | .512 | 86 | 129 | .667 | 129 | 352 | 481 | 64 | 28 | 88 | 53 | 460 | 7.0 | 0.9 | 6.7 |
| 02-03—L.A. Lakers ..... | 67 | 1243 | 115 | 274 | .420 | 66 | 101 | .653 | 115 | 253 | 368 | 64 | 20 | 55 | 56 | 296 | 5.5 | 1.0 | 4.4 |
| 03-04—Miami ............ | 33 | 418 | 38 | 99 | .384 | 29 | 44 | .659 | 42 | 70 | 112 | 6 | 9 | 11 | 15 | 105 | 3.4 | 0.2 | 3.2 |
| 04-05—Washington ... | 14 | 134 | 11 | 31 | .355 | 2 | 3 | .667 | 8 | 10 | 18 | 4 | 3 | 7 | 8 | 24 | 1.3 | 0.3 | 1.7 |
| Totals ............ | 438 | 7590 | 936 | 2024 | .462 | 501 | 796 | .629 | 627 | 1459 | 2086 | 252 | 134 | 315 | 401 | 2374 | 4.8 | 0.6 | 5.4 |

Three-point field goals: 1996-97, 0-for-1. 1997-98, 0-for-1. 1998-99, 0-for-1. 2000-01, 1-for-3 (.333). 2002-03, 0-for-1. 2003-04, 0-for-2. Totals, 1-for-9 (.111).

Personal fouls/disqualifications: 1996-97, 71/0. 1997-98, 127/2. 1998-99, 87/3. 1999-00, 108/1. 2000-01, 103/0. 2001-02, 170/1. 2002-03, 143/4. 2003-04, 54/0. 2004-05, 25/2. Totals, 888/13.

## NBA PLAYOFF RECORD

| Season Team | G | Min. | FGM | FGA | Pct. | FTM | FTA | Pct. | REBOUNDS Off. | Def. | Tot. | Ast. | St. | Blk. | TO | Pts. | AVERAGES RPG | APG | PPG |
|---|---|---|---|---|---|---|---|---|---|---|---|---|---|---|---|---|---|---|---|
| 99-00—San Antonio.... | 4 | 121 | 14 | 31 | .452 | 8 | 12 | .667 | 13 | 32 | 45 | 2 | 1 | 12 | 8 | 36 | 11.3 | 0.5 | 9.0 |
| 00-01—San Antonio.... | 12 | 76 | 5 | 15 | .333 | 4 | 8 | .500 | 5 | 9 | 14 | 3 | 1 | 1 | 1 | 14 | 1.2 | 0.3 | 1.2 |
| 01-02—L.A. Lakers ..... | 19 | 240 | 24 | 52 | .462 | 13 | 17 | .765 | 32 | 46 | 78 | 4 | 2 | 6 | 12 | 62 | 4.1 | 0.2 | 3.3 |
| 02-03—L.A. Lakers ..... | 9 | 49 | 2 | 5 | .400 | 0 | 0 | ... | 4 | 9 | 13 | 2 | 1 | 2 | 3 | 4 | 1.4 | 0.2 | 0.4 |
| 03-04—Miami ............ | 4 | 11 | 0 | 2 | .000 | 0 | 0 | ... | 0 | 1 | 1 | 0 | 0 | 0 | 0 | 0 | 0.3 | 0.0 | 0.0 |
| Totals .................. | 48 | 497 | 45 | 105 | .429 | 25 | 37 | .676 | 54 | 97 | 151 | 11 | 5 | 21 | 24 | 116 | 3.1 | 0.2 | 2.4 |

Three-point field goals: 2001-02, 1-for-1 (1.000). Totals, 1-for-1 (1.000).
Personal fouls/disqualifications: 1999-00, 13/0. 2000-01, 12/0. 2001-02, 42/0. 2002-03, 11/0. 2003-04, 2/0. Totals, 80/0.

# WALLACE, BEN    F    PISTONS

**PERSONAL:** Born September 10, 1974, in White Hall, Ala. ... 6-9/240. (2.06/108.9).
**HIGH SCHOOL:** Central (Ala.).
**JUNIOR COLLEGE:** Cuyahoga Community College (Ohio).
**COLLEGE:** Virginia Union.
**TRANSACTIONS/CAREER NOTES:** Not drafted by an NBA franchise. ... Signed as free agent by Washington Bullets (October 2, 1996). ... Bullets franchise renamed Washington Wizards for 1997-98 season. ... Traded by Wizards with F/C Terry Davis, G Tim Legler and G Jeff McInnis to Orlando Magic for C Isaac Austin (August 11, 1999). ... Traded by Magic with G Chucky Atkins to Detroit Pistons for F Grant Hill (August 3, 2000).
**MISCELLANEOUS:** Member of NBA championship team (2004).

## COLLEGIATE RECORD

| Season Team | G | Min. | FGM | FGA | Pct. | FTM | FTA | Pct. | Reb. | Ast. | Pts. | AVERAGES RPG | APG | PPG |
|---|---|---|---|---|---|---|---|---|---|---|---|---|---|---|
| 92-93—Cuyahoga ...................... | | | | | | | Statistics unavailable. | | | | | | | |
| 93-94—Cuyahoga ...................... | | | | | | | Statistics unavailable. | | | | | | | |
| 94-95—Virginia Union .............. | 31 | 858 | 180 | 330 | .545 | 85 | 209 | .407 | 295 | 27 | 445 | 9.5 | 0.9 | 14.4 |
| 95-96—Virginia Union .............. | 31 | 902 | 159 | 318 | .500 | 70 | 187 | .374 | 325 | 18 | 388 | 10.5 | 0.6 | 12.5 |
| Totals ...................... | 62 | 1760 | 339 | 648 | .523 | 155 | 396 | .391 | 620 | 45 | 833 | 10.0 | 0.7 | 13.4 |

## NBA REGULAR-SEASON RECORD

**HONORS:** NBA Defensive Player of the Year (2002, 2003, 2005). ... NBA All-Defensive first team (2002, 2003, 2004, 2005). ... All-NBA third team (2002, 2005). ... All-NBA second team (2003, 2004).
**NOTES:** Led NBA with 3.48 blocks per game (2002).

| Season Team | G | Min. | FGM | FGA | Pct. | FTM | FTA | Pct. | REBOUNDS Off. | Def. | Tot. | Ast. | St. | Blk. | TO | Pts. | AVERAGES RPG | APG | PPG |
|---|---|---|---|---|---|---|---|---|---|---|---|---|---|---|---|---|---|---|---|
| 96-97—Washington .... | 34 | 197 | 16 | 46 | .348 | 6 | 20 | .300 | 25 | 33 | 58 | 2 | 8 | 11 | 18 | 38 | 1.7 | 0.1 | 1.1 |
| 97-98—Washington .... | 67 | 1124 | 85 | 164 | .518 | 35 | 98 | .357 | 112 | 212 | 324 | 18 | 61 | 72 | 28 | 205 | 4.8 | 0.3 | 3.1 |
| 98-99—Washington .... | 46 | 1231 | 115 | 199 | .578 | 47 | 132 | .356 | 137 | 247 | 384 | 18 | 50 | 90 | 36 | 277 | 8.3 | 0.4 | 6.0 |
| 99-00—Orlando.......... | 81 | 1959 | 168 | 334 | .503 | 54 | 114 | .474 | 211 | 454 | 665 | 67 | 72 | 130 | 67 | 390 | 8.2 | 0.8 | 4.8 |
| 00-01—Detroit .......... | 80 | 2760 | 215 | 439 | .490 | 80 | 238 | .336 | *303 | *749 | 1052 | 123 | 107 | 186 | 117 | 511 | 13.2 | 1.5 | 6.4 |
| 01-02—Detroit .......... | 80 | 2921 | 255 | 480 | .531 | 99 | 234 | .423 | 318 | 721 | 1039 | 115 | 138 | *278 | 70 | 609 | *13.0 | 1.4 | 7.6 |
| 02-03—Detroit .......... | 73 | 2873 | 210 | 437 | .481 | 85 | 189 | .450 | 293 | 833 | 1126 | 120 | 104 | 230 | 88 | 506 | 15.4 | 1.6 | 6.9 |
| 03-04—Detroit .......... | 81 | 3050 | 315 | 748 | .421 | 142 | 290 | .490 | 324 | 682 | 1006 | 138 | 143 | 246 | 123 | 773 | 12.4 | 1.7 | 9.5 |
| 04-05—Detroit .......... | 74 | 2671 | 295 | 651 | .453 | 130 | 304 | .428 | 292 | 610 | 902 | 123 | 106 | 176 | 82 | 721 | 12.2 | 1.7 | 9.7 |
| Totals .................. | 616 | 18786 | 1674 | 3498 | .479 | 678 | 1619 | .419 | 2015 | 4541 | 6556 | 724 | 789 | 1419 | 629 | 4030 | 10.6 | 1.2 | 6.5 |

Three-point field goals: 2000-01, 1-for-4 (.250). 2001-02, 0-for-3. 2002-03, 1-for-6 (.167). 2003-04, 1-for-8 (.125). 2004-05, 1-for-9 (.111). Totals, 4-for-30 (.133).
Personal fouls/disqualifications: 1996-97, 27/0. 1997-98, 116/1. 1998-99, 111/0. 1999-00, 162/0. 2000-01, 192/0. 2001-02, 178/2. 2002-03, 179/0. 2003-04, 162/0. 2004-05, 159/0. Totals, 1286/3.

## NBA PLAYOFF RECORD

| Season Team | G | Min. | FGM | FGA | Pct. | FTM | FTA | Pct. | REBOUNDS Off. | Def. | Tot. | Ast. | St. | Blk. | TO | Pts. | AVERAGES RPG | APG | PPG |
|---|---|---|---|---|---|---|---|---|---|---|---|---|---|---|---|---|---|---|---|
| 01-02—Detroit ........... | 10 | 408 | 28 | 59 | .475 | 17 | 39 | .436 | 48 | 113 | 161 | 12 | 19 | 26 | 19 | 73 | 16.1 | 1.2 | 7.3 |
| 02-03—Detroit ........... | 17 | 722 | 53 | 109 | .486 | 45 | 101 | .446 | 86 | 191 | 277 | 28 | 42 | 52 | 15 | 151 | 16.3 | 1.6 | 8.9 |
| 03-04—Detroit ........... | 23 | 924 | 93 | 205 | .454 | 50 | 117 | .427 | 95 | 233 | 328 | 44 | 44 | 56 | 37 | 236 | 14.3 | 1.9 | 10.3 |
| 04-05—Detroit ........... | 25 | 979 | 102 | 212 | .481 | 47 | 102 | .461 | 95 | 187 | 282 | 25 | 43 | 59 | 30 | 251 | 11.3 | 1.0 | 10.0 |
| Totals .................. | 75 | 3033 | 276 | 585 | .472 | 159 | 359 | .443 | 324 | 724 | 1048 | 109 | 148 | 193 | 101 | 711 | 14.0 | 1.5 | 9.5 |

W

Three-point field goals: 2002-03, 0-for-1. 2003-04, 0-for-3. 2004-05, 0-for-4. Totals, 0-for-8 (.000).
Personal fouls/disqualifications: 2001-02, 24/0. 2002-03, 50/0. 2003-04, 58/1. 2004-05, 65/0. Totals, 197/1.

### NBA ALL-STAR GAME RECORD

| Season Team | Min. | FGM | FGA | Pct. | FTM | FTA | Pct. | REBOUNDS Off. | Def. | Tot. | Ast. | PF | Dq. | St. | Blk. | TO | Pts. |
|---|---|---|---|---|---|---|---|---|---|---|---|---|---|---|---|---|---|
| 2003—Detroit.................. | 24 | 1 | 2 | .500 | 0 | 2 | .000 | 4 | 2 | 6 | 0 | 1 | 0 | 2 | 2 | 2 | 2 |
| 2004—Detroit.................. | 23 | 2 | 5 | .400 | 0 | 0 | ... | 2 | 5 | 7 | 0 | 0 | 0 | 3 | 1 | 0 | 4 |
| 2005—Detroit.................. | 15 | 3 | 7 | .429 | 0 | 0 | ... | 4 | 3 | 7 | 0 | 2 | 0 | 0 | 0 | 2 | 6 |
| Totals........................... | 62 | 6 | 14 | .429 | 0 | 2 | .000 | 10 | 10 | 20 | 0 | 3 | 0 | 5 | 3 | 4 | 12 |

Three-point field goals: 2004, 0-for-1. Totals, 0-for-1 (.000).

## WALLACE, GERALD          F          BOBCATS

**PERSONAL:** Born July 23, 1982, in Sylacauga, Ala. ... 6-7/215. (2.01/97.5). ... Full name: Gerald Jermaine Wallace
**HIGH SCHOOL:** Childersburg (Ala.).
**COLLEGE:** Alabama.
**TRANSACTIONS/CAREER NOTES:** Selected after freshman season by Sacramento Kings in first round (25th pick overall) of 2001 NBA Draft. ... Selected by Charlotte Bobcats from Kings in NBA Expansion Draft (June 22, 2004).

### COLLEGIATE RECORD

| Season Team | G | Min. | FGM | FGA | Pct. | FTM | FTA | Pct. | Reb. | Ast. | Pts. | AVERAGES RPG | APG | PPG |
|---|---|---|---|---|---|---|---|---|---|---|---|---|---|---|
| 00-01—Alabama ......................... | 36 | 824 | 126 | 288 | .438 | 88 | 155 | .568 | 216 | 55 | 351 | 6.0 | 1.5 | 9.8 |

Three-point field goals: 2000-01, 11-for-63 (.175). Totals, 11-for-63 (.175).
Personal fouls/disqualifications: 2000-01, 87/0. Totals, 87/0.

### NBA REGULAR-SEASON RECORD

| Season Team | G | Min. | FGM | FGA | Pct. | FTM | FTA | Pct. | REBOUNDS Off. | Def. | Tot. | Ast. | St. | Blk. | TO | Pts. | AVERAGES RPG | APG | PPG |
|---|---|---|---|---|---|---|---|---|---|---|---|---|---|---|---|---|---|---|---|
| 01-02—Sacramento .... | 54 | 430 | 75 | 175 | .429 | 23 | 46 | .500 | 49 | 40 | 89 | 27 | 19 | 6 | 22 | 173 | 1.6 | 0.5 | 3.2 |
| 02-03—Sacramento .... | 47 | 571 | 90 | 183 | .492 | 39 | 74 | .527 | 38 | 90 | 128 | 23 | 24 | 15 | 44 | 220 | 2.7 | 0.5 | 4.7 |
| 03-04—Sacramento .... | 37 | 337 | 32 | 89 | .360 | 11 | 24 | .458 | 35 | 39 | 74 | 19 | 14 | 14 | 8 | 75 | 2.0 | 0.5 | 2.0 |
| 04-05—Charlotte......... | 70 | 2147 | 286 | 637 | .449 | 191 | 289 | .661 | 118 | 268 | 386 | 137 | 117 | 91 | 159 | 780 | 5.5 | 2.0 | 11.1 |
| Totals ................... | 208 | 3485 | 483 | 1084 | .446 | 264 | 433 | .610 | 240 | 437 | 677 | 206 | 174 | 126 | 233 | 1248 | 3.3 | 1.0 | 6.0 |

Three-point field goals: 2001-02, 0-for-7. 2002-03, 1-for-4 (.250). 2003-04, 0-for-2. 2004-05, 17-for-62 (.274). Totals, 18-for-75 (.240).
Personal fouls/disqualifications: 2001-02, 46/0. 2002-03, 68/0. 2003-04, 37/0. 2004-05, 182/2. Totals, 333/2.

### NBA PLAYOFF RECORD

| Season Team | G | Min. | FGM | FGA | Pct. | FTM | FTA | Pct. | REBOUNDS Off. | Def. | Tot. | Ast. | St. | Blk. | TO | Pts. | AVERAGES RPG | APG | PPG |
|---|---|---|---|---|---|---|---|---|---|---|---|---|---|---|---|---|---|---|---|
| 01-02—Sacramento .... | 5 | 14 | 0 | 1 | .000 | 4 | 4 | 1.000 | 1 | 0 | 1 | 1 | 0 | 1 | 2 | 4 | 0.2 | 0.2 | 0.8 |
| 02-03—Sacramento .... | 7 | 18 | 2 | 5 | .400 | 2 | 2 | 1.000 | 0 | 5 | 5 | 0 | 0 | 1 | 2 | 6 | 0.7 | 0.0 | 0.9 |
| 03-04—Sacramento .... | 3 | 20 | 3 | 6 | .500 | 1 | 2 | .500 | 0 | 2 | 2 | 1 | 1 | 1 | 3 | 7 | 0.7 | 0.3 | 2.3 |
| Totals ................... | 15 | 52 | 5 | 12 | .417 | 7 | 8 | .875 | 1 | 7 | 8 | 2 | 1 | 3 | 7 | 17 | 0.5 | 0.1 | 1.1 |

Personal fouls/disqualifications: 2001-02, 3/0. 2002-03, 4/0. 2003-04, 4/0. Totals, 11/0.

## W

## WALLACE, RASHEED          F/C          PISTONS

**PERSONAL:** Born September 17, 1974, in Philadelphia. ... 6-11/230. (2.11/104.3). ... Full name: Rasheed Abdul Wallace
**HIGH SCHOOL:** Simon Gratz (Philadelphia).
**COLLEGE:** North Carolina.
**TRANSACTIONS/CAREER NOTES:** Selected after sophomore season by Washington Bullets in first round (fourth pick overall) of 1995 NBA Draft. ... Traded by Bullets with G Mitchell Butler to Portland Trail Blazers for G Rod Strickland and F Harvey Grant (July 15, 1996). ... Traded by Trail Blazers with G Wesley Person to Atlanta Hawks for F Shareef Abdur-Rahim, C Theo Ratliff and G Dan Dickau (February 9, 2004). ... Traded by Hawks to Detroit Pistons in three-team deal in which Pistons also received G Mike James from Boston Celtics for G Chucky Atkins, G Lindsey Hunter and 2004 first-round draft choice. Hawks received F Zeljko Rebraca, G Bob Sura and a future first-round draft choice from Pistons and F Chris Mills from Celtics (February 19, 2004).
**MISCELLANEOUS:** Member of NBA championship team (2004).

### COLLEGIATE RECORD

**NOTES:** THE SPORTING NEWS All-America first team (1995).

| Season Team | G | Min. | FGM | FGA | Pct. | FTM | FTA | Pct. | Reb. | Ast. | Pts. | AVERAGES RPG | APG | PPG |
|---|---|---|---|---|---|---|---|---|---|---|---|---|---|---|
| 93-94—North Carolina............... | 35 | 732 | 139 | 230 | .604 | 55 | 91 | .604 | 232 | 18 | 333 | 6.6 | 0.5 | 9.5 |
| 94-95—North Carolina............... | 34 | 1030 | 238 | 364 | .654 | 89 | 141 | .631 | 279 | 35 | 566 | 8.2 | 1.0 | 16.6 |
| Totals ................................. | 69 | 1762 | 377 | 594 | .635 | 144 | 232 | .621 | 511 | 53 | 899 | 7.4 | 0.8 | 13.0 |

Three-point field goals: 1993-94, 0-for-1. 1994-95, 1-for-3 (.333). Totals, 1-for-4 (.250).

### NBA REGULAR-SEASON RECORD

**HONORS:** NBA All-Rookie second team (1996).

| Season Team | G | Min. | FGM | FGA | Pct. | FTM | FTA | Pct. | REBOUNDS Off. | Def. | Tot. | Ast. | St. | Blk. | TO | Pts. | AVERAGES RPG | APG | PPG |
|---|---|---|---|---|---|---|---|---|---|---|---|---|---|---|---|---|---|---|---|
| 95-96—Washington .... | 65 | 1788 | 275 | 565 | .487 | 78 | 120 | .650 | 93 | 210 | 303 | 85 | 42 | 54 | 103 | 655 | 4.7 | 1.3 | 10.1 |
| 96-97—Portland.......... | 62 | 1892 | 380 | 681 | .558 | 169 | 265 | .638 | 122 | 297 | 419 | 74 | 48 | 59 | 114 | 938 | 6.8 | 1.2 | 15.1 |
| 97-98—Portland.......... | 77 | 2896 | 466 | 875 | .533 | 184 | 278 | .662 | 132 | 346 | 478 | 195 | 75 | 88 | 167 | 1124 | 6.2 | 2.5 | 14.6 |

| Season Team | G | Min. | FGM | FGA | Pct. | FTM | FTA | Pct. | REBOUNDS Off. | Def. | Tot. | Ast. | St. | Blk. | TO | Pts. | RPG | APG | PPG |
|---|---|---|---|---|---|---|---|---|---|---|---|---|---|---|---|---|---|---|---|
| 98-99—Portland | 49 | 1414 | 242 | 476 | .508 | 131 | 179 | .732 | 57 | 184 | 241 | 60 | 48 | 54 | 80 | 628 | 4.9 | 1.2 | 12.8 |
| 99-00—Portland | 81 | 2845 | 542 | 1045 | .519 | 233 | 331 | .704 | 129 | 437 | 566 | 142 | 87 | 107 | 157 | 1325 | 7.0 | 1.8 | 16.4 |
| 00-01—Portland | 77 | 2940 | 590 | 1178 | .501 | 245 | 320 | .766 | 147 | 455 | 602 | 212 | 90 | 135 | 158 | 1477 | 7.8 | 2.8 | 19.2 |
| 01-02—Portland | 79 | 2963 | 603 | 1287 | .469 | 201 | 274 | .734 | 136 | 509 | 645 | 152 | 101 | 101 | 131 | 1521 | 8.2 | 1.9 | 19.3 |
| 02-03—Portland | 74 | 2684 | 515 | 1094 | .471 | 200 | 272 | .735 | 113 | 435 | 548 | 153 | 70 | 77 | 140 | 1340 | 7.4 | 2.1 | 18.1 |
| 03-04—Port.-Atl.-Det. | 68 | 2390 | 425 | 974 | .436 | 156 | 212 | .736 | 102 | 357 | 459 | 156 | 61 | 122 | 119 | 1088 | 6.8 | 2.3 | 16.0 |
| 04-05—Detroit | 79 | 2687 | 467 | 1062 | .440 | 136 | 195 | .697 | 174 | 470 | 644 | 142 | 65 | 115 | 127 | 1145 | 8.2 | 1.8 | 14.5 |
| Totals | 711 | 24499 | 4505 | 9237 | .488 | 1733 | 2446 | .709 | 1205 | 3700 | 4905 | 1371 | 687 | 912 | 1296 | 11241 | 6.9 | 1.9 | 15.8 |

Three-point field goals: 1995-96, 27-for-82 (.329). 1996-97, 9-for-33 (.273). 1997-98, 8-for-39 (.205). 1998-99, 13-for-31 (.419). 1999-00, 8-for-50 (.160). 2000-01, 52-for-162 (.321). 2001-02, 114-for-317 (.360). 2002-03, 110-for-307 (.358). 2003-04, 82-for-248 (.331). 2004-05, 75-for-236 (.318). Totals, 498-for-1505 (.331).

Personal fouls/disqualifications: 1995-96, 206/4. 1996-97, 198/1. 1997-98, 268/6. 1998-99, 175/6. 1999-00, 216/2. 2000-01, 206/2. 2001-02, 212/0. 2002-03, 223/2. 2003-04, 190/1. 2004-05, 236/1. Totals, 2130/25.

## NBA PLAYOFF RECORD

| Season Team | G | Min. | FGM | FGA | Pct. | FTM | FTA | Pct. | REBOUNDS Off. | Def. | Tot. | Ast. | St. | Blk. | TO | Pts. | RPG | APG | PPG |
|---|---|---|---|---|---|---|---|---|---|---|---|---|---|---|---|---|---|---|---|
| 96-97—Portland | 4 | 148 | 33 | 56 | .589 | 11 | 20 | .550 | 8 | 16 | 24 | 6 | 2 | 2 | 6 | 79 | 6.0 | 1.5 | 19.8 |
| 97-98—Portland | 4 | 157 | 23 | 47 | .489 | 8 | 16 | .500 | 7 | 12 | 19 | 11 | 2 | 2 | 5 | 58 | 4.8 | 2.8 | 14.5 |
| 98-99—Portland | 13 | 468 | 75 | 146 | .514 | 42 | 58 | .724 | 17 | 46 | 63 | 20 | 20 | 11 | 16 | 193 | 4.8 | 1.5 | 14.8 |
| 99-00—Portland | 16 | 605 | 110 | 225 | .489 | 58 | 75 | .773 | 31 | 72 | 103 | 28 | 15 | 20 | 23 | 286 | 6.4 | 1.8 | 17.9 |
| 00-01—Portland | 3 | 128 | 19 | 51 | .373 | 8 | 14 | .571 | 5 | 19 | 24 | 7 | 1 | 3 | 4 | 50 | 8.0 | 2.3 | 16.7 |
| 01-02—Portland | 3 | 125 | 28 | 69 | .406 | 13 | 16 | .813 | 10 | 27 | 37 | 5 | 2 | 2 | 2 | 76 | 12.3 | 1.7 | 25.3 |
| 02-03—Portland | 7 | 260 | 44 | 97 | .454 | 20 | 28 | .714 | 10 | 26 | 36 | 18 | 4 | 5 | 6 | 122 | 5.1 | 2.6 | 17.4 |
| 03-04—Detroit | 23 | 804 | 118 | 286 | .413 | 46 | 60 | .767 | 47 | 132 | 179 | 37 | 13 | 45 | 43 | 299 | 7.8 | 1.6 | 13.0 |
| 04-05—Detroit | 25 | 826 | 136 | 310 | .439 | 40 | 54 | .741 | 39 | 134 | 173 | 32 | 26 | 44 | 38 | 341 | 6.9 | 1.3 | 13.6 |
| Totals | 98 | 3521 | 586 | 1287 | .455 | 246 | 341 | .721 | 174 | 484 | 658 | 164 | 85 | 134 | 143 | 1504 | 6.7 | 1.7 | 15.3 |

Three-point field goals: 1996-97, 2-for-5 (.400). 1997-98, 4-for-5 (.800). 1998-99, 1-for-9 (.111). 1999-00, 8-for-13 (.615). 2000-01, 4-for-11 (.364). 2001-02, 7-for-17 (.412). 2002-03, 14-for-35 (.400). 2003-04, 17-for-70 (.243). 2004-05, 29-for-86 (.337). Totals, 86-for-251 (.343).

Personal fouls/disqualifications: 1996-97, 17/1. 1997-98, 16/0. 1998-99, 50/1. 1999-00, 52/0. 2000-01, 9/0. 2001-02, 12/0. 2002-03, 26/1. 2003-04, 78/1. 2004-05, 95/1. Totals, 355/5.

## NBA ALL-STAR GAME RECORD

| Season Team | Min. | FGM | FGA | Pct. | FTM | FTA | Pct. | REBOUNDS Off. | Def. | Tot. | Ast. | PF | Dq. | St. | Blk. | TO | Pts. |
|---|---|---|---|---|---|---|---|---|---|---|---|---|---|---|---|---|---|
| 2000—Portland | 21 | 3 | 6 | .500 | 3 | 4 | .750 | 2 | 2 | 4 | 0 | 0 | 0 | 1 | 1 | 0 | 9 |
| 2001—Portland | 21 | 1 | 7 | .143 | 0 | 0 | ... | 1 | 3 | 4 | 2 | 0 | 0 | 1 | 0 | 2 | 2 |
| Totals | 42 | 4 | 13 | .308 | 3 | 4 | .750 | 3 | 5 | 8 | 2 | 0 | 0 | 2 | 1 | 2 | 11 |

Three-point field goals: 2001, 0-for-1. Totals, 0-for-1 (.000).

# WALTON, LUKE      F      LAKERS

**PERSONAL:** Born March 28, 1980, in San Diego, Calif. ... 6-8/245. (2.03/111.1). ... Full name: Luke Theodore Walton ... Full name: Luke Theodore Walton. ... Son of Bill Walton, center with Portland Trail Blazers (1974-75 through 1978-79), San Diego and Los Angeles Clippers (1979-80 through 1984-85) and Boston Celtics (1985-86 through 1987-88) and member of Naismith Memorial Basketball Hall of Fame.
**HIGH SCHOOL:** University (San Diego, Calif.).
**COLLEGE:** Arizona.
**TRANSACTIONS/CAREER NOTES:** Selected by Los Angeles Lakers in second round (32nd pick overall) of 2003 NBA Draft.

## COLLEGIATE RECORD

**NOTES:** The Sporting News All-America second team (2002).

| Season Team | G | Min. | FGM | FGA | Pct. | FTM | FTA | Pct. | Reb. | Ast. | Pts. | RPG | APG | PPG |
|---|---|---|---|---|---|---|---|---|---|---|---|---|---|---|
| 98-99—Arizona | | | | | | Did not play—redshirted | | | | | | | | |
| 99-00—Arizona | 34 | 868 | 65 | 184 | .353 | 52 | 73 | .712 | 138 | 131 | 193 | 4.1 | 3.9 | 5.7 |
| 00-01—Arizona | 36 | 736 | 74 | 176 | .420 | 41 | 61 | .672 | 140 | 115 | 198 | 3.9 | 3.2 | 5.5 |
| 01-02—Arizona | 31 | 1138 | 174 | 370 | .470 | 122 | 179 | .682 | 227 | 194 | 487 | 7.3 | 6.3 | 15.7 |
| 02-03—Arizona | 28 | 772 | 107 | 255 | .420 | 59 | 87 | .678 | 157 | 142 | 301 | 5.6 | 5.1 | 10.8 |
| Totals | 129 | 3514 | 420 | 985 | .426 | 274 | 400 | .685 | 662 | 582 | 1179 | 5.1 | 4.5 | 9.1 |

Three-point field goals: 1999-00, 11-for-55 (.200). 2000-01, 9-for-41 (.220). 2001-02, 17-for-60 (.283). 2002-03, 28-for-73 (.384). Totals, 65-for-229 (.284).

## NBA REGULAR-SEASON RECORD

| Season Team | G | Min. | FGM | FGA | Pct. | FTM | FTA | Pct. | REBOUNDS Off. | Def. | Tot. | Ast. | St. | Blk. | TO | Pts. | RPG | APG | PPG |
|---|---|---|---|---|---|---|---|---|---|---|---|---|---|---|---|---|---|---|---|
| 03-04—L.A. Lakers | 72 | 730 | 65 | 153 | .425 | 31 | 44 | .705 | 39 | 88 | 127 | 113 | 28 | 8 | 44 | 174 | 1.8 | 1.6 | 2.4 |
| 04-05—L.A. Lakers | 61 | 768 | 74 | 180 | .411 | 34 | 48 | .708 | 55 | 87 | 142 | 93 | 26 | 11 | 58 | 198 | 2.3 | 1.5 | 3.2 |
| Totals | 133 | 1498 | 139 | 333 | .417 | 65 | 92 | .707 | 94 | 175 | 269 | 206 | 54 | 19 | 102 | 372 | 2.0 | 1.5 | 2.8 |

Three-point field goals: 2003-04, 13-for-39 (.333). 2004-05, 16-for-61 (.262). Totals, 29-for-100 (.290).
Personal fouls/disqualifications: 2003-04, 70/1. 2004-05, 70/0. Totals, 140/1.

## NBA PLAYOFF RECORD

| Season Team | G | Min. | FGM | FGA | Pct. | FTM | FTA | Pct. | REBOUNDS Off. | Def. | Tot. | Ast. | St. | Blk. | TO | Pts. | RPG | APG | PPG |
|---|---|---|---|---|---|---|---|---|---|---|---|---|---|---|---|---|---|---|---|
| 03-04—L.A. Lakers | 17 | 134 | 10 | 29 | .345 | 7 | 10 | .700 | 5 | 17 | 22 | 26 | 7 | 2 | 14 | 32 | 1.3 | 1.5 | 1.9 |

Three-point field goals: 2003-04, 5-for-13 (.385). Totals, 5-for-13 (.385).
Personal fouls/disqualifications: 2003-04, 24/1. Totals, 24/1.

**W**

## WANG, ZHI-ZHI         C

**PERSONAL:** Born July 8, 1977, in Beijing, China. ... 7-0/255. (2.13/115.7).
**COLLEGE:** Beijing (China).
**TRANSACTIONS/CAREER NOTES:** Played in China (1996-2001). ... Selected by Dallas Mavericks in second round (36th pick overall) of 1999 NBA Draft. ... Signed as free agent by Los Angeles Clippers (October 1, 2002). ... Waived by Clippers (November 21, 2003). ... Signed as free agent by Miami Heat (December 1, 2003).
**MISCELLANEOUS:** Member of Chinese Olympic team (1996).

### CHINESE LEAGUE RECORD

| Season Team | G | Min. | FGM | FGA | Pct. | FTM | FTA | Pct. | Reb. | Ast. | Pts. | AVERAGES RPG | APG | PPG |
|---|---|---|---|---|---|---|---|---|---|---|---|---|---|---|
| 96-97—Bayi | 26 | ... | 163 | 298 | .547 | 97 | 117 | .829 | 189 | 26 | 429 | 7.3 | 1.0 | 16.5 |
| 97-98—Bayi | 22 | ... | 192 | 335 | .573 | 95 | 115 | .826 | 204 | 25 | 503 | 9.3 | 1.1 | 22.9 |
| 98-99—Bayi | 30 | ... | 262 | 456 | .575 | 112 | 135 | .830 | 184 | 24 | 656 | 6.1 | 0.8 | 21.9 |
| 99-00—Bayi | 30 | ... | 340 | 610 | .557 | 104 | 125 | .832 | 304 | 23 | 809 | 10.1 | 0.8 | 27.0 |
| 00-01—Bayi | 31 | ... | 330 | 539 | .612 | 93 | 123 | .756 | 354 | 51 | 773 | 11.4 | 1.6 | 24.9 |
| **Totals** | 139 | ... | 1287 | 2238 | .575 | 501 | 615 | .815 | 1235 | 149 | 3170 | 8.9 | 1.1 | 22.8 |

Three-point field goals: 1997-98, 16-for-42 (.381). Totals, 16-for-42 (.381).

### NBA REGULAR-SEASON RECORD

| Season Team | G | Min. | FGM | FGA | Pct. | FTM | FTA | Pct. | REBOUNDS Off. | Def. | Tot. | Ast. | St. | Blk. | TO | Pts. | AVERAGES RPG | APG | PPG |
|---|---|---|---|---|---|---|---|---|---|---|---|---|---|---|---|---|---|---|---|
| 00-01—Dallas | 5 | 38 | 8 | 19 | .421 | 8 | 10 | .800 | 1 | 6 | 7 | 0 | 0 | 0 | 1 | 24 | 1.4 | 0.0 | 4.8 |
| 01-02—Dallas | 55 | 600 | 109 | 248 | .440 | 42 | 57 | .737 | 19 | 92 | 111 | 22 | 11 | 18 | 25 | 308 | 2.0 | 0.4 | 5.6 |
| 02-03—L.A. Clippers | 41 | 412 | 62 | 162 | .383 | 42 | 58 | .724 | 26 | 51 | 77 | 10 | 8 | 10 | 31 | 182 | 1.9 | 0.2 | 4.4 |
| 03-04—L.A.C.-Miami | 16 | 114 | 17 | 46 | .370 | 9 | 10 | .900 | 4 | 14 | 18 | 2 | 3 | 5 | 6 | 47 | 1.1 | 0.1 | 2.9 |
| 04-05—Miami | 20 | 92 | 17 | 36 | .472 | 7 | 12 | .583 | 6 | 12 | 18 | 5 | 3 | 2 | 5 | 43 | 0.9 | 0.3 | 2.2 |
| **Totals** | 137 | 1256 | 213 | 511 | .417 | 108 | 147 | .735 | 56 | 175 | 231 | 39 | 25 | 35 | 68 | 604 | 1.7 | 0.3 | 4.4 |

Three-point field goals: 2000-01, 0-for-2. 2001-02, 48-for-116 (.414). 2002-03, 16-for-47 (.340). 2003-04, 4-for-14 (.286). 2004-05, 2-for-3 (.667). Totals, 70-for-182 (.385).
Personal fouls/disqualifications: 2000-01, 8/0. 2001-02, 84/0. 2002-03, 41/0. 2003-04, 13/0. 2004-05, 9/0. Totals, 155/0.

### NBA PLAYOFF RECORD

| Season Team | G | Min. | FGM | FGA | Pct. | FTM | FTA | Pct. | REBOUNDS Off. | Def. | Tot. | Ast. | St. | Blk. | TO | Pts. | AVERAGES RPG | APG | PPG |
|---|---|---|---|---|---|---|---|---|---|---|---|---|---|---|---|---|---|---|---|
| 00-01—Dallas | 5 | 23 | 3 | 8 | .375 | 3 | 3 | 1.000 | 0 | 2 | 2 | 1 | 1 | 1 | 1 | 10 | 0.4 | 0.2 | 2.0 |
| 01-02—Dallas | 8 | 44 | 7 | 16 | .438 | 3 | 6 | .500 | 5 | 3 | 8 | 3 | 0 | 1 | 0 | 20 | 1.0 | 0.4 | 2.5 |
| 03-04—Miami | 3 | 7 | 0 | 0 | ... | 0 | 0 | ... | 0 | 0 | 0 | 1 | 0 | 0 | 1 | 0 | 0.0 | 0.3 | 0.0 |
| **Totals** | 16 | 74 | 10 | 24 | .417 | 6 | 9 | .667 | 5 | 5 | 10 | 5 | 1 | 2 | 2 | 30 | 0.6 | 0.3 | 1.9 |

Three-point field goals: 2000-01, 1-for-2 (.500). 2001-02, 3-for-6 (.500). Totals, 4-for-8 (.500).
Personal fouls/disqualifications: 2000-01, 1/0. 2001-02, 11/0. 2003-04, 1/0. Totals, 13/0.

## WARD, CHARLIE         G

**W**

**PERSONAL:** Born October 12, 1970, in Tallahassee, Fla. ... 6-2/190. (1.88/86.2).
**HIGH SCHOOL:** Thomasville (Ga.) Central.
**JUNIOR COLLEGE:** Tallahassee (Fla.) Community College.
**COLLEGE:** Florida State.
**TRANSACTIONS/CAREER NOTES:** Selected by New York Knicks in first round (26th pick overall) of 1994 NBA Draft. ... Played in United States Basketball League with Jacksonville Hooters (1994). ... Traded by Knicks with G Howard Eisley, F Maciej Lampe, F Antonio McDyess, G Charlie Ward, draft rights to G Milos Vujanic, 2004 first-round draft choice and future first-round draft choice to Phoenix Suns for G Stephon Marbury, F/G Anfernee Hardaway and C Cezary Trybanski (January 5, 2004). ... Waived by Suns (January 6, 2004). ... Signed as free agent by San Antonio Spurs (January 9, 2004). ... Signed as free agent by Houston Rockets (August 9, 2004).
**MISCELLANEOUS:** Heisman Trophy winner (1993). ... Named College Football Player of the Year by THE SPORTING NEWS (1993). ... Named quarterback on THE SPORTING NEWS college All-America first team (1993). ... Named quarterback on THE SPORTING NEWS college All-America second team (1992). ... Selected by Milwaukee Brewers organization in 59th round of free-agent draft (June 3, 1993); did not sign. ... Selected by New York Yankees organization in 18th round of free-agent draft (June 2, 1994); did not sign.

### COLLEGIATE RECORD

| Season Team | G | Min. | FGM | FGA | Pct. | FTM | FTA | Pct. | Reb. | Ast. | Pts. | AVERAGES RPG | APG | PPG |
|---|---|---|---|---|---|---|---|---|---|---|---|---|---|---|
| 88-89—Tallahassee C.C. | | | | | | | Did not play. | | | | | | | |
| 89-90—Florida State | | | | | | | Did not play. | | | | | | | |
| 90-91—Florida State | 30 | 715 | 81 | 178 | .455 | 62 | 87 | .713 | 89 | 103 | 239 | 3.0 | 3.4 | 8.0 |
| 91-92—Florida State | 28 | 841 | 72 | 145 | .497 | 35 | 66 | .530 | 90 | 122 | 201 | 3.2 | 4.4 | 7.2 |
| 92-93—Florida State | 17 | 557 | 49 | 106 | .462 | 18 | 27 | .667 | 45 | 93 | 132 | 2.6 | 5.5 | 7.8 |
| 93-94—Florida State | 16 | 574 | 61 | 167 | .365 | 25 | 40 | .625 | 39 | 78 | 168 | 2.4 | 4.9 | 10.5 |
| **Totals** | 91 | 2687 | 263 | 596 | .441 | 140 | 220 | .636 | 263 | 396 | 740 | 2.9 | 4.4 | 8.1 |

Three-point field goals: 1990-91, 15-for-48 (.313). 1991-92, 22-for-48 (.458). 1992-93, 16-for-50 (.320). 1993-94, 21-for-83 (.253). Totals, 74-for-229 (.323).

### NBA REGULAR-SEASON RECORD

| Season Team | G | Min. | FGM | FGA | Pct. | FTM | FTA | Pct. | REBOUNDS Off. | Def. | Tot. | Ast. | St. | Blk. | TO | Pts. | AVERAGES RPG | APG | PPG |
|---|---|---|---|---|---|---|---|---|---|---|---|---|---|---|---|---|---|---|---|
| 94-95—New York | 10 | 44 | 4 | 19 | .211 | 7 | 10 | .700 | 1 | 5 | 6 | 4 | 2 | 0 | 8 | 16 | 0.6 | 0.4 | 1.6 |
| 95-96—New York | 62 | 787 | 87 | 218 | .399 | 37 | 54 | .685 | 29 | 73 | 102 | 132 | 54 | 6 | 79 | 244 | 1.6 | 2.1 | 3.9 |
| 96-97—New York | 79 | 1763 | 133 | 337 | .395 | 95 | 125 | .760 | 45 | 175 | 220 | 326 | 83 | 15 | 147 | 409 | 2.8 | 4.1 | 5.2 |
| 97-98—New York | 82 | 2317 | 235 | 516 | .455 | 91 | 113 | .805 | 32 | 242 | 274 | 466 | 144 | 37 | 175 | 642 | 3.3 | 5.7 | 7.8 |

| Season Team | G | Min. | FGM | FGA | Pct. | FTM | FTA | Pct. | REBOUNDS Off. | Def. | Tot. | Ast. | St. | Blk. | TO | Pts. | AVERAGES RPG | APG | PPG |
|---|---|---|---|---|---|---|---|---|---|---|---|---|---|---|---|---|---|---|---|
| 98-99—New York | 50 | 1556 | 135 | 334 | .404 | 55 | 78 | .705 | 23 | 149 | 172 | 271 | 103 | 8 | 131 | 378 | 3.4 | 5.4 | 7.6 |
| 99-00—New York | 72 | 1986 | 189 | 447 | .423 | 48 | 58 | .828 | 22 | 206 | 228 | 300 | 95 | 16 | 102 | 528 | 3.2 | 4.2 | 7.3 |
| 00-01—New York | 61 | 1492 | 155 | 373 | .416 | 56 | 70 | .800 | 32 | 127 | 159 | 273 | 70 | 10 | 112 | 433 | 2.6 | 4.5 | 7.1 |
| 01-02—New York | 63 | 1058 | 113 | 303 | .373 | 47 | 58 | .810 | 15 | 112 | 127 | 203 | 68 | 14 | 75 | 326 | 2.0 | 3.2 | 5.2 |
| 02-03—New York | 66 | 1465 | 165 | 414 | .399 | 41 | 53 | .774 | 25 | 152 | 177 | 306 | 78 | 11 | 95 | 472 | 2.7 | 4.6 | 7.2 |
| 04-05—Houston | 14 | 360 | 24 | 77 | .312 | 11 | 13 | .846 | 6 | 33 | 39 | 43 | 15 | 0 | 18 | 75 | 2.8 | 3.1 | 5.4 |
| Totals | 559 | 12828 | 1240 | 3038 | .408 | 488 | 632 | .772 | 230 | 1274 | 1504 | 2324 | 712 | 117 | 942 | 3523 | 2.7 | 4.2 | 6.3 |

Three-point field goals: 1994-95, 1-for-10 (.100). 1995-96, 33-for-99 (.333). 1996-97, 48-for-154 (.312). 1997-98, 81-for-215 (.377). 1998-99, 53-for-149 (.356). 1999-00, 102-for-264 (.386). 2000-01, 67-for-175 (.383). 2001-02, 53-for-164 (.323). 2002-03, 101-for-267 (.378). 2004-05, 16-for-51 (.314). Totals, 555-for-1548 (.359).

Personal fouls/disqualifications: 1994-95, 7/0. 1995-96, 98/0. 1996-97, 188/2. 1997-98, 195/3. 1998-99, 105/0. 1999-00, 176/3. 2000-01, 132/0. 2001-02, 100/0. 2002-03, 146/1. 2004-05, 22/0. Totals, 1169/9.

### NBA PLAYOFF RECORD

| Season Team | G | Min. | FGM | FGA | Pct. | FTM | FTA | Pct. | REBOUNDS Off. | Def. | Tot. | Ast. | St. | Blk. | TO | Pts. | AVERAGES RPG | APG | PPG |
|---|---|---|---|---|---|---|---|---|---|---|---|---|---|---|---|---|---|---|---|
| 95-96—New York | 7 | 92 | 13 | 27 | .481 | 3 | 7 | .429 | 2 | 7 | 9 | 17 | 11 | 0 | 6 | 32 | 1.3 | 2.4 | 4.6 |
| 96-97—New York | 9 | 182 | 8 | 27 | .296 | 3 | 4 | .750 | 3 | 22 | 25 | 39 | 13 | 0 | 15 | 20 | 2.8 | 4.3 | 2.2 |
| 97-98—New York | 10 | 261 | 23 | 55 | .418 | 11 | 16 | .688 | 3 | 25 | 28 | 60 | 20 | 2 | 17 | 66 | 2.8 | 6.0 | 6.6 |
| 98-99—New York | 20 | 494 | 34 | 93 | .366 | 6 | 8 | .750 | 12 | 34 | 46 | 75 | 35 | 3 | 24 | 92 | 2.3 | 3.8 | 4.6 |
| 99-00—New York | 16 | 439 | 57 | 113 | .504 | 15 | 21 | .714 | 11 | 57 | 68 | 65 | 22 | 5 | 20 | 150 | 4.3 | 4.1 | 9.4 |
| 00-01—New York | 5 | 86 | 8 | 27 | .296 | 6 | 6 | 1.000 | 2 | 5 | 7 | 7 | 2 | 0 | 8 | 25 | 1.4 | 1.4 | 5.0 |
| 03-04—San Antonio | 5 | 13 | 4 | 6 | .667 | 0 | 0 | ... | 0 | 0 | 0 | 1 | 2 | 0 | 2 | 11 | 0.0 | 0.2 | 2.2 |
| Totals | 72 | 1567 | 147 | 348 | .422 | 44 | 62 | .710 | 33 | 150 | 183 | 264 | 105 | 10 | 92 | 396 | 2.5 | 3.7 | 5.5 |

Three-point field goals: 1995-96, 3-for-12 (.250). 1996-97, 1-for-9 (.111). 1997-98, 9-for-21 (.429). 1998-99, 18-for-56 (.321). 1999-00, 21-for-53 (.396). 2000-01, 3-for-12 (.250). 2003-04, 3-for-3 (1.000). Totals, 58-for-166 (.349).

Personal fouls/disqualifications: 1995-96, 9/0. 1996-97, 18/1. 1997-98, 24/0. 1998-99, 45/0. 1999-00, 40/1. 2000-01, 8/0. 2003-04, 2/0. Totals, 146/2.

# WATSON, EARL     G

**PERSONAL:** Born June 12, 1979, in Kansas City, Kan. ... 6-1/195. (1.85/88.5). ... Full name: Earl Joseph Watson
**HIGH SCHOOL:** Washington (Kansas City, Kan.).
**COLLEGE:** UCLA.
**TRANSACTIONS/CAREER NOTES:** Selected by Seattle SuperSonics in second round (40th pick overall) of 2001 NBA Draft. ... Signed as free agent by Memphis Grizzlies (July 20, 2002).

### COLLEGIATE RECORD

| Season Team | G | Min. | FGM | FGA | Pct. | FTM | FTA | Pct. | Reb. | Ast. | Pts. | AVERAGES RPG | APG | PPG |
|---|---|---|---|---|---|---|---|---|---|---|---|---|---|---|
| 97-98—UCLA | 33 | 1057 | 65 | 166 | .392 | 40 | 66 | .606 | 122 | 104 | 191 | 3.7 | 3.2 | 5.8 |
| 98-99—UCLA | 31 | 1053 | 144 | 331 | .435 | 90 | 128 | .703 | 116 | 142 | 411 | 3.7 | 4.6 | 13.3 |
| 99-00—UCLA | 33 | 1146 | 137 | 304 | .451 | 61 | 94 | .649 | 129 | 195 | 376 | 3.9 | 5.9 | 11.4 |
| 00-01—UCLA | 32 | 1115 | 172 | 349 | .493 | 89 | 140 | .636 | 117 | 166 | 471 | 3.7 | 5.2 | 14.7 |
| Totals | 129 | 4371 | 518 | 1150 | .450 | 280 | 428 | .654 | 484 | 607 | 1449 | 3.8 | 4.7 | 11.2 |

Three-point field goals: 1997-98, 21-for-65 (.323). 1998-99, 33-for-103 (.320). 1999-00, 41-for-114 (.360). 2000-01, 38-for-108 (.352). Totals, 133-for-390 (.341).

Personal fouls/disqualifications: 1997-98, 84/0. 1998-99, 96/0. 1999-00, 92/0. 2000-01, 100/0. Totals, 372/0.

### NBA REGULAR-SEASON RECORD

| Season Team | G | Min. | FGM | FGA | Pct. | FTM | FTA | Pct. | REBOUNDS Off. | Def. | Tot. | Ast. | St. | Blk. | TO | Pts. | AVERAGES RPG | APG | PPG |
|---|---|---|---|---|---|---|---|---|---|---|---|---|---|---|---|---|---|---|---|
| 01-02—Seattle | 64 | 964 | 96 | 212 | .453 | 23 | 36 | .639 | 31 | 52 | 83 | 125 | 60 | 5 | 51 | 231 | 1.3 | 2.0 | 3.6 |
| 02-03—Memphis | 79 | 1366 | 170 | 391 | .435 | 62 | 86 | .721 | 46 | 118 | 164 | 225 | 89 | 14 | 88 | 433 | 2.1 | 2.8 | 5.5 |
| 03-04—Memphis | 81 | 1669 | 172 | 464 | .371 | 90 | 138 | .652 | 49 | 129 | 178 | 402 | 91 | 19 | 146 | 460 | 2.2 | 5.0 | 5.7 |
| 04-05—Memphis | 80 | 1808 | 236 | 554 | .426 | 91 | 138 | .659 | 35 | 129 | 164 | 359 | 83 | 19 | 167 | 615 | 2.1 | 4.5 | 7.7 |
| Totals | 304 | 5807 | 674 | 1621 | .416 | 266 | 398 | .668 | 161 | 428 | 589 | 1111 | 323 | 57 | 452 | 1739 | 1.9 | 3.7 | 5.7 |

Three-point field goals: 2001-02, 16-for-44 (.364). 2002-03, 31-for-91 (.341). 2003-04, 26-for-106 (.245). 2004-05, 52-for-163 (.319). Totals, 125-for-404 (.309).

Personal fouls/disqualifications: 2001-02, 93/0. 2002-03, 138/0. 2003-04, 175/3. 2004-05, 184/0. Totals, 590/3.

### NBA PLAYOFF RECORD

| Season Team | G | Min. | FGM | FGA | Pct. | FTM | FTA | Pct. | REBOUNDS Off. | Def. | Tot. | Ast. | St. | Blk. | TO | Pts. | AVERAGES RPG | APG | PPG |
|---|---|---|---|---|---|---|---|---|---|---|---|---|---|---|---|---|---|---|---|
| 03-04—Memphis | 4 | 62 | 8 | 15 | .533 | 3 | 3 | 1.000 | 4 | 5 | 9 | 7 | 5 | 0 | 6 | 19 | 2.3 | 1.8 | 4.8 |
| 04-05—Memphis | 4 | 74 | 8 | 24 | .333 | 2 | 2 | 1.000 | 3 | 7 | 10 | 15 | 3 | 1 | 2 | 19 | 2.5 | 3.8 | 4.8 |
| Totals | 8 | 136 | 16 | 39 | .410 | 5 | 5 | 1.000 | 7 | 12 | 19 | 22 | 8 | 1 | 8 | 38 | 2.4 | 2.8 | 4.8 |

Three-point field goals: 2003-04, 0-for-3. 2004-05, 1-for-9 (.111). Totals, 1-for-12 (.083).

Personal fouls/disqualifications: 2003-04, 8/0. 2004-05, 11/0. Totals, 19/0.

**W**

# WEATHERSPOON, CLARENCE     F

**PERSONAL:** Born September 8, 1970, in Crawford, Miss. ... 6-7/265. (2.01/120.2).
**HIGH SCHOOL:** Motley (Columbus, Miss.).
**COLLEGE:** Southern Mississippi.
**TRANSACTIONS/CAREER NOTES:** Selected by Philadelphia 76ers in first round (ninth pick overall) of 1992 NBA Draft. ... Traded by 76ers with C/F Michael Cage to Boston Celtics for C/F Dino Radja (June 20, 1997); trade voided because Radja failed physical (June 24, 1997). ... Traded by 76ers with G Jim Jackson to Golden State Warriors for F Joe Smith and G Brian Shaw (February 17, 1998). ... Signed as free agent by Miami Heat (January 24, 1999). ... Traded by Heat to Cleveland Cavaliers as part of three-way deal in which Cavaliers sent F Shawn Kemp to Portland Trail Blazers, Trail Blazers sent F Brian Grant to Heat, Heat sent F/C Chris Gatling, future first-

round draft choice and cash Cavaliers and Trail Blazers sent G Gary Grant to Cavaliers (August 30, 2000). ... Signed as free agent by New York Knicks (July 20, 2001). ... Traded by Knicks to Houston Rockets for F/C John Amaechi and G Moochie Norris (December 30, 2003). ... Waived by Rockets (August 15, 2005).

### COLLEGIATE RECORD

| Season Team | G | Min. | FGM | FGA | Pct. | FTM | FTA | Pct. | Reb. | Ast. | Pts. | RPG | APG | PPG |
|---|---|---|---|---|---|---|---|---|---|---|---|---|---|---|
| 88-89—Southern Mississippi...... | 27 | 915 | 152 | 279 | .545 | 92 | 156 | .590 | 289 | 30 | 397 | 10.7 | 1.1 | 14.7 |
| 89-90—Southern Mississippi...... | 32 | 1166 | 205 | 339 | .605 | 159 | 230 | .691 | 371 | 28 | 569 | 11.6 | 0.9 | 17.8 |
| 90-91—Southern Mississippi...... | 29 | 1019 | 195 | 331 | .589 | 120 | 161 | .745 | 355 | 66 | 517 | 12.2 | 2.3 | 17.8 |
| 91-92—Southern Mississippi...... | 29 | 1057 | 246 | 437 | .563 | 131 | 194 | .675 | 305 | 47 | 647 | 10.5 | 1.6 | 22.3 |
| Totals .................................. | 117 | 4157 | 798 | 1386 | .576 | 502 | 741 | .677 | 1320 | 171 | 2130 | 11.3 | 1.5 | 18.2 |

Three-point field goals: 1988-89, 1-for-3 (.333). 1989-90, 0-for-2. 1990-91, 7-for-14 (.500). 1991-92, 24-for-53 (.453). Totals, 32-for-72 (.444).

**HONORS:** NBA All-Rookie second team (1993).

### NBA REGULAR-SEASON RECORD

| Season Team | G | Min. | FGM | FGA | Pct. | FTM | FTA | Pct. | Off. | Def. | Tot. | Ast. | St. | Blk. | TO | Pts. | RPG | APG | PPG |
|---|---|---|---|---|---|---|---|---|---|---|---|---|---|---|---|---|---|---|---|
| 92-93—Philadelphia .... | 82 | 2654 | 494 | 1053 | .469 | 291 | 408 | .713 | 179 | 410 | 589 | 147 | 85 | 67 | 176 | 1280 | 7.2 | 1.8 | 15.6 |
| 93-94—Philadelphia .... | 82 | 3147 | 602 | 1246 | .483 | 298 | 430 | .693 | 254 | 578 | 832 | 192 | 100 | 116 | 195 | 1506 | 10.1 | 2.3 | 18.4 |
| 94-95—Philadelphia .... | 76 | 2991 | 543 | 1238 | .439 | 283 | 377 | .751 | 144 | 382 | 526 | 215 | 115 | 67 | 191 | 1373 | 6.9 | 2.8 | 18.1 |
| 95-96—Philadelphia .... | 78 | 3096 | 491 | 1015 | .484 | 318 | 426 | .746 | 237 | 516 | 753 | 158 | 112 | 108 | 179 | 1300 | 9.7 | 2.0 | 16.7 |
| 96-97—Philadelphia .... | 82 | 2949 | 398 | 811 | .491 | 206 | 279 | .738 | 219 | 460 | 679 | 140 | 74 | 86 | 137 | 1003 | 8.3 | 1.7 | 12.2 |
| 97-98—Phila.-G.S. ...... | 79 | 2325 | 268 | 608 | .441 | 200 | 277 | .722 | 198 | 396 | 594 | 89 | 85 | 74 | 119 | 736 | 7.5 | 1.1 | 9.3 |
| 98-99—Miami ............ | 49 | 1040 | 141 | 264 | .534 | 115 | 143 | .804 | 72 | 171 | 243 | 34 | 28 | 17 | 61 | 397 | 5.0 | 0.7 | 8.1 |
| 99-00—Miami ............ | 78 | 1615 | 215 | 419 | .513 | 135 | 183 | .738 | 128 | 321 | 449 | 93 | 51 | 49 | 100 | 565 | 5.8 | 1.2 | 7.2 |
| 00-01—Cleveland ........ | 82 | 2774 | 347 | 692 | .501 | 230 | 291 | .790 | 223 | 573 | 796 | 103 | 85 | 105 | 112 | 924 | 9.7 | 1.3 | 11.3 |
| 01-02—New York ....... | 56 | 1728 | 189 | 452 | .418 | 116 | 146 | .795 | 149 | 311 | 460 | 60 | 37 | 48 | 47 | 494 | 8.2 | 1.1 | 8.8 |
| 02-03—New York ....... | 79 | 2024 | 186 | 414 | .449 | 149 | 194 | .768 | 214 | 385 | 599 | 68 | 69 | 36 | 63 | 521 | 7.6 | 0.9 | 6.6 |
| 03-04—N.Y.-Houston ... | 52 | 868 | 104 | 211 | .493 | 53 | 72 | .736 | 74 | 130 | 204 | 30 | 30 | 15 | 35 | 261 | 3.9 | 0.6 | 5.0 |
| 04-05—Houston ......... | 40 | 525 | 47 | 114 | .412 | 29 | 35 | .829 | 35 | 87 | 122 | 17 | 9 | 6 | 15 | 123 | 3.1 | 0.4 | 3.1 |
| Totals .................. | 915 | 27736 | 4025 | 8537 | .471 | 2423 | 3261 | .743 | 2126 | 4720 | 6846 | 1346 | 880 | 794 | 1430 | 10483 | 7.5 | 1.5 | 11.5 |

Three-point field goals: 1992-93, 1-for-4 (.250). 1993-94, 4-for-17 (.235). 1994-95, 4-for-21 (.190). 1995-96, 0-for-2. 1996-97, 1-for-6 (.167). 2003-04, 0-for-1. Totals, 10-for-51 (.196).

Personal fouls/disqualifications: 1992-93, 188/1. 1993-94, 152/0. 1994-95, 195/1. 1995-96, 214/3. 1996-97, 187/0. 1997-98, 194/2. 1998-99, 107/0. 1999-00, 165/1. 2000-01, 171/0. 2001-02, 132/0. 2002-03, 174/0. 2003-04, 75/0. 2004-05, 74/1. Totals, 2028/9.

### NBA PLAYOFF RECORD

| Season Team | G | Min. | FGM | FGA | Pct. | FTM | FTA | Pct. | Off. | Def. | Tot. | Ast. | St. | Blk. | TO | Pts. | RPG | APG | PPG |
|---|---|---|---|---|---|---|---|---|---|---|---|---|---|---|---|---|---|---|---|
| 98-99—Miami ............ | 5 | 112 | 9 | 26 | .346 | 11 | 17 | .647 | 4 | 17 | 21 | 2 | 7 | 1 | 3 | 29 | 4.2 | 0.4 | 5.8 |
| 99-00—Miami ........... | 10 | 170 | 25 | 60 | .417 | 14 | 24 | .583 | 18 | 23 | 41 | 1 | 4 | 3 | 8 | 64 | 4.1 | 0.1 | 6.4 |
| 03-04—Houston .......... | 2 | 22 | 2 | 5 | .400 | 3 | 6 | .500 | 2 | 2 | 4 | 0 | 0 | 0 | 0 | 7 | 2.0 | 0.0 | 3.5 |
| 04-05—Houston ......... | 1 | 1 | 0 | 0 | ... | 0 | 0 | ... | 0 | 0 | 0 | 0 | 0 | 0 | 0 | 0 | 0.0 | 0.0 | 0.0 |
| Totals .................. | 18 | 305 | 36 | 91 | .396 | 28 | 47 | .596 | 24 | 42 | 66 | 3 | 11 | 4 | 11 | 100 | 3.7 | 0.2 | 5.6 |

Personal fouls/disqualifications: 1998-99, 8/0. 1999-00, 23/0. 2003-04, 3/0. 2004-05, 1/0. Totals, 35/0.

---

## WEBBER, CHRIS      F      76ERS

**W**

**PERSONAL:** Born March 1, 1973, in Detroit. ... 6-10/245. (2.08/111.1). ... Full name: Mayce Edward Christopher Webber.
**HIGH SCHOOL:** Detroit Country Day (Beverly Hills, Mich.).
**COLLEGE:** Michigan.
**TRANSACTIONS/CAREER NOTES:** Selected after sophomore season by Orlando Magic in first round (first pick overall) of 1993 NBA Draft. ... Draft rights traded by Magic to Golden State Warriors for draft rights to G Anfernee Hardaway and 1996, 1998 and 2000 first-round draft choices (June 30, 1993). ... Traded by Warriors to Washington Bullets for F Tom Gugliotta and 1996, 1998 and 2000 first-round draft choices (November 17, 1994). ... Bullets franchise renamed Wizards for 1997-98 season. ... Traded by Wizards to Sacramento Kings for G Mitch Richmond and F Otis Thorpe (May 14, 1998). ... Traded by Kings to Philadelphia 76ers with Fs Michael Bradley and Matt Barnes for Fs Kenny Thomas and Corliss Williamson and C Brian Skinner (February 23, 2005).

### COLLEGIATE RECORD

**NOTES:** THE SPORTING NEWS All-America first team (1993).

| Season Team | G | Min. | FGM | FGA | Pct. | FTM | FTA | Pct. | Reb. | Ast. | Pts. | RPG | APG | PPG |
|---|---|---|---|---|---|---|---|---|---|---|---|---|---|---|
| 91-92—Michigan ...................... | 34 | 1088 | 229 | 412 | .556 | 56 | 113 | .496 | 340 | 76 | 528 | 10.0 | 2.2 | 15.5 |
| 92-93—Michigan ...................... | 36 | 1143 | 281 | 454 | .619 | 101 | 183 | .552 | 362 | 90 | 690 | 10.1 | 2.5 | 19.2 |
| Totals .................................. | 70 | 2231 | 510 | 866 | .589 | 157 | 296 | .530 | 702 | 166 | 1218 | 10.0 | 2.4 | 17.4 |

Three-point field goals: 1991-92, 14-for-54 (.259). 1992-93, 27-for-80 (.338). Totals, 41-for-134 (.306).

### NBA REGULAR-SEASON RECORD

**HONORS:** NBA Rookie of the Year (1994). ... All-NBA first team (2001). ... All-NBA second team (1999, 2002, 2003). ... All-NBA third team (2000). ... NBA All-Rookie first team (1994).

| Season Team | G | Min. | FGM | FGA | Pct. | FTM | FTA | Pct. | Off. | Def. | Tot. | Ast. | St. | Blk. | TO | Pts. | RPG | APG | PPG |
|---|---|---|---|---|---|---|---|---|---|---|---|---|---|---|---|---|---|---|---|
| 93-94—Golden State ... | 76 | 2438 | 572 | 1037 | .552 | 189 | 355 | .532 | 305 | 389 | 694 | 272 | 93 | 164 | 206 | 1333 | 9.1 | 3.6 | 17.5 |
| 94-95—Washington ... | 54 | 2067 | 464 | 938 | .495 | 117 | 233 | .502 | 200 | 318 | 518 | 256 | 83 | 85 | 167 | 1085 | 9.6 | 4.7 | 20.1 |
| 95-96—Washington ... | 15 | 558 | 150 | 276 | .543 | 41 | 69 | .594 | 37 | 77 | 114 | 75 | 27 | 9 | 49 | 356 | 7.6 | 5.0 | 23.7 |
| 96-97—Washington ... | 72 | 2806 | 604 | 1167 | .518 | 177 | 313 | .565 | 238 | 505 | 743 | 331 | 122 | 137 | 230 | 1445 | 10.3 | 4.6 | 20.1 |
| 97-98—Washington ... | 71 | 2809 | 647 | 1341 | .482 | 196 | 333 | .589 | 176 | 498 | 674 | 273 | 111 | 124 | 185 | 1555 | 9.5 | 3.8 | 21.9 |
| 98-99—Sacramento ... | 42 | 1719 | 378 | 778 | .486 | 79 | 174 | .454 | 149 | 396 | 545 | 173 | 60 | 89 | 148 | 839 | *13.0 | 4.1 | 20.0 |
| 99-00—Sacramento ... | 75 | 2880 | 748 | 1548 | .483 | 311 | 414 | .751 | 189 | 598 | 787 | 345 | 120 | 128 | 218 | 1834 | 10.5 | 4.6 | 24.5 |

| Season Team | G | Min. | FGM | FGA | Pct. | FTM | FTA | Pct. | Off. | Def. | Tot. | Ast. | St. | Blk. | TO | Pts. | RPG | APG | PPG |
|---|---|---|---|---|---|---|---|---|---|---|---|---|---|---|---|---|---|---|---|
| 00-01—Sacramento .... | 70 | 2836 | 786 | 1635 | .481 | 324 | 461 | .703 | 179 | 598 | 777 | 294 | 93 | 118 | 195 | 1898 | 11.1 | 4.2 | 27.1 |
| 01-02—Sacramento .... | 54 | 2071 | 532 | 1075 | .495 | 253 | 338 | .749 | 150 | 396 | 546 | 258 | 90 | 76 | 158 | 1322 | 10.1 | 4.8 | 24.5 |
| 02-03—Sacramento .... | 67 | 2622 | 661 | 1433 | .461 | 215 | 354 | .607 | 160 | 544 | 704 | 364 | 106 | 88 | 215 | 1542 | 10.5 | 5.4 | 23.0 |
| 03-04—Sacramento .... | 23 | 831 | 174 | 421 | .413 | 81 | 114 | .711 | 48 | 152 | 200 | 105 | 31 | 20 | 60 | 430 | 8.7 | 4.6 | 18.7 |
| 04-05—Sac.-Phila. ...... | 67 | 2370 | 555 | 1283 | .433 | 181 | 228 | .794 | 130 | 482 | 612 | 318 | 94 | 53 | 182 | 1306 | 9.1 | 4.7 | 19.5 |
| Totals .................. | 686 | 26007 | 6271 | 12932 | .485 | 2164 | 3386 | .639 | 1961 | 4953 | 6914 | 3064 | 1030 | 1091 | 2013 | 14945 | 10.1 | 4.5 | 21.8 |

Three-point field goals: 1993-94, 0-for-14. 1994-95, 40-for-145 (.276). 1995-96, 15-for-34 (.441). 1996-97, 60-for-151 (.397). 1997-98, 65-for-205 (.317). 1998-99, 4-for-34 (.118). 1999-00, 27-for-95 (.284). 2000-01, 2-for-28 (.071). 2001-02, 5-for-19 (.263). 2002-03, 5-for-21 (.238). 2003-04, 1-for-5 (.200). 2004-05, 15-for-44 (.341). Totals, 239-for-795 (.301).

Personal fouls/disqualifications: 1993-94, 247/4. 1994-95, 186/2. 1995-96, 51/1. 1996-97, 258/6. 1997-98, 269/4. 1998-99, 145/1. 1999-00, 264/7. 2000-01, 226/1. 2001-02, 181/1. 2002-03, 204/1. 2003-04, 76/1. 2004-05, 214/6. Totals, 2321/35.

## NBA PLAYOFF RECORD

| Season Team | G | Min. | FGM | FGA | Pct. | FTM | FTA | Pct. | Off. | Def. | Tot. | Ast. | St. | Blk. | TO | Pts. | RPG | APG | PPG |
|---|---|---|---|---|---|---|---|---|---|---|---|---|---|---|---|---|---|---|---|
| 93-94—Golden State .... | 3 | 109 | 22 | 40 | .550 | 3 | 10 | .300 | 13 | 13 | 26 | 27 | 3 | 9 | 9 | 47 | 8.7 | 9.0 | 15.7 |
| 96-97—Washington .... | 3 | 106 | 19 | 30 | .633 | 4 | 8 | .500 | 7 | 17 | 24 | 10 | 2 | 7 | 16 | 47 | 8.0 | 3.3 | 15.7 |
| 98-99—Sacramento .... | 5 | 192 | 31 | 80 | .388 | 10 | 25 | .400 | 13 | 34 | 47 | 20 | 9 | 5 | 20 | 74 | 9.4 | 4.0 | 14.8 |
| 99-00—Sacramento .... | 5 | 196 | 47 | 110 | .427 | 27 | 34 | .794 | 14 | 34 | 48 | 27 | 8 | 10 | 8 | 122 | 9.6 | 5.4 | 24.4 |
| 00-01—Sacramento .... | 8 | 348 | 76 | 196 | .388 | 34 | 49 | .694 | 34 | 58 | 92 | 25 | 9 | 8 | 31 | 186 | 11.5 | 3.1 | 23.3 |
| 01-02—Sacramento .... | 16 | 667 | 160 | 319 | .502 | 59 | 99 | .596 | 49 | 124 | 173 | 75 | 14 | 25 | 46 | 379 | 10.8 | 4.7 | 23.7 |
| 02-03—Sacramento .... | 7 | 246 | 67 | 135 | .496 | 32 | 49 | .653 | 18 | 40 | 58 | 25 | 10 | 8 | 23 | 166 | 8.3 | 3.6 | 23.7 |
| 03-04—Sacramento .... | 12 | 446 | 90 | 199 | .452 | 40 | 65 | .615 | 24 | 75 | 99 | 44 | 16 | 10 | 38 | 221 | 8.3 | 3.7 | 18.4 |
| 04-05—Philadelphia .... | 5 | 186 | 39 | 95 | .411 | 12 | 16 | .750 | 12 | 17 | 29 | 14 | 6 | 1 | 11 | 95 | 5.8 | 2.8 | 19.0 |
| Totals .................. | 64 | 2496 | 551 | 1204 | .458 | 221 | 355 | .623 | 184 | 412 | 596 | 267 | 77 | 83 | 202 | 1337 | 9.3 | 4.2 | 20.9 |

Three-point field goals: 1993-94, 0-for-2. 1996-97, 5-for-11 (.455). 1998-99, 2-for-7 (.286). 1999-00, 1-for-5 (.200). 2000-01, 0-for-1. 2001-02, 0-for-4. 2002-03, 0-for-3. 2003-04, 1-for-4 (.250). 2004-05, 5-for-14 (.357). Totals, 14-for-51 (.275).

Personal fouls/disqualifications: 1993-94, 11/0. 1996-97, 18/3. 1998-99, 20/1. 1999-00, 14/1. 2000-01, 29/0. 2001-02, 64/2. 2002-03, 25/1. 2003-04, 34/0. 2004-05, 20/0. Totals, 235/8.

## NBA ALL-STAR GAME RECORD

| Season Team | Min. | FGM | FGA | Pct. | FTM | FTA | Pct. | Off. | Def. | Tot. | Ast. | PF | Dq. | St. | Blk. | TO | Pts. |
|---|---|---|---|---|---|---|---|---|---|---|---|---|---|---|---|---|---|
| 1997—Washington........... | 14 | 1 | 4 | .250 | 0 | 0 | ... | 1 | 3 | 4 | 3 | 3 | 0 | 1 | 0 | 3 | 2 |
| 2000—Sacramento........... | 13 | 3 | 10 | .300 | 0 | 0 | ... | 3 | 5 | 8 | 3 | 2 | 0 | 1 | 0 | 2 | 6 |
| 2001—Sacramento........... | 29 | 6 | 14 | .429 | 2 | 4 | .500 | 4 | 5 | 9 | 3 | 2 | 0 | 1 | 0 | 1 | 14 |
| 2002—Sacramento........... | 20 | 3 | 7 | .429 | 1 | 4 | .250 | 3 | 0 | 3 | 4 | 2 | 0 | 1 | 0 | 2 | 8 |
| 2003—Sacramento........... | | | | | | | Selected, did not play—injured | | | | | | | | | | |
| Totals........................... | 76 | 13 | 35 | .371 | 3 | 8 | .375 | 11 | 13 | 24 | 13 | 9 | 0 | 4 | 0 | 8 | 30 |

Three-point field goals: 2001, 0-for-1. 2002, 1-for-2 (.500). Totals, 1-for-3 (.333).

# WELLS, BONZI     G/F     KINGS

**PERSONAL:** Born September 20, 1976, in Muncie, Ind. ... 6-5/210. (1.96/95.3). ... Full name: Gawen Deangelo Wells

**HIGH SCHOOL:** Central (Muncie, Ind.).

**COLLEGE:** Ball State.

**TRANSACTIONS/CAREER NOTES:** Selected by Detroit Pistons in first round (11th pick overall) of 1998 NBA Draft. ... Rights traded by Pistons to Portland Trail Blazers for conditional first-round draft choice (January 21, 1999); Pistons received 2000 second-round draft choice to complete deal (June 13, 2000). ... Traded by Trail Blazers to Memphis Grizzlies for F/G Wesley Person and 2004 first-round draft choice (December 3, 2003). ... Traded by Grizzlies to Sacramento Kings for C Greg Ostertag and G Bobby Jackson (August 2, 2005).

## COLLEGIATE RECORD

**NOTES:** Led NCAA Division I with 3.6 steals per game (1998).

| Season Team | G | Min. | FGM | FGA | Pct. | FTM | FTA | Pct. | Reb. | Ast. | Pts. | RPG | APG | PPG |
|---|---|---|---|---|---|---|---|---|---|---|---|---|---|---|
| 94-95—Ball State ..................... | 30 | 887 | 177 | 380 | .466 | 87 | 141 | .617 | 183 | 84 | 474 | 6.1 | 2.8 | 15.8 |
| 95-96—Ball State ..................... | 28 | 910 | 269 | 544 | .494 | 143 | 202 | .708 | 246 | 80 | 712 | 8.8 | 2.9 | 25.4 |
| 96-97—Ball State ..................... | 29 | 900 | 229 | 492 | .465 | 154 | 223 | .691 | 230 | 127 | 637 | 7.9 | 4.4 | 22.0 |
| 97-98—Ball State ..................... | 29 | 843 | 238 | 486 | .490 | 133 | 193 | .689 | 184 | 95 | 662 | 6.3 | 3.3 | 22.8 |
| Totals .................. | 116 | 3540 | 913 | 1902 | .480 | 517 | 759 | .681 | 843 | 386 | 2485 | 7.3 | 3.3 | 21.4 |

Three-point field goals: 1994-95, 33-for-99 (.333). 1995-96, 31-for-92 (.337). 1996-97, 25-for-104 (.240). 1997-98, 53-for-142 (.373). Totals, 142-for-437 (.325).

## NBA REGULAR-SEASON RECORD

| Season Team | G | Min. | FGM | FGA | Pct. | FTM | FTA | Pct. | Off. | Def. | Tot. | Ast. | St. | Blk. | TO | Pts. | RPG | APG | PPG |
|---|---|---|---|---|---|---|---|---|---|---|---|---|---|---|---|---|---|---|---|
| 98-99—Portland......... | 7 | 35 | 11 | 20 | .550 | 8 | 18 | .444 | 4 | 5 | 9 | 3 | 1 | 1 | 6 | 31 | 1.3 | 0.4 | 4.4 |
| 99-00—Portland......... | 66 | 1162 | 236 | 480 | .492 | 88 | 129 | .682 | 78 | 104 | 182 | 97 | 69 | 12 | 97 | 580 | 2.8 | 1.5 | 8.8 |
| 00-01—Portland......... | 75 | 1995 | 387 | 726 | .533 | 159 | 240 | .663 | 120 | 247 | 367 | 208 | 94 | 20 | 169 | 950 | 4.9 | 2.8 | 12.7 |
| 01-02—Portland......... | 74 | 2348 | 487 | 1039 | .469 | 215 | 290 | .741 | 121 | 323 | 444 | 204 | 113 | 25 | 191 | 1255 | 6.0 | 2.8 | 17.0 |
| 02-03—Portland......... | 75 | 2396 | 437 | 990 | .441 | 226 | 313 | .722 | 98 | 296 | 394 | 246 | 123 | 18 | 215 | 1138 | 5.3 | 3.3 | 15.2 |
| 03-04—Portland-Mem. | 72 | 1872 | 363 | 850 | .427 | 138 | 183 | .754 | 78 | 182 | 260 | 139 | 91 | 19 | 161 | 886 | 3.6 | 1.9 | 12.3 |
| 04-05—Memphis........ | 69 | 1489 | 272 | 617 | .441 | 141 | 188 | .750 | 49 | 180 | 229 | 80 | 85 | 27 | 90 | 721 | 3.3 | 1.2 | 10.4 |
| Totals .................. | 438 | 11297 | 2193 | 4722 | .464 | 975 | 1361 | .716 | 548 | 1337 | 1885 | 977 | 576 | 122 | 929 | 5561 | 4.3 | 2.2 | 12.7 |

Three-point field goals: 1998-99, 1-for-3 (.333). 1999-00, 20-for-53 (.377). 2000-01, 17-for-50 (.340). 2001-02, 66-for-172 (.384). 2002-03, 38-for-130 (.292). 2003-04, 22-for-69 (.319). 2004-05, 36-for-104 (.346). Totals, 200-for-581 (.344).

Personal fouls/disqualifications: 1998-99, 5/0. 1999-00, 153/3. 2000-01, 203/1. 2001-02, 208/0. 2002-03, 220/2. 2003-04, 197/2. 2004-05, 165/0. Totals, 1151/8.

| Season Team | G | Min. | FGM | FGA | Pct. | FTM | FTA | Pct. | REBOUNDS Off. | Def. | Tot. | Ast. | St. | Blk. | TO | Pts. | AVERAGES RPG | APG | PPG |
|---|---|---|---|---|---|---|---|---|---|---|---|---|---|---|---|---|---|---|---|
| 99-00—Portland | 14 | 188 | 37 | 83 | .446 | 29 | 41 | .707 | 12 | 23 | 35 | 13 | 7 | 0 | 16 | 105 | 2.5 | 0.9 | 7.5 |
| 01-02—Portland | 3 | 106 | 14 | 38 | .368 | 9 | 13 | .692 | 4 | 8 | 12 | 13 | 6 | 1 | 11 | 37 | 4.0 | 4.3 | 12.3 |
| 02-03—Portland | 7 | 268 | 49 | 124 | .395 | 26 | 39 | .667 | 14 | 34 | 48 | 26 | 15 | 3 | 21 | 133 | 6.9 | 3.7 | 19.0 |
| 03-04—Memphis | 4 | 94 | 19 | 37 | .514 | 9 | 14 | .643 | 2 | 10 | 12 | 4 | 4 | 1 | 9 | 47 | 3.0 | 1.0 | 11.8 |
| 04-05—Memphis | 2 | 25 | 4 | 9 | .444 | 6 | 6 | 1.000 | 0 | 4 | 4 | 3 | 2 | 1 | 1 | 14 | 2.0 | 1.5 | 7.0 |
| **Totals** | 30 | 681 | 123 | 291 | .423 | 79 | 113 | .699 | 32 | 79 | 111 | 59 | 34 | 6 | 58 | 336 | 3.7 | 2.0 | 11.2 |

Three-point field goals: 1999-00, 2-for-10 (.200). 2001-02, 0-for-7. 2002-03, 9-for-30 (.300). 2003-04, 0-for-1. Totals, 11-for-48 (.229).
Personal fouls/disqualifications: 1999-00, 33/0. 2001-02, 11/1. 2002-03, 30/1. 2003-04, 8/0. 2004-05, 1/0. Totals, 83/2.

## WELSCH, JIRI      G      BUCKS

**PERSONAL:** Born January 27, 1980, in Pardubice, Czechoslovakia. ... 6-7/208. (2.01/94.3).
**TRANSACTIONS/CAREER NOTES:** Played in Czech Republic (1997-2000). ... Played in Slovenia (2000-02). ... Selected by Philadelphia 76ers in first round (16th pick overall) of 2002 NBA Draft. ... Draft rights traded by 76ers to Golden State Warriors for future first-round draft choice and future first- or second-round draft choice (June 26, 2002). ... Traded by Warriors with F Danny Fortson, F Chris Mills and F Antawn Jamison to Dallas Mavericks for G Nick Van Exel, G Avery Johnson, F Popeye Jones, F Antoine Rigaudeau and C Evan Eschmeyer (August 18, 2003). ... Traded by Mavericks with F/C Raef LaFrentz, F Chris Mills and 2004 first-round draft choice to Boston Celtics for G Tony Delk and F Antoine Walker (October 20, 2003). ... Traded by Celtics to Cleveland Cavaliers for first-round draft pick in 2007 draft (February 24, 2005). ... Traded by Cavaliers to Milwaukee Bucks for a 2006 second-round draft choice (June 28, 2005).

### CZECH LEAGUE RECORD

| Season Team | G | Min. | FGM | FGA | Pct. | FTM | FTA | Pct. | Reb. | Ast. | Pts. | AVERAGES RPG | APG | PPG |
|---|---|---|---|---|---|---|---|---|---|---|---|---|---|---|
| 97-98—Pardubice | 33 | 1073 | 169 | 384 | .440 | 127 | 156 | .814 | 90 | 30 | 482 | 2.7 | 0.9 | 14.6 |
| 98-99—Sparta Praha | 30 | 679 | 115 | 227 | .507 | 107 | 141 | .759 | 75 | 47 | 354 | 2.5 | 1.6 | 11.8 |
| 99-00—Sparta Praha | 35 | 1243 | 201 | 460 | .437 | 219 | 276 | .793 | 164 | 108 | 668 | 4.7 | 3.1 | 19.1 |
| **Totals** | 98 | 2995 | 485 | 1071 | .453 | 453 | 573 | .791 | 329 | 185 | 1504 | 3.4 | 1.9 | 15.3 |

Three-point field goals: 1997-98, 23-for-84 (.274). 1998-99, 17-for-38 (.447). 1999-00, 43-for-123 (.350). Totals, 83-for-245 (.339).

### SLOVENIAN LEAGUE RECORD

| Season Team | G | Min. | FGM | FGA | Pct. | FTM | FTA | Pct. | Reb. | Ast. | Pts. | AVERAGES RPG | APG | PPG |
|---|---|---|---|---|---|---|---|---|---|---|---|---|---|---|
| 00-01—Olimpija Ljubljana | 20 | 479 | 85 | 169 | .503 | 33 | 48 | .688 | 49 | 32 | 219 | 2.5 | 1.6 | 11.0 |
| 01-02—Olimpija Ljubljana | 22 | 565 | 109 | 196 | .556 | 95 | 114 | .833 | 49 | 36 | 341 | 2.2 | 1.6 | 15.5 |
| **Totals** | 42 | 1044 | 194 | 365 | .532 | 128 | 162 | .790 | 98 | 68 | 560 | 2.3 | 1.6 | 13.3 |

Three-point field goals: 2000-01, 16-for-47 (.340). 2001-02, 28-for-72 (.389). Totals, 44-for-119 (.370).

### NBA REGULAR-SEASON RECORD

| Season Team | G | Min. | FGM | FGA | Pct. | FTM | FTA | Pct. | REBOUNDS Off. | Def. | Tot. | Ast. | St. | Blk. | TO | Pts. | AVERAGES RPG | APG | PPG |
|---|---|---|---|---|---|---|---|---|---|---|---|---|---|---|---|---|---|---|---|
| 02-03—Golden State | 37 | 234 | 19 | 75 | .253 | 22 | 29 | .759 | 12 | 16 | 28 | 27 | 8 | 2 | 19 | 61 | 0.8 | 0.7 | 1.6 |
| 03-04—Boston | 81 | 2179 | 262 | 612 | .428 | 153 | 206 | .743 | 60 | 236 | 296 | 183 | 101 | 7 | 129 | 746 | 3.7 | 2.3 | 9.2 |
| 04-05—Boston-Cleve. | 71 | 1317 | 149 | 371 | .402 | 129 | 169 | .763 | 26 | 141 | 167 | 103 | 44 | 5 | 73 | 461 | 2.4 | 1.5 | 6.5 |
| **Totals** | 189 | 3730 | 430 | 1058 | .406 | 304 | 404 | .752 | 98 | 393 | 491 | 313 | 153 | 14 | 221 | 1268 | 2.6 | 1.7 | 6.7 |

Three-point field goals: 2002-03, 1-for-4 (.250). 2003-04, 69-for-181 (.381). 2004-05, 34-for-110 (.309). Totals, 104-for-295 (.353).
Personal fouls/disqualifications: 2002-03, 32/1. 2003-04, 176/0. 2004-05, 121/1. Totals, 329/2.

### NBA PLAYOFF RECORD

| Season Team | G | Min. | FGM | FGA | Pct. | FTM | FTA | Pct. | REBOUNDS Off. | Def. | Tot. | Ast. | St. | Blk. | TO | Pts. | AVERAGES RPG | APG | PPG |
|---|---|---|---|---|---|---|---|---|---|---|---|---|---|---|---|---|---|---|---|
| 03-04—Boston | 4 | 104 | 11 | 23 | .478 | 9 | 9 | 1.000 | 0 | 12 | 12 | 9 | 2 | 0 | 8 | 32 | 3.0 | 2.3 | 8.0 |

Three-point field goals: 2003-04, 1-for-4 (.250). Totals, 1-for-4 (.250).
Personal fouls/disqualifications: 2003-04, 7/0. Totals, 7/0.

**W**

## WESLEY, DAVID      G      ROCKETS

**PERSONAL:** Born November 14, 1970, in San Antonio. ... 6-1/203. (1.85/92.1). ... Full name: David Barakau Wesley
**HIGH SCHOOL:** Longview (Texas).
**JUNIOR COLLEGE:** Temple (Texas) Junior College.
**COLLEGE:** Baylor.
**TRANSACTIONS/CAREER NOTES:** Not drafted by an NBA franchise. ... Played in Continental Basketball Association with Wichita Falls Texans (1992-93). ... Signed as free agent by New Jersey Nets (July 27, 1993). ... Signed as unrestricted free agent by Boston Celtics (July 20, 1994). ... Signed as free agent by Charlotte Hornets (July 1, 1997). ... Hornets franchise moved to New Orleans for 2002-03 season. ... Traded by Hornets to Houston Rockets for G Jim Jackson and F Bostjan Nachbar (December 27, 2004).

### COLLEGIATE RECORD

| Season Team | G | Min. | FGM | FGA | Pct. | FTM | FTA | Pct. | Reb. | Ast. | Pts. | AVERAGES RPG | APG | PPG |
|---|---|---|---|---|---|---|---|---|---|---|---|---|---|---|
| 88-89—Temple J.C. | 31 | ... | 155 | 331 | .468 | 88 | 125 | .704 | 106 | 184 | 455 | 3.4 | 5.9 | 14.7 |
| 89-90—Baylor | 18 | 394 | 61 | 134 | .455 | 61 | 73 | .836 | 39 | 37 | 208 | 2.2 | 2.1 | 11.6 |
| 90-91—Baylor | 26 | 837 | 133 | 314 | .424 | 125 | 149 | .839 | 76 | 148 | 430 | 2.9 | 5.7 | 16.5 |
| 91-92—Baylor | 28 | 1020 | 174 | 387 | .450 | 179 | 219 | .817 | 136 | 131 | 586 | 4.9 | 4.7 | 20.9 |
| **Junior College Totals** | 31 | ... | 155 | 331 | .468 | 88 | 125 | .704 | 106 | 184 | 455 | 3.4 | 5.9 | 14.7 |
| **4-Year-College Totals** | 72 | 2251 | 368 | 835 | .441 | 365 | 441 | .828 | 251 | 316 | 1224 | 3.5 | 4.4 | 17.0 |

Three-point field goals: 1989-90, 25-for-56 (.446). 1990-91, 39-for-114 (.342). 1991-92, 59-for-156 (.378). Totals, 123-for-326 (.377).
Personal fouls/disqualifications: 1989-90, 35/1. 1990-91, 84/4. Totals, 119/5.

**NOTES:** CBA All-Rookie first team (1993).

| | | | | | | | | | | | | AVERAGES | | |
|---|---|---|---|---|---|---|---|---|---|---|---|---|---|---|
| Season Team | G | Min. | FGM | FGA | Pct. | FTM | FTA | Pct. | Reb. | Ast. | Pts. | RPG | APG | PPG |
| 92-93—Wichita Falls | 55 | 1830 | 350 | 759 | .461 | 282 | 360 | .783 | 218 | 225 | 948 | 4.0 | 4.1 | 17.2 |

Three-point field goals: 1992-93, 34-for-93 (.366). Totals, 34-for-93 (.366).
Personal fouls/disqualifications: 1992-93, 189/0. Totals, 189/0.

### NBA REGULAR-SEASON RECORD

| | | | | | | | | | REBOUNDS | | | | | | | | AVERAGES | | |
|---|---|---|---|---|---|---|---|---|---|---|---|---|---|---|---|---|---|---|---|---|
| Season Team | G | Min. | FGM | FGA | Pct. | FTM | FTA | Pct. | Off. | Def. | Tot. | Ast. | St. | Blk. | TO | Pts. | RPG | APG | PPG |
| 93-94—New Jersey | 60 | 542 | 64 | 174 | .368 | 44 | 53 | .830 | 10 | 34 | 44 | 123 | 38 | 4 | 52 | 183 | 0.7 | 2.1 | 3.1 |
| 94-95—Boston | 51 | 1380 | 128 | 313 | .409 | 71 | 94 | .755 | 31 | 86 | 117 | 266 | 82 | 9 | 87 | 378 | 2.3 | 5.2 | 7.4 |
| 95-96—Boston | 82 | 2104 | 338 | 736 | .459 | 217 | 288 | .753 | 68 | 196 | 264 | 390 | 100 | 11 | 159 | 1009 | 3.2 | 4.8 | 12.3 |
| 96-97—Boston | 74 | 2991 | 456 | 974 | .468 | 225 | 288 | .781 | 67 | 197 | 264 | 537 | 162 | 13 | 211 | 1240 | 3.6 | 7.3 | 16.8 |
| 97-98—Charlotte | 81 | 2845 | 383 | 864 | .443 | 229 | 288 | .795 | 49 | 164 | 213 | 529 | 140 | 30 | 226 | 1054 | 2.6 | 6.5 | 13.0 |
| 98-99—Charlotte | 50 | 1848 | 243 | 545 | .446 | 159 | 191 | .832 | 23 | 138 | 161 | 322 | 100 | 10 | 142 | 706 | 3.2 | 6.4 | 14.1 |
| 99-00—Charlotte | 82 | 2760 | 407 | 955 | .426 | 214 | 275 | .778 | 39 | 186 | 225 | 463 | 109 | 11 | 159 | 1116 | 2.7 | 5.6 | 13.6 |
| 00-01—Charlotte | 82 | 3106 | 523 | 1239 | .422 | 271 | 339 | .799 | 64 | 160 | 224 | 361 | 128 | 16 | 171 | 1414 | 2.7 | 4.4 | 17.2 |
| 01-02—Charlotte | 67 | 2487 | 364 | 910 | .400 | 138 | 188 | .734 | 44 | 99 | 143 | 236 | 74 | 15 | 119 | 951 | 2.1 | 3.5 | 14.2 |
| 02-03—New Orleans | 73 | 2710 | 449 | 1037 | .433 | 185 | 237 | .781 | 38 | 137 | 175 | 251 | 109 | 9 | 132 | 1217 | 2.4 | 3.4 | 16.7 |
| 03-04—New Orleans | 61 | 2001 | 311 | 800 | .389 | 137 | 182 | .753 | 28 | 106 | 134 | 175 | 71 | 14 | 100 | 851 | 2.2 | 2.9 | 14.0 |
| 04-05—N.O.-Houston | 80 | 2774 | 334 | 840 | .398 | 162 | 189 | .857 | 38 | 190 | 228 | 265 | 96 | 9 | 113 | 948 | 2.9 | 3.3 | 11.9 |
| **Totals** | 843 | 27548 | 4000 | 9387 | .426 | 2052 | 2612 | .786 | 499 | 1693 | 2192 | 3918 | 1209 | 151 | 1671 | 11067 | 2.6 | 4.6 | 13.1 |

Three-point field goals: 1993-94, 11-for-47 (.234). 1994-95, 51-for-119 (.429). 1995-96, 116-for-272 (.426). 1996-97, 103-for-286 (.360). 1997-98, 59-for-170 (.347). 1998-99, 61-for-170 (.359). 1999-00, 88-for-248 (.355). 2000-01, 97-for-258 (.376). 2001-02, 85-for-256 (.332). 2002-03, 134-for-316 (.424). 2003-04, 92-for-285 (.323). 2004-05, 118-for-315 (.375). Totals, 1015-for-2742 (.370).
Personal fouls/disqualifications: 1993-94, 47/0. 1994-95, 144/0. 1995-96, 207/0. 1996-97, 221/1. 1997-98, 229/3. 1998-99, 130/2. 1999-00, 186/2. 2000-01, 220/2. 2001-02, 147/0. 2002-03, 173/0. 2003-04, 147/1. 2004-05, 215/2. Totals, 2066/13.

### NBA PLAYOFF RECORD

| | | | | | | | | | REBOUNDS | | | | | | | | AVERAGES | | |
|---|---|---|---|---|---|---|---|---|---|---|---|---|---|---|---|---|---|---|---|---|
| Season Team | G | Min. | FGM | FGA | Pct. | FTM | FTA | Pct. | Off. | Def. | Tot. | Ast. | St. | Blk. | TO | Pts. | RPG | APG | PPG |
| 93-94—New Jersey | 3 | 18 | 3 | 7 | .429 | 2 | 2 | 1.000 | 0 | 0 | 0 | 3 | 2 | 0 | 4 | 9 | 0.0 | 1.0 | 3.0 |
| 97-98—Charlotte | 9 | 285 | 33 | 83 | .398 | 15 | 21 | .714 | 5 | 13 | 18 | 60 | 7 | 0 | 19 | 90 | 2.0 | 6.7 | 10.0 |
| 99-00—Charlotte | 4 | 152 | 16 | 48 | .333 | 9 | 9 | 1.000 | 3 | 9 | 12 | 19 | 8 | 0 | 6 | 44 | 3.0 | 4.8 | 11.0 |
| 00-01—Charlotte | 10 | 394 | 63 | 134 | .470 | 31 | 41 | .756 | 4 | 26 | 30 | 39 | 16 | 1 | 14 | 170 | 3.0 | 3.9 | 17.0 |
| 01-02—Charlotte | 9 | 377 | 52 | 129 | .403 | 21 | 23 | .913 | 3 | 14 | 17 | 31 | 10 | 2 | 21 | 142 | 1.9 | 3.4 | 15.8 |
| 02-03—New Orleans | 6 | 185 | 29 | 72 | .403 | 7 | 7 | 1.000 | 1 | 6 | 7 | 13 | 5 | 1 | 15 | 79 | 1.2 | 2.2 | 13.2 |
| 03-04—New Orleans | 7 | 243 | 24 | 74 | .324 | 15 | 21 | .714 | 1 | 15 | 16 | 17 | 5 | 0 | 16 | 74 | 2.3 | 2.4 | 10.6 |
| 04-05—Houston | 7 | 280 | 19 | 54 | .352 | 9 | 13 | .692 | 4 | 17 | 21 | 23 | 9 | 1 | 9 | 57 | 3.0 | 3.3 | 8.1 |
| **Totals** | 55 | 1934 | 239 | 601 | .398 | 109 | 137 | .796 | 21 | 100 | 121 | 205 | 62 | 5 | 104 | 665 | 2.2 | 3.7 | 12.1 |

Three-point field goals: 1993-94, 1-for-4 (.250). 1997-98, 9-for-21 (.429). 1999-00, 3-for-10 (.300). 2000-01, 13-for-33 (.394). 2001-02, 17-for-38 (.447). 2002-03, 14-for-34 (.412). 2003-04, 11-for-30 (.367). 2004-05, 10-for-21 (.476). Totals, 78-for-191 (.408).
Personal fouls/disqualifications: 1997-98, 25/0. 1999-00, 17/0. 2000-01, 28/0. 2001-02, 30/0. 2002-03, 23/1. 2003-04, 21/0. 2004-05, 20/0. Totals, 164/1.

# WEST, DAVID F HORNETS

**PERSONAL:** Born August 29, 1980, in Teaneck, N.J. ... 6-9/240. (2.06/108.9). ... Full name: David Moorer West
**HIGH SCHOOL:** Garner Senior (Garner, N.C.).
**COLLEGE:** Xavier.
**TRANSACTIONS/CAREER NOTES:** Selected by New Orleans Hornets in first round (18th pick overall) of 2003 NBA Draft.

### COLLEGIATE RECORD

**NOTES:** The Sporting News All-America first team (2003). ... The Sporting News All-America third team (2002).

| | | | | | | | | | | | | AVERAGES | | |
|---|---|---|---|---|---|---|---|---|---|---|---|---|---|---|
| Season Team | G | Min. | FGM | FGA | Pct. | FTM | FTA | Pct. | Reb. | Ast. | Pts. | RPG | APG | PPG |
| 99-00—Xavier | 33 | 970 | 143 | 269 | .532 | 100 | 150 | .667 | 301 | 57 | 386 | 9.1 | 1.7 | 11.7 |
| 00-01—Xavier | 29 | 978 | 174 | 316 | .551 | 168 | 227 | .740 | 316 | 58 | 516 | 10.9 | 2.0 | 17.8 |
| 01-02—Xavier | 32 | 1094 | 196 | 366 | .536 | 185 | 241 | .768 | 313 | 50 | 586 | 9.8 | 1.6 | 18.3 |
| 02-03—Xavier | 32 | 1168 | 213 | 415 | .513 | 209 | 256 | .816 | 378 | 102 | 644 | 11.8 | 3.2 | 20.1 |
| **Totals** | 126 | 4210 | 726 | 1366 | .531 | 662 | 874 | .757 | 1308 | 267 | 2132 | 10.4 | 2.1 | 16.9 |

Three-point field goals: 2000-01, 0-for-1. 2001-02, 9-for-28 (.321). 2002-03, 9-for-26 (.346). Totals, 18-for-55 (.327).

### NBA REGULAR-SEASON RECORD

| | | | | | | | | | REBOUNDS | | | | | | | | AVERAGES | | |
|---|---|---|---|---|---|---|---|---|---|---|---|---|---|---|---|---|---|---|---|---|
| Season Team | G | Min. | FGM | FGA | Pct. | FTM | FTA | Pct. | Off. | Def. | Tot. | Ast. | St. | Blk. | TO | Pts. | RPG | APG | PPG |
| 03-04—New Orleans | 71 | 930 | 108 | 228 | .474 | 57 | 80 | .713 | 117 | 180 | 297 | 60 | 27 | 28 | 48 | 273 | 4.2 | 0.8 | 3.8 |
| 04-05—New Orleans | 30 | 552 | 75 | 172 | .436 | 34 | 50 | .680 | 40 | 89 | 129 | 23 | 12 | 16 | 37 | 186 | 4.3 | 0.8 | 6.2 |
| **Totals** | 101 | 1482 | 183 | 400 | .458 | 91 | 130 | .700 | 157 | 269 | 426 | 83 | 39 | 44 | 85 | 459 | 4.2 | 0.8 | 4.5 |

Three-point field goals: 2003-04, 0-for-2. 2004-05, 2-for-5 (.400). Totals, 2-for-7 (.286).
Personal fouls/disqualifications: 2003-04, 117/0. 2004-05, 62/0. Totals, 179/0.

### NBA PLAYOFF RECORD

| | | | | | | | | | REBOUNDS | | | | | | | | AVERAGES | | |
|---|---|---|---|---|---|---|---|---|---|---|---|---|---|---|---|---|---|---|---|---|
| Season Team | G | Min. | FGM | FGA | Pct. | FTM | FTA | Pct. | Off. | Def. | Tot. | Ast. | St. | Blk. | TO | Pts. | RPG | APG | PPG |
| 03-04—New Orleans | 7 | 111 | 15 | 28 | .536 | 11 | 13 | .846 | 8 | 22 | 30 | 8 | 2 | 4 | 7 | 41 | 4.3 | 1.1 | 5.9 |

Personal fouls/disqualifications: 2003-04, 10/0. Totals, 10/0.

## WEST, DELONTE      G      CELTICS

**PERSONAL:** Born July 26, 1983, in Washington, D.C. ... 6-4/180. (1.93/81.6).
**HIGH SCHOOL:** Eleanor Roosevelt (Greenbelt, Md.).
**COLLEGE:** Saint Joseph's.
**TRANSACTIONS/CAREER NOTES:** Selected after junior season by Boston Celtics in first round (24th pick overall) of 2004 NBA Draft.

### COLLEGIATE RECORD

**NOTES:** The Sporting News All-America third team (2004).

| Season Team | G | Min. | FGM | FGA | Pct. | FTM | FTA | Pct. | Reb. | Ast. | Pts. | RPG | APG | PPG |
|---|---|---|---|---|---|---|---|---|---|---|---|---|---|---|
| 01-02—St. Joseph's | 31 | 526 | 76 | 162 | .469 | 28 | 42 | .667 | 92 | 36 | 182 | 3.0 | 1.2 | 5.9 |
| 02-03—St. Joseph's | 26 | 785 | 162 | 342 | .474 | 70 | 86 | .814 | 113 | 83 | 449 | 4.3 | 3.2 | 17.3 |
| 03-04—St. Joseph's | 32 | 1073 | 212 | 416 | .510 | 124 | 139 | .892 | 172 | 151 | 604 | 5.4 | 4.7 | 18.9 |
| **Totals** | 89 | 2384 | 450 | 920 | .489 | 222 | 267 | .831 | 377 | 270 | 1235 | 4.2 | 3.0 | 13.9 |

Three-point field goals: 2001-02, 2-for-17 (.118). 2002-03, 55-for-147 (.374). 2003-04, 56-for-136 (.412). Totals, 113-for-300 (.377).

### NBA REGULAR-SEASON RECORD

| Season Team | G | Min. | FGM | FGA | Pct. | FTM | FTA | Pct. | Off. | Def. | Tot. | Ast. | St. | Blk. | TO | Pts. | RPG | APG | PPG |
|---|---|---|---|---|---|---|---|---|---|---|---|---|---|---|---|---|---|---|---|
| 04-05—Boston | 39 | 507 | 66 | 155 | .426 | 19 | 27 | .704 | 14 | 51 | 65 | 53 | 21 | 8 | 24 | 175 | 1.7 | 1.4 | 4.5 |

Three-point field goals: 2004-05, 24-for-67 (.358). Totals, 24-for-67 (.358).
Personal fouls/disqualifications: 2004-05, 69/0. Totals, 69/0.

### NBA PLAYOFF RECORD

| Season Team | G | Min. | FGM | FGA | Pct. | FTM | FTA | Pct. | Off. | Def. | Tot. | Ast. | St. | Blk. | TO | Pts. | RPG | APG | PPG |
|---|---|---|---|---|---|---|---|---|---|---|---|---|---|---|---|---|---|---|---|
| 04-05—Boston | 7 | 115 | 11 | 21 | .524 | 2 | 4 | .500 | 2 | 7 | 9 | 4 | 7 | 1 | 2 | 29 | 1.3 | 0.6 | 4.1 |

Three-point field goals: 2004-05, 5-for-11 (.455). Totals, 5-for-11 (.455).
Personal fouls/disqualifications: 2004-05, 17/0. Totals, 17/0.

## WHITE, JAHIDI      C

**PERSONAL:** Born February 19, 1976, in St. Louis. ... 6-9/290. (2.06/131.5).
**HIGH SCHOOL:** Cardinal Ritter (St. Louis).
**COLLEGE:** Georgetown.
**TRANSACTIONS/CAREER NOTES:** Selected by Washington Wizards in second round (43rd pick overall) of 1998 NBA Draft. ... Traded by Wizards to Phoenix Suns for G Brevin Knight (November 5, 2003). ... Selected by Charlotte Bobcats from Suns in NBA Expansion Draft (June 22, 2004).

### COLLEGIATE RECORD

| Season Team | G | Min. | FGM | FGA | Pct. | FTM | FTA | Pct. | Reb. | Ast. | Pts. | RPG | APG | PPG |
|---|---|---|---|---|---|---|---|---|---|---|---|---|---|---|
| 94-95—Georgetown | 26 | 201 | 24 | 56 | .429 | 13 | 35 | .371 | 46 | 2 | 61 | 1.8 | 0.1 | 2.3 |
| 95-96—Georgetown | 37 | 409 | 70 | 125 | .560 | 43 | 89 | .483 | 138 | 5 | 183 | 3.7 | 0.1 | 4.9 |
| 96-97—Georgetown | 30 | 607 | 84 | 164 | .512 | 50 | 103 | .485 | 193 | 14 | 218 | 6.4 | 0.5 | 7.3 |
| 97-98—Georgetown | 12 | 259 | 52 | 82 | .634 | 22 | 50 | .440 | 100 | 2 | 126 | 8.3 | 0.2 | 10.5 |
| **Totals** | 105 | 1476 | 230 | 427 | .539 | 128 | 277 | .462 | 477 | 23 | 588 | 4.5 | 0.2 | 5.6 |

### NBA REGULAR-SEASON RECORD

| Season Team | G | Min. | FGM | FGA | Pct. | FTM | FTA | Pct. | Off. | Def. | Tot. | Ast. | St. | Blk. | TO | Pts. | RPG | APG | PPG |
|---|---|---|---|---|---|---|---|---|---|---|---|---|---|---|---|---|---|---|---|
| 98-99—Washington | 20 | 191 | 17 | 32 | .531 | 15 | 35 | .429 | 23 | 35 | 58 | 1 | 3 | 11 | 16 | 49 | 2.9 | 0.1 | 2.5 |
| 99-00—Washington | 80 | 1537 | 228 | 450 | .507 | 113 | 211 | .536 | 202 | 351 | 553 | 15 | 31 | 83 | 94 | 569 | 6.9 | 0.2 | 7.1 |
| 00-01—Washington | 68 | 1609 | 203 | 408 | .498 | 177 | 312 | .567 | 178 | 343 | 521 | 20 | 32 | 111 | 136 | 583 | 7.7 | 0.3 | 8.6 |
| 01-02—Washington | 71 | 1346 | 150 | 279 | .538 | 83 | 154 | .539 | 159 | 285 | 444 | 17 | 25 | 75 | 65 | 383 | 6.3 | 0.2 | 5.4 |
| 02-03—Washington | 16 | 230 | 25 | 53 | .472 | 17 | 25 | .680 | 37 | 36 | 73 | 2 | 1 | 12 | 9 | 67 | 4.6 | 0.1 | 4.2 |
| 03-04—Washington | 62 | 865 | 99 | 190 | .521 | 63 | 126 | .500 | 97 | 164 | 261 | 7 | 25 | 51 | 66 | 261 | 4.2 | 0.1 | 4.2 |
| 04-05—Charlotte | 17 | 135 | 14 | 31 | .452 | 14 | 40 | .350 | 11 | 23 | 34 | 1 | 2 | 12 | 11 | 42 | 2.0 | 0.1 | 2.5 |
| **Totals** | 334 | 5913 | 736 | 1443 | .510 | 482 | 903 | .534 | 707 | 1237 | 1944 | 63 | 119 | 355 | 397 | 1954 | 5.8 | 0.2 | 5.9 |

Three-point field goals: 2000-01, 0-for-1. Totals, 0-for-1 (.000).
Personal fouls/disqualifications: 1998-99, 39/1. 1999-00, 234/2. 2000-01, 211/3. 2001-02, 163/0. 2002-03, 33/1. 2003-04, 176/4. 2004-05, 31/1. Totals, 887/12.

## WHITE, RODNEY      F

**PERSONAL:** Born June 28, 1980, in Philadelphia. ... 6-9/238. (2.06/108.0). ... Full name: Rodney Charles White.
**HIGH SCHOOL:** Newport School (Silver Spring, Md.), then St. Peter's (New Brunswick, N.J.), then Mt. Zion Christian Academy (Durham, N.C.).
**COLLEGE:** Charlotte.
**TRANSACTIONS/CAREER NOTES:** Selected after freshman season by Detroit Pistons in first round (ninth pick overall) of 2001 NBA Draft. ... Traded by Pistons to Denver Nuggets for F Don Reid, C Bateer Mengke and future first-round draft choice (October 1, 2002). ... Traded by Nuggets with F Nikoloz Tskitishvili to Golden State Warriors for F Eduardo Najera, G Luis Flores and future first-round draft pick (February 24, 2005). ... Waived by Warriors (June 30, 2005).

### COLLEGIATE RECORD

| Season Team | G | Min. | FGM | FGA | Pct. | FTM | FTA | Pct. | Reb. | Ast. | Pts. | RPG | APG | PPG |
|---|---|---|---|---|---|---|---|---|---|---|---|---|---|---|
| 00-01—UNC Charlotte | 28 | 865 | 188 | 386 | .487 | 114 | 160 | .713 | 182 | 41 | 523 | 6.5 | 1.5 | 18.7 |

W

Three-point field goals: 2000-01, 33-for-95 (.347). Totals, 33-for-95 (.347).
Personal fouls/disqualifications: 2000-01, 73/0. Totals, 73/0.

### NBA REGULAR-SEASON RECORD

| | | | | | | | | REBOUNDS | | | | | | | | AVERAGES | | |
|---|---|---|---|---|---|---|---|---|---|---|---|---|---|---|---|---|---|---|
| Season Team | G | Min. | FGM | FGA | Pct. | FTM | FTA | Pct. | Off. | Def. | Tot. | Ast. | St. | Blk. | TO | Pts. | RPG | APG | PPG |
| 01-02—Detroit ........... | 16 | 129 | 21 | 60 | .350 | 12 | 14 | .857 | 2 | 16 | 18 | 12 | 9 | 2 | 14 | 56 | 1.1 | 0.8 | 3.5 |
| 02-03—Denver ........... | 72 | 1563 | 260 | 638 | .408 | 98 | 125 | .784 | 43 | 170 | 213 | 121 | 45 | 32 | 156 | 650 | 3.0 | 1.7 | 9.0 |
| 03-04—Denver ........... | 72 | 985 | 215 | 468 | .459 | 78 | 104 | .750 | 44 | 121 | 165 | 60 | 32 | 20 | 78 | 541 | 2.3 | 0.8 | 7.5 |
| 04-05—Denver-G.S. .... | 58 | 677 | 121 | 289 | .419 | 27 | 44 | .614 | 24 | 65 | 89 | 44 | 32 | 11 | 37 | 293 | 1.5 | 0.8 | 5.1 |
| Totals ................. | 218 | 3354 | 617 | 1455 | .424 | 215 | 287 | .749 | 113 | 372 | 485 | 237 | 118 | 65 | 285 | 1540 | 2.2 | 1.1 | 7.1 |

Three-point field goals: 2001-02, 2-for-9 (.222). 2002-03, 32-for-134 (.239). 2003-04, 33-for-87 (.379). 2004-05, 24-for-60 (.400). Totals, 91-for-290 (.314).
Personal fouls/disqualifications: 2001-02, 6/0. 2002-03, 134/1. 2003-04, 105/0. 2004-05, 64/0. Totals, 309/1.

### NBA PLAYOFF RECORD

| | | | | | | | | REBOUNDS | | | | | | | | AVERAGES | | |
|---|---|---|---|---|---|---|---|---|---|---|---|---|---|---|---|---|---|---|
| Season Team | G | Min. | FGM | FGA | Pct. | FTM | FTA | Pct. | Off. | Def. | Tot. | Ast. | St. | Blk. | TO | Pts. | RPG | APG | PPG |
| 01-02—Detroit ........... | 1 | 2 | 0 | 1 | .000 | 0 | 0 | ... | 0 | 0 | 0 | 0 | 0 | 0 | 1 | 0 | 0.0 | 0.0 | 0.0 |
| 03-04—Denver ........... | 4 | 26 | 4 | 15 | .267 | 0 | 0 | ... | 1 | 4 | 5 | 0 | 2 | 0 | 2 | 8 | 1.3 | 0.0 | 2.0 |
| Totals ................. | 5 | 28 | 4 | 16 | .250 | 0 | 0 | ... | 1 | 4 | 5 | 0 | 2 | 0 | 3 | 8 | 1.0 | 0.0 | 1.6 |

Three-point field goals: 2003-04, 0-for-3. Totals, 0-for-3 (.000).
Personal fouls/disqualifications: 2003-04, 3/0. Totals, 3/0.

## WILCOX, CHRIS — F — CLIPPERS

**PERSONAL:** Born August 3, 1982, in Raleigh, N.C. ... 6-10/221. (2.08/100.2). ... Full name: Chris Ray Wilcox
**HIGH SCHOOL:** Whitefield (N.C.), then West Columbus (Whitefield, N.C.), then Enloe (Raleigh, N.C.).
**COLLEGE:** Maryland.
**TRANSACTIONS/CAREER NOTES:** Selected after sophomore season by Los Angeles Clippers in first round (eighth pick overall) of 2002 NBA Draft.

### COLLEGIATE RECORD

| | | | | | | | | | | | AVERAGES | | |
|---|---|---|---|---|---|---|---|---|---|---|---|---|---|
| Season Team | G | Min. | FGM | FGA | Pct. | FTM | FTA | Pct. | Reb. | Ast. | Pts. | RPG | APG | PPG |
| 00-01—Maryland ...................... | 34 | 294 | 51 | 88 | .580 | 20 | 33 | .606 | 73 | 16 | 122 | 2.1 | 0.5 | 3.6 |
| 01-02—Maryland ...................... | 36 | 866 | 173 | 343 | .504 | 86 | 147 | .585 | 257 | 53 | 432 | 7.1 | 1.5 | 12.0 |
| Totals ...................... | 70 | 1160 | 224 | 431 | .520 | 106 | 180 | .589 | 330 | 69 | 554 | 4.7 | 1.0 | 7.9 |

Three-point field goals: 2001-02, 0-for-2. Totals, 0-for-2 (.000).

### NBA REGULAR-SEASON RECORD

| | | | | | | | | REBOUNDS | | | | | | | | AVERAGES | | |
|---|---|---|---|---|---|---|---|---|---|---|---|---|---|---|---|---|---|---|
| Season Team | G | Min. | FGM | FGA | Pct. | FTM | FTA | Pct. | Off. | Def. | Tot. | Ast. | St. | Blk. | TO | Pts. | RPG | APG | PPG |
| 02-03—L.A. Clippers ... | 46 | 479 | 73 | 140 | .521 | 25 | 50 | .500 | 32 | 72 | 104 | 21 | 7 | 12 | 26 | 171 | 2.3 | 0.5 | 3.7 |
| 03-04—L.A. Clippers ... | 65 | 1340 | 227 | 436 | .521 | 105 | 150 | .700 | 125 | 180 | 305 | 51 | 29 | 20 | 80 | 559 | 4.7 | 0.8 | 8.6 |
| 04-05—L.A. Clippers ... | 54 | 1005 | 169 | 329 | .514 | 88 | 144 | .611 | 63 | 165 | 228 | 38 | 26 | 24 | 77 | 426 | 4.2 | 0.7 | 7.9 |
| Totals ................. | 165 | 2824 | 469 | 905 | .518 | 218 | 344 | .634 | 220 | 417 | 637 | 110 | 62 | 56 | 183 | 1156 | 3.9 | 0.7 | 7.0 |

Three-point field goals: 2003-04, 0-for-1. Totals, 0-for-1 (.000).
Personal fouls/disqualifications: 2002-03, 65/2. 2003-04, 183/4. 2004-05, 129/2. Totals, 377/8.

## WILKINS, DAMIEN — F — SUPERSONICS

**W**

**PERSONAL:** Born January 11, 1980, in Washington, D.C. ... 6-6/225. (1.98/102.1). ... Full name: Damien Lamont Wilkins. Son of Gerald Wilkins, guard, New York Knicks (1986-86 to 1991-92), Cleveland Cavaliers (1992-94), Vancouver Grizzlies (1995-96) and Orlando Magic (1996-99). Nephew of Dominique Wilkins, forward, Atlanta Hawks (1982-1994), Los Angeles Clippers (1993-94), Boston Celtics (1994-95), San Antonio Spurs (1996-97) and Orlando Magic (1998-99).
**HIGH SCHOOL:** Dr. Phillips (Orlando, Fla.).
**COLLEGE:** North Caroline State, then Georgia.
**TRANSACTIONS/CAREER NOTES:** Not drafted by an NBA franchise. ... Signed as free agent by Seattle SuperSonics (November 3, 2004).

### COLLEGIATE RECORD

| | | | | | | | | | | | AVERAGES | | |
|---|---|---|---|---|---|---|---|---|---|---|---|---|---|
| Season Team | G | Min. | FGM | FGA | Pct. | FTM | FTA | Pct. | Reb. | Ast. | Pts. | RPG | APG | PPG |
| 99-00—NC State ...................... | 34 | 1083 | 127 | 311 | .408 | 106 | 159 | .667 | 197 | 77 | 389 | 5.8 | 2.3 | 11.4 |
| 00-01—NC State ...................... | 26 | 848 | 109 | 267 | .408 | 67 | 94 | .713 | 151 | 69 | 304 | 5.8 | 2.7 | 11.7 |
| 01-02—Georgia.......................... | | | | | Did Not Play - Transfer Student | | | | | | | | | |
| 02-03—Georgia.......................... | 27 | 569 | 65 | 158 | .411 | 67 | 91 | .736 | 79 | 71 | 203 | 2.9 | 2.6 | 7.5 |
| 03-04—Georgia.......................... | 30 | 1056 | 117 | 288 | .406 | 118 | 150 | .787 | 162 | 88 | 379 | 5.4 | 2.9 | 12.6 |
| Totals ...................... | 117 | 3556 | 418 | 1024 | .408 | 358 | 494 | .725 | 589 | 305 | 1275 | 5.0 | 2.6 | 10.9 |

Three-point field goals: 1999-00, 29-for-89 (.326). 2000-01, 19-for-71 (.268). 2002-03, 6-for-22 (.273). 2003-04, 27-for-84 (.321). Totals, 81-for-266 (.305).

### NBA REGULAR-SEASON RECORD

| | | | | | | | | REBOUNDS | | | | | | | | AVERAGES | | |
|---|---|---|---|---|---|---|---|---|---|---|---|---|---|---|---|---|---|---|
| Season Team | G | Min. | FGM | FGA | Pct. | FTM | FTA | Pct. | Off. | Def. | Tot. | Ast. | St. | Blk. | TO | Pts. | RPG | APG | PPG |
| 04-05—Seattle ........... | 29 | 520 | 73 | 168 | .435 | 21 | 34 | .618 | 29 | 37 | 66 | 26 | 22 | 10 | 16 | 183 | 2.3 | 0.9 | 6.3 |

Three-point field goals: 2004-05, 16-for-59 (.271). Totals, 16-for-59 (.271).
Personal fouls/disqualifications: 2004-05, 55/0. Totals, 55/0.

## NBA PLAYOFF RECORD

| Season Team | G | Min. | FGM | FGA | Pct. | FTM | FTA | Pct. | REBOUNDS Off. | Def. | Tot. | Ast. | St. | Blk. | TO | Pts. | AVERAGES RPG | APG | PPG |
|---|---|---|---|---|---|---|---|---|---|---|---|---|---|---|---|---|---|---|---|
| 04-05—Seattle ............ | 7 | 136 | 16 | 36 | .444 | 4 | 9 | .444 | 9 | 9 | 18 | 3 | 10 | 1 | 8 | 39 | 2.6 | 0.4 | 5.6 |

Three-point field goals: 2004-05, 3-for-11 (.273). Totals, 3-for-11 (.273).
Personal fouls/disqualifications: 2004-05, 17/0. Totals, 17/0.

## WILKS, MIKE                     G                     SPURS

**PERSONAL:** Born May 7, 1979, in Milwaukee, Wis. ... 5-11/180. (1.80/81.6).
**HIGH SCHOOL:** Rufus King (Milwaukee, Wis.).
**COLLEGE:** Rice.
**TRANSACTIONS/CAREER NOTES:** Not drafted by an NBA franchise. ... Signed as a free agent by Milwaukee Bucks (August 23, 2002). ... Signed by Atlanta Hawks from NBDL's Huntsville franchise (December 24, 2002). ... Signed by Atlanta Hawks to 10-day contract (January 9, 2003). ... Signed by Hawks to second 10-day contract (January 20, 2003). ... Signed by Minnesota Timberwolves to 10-day contract (February 12, 2003). ... Signed by Timberwolves for remainder of season (February 22, 2003). ... Signed as free agent by Houston Rockets (September 9, 2003). ... Traded by Rockets with G/F Eric Piatkowski and G/F Adrian Griffin to Chicago Bulls for C Dikembe Mutombo (September 8, 2004). ... Waived by Bulls (October 20, 2004). ... Signed as free agent by San Antonio Spurs (October 27, 2004).

### COLLEGIATE RECORD

| Season Team | G | Min. | FGM | FGA | Pct. | FTM | FTA | Pct. | Reb. | Ast. | Pts. | AVERAGES RPG | APG | PPG |
|---|---|---|---|---|---|---|---|---|---|---|---|---|---|---|
| 97-98—Rice ................. | 28 | 617 | 46 | 129 | .357 | 36 | 58 | .621 | 73 | 72 | 135 | 2.6 | 2.6 | 4.8 |
| 98-99—Rice ................. | 28 | 967 | 68 | 174 | .391 | 86 | 125 | .688 | 124 | 116 | 230 | 4.4 | 4.1 | 8.2 |
| 99-00—Rice ................. | 21 | 783 | 112 | 281 | .399 | 71 | 97 | .732 | 84 | 70 | 331 | 4.0 | 3.3 | 15.8 |
| 00-01—Rice ................. | 30 | 1114 | 190 | 434 | .438 | 168 | 215 | .781 | 147 | 90 | 604 | 4.9 | 3.0 | 20.1 |
| Totals ...................... | 107 | 3481 | 416 | 1018 | .409 | 361 | 495 | .729 | 428 | 348 | 1300 | 4.0 | 3.3 | 12.1 |

Three-point field goals: 1997-98, 7-for-23 (.304). 1998-99, 8-for-29 (.276). 1999-00, 36-for-112 (.321). 2000-01, 56-for-145 (.386). Totals, 107-for-309 (.346).

### NBDL RECORD

| Season Team | G | Min. | FGM | FGA | Pct. | FTM | FTA | Pct. | Reb. | Ast. | Pts. | AVERAGES RPG | APG | PPG |
|---|---|---|---|---|---|---|---|---|---|---|---|---|---|---|
| 01-02—Huntsville ...................... | 38 | 1136 | 121 | 292 | .414 | 122 | 155 | .787 | 143 | 172 | 387 | 3.8 | 4.5 | 10.2 |
| 02-03—Huntsville ...................... | 16 | 508 | 60 | 135 | .444 | 44 | 56 | .786 | 60 | 58 | 173 | 3.8 | 3.6 | 10.8 |
| Totals ...................... | 54 | 1644 | 181 | 427 | .424 | 166 | 211 | .787 | 203 | 230 | 560 | 3.8 | 4.3 | 10.4 |

Three-point field goals: 2001-02, 23-for-60 (.383). 2002-03, 9-for-28 (.321). Totals, 32-for-88 (.364).
Personal fouls/disqualifications: 2001-02, 102/0. 2002-03, 34/0. Totals, 136/0.

### NBA REGULAR-SEASON RECORD

| Season Team | G | Min. | FGM | FGA | Pct. | FTM | FTA | Pct. | REBOUNDS Off. | Def. | Tot. | Ast. | St. | Blk. | TO | Pts. | AVERAGES RPG | APG | PPG |
|---|---|---|---|---|---|---|---|---|---|---|---|---|---|---|---|---|---|---|---|
| 02-03—Atl.-Minn......... | 46 | 688 | 50 | 148 | .338 | 37 | 47 | .787 | 20 | 51 | 71 | 92 | 27 | 4 | 28 | 147 | 1.5 | 2.0 | 3.2 |
| 03-04—Houston.......... | 26 | 145 | 17 | 36 | .472 | 10 | 12 | .833 | 3 | 13 | 16 | 17 | 3 | 0 | 7 | 50 | 0.6 | 0.7 | 1.9 |
| 04-05—San Antonio.... | 48 | 278 | 32 | 77 | .416 | 12 | 16 | .750 | 4 | 21 | 25 | 33 | 14 | 1 | 14 | 81 | 0.5 | 0.7 | 1.7 |
| Totals ................... | 120 | 1111 | 99 | 261 | .379 | 59 | 75 | .787 | 27 | 85 | 112 | 142 | 44 | 5 | 49 | 278 | 0.9 | 1.2 | 2.3 |

Three-point field goals: 2002-03, 10-for-35 (.286). 2003-04, 6-for-10 (.600). 2004-05, 5-for-16 (.313). Totals, 21-for-61 (.344).
Personal fouls/disqualifications: 2002-03, 69/0. 2003-04, 15/0. 2004-05, 26/0. Totals, 110/0.

### NBA PLAYOFF RECORD

| Season Team | G | Min. | FGM | FGA | Pct. | FTM | FTA | Pct. | REBOUNDS Off. | Def. | Tot. | Ast. | St. | Blk. | TO | Pts. | AVERAGES RPG | APG | PPG |
|---|---|---|---|---|---|---|---|---|---|---|---|---|---|---|---|---|---|---|---|
| 02-03—Minnesota....... | 4 | 7 | 1 | 2 | .500 | 0 | 0 | ... | 0 | 0 | 0 | 0 | 0 | 0 | 0 | 3 | 0.0 | 0.0 | 0.8 |
| 03-04—Houston......... | 2 | 5 | 0 | 0 | ... | 0 | 0 | ... | 0 | 0 | 0 | 1 | 0 | 0 | 1 | 0 | 0.0 | 0.5 | 0.0 |
| Totals .................. | 6 | 12 | 1 | 2 | .500 | 0 | 0 | ... | 0 | 0 | 0 | 1 | 0 | 0 | 1 | 3 | 0.0 | 0.2 | 0.5 |

Three-point field goals: 2002-03, 1-for-1 (1.000). Totals, 1-for-1 (1.000).

## WILLIAMS, AARON                     F                     RAPTORS

**PERSONAL:** Born October 2, 1971, in Evanston, Ill. ... 6-9/225. (2.06/102.1).
**HIGH SCHOOL:** Rolling Meadows (Ill.).
**COLLEGE:** Xavier.
**TRANSACTIONS/CAREER NOTES:** Not drafted by an NBA franchise. ... Played in Continental Basketball Association with Grand Rapids Hoops (1993-94) and Connecticut Pride (1995-96 and 1996-97). ... Played in Italy (1993-94). ... Signed as free agent by Utah Jazz (November 29, 1993). ... Waived by Jazz (December 27, 1993). ... Signed as free agent by Milwaukee Bucks (October 6, 1994). ... Waived by Bucks (November 7, 1994). ... Re-signed as free agent by Bucks (November 9, 1994). ... Waived by Bucks (March 22, 1995). ... Played in Greece (1995-96). ... Signed as free agent by Denver Nuggets (December 22, 1996). ... Waived by Nuggets (January 6, 1997). ... Signed by Vancouver Grizzlies to first of two consecutive 10-day contracts (January 29, 1997). ... Signed by Grizzlies for remainder of season (February 20, 1997). ... Signed as free agent by Seattle SuperSonics (August 11, 1997). ... Signed as free agent by Washington Wizards (August 17, 1999). ... Signed as free agent by New Jersey Nets (August 5, 2000). ... Traded by Nets with C Alonzo Mourning and F Eric Williams and two first round draft picks to Toronto Raptors for F Vince Carter ( December 17, 2004).

W

## COLLEGIATE RECORD

| Season Team | G | Min. | FGM | FGA | Pct. | FTM | FTA | Pct. | Reb. | Ast. | Pts. | AVERAGES RPG | APG | PPG |
|---|---|---|---|---|---|---|---|---|---|---|---|---|---|---|
| 89-90—Xavier | 28 | 278 | 27 | 47 | .574 | 8 | 20 | .400 | 76 | 6 | 62 | 2.7 | 0.2 | 2.2 |
| 90-91—Xavier | 32 | 858 | 127 | 237 | .536 | 55 | 77 | .714 | 209 | 33 | 309 | 6.5 | 1.0 | 9.7 |
| 91-92—Xavier | 27 | 786 | 148 | 253 | .585 | 79 | 113 | .699 | 215 | 31 | 375 | 8.0 | 1.1 | 13.9 |
| 92-93—Xavier | 30 | 843 | 127 | 247 | .514 | 73 | 94 | .777 | 213 | 54 | 327 | 7.1 | 1.8 | 10.9 |
| Totals | 117 | 2765 | 429 | 771 | .556 | 215 | 304 | .707 | 713 | 124 | 1073 | 6.1 | 1.1 | 9.2 |

## CBA RECORD

**NOTES:** CBA All-Rookie second team (1994).

| Season Team | G | Min. | FGM | FGA | Pct. | FTM | FTA | Pct. | Reb. | Ast. | Pts. | AVERAGES RPG | APG | PPG |
|---|---|---|---|---|---|---|---|---|---|---|---|---|---|---|
| 93-94—Grand Rapids | 43 | 863 | 149 | 267 | .558 | 81 | 105 | .771 | 242 | 38 | 379 | 5.6 | 0.9 | 8.8 |
| 95-96—Connecticut | 13 | 235 | 51 | 90 | .567 | 8 | 16 | .500 | 80 | 4 | 110 | 6.2 | 0.3 | 8.5 |
| 96-97—Connecticut | 25 | 968 | 174 | 316 | .551 | 73 | 101 | .723 | 247 | 42 | 421 | 9.9 | 1.7 | 16.8 |
| Totals | 81 | 2066 | 374 | 673 | .556 | 162 | 222 | .730 | 569 | 84 | 910 | 7.0 | 1.0 | 11.2 |

Three-point field goals: 1993-94, 0-for-2. 1996-97, 0-for-2. Totals, 0-for-4 (.000).
Personal fouls/disqualifications: 1993-94, 106/0. 1995-96, 41/0. 1996-97, 104/0. Totals, 251/0.

## ITALIAN LEAGUE RECORD

| Season Team | G | Min. | FGM | FGA | Pct. | FTM | FTA | Pct. | Reb. | Ast. | Pts. | AVERAGES RPG | APG | PPG |
|---|---|---|---|---|---|---|---|---|---|---|---|---|---|---|
| 93-94—Teorematour Milan | 6 | 208 | 30 | 62 | .484 | 21 | 28 | .750 | 71 | 2 | 83 | 11.8 | 0.3 | 13.8 |

Three-point field goals: 1993-94, 2-for-8 (.250). Totals, 2-for-8 (.250).

## NBA REGULAR-SEASON RECORD

**NOTES:** Led NBA with 319 personal fouls (2001).

| Season Team | G | Min. | FGM | FGA | Pct. | FTM | FTA | Pct. | REBOUNDS Off. | Def. | Tot. | Ast. | St. | Blk. | TO | Pts. | AVERAGES RPG | APG | PPG |
|---|---|---|---|---|---|---|---|---|---|---|---|---|---|---|---|---|---|---|---|
| 93-94—Utah | 6 | 12 | 2 | 8 | .250 | 0 | 1 | .000 | 1 | 2 | 3 | 1 | 0 | 0 | 1 | 4 | 0.5 | 0.2 | 0.7 |
| 94-95—Milwaukee | 15 | 72 | 8 | 24 | .333 | 8 | 12 | .667 | 5 | 14 | 19 | 0 | 2 | 6 | 7 | 24 | 1.3 | 0.0 | 1.6 |
| 96-97—Denver-Van. | 33 | 563 | 85 | 148 | .574 | 33 | 49 | .673 | 62 | 81 | 143 | 15 | 16 | 29 | 32 | 203 | 4.3 | 0.5 | 6.2 |
| 97-98—Seattle | 65 | 757 | 115 | 220 | .523 | 66 | 85 | .776 | 48 | 99 | 147 | 14 | 19 | 38 | 50 | 296 | 2.3 | 0.2 | 4.6 |
| 98-99—Seattle | 40 | 458 | 52 | 123 | .423 | 54 | 74 | .730 | 54 | 74 | 128 | 22 | 14 | 24 | 30 | 158 | 3.2 | 0.6 | 4.0 |
| 99-00—Washington | 81 | 1545 | 235 | 450 | .522 | 146 | 201 | .726 | 159 | 250 | 409 | 58 | 41 | 92 | 80 | 616 | 5.0 | 0.7 | 7.6 |
| 00-01—New Jersey | 82 | 2336 | 297 | 650 | .457 | 244 | 310 | .787 | 211 | 379 | 590 | 88 | 59 | 113 | 132 | 838 | 7.2 | 1.1 | 10.2 |
| 01-02—New Jersey | 82 | 1546 | 231 | 439 | .526 | 130 | 186 | .699 | 115 | 224 | 339 | 77 | 29 | 76 | 79 | 592 | 4.1 | 0.9 | 7.2 |
| 02-03—New Jersey | 81 | 1597 | 199 | 439 | .453 | 102 | 130 | .785 | 137 | 194 | 331 | 88 | 27 | 57 | 85 | 500 | 4.1 | 1.1 | 6.2 |
| 03-04—New Jersey | 72 | 1337 | 172 | 342 | .503 | 105 | 155 | .677 | 101 | 193 | 294 | 81 | 34 | 46 | 89 | 450 | 4.1 | 1.1 | 6.3 |
| 04-05—N.J.-Tor. | 42 | 315 | 29 | 63 | .460 | 15 | 17 | .882 | 17 | 43 | 60 | 8 | 5 | 8 | 17 | 73 | 1.4 | 0.2 | 1.7 |
| Totals | 599 | 10538 | 1425 | 2906 | .490 | 903 | 1220 | .740 | 910 | 1553 | 2463 | 452 | 246 | 489 | 602 | 3754 | 4.1 | 0.8 | 6.3 |

Three-point field goals: 1994-95, 0-for-1. 1996-97, 0-for-1. 1997-98, 0-for-1. 1998-99, 0-for-1. 1999-00, 0-for-3. 2000-01, 0-for-2. 2001-02, 0-for-2. 2002-03, 0-for-1. 2003-04, 1-for-3 (.333). Totals, 1-for-15 (.067).
Personal fouls/disqualifications: 1993-94, 4/0. 1994-95, 14/0. 1996-97, 72/1. 1997-98, 119/0. 1998-99, 75/1. 1999-00, 234/3. 2000-01, 319/9. 2001-02, 212/5. 2002-03, 206/5. 2003-04, 187/0. 2004-05, 70/0. Totals, 1512/24.

## NBA PLAYOFF RECORD

| Season Team | G | Min. | FGM | FGA | Pct. | FTM | FTA | Pct. | REBOUNDS Off. | Def. | Tot. | Ast. | St. | Blk. | TO | Pts. | AVERAGES RPG | APG | PPG |
|---|---|---|---|---|---|---|---|---|---|---|---|---|---|---|---|---|---|---|---|
| 97-98—Seattle | 3 | 7 | 0 | 3 | .000 | 2 | 2 | 1.000 | 1 | 0 | 1 | 0 | 0 | 1 | 1 | 2 | 0.3 | 0.0 | 0.7 |
| 01-02—New Jersey | 20 | 416 | 46 | 96 | .479 | 38 | 46 | .826 | 24 | 46 | 70 | 16 | 8 | 16 | 23 | 130 | 3.5 | 0.8 | 6.5 |
| 02-03—New Jersey | 19 | 340 | 50 | 106 | .472 | 23 | 31 | .742 | 33 | 54 | 87 | 18 | 6 | 17 | 13 | 123 | 4.6 | 0.9 | 6.5 |
| 03-04—New Jersey | 11 | 149 | 18 | 33 | .545 | 6 | 10 | .600 | 7 | 15 | 22 | 4 | 0 | 7 | 15 | 42 | 2.0 | 0.4 | 3.8 |
| Totals | 53 | 912 | 114 | 238 | .479 | 69 | 89 | .775 | 65 | 115 | 180 | 38 | 14 | 41 | 52 | 297 | 3.4 | 0.7 | 5.6 |

Three-point field goals: 2001-02, 0-for-1. Totals, 0-for-1 (.000).
Personal fouls/disqualifications: 2001-02, 78/5. 2002-03, 54/0. 2003-04, 41/2. Totals, 173/7.

## GREEK LEAGUE RECORD

| Season Team | G | Min. | FGM | FGA | Pct. | FTM | FTA | Pct. | Reb. | Ast. | Pts. | AVERAGES RPG | APG | PPG |
|---|---|---|---|---|---|---|---|---|---|---|---|---|---|---|
| 95-96—Ambelokipi | 13 | ... | ... | ... | ... | ... | ... | ... | 111 | 11 | 178 | 8.5 | 0.8 | 13.7 |

**W**

# WILLIAMS, ERIC     F     RAPTORS

**PERSONAL:** Born July 17, 1972, in Newark, N.J. ... 6-8/220. (2.03/99.8). ... Full name: Eric C. Williams.
**HIGH SCHOOL:** M.X. Shabazz (Newark, N.J.).
**JUNIOR COLLEGE:** Burlington County (N.J.) College, then Vincennes (Ind.) University.
**COLLEGE:** Providence.
**TRANSACTIONS/CAREER NOTES:** Selected by Boston Celtics in first round (14th pick overall) of 1995 NBA Draft. ... Traded by Celtics to Denver Nuggets for a second-round draft choice in 1999 and a second-round draft choice in 2001 (August 21, 1997). ... Traded by Nuggets with F Danny Fortson, G Eric Washington and first-round draft choice within the next three years to Celtics for G/F Ron Mercer, F Popeye Jones and C Dwayne Schintzius (August 3, 1999). ... Traded by Celtics with F/C Tony Battie and F Kedrick Brown to Cleveland Cavaliers for G Ricky Davis, F/C Chris Mihm, C Michael Stewart and a second-round draft choice (December 15, 2003). ... Signed as free agent by New Jersey Nets (August 6, 2004). ... Traded by Nets with C Alonzo Mourning, F Aaron Williams and two first round draft picks to Toronto Raptors for F Vince Carter ( December 17, 2004).

## COLLEGIATE RECORD

| Season Team | G | Min. | FGM | FGA | Pct. | FTM | FTA | Pct. | Reb. | Ast. | Pts. | AVERAGES RPG | APG | PPG |
|---|---|---|---|---|---|---|---|---|---|---|---|---|---|---|
| 90-91—Burlington County J.C. | | | | | | | Did not play. | | | | | | | |
| 91-92—Vincennes | 25 | ... | 167 | 271 | .616 | 103 | 154 | .669 | 189 | ... | 437 | 7.6 | ... | 17.5 |

| Season Team | G | Min. | FGM | FGA | Pct. | FTM | FTA | Pct. | Reb. | Ast. | Pts. | RPG | APG | PPG |
|---|---|---|---|---|---|---|---|---|---|---|---|---|---|---|
| 92-93—Vincennes | 35 | ... | 273 | 485 | .563 | 182 | 273 | .667 | 323 | 96 | 729 | 9.2 | 2.7 | 20.8 |
| 93-94—Providence | 30 | 781 | 166 | 327 | .508 | 138 | 209 | .660 | 151 | 37 | 470 | 5.0 | 1.2 | 15.7 |
| 94-95—Providence | 30 | 1041 | 184 | 445 | .413 | 134 | 195 | .687 | 201 | 75 | 531 | 6.7 | 2.5 | 17.7 |
| Junior College Totals | 60 | ... | 440 | 756 | .582 | 285 | 427 | .667 | 512 | 96 | 1166 | 8.5 | 1.6 | 19.4 |
| 4-Year-College Totals | 60 | 1822 | 350 | 772 | .453 | 272 | 404 | .673 | 352 | 112 | 1001 | 5.9 | 1.9 | 16.7 |

Three-point field goals: 1991-92, 0-for-1. 1992-93, 1-for-2 (.500). 1993-94, 0-for-5. 1994-95, 29-for-78 (.372). Totals, 30-for-86 (.349).

## NBA REGULAR-SEASON RECORD

| Season Team | G | Min. | FGM | FGA | Pct. | FTM | FTA | Pct. | REBOUNDS Off. | Def. | Tot. | Ast. | St. | Blk. | TO | Pts. | RPG | APG | PPG |
|---|---|---|---|---|---|---|---|---|---|---|---|---|---|---|---|---|---|---|---|
| 95-96—Boston | 64 | 1470 | 241 | 546 | .441 | 200 | 298 | .671 | 92 | 125 | 217 | 70 | 56 | 11 | 88 | 685 | 3.4 | 1.1 | 10.7 |
| 96-97—Boston | 72 | 2435 | 374 | 820 | .456 | 328 | 436 | .752 | 126 | 203 | 329 | 129 | 72 | 13 | 139 | 1078 | 4.6 | 1.8 | 15.0 |
| 97-98—Denver | 4 | 145 | 24 | 61 | .393 | 31 | 45 | .689 | 10 | 11 | 21 | 12 | 4 | 0 | 9 | 79 | 5.3 | 3.0 | 19.8 |
| 98-99—Denver | 38 | 780 | 80 | 219 | .365 | 111 | 139 | .799 | 34 | 47 | 81 | 37 | 27 | 8 | 49 | 277 | 2.1 | 1.0 | 7.3 |
| 99-00—Boston | 68 | 1378 | 165 | 386 | .427 | 134 | 169 | .793 | 55 | 101 | 156 | 93 | 44 | 16 | 66 | 489 | 2.3 | 1.4 | 7.2 |
| 00-01—Boston | 81 | 1745 | 162 | 448 | .362 | 165 | 231 | .714 | 64 | 143 | 207 | 112 | 64 | 13 | 76 | 535 | 2.6 | 1.4 | 6.6 |
| 01-02—Boston | 74 | 1747 | 144 | 385 | .374 | 160 | 219 | .731 | 58 | 163 | 221 | 109 | 77 | 8 | 95 | 472 | 3.0 | 1.5 | 6.4 |
| 02-03—Boston | 82 | 2350 | 254 | 575 | .442 | 201 | 268 | .750 | 143 | 239 | 382 | 140 | 86 | 19 | 97 | 746 | 4.7 | 1.7 | 9.1 |
| 03-04—Boston-Cleve. | 71 | 1886 | 231 | 598 | .386 | 215 | 283 | .760 | 65 | 221 | 286 | 120 | 70 | 9 | 88 | 712 | 4.0 | 1.7 | 10.0 |
| 04-05—N.J.-Tor. | 55 | 1322 | 142 | 330 | .430 | 112 | 161 | .696 | 44 | 128 | 172 | 92 | 38 | 4 | 60 | 424 | 3.1 | 1.7 | 7.7 |
| Totals | 609 | 15258 | 1817 | 4368 | .416 | 1657 | 2249 | .737 | 691 | 1381 | 2072 | 914 | 538 | 101 | 767 | 5497 | 3.4 | 1.5 | 9.0 |

Three-point field goals: 1995-96, 3-for-10 (.300). 1996-97, 2-for-8 (.250). 1998-99, 6-for-26 (.231). 1999-00, 25-for-72 (.347). 2000-01, 46-for-139 (.331). 2001-02, 24-for-86 (.279). 2002-03, 37-for-110 (.336). 2003-04, 35-for-127 (.276). 2004-05, 28-for-73 (.384). Totals, 206-for-651 (.316).

---

## WILLIAMS, FRANK G BULLS

**PERSONAL:** Born February 25, 1980, in Peoria, Ill. ... 6-3/205. (1.91/93.0). ... Full name: Frank Lowell Williams.
**HIGH SCHOOL:** Peoria Manual (Peoria, Ill.).
**COLLEGE:** Illinois.
**TRANSACTIONS/CAREER NOTES:** Selected after junior season by Denver Nuggets in first round (25th pick overall) of 2002 NBA Draft. ... Draft rights traded by Nuggets with F Antonio McDyess and 2003 second-round draft choice to New York Knicks for F/C Marcus Camby, G Mark Jackson and draft rights to F/C Nene Hilario (June 26, 2002). ... Traded by Knicks with F Othella Harrington, C Dikembe Mutombo and C Cezary Trybanski to Chicago Bulls for G Jamal Crawford and F Jerome Williams (August 5, 2004).

## COLLEGIATE RECORD

| Season Team | G | Min. | FGM | FGA | Pct. | FTM | FTA | Pct. | Reb. | Ast. | Pts. | RPG | APG | PPG |
|---|---|---|---|---|---|---|---|---|---|---|---|---|---|---|
| 98-99—Illinois | | | | | | Did not play—ineligible. | | | | | | | | |
| 99-00—Illinois | 32 | 972 | 125 | 327 | .382 | 74 | 92 | .804 | 110 | 131 | 366 | 3.4 | 4.1 | 11.4 |
| 00-01—Illinois | 34 | 1095 | 168 | 410 | .410 | 133 | 165 | .806 | 126 | 148 | 508 | 3.7 | 4.4 | 14.9 |
| 01-02—Illinois | 35 | 1135 | 174 | 443 | .393 | 164 | 203 | .808 | 163 | 153 | 566 | 4.7 | 4.4 | 16.2 |
| Totals | 101 | 3202 | 467 | 1180 | .396 | 371 | 460 | .807 | 399 | 432 | 1440 | 4.0 | 4.3 | 14.3 |

Three-point field goals: 1999-00, 42-for-133 (.316). 2000-01, 39-for-122 (.320). 2001-02, 54-for-159 (.340). Totals, 135-for-414 (.326).

## NBA REGULAR-SEASON RECORD

| Season Team | G | Min. | FGM | FGA | Pct. | FTM | FTA | Pct. | REBOUNDS Off. | Def. | Tot. | Ast. | St. | Blk. | TO | Pts. | RPG | APG | PPG |
|---|---|---|---|---|---|---|---|---|---|---|---|---|---|---|---|---|---|---|---|
| 02-03—New York | 21 | 167 | 9 | 33 | .273 | 4 | 6 | .667 | 3 | 15 | 18 | 34 | 7 | 2 | 17 | 28 | 0.9 | 1.6 | 1.3 |
| 03-04—New York | 56 | 714 | 80 | 208 | .385 | 41 | 48 | .854 | 8 | 45 | 53 | 121 | 25 | 6 | 63 | 219 | 0.9 | 2.2 | 3.9 |
| 04-05—Chicago | 9 | 71 | 3 | 20 | .150 | 0 | 0 | ... | 2 | 4 | 6 | 11 | 2 | 3 | 3 | 6 | 0.7 | 1.2 | 0.7 |
| Totals | 86 | 952 | 92 | 261 | .352 | 45 | 54 | .833 | 13 | 64 | 77 | 166 | 34 | 11 | 83 | 253 | 0.9 | 1.9 | 2.9 |

Three-point field goals: 2002-03, 6-for-16 (.375). 2003-04, 18-for-60 (.300). 2004-05, 0-for-4. Totals, 24-for-80 (.300).
Personal fouls/disqualifications: 2002-03, 20/0. 2003-04, 58/0. 2004-05, 9/0. Totals, 87/0.

## NBA PLAYOFF RECORD

| Season Team | G | Min. | FGM | FGA | Pct. | FTM | FTA | Pct. | REBOUNDS Off. | Def. | Tot. | Ast. | St. | Blk. | TO | Pts. | RPG | APG | PPG |
|---|---|---|---|---|---|---|---|---|---|---|---|---|---|---|---|---|---|---|---|
| 03-04—New York | 4 | 74 | 6 | 22 | .273 | 3 | 5 | .600 | 1 | 1 | 2 | 5 | 3 | 0 | 4 | 19 | 0.5 | 1.3 | 4.8 |

Three-point field goals: 2003-04, 4-for-13 (.308). Totals, 4-for-13 (.308).
Personal fouls/disqualifications: 2003-04, 13/0. Totals, 13/0.

---

## WILLIAMS, JASON G HEAT

**PERSONAL:** Born November 18, 1975, in Belle, W.Va. ... 6-1/190. (1.85/86.2). ... Full name: Jason Chandler Williams.
**HIGH SCHOOL:** Dupont (Belle, W.Va.).
**COLLEGE:** Marshall, then Florida.
**TRANSACTIONS/CAREER NOTES:** Selected after junior season by Sacramento Kings in first round (seventh pick overall) of 1998 NBA Draft. ... Traded by Kings with G/F Nick Anderson to Vancouver Grizzlies for G Mike Bibby and G Brent Price (June 27, 2001). ... Grizzlies franchise moved to Memphis for 2001-02 season. ... Traded by Grizzlies with F James Posey and G Andre Emmett to Miami Heat in five-team trade (August 2, 2005).

## COLLEGIATE RECORD

| Season Team | G | Min. | FGM | FGA | Pct. | FTM | FTA | Pct. | Reb. | Ast. | Pts. | RPG | APG | PPG |
|---|---|---|---|---|---|---|---|---|---|---|---|---|---|---|
| 94-95—Marshall | | | | | | Did not play—redshirted. | | | | | | | | |
| 95-96—Marshall | 28 | 816 | 144 | 276 | .522 | 52 | 70 | .743 | 99 | 178 | 375 | 3.5 | 6.4 | 13.4 |

W

| Season Team | G | Min. | FGM | FGA | Pct. | FTM | FTA | Pct. | Reb. | Ast. | Pts. | RPG | APG | PPG |
|---|---|---|---|---|---|---|---|---|---|---|---|---|---|---|
| | | | | | | | | | | | | AVERAGES | | |
| 96-97—Florida ........................... | | | | | Did not play—transfer student. | | | | | | | | | |
| 97-98—Florida ........................... | 20 | 635 | 112 | 254 | .441 | 63 | 75 | .840 | 59 | 134 | 341 | 3.0 | 6.7 | 17.1 |
| Totals ................................... | 48 | 1451 | 256 | 530 | .483 | 115 | 145 | .793 | 158 | 312 | 716 | 3.3 | 6.5 | 14.9 |

Three-point field goals: 1995-96, 35-for-92 (.380). 1997-98, 54-for-134 (.403). Totals, 89-for-226 (.394).

**HONORS:** NBA All-Rookie first team (1999).

## NBA REGULAR-SEASON RECORD

| Season Team | G | Min. | FGM | FGA | Pct. | FTM | FTA | Pct. | REBOUNDS Off. | Def. | Tot. | Ast. | St. | Blk. | TO | Pts. | AVERAGES RPG | APG | PPG |
|---|---|---|---|---|---|---|---|---|---|---|---|---|---|---|---|---|---|---|---|
| 98-99—Sacramento .... | 50 | 1805 | 231 | 617 | .374 | 79 | 105 | .752 | 14 | 139 | 153 | 299 | 95 | 1 | 143 | 641 | 3.1 | 6.0 | 12.8 |
| 99-00—Sacramento .... | 81 | 2760 | 363 | 973 | .373 | 128 | 170 | .753 | 22 | 208 | 230 | 589 | 117 | 8 | 296 | 999 | 2.8 | 7.3 | 12.3 |
| 00-01—Sacramento .... | 77 | 2290 | 281 | 690 | .407 | 60 | 76 | .789 | 19 | 166 | 185 | 416 | 94 | 9 | 160 | 720 | 2.4 | 5.4 | 9.4 |
| 01-02—Memphis ........ | 65 | 2236 | 376 | 985 | .382 | 80 | 101 | .792 | 22 | 173 | 195 | 519 | 111 | 7 | 214 | 959 | 3.0 | 8.0 | 14.8 |
| 02-03—Memphis ........ | 76 | 2407 | 333 | 859 | .388 | 110 | 131 | .840 | 25 | 187 | 212 | 631 | 91 | 10 | 168 | 919 | 2.8 | 8.3 | 12.1 |
| 03-04—Memphis ........ | 72 | 2115 | 290 | 713 | .407 | 82 | 98 | .837 | 25 | 122 | 147 | 492 | 92 | 5 | 136 | 782 | 2.0 | 6.8 | 10.9 |
| 04-05—Memphis ........ | 71 | 1952 | 266 | 644 | .413 | 80 | 101 | .792 | 19 | 103 | 122 | 399 | 75 | 5 | 130 | 719 | 1.7 | 5.6 | 10.1 |
| Totals ................... | 492 | 15565 | 2140 | 5481 | .390 | 619 | 782 | .792 | 146 | 1098 | 1244 | 3345 | 675 | 45 | 1247 | 5739 | 2.5 | 6.8 | 11.7 |

Three-point field goals: 1998-99, 100-for-323 (.310). 1999-00, 145-for-505 (.287). 2000-01, 98-for-311 (.315). 2001-02, 127-for-430 (.295). 2002-03, 143-for-404 (.354). 2003-04, 120-for-364 (.330). 2004-05, 107-for-330 (.324). Totals, 840-for-2667 (.315).

Personal fouls/disqualifications: 1998-99, 91/0. 1999-00, 140/0. 2000-01, 114/0. 2001-02, 102/0. 2002-03, 130/0. 2003-04, 97/0. 2004-05, 91/0. Totals, 765/0.

## NBA PLAYOFF RECORD

| Season Team | G | Min. | FGM | FGA | Pct. | FTM | FTA | Pct. | REBOUNDS Off. | Def. | Tot. | Ast. | St. | Blk. | TO | Pts. | AVERAGES RPG | APG | PPG |
|---|---|---|---|---|---|---|---|---|---|---|---|---|---|---|---|---|---|---|---|
| 98-99—Sacramento .... | 5 | 163 | 16 | 45 | .356 | 9 | 9 | 1.000 | 2 | 16 | 18 | 20 | 8 | 1 | 13 | 50 | 3.6 | 4.0 | 10.0 |
| 99-00—Sacramento .... | 5 | 145 | 18 | 48 | .375 | 8 | 10 | .800 | 1 | 7 | 8 | 12 | 3 | 0 | 8 | 52 | 1.6 | 2.4 | 10.4 |
| 00-01—Sacramento .... | 8 | 191 | 26 | 61 | .426 | 7 | 7 | 1.000 | 0 | 18 | 18 | 23 | 8 | 0 | 21 | 70 | 2.3 | 2.9 | 8.8 |
| 03-04—Memphis ........ | 4 | 130 | 15 | 46 | .326 | 7 | 7 | 1.000 | 1 | 8 | 9 | 18 | 2 | 0 | 7 | 43 | 2.3 | 4.5 | 10.8 |
| 04-05—Memphis ........ | 4 | 114 | 28 | 53 | .528 | 2 | 2 | 1.000 | 1 | 8 | 9 | 21 | 6 | 0 | 8 | 68 | 2.3 | 5.3 | 17.0 |
| Totals ................... | 26 | 743 | 103 | 253 | .407 | 33 | 35 | .943 | 5 | 57 | 62 | 94 | 27 | 1 | 57 | 283 | 2.4 | 3.6 | 10.9 |

Three-point field goals: 1998-99, 9-for-29 (.310). 1999-00, 8-for-25 (.320). 2000-01, 11-for-30 (.367). 2003-04, 6-for-21 (.286). 2004-05, 10-for-21 (.476). Totals, 44-for-126 (.349).

Personal fouls/disqualifications: 1998-99, 15/0. 1999-00, 8/0. 2000-01, 14/0. 2003-04, 10/0. 2004-05, 7/0. Totals, 54/0.

# WILLIAMS, JEROME          F

**PERSONAL:** Born May 10, 1973, in Washington, D.C. ... 6-9/206. (2.06/93.4).
**HIGH SCHOOL:** Magruder (Germantown, Md.).
**JUNIOR COLLEGE:** Montgomery College (Md.).
**COLLEGE:** Georgetown.
**TRANSACTIONS/CAREER NOTES:** Selected by Detroit Pistons in first round (26th pick overall) of 1996 NBA Draft. ... Traded by Pistons with C Eric Montross to Toronto Raptors for F Corliss Williamson, F Tyrone Corbin, F Kornel David and future first-round draft choice (February 22, 2001). ... Traded by Raptors with F/C Antonio Davis and F Chris Jefferies to Chicago Bulls for F Lonny Baxter, F Donyell Marshall and G Jalen Rose (December 1, 2003). ... Traded by Bulls with G Jamal Crawford to New York Knicks for F Othella Harrington, C Dikembe Mutombo, C Cezary Trybanski and G Frank Williams (August 5, 2004). ... Waived by Knicks (August 15, 2005).

## COLLEGIATE RECORD

| Season Team | G | Min. | FGM | FGA | Pct. | FTM | FTA | Pct. | Reb. | Ast. | Pts. | AVERAGES RPG | APG | PPG |
|---|---|---|---|---|---|---|---|---|---|---|---|---|---|---|
| 92-93—Montgomery College...... | | | | | | Statistics unavailable. | | | | | | | | |
| 93-94—Montgomery College...... | | | | | | Statistics unavailable. | | | | | | | | |
| 94-95—Georgetown.................. | 31 | 939 | 126 | 252 | .500 | 83 | 132 | .629 | 310 | 45 | 337 | 10.0 | 1.5 | 10.9 |
| 95-96—Georgetown.................. | 37 | 1016 | 147 | 250 | .588 | 85 | 133 | .639 | 324 | 51 | 380 | 8.8 | 1.4 | 10.3 |
| Totals ....................................... | 68 | 1955 | 273 | 502 | .544 | 168 | 265 | .634 | 634 | 96 | 717 | 9.3 | 1.4 | 10.5 |

Three-point field goals: 1994-95, 2-for-11 (.182). 1995-96, 1-for-7 (.143). Totals, 3-for-18 (.167).

## NBA REGULAR-SEASON RECORD

| Season Team | G | Min. | FGM | FGA | Pct. | FTM | FTA | Pct. | REBOUNDS Off. | Def. | Tot. | Ast. | St. | Blk. | TO | Pts. | AVERAGES RPG | APG | PPG |
|---|---|---|---|---|---|---|---|---|---|---|---|---|---|---|---|---|---|---|---|
| 96-97—Detroit ........... | 33 | 177 | 20 | 51 | .392 | 9 | 17 | .529 | 22 | 28 | 50 | 7 | 13 | 1 | 13 | 49 | 1.5 | 0.2 | 1.5 |
| 97-98—Detroit ........... | 77 | 1305 | 151 | 288 | .524 | 108 | 166 | .651 | 170 | 209 | 379 | 48 | 51 | 10 | 60 | 410 | 4.9 | 0.6 | 5.3 |
| 98-99—Detroit ........... | 50 | 1154 | 124 | 248 | .500 | 107 | 159 | .673 | 158 | 191 | 349 | 23 | 63 | 7 | 41 | 355 | 7.0 | 0.5 | 7.1 |
| 99-00—Detroit ........... | 82 | 2102 | 257 | 456 | .564 | 175 | 284 | .616 | 277 | 512 | 789 | 68 | 95 | 21 | 105 | 689 | 9.6 | 0.8 | 8.4 |
| 00-01—Det.-Toronto ... | 59 | 1182 | 136 | 294 | .463 | 100 | 135 | .741 | 133 | 249 | 382 | 45 | 57 | 20 | 63 | 372 | 6.5 | 0.8 | 6.3 |
| 01-02—Toronto .......... | 68 | 1641 | 190 | 388 | .490 | 138 | 204 | .676 | 165 | 221 | 386 | 75 | 78 | 25 | 68 | 518 | 5.7 | 1.1 | 7.6 |
| 02-03—Toronto .......... | 71 | 2346 | 267 | 535 | .499 | 156 | 281 | .555 | 231 | 419 | 650 | 95 | 116 | 26 | 98 | 691 | 9.2 | 1.3 | 9.7 |
| 03-04—Tor.-Chi. ........ | 68 | 1637 | 158 | 336 | .470 | 106 | 155 | .684 | 177 | 298 | 475 | 72 | 90 | 8 | 74 | 422 | 7.0 | 1.1 | 6.2 |
| 04-05—New York ....... | 79 | 1211 | 122 | 243 | .502 | 115 | 172 | .669 | 115 | 168 | 283 | 41 | 55 | 10 | 65 | 359 | 3.6 | 0.5 | 4.5 |
| Totals ................... | 587 | 12755 | 1425 | 2839 | .502 | 1014 | 1573 | .645 | 1448 | 2295 | 3743 | 474 | 618 | 128 | 587 | 3865 | 6.4 | 0.8 | 6.6 |

Three-point field goals: 1997-98, 0-for-1. 1999-00, 0-for-3. 2000-01, 0-for-3. 2002-03, 1-for-6 (.167). 2003-04, 0-for-8. 2004-05, 0-for-5. Totals, 1-for-26 (.038).

Personal fouls/disqualifications: 1996-97, 18/0. 1997-98, 144/1. 1998-99, 108/0. 1999-00, 196/0. 2000-01, 124/0. 2001-02, 153/0. 2002-03, 197/2. 2003-04, 134/0. 2004-05, 155/0. Totals, 1229/3.

## NBA PLAYOFF RECORD

| Season Team | G | Min. | FGM | FGA | Pct. | FTM | FTA | Pct. | REBOUNDS Off. | Def. | Tot. | Ast. | St. | Blk. | TO | Pts. | AVERAGES RPG | APG | PPG |
|---|---|---|---|---|---|---|---|---|---|---|---|---|---|---|---|---|---|---|---|
| 96-97—Detroit ........... | 1 | 5 | 2 | 2 | 1.000 | 0 | 0 | ... | 0 | 3 | 3 | 0 | 1 | 0 | 1 | 4 | 3.0 | 0.0 | 4.0 |

| Season Team | G | Min. | FGM | FGA | Pct. | FTM | FTA | Pct. | REBOUNDS Off. | Def. | Tot. | Ast. | St. | Blk. | TO | Pts. | RPG | APG | PPG |
|---|---|---|---|---|---|---|---|---|---|---|---|---|---|---|---|---|---|---|---|
| 98-99—Detroit | 5 | 123 | 12 | 27 | .444 | 7 | 9 | .778 | 12 | 20 | 32 | 4 | 4 | 0 | 4 | 31 | 6.4 | 0.8 | 6.2 |
| 99-00—Detroit | 3 | 73 | 7 | 14 | .500 | 1 | 8 | .125 | 7 | 14 | 21 | 2 | 3 | 0 | 3 | 15 | 7.0 | 0.7 | 5.0 |
| 00-01—Toronto | 11 | 164 | 12 | 24 | .500 | 11 | 22 | .500 | 20 | 25 | 45 | 9 | 10 | 6 | 6 | 35 | 4.1 | 0.8 | 3.2 |
| 01-02—Toronto | 5 | 143 | 14 | 33 | .424 | 8 | 12 | .667 | 16 | 17 | 33 | 7 | 9 | 1 | 4 | 36 | 6.6 | 1.4 | 7.2 |
| Totals | 25 | 508 | 47 | 100 | .470 | 27 | 51 | .529 | 55 | 79 | 134 | 22 | 27 | 7 | 18 | 121 | 5.4 | 0.9 | 4.8 |

Personal fouls/disqualifications: 1998-99, 7/0. 1999-00, 8/0. 2000-01, 23/0. 2001-02, 19/0. Totals, 57/0.

# WILLIAMS, MAURICE　　　　　G　　　　　BUCKS

**PERSONAL:** Born December 19, 1982, in Jackson, Miss. ... 6-1/185. (1.85/83.9).
**HIGH SCHOOL:** William B.Murrah (Jackson, MS).
**COLLEGE:** Alabama.
**TRANSACTIONS/CAREER NOTES:** Selected after sophomore season by Utah Jazz in second round (47th pick overall) of 2003 NBA Draft. ... Signed as free agent by Milwaukee Bucks (August 21, 2004).

**NOTES:** The Sporting News Freshman of the Year (2002).

### COLLEGIATE RECORD

| Season Team | G | Min. | FGM | FGA | Pct. | FTM | FTA | Pct. | Reb. | Ast. | Pts. | RPG | APG | PPG |
|---|---|---|---|---|---|---|---|---|---|---|---|---|---|---|
| 01-02—Alabama | 35 | 1121 | 123 | 327 | .376 | 84 | 98 | .857 | 137 | 159 | 363 | 3.9 | 4.5 | 10.4 |
| 02-03—Alabama | 29 | 1038 | 160 | 371 | .431 | 98 | 117 | .838 | 113 | 112 | 475 | 3.9 | 3.9 | 16.4 |
| Totals | 64 | 2159 | 283 | 698 | .405 | 182 | 215 | .847 | 250 | 271 | 838 | 3.9 | 4.2 | 13.1 |

Three-point field goals: 2001-02, 33-for-126 (.262). 2002-03, 57-for-180 (.317). Totals, 90-for-306 (.294).

### NBA REGULAR-SEASON RECORD

| Season Team | G | Min. | FGM | FGA | Pct. | FTM | FTA | Pct. | REBOUNDS Off. | Def. | Tot. | Ast. | St. | Blk. | TO | Pts. | RPG | APG | PPG |
|---|---|---|---|---|---|---|---|---|---|---|---|---|---|---|---|---|---|---|---|
| 03-04—Utah | 57 | 772 | 115 | 303 | .380 | 44 | 56 | .786 | 23 | 49 | 72 | 76 | 28 | 2 | 51 | 284 | 1.3 | 1.3 | 5.0 |
| 04-05—Milwaukee | 80 | 2254 | 323 | 737 | .438 | 136 | 160 | .850 | 50 | 194 | 244 | 484 | 74 | 11 | 196 | 814 | 3.1 | 6.1 | 10.2 |
| Totals | 137 | 3026 | 438 | 1040 | .421 | 180 | 216 | .833 | 73 | 243 | 316 | 560 | 102 | 13 | 247 | 1098 | 2.3 | 4.1 | 8.0 |

Three-point field goals: 2003-04, 10-for-39 (.256). 2004-05, 32-for-99 (.323). Totals, 42-for-138 (.304).
Personal fouls/disqualifications: 2003-04, 87/0. 2004-05, 221/3. Totals, 308/3.

# WILLIAMS, SCOTT　　　　　C/F

**PERSONAL:** Born March 21, 1968, in Hacienda Heights, Calif. ... 6-10/245. (2.08/111.1). ... Full name: Scott Christopher Williams
**HIGH SCHOOL:** Woodrow Wilson (Los Angeles).
**COLLEGE:** North Carolina.
**TRANSACTIONS/CAREER NOTES:** Not drafted by an NBA franchise. ... Signed as free agent by Chicago Bulls (July 20, 1990). ... Signed as unrestricted free agent by Philadelphia 76ers (July 28, 1994). ... Traded by 76ers with F Tim Thomas to Milwaukee Bucks for F Tyrone Hill and F/G Jerald Honeycutt (March 11, 1999). ... Traded by Bucks with future first-round draft choice to Denver Nuggets for C Aleksander Radojevic and F/C Kevin Willis (October 22, 2001). ... Signed as free agent by Phoenix Suns (July 19, 2002). ... Waived by Suns (January 28, 2004). ... Signed as free agent by Dallas Mavericks (January 30, 2004). ... Signed as free agent by Cleveland Cavaliers (September 28, 2004).
**MISCELLANEOUS:** Member of NBA championship team (1991, 1992, 1993).

### COLLEGIATE RECORD

| Season Team | G | Min. | FGM | FGA | Pct. | FTM | FTA | Pct. | Reb. | Ast. | Pts. | RPG | APG | PPG |
|---|---|---|---|---|---|---|---|---|---|---|---|---|---|---|
| 86-87—North Carolina | 36 | 540 | 78 | 157 | .497 | 43 | 77 | .558 | 150 | 31 | 199 | 4.2 | 0.9 | 5.5 |
| 87-88—North Carolina | 34 | 900 | 162 | 283 | .572 | 107 | 159 | .673 | 217 | 42 | 434 | 6.4 | 1.2 | 12.8 |
| 88-89—North Carolina | 35 | 802 | 165 | 297 | .556 | 68 | 104 | .654 | 254 | 26 | 398 | 7.3 | 0.7 | 11.4 |
| 89-90—North Carolina | 33 | 813 | 190 | 343 | .554 | 96 | 156 | .615 | 240 | 25 | 477 | 7.3 | 0.8 | 14.5 |
| Totals | 138 | 3055 | 595 | 1080 | .551 | 314 | 496 | .633 | 861 | 124 | 1508 | 6.2 | 0.9 | 10.9 |

Three-point field goals: 1986-87, 0-for-1. 1987-88, 3-for-7 (.429). 1988-89, 0-for-2. 1989-90, 1-for-7 (.143). Totals, 4-for-17 (.235).
Personal fouls/disqualifications: 1989-90, 114/6. Totals, 114/6.

### NBA REGULAR-SEASON RECORD

| Season Team | G | Min. | FGM | FGA | Pct. | FTM | FTA | Pct. | REBOUNDS Off. | Def. | Tot. | Ast. | St. | Blk. | TO | Pts. | RPG | APG | PPG |
|---|---|---|---|---|---|---|---|---|---|---|---|---|---|---|---|---|---|---|---|
| 90-91—Chicago | 51 | 337 | 53 | 104 | .510 | 20 | 28 | .714 | 42 | 56 | 98 | 16 | 12 | 13 | 23 | 127 | 1.9 | 0.3 | 2.5 |
| 91-92—Chicago | 63 | 690 | 83 | 172 | .483 | 48 | 74 | .649 | 90 | 157 | 247 | 50 | 13 | 36 | 35 | 214 | 3.9 | 0.8 | 3.4 |
| 92-93—Chicago | 71 | 1369 | 166 | 356 | .466 | 90 | 126 | .714 | 168 | 283 | 451 | 68 | 55 | 66 | 73 | 422 | 6.4 | 1.0 | 5.9 |
| 93-94—Chicago | 38 | 638 | 114 | 236 | .483 | 60 | 98 | .612 | 69 | 112 | 181 | 39 | 16 | 21 | 44 | 289 | 4.8 | 1.0 | 7.6 |
| 94-95—Philadelphia | 77 | 1781 | 206 | 434 | .475 | 79 | 107 | .738 | 173 | 312 | 485 | 59 | 71 | 40 | 84 | 491 | 6.3 | 0.8 | 6.4 |
| 95-96—Philadelphia | 13 | 193 | 15 | 29 | .517 | 10 | 12 | .833 | 13 | 33 | 46 | 5 | 4 | 7 | 8 | 40 | 3.5 | 0.4 | 3.1 |
| 96-97—Philadelphia | 62 | 1317 | 162 | 318 | .509 | 38 | 55 | .691 | 155 | 242 | 397 | 41 | 44 | 41 | 50 | 362 | 6.4 | 0.7 | 5.8 |
| 97-98—Philadelphia | 58 | 801 | 93 | 213 | .437 | 51 | 63 | .810 | 87 | 124 | 211 | 29 | 17 | 21 | 30 | 237 | 3.6 | 0.5 | 4.1 |
| 98-99—Phila.-Mil. | 7 | 46 | 5 | 17 | .294 | 4 | 7 | .571 | 3 | 11 | 14 | 1 | 3 | 2 | 4 | 14 | 2.0 | 0.1 | 2.0 |
| 99-00—Milwaukee | 68 | 1488 | 213 | 426 | .500 | 94 | 129 | .729 | 177 | 271 | 448 | 28 | 40 | 66 | 65 | 520 | 6.6 | 0.4 | 7.6 |
| 00-01—Milwaukee | 66 | 1272 | 171 | 361 | .474 | 60 | 70 | .857 | 97 | 267 | 364 | 35 | 48 | 32 | 41 | 403 | 5.5 | 0.5 | 6.1 |
| 01-02—Denver | 41 | 737 | 86 | 217 | .396 | 30 | 41 | .732 | 82 | 127 | 209 | 13 | 17 | 33 | 35 | 202 | 5.1 | 0.3 | 4.9 |
| 02-03—Phoenix | 69 | 872 | 120 | 292 | .411 | 33 | 42 | .786 | 72 | 121 | 193 | 22 | 27 | 21 | 32 | 273 | 2.8 | 0.3 | 4.0 |
| 03-04—Pho.-Dal. | 43 | 527 | 90 | 186 | .484 | 16 | 27 | .593 | 38 | 94 | 132 | 17 | 20 | 16 | 16 | 198 | 3.1 | 0.4 | 4.6 |
| 04-05—Cleveland | 19 | 152 | 12 | 41 | .293 | 9 | 11 | .818 | 15 | 15 | 30 | 8 | 4 | 6 | 5 | 33 | 1.6 | 0.4 | 1.7 |
| Totals | 746 | 12220 | 1589 | 3402 | .467 | 642 | 890 | .721 | 1281 | 2225 | 3506 | 431 | 393 | 421 | 545 | 3825 | 4.7 | 0.6 | 5.1 |

Three-point field goals: 1990-91, 1-for-2 (.500). 1991-92, 0-for-3. 1992-93, 0-for-7. 1993-94, 1-for-5 (.200). 1994-95, 0-for-7. 1995-96, 0-for-2. 1996-97, 0-for-2. 1997-98, 0-for-5. 2000-01, 1-for-4 (.250). 2001-02, 0-for-2. 2002-03, 0-for-2. 2003-04, 2-for-3 (.667). 2004-05, 0-for-1. Totals, 5-for-45 (.111).
Personal fouls/disqualifications: 1990-91, 51/0. 1991-92, 122/0. 1992-93, 230/3. 1993-94, 112/1. 1994-95, 237/4. 1995-96, 27/0. 1996-97, 206/5. 1997-98, 132/0. 1998-99, 9/0. 1999-00, 230/3. 2000-01, 178/1. 2001-02, 98/1. 2002-03, 159/2. 2003-04, 95/0. Totals, 1916/20.

### NBA PLAYOFF RECORD

| Season Team | G | Min. | FGM | FGA | Pct. | FTM | FTA | Pct. | REBOUNDS Off. | Def. | Tot. | Ast. | St. | Blk. | TO | Pts. | RPG | APG | PPG |
|---|---|---|---|---|---|---|---|---|---|---|---|---|---|---|---|---|---|---|---|
| 90-91—Chicago | 12 | 72 | 6 | 13 | .462 | 11 | 20 | .550 | 4 | 16 | 20 | 3 | 1 | 3 | 4 | 23 | 1.7 | 0.3 | 1.9 |

| Season Team | G | Min. | FGM | FGA | Pct. | FTM | FTA | Pct. | REBOUNDS Off. | Def. | Tot. | Ast. | St. | Blk. | TO | Pts. | AVERAGES RPG | APG | PPG |
|---|---|---|---|---|---|---|---|---|---|---|---|---|---|---|---|---|---|---|---|
| 91-92—Chicago ......... | 22 | 321 | 34 | 70 | .486 | 20 | 28 | .714 | 33 | 62 | 95 | 7 | 6 | 18 | 15 | 88 | 4.3 | 0.3 | 4.0 |
| 92-93—Chicago ......... | 19 | 395 | 44 | 87 | .506 | 16 | 29 | .552 | 40 | 71 | 111 | 26 | 7 | 17 | 24 | 104 | 5.8 | 1.4 | 5.5 |
| 93-94—Chicago ......... | 10 | 151 | 24 | 57 | .421 | 15 | 21 | .714 | 15 | 24 | 39 | 7 | 7 | 3 | 9 | 63 | 3.9 | 0.7 | 6.3 |
| 99-00—Milwaukee ..... | 5 | 93 | 23 | 36 | .639 | 5 | 6 | .833 | 9 | 19 | 28 | 2 | 2 | 5 | 4 | 51 | 5.6 | 0.4 | 10.2 |
| 00-01—Milwaukee ..... | 17 | 378 | 59 | 120 | .492 | 16 | 28 | .571 | 45 | 77 | 122 | 12 | 11 | 24 | 12 | 134 | 7.2 | 0.7 | 7.9 |
| 02-03—Phoenix ......... | 6 | 83 | 11 | 32 | .344 | 2 | 2 | 1.000 | 6 | 9 | 15 | 1 | 4 | 3 | 1 | 24 | 2.5 | 0.2 | 4.0 |
| 03-04—Dallas.............. | 3 | 11 | 0 | 4 | .000 | 0 | 0 | | 0 | 2 | 2 | 4 | 0 | 0 | 1 | 0 | 1.3 | 0.0 | 0.0 |
| Totals ........................ | 94 | 1504 | 201 | 419 | .480 | 85 | 134 | .634 | 154 | 280 | 434 | 58 | 38 | 74 | 69 | 487 | 4.6 | 0.6 | 5.2 |

Three-point field goals: 1990-91, 0-for-1. 1991-92, 0-for-1. 1992-93, 0-for-2. Totals, 0-for-4 (.000).
Personal fouls/disqualifications: 1990-91, 15/0. 1991-92, 65/0. 1992-93, 58/2. 1993-94, 23/0. 1999-00, 16/0. 2000-01, 57/1. 2002-03, 17/0. 2003-04, 3/0. Totals, 254/3.

## WILLIAMSON, CORLISS        F        KINGS

**PERSONAL:** Born December 4, 1973, in Russellville, Ark. ... 6-7/245. (2.01/111.1). ... Full name: Corliss Mondari Williamson
**HIGH SCHOOL:** Russellville (Ark.).
**COLLEGE:** Arkansas.
**TRANSACTIONS/CAREER NOTES:** Selected after junior season by Sacramento Kings in first round (13th pick overall) of 1995 NBA Draft. ... Traded by Kings to Toronto Raptors for G/F Doug Christie (September 29, 2000). ... Traded by Raptors with F Tyrone Corbin, F Kornel David and future first-round draft choice to Detroit Pistons for F Jerome Williams and C Eric Montross (February 22, 2001). ... Traded by Pistons to Philadelphia 76ers for F Derrick Coleman and F/C Amal McCaskill (August 4, 2004). ... Traded by 76ers with F Kenny Thomas and C Brian Skinner to Sacramento Kings for Fs Chris Webber, Michael Bradley and Matt Barnes (February 23, 2005).
**MISCELLANEOUS:** Member of NBA championship team (2004).

### COLLEGIATE RECORD

**NOTES:** Member of NCAA Division I championship team (1994). ... THE SPORTING NEWS All-America first team (1995). ... NCAA Division I Tournament Most Outstanding Player (1994).

| Season Team | G | Min. | FGM | FGA | Pct. | FTM | FTA | Pct. | Reb. | Ast. | Pts. | AVERAGES RPG | APG | PPG |
|---|---|---|---|---|---|---|---|---|---|---|---|---|---|---|
| 92-93—Arkansas ...................... | 18 | 454 | 101 | 176 | .574 | 61 | 98 | .622 | 92 | 30 | 263 | 5.1 | 1.7 | 14.6 |
| 93-94—Arkansas ...................... | 34 | 989 | 273 | 436 | .626 | 149 | 213 | .700 | 262 | 74 | 695 | 7.7 | 2.2 | 20.4 |
| 94-95—Arkansas ...................... | 39 | 1208 | 283 | 515 | .550 | 203 | 304 | .668 | 293 | 89 | 770 | 7.5 | 2.3 | 19.7 |
| Totals ...................................... | 91 | 2651 | 657 | 1127 | .583 | 413 | 615 | .672 | 647 | 193 | 1728 | 7.1 | 2.1 | 19.0 |

Three-point field goals: 1994-95, 1-for-6 (.167). Totals, 1-for-6 (.167).

### NBA REGULAR-SEASON RECORD

**HONORS:** NBA Sixth Man Award (2002).

| Season Team | G | Min. | FGM | FGA | Pct. | FTM | FTA | Pct. | REBOUNDS Off. | Def. | Tot. | Ast. | St. | Blk. | TO | Pts. | AVERAGES RPG | APG | PPG |
|---|---|---|---|---|---|---|---|---|---|---|---|---|---|---|---|---|---|---|---|
| 95-96—Sacramento .... | 53 | 609 | 125 | 268 | .466 | 47 | 84 | .560 | 56 | 58 | 114 | 23 | 11 | 9 | 76 | 297 | 2.2 | 0.4 | 5.6 |
| 96-97—Sacramento .... | 79 | 1992 | 371 | 745 | .498 | 173 | 251 | .689 | 139 | 187 | 326 | 124 | 60 | 49 | 157 | 915 | 4.1 | 1.6 | 11.6 |
| 97-98—Sacramento .... | 79 | 2819 | 561 | 1134 | .495 | 279 | 443 | .630 | 162 | 284 | 446 | 230 | 76 | 48 | 199 | 1401 | 5.6 | 2.9 | 17.7 |
| 98-99—Sacramento .... | 50 | 1374 | 269 | 555 | .485 | 120 | 188 | .638 | 85 | 121 | 206 | 66 | 30 | 8 | 75 | 659 | 4.1 | 1.3 | 13.2 |
| 99-00—Sacramento .... | 76 | 1707 | 311 | 622 | .500 | 163 | 212 | .769 | 122 | 168 | 290 | 82 | 38 | 19 | 110 | 785 | 3.8 | 1.1 | 10.3 |
| 00-01—Sacra.-Det. ..... | 69 | 1686 | 325 | 647 | .502 | 151 | 237 | .637 | 110 | 211 | 321 | 61 | 50 | 21 | 110 | 801 | 4.7 | 0.9 | 11.6 |
| 01-02—Detroit ........... | 78 | 1701 | 411 | 806 | .510 | 240 | 298 | .805 | 117 | 202 | 319 | 94 | 49 | 26 | 137 | 1063 | 4.4 | 1.2 | 13.6 |
| 02-03—Detroit ........... | 82 | 2061 | 374 | 826 | .453 | 237 | 300 | .790 | 147 | 211 | 358 | 104 | 44 | 27 | 126 | 987 | 4.4 | 1.3 | 12.0 |
| 03-04—Detroit ........... | 79 | 1574 | 304 | 602 | .505 | 144 | 197 | .731 | 88 | 168 | 256 | 57 | 30 | 20 | 113 | 752 | 3.2 | 0.7 | 9.5 |
| 04-05—Phila.-Sac. ..... | 72 | 1527 | 273 | 584 | .467 | 195 | 244 | .799 | 104 | 155 | 259 | 78 | 38 | 15 | 86 | 741 | 3.6 | 1.1 | 10.3 |
| Totals ...................... | 717 | 17050 | 3324 | 6789 | .490 | 1749 | 2454 | .713 | 1130 | 1765 | 2895 | 919 | 426 | 242 | 1189 | 8401 | 4.0 | 1.3 | 11.7 |

Three-point field goals: 1995-96, 0-for-3. 1996-97, 0-for-3. 1997-98, 0-for-9. 1998-99, 1-for-5 (.200). 2000-01, 0-for-2. 2001-02, 1-for-5 (.200). 2002-03, 2-for-11 (.182). 2004-05, 0-for-2. Totals, 4-for-40 (.100).
Personal fouls/disqualifications: 1995-96, 115/2. 1996-97, 263/4. 1997-98, 252/4. 1998-99, 118/1. 1999-00, 192/0. 2000-01, 185/0. 2001-02, 226/1. 2002-03, 238/1. 2003-04, 204/2. 2004-05, 218/3. Totals, 2011/18.

### NBA PLAYOFF RECORD

| Season Team | G | Min. | FGM | FGA | Pct. | FTM | FTA | Pct. | REBOUNDS Off. | Def. | Tot. | Ast. | St. | Blk. | TO | Pts. | AVERAGES RPG | APG | PPG |
|---|---|---|---|---|---|---|---|---|---|---|---|---|---|---|---|---|---|---|---|
| 95-96—Sacramento .... | 1 | 2 | 0 | 1 | .000 | 1 | 1 | 1.000 | 0 | 0 | 0 | 0 | 0 | 0 | 1 | 1 | 0.0 | 0.0 | 1.0 |
| 98-99—Sacramento .... | 5 | 130 | 23 | 40 | .575 | 7 | 10 | .700 | 7 | 9 | 16 | 6 | 2 | 1 | 6 | 53 | 3.2 | 1.2 | 10.6 |
| 99-00—Sacramento .... | 5 | 87 | 11 | 16 | .688 | 11 | 12 | .917 | 4 | 11 | 15 | 1 | 1 | 0 | 5 | 33 | 3.0 | 0.2 | 6.6 |
| 01-02—Detroit ........... | 10 | 269 | 52 | 112 | .464 | 29 | 38 | .763 | 19 | 34 | 53 | 10 | 9 | 2 | 22 | 133 | 5.3 | 1.0 | 13.3 |
| 02-03—Detroit ........... | 15 | 233 | 37 | 90 | .411 | 43 | 58 | .741 | 13 | 20 | 33 | 15 | 4 | 3 | 20 | 117 | 2.2 | 1.0 | 7.8 |
| 03-04—Detroit ........... | 22 | 327 | 44 | 121 | .364 | 38 | 47 | .809 | 20 | 29 | 49 | 15 | 6 | 3 | 24 | 126 | 2.2 | 0.7 | 5.7 |
| 04-05—Sacramento .... | 5 | 40 | 6 | 16 | .375 | 14 | 18 | .778 | 4 | 2 | 6 | 3 | 1 | 2 | 4 | 26 | 1.2 | 0.6 | 5.2 |
| Totals ...................... | 63 | 1088 | 173 | 396 | .437 | 143 | 184 | .777 | 67 | 105 | 172 | 50 | 23 | 11 | 81 | 489 | 2.7 | 0.8 | 7.8 |

Three-point field goals: 2001-02, 0-for-2. 2003-04, 0-for-1. 2004-05, 0-for-1. Totals, 0-for-4 (.000).
Personal fouls/disqualifications: 1998-99, 13/0. 1999-00, 8/0. 2001-02, 31/0. 2002-03, 38/1. 2003-04, 59/0. 2004-05, 11/0. Totals, 160/1.

## WILLIS, KEVIN        F/C        HAWKS

**PERSONAL:** Born September 6, 1962, in Los Angeles. ... 7-0/245. (2.13/111.1). ... Full name: Kevin Alvin Willis
**HIGH SCHOOL:** Pershing (Detroit).
**JUNIOR COLLEGE:** Jackson Community College (Mich.).
**COLLEGE:** Michigan State.
**TRANSACTIONS/CAREER NOTES:** Selected by Atlanta Hawks in first round (11th pick overall) of 1984 NBA Draft. ... Traded by Hawks with conditional first-round draft choice to Miami Heat for G Steve Smith, F Grant Long and conditional second-round draft choice (November 7, 1994). ... Traded by Heat with G Bimbo Coles to Golden State Warriors for G Tim Hardaway and F/C Chris Gatling (February 22, 1996). ... Signed as free agent by Houston Rockets (August 19, 1996). ... Traded by Rockets to Toronto Raptors for F Roy Rogers and two first-round picks in 1998 draft (June 9, 1998). ... Traded by Raptors with C Aleksander Radojevic, C Garth Joseph and 2001 or 2002 second-round draft choice to Denver Nuggets for F Tracy Murray, F/C Keon Clark and C Mamadou N'diaye (January 12, 2001). ... Traded by Nuggets with C Aleksander Radojevic to Milwaukee Bucks for F/C Scott Williams and future first-round draft choice (October 22, 2001). ... Traded by Bucks to Houston Rockets for 2002 second-round draft choice (October 22, 2001). ... Signed as free agent by San Antonio Spurs (August 26, 2002). ... Signed as free agent by Atlanta Hawks (September 22, 2004).
**MISCELLANEOUS:** Member of NBA championship team (2003).

**W**

## COLLEGIATE RECORD

| Season Team | G | Min. | FGM | FGA | Pct. | FTM | FTA | Pct. | Reb. | Ast. | Pts. | AVERAGES RPG | APG | PPG |
|---|---|---|---|---|---|---|---|---|---|---|---|---|---|---|
| 80-81—Jackson C.C. .......... | ... | ... | ... | ... | ... | ... | ... | ... | ... | ... | ... | ... | ... | ... |
| 81-82—Michigan State .............. | 27 | 518 | 73 | 154 | .474 | 17 | 30 | .567 | 113 | 2 | 163 | 4.2 | 0.1 | 6.0 |
| 82-83—Michigan State .............. | 27 | 865 | 162 | 272 | .596 | 36 | 70 | .514 | 258 | 8 | 360 | 9.6 | 0.3 | 13.3 |
| 83-84—Michigan State .............. | 25 | 738 | 118 | 240 | .492 | 39 | 59 | .661 | 192 | 7 | 275 | 7.7 | 0.3 | 11.0 |
| Junior College Totals............. | ... | ... | ... | ... | ... | ... | ... | ... | ... | ... | ... | ... | ... | ... |
| 4-Year-College Totals............. | 79 | 2121 | 353 | 666 | .530 | 92 | 159 | .579 | 563 | 17 | 798 | 7.1 | 0.2 | 10.1 |

Three-point field goals: 1982-83, 0-for-1. Totals, 0-for-1 (.000).

**HONORS:** All-NBA Third Team (1992).

## NBA REGULAR-SEASON RECORD

| Season Team | G | Min. | FGM | FGA | Pct. | FTM | FTA | Pct. | REBOUNDS Off. | Def. | Tot. | Ast. | St. | Blk. | TO | Pts. | AVERAGES RPG | APG | PPG |
|---|---|---|---|---|---|---|---|---|---|---|---|---|---|---|---|---|---|---|---|
| 84-85—Atlanta .......... | 82 | 1785 | 322 | 690 | .467 | 119 | 181 | .657 | 177 | 345 | 522 | 36 | 31 | 49 | 104 | 765 | 6.4 | 0.4 | 9.3 |
| 85-86—Atlanta .......... | 82 | 2300 | 419 | 811 | .517 | 172 | 263 | .654 | 243 | 461 | 704 | 45 | 66 | 44 | 177 | 1010 | 8.6 | 0.5 | 12.3 |
| 86-87—Atlanta .......... | 81 | 2626 | 538 | 1003 | .536 | 227 | 320 | .709 | 321 | 528 | 849 | 62 | 65 | 61 | 173 | 1304 | 10.5 | 0.8 | 16.1 |
| 87-88—Atlanta .......... | 75 | 2091 | 356 | 687 | .518 | 159 | 245 | .649 | 235 | 312 | 547 | 28 | 68 | 42 | 138 | 871 | 7.3 | 0.4 | 11.6 |
| 88-89—Atlanta .......... | | | | | | | | Did not play—injured. | | | | | | | | | | |
| 89-90—Atlanta .......... | 81 | 2273 | 418 | 805 | .519 | 168 | 246 | .683 | 253 | 392 | 645 | 57 | 63 | 47 | 144 | 1006 | 8.0 | 0.7 | 12.4 |
| 90-91—Atlanta .......... | 80 | 2373 | 444 | 881 | .504 | 159 | 238 | .668 | 259 | 445 | 704 | 99 | 60 | 40 | 153 | 1051 | 8.8 | 1.2 | 13.1 |
| 91-92—Atlanta .......... | 81 | 2962 | 591 | 1224 | .483 | 292 | 363 | .804 | 418 | 840 | 1258 | 173 | 72 | 54 | 197 | 1480 | 15.5 | 2.1 | 18.3 |
| 92-93—Atlanta .......... | 80 | 2878 | 616 | 1218 | .506 | 196 | 300 | .653 | 335 | 693 | 1028 | 165 | 68 | 41 | 213 | 1435 | 12.9 | 2.1 | 17.9 |
| 93-94—Atlanta .......... | 80 | 2867 | 627 | 1257 | .499 | 268 | 376 | .713 | 335 | 628 | 963 | 150 | 79 | 38 | 188 | 1531 | 12.0 | 1.9 | 19.1 |
| 94-95—Atlanta-Miami. | 67 | 2390 | 473 | 1015 | .466 | 205 | 297 | .690 | 227 | 505 | 732 | 86 | 60 | 36 | 162 | 1154 | 10.9 | 1.3 | 17.2 |
| 95-96—Mia.-G.S. ....... | 75 | 2135 | 325 | 712 | .456 | 143 | 202 | .708 | 208 | 430 | 638 | 53 | 32 | 41 | 161 | 794 | 8.5 | 0.7 | 10.6 |
| 96-97—Houston ......... | 75 | 1964 | 350 | 728 | .481 | 140 | 202 | .693 | 146 | 415 | 561 | 71 | 42 | 32 | 119 | 842 | 7.5 | 0.9 | 11.2 |
| 97-98—Houston ......... | 81 | 2528 | 531 | 1041 | .510 | 242 | 305 | .793 | 232 | 447 | 679 | 78 | 55 | 38 | 170 | 1305 | 8.4 | 1.0 | 16.1 |
| 98-99—Toronto .......... | 42 | 1216 | 187 | 447 | .418 | 130 | 155 | .839 | 109 | 241 | 350 | 67 | 28 | 28 | 86 | 504 | 8.3 | 1.6 | 12.0 |
| 99-00—Toronto .......... | 79 | 1679 | 236 | 569 | .415 | 131 | 164 | .799 | 201 | 281 | 482 | 49 | 36 | 48 | 98 | 604 | 6.1 | 0.6 | 7.6 |
| 00-01—Toronto-Den. .. | 78 | 1830 | 304 | 690 | .441 | 113 | 147 | .769 | 177 | 355 | 532 | 50 | 57 | 52 | 87 | 722 | 6.8 | 0.6 | 9.3 |
| 01-02—Houston ......... | 52 | 865 | 125 | 284 | .440 | 65 | 87 | .747 | 105 | 194 | 299 | 14 | 25 | 23 | 41 | 315 | 5.8 | 0.3 | 6.1 |
| 02-03—San Antonio ... | 71 | 840 | 123 | 257 | .479 | 51 | 83 | .614 | 83 | 143 | 226 | 24 | 20 | 20 | 60 | 297 | 3.2 | 0.3 | 4.2 |
| 03-04—San Antonio ... | 48 | 373 | 70 | 150 | .467 | 24 | 39 | .615 | 37 | 61 | 98 | 11 | 21 | 9 | 32 | 164 | 2.0 | 0.2 | 3.4 |
| 04-05—Atlanta .......... | 29 | 344 | 35 | 90 | .389 | 17 | 23 | .739 | 29 | 47 | 76 | 9 | 8 | 7 | 15 | 87 | 2.6 | 0.3 | 3.0 |
| **Totals .................** | 1419 | 38319 | 7090 | 14559 | .487 | 3021 | 4236 | .713 | 4130 | 7763 | 11893 | 1327 | 956 | 750 | 2518 | 17241 | 8.4 | 0.9 | 12.2 |

Three-point field goals: 1984-85, 2-for-9 (.222). 1985-86, 0-for-6. 1986-87, 1-for-4 (.250). 1987-88, 0-for-2. 1989-90, 2-for-7 (.286). 1990-91, 4-for-10 (.400). 1991-92, 6-for-37 (.162). 1992-93, 7-for-29 (.241). 1993-94, 9-for-24 (.375). 1994-95, 3-for-15 (.200). 1995-96, 1-for-9 (.111). 1996-97, 2-for-14 (.143). 1997-98, 1-for-7 (.143). 1998-99, 0-for-2. 1999-00, 1-for-3 (.333). 2000-01, 1-for-6 (.167). 2001-02, 0-for-1. 2002-03, 0-for-1. 2003-04, 0-for-1. 2004-05, 0-for-2. Totals, 40-for-190 (.211).

Personal fouls/disqualifications: 1984-85, 226/4. 1985-86, 294/6. 1986-87, 313/4. 1987-88, 240/2. 1989-90, 259/4. 1990-91, 235/2. 1991-92, 223/0. 1992-93, 264/1. 1993-94, 250/2. 1994-95, 215/3. 1995-96, 253/4. 1996-97, 216/1. 1997-98, 235/1. 1998-99, 134/1. 1999-00, 256/3. 2000-01, 216/0. 2001-02, 98/0. 2002-03, 120/1. 2003-04, 61/0. 2004-05, 53/0. Totals, 4161/39.

## NBA PLAYOFF RECORD

| Season Team | G | Min. | FGM | FGA | Pct. | FTM | FTA | Pct. | REBOUNDS Off. | Def. | Tot. | Ast. | St. | Blk. | TO | Pts. | AVERAGES RPG | APG | PPG |
|---|---|---|---|---|---|---|---|---|---|---|---|---|---|---|---|---|---|---|---|
| 85-86—Atlanta ......... | 9 | 280 | 55 | 98 | .561 | 15 | 23 | .652 | 31 | 34 | 65 | 5 | 7 | 8 | 15 | 125 | 7.2 | 0.6 | 13.9 |
| 86-87—Atlanta ......... | 9 | 356 | 60 | 115 | .522 | 21 | 31 | .677 | 33 | 50 | 83 | 6 | 9 | 7 | 17 | 141 | 9.2 | 0.7 | 15.7 |
| 87-88—Atlanta ......... | 12 | 462 | 80 | 138 | .580 | 34 | 50 | .680 | 36 | 72 | 108 | 11 | 10 | 10 | 25 | 194 | 9.0 | 0.9 | 16.2 |
| 90-91—Atlanta ......... | 5 | 159 | 27 | 67 | .403 | 21 | 30 | .700 | 18 | 27 | 45 | 5 | 3 | 1 | 2 | 77 | 9.0 | 1.0 | 15.4 |
| 92-93—Atlanta ......... | 3 | 103 | 21 | 45 | .467 | 8 | 14 | .571 | 13 | 13 | 26 | 3 | 2 | 0 | 7 | 50 | 8.7 | 1.0 | 16.7 |
| 93-94—Atlanta ......... | 11 | 362 | 59 | 129 | .457 | 16 | 21 | .762 | 38 | 81 | 119 | 11 | 8 | 5 | 19 | 134 | 10.8 | 1.0 | 12.2 |
| 96-97—Houston ......... | 16 | 295 | 38 | 95 | .400 | 26 | 38 | .684 | 22 | 53 | 75 | 11 | 9 | 4 | 22 | 102 | 4.7 | 0.6 | 6.4 |
| 97-98—Houston ......... | 5 | 168 | 22 | 55 | .400 | 12 | 16 | .750 | 18 | 35 | 53 | 5 | 8 | 3 | 12 | 56 | 10.6 | 1.0 | 11.2 |
| 99-00—Toronto .......... | 3 | 76 | 12 | 33 | .364 | 15 | 20 | .750 | 6 | 20 | 26 | 1 | 2 | 0 | 2 | 39 | 8.7 | 0.3 | 13.0 |
| 02-03—San Antonio ... | 18 | 91 | 21 | 40 | .525 | 3 | 3 | 1.000 | 19 | 12 | 31 | 2 | 1 | 1 | 8 | 46 | 1.7 | 0.1 | 2.6 |
| 03-04—San Antonio .... | 7 | 25 | 3 | 8 | .375 | 0 | 1 | .000 | 6 | 6 | 6 | 1 | 1 | 0 | 6 | 6 | 0.9 | 0.0 | 0.9 |
| **Totals .................** | 98 | 2377 | 398 | 823 | .484 | 171 | 247 | .692 | 234 | 403 | 637 | 60 | 60 | 39 | 129 | 970 | 6.5 | 0.6 | 9.9 |

Three-point field goals: 1987-88, 0-for-1. 1990-91, 2-for-3 (.667). 1992-93, 0-for-1. 1993-94, 0-for-5. 1996-97, 0-for-1. 1997-98, 0-for-1. 2002-03, 1-for-1 (1.000). 2003-04, 0-for-1. Totals, 3-for-14 (.214).

Personal fouls/disqualifications: 1985-86, 38/2. 1986-87, 33/0. 1987-88, 51/1. 1990-91, 22/0. 1992-93, 13/0. 1993-94, 37/0. 1996-97, 47/0. 1997-98, 21/0. 1999-00, 11/0. 2002-03, 16/0. 2003-04, 5/0. Totals, 294/3.

## NBA ALL-STAR GAME RECORD

| Season Team | Min. | FGM | FGA | Pct. | FTM | FTA | Pct. | REBOUNDS Off. | Def. | Tot. | Ast. | PF | Dq. | St. | Blk. | TO | Pts. |
|---|---|---|---|---|---|---|---|---|---|---|---|---|---|---|---|---|---|
| 1992—Atlanta.................. | 14 | 4 | 10 | .400 | 0 | 0 | ... | 4 | 0 | 4 | 0 | 1 | 0 | 0 | 0 | 0 | 8 |

# WOODS, LOREN      C      RAPTORS

**PERSONAL:** Born June 21, 1978, in St. Louis. ... 7-1/245. (2.16/111.1). ... Full name: Loren Gerard Woods.
**HIGH SCHOOL:** Cardinal Ritter (St. Louis).
**COLLEGE:** Wake Forest, then Arizona.
**TRANSACTIONS/CAREER NOTES:** Selected by Minnesota Timberwolves in second round (46th pick overall) of 2001 NBA Draft. ... Signed as free agent by Miami Heat (August 8, 2003) ... Selected by Charlotte Bobcats from Heat in NBA Expansion Draft (June 22, 2004). ... Signed as free agent by Toronto Raptors (August 18, 2004).

## COLLEGIATE RECORD

| Season Team | G | Min. | FGM | FGA | Pct. | FTM | FTA | Pct. | Reb. | Ast. | Pts. | AVERAGES RPG | APG | PPG |
|---|---|---|---|---|---|---|---|---|---|---|---|---|---|---|
| 96-97—Wake Forest ................. | 30 | 525 | 71 | 147 | .483 | 63 | 93 | .677 | 157 | 16 | 205 | 5.2 | 0.5 | 6.8 |
| 97-98—Wake Forest ................. | 22 | 554 | 63 | 157 | .401 | 67 | 100 | .670 | 157 | 19 | 194 | 7.1 | 0.9 | 8.8 |
| 98-99—Arizona............................ | | | | | | | | Did not play—transfer student. | | | | | | |
| 99-00—Arizona............................ | 26 | 820 | 154 | 286 | .538 | 97 | 128 | .758 | 194 | 38 | 405 | 7.5 | 1.5 | 15.6 |
| 00-01—Arizona............................ | 29 | 879 | 133 | 264 | .504 | 117 | 141 | .830 | 189 | 62 | 384 | 6.5 | 2.1 | 13.2 |
| **Totals ................................** | 107 | 2778 | 421 | 854 | .493 | 344 | 462 | .745 | 697 | 135 | 1188 | 6.5 | 1.3 | 11.1 |

Three-point field goals: 1997-98, 1-for-4 (.250). 1999-00, 0-for-2. 2000-01, 1-for-3 (.333). Totals, 2-for-9 (.222).
Personal fouls/disqualifications: 1996-97, 45/0. 1997-98, 50/0. 1999-00, 50/0. 2000-01, 64/0. Totals, 209/0.

**W**

### NBA REGULAR-SEASON RECORD

| Season Team | G | Min. | FGM | FGA | Pct. | FTM | FTA | Pct. | REBOUNDS Off. | Def. | Tot. | Ast. | St. | Blk. | TO | Pts. | AVERAGES RPG | APG | PPG |
|---|---|---|---|---|---|---|---|---|---|---|---|---|---|---|---|---|---|---|---|
| 01-02—Minnesota | 60 | 516 | 33 | 96 | .344 | 44 | 60 | .733 | 46 | 76 | 122 | 22 | 17 | 34 | 36 | 110 | 2.0 | 0.4 | 1.8 |
| 02-03—Minnesota | 38 | 353 | 29 | 76 | .382 | 21 | 27 | .778 | 27 | 68 | 95 | 19 | 10 | 13 | 23 | 80 | 2.5 | 0.5 | 2.1 |
| 03-04—Miami | 38 | 506 | 44 | 96 | .458 | 33 | 55 | .600 | 65 | 69 | 134 | 10 | 11 | 19 | 26 | 121 | 3.5 | 0.3 | 3.2 |
| 04-05—Toronto | 45 | 712 | 71 | 164 | .433 | 34 | 59 | .576 | 81 | 139 | 220 | 17 | 8 | 39 | 37 | 176 | 4.9 | 0.4 | 3.9 |
| Totals | 181 | 2087 | 177 | 432 | .410 | 132 | 201 | .657 | 219 | 352 | 571 | 68 | 46 | 105 | 122 | 487 | 3.2 | 0.4 | 2.7 |

Three-point field goals: 2001-02, 0-for-2. 2002-03, 1-for-3 (.333). 2004-05, 0-for-1. Totals, 1-for-6 (.167).
Personal fouls/disqualifications: 2001-02, 60/0. 2002-03, 37/0. 2003-04, 52/0. 2004-05, 78/0. Totals, 227/0.

### NBA PLAYOFF RECORD

| Season Team | G | Min. | FGM | FGA | Pct. | FTM | FTA | Pct. | REBOUNDS Off. | Def. | Tot. | Ast. | St. | Blk. | TO | Pts. | AVERAGES RPG | APG | PPG |
|---|---|---|---|---|---|---|---|---|---|---|---|---|---|---|---|---|---|---|---|
| 02-03—Minnesota | 2 | 2 | 1 | 3 | .333 | 0 | 0 | ... | 1 | 0 | 1 | 0 | 0 | 0 | 0 | 2 | 0.5 | 0.0 | 1.0 |
| 03-04—Miami | 1 | 2 | 0 | 0 | ... | 0 | 0 | ... | 0 | 0 | 0 | 0 | 0 | 0 | 0 | 0 | 0.0 | 0.0 | 0.0 |
| Totals | 3 | 4 | 1 | 3 | .333 | 0 | 0 | ... | 1 | 0 | 1 | 0 | 0 | 0 | 0 | 2 | 0.3 | 0.0 | 0.7 |

# WOODS, QYNTEL     F/G     CELTICS

**PERSONAL:** Born February 16, 1981, in Memphis. ... 6-8/221. (2.03/100.2). ... Full name: Qyntel Deon Woods
**HIGH SCHOOL:** Carver (Memphis).
**JUNIOR COLLEGE:** Moberly (Mo.) Area Junior College, then Northeast .
**TRANSACTIONS/CAREER NOTES:** Selected after sophomore season by Portland Trail Blazers in first round (21st pick overall) of 2002 NBA Draft. ... Waived by Trail Blazers (January 21, 2005). ... Signed as free agent by Miami Heat (January 26, 2005). ... Traded by Heat with two second-round draft picks and draft rights to Albert Miralles to Boston Celtics in five-team deal (August 2, 2005).

### COLLEGIATE RECORD

| Season Team | G | Min. | FGM | FGA | Pct. | FTM | FTA | Pct. | Reb. | Ast. | Pts. | AVERAGES RPG | APG | PPG |
|---|---|---|---|---|---|---|---|---|---|---|---|---|---|---|
| 99-00—Moberly Area J.C. | | | | | | Did not play—redshirted. | | | | | | | | |
| 00-01—Moberly Area J.C. | 32 | 867 | 256 | 534 | .479 | 205 | 262 | .782 | 264 | 66 | 749 | 8.3 | 2.1 | 23.4 |
| 01-02—NE Mississippi CC | 23 | 722 | 239 | 495 | .483 | 230 | 285 | .807 | 229 | 42 | 742 | 10.0 | 1.8 | 32.3 |
| Totals | 55 | 1589 | 495 | 1029 | .481 | 435 | 547 | .795 | 493 | 108 | 1491 | 9.0 | 2.0 | 27.1 |

Three-point field goals: 2000-01, 32-for-111 (.288). 2001-02, 34-for-113 (.301). Totals, 66-for-224 (.295).

### NBA REGULAR-SEASON RECORD

| Season Team | G | Min. | FGM | FGA | Pct. | FTM | FTA | Pct. | REBOUNDS Off. | Def. | Tot. | Ast. | St. | Blk. | TO | Pts. | AVERAGES RPG | APG | PPG |
|---|---|---|---|---|---|---|---|---|---|---|---|---|---|---|---|---|---|---|---|
| 02-03—Portland | 53 | 334 | 59 | 118 | .500 | 7 | 20 | .350 | 15 | 38 | 53 | 12 | 15 | 1 | 23 | 128 | 1.0 | 0.2 | 2.4 |
| 03-04—Portland | 62 | 673 | 88 | 237 | .371 | 38 | 60 | .633 | 46 | 90 | 136 | 46 | 20 | 14 | 52 | 224 | 2.2 | 0.7 | 3.6 |
| 04-05—Miami | 3 | 40 | 5 | 12 | .417 | 0 | 0 | ... | 2 | 4 | 6 | 0 | 4 | 0 | 2 | 10 | 2.0 | 0.0 | 3.3 |
| Totals | 118 | 1047 | 152 | 367 | .414 | 45 | 80 | .563 | 63 | 132 | 195 | 58 | 39 | 15 | 77 | 362 | 1.7 | 0.5 | 3.1 |

Three-point field goals: 2002-03, 3-for-9 (.333). 2003-04, 10-for-29 (.345). Totals, 13-for-38 (.342).
Personal fouls/disqualifications: 2002-03, 36/1. 2003-04, 88/1. 2004-05, 6/0. Totals, 130/2.

### NBA PLAYOFF RECORD

| Season Team | G | Min. | FGM | FGA | Pct. | FTM | FTA | Pct. | REBOUNDS Off. | Def. | Tot. | Ast. | St. | Blk. | TO | Pts. | AVERAGES RPG | APG | PPG |
|---|---|---|---|---|---|---|---|---|---|---|---|---|---|---|---|---|---|---|---|
| 02-03—Portland | 4 | 18 | 3 | 9 | .333 | 1 | 2 | .500 | 1 | 1 | 2 | 0 | 0 | 0 | 1 | 7 | 0.5 | 0.0 | 1.8 |

Three-point field goals: 2002-03, 0-for-1. Totals, 0-for-1 (.000).
Personal fouls/disqualifications: 2002-03, 3/0. Totals, 3/0.

# WRIGHT, DORELL     F     HEAT

**PERSONAL:** Born December 2, 1985, in Los Angeles. ... 6-7/210. (2.01/95.3).
**HIGH SCHOOL:** Leuzinger (Lawndale, Calif.), then South Kent Prep (Conn.)
**COLLEGE:** Did not attend college.
**TRANSACTIONS/CAREER NOTES:** Selected out of high school by Miami Heat in first round (19th pick overall) of 2004 NBA Draft.

### NBA REGULAR-SEASON RECORD

| Season Team | G | Min. | FGM | FGA | Pct. | FTM | FTA | Pct. | REBOUNDS Off. | Def. | Tot. | Ast. | St. | Blk. | TO | Pts. | AVERAGES RPG | APG | PPG |
|---|---|---|---|---|---|---|---|---|---|---|---|---|---|---|---|---|---|---|---|
| 04-05—Miami | 3 | 27 | 3 | 11 | .273 | 1 | 1 | 1.000 | 0 | 1 | 1 | 3 | 4 | 0 | 3 | 7 | 0.3 | 1.0 | 2.3 |

Three-point field goals: 2004-05, 0-for-4. Totals, 0-for-4 (.000).
Personal fouls/disqualifications: 2004-05, 2/0. Totals, 2/0.
Personal fouls/disqualifications: 1995-96, 147/1. 1996-97, 213/0. 1997-98, 9/0. 1998-99, 76/0. 1999-00, 165/3. 2000-01, 179/1. 2001-02, 179/1. 2002-03, 234/0. 2003-04, 180/0. 2004-05, 147/2. Totals, 1529/8.

# WRIGHT, LORENZEN     F/C     GRIZZLIES

**PERSONAL:** Born November 4, 1975, in Memphis, Tenn. ... 6-11/240. (2.11/108.9). ... Full name: Lorenzen Vern-Gagne Wright
**HIGH SCHOOL:** Booker T. Washington (Memphis, Tenn.).
**COLLEGE:** Memphis.
**TRANSACTIONS/CAREER NOTES:** Selected after sophomore season by Los Angeles Clippers in first round (seventh pick overall) of 1996 NBA Draft. ... Traded by Clippers to Atlanta Hawks for two future first-round draft choices (August 8, 1999). ... Traded by Hawks with G Brevin Knight and draft rights to Pau Gasol to Memphis Grizzlies for F Shareef Abdur-Rahim and draft rights to G Jamaal Tinsley (July 19, 2001).

W

| Season Team | G | Min. | FGM | FGA | Pct. | FTM | FTA | Pct. | Reb. | Ast. | Pts. | RPG | APG | PPG |
|---|---|---|---|---|---|---|---|---|---|---|---|---|---|---|
| 94-95—Memphis | 34 | 1170 | 198 | 353 | .561 | 107 | 171 | .626 | 345 | 50 | 503 | 10.1 | 1.5 | 14.8 |
| 95-96—Memphis | 30 | 1058 | 207 | 382 | .542 | 109 | 169 | .645 | 313 | 35 | 523 | 10.4 | 1.2 | 17.4 |
| **Totals** | 64 | 2228 | 405 | 735 | .551 | 216 | 340 | .635 | 658 | 85 | 1026 | 10.3 | 1.3 | 16.0 |

Three-point field goals: 1994-95, 0-for-1. 1995-96, 0-for-1. Totals, 0-for-2 (.000).

## NBA REGULAR-SEASON RECORD

| Season Team | G | Min. | FGM | FGA | Pct. | FTM | FTA | Pct. | Off. | Def. | Tot. | Ast. | St. | Blk. | TO | Pts. | RPG | APG | PPG |
|---|---|---|---|---|---|---|---|---|---|---|---|---|---|---|---|---|---|---|---|
| 96-97—L.A. Clippers | 77 | 1936 | 236 | 491 | .481 | 88 | 150 | .587 | 206 | 265 | 471 | 49 | 48 | 60 | 79 | 561 | 6.1 | 0.6 | 7.3 |
| 97-98—L.A. Clippers | 69 | 2067 | 241 | 542 | .445 | 141 | 214 | .659 | 180 | 426 | 606 | 55 | 55 | 87 | 81 | 623 | 8.8 | 0.8 | 9.0 |
| 98-99—L.A. Clippers | 48 | 1135 | 119 | 260 | .458 | 81 | 117 | .692 | 142 | 219 | 361 | 33 | 26 | 36 | 48 | 319 | 7.5 | 0.7 | 6.6 |
| 99-00—Atlanta | 75 | 1205 | 180 | 361 | .499 | 87 | 135 | .644 | 117 | 188 | 305 | 21 | 29 | 40 | 66 | 448 | 4.1 | 0.3 | 6.0 |
| 00-01—Atlanta | 71 | 1988 | 363 | 811 | .448 | 155 | 216 | .718 | 180 | 355 | 535 | 87 | 42 | 63 | 125 | 881 | 7.5 | 1.2 | 12.4 |
| 01-02—Memphis | 43 | 1251 | 223 | 486 | .459 | 70 | 123 | .569 | 130 | 275 | 405 | 44 | 30 | 23 | 72 | 516 | 9.4 | 1.0 | 12.0 |
| 02-03—Memphis | 70 | 1982 | 325 | 716 | .454 | 147 | 223 | .659 | 170 | 358 | 528 | 80 | 51 | 54 | 110 | 797 | 7.5 | 1.1 | 11.4 |
| 03-04—Memphis | 65 | 1674 | 257 | 586 | .439 | 96 | 131 | .733 | 144 | 301 | 445 | 71 | 45 | 58 | 77 | 610 | 6.8 | 1.1 | 9.4 |
| 04-05—Memphis | 80 | 2287 | 320 | 683 | .469 | 131 | 198 | .662 | 177 | 436 | 613 | 87 | 58 | 69 | 100 | 771 | 7.7 | 1.1 | 9.6 |
| **Totals** | 598 | 15525 | 2264 | 4936 | .459 | 996 | 1507 | .661 | 1446 | 2823 | 4269 | 527 | 384 | 490 | 758 | 5526 | 7.1 | 0.9 | 9.2 |

Three-point field goals: 1996-97, 1-for-4 (.250). 1997-98, 0-for-2. 1998-99, 0-for-1. 1999-00, 1-for-3 (.333). 2000-01, 0-for-2. 2001-02, 0-for-2. 2002-03, 0-for-5. 2003-04, 0-for-5. 2004-05, 0-for-3. Totals, 2-for-27 (.074).

Personal fouls/disqualifications: 1996-97, 211/2. 1997-98, 237/2. 1998-99, 162/2. 1999-00, 203/3. 2000-01, 232/2. 2001-02, 126/0. 2002-03, 209/7. 2003-04, 192/4. 2004-05, 251/1. Totals, 1823/23.

## NBA PLAYOFF RECORD

| Season Team | G | Min. | FGM | FGA | Pct. | FTM | FTA | Pct. | Off. | Def. | Tot. | Ast. | St. | Blk. | TO | Pts. | RPG | APG | PPG |
|---|---|---|---|---|---|---|---|---|---|---|---|---|---|---|---|---|---|---|---|
| 96-97—L.A. Clippers | 3 | 92 | 13 | 32 | .406 | 5 | 5 | 1.000 | 7 | 15 | 22 | 2 | 3 | 2 | 1 | 31 | 7.3 | 0.7 | 10.3 |
| 03-04—Memphis | 4 | 100 | 10 | 23 | .435 | 2 | 6 | .333 | 5 | 12 | 17 | 2 | 4 | 2 | 5 | 22 | 4.3 | 0.5 | 5.5 |
| 04-05—Memphis | 4 | 85 | 16 | 28 | .571 | 1 | 2 | .500 | 6 | 14 | 20 | 9 | 1 | 1 | 2 | 33 | 5.0 | 2.3 | 8.3 |
| **Totals** | 11 | 277 | 39 | 83 | .470 | 8 | 13 | .615 | 18 | 41 | 59 | 13 | 8 | 5 | 8 | 86 | 5.4 | 1.2 | 7.8 |

Personal fouls/disqualifications: 1996-97, 6/0. 2003-04, 15/0. 2004-05, 10/0. Totals, 31/0.

# YAO, MING — C — ROCKETS

**PERSONAL:** Born September 12, 1980, in Shanghai, China. ... 7-5/296. (2.26/134.3).
**TRANSACTIONS/CAREER NOTES:** Played in China (1997-2002). ... Selected by Houston Rockets in first round (first pick overall) of 2002 NBA Draft.
**MISCELLANEOUS:** Member of Chinese Olympic team (2000, 2004).

## CHINESE LEAGUE RECORD

| Season Team | G | Min. | FGM | FGA | Pct. | FTM | FTA | Pct. | Reb. | Ast. | Pts. | RPG | APG | PPG |
|---|---|---|---|---|---|---|---|---|---|---|---|---|---|---|
| 97-98—Shanghai | 21 | ... | 91 | 148 | .615 | 32 | 66 | .485 | 175 | 13 | 214 | 8.3 | 0.6 | 10.2 |
| 98-99—Shanghai | 12 | ... | 100 | 171 | .585 | 51 | 73 | .699 | 155 | 7 | 251 | 12.9 | 0.6 | 20.9 |
| 99-00—Shanghai | 33 | ... | 285 | 497 | .573 | 127 | 186 | .683 | 480 | 57 | 703 | 14.5 | 1.7 | 21.3 |
| 00-01—Shanghai | 22 | ... | 226 | 340 | .665 | 139 | 174 | .799 | 426 | 48 | 596 | 19.4 | 2.2 | 27.1 |
| 01-02—Shanghai | 34 | ... | 421 | 595 | .708 | 255 | 336 | .759 | 645 | 98 | 1107 | 19.0 | 2.9 | 32.6 |
| **Totals** | 122 | | 1123 | 1751 | .641 | 604 | 835 | .723 | 1881 | 223 | 2871 | 15.4 | 1.8 | 23.5 |

Three-point field goals: 1999-00, 2-for-10 (.200). 2000-01, 5-for-14 (.357). 2001-02, 10-for-25 (.400). Totals, 17-for-49 (.347).

## NBA REGULAR-SEASON RECORD

**HONORS:** All-NBA third team (2004). ... NBA All-Rookie first team (2003).

| Season Team | G | Min. | FGM | FGA | Pct. | FTM | FTA | Pct. | Off. | Def. | Tot. | Ast. | St. | Blk. | TO | Pts. | RPG | APG | PPG |
|---|---|---|---|---|---|---|---|---|---|---|---|---|---|---|---|---|---|---|---|
| 02-03—Houston | 82 | 2382 | 401 | 805 | .498 | 301 | 371 | .811 | 196 | 479 | 675 | 137 | 31 | 147 | 173 | 1104 | 8.2 | 1.7 | 13.5 |
| 03-04—Houston | 82 | 2692 | 535 | 1025 | .522 | 361 | 446 | .809 | 197 | 538 | 735 | 122 | 22 | 156 | 204 | 1431 | 9.0 | 1.5 | 17.5 |
| 04-05—Houston | 80 | 2447 | 538 | 975 | .552 | 389 | 497 | .783 | 208 | 461 | 669 | 61 | 34 | 160 | 196 | 1465 | 8.4 | 0.8 | 18.3 |
| **Totals** | 244 | 7521 | 1474 | 2805 | .525 | 1051 | 1314 | .800 | 601 | 1478 | 2079 | 320 | 87 | 463 | 573 | 4000 | 8.5 | 1.3 | 16.4 |

Three-point field goals: 2002-03, 1-for-2 (.500). 2003-04, 0-for-2. Totals, 1-for-4 (.250).
Personal fouls/disqualifications: 2002-03, 230/1. 2003-04, 273/4. 2004-05, 298/8. Totals, 801/13.

## NBA PLAYOFF RECORD

| Season Team | G | Min. | FGM | FGA | Pct. | FTM | FTA | Pct. | Off. | Def. | Tot. | Ast. | St. | Blk. | TO | Pts. | RPG | APG | PPG |
|---|---|---|---|---|---|---|---|---|---|---|---|---|---|---|---|---|---|---|---|
| 03-04—Houston | 5 | 185 | 31 | 68 | .456 | 13 | 17 | .765 | 11 | 26 | 37 | 9 | 2 | 7 | 13 | 75 | 7.4 | 1.8 | 15.0 |
| 04-05—Houston | 7 | 220 | 55 | 84 | .655 | 40 | 55 | .727 | 23 | 31 | 54 | 5 | 2 | 19 | 19 | 150 | 7.7 | 0.7 | 21.4 |
| **Totals** | 12 | 405 | 86 | 152 | .566 | 53 | 72 | .736 | 34 | 57 | 91 | 14 | 4 | 26 | 32 | 225 | 7.6 | 1.2 | 18.8 |

Personal fouls/disqualifications: 2003-04, 20/2. 2004-05, 31/1. Totals, 51/3.

## NBA ALL-STAR GAME RECORD

| Season Team | Min. | FGM | FGA | Pct. | FTM | FTA | Pct. | Off. | Def. | Tot. | Ast. | PF | Dq. | St. | Blk. | TO | Pts. |
|---|---|---|---|---|---|---|---|---|---|---|---|---|---|---|---|---|---|
| 2003—Houston | 17 | 1 | 1 | 1.000 | 0 | 0 | ... | 0 | 2 | 2 | 0 | 1 | 0 | 0 | 0 | 0 | 2 |
| 2004—Houston | 19 | 8 | 14 | .571 | 0 | 0 | ... | 2 | 2 | 4 | 1 | 2 | 0 | 0 | 0 | 0 | 16 |
| 2005—Houston | 22 | 5 | 9 | .556 | 1 | 2 | .500 | 3 | 5 | 8 | 5 | 1 | 0 | 0 | 1 | 1 | 11 |
| **Totals** | 58 | 14 | 24 | .583 | 1 | 2 | .500 | 5 | 9 | 14 | 6 | 4 | 0 | 0 | 1 | 1 | 29 |

Three-point field goals: 2004, 0-for-2. Totals, 0-for-2 (.000).

**Y**

## ACKER, ALEX     G      PISTONS

**PERSONAL:** Born January 21, 1983, in Compton, Calif. ... 6-5/185. (1.96/83.9).
**HIGH SCHOOL:** Cajon (San Bernardino, Calif.), then Eisenhower (Rialto, Calif.)
**COLLEGE:** Pepperdine.
**TRANSACTIONS/CAREER NOTES:** Selected after junior season by Detroit Pistons in second round (60th pick overall) of 2005 NBA draft.

### COLLEGIATE RECORD

| Season Team | G | Min. | FGM | FGA | Pct. | FTM | FTA | Pct. | Reb. | Ast. | Pts. | RPG | APG | PPG |
|---|---|---|---|---|---|---|---|---|---|---|---|---|---|---|
| 01-02—Pepperdine | | | | | | | | Did Not Play - Ineligible | | | | | | |
| 02-03—Pepperdine | 28 | 931 | 128 | 269 | .476 | 79 | 97 | .814 | 139 | 24 | 364 | 5.0 | 0.9 | 13.0 |
| 03-04—Pepperdine | 29 | 940 | 138 | 307 | .450 | 85 | 107 | .794 | 155 | 111 | 393 | 5.3 | 3.8 | 13.6 |
| 04-05—Pepperdine | 31 | 1152 | 183 | 407 | .450 | 91 | 106 | .858 | 201 | 114 | 516 | 6.5 | 3.7 | 16.6 |
| Totals | 88 | 3023 | 449 | 983 | .457 | 255 | 310 | .823 | 495 | 249 | 1273 | 5.6 | 2.8 | 14.5 |

Three-point field goals: 2002-03, 29-for-68 (.426). 2003-04, 32-for-87 (.368). 2004-05, 59-for-137 (.431). Totals, 120-for-292 (.411).

## AKYOL, CENK     G      HAWKS

**PERSONAL:** Born April 16, 1987, in Kadikoy, Turkey. ... 6-4/195. (1.93/88.5).
**COLLEGE:** Did not attend.
**TRANSACTIONS/CAREER NOTES:** Played for Efes Pilsen of Turkish league. ... Selected by Atlanta Hawks in second round (59th pick overall) of 2005 NBA Draft.

### TURKISH LEAGUE RECORD

| Season Team | G | Min. | FGM | FGA | Pct. | FTM | FTA | Pct. | Reb. | Ast. | Pts. | RPG | APG | PPG |
|---|---|---|---|---|---|---|---|---|---|---|---|---|---|---|
| 03-04—Efes Pilsen | 3 | 6 | 2 | 2 | 1.000 | 1 | 2 | .500 | 4 | 6 | 6 | 1.3 | 2.0 | 2.0 |
| 04-05—Efes Pilsen | 18 | 236 | 24 | 57 | .421 | 21 | 26 | .808 | 29 | 19 | 80 | 1.6 | 1.1 | 4.4 |
| Totals | 21 | 242 | 26 | 59 | .441 | 22 | 28 | .786 | 33 | 25 | 86 | 1.6 | 1.2 | 4.1 |

Three-point field goals: 2003-04, 1-for-1 (1.000). 2004-05, 11-for-29 (.379). Totals, 12-for-30 (.400).

## ANDERSON, ALAN     G/F      BOBCATS

**PERSONAL:** Born October 16, 1982, in Minneapolis, Minn. ... 6-6/220. (1.98/99.8). ... Full name: Alan Jeffery Anderson.
**HIGH SCHOOL:** DeLaSalle (Minneapolis, Minn.).
**COLLEGE:** Michigan State.
**TRANSACTIONS/CAREER NOTES:** Not drafted by an NBA franchise. ... Signed as free agent by Charlotte Bobcats (August 9, 2005).

### COLLEGIATE RECORD

| Season Team | G | Min. | FGM | FGA | Pct. | FTM | FTA | Pct. | Reb. | Ast. | Pts. | RPG | APG | PPG |
|---|---|---|---|---|---|---|---|---|---|---|---|---|---|---|
| 01-02—Michigan State | 31 | 759 | 67 | 149 | .450 | 67 | 87 | .770 | 130 | 51 | 203 | 4.2 | 1.6 | 6.5 |
| 02-03—Michigan State | 32 | 883 | 90 | 179 | .503 | 128 | 152 | .842 | 117 | 104 | 312 | 3.7 | 3.3 | 9.8 |
| 03-04—Michigan State | 30 | 861 | 78 | 167 | .467 | 70 | 87 | .805 | 93 | 96 | 243 | 3.1 | 3.2 | 8.1 |
| 04-05—Michigan State | 33 | 877 | 149 | 268 | .556 | 114 | 130 | .877 | 184 | 56 | 437 | 5.6 | 1.7 | 13.2 |
| Totals | 126 | 3380 | 384 | 763 | .503 | 379 | 456 | .831 | 524 | 307 | 1195 | 4.2 | 2.4 | 9.5 |

Three-point field goals: 2001-02, 2-for-5 (.400). 2002-03, 4-for-13 (.308). 2003-04, 17-for-48 (.354). 2004-05, 25-for-65 (.385). Totals, 48-for-131 (.366).

## ANDRIUSKEVICIUS, MARTYNAS     C      CAVALIERS

**PERSONAL:** Born March 12, 1986, in Kaunas, Lithuania. ... 7-2/240. (2.18/108.9).
**COLLEGE:** Did not attend.
**TRANSACTIONS/CAREER NOTES:** Played for Zalgiris of Lithuanian league. ... Selected by Orlando Magic in second round (44th pick overall) of 2005 NBA Draft. ... Draft rights traded by Magic to Cleveland Cavaliers for 2006 second-round pick and future considerations (June 28, 2005).

### LITHUANIAN LEAGUE RECORD

| Season Team | G | Min. | FGM | FGA | Pct. | FTM | FTA | Pct. | Reb. | Ast. | Pts. | RPG | APG | PPG |
|---|---|---|---|---|---|---|---|---|---|---|---|---|---|---|
| 04-05—Zalgiris Kaunas | 21 | 202 | 30 | 60 | .500 | 29 | 46 | .630 | 53 | 4 | 93 | 2.5 | 0.2 | 4.4 |

Three-point field goals: 2004-05, 4-for-8 (.500). Totals, 4-for-8 (.500).

## BASDEN, EDDIE     G      BULLS

**PERSONAL:** Born February 15, 1983, in New York, N.Y. ... 6-5/215. (1.96/97.5). ... Full name: Edward Richard Basden.
**HIGH SCHOOL:** Eleanor Roosevelt (Greenbelt, Md.).
**COLLEGE:** Charlotte.
**TRANSACTIONS/CAREER NOTES:** Not drafted by an NBA franchise. ... Signed as free agent by Chicago Bulls (August 9, 2005).

## COLLEGIATE RECORD

| Season Team | G | Min. | FGM | FGA | Pct. | FTM | FTA | Pct. | Reb. | Ast. | Pts. | RPG | APG | PPG |
|---|---|---|---|---|---|---|---|---|---|---|---|---|---|---|
| 01-02—Charlotte | 30 | 566 | 45 | 96 | .469 | 37 | 58 | .638 | 128 | 39 | 128 | 4.3 | 1.3 | 4.3 |
| 02-03—Charlotte | 29 | 742 | 60 | 133 | .451 | 60 | 83 | .723 | 200 | 74 | 183 | 6.9 | 2.6 | 6.3 |
| 03-04—Charlotte | 30 | 850 | 105 | 196 | .536 | 87 | 135 | .644 | 192 | 93 | 313 | 6.4 | 3.1 | 10.4 |
| 04-05—Charlotte | 29 | 1049 | 155 | 318 | .487 | 110 | 152 | .724 | 245 | 108 | 442 | 8.4 | 3.7 | 15.2 |
| Totals | 118 | 3207 | 365 | 743 | .491 | 294 | 428 | .687 | 765 | 314 | 1066 | 6.5 | 2.7 | 9.0 |

Three-point field goals: 2001-02, 1-for-8 (.125). 2002-03, 3-for-12 (.250). 2003-04, 16-for-42 (.381). 2004-05, 22-for-57 (.386). Totals, 42-for-119 (.353).

## BASS, BRANDON    F    HORNETS

**PERSONAL:** Born April 30, 1985, in Baton Rouge, La. ... 6-8/240. (2.03/108.9). ... Full name: Brandon Sam Bass
**HIGH SCHOOL:** Capitol (Baton Rouge, La.).
**COLLEGE:** LSU.
**TRANSACTIONS/CAREER NOTES:** Selected after sophomore season by New Orleans Hornets in second round (33rd overall pick) of 2005 NBA draft.

### COLLEGIATE RECORD

| Season Team | G | Min. | FGM | FGA | Pct. | FTM | FTA | Pct. | Reb. | Ast. | Pts. | RPG | APG | PPG |
|---|---|---|---|---|---|---|---|---|---|---|---|---|---|---|
| 03-04—LSU | 29 | 1013 | 121 | 240 | .504 | 123 | 157 | .783 | 214 | 17 | 370 | 7.4 | 0.6 | 12.8 |
| 04-05—LSU | 30 | 1007 | 181 | 319 | .567 | 146 | 188 | .777 | 272 | 25 | 520 | 9.1 | 0.8 | 17.3 |
| Totals | 59 | 2020 | 302 | 559 | .540 | 269 | 345 | .780 | 486 | 42 | 890 | 8.2 | 0.7 | 15.1 |

Three-point field goals: 2003-04, 5-for-19 (.263). 2004-05, 12-for-26 (.462). Totals, 17-for-45 (.378).

## BLATCHE, ANDRAY    F    WIZARDS

**PERSONAL:** Born August 22, 1986, in Syracuse, N.Y. ... 6-11/235. (2.11/106.6).
**HIGH SCHOOL:** Henninger (Syracuse, N.Y.) then South Kent Prep (Conn.).
**COLLEGE:** Did not attend college.
**TRANSACTIONS/CAREER NOTES:** Selected out of high school by Washington Wizards in second round (49th pick overall) of 2005 NBA draft.

## BOGUT, ANDREW    C    BUCKS

**PERSONAL:** Born November 28, 1984, in Melbourne, Australia. ... 7-0/245. (2.13/111.1). ... Full name: Andrew Michael Bogut
**HIGH SCHOOL:** Australian Institute of Sport (Melbourne, Australia).
**COLLEGE:** Utah.
**TRANSACTIONS/CAREER NOTES:** Selected after sophomore season by Milwaukee Bucks in first round (first pick overall) of 2005 NBA draft.
**MISCELLANEOUS:** Member of Australian Olympic Team (2004).

### COLLEGIATE RECORD

**NOTES:** National player of the year (2005). ... The SPORTING NEWS All-America first team (2005).

| Season Team | G | Min. | FGM | FGA | Pct. | FTM | FTA | Pct. | Reb. | Ast. | Pts. | RPG | APG | PPG |
|---|---|---|---|---|---|---|---|---|---|---|---|---|---|---|
| 03-04—Utah | 33 | 1002 | 168 | 291 | .577 | 71 | 111 | .640 | 326 | 73 | 411 | 9.9 | 2.2 | 12.5 |
| 04-05—Utah | 35 | 1224 | 281 | 453 | .620 | 144 | 208 | .692 | 427 | 82 | 715 | 12.2 | 2.3 | 20.4 |
| Totals | 68 | 2226 | 449 | 744 | .603 | 215 | 319 | .674 | 753 | 155 | 1126 | 11.1 | 2.3 | 16.6 |

Three-point field goals: 2003-04, 4-for-11 (.364). 2004-05, 9-for-25 (.360). Totals, 13-for-36 (.361).

## BYNUM, ANDREW    C    LAKERS

**PERSONAL:** Born October 27, 1987, in Plainsboro, N.J. ... 7-0/285. (2.13/129.3).
**HIGH SCHOOL:** Solebury Prep (New Hope, Pa.), then St. Joseph (Metuchen, N.J.).
**COLLEGE:** Did not attend college.
**TRANSACTIONS/CAREER NOTES:** Selected out of high school by Los Angeles Lakers in first round (10th pick overall) of 2005 NBA draft.

## BYNUM, WILL    G    CELTICS

**PERSONAL:** Born January 4, 1983 ... 6-0/185. (1.83/83.9).
**HIGH SCHOOL:** Crane Tech (Chicago).
**COLLEGE:** Arizona, then Georgia Tech.
**TRANSACTIONS/CAREER NOTES:** Not drafted by an NBA franchise. ... Signed as free agent by Boston Celtics (August 19, 2005).

### COLLEGIATE RECORD

| Season Team | G | Min. | FGM | FGA | Pct. | FTM | FTA | Pct. | Reb. | Ast. | Pts. | RPG | APG | PPG |
|---|---|---|---|---|---|---|---|---|---|---|---|---|---|---|
| 01-02—Arizona | 31 | 584 | 73 | 212 | .344 | 26 | 40 | .650 | 48 | 44 | 197 | 1.5 | 1.4 | 6.4 |

*PROMISING NEWCOMERS*

| Season Team | G | Min. | FGM | FGA | Pct. | FTM | FTA | Pct. | Reb. | Ast. | Pts. | RPG | APG | PPG |
|---|---|---|---|---|---|---|---|---|---|---|---|---|---|---|
| 02-03—Arizona | 8 | 133 | 21 | 59 | .356 | 7 | 12 | .583 | 22 | 12 | 62 | 2.8 | 1.5 | 7.8 |
| 03-04—Georgia Tech | 30 | 616 | 92 | 223 | .413 | 69 | 90 | .767 | 65 | 75 | 287 | 2.2 | 2.5 | 9.6 |
| 04-05—Georgia Tech | 32 | 873 | 128 | 322 | .398 | 96 | 126 | .762 | 80 | 79 | 401 | 2.5 | 2.5 | 12.5 |
| Totals | 101 | 2206 | 314 | 816 | .385 | 198 | 268 | .739 | 215 | 210 | 947 | 2.1 | 2.1 | 9.4 |

Three-point field goals: 2001-02, 25-for-98 (.255). 2002-03, 13-for-37 (.351). 2003-04, 34-for-97 (.351). 2004-05, 49-for-158 (.310). Totals, 121-for-390 (.310).

## CALDERON, JOSE — RAPTORS

**PERSONAL:** Born September 28, 1981, in Villanueva de la Serena, Spain. ...6-3/210. ... Full name: Jose Manuel Calderon Borrallo.
**TRANSACTIONS/CAREER NOTES:** Played for Tau Ceramic of Spanish league. ... Not drafted by an NBA franchise. ... Signed as free agent by Toronto Raptors (August 3, 2005).
**MISCELLANEOUS:** Member of Spanish Olympic Team (2004).

### SPANISH RECORD

| Season Team | G | Min. | FGM | FGA | Pct. | FTM | FTA | Pct. | Reb. | Ast. | Pts. | RPG | APG | PPG |
|---|---|---|---|---|---|---|---|---|---|---|---|---|---|---|
| 00-01—Lucentum Alicante | 34 | 861 | 111 | 238 | .466 | 48 | 74 | .649 | 78 | 48 | 294 | 2.3 | 1.4 | 8.6 |
| 01-02—Fuenlabrada | 32 | 587 | 94 | 224 | .420 | 87 | 104 | .837 | 49 | 51 | 306 | 1.5 | 1.6 | 9.6 |
| 02-03—Tau Ceramica | 32 | 623 | 58 | 134 | .433 | 58 | 67 | .866 | 59 | 56 | 193 | 1.8 | 1.8 | 6.0 |
| 03-04—Tau Ceramica | 33 | 678 | 89 | 168 | .530 | 52 | 63 | .825 | 93 | 72 | 251 | 2.8 | 2.2 | 7.6 |
| 04-05—Tau Ceramica | 31 | 926 | 140 | 261 | .536 | 90 | 111 | .811 | 83 | 97 | 411 | 2.7 | 3.1 | 13.3 |
| Totals | 162 | 3675 | 492 | 1025 | .480 | 335 | 419 | .800 | 362 | 324 | 1455 | 2.2 | 2.0 | 9.0 |

Three-point field goals: 2000-01, 24-for-67 (.358). 2001-02, 31-for-89 (.348). 2002-03, 19-for-52 (.365). 2003-04, 21-for-58 (.362). 2004-05, 41-for-89 (.461). Totals, 136-for-355 (.383).

## DIENER, TRAVIS — G — MAGIC

**PERSONAL:** Born March 1, 1982, in Fond du Lac, Wisc. ... 6-1/175. (1.85/79.4). ... Full name: Travis Lyle Diener.
**HIGH SCHOOL:** Goodrich (Fond du Lac, Wisc.).
**COLLEGE:** Marquette.
**TRANSACTIONS/CAREER NOTES:** Selected by Orlando Magic in second round (38th pick overall) of 2005 NBA draft.

### COLLEGIATE RECORD

| Season Team | G | Min. | FGM | FGA | Pct. | FTM | FTA | Pct. | Reb. | Ast. | Pts. | RPG | APG | PPG |
|---|---|---|---|---|---|---|---|---|---|---|---|---|---|---|
| 01-02—Marquette | 33 | 781 | 77 | 179 | .430 | 51 | 67 | .761 | 81 | 86 | 262 | 2.5 | 2.6 | 7.9 |
| 02-03—Marquette | 33 | 1146 | 124 | 313 | .396 | 74 | 91 | .813 | 105 | 184 | 391 | 3.2 | 5.6 | 11.8 |
| 03-04—Marquette | 31 | 1060 | 179 | 424 | .422 | 136 | 154 | .883 | 97 | 187 | 584 | 3.1 | 6.0 | 18.8 |
| 04-05—Marquette | 23 | 783 | 131 | 312 | .420 | 124 | 148 | .838 | 90 | 160 | 454 | 3.9 | 7.0 | 19.7 |
| Totals | 120 | 3770 | 511 | 1228 | .416 | 385 | 460 | .837 | 373 | 617 | 1691 | 3.1 | 5.1 | 14.1 |

Three-point field goals: 2001-02, 57-for-129 (.442). 2002-03, 69-for-190 (.363). 2003-04, 90-for-200 (.450). 2004-05, 68-for-168 (.405). Totals, 284-for-687 (.413).

## DIOGU, IKE — F — WARRIORS

**PERSONAL:** Born September 11, 1983, in Buffalo, N.Y. ... 6-8/250. (2.03/113.4). ... Full name: Ikechukwa Somotochukwa Diogu
**HIGH SCHOOL:** Garland (Texas).
**COLLEGE:** Arizona State.
**TRANSACTIONS/CAREER NOTES:** Selected after junior season by Golden State Warriors in first round (ninth pick overall) of 2005 NBA draft.

### COLLEGIATE RECORD

**NOTES:** The SPORTING NEWS All-America second team (2005).

| Season Team | G | Min. | FGM | FGA | Pct. | FTM | FTA | Pct. | Reb. | Ast. | Pts. | RPG | APG | PPG |
|---|---|---|---|---|---|---|---|---|---|---|---|---|---|---|
| 02-03—Arizona State | 32 | 1030 | 209 | 344 | .608 | 180 | 245 | .735 | 249 | 26 | 607 | 7.8 | 0.8 | 19.0 |
| 03-04—Arizona State | 27 | 996 | 179 | 338 | .530 | 243 | 298 | .815 | 241 | 44 | 615 | 8.9 | 1.6 | 22.8 |
| 04-05—Arizona State | 32 | 164 | 229 | 398 | .575 | 248 | 311 | .797 | 312 | 43 | 724 | 9.8 | 1.3 | 22.6 |
| Totals | 91 | 2190 | 617 | 1080 | .571 | 671 | 854 | .786 | 802 | 113 | 1946 | 8.8 | 1.2 | 21.4 |

Three-point field goals: 2002-03, 9-for-24 (.375). 2003-04, 14-for-37 (.378). 2004-05, 18-for-45 (.400). Totals, 41-for-106 (.387).

## ELLIS, MONTA — G — WARRIORS

**PERSONAL:** Born October 26, 1985 ... 6-3/175. (1.91/79.4).
**HIGH SCHOOL:** Lanier (Jackson, Miss.).
**COLLEGE:** Did not attend college.
**TRANSACTIONS/CAREER NOTES:** Selected out of high school by Golden State Warriors in second round (40th pick overall) of 2005 NBA draft.

## EWING, DANIEL　　　　G　　　　CLIPPERS

**PERSONAL:** Born March 26, 1983, in Milton, Fla. ... 6-3/185. (1.91/83.9). ... Full name: Daniel George Ewing
**HIGH SCHOOL:** Willowridge (Missouri City, Texas).
**COLLEGE:** Duke.
**TRANSACTIONS/CAREER NOTES:** Selected by Los Angeles Clippers in second round (32nd overall pick) of 2005 NBA draft.

### COLLEGIATE RECORD

| Season Team | G | Min. | FGM | FGA | Pct. | FTM | FTA | Pct. | Reb. | Ast. | Pts. | AVERAGES RPG | APG | PPG |
|---|---|---|---|---|---|---|---|---|---|---|---|---|---|---|
| 01-02—Duke | 35 | 638 | 80 | 167 | .479 | 35 | 51 | .686 | 78 | 47 | 227 | 2.2 | 1.3 | 6.5 |
| 02-03—Duke | 33 | 920 | 126 | 293 | .430 | 101 | 123 | .821 | 104 | 45 | 395 | 3.2 | 1.4 | 12.0 |
| 03-04—Duke | 37 | 1131 | 151 | 362 | .417 | 92 | 124 | .742 | 96 | 69 | 468 | 2.6 | 1.9 | 12.6 |
| 04-05—Duke | 33 | 1138 | 181 | 424 | .427 | 74 | 107 | .692 | 104 | 132 | 505 | 3.2 | 4.0 | 15.3 |
| **Totals** | 138 | 3827 | 538 | 1246 | .432 | 302 | 405 | .746 | 382 | 293 | 1595 | 2.8 | 2.1 | 11.6 |

Three-point field goals: 2001-02, 32-for-70 (.457). 2002-03, 42-for-105 (.400). 2003-04, 74-for-180 (.411). 2004-05, 69-for-199 (.347). Totals, 217-for-554 (.392).

## FELTON, RAYMOND　　　　G　　　　BOBCATS

**PERSONAL:** Born June 26, 1984, in Marion, S.C. ... 6-1/198. (1.85/89.8). ... Full name: Raymond Bernard Felton
**HIGH SCHOOL:** Latta (S.C.).
**COLLEGE:** North Carolina.
**TRANSACTIONS/CAREER NOTES:** Selected after junior season by Charlotte Bobcats in first round (fifth pick overall) of 2005 NBA draft.

### COLLEGIATE RECORD

**NOTES:** Member of NCAA Division I championship team (2005).

| Season Team | G | Min. | FGM | FGA | Pct. | FTM | FTA | Pct. | Reb. | Ast. | Pts. | AVERAGES RPG | APG | PPG |
|---|---|---|---|---|---|---|---|---|---|---|---|---|---|---|
| 02-03—North Carolina | 35 | 1240 | 151 | 379 | .398 | 79 | 114 | .693 | 143 | 236 | 450 | 4.1 | 6.7 | 12.9 |
| 03-04—North Carolina | 30 | 1039 | 113 | 269 | .420 | 85 | 105 | .810 | 119 | 213 | 346 | 4.0 | 7.1 | 11.5 |
| 04-05—North Carolina | 36 | 1142 | 150 | 330 | .455 | 94 | 134 | .701 | 155 | 249 | 464 | 4.3 | 6.9 | 12.9 |
| **Totals** | 101 | 3421 | 414 | 978 | .423 | 258 | 353 | .731 | 417 | 698 | 1260 | 4.1 | 6.9 | 12.5 |

Three-point field goals: 2002-03, 69-for-193 (.358). 2003-04, 35-for-112 (.313). 2004-05, 70-for-159 (.440). Totals, 174-for-464 (.375).

## FRYE, CHANNING　　　　C　　　　KNICKS

**PERSONAL:** Born May 17, 1983, in White Plains, N.Y. ... 6-11/248. (2.11/112.5). ... Full name: Channing Thomas Frye
**HIGH SCHOOL:** St. Mary's (Phoenix, Ariz.).
**COLLEGE:** Arizona.
**TRANSACTIONS/CAREER NOTES:** Selected by New York Knicks in first round (eighth pick overall) of 2005 NBA Draft.

### COLLEGIATE RECORD

| Season Team | G | Min. | FGM | FGA | Pct. | FTM | FTA | Pct. | Reb. | Ast. | Pts. | AVERAGES RPG | APG | PPG |
|---|---|---|---|---|---|---|---|---|---|---|---|---|---|---|
| 01-02—Arizona | 34 | 814 | 122 | 205 | .595 | 80 | 110 | .727 | 214 | 25 | 324 | 6.3 | 0.7 | 9.5 |
| 02-03—Arizona | 32 | 814 | 165 | 290 | .569 | 73 | 110 | .664 | 257 | 23 | 403 | 8.0 | 0.7 | 12.6 |
| 03-04—Arizona | 30 | 910 | 193 | 352 | .548 | 89 | 113 | .788 | 222 | 56 | 478 | 7.4 | 1.9 | 15.9 |
| 04-05—Arizona | 37 | 1148 | 227 | 410 | .554 | 127 | 153 | .830 | 282 | 71 | 584 | 7.6 | 1.9 | 15.8 |
| **Totals** | 133 | 3686 | 707 | 1257 | .562 | 369 | 486 | .759 | 975 | 175 | 1789 | 7.3 | 1.3 | 13.5 |

Three-point field goals: 2001-02, 0-for-0. 2002-03, 0-for-1. 2003-04, 3-for-5 (.600). 2004-05, 3-for-17 (.176). Totals, 6-for-23 (.261).

## GARCIA, FRANCISCO　　　　G/F　　　　KINGS

**PERSONAL:** Born December 31, 1981, in Santo Domingo, Dominican Republic. ... 6-7/195. (2.01/88.5). ... Full name: Francisco Alberto Garcia
**HIGH SCHOOL:** Winchendon School (Mass.).
**COLLEGE:** Louisville.
**TRANSACTIONS/CAREER NOTES:** Selected after junior season by Sacramento Kings in first round (23rd pick overall) of 2005 NBA draft.

### COLLEGIATE RECORD

| Season Team | G | Min. | FGM | FGA | Pct. | FTM | FTA | Pct. | Reb. | Ast. | Pts. | AVERAGES RPG | APG | PPG |
|---|---|---|---|---|---|---|---|---|---|---|---|---|---|---|
| 02-03—Louisville | 32 | 696 | 126 | 258 | .488 | 49 | 55 | .891 | 94 | 67 | 358 | 2.9 | 2.1 | 11.2 |
| 03-04—Louisville | 28 | 850 | 149 | 345 | .432 | 110 | 138 | .797 | 127 | 131 | 460 | 4.5 | 4.7 | 16.4 |
| 04-05—Louisville | 38 | 1211 | 187 | 428 | .437 | 150 | 171 | .877 | 158 | 148 | 595 | 4.2 | 3.9 | 15.7 |
| **Totals** | 98 | 2757 | 462 | 1031 | .448 | 309 | 364 | .849 | 379 | 346 | 1413 | 3.9 | 3.5 | 14.4 |

Three-point field goals: 2002-03, 57-for-134 (.425). 2003-04, 52-for-160 (.325). 2004-05, 71-for-194 (.366). Totals, 180-for-488 (.369).

# GELABALE, MICKAEL          F          SUPERSONICS

**PERSONAL:** Born May 22, 1983, in Pointe Noire, France. ... 6-7/215. (2.01/97.5).
**TRANSACTIONS/CAREER NOTES:** Played for Cholet of French League. ... Played for Real Madrid of Spanish League. ... Selected by Seattle SuperSonics in second round (48th pick overall) of 2005 NBA Draft.

## FRENCH LEAGUE RECORD

| Season Team | G | Min. | FGM | FGA | Pct. | FTM | FTA | Pct. | Reb. | Ast. | Pts. | RPG | APG | PPG |
|---|---|---|---|---|---|---|---|---|---|---|---|---|---|---|
| 01-02—Cholet | 6 | 24 | 3 | 5 | .600 | 2 | 2 | 1.000 | 4 | 0 | 8 | 0.7 | 0.0 | 1.3 |
| 02-03—Cholet | 18 | 276 | 45 | 89 | .506 | 12 | 19 | .632 | 46 | 17 | 108 | 2.6 | 0.9 | 6.0 |
| 03-04—Cholet | 34 | 1005 | 128 | 246 | .520 | 78 | 96 | .813 | 50 | 75 | 353 | 1.5 | 2.2 | 10.4 |
| **Totals** | 58 | 1305 | 176 | 340 | .518 | 92 | 117 | .786 | 100 | 92 | 469 | 1.7 | 1.6 | 8.1 |

Three-point field goals: 2001-02, 0-for-1. 2002-03, 6-for-23 (.261). 2003-04, 19-for-52 (.365). Totals, 25-for-76 (.329).

## SPANISH LEAGUE RECORD

| Season Team | G | Min. | FGM | FGA | Pct. | FTM | FTA | Pct. | Reb. | Ast. | Pts. | RPG | APG | PPG |
|---|---|---|---|---|---|---|---|---|---|---|---|---|---|---|
| 04-05—Real Madrid | 34 | 820 | 103 | 185 | .557 | 52 | 67 | .776 | 120 | 37 | 275 | 3.5 | 1.1 | 8.1 |

Three-point field goals: 2004-05, 17-for-47 (.362).

# GOMES, RYAN          F          CELTICS

**PERSONAL:** Born September 1, 1982, in Waterbury, Conn. ... 6-7/250. (2.01/113.4). ... Full name: Ryan Anthony Gomes
**HIGH SCHOOL:** Wilby (Waterbury, Conn.).
**COLLEGE:** Providence.
**TRANSACTIONS/CAREER NOTES:** Selected by Boston Celtics in second round (50th pick overall) of 2005 NBA draft.

## COLLEGIATE RECORD

**NOTES:** The SPORTING NEWS All-America first team (2004).

| Season Team | G | Min. | FGM | FGA | Pct. | FTM | FTA | Pct. | Reb. | Ast. | Pts. | RPG | APG | PPG |
|---|---|---|---|---|---|---|---|---|---|---|---|---|---|---|
| 01-02—Providence | 24 | 756 | 132 | 236 | .559 | 68 | 111 | .613 | 188 | 37 | 332 | 7.8 | 1.5 | 13.8 |
| 02-03—Providence | 32 | 1152 | 213 | 397 | .537 | 163 | 194 | .840 | 311 | 66 | 589 | 9.7 | 2.1 | 18.4 |
| 03-04—Providence | 29 | 1008 | 192 | 379 | .507 | 163 | 154 | .870 | 274 | 67 | 547 | 9.4 | 2.3 | 18.9 |
| 04-05—Providence | 31 | 1161 | 247 | 498 | .496 | 124 | 161 | .770 | 255 | 100 | 670 | 8.2 | 3.2 | 21.6 |
| **Totals** | 116 | 4077 | 784 | 1510 | .519 | 489 | 620 | .789 | 1028 | 270 | 2138 | 8.9 | 2.3 | 18.4 |

Three-point field goals: 2001-02, 0-for-3. 2002-03, 0-for-3. 2003-04, 29-for-87 (.333). 2004-05, 52-for-137 (.380). Totals, 81-for-230 (.352).

# GORTAT, MARCIN          F/C          MAGIC

**PERSONAL:** Born February 17, 1984, in Lodz, Poland. ... 6-11/240. (2.11/108.9).
**COLLEGE:** Did not attend.
**TRANSACTIONS/CAREER NOTES:** Played for RheinEnergy Koln of German league. ... Selected by Phoenix Suns in second round (57th pick overall) of 2005 NBA Draft. ... Draft rights traded by Suns to Orlando Magic for future considerations (June 28, 2005).

## GERMAN LEAGUE RECORD

| Season Team | G | Min. | FGM | FGA | Pct. | FTM | FTA | Pct. | Reb. | Ast. | Pts. | RPG | APG | PPG |
|---|---|---|---|---|---|---|---|---|---|---|---|---|---|---|
| 03-04—RheinEnergie Koln | 5 | 14 | 0 | 0 | ... | 2 | 4 | .500 | 3 | 0 | 2 | 0.6 | 0.0 | 0.4 |
| 04-05—RheinEnergie Koln | 29 | 458 | 65 | 91 | .714 | 20 | 43 | .465 | 110 | 10 | 150 | 3.8 | 0.3 | 5.2 |
| **Totals** | 34 | 472 | 65 | 91 | .714 | 22 | 47 | .468 | 113 | 10 | 152 | 3.3 | 0.3 | 4.5 |

# GRAHAM, JOEY          F          RAPTORS

**PERSONAL:** Born June 11, 1982, in Wilmington, Del. ... 6-7/225. (2.01/102.1). ... Full name: Joey Joseph Graham
**HIGH SCHOOL:** Brandon (Fla.).
**COLLEGE:** Central Florida, then Oklahoma State.
**TRANSACTIONS/CAREER NOTES:** Selected by Toronto Raptors in first round (16th pick overall) of 2005 NBA draft.

## COLLEGIATE RECORD

| Season Team | G | Min. | FGM | FGA | Pct. | FTM | FTA | Pct. | Reb. | Ast. | Pts. | RPG | APG | PPG |
|---|---|---|---|---|---|---|---|---|---|---|---|---|---|---|
| 00-01—Central Florida | 31 | 632 | 91 | 192 | .474 | 69 | 82 | .841 | 117 | 33 | 262 | 3.8 | 1.1 | 8.5 |
| 01-02—Central Florida | 29 | 832 | 134 | 263 | .510 | 98 | 128 | .766 | 163 | 70 | 386 | 5.6 | 2.4 | 13.3 |
| 02-03—Oklahoma State | | | | | Did Not Play - Transfer Student | | | | | | | | | |
| 03-04—Oklahoma State | 35 | 864 | 171 | 297 | .576 | 78 | 110 | .709 | 183 | 40 | 434 | 5.2 | 1.1 | 12.4 |
| 04-05—Oklahoma State | 33 | 1009 | 201 | 380 | .529 | 157 | 177 | .887 | 204 | 67 | 585 | 6.2 | 2.0 | 17.7 |
| **Totals** | 128 | 3337 | 597 | 1132 | .527 | 402 | 497 | .809 | 667 | 210 | 1667 | 5.2 | 1.6 | 13.0 |

Three-point field goals: 2000-01, 11-for-52 (.212). 2001-02, 20-for-52 (.385). 2003-04, 14-for-29 (.483). 2004-05, 26-for-55 (.473). Totals, 71-for-188 (.378).

PROMISING NEWCOMERS

## GRANGER, DANNY  F  PACERS

**PERSONAL:** Born April 20, 1983, in New Orleans, La. ... 6-8/225. (2.03/102.1).
**HIGH SCHOOL:** Grace King (Metairie, La.) .
**COLLEGE:** Bradley, then New Mexico.
**TRANSACTIONS/CAREER NOTES:** Selected by Indiana Pacers in first round (17th pick overall) of 2005 NBA draft.

### COLLEGIATE RECORD

| Season Team | G | Min. | FGM | FGA | Pct. | FTM | FTA | Pct. | Reb. | Ast. | Pts. | AVERAGES RPG | APG | PPG |
|---|---|---|---|---|---|---|---|---|---|---|---|---|---|---|
| 01-02—Bradley | 29 | 712 | 111 | 249 | .446 | 98 | 124 | .790 | 207 | 21 | 323 | 7.1 | 0.7 | 11.1 |
| 02-03—Bradley | 14 | 380 | 99 | 191 | .518 | 65 | 95 | .684 | 111 | 16 | 269 | 7.9 | 1.1 | 19.2 |
| 03-04—New Mexico | 22 | 703 | 136 | 277 | .491 | 133 | 175 | .760 | 197 | 46 | 429 | 9.0 | 2.1 | 19.5 |
| 04-05—New Mexico | 30 | 900 | 183 | 349 | .524 | 154 | 204 | .755 | 266 | 71 | 565 | 8.9 | 2.4 | 18.8 |
| Totals | 95 | 2695 | 529 | 1066 | .496 | 450 | 598 | .753 | 781 | 154 | 1586 | 8.2 | 1.6 | 16.7 |

Three-point field goals: 2001-02, 3-for-17 (.176). 2002-03, 6-for-20 (.300). 2003-04, 24-for-72 (.333). 2004-05, 45-for-104 (.433). Totals, 78-for-213 (.366).

## GREEN, GERALD  F  CELTICS

**PERSONAL:** Born January 26, 1986, in Houston, Texas. ... 6-8/200. (2.03/90.7).
**HIGH SCHOOL:** Dobie (Houston), then Gulf Shores Academy (Texas).
**COLLEGE:** Did not attend college.
**TRANSACTIONS/CAREER NOTES:** Selected out of high school by Boston Celtics in first round (18th pick overall) of 2005 NBA draft.

## GREENE, ORIEN  G  CELTICS

**PERSONAL:** Born February 4, 1982, in Gainesville, Fla. ... 6-4/208. (1.93/94.3). ... Full name: Orien Randolph Greene.
**COLLEGE:** Florida, then La.-Lafayette.
**TRANSACTIONS/CAREER NOTES:** Selected by Boston Celtics in second round (53rd pick overall) of 2005 NBA draft.

### COLLEGIATE RECORD

| Season Team | G | Min. | FGM | FGA | Pct. | FTM | FTA | Pct. | Reb. | Ast. | Pts. | AVERAGES RPG | APG | PPG |
|---|---|---|---|---|---|---|---|---|---|---|---|---|---|---|
| 00-01—Florida | 31 | 591 | 35 | 99 | .354 | 21 | 28 | .750 | 72 | 85 | 104 | 2.3 | 2.7 | 3.4 |
| 01-02—Florida | 31 | 737 | 63 | 145 | .434 | 14 | 22 | .636 | 88 | 89 | 160 | 2.8 | 2.9 | 5.2 |
| 02-03—La-Lafayette | | | | | Did Not Play - Transfer Student | | | | | | | | | |
| 03-04—La-Lafayette | 18 | 464 | 68 | 150 | .453 | 22 | 32 | .688 | 82 | 54 | 188 | 4.6 | 3.0 | 10.4 |
| 04-05—La-Lafayette | 24 | 775 | 92 | 237 | .388 | 62 | 82 | .756 | 113 | 98 | 280 | 4.7 | 4.1 | 11.7 |
| Totals | 104 | 2567 | 258 | 631 | .409 | 119 | 164 | .726 | 355 | 326 | 732 | 3.4 | 3.1 | 7.0 |

Three-point field goals: 2000-01, 13-for-52 (.250). 2001-02, 20-for-66 (.303). 2003-04, 30-for-83 (.361). 2004-05, 34-for-106 (.321). Totals, 97-for-307 (.316).

## HEAD, LUTHER  G  ROCKETS

**PERSONAL:** Born November 26, 1982, in Chicago, Ill. ... 6-3/185. (1.91/83.9). ... Full name: Luther D. Head
**HIGH SCHOOL:** Manley Career Academy (Chicago).
**COLLEGE:** Illinois.
**TRANSACTIONS/CAREER NOTES:** Selected by Houston Rockets in first round (24th pick overall) of 2005 NBA draft.

### COLLEGIATE RECORD

| Season Team | G | Min. | FGM | FGA | Pct. | FTM | FTA | Pct. | Reb. | Ast. | Pts. | AVERAGES RPG | APG | PPG |
|---|---|---|---|---|---|---|---|---|---|---|---|---|---|---|
| 01-02—Illinois | 35 | 581 | 63 | 124 | .508 | 14 | 25 | .560 | 67 | 59 | 156 | 1.9 | 1.7 | 4.5 |
| 02-03—Illinois | 25 | 509 | 68 | 131 | .519 | 34 | 46 | .739 | 71 | 42 | 198 | 2.8 | 1.7 | 7.9 |
| 03-04—Illinois | 29 | 863 | 107 | 239 | .448 | 56 | 72 | .778 | 110 | 75 | 319 | 3.8 | 2.6 | 11.0 |
| 04-05—Illinois | 39 | 1297 | 214 | 462 | .463 | 78 | 99 | .788 | 155 | 150 | 622 | 4.0 | 3.8 | 15.9 |
| Totals | 128 | 3250 | 452 | 956 | .473 | 182 | 242 | .752 | 403 | 326 | 1295 | 3.1 | 2.5 | 10.1 |

Three-point field goals: 2001-02, 16-for-55 (.291). 2002-03, 28-for-66 (.424). 2003-04, 49-for-143 (.343). 2004-05, 116-for-283 (.410). Totals, 209-for-547 (.382).

## HERVELLE, AXEL  F  NUGGETS

**PERSONAL:** Born May 12, 1983, in Liege, Belgium. ... 6-8/230. (2.03/104.3).
**COLLEGE:** Did not attend.
**TRANSACTIONS/CAREER NOTES:** Played for Real Madrid of Spanish league. ... Selected by Denver Nuggets in second round (52nd pick overall) of 2005 NBA Draft.

### BELGIAN LEAGUE RECORD

| Season Team | G | Min. | FGM | FGA | Pct. | FTM | FTA | Pct. | Reb. | Ast. | Pts. | AVERAGES RPG | APG | PPG |
|---|---|---|---|---|---|---|---|---|---|---|---|---|---|---|
| 00-01—Pepinster | 6 | 32 | 4 | 7 | .571 | 2 | 2 | 1.000 | 6 | 0 | 10 | 1.0 | 0.0 | 1.7 |
| 01-02—Pepinster | 24 | 279 | 35 | 74 | .473 | 22 | 31 | .710 | 69 | 13 | 97 | 2.9 | 0.5 | 4.0 |

| Season Team | G | Min. | FGM | FGA | Pct. | FTM | FTA | Pct. | Reb. | Ast. | Pts. | AVERAGES RPG | APG | PPG |
|---|---|---|---|---|---|---|---|---|---|---|---|---|---|---|
| 02-03—Pepinster | 25 | 637 | 80 | 162 | .494 | 52 | 81 | .642 | 186 | 34 | 219 | 7.4 | 1.4 | 8.8 |
| 03-04—Pepinster | 16 | 419 | 60 | 121 | .496 | 50 | 71 | .704 | 169 | 18 | 182 | 10.6 | 1.1 | 11.4 |
| 04-05—Pepinster | 3 | 90 | 15 | 31 | .484 | 6 | 9 | .667 | 31 | 3 | 36 | 10.3 | 1.0 | 12.0 |
| Totals | 74 | 1457 | 194 | 395 | .491 | 132 | 194 | .680 | 461 | 68 | 544 | 6.2 | 0.9 | 7.4 |

Three-point field goals: 2001-02, 5-for-18 (.278). 2002-03, 7-for-34 (.206). 2003-04, 12-for-29 (.414). 2004-05, 0-for-8. Totals, 24-for-89 (.270).

# HODGE, JULIUS      G      NUGGETS

**PERSONAL:** Born November 18, 1983, in New York, N.Y. ... 6-7/210. (2.01/95.3). ... Full name: Julius Melvin Hodge.
**HIGH SCHOOL:** St. Raymond's (Bronx, N.Y.).
**COLLEGE:** North Carolina State.
**TRANSACTIONS/CAREER NOTES:** Selected by Denver Nuggets in first round (20th pick overall) of 2005 NBA draft.

### COLLEGIATE RECORD

**NOTES:** The SPORTING NEWS All-America first team (2004).

| Season Team | G | Min. | FGM | FGA | Pct. | FTM | FTA | Pct. | Reb. | Ast. | Pts. | AVERAGES RPG | APG | PPG |
|---|---|---|---|---|---|---|---|---|---|---|---|---|---|---|
| 01-02—North Carolina State | 33 | 907 | 115 | 260 | .442 | 89 | 120 | .742 | 160 | 71 | 352 | 4.8 | 2.2 | 10.7 |
| 02-03—North Carolina State | 31 | 1093 | 164 | 374 | .439 | 179 | 219 | .817 | 190 | 109 | 548 | 6.1 | 3.5 | 17.7 |
| 03-04—North Carolina State | 31 | 1081 | 189 | 373 | .507 | 159 | 192 | .828 | 198 | 112 | 563 | 6.4 | 3.6 | 18.2 |
| 04-05—North Carolina State | 34 | 1177 | 197 | 400 | .493 | 169 | 253 | .668 | 225 | 162 | 577 | 6.6 | 4.8 | 17.0 |
| Totals | 129 | 4258 | 665 | 1407 | .473 | 507 | 664 | .764 | 773 | 454 | 2040 | 6.0 | 3.5 | 15.8 |

Three-point field goals: 2001-02, 33-for-95 (.347). 2002-03, 41-for-125 (.328). 2003-04, 26-for-72 (.361). 2004-05, 14-for-55 (.255). Totals, 114-for-347 (.329).

# ILIC, MILE      C      NETS

**PERSONAL:** Born June 2, 1984, in Tuzla, Bosnia-Herzegovina. ... 7-1/230. (2.16/104.3).
**COLLEGE:** Did not attend.
**TRANSACTIONS/CAREER NOTES:** Played for FMP Zeleznik of the Yugoslavian league. ... Selected by New Jersey Nets in second round (43rd pick overall) of 2005 NBA Draft.

### YUGOSLAVIAN LEAGUE RECORD

| Season Team | G | Min. | FGM | FGA | Pct. | FTM | FTA | Pct. | Reb. | Ast. | Pts. | AVERAGES RPG | APG | PPG |
|---|---|---|---|---|---|---|---|---|---|---|---|---|---|---|
| 01-02—FMP Zeleznik | 1 | 2 | 1 | 3 | .333 | 0 | 0 | ... | 0 | 0 | 2 | 0.0 | 0.0 | 2.0 |
| 02-03—FMP Zeleznik | 8 | 16 | 3 | 7 | .429 | 3 | 4 | .750 | 5 | 3 | 9 | 0.6 | 0.4 | 1.1 |
| Totals | 9 | 18 | 4 | 10 | .400 | 3 | 4 | .750 | 5 | 3 | 11 | 0.6 | 0.3 | 1.2 |

Three-point field goals: 2001-02, 0-for-1. 2002-03, 0-for-1. Totals, 0-for-2 (.000).

### ADRIATIC LEAGUE RECORD

| Season Team | G | Min. | FGM | FGA | Pct. | FTM | FTA | Pct. | Reb. | Ast. | Pts. | AVERAGES RPG | APG | PPG |
|---|---|---|---|---|---|---|---|---|---|---|---|---|---|---|
| 03-04—KK Reflex | 14 | 115 | 15 | 29 | .517 | 13 | 17 | .765 | 13 | 3 | 43 | 0.9 | 0.2 | 3.1 |
| 04-05—KK Reflex | 31 | 486 | 97 | 143 | .678 | 32 | 49 | .653 | 106 | 16 | 226 | 3.4 | 0.5 | 7.3 |
| Totals | 45 | 601 | 112 | 172 | .651 | 45 | 66 | .682 | 119 | 19 | 269 | 2.6 | 0.4 | 6.0 |

Three-point field goals: 2003-04, 0-for-1. 2004-05, 0-for-2. Totals, 0-for-3 (.000).

# ILYASOVA, ERSAN      F      BUCKS

**PERSONAL:** Born May 15, 1987, in Ekisehir, Turkey. ... 6-9/235. (2.06/106.6).
**HIGH SCHOOL:** Did not attend.
**COLLEGE:** Did not attend.
**TRANSACTIONS/CAREER NOTES:** Played for Ulker of the Turkish league. ... Selected by Milwaukee Bucks in second round (36th pick overall) of 2005 NBA Draft.

### TURKISH LEAGUE RECORD

| Season Team | G | Min. | FGM | FGA | Pct. | FTM | FTA | Pct. | Reb. | Ast. | Pts. | AVERAGES RPG | APG | PPG |
|---|---|---|---|---|---|---|---|---|---|---|---|---|---|---|
| 04-05—Ulker | 15 | 186 | 21 | 49 | .429 | 5 | 11 | .455 | 52 | 8 | 58 | 3.5 | 0.5 | 3.9 |

Three-point field goals: 2004-05, 11-for-29 (.379). Totals, 11-for-29 (.379).

# JACK, JARRETT      G      TRAIL BLAZERS

**PERSONAL:** Born October 28, 1983, in Fort Washington, Md. ... 6-3/202. (1.91/91.6). ... Full name: Jarrett Matthew Jack
**HIGH SCHOOL:** Worcester Academy (Worcester, Mass.).
**COLLEGE:** Georgia Tech.
**TRANSACTIONS/CAREER NOTES:** Selected after junior season by Denver Nuggets in first round (22nd pick overall) of 2005 NBA draft. ... Draft rights traded by Nuggets to Portland Trail Blazers for draft rights to Fs Linas Kleiza and Ricky Sanchez (June 28, 2005).

| | | | | | | | | | | | | AVERAGES | | |
| Season Team | G | Min. | FGM | FGA | Pct. | FTM | FTA | Pct. | Reb. | Ast. | Pts. | RPG | APG | PPG |
|---|---|---|---|---|---|---|---|---|---|---|---|---|---|---|
| 02-03—Georgia Tech............... | 31 | 984 | 97 | 213 | .455 | 83 | 118 | .703 | 110 | 185 | 294 | 3.5 | 6.0 | 9.5 |
| 03-04—Georgia Tech............... | 38 | 1185 | 145 | 318 | .456 | 154 | 192 | .802 | 185 | 213 | 474 | 4.9 | 5.6 | 12.5 |
| 04-05—Georgia Tech............... | 32 | 1091 | 164 | 319 | .514 | 123 | 142 | .866 | 155 | 145 | 497 | 4.8 | 4.5 | 15.5 |
| Totals ................................. | 101 | 3260 | 406 | 850 | .478 | 360 | 452 | .796 | 450 | 543 | 1265 | 4.5 | 5.4 | 12.5 |

Three-point field goals: 2002-03, 17-for-60 (.283). 2003-04, 30-for-95 (.316). 2004-05, 46-for-104 (.442). Totals, 93-for-259 (.359).

# JASIKEVICIUS, SARUNAS  G                                          PACERS

**PERSONAL:** Born March 5, 1976, in Kaunas, Lithuania. ... 6-4/195. (1.93/88.5).
**HIGH SCHOOL:** Solanco (Quarryville, Pa).
**COLLEGE:** Maryland.
**TRANSACTIONS/CAREER NOTES:** Not drafted by an NBA franchise. ... Signed as free agent by Indiana Pacers (August 11, 2005).
**MISCELLANEOUS:** Member of bronze-medal-winning Lithuanian Olympic team (2000). ... Member of Lithuanian Olympic team (2004).

| | | | | | | | | | | | | AVERAGES | | |
| Season Team | G | Min. | FGM | FGA | Pct. | FTM | FTA | Pct. | Reb. | Ast. | Pts. | RPG | APG | PPG |
|---|---|---|---|---|---|---|---|---|---|---|---|---|---|---|
| 94-95—Maryland ..................... | 29 | 177 | 29 | 65 | .446 | 17 | 21 | .810 | 19 | 16 | 89 | 0.7 | 0.6 | 3.1 |
| 95-96—Maryland ..................... | 27 | 261 | 38 | 89 | .427 | 10 | 20 | .500 | 31 | 21 | 106 | 1.1 | 0.8 | 3.9 |
| 96-97—Maryland ..................... | 32 | 928 | 115 | 275 | .418 | 66 | 89 | .742 | 80 | 78 | 338 | 2.5 | 2.4 | 10.6 |
| 97-98—Maryland ..................... | 32 | 937 | 135 | 296 | .456 | 66 | 87 | .759 | 104 | 80 | 396 | 3.3 | 2.5 | 12.4 |
| Totals ................................. | 120 | 2303 | 317 | 725 | .437 | 159 | 217 | .733 | 234 | 195 | 929 | 2.0 | 1.6 | 7.7 |

Three-point field goals: 1994-95, 14-for-37 (.378). 1995-96, 20-for-44 (.455). 1996-97, 42-for-131 (.321). 1997-98, 60-for-151 (.397). Totals, 136-for-363 (.375).

| | | | | | | | | | | | | AVERAGES | | |
| Season Team | G | Min. | FGM | FGA | Pct. | FTM | FTA | Pct. | Reb. | Ast. | Pts. | RPG | APG | PPG |
|---|---|---|---|---|---|---|---|---|---|---|---|---|---|---|
| 98-99—Lietuvos ..................... | 30 | 945 | 180 | 353 | .510 | 89 | 110 | .809 | 103 | 151 | 526 | 3.4 | 5.0 | 17.5 |

Three-point field goals: 1998-99, 77-for-166 (.464). Totals, 77-for-166 (.464).

| | | | | | | | | | | | | AVERAGES | | |
| Season Team | G | Min. | FGM | FGA | Pct. | FTM | FTA | Pct. | Reb. | Ast. | Pts. | RPG | APG | PPG |
|---|---|---|---|---|---|---|---|---|---|---|---|---|---|---|
| 98-99—Olimpija Ljubljana.......... | 30 | 945 | 180 | 353 | .510 | 89 | 110 | .809 | 103 | 151 | 526 | 3.4 | 5.0 | 17.5 |

Three-point field goals: 1998-99, 77-for-166 (.464). Totals, 77-for-166 (.464).

| | | | | | | | | | | | | AVERAGES | | |
| Season Team | G | Min. | FGM | FGA | Pct. | FTM | FTA | Pct. | Reb. | Ast. | Pts. | RPG | APG | PPG |
|---|---|---|---|---|---|---|---|---|---|---|---|---|---|---|
| 00-01—FC Barcelona ................ | 28 | 753 | 135 | 265 | .509 | 56 | 69 | .812 | 60 | 140 | 388 | 2.1 | 5.0 | 13.9 |
| 01-02—FC Barcelona ................ | 30 | 730 | 138 | 286 | .483 | 102 | 121 | .843 | 77 | 131 | 444 | 2.6 | 4.4 | 14.8 |
| 02-03—FC Barcelona ................ | 34 | 832 | 129 | 272 | .474 | 74 | 83 | .892 | 43 | 113 | 402 | 1.3 | 3.3 | 11.8 |
| Totals ................................. | 92 | 2315 | 402 | 823 | .488 | 232 | 273 | .850 | 180 | 384 | 1234 | 2.0 | 4.2 | 13.4 |

Three-point field goals: 2000-01, 62-for-142 (.437). 2001-02, 66-for-158 (.418). 2002-03, 70-for-150 (.467). Totals, 198-for-450 (.440).

| | | | | | | | | | | | | AVERAGES | | |
| Season Team | G | Min. | FGM | FGA | Pct. | FTM | FTA | Pct. | Reb. | Ast. | Pts. | RPG | APG | PPG |
|---|---|---|---|---|---|---|---|---|---|---|---|---|---|---|
| 03-04—Maccabi Tel-Aviv ........... | 21 | 547 | 88 | 162 | .543 | 19 | 29 | .655 | 35 | 110 | 251 | 1.7 | 5.2 | 12.0 |
| 04-05—Maccabi Tel-Aviv ........... | 17 | 411 | 69 | 131 | .527 | 29 | 34 | .853 | 36 | 85 | 211 | 2.1 | 5.0 | 12.4 |
| Totals ................................. | 38 | 958 | 157 | 293 | .536 | 48 | 63 | .762 | 71 | 195 | 462 | 1.9 | 5.1 | 12.2 |

Three-point field goals: 2003-04, 56-for-99 (.566). 2004-05, 44-for-86 (.512). Totals, 100-for-185 (.541).

# JOHNSON, AMIR                    F                                 PISTONS

**PERSONAL:** Born May 1, 1987, in Los Angeles, Calif. ... 6-9/210. (2.06/95.3).
**HIGH SCHOOL:** Westchester (Los Angeles, Calif.).
**COLLEGE:** Did not attend college.
**TRANSACTIONS/CAREER NOTES:** Selected out of high school by Detroit Pistons in second round (56th pick overall) of 2005 NBA draft.

# KLEIZA, LINAS                    F                                 NUGGETS

**PERSONAL:** Born January 3, 1985, in Kaunas, Lithuania. ... 6-8/245. (2.03/111.1).
**HIGH SCHOOL:** Montrose Christian (Rockville, Md.) .
**COLLEGE:** Missouri.
**TRANSACTIONS/CAREER NOTES:** Selected after sophomore season by Portland Trail Blazers in first round (27th pick overall) of 2005 NBA draft. ... Draft rights traded by Trail Blazers with draft rights to F Ricky Sanchez to Denver Nuggets for draft rights to G Jarrett Jack (June 28, 2005).

| | | | | | | | | | | | | AVERAGES | | |
| Season Team | G | Min. | FGM | FGA | Pct. | FTM | FTA | Pct. | Reb. | Ast. | Pts. | RPG | APG | PPG |
|---|---|---|---|---|---|---|---|---|---|---|---|---|---|---|
| 03-04—Missouri ....................... | 16 | 370 | 64 | 146 | .438 | 41 | 66 | .621 | 135 | 13 | 177 | 8.4 | 0.8 | 11.1 |
| 04-05—Missouri ....................... | 33 | 1038 | 165 | 409 | .403 | 169 | 231 | .732 | 250 | 53 | 530 | 7.6 | 1.6 | 16.1 |
| Totals ................................. | 49 | 1408 | 229 | 555 | .413 | 210 | 297 | .707 | 385 | 66 | 707 | 7.9 | 1.3 | 14.4 |

Three-point field goals: 2003-04, 8-for-23 (.348). 2004-05, 31-for-113 (.274). Totals, 39-for-136 (.287).

PROMISING NEWCOMERS

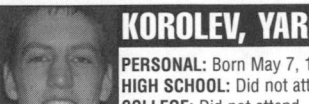

## KOROLEV, YAROSLAV    F          CLIPPERS

**PERSONAL:** Born May 7, 1987, in Moscow, Russia. ... 6-9/203. (2.06/92.1).
**HIGH SCHOOL:** Did not attend.
**COLLEGE:** Did not attend.
**TRANSACTIONS/CAREER NOTES:** Played for CSKA of the Russian league. ... Selected by Los Angeles Clippers in first round (12th pick overall) of 2005 NBA Draft.

### RUSSIAN LEAGUE RECORD

| | | | | | | | | | | | AVERAGES | | |
| Season Team | G | Min. | FGM | FGA | Pct. | FTM | FTA | Pct. | Reb. | Ast. | Pts. | RPG | APG | PPG |
| --- | --- | --- | --- | --- | --- | --- | --- | --- | --- | --- | --- | --- | --- | --- |
| 03-04—Avtodor Saratov ............ | 22 | 400 | 34 | 103 | .330 | 31 | 50 | .620 | 62 | 19 | 106 | 2.8 | 0.9 | 4.8 |
| 04-05—CSKA............................. | 4 | 24 | 4 | 6 | .667 | 3 | 4 | .750 | 3 | 2 | 12 | 0.8 | 0.5 | 3.0 |
| Totals .................................. | 26 | 424 | 38 | 109 | .349 | 34 | 54 | .630 | 65 | 21 | 118 | 2.5 | 0.8 | 4.5 |

Three-point field goals: 2003-04, 7-for-25 (.280). 2004-05, 1-for-3 (.333). Totals, 8-for-28 (.286).

## LEE, DAVID    F          KNICKS

**PERSONAL:** Born April 29, 1983, in St. Louis, Mo. ... 6-9/249. (2.06/112.9).
**HIGH SCHOOL:** Chaminade Prep (St. Louis, Mo.).
**COLLEGE:** Florida.
**TRANSACTIONS/CAREER NOTES:** Selected by New York Knicks in first round (30th pick overall) of 2005 NBA draft.

### COLLEGIATE RECORD

| | | | | | | | | | | | AVERAGES | | |
| Season Team | G | Min. | FGM | FGA | Pct. | FTM | FTA | Pct. | Reb. | Ast. | Pts. | RPG | APG | PPG |
| --- | --- | --- | --- | --- | --- | --- | --- | --- | --- | --- | --- | --- | --- | --- |
| 01-02—Florida ........................ | 31 | 557 | 84 | 145 | .579 | 50 | 91 | .549 | 145 | 32 | 218 | 4.7 | 1.0 | 7.0 |
| 02-03—Florida ........................ | 33 | 866 | 149 | 230 | .648 | 73 | 117 | .624 | 224 | 61 | 371 | 6.8 | 1.8 | 11.2 |
| 03-04—Florida ........................ | 31 | 851 | 150 | 255 | .588 | 112 | 145 | .772 | 212 | 88 | 412 | 6.8 | 2.8 | 13.3 |
| 04-05—Florida ........................ | 32 | 897 | 160 | 305 | .525 | 115 | 161 | .714 | 288 | 70 | 435 | 9.0 | 2.2 | 13.6 |
| Totals ................................. | 127 | 3171 | 543 | 935 | .581 | 350 | 514 | .681 | 869 | 251 | 1436 | 6.8 | 2.0 | 11.3 |

Three-point field goals: 2003-04, 0-for-2. 2004-05, 0-for-4. Totals, 0-for-6 (.000).

## LORBEK, ERAZEM    F          PACERS

**PERSONAL:** Born February 21, 1984, in Ljubljana, Slovenia. ... 6-10/240. (2.08/108.9).
**HIGH SCHOOL:** Gimnazija Bezigrad (Ljubljana, Slovenia).
**COLLEGE:** Michigan State.
**TRANSACTIONS/CAREER NOTES:** Played for Skipper Bologna of Italian League. ... Selected by Indiana Pacers in second round (45th pick overall) of 2005 NBA Draft.

### COLLEGIATE RECORD

| | | | | | | | | | | | AVERAGES | | |
| Season Team | G | Min. | FGM | FGA | Pct. | FTM | FTA | Pct. | Reb. | Ast. | Pts. | RPG | APG | PPG |
| --- | --- | --- | --- | --- | --- | --- | --- | --- | --- | --- | --- | --- | --- | --- |
| 02-03—Michigan State .............. | 35 | 551 | 87 | 163 | .534 | 37 | 57 | .649 | 115 | 20 | 223 | 3.3 | 0.6 | 6.4 |

Three-point field goals: 2002-03, 12-for-26 (.462). Totals, 12-for-26 (.462).

### ITALIAN LEAGUE RECORD

| | | | | | | | | | | | AVERAGES | | |
| Season Team | G | Min. | FGM | FGA | Pct. | FTM | FTA | Pct. | Reb. | Ast. | Pts. | RPG | APG | PPG |
| --- | --- | --- | --- | --- | --- | --- | --- | --- | --- | --- | --- | --- | --- | --- |
| 03-04—Skipper Bologna .......... | 31 | 406 | 55 | 94 | .585 | 14 | 22 | .636 | 105 | 15 | 129 | 3.4 | 0.5 | 4.2 |
| 04-05—Climamio Bologna........ | 34 | 770 | 109 | 195 | .559 | 38 | 54 | .704 | 174 | 30 | 266 | 5.1 | 0.9 | 7.8 |
| Totals ................................. | 65 | 1176 | 164 | 289 | .567 | 52 | 76 | .684 | 279 | 45 | 395 | 4.3 | 0.7 | 6.1 |

Three-point field goals: 2003-04, 5-for-14 (.357). 2004-05, 10-for-28 (.357). Totals, 15-for-42 (.357).

## MACIJAUSKAS, ARVYDAS G          HORNETS

**PERSONAL:** Born January 19, 1980, in Klaipeda, Lithuania. ... 6-4/214. (1.93/97.1).
**TRANSACTIONS/CAREER NOTES:** Played for Tau Ceramica of Spanish League. ... Not drafted by an NBA franchise. ... Signed as free agent by New Orleans Hornets (August 2, 2005).
**MISCELLANEOUS:** Member of bronze medal-winning Lithuanian Olympic team (2000). ... Member of Lithuanian Olympic team (2004).

### LITHUANIAN LEAGUE RECORD

| | | | | | | | | | | | AVERAGES | | |
| Season Team | G | Min. | FGM | FGA | Pct. | FTM | FTA | Pct. | Reb. | Ast. | Pts. | RPG | APG | PPG |
| --- | --- | --- | --- | --- | --- | --- | --- | --- | --- | --- | --- | --- | --- | --- |
| 96-97—Neptunas Klaibeda ....... | 3 | 9 | 1 | 4 | .250 | 0 | 0 | ... | 0 | 0 | 2 | 0.0 | 0.0 | 0.7 |
| 97-98—Neptunas Klaibeda ....... | 28 | 501 | 93 | 186 | .500 | 65 | 73 | .890 | 63 | 40 | 301 | 2.3 | 1.4 | 10.8 |
| 98-99—Neptunas Klaibeda ....... | 34 | 847 | 171 | 330 | .518 | 118 | 141 | .837 | 81 | 59 | 525 | 2.4 | 1.7 | 15.4 |
| 99-00—Lietuvos Rytas............. | 31 | 577 | 108 | 186 | .581 | 102 | 113 | .903 | 55 | 24 | 353 | 1.8 | 0.8 | 11.4 |
| 00-01—Lietuvos Rytas............. | 25 | 650 | 154 | 262 | .588 | 91 | 103 | .883 | 56 | 42 | 456 | 2.2 | 1.7 | 18.2 |
| 01-02—Lietuvos Rytas............. | 31 | 639 | 170 | 307 | .554 | 73 | 81 | .901 | 88 | 47 | 488 | 2.8 | 1.5 | 15.7 |
| 02-03—Lietuvos Rytas............. | 36 | 880 | 217 | 380 | .571 | 147 | 159 | .925 | 110 | 82 | 672 | 3.1 | 2.3 | 18.7 |
| Totals ................................. | 188 | 4103 | 914 | 1655 | .552 | 596 | 670 | .890 | 453 | 294 | 2797 | 2.4 | 1.6 | 14.9 |

Three-point field goals: 1996-97, 0-for-1. 1997-98, 50-for-107 (.467). 1998-99, 65-for-130 (.500). 1999-00, 35-for-67 (.522). 2000-01, 57-for-105 (.543). 2001-02, 75-for-156 (.481). 2002-03, 91-for-171 (.532). Totals, 373-for-737 (.506).

| Season Team | G | Min. | FGM | FGA | Pct. | FTM | FTA | Pct. | Reb. | Ast. | Pts. | AVERAGES | | |
|---|---|---|---|---|---|---|---|---|---|---|---|---|---|---|
| | | | | | | | | | | | | RPG | APG | PPG |
| 03-04—Tau Ceramica.............. | 32 | 953 | 190 | 377 | .504 | 161 | 176 | .915 | 92 | 47 | 599 | 2.9 | 1.5 | 18.7 |
| 04-05—Tau Ceramica.............. | 31 | 775 | 161 | 312 | .516 | 94 | 102 | .922 | 57 | 61 | 503 | 1.8 | 2.0 | 16.2 |
| Totals ................................. | 63 | 1728 | 351 | 689 | .509 | 255 | 278 | .917 | 149 | 108 | 1102 | 2.4 | 1.7 | 17.5 |

Three-point field goals: 2003-04, 58-for-149 (.389). 2004-05, 87-for-146 (.596). Totals, 145-for-295 (.492).

## MAHINMI, IAN — SPURS

**PERSONAL:** Born November 5, 1986, in Rouen, France. ... 6-10, 230 (2.08/104.3).
**TRANSACTIONS/CAREER NOTES:** Played for Le Haure of the French league. ... Selected by San Antonio Spurs in first round (28th pick overall) of 2005 NBA Draft.

### FRENCH LEAGUE RECORD

| Season Team | G | Min. | FGM | FGA | Pct. | FTM | FTA | Pct. | Reb. | Ast. | Pts. | AVERAGES | | |
|---|---|---|---|---|---|---|---|---|---|---|---|---|---|---|
| | | | | | | | | | | | | RPG | APG | PPG |
| 03-04—LE Haure ..................... | 3 | 12 | 2 | 3 | .667 | 1 | 1 | 1.000 | 3 | 0 | 5 | 1.0 | 0.0 | 1.7 |
| 04-05—LE Haure ..................... | 32 | 521 | 71 | 119 | .597 | 45 | 68 | .662 | 124 | 3 | 187 | 3.9 | 0.1 | 5.8 |
| Totals ..................................... | 35 | 533 | 73 | 122 | .598 | 46 | 69 | .667 | 127 | 3 | 192 | 3.6 | 0.1 | 5.5 |

## MAXIELL, JASON — F — PISTONS

**PERSONAL:** Born February 18, 1983, in Chicago, Ill. ... 6-7/260. (2.01/117.9). ... Full name: Jason Dior Maxiell
**HIGH SCHOOL:** Newman Smith (Carrollton, Texas).
**COLLEGE:** Cincinnati.
**TRANSACTIONS/CAREER NOTES:** Selected by Detroit Pistons in first round (26th pick overall) of 2005 NBA draft.

### COLLEGIATE RECORD

| Season Team | G | Min. | FGM | FGA | Pct. | FTM | FTA | Pct. | Reb. | Ast. | Pts. | AVERAGES | | |
|---|---|---|---|---|---|---|---|---|---|---|---|---|---|---|
| | | | | | | | | | | | | RPG | APG | PPG |
| 01-02—Cincinnati ..................... | 35 | 732 | 117 | 212 | .552 | 48 | 82 | .585 | 237 | 3 | 282 | 6.8 | 0.1 | 8.1 |
| 02-03—Cincinnati ..................... | 29 | 879 | 129 | 290 | .445 | 86 | 128 | .672 | 195 | 13 | 344 | 6.7 | 0.4 | 11.9 |
| 03-04—Cincinnati ..................... | 32 | 915 | 152 | 304 | .500 | 130 | 191 | .681 | 222 | 43 | 434 | 6.9 | 1.3 | 13.6 |
| 04-05—Cincinnati ..................... | 33 | 1037 | 164 | 302 | .543 | 176 | 273 | .645 | 254 | 28 | 506 | 7.7 | 0.8 | 15.3 |
| Totals ..................................... | 129 | 3563 | 562 | 1108 | .507 | 440 | 674 | .653 | 908 | 87 | 1566 | 7.0 | 0.7 | 12.2 |

Three-point field goals: 2001-02, 0-for-0. 2002-03, 0-for-1. 2003-04, 0-for-1. 2004-05, 2-for-5. Totals, 2-for-7 (.286).

## MAY, SEAN — F — BOBCATS

**PERSONAL:** Born April 4, 1984, in Chicago, Ill. ... 6-9/266. (2.06/120.7). ... Full name: Sean Gregory May
**HIGH SCHOOL:** Bloomington North (Ill.).
**COLLEGE:** North Carolina.
**TRANSACTIONS/CAREER NOTES:** Selected after junior season by Charlotte Bobcats in first round (13th pick overall) of 2005 NBA draft.

### COLLEGIATE RECORD

**NOTES:** Member of NCAA Division I championship team (2005). ... NCAA Division I Tournament Most Outstanding Player (2005). ... The SPORTING NEWS All-America second team (2005).

| Season Team | G | Min. | FGM | FGA | Pct. | FTM | FTA | Pct. | Reb. | Ast. | Pts. | AVERAGES | | |
|---|---|---|---|---|---|---|---|---|---|---|---|---|---|---|
| | | | | | | | | | | | | RPG | APG | PPG |
| 02-03—North Carolina.............. | 11 | 308 | 51 | 108 | .472 | 23 | 40 | .575 | 89 | 11 | 125 | 8.1 | 1.0 | 11.4 |
| 03-04—North Carolina.............. | 29 | 839 | 163 | 352 | .463 | 115 | 167 | .689 | 285 | 40 | 441 | 9.8 | 1.4 | 15.2 |
| 04-05—North Carolina.............. | 37 | 992 | 228 | 402 | .567 | 191 | 252 | .758 | 397 | 62 | 647 | 10.7 | 1.7 | 17.5 |
| Totals ..................................... | 77 | 2139 | 442 | 862 | .513 | 329 | 459 | .717 | 771 | 113 | 1213 | 10.0 | 1.5 | 15.8 |

Three-point field goals: 2002-03, 0-for-4. 2003-04, 0-for-4. 2004-05, 0-for-3. Totals, 0-for-11 (.000).

## MCCANTS, RASHAD — G — TIMBERWOLVES

**PERSONAL:** Born September 25, 1984, in Asheville, N.C. ... 6-4/207. (1.93/93.9). ... Full name: Rashad Dion McCants
**HIGH SCHOOL:** Erwin (Ashville, N.C.), then New Hampton Prep (N.H.).
**COLLEGE:** North Carolina.
**TRANSACTIONS/CAREER NOTES:** Selected after junior season by Minnesota Timberwolves in first round (14th pick overall) of 2005 NBA draft.

### COLLEGIATE RECORD

**NOTES:** Member of NCAA Division I championship team (2005). ... THE SPORTING NEWS All-America third team (2004).

| Season Team | G | Min. | FGM | FGA | Pct. | FTM | FTA | Pct. | Reb. | Ast. | Pts. | AVERAGES | | |
|---|---|---|---|---|---|---|---|---|---|---|---|---|---|---|
| | | | | | | | | | | | | RPG | APG | PPG |
| 02-03—North Carolina.............. | 35 | 1046 | 215 | 438 | .491 | 92 | 132 | .697 | 162 | 51 | 594 | 4.6 | 1.5 | 17.0 |
| 03-04—North Carolina.............. | 30 | 961 | 216 | 451 | .479 | 89 | 119 | .748 | 137 | 65 | 599 | 4.6 | 2.2 | 20.0 |
| 04-05—North Carolina.............. | 33 | 856 | 183 | 374 | .489 | 91 | 126 | .722 | 99 | 88 | 528 | 3.0 | 2.7 | 16.0 |
| Totals ..................................... | 98 | 2863 | 614 | 1263 | .486 | 272 | 377 | .721 | 398 | 204 | 1721 | 4.1 | 2.1 | 17.6 |

Three-point field goals: 2002-03, 72-for-174 (.414). 2003-04, 78-for-191 (.408). 2004-05, 71-for-168 (.423). Totals, 221-for-533 (.415).

## MILES, C.J.       G       JAZZ

**PERSONAL:** Born March 18, 1987, in Dallas, Texas. ... 6-6/210. (1.98/95.3).
**HIGH SCHOOL:** Skyline (Dallas, Texas).
**COLLEGE:** Did not attend college.
**TRANSACTIONS/CAREER NOTES:** Selected out of high school by Utah Jazz in second round (34th pick overall) of 2005 NBA draft.

## MONIA, SERGEI       TRAIL BLAZERS

**PERSONAL:** Born April 15, 1983, in Saratov, Russia. ... 6-8/220. (2.03/99.8).
**TRANSACTIONS/CAREER NOTES:** Played in Russia (2000-04). ... Selected by Portland Trail Blazers in first round (23rd pick overall) of 2004 NBA Draft.

### RUSSIAN LEAGUE RECORD

| | | | | | | | | | | | | AVERAGES | | |
|---|---|---|---|---|---|---|---|---|---|---|---|---|---|---|
| Season Team | G | Min. | FGM | FGA | Pct. | FTM | FTA | Pct. | Reb. | Ast. | Pts. | RPG | APG | PPG |
| 00-01—Avtodor Saratov | 2 | 21 | 3 | 8 | .375 | 0 | 0 | ... | 6 | 6 | 6 | 3.0 | 0.0 | 3.0 |
| 01-02—Avtodor Saratov | 40 | 785 | 115 | 284 | .405 | 59 | 93 | .634 | 182 | 47 | 309 | 4.6 | 1.2 | 7.7 |
| 02-03—CSKA | 28 | 436 | 75 | 151 | .497 | 23 | 32 | .719 | 89 | 22 | 205 | 3.2 | 0.8 | 7.3 |
| 03-04—CSKA | 32 | 577 | 77 | 174 | .443 | 50 | 68 | .735 | 123 | 35 | 232 | 3.8 | 1.1 | 7.3 |
| 04-05—CSKA | 32 | 536 | 67 | 151 | .444 | 27 | 39 | .692 | 102 | 43 | 186 | 3.2 | 1.3 | 5.8 |
| Totals | 134 | 2355 | 337 | 768 | .439 | 159 | 232 | .685 | 502 | 147 | 938 | 3.7 | 1.1 | 7.0 |

Three-point field goals: 2000-01, 0-for-3. 2001-02, 20-for-73 (.274). 2002-03, 32-for-76 (.421). 2003-04, 28-for-81 (.346). 2004-05, 25-for-64 (.391). Totals, 105-for-297 (.354).

## OBERTO, FABRICIO       F       SPURS

**PERSONAL:** Born March 21, 1975, in Las Varillas, Argentina. ... 6-10/245. (2.08/111.1). ... Full name: Fabricio Raul Jesus Oberto.
**TRANSACTIONS/CAREER NOTES:** Played in Spain. ... Not drafted by an NBA franchise. ... Signed as free agent by San Antonio Spurs (August 2, 2005).

### GREEK LEAGUE RECORD

| | | | | | | | | | | | | AVERAGES | | |
|---|---|---|---|---|---|---|---|---|---|---|---|---|---|---|
| Season Team | G | Min. | FGM | FGA | Pct. | FTM | FTA | Pct. | Reb. | Ast. | Pts. | RPG | APG | PPG |
| 98-99—Olympiakos S.F.P. | 24 | 436 | 66 | 107 | .617 | 30 | 49 | .612 | 132 | 20 | 163 | 5.5 | 0.8 | 6.8 |

Three-point field goals: 1998-99, 1-for-2 (.500). Totals, 1-for-2 (.500).

### SPANISH RECORD

| | | | | | | | | | | | | AVERAGES | | |
|---|---|---|---|---|---|---|---|---|---|---|---|---|---|---|
| Season Team | G | Min. | FGM | FGA | Pct. | FTM | FTA | Pct. | Reb. | Ast. | Pts. | RPG | APG | PPG |
| 99-00—Tau Ceramica | 12 | 240 | 50 | 74 | .676 | 9 | 23 | .391 | 44 | 11 | 109 | 3.7 | 0.9 | 9.1 |
| 00-01—Tau Ceramica | 34 | 802 | 131 | 193 | .679 | 44 | 96 | .458 | 209 | 41 | 306 | 6.1 | 1.2 | 9.0 |
| 01-02—Tau Ceramica | 32 | 905 | 155 | 249 | .622 | 43 | 88 | .489 | 202 | 48 | 353 | 6.3 | 1.5 | 11.0 |
| 02-03—Pamesa Valencia | 34 | 910 | 188 | 296 | .635 | 58 | 105 | .552 | 180 | 69 | 434 | 5.3 | 2.0 | 12.8 |
| 03-04—Pamesa Valencia | 34 | 898 | 177 | 290 | .610 | 39 | 90 | .433 | 182 | 62 | 393 | 5.4 | 1.8 | 11.6 |
| 04-05—Pamesa Valencia | 30 | 856 | 191 | 292 | .654 | 43 | 95 | .453 | 218 | 64 | 425 | 7.3 | 2.1 | 14.2 |
| Totals | 176 | 4611 | 892 | 1394 | .640 | 236 | 497 | .475 | 1035 | 295 | 2020 | 5.9 | 1.7 | 11.5 |

Three-point field goals: 2002-03, 0-for-3. 2003-04, 0-for-1. Totals, 0-for-4 (.000).

## PAUL, CHRIS       G       HORNETS

**PERSONAL:** Born May 6, 1985, in Winston-Salem, N.C. ... 6-0/175. (1.83/79.4). ... Full name: Christopher Emmanuel Paul
**HIGH SCHOOL:** West Forsyth (Winston-Salem, N.C.).
**COLLEGE:** Wake Forest.
**TRANSACTIONS/CAREER NOTES:** Selected after sophomore season by New Orleans Hornets in first round (fourth pick overall) of 2005 NBA draft.

### COLLEGIATE RECORD

**NOTES:** The SPORTING NEWS All-America first team (2005).

| | | | | | | | | | | | | AVERAGES | | |
|---|---|---|---|---|---|---|---|---|---|---|---|---|---|---|
| Season Team | G | Min. | FGM | FGA | Pct. | FTM | FTA | Pct. | Reb. | Ast. | Pts. | RPG | APG | PPG |
| 03-04—Wake Forest | 31 | 1041 | 135 | 272 | .496 | 150 | 178 | .843 | 101 | 183 | 460 | 3.3 | 5.9 | 14.8 |
| 04-05—Wake Forest | 32 | 1069 | 143 | 317 | .451 | 156 | 187 | .834 | 144 | 212 | 488 | 4.5 | 6.6 | 15.3 |
| Totals | 63 | 2110 | 278 | 589 | .472 | 306 | 365 | .838 | 245 | 395 | 948 | 3.9 | 6.3 | 15.0 |

Three-point field goals: 2003-04, 40-for-86 (.465). 2004-05, 46-for-97 (.474). Totals, 86-for-183 (.470).

## PETRO, JOHAN       C       SUPERSONICS

**PERSONAL:** Born January 27, 1986, in Paris, France. ... 7-0/247. (2.13/112.0).
**COLLEGE:** Did not attend.
**TRANSACTIONS/CAREER NOTES:** Played for Pau-Orthez of the French league. ... Selected by Seattle SuperSonics in the first round (25th pick overall) of the 2005 NBA Draft.

| Season Team | G | Min. | FGM | FGA | Pct. | FTM | FTA | Pct. | Reb. | Ast. | Pts. | AVERAGES RPG | APG | PPG |
|---|---|---|---|---|---|---|---|---|---|---|---|---|---|---|
| 01-02—INSEP | 22 | 510 | 76 | 138 | .551 | 31 | 67 | .463 | 148 | 11 | 183 | 6.7 | 0.5 | 8.3 |
| 02-03—INSEP | 13 | 332 | 56 | 109 | .514 | 24 | 41 | .585 | 81 | 10 | 136 | 6.2 | 0.8 | 10.5 |
| 03-04—Pau Orthez | 16 | 130 | 20 | 47 | .426 | 6 | 12 | .500 | 49 | 6 | 46 | 3.1 | 0.4 | 2.9 |
| 04-05—Pau Orthez | 31 | 365 | 70 | 134 | .522 | 31 | 43 | .721 | 92 | 14 | 171 | 3.0 | 0.5 | 5.5 |
| Totals | 82 | 1337 | 222 | 428 | .519 | 92 | 163 | .564 | 370 | 41 | 536 | 4.5 | 0.5 | 6.5 |

Three-point field goals: 2002-03, 0-for-1. Totals, 0-for-1 (.000).

## POWELL, JOSH      F      MAVERICKS

**PERSONAL:** Born December 5, 1983, in Charleston, S.C. ... 6-9/225. (2.06/102.1).
**HIGH SCHOOL:** Riverdale (Ga.)
**COLLEGE:** N.C. State.
**TRANSACTIONS/CAREER NOTES:** Not drafted by an NBA franchise. ... Signed as free agent by Dallas Mavericks (August 2, 2005).

### COLLEGIATE RECORD

| Season Team | G | Min. | FGM | FGA | Pct. | FTM | FTA | Pct. | Reb. | Ast. | Pts. | AVERAGES RPG | APG | PPG |
|---|---|---|---|---|---|---|---|---|---|---|---|---|---|---|
| 01-02—NC State | 34 | 662 | 95 | 180 | .528 | 52 | 73 | .712 | 131 | 31 | 244 | 3.9 | 0.9 | 7.2 |
| 02-03—NC State | 31 | 838 | 144 | 252 | .571 | 88 | 119 | .739 | 163 | 31 | 385 | 5.3 | 1.0 | 12.4 |
| Totals | 65 | 1500 | 239 | 432 | .553 | 140 | 192 | .729 | 294 | 62 | 629 | 4.5 | 1.0 | 9.7 |

Three-point field goals: 2001-02, 2-for-14 (.143). 2002-03, 9-for-24 (.375). Totals, 11-for-38 (.289).

### ITALIAN LEAGUE RECORD

| Season Team | G | Min. | FGM | FGA | Pct. | FTM | FTA | Pct. | Reb. | Ast. | Pts. | AVERAGES RPG | APG | PPG |
|---|---|---|---|---|---|---|---|---|---|---|---|---|---|---|
| 03-04—Euroride Scafati | 18 | 564 | 95 | 162 | .586 | 58 | 77 | .753 | 163 | 8 | 248 | 9.1 | 0.4 | 13.8 |
| 04-05—Pepsi Caserta | 30 | 1056 | 191 | 326 | .586 | 113 | 165 | .685 | 356 | 22 | 498 | 11.9 | 0.7 | 16.6 |
| Totals | 48 | 1620 | 286 | 488 | .586 | 171 | 242 | .707 | 519 | 30 | 746 | 10.8 | 0.6 | 15.5 |

Three-point field goals: 2003-04, 0-for-5. 2004-05, 3-for-24 (.125). Totals, 3-for-29 (.103).

### RUSSIAN LEAGUE RECORD

| Season Team | G | Min. | FGM | FGA | Pct. | FTM | FTA | Pct. | Reb. | Ast. | Pts. | AVERAGES RPG | APG | PPG |
|---|---|---|---|---|---|---|---|---|---|---|---|---|---|---|
| 03-04—Lokomotiv-Rostov | 2 | 11 | 0 | 2 | .000 | 3 | 4 | .750 | 2 | 1 | 3 | 1.0 | 0.5 | 1.5 |

## PRICE, RONNIE      G      KINGS

**PERSONAL:** Born June 21, 1983, in Friendswood, Texas. ... 6-2/190. (1.88/86.2).
**HIGH SCHOOL:** Clear Brook (Friendswood, Texas).
**COLLEGE:** Nicholls State, then Utah Valley State College.
**TRANSACTIONS/CAREER NOTES:** Not drafted by an NBA franchise. ... Signed as free agent by Sacramento Kings (August 2, 2005).

### COLLEGIATE RECORD

| Season Team | G | Min. | FGM | FGA | Pct. | FTM | FTA | Pct. | Reb. | Ast. | Pts. | AVERAGES RPG | APG | PPG |
|---|---|---|---|---|---|---|---|---|---|---|---|---|---|---|
| 01-02—Nicholls State | 25 | 746 | 99 | 267 | .371 | 47 | 61 | .770 | 58 | 72 | 282 | 2.3 | 2.9 | 11.3 |
| 02-03—Utah Valley State (J.C.) | 33 | 893 | 175 | 423 | .414 | 78 | 100 | .780 | 119 | 75 | 505 | 3.6 | 2.3 | 15.3 |
| 03-04—Utah Valley State | 28 | 876 | 197 | 454 | .434 | 90 | 112 | .804 | 108 | 86 | 565 | 3.9 | 3.1 | 20.2 |
| 04-05—Utah Valley State | 28 | 1042 | 229 | 536 | .427 | 142 | 180 | .789 | 117 | 84 | 680 | 4.2 | 3.0 | 24.3 |
| Junior College Totals | 33 | 893 | 175 | 423 | .414 | 78 | 100 | .780 | 119 | 75 | 505 | 3.6 | 2.3 | 15.3 |
| 4-Year-College Totals | 81 | 2664 | 525 | 1257 | .418 | 279 | 353 | .790 | 283 | 242 | 1527 | 3.5 | 3.0 | 18.9 |

Three-point field goals: 2001-02, 37-for-134 (.276). 2002-03, 77-for-227 (.339). 2003-04, 81-for-214 (.379). 2004-05, 80-for-223 (.359). Totals, 275-for-798 (.345).

## ROBERTS, LAWRENCE      F      GRIZZLIES

**PERSONAL:** Born October 20, 1982, in Houston, Texas. ... 6-9/240. (2.06/108.9). ... Full name: Lawrence Edward Roberts
**HIGH SCHOOL:** Lamar (Houston, Texas).
**COLLEGE:** Baylor, then Mississippi State.
**TRANSACTIONS/CAREER NOTES:** Selected by Seattle Supersonics in second round (55th pick overall) of 2005 NBA draft. ... Draft rights traded by Supersonics to Memphis Grizzlies for two future second-round picks and cash (June 28, 2005).

### COLLEGIATE RECORD

**NOTES:** The SPORTING NEWS All-America second team (2004).

| Season Team | G | Min. | FGM | FGA | Pct. | FTM | FTA | Pct. | Reb. | Ast. | Pts. | AVERAGES RPG | APG | PPG |
|---|---|---|---|---|---|---|---|---|---|---|---|---|---|---|
| 01-02—Baylor | 30 | 858 | 174 | 391 | .445 | 124 | 183 | .678 | 247 | 39 | 498 | 8.2 | 1.3 | 16.6 |
| 02-03—Baylor | 26 | 838 | 133 | 316 | .421 | 119 | 174 | .684 | 271 | 40 | 396 | 10.4 | 1.5 | 15.2 |
| 03-04—Mississippi State | 30 | 982 | 175 | 337 | .519 | 144 | 227 | .634 | 303 | 37 | 506 | 10.1 | 1.2 | 16.9 |
| 04-05—Mississippi State | 32 | 1023 | 171 | 382 | .448 | 188 | 288 | .653 | 351 | 61 | 542 | 11.0 | 1.9 | 16.9 |
| Totals | 118 | 3701 | 653 | 1426 | .458 | 575 | 872 | .659 | 1172 | 177 | 1942 | 9.9 | 1.5 | 16.5 |

Three-point field goals: 2001-02, 26-for-79 (.329). 2002-03, 11-for-42 (.262). 2003-04, 12-for-40 (.300). 2004-05, 12-for-41 (.293). Totals, 61-for-202 (.302).

**PROMISING NEWCOMERS**

## ROBINSON, NATE — G — KNICKS

**PERSONAL:** Born May 31, 1984, in Seattle, Wash. ... 5-9/180. (1.75/81.6).
**HIGH SCHOOL:** Logan (Oakland, Calif.), then Rainier Beach (Seattle).
**COLLEGE:** Washington.
**TRANSACTIONS/CAREER NOTES:** Selected after junior season by Phoenix Suns in first round (21st pick overall) of 2005 NBA draft. ... Draft rights traded by Suns with G Quentin Richardson and cash to New York Knicks for F Kurt Thomas and draft rights to G/F Dijon Thompson (June 28, 2005).

### COLLEGIATE RECORD

| Season Team | G | Min. | FGM | FGA | Pct. | FTM | FTA | Pct. | Reb. | Ast. | Pts. | RPG | APG | PPG |
|---|---|---|---|---|---|---|---|---|---|---|---|---|---|---|
| 02-03—Washington | 23 | 576 | 120 | 260 | .462 | 41 | 57 | .719 | 89 | 52 | 300 | 3.9 | 2.3 | 13.0 |
| 03-04—Washington | 31 | 833 | 138 | 309 | .447 | 87 | 102 | .853 | 121 | 84 | 409 | 3.9 | 2.7 | 13.2 |
| 04-05—Washington | 35 | 1101 | 188 | 406 | .463 | 136 | 174 | .782 | 135 | 159 | 574 | 3.9 | 4.5 | 16.4 |
| Totals | 89 | 2510 | 446 | 975 | .457 | 264 | 333 | .793 | 345 | 295 | 1283 | 3.9 | 3.3 | 14.4 |

Three-field goals: 2002-03, 19-for-74 (.257). 2003-04, 46-for-130 (.354). 2004-05, 62-for-161 (.385). Totals, 127-for-365 (.348).

## SANCHEZ, RICKY — F — NUGGETS

**PERSONAL:** Born July 6, 1987 ... 6-11/215. (2.11/97.5).
**HIGH SCHOOL:** IMG Academy (Bradenton, Fla.).
**COLLEGE:** Did not attend.
**TRANSACTIONS/CAREER NOTES:** Selected out of high school by Portland Trail Blazers in second round (35th pick overall) of 2005 NBA draft. ... Draft rights traded by Trail Blazers with draft rights to F Linas Kleiza to Denver Nuggets for draft rights to G Jarrett Jack (June 28, 2005).

## SIMIEN, WAYNE — F — HEAT

**PERSONAL:** Born March 9, 1983, in Leavenworth, Kan. ... 6-9/255. (2.06/115.7). ... Full name: Wayne Anthony Simien
**HIGH SCHOOL:** Leavenworth (Kan.).
**COLLEGE:** Kansas.
**TRANSACTIONS/CAREER NOTES:** Selected by Miami Heat in first round (29th pick overall) of 2005 NBA draft.

### COLLEGIATE RECORD

**NOTES:** The SPORTING NEWS All-America first team (2005).

| Season Team | G | Min. | FGM | FGA | Pct. | FTM | FTA | Pct. | Reb. | Ast. | Pts. | RPG | APG | PPG |
|---|---|---|---|---|---|---|---|---|---|---|---|---|---|---|
| 01-02—Kansas | 32 | 490 | 99 | 179 | .553 | 62 | 84 | .738 | 169 | 9 | 260 | 5.3 | 0.3 | 8.1 |
| 02-03—Kansas | 16 | 390 | 95 | 147 | .646 | 46 | 68 | .676 | 131 | 9 | 236 | 8.2 | 0.6 | 14.8 |
| 03-04—Kansas | 32 | 1045 | 200 | 376 | .532 | 167 | 206 | .811 | 297 | 39 | 569 | 9.3 | 1.2 | 17.8 |
| 04-05—Kansas | 26 | 892 | 191 | 346 | .552 | 142 | 174 | .816 | 287 | 36 | 528 | 11.0 | 1.4 | 20.3 |
| Totals | 106 | 2817 | 585 | 1048 | .558 | 417 | 532 | .784 | 884 | 93 | 1593 | 8.3 | 0.9 | 15.0 |

Three-point field goals: 2003-04, 2-for-11 (.182). 2004-05, 4-for-14 (.286). Totals, 6-for-25 (.240).

## SINGLETON, JAMES — CLIPPERS

**PERSONAL:** Born July 20, 1981
**HIGH SCHOOL:** Hirsch Metro (Chicago).
**JUNIOR COLLEGE:** Pearl River (Miss.).
**COLLEGE:** Murray State.
**TRANSACTIONS/CAREER NOTES:** Played in Italy. ... Not drafted by an NBA franchise. ... Signed as free agent by Los Angeles Clippers (August 11, 2005).

### COLLEGIATE RECORD

| Season Team | G | Min. | FGM | FGA | Pct. | FTM | FTA | Pct. | Reb. | Ast. | Pts. | RPG | APG | PPG |
|---|---|---|---|---|---|---|---|---|---|---|---|---|---|---|
| 99-00—Pearl River CC | | | | | | | | Statistics Unavailable | | | | | | |
| 00-01—Pearl River CC | 27 | 827 | 146 | 238 | .613 | 84 | 123 | .683 | 373 | 30 | 376 | 13.8 | 1.1 | 13.9 |
| 01-02—Murray State | 31 | 931 | 145 | 243 | .597 | 85 | 108 | .787 | 312 | 36 | 378 | 10.1 | 1.2 | 12.2 |
| 02-03—Murray State | 29 | 953 | 153 | 283 | .541 | 112 | 140 | .800 | 320 | 54 | 433 | 11.0 | 1.9 | 14.9 |
| Junior College Totals | 27 | 827 | 146 | 238 | .613 | 84 | 123 | .683 | 373 | 30 | 376 | 13.8 | 1.1 | 13.9 |
| 4-Year-College Totals | 60 | 1884 | 298 | 526 | .567 | 197 | 248 | .794 | 632 | 90 | 811 | 10.5 | 1.5 | 13.5 |

Three-point field goals: 2000-01, 0-for-2. 2001-02, 3-for-8 (.375). 2002-03, 15-for-34 (.441). Totals, 18-for-44 (.409).

### ITALIAN LEAGUE RECORD

| Season Team | G | Min. | FGM | FGA | Pct. | FTM | FTA | Pct. | Reb. | Ast. | Pts. | RPG | APG | PPG |
|---|---|---|---|---|---|---|---|---|---|---|---|---|---|---|
| 03-04—Sicc Cucine Jesi-A2 | 32 | 1016 | 166 | 325 | .511 | 62 | 89 | .697 | 386 | 24 | 426 | 12.1 | 0.8 | 13.3 |
| 04-05—Armani Jeans Milano-A1 | 34 | 892 | 160 | 325 | .492 | 72 | 98 | .735 | 284 | 21 | 414 | 8.4 | 0.6 | 12.2 |
| Totals | 66 | 1908 | 326 | 650 | .502 | 134 | 187 | .717 | 670 | 45 | 840 | 10.2 | 0.7 | 12.7 |

Three-point field goals: 2003-04, 32-for-89 (.360). 2004-05, 22-for-74 (.297). Totals, 54-for-163 (.331).

## SLOKAR, UROS     F      RAPTORS

**PERSONAL:** Born May 14, 1983, in Ljubljana, Slovenia. ... 6-10/238. (2.08/108.0).
**COLLEGE:** Did not attend.
**TRANSACTIONS/CAREER NOTES:** Played for Benetton Treviso of Italian league. ... Selected by Toronto Raptors in second round (58th pick overall) of 2005 NBA Draft.

### ADRIATIC LEAGUE RECORD

| Season Team | G | Min. | FGM | FGA | Pct. | FTM | FTA | Pct. | Reb. | Ast. | Pts. | RPG | APG | PPG |
|---|---|---|---|---|---|---|---|---|---|---|---|---|---|---|
| 01-02—KD Slovan | 15 | 307 | 46 | 83 | .554 | 41 | 66 | .621 | 48 | 9 | 133 | 3.2 | 0.6 | 8.9 |

Three-point field goals: 2001-02, 0-for-5. Totals, 0-for-5 (.000).

### SLOVENIAN LEAGUE RECORD

| Season Team | G | Min. | FGM | FGA | Pct. | FTM | FTA | Pct. | Reb. | Ast. | Pts. | RPG | APG | PPG |
|---|---|---|---|---|---|---|---|---|---|---|---|---|---|---|
| 02-03—KD Slovan | 20 | 613 | 115 | 208 | .553 | 99 | 128 | .773 | 128 | 14 | 345 | 6.4 | 0.7 | 17.3 |

Three-point field goals: 2002-03, 16-for-32 (.500). Totals, 16-for-32 (.500).

### ITALIAN LEAGUE RECORD

| Season Team | G | Min. | FGM | FGA | Pct. | FTM | FTA | Pct. | Reb. | Ast. | Pts. | RPG | APG | PPG |
|---|---|---|---|---|---|---|---|---|---|---|---|---|---|---|
| 03-04—Benetton Treviso | 25 | 267 | 41 | 76 | .539 | 24 | 36 | .667 | 37 | 7 | 112 | 1.5 | 0.3 | 4.5 |
| 04-05—Benetton Treviso | 28 | 426 | 53 | 92 | .576 | 46 | 60 | .767 | 121 | 9 | 159 | 4.3 | 0.3 | 5.7 |
| Totals | 53 | 693 | 94 | 168 | .560 | 70 | 96 | .729 | 158 | 16 | 271 | 3.0 | 0.3 | 5.1 |

Three-point field goals: 2003-04, 6-for-15 (.400). 2004-05, 7-for-17 (.412). Totals, 13-for-32 (.406).

## STOUDAMIRE, SALIM     G      HAWKS

**PERSONAL:** Born October 11, 1982, in Portland, Ore. ... 6-1/179. (1.85/81.2). ... Full name: Charles Salim Stoudamire. ... Cousin of Damon Stoudamire, guard, Memphis Grizzlies.
**HIGH SCHOOL:** Lincoln (Portland, Ore.), then Lake Oswego (Ore.) .
**COLLEGE:** Arizona.
**TRANSACTIONS/CAREER NOTES:** Selected by Atlanta Hawks in second round (31st pick overall) of 2005 NBA draft.

### COLLEGIATE RECORD

**NOTES:** The SPORTING NEWS All-America second team (2005). ... Led NCAA Division I with .503 three-point shooting percentage (2005).

| Season Team | G | Min. | FGM | FGA | Pct. | FTM | FTA | Pct. | Reb. | Ast. | Pts. | RPG | APG | PPG |
|---|---|---|---|---|---|---|---|---|---|---|---|---|---|---|
| 01-02—Arizona | 34 | 1021 | 129 | 291 | .443 | 103 | 114 | .904 | 72 | 38 | 434 | 2.1 | 1.1 | 12.8 |
| 02-03—Arizona | 30 | 774 | 125 | 264 | .473 | 70 | 81 | .864 | 49 | 54 | 391 | 1.6 | 1.8 | 13.0 |
| 03-04—Arizona | 29 | 927 | 151 | 334 | .452 | 93 | 117 | .795 | 79 | 86 | 473 | 2.7 | 3.0 | 16.3 |
| 04-05—Arizona | 36 | 1126 | 210 | 417 | .504 | 122 | 134 | .910 | 83 | 78 | 662 | 2.3 | 2.2 | 18.4 |
| Totals | 129 | 3848 | 615 | 1306 | .471 | 388 | 446 | .870 | 283 | 256 | 1960 | 2.2 | 2.0 | 15.2 |

Three-point field goals: 2001-02, 73-for-161 (.453). 2002-03, 71-for-160 (.444). 2003-04, 78-for-188 (.415). 2004-05, 120-for-238 (.504). Totals, 342-for-747 (.458).

## TAFT, CHRIS     F      WARRIORS

**PERSONAL:** Born March 10, 1985, in Brooklyn, N.Y. ... 6-10/260. (2.08/117.9).
**HIGH SCHOOL:** Xaverian Prep (Brooklyn, N.Y.).
**COLLEGE:** Pittsburgh.
**TRANSACTIONS/CAREER NOTES:** Selected after sophomore season by Golden State Warriors in second round (42nd pick overall) of 2005 NBA Draft.

### COLLEGIATE RECORD

| Season Team | G | Min. | FGM | FGA | Pct. | FTM | FTA | Pct. | Reb. | Ast. | Pts. | RPG | APG | PPG |
|---|---|---|---|---|---|---|---|---|---|---|---|---|---|---|
| 03-04—Pittsburgh | 36 | 923 | 162 | 290 | .559 | 68 | 125 | .544 | 270 | 45 | 392 | 7.5 | 1.3 | 10.9 |
| 04-05—Pittsburgh | 29 | 769 | 159 | 274 | .580 | 68 | 116 | .586 | 218 | 24 | 386 | 7.5 | 0.8 | 13.3 |
| Totals | 65 | 1692 | 321 | 564 | .569 | 136 | 241 | .564 | 488 | 69 | 778 | 7.5 | 1.1 | 12.0 |

## THOMPSON, DIJON     G/F      SUNS

**PERSONAL:** Born February 23, 1983, in Los Angeles, Calif. ... 6-7/195. (2.01/88.5). ... Full name: Dijon Lynn Thompson.
**HIGH SCHOOL:** Redondo Union (Redondo Beach, Calif.).
**COLLEGE:** UCLA.
**TRANSACTIONS/CAREER NOTES:** Selected by New York Knicks in second round (54th pick overall) of 2005 NBA draft. ... Draft rights traded by Knicks with F Kurt Thomas to Phoenix Suns for G Quentin Richardson and draft rights to G Nate Robinson and cash (June 28, 2005).

### COLLEGIATE RECORD

| Season Team | G | Min. | FGM | FGA | Pct. | FTM | FTA | Pct. | Reb. | Ast. | Pts. | RPG | APG | PPG |
|---|---|---|---|---|---|---|---|---|---|---|---|---|---|---|
| 01-02—UCLA | 33 | 494 | 57 | 133 | .429 | 20 | 23 | .870 | 73 | 35 | 147 | 2.2 | 1.1 | 4.5 |

| Season Team | G | Min. | FGM | FGA | Pct. | FTM | FTA | Pct. | Reb. | Ast. | Pts. | AVERAGES | | |
|---|---|---|---|---|---|---|---|---|---|---|---|---|---|---|
| | | | | | | | | | | | | RPG | APG | PPG |
| 02-03—UCLA | 28 | 828 | 155 | 312 | .497 | 55 | 74 | .743 | 131 | 78 | 393 | 4.7 | 2.8 | 14.0 |
| 03-04—UCLA | 28 | 960 | 146 | 336 | .435 | 61 | 78 | .782 | 120 | 63 | 402 | 4.3 | 2.3 | 14.4 |
| 04-05—UCLA | 28 | 970 | 183 | 386 | .474 | 107 | 136 | .787 | 222 | 63 | 516 | 7.9 | 2.3 | 18.4 |
| Totals | 117 | 3252 | 541 | 1167 | .464 | 243 | 311 | .781 | 546 | 239 | 1458 | 4.7 | 2.0 | 12.5 |

Three-point field goals: 2001-02, 13-for-48 (.271). 2002-03, 28-for-76 (.368). 2003-04, 49-for-128 (.383). 2004-05, 43-for-115 (.374). Totals, 133-for-367 (.362).

## TURIAF, RONNY — F — LAKERS

**PERSONAL:** Born January 13, 1983, in Le Robert, Martinique. ... 6-10/249. (2.08/112.9).
**HIGH SCHOOL:** Sporting Club Lamentinois (Le Robert, Martinique),.
**COLLEGE:** Gonzaga.
**TRANSACTIONS/CAREER NOTES:** Selected by Los Angeles Lakers in second round (37th pick overall) of 2005 NBA draft.

### COLLEGIATE RECORD

| Season Team | G | Min. | FGM | FGA | Pct. | FTM | FTA | Pct. | Reb. | Ast. | Pts. | AVERAGES | | |
|---|---|---|---|---|---|---|---|---|---|---|---|---|---|---|
| | | | | | | | | | | | | RPG | APG | PPG |
| 01-02—Gonzaga | 32 | 624 | 73 | 139 | .525 | 89 | 128 | .695 | 161 | 16 | 235 | 5.0 | 0.5 | 7.3 |
| 02-03—Gonzaga | 33 | 814 | 151 | 291 | .519 | 212 | 279 | .760 | 206 | 19 | 515 | 6.2 | 0.6 | 15.6 |
| 03-04—Gonzaga | 31 | 834 | 157 | 299 | .525 | 165 | 233 | .708 | 197 | 47 | 480 | 6.4 | 1.5 | 15.5 |
| 04-05—Gonzaga | 31 | 967 | 157 | 309 | .508 | 177 | 259 | .683 | 295 | 48 | 493 | 9.5 | 1.5 | 15.9 |
| Totals | 127 | 3239 | 538 | 1038 | .518 | 643 | 899 | .715 | 859 | 130 | 1723 | 6.8 | 1.0 | 13.6 |

Three-point field goals: 2001-02, 0-for-2. 2002-03, 1-for-6 (.167). 2003-04, 1-for-3 (.333). 2004-05, 2-for-7 (.286). Totals, 4-for-18 (.222).

## UKIC, ROKO — G — RAPTORS

**PERSONAL:** Born May 12, 1984, in Split, Croatia. ... 6-5/183. (1.96/83.0). ... Full name: Roko Leni Ukic
**COLLEGE:** Did not attend.
**TRANSACTIONS/CAREER NOTES:** Played for KK Split of the Croatian league. ... Selected by Toronto Raptors in second round (41st pick overall) of 2005 NBA Draft.

### CROATION RECORD

| Season Team | G | Min. | FGM | FGA | Pct. | FTM | FTA | Pct. | Reb. | Ast. | Pts. | AVERAGES | | |
|---|---|---|---|---|---|---|---|---|---|---|---|---|---|---|
| | | | | | | | | | | | | RPG | APG | PPG |
| 00-01—KK Split | 17 | 122 | 19 | 53 | .358 | 9 | 18 | .500 | 6 | 10 | 51 | 0.4 | 0.6 | 3.0 |
| 01-02—KK Split | 22 | 394 | 46 | 121 | .380 | 22 | 31 | .710 | 22 | 20 | 129 | 1.0 | 0.9 | 5.9 |
| 02-03—KK Split | 16 | ... | 53 | 115 | .461 | 15 | 20 | .750 | 27 | 22 | 139 | 1.7 | 1.4 | 8.7 |
| 03-04—KK Split | 7 | ... | 26 | 75 | .347 | 15 | 22 | .682 | 15 | 28 | 78 | 2.1 | 4.0 | 11.1 |
| 04-05—KK Split | 11 | 346 | 56 | 140 | .400 | 51 | 61 | .836 | 41 | 51 | 176 | 3.7 | 4.6 | 16.0 |
| Totals | 73 | 862 | 200 | 504 | .397 | 112 | 152 | .737 | 111 | 131 | 573 | 1.5 | 1.8 | 7.8 |

Three-point field goals: 2000-01, 4-for-22 (.182). 2001-02, 15-for-36 (.417). 2002-03, 18-for-50 (.360). 2003-04, 11-for-38 (.289). 2004-05, 13-for-62 (.210). Totals, 61-for-208 (.293).

### ADRIATIC LEAGUE RECORD

| Season Team | G | Min. | FGM | FGA | Pct. | FTM | FTA | Pct. | Reb. | Ast. | Pts. | AVERAGES | | |
|---|---|---|---|---|---|---|---|---|---|---|---|---|---|---|
| | | | | | | | | | | | | RPG | APG | PPG |
| 01-02—KK Split | 22 | 392 | 46 | 121 | .380 | 22 | 31 | .710 | 30 | 20 | 129 | 1.4 | 0.9 | 5.9 |
| 02-03—KK Split | 22 | 688 | 95 | 287 | .331 | 66 | 87 | .759 | 47 | 47 | 287 | 2.1 | 2.1 | 13.0 |
| 03-04—KK Split | 24 | 814 | 138 | 370 | .373 | 64 | 91 | .703 | 58 | 66 | 370 | 2.4 | 2.8 | 15.4 |
| 04-05—KK Split | 26 | 919 | 150 | 239 | .628 | 140 | 164 | .854 | 72 | 113 | 481 | 2.8 | 4.3 | 18.5 |
| Totals | 94 | 2813 | 429 | 1017 | .422 | 292 | 373 | .783 | 207 | 246 | 1267 | 2.2 | 2.6 | 13.5 |

Three-point field goals: 2001-02, 15-for-36 (.417). 2002-03, 31-for-106 (.292). 2003-04, 30-for-114 (.263). 2004-05, 41-for-137 (.299). Totals, 117-for-393 (.298).

## VAZQUEZ, FRAN — F/C — MAGIC

**PERSONAL:** Born May 1, 1983, in Carbelledo Lugo, Spain. ... 6-10/238. (2.08/108.0).
**HIGH SCHOOL:** Did not attend high school.
**COLLEGE:** Did not attend college.
**TRANSACTIONS/CAREER NOTES:** Played for Unicaja Malaga of the Spanish league. ... Selected by Orlando Magic in first round (11th pick overall) of 2005 NBA Draft.

### SPANISH RECORD

| Season Team | G | Min. | FGM | FGA | Pct. | FTM | FTA | Pct. | Reb. | Ast. | Pts. | AVERAGES | | |
|---|---|---|---|---|---|---|---|---|---|---|---|---|---|---|
| | | | | | | | | | | | | RPG | APG | PPG |
| 01-02—Unicaja | 5 | 21 | 3 | 5 | .600 | 0 | 0 | ... | 4 | 0 | 6 | 0.8 | 0.0 | 1.2 |
| 02-03—Unicaja | 9 | 51 | 5 | 16 | .313 | 2 | 6 | .333 | 10 | 0 | 12 | 1.1 | 0.0 | 1.3 |
| 03-04—Granada Canaria | 33 | 621 | 93 | 173 | .538 | 46 | 73 | .630 | 138 | 7 | 232 | 4.2 | 0.2 | 7.0 |
| 04-05—Unicaja | 34 | 825 | 153 | 249 | .614 | 63 | 102 | .618 | 203 | 10 | 370 | 6.0 | 0.3 | 10.9 |
| Totals | 81 | 1518 | 254 | 443 | .573 | 111 | 181 | .613 | 355 | 17 | 620 | 4.4 | 0.2 | 7.7 |

Three-point field goals: 2004-05, 1-for-3 (.333). Totals, 1-for-3 (.333).

## VILLANUEVA, CHARLIE    F       RAPTORS

**PERSONAL:** Born August 24, 1984, in Queens, N.Y. ... 6-11/240. (2.11/108.9).
**HIGH SCHOOL:** Blair Academy (Blairstown, N.J.).
**COLLEGE:** Connecticut.
**TRANSACTIONS/CAREER NOTES:** Selected after sophomore season by Toronto Raptors in first round (seventh pick overall) of 2005 NBA draft.

### COLLEGIATE RECORD

**NOTES:** Member of NCAA Division I championship team (2004).

| Season Team | G | Min. | FGM | FGA | Pct. | FTM | FTA | Pct. | Reb. | Ast. | Pts. | RPG | APG | PPG |
|---|---|---|---|---|---|---|---|---|---|---|---|---|---|---|
| 03-04—Connecticut | 32 | 607 | 113 | 220 | .514 | 42 | 63 | .667 | 168 | 23 | 286 | 5.3 | 0.7 | 8.9 |
| 04-05—Connecticut | 31 | 798 | 159 | 305 | .521 | 97 | 141 | .688 | 257 | 40 | 421 | 8.3 | 1.3 | 13.6 |
| Totals | 63 | 1405 | 272 | 525 | .518 | 139 | 204 | .681 | 425 | 63 | 707 | 6.7 | 1.0 | 11.2 |

Three-point field goals: 2003-04, 18-for-49 (.367). 2004-05, 6-for-12 (.500). Totals, 24-for-61 (.393).

## WAFER, VON      G       LAKERS

**PERSONAL:** Born July 21, 1985, in Homer, La. ... 6-5/210. (1.96/95.3). ... Full name: Vakeaton Quamar Wafer
**HIGH SCHOOL:** Pineview (Lisbon, La.), then Heritage Christian Academy (Cleveland, Texas) .
**COLLEGE:** Florida State.
**TRANSACTIONS/CAREER NOTES:** Selected after sophomore season by Los Angeles Lakers in second round (39th pick overall) of 2005 NBA draft.

### COLLEGIATE RECORD

| Season Team | G | Min. | FGM | FGA | Pct. | FTM | FTA | Pct. | Reb. | Ast. | Pts. | RPG | APG | PPG |
|---|---|---|---|---|---|---|---|---|---|---|---|---|---|---|
| 03-04—Florida State | 32 | 560 | 90 | 244 | .369 | 30 | 50 | .600 | 60 | 36 | 253 | 1.9 | 1.1 | 7.9 |
| 04-05—Florida State | 29 | 758 | 124 | 284 | .437 | 49 | 68 | .721 | 73 | 48 | 362 | 2.5 | 1.7 | 12.5 |
| Totals | 61 | 1318 | 214 | 528 | .405 | 79 | 118 | .669 | 133 | 84 | 615 | 2.2 | 1.4 | 10.1 |

Three-point field goals: 2003-04, 43-for-132 (.326). 2004-05, 65-for-164 (.396). Totals, 108-for-296 (.365).

## WARRICK, HAKIM      F       GRIZZLIES

**PERSONAL:** Born July 8, 1982, in Philadelphia, Pa. ... 6-9/219. (2.06/99.3). ... Full name: Hakim Hanif Warrick
**HIGH SCHOOL:** Friends Central (Wynnewood, Pa.).
**COLLEGE:** Syracuse.
**TRANSACTIONS/CAREER NOTES:** Selected by Memphis Grizzlies in first round (19th pick overall) of 2005 NBA draft.

### COLLEGIATE RECORD

**NOTES:** Member of NCAA Division I championship team (2003). ... The SPORTING NEWS All-America second team (2004, 2005).

| Season Team | G | Min. | FGM | FGA | Pct. | FTM | FTA | Pct. | Reb. | Ast. | Pts. | RPG | APG | PPG |
|---|---|---|---|---|---|---|---|---|---|---|---|---|---|---|
| 01-02—Syracuse | 35 | 609 | 95 | 172 | .552 | 23 | 60 | .383 | 168 | 18 | 214 | 4.8 | 0.5 | 6.1 |
| 02-03—Syracuse | 35 | 1146 | 197 | 364 | .541 | 124 | 186 | .667 | 297 | 57 | 518 | 8.5 | 1.6 | 14.8 |
| 03-04—Syracuse | 31 | 1156 | 222 | 434 | .512 | 171 | 247 | .692 | 266 | 82 | 615 | 8.6 | 2.6 | 19.8 |
| 04-05—Syracuse | 34 | 1275 | 253 | 462 | .548 | 211 | 310 | .681 | 294 | 50 | 726 | 8.6 | 1.5 | 21.4 |
| Totals | 135 | 4186 | 767 | 1432 | .536 | 529 | 803 | .659 | 1025 | 207 | 2073 | 7.6 | 1.5 | 15.4 |

Three-point field goals: 2001-02, 1-for-2 (.500). 2002-03, 0-for-1. 2003-04, 0-for-6. 2004-05, 9-for-31 (.290). Totals, 10-for-40 (.250).

## WEBSTER, MARTELL      F/G       TRAIL BLAZERS

**PERSONAL:** Born December 4, 1986, in Edmond, Wash. ... 6-7/210. (2.01/95.3).
**HIGH SCHOOL:** Seattle Prep (Seattle, Wash.).
**COLLEGE:** Did not attend college.
**TRANSACTIONS/CAREER NOTES:** Selected out of high school by Portland Trail Blazers in first round (sixth pick overall) of 2005 NBA draft.

## WHALEY, ROBERT      C       JAZZ

**PERSONAL:** Born April 16, 1982 ... 6-10/260. (2.08/117.9). ... Full name: Robert Antawon Whaley.
**HIGH SCHOOL:** Benton Harbor (Mich.)
**JUNIOR COLLEGE:** Barton County (Kan.).
**COLLEGE:** Cincinnati, then Walsh.
**TRANSACTIONS/CAREER NOTES:** Selected by Utah Jazz in second round (51st pick overall) of 2005 NBA Draft.

### COLLEGIATE RECORD

| Season Team | G | Min. | FGM | FGA | Pct. | FTM | FTA | Pct. | Reb. | Ast. | Pts. | RPG | APG | PPG |
|---|---|---|---|---|---|---|---|---|---|---|---|---|---|---|
| 01-02—Barton County | 32 | 784 | 229 | 405 | .565 | 79 | 138 | .572 | 216 | 34 | 538 | 6.8 | 1.1 | 16.8 |
| 02-03—Barton County | 29 | 801 | 203 | 408 | .498 | 84 | 146 | .575 | 224 | 30 | 491 | 7.7 | 1.0 | 16.9 |
| 03-04—Cincinnati | 22 | 286 | 48 | 138 | .348 | 31 | 47 | .660 | 54 | 14 | 127 | 2.5 | 0.6 | 5.8 |
| 04-05—Walsh | 35 | 1049 | 194 | 574 | .512 | 105 | 183 | .574 | 263 | 48 | 696 | 7.5 | 1.4 | 19.9 |
| Junior college totals | 61 | 1585 | 432 | 813 | .531 | 163 | 284 | .574 | 440 | 64 | 1029 | 7.2 | 1.0 | 16.9 |
| Totals | 57 | 1335 | 342 | 712 | .480 | 136 | 230 | .591 | 317 | 62 | 823 | 5.6 | 1.1 | 14.4 |

Three-point field goals: 2001-02, 1-for-2 (.500). 2002-03, 1-for-4 (.250). 2003-04, 0-for-1 (.000). 2004-05, 3-for-14 (.214). Totals, 5-for-21 (.238).

## WILLIAMS, DERON     G     JAZZ

**PERSONAL:** Born July 26, 1984, in Parkersburg, W.V. ... 6-3/210. (1.91/95.3). ... Full name: Deron Michael Williams
**HIGH SCHOOL:** The Colony (Texas).
**COLLEGE:** Illinois.
**TRANSACTIONS/CAREER NOTES:** Selected after junior season by Utah Jazz in first round (third pick overall) in 2005 N draft.

### COLLEGIATE RECORD

**NOTES:** The SPORTING NEWS All-America second team (2005).

| Season Team | G | Min. | FGM | FGA | Pct. | FTM | FTA | Pct. | Reb. | Ast. | Pts. | RPG | APG | PP |
|---|---|---|---|---|---|---|---|---|---|---|---|---|---|---|
| 02-03—Illinois | 32 | 868 | 75 | 176 | .426 | 24 | 45 | .533 | 95 | 145 | 202 | 3.0 | 4.5 | 6. |
| 03-04—Illinois | 30 | 1017 | 147 | 360 | .408 | 59 | 75 | .787 | 97 | 185 | 420 | 3.2 | 6.2 | 14. |
| 04-05—Illinois | 39 | 1315 | 178 | 411 | .433 | 65 | 96 | .677 | 142 | 264 | 489 | 3.6 | 6.8 | 12. |
| Totals | 101 | 3200 | 400 | 947 | .422 | 148 | 216 | .685 | 334 | 594 | 1111 | 3.3 | 5.9 | 11. |

Three-point field goals: 2002-03, 28-for-79 (.354). 2003-04, 67-for-170 (.394). 2004-05, 68-for-187 (.364). Totals, 163-for-436 (.374).

## WILLIAMS, LOUIS     G     76ERS

**PERSONAL:** Born October 27, 1986, in Lithonia, Ga. ... 6-2/175. (1.88/79.4).
**HIGH SCHOOL:** South Gwinnett (Snellville, Ga.).
**COLLEGE:** Did not attend college.
**TRANSACTIONS/CAREER NOTES:** Selected out of high school by Philadelphia 76ers in second round (45th pick overall) 2005 NBA draft.

## WILLIAMS, MARVIN     F     HAWKS

**PERSONAL:** Born June 19, 1986, in Bremerton, Wash. ... 6-9/230. (2.06/104.3). ... Full name: Marvin Gaye Williams
**HIGH SCHOOL:** Bremerton (Wash.).
**COLLEGE:** North Carolina.
**TRANSACTIONS/CAREER NOTES:** Selected after freshman season by Atlanta Hawks in first round (second pick overall) 2005 draft.

### COLLEGIATE RECORD

**NOTES:** Member of NCAA Division I championship team (2005).

| Season Team | G | Min. | FGM | FGA | Pct. | FTM | FTA | Pct. | Reb. | Ast. | Pts. | RPG | APG | PPG |
|---|---|---|---|---|---|---|---|---|---|---|---|---|---|---|
| 04-05—North Carolina | 36 | 800 | 125 | 247 | .506 | 138 | 163 | .847 | 236 | 26 | 407 | 6.6 | 0.7 | 11.3 |

Three-point field goals: 2004-05, 19-for-44 (.432). Totals, 19-for-44 (.432).

## WRIGHT, ANTOINE     F/G     NETS

**PERSONAL:** Born February 6, 1984, in West Covina, Calif. ... 6-7/210. (2.01/95.3). ... Full name: Antoine Domonick Wright
**HIGH SCHOOL:** Lawrence Academy (Groton, Mass.) .
**COLLEGE:** Texas A&M.
**TRANSACTIONS/CAREER NOTES:** Selected after junior season by New Jersey Nets in first round (15th pick overall) of 2005 NBA draft.

### COLLEGIATE RECORD

| Season Team | G | Min. | FGM | FGA | Pct. | FTM | FTA | Pct. | Reb. | Ast. | Pts. | RPG | APG | PPG |
|---|---|---|---|---|---|---|---|---|---|---|---|---|---|---|
| 02-03—Texas A&M | 28 | 889 | 144 | 396 | .364 | 55 | 90 | .611 | 186 | 50 | 406 | 6.6 | 1.8 | 14.5 |
| 03-04—Texas A&M | 28 | 852 | 130 | 353 | .368 | 72 | 115 | .626 | 116 | 65 | 379 | 4.1 | 2.3 | 13.5 |
| 04-05—Texas A&M | 31 | 1052 | 193 | 385 | .501 | 96 | 139 | .691 | 185 | 69 | 553 | 6.0 | 2.2 | 17.8 |
| Totals | 87 | 2793 | 467 | 1134 | .412 | 223 | 344 | .648 | 487 | 184 | 1338 | 5.6 | 2.1 | 15.4 |

Three-point field goals: 2002-03, 63-for-165 (.382). 2003-04, 47-for-158 (.297). 2004-05, 71-for-159 (.447). Totals, 181-for-482 (.376).

## WRIGHT, BRACEY     G     TIMBERWOLVES

**PERSONAL:** Born July 1, 1984, in The Colony, Texas. ... 6-3/210. (1.91/95.3).
**HIGH SCHOOL:** The Colony (Texas).
**COLLEGE:** Indiana.
**TRANSACTIONS/CAREER NOTES:** Selected after junior season by Minnesota Timberwolves in second round (47th pick overall) of 2005 NBA draft.

### COLLEGIATE RECORD

| Season Team | G | Min. | FGM | FGA | Pct. | FTM | FTA | Pct. | Reb. | Ast. | Pts. | RPG | APG | PPG |
|---|---|---|---|---|---|---|---|---|---|---|---|---|---|---|
| 02-03—Indiana | 30 | 1007 | 157 | 363 | .433 | 106 | 141 | .752 | 151 | 64 | 486 | 5.0 | 2.1 | 16.2 |
| 03-04—Indiana | 29 | 1111 | 162 | 433 | .374 | 142 | 180 | .789 | 157 | 70 | 536 | 5.4 | 2.4 | 18.5 |
| 04-05—Indiana | 26 | 917 | 150 | 363 | .413 | 126 | 161 | .783 | 125 | 70 | 476 | 4.8 | 2.7 | 18.3 |
| Totals | 85 | 3035 | 469 | 1159 | .405 | 374 | 482 | .776 | 433 | 204 | 1498 | 5.1 | 2.4 | 17.6 |

Three-point field goals: 2002-03, 66-for-176 (.375). 2003-04, 70-for-204 (.343). 2004-05, 50-for-152 (.329). Totals, 186-for-532 (.350).

## ADELMAN, RICK — KINGS

**PERSONAL:** Born June 16, 1946, in Lynwood, Calif. ... 6-2/180. (1,88/81,6). ... Full name: Richard Leonard Adelman. ... Name pronounced ADD-el-mun.
**HIGH SCHOOL:** St. Pius X (Downey, Calif.).
**COLLEGE:** Loyola Marymount.
**TRANSACTIONS/CAREER NOTES:** Selected by San Diego Rockets in seventh round (79th pick overall) of 1968 NBA Draft. ... Selected by Portland Trail Blazers from Rockets in NBA expansion draft (May 11, 1970). ... Traded by Trail Blazers to Chicago Bulls for cash and 1974 second-round draft choice (September 14, 1973). ... Traded by Bulls to New Orleans Jazz for F/C John Block (November 11, 1974). ... Traded by Jazz with F Ollie Johnson to Kansas City/Omaha Kings for F Nate Williams (February 1, 1975). ... Kings franchise moved from Kansas City/Omaha to Kansas City for 1975-76 season. ... Released by Kings (October 21, 1975).

### COLLEGIATE RECORD

| Season Team | G | Min. | FGM | FGA | Pct. | FTM | FTA | Pct. | Reb. | Ast. | Pts. | RPG | APG | PPG |
|---|---|---|---|---|---|---|---|---|---|---|---|---|---|---|
| 64-65—Loyola (Calif.)‡ | | | | | | Freshman team statistics unavailable. | | | | | | | | |
| 65-66—Loyola (Calif.) | 26 | ... | 149 | 376 | .396 | 129 | 152 | .849 | 113 | ... | 427 | 4.3 | ... | 16.4 |
| 66-67—Loyola (Calif.) | 25 | ... | 151 | 349 | .433 | 171 | 214 | .799 | 124 | ... | 473 | 5.0 | ... | 18.9 |
| 67-68—Loyola (Calif.) | 25 | ... | 177 | 420 | .421 | 171 | 216 | .792 | 127 | ... | 525 | 5.1 | ... | 21.0 |
| Varsity totals | 76 | ... | 477 | 1145 | .417 | 471 | 582 | .809 | 364 | ... | 1425 | 4.8 | ... | 18.8 |

### NBA REGULAR-SEASON RECORD

| Season Team | G | Min. | FGM | FGA | Pct. | FTM | FTA | Pct. | Reb. | Ast. | PF | Dq. | Pts. | RPG | APG | PPG |
|---|---|---|---|---|---|---|---|---|---|---|---|---|---|---|---|---|
| 68-69—San Diego | 77 | 1448 | 177 | 449 | .394 | 131 | 204 | .642 | 216 | 238 | 158 | 1 | 485 | 2.8 | 3.1 | 6.3 |
| 69-70—San Diego | 35 | 717 | 96 | 247 | .389 | 68 | 91 | .747 | 81 | 113 | 90 | 0 | 260 | 2.3 | 3.2 | 7.4 |
| 70-71—Portland | 81 | 2303 | 378 | 895 | .422 | 267 | 369 | .724 | 282 | 380 | 214 | 2 | 1023 | 3.5 | 4.7 | 12.6 |
| 71-72—Portland | 80 | 2445 | 329 | 753 | .437 | 151 | 201 | .751 | 229 | 413 | 209 | 2 | 808 | 2.9 | 5.2 | 10.1 |
| 72-73—Portland | 76 | 1822 | 214 | 525 | .408 | 73 | 102 | .716 | 157 | 294 | 155 | 2 | 591 | 2.1 | 3.9 | 7.8 |

| Season Team | G | Min. | FGM | FGA | Pct. | FTM | FTA | Pct. | Off. | Def. | Tot. | Ast. | St. | Blk. | TO | Pts. | RPG | APG | PPG |
|---|---|---|---|---|---|---|---|---|---|---|---|---|---|---|---|---|---|---|---|
| 73-74—Chicago | 55 | 618 | 64 | 170 | .376 | 54 | 76 | .711 | 16 | 53 | 69 | 56 | 36 | 1 | ... | 182 | 1.3 | 1.0 | 3.3 |
| 74-75—Ch-NO-KC/O | 58 | 1074 | 123 | 291 | .423 | 73 | 103 | .709 | 25 | 70 | 95 | 112 | 70 | 8 | ... | 319 | 1.6 | 1.9 | 5.5 |
| Totals | 462 | 10427 | 1381 | 3330 | .415 | 817 | 1146 | .713 | ... | ... | 1129 | 1606 | 106 | 9 | ... | 3668 | 2.4 | 3.5 | 7.9 |

Personal fouls/disqualifications: 1973-74, 63/0. 1974-75, 101/1. Totals, 990/8.

### NBA PLAYOFF RECORD

| Season Team | G | Min. | FGM | FGA | Pct. | FTM | FTA | Pct. | Reb. | Ast. | PF | Dq. | Pts. | RPG | APG | PPG |
|---|---|---|---|---|---|---|---|---|---|---|---|---|---|---|---|---|
| 68-69—San Diego | 6 | 187 | 24 | 53 | .453 | 22 | 37 | .595 | 15 | 29 | 18 | 0 | 70 | 2.5 | 4.8 | 11.7 |

| Season Team | G | Min. | FGM | FGA | Pct. | FTM | FTA | Pct. | Off. | Def. | Tot. | Ast. | St. | Blk. | TO | Pts. | RPG | APG | PPG |
|---|---|---|---|---|---|---|---|---|---|---|---|---|---|---|---|---|---|---|---|
| 73-74—Chicago | 9 | 108 | 16 | 34 | .471 | 7 | 11 | .636 | 1 | 9 | 10 | 7 | 7 | 0 | ... | 39 | 1.1 | 0.8 | 4.3 |
| 74-75—K.C./Omaha | 6 | 34 | 3 | 9 | .333 | 6 | 8 | .750 | 1 | 1 | 2 | 3 | 1 | 0 | ... | 12 | 0.3 | 0.5 | 2.0 |
| Totals | 21 | 329 | 43 | 96 | .448 | 35 | 56 | .625 | ... | ... | 27 | 39 | 8 | 0 | ... | 121 | 1.3 | 1.9 | 5.8 |

Personal fouls/disqualifications: 1973-74, 5/0. 1974-75, 9/0. Totals, 32/0.

### HEAD COACHING RECORD

**BACKGROUND:** Head coach, Chemeketa Community College, Ore. (1977-78 through 1982-83; record: 141-39, .783). ... Assistant coach, Portland Trail Blazers (1983-84 to February 18, 1989).

### NBA COACHING RECORD

| Season Team | REGULAR SEASON | | | | PLAYOFFS | | |
|---|---|---|---|---|---|---|---|
| | W | L | Pct. | Finish | W | L | Pct. |
| 88-89—Portland | 14 | 21 | .400 | 5th/Pacific Division | 0 | 3 | .000 |
| 89-90—Portland | 59 | 23 | .720 | 2nd/Pacific Division | 12 | 9 | .571 |
| 90-91—Portland | 63 | 19 | .768 | 1st/Pacific Division | 9 | 7 | .563 |
| 91-92—Portland | 57 | 25 | .695 | 1st/Pacific Division | 13 | 8 | .619 |
| 92-93—Portland | 51 | 31 | .622 | 3rd/Pacific Division | 1 | 3 | .250 |
| 93-94—Portland | 47 | 35 | .573 | 4th/Pacific Division | 1 | 3 | .250 |
| 95-96—Golden State | 36 | 46 | .439 | 6th/Pacific Division | — | — | — |
| 96-97—Golden State | 30 | 52 | .366 | 7th Pacific Divison | — | — | — |
| 98-99—Sacramento | 27 | 23 | .540 | T3rd/Pacific Division | 2 | 3 | .400 |
| 99-00—Sacramento | 44 | 38 | .537 | 5th/Pacific Division | 2 | 3 | .400 |
| 00-01—Sacramento | 55 | 27 | .671 | 2nd/Pacific Division | 3 | 5 | .375 |
| 01-02—Sacramento | 61 | 21 | .744 | 1st/Pacific Division | 10 | 6 | .625 |
| 02-03—Sacramento | 59 | 23 | .719 | 1st/Pacific Division | 7 | 5 | .583 |
| 03-04—Sacramento | 55 | 27 | .671 | 2nd/Pacific Division | 7 | 5 | .583 |
| 04-05—Sacramento | 50 | 32 | .610 | 2nd/Pacific Division | 1 | 4 | .200 |
| Totals (15 years) | 708 | 443 | .615 | Totals (13 years) | 68 | 64 | .515 |

**NOTES:**

1989—Replaced Mike Schuler as Portland head coach (February 18), with record of 25-22. Lost to Los Angeles Lakers in Western Conference first round.

1990—Defeated Dallas, 3-0, in Western Conference first round; defeated San Antonio, 4-3, in Western Conference semifinals; defeated Phoenix, 4-2, in Western Conference finals; lost to Detroit, 4-1, in NBA Finals.

1991—Defeated Seattle, 3-2, in Western Conference first round; defeated Utah, 4-1, in Western Conference semifinals; lost to Los Angeles Lakers, 4-2, in Western Conference finals.

1992—Defeated Los Angeles Lakers, 3-1, in Western Conference first round; defeated Phoenix, 4-1, in Western Conference semifinals; defeated Utah, 4-2, in Western Conference finals; lost to Chicago, 4-2, in NBA Finals.

1993—Lost to San Antonio in Western Conference first round.

1994—Lost to Houston in Western Conference first round.
1999—Lost to Utah in Western Conference first round.
2000—Lost to Los Angeles Lakers in Western Conference first round.
2001—Defeated Phoenix, 3-1, in Western Conference first round; lost to Los Angeles Lakers, 4-0, in Western Conference semifinals.
2002—Defeated Utah, 3-1, in Western Conference first round; defeated Dallas, 4-1, in Western Conference semifinals; lost to Los Angeles Lakers, 4-3, in Western Conference finals.
2003—Defeated Utah, 4-1, in Western Conference first round; lost to Dallas, 4-3, in Western Conference semifinals.
2004—Defeated Dallas, 4-1, in Western Conference first round; lost to Minnesota, 4-3, in Western Conference semifinals.
2005—Lost to Seattle SuperSonics in Western Conference first round.

# BICKERSTAFF, BERNIE                        BOBCATS

**PERSONAL:** Born February 11, 1944, in Benham, Ky. ... 6-3/185 (1,90/83,9). ... Full name: Bernard Tyrone Bickerstaff.
**HIGH SCHOOL:** East Benham (Benham, Ky.).
**COLLEGE:** Rio Grande (Ohio), then San Diego.
**CAREER NOTES:** Vice president/general manager, Denver Nuggets (July 1990 through 1995-96). ... President, Nuggets (1996 through February 10, 1997). ... General manager, Charlotte Bobcats (2003-present).

## COLLEGIATE RECORD

| Season Team | G | Min. | FGM | FGA | Pct. | FTM | FTA | Pct. | Reb. | Ast. | Pts. | RPG | APG | PPG |
|---|---|---|---|---|---|---|---|---|---|---|---|---|---|---|
| 64-65—San Diego | 26 | ... | 78 | 211 | .370 | 46 | 91 | .506 | 135 | ... | 202 | 5.2 | ... | 7.8 |
| 65-66—San Diego | 28 | ... | 88 | 249 | .353 | 82 | 116 | .707 | 201 | ... | 248 | 7.2 | ... | 8.9 |
| Totals | 54 | ... | 166 | 460 | .361 | 128 | 207 | .618 | 336 | ... | 450 | 6.2 | ... | 8.3 |

## HEAD COACHING RECORD

**BACKGROUND:** Assistant coach, University of San Diego (1967-68 and 1968-69). ... Assistant coach, Capital Bullets of NBA (1973-74). ... Assistant coach, Washington Bullets (1974-75 through 1984-85). ... Bullets franchise renamed Washington Wizards for 1997-98 season.

### COLLEGIATE COACHING RECORD

| Season Team | W | L | Pct. | Finish |
|---|---|---|---|---|
| 69-70—San Diego | 14 | 12 | .538 | Division II Independent |
| 70-71—San Diego | 10 | 14 | .417 | Division II Independent |
| 71-72—San Diego | 12 | 14 | .462 | Division II Independent |
| 72-73—San Diego | 19 | 9 | .679 | Division II Independent |
| Totals (4 years) | 55 | 49 | .529 | |

### NBA COACHING RECORD

| | REGULAR SEASON | | | | PLAYOFFS | | |
|---|---|---|---|---|---|---|---|
| Season Team | W | L | Pct. | Finish | W | L | Pct. |
| 85-86—Seattle | 31 | 51 | .378 | 5th/Pacific Division | — | — | — |
| 86-87—Seattle | 39 | 43 | .476 | 4th/Pacific Division | 7 | 7 | .500 |
| 87-88—Seattle | 44 | 38 | .537 | 3rd/Pacific Division | 2 | 3 | .400 |
| 88-89—Seattle | 47 | 35 | .573 | 3rd/Pacific Division | 3 | 5 | .375 |
| 89-90—Seattle | 41 | 41 | .500 | 4th/Pacific Division | — | — | — |
| 94-95—Denver | 20 | 12 | .625 | 4th/Midwest Division | 0 | 3 | .000 |
| 95-96—Denver | 35 | 47 | .427 | 4th/Midwest Division | — | — | — |
| 96-97—Denver | 4 | 9 | .308 | | — | — | — |
| —Washington | 22 | 13 | .629 | 4th/Atlantic Division | 0 | 3 | .000 |
| 97-98—Washington | 42 | 40 | .512 | 4th/Atlantic Division | — | — | — |
| 98-99—Washington | 13 | 19 | .406 | | — | — | — |
| 04-05—Charlotte | 18 | 64 | .220 | 4th/Southeast Division | — | — | — |
| Totals (11 years) | 356 | 412 | .464 | Totals (5 years) | 12 | 21 | .364 |

**NOTES:**
1987—Defeated Dallas, 3-1, in Western Conference first round; defeated Houston, 4-2, in Western Conference semifinals; lost to Los Angeles Lakers, 4-0, in Western Conference finals.
1988—Lost to Denver in Western Conference first round.
1989—Defeated Houston, 3-1, in Western Conference first round; lost to Los Angeles Lakers, 4-0, in Western Conference semifinals.
1995—Replaced Dan Issel (18-16) and Gene Littles (interim head coach, 3-13) as Denver head coach (February 20), with record of 21-29 and club in fourth place. Lost to San Antonio in Western Conference first round.
1996—Replaced as Denver head coach by Dick Motta (November 26).
1997—Replaced Jim Lynam (22-24) and Bob Staak (interim head coach, 0-1) as Washington head coach (February 10); with record of 22-25 and club in fourth place. Lost to Chicago in Eastern Conference first round.

# BROWN, LARRY                        KNICKS

**PERSONAL:** Born September 14, 1940, in Brooklyn, N.Y. ... 5-9/160. (1,76/72,6). ... Full name: Lawrence Harvey Brown. ... Brother of Herb Brown, head coach with Detroit Pistons (1975-76 through 1977-78).
**HIGH SCHOOL:** Long Beach (N.Y.).
**COLLEGE:** North Carolina.
**TRANSACTIONS/CAREER NOTES:** Signed by New Orleans Buccaneers of American Basketball Association (1967). ... Traded by Buccaneers with F/G Doug Moe to Oakland Oaks for F Steve Jones, F Ron Franz and G Barry Leibowitz (June 18, 1968). ... Oaks franchise moved from Oakland to Washington and renamed Capitols for 1969-70 season. ... Capitols franchise moved from Washington to Virginia and renamed Squires for 1970-71 season. ... Contract sold by Squires to Denver Rockets (January 23, 1971).
**CAREER HONORS:** Elected to Naismith Memorial Basketball Hall of Fame (2002).
**MISCELLANEOUS:** Member of gold-medal-winning U.S. Olympic team (1964).

HEAD COACHES

## COLLEGIATE RECORD

| Season Team | G | Min. | FGM | FGA | Pct. | FTM | FTA | Pct. | Reb. | Ast. | Pts. | AVERAGES RPG | APG | PPG |
|---|---|---|---|---|---|---|---|---|---|---|---|---|---|---|
| 59-60—North Carolina‡ | 15 | ... | 88 | ... | ... | 100 | 143 | .699 | ... | ... | 276 | ... | ... | 18.4 |
| 60-61—North Carolina | 18 | ... | 28 | 54 | .519 | 25 | 34 | .735 | 28 | ... | 81 | 1.6 | ... | 4.5 |
| 61-62—North Carolina | 17 | ... | 90 | 204 | .441 | 101 | 127 | .795 | 52 | ... | 281 | 3.1 | ... | 16.5 |
| 62-63—North Carolina | 21 | ... | 102 | 231 | .442 | 95 | 122 | .779 | 50 | ... | 299 | 2.4 | ... | 14.2 |
| Varsity totals | 56 | ... | 220 | 489 | .450 | 221 | 283 | .781 | 130 | ... | 661 | 2.3 | ... | 11.8 |

## AMATEUR PLAYING RECORD

| Season Team | G | Min. | FGM | FGA | Pct. | FTM | FTA | Pct. | Reb. | Ast. | Pts. | AVERAGES RPG | APG | PPG |
|---|---|---|---|---|---|---|---|---|---|---|---|---|---|---|
| 63-64—Akron (Ohio) | 33 | ... | 149 | ... | ... | 31 | ... | ... | ... | ... | 329 | ... | ... | 10.0 |
| 64-65—Akron (Ohio) | 32 | ... | 144 | 297 | .485 | 139 | 167 | .832 | 90 | ... | 427 | 2.8 | ... | 13.3 |
| Totals | 65 | ... | 293 | ... | ... | 170 | ... | ... | ... | ... | 756 | ... | ... | 11.6 |

## ABA REGULAR-SEASON RECORD

**NOTES:** ABA All-Star second team (1968). ... Member of ABA championship team (1969). ... Holds single-game record for most assists—23 (February 20, 1972, vs. Pittsburgh).

| Season Team | G | Min. | 2-POINT FGM | FGA | Pct. | 3-POINT FGM | FGA | Pct. | FTM | FTA | Pct. | Reb. | Ast. | Pts. | AVERAGES RPG | APG | PPG |
|---|---|---|---|---|---|---|---|---|---|---|---|---|---|---|---|---|---|
| 67-68—New Orleans | 78 | 2807 | 311 | 812 | .383 | 19 | 89 | .213 | 366 | 450 | .813 | 249 | *506 | 1045 | 3.2 | 6.5 | 13.4 |
| 68-69—Oakland | 77 | 2381 | 300 | 671 | .447 | 8 | 35 | .229 | 301 | 379 | .794 | 235 | *544 | 925 | 3.1 | 7.1 | 12.0 |
| 69-70—Washington | 82 | 2766 | 366 | 815 | .449 | 10 | 39 | .256 | 362 | 439 | .825 | 246 | *580 | 1124 | 3.0 | 7.1 | 13.7 |
| 70-71—Virginia-Denver | 63 | 1343 | 121 | 319 | .379 | 6 | 21 | .286 | 186 | 225 | .827 | 109 | 330 | 446 | 1.7 | 5.2 | 7.1 |
| 71-72—Denver | 76 | 2012 | 238 | 531 | .448 | 5 | 25 | .200 | 198 | 244 | .811 | 166 | 549 | 689 | 2.2 | 7.2 | 9.1 |
| Totals | 376 | 11309 | 1336 | 3148 | .424 | 48 | 209 | .230 | 1413 | 1737 | .813 | 1005 | 2509 | 4229 | 2.7 | 6.7 | 11.2 |

## ABA PLAYOFF RECORD

| Season Team | G | Min. | 2-POINT FGM | FGA | Pct. | 3-POINT FGM | FGA | Pct. | FTM | FTA | Pct. | Reb. | Ast. | Pts. | AVERAGES RPG | APG | PPG |
|---|---|---|---|---|---|---|---|---|---|---|---|---|---|---|---|---|---|
| 67-68—New Orleans | 17 | 696 | 86 | 194 | .443 | 4 | 18 | .222 | 100 | 122 | .820 | 59 | 129 | 284 | 3.5 | 7.6 | 16.7 |
| 68-69—Oakland | 16 | 534 | 74 | 170 | .435 | 0 | 3 | .000 | 76 | 90 | .844 | 52 | 87 | 224 | 3.3 | 5.4 | 14.0 |
| 69-70—Washington | 7 | 269 | 32 | 68 | .471 | 1 | 5 | .200 | 30 | 34 | .882 | 35 | 68 | 97 | 5.0 | 9.7 | 13.9 |
| 71-72—Denver | 7 | 211 | 21 | 47 | .447 | 0 | 3 | .000 | 23 | 24 | .958 | 10 | 36 | 65 | 1.4 | 5.1 | 9.3 |
| Totals | 47 | 1710 | 213 | 479 | .445 | 5 | 29 | .172 | 229 | 270 | .848 | 156 | 320 | 670 | 3.3 | 6.8 | 14.3 |

## ABA ALL-STAR GAME RECORD

**NOTES:** ABA All-Star Game Most Valuable Player (1968).

| Season Team | Min. | 2-POINT FGM | FGA | Pct. | 3-POINT FGM | FGA | Pct. | FTM | FTA | Pct. | Reb. | Ast. | Pts. |
|---|---|---|---|---|---|---|---|---|---|---|---|---|---|
| 1968—New Orleans | 22 | 5 | 7 | .714 | 2 | 2 | 1.000 | 1 | 1 | 1.000 | 3 | 5 | 17 |
| 1969—Oakland | 25 | 1 | 6 | .167 | 0 | 1 | .000 | 3 | 5 | .600 | 0 | 7 | 5 |
| 1970—Washington | 15 | 0 | 2 | .000 | 0 | 0 | ... | 3 | 3 | 1.000 | 3 | 3 | 3 |
| Totals | 62 | 6 | 15 | .400 | 2 | 3 | .667 | 7 | 9 | .778 | 6 | 15 | 25 |

## HEAD COACHING RECORD

**BACKGROUND:** Assistant coach, University of North Carolina (1965-66 and 1966-67). ... Assistant coach, U.S. Olympic team (1980).
**HONORS:** ABA Coach of the Year (1973, 1975, 1976). ... NBA Coach of the Year (2001).

## ABA COACHING RECORD

| Season Team | REGULAR SEASON W | L | Pct. | Finish | PLAYOFFS W | L | Pct. |
|---|---|---|---|---|---|---|---|
| 72-73—Carolina | 57 | 27 | .679 | 1st/Eastern Division | 7 | 5 | .583 |
| 73-74—Carolina | 47 | 37 | .560 | 3rd/Eastern Division | 0 | 4 | .000 |
| 74-75—Denver | 65 | 19 | .774 | 1st/Western Division | 7 | 6 | .538 |
| 75-76—Denver | 60 | 24 | .714 | 1st/Western Division | 6 | 7 | .462 |
| Totals (4 years) | 229 | 107 | .682 | Totals (4 years) | 20 | 22 | .476 |

## NBA COACHING RECORD

| Season Team | REGULAR SEASON W | L | Pct. | Finish | PLAYOFFS W | L | Pct. |
|---|---|---|---|---|---|---|---|
| 76-77—Denver | 50 | 32 | .610 | 1st/Midwest Division | 2 | 4 | .500 |
| 77-78—Denver | 48 | 34 | .585 | 1st/Midwest Division | 6 | 7 | .462 |
| 78-79—Denver | 28 | 25 | .528 | | — | — | — |
| 81-82—New Jersey | 44 | 38 | .537 | 3rd/Atlantic Division | 0 | 2 | .000 |
| 82-83—New Jersey | 47 | 29 | .618 | | — | — | — |
| 88-89—San Antonio | 21 | 61 | .256 | | — | — | — |
| 89-90—San Antonio | 56 | 26 | .683 | 1st/Midwest Division | 6 | 4 | .600 |
| 90-91—San Antonio | 55 | 27 | .671 | 1st/Midwest Division | 1 | 3 | .250 |
| 91-92—San Antonio | 21 | 17 | .553 | | — | — | — |
| —Los Angeles Clippers | 23 | 12 | .657 | 5th/Pacific Division | 2 | 3 | .400 |
| 92-93—Los Angeles Clippers | 41 | 41 | .500 | 4th/Pacific Division | 2 | 3 | .400 |
| 93-94—Indiana | 47 | 35 | .573 | T3rd/Central Division | 10 | 6 | .625 |
| 94-95—Indiana | 52 | 30 | .634 | 1st/Central Division | 10 | 7 | .588 |
| 95-96—Indiana | 52 | 30 | .634 | 2nd/Central Division | 2 | 3 | .400 |
| 96-97—Indiana | 39 | 43 | .476 | 6th/Central Division | — | — | — |
| 97-98—Philadelphia | 31 | 51 | .378 | 7th/Atlantic Division | — | — | — |
| 98-99—Philadelphia | 28 | 22 | .560 | 3rd/Atlantic Division | 3 | 5 | .375 |
| 99-00—Philadelphia | 49 | 33 | .598 | 3rd/Atlantic Division | 5 | 5 | .500 |
| 00-01—Philadelphia | 56 | 26 | .683 | 1st/Atlantic Division | 12 | 11 | .522 |

| Season | Team | W | L | Pct. | Finish | | W | L | Pct. |
|--------|------|---|---|------|--------|---|---|---|------|
| | | | | | **REGULAR SEASON** | | | **PLAYOFFS** | |
| 01-02 | Philadelphia | 43 | 39 | .521 | 4th/Atlantic Division | | 2 | 3 | .400 |
| 02-03 | Philadelphia | 48 | 34 | .585 | 2nd/Atlantic Division | | 6 | 6 | .500 |
| 03-04 | Detroit | 54 | 28 | .659 | 2nd/Central Division | | 16 | 7 | .696 |
| 04-05 | Detroit | 54 | 28 | .659 | 1st/Central Division | | 15 | 10 | .600 |
| | Totals (22 years) | 987 | 741 | .571 | Totals (17 years) | | 100 | 89 | .529 |

## COLLEGIATE COACHING RECORD

| Season | Team | W | L | Pct. | Finish |
|--------|------|---|---|------|--------|
| 79-80 | UCLA | 22 | 10 | .688 | 4th/Pacific-10 Conference |
| 80-81 | UCLA | 20 | 7 | .741 | 3rd/Pacific-10 Conference |
| 83-84 | Kansas | 22 | 10 | .688 | 2nd/Big Eight Conference |
| 84-85 | Kansas | 26 | 8 | .765 | 2nd/Big Eight Conference |
| 85-86 | Kansas | 35 | 4 | .897 | 1st/Big Eight Conference |
| 86-87 | Kansas | 25 | 11 | .694 | T2nd/Big Eight Conference |
| 87-88 | Kansas | 27 | 11 | .711 | 3rd/Big Eight Conference |
| | Totals (7 years) | 177 | 61 | .744 | |

**NOTES:**

1973—Defeated New York, 4-1, in Eastern Division semifinals; lost to Kentucky, 4-3, in Eastern Division finals.

1974—Lost to Kentucky in Eastern Division semifinals.

1975—Defeated Utah, 4-2, in Western Division semifinals; lost to Indiana, 4-3, in Western Division finals.

1976—Defeated Kentucky, 4-3, in semifinals; lost to New York, 4-2, in ABA Finals.

1977—Lost to Portland in Western Conference semifinals.

1978—Defeated Milwaukee, 4-3, in Western Conference semifinals; lost to Seattle, 4-2, in Western Conference finals.

1979—Resigned as Denver head coach (February 1); replaced by Donnie Walsh with club in second place.

1980—Defeated Old Dominion, 87-74, in NCAA Tournament first round; defeated DePaul, 77-71, in second round; defeated Ohio State, 72-68, in regional semifinals; defeated Clemson, 85-74, in regional finals; defeated Purdue, 67-62, in semifinals; lost to Louisville, 59-54, in championship game.

1981—Lost to Brigham Young, 78-55, in NCAA Tournament second round.

1982—Lost to Washington in Eastern Conference first round.

1983—Resigned as New Jersey head coach (April 7); replaced by Bill Blair with club in third place.

1984—Defeated Alcorn State, 57-56, in NCAA Tournament first round; lost to Wake Forest, 69-59, in second round.

1985—Defeated Ohio University, 49-38, in NCAA Tournament first round; lost to Auburn, 66-64, in second round.

1986—Defeated North Carolina A&T, 71-46, in NCAA Tournament first round; defeated Temple, 65-43, in second round; defeated Michigan State, 96-86 (OT), in regional semifinals; defeated North Carolina State, 75-67, in regional finals; lost to Duke, 71-67, in semifinals.

1987—Defeated Houston, 66-55, in NCAA Tournament first round; defeated Southwest Missouri State, 67-63, in second round; lost to Georgetown, 70-57, in regional semifinals.

1988—Defeated Xavier, 85-72, in NCAA Tournament first round; defeated Murray State, 61-58, in second round; defeated Vanderbilt, 77-64, in regional semifinals; defeated Kansas State, 71-58, in regional finals; defeated Duke, 66-59, in semifinals; defeated Oklahoma, 83-79, in championship game.

1990—Defeated Denver, 3-0, in Western Conference first round; lost to Portland, 4-3, in Western Conference semifinals.

1991—Lost to Golden State in Western Conference first round.

1992—Replaced as San Antonio head coach by Bob Bass with club in second place (January 21); replaced Mike Schuler (21-24) and Mack Calvin (interim head coach, 1-1) as Los Angeles Clippers head coach (February 6), with record of 22-25 and club in sixth place. Lost to Utah in Western Conference first round.

1993—Lost to Houston in Western Conference first round.

1994—Defeated Orlando, 3-0, in Eastern Conference first round; defeated Atlanta, 4-2, in Eastern Conference semifinals; lost to New York, 4-3, in Eastern Conference finals.

1995—Defeated Atlanta, 3-0, in Eastern Conference first round; defeated New York, 4-3, Eastern Conference semifinals; lost to Orlando, 4-3, in Eastern Conference finals.

1996—Lost to Atlanta in Eastern Conference first round.

1999—Defeated Orlando, 3-1, in Eastern Conference first round; lost to Indiana, 4-0, in Eastern Conference semifinals.

2000—Defeated Charlotte, 3-1, in Eastern Conference first round; lost to Indiana, 4-2, in Eastern Conference semifinals.

2001—Defeated Indiana, 3-1, in Eastern Conference first round; defeated Toronto, 4-3, in Eastern Conference semifinals; defeated Milwaukee, 4-3, in Eastern Conferene finals; lost to Los Angeles Lakers, 4-1, in NBA Finals.

2002—Lost to Boston in Eastern Conference first round.

2003—Defeated New Orleans, 4-2, in Eastern Conference first round; lost to Detroit, 4-2, in Eastern Conference semifinals.

2004—Defeated Milwaukee, 4-1, in Eastern Conference first round; defeated New Jersey, 4-3, in Eastern Conference semifinals; defeated Indiana, 4-2, in Eastern Conference finals; defeated Los Angeles Lakers, 4-1, in NBA Finals.

2005—Defeated Philadelphia, 4-1, in Eastern Conference first round; defeated Indiana, 4-2, in Eastern Conference semifinals; defeated Miami, 4-3, in Eastern Conference finals; lost to San Antonio, 4-3, in NBA Finals.

# BROWN, MIKE                    CAVALIERS

**PERSONAL:** Born March 5, 1970 in Columbus, Ohio. ... 6-3/200
**HIGH SCHOOL:** Wurzburg American (Germany).
**JUNIOR COLLEGE:** Mesa Community College.
**COLLEGE:** University of San Diego.

HEAD COACHES

## COLLEGIATE RECORD

| Season Team | G | Min. | FGM | FGA | Pct. | FTM | FTA | Pct. | Reb. | Ast. | Pts. | AVERAGES RPG | APG | PPG |
|---|---|---|---|---|---|---|---|---|---|---|---|---|---|---|
| 88-89—Mesa C.C. | | | | | | Statistics unavailable | | | | | | | | |
| 89-90—Mesa C.C. | 35 | ... | 156 | 319 | .489 | 117 | 158 | .741 | 148 | 113 | 485 | 4.2 | 3.2 | 13.9 |
| 90-91—San Diego | 29 | 740 | 79 | 183 | .432 | 64 | 100 | .640 | 100 | 75 | 258 | 3.4 | 2.6 | 8.9 |
| 91-92—San Diego | 28 | 695 | 52 | 135 | .385 | 99 | 127 | .780 | 86 | 32 | 212 | 3.1 | 1.1 | 7.6 |
| Totals | 57 | 1435 | 131 | 318 | .412 | 163 | 227 | .718 | 186 | 107 | 470 | 3.3 | 1.9 | 8.2 |

## HEAD COACHING RECORD

**BACKGROUND:** Video coordinator/scout, Nuggets (1992-97). ... Assistant coach/scout Wizards (1997-2000). ... Assistant coach, Spurs (2000-03). ... Assistant coach, Pacers (2003-04 season-June 2, 2005).

# CARLISLE, RICK                                    PACERS

**PERSONAL:** Born October 27, 1959, in Ogdensburg, N.Y. ... 6-5/210. (1,96/95,3). ... Full Name: Richard Preston Carlisle.
**HIGH SCHOOL:** Central.
**COLLEGE:** Maine, then Virginia.
**TRANSACTIONS/CAREER NOTES:** Selected by Boston Celtics in third round (69th pick overall) of 1984 NBA Draft. ... Waived by Celtics (November 3, 1987). ... Signed as free agent by New York Knicks (November 30, 1987). ... Played in Continental Basketball Association with Albany Patroons (1987-88). ... Signed as free agent by New Jersey Nets (October 4, 1989). ... Waived by Nets (December 1, 1989).

## COLLEGIATE RECORD

| Season Team | G | Min. | FGM | FGA | Pct. | FTM | FTA | Pct. | Reb. | Ast. | Pts. | AVERAGES RPG | APG | PPG |
|---|---|---|---|---|---|---|---|---|---|---|---|---|---|---|
| 79-80—Maine | 28 | ... | 131 | 236 | .555 | 83 | 97 | .856 | 96 | 118 | 345 | 3.4 | 4.2 | 12.3 |
| 80-81—Maine | 28 | ... | 176 | 322 | .547 | 102 | 126 | .810 | 118 | 132 | 454 | 4.2 | 4.7 | 16.2 |
| 81-82—Virginia | | | | | | Did not play—transfer student. | | | | | | | | |
| 82-83—Virginia | 33 | 956 | 142 | 277 | .513 | 87 | 104 | .837 | 100 | 98 | 379 | 3.0 | 3.0 | 11.5 |
| 83-84—Virginia | 33 | 959 | 149 | 289 | .516 | 67 | 96 | .698 | 93 | 95 | 365 | 2.8 | 2.9 | 11.1 |
| Totals | 122 | ... | 598 | 1124 | .532 | 339 | 423 | .801 | 407 | 443 | 1543 | 3.3 | 3.6 | 12.6 |

Three-point field goals: 1982-83, 8-for-12 (.667).

## NBA REGULAR-SEASON RECORD

| Season Team | G | Min. | FGM | FGA | Pct. | FTM | FTA | Pct. | REBOUNDS Off. | Def. | Tot. | Ast. | St. | Blk. | TO | Pts. | AVERAGES RPG | APG | PPG |
|---|---|---|---|---|---|---|---|---|---|---|---|---|---|---|---|---|---|---|---|
| 84-85—Boston | 38 | 179 | 26 | 67 | .388 | 15 | 17 | .882 | 8 | 13 | 21 | 25 | 3 | 0 | ... | 67 | 0.6 | 0.7 | 1.8 |
| 85-86—Boston | 77 | 760 | 92 | 189 | .487 | 15 | 23 | .652 | 22 | 55 | 77 | 104 | 19 | 4 | ... | 199 | 1.0 | 1.4 | 2.6 |
| 86-87—Boston | 42 | 297 | 30 | 92 | .326 | 15 | 20 | .750 | 8 | 22 | 30 | 35 | 8 | 0 | ... | 80 | 0.7 | 0.8 | 1.9 |
| 87-88—New York | 26 | 204 | 29 | 67 | .433 | 10 | 11 | .909 | 6 | 7 | 13 | 32 | 11 | 4 | ... | 74 | 0.5 | 1.2 | 2.8 |
| 89-90—New Jersey | 5 | 21 | 1 | 7 | .143 | 0 | 0 | ... | 0 | 0 | 0 | 5 | 1 | 1 | ... | 2 | 0.0 | 1.0 | 0.4 |
| Totals | 188 | 1461 | 178 | 422 | .422 | 55 | 71 | .775 | 44 | 97 | 141 | 201 | 42 | 9 | ... | 422 | 0.8 | 1.1 | 2.2 |

Three-point field goals: 1984-85, 0-for-2. 1985-86, 0-for-10. 1986-87, 5-for-16 (.313). 1987-88, 6-for-17 (.353). 1989-90, 0-for-3. Totals, 11-for-48 (.229).

Personal fouls/disqualifications: 1984-85, 21/0. 1985-86, 92/1. 1986-87, 28/0. 1987-88, 39/1. 1989-90, 7/0. Totals, 187/2.

## NBA PLAYOFF RECORD

| Season Team | G | Min. | FGM | FGA | Pct. | FTM | FTA | Pct. | REBOUNDS Off. | Def. | Tot. | Ast. | St. | Blk. | TO | Pts. | AVERAGES RPG | APG | PPG |
|---|---|---|---|---|---|---|---|---|---|---|---|---|---|---|---|---|---|---|---|
| 85-86—Boston | 10 | 54 | 8 | 15 | .533 | 3 | 4 | .750 | 3 | 2 | 5 | 8 | 2 | 0 | ... | 19 | 0.5 | 0.8 | 1.9 |
| 87-88—New York | 2 | 8 | 1 | 4 | .250 | 0 | 0 | ... | 1 | 1 | 2 | 0 | 1 | 0 | ... | 2 | 1.0 | 0.0 | 1.0 |
| Totals | 12 | 62 | 9 | 19 | .474 | 3 | 4 | .750 | 4 | 3 | 7 | 8 | 3 | 0 | ... | 21 | 0.6 | 0.7 | 1.8 |

Three-point field goals: 1987-88, 0-for-2. Totals, 0-for-2 (.000).

Personal fouls/disqualifications: 1985-86, 9/0. 1987-88, 1/0. Totals, 10/0.

## CBA REGULAR-SEASON RECORD

| Season Team | G | Min. | FGM | FGA | Pct. | FTM | FTA | Pct. | Reb. | Ast. | Pts. | AVERAGES RPG | APG | PPG |
|---|---|---|---|---|---|---|---|---|---|---|---|---|---|---|
| 87-88—Albany | 6 | 172 | 38 | 74 | .514 | 16 | 19 | .842 | 11 | 14 | 104 | 1.8 | 2.3 | 17.3 |

Three-point field goals: 1987-88, 4-for-8 (.500).

## HEAD COACHING RECORD

**NOTES:** Assistant coach, New Jersey Nets (1989-90 through 1993-94). ... Assistant coach, Portland Trail Blazers (1994-95 through 1996-97). ... Assistant coach, Indiana Pacers (1997-98 through 2000-01).
**HONORS:** NBA Coach of the Year (2002).

## NBA COACHING RECORD

| Season Team | REGULAR SEASON W | L | Pct. | Finish | PLAYOFFS W | L | Pct. |
|---|---|---|---|---|---|---|---|
| 01-02—Detroit | 50 | 32 | .610 | 1st/Central Division | 4 | 6 | .400 |
| 02-03—Detroit | 50 | 32 | .610 | 1st/Central Division | 8 | 9 | .471 |
| 03-04—Indiana | 61 | 21 | .744 | 1st/Central Division | 10 | 6 | .625 |
| 04-05—Indiana | 44 | 38 | .537 | 3rd/Central Division | 6 | 7 | .462 |
| Totals (4 years) | 205 | 123 | .625 | Totals (4 years) | 28 | 28 | .500 |

**NOTES:**
2002—Defeated Toronto, 3-2, in Eastern Conference first round; lost to Boston, 4-1, in Eastern Conference semifinals.

2003—Defeated Orlando, 4-3, in Eastern Conference first round; defeated Philadelphia, 4-2, in Eastern Conference semifinals; lost to New Jersey, 4-0, in Eastern Conference finals.
2004—Defeated Boston, 4-0, in Eastern Conference first round; defeated Miami, 4-2, in Eastern Conference semifinals; lost to Detroit, 4-2, in Eastern Conference finals.
2005—Defeated Boston, 4-3, in Eastern Conference first round; lost to Detroit, 4-2, in Eastern Conference semifinals.

## CASEY, DWANE — TIMBERWOLVES

**PERSONAL:** Born April 17, 1957, in Morganfield, Ky. ... 6-2/195
**HIGH SCHOOL:** Union County (Ky.)
**COLLEGE:** Kentucky.

### COLLEGIATE RECORD

| Season Team | G | Min. | FGM | FGA | Pct. | FTM | FTA | Pct. | Reb. | Ast. | Pts. | RPG | APG | PPG |
|---|---|---|---|---|---|---|---|---|---|---|---|---|---|---|
| 75-76—Kentucky | 20 | 144 | 10 | 27 | .370 | 5 | 9 | .556 | 13 | 12 | 25 | 0.7 | 0.6 | 1.3 |
| 76-77—Kentucky | 27 | 196 | 16 | 51 | .314 | 17 | 25 | .680 | 11 | 21 | 49 | 0.4 | 0.9 | 3.2 |
| 77-78—Kentucky | 26 | 177 | 13 | 34 | .382 | 6 | 10 | .600 | 17 | 21 | 32 | 0.6 | 0.8 | 2.3 |
| 78-79—Kentucky | 22 | 99 | 7 | 18 | .389 | 5 | 7 | .714 | 10 | 8 | 19 | 0.5 | 0.4 | 1.0 |
| Totals | 95 | 616 | 46 | 130 | .354 | 33 | 51 | .647 | 51 | 62 | 125 | 0.5 | 0.6 | 1.3 |

### HEAD COACHING RECORD

**BACKGROUND:** Assistant coach, Western Kentucky University (1980-85). ... Assistant coach, University of Kentucky (1985-90). ... Head coach in Japan (1990-94). ... Assistant coach, SuperSonics (1994-95 season-June 17, 2005).

## CHEEKS, MAURICE — 76ERS

**PERSONAL:** Born September 8, 1956, in Chicago. ... 6-1/180. (1,85/81,6). ... Full name: Maurice Edward Cheeks.
**HIGH SCHOOL:** Du Sable (Chicago).
**COLLEGE:** West Texas State.
**TRANSACTIONS:** Selected by Philadelphia 76ers in second round (36th pick overall) of 1978 NBA Draft. ... Traded by 76ers with C Christian Welp and G David Wingate to San Antonio Spurs for G Johnny Dawkins and F Jay Vincent (August 28, 1989). ... Traded by Spurs to New York Knicks for G Rod Strickland (February 21, 1990). ... Traded by Knicks to Atlanta Hawks for C Tim McCormick (October 3, 1991). ... Signed as free agent by New Jersey Nets (January 7, 1993).
**CAREER NOTES:** Assistant coach, 76ers (1994-95 to 2000-01).
**MISCELLANEOUS:** Member of NBA championship team (1983). ... Philadelphia 76ers franchise all-time assists leader with 6,212 and all-time steals leader with 1,942 (1978-79 through 1988-89).

### COLLEGIATE RECORD

| Season Team | G | Min. | FGM | FGA | Pct. | FTM | FTA | Pct. | Reb. | Ast. | Pts. | RPG | APG | PPG |
|---|---|---|---|---|---|---|---|---|---|---|---|---|---|---|
| 74-75—West Texas State | 26 | ... | 35 | 75 | .467 | 31 | 53 | .585 | 56 | ... | 101 | 2.2 | ... | 3.9 |
| 75-76—West Texas State | 23 | 767 | 102 | 170 | .600 | 52 | 84 | .619 | 91 | ... | 256 | 4.0 | ... | 11.1 |
| 76-77—West Texas State | 30 | 1095 | 149 | 246 | .606 | 119 | 169 | .704 | 119 | 212 | 417 | 4.0 | 7.1 | 13.9 |
| 77-78—West Texas State | 27 | 941 | 174 | 319 | .545 | 105 | 147 | .714 | 152 | 153 | 453 | 5.6 | 5.7 | 16.8 |
| Totals | 106 | ... | 460 | 810 | .568 | 307 | 453 | .678 | 418 | ... | 1227 | 3.9 | ... | 11.6 |

### NBA REGULAR-SEASON RECORD

**HONORS:** NBA All-Defensive first team (1983, 1984, 1985, 1986). ... NBA All-Defensive second team (1987).

| Season Team | G | Min. | FGM | FGA | Pct. | FTM | FTA | Pct. | Off. | Def. | Tot. | Ast. | St. | Blk. | TO | Pts. | RPG | APG | PPG |
|---|---|---|---|---|---|---|---|---|---|---|---|---|---|---|---|---|---|---|---|
| 78-79—Philadelphia | 82 | 2409 | 292 | 572 | .510 | 101 | 140 | .721 | 63 | 191 | 254 | 431 | 174 | 12 | 193 | 685 | 3.1 | 5.3 | 8.4 |
| 79-80—Philadelphia | 79 | 2623 | 357 | 661 | .540 | 180 | 231 | .779 | 75 | 199 | 274 | 556 | 183 | 32 | 216 | 898 | 3.5 | 7.0 | 11.4 |
| 80-81—Philadelphia | 81 | 2415 | 310 | 581 | .534 | 140 | 178 | .787 | 67 | 178 | 245 | 560 | 193 | 39 | 174 | 763 | 3.0 | 6.9 | 9.4 |
| 81-82—Philadelphia | 79 | 2498 | 352 | 676 | .521 | 171 | 220 | .777 | 51 | 197 | 248 | 667 | 209 | 33 | 184 | 881 | 3.1 | 8.4 | 11.2 |
| 82-83—Philadelphia | 79 | 2465 | 404 | 745 | .542 | 181 | 240 | .754 | 53 | 156 | 209 | 543 | 184 | 31 | 179 | 990 | 2.6 | 6.9 | 12.5 |
| 83-84—Philadelphia | 75 | 2494 | 386 | 702 | .550 | 170 | 232 | .733 | 44 | 161 | 205 | 478 | 171 | 20 | 182 | 950 | 2.7 | 6.4 | 12.7 |
| 84-85—Philadelphia | 78 | 2616 | 422 | 741 | .570 | 175 | 199 | .879 | 54 | 163 | 217 | 497 | 169 | 24 | 155 | 1025 | 2.8 | 6.4 | 13.1 |
| 85-86—Philadelphia | 82 | *3270 | 490 | 913 | .537 | 282 | 335 | .842 | 55 | 180 | 235 | 753 | 207 | 27 | 238 | 1266 | 2.9 | 9.2 | 15.4 |
| 86-87—Philadelphia | 68 | 2624 | 415 | 788 | .527 | 227 | 292 | .777 | 47 | 168 | 215 | 538 | 180 | 15 | 173 | 1061 | 3.2 | 7.9 | 15.6 |
| 87-88—Philadelphia | 79 | 2871 | 428 | 865 | .495 | 227 | 275 | .825 | 59 | 194 | 253 | 635 | 167 | 22 | 160 | 1086 | 3.2 | 8.0 | 13.7 |
| 88-89—Philadelphia | 71 | 2298 | 336 | 696 | .483 | 151 | 195 | .774 | 39 | 144 | 183 | 554 | 105 | 17 | 116 | 824 | 2.6 | 7.8 | 11.6 |
| 89-90—S.A.-N.Y. | 81 | 2519 | 307 | 609 | .504 | 171 | 202 | .847 | 50 | 190 | 240 | 453 | 124 | 10 | 121 | 789 | 3.0 | 5.6 | 9.7 |
| 90-91—New York | 76 | 2147 | 241 | 483 | .499 | 105 | 129 | .814 | 22 | 151 | 173 | 435 | 128 | 10 | 108 | 592 | 2.3 | 5.7 | 7.8 |
| 91-92—Atlanta | 56 | 1086 | 115 | 249 | .462 | 26 | 43 | .605 | 29 | 66 | 95 | 185 | 83 | 0 | 36 | 259 | 1.7 | 3.3 | 4.6 |
| 92-93—New Jersey | 35 | 510 | 51 | 93 | .548 | 24 | 27 | .889 | 5 | 37 | 42 | 107 | 33 | 2 | 33 | 126 | 1.2 | 3.1 | 3.6 |
| Totals | 1101 | 34845 | 4906 | 9374 | .523 | 2331 | 2938 | .793 | 713 | 2375 | 3088 | 7392 | 2310 | 294 | 2268 | 12195 | 2.8 | 6.7 | 11.1 |

Three-point field goals: 1979-80, 4-for-9 (.444). 1980-81, 3-for-8 (.375). 1981-82, 6-for-22 (.273). 1982-83, 1-for-6 (.167). 1983-84, 8-for-20 (.400). 1984-85, 6-for-26 (.231). 1985-86, 4-for-17 (.235). 1986-87, 4-for-17 (.235). 1987-88, 3-for-22 (.136). 1988-89, 1-for-13 (.077). 1989-90, 4-for-16 (.250). 1990-91, 5-for-20 (.250). 1991-92, 3-for-6 (.500). 1992-93, 0-for-2. Totals, 52-for-204 (.255).

Personal fouls/disqualifications: 1978-79, 198/2. 1979-80, 197/1. 1980-81, 231/1. 1981-82, 247/0. 1982-83, 182/0. 1983-84, 196/1. 1984-85, 184/0. 1985-86, 160/0. 1986-87, 109/0. 1987-88, 116/0. 1988-89, 114/0. 1989-90, 78/0. 1990-91, 138/0. 1991-92, 73/0. 1992-93, 35/0. Totals, 2258/5.

### NBA PLAYOFF RECORD

| Season Team | G | Min. | FGM | FGA | Pct. | FTM | FTA | Pct. | Off. | Def. | Tot. | Ast. | St. | Blk. | TO | Pts. | RPG | APG | PPG |
|---|---|---|---|---|---|---|---|---|---|---|---|---|---|---|---|---|---|---|---|
| 78-79—Philadelphia | 9 | 330 | 66 | 121 | .545 | 37 | 56 | .661 | 13 | 22 | 35 | 63 | 37 | 4 | 29 | 169 | 3.9 | 7.0 | 18.8 |

**HEAD COACHES**

| Season Team | G | Min. | FGM | FGA | Pct. | FTM | FTA | Pct. | REBOUNDS Off. | Def. | Tot. | Ast. | St. | Blk. | TO | Pts. | AVERAGES RPG | APG | PPG |
|---|---|---|---|---|---|---|---|---|---|---|---|---|---|---|---|---|---|---|---|
| 79-80—Philadelphia.... | 18 | 675 | 89 | 174 | .512 | 29 | 41 | .707 | 22 | 52 | 74 | 111 | 45 | 4 | 45 | 208 | 4.1 | 6.2 | 11.6 |
| 80-81—Philadelphia.... | 16 | 513 | 68 | 125 | .544 | 32 | 42 | .762 | 4 | 47 | 51 | 116 | 40 | 12 | 36 | 168 | 3.2 | 7.3 | 10.5 |
| 81-82—Philadelphia... | 21 | 765 | 125 | 265 | .472 | 50 | 65 | .769 | 15 | 47 | 62 | 172 | 48 | 6 | 49 | 301 | 3.0 | 8.2 | 14.3 |
| 82-83—Philadelphia... | 13 | 483 | 83 | 165 | .503 | 45 | 64 | .703 | 11 | 28 | 39 | 91 | 26 | 2 | 34 | 212 | 3.0 | 7.0 | 16.3 |
| 83-84—Philadelphia... | 5 | 171 | 35 | 67 | .522 | 13 | 15 | .867 | 2 | 10 | 12 | 19 | 13 | 0 | 10 | 83 | 2.4 | 3.8 | 16.6 |
| 84-85—Philadelphia... | 13 | 483 | 81 | 153 | .529 | 36 | 42 | .857 | 12 | 34 | 46 | 67 | 31 | 5 | 34 | 198 | 3.5 | 5.2 | 15.2 |
| 85-86—Philadelphia... | 12 | 519 | 94 | 182 | .516 | 62 | 73 | .849 | 13 | 43 | 56 | 85 | 13 | 3 | 32 | 250 | 4.7 | 7.1 | 20.8 |
| 86-87—Philadelphia... | 5 | 210 | 35 | 66 | .530 | 18 | 21 | .857 | 1 | 12 | 13 | 44 | 9 | 4 | 12 | 88 | 2.6 | 8.8 | 17.6 |
| 88-89—Philadelphia... | 3 | 128 | 21 | 41 | .512 | 11 | 13 | .846 | 3 | 8 | 11 | 39 | 7 | 1 | 3 | 53 | 3.7 | 13.0 | 17.7 |
| 89-90—New York...... | 10 | 388 | 50 | 104 | .481 | 28 | 31 | .903 | 12 | 27 | 39 | 85 | 17 | 2 | 19 | 128 | 3.9 | 8.5 | 12.8 |
| 90-91—New York...... | 3 | 101 | 14 | 23 | .609 | 1 | 2 | .500 | 3 | 6 | 9 | 16 | 3 | 1 | 8 | 30 | 3.0 | 5.3 | 10.0 |
| 92-93—New Jersey..... | 5 | 82 | 11 | 23 | .478 | 0 | 1 | .000 | 3 | 3 | 6 | 14 | 6 | 1 | 7 | 22 | 1.2 | 2.8 | 4.4 |
| Totals.............. | 133 | 4848 | 772 | 1509 | .512 | 362 | 466 | .777 | 114 | 339 | 453 | 922 | 295 | 45 | 318 | 1910 | 3.4 | 6.9 | 14.4 |

Three-point field goals: 1979-80, 1-for-5 (.200). 1980-81, 0-for-3. 1981-82, 1-for-9 (.111). 1982-83, 1-for-2 (.500). 1983-84, 0-for-1. 1984-85, 0-for-5. 1985-86, 0-for-7. 1986-87, 0-for-1. 1988-89, 0-for-1. 1989-90, 0-for-4. 1990-91, 1-for-3 (.333). Totals, 4-for-41 (.098).

Personal fouls/disqualifications: 1978-79, 29/0. 1979-80, 43/0. 1980-81, 55/1. 1981-82, 58/0. 1982-83, 23/0. 1983-84, 18/0. 1984-85, 29/0. 1985-86, 18/0. 1986-87, 14/0. 1988-89, 4/0. 1989-90, 21/0. 1990-91, 9/0. 1992-93, 3/0. Totals, 324/1.

## NBA ALL-STAR GAME RECORD

| Season Team | Min. | FGM | FGA | Pct. | FTM | FTA | Pct. | REBOUNDS Off. | Def. | Tot. | Ast. | PF | Dq. | St. | Blk. | TO | Pts. |
|---|---|---|---|---|---|---|---|---|---|---|---|---|---|---|---|---|---|
| 1983—Philadelphia .......... | 18 | 3 | 8 | .375 | 0 | 0 | ... | 0 | 1 | 1 | 1 | 0 | 0 | 0 | 0 | 0 | 6 |
| 1986—Philadelphia .......... | 14 | 3 | 6 | .500 | 0 | 0 | ... | 0 | 0 | 0 | 2 | 0 | 0 | 2 | 0 | 3 | 6 |
| 1987—Philadelphia .......... | 8 | 1 | 2 | .500 | 2 | 2 | 1.000 | 0 | 0 | 0 | 0 | 1 | 0 | 1 | 0 | 1 | 4 |
| 1988—Philadelphia .......... | 4 | 0 | 0 | ... | 0 | 0 | ... | 0 | 2 | 2 | 1 | 1 | 0 | 0 | 0 | 0 | 0 |
| Totals........................... | 44 | 7 | 16 | .438 | 2 | 2 | 1.000 | 0 | 3 | 3 | 4 | 2 | 0 | 3 | 0 | 4 | 16 |

## HEAD COACHING RECORD

**NOTES:** Assistant coach, 76ers (1994-95 to 2000-01).

## NBA COACHING RECORD

| Season Team | REGULAR SEASON W | L | Pct. | Finish | PLAYOFFS W | L | Pct. |
|---|---|---|---|---|---|---|---|
| 01-02—Portland .................................................... | 49 | 33 | .598 | 3rd/Pacific Division | 0 | 3 | .000 |
| 02-03—Portland .................................................... | 50 | 32 | .610 | T2nd/Pacific Division | 3 | 4 | .429 |
| 03-04—Portland .................................................... | 41 | 41 | .500 | 3rd/Pacific Division | — | — | — |
| 04-05—Portland .................................................... | 22 | 33 | .400 | 4th/Northwest Division | | | |
| Totals (4 years)..................................... | 162 | 139 | .538 | Totals (2 years)....... | 3 | 7 | .300 |

**NOTES:**
2002—Lost to Los Angeles Lakers in Western Conference first round.
2003—Lost to Dallas, 4-3, in Western Conference first round.
2005—Replaced by Kevin Pritchard as head coach (March 2) with club in fourth place.

# D'ANTONI, MIKE

# SUNS

**PERSONAL:** Born May 8, 1951, in Mullens, W.Va. ... 6-3/190 (1,90/86,2). ... Full name: Michael Andrew D'Antoni.
**COLLEGE:** Marshall.
**TRANSACTIONS/CAREER NOTES:** Selected by Kansas City/Omaha Kings in second round (20th pick overall) of 1973 NBA Draft. ... Waived by Kings (November 27, 1975). ... Signed by St. Louis Spirits of American Basketball Association for remainder of 1975-76 season. ... Signed as free agent by San Antonio Spurs (August 12, 1976). ... Released by Spurs (November 22, 1976). ... Played in Italy (1977-78 through 1988-89).

## COLLEGIATE RECORD

| Season Team | G | Min. | FGM | FGA | Pct. | FTM | FTA | Pct. | Reb. | Ast. | Pts. | AVERAGES RPG | APG | PPG |
|---|---|---|---|---|---|---|---|---|---|---|---|---|---|---|
| 69-70—Marshall ......................... | | | | | Freshman team statistics unavailable. | | | | | | | | | |
| 70-71—Marshall ......................... | 26 | ... | 162 | 341 | .475 | 68 | 91 | .747 | 106 | 190 | 392 | 4.1 | 7.3 | 15.1 |
| 71-72—Marshall ......................... | 27 | ... | 177 | 388 | .456 | 99 | 125 | .792 | 127 | 241 | 453 | 4.7 | 8.9 | 16.8 |
| 72-73—Marshall ......................... | 27 | ... | 152 | 352 | .432 | 78 | 99 | .788 | 126 | 228 | 382 | 4.7 | 8.4 | 14.1 |
| Varsity totals......................... | 80 | ... | 491 | 1081 | .454 | 245 | 315 | .778 | 359 | 659 | 1227 | 4.5 | 8.2 | 15.3 |

## ABA REGULAR-SEASON RECORD

| Season Team | G | Min. | 2-POINT FGM | FGA | Pct. | 3-POINT FGM | FGA | Pct. | FTM | FTA | Pct. | Reb. | Ast. | Pts. | AVERAGES RPG | APG | PPG |
|---|---|---|---|---|---|---|---|---|---|---|---|---|---|---|---|---|---|
| 75-76—St. Louis ................. | 50 | 708 | 77 | 158 | .487 | 0 | 4 | .000 | 19 | 26 | .731 | 76 | 115 | 173 | 1.5 | 2.3 | 3.5 |

## NBA REGULAR-SEASON RECORD

| Season Team | G | Min. | FGM | FGA | Pct. | FTM | FTA | Pct. | REBOUNDS Off. | Def. | Tot. | Ast. | St. | Blk. | TO | Pts. | AVERAGES RPG | APG | PPG |
|---|---|---|---|---|---|---|---|---|---|---|---|---|---|---|---|---|---|---|---|
| 73-74—K.C./Omaha .... | 52 | 989 | 107 | 266 | .402 | 33 | 47 | .702 | 24 | 69 | 93 | 123 | 75 | 15 | ... | 247 | 1.8 | 2.4 | 4.8 |
| 74-75—K.C./Omaha .... | 67 | 759 | 69 | 173 | .399 | 28 | 36 | .778 | 13 | 64 | 77 | 107 | 67 | 12 | ... | 166 | 1.2 | 1.6 | 2.5 |
| 75-76—Kansas City .... | 9 | 101 | 7 | 27 | .259 | 2 | 2 | 1.000 | 4 | 10 | 14 | 16 | 10 | 0 | ... | 16 | 1.6 | 1.8 | 1.8 |
| 76-77—San Antonio .... | 2 | 9 | 1 | 3 | .333 | 1 | 2 | .500 | 0 | 2 | 2 | 2 | 0 | 0 | ... | 3 | 1.0 | 1.0 | 1.5 |
| Totals .................... | 130 | 1858 | 184 | 469 | .392 | 64 | 87 | .736 | 41 | 145 | 186 | 248 | 152 | 27 | ... | 432 | 1.4 | 1.9 | 3.3 |

Personal fouls/disqualifications: 1973-74, 112/0. 1974-75, 106/0. 1975-76, 18/0. 1976-77, 3/0. Totals, 239/0.

## NBA PLAYOFF RECORD

| | | | | | | | | REBOUNDS | | | | | | | | AVERAGES | | |
|---|---|---|---|---|---|---|---|---|---|---|---|---|---|---|---|---|---|---|
| Season Team | G | Min. | FGM | FGA | Pct. | FTM | FTA | Pct. | Off. | Def. | Tot. | Ast. | St. | Blk. | TO | Pts. | RPG | APG | PPG |
| 74-75—K.C./Omaha.... | 4 | 42 | 7 | 14 | .500 | 4 | 4 | 1.000 | 2 | 5 | 7 | 1 | 4 | 1 | ... | 18 | 1.8 | 0.3 | 4.5 |

Personal fouls/disqualifications: 1974-75, 6/0.

## COMBINED ABA AND NBA REGULAR-SEASON RECORDS

| | | | | | | | | REBOUNDS | | | | | | | | AVERAGES | | |
|---|---|---|---|---|---|---|---|---|---|---|---|---|---|---|---|---|---|---|
| | G | Min. | FGM | FGA | Pct. | FTM | FTA | Pct. | Off. | Def. | Tot. | Ast. | Stl. | Blk. | TO | Pts. | RPG | APG | PPG |
| Totals ........... | 180 | 2656 | 261 | 631 | .414 | 83 | 113 | .735 | 57 | 205 | 262 | 363 | 215 | 14 | ... | 605 | 1.5 | 2.0 | 3.4 |

Three-point field goals: 0-for-4 (.000).
Personal fouls/disqualifications: 373/0.

## ITALIAN LEAGUE RECORD

| | | | | | | | | | | | AVERAGES | | |
|---|---|---|---|---|---|---|---|---|---|---|---|---|---|
| Season Team | G | Min. | FGM | FGA | Pct. | FTM | FTA | Pct. | Reb. | Ast. | Pts. | RPG | APG | PPG |
| 77-78—Milan .......................... | 24 | ... | 111 | 242 | .459 | 31 | 45 | .689 | 67 | 37 | 253 | 2.8 | 1.5 | 10.5 |
| 78-79—Milan .......................... | 28 | 1032 | 114 | 266 | .429 | 52 | 65 | .800 | 87 | 33 | 280 | 3.1 | 1.2 | 10.0 |
| 79-80—Milan .......................... | 31 | 1147 | 176 | 359 | .490 | 60 | 73 | .822 | 115 | 73 | 412 | 3.7 | 2.4 | 13.3 |
| 80-81—Milan .......................... | 37 | 1438 | 260 | 545 | .477 | 89 | 112 | .795 | 109 | 56 | 609 | 3.0 | 1.5 | 16.5 |
| 81-82—Milan .......................... | 39 | 1524 | 253 | 585 | .432 | 89 | 107 | .832 | 119 | 62 | 595 | 3.1 | 1.6 | 15.3 |
| 82-83—Milan .......................... | 38 | 1447 | 221 | 484 | .457 | 106 | 121 | .876 | 113 | 100 | 548 | 3.0 | 2.6 | 14.4 |
| 83-84—Milan .......................... | 31 | 985 | 159 | 333 | .478 | 73 | 86 | .849 | 87 | 73 | 391 | 2.8 | 2.4 | 12.6 |
| 84-85—Milan .......................... | 36 | 1393 | 175 | 389 | .450 | 86 | 97 | .887 | 138 | 134 | 555 | 3.8 | 3.7 | 15.4 |
| 85-86—Milan .......................... | 40 | 1525 | 158 | 393 | .402 | 100 | 117 | .855 | 115 | 161 | 524 | 2.9 | 4.0 | 13.1 |
| 86-87—Milan .......................... | 38 | 1358 | 127 | 347 | .366 | 57 | 66 | .864 | 93 | 110 | 397 | 2.5 | 2.9 | 10.5 |
| 87-88—Milan .......................... | 38 | 1354 | 144 | 306 | .471 | 70 | 76 | .921 | 67 | 117 | 450 | 1.8 | 3.1 | 11.8 |
| 88-89—Milan .......................... | 42 | 1497 | 102 | 246 | .415 | 68 | 79 | .861 | 127 | 104 | 340 | 3.0 | 2.5 | 8.1 |
| Totals ...................................... | 422 | 2000 | 4495 | | .445 | 881 | 1044 | .844 | 1237 | 1060 | 5354 | 2.9 | 2.5 | 12.7 |

Three-point field goals: 1984-85, 119-for-254 (.469). 1985-86, 108-for-281 (.384). 1986-87, 86-for-231 (.372). 1987-88, 92-for-223 (.413). 1988-89, 68-for-174 (.391). Totals, 473-for-1163 (.407).

## HEAD COACHING RECORD

**BACKGROUND:** Head coach, Philips Milan of Italian League (1990-91 through 1993-94). ... Head coach, Benetton Treviso of Italian League (1994-95 through 1996-97). ... Director of Player Personnel, Denver Nuggets (1997-98). ... Scout, San Antonio Spurs (1999-2000). ... Assistant, Portland Trail Blazers (2000-01).

## EUROPEAN COACHING RECORD

| | REGULAR SEASON | | | |
|---|---|---|---|---|
| Season Team | W | L | Pct. | Finish |
| 90-91—Philips Milan ............................................... | 21 | 9 | .700 | 1st |
| 91-92—Philips Milan ............................................... | 22 | 8 | .733 | 1st |
| 92-93—Philips Milan ............................................... | 21 | 9 | .700 | 2nd |
| 93-94—Philips Milan ............................................... | 22 | 8 | .733 | 4th |
| 94-95—Benetton Treviso ....................................... | 20 | 10 | .667 | 3rd |
| 95-96—Benetton Treviso ....................................... | 22 | 8 | .733 | 3rd |
| 96-97—Benetton Treviso ....................................... | 22 | 4 | .846 | 1st |
| 01-02—Benetton Treviso ....................................... | 28 | 8 | .778 | 1st |
| Totals ................................................................ | 178 | 64 | .736 | |

## NBA COACHING RECORD

| | REGULAR SEASON | | | | PLAYOFFS | | |
|---|---|---|---|---|---|---|---|
| Season Team | W | L | Pct. | Finish | W | L | Pct. |
| 98-99—Denver................................................. | 14 | 36 | .280 | 6th/Midwest Division | — | — | — |
| 03-04—Phoenix............................................... | 21 | 40 | .344 | 6th/Pacific Division | — | — | — |
| 04-05—Phoenix............................................... | 62 | 20 | .756 | 1st/Pacific Division | 9 | 6 | .600 |
| Totals (3 years) ............................................ | 97 | 96 | .503 | Totals (1 year) | 9 | 6 | .600 |

**NOTES:**
2003—Replaced Frank Johnson as Phoenix head coach (December 10) with 8-17 record and club in seventh place.
2005—Defeated Memphis, 4-0, in Western Conference first round; defeated Dallas, 4-2, in Western Conference semifinals; lost to San Antonio, 4-1, in Western Conference finals.

# DUNLEAVY, MIKE                                    CLIPPERS

**PERSONAL:** Born March 21, 1954, in Brooklyn, N.Y. ... 6-3/180 (1,90/81,6). ... Full name: Michael Joseph Dunleavy. ... Name pronounced DONE-lee-vee. ... Father of Mike Dunleavy, a guard/forward with the Golden State Warriors.

**HIGH SCHOOL:** Nazareth Regional (Brooklyn, N.Y.).

**COLLEGE:** South Carolina.

**TRANSACTIONS/CAREER NOTES:** Selected by Philadelphia 76ers in sixth round (99th pick overall) of 1976 NBA Draft. ... Waived by 76ers (November 14, 1977). ... Player/head coach with Carolina Lightning of All-America Basketball Alliance (1977-78). ... Signed as free agent by Houston Rockets (March 10, 1978). ... Signed as veteran free agent by San Antonio Spurs (October 16, 1982); Rockets waived their right of first refusal in exchange for 1983 third-round draft choice. ... Signed as veteran free agent by Milwaukee Bucks (March 8, 1984); Spurs waived their right of first refusal in exchange for 1984 fourth-round draft choice and cash. ... Waived by Bucks (October 24, 1985). ... Re-signed by Bucks to 10-day contract (February 19, 1989). ... Waived by Bucks (February 24, 1989). ... Re-signed as free agent by Bucks (December 10, 1989). ... Waived by Bucks (December 15, 1989). ... Re-signed by Bucks to 10-day contract (March 2, 1990). ... Waived by Bucks (March 9, 1990).

**CAREER NOTES:** Vice president of basketball operations/head coach, Bucks (1992-93 through 1995-96). ... Vice president of basketball operations/general manager, Bucks (1996-97).

## COLLEGIATE RECORD

| Season Team | G | Min. | FGM | FGA | Pct. | FTM | FTA | Pct. | Reb. | Ast. | Pts. | AVERAGES RPG | APG | PPG |
|---|---|---|---|---|---|---|---|---|---|---|---|---|---|---|
| 72-73—South Carolina.............. | 29 | 803 | 122 | 236 | .517 | 59 | 72 | .819 | 60 | 73 | 303 | 2.1 | 2.5 | 10.4 |
| 73-74—South Carolina.............. | 27 | 983 | 167 | 369 | .453 | 97 | 116 | .836 | 85 | 95 | 431 | 3.1 | 3.5 | 16.0 |
| 74-75—South Carolina.............. | 28 | 1016 | 182 | 368 | .495 | 91 | 119 | .765 | 110 | 89 | 455 | 3.9 | 3.2 | 16.3 |
| 75-76—South Carolina.............. | 27 | 962 | 144 | 297 | .485 | 109 | 139 | .784 | 87 | 113 | 397 | 3.2 | 4.2 | 14.7 |
| Totals ................. | 111 | 3764 | 615 | 1270 | .484 | 356 | 446 | .798 | 342 | 370 | 1586 | 3.1 | 3.3 | 14.3 |

## NBA REGULAR-SEASON RECORD

**NOTES:** Led NBA with .345 three-point field-goal percentage (1983).

| Season Team | G | Min. | FGM | FGA | Pct. | FTM | FTA | Pct. | REBOUNDS Off. | Def. | Tot. | Ast. | St. | Blk. | TO | Pts. | AVERAGES RPG | APG | PPG |
|---|---|---|---|---|---|---|---|---|---|---|---|---|---|---|---|---|---|---|---|
| 76-77—Philadelphia .. | 32 | 359 | 60 | 145 | .414 | 34 | 45 | .756 | 10 | 24 | 34 | 56 | 13 | 2 | ... | 154 | 1.1 | 1.8 | 4.8 |
| 77-78—Phil.-Hou. ...... | 15 | 119 | 20 | 50 | .400 | 13 | 18 | .722 | 1 | 9 | 10 | 28 | 9 | 1 | 12 | 53 | 0.7 | 1.9 | 3.5 |
| 78-79—Houston ........ | 74 | 1486 | 215 | 425 | .506 | 159 | 184 | .864 | 28 | 100 | 128 | 324 | 56 | 5 | 130 | 589 | 1.7 | 4.4 | 8.0 |
| 79-80—Houston ........ | 51 | 1036 | 148 | 319 | .464 | 111 | 134 | .828 | 26 | 74 | 100 | 210 | 40 | 4 | 110 | 410 | 2.0 | 4.1 | 8.0 |
| 80-81—Houston ........ | 74 | 1609 | 310 | 632 | .491 | 156 | 186 | .839 | 28 | 90 | 118 | 268 | 64 | 2 | 137 | 777 | 1.6 | 3.6 | 10.5 |
| 81-82—Houston ........ | 70 | 1315 | 206 | 450 | .458 | 75 | 106 | .708 | 24 | 80 | 104 | 227 | 45 | 3 | 80 | 520 | 1.5 | 3.2 | 7.4 |
| 82-83—San Antonio .. | 79 | 1619 | 213 | 510 | .418 | 120 | 154 | .779 | 18 | 116 | 134 | 437 | 74 | 4 | 160 | 613 | 1.7 | 5.5 | 7.8 |
| 83-84—Milwaukee...... | 17 | 404 | 70 | 127 | .551 | 32 | 40 | .800 | 6 | 22 | 28 | 78 | 12 | 1 | 36 | 191 | 1.6 | 4.6 | 11.2 |
| 84-85—Milwaukee...... | 19 | 433 | 64 | 135 | .474 | 25 | 29 | .862 | 6 | 25 | 31 | 85 | 15 | 3 | 40 | 169 | 1.6 | 4.5 | 8.9 |
| 85-86— ...................... | | | | | | | Did not play. | | | | | | | | | | | | |
| 86-87— ...................... | | | | | | | Did not play. | | | | | | | | | | | | |
| 87-88— ...................... | | | | | | | Did not play. | | | | | | | | | | | | |
| 88-89—Milwaukee...... | 2 | 5 | 1 | 2 | .500 | 0 | 0 | ... | 0 | 0 | 0 | 0 | 0 | 0 | 0 | 3 | 0.0 | 0.0 | 1.5 |
| 89-90—Milwaukee...... | 5 | 43 | 4 | 14 | .286 | 7 | 8 | .875 | 0 | 2 | 2 | 10 | 1 | 0 | 8 | 17 | 0.4 | 2.0 | 3.4 |
| Totals ................... | 438 | 8428 | 1311 | 2809 | .467 | 732 | 904 | .810 | 147 | 542 | 689 | 1723 | 329 | 25 | 713 | 3496 | 1.6 | 3.9 | 8.0 |

Three-point field goals: 1979-80, 3-for-20 (.150). 1980-81, 1-for-16 (.063). 1981-82, 33-for-86 (.384). 1982-83, 67-for-194 (.345). 1983-84, 19-for-45 (.422). 1984-85, 16-for-47 (.340). 1988-89, 1-for-2 (.500). 1989-90, 2-for-9 (.222). Totals, 142-for-419 (.339).

Personal fouls/disqualifications: 1976-77, 64/1. 1977-78, 12/0. 1978-79, 168/2. 1979-80, 120/2. 1980-81, 165/1. 1981-82, 161/0. 1982-83, 210/1. 1983-84, 51/0. 1984-85, 55/1. 1989-90, 7/0. Totals, 1013/8.

## NBA PLAYOFF RECORD

| Season Team | G | Min. | FGM | FGA | Pct. | FTM | FTA | Pct. | REBOUNDS Off. | Def. | Tot. | Ast. | St. | Blk. | TO | Pts. | AVERAGES RPG | APG | PPG |
|---|---|---|---|---|---|---|---|---|---|---|---|---|---|---|---|---|---|---|---|
| 76-77—Philadelphia .. | 11 | 68 | 9 | 25 | .360 | 4 | 5 | .800 | 1 | 3 | 4 | 9 | 3 | 0 | ... | 22 | 0.4 | 0.8 | 2.0 |
| 78-79—Houston ........ | 1 | 10 | 0 | 2 | .000 | 0 | 0 | ... | 0 | 1 | 1 | 0 | 0 | 0 | 0 | 0 | 1.0 | 0.0 | 0.0 |
| 79-80—Houston ........ | 6 | 45 | 6 | 12 | .500 | 5 | 6 | .833 | 2 | 3 | 5 | 13 | 5 | 0 | 6 | 17 | 0.8 | 2.2 | 2.8 |
| 80-81—Houston ........ | 20 | 472 | 69 | 152 | .454 | 33 | 38 | .868 | 9 | 33 | 42 | 68 | 15 | 1 | 30 | 177 | 2.1 | 3.4 | 8.9 |
| 81-82—Houston ........ | 3 | 66 | 9 | 22 | .409 | 5 | 6 | .833 | 0 | 3 | 3 | 9 | 2 | 0 | 1 | 23 | 1.0 | 3.0 | 7.7 |
| 82-83—San Antonio .. | 11 | 174 | 22 | 65 | .338 | 9 | 13 | .692 | 3 | 10 | 13 | 49 | 9 | 1 | 14 | 61 | 1.2 | 4.5 | 5.5 |
| 83-84—Milwaukee...... | 15 | 393 | 59 | 129 | .457 | 33 | 36 | .917 | 10 | 25 | 35 | 46 | 17 | 0 | 35 | 169 | 2.3 | 3.1 | 11.3 |
| Totals ................... | 67 | 1228 | 174 | 407 | .428 | 89 | 104 | .856 | 25 | 78 | 103 | 194 | 51 | 2 | 86 | 469 | 1.5 | 2.9 | 7.0 |

Three-point field goals: 1979-80, 0-for-2. 1980-81, 6-for-15 (.400). 1981-82, 0-for-4. 1982-83, 8-for-30 (.267). 1983-84, 18-for-50 (.360). Totals, 32-for-101 (.317).

Personal fouls/disqualifications: 1976-77, 14/0. 1978-79, 1/0. 1979-80, 11/0. 1980-81, 59/1. 1981-82, 7/0. 1982-83, 22/0. 1983-84, 59/2. Totals, 173/3.

## ABA REGULAR-SEASON RECORD

| Season Team | G | Min. | 2-POINT FGM | FGA | Pct. | 3-POINT FGM | FGA | Pct. | FTM | FTA | Pct. | Reb. | Ast. | Pts. | AVERAGES RPG | APG | PPG |
|---|---|---|---|---|---|---|---|---|---|---|---|---|---|---|---|---|---|
| 77-78—Carolina ................... | 10 | 332 | 66 | 123 | .537 | 2 | 5 | .400 | 53 | 60 | .883 | 52 | 50 | 191 | 5.2 | 5.0 | 19.1 |

## HEAD COACHING RECORD

**BACKGROUND:** Player/head coach, Carolina Lightning of All-American Basketball Association (1977-78). ... Assistant coach, Milwaukee Bucks (1986-87 through 1989-90).

## ABA COACHING RECORD

| Season Team | REGULAR SEASON W | L | Pct. | Finish | PLAYOFFS W | L | Pct. |
|---|---|---|---|---|---|---|---|
| 77-78—Carolina............................................... | 8 | 2 | .800 | 1st/South Division | — | — | — |

**HONORS:** NBA Coach of the Year (1999).

## NBA COACHING RECORD

| Season Team | REGULAR SEASON W | L | Pct. | Finish | PLAYOFFS W | L | Pct. |
|---|---|---|---|---|---|---|---|
| 90-91—L.A. Lakers..................................................... | 58 | 24 | .707 | 2nd/Pacific Division | 12 | 7 | .632 |
| 91-92—L.A. Lakers..................................................... | 43 | 39 | .524 | 6th/Pacific Division | 1 | 3 | .250 |
| 92-93—Milwaukee..................................................... | 28 | 54 | .341 | 7th/Central Division | — | — | — |
| 93-94—Milwaukee..................................................... | 20 | 62 | .244 | T6th/Central Division | — | — | — |
| 94-95—Milwaukee..................................................... | 34 | 48 | .415 | 6th/Central Division | — | — | — |
| 95-96—Milwaukee..................................................... | 25 | 57 | .305 | 7th/Central Division | — | — | — |
| 97-98—Portland ....................................................... | 46 | 36 | .561 | 4th/Pacific Division | 1 | 3 | .250 |
| 98-99—Portland ....................................................... | 35 | 15 | .700 | 1st/Pacific Division | 7 | 6 | .538 |

| Season Team | W | L | Pct. | Finish | | W | L | Pct. |
|---|---|---|---|---|---|---|---|---|
| | **REGULAR SEASON** | | | | | **PLAYOFFS** | | |
| 99-00—Portland | 59 | 23 | .720 | 2nd/Pacific Division | | 10 | 6 | .625 |
| 00-01—Portland | 50 | 32 | .610 | 4th/Pacific Division | | 0 | 3 | .000 |
| 03-04—L.A. Clippers | 28 | 54 | .341 | 7th/Pacific Division | | — | — | — |
| 04-05—L.A. Clippers | 37 | 45 | .451 | 3rd/Pacific Division | | — | — | — |
| Totals (12 years) | 463 | 489 | .486 | Totals (6 years) | | 31 | 28 | .525 |

**NOTES:**

1991—Defeated Houston, 3-0, in Western Conference first round; defeated Golden State, 4-1, in Western Conference semifinals; defeated Portland, 4-2, in Western Conference finals; lost to Chicago, 4-1, in NBA Finals.

1992—Lost to Portland, 3-1, in Western Conference first round.

1998—Lost to Los Angeles Lakers, 3-1, in Western Conference first round.

1999—Defeated Phoenix, 3-0, in Western Conference first round; defeated Utah, 4-2, in Western Conference semifinals; lost to San Antonio, 4-0, in Western Conference finals.

2000—Defeated Minnesota, 3-1, in Western Conference first round; defeated Utah, 4-1, in Western Conference semifinals; lost to Los Angeles Lakers, 4-3, in Western Conference finals.

2001—Lost to Los Angeles Lakers, 3-0, in Western Conference first round.

## FRANK, LAWRENCE — NETS

**PERSONAL:** Born August 23, 1970, in Teaneck, N.J.
**HIGH SCHOOL:** Teaneck (N.J.).
**COLLEGE:** Indiana.

### HEAD COACHING RECORD

**BACKGROUND:** Staff assistant, Marquette University (1992-94). ... Assistant coach, University of Tennessee (1994-97). ... Assistant coach, Vancouver Grizzlies (1997-2000) ... Assistant coach, Nets (2000-01 through January 26, 2004).

### NBA COACHING RECORD

| Season Team | W | L | Pct. | Finish | | W | L | Pct. |
|---|---|---|---|---|---|---|---|---|
| | **REGULAR SEASON** | | | | | **PLAYOFFS** | | |
| 03-04—New Jersey | 25 | 15 | .625 | 1st/Atlantic Division | | 7 | 4 | .636 |
| 04-05—New Jersey | 42 | 40 | .512 | 3rd/Atlantic Division | | 0 | 4 | .000 |
| Totals (2 years) | 67 | 55 | .549 | Totals (2 years) | | 7 | 8 | .467 |

**NOTES:**

2004—Replaced Byron Scott as New Jersey head coach (January 26) with record of 22-20 and club in first place.

2005—Lost to Miami in Eastern Conference first round.

## FRATELLO, MIKE — GRIZZLIES

**PERSONAL:** Born February 24, 1947, in Hackensack, N.J. ... 5-7/150 (1,70/68,0). ... Full name: Michael Robert Fratello.
**HIGH SCHOOL:** Hackensack (N.J.).
**COLLEGE:** Montclair (N.J.) State College, then graduate work at Rhode Island.

### HEAD COACHING RECORD

**BACKGROUND:** Football and basketball coach, Hackensack (N.J.) High (1969-70). ... Assistant coach/freshman coach, University of Rhode Island (1970-71 and 1971-72). ... Assistant coach, James Madison University (1972-73 through 1974-75). ... Assistant coach, Villanova University (1975-76 through 1977-78). ... Assistant coach, Atlanta Hawks (1978-79 through 1981-82). ... Assistant coach, New York Knicks (1982-83). ... Vice president/head coach, Hawks (1986-87 through 1989-90).
**CAREER NOTES:** Broadcaster, NBC Sports (1990-91 through 1992-93); TNT Sports (1999-2004).
**HONORS:** NBA Coach of the Year (1986).

### NBA COACHING RECORD

| Season Team | W | L | Pct. | Finish | | W | L | Pct. |
|---|---|---|---|---|---|---|---|---|
| | **REGULAR SEASON** | | | | | **PLAYOFFS** | | |
| 80-81—Atlanta | 0 | 3 | .000 | 4th/Central Division | | — | — | — |
| 83-84—Atlanta | 40 | 42 | .488 | 3rd/Central Division | | 2 | 3 | .400 |
| 84-85—Atlanta | 34 | 48 | .415 | 5th/Central Division | | — | — | — |
| 85-86—Atlanta | 50 | 32 | .610 | 2nd/Central Division | | 4 | 5 | .444 |
| 86-87—Atlanta | 57 | 25 | .695 | 1st/Central Division | | 4 | 5 | .444 |
| 87-88—Atlanta | 50 | 32 | .610 | T2nd/Central Division | | 6 | 6 | .500 |
| 88-89—Atlanta | 52 | 30 | .634 | 3rd/Central Division | | 2 | 3 | .400 |
| 89-90—Atlanta | 41 | 41 | .500 | 6th/Central Division | | — | — | — |
| 93-94—Cleveland | 47 | 35 | .573 | T3rd/Central Division | | 0 | 3 | .000 |
| 94-95—Cleveland | 43 | 39 | .524 | 4th/Central Division | | 1 | 3 | .250 |
| 95-96—Cleveland | 47 | 35 | .573 | 3rd/Central Division | | 0 | 3 | .000 |
| 96-97—Cleveland | 42 | 40 | .512 | 5th/Central Division | | — | — | — |
| 97-98—Cleveland | 47 | 35 | .573 | 5th/Central Division | | 1 | 3 | .250 |
| 98-99—Cleveland | 22 | 28 | .440 | | | — | — | — |
| 04-05—Memphis | 45 | 37 | .549 | 4th/Southwest Division | | 0 | 4 | .000 |
| Totals (15 years) | 612 | 491 | .555 | Totals (10 years) | | 20 | 38 | .345 |

**NOTES:**

1981—Replaced Hubie Brown as Atlanta head coach (March 26), with record of 31-48 and club in fourth place. Served as interim co-head coach with Brendan Suhr for remainder of season.

1984—Lost to Milwaukee in Eastern Conference first round.
1986—Defeated Detroit, 3-1, in Eastern Conference first round; lost to Boston, 4-1, in Eastern Conference semifinals.
1987—Defeated Indiana, 3-1, in Eastern Conference first round; lost to Detroit, 4-1, in Eastern Conference semifinals.
1988—Defeated Milwaukee, 3-2, in Eastern Conference first round; lost to Boston, 4-3, in Eastern Conference semifinals.
1989—Lost to Milwaukee in Eastern Conference first round.
1994—Lost to Chicago in Eastern Conference first round.
1995—Lost to New York in Eastern Conference first round.
1996—Lost to New York in Eastern Conference first round.
1998—Lost to Indiana in Eastern Conference first round.
2005—Lost to Phoenix in Western Conference first round.

# HILL, BRIAN — MAGIC

**PERSONAL:** Born September 19, 1947, in East Orange, N.J. ... 5-9/175 (1,76/79,4). ... Full name: Brian Alfred Hill. ... Brother of Fred Hill, head baseball coach, Rutgers University.
**HIGH SCHOOL:** Our Lady of the Valley (East Orange, N.J.).
**COLLEGE:** Kennedy (Neb.).

### HEAD COACHING RECORD

**BACKGROUND:** Assistant coach, Piscataway (N.J.) Township High School (1969-70 and 1970-71). ... Assistant coach, Clifford J. Scott High School, N.J (1971-72). ... Assistant coach, Montclair (N.J.) State University (1972-73 and 1973-74). ... Assistant coach, Lehigh University (1974-75). ... Assistant coach, Penn State University (1983-84 through 1985-86). ... Assistant coach, Atlanta Hawks (1986-87 through 1989-90). ... Assistant coach, Orlando Magic (1990-91 through 1992-93).

### COLLEGIATE COACHING RECORD

| Season Team | W | L | Pct. | Finish |
|---|---|---|---|---|
| 75-76—Lehigh | 9 | 15 | .375 | 6th/East Coast Conference Western section |
| 76-77—Lehigh | 12 | 15 | .444 | 3rd/East Coast Conference Western section |
| 77-78—Lehigh | 8 | 18 | .308 | 4th/East Coast Conference Western section |
| 78-79—Lehigh | 8 | 18 | .308 | 5th/East Coast Conference Western section |
| 79-80—Lehigh | 5 | 20 | .200 | 5th/East Coast Conference Western section |
| 80-81—Lehigh | 14 | 12 | .538 | 4th/East Coast Conference Western section |
| 81-82—Lehigh | 9 | 17 | .346 | 6th/East Coast Conference Western section |
| 82-83—Lehigh | 10 | 16 | .384 | 5th/East Coast Conference Western section |
| Totals (8 years) | 75 | 131 | .364 | |

### NBA COACHING RECORD

| Season Team | REGULAR SEASON W | L | Pct. | Finish | PLAYOFFS W | L | Pct. |
|---|---|---|---|---|---|---|---|
| 93-94—Orlando | 50 | 32 | .610 | 2nd/Atlantic Division | 0 | 3 | .000 |
| 94-95—Orlando | 57 | 25 | .695 | 1st/Atlantic Division | 11 | 10 | .524 |
| 95-96—Orlando | 60 | 22 | .732 | 1st/Atlantic Division | 7 | 5 | .583 |
| 96-97—Orlando | 24 | 25 | .490 | | — | — | — |
| 97-98—Vancouver | 19 | 63 | .232 | 6th/Midwest Division | — | — | — |
| 98-99—Vancouver | 8 | 42 | .160 | 7th/Midwest Division | — | — | — |
| 99-00—Vancouver | 4 | 18 | .182 | | — | — | — |
| Totals (7 years) | 222 | 227 | .494 | Totals (3 years) | 18 | 18 | .500 |

**NOTES:**
1994—Lost to Indiana in Eastern Conference first round.
1995—Defeated Boston, 3-1, in Eastern Conference first round; defeated Chicago, 4-2, in Eastern Conference semifinals; defeated Indiana, 4-3, in Eastern Conference finals; lost to Houston, 4-0, in NBA Finals.
1996—Defeated Detroit, 3-0, in Eastern Conference first round; defeated Atlanta, 4-1, in Eastern Conference semifinals; lost to Chicago, 4-0, in Eastern Conference finals.
1997—Replaced as Orlando head coach by Richie Adubato (February 18) with club in third place.

# JACKSON, PHIL — LAKERS

**PERSONAL:** Born September 17, 1945, in Deer Lodge, Mont. ... 6-8/230. (2,03/104,3). ... Full name: Philip D. Jackson.
**HIGH SCHOOL:** Williston (N.D.).
**COLLEGE:** North Dakota.
**TRANSACTIONS/CAREER NOTES:** Selected by New York Knicks in second round (17th pick overall) of 1967 NBA Draft. ... Traded by Knicks with future draft choice to New Jersey Nets for future draft choices (June 8, 1978). ... Waived by Nets (October 11, 1978). ... Re-signed as free agent by Nets (November 10, 1978). ... Waived by Nets (October 12, 1979). ... Re-signed as free agent by Nets (February 15, 1980).
**MISCELLANEOUS:** Member of NBA championship team (1973).

### COLLEGIATE RECORD

| Season Team | G | Min. | FGM | FGA | Pct. | FTM | FTA | Pct. | Reb. | Ast. | Pts. | AVERAGES RPG | APG | PPG |
|---|---|---|---|---|---|---|---|---|---|---|---|---|---|---|
| 63-64—North Dakota‡ | ... | ... | ... | ... | ... | ... | ... | ... | ... | ... | ... | ... | ... | 24.3 |
| 64-65—North Dakota | 31 | ... | 129 | 307 | .420 | 107 | 156 | .686 | 361 | ... | 365 | 11.6 | ... | 11.8 |
| 65-66—North Dakota | 29 | ... | 238 | 439 | .542 | 155 | 203 | .764 | 374 | ... | 631 | 12.9 | ... | 21.8 |
| 66-67—North Dakota | 26 | ... | 252 | 468 | .538 | 208 | 278 | .748 | 374 | ... | 712 | 14.4 | ... | 27.4 |
| Varsity totals | 86 | ... | 619 | 1214 | .510 | 470 | 637 | .738 | 1109 | ... | 1708 | 12.9 | ... | 19.9 |

### NBA REGULAR-SEASON RECORD

**HONORS:** NBA All-Rookie team (1968).
**NOTES:** Led NBA with 330 personal fouls (1975).

HEAD COACHES

## NBA REGULAR SEASON

| Season Team | G | Min. | FGM | FGA | Pct. | FTM | FTA | Pct. | Reb. | Ast. | PF | Dq. | Pts. | AVERAGES RPG | APG | PPG |
|---|---|---|---|---|---|---|---|---|---|---|---|---|---|---|---|---|
| 67-68—New York | 75 | 1093 | 182 | 455 | .400 | 99 | 168 | .589 | 338 | 55 | 212 | 3 | 463 | 4.5 | 0.7 | 6.2 |
| 68-69—New York | 47 | 924 | 126 | 294 | .429 | 80 | 119 | .672 | 246 | 43 | 168 | 6 | 332 | 5.2 | 0.9 | 7.1 |
| 69-70—New York | | | | | Did not play—injured. | | | | | | | | | | | |
| 70-71—New York | 71 | 771 | 118 | 263 | .449 | 95 | 133 | .714 | 238 | 31 | 169 | 4 | 331 | 3.4 | 0.4 | 4.7 |
| 71-72—New York | 80 | 1273 | 205 | 466 | .440 | 167 | 228 | .732 | 326 | 72 | 224 | 4 | 577 | 4.1 | 0.9 | 7.2 |
| 72-73—New York | 80 | 1393 | 245 | 553 | .443 | 154 | 195 | .790 | 344 | 94 | 218 | 2 | 644 | 4.3 | 1.2 | 8.1 |

| Season Team | G | Min. | FGM | FGA | Pct. | FTM | FTA | Pct. | REBOUNDS Off. | Def. | Tot. | Ast. | St. | Blk. | TO | Pts. | AVERAGES RPG | APG | PPG |
|---|---|---|---|---|---|---|---|---|---|---|---|---|---|---|---|---|---|---|---|
| 73-74—New York | 82 | 2050 | 361 | 757 | .477 | 191 | 246 | .776 | 123 | 355 | 478 | 134 | 42 | 67 | ... | 913 | 5.8 | 1.6 | 11.1 |
| 74-75—New York | 78 | 2285 | 324 | 712 | .455 | 193 | 253 | .763 | 137 | 463 | 600 | 136 | 84 | 53 | ... | 841 | 7.7 | 1.7 | 10.8 |
| 75-76—New York | 80 | 1461 | 185 | 387 | .478 | 110 | 150 | .733 | 80 | 263 | 343 | 105 | 41 | 20 | ... | 480 | 4.3 | 1.3 | 6.0 |
| 76-77—N.Y. Knicks | 76 | 1033 | 102 | 232 | .440 | 51 | 71 | .718 | 75 | 154 | 229 | 85 | 33 | 18 | ... | 255 | 3.0 | 1.1 | 3.4 |
| 77-78—New York | 63 | 654 | 55 | 115 | .478 | 43 | 56 | .768 | 29 | 81 | 110 | 46 | 31 | 15 | 47 | 153 | 1.7 | 0.7 | 2.4 |
| 78-79—New Jersey | 59 | 1070 | 144 | 303 | .475 | 86 | 105 | .819 | 59 | 119 | 178 | 85 | 45 | 22 | 78 | 374 | 3.0 | 1.4 | 6.3 |
| 79-80—New Jersey | 16 | 194 | 29 | 46 | .630 | 7 | 10 | .700 | 12 | 12 | 24 | 12 | 5 | 4 | 9 | 65 | 1.5 | 0.8 | 4.1 |
| Totals | 807 | 14201 | 2076 | 4583 | .453 | 1276 | 1734 | .736 | ... | ... | 3454 | 898 | 281 | 199 | 134 | 5428 | 4.3 | 1.1 | 6.7 |

Three-point field goals: 1979-80, 0-for-2.

Personal fouls/disqualifications: 1973-74, 277/7. 1974-75, 330/10. 1975-76, 275/3. 1976-77, 184/4. 1977-78, 106/0. 1978-79, 168/7. 1979-80, 35/1. Totals, 2366/51.

## NBA PLAYOFF RECORD

| Season Team | G | Min. | FGM | FGA | Pct. | FTM | FTA | Pct. | Reb. | Ast. | PF | Dq. | Pts. | AVERAGES RPG | APG | PPG |
|---|---|---|---|---|---|---|---|---|---|---|---|---|---|---|---|---|
| 67-68—New York | 6 | 90 | 10 | 35 | .286 | 4 | 5 | .800 | 25 | 2 | 23 | 0 | 24 | 4.2 | 0.3 | 4.0 |
| 68-69—New York | | | | | Did not play—injured. | | | | | | | | | | | |
| 70-71—New York | 5 | 30 | 4 | 14 | .286 | 1 | 1 | 1.000 | 10 | 2 | 8 | 0 | 9 | 2.0 | 0.4 | 1.8 |
| 71-72—New York | 16 | 320 | 57 | 120 | .475 | 42 | 57 | .737 | 82 | 15 | 51 | 1 | 156 | 5.1 | 0.9 | 9.8 |
| 72-73—New York | 17 | 338 | 60 | 120 | .500 | 28 | 38 | .737 | 72 | 24 | 59 | 3 | 148 | 4.2 | 1.4 | 8.7 |

| Season Team | G | Min. | FGM | FGA | Pct. | FTM | FTA | Pct. | REBOUNDS Off. | Def. | Tot. | Ast. | St. | Blk. | TO | Pts. | AVERAGES RPG | APG | PPG |
|---|---|---|---|---|---|---|---|---|---|---|---|---|---|---|---|---|---|---|---|
| 73-74—New York | 12 | 297 | 54 | 116 | .466 | 27 | 30 | .900 | 15 | 42 | 57 | 15 | 10 | 5 | ... | 135 | 4.8 | 1.3 | 11.3 |
| 74-75—New York | 3 | 78 | 10 | 21 | .476 | 7 | 8 | .875 | 5 | 20 | 25 | 2 | 4 | 3 | ... | 27 | 8.3 | 0.7 | 9.0 |
| 77-78—New York | 6 | 50 | 4 | 8 | .500 | 4 | 6 | .667 | 4 | 6 | 10 | 3 | 3 | 0 | 4 | 12 | 1.7 | 0.5 | 2.0 |
| 78-79—New Jersey | 2 | 20 | 1 | 3 | .333 | 2 | 2 | 1.000 | 2 | 1 | 3 | 0 | 1 | 0 | 0 | 4 | 1.5 | 0.0 | 2.0 |
| Totals | 67 | 1223 | 200 | 437 | .458 | 115 | 147 | .782 | ... | ... | 284 | 63 | 18 | 8 | 4 | 515 | 4.2 | 0.9 | 7.7 |

Personal fouls/disqualifications: 1973-74, 40/0. 1974-75, 15/0. 1977-78, 11/0. 1978-79, 1/0. Totals, 208/4.

## HEAD COACHING RECORD

**BACKGROUND:** Player/assistant coach, New Jersey Nets (1978-79 and 1979-80). ... Assistant coach, Nets (1980-81). ... Broadcaster, Nets (1981-82). ... Assistant coach, Chicago Bulls (1987-88 and 1988-89).

**HONORS:** NBA Coach of the Year (1996). ... One of the Top 10 Coaches in NBA History (1996). ... CBA Coach of the Year (1985).

**RECORDS:** Holds NBA regular season record for highest winning percentage—.728. ... Holds NBA playoff record for highest winning percentage (minimum 25 games)—.730 ... Holds NBA career record for playoff wins—162.

### CBA COACHING RECORD

| Season Team | REGULAR SEASON W | L | Pct. | Finish | PLAYOFFS W | L | Pct. |
|---|---|---|---|---|---|---|---|
| 82-83—Albany | 8 | 11 | .421 | 4th/Eastern Division | — | — | — |
| 83-84—Albany | 25 | 19 | .568 | 2nd/Eastern Division | 9 | 5 | .643 |
| 84-85—Albany | 34 | 14 | .708 | 1st/Eastern Division | 5 | 5 | .500 |
| 85-86—Albany | 24 | 24 | .500 | 4th/Eastern Division | 3 | 4 | .429 |
| 86-87—Albany | 26 | 22 | .542 | T2nd/Eastern Division | 4 | 4 | .500 |
| Totals (5 years) | 117 | 90 | .565 | Totals (4 years) | 21 | 18 | .538 |

### NBA COACHING RECORD

| Season Team | REGULAR SEASON W | L | Pct. | Finish | PLAYOFFS W | L | Pct. |
|---|---|---|---|---|---|---|---|
| 89-90—Chicago | 55 | 27 | .671 | 2nd/Central Division | 10 | 6 | .625 |
| 90-91—Chicago | 61 | 21 | .744 | 1st/Central Division | 15 | 2 | .882 |
| 91-92—Chicago | 67 | 15 | .817 | 1st/Central Division | 15 | 7 | .682 |
| 92-93—Chicago | 57 | 25 | .695 | 1st/Central Division | 15 | 4 | .789 |
| 93-94—Chicago | 55 | 27 | .671 | 2nd/Central Division | 6 | 4 | .600 |
| 94-95—Chicago | 47 | 35 | .573 | 2nd/Central Division | 5 | 5 | .500 |
| 95-96—Chicago | 72 | 10 | .878 | 1st/Central Division | 15 | 3 | .833 |
| 96-97—Chicago | 69 | 13 | .841 | 1st/Central Division | 15 | 4 | .789 |
| 97-98—Chicago | 62 | 20 | .756 | 1st/Central Division | 15 | 6 | .714 |
| 99-00—Los Angeles Lakers | 67 | 15 | .817 | 1st/Pacific Division | 15 | 8 | .652 |
| 00-01—Los Angeles Lakers | 56 | 26 | .817 | 1st/Pacific Division | 15 | 1 | .938 |
| 01-02—Los Angeles Lakers | 58 | 24 | .707 | 1st/Pacific Division | 15 | 4 | .789 |
| 02-03—Los Angeles Lakers | 50 | 32 | .610 | T2nd/Pacific Division | 6 | 6 | .500 |
| 03-04—Los Angeles Lakers | 56 | 26 | .683 | 1st/Pacific Division | 13 | 9 | .592 |
| Totals (14 years) | 832 | 316 | .725 | Totals (14 years) | 175 | 69 | .717 |

**NOTES:**

1983—Replaced Dean Meminger (8-15) and player/interim coach Sam Worthen (0-2) as Albany Patroons head coach (January 29), with record of 8-17.

1984—Defeated Bay State, 3-2, in Eastern semifinals; defeated Puerto Rico, 3-1, in Eastern finals; defeated Wyoming, 3-2, in CBA Championship Series.

1985—Defeated Toronto, 3-2, in Eastern semifinals; lost to Tampa Bay, 3-2, in Eastern finals.

1986—Lost to Tampa Bay in Eastern semifinals.

1987—Defeated Mississippi, 4-0, in Eastern semifinals; lost to Rapid City, 4-0, in Eastern finals.

1990—Defeated Milwaukee, 3-1, in Eastern Conference first round; defeated Philadelphia, 4-1, in Eastern Conference semifinals; lost to Detroit, 4-3, in Eastern Conference finals.

1991—Defeated New York, 3-0, in Eastern Conference first round; defeated Philadelphia, 4-1, in Eastern Conference semifinals; defeated Detroit, 4-0, in Eastern Conference finals; defeated Los Angeles Lakers, 4-1, in NBA Finals.

1992—Defeated Miami, 3-0, in Eastern Conference first round; defeated New York, 4-3, in Eastern Conference semifinals; defeated Cleveland, 4-2, in Eastern Conference finals; defeated Portland, 4-2, in NBA Finals.

1993—Defeated Atlanta, 3-0, in Eastern Conference first round; defeated Cleveland, 4-0, in Eastern Conference semifinals; defeated New York, 4-2, in Eastern Conference finals; defeated Phoenix, 4-2, in NBA Finals.

1994—Defeated Cleveland, 3-0, in Eastern Conference first round; lost to New York, 4-3, in Eastern Conference semifinals.

1995—Defeated Charlotte, 3-1, in Eastern Conference first round; lost to Orlando, 4-2, in Eastern Conference semifinals.

1996—Defeated Miami, 3-0, in Eastern Conference first round; defeated New York, 4-1, in Eastern Conference semifinals; defeated Orlando, 4-0, in Eastern Conference finals; defeated Seattle, 4-2, in NBA Finals.

1997—Defeated Washington, 3-0, in Eastern Conference first round; defeated Atlanta, 4-1, in Eastern Conference semifinals; defeated Miami, 4-1, in Eastern Conference finals; defeated Utah, 4-2, in NBA Finals.

1998—Defeated New Jersey, 3-0, in Eastern Conference first round; defeated Charlotte, 4-1, in Eastern Conference semifinals; defeated Indiana, 4-3, in Eastern Conference finals; defeated Utah, 4-2, in NBA Finals.

2000—Defeated Sacramento, 3-2, in Western Conference first round; defeated Phoenix, 4-1, in Western Conference semifinals; defeated Portland, 4-3, in Western Conference finals; defeated Indiana, 4-2, in NBA Finals.

2001—Defeated Portland, 3-0, in Western Conference first round; defeated Sacramento, 4-0, in Western Conference semifinals; defeated San Antonio, 4-0, in Western Conference finals; defeated Philadelphia, 4-1, in NBA Finals.

2002—Defeated Portland, 3-0, in Western Conference first round; defeated San Antonio, 4-1, in Western Conference semifinals; defeated Sacramento, 4-3, in Western Conference finals; defeated New Jersey, 4-0, in NBA Finals.

2003—Defeated Minnesota, 4-2, in Western Conference first round; lost to San Antonio, 4-2, in Western Conference semifinals.

2004—Defeated Houston, 4-1, in Western Conference first round; defeated San Antonio, 4-2, in Western Conference semifinals; defeated Minnesota, 4-2, in Western Conference finals; lost to Detroit, 4-1, in NBA Finals.

## JOHNSON, AVERY — MAVERICKS

**PERSONAL:** Born March 25, 1965, in New Orleans. ... 5-11/180. (1,80/81,6).
**HIGH SCHOOL:** St. Augustine (New Orleans).
**JUNIOR COLLEGE:** New Mexico Junior College.
**COLLEGE:** Cameron (Okla.), then Southern (La.).
**TRANSACTIONS/CAREER NOTES:** Not drafted by an NBA franchise. ... Played in United States Basketball League with Palm Beach Stingrays (1988). ... Signed as free agent by Seattle SuperSonics (August 2, 1988). ... Traded by SuperSonics to Denver Nuggets for 1997 second-round draft choice (October 24, 1990). ... Waived by Nuggets (December 24, 1990). ... Signed as free agent by San Antonio Spurs (January 17, 1991). ... Waived by Spurs (December 17, 1991). ... Signed by Houston Rockets to first of two consecutive 10-day contracts (January 10, 1992). ... Re-signed by Rockets for remainder of season (January 31, 1992). ... Signed as free agent by Spurs (November 19, 1992). ... Signed as free agent by Golden State Warriors (October 25, 1993). ... Signed as unrestricted free agent by Spurs (July 21, 1994). ... Signed as free agent by Nuggets (July 18, 2001). ... Traded by Nuggets with G Nick Van Exel, F/C Raef LaFrentz and G/F Tariq Abdul-Wahad to Dallas Mavericks for F Juwan Howard, G Tim Hardaway, F Donnell Harvey, cash considerations and first-round draft choice (February 21, 2002). ... Traded by Mavericks with G Nick Van Exel, F Popeye Jones, F Antoine Rigaudeau and C Evan Eschmeyer to Golden State Warriors for F Antawn Jamison, F Chris Mills, F Danny Fortson and G Jiri Welsch (August 18, 2003).
**MISCELLANEOUS:** Member of NBA championship team (1999). ... San Antonio Spurs all-time assist leader with 4,474 (1990-91 through 1992-93, and 1994-95 through 2000-01).

### COLLEGIATE RECORD

**NOTES:** Holds NCAA Division I career record for highest assists-per-game average—12.0. ... Holds NCAA Division I single-season record for highest assists-per-game average—13.3 (1988). ... Shares NCAA Division I single-game record for most assists—22 (January 25, 1988, vs. Texas Southern). ... Led NCAA Division I with 10.74 assists per game (1987) and 13.30 assists per game (1988).

| | | | | | | | | | | | AVERAGES | | |
| Season Team | G | Min. | FGM | FGA | Pct. | FTM | FTA | Pct. | Reb. | Ast. | Pts. | RPG | APG | PPG |
| --- | --- | --- | --- | --- | --- | --- | --- | --- | --- | --- | --- | --- | --- | --- |
| 83-84—New Mexico J.C. ........... | 26 | 583 | 66 | 102 | .647 | 28 | 39 | .718 | 30 | 159 | 160 | 1.2 | 6.1 | 6.2 |
| 84-85—Cameron........................ | 33 | ... | 54 | 106 | .509 | 34 | 55 | .618 | 31 | 111 | 142 | 0.9 | 3.4 | 4.3 |
| 85-86—Southern ...................... | | | | | | Did not play—transfer student. | | | | | | | | |
| 86-87—Southern ...................... | 31 | 1111 | 86 | 196 | .439 | 40 | 65 | .615 | 73 | 333 | 219 | 2.4 | 10.7 | 7.1 |
| 87-88—Southern ...................... | 30 | 1145 | 138 | 257 | .537 | 44 | 64 | .688 | 84 | 399 | 342 | 2.8 | 13.3 | 11.4 |
| Junior College Totals............ | 26 | 583 | 66 | 102 | .647 | 28 | 39 | .718 | 30 | 159 | 160 | 1.2 | 6.1 | 6.2 |
| 4-Year-College Totals ........... | 94 | ... | 278 | 559 | .497 | 118 | 184 | .641 | 188 | 843 | 703 | 2.0 | 9.0 | 7.5 |

Three-point field goals: 1986-87, 7-for-24 (.292). 1987-88, 22-for-47 (.468). Totals, 29-for-71 (.408).

### NBA REGULAR-SEASON RECORD

**HONORS:** NBA Sportsmanship Award (1998).

| | | | | | | | | | REBOUNDS | | | | | | | | AVERAGES | | |
| Season Team | G | Min. | FGM | FGA | Pct. | FTM | FTA | Pct. | Off. | Def. | Tot. | Ast. | St. | Blk. | TO | Pts. | RPG | APG | PPG |
| --- | --- | --- | --- | --- | --- | --- | --- | --- | --- | --- | --- | --- | --- | --- | --- | --- | --- | --- | --- |
| 88-89—Seattle ........... | 43 | 291 | 29 | 83 | .349 | 9 | 16 | .563 | 11 | 13 | 24 | 73 | 21 | 3 | 18 | 68 | 0.6 | 1.7 | 1.6 |
| 89-90—Seattle ........... | 53 | 575 | 55 | 142 | .387 | 29 | 40 | .725 | 21 | 22 | 43 | 162 | 26 | 1 | 48 | 140 | 0.8 | 3.1 | 2.6 |
| 90-91—Denver-S.A. .... | 68 | 959 | 130 | 277 | .469 | 59 | 87 | .678 | 22 | 55 | 77 | 230 | 47 | 4 | 74 | 320 | 1.1 | 3.4 | 4.7 |
| 91-92—S.A.-Hou........ | 69 | 1235 | 158 | 330 | .479 | 66 | 101 | .653 | 13 | 67 | 80 | 266 | 61 | 9 | 110 | 386 | 1.2 | 3.9 | 5.6 |
| 92-93—San Antonio .... | 75 | 2030 | 256 | 510 | .502 | 144 | 182 | .791 | 20 | 126 | 146 | 561 | 85 | 16 | 145 | 656 | 1.9 | 7.5 | 8.7 |
| 93-94—Golden State ... | 82 | 2332 | 356 | 724 | .492 | 178 | 253 | .704 | 41 | 135 | 176 | 433 | 113 | 8 | 172 | 890 | 2.1 | 5.3 | 10.9 |
| 94-95—San Antonio .... | 82 | 3011 | 448 | 863 | .519 | 202 | 295 | .685 | 49 | 159 | 208 | 670 | 114 | 13 | 207 | 1101 | 2.5 | 8.2 | 13.4 |
| 95-96—San Antonio .... | 82 | 3084 | 438 | 887 | .494 | 189 | 262 | .721 | 37 | 169 | 206 | 789 | 119 | 21 | 195 | 1071 | 2.5 | 9.6 | 13.1 |
| 96-97—San Antonio .... | 76 | 2472 | 327 | 685 | .477 | 140 | 203 | .690 | 32 | 115 | 147 | 513 | 96 | 15 | 146 | 800 | 1.9 | 6.8 | 10.5 |
| 97-98—San Antonio .... | 75 | 2674 | 321 | 671 | .478 | 122 | 168 | .726 | 30 | 120 | 150 | 591 | 84 | 18 | 165 | 766 | 2.0 | 7.9 | 10.2 |
| 98-99—San Antonio .... | 50 | 1672 | 218 | 461 | .473 | 50 | 88 | .568 | 22 | 96 | 118 | 369 | 51 | 11 | 112 | 487 | 2.4 | 7.4 | 9.7 |
| 99-00—San Antonio .... | 82 | 2571 | 400 | 850 | .473 | 114 | 155 | .735 | 33 | 125 | 158 | 491 | 76 | 18 | 140 | 919 | 1.9 | 6.0 | 11.2 |
| 00-01—San Antonio .... | 55 | 1290 | 134 | 300 | .447 | 41 | 60 | .683 | 21 | 64 | 85 | 237 | 33 | 4 | 60 | 310 | 1.5 | 4.3 | 5.6 |
| 01-02—Denver-Dallas... | 68 | 1352 | 207 | 432 | .479 | 121 | 163 | .742 | 14 | 55 | 69 | 286 | 40 | 9 | 76 | 535 | 1.0 | 4.2 | 7.9 |
| 02-03—Dallas............. | 48 | 430 | 63 | 150 | .420 | 30 | 39 | .769 | 10 | 21 | 31 | 64 | 15 | 1 | 29 | 156 | 0.6 | 1.3 | 3.3 |
| 03-04—Golden State ... | 46 | 637 | 80 | 199 | .402 | 52 | 78 | .667 | 3 | 30 | 33 | 111 | 26 | 3 | 51 | 212 | 0.7 | 2.4 | 4.6 |
| Totals ................... | 1054 | 26615 | 3622 | 7564 | .479 | 1546 | 2190 | .706 | 379 | 1372 | 1751 | 5846 | 1007 | 154 | 1748 | 8817 | 1.7 | 5.5 | 8.4 |

Three-point field goals: 1988-89, 1-for-9 (.111). 1989-90, 1-for-4 (.250). 1990-91, 1-for-9 (.111). 1991-92, 4-for-15 (.267). 1992-93, 0-for-8. 1993-94, 0-for-12. 1994-95, 3-for-22 (.136). 1995-96, 6-for-31 (.194). 1996-97, 6-for-26 (.231). 1997-98, 2-for-13 (.154). 1998-99, 1-for-12 (.083). 1999-00, 1-for-9 (.111). 2000-01, 1-for-6 (.167). 2001-02, 0-for-5. 2002-03, 0-for-2. 2003-04, 0-for-5. Totals, 27-for-186 (.145).

Personal fouls/disqualifications: 1988-89, 34/0. 1989-90, 55/0. 1990-91, 62/0. 1991-92, 89/1. 1992-93, 141/0. 1993-94, 160/0. 1994-95, 154/0. 1995-96, 179/1. 1996-97, 158/1. 1997-98, 140/0. 1998-99, 101/0. 1999-00, 150/0. 2000-01, 90/0. 2001-02, 86/0. 2002-03, 26/0. 2003-04, 34/0. Totals, 1659/3.

## NBA PLAYOFF RECORD

| Season Team | G | Min. | FGM | FGA | Pct. | FTM | FTA | Pct. | REBOUNDS | | | Ast. | St. | Blk. | TO | Pts. | AVERAGES | | |
| | | | | | | | | | Off. | Def. | Tot. | | | | | | RPG | APG | PPG |
|---|---|---|---|---|---|---|---|---|---|---|---|---|---|---|---|---|---|---|---|
| 88-89—Seattle ......... | 6 | 31 | 5 | 12 | .417 | 1 | 2 | .500 | 2 | 2 | 4 | 5 | 4 | 0 | 0 | 11 | 0.7 | 0.8 | 1.8 |
| 90-91—San Antonio.... | 3 | 19 | 0 | 5 | .000 | 2 | 2 | 1.000 | 0 | 0 | 0 | 4 | 1 | 0 | 0 | 2 | 0.0 | 1.3 | 0.7 |
| 92-93—San Antonio.... | 10 | 314 | 36 | 70 | .514 | 10 | 14 | .714 | 8 | 23 | 31 | 81 | 10 | 1 | 23 | 82 | 3.1 | 8.1 | 8.2 |
| 93-94—Golden State ... | 3 | 41 | 9 | 17 | .529 | 0 | 0 | ... | 0 | 3 | 3 | 10 | 4 | 1 | 3 | 18 | 1.0 | 3.3 | 6.0 |
| 94-95—San Antonio.... | 15 | 575 | 91 | 176 | .517 | 36 | 58 | .621 | 9 | 23 | 32 | 125 | 20 | 6 | 30 | 218 | 2.1 | 8.3 | 14.5 |
| 95-96—San Antonio.... | 10 | 407 | 52 | 121 | .430 | 19 | 27 | .704 | 6 | 30 | 36 | 94 | 20 | 1 | 24 | 123 | 3.6 | 9.4 | 12.3 |
| 97-98—San Antonio.... | 9 | 342 | 61 | 101 | .604 | 34 | 51 | .667 | 3 | 10 | 13 | 55 | 9 | 0 | 21 | 156 | 1.4 | 6.1 | 17.3 |
| 98-99—San Antonio.... | 17 | 653 | 91 | 187 | .487 | 32 | 47 | .681 | 9 | 33 | 42 | 126 | 20 | 1 | 50 | 215 | 2.5 | 7.4 | 12.6 |
| 99-00—San Antonio.... | 4 | 144 | 19 | 42 | .452 | 10 | 14 | .714 | 2 | 7 | 9 | 21 | 4 | 0 | 10 | 48 | 2.3 | 5.3 | 12.0 |
| 00-01—San Antonio.... | 13 | 281 | 34 | 88 | .386 | 8 | 15 | .533 | 3 | 13 | 16 | 41 | 10 | 1 | 10 | 76 | 1.2 | 3.2 | 5.8 |
| Totals .................. | 90 | 2807 | 398 | 819 | .486 | 152 | 230 | .661 | 42 | 144 | 186 | 562 | 102 | 11 | 171 | 949 | 2.1 | 6.2 | 10.5 |

Three-point field goals: 1988-89, 0-for-4. 1990-91, 0-for-1. 1992-93, 0-for-1. 1993-94, 0-for-1. 1994-95, 0-for-1. 1995-96, 0-for-2. 1997-98, 0-for-2. 1998-99, 1-for-3 (.333). 2000-01, 0-for-1. Totals, 1-for-16 (.063).

Personal fouls/disqualifications: 1988-89, 1/0. 1990-91, 3/0. 1992-93, 27/0. 1993-94, 2/0. 1994-95, 29/0. 1995-96, 21/0. 1997-98, 27/0. 1998-99, 30/0. 1999-00, 10/0. 2000-01, 24/1. Totals, 174/1.

## HEAD COACHING RECORD

**NOTES:** Assistant coach, Mavericks (October 28, 2004-March 19, 2005).

## NBA COACHING RECORD

| Season Team | REGULAR SEASON | | | | PLAYOFFS | | |
| | W | L | Pct. | Finish | W | L | Pct. |
|---|---|---|---|---|---|---|---|
| 04-05—Dallas ........................................................ | 16 | 2 | .889 | 2nd/Southwest Division | 6 | 7 | .462 |

**NOTES:**
2005—Defeated Houston, 4-3, in Western Conference first round; lost to Phoenix, 4-2, in Western Conference semifinals.

# JORDAN, EDDIE — WIZARDS

**PERSONAL:** Born January 29, 1955, in Washington D.C. ... 6-1/170. ... Full name: Edward Montgomery Jordan.
**HIGH SCHOOL:** Archbishop Carroll (Washington D.C.).
**COLLEGE:** Rutgers.
**TRANSACTIONS/CAREER NOTES:** Selected by Cleveland Cavaliers in second round (33rd pick overall) of 1977 NBA Draft. ... Claimed on waivers by New Jersey Nets (December 12, 1977). ... Traded by Nets to Los Angeles Lakers for 1982 first-round draft choice (November 20, 1980). ... Traded by Lakers with G Norm Nixon and two future second-round draft choices to San Diego Clippers for C Swen Nater and draft rights to G Byron Scott (October 10, 1983). ... Signed as free agent by Portland Trail Blazers (January 4, 1984). ... Signed as free agent by Lakers (April 11, 1984).
**MISCELLANEOUS:** Member of NBA championship team (1982).

## COLLEGIATE RECORD

| Season Team | G | Min. | FGM | FGA | Pct. | FTM | FTA | Pct. | Reb. | Ast. | Pts. | AVERAGES | | |
| | | | | | | | | | | | | RPG | APG | PPG |
|---|---|---|---|---|---|---|---|---|---|---|---|---|---|---|
| 73-74—Rutgers ......................... | 26 | ... | 124 | 278 | .446 | 40 | 56 | .714 | 82 | 28 | 288 | 3.2 | 1.1 | 11.1 |
| 74-75—Rutgers ......................... | 29 | 958 | 164 | 337 | .487 | 57 | 80 | .713 | 98 | 131 | 385 | 3.4 | 4.5 | 13.3 |
| 75-76—Rutgers ......................... | 33 | 939 | 187 | 397 | .471 | 90 | 113 | .796 | 102 | 174 | 464 | 3.1 | 5.3 | 14.1 |
| 76-77—Rutgers ......................... | 28 | 1025 | 190 | 413 | .460 | 116 | 170 | .682 | 124 | 202 | 496 | 4.4 | 7.2 | 17.7 |
| Totals ................. | 116 | ... | 754 | 1633 | .462 | 346 | 473 | .732 | 449 | 535 | 1855 | 2.6 | 4.6 | 10.7 |

## NBA REGULAR-SEASON RECORD

| Season Team | G | Min. | FGM | FGA | Pct. | FTM | FTA | Pct. | REBOUNDS | | | Ast. | St. | Blk. | TO | Pts. | AVERAGES | | |
| | | | | | | | | | Off. | Def. | Tot. | | | | | | RPG | APG | PPG |
|---|---|---|---|---|---|---|---|---|---|---|---|---|---|---|---|---|---|---|---|
| 77-78—Clev.-N.J. ...... | 73 | 1213 | 215 | 538 | .400 | 131 | 167 | .784 | 35 | 84 | 119 | 177 | 126 | 19 | 106 | 561 | 1.6 | 2.4 | 7.7 |
| 78-79—New Jersey .... | 82 | 2260 | 401 | 960 | .418 | 213 | 274 | .777 | 74 | 141 | 215 | 365 | 201 | 40 | 244 | 1015 | 2.6 | 4.5 | 12.4 |
| 79-80—New Jersey .... | 82 | 2657 | 437 | 1017 | .430 | 201 | 258 | .779 | 62 | 208 | 270 | 557 | 223 | 27 | 258 | 1087 | 3.3 | 6.8 | 13.3 |
| 80-81—N.J.-L.A. ........ | 74 | 1226 | 150 | 352 | .426 | 87 | 127 | .685 | 30 | 68 | 98 | 241 | 98 | 8 | 143 | 393 | 1.3 | 3.3 | 5.3 |
| 81-82—Los Angeles .. | 58 | 608 | 89 | 208 | .428 | 43 | 54 | .796 | 4 | 39 | 43 | 131 | 62 | 1 | 66 | 222 | 0.7 | 2.3 | 3.8 |
| 82-83—Los Angeles .. | 35 | 333 | 40 | 132 | .303 | 11 | 17 | .647 | 8 | 18 | 26 | 80 | 31 | 1 | 54 | 94 | 0.7 | 2.3 | 2.7 |
| 83-84—Port.-L.A. ...... | 16 | 210 | 17 | 49 | .347 | 8 | 12 | .667 | 3 | 14 | 17 | 44 | 25 | 0 | 26 | 42 | 1.1 | 2.8 | 2.6 |
| Totals .................. | 420 | 8507 | 1349 | 3256 | .414 | 694 | 909 | .763 | 216 | 572 | 788 | 1595 | 766 | 95 | 897 | 3192 | 2.1 | 4.0 | 8.8 |

Three-point field goals: 1979-80, 12-for-48 (.250). 1980-81, 6-for-22 (.273). 1981-82, 1-for-9 (.111). 1982-83, 3-for-16 (.188). 1983-84, 0-for-3. Totals, 22-for-98 (.224).

Personal fouls/disqualifications: 1977-78, 94/0. 1978-79, 209/0. 1979-80, 238/7. 1980-81, 165/0. 1981-82, 98/0. 1982-83, 52/0. 1983-84, 37/0. Totals, 893/7.

## NBA PLAYOFF RECORD

| Season Team | G | Min. | FGM | FGA | Pct. | FTM | FTA | Pct. | REBOUNDS | | | Ast. | St. | Blk. | TO | Pts. | AVERAGES | | |
| | | | | | | | | | Off. | Def. | Tot. | | | | | | RPG | APG | PPG |
|---|---|---|---|---|---|---|---|---|---|---|---|---|---|---|---|---|---|---|---|
| 78-79—New Jersey .... | 2 | 83 | 15 | 38 | .395 | 8 | 9 | .889 | 6 | 9 | 15 | 17 | 8 | 3 | ... | 38 | 7.5 | 8.5 | 19.0 |
| 80-81—Los Angeles .. | 2 | 4 | 0 | 0 | ... | 0 | 0 | ... | 0 | 0 | 0 | 1 | 0 | 0 | ... | 0 | 0.0 | 0.5 | 0.0 |
| 81-82—Los Angeles .. | 3 | 6 | 0 | 2 | .000 | 0 | 0 | ... | 0 | 0 | 0 | 5 | 2 | 0 | ... | 0 | 0.0 | 1.7 | 0.0 |
| Totals .................. | 7 | 93 | 15 | 40 | .375 | 8 | 9 | .889 | 6 | 9 | 15 | 23 | 10 | 3 | ... | 38 | 2.1 | 3.3 | 5.4 |

Three-point field goals: 1981-82, 0-for-1.
Personal fouls/disqualifications: 1978-79, 6/0.

## HEAD COACHING RECORD

**BACKGROUND:** Assistant coach, Sacramento Kings (1992-93 through March 10, 1997). ... Assistant coach, New Jersey Nets (1999-2000 through 2002-03).

### NBA COACHING RECORD

| Season Team | REGULAR SEASON | | | | PLAYOFFS | | |
|---|---|---|---|---|---|---|---|
| | W | L | Pct. | Finish | W | L | Pct. |
| 96-97—Sacramento | 6 | 9 | .400 | 6th/Pacific Division | — | — | — |
| 97-98—Sacramento | 27 | 55 | .329 | 5th/Pacific Division | — | — | — |
| 03-04—Washington | 25 | 57 | .305 | 6th/Atlantic Division | — | — | — |
| 04-05—Washington | 45 | 37 | .549 | 2nd/Southeast Division | 4 | 6 | .400 |
| Totals (4 years) | 103 | 158 | .395 | | | | |
| Totals (1 year) | | | | | 4 | 6 | .400 |

**NOTES:**

1997—Replaced Garry St. Jean as Sacramento head coach (March 20), with record of 28-39 and club in fifth place.
2005—Defeated Chicago, 4-2, in Eastern Conference first round; lost to Miami, 4-0, in Eastern Conference semifinals.

# KARL, GEORGE                                                      NUGGETS

**PERSONAL:** Born May 12, 1951, in Penn Hills, Pa. ... 6-2/190. (1,88/86,2). ... Full name: George Matthew Karl.
**HIGH SCHOOL:** Penn Hills (Pa.).
**COLLEGE:** North Carolina.
**TRANSACTIONS/CAREER NOTES:** Selected by New York Knicks in fourth round of 1973 NBA Draft. ... Signed as free agent by San Antonio Spurs of American Basketball Association (1973). ... Spurs franchise became part of NBA for 1976-77 season.

### COLLEGIATE RECORD

| Season Team | G | Min. | FGM | FGA | Pct. | FTM | FTA | Pct. | Reb. | Ast. | Pts. | RPG | APG | PPG |
|---|---|---|---|---|---|---|---|---|---|---|---|---|---|---|
| 69-70—North Carolina‡ | 6 | ... | 56 | 97 | .577 | 20 | 23 | .870 | 29 | ... | 132 | 4.8 | ... | 22.0 |
| 70-71—North Carolina | 32 | ... | 150 | 286 | .524 | 92 | 115 | .800 | 104 | 78 | 392 | 3.3 | 2.4 | 12.3 |
| 71-72—North Carolina | 29 | ... | 125 | 241 | .519 | 89 | 113 | .788 | 72 | 124 | 339 | 2.5 | 4.3 | 11.7 |
| 72-73—North Carolina | 33 | ... | 219 | 437 | .501 | 124 | 163 | .761 | 103 | 192 | 562 | 3.1 | 5.8 | 17.0 |
| Varsity totals | 94 | ... | 494 | 964 | .512 | 305 | 391 | .780 | 279 | 394 | 1293 | 3.0 | 4.2 | 13.8 |

### ABA REGULAR-SEASON RECORD

| Season Team | G | Min. | 2-POINT | | | 3-POINT | | | FTM | FTA | Pct. | Reb. | Ast. | Pts. | AVERAGES | | |
|---|---|---|---|---|---|---|---|---|---|---|---|---|---|---|---|---|---|
| | | | FGM | FGA | Pct. | FGM | FGA | Pct. | | | | | | | RPG | APG | PPG |
| 73-74—San Antonio | 74 | 1339 | 228 | 480 | .475 | 8 | 22 | .364 | 94 | 113 | .832 | 126 | 160 | 574 | 1.7 | 2.2 | 7.8 |
| 74-75—San Antonio | 82 | 1629 | 257 | 511 | .503 | 4 | 23 | .174 | 137 | 177 | .774 | 155 | 334 | 663 | 1.9 | 4.1 | 8.1 |
| 75-76—San Antonio | 75 | 1200 | 150 | 325 | .462 | 0 | 9 | .000 | 81 | 106 | .764 | 66 | 250 | 381 | 0.9 | 3.3 | 5.1 |
| Totals | 231 | 4168 | 635 | 1316 | .483 | 12 | 54 | .222 | 312 | 396 | .788 | 347 | 744 | 1618 | 1.5 | 3.2 | 7.0 |

### ABA PLAYOFF RECORD

| Season Team | G | Min. | 2-POINT | | | 3-POINT | | | FTM | FTA | Pct. | Reb. | Ast. | Pts. | AVERAGES | | |
|---|---|---|---|---|---|---|---|---|---|---|---|---|---|---|---|---|---|
| | | | FGM | FGA | Pct. | FGM | FGA | Pct. | | | | | | | RPG | APG | PPG |
| 73-74—San Antonio | 7 | 141 | 13 | 27 | .481 | 0 | 1 | .000 | 2 | 5 | .400 | 15 | 23 | 28 | 2.1 | 3.3 | 4.0 |
| 74-75—San Antonio | 4 | 40 | 1 | 7 | .143 | 0 | 1 | .000 | 3 | 4 | .750 | 3 | 5 | 5 | 0.8 | 1.3 | 1.3 |
| 75-76—San Antonio | 6 | 64 | 10 | 21 | .476 | 0 | 1 | .000 | 6 | 9 | .667 | 4 | 17 | 26 | 0.7 | 2.8 | 4.3 |
| Totals | 17 | 245 | 24 | 55 | .436 | 0 | 3 | .000 | 11 | 18 | .611 | 22 | 45 | 59 | 1.3 | 2.6 | 3.5 |

### NBA REGULAR-SEASON RECORD

| Season Team | G | Min. | FGM | FGA | Pct. | FTM | FTA | Pct. | REBOUNDS | | | Ast. | St. | Blk. | TO | Pts. | AVERAGES | | |
|---|---|---|---|---|---|---|---|---|---|---|---|---|---|---|---|---|---|---|---|
| | | | | | | | | | Off. | Def. | Tot. | | | | | | RPG | APG | PPG |
| 76-77—San Antonio .. | 29 | 251 | 25 | 73 | .342 | 29 | 42 | .690 | 4 | 13 | 17 | 46 | 10 | 0 | ... | 79 | 0.6 | 1.6 | 2.7 |
| 77-78—San Antonio .. | 4 | 30 | 2 | 6 | .333 | 2 | 2 | 1.000 | 0 | 5 | 5 | 5 | 1 | 0 | 4 | 6 | 1.3 | 1.3 | 1.5 |
| Totals | 33 | 281 | 27 | 79 | .342 | 31 | 44 | .705 | 4 | 18 | 22 | 51 | 11 | 0 | 4 | 85 | 0.7 | 1.5 | 2.6 |

Personal fouls/disqualifications: 1976-77, 36/0. 1977-78, 6/0. Totals, 42/0.

### NBA PLAYOFF RECORD

| Season Team | G | Min. | FGM | FGA | Pct. | FTM | FTA | Pct. | REBOUNDS | | | Ast. | St. | Blk. | TO | Pts. | AVERAGES | | |
|---|---|---|---|---|---|---|---|---|---|---|---|---|---|---|---|---|---|---|---|
| | | | | | | | | | Off. | Def. | Tot. | | | | | | RPG | APG | PPG |
| 76-77—San Antonio .. | 1 | 1 | 0 | 0 | ... | 0 | 0 | ... | 0 | 0 | 0 | 0 | 0 | 0 | ... | 0 | 0.0 | 0.0 | 0.0 |

### COMBINED ABA AND NBA REGULAR-SEASON RECORDS

| | G | Min. | FGM | FGA | Pct. | FTM | FTA | Pct. | REBOUNDS | | | Ast. | Stl. | Blk. | TO | Pts. | AVERAGES | | |
|---|---|---|---|---|---|---|---|---|---|---|---|---|---|---|---|---|---|---|---|
| | | | | | | | | | Off. | Def. | Tot. | | | | | | RPG | APG | PPG |
| Totals | 264 | 4449 | 674 | 1449 | .465 | 343 | 440 | .780 | 105 | 264 | 369 | 795 | 232 | 20 | ... | 1703 | 1.4 | 3.0 | 6.5 |

Three-point field goals: 12-for-54 (.222).
Personal fouls/disqualifications: 559.

### HEAD COACHING RECORD

**BACKGROUND:** Assistant coach, San Antonio Spurs (1978-79 and 1979-80). ... Director of player acquisition, Cleveland Cavaliers (1983-84). ... Head coach, Real Madrid of Spanish League (1989-90 and 1991-January 1992).
**HONORS:** CBA Coach of the Year (1981, 1983, 1991).

### CBA COACHING RECORD

| Season Team | REGULAR SEASON | | | | PLAYOFFS | | |
|---|---|---|---|---|---|---|---|
| | W | L | Pct. | Finish | W | L | Pct. |
| 80-81—Montana | 27 | 15 | .643 | 1st/Western Division | 5 | 5 | .500 |
| 81-82—Montana | 30 | 16 | .652 | 2nd/Western Division | 2 | 3 | .400 |

| Season  Team | | REGULAR SEASON | | | | | PLAYOFFS | | |
|---|---|---|---|---|---|---|---|---|---|
| | W | L | Pct. | Finish | | | W | L | Pct. |
| 82-83—Montana | 33 | 11 | .750 | 1st/Western Division | | | 6 | 5 | .545 |
| 88-89—Albany | 36 | 18 | .667 | 1st/Eastern Division | | | 2 | 4 | .333 |
| 90-91—Albany | 50 | 6 | .893 | 1st/Eastern Division | | | 5 | 6 | .455 |
| Totals (5 years) | 176 | 66 | .727 | | Totals (5 years) | | 20 | 23 | .465 |

## NBA COACHING RECORD

| Season  Team | | REGULAR SEASON | | | | | PLAYOFFS | | |
|---|---|---|---|---|---|---|---|---|---|
| | W | L | Pct. | Finish | | | W | L | Pct. |
| 84-85—Cleveland | 36 | 46 | .439 | 4th/Central Division | | | 1 | 3 | .250 |
| 85-86—Cleveland | 25 | 42 | .373 | | | | — | — | — |
| 86-87—Golden State | 42 | 40 | .512 | 3rd/Pacific Division | | | 4 | 6 | .400 |
| 87-88—Golden State | 16 | 48 | .250 | | | | — | — | — |
| 91-92—Seattle | 27 | 15 | .643 | 4th/Pacific Division | | | 4 | 5 | .444 |
| 92-93—Seattle | 55 | 27 | .671 | 2nd/Pacific Division | | | 10 | 9 | .526 |
| 93-94—Seattle | 63 | 19 | .768 | 1st/Pacific Division | | | 2 | 3 | .400 |
| 94-95—Seattle | 57 | 25 | .695 | 2nd/Pacific Division | | | 1 | 3 | .250 |
| 95-96—Seattle | 64 | 18 | .780 | 1st/Pacific Division | | | 13 | 8 | .619 |
| 96-97—Seattle | 57 | 25 | .695 | 1st/Pacific Division | | | 6 | 6 | .500 |
| 97-98—Seattle | 61 | 21 | .744 | 1st/Pacific Division | | | 4 | 6 | .400 |
| 98-99—Milwaukee | 28 | 22 | .560 | 4th/Central Division | | | 0 | 3 | .000 |
| 99-00—Milwaukee | 42 | 40 | .512 | T-5th/Central Division | | | 2 | 3 | .400 |
| 00-01—Milwaukee | 52 | 30 | .634 | 1st/Central Division | | | 10 | 8 | .556 |
| 01-02—Milwaukee | 41 | 41 | .500 | 5th/Central Division | | | — | — | — |
| 02-03—Milwaukee | 42 | 40 | .512 | 4th/Central Division | | | 2 | 4 | .333 |
| 04-05—Denver | 32 | 8 | .800 | 2nd/Northwest Division | | | 1 | 4 | .200 |
| Totals (17 years) | 740 | 507 | .593 | | Totals (14 years) | | 60 | 71 | .458 |

**NOTES:**

1981—Defeated Alberta, 2-0, in Western semifinals; defeated Billings, 3-1, in Western finals; lost to Rochester, 4-0, in CBA Championship Series.

1982—Lost to Billings in Western finals.

1983—Defeated Wyoming, 3-1, in Western finals; lost to Detroit, 4-3, in CBA Championship Series.

1985—Lost to Boston in Eastern Conference first round.

1986—Replaced as Cleveland head coach by Gene Littles (March 16).

1987—Defeated Utah, 3-2, in Western Conference first round; lost to Los Angeles Lakers, 4-1, in Western Conference semifinals.

1988—Resigned as Golden State head coach (March 23).

1989—Lost to Wichita Falls in Eastern semifinals.

1991—Defeated Grand Rapids, 3-2, in National Conference first round; lost to Wichita Falls, 4-2, in National Conference finals.

1992—Replaced K.C. Jones (18-18) and Bob Kloppenburg (2-2) as Seattle head coach (January 23), with record of 20-20 and club in fifth place. Defeated Golden State, 3-1, in Western Conference first round; lost to Utah, 4-1, in Western Conference semifinals.

1993—Defeated Utah, 3-2, in Western Conference first round; defeated Houston, 4-3, in Western Conference semifinals; lost to Phoenix, 4-3, in Western Conference finals.

1994—Lost to Denver in Western Conference first round.

1995—Lost to Los Angeles Lakers in Western Conference first round.

1996—Defeated Sacramento, 3-1, in Western Conference first round; defeated Houston, 4-0, in Western Conference semifinals; defeated Utah, 4-3, in Western Conference finals; lost to Chicago, 4-2, in NBA Finals.

1997—Defeated Phoenix, 3-2, in Western Conference first round; lost to Houston, 4-3, in Western Conference semifinals.

1998—Defeated Minnesota, 3-2, in Western Conference first round; lost to Los Angeles Lakers, 4-1, in Western Conference semifinals.

1999—Lost to Indiana in Eastern Conference first round.

2000—Lost to Indiana in Eastern Conference first round.

2001—Defeated Orlando, 3-1, in Eastern Conference first round; defeated Charlotte, 4-3, in Eastern Conference semifinals; lost to Philadelphia, 4-3, in Eastern Conference finals.

2002—Lost to New Jersey in Eastern Conference first round.

2005—Lost to San Antonio in Eastern Conference first round.

# McMILLAN, NATE     TRAIL BLAZERS

**PERSONAL:** Born August 3, 1964, in Raleigh, N.C. ... 6-5/200. (1,96/90,7). ... Full Name: Nathaniel McMillan.
**HIGH SCHOOL:** Enloe (Raleigh, N.C.).
**JUNIOR COLLEGE:** Chowan College (N.C.).
**COLLEGE:** North Carolina State.
**TRANSACTIONS/CAREER NOTES:** Selected by Seattle SuperSonics in second round (30th pick overall) of 1986 NBA Draft. ... Announced retirement to become assistant coach of SuperSonics (September 29, 1998).

## COLLEGIATE RECORD

| Season  Team | G | Min. | FGM | FGA | Pct. | FTM | FTA | Pct. | Reb. | Ast. | Pts. | AVERAGES | | |
|---|---|---|---|---|---|---|---|---|---|---|---|---|---|---|
| | | | | | | | | | | | | RPG | APG | PPG |
| 82-83—Chowan College | 27 | ... | 101 | 174 | .580 | 64 | 92 | .696 | 134 | 191 | 266 | 5.0 | 7.1 | 9.9 |
| 83-84—Chowan College | 35 | ... | 180 | 331 | .544 | 100 | 130 | .769 | 342 | 411 | 460 | 9.8 | 11.7 | 13.1 |
| 84-85—North Carolina State | 33 | 973 | 94 | 207 | .454 | 64 | 95 | .674 | 189 | 169 | 252 | 5.7 | 5.1 | 7.6 |
| 85-86—North Carolina State | 34 | 1208 | 127 | 262 | .485 | 66 | 90 | .733 | 155 | 233 | 320 | 4.6 | 6.9 | 9.4 |
| Junior College Totals | 62 | ... | 281 | 505 | .556 | 164 | 222 | .739 | 476 | 602 | 726 | 7.7 | 9.7 | 11.7 |
| 4-Year-College Totals | 67 | 2181 | 221 | 469 | .471 | 130 | 185 | .703 | 344 | 402 | 572 | 5.1 | 6.0 | 8.5 |

## NBA REGULAR-SEASON RECORD

**RECORDS:** Shares single-game record for most assists by a rookie—25 (February 23, 1987, vs. Los Angeles Clippers).
**HONORS:** NBA All-Defensive second team (1994, 1995).
**NOTES:** Led NBA with 2.96 steals per game (1994).

| Season Team | G | Min. | FGM | FGA | Pct. | FTM | FTA | Pct. | Off. | Def. | Tot. | Ast. | St. | Blk. | TO | Pts. | RPG | APG | PPG |
|---|---|---|---|---|---|---|---|---|---|---|---|---|---|---|---|---|---|---|---|
| 86-87—Seattle.......... | 71 | 1972 | 143 | 301 | .475 | 87 | 141 | .617 | 101 | 230 | 331 | 583 | 125 | 45 | 155 | 373 | 4.7 | 8.2 | 5.3 |
| 87-88—Seattle.......... | 82 | 2453 | 235 | 496 | .474 | 145 | 205 | .707 | 117 | 221 | 338 | 702 | 169 | 47 | 189 | 624 | 4.1 | 8.6 | 7.6 |
| 88-89—Seattle.......... | 75 | 2341 | 199 | 485 | .410 | 119 | 189 | .630 | 143 | 245 | 388 | 696 | 156 | 42 | 211 | 532 | 5.2 | 9.3 | 7.1 |
| 89-90—Seattle.......... | 82 | 2338 | 207 | 438 | .473 | 98 | 153 | .641 | 127 | 276 | 403 | 598 | 140 | 37 | 187 | 523 | 4.9 | 7.3 | 6.4 |
| 90-91—Seattle.......... | 78 | 1434 | 132 | 305 | .433 | 57 | 93 | .613 | 71 | 180 | 251 | 371 | 104 | 20 | 122 | 338 | 3.2 | 4.8 | 4.3 |
| 91-92—Seattle.......... | 72 | 1652 | 177 | 405 | .437 | 54 | 84 | .643 | 92 | 160 | 252 | 359 | 129 | 29 | 112 | 435 | 3.5 | 5.0 | 6.0 |
| 92-93—Seattle.......... | 73 | 1977 | 213 | 459 | .464 | 95 | 134 | .709 | 84 | 222 | 306 | 384 | 173 | 33 | 139 | 546 | 4.2 | 5.3 | 7.5 |
| 93-94—Seattle.......... | 73 | 1887 | 177 | 396 | .447 | 31 | 55 | .564 | 50 | 233 | 283 | 387 | *216 | 22 | 126 | 437 | 3.9 | 5.3 | 6.0 |
| 94-95—Seattle.......... | 80 | 2070 | 166 | 397 | .418 | 34 | 58 | .586 | 65 | 237 | 302 | 421 | 165 | 53 | 126 | 419 | 3.8 | 5.3 | 5.2 |
| 95-96—Seattle.......... | 55 | 1261 | 100 | 238 | .420 | 29 | 41 | .707 | 41 | 169 | 210 | 197 | 95 | 18 | 75 | 275 | 3.8 | 3.6 | 5.0 |
| 96-97—Seattle.......... | 37 | 798 | 61 | 149 | .409 | 19 | 29 | .655 | 15 | 103 | 118 | 140 | 58 | 6 | 32 | 169 | 3.2 | 3.8 | 4.6 |
| 97-98—Seattle.......... | 18 | 279 | 23 | 67 | .343 | 1 | 1 | 1.000 | 1 | 27 | 40 | 55 | 14 | 4 | 12 | 62 | 2.2 | 3.1 | 3.4 |
| Totals ................. | 796 | 20462 | 1833 | 4136 | .443 | 769 | 1183 | .650 | 919 | 2303 | 3222 | 4893 | 1544 | 356 | 1486 | 4733 | 4.0 | 6.1 | 5.9 |

Three-point field goals: 1986-87, 0-for-7. 1987-88, 9-for-24 (.375). 1988-89, 15-for-70 (.214). 1989-90, 11-for-31 (.355). 1990-91, 17-for-48 (.354). 1991-92, 27-for-98 (.276). 1992-93, 25-for-65 (.385). 1993-94, 52-for-133 (.391). 1994-95, 53-for-155 (.342). 1995-96, 46-for-121 (.380). 1996-97, 28-for-84 (.333). 1997-98, 15-for-34 (.441). Totals, 298-for-870 (.343).

Personal fouls/disqualifications: 1986-87, 238/4. 1987-88, 238/1. 1988-89, 236/3. 1989-90, 289/7. 1990-91, 211/6. 1991-92, 218/4. 1992-93, 240/6. 1993-94, 201/1. 1994-95, 275/8. 1995-96, 143/3. 1996-97, 78/0. 1997-98, 41/0. Totals, 2408/43.

## NBA PLAYOFF RECORD

| Season Team | G | Min. | FGM | FGA | Pct. | FTM | FTA | Pct. | Off. | Def. | Tot. | Ast. | St. | Blk. | TO | Pts. | RPG | APG | PPG |
|---|---|---|---|---|---|---|---|---|---|---|---|---|---|---|---|---|---|---|---|
| 86-87—Seattle.......... | 14 | 356 | 27 | 62 | .435 | 17 | 24 | .708 | 13 | 41 | 54 | 112 | 14 | 10 | 26 | 71 | 3.9 | 8.0 | 5.1 |
| 87-88—Seattle.......... | 5 | 127 | 12 | 35 | .343 | 9 | 14 | .643 | 6 | 15 | 21 | 33 | 2 | 3 | 8 | 33 | 4.2 | 6.6 | 6.6 |
| 88-89—Seattle.......... | 8 | 200 | 19 | 40 | .475 | 16 | 25 | .640 | 9 | 16 | 25 | 63 | 10 | 5 | 19 | 54 | 3.1 | 7.9 | 6.8 |
| 90-91—Seattle.......... | 5 | 95 | 6 | 23 | .261 | 2 | 4 | .500 | 6 | 12 | 18 | 22 | 6 | 1 | 3 | 14 | 3.6 | 4.4 | 2.8 |
| 91-92—Seattle.......... | 9 | 246 | 35 | 83 | .422 | 10 | 14 | .714 | 14 | 19 | 33 | 63 | 16 | 3 | 22 | 86 | 3.7 | 7.0 | 9.6 |
| 92-93—Seattle.......... | 19 | 415 | 35 | 103 | .340 | 16 | 30 | .533 | 21 | 46 | 67 | 103 | 40 | 11 | 25 | 91 | 3.5 | 5.4 | 4.8 |
| 93-94—Seattle.......... | 5 | 109 | 8 | 25 | .320 | 1 | 4 | .250 | 6 | 10 | 16 | 10 | 6 | 1 | 5 | 21 | 3.2 | 2.0 | 4.2 |
| 94-95—Seattle.......... | 4 | 113 | 8 | 23 | .348 | 2 | 2 | 1.000 | 7 | 11 | 18 | 29 | 10 | 2 | 7 | 19 | 4.5 | 7.3 | 4.8 |
| 95-96—Seattle.......... | 19 | 385 | 28 | 69 | .406 | 9 | 14 | .643 | 13 | 57 | 70 | 52 | 23 | 5 | 20 | 84 | 3.7 | 2.7 | 4.4 |
| 96-97—Seattle.......... | 3 | 41 | 0 | 2 | .000 | 0 | 0 | ... | 1 | 4 | 5 | 3 | 1 | 0 | 2 | 0 | 1.7 | 1.0 | 0.0 |
| 97-98—Seattle.......... | 7 | 99 | 6 | 18 | .333 | 2 | 2 | 1.000 | 2 | 14 | 16 | 15 | 3 | 2 | 2 | 16 | 2.3 | 2.1 | 2.3 |
| Totals ................. | 98 | 2186 | 184 | 483 | .381 | 84 | 133 | .632 | 98 | 245 | 343 | 505 | 131 | 43 | 139 | 489 | 3.5 | 5.2 | 5.0 |

Three-point field goals: 1987-88, 0-for-1. 1988-89, 0-for-2. 1990-91, 0-for-2. 1991-92, 6-for-26 (.231). 1992-93, 5-for-24 (.208). 1993-94, 4-for-11 (.364). 1994-95, 1-for-8 (.125). 1995-96, 19-for-40 (.475). 1996-97, 0-for-2. 1997-98, 2-for-12 (.167). Totals, 37-for-128 (.289).

Personal fouls/disqualifications: 1986-87, 42/1. 1987-88, 11/0. 1988-89, 21/0. 1990-91, 15/0. 1991-92, 35/1. 1992-93, 54/2. 1993-94, 18/1. 1994-95, 13/0. 1995-96, 34/0. 1996-97, 11/0. 1997-98, 17/0. Totals, 271/5.

## HEAD COACHING RECORD

**NOTES:** Assistant coach, SuperSonics (1998-99 through November 27, 2000).

## NBA COACHING RECORD

| Season Team | REGULAR SEASON | | | | PLAYOFFS | | |
|---|---|---|---|---|---|---|---|
| | W | L | Pct. | Finish | W | L | Pct. |
| 00-01—Seattle................................ | 38 | 29 | .567 | 5th Pacific Division | — | — | — |
| 01-02—Seattle................................ | 45 | 37 | .549 | 4th/Pacific Division | 2 | 3 | .400 |
| 02-03—Seattle................................ | 40 | 42 | .488 | 5th/Pacific Division | — | — | — |
| 03-04—Seattle................................ | 37 | 45 | .451 | 5th/Pacific Division | — | — | — |
| 04-05—Seattle................................ | 52 | 30 | .634 | 1st/Northwest Division | 6 | 5 | .545 |
| Totals (5 years)............................ | 212 | 183 | .537 | | | | |
| | | | | Totals (2 years)....... | 8 | 8 | .500 |

**NOTES:**

2001—Replaced Paul Westphal as Seattle head coach (November 27), with record of 6-9 and club in fifth place.
2002—Lost to San Antonio, 3-2, in Western Conference first round.
2005—Defeated Sacramento, 4-1, in Western Conference first round; lost to San Antonio, 4-2, in Western Conference semifinals.

---

# MITCHELL, SAM — RAPTORS

**PERSONAL:** Born September 2, 1963, in Columbus, Ga. ... 6-7/215. (2,01/97,5). ... Full Name: Samuel E. Mitchell Jr.
**HIGH SCHOOL:** Columbus (Ga.).
**COLLEGE:** Mercer (Ga.).
**TRANSACTIONS/CAREER NOTES:** Selected by Houston Rockets in third round (54th pick overall) of 1985 NBA Draft. ... Waived by Rockets (October 22, 1985). ... Played in Continental Basketball Association with Wisconsin Flyers (1985-86 and 1986-87) and Rapid City Thrillers (1986-87). ... Played in United States Basketball League with Tampa Bay Flash (1986). ... Signed as free agent by Rockets (October 7, 1986). ... Waived by Rockets (October 28, 1986). ... Played in France (1987-88 and 1988-89). ... Signed as free agent by Minnesota Timberwolves (July 23, 1989). ... Traded by Timberwolves with G Pooh Richardson to Indiana Pacers for F Chuck Person and G Micheal Williams (September 8, 1992). ... Signed as unrestricted free agent by Timberwolves (September 29, 1995).

## COLLEGIATE RECORD

| Season Team | G | Min. | FGM | FGA | Pct. | FTM | FTA | Pct. | Reb. | Ast. | Pts. | RPG | APG | PPG |
|---|---|---|---|---|---|---|---|---|---|---|---|---|---|---|
| 81-82—Mercer.............. | 27 | ... | 77 | 155 | .497 | 38 | 53 | .717 | 100 | 13 | 192 | 3.7 | 0.5 | 7.1 |
| 82-83—Mercer.............. | 28 | 964 | 178 | 343 | .519 | 105 | 134 | .784 | 164 | 47 | 461 | 5.9 | 1.7 | 16.5 |
| 83-84—Mercer.............. | 26 | 935 | 219 | 432 | .507 | 121 | 155 | .781 | 184 | 46 | 559 | 7.1 | 1.8 | 21.5 |
| 84-85—Mercer.............. | 31 | 1157 | 294 | 570 | .516 | 186 | 248 | .750 | 255 | 43 | 774 | 8.2 | 1.4 | 25.0 |
| Totals ................. | 112 | ... | 768 | 1500 | .512 | 450 | 590 | .763 | 703 | 149 | 1986 | 6.3 | 1.3 | 17.7 |

## CBA REGULAR-SEASON RECORD

| Season Team | G | Min. | FGM | FGA | Pct. | FTM | FTA | Pct. | Reb. | Ast. | Pts. | AVERAGES RPG | APG | PPG |
|---|---|---|---|---|---|---|---|---|---|---|---|---|---|---|
| 85-86—Wisconsin | 13 | 450 | 107 | 238 | .450 | 55 | 83 | .663 | 95 | 16 | 270 | 7.3 | 1.2 | 20.8 |
| 86-87—Wisconsin-Rapid City | 42 | 1370 | 253 | 554 | .457 | 154 | 210 | .733 | 256 | 31 | 663 | 6.1 | 0.7 | 15.8 |
| **Totals** | 55 | 1820 | 360 | 792 | .455 | 209 | 293 | .713 | 351 | 47 | 933 | 6.4 | 0.9 | 17.0 |

Three-point field goals: 1985-86, 1-for-3 (.333). 1986-87, 3-for-12 (.250). Totals, 4-for-15 (.267).

## NBA REGULAR-SEASON RECORD

**NOTES:** Led NBA with 338 personal fouls (1991).

| Season Team | G | Min. | FGM | FGA | Pct. | FTM | FTA | Pct. | Off. | Def. | Tot. | Ast. | St. | Blk. | TO | Pts. | RPG | APG | PPG |
|---|---|---|---|---|---|---|---|---|---|---|---|---|---|---|---|---|---|---|---|
| 89-90—Minnesota | 80 | 2414 | 372 | 834 | .446 | 268 | 349 | .768 | 180 | 282 | 462 | 89 | 66 | 54 | 96 | 1012 | 5.8 | 1.1 | 12.7 |
| 90-91—Minnesota | 82 | 3121 | 445 | 1010 | .441 | 307 | 396 | .775 | 188 | 332 | 520 | 133 | 66 | 57 | 104 | 1197 | 6.3 | 1.6 | 14.6 |
| 91-92—Minnesota | 82 | 2151 | 307 | 725 | .423 | 209 | 266 | .786 | 158 | 315 | 473 | 94 | 53 | 39 | 97 | 825 | 5.8 | 1.1 | 10.1 |
| 92-93—Indiana | 81 | 1402 | 215 | 483 | .445 | 150 | 185 | .811 | 93 | 155 | 248 | 76 | 23 | 10 | 51 | 584 | 3.1 | 0.9 | 7.2 |
| 93-94—Indiana | 75 | 1084 | 140 | 306 | .458 | 82 | 110 | .745 | 71 | 119 | 190 | 65 | 33 | 9 | 50 | 362 | 2.5 | 0.9 | 4.8 |
| 94-95—Indiana | 81 | 1377 | 201 | 413 | .487 | 126 | 174 | .724 | 95 | 148 | 243 | 61 | 43 | 20 | 54 | 529 | 3.0 | 0.8 | 6.5 |
| 95-96—Minnesota | 78 | 2145 | 303 | 618 | .490 | 237 | 291 | .814 | 107 | 232 | 339 | 74 | 49 | 26 | 87 | 844 | 4.3 | 0.9 | 10.8 |
| 96-97—Minnesota | 82 | 2044 | 269 | 603 | .446 | 224 | 295 | .759 | 112 | 214 | 326 | 79 | 51 | 20 | 93 | 766 | 4.0 | 1.0 | 9.3 |
| 97-98—Minnesota | 81 | 2239 | 371 | 800 | .464 | 243 | 292 | .832 | 118 | 267 | 385 | 107 | 64 | 22 | 66 | 1000 | 4.8 | 1.3 | 12.3 |
| 98-99—Minnesota | 50 | 1344 | 213 | 522 | .408 | 126 | 165 | .764 | 55 | 127 | 182 | 98 | 35 | 16 | 34 | 561 | 3.6 | 2.0 | 11.2 |
| 99-00—Minnesota | 66 | 1227 | 168 | 376 | .447 | 81 | 92 | .880 | 28 | 110 | 138 | 111 | 27 | 14 | 44 | 427 | 2.1 | 1.7 | 6.5 |
| 00-01—Minnesota | 82 | 983 | 118 | 289 | .408 | 40 | 55 | .727 | 28 | 95 | 123 | 57 | 26 | 10 | 36 | 285 | 1.5 | 0.7 | 3.5 |
| 01-02—Minnesota | 74 | 726 | 98 | 227 | .432 | 38 | 49 | .776 | 18 | 64 | 82 | 45 | 12 | 4 | 26 | 244 | 1.1 | 0.6 | 3.3 |
| **Totals** | 994 | 22257 | 3220 | 7206 | .447 | 2131 | 2719 | .784 | 1251 | 2460 | 3711 | 1089 | 548 | 301 | 838 | 8636 | 3.7 | 1.1 | 8.7 |

Three-point field goals: 1989-90, 0-for-9. 1990-91, 0-for-9. 1991-92, 2-for-11 (.182). 1992-93, 4-for-23 (.174). 1993-94, 0-for-5. 1994-95, 1-for-10 (.100). 1995-96, 1-for-18 (.056). 1996-97, 4-for-25 (.160). 1997-98, 15-for-43 (.349). 1998-99, 9-for-38 (.237). 1999-00, 10-for-23 (.435). 2000-01, 9-for-43 (.209). 2001-02, 10-for-35 (.286). Totals, 65-for-292 (.223).

Personal fouls/disqualifications: 1989-90, 301/7. 1990-91, 338/13. 1991-92, 230/3. 1992-93, 207/1. 1993-94, 152/1. 1994-95, 206/0. 1995-96, 220/3. 1996-97, 232/1. 1997-98, 200/0. 1998-99, 111/1. 1999-00, 116/0. 2000-01, 117/0. 2001-02, 79/0. Totals, 2509/30.

## NBA PLAYOFF RECORD

| Season Team | G | Min. | FGM | FGA | Pct. | FTM | FTA | Pct. | Off. | Def. | Tot. | Ast. | St. | Blk. | TO | Pts. | RPG | APG | PPG |
|---|---|---|---|---|---|---|---|---|---|---|---|---|---|---|---|---|---|---|---|
| 92-93—Indiana | 4 | 25 | 5 | 8 | .625 | 2 | 2 | 1.000 | 0 | 1 | 1 | 0 | 0 | 0 | 2 | 12 | 0.3 | 0.0 | 3.0 |
| 93-94—Indiana | 15 | 99 | 9 | 26 | .346 | 3 | 4 | .750 | 5 | 12 | 17 | 5 | 2 | 2 | 4 | 21 | 1.1 | 0.3 | 1.4 |
| 94-95—Indiana | 17 | 223 | 23 | 64 | .359 | 22 | 28 | .786 | 17 | 31 | 48 | 6 | 3 | 1 | 14 | 68 | 2.8 | 0.4 | 4.0 |
| 96-97—Minnesota | 3 | 47 | 6 | 13 | .462 | 5 | 8 | .625 | 2 | 5 | 7 | 1 | 1 | 1 | 1 | 17 | 2.3 | 0.3 | 5.7 |
| 97-98—Minnesota | 5 | 177 | 26 | 58 | .448 | 17 | 19 | .895 | 7 | 20 | 27 | 8 | 1 | 1 | 5 | 72 | 5.4 | 1.6 | 14.4 |
| 98-99—Minnesota | 4 | 131 | 15 | 40 | .375 | 9 | 12 | .750 | 5 | 9 | 14 | 6 | 1 | 2 | 8 | 40 | 3.5 | 1.5 | 10.0 |
| 99-00—Minnesota | 4 | 68 | 9 | 18 | .500 | 3 | 3 | 1.000 | 2 | 5 | 7 | 2 | 0 | 1 | 4 | 23 | 1.8 | 0.5 | 5.8 |
| 00-01—Minnesota | 4 | 50 | 2 | 10 | .200 | 2 | 2 | 1.000 | 1 | 6 | 7 | 3 | 1 | 0 | 1 | 6 | 1.8 | 0.8 | 1.5 |
| 01-02—Minnesota | 3 | 34 | 3 | 9 | .333 | 2 | 2 | 1.000 | 0 | 2 | 2 | 3 | 1 | 1 | 0 | 8 | 0.7 | 1.0 | 2.7 |
| **Totals** | 52 | 770 | 93 | 227 | .410 | 61 | 76 | .803 | 38 | 83 | 121 | 28 | 8 | 8 | 38 | 253 | 2.3 | 0.5 | 4.9 |

Three-point field goals: 1993-94, 0-for-1. 1994-95, 0-for-2. 1997-98, 3-for-14 (.214). 1998-99, 1-for-6 (.167). 1999-00, 2-for-5 (.400). 2000-01, 0-for-1. Totals, 6-for-29 (.207).

Personal fouls/disqualifications: 1992-93, 4/0. 1993-94, 22/0. 1994-95, 41/0. 1996-97, 9/0. 1997-98, 18/0. 1998-99, 13/0. 1999-00, 5/0. 2000-01, 5/0. 2001-02, 5/0. Totals, 122/0.

## HEAD COACHING RECORD

**NOTES:** Assistant coach, Bucks (2002-03 through 2003-04).

### NBA COACHING RECORD

| | | | REGULAR SEASON | | | PLAYOFFS | | |
|---|---|---|---|---|---|---|---|---|
| Season Team | W | L | Pct. | Finish | | W | L | Pct. |
| 04-05—Toronto | 33 | 49 | .402 | 4th/Atlantic Division | | — | — | — |

# MONTGOMERY, MIKE      WARRIORS

**PERSONAL:** Born February 27, 1947, in Long Beach, Calif. ... Full name: Mike John Montgomery.
**HIGH SCHOOL:** Millikan (Long Beach, Calif.)
**COLLEGE:** Long Beach State.
**CAREER HONORS:** John R. Wooden "Legends of Coaching" Lifetime Achievement Award (2004).
**MISCELLANEOUS:** Assistant coach, U.S. men's basketball team (2002) ... Head coach, USA men's 22-and-Under Select team (1996). ... Assistant coach, U.S. junior men's basketball team (1994).

## COLLEGIATE RECORD

| Season Team | G | Min. | FGM | FGA | Pct. | FTM | FTA | Pct. | Reb. | Ast. | Pts. | AVERAGES RPG | APG | PPG |
|---|---|---|---|---|---|---|---|---|---|---|---|---|---|---|
| 64-65—Long Beach State | | | | | | Statistics Unavailable. | | | | | | | | |
| 65-66—Long Beach State | 5 | ... | 2 | 9 | .222 | 3 | 4 | .750 | 2 | ... | 7 | 0.4 | ... | 1.4 |
| 66-67—Long Beach State | | | | | | Did not play. | | | | | | | | |
| 67-68—Long Beach State | 25 | ... | 81 | 91 | .424 | 82 | 124 | .660 | 52 | ... | 224 | 2.1 | ... | 9.8 |
| **Totals** | 30 | ... | 83 | 200 | .415 | 85 | 128 | .781 | 54 | ... | 231 | 1.8 | ... | 7.7 |

## COLLEGIATE COACHING RECORD

**BACKGROUND:** Assistant coach, Boise State (1975-76 through 1977-1978).
**HONORS:** Pac-10 Coach of the Year (1999, 2000, 2003, 2004) ... Naismith Coach of the Year (2000) ... John & Nellie Wooden Award winner (2001).

| Season Team | W | L | Pct. | Finish |
|---|---|---|---|---|
| 78-79—Montana | 14 | 13 | .519 | 4th/Big Sky Conference |
| 79-80—Montana | 17 | 11 | .607 | 3rd/Big Sky Conference |

| Season Team | W | L | Pct. | Finish |
|---|---|---|---|---|
| 80-81—Montana | 19 | 9 | .679 | 2nd/Big Sky Conference |
| 81-82—Montana | 17 | 10 | .630 | 2nd/Big Sky Conference |
| 82-83—Montana | 21 | 8 | .724 | 3rd/Big Sky Conference |
| 83-84—Montana | 23 | 7 | .767 | 2ndt/Big Sky Conference |
| 84-85—Montana | 22 | 8 | .733 | 2nd/Big Sky Conference |
| 85-86—Montana | 21 | 11 | .656 | 2nd/Big Sky Conference |
| 86-87—Stanford | 15 | 13 | .536 | 6th/Pacific-10 Conference |
| 87-88—Stanford | 21 | 12 | .636 | 4th/Pacific-10 Conference |
| 88-89—Stanford | 26 | 7 | .788 | 2nd/Pacific-10 Conference |
| 89-90—Stanford | 18 | 12 | .600 | 6th/Pacific-10 Conference |
| 90-91—Stanford | 20 | 13 | .606 | 5th/Pacific-10 Conference |
| 91-92—Stanford | 18 | 11 | .621 | 4th/Pacific-10 Conference |
| 92-93—Stanford | 7 | 23 | .233 | 10th/Pacific-10 Conference |
| 93-94—Stanford | 17 | 11 | .607 | 5th/Pacific-10 Conference |
| 94-95—Stanford | 20 | 9 | .690 | 5th/Pacific-10 Conference |
| 95-96—Stanford | 21 | 8 | .724 | 3rd/Pacific-10 Conference |
| 96-97—Stanford | 22 | 8 | .733 | T2nd/Pacific-10 Conference |
| 97-98—Stanford | 30 | 5 | .857 | 2nd/Pacific-10 Conference |
| 98-99—Stanford | 26 | 7 | .789 | 1st/Pacific-10 Conference |
| 99-00—Stanford | 27 | 4 | .871 | T1st/Pacific-10 Conference |
| 00-01—Stanford | 31 | 3 | .912 | 1st/Pacific-10 Conference |
| 01-02—Stanford | 20 | 10 | .667 | T2nd/Pacific-10 Conference |
| 02-03—Stanford | 24 | 9 | .727 | 2nd/Pacific-10 Conference |
| 03-04—Stanford | 30 | 2 | .934 | 1st/Pacific-10 Conference |
| Totals (26 years) | 547 | 244 | .692 | |

**NOTES:**

1985—Lost to UCLA in NIT first round.

1986—Lost to Texas Christian in NIT first round.

1988—Defeated Long Beach State in NIT first round; lost to Arkansas State in second round

1989—Lost to Siena College in NCAA Tournament first round.

1990—Lost to Hawaii in NIT first round.

1991—Defeated Houston in NIT first round; defeated Wisconsin in second round; defeated Southern Illinois in third round; defeated Massachusetts in semi finals; defeated Oklahoma in title game.

1992—Lost to Alabama in NCAA Tournament first round.

1994—Lost to Gonzaga in NIT first round.

1995—Defeated UNC-Charlotte in NCAA Tournament first round; lost to Massachusetts in second round.

1996—Defeated Bradley in NCAA Tournament first round; lost to Massachusetts in second round.

1997—Defeated Oklahoma in NCAA Tournament first round; defeated Wake Forest in second round; lost to Utah in regional semifinals

1998—Defeated College of Charleston in NCAA Tournament first round; defeated Western Michigan in second round; defeated Purdue in regional semifinals; defeated Rhode Island in regional final; lost to Kentucky in Final Four.

1999—Defeated Alcorn State in NCAA Tournament first round; lost to Gonzaga in second round.

2000—Defeated South Carolina State in NCAA Tournament first round; lost to North Carolina in second round.

2001—Defeated UNC-Greensboro in NCAA Tournament first round; defeated Saint Joseph's in second round; defeated Cincinnati in regional semifinals; lost to Maryland in regional final.

2002—Defeated Western Kentucky in NCAA Tournament first round; lost to Kansas in second round.

2003—Defeated San Diego in NCAA Tournament first round; lost to Connecticut in second round.

2004—Defeated Texas-San Antonio in NCAA Tournament first round; lost to Alabama in second round.

### NBA COACHING RECORD

| Season Team | REGULAR SEASON | | | | PLAYOFFS | | |
|---|---|---|---|---|---|---|---|
| | W | L | Pct. | Finish | W | L | Pct. |
| 04-05—Golden State | 34 | 48 | .415 | 5th/Pacific Division | — | — | — |

## POPOVICH, GREGG                    SPURS

**PERSONAL:** Born January 28, 1949, in East Chicago, Ind. ... 6-2/200. (1,88/90,7). ... Full name: Gregg Charles Popovich.
**HIGH SCHOOL:** Merrilville (Ind.).
**COLLEGE:** Air Force, Denver (master's degree).
**CAREER NOTES:** Executive vice president of basketball operations/general manager, Spurs (1994-95 to present).

### COLLEGIATE RECORD

| Season Team | G | Min. | FGM | FGA | Pct. | FTM | FTA | Pct. | Reb. | Ast. | Pts. | RPG | APG | PPG |
|---|---|---|---|---|---|---|---|---|---|---|---|---|---|---|
| 66-67—Air Force | | | | Freshman statistics unavailable | | | | | | | | | | |
| 67-68—Air Force | | | | Junior-varsity statistics unavailable | | | | | | | | | | |
| 68-69—Air Force | 19 | ... | 38 | 79 | .481 | 26 | 40 | .650 | 36 | ... | 102 | 1.9 | ... | 5.4 |
| 69-70—Air Force | 24 | ... | 132 | 236 | .559 | 78 | 98 | .796 | 109 | ... | 342 | 4.5 | ... | 14.3 |
| Varsity totals | 43 | ... | 170 | 315 | .540 | 104 | 138 | .754 | 145 | ... | 444 | 3.4 | ... | 10.3 |

### COLLEGIATE COACHING RECORD

| Season Team | W | L | Pct. | Finish |
|---|---|---|---|---|
| 79-80—Pomona-Pitzer | 2 | 22 | .083 | T6th/Southern California I.A.C. |
| 80-81—Pomona-Pitzer | 10 | 15 | .400 | 6th/Southern California I.A.C. |
| 81-82—Pomona-Pitzer | 9 | 17 | .346 | 4th/Southern California I.A.C. |

| Season Team | W | L | Pct. | Finish |
|---|---|---|---|---|
| 82-83—Pomona-Pitzer | 12 | 13 | .480 | 5th/Southern California I.A.C. |
| 83-84—Pomona-Pitzer | 9 | 17 | .346 | T4th/Southern California I.A.C. |
| 84-85—Pomona-Pitzer | 11 | 14 | .440 | 4th/Southern California I.A.C. |
| 85-86—Pomona-Pitzer | 16 | 12 | .571 | 1st/Southern California I.A.C. |
| Totals (7 years) | 69 | 110 | .385 | |

## NBA COACHING RECORD

**BACKGROUND:** Assistant coach, Air Force (1972-73 through 1977-78). ... Assistant coach, San Antonio Spurs (1988-89 through 1991-92). ... Assistant coach, Golden State Warriors (1992-93 and 1993-94).

**HONORS:** NBA Coach of the Year (2003).

| Season Team | REGULAR SEASON | | | | PLAYOFFS | | |
|---|---|---|---|---|---|---|---|
| | W | L | Pct. | Finish | W | L | Pct. |
| 96-97—San Antonio | 17 | 47 | .266 | 6th/Midwest Division | — | — | — |
| 97-98—San Antonio | 56 | 26 | .683 | 2nd/Midwest Division | 4 | 5 | .444 |
| 98-99—San Antonio | 37 | 13 | .740 | T1st/Midwest Division | 15 | 2 | .882 |
| 99-00—San Antonio | 53 | 29 | .646 | 2nd/Midwest Division | 1 | 3 | .250 |
| 00-01—San Antonio | 58 | 24 | .707 | 1st/Midwest Division | 7 | 6 | .539 |
| 01-02—San Antonio | 58 | 24 | .707 | 1st/Midwest Division | 4 | 6 | .400 |
| 02-03—San Antonio | 60 | 22 | .732 | 1st/Midwest Division | 16 | 8 | .666 |
| 03-04—San Antonio | 57 | 25 | .695 | 2nd/Midwest Division | 6 | 4 | .600 |
| 04-05—San Antonio | 59 | 23 | .720 | 1st/Southwest Division | 16 | 7 | .696 |
| Totals (9 years) | 455 | 233 | .661 | Totals (8 years) | 69 | 41 | .627 |

**NOTES:**

1996—Replaced Bob Hill as San Antonio head coach (December 10), with record of 3-15 and club in seventh place.

1998—Defeated Phoenix, 3-1, in Western Conference first round; lost to Utah, 4-1, in Western Conference semifinals.

1999—Defeated Minnesota, 3-1, in Western Conference first round; defeated Los Angeles Lakers, 4-0, in Western Conference semifinals; defeated Portland, 4-0, in Western Conference finals; defeated New York, 4-1, in NBA Finals.

2000—Lost to Phoenix in Western Conference first round.

2001—Defeated Minnesota, 3-1, in Western Conference first round; defeated Dallas, 4-1, in Western Conference semifinals; lost to Los Angeles Lakers, 4-0, in Western Conference finals.

2002—Defeated Seattle, 3-2, in Western Conference first round; lost to Los Angeles Lakers, 4-1, in Western Conference semifinals.

2003—Defeated Phoenix, 4-2, in Western Conference first round; defeated Los Angeles Lakers, 4-2, in Western Conference semifinals; defeated Dallas, 4-2, in Western Conference finals; defeated New Jersey, 4-2, in NBA Finals.

2004—Defeated Memphis, 4-0, in Western Conference first round; lost to Los Angeles Lakers, 4-2, in Western Conference semifinals.

2005—Defeated Denver, 4-1, in Western Conference first round; defeated Seattle, 4-2, in Western Conference semifinals; defeated Phoenix, 4-1, in Western Conference finals; defeated Detroit, 4-3, in NBA Finals.

# RIVERS, DOC          CELTICS

**PERSONAL:** Born October 13, 1961, in Chicago. ... 6-4/210. (1,93/95,3). ... Full name: Glenn Anton Rivers. ... Nephew of Jim Brewer, forward with Cleveland Cavaliers, Detroit Pistons, Portland Trail Blazers and Los Angeles Lakers (1973-74 through 1981-82); cousin of Byron Irvin, guard with Portland Trail Blazers and Washington Bullets (1989-90, 1990-91 and 1992-93); and cousin of Ken Singleton, outfielder/designated hitter with New York Mets, Montreal Expos and Baltimore Orioles (1970 through 1984).

**HIGH SCHOOL:** Proviso East (Maywood, Ill.).

**COLLEGE:** Marquette.

**TRANSACTIONS:** Selected after junior season by Atlanta Hawks in second round (31st pick overall) of 1983 NBA Draft. ... Traded by Hawks to Los Angeles Clippers for 1991 first-round draft choice and 1993 and 1994 second-round draft choices (June 26, 1991). ... Traded by Clippers with C/F Charles Smith and G Bo Kimble to New York Knicks in three-way deal in which Clippers received G Mark Jackson and 1995 second-round draft choice from Knicks and C Stanley Roberts from Orlando Magic and Magic received 1993 first-round draft choice from Knicks and 1994 first-round draft choice from Clippers (September 22, 1992). ... Waived by Knicks (December 15, 1994). ... Signed as free agent by San Antonio Spurs (December 26, 1994). ... Announced retirement (July 11, 1996).

**CAREER NOTES:** Broadcaster, Turner Sports (1998-99). ...Broadcaster, ABC Sports (2003-04).

**MISCELLANEOUS:** Member of silver-medal-winning U.S. World Championship team (1982). ... Atlanta Hawks franchise all-time assists leader with 3,866 (1983-84 through 1990-91).

## COLLEGIATE RECORD

| Season Team | G | Min. | FGM | FGA | Pct. | FTM | FTA | Pct. | Reb. | Ast. | Pts. | AVERAGES | | |
|---|---|---|---|---|---|---|---|---|---|---|---|---|---|---|
| | | | | | | | | | | | | RPG | APG | PPG |
| 80-81—Marquette | 31 | 921 | 182 | 329 | .553 | 70 | 119 | .588 | 99 | 113 | 434 | 3.2 | 3.6 | 14.0 |
| 81-82—Marquette | 29 | 987 | 173 | 382 | .453 | 70 | 108 | .648 | 99 | 170 | 416 | 3.4 | 5.9 | 14.3 |
| 82-83—Marquette | 29 | 1012 | 163 | 373 | .437 | 58 | 95 | .611 | 94 | 126 | 384 | 3.2 | 4.3 | 13.2 |
| Totals | 89 | 2920 | 518 | 1084 | .478 | 198 | 322 | .615 | 292 | 409 | 1234 | 3.3 | 4.6 | 13.9 |

## NBA REGULAR-SEASON RECORD

**HONORS:** J. Walter Kennedy Citizenship Award (1990).

| Season Team | G | Min. | FGM | FGA | Pct. | FTM | FTA | Pct. | REBOUNDS | | | Ast. | St. | Blk. | TO | Pts. | AVERAGES | | |
|---|---|---|---|---|---|---|---|---|---|---|---|---|---|---|---|---|---|---|---|
| | | | | | | | | | Off. | Def. | Tot. | | | | | | RPG | APG | PPG |
| 83-84—Atlanta | 81 | 1938 | 250 | 541 | .462 | 255 | 325 | .785 | 72 | 148 | 220 | 314 | 127 | 30 | 174 | 757 | 2.7 | 3.9 | 9.3 |
| 84-85—Atlanta | 69 | 2126 | 334 | 701 | .476 | 291 | 378 | .770 | 66 | 148 | 214 | 410 | 163 | 53 | 176 | 974 | 3.1 | 5.9 | 14.1 |
| 85-86—Atlanta | 53 | 1571 | 220 | 464 | .474 | 172 | 283 | .608 | 49 | 113 | 162 | 443 | 120 | 13 | 141 | 612 | 3.1 | 8.4 | 11.5 |
| 86-87—Atlanta | 82 | 2590 | 342 | 758 | .451 | 365 | 441 | .828 | 83 | 216 | 299 | 823 | 171 | 30 | 217 | 1053 | 3.6 | 10.0 | 12.8 |

| Season Team | G | Min. | FGM | FGA | Pct. | FTM | FTA | Pct. | Off. | Def. | Tot. | Ast. | St. | Blk. | TO | Pts. | RPG | APG | PPG |
|---|---|---|---|---|---|---|---|---|---|---|---|---|---|---|---|---|---|---|---|
| | | | | | | | | | REBOUNDS | | | | | | | | AVERAGES | | |
| 87-88—Atlanta ........... | 80 | 2502 | 403 | 890 | .453 | 319 | 421 | .758 | 83 | 283 | 366 | 747 | 140 | 41 | 210 | 1134 | 4.6 | 9.3 | 14.2 |
| 88-89—Atlanta ........... | 76 | 2462 | 371 | 816 | .455 | 247 | 287 | .861 | 89 | 197 | 286 | 525 | 181 | 40 | 158 | 1032 | 3.8 | 6.9 | 13.6 |
| 89-90—Atlanta ........... | 48 | 1526 | 218 | 480 | .454 | 138 | 170 | .812 | 47 | 153 | 200 | 264 | 116 | 22 | 98 | 598 | 4.2 | 5.5 | 12.5 |
| 90-91—Atlanta ........... | 79 | 2586 | 444 | 1020 | .435 | 221 | 262 | .844 | 47 | 206 | 253 | 340 | 148 | 47 | 125 | 1197 | 3.2 | 4.3 | 15.2 |
| 91-92—L.A. Clippers ... | 59 | 1657 | 226 | 533 | .424 | 163 | 196 | .832 | 23 | 124 | 147 | 233 | 111 | 19 | 92 | 641 | 2.5 | 3.9 | 10.9 |
| 92-93—New York ........ | 77 | 1886 | 216 | 494 | .437 | 133 | 162 | .821 | 26 | 166 | 192 | 405 | 123 | 9 | 114 | 604 | 2.5 | 5.3 | 7.8 |
| 93-94—New York ........ | 19 | 499 | 55 | 127 | .433 | 14 | 22 | .636 | 4 | 35 | 39 | 100 | 25 | 5 | 29 | 143 | 2.1 | 5.3 | 7.5 |
| 94-95—N.Y.-S.A. ........ | 63 | 989 | 108 | 302 | .358 | 60 | 82 | .732 | 15 | 94 | 109 | 162 | 65 | 21 | 60 | 321 | 1.7 | 2.6 | 5.1 |
| 95-96—San Antonio .... | 78 | 1235 | 108 | 290 | .372 | 48 | 64 | .750 | 30 | 108 | 138 | 123 | 73 | 21 | 57 | 311 | 1.8 | 1.6 | 4.0 |
| Totals ................... | 864 | 23567 | 3295 | 7416 | .444 | 2426 | 3093 | .784 | 634 | 1991 | 2625 | 4889 | 1563 | 351 | 1651 | 9377 | 3.0 | 5.7 | 10.9 |

Three-point field goals: 1983-84, 2-for-12 (.167). 1984-85, 15-for-36 (.417). 1985-86, 0-for-16. 1986-87, 4-for-21 (.190). 1987-88, 9-for-33 (.273). 1988-89, 43-for-124 (.347). 1989-90, 24-for-66 (.364). 1990-91, 88-for-262 (.336). 1991-92, 26-for-92 (.283). 1992-93, 39-for-123 (.317). 1993-94, 19-for-52 (.365). 1994-95, 45-for-127 (.354). 1995-96, 47-for-137 (.343). Totals, 361-for-1101 (.328).

Personal fouls/disqualifications: 1983-84, 286/8. 1984-85, 250/7. 1985-86, 185/2. 1986-87, 287/5. 1987-88, 272/3. 1988-89, 263/6. 1989-90, 151/2. 1990-91, 216/2. 1991-92, 166/2. 1992-93, 215/2. 1993-94, 64/0. 1994-95, 92/0. 1995-96, 175/0. Totals, 2660/41.

## NBA PLAYOFF RECORD

NOTES: Shares single-game playoff record for most assists in one half—15 (May 16, 1988, vs. Boston).

| Season Team | G | Min. | FGM | FGA | Pct. | FTM | FTA | Pct. | Off. | Def. | Tot. | Ast. | St. | Blk. | TO | Pts. | RPG | APG | PPG |
|---|---|---|---|---|---|---|---|---|---|---|---|---|---|---|---|---|---|---|---|
| | | | | | | | | | REBOUNDS | | | | | | | | AVERAGES | | |
| 83-84—Atlanta ........... | 5 | 130 | 16 | 32 | .500 | 36 | 41 | .878 | 7 | 3 | 10 | 16 | 12 | 4 | 9 | 68 | 2.0 | 3.2 | 13.6 |
| 85-86—Atlanta ........... | 9 | 262 | 40 | 92 | .435 | 31 | 42 | .738 | 10 | 32 | 42 | 78 | 18 | 0 | 26 | 114 | 4.7 | 8.7 | 12.7 |
| 86-87—Atlanta ........... | 8 | 245 | 18 | 47 | .383 | 26 | 52 | .500 | 6 | 21 | 27 | 90 | 9 | 3 | 25 | 62 | 3.4 | 11.3 | 7.8 |
| 87-88—Atlanta ........... | 12 | 409 | 71 | 139 | .511 | 39 | 43 | .907 | 8 | 51 | 59 | 115 | 25 | 2 | 25 | 188 | 4.9 | 9.6 | 15.7 |
| 88-89—Atlanta ........... | 5 | 191 | 22 | 57 | .386 | 17 | 24 | .708 | 4 | 20 | 24 | 34 | 7 | 2 | 12 | 67 | 4.8 | 6.8 | 13.4 |
| 90-91—Atlanta ........... | 5 | 173 | 30 | 64 | .469 | 17 | 19 | .895 | 6 | 14 | 20 | 15 | 5 | 2 | 4 | 78 | 4.0 | 3.0 | 15.6 |
| 91-92—L.A. Clippers ... | 5 | 187 | 25 | 56 | .446 | 22 | 27 | .815 | 4 | 15 | 19 | 21 | 6 | 0 | 3 | 76 | 3.8 | 4.2 | 15.2 |
| 92-93—New York ........ | 15 | 458 | 48 | 106 | .453 | 46 | 60 | .767 | 6 | 33 | 39 | 86 | 29 | 1 | 30 | 153 | 2.6 | 5.7 | 10.2 |
| 94-95—San Antonio .... | 15 | 318 | 37 | 95 | .389 | 26 | 31 | .839 | 3 | 26 | 29 | 24 | 14 | 9 | 18 | 117 | 1.9 | 1.6 | 7.8 |
| 95-96—San Antonio .... | 2 | 20 | 1 | 3 | .333 | 0 | 0 | ... | 0 | 1 | 1 | 0 | 0 | 0 | 1 | 3 | 0.5 | 0.0 | 1.5 |
| Totals ................... | 81 | 2393 | 308 | 691 | .446 | 260 | 339 | .767 | 54 | 216 | 270 | 479 | 125 | 23 | 153 | 926 | 3.3 | 5.9 | 11.4 |

Three-point field goals: 1983-84, 0-for-3. 1985-86, 3-for-6 (.500). 1987-88, 7-for-22 (.318). 1988-89, 6-for-19 (.316). 1990-91, 1-for-11 (.091). 1991-92, 4-for-8 (.500). 1992-93, 11-for-31 (.355). 1994-95, 17-for-46 (.370). 1995-96, 1-for-2 (.500). Totals, 50-for-148 (.338).

Personal fouls/disqualifications: 1983-84, 16/0. 1985-86, 38/2. 1986-87, 32/0. 1987-88, 40/1. 1988-89, 22/2. 1990-91, 14/0. 1991-92, 16/0. 1992-93, 44/0. 1994-95, 40/0. 1995-96, 3/0. Totals, 265/5.

## NBA ALL-STAR GAME RECORD

| Season Team | Min. | FGM | FGA | Pct. | FTM | FTA | Pct. | Off. | Def. | Tot. | Ast. | PF | Dq. | St. | Blk. | TO | Pts. |
|---|---|---|---|---|---|---|---|---|---|---|---|---|---|---|---|---|---|
| | | | | | | | | REBOUNDS | | | | | | | | | |
| 1988—Atlanta.................. | 16 | 2 | 4 | .500 | 5 | 11 | .455 | 0 | 3 | 3 | 6 | 3 | 0 | 0 | 0 | 3 | 9 |

## NBA COACHING RECORD

HONORS: NBA Coach of the Year (2000).

| Season Team | W | L | Pct. | Finish | W | L | Pct. |
|---|---|---|---|---|---|---|---|
| | REGULAR SEASON | | | | PLAYOFFS | | |
| 99-00—Orlando ....................................... | 41 | 41 | .500 | 4th/Atlantic Division | — | — | — |
| 00-01—Orlando ....................................... | 43 | 39 | .524 | 4th/Atlantic Division | 1 | 3 | .250 |
| 01-02—Orlando ....................................... | 44 | 38 | .537 | 3rd/Atlantic Division | 1 | 3 | .250 |
| 02-03—Orlando ....................................... | 42 | 40 | .512 | 4th/Atlantic Division | 3 | 4 | .429 |
| 03-04—Orlando ....................................... | 1 | 10 | .091 | | — | — | — |
| 04-05—Boston.......................................... | 45 | 37 | .549 | 1st/Atlantic Division | 3 | 4 | .429 |
| Totals (6 years)...................................... | 216 | 205 | .513 | Totals (4 years)....... | 8 | 14 | .364 |

NOTES:
2001—Lost to Milwaukee, 3-1, in Eastern Conference first round.
2002—Lost to Charlotte, 3-1, in Eastern Conference first round.
2003—Lost to Detroit, 4-3, in Eastern Conference first round; replaced as Orlando head coach by Johnny Davis (November 17) with club in seventh place.
2005—Lost to Indiana in Eastern Conference first round.

# SAUNDERS, FLIP — PISTONS

PERSONAL: Born February 23, 1955, in Cleveland. ... 5-11/175. (1,81/79,4). ... Full name: Philip D. Saunders.
HIGH SCHOOL: Cuyahoga Heights (Ohio).
COLLEGE: Minnesota.
CAREER NOTES: General manager, Minnesota Timberwolves (1994-95 to present).

## COLLEGIATE RECORD

| Season Team | G | Min. | FGM | FGA | Pct. | FTM | FTA | Pct. | Reb. | Ast. | Pts. | RPG | APG | PPG |
|---|---|---|---|---|---|---|---|---|---|---|---|---|---|---|
| | | | | | | | | | | | | AVERAGES | | |
| 73-74—Minnesota ..................... | 24 | ... | 93 | 209 | .445 | 53 | 61 | .869 | 93 | ... | 239 | 3.9 | ... | 9.9 |
| 74-75—Minnesota ..................... | 26 | ... | 67 | 154 | .435 | 54 | 74 | .730 | 74 | ... | 188 | 2.8 | ... | 7.2 |
| 75-76—Minnesota ..................... | 26 | ... | 99 | 209 | .474 | 47 | 55 | .854 | 95 | 95 | 245 | 3.8 | 3.7 | 9.4 |
| 76-77—Minnesota ..................... | 27 | ... | 77 | 172 | .448 | 16 | 20 | .800 | 103 | 107 | 170 | 3.8 | 4.0 | 6.3 |
| Varsity totals.......................... | 103 | ... | 336 | 744 | .452 | 170 | 210 | .810 | 365 | ... | 842 | 3.5 | ... | 8.2 |

## HEAD COACHING RECORD

BACKGROUND: Assistant coach, University of Minnesota (1981-82 through 1985-86). ... Assistant coach, University of Tulsa (1986-87 and 1987-88).
HONORS: CBA Coach of the Year (1990, 1992).

## COLLEGIATE COACHING RECORD

| Season Team | W | L | Pct. |
|---|---|---|---|
| 77-78—Golden Valley Lutheran College .................. | 19 | 5 | .792 |

| Season Team | W | L | Pct. |
|---|---|---|---|
| 78-79—Golden Valley Lutheran College | 21 | 4 | .840 |
| 79-80—Golden Valley Lutheran College | 23 | 2 | .920 |
| 80-81—Golden Valley Lutheran College | 28 | 2 | .933 |
| Totals (4 years) | 91 | 13 | .875 |

## CBA COACHING RECORD

| Season Team | REGULAR SEASON W | L | Pct. | Finish | | PLAYOFFS W | L | Pct. |
|---|---|---|---|---|---|---|---|---|
| 88-89—Rapid City | 38 | 16 | .704 | 1st/Western Division | | 6 | 5 | .545 |
| 89-90—La Crosse | 42 | 14 | .750 | 1st/Central Division | | 11 | 4 | .733 |
| 90-91—La Crosse | 32 | 24 | .571 | 2nd/Central Division | | 2 | 3 | .400 |
| 91-92—La Crosse | 40 | 16 | .714 | 2nd/Midwest Division | | 10 | 6 | .625 |
| 92-93—La Crosse | 32 | 24 | .571 | 3rd/Mideast Division | | 2 | 3 | .400 |
| 93-94—La Crosse | 35 | 21 | .625 | 1st/Mideast Division | | 3 | 3 | .500 |
| 94-95—Sioux Falls | 34 | 22 | .607 | 2nd/Western Division | | 1 | 2 | .333 |
| Totals (7 years) | 253 | 137 | .649 | | Totals (7 years) | 35 | 26 | .574 |

## NBA COACHING RECORD

| Season Team | REGULAR SEASON W | L | Pct. | Finish | | PLAYOFFS W | L | Pct. |
|---|---|---|---|---|---|---|---|---|
| 95-96—Minnesota | 20 | 42 | .323 | T5th/Midwest Division | | — | — | — |
| 96-97—Minnesota | 40 | 42 | .488 | 3rd/Midwest Division | | 0 | 3 | .000 |
| 97-98—Minnesota | 45 | 37 | .549 | 3rd/Midwest Division | | 2 | 3 | .400 |
| 98-99—Minnesota | 25 | 25 | .500 | 4th/Midwest Division | | 1 | 3 | .250 |
| 99-00—Minnesota | 50 | 32 | .610 | 3rd/Midwest Division | | 1 | 3 | .250 |
| 00-01—Minnesota | 47 | 35 | .573 | 4th/Midwest Division | | 1 | 3 | .250 |
| 01-02—Minnesota | 50 | 32 | .610 | 3rd/Midwest Division | | 0 | 3 | .000 |
| 02-03—Minnesota | 51 | 31 | .622 | 3rd/Midwest Division | | 2 | 4 | .333 |
| 03-04—Minnesota | 58 | 24 | .707 | 1st/Midwest Division | | 10 | 8 | .556 |
| 04-05—Minnesota | 25 | 26 | .490 | 3rd/Northwest Division | | | | |
| Totals (10 years) | 411 | 326 | .558 | | Totals (8 years) | 17 | 30 | .362 |

NOTES:
1989—Defeated Cedar Rapids, 4-1, in Western semifinals; lost to Rockford, 4-2, in Western finals.
1990—Defeated Quad City, 3-0, in American semifinals; defeated Albany, 4-3, in American finals; defeated Rapid City, 4-1, in CBA Championship Series.
1991—Lost to Quad City, 3-2, in American first round.
1992—Defeated Grand Rapids, 3-1, in American second round; defeated Quad City, 3-2, in American finals; defeated Rapid City, 4-3, in CBA Championship Series.
1993—Lost to Rockford, 3-2, in American first round.
1994—Defeated Rockford, 3-0, in American first round; lost to Quad City, 3-0, in American finals.
1995—Lost to Omaha, 2-1, in National first round. Replaced Bill Blair as Minnesota head coach (December 18), with record of 6-14 and club in sixth place.
1997—Lost to Houston, 3-0, in Western Conference first round.
1998—Lost to Seattle, 3-2, in Western Conference first round.
1999—Lost to San Antonio, 3-1, in Western Conference first round.
2000—Lost to Portland, 3-1, in Western Conference first round.
2001—Lost to San Antonio, 3-1, in Western Conference first round.
2002—Lost to Dallas, 3-0, in Western Conference first round.
2003—Lost to Los Angeles Lakers, 4-2, in Western Conference first round.
2004—Defeated Denver, 4-1, in Western Conference first round; defeated Sacramento, 4-3, in Western Conference semifinals; lost to Los Angeles Lakers, 4-2, in Western Conference finals.
2005—Replaced as head coach by Kevin McHale (February 12) with team in third place.

# SCOTT, BYRON                                    HORNETS

**PERSONAL:** Born March 28, 1961, in Ogden, Utah. ... 6-4/200. (1,93/90,7). ... Full Name: Byron Antom Scott.
**HIGH SCHOOL:** Morningside (Inglewood, Calif.).
**COLLEGE:** Arizona State.
**TRANSACTIONS/CAREER NOTES:** Selected by San Diego Clippers in first round (fourth pick overall) of 1983 NBA Draft. ... Draft rights traded by Clippers with C Swen Nater to Los Angeles Lakers for G Norm Nixon, G Eddie Jordan and 1986 and 1987 second-round draft choices (October 10, 1983). ... Signed as free agent by Indiana Pacers (December 6, 1993). ... Selected by Vancouver Grizzlies from Pacers in NBA Expansion Draft (June 24, 1995). ... Waived by Grizzlies (July 22, 1996). ... Signed as free agent by Lakers (September 30, 1996). ... Played in Greece (1997-98).
**MISCELLANEOUS:** Member of NBA championship team (1985, 1987, 1988).

## COLLEGIATE RECORD

| Season Team | G | Min. | FGM | FGA | Pct. | FTM | FTA | Pct. | Reb. | Ast. | Pts. | AVERAGES RPG | APG | PPG |
|---|---|---|---|---|---|---|---|---|---|---|---|---|---|---|
| 79-80—Arizona State | 29 | 936 | 166 | 332 | .500 | 63 | 86 | .733 | 79 | 65 | 395 | 2.7 | 2.2 | 13.6 |
| 80-81—Arizona State | 28 | 1003 | 197 | 390 | .505 | 70 | 101 | .693 | 106 | 78 | 464 | 3.8 | 2.8 | 16.6 |
| 81-82—Arizona State | | | | | Did not play—academic and personal reasons. | | | | | | | | | |
| 82-83—Arizona State | 33 | 1206 | 283 | 552 | .513 | 147 | 188 | .782 | 177 | 140 | 713 | 5.4 | 4.2 | 21.6 |
| Totals | 90 | 3145 | 646 | 1274 | .507 | 280 | 375 | .747 | 362 | 283 | 1572 | 4.0 | 3.1 | 17.5 |

## NBA REGULAR-SEASON RECORD

**HONORS:** NBA All-Rookie team (1984).
**NOTES:** Led NBA with .433 three-point field goal percentage (1985).

| Season Team | G | Min. | FGM | FGA | Pct. | FTM | FTA | Pct. | REBOUNDS Off. | Def. | Tot. | Ast. | St. | Blk. | TO | Pts. | AVERAGES RPG | APG | PPG |
|---|---|---|---|---|---|---|---|---|---|---|---|---|---|---|---|---|---|---|---|
| 83-84—L.A. Lakers | 74 | 1637 | 334 | 690 | .484 | 112 | 139 | .806 | 50 | 114 | 164 | 177 | 81 | 19 | 116 | 788 | 2.2 | 2.4 | 10.6 |
| 84-85—L.A. Lakers | 81 | 2305 | 541 | 1003 | .539 | 187 | 228 | .820 | 57 | 153 | 210 | 244 | 100 | 17 | 138 | 1295 | 2.6 | 3.0 | 16.0 |

<table>
<thead>
<tr><th>Season Team</th><th>G</th><th>Min.</th><th>FGM</th><th>FGA</th><th>Pct.</th><th>FTM</th><th>FTA</th><th>Pct.</th><th>Off.</th><th>Def.</th><th>Tot.</th><th>Ast.</th><th>St.</th><th>Blk.</th><th>TO</th><th>Pts.</th><th>RPG</th><th>APG</th><th>PPG</th></tr>
</thead>
<tbody>
<tr><td>85-86—L.A. Lakers .....</td><td>76</td><td>2190</td><td>507</td><td>989</td><td>.513</td><td>138</td><td>176</td><td>.784</td><td>55</td><td>134</td><td>189</td><td>164</td><td>85</td><td>15</td><td>110</td><td>1174</td><td>2.5</td><td>2.2</td><td>15.4</td></tr>
<tr><td>86-87—L.A. Lakers .....</td><td>82</td><td>2729</td><td>554</td><td>1134</td><td>.489</td><td>224</td><td>251</td><td>.892</td><td>63</td><td>223</td><td>286</td><td>281</td><td>125</td><td>18</td><td>144</td><td>1397</td><td>3.5</td><td>3.4</td><td>17.0</td></tr>
<tr><td>87-88—L.A. Lakers .....</td><td>81</td><td>3048</td><td>710</td><td>1348</td><td>.527</td><td>272</td><td>317</td><td>.858</td><td>76</td><td>257</td><td>333</td><td>335</td><td>155</td><td>27</td><td>161</td><td>1754</td><td>4.1</td><td>4.1</td><td>21.7</td></tr>
<tr><td>88-89—L.A. Lakers .....</td><td>74</td><td>2605</td><td>588</td><td>1198</td><td>.491</td><td>195</td><td>226</td><td>.863</td><td>72</td><td>230</td><td>302</td><td>231</td><td>114</td><td>27</td><td>157</td><td>1448</td><td>4.1</td><td>3.1</td><td>19.6</td></tr>
<tr><td>89-90—L.A. Lakers .....</td><td>77</td><td>2593</td><td>472</td><td>1005</td><td>.470</td><td>160</td><td>209</td><td>.766</td><td>51</td><td>191</td><td>242</td><td>274</td><td>77</td><td>31</td><td>122</td><td>1197</td><td>3.1</td><td>3.6</td><td>15.5</td></tr>
<tr><td>90-91—L.A. Lakers .....</td><td>82</td><td>2630</td><td>501</td><td>1051</td><td>.477</td><td>118</td><td>148</td><td>.797</td><td>54</td><td>192</td><td>246</td><td>177</td><td>95</td><td>21</td><td>85</td><td>1191</td><td>3.0</td><td>2.2</td><td>14.5</td></tr>
<tr><td>91-92—L.A. Lakers .....</td><td>82</td><td>2679</td><td>460</td><td>1005</td><td>.458</td><td>244</td><td>291</td><td>.838</td><td>74</td><td>236</td><td>310</td><td>226</td><td>105</td><td>28</td><td>119</td><td>1218</td><td>3.8</td><td>2.8</td><td>14.9</td></tr>
<tr><td>92-93—L.A. Lakers .....</td><td>58</td><td>1677</td><td>296</td><td>659</td><td>.449</td><td>156</td><td>184</td><td>.848</td><td>27</td><td>107</td><td>134</td><td>157</td><td>55</td><td>13</td><td>70</td><td>792</td><td>2.3</td><td>2.7</td><td>13.7</td></tr>
<tr><td>93-94—Indiana...........</td><td>67</td><td>1197</td><td>256</td><td>548</td><td>.467</td><td>157</td><td>195</td><td>.805</td><td>19</td><td>91</td><td>110</td><td>133</td><td>62</td><td>9</td><td>103</td><td>696</td><td>1.6</td><td>2.0</td><td>10.4</td></tr>
<tr><td>94-95—Indiana...........</td><td>80</td><td>1528</td><td>265</td><td>583</td><td>.455</td><td>193</td><td>227</td><td>.850</td><td>18</td><td>133</td><td>151</td><td>108</td><td>61</td><td>13</td><td>119</td><td>802</td><td>1.9</td><td>1.4</td><td>10.0</td></tr>
<tr><td>95-96—Vancouver.....</td><td>80</td><td>1894</td><td>271</td><td>676</td><td>.401</td><td>203</td><td>243</td><td>.835</td><td>40</td><td>152</td><td>192</td><td>123</td><td>63</td><td>22</td><td>100</td><td>819</td><td>2.4</td><td>1.5</td><td>10.2</td></tr>
<tr><td>96-97—Indiana...........</td><td>79</td><td>1440</td><td>163</td><td>379</td><td>.430</td><td>127</td><td>151</td><td>.841</td><td>21</td><td>97</td><td>118</td><td>99</td><td>46</td><td>16</td><td>53</td><td>526</td><td>1.5</td><td>1.3</td><td>6.7</td></tr>
<tr><td>Totals ...................</td><td>1073</td><td>30152</td><td>5918</td><td>12268</td><td>.482</td><td>2486</td><td>2985</td><td>.833</td><td>677</td><td>2310</td><td>2987</td><td>2729</td><td>1224</td><td>276</td><td>1597</td><td>15097</td><td>2.8</td><td>2.5</td><td>14.1</td></tr>
</tbody>
</table>

Three-point field goals: 1983-84, 8-for-34 (.235). 1984-85, 26-for-60 (.433). 1985-86, 22-for-61 (.361). 1986-87, 65-for-149 (.436). 1987-88, 62-for-179 (.346). 1988-89, 77-for-193 (.399). 1989-90, 93-for-220 (.423). 1990-91, 71-for-219 (.324). 1991-92, 54-for-157 (.344). 1992-93, 44-for-135 (.326). 1993-94, 27-for-74 (.365). 1994-95, 79-for-203 (.389). 1995-96, 74-for-221 (.335). 1996-97, 73-for-188 (.388). Totals, 775-for-2093 (.370).

Personal fouls/disqualifications: 1983-84, 174/0. 1984-85, 197/1. 1985-86, 167/0. 1986-87, 163/0. 1987-88, 204/2. 1988-89, 181/1. 1989-90, 180/2. 1990-91, 146/0. 1991-92, 140/0. 1992-93, 98/0. 1993-94, 80/0. 1994-95, 123/1. 1995-96, 126/0. 1996-97, 72/0. Totals, 2051/7.

## NBA PLAYOFF RECORD

<table>
<thead>
<tr><th>Season Team</th><th>G</th><th>Min.</th><th>FGM</th><th>FGA</th><th>Pct.</th><th>FTM</th><th>FTA</th><th>Pct.</th><th>Off.</th><th>Def.</th><th>Tot.</th><th>Ast.</th><th>St.</th><th>Blk.</th><th>TO</th><th>Pts.</th><th>RPG</th><th>APG</th><th>PPG</th></tr>
</thead>
<tbody>
<tr><td>83-84—Los Angeles....</td><td>20</td><td>404</td><td>74</td><td>161</td><td>.460</td><td>21</td><td>35</td><td>.600</td><td>11</td><td>26</td><td>37</td><td>34</td><td>18</td><td>2</td><td>26</td><td>171</td><td>1.9</td><td>1.7</td><td>8.6</td></tr>
<tr><td>84-85—L.A. Lakers ....</td><td>19</td><td>585</td><td>138</td><td>267</td><td>.517</td><td>35</td><td>44</td><td>.795</td><td>16</td><td>36</td><td>52</td><td>50</td><td>41</td><td>4</td><td>24</td><td>321</td><td>2.7</td><td>2.6</td><td>16.9</td></tr>
<tr><td>85-86—L.A. Lakers ....</td><td>14</td><td>470</td><td>90</td><td>181</td><td>.497</td><td>38</td><td>42</td><td>.905</td><td>15</td><td>40</td><td>55</td><td>42</td><td>19</td><td>2</td><td>30</td><td>224</td><td>3.9</td><td>3.0</td><td>16.0</td></tr>
<tr><td>86-87—L.A. Lakers ....</td><td>18</td><td>608</td><td>103</td><td>210</td><td>.490</td><td>53</td><td>67</td><td>.791</td><td>20</td><td>42</td><td>62</td><td>57</td><td>19</td><td>4</td><td>25</td><td>266</td><td>3.4</td><td>3.2</td><td>14.8</td></tr>
<tr><td>87-88—L.A. Lakers ....</td><td>24</td><td>897</td><td>178</td><td>357</td><td>.499</td><td>90</td><td>104</td><td>.865</td><td>26</td><td>74</td><td>100</td><td>60</td><td>34</td><td>5</td><td>47</td><td>470</td><td>4.2</td><td>2.5</td><td>19.6</td></tr>
<tr><td>88-89—L.A. Lakers ....</td><td>11</td><td>402</td><td>79</td><td>160</td><td>.494</td><td>46</td><td>55</td><td>.836</td><td>10</td><td>35</td><td>45</td><td>25</td><td>18</td><td>2</td><td>20</td><td>219</td><td>4.1</td><td>2.3</td><td>19.9</td></tr>
<tr><td>89-90—L.A. Lakers ....</td><td>9</td><td>325</td><td>49</td><td>106</td><td>.462</td><td>10</td><td>13</td><td>.769</td><td>7</td><td>30</td><td>37</td><td>23</td><td>20</td><td>3</td><td>13</td><td>121</td><td>4.1</td><td>2.6</td><td>13.4</td></tr>
<tr><td>90-91—L.A. Lakers ....</td><td>18</td><td>678</td><td>95</td><td>186</td><td>.511</td><td>27</td><td>34</td><td>.794</td><td>13</td><td>44</td><td>57</td><td>29</td><td>23</td><td>4</td><td>17</td><td>237</td><td>3.2</td><td>1.6</td><td>13.2</td></tr>
<tr><td>91-92—L.A. Lakers ....</td><td>4</td><td>148</td><td>22</td><td>44</td><td>.500</td><td>24</td><td>27</td><td>.889</td><td>3</td><td>7</td><td>10</td><td>14</td><td>6</td><td>1</td><td>5</td><td>75</td><td>2.5</td><td>3.5</td><td>18.8</td></tr>
<tr><td>92-93—L.A. Lakers ....</td><td>5</td><td>177</td><td>21</td><td>42</td><td>.500</td><td>18</td><td>23</td><td>.783</td><td>0</td><td>11</td><td>11</td><td>9</td><td>5</td><td>0</td><td>4</td><td>68</td><td>2.2</td><td>1.8</td><td>13.6</td></tr>
<tr><td>93-94—Indiana...........</td><td>16</td><td>239</td><td>38</td><td>96</td><td>.396</td><td>40</td><td>51</td><td>.784</td><td>10</td><td>23</td><td>33</td><td>20</td><td>12</td><td>2</td><td>25</td><td>125</td><td>2.1</td><td>1.3</td><td>7.8</td></tr>
<tr><td>94-95—Indiana...........</td><td>17</td><td>298</td><td>32</td><td>94</td><td>.340</td><td>30</td><td>34</td><td>.882</td><td>5</td><td>20</td><td>25</td><td>16</td><td>10</td><td>1</td><td>22</td><td>103</td><td>1.5</td><td>0.9</td><td>6.1</td></tr>
<tr><td>96-97—L.A. Lakers ....</td><td>8</td><td>134</td><td>15</td><td>33</td><td>.455</td><td>17</td><td>19</td><td>.895</td><td>0</td><td>12</td><td>12</td><td>11</td><td>1</td><td>0</td><td>8</td><td>51</td><td>1.5</td><td>1.4</td><td>6.4</td></tr>
<tr><td>Totals ...................</td><td>183</td><td>5365</td><td>934</td><td>1937</td><td>.482</td><td>449</td><td>548</td><td>.819</td><td>136</td><td>400</td><td>536</td><td>390</td><td>226</td><td>30</td><td>266</td><td>2451</td><td>2.9</td><td>2.1</td><td>13.4</td></tr>
</tbody>
</table>

Three-point field goals: 1983-84, 2-for-10 (.200). 1984-85, 10-for-21 (.476). 1985-86, 6-for-17 (.353). 1986-87, 7-for-34 (.206). 1987-88, 24-for-55 (.436). 1988-89, 15-for-39 (.385). 1989-90, 13-for-34 (.382). 1990-91, 20-for-38 (.526). 1991-92, 7-for-12 (.583). 1992-93, 8-for-15 (.533). 1993-94, 9-for-19 (.474). 1994-95, 9-for-34 (.265). 1996-97, 4-for-11 (.364). Totals, 134-for-339 (.395).

Personal fouls/disqualifications: 1983-84, 39/1. 1984-85, 47/0. 1985-86, 38/0. 1986-87, 52/0. 1987-88, 65/0. 1988-89, 31/0. 1989-90, 32/1. 1990-91, 53/0. 1991-92, 10/0. 1992-93, 11/0. 1993-94, 22/0. 1994-95, 30/0. 1996-97, 15/0. Totals, 445/2.

## GREEK LEAGUE RECORD

<table>
<thead>
<tr><th>Season Team</th><th>G</th><th>Min.</th><th>FGM</th><th>FGA</th><th>Pct.</th><th>FTM</th><th>FTA</th><th>Pct.</th><th>Reb.</th><th>Ast.</th><th>Pts.</th><th>RPG</th><th>APG</th><th>PPG</th></tr>
</thead>
<tbody>
<tr><td>97-98—Panathinaikos</td><td>17</td><td>436</td><td>82</td><td>171</td><td>.480</td><td>44</td><td>49</td><td>.898</td><td>40</td><td>36</td><td>228</td><td>2.4</td><td>2.1</td><td>13.4</td></tr>
</tbody>
</table>

Three-point field goals: 1997-98, 20-for-60 (.333).

## HEAD COACHING RECORD

**NOTES:** Assistant coach, Sacramento Kings (1998-99 and 1999-2000).

### NBA COACHING RECORD

<table>
<thead>
<tr><th rowspan="2">Season  Team</th><th colspan="4">REGULAR SEASON</th><th colspan="3">PLAYOFFS</th></tr>
<tr><th>W</th><th>L</th><th>Pct.</th><th>Finish</th><th>W</th><th>L</th><th>Pct.</th></tr>
</thead>
<tbody>
<tr><td>00-01—New Jersey .................</td><td>26</td><td>56</td><td>.317</td><td>6th/Atlantic Division</td><td>—</td><td>—</td><td>—</td></tr>
<tr><td>01-02—New Jersey .................</td><td>52</td><td>30</td><td>.634</td><td>1st/Atlantic Division</td><td>11</td><td>9</td><td>.550</td></tr>
<tr><td>02-03—New Jersey .................</td><td>49</td><td>33</td><td>.598</td><td>1st/Atlantic Division</td><td>14</td><td>6</td><td>.700</td></tr>
<tr><td>03-04—New Jersey .................</td><td>22</td><td>20</td><td>.524</td><td></td><td>—</td><td>—</td><td>—</td></tr>
<tr><td>04-05—New Orleans ...............</td><td>18</td><td>64</td><td>.220</td><td>5th/Southwest Division</td><td>—</td><td>—</td><td>—</td></tr>
<tr><td>Totals (5 years).......................</td><td>167</td><td>203</td><td>.451</td><td>Totals (2 years).......</td><td>25</td><td>15</td><td>.625</td></tr>
</tbody>
</table>

**NOTES:**

2002—Defeated Indiana, 3-2, in Eastern Conference first round; defeated Charlotte, 4-1, in Eastern Conference semifinals; defeated Boston, 4-2, in Eastern Conference finals; lost to Los Angeles Lakers, 4-0, in NBA Finals.

2003—Defeated Milwaukee, 4-2, in Eastern Conference first round; defeated Boston, 4-0, in Eastern Conference semifinals; defeated Detroit, 4-0, in Eastern Conference finals; lost to San Antonio, 4-2, in NBA Finals.

2004—Replaced as New Jersey coach by Lawrence Frank (January 26) with club in first place.

# SKILES, SCOTT — BULLS

**PERSONAL:** Born March 5, 1964, in LaPorte, Ind. ... 6-1/180. (1,85/81,6). ... Full Name: Scott Allen Skiles.
**HIGH SCHOOL:** Plymouth (Ind.).
**COLLEGE:** Michigan State.
**TRANSACTIONS/CAREER NOTES:** Selected by Milwaukee Bucks in first round (22nd pick overall) of 1986 NBA Draft. ... Traded by Bucks to Indiana Pacers for second-round draft choice (June 22, 1987). ... Selected by Orlando Magic from Pacers in NBA Expansion Draft (June 15, 1989). ... Traded by Magic with 1996 first-round draft choice and future considerations to Washington Bullets for 1996 second-round draft choice and future considerations (July 29, 1994). ... Signed by Philadelphia 76ers for remainder of season (December 12, 1995). ... Announced retirement (January 6, 1996).
**MISCELLANEOUS:** Orlando Magic all-time assists leader with 2,776 (1989-90 through 1993-94).

## COLLEGIATE RECORD

**NOTES:** THE SPORTING NEWS All-America first team (1986).

| Season Team | G | Min. | FGM | FGA | Pct. | FTM | FTA | Pct. | Reb. | Ast. | Pts. | RPG | APG | PPG |
|---|---|---|---|---|---|---|---|---|---|---|---|---|---|---|
| 82-83—Michigan State | 30 | 1023 | 141 | 286 | .493 | 69 | 83 | .831 | 63 | 146 | 376 | 2.1 | 4.9 | 12.5 |
| 83-84—Michigan State | 28 | 983 | 153 | 319 | .480 | 99 | 119 | .832 | 62 | 128 | 405 | 2.2 | 4.6 | 14.5 |
| 84-85—Michigan State | 29 | 1107 | 212 | 420 | .505 | 90 | 114 | .789 | 93 | 168 | 514 | 3.2 | 5.8 | 17.7 |
| 85-86—Michigan State | 31 | 1172 | 331 | 598 | .554 | 188 | 209 | .900 | 135 | 203 | 850 | 4.4 | 6.5 | 27.4 |
| Totals | 118 | 4285 | 837 | 1623 | .516 | 446 | 525 | .850 | 353 | 645 | 2145 | 3.0 | 5.5 | 18.2 |

Three-point field goals: 1982-83, 25-for-50 (.500).

## NBA REGULAR-SEASON RECORD

**RECORDS:** Holds single-game record for most assists—30 (December 30, 1990, vs. Denver).

**HONORS:** NBA Most Improved Player (1991).

| Season Team | G | Min. | FGM | FGA | Pct. | FTM | FTA | Pct. | Off. | Def. | Tot. | Ast. | St. | Blk. | TO | Pts. | RPG | APG | PPG |
|---|---|---|---|---|---|---|---|---|---|---|---|---|---|---|---|---|---|---|---|
| 86-87—Milwaukee | 13 | 205 | 18 | 62 | .290 | 10 | 12 | .833 | 6 | 20 | 26 | 45 | 5 | 1 | 21 | 49 | 2.0 | 3.5 | 3.8 |
| 87-88—Indiana | 51 | 760 | 86 | 209 | .411 | 45 | 54 | .833 | 11 | 55 | 66 | 180 | 22 | 3 | 76 | 223 | 1.3 | 3.5 | 4.4 |
| 88-89—Indiana | 80 | 1571 | 198 | 442 | .448 | 130 | 144 | .903 | 21 | 128 | 149 | 390 | 64 | 2 | 177 | 546 | 1.9 | 4.9 | 6.8 |
| 89-90—Orlando | 70 | 1460 | 190 | 464 | .409 | 104 | 119 | .874 | 23 | 136 | 159 | 334 | 36 | 4 | 90 | 536 | 2.3 | 4.8 | 7.7 |
| 90-91—Orlando | 79 | 2714 | 462 | 1039 | .445 | 340 | 377 | .902 | 57 | 213 | 270 | 660 | 89 | 4 | 252 | 1357 | 3.4 | 8.4 | 17.2 |
| 91-92—Orlando | 75 | 2377 | 359 | 868 | .414 | 248 | 277 | .895 | 36 | 166 | 202 | 544 | 74 | 5 | 233 | 1057 | 2.7 | 7.3 | 14.1 |
| 92-93—Orlando | 78 | 3086 | 416 | 891 | .467 | 289 | 324 | .892 | 52 | 238 | 290 | 735 | 86 | 2 | 267 | 1201 | 3.7 | 9.4 | 15.4 |
| 93-94—Orlando | 82 | 2303 | 276 | 644 | .429 | 195 | 222 | .878 | 42 | 147 | 189 | 503 | 47 | 2 | 193 | 815 | 2.3 | 6.1 | 9.9 |
| 94-95—Washington | 62 | 2077 | 265 | 583 | .455 | 179 | 202 | .886 | 26 | 133 | 159 | 452 | 70 | 6 | 172 | 805 | 2.6 | 7.3 | 13.0 |
| 95-96—Philadelphia | 10 | 236 | 20 | 57 | .351 | 8 | 10 | .800 | 1 | 15 | 16 | 38 | 7 | 0 | 16 | 63 | 1.6 | 3.8 | 6.3 |
| Totals | 600 | 16789 | 2290 | 5259 | .435 | 1548 | 1741 | .889 | 275 | 1251 | 1526 | 3881 | 500 | 29 | 1497 | 6652 | 2.5 | 6.5 | 11.1 |

Three-point field goals: 1986-87, 3-for-14 (.214). 1987-88, 6-for-20 (.300). 1988-89, 20-for-75 (.267). 1989-90, 52-for-132 (.394). 1990-91, 93-for-228 (.408). 1991-92, 91-for-250 (.364). 1992-93, 80-for-235 (.340). 1993-94, 68-for-165 (.412). 1994-95, 96-for-228 (.421). 1995-96, 15-for-34 (.441). Totals, 524-for-1381 (.379).

Personal fouls/disqualifications: 1986-87, 18/0. 1987-88, 97/0. 1988-89, 151/1. 1989-90, 126/0. 1990-91, 192/2. 1991-92, 188/0. 1992-93, 244/4. 1993-94, 171/1. 1994-95, 135/2. 1995-96, 21/0. Totals, 1343/10.

## NBA PLAYOFF RECORD

| Season Team | G | Min. | FGM | FGA | Pct. | FTM | FTA | Pct. | Off. | Def. | Tot. | Ast. | St. | Blk. | TO | Pts. | RPG | APG | PPG |
|---|---|---|---|---|---|---|---|---|---|---|---|---|---|---|---|---|---|---|---|
| 93-94—Orlando | 2 | 23 | 4 | 8 | .500 | 1 | 1 | 1.000 | 1 | 0 | 1 | 3 | 0 | 0 | 5 | 9 | 0.5 | 1.5 | 4.5 |

Three-point field goals: 1993-94, 0-for-2.

Personal fouls/disqualifications: 1993-94, 2/0.

## HEAD COACHING RECORD

**NOTES:** Assistant coach, Phoenix Suns (1997-98 through December 13, 1999).

## NBA COACHING RECORD

| Season Team | REGULAR SEASON | | | | PLAYOFFS | | |
|---|---|---|---|---|---|---|---|
| | W | L | Pct. | Finish | W | L | Pct. |
| 99-00—Phoenix | 40 | 22 | .645 | 3rd/Pacific Division | 4 | 5 | .444 |
| 00-01—Phoenix | 51 | 31 | .622 | 3rd/Pacific Division | 1 | 3 | .250 |
| 01-02—Phoenix | 25 | 26 | .490 | | — | — | — |
| 03-04—Chicago | 19 | 47 | .288 | 8th/Central Division | — | — | — |
| 04-05—Chicago | 47 | 35 | .573 | 2nd/Central Division | 2 | 4 | .333 |
| Totals (5 years) | 182 | 161 | .531 | Totals (3 years) | 7 | 12 | .368 |

## NOTES:

1999—Replaced Danny Ainge as head coach (December 13), with a record of 13-7 and club in fourth place.

2000—Defeated San Antonio, 3-1, in Western Conference first round; lost to Los Angeles Lakers, 4-1, in Western Conference semifinals.

2001—Lost to Sacramento, 3-1, in Western Conference first round.

2002—Replaced as Phoenix head coach by Frank Johnson (February 17) with club in sixth place.

2003—Replaced Bill Cartwright as Chicago head coach (November 28) with 4-12 record and club in 8th place.

2005—Lost to Washington in Eastern Conference first round.

# SLOAN, JERRY    JAZZ

**PERSONAL:** Born March 28, 1942, in McLeansboro, Ill. ... 6-5/200. (1,96/90,7). ... Full name: Gerald Eugene Sloan.

**HIGH SCHOOL:** McLeansboro (Ill.).

**COLLEGE:** Illinois, then Evansville.

**TRANSACTIONS/CAREER NOTES:** Selected by Baltimore Bullets in third round of 1964 NBA Draft. ... Selected by Bullets in second round of 1965 NBA Draft. ... Selected by Chicago Bulls from Bullets in NBA expansion draft (April 30, 1966).

**CAREER NOTES:** Scout, Chicago Bulls (1976-77). ... Scout, Utah Jazz (1983-84).

## COLLEGIATE RECORD

**NOTES:** Left Illinois before 1961 basketball season. ... Outstanding Player in NCAA College Division Tournament (1964, 1965). ... THE SPORTING NEWS All-America second team (1965).

| Season Team | G | Min. | FGM | FGA | Pct. | FTM | FTA | Pct. | Reb. | Ast. | Pts. | RPG | APG | PPG |
|---|---|---|---|---|---|---|---|---|---|---|---|---|---|---|
| 61-62—Evansville | | | | | | Did not play—transfer student. | | | | | | | | |
| 62-63—Evansville | 27 | ... | 152 | 446 | .341 | 103 | 151 | .682 | 293 | ... | 407 | 10.9 | ... | 15.1 |

| Season Team | G | Min. | FGM | FGA | Pct. | FTM | FTA | Pct. | Reb. | Ast. | Pts. | RPG | APG | PPG |
|---|---|---|---|---|---|---|---|---|---|---|---|---|---|---|
| 63-64—Evansville | 29 | ... | 160 | 385 | .416 | 84 | 114 | .737 | 335 | ... | 404 | 11.6 | ... | 13.9 |
| 64-65—Evansville | 29 | ... | 207 | 458 | .452 | 95 | 126 | .754 | 425 | ... | 509 | 14.7 | ... | 17.6 |
| Totals | 85 | ... | 519 | 1289 | .403 | 282 | 391 | .721 | 1053 | ... | 1320 | 12.4 | ... | 15.5 |

## NBA REGULAR-SEASON RECORD

**HONORS:** NBA All-Defensive first team (1969, 1972, 1974, 1975). ... NBA All-Defensive second team (1970, 1971).

| Season Team | G | Min. | FGM | FGA | Pct. | FTM | FTA | Pct. | Reb. | Ast. | PF | Dq. | Pts. | RPG | APG | PPG |
|---|---|---|---|---|---|---|---|---|---|---|---|---|---|---|---|---|
| 65-66—Baltimore | 59 | 952 | 120 | 289 | .415 | 98 | 139 | .705 | 230 | 110 | 176 | 7 | 338 | 3.9 | 1.9 | 5.7 |
| 66-67—Chicago | 80 | 2942 | 525 | 1214 | .432 | 340 | 427 | .796 | 726 | 170 | 293 | 7 | 1390 | 9.1 | 2.1 | 17.4 |
| 67-68—Chicago | 77 | 2454 | 369 | 959 | .385 | 280 | 386 | .725 | 591 | 229 | 291 | 11 | 1027 | 7.7 | 3.0 | 13.3 |
| 68-69—Chicago | 78 | 2939 | 488 | 1179 | .414 | 333 | 447 | .745 | 619 | 276 | 313 | 6 | 1309 | 7.9 | 3.5 | 16.8 |
| 69-70—Chicago | 53 | 1822 | 310 | 737 | .421 | 207 | 318 | .651 | 372 | 165 | 179 | 3 | 827 | 7.0 | 3.1 | 15.6 |
| 70-71—Chicago | 80 | 3140 | 592 | 1342 | .441 | 278 | 389 | .715 | 701 | 281 | 289 | 5 | 1462 | 8.8 | 3.5 | 18.3 |
| 71-72—Chicago | 82 | 3035 | 535 | 1206 | .444 | 258 | 391 | .660 | 691 | 211 | 309 | 8 | 1328 | 8.4 | 2.6 | 16.2 |
| 72-73—Chicago | 69 | 2412 | 301 | 733 | .411 | 94 | 133 | .707 | 475 | 151 | 235 | 5 | 696 | 6.9 | 2.2 | 10.1 |

| Season Team | G | Min. | FGM | FGA | Pct. | FTM | FTA | Pct. | REBOUNDS | | | Ast. | St. | Blk. | TO | Pts. | AVERAGES | | |
|---|---|---|---|---|---|---|---|---|---|---|---|---|---|---|---|---|---|---|---|
| | | | | | | | | | Off. | Def. | Tot. | | | | | | RPG | APG | PPG |
| 73-74—Chicago | 77 | 2860 | 412 | 921 | .447 | 194 | 273 | .711 | 150 | 406 | 556 | 149 | 183 | 10 | ... | 1018 | 7.2 | 1.9 | 13.2 |
| 74-75—Chicago | 78 | 2577 | 380 | 865 | .439 | 193 | 258 | .748 | 177 | 361 | 538 | 161 | 171 | 17 | ... | 953 | 6.9 | 2.1 | 12.2 |
| 75-76—Chicago | 22 | 617 | 84 | 210 | .400 | 55 | 78 | .705 | 40 | 76 | 116 | 22 | 27 | 5 | ... | 223 | 5.3 | 1.0 | 10.1 |
| Totals | 755 | 25750 | 4116 | 9655 | .426 | 2330 | 3239 | .719 | ... | ... | 5615 | 1925 | 381 | 32 | ... | 10571 | 7.4 | 2.5 | 14.0 |

Personal fouls/disqualifications: 1973-74, 273/3. 1974-75, 265/5. 1975-76, 77/1. Totals, 2700/61.

## NBA PLAYOFF RECORD

| Season Team | G | Min. | FGM | FGA | Pct. | FTM | FTA | Pct. | Reb. | Ast. | PF | Dq. | Pts. | RPG | APG | PPG |
|---|---|---|---|---|---|---|---|---|---|---|---|---|---|---|---|---|
| 65-66—Baltimore | 2 | 34 | 5 | 12 | .417 | 3 | 4 | .750 | 16 | 6 | 6 | 1 | 13 | 8.0 | 3.0 | 6.5 |
| 66-67—Chicago | 3 | 71 | 12 | 31 | .387 | 6 | 9 | .667 | 10 | 1 | 7 | 0 | 30 | 3.3 | 0.3 | 10.0 |
| 67-68—Chicago | 5 | 137 | 12 | 37 | .324 | 19 | 25 | .760 | 32 | 12 | 19 | 0 | 43 | 6.4 | 2.4 | 8.6 |
| 69-70—Chicago | 5 | 190 | 29 | 74 | .392 | 16 | 25 | .640 | 39 | 11 | 18 | 0 | 74 | 7.8 | 2.2 | 14.8 |
| 70-71—Chicago | 7 | 284 | 51 | 117 | .436 | 17 | 23 | .739 | 63 | 17 | 25 | 1 | 119 | 9.0 | 2.4 | 17.0 |
| 71-72—Chicago | 4 | 170 | 26 | 64 | .406 | 11 | 19 | .579 | 35 | 10 | 18 | 1 | 63 | 8.8 | 2.5 | 15.8 |
| 72-73—Chicago | 7 | 292 | 45 | 103 | .437 | 14 | 19 | .737 | 59 | 14 | 31 | 1 | 104 | 8.4 | 2.0 | 14.9 |

| Season Team | G | Min. | FGM | FGA | Pct. | FTM | FTA | Pct. | REBOUNDS | | | Ast. | St. | Blk. | TO | Pts. | AVERAGES | | |
|---|---|---|---|---|---|---|---|---|---|---|---|---|---|---|---|---|---|---|---|
| | | | | | | | | | Off. | Def. | Tot. | | | | | | RPG | APG | PPG |
| 73-74—Chicago | 6 | 240 | 39 | 88 | .443 | 22 | 29 | .759 | 18 | 44 | 62 | 12 | 7 | 1 | ... | 100 | 10.3 | 2.0 | 16.7 |
| 74-75—Chicago | 13 | 470 | 75 | 163 | .460 | 20 | 36 | .556 | 24 | 72 | 96 | 26 | 20 | 0 | ... | 170 | 7.4 | 2.0 | 13.1 |
| Totals | 52 | 1888 | 294 | 689 | .427 | 128 | 189 | .677 | ... | ... | 412 | 109 | 27 | 1 | ... | 716 | 7.9 | 2.1 | 13.8 |

Personal fouls/disqualifications: 1973-74, 17/0. 1974-75, 46/0. Totals, 187/4.

## NBA ALL-STAR GAME RECORD

| Season Team | Min. | FGM | FGA | Pct. | FTM | FTA | Pct. | Reb | Ast. | PF | Dq. | Pts. |
|---|---|---|---|---|---|---|---|---|---|---|---|---|
| 1967—Chicago | 22 | 4 | 9 | .444 | 0 | 0 | ... | 4 | 4 | 5 | 0 | 8 |
| 1969—Chicago | 18 | 2 | 8 | .250 | 0 | 1 | .000 | 3 | 0 | 5 | 0 | 4 |
| Totals | 40 | 6 | 17 | .353 | 0 | 1 | .000 | 7 | 4 | 10 | 0 | 12 |

## HEAD COACHING RECORD

**BACKGROUND:** Assistant coach, Bulls (1977-78 and 1978-79). ... Head coach, Evansville Thunder of CBA (1984-November 19, 1984; no record). ... Assistant coach, Jazz (November 19, 1984-December 9, 1988).

## NBA COACHING RECORD

| Season Team | REGULAR SEASON | | | | PLAYOFFS | | |
|---|---|---|---|---|---|---|---|
| | W | L | Pct. | Finish | W | L | Pct. |
| 79-80—Chicago | 30 | 52 | .366 | 4th/Midwest Division | — | — | — |
| 80-81—Chicago | 45 | 37 | .549 | 2nd/Central Division | 2 | 4 | .333 |
| 81-82—Chicago | 19 | 32 | .373 | | — | — | — |
| 88-89—Utah | 40 | 25 | .615 | 1st/Midwest Division | 0 | 3 | .000 |
| 89-90—Utah | 55 | 27 | .671 | 2nd/Midwest Division | 2 | 3 | .400 |
| 90-91—Utah | 54 | 28 | .659 | 2nd/Midwest Division | 4 | 5 | .444 |
| 91-92—Utah | 55 | 27 | .671 | 1st/Midwest Division | 9 | 7 | .563 |
| 92-93—Utah | 47 | 35 | .573 | 3rd/Midwest Division | 2 | 3 | .400 |
| 93-94—Utah | 53 | 29 | .646 | 3rd/Midwest Division | 8 | 8 | .500 |
| 94-95—Utah | 60 | 22 | .732 | 2nd/Midwest Division | 2 | 3 | .400 |
| 95-96—Utah | 55 | 27 | .671 | 2nd/Midwest Division | 10 | 8 | .556 |
| 96-97—Utah | 64 | 18 | .780 | 1st/Midwest Division | 13 | 7 | .650 |
| 97-98—Utah | 62 | 20 | .756 | 1st/Midwest Division | 13 | 7 | .650 |
| 98-99—Utah | 37 | 13 | .740 | T1st/Midwest Division | 5 | 6 | .455 |
| 99-00—Utah | 55 | 27 | .671 | 1st/Midwest Division | 4 | 6 | .400 |

HEAD COACHES

| | | REGULAR SEASON | | | | | PLAYOFFS | | |
|---|---|---|---|---|---|---|---|---|---|
| Season Team | W | L | Pct. | Finish | | W | L | Pct. |
| 00-01—Utah | 53 | 29 | .646 | 2nd/Midwest Division | | 2 | 3 | .400 |
| 01-02—Utah | 44 | 38 | .537 | 4th/Midwest Division | | 1 | 3 | .250 |
| 02-03—Utah | 47 | 35 | .573 | 4th/Midwest Division | | 1 | 4 | .200 |
| 03-04—Utah | 42 | 40 | .512 | 7th/Midwest Division | | — | — | — |
| 04-05—Utah | 26 | 56 | .317 | 5th/Northwest Division | | — | — | — |
| Totals (20 years) | 943 | 617 | .604 | Totals (16 years) | | 78 | 80 | .494 |

**NOTES:**

1981—Defeated New York, 2-0, in Eastern Conference first round; lost to Boston, 4-0, in Eastern Conference semifinals.

1982—Replaced as Chicago head coach by Rod Thorn (February 17).

1988—Replaced retiring Utah head coach Frank Layden (December 9), with record of 11-6.

1989—Lost to Golden State in Western Conference first round.

1990—Lost to Phoenix in Western Conference first round.

1991—Defeated Phoenix, 3-1, in Western Conference first round; lost to Portland, 4-1, in Western Conference semifinals.

1992—Defeated Los Angeles Clippers, 3-2, in Western Conference first round; defeated Seattle, 4-1, in Western Conference semifinals; lost to Portland, 4-2, in Western Conference finals.

1993—Lost to Seattle in Western Conference first round.

1994—Defeated San Antonio, 3-1, in Western Conference first round; defeated Denver, 4-3, in Western Conference semifinals; lost to Houston, 4-1, in Western Conference finals.

1995—Lost to Houston in Western Conference first round.

1996—Defeated Portland, 3-2, in Western Conference first round; Defeated San Antonio, 4-2, in Western Conference semifinals; lost to Seattle, 4-3, in Western Conference finals.

1997—Defeated Los Angeles Clippers, 3-0, in Western Conference first round; defeated Los Angeles Lakers, 4-1, in Western Conference semifinals; defeated Houston, 4-2, in Western Conference finals; lost to Chicago, 4-2, in NBA Finals.

1998—Defeated Houston, 3-2, in Western Conference first round; defeated San Antonio, 4-1, in Western Conference semifinals; defeated Los Angeles Lakers, 4-0, in Western Conference finals; lost to Chicago, 4-2, in NBA Finals.

1999—Defeated Sacramento, 3-2, in Western Conference first round; lost to Portland, 4-2, in Western Conference semifinals.

2000—Defeated Seattle, 3-2, in Western Conference first round; lost to Portland, 4-1, in Western Conference semifinals.

2001—Lost to Dallas, 3-2, in Western Conference first round.

2002—Lost to Sacramento, 3-1, in Western Conference first round.

2003—Lost to Sacramento, 4-1, in Western Conference first round.

## STOTTS, TERRY — BUCKS

**PERSONAL:** Born November 25, 1957, in Cedar Falls, Iowa. ... 6-8/220. (2,03/99,8).
**HIGH SCHOOL:** North High (Bloomington, Ind.).
**COLLEGE:** Oklahoma.
**TRANSACTIONS/CAREER NOTES:** Selected by Houston Rockets in second round (38th pick overall) of 1980 NBA Draft.... Played in Continental Basketball Association (1980-81 through 1982-83, 1990-91).

### COLLEGIATE RECORD

| | | | | | | | | | | | | | AVERAGES | | |
|---|---|---|---|---|---|---|---|---|---|---|---|---|---|---|---|
| Season Team | G | Min. | FGM | FGA | Pct. | FTM | FTA | Pct. | Reb. | Ast. | Pts. | | RPG | APG | PPG |
| 76-77—Oklahoma | 20 | ... | 34 | 104 | .327 | 13 | 17 | .765 | 59 | 18 | 81 | | 3.0 | 0.9 | 4.1 |
| 77-78—Oklahoma | 13 | ... | 50 | 96 | .521 | 20 | 28 | .714 | 55 | 11 | 120 | | 4.2 | 0.8 | 9.2 |
| 78-79—Oklahoma | 31 | 1102 | 186 | 373 | .499 | 76 | 98 | .776 | 175 | 83 | 448 | | 5.6 | 2.7 | 14.5 |
| 79-80—Oklahoma | 27 | 1002 | 184 | 355 | .518 | 87 | 110 | .791 | 125 | 106 | 455 | | 4.6 | 3.9 | 16.9 |
| Totals | 91 | ... | 454 | 928 | .489 | 196 | 253 | .775 | 414 | 218 | 1104 | | 4.5 | 2.4. | 12.1 |

### CBA REGULAR-SEASON RECORD

| | | | | | | | | | | | | | | AVERAGES | | |
|---|---|---|---|---|---|---|---|---|---|---|---|---|---|---|---|---|
| Season Team | G | Min. | FGM | FGA | Pct. | FTM | FTA | Pct. | Reb. | Ast. | PF | St. | Pts. | RPG | APG | PPG |
| 80-81—Montana | 36 | 1088 | 186 | 440 | .423 | 99 | 131 | .756 | 172 | 84 | 110 | 41 | 475 | 4.8 | 2.3 | 13.2 |
| 81-82—Montana | 46 | 1674 | 301 | 656 | .459 | 124 | 162 | .765 | 223 | 189 | 164 | 65 | 741 | 4.8 | 4.1 | 16.1 |
| 82-83—Montana | 44 | 1546 | 227 | 431 | .522 | 102 | 119 | .857 | 200 | 150 | 156 | 62 | 561 | 4.5 | 3.4 | 12.8 |
| 90-91—Albany | 78 | 2939 | 488 | 1179 | .414 | 333 | 447 | .745 | 619 | 276 | 313 | 6 | 1309 | 7.9 | 3.5 | 16.8 |
| Totals | 137 | 4603 | 751 | 1600 | .469 | 340 | 432 | .787 | 632 | 466 | 473 | 186 | 1871 | 4.6 | 3.4 | 13.7 |

### CBA PLAYOFF RECORD

| | | | | | | | | | | | | | | AVERAGES | | |
|---|---|---|---|---|---|---|---|---|---|---|---|---|---|---|---|---|
| Season Team | G | Min. | FGM | FGA | Pct. | FTM | FTA | Pct. | Reb. | Ast. | PF | St.. | Pts. | RPG | APG | PPG |
| 80-81—Montana | 10 | 314 | 51 | 118 | .432 | 27 | 35 | .771 | 42 | 27 | 33 | 9 | 130 | 4.2 | 2.7 | 13.0 |
| 81-82—Montana | 5 | 173 | 22 | 48 | .458 | 7 | 9 | .778 | 24 | 27 | 17 | 6 | 55 | 4.8 | 5.4 | 11.0 |
| 82-83—Montana | 11 | 444 | 72 | 138 | .522 | 24 | 40 | .600 | 69 | 39 | 42 | 22 | 170 | 6.3 | 3.6 | 15.5 |
| 90-91—Albany | 10 | 290 | 34 | 68 | .500 | 16 | 20 | .800 | 38 | 32 | 36 | 15 | 94 | 3.8 | 3.2 | 9.4 |
| Totals | 36 | 1221 | 179 | 372 | .481 | 74 | 104 | .712 | 173 | 125 | 128 | 52 | 449 | 4.8 | 3.5 | 112.5 |

### HEAD COACHING RECORD

**BACKGROUND:** Assistant coach, Seattle SuperSonics (1993-94 through 1997-98). ... Assistant coach, Milwaukee Bucks (1998-99 through 2001-02). ... Assistant coach, Atlanta Hawks (August 2002-December 26, 2002).

## NBA COACHING RECORD

| Season Team | W | L | Pct. | REGULAR SEASON Finish | W | L | PLAYOFFS Pct. |
|---|---|---|---|---|---|---|---|
| 02-03—Atlanta | 24 | 31 | .436 | 5th/Central Division | — | — | — |
| 03-04—Atlanta | 28 | 54 | .341 | 7th/Central Division | — | — | — |
| Totals (2 years) | 52 | 85 | .380 | | | | |

**NOTES:**

2002—Replaced Lon Kruger as Atlanta interim head coach (December 26) with a record of 11-16 and club in fifth place.

# VAN GUNDY, JEFF        ROCKETS

**PERSONAL:** Born January 19, 1962, in Hemet, Calif. ... 5-9/150. (1,76/68,0). ... Brother of Stan Van Gundy, head coach, Miami Heat.
**HIGH SCHOOL:** Brockport (N.Y.).
**JUNIOR COLLEGE:** Menlo Junior College (Palo Alto, Calif.).
**COLLEGE:** SUNY-Brockport (N.Y.), then Nazareth (Rochester, N.Y.).

### COLLEGIATE RECORD

| Season Team | G | Min. | FGM | FGA | Pct. | FTM | FTA | Pct. | Reb. | Ast. | Pts. | RPG | AVERAGES APG | PPG |
|---|---|---|---|---|---|---|---|---|---|---|---|---|---|---|
| 81-82—Menlo Junior College | | | | | | Statistics unavailable. | | | | | | | | |
| 82-83—SUNY-Brockport | 24 | ... | 125 | 222 | .536 | 57 | 78 | .731 | 80 | 85 | 307 | 3.3 | 3.5 | 12.8 |
| 83-84—Nazareth | 28 | ... | 84 | 146 | .575 | 41 | 48 | .854 | 42 | 118 | 209 | 1.5 | 4.2 | 7.5 |
| 84-85—Nazareth | 26 | ... | 88 | 156 | .564 | 91 | 104 | .875 | 64 | 133 | 267 | 2.5 | 5.1 | 10.3 |
| Varsity totals | 54 | ... | 172 | 302 | .570 | 132 | 152 | .868 | 106 | 251 | 476 | 2.0 | 4.6 | 8.8 |

### HEAD COACHING RECORD

**BACKGROUND:** Head coach, McQuaid Jesuit (Rochester, N.Y.) High School (1985-86). ... Graduate assistant, Providence College (1986-87). ... Assistant coach, Providence (1987-88). ... Assistant coach, Rutgers University (1988-89). ... Assistant coach, New York Knicks (1989-90 to March 8, 1996).

### NBA COACHING RECORD

| Season Team | W | L | Pct. | REGULAR SEASON Finish | W | L | PLAYOFFS Pct. |
|---|---|---|---|---|---|---|---|
| 95-96—New York | 13 | 10 | .565 | 2nd/Atlantic Division | 4 | 4 | .500 |
| 96-97—New York | 57 | 25 | .695 | 2nd/Atlantic Division | 6 | 4 | .600 |
| 97-98—New York | 43 | 39 | .524 | 2nd/Atlantic Division | 4 | 6 | .400 |
| 98-99—New York | 27 | 23 | .540 | 4th/Atlantic Division | 12 | 8 | .600 |
| 99-00—New York | 50 | 32 | .610 | 2nd/Atlantic Division | 9 | 7 | .563 |
| 00-01—New York | 48 | 34 | .585 | 3rd/Atlantic Division | 2 | 3 | .400 |
| 01-02—New York | 10 | 9 | .526 | | | | |
| 03-04—Houston | 45 | 37 | .549 | 5th/Midwest Division | 1 | 4 | .200 |
| 04-05—Houston | 51 | 31 | .622 | 3rd/Southwest Division | 3 | 4 | .429 |
| Totals (9 years) | 344 | 240 | .589 | Totals (8 years) | 41 | 40 | .506 |

**NOTES:**

1996—Replaced Don Nelson as New York Knicks head coach (March 8), with record of 34-26 and club in second place. Defeated Cleveland, 3-0, in Eastern Conference first round; lost to Chicago, 4-1, in Eastern Conference semifinals.

1997—Defeated Charlotte, 3-0, in Eastern Conference first round; lost to Miami, 4-3, in Eastern Conference semifinals.

1998—Defeated Miami, 3-2, in Eastern Conference first round; lost to Indiana, 4-1, in Eastern Conference semifinals.

1999—Defeated Miami, 3-2, in Eastern Conference first round; defeated Atlanta, 4-0, in Eastern Conference semifinals; defeated Indiana, 4-2, in Eastern Conference finals; lost to San Antonio, 4-1, in NBA Finals.

2000—Defeated Toronto, 3-0, in Eastern Conference first round; defeated Miami, 4-3, in Eastern Conference semifinals; lost to Indiana, 4-2, in Eastern Conference finals.

2001—Lost to Toronto in Eastern Conference first round.

2001—Replaced by Don Chaney as New York head coach (December 10) with record of 10-9 and club in third place.

2004—Lost to Los Angeles Lakers in Western Conference first round.

2005—Lost to Dallas in Western Conference first round.

# VAN GUNDY, STAN        HEAT

**PERSONAL:** Born in Indio, Calif. ... Brother of Jeff Van Gundy, head coach, Houston Rockets.
**HIGH SCHOOL:** Alhambra (N.Y.).
**COLLEGE:** SUNY-Brockport (N.Y.).
**MISCELLANEOUS:** Holds SUNY-Brockport record for career free throw percentage (.859).

### COLLEGIATE RECORD

| Season Team | G | Min. | FGM | FGA | Pct. | FTM | FTA | Pct. | Reb. | Ast. | Pts. | RPG | AVERAGES APG | PPG |
|---|---|---|---|---|---|---|---|---|---|---|---|---|---|---|
| 77-78—SUNY-Brockport | 20 | ... | 29 | 59 | .491 | 28 | 35 | .800 | 32 | ... | 86 | 1.6 | ... | 4.3 |
| 78-79—SUNY-Brockport | 27 | ... | 65 | 136 | .478 | 33 | 33 | 1.000 | 45 | ... | 163 | 1.7 | ... | 6.0 |
| 80-81—SUNY-Brockport | 23 | ... | 70 | 136 | .515 | 40 | 53 | .755 | 29 | ... | 180 | 1.3 | ... | 7.8 |
| 81-82—SUNY-Brockport | 24 | ... | 103 | 190 | .542 | 51 | 56 | .911 | 55 | ... | 257 | 2.3 | ... | 10.7 |
| Totals | 94 | ... | 267 | 521 | .512 | 152 | 177 | .859 | 161 | ... | 686 | 1.7 | ... | 7.3 |

**HEAD COACHES**

## HEAD COACHING RECORD

**BACKGROUND:** Assistant coach, University of Vermont (1981-83). ... Assistant coach, Canisus College (1987). ... Assistant coach, Fordham University (1998). ... Assistant coach, University of Wisconsin (1992-94).

### COLLEGIATE COACHING RECORD

| Season Team | W | L | Pct. |
|---|---|---|---|
| 83-84—Castleton State College | 26 | 2 | .923 |
| 84-85—Castleton State College | 23 | 7 | .767 |
| 85-86—Castleton State College | 19 | 9 | .679 |
| 88-89—Massachusetts-Lowell | 16 | 13 | .552 |
| 89-90—Massachusetts-Lowell | 13 | 15 | .464 |
| 90-91—Massachusetts-Lowell | 11 | 17 | .393 |
| 91-92—Massachusetts-Lowell | 14 | 15 | .483 |
| 94-95—Wisconsin | 13 | 14 | .482 |
| Totals (8 years) | 135 | 92 | .595 |

### NBA COACHING RECORD

| Season Team | REGULAR SEASON | | | | | PLAYOFFS | | |
|---|---|---|---|---|---|---|---|---|
| | W | L | Pct. | Finish | | W | L | Pct. |
| 03-04—Miami | 42 | 40 | .512 | 2nd/Atlantic Division | | 6 | 7 | .462 |
| 04-05—Miami | 59 | 23 | .720 | 1st/Atlantic Division | | 11 | 4 | .733 |
| Totals (2 years) | 101 | 63 | .616 | Totals (2 years) | | 17 | 11 | .607 |

**NOTES:**

2004—Defeated New Orleans, 4-3, in Eastern Conference first round; lost to Indiana, 4-2, in Eastern Conference semifinals.

2005—Defeated New Jersey, 4-0, in Eastern Conference first round; defeated Washington, 4-0, in Eastern Conference semifinals; lost to Detroit, 4-3, in Eastern Conference finals.

# WEISS, BOB                                        SUPERSONICS

**PERSONAL:** Born March 7, 1942, in Easton, Pa.
**HIGH SCHOOL:** Athens Area (Pa.).
**COLLEGE:** Penn State.
**TRANSACTIONS/CAREER NOTES:** Selected by Philadelphia 76ers in third round (25th pick overall) of 1965 NBA Draft. ... Played with Wilmington Blue Bombers in Eastern Basketball League (1965-66 and 1966-67). ... Selected by Seattle SuperSonics from 76ers in NBA Expansion Draft (May 1, 1967). ... Traded by Bucks with Bob Love to Chicago Bulls for Flynn Robinson (November 23, 1968). ... Traded by Bulls to Buffalo Braves for Matt Guokas and future draft choice (September 4, 1974). ... Waived by Braves (September 29, 1976). ... Signed as free agent by Washington Bullets (November 15, 1976).
**MISCELLANEOUS:** Member of NBA championship team (1967).

### COLLEGIATE RECORD

| Season Team | G | Min. | FGM | FGA | Pct. | FTM | FTA | Pct. | Reb. | Ast. | Pts. | AVERAGES | | |
|---|---|---|---|---|---|---|---|---|---|---|---|---|---|---|
| | | | | | | | | | | | | RPG | APG | PPG |
| 61-62—Penn State | | | | Freshman team statistics unavailable. | | | | | | | | | | |
| 62-63—Penn State | 20 | ... | 124 | 293 | .423 | 57 | 81 | .701 | 90 | ... | 305 | 4.5 | ... | 15.3 |
| 63-64—Penn State | 23 | ... | 154 | 353 | .436 | 84 | 105 | .800 | 90 | ... | 392 | 7.0 | ... | 17.0 |
| 64-65—Penn State | 24 | ... | 152 | 362 | .420 | 90 | 117 | .769 | 114 | ... | 394 | 5.4 | ... | 16.4 |
| Varsity totals | 67 | ... | 430 | 1008 | .427 | 231 | 303 | .762 | 294 | ... | 1091 | 4.4 | ... | 16.3 |

### EBL REGULAR-SEASON RECORD

| Season Team | G | Min. | FGM | FGA | Pct. | FTM | FTA | Pct. | Reb. | Ast. | Pts. | AVERAGES | | |
|---|---|---|---|---|---|---|---|---|---|---|---|---|---|---|
| | | | | | | | | | | | | RPG | APG | PPG |
| 65-66—Wilmington | 19 | ... | 56 | ... | ... | 32 | 44 | .727 | 55 | 83 | 146 | 3.0 | 4.4 | 7.7 |
| 66-67—Wilmington | 27 | ... | 151 | ... | ... | 100 | 118 | .847 | 103 | *238 | 403 | 3.8 | 8.8 | 14.9 |
| Totals | 46 | ... | 207 | ... | ... | 132 | 162 | .815 | 158 | 321 | 549 | 3.4 | 7.0 | 11.9 |

### NBA REGULAR-SEASON RECORD

| Season Team | G | Min. | FGM | FGA | Pct. | FTM | FTA | Pct. | Reb. | Ast. | Pts. | AVERAGES | | |
|---|---|---|---|---|---|---|---|---|---|---|---|---|---|---|
| | | | | | | | | | | | | RPG | APG | PPG |
| 65-66—Philadelphia | 7 | 30 | 3 | 9 | .333 | 0 | 0 | .000 | 7 | 4 | 6 | 1.0 | 0.6 | 0.9 |
| 66-67—Philadelphia | 6 | 29 | 5 | 10 | .500 | 2 | 5 | .400 | 3 | 10 | 12 | 0.5 | 1.7 | 2.0 |
| 67-68—Seattle | 82 | 1614 | 295 | 686 | .430 | 213 | 254 | .839 | 150 | 342 | 803 | 1.8 | 4.2 | 9.8 |
| 68-69—Milwaukee-Chicago | 77 | 1478 | 189 | 499 | .379 | 128 | 160 | .800 | 162 | 199 | 506 | 2.1 | 2.6 | 6.6 |
| 69-70—Chicago | 82 | 2544 | 365 | 855 | .427 | 213 | 253 | .842 | 227 | 474 | 943 | 2.8 | 5.8 | 11.5 |
| 70-71—Chicago | 82 | 2237 | 278 | 659 | .422 | 226 | 269 | .840 | 189 | 387 | 782 | 2.3 | 4.7 | 9.5 |
| 71-72—Chicago | 82 | 2450 | 358 | 832 | .430 | 212 | 254 | .835 | 170 | 377 | 212 | 2.1 | 4.6 | 11.3 |
| 72-73—Chicago | 82 | 2086 | 279 | 655 | .426 | 159 | 189 | .841 | 148 | 295 | 717 | 1.8 | 3.6 | 8.7 |

| Season Team | G | Min. | FGM | FGA | Pct. | FTM | FTA | Pct. | REBOUNDS | | | Ast. | St. | Blk. | TO | Pts. | AVERAGES | | |
|---|---|---|---|---|---|---|---|---|---|---|---|---|---|---|---|---|---|---|---|
| | | | | | | | | | Off. | Def. | Tot. | | | | | | RPG | APG | PPG |
| 73-74—Chicago | 79 | 1708 | 263 | 564 | .466 | 142 | 170 | .835 | 32 | 71 | 103 | 303 | 104 | 12 | ... | 668 | 1.3 | 3.8 | 8.5 |
| 74-75—Buffalo | 76 | 1338 | 102 | 261 | .391 | 54 | 67 | .806 | 21 | 83 | 104 | 260 | 82 | 19 | ... | 258 | 1.4 | 3.4 | 3.4 |
| 75-76—Buffalo | 66 | 995 | 89 | 183 | .486 | 35 | 48 | .729 | 13 | 53 | 66 | 150 | 48 | 14 | ... | 213 | 1.0 | 2.3 | 3.2 |
| 76-77—Washington | 62 | 768 | 62 | 133 | .466 | 29 | 37 | .784 | 15 | 54 | 69 | 130 | 53 | 7 | ... | 153 | 1.1 | 2.1 | 2.5 |
| Totals | 783 | 17277 | 2288 | 5346 | .428 | 1413 | 1706 | .828 | | | 1398 | 2931 | 287 | 52 | ... | 5989 | 1.8 | 3.7 | 7.6 |

Personal fouls/disqualifications: 1965-66, 10/0. 1966-67, 8/0. 1967-68, 137/1. 1968-69, 174/0. 1969-70, 206/0. 1970-71, 216/1. 1971-72, 212/1. 1972-73, 151/1. 1973-74, 156/0. 1974-75, 146/0. 1975-76, 94/0. 1976-77, 66/0. Totals, 1576/4.

## NBA PLAYOFF RECORD

| Season Team | G | Min. | FGM | FGA | Pct. | FTM | FTA | Pct. | Reb. | Ast. | Pts. | AVERAGES | | |
| --- | --- | --- | --- | --- | --- | --- | --- | --- | --- | --- | --- | --- | --- | --- |
| | | | | | | | | | | | | RPG | APG | PPG |
| 65-66—Philadelphia | 1 | 4 | 2 | 3 | .667 | 0 | 0 | ... | 2 | 2 | 4 | 2.0 | 2.0 | 4.0 |
| 69-70—Chicago | 5 | 121 | 25 | 59 | .424 | 8 | 10 | .800 | 6 | 24 | 58 | 1.2 | 4.8 | 11.6 |
| 70-71—Chicago | 7 | 250 | 42 | 92 | .457 | 26 | 30 | .867 | 18 | 57 | 110 | 2.6 | 8.1 | 15.7 |
| 71-72—Chicago | 4 | 119 | 24 | 49 | .490 | 7 | 8 | .875 | 13 | 12 | 55 | 3.3 | 3.0 | 13.8 |
| 72-73—Chicago | 7 | 175 | 34 | 79 | .430 | 16 | 21 | .762 | 16 | 15 | 84 | 2.3 | 2.1 | 12.0 |

| Season Team | G | Min. | FGM | FGA | Pct. | FTM | FTA | Pct. | REBOUNDS | | | Ast. | St. | Blk. | TO | Pts. | AVERAGES | | |
| --- | --- | --- | --- | --- | --- | --- | --- | --- | --- | --- | --- | --- | --- | --- | --- | --- | --- | --- | --- |
| | | | | | | | | | Off. | Def. | Tot. | | | | | | RPG | APG | PPG |
| 73-74—Chicago | 11 | 251 | 23 | 74 | .311 | 6 | 6 | 1.000 | 5 | 15 | 20 | 32 | 7 | 1 | ... | 52 | 1.8 | 2.9 | 4.7 |
| 74-75—Buffalo | 7 | 113 | 11 | 23 | .478 | 8 | 12 | .667 | 2 | 5 | 7 | 17 | 4 | 1 | ... | 30 | 1.0 | 2.4 | 4.3 |
| 75-76—Buffalo | 7 | 36 | 3 | 8 | .375 | 2 | 3 | .667 | 0 | 4 | 4 | 3 | 2 | 0 | ... | 8 | 0.6 | 0.4 | 1.1 |
| 76-77—Washington | 4 | 34 | 3 | 5 | .600 | 0 | 1 | .000 | 1 | 2 | 3 | 2 | 1 | 0 | ... | 6 | 0.8 | 0.5 | 1.5 |
| Totals | 53 | 1103 | 167 | 392 | .426 | 73 | 91 | .802 | ... | ... | 89 | 164 | 14 | 2 | | 407 | 1.7 | 3.1 | 7.7 |

Personal fouls/disqualifications: 1966-67, 1/0. 1969-70,11/0. 1970-71, 19/0. 1971-72, 15/1. 1972-73, 20/0. 1973-74, 20/0. 1974-75, 15/0. 1975-76, 5/0. 1976-77, 5/0. Totals, 111/1.

## HEAD COACHING RECORD

**NOTES:** Assistant coach, San Diego Clippers (1977-78 and 1978-79) ... Assistant coach, Dallas Mavericks (1980-81 through 1985-86) ... Assistant coach, Orlando Magic (1989-90) ... Assistant coach, Detroit Pistons (May 27-July 12, 1993).

### NBA COACHING RECORD

| Season Team | REGULAR SEASON | | | | PLAYOFFS | | |
| --- | --- | --- | --- | --- | --- | --- | --- |
| | W | L | Pct. | Finish | W | L | Pct. |
| 86-87—San Antonio | 28 | 54 | .341 | 6th/Midwest Division | — | — | — |
| 87-88—San Antonio | 31 | 51 | .378 | 5th/Midwest Division | 0 | 3 | .000 |
| 90-91—Atlanta | 43 | 39 | .524 | 4th/Central Division | 2 | 3 | .400 |
| 91-92—Atlanta | 38 | 44 | .463 | 5th/Central Division | — | — | — |
| 92-93—Atlanta | 43 | 39 | .524 | 4th/Central Division | 0 | 3 | .000 |
| 93-94—Los Angeles Clippers | 27 | 55 | .329 | 7th/Pacific Division | — | — | — |
| Totals (6 years) | 210 | 282 | .427 | Totals (3 years) | 2 | 9 | .182 |

**NOTES:**

1988—Lost to Los Angeles Lakers in Western Conference first round.
1991—Lost to Detroit in Eastern Conference first round.
1993—Lost to Chicago in Eastern Conference first round.

## WOODSON, MIKE                                                 HAWKS

**PERSONAL:** Born March 24, 1958, in Indianapolis ... 6-5/198.
**HIGH SCHOOL:** Broad Ripple (Indianapolis).
**COLLEGE:** Indiana.
**TRANSACTIONS/CAREER NOTES:** Selected by New York Knicks in first round (12th pick overall) of 1980 NBA Draft. ... Traded by Knicks to New Jersey Nets for Mike Newlin (June 10, 1981). ... Traded by Nets with 1982 first-round draft choice to Kansas City Kings for Sam Lacey (November 12, 1981). ... Traded by Kings with Larry Drew, a 1988 first-round draft choice and a 1989 first-round draft choice to Los Angeles Clippers for Junior Bridgeman, Franklin Edwards and Derek Smith (August 19, 1986). ... Signed as free agent by Houston Rockets (July 19, 1988). ... Waived by Rockets (December 4, 1990). ... Signed as free agent by Cleveland Cavaliers (December 13, 1990). ... Waived by Cavaliers (December 24, 1990).

### COLLEGIATE RECORD

| Season Team | G | Min. | FGM | FGA | Pct. | FTM | FTA | Pct. | Reb. | Ast. | Pts. | AVERAGES | | |
| --- | --- | --- | --- | --- | --- | --- | --- | --- | --- | --- | --- | --- | --- | --- |
| | | | | | | | | | | | | RPG | APG | PPG |
| 76-77—Indiana | 27 | ... | 212 | 407 | .521 | 76 | 96 | .792 | 182 | 43 | 500 | 6.7 | 1.6 | 18.5 |
| 77-78—Indiana | 29 | ... | 242 | 462 | .524 | 93 | 121 | .769 | 157 | 41 | 577 | 5.4 | 1.4 | 19.9 |
| 78-79—Indiana | 34 | ... | 265 | 532 | .498 | 184 | 241 | .763 | 193 | 100 | 714 | 5.7 | 2.9 | 21.0 |
| 79-80—Indiana | 14 | ... | 102 | 225 | .453 | 66 | 79 | .835 | 49 | 36 | 270 | 3.5 | 2.6 | 19.3 |
| Totals | 104 | ... | 821 | 1626 | .505 | 419 | 537 | .780 | 581 | 220 | 2061 | 5.6 | 2.1 | 19.8 |

### NBA REGULAR-SEASON RECORD

| Season Team | G | Min. | FGM | FGA | Pct. | FTM | FTA | Pct. | REBOUNDS | | | Ast. | St. | Blk. | TO | Pts. | AVERAGES | | |
| --- | --- | --- | --- | --- | --- | --- | --- | --- | --- | --- | --- | --- | --- | --- | --- | --- | --- | --- | --- |
| | | | | | | | | | Off. | Def. | Tot. | | | | | | RPG | APG | PPG |
| 80-81—New York | 81 | 949 | 165 | 373 | .442 | 49 | 64 | .766 | 33 | 64 | 97 | 75 | 36 | 12 | ... | 380 | 1.2 | 0.9 | 4.7 |
| 81-82—N.J.-K.C. | 83 | 2331 | 538 | 1069 | .503 | 221 | 286 | .773 | 102 | 145 | 247 | 222 | 142 | 35 | ... | 1304 | 3.0 | 2.7 | 15.7 |
| 82-83—Kansas City | 81 | 2426 | 584 | 1154 | .506 | 298 | 377 | .790 | 84 | 164 | 248 | 254 | 137 | 59 | ... | 1473 | 3.1 | 3.1 | 18.2 |
| 83-84—Kansas City | 71 | 1838 | 389 | 816 | .477 | 247 | 302 | .818 | 62 | 113 | 175 | 175 | 83 | 28 | ... | 1027 | 2.5 | 2.5 | 14.5 |
| 84-85—Kansas City | 78 | 1998 | 530 | 1068 | .496 | 264 | 330 | .800 | 69 | 129 | 198 | 143 | 117 | 28 | ... | 1329 | 2.5 | 1.8 | 17.0 |
| 85-86—Sacramento | 81 | 2417 | 510 | 1073 | .475 | 242 | 289 | .837 | 94 | 132 | 226 | 197 | 92 | 37 | ... | 1264 | 2.8 | 2.4 | 15.6 |
| 86-87—L.A. Clippers | 74 | 2126 | 494 | 1130 | .437 | 240 | 290 | .828 | 68 | 94 | 162 | 196 | 100 | 16 | ... | 1262 | 2.2 | 2.6 | 17.1 |
| 87-88—L.A. Clippers | 80 | 2534 | 562 | 1263 | .445 | 296 | 341 | .868 | 64 | 126 | 190 | 273 | 109 | 26 | ... | 1438 | 2.4 | 3.4 | 18.0 |
| 88-89—Houston | 81 | 2259 | 410 | 936 | .438 | 195 | 237 | .823 | 51 | 143 | 194 | 206 | 89 | 18 | ... | 1046 | 2.4 | 2.5 | 12.9 |
| 89-90—Houston | 61 | 972 | 160 | 405 | .395 | 62 | 86 | .721 | 25 | 53 | 88 | 66 | 42 | 11 | ... | 394 | 1.4 | 1.1 | 6.5 |
| 90-91—Hous.-Cleve. | 15 | 171 | 26 | 77 | .338 | 11 | 13 | .846 | 3 | 10 | 13 | 15 | 5 | 5 | ... | 64 | 0.9 | 1.0 | 4.3 |
| Totals | 786 | 20021 | 4368 | 9364 | .466 | 2125 | 2615 | .813 | 655 | 1183 | 1838 | 1822 | 952 | 275 | ... | 10981 | 2.3 | 2.3 | 14.0 |

HEAD COACHES

Three-point field goals: 1980-81, 1-for-5 (.200). 1981-82, 7-for-25 (.280). 1982-83, 7-for-33 (.212). 1983-84, 2-for-8 (.250). 1984-85, 5-for-21 (.238). 1985-86, 2-for-13 (.154). 1986-87, 34-for-123 (.276). 1987-88, 18-for-78 (.231). 1988-89, 31-for-89 (.348). 1989-90, 12-for-41 (.293). 1990-91, 1-for-7 (.143). Totals: 120-for-443 (.271).

## NBA PLAYOFF RECORD

| Season  Team | G | Min. | FGM | FGA | Pct. | FTM | FTA | Pct. | Reb. | Ast. | PF | Dq. | Pts. | AVERAGES RPG | APG | PPG |
|---|---|---|---|---|---|---|---|---|---|---|---|---|---|---|---|---|
| 80-81—New York | 2 | 8 | 1 | 3 | .333 | 2 | 2 | 1.000 | 2 | 0 | 3 | 0 | 4 | 1.0 | 0.0 | 2.0 |
| 83-84—Kansas City | 3 | 87 | 18 | 44 | .409 | 13 | 15 | .867 | 8 | 9 | 11 | 0 | 49 | 2.7 | 3.0 | 16.3 |
| 85-86—Sacramento | 3 | 110 | 22 | 49 | .449 | 12 | 12 | 1.000 | 11 | 5 | 13 | 0 | 56 | 3.7 | 1.7 | 18.7 |
| 88-89—Houston | 4 | 137 | 17 | 49 | .347 | 10 | 12 | .833 | 9 | 18 | 7 | 0 | 47 | 2.3 | 4.5 | 11.8 |
| 89-90—Houston | 1 | 6 | 1 | 3 | .333 | 0 | 0 | ... | 0 | 2 | 1 | 0 | 2 | 0.0 | 2.0 | 2.0 |
| **Totals** | 13 | 348 | 59 | 148 | .399 | 37 | 41 | .902 | 30 | 34 | 35 | 0 | 158 | 2.3 | 2.6 | 12.2 |

Three-point field goals: 1983-84, 0-for-1. 1985-86, 0-for-2. 1988-89, 3-for-9, (.333). 1989-90, 0-for-1. Totals: 3-for-13 (.231).

## HEAD COACHING RECORD

**BACKGROUND:** Assistant coach, Bucks (1996-99). ... Assistant coach, Cavaliers (1999-2001). ... Assistant coach, 76ers (2001-03). ... Assistant coach, Pistons (2003-04).

### NBA COACHING RECORD

| Season  Team | REGULAR SEASON W | L | Pct. | Finish | PLAYOFFS W | L | Pct. |
|---|---|---|---|---|---|---|---|
| 04-05—Atlanta | 13 | 69 | .159 | 5th/Southeast Division | — | — | — |

HEAD COACHES

## ABDUL-JABBAR, KAREEM      C

**PERSONAL:** Born April 16, 1947, in New York. ... 7-2/267 (2,18/121,1). ... Full name: Kareem Abdul-Jabbar. ... Formerly known as Lew Alcindor.
**HIGH SCHOOL:** Power Memorial (New York).
**COLLEGE:** UCLA.
**TRANSACTIONS:** Selected by Milwaukee Bucks in first round (first pick overall) of 1969 NBA Draft. ... Traded by Bucks with C Walt Wesley to Los Angeles Lakers for C Elmore Smith, G/F Brian Winters, F Dave Meyers and F/G Junior Bridgeman (June 16, 1975).
**CAREER HONORS:** Elected to Naismith Memorial Basketball Hall of Fame (1995). ... NBA 35th Anniversary All-Time Team (1980) and One of the 50 Greatest Players in NBA History (1996).
**CAREER NOTES:** Assistant coach, Los Angeles Clippers (February 18, 2000-July 1, 2000). ... Head coach, Oklahoma Storm, USBL (2002). ... Scout, New York Knicks.
**MISCELLANEOUS:** Member of NBA championship team (1971, 1980, 1982, 1985, 1987, 1988). ... Milwaukee Bucks all-time leading scorer with 14,211 points and all-time leading rebounder with 7,161 (1969-70 through 1974-75). ... Los Angeles Lakers franchise all-time blocked shots leader with 2,694 (1975-76 through 1988-89).

### COLLEGIATE RECORD

**NOTES:** Member of NCAA championship team (1967, 1968, 1969). ... THE SPORTING NEWS College Player of the Year (1967, 1969). ... Naismith Award winner (1969). ... THE SPORTING NEWS All-America first team (1967, 1968, 1969). ... NCAA Tournament Most Outstanding Player (1967, 1968, 1969). ... Led NCAA Division I with .667 field goal percentage (1967) and .635 field goal percentage (1969).

| | | | | | | | | | | | | | AVERAGES | |
| Season Team | G | Min. | FGM | FGA | Pct. | FTM | FTA | Pct. | Reb. | Ast. | Pts. | RPG | APG | PPG |
|---|---|---|---|---|---|---|---|---|---|---|---|---|---|---|
| 65-66—UCLA‡ | 21 | ... | 295 | 432 | .683 | 106 | 179 | .592 | 452 | ... | 696 | 21.5 | ... | 33.1 |
| 66-67—UCLA | 30 | ... | 346 | 519 | .667 | 178 | 274 | .650 | 466 | ... | 870 | 15.5 | ... | 29.0 |
| 67-68—UCLA | 28 | ... | 294 | 480 | .613 | 146 | 237 | .616 | 461 | ... | 734 | 16.5 | ... | 26.2 |
| 68-69—UCLA | 30 | ... | 303 | 477 | .635 | 115 | 188 | .612 | 440 | ... | 721 | 14.7 | ... | 24.0 |
| Varsity totals | 88 | ... | 943 | 1476 | .639 | 439 | 699 | .628 | 1367 | ... | 2325 | 15.5 | ... | 26.4 |

### NBA REGULAR-SEASON RECORD

**RECORDS:** Holds career records for most minutes played—57,446; most points—38,387; most field goals made—15,837; most field goals attempted—28,307. ... Holds single-season record for most defensive rebounds—1,111 (1976). ... Holds single-game record for most defensive rebounds—29 (December 14, 1975, vs. Detroit).
**HONORS:** NBA Most Valuable Player (1971, 1972, 1974, 1976, 1977, 1980). ... NBA Rookie of the Year (1970). ... All-NBA first team (1971, 1972, 1973, 1974, 1976, 1977, 1980, 1981, 1984, 1986). ... All-NBA second team (1970, 1978, 1979, 1983, 1985). ... NBA All-Defensive first team (1974, 1975, 1979, 1980, 1981). ... NBA All-Defensive second team (1970, 1971, 1976, 1977, 1978, 1984). ... NBA All-Rookie team (1970).
**NOTES:** Led NBA with 3.26 blocked shots per game (1975), 4.12 blocked shots per game (1976), 3.95 blocked shots per game (1979) and 3.41 blocked shots per game (1980).

| | | | | | | | | | | | | | | AVERAGES | | |
| Season Team | G | Min. | FGM | FGA | Pct. | FTM | FTA | Pct. | Reb. | Ast. | PF | Dq. | Pts. | RPG | APG | PPG |
|---|---|---|---|---|---|---|---|---|---|---|---|---|---|---|---|---|
| 69-70—Milwaukee | 82 | 3534 | *938 | 1810 | .518 | 485 | 743 | .653 | 1190 | 337 | 283 | 8 | *2361 | 14.5 | 4.1 | 28.8 |
| 70-71—Milwaukee | 82 | 3288 | *1063 | 1843 | .577 | 470 | 681 | .690 | 1311 | 272 | 264 | 4 | *2596 | 16.0 | 3.3 | *31.7 |
| 71-72—Milwaukee | 81 | 3583 | *1159 | *2019 | .574 | 504 | 732 | .689 | 1346 | 370 | 235 | 1 | *2822 | 16.6 | 4.6 | *34.8 |
| 72-73—Milwaukee | 76 | 3254 | 982 | 1772 | .554 | 328 | 460 | .713 | 1224 | 379 | 208 | 0 | 2292 | 16.1 | 5.0 | 30.2 |

| | | | | | | | | | REBOUNDS | | | | | | | AVERAGES | | |
| Season Team | G | Min. | FGM | FGA | Pct. | FTM | FTA | Pct. | Off. | Def. | Tot. | Ast. | St. | Blk. | TO | Pts. | RPG | APG | PPG |
|---|---|---|---|---|---|---|---|---|---|---|---|---|---|---|---|---|---|---|---|
| 73-74—Milwaukee | 81 | 3548 | *948 | 1759 | .539 | 295 | 420 | .702 | 287 | 891 | 1178 | 386 | 112 | 283 | ... | 2191 | 14.5 | 4.8 | 27.0 |
| 74-75—Milwaukee | 65 | 2747 | 812 | 1584 | .513 | 325 | 426 | .763 | 194 | 718 | 912 | 264 | 65 | 212 | ... | 1949 | 14.0 | 4.1 | 30.0 |
| 75-76—Los Angeles | 82 | *3379 | 914 | 1728 | .529 | 447 | 636 | .703 | 272 | *1111 | *1383 | 413 | 119 | *338 | ... | 2275 | *16.9 | 5.0 | 27.7 |
| 76-77—Los Angeles | 82 | 3016 | *888 | 1533 | *.579 | 376 | 536 | .702 | 266 | *824 | *1090 | 319 | 101 | *261 | ... | 2152 | 13.3 | 3.9 | 26.2 |
| 77-78—Los Angeles | 62 | 2265 | 663 | 1205 | .550 | 274 | 350 | .783 | 186 | 615 | 801 | 269 | 103 | 185 | 208 | 1600 | 12.9 | 4.3 | 25.8 |
| 78-79—Los Angeles | 80 | 3157 | 777 | 1347 | .577 | 349 | 474 | .736 | 207 | 818 | 1025 | 431 | 76 | *316 | 282 | 1903 | 12.8 | 5.4 | 23.8 |
| 79-80—Los Angeles | 82 | 3143 | 835 | 1383 | .604 | 364 | 476 | .765 | 190 | 696 | 886 | 371 | 81 | *280 | 297 | 2034 | 10.8 | 4.5 | 24.8 |
| 80-81—Los Angeles | 80 | 2976 | 836 | 1457 | .574 | 423 | 552 | .766 | 197 | 624 | 821 | 272 | 59 | 228 | 249 | 2095 | 10.3 | 3.4 | 26.2 |
| 81-82—Los Angeles | 76 | 2677 | 753 | 1301 | .579 | 312 | 442 | .706 | 172 | 487 | 659 | 225 | 63 | 207 | 230 | 1818 | 8.7 | 3.0 | 23.9 |
| 82-83—Los Angeles | 79 | 2554 | 722 | 1228 | .588 | 278 | 371 | .749 | 167 | 425 | 592 | 200 | 61 | 170 | 200 | 1722 | 7.5 | 2.5 | 21.8 |
| 83-84—Los Angeles | 80 | 2622 | 716 | 1238 | .578 | 285 | 394 | .723 | 169 | 418 | 587 | 211 | 55 | 143 | 221 | 1717 | 7.3 | 2.6 | 21.5 |
| 84-85—L.A. Lakers | 79 | 2630 | 723 | 1207 | .599 | 289 | 395 | .732 | 162 | 460 | 622 | 249 | 63 | 162 | 197 | 1735 | 7.9 | 3.2 | 22.0 |
| 85-86—L.A. Lakers | 79 | 2629 | 755 | 1338 | .564 | 336 | 439 | .765 | 133 | 345 | 478 | 280 | 67 | 130 | 203 | 1846 | 6.1 | 3.5 | 23.4 |
| 86-87—L.A. Lakers | 78 | 2441 | 560 | 993 | .564 | 245 | 343 | .714 | 152 | 371 | 523 | 203 | 49 | 97 | 186 | 1366 | 6.7 | 2.6 | 17.5 |
| 87-88—L.A. Lakers | 80 | 2308 | 480 | 903 | .532 | 205 | 269 | .762 | 118 | 360 | 478 | 135 | 48 | 92 | 159 | 1165 | 6.0 | 1.7 | 14.6 |
| 88-89—L.A. Lakers | 74 | 1695 | 313 | 659 | .475 | 122 | 165 | .739 | 103 | 231 | 334 | 74 | 38 | 85 | 95 | 748 | 4.5 | 1.0 | 10.1 |
| Totals | 1560 | 57446 | 15837 | 28307 | .559 | 6712 | 9304 | .721 | ... | ... | 17440 | 5660 | 1160 | 3189 | 2527 | 38387 | 11.2 | 3.6 | 24.6 |

Three-point field goals: 1979-80, 0-for-1. 1980-81, 0-for-1. 1981-82, 0-for-3. 1982-83, 0-for-2. 1983-84, 0-for-1. 1984-85, 0-for-1. 1985-86, 0-for-2. 1986-87, 1-for-3 (.333). 1987-88, 0-for-1. 1988-89, 0-for-3. Totals, 1-for-18 (.056).
Personal fouls/disqualifications: 1973-74, 238/2. 1974-75, 205/2. 1975-76, 292/6. 1976-77, 262/4. 1977-78, 182/1. 1978-79, 230/3. 1979-80, 216/2. 1980-81, 244/4. 1981-82, 224/0. 1982-83, 220/1. 1983-84, 211/1. 1984-85, 238/3. 1985-86, 248/2. 1986-87, 245/2. 1987-88, 216/1. 1988-89, 196/1. Totals, 4657/48.

### NBA PLAYOFF RECORD

**NOTES:** NBA Finals Most Valuable Player (1971, 1985). ... Holds career playoff records for most seasons played—18; most games played—237; most minutes played—8,851; most field goals made—2,356; most blocked shots—476; and most personal fouls—797.

| | | | | | | | | | | | | | AVERAGES | | |
| Season Team | G | Min. | FGM | FGA | Pct. | FTM | FTA | Pct. | Reb. | Ast. | PF | Dq. | Pts. | RPG | APG | PPG |
|---|---|---|---|---|---|---|---|---|---|---|---|---|---|---|---|---|
| 69-70—Milwaukee | 10 | 435 | 139 | 245 | .567 | 74 | 101 | .733 | 168 | 41 | 25 | 1 | 352 | 16.8 | 4.1 | 35.2 |
| 70-71—Milwaukee | 14 | 577 | 152 | 295 | .515 | 68 | 101 | .673 | 238 | 35 | 45 | 0 | 372 | 17.0 | 2.5 | 26.6 |
| 71-72—Milwaukee | 11 | 510 | 139 | 318 | .437 | 38 | 54 | .704 | 200 | 56 | 35 | 0 | 316 | 18.2 | 5.1 | 28.7 |
| 72-73—Milwaukee | 6 | 276 | 59 | 138 | .428 | 19 | 35 | .543 | 97 | 17 | 26 | 0 | 137 | 16.2 | 2.8 | 22.8 |

| Season Team | G | Min. | FGM | FGA | Pct. | FTM | FTA | Pct. | Off. | Def. | Tot. | Ast. | St. | Blk. | TO | Pts. | RPG | APG | PPG |
|---|---|---|---|---|---|---|---|---|---|---|---|---|---|---|---|---|---|---|---|
| 73-74—Milwaukee ...... | 16 | 758 | 224 | 402 | .557 | 67 | 91 | .736 | 67 | 186 | 253 | 78 | 20 | 39 | ... | 515 | 15.8 | 4.9 | 32.2 |
| 76-77—Los Angeles .... | 11 | 467 | 147 | 242 | .607 | 87 | 120 | .725 | 51 | 144 | 195 | 45 | 19 | 38 | ... | 381 | 17.7 | 4.1 | 34.6 |
| 77-78—Los Angeles.... | 3 | 134 | 38 | 73 | .521 | 5 | 9 | .556 | 14 | 27 | 41 | 11 | 2 | 12 | 14 | 81 | 13.7 | 3.7 | 27.0 |
| 78-79—Los Angeles .... | 8 | 367 | 88 | 152 | .579 | 52 | 62 | .839 | 18 | 83 | 101 | 38 | 8 | 33 | 29 | 228 | 12.6 | 4.8 | 28.5 |
| 79-80—Los Angeles .... | 15 | 618 | 198 | 346 | .572 | 83 | 105 | .790 | 51 | 130 | 181 | 46 | 17 | 58 | 55 | 479 | 12.1 | 3.1 | 31.9 |
| 80-81—Los Angeles .... | 3 | 134 | 30 | 65 | .462 | 20 | 28 | .714 | 13 | 37 | 50 | 12 | 3 | 8 | 11 | 80 | 16.7 | 4.0 | 26.7 |
| 81-82—Los Angeles .... | 14 | 493 | 115 | 221 | .520 | 55 | 87 | .632 | 33 | 86 | 119 | 51 | 14 | 45 | 41 | 285 | 8.5 | 3.6 | 20.4 |
| 82-83—Los Angeles .... | 15 | 588 | 163 | 287 | .568 | 80 | 106 | .755 | 25 | 90 | 115 | 42 | 17 | 55 | 50 | 406 | 7.7 | 2.8 | 27.1 |
| 83-84—Los Angeles .... | 21 | 767 | 206 | 371 | .555 | 90 | 120 | .750 | 56 | 117 | 173 | 79 | 23 | 45 | 45 | 502 | 8.2 | 3.8 | 23.9 |
| 84-85—L.A. Lakers .... | 19 | 610 | 168 | 300 | .560 | 80 | 103 | .777 | 50 | 104 | 154 | 76 | 23 | 36 | 52 | 416 | 8.1 | 4.0 | 21.9 |
| 85-86—L.A. Lakers .... | 14 | 489 | 157 | 282 | .557 | 48 | 61 | .787 | 26 | 57 | 83 | 49 | 15 | 24 | 42 | 362 | 5.9 | 3.5 | 25.9 |
| 86-87—L.A. Lakers .... | 18 | 559 | 124 | 234 | .530 | 97 | 122 | .795 | 39 | 84 | 123 | 36 | 8 | 35 | 40 | 345 | 6.8 | 2.0 | 19.2 |
| 87-88—L.A. Lakers .... | 24 | 718 | 141 | 304 | .464 | 56 | 71 | .789 | 49 | 82 | 131 | 36 | 15 | 37 | 46 | 338 | 5.5 | 1.5 | 14.1 |
| 88-89—L.A. Lakers .... | 15 | 351 | 68 | 147 | .463 | 31 | 43 | .721 | 13 | 46 | 59 | 15 | 5 | 11 | 22 | 167 | 3.9 | 1.3 | 11.1 |
| Totals .................. | 237 | 8851 | 2356 | 4422 | .533 | 1050 | 1419 | .740 | ... | ... | 2481 | 767 | 189 | 476 | 447 | 5762 | 10.5 | 3.2 | 24.3 |

Three-point field goals: 1982-83, 0-for-1. 1986-87, 0-for-1. 1987-88, 0-for-2. 1988-89, 0-for-1. Totals, 0-for-5.

Personal fouls/disqualifications: 1973-74, 41/0. 1976-77, 42/0. 1977-78, 14/1. 1978-79, 26/0. 1979-80, 51/0. 1980-81, 14/0. 1981-82, 45/0. 1982-83, 61/1. 1983-84, 71/2. 1984-85, 67/1. 1985-86, 54/0. 1986-87, 56/0. 1987-88, 81/1. 1988-89, 43/0. Totals, 797/7.

## NBA ALL-STAR GAME RECORD

**NOTES:** Holds career records for most games played—18; most minutes played—449; most field goals made—105; most field goals attempted—213; most points—251; most blocked shots—31; and most personal fouls—57. ... Holds single-game record for most blocked shots—6 (1980, OT).

| Season Team | Min. | FGM | FGA | Pct. | FTM | FTA | Pct. | Reb. | Ast. | PF | Dq. | Pts. |
|---|---|---|---|---|---|---|---|---|---|---|---|---|
| 1970—Milwaukee ................... | 18 | 4 | 8 | .500 | 2 | 2 | 1.000 | 11 | 4 | 6 | 1 | 10 |
| 1971—Milwaukee ................... | 30 | 8 | 16 | .500 | 3 | 4 | .750 | 14 | 1 | 2 | 0 | 19 |
| 1972—Milwaukee ................... | 19 | 5 | 10 | .500 | 2 | 2 | 1.000 | 7 | 2 | 0 | 0 | 12 |
| 1973—Milwaukee | | | | | | Selected, did not play. | | | | | | |
| 1974—Milwaukee ............ | 23 | 7 | 11 | .636 | 0 | 0 | ... | 1 | 7 | 8 | 6 | 2 | 0 | 1 | 1 | ... | 14 |
| 1975—Milwaukee............ | 19 | 3 | 10 | .300 | 1 | 2 | .500 | 5 | 5 | 10 | 3 | 2 | 0 | 0 | 1 | ... | 7 |
| 1976—Los Angeles ......... | 36 | 9 | 16 | .563 | 4 | 4 | 1.000 | 2 | 13 | 15 | 3 | 3 | 0 | 3 | ... | 22 |
| 1977—Los Angeles ......... | 23 | 8 | 14 | .571 | 5 | 6 | .833 | 3 | 1 | 4 | 2 | 1 | 0 | 1 | 1 | ... | 21 |
| 1979—Los Angeles ......... | 28 | 5 | 12 | .417 | 1 | 2 | .500 | 1 | 7 | 8 | 3 | 4 | 0 | 1 | 1 | 3 | 11 |
| 1980—Los Angeles ......... | 30 | 6 | 17 | .353 | 5 | 6 | .833 | 5 | 11 | 16 | 9 | 5 | 0 | 6 | 9 | 17 |
| 1981—Los Angeles ......... | 23 | 6 | 9 | .667 | 3 | 3 | 1.000 | 2 | 4 | 6 | 4 | 3 | 0 | 4 | 3 | 15 |
| 1982—Los Angeles ......... | 22 | 1 | 10 | .100 | 0 | 0 | ... | 1 | 2 | 3 | 1 | 3 | 0 | 2 | 1 | 2 |
| 1983—Los Angeles ......... | 32 | 9 | 12 | .750 | 2 | 3 | .667 | 2 | 4 | 6 | 5 | 1 | 0 | 1 | 4 | 20 |
| 1984—Los Angeles ......... | 37 | 11 | 19 | .579 | 3 | 4 | .750 | 5 | 8 | 13 | 2 | 5 | 0 | 1 | 4 | 25 |
| 1985—L.A. Lakers ......... | 23 | 5 | 10 | .500 | 1 | 2 | .500 | 0 | 6 | 6 | 1 | 5 | 0 | 1 | 1 | 11 |
| 1986—L.A. Lakers ......... | 32 | 9 | 15 | .600 | 3 | 4 | .750 | 2 | 5 | 7 | 2 | 4 | 0 | 2 | 5 | 21 |
| 1987—L.A. Lakers ......... | 27 | 4 | 9 | .444 | 2 | 2 | 1.000 | 2 | 6 | 8 | 3 | 5 | 0 | 2 | 1 | 10 |
| 1988—L.A. Lakers ......... | 14 | 4 | 9 | .444 | 2 | 2 | 1.000 | 2 | 2 | 4 | 0 | 3 | 0 | 0 | 0 | 10 |
| 1989—L.A. Lakers ......... | 13 | 1 | 6 | .167 | 2 | 2 | 1.000 | 0 | 3 | 3 | 0 | 3 | 0 | 2 | 0 | 4 |
| Totals ........................... | 449 | 105 | 213 | .493 | 41 | 50 | .820 | ... | ... | 149 | 51 | 57 | 1 | 6 | 31 | 28 | 251 |

Three-point field goals: 1989, 0-for-1.

## USBL COACHING RECORD

| | | REGULAR SEASON | | | | | PLAYOFFS | | |
|---|---|---|---|---|---|---|---|---|---|
| Season Team | W | L | Pct. | Finish | | W | L | Pct. |
| 2002—Oklahoma ...................................... | 17 | 13 | .567 | 2nd/Midwest Division | | 3 | 0 | 1.000 |

**NOTES:**
2002—Defeated St. Joseph in quarterfinals; defeated Brevard in semifinals; defeated Kansas in USBL Finals.

---

## AGUIRRE, MARK                    F

**PERSONAL:** Born December 10, 1959, in Chicago. ... 6-6/232 (1,98/105,2). ... Full name: Mark Anthony Aguirre. ... Name pronounced a-GWIRE.
**HIGH SCHOOL:** Austin (Chicago), then Westinghouse Vocational (Chicago).
**COLLEGE:** DePaul.
**TRANSACTIONS:** Selected after junior season by Dallas Mavericks in first round (first pick overall) of 1981 NBA Draft. ... Traded by Mavericks to Detroit Pistons for F Adrian Dantley and 1991 first-round draft choice (February 15, 1989). ... Waived by Pistons (October 7, 1993). ... Signed as free agent by Los Angeles Clippers (October 25, 1993). ... Waived by Clippers (February 1, 1994).
**CAREER NOTES:** Director of player development and scouting, Dallas Mavericks (1996-97). ... Special assistant, Indiana Pacers (2002-03). ... Assistant coach, New York Knicks (2003-04).
**MISCELLANEOUS:** Member of NBA championship team (1989, 1990). ... Member of U.S. Olympic team (1980).

## COLLEGIATE RECORD

**NOTES:** The Sporting News College Player of the Year (1981). ... Naismith Award winner (1980). ... The Sporting News All-America first team (1980, 1981).

| Season Team | G | Min. | FGM | FGA | Pct. | FTM | FTA | Pct. | Reb. | Ast. | Pts. | RPG | APG | PPG |
|---|---|---|---|---|---|---|---|---|---|---|---|---|---|---|
| 78-79—DePaul.......................... | 32 | 1206 | 302 | 581 | .520 | 163 | 213 | .765 | 244 | 86 | 767 | 7.6 | 2.7 | 24.0 |
| 79-80—DePaul.......................... | 28 | 1049 | 281 | 520 | .540 | 187 | 244 | .766 | 213 | 77 | 749 | 7.6 | 2.8 | 26.8 |
| 80-81—DePaul.......................... | 29 | 1069 | 280 | 481 | .582 | 106 | 137 | .774 | 249 | 131 | 666 | 8.6 | 4.5 | 23.0 |
| Totals ..................... | 89 | 3324 | 863 | 1582 | .546 | 456 | 594 | .768 | 706 | 294 | 2182 | 7.9 | 3.3 | 24.5 |

## NBA REGULAR-SEASON RECORD

| Season Team | G | Min. | FGM | FGA | Pct. | FTM | FTA | Pct. | REBOUNDS Off. | Def. | Tot. | Ast. | St. | Blk. | TO | Pts. | RPG | APG | PPG |
|---|---|---|---|---|---|---|---|---|---|---|---|---|---|---|---|---|---|---|---|
| 81-82—Dallas | 51 | 1468 | 381 | 820 | .465 | 168 | 247 | .680 | 89 | 160 | 249 | 164 | 37 | 22 | 135 | 955 | 4.9 | 3.2 | 18.7 |
| 82-83—Dallas | 81 | 2784 | 767 | 1589 | .483 | 429 | 589 | .728 | 191 | 317 | 508 | 332 | 80 | 26 | 261 | 1979 | 6.3 | 4.1 | 24.4 |
| 83-84—Dallas | 79 | 2900 | *925 | *1765 | .524 | 465 | 621 | .749 | 161 | 308 | 469 | 358 | 80 | 22 | 285 | 2330 | 5.9 | 4.5 | 29.5 |
| 84-85—Dallas | 80 | 2699 | 794 | 1569 | .506 | 440 | 580 | .759 | 188 | 289 | 477 | 249 | 60 | 24 | 253 | 2055 | 6.0 | 3.1 | 25.7 |
| 85-86—Dallas | 74 | 2501 | 668 | 1327 | .503 | 318 | 451 | .705 | 177 | 268 | 445 | 339 | 62 | 14 | 252 | 1670 | 6.0 | 4.6 | 22.6 |
| 86-87—Dallas | 80 | 2663 | 787 | 1590 | .495 | 429 | 557 | .770 | 181 | 246 | 427 | 254 | 84 | 30 | 217 | 2056 | 5.3 | 3.2 | 25.7 |
| 87-88—Dallas | 77 | 2610 | 746 | 1571 | .475 | 388 | 504 | .770 | 182 | 252 | 434 | 278 | 70 | 57 | 203 | 1932 | 5.6 | 3.6 | 25.1 |
| 88-89—Dallas-Det. | 80 | 2597 | 586 | 1270 | .461 | 288 | 393 | .733 | 146 | 240 | 386 | 278 | 45 | 36 | 208 | 1511 | 4.8 | 3.5 | 18.9 |
| 89-90—Detroit | 78 | 2005 | 438 | 898 | .488 | 192 | 254 | .756 | 117 | 188 | 305 | 145 | 34 | 19 | 121 | 1099 | 3.9 | 1.9 | 14.1 |
| 90-91—Detroit | 78 | 2006 | 420 | 909 | .462 | 240 | 317 | .757 | 134 | 240 | 374 | 139 | 47 | 20 | 128 | 1104 | 4.8 | 1.8 | 14.2 |
| 91-92—Detroit | 75 | 1582 | 339 | 787 | .431 | 158 | 230 | .687 | 67 | 169 | 236 | 126 | 51 | 11 | 105 | 851 | 3.1 | 1.7 | 11.3 |
| 92-93—Detroit | 51 | 1056 | 187 | 422 | .443 | 99 | 129 | .767 | 43 | 109 | 152 | 105 | 16 | 7 | 68 | 503 | 3.0 | 2.1 | 9.9 |
| 93-94—L.A. Clippers | 39 | 859 | 163 | 348 | .468 | 50 | 72 | .694 | 28 | 88 | 116 | 104 | 21 | 8 | 70 | 413 | 3.0 | 2.7 | 10.6 |
| **Totals** | 923 | 27730 | 7201 | 14865 | .484 | 3664 | 4944 | .741 | 1704 | 2874 | 4578 | 2871 | 687 | 296 | 2306 | 18458 | 5.0 | 3.1 | 20.0 |

Three-point field goals: 1981-82, 25-for-71 (.352). 1982-83, 16-for-76 (.211). 1983-84, 15-for-56 (.268). 1984-85, 27-for-85 (.318). 1985-86, 16-for-56 (.286). 1986-87, 53-for-150 (.353). 1987-88, 52-for-172 (.302). 1988-89, 51-for-174 (.293). 1989-90, 31-for-93 (.333). 1990-91, 24-for-78 (.308). 1991-92, 15-for-71 (.211). 1992-93, 30-for-83 (.361). 1993-94, 37-for-93 (.398). Totals, 392-for-1258 (.312).

Personal fouls/disqualifications: 1981-82, 152/0. 1982-83, 247/5. 1983-84, 246/5. 1984-85, 250/3. 1985-86, 229/6. 1986-87, 243/4. 1987-88, 223/1. 1988-89, 229/2. 1989-90, 201/2. 1990-91, 209/2. 1991-92, 171/0. 1992-93, 101/1. 1993-94, 98/1. Totals, 2599/33.

## NBA PLAYOFF RECORD

| Season Team | G | Min. | FGM | FGA | Pct. | FTM | FTA | Pct. | REBOUNDS Off. | Def. | Tot. | Ast. | St. | Blk. | TO | Pts. | RPG | APG | PPG |
|---|---|---|---|---|---|---|---|---|---|---|---|---|---|---|---|---|---|---|---|
| 83-84—Dallas | 10 | 350 | 88 | 184 | .478 | 44 | 57 | .772 | 21 | 55 | 76 | 32 | 5 | 5 | 27 | 220 | 7.6 | 3.2 | 22.0 |
| 84-85—Dallas | 4 | 164 | 44 | 89 | .494 | 27 | 32 | .844 | 16 | 14 | 30 | 16 | 3 | 0 | 15 | 116 | 7.5 | 4.0 | 29.0 |
| 85-86—Dallas | 10 | 345 | 105 | 214 | .491 | 35 | 55 | .636 | 21 | 50 | 71 | 54 | 9 | 0 | 23 | 247 | 7.1 | 5.4 | 24.7 |
| 86-87—Dallas | 4 | 130 | 31 | 62 | .500 | 23 | 30 | .767 | 11 | 13 | 24 | 8 | 8 | 0 | 9 | 85 | 6.0 | 2.0 | 21.3 |
| 87-88—Dallas | 17 | 558 | 147 | 294 | .500 | 60 | 86 | .698 | 34 | 66 | 100 | 56 | 14 | 9 | 41 | 367 | 5.9 | 3.3 | 21.6 |
| 88-89—Detroit | 17 | 462 | 89 | 182 | .489 | 28 | 38 | .737 | 26 | 49 | 75 | 28 | 8 | 3 | 20 | 214 | 4.4 | 1.6 | 12.6 |
| 89-90—Detroit | 20 | 439 | 86 | 184 | .467 | 39 | 52 | .750 | 31 | 60 | 91 | 27 | 10 | 3 | 30 | 219 | 4.6 | 1.4 | 11.0 |
| 90-91—Detroit | 15 | 397 | 90 | 178 | .506 | 42 | 51 | .824 | 17 | 44 | 61 | 29 | 12 | 1 | 20 | 234 | 4.1 | 1.9 | 15.6 |
| 91-92—Detroit | 5 | 113 | 16 | 48 | .333 | 12 | 16 | .750 | 4 | 5 | 9 | 12 | 2 | 1 | 13 | 45 | 1.8 | 2.4 | 9.0 |
| **Totals** | 102 | 2958 | 696 | 1435 | .485 | 310 | 417 | .743 | 181 | 356 | 537 | 262 | 71 | 22 | 198 | 1747 | 5.3 | 2.6 | 17.1 |

Three-point field goals: 1983-84, 0-for-5. 1984-85, 1-for-2 (.500). 1985-86, 2-for-6 (.333). 1986-87, 0-for-4. 1987-88, 13-for-34 (.382). 1988-89, 8-for-29 (.276). 1989-90, 8-for-24 (.333). 1990-91, 12-for-33 (.364). 1991-92, 1-for-5 (.200). Totals, 45-for-142 (.317).

Personal fouls/disqualifications: 1983-84, 34/2. 1984-85, 16/1. 1985-86, 28/1. 1986-87, 15/1. 1987-88, 49/0. 1988-89, 38/0. 1989-90, 51/0. 1990-91, 41/0. 1991-92, 9/0. Totals, 281/5.

## NBA ALL-STAR GAME RECORD

| Season Team | Min. | FGM | FGA | Pct. | FTM | FTA | Pct. | REBOUNDS Off. | Def. | Tot. | Ast. | PF | Dq. | St. | Blk. | TO | Pts. |
|---|---|---|---|---|---|---|---|---|---|---|---|---|---|---|---|---|---|
| 1984—Dallas | 13 | 5 | 8 | .625 | 3 | 4 | .750 | 1 | 0 | 1 | 2 | 1 | 0 | 1 | 1 | 2 | 13 |
| 1987—Dallas | 17 | 3 | 6 | .500 | 2 | 3 | .667 | 1 | 1 | 2 | 1 | 1 | 0 | 0 | 0 | 2 | 9 |
| 1988—Dallas | 12 | 5 | 10 | .500 | 3 | 3 | 1.000 | 0 | 1 | 1 | 1 | 3 | 0 | 1 | 0 | 3 | 14 |
| **Totals** | 42 | 13 | 24 | .542 | 8 | 10 | .800 | 2 | 2 | 4 | 4 | 5 | 0 | 2 | 1 | 7 | 36 |

Three-point field goals: 1987, 1-for-2 (.500). 1988, 1-for-3 (.333). Totals, 2-for-5 (.400).

# ARCHIBALD, NATE     G

**PERSONAL:** Born September 2, 1948, in New York. ... 6-1/160 (1,85/72,6). ... Full name: Nathaniel Archibald. ... Nickname: Tiny.
**HIGH SCHOOL:** DeWitt Clinton (Bronx, N.Y.).
**JUNIOR COLLEGE:** Arizona Western College.
**COLLEGE:** Texas-El Paso.
**TRANSACTIONS:** Selected by Cincinnati Royals in second round (19th pick overall) of 1970 NBA Draft. ... Royals franchise moved from Cincinnati to Kansas City/Omaha and renamed Kings for 1972-73 season. ... Kings franchise moved from Kansas City/Omaha to Kansas City for 1975-76 season. ... Traded by Kings to New York Nets for G Brian Taylor, C Jim Eakins and 1977 and 1978 first-round draft choices (September 10, 1976). ... Nets franchise moved from New York to New Jersey for 1977-78 season. ... Traded by Nets to Buffalo Braves for C George Johnson and 1979 first-round draft choice (September 1, 1977). ... Braves franchise moved from Buffalo to San Diego and renamed Clippers for 1978-79 season. ... Traded by Clippers with F Marvin Barnes, F/G Billy Knight and 1981 and 1983 second-round draft choices to Boston Celtics for F Kermit Washington, C Kevin Kunnert, F Sidney Wicks and draft rights to G Freeman Williams (August 4, 1978). ... Waived by Celtics (July 22, 1983). ... Signed as free agent by Milwaukee Bucks (August 1, 1983).
**CAREER HONORS:** Elected to Naismith Memorial Basketball Hall of Fame (1991). ... One of the 50 Greatest Players in NBA History (1996).
**CAREER NOTES:** Head coach, Fayetteville Patriots, NBDL (January 31, 2001-January 8, 2002). ... Liaison, NBA Community Relations (2002).
**MISCELLANEOUS:** Member of NBA championship team (1981).

## COLLEGIATE RECORD

| Season Team | G | Min. | FGM | FGA | Pct. | FTM | FTA | Pct. | Reb. | Ast. | Pts. | AVERAGES RPG | APG | PPG |
|---|---|---|---|---|---|---|---|---|---|---|---|---|---|---|
| 66-67—Arizona Western College | 27 | ... | 303 | ... | ... | 190 | ... | ... | ... | ... | 796 | ... | ... | 29.5 |
| 67-68—Texas-El Paso | 23 | ... | 131 | 281 | .466 | 102 | 140 | .729 | 81 | ... | 364 | 3.5 | ... | 15.8 |
| 68-69—Texas-El Paso | 25 | ... | 199 | 374 | .532 | 161 | 194 | .830 | 69 | ... | 559 | 2.8 | ... | 22.4 |
| 69-70—Texas-El Paso | 25 | ... | 180 | 351 | .513 | 176 | 225 | .782 | 66 | ... | 536 | 2.6 | ... | 21.4 |
| **Junior college totals** | 27 | ... | 303 | ... | ... | 190 | ... | ... | ... | ... | 796 | ... | ... | 29.5 |
| **4-year-college totals** | 73 | ... | 510 | 1006 | .507 | 439 | 559 | .785 | 216 | ... | 1459 | 3.0 | ... | 20.0 |

## NBA REGULAR-SEASON RECORD

**HONORS:** All-NBA first team (1973, 1975, 1976). ... All-NBA second team (1972, 1981).

| Season Team | G | Min. | FGM | FGA | Pct. | FTM | FTA | Pct. | Reb. | Ast. | PF | Dq. | Pts. | RPG | APG | PPG |
|---|---|---|---|---|---|---|---|---|---|---|---|---|---|---|---|---|
| | | | | | | | | | | | | | | **AVERAGES** | | |
| 70-71—Cincinnati | 82 | 2867 | 486 | 1095 | .444 | 336 | 444 | .757 | 242 | 450 | 218 | 2 | 1308 | 3.0 | 5.5 | 16.0 |
| 71-72—Cincinnati | 76 | 3272 | 734 | 1511 | .486 | *677 | *824 | .822 | 222 | 701 | 198 | 3 | 2145 | 2.9 | 9.2 | 28.2 |
| 72-73—K.C./Omaha | 80 | *3681 | *1028 | *2106 | .488 | *663 | *783 | .847 | 223 | *910 | 207 | 2 | *2719 | 2.8 | *11.4 | *34.0 |

| Season Team | G | Min. | FGM | FGA | Pct. | FTM | FTA | Pct. | Off. | Def. | Tot. | Ast. | St. | Blk. | TO | Pts. | RPG | APG | PPG |
|---|---|---|---|---|---|---|---|---|---|---|---|---|---|---|---|---|---|---|---|
| | | | | | | | | | **REBOUNDS** | | | | | | | | **AVERAGES** | | |
| 73-74—K.C./Omaha | 35 | 1272 | 222 | 492 | .451 | 173 | 211 | .820 | 21 | 64 | 85 | 266 | 56 | 7 | ... | 617 | 2.4 | 7.6 | 17.6 |
| 74-75—K.C./Omaha | 82 | 3244 | 759 | 1664 | .456 | *652 | 748 | .872 | 48 | 174 | 222 | 557 | 119 | 7 | ... | 2170 | 2.7 | 6.8 | 26.5 |
| 75-76—Kansas City | 78 | 3184 | 717 | 1583 | .453 | 501 | 625 | .802 | 67 | 146 | 213 | 615 | 126 | 15 | ... | 1935 | 2.7 | 7.9 | 24.8 |
| 76-77—N.Y. Nets | 34 | 1277 | 250 | 560 | .446 | 197 | 251 | .785 | 22 | 58 | 80 | 254 | 59 | 11 | ... | 697 | 2.4 | 7.5 | 20.5 |
| 77-78—Buffalo | | | | | | | Did not play—torn Achilles' tendon. | | | | | | | | | | | | |
| 78-79—Boston | 69 | 1662 | 259 | 573 | .452 | 242 | 307 | .788 | 25 | 78 | 103 | 324 | 55 | 6 | 197 | 760 | 1.5 | 4.7 | 11.0 |
| 79-80—Boston | 80 | 2864 | 383 | 794 | .482 | 361 | 435 | .830 | 59 | 138 | 197 | 671 | 106 | 10 | 242 | 1131 | 2.5 | 8.4 | 14.1 |
| 80-81—Boston | 80 | 2820 | 382 | 766 | .499 | 342 | 419 | .816 | 36 | 140 | 176 | 618 | 75 | 18 | 265 | 1106 | 2.2 | 7.7 | 13.8 |
| 81-82—Boston | 68 | 2167 | 308 | 652 | .472 | 236 | 316 | .747 | 25 | 91 | 116 | 541 | 52 | 3 | 178 | 858 | 1.7 | 8.0 | 12.6 |
| 82-83—Boston | 66 | 1811 | 235 | 553 | .425 | 220 | 296 | .743 | 25 | 66 | 91 | 409 | 38 | 4 | 163 | 695 | 1.4 | 6.2 | 10.5 |
| 83-84—Milwaukee | 46 | 1038 | 136 | 279 | .487 | 64 | 101 | .634 | 16 | 60 | 76 | 160 | 33 | 0 | 78 | 340 | 1.7 | 3.5 | 7.4 |
| Totals | 876 | 31159 | 5899 | 12628 | .467 | 4664 | 5760 | .810 | ... | ... | 2046 | 6476 | 719 | 81 | 1123 | 16481 | 2.3 | 7.4 | 18.8 |

Three-point field goals: 1979-80, 4-for-18 (.222). 1980-81, 0-for-9. 1981-82, 6-for-16 (.375). 1982-83, 5-for-24 (.208). 1983-84, 4-for-18 (.222). Totals, 19-for-85 (.224).

Personal fouls/disqualifications: 1973-74, 76/0. 1974-75, 187/0. 1975-76, 169/0. 1976-77, 77/1. 1978-79, 132/2. 1979-80, 218/2. 1980-81, 201/1. 1981-82, 131/1. 1982-83, 110/1. 1983-84, 78/0. Totals, 2002/15.

## NBA PLAYOFF RECORD

| Season Team | G | Min. | FGM | FGA | Pct. | FTM | FTA | Pct. | Off. | Def. | Tot. | Ast. | St. | Blk. | TO | Pts. | RPG | APG | PPG |
|---|---|---|---|---|---|---|---|---|---|---|---|---|---|---|---|---|---|---|---|
| | | | | | | | | | **REBOUNDS** | | | | | | | | **AVERAGES** | | |
| 74-75—K.C./Omaha | 6 | 242 | 43 | 118 | .364 | 35 | 43 | .814 | 2 | 9 | 11 | 32 | 4 | 0 | ... | 121 | 1.8 | 5.3 | 20.2 |
| 79-80—Boston | 9 | 332 | 45 | 89 | .506 | 37 | 42 | .881 | 3 | 8 | 11 | 71 | 10 | 0 | 38 | 128 | 1.2 | 7.9 | 14.2 |
| 80-81—Boston | 17 | 630 | 95 | 211 | .450 | 76 | 94 | .809 | 6 | 22 | 28 | 107 | 13 | 0 | 50 | 266 | 1.6 | 6.3 | 15.6 |
| 81-82—Boston | 8 | 277 | 30 | 70 | .429 | 25 | 28 | .893 | 1 | 16 | 17 | 52 | 5 | 2 | 23 | 85 | 2.1 | 6.5 | 10.6 |
| 82-83—Boston | 7 | 161 | 22 | 68 | .324 | 22 | 29 | .759 | 3 | 7 | 10 | 44 | 2 | 0 | 11 | 67 | 1.4 | 6.3 | 9.6 |
| Totals | 47 | 1642 | 235 | 556 | .423 | 195 | 236 | .826 | 15 | 62 | 77 | 306 | 34 | 2 | 122 | 667 | 1.6 | 6.5 | 14.2 |

Three-point field goals: 1979-80, 1-for-2 (.500). 1980-81, 0-for-5. 1981-82, 0-for-4. 1982-83, 1-for-6 (.167). Totals, 2-for-17 (.118).

Personal fouls/disqualifications: 1974-75, 18/0. 1979-80, 28/1. 1980-81, 39/0. 1981-82, 21/0. 1982-83, 12/0. Totals, 118/1.

## NBA ALL-STAR GAME RECORD

**NOTES:** NBA All-Star Game Most Valuable Player (1981).

| Season Team | Min. | FGM | FGA | Pct. | FTM | FTA | Pct. | Reb | Ast. | PF | Dq. | Pts. |
|---|---|---|---|---|---|---|---|---|---|---|---|---|
| 1973—Kansas City/Omaha | 27 | 6 | 12 | .500 | 5 | 5 | 1.000 | 1 | 5 | 1 | 0 | 17 |

| Season Team | Min. | FGM | FGA | Pct. | FTM | FTA | Pct. | Off. | Def. | Tot. | Ast. | PF | Dq. | St. | Blk. | TO | Pts. |
|---|---|---|---|---|---|---|---|---|---|---|---|---|---|---|---|---|---|
| | | | | | | | | **REBOUNDS** | | | | | | | | | |
| 1975—K.C./Omaha | 36 | 10 | 15 | .667 | 7 | 8 | .875 | 1 | 1 | 2 | 6 | 2 | 0 | 3 | 1 | ... | 27 |
| 1976—Kansas City | 30 | 5 | 13 | .385 | 3 | 3 | 1.000 | 2 | 3 | 5 | 7 | 0 | 0 | 2 | 0 | ... | 13 |
| 1980—Boston | 21 | 0 | 8 | .000 | 2 | 3 | .667 | 1 | 2 | 3 | 6 | 1 | 0 | 2 | 0 | 2 | 2 |
| 1981—Boston | 25 | 4 | 7 | .571 | 1 | 3 | .333 | 0 | 5 | 5 | 9 | 3 | 0 | 3 | 0 | 2 | 9 |
| 1982—Boston | 23 | 2 | 5 | .400 | 2 | 2 | 1.000 | 1 | 1 | 2 | 7 | 3 | 0 | 1 | 0 | 2 | 6 |
| Totals | 162 | 27 | 60 | .450 | 20 | 24 | .833 | ... | ... | 18 | 40 | 10 | 0 | 11 | 1 | 6 | 74 |

## NBDL COACHING RECORD

| | REGULAR SEASON | | | |
|---|---|---|---|---|
| Season Team | W | L | Pct. | Finish |
| 01-02—Fayetteville | 5 | 16 | .238 | |

# ARIZIN, PAUL      F

**PERSONAL:** Born April 9, 1928, in Philadelphia. ... 6-4/200 (1,93/90,7). ... Full name: Paul Joseph Arizin.
**HIGH SCHOOL:** La Salle (Philadelphia).
**COLLEGE:** Villanova.
**TRANSACTIONS:** Selected by Philadelphia Warriors in first round of 1950 NBA Draft. ... Played in Eastern Basketball League with Camden Bullets (1962-63 through 1964-65).
**CAREER HONORS:** Elected to Naismith Memorial Basketball Hall of Fame (1978). ... NBA 25th Anniversary All-Time Team (1970) and One of the 50 Greatest Players in NBA History (1996).
**MISCELLANEOUS:** Member of NBA championship team (1956).

## COLLEGIATE RECORD

**NOTES:** THE SPORTING NEWS College Player of the Year (1950). ... THE SPORTING NEWS All-America first team (1950). ... Led NCAA Division I with 25.3 points per game (1950).

| Season Team | G | Min. | FGM | FGA | Pct. | FTM | FTA | Pct. | Reb. | Ast. | Pts. | RPG | APG | PPG |
|---|---|---|---|---|---|---|---|---|---|---|---|---|---|---|
| | | | | | | | | | | | | | **AVERAGES** | |
| 46-47—Villanova | | | | | | Did not play. | | | | | | | | |
| 47-48—Villanova | 24 | ... | 101 | ... | ... | 65 | | | ... | ... | 267 | ... | ... | 11.1 |
| 48-49—Villanova | 27 | ... | 210 | ... | ... | 174 | 233 | .747 | ... | ... | 594 | ... | ... | 22.0 |
| 49-50—Villanova | 29 | ... | 260 | 527 | .493 | 215 | 277 | .776 | ... | ... | 735 | ... | ... | 25.3 |
| Totals | 80 | ... | 571 | ... | ... | 454 | ... | ... | ... | ... | 1596 | ... | ... | 20.0 |

## NBA REGULAR-SEASON RECORD

**HONORS:** All-NBA first team (1952, 1956, 1957). ... All-NBA second team (1959).

| Season Team | G | Min. | FGM | FGA | Pct. | FTM | FTA | Pct. | Reb. | Ast. | PF | Dq. | Pts. | AVERAGES RPG | APG | PPG |
|---|---|---|---|---|---|---|---|---|---|---|---|---|---|---|---|---|
| 50-51—Philadelphia | 65 | ... | 352 | 864 | .407 | 417 | 526 | .793 | 640 | 138 | 284 | 18 | 1121 | 9.8 | 2.1 | 17.2 |
| 51-52—Philadelphia | 66 | *2939 | *548 | 1222 | *.448 | *578 | *707 | .818 | 745 | 170 | 250 | 5 | *1674 | 11.3 | 2.6 | *25.4 |
| 52-53—Philadelphia | | | | | | Did not play—in military service. | | | | | | | | | | |
| 53-54—Philadelphia | | | | | | Did not play—in military service. | | | | | | | | | | |
| 54-55—Philadelphia | 72 | *2953 | *529 | *1325 | .399 | 454 | 585 | .776 | 675 | 210 | 270 | 5 | 1512 | 9.4 | 2.9 | 21.0 |
| 55-56—Philadelphia | 72 | 2724 | 617 | 1378 | .448 | 507 | 626 | .810 | 539 | 189 | 282 | 11 | 1741 | 7.5 | 2.6 | 24.2 |
| 56-57—Philadelphia | 71 | 2767 | 613 | 1451 | .422 | 591 | *713 | .829 | 561 | 150 | 274 | 13 | *1817 | 7.9 | 2.1 | *25.6 |
| 57-58—Philadelphia | 68 | 2377 | 483 | 1229 | .393 | 440 | 544 | .809 | 503 | 135 | 235 | 7 | 1406 | 7.4 | 2.0 | 20.7 |
| 58-59—Philadelphia | 70 | 2799 | 632 | 1466 | .431 | 587 | 722 | .813 | 637 | 119 | 264 | 7 | 1851 | 9.1 | 1.7 | 26.4 |
| 59-60—Philadelphia | 72 | 2618 | 593 | 1400 | .424 | 420 | 526 | .798 | 621 | 165 | 263 | 6 | 1606 | 8.6 | 2.3 | 22.3 |
| 60-61—Philadelphia | 79 | 2935 | 650 | 1529 | .425 | 532 | 639 | .833 | 681 | 188 | *335 | 11 | 1832 | 8.6 | 2.4 | 23.2 |
| 61-62—Philadelphia | 78 | 2785 | 611 | 1490 | .410 | 484 | 601 | .805 | 527 | 201 | 307 | 18 | 1706 | 6.8 | 2.6 | 21.9 |
| Totals | 713 | ... | 5628 | 13354 | .421 | 5010 | 6189 | .810 | 6129 | 1665 | 2764 | 101 | 16266 | 8.6 | 2.3 | 22.8 |

## NBA PLAYOFF RECORD

| Season Team | G | Min. | FGM | FGA | Pct. | FTM | FTA | Pct. | Reb. | Ast. | PF | Dq. | Pts. | AVERAGES RPG | APG | PPG |
|---|---|---|---|---|---|---|---|---|---|---|---|---|---|---|---|---|
| 50-51—Philadelphia | 2 | ... | 14 | 27 | .519 | 13 | 16 | .813 | 20 | 3 | 10 | 1 | 41 | 10.0 | 1.5 | 20.5 |
| 51-52—Philadelphia | 3 | 120 | 24 | 53 | .453 | 29 | 33 | .879 | 38 | 8 | 17 | 2 | 77 | 12.7 | 2.7 | 25.7 |
| 55-56—Philadelphia | 10 | 409 | 103 | 229 | .450 | 83 | 99 | .838 | 84 | 29 | 31 | 1 | 289 | 8.4 | 2.9 | 28.9 |
| 56-57—Philadelphia | 2 | 22 | 3 | 8 | .375 | 3 | 5 | .600 | 8 | 1 | 3 | 0 | 9 | 4.0 | 0.5 | 4.5 |
| 57-58—Philadelphia | 8 | 309 | 66 | 169 | .391 | 56 | 72 | .778 | 62 | 16 | 26 | 1 | 188 | 7.8 | 2.0 | 23.5 |
| 59-60—Philadelphia | 9 | 371 | 84 | 195 | .431 | 69 | 79 | .873 | 86 | 33 | 29 | 0 | 237 | 9.6 | 3.7 | 26.3 |
| 60-61—Philadelphia | 3 | 125 | 22 | 67 | .328 | 23 | 33 | .697 | 26 | 12 | 17 | 2 | 67 | 8.7 | 4.0 | 22.3 |
| 61-62—Philadelphia | 12 | 459 | 95 | 253 | .376 | 88 | 102 | .863 | 80 | 26 | 44 | 1 | 278 | 6.7 | 2.2 | 23.2 |
| Totals | 49 | ... | 411 | 1001 | .411 | 364 | 439 | .829 | 404 | 128 | 177 | 8 | 1186 | 8.2 | 2.6 | 24.2 |

## NBA ALL-STAR GAME RECORD

**NOTES:** NBA All-Star Game Most Valuable Player (1952).

| Season Team | Min. | FGM | FGA | Pct. | FTM | FTA | Pct. | Reb | Ast. | PF | Dq. | Pts. |
|---|---|---|---|---|---|---|---|---|---|---|---|---|
| 1951—Philadelphia | ... | 7 | 12 | .583 | 1 | 2 | .500 | 7 | 0 | 2 | 0 | 15 |
| 1952—Philadelphia | 32 | 9 | 13 | .692 | 8 | 8 | 1.000 | 6 | 0 | 1 | 0 | 26 |
| 1955—Philadelphia | 23 | 4 | 9 | .444 | 1 | 2 | .500 | 2 | 2 | 5 | 0 | 9 |
| 1956—Philadelphia | 28 | 5 | 13 | .385 | 3 | 5 | .600 | 7 | 1 | 6 | 1 | 13 |
| 1957—Philadelphia | 26 | 6 | 13 | .462 | 1 | 2 | .500 | 5 | 0 | 2 | 0 | 13 |
| 1958—Philadelphia | 29 | 11 | 17 | .647 | 2 | 2 | 1.000 | 8 | 2 | 3 | 0 | 24 |
| 1959—Philadelphia | 30 | 4 | 15 | .267 | 8 | 9 | .889 | 8 | 0 | 2 | 0 | 16 |
| 1960—Philadelphia | | | | | Selected, did not play—injured. | | | | | | | |
| 1961—Philadelphia | 17 | 6 | 12 | .500 | 5 | 6 | .833 | 2 | 1 | 4 | 0 | 17 |
| 1962—Philadelphia | 21 | 2 | 12 | .167 | 0 | 0 | ... | 2 | 0 | 4 | 0 | 4 |
| Totals | ... | 54 | 116 | .466 | 29 | 36 | .806 | 47 | 6 | 29 | 1 | 137 |

## EBL REGULAR-SEASON RECORD

**NOTES:** Eastern Basketball League Most Valuable Player (1963). ... EBL All-Star first team (1963, 1964). ... EBL All-Star second team (1965).

| Season Team | G | Min. | FGM | FGA | Pct. | FTM | FTA | Pct. | Reb. | Ast. | PF | Dq. | Pts. | AVERAGES RPG | APG | PPG |
|---|---|---|---|---|---|---|---|---|---|---|---|---|---|---|---|---|
| 62-63—Camden | 28 | ... | 264 | ... | ... | 196 | 249 | .787 | 203 | 42 | ... | ... | 724 | 7.3 | 1.5 | 25.9 |
| 63-64—Camden | 27 | ... | 261 | ... | ... | 174 | 218 | .798 | 226 | 52 | ... | ... | 696 | 8.4 | 1.9 | 25.8 |
| 64-65—Camden | 28 | ... | 226 | ... | ... | 196 | 244 | .803 | 164 | 50 | ... | ... | 657 | 5.9 | 1.8 | 23.5 |
| Totals | 83 | ... | 751 | ... | ... | 566 | 711 | .796 | 593 | 144 | ... | ... | 2077 | 7.1 | 1.7 | 25.0 |

# BARKLEY, CHARLES          F

**PERSONAL:** Born February 20, 1963, in Leeds, Ala. ... 6-6/252. (1.98 m/114 kg). ... Full Name: Charles Wade Barkley.
**HIGH SCHOOL:** Leeds (Ala.).
**COLLEGE:** Auburn.
**TRANSACTIONS/CAREER NOTES:** Selected after junior season by Philadelphia 76ers in first round (fifth pick overall) of 1984 NBA Draft. ... Traded by 76ers to Phoenix Suns for G Jeff Hornacek, F Tim Perry and C Andrew Lang (June 17, 1992). ... Traded by Suns with 1999 second-round draft choice to Houston Rockets for G Sam Cassell, F Chucky Brown, F Robert Horry and F Mark Bryant (August 19, 1996).
**CAREER HONORS:** NBA 50th Anniversary All-Time Team (1996).
**CAREER NOTES:** Broadcaster, Turner Sports (2001-present).
**MISCELLANEOUS:** Member of gold-medal-winning U.S. Olympic teams (1992, 1996).

## COLLEGIATE RECORD

| Season Team | G | Min. | FGM | FGA | Pct. | FTM | FTA | Pct. | Reb. | Ast. | Pts. | AVERAGES RPG | APG | PPG |
|---|---|---|---|---|---|---|---|---|---|---|---|---|---|---|
| 81-82—Auburn | 28 | 746 | 144 | 242 | .595 | 68 | 107 | .636 | 275 | 30 | 356 | 9.8 | 1.1 | 12.7 |
| 82-83—Auburn | 28 | 782 | 161 | 250 | .644 | 82 | 130 | .631 | 266 | 49 | 404 | 9.5 | 1.8 | 14.4 |
| 83-84—Auburn | 28 | 794 | 162 | 254 | .638 | 99 | 145 | .683 | 265 | 58 | 423 | 9.5 | 2.1 | 15.1 |
| Totals | 84 | 2322 | 467 | 746 | .626 | 249 | 382 | .652 | 806 | 137 | 1183 | 9.6 | 1.6 | 14.1 |

## NBA REGULAR-SEASON RECORD

**RECORDS:** Holds single-game records for most offensive rebounds in one quarter—11; and most offensive rebounds in one half—13 (March 4, 1987, vs. New York).
**HONORS:** NBA Most Valuable Player (1993). ... IBM Award, for all-around contributions to team's success (1986, 1987, 1988). ... All-NBA first team (1988, 1989, 1990, 1991, 1993). ... All-NBA second team (1986, 1987, 1992, 1994, 1995). ... All-NBA third team (1996). ... NBA All-Rookie team (1985).
**NOTES:** Led NBA with 333 personal fouls (1986).

| Season Team | G | Min. | FGM | FGA | Pct. | FTM | FTA | Pct. | REBOUNDS Off. | Def. | Tot. | Ast. | St. | Blk. | TO | Pts. | AVERAGES RPG | APG | PPG |
|---|---|---|---|---|---|---|---|---|---|---|---|---|---|---|---|---|---|---|---|
| 84-85—Philadelphia.... | 82 | 2347 | 427 | 783 | .545 | 293 | 400 | .733 | 266 | 437 | 703 | 155 | 95 | 80 | 209 | 1148 | 8.6 | 1.9 | 14.0 |
| 85-86—Philadelphia.... | 80 | 2952 | 595 | 1041 | .572 | 396 | 578 | .685 | 354 | 672 | 1026 | 312 | 173 | 125 | *350 | 1603 | 12.8 | 3.9 | 20.0 |
| 86-87—Philadelphia.... | 68 | 2740 | 557 | 937 | .594 | 429 | 564 | .761 | *390 | 604 | 994 | 331 | 119 | 104 | 322 | 1564 | *14.6 | 4.9 | 23.0 |
| 87-88—Philadelphia.... | 80 | 3170 | 753 | 1283 | .587 | 714 | *951 | .751 | *385 | 566 | 951 | 254 | 100 | 103 | 304 | 2264 | 11.9 | 3.2 | 28.3 |
| 88-89—Philadelphia.... | 79 | 3088 | 700 | 1208 | .579 | 602 | 799 | .753 | *403 | 583 | 986 | 325 | 126 | 67 | 254 | 2037 | 12.5 | 4.1 | 25.8 |
| 89-90—Philadelphia.... | 79 | 3085 | 706 | 1177 | .600 | 557 | 744 | .749 | 361 | 548 | 909 | 307 | 148 | 50 | 243 | 1989 | 11.5 | 3.9 | 25.2 |
| 90-91—Philadelphia.... | 67 | 2498 | 665 | 1167 | .570 | 475 | 658 | .722 | 258 | 422 | 680 | 284 | 110 | 33 | 210 | 1849 | 10.1 | 4.2 | 27.6 |
| 91-92—Philadelphia.... | 75 | 2881 | 622 | 1126 | .552 | 454 | 653 | .695 | 271 | 559 | 830 | 308 | 136 | 44 | 235 | 1730 | 11.1 | 4.1 | 23.1 |
| 92-93—Phoenix ........ | 76 | 2859 | 716 | 1376 | .520 | 445 | 582 | .765 | 237 | 691 | 928 | 385 | 119 | 74 | 233 | 1944 | 12.2 | 5.1 | 25.6 |
| 93-94—Phoenix ........ | 65 | 2298 | 518 | 1046 | .495 | 318 | 452 | .704 | 198 | 529 | 727 | 296 | 101 | 37 | 206 | 1402 | 11.2 | 4.6 | 21.6 |
| 94-95—Phoenix ........ | 68 | 2382 | 554 | 1141 | .486 | 379 | 507 | .748 | 203 | 553 | 756 | 276 | 110 | 45 | 150 | 1561 | 11.1 | 4.1 | 23.0 |
| 95-96—Phoenix ........ | 71 | 2632 | 580 | 1160 | .500 | 440 | 566 | .777 | 243 | 578 | 821 | 262 | 114 | 56 | 218 | 1649 | 11.6 | 3.7 | 23.2 |
| 96-97—Houston......... | 53 | 2009 | 335 | 692 | .484 | 288 | 415 | .694 | 212 | 504 | 716 | 248 | 69 | 25 | 151 | 1016 | 13.5 | 4.7 | 19.2 |
| 97-98—Houston......... | 68 | 2243 | 361 | 744 | .485 | 296 | 397 | .746 | 241 | 553 | 794 | 217 | 71 | 28 | 147 | 1036 | 11.7 | 3.2 | 15.2 |
| 98-99—Houston......... | 42 | 1526 | 240 | 502 | .478 | 192 | 267 | .719 | 167 | 349 | 516 | 192 | 43 | 13 | 100 | 676 | 12.3 | 4.6 | 16.1 |
| 99-00—Houston......... | 20 | 620 | 106 | 222 | .477 | 71 | 110 | .645 | 71 | 138 | 209 | 63 | 14 | 4 | 44 | 289 | 10.5 | 3.2 | 14.5 |
| Totals .................. | 1073 | 39330 | 8435 | 15605 | .541 | 6349 | 8643 | .735 | 4260 | 8286 | 12546 | 4215 | 1648 | 888 | 3376 | 23757 | 11.7 | 3.9 | 22.1 |

Three-point field goals: 1984-85, 1-for-6 (.167). 1985-86, 17-for-75 (.227). 1986-87, 21-for-104 (.202). 1987-88, 44-for-157 (.280). 1988-89, 35-for-162 (.216). 1989-90, 20-for-92 (.217). 1990-91, 44-for-155 (.284). 1991-92, 32-for-137 (.234). 1992-93, 67-for-220 (.305). 1993-94, 48-for-178 (.270). 1994-95, 74-for-219 (.338). 1995-96, 49-for-175 (.280). 1996-97, 58-for-205 (.283). 1997-98, 18-for-84 (.214). 1998-99, 4-for-25 (.160). 1999-00, 6-for-26 (.231). Totals, 538-for-2020 (.266).

Personal fouls/disqualifications: 1984-85, 301/5. 1985-86, 333/8. 1986-87, 252/5. 1987-88, 278/6. 1988-89, 262/3. 1989-90, 250/2. 1990-91, 173/2. 1991-92, 196/2. 1992-93, 196/0. 1993-94, 160/1. 1994-95, 201/3. 1995-96, 208/3. 1996-97, 153/2. 1997-98, 187/2. 1998-99, 89/0. 1999-00, 48/0. Totals, 3287/44.

## NBA PLAYOFF RECORD

NOTES: Shares single-game playoff records for most free throws made in one half—19 (June 5, 1993, vs. Seattle); and most field goals made in one half—15 (May 4, 1994, at Golden State).

| Season Team | G | Min. | FGM | FGA | Pct. | FTM | FTA | Pct. | REBOUNDS Off. | Def. | Tot. | Ast. | St. | Blk. | TO | Pts. | AVERAGES RPG | APG | PPG |
|---|---|---|---|---|---|---|---|---|---|---|---|---|---|---|---|---|---|---|---|
| 84-85—Philadelphia.... | 13 | 408 | 75 | 139 | .540 | 40 | 63 | .635 | 52 | 92 | 144 | 26 | 23 | 15 | 35 | 194 | 11.1 | 2.0 | 14.9 |
| 85-86—Philadelphia.... | 12 | 497 | 104 | 180 | .578 | 91 | 131 | .695 | 60 | 129 | 189 | 67 | 27 | 15 | 65 | 300 | 15.8 | 5.6 | 25.0 |
| 86-87—Philadelphia.... | 5 | 210 | 43 | 75 | .573 | 36 | 45 | .800 | 27 | 36 | 63 | 12 | 4 | 8 | 22 | 123 | 12.6 | 2.4 | 24.6 |
| 88-89—Philadelphia.... | 3 | 135 | 29 | 45 | .644 | 22 | 31 | .710 | 8 | 27 | 35 | 16 | 5 | 2 | 11 | 81 | 11.7 | 5.3 | 27.0 |
| 89-90—Philadelphia.... | 10 | 419 | 88 | 162 | .543 | 65 | 108 | .602 | 66 | 89 | 155 | 43 | 8 | 7 | 30 | 247 | 15.5 | 4.3 | 24.7 |
| 90-91—Philadelphia.... | 8 | 326 | 74 | 125 | .592 | 49 | 75 | .653 | 31 | 53 | 84 | 48 | 15 | 3 | 25 | 199 | 10.5 | 6.0 | 24.9 |
| 92-93—Phoenix ........ | 24 | 1026 | 230 | 482 | .477 | 168 | 218 | .771 | 93 | 233 | 326 | 102 | 39 | 25 | 50 | 638 | 13.6 | 4.3 | 26.6 |
| 93-94—Phoenix ........ | 10 | 425 | 110 | 216 | .509 | 42 | 55 | .764 | 34 | 96 | 130 | 48 | 25 | 9 | 27 | 276 | 13.0 | 4.8 | 27.6 |
| 94-95—Phoenix ........ | 10 | 390 | 91 | 182 | .500 | 66 | 90 | .733 | 39 | 95 | 134 | 32 | 13 | 11 | 25 | 257 | 13.4 | 3.2 | 25.7 |
| 95-96—Phoenix ........ | 4 | 164 | 31 | 70 | .443 | 37 | 47 | .787 | 18 | 36 | 54 | 15 | 4 | 4 | 6 | 102 | 13.5 | 3.8 | 25.5 |
| 96-97—Houston......... | 16 | 605 | 86 | 198 | .434 | 103 | 134 | .769 | 64 | 128 | 192 | 54 | 19 | 7 | 43 | 286 | 12.0 | 3.4 | 17.9 |
| 97-98—Houston......... | 4 | 87 | 12 | 23 | .522 | 12 | 21 | .571 | 5 | 16 | 21 | 4 | 5 | 0 | 6 | 36 | 5.3 | 1.0 | 9.0 |
| 98-99—Houston......... | 4 | 157 | 36 | 68 | .529 | 20 | 30 | .667 | 13 | 42 | 55 | 15 | 6 | 2 | 8 | 94 | 13.8 | 3.8 | 23.5 |
| Totals .................. | 123 | 4849 | 1009 | 1965 | .513 | 751 | 1048 | .717 | 510 | 1072 | 1582 | 482 | 193 | 108 | 353 | 2833 | 12.9 | 3.9 | 23.0 |

Three-point field goals: 1984-85, 4-for-6 (.667). 1985-86, 1-for-15 (.067). 1988-89, 1-for-5 (.200). 1989-90, 6-for-18 (.333). 1990-91, 2-for-20 (.100). 1992-93, 10-for-45 (.222). 1993-94, 14-for-40 (.350). 1994-95, 9-for-35 (.257). 1995-96, 3-for-12 (.250). 1996-97, 11-for-38 (.289). 1997-98, 0-for-2. 1998-99, 2-for-7 (.286). Totals, 63-for-243 (.259).

Personal fouls/disqualifications: 1984-85, 49/0. 1985-86, 52/2. 1988-89, 9/0. 1989-90, 36/0. 1990-91, 23/0. 1992-93, 73/0. 1993-94, 26/0. 1994-95, 28/0. 1995-96, 15/0. 1996-97, 52/1. 1997-98, 12/1. 1998-99, 12/0. Totals, 408/4.

## NBA ALL-STAR GAME RECORD

NOTES: NBA All-Star Game Most Valuable Player (1991).

| Season Team | Min. | FGM | FGA | Pct. | FTM | FTA | Pct. | REBOUNDS Off. | Def. | Tot. | Ast. | PF | Dq. | St. | Blk. | TO | Pts. |
|---|---|---|---|---|---|---|---|---|---|---|---|---|---|---|---|---|---|
| 1987—Philadelphia .......... | 16 | 2 | 6 | .333 | 3 | 6 | .500 | 1 | 3 | 4 | 1 | 2 | 0 | 1 | 0 | 0 | 7 |
| 1988—Philadelphia .......... | 15 | 1 | 4 | .250 | 2 | 2 | 1.000 | 1 | 2 | 3 | 0 | 2 | 0 | 1 | 1 | 3 | 4 |
| 1989—Philadelphia .......... | 20 | 6 | 11 | .545 | 5 | 8 | .625 | 3 | 2 | 5 | 0 | 0 | 0 | 2 | 1 | 1 | 17 |
| 1990—Philadelphia .......... | 22 | 7 | 12 | .583 | 2 | 3 | .667 | 2 | 2 | 4 | 0 | 1 | 0 | 1 | 1 | 2 | 17 |
| 1991—Philadelphia .......... | 35 | 7 | 15 | .467 | 3 | 6 | .500 | 8 | 14 | 22 | 4 | 5 | 0 | 1 | 1 | 3 | 17 |
| 1992—Philadelphia .......... | 28 | 6 | 14 | .429 | 0 | 0 | ... | 2 | 7 | 9 | 1 | 3 | 0 | 0 | 0 | 3 | 12 |
| 1993—Phoenix .............. | 34 | 5 | 11 | .455 | 5 | 7 | .714 | 0 | 4 | 4 | 7 | 3 | 0 | 4 | 0 | 4 | 16 |
| 1994—.................... | | | | | | | | Selected, did not play—injured. | | | | | | | | | |
| 1995—Phoenix .............. | 23 | 7 | 12 | .583 | 0 | 0 | ... | 5 | 4 | 9 | 2 | 1 | 0 | 2 | 0 | 2 | 15 |
| 1996—Phoenix .............. | 16 | 4 | 6 | .667 | 0 | 0 | ... | 0 | 0 | 0 | 1 | 1 | 0 | 0 | 0 | 2 | 8 |
| 1997—Houston .............. | | | | | | | | Selected, did not play—injured. | | | | | | | | | |
| Totals .......................... | 209 | 45 | 91 | .495 | 20 | 32 | .625 | 22 | 38 | 60 | 16 | 18 | 0 | 12 | 4 | 20 | 113 |

Three-point field goals: 1987, 0-for-2. 1988, 0-for-1. 1990, 1-for-1. 1992, 0-for-2. 1993, 1-for-2 (.500). 1995, 1-for-4 (.250). Totals, 3-for-12 (.250)

## BARRY, RICK                                     F

**PERSONAL:** Born March 28, 1944, in Elizabeth, N.J. ... 6-7/220 (2,00/99,8). ... Full name: Richard Francis Dennis Barry III. ... Father of Jon Barry, guard with Houston Rockets; father of Brent Barry, guard with San Antonio Spurs; and father of Drew Barry, guard with Atlanta Hawks (1997-98 and 1999-2000), Seattle SuperSonics (1998-99) and Golden State Warriors (1999-2000).
**HIGH SCHOOL:** Roselle Park (N.J.).
**COLLEGE:** Miami (Fla.).
**TRANSACTIONS:** Selected by San Francisco Warriors in first round of 1965 NBA Draft. ... Signed as free agent by Oakland Oaks of American Basketball Association (1967); court order required him to sit out option season with Warriors (1967-68). ... Oaks franchise moved to Washington and renamed Capitols for 1969-70 season. ... Capitols franchise moved from Washington to Virginia and renamed Squires for

1970-71 season. ... Traded by Squires to New York Nets for first-round draft choice and cash (August 1970). ... Returned to NBA with Golden State Warriors for 1972-73 season. ... Signed as veteran free agent by Houston Rockets (June 17, 1978); Warriors waived their right of first refusal in exchange for G John Lucas and cash.

**CAREER HONORS:** Elected to Naismith Memorial Basketball Hall of Fame (1987). ... One of the 50 Greatest Players in NBA History (1996).

**MISCELLANEOUS:** Member of NBA championship team (1975).

## COLLEGIATE RECORD

**NOTES:** THE SPORTING NEWS All-America second team (1965). ... Led NCAA Division I with 37.4 points per game (1965).

| Season Team | G | Min. | FGM | FGA | Pct. | FTM | FTA | Pct. | Reb. | Ast. | Pts. | RPG | APG | PPG |
|---|---|---|---|---|---|---|---|---|---|---|---|---|---|---|
| 61-62—Miami (Fla.)‡ | 17 | ... | 208 | ... | ... | 73 | ... | ... | ... | ... | 489 | ... | ... | 28.8 |
| 62-63—Miami (Fla.) | 24 | ... | 162 | 341 | .475 | 131 | 158 | .829 | 351 | ... | 455 | 14.6 | ... | 19.0 |
| 63-64—Miami (Fla.) | 27 | ... | 314 | 572 | .549 | 242 | 287 | .843 | 448 | ... | 870 | 16.6 | ... | 32.2 |
| 64-65—Miami (Fla.) | 26 | ... | 340 | 651 | .522 | 293 | 341 | .859 | 475 | ... | 973 | 18.3 | ... | 37.4 |
| Varsity totals | 77 | ... | 816 | 1564 | .522 | 666 | 786 | .847 | 1274 | ... | 2298 | 16.5 | ... | 29.8 |

## NBA REGULAR-SEASON RECORD

**RECORDS:** Shares single-game record for most free throws made in one quarter—14 (December 6, 1966, vs. New York).

**HONORS:** NBA Rookie of the Year (1966). ... All-NBA first team (1966, 1967, 1974, 1975, 1976). ... All-NBA second team (1973). ... NBA All-Rookie team (1966).

**NOTES:** Led NBA with 2.85 steals per game (1975).

| Season Team | G | Min. | FGM | FGA | Pct. | FTM | FTA | Pct. | Reb. | Ast. | PF | Dq. | Pts. | RPG | APG | PPG |
|---|---|---|---|---|---|---|---|---|---|---|---|---|---|---|---|---|
| 65-66—San Francisco | 80 | 2990 | 745 | 1698 | .439 | 569 | 660 | .862 | 850 | 173 | 297 | 2 | 2059 | 10.6 | 2.2 | 25.7 |
| 66-67—San Francisco | 78 | 3175 | *1011 | *2240 | .451 | *753 | 852 | .884 | 714 | 282 | 258 | 1 | *2775 | 9.2 | 3.6 | *35.6 |
| 72-73—Golden State | 82 | 3075 | 737 | 1630 | .452 | 358 | 397 | *.902 | 728 | 399 | 245 | 2 | 1832 | 8.9 | 4.9 | 22.3 |

| | | | | | | | | | REBOUNDS | | | | | | | | AVERAGES | | |
| Season Team | G | Min. | FGM | FGA | Pct. | FTM | FTA | Pct. | Off. | Def. | Tot. | Ast. | St. | Blk. | TO | Pts. | RPG | APG | PPG |
|---|---|---|---|---|---|---|---|---|---|---|---|---|---|---|---|---|---|---|---|
| 73-74—Golden State | 80 | 2918 | 796 | 1746 | .456 | 417 | 464 | .899 | 103 | 437 | 540 | 484 | 169 | 40 | ... | 2009 | 6.8 | 6.1 | 25.1 |
| 74-75—Golden State | 80 | 3235 | 1028 | *2217 | .464 | 394 | 436 | *.904 | 92 | 364 | 456 | 492 | *228 | 33 | ... | 2450 | 5.7 | 6.2 | 30.6 |
| 75-76—Golden State | 81 | 3122 | 707 | 1624 | .435 | 287 | 311 | *.923 | 74 | 422 | 496 | 496 | 202 | 27 | ... | 1701 | 6.1 | 6.1 | 21.0 |
| 76-77—Golden State | 79 | 2904 | 682 | 1551 | .440 | 359 | 392 | .916 | 73 | 349 | 422 | 475 | 172 | 58 | ... | 1723 | 5.3 | 6.0 | 21.8 |
| 77-78—Golden State | 82 | 3024 | 760 | 1686 | .451 | 378 | 409 | *.924 | 75 | 374 | 449 | 446 | 158 | 45 | 224 | 1898 | 5.5 | 5.4 | 23.1 |
| 78-79—Houston | 80 | 2566 | 461 | 1000 | .461 | 160 | 169 | *.947 | 40 | 237 | 277 | 502 | 95 | 38 | 198 | 1082 | 3.5 | 6.3 | 13.5 |
| 79-80—Houston | 72 | 1816 | 325 | 771 | .422 | 143 | 153 | *.935 | 53 | 183 | 236 | 268 | 80 | 28 | 152 | 866 | 3.3 | 3.7 | 12.0 |
| Totals | 794 | 28825 | 7252 | 16163 | .449 | 3818 | 4243 | .900 | ... | ... | 5168 | 4017 | 1104 | 269 | 574 | 18395 | 6.5 | 5.1 | 23.2 |

Three-point field goals: 1979-80, 73-for-221 (.330).

Personal fouls/disqualifications: 1973-74, 265/4. 1974-75, 225/0. 1975-76, 215/1. 1976-77, 194/2. 1977-78, 188/1. 1978-79, 195/0. 1979-80, 182/0. Totals, 2264/13.

## NBA PLAYOFF RECORD

**NOTES:** NBA Finals Most Valuable Player (1975). ... Holds NBA Finals single-game records for most field goals attempted—48 (April 18, 1967, vs. Philadelphia); and most field goals attempted in one quarter—17 (April 14, 1967, vs. Philadelphia). ... Shares NBA Finals single-game record for most field goals made—22 (April 18, 1967, vs. Philadelphia). ... Holds single-game playoff record for most field goals attempted in one quarter—17 (April 14, 1967, vs. Philadelphia).

| Season Team | G | Min. | FGM | FGA | Pct. | FTM | FTA | Pct. | Reb. | Ast. | PF | Dq. | Pts. | RPG | APG | PPG |
|---|---|---|---|---|---|---|---|---|---|---|---|---|---|---|---|---|---|
| 66-67—San Francisco | 15 | 614 | 197 | 489 | .403 | 127 | 157 | .809 | 113 | 58 | 49 | 0 | 521 | 7.5 | 3.9 | 34.7 |
| 72-73—Golden State | 11 | 292 | 65 | 164 | .396 | 50 | 55 | .909 | 54 | 24 | 41 | 1 | 180 | 4.9 | 2.2 | 16.4 |

| | | | | | | | | | REBOUNDS | | | | | | | | AVERAGES | | |
| Season Team | G | Min. | FGM | FGA | Pct. | FTM | FTA | Pct. | Off. | Def. | Tot. | Ast. | St. | Blk. | TO | Pts. | RPG | APG | PPG |
|---|---|---|---|---|---|---|---|---|---|---|---|---|---|---|---|---|---|---|---|
| 74-75—Golden State | 17 | 726 | 189 | 426 | .444 | 101 | 110 | .918 | 22 | 72 | 94 | 103 | 50 | 15 | ... | 479 | 5.5 | 6.1 | 28.2 |
| 75-76—Golden State | 13 | 532 | 126 | 289 | .436 | 60 | 68 | .882 | 20 | 64 | 84 | 84 | 38 | 14 | ... | 312 | 6.5 | 6.5 | 24.0 |
| 76-77—Golden State | 10 | 415 | 122 | 262 | .466 | 40 | 44 | .909 | 25 | 34 | 59 | 47 | 17 | 7 | ... | 284 | 5.9 | 4.7 | 28.4 |
| 78-79—Houston | 2 | 65 | 8 | 25 | .320 | 8 | 8 | 1.000 | 2 | 6 | 8 | 9 | 0 | 2 | 2 | 24 | 4.0 | 4.5 | 12.0 |
| 79-80—Houston | 6 | 79 | 12 | 33 | .364 | 6 | 6 | 1.000 | 0 | 6 | 6 | 15 | 1 | 1 | 10 | 33 | 1.0 | 2.5 | 5.5 |
| Totals | 74 | 2723 | 719 | 1688 | .426 | 392 | 448 | .875 | ... | ... | 418 | 340 | 106 | 39 | 12 | 1833 | 5.6 | 4.6 | 24.8 |

Three-point field goals: 1979-80, 3-for-12 (.250).

Personal fouls/disqualifications: 1974-75, 51/1. 1975-76, 40/1. 1976-77, 32/0. 1978-79, 8/0. 1979-80, 11/0. Totals, 232/3.

## NBA ALL-STAR GAME RECORD

**NOTES:** NBA All-Star Game Most Valuable Player (1967). ... Holds single-game records for most field goals attempted—27 (1967); and most steals—8 (1975).

| Season Team | Min. | FGM | FGA | Pct. | FTM | FTA | Pct. | Reb. | Ast. | PF | Dq. | Pts. |
|---|---|---|---|---|---|---|---|---|---|---|---|---|
| 1966—San Francisco | 17 | 4 | 10 | .400 | 2 | 4 | .500 | 2 | 2 | 6 | 1 | 10 |
| 1967—San Francisco | 34 | 16 | 27 | .593 | 6 | 8 | .750 | 6 | 3 | 5 | 0 | 38 |
| 1973—Golden State | | | | | Selected, did not play—injured. | | | | | | | |

| | | | | | | | | REBOUNDS | | | | | | | |
| Season Team | Min. | FGM | FGA | Pct. | FTM | FTA | Pct. | Off. | Def. | Tot. | Ast. | PF | Dq. | St. | Blk. | TO | Pts. |
|---|---|---|---|---|---|---|---|---|---|---|---|---|---|---|---|---|---|
| 1974—Golden State | 19 | 3 | 6 | .500 | 2 | 2 | 1.000 | 1 | 3 | 4 | 3 | 3 | 0 | 1 | 0 | ... | 8 |
| 1975—Golden State | 38 | 11 | 20 | .550 | 0 | 0 | | 1 | 4 | 5 | 8 | 4 | 0 | 8 | 1 | ... | 22 |
| 1976—Golden State | 28 | 6 | 15 | .400 | 5 | 5 | 1.000 | 2 | 2 | 4 | 2 | 5 | 0 | 2 | 0 | ... | 17 |
| 1977—Golden State | 29 | 7 | 16 | .438 | 4 | 4 | 1.000 | 1 | 3 | 4 | 8 | 1 | 0 | 2 | 0 | ... | 18 |
| 1978—Golden State | 30 | 7 | 17 | .412 | 1 | 1 | 1.000 | 2 | 2 | 4 | 5 | 6 | 1 | 3 | 0 | 5 | 15 |
| Totals | 195 | 54 | 111 | .486 | 20 | 24 | .833 | ... | ... | 29 | 31 | 30 | 2 | 16 | 1 | 5 | 128 |

## ABA REGULAR-SEASON RECORD

**NOTES:** Member of ABA championship team (1969). ... ABA All-Star first team (1969, 1970, 1971, 1972).

| | | | 2-POINT | | | 3-POINT | | | | | | | | | AVERAGES | | |
| Season Team | G | Min. | FGM | FGA | Pct. | FGM | FGA | Pct. | FTM | FTA | Pct. | Reb. | Ast. | Pts. | RPG | APG | PPG |
|---|---|---|---|---|---|---|---|---|---|---|---|---|---|---|---|---|---|
| 67-68— | | | | | Did not play—sat out option year. | | | | | | | | | | | | |
| 68-69—Oakland | 35 | 1361 | 389 | 757 | .514 | 3 | 10 | .300 | 403 | 454 | *.888 | 329 | 136 | *1190 | 9.4 | 3.9 | *34.0 |
| 69-70—Washington | 52 | 1849 | 509 | 907 | .561 | 8 | 39 | .205 | 400 | 463 | .864 | 363 | 178 | 1442 | 7.0 | 3.4 | 27.7 |
| 70-71—New York | 59 | 2502 | 613 | 1262 | .486 | 19 | 86 | .221 | 451 | 507 | *.890 | 401 | 294 | 1734 | 6.8 | 5.0 | 29.4 |
| 71-72—New York | 80 | 3616 | 829 | 1732 | .479 | 73 | 237 | .308 | *641 | 730 | .878 | 602 | 327 | 2518 | 7.5 | 4.1 | 31.5 |
| Totals | 226 | 9328 | 2340 | 4658 | .502 | 103 | 372 | .277 | 1895 | 2154 | .880 | 1695 | 935 | 6884 | 7.5 | 4.1 | 30.5 |

## ABA PLAYOFF RECORD

| | | | 2-POINT | | | 3-POINT | | | | | | | | | AVERAGES | | |
|---|---|---|---|---|---|---|---|---|---|---|---|---|---|---|---|---|---|
| Season Team | G | Min. | FGM | FGA | Pct. | FGM | FGA | Pct. | FTM | FTA | Pct. | Reb. | Ast. | Pts. | RPG | APG | PPG |
| 69-70—Washington | 7 | 302 | 105 | 194 | .541 | .3 | 9 | .333 | 62 | 68 | .912 | 70 | 23 | 281 | 10.0 | 3.3 | 40.1 |
| 70-71—New York | 6 | 287 | 46 | 108 | .426 | 14 | 27 | .519 | 48 | 59 | .814 | 70 | 24 | 202 | 11.7 | 4.0 | 33.7 |
| 71-72—New York | 18 | 749 | 180 | 368 | .489 | 23 | 61 | .377 | 125 | 146 | .856 | 117 | 69 | 554 | 6.5 | 3.8 | 30.8 |
| Totals | 31 | 1338 | 331 | 670 | .494 | 40 | 97 | .412 | 235 | 273 | .861 | 257 | 116 | 1037 | 8.3 | 3.7 | 33.5 |

## ABA ALL-STAR GAME RECORD

| | | 2-POINT | | | 3-POINT | | | | | | | |
|---|---|---|---|---|---|---|---|---|---|---|---|---|
| Season Team | Min. | FGM | FGA | Pct. | FGM | FGA | Pct. | FTM | FTA | Pct. | Reb. | Ast. | Pts. |
| 1968—Oakland | 12 | 3 | 9 | .333 | 0 | 0 | ... | 4 | 5 | .800 | 3 | 1 | 10 |
| 1969—Washington | 27 | 7 | 12 | .583 | 0 | 0 | ... | 2 | 2 | 1.000 | 7 | 7 | 16 |
| 1970—New York | 17 | 4 | 6 | .667 | 0 | 0 | ... | 6 | 6 | 1.000 | 2 | 2 | 14 |
| 1971—New York | 26 | 2 | 10 | .200 | 0 | 0 | ... | 0 | 1 | .000 | 12 | 8 | 4 |
| Totals | 82 | 16 | 37 | .432 | 0 | 0 | ... | 12 | 14 | .857 | 24 | 18 | 44 |

## COMBINED ABA AND NBA REGULAR-SEASON RECORDS

| | | | | | | | REBOUNDS | | | | | | | AVERAGES | | |
|---|---|---|---|---|---|---|---|---|---|---|---|---|---|---|---|---|
| | G | Min. | FGM | FGA | Pct. | FTM | FTA | Pct. | Off. | Def. | Tot. | Ast. | Stl. | Blk. | TO | Pts. | RPG | APG | PPG |
| Totals | 1020 | 38153 | 9695 | 21193 | .457 | 5713 | 6397 | .893 | ... | ... | 6863 | 4952 | ... | ... | ... | 25279 | 6.7 | 4.9 | 24.8 |

Three-point field goals: 176-for-593 (.297).
Personal fouls/disqualifications: 3028.

## CBA COACHING RECORD

| | REGULAR SEASON | | | | | PLAYOFFS | | |
|---|---|---|---|---|---|---|---|---|
| Season Team | W | L | Pct. | Finish | | W | L | Pct. |
| 92-93—Fort Wayne | 11 | 16 | .407 | 4th/Eastern Division——— | | | | |
| 93-94—Fort Wayne | 14 | 30 | .318 | | | | | |
| Totals (2 years) | 25 | 46 | .352 | | | | | |

## USBL COACHING RECORD

| | REGULAR SEASON | | | | | PLAYOFFS | | |
|---|---|---|---|---|---|---|---|---|
| Season Team | W | L | Pct. | Finish | | W | L | Pct. |
| 97-98—New Jersey | 14 | 12 | .538 | 3rd/Mid-Atlantic Division | | 1 | 1 | .500 |
| 98-99—New Jersey | 23 | 6 | .793 | 1st/Mid-Atlantic Division | | 3 | 0 | 1.000 |
| 99-00—Florida | 16 | 14 | .533 | 3rd/Southern Division | | 0 | 1 | .000 |
| Totals (3 years) | 53 | 32 | .624 | | Totals (3 years) | 4 | 2 | .667 |

**NOTES:**
1998—Defeated Tampa Bay in play-in game; lost to Jacksonville in quarterfinals.
1999—Defeated Tampa Bay in quarterfinals; defeated Pennsylvania in semifinals; defeated Connecticut in USBL Finals.
2000—Lost to Kansas in quarterfinals.

# BAYLOR, ELGIN                    F

**PERSONAL:** Born September 16, 1934, in Washington, D.C. ... 6-5/225 (1,96/102,1). ... Full name: Elgin Gay Baylor.
**HIGH SCHOOL:** Phelps Vocational (Washington, D.C.), then Spingarn (Washington, D.C.).
**COLLEGE:** The College of Idaho, then Seattle.
**TRANSACTIONS:** Selected after junior season by Minneapolis Lakers in first round (first pick overall) of 1958 NBA Draft. ... Lakers franchise moved to Los Angeles for 1960-61 season.
**CAREER HONORS:** Elected to Naismith Memorial Basketball Hall of Fame (1977). ... NBA 35th Anniversary All-Time Team (1980) and One of the 50 Greatest Players in NBA History (1996).
**CAREER NOTES:** Vice president of basketball operations, Los Angeles Clippers (1986 to present).
**MISCELLANEOUS:** Los Angeles Lakers franchise all-time leading rebounder with 11,463 (1958-59 through 1971-72).

## COLLEGIATE RECORD

**NOTES:** THE SPORTING NEWS All-America first team (1958). ... NCAA University Division Tournament Most Valuable Player (1958). ... Led NCAA Division I with .235 rebound average (1957), when championship was determined by highest individual recoveries as percentage of total recoveries by both teams in all games. ... Played for Westside Ford (AAU team in Seattle) averaging 34 points per game (1955-56).

| | | | | | | | | | | | | AVERAGES | | |
|---|---|---|---|---|---|---|---|---|---|---|---|---|---|---|
| Season Team | G | Min. | FGM | FGA | Pct. | FTM | FTA | Pct. | Reb. | Ast. | Pts. | RPG | APG | PPG |
| 54-55—The College of Idaho | 26 | ... | 332 | 651 | .510 | 150 | 232 | .647 | 492 | ... | 814 | 18.9 | ... | 31.3 |
| 55-56—Seattle | | | | | | Did not play—transfer student. | | | | | | | | |
| 56-57—Seattle | 25 | ... | 271 | 555 | .488 | 201 | 251 | .801 | 508 | ... | 743 | 20.3 | ... | 29.7 |
| 57-58—Seattle | 29 | ... | 353 | 697 | .506 | 237 | 308 | .769 | 559 | ... | 943 | 19.3 | ... | 32.5 |
| Totals | 80 | ... | 956 | 1903 | .502 | 588 | 791 | .743 | 1559 | ... | 2500 | 19.5 | ... | 31.3 |

## NBA REGULAR-SEASON RECORD

**HONORS:** NBA Rookie of the Year (1959). ... All-NBA first team (1959, 1960, 1961, 1962, 1963, 1964, 1965, 1967, 1968, 1969).

| | | | | | | | | | | | | | | AVERAGES | | |
|---|---|---|---|---|---|---|---|---|---|---|---|---|---|---|---|---|
| Season Team | G | Min. | FGM | FGA | Pct. | FTM | FTA | Pct. | Reb. | Ast. | PF | Dq. | Pts. | RPG | APG | PPG |
| 58-59—Minneapolis | 70 | 2855 | 605 | 1482 | .408 | 532 | 685 | .777 | 1050 | 287 | 270 | 4 | 1742 | 15.0 | 4.1 | 24.9 |
| 59-60—Minneapolis | 70 | 2873 | 755 | 1781 | .424 | 564 | 770 | .732 | 1150 | 243 | 234 | 2 | 2074 | 16.4 | 3.5 | 29.6 |
| 60-61—Los Angeles | 73 | 3133 | 931 | 2166 | .430 | 676 | 863 | .783 | 1447 | 371 | 279 | 3 | 2538 | 19.8 | 5.1 | 34.8 |
| 61-62—Los Angeles | 48 | 2129 | 680 | 1588 | .428 | 476 | 631 | .754 | 892 | 222 | 155 | 1 | 1836 | 18.6 | 4.6 | 38.3 |
| 62-63—Los Angeles | 80 | 3370 | 1029 | 2273 | .453 | 661 | 790 | .837 | 1146 | 386 | 226 | 1 | 2719 | 14.3 | 4.8 | 34.0 |
| 63-64—Los Angeles | 78 | 3164 | 756 | 1778 | .425 | 471 | 586 | .804 | 936 | 347 | 235 | 1 | 1983 | 12.0 | 4.4 | 25.4 |
| 64-65—Los Angeles | 74 | 3056 | 763 | 1903 | .401 | 483 | 610 | .792 | 950 | 280 | 235 | 0 | 2009 | 12.8 | 3.8 | 27.1 |
| 65-66—Los Angeles | 65 | 1975 | 415 | 1034 | .401 | 249 | 337 | .739 | 621 | 224 | 157 | 0 | 1079 | 9.6 | 3.4 | 16.6 |
| 66-67—Los Angeles | 70 | 2706 | 711 | 1658 | .429 | 440 | 541 | .813 | 898 | 215 | 211 | 1 | 1862 | 12.8 | 3.1 | 26.6 |
| 67-68—Los Angeles | 77 | 3029 | 757 | 1709 | .443 | 488 | 621 | .786 | 941 | 355 | 232 | 0 | 2002 | 12.2 | 4.6 | 26.0 |

| Season Team | G | Min. | FGM | FGA | Pct. | FTM | FTA | Pct. | Reb. | Ast. | PF | Dq. | Pts. | RPG | APG | PPG |
|---|---|---|---|---|---|---|---|---|---|---|---|---|---|---|---|---|
| 68-69—Los Angeles | 76 | 3064 | 730 | 1632 | .447 | 421 | 567 | .743 | 805 | 408 | 204 | 0 | 1881 | 10.6 | 5.4 | 24.8 |
| 69-70—Los Angeles | 54 | 2213 | 511 | 1051 | .486 | 276 | 357 | .773 | 559 | 292 | 132 | 1 | 1298 | 10.4 | 5.4 | 24.0 |
| 70-71—Los Angeles | 2 | 57 | 8 | 19 | .421 | 4 | 6 | .667 | 11 | 2 | 6 | 0 | 20 | 5.5 | 1.0 | 10.0 |
| 71-72—Los Angeles | 9 | 239 | 42 | 97 | .433 | 22 | 27 | .815 | 57 | 18 | 20 | 0 | 106 | 6.3 | 2.0 | 11.8 |
| Totals | 846 | 33863 | 8693 | 20171 | .431 | 5763 | 7391 | .780 | 11463 | 3650 | 2596 | 14 | 23149 | 13.5 | 4.3 | 27.4 |

### NBA PLAYOFF RECORD

**RECORDS:** Holds NBA Finals single-game records for most points—61; and most field goals attempted in one half—25 (April 14, 1962, vs. Boston). ... Shares NBA Finals single-game record for most field goals made—22 (April 14, 1962, vs. Boston). ... Shares single-game play-off record for most field goals attempted in one half—25 (April 14, 1962, vs. Boston).

| Season Team | G | Min. | FGM | FGA | Pct. | FTM | FTA | Pct. | Reb. | Ast. | PF | Dq. | Pts. | RPG | APG | PPG |
|---|---|---|---|---|---|---|---|---|---|---|---|---|---|---|---|---|
| 58-59—Minneapolis | 13 | 556 | 122 | 303 | .403 | 87 | 113 | .770 | 156 | 43 | 52 | 0 | 331 | 12.0 | 3.3 | 25.5 |
| 59-60—Minneapolis | 9 | 408 | 111 | 234 | .474 | 79 | 94 | .840 | 127 | 31 | 38 | 0 | 301 | 14.1 | 3.4 | 33.4 |
| 60-61—Los Angeles | 12 | 540 | 170 | 362 | .470 | 117 | 142 | .824 | 183 | 55 | 44 | 1 | 457 | 15.3 | 4.6 | 38.1 |
| 61-62—Los Angeles | 13 | 571 | 186 | 425 | .438 | 130 | 168 | .774 | 230 | 47 | 45 | 1 | 502 | 17.7 | 3.6 | 38.6 |
| 62-63—Los Angeles | 13 | 562 | 160 | 362 | .442 | 104 | 126 | .825 | 177 | 58 | 48 | 0 | 424 | 13.6 | 4.5 | 32.6 |
| 63-64—Los Angeles | 5 | 221 | 45 | 119 | .378 | 31 | 40 | .775 | 58 | 28 | 17 | 0 | 121 | 11.6 | 5.6 | 24.2 |
| 64-65—Los Angeles | 1 | 5 | 0 | 2 | .000 | 0 | 0 | ... | 0 | 1 | 0 | 0 | 0 | 0.0 | 1.0 | 0.0 |
| 65-66—Los Angeles | 14 | 586 | 145 | 328 | .442 | 85 | 105 | .810 | 197 | 52 | 38 | 0 | 375 | 14.1 | 3.7 | 26.8 |
| 66-67—Los Angeles | 3 | 121 | 28 | 76 | .368 | 15 | 20 | .750 | 39 | 9 | 6 | 0 | 71 | 13.0 | 3.0 | 23.7 |
| 67-68—Los Angeles | 15 | 633 | 176 | 376 | .468 | 76 | 112 | .679 | 218 | 60 | 41 | 0 | 428 | 14.5 | 4.0 | 28.5 |
| 68-69—Los Angeles | 18 | 640 | 107 | 278 | .385 | 63 | 97 | .649 | 166 | 74 | 56 | 0 | 277 | 9.2 | 4.1 | 15.4 |
| 69-70—Los Angeles | 18 | 667 | 138 | 296 | .466 | 60 | 81 | .741 | 173 | 83 | 50 | 1 | 336 | 9.6 | 4.6 | 18.7 |
| Totals | 134 | 5510 | 1388 | 3161 | .439 | 847 | 1098 | .771 | 1724 | 541 | 435 | 3 | 3623 | 12.9 | 4.0 | 27.0 |

### NBA ALL-STAR GAME RECORD

**NOTES:** NBA All-Star Game co-Most Valuable Player (1959). ... Holds career record for most free throws made—78. ... Shares career record for most free throws attempted—98. ... Shares single-game record for most free throws made—12 (1962).

| Season Team | Min. | FGM | FGA | Pct. | FTM | FTA | Pct. | Reb | Ast. | PF | Dq. | Pts. |
|---|---|---|---|---|---|---|---|---|---|---|---|---|
| 1959—Minneapolis | 32 | 10 | 20 | .500 | 4 | 5 | .800 | 11 | 1 | 3 | 0 | 24 |
| 1960—Minneapolis | 28 | 10 | 18 | .556 | 5 | 7 | .714 | 13 | 3 | 4 | 0 | 25 |
| 1961—Los Angeles | 27 | 3 | 11 | .273 | 9 | 10 | .900 | 10 | 4 | 5 | 0 | 15 |
| 1962—Los Angeles | 37 | 10 | 23 | .435 | 12 | 14 | .857 | 9 | 4 | 2 | 0 | 32 |
| 1963—Los Angeles | 36 | 4 | 15 | .267 | 9 | 13 | .692 | 14 | 7 | 0 | 0 | 17 |
| 1964—Los Angeles | 29 | 5 | 15 | .333 | 5 | 11 | .455 | 8 | 5 | 1 | 0 | 15 |
| 1965—Los Angeles | 27 | 5 | 13 | .385 | 8 | 8 | 1.000 | 7 | 0 | 4 | 0 | 18 |
| 1967—Los Angeles | 20 | 8 | 14 | .571 | 4 | 4 | 1.000 | 5 | 5 | 2 | 0 | 20 |
| 1968—Los Angeles | 27 | 8 | 13 | .615 | 6 | 7 | .857 | 6 | 1 | 5 | 0 | 22 |
| 1969—Los Angeles | 32 | 5 | 13 | .385 | 11 | 12 | .917 | 9 | 5 | 2 | 0 | 21 |
| 1970—Los Angeles | 26 | 2 | 9 | .222 | 5 | 7 | .714 | 7 | 3 | 3 | 0 | 9 |
| Totals | 321 | 70 | 164 | .427 | 78 | 98 | .796 | 99 | 38 | 31 | 0 | 218 |

### NBA COACHING RECORD

**BACKGROUND:** Assistant coach, New Orleans Jazz (1974-75 and 1975-76).

| Season Team | REGULAR SEASON | | | | PLAYOFFS | | |
|---|---|---|---|---|---|---|---|
| | W | L | Pct. | Finish | W | L | Pct. |
| 74-75—New Orleans | 0 | 1 | .000 | | — | — | — |
| 76-77—New Orleans | 21 | 35 | .375 | 5th/Central Division | — | — | — |
| 77-78—New Orleans | 39 | 43 | .476 | 5th/Central Division | — | — | — |
| 78-79—New Orleans | 26 | 56 | .317 | 6th/Central Division | — | — | — |
| Totals (4 years) | 86 | 135 | .389 | | | | |

**NOTES:**
1974—Replaced Scotty Robertson as New Orleans head coach (November), with record of 1-14; replaced as New Orleans head coach by Bill van Breda Kolff (November).
1976—Replaced Bill van Breda Kolff as New Orleans head coach (December), with record of 14-12.

## BELLAMY, WALT      C

**PERSONAL:** Born July 24, 1939, in New Bern, N.C. ... 6-11/245 (2,11/111). ... Full name: Walter Jones Bellamy. ... Nickname: Bells.
**HIGH SCHOOL:** J.T. Barber (New Bern, N.C.).
**COLLEGE:** Indiana.
**TRANSACTIONS:** Selected by Chicago Packers in first round (first pick overall) of 1961 NBA Draft. ... Packers franchise renamed Zephyrs for 1962-63 season. ... Zephyrs franchise moved to Baltimore and renamed Bullets for 1963-64 season. ... Traded by Bullets to New York Knicks for F John Green, G John Egan, F/C Jim Barnes and cash (November 2, 1965). ... Traded by Knicks with G Howard Komives to Detroit Pistons for F Dave DeBusschere (December 19, 1968). ... Traded by Pistons to Atlanta Hawks for future considerations (February 1, 1970); Pistons received G John Arthurs from Milwaukee Bucks to complete deal. ... Selected by New Orleans Jazz from Hawks in NBA Expansion Draft (May 20, 1974). ... Waived by Jazz (October 18, 1974).
**CAREER HONORS:** Elected to Naismith Memorial Basketball Hall of Fame (1993).
**MISCELLANEOUS:** Member of gold-medal-winning U.S. Olympic Team (1960).

### COLLEGIATE RECORD

**NOTES:** THE SPORTING NEWS All-America second team (1961).

| Season Team | G | Min. | FGM | FGA | Pct. | FTM | FTA | Pct. | Reb. | Ast. | Pts. | RPG | APG | PPG |
|---|---|---|---|---|---|---|---|---|---|---|---|---|---|---|
| 57-58—Indiana‡ | | | | | Freshman team did not play intercollegiate schedule. | | | | | | | | | |
| 58-59—Indiana | 22 | ... | 148 | 289 | .512 | 86 | 141 | .610 | 335 | ... | 382 | 15.2 | ... | 17.4 |
| 59-60—Indiana | 24 | ... | 212 | 396 | .535 | 113 | 161 | .702 | 324 | ... | 537 | 13.5 | ... | 22.4 |
| 60-61—Indiana | 24 | ... | 195 | 389 | .501 | 132 | 204 | .647 | 428 | ... | 522 | 17.8 | ... | 21.8 |
| Varsity totals | 70 | ... | 555 | 1074 | .517 | 331 | 506 | .654 | 1087 | ... | 1441 | 15.5 | ... | 20.6 |

# NBA REGULAR-SEASON RECORD

**RECORDS:** Holds single-season record for most games played—88 (1969).
**HONORS:** NBA Rookie of the Year (1962).

| Season Team | G | Min. | FGM | FGA | Pct. | FTM | FTA | Pct. | Reb. | Ast. | PF | Dq. | Pts. | AVERAGES RPG | APG | PPG |
|---|---|---|---|---|---|---|---|---|---|---|---|---|---|---|---|---|
| 61-62—Chicago | 79 | 3344 | 973 | 1875 *.519 | | 549 | 853 | .644 | 1500 | 210 | 281 | 6 | 2495 | 19.0 | 2.7 | 31.6 |
| 62-63—Chicago | 80 | 3306 | 840 | 1595 | .527 | 553 | 821 | .674 | 1309 | 233 | 283 | 7 | 2233 | 16.4 | 2.9 | 27.9 |
| 63-64—Baltimore | 80 | 3394 | 811 | 1582 | .513 | 537 | 825 | .651 | 1361 | 126 | 300 | 7 | 2159 | 17.0 | 1.6 | 27.0 |
| 64-65—Baltimore | 80 | 3301 | 733 | 1441 | .509 | 515 | 752 | .685 | 1254 | 191 | 260 | 2 | 1981 | 14.6 | 2.4 | 24.8 |
| 65-66—Balt.-N.Y. | 80 | 3352 | 695 | 1373 | .506 | 430 | 689 | .624 | 1254 | 235 | 294 | 9 | 1820 | 15.7 | 2.9 | 22.8 |
| 66-67—New York | 79 | 3010 | 565 | 1084 | .521 | 369 | 580 | .636 | 1064 | 206 | 275 | 5 | 1499 | 13.5 | 2.6 | 19.0 |
| 67-68—New York | 82 | 2695 | 511 | 944 | .541 | 350 | 529 | .662 | 961 | 164 | 259 | 3 | 1372 | 11.7 | 2.0 | 16.7 |
| 68-69—N.Y.-Detroit | 88 | 3159 | 563 | 1103 | .510 | 401 | 618 | .649 | 1101 | 176 | 320 | 5 | 1527 | 12.5 | 2.0 | 17.4 |
| 69-70—Detroit-Atl. | 79 | 2028 | 351 | 671 | .523 | 215 | 373 | .576 | 707 | 143 | 260 | 5 | 917 | 8.9 | 1.8 | 11.6 |
| 70-71—Atlanta | 82 | 2908 | 433 | 879 | .493 | 336 | 556 | .604 | 1060 | 230 | 271 | 4 | 1202 | 12.9 | 2.8 | 14.7 |
| 71-72—Atlanta | 82 | 3187 | 593 | 1089 | .545 | 340 | 581 | .585 | 1049 | 262 | 255 | 2 | 1526 | 12.8 | 3.2 | 18.6 |
| 72-73—Atlanta | 74 | 2802 | 455 | 901 | .505 | 283 | 526 | .538 | 964 | 179 | 244 | 1 | 1193 | 13.0 | 2.4 | 16.1 |

| Season Team | G | Min. | FGM | FGA | Pct. | FTM | FTA | Pct. | REBOUNDS Off. | Def. | Tot. | Ast. | St. | Blk. | TO | Pts. | AVERAGES RPG | APG | PPG |
|---|---|---|---|---|---|---|---|---|---|---|---|---|---|---|---|---|---|---|---|
| 73-74—Atlanta | 77 | 2440 | 389 | 801 | .486 | 233 | 383 | .608 | 264 | 476 | 740 | 189 | 52 | 48 | ... | 1011 | 9.6 | 2.5 | 13.1 |
| 74-75—New Orleans | 1 | 14 | 2 | 2 | 1.000 | 2 | 2 | 1.000 | 0 | 5 | 5 | 0 | 0 | 0 | ... | 6 | 5.0 | 0.0 | 6.0 |
| Totals | 1043 | 38940 | 7914 | 15340 | .516 | 5113 | 8088 | .632 | ... | | 14241 | 2544 | 52 | 48 | ... | 20941 | 13.7 | 2.4 | 20.1 |

Personal fouls/disqualifications: 1973-74, 232/2. 1974-75, 2/0. Totals, 3536/58.

## NBA PLAYOFF RECORD

| Season Team | G | Min. | FGM | FGA | Pct. | FTM | FTA | Pct. | Reb. | Ast. | PF | Dq. | Pts. | AVERAGES RPG | APG | PPG |
|---|---|---|---|---|---|---|---|---|---|---|---|---|---|---|---|---|
| 64-65—Baltimore | 10 | 427 | 74 | 158 | .468 | 61 | 92 | .663 | 151 | 34 | 38 | 0 | 209 | 15.1 | 3.4 | 20.9 |
| 66-67—New York | 4 | 157 | 28 | 54 | .519 | 17 | 29 | .586 | 66 | 12 | 15 | 0 | 73 | 16.5 | 3.0 | 18.3 |
| 67-68—New York | 6 | 277 | 45 | 107 | .421 | 30 | 48 | .625 | 96 | 21 | 22 | 0 | 120 | 16.0 | 3.5 | 20.0 |
| 69-70—Atlanta | 9 | 368 | 59 | 126 | .468 | 33 | 46 | .717 | 140 | 35 | 32 | 0 | 151 | 15.6 | 3.9 | 16.8 |
| 70-71—Atlanta | 5 | 216 | 41 | 69 | .594 | 22 | 29 | .759 | 72 | 10 | 16 | 0 | 104 | 14.4 | 2.0 | 20.8 |
| 71-72—Atlanta | 6 | 247 | 42 | 86 | .488 | 27 | 43 | .628 | 82 | 11 | 20 | 0 | 111 | 13.7 | 1.8 | 18.5 |
| 72-73—Atlanta | 6 | 247 | 34 | 86 | .395 | 14 | 31 | .452 | 73 | 13 | 17 | 0 | 82 | 12.2 | 2.2 | 13.7 |
| Totals | 46 | 1939 | 323 | 686 | .471 | 204 | 318 | .642 | 680 | 136 | 160 | 0 | 850 | 14.8 | 3.0 | 18.5 |

## NBA ALL-STAR GAME RECORD

| Season Team | Min. | FGM | FGA | Pct. | FTM | FTA | Pct. | Reb | Ast. | PF | Dq. | Pts. |
|---|---|---|---|---|---|---|---|---|---|---|---|---|
| 1962—Chicago | 29 | 10 | 18 | .556 | 3 | 8 | .375 | 17 | 1 | 6 | 1 | 23 |
| 1963—Chicago | 14 | 1 | 4 | .250 | 0 | 2 | .000 | 1 | 2 | 3 | 0 | 2 |
| 1964—Baltimore | 23 | 4 | 11 | .364 | 3 | 5 | .600 | 7 | 0 | 3 | 0 | 11 |
| 1965—Baltimore | 17 | 4 | 5 | .800 | 4 | 4 | 1.000 | 5 | 1 | 3 | 0 | 12 |
| Totals | 83 | 19 | 38 | .500 | 10 | 19 | .526 | 30 | 4 | 15 | 1 | 48 |

# BING, DAVE                    G

**PERSONAL:** Born November 24, 1943, in Washington, D.C. ... 6-3/185 (1,90/84). ... Full name: David Bing.
**HIGH SCHOOL:** Spingarn (Washington, D.C.).
**COLLEGE:** Syracuse.
**TRANSACTIONS:** Selected by Detroit Pistons in first round (second pick overall) of 1966 NBA Draft. ... Traded by Pistons with 1977 first-round draft choice to Washington Bullets for G Kevin Porter (August 28, 1975). ... Waived by Bullets (September 20, 1977). ... Signed as free agent by Boston Celtics (September 28, 1977).
**CAREER HONORS:** Elected to Naismith Memorial Basketball Hall of Fame (1990). ... One of the 50 Greatest Players in NBA History (1996).

## COLLEGIATE RECORD

**NOTES:** The Sporting News All-America first team (1966).

| Season Team | G | Min. | FGM | FGA | Pct. | FTM | FTA | Pct. | Reb. | Ast. | Pts. | AVERAGES RPG | APG | PPG |
|---|---|---|---|---|---|---|---|---|---|---|---|---|---|---|
| 62-63—Syracuse‡ | 17 | ... | 170 | 341 | .499 | 97 | 131 | .740 | 192 | ... | 437 | 11.3 | ... | 25.7 |
| 63-64—Syracuse | 25 | ... | 215 | 460 | .467 | 126 | 172 | .733 | 206 | ... | 556 | 8.2 | ... | 22.2 |
| 64-65—Syracuse | 23 | ... | 206 | 444 | .464 | 121 | 162 | .747 | 277 | ... | 533 | 12.0 | ... | 23.2 |
| 65-66—Syracuse | 28 | ... | 308 | 569 | .541 | 178 | 222 | .802 | 303 | ... | 794 | 10.8 | ... | 28.4 |
| Varsity totals | 76 | | 729 | 1473 | .495 | 425 | 556 | .764 | 786 | ... | 1883 | 10.3 | ... | 24.8 |

## NBA REGULAR-SEASON RECORD

**HONORS:** NBA Rookie of the Year (1967). ... All-NBA first team (1968, 1971). ... All-NBA second team (1974). ... NBA All-Rookie team (1967). ... J. Walter Kennedy Citizenship Award (1977).

| Season Team | G | Min. | FGM | FGA | Pct. | FTM | FTA | Pct. | Reb. | Ast. | PF | Dq. | Pts. | AVERAGES RPG | APG | PPG |
|---|---|---|---|---|---|---|---|---|---|---|---|---|---|---|---|---|
| 66-67—Detroit | 80 | 2762 | 664 | 1522 | .436 | 273 | 370 | .738 | 359 | 330 | 217 | 2 | 1601 | 4.5 | 4.1 | 20.0 |
| 67-68—Detroit | 79 | 3209 | *835 | *1893 | .441 | 472 | 668 | .707 | 373 | 509 | 254 | 2 | *2142 | 4.7 | 6.4 | *27.1 |
| 68-69—Detroit | 77 | 3039 | 678 | 1594 | .425 | 444 | 623 | .713 | 382 | 546 | 256 | 3 | 1800 | 5.0 | 7.1 | 23.4 |
| 69-70—Detroit | 70 | 2334 | 575 | 1295 | .444 | 454 | 580 | .783 | 299 | 418 | 196 | 0 | 1604 | 4.3 | 6.0 | 22.9 |
| 70-71—Detroit | 82 | 3065 | 799 | 1710 | .467 | *615 | *772 | .797 | 364 | 408 | 228 | 4 | 2213 | 4.4 | 5.0 | 27.0 |
| 71-72—Detroit | 45 | 1936 | 369 | 891 | .414 | 278 | 354 | .785 | 186 | 317 | 138 | 3 | 1016 | 4.1 | 7.0 | 22.6 |
| 72-73—Detroit | 82 | 3361 | 692 | 1545 | .448 | 456 | 560 | .814 | 298 | 637 | 229 | 1 | 1840 | 3.6 | 7.8 | 22.4 |

| Season Team | G | Min. | FGM | FGA | Pct. | FTM | FTA | Pct. | REBOUNDS Off. | Def. | Tot. | Ast. | St. | Blk. | TO | Pts. | AVERAGES RPG | APG | PPG |
|---|---|---|---|---|---|---|---|---|---|---|---|---|---|---|---|---|---|---|---|
| 73-74—Detroit .......... | 81 | 3124 | 582 | 1336 | .436 | 356 | 438 | .813 | 108 | 173 | 281 | 555 | 109 | 17 | ... | 1520 | 3.5 | 6.9 | 18.8 |
| 74-75—Detroit .......... | 79 | 3222 | 578 | 1333 | .434 | 343 | 424 | .809 | 86 | 200 | 286 | 610 | 116 | 26 | ... | 1499 | 3.6 | 7.7 | 19.0 |
| 75-76—Washington ... | 82 | 2945 | 497 | 1113 | .447 | 332 | 422 | .787 | 94 | 143 | 237 | 492 | 118 | 23 | ... | 1326 | 2.9 | 6.0 | 16.2 |
| 76-77—Washington ... | 64 | 1516 | 271 | 597 | .454 | 136 | 176 | .773 | 54 | 89 | 143 | 275 | 61 | 5 | ... | 678 | 2.2 | 4.3 | 10.6 |
| 77-78—Boston .......... | 80 | 2256 | 422 | 940 | .449 | 244 | 296 | .824 | 76 | 136 | 212 | 300 | 79 | 18 | 216 | 1088 | 2.7 | 3.8 | 13.6 |
| Totals ................. | 901 | 32769 | 6962 | 15769 | .441 | 4403 | 5683 | .775 | ... | ... | 3420 | 5397 | 483 | 89 | 216 | 18327 | 3.8 | 6.0 | 20.3 |

Personal fouls/disqualifications: 1973-74, 216/1. 1974-75, 222/3. 1975-76, 262/0. 1976-77, 150/1. 1977-78, 247/2. Totals, 2615/22.

### NBA PLAYOFF RECORD

| Season Team | G | Min. | FGM | FGA | Pct. | FTM | FTA | Pct. | REBOUNDS Off. | Def. | Tot. | Ast. | St. | Blk. | TO | Pts. | AVERAGES RPG | APG | PPG |
|---|---|---|---|---|---|---|---|---|---|---|---|---|---|---|---|---|---|---|---|
| 67-68—Detroit .......... | 6 | 254 | 68 | 166 | .410 | 33 | 45 | .733 | ... | ... | 24 | 29 | ... | ... | ... | 169 | 4.0 | 4.8 | 28.2 |
| 73-74—Detroit .......... | 7 | 312 | 55 | 131 | .420 | 22 | 30 | .733 | 6 | 20 | 26 | 42 | 3 | 1 | ... | 132 | 3.7 | 6.0 | 18.9 |
| 74-75—Detroit .......... | 3 | 134 | 20 | 47 | .426 | 8 | 13 | .615 | 3 | 8 | 11 | 29 | 5 | 0 | ... | 48 | 3.7 | 9.7 | 16.0 |
| 75-76—Washington ... | 7 | 209 | 34 | 76 | .447 | 28 | 35 | .800 | 6 | 12 | 18 | 28 | 7 | 2 | ... | 96 | 2.6 | 4.0 | 13.7 |
| 76-77—Washington ... | 8 | 55 | 14 | 32 | .438 | 4 | 4 | 1.000 | 3 | 3 | 6 | 5 | 0 | 1 | ... | 32 | 0.8 | 0.6 | 4.0 |
| Totals ................. | 31 | 964 | 191 | 452 | .423 | 95 | 127 | .748 | ... | ... | 85 | 133 | 15 | 4 | ... | 477 | 2.7 | 4.3 | 15.4 |

Personal fouls/disqualifications: 1967-68, 21/0. 1973-74, 20/0. 1974-75, 12/0. 1975-76, 18/0. 1976-77, 5/0. Totals, 76/0.

### NBA ALL-STAR GAME RECORD

**NOTES:** NBA All-Star Game Most Valuable Player (1976).

| Season Team | Min. | FGM | FGA | Pct. | FTM | FTA | Pct. | Reb. | Ast. | PF | Dq. | Pts. |
|---|---|---|---|---|---|---|---|---|---|---|---|---|
| 1968—Detroit ................. | 20 | 4 | 7 | .571 | 1 | 1 | 1.000 | 2 | 4 | 3 | 0 | 9 |
| 1969—Detroit ................. | 13 | 1 | 3 | .333 | 1 | 1 | 1.000 | 0 | 3 | 0 | 0 | 3 |
| 1971—Detroit ................. | 19 | 2 | 7 | .286 | 0 | 0 | ... | 2 | 2 | 1 | 0 | 4 |
| 1973—Detroit ................. | 19 | 0 | 4 | .000 | 2 | 2 | 1.000 | 3 | 0 | 1 | 0 | 2 |

| Season Team | Min. | FGM | FGA | Pct. | FTM | FTA | Pct. | REBOUNDS Off. | Def. | Tot. | Ast. | PF | Dq. | St. | Blk. | TO | Pts. |
|---|---|---|---|---|---|---|---|---|---|---|---|---|---|---|---|---|---|
| 1974—Detroit ................. | 16 | 2 | 9 | .222 | 1 | 1 | 1.000 | 1 | 5 | 6 | 2 | 1 | 0 | 0 | 0 | ... | 5 |
| 1975—Detroit ................. | 12 | 0 | 2 | .000 | 2 | 2 | 1.000 | 0 | 0 | 0 | 1 | 0 | 0 | 0 | 0 | ... | 2 |
| 1976—Washington ........... | 26 | 7 | 11 | .636 | 2 | 2 | 1.000 | 1 | 2 | 3 | 4 | 1 | 0 | 0 | 0 | ... | 16 |
| Totals ................. | 125 | 16 | 43 | .372 | 9 | 9 | 1.000 | ... | ... | 16 | 16 | 7 | 0 | 0 | 0 | ... | 41 |

## BIRD, LARRY

**PERSONAL:** Born December 7, 1956, in West Baden, Ind. ... 6-9/220 (2,05/99,8). ... Full name: Larry Joe Bird.
**HIGH SCHOOL:** Springs Valley (French Lick, Ind.).
**COLLEGE:** Indiana, then Northwood Institute (Ind.), then Indiana State.
**TRANSACTIONS/CAREER NOTES:** Selected after junior season by Boston Celtics in first round (sixth pick overall) of 1978 NBA Draft. ... Announced retirement (August 18, 1992).
**CAREER NOTES:** President of Basketball Operations, Indiana Pacers (July 11, 2003-present).
**CAREER HONORS:** Elected to Naismith Memorial Basketball Hall of Fame (1998). ... One of the 50 Greatest Players in NBA History (1996).
**MISCELLANEOUS:** Member of NBA championship team (1981, 1984, 1986). ... Member of gold-medal-winning U.S. Olympic team (1992). ... Boston Celtics all-time steals leader with 1,556 (1979-80 through 1991-92).

### COLLEGIATE RECORD

**NOTES:** THE SPORTING NEWS College Player of the Year (1979). ... Naismith Award winner (1979). ... Wooden Award winner (1979). ... THE SPORTING NEWS All-America first team (1978, 1979).

| Season Team | G | Min. | FGM | FGA | Pct. | FTM | FTA | Pct. | Reb. | Ast. | Pts. | AVERAGES RPG | APG | PPG |
|---|---|---|---|---|---|---|---|---|---|---|---|---|---|---|
| 74-75—Indiana ........................... | | | | | | | Did not play. | | | | | | | |
| 75-76—Indiana State ................. | | | | | | Did not play—transfer student. | | | | | | | | |
| 76-77—Indiana State ................. | 28 | 1033 | 375 | 689 | .544 | 168 | 200 | .840 | 373 | 122 | 918 | 13.3 | 4.4 | 32.8 |
| 77-78—Indiana State ................. | 32 | ... | 403 | 769 | .524 | 153 | 193 | .793 | 369 | 125 | 959 | 11.5 | 3.9 | 30.0 |
| 78-79—Indiana State ................. | 34 | ... | 376 | 707 | .532 | 221 | 266 | .831 | 505 | 187 | 973 | 14.9 | 5.5 | 28.6 |
| Totals ................................. | 94 | ... | 1154 | 2165 | .533 | 542 | 659 | .822 | 1247 | 434 | 2850 | 13.3 | 4.6 | 30.3 |

### NBA REGULAR-SEASON RECORD

**HONORS:** NBA Most Valuable Player (1984, 1985, 1986). ... NBA Rookie of the Year (1980). ... All-NBA first team (1980, 1981, 1982, 1983, 1984, 1985, 1986, 1987, 1988). ... All-NBA second team (1990). ... NBA All-Defensive second team (1982, 1983, 1984). ... NBA All-Rookie team (1980). ... Long Distance Shootout winner (1986, 1987, 1988).

| Season Team | G | Min. | FGM | FGA | Pct. | FTM | FTA | Pct. | REBOUNDS Off. | Def. | Tot. | Ast. | St. | Blk. | TO | Pts. | AVERAGES RPG | APG | PPG |
|---|---|---|---|---|---|---|---|---|---|---|---|---|---|---|---|---|---|---|---|
| 79-80—Boston .......... | 82 | 2955 | 693 | 1463 | .474 | 301 | 360 | .836 | 216 | 636 | 852 | 370 | 143 | 53 | 263 | 1745 | 10.4 | 4.5 | 21.3 |
| 80-81—Boston .......... | 82 | 3239 | 719 | 1503 | .478 | 283 | 328 | .863 | 191 | 704 | 895 | 451 | 161 | 63 | 289 | 1741 | 10.9 | 5.5 | 21.2 |
| 81-82—Boston .......... | 77 | 2923 | 711 | 1414 | .503 | 328 | 380 | .863 | 200 | 637 | 837 | 447 | 143 | 66 | 254 | 1761 | 10.9 | 5.8 | 22.9 |
| 82-83—Boston .......... | 79 | 2982 | 747 | 1481 | .504 | 351 | 418 | .840 | 193 | 677 | 870 | 458 | 148 | 71 | 240 | 1867 | 11.0 | 5.8 | 23.6 |
| 83-84—Boston .......... | 79 | 3028 | 758 | 1542 | .492 | 374 | 421 | *.888 | 181 | 615 | 796 | 520 | 144 | 69 | 237 | 1908 | 10.1 | 6.6 | 24.2 |
| 84-85—Boston .......... | 80 | 3161 | 918 | 1760 | .522 | 403 | 457 | *.882 | 164 | 678 | 842 | 531 | 129 | 98 | 248 | 2295 | 10.5 | 6.6 | 28.7 |
| 85-86—Boston .......... | 82 | 3113 | 796 | 1606 | .496 | 441 | 492 | *.896 | 190 | 615 | 805 | 557 | 166 | 51 | 266 | 2115 | 9.8 | 6.8 | 25.8 |
| 86-87—Boston .......... | 74 | 3005 | 786 | 1497 | .525 | 414 | 455 | *.910 | 124 | 558 | 682 | 566 | 135 | 70 | 240 | 2076 | 9.2 | 7.6 | 28.1 |
| 87-88—Boston .......... | 76 | 2965 | 881 | 1672 | .527 | 415 | 453 | .916 | 108 | 595 | 703 | 467 | 125 | 57 | 213 | 2275 | 9.3 | 6.1 | 29.9 |
| 88-89—Boston .......... | 6 | 189 | 49 | 104 | .471 | 18 | 19 | .947 | 1 | 36 | 37 | 29 | 6 | 5 | 11 | 116 | 6.2 | 4.8 | 19.3 |
| 89-90—Boston .......... | 75 | 2944 | 718 | 1517 | .473 | 319 | 343 | *.930 | 90 | 622 | 712 | 562 | 106 | 61 | 243 | 1820 | 9.5 | 7.5 | 24.3 |
| 90-91—Boston .......... | 60 | 2277 | 462 | 1017 | .454 | 163 | 183 | .891 | 53 | 456 | 509 | 431 | 108 | 58 | 187 | 1164 | 8.5 | 7.2 | 19.4 |
| 91-92—Boston .......... | 45 | 1662 | 353 | 758 | .466 | 150 | 162 | .926 | 46 | 388 | 434 | 306 | 42 | 33 | 125 | 908 | 9.6 | 6.8 | 20.2 |
| Totals ................. | 897 | 34443 | 8591 | 17334 | .496 | 3960 | 4471 | .886 | 1757 | 7217 | 8974 | 5695 | 1556 | 755 | 2816 | 21791 | 10.0 | 6.3 | 24.3 |

Three-point field goals: 1979-80, 58-for-143 (.406). 1980-81, 20-for-74 (.270). 1981-82, 11-for-52 (.212). 1982-83, 22-for-77 (.286). 1983-84, 18-for-73 (.247). 1984-85, 56-for-131 (.427). 1985-86, 82-for-194 (.423). 1986-87, 90-for-225 (.400). 1987-88, 98-for-237 (.414). 1989-90, 65-for-195 (.333). 1990-91, 77-for-198 (.389). 1991-92, 52-for-128 (.406). Totals, 649-for-1727 (.376).
Personal fouls/disqualifications: 1979-80, 279/4. 1980-81, 239/2. 1981-82, 244/0. 1982-83, 197/0. 1983-84, 197/0. 1984-85, 208/0. 1985-86, 182/0. 1986-87, 185/3. 1987-88, 157/0. 1988-89, 18/0. 1989-90, 173/2. 1990-91, 118/0. 1991-92, 82/0. Totals, 2279/11.

## NBA PLAYOFF RECORD

**NOTES:** NBA Finals Most Valuable Player (1984, 1986). ... Holds career playoff record for most defensive rebounds—1,323.

| Season Team | G | Min. | FGM | FGA | Pct. | FTM | FTA | Pct. | Off. | Def. | Tot. | Ast. | St. | Blk. | TO | Pts. | RPG | APG | PPG |
|---|---|---|---|---|---|---|---|---|---|---|---|---|---|---|---|---|---|---|---|
| 79-80—Boston ........... | 9 | 372 | 83 | 177 | .469 | 22 | 25 | .880 | 22 | 79 | 101 | 42 | 14 | 8 | 33 | 192 | 11.2 | 4.7 | 21.3 |
| 80-81—Boston ........... | 17 | 750 | 147 | 313 | .470 | 76 | 85 | .894 | 49 | 189 | 238 | 103 | 39 | 17 | 62 | 373 | 14.0 | 6.1 | 21.9 |
| 81-82—Boston ........... | 12 | 490 | 88 | 206 | .427 | 37 | 45 | .822 | 33 | 117 | 150 | 67 | 23 | 17 | 38 | 214 | 12.5 | 5.6 | 17.8 |
| 82-83—Boston ........... | 6 | 240 | 49 | 116 | .422 | 24 | 29 | .828 | 20 | 55 | 75 | 41 | 13 | 3 | 19 | 123 | 12.5 | 6.8 | 20.5 |
| 83-84—Boston ........... | 23 | 961 | 229 | 437 | .524 | 167 | 190 | .879 | 62 | 190 | 252 | 136 | 54 | 27 | 87 | 632 | 11.0 | 5.9 | 27.5 |
| 84-85—Boston ........... | 20 | 815 | 196 | 425 | .461 | 121 | 136 | .890 | 53 | 129 | 182 | 115 | 34 | 19 | 57 | 520 | 9.1 | 5.8 | 26.0 |
| 85-86—Boston ........... | 18 | 770 | 171 | 331 | .517 | 101 | 109 | .927 | 34 | 134 | 168 | 148 | 37 | 11 | 47 | 466 | 9.3 | 8.2 | 25.9 |
| 86-87—Boston ........... | 23 | 1015 | 216 | 454 | .476 | 176 | 193 | .912 | 41 | 190 | 231 | 165 | 27 | 19 | 71 | 622 | 10.0 | 7.2 | 27.0 |
| 87-88—Boston ........... | 17 | 763 | 152 | 338 | .450 | 101 | 113 | .894 | 29 | 121 | 150 | 115 | 36 | 14 | 49 | 417 | 8.8 | 6.8 | 24.5 |
| 89-90—Boston ........... | 5 | 207 | 44 | 99 | .444 | 29 | 32 | .906 | 7 | 39 | 46 | 44 | 5 | 5 | 18 | 122 | 9.2 | 8.8 | 24.4 |
| 90-91—Boston ........... | 10 | 396 | 62 | 152 | .408 | 44 | 51 | .863 | 8 | 64 | 72 | 65 | 13 | 3 | 19 | 171 | 7.2 | 6.5 | 17.1 |
| 91-92—Boston ........... | 4 | 107 | 21 | 42 | .500 | 3 | 4 | .750 | 2 | 16 | 18 | 21 | 1 | 2 | 6 | 45 | 4.5 | 5.3 | 11.3 |
| Totals ................... | 164 | 6886 | 1458 | 3090 | .472 | 901 | 1012 | .890 | 360 | 1323 | 1683 | 1062 | 296 | 145 | 506 | 3897 | 10.3 | 6.5 | 23.8 |

Three-point field goals: 1979-80, 4-for-15 (.267). 1980-81, 3-for-8 (.375). 1981-82, 1-for-6 (.167). 1982-83, 1-for-4 (.250). 1983-84, 7-for-17 (.412). 1984-85, 7-for-25 (.280). 1985-86, 23-for-56 (.411). 1986-87, 14-for-41 (.341). 1987-88, 12-for-32 (.375). 1989-90, 5-for-19 (.263). 1990-91, 3-for-21 (.143). 1991-92, 0-for-5. Totals, 80-for-249 (.321).

Personal fouls/disqualifications: 1979-80, 30/0. 1980-81, 53/0. 1981-82, 43/0. 1982-83, 15/0. 1983-84, 71/0. 1984-85, 54/0. 1985-86, 55/0. 1986-87, 55/1. 1987-88, 45/0. 1989-90, 10/0. 1990-91, 28/0. 1991-92, 7/0. Totals, 466/1.

## NBA ALL-STAR GAME RECORD

**NOTES:** NBA All-Star Game Most Valuable Player (1982).

| Season Team | Min. | FGM | FGA | Pct. | FTM | FTA | Pct. | Off. | Def. | Tot. | Ast. | PF | Dq. | St. | Blk. | TO | Pts. |
|---|---|---|---|---|---|---|---|---|---|---|---|---|---|---|---|---|---|
| 1980—Boston ................ | 23 | 3 | 6 | .500 | 0 | 0 | ... | 3 | 3 | 6 | 7 | 1 | 0 | 1 | 0 | 3 | 7 |
| 1981—Boston ................ | 18 | 1 | 5 | .200 | 0 | 0 | ... | 1 | 3 | 4 | 3 | 1 | 0 | 1 | 0 | 2 | 2 |
| 1982—Boston ................ | 28 | 7 | 12 | .583 | 5 | 8 | .625 | 0 | 12 | 12 | 5 | 3 | 0 | 1 | 1 | 4 | 19 |
| 1983—Boston ................ | 29 | 7 | 14 | .500 | 0 | 0 | ... | 3 | 10 | 13 | 7 | 4 | 0 | 2 | 0 | 5 | 14 |
| 1984—Boston ................ | 33 | 6 | 18 | .333 | 4 | 4 | 1.000 | 1 | 6 | 7 | 3 | 1 | 0 | 2 | 0 | 2 | 16 |
| 1985—Boston ................ | 31 | 8 | 16 | .500 | 5 | 6 | .833 | 5 | 3 | 8 | 2 | 3 | 0 | 0 | 1 | 4 | 21 |
| 1986—Boston ................ | 35 | 8 | 18 | .444 | 5 | 6 | .833 | 2 | 6 | 8 | 5 | 5 | 0 | 7 | 0 | 4 | 23 |
| 1987—Boston ................ | 35 | 7 | 18 | .389 | 4 | 4 | 1.000 | 2 | 4 | 6 | 5 | 5 | 0 | 2 | 0 | 2 | 18 |
| 1988—Boston ................ | 32 | 2 | 8 | .250 | 2 | 2 | 1.000 | 0 | 7 | 7 | 1 | 4 | 0 | 4 | 1 | 2 | 6 |
| 1990—Boston ................ | 23 | 3 | 8 | .375 | 2 | 2 | 1.000 | 2 | 6 | 8 | 3 | 1 | 0 | 3 | 0 | 3 | 8 |
| 1991—Boston ................ | | | | | | | Selected, did not play—injured. | | | | | | | | | | |
| 1992—Boston ................ | | | | | | | Selected, did not play—injured. | | | | | | | | | | |
| Totals ........................... | 287 | 52 | 123 | .423 | 27 | 32 | .844 | 19 | 60 | 79 | 41 | 28 | 0 | 23 | 3 | 31 | 134 |

Three-point field goals: 1980, 1-for-2 (.500). 1983, 0-for-1. 1985, 0-for-1. 1986, 2-for-4 (.500). 1987, 0-for-3. 1988, 0-for-1. 1990, 0-for-1. Totals, 3-for-13 (.231).

## HEAD COACHING RECORD

**BACKGROUND:** Special assistant, Boston Celtics (1992-93 through 1996-97).

## NBA COACHING RECORD

**HONORS:** NBA Coach of the Year (1998).

| | REGULAR SEASON | | | | PLAYOFFS | | |
|---|---|---|---|---|---|---|---|
| Season Team | W | L | Pct. | Finish | W | L | Pct. |
| 97-98—Indiana ...................................... | 58 | 24 | .707 | 2nd/Central Division | 10 | 6 | .625 |
| 98-99—Indiana ...................................... | 33 | 17 | .660 | 1st/Central Division | 9 | 4 | .692 |
| 99-00—Indiana ...................................... | 56 | 26 | .683 | 1st/Central Division | 13 | 10 | .565 |
| Totals (3 years) .................................... | 147 | 67 | .687 | Totals (3 years) ....... | 32 | 20 | .615 |

**NOTES:**

1998—Defeated Cleveland, 3-1, in Eastern Conference First Round; defeated New York, 4-1, in Eastern Conference Semifinals; lost to Chicago, 4-3, in Eastern Conference Finals.

1999—Defeated Milwaukee, 3-0, in Eastern Conference First Round; defeated Philadelphia, 4-0, in Eastern Conference Semifinals; lost to New York, 4-2, in Eastern Conference Finals.

2000—Defeated Milwaukee, 3-2, in Eastern Conference First Round; defeated Philadelphia, 4-2, in Eastern Conference Semifinals; defeated New York, 4-2, in Eastern Conference Finals; lost to Los Angeles Lakers, 4-2, in NBA Finals.

# BLACKMAN, ROLANDO     G

**PERSONAL:** Born February 26, 1959, in Panama City, Panama. ... 6-6/206 (1,98/93,4). ... Full name: Rolando Antonio Blackman. ... Name pronounced roll-ON-doe.

**HIGH SCHOOL:** William E. Grady Vocational Technical School (Brooklyn, N.Y.).

**COLLEGE:** Kansas State.

**TRANSACTIONS:** Selected by Dallas Mavericks in first round (ninth pick overall) of 1981 NBA Draft. ... Traded by Mavericks to New York Knicks for 1995 first-round draft choice (June 24, 1992). ... Waived by Knicks (July 4, 1994). ... Played in Greece (1994-95). ... Played in Italy (1995-96).

**CAREER NOTES:** Player development, Dallas Mavericks (2000-01-present).

**MISCELLANEOUS:** Member of U.S. Olympic team (1980). ... Dallas Mavericks all-time leading scorer with 16,643 points (1981-82 through 1991-92).

## COLLEGIATE RECORD

**NOTES:** THE SPORTING NEWS All-America first team (1981).

| Season Team | G | Min. | FGM | FGA | Pct. | FTM | FTA | Pct. | Reb. | Ast. | Pts. | RPG | APG | PPG |
|---|---|---|---|---|---|---|---|---|---|---|---|---|---|---|
| 77-78—Kansas State ................ | 29 | 967 | 127 | 269 | .472 | 61 | 93 | .656 | 187 | 45 | 315 | 6.4 | 1.6 | 10.9 |
| 78-79—Kansas State ................ | 28 | 1056 | 200 | 392 | .510 | 83 | 113 | .735 | 110 | 79 | 483 | 3.9 | 2.8 | 17.3 |
| 79-80—Kansas State ................ | 31 | 1103 | 226 | 419 | .539 | 100 | 145 | .690 | 145 | 97 | 552 | 4.7 | 3.1 | 17.8 |
| 80-81—Kansas State ................ | 33 | 1239 | 202 | 380 | .532 | 90 | 115 | .783 | 165 | 102 | 494 | 5.0 | 3.1 | 15.0 |
| Totals ..................... | 121 | 4365 | 755 | 1460 | .517 | 334 | 466 | .717 | 607 | 323 | 1844 | 5.0 | 2.7 | 15.2 |

## NBA REGULAR-SEASON RECORD

| Season Team | G | Min. | FGM | FGA | Pct. | FTM | FTA | Pct. | REBOUNDS Off. | Def. | Tot. | Ast. | St. | Blk. | TO | Pts. | AVERAGES RPG | APG | PPG |
|---|---|---|---|---|---|---|---|---|---|---|---|---|---|---|---|---|---|---|---|
| 81-82—Dallas | 82 | 1979 | 439 | 855 | .513 | 212 | 276 | .768 | 97 | 157 | 254 | 105 | 46 | 30 | 113 | 1091 | 3.1 | 1.3 | 13.3 |
| 82-83—Dallas | 75 | 2349 | 513 | 1042 | .492 | 297 | 381 | .780 | 108 | 185 | 293 | 185 | 37 | 29 | 118 | 1326 | 3.9 | 2.5 | 17.7 |
| 83-84—Dallas | 81 | 3025 | 721 | 1320 | .546 | 372 | 458 | .812 | 124 | 249 | 373 | 288 | 56 | 37 | 169 | 1815 | 4.6 | 3.6 | 22.4 |
| 84-85—Dallas | 81 | 2834 | 625 | 1230 | .508 | 342 | 413 | .828 | 107 | 193 | 300 | 289 | 61 | 16 | 162 | 1598 | 3.7 | 3.6 | 19.7 |
| 85-86—Dallas | 82 | 2787 | 677 | 1318 | .514 | 404 | 483 | .836 | 88 | 203 | 291 | 271 | 79 | 25 | 189 | 1762 | 3.5 | 3.3 | 21.5 |
| 86-87—Dallas | 80 | 2758 | 626 | 1264 | .495 | 419 | 474 | .884 | 96 | 182 | 278 | 266 | 64 | 21 | 174 | 1676 | 3.5 | 3.3 | 21.0 |
| 87-88—Dallas | 71 | 2580 | 497 | 1050 | .473 | 331 | 379 | .873 | 82 | 164 | 246 | 262 | 64 | 18 | 144 | 1325 | 3.5 | 3.7 | 18.7 |
| 88-89—Dallas | 78 | 2946 | 594 | 1249 | .476 | 316 | 370 | .854 | 70 | 203 | 273 | 288 | 65 | 20 | 165 | 1534 | 3.5 | 3.7 | 19.7 |
| 89-90—Dallas | 80 | 2934 | 626 | 1256 | .498 | 287 | 340 | .844 | 88 | 192 | 280 | 289 | 77 | 21 | 174 | 1552 | 3.5 | 3.6 | 19.4 |
| 90-91—Dallas | 80 | 2965 | 634 | 1316 | .482 | 282 | 326 | .865 | 63 | 193 | 256 | 301 | 69 | 19 | 159 | 1590 | 3.2 | 3.8 | 19.9 |
| 91-92—Dallas | 75 | 2527 | 535 | 1161 | .461 | 239 | 266 | .899 | 78 | 161 | 239 | 204 | 50 | 22 | 153 | 1374 | 3.2 | 2.7 | 18.3 |
| 92-93—New York | 60 | 1434 | 239 | 539 | .443 | 71 | 90 | .789 | 23 | 79 | 102 | 157 | 22 | 10 | 65 | 580 | 1.7 | 2.6 | 9.7 |
| 93-94—New York | 55 | 969 | 161 | 369 | .436 | 48 | 53 | .906 | 23 | 70 | 93 | 76 | 25 | 6 | 44 | 400 | 1.7 | 1.4 | 7.3 |
| **Totals** | 980 | 32087 | 6887 | 13969 | .493 | 3620 | 4309 | .840 | 1047 | 2231 | 3278 | 2981 | 715 | 274 | 1829 | 17623 | 3.3 | 3.0 | 18.0 |

Three-point field goals: 1981-82, 1-for-4 (.250). 1982-83, 3-for-15 (.200). 1983-84, 1-for-11 (.091). 1984-85, 6-for-20 (.300). 1985-86, 4-for-29 (.138). 1986-87, 5-for-15 (.333). 1987-88, 0-for-5. 1988-89, 30-for-85 (.353). 1989-90, 13-for-43 (.302). 1990-91, 40-for-114 (.351). 1991-92, 65-for-169 (.385). 1992-93, 31-for-73 (.425). 1993-94, 30-for-84 (.357). Totals, 229-for-667 (.343).

Personal fouls/disqualifications: 1981-82, 122/0. 1982-83, 116/0. 1983-84, 127/0. 1984-85, 96/0. 1985-86, 138/0. 1986-87, 142/0. 1987-88, 112/0. 1988-89, 137/0. 1989-90, 128/0. 1990-91, 153/0. 1991-92, 134/0. 1992-93, 129/1. 1993-94, 100/0. Totals, 1634/1.

## NBA PLAYOFF RECORD

| Season Team | G | Min. | FGM | FGA | Pct. | FTM | FTA | Pct. | REBOUNDS Off. | Def. | Tot. | Ast. | St. | Blk. | TO | Pts. | AVERAGES RPG | APG | PPG |
|---|---|---|---|---|---|---|---|---|---|---|---|---|---|---|---|---|---|---|---|
| 83-84—Dallas | 10 | 397 | 93 | 175 | .531 | 53 | 63 | .841 | 15 | 26 | 41 | 40 | 6 | 4 | 24 | 239 | 4.1 | 4.0 | 23.9 |
| 84-85—Dallas | 4 | 169 | 47 | 92 | .511 | 36 | 38 | .947 | 11 | 15 | 26 | 19 | 2 | 2 | 14 | 131 | 6.5 | 4.8 | 32.8 |
| 85-86—Dallas | 10 | 371 | 83 | 167 | .497 | 42 | 53 | .792 | 15 | 20 | 35 | 32 | 8 | 1 | 20 | 208 | 3.5 | 3.2 | 20.8 |
| 86-87—Dallas | 4 | 153 | 36 | 73 | .493 | 22 | 24 | .917 | 4 | 10 | 14 | 17 | 2 | 0 | 8 | 94 | 3.5 | 4.3 | 23.5 |
| 87-88—Dallas | 17 | 672 | 126 | 261 | .483 | 55 | 62 | .887 | 26 | 29 | 55 | 77 | 15 | 3 | 25 | 307 | 3.2 | 4.5 | 18.1 |
| 89-90—Dallas | 3 | 127 | 24 | 54 | .444 | 10 | 10 | 1.000 | 2 | 7 | 9 | 13 | 6 | 2 | 13 | 60 | 3.0 | 4.3 | 20.0 |
| 92-93—New York | 15 | 214 | 22 | 64 | .344 | 15 | 18 | .833 | 4 | 13 | 17 | 16 | 3 | 2 | 21 | 63 | 1.1 | 1.1 | 4.2 |
| 93-94—New York | 6 | 34 | 3 | 11 | .273 | 0 | 0 | ... | 1 | 2 | 3 | 3 | 0 | 0 | 1 | 8 | 0.5 | 0.5 | 1.3 |
| **Totals** | 69 | 2137 | 434 | 897 | .484 | 233 | 268 | .869 | 78 | 122 | 200 | 217 | 42 | 14 | 126 | 1110 | 2.9 | 3.1 | 16.1 |

Three-point field goals: 1984-85, 1-for-2 (.500). 1985-86, 0-for-1. 1986-87, 0-for-1. 1987-88, 0-for-3. 1989-90, 2-for-5 (.400). 1992-93, 4-for-15 (.267). 1993-94, 2-for-4 (.500). Totals, 9-for-31 (.290).

Personal fouls/disqualifications: 1983-84, 15/0. 1984-85, 8/0. 1985-86, 26/1. 1986-87, 7/0. 1987-88, 28/0. 1989-90, 7/0. 1992-93, 22/0. 1993-94, 6/0. Totals, 119/1.

## NBA ALL-STAR GAME RECORD

| Season Team | Min. | FGM | FGA | Pct. | FTM | FTA | Pct. | REBOUNDS Off. | Def. | Tot. | Ast. | PF | Dq. | St. | Blk. | TO | Pts. |
|---|---|---|---|---|---|---|---|---|---|---|---|---|---|---|---|---|---|
| 1985—Dallas | 23 | 7 | 14 | .500 | 1 | 2 | .500 | 1 | 2 | 3 | 2 | 1 | 0 | 1 | 1 | 0 | 15 |
| 1986—Dallas | 22 | 6 | 11 | .545 | 0 | 0 | ... | 1 | 3 | 4 | 8 | 1 | 0 | 2 | 1 | 1 | 12 |
| 1987—Dallas | 22 | 9 | 15 | .600 | 11 | 13 | .846 | 1 | 3 | 4 | 1 | 2 | 0 | 0 | 0 | 2 | 29 |
| 1990—Dallas | 21 | 7 | 9 | .778 | 1 | 1 | 1.000 | 1 | 1 | 2 | 2 | 1 | 0 | 2 | 0 | 2 | 15 |
| **Totals** | 88 | 29 | 49 | .592 | 13 | 16 | .813 | 4 | 9 | 13 | 13 | 5 | 0 | 5 | 2 | 5 | 71 |

## GREEK LEAGUE RECORD

| Season Team | G | Min. | FGM | FGA | Pct. | FTM | FTA | Pct. | Reb. | Ast. | Pts. | AVERAGES RPG | APG | PPG |
|---|---|---|---|---|---|---|---|---|---|---|---|---|---|---|
| 94-95—A.E.K. | 14 | ... | 69 | 150 | .460 | 55 | 63 | .873 | ... | 19 | 265 | ... | 1.4 | 18.9 |

## ITALIAN LEAGUE RECORD

| Season Team | G | Min. | FGM | FGA | Pct. | FTM | FTA | Pct. | Reb. | Ast. | Pts. | AVERAGES RPG | APG | PPG |
|---|---|---|---|---|---|---|---|---|---|---|---|---|---|---|
| 95-96—Stefanel Milano | 24 | 762 | 141 | 302 | .467 | 55 | 64 | .859 | 62 | 19 | 382 | 2.6 | 0.8 | 15.9 |

## BLAYLOCK, MOOKIE     G

**PERSONAL:** Born March 20, 1967, in Garland, Texas. ... 6-1/185. (1,85/83,9). ... Full Name: Daron Oshay Blaylock.
**HIGH SCHOOL:** Garland (Texas).
**JUNIOR COLLEGE:** Midland (Texas) College.
**COLLEGE:** Oklahoma.
**TRANSACTIONS/CAREER NOTES:** Selected by New Jersey Nets in first round (12th pick overall) of 1989 NBA Draft. ... Traded by Nets with F Roy Hinson to Atlanta Hawks for G Rumeal Robinson (November 3, 1992). ... Traded by Hawks with 1999 first-round draft choice to Golden State Warriors for G Bimbo Coles, F Duane Ferrell and 1999 first-round draft choice (June 29, 1999).
**MISCELLANEOUS:** Atlanta Hawks franchise all-time steals leader with 1,321 (1992-93 through 1998-99).

### COLLEGIATE RECORD

**NOTES:** THE SPORTING NEWS All-America second team (1989). ... Holds NCAA Division I career record for for most steals per game—3.8. ... Holds NCAA Division I single-season record for most steals—150 (1988). ... Holds NCAA Division I single-game record for most steals—13 (December 12, 1987, vs. Centenary; and December 17, 1988, vs. Loyola Marymount).

| Season Team | G | Min. | FGM | FGA | Pct. | FTM | FTA | Pct. | Reb. | Ast. | Pts. | AVERAGES RPG | APG | PPG |
|---|---|---|---|---|---|---|---|---|---|---|---|---|---|---|
| 85-86—Midland College | 34 | ... | 254 | 449 | .566 | 62 | 84 | .738 | 109 | 158 | 570 | 3.2 | 4.6 | 16.8 |
| 86-87—Midland College | 33 | ... | 258 | 500 | .516 | 60 | 83 | .723 | 138 | 161 | 647 | 4.2 | 4.9 | 19.6 |
| 87-88—Oklahoma | 39 | 1347 | 241 | 524 | .460 | 78 | 114 | .684 | 162 | 232 | 638 | 4.2 | 5.9 | 16.4 |
| 88-89—Oklahoma | 35 | 1359 | 272 | 598 | .455 | 65 | 100 | .650 | 164 | 233 | 700 | 4.7 | 6.7 | 20.0 |
| **Junior College Totals** | 67 | ... | 512 | 949 | .540 | 122 | 167 | .731 | 247 | 319 | 1217 | 3.7 | 4.8 | 18.2 |
| **4-Year-College Totals** | 74 | 2706 | 513 | 1122 | .457 | 143 | 214 | .668 | 326 | 465 | 1338 | 4.4 | 6.3 | 18.1 |

Three-point field goals: 1987-88, 78-for-201 (.388). 1988-89, 91-for-245 (.371). Totals, 169-for-446 (.379).

**RECORDS:** Shares career record for most consecutive seasons leading league in steals—2 (1996-97 and 1997-98).
**HONORS:** NBA All-Defensive first team (1994, 1995). ... NBA All-Defensive second team (1996, 1997, 1998, 1999).
**NOTES:** Led NBA with 2.72 steals per game (1997) and 2.61 steals per game (1998).

| | | | | | | | | REBOUNDS | | | | | | | | AVERAGES | | |
|---|---|---|---|---|---|---|---|---|---|---|---|---|---|---|---|---|---|---|
| Season Team | G | Min. | FGM | FGA | Pct. | FTM | FTA | Pct. | Off. | Def. | Tot. | Ast. | St. | Blk. | TO | Pts. | RPG | APG | PPG |
| 89-90—New Jersey..... | 50 | 1267 | 212 | 571 | .371 | 63 | 81 | .778 | 42 | 98 | 140 | 210 | 82 | 14 | 111 | 505 | 2.8 | 4.2 | 10.1 |
| 90-91—New Jersey..... | 72 | 2585 | 432 | 1039 | .416 | 139 | 176 | .790 | 67 | 182 | 249 | 441 | 169 | 40 | 207 | 1017 | 3.5 | 6.1 | 14.1 |
| 91-92—New Jersey..... | 72 | 2548 | 429 | 993 | .432 | 126 | 177 | .712 | 101 | 168 | 269 | 492 | 170 | 40 | 152 | 996 | 3.7 | 6.8 | 13.8 |
| 92-93—Atlanta ........... | 80 | 2820 | 414 | 964 | .429 | 123 | 169 | .728 | 89 | 191 | 280 | 671 | 203 | 23 | 187 | 1069 | 3.5 | 8.4 | 13.4 |
| 93-94—Atlanta ........... | 81 | 2915 | 444 | 1079 | .411 | 116 | 159 | .730 | 117 | 307 | 424 | 789 | 212 | 44 | 196 | 1118 | 5.2 | 9.7 | 13.8 |
| 94-95—Atlanta ........... | 80 | 3069 | 509 | 1198 | .425 | 156 | 214 | .729 | 117 | 276 | 393 | 616 | 200 | 26 | 242 | 1373 | 4.9 | 7.7 | 17.2 |
| 95-96—Atlanta ........... | 81 | 2893 | 455 | 1123 | .405 | 127 | 170 | .747 | 110 | 222 | 332 | 478 | 212 | 17 | 188 | 1268 | 4.1 | 5.9 | 15.7 |
| 96-97—Atlanta ........... | 78 | 3056 | 501 | 1159 | .432 | 131 | 174 | .753 | 114 | 299 | 413 | 463 | *212 | 20 | 185 | 1354 | 5.3 | 5.9 | 17.4 |
| 97-98—Atlanta ........... | 70 | 2700 | 368 | 938 | .392 | 95 | 134 | .709 | 81 | 260 | 341 | 469 | *183 | 21 | 176 | 921 | 4.9 | 6.7 | 13.2 |
| 98-99—Atlanta ........... | 48 | 1763 | 247 | 651 | .379 | 69 | 91 | .758 | 45 | 179 | 224 | 278 | 99 | 9 | 115 | 640 | 4.7 | 5.8 | 13.3 |
| 99-00—Golden State ... | 73 | 2459 | 327 | 837 | .391 | 67 | 95 | .705 | 55 | 215 | 270 | 489 | 146 | 22 | 143 | 822 | 3.7 | 6.7 | 11.3 |
| 00-01—Golden State ... | 69 | 2352 | 317 | 801 | .396 | 53 | 76 | .697 | 71 | 201 | 272 | 462 | 163 | 20 | 128 | 760 | 3.9 | 6.7 | 11.0 |
| 01-02—Golden State ... | 35 | 599 | 50 | 146 | .342 | 4 | 8 | .500 | 8 | 44 | 52 | 114 | 24 | 4 | 37 | 119 | 1.5 | 3.3 | 3.4 |
| **Totals** ................... | 889 | 31026 | 4705 | 11499 | .409 | 1269 | 1724 | .736 | 1017 | 2642 | 3659 | 5972 | 2075 | 300 | 2067 | 11962 | 4.1 | 6.7 | 13.5 |

Three-point field goals: 1989-90, 18-for-80 (.225). 1990-91, 14-for-91 (.154). 1991-92, 12-for-54 (.222). 1992-93, 118-for-315 (.375). 1993-94, 114-for-341 (.334). 1994-95, 199-for-555 (.359). 1995-96, 231-for-623 (.371). 1996-97, 221-for-604 (.366). 1997-98, 90-for-334 (.269). 1998-99, 77-for-251 (.307). 1999-00, 101-for-301 (.336). 2000-01, 73-for-225 (.324). 2001-02, 15-for-42 (.357). Totals, 1283-for-3816 (.336).

Personal fouls/disqualifications: 1989-90, 110/0. 1990-91, 180/0. 1991-92, 182/1. 1992-93, 156/0. 1993-94, 144/0. 1994-95, 164/3. 1995-96, 151/1. 1996-97, 141/0. 1997-98, 122/0. 1998-99, 61/0. 1999-00, 122/0. 2000-01, 134/1. 2001-02, 20/0. Totals, 1687/6.

## NBA PLAYOFF RECORD

| | | | | | | | | REBOUNDS | | | | | | | | AVERAGES | | |
|---|---|---|---|---|---|---|---|---|---|---|---|---|---|---|---|---|---|---|
| Season Team | G | Min. | FGM | FGA | Pct. | FTM | FTA | Pct. | Off. | Def. | Tot. | Ast. | St. | Blk. | TO | Pts. | RPG | APG | PPG |
| 91-92—New Jersey..... | 4 | 148 | 17 | 55 | .309 | 3 | 4 | .750 | 5 | 11 | 16 | 31 | 15 | 2 | 7 | 38 | 4.0 | 7.8 | 9.5 |
| 92-93—Atlanta ........... | 3 | 99 | 9 | 25 | .360 | 5 | 6 | .833 | 2 | 11 | 13 | 13 | 3 | 4 | 11 | 27 | 4.3 | 4.3 | 9.0 |
| 93-94—Atlanta ........... | 11 | 415 | 48 | 141 | .340 | 25 | 30 | .833 | 16 | 39 | 55 | 98 | 24 | 5 | 32 | 143 | 5.0 | 8.9 | 13.0 |
| 94-95—Atlanta ........... | 3 | 121 | 18 | 49 | .367 | 7 | 11 | .636 | 7 | 6 | 13 | 17 | 4 | 0 | 9 | 54 | 4.3 | 5.7 | 18.0 |
| 95-96—Atlanta ........... | 10 | 426 | 61 | 145 | .421 | 16 | 24 | .667 | 13 | 30 | 43 | 64 | 22 | 8 | 29 | 171 | 4.3 | 6.4 | 17.1 |
| 96-97—Atlanta ........... | 10 | 441 | 61 | 154 | .396 | 14 | 21 | .667 | 12 | 58 | 70 | 65 | 21 | 2 | 35 | 164 | 7.0 | 6.5 | 16.4 |
| 97-98—Atlanta ........... | 4 | 153 | 22 | 53 | .415 | 7 | 12 | .583 | 6 | 14 | 20 | 33 | 9 | 1 | 9 | 59 | 5.0 | 8.3 | 14.8 |
| 98-99—Atlanta ........... | 9 | 358 | 44 | 135 | .326 | 7 | 15 | .467 | 6 | 30 | 36 | 36 | 18 | 2 | 30 | 113 | 4.0 | 4.0 | 12.6 |
| **Totals** ................... | 54 | 2161 | 280 | 757 | .370 | 84 | 123 | .683 | 67 | 199 | 266 | 357 | 116 | 24 | 162 | 769 | 4.9 | 6.6 | 14.2 |

Three-point field goals: 1991-92, 1-for-6 (.167). 1992-93, 4-for-12 (.333). 1993-94, 22-for-64 (.344). 1994-95, 11-for-28 (.393). 1995-96, 33-for-84 (.393). 1996-97, 28-for-85 (.329). 1997-98, 8-for-27 (.296). 1998-99, 18-for-51 (.353). Totals, 125-for-357 (.350).

Personal fouls/disqualifications: 1991-92, 16/0. 1992-93, 9/0. 1993-94, 22/0. 1994-95, 6/0. 1995-96, 15/0. 1996-97, 15/0. 1997-98, 8/0. 1998-99, 11/0. Totals, 102/0.

## NBA ALL-STAR GAME RECORD

| | | | | | | | REBOUNDS | | | | | | | | |
|---|---|---|---|---|---|---|---|---|---|---|---|---|---|---|---|
| Season Team | Min. | FGM | FGA | Pct. | FTM | FTA | Pct. | Off. | Def. | Tot. | Ast. | PF | Dq. | St. | Blk. | TO | Pts. |
| 1994—Atlanta................... | 16 | 2 | 5 | .400 | 0 | 0 | ... | 0 | 1 | 1 | 2 | 3 | 0 | 0 | 0 | 1 | 5 |

Three-point field goals: 1994, 1-for-2 (.500).

---

## BOONE, RON                                    G

**PERSONAL:** Born September 6, 1946, in Oklahoma City. ... 6-2/200 (1,88/90,7). ... Full name: Ronald Bruce Boone.
**HIGH SCHOOL:** Tech (Omaha, Neb.).
**JUNIOR COLLEGE:** Iowa Western Community College.
**COLLEGE:** Idaho State.
**TRANSACTIONS:** Selected by Phoenix Suns in 11th round (147th pick overall) of 1968 NBA Draft. ... Selected by Dallas Chaparrals in eighth round of 1968 ABA Draft. ... Traded by Chaparrals with G Glen Combs to Utah Stars for G Donnie Freeman and C Wayne Hightower (January 8, 1971). ... Contract sold by Stars to Spirits of St. Louis (December 2, 1975). ... Selected by Kansas City Kings of NBA from Spirits in ABA dispersal draft (August 5, 1976). ... Traded by Kings with 1979 second-round draft choice to Denver Nuggets for F Darnell Hillman and draft rights to G Mike Evans (June 26, 1978). ... Traded by Nuggets with two 1979 second-round draft choices to Los Angeles Lakers for G Charlie Scott (June 26, 1978). ... Traded by Lakers to Utah Jazz for 1981 third-round draft choice (October 25, 1979). ... Waived by Jazz (January 26, 1981).

## COLLEGIATE RECORD

| | | | | | | | | | | | | AVERAGES | | |
|---|---|---|---|---|---|---|---|---|---|---|---|---|---|---|
| Season Team | G | Min. | FGM | FGA | Pct. | FTM | FTA | Pct. | Reb. | Ast. | Pts. | RPG | APG | PPG |
| 64-65—Iowa Western C.C.......... | 9 | ... | ... | ... | ... | ... | ... | ... | ... | ... | 227 | ... | ... | 25.2 |
| 65-66—Idaho State.................... | 10 | ... | 46 | 119 | .387 | 17 | 26 | .654 | 95 | ... | 109 | 9.5 | ... | 10.9 |
| 66-67—Idaho State.................... | 25 | ... | 199 | 416 | .478 | 160 | 215 | .744 | 128 | ... | 558 | 5.1 | ... | 22.3 |
| 67-68—Idaho State.................... | 26 | ... | 223 | 519 | .430 | 108 | 159 | .679 | 110 | ... | 554 | 4.2 | ... | 21.3 |
| **Junior college totals** ............. | 9 | ... | ... | ... | ... | ... | ... | ... | ... | ... | 227 | ... | ... | 25.2 |
| **4-year-college totals** ............. | 61 | ... | 468 | 1054 | .444 | 285 | 400 | .713 | 333 | ... | 1221 | 5.5 | ... | 20.0 |

## ABA REGULAR-SEASON RECORD

**NOTES:** ABA All-Star first team (1975). ... ABA All-Star second team (1974). ... ABA All-Rookie team (1969). ... Member of ABA championship team (1971).

| Season Team | G | Min. | 2-POINT | | | 3-POINT | | | FTM | FTA | Pct. | Reb. | Ast. | Pts. | AVERAGES | | |
|---|---|---|---|---|---|---|---|---|---|---|---|---|---|---|---|---|---|
| | | | FGM | FGA | Pct. | FGM | FGA | Pct. | | | | | | | RPG | APG | PPG |
| 68-69—Dallas | 78 | 2682 | 518 | 1182 | .438 | 2 | 15 | .133 | 436 | 537 | .812 | 394 | 279 | 1478 | 5.1 | 3.6 | 18.9 |
| 69-70—Dallas | 84 | 2340 | 406 | 925 | .439 | 17 | 55 | .309 | 300 | 382 | .785 | 366 | 272 | 1163 | 4.4 | 3.2 | 13.8 |
| 70-71—Dallas-Utah | 86 | 2476 | 561 | 1257 | .446 | 49 | 138 | .355 | 278 | 357 | .779 | 564 | 256 | 1547 | 6.6 | 3.0 | 18.0 |
| 71-72—Utah | 84 | 2040 | 391 | 897 | .436 | 13 | 65 | .200 | 271 | 341 | .795 | 393 | 233 | 1092 | 4.7 | 2.8 | 13.0 |
| 72-73—Utah | 84 | 2585 | 556 | 1096 | .507 | 10 | 40 | .250 | 415 | 479 | .866 | 423 | 353 | 1557 | 5.0 | 4.2 | 18.5 |
| 73-74—Utah | 84 | 3098 | 581 | 1162 | .500 | 6 | 26 | .231 | 300 | 343 | .875 | 435 | 417 | 1480 | 5.2 | 5.0 | 17.6 |
| 74-75—Utah | 84 | 3414 | 862 | 1743 | .495 | 10 | 33 | .303 | 363 | 422 | .860 | 406 | 372 | 2117 | 4.8 | 4.4 | 25.2 |
| 75-76—Utah-St. Louis | 78 | 2961 | 697 | 1424 | .489 | 16 | 43 | .372 | 277 | 318 | .871 | 319 | 387 | 1719 | 4.1 | 5.0 | 22.0 |
| Totals | 662 | 21596 | 4572 | 9686 | .472 | 123 | 415 | .296 | 2640 | 3179 | .830 | 3300 | 2569 | 12153 | 5.0 | 3.9 | 18.4 |

## ABA PLAYOFF RECORD

| Season Team | G | Min. | 2-POINT | | | 3-POINT | | | FTM | FTA | Pct. | Reb. | Ast. | Pts. | AVERAGES | | |
|---|---|---|---|---|---|---|---|---|---|---|---|---|---|---|---|---|---|
| | | | FGM | FGA | Pct. | FGM | FGA | Pct. | | | | | | | RPG | APG | PPG |
| 68-69—Dallas | 7 | 196 | 38 | 81 | .469 | 0 | 4 | .000 | 21 | 25 | .840 | 22 | 27 | 97 | 3.1 | 3.9 | 13.9 |
| 69-70—Dallas | 6 | 193 | 43 | 89 | .483 | 3 | 8 | .375 | 15 | 21 | .714 | 27 | 27 | 110 | 4.5 | 4.5 | 18.3 |
| 70-71—Utah | 18 | 569 | 104 | 229 | .454 | 9 | 27 | .333 | 74 | 86 | .860 | 110 | 94 | 309 | 6.1 | 5.2 | 17.2 |
| 71-72—Utah | 11 | 209 | 49 | 100 | .490 | 1 | 5 | .200 | 25 | 29 | .862 | 24 | 26 | 126 | 2.2 | 2.4 | 11.5 |
| 72-73—Utah | 10 | 360 | 68 | 132 | .515 | 0 | 3 | .000 | 33 | 34 | .971 | 43 | 47 | 169 | 4.3 | 4.7 | 16.9 |
| 73-74—Utah | 18 | 747 | 137 | 282 | .486 | 0 | 7 | .000 | 34 | 37 | .919 | 108 | 109 | 308 | 6.0 | 6.1 | 17.1 |
| 74-75—Utah | 6 | 219 | 54 | 127 | .425 | 0 | 0 | ... | 34 | 38 | .895 | 24 | 41 | 142 | 4.0 | 6.8 | 23.7 |
| Totals | 76 | 2493 | 493 | 1040 | .474 | 13 | 54 | .241 | 236 | 270 | .874 | 358 | 371 | 1261 | 4.7 | 4.9 | 16.6 |

## ABA ALL-STAR GAME RECORD

| Season Team | Min. | 2-POINT | | | 3-POINT | | | FTM | FTA | Pct. | Reb. | Ast. | Pts. |
|---|---|---|---|---|---|---|---|---|---|---|---|---|---|
| | | FGM | FGA | Pct. | FGM | FGA | Pct. | | | | | | |
| 1971—Utah | 4 | 2 | 4 | .500 | 0 | 0 | ... | 2 | 3 | .667 | 2 | 0 | 6 |
| 1974—Utah | 24 | 6 | 11 | .545 | 1 | 2 | .500 | 0 | 0 | ... | 3 | 5 | 15 |
| 1975—Utah | 23 | 4 | 8 | .500 | 0 | 0 | ... | 2 | 2 | 1.000 | 2 | 2 | 10 |
| 1976—St. Louis | 16 | 5 | 11 | .455 | 0 | 0 | ... | 0 | 0 | ... | 3 | 2 | 10 |
| Totals | 67 | 17 | 34 | .500 | 1 | 2 | .500 | 4 | 5 | .800 | 10 | 9 | 41 |

## NBA REGULAR-SEASON RECORD

| Season Team | G | Min. | FGM | FGA | Pct. | FTM | FTA | Pct. | REBOUNDS | | | Ast. | St. | Blk. | TO | Pts. | AVERAGES | | |
|---|---|---|---|---|---|---|---|---|---|---|---|---|---|---|---|---|---|---|---|
| | | | | | | | | | Off. | Def. | Tot. | | | | | | RPG | APG | PPG |
| 76-77—Kansas City | 82 | 3021 | 747 | 1577 | .474 | 324 | 384 | .844 | 128 | 193 | 321 | 338 | 119 | 19 | ... | 1818 | 3.9 | 4.1 | 22.2 |
| 77-78—Kansas City | 82 | 2653 | 563 | 1271 | .443 | 322 | 377 | .854 | 112 | 157 | 269 | 311 | 105 | 11 | 303 | 1448 | 3.3 | 3.8 | 17.7 |
| 78-79—Los Angeles | 82 | 1583 | 259 | 569 | .455 | 90 | 104 | .865 | 53 | 92 | 145 | 154 | 66 | 11 | 147 | 608 | 1.8 | 1.9 | 7.4 |
| 79-80—L.A.-Utah | 81 | 2392 | 405 | 915 | .443 | 175 | 196 | .893 | 54 | 173 | 227 | 309 | 97 | 3 | 197 | 1004 | 2.8 | 3.8 | 12.4 |
| 80-81—Utah | 52 | 1146 | 160 | 371 | .431 | 75 | 94 | .798 | 17 | 67 | 84 | 161 | 33 | 8 | 111 | 406 | 1.6 | 3.1 | 7.8 |
| Totals | 379 | 10795 | 2134 | 4703 | .454 | 986 | 1155 | .854 | 364 | 682 | 1046 | 1273 | 420 | 52 | 758 | 5284 | 2.8 | 3.4 | 13.9 |

Three-point field goals: 1979-80, 19-for-50 (.380). 1980-81, 11-for-39 (.282). Totals, 30-for-89 (.337).

Personal fouls/disqualifications: 1976-77, 258/1. 1977-78, 232/3. 1978-79, 171/1. 1979-80, 232/3. 1980-81, 126/0. Totals, 1020/8.

## NBA PLAYOFF RECORD

| Season Team | G | Min. | FGM | FGA | Pct. | FTM | FTA | Pct. | REBOUNDS | | | Ast. | St. | Blk. | TO | Pts. | AVERAGES | | |
|---|---|---|---|---|---|---|---|---|---|---|---|---|---|---|---|---|---|---|---|
| | | | | | | | | | Off. | Def. | Tot. | | | | | | RPG | APG | PPG |
| 78-79—Los Angeles | 8 | 226 | 37 | 77 | .481 | 20 | 21 | .952 | 7 | 8 | 15 | 14 | 9 | 0 | 14 | 94 | 1.9 | 1.8 | 11.8 |

Personal fouls/disqualifications: 1978-79, 28/0.

## COMBINED ABA AND NBA REGULAR-SEASON RECORDS

| | G | Min. | FGM | FGA | Pct. | FTM | FTA | Pct. | REBOUNDS | | | Ast. | Stl. | Blk. | TO | Pts. | AVERAGES | | |
|---|---|---|---|---|---|---|---|---|---|---|---|---|---|---|---|---|---|---|---|
| | | | | | | | | | Off. | Def. | Tot. | | | | | | RPG | APG | PPG |
| Totals | 1041 | 32391 | 6829 | 14804 | .461 | 3626 | 4334 | .837 | ... | ... | 4346 | 3842 | ... | ... | ... | 17437 | 4.2 | 3.7 | 16.8 |

Three-point field goals: 153-for-504 (.304).

## BRIAN, FRANK                    G

**PERSONAL:** Born May 1, 1923, in Zachary, La. ... 6-1/180 (1,85/81,6). ... Full name: Frank Sands Brian. ... Nickname: Flash.
**HIGH SCHOOL:** Zachary (La.).
**COLLEGE:** Louisiana State.
**TRANSACTIONS:** Signed by Anderson of National Basketball League (1947). ... Selected by Chicago from Anderson in NBL dispersal draft (April 25, 1950). ... Traded by Chicago to Tri-Cities (1950). ... Traded by Tri-Cities to Fort Wayne for C/F Howie Schultz, F/C/G Dick Mehen and cash (May 31, 1951).
**MISCELLANEOUS:** Member of NBL championship team (1949).

## COLLEGIATE RECORD

| Season Team | G | Min. | FGM | FGA | Pct. | FTM | FTA | Pct. | Reb. | Ast. | Pts. | AVERAGES | | |
|---|---|---|---|---|---|---|---|---|---|---|---|---|---|---|
| | | | | | | | | | | | | RPG | APG | PPG |
| 42-43—Louisiana State | 15 | ... | 77 | ... | ... | 56 | ... | ... | ... | ... | 210 | ... | ... | 14.0 |
| 43-44—Louisiana State | | | | | | Did not play—in military service. | | | | | | | | |
| 44-45—Louisiana State | | | | | | Did not play—in military service. | | | | | | | | |
| 45-46—Louisiana State | | | | | | Did not play—in military service. | | | | | | | | |
| 46-47—Louisiana State | 21 | ... | 127 | ... | ... | 86 | ... | ... | ... | ... | 340 | ... | ... | 16.2 |
| Totals | 36 | ... | 204 | ... | ... | 142 | ... | ... | ... | ... | 550 | ... | ... | 15.3 |

## NBL AND NBA REGULAR-SEASON RECORD

**HONORS:** All-NBA second team (1950, 1951). ... All-NBL first team (1949). ... All-NBL second team (1948).

| Season Team | G | Min. | FGM | FGA | Pct. | FTM | FTA | Pct. | Reb. | Ast. | PF | Dq. | Pts. | AVERAGES RPG | APG | PPG |
|---|---|---|---|---|---|---|---|---|---|---|---|---|---|---|---|---|
| 47-48—And. (NBL) | 59 | ... | 248 | ... | ... | 155 | 210 | .738 | ... | ... | 148 | ... | 651 | ... | ... | 11.0 |
| 48-49—And. (NBL) | 64 | ... | 216 | ... | ... | 201 | 256 | .785 | ... | ... | 144 | ... | 633 | ... | ... | 9.9 |
| 49-50—Anderson | 64 | ... | 368 | 1156 | .318 | 402 | 488 | *.824 | ... | 189 | 192 | ... | 1138 | ... | 3.0 | 17.8 |
| 50-51—Tri-Cities | 68 | ... | 363 | 1127 | .322 | 418 | 508 | .823 | 244 | 266 | 215 | 4 | 1144 | 3.6 | 3.9 | 16.8 |
| 51-52—Fort Wayne | 66 | 2672 | 342 | 972 | .352 | 367 | 433 | .848 | 232 | 233 | 220 | 6 | 1051 | 3.5 | 3.5 | 15.9 |
| 52-53—Fort Wayne | 68 | 1910 | 245 | 699 | .351 | 236 | 297 | .795 | 133 | 142 | 205 | 8 | 726 | 2.0 | 2.1 | 10.7 |
| 53-54—Fort Wayne | 64 | 973 | 132 | 352 | .375 | 137 | 182 | .753 | 79 | 92 | 100 | 2 | 401 | 1.2 | 1.4 | 6.3 |
| 54-55—Fort Wayne | 71 | 1381 | 237 | 623 | .380 | 217 | 255 | .851 | 127 | 142 | 133 | 0 | 691 | 1.8 | 2.0 | 9.7 |
| 55-56—Fort Wayne | 37 | 680 | 78 | 263 | .297 | 72 | 88 | .818 | 88 | 74 | 62 | 0 | 228 | 2.4 | 2.0 | 6.2 |
| Totals | 561 | ... | 2229 | ... | ... | 2205 | 2717 | .812 | ... | ... | 1419 | ... | 6663 | ... | ... | 11.9 |

## NBL AND NBA PLAYOFF RECORD

| Season Team | G | Min. | FGM | FGA | Pct. | FTM | FTA | Pct. | Reb. | Ast. | PF | Dq. | Pts. | AVERAGES RPG | APG | PPG |
|---|---|---|---|---|---|---|---|---|---|---|---|---|---|---|---|---|
| 47-48—And. (NBL) | 6 | ... | 18 | ... | ... | 11 | 16 | .688 | ... | ... | ... | ... | 47 | ... | ... | 7.8 |
| 48-49—And. (NBL) | 7 | ... | 26 | ... | ... | 27 | 32 | .844 | ... | ... | ... | ... | 79 | ... | ... | 11.3 |
| 49-50—Anderson | 8 | ... | 26 | 96 | .271 | 43 | 48 | .896 | ... | 19 | 24 | ... | 95 | ... | 2.4 | 11.9 |
| 51-52—Fort Wayne | 2 | 81 | 6 | 24 | .250 | 5 | 6 | .833 | 6 | 9 | 10 | 0 | 17 | 3.0 | 4.5 | 8.5 |
| 52-53—Fort Wayne | 8 | 146 | 13 | 42 | .310 | 19 | 25 | .760 | 9 | 11 | 23 | 1 | 45 | 1.1 | 1.4 | 5.6 |
| 53-54—Fort Wayne | 4 | 106 | 15 | 36 | .417 | 11 | 16 | .688 | 12 | 10 | 7 | 0 | 41 | 3.0 | 2.5 | 10.3 |
| 54-55—Fort Wayne | 11 | 269 | 48 | 120 | .400 | 31 | 38 | .816 | 22 | 27 | 26 | 0 | 127 | 2.0 | 2.5 | 11.5 |
| 55-56—Fort Wayne | 10 | 166 | 26 | 68 | .382 | 17 | 21 | .810 | 12 | 17 | 15 | 0 | 69 | 1.2 | 1.7 | 6.9 |
| Totals | 56 | ... | 178 | ... | ... | 164 | 202 | .812 | ... | ... | ... | ... | 520 | ... | ... | 9.3 |

## NBA ALL-STAR GAME RECORD

| Season Team | Min. | FGM | FGA | Pct. | FTM | FTA | Pct. | Reb | Ast. | PF | Dq. | Pts. |
|---|---|---|---|---|---|---|---|---|---|---|---|---|
| 1951—Tri-Cities | ... | 5 | 14 | .357 | 4 | 5 | .800 | 6 | 3 | 2 | ... | 14 |
| 1952—Fort Wayne | 25 | 4 | 10 | .400 | 5 | 6 | .833 | 7 | 4 | 2 | ... | 13 |
| Totals | ... | 9 | 24 | .375 | 9 | 11 | .818 | 13 | 7 | 4 | ... | 27 |

## BRIDGES, BILL                                           F

**PERSONAL:** Born April 4, 1939, in Hobbs, N.M. ... 6-6/235 (1,98/106,6). ... Full name: William C. Bridges.
**HIGH SCHOOL:** Hobbs (N.M.).
**COLLEGE:** Kansas.
**TRANSACTIONS:** Selected by Chicago Packers in third round (32nd pick overall) of 1961 NBA Draft. ... Played in American Basketball League with Kansas City Steers (1961-62 and 1962-63). ... Draft rights traded by Packers with G Ralph Davis to St. Louis Hawks for G Al Ferrari and F Shellie McMillion (June 14, 1962). ... Hawks franchise moved to Atlanta for 1968-69 season. ... Traded by Hawks to Philadelphia 76ers for F/C Jim Washington (November 19, 1971). ... Traded by 76ers with C/F Mel Counts to Los Angeles Lakers for F/C Leroy Ellis and F John Q. Trapp (November 2, 1972). ... Waived by Lakers (December 6, 1974). ... Signed as free agent by Golden State Warriors (March 1, 1975).
**MISCELLANEOUS:** Member of NBA championship team (1975).

### COLLEGIATE RECORD

| Season Team | G | Min. | FGM | FGA | Pct. | FTM | FTA | Pct. | Reb. | Ast. | Pts. | AVERAGES RPG | APG | PPG |
|---|---|---|---|---|---|---|---|---|---|---|---|---|---|---|
| 57-58—Kansas‡ | | | | | Freshman team did not play intercollegiate schedule. | | | | | | | | | |
| 58-59—Kansas | 25 | ... | 117 | 307 | .381 | 74 | 129 | .574 | 343 | ... | 308 | 13.7 | ... | 12.3 |
| 59-60—Kansas | 28 | ... | 112 | 293 | .382 | 94 | 142 | .662 | 385 | ... | 318 | 13.8 | ... | 11.4 |
| 60-61—Kansas | 25 | ... | 146 | 334 | .437 | 110 | 155 | .710 | 353 | ... | 402 | 14.1 | ... | 16.1 |
| Varsity totals | 78 | ... | 375 | 934 | .401 | 278 | 426 | .653 | 1081 | ... | 1028 | 13.9 | ... | 13.2 |

### ABL REGULAR-SEASON RECORD

**ABL:** ABL All-Star first team (1962). ... Holds single-game record for most points—55 (December 9, 1962, vs. Oakland).

| Season Team | G | Min. | FGM | FGA | Pct. | FTM | FTA | Pct. | Reb. | Ast. | Pts. | AVERAGES RPG | APG | PPG |
|---|---|---|---|---|---|---|---|---|---|---|---|---|---|---|
| 61-62—Kansas City | 79 | 3259 | 638 | 1400 | .456 | 412 | 587 | .702 | *1059 | 181 | 1697 | 13.4 | 2.3 | 21.5 |
| 62-63—Kansas City | 29 | 1185 | 312 | 606 | .515 | 225 | 289 | .779 | *437 | 87 | *849 | 15.1 | 3.0 | 29.3 |
| Totals | 108 | 4444 | 950 | 2006 | .474 | 637 | 876 | .727 | 1496 | 268 | 2546 | 13.9 | 2.5 | 23.6 |

### NBA REGULAR-SEASON RECORD

**HONORS:** NBA All-Defensive second team (1969, 1970).

| Season Team | G | Min. | FGM | FGA | Pct. | FTM | FTA | Pct. | Reb. | Ast. | PF | Dq. | Pts. | AVERAGES RPG | APG | PPG |
|---|---|---|---|---|---|---|---|---|---|---|---|---|---|---|---|---|
| 62-63—St. Louis | 27 | 374 | 66 | 160 | .413 | 32 | 51 | .627 | 144 | 23 | 58 | 0 | 164 | 5.3 | 0.9 | 6.1 |
| 63-64—St. Louis | 80 | 1949 | 268 | 675 | .397 | 146 | 224 | .652 | 680 | 181 | 269 | 6 | 682 | 8.5 | 2.3 | 8.5 |
| 64-65—St. Louis | 79 | 2362 | 362 | 938 | .386 | 186 | 275 | .676 | 853 | 187 | 276 | 3 | 910 | 10.8 | 2.4 | 11.5 |
| 65-66—St. Louis | 78 | 2677 | 377 | 927 | .407 | 257 | 364 | .706 | 951 | 208 | 333 | 11 | 1011 | 12.2 | 2.7 | 13.0 |
| 66-67—St. Louis | 79 | 3130 | 503 | 1106 | .455 | 367 | 523 | .702 | 1190 | 222 | 325 | 12 | 1373 | 15.1 | 2.8 | 17.4 |
| 67-68—St. Louis | 82 | 3197 | 466 | 1009 | .462 | 347 | 484 | .717 | 1102 | 253 | *366 | 12 | 1279 | 13.4 | 3.1 | 15.6 |
| 68-69—Atlanta | 80 | 2930 | 351 | 775 | .453 | 239 | 353 | .677 | 1132 | 298 | 290 | 3 | 941 | 14.2 | 3.7 | 11.8 |
| 69-70—Atlanta | 82 | 3269 | 443 | 932 | .475 | 331 | 451 | .734 | 1181 | 345 | 292 | 6 | 1217 | 14.4 | 4.2 | 14.8 |
| 70-71—Atlanta | 82 | 3410 | 382 | 834 | .458 | 211 | 330 | .639 | 1233 | 240 | 317 | 7 | 975 | 15.0 | 2.9 | 11.9 |
| 71-72—Atl.-Phil. | 78 | 2756 | 379 | 779 | .487 | 222 | 316 | .703 | 1051 | 198 | 269 | 6 | 980 | 13.5 | 2.5 | 12.6 |
| 72-73—Phil.-L.A. | 82 | 2867 | 333 | 722 | .461 | 179 | 255 | .702 | 904 | 219 | 296 | 3 | 845 | 11.0 | 2.7 | 10.3 |

| Season Team | G | Min. | FGM | FGA | Pct. | FTM | FTA | Pct. | REBOUNDS Off. | Def. | Tot. | Ast. | St. | Blk. | TO | Pts. | AVERAGES RPG | APG | PPG |
|---|---|---|---|---|---|---|---|---|---|---|---|---|---|---|---|---|---|---|---|
| 73-74—Los Angeles.... | 65 | 1812 | 216 | 513 | .421 | 116 | 164 | .707 | 193 | 306 | 499 | 148 | 58 | 31 | ... | 548 | 7.7 | 2.3 | 8.4 |
| 74-75—L.A.-G.S......... | 32 | 415 | 35 | 93 | .376 | 17 | 34 | .500 | 64 | 70 | 134 | 31 | 11 | 5 | ... | 87 | 4.2 | 1.0 | 2.7 |
| Totals ................... | 926 | 30878 | 4181 | 9463 | .442 | 2650 | 3824 | .693 | ... | ... | 11054 | 2553 | 69 | 36 | ... | 11012 | 11.9 | 2.8 | 11.9 |

Personal fouls/disqualifications: 1973-74, 219/3. 1974-75, 65/1. Totals, 3375/73.

### NBA PLAYOFF RECORD

| Season Team | G | Min. | FGM | FGA | Pct. | FTM | FTA | Pct. | Reb. | Ast. | PF | Dq. | Pts. | AVERAGES RPG | APG | PPG |
|---|---|---|---|---|---|---|---|---|---|---|---|---|---|---|---|---|
| 62-63—St. Louis............................ | 11 | 204 | 41 | 96 | .427 | 20 | 27 | .741 | 86 | 9 | 31 | 0 | 102 | 7.8 | 0.8 | 9.3 |
| 63-64—St. Louis............................ | 12 | 240 | 26 | 83 | .313 | 12 | 19 | .632 | 84 | 24 | 40 | 0 | 64 | 7.0 | 2.0 | 5.3 |
| 64-65—St. Louis............................ | 4 | 145 | 21 | 59 | .356 | 10 | 15 | .667 | 67 | 9 | 19 | 1 | 52 | 16.8 | 2.3 | 13.0 |
| 65-66—St. Louis............................ | 10 | 421 | 86 | 170 | .506 | 31 | 43 | .721 | 149 | 28 | 47 | 2 | 203 | 14.9 | 2.8 | 20.3 |
| 66-67—St. Louis............................ | 9 | 369 | 48 | 128 | .375 | 45 | 67 | .672 | 169 | 22 | 36 | 2 | 141 | 18.8 | 2.4 | 15.7 |
| 67-68—St. Louis............................ | 6 | 216 | 38 | 75 | .507 | 18 | 25 | .720 | 77 | 14 | 23 | 0 | 94 | 12.8 | 2.3 | 15.7 |
| 68-69—Atlanta ............................ | 11 | 442 | 69 | 156 | .442 | 34 | 48 | .708 | 178 | 37 | 48 | 2 | 172 | 16.2 | 3.4 | 15.6 |
| 69-70—Atlanta ............................ | 9 | 381 | 44 | 110 | .400 | 16 | 27 | .593 | 154 | 29 | 37 | 1 | 104 | 17.1 | 3.2 | 11.6 |
| 70-71—Atlanta ............................ | 5 | 229 | 23 | 58 | .397 | 3 | 9 | .333 | 104 | 5 | 17 | 0 | 49 | 20.8 | 1.0 | 9.8 |
| 72-73—Los Angeles...................... | 17 | 582 | 57 | 136 | .419 | 38 | 49 | .776 | 158 | 29 | 68 | 2 | 152 | 9.3 | 1.7 | 8.9 |

| Season Team | G | Min. | FGM | FGA | Pct. | FTM | FTA | Pct. | REBOUNDS Off. | Def. | Tot. | Ast. | St. | Blk. | TO | Pts. | AVERAGES RPG | APG | PPG |
|---|---|---|---|---|---|---|---|---|---|---|---|---|---|---|---|---|---|---|---|
| 73-74—Los Angeles ... | 5 | 144 | 12 | 41 | .293 | 6 | 13 | .462 | 14 | 16 | 30 | 6 | 7 | 0 | ... | 30 | 6.0 | 1.2 | 6.0 |
| 74-75—Golden State... | 14 | 148 | 10 | 23 | .435 | 2 | 7 | .286 | 13 | 36 | 49 | 7 | 9 | 4 | ... | 22 | 3.5 | 0.5 | 1.6 |
| Totals ................... | 113 | 3521 | 475 | 1135 | .419 | 235 | 349 | .673 | ... | ... | 1305 | 219 | 16 | 4 | ... | 1185 | 11.5 | 1.9 | 10.5 |

Personal fouls/disqualifications: 1973-74, 19/0. 1974-75, 23/0. Totals, 408/10.

### NBA ALL-STAR GAME RECORD

| Season Team | Min. | FGM | FGA | Pct. | FTM | FTA | Pct. | Reb. | Ast. | PF | Dq. | Pts. |
|---|---|---|---|---|---|---|---|---|---|---|---|---|
| 1967—St. Louis ...................... | 17 | 4 | 5 | .800 | 0 | 2 | .000 | 3 | 3 | 1 | 0 | 8 |
| 1968—St. Louis ...................... | 21 | 7 | 9 | .778 | 1 | 4 | .250 | 7 | 1 | 4 | 0 | 15 |
| 1970—Atlanta ........................ | 15 | 2 | 2 | 1.000 | 1 | 5 | .200 | 4 | 2 | 1 | 0 | 5 |
| Totals ................................ | 53 | 13 | 16 | .813 | 2 | 11 | .182 | 14 | 6 | 6 | 0 | 28 |

## CERVI, AL      G

**PERSONAL:** Born February 12, 1917, in Buffalo, N.Y. ... 5-11/185 (1,80/83,9). ... Full name: Alfred Nicholas Cervi. ... Nickname: Digger.
**HIGH SCHOOL:** East (Buffalo).
**COLLEGE:** Did not attend college.
**TRANSACTIONS:** Played with independent teams (1935-36, 1936-37 and 1938-39 through 1944-45 seasons). ... Syracuse Nationals franchise became part of NBA for 1949-50 season.
**CAREER HONORS:** Elected to Naismith Memorial Basketball Hall of Fame (1985).
**MISCELLANEOUS:** Member of NBL championship team (1946).

### NBL AND NBA REGULAR-SEASON RECORD

**HONORS:** All-NBA second team (1950). ... All-NBL first team (1947, 1948, 1949). ... All-NBL second team (1946).

| Season Team | G | Min. | FGM | FGA | Pct. | FTM | FTA | Pct. | Reb. | Ast. | PF | Dq. | Pts. | AVERAGES RPG | APG | PPG |
|---|---|---|---|---|---|---|---|---|---|---|---|---|---|---|---|---|
| 37-38—Buff. (NBL) ........................ | 9 | ... | 19 | ... | ... | 6 | ... | ... | ... | ... | ... | ... | 44 | ... | ... | 4.9 |
| 45-46—Roc. (NBL) ........................ | 28 | ... | 112 | ... | ... | 76 | 108 | .704 | ... | ... | 21 | ... | 300 | ... | ... | 10.7 |
| 46-47—Roc. (NBL) ........................ | 44 | ... | 228 | ... | ... | 176 | 236 | .746 | ... | ... | 127 | ... | *632 | ... | ... | 14.4 |
| 47-48—Roc. (NBL) ........................ | 49 | ... | 234 | ... | ... | 187 | 242 | .773 | ... | ... | 118 | ... | 655 | ... | ... | 13.4 |
| 48-49—Syr. (NBL) ........................ | 57 | ... | 204 | ... | ... | 287 | 382 | .751 | ... | ... | 170 | ... | 695 | ... | ... | 12.2 |
| 49-50—Syracuse............................ | 56 | ... | 143 | 431 | .332 | 287 | 346 | .829 | ... | 264 | 223 | ... | 573 | ... | 4.7 | 10.2 |
| 50-51—Syracuse............................ | 53 | ... | 132 | 346 | .382 | 194 | 237 | .819 | 152 | 208 | 180 | 9 | 458 | 2.9 | 3.9 | 8.6 |
| 51-52—Syracuse............................ | 55 | 850 | 99 | 280 | .354 | 219 | 248 | .883 | 87 | 148 | 176 | 7 | 417 | 1.6 | 2.7 | 7.6 |
| 52-53—Syracuse............................ | 38 | 301 | 31 | 71 | .437 | 81 | 100 | .810 | 22 | 28 | 90 | 2 | 143 | 0.6 | 0.7 | 3.8 |
| Totals............................... | 389 | ... | 1202 | ... | ... | 1513 | ... | ... | ... | ... | ... | ... | 3917 | ... | ... | 10.1 |

### NBL AND NBA PLAYOFF RECORD

| Season Team | G | Min. | FGM | FGA | Pct. | FTM | FTA | Pct. | Reb. | Ast. | PF | Dq. | Pts. | AVERAGES RPG | APG | PPG |
|---|---|---|---|---|---|---|---|---|---|---|---|---|---|---|---|---|
| 45-46—Roc. (NBL)........................ | 7 | ... | 23 | ... | ... | 24 | 30 | .800 | ... | ... | 21 | ... | 70 | ... | ... | 10.0 |
| 46-47—Roc. (NBL)........................ | 11 | ... | 49 | ... | ... | 50 | 68 | .735 | ... | ... | 41 | ... | 148 | ... | ... | 13.5 |
| 47-48—Roc. (NBL)........................ | 6 | ... | 18 | ... | ... | 14 | 19 | .737 | 13 | ... | ... | ... | 50 | 2.2 | ... | 8.3 |
| 48-49—Syr. (NBL)........................ | 6 | ... | 12 | ... | ... | 22 | 30 | .733 | ... | ... | 23 | ... | 46 | ... | ... | 7.7 |
| 49-50—Syracuse............................ | 11 | ... | 23 | 68 | .338 | 38 | 46 | .826 | ... | 52 | 36 | ... | 84 | ... | 4.7 | 7.6 |
| 50-51—Syracuse............................ | 7 | ... | 17 | 56 | .304 | 44 | 50 | .880 | 33 | 38 | 31 | 1 | 78 | 4.7 | 5.4 | 11.1 |
| 51-52—Syracuse............................ | 7 | 88 | 7 | 30 | .233 | 22 | 23 | .957 | 10 | 15 | 23 | 1 | 36 | 1.4 | 2.1 | 5.1 |
| 52-53—Syracuse............................ | 2 | ... | 3 | 5 | .600 | 12 | 15 | .800 | 0 | 1 | 12 | 1 | 18 | 0.0 | 0.5 | 9.0 |
| Totals............................... | 57 | ... | 152 | ... | ... | 226 | 281 | .804 | ... | ... | ... | ... | 530 | ... | ... | 9.3 |

### HEAD COACHING RECORD

**HONORS:** NBL Coach of the Year (1949).

### NBL AND NBA COACHING RECORD

| Season Team | REGULAR SEASON W | L | Pct. | Finish | PLAYOFFS W | L | Pct. |
|---|---|---|---|---|---|---|---|
| 48-49—Syracuse (NBL).............................................. | 40 | 23 | .635 | 2nd/Eastern Division | 3 | 3 | .500 |
| 49-50—Syracuse ..................................................... | 51 | 13 | .797 | 1st/Eastern Division | 6 | 5 | .545 |
| 50-51—Syracuse ..................................................... | 32 | 34 | .485 | 4th/Eastern Division | 4 | 3 | .571 |

| Season  Team | REGULAR SEASON | | | | | PLAYOFFS | | |
|---|---|---|---|---|---|---|---|---|
| | W | L | Pct. | Finish | | W | L | Pct. |
| 51-52—Syracuse | 40 | 26 | .606 | 1st/Eastern Division | | 3 | 4 | .429 |
| 52-53—Syracuse | 47 | 24 | .662 | 2nd/Eastern Division | | 0 | 2 | .000 |
| 53-54—Syracuse | 42 | 30 | .583 | 3rd/Eastern Division | | 9 | 4 | .692 |
| 54-55—Syracuse | 43 | 29 | .597 | 1st/Eastern Division | | 7 | 4 | .636 |
| 55-56—Syracuse | 35 | 37 | .493 | 3rd/Eastern Division | | 5 | 4 | .555 |
| 56-57—Syracuse | 4 | 8 | .333 | | | — | — | — |
| 58-59—Philadelphia | 32 | 40 | .444 | 4th/Eastern Division | | — | — | — |
| Totals (10 years) | 366 | 264 | .581 | | Totals (8 years) | 37 | 29 | .561 |

**NOTES:**
1949—Defeated Hammond, 2-0, in Eastern Division First Round; lost to Anderson, 3-1, in Eastern Division Finals.
1950—Defeated Philadelphia, 2-0, in Eastern Division Semifinals; defeated New York, 2-1, in Eastern Division Finals; lost to Minneapolis, 4-2, in NBA Finals.
1951—Defeated Philadelphia, 2-0, in Eastern Division Semifinals; lost to New York, 3-2, in Eastern Division Finals.
1952—Defeated Philadelphia, 2-1, in Eastern Division Semifinals; lost to New York, 3-1, in Eastern Division Finals.
1953—Lost to Boston in Eastern Division Semifinals.
1954—Defeated Boston, 96-95 (OT); defeated New York, 75-68; defeated New York, 103-99; and defeated Boston, 98-85, in Eastern Division round robin; defeated Boston, 2-0, in Eastern Division Finals; lost to Minneapolis, 4-3, in World Championship Series.
1955—Defeated Boston, 3-1, in Eastern Division Finals; defeated Fort Wayne, 4-3, in World Championship Series.
1956—Defeated New York, 82-77, in Eastern Division third-place game; defeated Boston, 2-1, in Eastern Division Semifinals; lost to Philadelphia, 3-2, in Eastern Division Finals. Replaced as Syracuse head coach by Paul Seymour (November).

## CHAMBERLAIN, WILT    C

**PERSONAL:** Born August 21, 1936, in Philadelphia. ... Died October 12, 1999. ... 7-1/275 (2,16/124,7). ... Full name: Wilton Norman Chamberlain. ... Nickname: Wilt the Stilt and The Big Dipper.
**HIGH SCHOOL:** Overbrook (Philadelphia).
**COLLEGE:** Kansas.
**TRANSACTIONS:** Played with Harlem Globetrotters during 1958-59 season. ... Selected by Philadelphia Warriors in 1959 NBA Draft (territorial pick). ... Warriors franchise moved from Philadelphia to San Francisco for 1962-63 season. ... Traded by Warriors to Philadelphia 76ers for G Paul Neumann, C/F Connie Dierking, F Lee Shaffer and cash (January 15, 1965). ... Traded by 76ers to Los Angeles Lakers for F Jerry Chambers, G Archie Clark and C Darrall Imhoff (July 9, 1968).
**CAREER HONORS:** Elected to Naismith Memorial Basketball Hall of Fame (1978). ... NBA 35th Anniversary All-Time Team (1980) and One of the 50 Greatest Players in NBA History (1996).
**MISCELLANEOUS:** Member of NBA championship team (1967, 1972). ... Golden State Warriors franchise all-time leading scorer with 17,783 points (1959-60 through 1964-65).

### COLLEGIATE RECORD

**NOTES:** The Sporting News All-America first team (1958).

| Season Team | G | Min. | FGM | FGA | Pct. | FTM | FTA | Pct. | Reb. | Ast. | Pts. | AVERAGES | | |
|---|---|---|---|---|---|---|---|---|---|---|---|---|---|---|
| | | | | | | | | | | | | RPG | APG | PPG |
| 55-56—Kansas‡ | | | | | Freshman team did not play intercollegiate schedule. | | | | | | | | | |
| 56-57—Kansas | 27 | ... | 275 | 588 | .468 | 250 | 399 | .627 | 510 | ... | 800 | 18.9 | ... | 29.6 |
| 57-58—Kansas | 21 | ... | 228 | 482 | .473 | 177 | 291 | .608 | 367 | ... | 633 | 17.5 | ... | 30.1 |
| Varsity totals | 48 | | 503 | 1070 | .470 | 427 | 690 | .619 | 877 | ... | 1433 | 18.3 | ... | 29.9 |

### NBA REGULAR-SEASON RECORD

**RECORDS:** Holds career records for most games with 50 or more points—118; most seasons leading league in field goal percentage—9; most free throws attempted—11,862; most rebounds—23,924; and highest rebounds-per-game average (minimum 400 games)—22.9. ... Shares career records for most consecutive seasons leading league in scoring—7 (1959-60 through 1965-66). ... Holds single-season records for most games with 50 or more points—45 (1962); most minutes played—3,882 (1962); most points—4,029 (1962); highest points-per-game average—50.4 (1962); most points by a rookie—2,707 (1960); most field goals made—1,597 (1962); most consecutive field goals made—35 (February 17 through February 28, 1967); most field goals attempted—3,159 (1962); highest field goal percentage—.727 (1973); most free throws attempted—1,363 (1962); most rebounds—2,149 (1961); most rebounds by a rookie—1,941 (1960); and highest rebounds-per-game average—27.2 (1961). ... Holds single-game records for most points—100; most points in one half—59; most field goals made—36; most field goals made in one half—22; most field goals attempted—63; most field goals attempted in one half—37; and most field goals attempted in one quarter—21 (March 2, 1962, vs. New York at Hershey, Pa.). ... Holds single-game records for most points by a rookie—58 (January 25, 1960, vs. Detroit); highest field goal percentage (minimum 15 made)—1.000 (January 20, 1967, vs. Los Angeles, 15-for-15; February 24, 1967, vs. Baltimore, 18-for-18; and March 19, 1967, vs. Baltimore, 16-for-16); most rebounds—55 (November 24, 1960, vs. Boston); and most rebounds by a rookie—45 (February 6, 1960, vs. Syracuse). ... Shares single-game record for most free throws made—28 (March 2, 1962, vs. New York at Hershey, Pa.).
**HONORS:** NBA Most Valuable Player (1960, 1966, 1967, 1968). ... NBA Rookie of the Year (1960). ... All-NBA first team (1960, 1961, 1962, 1964, 1966, 1967, 1968). ... All-NBA second team (1963, 1965, 1972). ... NBA All-Defensive first team (1972, 1973).

| Season Team | G | Min. | FGM | FGA | Pct. | FTM | FTA | Pct. | Reb. | Ast. | PF | Dq. | Pts. | AVERAGES | | |
|---|---|---|---|---|---|---|---|---|---|---|---|---|---|---|---|---|
| | | | | | | | | | | | | | | RPG | APG | PPG |
| 59-60—Philadelphia | 72 | †3338 | *1065 | *2311 | .461 | 577 | *991 | .582 | *1941 | 168 | 150 | 0 | *2707 | *27.0 | 2.3 | *37.6 |
| 60-61—Philadelphia | 79 | *3773 | *1251 | *2457 | *.509 | 531 | *1054 | .504 | *2149 | 148 | 130 | 0 | *3033 | *27.2 | 1.9 | *38.4 |
| 61-62—Philadelphia | 80 | *3882 | *1597 | *3159 | .506 | *835 | *1363 | .613 | *2052 | 192 | 123 | 0 | *4029 | *25.7 | 2.4 | *50.4 |
| 62-63—San Francisco | 80 | *3806 | *1463 | *2770 | .528 | 660 | *1113 | .593 | *1946 | 275 | 136 | 0 | *3586 | *24.3 | 3.4 | *44.8 |
| 63-64—San Francisco | 80 | *3689 | *1204 | *2298 | .524 | 540 | *1016 | .532 | 1787 | 403 | 182 | 0 | *2948 | 22.3 | 5.0 | *36.9 |
| 64-65—S.F.-Phil. | 73 | *3301 | *1063 | *2083 | *.510 | 408 | *880 | .464 | 1673 | 250 | 146 | 0 | *2534 | 22.9 | 3.4 | *34.7 |
| 65-66—Philadelphia | 79 | *3737 | *1074 | *1990 | *.540 | 501 | 976 | .513 | *1943 | 414 | 171 | 0 | *2649 | *24.6 | 5.2 | *33.5 |
| 66-67—Philadelphia | 81 | *3682 | 785 | 1150 | *.683 | 386 | *875 | .441 | *1957 | 630 | 143 | 0 | 1956 | *24.2 | 7.8 | 24.1 |
| 67-68—Philadelphia | 82 | *3836 | 819 | 1377 | *.595 | 354 | *932 | .380 | *1952 | *702 | 160 | 0 | 1992 | *23.8 | 8.6 | 24.3 |
| 68-69—Los Angeles | 81 | 3669 | 641 | 1099 | *.583 | 382 | *857 | .446 | *1712 | 366 | 142 | 0 | 1664 | *21.1 | 4.5 | 20.5 |
| 69-70—Los Angeles | 12 | 505 | 129 | 227 | .568 | 70 | 157 | .446 | 221 | 49 | 31 | 0 | 328 | 18.4 | 4.1 | 27.3 |
| 70-71—Los Angeles | 82 | 3630 | 668 | 1226 | .545 | 360 | 669 | .538 | *1493 | 352 | 174 | 0 | 1696 | *18.2 | 4.3 | 20.7 |
| 71-72—Los Angeles | 82 | 3469 | 496 | 764 | *.649 | 221 | 524 | .422 | *1572 | 329 | 196 | 0 | 1213 | *19.2 | 4.0 | 14.8 |
| 72-73—Los Angeles | 82 | 3542 | 426 | 586 | *.727 | 232 | 455 | .510 | *1526 | 365 | 191 | 0 | 1084 | *18.6 | 4.5 | 13.2 |
| Totals | 1045 | 47859 | 12681 | 23497 | .540 | 6057 | 11862 | .511 | 23924 | 4643 | 2075 | 0 | 31419 | 22.9 | 4.4 | 30.1 |

## NBA PLAYOFF RECORD

**NOTES:** NBA Finals Most Valuable Player (1972). ... Holds NBA Finals single-game record for most rebounds in one half—26 (April 16, 1967, vs. San Francisco). ... Holds single-series playoff record for highest rebounds-per-game average—32.0 (1967). ... Holds single-game playoff records for most rebounds—41 (April 5, 1967, vs. Boston); most rebounds in one half—26 (April 16, 1967, vs. San Francisco); and most points by a rookie—53 (March 14, 1960, vs. Syracuse). ... Shares single-game playoff records for most field goals made—24 (March 14, 1960, vs. Syracuse); most field goals attempted—48 (March 22, 1962, vs. Syracuse); and most field goals attempted in one half—25 (March 22, 1962, vs. Syracuse).

| Season Team | G | Min. | FGM | FGA | Pct. | FTM | FTA | Pct. | Reb. | Ast. | PF | Dq. | Pts. | RPG | APG | PPG |
|---|---|---|---|---|---|---|---|---|---|---|---|---|---|---|---|---|
| 59-60—Philadelphia | 9 | 415 | 125 | 252 | .496 | 49 | 110 | .445 | 232 | 19 | 17 | 0 | 299 | 25.8 | 2.1 | 33.2 |
| 60-61—Philadelphia | 3 | 144 | 45 | 96 | .469 | 21 | 38 | .553 | 69 | 6 | 10 | 0 | 111 | 23.0 | 2.0 | 37.0 |
| 61-62—Philadelphia | 12 | 576 | 162 | 347 | .467 | 96 | 151 | .636 | 319 | 37 | 27 | 0 | 420 | 26.6 | 3.1 | 35.0 |
| 63-64—San Francisco | 12 | 558 | 175 | 322 | .543 | 66 | 139 | .475 | 302 | 39 | 27 | 0 | 416 | 25.2 | 3.3 | 34.7 |
| 64-65—Philadelphia | 11 | 536 | 123 | 232 | .530 | 76 | 136 | .559 | 299 | 48 | 29 | 0 | 322 | 27.2 | 4.4 | 29.3 |
| 65-66—Philadelphia | 5 | 240 | 56 | 110 | .509 | 28 | 68 | .412 | 151 | 15 | 10 | 0 | 140 | 30.2 | 3.0 | 28.0 |
| 66-67—Philadelphia | 15 | 718 | 132 | 228 | .579 | 62 | 160 | .388 | 437 | 135 | 37 | 0 | 326 | 29.1 | 9.0 | 21.7 |
| 67-68—Philadelphia | 13 | 631 | 124 | 232 | .534 | 60 | 158 | .380 | 321 | 85 | 29 | 0 | 308 | 24.7 | 6.5 | 23.7 |
| 68-69—Los Angeles | 18 | 832 | 96 | 176 | .545 | 58 | 148 | .392 | 444 | 46 | 56 | 0 | 250 | 24.7 | 2.6 | 13.9 |
| 69-70—Los Angeles | 18 | 851 | 158 | 288 | .549 | 82 | 202 | .406 | 399 | 81 | 42 | 0 | 398 | 22.2 | 4.5 | 22.1 |
| 70-71—Los Angeles | 12 | 554 | 85 | 187 | .455 | 50 | 97 | .515 | 242 | 53 | 33 | 0 | 220 | 20.2 | 4.4 | 18.3 |
| 71-72—Los Angeles | 15 | 703 | 80 | 142 | .563 | 60 | 122 | .492 | 315 | 49 | 47 | 0 | 220 | 21.0 | 3.3 | 14.7 |
| 72-73—Los Angeles | 17 | 801 | 64 | 116 | .552 | 49 | 98 | .500 | 383 | 60 | 48 | 0 | 177 | 22.5 | 3.5 | 10.4 |
| Totals | 160 | 7559 | 1425 | 2728 | .522 | 757 | 1627 | .465 | 3913 | 673 | 412 | 0 | 3607 | 24.5 | 4.2 | 22.5 |

## NBA ALL-STAR GAME RECORD

**NOTES:** NBA All-Star Game Most Valuable Player (1960). ... Holds career record for most rebounds—197. ... Holds single-game records for most points—42 (1962); most free throws attempted—16 (1962); and most field goals made in one half—10 (1962). ... Shares single-game records for most field goals made—17 (1962); and most rebounds in one half—16 (1960).

| Season Team | Min. | FGM | FGA | Pct. | FTM | FTA | Pct. | Reb | Ast. | PF | Dq. | Pts. |
|---|---|---|---|---|---|---|---|---|---|---|---|---|
| 1960—Philadelphia | 30 | 9 | 20 | .450 | 5 | 7 | .714 | 25 | 2 | 1 | 0 | 23 |
| 1961—Philadelphia | 38 | 2 | 8 | .250 | 8 | 15 | .533 | 18 | 5 | 1 | 0 | 12 |
| 1962—Philadelphia | 37 | 17 | 23 | .739 | 8 | 16 | .500 | 24 | 1 | 4 | 0 | 42 |
| 1963—San Francisco | 35 | 7 | 11 | .636 | 3 | 7 | .429 | 19 | 0 | 2 | 0 | 17 |
| 1964—San Francisco | 37 | 4 | 14 | .286 | 11 | 14 | .786 | 20 | 1 | 2 | 0 | 19 |
| 1965—San Francisco | 31 | 9 | 15 | .600 | 2 | 8 | .250 | 16 | 1 | 4 | 0 | 20 |
| 1966—Philadelphia | 25 | 8 | 11 | .727 | 5 | 9 | .556 | 9 | 3 | 2 | 0 | 21 |
| 1967—Philadelphia | 39 | 6 | 7 | .857 | 2 | 5 | .400 | 22 | 4 | 1 | 0 | 14 |
| 1968—Philadelphia | 25 | 3 | 4 | .750 | 1 | 4 | .250 | 7 | 6 | 2 | 0 | 7 |
| 1969—Los Angeles | 27 | 2 | 3 | .667 | 0 | 1 | .000 | 12 | 2 | 2 | 0 | 4 |
| 1971—Los Angeles | 18 | 1 | 1 | 1.000 | 0 | 0 | ... | 8 | 5 | 0 | 0 | 2 |
| 1972—Los Angeles | 24 | 3 | 3 | 1.000 | 2 | 8 | .250 | 10 | 3 | 2 | 0 | 8 |
| 1973—Los Angeles | 22 | 1 | 2 | .500 | 0 | 0 | ... | 7 | 3 | 0 | 0 | 2 |
| Totals | 388 | 72 | 122 | .590 | 47 | 94 | .500 | 197 | 36 | 23 | 0 | 191 |

## ABA COACHING RECORD

| Season Team | REGULAR SEASON | | | | PLAYOFFS | | |
|---|---|---|---|---|---|---|---|
| | W | L | Pct. | Finish | W | L | Pct. |
| 73-74—San Diego | 37 | 47 | .440 | T4th/Western Division | 2 | 4 | .333 |

**NOTES:**
1974—Lost to Utah in Western Division Semifinals.

---

## CHAMBERS, TOM                    F

**PERSONAL:** Born June 21, 1959, in Ogden, Utah. ... 6-10/230 (2,08/104,3). ... Full name: Thomas Doane Chambers.
**HIGH SCHOOL:** Fairview (Boulder, Colo.).
**COLLEGE:** Utah.
**TRANSACTIONS:** Selected by San Diego Clippers in first round (eighth pick overall) of 1981 NBA Draft. ... Traded by Clippers with F Al Wood, 1987 second-round draft choice and future third-round draft choice to Seattle SuperSonics for C James Donaldson, F Greg Kelser, G Mark Radford, 1984 first-round draft choice and 1985 second-round draft choice (August 18, 1983). ... Signed as unrestricted free agent by Phoenix Suns (July 5, 1988). ... Signed as unrestricted free agent by Utah Jazz (August 12, 1993). ... Played in Israel (1995-96). ... Signed as free agent by Charlotte Hornets (January 30, 1997). ... Waived by Hornets (April 8, 1997). ... Signed as free agent by Suns (August 22, 1997). ... Traded by Suns to Philadelphia 76ers for G/F Marko Milic (November 21, 1997). ... Announced retirement (December 11, 1997).
**CAREER NOTES:** Community relations representative, Phoenix Suns (1997-present).

### COLLEGIATE RECORD

| Season Team | G | Min. | FGM | FGA | Pct. | FTM | FTA | Pct. | Reb. | Ast. | Pts. | RPG | APG | PPG |
|---|---|---|---|---|---|---|---|---|---|---|---|---|---|---|
| 77-78—Utah | 28 | 355 | 69 | 139 | .496 | 40 | 64 | .625 | 104 | 7 | 178 | 3.7 | 0.3 | 6.4 |
| 78-79—Utah | 30 | 853 | 206 | 379 | .544 | 69 | 127 | .543 | 266 | 28 | 481 | 8.9 | 0.9 | 16.0 |
| 79-80—Utah | 28 | 792 | 195 | 359 | .543 | 92 | 129 | .713 | 244 | 23 | 482 | 8.7 | 0.8 | 17.2 |
| 80-81—Utah | 30 | 959 | 221 | 372 | .594 | 115 | 155 | .742 | 262 | 24 | 557 | 8.7 | 0.8 | 18.6 |
| Totals | 116 | 2959 | 691 | 1249 | .553 | 316 | 475 | .665 | 876 | 82 | 1698 | 7.6 | 0.7 | 14.6 |

**HONORS:** All-NBA second team (1989, 1990).

### NBA REGULAR-SEASON RECORD

| Season Team | G | Min. | FGM | FGA | Pct. | FTM | FTA | Pct. | REBOUNDS | | | Ast. | St. | Blk. | TO | Pts. | AVERAGES | | |
|---|---|---|---|---|---|---|---|---|---|---|---|---|---|---|---|---|---|---|---|
| | | | | | | | | | Off. | Def. | Tot. | | | | | | RPG | APG | PPG |
| 81-82—San Diego | 81 | 2682 | 554 | 1056 | .525 | 284 | 458 | .620 | 211 | 350 | 561 | 146 | 58 | 46 | 220 | 1392 | 6.9 | 1.8 | 17.2 |
| 82-83—San Diego | 79 | 2665 | 519 | 1099 | .472 | 353 | 488 | .723 | 218 | 301 | 519 | 192 | 79 | 57 | 234 | 1391 | 6.6 | 2.4 | 17.6 |
| 83-84—Seattle | 82 | 2570 | 554 | 1110 | .499 | 375 | 469 | .800 | 219 | 313 | 532 | 133 | 47 | 51 | 192 | 1483 | 6.5 | 1.6 | 18.1 |
| 84-85—Seattle | 81 | 2923 | 629 | 1302 | .483 | 475 | 571 | .832 | 164 | 415 | 579 | 209 | 70 | 57 | 260 | 1739 | 7.1 | 2.6 | 21.5 |
| 85-86—Seattle | 66 | 2019 | 432 | 928 | .466 | 346 | 414 | .836 | 126 | 305 | 431 | 132 | 55 | 37 | 194 | 1223 | 6.5 | 2.0 | 18.5 |
| 86-87—Seattle | 82 | 3018 | 660 | 1446 | .456 | 535 | 630 | .849 | 163 | 382 | 545 | 245 | 81 | 50 | 268 | 1909 | 6.6 | 3.0 | 23.3 |
| 87-88—Seattle | 82 | 2680 | 611 | 1364 | .448 | 419 | 519 | .807 | 135 | 355 | 490 | 212 | 87 | 53 | 209 | 1674 | 6.0 | 2.6 | 20.4 |
| 88-89—Phoenix | 81 | 3002 | 774 | 1643 | .471 | 509 | 598 | .851 | 143 | 541 | 684 | 231 | 87 | 55 | 231 | 2085 | 8.4 | 2.9 | 25.7 |

| Season Team | G | Min. | FGM | FGA | Pct. | FTM | FTA | Pct. | REBOUNDS Off. | Def. | Tot. | Ast. | St. | Blk. | TO | Pts. | AVERAGES RPG | APG | PPG |
|---|---|---|---|---|---|---|---|---|---|---|---|---|---|---|---|---|---|---|---|
| 89-90—Phoenix | 81 | 3046 | 810 | 1617 | .501 | 557 | 647 | .861 | 121 | 450 | 571 | 190 | 88 | 47 | 218 | 2201 | 7.0 | 2.3 | 27.2 |
| 90-91—Phoenix | 76 | 2475 | 556 | 1271 | .437 | 379 | 459 | .826 | 104 | 386 | 490 | 194 | 65 | 52 | 177 | 1511 | 6.4 | 2.6 | 19.9 |
| 91-92—Phoenix | 69 | 1948 | 426 | 989 | .431 | 258 | 311 | .830 | 86 | 315 | 401 | 142 | 57 | 37 | 103 | 1128 | 5.8 | 2.1 | 16.3 |
| 92-93—Phoenix | 73 | 1723 | 320 | 716 | .447 | 241 | 288 | .837 | 96 | 249 | 345 | 101 | 43 | 23 | 92 | 892 | 4.7 | 1.4 | 12.2 |
| 93-94—Utah | 80 | 1838 | 329 | 748 | .440 | 221 | 281 | .786 | 87 | 239 | 326 | 79 | 40 | 32 | 89 | 893 | 4.1 | 1.0 | 11.2 |
| 94-95—Utah | 81 | 1240 | 195 | 427 | .457 | 109 | 135 | .807 | 66 | 147 | 213 | 73 | 25 | 30 | 52 | 503 | 2.6 | 0.9 | 6.2 |
| 95-96— | | | | | | | | Played in Israel. | | | | | | | | | | | |
| 96-97—Charlotte | 12 | 83 | 7 | 31 | .226 | 3 | 4 | .750 | 3 | 11 | 14 | 4 | 1 | 0 | 9 | 19 | 1.2 | 0.3 | 1.6 |
| 97-98—Philadelphia | 1 | 10 | 2 | 2 | 1.000 | 0 | 2 | 1.000 | 0 | 2 | 2 | 0 | 2 | 0 | 1 | 6 | 2.0 | 0.0 | 6.0 |
| Totals | 1107 | 33922 | 7378 | 15749 | .468 | 5066 | 6274 | .807 | 1942 | 4761 | 6703 | 2283 | 885 | 627 | 2549 | 20049 | 6.1 | 2.1 | 18.1 |

Three-point field goals: 1981-82, 0-for-2. 1982-83, 0-for-8. 1983-84, 0-for-12. 1984-85, 6-for-22 (.273). 1985-86, 13-for-48 (.271). 1986-87, 54-for-145 (.372). 1987-88, 33-for-109 (.303). 1988-89, 28-for-86 (.326). 1989-90, 24-for-86 (.279). 1990-91, 20-for-73 (.274). 1991-92, 18-for-49 (.367). 1992-93, 11-for-28 (.393). 1993-94, 14-for-45 (.311). 1994-95, 4-for-24 (.167). 1996-97, 2-for-3 (.667). Totals, 227-for-740 (.307).

Personal fouls/disqualifications: 1981-82, 341/17. 1982-83, 333/15. 1983-84, 309/8. 1984-85, 312/4. 1985-86, 248/6. 1986-87, 307/9. 1987-88, 297/4. 1988-89, 271/2. 1989-90, 260/1. 1990-91, 235/3. 1991-92, 196/1. 1992-93, 212/2. 1993-94, 232/2. 1994-95, 173/1. 1996-97, 14/0. 1997-98, 2/0. Totals, 3742/75.

## NBA PLAYOFF RECORD

| Season Team | G | Min. | FGM | FGA | Pct. | FTM | FTA | Pct. | REBOUNDS Off. | Def. | Tot. | Ast. | St. | Blk. | TO | Pts. | AVERAGES RPG | APG | PPG |
|---|---|---|---|---|---|---|---|---|---|---|---|---|---|---|---|---|---|---|---|
| 83-84—Seattle | 5 | 191 | 28 | 59 | .475 | 12 | 18 | .667 | 4 | 29 | 33 | 8 | 5 | 3 | 9 | 68 | 6.6 | 1.6 | 13.6 |
| 86-87—Seattle | 14 | 498 | 118 | 263 | .449 | 80 | 99 | .808 | 32 | 58 | 90 | 32 | 12 | 13 | 34 | 322 | 6.4 | 2.3 | 23.0 |
| 87-88—Seattle | 5 | 168 | 50 | 91 | .549 | 29 | 35 | .829 | 8 | 23 | 31 | 11 | 3 | 1 | 13 | 129 | 6.2 | 2.2 | 25.8 |
| 88-89—Phoenix | 12 | 495 | 118 | 257 | .459 | 67 | 78 | .859 | 22 | 109 | 131 | 46 | 13 | 15 | 39 | 312 | 10.9 | 3.8 | 26.0 |
| 89-90—Phoenix | 16 | 612 | 117 | 275 | .425 | 116 | 132 | .879 | 20 | 87 | 107 | 31 | 7 | 7 | 49 | 355 | 6.7 | 1.9 | 22.2 |
| 90-91—Phoenix | 4 | 142 | 27 | 66 | .409 | 14 | 19 | .737 | 2 | 21 | 23 | 10 | 7 | 5 | 12 | 68 | 5.8 | 2.5 | 17.0 |
| 91-92—Phoenix | 7 | 194 | 39 | 85 | .459 | 27 | 32 | .844 | 8 | 23 | 31 | 19 | 2 | 5 | 15 | 109 | 4.4 | 2.7 | 15.6 |
| 92-93—Phoenix | 24 | 376 | 64 | 165 | .388 | 44 | 54 | .815 | 23 | 42 | 65 | 12 | 6 | 10 | 26 | 174 | 2.7 | 0.5 | 7.3 |
| 93-94—Utah | 16 | 325 | 35 | 97 | .361 | 23 | 29 | .793 | 16 | 29 | 45 | 12 | 5 | 9 | 8 | 93 | 2.8 | 0.8 | 5.8 |
| 94-95—Utah | 5 | 60 | 11 | 22 | .500 | 9 | 13 | .692 | 3 | 10 | 13 | 2 | 2 | 0 | 3 | 32 | 2.6 | 0.4 | 6.4 |
| Totals | 108 | 3061 | 607 | 1380 | .440 | 421 | 509 | .827 | 138 | 431 | 569 | 183 | 62 | 68 | 208 | 1662 | 5.3 | 1.7 | 15.4 |

Three-point field goals: 1983-84, 0-for-1. 1986-87, 6-for-17 (.353). 1987-88, 0-for-2. 1988-89, 9-for-22 (.409). 1989-90, 5-for-19 (.263). 1990-91, 0-for-5. 1991-92, 4-for-7 (.571). 1992-93, 2-for-5 (.400). 1993-94, 0-for-7. 1994-95, 1-for-3 (.333). Totals, 27-for-88 (.307).

Personal fouls/disqualifications: 1983-84, 23/0. 1986-87, 51/0. 1987-88, 24/1. 1988-89, 44/0. 1989-90, 54/0. 1990-91, 12/1. 1991-92, 25/1. 1992-93, 58/0. 1993-94, 50/1. 1994-95, 18/1. Totals, 359/5.

## NBA ALL-STAR GAME RECORD

**NOTES:** NBA All-Star Game Most Valuable Player (1987).

| Season Team | Min. | FGM | FGA | Pct. | FTM | FTA | Pct. | REBOUNDS Off. | Def. | Tot. | Ast. | PF | Dq. | St. | Blk. | TO | Pts. |
|---|---|---|---|---|---|---|---|---|---|---|---|---|---|---|---|---|---|
| 1987—Seattle | 29 | 13 | 25 | .520 | 6 | 9 | .667 | 3 | 1 | 4 | 2 | 5 | 0 | 4 | 0 | 3 | 34 |
| 1989—Phoenix | 16 | 4 | 8 | .500 | 6 | 6 | 1.000 | 2 | 3 | 5 | 1 | 3 | 0 | 0 | 0 | 2 | 14 |
| 1990—Phoenix | 21 | 8 | 12 | .667 | 5 | 7 | .714 | 2 | 1 | 3 | 1 | 0 | 0 | 1 | 0 | 3 | 21 |
| 1991—Phoenix | 18 | 4 | 11 | .364 | 0 | 0 | | 2 | 2 | 4 | 1 | 3 | 0 | 1 | 0 | 4 | 8 |
| Totals | 84 | 29 | 56 | .518 | 17 | 22 | .773 | 9 | 7 | 16 | 5 | 11 | 0 | 6 | 0 | 12 | 77 |

Three-point field goals: 1987, 2-for-3 (.667). 1990, 0-for-1. 1991, 0-for-1. Totals, 2-for-5 (.400).

## ISRAELI LEAGUE RECORD

| Season Team | G | Min. | FGM | FGA | Pct. | FTM | FTA | Pct. | Reb. | Ast. | Pts. | AVERAGES RPG | APG | PPG |
|---|---|---|---|---|---|---|---|---|---|---|---|---|---|---|
| 95-96—Maccabo Tel-Aviv | 16 | ... | 117 | 197 | .594 | 44 | 60 | .733 | 101 | 36 | 283 | 6.3 | 2.3 | 17.7 |

# CHEEKS, MAURICE — G

See Head Coaches, page 295.

# COSTELLO, LARRY — G

See All-Time Great Coaches, page 457.

# COUSY, BOB — G

**PERSONAL:** Born August 9, 1928, in New York. ... 6-1/175 (1,85/79,4). ... Full name: Robert Joseph Cousy. ... Nickname: Houdini of the Hardwood.

**HIGH SCHOOL:** Andrew Jackson (Queens, N.Y.).

**COLLEGE:** Holy Cross.

**TRANSACTIONS:** Selected by Tri-Cities Blackhawks in first round of 1950 NBA Draft. ... Traded by Blackhawks to Chicago Stags for F/G Gene Vance (1950). ... NBA rights drawn out of a hat by Boston Celtics in dispersal of Stags franchise (1950). ... Traded by Celtics to Cincinnati Royals for F Bill Dinwiddie (November 18, 1969).

**CAREER HONORS:** Elected to Naismith Memorial Basketball Hall of Fame (1971). ... NBA 25th Anniversary All-Time Team (1970), 35th Anniversary All-Time Team (1980) and One of the 50 Greatest Players in NBA History (1996).

**MISCELLANEOUS:** Member of NBA championship team (1957, 1959, 1960, 1961, 1962, 1963). ... Commissioner of American Soccer League (1975 through mid-1980 season). ... Boston Celtics all-time assists leader with 6,945 (1950-51 through 1962-63).

## COLLEGIATE RECORD

**NOTES:** Member of NCAA championship team (1947). ... THE SPORTING NEWS All-America first team (1950). ... THE SPORTING NEWS All-America second team (1949).

| Season Team | G | Min. | FGM | FGA | Pct. | FTM | FTA | Pct. | Reb. | Ast. | Pts. | AVERAGES RPG | APG | PPG |
|---|---|---|---|---|---|---|---|---|---|---|---|---|---|---|
| 46-47—Holy Cross | 30 | ... | 91 | ... | ... | 45 | ... | ... | ... | ... | 227 | ... | ... | 7.6 |
| 47-48—Holy Cross | 30 | ... | 207 | ... | ... | 72 | 108 | .667 | ... | ... | 486 | ... | ... | 16.2 |
| 48-49—Holy Cross | 27 | ... | 195 | ... | ... | 90 | 134 | .672 | ... | ... | 480 | ... | ... | 17.8 |
| 49-50—Holy Cross | 30 | ... | 216 | 659 | .328 | 150 | 199 | .754 | ... | ... | 582 | ... | ... | 19.4 |
| Totals | 117 | ... | 709 | ... | ... | 357 | ... | ... | ... | ... | 1775 | ... | ... | 15.2 |

## NBA REGULAR-SEASON RECORD

**RECORDS:** Holds single-game record for most assists in one half—19 (February 27, 1959, vs. Minneapolis).

**HONORS:** NBA Most Valuable Player (1957). ... All-NBA first team (1952, 1953, 1954, 1955, 1956, 1957, 1958, 1959, 1960, 1961). ... All-NBA second team (1962, 1963).

| Season Team | G | Min. | FGM | FGA | Pct. | FTM | FTA | Pct. | Reb. | Ast. | PF | Dq. | Pts. | AVERAGES RPG | APG | PPG |
|---|---|---|---|---|---|---|---|---|---|---|---|---|---|---|---|---|
| 50-51—Boston | 69 | ... | 401 | 1138 | .352 | 276 | 365 | .756 | 474 | 341 | 185 | 2 | 1078 | 6.9 | 4.9 | 15.6 |
| 51-52—Boston | 66 | 2681 | 512 | 1388 | .369 | 409 | 506 | .808 | 421 | 441 | 190 | 5 | 1433 | 6.4 | 6.7 | 21.7 |
| 52-53—Boston | 71 | 2945 | 464 | *1320 | .352 | 479 | 587 | .816 | 449 | *547 | 227 | 4 | 1407 | 6.3 | *7.7 | 19.8 |
| 53-54—Boston | 72 | 2857 | 486 | 1262 | .385 | 411 | 522 | .787 | 394 | *518 | 201 | 3 | 1383 | 5.5 | *7.2 | 19.2 |
| 54-55—Boston | 71 | 2747 | 522 | 1316 | .397 | 460 | 570 | .807 | 424 | *557 | 165 | 1 | 1504 | 6.0 | *7.8 | 21.2 |
| 55-56—Boston | 72 | 2767 | 440 | 1223 | .360 | 476 | 564 | .844 | 492 | *642 | 206 | 2 | 1356 | 6.8 | *8.9 | 18.8 |
| 56-57—Boston | 64 | 2364 | 478 | 1264 | .378 | 363 | 442 | .821 | 309 | *478 | 134 | 0 | 1319 | 4.8 | *7.5 | 20.6 |
| 57-58—Boston | 65 | 2222 | 445 | 1262 | .353 | 277 | 326 | .850 | 322 | *463 | 136 | 1 | 1167 | 5.0 | *7.1 | 18.0 |
| 58-59—Boston | 65 | 2403 | 484 | 1260 | .384 | 329 | 385 | .855 | 359 | *557 | 135 | 0 | 1297 | 5.5 | *8.6 | 20.0 |
| 59-60—Boston | 75 | 2588 | 568 | 1481 | .384 | 319 | 403 | .792 | 352 | *715 | 146 | 2 | 1455 | 4.7 | *9.5 | 19.4 |
| 60-61—Boston | 76 | 2468 | 513 | 1382 | .371 | 352 | 452 | .779 | 331 | 587 | 196 | 0 | 1378 | 4.4 | 7.7 | 18.1 |
| 61-62—Boston | 75 | 2114 | 462 | 1181 | .391 | 251 | 333 | .754 | 261 | 584 | 135 | 0 | 1175 | 3.5 | 7.8 | 15.7 |
| 62-63—Boston | 76 | 1975 | 392 | 988 | .397 | 219 | 298 | .735 | 193 | 515 | 175 | 0 | 1003 | 2.5 | 6.8 | 13.2 |
| 69-70—Cincinnati | 7 | 34 | 1 | 3 | .333 | 3 | 3 | 1.000 | 5 | 10 | 11 | 0 | 5 | 0.7 | 1.4 | 0.7 |
| Totals | 924 | ... | 6168 | 16468 | .375 | 4624 | 5756 | .803 | 4786 | 6955 | 2242 | 20 | 16960 | 5.2 | 7.5 | 18.4 |

## NBA PLAYOFF RECORD

**NOTES:** Shares NBA Finals single-game record for most assists in one quarter—8 (April 9, 1957, vs. St. Louis). ... Holds single-game play-off record for most free throws made—30 (March 21, 1953, vs. Syracuse).

| Season Team | G | Min. | FGM | FGA | Pct. | FTM | FTA | Pct. | Reb. | Ast. | PF | Dq. | Pts. | AVERAGES RPG | APG | PPG |
|---|---|---|---|---|---|---|---|---|---|---|---|---|---|---|---|---|
| 50-51—Boston | 2 | ... | 9 | 42 | .214 | 10 | 12 | .833 | 15 | 12 | 8 | ... | 28 | 7.5 | 6.0 | 14.0 |
| 51-52—Boston | 3 | 138 | 26 | 65 | .400 | 41 | 44 | .932 | 12 | 19 | 13 | 1 | 93 | 4.0 | 6.3 | 31.0 |
| 52-53—Boston | 6 | 270 | 46 | 120 | .383 | 61 | 73 | .836 | 25 | 37 | 21 | 0 | 153 | 4.2 | 6.2 | 25.5 |
| 53-54—Boston | 6 | 259 | 33 | 116 | .284 | 60 | 75 | .800 | 32 | 38 | 20 | 0 | 126 | 5.3 | 6.3 | 21.0 |
| 54-55—Boston | 7 | 299 | 53 | 139 | .381 | 46 | 48 | .958 | 43 | 65 | 26 | 0 | 152 | 6.1 | 9.3 | 21.7 |
| 55-56—Boston | 3 | 124 | 28 | 56 | .500 | 23 | 25 | .920 | 24 | 26 | 4 | 0 | 79 | 8.0 | 8.7 | 26.3 |
| 56-57—Boston | 10 | 440 | 67 | 207 | .324 | 68 | 91 | .747 | 61 | 93 | 27 | 0 | 202 | 6.1 | 9.3 | 20.2 |
| 57-58—Boston | 11 | 457 | 67 | 196 | .342 | 64 | 75 | .853 | 71 | 82 | 20 | 0 | 198 | 6.5 | 7.5 | 18.0 |
| 58-59—Boston | 11 | 460 | 72 | 221 | .326 | 70 | 94 | .745 | 76 | 119 | 28 | 0 | 214 | 6.9 | 10.8 | 19.5 |
| 59-60—Boston | 13 | 468 | 80 | 262 | .305 | 39 | 51 | .765 | 48 | 116 | 27 | 0 | 199 | 3.7 | 8.9 | 15.3 |
| 60-61—Boston | 10 | 337 | 50 | 147 | .340 | 67 | 88 | .761 | 43 | 91 | 33 | 1 | 167 | 4.3 | 9.1 | 16.7 |
| 61-62—Boston | 14 | 474 | 86 | 241 | .357 | 52 | 76 | .684 | 64 | 123 | 43 | 0 | 224 | 4.6 | 8.8 | 16.0 |
| 62-63—Boston | 13 | 393 | 72 | 204 | .353 | 39 | 47 | .830 | 32 | 116 | 44 | 2 | 183 | 2.5 | 8.9 | 14.1 |
| Totals | 109 | ... | 689 | 2016 | .342 | 640 | 799 | .801 | 546 | 937 | 314 | ... | 2018 | 5.0 | 8.6 | 18.5 |

## NBA ALL-STAR GAME RECORD

**NOTES:** NBA All-Star Game Most Valuable Player (1954, 1957).

| Season Team | Min. | FGM | FGA | Pct. | FTM | FTA | Pct. | Reb | Ast. | PF | Dq. | Pts. |
|---|---|---|---|---|---|---|---|---|---|---|---|---|
| 1951—Boston | ... | 2 | 12 | .167 | 4 | 5 | .800 | 9 | 8 | 3 | 0 | 8 |
| 1952—Boston | 33 | 4 | 14 | .286 | 1 | 2 | .500 | 4 | 13 | 3 | 0 | 9 |
| 1953—Boston | 36 | 4 | 11 | .364 | 7 | 7 | 1.000 | 5 | 3 | 1 | 0 | 15 |
| 1954—Boston | 34 | 6 | 15 | .400 | 8 | 8 | 1.000 | 11 | 4 | 1 | 0 | 20 |
| 1955—Boston | 35 | 7 | 14 | .500 | 6 | 7 | .857 | 9 | 5 | 1 | 0 | 20 |
| 1956—Boston | 24 | 2 | 8 | .250 | 3 | 4 | .750 | 7 | 2 | 6 | 1 | 7 |
| 1957—Boston | 28 | 4 | 14 | .286 | 2 | 2 | 1.000 | 5 | 7 | 0 | 0 | 10 |
| 1958—Boston | 31 | 8 | 20 | .400 | 4 | 6 | .667 | 5 | 10 | 0 | 0 | 20 |
| 1959—Boston | 32 | 4 | 8 | .500 | 5 | 6 | .833 | 5 | 4 | 0 | 0 | 13 |
| 1960—Boston | 26 | 1 | 7 | .143 | 0 | 0 | ... | 5 | 8 | 2 | 0 | 2 |
| 1961—Boston | 33 | 2 | 11 | .182 | 0 | 0 | ... | 3 | 8 | 6 | 1 | 4 |
| 1962—Boston | 31 | 4 | 13 | .308 | 3 | 4 | .750 | 6 | 8 | 2 | 0 | 11 |
| 1963—Boston | 25 | 4 | 11 | .364 | 0 | 0 | ... | 4 | 6 | 2 | 0 | 8 |
| Totals | ... | 52 | 158 | .329 | 43 | 51 | .843 | 78 | 86 | 27 | 2 | 147 |

## COLLEGIATE COACHING RECORD

| Season Team | W | L | Pct. |
|---|---|---|---|
| 63-64—Boston College | 10 | 11 | .476 |
| 64-65—Boston College | 22 | 7 | .759 |
| 65-66—Boston College | 21 | 5 | .808 |
| 66-67—Boston College | 23 | 3 | .885 |
| 67-68—Boston College | 17 | 8 | .680 |
| 68-69—Boston College | 24 | 4 | .857 |
| Totals (6 years) | 117 | 38 | .755 |

## NBA COACHING RECORD

| Season Team | REGULAR SEASON W | L | Pct. | Finish | PLAYOFFS W | L | Pct. |
|---|---|---|---|---|---|---|---|
| 69-70—Cincinnati | 36 | 46 | .439 | 5th/Eastern Division | — | — | — |
| 70-71—Cincinnati | 33 | 49 | .402 | 3rd/Central Division | — | — | — |
| 71-72—Cincinnati | 30 | 52 | .366 | 3rd/Central Division | — | — | — |
| 72-73—Kansas City/Omaha | 36 | 46 | .439 | 4th/Midwest Division | — | — | — |
| 73-74—Kansas City/Omaha | 6 | 16 | .273 | | — | — | — |
| Totals (5 years) | 141 | 209 | .403 | | | | |

**NOTES:**
1965—Lost to St. John's, 114-92, in NIT first round.
1966—Defeated Louisville, 96-90 (3 OT), in NIT first round; lost to Villanova, 86-85, in quarterfinals.
1967—Defeated Connecticut, 48-42, in NCAA Tournament first round; defeated St. John's, 63-62, in regional semifinal; lost to North Carolina, 96-80, in regional final.
1968—Lost to St. Bonaventure, 102-93, in NCAA Tournament first round.
1969—Defeated Kansas, 78-62, in NIT first round; defeated Louisville, 88-83, in quarterfinals; defeated Army, 73-61, in semifinals; lost to Temple 89-76, in championship game.
1973—Replaced as Kansas City/Omaha head coach by Draff Young (November).

# COWENS, DAVE                    C

**PERSONAL:** Born October 25, 1948, in Newport, Ky. ... 6-9/230. (2,05/104,3). ... Full name: David William Cowens.
**HIGH SCHOOL:** Newport (Ky.) Central Catholic.
**COLLEGE:** Florida State.
**TRANSACTIONS/CAREER NOTES:** Selected by Boston Celtics in first round (fourth pick overall) of 1970 NBA Draft. ... Traded by Celtics to Milwaukee Bucks for G Quinn Buckner (September 9, 1982).
**CAREER HONORS:** Elected to Naismith Memorial Basketball Hall of Fame (1990). ... One of the 50 Greatest Players in NBA History (1996).
**MISCELLANEOUS:** Member of NBA championship team (1974, 1976).

## COLLEGIATE RECORD

**NOTES:** THE SPORTING NEWS All-America second team (1970).

| Season Team | G | Min. | FGM | FGA | Pct. | FTM | FTA | Pct. | Reb. | Ast. | Pts. | RPG | APG | PPG |
|---|---|---|---|---|---|---|---|---|---|---|---|---|---|---|
| | | | | | | | | | | | | AVERAGES | | |
| 66-67—Florida State‡ | 18 | ... | 105 | 208 | .505 | 49 | 90 | .544 | 357 | ... | 259 | 19.8 | ... | 14.4 |
| 67-68—Florida State | 27 | ... | 206 | 383 | .538 | 96 | 131 | .733 | 456 | ... | 508 | 16.9 | ... | 18.8 |
| 68-69—Florida State | 25 | ... | 202 | 384 | .526 | 104 | 164 | .634 | 437 | ... | 508 | 17.5 | ... | 20.3 |
| 69-70—Florida State | 26 | ... | 174 | 355 | .490 | 115 | 169 | .680 | 447 | ... | 463 | 17.2 | ... | 17.8 |
| Varsity totals | 78 | ... | 582 | 1122 | .519 | 315 | 464 | .679 | 1340 | ... | 1479 | 17.2 | ... | 19.0 |

## NBA REGULAR-SEASON RECORD

**HONORS:** NBA Most Valuable Player (1973). ... NBA co-Rookie of the Year (1971). ... All-NBA second team (1973, 1975, 1976). ... NBA All-Defensive first team (1976). ... NBA All-Defensive second team (1975, 1980). ... NBA All-Rookie team (1971).

| Season Team | G | Min. | FGM | FGA | Pct. | FTM | FTA | Pct. | Reb. | Ast. | PF | Dq. | Pts. | RPG | APG | PPG |
|---|---|---|---|---|---|---|---|---|---|---|---|---|---|---|---|---|
| 70-71—Boston | 81 | 3076 | 550 | 1302 | .422 | 273 | 373 | .732 | 1216 | 228 | *350 | 15 | 1373 | 15.0 | 2.8 | 17.0 |
| 71-72—Boston | 79 | 3186 | 657 | 1357 | .484 | 175 | 243 | .720 | 1203 | 245 | *314 | 10 | 1489 | 15.2 | 3.1 | 18.8 |
| 72-73—Boston | 82 | 3425 | 740 | 1637 | .452 | 204 | 262 | .779 | 1329 | 333 | 311 | 7 | 1684 | 16.2 | 4.1 | 20.5 |

| | | | | | | | | | REBOUNDS | | | | | | AVERAGES | | |
|---|---|---|---|---|---|---|---|---|---|---|---|---|---|---|---|---|---|---|
| Season Team | G | Min. | FGM | FGA | Pct. | FTM | FTA | Pct. | Off. | Def. | Tot. | Ast. | St. | Blk. | TO | Pts. | RPG APG PPG |
| 73-74—Boston | 80 | 3352 | 645 | 1475 | .437 | 228 | 274 | .832 | 264 | 993 | 1257 | 354 | 95 | 101 | ... | 1518 | 15.7 4.4 19.0 |
| 74-75—Boston | 65 | 2632 | 569 | 1199 | .475 | 191 | 244 | .783 | 229 | 729 | 958 | 296 | 87 | 73 | ... | 1329 | 14.7 4.6 20.4 |
| 75-76—Boston | 78 | 3101 | 611 | 1305 | .468 | 257 | 340 | .756 | 335 | 911 | 1246 | 325 | 94 | 71 | ... | 1479 | 16.0 4.2 19.0 |
| 76-77—Boston | 50 | 1888 | 328 | 756 | .434 | 162 | 198 | .818 | 147 | 550 | 697 | 248 | 46 | 49 | ... | 818 | 13.9 5.0 16.4 |
| 77-78—Boston | 77 | 3215 | 598 | 1220 | .490 | 239 | 284 | .842 | 248 | 830 | 1078 | 351 | 102 | 67 | 217 | 1435 | 14.0 4.6 18.6 |
| 78-79—Boston | 68 | 2517 | 488 | 1010 | .483 | 151 | 187 | .807 | 152 | 500 | 652 | 242 | 76 | 51 | 174 | 1127 | 9.6 3.6 16.6 |
| 79-80—Boston | 66 | 2159 | 422 | 932 | .453 | 95 | 122 | .779 | 126 | 408 | 534 | 206 | 69 | 61 | 108 | 940 | 8.1 3.1 14.2 |
| 80-81— | | | | | | | | Did not play—retired. | | | | | | | | | |
| 81-82— | | | | | | | | Did not play—retired. | | | | | | | | | |
| 82-83—Milwaukee | 40 | 1014 | 136 | 306 | .444 | 52 | 63 | .825 | 73 | 201 | 274 | 82 | 30 | 15 | 44 | 324 | 6.9 2.1 8.1 |
| Totals | 766 | 29565 | 5744 | 12499 | .460 | 2027 | 2590 | .783 | ... | ... | 10444 | 2910 | 599 | 488 | 543 | 13516 | 13.6 3.8 17.6 |

Three-point field goals: 1979-80, 1-for-12 (.083). 1982-83, 0-for-2. Totals, 1-for-14 (.071).
Personal fouls/disqualifications: 1973-74, 294/7. 1974-75, 243/7. 1975-76, 314/10. 1976-77, 181/7. 1977-78, 297/5. 1978-79, 263/16. 1979-80, 216/2. 1982-83, 137/4. Totals, 2920/90.

## NBA PLAYOFF RECORD

**NOTES:** Shares single-game playoff record for most defensive rebounds—20 (April 22, 1975, vs. Houston; and May 1, 1977, vs. Philadelphia).

| Season Team | G | Min. | FGM | FGA | Pct. | FTM | FTA | Pct. | Reb. | Ast. | PF | Dq. | Pts. | RPG | APG | PPG |
|---|---|---|---|---|---|---|---|---|---|---|---|---|---|---|---|---|
| 71-72—Boston | 11 | 441 | 71 | 156 | .455 | 28 | 47 | .596 | 152 | 33 | 50 | 2 | 170 | 13.8 | 3.0 | 15.5 |
| 72-73—Boston | 13 | 598 | 129 | 273 | .473 | 27 | 41 | .659 | 216 | 48 | 54 | 2 | 285 | 16.6 | 3.7 | 21.9 |

| | | | | | | | | | REBOUNDS | | | | | | AVERAGES | | |
|---|---|---|---|---|---|---|---|---|---|---|---|---|---|---|---|---|---|---|
| Season Team | G | Min. | FGM | FGA | Pct. | FTM | FTA | Pct. | Off. | Def. | Tot. | Ast. | St. | Blk. | TO | Pts. | RPG APG PPG |
| 73-74—Boston | 18 | 772 | 161 | 370 | .435 | 47 | 59 | .797 | 60 | 180 | 240 | 66 | 21 | 17 | ... | 369 | 13.3 3.7 20.5 |
| 74-75—Boston | 11 | 479 | 101 | 236 | .428 | 23 | 26 | .885 | 49 | 132 | 181 | 46 | 18 | 6 | ... | 225 | 16.5 4.2 20.5 |
| 75-76—Boston | 18 | 798 | 156 | 341 | .457 | 66 | 87 | .759 | 87 | 209 | 296 | 83 | 22 | 13 | ... | 378 | 16.4 4.6 21.0 |
| 76-77—Boston | 9 | 379 | 66 | 148 | .446 | 17 | 22 | .773 | 29 | 105 | 134 | 36 | 8 | 13 | ... | 149 | 14.9 4.0 16.6 |
| 79-80—Boston | 9 | 301 | 49 | 103 | .476 | 10 | 11 | .909 | 18 | 48 | 66 | 21 | 9 | 7 | 8 | 108 | 7.3 2.3 12.0 |
| Totals | 89 | 3768 | 733 | 1627 | .451 | 218 | 293 | .744 | ... | ... | 1285 | 333 | 78 | 56 | 8 | 1684 | 14.4 3.7 18.9 |

Three-point field goals: 1979-80, 0-for-2.
Personal fouls/disqualifications: 1973-74, 85/2. 1974-75, 50/2. 1975-76, 85/4. 1976-77, 37/3. 1979-80, 37/0. Totals, 398/15.

## NBA ALL-STAR GAME RECORD

**NOTES:** NBA All-Star Game Most Valuable Player (1973).

| Season Team | Min. | FGM | FGA | Pct. | FTM | FTA | Pct. | Reb | Ast. | PF | Dq. | Pts. |
|---|---|---|---|---|---|---|---|---|---|---|---|---|
| 1972—Boston | 32 | 5 | 12 | .417 | 4 | 5 | .800 | 20 | 1 | 4 | 0 | 14 |
| 1973—Boston | 30 | 7 | 15 | .467 | 1 | 1 | 1.000 | 13 | 1 | 2 | 0 | 15 |

| Season Team | Min. | FGM | FGA | Pct. | FTM | FTA | Pct. | REBOUNDS Off. | Def. | Tot. | Ast. | PF | Dq. | St. | Blk. | TO | Pts. |
|---|---|---|---|---|---|---|---|---|---|---|---|---|---|---|---|---|---|
| 1974—Boston | 26 | 5 | 10 | .500 | 1 | 3 | .333 | 6 | 6 | 12 | 1 | 3 | 0 | 0 | 1 | ... | 11 |
| 1975—Boston | 15 | 3 | 7 | .429 | 0 | 0 | ... | 0 | 6 | 6 | 3 | 4 | 0 | 1 | 0 | ... | 6 |
| 1976—Boston | 23 | 6 | 13 | .462 | 4 | 5 | .800 | 8 | 8 | 16 | 1 | 3 | 0 | 1 | 0 | ... | 16 |
| 1977—Boston | | | | | | | | Selected, did not play—injured. | | | | | | | | | |
| 1978—Boston | 28 | 7 | 9 | .778 | 0 | 0 | ... | 6 | 8 | 14 | 5 | 5 | 0 | 2 | 0 | 2 | 14 |
| Totals | 154 | 33 | 66 | .500 | 10 | 14 | .714 | ... | ... | 81 | 12 | 21 | 0 | 4 | 1 | 2 | 76 |

## HEAD COACHING RECORD

**BACKGROUND:** Assistant coach, San Antonio Spurs (1994-95 and 1995-96). ... Assistant coach, Golden State Warriors (January 31-April 20, 2000).

## NBA COACHING RECORD

| Season Team | REGULAR SEASON W | L | Pct. | Finish | PLAYOFFS W | L | Pct. |
|---|---|---|---|---|---|---|---|
| 78-79—Boston | 27 | 41 | .397 | 5th/Atlantic Division | — | — | — |
| 96-97—Charlotte | 54 | 28 | .659 | 6th/Central Division | 0 | 3 | .000 |
| 97-98—Charlotte | 51 | 31 | .622 | 3rd/Central Division | 4 | 5 | .444 |
| 98-99—Charlotte | 4 | 11 | .267 | | — | — | — |
| 00-01—Golden State | 17 | 65 | .207 | 7th/Pacific Division | — | — | — |
| 01-02—Golden State | 8 | 15 | .348 | | — | — | — |
| Totals (6 years) | 161 | 191 | .457 | Totals (2 years) | 4 | 8 | .333 |

## CBA COACHING RECORD

| Season Team | REGULAR SEASON W | L | Pct. | Finish | PLAYOFFS W | L | Pct. |
|---|---|---|---|---|---|---|---|
| 84-85—Bay State | 20 | 28 | .417 | 6th/Atlantic Division | — | — | — |

**NOTES:**
1978—Replaced Tom Sanders as Boston head coach (November), with record of 2-12.
1997—Lost to New York in Eastern Conference First Round.
1998—Defeated New Jersey, 3-1, in Eastern Conference First Round; lost to Chicago, 4-1, in Eastern Conference Semifinals.
1999—Resigned as Charlotte head coach (March 7); replaced by Paul Silas with club in seventh place.
2001—Replaced as head coach by Brian Winters (December 15) with club in seventh place.

# CUMMINGS, TERRY                    F

**PERSONAL:** Born March 15, 1961, in Chicago. ... 6-9/250. (2.06 m/113 kg). ... Full Name: Robert Terrell Cummings.
**HIGH SCHOOL:** Carver (Chicago).
**COLLEGE:** DePaul.
**TRANSACTIONS/CAREER NOTES:** Selected after junior season by San Diego Clippers in first round (second pick overall) of 1982 NBA Draft. ... Clippers franchise moved from San Diego to Los Angeles for 1984-85 season. ... Traded by Clippers with G Craig Hodges and G/F Ricky Pierce to Milwaukee Bucks for F Marques Johnson, C/F Harvey Catchings, G/F Junior Bridgeman and cash (September 29, 1984). ... Traded by Bucks with future considerations to San Antonio Spurs for G Alvin Robertson, F/C Greg Anderson and future considerations (May 28, 1989). ... Signed as unrestricted free agent by Milwaukee Bucks (November 2, 1995). ... Signed as free agent by Seattle SuperSonics (January 13, 1997). ... Signed as free agent by Philadelphia 76ers (September 4, 1997). ... Traded by 76ers to New York Knicks for F Ronnie Grandison and C Herb Williams (February 19, 1998). ... Traded by Knicks with G John Starks and F Chris Mills to Golden State Warriors for G Latrell Sprewell (January 21, 1999). ... Announced retirement (October 2, 2000).

## COLLEGIATE RECORD

**NOTES:** THE SPORTING NEWS All-America first team (1982).

| Season Team | G | Min. | FGM | FGA | Pct. | FTM | FTA | Pct. | Reb. | Ast. | Pts. | AVERAGES RPG | APG | PPG |
|---|---|---|---|---|---|---|---|---|---|---|---|---|---|---|
| 79-80—DePaul | 28 | 861 | 154 | 303 | .508 | 89 | 107 | .832 | 263 | 40 | 397 | 9.4 | 1.4 | 14.2 |
| 80-81—DePaul | 29 | 994 | 151 | 303 | .498 | 75 | 100 | .750 | 260 | 47 | 377 | 9.0 | 1.6 | 13.0 |
| 81-82—DePaul | 28 | 1031 | 244 | 430 | .567 | 136 | 180 | .756 | 334 | 57 | 624 | 11.9 | 2.0 | 22.3 |
| Totals | 85 | 2886 | 549 | 1036 | .530 | 300 | 387 | .775 | 857 | 144 | 1398 | 10.1 | 1.7 | 16.4 |

## NBA REGULAR-SEASON RECORD

**HONORS:** NBA Rookie of the Year (1983). ... All-NBA second team (1985). ... All-NBA third team (1989). ... NBA All-Rookie team (1983).

| Season Team | G | Min. | FGM | FGA | Pct. | FTM | FTA | Pct. | REBOUNDS Off. | Def. | Tot. | Ast. | St. | Blk. | TO | Pts. | AVERAGES RPG | APG | PPG |
|---|---|---|---|---|---|---|---|---|---|---|---|---|---|---|---|---|---|---|---|
| 82-83—San Diego | 70 | 2531 | 684 | 1309 | .523 | 292 | 412 | .709 | 303 | 441 | 744 | 177 | 129 | 62 | 204 | 1660 | 10.6 | 2.5 | 23.7 |
| 83-84—San Diego | 81 | 2907 | 737 | 1491 | .494 | 380 | 528 | .720 | 323 | 454 | 777 | 139 | 92 | 57 | 218 | 1854 | 9.6 | 1.7 | 22.9 |
| 84-85—Milwaukee | 79 | 2722 | 759 | 1532 | .495 | 343 | 463 | .741 | 244 | 472 | 716 | 228 | 117 | 67 | 190 | 1861 | 9.1 | 2.9 | 23.6 |
| 85-86—Milwaukee | 82 | 2669 | 681 | 1438 | .474 | 265 | 404 | .656 | 222 | 472 | 694 | 193 | 121 | 51 | 191 | 1627 | 8.5 | 2.4 | 19.8 |
| 86-87—Milwaukee | 82 | 2770 | 729 | 1426 | .511 | 249 | 376 | .662 | 214 | 486 | 700 | 229 | 129 | 81 | 172 | 1707 | 8.5 | 2.8 | 20.8 |
| 87-88—Milwaukee | 76 | 2629 | 675 | 1392 | .485 | 270 | 406 | .665 | 184 | 369 | 553 | 181 | 78 | 46 | 170 | 1621 | 7.3 | 2.4 | 21.3 |
| 88-89—Milwaukee | 80 | 2824 | 730 | 1563 | .467 | 362 | 460 | .787 | 281 | 369 | 650 | 198 | 106 | 72 | 201 | 1829 | 8.1 | 2.5 | 22.9 |
| 89-90—San Antonio | 81 | 2821 | 728 | 1532 | .475 | 343 | 440 | .780 | 226 | 451 | 677 | 219 | 110 | 52 | 202 | 1818 | 8.4 | 2.7 | 22.4 |
| 90-91—San Antonio | 67 | 2195 | 503 | 1039 | .484 | 164 | 240 | .683 | 194 | 327 | 521 | 157 | 61 | 30 | 131 | 1177 | 7.8 | 2.3 | 17.6 |
| 91-92—San Antonio | 70 | 2149 | 514 | 1053 | .488 | 177 | 249 | .711 | 247 | 384 | 631 | 102 | 58 | 34 | 115 | 1210 | 9.0 | 1.5 | 17.3 |
| 92-93—San Antonio | 8 | 76 | 11 | 29 | .379 | 5 | 10 | .500 | 6 | 13 | 19 | 4 | 1 | 1 | 2 | 27 | 2.4 | 0.5 | 3.4 |
| 93-94—San Antonio | 59 | 1133 | 183 | 428 | .428 | 63 | 107 | .589 | 132 | 165 | 297 | 50 | 31 | 13 | 59 | 429 | 5.0 | 0.8 | 7.3 |
| 94-95—San Antonio | 76 | 1273 | 224 | 464 | .483 | 72 | 123 | .585 | 138 | 240 | 378 | 59 | 36 | 19 | 95 | 520 | 5.0 | 0.8 | 6.8 |
| 95-96—Milwaukee | 81 | 1777 | 270 | 584 | .462 | 104 | 160 | .650 | 162 | 283 | 445 | 89 | 56 | 30 | 69 | 645 | 5.5 | 1.1 | 8.0 |

| Season Team | G | Min. | FGM | FGA | Pct. | FTM | FTA | Pct. | REBOUNDS Off. | Def. | Tot. | Ast. | St. | Blk. | TO | Pts. | RPG | APG | PPG |
|---|---|---|---|---|---|---|---|---|---|---|---|---|---|---|---|---|---|---|---|
| 96-97—Seattle ......... | 45 | 828 | 155 | 319 | .486 | 57 | 82 | .695 | 70 | 113 | 183 | 39 | 33 | 7 | 45 | 370 | 4.1 | 0.9 | 8.2 |
| 97-98—Phil.-New York | 74 | 1185 | 200 | 428 | .467 | 67 | 98 | .684 | 97 | 186 | 283 | 47 | 38 | 10 | 51 | 467 | 3.8 | 0.6 | 6.3 |
| 98-99—Golden State... | 50 | 1011 | 186 | 424 | .439 | 81 | 114 | .711 | 95 | 160 | 255 | 58 | 46 | 10 | 58 | 454 | 5.1 | 1.2 | 9.1 |
| 99-00—Golden State.. | 22 | 398 | 76 | 177 | .429 | 32 | 39 | .821 | 45 | 62 | 107 | 21 | 13 | 8 | 27 | 184 | 4.9 | 1.0 | 8.4 |
| **Totals** ................. | 1183 | 33898 | 8045 | 16628 | .484 | 3326 | 4711 | .706 | 3183 | 5447 | 8630 | 2190 | 1255 | 650 | 2200 | 19460 | 7.3 | 1.9 | 16.4 |

Three-point field goals: 1982-83, 0-for-1. 1983-84, 0-for-3. 1984-85, 0-for-1. 1985-86, 0-for-2. 1986-87, 0-for-3. 1987-88, 1-for-3 (.333). 1988-89, 7-for-15 (.467). 1989-90, 19-for-59 (.322). 1990-91, 7-for-33 (.212). 1991-92, 5-for-13 (.385). 1993-94, 0-for-2. 1995-96, 1-for-7 (.143). 1996-97, 3-for-5 (.600). 1997-98, 0-for-1. 1998-99, 1-for-1. Totals, 44-for-149 (.295).

Personal fouls/disqualifications: 1982-83, 294/10. 1983-84, 298/6. 1984-85, 264/4. 1985-86, 283/4. 1986-87, 296/3. 1987-88, 274/6. 1988-89, 265/5. 1989-90, 286/1. 1990-91, 225/5. 1991-92, 210/4. 1993-94, 137/0. 1995-96, 263/2. 1996-97, 113/0. 1997-98, 181/1. 1998-99, 168/4. Totals, 3836/56.

### NBA PLAYOFF RECORD

| Season Team | G | Min. | FGM | FGA | Pct. | FTM | FTA | Pct. | REBOUNDS Off. | Def. | Tot. | Ast. | St. | Blk. | TO | Pts. | RPG | APG | PPG |
|---|---|---|---|---|---|---|---|---|---|---|---|---|---|---|---|---|---|---|---|
| 84-85—Milwaukee ...... | 8 | 311 | 86 | 149 | .577 | 48 | 58 | .828 | 21 | 49 | 70 | 20 | 12 | 7 | 26 | 220 | 8.8 | 2.5 | 27.5 |
| 85-86—Milwaukee ...... | 14 | 510 | 130 | 253 | .514 | 43 | 62 | .694 | 33 | 105 | 138 | 42 | 20 | 16 | 39 | 303 | 9.9 | 3.0 | 21.6 |
| 86-87—Milwaukee ...... | 12 | 443 | 105 | 215 | .488 | 57 | 83 | .687 | 29 | 66 | 95 | 28 | 12 | 13 | 15 | 267 | 7.9 | 2.3 | 22.3 |
| 87-88—Milwaukee ...... | 5 | 193 | 50 | 89 | .562 | 29 | 44 | .659 | 12 | 27 | 39 | 13 | 9 | 3 | 12 | 129 | 7.8 | 2.6 | 25.8 |
| 88-89—Milwaukee ...... | 5 | 124 | 25 | 69 | .362 | 14 | 16 | .875 | 19 | 14 | 33 | 7 | 3 | 0 | 4 | 64 | 6.6 | 1.4 | 12.8 |
| 89-90—San Antonio.... | 10 | 375 | 103 | 195 | .528 | 42 | 52 | .808 | 31 | 63 | 94 | 22 | 7 | 4 | 19 | 249 | 9.4 | 2.2 | 24.9 |
| 90-91—San Antonio.... | 4 | 124 | 25 | 49 | .510 | 9 | 18 | .500 | 14 | 23 | 37 | 4 | 3 | 2 | 9 | 59 | 9.3 | 1.0 | 14.8 |
| 91-92—San Antonio.... | 3 | 122 | 34 | 66 | .515 | 10 | 20 | .500 | 15 | 19 | 34 | 7 | 4 | 4 | 7 | 78 | 11.3 | 2.3 | 26.0 |
| 92-93—San Antonio.... | 10 | 138 | 31 | 70 | .443 | 5 | 8 | .625 | 17 | 22 | 39 | 5 | 3 | 1 | 8 | 67 | 3.9 | 0.5 | 6.7 |
| 93-94—San Antonio.... | 4 | 72 | 11 | 22 | .500 | 10 | 12 | .833 | 10 | 15 | 25 | 2 | 5 | 3 | 4 | 32 | 6.3 | 0.5 | 8.0 |
| 94-95—San Antonio.... | 15 | 135 | 18 | 48 | .375 | 22 | 30 | .733 | 12 | 19 | 31 | 4 | 5 | 1 | 7 | 58 | 2.1 | 0.3 | 3.9 |
| 96-97—Seattle ...... | 12 | 292 | 45 | 92 | .489 | 16 | 24 | .667 | 28 | 44 | 72 | 14 | 11 | 6 | 14 | 106 | 6.0 | 1.2 | 8.8 |
| 97-98—New York ..... | 8 | 120 | 15 | 34 | .441 | 2 | 8 | .250 | 11 | 24 | 35 | 5 | 4 | 2 | 7 | 32 | 4.4 | 0.6 | 4.0 |
| **Totals** ................. | 110 | 2959 | 678 | 1351 | .502 | 307 | 435 | .706 | 252 | 490 | 742 | 173 | 98 | 62 | 171 | 1664 | 6.7 | 1.6 | 15.1 |

Three-point field goals: 1984-85, 0-for-1. 1988-89, 0-for-1. 1989-90, 1-for-5 (.200). 1990-91, 0-for-1. 1991-92, 0-for-1. 1992-93, 0-for-1. 1994-95, 0-for-1. Totals, 1-for-11 (.091).

Personal fouls/disqualifications: 1984-85, 33/1. 1988-89, 16/0. 1989-90, 39/0. 1990-91, 13/0. 1991-92, 9/0. 1992-93, 27/0. 1994-95, 25/0. Totals, 353/3.

### NBA ALL-STAR GAME RECORD

| Season Team | Min. | FGM | FGA | Pct. | FTM | FTA | Pct. | REBOUNDS Off. | Def. | Tot. | Ast. | PF | Dq. | St. | Blk. | TO | Pts. |
|---|---|---|---|---|---|---|---|---|---|---|---|---|---|---|---|---|---|
| 1985—Milwaukee............ | 16 | 7 | 17 | .412 | 3 | 4 | .750 | 4 | 3 | 7 | 0 | 1 | 0 | 0 | 1 | 0 | 17 |
| 1989—Milwaukee............ | 19 | 4 | 9 | .444 | 2 | 2 | 1.000 | 2 | 3 | 5 | 1 | 4 | 0 | 3 | 1 | 0 | 10 |
| **Totals**............................ | 35 | 11 | 26 | .423 | 5 | 6 | .833 | 6 | 6 | 12 | 1 | 5 | 0 | 3 | 2 | 0 | 27 |

## CUNNINGHAM, BILLY                                      F

See All-Time Great Coaches, page 458.

## DANIELS, MEL                                      C

**PERSONAL:** Born July 20, 1944, in Detroit. ... 6-9/225 (2,06/102,1). ... Full name: Melvin Joe Daniels.
**HIGH SCHOOL:** Pershing (Detroit).
**JUNIOR COLLEGE:** Burlington (Iowa) Junior College.
**COLLEGE:** New Mexico.
**TRANSACTIONS:** Selected by Minnesota Muskies in first round of 1967 ABA draft. ... Traded by Muskies to Indiana Pacers for 1969 first-round draft choice, G James Dawson, F Ron Kozlicki and cash (May 1968). ... Traded by Pacers with G Freddie Lewis to Memphis Sounds for F Charlie Edge and cash (July 26, 1974). ... Memphis franchise transferred to Baltimore and renamed Claws for 1975-76 season. ... Baltimore franchise folded prior to 1975-76 season. ... Signed as free agent by New York Nets of NBA (October 19, 1976). ... Waived by Nets (December 13, 1976).
**CAREER NOTES:** Scout, Pacers (1984-85 to 1995-96). ... Director of player personnel (1996 to present).
**MISCELLANEOUS:** Indiana Pacers franchise all-time leading rebounder with 7,643 (1986-74).

### COLLEGIATE RECORD

| Season Team | G | Min. | FGM | FGA | Pct. | FTM | FTA | Pct. | Reb. | Ast. | Pts. | AVERAGES RPG | APG | PPG |
|---|---|---|---|---|---|---|---|---|---|---|---|---|---|---|
| 63-64—Burlington County J.C.... | 34 | ... | 334 | ... | ... | 100 | ... | ... | ... | ... | 768 | ... | ... | 22.6 |
| 64-65—New Mexico................. | 27 | ... | 178 | 366 | .486 | 111 | 182 | .610 | 302 | ... | 467 | 11.2 | ... | 17.3 |
| 65-66—New Mexico................. | 23 | ... | 191 | 394 | .485 | 107 | 145 | .738 | 238 | ... | 489 | 10.3 | ... | 21.3 |
| 66-67—New Mexico................. | 27 | ... | 225 | 468 | .481 | 131 | 191 | .686 | 313 | ... | 581 | 11.6 | ... | 21.5 |
| **Totals** ...................................... | 111 | ... | 928 | ... | ... | 449 | ... | ... | ... | ... | 2305 | ... | ... | 20.8 |

### ABA REGULAR-SEASON RECORD

**NOTES:** ABA Most Valuable Player (1969, 1971). ... ABA Rookie of the Year (1968). ... All-ABA first team (1968, 1969, 1970, 1971). ... All-ABA second team (1973). ... ABA All-Rookie team (1968). ... Member of ABA championship team (1970, 1972, 1973).

| Season Team | G | Min. | 2-POINT FGM | FGA | Pct. | 3-POINT FGM | FGA | Pct. | FTM | FTA | Pct. | Reb. | Ast. | Pts. | AVERAGES RPG | APG | PPG |
|---|---|---|---|---|---|---|---|---|---|---|---|---|---|---|---|---|---|
| 67-68—Minnesota | 78 | 2938 | 669 | 1640 | .408 | 1 | 5 | .200 | 390 | 678 | .575 | 1213 | 109 | 1729 | *15.6 | 1.4 | 22.2 |
| 68-69—Indiana | 76 | 2934 | 712 | 1496 | .476 | 0 | 4 | .000 | 400 | 662 | .604 | 1256 | 116 | 1824 | *16.5 | 1.5 | 24.0 |
| 69-70—Indiana | 83 | 3039 | 613 | 1295 | .473 | 0 | 2 | .000 | 330 | 489 | .675 | 1462 | 131 | 1556 | 17.6 | 1.6 | 18.7 |
| 70-71—Indiana | 82 | 3170 | 698 | 1357 | .514 | 1 | 13 | .077 | 326 | 480 | .679 | 1475 | 178 | 1723 | *18.0 | 2.2 | 21.0 |
| 71-72—Indiana | 79 | 2971 | 598 | 1184 | .505 | 0 | 6 | .000 | 317 | 451 | .703 | 1297 | 176 | 1513 | 16.4 | 2.2 | 19.2 |
| 72-73—Indiana | 81 | 3103 | 587 | 1217 | .482 | 1 | 4 | .250 | 322 | 446 | .722 | 1247 | 177 | 1497 | 15.4 | 2.2 | 18.5 |
| 73-74—Indiana | 78 | 2539 | 492 | 1117 | .440 | 0 | 0 | ... | 217 | 287 | .756 | 906 | 120 | 1201 | 11.6 | 1.5 | 15.4 |
| 74-75—Memphis | 71 | 1646 | 290 | 644 | .450 | 0 | 0 | ... | 116 | 183 | .634 | 638 | 125 | 696 | 9.0 | 1.8 | 9.8 |
| Totals | 628 | 22340 | 4659 | 9950 | .468 | 3 | 34 | .088 | 2418 | 3676 | .658 | 9494 | 1132 | 11739 | 15.1 | 1.8 | 18.7 |

## ABA PLAYOFF RECORD

| Season Team | G | Min. | 2-POINT FGM | FGA | Pct. | 3-POINT FGM | FGA | Pct. | FTM | FTA | Pct. | Reb. | Ast. | Pts. | AVERAGES RPG | APG | PPG |
|---|---|---|---|---|---|---|---|---|---|---|---|---|---|---|---|---|---|
| 67-68—Minnesota | 10 | 409 | 98 | 226 | .434 | 0 | 0 | ... | 54 | 94 | .574 | 161 | 19 | 253 | 16.1 | 1.9 | 25.3 |
| 68-69—Indiana | 17 | 570 | 127 | 300 | .423 | 0 | 1 | .000 | 79 | 130 | .608 | 237 | 22 | 333 | 13.9 | 1.3 | 19.6 |
| 69-70—Indiana | 15 | 533 | 108 | 242 | .446 | 0 | 1 | .000 | 74 | 111 | .667 | 265 | 15 | 290 | 17.7 | 1.0 | 19.3 |
| 70-71—Indiana | 11 | 457 | 94 | 194 | .485 | 0 | 0 | ... | 47 | 63 | .746 | 211 | 16 | 235 | 19.2 | 1.5 | 21.4 |
| 71-72—Indiana | 20 | 744 | 121 | 249 | .486 | 0 | 3 | .000 | 64 | 85 | .753 | 302 | 28 | 306 | 15.1 | 1.4 | 15.3 |
| 72-73—Indiana | 18 | 636 | 112 | 238 | .471 | 0 | 0 | ... | 62 | 81 | .765 | 248 | 40 | 286 | 13.8 | 2.2 | 15.9 |
| 73-74—Indiana | 14 | 498 | 69 | 172 | .401 | 0 | 0 | ... | 33 | 43 | .767 | 160 | 27 | 171 | 11.4 | 1.9 | 12.2 |
| 74-75—Indiana | 4 | 54 | 11 | 22 | .500 | 0 | 0 | ... | 5 | 9 | .556 | 24 | 1 | 27 | 6.0 | 0.3 | 6.8 |
| Totals | 109 | 3901 | 740 | 1643 | .450 | 0 | 5 | .000 | 418 | 616 | .679 | 1608 | 168 | 1901 | 14.8 | 1.5 | 17.4 |

## ABA ALL-STAR GAME RECORD

NOTES: ABA All-Star Game Most Valuable Player (1971).

| Season Team | Min. | 2-POINT FGM | FGA | Pct. | 3-POINT FGM | FGA | Pct. | FTM | FTA | Pct. | Reb. | Ast. | Pts. |
|---|---|---|---|---|---|---|---|---|---|---|---|---|---|
| 1968—Minnesota | 29 | 9 | 18 | .500 | 0 | 0 | ... | 4 | 11 | .364 | 15 | 0 | 22 |
| 1969—Indiana | 31 | 5 | 16 | .313 | 0 | 0 | ... | 7 | 10 | .700 | 10 | 2 | 17 |
| 1970—Indiana | 26 | 6 | 14 | .429 | 0 | 0 | ... | 1 | 3 | .333 | 12 | 1 | 13 |
| 1971—Indiana | 30 | 12 | 19 | .632 | 0 | 0 | ... | 5 | 7 | .714 | 13 | 3 | 29 |
| 1972—Indiana | 26 | 8 | 14 | .571 | 0 | 0 | ... | 5 | 8 | .625 | 9 | 1 | 21 |
| 1973—Indiana | 33 | 8 | 19 | .421 | 0 | 0 | ... | 9 | 12 | .750 | 11 | 1 | 25 |
| 1974—Indiana | 20 | 2 | 11 | .182 | 0 | 0 | ... | 1 | 2 | .500 | 7 | 0 | 5 |
| Totals | 195 | 50 | 111 | .450 | 0 | 0 | ... | 32 | 53 | .604 | 77 | 8 | 132 |

## NBA REGULAR-SEASON RECORD

| Season Team | G | Min. | FGM | FGA | Pct. | FTM | FTA | Pct. | REBOUNDS Off. | Def. | Tot. | Ast. | St. | Blk. | TO | Pts. | AVERAGES RPG | APG | PPG |
|---|---|---|---|---|---|---|---|---|---|---|---|---|---|---|---|---|---|---|---|
| 76-77—N.Y. Nets | 11 | 126 | 13 | 35 | .371 | 13 | 23 | .565 | 10 | 24 | 34 | 6 | 3 | 11 | ... | 39 | 3.1 | 0.5 | 3.5 |

Personal fouls/disqualifications: 1976-77, 29/0.

## COMBINED ABA AND NBA REGULAR-SEASON RECORDS

| | G | Min. | FGM | FGA | Pct. | FTM | FTA | Pct. | REBOUNDS Off. | Def. | Tot. | Ast. | Stl. | Blk. | TO | Pts. | AVERAGES RPG | APG | PPG |
|---|---|---|---|---|---|---|---|---|---|---|---|---|---|---|---|---|---|---|---|
| Totals | 639 | 22466 | 4675 | 10019 | .467 | 2431 | 3699 | .657 | ... | ... | 9528 | 1138 | ... | ... | ... | 11778 | 14.9 | 1.8 | 18.4 |

Three-point field goals: 3-for-34 (.088).
Personal fouls/disqualifications: 2309.

## HEAD COACHING RECORD

BACKGROUND: Assistant coach, Indiana State (1978-79 through 1981-82). ... Assistant coach, Indiana Pacers (1984-85 through 1988-89 and 1991-92 and 1992-93).
HONORS: USBL Coach of the Year (1993).

## NBA COACHING RECORD

| Season Team | REGULAR SEASON W | L | Pct. | Finish | PLAYOFFS W | L | Pct. |
|---|---|---|---|---|---|---|---|
| 88-89—Indiana | 0 | 2 | .000 | | — | — | — |

NOTES:
1988—Replaced Jack Ramsay as Indiana head coach (November 17), with record of 0-7 and club in sixth place. Replaced as Indiana interim coach by George Irvine (November 21).

---

# DANTLEY, ADRIAN  F/G

PERSONAL: Born February 28, 1956, in Washington, D.C. ... 6-5/210 (1,96/95,3). ... Full name: Adrian Delano Dantley.
HIGH SCHOOL: DeMatha Catholic (Hyattsville, Md.).
COLLEGE: Notre Dame.
TRANSACTIONS: Selected after junior season by Buffalo Braves in first round (sixth pick overall) of 1976 NBA Draft. ... Traded by Braves with F Mike Bantom to Indiana Pacers for G/F Billy Knight (September 1, 1977). ... Traded by Pacers with C/F Dave Robisch to Los Angeles Lakers for C James Edwards, G Earl Tatum and cash (December 13, 1977). ... Traded by Lakers to Utah Jazz for F Spencer Haywood (September 13, 1979). ... Traded by Jazz with 1987 and 1990 second-round draft choices to Detroit Pistons for F Kelly Tripucka and F/C Kent Benson (August 21, 1986). ... Traded by Pistons with 1991 first-round draft choice to Dallas Mavericks for F Mark Aguirre (February 15, 1989). ... Waived by Mavericks (April 2, 1990). ... Signed as free agent by Milwaukee Bucks (April 2, 1991). ... Played in Italy (1991-92).
MISCELLANEOUS: Member of gold-medal-winning U.S. Olympic team (1976).

## COLLEGIATE RECORD

**NOTES:** THE SPORTING NEWS All-America first team (1975, 1976).

| | | | | | | | | | | | | AVERAGES | | |
|---|---|---|---|---|---|---|---|---|---|---|---|---|---|---|
| Season Team | G | Min. | FGM | FGA | Pct. | FTM | FTA | Pct. | Reb. | Ast. | Pts. | RPG | APG | PPG |
| 73-74—Notre Dame | 28 | 795 | 189 | 339 | .558 | 133 | 161 | .826 | 255 | 40 | 511 | 9.1 | 1.4 | 18.3 |
| 74-75—Notre Dame | 29 | 1091 | 315 | 581 | .542 | 253 | 314 | .806 | 296 | 47 | 883 | 10.2 | 1.6 | 30.4 |
| 75-76—Notre Dame | 29 | 1056 | 300 | 510 | .588 | 229 | 294 | .779 | 292 | 49 | 829 | 10.1 | 1.7 | 28.6 |
| Totals | 86 | 2942 | 804 | 1430 | .562 | 615 | 769 | .800 | 843 | 136 | 2223 | 9.8 | 1.6 | 25.8 |

## NBA REGULAR-SEASON RECORD

**RECORDS:** Shares single-game records for most free throws made—28 (January 4, 1984, vs. Houston); and most free throws made in one quarter—14 (December 10, 1986, vs. Sacramento).

**HONORS:** NBA Rookie of the Year (1977). ... All-NBA second team (1981, 1984). ... NBA All-Rookie team (1977). ... NBA Comeback Player of the Year (1984).

| | | | | | | | | | REBOUNDS | | | | | | | | AVERAGES | | |
|---|---|---|---|---|---|---|---|---|---|---|---|---|---|---|---|---|---|---|---|
| Season Team | G | Min. | FGM | FGA | Pct. | FTM | FTA | Pct. | Off. | Def. | Tot. | Ast. | St. | Blk. | TO | Pts. | RPG | APG | PPG |
| 76-77—Buffalo | 77 | 2816 | 544 | 1046 | .520 | 476 | 582 | .818 | 251 | 336 | 587 | 144 | 91 | 15 | ... | 1564 | 7.6 | 1.9 | 20.3 |
| 77-78—Ind.-L.A. | 79 | 2933 | 578 | 1128 | .512 | *541 | 680 | .796 | 265 | 355 | 620 | 253 | 118 | 24 | 228 | 1697 | 7.8 | 3.2 | 21.5 |
| 78-79—Los Angeles | 60 | 1775 | 374 | 733 | .510 | 292 | 342 | .854 | 131 | 211 | 342 | 138 | 63 | 12 | 155 | 1040 | 5.7 | 2.3 | 17.3 |
| 79-80—Utah | 68 | 2674 | 730 | 1267 | .576 | 443 | 526 | .842 | 183 | 333 | 516 | 191 | 96 | 14 | 233 | 1903 | 7.6 | 2.8 | 28.0 |
| 80-81—Utah | 80 | *3417 | *909 | 1627 | .559 | *632 | 784 | .806 | 192 | 317 | 509 | 322 | 109 | 18 | 282 | *2452 | 6.4 | 4.0 | *30.7 |
| 81-82—Utah | 81 | 3222 | 904 | 1586 | .570 | *648 | 818 | .792 | 231 | 283 | 514 | 324 | 95 | 14 | †299 | 2457 | 6.3 | 4.0 | 30.3 |
| 82-83—Utah | 22 | 887 | 233 | 402 | .580 | 210 | 248 | .847 | 58 | 82 | 140 | 105 | 20 | 0 | 81 | 676 | 6.4 | 4.8 | 30.7 |
| 83-84—Utah | 79 | 2984 | 802 | 1438 | .558 | *813 | *946 | .859 | 179 | 269 | 448 | 310 | 61 | 4 | 263 | *2418 | 5.7 | 3.9 | *30.6 |
| 84-85—Utah | 55 | 1971 | 512 | 964 | .531 | 438 | 545 | .804 | 148 | 175 | 323 | 186 | 57 | 8 | 171 | 1462 | 5.9 | 3.4 | 26.6 |
| 85-86—Utah | 76 | 2744 | 818 | 1453 | .563 | *630 | 796 | .791 | 178 | 217 | 395 | 264 | 64 | 4 | 231 | 2267 | 5.2 | 3.5 | |
| 29.886-87—Detroit | 81 | 2736 | 601 | 1126 | .534 | 539 | 664 | .812 | 104 | 228 | 332 | 162 | 63 | 7 | 181 | 1742 | 4.1 | 2.0 | 21.5 |
| 87-88—Detroit | 69 | 2144 | 444 | 863 | .514 | 492 | 572 | .860 | 84 | 143 | 227 | 171 | 39 | 10 | 135 | 1380 | 3.3 | 2.5 | 20.0 |
| 88-89—Detroit-Dal. | 73 | 2422 | 470 | 954 | .493 | 460 | 568 | .810 | 117 | 200 | 317 | 171 | 43 | 13 | 163 | 1400 | 4.3 | 2.3 | 19.2 |
| 89-90—Dallas | 45 | 1300 | 231 | 484 | .477 | 200 | 254 | .787 | 78 | 94 | 172 | 80 | 20 | 7 | 75 | 662 | 3.8 | 1.8 | 14.7 |
| 90-91—Milwaukee | 10 | 126 | 19 | 50 | .380 | 18 | 26 | .692 | 8 | 5 | 13 | 9 | 5 | 0 | 6 | 57 | 1.3 | 0.9 | 5.7 |
| Totals | 955 | 34151 | 8169 | 15121 | .540 | 6832 | 8351 | .818 | 2207 | 3248 | 5455 | 2830 | 944 | 150 | 2503 | 23177 | 5.7 | 3.0 | 24.3 |

Three-point field goals: 1979-80, 0-for-2. 1980-81, 2-for-7 (.286). 1981-82, 1-for-3 (.333). 1983-84, 1-for-4 (.250). 1985-86, 1-for-11 (.091). 1986-87, 1-for-6 (.167). 1987-88, 0-for-2. 1988-89, 0-for-1. 1989-90, 0-for-2. 1990-91, 1-for-3 (.333). Totals, 7-for-41 (.171).

Personal fouls/disqualifications: 1976-77, 215/2. 1977-78, 233/2. 1978-79, 162/0. 1979-80, 211/2. 1980-81, 245/1. 1981-82, 252/1. 1982-83, 62/2. 1983-84, 201/0. 1984-85, 133/0. 1985-86, 206/2. 1986-87, 193/1. 1987-88, 144/0. 1988-89, 186/1. 1989-90, 99/0. 1990-91, 8/0. Totals, 2550/14.

## NBA PLAYOFF RECORD

| | | | | | | | | | REBOUNDS | | | | | | | | AVERAGES | | |
|---|---|---|---|---|---|---|---|---|---|---|---|---|---|---|---|---|---|---|---|
| Season Team | G | Min. | FGM | FGA | Pct. | FTM | FTA | Pct. | Off. | Def. | Tot. | Ast. | St. | Bik. | TO | Pts. | RPG | APG | PPG |
| 77-78—Los Angeles | 3 | 104 | 20 | 35 | .571 | 11 | 17 | .647 | 9 | 16 | 25 | 11 | 5 | 3 | 6 | 51 | 8.3 | 3.7 | 17.0 |
| 78-79—Los Angeles | 8 | 236 | 50 | 89 | .562 | 41 | 52 | .788 | 10 | 23 | 33 | 11 | 6 | 1 | 19 | 141 | 4.1 | 1.4 | 17.6 |
| 83-84—Utah | 11 | 454 | 117 | 232 | .504 | 120 | 139 | .863 | 37 | 46 | 83 | 46 | 10 | 1 | 38 | 354 | 7.5 | 4.2 | 32.2 |
| 84-85—Utah | 10 | 398 | 79 | 151 | .523 | 95 | 122 | .779 | 25 | 50 | 75 | 20 | 16 | 0 | 36 | 253 | 7.5 | 2.0 | 25.3 |
| 85-86—Utah | | | | | Did not play—injured. | | | | | | | | | | | | | | |
| 86-87—Detroit | 15 | 500 | 111 | 206 | .539 | 86 | 111 | .775 | 29 | 39 | 68 | 35 | 13 | 0 | 33 | 308 | 4.5 | 2.3 | 20.5 |
| 87-88—Detroit | 23 | 804 | 153 | 292 | .524 | 140 | 178 | .787 | 37 | 70 | 107 | 46 | 19 | 1 | 51 | 446 | 4.7 | 2.0 | 19.4 |
| 90-91—Milwaukee | 3 | 19 | 1 | 7 | .143 | 3 | 4 | .750 | 2 | 2 | 4 | 0 | 0 | 0 | 2 | 5 | 1.3 | 0.0 | 1.7 |
| Totals | 73 | 2515 | 531 | 1012 | .525 | 496 | 623 | .796 | 149 | 246 | 395 | 169 | 69 | 6 | 185 | 1558 | 5.4 | 2.3 | 21.3 |

Three-point field goals: 1984-85, 0-for-1. 1987-88, 0-for-2. Totals, 0-for-3.

Personal fouls/disqualifications: 1977-78, 9/0. 1978-79, 24/0. 1983-84, 30/0. 1984-85, 39/1. 1986-87, 36/0. 1987-88, 50/0. Totals, 188/1.

## NBA ALL-STAR GAME RECORD

| | | | | | | | | REBOUNDS | | | | | | | | | |
|---|---|---|---|---|---|---|---|---|---|---|---|---|---|---|---|---|---|
| Season Team | Min. | FGM | FGA | Pct. | FTM | FTA | Pct. | Off. | Def. | Tot. | Ast. | PF | Dq. | St. | Blk. | TO | Pts. |
| 1980—Utah | 30 | 8 | 15 | .533 | 7 | 8 | .875 | 4 | 1 | 5 | 2 | 1 | 0 | 2 | 0 | 2 | 23 |
| 1981—Utah | 21 | 3 | 9 | .333 | 2 | 2 | 1.000 | 2 | 3 | 5 | 0 | 1 | 0 | 1 | 0 | 0 | 8 |
| 1982—Utah | 21 | 6 | 8 | .750 | 0 | 1 | .000 | 1 | 1 | 2 | 0 | 2 | 0 | 0 | 1 | 1 | 12 |
| 1984—Utah | 18 | 1 | 8 | .125 | 0 | 0 | ... | 0 | 2 | 2 | 1 | 4 | 0 | 1 | 0 | 1 | 2 |
| 1985—Utah | 23 | 2 | 6 | .333 | 6 | 6 | 1.000 | 0 | 2 | 2 | 1 | 4 | 0 | 1 | 0 | 2 | 10 |
| 1986—Utah | 17 | 3 | 8 | .375 | 2 | 2 | 1.000 | 1 | 6 | 7 | 3 | 1 | 0 | 1 | 0 | 0 | 8 |
| Totals | 130 | 23 | 54 | .426 | 17 | 19 | .895 | 8 | 15 | 23 | 7 | 13 | 0 | 6 | 0 | 6 | 63 |

## ITALIAN LEAGUE RECORD

| | | | | | | | | | | | | AVERAGES | | |
|---|---|---|---|---|---|---|---|---|---|---|---|---|---|---|
| Season Team | G | Min. | FGM | FGA | Pct. | FTM | FTA | Pct. | Reb. | Ast. | Pts. | RPG | APG | PPG |
| 91-92—Breeze Milan | 27 | 906 | 253 | 427 | .593 | 179 | 221 | .810 | 152 | 10 | 721 | 5.6 | 0.4 | 26.7 |

## DAVIES, BOB     G

**PERSONAL:** Born January 15, 1920, in Harrisburg, Pa. ... Died April 22, 1990. ... 6-1/175 (1,85/79,4). ... Full name: Robert Edris Davies. ... Nickname: The Harrisburg Houdini.
**HIGH SCHOOL:** John Harris (Harrisburg, Pa.).
**COLLEGE:** Franklin & Marshall (Pa.), then Seton Hall.
**TRANSACTIONS:** Played with Great Lakes (Ill.) Naval Training Station during 1942-43 season (led team in scoring—269 points, 114 field goals and 41 free throws). ... In military service during 1942-43, 1943-44 and 1944-45 seasons. ... Played in American

Basketball League with Brooklyn Indians (1943-44) and New York Gothams (1944-45). ... Signed as free agent by Rochester Royals of National Basketball League (1945). ... Royals franchise transferred to Basketball Association of America for 1948-49 season.

**CAREER HONORS:** Elected to Naismith Memorial Basketball Hall of Fame (1970). ... NBA 25th Anniversary All-Time Team (1970).

**MISCELLANEOUS:** Member of NBA championship team (1951). ... Member of NBL championship team (1946).

## COLLEGIATE RECORD

| Season Team | G | Min. | FGM | FGA | Pct. | FTM | FTA | Pct. | Reb. | Ast. | Pts. | AVERAGES RPG | APG | PPG |
|---|---|---|---|---|---|---|---|---|---|---|---|---|---|---|
| 37-38—Frank. & Marshall‡ | | | | | Freshman team statistics unavailable. | | | | | | | | | |
| 38-39—Seton Hall‡ | | | | | Freshman team statistics unavailable. | | | | | | | | | |
| 39-40—Seton Hall | 18 | ... | 78 | ... | ... | 56 | ... | ... | ... | ... | 212 | ... | ... | 11.8 |
| 40-41—Seton Hall | 22 | ... | 91 | ... | ... | 42 | ... | ... | ... | ... | 224 | ... | ... | 10.2 |
| 41-42—Seton Hall | 19 | ... | 81 | ... | ... | 63 | ... | ... | ... | ... | 225 | ... | ... | 11.8 |
| Varsity totals | 59 | ... | 250 | ... | ... | 161 | ... | ... | ... | ... | 661 | ... | ... | 11.2 |

## ABL REGULAR-SEASON RECORD

| Season Team | G | Min. | FGM | FGA | Pct. | FTM | FTA | Pct. | Reb. | Ast. | Pts. | AVERAGES RPG | APG | PPG |
|---|---|---|---|---|---|---|---|---|---|---|---|---|---|---|
| 43-44—Brooklyn | 4 | ... | 8 | ... | ... | 8 | ... | ... | ... | ... | 24 | ... | ... | 6.0 |
| 44-45—New York | 5 | ... | 21 | ... | ... | 21 | ... | ... | ... | ... | 63 | ... | ... | 12.6 |
| Totals | 9 | ... | 29 | ... | ... | 29 | ... | ... | ... | ... | 87 | ... | ... | 9.7 |

## NBL AND NBA REGULAR-SEASON RECORD

**HONORS:** All-NBA first team (1950, 1951, 1952). ... All-NBA second team (1953). ... All-BAA first team (1949). ... NBL Most Valuable Player (1947). ... All-NBL first team (1947). ... All-NBL second team (1948).

| Season Team | G | Min. | FGM | FGA | Pct. | FTM | FTA | Pct. | Reb. | Ast. | PF | Dq. | Pts. | AVERAGES RPG | APG | PPG |
|---|---|---|---|---|---|---|---|---|---|---|---|---|---|---|---|---|
| 45-46—Rochester (NBL) | 27 | ... | 86 | ... | ... | 70 | 103 | .680 | ... | ... | 85 | ... | 242 | ... | ... | 9.0 |
| 46-47—Rochester (NBL) | 32 | ... | 166 | ... | ... | 130 | 166 | .783 | ... | ... | 90 | ... | 462 | ... | ... | 14.4 |
| 47-48—Rochester (NBL) | 48 | ... | 176 | ... | ... | 120 | 160 | .750 | ... | ... | 111 | ... | 472 | ... | ... | 9.8 |
| 48-49—Rochester (BAA) | 60 | ... | 317 | 871 | .364 | 270 | 348 | .776 | ... | *321 | 197 | ... | 904 | ... | *5.4 | 15.1 |
| 49-50—Rochester | 64 | ... | 317 | 887 | .357 | 261 | 347 | .752 | ... | 294 | 187 | ... | 895 | ... | 4.6 | 14.0 |
| 50-51—Rochester | 63 | ... | 326 | 877 | .372 | 303 | 381 | .795 | 197 | 287 | 208 | 7 | 955 | 3.1 | 4.6 | 15.2 |
| 51-52—Rochester | 65 | 2394 | 379 | 990 | .383 | 294 | 379 | .776 | 189 | 390 | 269 | 10 | 1052 | 2.9 | 6.0 | 16.2 |
| 52-53—Rochester | 66 | 2216 | 339 | 880 | .385 | 351 | 466 | .753 | 195 | 280 | 261 | 7 | 1029 | 3.0 | 4.2 | 15.6 |
| 53-54—Rochester | 72 | 2137 | 288 | 777 | .371 | 311 | 433 | .718 | 194 | 323 | 224 | 4 | 887 | 2.7 | 4.5 | 12.3 |
| 54-55—Rochester | 72 | 1870 | 326 | 785 | .415 | 220 | 293 | .751 | 205 | 355 | 220 | 2 | 872 | 2.8 | 4.9 | 12.1 |
| Totals | 569 | ... | 2720 | ... | ... | 2330 | 3076 | .757 | ... | ... | 1852 | ... | 7770 | ... | ... | 13.7 |

## NBL AND NBA PLAYOFF RECORD

| Season Team | G | Min. | FGM | FGA | Pct. | FTM | FTA | Pct. | Reb. | Ast. | PF | Dq. | Pts. | AVERAGES RPG | APG | PPG |
|---|---|---|---|---|---|---|---|---|---|---|---|---|---|---|---|---|
| 45-46—Rochester (NBL) | 7 | ... | 28 | ... | ... | 30 | 41 | .732 | ... | ... | 17 | ... | 86 | ... | ... | 12.3 |
| 46-47—Rochester (NBL) | 11 | ... | 54 | ... | ... | 43 | 63 | .683 | ... | ... | 30 | ... | 151 | ... | ... | 13.7 |
| 47-48—Rochester (NBL) | 11 | ... | 56 | ... | ... | 49 | 64 | .766 | ... | ... | 24 | ... | 161 | ... | ... | 14.6 |
| 48-49—Rochester (BAA) | 4 | ... | 19 | 51 | .373 | 10 | 13 | .769 | ... | 13 | 11 | ... | 48 | ... | 3.3 | 12.0 |
| 49-50—Rochester | 2 | ... | 4 | 17 | .235 | 7 | 8 | .875 | ... | 9 | 11 | ... | 15 | ... | 4.5 | 7.5 |
| 50-51—Rochester | 14 | ... | 79 | 234 | .338 | 64 | 80 | .800 | 43 | 75 | 45 | 1 | 222 | 3.1 | 5.4 | 15.9 |
| 51-52—Rochester | 6 | 233 | 37 | 92 | .402 | 45 | 55 | .818 | 13 | 28 | 18 | 0 | 119 | 2.2 | 4.7 | 19.8 |
| 52-53—Rochester | 3 | 91 | 6 | 29 | .207 | 14 | 20 | .700 | 4 | 14 | 11 | 0 | 26 | 1.3 | 4.7 | 8.7 |
| 53-54—Rochester | 6 | 172 | 17 | 52 | .327 | 17 | 23 | .739 | 12 | 14 | 16 | 0 | 51 | 2.0 | 2.3 | 8.5 |
| 54-55—Rochester | 3 | 75 | 11 | 33 | .333 | 3 | 4 | .750 | 6 | 9 | 11 | 0 | 25 | 2.0 | 3.0 | 8.3 |
| Totals | 67 | ... | 311 | ... | ... | 282 | 371 | .760 | ... | ... | 194 | ... | 904 | ... | ... | 13.5 |

## NBA ALL-STAR GAME RECORD

| Season Team | Min. | FGM | FGA | Pct. | FTM | FTA | Pct. | Reb | Ast. | PF | Dq. | Pts. |
|---|---|---|---|---|---|---|---|---|---|---|---|---|
| 1951—Rochester | ... | 4 | 6 | .667 | 5 | 5 | 1.000 | 5 | 5 | 3 | 0 | 13 |
| 1952—Rochester | 27 | 4 | 11 | .364 | 0 | 0 | | 0 | 5 | 4 | 0 | 8 |
| 1953—Rochester | 17 | 3 | 7 | .429 | 3 | 6 | .500 | 3 | 2 | 2 | 0 | 9 |
| 1954—Rochester | 31 | 8 | 16 | .500 | 2 | 3 | .667 | 5 | 5 | 4 | 0 | 18 |
| Totals | ... | 19 | 40 | .475 | 10 | 14 | .714 | 13 | 17 | 13 | 0 | 48 |

## COLLEGIATE COACHING RECORD

| Season Team | W | L | Pct. |
|---|---|---|---|
| 46-47—Seton Hall | 24 | 3 | .889 |
| 55-56—Gettysburg | 11 | 17 | .393 |
| 56-57—Gettysburg | 7 | 18 | .280 |
| Totals (3 years) | 42 | 38 | .525 |

## DAVIS, WALTER     G

**PERSONAL:** Born September 9, 1954, in Pineville, N.C. ... 6-6/200 (1,98/90,7). ... Full name: Walter Paul Davis. ... Uncle of Hubert Davis, guard with Washington Wizards.

**HIGH SCHOOL:** South Mecklenburg (Charlotte).

**COLLEGE:** North Carolina.

**TRANSACTIONS:** Selected by Phoenix Suns in first round (fifth pick overall) of 1977 NBA Draft. ... Signed as unrestricted free agent by Denver Nuggets (July 6, 1988). ... Traded by Nuggets to Portland Trail Blazers in three-way deal in which Trail Blazers sent G

Drazen Petrovic to New Jersey Nets, Nets sent F Greg Anderson to Nuggets, and Nuggets sent F Terry Mills to Nets (January 23, 1991); Nuggets also received 1992 first-round draft choice from Nets and 1993 second-round draft choice from Trail Blazers and Trail Blazers also received 1992 second-round draft choice from Nuggets. ... Waived by Trail Blazers (October 29, 1991). ... Signed as free agent by Nuggets (November 1, 1991).

**MISCELLANEOUS:** Member of gold-medal-winning U.S. Olympic team (1976). ... Phoenix Suns all-time leading scorer with 15,666 points (1977-78 through 1987-88).

## COLLEGIATE RECORD

| Season Team | G | Min. | FGM | FGA | Pct. | FTM | FTA | Pct. | Reb. | Ast. | Pts. | AVERAGES RPG | APG | PPG |
|---|---|---|---|---|---|---|---|---|---|---|---|---|---|---|
| 73-74—North Carolina | 27 | ... | 161 | 322 | .500 | 65 | 82 | .793 | 126 | 72 | 387 | 4.7 | 2.7 | 14.3 |
| 74-75—North Carolina | 31 | ... | 200 | 396 | .505 | 98 | 130 | .754 | 195 | 137 | 498 | 6.3 | 4.4 | 16.1 |
| 75-76—North Carolina | 29 | ... | 190 | 351 | .541 | 101 | 130 | .777 | 166 | 96 | 481 | 5.7 | 3.3 | 16.6 |
| 76-77—North Carolina | 32 | ... | 203 | 351 | .578 | 91 | 117 | .778 | 183 | 104 | 497 | 5.7 | 3.3 | 15.5 |
| Totals | 119 | ... | 754 | 1420 | .531 | 355 | 459 | .773 | 670 | 409 | 1863 | 5.6 | 3.4 | 15.7 |

## NBA REGULAR-SEASON RECORD

**HONORS:** NBA Rookie of the Year (1978). ... All-NBA second team (1978, 1979). ... NBA All-Rookie team (1978).

| Season Team | G | Min. | FGM | FGA | Pct. | FTM | FTA | Pct. | REBOUNDS Off. | Def. | Tot. | Ast. | St. | Blk. | TO | Pts. | AVERAGES RPG | APG | PPG |
|---|---|---|---|---|---|---|---|---|---|---|---|---|---|---|---|---|---|---|---|
| 77-78—Phoenix | 81 | 2590 | 786 | 1494 | .526 | 387 | 466 | .830 | 158 | 326 | 484 | 273 | 113 | 20 | 283 | 1959 | 6.0 | 3.4 | 24.2 |
| 78-79—Phoenix | 79 | 2437 | 764 | 1362 | .561 | 340 | 409 | .831 | 111 | 262 | 373 | 339 | 147 | 26 | 293 | 1868 | 4.7 | 4.3 | 23.6 |
| 79-80—Phoenix | 75 | 2309 | 657 | 1166 | .563 | 299 | 365 | .819 | 75 | 197 | 272 | 337 | 114 | 19 | 242 | 1613 | 3.6 | 4.5 | 21.5 |
| 80-81—Phoenix | 78 | 2182 | 593 | 1101 | .539 | 209 | 250 | .836 | 63 | 137 | 200 | 302 | 97 | 12 | 222 | 1402 | 2.6 | 3.9 | 18.0 |
| 81-82—Phoenix | 55 | 1182 | 350 | 669 | .523 | 91 | 111 | .820 | 21 | 82 | 103 | 162 | 46 | 3 | 112 | 794 | 1.9 | 2.9 | 14.4 |
| 82-83—Phoenix | 80 | 2491 | 665 | 1289 | .516 | 184 | 225 | .818 | 63 | 134 | 197 | 397 | 117 | 12 | 188 | 1521 | 2.5 | 5.0 | 19.0 |
| 83-84—Phoenix | 78 | 2546 | 652 | 1274 | .512 | 233 | 270 | .863 | 38 | 164 | 202 | 429 | 107 | 12 | 213 | 1557 | 2.6 | 5.5 | 20.0 |
| 84-85—Phoenix | 23 | 570 | 139 | 309 | .450 | 64 | 73 | .877 | 6 | 29 | 35 | 98 | 18 | 0 | 50 | 345 | 1.5 | 4.3 | 15.0 |
| 85-86—Phoenix | 70 | 2239 | 624 | 1287 | .485 | 257 | 305 | .843 | 54 | 149 | 203 | 361 | 99 | 3 | 219 | 1523 | 2.9 | 5.2 | 21.8 |
| 86-87—Phoenix | 79 | 2646 | 779 | 1515 | .514 | 288 | 334 | .862 | 90 | 154 | 244 | 364 | 96 | 5 | 226 | 1867 | 3.1 | 4.6 | 23.6 |
| 87-88—Phoenix | 68 | 1951 | 488 | 1031 | .473 | 205 | 231 | .887 | 32 | 127 | 159 | 278 | 86 | 3 | 126 | 1217 | 2.3 | 4.1 | 17.9 |
| 88-89—Denver | 81 | 1857 | 536 | 1076 | .498 | 175 | 199 | .879 | 41 | 110 | 151 | 190 | 72 | 5 | 132 | 1267 | 1.9 | 2.3 | 15.6 |
| 89-90—Denver | 69 | 1635 | 497 | 1033 | .481 | 207 | 227 | .912 | 46 | 133 | 179 | 155 | 59 | 9 | 102 | 1207 | 2.6 | 2.2 | 17.5 |
| 90-91—Den.-Port. | 71 | 1483 | 403 | 862 | .468 | 107 | 117 | .915 | 71 | 110 | 181 | 125 | 80 | 3 | 88 | 924 | 2.5 | 1.8 | 13.0 |
| 91-92—Denver | 46 | 741 | 185 | 403 | .459 | 82 | 94 | .872 | 20 | 50 | 70 | 68 | 29 | 1 | 45 | 457 | 1.5 | 1.5 | 9.9 |
| Totals | 1033 | 28859 | 8118 | 15871 | .511 | 3128 | 3676 | .851 | 889 | 2164 | 3053 | 3878 | 1280 | 133 | 2541 | 19521 | 3.0 | 3.8 | 18.9 |

Three-point field goals: 1979-80, 0-for-4. 1980-81, 7-for-17 (.412). 1981-82, 3-for-16 (.188). 1982-83, 7-for-23 (.304). 1983-84, 20-for-87 (.230). 1984-85, 3-for-10 (.300). 1985-86, 18-for-76 (.237). 1986-87, 21-for-81 (.259). 1987-88, 36-for-96 (.375). 1988-89, 20-for-69 (.290). 1989-90, 6-for-46 (.130). 1990-91, 11-for-36 (.306). 1991-92, 5-for-16 (.313). Totals, 157-for-577 (.272).

Personal fouls/disqualifications: 1977-78, 242/2. 1978-79, 250/5. 1979-80, 202/2. 1980-81, 192/3. 1981-82, 104/1. 1982-83, 186/2. 1983-84, 202/0. 1984-85, 42/0. 1985-86, 153/1. 1986-87, 184/1. 1987-88, 131/0. 1988-89, 187/1. 1989-90, 160/1. 1990-91, 150/2. 1991-92, 69/0. Totals, 2454/21.

## NBA PLAYOFF RECORD

| Season Team | G | Min. | FGM | FGA | Pct. | FTM | FTA | Pct. | REBOUNDS Off. | Def. | Tot. | Ast. | St. | Blk. | TO | Pts. | AVERAGES RPG | APG | PPG |
|---|---|---|---|---|---|---|---|---|---|---|---|---|---|---|---|---|---|---|---|
| 77-78—Phoenix | 2 | 66 | 19 | 40 | .475 | 12 | 16 | .750 | 4 | 13 | 17 | 8 | 3 | 0 | 6 | 50 | 8.5 | 4.0 | 25.0 |
| 78-79—Phoenix | 15 | 490 | 127 | 244 | .521 | 78 | 96 | .813 | 24 | 45 | 69 | 79 | 26 | 5 | 66 | 332 | 4.6 | 5.3 | 22.1 |
| 79-80—Phoenix | 8 | 245 | 69 | 137 | .504 | 28 | 38 | .737 | 9 | 14 | 23 | 35 | 4 | 1 | 20 | 166 | 2.9 | 4.4 | 20.8 |
| 80-81—Phoenix | 7 | 199 | 51 | 106 | .481 | 10 | 17 | .588 | 7 | 12 | 19 | 22 | 7 | 1 | 17 | 112 | 2.7 | 3.1 | 16.0 |
| 81-82—Phoenix | 7 | 173 | 52 | 116 | .448 | 22 | 24 | .917 | 5 | 17 | 22 | 30 | 5 | 1 | 12 | 127 | 3.1 | 4.3 | 18.1 |
| 82-83—Phoenix | 3 | 113 | 30 | 69 | .435 | 17 | 21 | .810 | 5 | 10 | 15 | 13 | 6 | 5 | 5 | 78 | 5.0 | 4.3 | 26.0 |
| 83-84—Phoenix | 17 | 623 | 175 | 327 | .535 | 70 | 78 | .897 | 15 | 31 | 46 | 109 | 29 | 3 | 43 | 423 | 2.7 | 6.4 | 24.9 |
| 88-89—Denver | 3 | 94 | 31 | 60 | .517 | 15 | 15 | 1.000 | 2 | 3 | 5 | 4 | 3 | 0 | 8 | 77 | 1.7 | 1.3 | 25.7 |
| 89-90—Denver | 3 | 70 | 18 | 45 | .400 | 6 | 6 | 1.000 | 4 | 5 | 9 | 6 | 1 | 0 | 5 | 42 | 3.0 | 2.0 | 14.0 |
| 90-91—Portland | 13 | 111 | 19 | 48 | .396 | 5 | 6 | .833 | 7 | 8 | 15 | 6 | 4 | 0 | 7 | 43 | 1.2 | 0.5 | 3.3 |
| Totals | 78 | 2184 | 591 | 1192 | .496 | 263 | 317 | .830 | 82 | 158 | 240 | 312 | 88 | 16 | 189 | 1450 | 3.1 | 4.0 | 18.6 |

Three-point field goals: 1979-80, 0-for-3. 1980-81, 0-for-1. 1981-82, 1-for-3 (.333). 1982-83, 1-for-2 (.500). 1983-84, 3-for-11 (.273). 1988-89, 0-for-4. 1989-90, 0-for-1. 1990-91, 0-for-1. Totals, 5-for-26 (.192).

Personal fouls/disqualifications: 1977-78, 8/0. 1978-79, 41/0. 1979-80, 20/0. 1980-81, 17/0. 1981-82, 19/0. 1982-83, 6/0. 1983-84, 55/0. 1988-89, 11/0. 1989-90, 4/0. 1990-91, 5/0. Totals, 186/0.

## NBA ALL-STAR GAME RECORD

| Season Team | Min. | FGM | FGA | Pct. | FTM | FTA | Pct. | REBOUNDS Off. | Def. | Tot. | Ast. | PF | Dq. | St. | Blk. | TO | Pts. |
|---|---|---|---|---|---|---|---|---|---|---|---|---|---|---|---|---|---|
| 1978—Phoenix | 15 | 3 | 6 | .500 | 4 | 4 | 1.000 | 0 | 1 | 1 | 6 | 1 | 0 | 1 | 0 | 0 | 10 |
| 1979—Phoenix | 19 | 4 | 9 | .444 | 0 | 0 | ... | 1 | 3 | 4 | 4 | 0 | 0 | 1 | 0 | 2 | 8 |
| 1980—Phoenix | 23 | 5 | 10 | .500 | 2 | 2 | 1.000 | 2 | 2 | 4 | 2 | 2 | 0 | 4 | 0 | 3 | 12 |
| 1981—Phoenix | 22 | 5 | 9 | .556 | 2 | 2 | 1.000 | 1 | 6 | 7 | 1 | 2 | 0 | 0 | 1 | 2 | 12 |
| 1984—Phoenix | 15 | 5 | 9 | .556 | 0 | 0 | ... | 0 | 2 | 2 | 1 | 0 | 0 | 1 | 0 | 0 | 10 |
| 1987—Phoenix | 15 | 3 | 12 | .250 | 0 | 0 | ... | 2 | 0 | 2 | 1 | 0 | 0 | 0 | 0 | 0 | 7 |
| Totals | 109 | 25 | 55 | .455 | 8 | 8 | 1.000 | 6 | 14 | 20 | 15 | 5 | 0 | 7 | 0 | 6 | 59 |

Three-point field goals: 1987, 1-for-1.

## DeBUSSCHERE, DAVE          F

**PERSONAL:** Born October 16, 1940, in Detroit. ... Died May 14, 2003. ... 6-6/235 (1,98/106,6). ... Full name: David Albert DeBusschere.
**HIGH SCHOOL:** Austin Catholic (Detroit).
**COLLEGE:** Detroit.
**TRANSACTIONS:** Selected by Detroit Pistons in 1962 NBA Draft (territorial pick). ... Traded by Pistons to New York Knicks for C Walt Bellamy and G Howard Komives (December 19, 1968).
**CAREER HONORS:** Elected to Naismith Memorial Basketball Hall of Fame (1983). ... One of the 50 Greatest Players in NBA History (1996).
**CAREER NOTES:** General manager, New York Knicks (May 1982 through January 1986).
**MISCELLANEOUS:** Member of NBA championship team (1970, 1973).

## COLLEGIATE RECORD

| Season Team | G | Min. | FGM | FGA | Pct. | FTM | FTA | Pct. | Reb. | Ast. | Pts. | RPG | APG | PPG |
|---|---|---|---|---|---|---|---|---|---|---|---|---|---|---|
| 58-59—Detroit‡ | 15 | ... | 144 | 306 | .471 | 68 | 101 | .673 | 305 | ... | 356 | 20.3 | ... | 23.7 |
| 59-60—Detroit | 27 | ... | 288 | 665 | .433 | 115 | 196 | .587 | 540 | ... | 691 | 20.0 | ... | 25.6 |
| 60-61—Detroit | 27 | ... | 256 | 636 | .403 | 86 | 155 | .555 | 514 | ... | 598 | 19.0 | ... | 22.1 |
| 61-62—Detroit | 26 | ... | 267 | 616 | .433 | 162 | 242 | .669 | 498 | ... | 696 | 19.2 | ... | 26.8 |
| Varsity totals | 80 | ... | 811 | 1917 | .423 | 363 | 593 | .612 | 1552 | ... | 1985 | 19.4 | ... | 24.8 |

## NBA REGULAR-SEASON RECORD

**HONORS:** All-NBA second team (1969). ... NBA All-Defensive first team (1969, 1970, 1971, 1972, 1973, 1974). ... NBA All-Rookie team (1963).

| Season Team | G | Min. | FGM | FGA | Pct. | FTM | FTA | Pct. | Reb. | Ast. | PF | Dq. | Pts. | RPG | APG | PPG |
|---|---|---|---|---|---|---|---|---|---|---|---|---|---|---|---|---|
| 62-63—Detroit | 80 | 2352 | 406 | 944 | .430 | 206 | 287 | .718 | 694 | 207 | 247 | 5 | 1018 | 8.7 | 2.6 | 12.7 |
| 63-64—Detroit | 15 | 304 | 52 | 133 | .391 | 25 | 43 | .581 | 105 | 23 | 32 | 1 | 129 | 7.0 | 1.5 | 8.6 |
| 64-65—Detroit | 79 | 2769 | 508 | 1196 | .425 | 306 | 437 | .700 | 874 | 253 | 242 | 5 | 1322 | 11.1 | 3.2 | 16.7 |
| 65-66—Detroit | 79 | 2696 | 524 | 1284 | .408 | 249 | 378 | .659 | 916 | 209 | 252 | 5 | 1297 | 11.6 | 2.6 | 16.4 |
| 66-67—Detroit | 78 | 2897 | 531 | 1278 | .416 | 361 | 512 | .705 | 924 | 216 | 297 | 7 | 1423 | 11.8 | 2.8 | 18.2 |
| 67-68—Detroit | 80 | 3125 | 573 | 1295 | .442 | 289 | 435 | .664 | 1081 | 181 | 304 | 3 | 1435 | 13.5 | 2.3 | 17.9 |
| 68-69—Detroit-N.Y. | 76 | 2943 | 506 | 1140 | .444 | 229 | 328 | .698 | 888 | 191 | 290 | 6 | 1241 | 11.7 | 2.5 | 16.3 |
| 69-70—New York | 79 | 2627 | 488 | 1082 | .451 | 176 | 256 | .688 | 790 | 194 | 244 | 2 | 1152 | 10.0 | 2.5 | 14.6 |
| 70-71—New York | 81 | 2891 | 523 | 1243 | .421 | 217 | 312 | .696 | 901 | 220 | 237 | 2 | 1263 | 11.1 | 2.7 | 15.6 |
| 71-72—New York | 80 | 3072 | 520 | 1218 | .427 | 193 | 265 | .728 | 901 | 291 | 219 | 1 | 1233 | 11.3 | 3.6 | 15.4 |
| 72-73—New York | 77 | 2827 | 532 | 1224 | .435 | 194 | 260 | .746 | 787 | 259 | 215 | 1 | 1258 | 10.2 | 3.4 | 16.3 |

| Season Team | G | Min. | FGM | FGA | Pct. | FTM | FTA | Pct. | Off. | Def. | Tot. | Ast. | St. | Blk. | TO | Pts. | RPG | APG | PPG |
|---|---|---|---|---|---|---|---|---|---|---|---|---|---|---|---|---|---|---|---|
| 73-74—New York | 71 | 2699 | 559 | 1212 | .461 | 164 | 217 | .756 | 134 | 623 | 757 | 253 | 67 | 39 | ... | 1282 | 10.7 | 3.6 | 18.1 |
| Totals | 875 | 31202 | 5722 | 13249 | .432 | 2609 | 3730 | .699 | ... | ... | 9618 | 2497 | 67 | 39 | ... | 14053 | 11.0 | 2.9 | 16.1 |

Personal fouls/disqualifications: 1973-74, 222/2.

## NBA PLAYOFF RECORD

| Season Team | G | Min. | FGM | FGA | Pct. | FTM | FTA | Pct. | Reb. | Ast. | PF | Dq. | Pts. | RPG | APG | PPG |
|---|---|---|---|---|---|---|---|---|---|---|---|---|---|---|---|---|
| 62-63—Detroit | 4 | 159 | 25 | 59 | .424 | 30 | 44 | .682 | 63 | 6 | 14 | 1 | 80 | 15.8 | 1.5 | 20.0 |
| 67-68—Detroit | 6 | 263 | 45 | 106 | .425 | 26 | 45 | .578 | 97 | 13 | 23 | 0 | 116 | 16.2 | 2.2 | 19.3 |
| 68-69—New York | 10 | 419 | 61 | 174 | .351 | 41 | 50 | .820 | 148 | 33 | 43 | 0 | 163 | 14.8 | 3.3 | 16.3 |
| 69-70—New York | 19 | 701 | 130 | 309 | .421 | 45 | 68 | .662 | 220 | 46 | 63 | 1 | 305 | 11.6 | 2.4 | 16.1 |
| 70-71—New York | 12 | 488 | 84 | 202 | .416 | 29 | 44 | .659 | 156 | 22 | 40 | 1 | 197 | 13.0 | 1.8 | 16.4 |
| 71-72—New York | 16 | 616 | 109 | 242 | .450 | 48 | 64 | .750 | 193 | 37 | 51 | 2 | 266 | 12.1 | 2.3 | 16.6 |
| 72-73—New York | 17 | 632 | 117 | 265 | .442 | 31 | 40 | .775 | 179 | 58 | 57 | 0 | 265 | 10.5 | 3.4 | 15.6 |

| Season Team | G | Min. | FGM | FGA | Pct. | FTM | FTA | Pct. | Off. | Def. | Tot. | Ast. | St. | Blk. | TO | Pts. | RPG | APG | PPG |
|---|---|---|---|---|---|---|---|---|---|---|---|---|---|---|---|---|---|---|---|
| 73-74—New York | 12 | 404 | 63 | 166 | .380 | 18 | 29 | .621 | 25 | 74 | 99 | 38 | 7 | 4 | ... | 144 | 8.3 | 3.2 | 12.0 |
| Totals | 96 | 3682 | 634 | 1523 | .416 | 268 | 384 | .698 | ... | ... | 1155 | 253 | ... | ... | ... | 1536 | 12.0 | 2.6 | 16.0 |

Personal fouls/disqualifications: 1973-74, 36/0.

## NBA ALL-STAR GAME RECORD

**NOTES:** Shares single-game record for most field goals made in one quarter—8 (1967).

| Season Team | Min. | FGM | FGA | Pct. | FTM | FTA | Pct. | Reb | Ast. | PF | Dq. | Pts. |
|---|---|---|---|---|---|---|---|---|---|---|---|---|
| 1966—Detroit | 22 | 1 | 14 | .071 | 2 | 2 | 1.000 | 6 | 1 | 1 | 0 | 4 |
| 1967—Detroit | 25 | 11 | 17 | .647 | 0 | 0 | ... | 6 | 0 | 1 | 0 | 22 |
| 1968—Detroit | 12 | 0 | 3 | .000 | 0 | 0 | ... | 4 | 0 | 1 | 0 | 0 |
| 1970—New York | 14 | 5 | 10 | .500 | 0 | 0 | ... | 7 | 2 | 1 | 0 | 10 |
| 1971—New York | 19 | 4 | 7 | .571 | 0 | 0 | ... | 7 | 3 | 3 | 0 | 8 |
| 1972—New York | 26 | 4 | 8 | .500 | 0 | 0 | ... | 11 | 0 | 2 | 0 | 8 |
| 1973—New York | 25 | 4 | 8 | .500 | 1 | 2 | .500 | 7 | 2 | 1 | 0 | 9 |

| Season Team | Min. | FGM | FGA | Pct. | FTM | FTA | Pct. | Off. | Def. | Tot. | Ast. | PF | Dq. | St. | Blk. | TO | Pts. |
|---|---|---|---|---|---|---|---|---|---|---|---|---|---|---|---|---|---|
| 1974—New York | 24 | 8 | 14 | .571 | 0 | 0 | ... | 2 | 1 | 3 | 3 | 2 | 0 | 1 | 0 | ... | 16 |
| Totals | 167 | 37 | 81 | .457 | 3 | 4 | .750 | ... | ... | 51 | 11 | 12 | 0 | 1 | 0 | ... | 77 |

## NBA COACHING RECORD

**BACKGROUND:** Player/head coach, Detroit Pistons (November 1964 to March 1967).
**MISCELLANEOUS:** Youngest coach in NBA history.

| Season Team | W | L | Pct. | Finish | W | L | Pct. |
|---|---|---|---|---|---|---|---|
| | | | | | PLAYOFFS | | |
| | REGULAR SEASON | | | | | | |
| 64-65—Detroit | 29 | 40 | .420 | 4th/Western Division | — | — | — |
| 65-66—Detroit | 22 | 58 | .275 | 5th/Western Division | — | — | — |
| 66-67—Detroit | 28 | 45 | .384 | | — | — | — |
| Totals (3 years) | 79 | 143 | .356 | | | | |

**NOTES:**

1964—Replaced Charles Wolf as Detroit head coach (November), with record of 2-9.
1967—Replaced as Detroit head coach by Donnis Butcher (March).

## RECORD AS BASEBALL PLAYER

**TRANSACTIONS:** Signed by Chicago White Sox (April 1, 1962). ... On disabled list (June 4-20, 1964). ... On restricted list (September 7, 1965-December 19, 1968). ... Released by White Sox organization (December 23, 1968).

| Year Team (League) | W | L | Pct. | ERA | G | GS | CG | ShO | Sv. | IP | H | R | ER | BB | SO |
|---|---|---|---|---|---|---|---|---|---|---|---|---|---|---|---|
| 1962—Chicago (A.L.) | 0 | 0 | ... | 2.00 | 12 | 0 | 0 | 0 | ... | 18 | 5 | 7 | 4 | 23 | 8 |
| Savannah (S. Atl.) | 10 | 1 | .909 | 2.49 | 15 | 14 | 7 | 2 | ... | 94 | 62 | 35 | 26 | 53 | 93 |
| 1963—Chicago (A.L.) | 3 | 4 | .429 | 3.11 | 24 | 10 | 1 | 1 | ... | 84 | 80 | 35 | 29 | 34 | 53 |
| 1964—Indianapolis (PCL) | 15 | 8 | .652 | 3.93 | 32 | 30 | 10 | 2 | ... | 174 | 173 | 88 | 76 | 66 | 126 |
| 1965—Indianapolis (PCL) | 15 | 12 | .556 | 3.65 | 35 | *34 | 10 | 1 | ... | *244 | *255 | 120 | 99 | 66 | 176 |
| Major league totals (2 years) | 3 | 4 | .429 | 2.91 | 36 | 10 | 1 | 1 | ... | 102 | 85 | 42 | 33 | 57 | 61 |

# DREXLER, CLYDE                          G

**PERSONAL:** Born June 22, 1962, in New Orleans. ... 6-7/222 (2,00/100,7). ... Full name: Clyde Austin Drexler.
**HIGH SCHOOL:** Sterling (Houston).
**COLLEGE:** Houston.
**TRANSACTIONS:** Selected after junior season by Portland Trail Blazers in first round (14th pick overall) of 1983 NBA Draft. ... Traded by Trail Blazers with F Tracy Murray to Houston Rockets for F Otis Thorpe, rights to F Marcelo Nicola and 1995 first-round draft choice (February 14, 1995). ... Announced retirement, effective with the conclusion of 1997-98 season (March 18, 1998).
**CAREER HONORS:** One of the 50 Greatest Players in NBA History (1996). ... Elected to the Naismith Memorial Basketball Hall of Fame (2004).
**CAREER NOTES:** Head coach, University of Houston (1998-99 to 1999-2000). ... Special assistant to general manager, Denver Nuggets (September 27-December 30, 2001). ... Assistant coach, Nuggets (2002).
**MISCELLANEOUS:** Member of NBA championship team (1995). ... Member of gold-medal-winning U.S. Olympic team (1992). ... Portland Trail Blazers all-time leading scorer with 18,040 points, all-time leading rebounder with 5,339 and all-time steals leader with 1,795 (1983-84 through 1994-95).

## COLLEGIATE RECORD

| Season Team | G | Min. | FGM | FGA | Pct. | FTM | FTA | Pct. | Reb. | Ast. | Pts. | RPG | APG | PPG |
|---|---|---|---|---|---|---|---|---|---|---|---|---|---|---|
| 80-81—Houston | 30 | 992 | 153 | 303 | .505 | 50 | 85 | .588 | 314 | 78 | 356 | 10.5 | 2.6 | 11.9 |
| 81-82—Houston | 32 | 1077 | 206 | 362 | .569 | 73 | 120 | .608 | 336 | 96 | 485 | 10.5 | 3.0 | 15.2 |
| 82-83—Houston | 34 | 1186 | 236 | 440 | .536 | 70 | 95 | .737 | 298 | 129 | 542 | 8.8 | 3.8 | 15.9 |
| Totals | 96 | 3255 | 595 | 1105 | .538 | 193 | 300 | .643 | 948 | 303 | 1383 | 9.9 | 3.2 | 14.4 |

## NBA REGULAR-SEASON RECORD

**HONORS:** All-NBA first team (1992). ... All-NBA second team (1988, 1991). ... All-NBA third team (1990, 1995).

| Season Team | G | Min. | FGM | FGA | Pct. | FTM | FTA | Pct. | Off. | Def. | Tot. | Ast. | St. | Blk. | TO | Pts. | RPG | APG | PPG |
|---|---|---|---|---|---|---|---|---|---|---|---|---|---|---|---|---|---|---|---|
| 83-84—Portland | 82 | 1408 | 252 | 559 | .451 | 123 | 169 | .728 | 112 | 123 | 235 | 153 | 107 | 29 | 123 | 628 | 2.9 | 1.9 | 7.7 |
| 84-85—Portland | 80 | 2555 | 573 | 1161 | .494 | 223 | 294 | .759 | 217 | 259 | 476 | 441 | 177 | 68 | 223 | 1377 | 6.0 | 5.5 | 17.2 |
| 85-86—Portland | 75 | 2576 | 542 | 1142 | .475 | 293 | 381 | .769 | 171 | 250 | 421 | 600 | 197 | 46 | 282 | 1389 | 5.6 | 8.0 | 18.5 |
| 86-87—Portland | 82 | 3114 | 707 | 1408 | .502 | 357 | 470 | .760 | 227 | 291 | 518 | 566 | 204 | 71 | 253 | 1782 | 6.3 | 6.9 | 21.7 |
| 87-88—Portland | 81 | 3060 | 849 | 1679 | .506 | 476 | 587 | .811 | 261 | 272 | 533 | 467 | 203 | 52 | 236 | 2185 | 6.6 | 5.8 | 27.0 |
| 88-89—Portland | 78 | 3064 | 829 | 1672 | .496 | 438 | 548 | .799 | 289 | 326 | 615 | 450 | 213 | 54 | 250 | 2123 | 7.9 | 5.8 | 27.2 |
| 89-90—Portland | 73 | 2683 | 670 | 1357 | .494 | 333 | 430 | .774 | 208 | 299 | 507 | 432 | 145 | 51 | 191 | 1703 | 6.9 | 5.9 | 23.3 |
| 90-91—Portland | 82 | 2852 | 645 | 1338 | .482 | 416 | 524 | .794 | 212 | 334 | 546 | 493 | 144 | 60 | 232 | 1767 | 6.7 | 6.0 | 21.5 |
| 91-92—Portland | 76 | 2751 | 694 | 1476 | .470 | 401 | 505 | .794 | 166 | 334 | 500 | 512 | 138 | 70 | 240 | 1903 | 6.6 | 6.7 | 25.0 |
| 92-93—Portland | 49 | 1671 | 350 | 816 | .429 | 245 | 292 | .839 | 126 | 183 | 309 | 278 | 95 | 37 | 115 | 976 | 6.3 | 5.7 | 19.9 |
| 93-94—Portland | 68 | 2334 | 473 | 1105 | .428 | 286 | 368 | .777 | 154 | 291 | 445 | 333 | 98 | 34 | 167 | 1303 | 6.5 | 4.9 | 19.2 |
| 94-95—Port.-Hou. | 76 | 2728 | 571 | 1238 | .461 | 364 | 442 | .824 | 152 | 328 | 480 | 362 | 136 | 45 | 186 | 1653 | 6.3 | 4.8 | 21.8 |
| 95-96—Houston | 52 | 1997 | 331 | 764 | .433 | 265 | 338 | .784 | 97 | 276 | 373 | 302 | 105 | 24 | 134 | 1005 | 7.2 | 5.8 | 19.3 |
| 96-97—Houston | 62 | 2271 | 397 | 899 | .442 | 201 | 268 | .750 | 118 | 255 | 373 | 354 | 119 | 36 | 156 | 1114 | 6.0 | 5.7 | 18.0 |
| 97-98—Houston | 70 | 2473 | 452 | 1059 | .427 | 277 | 346 | .801 | 105 | 241 | 346 | 382 | 126 | 42 | 189 | 1287 | 4.9 | 5.5 | 18.4 |
| Totals | 1086 | 37537 | 8335 | 17673 | .472 | 4698 | 5962 | .788 | 2615 | 4062 | 6677 | 6125 | 2207 | 719 | 2977 | 22195 | 6.1 | 5.6 | 20.4 |

Three-point field goals: 1983-84, 1-for-4 (.250). 1984-85, 8-for-37 (.216). 1985-86, 12-for-60 (.200). 1986-87, 11-for-47 (.234). 1987-88, 11-for-52 (.212). 1988-89, 27-for-104 (.260). 1989-90, 30-for-106 (.283). 1990-91, 61-for-191 (.319). 1991-92, 114-for-338 (.337). 1992-93, 31-for-133 (.233). 1993-94, 71-for-219 (.324). 1994-95, 147-for-408 (.360). 1995-96, 78-for-235 (.332). 1996-97, 119-for-335 (.355). 1997-98, 106-for-334 (.317). Totals, 827-for-2603 (.318).

Personal fouls/disqualifications: 1983-84, 209/2. 1984-85, 265/3. 1985-86, 270/8. 1986-87, 281/7. 1987-88, 250/2. 1988-89, 269/2. 1989-90, 222/1. 1990-91, 226/2. 1991-92, 229/2. 1992-93, 159/1. 1993-94, 202/2. 1994-95, 206/1. 1995-96, 153/0. 1996-97, 151/0. 1997-98, 193/0. Totals, 3285/33.

## NBA PLAYOFF RECORD

**NOTES:** Holds single-game playoff record for most points in an overtime period—13 (April 29, 1992, vs. Los Angeles Lakers).

| Season Team | G | Min. | FGM | FGA | Pct. | FTM | FTA | Pct. | Off. | Def. | Tot. | Ast. | St. | Blk. | TO | Pts. | RPG | APG | PPG |
|---|---|---|---|---|---|---|---|---|---|---|---|---|---|---|---|---|---|---|---|
| 83-84—Portland | 5 | 85 | 15 | 35 | .429 | 6 | 7 | .857 | 7 | 10 | 17 | 8 | 5 | 1 | 7 | 36 | 3.4 | 1.6 | 7.2 |
| 84-85—Portland | 9 | 339 | 55 | 134 | .410 | 38 | 45 | .844 | 27 | 28 | 55 | 83 | 23 | 9 | 29 | 150 | 6.1 | 9.2 | 16.7 |
| 85-86—Portland | 4 | 145 | 26 | 57 | .456 | 18 | 23 | .783 | 9 | 16 | 25 | 26 | 6 | 3 | 19 | 72 | 6.3 | 6.5 | 18.0 |
| 86-87—Portland | 4 | 153 | 36 | 79 | .456 | 23 | 29 | .793 | 16 | 14 | 30 | 15 | 7 | 3 | 6 | 96 | 7.5 | 3.8 | 24.0 |
| 87-88—Portland | 4 | 170 | 32 | 83 | .386 | 21 | 29 | .724 | 12 | 16 | 28 | 21 | 12 | 2 | 12 | 88 | 7.0 | 5.3 | 22.0 |
| 88-89—Portland | 3 | 128 | 35 | 71 | .493 | 13 | 17 | .765 | 13 | 7 | 20 | 25 | 6 | 2 | 12 | 83 | 6.7 | 8.3 | 27.7 |
| 89-90—Portland | 21 | 853 | 172 | 390 | .441 | 96 | 124 | .774 | 63 | 88 | 151 | 150 | 53 | 18 | 67 | 449 | 7.2 | 7.1 | 21.4 |
| 90-91—Portland | 16 | 633 | 128 | 269 | .476 | 76 | 98 | .776 | 40 | 89 | 129 | 129 | 34 | 16 | 61 | 347 | 8.1 | 8.1 | 21.7 |
| 91-92—Portland | 21 | 847 | 198 | 425 | .466 | 138 | 171 | .807 | 60 | 95 | 155 | 147 | 31 | 20 | 58 | 553 | 7.4 | 7.0 | 26.3 |
| 92-93—Portland | 3 | 116 | 18 | 43 | .419 | 16 | 20 | .800 | 8 | 11 | 19 | 14 | 5 | 3 | 3 | 57 | 6.3 | 4.7 | 19.0 |
| 93-94—Portland | 4 | 157 | 31 | 73 | .425 | 19 | 23 | .826 | 10 | 31 | 41 | 22 | 8 | 2 | 9 | 84 | 10.3 | 5.5 | 21.0 |
| 94-95—Houston | 22 | 849 | 155 | 322 | .481 | 110 | 140 | .786 | 45 | 109 | 154 | 111 | 33 | 15 | 45 | 450 | 7.0 | 5.0 | 20.5 |
| 95-96—Houston | 8 | 292 | 49 | 118 | .415 | 26 | 34 | .765 | 15 | 47 | 62 | 40 | 21 | 4 | 20 | 133 | 7.8 | 5.0 | 16.6 |
| 96-97—Houston | 16 | 623 | 105 | 241 | .436 | 42 | 54 | .778 | 25 | 64 | 89 | 77 | 26 | 7 | 36 | 290 | 5.6 | 4.8 | 18.1 |
| 97-98—Houston | 5 | 182 | 21 | 68 | .309 | 28 | 37 | .757 | 9 | 18 | 27 | 23 | 8 | 3 | 13 | 75 | 5.4 | 4.6 | 15.0 |
| Totals | 145 | 5572 | 1076 | 2408 | .447 | 670 | 851 | .787 | 359 | 643 | 1002 | 891 | 278 | 108 | 397 | 2963 | 6.9 | 6.1 | 20.4 |

Three-point field goals: 1983-84, 0-for-1. 1984-85, 2-for-7 (.286). 1985-86, 2-for-5 (.400). 1986-87, 1-for-4 (.250). 1987-88, 3-for-6 (.500). 1988-89, 0-for-2. 1989-90, 9-for-41 (.220). 1990-91, 15-for-56 (.268). 1991-92, 19-for-81 (.235). 1992-93, 5-for-12 (.417). 1993-94, 3-for-13 (.231). 1994-95, 30-for-99 (.303). 1995-96, 9-for-34 (.265). 1996-97, 38-for-102 (.373). 1997-98, 5-for-26 (.192). Totals, 141-for-489 (.288).

Personal fouls/disqualifications: 1983-84, 11/0. 1984-85, 37/0. 1985-86, 19/1. 1986-87, 16/1. 1987-88, 14/0. 1988-89, 11/0. 1989-90, 72/2. 1990-91, 56/0. 1991-92, 77/2. 1992-93, 9/0. 1993-94, 7/0. 1994-95, 68/1. 1995-96, 22/0. 1996-97, 52/0. 1997-98, 15/0. Totals, 486/7.

## NBA ALL-STAR GAME RECORD

**NOTES:** Teamed with Cynthia Cooper to win inaugural Nestlé Crunch All-Star 2ball championship (1998).

| Season Team | Min. | FGM | FGA | Pct. | FTM | FTA | Pct. | Off. | Def. | Tot. | Ast. | PF | Dq. | St. | Blk. | TO | Pts. |
|---|---|---|---|---|---|---|---|---|---|---|---|---|---|---|---|---|---|
| 1986—Portland | 15 | 5 | 7 | .714 | 0 | 0 | ... | 0 | 4 | 4 | 4 | 3 | 0 | 3 | 1 | 3 | 10 |
| 1988—Portland | 15 | 3 | 5 | .600 | 6 | 6 | 1.000 | 2 | 3 | 5 | 0 | 3 | 0 | 1 | 0 | 1 | 12 |
| 1989—Portland | 25 | 7 | 19 | .368 | 0 | 0 | ... | 6 | 6 | 12 | 4 | 3 | 0 | 2 | 0 | 6 | 14 |
| 1990—Portland | 19 | 2 | 6 | .333 | 2 | 2 | 1.000 | 4 | 0 | 4 | 2 | 1 | 0 | 1 | 1 | 1 | 7 |
| 1991—Portland | 19 | 4 | 9 | .444 | 4 | 4 | 1.000 | 2 | 2 | 4 | 2 | 3 | 0 | 1 | 1 | 0 | 12 |
| 1992—Portland | 28 | 10 | 15 | .667 | 0 | 0 | ... | 2 | 7 | 9 | 6 | 2 | 0 | 0 | 2 | 1 | 22 |
| 1993—Portland | 11 | 1 | 3 | .333 | 0 | 0 | ... | 1 | 0 | 1 | 1 | 3 | 0 | 0 | 0 | 2 | 2 |
| 1994—Portland | 15 | 3 | 7 | .429 | 0 | 0 | ... | 0 | 3 | 3 | 1 | 1 | 0 | 1 | 1 | 1 | 6 |
| 1996—Houston | 19 | 5 | 8 | .625 | 0 | 0 | ... | 0 | 2 | 2 | 3 | 0 | 0 | 3 | 0 | 3 | 11 |
| 1997—Houston | | | | | | | Selected, did not play—injured. | | | | | | | | | | |
| **Totals** | 166 | 40 | 79 | .506 | 12 | 12 | 1.000 | 17 | 27 | 44 | 23 | 19 | 0 | 12 | 6 | 18 | 96 |

Three-point field goals: 1986, 0-for-1. 1988, 0-for-1. 1990, 1-for-1. 1992, 2-for-4 (.500). 1993, 0-for-1. 1994, 0-for-2. 1996, 1-for-4 (.250). Totals, 4-for-14 (.286).

## COLLEGIATE COACHING RECORD

| Season Team | W | L | Pct. | |
|---|---|---|---|---|
| 98-99—Houston | 10 | 17 | .370 | 6th/National Division/Conference USA |
| 99-00—Houston | 9 | 22 | .290 | 6th/National Division/Conference USA |

# DUMARS, JOE  G

**PERSONAL:** Born May 24, 1963, in Shreveport, La. ... 6-3/195 (1,90/88,5). ... Full name: Joe Dumars III.
**HIGH SCHOOL:** Natchitoches (La.) Central.
**COLLEGE:** McNeese State.
**TRANSACTIONS/CAREER NOTES:** Selected by Detroit Pistons in first round (18th pick overall) of 1985 NBA Draft. ... Announced retirement (April 28, 1999).
**MISCELLANEOUS:** Member of NBA championship team (1989, 1990).
**CAREER NOTES:** Vice President of Player Personnel, Detroit Pistons (1999-2000). ... President of Basketball Operations, Detroit Pistons (June 6, 2000-present).

## COLLEGIATE RECORD

**NOTES:** THE SPORTING NEWS All-America second team (1985).

| Season Team | G | Min. | FGM | FGA | Pct. | FTM | FTA | Pct. | Reb. | Ast. | Pts. | AVERAGES RPG | APG | PPG |
|---|---|---|---|---|---|---|---|---|---|---|---|---|---|---|
| 81-82—McNeese State | 29 | ... | 206 | 464 | .444 | 115 | 160 | .719 | 64 | 80 | 527 | 2.2 | 2.8 | 18.2 |
| 82-83—McNeese State | 29 | ... | 212 | 487 | .435 | 140 | 197 | .711 | 128 | 64 | 569 | 4.4 | 2.2 | 19.6 |
| 83-84—McNeese State | 31 | ... | 276 | 586 | .471 | 267 | 324 | .824 | 164 | 80 | 819 | 5.3 | 2.6 | 26.4 |
| 84-85—McNeese State | 27 | ... | 248 | 501 | .495 | 201 | 236 | .852 | 132 | 106 | 697 | 4.9 | 3.9 | 25.8 |
| **Totals** | 116 | ... | 942 | 2038 | .462 | 723 | 917 | .788 | 488 | 330 | 2612 | 4.2 | 2.8 | 22.5 |

Three-point field goals: 1982-83, 5-for-8 (.625).

## NBA REGULAR-SEASON RECORD

**HONORS:** J. Walter Kennedy Citizenship Award (1994). ... NBA Sportsmanship Award (1996). ... All-NBA second team (1993). ... All-NBA third team (1990, 1991). ... NBA All-Defensive first team (1989, 1990, 1992, 1993). ... NBA All-Defensive second team (1991). ... NBA All-Rookie team (1986).

| Season Team | G | Min. | FGM | FGA | Pct. | FTM | FTA | Pct. | Off. | Def. | Tot. | Ast. | St. | Blk. | TO | Pts. | RPG | APG | PPG |
|---|---|---|---|---|---|---|---|---|---|---|---|---|---|---|---|---|---|---|---|
| 85-86—Detroit | 82 | 1957 | 287 | 597 | .481 | 190 | 238 | .798 | 60 | 59 | 119 | 390 | 66 | 11 | 158 | 769 | 1.5 | 4.8 | 9.4 |
| 86-87—Detroit | 79 | 2439 | 369 | 749 | .493 | 184 | 246 | .748 | 50 | 117 | 167 | 352 | 83 | 5 | 171 | 931 | 2.1 | 4.5 | 11.8 |
| 87-88—Detroit | 82 | 2732 | 453 | 960 | .472 | 251 | 308 | .815 | 63 | 137 | 200 | 387 | 87 | 15 | 172 | 1161 | 2.4 | 4.7 | 14.2 |
| 88-89—Detroit | 69 | 2408 | 456 | 903 | .505 | 260 | 306 | .850 | 57 | 115 | 172 | 390 | 63 | 5 | 178 | 1186 | 2.5 | 5.7 | 17.2 |
| 89-90—Detroit | 75 | 2578 | 508 | 1058 | .480 | 297 | 330 | .900 | 60 | 152 | 212 | 368 | 63 | 2 | 145 | 1335 | 2.8 | 4.9 | 17.8 |
| 90-91—Detroit | 80 | 3046 | 622 | 1292 | .481 | 371 | 417 | .890 | 62 | 125 | 187 | 443 | 89 | 7 | 189 | 1629 | 2.3 | 5.5 | 20.4 |
| 91-92—Detroit | 82 | 3192 | 587 | 1311 | .448 | 412 | 475 | .867 | 82 | 106 | 188 | 375 | 71 | 12 | 193 | 1635 | 2.3 | 4.6 | 19.9 |
| 92-93—Detroit | 77 | 3094 | 677 | 1454 | .466 | 343 | 397 | .864 | 63 | 85 | 148 | 308 | 78 | 7 | 138 | 1809 | 1.9 | 4.0 | 23.5 |
| 93-94—Detroit | 69 | 2591 | 505 | 1118 | .452 | 276 | 330 | .836 | 35 | 116 | 151 | 261 | 63 | 4 | 159 | 1410 | 2.2 | 3.8 | 20.4 |
| 94-95—Detroit | 67 | 2544 | 417 | 970 | .430 | 277 | 344 | .805 | 47 | 111 | 158 | 368 | 72 | 7 | 219 | 1214 | 2.4 | 5.5 | 18.1 |
| 95-96—Detroit | 67 | 2193 | 255 | 598 | .426 | 162 | 197 | .822 | 28 | 110 | 138 | 265 | 43 | 3 | 97 | 793 | 2.1 | 4.0 | 11.8 |
| 96-97—Detroit | 79 | 2923 | 385 | 875 | .440 | 222 | 256 | .867 | 38 | 153 | 191 | 318 | 57 | 1 | 128 | 1158 | 2.4 | 4.0 | 14.7 |
| 97-98—Detroit | 72 | 2326 | 329 | 791 | .416 | 127 | 154 | .825 | 14 | 90 | 104 | 253 | 44 | 2 | 84 | 943 | 1.4 | 3.5 | 13.1 |
| 98-99—Detroit | 38 | 1116 | 144 | 350 | .411 | 51 | 61 | .836 | 12 | 56 | 68 | 134 | 23 | 2 | 53 | 428 | 1.8 | 3.5 | 11.3 |
| **Totals** | 1018 | 35139 | 5994 | 13026 | .460 | 3423 | 4059 | .843 | 671 | 1532 | 2203 | 4612 | 902 | 83 | 2084 | 16401 | 2.2 | 4.5 | 16.1 |

Three-point field goals: 1985-86, 5-for-16 (.313). 1986-87, 9-for-22 (.409). 1987-88, 4-for-19 (.211). 1988-89, 14-for-29 (.483). 1989-90, 22-for-55 (.400). 1990-91, 14-for-45 (.311). 1991-92, 49-for-120 (.408). 1992-93, 112-for-299 (.375). 1993-94, 124-for-320 (.388). 1994-95, 103-for-338 (.305). 1995-96, 121-for-298 (.406). 1996-97, 166-for-384 (.432). 1997-98, 158-for-426 (.371). 1998-99, 89-for-221 (.403). Totals, 990-for-2592 (.382).

Personal fouls/disqualifications: 1985-86, 200/1. 1986-87, 194/1. 1987-88, 155/1. 1988-89, 103/1. 1989-90, 129/1. 1990-91, 135/0. 1991-92, 145/0. 1992-93, 141/0. 1993-94, 118/0. 1994-95, 153/0. 1995-96, 106/0. 1996-97, 97/0. 1997-98, 99/0. 1998-99, 51/0. Totals, 1826/5.

## NBA PLAYOFF RECORD

**NOTES:** NBA Finals Most Valuable Player (1989).

| Season Team | G | Min. | FGM | FGA | Pct. | FTM | FTA | Pct. | Off. | Def. | Tot. | Ast. | St. | Blk. | TO | Pts. | RPG | APG | PPG |
|---|---|---|---|---|---|---|---|---|---|---|---|---|---|---|---|---|---|---|---|
| 85-86—Detroit | 4 | 147 | 25 | 41 | .610 | 10 | 15 | .667 | 6 | 7 | 13 | 25 | 4 | 0 | 7 | 60 | 3.3 | 6.3 | 15.0 |
| 86-87—Detroit | 15 | 473 | 78 | 145 | .538 | 32 | 41 | .780 | 8 | 11 | 19 | 72 | 12 | 1 | 27 | 190 | 1.3 | 4.8 | 12.7 |
| 87-88—Detroit | 23 | 804 | 113 | 247 | .457 | 56 | 63 | .889 | 18 | 32 | 50 | 112 | 13 | 2 | 40 | 284 | 2.2 | 4.9 | 12.3 |
| 88-89—Detroit | 17 | 620 | 106 | 233 | .455 | 87 | 101 | .861 | 11 | 33 | 44 | 96 | 12 | 1 | 31 | 300 | 2.6 | 5.6 | 17.6 |

| Season Team | G | Min. | FGM | FGA | Pct. | FTM | FTA | Pct. | Off. | Def. | Tot. | Ast. | St. | Blk. | TO | Pts. | RPG | APG | PPG |
|---|---|---|---|---|---|---|---|---|---|---|---|---|---|---|---|---|---|---|---|
| 89-90—Detroit | 20 | 754 | 130 | 284 | .458 | 99 | 113 | .876 | 18 | 26 | 44 | 95 | 22 | 0 | 54 | 364 | 2.2 | 4.8 | 18.2 |
| 90-91—Detroit | 15 | 588 | 105 | 245 | .429 | 82 | 97 | .845 | 21 | 29 | 50 | 62 | 16 | 1 | 17 | 309 | 3.3 | 4.1 | 20.6 |
| 91-92—Detroit | 5 | 221 | 32 | 68 | .471 | 15 | 19 | .789 | 5 | 3 | 8 | 16 | 5 | 1 | 7 | 84 | 1.6 | 3.2 | 16.8 |
| 95-96—Detroit | 3 | 123 | 16 | 35 | .457 | 4 | 4 | 1.000 | 5 | 8 | 13 | 11 | 0 | 0 | 7 | 41 | 4.3 | 3.7 | 13.7 |
| 96-97—Detroit | 5 | 214 | 22 | 61 | .361 | 19 | 20 | .950 | 2 | 7 | 9 | 10 | 5 | 0 | 6 | 69 | 1.8 | 2.0 | 13.8 |
| 98-99—Detroit | 5 | 153 | 19 | 39 | .487 | 3 | 3 | 1.000 | 1 | 6 | 7 | 13 | 2 | 0 | 9 | 51 | 1.4 | 2.6 | 10.2 |
| **Totals** | 112 | 4097 | 646 | 1398 | .462 | 407 | 476 | .855 | 95 | 162 | 257 | 512 | 91 | 6 | 205 | 1752 | 2.3 | 4.6 | 15.6 |

Three-point field goals: 1986-87, 2-for-3 (.667). 1987-88, 2-for-6 (.333). 1988-89, 1-for-12 (.083). 1989-90, 5-for-19 (.263). 1990-91, 17-for-42 (.405). 1991-92, 5-for-10 (.500). 1995-96, 5-for-14 (.357). 1996-97, 6-for-23 (.261). 1998-99, 10-for-19 (.526). Totals, 53-for-148 (.358).

Personal fouls/disqualifications: 1985-86, 16/0. 1986-87, 26/0. 1987-88, 50/1. 1988-89, 31/0. 1989-90, 37/0. 1990-91, 33/1. 1991-92, 11/0. 1995-96, 5/0. 1996-97, 9/0. 1998-99, 9/0. Totals, 227/2.

## NBA ALL-STAR GAME RECORD

| Season Team | Min. | FGM | FGA | Pct. | FTM | FTA | Pct. | Off. | Def. | Tot. | Ast. | PF | Dq. | St. | Blk. | TO | Pts. |
|---|---|---|---|---|---|---|---|---|---|---|---|---|---|---|---|---|---|
| 1990—Detroit | 18 | 3 | 4 | .750 | 1 | 2 | .500 | 0 | 1 | 1 | 5 | 0 | 0 | 0 | 0 | 3 | 9 |
| 1991—Detroit | 15 | 1 | 4 | .250 | 0 | 0 | ... | 1 | 1 | 2 | 1 | 1 | 0 | 0 | 0 | 4 | 2 |
| 1992—Detroit | 17 | 2 | 7 | .286 | 0 | 0 | ... | 0 | 1 | 1 | 3 | 0 | 0 | 0 | 0 | 2 | 4 |
| 1993—Detroit | 17 | 2 | 8 | .250 | 0 | 0 | ... | 0 | 2 | 2 | 4 | 1 | 0 | 0 | 0 | 1 | 5 |
| 1995—Detroit | 21 | 5 | 8 | .625 | 0 | 0 | ... | 0 | 0 | 0 | 6 | 1 | 0 | 1 | 0 | 1 | 11 |
| 1997—Detroit | 10 | 1 | 4 | .250 | 0 | 0 | ... | 0 | 1 | 1 | 1 | 0 | 0 | 0 | 0 | 0 | 3 |
| **Totals** | 98 | 14 | 35 | .400 | 1 | 2 | .500 | 1 | 6 | 7 | 20 | 3 | 0 | 1 | 0 | 11 | 34 |

Three-point field goals: 1990, 2-for-2. 1991, 0-for-1. 1992, 0-for-2. 1993, 1-for-4 (.250). 1995, 1-for-2 (.500). 1997, 1-for-4 (.250). Totals, 5-for-15 (.333).

## ELLIS, DALE                         G/F

**PERSONAL:** Born August 6, 1960, in Marietta, Ga. ... 6-7/215. (2.01 m/98 kg).
**HIGH SCHOOL:** Marietta (Ga.).
**COLLEGE:** Tennessee.
**TRANSACTIONS/CAREER NOTES:** Selected by Dallas Mavericks in first round (ninth pick overall) of 1983 NBA Draft. ... Traded by Mavericks to Seattle SuperSonics for G/F Al Wood (July 23, 1986). ... Traded by SuperSonics to Milwaukee Bucks for G/F Ricky Pierce (February 15, 1991). ... Traded by Bucks to San Antonio Spurs for draft rights to F Tracy Murray (July 1, 1992). ... Signed as free agent by Denver Nuggets (October 4, 1994). ... Traded by Nuggets to SuperSonics for G Greg Graham, C Steve Scheffler, 1998 second-round draft choice and 1999 or 2002 conditional second-round draft choice (October 2, 1997). ... Became a free agent when SuperSonics did not exercise option for 1998-99 season (June 30, 1998). ... Re-signed as free agent by SuperSonics (January 21, 1999). ... Traded by SuperSonics with F/G Billy Owens, F Don MacLean and draft rights to F Corey Maggette to Orlando Magic for F Horace Grant and 2001 and 2002 second-round draft choices (June 30, 1999). ... Traded by Magic with F/C Danny Manning to Milwaukee Bucks for F/C Chris Gatling and F Armen Gilliam (August 19, 1999). ... Traded by Bucks to Charlotte Hornets for 2000 and 2001 second-round draft choices (January 18, 2000). ... Traded by Hornets with G Eddie Jones, F Anthony Mason and G Ricky Davis to Miami Heat for F P.J. Brown, F Jamal Mashburn, F/C Otis Thorpe, F Tim James and G/F Rodney Buford (August 1, 2000). ... Waived by Heat (October 30, 2000).

### COLLEGIATE RECORD

**NOTES:** The Sporting News All-America first team (1983).

| Season Team | G | Min. | FGM | FGA | Pct. | FTM | FTA | Pct. | Reb. | Ast. | Pts. | RPG | APG | PPG |
|---|---|---|---|---|---|---|---|---|---|---|---|---|---|---|
| 79-80—Tennessee | 27 | 573 | 81 | 182 | .445 | 31 | 40 | .775 | 96 | 34 | 193 | 3.6 | 1.3 | 7.1 |
| 80-81—Tennessee | 29 | 1057 | 215 | 360 | .597 | 83 | 111 | .748 | 185 | 21 | 513 | 6.4 | 0.7 | 17.7 |
| 81-82—Tennessee | 30 | 1134 | 257 | 393 | .654 | 121 | 152 | .796 | 189 | 22 | 635 | 6.3 | 0.7 | 21.2 |
| 82-83—Tennessee | 32 | 1179 | 279 | 464 | .601 | 166 | 221 | .751 | 209 | 32 | 724 | 6.5 | 1.0 | 22.6 |
| **Totals** | 118 | 3943 | 832 | 1399 | .594 | 401 | 524 | .765 | 679 | 109 | 2065 | 5.8 | 0.9 | 17.5 |

### NBA REGULAR-SEASON RECORD

**RECORDS:** Holds single-game record for most minutes played—69 (November 9, 1989, vs. Milwaukee, 5 OT).
**HONORS:** NBA Most Improved Player (1987). ... Long Distance Shootout winner (1989). ... All-NBA third team (1989).
**NOTES:** Led NBA with .464 three-point field goal percentage (1998).

| Season Team | G | Min. | FGM | FGA | Pct. | FTM | FTA | Pct. | Off. | Def. | Tot. | Ast. | St. | Blk. | TO | Pts. | RPG | APG | PPG |
|---|---|---|---|---|---|---|---|---|---|---|---|---|---|---|---|---|---|---|---|
| 83-84—Dallas | 67 | 1059 | 225 | 493 | .456 | 87 | 121 | .719 | 106 | 144 | 250 | 56 | 41 | 9 | 78 | 549 | 3.7 | 0.8 | 8.2 |
| 84-85—Dallas | 72 | 1314 | 274 | 603 | .454 | 77 | 104 | .740 | 100 | 138 | 238 | 56 | 46 | 7 | 58 | 667 | 3.3 | 0.8 | 9.3 |
| 85-86—Dallas | 72 | 1086 | 193 | 470 | .411 | 59 | 82 | .720 | 86 | 82 | 168 | 37 | 40 | 9 | 38 | 508 | 2.3 | 0.5 | 7.1 |
| 86-87—Seattle | 82 | 3073 | 785 | 1520 | .516 | 385 | 489 | .787 | 187 | 260 | 447 | 238 | 104 | 32 | 238 | 2041 | 5.5 | 2.9 | 24.9 |
| 87-88—Seattle | 75 | 2790 | 764 | 1519 | .503 | 303 | 395 | .767 | 167 | 173 | 340 | 197 | 74 | 11 | 172 | 1938 | 4.5 | 2.6 | 25.8 |
| 88-89—Seattle | 82 | 3190 | 857 | 1710 | .501 | 377 | 462 | .816 | 156 | 186 | 342 | 164 | 108 | 22 | 218 | 2253 | 4.2 | 2.0 | 27.5 |
| 89-90—Seattle | 55 | 2033 | 502 | 1011 | .497 | 193 | 236 | .818 | 90 | 148 | 238 | 110 | 59 | 7 | 119 | 1293 | 4.3 | 2.0 | 23.5 |
| 90-91—Seattle-Mil. | 51 | 1424 | 340 | 718 | .474 | 120 | 166 | .723 | 66 | 107 | 173 | 95 | 49 | 8 | 81 | 857 | 3.4 | 1.9 | 16.8 |
| 91-92—Milwaukee | 81 | 2191 | 485 | 1034 | .469 | 164 | 212 | .774 | 92 | 161 | 253 | 104 | 57 | 18 | 119 | 1272 | 3.1 | 1.3 | 15.7 |
| 92-93—San Antonio | 82 | 2731 | 545 | 1092 | .499 | 157 | 197 | .797 | 81 | 231 | 312 | 107 | 78 | 18 | 111 | 1366 | 3.8 | 1.3 | 16.7 |
| 93-94—San Antonio | 77 | 2590 | 478 | 967 | .494 | 83 | 107 | .776 | 70 | 185 | 255 | 80 | 66 | 11 | 75 | 1170 | 3.3 | 1.0 | 15.2 |
| 94-95—Denver | 81 | 1996 | 351 | 774 | .453 | 110 | 127 | .866 | 56 | 166 | 222 | 57 | 37 | 9 | 81 | 918 | 2.7 | 0.7 | 11.3 |
| 95-96—Denver | 81 | 2626 | 459 | 959 | .479 | 136 | 179 | .760 | 88 | 227 | 315 | 139 | 57 | 7 | 98 | 1204 | 3.9 | 1.7 | 14.9 |
| 96-97—Denver | 82 | 2940 | 477 | 1151 | .414 | 215 | 263 | .817 | 99 | 194 | 293 | 165 | 60 | 7 | 146 | 1361 | 3.6 | 2.0 | 16.6 |
| 97-98—Seattle | 79 | 1939 | 348 | 700 | .497 | 111 | 142 | .782 | 51 | 133 | 184 | 89 | 60 | 5 | 74 | 934 | 2.3 | 1.1 | 11.8 |
| 98-99—Seattle | 48 | 1232 | 174 | 395 | .441 | 53 | 70 | .757 | 25 | 90 | 115 | 38 | 25 | 3 | 45 | 495 | 2.4 | 0.8 | 10.3 |
| 99-00—Mil.-Charlotte | 42 | 564 | 66 | 159 | .415 | 9 | 13 | .692 | 13 | 43 | 56 | 14 | 13 | 0 | 20 | 178 | 1.3 | 0.3 | 4.2 |
| **Totals** | 1209 | 34778 | 7323 | 15275 | .479 | 2639 | 3365 | .784 | 1533 | 2668 | 4201 | 1746 | 974 | 183 | 1771 | 19004 | 3.5 | 1.4 | 15.7 |

Three-point field goals: 1983-84, 12-for-29 (.414). 1984-85, 42-for-109 (.385). 1985-86, 63-for-173 (.364). 1986-87, 86-for-240 (.358). 1987-88, 107-for-259 (.413). 1988-89, 162-for-339 (.478). 1989-90, 96-for-256 (.375). 1990-91, 57-for-157 (.363). 1991-92, 138-for-329 (.419). 1992-93, 119-for-297 (.401). 1993-94, 131-for-332 (.395). 1994-95, 106-for-263 (.403). 1995-96, 150-for-364 (.412). 1996-97, 192-for-528 (.364). 1997-98, 127-for-274 (.464). 1998-99, 94-for-217 (.433). 1999-00, 27-for-73 (.370). Totals, 1719-for-4266 (.403).

Personal fouls/disqualifications: 1983-84, 118/0. 1984-85, 131/1. 1985-86, 78/0. 1986-87, 267/2. 1987-88, 221/1. 1988-89, 197/0. 1989-90, 124/3. 1990-91, 112/1. 1991-92, 151/0. 1992-93, 179/0. 1993-94, 141/0. 1994-95, 142/0. 1995-96, 191/1. 1996-97, 178/0. 1997-98, 128/0. 1998-99, 77/1. 1999-00, 45/0. Totals, 2480/10.

## NBA PLAYOFF RECORD

| Season Team | G | Min. | FGM | FGA | Pct. | FTM | FTA | Pct. | REBOUNDS Off. | Def. | Tot. | Ast. | St. | Blk. | TO | Pts. | AVERAGES RPG | APG | PPG |
|---|---|---|---|---|---|---|---|---|---|---|---|---|---|---|---|---|---|---|---|
| 83-84—Dallas.............. | 8 | 178 | 26 | 80 | .325 | 6 | 8 | .750 | 19 | 23 | 42 | 4 | 10 | 2 | 5 | 59 | 5.3 | 0.5 | 7.4 |
| 84-85—Dallas.............. | 4 | 68 | 10 | 23 | .435 | 1 | 2 | .500 | 4 | 3 | 7 | 3 | 4 | 0 | 4 | 23 | 1.8 | 0.8 | 5.8 |
| 85-86—Dallas.............. | 7 | 67 | 9 | 22 | .409 | 5 | 5 | 1.000 | 3 | 4 | 7 | 2 | 2 | 2 | 4 | 30 | 1.0 | 0.3 | 4.3 |
| 86-87—Seattle | 14 | 530 | 148 | 304 | .487 | 44 | 54 | .815 | 37 | 53 | 90 | 37 | 10 | 6 | 33 | 353 | 6.4 | 2.6 | 25.2 |
| 87-88—Seattle | 5 | 172 | 40 | 83 | .482 | 21 | 29 | .724 | 11 | 12 | 23 | 15 | 3 | 2 | 12 | 104 | 4.6 | 3.0 | 20.8 |
| 88-89—Seattle | 8 | 304 | 72 | 160 | .450 | 24 | 33 | .727 | 14 | 18 | 32 | 10 | 11 | 1 | 21 | 183 | 4.0 | 1.3 | 22.9 |
| 92-93—San Antonio.... | 10 | 305 | 51 | 113 | .451 | 13 | 16 | .813 | 9 | 26 | 35 | 11 | 4 | 0 | 10 | 125 | 3.5 | 1.1 | 12.5 |
| 93-94—San Antonio | 4 | 114 | 17 | 43 | .395 | 3 | 5 | .600 | 3 | 7 | 10 | 1 | 3 | 0 | 4 | 42 | 2.5 | 0.3 | 10.5 |
| 94-95—Denver | 3 | 73 | 10 | 28 | .357 | 12 | 13 | .923 | 6 | 8 | 14 | 3 | 2 | 1 | 2 | 36 | 4.7 | 1.0 | 12.0 |
| 97-98—Seattle | 10 | 170 | 20 | 53 | .377 | 5 | 6 | .833 | 4 | 9 | 13 | 6 | 2 | 0 | 2 | 56 | 1.3 | 0.6 | 5.6 |
| **Totals ...................** | 73 | 1981 | 403 | 909 | .443 | 134 | 171 | .784 | 110 | 163 | 273 | 92 | 51 | 14 | 97 | 1011 | 3.7 | 1.3 | 13.8 |

Three-point field goals: 1983-84, 1-for-12 (.083). 1984-85, 2-for-5 (.400). 1985-86, 7-for-12 (.583). 1986-87, 13-for-36 (.361). 1987-88, 3-for-12 (.250). 1988-89, 15-for-37 (.405). 1992-93, 10-for-32 (.313). 1993-94, 5-for-17 (.294). 1994-95, 4-for-13 (.308). 1997-98, 11-for-26 (.423). Totals, 71-for-202 (.351).

Personal fouls/disqualifications: 1983-84, 17/0. 1984-85, 3/0. 1985-86, 6/0. 1986-87, 54/1. 1987-88, 17/0. 1988-89, 19/1. 1992-93, 25/0. 1993-94, 6/0. 1994-95, 6/0. 1997-98, 10/0. Totals, 163/2.

## NBA ALL-STAR GAME RECORD

| Season Team | Min. | FGM | FGA | Pct. | FTM | FTA | Pct. | REBOUNDS Off. | Def. | Tot. | Ast. | PF | Dq. | St. | Blk. | TO | Pts. |
|---|---|---|---|---|---|---|---|---|---|---|---|---|---|---|---|---|---|
| 1989—Seattle.................. | 26 | 12 | 16 | .750 | 2 | 2 | 1.000 | 3 | 3 | 6 | 2 | 2 | 0 | 0 | 0 | 2 | 27 |
| **Totals..........................** | 26 | 12 | 16 | .750 | 2 | 2 | 1.000 | 3 | 3 | 6 | 2 | 2 | 0 | 0 | 0 | 2 | 27 |

Three-point field goals: 1989, 1-for-1.

# ENGLISH, ALEX                                    F

**PERSONAL:** Born January 5, 1954, in Columbia, S.C. ... 6-7/190 (2,00/86,2). ... Full name: Alexander English.
**HIGH SCHOOL:** Dreher (Columbia, S.C.).
**COLLEGE:** South Carolina.
**TRANSACTIONS:** Selected by Milwaukee Bucks in second round (23rd pick overall) of 1976 NBA Draft. ... Signed as veteran free agent by Indiana Pacers (June 8, 1978); Bucks waived their right of first refusal in exchange for 1979 first-round draft choice (October 3, 1978). ... Traded by Pacers with 1980 first-round draft choice to Denver Nuggets for F George McGinnis (February 1, 1980). ... Signed as unrestricted free agent by Dallas Mavericks (August 15, 1990). ... Played in Italy (1991-92).
**CAREER HONORS:** Elected to Naismith Memorial Basketball Hall of Fame (1997).
**CAREER NOTES:** Assistant coach, Philadelphia 76ers (2003-04). ... Named assistant coach, Toronto Raptors (July 2, 2004).
**MISCELLANEOUS:** Denver Nuggets franchise all-time leading scorer with 21,645 points and all-time assists leader with 3,679 (1979-80 through 1989-90).

## COLLEGIATE RECORD

**HONORS:** All-NBA second team (1982, 1983, 1986). ... J. Walter Kennedy Citizenship Award (1988).

| Season Team | G | Min. | FGM | FGA | Pct. | FTM | FTA | Pct. | Reb. | Ast. | Pts. | AVERAGES RPG | APG | PPG |
|---|---|---|---|---|---|---|---|---|---|---|---|---|---|---|
| 72-73—South Carolina............... | 29 | 1037 | 189 | 368 | .514 | 44 | 70 | .629 | 306 | 25 | 422 | 10.6 | 0.9 | 14.6 |
| 73-74—South Carolina............... | 27 | 1007 | 209 | 395 | .529 | 75 | 112 | .670 | 237 | 28 | 493 | 8.8 | 1.0 | 18.3 |
| 74-75—South Carolina............... | 28 | 1024 | 199 | 359 | .554 | 49 | 77 | .636 | 244 | 30 | 447 | 8.7 | 1.1 | 16.0 |
| 75-76—South Carolina............... | 27 | 1045 | 258 | 468 | .551 | 94 | 134 | .702 | 277 | 27 | 610 | 10.3 | 1.0 | 22.6 |
| **Totals .....................................** | 111 | 4113 | 855 | 1590 | .538 | 262 | 393 | .667 | 1064 | 110 | 1972 | 9.6 | 1.0 | 17.8 |

## NBA REGULAR-SEASON RECORD

| Season Team | G | Min. | FGM | FGA | Pct. | FTM | FTA | Pct. | REBOUNDS Off. | Def. | Tot. | Ast. | St. | Blk. | TO | Pts. | AVERAGES RPG | APG | PPG |
|---|---|---|---|---|---|---|---|---|---|---|---|---|---|---|---|---|---|---|---|
| 76-77—Milwaukee ...... | 60 | 648 | 132 | 277 | .477 | 46 | 60 | .767 | 68 | 100 | 168 | 25 | 17 | 18 | ... | 310 | 2.8 | 0.4 | 5.2 |
| 77-78—Milwaukee ...... | 82 | 1552 | 343 | 633 | .542 | 104 | 143 | .727 | 144 | 251 | 395 | 129 | 41 | 55 | 137 | 790 | 4.8 | 1.6 | 9.6 |
| 78-79—Indiana............ | 81 | 2696 | 563 | 1102 | .511 | 173 | 230 | .752 | 253 | 402 | 655 | 271 | 70 | 78 | 196 | 1299 | 8.1 | 3.3 | 16.0 |
| 79-80—Ind.-Denver..... | 78 | 2401 | 553 | 1113 | .497 | 210 | 266 | .789 | 269 | 336 | 605 | 224 | 73 | 62 | 214 | 1318 | 7.8 | 2.9 | 16.9 |
| 80-81—Denver............ | 81 | 3093 | 768 | 1555 | .494 | 390 | 459 | .850 | 273 | 373 | 646 | 290 | 106 | 100 | 241 | 1929 | 8.0 | 3.6 | 23.8 |
| 81-82—Denver............ | 82 | 3015 | 855 | 1553 | .551 | 372 | 443 | .840 | 210 | 348 | 558 | 433 | 87 | 120 | 261 | 2082 | 6.8 | 5.3 | 25.4 |
| 82-83—Denver............ | 82 | 2988 | *959 | *1857 | .516 | 406 | 490 | .829 | 263 | 338 | 601 | 397 | 116 | 126 | 263 | *2326 | 7.3 | 4.8 | *28.4 |
| 83-84—Denver............ | 82 | 2870 | 907 | 1714 | .529 | 352 | 427 | .824 | 216 | 248 | 464 | 406 | 83 | 95 | 222 | 2167 | 5.7 | 5.0 | 26.4 |
| 84-85—Denver............ | 81 | 2924 | *939 | 1812 | .518 | 383 | 462 | .829 | 203 | 255 | 458 | 344 | 101 | 46 | 251 | 2262 | 5.7 | 4.2 | 27.9 |
| 85-86—Denver............ | 81 | 3024 | *951 | 1888 | .504 | 511 | 593 | .862 | 192 | 213 | 405 | 320 | 73 | 29 | 249 | *2414 | 5.0 | 4.0 | 29.8 |
| 86-87—Denver............ | 82 | 3085 | 965 | 1920 | .503 | 411 | 487 | .844 | 146 | 198 | 344 | 422 | 73 | 21 | 214 | 2345 | 4.2 | 5.1 | 28.6 |
| 87-88—Denver............ | 80 | 2818 | 843 | 1704 | .495 | 314 | 379 | .829 | 166 | 207 | 373 | 377 | 70 | 23 | 181 | 2000 | 4.7 | 4.7 | 25.0 |
| 88-89—Denver............ | 82 | 2990 | 924 | 1881 | .491 | 325 | 379 | .858 | 148 | 178 | 326 | 383 | 66 | 12 | 198 | 2175 | 4.0 | 4.7 | 26.5 |
| 89-90—Denver............ | 80 | 2211 | 635 | 1293 | .491 | 161 | 183 | .880 | 119 | 167 | 286 | 225 | 51 | 23 | 93 | 1433 | 3.6 | 2.8 | 17.9 |
| 90-91—Dallas............. | 79 | 1748 | 322 | 734 | .439 | 119 | 140 | .850 | 108 | 146 | 254 | 105 | 40 | 25 | 101 | 763 | 3.2 | 1.3 | 9.7 |
| **Totals ...................** | 1193 | 38063 | 10659 | 21036 | .507 | 4277 | 5141 | .832 | 2778 | 3760 | 6538 | 4351 | 1067 | 833 | 2821 | 25613 | 5.5 | 3.6 | 21.5 |

Three-point field goals: 1979-80, 2-for-6 (.333). 1980-81, 3-for-5 (.600). 1981-82, 0-for-8. 1982-83, 2-for-12 (.167). 1983-84, 1-for-7 (.143). 1984-85, 1-for-5 (.200). 1985-86, 1-for-5 (.200). 1986-87, 4-for-15 (.267). 1987-88, 0-for-6. 1988-89, 2-for-8 (.250). 1989-90, 2-for-5 (.400). 1990-91, 0-for-1. Totals, 18-for-83 (.217).

Personal fouls/disqualifications: 1976-77, 78/0. 1977-78, 178/1. 1978-79, 214/3. 1979-80, 206/0. 1980-81, 255/2. 1981-82, 261/2. 1982-83, 235/1. 1983-84, 252/3. 1984-85, 259/1. 1985-86, 235/1. 1986-87, 216/0. 1987-88, 193/1. 1988-89, 174/0. 1989-90, 130/0. 1990-91, 141/0. Totals, 3027/15.

## NBA PLAYOFF RECORD

| Season Team | G | Min. | FGM | FGA | Pct. | FTM | FTA | Pct. | REBOUNDS Off. | Def. | Tot. | Ast. | St. | Blk. | TO | Pts. | AVERAGES RPG | APG | PPG |
|---|---|---|---|---|---|---|---|---|---|---|---|---|---|---|---|---|---|---|---|
| 77-78—Milwaukee ...... | 9 | 208 | 48 | 78 | .615 | 25 | 32 | .781 | 16 | 26 | 42 | 13 | 6 | 7 | 12 | 121 | 4.7 | 1.4 | 13.4 |
| 81-82—Denver............ | 3 | 118 | 26 | 55 | .473 | 6 | 7 | .857 | 8 | 15 | 23 | 17 | 3 | 3 | 4 | 58 | 7.7 | 5.7 | 19.3 |
| 82-83—Denver............ | 7 | 270 | 67 | 150 | .447 | 47 | 53 | .887 | 20 | 24 | 44 | 42 | 4 | 7 | 21 | 181 | 6.3 | 6.0 | 25.9 |
| 83-84—Denver............ | 5 | 203 | 60 | 102 | .588 | 25 | 28 | .893 | 16 | 24 | 40 | 28 | 3 | 2 | 7 | 145 | 8.0 | 5.6 | 29.0 |
| 84-85—Denver............ | 14 | 536 | 163 | 304 | .536 | 97 | 109 | .890 | 36 | 56 | 92 | 63 | 17 | 5 | 30 | 423 | 6.6 | 4.5 | 30.2 |

| Season Team | G | Min. | FGM | FGA | Pct. | FTM | FTA | Pct. | REBOUNDS Off. | Def. | Tot. | Ast. | St. | Blk. | TO | Pts. | AVERAGES RPG | APG | PPG |
|---|---|---|---|---|---|---|---|---|---|---|---|---|---|---|---|---|---|---|---|
| 85-86—Denver | 10 | 394 | 106 | 229 | .463 | 61 | 71 | .859 | 18 | 17 | 35 | 52 | 4 | 4 | 28 | 273 | 3.5 | 5.2 | 27.3 |
| 86-87—Denver | 3 | 76 | 25 | 49 | .510 | 6 | 7 | .857 | 10 | 4 | 14 | 10 | 0 | 0 | 8 | 56 | 4.7 | 3.3 | 18.7 |
| 87-88—Denver | 11 | 438 | 116 | 255 | .455 | 35 | 43 | .814 | 31 | 28 | 59 | 48 | 7 | 3 | 16 | 267 | 5.4 | 4.4 | 24.3 |
| 88-89—Denver | 3 | 108 | 32 | 62 | .516 | 14 | 16 | .875 | 8 | 5 | 13 | 11 | 1 | 0 | 14 | 78 | 4.3 | 3.7 | 26.0 |
| 89-90—Denver | 3 | 76 | 25 | 44 | .568 | 9 | 11 | .818 | 3 | 6 | 9 | 9 | 2 | 1 | 2 | 59 | 3.0 | 3.0 | 19.7 |
| Totals | 68 | 2427 | 668 | 1328 | .503 | 325 | 377 | .862 | 166 | 205 | 371 | 293 | 47 | 32 | 142 | 1661 | 5.5 | 4.3 | 24.4 |

Three-point field goals: 1982-83, 0-for-2. 1983-84, 0-for-1. 1984-85, 0-for-1. 1985-86, 0-for-1. 1987-88, 0-for-3. Totals, 0-for-8.
Personal fouls/disqualifications: 1977-78, 20/0. 1981-82, 6/0. 1982-83, 21/0. 1983-84, 17/0. 1984-85, 40/1. 1985-86, 29/0. 1986-87, 9/1. 1987-88, 34/0. 1988-89, 6/0. 1989-90, 6/0. Totals, 188/2.

### NBA ALL-STAR GAME RECORD

| Season Team | Min. | FGM | FGA | Pct. | FTM | FTA | Pct. | REBOUNDS Off. | Def. | Tot. | Ast. | PF | Dq. | St. | Blk. | TO | Pts. |
|---|---|---|---|---|---|---|---|---|---|---|---|---|---|---|---|---|---|
| 1982—Denver | 12 | 2 | 6 | .333 | 0 | 0 | ... | 2 | 3 | 5 | 1 | 2 | 0 | 1 | 0 | 1 | 4 |
| 1983—Denver | 23 | 7 | 14 | .500 | 0 | 1 | .000 | 2 | 2 | 4 | 0 | 2 | 0 | 1 | 2 | 2 | 14 |
| 1984—Denver | 19 | 6 | 8 | .750 | 1 | 1 | 1.000 | 0 | 0 | 0 | 2 | 2 | 0 | 1 | 1 | 3 | 13 |
| 1985—Denver | 14 | 0 | 3 | .000 | 0 | 0 | ... | 1 | 1 | 2 | 1 | 1 | 0 | 0 | 0 | 2 | 0 |
| 1986—Denver | 16 | 8 | 12 | .667 | 0 | 0 | ... | 1 | 0 | 1 | 2 | 0 | 0 | 0 | 1 | 1 | 16 |
| 1987—Denver | 13 | 0 | 6 | .000 | 0 | 0 | ... | 0 | 0 | 0 | 1 | 1 | 0 | 0 | 0 | 2 | 0 |
| 1988—Denver | 22 | 5 | 10 | .500 | 0 | 0 | ... | 2 | 1 | 3 | 4 | 0 | 0 | 1 | 0 | 0 | 10 |
| 1989—Denver | 29 | 8 | 13 | .615 | 1 | 2 | .500 | 1 | 2 | 3 | 4 | 0 | 0 | 2 | 0 | 3 | 16 |
| Totals | 148 | 36 | 72 | .500 | 2 | 4 | .500 | 9 | 9 | 18 | 15 | 8 | 0 | 6 | 4 | 14 | 73 |

### ITALIAN LEAGUE RECORD

| Season Team | G | Min. | FGM | FGA | Pct. | FTM | FTA | Pct. | Reb. | Ast. | Pts. | AVERAGES RPG | APG | PPG |
|---|---|---|---|---|---|---|---|---|---|---|---|---|---|---|
| 91-92—Depi Napoli | 18 | 566 | 103 | 214 | .481 | 44 | 55 | .800 | 86 | 5 | 251 | 4.8 | 0.3 | 13.9 |

### NBDL COACHING RECORD

| Season Team | REGULAR SEASON W | L | Pct. | Finish | PLAYOFFS W | L | Pct. |
|---|---|---|---|---|---|---|---|
| 01-02—North Charleston | 36 | 20 | .640 | 1st | 2 | 4 | .200 |

NOTES:
01-02—Defeated Mobile in semifinals; lost to Greenville in NBDL Finals.

## ERVING, JULIUS    F

**PERSONAL:** Born February 22, 1950, in Roosevelt, N.Y. ... 6-7/210 (2,00/95,3). ... Full name: Julius Winfield Erving II. ... Cousin of Mark Williams, linebacker with four NFL teams (1994-96). ... Nickname: Dr. J.
**HIGH SCHOOL:** Roosevelt (N.Y.).
**COLLEGE:** Massachusetts.
**TRANSACTIONS:** Signed as free agent after junior season by Virginia Squires of American Basketball Association (April 6, 1971). ... Selected by Milwaukee Bucks in first round (12th pick overall) of 1972 NBA draft. ... Traded by Squires with C Willie Sojourner to New York Nets for F George Carter, draft rights to F/C Kermit Washington and cash (August 1, 1973). ... Nets franchise became part of NBA for 1976-77 season. ... Contract sold by Nets to Philadelphia 76ers (October 20, 1976).
**CAREER HONORS:** Elected to Naismith Memorial Basketball Hall of Fame (1993). ... NBA 35th Anniversary All-Time Team (1980) and One of the 50 Greatest Players in NBA History (1996).
**CAREER NOTES:** Executive vice president, Orlando Magic (1997-98 to 2002-03).
**MISCELLANEOUS:** Member of NBA championship team (1983). ... Philadelphia 76ers franchise all-time blocked shots leader with 1,293 (1976-77 through 1986-87).

### COLLEGIATE RECORD

| Season Team | G | Min. | FGM | FGA | Pct. | FTM | FTA | Pct. | Reb. | Ast. | Pts. | AVERAGES RPG | APG | PPG |
|---|---|---|---|---|---|---|---|---|---|---|---|---|---|---|
| 68-69—Massachusetts‡ | 15 | | 112 | 216 | .519 | 49 | 81 | .605 | 214 | ... | 273 | 14.3 | ... | 18.2 |
| 69-70—Massachusetts | 25 | 969 | 238 | 468 | .509 | 167 | 230 | .726 | 522 | 89 | 643 | 20.9 | 3.6 | 25.7 |
| 70-71—Massachusetts | 27 | 1029 | 286 | 609 | .470 | 155 | 206 | .752 | 527 | 99 | 727 | 19.5 | 3.7 | 26.9 |
| Varsity totals | 52 | 1998 | 524 | 1077 | .487 | 322 | 436 | .739 | 1049 | 188 | 1370 | 20.2 | 3.6 | 26.3 |

### ABA REGULAR-SEASON RECORD

**NOTES:** ABA Most Valuable Player (1974, 1976). ... ABA co-Most Valuable Player (1975). ... ABA All-Star first team (1973, 1974, 1975, 1976). ... ABA All-Star second team (1972). ... ABA All-Defensive team (1976). ... ABA All-Rookie team (1972). ... Member of ABA championship team (1974, 1976). ... Holds career record for highest points-per-game average (minimum 250 games)—28.7.

| Season Team | G | Min. | 2-POINT FGM | FGA | Pct. | 3-POINT FGM | FGA | Pct. | FTM | FTA | Pct. | Reb. | Ast. | Pts. | AVERAGES RPG | APG | PPG |
|---|---|---|---|---|---|---|---|---|---|---|---|---|---|---|---|---|---|
| 71-72—Virginia | 84 | 3513 | 907 | 1810 | .501 | 3 | 16 | .188 | 467 | 627 | .745 | 1319 | 335 | 2290 | 15.7 | 4.0 | 27.3 |
| 72-73—Virginia | 71 | 2993 | 889 | 1780 | .499 | 5 | 24 | .208 | 475 | 612 | .776 | 867 | 298 | *2268 | 12.2 | 4.2 | *31.9 |
| 73-74—New York | 84 | 3398 | 897 | 1742 | .515 | 17 | 43 | .395 | 454 | 593 | .766 | 899 | 434 | *2299 | 10.7 | 5.2 | *27.4 |
| 74-75—New York | 84 | 3402 | 885 | 1719 | .515 | 29 | 87 | .333 | 486 | 608 | .799 | 914 | 462 | 2343 | 10.9 | 5.5 | 27.9 |
| 75-76—New York | 84 | 3244 | 915 | 1770 | .517 | 34 | 103 | .330 | 530 | 662 | .801 | 925 | 423 | *2462 | 11.0 | 5.0 | *29.3 |
| Totals | 407 | 16550 | 4493 | 8821 | .509 | 88 | 273 | .322 | 2412 | 3102 | .778 | 4924 | 1952 | 11662 | 12.1 | 4.8 | 28.7 |

### ABA PLAYOFF RECORD

**NOTES:** ABA Playoff Most Valuable Player (1974, 1976).

| Season Team | G | Min. | 2-POINT | | | 3-POINT | | | FTM | FTA | Pct. | Reb. | Ast. | Pts. | AVERAGES | | |
| | | | FGM | FGA | Pct. | FGM | FGA | Pct. | | | | | | | RPG | APG | PPG |
|---|---|---|---|---|---|---|---|---|---|---|---|---|---|---|---|---|---|
| 71-72—Virginia | 11 | 504 | 146 | 280 | .521 | 1 | 4 | .250 | 71 | 85 | .835 | 224 | 72 | 366 | 20.4 | 6.5 | 33.3 |
| 72-73—Virginia | 5 | 219 | 59 | 109 | .541 | 0 | 3 | .000 | 30 | 40 | .750 | 45 | 16 | 148 | 9.0 | 3.2 | 29.6 |
| 73-74—New York | 14 | 579 | 156 | 294 | .531 | 5 | 11 | .455 | 63 | 85 | .741 | 135 | 67 | 390 | 9.6 | 4.8 | 27.9 |
| 74-75—New York | 5 | 211 | 55 | 113 | .487 | 0 | 8 | .000 | 27 | 32 | .844 | 49 | 28 | 137 | 9.8 | 5.6 | 27.4 |
| 75-76—New York | 13 | 551 | 156 | 286 | .545 | 4 | 14 | .286 | 127 | 158 | .804 | 164 | 64 | 451 | 12.6 | 4.9 | 34.7 |
| Totals | 48 | 2064 | 572 | 1082 | .529 | 10 | 40 | .250 | 318 | 400 | .795 | 617 | 247 | 1492 | 12.9 | 5.1 | 31.1 |

## ABA ALL-STAR GAME RECORD

| Season Team | Min. | 2-POINT | | | 3-POINT | | | FTM | FTA | Pct. | Reb. | Ast. | Pts. |
| | | FGM | FGA | Pct. | FGM | FGA | Pct. | | | | | | |
|---|---|---|---|---|---|---|---|---|---|---|---|---|---|
| 1972—Virginia | 25 | 9 | 15 | .600 | 0 | 0 | ... | 2 | 2 | 1.000 | 6 | 3 | 20 |
| 1973—Virginia | 30 | 8 | 16 | .500 | 0 | 0 | ... | 6 | 8 | .750 | 5 | 1 | 22 |
| 1974—New York | 27 | 6 | 15 | .400 | 0 | 0 | ... | 2 | 2 | 1.000 | 11 | 8 | 14 |
| 1975—New York | 27 | 5 | 11 | .455 | 1 | 1 | 1.000 | 8 | 10 | .800 | 7 | 7 | 21 |
| 1976—New York | 25 | 9 | 12 | .750 | 0 | 1 | .000 | 5 | 7 | .714 | 7 | 5 | 23 |
| Totals | 134 | 37 | 69 | .536 | 1 | 2 | .500 | 23 | 29 | .793 | 36 | 24 | 100 |

HONORS: NBA Most Valuable Player (1981). ... All-NBA first team (1978, 1980, 1981, 1982, 1983). ... All-NBA second team (1977, 1984). ... J. Walter Kennedy Citizenship Award (1983).

## NBA REGULAR-SEASON RECORD

| Season Team | G | Min. | FGM | FGA | Pct. | FTM | FTA | Pct. | REBOUNDS | | | Ast. | St. | Blk. | TO | Pts. | AVERAGES | | |
| | | | | | | | | | Off. | Def. | Tot. | | | | | | RPG | APG | PPG |
|---|---|---|---|---|---|---|---|---|---|---|---|---|---|---|---|---|---|---|---|
| 76-77—Philadelphia | 82 | 2940 | 685 | 1373 | .499 | 400 | 515 | .777 | 192 | 503 | 695 | 306 | 159 | 113 | ... | 1770 | 8.5 | 3.7 | 21.6 |
| 77-78—Philadelphia | 74 | 2429 | 611 | 1217 | .502 | 306 | 362 | .845 | 179 | 302 | 481 | 279 | 135 | 97 | 238 | 1528 | 6.5 | 3.8 | 20.6 |
| 78-79—Philadelphia | 78 | 2802 | 715 | 1455 | .491 | 373 | 501 | .745 | 198 | 366 | 564 | 357 | 133 | 100 | 315 | 1803 | 7.2 | 4.6 | 23.1 |
| 79-80—Philadelphia | 78 | 2812 | 838 | 1614 | .519 | 420 | 534 | .787 | 215 | 361 | 576 | 355 | 170 | 140 | 284 | 2100 | 7.4 | 4.6 | 26.9 |
| 80-81—Philadelphia | 82 | 2874 | 794 | 1524 | .521 | 422 | 536 | .787 | 244 | 413 | 657 | 364 | 173 | 147 | 266 | 2014 | 8.0 | 4.4 | 24.6 |
| 81-82—Philadelphia | 81 | 2789 | 780 | 1428 | .546 | 411 | 539 | .763 | 220 | 337 | 557 | 319 | 161 | 141 | 214 | 1974 | 6.9 | 3.9 | 24.4 |
| 82-83—Philadelphia | 72 | 2421 | 605 | 1170 | .517 | 330 | 435 | .759 | 173 | 318 | 491 | 263 | 112 | 131 | 196 | 1542 | 6.8 | 3.7 | 21.4 |
| 83-84—Philadelphia | 77 | 2683 | 678 | 1324 | .512 | 364 | 483 | .754 | 190 | 342 | 532 | 309 | 141 | 139 | 230 | 1727 | 6.9 | 4.0 | 22.4 |
| 84-85—Philadelphia | 78 | 2535 | 610 | 1236 | .494 | 338 | 442 | .765 | 172 | 242 | 414 | 233 | 135 | 109 | 208 | 1561 | 5.3 | 3.0 | 20.0 |
| 85-86—Philadelphia | 74 | 2474 | 521 | 1085 | .480 | 289 | 368 | .785 | 169 | 201 | 370 | 248 | 113 | 82 | 214 | 1340 | 5.0 | 3.4 | 18.1 |
| 86-87—Philadelphia | 60 | 1918 | 400 | 850 | .471 | 191 | 235 | .813 | 115 | 149 | 264 | 191 | 76 | 94 | 158 | 1005 | 4.4 | 3.2 | 16.8 |
| Totals | 836 | 28677 | 7237 | 14276 | .507 | 3844 | 4950 | .777 | 2067 | 3534 | 5601 | 3224 | 1508 | 1293 | 2323 | 18364 | 6.7 | 3.9 | 22.0 |

Three-point field goals: 1979-80, 4-for-20 (.200). 1980-81, 4-for-18 (.222). 1981-82, 3-for-11 (.273). 1982-83, 2-for-7 (.286). 1983-84, 7-for-21 (.333). 1984-85, 3-for-14 (.214). 1985-86, 9-for-32 (.281). 1986-87, 14-for-53 (.264). Totals, 46-for-176 (.261).

Personal fouls/disqualifications: 1976-77, 251/1. 1977-78, 207/0. 1978-79, 207/0. 1979-80, 208/0. 1980-81, 233/0. 1981-82, 229/1. 1982-83, 202/1. 1983-84, 217/3. 1984-85, 199/0. 1985-86, 196/3. 1986-87, 137/0. Totals, 2286/9.

## NBA PLAYOFF RECORD

| Season Team | G | Min. | FGM | FGA | Pct. | FTM | FTA | Pct. | REBOUNDS | | | Ast. | St. | Blk. | TO | Pts. | AVERAGES | | |
| | | | | | | | | | Off. | Def. | Tot. | | | | | | RPG | APG | PPG |
|---|---|---|---|---|---|---|---|---|---|---|---|---|---|---|---|---|---|---|---|
| 76-77—Philadelphia | 19 | 758 | 204 | 390 | .523 | 110 | 134 | .821 | 41 | 81 | 122 | 85 | 41 | 23 | ... | 518 | 6.4 | 4.5 | 27.3 |
| 77-78—Philadelphia | 10 | 358 | 88 | 180 | .489 | 42 | 56 | .750 | 40 | 57 | 97 | 40 | 15 | 18 | 35 | 218 | 9.7 | 4.0 | 21.8 |
| 78-79—Philadelphia | 9 | 372 | 89 | 172 | .517 | 51 | 67 | .761 | 29 | 41 | 70 | 53 | 18 | 17 | 38 | 229 | 7.8 | 5.9 | 25.4 |
| 79-80—Philadelphia | 18 | 694 | 165 | 338 | .488 | 108 | 136 | .794 | 31 | 105 | 136 | 79 | 36 | 37 | 56 | 440 | 7.6 | 4.4 | 24.4 |
| 80-81—Philadelphia | 16 | 592 | 143 | 301 | .475 | 81 | 107 | .757 | 52 | 62 | 114 | 54 | 22 | 41 | 55 | 367 | 7.1 | 3.4 | 22.9 |
| 81-82—Philadelphia | 21 | 780 | 168 | 324 | .519 | 124 | 165 | .752 | 57 | 99 | 156 | 99 | 37 | 37 | 67 | 461 | 7.4 | 4.7 | 22.0 |
| 82-83—Philadelphia | 13 | 493 | 95 | 211 | .450 | 49 | 68 | .721 | 32 | 67 | 99 | 44 | 15 | 27 | 39 | 239 | 7.6 | 3.4 | 18.4 |
| 83-84—Philadelphia | 5 | 194 | 36 | 76 | .474 | 19 | 22 | .864 | 9 | 23 | 32 | 25 | 8 | 6 | 21 | 91 | 6.4 | 5.0 | 18.2 |
| 84-85—Philadelphia | 13 | 434 | 84 | 187 | .449 | 54 | 63 | .857 | 29 | 44 | 73 | 48 | 25 | 11 | 37 | 222 | 5.6 | 3.7 | 17.1 |
| 85-86—Philadelphia | 12 | 433 | 81 | 180 | .450 | 48 | 65 | .738 | 26 | 44 | 70 | 50 | 11 | 16 | 39 | 212 | 5.8 | 4.2 | 17.7 |
| 86-87—Philadelphia | 5 | 180 | 34 | 82 | .415 | 21 | 25 | .840 | 14 | 11 | 25 | 17 | 7 | 6 | 9 | 91 | 5.0 | 3.4 | 18.2 |
| Totals | 141 | 5288 | 1187 | 2441 | .486 | 707 | 908 | .779 | 360 | 634 | 994 | 594 | 235 | 239 | 396 | 3088 | 7.0 | 4.2 | 21.9 |

Three-point field goals: 1979-80, 2-for-9 (.222). 1980-81, 0-for-1. 1981-82, 1-for-6 (.167). 1982-83, 0-for-1. 1983-84, 0-for-1. 1984-85, 0-for-1. 1985-86, 2-for-11 (.182). 1986-87, 2-for-6 (.333). Totals, 7-for-36 (.194).

Personal fouls/disqualifications: 1976-77, 45/0. 1977-78, 30/0. 1978-79, 22/0. 1979-80, 56/0. 1980-81, 54/0. 1981-82, 55/0. 1982-83, 42/1. 1983-84, 14/0. 1984-85, 34/0. 1985-86, 32/0. 1986-87, 19/0. Totals, 403/1.

## NBA ALL-STAR GAME RECORD

NOTES: NBA All-Star Game Most Valuable Player (1977, 1983). ... Holds single-game record for most free throws attempted in one quarter—11 (1978). ... Shares single-game record for most free throws made in one quarter—9 (1978).

| Season Team | Min. | FGM | FGA | Pct. | FTM | FTA | Pct. | REBOUNDS | | | Ast. | PF | Dq. | St. | Blk. | TO | Pts. |
| | | | | | | | | Off. | Def. | Tot. | | | | | | | |
|---|---|---|---|---|---|---|---|---|---|---|---|---|---|---|---|---|---|
| 1977—Philadelphia | 30 | 12 | 20 | .600 | 6 | 6 | 1.000 | 5 | 7 | 12 | 3 | 2 | 0 | 4 | 1 | ... | 30 |
| 1978—Philadelphia | 27 | 3 | 14 | .214 | 10 | 12 | .833 | 2 | 6 | 8 | 3 | 1 | 0 | 1 | 2 | 16 |
| 1979—Philadelphia | 39 | 10 | 22 | .455 | 9 | 12 | .750 | 6 | 2 | 8 | 5 | 4 | 0 | 2 | 0 | 1 | 29 |
| 1980—Philadelphia | 20 | 4 | 12 | .333 | 3 | 4 | .750 | 2 | 3 | 5 | 2 | 5 | 0 | 2 | 1 | 2 | 11 |
| 1981—Philadelphia | 29 | 6 | 15 | .400 | 6 | 7 | .857 | 3 | 0 | 3 | 2 | 2 | 0 | 2 | 1 | 2 | 18 |
| 1982—Philadelphia | 32 | 7 | 16 | .438 | 2 | 4 | .500 | 3 | 5 | 8 | 2 | 4 | 0 | 1 | 2 | 4 | 16 |
| 1983—Philadelphia | 28 | 11 | 19 | .579 | 3 | 3 | 1.000 | 3 | 3 | 6 | 3 | 1 | 0 | 1 | 2 | 25 |
| 1984—Philadelphia | 36 | 14 | 22 | .636 | 6 | 8 | .750 | 4 | 4 | 8 | 5 | 4 | 0 | 2 | 2 | 1 | 34 |
| 1985—Philadelphia | 23 | 5 | 15 | .333 | 2 | 2 | 1.000 | 2 | 2 | 4 | 3 | 3 | 0 | 1 | 0 | 1 | 12 |
| 1986—Philadelphia | 19 | 4 | 10 | .400 | 0 | 2 | .000 | 1 | 3 | 4 | 2 | 2 | 0 | 2 | 0 | 2 | 8 |
| 1987—Philadelphia | 33 | 9 | 13 | .692 | 3 | 3 | 1.000 | 3 | 1 | 4 | 5 | 3 | 0 | 1 | 1 | 2 | 22 |
| Totals | 316 | 85 | 178 | .478 | 50 | 63 | .794 | 34 | 36 | 70 | 35 | 31 | 0 | 18 | 11 | 19 | 221 |

Three-point field goals: 1987, 1-for-1.

## COMBINED ABA AND NBA REGULAR-SEASON RECORDS

| | G | Min. | FGM | FGA | Pct. | FTM | FTA | Pct. | REBOUNDS | | | Ast. | Stl. | Blk. | TO | Pts. | AVERAGES | | |
| | | | | | | | | | Off. | Def. | Tot. | | | | | | RPG | APG | PPG |
|---|---|---|---|---|---|---|---|---|---|---|---|---|---|---|---|---|---|---|---|
| Totals | 1243 | 45227 | 11818 | 23370 | .506 | 6256 | 8052 | .777 | ... | ... | 10525 | 5176 | ... | ... | ... | 30026 | 8.5 | 4.2 | 24.2 |

Three-point field goals: 134-for-449 (.298).
Personal fouls/disqualifications: 3494.

# EWING, PATRICK       C

**PERSONAL:** Born August 5, 1962, in Kingston, Jamaica. ... 7-0/255. (2,13/115,7). ... Full Name: Patrick Aloysius Ewing.
**HIGH SCHOOL:** Cambridge (Mass.) Rindge & Latin School.
**COLLEGE:** Georgetown.
**TRANSACTIONS/CAREER NOTES:** Selected by New York Knicks in first round (first pick overall) of 1985 NBA Draft. ... Traded by Knicks to Seattle SuperSonics as part of four-team trade in which Knicks acquired F Glen Rice, C Luc Longley, F/C Travis Knight, G Vernon Maxwell, C Vladimir Stepania, F Lazaro Borrell, two 2001 first-round draft choices and two 2001 second-round draft choices, Phoenix Suns acquired C Chris Dudley and 2001 first-round draft choice and Los Angeles Lakers acquired F Horace Grant, C Greg Foster, F Chuck Person and G Emanual Davis (September 20, 2000). ... Signed as free agent by Orlando Magic (July 18, 2001).
**CAREER HONORS:** NBA 50th Anniversary All-Time Team (1996).
**CAREER NOTES:** Assistant coach, Washington Wizards (2002-03). ... Named assistant coach, Houston Rockets (July 2, 2003).
**MISCELLANEOUS:** Member of gold-medal-winning U.S. Olympic teams (1984, 1992). , ... New York Knicks all-time leading scorer with 23,665 points, all-time leading rebounder with 10,759, all-time steals leader with 1,061 and all-time blocked shots leader with 2,758 (1985-86 through 1999-2000).

## COLLEGIATE RECORD

**NOTES:** THE SPORTING NEWS College Player of the Year (1985). ... Naismith Award winner (1985). ... THE SPORTING NEWS All-America first team (1985). ... THE SPORTING NEWS All-America second team (1983, 1984). ... NCAA Division I Tournament Most Outstanding Player (1984). ... Member of NCAA Division I championship team (1984).

| Season Team | G | Min. | FGM | FGA | Pct. | FTM | FTA | Pct. | Reb. | Ast. | Pts. | AVERAGES RPG | APG | PPG |
|---|---|---|---|---|---|---|---|---|---|---|---|---|---|---|
| 81-82—Georgetown | 37 | 1064 | 183 | 290 | .631 | 103 | 167 | .617 | 279 | 23 | 469 | 7.5 | 0.6 | 12.7 |
| 82-83—Georgetown | 32 | 1024 | 212 | 372 | .570 | 141 | 224 | .629 | 325 | 26 | 565 | 10.2 | 0.8 | 17.7 |
| 83-84—Georgetown | 37 | 1179 | 242 | 368 | .658 | 124 | 189 | .656 | 371 | 31 | 608 | 10.0 | 0.8 | 16.4 |
| 84-85—Georgetown | 37 | 1132 | 220 | 352 | .625 | 102 | 160 | .638 | 341 | 48 | 542 | 9.2 | 1.3 | 14.6 |
| Totals | 143 | 4399 | 857 | 1382 | .620 | 470 | 740 | .635 | 1316 | 128 | 2184 | 9.2 | 0.9 | 15.3 |

## NBA REGULAR-SEASON RECORD

**HONORS:** NBA Rookie of the Year (1986). ... All-NBA first Team (1990). ... All-NBA second Team (1988, 1989, 1991, 1992, 1993, 1997). ... NBA All-Defensive second team (1988, 1989, 1992). ... NBA All-Rookie team (1986).
**NOTES:** Led NBA with 332 personal fouls (1988).

| Season Team | G | Min. | FGM | FGA | Pct. | FTM | FTA | Pct. | REBOUNDS Off. | Def. | Tot. | Ast. | St. | Blk. | TO | Pts. | AVERAGES RPG | APG | PPG |
|---|---|---|---|---|---|---|---|---|---|---|---|---|---|---|---|---|---|---|---|
| 85-86—New York | 50 | 1771 | 386 | 814 | .474 | 226 | 306 | .739 | 124 | 327 | 451 | 102 | 54 | 103 | 172 | 998 | 9.0 | 2.0 | 20.0 |
| 86-87—New York | 63 | 2206 | 530 | 1053 | .503 | 296 | 415 | .713 | 157 | 398 | 555 | 104 | 89 | 147 | 229 | 1356 | 8.8 | 1.7 | 21.5 |
| 87-88—New York | 82 | 2546 | 656 | 1183 | .555 | 341 | 476 | .716 | 245 | 431 | 676 | 125 | 104 | 245 | 287 | 1653 | 8.2 | 1.5 | 20.2 |
| 88-89—New York | 80 | 2896 | 727 | 1282 | .567 | 361 | 484 | .746 | 213 | 527 | 740 | 188 | 117 | 281 | 266 | 1815 | 9.3 | 2.4 | 22.7 |
| 89-90—New York | 82 | 3165 | 922 | 1673 | .551 | 502 | 648 | .775 | 235 | 658 | 893 | 182 | 78 | 327 | 278 | 2347 | 10.9 | 2.2 | 28.6 |
| 90-91—New York | 81 | 3104 | 845 | 1645 | .514 | 464 | 623 | .745 | 194 | 711 | 905 | 244 | 80 | 258 | 291 | 2154 | 11.2 | 3.0 | 26.6 |
| 91-92—New York | 82 | 3150 | 796 | 1525 | .522 | 377 | 511 | .738 | 228 | 693 | 921 | 156 | 88 | 245 | 209 | 1970 | 11.2 | 1.9 | 24.0 |
| 92-93—New York | 81 | 3003 | 779 | 1550 | .503 | 400 | 556 | .719 | 191 | *789 | 980 | 151 | 74 | 161 | 265 | 1959 | 12.1 | 1.9 | 24.2 |
| 93-94—New York | 79 | 2972 | 745 | 1503 | .496 | 445 | 582 | .765 | 219 | 666 | 885 | 179 | 90 | 217 | 260 | 1939 | 11.2 | 2.3 | 24.5 |
| 94-95—New York | 79 | 2920 | 730 | 1452 | .503 | 420 | 560 | .750 | 157 | 710 | 867 | 212 | 68 | 159 | 256 | 1886 | 11.0 | 2.7 | 23.9 |
| 95-96—New York | 76 | 2783 | 678 | 1456 | .466 | 351 | 461 | .761 | 157 | 649 | 806 | 160 | 68 | 184 | 221 | 1711 | 10.6 | 2.1 | 22.5 |
| 96-97—New York | 78 | 2887 | 655 | 1342 | .488 | 439 | 582 | .754 | 175 | 659 | 834 | 156 | 69 | 189 | 269 | 1751 | 10.7 | 2.0 | 22.4 |
| 97-98—New York | 26 | 848 | 203 | 403 | .504 | 134 | 186 | .720 | 59 | 206 | 265 | 28 | 16 | 58 | 77 | 540 | 10.2 | 1.1 | 20.8 |
| 98-99—New York | 38 | 1300 | 247 | 568 | .435 | 163 | 231 | .706 | 74 | 303 | 377 | 43 | 30 | 100 | 99 | 657 | 9.9 | 1.1 | 17.3 |
| 99-00—New York | 62 | 2035 | 361 | 775 | .466 | 207 | 283 | .731 | 140 | 464 | 604 | 58 | 36 | 84 | 142 | 929 | 9.7 | 0.9 | 15.0 |
| 00-01—Seattle | 79 | 2107 | 294 | 684 | .430 | 172 | 251 | .685 | 124 | 461 | 585 | 92 | 53 | 91 | 151 | 760 | 7.4 | 1.2 | 9.6 |
| 01-02—Orlando | 65 | 901 | 148 | 333 | .444 | 94 | 134 | .701 | 60 | 203 | 263 | 35 | 22 | 45 | 65 | 390 | 4.0 | 0.5 | 6.0 |
| Totals | 1183 | 40594 | 9702 | 19241 | .504 | 5392 | 7289 | .740 | 2752 | 8855 | 11607 | 2215 | 1136 | 2894 | 3537 | 24815 | 9.8 | 1.9 | 21.0 |

Three-point field goals: 1985-86, 0-for-5. 1986-87, 0-for-7. 1987-88, 0-for-3. 1988-89, 0-for-6. 1989-90, 1-for-4 (.250). 1990-91, 0-for-5. 1991-92, 1-for-6 (.167). 1992-93, 1-for-7 (.143). 1993-94, 4-for-14 (.286). 1994-95, 6-for-21 (.286). 1995-96, 4-for-28 (.143). 1996-97, 2-for-9 (.222). 1997-98, 0-for-2. 1998-99, 0-for-2. 1999-00, 0-for-2. 2000-01, 0-for-2. 2001-02, 0-for-1. Totals, 19-for-125 (.152).
Personal fouls/disqualifications: 1985-86, 191/7. 1986-87, 248/5. 1987-88, 332/5. 1988-89, 311/5. 1989-90, 325/7. 1990-91, 287/3. 1991-92, 277/2. 1992-93, 286/2. 1993-94, 275/3. 1994-95, 272/3. 1995-96, 247/2. 1996-97, 250/2. 1997-98, 74/0. 1998-99, 105/1. 1999-00, 196/1. 2000-01, 229/1. 2001-02, 129/0. Totals, 4034/49.

## NBA PLAYOFF RECORD

**NOTES:** Holds NBA Finals single-series record for most blocked shots—30 (1994, vs. Houston). ... Shares NBA Finals single-game record for most blocked shots—8 (June 17, 1994, vs. Houston).

| Season Team | G | Min. | FGM | FGA | Pct. | FTM | FTA | Pct. | REBOUNDS Off. | Def. | Tot. | Ast. | St. | Blk. | TO | Pts. | AVERAGES RPG | APG | PPG |
|---|---|---|---|---|---|---|---|---|---|---|---|---|---|---|---|---|---|---|---|
| 87-88—New York | 4 | 153 | 28 | 57 | .491 | 19 | 22 | .864 | 16 | 35 | 51 | 10 | 6 | 13 | 11 | 75 | 12.8 | 2.5 | 18.8 |
| 88-89—New York | 9 | 340 | 70 | 144 | .486 | 39 | 52 | .750 | 23 | 67 | 90 | 20 | 9 | 18 | 15 | 179 | 10.0 | 2.2 | 19.9 |
| 89-90—New York | 10 | 395 | 114 | 219 | .521 | 65 | 79 | .823 | 21 | 84 | 105 | 31 | 13 | 20 | 27 | 294 | 10.5 | 3.1 | 29.4 |
| 90-91—New York | 3 | 110 | 18 | 45 | .400 | 14 | 18 | .778 | 2 | 28 | 30 | 6 | 1 | 5 | 11 | 50 | 10.0 | 2.0 | 16.7 |
| 91-92—New York | 12 | 482 | 109 | 239 | .456 | 54 | 73 | .740 | 33 | 100 | 133 | 27 | 7 | 31 | 23 | 272 | 11.1 | 2.3 | 22.7 |
| 92-93—New York | 15 | 604 | 165 | 322 | .512 | 51 | 80 | .638 | 43 | 121 | 164 | 36 | 17 | 31 | 39 | 382 | 10.9 | 2.4 | 25.5 |
| 93-94—New York | 25 | 1032 | 210 | 481 | .437 | 123 | 163 | .755 | 88 | 205 | 293 | 65 | 32 | 76 | 83 | 547 | 11.7 | 2.6 | 21.9 |
| 94-95—New York | 11 | 399 | 80 | 156 | .513 | 48 | 70 | .686 | 17 | 89 | 106 | 27 | 6 | 25 | 30 | 209 | 9.6 | 2.5 | 19.0 |
| 95-96—New York | 8 | 328 | 65 | 137 | .474 | 41 | 63 | .651 | 11 | 74 | 85 | 15 | 1 | 25 | 30 | 172 | 10.6 | 1.9 | 21.5 |
| 96-97—New York | 9 | 357 | 88 | 167 | .527 | 27 | 42 | .643 | 26 | 69 | 95 | 17 | 3 | 22 | 27 | 203 | 10.6 | 1.9 | 22.6 |
| 97-98—New York | 4 | 132 | 20 | 56 | .357 | 16 | 27 | .593 | 9 | 23 | 32 | 5 | 3 | 5 | 10 | 56 | 8.0 | 1.3 | 14.0 |
| 98-99—New York | 11 | 347 | 58 | 135 | .430 | 28 | 36 | .778 | 14 | 82 | 96 | 6 | 7 | 8 | 10 | 144 | 8.7 | 0.5 | 13.1 |
| 99-00—New York | 14 | 461 | 71 | 170 | .418 | 62 | 89 | .697 | 29 | 104 | 133 | 6 | 16 | 20 | 27 | 204 | 9.5 | 0.4 | 14.6 |
| 01-02—Orlando | 4 | 67 | 8 | 25 | .320 | 10 | 17 | .588 | 5 | 17 | 22 | 4 | 1 | 4 | 2 | 26 | 5.5 | 1.0 | 6.5 |
| Totals | 139 | 5207 | 1104 | 2353 | .469 | 597 | 831 | .718 | 337 | 1098 | 1435 | 275 | 122 | 303 | 345 | 2813 | 10.3 | 2.0 | 20.2 |

Three-point field goals: 1987-88, 0-for-1. 1988-89, 0-for-1. 1991-92, 0-for-2 (.500). 1991-92, 0-for-1. 1992-93, 1-for-1. 1993-94, 4-for-11 (.364). 1994-95, 1-for-3 (.333). 1995-96, 1-for-2 (.500). 1996-97, 0-for-1. 2001-02, 0-for-1. Totals, 8-for-23 (.348).
Personal fouls/disqualifications: 1987-88, 17/0. 1988-89, 35/0. 1989-90, 41/0. 1990-91, 12/0. 1991-92, 49/1. 1992-93, 60/2. 1993-94, 94/1. 1994-95, 51/1. 1995-96, 22/0. 1996-97, 30/0. 1997-98, 16/0. 1998-99, 35/0. 1999-00, 48/0. 2001-02, 12/0. Totals, 522/5.

### NBA ALL-STAR GAME RECORD

| Season Team | Min. | FGM | FGA | Pct. | FTM | FTA | Pct. | REBOUNDS Off. | Def. | Tot. | Ast. | PF | Dq. | St. | Blk. | TO | Pts. |
|---|---|---|---|---|---|---|---|---|---|---|---|---|---|---|---|---|---|
| 1986—New York ............ | | | | | | | Selected, did not play—injured. | | | | | | | | | | |
| 1988—New York ............ | 16 | 4 | 8 | .500 | 1 | 1 | 1.000 | 1 | 5 | 6 | 0 | 1 | 0 | 0 | 1 | 1 | 9 |
| 1989—New York ............ | 17 | 2 | 8 | .250 | 0 | 4 | .000 | 1 | 5 | 6 | 2 | 2 | 0 | 1 | 2 | 3 | 4 |
| 1990—New York ............ | 27 | 5 | 9 | .556 | 2 | 2 | 1.000 | 1 | 9 | 10 | 1 | 5 | 0 | 1 | 5 | 5 | 12 |
| 1991—New York ............ | 30 | 8 | 10 | .800 | 2 | 2 | 1.000 | 2 | 8 | 10 | 0 | 5 | 0 | 1 | 4 | 2 | 18 |
| 1992—New York ............ | 17 | 4 | 7 | .571 | 2 | 5 | .400 | 2 | 2 | 4 | 0 | 3 | 0 | 2 | 1 | 2 | 10 |
| 1993—New York ............ | 25 | 7 | 11 | .636 | 1 | 1 | 1.000 | 3 | 7 | 10 | 1 | 4 | 0 | 2 | 2 | 4 | 15 |
| 1994—New York ............ | 24 | 7 | 15 | .467 | 6 | 7 | .857 | 4 | 4 | 8 | 1 | 2 | 0 | 0 | 0 | 1 | 20 |
| 1995—New York ............ | 22 | 4 | 7 | .571 | 2 | 2 | 1.000 | 0 | 3 | 3 | 1 | 3 | 0 | 1 | 0 | 5 | 10 |
| 1996—New York ............ | 12 | 3 | 7 | .429 | 2 | 2 | 1.000 | 1 | 2 | 3 | 1 | 2 | 0 | 3 | 1 | 0 | 8 |
| 1997—New York ............ | | | | | | | Selected, did not play—injured. | | | | | | | | | | |
| Totals ...................... | 190 | 44 | 82 | .537 | 18 | 26 | .692 | 15 | 45 | 60 | 7 | 27 | 0 | 11 | 16 | 23 | 106 |

## FLOYD, SLEEPY      G

**PERSONAL:** Born March 6, 1960, in Gastonia, N.C. ... 6-3/185 (1,90/83,9). ... Full name: Eric Augustus Floyd.
**HIGH SCHOOL:** Hunter Huss (Gastonia, N.C.).
**COLLEGE:** Georgetown.
**TRANSACTIONS:** Selected by New Jersey Nets in first round (13th pick overall) of 1982 NBA Draft. ... Traded by Nets with F Mickey Johnson to Golden State Warriors for G Micheal Ray Richardson (February 6, 1983). ... Traded by Warriors with C Joe Barry Carroll to Houston Rockets for C Ralph Sampson and G Steve Harris (December 12, 1987). ... Waived by Rockets (August 2, 1993). ... Signed as free agent by San Antonio Spurs (August 13, 1993). ... Signed as free agent by Nets (October 6, 1994).

### COLLEGIATE RECORD

**NOTES:** THE SPORTING NEWS All-America second team (1982).

| Season Team | G | Min. | FGM | FGA | Pct. | FTM | FTA | Pct. | Reb. | Ast. | Pts. | AVERAGES RPG | APG | PPG |
|---|---|---|---|---|---|---|---|---|---|---|---|---|---|---|
| 78-79—Georgetown.................. | 29 | 975 | 177 | 388 | .456 | 126 | 155 | .813 | 119 | 78 | 480 | 4.1 | 2.7 | 16.6 |
| 79-80—Georgetown.................. | 32 | 1052 | 246 | 444 | .554 | 106 | 140 | .757 | 98 | 95 | 598 | 3.1 | 3.0 | 18.7 |
| 80-81—Georgetown.................. | 32 | 1115 | 237 | 508 | .467 | 133 | 165 | .806 | 133 | 83 | 607 | 4.2 | 2.6 | 19.0 |
| 81-82—Georgetown.................. | 37 | 1200 | 249 | 494 | .504 | 121 | 168 | .720 | 127 | 99 | 619 | 3.4 | 2.7 | 16.7 |
| Totals ...................................... | 130 | 4342 | 909 | 1834 | .496 | 486 | 628 | .774 | 477 | 355 | 2304 | 3.7 | 2.7 | 17.7 |

### NBA REGULAR-SEASON RECORD

| Season Team | G | Min. | FGM | FGA | Pct. | FTM | FTA | Pct. | REBOUNDS Off. | Def. | Tot. | Ast. | St. | Blk. | TO | Pts. | AVERAGES RPG | APG | PPG |
|---|---|---|---|---|---|---|---|---|---|---|---|---|---|---|---|---|---|---|---|
| 82-83—N.J.-G.S......... | 76 | 1248 | 226 | 527 | .429 | 150 | 180 | .833 | 56 | 81 | 137 | 138 | 58 | 17 | 156 | 612 | 1.8 | 1.8 | 8.1 |
| 83-84—Golden State | 77 | 2555 | 484 | 1045 | .463 | 315 | 386 | .816 | 87 | 184 | 271 | 269 | 103 | 31 | 196 | 1291 | 3.5 | 3.5 | 16.8 |
| 84-85—Golden State ... | 82 | 2873 | 610 | 1372 | .445 | 336 | 415 | .810 | 62 | 140 | 202 | 406 | 134 | 41 | 251 | 1598 | 2.5 | 5.0 | 19.5 |
| 85-86—Golden State ... | 82 | 2764 | 510 | 1007 | .506 | 351 | 441 | .796 | 76 | 221 | 297 | 746 | 157 | 16 | 290 | 1410 | 3.6 | 9.1 | 17.2 |
| 86-87—Golden State ... | 82 | 3064 | 503 | 1030 | .488 | 462 | 537 | .860 | 56 | 212 | 268 | 848 | 146 | 18 | 280 | 1541 | 3.3 | 10.3 | 18.8 |
| 87-88—G.S.-Hou........ | 77 | 2514 | 420 | 969 | .433 | 301 | 354 | .850 | 77 | 219 | 296 | 544 | 95 | 12 | 223 | 1155 | 3.8 | 7.1 | 15.0 |
| 88-89—Houston ......... | 82 | 2788 | 396 | 893 | .443 | 261 | 309 | .845 | 48 | 258 | 306 | 709 | 124 | 11 | 253 | 1162 | 3.7 | 8.6 | 14.2 |
| 89-90—Houston ......... | 82 | 2630 | 362 | 803 | .451 | 187 | 232 | .806 | 46 | 152 | 198 | 600 | 94 | 11 | 204 | 1000 | 2.4 | 7.3 | 12.2 |
| 90-91—Houston ......... | 82 | 1850 | 386 | 939 | .411 | 185 | 246 | .752 | 52 | 107 | 159 | 317 | 95 | 17 | 140 | 1005 | 1.9 | 3.9 | 12.3 |
| 91-92—Houston ......... | 82 | 1662 | 286 | 704 | .406 | 135 | 170 | .794 | 34 | 116 | 150 | 239 | 57 | 21 | 128 | 744 | 1.8 | 2.9 | 9.1 |
| 92-93—Houston ......... | 52 | 867 | 124 | 305 | .407 | 81 | 102 | .794 | 14 | 72 | 86 | 132 | 32 | 6 | 68 | 345 | 1.7 | 2.5 | 6.6 |
| 93-94—San Antonio ... | 53 | 737 | 70 | 209 | .335 | 52 | 78 | .667 | 10 | 60 | 70 | 101 | 12 | 8 | 61 | 200 | 1.3 | 1.9 | 3.8 |
| 94-95—New Jersey ... | 48 | 831 | 71 | 212 | .335 | 30 | 43 | .698 | 8 | 46 | 54 | 126 | 13 | 6 | 51 | 197 | 1.1 | 2.6 | 4.1 |
| Totals ................... | 957 | 26383 | 4448 | 10015 | .444 | 2846 | 3493 | .815 | 626 | 1868 | 2494 | 5175 | 1120 | 215 | 2251 | 12260 | 2.6 | 5.4 | 12.8 |

Three-point field goals: 1982-83, 10-for-25 (.400). 1983-84, 8-for-45 (.178). 1984-85, 42-for-143 (.294). 1985-86, 39-for-119 (.328). 1986-87, 73-for-190 (.384). 1987-88, 14-for-72 (.194). 1988-89, 109-for-292 (.373). 1989-90, 89-for-234 (.380). 1990-91, 48-for-176 (.273). 1991-92, 37-for-123 (.301). 1992-93, 16-for-56 (.286). 1993-94, 8-for-36 (.222). 1994-95, 25-for-88 (.284). Totals, 518-for-1599 (.324).
Personal fouls/disqualifications: 1982-83, 134/3. 1983-84, 216/0. 1984-85, 226/1. 1985-86, 199/2. 1986-87, 199/1. 1987-88, 190/1. 1988-89, 196/1. 1989-90, 159/0. 1990-91, 122/0. 1991-92, 128/0. 1992-93, 59/0. 1993-94, 71/0. 1994-95, 73/0. Totals, 1972/9.

### NBA PLAYOFF RECORD

**NOTES:** Holds single-game playoff records for most points in one half—39; most points in one quarter—29; and most field goals in one quarter—12 (May 10, 1987, vs. Los Angeles Lakers). ... Shares single-game playoff record for most field goals made in one half—15 (May 10, 1987, vs. Los Angeles Lakers).

| Season Team | G | Min. | FGM | FGA | Pct. | FTM | FTA | Pct. | REBOUNDS Off. | Def. | Tot. | Ast. | St. | Blk. | TO | Pts. | AVERAGES RPG | APG | PPG |
|---|---|---|---|---|---|---|---|---|---|---|---|---|---|---|---|---|---|---|---|
| 86-87—Golden State ... | 10 | 414 | 77 | 152 | .507 | 47 | 51 | .922 | 9 | 21 | 30 | 102 | 18 | 2 | 35 | 214 | 3.0 | 10.2 | 21.4 |
| 87-88—Houston ......... | 4 | 154 | 26 | 61 | .426 | 19 | 22 | .864 | 3 | 4 | 7 | 34 | 8 | 0 | 12 | 75 | 1.8 | 8.5 | 18.8 |
| 88-89—Houston ......... | 4 | 160 | 22 | 46 | .478 | 10 | 14 | .714 | 3 | 15 | 18 | 26 | 8 | 1 | 10 | 62 | 4.5 | 6.5 | 15.5 |
| 89-90—Houston ......... | 4 | 172 | 30 | 64 | .469 | 11 | 17 | .647 | 7 | 8 | 15 | 41 | 5 | 1 | 15 | 74 | 3.8 | 10.3 | 18.5 |
| 90-91—Houston ......... | 3 | 41 | 8 | 24 | .333 | 0 | 0 | ... | 0 | 2 | 2 | 7 | 2 | 1 | 7 | 16 | 0.7 | 2.3 | 5.3 |
| 92-93—Houston ......... | 7 | 60 | 6 | 19 | .316 | 7 | 10 | .700 | 1 | 3 | 4 | 8 | 2 | 0 | 9 | 20 | 0.6 | 1.1 | 2.9 |
| 93-94—San Antonio ... | 4 | 37 | 2 | 8 | .250 | 2 | 4 | .500 | 0 | 1 | 1 | 1 | 0 | 0 | 4 | 6 | 0.3 | 0.3 | 1.5 |
| Totals ................... | 36 | 1038 | 171 | 374 | .457 | 96 | 118 | .814 | 23 | 54 | 77 | 219 | 43 | 5 | 92 | 467 | 2.1 | 6.1 | 13.0 |

Three-point field goals: 1986-87, 13-for-28 (.464). 1987-88, 4-for-8 (.500). 1988-89, 8-for-15 (.533). 1989-90, 3-for-12 (.250). 1990-91, 0-for-4. 1992-93, 1-for-3 (.333). Totals, 29-for-70 (.414).
Personal fouls/disqualifications: 1986-87, 24/0. 1987-88, 10/0. 1988-89, 10/0. 1989-90, 5/0. 1990-91, 4/0. 1992-93, 2/0. 1993-94, 3/0. Totals, 58/0.

### NBA ALL-STAR GAME RECORD

| Season Team | Min. | FGM | FGA | Pct. | FTM | FTA | Pct. | REBOUNDS Off. | Def. | Tot. | Ast. | PF | Dq. | St. | Blk. | TO | Pts. |
|---|---|---|---|---|---|---|---|---|---|---|---|---|---|---|---|---|---|
| 1987—Golden State ......... | 19 | 4 | 7 | .571 | 5 | 7 | .714 | 2 | 3 | 5 | 1 | 2 | 0 | 1 | 0 | 2 | 14 |

Three-point field goals: 1987, 1-for-3 (.333).

# FOUST, LARRY                    C/F

**PERSONAL:** Born June 24, 1928, in Painesville, Ohio. ... Died October 27, 1984. ... 6-9/250 (2,06/113,4). ... Full name: Lawrence Michael Foust.
**HIGH SCHOOL:** South Catholic (Philadelphia).
**COLLEGE:** La Salle.
**TRANSACTIONS:** Selected by Chicago Stags in first round of 1950 NBA Draft. ... Draft rights selected by Fort Wayne Pistons in dispersal of Stags franchise (1950). ... Pistons franchise moved from Fort Wayne to Detroit for 1957-58 season. ... Traded by Pistons with cash to Minneapolis Lakers for C Walt Dukes (September 12, 1957). ... Traded by Lakers to St. Louis Hawks for C Charlie Share, draft rights to G Nick Mantis, G Willie Merriweather and cash (February 1, 1960).

## COLLEGIATE RECORD

**NOTES:** The Sporting News All-America fifth team (1950).

| Season Team | G | Min. | FGM | FGA | Pct. | FTM | FTA | Pct. | Reb. | Ast. | Pts. | RPG | APG | PPG |
|---|---|---|---|---|---|---|---|---|---|---|---|---|---|---|
| 46-47—La Salle | 26 | ... | 103 | ... | ... | 49 | ... | ... | ... | ... | 255 | ... | ... | 9.8 |
| 47-48—La Salle | 24 | ... | 157 | ... | ... | 87 | ... | ... | ... | ... | 401 | ... | ... | 16.7 |
| 48-49—La Salle | 28 | ... | 177 | ... | ... | 99 | 164 | .604 | ... | ... | 453 | ... | ... | 16.2 |
| 49-50—La Salle | 25 | ... | 136 | ... | ... | 83 | 122 | .680 | ... | ... | 355 | ... | ... | 14.2 |
| Totals | 103 | ... | 573 | ... | ... | 318 | ... | ... | ... | ... | 1464 | ... | ... | 14.2 |

## NBA REGULAR-SEASON RECORD

**HONORS:** All-NBA first team (1955). ... All-NBA second team (1952).

| Season Team | G | Min. | FGM | FGA | Pct. | FTM | FTA | Pct. | Reb. | Ast. | PF | Dq. | Pts. | RPG | APG | PPG |
|---|---|---|---|---|---|---|---|---|---|---|---|---|---|---|---|---|
| 50-51—Fort Wayne | 68 | ... | 327 | 944 | .346 | 261 | 396 | .659 | 681 | 90 | 247 | 6 | 915 | 10.0 | 1.3 | 13.5 |
| 51-52—Fort Wayne | 66 | 2615 | 390 | 989 | .394 | 267 | 394 | .678 | †880 | 200 | 245 | 10 | 1047 | 13.3 | 3.0 | 15.9 |
| 52-53—Fort Wayne | 67 | 2303 | 311 | 865 | .360 | 336 | 465 | .723 | 769 | 151 | 267 | 16 | 958 | 11.5 | 2.3 | 14.3 |
| 53-54—Fort Wayne | 72 | 2693 | 376 | 919 | .409 | 338 | 475 | .712 | 967 | 161 | 258 | 4 | 1090 | 13.4 | 2.2 | 15.1 |
| 54-55—Fort Wayne | 70 | 2264 | 398 | 818 | *.487 | 393 | 513 | .766 | 700 | 118 | 264 | 9 | 1189 | 10.0 | 1.7 | 17.0 |
| 55-56—Fort Wayne | 72 | 2024 | 367 | 821 | .447 | 432 | 555 | .778 | 648 | 127 | 263 | 7 | 1166 | 9.0 | 1.8 | 16.2 |
| 56-57—Fort Wayne | 61 | 1533 | 243 | 617 | .394 | 273 | 380 | .718 | 555 | 71 | 221 | 7 | 759 | 9.1 | 1.2 | 12.4 |
| 57-58—Minneapolis | 72 | 2200 | 391 | 982 | .398 | 428 | 566 | .756 | 876 | 108 | 299 | 11 | 1210 | 12.2 | 1.5 | 16.8 |
| 58-59—Minneapolis | 72 | 1933 | 301 | 771 | .390 | 280 | 366 | .765 | 627 | 91 | 233 | 5 | 882 | 8.7 | 1.3 | 12.3 |
| 59-60—Minn.-St.L. | 72 | 1964 | 312 | 766 | .407 | 253 | 320 | .791 | 621 | 96 | 241 | 7 | 877 | 8.6 | 1.3 | 12.2 |
| 60-61—St. Louis | 68 | 1208 | 194 | 489 | .397 | 164 | 208 | .788 | 389 | 77 | 165 | 0 | 552 | 5.7 | 1.1 | 8.1 |
| 61-62—St. Louis | 57 | 1153 | 204 | 433 | .471 | 145 | 178 | .815 | 328 | 78 | 186 | 2 | 553 | 5.8 | 1.4 | 9.7 |
| Totals | 817 | ... | 3814 | 9414 | .405 | 3570 | 4816 | .741 | 8041 | 1368 | 2889 | 84 | 11198 | 9.8 | 1.7 | 13.7 |

## NBA PLAYOFF RECORD

| Season Team | G | Min. | FGM | FGA | Pct. | FTM | FTA | Pct. | Reb. | Ast. | PF | Dq. | Pts. | RPG | APG | PPG |
|---|---|---|---|---|---|---|---|---|---|---|---|---|---|---|---|---|
| 50-51—Fort Wayne | 3 | ... | 14 | 45 | .311 | 8 | 10 | .800 | 37 | 5 | 5 | ... | 36 | 12.3 | 1.7 | 12.0 |
| 51-52—Fort Wayne | 2 | 77 | 12 | 23 | .522 | 6 | 7 | .857 | 30 | 5 | 8 | 1 | 30 | 15.0 | 2.5 | 15.0 |
| 52-53—Fort Wayne | 8 | 332 | 48 | 121 | .397 | 57 | 68 | .838 | 111 | 6 | 34 | 2 | 153 | 13.9 | 0.8 | 19.1 |
| 53-54—Fort Wayne | 4 | 129 | 11 | 41 | .268 | 19 | 25 | .760 | 38 | 7 | 21 | 2 | 41 | 9.5 | 1.8 | 10.3 |
| 54-55—Fort Wayne | 11 | 331 | 60 | 152 | .395 | 52 | 73 | .712 | 107 | 26 | 43 | 0 | 172 | 9.7 | 2.4 | 15.6 |
| 55-56—Fort Wayne | 10 | 289 | 49 | 130 | .377 | 70 | 89 | .787 | 127 | 14 | 38 | 2 | 168 | 12.7 | 1.4 | 16.8 |
| 56-57—Fort Wayne | 2 | 64 | 13 | 23 | .565 | 19 | 23 | .826 | 25 | 6 | 10 | 0 | 45 | 12.5 | 3.0 | 22.5 |
| 58-59—Minneapolis | 13 | 404 | 56 | 134 | .418 | 41 | 50 | .820 | 136 | 12 | 47 | 2 | 153 | 10.5 | 0.9 | 11.8 |
| 59-60—St. Louis | 12 | 205 | 29 | 74 | .392 | 20 | 25 | .800 | 68 | 11 | 36 | 0 | 78 | 5.7 | 0.9 | 6.5 |
| 60-61—St. Louis | 8 | 89 | 9 | 20 | .450 | 8 | 14 | .571 | 28 | 2 | 13 | 0 | 26 | 3.5 | 0.3 | 3.3 |
| Totals | 73 | ... | 301 | 763 | .394 | 300 | 384 | .781 | 707 | 94 | 255 | ... | 902 | 9.7 | 1.3 | 12.4 |

## NBA ALL-STAR GAME RECORD

| Season Team | Min. | FGM | FGA | Pct. | FTM | FTA | Pct. | Reb | Ast. | PF | Dq. | Pts. |
|---|---|---|---|---|---|---|---|---|---|---|---|---|
| 1951—Fort Wayne | ... | 1 | 6 | .167 | 0 | 0 | ... | 5 | 2 | 3 | 0 | 2 |
| 1952—Fort Wayne | | | | | Selected, did not play—injured. | | | | | | | |
| 1953—Fort Wayne | 18 | 5 | 7 | .714 | 0 | 0 | ... | 6 | 0 | 4 | 0 | 10 |
| 1954—Fort Wayne | 27 | 1 | 9 | .111 | 1 | 1 | 1.000 | 15 | 0 | 1 | 0 | 3 |
| 1955—Fort Wayne | 24 | 3 | 10 | .300 | 1 | 1 | 1.000 | 7 | 1 | 1 | 0 | 7 |
| 1956—Fort Wayne | 20 | 3 | 9 | .333 | 3 | 4 | .750 | 4 | 0 | 1 | 0 | 9 |
| 1958—Minneapolis | 13 | 1 | 4 | .250 | 8 | 8 | 1.000 | 3 | 0 | 3 | 0 | 10 |
| 1959—Minneapolis | 16 | 3 | 9 | .333 | 2 | 2 | 1.000 | 9 | 0 | 3 | 0 | 8 |
| Totals | ... | 17 | 54 | .315 | 15 | 16 | .938 | 49 | 3 | 16 | 0 | 49 |

# FRAZIER, WALT                    G

**PERSONAL:** Born March 29, 1945, in Atlanta. ... 6-4/205 (1,93/93,0). ... Full name: Walter Frazier Jr. ... Nickname: Clyde.
**HIGH SCHOOL:** David Howard (Atlanta).
**COLLEGE:** Southern Illinois.
**TRANSACTIONS:** Selected by New York Knicks in first round (fifth pick overall) of 1967 NBA Draft. ... Acquired by Cleveland Cavaliers as compensation for Knicks signing veteran free agent G Jim Cleamons (October 7, 1977). ... Waived by Cavaliers (October 19, 1979).
**CAREER HONORS:** Elected to Naismith Memorial Basketball Hall of Fame (1987). ... One of the 50 Greatest Players in NBA History (1996).
**MISCELLANEOUS:** Member of NBA championship team (1970, 1973). ... New York Knicks all-time assists leader with 4,791 (1967-68 through 1976-77).

ALL-TIME GREAT PLAYERS

## COLLEGIATE RECORD

**NOTES:** THE SPORTING NEWS All-America second team (1967).

| Season Team | G | Min. | FGM | FGA | Pct. | FTM | FTA | Pct. | Reb. | Ast. | Pts. | RPG | APG | PPG |
|---|---|---|---|---|---|---|---|---|---|---|---|---|---|---|
| 63-64—Southern Illinois‡ | 14 | ... | 133 | 225 | .591 | 52 | 85 | .612 | 129 | ... | 318 | 9.2 | ... | 22.7 |
| 64-65—Southern Illinois | 24 | ... | 161 | 353 | .456 | 88 | 111 | .793 | 221 | ... | 410 | 9.2 | ... | 17.1 |
| 65-66—Southern Illinois | | | | | | Did not play—ineligible. | | | | | | | | |
| 66-67—Southern Illinois | 26 | ... | 192 | 397 | .484 | 90 | 126 | .714 | 310 | ... | 474 | 11.9 | ... | 18.2 |
| **Varsity totals** | 50 | ... | 353 | 750 | .471 | 178 | 237 | .751 | 531 | ... | 884 | 10.6 | ... | 17.7 |

## NBA REGULAR-SEASON RECORD

**HONORS:** All-NBA first team (1970, 1972, 1974, 1975). ... All-NBA second team (1971, 1973). ... NBA All-Defensive first team (1969, 1970, 1971, 1972, 1973, 1974, 1975). ... NBA All-Rookie team (1968).

| Season Team | G | Min. | FGM | FGA | Pct. | FTM | FTA | Pct. | Reb. | Ast. | PF | Dq. | Pts. | RPG | APG | PPG |
|---|---|---|---|---|---|---|---|---|---|---|---|---|---|---|---|---|
| 67-68—New York | 74 | 1588 | 256 | 568 | .451 | 154 | 235 | .655 | 313 | 305 | 199 | 2 | 666 | 4.2 | 4.1 | 9.0 |
| 68-69—New York | 80 | 2949 | 531 | 1052 | .505 | 341 | 457 | .746 | 499 | 635 | 245 | 2 | 1403 | 6.2 | 7.9 | 17.5 |
| 69-70—New York | 77 | 3040 | 600 | 1158 | .518 | 409 | 547 | .748 | 465 | 629 | 203 | 1 | 1609 | 6.0 | 8.2 | 20.9 |
| 70-71—New York | 80 | 3455 | 651 | 1317 | .494 | 434 | 557 | .779 | 544 | 536 | 240 | 1 | 1736 | 6.8 | 6.7 | 21.7 |
| 71-72—New York | 77 | 3126 | 669 | 1307 | .512 | 450 | 557 | .808 | 513 | 446 | 185 | 0 | 1788 | 6.7 | 5.8 | 23.2 |
| 72-73—New York | 78 | 3181 | 681 | 1389 | .490 | 286 | 350 | .817 | 570 | 461 | 186 | 0 | 1648 | 7.3 | 5.9 | 21.1 |

| Season Team | G | Min. | FGM | FGA | Pct. | FTM | FTA | Pct. | REBOUNDS Off. | Def. | Tot. | Ast. | St. | Blk. | TO | Pts. | AVERAGES RPG | APG | PPG |
|---|---|---|---|---|---|---|---|---|---|---|---|---|---|---|---|---|---|---|---|
| 73-74—New York | 80 | 3338 | 674 | 1429 | .472 | 295 | 352 | .838 | 120 | 416 | 536 | 551 | 161 | 15 | ... | 1643 | 6.7 | 6.9 | 20.5 |
| 74-75—New York | 78 | 3204 | 672 | 1391 | .483 | 331 | 400 | .828 | 90 | 375 | 465 | 474 | 190 | 14 | ... | 1675 | 6.0 | 6.1 | 21.5 |
| 75-76—New York | 59 | 2427 | 470 | 969 | .485 | 186 | 226 | .823 | 79 | 321 | 400 | 351 | 106 | 9 | ... | 1126 | 6.8 | 5.9 | 19.1 |
| 76-77—N.Y. Knicks | 76 | 2687 | 532 | 1089 | .489 | 259 | 336 | .771 | 52 | 241 | 293 | 403 | 132 | 9 | ... | 1323 | 3.9 | 5.3 | 17.4 |
| 77-78—Cleveland | 51 | 1664 | 336 | 714 | .471 | 153 | 180 | .850 | 54 | 155 | 209 | 209 | 77 | 9 | 113 | 825 | 4.1 | 4.1 | 16.2 |
| 78-79—Cleveland | 12 | 279 | 54 | 122 | .443 | 21 | 27 | .778 | 7 | 13 | 20 | 32 | 13 | 2 | 22 | 129 | 1.7 | 2.7 | 10.8 |
| 79-80—Cleveland | 3 | 27 | 4 | 11 | .364 | 2 | 2 | 1.000 | 1 | 2 | 3 | 8 | 2 | 1 | 4 | 10 | 1.0 | 2.7 | 3.3 |
| **Totals** | 825 | 30965 | 6130 | 12516 | .490 | 3321 | 4226 | .786 | ... | ... | 4830 | 5040 | 681 | 59 | 139 | 15581 | 5.9 | 6.1 | 18.9 |

Three-point field goals: 1979-80, 0-for-1.

Personal fouls/disqualifications: 1973-74, 212/2. 1974-75, 205/2. 1975-76, 163/1. 1976-77, 194/0. 1977-78, 124/1. 1978-79, 22/0. 1979-80, 2/0. Totals, 2180/12.

## NBA PLAYOFF RECORD

| Season Team | G | Min. | FGM | FGA | Pct. | FTM | FTA | Pct. | Reb. | Ast. | PF | Dq. | Pts. | RPG | APG | PPG |
|---|---|---|---|---|---|---|---|---|---|---|---|---|---|---|---|---|
| 67-68—New York | 4 | 119 | 12 | 33 | .364 | 14 | 18 | .778 | 22 | 25 | 12 | 0 | 38 | 5.5 | 6.3 | 9.5 |
| 68-69—New York | 10 | 415 | 89 | 177 | .503 | 34 | 57 | .597 | 74 | 91 | 30 | 0 | 212 | 7.4 | 9.1 | 21.2 |
| 69-70—New York | 19 | 834 | 118 | 247 | .478 | 68 | 89 | .764 | 149 | 156 | 53 | 0 | 304 | 7.8 | 8.2 | 16.0 |
| 70-71—New York | 12 | 501 | 108 | 204 | .529 | 55 | 75 | .733 | 70 | 54 | 45 | 0 | 271 | 5.8 | 4.5 | 22.6 |
| 71-72—New York | 16 | 704 | 148 | 276 | .536 | 92 | 125 | .736 | 112 | 98 | 48 | 0 | 388 | 7.0 | 6.1 | 24.3 |
| 72-73—New York | 17 | 765 | 150 | 292 | .514 | 73 | 94 | .777 | 124 | 124 | 52 | 1 | 373 | 7.3 | 6.2 | 21.9 |

| Season Team | G | Min. | FGM | FGA | Pct. | FTM | FTA | Pct. | REBOUNDS Off. | Def. | Tot. | Ast. | St. | Blk. | TO | Pts. | AVERAGES RPG | APG | PPG |
|---|---|---|---|---|---|---|---|---|---|---|---|---|---|---|---|---|---|---|---|
| 73-74—New York | 12 | 491 | 113 | 225 | .502 | 44 | 49 | .898 | 21 | 74 | 95 | 48 | 21 | 4 | ... | 270 | 7.9 | 4.0 | 22.5 |
| 74-75—New York | 3 | 124 | 29 | 46 | .630 | 13 | 16 | .813 | 3 | 17 | 20 | 21 | 11 | 0 | ... | 71 | 6.7 | 7.0 | 23.7 |
| **Totals** | 93 | 3953 | 767 | 1500 | .511 | 393 | 523 | .751 | ... | ... | 666 | 599 | 32 | 4 | ... | 1927 | 7.2 | 6.4 | 20.7 |

Personal fouls/disqualifications: 1973-74, 41/1. 1974-75, 4/0. Totals, 285/2.

## NBA ALL-STAR GAME RECORD

**NOTES:** NBA All-Star Game Most Valuable Player (1975).

| Season Team | Min. | FGM | FGA | Pct. | FTM | FTA | Pct. | Reb. | Ast. | PF | Dq. | Pts. |
|---|---|---|---|---|---|---|---|---|---|---|---|---|
| 1970—New York | 24 | 3 | 7 | .429 | 1 | 2 | .500 | 3 | 4 | 2 | 0 | 7 |
| 1971—New York | 26 | 3 | 9 | .333 | 0 | 0 | ... | 6 | 5 | 2 | 0 | 6 |
| 1972—New York | 25 | 7 | 11 | .636 | 1 | 2 | .500 | 3 | 5 | 2 | 0 | 15 |
| 1973—New York | 26 | 5 | 15 | .333 | 0 | 0 | ... | 6 | 2 | 1 | 0 | 10 |

| Season Team | Min. | FGM | FGA | Pct. | FTM | FTA | Pct. | REBOUNDS Off. | Def. | Tot. | Ast. | PF | Dq. | St. | Blk. | TO | Pts. |
|---|---|---|---|---|---|---|---|---|---|---|---|---|---|---|---|---|---|
| 1974—New York | 28 | 5 | 12 | .417 | 2 | 2 | 1.000 | 1 | 1 | 2 | 5 | 1 | 0 | 3 | 0 | ... | 12 |
| 1975—New York | 35 | 10 | 17 | .588 | 10 | 11 | .909 | 0 | 5 | 5 | 2 | 2 | 0 | 4 | 0 | ... | 30 |
| 1976—New York | 19 | 2 | 7 | .286 | 4 | 4 | 1.000 | 0 | 2 | 2 | 3 | 0 | 0 | 2 | 0 | ... | 8 |
| **Totals** | 183 | 35 | 78 | .449 | 18 | 21 | .857 | ... | ... | 27 | 26 | 10 | 0 | 9 | 0 | ... | 88 |

## FREE, WORLD B.                    G

**PERSONAL:** Born December 9, 1953, in Atlanta. ... 6-3/190 (1,90/86,2). ... Formerly known as Lloyd Free.
**HIGH SCHOOL:** Canarsie (Brooklyn, N.Y.).
**COLLEGE:** Guilford (N.C.).
**TRANSACTIONS:** Selected after junior season by Philadelphia 76ers in second round (23rd pick overall) of 1975 NBA Draft. ... Traded by 76ers to San Diego Clippers for 1984 first-round draft choice (October 12, 1978). ... Traded by Clippers to Golden State Warriors for G Phil Smith and 1984 first-round draft choice (August 28, 1980). ... Traded by Warriors to Cleveland Cavaliers for G Ron Brewer (December 15, 1982). ... Signed as veteran free agent by 76ers (December 30, 1986). ... Cavaliers waived their right of first refusal in exchange for 1990 second-round draft choice. ... Waived by 76ers (March 4, 1987). ... Played in United States Basketball League with Miami Tropics (1987). ... Signed as free agent by Houston Rockets (October 1, 1987).
**CAREER NOTES:** Named strength and conditioning coach of Philadelphia 76ers (September 28, 1994). ... Community relations player representative, Philadelphia 76ers (1996-97 to present).

## COLLEGIATE RECORD

**NOTES:** Member of NAIA championship team (1973). ... Most Valuable Player in NAIA tournament (1973).

| Season Team | G | Min. | FGM | FGA | Pct. | FTM | FTA | Pct. | Reb. | Ast. | Pts. | RPG | APG | PPG |
|---|---|---|---|---|---|---|---|---|---|---|---|---|---|---|
| 72-73—Guilford (N.C.) | 33 | ... | 272 | 572 | .476 | 153 | 217 | .705 | 191 | ... | 697 | 5.8 | ... | 21.1 |
| 73-74—Guilford (N.C.) | 24 | ... | 216 | 456 | .474 | 165 | 225 | .733 | 200 | ... | 597 | 8.3 | ... | 24.9 |
| 74-75—Guilford (N.C.) | 28 | ... | 247 | 486 | .508 | 218 | 291 | .749 | 163 | ... | 712 | 5.8 | ... | 25.4 |
| Totals | 85 | ... | 735 | 1514 | .485 | 536 | 733 | .731 | 554 | ... | 2006 | 6.5 | ... | 23.6 |

## NBA REGULAR-SEASON RECORD

**HONORS:** All-NBA second team (1979).

| Season Team | G | Min. | FGM | FGA | Pct. | FTM | FTA | Pct. | REBOUNDS Off. | Def. | Tot. | Ast. | St. | Blk. | TO | Pts. | AVERAGES RPG | APG | PPG |
|---|---|---|---|---|---|---|---|---|---|---|---|---|---|---|---|---|---|---|---|
| 75-76—Philadelphia | 71 | 1121 | 239 | 533 | .448 | 112 | 186 | .602 | 64 | 61 | 125 | 104 | 37 | 6 | ... | 590 | 1.8 | 1.5 | 8.3 |
| 76-77—Philadelphia | 78 | 2253 | 467 | 1022 | .457 | 334 | 464 | .720 | 97 | 140 | 237 | 266 | 75 | 25 | ... | 1268 | 3.0 | 3.4 | 16.3 |
| 77-78—Philadelphia | 76 | 2050 | 390 | 857 | .455 | 411 | 562 | .731 | 92 | 120 | 212 | 306 | 68 | 41 | 200 | 1191 | 2.8 | 4.0 | 15.7 |
| 78-79—San Diego | 78 | 2954 | 795 | 1653 | .481 | *654 | *865 | .756 | 127 | 174 | 301 | 340 | 111 | 35 | 297 | 2244 | 3.9 | 4.4 | 28.8 |
| 79-80—San Diego | 68 | 2585 | 737 | 1556 | .474 | *572 | 760 | .753 | 129 | 109 | 238 | 283 | 81 | 32 | 228 | 2055 | 3.5 | 4.2 | 30.2 |
| 80-81—Golden State | 65 | 2370 | 516 | 1157 | .446 | 528 | 649 | .814 | 48 | 111 | 159 | 361 | 85 | 11 | 195 | 1565 | 2.4 | 5.6 | 24.1 |
| 81-82—Golden State | 78 | 2796 | 650 | 1452 | .448 | 479 | 647 | .740 | 118 | 130 | 248 | 419 | 71 | 8 | 208 | 1789 | 3.2 | 5.4 | 22.9 |
| 82-83—G.S.-Clev. | 73 | 2638 | 649 | 1423 | .456 | 430 | 583 | .738 | 92 | 109 | 201 | 290 | 97 | 15 | 209 | 1743 | 2.8 | 4.0 | 23.9 |
| 83-84—Cleveland | 75 | 2375 | 626 | 1407 | .445 | 395 | 504 | .784 | 89 | 128 | 217 | 226 | 94 | 8 | 154 | 1669 | 2.9 | 3.0 | 22.3 |
| 84-85—Cleveland | 71 | 2249 | 609 | 1328 | .459 | 308 | 411 | .749 | 61 | 150 | 211 | 320 | 75 | 16 | 139 | 1597 | 3.0 | 4.5 | 22.5 |
| 85-86—Cleveland | 75 | 2535 | 652 | 1433 | .455 | 379 | 486 | .780 | 72 | 146 | 218 | 314 | 91 | 19 | 172 | 1754 | 2.9 | 4.2 | 23.4 |
| 86-87—Philadelphia | 20 | 285 | 39 | 123 | .317 | 36 | 47 | .766 | 5 | 14 | 19 | 30 | 5 | 4 | 18 | 116 | 1.0 | 1.5 | 5.8 |
| 87-88—Houston | 58 | 682 | 143 | 350 | .409 | 80 | 100 | .800 | 14 | 30 | 44 | 60 | 20 | 3 | 49 | 374 | 0.8 | 1.0 | 6.4 |
| Totals | 886 | 26893 | 6512 | 14294 | .456 | 4718 | 6264 | .753 | 1008 | 1422 | 2430 | 3319 | 910 | 223 | 1869 | 17955 | 2.7 | 3.7 | 20.3 |

Three-point field goals: 1979-80, 9-for-25 (.360). 1980-81, 5-for-31 (.161). 1981-82, 10-for-58 (.179). 1982-83, 15-for-45 (.333). 1983-84, 22-for-69 (.319). 1984-85, 71-for-193 (.368). 1985-86, 71-for-169 (.420). 1986-87, 2-for-9 (.222). 1987-88, 8-for-35 (.229). Totals, 213-for-632 (.337).
Personal fouls/disqualifications: 1975-76, 107/0. 1976-77, 207/2. 1977-78, 199/0. 1978-79, 253/8. 1979-80, 195/0. 1980-81, 183/1. 1981-82, 222/1. 1982-83, 241/4. 1983-84, 214/2. 1984-85, 163/0. 1985-86, 186/1. 1986-87, 26/0. 1987-88, 74/2. Totals, 2270/21.

## NBA PLAYOFF RECORD

| Season Team | G | Min. | FGM | FGA | Pct. | FTM | FTA | Pct. | REBOUNDS Off. | Def. | Tot. | Ast. | St. | Blk. | TO | Pts. | AVERAGES RPG | APG | PPG |
|---|---|---|---|---|---|---|---|---|---|---|---|---|---|---|---|---|---|---|---|
| 75-76—Philadelphia | 3 | 62 | 11 | 28 | .393 | 10 | 13 | .769 | 1 | 0 | 1 | 5 | 3 | 0 | ... | 32 | 0.3 | 1.7 | 10.7 |
| 76-77—Philadelphia | 15 | 281 | 63 | 170 | .371 | 53 | 77 | .688 | 10 | 22 | 32 | 29 | 12 | 8 | ... | 179 | 2.1 | 1.9 | 11.9 |
| 77-78—Philadelphia | 10 | 268 | 51 | 124 | .411 | 59 | 81 | .728 | 10 | 21 | 31 | 37 | 4 | 6 | 26 | 161 | 3.1 | 3.7 | 16.1 |
| 84-85—Cleveland | 4 | 150 | 41 | 93 | .441 | 23 | 25 | .920 | 4 | 6 | 10 | 31 | 6 | 0 | 6 | 105 | 2.5 | 7.8 | 26.3 |
| 87-88—Houston | 2 | 12 | 0 | 2 | .000 | 0 | 0 | ... | 1 | 1 | 2 | 1 | 0 | 0 | 3 | 0 | 1.0 | 0.5 | 0.0 |
| Totals | 34 | 773 | 166 | 417 | .398 | 145 | 196 | .740 | 26 | 50 | 76 | 103 | 25 | 14 | 35 | 477 | 2.2 | 3.0 | 14.0 |

Three-point field goals: 1984-85, 0-for-4. 1987-88, 0-for-1. Totals, 0-for-5.
Personal fouls/disqualifications: 1975-76, 6/0. 1976-77, 33/0. 1977-78, 26/0. 1984-85, 12/0. 1987-88, 2/0. Totals, 79/0.

## NBA ALL-STAR GAME RECORD

| Season Team | Min. | FGM | FGA | Pct. | FTM | FTA | Pct. | REBOUNDS Off. | Def. | Tot. | Ast. | PF | Dq. | St. | Blk. | TO | Pts. |
|---|---|---|---|---|---|---|---|---|---|---|---|---|---|---|---|---|---|
| 1980—San Diego | 21 | 7 | 13 | .538 | 0 | 1 | .000 | 1 | 2 | 3 | 5 | 1 | 0 | 0 | 1 | 5 | 14 |

# FULKS, JOE                              F/C

**PERSONAL:** Born October 26, 1921, in Birmingham, Ky. ... Died March 21, 1976. ... 6-5/190 (1,96/86,2). ... Full name: Joseph Franklin Fulks. ... Nickname: Jumpin' Joe.
**HIGH SCHOOL:** Birmingham (Ky.), then Kuttawa (Ky.).
**COLLEGE:** Murray State.
**TRANSACTIONS:** In military service (1943-44 through 1945-46 seasons). ... Signed by Philadelphia Warriors of Basketball Association of America (1946).
**CAREER HONORS:** Elected to Naismith Memorial Basketball Hall of Fame (1978). ... NBA 25th Anniversary All-Time Team (1970).
**MISCELLANEOUS:** Member of BAA championship team (1947).

## COLLEGIATE RECORD

**NOTES:** Elected to NAIA Basketball Hall of Fame (1952).

| Season Team | G | Min. | FGM | FGA | Pct. | FTM | FTA | Pct. | Reb. | Ast. | Pts. | RPG | APG | PPG |
|---|---|---|---|---|---|---|---|---|---|---|---|---|---|---|
| 41-42—Murray State | 22 | ... | 117 | ... | ... | 50 | 76 | .658 | ... | ... | 284 | ... | ... | 12.9 |
| 42-43—Murray State | 25 | ... | 135 | ... | ... | 67 | 100 | .670 | ... | ... | 337 | ... | ... | 13.5 |
| Totals | 47 | ... | 252 | ... | ... | 117 | 176 | .665 | ... | ... | 621 | ... | ... | 13.2 |

## NBA REGULAR-SEASON RECORD

**HONORS:** All-NBA second team (1951). ... All-BAA first team (1947, 1948, 1949).

| Season Team | G | Min. | FGM | FGA | Pct. | FTM | FTA | Pct. | Reb. | Ast. | PF | Dq. | Pts. | RPG | APG | PPG |
|---|---|---|---|---|---|---|---|---|---|---|---|---|---|---|---|---|
| 46-47—Philadelphia (BAA) | 60 | ... | *475 | *1557 | .305 | *439 | *601 | .730 | ... | 25 | 199 | ... | *1389 | ... | 0.4 | *23.2 |
| 47-48—Philadelphia (BAA) | 43 | ... | 326 | *1258 | .259 | *297 | 390 | .762 | ... | 26 | 162 | ... | 949 | ... | 0.6 | *22.1 |
| 48-49—Philadelphia (BAA) | 60 | ... | 529 | *1689 | .313 | 502 | 638 | .787 | ... | 74 | 262 | ... | 1560 | ... | 1.2 | 26.0 |
| 49-50—Philadelphia | 68 | ... | 336 | 1209 | .278 | 293 | 421 | .696 | ... | 56 | 240 | ... | 965 | ... | 0.8 | 14.2 |
| 50-51—Philadelphia | 66 | ... | 429 | 1358 | .316 | 378 | 442 | *.855 | 523 | 117 | 247 | 8 | 1236 | 7.9 | 1.8 | 18.7 |
| 51-52—Philadelphia | 61 | 1904 | 336 | 1078 | .312 | 250 | 303 | .825 | 368 | 123 | 255 | 13 | 922 | 6.0 | 2.0 | 15.1 |
| 52-53—Philadelphia | 70 | 2085 | 332 | 960 | .346 | 168 | 231 | .727 | 387 | 138 | 319 | 20 | 832 | 5.5 | 2.0 | 11.9 |
| 53-54—Philadelphia | 61 | 501 | 61 | 229 | .266 | 28 | 49 | .571 | 101 | 28 | 90 | 0 | 150 | 1.7 | 0.5 | 2.5 |
| Totals | 489 | ... | 2824 | 9338 | .302 | 2355 | 3075 | .766 | ... | 587 | 1774 | ... | 8003 | ... | 1.2 | 16.4 |

## NBA PLAYOFF RECORD

| | | | | | | | | | | | | | | AVERAGES | | |
|---|---|---|---|---|---|---|---|---|---|---|---|---|---|---|---|---|
| Season Team | G | Min. | FGM | FGA | Pct. | FTM | FTA | Pct. | Reb. | Ast. | PF | Dq. | Pts. | RPG | APG | PPG |
| 46-47—Philadelphia (BAA) | 10 | ... | 74 | 257 | .288 | 74 | 94 | .787 | ... | 3 | 32 | ... | 222 | ... | 0.3 | 22.2 |
| 47-48—Philadelphia (BAA) | 13 | ... | 92 | 380 | .242 | 98 | 121 | .810 | ... | 3 | 55 | ... | 282 | ... | 0.2 | 21.7 |
| 48-49—Philadelphia (BAA) | 1 | ... | 0 | 0 | ... | 0 | 0 | ... | ... | 0 | 1 | 0 | 0 | ... | 0.0 | 0.0 |
| 49-50—Philadelphia | 2 | ... | 5 | 26 | .192 | 5 | 10 | .500 | ... | 2 | 10 | ... | 15 | ... | 1.0 | 7.5 |
| 50-51—Philadelphia | 2 | ... | 16 | 49 | .327 | 20 | 27 | .741 | 16 | 1 | 9 | 0 | 52 | 8.0 | 0.5 | 26.0 |
| 51-52—Philadelphia | 3 | 70 | 5 | 33 | .152 | 7 | 9 | .778 | 12 | 2 | 13 | 1 | 17 | 4.0 | 0.7 | 5.7 |
| Totals | 31 | ... | 192 | 745 | .258 | 204 | 261 | .782 | ... | 11 | 120 | ... | 588 | ... | 0.4 | 19.0 |

## NBA ALL-STAR GAME RECORD

| Season Team | Min. | FGM | FGA | Pct. | FTM | FTA | Pct. | Reb | Ast. | PF | Dq. | Pts. |
|---|---|---|---|---|---|---|---|---|---|---|---|---|
| 1951—Philadelphia | ... | 6 | 15 | .400 | 7 | 9 | .778 | 7 | 3 | 5 | 0 | 19 |
| 1952—Philadelphia | 9 | 3 | 7 | .429 | 0 | 1 | .000 | 5 | 2 | 2 | 0 | 6 |
| Totals | ... | 9 | 22 | .409 | 7 | 10 | .700 | 12 | 5 | 7 | 0 | 25 |

# GALLATIN, HARRY     F/C

**PERSONAL:** Born April 26, 1927, in Roxana, Ill. ... 6-6/215 (1,98/97,5). ... Full name: Harry Junior Gallatin. ... Nickname: The Horse.
**HIGH SCHOOL:** Roxana (Ill.).
**COLLEGE:** Northeast Missouri State Teachers College.
**TRANSACTIONS:** Selected by New York Knicks in first round of 1948 BAA Draft. ... Knicks franchise became part of NBA for 1949-50 season. ... Traded by Knicks with G Dick Atha and C/F Nat Clifton to Detroit Pistons for F Mel Hutchins and first-round draft choice (April 3, 1957).
**CAREER HONORS:** Elected to Naismith Memorial Basketball Hall of Fame (1991).

## COLLEGIATE RECORD

**NOTES:** Elected to NAIA Basketball Hall of Fame (1957).

| | | | | | | | | | | | AVERAGES | | |
|---|---|---|---|---|---|---|---|---|---|---|---|---|---|
| Season Team | G | Min. | FGM | FGA | Pct. | FTM | FTA | Pct. | Reb. | Ast. | Pts. | RPG | APG | PPG |
| 46-47—NE Missouri St. | 31 | ... | 149 | ... | ... | 53 | 89 | .596 | ... | ... | 351 | ... | ... | 11.3 |
| 47-48—NE Missouri St. | 31 | ... | 178 | 465 | .383 | 109 | 162 | .673 | ... | ... | 465 | ... | ... | 15.0 |
| Totals | 62 | ... | 327 | ... | ... | 162 | 251 | .645 | ... | ... | 816 | ... | ... | 13.2 |

## NBA REGULAR-SEASON RECORD

**HONORS:** All-NBA first team (1954). ... All-NBA second team (1955).

| | | | | | | | | | | | | | | AVERAGES | | |
|---|---|---|---|---|---|---|---|---|---|---|---|---|---|---|---|---|
| Season Team | G | Min. | FGM | FGA | Pct. | FTM | FTA | Pct. | Reb. | Ast. | PF | Dq. | Pts. | RPG | APG | PPG |
| 48-49—New York (BAA) | 52 | ... | 157 | 479 | .328 | 120 | 169 | .710 | ... | 63 | 127 | ... | 434 | ... | 1.2 | 8.3 |
| 49-50—New York | 68 | ... | 263 | 664 | .396 | 277 | 366 | .757 | ... | 56 | 215 | ... | 803 | ... | 0.8 | 11.8 |
| 50-51—New York | 66 | ... | 293 | 705 | .416 | 259 | 354 | .732 | 800 | 180 | 244 | 4 | 845 | 12.1 | 2.7 | 12.8 |
| 51-52—New York | 66 | 1931 | 233 | 527 | .442 | 275 | 341 | .806 | 661 | 115 | 223 | 5 | 741 | 10.0 | 1.7 | 11.2 |
| 52-53—New York | 70 | 2333 | 282 | 635 | .444 | 301 | 430 | .700 | 916 | 126 | 224 | 6 | 865 | 13.1 | 1.8 | 12.4 |
| 53-54—New York | 72 | 2690 | 258 | 639 | .404 | 433 | 552 | .784 | *1098 | 153 | 208 | 2 | 949 | *15.3 | 2.1 | 13.2 |
| 54-55—New York | 72 | 2548 | 330 | 859 | .384 | 393 | 483 | .814 | 995 | 176 | 206 | 5 | 1053 | 13.8 | 2.4 | 14.6 |
| 55-56—New York | 72 | 2378 | 322 | 834 | .386 | 358 | 455 | .787 | 740 | 168 | 220 | 6 | 1002 | 10.3 | 2.3 | 13.9 |
| 56-57—New York | 72 | 1943 | 332 | 817 | .406 | 415 | 519 | .800 | 725 | 85 | 202 | 1 | 1079 | 10.1 | 1.2 | 15.0 |
| 57-58—Detroit | 72 | 1990 | 340 | 898 | .379 | 392 | 498 | .787 | 749 | 86 | 217 | 5 | 1072 | 10.4 | 1.2 | 14.9 |
| Totals | 682 | ... | 2810 | 7057 | .398 | 3223 | 4167 | .773 | ... | 1208 | 2086 | ... | 8843 | ... | 1.8 | 13.0 |

## NBA PLAYOFF RECORD

| | | | | | | | | | | | | | | AVERAGES | | |
|---|---|---|---|---|---|---|---|---|---|---|---|---|---|---|---|---|
| Season Team | G | Min. | FGM | FGA | Pct. | FTM | FTA | Pct. | Reb. | Ast. | PF | Dq. | Pts. | RPG | APG | PPG |
| 48-49—New York (BAA) | 6 | ... | 20 | 56 | .357 | 32 | 39 | .821 | ... | 10 | 31 | ... | 72 | ... | 1.7 | 12.0 |
| 49-50—New York | 5 | ... | 20 | 52 | .385 | 25 | 32 | .781 | ... | 6 | 23 | ... | 65 | ... | 1.2 | 13.0 |
| 50-51—New York | 14 | ... | 49 | 140 | .350 | 67 | 87 | .770 | 163 | 26 | 57 | 3 | 165 | 11.6 | 1.9 | 11.8 |
| 51-52—New York | 14 | 471 | 50 | 122 | .410 | 51 | 66 | .773 | 134 | 19 | 45 | 1 | 151 | 9.6 | 1.4 | 10.8 |
| 52-53—New York | 11 | 303 | 36 | 86 | .419 | 44 | 59 | .746 | 120 | 15 | 29 | 0 | 116 | 10.9 | 1.4 | 10.5 |
| 53-54—New York | 4 | 151 | 16 | 35 | .457 | 22 | 31 | .710 | 61 | 6 | 12 | 0 | 54 | 15.3 | 1.5 | 13.5 |
| 54-55—New York | 3 | 108 | 19 | 42 | .452 | 17 | 22 | .773 | 44 | 7 | 11 | 0 | 55 | 14.7 | 2.3 | 18.3 |
| 57-58—Detroit | 7 | 182 | 32 | 87 | .368 | 26 | 37 | .703 | 70 | 11 | 27 | 1 | 90 | 10.0 | 1.6 | 12.9 |
| Totals | 64 | ... | 242 | 620 | .390 | 284 | 373 | .761 | ... | 100 | 235 | ... | 768 | ... | 1.6 | 12.0 |

## NBA ALL-STAR GAME RECORD

| Season Team | Min. | FGM | FGA | Pct. | FTM | FTA | Pct. | Reb | Ast. | PF | Dq. | Pts. |
|---|---|---|---|---|---|---|---|---|---|---|---|---|
| 1951—New York | ... | 2 | 4 | .500 | 1 | 1 | 1.000 | 5 | 2 | 4 | 0 | 5 |
| 1952—New York | 22 | 3 | 5 | .600 | 1 | 4 | .250 | 9 | 3 | 3 | 0 | 7 |
| 1953—New York | 19 | 1 | 4 | .250 | 1 | 2 | .500 | 3 | 2 | 1 | 0 | 3 |
| 1954—New York | 28 | 0 | 2 | .000 | 5 | 6 | .833 | 18 | 3 | 0 | 0 | 5 |
| 1955—New York | 36 | 4 | 7 | .571 | 5 | 5 | 1.000 | 14 | 3 | 2 | 0 | 13 |
| 1956—New York | 30 | 5 | 12 | .417 | 6 | 7 | .857 | 5 | 2 | 4 | 0 | 16 |
| 1957—New York | 24 | 4 | 7 | .571 | 0 | 2 | .000 | 11 | 1 | 3 | 0 | 8 |
| Totals | ... | 19 | 41 | .463 | 19 | 27 | .704 | 65 | 16 | 17 | 0 | 57 |

## HEAD COACHING RECORD

**HONORS:** NBA Coach of the Year (1963).

### COLLEGIATE COACHING RECORD

| Season Team | W | L | Pct. | Finish |
|---|---|---|---|---|
| 58-59—Southern Illinois-Carbondale | 17 | 10 | .630 | 2nd/Interstate Intercollegiate Athletic Conference |
| 59-60—Southern Illinois-Carbondale | 20 | 9 | .690 | T1st/Interstate Intercollegiate Athletic Conference |
| 60-61—Southern Illinois-Carbondale | 21 | 6 | .778 | 1st/Interstate Intercollegiate Athletic Conference |
| 61-62—Southern Illinois-Carbondale | 21 | 10 | .677 | 1st/Interstate Intercollegiate Athletic Conference |
| 67-68—Southern Ill.-Edwardsville | 5 | 5 | .500 | |
| 68-69—Southern Ill.-Edwardsville | 7 | 10 | .412 | |
| 69-70—Southern Ill.-Edwardsville | 7 | 16 | .304 | |
| Totals (7 years) | 98 | 66 | .598 | |

### NBA COACHING RECORD

| | REGULAR SEASON | | | | PLAYOFFS | | |
|---|---|---|---|---|---|---|---|
| Season Team | W | L | Pct. | Finish | W | L | Pct. |
| 62-63—St. Louis | 48 | 32 | .600 | 2nd/Western Division | 6 | 5 | .545 |
| 63-64—St. Louis | 46 | 34 | .575 | 2nd/Western Division | 6 | 6 | .500 |
| 64-65—St. Louis | 17 | 16 | .515 | | — | — | — |
| —New York | 19 | 23 | .452 | 4th/Eastern Division | — | — | — |
| 65-66—New York | 6 | 15 | .286 | | — | — | — |
| Totals (4 years) | 136 | 120 | .531 | Totals (2 years) | 12 | 11 | .522 |

**NOTES:**

1959—Defeated Wittenberg, 90-80, in NCAA College Division Tournament regional semifinal; lost to Belmont Academy, 79-70, in regional final.

1960—Defeated McKendree, 97-71, in NCAA College Division Tournament regional; lost to Oklahoma Baptist, 75-71, in semifinal.

1961—Defeated Trinity (Tex.), 96-84, in NCAA College Division Tournament regional semifinal; lost to Southeast Missouri, 87-84, in regional final.

1962—Defeated Union, 78-56, in NCAA College Division Tournament regional semifinal; defeated Evansville, 88-83, in regional final; defeated Northeastern, 73-57, in quarterfinal; lost to Mount St. Mary's, 58-57, in semifinals; defeated Nebraska Wesleyan 98-81, in third-place game.

1963—Defeated Detroit, 3-1, in Western Division Semifinals; lost to Los Angeles, 4-3, in Western Division Finals.

1964—Defeated Los Angeles, 3-2, in Western Division Semifinals; lost to San Francisco, 4-3, in Western Division Finals. Replaced as St. Louis head coach by Richie Guerin (November).

1965—Replaced Eddie Donovan as New York head coach (January), with record of 12-26. Replaced as New York head coach by Dick McGuire (November 29).

### RECORD AS BASEBALL PLAYER

**TRANSACTIONS:** Signed by Erwin (Tenn.) of Appalachian League (January 1945). ... On military service list (July 1945-February 24, 1949). ... Placed on suspended list (July 13, 1950). ... Released (September 29, 1950).

| Year Team (League) | W | L | Pct. | ERA | G | GS | CG | ShO | Sv. | IP | H | R | ER | BB | SO |
|---|---|---|---|---|---|---|---|---|---|---|---|---|---|---|---|
| 1949—Decatur (Three I) | 7 | 9 | .438 | 4.28 | 32 | ... | 10 | 1 | ... | 166 | 171 | 88 | 79 | 85 | 78 |

## GERVIN, GEORGE      G/F

**PERSONAL:** Born April 27, 1952, in Detroit. ... 6-7/185 (2,00/83,9). ... Full name: George Gervin. ... Nickname: Iceman. ... Brother of Derrick Gervin, guard with New Jersey Nets (1989-90 and 1990-91).

**HIGH SCHOOL:** Martin Luther King (Detroit).

**COLLEGE:** Long Beach State, then Eastern Michigan.

**TRANSACTIONS:** Selected after sophomore season by Virginia Squires in first round of 1973 ABA special circumstance draft. ... Selected by Phoenix Suns in third round (40th pick overall) of 1974 NBA Draft. ... Contract sold by Squires to San Antonio Spurs (January 30, 1974). ... Spurs franchise became part of NBA for 1976-77 season. ... Traded by Spurs to Chicago Bulls for F David Greenwood (October 24, 1985). ... Played in Italy (1986-87). ... Played with Quad City Thunder of Continental Basketball Association (1989-90).

**CAREER NOTES:** Assistant coach, San Antonio Spurs (1992-93 and 1993-94). ... Community relations representative, Spurs (1993-94 to 1999-2000). ... Head coach, Detroit Dogs, ABA 2000. ... Vice president of basketball operations, Detroit Dogs (2001-present).

**CAREER HONORS:** Elected to Naismith Memorial Basketball Hall of Fame (1996). ... One of the 50 Greatest Players in NBA History (1996).

### COLLEGIATE RECORD

**NOTES:** Left Long Beach State before the start of 1969-70 season.

| Season Team | G | Min. | FGM | FGA | Pct. | FTM | FTA | Pct. | Reb. | Ast. | Pts. | RPG | APG | PPG |
|---|---|---|---|---|---|---|---|---|---|---|---|---|---|---|
| 70-71—Eastern Mich. | 9 | 300 | 65 | 123 | .528 | 28 | 39 | .718 | 104 | 29 | 158 | 11.6 | 3.2 | 17.6 |
| 71-72—Eastern Mich. | 30 | 1098 | 339 | 571 | .594 | 208 | 265 | .785 | 458 | 103 | 886 | 15.3 | 3.4 | 29.5 |
| Totals | 39 | 1398 | 404 | 694 | .582 | 236 | 304 | .776 | 562 | 132 | 1044 | 14.4 | 3.4 | 26.8 |

### ABA REGULAR-SEASON RECORD

**NOTES:** ABA All-Star second team (1975, 1976). ... ABA All-Rookie team (1973).

| | | | 2-POINT | | | 3-POINT | | | | | | | | | AVERAGES | | |
|---|---|---|---|---|---|---|---|---|---|---|---|---|---|---|---|---|---|
| Season Team | G | Min. | FGM | FGA | Pct. | FGM | FGA | Pct. | FTM | FTA | Pct. | Reb. | Ast. | Pts. | RPG | APG | PPG |
| 72-73—Virginia | 30 | 689 | 155 | 315 | .492 | 6 | 26 | .231 | 96 | 118 | .814 | 128 | 34 | 424 | 4.3 | 1.1 | 14.1 |
| 73-74—Virginia-San Antonio | 74 | 2511 | 664 | 1370 | .485 | 8 | 56 | .143 | 378 | 464 | .815 | 624 | 142 | 1730 | 8.4 | 1.9 | 23.4 |
| 74-75—San Antonio | 84 | 3113 | 767 | 1600 | .479 | 17 | 55 | .309 | 380 | 458 | .830 | 697 | 207 | 1965 | 8.3 | 2.5 | 23.4 |
| 75-76—San Antonio | 81 | 2748 | 692 | 1359 | .509 | 14 | 55 | .255 | 342 | 399 | .857 | 546 | 201 | 1768 | 6.7 | 2.5 | 21.8 |
| Totals | 269 | 9061 | 2278 | 4644 | .491 | 45 | 192 | .234 | 1196 | 1439 | .831 | 1995 | 584 | 5887 | 7.4 | 2.2 | 21.9 |

## ABA PLAYOFF RECORD

| Season Team | G | Min. | 2-POINT | | | 3-POINT | | | FTM | FTA | Pct. | Reb. | Ast. | Pts. | AVERAGES | | |
| | | | FGM | FGA | Pct. | FGM | FGA | Pct. | | | | | | | RPG | APG | PPG |
|---|---|---|---|---|---|---|---|---|---|---|---|---|---|---|---|---|---|
| 72-73—Virginia | 5 | 200 | 33 | 72 | .458 | 1 | 5 | .200 | 23 | 34 | .676 | 38 | 8 | 93 | 7.6 | 1.6 | 18.6 |
| 73-74—San Antonio | 7 | 226 | 56 | 114 | .491 | 1 | 1 | 1.000 | 29 | 31 | .935 | 52 | 19 | 144 | 7.4 | 2.7 | 20.6 |
| 74-75—San Antonio | 6 | 276 | 76 | 159 | .478 | 3 | 12 | .250 | 43 | 52 | .827 | 84 | 8 | 204 | 14.0 | 1.3 | 34.0 |
| 75-76—San Antonio | 7 | 288 | 67 | 125 | .536 | 0 | 3 | .000 | 56 | 69 | .812 | 64 | 19 | 190 | 9.1 | 2.7 | 27.1 |
| Totals | 25 | 990 | 232 | 470 | .494 | 5 | 21 | .238 | 151 | 186 | .812 | 238 | 54 | 631 | 9.5 | 2.2 | 25.2 |

## ABA ALL-STAR GAME RECORD

| Season Team | Min. | 2-POINT | | | 3-POINT | | | FTM | FTA | Pct. | Reb. | Ast. | Pts. |
| | | FGM | FGA | Pct. | FGM | FGA | Pct. | | | | | | |
|---|---|---|---|---|---|---|---|---|---|---|---|---|---|
| 1974—Virginia | 21 | 3 | 8 | .375 | 0 | 1 | .000 | 3 | 4 | .750 | 5 | 3 | 9 |
| 1975—San Antonio | 30 | 8 | 14 | .571 | 0 | 1 | .000 | 7 | 8 | .875 | 6 | 3 | 23 |
| 1976—San Antonio | 16 | 3 | 13 | .231 | 0 | 0 | ... | 1 | 2 | .500 | 6 | 1 | 8 |
| Totals | 67 | 14 | 35 | .400 | 0 | 2 | .000 | 11 | 14 | .786 | 17 | 7 | 40 |

## NBA REGULAR-SEASON RECORD

**RECORDS:** Holds single-game record for most points in one quarter—33 (April 9, 1978, vs. New Orleans).

**HONORS:** All-NBA first team (1978, 1979, 1980, 1981, 1982). ... All-NBA second team (1977, 1983).

| Season Team | G | Min. | FGM | FGA | Pct. | FTM | FTA | Pct. | REBOUNDS | | | Ast. | St. | Blk. | TO | Pts. | AVERAGES | | |
| | | | | | | | | | Off. | Def. | Tot. | | | | | | RPG | APG | PPG |
|---|---|---|---|---|---|---|---|---|---|---|---|---|---|---|---|---|---|---|---|
| 76-77—San Antonio | 82 | 2705 | 726 | 1335 | .544 | 443 | 532 | .833 | 134 | 320 | 454 | 238 | 105 | 104 | ... | 1895 | 5.5 | 2.9 | 23.1 |
| 77-78—San Antonio | 82 | 2857 | *864 | 1611 | .536 | 504 | 607 | .830 | 118 | 302 | 420 | 302 | 136 | 110 | 306 | *2232 | 5.1 | 3.7 | *27.2 |
| 78-79—San Antonio | 80 | 2888 | *947 | *1749 | .541 | 471 | 570 | .826 | 142 | 258 | 400 | 219 | 137 | 91 | 286 | *2365 | 5.0 | 2.7 | *29.6 |
| 79-80—San Antonio | 78 | 2934 | *1024 | *1940 | .528 | 505 | 593 | .852 | 154 | 249 | 403 | 202 | 110 | 79 | 254 | *2585 | 5.2 | 2.6 | *33.1 |
| 80-81—San Antonio | 82 | 2765 | 850 | 1729 | .492 | 512 | 620 | .826 | 126 | 293 | 419 | 260 | 94 | 56 | 251 | 2221 | 5.1 | 3.2 | 27.1 |
| 81-82—San Antonio | 79 | 2817 | *993 | *1987 | .500 | 555 | 642 | .864 | 138 | 254 | 392 | 187 | 77 | 45 | 210 | *2551 | 5.0 | 2.4 | *32.3 |
| 82-83—San Antonio | 78 | 2830 | 757 | 1553 | .487 | 517 | 606 | .853 | 111 | 246 | 357 | 264 | 88 | 67 | 247 | 2043 | 4.6 | 3.4 | 26.2 |
| 83-84—San Antonio | 76 | 2584 | 765 | 1561 | .490 | 427 | 507 | .842 | 106 | 207 | 313 | 220 | 79 | 47 | 224 | 1967 | 4.1 | 2.9 | 25.9 |
| 84-85—San Antonio | 72 | 2091 | 600 | 1182 | .508 | 324 | 384 | .844 | 79 | 155 | 234 | 178 | 66 | 48 | 198 | 1524 | 3.3 | 2.5 | 21.2 |
| 85-86—Chicago | 82 | 2065 | 519 | 1100 | .472 | 283 | 322 | .879 | 78 | 137 | 215 | 144 | 49 | 23 | 161 | 1325 | 2.6 | 1.8 | 16.2 |
| Totals | 791 | 26536 | 8045 | 15747 | .511 | 4541 | 5383 | .844 | 1186 | 2421 | 3607 | 2214 | 941 | 670 | 2137 | 20708 | 4.6 | 2.8 | 26.2 |

Three-point field goals: 1979-80, 32-for-102 (.314). 1980-81, 9-for-35 (.257). 1981-82, 10-for-36 (.278). 1982-83, 12-for-33 (.364). 1983-84, 10-for-24 (.417). 1984-85, 0-for-10. 1985-86, 4-for-19 (.211). Totals, 77-for-259 (.297).

Personal fouls/disqualifications: 1976-77, 286/12. 1977-78, 255/3. 1978-79, 275/5. 1979-80, 208/0. 1980-81, 212/4. 1981-82, 215/2. 1982-83, 243/5. 1983-84, 219/3. 1984-85, 208/2. 1985-86, 210/4. Totals, 2331/40.

## NBA PLAYOFF RECORD

| Season Team | G | Min. | FGM | FGA | Pct. | FTM | FTA | Pct. | REBOUNDS | | | Ast. | St. | Blk. | TO | Pts. | AVERAGES | | |
| | | | | | | | | | Off. | Def. | Tot. | | | | | | RPG | APG | PPG |
|---|---|---|---|---|---|---|---|---|---|---|---|---|---|---|---|---|---|---|---|
| 76-77—San Antonio | 2 | 62 | 19 | 44 | .432 | 12 | 15 | .800 | 5 | 6 | 11 | 3 | 1 | 2 | ... | 50 | 5.5 | 1.5 | 25.0 |
| 77-78—San Antonio | 6 | 227 | 78 | 142 | .549 | 43 | 56 | .768 | 11 | 23 | 34 | 19 | 6 | 16 | 19 | 199 | 5.7 | 3.2 | 33.2 |
| 78-79—San Antonio | 14 | 513 | 158 | 295 | .536 | 84 | 104 | .808 | 33 | 49 | 82 | 35 | 27 | 14 | 40 | 400 | 5.9 | 2.5 | 28.6 |
| 79-80—San Antonio | 3 | 122 | 37 | 74 | .500 | 26 | 30 | .867 | 9 | 11 | 20 | 12 | 5 | 3 | 9 | 100 | 6.7 | 4.0 | 33.3 |
| 80-81—San Antonio | 7 | 274 | 77 | 154 | .500 | 36 | 45 | .800 | 9 | 26 | 35 | 24 | 5 | 5 | 20 | 190 | 5.0 | 3.4 | 27.1 |
| 81-82—San Antonio | 9 | 373 | 103 | 228 | .452 | 59 | 71 | .831 | 19 | 47 | 66 | 41 | 10 | 4 | 31 | 265 | 7.3 | 4.6 | 29.4 |
| 82-83—San Antonio | 11 | 437 | 108 | 208 | .519 | 61 | 69 | .884 | 21 | 53 | 74 | 37 | 12 | 4 | 46 | 277 | 6.7 | 3.4 | 25.2 |
| 84-85—San Antonio | 5 | 183 | 42 | 79 | .532 | 27 | 34 | .794 | 3 | 15 | 18 | 14 | 3 | 3 | 20 | 111 | 3.6 | 2.8 | 22.2 |
| 85-86—Chicago | 2 | 11 | 0 | 1 | .000 | 0 | 0 | ... | 1 | 1 | 1 | 0 | 0 | 2 | 2 | 0 | 0.5 | 0.5 | 0.0 |
| Totals | 59 | 2202 | 622 | 1225 | .508 | 348 | 424 | .821 | 110 | 231 | 341 | 186 | 69 | 51 | 187 | 1592 | 5.8 | 3.2 | 27.0 |

Three-point field goals: 1979-80, 0-for-2. 1980-81, 0-for-3. 1981-82, 0-for-3. 1982-83, 0-for-2. 1984-85, 0-for-3. Totals, 0-for-13.

Personal fouls/disqualifications: 1976-77, 9/1. 1977-78, 23/0. 1978-79, 51/1. 1979-80, 8/0. 1980-81, 19/1. 1981-82, 36/1. 1982-83, 39/1. 1984-85, 19/0. 1985-86, 3/0. Totals, 207/5.

## NBA ALL-STAR GAME RECORD

**NOTES:** NBA All-Star Game Most Valuable Player (1980).

| Season Team | Min. | FGM | FGA | Pct. | FTM | FTA | Pct. | REBOUNDS | | | Ast. | PF | Dq. | St. | Blk. | TO | Pts. |
| | | | | | | | | Off. | Def. | Tot. | | | | | | | |
|---|---|---|---|---|---|---|---|---|---|---|---|---|---|---|---|---|---|
| 1977—San Antonio | 12 | 0 | 6 | .000 | 0 | 0 | ... | 0 | 1 | 1 | 0 | 1 | 0 | 0 | 1 | ... | 0 |
| 1978—San Antonio | 18 | 4 | 11 | .364 | 1 | 3 | .333 | 1 | 1 | 2 | 1 | 2 | 0 | 2 | 1 | 2 | 9 |
| 1979—San Antonio | 34 | 8 | 16 | .500 | 10 | 11 | .909 | 2 | 4 | 6 | 2 | 4 | 0 | 1 | 1 | 3 | 26 |
| 1980—San Antonio | 40 | 14 | 26 | .538 | 6 | 9 | .667 | 4 | 6 | 10 | 3 | 2 | 0 | 3 | 0 | 3 | 34 |
| 1981—San Antonio | 24 | 5 | 9 | .556 | 1 | 2 | .500 | 1 | 2 | 3 | 0 | 3 | 0 | 2 | 1 | 2 | 11 |
| 1982—San Antonio | 27 | 5 | 14 | .357 | 2 | 2 | 1.000 | 1 | 5 | 6 | 1 | 3 | 0 | 3 | 3 | 0 | 12 |
| 1983—San Antonio | 14 | 3 | 8 | .375 | 2 | 2 | 1.000 | 0 | 0 | 0 | 3 | 2 | 0 | 2 | 0 | 0 | 9 |
| 1984—San Antonio | 21 | 5 | 6 | .833 | 3 | 3 | 1.000 | 0 | 2 | 2 | 1 | 5 | 0 | 0 | 1 | 6 | 13 |
| 1985—San Antonio | 25 | 10 | 12 | .833 | 3 | 4 | .750 | 0 | 3 | 3 | 1 | 2 | 0 | 3 | 1 | 4 | 23 |
| Totals | 215 | 54 | 108 | .500 | 28 | 36 | .778 | 9 | 24 | 33 | 12 | 25 | 0 | 16 | 9 | 20 | 137 |

## COMBINED ABA AND NBA REGULAR-SEASON RECORDS

| | G | Min. | FGM | FGA | Pct. | FTM | FTA | Pct. | REBOUNDS | | | Ast. | Stl. | Blk. | TO | Pts. | AVERAGES | | |
| | | | | | | | | | Off. | Def. | Tot. | | | | | | RPG | APG | PPG |
|---|---|---|---|---|---|---|---|---|---|---|---|---|---|---|---|---|---|---|---|
| Totals | 1060 | 35597 | 10368 | 20583 | .504 | 5737 | 6822 | .841 | ... | ... | 5602 | 2798 | ... | ... | ... | 26595 | 5.3 | 2.6 | 25.1 |

Three-point field goals: 122-for-451 (.271).

Personal fouls/disqualifications: 3250.

## ITALIAN LEAGUE RECORD

| Season Team | G | Min. | FGM | FGA | Pct. | FTM | FTA | Pct. | Reb. | Ast. | Pts. | AVERAGES | | |
| | | | | | | | | | | | | RPG | APG | PPG |
|---|---|---|---|---|---|---|---|---|---|---|---|---|---|---|
| 86-87—Banco Roma | 27 | 893 | 263 | 525 | .501 | 159 | 190 | .837 | 134 | 9 | 704 | 5.0 | 0.3 | 26.1 |

## CBA REGULAR-SEASON RECORD

| | | | | | | | | | | | | AVERAGES | | |
|---|---|---|---|---|---|---|---|---|---|---|---|---|---|---|
| Season Team | G | Min. | FGM | FGA | Pct. | FTM | FTA | Pct. | Reb. | Ast. | Pts. | RPG | APG | PPG |
| 89-90—Quad City | 14 | 391 | 115 | 235 | .489 | 54 | 73 | .740 | 91 | 20 | 284 | 6.5 | 1.4 | 20.3 |

## ABA 2000 COACHING RECORD

| | REGULAR SEASON | | | | PLAYOFFS | | |
|---|---|---|---|---|---|---|---|
| Season Team | W | L | Pct. | Finish | W | L | Pct. |
| 00-01—Detroit | 21 | 20 | .512 | 1st | 3 | 0 | 1.000 |

**NOTES:**
2001—Defeated Tampa Bay in Eastern Division Semifinals; defeated Indiana in Eastern Division Finals; defeated Chicago in ABA 2000 Finals.

# GILMORE, ARTIS                                                    C

**PERSONAL:** Born September 21, 1949, in Chipley, Fla. ... 7-2/265 (2,18/120,2). ... Full name: Artis Gilmore.
**HIGH SCHOOL:** Roulhac (Chipley, Fla.), then Carver (Dothan, Ala.).
**JUNIOR COLLEGE:** Gardner-Webb Junior College (N.C.).
**COLLEGE:** Jacksonville.
**TRANSACTIONS:** Selected by Chicago Bulls in seventh round (117th pick overall) of 1971 NBA Draft. ... Selected by Kentucky Colonels in first round of 1971 ABA draft. ... Selected by Bulls from Colonels in ABA dispersal draft (August 5, 1976). ... Traded by Bulls to San Antonio Spurs for C Dave Corzine, F Mark Olberding and cash (July 22, 1982). ... Traded by Spurs to Bulls for 1988 second-round draft choice (June 22, 1987). ... Waived by Bulls (December 26, 1987). ... Signed as free agent by Boston Celtics (January 8, 1988). ... Played in Italy (1988-89).
**MISCELLANEOUS:** Chicago Bulls all-time blocked shots leader with 1,017 (1976-77 through 1981-82 and 1987-88).

## COLLEGIATE RECORD

**NOTES:** THE SPORTING NEWS All-America first team (1971). ... THE SPORTING NEWS All-America second team (1970). ... Holds NCAA career record for average rebounds per game—22.7. ... Led NCAA Division I with 22.2 rebounds per game (1970) and 23.2 rebounds per game (1971).

| | | | | | | | | | | | | AVERAGES | | |
|---|---|---|---|---|---|---|---|---|---|---|---|---|---|---|
| Season Team | G | Min. | FGM | FGA | Pct. | FTM | FTA | Pct. | Reb. | Ast. | Pts. | RPG | APG | PPG |
| 67-68—Gardner-Webb J.C. | 31 | ... | 296 | ... | ... | 121 | ... | ... | ... | ... | 713 | ... | ... | 23.0 |
| 68-69—Gardner-Webb J.C. | 36 | ... | 326 | ... | ... | 140 | ... | ... | ... | ... | 792 | ... | ... | 22.0 |
| 69-70—Jacksonville | 28 | ... | 307 | 529 | .580 | 128 | 202 | .634 | 621 | 51 | 742 | 22.2 | 1.8 | 26.5 |
| 70-71—Jacksonville | 26 | ... | 229 | 405 | .565 | 112 | 188 | .596 | 603 | 42 | 570 | 23.2 | 1.6 | 21.9 |
| Junior college totals | 67 | ... | 622 | ... | ... | 261 | ... | ... | ... | ... | 1505 | ... | ... | 22.5 |
| 4-year-college totals | 54 | ... | 536 | 934 | .574 | 240 | 390 | .615 | 1224 | 93 | 1312 | 22.7 | 1.7 | 24.3 |

## ABA REGULAR-SEASON RECORD

**NOTES:** ABA Most Valuable Player (1972). ... ABA Rookie of the Year (1972). ... ABA All-Star first team (1972, 1973, 1974, 1975, 1976). ... ABA All-Defensive team (1973, 1974, 1975, 1976). ... ABA All-Rookie team (1972). ... Member of ABA championship team (1975). ... Holds single-game record for most rebounds—40 (February 3, 1974, vs. New York). ... Holds single-season record for most blocked shots—422 (1972). ... Led ABA with 341 personal fouls (1976).

| | | | 2-POINT | | | 3-POINT | | | | | | | | | AVERAGES | | |
|---|---|---|---|---|---|---|---|---|---|---|---|---|---|---|---|---|---|
| Season Team | G | Min. | FGM | FGA | Pct. | FGM | FGA | Pct. | FTM | FTA | Pct. | Reb. | Ast. | Pts. | RPG | APG | PPG |
| 71-72—Kentucky | 84 | *3666 | 806 | 1348 | *.598 | 0 | 0 | ... | 391 | 605 | .646 | *1491 | 230 | 2003 | *17.8 | 2.7 | 23.8 |
| 72-73—Kentucky | 84 | 3502 | 686 | 1226 | *.560 | 1 | 2 | .500 | 368 | 572 | .643 | *1476 | 295 | 1743 | *17.6 | 3.5 | 20.8 |
| 73-74—Kentucky | 84 | *3502 | 621 | 1257 | .494 | 0 | 3 | .000 | 326 | 489 | .667 | *1538 | 329 | 1568 | *18.3 | 3.9 | 18.7 |
| 74-75—Kentucky | 84 | *3493 | 783 | 1349 | .580 | 1 | 2 | .500 | 412 | 592 | .696 | *1361 | 208 | 1981 | 16.2 | 2.5 | 23.6 |
| 75-76—Kentucky | 84 | 3286 | 773 | 1401 | .552 | 0 | 0 | ... | 521 | *764 | .682 | *1303 | 211 | 2067 | *15.5 | 2.5 | 24.6 |
| Totals | 420 | 17449 | 3669 | 6581 | .558 | 2 | 7 | .286 | 2018 | 3022 | .668 | 7169 | 1273 | 9362 | 17.1 | 3.0 | 22.3 |

## ABA PLAYOFF RECORD

**NOTES:** ABA Playoff Most Valuable Player (1975).

| | | | 2-POINT | | | 3-POINT | | | | | | | | | AVERAGES | | |
|---|---|---|---|---|---|---|---|---|---|---|---|---|---|---|---|---|---|
| Season Team | G | Min. | FGM | FGA | Pct. | FGM | FGA | Pct. | FTM | FTA | Pct. | Reb. | Ast. | Pts. | RPG | APG | PPG |
| 71-72—Kentucky | 6 | 285 | 52 | 90 | .578 | 0 | 1 | .000 | 27 | 38 | .711 | 106 | 25 | 131 | 17.7 | 4.2 | 21.8 |
| 72-73—Kentucky | 19 | 780 | 142 | 261 | .544 | 0 | 0 | ... | 77 | 123 | .626 | 260 | 75 | 361 | 13.7 | 3.9 | 19.0 |
| 73-74—Kentucky | 8 | 344 | 71 | 127 | .559 | 0 | 0 | ... | 38 | 66 | .576 | 149 | 28 | 180 | 18.6 | 3.5 | 22.5 |
| 74-75—Kentucky | 15 | 679 | 132 | 245 | .539 | 0 | 0 | ... | 98 | 127 | .772 | 264 | 38 | 362 | 17.6 | 2.5 | 24.1 |
| 75-76—Kentucky | 10 | 390 | 93 | 153 | .608 | 0 | 0 | ... | 56 | 74 | .757 | 152 | 19 | 242 | 15.2 | 1.9 | 24.2 |
| Totals | 58 | 2478 | 490 | 876 | .559 | 0 | 1 | .000 | 296 | 428 | .692 | 931 | 185 | 1276 | 16.1 | 3.2 | 22.0 |

## ABA ALL-STAR GAME RECORD

**NOTES:** ABA All-Star Game Most Valuable Player (1974).

| | | 2-POINT | | | 3-POINT | | | | | | | | |
|---|---|---|---|---|---|---|---|---|---|---|---|---|---|
| Season Team | Min. | FGM | FGA | Pct. | FGM | FGA | Pct. | FTM | FTA | Pct. | Reb. | Ast. | Pts. |
| 1972—Kentucky | 27 | 4 | 5 | .800 | 0 | 0 | ... | 6 | 10 | .600 | 10 | 2 | 14 |
| 1973—Kentucky | 31 | 3 | 8 | .375 | 0 | 0 | ... | 4 | 8 | .500 | 16 | 0 | 10 |
| 1974—Kentucky | 27 | 8 | 12 | .667 | 0 | 0 | ... | 2 | 3 | .667 | 13 | 1 | 18 |
| 1975—Kentucky | 28 | 4 | 8 | .500 | 0 | 0 | ... | 3 | 7 | .429 | 13 | 2 | 11 |
| 1976—Kentucky | 27 | 5 | 7 | .714 | 0 | 0 | ... | 4 | 6 | .667 | 7 | 1 | 14 |
| Totals | 140 | 24 | 40 | .600 | 0 | 0 | ... | 19 | 34 | .559 | 59 | 6 | 67 |

## NBA REGULAR-SEASON RECORD

**RECORDS:** Holds career record for highest field goal percentage (minimum 2,000 made)—.599.
**HONORS:** NBA All-Defensive second team (1978).

| Season Team | G | Min. | FGM | FGA | Pct. | FTM | FTA | Pct. | Off. | Def. | Tot. | Ast. | St. | Blk. | TO | Pts. | RPG | APG | PPG |
|---|---|---|---|---|---|---|---|---|---|---|---|---|---|---|---|---|---|---|---|
| 76-77—Chicago ......... | 82 | 2877 | 570 | 1091 | .522 | 387 | 586 | .660 | 313 | 757 | 1070 | 199 | 44 | 203 | ... | 1527 | 13.0 | 2.4 | 18.6 |
| 77-78—Chicago ......... | 82 | 3067 | 704 | 1260 | .559 | 471 | *669 | .704 | 318 | 753 | 1071 | 263 | 42 | 181 | *366 | 1879 | 13.1 | 3.2 | 22.9 |
| 78-79—Chicago ......... | 82 | 3265 | 753 | 1310 | .575 | 434 | 587 | .739 | 293 | 750 | 1043 | 274 | 50 | 156 | 310 | 1940 | 12.7 | 3.3 | 23.7 |
| 79-80—Chicago ......... | 48 | 1568 | 305 | 513 | .595 | 245 | 344 | .712 | 108 | 324 | 432 | 133 | 29 | 59 | 133 | 855 | 9.0 | 2.8 | 17.8 |
| 80-81—Chicago ......... | 82 | 2832 | 547 | 816 | *.670 | 375 | 532 | .705 | 220 | 608 | 828 | 172 | 47 | 198 | 236 | 1469 | 10.1 | 2.1 | 17.9 |
| 81-82—Chicago ......... | 82 | 2796 | 546 | 837 | *.652 | 424 | 552 | .768 | 224 | 611 | 835 | 136 | 49 | 220 | 227 | 1517 | 10.2 | 1.7 | 18.5 |
| 82-83—San Antonio.... | 82 | 2797 | 556 | 888 | *.626 | 367 | 496 | .740 | 299 | 685 | 984 | 126 | 40 | 192 | 254 | 1479 | 12.0 | 1.5 | 18.0 |
| 83-84—San Antonio.... | 64 | 2034 | 351 | 556 | *.631 | 280 | 390 | .718 | 213 | 449 | 662 | 70 | 36 | 132 | 149 | 982 | 10.3 | 1.1 | 15.3 |
| 84-85—San Antonio.... | 81 | 2756 | 532 | 854 | .623 | 484 | 646 | .749 | 231 | 615 | 846 | 131 | 40 | 173 | 241 | 1548 | 10.4 | 1.6 | 19.1 |
| 85-86—San Antonio.... | 71 | 2395 | 423 | 684 | .618 | 338 | 482 | .701 | 166 | 434 | 600 | 102 | 39 | 108 | 186 | 1184 | 8.5 | 1.4 | 16.7 |
| 86-87—San Antonio.... | 82 | 2405 | 346 | 580 | .597 | 242 | 356 | .680 | 185 | 394 | 579 | 150 | 39 | 95 | 178 | 934 | 7.1 | 1.8 | 11.4 |
| 87-88—Chi.-Boston..... | 71 | 893 | 99 | 181 | .547 | 67 | 128 | .523 | 69 | 142 | 211 | 21 | 15 | 30 | 67 | 265 | 3.0 | 0.3 | 3.7 |
| Totals ................... | 909 | 29685 | 5732 | 9570 | .599 | 4114 | 5768 | .713 | 2639 | 6522 | 9161 | 1777 | 470 | 1747 | 2347 | 15579 | 10.1 | 2.0 | 17.1 |

Three-point field goals: 1981-82, 1-for-1. 1982-83, 0-for-6. 1983-84, 0-for-3. 1984-85, 0-for-2. 1985-86, 0-for-1. Totals, 1-for-13 (.077).

Personal fouls/disqualifications: 1976-77, 266/4. 1977-78, 261/4. 1978-79, 280/2. 1979-80, 167/5. 1980-81, 295/2. 1981-82, 287/4. 1982-83, 273/4. 1983-84, 229/4. 1984-85, 306/4. 1985-86, 239/3. 1986-87, 235/2. 1987-88, 148/0. Totals, 2986/38.

### NBA PLAYOFF RECORD

| Season Team | G | Min. | FGM | FGA | Pct. | FTM | FTA | Pct. | Off. | Def. | Tot. | Ast. | St. | Blk. | TO | Pts. | RPG | APG | PPG |
|---|---|---|---|---|---|---|---|---|---|---|---|---|---|---|---|---|---|---|---|
| 76-77—Chicago ......... | 3 | 126 | 19 | 40 | .475 | 18 | 23 | .783 | 15 | 24 | 39 | 6 | 3 | 8 | ... | 56 | 13.0 | 2.0 | 18.7 |
| 80-81—Chicago ......... | 6 | 247 | 35 | 59 | .593 | 38 | 55 | .691 | 24 | 43 | 67 | 12 | 6 | 17 | 17 | 108 | 11.2 | 2.0 | 18.0 |
| 82-83—San Antonio.... | 11 | 401 | 76 | 132 | .576 | 32 | 46 | .696 | 37 | 105 | 142 | 18 | 9 | 34 | 27 | 184 | 12.9 | 1.6 | 16.7 |
| 84-85—San Antonio.... | 5 | 185 | 29 | 52 | .558 | 31 | 45 | .689 | 10 | 40 | 50 | 7 | 2 | 7 | 23 | 89 | 10.0 | 1.4 | 17.8 |
| 85-86—San Antonio.... | 3 | 107 | 16 | 24 | .667 | 8 | 14 | .571 | 7 | 11 | 18 | 3 | 7 | 1 | 10 | 40 | 6.0 | 1.0 | 13.3 |
| 87-88—Boston .......... | 14 | 86 | 4 | 8 | .500 | 7 | 14 | .500 | 4 | 16 | 20 | 1 | 0 | 4 | 4 | 15 | 1.4 | 0.1 | 1.1 |
| Totals ................... | 42 | 1152 | 179 | 315 | .568 | 134 | 197 | .680 | 97 | 239 | 336 | 47 | 27 | 71 | 81 | 492 | 8.0 | 1.1 | 11.7 |

Personal fouls/disqualifications: 1976-77, 9/0. 1980-81, 15/0. 1982-83, 46/1. 1984-85, 18/0. 1985-86, 11/0. 1987-88, 14/0. Totals, 113/1.

### NBA ALL-STAR GAME RECORD

| Season Team | Min. | FGM | FGA | Pct. | FTM | FTA | Pct. | Off. | Def. | Tot. | Ast. | PF | Dq. | St. | Blk. | TO | Pts. |
|---|---|---|---|---|---|---|---|---|---|---|---|---|---|---|---|---|---|
| 1978—Chicago ................. | 13 | 2 | 4 | .500 | 6 | 8 | .750 | 0 | 2 | 2 | 0 | 1 | 0 | 1 | 2 | 1 | 10 |
| 1979—Chicago ................. | 15 | 3 | 4 | .750 | 2 | 2 | 1.000 | 1 | 0 | 1 | 2 | 1 | 0 | 0 | 0 | 1 | 8 |
| 1981—Chicago ................. | 22 | 5 | 7 | .714 | 1 | 2 | .500 | 1 | 5 | 6 | 2 | 4 | 0 | 1 | 0 | 0 | 11 |
| 1982—Chicago ................. | 16 | 3 | 6 | .500 | 1 | 1 | 1.000 | 1 | 2 | 3 | 2 | 4 | 0 | 1 | 2 | 2 | 7 |
| 1983—San Antonio ......... | 16 | 2 | 4 | .500 | 1 | 2 | .500 | 1 | 4 | 5 | 1 | 4 | 0 | 1 | 0 | 1 | 5 |
| 1986—San Antonio ......... | 13 | 3 | 4 | .750 | 4 | 4 | 1.000 | 1 | 1 | 2 | 1 | 4 | 0 | 2 | 0 | 0 | 10 |
| Totals ...................... | 95 | 18 | 29 | .621 | 15 | 19 | .789 | 5 | 14 | 19 | 8 | 18 | 0 | 4 | 4 | 5 | 51 |

### COMBINED ABA AND NBA REGULAR-SEASON RECORDS

| | G | Min. | FGM | FGA | Pct. | FTM | FTA | Pct. | Off. | Def. | Tot. | Ast. | Stl. | Blk. | TO | Pts. | RPG | APG | PPG |
|---|---|---|---|---|---|---|---|---|---|---|---|---|---|---|---|---|---|---|---|
| Totals ........... | 1329 | 33356 | 9403 | 16158 | .582 | 6132 | 8790 | .698 | ... | ... | 16330 | 3050 | ... | ... | ... | 24041 | 12.3 | 2.3 | 18.1 |

Three-point field goals: 3-for-20 (.150).
Personal fouls/disqualifications: 4529.

### ITALIAN LEAGUE RECORD

| Season Team | G | Min. | FGM | FGA | Pct. | FTM | FTA | Pct. | Reb. | Ast. | Pts. | RPG | APG | PPG |
|---|---|---|---|---|---|---|---|---|---|---|---|---|---|---|
| 88-89—Bologna Arimo .............. | 30 | 952 | 144 | 226 | .637 | 85 | 131 | .649 | 333 | 20 | 373 | 11.1 | 0.7 | 12.4 |

# GOODRICH, GAIL     G

**PERSONAL:** Born April 23, 1943, in Los Angeles. ... 6-1/175 (1,85/79,4). ... Full name: Gail Charles Goodrich Jr.
**HIGH SCHOOL:** Los Angeles Polytechnic.
**COLLEGE:** UCLA.
**TRANSACTIONS:** Selected by Los Angeles Lakers in 1965 NBA Draft (territorial pick). ... Selected by Phoenix Suns from Lakers in NBA Expansion Draft (May 6, 1968). ... Traded by Suns to Lakers for F Mel Counts (May 20, 1970). ... Signed as veteran free agent by New Orleans Jazz (July 19, 1976); Lakers received 1977 and 1979 first-round draft choices and 1980 second-round draft choice as compensation; Jazz received 1977 second-round draft choice to complete transaction (October 6, 1976).
**CAREER HONORS:** Elected to Naismith Memorial Basketball Hall of Fame (1996).
**MISCELLANEOUS:** Member of NBA championship team (1972).

### COLLEGIATE RECORD

**NOTES:** The Sporting News All-America first team (1965). ... Member of NCAA Division I championship team (1964, 1965).

| Season Team | G | Min. | FGM | FGA | Pct. | FTM | FTA | Pct. | Reb. | Ast. | Pts. | RPG | APG | PPG |
|---|---|---|---|---|---|---|---|---|---|---|---|---|---|---|
| 61-62—UCLA‡ ........................... | 20 | ... | 189 | 385 | .491 | 110 | 155 | .710 | 122 | ... | 488 | 6.1 | ... | 24.4 |
| 62-63—UCLA ............................. | 29 | ... | 117 | 280 | .418 | 66 | 103 | .641 | 101 | ... | 300 | 3.5 | ... | 10.3 |
| 63-64—UCLA ............................. | 30 | ... | 243 | 530 | .459 | 160 | 225 | .711 | 156 | ... | 646 | 5.2 | ... | 21.5 |
| 64-65—UCLA ............................. | 30 | ... | 277 | 528 | .525 | 190 | 265 | .717 | 158 | ... | 744 | 5.3 | ... | 24.8 |
| Varsity totals ............... | 89 | ... | 637 | 1338 | .476 | 416 | 593 | .702 | 415 | ... | 1690 | 4.7 | ... | 19.0 |

**HONORS:** All-NBA first team (1974).

| Season Team | G | Min. | FGM | FGA | Pct. | FTM | FTA | Pct. | Reb. | Ast. | PF | Dq. | Pts. | AVERAGES RPG | APG | PPG |
|---|---|---|---|---|---|---|---|---|---|---|---|---|---|---|---|---|
| 65-66—Los Angeles | 65 | 1008 | 203 | 503 | .404 | 103 | 149 | .691 | 130 | 103 | 103 | 1 | 509 | 2.0 | 1.6 | 7.8 |
| 66-67—Los Angeles | 77 | 1780 | 352 | 776 | .454 | 253 | 337 | .751 | 251 | 210 | 194 | 3 | 957 | 3.3 | 2.7 | 12.4 |
| 67-68—Los Angeles | 79 | 2057 | 395 | 812 | .486 | 302 | 392 | .770 | 199 | 205 | 228 | 2 | 1092 | 2.5 | 2.6 | 13.8 |
| 68-69—Phoenix | 81 | 3236 | 718 | 1746 | .411 | 495 | 663 | .747 | 437 | 518 | 253 | 3 | 1931 | 5.4 | 6.4 | 23.8 |
| 69-70—Phoenix | 81 | 3234 | 568 | 1251 | .454 | 488 | 604 | .808 | 340 | 605 | 251 | 3 | 1624 | 4.2 | 7.5 | 20.0 |
| 70-71—Los Angeles | 79 | 2808 | 558 | 1174 | .475 | 264 | 343 | .770 | 260 | 380 | 258 | 3 | 1380 | 3.3 | 4.8 | 17.5 |
| 71-72—Los Angeles | 82 | 3040 | 826 | 1695 | .487 | 475 | 559 | .850 | 295 | 365 | 210 | 0 | 2127 | 3.6 | 4.5 | 25.9 |
| 72-73—Los Angeles | 76 | 2697 | 750 | 1615 | .464 | 314 | 374 | .840 | 263 | 332 | 193 | 1 | 1814 | 3.5 | 4.4 | 23.9 |

| Season Team | G | Min. | FGM | FGA | Pct. | FTM | FTA | Pct. | REBOUNDS Off. | Def. | Tot. | Ast. | St. | Blk. | TO | Pts. | AVERAGES RPG | APG | PPG |
|---|---|---|---|---|---|---|---|---|---|---|---|---|---|---|---|---|---|---|---|
| 73-74—Los Angeles | 82 | 3061 | 784 | 1773 | .442 | *508 | *588 | .864 | 95 | 155 | 250 | 427 | 126 | 12 | ... | 2076 | 3.0 | 5.2 | 25.3 |
| 74-75—Los Angeles | 72 | 2668 | 656 | 1429 | .459 | 318 | 378 | .841 | 96 | 123 | 219 | 420 | 102 | 6 | ... | 1630 | 3.0 | 5.8 | 22.6 |
| 75-76—Los Angeles | 75 | 2646 | 583 | 1321 | .441 | 293 | 346 | .847 | 94 | 120 | 214 | 421 | 123 | 17 | ... | 1459 | 2.9 | 5.6 | 19.5 |
| 76-77—New Orleans | 27 | 609 | 136 | 305 | .446 | 68 | 85 | .800 | 25 | 36 | 61 | 74 | 22 | 2 | ... | 340 | 2.3 | 2.7 | 12.6 |
| 77-78—New Orleans | 81 | 2553 | 520 | 1050 | .495 | 264 | 332 | .795 | 75 | 102 | 177 | 388 | 82 | 22 | 205 | 1304 | 2.2 | 4.8 | 16.1 |
| 78-79—New Orleans | 74 | 2130 | 382 | 850 | .449 | 174 | 204 | .853 | 68 | 115 | 183 | 357 | 90 | 13 | 185 | 938 | 2.5 | 4.8 | 12.7 |
| Totals | 1031 | 33527 | 7431 | 16300 | .456 | 4319 | 5354 | .807 | ... | ... | 3279 | 4805 | 545 | 72 | 390 | 19181 | 3.2 | 4.7 | 18.6 |

Personal fouls/disqualifications: 1973-74, 227/3. 1974-75, 214/1. 1975-76, 238/3. 1976-77, 43/0. 1977-78, 186/0. 1978-79, 177/1. Totals, 2775/24.

### NBA PLAYOFF RECORD

| Season Team | G | Min. | FGM | FGA | Pct. | FTM | FTA | Pct. | Reb. | Ast. | PF | Dq. | Pts. | AVERAGES RPG | APG | PPG |
|---|---|---|---|---|---|---|---|---|---|---|---|---|---|---|---|---|
| 65-66—Los Angeles | 11 | 290 | 43 | 92 | .467 | 29 | 43 | .674 | 42 | 33 | 35 | 0 | 115 | 3.8 | 3.0 | 10.5 |
| 66-67—Los Angeles | 3 | 81 | 11 | 31 | .355 | 11 | 18 | .611 | 9 | 10 | 5 | 0 | 33 | 3.0 | 3.3 | 11.0 |
| 67-68—Los Angeles | 10 | 100 | 23 | 47 | .489 | 14 | 18 | .778 | 14 | 14 | 10 | 0 | 60 | 1.4 | 1.4 | 6.0 |
| 69-70—Phoenix | 7 | 265 | 56 | 118 | .475 | 30 | 35 | .857 | 32 | 38 | 21 | 0 | 142 | 4.6 | 5.4 | 20.3 |
| 70-71—Los Angeles | 12 | 518 | 105 | 247 | .425 | 95 | 113 | .841 | 38 | 91 | 38 | 0 | 305 | 3.2 | 7.6 | 25.4 |
| 71-72—Los Angeles | 15 | 575 | 130 | 292 | .445 | 97 | 108 | .898 | 38 | 50 | 50 | 0 | 357 | 2.5 | 3.3 | 23.8 |
| 72-73—Los Angeles | 17 | 604 | 139 | 310 | .448 | 62 | 79 | .785 | 61 | 67 | 53 | 1 | 340 | 3.6 | 3.9 | 20.0 |

| Season Team | G | Min. | FGM | FGA | Pct. | FTM | FTA | Pct. | REBOUNDS Off. | Def. | Tot. | Ast. | St. | Blk. | TO | Pts. | AVERAGES RPG | APG | PPG |
|---|---|---|---|---|---|---|---|---|---|---|---|---|---|---|---|---|---|---|---|
| 73-74—Los Angeles | 5 | 189 | 35 | 90 | .389 | 28 | 33 | .848 | 7 | 9 | 16 | 30 | 7 | 1 | ... | 98 | 3.2 | 6.0 | 19.6 |
| Totals | 80 | 2622 | 542 | 1227 | .442 | 366 | 447 | .819 | ... | ... | 250 | 333 | 7 | 1 | ... | 1450 | 3.1 | 4.2 | 18.1 |

Personal fouls/disqualifications: 1973-74, 7/0.

### NBA ALL-STAR GAME RECORD

| Season Team | Min. | FGM | FGA | Pct. | FTM | FTA | Pct. | Reb | Ast. | PF | Dq. | Pts. |
|---|---|---|---|---|---|---|---|---|---|---|---|---|
| 1969—Phoenix | 6 | 2 | 4 | .500 | 1 | 2 | .500 | 1 | 1 | 1 | 0 | 5 |
| 1972—Los Angeles | 14 | 2 | 7 | .286 | 0 | 0 | ... | 1 | 2 | 2 | 0 | 4 |
| 1973—Los Angeles | 16 | 1 | 7 | .143 | 0 | 0 | ... | 2 | 1 | 2 | 0 | 2 |

| Season Team | Min. | FGM | FGA | Pct. | FTM | FTA | Pct. | REBOUNDS Off. | Def. | Tot. | Ast. | PF | Dq. | St. | Blk. | TO | Pts. |
|---|---|---|---|---|---|---|---|---|---|---|---|---|---|---|---|---|---|
| 1974—Los Angeles | 26 | 9 | 16 | .563 | 0 | 0 | ... | 1 | 3 | 4 | 6 | 2 | 0 | 1 | 0 | ... | 18 |
| 1975—Los Angeles | 15 | 2 | 4 | .500 | 0 | 0 | ... | 0 | 1 | 1 | 4 | 1 | 0 | 0 | 0 | ... | 4 |
| Totals | 77 | 16 | 38 | .421 | 1 | 2 | .500 | ... | ... | 9 | 14 | 8 | 0 | 1 | 0 | ... | 33 |

## GREER, HAL          G

**PERSONAL:** Born June 26, 1936, in Huntington, W.Va. ... 6-2/175 (1,88/79,4). ... Full name: Harold Everett Greer.
**HIGH SCHOOL:** Douglass (Huntington, W.Va.).
**COLLEGE:** Marshall.
**TRANSACTIONS:** Selected by Syracuse Nationals in second round (14th pick overall) of 1958 NBA Draft. ... Nationals franchise moved from Syracuse to Philadelphia and renamed 76ers for 1963-64 season.
**CAREER HONORS:** Elected to Naismith Memorial Basketball Hall of Fame (1982). ... One of the 50 Greatest Players in NBA History (1996).
**MISCELLANEOUS:** Member of NBA championship team (1967). ... Philadelphia 76ers franchise all-time leading scorer with 21,586 points (1958-59 through 1972-73).

### COLLEGIATE RECORD

| Season Team | G | Min. | FGM | FGA | Pct. | FTM | FTA | Pct. | Reb. | Ast. | Pts. | AVERAGES RPG | APG | PPG |
|---|---|---|---|---|---|---|---|---|---|---|---|---|---|---|
| 54-55—Marshall‡ | ... | ... | ... | ... | ... | ... | ... | ... | ... | ... | ... | ... | ... | 18.0 |
| 55-56—Marshall | 23 | ... | 128 | 213 | .601 | 101 | 145 | .697 | 153 | ... | 357 | 6.7 | ... | 15.5 |
| 56-57—Marshall | 24 | ... | 167 | 329 | .508 | 119 | 156 | .763 | 332 | ... | 453 | 13.8 | ... | 18.9 |
| 57-58—Marshall | 24 | ... | 236 | 432 | .546 | 95 | 114 | .833 | 280 | ... | 567 | 11.7 | ... | 23.6 |
| Varsity totals | 71 | ... | 531 | 974 | .545 | 315 | 415 | .759 | 765 | ... | 1377 | 10.8 | ... | 19.4 |

### NBA REGULAR-SEASON RECORD

**HONORS:** All-NBA second team (1963, 1964, 1965, 1966, 1967, 1968, 1969).

| Season Team | G | Min. | FGM | FGA | Pct. | FTM | FTA | Pct. | Reb. | Ast. | PF | Dq. | Pts. | AVERAGES RPG | APG | PPG |
|---|---|---|---|---|---|---|---|---|---|---|---|---|---|---|---|---|
| 58-59—Syracuse | 68 | 1625 | 308 | 679 | .454 | 137 | 176 | .778 | 196 | 101 | 189 | 1 | 753 | 2.9 | 1.5 | 11.1 |
| 59-60—Syracuse | 70 | 1918 | 388 | 815 | .476 | 148 | 189 | .783 | 303 | 188 | 208 | 4 | 924 | 4.3 | 2.7 | 13.2 |
| 60-61—Syracuse | 79 | 2763 | 623 | 1381 | .451 | 305 | 394 | .774 | 455 | 302 | 242 | 0 | 1551 | 5.8 | 3.8 | 19.6 |
| 61-62—Syracuse | 71 | 2705 | 644 | 1442 | .447 | 331 | 404 | .819 | 524 | 313 | 252 | 2 | 1619 | 7.4 | 4.4 | 22.8 |
| 62-63—Syracuse | 80 | 2631 | 600 | 1293 | .464 | 362 | 434 | .834 | 457 | 275 | 286 | 4 | 1562 | 5.7 | 3.4 | 19.5 |
| 63-64—Philadelphia | 80 | 3157 | 715 | 1611 | .444 | 435 | 525 | .829 | 484 | 374 | 291 | 6 | 1865 | 6.1 | 4.7 | 23.3 |

| Season Team | G | Min. | FGM | FGA | Pct. | FTM | FTA | Pct. | Reb. | Ast. | PF | Dq. | Pts. | RPG | APG | PPG |
|---|---|---|---|---|---|---|---|---|---|---|---|---|---|---|---|---|
| 64-65—Philadelphia | 70 | 2600 | 539 | 1245 | .433 | 335 | 413 | .811 | 355 | 313 | 254 | 7 | 1413 | 5.1 | 4.5 | 20.2 |
| 65-66—Philadelphia | 80 | 3326 | 703 | 1580 | .445 | 413 | 514 | .804 | 473 | 384 | 315 | 6 | 1819 | 5.9 | 4.8 | 22.7 |
| 66-67—Philadelphia | 80 | 3086 | 699 | 1524 | .459 | 367 | 466 | .788 | 422 | 303 | 302 | 5 | 1765 | 5.3 | 3.8 | 22.1 |
| 67-68—Philadelphia | 82 | 3263 | 777 | 1626 | .478 | 422 | 549 | .769 | 444 | 372 | 289 | 6 | 1976 | 5.4 | 4.5 | 24.1 |
| 68-69—Philadelphia | 82 | 3311 | 732 | 1595 | .459 | 432 | 543 | .796 | 435 | 414 | 294 | 8 | 1896 | 5.3 | 5.0 | 23.1 |
| 69-70—Philadelphia | 80 | 3024 | 705 | 1551 | .455 | 352 | 432 | .815 | 376 | 405 | 300 | 8 | 1762 | 4.7 | 5.1 | 22.0 |
| 70-71—Philadelphia | 81 | 3060 | 591 | 1371 | .431 | 326 | 405 | .805 | 364 | 369 | 289 | 4 | 1508 | 4.5 | 4.6 | 18.6 |
| 71-72—Philadelphia | 81 | 2410 | 389 | 866 | .449 | 181 | 234 | .774 | 271 | 316 | 268 | 10 | 959 | 3.3 | 3.9 | 11.8 |
| 72-73—Philadelphia | 38 | 848 | 91 | 232 | .392 | 32 | 39 | .821 | 106 | 111 | 76 | 1 | 214 | 2.8 | 2.9 | 5.6 |
| Totals | 1122 | 39788 | 8504 | 18811 | .452 | 4578 | 5717 | .801 | 5665 | 4540 | 3855 | 72 | 21586 | 5.0 | 4.0 | 19.2 |

### NBA PLAYOFF RECORD

| Season Team | G | Min. | FGM | FGA | Pct. | FTM | FTA | Pct. | Reb. | Ast. | PF | Dq. | Pts. | RPG | APG | PPG |
|---|---|---|---|---|---|---|---|---|---|---|---|---|---|---|---|---|
| 58-59—Syracuse | 9 | 277 | 39 | 93 | .419 | 26 | 32 | .813 | 47 | 20 | 35 | 2 | 104 | 5.2 | 2.2 | 11.6 |
| 59-60—Syracuse | 3 | 84 | 22 | 43 | .512 | 3 | 4 | .750 | 14 | 10 | 5 | 0 | 47 | 4.7 | 3.3 | 15.7 |
| 60-61—Syracuse | 8 | 232 | 41 | 106 | .387 | 33 | 40 | .825 | 33 | 19 | 32 | 1 | 115 | 4.1 | 2.4 | 14.4 |
| 61-62—Syracuse | 1 | 5 | 0 | 0 | ... | 0 | 0 | ... | 0 | 0 | 1 | 0 | 0 | 0.0 | 0.0 | 0.0 |
| 62-63—Syracuse | 5 | 214 | 44 | 87 | .506 | 29 | 35 | .829 | 27 | 21 | 21 | 1 | 117 | 5.4 | 4.2 | 23.4 |
| 63-64—Philadelphia | 5 | 211 | 37 | 95 | .389 | 33 | 39 | .846 | 28 | 30 | 19 | 1 | 107 | 5.6 | 6.0 | 21.4 |
| 64-65—Philadelphia | 11 | 505 | 101 | 222 | .455 | 69 | 87 | .793 | 81 | 55 | 45 | 2 | 271 | 7.4 | 5.0 | 24.6 |
| 65-66—Philadelphia | 5 | 226 | 32 | 91 | .352 | 18 | 23 | .783 | 36 | 21 | 21 | 0 | 82 | 7.2 | 4.2 | 16.4 |
| 66-67—Philadelphia | 15 | 688 | 161 | 375 | .429 | 94 | 118 | .797 | 88 | 79 | 55 | 1 | 416 | 5.9 | 5.3 | 27.7 |
| 67-68—Philadelphia | 13 | 553 | 120 | 278 | .432 | 95 | 111 | .856 | 79 | 55 | 49 | 1 | 335 | 6.1 | 4.2 | 25.8 |
| 68-69—Philadelphia | 5 | 204 | 26 | 81 | .321 | 28 | 36 | .778 | 30 | 23 | 23 | 0 | 80 | 6.0 | 4.6 | 16.0 |
| 69-70—Philadelphia | 5 | 178 | 33 | 74 | .446 | 11 | 13 | .846 | 17 | 27 | 16 | 0 | 77 | 3.4 | 5.4 | 15.4 |
| 70-71—Philadelphia | 7 | 265 | 49 | 112 | .438 | 27 | 36 | .750 | 25 | 33 | 35 | 4 | 125 | 3.6 | 4.7 | 17.9 |
| Totals | 92 | 3642 | 705 | 1657 | .425 | 466 | 574 | .812 | 505 | 393 | 357 | 13 | 1876 | 5.5 | 4.3 | 20.4 |

### NBA ALL-STAR GAME RECORD

NOTES: NBA All-Star Game Most Valuable Player (1968).

| Season Team | Min. | FGM | FGA | Pct. | FTM | FTA | Pct. | Reb | Ast. | PF | Dq. | Pts. |
|---|---|---|---|---|---|---|---|---|---|---|---|---|
| 1961—Syracuse | 18 | 7 | 11 | .636 | 0 | 0 | ... | 6 | 2 | 2 | 0 | 14 |
| 1962—Syracuse | 24 | 3 | 14 | .214 | 2 | 7 | .286 | 10 | 9 | 3 | 0 | 8 |
| 1963—Syracuse | 15 | 3 | 7 | .429 | 0 | 0 | ... | 3 | 2 | 4 | 0 | 6 |
| 1964—Philadelphia | 20 | 5 | 10 | .500 | 3 | 4 | .750 | 3 | 4 | 1 | 0 | 13 |
| 1965—Philadelphia | 21 | 5 | 11 | .455 | 3 | 4 | .750 | 4 | 1 | 2 | 0 | 13 |
| 1966—Philadelphia | 23 | 4 | 13 | .308 | 1 | 1 | 1.000 | 5 | 1 | 4 | 0 | 9 |
| 1967—Philadelphia | 31 | 5 | 16 | .313 | 7 | 8 | .875 | 4 | 1 | 5 | 0 | 17 |
| 1968—Philadelphia | 17 | 8 | 8 | 1.000 | 5 | 7 | .714 | 3 | 3 | 2 | 0 | 21 |
| 1969—Philadelphia | 17 | 0 | 1 | .000 | 4 | 5 | .800 | 3 | 2 | 2 | 0 | 4 |
| 1970—Philadelphia | 21 | 7 | 11 | .636 | 1 | 1 | 1.000 | 4 | 3 | 4 | 0 | 15 |
| Totals | 207 | 47 | 102 | .461 | 26 | 37 | .703 | 45 | 28 | 29 | 0 | 120 |

### CBA COACHING RECORD

| Season Team | REGULAR SEASON | | | | PLAYOFFS | | |
|---|---|---|---|---|---|---|---|
| | W | L | Pct. | Finish | W | L | Pct. |
| 80-81—Philadelphia | 17 | 23 | .425 | 3rd/Eastern Division | 3 | 3 | .500 |

NOTES:
1981—Defeated Atlantic City, 2-1, in Eastern Division Semifinals; lost to Rochester, 2-1, in Eastern Division Finals.

## GUERIN, RICHIE  G

PERSONAL: Born May 29, 1932, in New York. ... 6-4/210 (1,93/95,3). ... Full name: Richard V. Guerin.
HIGH SCHOOL: Mount St. Michael Academy (Bronx, N.Y.).
COLLEGE: Iona.
TRANSACTIONS: Selected by New York Knicks in second round of 1954 NBA Draft. ... In military service during 1954-55 and 1955-56 seasons; played with Quantico Marines and Marine All-Star teams. ... Traded by Knicks to St. Louis Hawks for cash and second-round draft choice (October 18, 1963). ... Selected by Seattle SuperSonics from Hawks in NBA Expansion Draft (1967). ... Traded by SuperSonics to Atlanta Hawks for Dick Smith (November 15, 1968).

### COLLEGIATE RECORD

| Season Team | G | Min. | FGM | FGA | Pct. | FTM | FTA | Pct. | Reb. | Ast. | Pts. | RPG | APG | PPG |
|---|---|---|---|---|---|---|---|---|---|---|---|---|---|---|
| 50-51—Iona‡ | | | | | | Freshman team statistics unavailable. | | | | | | | | |
| 51-52—Iona | 27 | ... | 159 | ... | ... | 146 | ... | ... | ... | ... | 464 | ... | ... | 17.2 |
| 52-53—Iona | 21 | ... | 139 | 283 | .491 | 114 | 172 | .663 | ... | ... | 392 | ... | ... | 18.7 |
| 53-54—Iona | 21 | ... | 171 | 405 | .422 | 177 | 249 | .711 | ... | ... | 519 | ... | ... | 24.7 |
| Varsity totals | 69 | ... | 469 | ... | ... | 437 | ... | ... | ... | ... | 1375 | ... | ... | 19.9 |

### NBA REGULAR-SEASON RECORD

HONORS: All-NBA second team (1959, 1960, 1962).

| Season Team | G | Min. | FGM | FGA | Pct. | FTM | FTA | Pct. | Reb. | Ast. | PF | Dq. | Pts. | RPG | APG | PPG |
|---|---|---|---|---|---|---|---|---|---|---|---|---|---|---|---|---|
| 56-57—New York | 72 | 1793 | 257 | 699 | .368 | 181 | 292 | .620 | 334 | 182 | 186 | 3 | 695 | 4.6 | 2.5 | 9.7 |
| 57-58—New York | 63 | 2368 | 344 | 973 | .354 | 353 | 511 | .691 | 489 | 317 | 202 | 3 | 1041 | 7.8 | 5.0 | 16.5 |
| 58-59—New York | 71 | 2558 | 443 | 1046 | .424 | 405 | 505 | .802 | 518 | 364 | 255 | 1 | 1291 | 7.3 | 5.1 | 18.2 |

| Season Team | G | Min. | FGM | FGA | Pct. | FTM | FTA | Pct. | Reb. | Ast. | PF | Dq. | Pts. | AVERAGES RPG | APG | PPG |
|---|---|---|---|---|---|---|---|---|---|---|---|---|---|---|---|---|
| 59-60—New York | 74 | 2429 | 579 | 1379 | .420 | 457 | 591 | .773 | 505 | 468 | 242 | 3 | 1615 | 6.8 | 6.3 | 21.8 |
| 60-61—New York | 79 | 3023 | 612 | 1545 | .396 | 496 | 626 | .792 | 628 | 503 | 310 | 3 | 1720 | 7.9 | 6.4 | 21.8 |
| 61-62—New York | 78 | 3348 | 839 | 1897 | .442 | 625 | 762 | .820 | 501 | 539 | 299 | 3 | 2303 | 6.4 | 6.9 | 29.5 |
| 62-63—New York | 79 | 2712 | 596 | 1380 | .432 | 509 | 600 | .848 | 331 | 348 | 228 | 2 | 1701 | 4.2 | 4.4 | 21.5 |
| 63-64—N.Y.-St.L. | 80 | 2366 | 351 | 846 | .415 | 347 | 424 | .818 | 256 | 375 | 276 | 4 | 1049 | 3.2 | 4.7 | 13.1 |
| 64-65—St. Louis | 57 | 1678 | 295 | 662 | .446 | 231 | 301 | .767 | 149 | 271 | 193 | 1 | 821 | 2.6 | 4.8 | 14.4 |
| 65-66—St. Louis | 80 | 2363 | 414 | 998 | .415 | 362 | 446 | .812 | 314 | 388 | 256 | 4 | 1190 | 3.9 | 4.9 | 14.9 |
| 66-67—St. Louis | 80 | 2275 | 394 | 904 | .436 | 304 | 416 | .731 | 192 | 345 | 247 | 2 | 1092 | 2.4 | 4.3 | 13.7 |
| 67-68— | | | | | | Did not play—retired. | | | | | | | | | | |
| 68-69—Atlanta | 27 | 472 | 47 | 111 | .423 | 57 | 74 | .770 | 59 | 99 | 66 | 0 | 151 | 2.2 | 3.7 | 5.6 |
| 69-70—Atlanta | 8 | 64 | 3 | 11 | .273 | 1 | 1 | 1.000 | 2 | 12 | 9 | 0 | 7 | 0.3 | 1.5 | 0.9 |
| Totals | 848 | 27449 | 5174 | 12451 | .416 | 4328 | 5549 | .780 | 4278 | 4211 | 2769 | 29 | 14676 | 5.0 | 5.0 | 17.3 |

## NBA PLAYOFF RECORD

| Season Team | G | Min. | FGM | FGA | Pct. | FTM | FTA | Pct. | Reb. | Ast. | PF | Dq. | Pts. | AVERAGES RPG | APG | PPG |
|---|---|---|---|---|---|---|---|---|---|---|---|---|---|---|---|---|
| 58-59—New York | 2 | 77 | 9 | 35 | .257 | 12 | 14 | .857 | 18 | 15 | 11 | 1 | 30 | 9.0 | 7.5 | 15.0 |
| 63-64—St. Louis | 12 | 428 | 75 | 169 | .444 | 67 | 85 | .788 | 50 | 49 | 54 | 1 | 217 | 4.2 | 4.1 | 18.1 |
| 64-65—St. Louis | 4 | 125 | 25 | 65 | .385 | 19 | 25 | .760 | 8 | 21 | 14 | 0 | 69 | 2.0 | 5.3 | 17.3 |
| 65-66—St. Louis | 10 | 399 | 72 | 159 | .453 | 62 | 76 | .816 | 37 | 79 | 41 | 0 | 206 | 3.7 | 7.9 | 20.6 |
| 66-67—St. Louis | 9 | 228 | 36 | 86 | .419 | 24 | 30 | .800 | 23 | 39 | 23 | 0 | 96 | 2.6 | 4.3 | 10.7 |
| 68-69—Atlanta | 3 | 32 | 1 | 4 | .250 | 1 | 2 | .500 | 5 | 7 | 8 | 0 | 3 | 1.7 | 2.3 | 1.0 |
| 69-70—Atlanta | 2 | 56 | 13 | 21 | .619 | 7 | 7 | 1.000 | 8 | 4 | 6 | 0 | 33 | 4.0 | 2.0 | 16.5 |
| Totals | 42 | 1345 | 231 | 539 | .429 | 192 | 239 | .803 | 149 | 214 | 157 | 2 | 654 | 3.5 | 5.1 | 15.6 |

## NBA ALL-STAR GAME RECORD

| Season Team | Min. | FGM | FGA | Pct. | FTM | FTA | Pct. | Reb | Ast. | PF | Dq. | Pts. |
|---|---|---|---|---|---|---|---|---|---|---|---|---|
| 1958—New York | 22 | 2 | 10 | .200 | 3 | 4 | .750 | 8 | 7 | 3 | 0 | 7 |
| 1959—New York | 22 | 1 | 7 | .143 | 3 | 5 | .600 | 3 | 3 | 1 | 0 | 5 |
| 1960—New York | 22 | 5 | 11 | .455 | 2 | 2 | 1.000 | 4 | 4 | 4 | 0 | 12 |
| 1961—New York | 15 | 3 | 8 | .375 | 5 | 6 | .833 | 0 | 2 | 1 | 0 | 11 |
| 1962—New York | 27 | 10 | 17 | .588 | 3 | 6 | .500 | 3 | 1 | 6 | 1 | 23 |
| 1963—New York | 14 | 2 | 3 | .667 | 1 | 3 | .333 | 1 | 1 | 2 | 0 | 5 |
| Totals | 122 | 23 | 56 | .411 | 17 | 26 | .654 | 19 | 18 | 17 | 1 | 63 |

## NBA COACHING RECORD

HONORS: NBA Coach of the Year (1968).

| Season Team | REGULAR SEASON W | L | Pct. | Finish | PLAYOFFS W | L | Pct. |
|---|---|---|---|---|---|---|---|
| 64-65—St. Louis | 28 | 19 | .596 | 2nd/Western Division | 1 | 3 | .250 |
| 65-66—St. Louis | 36 | 44 | .450 | 3rd/Western Division | 6 | 4 | .600 |
| 66-67—St. Louis | 39 | 42 | .481 | 2nd/Western Division | 5 | 4 | .556 |
| 67-68—St. Louis | 56 | 26 | .683 | 1st/Western Division | 2 | 4 | .333 |
| 68-69—Atlanta | 48 | 34 | .585 | 2nd/Western Division | 5 | 6 | .455 |
| 69-70—Atlanta | 48 | 34 | .585 | 1st/Western Division | 4 | 5 | .444 |
| 70-71—Atlanta | 36 | 46 | .439 | 2nd/Central Division | 1 | 4 | .200 |
| 71-72—Atlanta | 36 | 46 | .439 | 2nd/Central Division | 2 | 4 | .333 |
| Totals (8 years) | 327 | 291 | .529 | Totals (8 years) | 26 | 34 | .433 |

NOTES:

1964—Replaced Harry Gallatin as St. Louis head coach (November), with record of 17-16.

1965—Lost to Baltimore in Western Division Semifinals.

1966—Defeated Baltimore, 3-0, in Western Division Semifinals; lost to Los Angeles, 4-3, in Western Division Finals.

1967—Defeated Chicago, 3-0, in Western Division Semifinals; lost to San Francisco, 4-2, in Western Division Finals.

1968—Lost to San Francisco in Western Division Semifinals. Hawks franchise moved to Atlanta for 1968-69 season.

1969—Defeated San Diego, 4-2, in Western Division Semifinals; lost to Los Angeles, 4-1, in Western Division Finals.

1970—Defeated Chicago, 4-1, in Western Division Semifinals; lost to Los Angeles, 4-0, in Western Division Finals.

1971—Lost to New York in Eastern Conference Semifinals.

1972—Lost to Boston in Eastern Conference Semifinals.

# HAGAN, CLIFF                                    F

PERSONAL: Born December 9, 1931, in Owensboro, Ky. ... 6-4/215 (1,93/97,5). ... Full name: Clifford Oldham Hagan. ... Nickname: Li'l Abner.
HIGH SCHOOL: Owensboro (Ky.).
COLLEGE: Kentucky.
TRANSACTIONS: Selected by Boston Celtics in third round of 1953 NBA Draft. ... In military service during 1954-55 and 1955-56 seasons; played at Andrews Air Force Base. ... Draft rights traded by Celtics with C/F Ed Macauley to St. Louis Hawks for draft rights to C Bill Russell (April 29, 1956). ... Signed as player/head coach for Dallas Chaparrals of American Basketball Association (June 1967).
CAREER HONORS: Elected to Naismith Memorial Basketball Hall of Fame (1978).
MISCELLANEOUS: Member of NBA championship team (1958).

## COLLEGIATE RECORD

**NOTES:** Member of NCAA championship team (1951).

| Season Team | G | Min. | FGM | FGA | Pct. | FTM | FTA | Pct. | Reb. | Ast. | Pts. | RPG | APG | PPG |
|---|---|---|---|---|---|---|---|---|---|---|---|---|---|---|
| | | | | | | | | | | | | AVERAGES | | |
| 49-50—Kentucky‡ | 12 | ... | 114 | 244 | .467 | 42 | 58 | .724 | ... | ... | 270 | ... | ... | 22.5 |
| 50-51—Kentucky | 20 | ... | 69 | 188 | .367 | 45 | 61 | .738 | 169 | ... | 183 | 8.5 | ... | 9.2 |
| 51-52—Kentucky | 32 | ... | 264 | 633 | .417 | 164 | 235 | .698 | 528 | ... | 692 | 16.5 | ... | 21.6 |
| 52-53—Kentucky | | | | | Did not play—team suspended for season. | | | | | | | | | |
| 53-54—Kentucky | 25 | ... | 234 | 514 | .455 | 132 | 191 | .691 | 338 | ... | 600 | 13.5 | ... | 24.0 |
| Varsity totals | 77 | ... | 567 | 1335 | .425 | 341 | 487 | .700 | 1035 | ... | 1475 | 13.4 | ... | 19.2 |

## NBA REGULAR-SEASON RECORD

**HONORS:** All-NBA second team (1958, 1959).

| Season Team | G | Min. | FGM | FGA | Pct. | FTM | FTA | Pct. | Reb. | Ast. | PF | Dq. | Pts. | RPG | APG | PPG |
|---|---|---|---|---|---|---|---|---|---|---|---|---|---|---|---|---|
| | | | | | | | | | | | | | | AVERAGES | | |
| 56-57—St. Louis | 67 | 971 | 134 | 371 | .361 | 100 | 145 | .690 | 247 | 86 | 165 | 3 | 368 | 3.7 | 1.3 | 5.5 |
| 57-58—St. Louis | 70 | 2190 | 503 | 1135 | .443 | 385 | 501 | .768 | 707 | 175 | 267 | 9 | 1391 | 10.1 | 2.5 | 19.9 |
| 58-59—St. Louis | 72 | 2702 | 646 | 1417 | .456 | 415 | 536 | .774 | 783 | 245 | 275 | 10 | 1707 | 10.9 | 3.4 | 23.7 |
| 59-60—St. Louis | 75 | 2798 | 719 | 1549 | .464 | 421 | 524 | .803 | 803 | 299 | 270 | 4 | 1859 | 10.7 | 4.0 | 24.8 |
| 60-61—St. Louis | 77 | 2701 | 661 | 1490 | .444 | 383 | 467 | .820 | 715 | 381 | 286 | 9 | 1705 | 9.3 | 4.9 | 22.1 |
| 61-62—St. Louis | 77 | 2784 | 701 | 1490 | .470 | 362 | 439 | .825 | 633 | 370 | 282 | 8 | 1764 | 8.2 | 4.8 | 22.9 |
| 62-63—St. Louis | 79 | 1716 | 491 | 1055 | .465 | 244 | 305 | .800 | 341 | 193 | 211 | 2 | 1226 | 4.3 | 2.4 | 15.5 |
| 63-64—St. Louis | 77 | 2279 | 572 | 1280 | .447 | 269 | 331 | .813 | 377 | 193 | 273 | 4 | 1413 | 4.9 | 2.5 | 18.4 |
| 64-65—St. Louis | 77 | 1739 | 393 | 901 | .436 | 214 | 268 | .799 | 276 | 136 | 182 | 0 | 1000 | 3.6 | 1.8 | 13.0 |
| 65-66—St. Louis | 74 | 1851 | 419 | 942 | .445 | 176 | 206 | .854 | 234 | 164 | 177 | 1 | 1014 | 3.2 | 2.2 | 13.7 |
| Totals | 745 | 21731 | 5239 | 11630 | .450 | 2969 | 3722 | .798 | 5116 | 2242 | 2388 | 50 | 13447 | 6.9 | 3.0 | 18.0 |

## NBA PLAYOFF RECORD

| Season Team | G | Min. | FGM | FGA | Pct. | FTM | FTA | Pct. | Reb. | Ast. | PF | Dq. | Pts. | RPG | APG | PPG |
|---|---|---|---|---|---|---|---|---|---|---|---|---|---|---|---|---|
| | | | | | | | | | | | | | | AVERAGES | | |
| 56-57—St. Louis | 10 | 319 | 62 | 143 | .434 | 46 | 63 | .730 | 112 | 28 | 47 | 3 | 170 | 11.2 | 2.8 | 17.0 |
| 57-58—St. Louis | 11 | 418 | 111 | 221 | .502 | 83 | 99 | .838 | 115 | 37 | 48 | 3 | 305 | 10.5 | 3.4 | 27.7 |
| 58-59—St. Louis | 6 | 259 | 63 | 123 | .512 | 45 | 54 | .833 | 72 | 16 | 21 | 0 | 171 | 12.0 | 2.7 | 28.5 |
| 59-60—St. Louis | 14 | 544 | 125 | 296 | .422 | 89 | 109 | .817 | 138 | 54 | 54 | 1 | 339 | 9.9 | 3.9 | 24.2 |
| 60-61—St. Louis | 12 | 455 | 104 | 235 | .443 | 56 | 69 | .812 | 118 | 54 | 45 | 1 | 264 | 9.8 | 4.5 | 22.0 |
| 62-63—St. Louis | 11 | 255 | 83 | 179 | .464 | 37 | 53 | .698 | 55 | 34 | 42 | 4 | 203 | 5.0 | 3.1 | 18.5 |
| 63-64—St. Louis | 12 | 392 | 75 | 175 | .429 | 45 | 54 | .833 | 74 | 57 | 34 | 0 | 195 | 6.2 | 4.8 | 16.3 |
| 64-65—St. Louis | 4 | 123 | 34 | 75 | .453 | 6 | 12 | .500 | 26 | 7 | 14 | 0 | 74 | 6.5 | 1.8 | 18.5 |
| 65-66—St. Louis | 10 | 200 | 44 | 97 | .454 | 25 | 27 | .926 | 34 | 18 | 15 | 0 | 113 | 3.4 | 1.8 | 11.3 |
| Totals | 90 | 2965 | 701 | 1544 | .454 | 432 | 540 | .800 | 744 | 305 | 320 | 12 | 1834 | 8.3 | 3.4 | 20.4 |

## NBA ALL-STAR GAME RECORD

| Season Team | Min. | FGM | FGA | Pct. | FTM | FTA | Pct. | Reb | Ast. | PF | Dq. | Pts. |
|---|---|---|---|---|---|---|---|---|---|---|---|---|
| 1958—St. Louis | | | | | Selected, did not play—injured. | | | | | | | |
| 1959—St. Louis | 22 | 6 | 12 | .500 | 3 | 3 | 1.000 | 8 | 3 | 5 | 0 | 15 |
| 1960—St. Louis | 21 | 1 | 9 | .111 | 0 | 0 | ... | 3 | 2 | 1 | 0 | 2 |
| 1961—St. Louis | 13 | 0 | 2 | .000 | 2 | 2 | 1.000 | 2 | 0 | 1 | 0 | 2 |
| 1962—St. Louis | 9 | 1 | 3 | .333 | 0 | 0 | ... | 2 | 1 | 1 | 0 | 2 |
| Totals | 65 | 8 | 26 | .308 | 5 | 5 | 1.000 | 15 | 6 | 8 | 0 | 21 |

## ABA REGULAR-SEASON RECORD

| Season Team | G | Min. | 2-POINT | | | 3-POINT | | | FTM | FTA | Pct. | Reb. | Ast. | Pts. | AVERAGES | | |
|---|---|---|---|---|---|---|---|---|---|---|---|---|---|---|---|---|---|
| | | | FGM | FGA | Pct. | FGM | FGA | Pct. | | | | | | | RPG | APG | PPG |
| 67-68—Dallas | 56 | 1737 | 371 | 756 | .491 | 0 | 3 | .000 | 277 | 351 | .789 | 334 | 276 | 1019 | 6.0 | 4.9 | 18.2 |
| 68-69—Dallas | 35 | 579 | 132 | 258 | .512 | 0 | 1 | .000 | 123 | 144 | .854 | 102 | 122 | 387 | 2.9 | 3.5 | 11.1 |
| 69-70—Dallas | 3 | 27 | 8 | 12 | .667 | 0 | 1 | .000 | 1 | 2 | .500 | 3 | 6 | 17 | 1.0 | 2.0 | 5.7 |
| Totals | 94 | 2343 | 511 | 1026 | .498 | 0 | 5 | .000 | 401 | 497 | .807 | 439 | 404 | 1423 | 4.7 | 4.3 | 15.1 |

## ABA PLAYOFF RECORD

| Season Team | G | Min. | 2-POINT | | | 3-POINT | | | FTM | FTA | Pct. | Reb. | Ast. | Pts. | AVERAGES | | |
|---|---|---|---|---|---|---|---|---|---|---|---|---|---|---|---|---|---|
| | | | FGM | FGA | Pct. | FGM | FGA | Pct. | | | | | | | RPG | APG | PPG |
| 67-68—Dallas | 3 | 70 | 14 | 37 | .378 | 0 | 0 | ... | 9 | 13 | .692 | 13 | 9 | 37 | 4.3 | 3.0 | 12.3 |
| 68-69—Dallas | 2 | 45 | 5 | 14 | .357 | 0 | 0 | ... | 8 | 10 | .800 | 6 | 14 | 18 | 3.0 | 7.0 | 9.0 |
| Totals | 5 | 115 | 19 | 51 | .373 | 0 | 0 | ... | 17 | 23 | .739 | 19 | 23 | 55 | 3.8 | 4.6 | 11.0 |

## ABA ALL-STAR GAME RECORD

| Season Team | Min. | 2-POINT | | | 3-POINT | | | FTM | FTA | Pct. | Reb. | Ast. | Pts. |
|---|---|---|---|---|---|---|---|---|---|---|---|---|---|
| | | FGM | FGA | Pct. | FGM | FGA | Pct. | | | | | | |
| 1968—Dallas | 24 | 4 | 11 | .364 | 0 | 0 | ... | 2 | 2 | 1.000 | 0 | 5 | 10 |

## COMBINED ABA AND NBA REGULAR-SEASON RECORDS

| | G | Min. | FGM | FGA | Pct. | FTM | FTA | Pct. | REBOUNDS | | | Ast. | Stl. | Blk. | TO | Pts. | AVERAGES | | |
|---|---|---|---|---|---|---|---|---|---|---|---|---|---|---|---|---|---|---|---|
| | | | | | | | | | Off. | Def. | Tot. | | | | | | RPG | APG | PPG |
| Totals | 839 | 24074 | 5750 | 12661 | .454 | 3370 | 4219 | .799 | ... | ... | 5555 | 2646 | ... | ... | ... | 14870 | 6.6 | 3.2 | 17.7 |

Three-point field goals: 0-for-5.
Personal fouls/disqualifications: 2678/58.

## ABA COACHING RECORD

**BACKGROUND:** Player/head coach, Dallas Chaparrals of American Basketball Association (1967-68 to January 1970).

| Season Team | REGULAR SEASON | | | | PLAYOFFS | | |
|---|---|---|---|---|---|---|---|
| | W | L | Pct. | Finish | W | L | Pct. |
| 67-68—Dallas | 46 | 32 | .590 | 2nd/Western Division | 4 | 4 | .500 |
| 68-69—Dallas | 41 | 37 | .526 | 4th/Western Division | 3 | 4 | .426 |
| 69-70—Dallas | 22 | 21 | .512 | | — | — | — |
| Totals (3 years) | 109 | 90 | .548 | Totals (2 years) | 7 | 8 | .467 |

**NOTES:**
1968—Defeated Houston, 3-0, in Western Division Semifinals; lost to New Orleans, 4-1, in Western Division Finals.
1969—Lost to New Orleans in Western Division Semifinals.
1970—Replaced as Dallas head coach by Max Williams (January).

# HARDAWAY, TIM                         G

**PERSONAL:** Born September 1, 1966, in Chicago ... 6-0/195. (1,83/88,5). ... Full Name: Timothy Duane Hardaway.
**HIGH SCHOOL:** Carver (Chicago).
**COLLEGE:** Texas-El Paso.
**TRANSACTIONS/CAREER NOTES:** Selected by Golden State Warriors in first round (14th pick overall) of 1989 NBA Draft. ... Traded by Warriors with F/C Chris Gatling to Miami Heat for F/C Kevin Willis and G Bimbo Coles (February 22, 1996). ... Traded by Heat to Dallas Mavericks for 2003 or 2004 second-round draft choice (August 22, 2001). ... Traded by Mavericks with F Juwan Howard, F Donnell Harvey, cash considerations and first-round draft choice to Denver Nuggets for G Nick Van Exel, F/C Raef LaFrentz, G Avery Johnson and G/F Tariq Abdul-Wahad (February 21, 2002). ... Waived by Nuggets (June 25, 2002). ... Signed as free agent by Indiana Pacers (March 27, 2003).
**MISCELLANEOUS:** Member of gold-medal-winning U.S. Olympic team (2000). ... Member of gold-medal-winning U.S. World Championship team (1994). ... Miami Heat all-time assists leader with 2,867 (1995-96 through 2000-01).

## COLLEGIATE RECORD

**NOTES:** Frances Pomeroy Naismith Award winner (1989).

| Season Team | G | Min. | FGM | FGA | Pct. | FTM | FTA | Pct. | Reb. | Ast. | Pts. | AVERAGES | | |
|---|---|---|---|---|---|---|---|---|---|---|---|---|---|---|
| | | | | | | | | | | | | RPG | APG | PPG |
| 85-86—Texas-El Paso | 28 | 435 | 37 | 71 | .521 | 41 | 63 | .651 | 35 | 53 | 115 | 1.3 | 1.9 | 4.1 |
| 86-87—Texas-El Paso | 31 | 922 | 120 | 245 | .490 | 67 | 101 | .663 | 62 | 148 | 310 | 2.0 | 4.8 | 10.0 |
| 87-88—Texas-El Paso | 32 | 1036 | 159 | 354 | .449 | 98 | 130 | .754 | 93 | 183 | 434 | 2.9 | 5.7 | 13.6 |
| 88-89—Texas-El Paso | 33 | 1182 | 255 | 509 | .501 | 169 | 228 | .741 | 131 | 179 | 727 | 4.0 | 5.4 | 22.0 |
| Totals | 124 | 3575 | 571 | 1179 | .484 | 375 | 522 | .718 | 321 | 563 | 1586 | 2.6 | 4.5 | 12.8 |

Three-point field goals: 1986-87, 3-for-12 (.250). 1987-88, 18-for-53 (.340). 1988-89, 48-for-131 (.366). Totals, 69-for-196 (.352).

## NBA REGULAR-SEASON RECORD

**RECORDS:** Holds single-game record for most field goals attempted, none made—17 (December 27, 1991, OT, at San Antonio).
**HONORS:** All-NBA first team (1997). ... All-NBA second team (1992, 1998, 1999). ... All-NBA third team (1993). ... NBA All-Rookie first team (1990).

| Season Team | G | Min. | FGM | FGA | Pct. | FTM | FTA | Pct. | REBOUNDS | | | Ast. | St. | Blk. | TO | Pts. | AVERAGES | | |
|---|---|---|---|---|---|---|---|---|---|---|---|---|---|---|---|---|---|---|---|
| | | | | | | | | | Off. | Def. | Tot. | | | | | | RPG | APG | PPG |
| 89-90—Golden State | 79 | 2663 | 464 | 985 | .471 | 211 | 276 | .764 | 57 | 253 | 310 | 689 | 165 | 12 | 260 | 1162 | 3.9 | 8.7 | 14.7 |
| 90-91—Golden State | 82 | 3215 | 739 | 1551 | .476 | 306 | 381 | .803 | 87 | 245 | 332 | 793 | 214 | 12 | 270 | 1881 | 4.0 | 9.7 | 22.9 |
| 91-92—Golden State | 81 | 3332 | 734 | 1592 | .461 | 298 | 389 | .766 | 81 | 229 | 310 | 807 | 164 | 13 | 267 | 1893 | 3.8 | 10.0 | 23.4 |
| 92-93—Golden State | 66 | 2609 | 522 | 1168 | .447 | 273 | 367 | .744 | 60 | 203 | 263 | 699 | 116 | 12 | 220 | 1419 | 4.0 | 10.6 | 21.5 |
| 93-94—Golden State | | | | | | | Did not play—knee injury. | | | | | | | | | | | | |
| 94-95—Golden State | 62 | 2321 | 430 | 1007 | .427 | 219 | 288 | .760 | 46 | 144 | 190 | 578 | 88 | 12 | 214 | 1247 | 3.1 | 9.3 | 20.1 |
| 95-96—G.S.-Miami | 80 | 2534 | 419 | 992 | .422 | 241 | 305 | .790 | 35 | 194 | 229 | 640 | 132 | 17 | 235 | 1217 | 2.9 | 8.0 | 15.2 |
| 96-97—Miami | 81 | 3136 | 575 | 1384 | .415 | 291 | 364 | .799 | 49 | 228 | 277 | 695 | 151 | 9 | 230 | 1644 | 3.4 | 8.6 | 20.3 |
| 97-98—Miami | 81 | 3031 | 558 | 1296 | .431 | 257 | 329 | .781 | 48 | 251 | 299 | 672 | 136 | 16 | 224 | 1528 | 3.7 | 8.3 | 18.9 |
| 98-99—Miami | 48 | 1772 | 301 | 752 | .400 | 121 | 149 | .812 | 15 | 137 | 152 | 352 | 57 | 6 | 131 | 835 | 3.2 | 7.3 | 17.4 |
| 99-00—Miami | 52 | 1672 | 246 | 638 | .386 | 110 | 133 | .827 | 25 | 125 | 150 | 385 | 49 | 4 | 119 | 666 | 2.9 | 7.4 | 13.4 |
| 00-01—Miami | 77 | 2613 | 408 | 1042 | .392 | 145 | 181 | .801 | 26 | 178 | 204 | 483 | 90 | 6 | 189 | 1150 | 2.6 | 6.3 | 14.9 |
| 01-02—Dallas-Denver | 68 | 1601 | 226 | 620 | .365 | 77 | 97 | .794 | 14 | 110 | 124 | 278 | 57 | 10 | 111 | 652 | 1.8 | 4.1 | 9.6 |
| 02-03—Indiana | 10 | 127 | 18 | 49 | .367 | 2 | 4 | .500 | 1 | 14 | 15 | 24 | 9 | 0 | 11 | 49 | 1.5 | 2.4 | 4.9 |
| Totals | 867 | 30626 | 5640 | 13076 | .431 | 2551 | 3263 | .782 | 544 | 2311 | 2855 | 7095 | 1428 | 129 | 2481 | 15373 | 3.3 | 8.2 | 17.7 |

Three-point field goals: 1989-90, 23-for-84 (.274). 1990-91, 97-for-252 (.385). 1991-92, 127-for-376 (.338). 1992-93, 102-for-309 (.330). 1994-95, 168-for-444 (.378). 1995-96, 138-for-379 (.364). 1996-97, 203-for-590 (.344). 1997-98, 158-for-442 (.351). 1998-99, 112-for-311 (.360). 1999-00, 94-for-256 (.367). 2000-01, 189-for-517 (.366). 2001-02, 123-for-354 (.347). 2002-03, 11-for-31 (.355). Totals, 1542-for-4345 (.355).
Personal fouls/disqualifications: 1989-90, 232/6. 1990-91, 228/7. 1991-92, 208/1. 1992-93, 152/0. 1994-95, 155/1. 1995-96, 201/3. 1996-97, 165/2. 1997-98, 200/2. 1998-99, 102/1. 1999-00, 112/0. 2000-01, 155/1. 2001-02, 109/0. 2002-03, 8/0. Totals, 2027/24.

## NBA PLAYOFF RECORD

| Season Team | G | Min. | FGM | FGA | Pct. | FTM | FTA | Pct. | REBOUNDS | | | Ast. | St. | Blk. | TO | Pts. | AVERAGES | | |
|---|---|---|---|---|---|---|---|---|---|---|---|---|---|---|---|---|---|---|---|
| | | | | | | | | | Off. | Def. | Tot. | | | | | | RPG | APG | PPG |
| 90-91—Golden State | 9 | 396 | 90 | 185 | .486 | 30 | 38 | .789 | 5 | 28 | 33 | 101 | 28 | 7 | 25 | 227 | 3.7 | 11.2 | 25.2 |
| 91-92—Golden State | 4 | 176 | 32 | 80 | .400 | 24 | 37 | .649 | 6 | 9 | 15 | 29 | 13 | 0 | 14 | 98 | 3.8 | 7.3 | 24.5 |
| 95-96—Miami | 3 | 110 | 20 | 43 | .465 | 5 | 7 | .714 | 1 | 4 | 5 | 17 | 3 | 0 | 15 | 53 | 1.7 | 5.7 | 17.7 |
| 96-97—Miami | 17 | 701 | 103 | 287 | .359 | 70 | 88 | .795 | 13 | 56 | 69 | 119 | 27 | 1 | 53 | 318 | 4.1 | 7.0 | 18.7 |
| 97-98—Miami | 5 | 222 | 42 | 94 | .447 | 29 | 37 | .784 | 3 | 14 | 17 | 33 | 6 | 0 | 18 | 130 | 3.4 | 6.6 | 26.0 |
| 98-99—Miami | 5 | 182 | 15 | 56 | .268 | 10 | 16 | .625 | 3 | 11 | 14 | 32 | 5 | 1 | 18 | 45 | 2.8 | 6.4 | 9.0 |
| 99-00—Miami | 7 | 182 | 20 | 68 | .294 | 7 | 10 | .700 | 1 | 14 | 15 | 33 | 5 | 0 | 11 | 54 | 2.1 | 4.7 | 7.7 |
| 00-01—Miami | 2 | 36 | 2 | 9 | .222 | 0 | 0 | ... | 1 | 1 | 2 | 9 | 0 | 0 | 8 | 5 | 1.0 | 4.5 | 2.5 |
| 02-03—Indiana | 4 | 47 | 5 | 15 | .333 | 0 | 0 | ... | 0 | 2 | 2 | 9 | 1 | 0 | 3 | 13 | 0.5 | 2.3 | 3.3 |
| Totals | 56 | 2052 | 329 | 837 | .393 | 175 | 233 | .751 | 33 | 139 | 172 | 382 | 88 | 9 | 165 | 943 | 3.1 | 6.8 | 16.8 |

ALL-TIME GREAT PLAYERS

Three-point field goals: 1990-91, 17-for-48 (.354). 1991-92, 10-for-29 (.345). 1995-96, 8-for-22 (.364). 1996-97, 42-for-134 (.313). 1997-98, 17-for-39 (.436). 1998-99, 5-for-25 (.200). 1999-00, 7-for-34 (.206). 2000-01, 1-for-3 (.333). 2002-03, 3-for-10 (.300). Totals, 110-for-344 (.320).

Personal fouls/disqualifications: 1990-91, 22/0. 1991-92, 14/0. 1995-96, 10/0. 1996-97, 37/0. 1997-98, 9/0. 1998-99, 14/0. 1999-00, 10/0. 2000-01, 4/0. 2002-03, 2/0. Totals, 122/0.

## NBA ALL-STAR GAME RECORD

| Season Team | Min. | FGM | FGA | Pct. | FTM | FTA | Pct. | REBOUNDS Off. | Def. | Tot. | Ast. | PF | Dq. | St. | Blk. | TO | Pts. |
|---|---|---|---|---|---|---|---|---|---|---|---|---|---|---|---|---|---|
| 1991—Golden State | 12 | 2 | 7 | .286 | 0 | 0 | ... | 2 | 1 | 3 | 4 | 1 | 0 | 2 | 0 | 0 | 5 |
| 1992—Golden State | 20 | 5 | 10 | .500 | 2 | 2 | 1.000 | 0 | 0 | 0 | 7 | 2 | 0 | 1 | 0 | 2 | 14 |
| 1993—Golden State | 21 | 3 | 9 | .333 | 9 | 12 | .750 | 1 | 5 | 6 | 4 | 1 | 0 | 1 | 0 | 3 | 16 |
| 1997—Miami | 14 | 4 | 10 | .400 | 0 | 0 | ... | 0 | 3 | 3 | 2 | 1 | 0 | 1 | 0 | 2 | 10 |
| 1998—Miami | 17 | 3 | 8 | .375 | 0 | 0 | ... | 0 | 1 | 1 | 6 | 0 | 0 | 0 | 0 | 6 | 8 |
| Totals | 84 | 17 | 44 | .386 | 11 | 14 | .786 | 3 | 10 | 13 | 23 | 5 | 0 | 5 | 0 | 13 | 53 |

Three-point field goals: 1991, 1-for-2 (.500). 1992, 2-for-5 (.400). 1993, 1-for-3 (.333). 1997, 2-for-6 (.333). 1998, 2-for-5 (.400). Totals, 8-for-21 (.381).

# HARPER, DEREK                          G

**PERSONAL:** Born October 13, 1961, in Elberton, Ga. ... 6-4/206 (1,93/93,4). ... Full name: Derek Ricardo Harper.
**HIGH SCHOOL:** North Shore (West Palm Beach, Fla.).
**COLLEGE:** Illinois.
**TRANSACTIONS/CAREER NOTES:** Selected after junior season by Dallas Mavericks in first round (11th pick overall) of 1983 NBA Draft. ... Traded by Mavericks to New York Knicks for G/F Tony Campbell and 1997 first-round draft choice (January 6, 1994). ... Signed as free agent by Mavericks (July 26, 1996). ... Traded by Mavericks with F Ed O'Bannon to Orlando Magic for G Dennis Scott and cash (September 24, 1997). ... Signed as free agent by Los Angeles Lakers (January 21, 1999). ... Traded by Lakers to Detroit Pistons for draft rights to G Melvin Levett (September 21, 1999). ... Placed on suspension by Pistons (did not report) (October 5, 1999). ... Announced retirement (January 30, 2000).
**CAREER NOTES:** Vice president of business relations, Dallas Mavericks (February-April 2000).
**MISCELLANEOUS:** Dallas Mavericks all-time assists leader with 5,111 and all-time steals leader with 1,551 (1983-84 through 1993-94 and 1996-97).

## COLLEGIATE RECORD

| Season Team | G | Min. | FGM | FGA | Pct. | FTM | FTA | Pct. | Reb. | Ast. | Pts. | AVERAGES RPG | APG | PPG |
|---|---|---|---|---|---|---|---|---|---|---|---|---|---|---|
| 80-81—Illinois | 29 | 934 | 104 | 252 | .413 | 33 | 46 | .717 | 75 | 156 | 241 | 2.6 | 5.4 | 8.3 |
| 81-82—Illinois | 29 | 1059 | 105 | 230 | .457 | 34 | 45 | .756 | 133 | 145 | 244 | 4.6 | 5.0 | 8.4 |
| 82-83—Illinois | 32 | 1182 | 198 | 369 | .537 | 83 | 123 | .675 | 112 | 118 | 492 | 3.5 | 3.7 | 15.4 |
| Totals | 90 | 3175 | 407 | 851 | .478 | 150 | 214 | .701 | 320 | 419 | 977 | 3.6 | 4.7 | 10.9 |

Three-point field goals: 1982-83, 13-for-24 (.542).

## NBA REGULAR-SEASON RECORD

**HONORS:** NBA All-Defensive second team (1987, 1990).

| Season Team | G | Min. | FGM | FGA | Pct. | FTM | FTA | Pct. | REBOUNDS Off. | Def. | Tot. | Ast. | St. | Blk. | TO | Pts. | AVERAGES RPG | APG | PPG |
|---|---|---|---|---|---|---|---|---|---|---|---|---|---|---|---|---|---|---|---|
| 83-84—Dallas | 82 | 1712 | 200 | 451 | .443 | 66 | 98 | .673 | 53 | 119 | 172 | 239 | 95 | 21 | 111 | 469 | 2.1 | 2.9 | 5.7 |
| 84-85—Dallas | 82 | 2218 | 329 | 633 | .520 | 111 | 154 | .721 | 47 | 152 | 199 | 360 | 144 | 37 | 123 | 790 | 2.4 | 4.4 | 9.6 |
| 85-86—Dallas | 79 | 2150 | 390 | 730 | .534 | 171 | 229 | .747 | 75 | 151 | 226 | 416 | 153 | 24 | 144 | 963 | 2.9 | 5.3 | 12.2 |
| 86-87—Dallas | 77 | 2556 | 497 | 993 | .501 | 160 | 234 | .684 | 51 | 148 | 199 | 609 | 167 | 25 | 138 | 1230 | 2.6 | 7.9 | 16.0 |
| 87-88—Dallas | 82 | 3032 | 536 | 1167 | .459 | 261 | 344 | .759 | 71 | 175 | 246 | 634 | 168 | 35 | 190 | 1393 | 3.0 | 7.7 | 17.0 |
| 88-89—Dallas | 81 | 2968 | 538 | 1127 | .477 | 229 | 284 | .806 | 46 | 182 | 228 | 570 | 172 | 41 | 205 | 1404 | 2.8 | 7.0 | 17.3 |
| 89-90—Dallas | 82 | 3007 | 567 | 1161 | .488 | 250 | 315 | .794 | 54 | 190 | 244 | 609 | 187 | 26 | 207 | 1473 | 3.0 | 7.4 | 18.0 |
| 90-91—Dallas | 77 | 2879 | 572 | 1226 | .467 | 286 | 391 | .731 | 59 | 174 | 233 | 548 | 147 | 14 | 177 | 1519 | 3.0 | 7.1 | 19.7 |
| 91-92—Dallas | 65 | 2252 | 448 | 1011 | .443 | 198 | 261 | .759 | 49 | 121 | 170 | 373 | 101 | 17 | 154 | 1152 | 2.6 | 5.7 | 17.7 |
| 92-93—Dallas | 62 | 2108 | 393 | 939 | .419 | 239 | 316 | .756 | 42 | 81 | 123 | 334 | 80 | 16 | 136 | 1126 | 2.0 | 5.4 | 18.2 |
| 93-94—Dallas-N.Y. | 82 | 2204 | 303 | 744 | .407 | 112 | 163 | .687 | 20 | 121 | 141 | 334 | 125 | 8 | 135 | 791 | 1.7 | 4.1 | 9.6 |
| 94-95—New York | 80 | 2716 | 337 | 756 | .446 | 139 | 192 | .724 | 31 | 163 | 194 | 458 | 79 | 10 | 151 | 919 | 2.4 | 5.7 | 11.5 |
| 95-96—New York | 82 | 2893 | 436 | 939 | .464 | 156 | 206 | .757 | 32 | 170 | 202 | 352 | 131 | 5 | 178 | 1149 | 2.5 | 4.3 | 14.0 |
| 96-97—Dallas | 75 | 2210 | 299 | 674 | .444 | 95 | 128 | .742 | 30 | 107 | 137 | 321 | 92 | 12 | 132 | 753 | 1.8 | 4.3 | 10.0 |
| 97-98—Orlando | 66 | 1761 | 226 | 542 | .417 | 55 | 79 | .696 | 23 | 80 | 103 | 233 | 72 | 10 | 101 | 566 | 1.6 | 3.5 | 8.6 |
| 98-99—L.A. Lakers | 45 | 1120 | 120 | 291 | .412 | 26 | 32 | .813 | 13 | 54 | 67 | 187 | 44 | 4 | 52 | 309 | 1.5 | 4.2 | 6.9 |
| Totals | 1199 | 37786 | 6191 | 13384 | .463 | 2554 | 3426 | .745 | 696 | 2188 | 2884 | 6577 | 1957 | 304 | 2334 | 16006 | 2.4 | 5.5 | 13.3 |

Three-point field goals: 1983-84, 3-for-26 (.115). 1984-85, 21-for-61 (.344). 1985-86, 12-for-51 (.235). 1986-87, 76-for-212 (.358). 1987-88, 66-for-192 (.313). 1988-89, 99-for-278 (.356). 1989-90, 89-for-240 (.371). 1990-91, 89-for-246 (.362). 1991-92, 58-for-186 (.312). 1992-93, 101-for-257 (.393). 1993-94, 73-for-203 (.360). 1994-95, 106-for-292 (.363). 1995-96, 121-for-325 (.372). 1996-97, 60-for-176 (.341). 1997-98, 59-for-164 (.360). 1998-99, 43-for-117 (.368). Totals, 1070-for-3026 (.354).

Personal fouls/disqualifications: 1983-84, 143/0. 1984-85, 194/1. 1985-86, 166/1. 1986-87, 195/0. 1987-88, 164/0. 1988-89, 219/3. 1989-90, 224/1. 1990-91, 222/1. 1991-92, 150/0. 1992-93, 145/1. 1993-94, 163/0. 1994-95, 201/0. 1996-97, 144/0. 1997-98, 140/0. 1998-99, 66/0. Totals, 2755/8.

## NBA PLAYOFF RECORD

**NOTES:** Shares NBA Finals single-series record for most three-point field goals made—17 (1994, vs. Houston).

| Season Team | G | Min. | FGM | FGA | Pct. | FTM | FTA | Pct. | REBOUNDS Off. | Def. | Tot. | Ast. | St. | Blk. | TO | Pts. | AVERAGES RPG | APG | PPG |
|---|---|---|---|---|---|---|---|---|---|---|---|---|---|---|---|---|---|---|---|
| 83-84—Dallas | 10 | 226 | 21 | 54 | .389 | 5 | 7 | .714 | 8 | 12 | 20 | 28 | 11 | 2 | 6 | 50 | 2.0 | 2.8 | 5.0 |
| 84-85—Dallas | 4 | 132 | 10 | 21 | .476 | 5 | 7 | .714 | 1 | 11 | 12 | 20 | 6 | 1 | 4 | 26 | 3.0 | 5.0 | 6.5 |
| 85-86—Dallas | 10 | 348 | 57 | 107 | .533 | 12 | 16 | .750 | 13 | 6 | 19 | 76 | 23 | 0 | 23 | 134 | 1.9 | 7.6 | 13.4 |
| 86-87—Dallas | 4 | 123 | 20 | 40 | .500 | 24 | 30 | .800 | 2 | 10 | 12 | 27 | 7 | 0 | 5 | 66 | 3.0 | 6.8 | 16.5 |
| 87-88—Dallas | 17 | 602 | 89 | 202 | .441 | 43 | 59 | .729 | 11 | 32 | 43 | 121 | 32 | 5 | 32 | 230 | 2.5 | 7.1 | 13.5 |
| 89-90—Dallas | 3 | 119 | 21 | 48 | .438 | 11 | 16 | .688 | 2 | 6 | 8 | 23 | 4 | 0 | 12 | 58 | 2.7 | 7.7 | 19.3 |
| 93-94—New York | 23 | 750 | 99 | 231 | .429 | 36 | 56 | .643 | 13 | 41 | 54 | 103 | 42 | 1 | 41 | 263 | 2.3 | 4.5 | 11.4 |
| 94-95—New York | 11 | 346 | 56 | 109 | .514 | 18 | 24 | .750 | 5 | 33 | 38 | 62 | 11 | 1 | 26 | 157 | 3.5 | 5.6 | 14.3 |
| 95-96—New York | 8 | 293 | 29 | 82 | .354 | 11 | 15 | .733 | 0 | 17 | 17 | 38 | 10 | 1 | 14 | 80 | 2.1 | 4.8 | 10.0 |
| 98-99—L.A. Lakers | 7 | 155 | 13 | 31 | .419 | 3 | 6 | .500 | 1 | 9 | 10 | 15 | 2 | 0 | 4 | 30 | 1.4 | 2.1 | 4.3 |
| Totals | 97 | 3094 | 415 | 925 | .449 | 168 | 236 | .712 | 56 | 177 | 233 | 513 | 148 | 11 | 167 | 1094 | 2.4 | 5.3 | 11.3 |

Three-point field goals: 1983-84, 3-for-8 (.375). 1984-85, 1-for-3 (.333). 1985-86, 8-for-14 (.571). 1986-87, 2-for-9 (.222). 1987-88, 9-for-36 (.250). 1989-90, 5-for-16 (.313). 1993-94, 29-for-85 (.341). 1994-95, 27-for-47 (.574). 1995-96, 11-for-35 (.314). 1998-99, 1-for-10 (.100). Totals, 96-for-263 (.365).
Personal fouls/disqualifications: 1983-84, 16/0. 1984-85, 12/0. 1985-86, 27/0. 1986-87, 7/0. 1987-88, 44/0. 1989-90, 13/0. 1993-94, 63/1. 1994-95, 29/0. 1995-96, 24/0. 1998-99, 2/0. Totals, 237/1.

# HAVLICEK, JOHN        F/G

**PERSONAL:** Born April 8, 1940, in Martins Ferry, Ohio. ... 6-5/205 (1,96/93,0). ... Full name: John J. Havlicek. ... Nickname: Hondo.
**HIGH SCHOOL:** Bridgeport (Ohio).
**COLLEGE:** Ohio State.
**TRANSACTIONS:** Selected by Boston Celtics in first round of 1962 NBA Draft.
**CAREER HONORS:** Elected to Naismith Memorial Basketball Hall of Fame (1984). ... NBA 35th Anniversary All-Time Team (1980) and One of the 50 Greatest Players in NBA History (1996).
**MISCELLANEOUS:** Member of NBA championship team (1963, 1964, 1965, 1966, 1968, 1969, 1974, 1976). ... Selected as wide receiver by Cleveland Browns in seventh round of 1962 National Football League draft. ... Boston Celtics all-time leading scorer with 26,395 points (1962-63 through 1977-78).

## COLLEGIATE RECORD

**NOTES:** The Sporting News All-America second team (1962). ... Member of NCAA championship team (1960).

| Season Team | G | Min. | FGM | FGA | Pct. | FTM | FTA | Pct. | Reb. | Ast. | Pts. | RPG | APG | PPG |
|---|---|---|---|---|---|---|---|---|---|---|---|---|---|---|
| 58-59—Ohio State‡ | | | | Freshman team did not play intercollegiate schedule. | | | | | | | | | | |
| 59-60—Ohio State | 28 | ... | 144 | 312 | .462 | 53 | 74 | .716 | 205 | ... | 341 | 7.3 | ... | 12.2 |
| 60-61—Ohio State | 28 | ... | 173 | 321 | .539 | 61 | 87 | .701 | 244 | ... | 407 | 8.7 | ... | 14.5 |
| 61-62—Ohio State | 28 | ... | 196 | 377 | .520 | 83 | 109 | .761 | 271 | ... | 475 | 9.7 | ... | 17.0 |
| Varsity totals | 84 | ... | 513 | 1010 | .508 | 197 | 270 | .730 | 720 | ... | 1223 | 8.6 | ... | 14.6 |

## NBA REGULAR-SEASON RECORD

**HONORS:** All-NBA first team (1971, 1972, 1973, 1974). ... All-NBA second team (1964, 1966, 1968, 1969, 1970, 1975, 1976). ... NBA All-Defensive first team (1972, 1973, 1974, 1975, 1976). ... NBA All-Defensive second team (1969, 1970, 1971).

| Season Team | G | Min. | FGM | FGA | Pct. | FTM | FTA | Pct. | Reb. | Ast. | PF | Dq. | Pts. | RPG | APG | PPG |
|---|---|---|---|---|---|---|---|---|---|---|---|---|---|---|---|---|
| 62-63—Boston | 80 | 2200 | 483 | 1085 | .445 | 174 | 239 | .728 | 534 | 179 | 189 | 2 | 1140 | 6.7 | 2.2 | 14.3 |
| 63-64—Boston | 80 | 2587 | 640 | 1535 | .417 | 315 | 422 | .746 | 428 | 238 | 227 | 1 | 1595 | 5.4 | 3.0 | 19.9 |
| 64-65—Boston | 75 | 2169 | 570 | 1420 | .401 | 235 | 316 | .744 | 371 | 199 | 200 | 2 | 1375 | 4.9 | 2.7 | 18.3 |
| 65-66—Boston | 71 | 2175 | 530 | 1328 | .399 | 274 | 349 | .785 | 423 | 210 | 158 | 1 | 1334 | 6.0 | 3.0 | 18.8 |
| 66-67—Boston | 81 | 2602 | 684 | 1540 | .444 | 365 | 441 | .828 | 532 | 278 | 210 | 0 | 1733 | 6.6 | 3.4 | 21.4 |
| 67-68—Boston | 82 | 2921 | 666 | 1551 | .429 | 368 | 453 | .812 | 546 | 384 | 237 | 2 | 1700 | 6.7 | 4.7 | 20.7 |
| 68-69—Boston | 82 | 3174 | 692 | 1709 | .405 | 387 | 496 | .780 | 570 | 441 | 247 | 0 | 1771 | 7.0 | 5.4 | 21.6 |
| 69-70—Boston | 81 | 3369 | 736 | 1585 | .464 | 488 | 578 | .844 | 635 | 550 | 211 | 1 | 1960 | 7.8 | 6.8 | 24.2 |
| 70-71—Boston | 81 | *3678 | 892 | 1982 | .450 | 554 | 677 | .818 | 730 | 607 | 200 | 0 | 2338 | 9.0 | 7.5 | 28.9 |
| 71-72—Boston | 82 | *3698 | 897 | 1957 | .458 | 458 | 549 | .834 | 672 | 614 | 183 | 1 | 2252 | 8.2 | 7.5 | 27.5 |
| 72-73—Boston | 80 | 3367 | 766 | 1704 | .450 | 370 | 431 | .858 | 567 | 529 | 195 | 1 | 1902 | 7.1 | 6.6 | 23.8 |

| | | | | | | | | | REBOUNDS | | | | | | | AVERAGES | | |
|---|---|---|---|---|---|---|---|---|---|---|---|---|---|---|---|---|---|---|
| Season Team | G | Min. | FGM | FGA | Pct. | FTM | FTA | Pct. | Off. | Def. | Tot. | Ast. | St. | Blk. | TO | Pts. | RPG | APG | PPG |
| 73-74—Boston | 76 | 3091 | 685 | 1502 | .456 | 346 | 416 | .832 | 138 | 349 | 487 | 447 | 95 | 32 | ... | 1716 | 6.4 | 5.9 | 22.6 |
| 74-75—Boston | 82 | 3132 | 642 | 1411 | .455 | 289 | 332 | .870 | 154 | 330 | 484 | 432 | 110 | 16 | ... | 1573 | 5.9 | 5.3 | 19.2 |
| 75-76—Boston | 76 | 2598 | 504 | 1121 | .450 | 281 | 333 | .844 | 116 | 198 | 314 | 278 | 97 | 29 | ... | 1289 | 4.1 | 3.7 | 17.0 |
| 76-77—Boston | 79 | 2913 | 580 | 1283 | .452 | 235 | 288 | .816 | 109 | 273 | 382 | 400 | 84 | 18 | ... | 1395 | 4.8 | 5.1 | 17.7 |
| 77-78—Boston | 82 | 2797 | 546 | 1217 | .449 | 230 | 269 | .855 | 93 | 239 | 332 | 328 | 90 | 22 | 204 | 1322 | 4.0 | 4.0 | 16.1 |
| Totals | 1270 | 46471 | 10513 | 23930 | .439 | 5369 | 6589 | .815 | ... | ... | 8007 | 6114 | 476 | 117 | 204 | 26395 | 6.3 | 4.8 | 20.8 |

Personal fouls/disqualifications: 1973-74, 196/1. 1974-75, 231/2. 1975-76, 204/1. 1976-77, 208/4. 1977-78, 185/2. Totals, 3281/21.

## NBA PLAYOFF RECORD

**NOTES:** NBA Finals Most Valuable Player (1974). ... Shares NBA Finals single-game record for most points in an overtime period—9 (May 10, 1974, vs. Milwaukee). ... Shares single-game playoff record for most field goals made—24 (April 1, 1973, vs. Atlanta).

| Season Team | G | Min. | FGM | FGA | Pct. | FTM | FTA | Pct. | Reb. | Ast. | PF | Dq. | Pts. | RPG | APG | PPG |
|---|---|---|---|---|---|---|---|---|---|---|---|---|---|---|---|---|
| 62-63—Boston | 11 | 254 | 56 | 125 | .448 | 18 | 27 | .667 | 53 | 17 | 28 | 1 | 130 | 4.8 | 1.5 | 11.8 |
| 63-64—Boston | 10 | 289 | 61 | 159 | .384 | 35 | 44 | .795 | 43 | 32 | 26 | 0 | 157 | 4.3 | 3.2 | 15.7 |
| 64-65—Boston | 12 | 405 | 88 | 250 | .352 | 46 | 55 | .836 | 88 | 29 | 44 | 1 | 222 | 7.3 | 2.4 | 18.5 |
| 65-66—Boston | 17 | 719 | 153 | 374 | .409 | 95 | 113 | .841 | 154 | 70 | 69 | 2 | 401 | 9.1 | 4.1 | 23.6 |
| 66-67—Boston | 9 | 330 | 95 | 212 | .448 | 57 | 71 | .803 | 73 | 28 | 30 | 0 | 247 | 8.1 | 3.1 | 27.4 |
| 67-68—Boston | 19 | 862 | 184 | 407 | .452 | 125 | 151 | .828 | 164 | 142 | 67 | 1 | 493 | 8.6 | 7.5 | 25.9 |
| 68-69—Boston | 18 | 850 | 170 | 382 | .445 | 118 | 138 | .855 | 179 | 100 | 58 | 2 | 458 | 9.9 | 5.6 | 25.4 |
| 71-72—Boston | 11 | 517 | 108 | 235 | .460 | 85 | 99 | .859 | 92 | 70 | 35 | 1 | 301 | 8.4 | 6.4 | 27.4 |
| 72-73—Boston | 12 | 479 | 112 | 235 | .477 | 61 | 74 | .824 | 62 | 65 | 24 | 0 | 285 | 5.2 | 5.4 | 23.8 |

| | | | | | | | | | REBOUNDS | | | | | | | AVERAGES | | |
|---|---|---|---|---|---|---|---|---|---|---|---|---|---|---|---|---|---|---|
| Season Team | G | Min. | FGM | FGA | Pct. | FTM | FTA | Pct. | Off. | Def. | Tot. | Ast. | St. | Blk. | TO | Pts. | RPG | APG | PPG |
| 73-74—Boston | 18 | 811 | 199 | 411 | .484 | 89 | 101 | .881 | 28 | 88 | 116 | 108 | 24 | 6 | ... | 487 | 6.4 | 6.0 | 27.1 |
| 74-75—Boston | 11 | 464 | 83 | 192 | .432 | 66 | 76 | .868 | 18 | 39 | 57 | 51 | 16 | 1 | ... | 232 | 5.2 | 4.6 | 21.1 |
| 75-76—Boston | 15 | 505 | 80 | 180 | .444 | 38 | 47 | .809 | 18 | 38 | 56 | 51 | 12 | 5 | ... | 198 | 3.7 | 3.4 | 13.2 |
| 76-77—Boston | 9 | 375 | 62 | 167 | .371 | 41 | 50 | .820 | 15 | 34 | 49 | 62 | 8 | 4 | ... | 165 | 5.4 | 6.9 | 18.3 |
| Totals | 172 | 6860 | 1451 | 3329 | .436 | 874 | 1046 | .836 | ... | ... | 1186 | 825 | 60 | 16 | ... | 3776 | 6.9 | 4.8 | 22.0 |

Personal fouls/disqualifications: 1973-74, 43/0. 1974-75, 38/1. 1975-76, 22/0. 1976-77, 33/0. Totals, 517/9.

## NBA ALL-STAR GAME RECORD

| Season Team | Min. | FGM | FGA | Pct. | FTM | FTA | Pct. | Reb | Ast. | PF | Dq. | Pts. |
|---|---|---|---|---|---|---|---|---|---|---|---|---|
| 1966—Boston | 25 | 6 | 16 | .375 | 6 | 6 | 1.000 | 6 | 1 | 2 | 0 | 18 |
| 1967—Boston | 17 | 7 | 14 | .500 | 0 | 0 | ... | 2 | 1 | 1 | 0 | 14 |
| 1968—Boston | 22 | 9 | 15 | .600 | 8 | 11 | .727 | 5 | 4 | 0 | 0 | 26 |
| 1969—Boston | 31 | 6 | 14 | .429 | 2 | 2 | 1.000 | 7 | 2 | 2 | 0 | 14 |
| 1970—Boston | 29 | 7 | 15 | .467 | 3 | 3 | 1.000 | 5 | 7 | 2 | 0 | 17 |
| 1971—Boston | 24 | 6 | 12 | .500 | 0 | 2 | .000 | 3 | 2 | 3 | 0 | 12 |
| 1972—Boston | 24 | 5 | 13 | .385 | 5 | 5 | 1.000 | 3 | 2 | 2 | 0 | 15 |
| 1973—Boston | 22 | 6 | 10 | .600 | 2 | 5 | .400 | 3 | 5 | 1 | 0 | 14 |

| Season Team | Min. | FGM | FGA | Pct. | FTM | FTA | Pct. | REBOUNDS Off. | Def. | Tot. | Ast. | PF | Dq. | St. | Blk. | TO | Pts. |
|---|---|---|---|---|---|---|---|---|---|---|---|---|---|---|---|---|---|
| 1974—Boston | 18 | 5 | 10 | .500 | 0 | 2 | .000 | 0 | 0 | 0 | 2 | 2 | 0 | 1 | 0 | ... | 10 |
| 1975—Boston | 31 | 7 | 12 | .583 | 2 | 2 | 1.000 | 1 | 5 | 6 | 1 | 2 | 0 | 2 | 0 | ... | 16 |
| 1976—Boston | 21 | 3 | 10 | .300 | 3 | 3 | 1.000 | 1 | 1 | 2 | 2 | 0 | 0 | 1 | 0 | ... | 9 |
| 1977—Boston | 17 | 2 | 5 | .400 | 0 | 0 | ... | 0 | 1 | 1 | 1 | 1 | 0 | 0 | 0 | ... | 9 |
| 1978—Boston | 22 | 5 | 8 | .625 | 0 | 0 | ... | 0 | 3 | 3 | 1 | 2 | 0 | 0 | 0 | 4 | 10 |
| Totals | 303 | 74 | 154 | .481 | 31 | 41 | .756 | ... | ... | 46 | 31 | 20 | 0 | 4 | 0 | 4 | 179 |

## HAWKINS, CONNIE    F/C

**PERSONAL:** Born July 17, 1942, in Brooklyn, N.Y. ... 6-8/215 (2,03/97,5). ... Full name: Cornelius L. Hawkins.
**HIGH SCHOOL:** Boys (Brooklyn, N.Y.).
**COLLEGE:** Iowa.
**TRANSACTIONS:** Signed after freshman season by Pittsburgh Rens of American Basketball League (1961). ... ABL ceased operations (December 31, 1962). ... Played with Harlem Globetrotters (1963-64 through 1966-67). ... Signed by Pittsburgh Pipers of the American Basketball Association (1967). ... Pipers franchise transferred to Minnesota (1968). ... Signed as free agent by Phoenix Suns of NBA (June 20, 1969). ... Traded by Suns to Los Angeles Lakers for Keith Erickson and second-round draft choice (October 30, 1973). ... Traded by Lakers to Atlanta Hawks for draft choices (August 8, 1975). ... Waived by Hawks (1976).
**CAREER NOTES:** Community relations representative, Phoenix Suns (1992-93 to present).

### COLLEGIATE RECORD

| Season Team | G | Min. | FGM | FGA | Pct. | FTM | FTA | Pct. | Reb. | Ast. | Pts. | AVERAGES RPG | APG | PPG |
|---|---|---|---|---|---|---|---|---|---|---|---|---|---|---|
| 60-61—Iowa | | | | | Freshman team did not play intercollegiate schedule. | | | | | | | | | |

### ABL REGULAR-SEASON RECORD

**ABL:** ABL Most Valuable Player (1962). ... ABL All-Star first team (1962).

| Season Team | G | Min. | FGM | FGA | Pct. | FTM | FTA | Pct. | Reb. | Ast. | Pts. | AVERAGES RPG | APG | PPG |
|---|---|---|---|---|---|---|---|---|---|---|---|---|---|---|
| 61-62—Pittsburgh | 78 | 3349 | 760 | 1490 | .510 | 622 | 787 | .790 | 1038 | 183 | 2145 | 13.3 | 2.3 | *27.5 |
| 62-63—Pittsburgh | 16 | 668 | 160 | 326 | .491 | 127 | 165 | .770 | 205 | 42 | 447 | 12.8 | 2.6 | 27.9 |
| Totals | 94 | 4017 | 920 | 1816 | .507 | 749 | 952 | .787 | 1243 | 225 | 2592 | 13.2 | 2.4 | 27.6 |

### ABL PLAYOFF RECORD

| Season Team | G | Min. | FGM | FGA | Pct. | FTM | FTA | Pct. | Reb. | Ast. | Pts. | AVERAGES RPG | APG | PPG |
|---|---|---|---|---|---|---|---|---|---|---|---|---|---|---|
| 61-62—Pittsburgh | 1 | 53 | 14 | 23 | .609 | 13 | 14 | .929 | 17 | 4 | 41 | 17.0 | 4.0 | 41.0 |

### ABA REGULAR-SEASON RECORD

**NOTES:** ABA Most Valuable Player (1968). ... ABA All-Star first team (1968 and 1969). ... Member of ABA championship team (1968). ... Led ABA in scoring with 26.79 average (1968).

| Season Team | G | Min. | 2-POINT FGM | FGA | Pct. | 3-POINT FGM | FGA | Pct. | FTM | FTA | Pct. | Reb. | Ast. | Pts. | AVERAGES RPG | APG | PPG |
|---|---|---|---|---|---|---|---|---|---|---|---|---|---|---|---|---|---|
| 67-68—Pittsburgh | 70 | 3146 | 633 | 1214 | .521 | 2 | 9 | .222 | 603 | 789 | .764 | 945 | 320 | 1875 | 13.5 | 4.6 | *26.8 |
| 68-69—Minnesota | 47 | 1852 | 493 | 949 | .520 | 3 | 22 | .136 | 425 | 554 | .767 | 534 | 184 | 1420 | 11.4 | 3.9 | 30.2 |
| Totals | 117 | 4998 | 1126 | 2163 | .521 | 5 | 31 | .161 | 1028 | 1343 | .765 | 1479 | 504 | 3295 | 12.6 | 4.3 | 28.2 |

### ABA PLAYOFF RECORD

| Season Team | G | Min. | 2-POINT FGM | FGA | Pct. | 3-POINT FGM | FGA | Pct. | FTM | FTA | Pct. | Reb. | Ast. | Pts. | AVERAGES RPG | APG | PPG |
|---|---|---|---|---|---|---|---|---|---|---|---|---|---|---|---|---|---|
| 67-68—Pittsburgh | 14 | 616 | 145 | 244 | .594 | 0 | 0 | ... | 129 | 177 | .729 | 172 | 64 | 419 | 12.3 | 4.6 | 29.9 |
| 68-69—Minnesota | 7 | 320 | 61 | 164 | .372 | 4 | 8 | .500 | 40 | 62 | .645 | 86 | 27 | 174 | 12.3 | 3.9 | 24.9 |
| Totals | 21 | 936 | 206 | 408 | .505 | ... | 4 | ... | 169 | 239 | .707 | 258 | 91 | 593 | 12.3 | 4.3 | 28.2 |

### NBA REGULAR-SEASON RECORD

**HONORS:** All-NBA first team (1970).

| Season Team | G | Min. | FGM | FGA | Pct. | FTM | FTA | Pct. | Reb. | Ast. | PF | Dq. | Pts. | AVERAGES RPG | APG | PPG |
|---|---|---|---|---|---|---|---|---|---|---|---|---|---|---|---|---|
| 69-70—Phoenix | 81 | 3312 | 709 | 1447 | .490 | 577 | 741 | .779 | 846 | 391 | 287 | 4 | 1995 | 10.4 | 4.8 | 24.6 |
| 70-71—Phoenix | 71 | 2662 | 512 | 1181 | .434 | 457 | 560 | .816 | 643 | 322 | 197 | 2 | 1481 | 9.1 | 4.5 | 20.9 |
| 71-72—Phoenix | 76 | 2798 | 571 | 1244 | .459 | 456 | 565 | .807 | 633 | 296 | 235 | 2 | 1598 | 8.3 | 3.9 | 21.0 |
| 72-73—Phoenix | 75 | 2768 | 441 | 920 | .479 | 322 | 404 | .797 | 641 | 304 | 229 | 5 | 1204 | 8.5 | 4.1 | 16.1 |

| Season Team | G | Min. | FGM | FGA | Pct. | FTM | FTA | Pct. | REBOUNDS Off. | Def. | Tot. | Ast. | St. | Blk. | TO | Pts. | AVERAGES RPG | APG | PPG |
|---|---|---|---|---|---|---|---|---|---|---|---|---|---|---|---|---|---|---|---|
| 73-74—Pho-Lakers | 79 | 2761 | 404 | 807 | .501 | 191 | 251 | .761 | 146 | 389 | 565 | 407 | 113 | 81 | ... | 999 | 7.2 | 5.2 | 12.6 |
| 74-75—Los Angeles | 43 | 1026 | 139 | 324 | .429 | 68 | 99 | .687 | 54 | 144 | 198 | 120 | 51 | 23 | ... | 346 | 4.6 | 2.8 | 8.0 |
| 75-76—Atlanta | 74 | 1907 | 237 | 530 | .447 | 136 | 191 | .712 | 102 | 343 | 445 | 212 | 80 | 46 | ... | 610 | 6.0 | 2.9 | 8.2 |
| Totals | 499 | 17234 | 3013 | 6453 | .467 | 2207 | 2811 | .785 | ... | ... | 3971 | 2052 | ... | ... | ... | 8233 | 8.0 | 4.1 | 16.5 |

Personal fouls/disqualifications: 1973-74, 223/1. 1974-75, 116/1. 1975-76, 172/2. Totals, 1459/17.

### NBA PLAYOFF RECORD

| Season Team | G | Min. | FGM | FGA | Pct. | FTM | FTA | Pct. | Reb. | Ast. | PF | Dq. | Pts. | AVERAGES RPG | APG | PPG |
|---|---|---|---|---|---|---|---|---|---|---|---|---|---|---|---|---|
| 69-70—Phoenix | 7 | 328 | 62 | 150 | .413 | 54 | 66 | .818 | 97 | 41 | 22 | 0 | 178 | 13.9 | 5.9 | 25.4 |

| Season Team | G | Min. | FGM | FGA | Pct. | FTM | FTA | Pct. | REBOUNDS Off. | Def. | Tot. | Ast. | St. | Blk. | TO | Pts. | AVERAGES RPG | APG | PPG |
|---|---|---|---|---|---|---|---|---|---|---|---|---|---|---|---|---|---|---|---|
| 73-74—Los Angeles | 5 | 172 | 21 | 60 | .350 | 12 | 15 | .800 | 14 | 26 | 40 | 16 | 7 | 1 | ... | 54 | 8.0 | 3.2 | 10.8 |
| Totals | 12 | 500 | 83 | 210 | .395 | 66 | 81 | .815 | ... | ... | 137 | 57 | 7 | 1 | ... | 232 | 11.4 | 4.8 | 19.3 |

Personal fouls/disqualifications: 1973-74, 13/0.

| Season Team | Min. | FGM | FGA | Pct. | FTM | FTA | Pct. | Reb. | Ast. | PF | Dq. | Pts. |
|---|---|---|---|---|---|---|---|---|---|---|---|---|
| 1970—Phoenix | 19 | 2 | 4 | .500 | 6 | 6 | 1.000 | 4 | 2 | 3 | ... | 10 |
| 1971—Phoenix | 1 | 0 | 0 | ... | 0 | 0 | ... | 0 | 0 | 0 | ... | 0 |
| 1972—Phoenix | 14 | 5 | 7 | .714 | 3 | 4 | .750 | 4 | 0 | 1 | 0 | 13 |
| 1973—Phoenix | 11 | 1 | 5 | .200 | 0 | 0 | ... | 2 | 3 | 1 | 0 | 2 |
| Totals | 45 | 8 | 16 | .500 | 9 | 10 | .900 | 10 | 5 | 5 | ... | 25 |

## COMBINED ABA AND NBA REGULAR-SEASON RECORDS

| | G | Min. | FGM | FGA | Pct. | FTM | FTA | Pct. | REBOUNDS Off. | Def. | Tot. | Ast. | Stl. | Blk. | TO | Pts. | AVERAGES RPG | APG | PPG |
|---|---|---|---|---|---|---|---|---|---|---|---|---|---|---|---|---|---|---|---|
| Totals | 616 | 22232 | 4144 | 8647 | .479 | 3235 | 4154 | .779 | ... | ... | 5450 | 2556 | ... | ... | ... | 11528 | 8.8 | 4.1 | 18.7 |

Three-point field goals: 5-for-31 (.161).
Personal fouls/disqualifications: 1873/22.

# HAYES, ELVIN                     F/C

**PERSONAL:** Born November 17, 1945, in Rayville, La. ... 6-9/235 (2,06/106,6). ... Full name: Elvin Ernest Hayes.
**HIGH SCHOOL:** Eula D. Britton (Rayville, La.).
**COLLEGE:** Houston.
**TRANSACTIONS:** Selected by San Diego Rockets in first round (first pick overall) of 1968 NBA Draft. ... Rockets franchise moved from San Diego to Houston for 1971-72 season. ... Traded by Rockets to Baltimore Bullets for F Jack Marin and future considerations (June 23, 1972). ... Bullets franchise moved from Baltimore to Washington and renamed Capital Bullets for 1973-74 season. ... Bullets franchise renamed Washington Bullets for 1974-75 season. ... Traded by Bullets to Rockets for 1981 and 1983 second-round draft choices (June 8, 1981).
**CAREER HONORS:** Elected to Naismith Memorial Basketball Hall of Fame (1990). ... One of the 50 Greatest Players in NBA History (1996).
**MISCELLANEOUS:** Member of NBA championship team (1978). ... Washington Wizards franchise all-time leading scorer with 15,551 points and all-time blocked shots leader with 1,558 (1973-74 through 1980-81).

## COLLEGIATE RECORD

**NOTES:** The Sporting News College Player of the Year (1968). ... The Sporting News All-America first team (1967, 1968). ... The Sporting News All-America second team (1966).

| Season Team | G | Min. | FGM | FGA | Pct. | FTM | FTA | Pct. | Reb. | Ast. | Pts. | AVERAGES RPG | APG | PPG |
|---|---|---|---|---|---|---|---|---|---|---|---|---|---|---|
| 64-65—Houston‡ | 21 | ... | 217 | 478 | .454 | 93 | 176 | .528 | 500 | 43 | 527 | 23.8 | 2.0 | 25.1 |
| 65-66—Houston | 29 | 946 | 323 | 570 | .567 | 143 | 257 | .556 | 490 | 6 | 789 | 16.9 | 0.2 | 27.2 |
| 66-67—Houston | 31 | 1119 | 373 | 750 | .497 | 135 | 227 | .595 | 488 | 33 | 881 | 15.7 | 1.1 | 28.4 |
| 67-68—Houston | 33 | 1270 | 519 | 945 | .549 | 176 | 285 | .618 | 624 | 59 | 1214 | 18.9 | 1.8 | 36.8 |
| Varsity totals | 93 | 3335 | 1215 | 2265 | .536 | 454 | 769 | .590 | 1602 | 98 | 2884 | 17.2 | 1.1 | 31.0 |

## NBA REGULAR-SEASON RECORD

**RECORDS:** Holds single-season record for most minutes played by a rookie—3,695 (1969).
**HONORS:** All-NBA first team (1975, 1977, 1979). ... All-NBA second team (1973, 1974, 1976). ... NBA All-Defensive second team (1974, 1975). ... NBA All-Rookie team (1969).

| Season Team | G | Min. | FGM | FGA | Pct. | FTM | FTA | Pct. | Reb. | Ast. | PF | Dq. | Pts. | AVERAGES RPG | APG | PPG |
|---|---|---|---|---|---|---|---|---|---|---|---|---|---|---|---|---|
| 68-69—San Diego | 82 | *3695 | *930 | *2082 | .447 | 467 | 746 | .626 | 1406 | 113 | 266 | 2 | *2327 | 17.1 | 1.4 | *28.4 |
| 69-70—San Diego | 82 | *3665 | 914 | *2020 | .452 | 428 | 622 | .688 | *1386 | 162 | 270 | 5 | 2256 | 16.9 | 2.0 | 27.5 |
| 70-71—San Diego | 82 | 3633 | 948 | *2215 | .428 | 454 | 676 | .672 | 1362 | 186 | 225 | 1 | 2350 | 16.6 | 2.3 | 28.7 |
| 71-72—Houston | 82 | 3461 | 832 | 1918 | .434 | 399 | 615 | .649 | 1197 | 270 | 233 | 1 | 2063 | 14.6 | 3.3 | 25.2 |
| 72-73—Baltimore | 81 | 3347 | 713 | 1607 | .444 | 291 | 434 | .671 | 1177 | 127 | 232 | 3 | 1717 | 14.5 | 1.6 | 21.2 |

| Season Team | G | Min. | FGM | FGA | Pct. | FTM | FTA | Pct. | REBOUNDS Off. | Def. | Tot. | Ast. | St. | Blk. | TO | Pts. | AVERAGES RPG | APG | PPG |
|---|---|---|---|---|---|---|---|---|---|---|---|---|---|---|---|---|---|---|---|
| 73-74—Capital | 81 | *3602 | 689 | 1627 | .423 | 357 | 495 | .721 | *354 | *1109 | *1463 | 163 | 86 | 240 | ... | 1735 | 18.1 | 2.0 | 21.4 |
| 74-75—Washington | 82 | 3465 | 739 | 1668 | .443 | 409 | 534 | .766 | 221 | 783 | 1004 | 206 | 158 | 187 | ... | 1887 | 12.2 | 2.5 | 23.0 |
| 75-76—Washington | 80 | 2975 | 649 | 1381 | .470 | 287 | 457 | .628 | 210 | 668 | 878 | 121 | 104 | 202 | ... | 1585 | 11.0 | 1.5 | 19.8 |
| 76-77—Washington | 82 | *3364 | 760 | 1516 | .501 | 422 | 614 | .687 | 289 | 740 | 1029 | 158 | 87 | 220 | ... | 1942 | 12.5 | 1.9 | 23.7 |
| 77-78—Washington | 81 | 3246 | 636 | 1409 | .451 | 326 | 514 | .634 | 335 | 740 | 1075 | 149 | 96 | 159 | 229 | 1598 | 13.3 | 1.8 | 19.7 |
| 78-79—Washington | 82 | 3105 | 720 | 1477 | .487 | 349 | 534 | .654 | 312 | 682 | 994 | 143 | 75 | 190 | 235 | 1789 | 12.1 | 1.7 | 21.8 |
| 79-80—Washington | 81 | 3183 | 761 | 1677 | .454 | 334 | 478 | .699 | 269 | 627 | 896 | 129 | 62 | 189 | 215 | 1859 | 11.1 | 1.6 | 23.0 |
| 80-81—Washington | 81 | 2931 | 584 | 1296 | .451 | 271 | 439 | .617 | 235 | 554 | 789 | 98 | 68 | 171 | 189 | 1439 | 9.7 | 1.2 | 17.8 |
| 81-82—Houston | 82 | 3032 | 519 | 1100 | .472 | 280 | 422 | .664 | 267 | 480 | 747 | 144 | 62 | 104 | 208 | 1318 | 9.1 | 1.8 | 16.1 |
| 82-83—Houston | 81 | 2302 | 424 | 890 | .476 | 196 | 287 | .683 | 199 | 417 | 616 | 158 | 50 | 81 | 200 | 1066 | 7.6 | 2.0 | 12.9 |
| 83-84—Houston | 81 | 994 | 158 | 389 | .406 | 86 | 132 | .652 | 87 | 173 | 260 | 71 | 16 | 28 | 82 | 402 | 3.2 | 0.9 | 5.0 |
| Totals | 1303 | 50000 | 10976 | 24272 | .452 | 5356 | 7999 | .670 | ... | ... | 16279 | 2398 | 864 | 1771 | 1358 | 27313 | 12.5 | 1.8 | 21.0 |

Three-point field goals: 1979-80, 3-for-13 (.231). 1980-81, 0-for-10. 1981-82, 0-for-5. 1982-83, 2-for-4 (.500). 1983-84, 0-for-2. Totals, 5-for-34 (.147).
Personal fouls/disqualifications: 1973-74, 252/1. 1974-75, 238/0. 1975-76, 293/5. 1976-77, 312/1. 1977-78, 313/7. 1978-79, 308/5. 1979-80, 309/9. 1980-81, 300/6. 1981-82, 287/4. 1982-83, 232/2. 1983-84, 123/1. Totals, 4193/53.

## NBA PLAYOFF RECORD

**NOTES:** Shares NBA Finals single-game record for most offensive rebounds—11 (May 27, 1979, vs. Seattle).

| Season Team | G | Min. | FGM | FGA | Pct. | FTM | FTA | Pct. | Reb. | Ast. | PF | Dq. | Pts. | AVERAGES RPG | APG | PPG |
|---|---|---|---|---|---|---|---|---|---|---|---|---|---|---|---|---|
| 68-69—San Diego | 6 | 278 | 60 | 114 | .526 | 35 | 53 | .660 | 83 | 5 | 21 | 0 | 155 | 13.8 | 0.8 | 25.8 |
| 72-73—Baltimore | 5 | 228 | 53 | 105 | .505 | 23 | 33 | .697 | 57 | 5 | 16 | 0 | 129 | 11.4 | 1.0 | 25.8 |

| Season Team | G | Min. | FGM | FGA | Pct. | FTM | FTA | Pct. | Off. | Def. | Tot. | Ast. | St. | Blk. | TO | Pts. | RPG | APG | PPG |
|---|---|---|---|---|---|---|---|---|---|---|---|---|---|---|---|---|---|---|---|
| 73-74—Capital ............ | 7 | 323 | 76 | 143 | .531 | 29 | 41 | .707 | 31 | 80 | 111 | 21 | 5 | 15 | ... | 181 | 15.9 | 3.0 | 25.9 |
| 74-75—Washington .... | 17 | 751 | 174 | 372 | .468 | 86 | 127 | .677 | 46 | 140 | 186 | 37 | 26 | 39 | ... | 434 | 10.9 | 2.2 | 25.5 |
| 75-76—Washington .... | 7 | 305 | 54 | 122 | .443 | 32 | 55 | .582 | 16 | 72 | 88 | 10 | 5 | 28 | ... | 140 | 12.6 | 1.4 | 20.0 |
| 76-77—Washington .... | 9 | 405 | 74 | 173 | .428 | 41 | 59 | .695 | 29 | 93 | 122 | 17 | 10 | 22 | ... | 189 | 13.6 | 1.9 | 21.0 |
| 77-78—Washington .... | 21 | 868 | 189 | 385 | .491 | 79 | 133 | .594 | 103 | 176 | 279 | 43 | 32 | 52 | 58 | 457 | 13.3 | 2.0 | 21.8 |
| 78-79—Washington .... | 19 | 786 | 170 | 396 | .429 | 87 | 130 | .669 | 94 | 172 | 266 | 38 | 17 | 52 | 56 | 427 | 14.0 | 2.0 | 22.5 |
| 79-80—Washington .... | 2 | 92 | 16 | 41 | .390 | 8 | 10 | .800 | 10 | 12 | 22 | 6 | 0 | 4 | 4 | 40 | 11.0 | 3.0 | 20.0 |
| 81-82—Houston .......... | 3 | 124 | 17 | 50 | .340 | 8 | 15 | .533 | 7 | 23 | 30 | 3 | 2 | 10 | 6 | 42 | 10.0 | 1.0 | 14.0 |
| Totals ................... | 96 | 4160 | 883 | 1901 | .464 | 428 | 656 | .652 | ... | ... | 1244 | 185 | 77 | 222 | 124 | 2194 | 13.0 | 1.9 | 22.9 |

Personal fouls/disqualifications: 1973-74, 23/0. 1974-75, 70/3. 1975-76, 24/0. 1976-77, 39/0. 1977-78, 86/2. 1978-79, 79/3. 1979-80, 8/0. 1981-82, 12/0. Totals, 378/8.

### NBA ALL-STAR GAME RECORD

| Season Team | Min. | FGM | FGA | Pct. | FTM | FTA | Pct. | Reb. | Ast. | PF | Dq. | Pts. |
|---|---|---|---|---|---|---|---|---|---|---|---|---|
| 1969—San Diego .................... | 21 | 4 | 9 | .444 | 3 | 3 | 1.000 | 5 | 0 | 4 | 0 | 11 |
| 1970—San Diego .................... | 35 | 9 | 21 | .429 | 6 | 12 | .500 | 15 | 1 | 1 | 0 | 24 |
| 1971—San Diego .................... | 19 | 4 | 13 | .308 | 2 | 3 | .667 | 4 | 2 | 1 | 0 | 10 |
| 1972—Houston ........................ | 11 | 1 | 6 | .167 | 2 | 2 | 1.000 | 2 | 0 | 2 | 0 | 4 |
| 1973—Baltimore ..................... | 16 | 4 | 13 | .308 | 2 | 2 | 1.000 | 12 | 0 | 0 | 0 | 10 |

| Season Team | Min. | FGM | FGA | Pct. | FTM | FTA | Pct. | Off. | Def. | Tot. | Ast. | PF | Dq. | St. | Blk. | TO | Pts. |
|---|---|---|---|---|---|---|---|---|---|---|---|---|---|---|---|---|---|
| 1974—Capital .................. | 35 | 5 | 13 | .385 | 2 | 3 | .667 | 4 | 11 | 15 | 6 | 4 | 0 | 0 | 1 | ... | 12 |
| 1975—Washington .......... | 17 | 2 | 6 | .333 | 0 | 0 | ... | 0 | 5 | 5 | 2 | 1 | 0 | 1 | 0 | ... | 4 |
| 1976—Washington .......... | 31 | 6 | 14 | .429 | 0 | 2 | .000 | 3 | 7 | 10 | 1 | 5 | 0 | 1 | 0 | ... | 12 |
| 1977—Washington .......... | 11 | 6 | 6 | 1.000 | 0 | 0 | ... | 0 | 2 | 2 | 1 | 5 | 0 | 0 | 0 | ... | 12 |
| 1978—Washington .......... | 11 | 1 | 7 | .143 | 0 | 0 | ... | 3 | 1 | 4 | 0 | 4 | 0 | 1 | 0 | 1 | 2 |
| 1979—Washington .......... | 28 | 5 | 11 | .455 | 3 | 5 | .600 | 4 | 9 | 13 | 0 | 5 | 0 | 1 | 1 | 1 | 13 |
| 1980—Washington .......... | 29 | 5 | 10 | .500 | 2 | 2 | 1.000 | 2 | 3 | 5 | 4 | 5 | 0 | 1 | 4 | 3 | 12 |
| Totals.......................... | 264 | 52 | 129 | .403 | 22 | 34 | .647 | ... | ... | 92 | 17 | 37 | 0 | 5 | 6 | 5 | 126 |

# HAYWOOD, SPENCER     F/C

**PERSONAL:** Born April 22, 1949, in Silver City, Miss. ... 6-9/225 (2,05/102,1). ... Full name: Spencer Haywood.
**HIGH SCHOOL:** Pershing (Detroit).
**JUNIOR COLLEGE:** Trinidad State Junior College (Colo.).
**COLLEGE:** Detroit.
**TRANSACTIONS:** Signed as free agent after sophomore season by Denver Rockets of American Basketball Association (August 16, 1969). ... Selected by Buffalo Braves in second round (30th pick overall) of 1971 NBA Draft. ... Terminated contract with Rockets and signed by Seattle SuperSonics (1971). ... Traded by SuperSonics to New York Knicks for cash and the option of F Eugene Short or future draft choice (October 24, 1975). ... Traded by Knicks to New Orleans Jazz for C Joe C. Meriweather (January 5, 1979). ... Jazz franchise moved from New Orleans to Utah for 1979-80 season. ... Traded by Jazz to Los Angeles Lakers for F Adrian Dantley (September 13, 1979). ... Waived by Lakers (August 19, 1980). ... Played in Italy (1980-81 and 1981-82). ... Signed as free agent by Washington Bullets (October 24, 1981). ... Waived by Bullets (March 9, 1983).
**MISCELLANEOUS:** Member of NBA championship team (1980). ... Member of gold-medal-winning U.S. Olympic team (1968).

### COLLEGIATE RECORD

**NOTES:** The Sporting News All-America first team (1969). ... Led NCAA Division I with 22.1 rebounds per game (1969).

| Season Team | G | Min. | FGM | FGA | Pct. | FTM | FTA | Pct. | Reb. | Ast. | Pts. | RPG | APG | PPG |
|---|---|---|---|---|---|---|---|---|---|---|---|---|---|---|
| 67-68—Trinidad State J.C. .......... | 30 | ... | 358 | 675 | .530 | 129 | 195 | .662 | 663 | ... | 845 | 22.1 | ... | 28.2 |
| 68-69—Detroit .......................... | 24 | ... | 288 | 508 | .567 | 195 | 254 | .768 | 530 | ... | 771 | 22.1 | ... | 32.1 |
| Junior college totals .............. | 30 | ... | 358 | 675 | .530 | 129 | 195 | .662 | 663 | ... | 845 | 22.1 | ... | 28.2 |
| 4-year-college totals .............. | 24 | ... | 288 | 508 | .567 | 195 | 254 | .768 | 530 | ... | 771 | 22.1 | ... | 32.1 |

### ABA REGULAR-SEASON RECORD

**NOTES:** ABA Most Valuable Player (1970). ... ABA Rookie of the Year (1970). ... ABA All-Star first team (1970). ... ABA All-Rookie team (1970). ... Holds single-season records for most minutes played—3,808; most field goals made—986; most rebounds—1,637; and highest rebounds-per-game average—19.5 (1970).

| Season Team | G | Min. | FGM | FGA | Pct. | FGM | FGA | Pct. | FTM | FTA | Pct. | Reb. | Ast. | Pts. | RPG | APG | PPG |
|---|---|---|---|---|---|---|---|---|---|---|---|---|---|---|---|---|---|
| | | | 2-POINT | | | 3-POINT | | | | | | | | | AVERAGES | | |
| 69-70—Denver ..................... | 84 | *3808 | *986 | 1987 | .496 | 0 | 11 | .000 | 547 | 705 | .776 | *1637 | 190 | *2519 | *19.5 | 2.3 | *30.0 |

### ABA PLAYOFF RECORD

| Season Team | G | Min. | FGM | FGA | Pct. | FGM | FGA | Pct. | FTM | FTA | Pct. | Reb. | Ast. | Pts. | RPG | APG | PPG |
|---|---|---|---|---|---|---|---|---|---|---|---|---|---|---|---|---|---|
| | | | 2-POINT | | | 3-POINT | | | | | | | | | AVERAGES | | |
| 69-70—Denver ..................... | 12 | 568 | 185 | 362 | .511 | 1 | 5 | .200 | 69 | 83 | .831 | 237 | 39 | 440 | 19.8 | 3.3 | 36.7 |

### ABA ALL-STAR GAME RECORD

**NOTES:** ABA All-Star Game Most Valuable Player (1970).

| Season Team | Min. | FGM | FGA | Pct. | FGM | FGA | Pct. | FTM | FTA | Pct. | Reb. | Ast. | Pts. |
|---|---|---|---|---|---|---|---|---|---|---|---|---|---|---|
| | | 2-POINT | | | 3-POINT | | | | | | | | |
| 1970—Denver............................... | 39 | 10 | 19 | .526 | 0 | 0 | ... | 3 | 4 | .750 | 19 | 2 | 23 |

**HONORS:** All-NBA first team (1972, 1973). ... All-NBA second team (1974, 1975).

| Season Team | G | Min. | FGM | FGA | Pct. | FTM | FTA | Pct. | Reb. | Ast. | PF | Dq. | Pts. | AVERAGES RPG | APG | PPG |
|---|---|---|---|---|---|---|---|---|---|---|---|---|---|---|---|---|
| 70-71—Seattle | 33 | 1162 | 260 | 579 | .449 | 160 | 218 | .734 | 396 | 48 | 84 | 1 | 680 | 12.0 | 1.5 | 20.6 |
| 71-72—Seattle | 73 | 3167 | 717 | 1557 | .461 | 480 | 586 | .819 | 926 | 148 | 208 | 0 | 1914 | 12.7 | 2.0 | 26.2 |
| 72-73—Seattle | 77 | 3259 | 889 | 1868 | .476 | 473 | 564 | .839 | 995 | 196 | 213 | 2 | 2251 | 12.9 | 2.5 | 29.2 |

| Season Team | G | Min. | FGM | FGA | Pct. | FTM | FTA | Pct. | REBOUNDS Off. | Def. | Tot. | Ast. | St. | Blk. | TO | Pts. | AVERAGES RPG | APG | PPG |
|---|---|---|---|---|---|---|---|---|---|---|---|---|---|---|---|---|---|---|---|
| 73-74—Seattle | 75 | 3039 | 694 | 1520 | .457 | 373 | 458 | .814 | 318 | 689 | 1007 | 240 | 65 | 106 | ... | 1761 | 13.4 | 3.2 | 23.5 |
| 74-75—Seattle | 68 | 2529 | 608 | 1325 | .459 | 309 | 381 | .811 | 198 | 432 | 630 | 137 | 54 | 108 | ... | 1525 | 9.3 | 2.0 | 22.4 |
| 75-76—Seattle | 78 | 2892 | 605 | 1360 | .445 | 339 | 448 | .757 | 234 | 644 | 878 | 92 | 53 | 80 | ... | 1549 | 11.3 | 1.2 | 19.9 |
| 76-77—N.Y. Knicks | 31 | 1021 | 202 | 449 | .450 | 109 | 131 | .832 | 77 | 203 | 280 | 50 | 14 | 29 | ... | 513 | 9.0 | 1.6 | 16.5 |
| 77-78—New York | 67 | 1765 | 412 | 852 | .484 | 96 | 135 | .711 | 141 | 301 | 442 | 126 | 37 | 72 | 140 | 920 | 6.6 | 1.9 | 13.7 |
| 78-79—N.Y.-N.O. | 68 | 2361 | 595 | 1205 | .494 | 231 | 292 | .791 | 172 | 361 | 533 | 127 | 40 | 82 | 200 | 1421 | 7.8 | 1.9 | 20.9 |
| 79-80—Los Angeles | 76 | 1544 | 288 | 591 | .487 | 159 | 206 | .772 | 132 | 214 | 346 | 93 | 35 | 57 | 134 | 736 | 4.6 | 1.2 | 9.7 |
| 81-82—Washington | 76 | 2086 | 395 | 829 | .476 | 219 | 260 | .842 | 144 | 278 | 422 | 64 | 45 | 68 | 175 | 1009 | 5.6 | 0.8 | 13.3 |
| 82-83—Washington | 38 | 775 | 125 | 312 | .401 | 63 | 87 | .724 | 77 | 106 | 183 | 30 | 12 | 27 | 67 | 313 | 4.8 | 0.8 | 8.2 |
| **Totals** | 760 | 25600 | 5790 | 12447 | .465 | 3011 | 3766 | .800 | ... | ... | 7038 | 1351 | 355 | 629 | 716 | 14592 | 9.3 | 1.8 | 19.2 |

Three-point field goals: 1979-80, 1-for-4 (.250). 1981-82, 0-for-3. 1982-83, 0-for-1. Totals, 1-for-8 (.125).
Personal fouls/disqualifications: 1973-74, 198/2. 1974-75, 173/1. 1975-76, 255/1. 1976-77, 72/0. 1977-78, 188/1. 1978-79, 236/8. 1979-80, 197/2. 1981-82, 249/6. 1982-83, 94/2. Totals, 2167/26.

### NBA PLAYOFF RECORD

| Season Team | G | Min. | FGM | FGA | Pct. | FTM | FTA | Pct. | REBOUNDS Off. | Def. | Tot. | Ast. | St. | Blk. | TO | Pts. | AVERAGES RPG | APG | PPG |
|---|---|---|---|---|---|---|---|---|---|---|---|---|---|---|---|---|---|---|---|
| 74-75—Seattle | 9 | 337 | 47 | 131 | .359 | 47 | 61 | .771 | 20 | 61 | 81 | 18 | 7 | 11 | ... | 141 | 9.0 | 2.0 | 15.7 |
| 77-78—New York | 6 | 177 | 43 | 85 | .506 | 11 | 11 | 1.000 | 19 | 23 | 42 | 12 | 2 | 5 | 10 | 97 | 7.0 | 2.0 | 16.2 |
| 79-80—Los Angeles | 11 | 145 | 25 | 53 | .472 | 13 | 16 | .813 | 14 | 12 | 26 | 4 | 0 | 6 | 20 | 63 | 2.4 | 0.4 | 5.7 |
| 81-82—Washington | 7 | 231 | 57 | 115 | .496 | 26 | 35 | .743 | 16 | 23 | 39 | 7 | 4 | 14 | 15 | 140 | 5.6 | 1.0 | 20.0 |
| **Totals** | 33 | 890 | 172 | 384 | .448 | 97 | 123 | .789 | 69 | 119 | 188 | 41 | 13 | 36 | 45 | 441 | 5.7 | 1.2 | 13.4 |

Three-point field goals: 1979-80, 0-for-1.
Personal fouls/disqualifications: 1974-75, 29/0. 1977-78, 24/1. 1979-80, 17/0. 1981-82, 28/0. Totals, 98/1.

### NBA ALL-STAR GAME RECORD

| Season Team | Min. | FGM | FGA | Pct. | FTM | FTA | Pct. | Reb. | Ast. | PF | Dq. | Pts. |
|---|---|---|---|---|---|---|---|---|---|---|---|---|
| 1972—Seattle | 25 | 4 | 10 | .400 | 3 | 4 | .750 | 7 | 1 | 2 | 0 | 11 |
| 1973—Seattle | 22 | 5 | 10 | .500 | 2 | 2 | 1.000 | 10 | 0 | 5 | 0 | 12 |

| Season Team | Min. | FGM | FGA | Pct. | FTM | FTA | Pct. | REBOUNDS Off. | Def. | Tot. | Ast. | PF | Dq. | St. | Blk. | TO | Pts. |
|---|---|---|---|---|---|---|---|---|---|---|---|---|---|---|---|---|---|
| 1974—Seattle | 33 | 10 | 17 | .588 | 3 | 3 | 1.000 | 2 | 9 | 11 | 5 | 5 | 0 | 0 | 3 | ... | 23 |
| 1975—Seattle | 17 | 1 | 9 | .111 | 0 | 0 | ... | 1 | 2 | 3 | 0 | 1 | 0 | 0 | 0 | ... | 2 |
| **Totals** | 97 | 20 | 46 | .435 | 8 | 9 | .889 | ... | ... | 31 | 6 | 13 | 0 | 0 | 3 | | 48 |

### COMBINED ABA AND NBA REGULAR-SEASON RECORDS

| | G | Min. | FGM | FGA | Pct. | FTM | FTA | Pct. | REBOUNDS Off. | Def. | Tot. | Ast. | Stl. | Blk. | TO | Pts. | AVERAGES RPG | APG | PPG |
|---|---|---|---|---|---|---|---|---|---|---|---|---|---|---|---|---|---|---|---|
| Totals | 844 | 29408 | 6776 | 14445 | .470 | 3558 | 4471 | .796 | ... | ... | 8675 | 1541 | ... | ... | ... | 17111 | 10.3 | 1.8 | 20.3 |

Three-point field goals: 1-for-19 (.053).
Personal fouls/disqualifications: 2388/27.

### ITALIAN LEAGUE RECORD

| Season Team | G | Min. | FGM | FGA | Pct. | FTM | FTA | Pct. | Reb. | Ast. | Pts. | AVERAGES RPG | APG | PPG |
|---|---|---|---|---|---|---|---|---|---|---|---|---|---|---|
| 80-81—Venezia | 34 | ... | 334 | 601 | .556 | 132 | 179 | .737 | 354 | ... | 800 | 10.4 | ... | 23.5 |
| 81-82—Carrera | 5 | 175 | 63 | 100 | .630 | 24 | 32 | .750 | 37 | ... | 150 | 7.4 | ... | 30.0 |
| **Totals** | 39 | | 397 | 701 | .566 | 156 | 211 | .739 | 391 | ... | 950 | 10.0 | ... | 24.4 |

## HEINSOHN, TOM                                        F

See All-Time Great Coaches, page 466.

## HORNACEK, JEFF                                       G

**PERSONAL:** Born May 3, 1963, in Elmhurst, Ill. ... 6-4/190. (1.93 m/86 kg). ... Full Name: Jeffrey John Hornacek. ... Name pronounced HORN-a-sek.
**HIGH SCHOOL:** Lyons Township (La Grange, Ill.).
**COLLEGE:** Iowa State.
**TRANSACTIONS/CAREER NOTES:** Selected by Phoenix Suns in second round (46th pick overall) of 1986 NBA Draft. ... Traded by Suns with C Andrew Lang and F Tim Perry to Philadelphia 76ers for F Charles Barkley (June 17, 1992). ... Traded by 76ers with G Sean Green and 1995 or 1996 second-round draft choice to Utah Jazz for G Jeff Malone and 1994 conditional first-round draft choice (February 24, 1994). ... Announced retirement effective at end of 1999-2000 season.

### COLLEGIATE RECORD

| Season Team | G | Min. | FGM | FGA | Pct. | FTM | FTA | Pct. | Reb. | Ast. | Pts. | AVERAGES RPG | APG | PPG |
|---|---|---|---|---|---|---|---|---|---|---|---|---|---|---|
| 81-82—Iowa State | | | | | | Did not play—redshirted. | | | | | | | | |
| 82-83—Iowa State | 27 | 583 | 57 | 135 | .422 | 32 | 45 | .711 | 62 | 82 | 146 | 2.3 | 3.0 | 5.4 |
| 83-84—Iowa State | 29 | 1065 | 104 | 208 | .500 | 83 | 105 | .790 | 101 | 198 | 291 | 3.5 | 6.8 | 10.0 |
| 84-85—Iowa State | 34 | 1224 | 172 | 330 | .521 | 81 | 96 | .844 | 122 | 166 | 425 | 3.6 | 4.9 | 12.5 |
| 85-86—Iowa State | 33 | 1229 | 177 | 370 | .478 | 97 | 125 | .776 | 127 | 219 | 451 | 3.8 | 6.6 | 13.7 |
| **Totals** | 123 | 4101 | 510 | 1043 | .489 | 293 | 371 | .790 | 412 | 665 | 1313 | 3.3 | 5.4 | 10.7 |

**RECORDS:** Shares single-game record for most three-point field goals without a miss—8 (November 23, 1994, vs. Seattle).

**HONORS:** Long Distance Shootout winner (1998 and 2000).

| Season Team | G | Min. | FGM | FGA | Pct. | FTM | FTA | Pct. | Off. | Def. | Tot. | Ast. | St. | Blk. | TO | Pts. | RPG | APG | PPG |
|---|---|---|---|---|---|---|---|---|---|---|---|---|---|---|---|---|---|---|---|
| | | | | | | | | | REBOUNDS | | | | | | | | AVERAGES | | |
| 86-87—Phoenix ......... | 80 | 1561 | 159 | 350 | .454 | 94 | 121 | .777 | 41 | 143 | 184 | 361 | 70 | 5 | 153 | 424 | 2.3 | 4.5 | 5.3 |
| 87-88—Phoenix ......... | 82 | 2243 | 306 | 605 | .506 | 152 | 185 | .822 | 71 | 191 | 262 | 540 | 107 | 10 | 156 | 781 | 3.2 | 6.6 | 9.5 |
| 88-89—Phoenix ......... | 78 | 2487 | 440 | 889 | .495 | 147 | 178 | .826 | 75 | 191 | 266 | 465 | 129 | 8 | 111 | 1054 | 3.4 | 6.0 | 13.5 |
| 89-90—Phoenix ......... | 67 | 2278 | 483 | 901 | .536 | 173 | 202 | .856 | 86 | 227 | 313 | 337 | 117 | 14 | 125 | 1179 | 4.7 | 5.0 | 17.6 |
| 90-91—Phoenix ......... | 80 | 2733 | 544 | 1051 | .518 | 201 | 224 | .897 | 74 | 247 | 321 | 409 | 111 | 16 | 130 | 1350 | 4.0 | 5.1 | 16.9 |
| 91-92—Phoenix ......... | 81 | 3078 | 635 | 1240 | .512 | 279 | 315 | .886 | 106 | 301 | 407 | 411 | 158 | 31 | 170 | 1632 | 5.0 | 5.1 | 20.1 |
| 92-93—Philadelphia .... | 79 | 2860 | 582 | 1239 | .470 | 259 | 289 | .865 | 84 | 258 | 342 | 548 | 131 | 21 | 222 | 1511 | 4.3 | 6.9 | 19.1 |
| 93-94—Phil.-Utah ....... | 80 | 2820 | 472 | 1004 | .470 | 260 | 296 | .878 | 60 | 219 | 279 | 419 | 127 | 13 | 171 | 1274 | 3.5 | 5.2 | 15.9 |
| 94-95—Utah............... | 81 | 2696 | 482 | 937 | .514 | 284 | 322 | .882 | 53 | 157 | 210 | 347 | 129 | 17 | 145 | 1337 | 2.6 | 4.3 | 16.5 |
| 95-96—Utah............... | 82 | 2588 | 442 | 880 | .502 | 259 | 290 | .893 | 62 | 147 | 209 | 340 | 106 | 20 | 127 | 1247 | 2.5 | 4.1 | 15.2 |
| 96-97—Utah............... | 82 | 2592 | 413 | 856 | .482 | 293 | 326 | .899 | 60 | 181 | 241 | 361 | 124 | 26 | 134 | 1191 | 2.9 | 4.4 | 14.5 |
| 97-98—Utah............... | 80 | 2460 | 399 | 828 | .482 | 285 | 322 | .885 | 65 | 205 | 270 | 349 | 109 | 15 | 132 | 1139 | 3.4 | 4.4 | 14.2 |
| 98-99—Utah............... | 48 | 1435 | 214 | 449 | .477 | 125 | 140 | .893 | 33 | 127 | 160 | 192 | 52 | 14 | 82 | 587 | 3.3 | 4.0 | 12.2 |
| 99-00—Utah............... | 77 | 2133 | 358 | 728 | .492 | 171 | 180 | *.950 | 49 | 133 | 182 | 202 | 66 | 16 | 113 | 953 | 2.4 | 2.6 | 12.4 |
| Totals ................. | 1077 | 33964 | 5929 | 11957 | .496 | 2973 | 3390 | .877 | 919 | 2727 | 3646 | 5281 | 1536 | 226 | 1971 | 15659 | 3.4 | 4.9 | 14.5 |

Three-point field goals: 1986-87, 12-for-43 (.279). 1987-88, 17-for-58 (.293). 1988-89, 27-for-81 (.333). 1989-90, 40-for-98 (.408). 1990-91, 61-for-146 (.418). 1991-92, 83-for-189 (.439). 1992-93, 97-for-249 (.390). 1993-94, 70-for-208 (.337). 1994-95, 89-for-219 (.406). 1995-96, 104-for-223 (.466). 1996-97, 72-for-195 (.369). 1997-98, 56-for-127 (.441). 1998-99, 34-for-81 (.420). 1999-00, 66-for-138 (.478). Totals, 828-for-2055 (.403).

Personal fouls/disqualifications: 1986-87, 130/0. 1987-88, 151/0. 1988-89, 188/0. 1989-90, 144/2. 1990-91, 185/1. 1991-92, 218/1. 1992-93, 203/2. 1993-94, 186/0. 1994-95, 181/1. 1995-96, 171/1. 1996-97, 188/1. 1997-98, 175/1. 1998-99, 95/0. 1999-00, 149/1. Totals, 2364/11.

### NBA PLAYOFF RECORD

| Season Team | G | Min. | FGM | FGA | Pct. | FTM | FTA | Pct. | Off. | Def. | Tot. | Ast. | St. | Blk. | TO | Pts. | RPG | APG | PPG |
|---|---|---|---|---|---|---|---|---|---|---|---|---|---|---|---|---|---|---|---|
| | | | | | | | | | REBOUNDS | | | | | | | | AVERAGES | | |
| 88-89—Phoenix ......... | 12 | 374 | 74 | 149 | .497 | 21 | 25 | .840 | 25 | 44 | 69 | 62 | 16 | 3 | 18 | 169 | 5.8 | 5.2 | 14.1 |
| 89-90—Phoenix ......... | 16 | 583 | 112 | 219 | .511 | 68 | 73 | .932 | 13 | 49 | 62 | 73 | 24 | 0 | 34 | 298 | 3.9 | 4.6 | 18.6 |
| 90-91—Phoenix ......... | 4 | 145 | 22 | 51 | .431 | 26 | 28 | .929 | 3 | 22 | 25 | 8 | 3 | 2 | 3 | 73 | 6.3 | 2.0 | 18.3 |
| 91-92—Phoenix ......... | 8 | 343 | 62 | 128 | .484 | 31 | 34 | .912 | 12 | 39 | 51 | 42 | 14 | 2 | 19 | 163 | 6.4 | 5.3 | 20.4 |
| 93-94—Utah ............. | 16 | 558 | 85 | 179 | .475 | 62 | 68 | .912 | 11 | 28 | 39 | 64 | 24 | 6 | 28 | 247 | 2.4 | 4.0 | 15.4 |
| 94-95—Utah ............. | 5 | 178 | 26 | 51 | .510 | 11 | 14 | .786 | 3 | 3 | 6 | 20 | 8 | 1 | 7 | 70 | 1.2 | 4.0 | 14.0 |
| 95-96—Utah ............. | 18 | 644 | 104 | 207 | .502 | 73 | 82 | .890 | 22 | 43 | 65 | 60 | 19 | 3 | 27 | 315 | 3.6 | 3.3 | 17.5 |
| 96-97—Utah ............. | 20 | 704 | 90 | 208 | .433 | 92 | 105 | .876 | 22 | 67 | 89 | 73 | 21 | 4 | 36 | 291 | 4.5 | 3.7 | 14.6 |
| 97-98—Utah ............. | 20 | 636 | 74 | 178 | .416 | 55 | 65 | .846 | 7 | 43 | 50 | 64 | 20 | 4 | 32 | 217 | 2.5 | 3.2 | 10.9 |
| 98-99—Utah ............. | 11 | 304 | 49 | 106 | .462 | 29 | 33 | .879 | 9 | 32 | 41 | 26 | 11 | 0 | 12 | 134 | 3.7 | 2.4 | 12.2 |
| 99-00—Utah ............. | 10 | 297 | 43 | 102 | .422 | 20 | 24 | .833 | 9 | 21 | 30 | 33 | 10 | 0 | 15 | 115 | 3.0 | 3.3 | 11.5 |
| Totals ................. | 140 | 4766 | 741 | 1578 | .470 | 488 | 551 | .886 | 136 | 391 | 527 | 525 | 170 | 25 | 231 | 2092 | 3.8 | 3.8 | 14.9 |

Three-point field goals: 1988-89, 0-for-7. 1989-90, 6-for-24 (.250). 1990-91, 3-for-6 (.500). 1991-92, 8-for-17 (.471). 1993-94, 15-for-34 (.441). 1994-95, 7-for-13 (.538). 1995-96, 34-for-58 (.586). 1996-97, 19-for-53 (.358). 1997-98, 14-for-30 (.467). 1998-99, 7-for-18 (.389). 1999-00, 9-for-22 (.409). Totals, 122-for-282 (.433).

Personal fouls/disqualifications: 1988-89, 34/0. 1989-90, 43/1. 1990-91, 13/0. 1991-92, 23/0. 1993-94, 45/0. 1994-95, 19/1. 1995-96, 41/1. 1996-97, 53/1. 1997-98, 51/1. 1998-99, 34/1. 1999-00, 28/0. Totals, 384/6.

### NBA ALL-STAR GAME RECORD

| Season Team | Min. | FGM | FGA | Pct. | FTM | FTA | Pct. | Off. | Def. | Tot. | Ast. | PF | Dq. | St. | Blk. | TO | Pts. |
|---|---|---|---|---|---|---|---|---|---|---|---|---|---|---|---|---|---|
| | | | | | | | | REBOUNDS | | | | | | | | | |
| 1992—Phoenix................. | 24 | 5 | 7 | .714 | 0 | 0 | ... | 1 | 1 | 2 | 3 | 0 | 0 | 1 | 0 | 0 | 11 |
| Totals........................... | 24 | 5 | 7 | .714 | 0 | 0 | ... | 1 | 1 | 2 | 3 | 0 | 0 | 1 | 0 | 0 | 11 |

Three-point field goals: 1992, 1-for-2 (.500). Totals, 1-for-2 (.500).

## HOWELL, BAILEY                                      F

**PERSONAL:** Born January 20, 1937, in Middleton, Tenn. ... 6-7/220 (2,00/99,8). ... Full name: Bailey E. Howell.

**HIGH SCHOOL:** Middleton (Tenn.).

**COLLEGE:** Mississippi State.

**TRANSACTIONS:** Selected by Detroit Pistons in first round of 1959 NBA Draft. ... Traded by Pistons with C/F Bob Ferry, G Don Ohl, G Wali Jones and F Les Hunter to Baltimore Bullets for F/G Terry Dischinger, F Don Kojis and G Rod Thorn (June 18, 1964). ... Traded by Bullets to Boston Celtics for F/C Mel Counts (September 1, 1966). ... Selected by Buffalo Braves from Celtics in NBA Expansion Draft (May 11, 1970). ... Traded by Braves to Philadelphia 76ers for C Bob Kauffman and cash or future draft choice (May 11, 1970).

**CAREER HONORS:** Elected to Naismith Memorial Basketball Hall of Fame (1997).

**MISCELLANEOUS:** Member of NBA championship team (1968, 1969).

### COLLEGIATE RECORD

**NOTES:** The Sporting News All-America first team (1959). ... Led NCAA major college division with .568 field goal percentage (1957).

| Season Team | G | Min. | FGM | FGA | Pct. | FTM | FTA | Pct. | Reb. | Ast. | Pts. | RPG | APG | PPG |
|---|---|---|---|---|---|---|---|---|---|---|---|---|---|---|
| | | | | | | | | | | | | AVERAGES | | |
| 55-56—Mississippi State‡ .......... | | | | | Freshman team statistics unavailable. | | | | | | | | | |
| 56-57—Mississippi State ........... | 25 | ... | 217 | 382 | .568 | 213 | 285 | .747 | 492 | ... | 647 | 19.7 | ... | 25.9 |
| 57-58—Mississippi State ........... | 25 | ... | 226 | 439 | .515 | 243 | 315 | .771 | 406 | ... | 695 | 16.2 | ... | 27.8 |
| 58-59—Mississippi State ........... | 25 | ... | 231 | 464 | .498 | 226 | 292 | .774 | 379 | ... | 688 | 15.2 | ... | 27.5 |
| Varsity totals ........................ | 75 | ... | 674 | 1285 | .525 | 682 | 892 | .765 | 1277 | ... | 2030 | 17.0 | ... | 27.1 |

ALL-TIME GREAT PLAYERS

## NBA REGULAR-SEASON RECORD

**HONORS:** All-NBA second team (1963).

| Season Team | G | Min. | FGM | FGA | Pct. | FTM | FTA | Pct. | Reb. | Ast. | PF | Dq. | Pts. | RPG | APG | PPG |
|---|---|---|---|---|---|---|---|---|---|---|---|---|---|---|---|---|
| 59-60—Detroit | 75 | 2346 | 510 | 1119 | .456 | 312 | 422 | .739 | 790 | 63 | 282 | 13 | 1332 | 10.5 | 0.8 | 17.8 |
| 60-61—Detroit | 77 | 2952 | 607 | 1293 | .469 | 601 | 798 | .753 | 1111 | 196 | 297 | 10 | 1815 | 14.4 | 2.5 | 23.6 |
| 61-62—Detroit | 79 | 2857 | 553 | 1193 | .464 | 470 | 612 | .768 | 996 | 186 | 317 | 10 | 1576 | 12.6 | 2.4 | 19.9 |
| 62-63—Detroit | 79 | 2971 | 637 | 1235 | .516 | 519 | 650 | .798 | 910 | 232 | 300 | 9 | 1793 | 11.5 | 2.9 | 22.7 |
| 63-64—Detroit | 77 | 2700 | 598 | 1267 | .472 | 470 | 581 | .809 | 776 | 205 | 290 | 9 | 1666 | 10.1 | 2.7 | 21.6 |
| 64-65—Baltimore | 80 | 2975 | 515 | 1040 | .495 | 504 | 629 | .801 | 869 | 208 | *345 | 10 | 1534 | 10.9 | 2.6 | 19.2 |
| 65-66—Baltimore | 78 | 2328 | 481 | 986 | .488 | 402 | 551 | .730 | 773 | 155 | 306 | 12 | 1364 | 9.9 | 2.0 | 17.5 |
| 66-67—Boston | 81 | 2503 | 636 | 1242 | .512 | 349 | 471 | .741 | 677 | 103 | 296 | 4 | 1621 | 8.4 | 1.3 | 20.0 |
| 67-68—Boston | 82 | 2801 | 643 | 1336 | .481 | 335 | 461 | .727 | 805 | 133 | 285 | 4 | 1621 | 9.8 | 1.6 | 19.8 |
| 68-69—Boston | 78 | 2527 | 612 | 1257 | .487 | 313 | 426 | .735 | 685 | 137 | 285 | 3 | 1537 | 8.8 | 1.8 | 19.7 |
| 69-70—Boston | 82 | 2078 | 399 | 931 | .429 | 235 | 308 | .763 | 550 | 120 | 261 | 4 | 1033 | 6.7 | 1.5 | 12.6 |
| 70-71—Philadelphia | 82 | 1589 | 324 | 686 | .472 | 230 | 315 | .730 | 441 | 115 | 234 | 2 | 878 | 5.4 | 1.4 | 10.7 |
| Totals | 950 | 30627 | 6515 | 13585 | .480 | 4740 | 6224 | .762 | 9383 | 1853 | 3498 | 90 | 17770 | 9.9 | 2.0 | 18.7 |

## NBA PLAYOFF RECORD

| Season Team | G | Min. | FGM | FGA | Pct. | FTM | FTA | Pct. | Reb. | Ast. | PF | Dq. | Pts. | RPG | APG | PPG |
|---|---|---|---|---|---|---|---|---|---|---|---|---|---|---|---|---|
| 59-60—Detroit | 2 | 72 | 14 | 41 | .341 | 6 | 8 | .750 | 17 | 3 | 8 | 0 | 34 | 8.5 | 1.5 | 17.0 |
| 60-61—Detroit | 5 | 144 | 20 | 57 | .351 | 16 | 23 | .696 | 46 | 22 | 22 | 1 | 56 | 9.2 | 4.4 | 11.2 |
| 61-62—Detroit | 10 | 378 | 69 | 163 | .423 | 62 | 75 | .827 | 96 | 23 | 48 | 3 | 200 | 9.6 | 2.3 | 20.0 |
| 62-63—Detroit | 4 | 163 | 24 | 64 | .375 | 23 | 27 | .852 | 42 | 11 | 19 | 1 | 71 | 10.5 | 2.8 | 17.8 |
| 64-65—Baltimore | 9 | 350 | 67 | 130 | .515 | 53 | 70 | .757 | 105 | 19 | 38 | 3 | 187 | 11.7 | 2.1 | 20.8 |
| 65-66—Baltimore | 3 | 94 | 23 | 50 | .460 | 8 | 11 | .727 | 30 | 2 | 13 | 1 | 54 | 10.0 | 0.7 | 18.0 |
| 66-67—Boston | 9 | 241 | 59 | 122 | .484 | 20 | 30 | .667 | 66 | 5 | 35 | 2 | 138 | 7.3 | 0.6 | 15.3 |
| 67-68—Boston | 19 | 597 | 135 | 264 | .511 | 74 | 107 | .692 | 146 | 22 | 84 | 6 | 344 | 7.7 | 1.2 | 18.1 |
| 68-69—Boston | 18 | 551 | 112 | 229 | .489 | 46 | 64 | .719 | 118 | 19 | 84 | 3 | 270 | 6.6 | 1.1 | 15.0 |
| 70-71—Philadelphia | 7 | 122 | 19 | 45 | .422 | 9 | 18 | .500 | 31 | 4 | 25 | 1 | 47 | 4.4 | 0.6 | 6.7 |
| Totals | 86 | 2712 | 542 | 1165 | .465 | 317 | 433 | .732 | 697 | 130 | 376 | 21 | 1401 | 8.1 | 1.5 | 16.3 |

## NBA ALL-STAR GAME RECORD

| Season Team | Min. | FGM | FGA | Pct. | FTM | FTA | Pct. | Reb | Ast. | PF | Dq. | Pts. |
|---|---|---|---|---|---|---|---|---|---|---|---|---|
| 1961—Detroit | 16 | 5 | 10 | .500 | 3 | 4 | .750 | 3 | 3 | 4 | 0 | 13 |
| 1962—Detroit | 8 | 1 | 2 | .500 | 0 | 0 | ... | 0 | 1 | 1 | 0 | 2 |
| 1963—Detroit | 11 | 2 | 3 | .667 | 0 | 0 | ... | 1 | 1 | 2 | 0 | 4 |
| 1964—Detroit | 6 | 1 | 3 | .333 | 0 | 0 | ... | 2 | 0 | 0 | 0 | 2 |
| 1966—Baltimore | 26 | 3 | 11 | .273 | 1 | 2 | .500 | 2 | 2 | 4 | 0 | 7 |
| 1967—Boston | 14 | 1 | 4 | .250 | 2 | 2 | 1.000 | 2 | 1 | 1 | 0 | 4 |
| Totals | 81 | 13 | 33 | .394 | 6 | 8 | .750 | 10 | 8 | 12 | 0 | 32 |

# HUDSON, LOU     F/G

**PERSONAL:** Born July 11, 1944, in Greensboro, N.C. ... 6-5/210 (1,96/95,3). ... Full name: Louis Clyde Hudson. ... Nickname: Sweet Lou.
**HIGH SCHOOL:** Dudley Senior (Greensboro, N.C.).
**COLLEGE:** Minnesota.
**TRANSACTIONS:** Selected by St. Louis Hawks in first round (fourth pick overall) of 1966 NBA Draft. ... Hawks franchise moved from St. Louis to Atlanta for 1968-69 season. ... Traded by Hawks to Los Angeles Lakers for F Ollie Johnson (September 30, 1977).

## COLLEGIATE RECORD

| Season Team | G | Min. | FGM | FGA | Pct. | FTM | FTA | Pct. | Reb. | Ast. | Pts. | RPG | APG | PPG |
|---|---|---|---|---|---|---|---|---|---|---|---|---|---|---|
| 62-63—Minnesota‡ | | | | | Freshman team did not play intercollegiate schedule. | | | | | | | | | |
| 63-64—Minnesota | 24 | ... | 191 | 435 | .439 | 53 | 85 | .624 | 191 | ... | 435 | 8.0 | ... | 18.1 |
| 64-65—Minnesota | 24 | ... | 231 | 463 | .499 | 96 | 123 | .780 | 247 | ... | 558 | 10.3 | ... | 23.3 |
| 65-66—Minnesota | 17 | ... | 143 | 303 | .472 | 50 | 77 | .649 | 138 | ... | 336 | 8.1 | ... | 19.8 |
| Varsity totals | 65 | ... | 565 | 1201 | .470 | 199 | 285 | .698 | 576 | ... | 1329 | 8.9 | ... | 20.4 |

## NBA REGULAR-SEASON RECORD

**HONORS:** All-NBA second team (1970). ... NBA All-Rookie team (1967).

| Season Team | G | Min. | FGM | FGA | Pct. | FTM | FTA | Pct. | Reb. | Ast. | PF | Dq. | Pts. | RPG | APG | PPG |
|---|---|---|---|---|---|---|---|---|---|---|---|---|---|---|---|---|
| 66-67—St. Louis | 80 | 2446 | 620 | 1328 | .467 | 231 | 327 | .706 | 435 | 95 | 277 | 3 | 1471 | 5.4 | 1.2 | 18.4 |
| 67-68—St. Louis | 46 | 966 | 227 | 500 | .454 | 120 | 164 | .732 | 193 | 65 | 113 | 2 | 574 | 4.2 | 1.4 | 12.5 |
| 68-69—Atlanta | 81 | 2869 | 716 | 1455 | .492 | 338 | 435 | .777 | 533 | 216 | 248 | 0 | 1770 | 6.6 | 2.7 | 21.9 |
| 69-70—Atlanta | 80 | 3091 | 830 | 1564 | .531 | 371 | 450 | .824 | 373 | 276 | 225 | 1 | 2031 | 4.7 | 3.5 | 25.4 |
| 70-71—Atlanta | 76 | 3113 | 829 | 1713 | .484 | 381 | 502 | .759 | 386 | 257 | 186 | 0 | 2039 | 5.1 | 3.4 | 26.8 |
| 71-72—Atlanta | 77 | 3042 | 775 | 1540 | .503 | 349 | 430 | .812 | 385 | 309 | 225 | 0 | 1899 | 5.0 | 4.0 | 24.7 |
| 72-73—Atlanta | 75 | 3027 | 816 | 1710 | .477 | 397 | 481 | .825 | 467 | 258 | 197 | 1 | 2029 | 6.2 | 3.4 | 27.1 |

| Season Team | G | Min. | FGM | FGA | Pct. | FTM | FTA | Pct. | Off. | Def. | Tot. | Ast. | St. | Blk. | TO | Pts. | RPG | APG | PPG |
|---|---|---|---|---|---|---|---|---|---|---|---|---|---|---|---|---|---|---|---|
| 73-74—Atlanta | 65 | 2588 | 678 | 1356 | .500 | 295 | 353 | .836 | 126 | 224 | 350 | 213 | 160 | 29 | ... | 1651 | 5.4 | 3.3 | 25.4 |
| 74-75—Atlanta | 11 | 380 | 97 | 225 | .431 | 48 | 57 | .842 | 14 | 33 | 47 | 40 | 13 | 2 | ... | 242 | 4.3 | 3.6 | 22.0 |
| 75-76—Atlanta | 81 | 2558 | 569 | 1205 | .472 | 237 | 291 | .814 | 104 | 196 | 300 | 214 | 124 | 17 | ... | 1375 | 3.7 | 2.6 | 17.0 |
| 76-77—Atlanta | 58 | 1745 | 413 | 905 | .456 | 142 | 169 | .840 | 48 | 81 | 129 | 155 | 67 | 19 | ... | 968 | 2.2 | 2.7 | 16.7 |
| 77-78—Los Angeles | 82 | 2283 | 493 | 992 | .497 | 137 | 177 | .774 | 80 | 108 | 188 | 193 | 94 | 14 | 150 | 1123 | 2.3 | 2.4 | 13.7 |
| 78-79—Los Angeles | 78 | 1686 | 329 | 636 | .517 | 110 | 124 | .887 | 64 | 76 | 140 | 141 | 58 | 17 | 99 | 768 | 1.8 | 1.8 | 9.8 |
| Totals | 890 | 29794 | 7392 | 15129 | .489 | 3156 | 3960 | .797 | ... | ... | 3926 | 2432 | 516 | 98 | 249 | 17940 | 4.4 | 2.7 | 20.2 |

Personal fouls/disqualifications: 1973-74, 205/3. 1974-75, 33/1. 1975-76, 241/3. 1976-77, 160/2. 1977-78, 196/0. 1978-79, 133/1. Totals, 2439/17.

| Season Team | G | Min. | FGM | FGA | Pct. | FTM | FTA | Pct. | Reb. | Ast. | PF | Dq. | Pts. | AVERAGES RPG | APG | PPG |
|---|---|---|---|---|---|---|---|---|---|---|---|---|---|---|---|---|
| 66-67—St. Louis | 9 | 317 | 77 | 179 | .430 | 49 | 68 | .721 | 48 | 15 | 35 | 1 | 203 | 5.3 | 1.7 | 22.6 |
| 67-68—St. Louis | 6 | 181 | 44 | 99 | .444 | 42 | 47 | .894 | 43 | 14 | 21 | 0 | 130 | 7.2 | 2.3 | 21.7 |
| 68-69—Atlanta | 11 | 424 | 101 | 216 | .468 | 40 | 52 | .769 | 59 | 32 | 43 | 1 | 242 | 5.4 | 2.9 | 22.0 |
| 69-70—Atlanta | 9 | 360 | 78 | 187 | .417 | 41 | 50 | .820 | 40 | 33 | 34 | 2 | 197 | 4.4 | 3.7 | 21.9 |
| 70-71—Atlanta | 5 | 213 | 49 | 108 | .454 | 29 | 39 | .744 | 35 | 15 | 19 | 0 | 127 | 7.0 | 3.0 | 25.4 |
| 71-72—Atlanta | 6 | 266 | 63 | 139 | .453 | 24 | 29 | .828 | 33 | 21 | 13 | 0 | 150 | 5.5 | 3.5 | 25.0 |
| 72-73—Atlanta | 6 | 255 | 76 | 166 | .458 | 26 | 29 | .897 | 47 | 17 | 16 | 0 | 178 | 7.8 | 2.8 | 29.7 |

| Season Team | G | Min. | FGM | FGA | Pct. | FTM | FTA | Pct. | REBOUNDS Off. | Def. | Tot. | Ast. | St. | Blk. | TO | Pts. | AVERAGES RPG | APG | PPG |
|---|---|---|---|---|---|---|---|---|---|---|---|---|---|---|---|---|---|---|---|
| 77-78—Los Angeles | 3 | 93 | 14 | 38 | .368 | 7 | 8 | .875 | 7 | 2 | 9 | 9 | 5 | 0 | 5 | 35 | 3.0 | 3.0 | 11.7 |
| 78-79—Los Angeles | 6 | 90 | 17 | 32 | .531 | 4 | 4 | 1.000 | 1 | 3 | 4 | 8 | 1 | 0 | 5 | 38 | 0.7 | 1.3 | 6.3 |
| Totals | 61 | 2199 | 519 | 1164 | .446 | 262 | 326 | .804 | ... | ... | 318 | 164 | 6 | 0 | 10 | 1300 | 5.2 | 2.7 | 21.3 |

Personal fouls/disqualifications: 1977-78, 9/0. 1978-79, 6/0. Totals, 196/4.

## NBA ALL-STAR GAME RECORD

| Season Team | Min. | FGM | FGA | Pct. | FTM | FTA | Pct. | Reb | Ast. | PF | Dq. | Pts. |
|---|---|---|---|---|---|---|---|---|---|---|---|---|
| 1969—Atlanta | 20 | 6 | 13 | .462 | 1 | 1 | 1.000 | 1 | 1 | 0 | 0 | 13 |
| 1970—Atlanta | 18 | 5 | 12 | .417 | 5 | 5 | 1.000 | 1 | 0 | 1 | 0 | 15 |
| 1971—Atlanta | 17 | 6 | 13 | .462 | 2 | 3 | .667 | 3 | 1 | 3 | 0 | 14 |
| 1972—Atlanta | 18 | 2 | 7 | .286 | 2 | 2 | 1.000 | 3 | 3 | 3 | 0 | 6 |
| 1973—Atlanta | 9 | 2 | 8 | .250 | 2 | 2 | 1.000 | 2 | 0 | 2 | 0 | 6 |

| Season Team | Min. | FGM | FGA | Pct. | FTM | FTA | Pct. | REBOUNDS Off. | Def. | Tot. | Ast. | PF | Dq. | St. | Blk. | TO | Pts. |
|---|---|---|---|---|---|---|---|---|---|---|---|---|---|---|---|---|---|
| 1974—Atlanta | 17 | 5 | 8 | .625 | 2 | 2 | 1.000 | 1 | 2 | 3 | 1 | 2 | 0 | 0 | 1 | ... | 12 |
| Totals | 99 | 26 | 61 | .426 | 14 | 15 | .933 | ... | ... | 13 | 6 | 11 | 0 | 0 | 1 | ... | 66 |

# ISSEL, DAN　　　　　　　　　　　　　　F

**PERSONAL:** Born October 25, 1948, in Batavia, Ill. ... 6-9/240. (2,06/108,4). ... Full name: Daniel Paul Issel.
**HIGH SCHOOL:** Batavia (Ill.).
**COLLEGE:** Kentucky.
**TRANSACTIONS:** Selected by Detroit Pistons in eighth round (122nd pick overall) of 1970 NBA Draft. ... Selected by Kentucky Colonels in first round of 1970 ABA draft. ... Traded by Colonels to Baltimore Claws for C Tom Owens and cash (September 19, 1975). ... Traded by Claws to Denver Nuggets for C Dave Robisch and cash (October 8, 1975). ... Nuggets franchise became part of NBA for 1976-77 season.
**CAREER HONORS:** Elected to Naismith Memorial Basketball Hall of Fame (1993).
**MISCELLANEOUS:** Denver Nuggets franchise all-time leading rebounder with 6,630 (1976-77 through 1984-85).
**CAREER NOTES:** Vice president, Denver Nuggets (March 1998 to August 2001).

## COLLEGIATE RECORD

NOTES: The Sporting News All-America first team (1970). ... The Sporting News All-America second team (1969).

| Season Team | G | Min. | FGM | FGA | Pct. | FTM | FTA | Pct. | Reb. | Ast. | Pts. | AVERAGES RPG | APG | PPG |
|---|---|---|---|---|---|---|---|---|---|---|---|---|---|---|
| 66-67—Kentucky‡ | 20 | ... | 168 | 332 | .506 | 80 | 111 | .721 | 355 | ... | 416 | 17.8 | ... | 20.8 |
| 67-68—Kentucky | 27 | 836 | 171 | 390 | .438 | 102 | 154 | .662 | 328 | 10 | 444 | 12.1 | 0.4 | 16.4 |
| 68-69—Kentucky | 28 | 1063 | 285 | 534 | .534 | 176 | 232 | .759 | 381 | 49 | 746 | 13.6 | 1.8 | 26.6 |
| 69-70—Kentucky | 28 | 1044 | 369 | 667 | .553 | 210 | 275 | .764 | 369 | 39 | 948 | 13.2 | 1.4 | 33.9 |
| Varsity totals | 83 | 2943 | 825 | 1591 | .519 | 468 | 661 | .738 | 1078 | 98 | 2138 | 13.0 | 1.2 | 25.8 |

## ABA REGULAR-SEASON RECORD

NOTES: ABA co-Rookie of the Year (1971). ... ABA All-Star first team (1972). ... ABA All-Star second team (1971, 1973, 1974, 1976). ... ABA All-Rookie team (1971). ... Member of ABA championship team (1975). ... Holds single-season record for most points—2,538 (1972).

| Season Team | G | Min. | 2-POINT FGM | FGA | Pct. | 3-POINT FGM | FGA | Pct. | FTM | FTA | Pct. | Reb. | Ast. | Pts. | AVERAGES RPG | APG | PPG |
|---|---|---|---|---|---|---|---|---|---|---|---|---|---|---|---|---|---|
| 70-71—Kentucky | 83 | 3274 | 938 | 1989 | .472 | 0 | 5 | .000 | 604 | 748 | .807 | 1093 | 162 | *2480 | 13.2 | 2.0 | *29.9 |
| 71-72—Kentucky | 83 | 3570 | 969 | 1990 | .487 | 3 | 11 | .273 | 591 | *753 | .785 | 931 | 195 | *2538 | 11.2 | 2.3 | 30.6 |
| 72-73—Kentucky | 84 | *3531 | 899 | 1742 | .516 | 3 | 15 | .200 | 485 | 635 | .764 | 922 | 220 | *2292 | 11.0 | 2.6 | 27.3 |
| 73-74—Kentucky | 83 | 3347 | 826 | 1709 | .483 | 3 | 17 | .176 | 457 | 581 | .787 | 847 | 137 | 2118 | 10.2 | 1.7 | 25.5 |
| 74-75—Kentucky | 83 | 2864 | 614 | 1298 | .473 | 0 | 5 | .000 | 237 | 321 | .738 | 710 | 188 | 1465 | 8.6 | 2.3 | 17.7 |
| 75-76—Denver | 84 | 2858 | 751 | 1468 | .512 | 1 | 4 | .250 | 425 | 521 | .816 | 923 | 201 | 1930 | 11.0 | 2.4 | 23.0 |
| Totals | 500 | 19444 | 4997 | 10196 | .490 | 10 | 57 | .175 | 2799 | 3559 | .786 | 5426 | 1103 | 12823 | 10.9 | 2.2 | 25.6 |

## ABA PLAYOFF RECORD

| Season Team | G | Min. | 2-POINT FGM | FGA | Pct. | 3-POINT FGM | FGA | Pct. | FTM | FTA | Pct. | Reb. | Ast. | Pts. | AVERAGES RPG | APG | PPG |
|---|---|---|---|---|---|---|---|---|---|---|---|---|---|---|---|---|---|
| 70-71—Kentucky | 19 | 670 | 207 | 408 | .507 | 0 | 0 | ... | 123 | 141 | .872 | 221 | 28 | 536 | 11.6 | 1.5 | 28.2 |
| 71-72—Kentucky | 6 | 269 | 47 | 113 | .416 | 0 | 1 | .000 | 38 | 50 | .760 | 54 | 5 | 132 | 9.0 | 0.8 | 22.0 |
| 72-73—Kentucky | 19 | 821 | 197 | 392 | .503 | 1 | 6 | .167 | 124 | 156 | .795 | 225 | 28 | 521 | 11.8 | 1.5 | 27.4 |
| 73-74—Kentucky | 8 | 311 | 60 | 135 | .444 | 0 | 0 | ... | 28 | 33 | .848 | 87 | 14 | 148 | 10.9 | 1.8 | 18.5 |
| 74-75—Kentucky | 15 | 578 | 122 | 261 | .467 | 0 | 0 | ... | 60 | 74 | .811 | 119 | 29 | 304 | 7.9 | 1.9 | 20.3 |
| 75-76—Denver | 13 | 470 | 111 | 226 | .491 | 0 | 1 | .000 | 44 | 56 | .786 | 156 | 32 | 266 | 12.0 | 2.5 | 20.5 |
| Totals | 80 | 3119 | 744 | 1535 | .485 | 1 | 8 | .125 | 417 | 510 | .818 | 862 | 136 | 1907 | 10.8 | 1.7 | 23.8 |

# ABA ALL-STAR GAME RECORD

**NOTES:** ABA All-Star Game Most Valuable Player (1972).

| Season Team | Min. | 2-POINT | | | 3-POINT | | | FTM | FTA | Pct. | Reb. | Ast. | Pts. |
| | | FGM | FGA | Pct. | FGM | FGA | Pct. | | | | | | |
| --- | --- | --- | --- | --- | --- | --- | --- | --- | --- | --- | --- | --- | --- |
| 1971—Kentucky | 34 | 8 | 15 | .533 | 0 | 0 | ... | 5 | 8 | .625 | 11 | 0 | 21 |
| 1972—Kentucky | 23 | 9 | 13 | .692 | 0 | 0 | ... | 3 | 4 | .750 | 9 | 5 | 21 |
| 1973—Kentucky | 29 | 6 | 14 | .429 | 0 | 0 | ... | 2 | 2 | 1.000 | 7 | 4 | 14 |
| 1974—Kentucky | 26 | 10 | 15 | .667 | 0 | 0 | ... | 1 | 1 | 1.000 | 4 | 1 | 21 |
| 1975—Kentucky | 20 | 3 | 6 | .500 | 0 | 0 | ... | 1 | 2 | .500 | 7 | 1 | 7 |
| 1976—Denver | 31 | 6 | 16 | .375 | 0 | 0 | ... | 7 | 9 | .778 | 9 | 5 | 19 |
| **Totals** | 163 | 42 | 79 | .532 | 0 | 0 | ... | 19 | 26 | .731 | 47 | 16 | 103 |

# NBA REGULAR-SEASON RECORD

**HONORS:** J. Walter Kennedy Citizenship Award (1985).

| Season Team | G | Min. | FGM | FGA | Pct. | FTM | FTA | Pct. | REBOUNDS | | | Ast. | St. | Blk. | TO | Pts. | AVERAGES | | |
| | | | | | | | | | Off. | Def. | Tot. | | | | | | RPG | APG | PPG |
| --- | --- | --- | --- | --- | --- | --- | --- | --- | --- | --- | --- | --- | --- | --- | --- | --- | --- | --- | --- |
| 76-77—Denver | 79 | 2507 | 660 | 1282 | .515 | 445 | 558 | .798 | 211 | 485 | 696 | 177 | 91 | 29 | ... | 1765 | 8.8 | 2.2 | 22.3 |
| 77-78—Denver | 82 | 2851 | 659 | 1287 | .512 | 428 | 547 | .782 | 253 | 577 | 830 | 304 | 100 | 41 | 259 | 1746 | 10.1 | 3.7 | 21.3 |
| 78-79—Denver | 81 | 2742 | 532 | 1030 | .517 | 316 | 419 | .754 | 240 | 498 | 738 | 255 | 61 | 46 | 171 | 1380 | 9.1 | 3.1 | 17.0 |
| 79-80—Denver | 82 | 2938 | 715 | 1416 | .505 | 517 | 667 | .775 | 236 | 483 | 719 | 198 | 88 | 54 | 163 | 1951 | 8.8 | 2.4 | 23.8 |
| 80-81—Denver | 80 | 2641 | 614 | 1220 | .503 | 519 | 684 | .759 | 229 | 447 | 676 | 158 | 83 | 53 | 130 | 1749 | 8.5 | 2.0 | 21.9 |
| 81-82—Denver | 81 | 2472 | 651 | 1236 | .527 | 546 | 655 | .834 | 174 | 434 | 608 | 179 | 67 | 55 | 169 | 1852 | 7.5 | 2.2 | 22.9 |
| 82-83—Denver | 80 | 2431 | 661 | 1296 | .510 | 400 | 479 | .835 | 151 | 445 | 596 | 223 | 83 | 43 | 174 | 1726 | 7.5 | 2.8 | 21.6 |
| 83-84—Denver | 76 | 2076 | 569 | 1153 | .494 | 364 | 428 | .850 | 112 | 401 | 513 | 173 | 60 | 44 | 122 | 1506 | 6.8 | 2.3 | 19.8 |
| 84-85—Denver | 77 | 1684 | 363 | 791 | .459 | 257 | 319 | .806 | 80 | 251 | 331 | 137 | 65 | 31 | 93 | 984 | 4.3 | 1.8 | 12.8 |
| **Totals** | 718 | 22342 | 5424 | 10711 | .506 | 3792 | 4756 | .797 | 1686 | 4021 | 5707 | 1804 | 698 | 396 | 1281 | 14659 | 7.9 | 2.5 | 20.4 |

Three-point field goals: 1979-80, 4-for-12 (.333). 1980-81, 2-for-12 (.167). 1981-82, 4-for-6 (.667). 1982-83, 4-for-19 (.211). 1983-84, 4-for-19 (.211). 1984-85, 1-for-7 (.143). Totals, 19-for-75 (.253).

Personal fouls/disqualifications: 1976-77, 246/7. 1977-78, 279/5. 1978-79, 233/6. 1979-80, 190/1. 1980-81, 249/6. 1981-82, 245/4. 1982-83, 227/0. 1983-84, 182/2. 1984-85, 171/1. Totals, 2022/32.

# NBA PLAYOFF RECORD

| Season Team | G | Min. | FGM | FGA | Pct. | FTM | FTA | Pct. | REBOUNDS | | | Ast. | St. | Blk. | TO | Pts. | AVERAGES | | |
| | | | | | | | | | Off. | Def. | Tot. | | | | | | RPG | APG | PPG |
| --- | --- | --- | --- | --- | --- | --- | --- | --- | --- | --- | --- | --- | --- | --- | --- | --- | --- | --- | --- |
| 76-77—Denver | 6 | 222 | 49 | 96 | .510 | 34 | 45 | .756 | 18 | 40 | 58 | 17 | 5 | 4 | ... | 132 | 9.7 | 2.8 | 22.0 |
| 77-78—Denver | 13 | 460 | 103 | 212 | .486 | 56 | 65 | .862 | 41 | 93 | 134 | 53 | 7 | 3 | 39 | 262 | 10.3 | 4.1 | 20.2 |
| 78-79—Denver | 3 | 109 | 24 | 45 | .533 | 25 | 31 | .806 | 7 | 21 | 28 | 10 | 0 | 0 | 9 | 73 | 9.3 | 3.3 | 24.3 |
| 81-82—Denver | 3 | 103 | 32 | 60 | .533 | 12 | 12 | 1.000 | 8 | 13 | 21 | 5 | 3 | 1 | 7 | 76 | 7.0 | 1.7 | 25.3 |
| 82-83—Denver | 8 | 227 | 69 | 136 | .507 | 25 | 29 | .862 | 13 | 45 | 58 | 25 | 9 | 5 | 10 | 163 | 7.3 | 3.1 | 20.4 |
| 83-84—Denver | 5 | 153 | 52 | 102 | .510 | 32 | 39 | .821 | 10 | 30 | 40 | 8 | 6 | 6 | 15 | 137 | 8.0 | 1.6 | 27.4 |
| 84-85—Denver | 15 | 325 | 73 | 159 | .459 | 39 | 48 | .813 | 14 | 40 | 54 | 27 | 12 | 5 | 13 | 186 | 3.6 | 1.8 | 12.4 |
| **Totals** | 53 | 1599 | 402 | 810 | .496 | 223 | 269 | .829 | 111 | 282 | 393 | 145 | 42 | 24 | 93 | 1029 | 7.4 | 2.7 | 19.4 |

Three-point field goals: 1982-83, 0-for-1. 1983-84, 1-for-2 (.500). 1984-85, 1-for-1. Totals, 2-for-4 (.500).

Personal fouls/disqualifications: 1976-77, 20/0. 1977-78, 43/1. 1978-79, 15/0. 1981-82, 10/0. 1982-83, 18/0. 1983-84, 15/0. 1984-85, 36/0. Totals, 157/1.

# NBA ALL-STAR GAME RECORD

| Season Team | Min. | FGM | FGA | Pct. | FTM | FTA | Pct. | REBOUNDS | | | Ast. | PF | Dq. | St. | Blk. | TO | Pts. |
| | | | | | | | | Off. | Def. | Tot. | | | | | | | |
| --- | --- | --- | --- | --- | --- | --- | --- | --- | --- | --- | --- | --- | --- | --- | --- | --- | --- |
| 1977—Denver | 10 | 0 | 3 | .000 | 0 | 0 | ... | 1 | 0 | 1 | 0 | 0 | 0 | 0 | 0 | ... | 0 |

# COMBINED ABA AND NBA REGULAR-SEASON RECORDS

| | G | Min. | FGM | FGA | Pct. | FTM | FTA | Pct. | REBOUNDS | | | Ast. | Stl. | Blk. | TO | Pts. | AVERAGES | | |
| | | | | | | | | | Off. | Def. | Tot. | | | | | | RPG | APG | PPG |
| --- | --- | --- | --- | --- | --- | --- | --- | --- | --- | --- | --- | --- | --- | --- | --- | --- | --- | --- | --- |
| **Totals** | 1218 | 41786 | 10431 | 20964 | .498 | 6591 | 8315 | .793 | ... | ... | 11133 | 2907 | ... | ... | ... | 27482 | 9.1 | 2.4 | 22.6 |

Three-point field goals: 29-for-132 (.220).

Personal fouls/disqualifications: 3504.

# NBA COACHING RECORD

| Season Team | REGULAR SEASON | | | | PLAYOFFS | | |
| | W | L | Pct. | Finish | W | L | Pct. |
| --- | --- | --- | --- | --- | --- | --- | --- |
| 92-93—Denver | 36 | 46 | .439 | 4th/Midwest Division | — | — | — |
| 93-94—Denver | 42 | 40 | .512 | 4th/Midwest Division | 6 | 6 | .500 |
| 94-95—Denver | 18 | 16 | .529 | | — | — | — |
| 99-00—Denver | 35 | 47 | .427 | 5th/Midwest Division | — | — | — |
| 00-01—Denver | 40 | 42 | .488 | 6th/Midwest Division | — | — | — |
| 01-02—Denver | 9 | 17 | .346 | | — | — | — |
| **Totals (6 years)** | 180 | 208 | .464 | **Totals (1 year)** | 6 | 6 | .500 |

**NOTES:**

1994—Defeated Seattle, 3-2, in Western Conference First Round; lost to Utah, 4-3, in Western Conference Semifinals.

1995—Resigned as Denver head coach (January 15); replaced by Gene Littles with club in fourth place.

2001—Resigned as head coach (December 26); replaced by Mike Evans with club in fifth place.

ALL-TIME GREAT PLAYERS

# JACKSON, MARK     G

**PERSONAL:** Born April 1, 1965, in Brooklyn, N.Y. ... 6-3/205. (1,91/93,0). ... Full Name: Mark A. Jackson.
**HIGH SCHOOL:** Bishop Loughlin Memorial (Brooklyn, N.Y.).
**COLLEGE:** St. John's.
**TRANSACTIONS/CAREER NOTES:** Selected by New York Knicks in first round (18th pick overall) of 1987 NBA Draft. ... Traded by Knicks with 1995 second-round draft choice to Los Angeles Clippers in three-way deal in which Clippers also received C Stanley Roberts from Orlando Magic, Knicks received G Doc Rivers, F Charles Smith and G Bo Kimble from Clippers and Magic received 1993 first-round draft choice from Clippers (September 22, 1992). ... Traded by Clippers with draft rights to G Greg Minor to Indiana Pacers for G Pooh Richardson, F Malik Sealy and draft rights to F Eric Piatkowski (June 30, 1994). ... Traded by Pacers with G Ricky Pierce and 1996 first-round draft choice to Denver Nuggets for G Jalen Rose, F Reggie Williams and 1996 first-round draft choice (June 13, 1996). ... Traded by Nuggets with F/C LaSalle Thompson to Pacers for G Vincent Askew, F Eddie Johnson and 1997 and 1998 second-round draft choices (February 20, 1997). ... Signed as free agent by Toronto Raptors (August 11, 2000). ... Traded by Raptors with G Muggsy Bogues to Knicks for G Chris Childs and 2001 first-round draft choice (February 22, 2001). ... Traded by Knicks with F/C Marcus Camby and draft rights to F/C Nene Hilario to Nuggets for F Antonio McDyess, draft rights to G Frank Williams and 2003 second-round draft choice (June 26, 2002). ... Waived by Nuggets (September 27, 2002). ... Signed as free agent by Utah Jazz (October 2, 2002). ... Signed as free agent by Houston Rockets (January 15, 2004).

## COLLEGIATE RECORD

**NOTES:** THE SPORTING NEWS All-America second team (1987). ... Led NCAA Division I with 9.11 assists per game (1986).

| Season Team | G | Min. | FGM | FGA | Pct. | FTM | FTA | Pct. | Reb. | Ast. | Pts. | RPG | APG | PPG |
|---|---|---|---|---|---|---|---|---|---|---|---|---|---|---|
| 83-84—St. John's | 30 | 855 | 61 | 106 | .575 | 53 | 77 | .688 | 59 | 108 | 175 | 2.0 | 3.6 | 5.8 |
| 84-85—St. John's | 35 | 601 | 57 | 101 | .564 | 66 | 91 | .725 | 44 | 109 | 180 | 1.3 | 3.1 | 5.1 |
| 85-86—St. John's | 36 | 1340 | 151 | 316 | .478 | 105 | 142 | .739 | 125 | 328 | 407 | 3.5 | 9.1 | 11.3 |
| 86-87—St. John's | 30 | 1184 | 196 | 389 | .504 | 125 | 155 | .806 | 110 | 193 | 566 | 3.7 | 6.4 | 18.9 |
| **Totals** | 131 | 3980 | 465 | 912 | .510 | 349 | 465 | .751 | 338 | 738 | 1328 | 2.6 | 5.6 | 10.1 |

Three-point field goals: 1986-87, 49-for-117 (.419). .

## NBA REGULAR-SEASON RECORD

**RECORDS:** Holds single-season record for most assists by a rookie—868 (1988).
**HONORS:** NBA Rookie of the Year (1988). ... NBA All-Rookie team (1988).

| Season Team | G | Min. | FGM | FGA | Pct. | FTM | FTA | Pct. | Off. | Def. | Tot. | Ast. | St. | Blk. | TO | Pts. | RPG | APG | PPG |
|---|---|---|---|---|---|---|---|---|---|---|---|---|---|---|---|---|---|---|---|
| 87-88—New York | 82 | 3249 | 438 | 1013 | .432 | 206 | 266 | .774 | 120 | 276 | 396 | 868 | 205 | 6 | 258 | 1114 | 4.8 | 10.6 | 13.6 |
| 88-89—New York | 72 | 2477 | 479 | 1025 | .467 | 180 | 258 | .698 | 106 | 235 | 341 | 619 | 139 | 7 | 226 | 1219 | 4.7 | 8.6 | 16.9 |
| 89-90—New York | 82 | 2428 | 327 | 749 | .437 | 120 | 165 | .727 | 106 | 212 | 318 | 604 | 109 | 4 | 211 | 809 | 3.9 | 7.4 | 9.9 |
| 90-91—New York | 72 | 1595 | 250 | 508 | .492 | 117 | 160 | .731 | 62 | 135 | 197 | 452 | 60 | 9 | 135 | 630 | 2.7 | 6.3 | 8.8 |
| 91-92—New York | 81 | 2461 | 367 | 747 | .491 | 171 | 222 | .770 | 95 | 210 | 305 | 694 | 112 | 13 | 211 | 916 | 3.8 | 8.6 | 11.3 |
| 92-93—L.A. Clippers | 82 | 3117 | 459 | 945 | .486 | 241 | 300 | .803 | 129 | 259 | 388 | 724 | 136 | 12 | 220 | 1181 | 4.7 | 8.8 | 14.4 |
| 93-94—L.A. Clippers | 79 | 2711 | 331 | 732 | .452 | 167 | 211 | .791 | 107 | 241 | 348 | 678 | 120 | 6 | 232 | 865 | 4.4 | 8.6 | 10.9 |
| 94-95—Indiana | 82 | 2402 | 239 | 566 | .422 | 119 | 153 | .778 | 73 | 233 | 306 | 616 | 105 | 16 | 210 | 624 | 3.7 | 7.5 | 7.6 |
| 95-96—Indiana | 81 | 2643 | 296 | 626 | .473 | 150 | 191 | .785 | 66 | 241 | 307 | 635 | 100 | 5 | 201 | 806 | 3.8 | 7.8 | 10.0 |
| 96-97—Den.-Indiana | 82 | 3054 | 289 | 679 | .426 | 168 | 213 | .789 | 91 | 304 | 395 | *935 | 97 | 12 | 274 | 812 | 4.8 | *11.4 | 9.9 |
| 97-98—Indiana | 82 | 2413 | 249 | 598 | .416 | 137 | 180 | .761 | 67 | 255 | 322 | 713 | 84 | 2 | 174 | 678 | 3.9 | 8.7 | 8.3 |
| 98-99—Indiana | 49 | 1382 | 138 | 329 | .419 | 65 | 79 | .823 | 33 | 151 | 184 | 386 | 42 | 3 | 99 | 373 | 3.8 | 7.9 | 7.6 |
| 99-00—Indiana | 81 | 2190 | 246 | 570 | .432 | 79 | 98 | .806 | 63 | 233 | 296 | 650 | 76 | 10 | 174 | 660 | 3.7 | 8.0 | 8.1 |
| 00-01—Toronto-N.Y. | *83 | 2588 | 244 | 583 | .419 | 73 | 93 | .785 | 63 | 242 | 305 | 661 | 84 | 7 | 175 | 631 | 3.7 | 8.0 | 7.6 |
| 01-02—New York | 82 | 2367 | 260 | 592 | .439 | 87 | 110 | .791 | 56 | 253 | 309 | 605 | 74 | 1 | 150 | 686 | 3.8 | 7.4 | 8.4 |
| 02-03—Utah | 82 | 1467 | 147 | 369 | .398 | 61 | 80 | .763 | 34 | 142 | 176 | 375 | 48 | 3 | 152 | 382 | 2.1 | 4.6 | 4.7 |
| 03-04—Houston | 42 | 577 | 34 | 100 | .340 | 28 | 39 | .718 | 10 | 60 | 70 | 119 | 17 | 1 | 53 | 103 | 1.7 | 2.8 | 2.5 |
| **Totals** | 1296 | 39121 | 4793 | 10731 | .447 | 2169 | 2818 | .770 | 1281 | 3682 | 4963 | 10334 | 1608 | 117 | 3155 | 12489 | 3.8 | 8.0 | 9.6 |

Three-point field goals: 1987-88, 32-for-126 (.254). 1988-89, 81-for-240 (.338). 1989-90, 35-for-131 (.267). 1990-91, 13-for-51 (.255). 1991-92, 11-for-43 (.256). 1992-93, 22-for-82 (.268). 1993-94, 36-for-127 (.283). 1994-95, 27-for-87 (.310). 1995-96, 64-for-149 (.430). 1996-97, 66-for-178 (.371). 1997-98, 43-for-137 (.314). 1998-99, 32-for-103 (.311). 1999-00, 89-for-221 (.403). 2000-01, 70-for-207 (.338). 2001-02, 79-for-195 (.405). 2002-03, 27-for-95 (.284). 2003-04, 7-for-41 (.171). Totals, 734-for-2213 (.332).

Personal fouls/disqualifications: 1987-88, 244/2. 1988-89, 163/1. 1989-90, 121/0. 1990-91, 81/0. 1991-92, 153/0. 1992-93, 158/0. 1993-94, 115/0. 1994-95, 148/0. 1995-96, 153/0. 1996-97, 161/0. 1997-98, 132/0. 1998-99, 58/0. 1999-00, 111/0. 2000-01, 139/0. 2001-02, 162/0. 2002-03, 90/0. 2003-04, 41/0. Totals, 2230/3.

## NBA PLAYOFF RECORD

| Season Team | G | Min. | FGM | FGA | Pct. | FTM | FTA | Pct. | Off. | Def. | Tot. | Ast. | St. | Blk. | TO | Pts. | RPG | APG | PPG |
|---|---|---|---|---|---|---|---|---|---|---|---|---|---|---|---|---|---|---|---|
| 87-88—New York | 4 | 171 | 22 | 60 | .367 | 8 | 11 | .727 | 6 | 13 | 19 | 39 | 10 | 0 | 14 | 57 | 4.8 | 9.8 | 14.3 |
| 88-89—New York | 9 | 336 | 51 | 100 | .510 | 19 | 28 | .679 | 7 | 24 | 31 | 91 | 10 | 3 | 28 | 132 | 3.4 | 10.1 | 14.7 |
| 89-90—New York | 9 | 81 | 13 | 31 | .419 | 8 | 11 | .727 | 1 | 4 | 5 | 21 | 2 | 0 | 7 | 34 | 0.6 | 2.3 | 3.8 |
| 90-91—New York | 3 | 36 | 1 | 3 | .333 | 0 | 0 | ... | 0 | 0 | 0 | 8 | 1 | 1 | 5 | 2 | 0.0 | 2.7 | 0.7 |
| 91-92—New York | 12 | 368 | 37 | 92 | .402 | 22 | 27 | .815 | 12 | 15 | 27 | 86 | 10 | 0 | 30 | 100 | 2.3 | 7.2 | 8.3 |
| 92-93—L.A. Clippers | 5 | 188 | 28 | 64 | .438 | 19 | 22 | .864 | 8 | 21 | 29 | 38 | 8 | 1 | 13 | 76 | 5.8 | 7.6 | 15.2 |
| 94-95—Indiana | 17 | 553 | 59 | 130 | .454 | 34 | 46 | .739 | 27 | 62 | 89 | 121 | 15 | 0 | 41 | 168 | 5.2 | 7.1 | 9.9 |
| 95-96—Indiana | 5 | 186 | 18 | 51 | .353 | 13 | 17 | .765 | 3 | 22 | 25 | 30 | 6 | 0 | 13 | 53 | 5.0 | 6.0 | 10.6 |
| 97-98—Indiana | 16 | 494 | 53 | 127 | .417 | 27 | 34 | .794 | 18 | 55 | 73 | 133 | 23 | 0 | 47 | 147 | 4.6 | 8.3 | 9.2 |
| 98-99—Indiana | 13 | 451 | 51 | 103 | .495 | 30 | 42 | .714 | 14 | 45 | 59 | 112 | 14 | 1 | 35 | 146 | 4.5 | 8.6 | 11.2 |
| 99-00—Indiana | 23 | 634 | 69 | 176 | .392 | 28 | 31 | .903 | 12 | 74 | 86 | 178 | 19 | 2 | 43 | 187 | 3.7 | 7.7 | 8.1 |
| 00-01—New York | 5 | 156 | 20 | 40 | .500 | 3 | 3 | 1.000 | 3 | 23 | 26 | 26 | 8 | 0 | 10 | 45 | 5.2 | 5.2 | 9.0 |
| 02-03—Utah | 5 | 83 | 15 | 30 | .500 | 1 | 1 | 1.000 | 2 | 3 | 5 | 16 | 3 | 0 | 4 | 36 | 1.0 | 3.2 | 7.2 |
| 03-04—Houston | 5 | 38 | 1 | 6 | .167 | 0 | 0 | ... | 0 | 3 | 3 | 5 | 2 | 0 | 2 | 2 | 0.6 | 1.0 | 0.4 |
| **Totals** | 131 | 3775 | 438 | 1013 | .432 | 212 | 273 | .777 | 113 | 364 | 477 | 904 | 131 | 8 | 292 | 1185 | 3.6 | 6.9 | 9.0 |

Three-point field goals: 1987-88, 5-for-12 (.417). 1988-89, 11-for-28 (.393). 1989-90, 0-for-2. 1991-92, 4-for-21 (.190). 1992-93, 1-for-2 (.500). 1994-95, 16-for-40 (.400). 1995-96, 4-for-18 (.222). 1997-98, 14-for-37 (.378). 1998-99, 14-for-34 (.412). 1999-00, 21-for-67 (.313). 2000-01, 2-for-8 (.250). 2002-03, 5-for-9 (.556). 2003-04, 0-for-3. Totals, 97-for-281 (.345).

Personal fouls/disqualifications: 1987-88, 13/0. 1988-89, 9/0. 1989-90, 5/0. 1990-91, 1/0. 1991-92, 26/0. 1992-93, 8/0. 1994-95, 34/0. 1995-96, 9/0. 1997-98, 28/0. 1998-99, 32/0. 1999-00, 42/0. 2000-01, 6/0. 2002-03, 11/0. 2003-04, 1/0. Totals, 225/0.

## NBA ALL-STAR GAME RECORD

| Season Team | Min. | FGM | FGA | Pct. | FTM | FTA | Pct. | Off. | REBOUNDS Def. | Tot. | Ast. | PF | Dq. | St. | Blk. | TO | Pts. |
|---|---|---|---|---|---|---|---|---|---|---|---|---|---|---|---|---|---|
| 1989—New York ............. | 16 | 3 | 5 | .600 | 2 | 4 | .500 | 1 | 1 | 2 | 4 | 1 | 0 | 1 | 1 | 2 | 9 |

Three-point field goals: 1989, 1-for-1.

## JEANNETTE, BUDDY                                    G

**PERSONAL:** Born September 15, 1917, in New Kensington, Pa. ... Died March 11, 1998. ... 5-11/175 (1,81/79,4). ... Full name: Harry Edward Jeannette.
**HIGH SCHOOL:** New Kensington (Pa.).
**COLLEGE:** Washington & Jefferson (Pa.).
**TRANSACTIONS:** Warren Penns franchise transferred to Cleveland and renamed White Horses (February 10, 1939). ... Played in New York-Penn League with Elmira in 1939 and New York State League with Saratoga in 1942.
**CAREER HONORS:** Elected to Naismith Memorial Basketball Basketball Hall of Fame (1994).
**MISCELLANEOUS:** Member of BAA championship team (1948). ... Member of NBL championship team (1943, 1944, 1945).

### COLLEGIATE RECORD

| Season Team | G | Min. | FGM | FGA | Pct. | FTM | FTA | Pct. | Reb. | Ast. | Pts. | AVERAGES RPG | APG | PPG |
|---|---|---|---|---|---|---|---|---|---|---|---|---|---|---|
| 34-35—Wash. & Jefferson ........ | 14 | ... | 62 | ... | ... | 35 | ... | ... | ... | ... | 159 | ... | ... | 11.4 |
| 35-36—Wash. & Jefferson ........ | 20 | ... | 92 | ... | ... | 42 | ... | ... | ... | ... | 226 | ... | ... | 11.3 |
| 36-37—Wash. & Jefferson ........ | 18 | ... | 92 | ... | ... | 56 | ... | ... | ... | ... | 240 | ... | ... | 13.3 |
| 37-38—Wash. & Jefferson ........ | 20 | ... | ... | ... | ... | ... | ... | ... | ... | ... | 240 | ... | ... | 12.0 |
| Totals .................................... | 72 | ... | ... | ... | ... | ... | ... | ... | ... | ... | 865 | ... | ... | 12.0 |

### NBL AND NBA REGULAR-SEASON RECORD

**HONORS:** All-BAA second team (1948). ... All-NBL first team (1941, 1944, 1945, 1946). ... All-NBL second team (1943).

| Season Team | G | Min. | FGM | FGA | Pct. | FTM | FTA | Pct. | Reb. | Ast. | PF | Dq. | Pts. | AVERAGES RPG | APG | PPG |
|---|---|---|---|---|---|---|---|---|---|---|---|---|---|---|---|---|
| 38-39—W-Cl (NBL) ......................... | 26 | ... | 54 | ... | ... | 65 | ... | ... | ... | ... | 57 | ... | 173 | ... | ... | 6.7 |
| 39-40—Det. (NBL) ......................... | 25 | ... | 45 | ... | ... | 52 | 80 | .650 | ... | ... | 62 | ... | 142 | ... | ... | 5.7 |
| 40-41—Det. (NBL) ......................... | 23 | ... | 75 | ... | ... | 54 | 86 | .628 | ... | ... | 56 | ... | 204 | ... | ... | 8.9 |
| 42-43—Shb. (NBL) ......................... | 4 | ... | 24 | ... | ... | 14 | 17 | .824 | ... | ... | 8 | ... | 62 | ... | ... | 15.5 |
| 43-44—F.W. (NBL) ......................... | 22 | ... | 68 | ... | ... | 48 | 65 | .738 | ... | ... | 46 | ... | 184 | ... | ... | 8.4 |
| 44-45—F.W. (NBL) ......................... | 27 | ... | 85 | ... | ... | 82 | 111 | *.739 | ... | ... | 67 | ... | 252 | ... | ... | 9.3 |
| 45-46—F.W. (NBL) ......................... | 34 | ... | 99 | ... | ... | 105 | 136 | .772 | ... | ... | 184 | ... | 303 | ... | ... | 8.9 |
| 47-48—Baltimore (BAA) ................. | 46 | ... | 150 | 430 | .349 | 191 | 252 | .758 | ... | 70 | 147 | ... | 491 | ... | 1.5 | 10.7 |
| 48-49—Baltimore (BAA) ................. | 56 | ... | 73 | 199 | .367 | 167 | 213 | .784 | ... | 124 | 157 | ... | 313 | ... | 2.2 | 5.6 |
| 49-50—Baltimore ............................ | 37 | ... | 42 | 148 | .284 | 109 | 133 | .820 | ... | 93 | 82 | ... | 193 | ... | 2.5 | 5.2 |
| Totals............................................. | 300 | ... | 715 | ... | ... | 887 | ... | ... | ... | ... | 866 | ... | 2317 | ... | ... | 7.7 |

### NBL AND NBA PLAYOFF RECORD

| Season Team | G | Min. | FGM | FGA | Pct. | FTM | FTA | Pct. | Reb. | Ast. | PF | Dq. | Pts. | AVERAGES RPG | APG | PPG |
|---|---|---|---|---|---|---|---|---|---|---|---|---|---|---|---|---|
| 39-40—Det. (NBL) ......................... | 3 | ... | 6 | ... | ... | 8 | ... | ... | ... | ... | ... | ... | 20 | ... | ... | 6.7 |
| 40-41—Det. (NBL) ......................... | 3 | ... | 8 | ... | ... | 5 | ... | ... | ... | ... | ... | ... | 21 | ... | ... | 7.0 |
| 42-43—Shb. (NBL) ......................... | 5 | ... | 16 | ... | ... | 17 | ... | ... | ... | ... | ... | ... | 49 | ... | ... | 9.8 |
| 43-44—F.W. (NBL) ......................... | 5 | ... | 12 | ... | ... | 10 | ... | ... | ... | ... | ... | ... | 34 | ... | ... | 6.8 |
| 44-45—F.W. (NBL) ......................... | 7 | ... | 22 | ... | ... | 23 | ... | ... | ... | ... | ... | ... | 67 | ... | ... | 9.6 |
| 45-46—F.W. (NBL) ......................... | 4 | ... | 7 | ... | ... | 5 | 6 | .833 | ... | ... | ... | ... | 19 | ... | ... | 4.8 |
| 47-48—Baltimore (BAA) ................. | 11 | ... | 30 | 61 | .492 | 37 | 42 | .881 | ... | 12 | 45 | ... | 97 | ... | 1.1 | 8.8 |
| 48-49—Baltimore (BAA) ................. | 3 | ... | 2 | 13 | .154 | 4 | 4 | 1.000 | ... | 5 | 11 | ... | 8 | ... | 1.7 | 2.7 |
| Totals............................................. | 41 | ... | 103 | ... | ... | 109 | ... | ... | ... | ... | ... | ... | 315 | ... | ... | 7.7 |

### ABL REGULAR-SEASON RECORD

| Season Team | G | Min. | FGM | FGA | Pct. | FTM | FTA | Pct. | Reb. | Ast. | Pts. | AVERAGES RPG | APG | PPG |
|---|---|---|---|---|---|---|---|---|---|---|---|---|---|---|
| 46-47—Baltimore...................... | 29 | ... | 113 | ... | ... | 118 | ... | ... | ... | ... | 344 | ... | ... | 11.9 |

### HEAD COACHING RECORD

**BACKGROUND:** Player/head coach, Baltimore Bullets of ABL (1946-47). ... Assistant coach, Pittsburgh Condors of ABA (1970-71).

### ABL COACHING RECORD

| Season Team | REGULAR SEASON W | L | Pct. | Finish | PLAYOFFS W | L | Pct. |
|---|---|---|---|---|---|---|---|
| 46-47—Baltimore................................ | 31 | 3 | .912 | 1st/Southern Division | 2 | 1 | .667 |

### COLLEGIATE COACHING RECORD

| Season Team | W | L | Pct. |
|---|---|---|---|
| 52-53—Georgetown................................ | 13 | 7 | .650 |
| 53-54—Georgetown................................ | 11 | 18 | .379 |
| 54-55—Georgetown................................ | 12 | 13 | .480 |
| 55-56—Georgetown................................ | 13 | 11 | .542 |
| Totals (4 years)................................ | 49 | 49 | .500 |

### NBA COACHING RECORD

| Season Team | REGULAR SEASON W | L | Pct. | Finish | PLAYOFFS W | L | Pct. |
|---|---|---|---|---|---|---|---|
| 47-48—Baltimore (BAA) ................................ | 28 | 20 | .583 | 2nd/Western Division | 9 | 3 | .750 |
| 48-49—Baltimore (BAA) ................................ | 29 | 31 | .483 | 3rd/Eastern Division | 1 | 2 | .333 |
| 49-50—Baltimore................................ | 25 | 43 | .368 | 5th/Eastern Division | — | — | — |
| 50-51—Baltimore................................ | 14 | 23 | .378 | | — | — | — |
| 64-65—Baltimore................................ | 37 | 43 | .463 | 3rd/Western Division | 5 | 5 | .500 |
| 66-67—Baltimore................................ | 3 | 13 | .188 | | — | — | — |
| Totals (6 years)................................ | 136 | 173 | .440 | Totals (3 years)....... | 15 | 10 | .600 |

ALL-TIME GREAT PLAYERS

## EBL COACHING RECORD

| Season  Team | W | L | Pct. | Finish | | W | L | Pct. |
|---|---|---|---|---|---|---|---|---|
| | | | **REGULAR SEASON** | | | | **PLAYOFFS** | |
| 59-60—Baltimore.................................................. | 20 | 8 | .714 | 2nd | | 2 | 2 | .500 |
| 60-61—Baltimore.................................................. | 19 | 9 | .679 | 1st | | 2 | 0 | 1.000 |
| Totals (2 years)................... | 39 | 17 | .696 | Totals (2 years)....... | | 4 | 2 | .667 |

## ABA COACHING RECORD

| Season  Team | W | L | Pct. | Finish | | W | L | Pct. |
|---|---|---|---|---|---|---|---|---|
| | | | **REGULAR SEASON** | | | | **PLAYOFFS** | |
| 69-70—Pittsburgh ................................ | 15 | 30 | .333 | 5th/Eastern Division | | — | — | — |

**NOTES:**

1948—Defeated Chicago, 75-72, in Western Division tiebreaker; defeated New York, 2-1, in quarterfinals; defeated Chicago, 2-0, in semifinals; defeated Philadelphia, 4-2, in NBA Finals.

1949—Lost to New York in Eastern Division Semifinals.

1951—Replaced as Baltimore head coach by Walt Budko (January).

1960—Defeated Allentown, 103-89, in semifinal; lost to Easton, 2-1, in EBL Finals.

1961—Defeated Scranton, 132-107, in semifinal; defeated Allentown, 119-104, in EBL Final.

1965—Defeated St. Louis, 3-1, in Western Division Semifinals; lost to Los Angeles, 4-2, in Western Division Finals.

1966—Replaced Michael Farmer as Baltimore coach, with 1-8 record (November). Replaced as Baltimore coach by Gene Shue (December).

# JOHNSON, DENNIS                    G

**PERSONAL:** Born September 18, 1954, in San Pedro, Calif. ... 6-4/202 (1,93/91,6). ... Full name: Dennis Wayne Johnson. ... Nickname: D.J.
**HIGH SCHOOL:** Dominquez (Compton, Calif.).
**JUNIOR COLLEGE:** Los Angeles Harbor Junior College.
**COLLEGE:** Pepperdine.
**TRANSACTIONS:** Selected after junior season by Seattle SuperSonics in second round (29th pick overall) of 1976 NBA Draft. ... Traded by SuperSonics to Phoenix Suns for G Paul Westphal (June 4, 1980). ... Traded by Suns with 1983 first- and third-round draft choices to Boston Celtics for F/C Rick Robey and two 1983 second-round draft choices (June 27, 1983).
**CAREER NOTES:** Assistant coach, Boston Celtics (1993-94 through 1996-97). ... Head coach, La Crosse Catbirds of CBA (1999-February 3, 2000). ... Assistant coach, Los Angeles Clippers (February 4, 2000 to present). ... Replaced Alvin Gentry (March 3, 2003) as head coach of Clippers and compiled 8-16 record through end of season. ... Named head coach of NBDL's Florida Flame (August 24, 2004).
**MISCELLANEOUS:** Member of NBA championship team (1979, 1984, 1986).

## COLLEGIATE RECORD

| Season Team | G | Min. | FGM | FGA | Pct. | FTM | FTA | Pct. | Reb. | Ast. | Pts. | RPG | APG | PPG |
|---|---|---|---|---|---|---|---|---|---|---|---|---|---|---|
| | | | | | | | | | | | | **AVERAGES** | | |
| 73-74—Los Angeles Harbor J.C. | ... | 699 | 103 | 191 | .539 | 45 | 82 | .549 | 230 | ... | 251 | ... | ... | ... |
| 74-75—Los Angeles Harbor J.C. | 28 | 967 | ... | ... | ... | ... | ... | ... | 336 | ... | 511 | 12.0 | ... | 18.3 |
| 75-76—Pepperdine .................... | 27 | 930 | 181 | 378 | .479 | 63 | 112 | .563 | 156 | 88 | 425 | 5.8 | 3.3 | 15.7 |
| Junior college totals .............. | ... | 1666 | ... | ... | ... | ... | ... | ... | 566 | ... | 762 | ... | ... | ... |
| 4-year-college totals .............. | 27 | 930 | 181 | 378 | .479 | 63 | 112 | .563 | 156 | 88 | 425 | 5.8 | 3.3 | 15.7 |

## NBA REGULAR-SEASON RECORD

**HONORS:** All-NBA first team (1981). ... All-NBA second team (1980). ... NBA All-Defensive first team (1979, 1980, 1981, 1982, 1983, 1987). ... NBA All-Defensive second team (1984, 1985, 1986).

| Season Team | G | Min. | FGM | FGA | Pct. | FTM | FTA | Pct. | Off. | Def. | Tot. | Ast. | St. | Blk. | TO | Pts. | RPG | APG | PPG |
|---|---|---|---|---|---|---|---|---|---|---|---|---|---|---|---|---|---|---|---|
| | | | | | | | | | | **REBOUNDS** | | | | | | | | **AVERAGES** | |
| 76-77—Seattle ........... | 81 | 1667 | 285 | 566 | .504 | 179 | 287 | .624 | 161 | 141 | 302 | 123 | 123 | 57 | ... | 749 | 3.7 | 1.5 | 9.2 |
| 77-78—Seattle ........... | 81 | 2209 | 367 | 881 | .417 | 297 | 406 | .732 | 152 | 142 | 294 | 230 | 118 | 51 | 164 | 1031 | 3.6 | 2.8 | 12.7 |
| 78-79—Seattle ........... | 80 | 2717 | 482 | 1110 | .434 | 306 | 392 | .781 | 146 | 228 | 374 | 280 | 100 | 97 | 191 | 1270 | 4.7 | 3.5 | 15.9 |
| 79-80—Seattle ........... | 81 | 2937 | 574 | 1361 | .422 | 380 | 487 | .780 | 173 | 241 | 414 | 332 | 144 | 82 | 227 | 1540 | 5.1 | 4.1 | 19.0 |
| 80-81—Phoenix .......... | 79 | 2615 | 532 | 1220 | .436 | 411 | 501 | .820 | 160 | 203 | 363 | 291 | 136 | 61 | 208 | 1486 | 4.6 | 3.7 | 18.8 |
| 81-82—Phoenix .......... | 80 | 2937 | 577 | 1228 | .470 | 399 | 495 | .806 | 142 | 268 | 410 | 369 | 105 | 55 | 233 | 1561 | 5.1 | 4.6 | 19.5 |
| 82-83—Phoenix .......... | 77 | 2551 | 398 | 861 | .462 | 292 | 369 | .791 | 92 | 243 | 335 | 388 | 97 | 39 | 204 | 1093 | 4.4 | 5.0 | 14.2 |
| 83-84—Boston ............ | 80 | 2665 | 384 | 878 | .437 | 281 | 330 | .852 | 87 | 193 | 280 | 338 | 93 | 57 | 172 | 1053 | 3.5 | 4.2 | 13.2 |
| 84-85—Boston ............ | 80 | 2976 | 493 | 1066 | .462 | 261 | 306 | .853 | 91 | 226 | 317 | 543 | 96 | 39 | 212 | 1254 | 4.0 | 6.8 | 15.7 |
| 85-86—Boston ............ | 78 | 2732 | 482 | 1060 | .455 | 243 | 297 | .818 | 69 | 199 | 268 | 456 | 110 | 35 | 173 | 1213 | 3.4 | 5.8 | 15.6 |
| 86-87—Boston ............ | 79 | 2933 | 423 | 953 | .444 | 209 | 251 | .833 | 45 | 216 | 261 | 594 | 87 | 38 | 177 | 1062 | 3.3 | 7.5 | 13.4 |
| 87-88—Boston ............ | 77 | 2670 | 352 | 803 | .438 | 255 | 298 | .856 | 62 | 178 | 240 | 598 | 93 | 29 | 195 | 971 | 3.1 | 7.8 | 12.6 |
| 88-89—Boston ............ | 72 | 2309 | 277 | 638 | .434 | 160 | 195 | .821 | 31 | 159 | 190 | 472 | 94 | 21 | 175 | 721 | 2.6 | 6.6 | 10.0 |
| 89-90—Boston ............ | 75 | 2036 | 206 | 475 | .434 | 118 | 140 | .843 | 48 | 153 | 201 | 485 | 81 | 14 | 117 | 531 | 2.7 | 6.5 | 7.1 |
| Totals .................. | 1100 | 35954 | 5832 | 13100 | .445 | 3791 | 4754 | .797 | 1459 | 2790 | 4249 | 5499 | 1477 | 675 | 2448 | 15535 | 3.9 | 5.0 | 14.1 |

Three-point field goals: 1979-80, 12-for-58 (.207). 1980-81, 11-for-51 (.216). 1981-82, 8-for-42 (.190). 1982-83, 5-for-31 (.161). 1983-84, 4-for-32 (.125). 1984-85, 7-for-26 (.269). 1985-86, 6-for-42 (.143). 1986-87, 7-for-62 (.113). 1987-88, 12-for-46 (.261). 1988-89, 7-for-50 (.140). 1989-90, 1-for-24 (.042). Totals, 80-for-464 (.172).

Personal fouls/disqualifications: 1976-77, 221/3. 1977-78, 213/2. 1978-79, 209/2. 1979-80, 267/6. 1980-81, 244/2. 1981-82, 253/6. 1982-83, 204/1. 1983-84, 251/6. 1984-85, 224/2. 1985-86, 206/3. 1986-87, 201/0. 1987-88, 204/0. 1988-89, 211/3. 1989-90, 179/2. Totals, 3087/38.

## NBA PLAYOFF RECORD

**NOTES:** NBA Finals Most Valuable Player (1979).

| Season Team | G | Min. | FGM | FGA | Pct. | FTM | FTA | Pct. | Off. | Def. | Tot. | Ast. | St. | Blk. | TO | Pts. | RPG | APG | PPG |
|---|---|---|---|---|---|---|---|---|---|---|---|---|---|---|---|---|---|---|---|
| | | | | | | | | | | **REBOUNDS** | | | | | | | | **AVERAGES** | |
| 77-78—Seattle ........... | 22 | 827 | 121 | 294 | .412 | 112 | 159 | .704 | 47 | 54 | 101 | 72 | 23 | 23 | 56 | 354 | 4.6 | 3.3 | 16.1 |
| 78-79—Seattle ........... | 17 | 681 | 136 | 302 | .450 | 84 | 109 | .771 | 44 | 60 | 104 | 69 | 28 | 26 | 51 | 356 | 6.1 | 4.1 | 20.9 |
| 79-80—Seattle ........... | 15 | 582 | 100 | 244 | .410 | 52 | 62 | .839 | 25 | 39 | 64 | 57 | 27 | 10 | 43 | 257 | 4.3 | 3.8 | 17.1 |
| 80-81—Phoenix ......... | 7 | 267 | 52 | 110 | .473 | 32 | 42 | .762 | 7 | 26 | 33 | 20 | 9 | 9 | 19 | 137 | 4.7 | 2.9 | 19.6 |
| 81-82—Phoenix ......... | 7 | 271 | 63 | 132 | .477 | 30 | 39 | .769 | 13 | 18 | 31 | 32 | 15 | 4 | 25 | 156 | 4.4 | 4.6 | 22.3 |
| 82-83—Phoenix ......... | 3 | 108 | 22 | 48 | .458 | 10 | 12 | .833 | 6 | 17 | 23 | 17 | 5 | 2 | 8 | 54 | 7.7 | 5.7 | 18.0 |
| 83-84—Boston ........... | 22 | 808 | 129 | 319 | .404 | 104 | 120 | .867 | 30 | 49 | 79 | 97 | 25 | 7 | 53 | 365 | 3.6 | 4.4 | 16.6 |

| Season Team | G | Min. | FGM | FGA | Pct. | FTM | FTA | Pct. | REBOUNDS Off. | Def. | Tot. | Ast. | St. | Blk. | TO | Pts. | AVERAGES RPG | APG | PPG |
|---|---|---|---|---|---|---|---|---|---|---|---|---|---|---|---|---|---|---|---|
| 84-85—Boston | 21 | 848 | 142 | 319 | .445 | 80 | 93 | .860 | 24 | 60 | 84 | 154 | 31 | 9 | 72 | 364 | 4.0 | 7.3 | 17.3 |
| 85-86—Boston | 18 | 715 | 109 | 245 | .445 | 67 | 84 | .798 | 23 | 53 | 76 | 107 | 39 | 5 | 51 | 291 | 4.2 | 5.9 | 16.2 |
| 86-87—Boston | 23 | 964 | 168 | 361 | .465 | 96 | 113 | .850 | 24 | 67 | 91 | 205 | 16 | 8 | 44 | 435 | 4.0 | 8.9 | 18.9 |
| 87-88—Boston | 17 | 702 | 91 | 210 | .433 | 82 | 103 | .796 | 15 | 62 | 77 | 139 | 24 | 8 | 45 | 270 | 4.5 | 8.2 | 15.9 |
| 88-89—Boston | 3 | 59 | 4 | 15 | .267 | 0 | 0 | ... | 2 | 2 | 4 | 9 | 3 | 0 | 3 | 8 | 1.3 | 3.0 | 2.7 |
| 89-90—Boston | 5 | 162 | 30 | 62 | .484 | 7 | 7 | 1.000 | 2 | 12 | 14 | 28 | 2 | 2 | 10 | 69 | 2.8 | 5.6 | 13.8 |
| Totals | 180 | 6994 | 1167 | 2661 | .439 | 756 | 943 | .802 | 262 | 519 | 781 | 1006 | 247 | 113 | 480 | 3116 | 4.3 | 5.6 | 17.3 |

Three-point field goals: 1979-80, 5-for-15 (.333). 1980-81, 1-for-5 (.200). 1981-82, 0-for-4. 1982-83, 0-for-1. 1983-84, 3-for-7 (.429). 1984-85, 0-for-14. 1985-86, 6-for-16 (.375). 1986-87, 3-for-26 (.115). 1987-88, 6-for-16 (.375). 1989-90, 2-for-6 (.333). Totals, 26-for-110 (.236).

Personal fouls/disqualifications: 1977-78, 63/0. 1978-79, 63/0. 1979-80, 48/2. 1980-81, 18/0. 1981-82, 28/2. 1982-83, 9/0. 1983-84, 75/1. 1984-85, 66/0. 1985-86, 58/2. 1986-87, 71/0. 1987-88, 51/0. 1989-90, 17/1. Totals, 575/8.

## NBA ALL-STAR GAME RECORD

| Season Team | Min. | FGM | FGA | Pct. | FTM | FTA | Pct. | REBOUNDS Off. | Def. | Tot. | Ast. | PF | Dq. | St. | Blk. | TO | Pts. |
|---|---|---|---|---|---|---|---|---|---|---|---|---|---|---|---|---|---|
| 1979—Seattle | 27 | 5 | 7 | .714 | 2 | 2 | 1.000 | 1 | 0 | 1 | 3 | 3 | 0 | 0 | 1 | 1 | 12 |
| 1980—Seattle | 20 | 7 | 13 | .538 | 5 | 6 | .833 | 2 | 2 | 4 | 1 | 3 | 0 | 2 | 1 | 2 | 19 |
| 1981—Phoenix | 24 | 5 | 8 | .625 | 9 | 10 | .900 | 1 | 1 | 2 | 1 | 1 | 0 | 3 | 0 | 2 | 19 |
| 1982—Phoenix | 15 | 0 | 2 | .000 | 1 | 2 | .500 | 2 | 3 | 5 | 1 | 1 | 0 | 0 | 2 | 3 | 1 |
| 1985—Boston | 12 | 3 | 7 | .429 | 2 | 2 | 1.000 | 1 | 5 | 6 | 3 | 2 | 0 | 0 | 0 | 1 | 8 |
| Totals | 98 | 20 | 37 | .541 | 19 | 22 | .864 | 7 | 11 | 18 | 9 | 10 | 0 | 5 | 4 | 9 | 59 |

## CBA COACHING RECORD

| Season Team | REGULAR SEASON W | L | Pct. | Finish | PLAYOFFS W | L | Pct. |
|---|---|---|---|---|---|---|---|
| 99-00—La Crosse | 14 | 22 | .389 | | — | — | — |

NOTES:
2000—Named assistant coach by Los Angeles Clippers (February 4).

# JOHNSON, EDDIE    G/F

**PERSONAL:** Born May 1, 1959, in Chicago. ... 6-7/215 (2,00/97,5). ... Full name: Edward Arnet Johnson.
**HIGH SCHOOL:** Westinghouse Vocational (Chicago).
**COLLEGE:** Illinois.
**TRANSACTIONS/CAREER NOTES:** Selected by Kansas City Kings in second round (29th pick overall) of 1981 NBA Draft. ... Kings franchise moved from Kansas City to Sacramento for 1985-86 season. ... Traded by Kings to Phoenix Suns for F Ed Pinckney and 1988 second-round draft choice (June 21, 1987). ... Traded by Suns with 1991 first-round draft choice and 1993 or 1994 first-round draft choice to Seattle SuperSonics for F Xavier McDaniel (December 7, 1990). ... Traded by SuperSonics with G Dana Barros and option to switch 1994 first-round draft choices to Charlotte Hornets for G Kendall Gill (September 1, 1993). ... Played in Greece (1994-95). ... Signed as free agent by Indiana Pacers (October 3, 1995). ... Traded by Pacers with G Vincent Askew and 1997 and 1998 second-round draft choices to Denver Nuggets for F/C LaSalle Thompson and G Mark Jackson (February 20, 1997). ... Waived by Nuggets (February 27, 1997). ... Signed by Houston Rockets for remainder of season (March 3, 1997).

## COLLEGIATE RECORD

| Season Team | G | Min. | FGM | FGA | Pct. | FTM | FTA | Pct. | Reb. | Ast. | Pts. | AVERAGES RPG | APG | PPG |
|---|---|---|---|---|---|---|---|---|---|---|---|---|---|---|
| 77-78—Illinois | 27 | 469 | 100 | 234 | .427 | 20 | 27 | .741 | 84 | 16 | 220 | 3.1 | 0.6 | 8.1 |
| 78-79—Illinois | 30 | 786 | 168 | 405 | .415 | 26 | 49 | .531 | 170 | 52 | 362 | 5.7 | 1.7 | 12.1 |
| 79-80—Illinois | 35 | 1215 | 266 | 576 | .462 | 78 | 119 | .655 | 310 | 71 | 610 | 8.9 | 2.0 | 17.4 |
| 80-81—Illinois | 29 | 1009 | 219 | 443 | .494 | 62 | 82 | .756 | 267 | 70 | 500 | 9.2 | 2.4 | 17.2 |
| Totals | 121 | 3479 | 753 | 1658 | .454 | 186 | 277 | .671 | 831 | 209 | 1692 | 6.9 | 1.7 | 14.0 |

HONORS: NBA Sixth Man Award (1989).

## NBA REGULAR-SEASON RECORD

| Season Team | G | Min. | FGM | FGA | Pct. | FTM | FTA | Pct. | REBOUNDS Off. | Def. | Tot. | Ast. | St. | Blk. | TO | Pts. | AVERAGES RPG | APG | PPG |
|---|---|---|---|---|---|---|---|---|---|---|---|---|---|---|---|---|---|---|---|
| 81-82—Kansas City | 74 | 1517 | 295 | 643 | .459 | 99 | 149 | .664 | 128 | 194 | 322 | 109 | 50 | 14 | 97 | 690 | 4.4 | 1.5 | 9.3 |
| 82-83—Kansas City | 82 | 2933 | 677 | 1370 | .494 | 247 | 317 | .779 | 191 | 310 | 501 | 216 | 70 | 20 | 181 | 1621 | 6.1 | 2.6 | 19.8 |
| 83-84—Kansas City | 82 | 2920 | 753 | 1552 | .485 | 268 | 331 | .810 | 165 | 290 | 455 | 296 | 76 | 21 | 213 | 1794 | 5.5 | 3.6 | 21.9 |
| 84-85—Kansas City | 82 | 3029 | 769 | 1565 | .491 | 325 | 373 | .871 | 151 | 256 | 407 | 273 | 83 | 22 | 225 | 1876 | 5.0 | 3.3 | 22.9 |
| 85-86—Sacramento | 82 | 2514 | 623 | 1311 | .475 | 280 | 343 | .816 | 173 | 246 | 419 | 214 | 54 | 17 | 191 | 1530 | 5.1 | 2.6 | 18.7 |
| 86-87—Sacramento | 81 | 2457 | 606 | 1309 | .463 | 267 | 322 | .829 | 146 | 207 | 353 | 251 | 42 | 19 | 163 | 1516 | 4.4 | 3.1 | 18.7 |
| 87-88—Phoenix | 73 | 2177 | 533 | 1110 | .480 | 204 | 240 | .850 | 121 | 197 | 318 | 180 | 33 | 9 | 139 | 1294 | 4.4 | 2.5 | 17.7 |
| 88-89—Phoenix | 70 | 2043 | 608 | 1224 | .497 | 217 | 250 | .868 | 91 | 215 | 306 | 162 | 47 | 7 | 122 | 1504 | 4.4 | 2.3 | 21.5 |
| 89-90—Phoenix | 64 | 1811 | 411 | 907 | .453 | 188 | 205 | .917 | 69 | 177 | 246 | 107 | 32 | 10 | 108 | 1080 | 3.8 | 1.7 | 16.9 |
| 90-91—Pho.-Seattle | 81 | 2085 | 543 | 1122 | .484 | 229 | 257 | .891 | 107 | 164 | 271 | 111 | 58 | 9 | 122 | 1354 | 3.3 | 1.4 | 16.7 |
| 91-92—Seattle | 81 | 2366 | 534 | 1164 | .459 | 291 | 338 | .861 | 118 | 174 | 292 | 161 | 55 | 11 | 130 | 1386 | 3.6 | 2.0 | 17.1 |
| 92-93—Seattle | 82 | 1869 | 463 | 991 | .467 | 234 | 257 | .911 | 124 | 148 | 272 | 135 | 36 | 4 | 134 | 1177 | 3.3 | 1.6 | 14.4 |
| 93-94—Charlotte | 73 | 1460 | 339 | 738 | .459 | 99 | 127 | .780 | 80 | 144 | 224 | 125 | 36 | 8 | 84 | 836 | 3.1 | 1.7 | 11.5 |
| 95-96—Indiana | 62 | 1002 | 180 | 436 | .413 | 70 | 79 | .886 | 45 | 108 | 153 | 69 | 20 | 4 | 56 | 475 | 2.5 | 1.1 | 7.7 |
| 96-97—Ind.-Hou. | 52 | 913 | 160 | 362 | .442 | 55 | 68 | .809 | 27 | 111 | 138 | 52 | 15 | 2 | 47 | 424 | 2.7 | 1.0 | 8.2 |
| 97-98—Houston | 75 | 1490 | 227 | 544 | .417 | 113 | 136 | .831 | 50 | 103 | 153 | 88 | 32 | 3 | 62 | 633 | 2.0 | 1.2 | 8.4 |
| 98-99—Houston | 3 | 18 | 6 | 13 | .462 | 0 | 0 | ... | 0 | 2 | 2 | 1 | 0 | 0 | 2 | 12 | 0.7 | 0.3 | 4.0 |
| Totals | 1199 | 32604 | 7727 | 16361 | .472 | 3186 | 3792 | .840 | 1786 | 3046 | 4832 | 2550 | 739 | 180 | 2076 | 19202 | 4.0 | 2.1 | 16.0 |

Three-point field goals: 1981-82, 1-for-11 (.091). 1982-83, 20-for-71 (.282). 1983-84, 20-for-64 (.313). 1984-85, 13-for-54 (.241). 1985-86, 4-for-20 (.200). 1986-87, 37-for-118 (.314). 1987-88, 24-for-94 (.255). 1988-89, 71-for-172 (.413). 1989-90, 70-for-184 (.380). 1990-91, 39-for-120 (.325). 1991-92, 27-for-107 (.252). 1992-93, 17-for-56 (.304). 1993-94, 59-for-150 (.393). 1995-96, 45-for-128 (.352). 1996-97, 49-for-131 (.374). 1997-98, 66-for-198 (.333). 1998-99, 0-for-1. Totals, 562-for-1679 (.335).

Personal fouls/disqualifications: 1981-82, 210/6. 1982-83, 259/3. 1983-84, 266/4. 1984-85, 237/2. 1985-86, 237/0. 1986-87, 218/4. 1987-88, 190/0. 1988-89, 198/0. 1989-90, 174/4. 1990-91, 181/0. 1991-92, 199/0. 1992-93, 173/0. 1993-94, 143/2. 1995-96, 104/1. 1996-97, 81/0. 1997-98, 89/0. 1998-99, 3/0. Totals, 2962/26.

## NBA PLAYOFF RECORD

| Season Team | G | Min. | FGM | FGA | Pct. | FTM | FTA | Pct. | REBOUNDS Off. | Def. | Tot. | Ast. | St. | Blk. | TO | Pts. | AVERAGES RPG | APG | PPG |
|---|---|---|---|---|---|---|---|---|---|---|---|---|---|---|---|---|---|---|---|
| 83-84—Kansas City..... | 3 | 107 | 21 | 48 | .438 | 7 | 7 | 1.000 | 4 | 6 | 10 | 12 | 3 | 1 | 2 | 51 | 3.3 | 4.0 | 17.0 |
| 85-86—Sacramento .... | 3 | 96 | 24 | 55 | .436 | 8 | 9 | .889 | 10 | 11 | 21 | 4 | 3 | 1 | 6 | 56 | 7.0 | 1.3 | 18.7 |
| 88-89—Phoenix ......... | 12 | 392 | 85 | 206 | .413 | 30 | 39 | .769 | 28 | 59 | 87 | 25 | 12 | 2 | 18 | 213 | 7.3 | 2.1 | 17.8 |
| 89-90—Phoenix ......... | 16 | 337 | 72 | 160 | .450 | 37 | 47 | .787 | 15 | 42 | 57 | 17 | 10 | 4 | 20 | 196 | 3.6 | 1.1 | 12.3 |

| Season Team | G | Min. | FGM | FGA | Pct. | FTM | FTA | Pct. | REBOUNDS Off. | Def. | Tot. | Ast. | St. | Blk. | TO | Pts. | AVERAGES RPG | APG | PPG |
|---|---|---|---|---|---|---|---|---|---|---|---|---|---|---|---|---|---|---|---|
| 90-91—Seattle ............ | 5 | 171 | 46 | 89 | .517 | 24 | 29 | .828 | 12 | 9 | 21 | 7 | 7 | 1 | 8 | 120 | 4.2 | 1.4 | 24.0 |
| 91-92—Seattle ............ | 9 | 247 | 65 | 137 | .474 | 32 | 34 | .941 | 8 | 19 | 27 | 8 | 3 | 3 | 15 | 166 | 3.0 | 0.9 | 18.4 |
| 92-93—Seattle ............ | 19 | 382 | 82 | 210 | .390 | 29 | 31 | .935 | 17 | 28 | 45 | 17 | 3 | 1 | 19 | 205 | 2.4 | 0.9 | 10.8 |
| 95-96—Indiana............ | 1 | 9 | 0 | 5 | .000 | 0 | 0 | ... | 0 | 0 | 0 | 1 | 0 | 0 | 0 | 0 | 0.0 | 1.0 | 0.0 |
| 96-97—Houston ......... | 16 | 284 | 48 | 117 | .410 | 23 | 24 | .958 | 15 | 21 | 36 | 10 | 5 | 0 | 7 | 133 | 2.3 | 0.6 | 8.3 |
| 97-98—Houston ......... | 5 | 89 | 9 | 27 | .333 | 7 | 8 | .875 | 4 | 4 | 8 | 1 | 0 | 0 | 3 | 28 | 1.6 | 0.2 | 5.6 |
| Totals .................. | 89 | 2114 | 452 | 1054 | .429 | 197 | 228 | .864 | 113 | 199 | 312 | 102 | 46 | 13 | 98 | 1168 | 3.5 | 1.1 | 13.1 |

Three-point field goals: 1983-84, 2-for-5 (.400). 1985-86, 0-for-3. 1988-89, 13-for-38 (.342). 1989-90, 15-for-38 (.395). 1990-91, 4-for-15 (.267). 1991-92, 4-for-22 (.182). 1992-93, 12-for-36 (.333). 1995-96, 0-for-2. 1996-97, 14-for-47 (.298). 1997-98, 3-for-10 (.300). Totals, 67-for-216 (.310).

Personal fouls/disqualifications: 1983-84, 8/0. 1985-86, 7/0. 1988-89, 41/1. 1989-90, 40/0. 1990-91, 13/0. 1991-92, 19/0. 1992-93, 44/2. 1996-97, 17/0. 1997-98, 10/0. Totals, 199/3.

## GREEK LEAGUE RECORD

| Season Team | G | Min. | FGM | FGA | Pct. | FTM | FTA | Pct. | Reb. | Ast. | Pts. | AVERAGES RPG | APG | PPG |
|---|---|---|---|---|---|---|---|---|---|---|---|---|---|---|
| 94-95—Olympiakos S.F.P. ........... | 25 | 829 | 188 | 419 | .449 | 92 | 109 | .844 | 122 | 48 | 527 | 4.9 | 1.9 | 21.1 |

# JOHNSON, GUS · F

**PERSONAL:** Born December 13, 1938, in Akron, Ohio. ... Died April 29, 1987. ... 6-6/235 (1,98/106,6). ... Full name: Gus Johnson Jr. ... Nickname: Honeycomb.
**HIGH SCHOOL:** Central Hower (Akron, Ohio).
**JUNIOR COLLEGE:** Boise (Idaho) Junior College.
**COLLEGE:** Akron, then Idaho.

**TRANSACTIONS:** Selected by Baltimore Bullets in second round (11th pick overall) of 1963 NBA Draft. ... Traded by Bullets to Phoenix Suns for second-round draft choice (April 10, 1972). ... Waived by Suns (December 1, 1972). ... Signed as free agent by Indiana Pacers of American Basketball Association (December 15, 1972).

## COLLEGIATE RECORD

**NOTES:** Left Akron before start of 1959-60 basketball season.

| Season Team | G | Min. | FGM | FGA | Pct. | FTM | FTA | Pct. | Reb. | Ast. | Pts. | AVERAGES RPG | APG | PPG |
|---|---|---|---|---|---|---|---|---|---|---|---|---|---|---|
| 62-63—Idaho ............................. | 23 | ... | 188 | 438 | .429 | 62 | 105 | .590 | 466 | ... | 438 | 20.3 | ... | 19.0 |

## NBA REGULAR-SEASON RECORD

**HONORS:** All-NBA second team (1965, 1966, 1970, 1971). ... NBA All-Defensive first team (1970, 1971). ... NBA All-Rookie team (1964).

| Season Team | G | Min. | FGM | FGA | Pct. | FTM | FTA | Pct. | Reb. | Ast. | PF | Dq. | Pts. | AVERAGES RPG | APG | PPG |
|---|---|---|---|---|---|---|---|---|---|---|---|---|---|---|---|---|
| 63-64—Baltimore ......................... | 78 | 2847 | 571 | 1329 | .430 | 210 | 319 | .658 | 1064 | 169 | 321 | †11 | 1352 | 13.6 | 2.2 | 17.3 |
| 64-65—Baltimore ......................... | 76 | 2899 | 577 | 1379 | .418 | 261 | 386 | .676 | 988 | 270 | 258 | 4 | 1415 | 13.0 | 3.6 | 18.6 |
| 65-66—Baltimore ......................... | 41 | 1284 | 273 | 661 | .413 | 131 | 178 | .736 | 546 | 114 | 136 | 3 | 677 | 13.3 | 2.8 | 16.5 |
| 66-67—Baltimore ......................... | 73 | 2626 | 620 | 1377 | .450 | 271 | 383 | .708 | 855 | 194 | 281 | 7 | 1511 | 11.7 | 2.7 | 20.7 |
| 67-68—Baltimore ......................... | 60 | 2271 | 482 | 1033 | .467 | 180 | 270 | .667 | 782 | 159 | 223 | 7 | 1144 | 13.0 | 2.7 | 19.1 |
| 68-69—Baltimore ......................... | 49 | 1671 | 359 | 782 | .459 | 160 | 223 | .717 | 568 | 97 | 176 | 1 | 878 | 11.6 | 2.0 | 17.9 |
| 69-70—Baltimore ......................... | 78 | 2919 | 578 | 1282 | .451 | 197 | 272 | .724 | 1086 | 264 | 269 | 6 | 1353 | 13.9 | 3.4 | 17.3 |
| 70-71—Baltimore ......................... | 66 | 2538 | 494 | 1090 | .453 | 214 | 290 | .738 | 1128 | 192 | 227 | 4 | 1202 | 17.1 | 2.9 | 18.2 |
| 71-72—Baltimore ......................... | 39 | 668 | 103 | 269 | .383 | 43 | 63 | .683 | 226 | 51 | 91 | 0 | 249 | 5.8 | 1.3 | 6.4 |
| 72-73—Phoenix ........................... | 21 | 417 | 69 | 181 | .381 | 25 | 36 | .694 | 136 | 31 | 55 | 0 | 163 | 6.5 | 1.5 | 7.8 |
| Totals ......................... | 581 | 20140 | 4126 | 9383 | .440 | 1692 | 2420 | .699 | 7379 | 1541 | 2037 | 43 | 9944 | 12.7 | 2.7 | 17.1 |

## NBA PLAYOFF RECORD

| Season Team | G | Min. | FGM | FGA | Pct. | FTM | FTA | Pct. | Reb. | Ast. | PF | Dq. | Pts. | AVERAGES RPG | APG | PPG |
|---|---|---|---|---|---|---|---|---|---|---|---|---|---|---|---|---|
| 64-65—Baltimore ......................... | 10 | 377 | 62 | 173 | .358 | 34 | 46 | .739 | 111 | 34 | 38 | 1 | 158 | 11.1 | 3.4 | 15.8 |
| 65-66—Baltimore ......................... | 1 | 8 | 1 | 4 | .250 | 0 | 0 | ... | 0 | 0 | 1 | 0 | 2 | 0.0 | 0.0 | 2.0 |
| 69-70—Baltimore ......................... | 7 | 298 | 51 | 111 | .459 | 27 | 34 | .794 | 80 | 9 | 20 | 0 | 129 | 11.4 | 1.3 | 18.4 |
| 70-71—Baltimore ......................... | 11 | 365 | 54 | 128 | .422 | 35 | 47 | .745 | 114 | 30 | 34 | 0 | 143 | 10.4 | 2.7 | 13.0 |
| 71-72—Baltimore ......................... | 5 | 77 | 9 | 30 | .300 | 2 | 2 | 1.000 | 25 | 3 | 17 | 0 | 20 | 5.0 | 0.6 | 4.0 |
| Totals ......................... | 34 | 1125 | 177 | 446 | .397 | 98 | 129 | .760 | 330 | 76 | 110 | 1 | 452 | 9.7 | 2.2 | 13.3 |

## NBA ALL-STAR GAME RECORD

| Season Team | Min. | FGM | FGA | Pct. | FTM | FTA | Pct. | Reb | Ast. | PF | Dq. | Pts. |
|---|---|---|---|---|---|---|---|---|---|---|---|---|
| 1965—Baltimore ...................... | 25 | 7 | 13 | .538 | 11 | 13 | .846 | 8 | 2 | 2 | 0 | 25 |
| 1968—Baltimore ...................... | 16 | 3 | 9 | .333 | 1 | 2 | .500 | 6 | 1 | 2 | 0 | 7 |
| 1969—Baltimore ...................... | 18 | 4 | 10 | .400 | 5 | 8 | .625 | 10 | 0 | 3 | 0 | 13 |
| 1970—Baltimore ...................... | 17 | 5 | 12 | .417 | 0 | 0 | ... | 7 | 1 | 2 | 0 | 10 |
| 1971—Baltimore ...................... | 23 | 5 | 12 | .417 | 2 | 2 | 1.000 | 4 | 2 | 3 | 0 | 12 |
| Totals ................... | 99 | 24 | 56 | .429 | 19 | 25 | .760 | 35 | 6 | 12 | 0 | 67 |

## ABA REGULAR-SEASON RECORD

**NOTES:** Member of ABA championship team (1973).

| Season Team | G | Min. | 2-POINT | | | 3-POINT | | | FTM | FTA | Pct. | Reb. | Ast. | Pts. | AVERAGES | | |
|---|---|---|---|---|---|---|---|---|---|---|---|---|---|---|---|---|---|
| | | | FGM | FGA | Pct. | FGM | FGA | Pct. | | | | | | | RPG | APG | PPG |
| 72-73—Indiana | 50 | 753 | 128 | 278 | .460 | 4 | 21 | .190 | 31 | 42 | .738 | 245 | 62 | 299 | 4.9 | 1.2 | 6.0 |

## ABA PLAYOFF RECORD

| Season Team | G | Min. | 2-POINT | | | 3-POINT | | | FTM | FTA | Pct. | Reb. | Ast. | Pts. | AVERAGES | | |
|---|---|---|---|---|---|---|---|---|---|---|---|---|---|---|---|---|---|
| | | | FGM | FGA | Pct. | FGM | FGA | Pct. | | | | | | | RPG | APG | PPG |
| 72-73—Indiana | 17 | 184 | 15 | 56 | .268 | 0 | 3 | .000 | 12 | 16 | .750 | 69 | 15 | 42 | 4.1 | 0.9 | 2.5 |

## COMBINED ABA AND NBA REGULAR-SEASON RECORDS

| | G | Min. | FGM | FGA | Pct. | FTM | FTA | Pct. | REBOUNDS | | | Ast. | Stl. | Blk. | TO | Pts. | AVERAGES | | |
|---|---|---|---|---|---|---|---|---|---|---|---|---|---|---|---|---|---|---|---|
| | | | | | | | | | Off. | Def. | Tot. | | | | | | RPG | APG | PPG |
| Totals | 631 | 20893 | 4258 | 9682 | .440 | 1723 | 2462 | .700 | ... | ... | 7624 | 1603 | ... | ... | | 10243 | 12.1 | 2.5 | 16.2 |

Three-point field goals: 4-for-21 (.190).
Personal fouls/disqualifications: 2150.

---

# JOHNSON, KEVIN     G

**PERSONAL:** Born March 4, 1966, in Sacramento. ... 6-1/190. (1,85/86). ... Full Name: Kevin Maurice Johnson. ... Nickname: K.J.
**HIGH SCHOOL:** Sacramento.
**COLLEGE:** California.
**TRANSACTIONS/CAREER NOTES:** Selected by Cleveland Cavaliers in first round (seventh pick overall) of 1987 NBA Draft. ... Traded by Cavaliers with G/F Tyrone Corbin, F/C Mark West, 1988 first- and second-round draft choices and 1989 second-round draft choice to Phoenix Suns for F Larry Nance, F Mike Sanders and 1988 second-round draft choice (February 25, 1988). ... Announced retirement (October 12, 1999). ... Activated from retirement (March 25, 2000). ... Announced retirement (August 8, 2000).
**MISCELLANEOUS:** Member of gold-medal winning U.S. World Championship team (1994). ... Phoenix Suns all-time assists leader with 6,518 (1987-88 through 1997-98 and 1999-2000).

## COLLEGIATE RECORD

| Season Team | G | Min. | FGM | FGA | Pct. | FTM | FTA | Pct. | Reb. | Ast. | Pts. | AVERAGES | | |
|---|---|---|---|---|---|---|---|---|---|---|---|---|---|---|
| | | | | | | | | | | | | RPG | APG | PPG |
| 83-84—California | 28 | 773 | 98 | 192 | .510 | 75 | 104 | .721 | 83 | 65 | 271 | 3.0 | 2.3 | 9.7 |
| 84-85—California | 27 | 902 | 127 | 282 | .450 | 94 | 142 | .662 | 104 | 111 | 348 | 3.9 | 4.1 | 12.9 |
| 85-86—California | 29 | 1024 | 164 | 335 | .490 | 123 | 151 | .815 | 104 | 175 | 451 | 3.6 | 6.0 | 15.6 |
| 86-87—California | 34 | 1115 | 212 | 450 | .471 | 113 | 138 | .819 | 132 | 170 | 585 | 3.9 | 5.0 | 17.2 |
| Totals | 118 | 3814 | 601 | 1259 | .477 | 405 | 535 | .757 | 423 | 521 | 1655 | 3.6 | 4.4 | 14.0 |

Three-point field goals: 1986-87, 48-for-124 (.387).

## NBA REGULAR-SEASON RECORD

**HONORS:** NBA Most Improved Player (1989). ... All-NBA second team (1989, 1990, 1991, 1994). ... All-NBA third team (1992).

| Season Team | G | Min. | FGM | FGA | Pct. | FTM | FTA | Pct. | REBOUNDS | | | Ast. | St. | Blk. | TO | Pts. | AVERAGES | | |
|---|---|---|---|---|---|---|---|---|---|---|---|---|---|---|---|---|---|---|---|
| | | | | | | | | | Off. | Def. | Tot. | | | | | | RPG | APG | PPG |
| 87-88—Cle.-Phoenix | 80 | 1917 | 275 | 596 | .461 | 177 | 211 | .839 | 36 | 155 | 191 | 437 | 103 | 24 | 146 | 732 | 2.4 | 5.5 | 9.2 |
| 88-89—Phoenix | 81 | 3179 | 570 | 1128 | .505 | 508 | 576 | .882 | 46 | 294 | 340 | 991 | 135 | 24 | &322 | 1650 | 4.2 | 12.2 | 20.4 |
| 89-90—Phoenix | 74 | 2782 | 578 | 1159 | .499 | 501 | 598 | .838 | 42 | 228 | 270 | 846 | 95 | 14 | 263 | 1665 | 3.6 | 11.4 | 22.5 |
| 90-91—Phoenix | 77 | 2772 | 591 | 1145 | .516 | 519 | 616 | .843 | 54 | 217 | 271 | 781 | 163 | 11 | 269 | 1710 | 3.5 | 10.1 | 22.2 |
| 91-92—Phoenix | 78 | 2899 | 539 | 1125 | .479 | 448 | 555 | .807 | 61 | 231 | 292 | 836 | 116 | 23 | 272 | 1536 | 3.7 | 10.7 | 19.7 |
| 92-93—Phoenix | 49 | 1643 | 282 | 565 | .499 | 226 | 276 | .819 | 30 | 74 | 104 | 384 | 85 | 19 | 151 | 791 | 2.1 | 7.8 | 16.1 |
| 93-94—Phoenix | 67 | 2449 | 477 | 980 | .487 | 380 | 464 | .819 | 55 | 112 | 167 | 637 | 125 | 10 | 235 | 1340 | 2.5 | 9.5 | 20.0 |
| 94-95—Phoenix | 47 | 1352 | 246 | 523 | .470 | 234 | 289 | .810 | 32 | 83 | 115 | 360 | 47 | 18 | 105 | 730 | 2.4 | 7.7 | 15.5 |
| 95-96—Phoenix | 56 | 2007 | 342 | 674 | .507 | 342 | 398 | .859 | 42 | 179 | 221 | 517 | 82 | 13 | 170 | 1047 | 3.9 | 9.2 | 18.7 |
| 96-97—Phoenix | 70 | 2658 | 441 | 890 | .496 | 439 | 515 | .852 | 54 | 199 | 253 | 653 | 102 | 12 | 217 | 1410 | 3.6 | 9.3 | 20.1 |
| 97-98—Phoenix | 50 | 1290 | 155 | 347 | .447 | 162 | 186 | .871 | 35 | 129 | 164 | 245 | 27 | 8 | 101 | 476 | 3.3 | 4.9 | 9.5 |
| 99-00—Phoenix | 6 | 113 | 16 | 28 | .571 | 7 | 7 | 1.000 | 0 | 16 | 16 | 24 | 2 | 0 | 7 | 40 | 2.7 | 4.0 | 6.7 |
| Totals | 735 | 25061 | 4512 | 9160 | .493 | 3943 | 4691 | .841 | 487 | 1917 | 2404 | 6711 | 1082 | 176 | 2258 | 13127 | 3.3 | 9.1 | 17.9 |

Three-point field goals: 1987-88, 5-for-24 (.208). 1988-89, 2-for-22 (.091). 1989-90, 8-for-41 (.195). 1990-91, 9-for-44 (.205). 1991-92, 10-for-46 (.217). 1992-93, 1-for-8 (.125). 1993-94, 6-for-27 (.222). 1994-95, 4-for-26 (.154). 1995-96, 21-for-57 (.368). 1996-97, 89-for-202 (.441). 1997-98, 4-for-26 (.154). 1999-00, 1-for-1. Totals, 160-for-524 (.305).
Personal fouls/disqualifications: 1987-88, 155/1. 1988-89, 226/1. 1989-90, 143/0. 1990-91, 174/0. 1991-92, 180/0. 1992-93, 100/0. 1993-94, 127/1. 1994-95, 88/0. 1995-96, 144/0. 1996-97, 141/0. 1997-98, 57/0. 1999-00, 6/0. Totals, 1541/3.

## NBA PLAYOFF RECORD

**NOTES:** Holds NBA Finals single-game record for most minutes played—62 (June 13, 1993, at Chicago, 3 OT).

| Season Team | G | Min. | FGM | FGA | Pct. | FTM | FTA | Pct. | REBOUNDS | | | Ast. | St. | Blk. | TO | Pts. | AVERAGES | | |
|---|---|---|---|---|---|---|---|---|---|---|---|---|---|---|---|---|---|---|---|
| | | | | | | | | | Off. | Def. | Tot. | | | | | | RPG | APG | PPG |
| 88-89—Phoenix | 12 | 494 | 90 | 182 | .495 | 102 | 110 | .927 | 12 | 39 | 51 | 147 | 19 | 5 | 55 | 285 | 4.3 | 12.3 | 23.8 |
| 89-90—Phoenix | 16 | 582 | 123 | 257 | .479 | 92 | 112 | .821 | 9 | 44 | 53 | 170 | 25 | 0 | 62 | 340 | 3.3 | 10.6 | 21.3 |
| 90-91—Phoenix | 4 | 146 | 16 | 53 | .302 | 18 | 30 | .600 | 2 | 11 | 13 | 39 | 2 | 1 | 12 | 51 | 3.3 | 9.8 | 12.8 |
| 91-92—Phoenix | 8 | 335 | 62 | 128 | .484 | 62 | 72 | .861 | 8 | 25 | 33 | 93 | 12 | 2 | 25 | 189 | 4.1 | 11.6 | 23.6 |
| 92-93—Phoenix | 23 | 914 | 143 | 298 | .480 | 124 | 156 | .795 | 10 | 52 | 62 | 182 | 35 | 13 | 84 | 410 | 2.7 | 7.9 | 17.8 |
| 93-94—Phoenix | 10 | 427 | 97 | 212 | .458 | 69 | 81 | .852 | 10 | 25 | 35 | 96 | 10 | 1 | 34 | 266 | 3.5 | 9.6 | 26.6 |
| 94-95—Phoenix | 10 | 371 | 86 | 150 | .573 | 71 | 84 | .845 | 7 | 34 | 41 | 93 | 9 | 4 | 34 | 248 | 4.1 | 9.3 | 24.8 |
| 95-96—Phoenix | 4 | 151 | 27 | 57 | .474 | 14 | 17 | .824 | 2 | 15 | 17 | 43 | 2 | 1 | 11 | 69 | 4.3 | 10.8 | 17.3 |
| 96-97—Phoenix | 5 | 208 | 26 | 88 | .295 | 29 | 33 | .879 | 8 | 14 | 22 | 30 | 13 | 0 | 18 | 84 | 4.4 | 6.0 | 16.8 |
| 97-98—Phoenix | 4 | 122 | 23 | 42 | .548 | 8 | 12 | .667 | 2 | 7 | 9 | 19 | 2 | 1 | 6 | 55 | 2.3 | 4.8 | 13.8 |
| 99-00—Phoenix | 9 | 129 | 12 | 37 | .324 | 5 | 6 | .833 | 0 | 13 | 13 | 23 | 3 | 1 | 13 | 29 | 1.4 | 2.6 | 3.2 |
| Totals | 105 | 3879 | 705 | 1504 | .469 | 594 | 713 | .833 | 70 | 279 | 349 | 935 | 132 | 30 | 354 | 2026 | 3.3 | 8.9 | 19.3 |

Three-point field goals: 1988-89, 3-for-10 (.300). 1989-90, 2-for-11 (.182). 1990-91, 1-for-7 (.143). 1991-92, 3-for-6 (.500). 1992-93, 0-for-3. 1993-94, 3-for-10 (.300). 1994-95, 5-for-10 (.500). 1995-96, 1-for-4 (.250). 1996-97, 3-for-22 (.136). 1997-98, 1-for-4 (.250). 1999-00, 0-for-3. Totals, 22-for-90 (.244).

Personal fouls/disqualifications: 1988-89, 28/0. 1989-90, 28/0. 1990-91, 9/0. 1991-92, 24/1. 1992-93, 57/1. 1993-94, 23/0. 1994-95, 25/0. 1995-96, 8/0. 1996-97, 15/1. 1997-98, 6/0. 1999-00, 10/0. Totals, 233/3.

### NBA ALL-STAR GAME RECORD

| Season Team | Min. | FGM | FGA | Pct. | FTM | FTA | Pct. | REBOUNDS | | | Ast. | PF | Dq. | St. | Blk. | TO | Pts. |
|---|---|---|---|---|---|---|---|---|---|---|---|---|---|---|---|---|---|
| | | | | | | | | Off. | Def. | Tot. | | | | | | | |
| 1990—Phoenix | 14 | 1 | 1 | 1.000 | 0 | 0 | ... | 0 | 0 | 0 | 4 | 2 | 0 | 0 | 0 | 3 | 2 |
| 1991—Phoenix | 23 | 2 | 5 | .400 | 1 | 2 | .500 | 1 | 1 | 2 | 7 | 2 | 0 | 3 | 1 | 3 | 5 |
| 1994—Phoenix | 14 | 3 | 6 | .500 | 0 | 1 | .000 | 0 | 1 | 1 | 2 | 1 | 0 | 1 | 0 | 2 | 6 |
| Totals | 51 | 6 | 12 | .500 | 1 | 3 | .333 | 1 | 2 | 3 | 13 | 5 | 0 | 4 | 1 | 8 | 13 |

## JOHNSON, MAGIC     G

**PERSONAL:** Born August 14, 1959, in Lansing, Mich. ... 6-9/225 (2,05/102,1). ... Full name: Earvin Johnson Jr.
**HIGH SCHOOL:** Everett (Lansing, Mich.).
**COLLEGE:** Michigan State.
**TRANSACTIONS:** Selected after sophomore season by Los Angeles Lakers in first round (first pick overall) of 1979 NBA Draft. ... On voluntarily retired list (November 7, 1991-January 29, 1996). ... Activated from retirement by Lakers (January 29, 1996). ... Announced retirement (May 14, 1996). ... Rights renounced by Lakers (July 16, 1996).
**CAREER NOTES:** Broadcaster, NBC Sports (1992-1994). ... Vice president, Los Angeles Lakers (1994-95 to present). ... Analyst, Turner Sports.
**CAREER HONORS:** One of the 50 Greatest Players in NBA History (1996). ... Selected to Naismith Basketball Hall of Fame (2002).
**MISCELLANEOUS:** Member of NBA championship team (1980, 1982, 1985, 1987, 1988). ... Member of gold-medal-winning U.S. Olympic team (1992). ... Los Angeles Lakers franchise all-time assists leader with 10,141 and all-time steals leader with 1,724 (1979-80 through 1990-91 and 1995-96).

### COLLEGIATE RECORD

**NOTES:** Member of NCAA championship team (1979). ... NCAA Division I Tournament Most Outstanding Player (1979). ... THE SPORTING NEWS All-America first team (1979).

| Season Team | G | Min. | FGM | FGA | Pct. | FTM | FTA | Pct. | Reb. | Ast. | Pts. | AVERAGES | | |
|---|---|---|---|---|---|---|---|---|---|---|---|---|---|---|
| | | | | | | | | | | | | RPG | APG | PPG |
| 77-78—Michigan State | 30 | ... | 175 | 382 | .458 | 161 | 205 | .785 | 237 | 222 | 511 | 7.9 | 7.4 | 17.0 |
| 78-79—Michigan State | 32 | 1159 | 173 | 370 | .468 | 202 | 240 | .842 | 234 | 269 | 548 | 7.3 | 8.4 | 17.1 |
| Totals | 62 | ... | 348 | 752 | .463 | 363 | 445 | .816 | 471 | 491 | 1059 | 7.6 | 7.9 | 17.1 |

### NBA REGULAR-SEASON RECORD

**RECORDS:** Holds career record for highest assists-per-game average—11.2. ... Shares career record for most consecutive seasons leading league in steals—2.
**HONORS:** NBA Most Valuable Player (1987, 1989, 1990). ... IBM Award, for all-around contributions to team's success (1984). ... All-NBA first team (1983, 1984, 1985, 1986, 1987, 1988, 1989, 1990, 1991). ... All-NBA second team (1982). ... NBA All-Rookie team (1980). ... J. Walter Kennedy Citizenship Award (1992).
**NOTES:** Led NBA with 3.43 steals per game (1981) and 2.67 steals per game (1982).

| Season Team | G | Min. | FGM | FGA | Pct. | FTM | FTA | Pct. | REBOUNDS | | | Ast. | St. | Blk. | TO | Pts. | AVERAGES | | |
|---|---|---|---|---|---|---|---|---|---|---|---|---|---|---|---|---|---|---|---|
| | | | | | | | | | Off. | Def. | Tot. | | | | | | RPG | APG | PPG |
| 79-80—Los Angeles | 77 | 2795 | 503 | 949 | .530 | 374 | 462 | .810 | 166 | 430 | 596 | 563 | 187 | 41 | 305 | 1387 | 7.7 | 7.3 | 18.0 |
| 80-81—Los Angeles | 37 | 1371 | 312 | 587 | .532 | 171 | 225 | .760 | 101 | 219 | 320 | 317 | 127 | 27 | 143 | 798 | 8.6 | 8.6 | 21.6 |
| 81-82—Los Angeles | 78 | 2991 | 556 | 1036 | .537 | 329 | 433 | .760 | 252 | 499 | 751 | 743 | 208 | 34 | 286 | 1447 | 9.6 | 9.5 | 18.6 |
| 82-83—Los Angeles | 79 | 2907 | 511 | 933 | .548 | 304 | 380 | .800 | 214 | 469 | 683 | *829 | 176 | 47 | 301 | 1326 | 8.6 | *10.5 | 16.8 |
| 83-84—Los Angeles | 67 | 2567 | 441 | 780 | .565 | 290 | 358 | .810 | 99 | 392 | 491 | 875 | 150 | 49 | 306 | 1178 | 7.3 | *13.1 | 17.6 |
| 84-85—L.A. Lakers | 77 | 2781 | 504 | 899 | .561 | 391 | 464 | .843 | 90 | 386 | 476 | 968 | 113 | 25 | 305 | 1406 | 6.2 | 12.6 | 18.3 |
| 85-86—L.A. Lakers | 72 | 2578 | 483 | 918 | .526 | 378 | 434 | .871 | 85 | 341 | 426 | *907 | 113 | 16 | 273 | 1354 | 5.9 | 12.6 | 18.8 |
| 86-87—L.A. Lakers | 80 | 2904 | 683 | 1308 | .522 | 535 | 631 | .848 | 122 | 382 | 504 | *977 | 138 | 36 | 300 | 1909 | 6.3 | *12.2 | 23.9 |
| 87-88—L.A. Lakers | 72 | 2637 | 490 | 996 | .492 | 417 | 489 | .853 | 88 | 361 | 449 | 858 | 114 | 13 | 269 | 1408 | 6.2 | 11.9 | 19.6 |
| 88-89—L.A. Lakers | 77 | 2886 | 579 | 1137 | .509 | 513 | 563 | *.911 | 111 | 496 | 607 | 988 | 138 | 22 | 312 | 1730 | 7.9 | 12.8 | 22.5 |
| 89-90—L.A. Lakers | 79 | 2937 | 546 | 1138 | .480 | 567 | 637 | .890 | 128 | 394 | 522 | 907 | 132 | 34 | 289 | 1765 | 6.6 | 11.5 | 22.3 |
| 90-91—L.A. Lakers | 79 | 2933 | 466 | 976 | .477 | 519 | 573 | .906 | 105 | 446 | 551 | 989 | 102 | 17 | *314 | 1531 | 7.0 | 12.5 | 19.4 |
| 91-92—L.A. Lakers | | | | | | | | | Did not play—retired. | | | | | | | | | | |
| 92-93—L.A. Lakers | | | | | | | | | Did not play—retired. | | | | | | | | | | |
| 93-94—L.A. Lakers | | | | | | | | | Did not play—retired. | | | | | | | | | | |
| 94-95—L.A. Lakers | | | | | | | | | Did not play—retired. | | | | | | | | | | |
| 95-96—L.A. Lakers | 32 | 958 | 137 | 294 | .466 | 172 | 201 | .856 | 40 | 143 | 183 | 220 | 26 | 13 | 103 | 468 | 5.7 | 6.9 | 14.6 |
| Totals | 906 | 33245 | 6211 | 11951 | .520 | 4960 | 5850 | .848 | 1601 | 4958 | 6559 | 10141 | 1724 | 374 | 3506 | 17707 | 7.2 | 11.2 | 19.5 |

Three-point field goals: 1979-80, 7-for-31 (.226). 1980-81, 3-for-17 (.176). 1981-82, 6-for-29 (.207). 1982-83, 0-for-21. 1983-84, 6-for-29 (.207). 1984-85, 7-for-37 (.189). 1985-86, 10-for-43 (.233). 1986-87, 8-for-39 (.205). 1987-88, 11-for-56 (.196). 1988-89, 59-for-188 (.314). 1989-90, 106-for-276 (.384). 1990-91, 80-for-250 (.320). 1995-96, 22-for-58 (.379). Totals, 325-for-1074 (.303).

Personal fouls/disqualifications: 1979-80, 218/1. 1980-81, 100/0. 1981-82, 223/1. 1982-83, 200/1. 1983-84, 169/1. 1984-85, 155/0. 1985-86, 133/0. 1986-87, 168/0. 1987-88, 147/0. 1988-89, 172/0. 1989-90, 167/1. 1990-91, 150/0. 1995-96, 48/0. Totals, 2050/5.

### NBA PLAYOFF RECORD

**NOTES:** NBA Finals Most Valuable Player (1980, 1982, 1987). ... Holds career playoff record for most assists—2,346. ... Holds NBA Finals single-series records for highest assists-per-game average—14.0 (1985); and highest assists-per-game average by a rookie—8.7 (1980). ... Holds NBA Finals single-game records for most points by a rookie—42 (May 16, 1980, vs. Philadelphia); most assists—21 (June 3, 1984, vs. Boston); most assists by a rookie—11 (May 7, 1980, vs. Philadelphia); and most assists in one half—14 (June 19, 1988, vs. Detroit). ... Shares NBA Finals single-game record for most assists in one quarter—8 (four times). ... Holds single-series playoff record for highest assists-per-game average—17.0 (1985). ... Shares single-game playoff records for most free throws made in one game—19 (May 8, 1991, vs. Golden State); most assists—24 (May 15, 1984, vs. Phoenix); and most assists in one half—15 (May 3, 1985, vs. Portland).

| Season Team | G | Min. | FGM | FGA | Pct. | FTM | FTA | Pct. | REBOUNDS | | | Ast. | St. | Blk. | TO | Pts. | AVERAGES | | |
|---|---|---|---|---|---|---|---|---|---|---|---|---|---|---|---|---|---|---|---|
| | | | | | | | | | Off. | Def. | Tot. | | | | | | RPG | APG | PPG |
| 79-80—Los Angeles | 16 | 658 | 103 | 199 | .518 | 85 | 106 | .802 | 52 | 116 | 168 | 151 | 49 | 6 | 65 | 293 | 10.5 | 9.4 | 18.3 |
| 80-81—Los Angeles | 3 | 127 | 19 | 49 | .388 | 13 | 20 | .650 | 8 | 33 | 41 | 21 | 8 | 3 | 11 | 51 | 13.7 | 7.0 | 17.0 |

| Season Team | G | Min. | FGM | FGA | Pct. | FTM | FTA | Pct. | REBOUNDS Off. | Def. | Tot. | Ast. | St. | Blk. | TO | Pts. | AVERAGES RPG | APG | PPG |
|---|---|---|---|---|---|---|---|---|---|---|---|---|---|---|---|---|---|---|---|
| 81-82—Los Angeles.... | 14 | 562 | 83 | 157 | .529 | 77 | 93 | .828 | 54 | 104 | 158 | 130 | 40 | 3 | 44 | 243 | 11.3 | 9.3 | 17.4 |
| 82-83—Los Angeles.... | 15 | 643 | 100 | 206 | .485 | 68 | 81 | .840 | 51 | 77 | 128 | 192 | 34 | 12 | 64 | 268 | 8.5 | 12.8 | 17.9 |
| 83-84—Los Angeles.... | 21 | 837 | 151 | 274 | .551 | 80 | 100 | .800 | 26 | 113 | 139 | 284 | 42 | 20 | 79 | 382 | 6.6 | 13.5 | 18.2 |
| 84-85—L.A. Lakers.... | 19 | 687 | 116 | 226 | .513 | 100 | 118 | .847 | 19 | 115 | 134 | 289 | 32 | 4 | 76 | 333 | 7.1 | 15.2 | 17.5 |
| 85-86—L.A. Lakers.... | 14 | 541 | 110 | 205 | .537 | 82 | 107 | .766 | 21 | 79 | 100 | 211 | 27 | 1 | 45 | 302 | 7.1 | 15.1 | 21.6 |
| 86-87—L.A. Lakers.... | 18 | 666 | 146 | 271 | .539 | 98 | 118 | .831 | 28 | 111 | 139 | 219 | 31 | 7 | 51 | 392 | 7.7 | 12.2 | 21.8 |
| 87-88—L.A. Lakers.... | 24 | 965 | 169 | 329 | .514 | 132 | 155 | .852 | 32 | 98 | 130 | 303 | 34 | 4 | 83 | 477 | 5.4 | 12.6 | 19.9 |
| 88-89—L.A. Lakers.... | 14 | 518 | 85 | 174 | .489 | 78 | 86 | .907 | 15 | 68 | 83 | 165 | 27 | 3 | 53 | 258 | 5.9 | 11.8 | 18.4 |
| 89-90—L.A. Lakers.... | 9 | 376 | 76 | 155 | .490 | 70 | 79 | .886 | 12 | 45 | 57 | 115 | 11 | 1 | 36 | 227 | 6.3 | 12.8 | 25.2 |
| 90-91—L.A. Lakers.... | 19 | 823 | 118 | 268 | .440 | 157 | 178 | .882 | 23 | 131 | 154 | 240 | 23 | 0 | 77 | 414 | 8.1 | 12.6 | 21.8 |
| 95-96—L.A. Lakers.... | 4 | 135 | 15 | 39 | .385 | 28 | 33 | .848 | 8 | 26 | 34 | 26 | 0 | 0 | 12 | 61 | 8.5 | 6.5 | 15.3 |
| Totals | 190 | 7538 | 1291 | 2552 | .506 | 1068 | 1274 | .838 | 349 | 1116 | 1465 | 2346 | 358 | 64 | 696 | 3701 | 7.7 | 12.3 | 19.5 |

Three-point field goals: 1979-80, 2-for-8 (.250). 1981-82, 0-for-4. 1982-83, 0-for-11. 1983-84, 0-for-7. 1984-85, 1-for-7 (.143). 1985-86, 0-for-11. 1986-87, 2-for-10 (.200). 1987-88, 7-for-14 (.500). 1988-89, 10-for-35 (.286). 1989-90, 5-for-25 (.200). 1990-91, 21-for-71 (.296). 1995-96, 3-for-9 (.333). Totals, 51-for-212 (.241).

Personal fouls/disqualifications: 1979-80, 47/1. 1980-81, 14/1. 1981-82, 50/0. 1982-83, 49/0. 1983-84, 71/0. 1984-85, 48/0. 1985-86, 43/0. 1986-87, 37/0. 1987-88, 61/0. 1988-89, 30/1. 1989-90, 28/0. 1990-91, 43/0. 1995-96, 3/0. Totals, 524/3.

## NBA ALL-STAR GAME RECORD

**NOTES:** NBA All-Star Game Most Valuable Player (1990, 1992). ... Holds career records for most assists—127; and most three-point field goals made—10. ... Holds single-game record for most assists—22 (1984, OT).

| Season Team | Min. | FGM | FGA | Pct. | FTM | FTA | Pct. | REBOUNDS Off. | Def. | Tot. | Ast. | PF | Dq. | St. | Blk. | TO | Pts. |
|---|---|---|---|---|---|---|---|---|---|---|---|---|---|---|---|---|---|
| 1980—Los Angeles ......... | 24 | 5 | 8 | .625 | 2 | 2 | 1.000 | 2 | 0 | 2 | 4 | 3 | 0 | 3 | 2 | 2 | 12 |
| 1982—Los Angeles ......... | 23 | 5 | 9 | .556 | 6 | 7 | .857 | 3 | 1 | 4 | 7 | 5 | 0 | 0 | 0 | 1 | 16 |
| 1983—Los Angeles ......... | 33 | 7 | 16 | .438 | 3 | 4 | .750 | 3 | 2 | 5 | 16 | 2 | 0 | 5 | 0 | 7 | 17 |
| 1984—Los Angeles ......... | 37 | 6 | 13 | .462 | 2 | 2 | 1.000 | 4 | 5 | 9 | 22 | 3 | 0 | 3 | 2 | 4 | 15 |
| 1985—L.A. Lakers ........... | 31 | 7 | 14 | .500 | 7 | 8 | .875 | 2 | 3 | 5 | 15 | 2 | 0 | 1 | 0 | 3 | 21 |
| 1986—L.A. Lakers ........... | 28 | 1 | 3 | .333 | 4 | 4 | 1.000 | 0 | 4 | 4 | 15 | 4 | 0 | 1 | 0 | 9 | 6 |
| 1987—L.A. Lakers ........... | 34 | 4 | 10 | .400 | 1 | 2 | .500 | 1 | 6 | 7 | 13 | 2 | 0 | 4 | 0 | 1 | 9 |
| 1988—L.A. Lakers ........... | 39 | 4 | 15 | .267 | 9 | 9 | 1.000 | 1 | 5 | 6 | 19 | 2 | 0 | 2 | 2 | 8 | 17 |
| 1989—L.A. Lakers ........... | | | | | | | Selected, did not play—injured. | | | | | | | | | | |
| 1990—L.A. Lakers ........... | 25 | 9 | 15 | .600 | 0 | 0 | ... | 1 | 5 | 6 | 4 | 1 | 0 | 0 | 1 | 3 | 22 |
| 1991—L.A. Lakers ........... | 28 | 7 | 16 | .438 | 0 | 0 | ... | 1 | 3 | 4 | 3 | 1 | 0 | 0 | 0 | 3 | 16 |
| 1992—L.A. Lakers ........... | 29 | 9 | 12 | .750 | 4 | 4 | 1.000 | 3 | 2 | 5 | 9 | 0 | 0 | 2 | 0 | 7 | 25 |
| Totals | 331 | 64 | 131 | .489 | 38 | 42 | .905 | 21 | 36 | 57 | 127 | 25 | 0 | 21 | 7 | 48 | 176 |

Three-point field goals: 1980, 0-for-1. 1983, 0-for-1. 1984, 1-for-3 (.333). 1986, 0-for-1. 1988, 0-for-1. 1990, 4-for-6 (.667). 1991, 2-for-5 (.400). 1992, 3-for-3. Totals, 10-for-21 (.476).

## NBA COACHING RECORD

| Season Team | REGULAR SEASON W | L | Pct. | Finish | PLAYOFFS W | L | Pct. |
|---|---|---|---|---|---|---|---|
| 93-94—L.A. Lakers | 5 | 11 | .313 | 5th/Pacific Division | — | — | — |

**NOTES:**
1994—Replaced Randy Pfund (27-37) and Bill Bertka (1-1) as Los Angeles Lakers head coach (March 27), with record of 28-38 and club in fifth place.

# JOHNSTON, NEIL      C

**PERSONAL:** Born February 4, 1929, in Chillicothe, Ohio. ... Died September 27, 1978. ... 6-8/210 (2,03/95,3). ... Full name: Donald Neil Johnston. ... Nickname: Gabby.
**HIGH SCHOOL:** Chillicothe (Ohio).
**COLLEGE:** Ohio State.
**TRANSACTIONS:** Signed as free agent by Philadelphia Warriors (1951). ... Signed as player/head coach by Pittsburgh Rens of American Basketball League (1961).
**CAREER HONORS:** Elected to Naismith Memorial Basketball Hall of Fame (1990).
**MISCELLANEOUS:** Member of NBA championship team (1956).

### COLLEGIATE RECORD
**NOTES:** Signed pro baseball contract in 1948 and became ineligible for his final two years at Ohio State.

| Season Team | G | Min. | FGM | FGA | Pct. | FTM | FTA | Pct. | Reb. | Ast. | Pts. | AVERAGES RPG | APG | PPG |
|---|---|---|---|---|---|---|---|---|---|---|---|---|---|---|
| 46-47—Ohio State ..................... | 7 | ... | 5 | ... | ... | 3 | 8 | .375 | ... | ... | 13 | ... | ... | 1.9 |
| 47-48—Ohio State ..................... | 20 | ... | 67 | 219 | .306 | 46 | 87 | .529 | ... | ... | 180 | ... | ... | 9.0 |
| Totals ..................................... | 27 | ... | 72 | ... | ... | 49 | 95 | .516 | ... | ... | 193 | ... | ... | 7.1 |

### NBA REGULAR-SEASON RECORD
**HONORS:** All-NBA first team (1953, 1954, 1955, 1956). ... All-NBA second team (1957).

| Season Team | G | Min. | FGM | FGA | Pct. | FTM | FTA | Pct. | Reb. | Ast. | PF | Dq. | Pts. | AVERAGES RPG | APG | PPG |
|---|---|---|---|---|---|---|---|---|---|---|---|---|---|---|---|---|
| 51-52—Philadelphia | 64 | 993 | 141 | 299 | .472 | 100 | 151 | .662 | 342 | 39 | 154 | 5 | 382 | 5.3 | 0.6 | 6.0 |
| 52-53—Philadelphia | 70 | *3166 | *504 | 1114 | *.452 | *556 | *794 | .700 | 976 | 197 | 248 | 6 | *1564 | 13.9 | 2.8 | *22.3 |
| 53-54—Philadelphia | 72 | *3296 | *591 | *1317 | .449 | *577 | *772 | .747 | 797 | 203 | 259 | 7 | *1759 | 11.1 | 2.8 | *24.4 |
| 54-55—Philadelphia | 72 | 2917 | 521 | 1184 | .440 | *589 | *769 | .766 | *1085 | 215 | 255 | 4 | *1631 | *15.1 | 3.0 | *22.7 |
| 55-56—Philadelphia | 70 | 2594 | 499 | 1092 | *.457 | 549 | 685 | .801 | 872 | 225 | 251 | 4 | 1547 | 12.5 | 3.2 | 22.1 |
| 56-57—Philadelphia | 69 | 2531 | 520 | 1163 | *.447 | 535 | 648 | .826 | 855 | 203 | 231 | 2 | 1575 | 12.4 | 2.9 | 22.8 |
| 57-58—Philadelphia | 71 | 2408 | 473 | 1102 | .429 | 442 | 540 | .819 | 790 | 166 | 233 | 4 | 1388 | 11.1 | 2.3 | 19.5 |
| 58-59—Philadelphia | 28 | 393 | 54 | 164 | .329 | 69 | 88 | .784 | 139 | 21 | 50 | 0 | 177 | 5.0 | 0.8 | 6.3 |
| Totals | 516 | 18298 | 3303 | 7435 | .444 | 3417 | 4447 | .768 | 5856 | 1269 | 1681 | 36 | 10023 | 11.3 | 2.5 | 19.4 |

### NBA PLAYOFF RECORD

| Season Team | G | Min. | FGM | FGA | Pct. | FTM | FTA | Pct. | Reb. | Ast. | PF | Dq. | Pts. | AVERAGES RPG | APG | PPG |
|---|---|---|---|---|---|---|---|---|---|---|---|---|---|---|---|---|
| 51-52—Philadelphia ..................... | 3 | 32 | 5 | 10 | .500 | 6 | 8 | .750 | 10 | 1 | 8 | 0 | 16 | 3.3 | 0.3 | 5.3 |
| 55-56—Philadelphia ..................... | 10 | 397 | 69 | 169 | .408 | 65 | 92 | .707 | 143 | 51 | 44 | 0 | 203 | 14.3 | 5.1 | 20.3 |
| 56-57—Philadelphia ..................... | 2 | 84 | 17 | 53 | .321 | 4 | 6 | .667 | 35 | 9 | 9 | 0 | 38 | 17.5 | 4.5 | 19.0 |
| 57-58—Philadelphia ..................... | 8 | 189 | 30 | 78 | .385 | 27 | 33 | .818 | 69 | 14 | 18 | 0 | 87 | 8.6 | 1.8 | 10.9 |
| Totals ..................................... | 23 | 702 | 121 | 310 | .390 | 102 | 139 | .734 | 257 | 75 | 76 | 0 | 344 | 11.2 | 3.3 | 15.0 |

## NBA ALL-STAR GAME RECORD

| Season Team | Min. | FGM | FGA | Pct. | FTM | FTA | Pct. | Reb. | Ast. | PF | Dq. | Pts. |
|---|---|---|---|---|---|---|---|---|---|---|---|---|
| 1953—Philadelphia | 27 | 5 | 13 | .385 | 1 | 2 | .500 | 12 | 0 | 2 | 0 | 11 |
| 1954—Philadelphia | 20 | 2 | 9 | .222 | 2 | 4 | .500 | 7 | 2 | 1 | 0 | 6 |
| 1955—Philadelphia | 15 | 1 | 7 | .143 | 1 | 1 | 1.000 | 6 | 1 | 0 | 0 | 3 |
| 1956—Philadelphia | 25 | 5 | 9 | .556 | 7 | 11 | .636 | 10 | 1 | 3 | 0 | 17 |
| 1957—Philadelphia | 23 | 8 | 12 | .667 | 3 | 3 | 1.000 | 9 | 1 | 2 | 0 | 19 |
| 1958—Philadelphia | 22 | 6 | 13 | .462 | 2 | 2 | 1.000 | 8 | 1 | 5 | 0 | 14 |
| Totals | 132 | 27 | 63 | .429 | 16 | 23 | .696 | 52 | 6 | 13 | 0 | 70 |

## ABL REGULAR-SEASON RECORD

| Season Team | G | Min. | FGM | FGA | Pct. | FTM | FTA | Pct. | Reb. | Ast. | Pts. | RPG | APG | PPG |
|---|---|---|---|---|---|---|---|---|---|---|---|---|---|---|
| | | | | | | | | | | | | AVERAGES | | |
| 61-62—Pittsburgh | 5 | 106 | 15 | 37 | .405 | 24 | 16 | 1.500 | 18 | 10 | 49 | 3.6 | 2.0 | 9.8 |

## HEAD COACHING RECORD

**BACKGROUND:** Player/head coach, Pittsburgh Rens of American Basketball League (1961-62).

## NBA COACHING RECORD

| Season Team | REGULAR SEASON | | | | PLAYOFFS | | |
|---|---|---|---|---|---|---|---|
| | W | L | Pct. | Finish | W | L | Pct. |
| 59-60—Philadelphia | 49 | 26 | .653 | 2nd/Eastern Division | 4 | 5 | .444 |
| 60-61—Philadelphia | 46 | 33 | .582 | 2nd/Eastern Division | 0 | 3 | .000 |
| Totals (2 years) | 95 | 59 | .617 | Totals (2 years) | 4 | 8 | .333 |

## ABL COACHING RECORD

| Season Team | W | L | Pct. | Finish | W | L | Pct. |
|---|---|---|---|---|---|---|---|
| 61-62—Pittsburgh | 41 | 40 | .506 | 2nd/Eastern Division | 0 | 1 | .000 |
| 62-63—Pittsburgh | 12 | 10 | .545 | 3rd | — | — | — |
| Totals (2 years) | 53 | 50 | .515 | Totals (1 year) | 0 | 1 | .000 |

## EBL COACHING RECORD

| Season Team | W | L | Pct. | Finish | W | L | Pct. |
|---|---|---|---|---|---|---|---|
| 64-65—Wilmington | 12 | 16 | .429 | 5th | — | — | — |
| 65-66—Wilmington | 20 | 8 | .714 | 1st/Eastern Division | 4 | 2 | .667 |
| Totals (2 years) | 32 | 24 | .571 | Totals (1 year) | 4 | 2 | .667 |

**NOTES:**
1960—Defeated Syracuse, 2-1, in Eastern Division Semifinals; lost to Boston, 4-2, in Eastern Division Finals.
1961—Lost to Syracuse in Eastern Division Semifinals.
1962—ABL disbanded (December 31).
1966—Defeated Trenton, 2-1, in Eastern Finals; defeated Wilkes-Barre, 2-1, in EBL Finals.

## RECORD AS BASEBALL PLAYER

**TRANSACTION/CAREER NOTES:** Signed by Philadelphia Phillies organization (August 1948). ... Released by Phillies organization (June 1, 1952).

| Year Team (League) | G | W | L | Pct. | ERA | Sv. | IP | H | R | ER | BB | SO |
|---|---|---|---|---|---|---|---|---|---|---|---|---|
| 1949—Terre Haute (Three I) | 29 | 10 | 12 | .455 | 3.14 | ... | 166 | 159 | 85 | 58 | 73 | 129 |
| 1950—Terre Haute (Three I) | 28 | 11 | 12 | .478 | 2.89 | ... | 168 | 132 | 78 | 54 | 102 | 126 |
| 1951—Wilmington (Inter-State) | 27 | 3 | 9 | .250 | 5.40 | ... | 115 | 126 | 76 | 69 | 79 | 104 |

# JONES, BOBBY      F

**PERSONAL:** Born December 18, 1951, in Charlotte, N.C. ... 6-9/210 (2,05/95,3). ... Full name: Robert Clyde Jones.
**HIGH SCHOOL:** South Mecklenburg (Charlotte, N.C.).
**COLLEGE:** North Carolina
**TRANSACTIONS:** Selected by Carolina Cougars in second round of 1973 ABA special circumstance draft. ... Cougars franchise moved to St. Louis and renamed Spirits of St. Louis for 1974-75 season. ... Draft rights traded by Spirits of St. Louis to Denver Nuggets for draft rights to Marvin Barnes (1974). ... Nuggets franchise became part of NBA for 1976-77 season. ... Traded by Nuggets with Ralph Simpson to Philadelphia 76ers for F George McGinnis (August 16, 1978).
**MISCELLANEOUS:** Member of NBA championship team (1983). ... Member of silver-medal-winning U.S. Olympic team (1972).

## COLLEGIATE RECORD

| Season Team | G | Min. | FGM | FGA | Pct. | FTM | FTA | Pct. | Reb. | Ast. | Pts. | RPG | APG | PPG |
|---|---|---|---|---|---|---|---|---|---|---|---|---|---|---|
| | | | | | | | | | | | | AVERAGES | | |
| 70-71—North Carolina | 16 | ... | 136 | 237 | .574 | 86 | 113 | .761 | 236 | ... | 358 | 14.8 | ... | 22.4 |
| 71-72—North Carolina | 31 | ... | 127 | 190 | .668 | 62 | 95 | .653 | 195 | 75 | 316 | 6.3 | 2.4 | 10.2 |
| 72-73—North Carolina | 33 | ... | 206 | 343 | .601 | 84 | 128 | .656 | 348 | 130 | 496 | 10.5 | 3.9 | 15.0 |
| 73-74—North Carolina | 28 | ... | 189 | 326 | .580 | 74 | 120 | .617 | 274 | 80 | 452 | 9.8 | 2.9 | 16.1 |
| Totals | 108 | ... | 658 | 1096 | .600 | 306 | 456 | .671 | 1053 | ... | 1622 | 9.8 | ... | 15.0 |

## ABA REGULAR-SEASON RECORD

**NOTES:** ABA All-Star second team (1976). ... ABA All-Defensive Team (1975 and 1976). ... ABA All-Rookie team (1975). ... Holds ABA single-season record for highest field goal percentage—.605 (1975).

| Season Team | G | Min. | 2-POINT | | | 3-POINT | | | FTM | FTA | Pct. | Reb. | Ast. | Pts. | AVERAGES | | |
|---|---|---|---|---|---|---|---|---|---|---|---|---|---|---|---|---|---|
| | | | FGM | FGA | Pct. | FGM | FGA | Pct. | | | | | | | RPG | APG | PPG |
| 74-75—Denver | 84 | 2706 | 529 | 875 | *.605 | 0 | 1 | .000 | 187 | 269 | .695 | 692 | 303 | 1245 | 8.2 | 3.6 | 14.8 |
| 75-76—Denver | 83 | 2845 | 510 | 878 | *.581 | 0 | 0 | ... | 215 | 308 | .698 | 791 | 331 | 1235 | 9.5 | 4.0 | 14.9 |
| Totals | 167 | 5551 | 1039 | 1753 | .593 | 0 | 1 | .000 | 402 | 577 | .697 | 1483 | 634 | 2480 | 8.9 | 3.8 | 14.9 |

## ABA PLAYOFF RECORD

| Season Team | G | Min. | 2-POINT | | | 3-POINT | | | FTM | FTA | Pct. | Reb. | Ast. | Pts. | AVERAGES | | |
|---|---|---|---|---|---|---|---|---|---|---|---|---|---|---|---|---|---|
| | | | FGM | FGA | Pct. | FGM | FGA | Pct. | | | | | | | RPG | APG | PPG |
| 74-75—Denver | 13 | 428 | 69 | 128 | .539 | 0 | 1 | .000 | 31 | 40 | .775 | 111 | 38 | 169 | 8.5 | 2.9 | 13.0 |
| 75-76—Denver | 13 | 433 | 74 | 127 | .583 | 0 | 0 | ... | 30 | 41 | .732 | 112 | 59 | 178 | 8.6 | 4.5 | 13.7 |
| Totals | 26 | 861 | 143 | 255 | .561 | 0 | 1 | .000 | 61 | 81 | .753 | 223 | 97 | 347 | 8.6 | 3.7 | 13.3 |

## ABA ALL-STAR GAME RECORD

| Season Team | Min. | 2-POINT | | | 3-POINT | | | FTM | FTA | Pct. | Reb. | Ast. | Pts. |
| | | FGM | FGA | Pct. | FGM | FGA | Pct. | | | | | | |
| --- | --- | --- | --- | --- | --- | --- | --- | --- | --- | --- | --- | --- | --- |
| 1976—Denver.......................... | 29 | 8 | 12 | .667 | 0 | 0 | ... | 8 | 11 | .727 | 10 | 3 | 24 |

## NBA REGULAR-SEASON RECORD

**HONORS:** NBA Sixth Man Award (1983). ... NBA All-Defensive first team (1977, 1978, 1979, 1980, 1981, 1982, 1983, 1984) ... NBA All-Defensive second team (1985).

| Season Team | G | Min. | FGM | FGA | Pct. | FTM | FTA | Pct. | REBOUNDS | | | Ast. | St. | Blk. | TO | Pts. | AVERAGES | | |
| | | | | | | | | | Off. | Def. | Tot. | | | | | | RPG | APG | PPG |
| --- | --- | --- | --- | --- | --- | --- | --- | --- | --- | --- | --- | --- | --- | --- | --- | --- | --- | --- | --- |
| 76-77—Denver........... | 82 | 2419 | 501 | 879 | .570 | 236 | 329 | .717 | 174 | 504 | 678 | 264 | 186 | 162 | ... | 1238 | 8.3 | 3.2 | 15.1 |
| 77-78—Denver........... | 75 | 2440 | 440 | 761 | *.578 | 208 | 277 | .751 | 164 | 472 | 636 | 252 | 137 | 126 | 194 | 1088 | 8.5 | 3.4 | 14.5 |
| 78-79—Philadelphia.... | 80 | 2304 | 378 | 704 | .537 | 209 | 277 | .755 | 199 | 332 | 531 | 201 | 107 | 96 | 165 | 965 | 6.6 | 2.5 | 12.1 |
| 79-80—Philadelphia.... | 81 | 2125 | 398 | 748 | .532 | 257 | 329 | .781 | 152 | 298 | 450 | 146 | 102 | 118 | 146 | 1053 | 5.6 | 1.8 | 13.0 |
| 80-81—Philadelphia.... | 81 | 2046 | 407 | 755 | .539 | 282 | 347 | .813 | 142 | 293 | 435 | 226 | 95 | 74 | 149 | 1096 | 5.4 | 2.8 | 13.5 |
| 81-82—Philadelphia.... | 76 | 2181 | 416 | 737 | .564 | 263 | 333 | .790 | 109 | 284 | 393 | 189 | 99 | 112 | 145 | 1095 | 5.2 | 2.5 | 14.4 |
| 82-83—Philadelphia.... | 74 | 1749 | 250 | 460 | .543 | 165 | 208 | .793 | 102 | 242 | 344 | 142 | 85 | 91 | 109 | 665 | 4.6 | 1.9 | 9.0 |
| 83-84—Philadelphia.... | 75 | 1761 | 226 | 432 | .523 | 167 | 213 | .784 | 92 | 231 | 323 | 187 | 107 | 103 | 101 | 619 | 4.3 | 2.5 | 8.3 |
| 84-85—Philadelphia.... | 80 | 1633 | 207 | 385 | .538 | 186 | 216 | .861 | 105 | 192 | 297 | 155 | 84 | 50 | 118 | 600 | 3.7 | 1.9 | 7.5 |
| 85-86—Philadelphia.... | 70 | 1519 | 189 | 338 | .559 | 114 | 145 | .786 | 49 | 120 | 169 | 126 | 48 | 50 | 90 | 492 | 2.4 | 1.8 | 7.0 |
| Totals.................... | 774 | 20177 | 3412 | 6199 | .550 | 2087 | 2674 | .780 | 1288 | 2968 | 4256 | 1888 | 1050 | 982 | 1217 | 8911 | 5.5 | 2.4 | 11.5 |

Three-point field goals: 1979-80, 0-for-3. 1980-81, 0-for-3. 1981-82, 0-for-3. 1982-83, 0-for-1. 1983-84, 0-for-1. 1984-85, 0-for-4. 1985-86, 0-for-1. Totals, 0-for-16.

Personal fouls/disqualifications: 1976-77, 238/3. 1977-78, 221/2. 1978-79, 245/2. 1979-80, 223/3. 1980-81, 226/2. 1981-82, 211/3. 1982-83, 199/4. 1983-84, 199/1. 1984-85, 183/2. 1985-86, 159/0. Totals, 2104/22.

## NBA PLAYOFF RECORD

| Season Team | G | Min. | FGM | FGA | Pct. | FTM | FTA | Pct. | REBOUNDS | | | Ast. | St. | Blk. | TO | Pts. | AVERAGES | | |
| | | | | | | | | | Off. | Def. | Tot. | | | | | | RPG | APG | PPG |
| --- | --- | --- | --- | --- | --- | --- | --- | --- | --- | --- | --- | --- | --- | --- | --- | --- | --- | --- | --- |
| 76-77—Denver........... | 6 | 187 | 31 | 64 | .484 | 10 | 17 | .588 | 11 | 24 | 35 | 21 | 17 | 14 | ... | 72 | 5.8 | 3.5 | 12.0 |
| 77-78—Denver........... | 13 | 390 | 66 | 116 | .569 | 34 | 46 | .739 | 36 | 66 | 102 | 35 | 16 | 9 | 24 | 166 | 7.8 | 2.7 | 12.8 |
| 78-79—Philadelphia.... | 9 | 260 | 48 | 87 | .552 | 22 | 26 | .846 | 12 | 31 | 43 | 19 | 5 | 4 | 15 | 118 | 4.8 | 2.1 | 13.1 |
| 79-80—Philadelphia.... | 18 | 470 | 90 | 172 | .523 | 53 | 62 | .855 | 29 | 57 | 86 | 31 | 21 | 32 | 23 | 233 | 4.8 | 1.7 | 12.9 |
| 80-81—Philadelphia.... | 16 | 443 | 81 | 160 | .506 | 73 | 88 | .830 | 35 | 53 | 88 | 33 | 18 | 21 | 32 | 235 | 5.5 | 2.1 | 14.7 |
| 81-82—Philadelphia.... | 21 | 589 | 94 | 174 | .540 | 68 | 81 | .840 | 37 | 62 | 99 | 52 | 15 | 22 | 33 | 256 | 4.7 | 2.5 | 12.2 |
| 82-83—Philadelphia.... | 12 | 324 | 43 | 78 | .551 | 17 | 20 | .850 | 19 | 39 | 58 | 34 | 15 | 18 | 18 | 103 | 4.8 | 2.8 | 8.6 |
| 83-84—Philadelphia.... | 5 | 130 | 15 | 31 | .484 | 18 | 19 | .947 | 9 | 14 | 23 | 9 | 3 | 7 | 8 | 48 | 4.6 | 1.8 | 9.6 |
| 84-85—Philadelphia.... | 13 | 309 | 46 | 78 | .590 | 14 | 20 | .700 | 22 | 26 | 48 | 16 | 12 | 15 | 19 | 106 | 3.7 | 1.2 | 8.2 |
| 85-86—Philadelphia.... | 12 | 329 | 39 | 74 | .527 | 38 | 50 | .760 | 9 | 23 | 32 | 34 | 10 | 14 | 15 | 116 | 2.7 | 2.8 | 9.7 |
| Totals.................... | 125 | 3431 | 553 | 1034 | .535 | 347 | 429 | .809 | 219 | 395 | 614 | 284 | 132 | 156 | 187 | 1453 | 4.9 | 2.3 | 11.6 |

Three-point field goals: 1979-80, 0-for-1. 1982-83, 0-for-1. 1985-86, 0-for-1. Totals, 0-for-3.

Personal fouls/disqualifications: 1976-77, 25/1. 1977-78, 42/1. 1978-79, 30/0. 1979-80, 56/1. 1980-81, 60/1. 1981-82, 69/0. 1982-83, 29/0. 1983-84, 12/0. 1984-85, 38/0. 1985-86, 39/0. Totals, 400/4.

## NBA ALL-STAR GAME RECORD

| Season Team | Min. | FGM | FGA | Pct. | FTM | FTA | Pct. | REBOUNDS | | | Ast. | PF | Dq. | St. | Blk. | TO | Pts. |
| | | | | | | | | Off. | Def. | Tot. | | | | | | | |
| --- | --- | --- | --- | --- | --- | --- | --- | --- | --- | --- | --- | --- | --- | --- | --- | --- | --- |
| 1977—Denver ................. | 14 | 1 | 4 | .250 | 0 | 0 | ... | 0 | 0 | 0 | 3 | 0 | 0 | 0 | 1 | ... | 2 |
| 1978—Denver ................. | 18 | 1 | 3 | .333 | 0 | 0 | ... | 1 | 5 | 6 | 2 | 4 | 0 | 0 | 1 | 1 | 2 |
| 1981—Philadelphia ......... | 16 | 5 | 11 | .455 | 1 | 1 | 1.000 | 1 | 3 | 4 | 0 | 2 | 0 | 1 | 1 | 0 | 11 |
| 1982—Philadelphia ......... | 14 | 2 | 5 | .400 | 1 | 2 | .500 | 1 | 3 | 4 | 1 | 2 | 0 | 1 | 0 | 0 | 5 |
| Totals............................ | 62 | 9 | 23 | .391 | 2 | 3 | .667 | 3 | 11 | 14 | 6 | 8 | 0 | 2 | 3 | 1 | 20 |

## COMBINED ABA AND NBA REGULAR-SEASON RECORDS

| | G | Min. | FGM | FGA | Pct. | FTM | FTA | Pct. | REBOUNDS | | | Ast. | Stl. | Blk. | TO | Pts. | AVERAGES | | |
| | | | | | | | | | Off. | Def. | Tot. | | | | | | RPG | APG | PPG |
| --- | --- | --- | --- | --- | --- | --- | --- | --- | --- | --- | --- | --- | --- | --- | --- | --- | --- | --- | --- |
| Totals ........... | 941 | 25728 | 4451 | 7953 | .560 | 2489 | 3251 | .766 | 1759 | 3980 | 5739 | 2522 | 1387 | 1319 | 1683 | 11391 | 6.1 | 2.7 | 12.1 |

Three-point field goals: 0-for-17.
Personal fouls/disqualifications: 2620.

# JONES, CALDWELL                F/C

**PERSONAL:** Born August 4, 1950, in McGehee, Ark. ... 6-11/225 (2,10/102,1). ... Full name: Caldwell Jones. ... Brother of Charles Jones, forward/center with five NBA teams (1983-84 through 1997-98); brother of Major Jones, forward/center with Houston Rockets (1979-80 through 1984-85) and Detroit Pistons (1984-85); and brother of Wilbert Jones, forward with three ABA teams (1969-70 through 1975-76) and Indiana Pacers (1976-77) and Buffalo Braves of the NBA (1977-78).

**HIGH SCHOOL:** Desha Central (Rohwer, Ark.).

**COLLEGE:** Albany State College

**TRANSACTIONS:** Selected by Virginia Squires in third round of 1973 ABA draft. ... Selected by Philadelphia 76ers in second round (32nd pick overall) of 1973 NBA draft. ... Signed by San Diego Conquistadors; G Larry Miller sent by Conquistadors to Squires as compensation (October 29, 1973). ... Signed by 76ers (for future services) (February 25, 1975). ... Purchased by Kentucky Colonels from disbanded San Diego franchise (Novemeber 14, 1975). ... Traded by Kentucky Colonels to St. Louis for F Maurice Lucas (December 17, 1975). ... Traded by 76ers with 1983 first-round draft choice to Houston Rockets for C Moses Malone (September 15, 1982). ... Traded by Rockets to Chicago Bulls for G Mitchell Wiggins and 1985 second- and third-round draft choices (August 10, 1984). ... Signed by Portland Trail Blazers as veteran free agent (October 1, 1985); Bulls agreed not to exercise its right of first refusal in exchange for 1987 second-round draft choice. ... Signed by San Antonio Spurs as unrestricted free agent (July 20, 1989).

## COLLEGIATE RECORD

| Season Team | G | Min. | FGM | FGA | Pct. | FTM | FTA | Pct. | Reb. | Ast. | Pts. | RPG | APG | PPG |
|---|---|---|---|---|---|---|---|---|---|---|---|---|---|---|
| 69-70—Albany (Ga.) State ......... | 25 | ... | 185 | 367 | .504 | 80 | 108 | .741 | 440 | ... | 450 | 17.6 | ... | 18.0 |
| 70-71—Albany (Ga.) State ......... | 27 | ... | 206 | 437 | .471 | 76 | 137 | .555 | 576 | ... | 488 | 21.3 | ... | 18.1 |
| 71-72—Albany (Ga.) State ......... | 28 | ... | 288 | 539 | .534 | 156 | 219 | .712 | 567 | ... | 732 | 20.3 | ... | 26.1 |
| 72-73—Albany (Ga.) State ......... | 29 | ... | 238 | 470 | .506 | 91 | 134 | .679 | 633 | ... | 567 | 21.8 | ... | 19.6 |
| Totals ......... | 109 | ... | 917 | 1813 | .506 | 403 | 598 | .674 | 2216 | ... | 2237 | 20.3 | ... | 20.5 |

## ABA REGULAR-SEASON RECORD

**NOTES:** Shares ABA single-game record for most blocks—12 (January 6, 1974, vs. Carolina). ... Led ABA with 4.00 blocked shots per game (1974) and 3.24 blocked shots per game (1975).

| Season Team | G | Min. | 2-POINT FGM | 2-POINT FGA | 2-POINT Pct. | 3-POINT FGM | 3-POINT FGA | 3-POINT Pct. | FTM | FTA | Pct. | Reb. | Ast. | Pts. | RPG | APG | PPG |
|---|---|---|---|---|---|---|---|---|---|---|---|---|---|---|---|---|---|
| 73-74—San Diego ................ | 79 | 2929 | 505 | 1083 | .466 | 2 | 8 | .250 | 171 | 230 | .743 | 1095 | 144 | 1187 | 13.9 | 1.8 | 15.0 |
| 74-75—San Diego ................ | 76 | 3004 | 603 | 1229 | .491 | 3 | 11 | .273 | 264 | 335 | .788 | 1074 | 162 | 1479 | 14.1 | 2.1 | 19.5 |
| 75-76—SD-Kty.-St.L. ............ | 76 | 2674 | 423 | 893 | .474 | 0 | 7 | .000 | 140 | 186 | .753 | 853 | 147 | 986 | 11.2 | 1.9 | 13.0 |
| Totals ................ | 231 | 8607 | 1531 | 3205 | .478 | 5 | 26 | .192 | 575 | 751 | .766 | 3022 | 453 | 3652 | 13.1 | 2.0 | 15.8 |

## ABA PLAYOFF RECORD

| Season Team | G | Min. | 2-POINT FGM | 2-POINT FGA | 2-POINT Pct. | 3-POINT FGM | 3-POINT FGA | 3-POINT Pct. | FTM | FTA | Pct. | Reb. | Ast. | Pts. | RPG | APG | PPG |
|---|---|---|---|---|---|---|---|---|---|---|---|---|---|---|---|---|---|
| 73-74—San Diego ................ | 6 | 277 | 36 | 88 | .409 | 0 | 0 | ... | 11 | 16 | .688 | 94 | 15 | 83 | 15.7 | 2.5 | 13.8 |

## ABA ALL-STAR GAME RECORD

| Season Team | Min. | 2-POINT FGM | 2-POINT FGA | 2-POINT Pct. | 3-POINT FGM | 3-POINT FGA | 3-POINT Pct. | FTM | FTA | Pct. | Reb. | Ast. | Pts. |
|---|---|---|---|---|---|---|---|---|---|---|---|---|---|
| 1975—San Diego .................... | 15 | 2 | 4 | .500 | 0 | 0 | ... | 1 | 1 | 1.000 | 4 | 0 | 5 |

## NBA REGULAR-SEASON RECORD

**NOTES:** NBA All-Defensive first team (1981, 1982).

| Season Team | G | Min. | FGM | FGA | Pct. | FTM | FTA | Pct. | REBOUNDS Off. | REBOUNDS Def. | REBOUNDS Tot. | Ast. | St. | Blk. | TO | Pts. | RPG | APG | PPG |
|---|---|---|---|---|---|---|---|---|---|---|---|---|---|---|---|---|---|---|---|
| 76-77—Philadelphia .. | 82 | 2023 | 215 | 424 | .507 | 64 | 116 | .552 | 190 | 476 | 666 | 92 | 43 | 200 | ... | 494 | 8.1 | 1.1 | 6.0 |
| 77-78—Philadelphia .. | 80 | 1636 | 169 | 359 | .471 | 96 | 153 | .627 | 165 | 405 | 570 | 92 | 26 | 127 | ... | 434 | 7.1 | 1.2 | 5.4 |
| 78-79—Philadelphia .. | 78 | 2171 | 302 | 637 | .474 | 121 | 162 | .747 | 177 | 570 | 747 | 151 | 39 | 157 | ... | 725 | 9.6 | 1.9 | 9.3 |
| 79-80—Philadelphia .. | 80 | 2771 | 232 | 532 | .436 | 124 | 178 | .697 | 219 | 731 | 950 | 164 | 43 | 162 | ... | 588 | 11.9 | 2.1 | 7.4 |
| 80-81—Philadelphia .. | 81 | 2639 | 218 | 485 | .449 | 148 | 193 | .767 | 200 | 613 | 813 | 122 | 53 | 134 | 168 | 584 | 10.0 | 1.5 | 7.2 |
| 81-82—Philadelphia .. | 81 | 2446 | 231 | 465 | .497 | 179 | 219 | .817 | 164 | 544 | 708 | 100 | 38 | 146 | 155 | 641 | 8.7 | 1.2 | 7.9 |
| 82-83—Houston ........ | 82 | 2440 | 307 | 677 | .453 | 162 | 206 | .786 | 222 | 446 | 668 | 138 | 46 | 131 | 171 | 776 | 8.1 | 1.7 | 9.5 |
| 83-84—Houston ........ | 81 | 2506 | 318 | 633 | .502 | 164 | 196 | .837 | 168 | 414 | 582 | 156 | 46 | 80 | 158 | 801 | 7.2 | 1.9 | 9.9 |
| 84-85—Chicago ......... | 42 | 885 | 53 | 115 | .461 | 36 | 47 | .766 | 49 | 162 | 211 | 34 | 12 | 31 | 40 | 142 | 5.0 | 0.8 | 3.4 |
| 85-86—Portland ........ | 80 | 1437 | 126 | 254 | .496 | 124 | 150 | .827 | 105 | 250 | 355 | 74 | 38 | 61 | 102 | 376 | 4.4 | 0.9 | 4.7 |
| 86-87—Portland ........ | 78 | 1578 | 111 | 224 | .496 | 97 | 124 | .782 | 114 | 341 | 455 | 64 | 23 | 77 | 87 | 319 | 5.8 | 0.8 | 4.1 |
| 87-88—Portland ........ | 79 | 1778 | 128 | 263 | .487 | 78 | 106 | .736 | 105 | 303 | 408 | 81 | 29 | 99 | 82 | 334 | 5.2 | 1.0 | 4.2 |
| 88-89—Portland ........ | 72 | 1279 | 77 | 183 | .421 | 48 | 61 | .787 | 88 | 212 | 300 | 59 | 24 | 85 | 83 | 202 | 4.2 | 0.8 | 2.8 |
| 89-90—San Antonio .. | 72 | 885 | 67 | 144 | .465 | 38 | 54 | .704 | 76 | 154 | 230 | 20 | 20 | 27 | 48 | 173 | 3.2 | 0.3 | 2.4 |
| Totals ................... | 1068 | 26474 | 2554 | 5395 | .473 | 1479 | 1965 | .753 | 2042 | 5621 | 7663 | 1347 | 480 | 1517 | ... | 6589 | 7.2 | 1.3 | 6.2 |

Three-point field goals: 1979-80, 0-for-2. 1981-82, 0-for-3. 1982-83, 0-for-2. 1983-84, 1-for-3 (.333). 1984-85, 0-for-2. 1985-86, 0-for-7. 1986-87, 0-for-2. 1987-88, 0-for-4. 1988-89, 0-for-1. 1989-90, 1-for-5 (.200). Totals, 2-for-31 (.065).

Personal fouls/disqualifications: 1976-77, 301/3. 1977-78, 281/4. 1978-79, 303/10. 1979-80, 298/5. 1980-81, 271/2. 1981-82, 301/3. 1982-83, 278/2. 1983-84, 335/7. 1984-85, 125/3. 1985-86, 244/2. 1986-87, 227/5. 1987-88, 251/0. 1988-89, 166/0. 1989-90, 146/2. Totals, 3527/48.

## NBA PLAYOFF RECORD

| Season Team | G | Min. | FGM | FGA | Pct. | FTM | FTA | Pct. | REBOUNDS Off. | REBOUNDS Def. | REBOUNDS Tot. | Ast. | St. | Blk. | TO | Pts. | RPG | APG | PPG |
|---|---|---|---|---|---|---|---|---|---|---|---|---|---|---|---|---|---|---|---|
| 76-77—Philadelphia .. | 19 | 513 | 37 | 73 | .507 | 18 | 30 | .600 | 38 | 112 | 150 | 20 | 9 | 40 | ... | 92 | 7.9 | 1.1 | 4.8 |
| 77-78—Philadelphia .. | 10 | 301 | 28 | 56 | .500 | 8 | 10 | .800 | 22 | 84 | 106 | 14 | 5 | 30 | ... | 64 | 10.6 | 1.4 | 6.4 |
| 78-79—Philadelphia .. | 9 | 320 | 43 | 89 | .483 | 28 | 36 | .778 | 37 | 84 | 121 | 21 | 4 | 22 | ... | 114 | 13.4 | 2.3 | 12.7 |
| 79-80—Philadelphia .. | 18 | 639 | 58 | 129 | .450 | 42 | 52 | .808 | 50 | 135 | 185 | 34 | 13 | 37 | ... | 158 | 10.3 | 1.9 | 8.8 |
| 80-81—Philadelphia .. | 16 | 580 | 54 | 95 | .568 | 31 | 42 | .738 | 37 | 118 | 155 | 27 | 7 | 31 | ... | 139 | 9.7 | 1.7 | 8.7 |
| 81-82—Philadelphia .. | 21 | 679 | 74 | 160 | .463 | 35 | 41 | .854 | 52 | 137 | 189 | 19 | 11 | 40 | ... | 183 | 9.0 | 0.9 | 8.7 |
| 84-85—Chicago ......... | 2 | 18 | 5 | 6 | .833 | 0 | 0 | ... | 1 | 4 | 5 | 0 | 0 | 1 | ... | 10 | 2.5 | 0.0 | 5.0 |
| 85-86—Portland ........ | 4 | 73 | 6 | 17 | .353 | 2 | 4 | .500 | 9 | 10 | 19 | 3 | 0 | 2 | ... | 14 | 4.8 | 0.8 | 3.5 |
| 86-87—Portland ........ | 4 | 129 | 5 | 12 | .417 | 5 | 6 | .833 | 9 | 22 | 31 | 6 | 0 | 6 | ... | 15 | 7.8 | 1.5 | 3.8 |
| 87-88—Portland ........ | 4 | 98 | 6 | 16 | .375 | 1 | 2 | .500 | 4 | 13 | 17 | 1 | 2 | 8 | ... | 13 | 4.3 | 0.3 | 3.3 |
| 88-89—Portland ........ | 3 | 50 | 2 | 3 | .667 | 0 | 0 | ... | 2 | 6 | 8 | 0 | 0 | 3 | ... | 4 | 2.7 | 0.0 | 1.3 |
| 89-90—San Antonio .. | 9 | 66 | 4 | 9 | .444 | 0 | 1 | .000 | 6 | 7 | 13 | 2 | 0 | 3 | ... | 8 | 1.4 | 0.2 | 0.9 |
| Totals ................... | 119 | 3466 | 322 | 665 | .484 | 170 | 224 | .759 | 267 | 732 | 999 | 147 | 51 | 223 | ... | 814 | 8.4 | 1.2 | 6.8 |

Three-point field goals: 1979-80, 0-for-3. 1984-85, 0-for-1. Totals, 0-for-4.

Personal fouls/disqualifications: 1976-77, 81/4. 1977-78, 36/2. 1978-79, 36/0. 1979-80, 75/1. 1980-81, 53/0. 1981-82, 77/1. 1984-85, 7/1. 1985-86, 13/0. 1986-87, 15/0. 1987-88, 17/0. 1988-89, 6/0. 1989-90, 10/0. Totals, 426/9.

## COMBINED ABA AND NBA REGULAR-SEASON RECORDS

| | G | Min. | FGM | FGA | Pct. | FTM | FTA | Pct. | REBOUNDS Off. | REBOUNDS Def. | REBOUNDS Tot. | Ast. | Stl. | Blk. | TO | Pts. | RPG | APG | PPG |
|---|---|---|---|---|---|---|---|---|---|---|---|---|---|---|---|---|---|---|---|
| Totals ............ | 1299 | 35081 | 4090 | 8626 | .474 | 2054 | 2716 | .756 | 2921 | 7764 | 10685 | 1800 | 685 | 2297 | ... | 10241 | 8.2 | 1.4 | 7.9 |

# JONES, SAM      G

**PERSONAL:** Born June 24, 1933, in Wilmington, N.C. ... 6-4/205 (1,93/93,0). ... Full name: Samuel Jones.
**HIGH SCHOOL:** Laurinburg Institute (N.C.).
**COLLEGE:** North Carolina Central.
**TRANSACTIONS:** Selected by Boston Celtics in first round (eighth pick overall) of 1957 NBA Draft.
**CAREER HONORS:** Elected to Naismith Memorial Basketball Hall of Fame (1984). ... NBA 25th Anniversary All-Time Team
(1970) and One of the 50 Greatest Players in NBA History (1996).
**MISCELLANEOUS:** Member of NBA championship team (1959, 1960, 1961, 1962, 1963, 1964, 1965, 1966, 1968, 1969).

## COLLEGIATE RECORD

**NOTES:** Elected to NAIA Basketball Hall of Fame (1962).

| Season Team | G | Min. | FGM | FGA | Pct. | FTM | FTA | Pct. | Reb. | Ast. | Pts. | RPG | APG | PPG |
|---|---|---|---|---|---|---|---|---|---|---|---|---|---|---|
| 51-52—North Carolina Central.... | 22 | ... | 126 | 263 | .479 | 48 | 78 | .615 | 150 | ... | 300 | 6.8 | ... | 13.6 |
| 52-53—North Carolina Central.... | 24 | ... | 169 | 370 | .457 | 115 | 180 | .639 | 248 | ... | 453 | 10.3 | ... | 18.9 |
| 53-54—North Carolina Central.... | 27 | ... | 208 | 432 | .481 | 98 | 137 | .715 | 223 | ... | 514 | 8.3 | ... | 19.0 |
| 54-55— | | | | | | Did not play—in military service. | | | | | | | | |
| 55-56— | | | | | | Did not play—in military service. | | | | | | | | |
| 56-57—North Carolina Central.... | 27 | ... | 174 | 398 | .437 | 155 | 202 | .767 | 288 | ... | 503 | 10.7 | ... | 18.6 |
| Totals | 100 | ... | 677 | 1463 | .463 | 416 | 597 | .697 | 909 | ... | 1770 | 9.1 | ... | 17.7 |

*(AVERAGES columns: RPG, APG, PPG)*

## NBA REGULAR-SEASON RECORD

**HONORS:** All-NBA second team (1965, 1966, 1967).

| Season Team | G | Min. | FGM | FGA | Pct. | FTM | FTA | Pct. | Reb. | Ast. | PF | Dq. | Pts. | RPG | APG | PPG |
|---|---|---|---|---|---|---|---|---|---|---|---|---|---|---|---|---|
| 57-58—Boston | 56 | 594 | 100 | 233 | .429 | 60 | 84 | .714 | 160 | 37 | 42 | 0 | 260 | 2.9 | 0.7 | 4.6 |
| 58-59—Boston | 71 | 1466 | 305 | 703 | .434 | 151 | 196 | .770 | 428 | 101 | 102 | 0 | 761 | 6.0 | 1.4 | 10.7 |
| 59-60—Boston | 74 | 1512 | 355 | 782 | .454 | 168 | 220 | .764 | 375 | 125 | 101 | 1 | 878 | 5.1 | 1.7 | 11.9 |
| 60-61—Boston | 78 | 2028 | 480 | 1069 | .449 | 211 | 268 | .787 | 421 | 217 | 148 | 1 | 1171 | 5.4 | 2.8 | 15.0 |
| 61-62—Boston | 78 | 2388 | 596 | 1284 | .464 | 243 | 297 | .818 | 458 | 232 | 149 | 0 | 1435 | 5.9 | 3.0 | 18.4 |
| 62-63—Boston | 76 | 2323 | 621 | 1305 | .476 | 257 | 324 | .793 | 396 | 241 | 162 | 1 | 1499 | 5.2 | 3.2 | 19.7 |
| 63-64—Boston | 76 | 2381 | 612 | 1359 | .450 | 249 | 318 | .783 | 349 | 202 | 192 | 1 | 1473 | 4.6 | 2.7 | 19.4 |
| 64-65—Boston | 80 | 2885 | 821 | 1818 | .452 | 428 | 522 | .820 | 411 | 223 | 176 | 0 | 2070 | 5.1 | 2.8 | 25.9 |
| 65-66—Boston | 67 | 2155 | 626 | 1335 | .469 | 325 | 407 | .799 | 347 | 216 | 170 | 1 | 1577 | 5.2 | 3.2 | 23.5 |
| 66-67—Boston | 72 | 2325 | 638 | 1406 | .454 | 318 | 371 | .857 | 338 | 217 | 191 | 1 | 1594 | 4.7 | 3.0 | 22.1 |
| 67-68—Boston | 73 | 2408 | 621 | 1348 | .461 | 311 | 376 | .827 | 357 | 216 | 181 | 0 | 1553 | 4.9 | 3.0 | 21.3 |
| 68-69—Boston | 70 | 1820 | 496 | 1103 | .450 | 148 | 189 | .783 | 265 | 182 | 121 | 0 | 1140 | 3.8 | 2.6 | 16.3 |
| Totals | 871 | 24285 | 6271 | 13745 | .456 | 2869 | 3572 | .803 | 4305 | 2209 | 1735 | 5 | 15411 | 4.9 | 2.5 | 17.7 |

*(AVERAGES columns: RPG, APG, PPG)*

## NBA PLAYOFF RECORD

| Season Team | G | Min. | FGM | FGA | Pct. | FTM | FTA | Pct. | Reb. | Ast. | PF | Dq. | Pts. | RPG | APG | PPG |
|---|---|---|---|---|---|---|---|---|---|---|---|---|---|---|---|---|
| 57-58—Boston | 8 | 75 | 10 | 22 | .455 | 11 | 16 | .688 | 24 | 4 | 7 | 0 | 31 | 3.0 | 0.5 | 3.9 |
| 58-59—Boston | 11 | 192 | 40 | 108 | .370 | 33 | 39 | .846 | 63 | 17 | 14 | 0 | 113 | 5.7 | 1.5 | 10.3 |
| 59-60—Boston | 13 | 197 | 45 | 117 | .385 | 17 | 21 | .810 | 41 | 18 | 15 | 0 | 107 | 3.2 | 1.4 | 8.2 |
| 60-61—Boston | 10 | 258 | 50 | 112 | .446 | 31 | 35 | .886 | 54 | 22 | 22 | 0 | 131 | 5.4 | 2.2 | 13.1 |
| 61-62—Boston | 14 | 504 | 123 | 277 | .444 | 42 | 60 | .700 | 99 | 44 | 30 | 0 | 288 | 7.1 | 3.1 | 20.6 |
| 62-63—Boston | 13 | 450 | 120 | 248 | .484 | 69 | 83 | .831 | 81 | 32 | 42 | 1 | 309 | 6.2 | 2.5 | 23.8 |
| 63-64—Boston | 10 | 356 | 91 | 180 | .506 | 50 | 68 | .735 | 47 | 23 | 24 | 0 | 232 | 4.7 | 2.3 | 23.2 |
| 64-65—Boston | 12 | 495 | 135 | 294 | .459 | 73 | 84 | .869 | 55 | 30 | 39 | 1 | 343 | 4.6 | 2.5 | 28.6 |
| 65-66—Boston | 17 | 602 | 154 | 343 | .449 | 114 | 136 | .838 | 86 | 53 | 65 | 1 | 422 | 5.1 | 3.1 | 24.8 |
| 66-67—Boston | 9 | 326 | 95 | 207 | .459 | 50 | 58 | .862 | 46 | 28 | 30 | 1 | 240 | 5.1 | 3.1 | 26.7 |
| 67-68—Boston | 19 | 685 | 162 | 367 | .441 | 66 | 84 | .786 | 64 | 50 | 58 | 0 | 390 | 3.4 | 2.6 | 20.5 |
| 68-69—Boston | 18 | 514 | 124 | 296 | .419 | 55 | 69 | .797 | 58 | 37 | 45 | 1 | 303 | 3.2 | 2.1 | 16.8 |
| Totals | 154 | 4654 | 1149 | 2571 | .447 | 611 | 753 | .811 | 718 | 358 | 391 | 5 | 2909 | 4.7 | 2.3 | 18.9 |

*(AVERAGES columns: RPG, APG, PPG)*

## NBA ALL-STAR GAME RECORD

| Season Team | Min. | FGM | FGA | Pct. | FTM | FTA | Pct. | Reb | Ast. | PF | Dq. | Pts. |
|---|---|---|---|---|---|---|---|---|---|---|---|---|
| 1962—Boston | 14 | 1 | 8 | .125 | 0 | 1 | .000 | 1 | 0 | 1 | 0 | 2 |
| 1964—Boston | 27 | 8 | 20 | .400 | 0 | 0 | ... | 4 | 3 | 2 | 0 | 16 |
| 1965—Boston | 24 | 2 | 12 | .167 | 2 | 2 | 1.000 | 5 | 3 | 2 | 0 | 6 |
| 1966—Boston | 22 | 5 | 11 | .455 | 2 | 2 | 1.000 | 2 | 5 | 0 | 0 | 12 |
| 1968—Boston | 15 | 2 | 5 | .400 | 1 | 1 | 1.000 | 2 | 4 | 1 | 0 | 5 |
| Totals | 102 | 18 | 56 | .321 | 5 | 6 | .833 | 14 | 15 | 6 | 0 | 41 |

## HEAD COACHING RECORD

**BACKGROUND:** Athletic director/head coach, Federal City College, Washington, D.C. (1969-1973). ... Assistant coach, New Orleans Jazz
(1974-75).

### COLLEGIATE COACHING RECORD

| Season Team | W | L | Pct. | Finish |
|---|---|---|---|---|
| 69-70—Federal City College | 5 | 8 | .385 | |
| 70-71—Federal City College | 12 | 9 | .571 | |
| 71-72—Federal City College | 11 | 9 | .550 | |
| 72-73—Federal City College | 11 | 13 | .458 | |
| 73-74—North Carolina Central | 5 | 16 | .238 | 7th/Mid-Eastern Athletic Conference |
| Totals (5 years) | 44 | 55 | .444 | |

# JORDAN, MICHAEL  G

**PERSONAL:** Born February 17, 1963, in Brooklyn, N.Y. ... 6-6/216. (1,98/98,0). ... Full Name: Michael Jeffrey Jordan.
**HIGH SCHOOL:** Emsley A. Laney (Wilmington, N.C.).
**COLLEGE:** North Carolina.
**TRANSACTIONS/CAREER NOTES:** Selected after junior season by Chicago Bulls in first round (third pick overall) of 1984 NBA Draft. ... On voluntarily retired list (October 6, 1993-March 18, 1995). ... Activated from retirement (March 18, 1995). ... Announced retirement (January 13, 1999). ... Signed as free agent by Washington Wizards (September 25, 2001).
**CAREER HONORS:** NBA 50th Anniversary All-Time Team (1996).
**MISCELLANEOUS:** Member of NBA championship team (1991, 1992, 1993, 1996, 1997, 1998). ... Member of gold-medal-winning U.S. Olympic team (1984, 1992). ... Chicago Bulls all-time leading scorer with 29,277 points, all-time leading rebounder with 5,836, all-time assists leader with 5,012 and all-time steals leader with 2,306 (1984-85 through 1992-93 and 1994-95 through 1997-98). ... President of Basketball Operations, Washington Wizards and minority owner, Washington Wizards Sports and Entertainment (January 19, 2000-September 25, 2001).

## COLLEGIATE RECORD

**NOTES:** THE SPORTING NEWS College Player of the Year (1983, 1984). ... Naismith Award winner (1984). ... Wooden Award winner (1984). ... THE SPORTING NEWS All-America first team (1983, 1984). ... Member of NCAA Division I championship team (1982).

| Season Team | G | Min. | FGM | FGA | Pct. | FTM | FTA | Pct. | Reb. | Ast. | Pts. | AVERAGES | | |
|---|---|---|---|---|---|---|---|---|---|---|---|---|---|---|
| | | | | | | | | | | | | RPG | APG | PPG |
| 81-82—North Carolina | 34 | 1079 | 191 | 358 | .534 | 78 | 108 | .722 | 149 | 61 | 460 | 4.4 | 1.8 | 13.5 |
| 82-83—North Carolina | 36 | 1113 | 282 | 527 | .535 | 123 | 167 | .737 | 197 | 56 | 721 | 5.5 | 1.6 | 20.0 |
| 83-84—North Carolina | 31 | 915 | 247 | 448 | .551 | 113 | 145 | .779 | 163 | 64 | 607 | 5.3 | 2.1 | 19.6 |
| Totals | 101 | 3107 | 720 | 1333 | .540 | 314 | 420 | .748 | 509 | 181 | 1788 | 5.0 | 1.8 | 17.7 |

Three-point field goals: 1982-83, 34-for-76 (.447).

## NBA REGULAR-SEASON RECORD

**RECORDS:** Holds career record for most seasons leading league in scoring—10; highest points-per-game average (minimum 400 games or 10,000 points)—30.12; most seasons leading league in field goals made—10; and most seasons leading league in field goals attempted—10. ... Shares career records for most consecutive seasons leading league in scoring—7 (1986-87 through 1992-93). ... Holds single-game records for most free throws made in one half—20 (December 30, 1992, at Miami); and most free-throws attempted in one half—23 (December 30, 1992, at Miami). ... Shares single-game records for most free throws made in one quarter—14 (November 15, 1989, vs. Utah and December 30, 1992, at Miami); and most free throws attempted in one quarter—16 (December 30, 1992, at Miami).

**HONORS:** NBA Most Valuable Player (1988, 1991, 1992, 1996, 1998). ... NBA Defensive Player of the Year (1988). ... NBA Rookie of the Year (1985). ... IBM Award, for all-around contribution to team's success (1985, 1989). ... Slam Dunk championship winner (1987, 1988). ... All-NBA First Team (1987, 1988, 1989, 1990, 1991, 1992, 1993, 1996, 1997, 1998). ... All-NBA Second Team (1985). ... NBA All-Defensive first team (1988, 1989, 1990, 1991, 1992, 1993, 1996, 1997, 1998). ... NBA All-Rookie team (1985).

**NOTES:** Led NBA with 3.16 steals per game (1988), 2.77 steals per game (1991) and 2.83 steals per game (1993).

| Season Team | G | Min. | FGM | FGA | Pct. | FTM | FTA | Pct. | REBOUNDS | | | Ast. | St. | Blk. | TO | Pts. | AVERAGES | | |
|---|---|---|---|---|---|---|---|---|---|---|---|---|---|---|---|---|---|---|---|
| | | | | | | | | | Off. | Def. | Tot. | | | | | | RPG | APG | PPG |
| 84-85—Chicago | 82 | 3144 | 837 | 1625 | .515 | 630 | 746 | .845 | 167 | 367 | 534 | 481 | 196 | 69 | 291 | *2313 | 6.5 | 5.9 | 28.2 |
| 85-86—Chicago | 18 | 451 | 150 | 328 | .457 | 105 | 125 | .840 | 23 | 41 | 64 | 53 | 37 | 21 | 45 | 408 | 3.6 | 2.9 | 22.7 |
| 86-87—Chicago | 82 | *3281 | *1098 | *2279 | .482 | *833 | *972 | .857 | 166 | 264 | 430 | 377 | 236 | 125 | 272 | *3041 | 5.2 | 4.6 | *37.1 |
| 87-88—Chicago | 82 | *3311 | *1069 | *1998 | .535 | *723 | 860 | .841 | 139 | 310 | 449 | 485 | *259 | 131 | 252 | *2868 | 5.5 | 5.9 | *35.0 |
| 88-89—Chicago | 81 | *3255 | *966 | *1795 | .538 | 674 | 793 | .850 | 149 | 503 | 652 | 650 | 234 | 65 | 290 | *2633 | 8.0 | 8.0 | *32.5 |
| 89-90—Chicago | 82 | 3197 | *1034 | *1964 | .526 | 593 | 699 | .848 | 143 | 422 | 565 | 519 | *227 | 54 | 247 | *2753 | 6.9 | 6.3 | *33.6 |
| 90-91—Chicago | 82 | 3034 | *990 | *1837 | .539 | 571 | 671 | .851 | 118 | 374 | 492 | 453 | 223 | 83 | 202 | *2580 | 6.0 | 5.5 | *31.5 |
| 91-92—Chicago | 80 | 3102 | *943 | *1818 | .519 | 491 | 590 | .832 | 91 | 420 | 511 | 489 | 182 | 75 | 200 | *2404 | 6.4 | 6.1 | *30.1 |
| 92-93—Chicago | 78 | 3067 | *992 | *2003 | .495 | 476 | 569 | .837 | 135 | 387 | 522 | 428 | *221 | 61 | 207 | *2541 | 6.7 | 5.5 | *32.6 |
| 93-94—Chicago | | | | | | | Did not play—retired. | | | | | | | | | | | | |
| 94-95—Chicago | 17 | 668 | 166 | 404 | .411 | 109 | 136 | .801 | 25 | 92 | 117 | 90 | 30 | 13 | 35 | 457 | 6.9 | 5.3 | 26.9 |
| 95-96—Chicago | 82 | 3090 | *916 | *1850 | .495 | 548 | 657 | .834 | 148 | 395 | 543 | 352 | 180 | 42 | 197 | *2491 | 6.6 | 4.3 | *30.4 |
| 96-97—Chicago | 82 | 3106 | *920 | *1892 | .486 | 480 | 576 | .833 | 113 | 369 | 482 | 352 | 140 | 44 | 166 | *2431 | 5.9 | 4.3 | *29.6 |
| 97-98—Chicago | 82 | 3181 | *881 | *1893 | .465 | 565 | 721 | .784 | 130 | 345 | 475 | 283 | 141 | 45 | 185 | *2357 | 5.8 | 3.5 | *28.7 |
| 98-99— | | | | | | | Did not play—retired. | | | | | | | | | | | | |
| 99-00— | | | | | | | Did not play—retired. | | | | | | | | | | | | |
| 00-01— | | | | | | | Did not play—retired. | | | | | | | | | | | | |
| 01-02—Washington | 60 | 2093 | 551 | 1324 | .416 | 263 | 333 | .790 | 50 | 289 | 339 | 310 | 85 | 26 | 162 | 1375 | 5.7 | 5.2 | 22.9 |
| 02-03—Washington | 82 | 3031 | 679 | 1527 | .445 | 266 | 324 | .821 | 71 | 426 | 497 | 311 | 123 | 39 | 173 | 1640 | 6.1 | 3.8 | 20.0 |
| Totals | 1072 | 41011 | 12192 | 24537 | .497 | 7327 | 8772 | .835 | 1668 | 5004 | 6672 | 5633 | 2514 | 893 | 2924 | 32292 | 6.2 | 5.3 | 30.1 |

Three-point field goals: 1984-85, 9-for-52 (.173). 1985-86, 3-for-18 (.167). 1986-87, 12-for-66 (.182). 1987-88, 7-for-53 (.132). 1988-89, 27-for-98 (.276). 1989-90, 92-for-245 (.376). 1990-91, 29-for-93 (.312). 1991-92, 27-for-100 (.270). 1992-93, 81-for-230 (.352). 1994-95, 16-for-32 (.500). 1995-96, 111-for-260 (.427). 1996-97, 111-for-297 (.374). 1997-98, 30-for-126 (.238). 2001-02, 10-for-53 (.189). 2002-03, 16-for-55 (.291). Totals, 581-for-1778 (.327).

Personal fouls/disqualifications: 1984-85, 285/4. 1985-86, 46/0. 1986-87, 237/0. 1987-88, 270/2. 1988-89, 247/2. 1989-90, 241/0. 1990-91, 229/1. 1991-92, 201/1. 1992-93, 188/0. 1994-95, 47/0. 1995-96, 195/0. 1996-97, 156/0. 1997-98, 151/0. 2001-02, 119/0. 2002-03, 171/1. Totals, 2783/11.

## NBA PLAYOFF RECORD

**NOTES:** NBA Finals Most Valuable Player (1991, 1992, 1993, 1996, 1997, 1998). ... Holds NBA Finals career records for most three-point field goals made—42; and most consecutive games with 20 or more points—35 (June 2, 1991 through June 14, 1998). ... Holds NBA Finals single-series record for highest points-per-game average—41.0 (1993). ... Holds NBA Finals single-game record for most points in one half—35 (June 3, 1992, vs. Portland). ... Shares NBA Finals single-game records for most field goals made in one half—14; and most three-point field goals made in one half—6 (June 3, 1992, vs. Portland); most free throws made in one quarter—9 (June 11, 1997, vs. Utah); and most free throws attempted in one half—15 (June 4, 1997, vs. Utah). ... Holds career playoff record for most points—5,987; highest points-per-game average (minimum 25 games or 625 points)—33.4; most field goals attempted—4,497; most free throws made—1,463; most free throws attempted—1,766; and most steals—376. ... Holds single-game playoff records for most points—63 (April 20, 1986, at Boston); and most free throws made in one quarter—13 (May 21, 1991, vs. Detroit). ... Shares single-game playoff records for most field goals made—24 (May 1, 1988, vs. Cleveland); most field goals attempted in one half—25 (May 1, 1988, vs. Cleveland); and most three-point field goals made in one half—6 (June 3, 1992, vs. Portland).

| Season Team | G | Min. | FGM | FGA | Pct. | FTM | FTA | Pct. | Off. | Def. | Tot. | Ast. | St. | Blk. | TO | Pts. | RPG | APG | PPG |
|---|---|---|---|---|---|---|---|---|---|---|---|---|---|---|---|---|---|---|---|
| 84-85—Chicago ........ | 4 | 171 | 34 | 78 | .436 | 48 | 58 | .828 | 7 | 16 | 23 | 34 | 11 | 4 | 15 | 117 | 5.8 | 8.5 | 29.3 |
| 85-86—Chicago ........ | 3 | 135 | 48 | 95 | .505 | 34 | 39 | .872 | 5 | 14 | 19 | 17 | 7 | 4 | 14 | 131 | 6.3 | 5.7 | 43.7 |
| 86-87—Chicago ........ | 3 | 128 | 35 | 84 | .417 | 35 | 39 | .897 | 7 | 14 | 21 | 18 | 6 | 7 | 8 | 107 | 7.0 | 6.0 | 35.7 |
| 87-88—Chicago ........ | 10 | 427 | 138 | 260 | .531 | 86 | 99 | .869 | 23 | 48 | 71 | 47 | 24 | 11 | 39 | 363 | 7.1 | 4.7 | 36.3 |
| 88-89—Chicago ........ | 17 | 718 | 199 | 390 | .510 | 183 | 229 | .799 | 26 | 93 | 119 | 130 | 42 | 13 | 68 | 591 | 7.0 | 7.6 | 34.8 |
| 89-90—Chicago ........ | 16 | 674 | 219 | 426 | .514 | 133 | 159 | .836 | 24 | 91 | 115 | 109 | 45 | 14 | 56 | 587 | 7.2 | 6.8 | 36.7 |
| 90-91—Chicago ........ | 17 | 689 | 197 | 376 | .524 | 125 | 148 | .845 | 18 | 90 | 108 | 142 | 40 | 23 | 43 | 529 | 6.4 | 8.4 | 31.1 |
| 91-92—Chicago ........ | 22 | 920 | 290 | 581 | .499 | 162 | 189 | .857 | 37 | 100 | 137 | 127 | 44 | 16 | 81 | 759 | 6.2 | 5.8 | 34.5 |
| 92-93—Chicago ........ | 19 | 783 | 251 | 528 | .475 | 136 | 169 | .805 | 32 | 96 | 128 | 114 | 39 | 17 | 45 | 666 | 6.7 | 6.0 | 35.1 |
| 94-95—Chicago ........ | 10 | 420 | 120 | 248 | .484 | 64 | 79 | .810 | 20 | 45 | 65 | 45 | 23 | 14 | 41 | 315 | 6.5 | 4.5 | 31.5 |
| 95-96—Chicago ........ | 18 | 733 | 187 | 407 | .459 | 153 | 187 | .818 | 31 | 58 | 89 | 74 | 33 | 6 | 42 | 552 | 4.9 | 4.1 | 30.7 |
| 96-97—Chicago ........ | 19 | 804 | 227 | 498 | .456 | 123 | 148 | .831 | 42 | 108 | 150 | 91 | 30 | 17 | 49 | 590 | 7.9 | 4.8 | 31.1 |
| 97-98—Chicago ........ | 21 | 872 | 243 | 526 | .462 | 181 | 223 | .812 | 33 | 74 | 107 | 74 | 32 | 12 | 45 | 680 | 5.1 | 3.5 | 32.4 |
| **Totals** ................. | 179 | 7474 | 2188 | 4497 | .487 | 1463 | 1766 | .828 | 305 | 847 | 1152 | 1022 | 376 | 158 | 546 | 5987 | 6.4 | 5.7 | 33.4 |

Three-point field goals: 1984-85, 1-for-8 (.125). 1985-86, 1-for-1. 1986-87, 2-for-5 (.400). 1987-88, 1-for-3 (.333). 1988-89, 10-for-35 (.286). 1989-90, 16-for-50 (.320). 1990-91, 10-for-26 (.385). 1991-92, 17-for-44 (.386). 1992-93, 28-for-72 (.389). 1994-95, 11-for-30 (.367). 1995-96, 25-for-62 (.403). 1996-97, 13-for-67 (.194). 1997-98, 13-for-43 (.302). Totals, 148-for-446 (.332).

Personal fouls/disqualifications: 1984-85, 15/0. 1985-86, 13/1. 1986-87, 11/0. 1987-88, 38/1. 1988-89, 65/1. 1989-90, 54/0. 1990-91, 53/0. 1991-92, 62/0. 1992-93, 58/0. 1994-95, 30/0. 1995-96, 49/0. 1996-97, 46/0. 1997-98, 47/0. Totals, 543/3.

## NBA ALL-STAR GAME RECORD

**NOTES:** NBA All-Star Game Most Valuable Player (1988, 1996, 1998). ... Holds career record for field goals (110), field goal attempts (233) and steals (37). Shares record for most field goal attempts in one game—27 (2003). ... Recorded only triple-double in All-Star Game history (February 9, 1997).

| Season Team | Min. | FGM | FGA | Pct. | FTM | FTA | Pct. | Off. | Def. | Tot. | Ast. | PF | Dq. | St. | Blk. | TO | Pts. |
|---|---|---|---|---|---|---|---|---|---|---|---|---|---|---|---|---|---|
| 1985—Chicago ................ | 22 | 2 | 9 | .222 | 3 | 4 | .750 | 3 | 3 | 6 | 2 | 4 | 0 | 3 | 1 | 1 | 7 |
| 1986—Chicago ................ | | | | | | Selected, did not play—injured. | | | | | | | | | | | |
| 1987—Chicago ................ | 28 | 5 | 12 | .417 | 1 | 2 | .500 | 0 | 0 | 0 | 4 | 2 | 0 | 2 | 0 | 5 | 11 |
| 1988—Chicago ................ | 29 | 17 | 23 | .739 | 6 | 6 | 1.000 | 3 | 5 | 8 | 3 | 5 | 0 | 4 | 4 | 2 | 40 |
| 1989—Chicago ................ | 33 | 13 | 23 | .565 | 2 | 4 | .500 | 1 | 1 | 2 | 3 | 1 | 0 | 5 | 0 | 4 | 28 |
| 1990—Chicago ................ | 29 | 8 | 17 | .471 | 0 | 0 | ... | 1 | 4 | 5 | 2 | 1 | 0 | 5 | 1 | 5 | 17 |
| 1991—Chicago ................ | 36 | 10 | 25 | .400 | 6 | 7 | .857 | 3 | 2 | 5 | 5 | 2 | 0 | 2 | 0 | 10 | 26 |
| 1992—Chicago ................ | 31 | 9 | 17 | .529 | 0 | 0 | ... | 1 | 0 | 1 | 5 | 2 | 0 | 2 | 0 | 1 | 18 |
| 1993—Chicago ................ | 36 | 10 | 24 | .417 | 9 | 13 | .692 | 3 | 1 | 4 | 5 | 5 | 0 | 4 | 0 | 6 | 30 |
| 1996—Chicago ................ | 22 | 8 | 11 | .727 | 4 | 4 | 1.000 | 1 | 3 | 4 | 1 | 1 | 0 | 1 | 0 | 0 | 20 |
| 1997—Chicago ................ | 26 | 5 | 14 | .357 | 4 | 7 | .571 | 3 | 8 | 11 | 11 | 4 | 0 | 2 | 0 | 3 | 14 |
| 1998—Chicago ................ | 32 | 10 | 18 | .556 | 2 | 3 | .667 | 1 | 5 | 6 | 8 | 0 | 0 | 3 | 0 | 2 | 23 |
| 2002—Washington .......... | 22 | 4 | 13 | .308 | 0 | 0 | ... | 0 | 4 | 4 | 3 | 1 | 0 | 2 | 0 | 1 | 8 |
| 2003—Washington .......... | 36 | 9 | 27 | .333 | 2 | 2 | 1.000 | 2 | 3 | 5 | 2 | 3 | 0 | 2 | 0 | 2 | 20 |
| **Totals** .......................... | 382 | 110 | 233 | .472 | 39 | 52 | .750 | 22 | 39 | 61 | 54 | 31 | 0 | 37 | 6 | 42 | 262 |

Three-point field goals: 1985, 0-for-1. 1987, 0-for-1. 1989, 0-for-1. 1990, 1-for-1. 1991, 0-for-2. 1993, 1-for-2 (.500). 1998, 1-for-1. 2003, 0-for-2. Totals, 3-for-11 (.273).

# KERR, RED     C

**PERSONAL:** Born July 17, 1932, in Chicago. ... 6-9/230 (2,05/104,3). ... Full name: John G. Kerr.
**HIGH SCHOOL:** Tilden Technical School (Chicago).
**COLLEGE:** Illinois.
**TRANSACTIONS:** Selected by Syracuse Nationals in first round (sixth pick overall) of 1954 NBA Draft. ... Nationals franchise moved from Syracuse to Philadelphia and renamed 76ers for 1963-64 season. ... Traded by 76ers to Baltimore Bullets for G Wali Jones (September 22, 1965). ... Selected by Chicago Bulls from Bullets in NBA Expansion Draft (April 30, 1966).
**MISCELLANEOUS:** Member of NBA championship team (1955).

## COLLEGIATE RECORD

| Season Team | G | Min. | FGM | FGA | Pct. | FTM | FTA | Pct. | Reb. | Ast. | Pts. | RPG | APG | PPG |
|---|---|---|---|---|---|---|---|---|---|---|---|---|---|---|
| 50-51—Illinois‡ .......................... | | | | | Freshman team did not play intercollegiate schedule. | | | | | | | | | |
| 51-52—Illinois .......................... | 26 | ... | 143 | 365 | .392 | 71 | 124 | .573 | ... | ... | 357 | ... | ... | 13.7 |
| 52-53—Illinois .......................... | 22 | ... | 153 | 397 | .385 | 80 | 123 | .650 | ... | ... | 386 | ... | ... | 17.5 |
| 53-54—Illinois .......................... | 22 | ... | 210 | 520 | .404 | 136 | 214 | .636 | ... | ... | 556 | ... | ... | 25.3 |
| **Varsity totals** .......................... | 70 | ... | 506 | 1282 | .395 | 287 | 461 | .623 | ... | ... | 1299 | ... | ... | 18.6 |

## NBA REGULAR-SEASON RECORD

| Season Team | G | Min. | FGM | FGA | Pct. | FTM | FTA | Pct. | Reb. | Ast. | PF | Dq. | Pts. | RPG | APG | PPG |
|---|---|---|---|---|---|---|---|---|---|---|---|---|---|---|---|---|
| 54-55—Syracuse ..................... | 72 | 1529 | 301 | 718 | .419 | 152 | 223 | .682 | 474 | 80 | 165 | 2 | 754 | 6.6 | 1.1 | 10.5 |
| 55-56—Syracuse ..................... | 72 | 2114 | 377 | 935 | .403 | 207 | 316 | .655 | 607 | 84 | 168 | 3 | 961 | 8.4 | 1.2 | 13.3 |
| 56-57—Syracuse ..................... | 72 | 2191 | 333 | 827 | .403 | 225 | 313 | .719 | 807 | 90 | 190 | 3 | 891 | 11.2 | 1.3 | 12.4 |
| 57-58—Syracuse ..................... | 72 | 2384 | 407 | 1020 | .399 | 280 | 422 | .664 | 963 | 88 | 197 | 4 | 1094 | 13.4 | 1.2 | 15.2 |
| 58-59—Syracuse ..................... | 72 | 2671 | 502 | 1139 | .441 | 281 | 367 | .766 | 1008 | 142 | 183 | 1 | 1285 | 14.0 | 2.0 | 17.8 |
| 59-60—Syracuse ..................... | 75 | 2372 | 436 | 1111 | .392 | 233 | 310 | .752 | 913 | 167 | 207 | 4 | 1105 | 12.2 | 2.2 | 14.7 |
| 60-61—Syracuse ..................... | 79 | 2676 | 419 | 1056 | .397 | 218 | 299 | .729 | 951 | 199 | 230 | 4 | 1056 | 12.0 | 2.5 | 13.4 |
| 61-62—Syracuse ..................... | 80 | 2768 | 541 | 1220 | .443 | 222 | 302 | .735 | 1176 | 243 | 272 | 7 | 1304 | 14.7 | 3.0 | 16.3 |
| 62-63—Syracuse ..................... | 80 | 2561 | 507 | 1069 | .474 | 241 | 320 | .753 | 1039 | 214 | 208 | 3 | 1255 | 13.0 | 2.7 | 15.7 |
| 63-64—Philadelphia ................ | 80 | 2938 | 536 | 1250 | .429 | 268 | 357 | .751 | 1017 | 275 | 187 | 2 | 1340 | 12.7 | 3.4 | 16.8 |
| 64-65—Philadelphia ................ | 80 | 1810 | 264 | 714 | .370 | 126 | 181 | .696 | 551 | 197 | 132 | 1 | 654 | 6.9 | 2.5 | 8.2 |
| 65-66—Baltimore ..................... | 71 | 1770 | 286 | 692 | .413 | 209 | 272 | .768 | 586 | 225 | 148 | 0 | 781 | 8.3 | 3.2 | 11.0 |
| **Totals** ................................... | 905 | 27784 | 4909 | 11751 | .418 | 2662 | 3682 | .723 | 10092 | 2004 | 2287 | 34 | 12480 | 11.2 | 2.2 | 13.8 |

## NBA PLAYOFF RECORD

| Season Team | G | Min. | FGM | FGA | Pct. | FTM | FTA | Pct. | Reb. | Ast. | PF | Dq. | Pts. | RPG | APG | PPG |
|---|---|---|---|---|---|---|---|---|---|---|---|---|---|---|---|---|
| 54-55—Syracuse | 11 | 363 | 59 | 151 | .391 | 34 | 61 | .557 | 118 | 13 | 27 | 0 | 152 | 10.7 | 1.2 | 13.8 |
| 55-56—Syracuse | 8 | 213 | 37 | 77 | .481 | 15 | 33 | .455 | 68 | 10 | 23 | 0 | 89 | 8.5 | 1.3 | 11.1 |
| 56-57—Syracuse | 5 | 162 | 28 | 65 | .431 | 20 | 29 | .690 | 69 | 6 | 7 | 0 | 76 | 13.8 | 1.2 | 15.2 |
| 57-58—Syracuse | 3 | 116 | 18 | 55 | .327 | 14 | 18 | .778 | 61 | 3 | 5 | 0 | 50 | 20.3 | 1.0 | 16.7 |
| 58-59—Syracuse | 9 | 312 | 50 | 142 | .352 | 30 | 33 | .909 | 108 | 24 | 20 | 0 | 130 | 12.0 | 2.7 | 14.4 |
| 59-60—Syracuse | 3 | 104 | 15 | 51 | .294 | 11 | 12 | .917 | 25 | 9 | 9 | 0 | 41 | 8.3 | 3.0 | 13.7 |
| 60-61—Syracuse | 8 | 210 | 30 | 88 | .341 | 16 | 23 | .696 | 99 | 20 | 18 | 0 | 76 | 12.4 | 2.5 | 9.5 |
| 61-62—Syracuse | 5 | 193 | 41 | 109 | .376 | 6 | 8 | .750 | 80 | 10 | 15 | 0 | 88 | 16.0 | 2.0 | 17.6 |
| 62-63—Syracuse | 5 | 187 | 26 | 60 | .433 | 16 | 21 | .762 | 75 | 9 | 12 | 0 | 68 | 15.0 | 1.8 | 13.6 |
| 63-64—Philadelphia | 5 | 185 | 40 | 83 | .482 | 15 | 20 | .750 | 69 | 16 | 12 | 0 | 95 | 13.8 | 3.2 | 19.0 |
| 64-65—Philadelphia | 11 | 181 | 24 | 67 | .358 | 15 | 21 | .714 | 38 | 28 | 20 | 0 | 63 | 3.5 | 2.5 | 5.7 |
| 65-66—Baltimore | 3 | 49 | 2 | 11 | .182 | 1 | 2 | .500 | 17 | 4 | 5 | 0 | 5 | 5.7 | 1.3 | 1.7 |
| Totals | 76 | 2275 | 370 | 959 | .386 | 193 | 281 | .687 | 827 | 152 | 173 | 0 | 933 | 10.9 | 2.0 | 12.3 |

## NBA ALL-STAR GAME RECORD

| Season Team | Min. | FGM | FGA | Pct. | FTM | FTA | Pct. | Reb | Ast. | PF | Dq. | Pts. |
|---|---|---|---|---|---|---|---|---|---|---|---|---|
| 1956—Syracuse | 16 | 2 | 4 | .500 | 0 | 1 | .000 | 8 | 0 | 2 | 0 | 4 |
| 1959—Syracuse | 21 | 3 | 14 | .214 | 1 | 2 | .500 | 9 | 2 | 0 | 0 | 7 |
| 1963—Syracuse | 11 | 0 | 4 | .000 | 2 | 2 | 1.000 | 2 | 1 | 3 | 0 | 2 |
| Totals | 48 | 5 | 22 | .227 | 3 | 5 | .600 | 19 | 3 | 5 | 0 | 13 |

## NBA COACHING RECORD

**HONORS:** NBA Coach of the Year (1967).

| Season Team | REGULAR SEASON | | | | PLAYOFFS | | |
|---|---|---|---|---|---|---|---|
| | W | L | Pct. | Finish | W | L | Pct. |
| 66-67—Chicago | 33 | 48 | .407 | 4th/Western Division | 0 | 3 | .000 |
| 67-68—Chicago | 29 | 53 | .354 | 4th/Western Division | 1 | 4 | .200 |
| 68-69—Phoenix | 16 | 66 | .195 | 7th/Western Division | — | — | — |
| 69-70—Phoenix | 15 | 23 | .395 | | — | — | — |
| Totals (4 years) | 93 | 190 | .329 | Totals (2 years) | 1 | 7 | .125 |

**NOTES:**

1967—Lost to St. Louis in Western Division Semifinals.
1968—Lost to Los Angeles in Western Division Semifinals.
1970—Resigned as Phoenix head coach (January 2); replaced by Jerry Colangelo.

# KING, BERNARD                    F

**PERSONAL:** Born December 4, 1956, in Brooklyn, N.Y. ... 6-7/205 (2,00/93,0). ... Brother of Albert King, guard/forward with New Jersey Nets, Philadelphia 76ers, San Antonio Spurs and Washington Bullets (1981-82 through 1988-89 and 1991-92).
**HIGH SCHOOL:** Fort Hamilton (Brooklyn, N.Y.).
**COLLEGE:** Tennessee.

**TRANSACTIONS:** Selected after junior season by New Jersey Nets in first round (seventh pick overall) of 1977 NBA Draft. ... Traded by Nets with C/F John Gianelli and G Jim Boylan to Utah Jazz for C Rich Kelley (October 2, 1979). ... Traded by Jazz to Golden State Warriors for C/F Wayne Cooper and 1981 second-round draft choice (September 11, 1980). ... Signed as veteran free agent by New York Knicks (September 28, 1982); Warriors matched offer and traded King to Knicks for G Micheal Ray Richardson and 1984 fifth-round draft choice (October 22, 1982). ... Signed as free agent by Washington Bullets (October 16, 1987). ... Waived by Bullets (January 22, 1993). ... Signed as free agent by New Jersey Nets (February 6, 1993).

## COLLEGIATE RECORD

**NOTES:** The Sporting News All-America second team (1977). ... Led NCAA Division I with .622 field goal percentage (1975).

| Season Team | G | Min. | FGM | FGA | Pct. | FTM | FTA | Pct. | Reb. | Ast. | Pts. | RPG | APG | PPG |
|---|---|---|---|---|---|---|---|---|---|---|---|---|---|---|
| 74-75—Tennessee | 25 | ... | 273 | 439 | .622 | 115 | 147 | .782 | 308 | 39 | 661 | 12.3 | 1.6 | 26.4 |
| 75-76—Tennessee | 25 | ... | 260 | 454 | .573 | 109 | 163 | .669 | 325 | 40 | 629 | 13.0 | 1.6 | 25.2 |
| 76-77—Tennessee | 26 | ... | 278 | 481 | .578 | 116 | 163 | .712 | 371 | 82 | 672 | 14.3 | 3.2 | 25.8 |
| Totals | 76 | | 811 | 1374 | .590 | 340 | 473 | .719 | 1004 | 161 | 1962 | 13.2 | 2.1 | 25.8 |

## NBA REGULAR-SEASON RECORD

**HONORS:** NBA Comeback Player of the Year (1981). ... All-NBA first team (1984, 1985). ... All-NBA second team (1982). ... All-NBA third team (1991). ... NBA All-Rookie team (1978).

| Season Team | G | Min. | FGM | FGA | Pct. | FTM | FTA | Pct. | REBOUNDS | | | Ast. | St. | Blk. | TO | Pts. | AVERAGES | | |
|---|---|---|---|---|---|---|---|---|---|---|---|---|---|---|---|---|---|---|---|
| | | | | | | | | | Off. | Def. | Tot. | | | | | | RPG | APG | PPG |
| 77-78—New Jersey | 79 | 3092 | 798 | 1665 | .479 | 313 | 462 | .677 | 265 | 486 | 751 | 193 | 122 | 36 | 311 | 1909 | 9.5 | 2.4 | 24.2 |
| 78-79—New Jersey | 82 | 2859 | 710 | 1359 | .522 | 349 | 619 | .564 | 251 | 418 | 669 | 295 | 118 | 39 | 323 | 1769 | 8.2 | 3.6 | 21.6 |
| 79-80—Utah | 19 | 419 | 71 | 137 | .518 | 34 | 63 | .540 | 24 | 64 | 88 | 52 | 7 | 4 | 50 | 176 | 4.6 | 2.7 | 9.3 |
| 80-81—Golden State | 81 | 2914 | 731 | 1244 | .588 | 307 | 437 | .703 | 178 | 373 | 551 | 287 | 72 | 34 | 265 | 1771 | 6.8 | 3.5 | 21.9 |
| 81-82—Golden State | 79 | 2861 | 740 | 1307 | .566 | 352 | 499 | .705 | 140 | 329 | 469 | 282 | 78 | 23 | 267 | 1833 | 5.9 | 3.6 | 23.2 |
| 82-83—New York | 68 | 2207 | 603 | 1142 | .528 | 280 | 388 | .722 | 99 | 227 | 326 | 195 | 90 | 13 | 197 | 1486 | 4.8 | 2.9 | 21.9 |
| 83-84—New York | 77 | 2667 | 795 | 1391 | .572 | 437 | 561 | .779 | 123 | 271 | 394 | 164 | 75 | 17 | 197 | 2027 | 5.1 | 2.1 | 26.3 |
| 84-85—New York | 55 | 2063 | 691 | 1303 | .530 | 426 | 552 | .772 | 114 | 203 | 317 | 204 | 71 | 15 | 204 | 1809 | 5.8 | 3.7 | *32.9 |
| 85-86—New York | | | | | | Did not play—injured. | | | | | | | | | | | | | |
| 86-87—New York | 6 | 214 | 52 | 105 | .495 | 32 | 43 | .744 | 13 | 19 | 32 | 19 | 2 | 0 | 15 | 136 | 5.3 | 3.2 | 22.7 |

| Season Team | G | Min. | FGM | FGA | Pct. | FTM | FTA | Pct. | REBOUNDS Off. | Def. | Tot. | Ast. | St. | Blk. | TO | Pts. | AVERAGES RPG | APG | PPG |
|---|---|---|---|---|---|---|---|---|---|---|---|---|---|---|---|---|---|---|---|
| 87-88—Washington .... | 69 | 2044 | 470 | 938 | .501 | 247 | 324 | .762 | 86 | 194 | 280 | 192 | 49 | 10 | 211 | 1188 | 4.1 | 2.8 | 17.2 |
| 88-89—Washington .... | 81 | 2559 | 654 | 1371 | .477 | 361 | 441 | .819 | 133 | 251 | 384 | 294 | 64 | 13 | 227 | 1674 | 4.7 | 3.6 | 20.7 |
| 89-90—Washington .... | 82 | 2687 | 711 | 1459 | .487 | 412 | 513 | .803 | 129 | 275 | 404 | 376 | 51 | 7 | 248 | 1837 | 4.9 | 4.6 | 22.4 |
| 90-91—Washington .... | 64 | 2401 | 713 | 1511 | .472 | 383 | 485 | .790 | 114 | 205 | 319 | 292 | 56 | 16 | 255 | 1817 | 5.0 | 4.6 | 28.4 |
| 91-92—Washington .... | | | | | | | | Did not play—injured. | | | | | | | | | | | |
| 92-93—New Jersey ..... | 32 | 430 | 91 | 177 | .514 | 39 | 57 | .684 | 35 | 41 | 76 | 18 | 11 | 3 | 21 | 223 | 2.4 | 0.6 | 7.0 |
| Totals .................. | 874 | 29417 | 7830 | 15109 | .518 | 3972 | 5444 | .730 | 1704 | 3356 | 5060 | 2863 | 866 | 230 | 2791 | 19655 | 5.8 | 3.3 | 22.5 |

Three-point field goals: 1980-81, 2-for-6 (.333). 1981-82, 1-for-5 (.200). 1982-83, 0-for-6. 1983-84, 0-for-4. 1984-85, 1-for-10 (.100). 1987-88, 1-for-6 (.167). 1988-89, 5-for-30 (.167). 1989-90, 3-for-23 (.130). 1990-91, 6-for-37 (.216). 1992-93, 2-for-7 (.286). Totals, 23-for-134 (.172).

Personal fouls/disqualifications: 1977-78, 302/5. 1978-79, 326/10. 1979-80, 66/3. 1980-81, 304/5. 1981-82, 285/6. 1982-83, 233/5. 1983-84, 273/2. 1984-85, 191/3. 1986-87, 14/0. 1987-88, 202/3. 1988-89, 219/1. 1989-90, 230/1. 1990-91, 187/1. 1992-93, 53/0. Totals, 2885/45.

## NBA PLAYOFF RECORD

| Season Team | G | Min. | FGM | FGA | Pct. | FTM | FTA | Pct. | REBOUNDS Off. | Def. | Tot. | Ast. | St. | Blk. | TO | Pts. | AVERAGES RPG | APG | PPG |
|---|---|---|---|---|---|---|---|---|---|---|---|---|---|---|---|---|---|---|---|
| 78-79—New Jersey ..... | 2 | 81 | 21 | 42 | .500 | 10 | 24 | .417 | 5 | 6 | 11 | 7 | 4 | 0 | 6 | 52 | 5.5 | 3.5 | 26.0 |
| 82-83—New York ........ | 6 | 184 | 56 | 97 | .577 | 28 | 35 | .800 | 8 | 16 | 24 | 13 | 2 | 0 | 10 | 141 | 4.0 | 2.2 | 23.5 |
| 83-84—New York ........ | 12 | 477 | 162 | 282 | .574 | 93 | 123 | .756 | 28 | 46 | 74 | 36 | 14 | 6 | 31 | 417 | 6.2 | 3.0 | 34.8 |
| 87-88—Washington .... | 5 | 168 | 26 | 53 | .491 | 17 | 21 | .810 | 3 | 8 | 11 | 9 | 3 | 0 | 14 | 69 | 2.2 | 1.8 | 13.8 |
| 92-93—New Jersey ..... | 3 | 24 | 4 | 7 | .571 | 0 | 0 | | 1 | 0 | 1 | 0 | 1 | 0 | 1 | 8 | 0.3 | 0.0 | 2.7 |
| Totals .................. | 28 | 934 | 269 | 481 | .559 | 148 | 203 | .729 | 45 | 76 | 121 | 65 | 24 | 6 | 62 | 687 | 4.3 | 2.3 | 24.5 |

Three-point field goals: 1982-83, 1-for-3 (.333). 1983-84, 0-for-1. Totals, 1-for-4 (.250).

Personal fouls/disqualifications: 1978-79, 10/0. 1982-83, 16/0. 1983-84, 48/0. 1987-88, 17/0. 1992-93, 3/0. Totals, 94/0.

## NBA ALL-STAR GAME RECORD

| Season Team | Min. | FGM | FGA | Pct. | FTM | FTA | Pct. | REBOUNDS Off. | Def. | Tot. | Ast. | PF | Dq. | St. | Blk. | TO | Pts. |
|---|---|---|---|---|---|---|---|---|---|---|---|---|---|---|---|---|---|
| 1982—Golden State ......... | 14 | 2 | 7 | .286 | 2 | 2 | 1.000 | 0 | 4 | 4 | 1 | 2 | 0 | 3 | 1 | 2 | 6 |
| 1984—New York ............. | 22 | 8 | 13 | .615 | 2 | 5 | .400 | 2 | 1 | 3 | 4 | 2 | 0 | 0 | 0 | 0 | 18 |
| 1985—New York ............. | 22 | 6 | 10 | .600 | 1 | 2 | .500 | 4 | 3 | 7 | 1 | 5 | 0 | 0 | 1 | 1 | 13 |
| 1991—Washington .......... | 26 | 2 | 8 | .250 | 4 | 4 | 1.000 | 2 | 1 | 3 | 3 | 1 | 0 | 0 | 1 | 1 | 8 |
| Totals .......................... | 84 | 18 | 38 | .474 | 9 | 13 | .692 | 8 | 9 | 17 | 9 | 10 | 0 | 3 | 2 | 4 | 45 |

# LAIMBEER, BILL                    C

**PERSONAL:** Born May 19, 1957, in Boston. ... 6-11/260 (2,10/117,9). ... Full name: William Laimbeer Jr. ... Name pronounced lam-BEER.

**HIGH SCHOOL:** Palos Verdes (Calif.).

**JUNIOR COLLEGE:** Owens Technical (Ohio).

**COLLEGE:** Notre Dame.

**TRANSACTIONS:** Selected by Cleveland Cavaliers in third round (65th pick overall) of 1979 NBA Draft. ... Played in Italy (1979-80). ... Traded by Cavaliers with F Kenny Carr to Detroit Pistons for F Phil Hubbard, C Paul Mokeski and 1982 first- and second-round draft choices (February 16, 1982). ... Announced retirement (December 1, 1993).

**CAREER NOTES:** Special consultant, Detroit Shock, WNBA (April 18-June 19, 2002). ... Head coach, Detroit Shock (2002-present).

**MISCELLANEOUS:** Member of NBA championship team (1989, 1990). ... Detroit Pistons franchise all-time leading rebounder with 9,430 (1981-82 through 1993-94).

## COLLEGIATE RECORD

| Season Team | G | Min. | FGM | FGA | Pct. | FTM | FTA | Pct. | Reb. | Ast. | Pts. | AVERAGES RPG | APG | PPG |
|---|---|---|---|---|---|---|---|---|---|---|---|---|---|---|
| 76-77—Owens Tech................. | | | | | | | Did not play. | | | | | | | |
| 75-76—Notre Dame................. | 10 | 190 | 32 | 65 | .492 | 18 | 23 | .783 | 79 | 10 | 82 | 7.9 | 1.0 | 8.2 |
| 77-78—Notre Dame................. | 29 | 654 | 97 | 175 | .554 | 42 | 62 | .677 | 190 | 31 | 236 | 6.6 | 1.1 | 8.1 |
| 78-79—Notre Dame................. | 30 | 614 | 78 | 145 | .538 | 35 | 50 | .700 | 164 | 30 | 191 | 5.5 | 1.0 | 6.4 |
| Totals ...................................... | 69 | 1458 | 207 | 385 | .538 | 95 | 135 | .704 | 433 | 71 | 509 | 6.3 | 1.0 | 7.4 |

## ITALIAN LEAGUE RECORD

| Season Team | G | Min. | FGM | FGA | Pct. | FTM | FTA | Pct. | Reb. | Ast. | Pts. | AVERAGES RPG | APG | PPG |
|---|---|---|---|---|---|---|---|---|---|---|---|---|---|---|
| 79-80—Brescia ......................... | 29 | ... | 258 | 465 | .555 | 97 | 124 | .782 | 363 | ... | 613 | 12.5 | ... | 21.1 |

## NBA REGULAR-SEASON RECORD

| Season Team | G | Min. | FGM | FGA | Pct. | FTM | FTA | Pct. | REBOUNDS Off. | Def. | Tot. | Ast. | St. | Blk. | TO | Pts. | AVERAGES RPG | APG | PPG |
|---|---|---|---|---|---|---|---|---|---|---|---|---|---|---|---|---|---|---|---|
| 80-81—Cleveland ........ | 81 | 2460 | 337 | 670 | .503 | 117 | 153 | .765 | 266 | 427 | 693 | 216 | 56 | 78 | 132 | 791 | 8.6 | 2.7 | 9.8 |
| 81-82—Clev.-Det.......... | 80 | 1829 | 265 | 536 | .494 | 184 | 232 | .793 | 234 | 383 | 617 | 100 | 39 | 64 | 121 | 718 | 7.7 | 1.3 | 9.0 |
| 82-83—Detroit ............ | 82 | 2871 | 436 | 877 | .497 | 245 | 310 | .790 | 282 | 711 | 993 | 263 | 51 | 118 | 176 | 1119 | 12.1 | 3.2 | 13.6 |
| 83-84—Detroit ............ | 82 | 2864 | 553 | 1044 | .530 | 316 | 365 | .866 | 329 | 674*1003 | | 149 | 49 | 84 | 151 | 1422 | 12.2 | 1.8 | 17.3 |
| 84-85—Detroit ............ | 82 | 2892 | 595 | 1177 | .506 | 244 | 306 | .797 | 295 | 718 | 1013 | 154 | 69 | 71 | 129 | 1438 | 12.4 | 1.9 | 17.5 |
| 85-86—Detroit ............ | 82 | 2891 | 545 | 1107 | .492 | 266 | 319 | .834 | 305 | *770*1075 | | 146 | 59 | 65 | 133 | 1360 | *13.1 | 1.8 | 16.6 |
| 86-87—Detroit ............ | 82 | 2854 | 506 | 1010 | .501 | 245 | 274 | .894 | 243 | 712 | 955 | 151 | 72 | 69 | 120 | 1263 | 11.6 | 1.8 | 15.4 |
| 87-88—Detroit ............ | 82 | 2897 | 455 | 923 | .493 | 187 | 214 | .874 | 165 | 667 | 832 | 199 | 66 | 78 | 136 | 1110 | 10.1 | 2.4 | 13.5 |
| 88-89—Detroit ............ | 81 | 2640 | 449 | 900 | .499 | 178 | 212 | .840 | 138 | 638 | 776 | 177 | 51 | 100 | 129 | 1106 | 9.6 | 2.2 | 13.7 |
| 89-90—Detroit ............ | 81 | 2675 | 380 | 785 | .484 | 164 | 192 | .854 | 166 | 614 | 780 | 171 | 57 | 84 | 98 | 981 | 9.6 | 2.1 | 12.1 |
| 90-91—Detroit ............ | 82 | 2668 | 372 | 778 | .478 | 123 | 147 | .837 | 173 | 564 | 737 | 157 | 38 | 56 | 98 | 904 | 9.0 | 1.9 | 11.0 |
| 91-92—Detroit ............ | 81 | 2234 | 342 | 727 | .470 | 67 | 75 | .893 | 104 | 347 | 451 | 160 | 51 | 54 | 102 | 783 | 5.6 | 2.0 | 9.7 |
| 92-93—Detroit ............ | 79 | 1933 | 292 | 574 | .509 | 93 | 104 | .894 | 110 | 309 | 419 | 127 | 46 | 40 | 59 | 687 | 5.3 | 1.6 | 8.7 |
| 93-94—Detroit ............ | 11 | 248 | 47 | 90 | .522 | 11 | 13 | .846 | 9 | 47 | 56 | 14 | 6 | 4 | 10 | 108 | 5.1 | 1.3 | 9.8 |
| Totals .................. | 1068 | 33956 | 5574 | 11198 | .498 | 2440 | 2916 | .837 | 2819 | 7581 | 10400 | 2184 | 710 | 965 | 1594 | 13790 | 9.7 | 2.0 | 12.9 |

Three-point field goals: 1981-82, 0-for-13 (.308). 1982-83, 2-for-13 (.154). 1983-84, 0-for-11. 1984-85, 4-for-18 (.222). 1985-86, 4-for-14 (.286). 1986-87, 6-for-21 (.286). 1987-88, 13-for-39 (.333). 1988-89, 30-for-86 (.349). 1989-90, 57-for-158 (.361). 1990-91, 37-for-125 (.296). 1991-92, 32-for-85 (.376). 1992-93, 10-for-27 (.370). 1993-94, 9-for-14 (.326). Totals, 202-for-619 (.326).

Personal fouls/disqualifications: 1980-81, 332/14. 1981-82, 296/5. 1982-83, 320/9. 1983-84, 273/4. 1984-85, 308/4. 1985-86, 291/4. 1986-87, 283/4. 1987-88, 284/6. 1988-89, 259/2. 1989-90, 278/4. 1990-91, 242/3. 1991-92, 225/0. 1992-93, 212/4. 1993-94, 30/0. Totals, 3633/63.

## NBA PLAYOFF RECORD

**NOTES:** Shares NBA Finals single-game record for most points in an overtime period—9 (June 7, 1990, vs. Portland).

| Season Team | G | Min. | FGM | FGA | Pct. | FTM | FTA | Pct. | REBOUNDS Off. | Def. | Tot. | Ast. | St. | Blk. | TO | Pts. | AVERAGES RPG | APG | PPG |
|---|---|---|---|---|---|---|---|---|---|---|---|---|---|---|---|---|---|---|---|
| 83-84—Detroit ........... | 5 | 165 | 29 | 51 | .569 | 18 | 20 | .900 | 14 | 48 | 62 | 12 | 4 | 3 | 12 | 76 | 12.4 | 2.4 | 15.2 |
| 84-85—Detroit ........... | 9 | 325 | 48 | 107 | .449 | 36 | 51 | .706 | 36 | 60 | 96 | 15 | 7 | 7 | 16 | 132 | 10.7 | 1.5 | 14.7 |
| 85-86—Detroit ........... | 4 | 168 | 34 | 68 | .500 | 21 | 23 | .913 | 20 | 36 | 56 | 1 | 2 | 3 | 8 | 90 | 14.0 | 0.3 | 22.5 |
| 86-87—Detroit ........... | 15 | 543 | 84 | 163 | .515 | 15 | 24 | .625 | 30 | 126 | 156 | 37 | 15 | 12 | 20 | 184 | 10.4 | 2.5 | 12.3 |
| 87-88—Detroit ........... | 23 | 779 | 114 | 250 | .456 | 40 | 45 | .889 | 43 | 178 | 221 | 44 | 18 | 19 | 30 | 273 | 9.6 | 1.9 | 11.9 |
| 88-89—Detroit ........... | 17 | 497 | 66 | 142 | .465 | 25 | 31 | .806 | 26 | 114 | 140 | 31 | 6 | 8 | 19 | 172 | 8.2 | 1.8 | 10.1 |
| 89-90—Detroit ........... | 20 | 667 | 91 | 199 | .457 | 25 | 29 | .862 | 41 | 170 | 211 | 28 | 23 | 18 | 16 | 222 | 10.6 | 1.4 | 11.1 |
| 90-91—Detroit ........... | 15 | 446 | 66 | 148 | .446 | 27 | 31 | .871 | 42 | 80 | 122 | 19 | 5 | 12 | 17 | 164 | 8.1 | 1.3 | 10.9 |
| 91-92—Detroit ........... | 5 | 145 | 17 | 46 | .370 | 5 | 5 | 1.000 | 5 | 28 | 33 | 8 | 4 | 1 | 5 | 41 | 6.6 | 1.6 | 8.2 |
| **Totals** .................. | 113 | 3735 | 549 | 1174 | .468 | 212 | 259 | .819 | 257 | 840 | 1097 | 195 | 84 | 83 | 143 | 1354 | 9.7 | 1.7 | 12.0 |

Three-point field goals: 1984-85, 0-for-2. 1985-86, 1-for-1. 1986-87, 1-for-5 (.200). 1987-88, 5-for-17 (.294). 1988-89, 15-for-42 (.357). 1989-90, 15-for-43 (.349). 1990-91, 5-for-17 (.294). 1991-92, 2-for-10 (.200). Totals, 44-for-137 (.321).

Personal fouls/disqualifications: 1983-84, 23/2. 1984-85, 32/1. 1985-86, 19/1. 1986-87, 53/2. 1987-88, 77/2. 1988-89, 55/1. 1989-90, 77/3. 1990-91, 54/0. 1991-92, 18/1. Totals, 408/13.

## NBA ALL-STAR GAME RECORD

| Season Team | Min. | FGM | FGA | Pct. | FTM | FTA | Pct. | REBOUNDS Off. | Def. | Tot. | Ast. | PF | Dq. | St. | Blk. | TO | Pts. |
|---|---|---|---|---|---|---|---|---|---|---|---|---|---|---|---|---|---|
| 1983—Detroit.................. | 6 | 1 | 1 | 1.000 | 0 | 0 | ... | 1 | 0 | 1 | 0 | 1 | 0 | 0 | 0 | 1 | 2 |
| 1984—Detroit.................. | 17 | 6 | 8 | .750 | 1 | 1 | 1.000 | 1 | 4 | 5 | 0 | 3 | 0 | 1 | 2 | 0 | 13 |
| 1985—Detroit.................. | 11 | 2 | 4 | .500 | 1 | 2 | .500 | 1 | 2 | 3 | 1 | 1 | 0 | 0 | 0 | 0 | 5 |
| 1987—Detroit.................. | 11 | 4 | 7 | .571 | 0 | 0 | ... | 0 | 2 | 2 | 1 | 2 | 0 | 1 | 0 | 0 | 8 |
| **Totals**.......................... | 45 | 13 | 20 | .650 | 2 | 3 | .667 | 3 | 8 | 11 | 2 | 7 | 0 | 2 | 2 | 1 | 28 |

## WNBA COACHING RECORD

| Season Team | REGULAR SEASON W | L | Pct. | Finish | | PLAYOFFS W | L | Pct. |
|---|---|---|---|---|---|---|---|---|
| 2002—Detroit .................................................... | 9 | 13 | .409 | 8th/Eastern Conference | | — | — | — |
| 2003—Detroit .................................................... | 25 | 9 | .735 | 1st/Eastern Conference | | 6 | 2 | .750 |
| **Totals (2 years)**.......................................... | 34 | 22 | .607 | | **Totals (1 year)**......... | 6 | 2 | .750 |

# LANIER, BOB                                    C

**PERSONAL:** Born September 10, 1948, in Buffalo, N.Y. ... 6-11/265 (2,10/120,2). ... Full name: Robert Jerry Lanier Jr.
**HIGH SCHOOL:** Bennett (Buffalo).
**COLLEGE:** St. Bonaventure.
**TRANSACTIONS:** Selected by Detroit Pistons in first round (first pick overall) of 1970 NBA Draft. ... Traded by Pistons to Milwaukee Bucks for C Kent Benson and 1980 first-round draft choice (February 4, 1980).
**CAREER NOTES:** Chairman, NBA Stay in School Program (1989-94). ... Special assistant to the Commissioner/ Chairman, NBA Team-Up Program (1996-present).
**CAREER HONORS:** Elected to Naismith Memorial Basketball Hall of Fame (1992).

## COLLEGIATE RECORD

**NOTES:** The Sporting News All-America first team (1970).

| Season Team | G | Min. | FGM | FGA | Pct. | FTM | FTA | Pct. | Reb. | Ast. | Pts. | AVERAGES RPG | APG | PPG |
|---|---|---|---|---|---|---|---|---|---|---|---|---|---|---|
| 66-67—St. Bonaventure‡........... | 15 | ... | ... | ... | ... | ... | ... | ... | ... | ... | 450 | ... | ... | 30.0 |
| 67-68—St. Bonaventure............. | 25 | ... | 272 | 466 | .584 | 112 | 175 | .640 | 390 | ... | 656 | 15.6 | ... | 26.2 |
| 68-69—St. Bonaventure............. | 24 | ... | 270 | 460 | .587 | 114 | 181 | .630 | 374 | ... | 654 | 15.6 | ... | 27.3 |
| 69-70—St. Bonaventure............. | 26 | ... | 308 | 549 | .561 | 141 | 194 | .727 | 416 | ... | 757 | 16.0 | ... | 29.1 |
| **Varsity totals** ........................ | 75 | ... | 850 | 1475 | .576 | 367 | 550 | .667 | 1180 | ... | 2067 | 15.7 | ... | 27.6 |

## NBA REGULAR-SEASON RECORD

**HONORS:** NBA All-Rookie team (1971). ... J. Walter Kennedy Citizenship Award (1978).

| Season Team | G | Min. | FGM | FGA | Pct. | FTM | FTA | Pct. | Reb. | Ast. | PF | Dq. | Pts. | AVERAGES RPG | APG | PPG |
|---|---|---|---|---|---|---|---|---|---|---|---|---|---|---|---|---|
| 70-71—Detroit ............................. | 82 | 2017 | 504 | 1108 | .455 | 273 | 376 | .726 | 665 | 146 | 272 | 4 | 1281 | 8.1 | 1.8 | 15.6 |
| 71-72—Detroit ............................. | 80 | 3092 | 834 | 1690 | .494 | 388 | 505 | .768 | 1132 | 248 | 297 | 6 | 2056 | 14.2 | 3.1 | 25.7 |
| 72-73—Detroit ............................. | 81 | 3150 | 810 | 1654 | .490 | 307 | 397 | .773 | 1205 | 260 | 278 | 4 | 1927 | 14.9 | 3.2 | 23.8 |

| Season Team | G | Min. | FGM | FGA | Pct. | FTM | FTA | Pct. | REBOUNDS Off. | Def. | Tot. | Ast. | St. | Blk. | TO | Pts. | AVERAGES RPG | APG | PPG |
|---|---|---|---|---|---|---|---|---|---|---|---|---|---|---|---|---|---|---|---|
| 73-74—Detroit ........... | 81 | 3047 | 748 | 1483 | .504 | 326 | 409 | .797 | 269 | 805 | 1074 | 343 | 110 | 247 | ... | 1822 | 13.3 | 4.2 | 22.5 |
| 74-75—Detroit ........... | 76 | 2987 | 731 | 1433 | .510 | 361 | 450 | .802 | 225 | 689 | 914 | 350 | 75 | 172 | ... | 1823 | 12.0 | 4.6 | 24.0 |
| 75-76—Detroit ........... | 64 | 2363 | 541 | 1017 | .532 | 284 | 370 | .768 | 217 | 529 | 746 | 217 | 79 | 86 | ... | 1366 | 11.7 | 3.4 | 21.3 |
| 76-77—Detroit ........... | 64 | 2446 | 678 | 1269 | .534 | 260 | 318 | .818 | 200 | 545 | 745 | 214 | 70 | 126 | ... | 1616 | 11.6 | 3.3 | 25.3 |
| 77-78—Detroit ........... | 63 | 2311 | 622 | 1159 | .537 | 298 | 386 | .772 | 197 | 518 | 715 | 216 | 82 | 93 | 225 | 1542 | 11.3 | 3.4 | 24.5 |
| 78-79—Detroit ........... | 53 | 1835 | 489 | 950 | .515 | 275 | 367 | .749 | 164 | 330 | 494 | 140 | 50 | 75 | 175 | 1253 | 9.3 | 2.6 | 23.6 |
| 79-80—Detroit-Mil. ..... | 63 | 2131 | 466 | 867 | .537 | 277 | 354 | .782 | 152 | 400 | 552 | 184 | 74 | 89 | 162 | 1210 | 8.8 | 2.9 | 19.2 |
| 80-81—Milwaukee ...... | 67 | 1753 | 376 | 716 | .525 | 208 | 277 | .751 | 128 | 285 | 413 | 179 | 73 | 47 | 139 | 961 | 6.2 | 2.7 | 14.3 |
| 81-82—Milwaukee ...... | 74 | 1986 | 407 | 729 | .558 | 182 | 242 | .752 | 92 | 296 | 388 | 219 | 72 | 56 | 166 | 996 | 5.2 | 3.0 | 13.5 |
| 82-83—Milwaukee ...... | 39 | 978 | 163 | 332 | .491 | 91 | 133 | .684 | 58 | 142 | 200 | 105 | 34 | 24 | 82 | 417 | 5.1 | 2.7 | 10.7 |
| 83-84—Milwaukee ...... | 72 | 2007 | 392 | 685 | .572 | 194 | 274 | .708 | 141 | 314 | 455 | 186 | 58 | 51 | 163 | 978 | 6.3 | 2.6 | 13.6 |
| **Totals** .................. | 959 | 32103 | 7761 | 15092 | .514 | 3724 | 4858 | .767 | ... | ... | 9698 | 3007 | 777 | 1100 | 1112 | 19248 | 10.1 | 3.1 | 20.1 |

Three-point field goals: 1979-80, 1-for-6 (.167). 1980-81, 1-for-1. 1981-82, 0-for-2. 1982-83, 0-for-1. 1983-84, 0-for-3. Totals, 2-for-13 (.154).
Personal fouls/disqualifications: 1973-74, 273/7. 1974-75, 237/1. 1975-76, 203/2. 1976-77, 174/0. 1977-78, 185/2. 1978-79, 181/5. 1979-80, 200/3. 1980-81, 184/0. 1981-82, 211/3. 1982-83, 125/2. 1983-84, 228/8. Totals, 3048/47.

## NBA PLAYOFF RECORD

| Season Team | G | Min. | FGM | FGA | Pct. | FTM | FTA | Pct. | REBOUNDS Off. | Def. | Tot. | Ast. | St. | Blk. | TO | Pts. | AVERAGES RPG | APG | PPG |
|---|---|---|---|---|---|---|---|---|---|---|---|---|---|---|---|---|---|---|---|
| 73-74—Detroit ........... | 7 | 303 | 77 | 152 | .507 | 30 | 38 | .789 | 26 | 81 | 107 | 21 | 4 | 14 | ... | 184 | 15.3 | 3.0 | 26.3 |
| 74-75—Detroit ........... | 3 | 128 | 26 | 51 | .510 | 9 | 12 | .750 | 5 | 27 | 32 | 19 | 4 | 12 | ... | 61 | 10.7 | 6.3 | 20.3 |
| 75-76—Detroit ........... | 9 | 359 | 95 | 172 | .552 | 45 | 50 | .900 | 39 | 75 | 114 | 30 | 8 | 21 | ... | 235 | 12.7 | 3.3 | |
| 26.176-77—Detroit ..... | 3 | 118 | 34 | 54 | .630 | 16 | 19 | .842 | 13 | 37 | 50 | 6 | 3 | 7 | ... | 84 | 16.7 | 2.0 | 28.0 |
| 79-80—Milwaukee ..... | 7 | 256 | 52 | 101 | .515 | 31 | 42 | .738 | 17 | 48 | 65 | 31 | 7 | 8 | 17 | 135 | 9.3 | 4.4 | 19.3 |
| 80-81—Milwaukee ..... | 7 | 236 | 50 | 85 | .588 | 23 | 32 | .719 | 12 | 40 | 52 | 28 | 12 | 8 | 15 | 123 | 7.4 | 4.0 | 17.6 |
| 81-82—Milwaukee ..... | 6 | 212 | 41 | 80 | .513 | 14 | 25 | .560 | 18 | 27 | 45 | 22 | 8 | 5 | 14 | 96 | 7.5 | 3.7 | 16.0 |
| 82-83—Milwaukee ..... | 9 | 250 | 51 | 89 | .573 | 21 | 35 | .600 | 17 | 46 | 63 | 23 | 5 | 14 | 21 | 123 | 7.0 | 2.6 | 13.7 |
| 83-84—Milwaukee ..... | 16 | 499 | 82 | 171 | .480 | 39 | 44 | .886 | 32 | 85 | 117 | 55 | 11 | 10 | 38 | 203 | 7.3 | 3.4 | 12.7 |
| Totals ................... | 67 | 2361 | 508 | 955 | .532 | 228 | 297 | .768 | 179 | 466 | 645 | 235 | 62 | 99 | 105 | 1244 | 9.6 | 3.5 | 18.6 |

Three-point field goals: 1981-82, 0-for-1.
Personal fouls/disqualifications: 1973-74, 28/1. 1974-75, 10/0. 1975-76, 34/1. 1976-77, 10/0. 1979-80, 23/0. 1980-81, 18/0. 1981-82, 21/2. 1982-83, 32/2. 1983-84, 57/1. Totals, 233/7.

## NBA ALL-STAR GAME RECORD

NOTES: NBA All-Star Game Most Valuable Player (1974).

| Season Team | Min. | FGM | FGA | Pct. | FTM | FTA | Pct. | Reb. | Ast. | PF | Dq. | Pts. |
|---|---|---|---|---|---|---|---|---|---|---|---|---|
| 1972—Detroit ........................... | 5 | 0 | 2 | .000 | 2 | 3 | .667 | 3 | 0 | 0 | 0 | 2 |
| 1973—Detroit ........................... | 12 | 5 | 9 | .556 | 0 | 0 | ... | 6 | 0 | 1 | 0 | 10 |

| Season Team | Min. | FGM | FGA | Pct. | FTM | FTA | Pct. | REBOUNDS Off. | Def. | Tot. | Ast. | PF | Dq. | St. | Blk. | TO | Pts. |
|---|---|---|---|---|---|---|---|---|---|---|---|---|---|---|---|---|---|
| 1974—Detroit................... | 26 | 11 | 15 | .733 | 2 | 2 | 1.000 | 2 | 8 | 10 | 2 | 1 | 0 | 0 | 2 | ... | 24 |
| 1975—Detroit.................. | 12 | 1 | 4 | .250 | 0 | 0 | ... | 2 | 5 | 7 | 2 | 3 | 0 | 2 | 0 | ... | 2 |
| 1977—Detroit.................. | 20 | 7 | 8 | .875 | 3 | 3 | 1.000 | 5 | 5 | 10 | 4 | 3 | 0 | 1 | 1 | ... | 17 |
| 1978—Detroit.................. | 4 | 0 | 0 | ... | 1 | 2 | .500 | 2 | 0 | 2 | 0 | 0 | 0 | 0 | 0 | 1 | 1 |
| 1979—Detroit.................. | 31 | 5 | 10 | .500 | 0 | 0 | ... | 1 | 3 | 4 | 4 | 4 | 0 | 1 | 1 | 0 | 10 |
| 1982—Milwaukee............. | 11 | 3 | 7 | .429 | 2 | 2 | 1.000 | 2 | 1 | 3 | 0 | 3 | 0 | 0 | 1 | 1 | 8 |
| Totals........................... | 121 | 32 | 55 | .582 | 10 | 12 | .833 | ... | ... | 45 | 12 | 15 | 0 | 4 | 5 | 2 | 74 |

## NBA COACHING RECORD

BACKGROUND: Assistant coach, Golden State Warriors (beginning of 1994-95 season-February 13, 1995).

| Season Team | REGULAR SEASON W | L | Pct. | Finish | PLAYOFFS W | L | Pct. |
|---|---|---|---|---|---|---|---|
| 94-95—Golden State .................................................. | 12 | 25 | .324 | 6th/Pacific Division | — | — | — |

NOTES:
1995—Replaced Don Nelson as head coach (February 13), with record of 14-31 and club in sixth place.

# LUCAS, JERRY                    F/C

PERSONAL: Born March 30, 1940, in Middletown, Ohio. ... 6-8/235 (2,03/106,6). ... Full name: Jerry Ray Lucas. ... Nickname: Luke.
HIGH SCHOOL: Middletown (Ohio).
COLLEGE: Ohio State.
TRANSACTIONS: Selected by Cincinnati Royals in 1962 NBA Draft (territorial pick). ... Signed by Cleveland Pipers of American Basketball League (1962); Pipers dropped out of ABL prior to 1962-63 season. ... Did not play pro basketball (1962-63). ... Traded by Royals to San Francisco Warriors for G Jim King and F Bill Turner (October 25, 1969). ... Traded by Warriors to New York Knicks for F Cazzie Russell (May 7, 1971).
CAREER HONORS: Elected to Naismith Memorial Basketball Hall of Fame (1980). ... One of the 50 Greatest Players in NBA History (1996).
MISCELLANEOUS: Member of NBA championship team (1973). ... Member of gold-medal-winning U.S. Olympic team (1960).

## COLLEGIATE RECORD

NOTES: THE SPORTING NEWS College Player of the Year (1961, 1962). ... THE SPORTING NEWS All-America first team (1960, 1961, 1962). ... Member of NCAA championship team (1960). ... Led NCAA Division I with .637 field-goal percentage (1960), .623 field-goal percentage (1961) and .611 field-goal percentage (1962). ... Led NCAA Division I with .198 rebound average (1960-61) and .211 rebound average (1961-62), when championship was determined by highest individual recoveries as percentage of total recoveries by both teams in all games.

| Season Team | G | Min. | FGM | FGA | Pct. | FTM | FTA | Pct. | Reb. | Ast. | Pts. | AVERAGES RPG | APG | PPG |
|---|---|---|---|---|---|---|---|---|---|---|---|---|---|---|
| 58-59—Ohio State‡ .................... | | | | | Freshman team did not play intercollegiate schedule. | | | | | | | | | |
| 59-60—Ohio State ..................... | 27 | ... | 283 | 444 | .637 | 144 | 187 | .770 | 442 | ... | 710 | 16.4 | ... | 26.3 |
| 60-61—Ohio State ..................... | 27 | ... | 256 | 411 | .623 | 159 | 208 | .764 | 470 | ... | 671 | 17.4 | ... | 24.9 |
| 61-62—Ohio State ..................... | 28 | ... | 237 | 388 | .611 | 135 | 169 | .799 | 499 | ... | 609 | 17.8 | ... | 21.8 |
| Varsity totals ......................... | 82 | | 776 | 1243 | .624 | 438 | 564 | .777 | 1411 | ... | 1990 | 17.2 | ... | 24.3 |

## NBA REGULAR-SEASON RECORD

HONORS: NBA Rookie of the Year (1964). ... All-NBA first team (1965, 1966, 1968). ... All-NBA second team (1964, 1967). ... NBA All-Rookie team (1964).

| Season Team | G | Min. | FGM | FGA | Pct. | FTM | FTA | Pct. | Reb. | Ast. | PF | Dq. | Pts. | AVERAGES RPG | APG | PPG |
|---|---|---|---|---|---|---|---|---|---|---|---|---|---|---|---|---|
| 63-64—Cincinnati...................... | 79 | 3273 | 545 | 1035 | *.527 | 310 | 398 | .779 | 1375 | 204 | 300 | 6 | 1400 | 17.4 | 2.6 | 17.7 |
| 64-65—Cincinnati...................... | 66 | 2864 | 558 | 1121 | .498 | 298 | 366 | .814 | 1321 | 157 | 214 | 1 | 1414 | 20.0 | 2.4 | 21.4 |
| 65-66—Cincinnati...................... | 79 | 3517 | 690 | 1523 | .453 | 317 | 403 | .787 | 1668 | 213 | 274 | 5 | 1697 | 21.1 | 2.7 | 21.5 |
| 66-67—Cincinnati...................... | 81 | 3558 | 577 | 1257 | .459 | 284 | 359 | .791 | 1547 | 268 | 280 | 2 | 1438 | 19.1 | 3.3 | 17.8 |
| 67-68—Cincinnati...................... | 82 | 3416 | 707 | 1361 | .519 | 346 | 445 | .778 | 1560 | 251 | 243 | 3 | 1760 | 19.0 | 3.1 | 21.5 |
| 68-69—Cincinnati...................... | 74 | 3075 | 555 | 1007 | .551 | 247 | 327 | .755 | 1360 | 306 | 206 | 0 | 1357 | 18.4 | 4.1 | 18.3 |
| 69-70—Cin.-San Francisco............. | 67 | 2420 | 405 | 799 | .507 | 200 | 255 | .784 | 951 | 173 | 166 | 2 | 1010 | 14.2 | 2.6 | 15.1 |
| 70-71—San Francisco .................. | 80 | 3251 | 623 | 1250 | .498 | 289 | 367 | .787 | 1265 | 293 | 197 | 0 | 1535 | 15.8 | 3.7 | 19.2 |
| 71-72—New York ...................... | 77 | 2926 | 543 | 1060 | .512 | 197 | 249 | .791 | 1011 | 318 | 218 | 1 | 1283 | 13.1 | 4.1 | 16.7 |
| 72-73—New York ...................... | 71 | 2001 | 312 | 608 | .513 | 80 | 100 | .800 | 510 | 317 | 157 | 0 | 704 | 7.2 | 4.5 | 9.9 |

| Season Team | G | Min. | FGM | FGA | Pct. | FTM | FTA | Pct. | REBOUNDS Off. | REBOUNDS Def. | REBOUNDS Tot. | Ast. | St. | Blk. | TO | Pts. | AVERAGES RPG | AVERAGES APG | AVERAGES PPG |
|---|---|---|---|---|---|---|---|---|---|---|---|---|---|---|---|---|---|---|---|
| 73-74—New York | 73 | 1627 | 194 | 420 | .462 | 67 | 96 | .698 | 62 | 312 | 374 | 230 | 28 | 24 | ... | 455 | 5.1 | 3.2 | 6.2 |
| Totals | 829 | 32131 | 5709 | 11441 | .499 | 2635 | 3365 | .783 | ... | ... | 12942 | 2730 | 28 | 24 | ... | 14053 | 15.6 | 3.3 | 17.0 |

Personal fouls/disqualifications: 1973-74, 134/0.

## NBA PLAYOFF RECORD

| Season Team | G | Min. | FGM | FGA | Pct. | FTM | FTA | Pct. | Reb. | Ast. | PF | Dq. | Pts. | AVERAGES RPG | AVERAGES APG | AVERAGES PPG |
|---|---|---|---|---|---|---|---|---|---|---|---|---|---|---|---|---|
| 63-64—Cincinnati | 10 | 370 | 48 | 123 | .390 | 26 | 37 | .703 | 125 | 34 | 37 | 1 | 122 | 12.5 | 3.4 | 12.2 |
| 64-65—Cincinnati | 4 | 195 | 38 | 75 | .507 | 17 | 22 | .773 | 84 | 9 | 12 | 0 | 93 | 21.0 | 2.3 | 23.3 |
| 65-66—Cincinnati | 5 | 231 | 40 | 85 | .471 | 27 | 35 | .771 | 101 | 14 | 14 | 0 | 107 | 20.2 | 2.8 | 21.4 |
| 66-67—Cincinnati | 4 | 183 | 24 | 55 | .436 | 2 | 2 | 1.000 | 77 | 8 | 15 | 0 | 50 | 19.3 | 2.0 | 12.5 |
| 70-71—San Francisco | 5 | 171 | 39 | 77 | .507 | 11 | 16 | .688 | 50 | 16 | 14 | 0 | 89 | 10.0 | 3.2 | 17.8 |
| 71-72—New York | 16 | 737 | 119 | 238 | .500 | 59 | 71 | .831 | 173 | 85 | 49 | 1 | 297 | 10.8 | 5.3 | 18.6 |
| 72-73—New York | 17 | 368 | 54 | 112 | .482 | 20 | 23 | .870 | 85 | 39 | 47 | 0 | 128 | 5.0 | 2.3 | 7.5 |

| Season Team | G | Min. | FGM | FGA | Pct. | FTM | FTA | Pct. | REBOUNDS Off. | REBOUNDS Def. | REBOUNDS Tot. | Ast. | St. | Blk. | TO | Pts. | AVERAGES RPG | AVERAGES APG | AVERAGES PPG |
|---|---|---|---|---|---|---|---|---|---|---|---|---|---|---|---|---|---|---|---|
| 73-74—New York | 11 | 115 | 5 | 21 | .238 | 0 | 0 | ... | 6 | 16 | 22 | 9 | 4 | 0 | ... | 10 | 2.0 | 0.8 | 0.9 |
| Totals | 72 | 2370 | 367 | 786 | .467 | 162 | 206 | .786 | ... | ... | 717 | 214 | 4 | 0 | ... | 896 | 10.0 | 3.0 | 12.4 |

Personal fouls/disqualifications: 1973-74, 9/0.

## NBA ALL-STAR GAME RECORD

NOTES: NBA All-Star Game Most Valuable Player (1965).

| Season Team | Min. | FGM | FGA | Pct. | FTM | FTA | Pct. | Reb. | Ast. | PF | Dq. | Pts. |
|---|---|---|---|---|---|---|---|---|---|---|---|---|
| 1964—Cincinnati | 36 | 3 | 6 | .500 | 5 | 6 | .833 | 8 | 0 | 5 | 0 | 11 |
| 1965—Cincinnati | 35 | 12 | 19 | .632 | 1 | 1 | 1.000 | 10 | 1 | 2 | 0 | 25 |
| 1966—Cincinnati | 23 | 4 | 11 | .364 | 2 | 2 | 1.000 | 19 | 0 | 2 | 0 | 10 |
| 1967—Cincinnati | 22 | 3 | 5 | .600 | 1 | 1 | 1.000 | 7 | 2 | 3 | 0 | 7 |
| 1968—Cincinnati | 21 | 6 | 9 | .667 | 4 | 4 | 1.000 | 5 | 4 | 3 | 0 | 16 |
| 1969—Cincinnati | 17 | 2 | 5 | .400 | 4 | 5 | .800 | 6 | 1 | 3 | 0 | 8 |
| 1971—San Francisco | 29 | 5 | 9 | .556 | 2 | 2 | 1.000 | 9 | 4 | 2 | 0 | 12 |
| Totals | 183 | 35 | 64 | .547 | 19 | 21 | .905 | 64 | 12 | 20 | 0 | 89 |

# MACAULEY, ED    C/F

PERSONAL: Born March 22, 1928, in St. Louis. ... 6-8/190 (2,03/86,2). ... Full name: Charles Edward Macauley Jr. ... Nickname: Easy Ed.
HIGH SCHOOL: St. Louis University High School (St. Louis).
COLLEGE: St. Louis.
TRANSACTIONS: Selected by St. Louis Bombers in 1949 Basketball Association of America Draft (territorial pick). ... Selected by Boston Celtics in NBA dispersal draft (April 25, 1950). ... Traded by Celtics with draft rights to F/G Cliff Hagan to St. Louis Hawks for draft rights to C Bill Russell (April 29, 1956).
CAREER HONORS: Elected to Naismith Memorial Basketball Hall of Fame (1960).
MISCELLANEOUS: Member of NBA championship team (1958).

## COLLEGIATE RECORD

NOTES: THE SPORTING NEWS All-America first team (1949). ... Led NCAA Division I with .524 field-goal percentage (1949).

| Season Team | G | Min. | FGM | FGA | Pct. | FTM | FTA | Pct. | Reb. | Ast. | Pts. | AVERAGES RPG | AVERAGES APG | AVERAGES PPG |
|---|---|---|---|---|---|---|---|---|---|---|---|---|---|---|
| 45-46—St. Louis | 23 | ... | 94 | ... | ... | 71 | ... | ... | ... | ... | 259 | ... | ... | 11.3 |
| 46-47—St. Louis | 28 | ... | 141 | ... | ... | 104 | ... | ... | ... | ... | 386 | ... | ... | 13.8 |
| 47-48—St. Louis | 27 | ... | 132 | 324 | .407 | 104 | 159 | .654 | ... | ... | 368 | ... | ... | 13.6 |
| 48-49—St. Louis | 26 | ... | 144 | 275 | .524 | 116 | 153 | .758 | ... | ... | 404 | ... | ... | 15.5 |
| Totals | 104 | ... | 511 | ... | ... | 395 | ... | ... | ... | ... | 1417 | ... | ... | 13.6 |

## NBA REGULAR-SEASON RECORD

HONORS: All-NBA first team (1951, 1952, 1953). ... All-NBA second team (1954).

| Season Team | G | Min. | FGM | FGA | Pct. | FTM | FTA | Pct. | Reb. | Ast. | PF | Dq. | Pts. | AVERAGES RPG | AVERAGES APG | AVERAGES PPG |
|---|---|---|---|---|---|---|---|---|---|---|---|---|---|---|---|---|
| 49-50—St. Louis | 67 | ... | 351 | 882 | .398 | 379 | 528 | .718 | ... | 200 | 221 | ... | 1081 | ... | 3.0 | 16.1 |
| 50-51—Boston | 68 | ... | 459 | 985 | .466 | 466 | 614 | .759 | 616 | 252 | 205 | 4 | 1384 | 9.1 | 3.7 | 20.4 |
| 51-52—Boston | 66 | 2631 | 384 | 888 | .432 | 496 | 621 | .799 | 529 | 232 | 174 | 0 | 1264 | 8.0 | 3.5 | 19.2 |
| 52-53—Boston | 69 | 2902 | 451 | 997 | .452 | 500 | 667 | .750 | 629 | 280 | 188 | 0 | 1402 | 9.1 | 4.1 | 20.3 |
| 53-54—Boston | 71 | 2792 | 462 | 950 *| .486 | 420 | 554 | .758 | 571 | 271 | 168 | 1 | 1344 | 8.0 | 3.8 | 18.9 |
| 54-55—Boston | 71 | 2706 | 403 | 951 | .424 | 442 | 558 | .792 | 600 | 275 | 171 | 0 | 1248 | 8.5 | 3.9 | 17.6 |
| 55-56—Boston | 71 | 2354 | 420 | 995 | .422 | 400 | 504 | .794 | 422 | 211 | 158 | 2 | 1240 | 5.9 | 3.0 | 17.5 |
| 56-57—St. Louis | 72 | 2582 | 414 | 987 | .419 | 359 | 479 | .749 | 440 | 202 | 206 | 2 | 1187 | 6.1 | 2.8 | 16.5 |
| 57-58—St. Louis | 72 | 1908 | 376 | 879 | .428 | 267 | 369 | .724 | 478 | 143 | 156 | 2 | 1019 | 6.6 | 2.0 | 14.2 |
| 58-59—St. Louis | 14 | 196 | 22 | 75 | .293 | 21 | 35 | .600 | 40 | 13 | 20 | 1 | 65 | 2.9 | 0.9 | 4.6 |
| Totals | 641 | ... | 3742 | 8589 | .436 | 3750 | 4929 | .761 | ... | 2079 | 1667 | ... | 11234 | ... | 3.2 | 17.5 |

## NBA PLAYOFF RECORD

| Season Team | G | Min. | FGM | FGA | Pct. | FTM | FTA | Pct. | Reb. | Ast. | PF | Dq. | Pts. | AVERAGES RPG | AVERAGES APG | AVERAGES PPG |
|---|---|---|---|---|---|---|---|---|---|---|---|---|---|---|---|---|
| 50-51—Boston | 2 | ... | 17 | 36 | .472 | 10 | 16 | .625 | 18 | 8 | 4 | 0 | 44 | 9.0 | 4.0 | 22.0 |
| 51-52—Boston | 3 | 129 | 27 | 49 | .551 | 16 | 19 | .842 | 33 | 11 | 11 | 1 | 70 | 11.0 | 3.7 | 23.3 |
| 52-53—Boston | 6 | 278 | 31 | 71 | .437 | 39 | 54 | .722 | 58 | 21 | 23 | 2 | 101 | 9.7 | 3.5 | 16.8 |
| 53-54—Boston | 5 | 127 | 8 | 22 | .364 | 9 | 13 | .692 | 21 | 21 | 14 | 0 | 25 | 4.2 | 4.2 | 5.0 |
| 54-55—Boston | 7 | 283 | 43 | 93 | .462 | 41 | 54 | .759 | 52 | 32 | 21 | 0 | 127 | 7.4 | 4.6 | 18.1 |
| 55-56—Boston | 3 | 73 | 12 | 30 | .400 | 7 | 11 | .636 | 15 | 5 | 6 | 0 | 31 | 5.0 | 1.7 | 10.3 |
| 56-57—St. Louis | 10 | 297 | 44 | 109 | .404 | 54 | 74 | .730 | 62 | 22 | 39 | 3 | 142 | 6.2 | 2.2 | 14.2 |
| 57-58—St. Louis | 11 | 227 | 36 | 89 | .405 | 36 | 50 | .720 | 62 | 18 | 23 | 0 | 108 | 5.6 | 1.6 | 9.8 |
| Totals | 47 | ... | 218 | 499 | .437 | 212 | 291 | .729 | 321 | 138 | 141 | 6 | 648 | 6.8 | 2.9 | 13.8 |

ALL-TIME GREAT PLAYERS

# NBA ALL-STAR GAME RECORD

NOTES: NBA All-Star Game Most Valuable Player (1951).

| Season Team | Min. | FGM | FGA | Pct. | FTM | FTA | Pct. | Reb | Ast. | PF | Dq. | Pts. |
|---|---|---|---|---|---|---|---|---|---|---|---|---|
| 1951—Boston | ... | 7 | 12 | .583 | 6 | 7 | .857 | 6 | 1 | 3 | 0 | 20 |
| 1952—Boston | 28 | 3 | 7 | .429 | 9 | 9 | 1.000 | 7 | 3 | 2 | 0 | 15 |
| 1953—Boston | 35 | 5 | 12 | .417 | 8 | 8 | 1.000 | 7 | 3 | 2 | 0 | 18 |
| 1954—Boston | 25 | 4 | 11 | .364 | 5 | 6 | .833 | 1 | 3 | 2 | 0 | 13 |
| 1955—Boston | 27 | 1 | 5 | .200 | 4 | 5 | .800 | 4 | 2 | 1 | 0 | 6 |
| 1956—Boston | 20 | 1 | 9 | .111 | 2 | 4 | .500 | 2 | 3 | 3 | 0 | 4 |
| 1957—St. Louis | 19 | 3 | 6 | .500 | 1 | 2 | .500 | 5 | 3 | 0 | 0 | 7 |
| Totals | ... | 24 | 62 | .387 | 35 | 41 | .854 | 32 | 18 | 13 | 0 | 83 |

# NBA COACHING RECORD

| Season Team | REGULAR SEASON | | | | PLAYOFFS | | |
|---|---|---|---|---|---|---|---|
| | W | L | Pct. | Finish | W | L | Pct. |
| 58-59—St. Louis | 43 | 19 | .694 | 1st/Western Division | 2 | 4 | .333 |
| 59-60—St. Louis | 46 | 29 | .613 | 1st/Western Division | 7 | 7 | .500 |
| Totals (2 years) | 89 | 48 | .650 | | 9 | 11 | .450 |

NOTES:
1958—Replaced Andy Phillip as St. Louis head coach (November), with record of 6-4.
1959—Lost to Minneapolis in Western Division Finals.
1960—Defeated Minneapolis, 4-3, in Western Division Finals; lost to Boston, 4-3, in NBA Finals.

---

# MALONE, JEFF          G

PERSONAL: Born June 28, 1961, in Mobile, Ala. ... 6-4/205 (1,93/93,0). ... Full name: Jeffrey Nigel Malone.
HIGH SCHOOL: Southwest (Macon, Ga.).
COLLEGE: Mississippi State.
TRANSACTIONS: Selected by Washington Bullets in first round (10th pick overall) of 1983 NBA Draft. ... Traded by Bullets to Utah Jazz in three-way deal in which Sacramento Kings sent F Pervis Ellison to Bullets and Jazz sent G Bob Hansen, F/C Eric Leckner and 1990 first- and second-round draft choices to Kings (June 25, 1990); Jazz also received 1990 second-round draft choice from Kings and Kings also received 1991 second-round draft choice from Bullets. ... Traded by Jazz with 1994 conditional first-round draft choice to Philadelphia 76ers for G Jeff Hornacek and G Sean Green (February 24, 1994). ... Waived by 76ers (January 4, 1996). ... Signed by Miami Heat to first of two consecutive 10-day contracts (February 12, 1996). ... Re-signed by Heat for remainder of season (March 3, 1996). ... Played in Greece (1996-97).
CAREER NOTES: Head coach, Columbus Riverdragons (NBDL).

## COLLEGIATE RECORD

NOTES: The Sporting News All-America first team (1983).

| Season Team | G | Min. | FGM | FGA | Pct. | FTM | FTA | Pct. | Reb. | Ast. | Pts. | RPG | APG | PPG |
|---|---|---|---|---|---|---|---|---|---|---|---|---|---|---|
| 79-80—Mississippi State | 27 | 781 | 139 | 303 | .459 | 42 | 51 | .824 | 90 | 39 | 320 | 3.3 | 1.4 | 11.9 |
| 80-81—Mississippi State | 27 | 999 | 219 | 447 | .490 | 105 | 128 | .820 | 113 | 43 | 543 | 4.2 | 1.6 | 20.1 |
| 81-82—Mississippi State | 27 | 1001 | 225 | 410 | .549 | 52 | 70 | .743 | 111 | 20 | 502 | 4.1 | 0.7 | 18.6 |
| 82-83—Mississippi State | 29 | 1070 | 323 | 608 | .531 | 131 | 159 | .824 | 106 | 66 | 777 | 3.7 | 2.3 | 26.8 |
| Totals | 110 | 3851 | 906 | 1768 | .512 | 330 | 408 | .809 | 420 | 168 | 2142 | 3.8 | 1.5 | 19.5 |

## NBA REGULAR-SEASON RECORD

HONORS: NBA All-Rookie team (1984).

| Season Team | G | Min. | FGM | FGA | Pct. | FTM | FTA | Pct. | Off. | Def. | Tot. | Ast. | St. | Blk. | TO | Pts. | RPG | APG | PPG |
|---|---|---|---|---|---|---|---|---|---|---|---|---|---|---|---|---|---|---|---|
| 83-84—Washington | 81 | 1976 | 408 | 918 | .444 | 142 | 172 | .826 | 57 | 98 | 155 | 151 | 23 | 13 | 110 | 982 | 1.9 | 1.9 | 12.1 |
| 84-85—Washington | 76 | 2613 | 605 | 1213 | .499 | 211 | 250 | .844 | 60 | 146 | 206 | 184 | 52 | 9 | 107 | 1436 | 2.7 | 2.4 | 18.9 |
| 85-86—Washington | 80 | 2992 | 735 | 1522 | .483 | 322 | 371 | .868 | 66 | 222 | 288 | 191 | 70 | 12 | 168 | 1795 | 3.6 | 2.4 | 22.4 |
| 86-87—Washington | 80 | 2763 | 689 | 1509 | .457 | 376 | 425 | .885 | 50 | 168 | 218 | 298 | 75 | 13 | 182 | 1758 | 2.7 | 3.7 | 22.0 |
| 87-88—Washington | 80 | 2655 | 648 | 1360 | .476 | 335 | 380 | .882 | 44 | 162 | 206 | 237 | 51 | 13 | 172 | 1641 | 2.6 | 3.0 | 20.5 |
| 88-89—Washington | 76 | 2418 | 677 | 1410 | .480 | 296 | 340 | .871 | 55 | 124 | 179 | 219 | 39 | 14 | 165 | 1651 | 2.4 | 2.9 | 21.7 |
| 89-90—Washington | 75 | 2567 | 781 | 1592 | .491 | 257 | 293 | .877 | 54 | 152 | 206 | 243 | 48 | 6 | 125 | 1820 | 2.7 | 3.2 | 24.3 |
| 90-91—Utah | 69 | 2466 | 525 | 1034 | .508 | 231 | 252 | .917 | 36 | 170 | 206 | 143 | 50 | 6 | 108 | 1282 | 3.0 | 2.1 | 18.6 |
| 91-92—Utah | 81 | 2922 | 691 | 1353 | .511 | 256 | 285 | .898 | 49 | 184 | 233 | 180 | 56 | 5 | 140 | 1639 | 2.9 | 2.2 | 20.2 |
| 92-93—Utah | 79 | 2558 | 595 | 1205 | .494 | 236 | 277 | .852 | 31 | 142 | 173 | 128 | 42 | 4 | 125 | 1429 | 2.2 | 1.6 | 18.1 |
| 93-94—Utah-Phil. | 77 | 2560 | 525 | 1081 | .486 | 205 | 247 | .830 | 51 | 148 | 199 | 125 | 40 | 5 | 85 | 1262 | 2.6 | 1.6 | 16.4 |
| 94-95—Philadelphia | 19 | 660 | 144 | 284 | .507 | 51 | 59 | .864 | 11 | 44 | 55 | 29 | 15 | 0 | 29 | 350 | 2.9 | 1.5 | 18.4 |
| 95-96—Phil.-Miami | 32 | 510 | 76 | 193 | .394 | 32 | 35 | .906 | 8 | 32 | 40 | 26 | 16 | 0 | 22 | 186 | 1.3 | 0.8 | 5.8 |
| Totals | 905 | 29660 | 7099 | 14674 | .484 | 2947 | 3383 | .871 | 572 | 1792 | 2364 | 2154 | 577 | 100 | 1538 | 17231 | 2.6 | 2.4 | 19.0 |

Three-point field goals: 1983-84, 24-for-74 (.324). 1984-85, 15-for-72 (.208). 1985-86, 3-for-17 (.176). 1986-87, 4-for-26 (.154). 1987-88, 10-for-24 (.417). 1988-89, 1-for-19 (.053). 1989-90, 1-for-6 (.167). 1990-91, 1-for-6 (.167). 1991-92, 1-for-12 (.083). 1992-93, 3-for-9 (.333). 1993-94, 7-for-12 (.583). 1994-95, 11-for-28 (.393). 1995-96, 5-for-16 (.313). Totals, 86-for-321 (.268).
Personal fouls/disqualifications: 1983-84, 162/1. 1984-85, 176/1. 1985-86, 180/2. 1986-87, 154/0. 1987-88, 198/1. 1988-89, 155/0. 1989-90, 116/1. 1990-91, 128/0. 1991-92, 126/1. 1992-93, 117/0. 1993-94, 123/0. 1994-95, 35/0. 1995-96, 25/0. Totals, 1695/7.

## NBA PLAYOFF RECORD

| Season Team | G | Min. | FGM | FGA | Pct. | FTM | FTA | Pct. | Off. | Def. | Tot. | Ast. | St. | Blk. | TO | Pts. | RPG | APG | PPG |
|---|---|---|---|---|---|---|---|---|---|---|---|---|---|---|---|---|---|---|---|
| 83-84—Washington | 4 | 71 | 12 | 26 | .462 | 0 | 0 | ... | 2 | 3 | 5 | 2 | 1 | 0 | 3 | 24 | 1.3 | 0.5 | 6.0 |
| 84-85—Washington | 4 | 126 | 27 | 56 | .482 | 10 | 13 | .769 | 3 | 3 | 6 | 8 | 5 | 0 | 4 | 65 | 1.5 | 2.0 | 16.3 |
| 85-86—Washington | 5 | 197 | 42 | 103 | .408 | 26 | 29 | .897 | 4 | 12 | 16 | 17 | 7 | 3 | 11 | 110 | 3.2 | 3.4 | 22.0 |
| 86-87—Washington | 3 | 105 | 17 | 46 | .370 | 11 | 11 | 1.000 | 1 | 6 | 7 | 9 | 1 | 0 | 11 | 45 | 2.3 | 3.0 | 15.0 |
| 87-88—Washington | 5 | 199 | 50 | 97 | .515 | 28 | 37 | .757 | 3 | 14 | 17 | 11 | 5 | 5 | 14 | 128 | 3.4 | 2.2 | 25.6 |
| 90-91—Utah | 9 | 351 | 71 | 144 | .493 | 44 | 48 | .917 | 7 | 28 | 35 | 29 | 9 | 1 | 12 | 186 | 3.9 | 3.2 | 20.7 |
| 91-92—Utah | 16 | 610 | 134 | 275 | .487 | 62 | 72 | .861 | 12 | 27 | 39 | 31 | 8 | 2 | 26 | 331 | 2.4 | 1.9 | 20.7 |
| 92-93—Utah | 5 | 150 | 29 | 65 | .446 | 9 | 13 | .692 | 3 | 13 | 16 | 3 | 3 | 1 | 9 | 67 | 3.2 | 0.6 | 13.4 |
| Totals | 51 | 1809 | 382 | 812 | .470 | 190 | 223 | .852 | 35 | 106 | 141 | 110 | 39 | 12 | 90 | 956 | 2.8 | 2.2 | 18.7 |

Three-point field goals: 1983-84, 0-for-1. 1984-85, 1-for-3 (.333). 1985-86, 0-for-2. 1987-88, 0-for-1. 1990-91, 0-for-2. 1991-92, 1-for-3 (.333). Totals, 2-for-12 (.167).
Personal fouls/disqualifications: 1983-84, 6/0. 1984-85, 14/1. 1985-86, 13/0. 1986-87, 8/0. 1987-88, 16/0. 1990-91, 22/0. 1991-92, 33/0. 1992-93, 11/0. Totals, 123/1.

## NBA ALL-STAR GAME RECORD

| Season Team | Min. | FGM | FGA | Pct. | FTM | FTA | Pct. | Off. | Def. | Tot. | Ast. | PF | Dq. | St. | Blk. | TO | Pts. |
|---|---|---|---|---|---|---|---|---|---|---|---|---|---|---|---|---|---|
| 1986—Washington.......... | 12 | 3 | 5 | .600 | 0 | 0 | ... | 0 | 1 | 1 | 4 | 0 | 0 | 1 | 0 | 0 | 6 |
| 1987—Washington.......... | 13 | 3 | 5 | .600 | 0 | 0 | ... | 1 | 1 | 2 | 2 | 1 | 0 | 0 | 0 | 1 | 6 |
| Totals.......................... | 25 | 6 | 10 | .600 | 0 | 0 | ... | 1 | 2 | 3 | 6 | 1 | 0 | 1 | 0 | 1 | 12 |

Three-point field goals: 1987, 0-for-1.

## GREEK LEAGUE RECORD

| Season Team | G | Min. | FGM | FGA | Pct. | FTM | FTA | Pct. | Reb. | Ast. | Pts. | RPG | APG | PPG |
|---|---|---|---|---|---|---|---|---|---|---|---|---|---|---|
| 96-97—VAO ................................ | 12 | 423 | 65 | 165 | .394 | 35 | 46 | .761 | 29 | 12 | 175 | 2.4 | 1.0 | 14.6 |

# MALONE, KARL     F

**PERSONAL:** Born July 24, 1963, in Summerfield, La. ... 6-9/256. (2,06/116,1). ... Nickname: The Mailman.
**HIGH SCHOOL:** Summerfield (La.).
**COLLEGE:** Louisiana Tech.
**TRANSACTIONS/CAREER NOTES:** Selected after junior season by Utah Jazz in first round (13th pick overall) of 1985 NBA Draft. ... Signed as free agent by Los Angeles Lakers (July 16, 2003)
**CAREER HONORS:** NBA 50th Anniversary All-Time Team (1996).
**MISCELLANEOUS:** Member of gold-medal-winning U.S. Olympic teams (1992, 1996). ... Utah Jazz franchise all-time leading scorer with 36,374 points and all-time leading rebounder with 14,601 (1985-86 through 2002-03).

## COLLEGIATE RECORD

| Season Team | G | Min. | FGM | FGA | Pct. | FTM | FTA | Pct. | Reb. | Ast. | Pts. | RPG | APG | PPG |
|---|---|---|---|---|---|---|---|---|---|---|---|---|---|---|
| 81-82—Louisiana Tech .............. | | | | | | Did not play—redshirted. | | | | | | | | |
| 82-83—Louisiana Tech .............. | 28 | 894 | 217 | 373 | .582 | 152 | 244 | .623 | 289 | 10 | 586 | 10.3 | 0.4 | 20.9 |
| 83-84—Louisiana Tech .............. | 32 | 1011 | 220 | 382 | .576 | 161 | 236 | .682 | 282 | 42 | 601 | 8.8 | 1.3 | 18.8 |
| 84-85—Louisiana Tech .............. | 32 | 926 | 216 | 399 | .541 | 97 | 170 | .571 | 288 | 73 | 529 | 9.0 | 2.3 | 16.5 |
| Totals ...................................... | 92 | 2831 | 653 | 1154 | .566 | 410 | 650 | .631 | 859 | 125 | 1716 | 9.3 | 1.4 | 18.7 |

## NBA REGULAR-SEASON RECORD

**RECORDS:** Holds career records for most seasons with 2,000 or more points—12 (1987-88 through 1997-98 and 1999-2000); most consecutive seasons with 2,000 or more points—11 (1987-88 through 1997-98); most free throws made—9,619; most free throws attempted—12,963; most seasons leading league in free throws made—8; most consecutive seasons leading league in free throws made—5; and most turnovers—4,421.

**HONORS:** NBA Most Valuable Player (1997, 1999). ... IBM Award, for all-around contributions to team's success (1998). ... All-NBA first team (1989, 1990, 1991, 1992, 1993, 1994, 1995, 1996, 1997, 1998, 1999). ... All-NBA second team (1988, 2000). ... All-NBA third team (2001). ... NBA All-Defensive first team (1997, 1998, 1999). ... NBA All-Defensive second team (1988). ... NBA All-Rookie team (1986).

| | | | | | | | | | REBOUNDS | | | | | | | | AVERAGES | | |
|---|---|---|---|---|---|---|---|---|---|---|---|---|---|---|---|---|---|---|---|
| Season Team | G | Min. | FGM | FGA | Pct. | FTM | FTA | Pct. | Off. | Def. | Tot. | Ast. | St. | Blk. | TO | Pts. | RPG | APG | PPG |
| 85-86—Utah.............. | 81 | 2475 | 504 | 1016 | .496 | 195 | 405 | .481 | 174 | 544 | 718 | 236 | 105 | 44 | 279 | 1203 | 8.9 | 2.9 | 14.9 |
| 86-87—Utah.............. | 82 | 2857 | 728 | 1422 | .512 | 323 | 540 | .598 | 158 | 577 | 855 | 158 | 104 | 60 | 237 | 1779 | 10.4 | 1.9 | 21.7 |
| 87-88—Utah.............. | 82 | 3198 | 858 | 1650 | .520 | 552 | 789 | .700 | 277 | 709 | 986 | 199 | 117 | 50 | *325 | 2268 | 12.0 | 2.4 | 27.7 |
| 88-89—Utah.............. | 80 | 3126 | 809 | 1559 | .519 | *703 | *918 | .766 | 259 | 594 | 853 | 219 | 144 | 70 | 285 | 2326 | 10.7 | 2.7 | 29.1 |
| 89-90—Utah.............. | 82 | 3122 | 914 | 1627 | .562 | *696 | *913 | .762 | 232 | 679 | 911 | 226 | 121 | 50 | 304 | 2540 | 11.1 | 2.8 | 31.0 |
| 90-91—Utah.............. | 82 | 3302 | 847 | 1608 | .527 | *684 | *888 | .770 | 236 | *731 | 967 | 270 | 89 | 79 | 244 | 2382 | 11.8 | 3.3 | 29.0 |
| 91-92—Utah.............. | 81 | 3054 | 798 | 1516 | .526 | *673 | *865 | .778 | 225 | 684 | 909 | 241 | 108 | 51 | 248 | 2272 | 11.2 | 3.0 | 28.0 |
| 92-93—Utah.............. | 82 | 3099 | 797 | 1443 | .552 | *619 | *836 | .740 | 227 | 692 | 919 | 308 | 124 | 85 | 240 | 2217 | 11.2 | 3.8 | 27.0 |
| 93-94—Utah.............. | 82 | 3329 | 772 | 1552 | .497 | 511 | 736 | .694 | 235 | 705 | 940 | 328 | 125 | 126 | 234 | 2063 | 11.5 | 4.0 | 25.2 |
| 94-95—Utah.............. | 82 | 3126 | 830 | 1548 | .536 | 516 | 695 | .742 | 156 | *715 | 871 | 285 | 129 | 85 | 236 | 2187 | 10.6 | 3.5 | 26.7 |
| 95-96—Utah.............. | 82 | 3113 | 789 | 1520 | .519 | 512 | 708 | .723 | 175 | 629 | 804 | 345 | 138 | 56 | 199 | 2106 | 9.8 | 4.2 | 25.7 |
| 96-97—Utah.............. | 82 | 2998 | 864 | 1571 | .550 | *521 | *690 | .755 | 193 | 616 | 809 | 368 | 113 | 48 | 233 | 2249 | 9.9 | 4.5 | 27.4 |
| 97-98—Utah.............. | 81 | 3030 | 780 | 1472 | .530 | *628 | *825 | .761 | 189 | 645 | 834 | 316 | 96 | 70 | 247 | 2190 | 10.3 | 3.9 | 27.0 |
| 98-99—Utah.............. | 49 | 1832 | 393 | 797 | .493 | *378 | 480 | .788 | 107 | 356 | 463 | 201 | 62 | 28 | 162 | 1164 | 9.4 | 4.1 | 23.8 |
| 99-00—Utah.............. | 82 | 2947 | 752 | 1476 | .509 | 589 | 739 | .797 | 169 | 610 | 779 | 304 | 79 | 71 | 231 | 2095 | 9.5 | 3.7 | 25.5 |
| 00-01—Utah.............. | 81 | 2895 | 670 | 1345 | .498 | 536 | 676 | .793 | 114 | 555 | 669 | 361 | 93 | 62 | 244 | 1878 | 8.3 | 4.5 | 23.2 |
| 01-02—Utah.............. | 80 | 3040 | 635 | 1399 | .454 | 509 | 639 | .797 | 142 | 544 | 686 | 341 | 152 | 59 | 263 | 1788 | 8.6 | 4.3 | 22.4 |
| 02-03—Utah.............. | 81 | 2936 | 595 | 1289 | .462 | 474 | 621 | .763 | 113 | 515 | 628 | 379 | 136 | 31 | 210 | 1667 | 7.8 | 4.7 | 20.6 |
| 03-04—L.A. Lakers .... | 42 | 1373 | 193 | 400 | .483 | 168 | 225 | .747 | 61 | 306 | 367 | 163 | 50 | 20 | 103 | 554 | 8.7 | 3.9 | 13.2 |
| Totals ................... | 1476 | 54852 | 13528 | 26210 | .516 | 9787 | 13188 | .742 | 3562 | 11406 | 14968 | 5248 | 2085 | 1145 | 4524 | 36928 | 10.1 | 3.6 | 25.0 |

Three-point field goals: 1985-86, 0-for-2. 1986-87, 0-for-7. 1987-88, 0-for-5. 1988-89, 5-for-16 (.313). 1989-90, 16-for-43 (.372). 1990-91, 4-for-14 (.286). 1991-92, 3-for-17 (.176). 1992-93, 4-for-20 (.200). 1993-94, 8-for-32 (.250). 1994-95, 11-for-41 (.268). 1995-96, 16-for-40 (.400). 1996-97, 0-for-13. 1997-98, 2-for-6 (.333). 1998-99, 0-for-1. 1999-00, 2-for-8 (.250). 2000-01, 2-for-5 (.400). 2001-02, 9-for-25 (.360). 2002-03, 3-for-14 (.214). 2003-04, 1-for-1. Totals, 85-for-310 (.274).

Personal fouls/disqualifications: 1985-86, 295/2. 1986-87, 323/6. 1987-88, 296/2. 1988-89, 286/3. 1989-90, 259/1. 1990-91, 268/2. 1991-92, 226/2. 1992-93, 261/2. 1993-94, 268/2. 1994-95, 269/2. 1995-96, 245/1. 1996-97, 217/0. 1997-98, 237/0. 1998-99, 134/0. 1999-00, 229/1. 2000-01, 216/0. 2001-02, 229/1. 2002-03, 204/0. 2003-04, 116/1. Totals, 4578/28.

## NBA PLAYOFF RECORD

**NOTES:** Holds single-game playoff record for most free throws made, none missed—18 (May 10, 1997, at L.A. Lakers). ... Shares single-game playoff record for most free throws made in one half—19 (May 9, 1991, vs. Portland).

| | | | | | | | | | REBOUNDS | | | | | | | | AVERAGES | | |
|---|---|---|---|---|---|---|---|---|---|---|---|---|---|---|---|---|---|---|---|
| Season Team | G | Min. | FGM | FGA | Pct. | FTM | FTA | Pct. | Off. | Def. | Tot. | Ast. | St. | Blk. | TO | Pts. | RPG | APG | PPG |
| 85-86—Utah.............. | 4 | 144 | 38 | 72 | .528 | 11 | 26 | .423 | 6 | 24 | 30 | 4 | 8 | 0 | 6 | 87 | 7.5 | 1.0 | 21.8 |
| 86-87—Utah.............. | 5 | 200 | 37 | 88 | .420 | 26 | 36 | .722 | 15 | 33 | 48 | 6 | 11 | 4 | 17 | 100 | 9.6 | 1.2 | 20.0 |
| 87-88—Utah.............. | 11 | 494 | 123 | 255 | .482 | 81 | 112 | .723 | 33 | 97 | 130 | 17 | 13 | 7 | 39 | 327 | 11.8 | 1.5 | 29.7 |
| 88-89—Utah.............. | 3 | 136 | 33 | 66 | .500 | 26 | 32 | .813 | 22 | 27 | 49 | 4 | 3 | 1 | 13 | 92 | 16.3 | 1.3 | 30.7 |
| 89-90—Utah.............. | 5 | 203 | 46 | 105 | .438 | 34 | 45 | .756 | 16 | 35 | 51 | 11 | 11 | 5 | 12 | 126 | 10.2 | 2.2 | 25.2 |

| Season Team | G | Min. | FGM | FGA | Pct. | FTM | FTA | Pct. | Off. | Def. | Tot. | Ast. | St. | Blk. | TO | Pts. | RPG | APG | PPG |
|---|---|---|---|---|---|---|---|---|---|---|---|---|---|---|---|---|---|---|---|
| 90-91—Utah | 9 | 383 | 95 | 209 | .455 | 77 | 91 | .846 | 23 | 97 | 120 | 29 | 9 | 11 | 26 | 267 | 13.3 | 3.2 | 29.7 |
| 91-92—Utah | 16 | 688 | 148 | 284 | .521 | 169 | 210 | .805 | 43 | 138 | 181 | 42 | 22 | 19 | 46 | 465 | 11.3 | 2.6 | 29.1 |
| 92-93—Utah | 5 | 216 | 44 | 97 | .454 | 31 | 38 | .816 | 12 | 40 | 52 | 10 | 6 | 2 | 20 | 120 | 10.4 | 2.0 | 24.0 |
| 93-94—Utah | 16 | 703 | 158 | 338 | .467 | 118 | 160 | .738 | 52 | 146 | 198 | 54 | 23 | 13 | 34 | 434 | 12.4 | 3.4 | 27.1 |
| 94-95—Utah | 5 | 216 | 48 | 103 | .466 | 54 | 78 | .692 | 15 | 51 | 66 | 19 | 7 | 2 | 14 | 151 | 13.2 | 3.8 | 30.2 |
| 95-96—Utah | 18 | 725 | 188 | 401 | .469 | 101 | 176 | .574 | 47 | 139 | 186 | 79 | 34 | 10 | 45 | 477 | 10.3 | 4.4 | 26.5 |
| 96-97—Utah | 20 | 816 | 187 | 430 | .435 | 144 | 200 | .720 | 60 | 168 | 228 | 57 | 27 | 15 | 54 | 519 | 11.4 | 2.9 | 26.0 |
| 97-98—Utah | 20 | 795 | 198 | 420 | .471 | 130 | 165 | .788 | 47 | 170 | 217 | 68 | 22 | 20 | 60 | 526 | 10.9 | 3.4 | 26.3 |
| 98-99—Utah | 11 | 451 | 86 | 206 | .417 | 68 | 86 | .791 | 36 | 88 | 124 | 52 | 13 | 8 | 40 | 240 | 11.3 | 4.7 | 21.8 |
| 99-00—Utah | 10 | 386 | 103 | 198 | .520 | 64 | 79 | .810 | 19 | 70 | 89 | 31 | 7 | 7 | 27 | 272 | 8.9 | 3.1 | 27.2 |
| 00-01—Utah | 5 | 199 | 49 | 121 | .405 | 39 | 49 | .796 | 9 | 35 | 44 | 17 | 5 | 4 | 19 | 138 | 8.8 | 3.4 | 27.6 |
| 01-02—Utah | 4 | 163 | 30 | 73 | .411 | 20 | 28 | .714 | 3 | 27 | 30 | 18 | 5 | 3 | 11 | 80 | 7.5 | 4.5 | 20.0 |
| 02-03—Utah | 5 | 191 | 34 | 84 | .405 | 30 | 41 | .732 | 7 | 27 | 34 | 20 | 8 | 2 | 20 | 98 | 6.8 | 4.0 | 19.6 |
| 03-04—L.A. Lakers | 21 | 798 | 98 | 218 | .450 | 46 | 73 | .630 | 37 | 148 | 185 | 72 | 24 | 2 | 47 | 242 | 8.8 | 3.4 | 11.5 |
| Totals | 193 | 7907 | 1743 | 3768 | .463 | 1269 | 1725 | .736 | 502 | 1560 | 2062 | 610 | 258 | 135 | 550 | 4761 | 10.7 | 3.2 | 24.7 |

Three-point field goals: 1987-88, 0-for-1. 1989-90, 0-for-1. 1990-91, 0-for-8. 1991-92, 0-for-2. 1992-93, 1-for-2 (.500). 1993-94, 0-for-4. 1994-95, 1-for-3 (.333). 1995-96, 0-for-3. 1996-97, 1-for-2 (.500). 1997-98, 0-for-3. 1998-99, 0-for-1. 1999-00, 2-for-2. 2000-01, 1-for-2 (.500). 2001-02, 0-for-1. 2002-03, 0-for-4. 2003-04, 0-for-1. Totals, 6-for-37 (.162).

Personal fouls/disqualifications: 1985-86, 18/1. 1986-87, 20/1. 1987-88, 35/0. 1988-89, 16/1. 1989-90, 22/1. 1990-91, 35/0. 1991-92, 57/0. 1992-93, 21/0. 1993-94, 59/2. 1994-95, 18/0. 1995-96, 61/0. 1996-97, 59/0. 1997-98, 69/0. 1998-99, 37/0. 1999-00, 31/0. 2000-01, 13/0. 2001-02, 11/0. 2002-03, 15/0. 2003-04, 65/0. Totals, 662/6.

## NBA ALL-STAR GAME RECORD

**NOTES:** NBA All-Star Game Most Valuable Player (1989). ... NBA All-Star Game co-Most Valuable Player (1993).

| Season Team | Min. | FGM | FGA | Pct. | FTM | FTA | Pct. | Off. | Def. | Tot. | Ast. | PF | Dq. | St. | Blk. | TO | Pts. |
|---|---|---|---|---|---|---|---|---|---|---|---|---|---|---|---|---|---|
| 1988—Utah | 33 | 9 | 19 | .474 | 4 | 5 | .800 | 4 | 6 | 10 | 2 | 4 | 0 | 2 | 0 | 3 | 22 |
| 1989—Utah | 26 | 12 | 17 | .706 | 4 | 6 | .667 | 4 | 5 | 9 | 3 | 3 | 0 | 2 | 0 | 2 | 28 |
| 1990—Utah | | | | | | | Selected, did not play—injured. | | | | | | | | | | |
| 1991—Utah | 31 | 6 | 11 | .545 | 4 | 6 | .667 | 4 | 7 | 11 | 4 | 1 | 0 | 1 | 1 | 3 | 16 |
| 1992—Utah | 19 | 5 | 7 | .714 | 1 | 2 | .500 | 0 | 7 | 7 | 3 | 1 | 0 | 1 | 1 | 1 | 11 |
| 1993—Utah | 34 | 11 | 17 | .647 | 6 | 9 | .667 | 3 | 7 | 10 | 0 | 3 | 0 | 1 | 2 | 3 | 28 |
| 1994—Utah | 21 | 3 | 9 | .333 | 0 | 0 | ... | 3 | 4 | 7 | 2 | 2 | 0 | 1 | 0 | 1 | 6 |
| 1995—Utah | 16 | 6 | 6 | 1.000 | 3 | 4 | .750 | 0 | 3 | 3 | 1 | 0 | 0 | 0 | 0 | 1 | 15 |
| 1996—Utah | 20 | 2 | 6 | .333 | 7 | 8 | .875 | 0 | 9 | 9 | 2 | 1 | 0 | 1 | 0 | 1 | 11 |
| 1997—Utah | 20 | 2 | 8 | .250 | 0 | 0 | ... | 1 | 3 | 4 | 0 | 0 | 0 | 1 | 1 | 0 | 4 |
| 1998—Utah | 17 | 2 | 4 | .500 | 0 | 0 | ... | 0 | 3 | 3 | 2 | 1 | ... | 2 | 0 | 0 | 4 |
| 2000—Utah | 3 | 0 | 1 | .000 | 0 | 0 | ... | 0 | 0 | 0 | 0 | 0 | 0 | 0 | 0 | 0 | 0 |
| 2001—Utah | 4 | 0 | 2 | .000 | 0 | 0 | ... | 0 | 1 | 1 | 0 | 0 | 0 | 0 | 0 | 0 | 0 |
| 2002—Utah | | | | | | | Selected, did not play.. | | | | | | | | | | |
| Totals | 244 | 58 | 107 | .542 | 29 | 40 | .725 | 19 | 55 | 74 | 19 | 16 | 0 | 12 | 5 | 15 | 145 |

# MALONE, MOSES                    C

**PERSONAL:** Born March 23, 1955, in Petersburg, Va. ... 6-10/260 (2,08/117,9). ... Full name: Moses Eugene Malone.
**HIGH SCHOOL:** Petersburg (Va.).
**COLLEGE:** Did not attend college.
**TRANSACTIONS:** Selected out of high school by Utah Stars in third round of 1974 American Basketball Association Draft. ... Contract sold by Stars to Spirits of St. Louis (December 2, 1975). ... Selected by Portland Trail Blazers of NBA from Spirits in ABA dispersal draft (August 5, 1976). ... Traded by Trail Blazers to Buffalo Braves for 1978 first-round draft choice (October 18, 1976). ... Traded by Braves to Houston Rockets for 1977 and 1978 first-round draft choices (October 24, 1976). ... Signed as veteran free agent by Philadelphia 76ers (September 2, 1982); Rockets matched offer and traded Malone to 76ers for F/C Caldwell Jones and 1983 first-round draft choice (September 15, 1982). ... Traded by 76ers with F Terry Catledge and 1986 and 1988 first-round draft choices to Washington Bullets for C/F Jeff Ruland and F Cliff Robinson (June 16, 1986). ... Signed as unrestricted free agent by Atlanta Hawks (August 16, 1988). ... Signed as unrestricted free agent by Milwaukee Bucks (July 10, 1991). ... Signed as free agent by 76ers (August 12, 1993). ... Waived by 76ers (June 17, 1994). ... Signed as free agent by San Antonio Spurs (August 10, 1994).
**CAREER HONORS:** Elected to the Naismith Memorial Basketball Hall of Fame (2001). ... One of the 50 Greatest Players in NBA History (1996).
**MISCELLANEOUS:** Member of NBA championship team (1983).

**NOTES:** ABA All-Rookie team (1975).

### ABA REGULAR-SEASON RECORD

| Season Team | G | Min. | 2-POINT FGM | FGA | Pct. | 3-POINT FGM | FGA | Pct. | FTM | FTA | Pct. | Reb. | Ast. | Pts. | RPG | APG | PPG |
|---|---|---|---|---|---|---|---|---|---|---|---|---|---|---|---|---|---|
| 74-75—Utah | 83 | 3205 | 591 | 1034 | .572 | 0 | 1 | .000 | 375 | 591 | .635 | 1209 | 82 | 1557 | 14.6 | 1.0 | 18.8 |
| 75-76—St. Louis | 43 | 1168 | 251 | 488 | .514 | 0 | 2 | .000 | 112 | 183 | .612 | 413 | 58 | 614 | 9.6 | 1.3 | 14.3 |
| Totals | 126 | 4373 | 842 | 1522 | .553 | 0 | 3 | .000 | 487 | 774 | .629 | 1622 | 140 | 2171 | 12.9 | 1.1 | 17.2 |

### ABA PLAYOFF RECORD

| Season Team | G | Min. | 2-POINT FGM | FGA | Pct. | 3-POINT FGM | FGA | Pct. | FTM | FTA | Pct. | Reb. | Ast. | Pts. | RPG | APG | PPG |
|---|---|---|---|---|---|---|---|---|---|---|---|---|---|---|---|---|---|
| 74-75—Utah | 6 | 235 | 51 | 80 | .638 | 0 | 0 | ... | 34 | 51 | .667 | 105 | 9 | 136 | 17.5 | 1.5 | 22.7 |

### ABA ALL-STAR GAME RECORD

| Season Team | Min. | 2-POINT FGM | FGA | Pct. | 3-POINT FGM | FGA | Pct. | FTM | FTA | Pct. | Reb. | Ast. | Pts. |
|---|---|---|---|---|---|---|---|---|---|---|---|---|---|
| 1975—Utah | 20 | 2 | 3 | .667 | 0 | 0 | ... | 2 | 5 | .400 | 10 | 0 | 6 |

### NBA REGULAR-SEASON RECORD

**RECORDS:** Holds career records for most consecutive games without a disqualification—1,212 (January 7, 1978 through 1994-95 season); and most offensive rebounds—6,731. ... Holds single-season record for most offensive rebounds—587 (1979). ... Holds single-game record for most offensive rebounds—21 (February 11, 1982, vs. Seattle).
**HONORS:** NBA Most Valuable Player (1979, 1982, 1983). ... All-NBA first team (1979, 1982, 1983, 1985). ... All-NBA second team (1980, 1981, 1984, 1987). ... NBA All-Defensive first team (1983). ... NBA All-Defensive second team (1979).

| Season Team | G | Min. | FGM | FGA | Pct. | FTM | FTA | Pct. | REBOUNDS Off. | Def. | Tot. | Ast. | St. | Blk. | TO | Pts. | AVERAGES RPG | APG | PPG |
|---|---|---|---|---|---|---|---|---|---|---|---|---|---|---|---|---|---|---|---|
| 76-77—Buff.-Houston. | 82 | 2506 | 389 | 810 | .480 | 305 | 440 | .693 | *437 | 635 | 1072 | 89 | 67 | 181 | ... | 1083 | 13.1 | 1.1 | 13.2 |
| 77-78—Houston | 59 | 2107 | 413 | 828 | .499 | 318 | 443 | .718 | *380 | 506 | 886 | 31 | 48 | 76 | 220 | 1144 | 15.0 | 0.5 | 19.4 |
| 78-79—Houston | 82 | *3390 | 716 | 1325 | .540 | 599 | 811 | .739 | *587 | *857 | *1444 | 147 | 79 | 119 | 326 | 2031 | *17.6 | 1.8 | 24.8 |
| 79-80—Houston | 82 | 3140 | 778 | 1549 | .502 | 563 | 783 | .719 | *573 | 617 | 1190 | 147 | 80 | 107 | 300 | 2119 | 14.5 | 1.8 | 25.8 |
| 80-81—Houston | 80 | 3245 | 806 | 1545 | .522 | 609 | *804 | .757 | *474 | 706 | *1180 | 141 | 83 | 150 | *308 | 2222 | *14.8 | 1.8 | 27.8 |
| 81-82—Houston | 81 | *3398 | 945 | 1822 | .519 | 630 | *827 | .762 | *558 | 630 | *1188 | 142 | 76 | 125 | 294 | 2520 | *14.7 | 1.8 | 31.1 |
| 82-83—Philadelphia | 78 | 2922 | 654 | 1305 | .501 | *600 | *788 | .761 | *445 | *749 | *1194 | 101 | 89 | 157 | 264 | 1908 | *15.3 | 1.3 | 24.5 |
| 83-84—Philadelphia | 71 | 2613 | 532 | 1101 | .483 | 545 | 727 | .750 | 352 | 598 | 950 | 96 | 71 | 110 | 250 | 1609 | *13.4 | 1.4 | 22.7 |
| 84-85—Philadelphia | 79 | 2957 | 602 | 1284 | .469 | *737 | *904 | .815 | 385 | 646 | *1031 | 130 | 67 | 123 | 286 | 1941 | *13.1 | 1.6 | 24.6 |
| 85-86—Philadelphia | 74 | 2706 | 571 | 1246 | .458 | *617 | *784 | .787 | 339 | 533 | 872 | 90 | 67 | 71 | 261 | 1759 | 11.8 | 1.2 | 23.8 |
| 86-87—Washington | 73 | 2488 | 595 | 1311 | .454 | 570 | 692 | .824 | 340 | 484 | 824 | 120 | 59 | 92 | 202 | 1760 | 11.3 | 1.6 | 24.1 |
| 87-88—Washington | 79 | 2692 | 531 | 1090 | .487 | 543 | 689 | .788 | 372 | 512 | 884 | 112 | 59 | 72 | 249 | 1607 | 11.2 | 1.4 | 20.3 |
| 88-89—Atlanta | 81 | 2878 | 538 | 1096 | .491 | 561 | 711 | .789 | 386 | 570 | 956 | 112 | 79 | 100 | 245 | 1637 | 11.8 | 1.4 | 20.2 |
| 89-90—Atlanta | 81 | 2735 | 517 | 1077 | .480 | 493 | 631 | .781 | *364 | 448 | 812 | 130 | 47 | 84 | 232 | 1528 | 10.0 | 1.6 | 18.9 |
| 90-91—Atlanta | 82 | 1912 | 280 | 598 | .468 | 309 | 372 | .831 | 271 | 396 | 667 | 68 | 30 | 74 | 137 | 869 | 8.1 | 0.8 | 10.6 |
| 91-92—Milwaukee | 82 | 2511 | 440 | 929 | .474 | 396 | 504 | .786 | 320 | 424 | 744 | 93 | 74 | 64 | 150 | 1279 | 9.1 | 1.1 | 15.6 |
| 92-93—Milwaukee | 11 | 104 | 13 | 42 | .310 | 24 | 31 | .774 | 22 | 24 | 46 | 7 | 1 | 8 | 10 | 50 | 4.2 | 0.6 | 4.5 |
| 93-94—Milwaukee | 55 | 618 | 102 | 232 | .440 | 90 | 117 | .769 | 106 | 120 | 226 | 34 | 11 | 17 | 59 | 294 | 4.1 | 0.6 | 5.3 |
| 94-95—San Antonio | 17 | 149 | 13 | 35 | .371 | 22 | 32 | .688 | 20 | 26 | 46 | 6 | 2 | 3 | 11 | 49 | 2.7 | 0.4 | 2.9 |
| Totals | 1329 | 45071 | 9435 | 19225 | .491 | 8531 | 11090 | .769 | 6731 | 9481 | 16212 | 1796 | 1089 | 1733 | 3804 | 27409 | 12.2 | 1.4 | 20.6 |

Three-point field goals: 1979-80, 0-for-6. 1980-81, 1-for-3 (.333). 1981-82, 0-for-6. 1982-83, 0-for-1. 1983-84, 0-for-4. 1984-85, 0-for-2. 1985-86, 0-for-1. 1986-87, 0-for-11. 1987-88, 2-for-7 (.286). 1988-89, 0-for-12. 1989-90, 1-for-9 (.111). 1990-91, 0-for-7. 1991-92, 3-for-8 (.375). 1993-94, 0-for-1. 1994-95, 1-for-2 (.500). Totals, 8-for-80 (.100).

Personal fouls/disqualifications: 1976-77, 275/3. 1977-78, 179/2. 1978-79, 223/0. 1979-80, 210/0. 1980-81, 223/0. 1981-82, 208/0. 1982-83, 206/0. 1983-84, 188/0. 1984-85, 216/0. 1985-86, 194/0. 1986-87, 139/0. 1987-88, 160/0. 1988-89, 154/0. 1989-90, 158/0. 1990-91, 134/0. 1991-92, 136/0. 1992-93, 6/0. 1993-94, 52/0. 1994-95, 15/0. Totals, 3076/5.

### NBA PLAYOFF RECORD

NOTES: NBA Finals Most Valuable Player (1983). ... Holds single-game playoff record for most offensive rebounds—15 (April 21, 1977, vs. Washington).

| Season Team | G | Min. | FGM | FGA | Pct. | FTM | FTA | Pct. | REBOUNDS Off. | Def. | Tot. | Ast. | St. | Blk. | TO | Pts. | AVERAGES RPG | APG | PPG |
|---|---|---|---|---|---|---|---|---|---|---|---|---|---|---|---|---|---|---|---|
| 76-77—Houston | 12 | 518 | 81 | 162 | .500 | 63 | 91 | .692 | 84 | 119 | 203 | 7 | 13 | 21 | ... | 225 | 16.9 | 0.6 | 18.8 |
| 78-79—Houston | 2 | 78 | 18 | 41 | .439 | 13 | 18 | .722 | 25 | 16 | 41 | 2 | 1 | 8 | 8 | 49 | 20.5 | 1.0 | 24.5 |
| 79-80—Houston | 7 | 275 | 74 | 138 | .536 | 33 | 43 | .767 | 42 | 55 | 97 | 7 | 4 | 16 | 22 | 181 | 13.9 | 1.0 | 25.9 |
| 80-81—Houston | 21 | 955 | 207 | 432 | .479 | 148 | 208 | .712 | 125 | 180 | 305 | 35 | 13 | 34 | 59 | 562 | 14.5 | 1.7 | 26.8 |
| 81-82—Houston | 3 | 136 | 29 | 67 | .433 | 14 | 15 | .933 | 28 | 23 | 51 | 10 | 2 | 2 | 6 | 72 | 17.0 | 3.3 | 24.0 |
| 82-83—Philadelphia | 13 | 524 | 126 | 235 | .536 | 86 | 120 | .717 | 70 | 136 | 206 | 20 | 19 | 25 | 40 | 338 | 15.8 | 1.5 | 26.0 |
| 83-84—Philadelphia | 5 | 212 | 38 | 83 | .458 | 31 | 32 | .969 | 20 | 49 | 69 | 7 | 3 | 11 | 21 | 107 | 13.8 | 1.4 | 21.4 |
| 84-85—Philadelphia | 13 | 505 | 90 | 212 | .425 | 82 | 103 | .796 | 36 | 102 | 138 | 24 | 17 | 22 | 23 | 262 | 10.6 | 1.8 | 20.2 |
| 86-87—Washington | 3 | 114 | 21 | 47 | .447 | 20 | 21 | .952 | 15 | 23 | 38 | 5 | 0 | 3 | 8 | 62 | 12.7 | 1.7 | 20.7 |
| 87-88—Washington | 5 | 198 | 30 | 65 | .462 | 33 | 40 | .825 | 22 | 34 | 56 | 7 | 3 | 4 | 15 | 93 | 11.2 | 1.4 | 18.6 |
| 88-89—Atlanta | 5 | 197 | 32 | 64 | .500 | 40 | 51 | .784 | 27 | 33 | 60 | 9 | 7 | 4 | 11 | 105 | 12.0 | 1.8 | 21.0 |
| 90-91—Atlanta | 5 | 84 | 4 | 20 | .200 | 13 | 14 | .929 | 16 | 15 | 31 | 3 | 2 | 1 | 2 | 21 | 6.2 | 0.6 | 4.2 |
| Totals | 94 | 3796 | 750 | 1566 | .479 | 576 | 756 | .762 | 510 | 785 | 1295 | 136 | 84 | 151 | 215 | 2077 | 13.8 | 1.4 | 22.1 |

Three-point field goals: 1979-80, 0-for-1. 1980-81, 0-for-2. 1982-83, 0-for-1. 1984-85, 0-for-1. 1987-88, 0-for-1. 1988-89, 1-for-1. Totals, 1-for-7 (.143).
Personal fouls/disqualifications: 1976-77, 42/0. 1978-79, 5/0. 1979-80, 18/0. 1980-81, 54/0. 1981-82, 8/0. 1982-83, 40/0. 1983-84, 15/0. 1984-85, 39/0. 1986-87, 5/0. 1987-88, 9/0. 1988-89, 5/0. 1990-91, 4/0. Totals, 244/0.

### NBA ALL-STAR GAME RECORD

| Season Team | Min. | FGM | FGA | Pct. | FTM | FTA | Pct. | REBOUNDS Off. | Def. | Tot. | Ast. | PF | Dq. | St. | Blk. | TO | Pts. |
|---|---|---|---|---|---|---|---|---|---|---|---|---|---|---|---|---|---|
| 1978—Houston | 14 | 1 | 1 | 1.000 | 2 | 4 | .500 | 1 | 3 | 4 | 1 | 1 | 0 | 1 | 0 | 0 | 4 |
| 1979—Houston | 17 | 2 | 2 | 1.000 | 4 | 5 | .800 | 2 | 5 | 7 | 1 | 0 | 0 | 1 | 0 | 1 | 8 |
| 1980—Houston | 31 | 7 | 12 | .583 | 6 | 12 | .500 | 6 | 6 | 12 | 2 | 4 | 0 | 1 | 2 | 5 | 20 |
| 1981—Houston | 22 | 3 | 8 | .375 | 2 | 4 | .500 | 2 | 4 | 6 | 3 | 3 | 0 | 1 | 0 | 1 | 8 |
| 1982—Houston | 20 | 5 | 11 | .455 | 2 | 6 | .333 | 5 | 6 | 11 | 0 | 2 | 0 | 1 | 1 | 3 | 12 |
| 1983—Philadelphia | 24 | 3 | 8 | .375 | 4 | 6 | .667 | 2 | 6 | 8 | 3 | 1 | 0 | 0 | 1 | 1 | 10 |
| 1984—Philadelphia | | | | | | | | Selected, did not play—injured. | | | | | | | | | |
| 1985—Philadelphia | 33 | 2 | 10 | .200 | 3 | 6 | .500 | 5 | 7 | 12 | 1 | 4 | 0 | 0 | 0 | 3 | 7 |
| 1986—Philadelphia | 34 | 5 | 12 | .417 | 6 | 9 | .667 | 5 | 8 | 13 | 0 | 4 | 0 | 1 | 0 | 1 | 16 |
| 1987—Washington | 35 | 11 | 19 | .579 | 5 | 6 | .833 | 7 | 11 | 18 | 2 | 4 | 0 | 2 | 1 | 1 | 27 |
| 1988—Washington | 22 | 2 | 6 | .333 | 3 | 6 | .500 | 5 | 4 | 9 | 2 | 2 | 0 | 0 | 0 | 2 | 7 |
| 1989—Atlanta | 19 | 3 | 9 | .333 | 3 | 3 | 1.000 | 4 | 4 | 8 | 0 | 1 | 0 | 1 | 1 | 1 | 9 |
| Totals | 271 | 44 | 98 | .449 | 40 | 67 | .597 | 44 | 64 | 108 | 15 | 26 | 0 | 9 | 6 | 19 | 128 |

### COMBINED ABA AND NBA REGULAR-SEASON RECORDS

| | G | Min. | FGM | FGA | Pct. | FTM | FTA | Pct. | REBOUNDS Off. | Def. | Tot. | Ast. | Stl. | Blk. | TO | Pts. | AVERAGES RPG | APG | PPG |
|---|---|---|---|---|---|---|---|---|---|---|---|---|---|---|---|---|---|---|---|
| Totals | 1455 | 49444 | 10277 | 20750 | .495 | 9018 | 11864 | .760 | 7382 | 10452 | 17834 | 1936 | 1199 | 1889 | 4264 | 29580 | 12.3 | 1.3 | 20.3 |

Three-point field goals: 8-for-83 (.096).

## MARAVICH, PETE                    G

PERSONAL: Born June 22, 1947, in Aliquippa, Pa. ... Died January 5, 1988. ... 6-5/200 (1,96/90,7). ... Full name: Peter Press Maravich. ... Nickname: Pistol Pete. ... Son of Press Maravich, former college coach; and guard with Youngstown Bears of National Basketball League (1945-46) and Pittsburgh Ironmen of Basketball Association of America (1946-47).

HIGH SCHOOL: Daniel (Clemson, S.C.), then Needham Broughton (Raleigh, N.C.), then Edwards Military Institute (Salemburg, N.C.).

COLLEGE: Louisiana State.

TRANSACTIONS: Selected by Atlanta Hawks in first round (third pick overall) of 1970 NBA Draft. ... Traded by Hawks to New Orleans Jazz for G Dean Meminger, C/F Bob Kauffman, 1974 and 1975 first-round draft choices and 1975 and 1976 second-round draft choices (May 3, 1974). ... Jazz franchise moved from New Orleans to Utah for 1979-80 season. ... Waived by Jazz (January 17, 1980). ... Signed as free agent by Boston Celtics (January 22, 1980).

**CAREER HONORS:** Elected to Naismith Memorial Basketball Hall of Fame (1987). ... One of the 50 Greatest Players in NBA History (1996).

## COLLEGIATE RECORD

**NOTES:** THE SPORTING NEWS College Player of the Year (1970). ... Naismith Award winner (1970). ... THE SPORTING NEWS All-America first team (1968, 1969, 1970). ... Holds NCAA career records for most points—3667; highest points-per-game average—44.2; most field goals made—1387; most field goals attempted—3166; most free throws made (three-year career)—893; most free throws attempted (three-year career)—1152; and most games scoring at least 50 points—28. ... Holds NCAA single-season records for most points—1381; highest points-per-game average—44.5; most field goals made—522; most field goals attempted—1168; and most games scoring at least 50 points—10 (1970). ... Holds NCAA single-game record for most free throws made—30 (December 22, 1969, vs. Oregon State in 31 attempts). ... Led NCAA Division I with 43.8 points per game (1968), 44.2 points per game (1969) and 44.5 points per game (1970).

| Season Team | G | Min. | FGM | FGA | Pct. | FTM | FTA | Pct. | Reb. | Ast. | Pts. | AVERAGES RPG | APG | PPG |
|---|---|---|---|---|---|---|---|---|---|---|---|---|---|---|
| 66-67—Louisiana State‡ | 17 | ... | 273 | 604 | .452 | 195 | 234 | .833 | 176 | 124 | 741 | 10.4 | 7.3 | 43.6 |
| 67-68—Louisiana State | 26 | ... | 432 | 1022 | .423 | 274 | 338 | .811 | 195 | 105 | 1138 | 7.5 | 4.0 | 43.8 |
| 68-69—Louisiana State | 26 | ... | 433 | 976 | .444 | 282 | 378 | .746 | 169 | 128 | 1148 | 6.5 | 4.9 | 44.2 |
| 69-70—Louisiana State | 31 | ... | 522 | 1168 | .447 | 337 | 436 | .773 | 164 | 192 | 1381 | 5.3 | 6.2 | 44.5 |
| Varsity totals | 83 | ... | 1387 | 3166 | .438 | 893 | 1152 | .775 | 528 | 425 | 3667 | 6.4 | 5.1 | 44.2 |

## NBA REGULAR-SEASON RECORD

**RECORDS:** Shares single-game records for most free throws made in one quarter—14 (November 28, 1973, vs. Buffalo); and most free throws attempted in one quarter—16 (January 2, 1973, vs. Chicago).
**HONORS:** All-NBA first team (1976, 1977). ... All-NBA second team (1973, 1978). ... NBA All-Rookie team (1971).

| Season Team | G | Min. | FGM | FGA | Pct. | FTM | FTA | Pct. | Reb. | Ast. | PF | Dq. | Pts. | AVERAGES RPG | APG | PPG |
|---|---|---|---|---|---|---|---|---|---|---|---|---|---|---|---|---|
| 70-71—Atlanta | 81 | 2926 | 738 | 1613 | .458 | 404 | 505 | .800 | 298 | 355 | 238 | 1 | 1880 | 3.7 | 4.4 | 23.2 |
| 71-72—Atlanta | 66 | 2302 | 460 | 1077 | .427 | 355 | 438 | .811 | 256 | 393 | 207 | 0 | 1275 | 3.9 | 6.0 | 19.3 |
| 72-73—Atlanta | 79 | 3089 | 789 | 1788 | .441 | 485 | 606 | .800 | 346 | 546 | 245 | 1 | 2063 | 4.4 | 6.9 | 26.1 |

| Season Team | G | Min. | FGM | FGA | Pct. | FTM | FTA | Pct. | REBOUNDS Off. | Def. | Tot. | Ast. | St. | Blk. | TO | Pts. | AVERAGES RPG | APG | PPG |
|---|---|---|---|---|---|---|---|---|---|---|---|---|---|---|---|---|---|---|---|
| 73-74—Atlanta | 76 | 2903 | 819 | *1791 | .457 | 469 | 568 | .826 | 98 | 276 | 374 | 396 | 111 | 13 | ... | 2107 | 4.9 | 5.2 | 27.7 |
| 74-75—New Orleans | 79 | 2853 | 655 | 1562 | .419 | 390 | 481 | .811 | 93 | 329 | 422 | 488 | 120 | 18 | ... | 1700 | 5.3 | 6.2 | 21.5 |
| 75-76—New Orleans | 62 | 2373 | 604 | 1316 | .459 | 396 | 488 | .811 | 46 | 254 | 300 | 332 | 87 | 23 | ... | 1604 | 4.8 | 5.4 | 25.9 |
| 76-77—New Orleans | 73 | 3041 | 886 | *2047 | .433 | *501 | 600 | .835 | 90 | 284 | 374 | 392 | 84 | 22 | ... | *2273 | 5.1 | 5.4 | *31.1 |
| 77-78—New Orleans | 50 | 2041 | 556 | 1253 | .444 | 240 | 276 | .870 | 49 | 129 | 178 | 335 | 101 | 8 | 248 | 1352 | 3.6 | 6.7 | 27.0 |
| 78-79—New Orleans | 49 | 1824 | 436 | 1035 | .421 | 233 | 277 | .841 | 33 | 88 | 121 | 243 | 60 | 18 | 200 | 1105 | 2.5 | 5.0 | 22.6 |
| 79-80—Utah-Boston | 43 | 964 | 244 | 543 | .449 | 91 | 105 | .867 | 17 | 61 | 78 | 83 | 24 | 6 | 82 | 589 | 1.8 | 1.9 | 13.7 |
| Totals | 658 | 24316 | 6187 | 14025 | .441 | 3564 | 4344 | .820 | ... | ... | 2747 | 3563 | 587 | 108 | 530 | 15948 | 4.2 | 5.4 | 24.2 |

Three-point field goals: 1979-80, 10-for-15 (.667).
Personal fouls/disqualifications: 1973-74, 261/4. 1974-75, 227/4. 1975-76, 197/3. 1976-77, 191/1. 1977-78, 116/1. 1978-79, 104/2. 1979-80, 79/1. Totals, 1865/18.

## NBA PLAYOFF RECORD

| Season Team | G | Min. | FGM | FGA | Pct. | FTM | FTA | Pct. | Reb. | Ast. | PF | Dq. | Pts. | AVERAGES RPG | APG | PPG |
|---|---|---|---|---|---|---|---|---|---|---|---|---|---|---|---|---|
| 70-71—Atlanta | 5 | 199 | 46 | 122 | .377 | 18 | 26 | .692 | 26 | 24 | 14 | 0 | 110 | 5.2 | 4.8 | 22.0 |
| 71-72—Atlanta | 6 | 219 | 54 | 121 | .446 | 58 | 71 | .817 | 32 | 28 | 24 | 0 | 166 | 5.3 | 4.7 | 27.7 |
| 72-73—Atlanta | 6 | 234 | 65 | 155 | .419 | 27 | 34 | .794 | 29 | 40 | 24 | 1 | 157 | 4.8 | 6.7 | 26.2 |

| Season Team | G | Min. | FGM | FGA | Pct. | FTM | FTA | Pct. | REBOUNDS Off. | Def. | Tot. | Ast. | St. | Blk. | TO | Pts. | AVERAGES RPG | APG | PPG |
|---|---|---|---|---|---|---|---|---|---|---|---|---|---|---|---|---|---|---|---|
| 79-80—Boston | 9 | 104 | 25 | 51 | .490 | 2 | 3 | .667 | 0 | 8 | 8 | 6 | 3 | 0 | 9 | 54 | 0.9 | 0.7 | 6.0 |
| Totals | 26 | 756 | 190 | 449 | .423 | 105 | 134 | .784 | ... | ... | 95 | 98 | 3 | 0 | 9 | 487 | 3.7 | 3.8 | 18.7 |

Three-point field goals: 1979-80, 2-for-6 (.333).
Personal fouls/disqualifications: 1979-80, 12/0.

## NBA ALL-STAR GAME RECORD

| Season Team | Min. | FGM | FGA | Pct. | FTM | FTA | Pct. | Reb | Ast. | PF | Dq. | Pts. |
|---|---|---|---|---|---|---|---|---|---|---|---|---|
| 1973—Atlanta | 22 | 4 | 8 | .500 | 0 | 0 | ... | 3 | 5 | 4 | 0 | 8 |

| Season Team | Min. | FGM | FGA | Pct. | FTM | FTA | Pct. | REBOUNDS Off. | Def. | Tot. | Ast. | PF | Dq. | St. | Blk. | TO | Pts. |
|---|---|---|---|---|---|---|---|---|---|---|---|---|---|---|---|---|---|
| 1974—Atlanta | 22 | 4 | 15 | .267 | 7 | 9 | .778 | 1 | 2 | 3 | 4 | 2 | 0 | 0 | 0 | ... | 15 |
| 1977—New Orleans | 21 | 5 | 13 | .385 | 0 | 0 | ... | 0 | 0 | 0 | 4 | 1 | 0 | 4 | 0 | ... | 10 |
| 1978—New Orleans | | | | | | | Selected, did not play—injured. | | | | | | | | | | |
| 1979—New Orleans | 14 | 5 | 8 | .625 | 0 | 0 | ... | 0 | 2 | 2 | 2 | 1 | 0 | 0 | 0 | 4 | 10 |
| Totals | 79 | 18 | 44 | .409 | 7 | 9 | .778 | | | 8 | 15 | 8 | 0 | 4 | 0 | 4 | 43 |

## MARTIN, SLATER                    G

**PERSONAL:** Born October 22, 1925, in Houston. ... 5-10/170 (1,78/77,1). ... Full name: Slater Nelson Martin Jr. ... Nickname: Dugie.
**HIGH SCHOOL:** Jefferson Davis (Houston).
**COLLEGE:** Texas.
**TRANSACTIONS:** Selected by Minneapolis Lakers in 1949 Basketball Association of America Draft. ... Traded by Lakers with F Jerry Bird and player to be named later to New York Knicks for C Walter Dukes and draft rights to F/C Burdette Haldorson (October 26, 1956). ... Traded by Knicks to St. Louis Hawks for F Willie Naulls (December 10, 1956).
**CAREER HONORS:** Elected to Naismith Memorial Basketball Hall of Fame (1982).
**MISCELLANEOUS:** Member of NBA championship team (1950, 1952, 1953, 1954, 1958).

ALL-TIME GREAT PLAYERS

## COLLEGIATE RECORD

**NOTES:** THE SPORTING NEWS All-America fifth team (1949).

| Season Team | G | Min. | FGM | FGA | Pct. | FTM | FTA | Pct. | Reb. | Ast. | Pts. | AVERAGES | | |
|---|---|---|---|---|---|---|---|---|---|---|---|---|---|---|
| | | | | | | | | | | | | RPG | APG | PPG |
| 43-44—Texas | 14 | ... | 75 | ... | ... | 34 | ... | ... | ... | ... | 184 | ... | ... | 13.1 |
| 44-45— | | | | | | Did not play—in military service. | | | | | | | | |
| 45-46— | | | | | | Did not play—in military service. | | | | | | | | |
| 46-47—Texas | 27 | ... | 109 | ... | ... | 37 | ... | ... | ... | ... | 255 | ... | ... | 9.4 |
| 47-48—Texas | 25 | ... | 126 | ... | ... | 65 | 85 | .765 | ... | ... | 317 | ... | ... | 12.7 |
| 48-49—Texas | 24 | ... | 165 | ... | ... | 54 | ... | ... | ... | ... | 384 | ... | ... | 16.0 |
| Totals | 90 | ... | 475 | ... | ... | 190 | ... | ... | ... | ... | 1140 | ... | ... | 12.7 |

## NBA REGULAR-SEASON RECORD

**HONORS:** All-NBA second team (1954, 1956, 1957, 1958, 1959).

| Season Team | G | Min. | FGM | FGA | Pct. | FTM | FTA | Pct. | Reb. | Ast. | PF | Dq. | Pts. | AVERAGES | | |
|---|---|---|---|---|---|---|---|---|---|---|---|---|---|---|---|---|
| | | | | | | | | | | | | | | RPG | APG | PPG |
| 49-50—Minneapolis | 67 | ... | 106 | 302 | .351 | 59 | 93 | .634 | ... | 148 | 162 | ... | 271 | ... | 2.2 | 4.0 |
| 50-51—Minneapolis | 68 | ... | 227 | 627 | .362 | 121 | 177 | .684 | 246 | 235 | 199 | 3 | 575 | 3.6 | 3.5 | 8.5 |
| 51-52—Minneapolis | 66 | 2480 | 237 | 632 | .375 | 142 | 190 | .747 | 228 | 249 | 226 | 9 | 616 | 3.5 | 3.8 | 9.3 |
| 52-53—Minneapolis | 70 | 2556 | 260 | 634 | .410 | 224 | 287 | .780 | 186 | 250 | 246 | 4 | 744 | 2.7 | 3.6 | 10.6 |
| 53-54—Minneapolis | 69 | 2472 | 254 | 654 | .388 | 176 | 243 | .724 | 166 | 253 | 198 | 3 | 684 | 2.4 | 3.7 | 9.9 |
| 54-55—Minneapolis | 72 | 2784 | 350 | 919 | .381 | 276 | 359 | .769 | 260 | 427 | 221 | 7 | 976 | 3.6 | 5.9 | 13.6 |
| 55-56—Minneapolis | 72 | *2838 | 309 | 863 | .358 | 329 | 395 | .833 | 260 | 445 | 202 | 2 | 947 | 3.6 | 6.2 | 13.2 |
| 56-57—N.Y.-St.L. | 66 | 2401 | 244 | 736 | .332 | 230 | 291 | .790 | 288 | 269 | 193 | 1 | 718 | 4.4 | 4.1 | 10.9 |
| 57-58—St. Louis | 60 | 2098 | 258 | 768 | .336 | 206 | 276 | .746 | 228 | 218 | 187 | 0 | 722 | 3.8 | 3.6 | 12.0 |
| 58-59—St. Louis | 71 | 2504 | 245 | 706 | .347 | 197 | 254 | .776 | 253 | 336 | 230 | 8 | 687 | 3.6 | 4.7 | 9.7 |
| 59-60—St. Louis | 64 | 1756 | 142 | 383 | .371 | 113 | 155 | .729 | 187 | 330 | 174 | 2 | 397 | 2.9 | 5.2 | 6.2 |
| Totals | 745 | ... | 2632 | 7224 | .364 | 2073 | 2720 | .762 | ... | 3160 | 2238 | ... | 7337 | ... | 4.2 | 9.8 |

## NBA PLAYOFF RECORD

| Season Team | G | Min. | FGM | FGA | Pct. | FTM | FTA | Pct. | Reb. | Ast. | PF | Dq. | Pts. | AVERAGES | | |
|---|---|---|---|---|---|---|---|---|---|---|---|---|---|---|---|---|
| | | | | | | | | | | | | | | RPG | APG | PPG |
| 49-50—Minneapolis | 12 | ... | 21 | 50 | .420 | 14 | 24 | .583 | ... | 25 | 35 | ... | 56 | ... | 2.1 | 4.7 |
| 50-51—Minneapolis | 7 | ... | 18 | 51 | .353 | 14 | 27 | .519 | 42 | 25 | 20 | ... | 50 | 6.0 | 3.6 | 7.1 |
| 51-52—Minneapolis | 13 | 523 | 38 | 110 | .345 | 41 | 56 | .732 | 37 | 56 | 64 | 4 | 117 | 2.8 | 4.3 | 9.0 |
| 52-53—Minneapolis | 12 | 453 | 41 | 103 | .398 | 39 | 51 | .765 | 31 | 43 | 49 | 1 | 121 | 2.6 | 3.6 | 10.1 |
| 53-54—Minneapolis | 13 | 533 | 37 | 112 | .330 | 52 | 70 | .743 | 29 | 60 | 52 | 1 | 126 | 2.2 | 4.6 | 9.7 |
| 54-55—Minneapolis | 7 | 315 | 28 | 94 | .298 | 40 | 49 | .816 | 28 | 31 | 23 | 0 | 96 | 4.0 | 4.4 | 13.7 |
| 55-56—Minneapolis | 3 | 121 | 17 | 37 | .459 | 20 | 24 | .833 | 7 | 15 | 9 | 0 | 54 | 2.3 | 5.0 | 18.0 |
| 56-57—St. Louis | 10 | 439 | 55 | 155 | .355 | 56 | 74 | .757 | 42 | 49 | 39 | 2 | 166 | 4.2 | 4.9 | 16.6 |
| 57-58—St. Louis | 11 | 416 | 44 | 137 | .321 | 39 | 63 | .619 | 48 | 40 | 40 | 1 | 127 | 4.4 | 3.6 | 11.5 |
| 58-59—St. Louis | 1 | 18 | 4 | 5 | .800 | 0 | 0 | ... | 3 | 2 | 2 | 0 | 8 | 3.0 | 2.0 | 8.0 |
| 59-60—St. Louis | 3 | 58 | 1 | 13 | .077 | 1 | 4 | .250 | 3 | 8 | 9 | 0 | 3 | 1.0 | 2.7 | 1.0 |
| Totals | 92 | ... | 304 | 867 | .351 | 316 | 442 | .715 | ... | 354 | 342 | ... | 924 | ... | 3.8 | 10.0 |

## NBA ALL-STAR GAME RECORD

| Season Team | Min. | FGM | FGA | Pct. | FTM | FTA | Pct. | Reb | Ast. | PF | Dq. | Pts. |
|---|---|---|---|---|---|---|---|---|---|---|---|---|
| 1953—Minneapolis | 26 | 2 | 10 | .200 | 1 | 1 | 1.000 | 2 | 1 | 2 | 0 | 5 |
| 1954—Minneapolis | 23 | 1 | 5 | .200 | 0 | 0 | ... | 0 | 3 | 3 | 0 | 2 |
| 1955—Minneapolis | 23 | 2 | 5 | .400 | 1 | 2 | .500 | 2 | 5 | 3 | 0 | 5 |
| 1956—Minneapolis | 29 | 3 | 7 | .429 | 3 | 3 | 1.000 | 1 | 7 | 5 | 0 | 9 |
| 1957—St. Louis | 31 | 4 | 11 | .364 | 0 | 0 | ... | 2 | 3 | 1 | 0 | 8 |
| 1958—St. Louis | 26 | 2 | 9 | .222 | 2 | 4 | .500 | 2 | 8 | 3 | 0 | 6 |
| 1959—St. Louis | 22 | 2 | 6 | .333 | 1 | 2 | .500 | 6 | 1 | 2 | 0 | 5 |
| Totals | 180 | 16 | 53 | .302 | 8 | 12 | .667 | 15 | 28 | 19 | 0 | 40 |

## NBA COACHING RECORD

**BACKGROUND:** Player/head coach, St. Louis Hawks (1957). ... Head coach/general manager, Houston Mavericks of ABA (1967-68).

| Season Team | REGULAR SEASON | | | | PLAYOFFS | | |
|---|---|---|---|---|---|---|---|
| | W | L | Pct. | Finish | W | L | Pct. |
| 56-57—St. Louis | 5 | 3 | .625 | ——— | | | |

## ABA COACHING RECORD

| Season Team | REGULAR SEASON | | | | PLAYOFFS | | |
|---|---|---|---|---|---|---|---|
| | W | L | Pct. | Finish | W | L | Pct. |
| 67-68—Houston | 29 | 49 | .372 | 4th/Western Division | 0 | 3 | .000 |
| 68-69—Houston | 3 | 9 | .250 | | | | |
| Totals (2 years) | 32 | 58 | .356 | Totals (1 year) | 0 | 3 | .000> |

**NOTES:**

1957—Replaced Red Holzman as St. Louis head coach (January), with record of 14-19; replaced as St. Louis head coach by Alex Hannum (January).

1968—Lost to Dallas in Western Division Semifinals. Replaced as Houston head coach by Jim Weaver (November).

# McADOO, BOB                     C/F

**PERSONAL:** Born September 25, 1951, in Greensboro, N.C. ... 6-9/225 (2,05/102,1). ... Full name: Robert Allen McAdoo Jr.
**HIGH SCHOOL:** Ben Smith (Greensboro, N.C.).
**JUNIOR COLLEGE:** Vincennes (Ind.).University.
**COLLEGE:** North Carolina.
**TRANSACTIONS:** Selected after junior season by Buffalo Braves in first round (second pick overall) of 1972 NBA Draft. ... Traded by Braves with C/F Tom McMillen to New York Knicks for C/F John Gianelli and cash (December 9, 1976). ... Traded

by Knicks to Boston Celtics for three 1979 first-round draft choices and player to be named later (February 12, 1979); Knicks acquired C Tom Barker to complete deal (February 14, 1979). ... Acquired by Detroit Pistons for two 1980 first-round draft choices to complete compensation for Celtics signing of veteran free agent F/G M.L. Carr (September 6, 1979). ... Waived by Pistons (March 11, 1981). ... Signed as free agent by New Jersey Nets (March 13, 1981). ... Traded by Nets to Los Angeles Lakers for 1983 second-round draft choice and cash (December 24, 1981). ... Signed as veteran free agent by Philadelphia 76ers (January 31, 1986); Lakers waived their right of first refusal. ... Played in Italy (1986-87 through 1992-93).

**CAREER HONORS:** Elected to Naismith Memorial Basketball Hall of Fame (2000).
**CAREER NOTES:** Assistant coach, Miami Heat (September 20, 1995 to present).
**MISCELLANEOUS:** Member of NBA championship team (1982, 1985).

## COLLEGIATE RECORD

NOTES: THE SPORTING NEWS All-America first team (1972).

| Season Team | G | Min. | FGM | FGA | Pct. | FTM | FTA | Pct. | Reb. | Ast. | Pts. | RPG | APG | PPG |
|---|---|---|---|---|---|---|---|---|---|---|---|---|---|---|
| 69-70—Vincennes University...... | 32 | ... | 258 | ... | ... | 101 | 134 | .754 | 320 | ... | 617 | 10.0 | ... | 19.3 |
| 70-71—Vincennes University...... | 27 | ... | 273 | ... | ... | 129 | 164 | .787 | 297 | ... | 675 | 11.0 | ... | 25.0 |
| 71-72—North Carolina............... | 31 | ... | 243 | 471 | .516 | 118 | 167 | .707 | 312 | 72 | 604 | 10.1 | 2.3 | 19.5 |
| Junior college totals ............. | 59 | ... | 531 | ... | ... | 230 | 298 | .772 | 617 | ... | 1292 | 10.5 | ... | 21.9 |
| 4-year-college totals ............. | 31 | ... | 243 | 471 | .516 | 118 | 167 | .707 | 312 | 72 | 604 | 10.1 | 2.3 | 19.5 |

## NBA REGULAR-SEASON RECORD

HONORS: NBA Most Valuable Player (1975). ... NBA Rookie of the Year (1973). ... All-NBA first team (1975). ... All-NBA second team (1974). ... NBA All-Rookie team (1973).

| Season Team | G | Min. | FGM | FGA | Pct. | FTM | FTA | Pct. | Reb. | Ast. | PF | Dq. | Pts. | RPG | APG | PPG |
|---|---|---|---|---|---|---|---|---|---|---|---|---|---|---|---|---|
| 72-73—Buffalo............................ | 80 | 2562 | 585 | 1293 | .452 | 271 | 350 | .774 | 728 | 139 | 256 | 6 | 1441 | 9.1 | 1.7 | 18.0 |

| | | | | | | | | | REBOUNDS | | | | | | AVERAGES | | |
|---|---|---|---|---|---|---|---|---|---|---|---|---|---|---|---|---|---|
| Season Team | G | Min. | FGM | FGA | Pct. | FTM | FTA | Pct. | Off. | Def. | Tot. | Ast. | St. | Blk. | TO | Pts. | RPG | APG | PPG |
| 73-74—Buffalo ............ | 74 | 3185 | 901 | 1647 | *.547 | 459 | 579 | .793 | 281 | 836 | 1117 | 170 | 88 | 246 | ... | *2261 | 15.1 | 2.3 | *30.6 |
| 74-75—Buffalo ............ | 82 | *3539 | *1095 | 2138 | .512 | 641 | *796 | .805 | 307 | 848 | *1155 | 179 | 92 | 174 | ... | *2831 | 14.1 | 2.2 | *34.5 |
| 75-76—Buffalo ............ | 78 | 3328 | *934 | *1918 | .487 | *559 | *734 | .762 | 241 | 724 | 965 | 315 | 93 | 160 | ... | *2427 | 12.4 | 4.0 | *31.1 |
| 76-77—Buff.-Knicks ... | 72 | 2798 | 740 | 1445 | .512 | 381 | 516 | .738 | 199 | 727 | 926 | 205 | 77 | 99 | ... | 1861 | 12.9 | 2.8 | 25.8 |
| 77-78—New York ........ | 79 | 3182 | 814 | 1564 | .520 | 469 | 645 | .727 | 236 | 774 | 1010 | 298 | 105 | 126 | 346 | 2097 | 12.8 | 3.8 | 26.5 |
| 78-79—N.Y.-Boston ... | 60 | 2231 | 596 | 1127 | .529 | 295 | 450 | .656 | 130 | 390 | 520 | 168 | 74 | 67 | 217 | 1487 | 8.7 | 2.8 | 24.8 |
| 79-80—Detroit ............ | 58 | 2097 | 492 | 1025 | .480 | 235 | 322 | .730 | 100 | 367 | 467 | 200 | 73 | 65 | 238 | 1222 | 8.1 | 3.4 | 21.1 |
| 80-81—Detroit-N.J. .... | 16 | 321 | 68 | 157 | .433 | 29 | 41 | .707 | 17 | 50 | 67 | 30 | 17 | 13 | 32 | 165 | 4.2 | 1.9 | 10.3 |
| 81-82—Los Angeles.... | 41 | 746 | 151 | 330 | .458 | 90 | 126 | .714 | 45 | 114 | 159 | 32 | 22 | 36 | 51 | 392 | 3.9 | 0.8 | 9.6 |
| 82-83—Los Angeles .... | 47 | 1019 | 292 | 562 | .520 | 119 | 163 | .730 | 76 | 171 | 247 | 39 | 40 | 40 | 68 | 703 | 5.3 | 0.8 | 15.0 |
| 83-84—Los Angeles .... | 70 | 1456 | 352 | 748 | .471 | 212 | 264 | .803 | 82 | 207 | 289 | 74 | 42 | 50 | 127 | 916 | 4.1 | 1.1 | 13.1 |
| 84-85—L.A. Lakers ..... | 66 | 1254 | 284 | 546 | .520 | 122 | 162 | .753 | 79 | 216 | 295 | 67 | 18 | 53 | 95 | 690 | 4.5 | 1.0 | 10.5 |
| 85-86—Philadelphia .... | 29 | 609 | 116 | 251 | .462 | 62 | 81 | .765 | 25 | 78 | 103 | 35 | 10 | 18 | 49 | 294 | 3.6 | 1.2 | 10.1 |
| **Totals ........................** | 852 | 28327 | 7420 | 14751 | .503 | 3944 | 5229 | .754 | ... | ... | 8048 | 1951 | 751 | 1147 | 1223 | 18787 | 9.4 | 2.3 | 22.1 |

Three-point field goals: 1979-80, 3-for-24 (.125). 1980-81, 0-for-1. 1981-82, 0-for-5. 1982-83, 0-for-1. 1983-84, 0-for-5. 1984-85, 0-for-1. Totals, 3-for-37 (.081).

Personal fouls/disqualifications: 1973-74, 252/3. 1974-75, 278/3. 1975-76, 295/5. 1976-77, 262/3. 1977-78, 297/6. 1978-79, 189/3. 1979-80, 178/3. 1980-81, 38/0. 1981-82, 109/1. 1982-83, 153/2. 1983-84, 182/0. 1984-85, 170/0. 1985-86, 64/0. Totals, 2726/35.

## NBA PLAYOFF RECORD

| | | | | | | | | REBOUNDS | | | | | | | | AVERAGES | | |
|---|---|---|---|---|---|---|---|---|---|---|---|---|---|---|---|---|---|---|
| Season Team | G | Min. | FGM | FGA | Pct. | FTM | FTA | Pct. | Off. | Def. | Tot. | Ast. | St. | Blk. | TO | Pts. | RPG | APG | PPG |
| 73-74—Buffalo ............ | 6 | 271 | 76 | 159 | .478 | 38 | 47 | .809 | 14 | 68 | 82 | 9 | 6 | 13 | ... | 190 | 13.7 | 1.5 | 31.7 |
| 74-75—Buffalo ............ | 7 | 327 | 104 | 216 | .481 | 54 | 73 | .740 | 25 | 69 | 94 | 10 | 6 | 19 | ... | 262 | 13.4 | 1.4 | 37.4 |
| 75-76—Buffalo ............ | 9 | 406 | 97 | 215 | .451 | 58 | 82 | .707 | 31 | 97 | 128 | 29 | 7 | 18 | ... | 252 | 14.2 | 3.2 | 28.0 |
| 77-78—New York ........ | 6 | 238 | 61 | 126 | .484 | 21 | 35 | .600 | 11 | 47 | 58 | 23 | 7 | 12 | 23 | 143 | 9.7 | 3.8 | 23.8 |
| 81-82—Los Angeles.... | 14 | 388 | 101 | 179 | .564 | 32 | 47 | .681 | 21 | 74 | 95 | 22 | 10 | 21 | 35 | 234 | 6.8 | 1.6 | 16.7 |
| 82-83—Los Angeles .... | 8 | 166 | 37 | 84 | .440 | 11 | 14 | .786 | 15 | 31 | 46 | 5 | 11 | 10 | 14 | 87 | 5.8 | 0.6 | 10.9 |
| 83-84—Los Angeles .... | 20 | 447 | 111 | 215 | .516 | 57 | 81 | .704 | 30 | 78 | 108 | 12 | 12 | 27 | 39 | 279 | 5.4 | 0.6 | 14.0 |
| 84-85—L.A. Lakers ..... | 19 | 398 | 91 | 193 | .472 | 35 | 47 | .745 | 25 | 61 | 86 | 15 | 9 | 26 | 32 | 217 | 4.5 | 0.8 | 11.4 |
| 85-86—Philadelphia .... | 5 | 73 | 20 | 36 | .556 | 14 | 16 | .875 | 8 | 6 | 14 | 2 | 4 | 5 | 2 | 54 | 2.8 | 0.4 | 10.8 |
| **Totals ......................** | 94 | 2714 | 698 | 1423 | .491 | 320 | 442 | .724 | 180 | 531 | 711 | 127 | 72 | 151 | 145 | 1718 | 7.6 | 1.4 | 18.3 |

Three-point field goals: 1982-83, 2-for-6 (.333). 1983-84, 0-for-1. 1984-85, 0-for-1. Totals, 2-for-8 (.250).

Personal fouls/disqualifications: 1973-74, 25/1. 1974-75, 29/1. 1975-76, 37/3. 1977-78, 19/0. 1981-82, 43/2. 1982-83, 23/0. 1983-84, 60/0. 1984-85, 66/2. 1985-86, 13/0. Totals, 318/9.

## NBA ALL-STAR GAME RECORD

| | | | | | | | | REBOUNDS | | | | | | | | |
|---|---|---|---|---|---|---|---|---|---|---|---|---|---|---|---|---|
| Season   Team | Min. | FGM | FGA | Pct. | FTM | FTA | Pct. | Off. | Def. | Tot. | Ast. | PF | Dq. | St. | Blk. | TO | Pts. |
| 1974—Buffalo ................. | 13 | 3 | 4 | .750 | 5 | 8 | .625 | 1 | 2 | 3 | 1 | 4 | 0 | 0 | 1 | ... | 11 |
| 1975—Buffalo ................. | 26 | 4 | 9 | .444 | 3 | 3 | 1.000 | 4 | 2 | 6 | 2 | 4 | 0 | 0 | 0 | ... | 11 |
| 1976—Buffalo ................. | 29 | 10 | 14 | .714 | 2 | 4 | .500 | 2 | 5 | 7 | 1 | 5 | 0 | 0 | 0 | ... | 22 |
| 1977—N.Y. Knicks........... | 38 | 13 | 23 | .565 | 4 | 4 | 1.000 | 3 | 7 | 10 | 2 | 3 | 0 | 3 | 1 | ... | 30 |
| 1978—New York .............. | 20 | 7 | 14 | .500 | 0 | 0 | ... | 3 | 1 | 4 | 0 | 2 | 0 | 1 | 0 | 3 | 14 |
| **Totals...........................** | 126 | 37 | 64 | .578 | 14 | 19 | .737 | 13 | 17 | 30 | 6 | 18 | 0 | 4 | 2 | 3 | 88 |

## ITALIAN LEAGUE RECORD

| | | | | | | | | | | | | AVERAGES | | |
|---|---|---|---|---|---|---|---|---|---|---|---|---|---|---|
| Season Team | G | Min. | FGM | FGA | Pct. | FTM | FTA | Pct. | Reb. | Ast. | Pts. | RPG | APG | PPG |
| 86-87—Tracer Milan ................. | 38 | 1320 | 387 | 730 | .530 | 205 | 268 | .765 | 388 | 54 | 991 | 10.2 | 1.4 | 26.1 |
| 87-88—Tracer Milan ................. | 30 | 1064 | 325 | 561 | .579 | 175 | 211 | .829 | 260 | 56 | 838 | 8.7 | 1.9 | 27.9 |
| 88-89—Philips Milano ................ | 27 | 891 | 173 | 470 | .368 | 132 | 164 | .805 | 223 | 48 | 505 | 8.3 | 1.8 | 18.7 |
| 89-90—Philips Milano ................ | 28 | 906 | 296 | 523 | .566 | 160 | 195 | .821 | 219 | 37 | 764 | 7.8 | 1.3 | 27.3 |
| 90-91—Filanto Forli .................. | 23 | 858 | 278 | 490 | .567 | 179 | 225 | .796 | 219 | 28 | 759 | 9.5 | 1.2 | 33.0 |
| 91-92—Filanto Forli .................. | 20 | 700 | 199 | 399 | .499 | 129 | 159 | .811 | 188 | 20 | 538 | 9.4 | 1.0 | 26.9 |
| 92-93—Teamsystem Fabriano .... | 2 | 58 | 14 | 27 | .519 | 12 | 17 | .706 | 13 | 2 | 44 | 6.5 | 1.0 | 22.0 |
| **Totals ........................** | 168 | 5797 | 1672 | 3200 | .523 | 992 | 1239 | .801 | 1510 | 245 | 4439 | 8.7 | 1.4 | 26.6 |

ALL-TIME GREAT PLAYERS

# McGINNIS, GEORGE      F

**PERSONAL:** Born August 12, 1950, in Indianapolis. ... 6-8/235 (2,03/106,6). ... Full name: George F. McGinnis.
**HIGH SCHOOL:** George Washington (Indianapolis).
**COLLEGE:** Indiana.
**TRANSACTIONS:** Signed as free agent after sophomore season by Indiana Pacers of American Basketball Association in lieu of 1972 first-round draft choice (1971). ... Selected by Philadelphia 76ers in second round (22nd pick overall) of 1973 NBA Draft. ... Invoked proviso to buy his way out of contract with Pacers. ... Signed by 76ers (July 10, 1975) after Commissioner Larry O'Brien revoked contract McGinnis had signed with New York Knicks (May 30, 1975). ... Traded by 76ers to Denver Nuggets for F Bobby Jones and G Ralph Simpson (August 16, 1978). ... Traded by Nuggets to Pacers for F Alex English and 1980 first-round draft choice (February 1, 1980). ... Waived by Pacers (October 27, 1982).

## COLLEGIATE RECORD

| Season Team | G | Min. | FGM | FGA | Pct. | FTM | FTA | Pct. | Reb. | Ast. | Pts. | RPG | APG | PPG |
|---|---|---|---|---|---|---|---|---|---|---|---|---|---|---|
| 69-70—Indiana‡ | | | | | | Did not play—ineligible. | | | | | | | | |
| 70-71—Indiana | 24 | ... | 283 | 615 | .460 | 153 | 249 | .614 | 352 | 66 | 719 | 14.7 | 2.8 | 30.0 |
| Varsity totals | 24 | ... | 283 | 615 | .460 | 153 | 249 | .614 | 352 | 66 | 719 | 14.7 | 2.8 | 30.0 |

## ABA REGULAR-SEASON RECORD

**NOTES:** ABA co-Most Valuable Player (1975). ... ABA All-Star first team (1974, 1975). ... ABA All-Star second team (1973). ... ABA All-Rookie team (1972). ... Member of ABA championship team (1972, 1973).

| Season Team | G | Min. | 2-POINT FGM | FGA | Pct. | 3-POINT FGM | FGA | Pct. | FTM | FTA | Pct. | Reb. | Ast. | Pts. | RPG | APG | PPG |
|---|---|---|---|---|---|---|---|---|---|---|---|---|---|---|---|---|---|
| 71-72—Indiana | 73 | 2179 | 459 | 961 | .478 | 6 | 38 | .158 | 298 | 462 | .645 | 711 | 137 | 1234 | 9.7 | 1.9 | 16.9 |
| 72-73—Indiana | 82 | 3347 | 860 | 1723 | .499 | 8 | 32 | .250 | 517 | *778 | .665 | 1022 | 205 | 2261 | 12.5 | 2.5 | 27.6 |
| 73-74—Indiana | 80 | 3266 | 784 | 1652 | .475 | 5 | 34 | .147 | 488 | *715 | .683 | 1197 | 267 | 2071 | 15.0 | 3.3 | 25.9 |
| 74-75—Indiana | 79 | 3193 | 811 | 1759 | .461 | 62 | 175 | .354 | *545 | *753 | .724 | 1126 | 495 | *2353 | 14.3 | 6.3 | *29.8 |
| Totals | 314 | 11985 | 2914 | 6095 | .478 | 81 | 279 | .290 | 1848 | 2708 | .682 | 4056 | 1104 | 7919 | 12.9 | 3.5 | 25.2 |

## ABA PLAYOFF RECORD

**NOTES:** ABA Playoff Most Valuable Player (1973).

| Season Team | G | Min. | 2-POINT FGM | FGA | Pct. | 3-POINT FGM | FGA | Pct. | FTM | FTA | Pct. | Reb. | Ast. | Pts. | RPG | APG | PPG |
|---|---|---|---|---|---|---|---|---|---|---|---|---|---|---|---|---|---|
| 71-72—Indiana | 20 | 633 | 102 | 246 | .415 | 4 | 15 | .267 | 94 | 150 | .627 | 227 | 52 | 310 | 11.4 | 2.6 | 15.5 |
| 72-73—Indiana | 18 | 731 | 161 | 352 | .457 | 0 | 5 | .000 | 109 | 149 | .732 | 222 | 39 | 431 | 12.3 | 2.2 | 23.9 |
| 73-74—Indiana | 14 | 585 | 117 | 254 | .461 | 2 | 7 | .286 | 96 | 129 | .744 | 166 | 47 | 336 | 11.9 | 3.4 | 24.0 |
| 74-75—Indiana | 18 | 731 | 190 | 382 | .497 | 23 | 73 | .315 | 132 | 192 | .688 | 286 | 148 | 581 | 15.9 | 8.2 | 32.3 |
| Totals | 70 | 2680 | 570 | 1234 | .462 | 29 | 100 | .290 | 431 | 620 | .695 | 901 | 286 | 1658 | 12.9 | 4.1 | 23.7 |

## ABA ALL-STAR GAME RECORD

| Season Team | Min. | 2-POINT FGM | FGA | Pct. | 3-POINT FGM | FGA | Pct. | FTM | FTA | Pct. | Reb. | Ast. | Pts. |
|---|---|---|---|---|---|---|---|---|---|---|---|---|---|
| 1972—Indiana | 34 | 10 | 14 | .714 | 0 | 1 | .000 | 3 | 6 | .500 | 15 | 2 | 23 |
| 1973—Indiana | 30 | 7 | 21 | .333 | 0 | 0 | ... | 0 | 0 | ... | 11 | 1 | 14 |
| 1974—Indiana | 32 | 6 | 13 | .462 | 0 | 1 | .000 | 6 | 11 | .545 | 12 | 5 | 18 |
| Totals | 96 | 23 | 48 | .479 | 0 | 2 | .000 | 9 | 17 | .529 | 38 | 8 | 55 |

## NBA REGULAR-SEASON RECORD

**HONORS:** All-NBA first team (1976). ... All-NBA second team (1977).
**NOTES:** Tied for NBA lead with 12 disqualifications (1980).

| Season Team | G | Min. | FGM | FGA | Pct. | FTM | FTA | Pct. | REBOUNDS Off. | Def. | Tot. | Ast. | St. | Blk. | TO | Pts. | RPG | APG | PPG |
|---|---|---|---|---|---|---|---|---|---|---|---|---|---|---|---|---|---|---|---|
| 75-76—Philadelphia | 77 | 2946 | 647 | 1552 | .417 | 475 | 642 | .740 | 260 | 707 | 967 | 359 | 198 | 41 | ... | 1769 | 12.6 | 4.7 | 23.0 |
| 76-77—Philadelphia | 79 | 2769 | 659 | 1439 | .458 | 372 | 546 | .681 | 324 | 587 | 911 | 302 | 163 | 37 | ... | 1690 | 11.5 | 3.8 | 21.4 |
| 77-78—Philadelphia | 78 | 2533 | 588 | 1270 | .463 | 411 | 574 | .716 | 282 | 528 | 810 | 294 | 137 | 27 | 312 | 1587 | 10.4 | 3.8 | 20.3 |
| 78-79—Denver | 76 | 2552 | 603 | 1273 | .474 | 509 | 765 | .665 | 256 | 608 | 864 | 283 | 129 | 52 | *346 | 1715 | 11.4 | 3.7 | 22.6 |
| 79-80—Denver-Ind. | 73 | 2208 | 400 | 886 | .451 | 270 | 488 | .553 | 222 | 477 | 699 | 333 | 101 | 23 | 281 | 1072 | 9.6 | 4.6 | 14.7 |
| 80-81—Indiana | 69 | 1845 | 344 | 768 | .453 | 207 | 385 | .538 | 164 | 364 | 528 | 210 | 99 | 28 | 221 | 903 | 7.7 | 3.0 | 13.1 |
| 81-82—Indiana | 76 | 1341 | 141 | 378 | .373 | 72 | 159 | .453 | 93 | 305 | 398 | 204 | 96 | 28 | 131 | 354 | 5.2 | 2.7 | 4.7 |
| Totals | 528 | 16194 | 3386 | 7566 | .448 | 2316 | 3559 | .651 | 1601 | 3576 | 5177 | 1985 | 923 | 236 | 1291 | 9090 | 9.8 | 3.8 | 17.2 |

Three-point field goals: 1979-80, 2-for-15 (.133). 1980-81, 0-for-7. 1981-82, 0-for-3. Totals, 2-for-25 (.080).
Personal fouls/disqualifications: 1975-76, 334/13. 1976-77, 299/4. 1977-78, 287/6. 1978-79, 321/16. 1979-80, 303/12. 1980-81, 242/3. 1981-82, 98/4. Totals, 1884/58.

## NBA PLAYOFF RECORD

| Season Team | G | Min. | FGM | FGA | Pct. | FTM | FTA | Pct. | REBOUNDS Off. | Def. | Tot. | Ast. | St. | Blk. | TO | Pts. | RPG | APG | PPG |
|---|---|---|---|---|---|---|---|---|---|---|---|---|---|---|---|---|---|---|---|
| 75-76—Philadelphia | 3 | 120 | 29 | 61 | .475 | 11 | 18 | .611 | 9 | 32 | 41 | 12 | 1 | 4 | ... | 69 | 13.7 | 4.0 | 23.0 |
| 76-77—Philadelphia | 19 | 603 | 102 | 273 | .374 | 65 | 114 | .570 | 62 | 136 | 198 | 69 | 23 | 6 | ... | 269 | 10.4 | 3.6 | 14.2 |
| 77-78—Philadelphia | 10 | 273 | 53 | 125 | .424 | 41 | 49 | .837 | 24 | 54 | 78 | 30 | 15 | 1 | 38 | 147 | 7.8 | 3.0 | 14.7 |
| 80-81—Indiana | 2 | 39 | 3 | 15 | .200 | 4 | 8 | .500 | 2 | 8 | 10 | 7 | 2 | 0 | 5 | 10 | 5.0 | 3.5 | 5.0 |
| Totals | 34 | 1035 | 187 | 474 | .395 | 121 | 189 | .640 | 97 | 230 | 327 | 118 | 41 | 11 | 43 | 495 | 9.6 | 3.5 | 14.6 |

Personal fouls/disqualifications: 1975-76, 14/1. 1976-77, 83/2. 1977-78, 40/1. 1980-81, 6/0. Totals, 143/4.

## NBA ALL-STAR GAME RECORD

| Season Team | Min. | FGM | FGA | Pct. | FTM | FTA | Pct. | REBOUNDS Off. | Def. | Tot. | Ast. | PF | Dq. | St. | Blk. | TO | Pts. |
|---|---|---|---|---|---|---|---|---|---|---|---|---|---|---|---|---|---|
| 1976—Philadelphia | 19 | 4 | 9 | .444 | 2 | 4 | .500 | 1 | 6 | 7 | 2 | 2 | 0 | 0 | 0 | ... | 10 |
| 1977—Philadelphia | 26 | 2 | 9 | .222 | 0 | 2 | .000 | 5 | 2 | 7 | 2 | 3 | 0 | 4 | 0 | ... | 4 |
| 1979—Denver | 25 | 5 | 12 | .417 | 6 | 11 | .545 | 2 | 4 | 6 | 3 | 4 | 0 | 5 | 0 | 0 | 16 |
| Totals | 70 | 11 | 30 | .367 | 8 | 17 | .471 | 8 | 12 | 20 | 7 | 9 | 0 | 9 | 0 | 0 | 30 |

### COMBINED ABA AND NBA REGULAR-SEASON RECORDS

| | | | | | | | | | REBOUNDS | | | | | | | AVERAGES | | |
|---|---|---|---|---|---|---|---|---|---|---|---|---|---|---|---|---|---|---|
| | G | Min. | FGM | FGA | Pct. | FTM | FTA | Pct. | Off. | Def. | Tot. | Ast. | Stl. | Blk. | TO | Pts. | RPG | APG | PPG |
| Totals ........... | 842 | 28179 | 6381 | 13940 | .458 | 4164 | 6267 | .664 | ... | ... | 9233 | 3089 | 1448 | 332 | ... | 17009 | 11.0 | 3.7 | 20.2 |

Three-point field goals: 83-for-304 (.273).
Personal fouls/disqualifications: 3220.

# McGUIRE, DICK       G

**PERSONAL:** Born January 25, 1926, in New York. ... 6-0/180 (1,83/81,6). ... Full name: Richard Joseph McGuire. ... Brother of Al McGuire, guard with New York Knicks (1951-52 through 1953-54) and Baltimore Bullets (1954-55); and head coach, Belmont Abbey (1957-58 through 1963-64) and Marquette University (1964-65 through 1976-77). ... Nickname: Tricky Dick.
**HIGH SCHOOL:** LaSalle Academy (New York).
**COLLEGE:** St. John's and Dartmouth.
**TRANSACTIONS:** Selected by New York Knicks in first round of 1949 Basketball Association of America Draft. ... Traded by Knicks to Detroit Pistons for 1958 first-round draft choice (April 3, 1957).
**CAREER NOTES:** Director of scouting, New York Knicks (1967-68 to present).
**CAREER HONORS:** Elected to Naismith Memorial Basketball Hall of Fame (1993).

### COLLEGIATE RECORD

**NOTES:** THE SPORTING NEWS All-America second team (1944).

| | | | | | | | | | | | | AVERAGES | | |
|---|---|---|---|---|---|---|---|---|---|---|---|---|---|---|
| Season Team | G | Min. | FGM | FGA | Pct. | FTM | FTA | Pct. | Reb. | Ast. | Pts. | RPG | APG | PPG |
| 43-44—St. John's ...................... | 16 | ... | 43 | ... | ... | 20 | ... | ... | ... | ... | 106 | ... | ... | 6.6 |
| 44-45— | | | | | | Did not play—in military service. | | | | | | | | |
| 45-46— | | | | | | Did not play—in military service. | | | | | | | | |
| 46-47—St. John's ...................... | 21 | ... | 63 | ... | ... | 37 | ... | ... | ... | ... | 163 | ... | ... | 7.8 |
| 47-48—St. John's ...................... | 22 | ... | 75 | ... | ... | 72 | 115 | .626 | ... | ... | 222 | ... | ... | 10.1 |
| 48-49—St. John's ...................... | 25 | ... | 121 | ... | ... | 72 | 125 | .576 | ... | ... | 314 | ... | ... | 12.6 |
| Totals ...................... | 84 | ... | 302 | ... | ... | 201 | ... | ... | ... | ... | 805 | ... | ... | 9.6 |

### NBA REGULAR-SEASON RECORD

**HONORS:** All-NBA second team (1951).

| | | | | | | | | | | | | | | AVERAGES | | |
|---|---|---|---|---|---|---|---|---|---|---|---|---|---|---|---|---|---|
| Season Team | G | Min. | FGM | FGA | Pct. | FTM | FTA | Pct. | Reb. | Ast. | PF | Dq. | Pts. | RPG | APG | PPG |
| 49-50—New York .......................... | 68 | ... | 190 | 563 | .337 | 204 | 313 | .652 | ... | *386 | 160 | ... | 584 | ... | 5.7 | 8.6 |
| 50-51—New York .......................... | 64 | ... | 179 | 482 | .371 | 179 | 276 | .649 | 334 | 400 | 154 | 2 | 537 | 5.2 | †6.3 | 8.4 |
| 51-52—New York .......................... | 64 | 2018 | 204 | 474 | .430 | 183 | 290 | .631 | 332 | 388 | 181 | 4 | 591 | 5.2 | 6.1 | 9.2 |
| 52-53—New York .......................... | 61 | 1783 | 142 | 373 | .381 | 153 | 269 | .569 | 280 | 296 | 172 | 3 | 437 | 4.6 | 4.9 | 7.2 |
| 53-54—New York .......................... | 68 | 2343 | 201 | 493 | .408 | 220 | 345 | .638 | 310 | 354 | 179 | 3 | 622 | 4.6 | 5.2 | 9.1 |
| 54-55—New York .......................... | 71 | 2310 | 226 | 581 | .389 | 195 | 303 | .644 | 322 | 542 | 143 | 0 | 647 | 4.5 | 7.6 | 9.1 |
| 55-56—New York .......................... | 62 | 1685 | 152 | 438 | .347 | 121 | 193 | .627 | 220 | 362 | 146 | 0 | 425 | 3.5 | 5.8 | 6.9 |
| 56-57—New York .......................... | 72 | 1191 | 140 | 366 | .383 | 105 | 163 | .644 | 146 | 222 | 103 | 0 | 385 | 2.0 | 3.1 | 5.3 |
| 57-58—Detroit .......................... | 69 | 2311 | 203 | 544 | .373 | 150 | 225 | .667 | 291 | 454 | 178 | 0 | 556 | 4.2 | 6.6 | 8.1 |
| 58-59—Detroit .......................... | 71 | 2063 | 232 | 543 | .427 | 191 | 258 | .740 | 285 | 443 | 147 | 1 | 655 | 4.0 | 6.2 | 9.2 |
| 59-60—Detroit .......................... | 68 | 1466 | 179 | 402 | .445 | 124 | 201 | .617 | 264 | 358 | 112 | 0 | 482 | 3.9 | 5.3 | 7.1 |
| Totals.......................... | 738 | ... | 2048 | 5259 | .389 | 1825 | 2836 | .644 | ... | 4205 | 1695 | ... | 5921 | ... | 5.7 | 8.0 |

### NBA PLAYOFF RECORD

| | | | | | | | | | | | | | | AVERAGES | | |
|---|---|---|---|---|---|---|---|---|---|---|---|---|---|---|---|---|---|
| Season Team | G | Min. | FGM | FGA | Pct. | FTM | FTA | Pct. | Reb. | Ast. | PF | Dq. | Pts. | RPG | APG | PPG |
| 49-50—New York .......................... | 5 | ... | 22 | 52 | .423 | 19 | 26 | .731 | ... | 27 | 21 | ... | 63 | ... | 5.4 | 12.6 |
| 50-51—New York .......................... | 14 | ... | 25 | 80 | .313 | 24 | 53 | .453 | 83 | 78 | 50 | 1 | 74 | 5.9 | 5.6 | 5.3 |
| 51-52—New York .......................... | 14 | 546 | 48 | 107 | .449 | 49 | 86 | .570 | 71 | 90 | 46 | 1 | 145 | 5.1 | 6.4 | 10.4 |
| 52-53—New York .......................... | 11 | 360 | 24 | 59 | .407 | 35 | 55 | .636 | 63 | 70 | 25 | 0 | 83 | 5.7 | 6.4 | 7.5 |
| 53-54—New York .......................... | 4 | 68 | 4 | 16 | .250 | 3 | 5 | .600 | 4 | 5 | 12 | 0 | 11 | 1.0 | 1.3 | 2.8 |
| 54-55—New York .......................... | 3 | 75 | 6 | 19 | .316 | 8 | 12 | .667 | 9 | 12 | 7 | 0 | 20 | 3.0 | 4.0 | 6.7 |
| 57-58—Detroit .......................... | 7 | 236 | 25 | 60 | .417 | 17 | 24 | .708 | 33 | 40 | 13 | 0 | 67 | 4.7 | 5.7 | 9.6 |
| 58-59—Detroit .......................... | 3 | 109 | 20 | 32 | .625 | 7 | 11 | .636 | 17 | 19 | 10 | 0 | 47 | 5.7 | 6.3 | 15.7 |
| 59-60—Detroit .......................... | 2 | 42 | 5 | 12 | .417 | 1 | 3 | .333 | 4 | 9 | 3 | 0 | 11 | 2.0 | 4.5 | 5.5 |
| Totals.......................... | 63 | ... | 179 | 437 | .410 | 163 | 275 | .593 | ... | 350 | 187 | ... | 521 | ... | 5.6 | 8.3 |

### NBA ALL-STAR GAME RECORD

| Season Team | Min. | FGM | FGA | Pct. | FTM | FTA | Pct. | Reb | Ast. | PF | Dq. | Pts. |
|---|---|---|---|---|---|---|---|---|---|---|---|---|
| 1951—New York ...................... | ... | 3 | 4 | .750 | 0 | 0 | ... | 5 | 10 | 2 | 0 | 6 |
| 1952—New York ...................... | 18 | 0 | 0 | ... | 1 | 3 | .333 | 1 | 4 | 0 | 0 | 1 |
| 1954—New York ...................... | 24 | 2 | 5 | .400 | 0 | 0 | ... | 4 | 2 | 1 | 0 | 4 |
| 1955—New York ...................... | 25 | 1 | 2 | .500 | 1 | 2 | .500 | 3 | 6 | 1 | 0 | 3 |
| 1956—New York ...................... | 29 | 2 | 9 | .222 | 2 | 5 | .400 | 0 | 3 | 1 | 0 | 6 |
| 1958—Detroit ...................... | 31 | 2 | 4 | .500 | 0 | 0 | ... | 7 | 10 | 4 | 0 | 4 |
| 1959—Detroit ...................... | 24 | 2 | 7 | .286 | 1 | 2 | .500 | 3 | 3 | 2 | 0 | 5 |
| Totals ...................... | ... | 12 | 31 | .387 | 5 | 12 | .417 | 23 | 38 | 11 | 0 | 29 |

### NBA COACHING RECORD

**BACKGROUND:** Player/head coach, Detroit Pistons (December 28, 1959-remainder of season).

| | REGULAR SEASON | | | | PLAYOFFS | | |
|---|---|---|---|---|---|---|---|
| Season Team | W | L | Pct. | Finish | W | L | Pct. |
| 59-60—Detroit.......................................... | 17 | 24 | .415 | 2nd/Western Division | 0 | 2 | .000 |
| 60-61—Detroit.......................................... | 34 | 45 | .430 | 3rd/Western Division | 2 | 3 | .400 |

| Season Team | W | L | Pct. | Finish | | W | L | Pct. |
|---|---|---|---|---|---|---|---|---|
| | | | | REGULAR SEASON | | | PLAYOFFS | |
| 61-62—Detroit | 37 | 43 | .463 | 3rd/Western Division | | 5 | 5 | .500 |
| 62-63—Detroit | 34 | 46 | .425 | 3rd/Western Division | | 1 | 3 | .250 |
| 65-66—New York | 24 | 35 | .407 | 4th/Eastern Division | | — | — | — |
| 66-67—New York | 36 | 45 | .444 | 4th/Eastern Division | | 1 | 3 | .250 |
| 67-68—New York | 15 | 22 | .405 | | | — | — | — |
| Totals (7 years) | 197 | 260 | .431 | Totals (5 years) | | 9 | 16 | .360 |

**NOTES:**

1959—Replaced Detroit head coach Red Rocha (December 28), with record of 13-21.

1960—Lost to Minneapolis in Western Division Semifinals.

1961—Lost to Los Angeles in Western Division Semifinals.

1962—Defeated Cincinnati, 3-1, in Western Division Semifinals; lost to Los Angeles, 4-2, in Western Division Finals.

1963—Lost to St. Louis in Western Division Semifinals.

1965—Replaced Harry Gallatin as New York head coach (November 29), with record of 6-15 and in fourth place.

1967—Lost to Boston in Eastern Division Semifinals. Replaced as New York head coach by Red Holzman (December).

# McHALE, KEVIN          F/C

**PERSONAL:** Born December 19, 1957, in Hibbing, Minn. ... 6-10/225 (2,08/102,1). ... Full name: Kevin Edward McHale.
**HIGH SCHOOL:** Hibbing (Minn.).
**COLLEGE:** Minnesota.
**TRANSACTIONS:** Selected by Boston Celtics in first round (third pick overall) of 1980 NBA Draft.
**CAREER NOTES:** Assistant general manager, Minnesota Timberwolves (1994-95). ... Vice president of basketball operations, Timberwolves (May 1995 to present).
**CAREER HONORS:** One of the 50 Greatest Players in NBA History (1996). ... Elected to Naismith Memorial Basketball Hall of Fame (1999).
**MISCELLANEOUS:** Member of NBA championship team (1981, 1984, 1986).

## COLLEGIATE RECORD

| Season Team | G | Min. | FGM | FGA | Pct. | FTM | FTA | Pct. | Reb. | Ast. | Pts. | RPG | APG | PPG |
|---|---|---|---|---|---|---|---|---|---|---|---|---|---|---|
| | | | | | | | | | | | | AVERAGES | | |
| 76-77—Minnesota | 27 | ... | 133 | 241 | .552 | 58 | 77 | .753 | 218 | 36 | 324 | 8.1 | 1.3 | 12.0 |
| 77-78—Minnesota | 26 | ... | 143 | 242 | .591 | 54 | 77 | .701 | 192 | 27 | 340 | 7.4 | 1.0 | 13.1 |
| 78-79—Minnesota | 27 | ... | 202 | 391 | .517 | 79 | 96 | .823 | 259 | 33 | 483 | 9.6 | 1.2 | 17.9 |
| 79-80—Minnesota | 32 | ... | 236 | 416 | .567 | 85 | 107 | .794 | 281 | 28 | 557 | 8.8 | 0.9 | 17.4 |
| Totals | 112 | ... | 714 | 1290 | .553 | 276 | 357 | .773 | 950 | 124 | 1704 | 8.5 | 1.1 | 15.2 |

## NBA REGULAR-SEASON RECORD

**HONORS:** NBA Sixth Man Award (1984, 1985). ... All-NBA first team (1987). ... NBA All-Defensive first team (1986, 1987, 1988). ... NBA All-Defensive second team (1983, 1989, 1990). ... NBA All-Rookie team (1981).

| Season Team | G | Min. | FGM | FGA | Pct. | FTM | FTA | Pct. | Off. | Def. | Tot. | Ast. | St. | Blk. | TO | Pts. | RPG | APG | PPG |
|---|---|---|---|---|---|---|---|---|---|---|---|---|---|---|---|---|---|---|---|
| | | | | | | | | | | REBOUNDS | | | | | | | | AVERAGES | |
| 80-81—Boston | 82 | 1645 | 355 | 666 | .533 | 108 | 159 | .679 | 155 | 204 | 359 | 55 | 27 | 151 | 110 | 818 | 4.4 | 0.7 | 10.0 |
| 81-82—Boston | 82 | 2332 | 465 | 875 | .531 | 187 | 248 | .754 | 191 | 365 | 556 | 91 | 30 | 185 | 137 | 1117 | 6.8 | 1.1 | 13.6 |
| 82-83—Boston | 82 | 2345 | 483 | 893 | .541 | 193 | 269 | .717 | 215 | 338 | 553 | 104 | 34 | 192 | 159 | 1159 | 6.7 | 1.3 | 14.1 |
| 83-84—Boston | 82 | 2577 | 587 | 1055 | .556 | 336 | 439 | .765 | 208 | 402 | 610 | 104 | 23 | 126 | 150 | 1511 | 7.4 | 1.3 | 18.4 |
| 84-85—Boston | 79 | 2653 | 605 | 1062 | .570 | 355 | 467 | .760 | 229 | 483 | 712 | 141 | 28 | 120 | 157 | 1565 | 9.0 | 1.8 | 19.8 |
| 85-86—Boston | 68 | 2397 | 561 | 978 | .574 | 326 | 420 | .776 | 171 | 380 | 551 | 181 | 29 | 134 | 149 | 1448 | 8.1 | 2.7 | 21.3 |
| 86-87—Boston | 77 | 3060 | 790 | 1307 | *.604 | 428 | 512 | .836 | 247 | 516 | 763 | 198 | 38 | 172 | 197 | 2008 | 9.9 | 2.6 | 26.1 |
| 87-88—Boston | 64 | 2390 | 550 | 911 | *.604 | 346 | 434 | .797 | 159 | 377 | 536 | 171 | 27 | 92 | 141 | 1446 | 8.4 | 2.7 | 22.6 |
| 88-89—Boston | 78 | 2876 | 661 | 1211 | .546 | 436 | 533 | .818 | 223 | 414 | 637 | 172 | 26 | 97 | 196 | 1758 | 8.2 | 2.2 | 22.5 |
| 89-90—Boston | 82 | 2722 | 648 | 1181 | .549 | 393 | 440 | .893 | 201 | 476 | 677 | 172 | 30 | 157 | 183 | 1712 | 8.3 | 2.1 | 20.9 |
| 90-91—Boston | 68 | 2067 | 504 | 912 | .553 | 228 | 275 | .829 | 145 | 335 | 480 | 126 | 25 | 146 | 140 | 1251 | 7.1 | 1.9 | 18.4 |
| 91-92—Boston | 56 | 1398 | 323 | 634 | .509 | 134 | 163 | .822 | 119 | 211 | 330 | 82 | 11 | 59 | 82 | 780 | 5.9 | 1.5 | 13.9 |
| 92-93—Boston | 71 | 1656 | 298 | 649 | .459 | 164 | 195 | .841 | 95 | 263 | 358 | 73 | 16 | 59 | 92 | 762 | 5.0 | 1.0 | 10.7 |
| Totals | 971 | 30118 | 6830 | 12334 | .554 | 3634 | 4554 | .798 | 2358 | 4764 | 7122 | 1670 | 344 | 1690 | 1893 | 17335 | 7.3 | 1.7 | 17.9 |

Three-point field goals: 1980-81, 0-for-2. 1982-83, 0-for-1. 1983-84, 1-for-3 (.333). 1984-85, 0-for-6. 1986-87, 0-for-4. 1988-89, 0-for-4. 1989-90, 23-for-69 (.333). 1990-91, 15-for-37 (.405). 1991-92, 0-for-13. 1992-93, 2-for-18 (.111). Totals, 41-for-157 (.261).

Personal fouls/disqualifications: 1980-81, 260/3. 1981-82, 264/1. 1982-83, 241/3. 1983-84, 243/5. 1984-85, 234/3. 1985-86, 192/2. 1986-87, 240/1. 1987-88, 179/1. 1988-89, 223/2. 1989-90, 250/3. 1990-91, 194/2. 1991-92, 112/1. 1992-93, 126/0. Totals, 2758/27.

## NBA PLAYOFF RECORD

| Season Team | G | Min. | FGM | FGA | Pct. | FTM | FTA | Pct. | Off. | Def. | Tot. | Ast. | St. | Blk. | TO | Pts. | RPG | APG | PPG |
|---|---|---|---|---|---|---|---|---|---|---|---|---|---|---|---|---|---|---|---|
| | | | | | | | | | | REBOUNDS | | | | | | | | AVERAGES | |
| 80-81—Boston | 17 | 296 | 61 | 113 | .540 | 23 | 36 | .639 | 29 | 30 | 59 | 14 | 4 | 25 | 15 | 145 | 3.5 | 0.8 | 8.5 |
| 81-82—Boston | 12 | 344 | 77 | 134 | .575 | 40 | 53 | .755 | 41 | 44 | 85 | 11 | 5 | 27 | 16 | 194 | 7.1 | 0.9 | 16.2 |
| 82-83—Boston | 7 | 177 | 34 | 62 | .548 | 10 | 18 | .556 | 15 | 27 | 42 | 5 | 3 | 7 | 10 | 78 | 6.0 | 0.7 | 11.1 |
| 83-84—Boston | 23 | 702 | 123 | 244 | .504 | 94 | 121 | .777 | 62 | 81 | 143 | 27 | 3 | 35 | 38 | 340 | 6.2 | 1.2 | 14.8 |
| 84-85—Boston | 21 | 837 | 172 | 303 | .568 | 121 | 150 | .807 | 74 | 134 | 208 | 32 | 13 | 46 | 60 | 465 | 9.9 | 1.5 | 22.1 |
| 85-86—Boston | 18 | 715 | 168 | 290 | .579 | 112 | 141 | .794 | 51 | 104 | 155 | 48 | 8 | 43 | 48 | 448 | 8.6 | 2.7 | 24.9 |
| 86-87—Boston | 21 | 827 | 174 | 298 | .584 | 96 | 126 | .762 | 66 | 128 | 194 | 39 | 7 | 30 | 54 | 444 | 9.2 | 1.9 | 21.1 |
| 87-88—Boston | 17 | 716 | 158 | 262 | .603 | 115 | 137 | .839 | 55 | 81 | 136 | 40 | 7 | 30 | 39 | 432 | 8.0 | 2.4 | 25.4 |
| 88-89—Boston | 3 | 115 | 20 | 41 | .488 | 17 | 23 | .739 | 7 | 17 | 24 | 9 | 1 | 2 | 4 | 57 | 8.0 | 3.0 | 19.0 |
| 89-90—Boston | 5 | 192 | 42 | 69 | .609 | 25 | 29 | .862 | 8 | 31 | 39 | 13 | 2 | 10 | 14 | 110 | 7.8 | 2.6 | 22.0 |
| 90-91—Boston | 11 | 376 | 78 | 148 | .527 | 66 | 80 | .825 | 18 | 54 | 72 | 20 | 5 | 14 | 14 | 228 | 6.5 | 1.8 | 20.7 |

| Season Team | G | Min. | FGM | FGA | Pct. | FTM | FTA | Pct. | REBOUNDS Off. | REBOUNDS Def. | REBOUNDS Tot. | Ast. | St. | Blk. | TO | Pts. | AVERAGES RPG | AVERAGES APG | AVERAGES PPG |
|---|---|---|---|---|---|---|---|---|---|---|---|---|---|---|---|---|---|---|---|
| 91-92—Boston | 10 | 306 | 65 | 126 | .516 | 35 | 44 | .795 | 21 | 46 | 67 | 13 | 5 | 5 | 9 | 165 | 6.7 | 1.3 | 16.5 |
| 92-93—Boston | 4 | 113 | 32 | 55 | .582 | 12 | 14 | .857 | 9 | 20 | 29 | 3 | 2 | 7 | 5 | 76 | 7.3 | 0.8 | 19.0 |
| Totals | 169 | 5716 | 1204 | 2145 | .561 | 766 | 972 | .788 | 456 | 797 | 1253 | 274 | 65 | 281 | 326 | 3182 | 7.4 | 1.6 | 18.8 |

Three-point field goals: 1982-83, 0-for-1. 1983-84, 0-for-3. 1985-86, 0-for-1. 1987-88, 1-for-1. 1989-90, 1-for-3 (.333). 1990-91, 6-for-11 (.545). 1991-92, 0-for-1. Totals, 8-for-21 (.381).

Personal fouls/disqualifications: 1980-81, 51/1. 1981-82, 44/0. 1982-83, 16/0. 1983-84, 75/1. 1984-85, 73/3. 1985-86, 64/0. 1986-87, 71/2. 1987-88, 65/1. 1988-89, 13/0. 1989-90, 17/0. 1990-91, 42/0. 1991-92, 34/0. 1992-93, 6/0. Totals, 571/8.

## NBA ALL-STAR GAME RECORD

| Season Team | Min. | FGM | FGA | Pct. | FTM | FTA | Pct. | REBOUNDS Off. | REBOUNDS Def. | REBOUNDS Tot. | Ast. | PF | Dq. | St. | Blk. | TO | Pts. |
|---|---|---|---|---|---|---|---|---|---|---|---|---|---|---|---|---|---|
| 1984—Boston | 11 | 3 | 7 | .429 | 4 | 6 | .667 | 2 | 3 | 5 | 0 | 1 | 0 | 0 | 0 | 2 | 10 |
| 1986—Boston | 20 | 3 | 8 | .375 | 2 | 2 | 1.000 | 3 | 7 | 10 | 2 | 4 | 0 | 0 | 4 | 0 | 8 |
| 1987—Boston | 30 | 7 | 11 | .636 | 2 | 2 | 1.000 | 4 | 3 | 7 | 2 | 5 | 0 | 0 | 4 | 0 | 16 |
| 1988—Boston | 14 | 0 | 1 | .000 | 2 | 2 | 1.000 | 0 | 1 | 1 | 1 | 2 | 0 | 0 | 2 | 2 | 2 |
| 1989—Boston | 16 | 5 | 7 | .714 | 0 | 0 | ... | 1 | 2 | 3 | 0 | 3 | 0 | 0 | 2 | 1 | 10 |
| 1990—Boston | 20 | 6 | 11 | .545 | 0 | 0 | ... | 2 | 6 | 8 | 1 | 4 | 0 | 0 | 0 | 0 | 13 |
| 1991—Boston | 14 | 0 | 3 | .000 | 2 | 2 | 1.000 | 1 | 2 | 3 | 2 | 2 | 0 | 1 | 0 | 0 | 2 |
| Totals | 125 | 24 | 48 | .500 | 12 | 14 | .857 | 13 | 24 | 37 | 8 | 21 | 0 | 1 | 12 | 5 | 61 |

Three-point field goals: 1990, 1-for-1. 1991, 0-for-1. Totals, 1-for-2 (.500).

# MIKAN, GEORGE                    C

**PERSONAL:** Born June 18, 1924, in Joliet, Ill. ... 6-10/245 (2,08/111,1). ... Full name: George Lawrence Mikan Jr. ... Brother of Ed Mikan, forward/center with Chicago Stags of Basketball Association of America (1948-49) and six NBA teams (1949-50 through 1953-54); and father of Larry Mikan, forward with Cleveland Cavaliers (1970-71).
**HIGH SCHOOL:** Joliet (Ill.) Catholic, then Quigley Prep (Chicago).
**COLLEGE:** DePaul.
**TRANSACTIONS:** Signed by Chicago Gears of National Basketball League (March 16, 1946). ... Gears dropped out of NBL and entered Professional Basketball League of America for 1947-48 season. ... PBLA disbanded (November 13, 1947); Chicago was refused a franchise in the NBL and Mikan was awarded to Minneapolis Lakers at NBL meeting (November 17, 1947). Mikan scored 193 points in the eight PBLA games played by Gears before the league folded and led the league in total points and scoring average. ... Signed by Minneapolis Lakers of NBL (November 1947). ... Lakers franchise transferred to Basketball Association of America for 1948-49 season. ... Lakers franchise became part of NBA upon merger of BAA and NBL for 1949-50 season.
**CAREER HONORS:** Elected to Naismith Memorial Basketball Hall of Fame (1959). ... NBA 25th Anniversary All-Time Team (1970), 35th Anniversary All-Time Team (1980) and One of the 50 Greatest Players in NBA History (1996).
**MISCELLANEOUS:** Member of NBA championship team (1950, 1952, 1953, 1954). ... Member of BAA championship team (1949). ... Member of NBL championship team (1947, 1948).

**NOTES:** THE SPORTING NEWS All-America first team (1944, 1945).

## COLLEGIATE RECORD

| Season Team | G | Min. | FGM | FGA | Pct. | FTM | FTA | Pct. | Reb. | Ast. | Pts. | AVERAGES RPG | AVERAGES APG | AVERAGES PPG |
|---|---|---|---|---|---|---|---|---|---|---|---|---|---|---|
| 41-42—DePaul‡ | | | | | Freshman team statistics unavailable. | | | | | | | | | |
| 42-43—DePaul | 24 | ... | 97 | ... | ... | 77 | 111 | .694 | ... | ... | 271 | ... | ... | 11.3 |
| 43-44—DePaul | 26 | ... | 188 | ... | ... | 110 | 169 | .651 | ... | ... | 486 | ... | ... | 18.7 |
| 44-45—DePaul | 24 | ... | 218 | ... | ... | 122 | 199 | .613 | ... | ... | 558 | ... | ... | 23.3 |
| 45-46—DePaul | 24 | ... | 206 | ... | ... | 143 | 186 | .769 | ... | ... | 555 | ... | ... | 23.1 |
| Varsity totals | 98 | ... | 709 | ... | ... | 452 | 665 | .680 | ... | ... | 1870 | ... | ... | 19.1 |

### NBL AND NBA REGULAR-SEASON RECORD

**HONORS:** All-NBA first team (1950, 1951, 1952, 1953, 1954). ... NBL Most Valuable Player (1948). ... All-NBL first team (1947, 1948). ... All-BAA first team (1949).

| Season Team | G | Min. | FGM | FGA | Pct. | FTM | FTA | Pct. | Reb. | Ast. | PF | Dq. | Pts. | AVERAGES RPG | AVERAGES APG | AVERAGES PPG |
|---|---|---|---|---|---|---|---|---|---|---|---|---|---|---|---|---|
| 46-47—Chicago (NBL) | 25 | ... | 147 | ... | ... | 119 | 164 | .726 | ... | ... | 90 | ... | 413 | ... | ... | *16.5 |
| 47-48—Minneapolis. (NBL) | 56 | ... | *406 | ... | ... | *383 | *509 | .752 | ... | ... | 210 | ... | *1195 | ... | ... | *21.3 |
| 48-49—Minneapolis (BAA) | 60 | ... | *583 | 1403 | .416 | *532 | *689 | .772 | ... | 218 | 260 | ... | *1698 | ... | 3.6 | *28.3 |
| 49-50—Minneapolis | 68 | ... | *649 | *1595 | .407 | *567 | 728 | .779 | ... | 197 | *297 | ... | *1865 | ... | 2.9 | *27.4 |
| 50-51—Minneapolis | 68 | ... | *678 | *1584 | .428 | *576 | *717 | .803 | 958 | 208 | *308 | 14 | *1932 | 14.1 | 3.1 | *28.4 |
| 51-52—Minneapolis | 64 | 2572 | 545 | *1414 | .385 | 433 | 555 | .780 | 866 | 194 | *286 | 14 | *1523 | *13.5 | 3.0 | *23.8 |
| 52-53—Minneapolis | 70 | 2651 | 500 | 1252 | .399 | 442 | 567 | .780 | *1007 | 201 | 290 | 12 | 1442 | *14.4 | 2.9 | 20.6 |
| 53-54—Minneapolis | 72 | 2362 | 441 | 1160 | .380 | 424 | 546 | .777 | 1028 | 174 | 268 | 4 | 1306 | 14.3 | 2.4 | 18.1 |
| 54-55— | | | | | | Did not play—retired. | | | | | | | | | | |
| 55-56—Minneapolis | 37 | 765 | 148 | 375 | .395 | 94 | 122 | .771 | 308 | 53 | 153 | 6 | 390 | 8.3 | 1.4 | 10.5 |
| Totals | 520 | ... | 4097 | ... | ... | 3570 | 4597 | .777 | ... | ... | 2162 | ... | 11764 | ... | ... | 22.6 |

### NBL AND NBA PLAYOFF RECORD

| Season Team | G | Min. | FGM | FGA | Pct. | FTM | FTA | Pct. | Reb. | Ast. | PF | Dq. | Pts. | AVERAGES RPG | AVERAGES APG | AVERAGES PPG |
|---|---|---|---|---|---|---|---|---|---|---|---|---|---|---|---|---|
| 46-47—Chi. (NBL) | 11 | ... | 72 | ... | ... | 73 | 104 | .702 | ... | ... | 48 | ... | 217 | ... | ... | 19.7 |
| 47-48—Minn. (NBL) | 10 | ... | 88 | ... | ... | 68 | 97 | .701 | ... | ... | 37 | ... | 244 | ... | ... | 24.4 |
| 48-49—Minneapolis (BAA) | 10 | ... | 103 | 227 | .454 | 97 | 121 | .802 | ... | 21 | 44 | ... | 303 | ... | 2.1 | 30.3 |
| 49-50—Minneapolis | 12 | ... | 121 | 316 | .383 | 134 | 170 | .788 | ... | 36 | 47 | ... | 376 | ... | 3.0 | 31.3 |
| 50-51—Minneapolis | 7 | ... | 62 | 152 | .408 | 44 | 55 | .800 | 74 | 9 | 25 | 1 | 168 | 10.6 | 1.3 | 24.0 |
| 51-52—Minneapolis | 13 | 553 | 99 | 261 | .379 | 109 | 138 | .790 | 207 | 36 | 63 | 3 | 307 | 15.9 | 2.8 | 23.6 |
| 52-53—Minneapolis | 12 | 463 | 78 | 213 | .366 | 82 | 112 | .732 | 185 | 23 | 56 | 5 | 238 | 15.4 | 1.9 | 19.8 |
| 53-54—Minneapolis | 13 | 424 | 87 | 190 | .458 | 78 | 96 | .813 | 171 | 25 | 56 | 1 | 252 | 13.2 | 1.9 | 19.4 |
| 55-56—Minneapolis | 3 | 60 | 13 | 35 | .371 | 10 | 13 | .769 | 28 | 5 | 14 | 0 | 36 | 9.3 | 1.7 | 12.0 |
| Totals | 91 | ... | 723 | ... | ... | 695 | 906 | .767 | ... | ... | 390 | ... | 2141 | ... | ... | 23.5 |

## NBA ALL-STAR GAME RECORD

**NOTES:** NBA All-Star Game Most Valuable Player (1953).

| Season Team | Min. | FGM | FGA | Pct. | FTM | FTA | Pct. | Reb | Ast. | PF | Dq. | Pts. |
|---|---|---|---|---|---|---|---|---|---|---|---|---|
| 1951—Minneapolis | ... | 4 | 17 | .235 | 4 | 6 | .667 | 11 | 3 | 2 | 0 | 12 |
| 1952—Minneapolis | 29 | 9 | 19 | .474 | 8 | 9 | .889 | 15 | 1 | 5 | 0 | 26 |
| 1953—Minneapolis | 40 | 9 | 26 | .346 | 4 | 4 | 1.000 | 16 | 2 | 2 | 0 | 22 |
| 1954—Minneapolis | 31 | 6 | 18 | .333 | 6 | 8 | .750 | 9 | 1 | 5 | 0 | 18 |
| Totals | ... | 28 | 80 | .350 | 22 | 27 | .815 | 51 | 7 | 14 | 0 | 78 |

## NBA COACHING RECORD

| | | REGULAR SEASON | | | | PLAYOFFS | |
|---|---|---|---|---|---|---|---|
| Season Team | W | L | Pct. | | W | L | Pct. |
| 57-58—Minneapolis | 9 | 30 | .231 | | — | — | — |

**NOTES:**
1958—Resigned as Minneapolis head coach and replaced by John Kundla (January).

# MIKKELSEN, VERN          F/C

**PERSONAL:** Born October 21, 1928, in Fresno, Calif. ... 6-7/230 (2,00/104,3). ... Full name: Arild Verner Agerskov Mikkelsen.
**HIGH SCHOOL:** Askov (Minn.).
**COLLEGE:** Hamline University (Minn.).
**TRANSACTIONS:** Selected by Minneapolis Lakers in first round of 1949 NBA Draft.
**CAREER HONORS:** Elected to Naismith Memorial Basketball Hall of Fame (1995).
**MISCELLANEOUS:** Member of NBA championship team (1950, 1952, 1953, 1954).

## COLLEGIATE RECORD

**NOTES:** THE SPORTING NEWS All-America fourth team (1949). ... Inducted into NAIA Basketball Hall of Fame (1956). ... Led NCAA Division II with .538 field-goal percentage (1949).

| Season Team | G | Min. | FGM | FGA | Pct. | FTM | FTA | Pct. | Reb. | Ast. | Pts. | RPG | APG | PPG |
|---|---|---|---|---|---|---|---|---|---|---|---|---|---|---|
| 45-46—Hamline University | 17 | ... | 49 | ... | ... | 25 | ... | ... | ... | ... | 123 | ... | ... | 7.2 |
| 46-47—Hamline University | 26 | ... | 102 | ... | ... | 52 | ... | ... | ... | ... | 256 | ... | ... | 9.8 |
| 47-48—Hamline University | 31 | ... | 199 | ... | ... | 119 | ... | ... | ... | ... | 517 | ... | ... | 16.7 |
| 48-49—Hamline University | 30 | ... | 203 | 377 | .538 | 113 | 177 | .638 | ... | ... | 519 | ... | ... | 17.3 |
| Totals | 104 | ... | 553 | ... | ... | 309 | ... | ... | ... | ... | 1415 | ... | ... | 13.6 |

## NBA REGULAR-SEASON RECORD

**RECORDS:** Holds career record for most disqualifications—127.
**HONORS:** All-NBA second team (1951, 1952, 1953, 1955).

| | | | | | | | | | | | | | | AVERAGES | | |
|---|---|---|---|---|---|---|---|---|---|---|---|---|---|---|---|---|
| Season Team | G | Min. | FGM | FGA | Pct. | FTM | FTA | Pct. | Reb. | Ast. | PF | Dq. | Pts. | RPG | APG | PPG |
| 49-50—Minneapolis | 68 | ... | 288 | 722 | .399 | 215 | 286 | .752 | ... | 123 | 222 | ... | 791 | ... | 1.8 | 11.6 |
| 50-51—Minneapolis | 64 | ... | 359 | 893 | .402 | 186 | 275 | .676 | 655 | 181 | 260 | 13 | 904 | 10.2 | 2.8 | 14.1 |
| 51-52—Minneapolis | 66 | 2345 | 363 | 866 | .419 | 283 | 372 | .761 | 681 | 180 | 282 | 16 | 1009 | 10.3 | 2.7 | 15.3 |
| 52-53—Minneapolis | 70 | 2465 | 378 | 868 | .435 | 291 | 387 | .752 | 654 | 148 | 289 | 14 | 1047 | 9.3 | 2.1 | 15.0 |
| 53-54—Minneapolis | 72 | 2247 | 288 | 771 | .374 | 221 | 298 | .742 | 615 | 119 | 264 | 7 | 797 | 8.5 | 1.7 | 11.1 |
| 54-55—Minneapolis | 71 | 2559 | 440 | 1043 | .422 | 447 | 598 | .748 | 722 | 145 | *319 | 14 | 1327 | 10.2 | 2.0 | 18.7 |
| 55-56—Minneapolis | 72 | 2100 | 317 | 821 | .386 | 328 | 408 | .804 | 608 | 173 | *319 | †17 | 962 | 8.4 | 2.4 | 13.4 |
| 56-57—Minneapolis | 72 | 2198 | 322 | 854 | .377 | 342 | 424 | .807 | 630 | 121 | *312 | *18 | 986 | 8.8 | 1.7 | 13.7 |
| 57-58—Minneapolis | 72 | 2390 | 439 | 1070 | .410 | 370 | 471 | .786 | 805 | 166 | 299 | *20 | 1248 | 11.2 | 2.3 | 17.3 |
| 58-59—Minneapolis | 72 | 2139 | 353 | 904 | .390 | 286 | 355 | .806 | 570 | 159 | 246 | 8 | 992 | 7.9 | 2.2 | 13.8 |
| Totals | 699 | ... | 3547 | 8812 | .403 | 2969 | 3874 | .766 | ... | 1515 | 2812 | ... | 10063 | ... | 2.2 | 14.4 |

## NBA PLAYOFF RECORD

| | | | | | | | | | | | | | | AVERAGES | | |
|---|---|---|---|---|---|---|---|---|---|---|---|---|---|---|---|---|
| Season Team | G | Min. | FGM | FGA | Pct. | FTM | FTA | Pct. | Reb. | Ast. | PF | Dq. | Pts. | RPG | APG | PPG |
| 49-50—Minneapolis | 12 | ... | 55 | 149 | .369 | 46 | 60 | .767 | ... | 18 | 52 | ... | 156 | ... | 1.5 | 13.0 |
| 50-51—Minneapolis | 7 | ... | 39 | 96 | .406 | 31 | 47 | .660 | 67 | 17 | 35 | 3 | 109 | 9.6 | 2.4 | 15.6 |
| 51-52—Minneapolis | 13 | 496 | 60 | 139 | .432 | 53 | 64 | .828 | 110 | 20 | 66 | 4 | 173 | 8.5 | 1.5 | 13.3 |
| 52-53—Minneapolis | 12 | 400 | 44 | 133 | .331 | 56 | 66 | .848 | 104 | 24 | 59 | 3 | 144 | 8.7 | 2.0 | 12.0 |
| 53-54—Minneapolis | 13 | 375 | 51 | 111 | .459 | 31 | 36 | .861 | 73 | 17 | 52 | 1 | 133 | 5.6 | 1.3 | 10.2 |
| 54-55—Minneapolis | 7 | 209 | 30 | 85 | .353 | 36 | 46 | .783 | 78 | 13 | 36 | 4 | 96 | 11.1 | 1.9 | 13.7 |
| 55-56—Minneapolis | 3 | 90 | 11 | 26 | .423 | 18 | 20 | .900 | 17 | 2 | 14 | 2 | 40 | 5.7 | 0.7 | 13.3 |
| 56-57—Minneapolis | 5 | 162 | 33 | 83 | .398 | 22 | 34 | .647 | 43 | 17 | 29 | 4 | 88 | 8.6 | 3.4 | 17.6 |
| 58-59—Minneapolis | 13 | 371 | 73 | 177 | .412 | 56 | 73 | .767 | 93 | 24 | 54 | 3 | 202 | 7.2 | 1.8 | 15.5 |
| Totals | 85 | ... | 396 | 999 | .396 | 349 | 446 | .783 | ... | 152 | 397 | ... | 1141 | ... | 1.8 | 13.4 |

## NBA ALL-STAR GAME RECORD

| Season Team | Min. | FGM | FGA | Pct. | FTM | FTA | Pct. | Reb | Ast. | PF | Dq. | Pts. |
|---|---|---|---|---|---|---|---|---|---|---|---|---|
| 1951—Minneapolis | ... | 4 | 11 | .364 | 3 | 4 | .750 | 9 | 1 | 3 | 0 | 11 |
| 1952—Minneapolis | 23 | 5 | 8 | .625 | 2 | 2 | 1.000 | 10 | 0 | 2 | 0 | 12 |
| 1953—Minneapolis | 19 | 3 | 13 | .231 | 0 | 0 | ... | 6 | 3 | 3 | 0 | 6 |
| 1955—Minneapolis | 25 | 7 | 15 | .467 | 2 | 3 | .667 | 9 | 1 | 5 | 0 | 16 |
| 1956—Minneapolis | 22 | 5 | 13 | .385 | 6 | 7 | .857 | 9 | 2 | 4 | 0 | 16 |
| 1957—Minneapolis | 21 | 3 | 10 | .300 | 0 | 4 | .000 | 9 | 1 | 3 | 0 | 6 |
| Totals | ... | 27 | 70 | .386 | 13 | 20 | .650 | 52 | 8 | 20 | 0 | 67 |

## ABA COACHING RECORD

**BACKGROUND:** General manager, Minnesota Pipers of ABA (1968-69).

| | | REGULAR SEASON | | | | PLAYOFFS | |
|---|---|---|---|---|---|---|---|
| Season Team | W | L | Pct. | Finish | W | L | Pct. |
| 68-69—Minnesota | 6 | 7 | .462 | | — | — | — |

**NOTES:**
1969—Replaced Jim Harding as Minnesota head coach (January), with record of 20-12; later replaced by Gus Young.

# MONCRIEF, SIDNEY                                    G

**PERSONAL:** Born September 21, 1957, in Little Rock, Ark. ... 6-3/183 (1,90/83,0). ... Full name: Sidney A. Moncrief. ... Nickname: The Squid.
**HIGH SCHOOL:** Hall (Little Rock, Ark.).
**COLLEGE:** Arkansas.
**TRANSACTIONS:** Selected by Milwaukee Bucks in first round (fifth pick overall) of 1979 NBA Draft. ... Signed as unrestricted free agent by Atlanta Hawks (October 4, 1990). ... Rights renounced by Hawks (September 29, 1991).
**CAREER NOTES:** Head coach, University of Arkansas-Little Rock (1999-2000). ... Assistant coach, Dallas Mavericks (2000-present).

## COLLEGIATE RECORD

**NOTES:** The Sporting News All-America second team (1979). ... Led NCAA Division I with .665 field goal percentage (1976).

| | | | | | | | | | | | | AVERAGES | | |
|---|---|---|---|---|---|---|---|---|---|---|---|---|---|---|
| Season Team | G | Min. | FGM | FGA | Pct. | FTM | FTA | Pct. | Reb. | Ast. | Pts. | RPG | APG | PPG |
| 75-76—Arkansas | 28 | | 149 | 224 | .665 | 56 | 77 | .727 | 213 | 59 | 354 | 7.6 | 2.1 | 12.6 |
| 76-77—Arkansas | 28 | 997 | 157 | 242 | .649 | 117 | 171 | .684 | 235 | 41 | 431 | 8.4 | 1.5 | 15.4 |
| 77-78—Arkansas | 36 | 1293 | 209 | 354 | .590 | 203 | 256 | .793 | 278 | 60 | 621 | 7.7 | 1.7 | 17.3 |
| 78-79—Arkansas | 30 | 1157 | 224 | 400 | .560 | 212 | 248 | .855 | 289 | 80 | 660 | 9.6 | 2.7 | 22.0 |
| Totals | 122 | ... | 739 | 1220 | .606 | 588 | 752 | .782 | 1015 | 240 | 2066 | 8.3 | 2.0 | 16.9 |

## NBA REGULAR-SEASON RECORD

**HONORS:** NBA Defensive Player of the Year (1983, 1984). ... All-NBA first team (1983). ... All-NBA second team (1982, 1984, 1985, 1986). ... NBA All-Defensive first team (1983, 1984, 1985, 1986). ... NBA All-Defensive second team (1982).

| | | | | | | | | REBOUNDS | | | | | | | | AVERAGES | | |
|---|---|---|---|---|---|---|---|---|---|---|---|---|---|---|---|---|---|---|
| Season Team | G | Min. | FGM | FGA | Pct. | FTM | FTA | Pct. | Off. | Def. | Tot. | Ast. | St. | Blk. | TO | Pts. | RPG | APG | PPG |
| 79-80—Milwaukee | 77 | 1557 | 211 | 451 | .468 | 232 | 292 | .795 | 154 | 184 | 338 | 133 | 72 | 16 | 117 | 654 | 4.4 | 1.7 | 8.5 |
| 80-81—Milwaukee | 80 | 2417 | 400 | 739 | .541 | 320 | 398 | .804 | 186 | 220 | 406 | 264 | 90 | 37 | 145 | 1122 | 5.1 | 3.3 | 14.0 |
| 81-82—Milwaukee | 80 | 2980 | 556 | 1063 | .523 | 468 | 573 | .817 | 221 | 313 | 534 | 382 | 138 | 22 | 208 | 1581 | 6.7 | 4.8 | 19.8 |
| 82-83—Milwaukee | 76 | 2710 | 606 | 1156 | .524 | 499 | 604 | .826 | 192 | 245 | 437 | 300 | 113 | 23 | 197 | 1712 | 5.8 | 3.9 | 22.5 |
| 83-84—Milwaukee | 79 | 3075 | 560 | 1125 | .498 | 529 | 624 | .848 | 215 | 313 | 528 | 358 | 108 | 27 | 217 | 1654 | 6.7 | 4.5 | 20.9 |
| 84-85—Milwaukee | 73 | 2734 | 561 | 1162 | .483 | 454 | 548 | .828 | 149 | 242 | 391 | 382 | 117 | 39 | 184 | 1585 | 5.4 | 5.2 | 21.7 |
| 85-86—Milwaukee | 73 | 2567 | 470 | 962 | .489 | 498 | 580 | .859 | 115 | 219 | 334 | 357 | 103 | 18 | 174 | 1471 | 4.6 | 4.9 | 20.2 |
| 86-87—Milwaukee | 39 | 992 | 158 | 324 | .488 | 136 | 162 | .840 | 57 | 70 | 127 | 121 | 27 | 10 | 63 | 460 | 3.3 | 3.1 | 11.8 |
| 87-88—Milwaukee | 56 | 1428 | 217 | 444 | .489 | 164 | 196 | .837 | 58 | 122 | 180 | 204 | 41 | 12 | 86 | 603 | 3.2 | 3.6 | 10.8 |
| 88-89—Milwaukee | 62 | 1594 | 261 | 532 | .491 | 205 | 237 | .865 | 46 | 126 | 172 | 188 | 65 | 13 | 94 | 752 | 2.8 | 3.0 | 12.1 |
| 89-90— | | | | | | | Did not play—retired. | | | | | | | | | | | | |
| 90-91—Atlanta | 72 | 1096 | 117 | 240 | .488 | 82 | 105 | .781 | 31 | 97 | 128 | 104 | 50 | 9 | 66 | 337 | 1.8 | 1.4 | 4.7 |
| Totals | 767 | 23150 | 4117 | 8198 | .502 | 3587 | 4319 | .831 | 1424 | 2151 | 3575 | 2793 | 924 | 226 | 1551 | 11931 | 4.7 | 3.6 | 15.6 |

Three-point field goals: 1979-80, 0-for-1. 1980-81, 2-for-9 (.222). 1981-82, 1-for-14 (.071). 1982-83, 1-for-10 (.100). 1983-84, 5-for-18 (.278). 1984-85, 9-for-33 (.273). 1985-86, 33-for-103 (.320). 1986-87, 8-for-31 (.258). 1987-88, 5-for-31 (.161). 1988-89, 25-for-73 (.342). 1990-91, 21-for-64 (.328). Totals, 110-for-387 (.284).
Personal fouls/disqualifications: 1979-80, 106/0. 1980-81, 156/1. 1981-82, 206/3. 1982-83, 180/1. 1983-84, 204/2. 1984-85, 197/1. 1985-86, 178/1. 1986-87, 73/0. 1987-88, 109/0. 1988-89, 114/1. 1990-91, 112/0. Totals, 1635/10.

## NBA PLAYOFF RECORD

| | | | | | | | | REBOUNDS | | | | | | | | AVERAGES | | |
|---|---|---|---|---|---|---|---|---|---|---|---|---|---|---|---|---|---|---|
| Season Team | G | Min. | FGM | FGA | Pct. | FTM | FTA | Pct. | Off. | Def. | Tot. | Ast. | St. | Blk. | TO | Pts. | RPG | APG | PPG |
| 79-80—Milwaukee | 7 | 182 | 30 | 51 | .588 | 27 | 31 | .871 | 17 | 14 | 31 | 11 | 5 | 1 | 14 | 87 | 4.4 | 1.6 | 12.4 |
| 80-81—Milwaukee | 7 | 277 | 30 | 69 | .435 | 38 | 51 | .745 | 19 | 28 | 47 | 20 | 12 | 3 | 21 | 98 | 6.7 | 2.9 | 14.0 |
| 81-82—Milwaukee | 6 | 252 | 31 | 74 | .419 | 30 | 38 | .789 | 15 | 15 | 30 | 24 | 9 | 2 | 12 | 92 | 5.0 | 4.0 | 15.3 |
| 82-83—Milwaukee | 9 | 377 | 62 | 142 | .437 | 46 | 61 | .754 | 28 | 32 | 60 | 33 | 18 | 3 | 27 | 170 | 6.7 | 3.7 | 18.9 |
| 83-84—Milwaukee | 16 | 618 | 99 | 191 | .518 | 106 | 134 | .791 | 44 | 67 | 111 | 68 | 28 | 9 | 61 | 305 | 6.9 | 4.3 | 19.1 |
| 84-85—Milwaukee | 8 | 319 | 55 | 99 | .556 | 70 | 75 | .933 | 10 | 24 | 34 | 40 | 5 | 4 | 20 | 184 | 4.3 | 5.0 | 23.0 |
| 85-86—Milwaukee | 9 | 327 | 52 | 122 | .426 | 44 | 63 | .698 | 15 | 26 | 41 | 44 | 5 | 5 | 21 | 152 | 4.6 | 4.9 | 16.9 |
| 86-87—Milwaukee | 12 | 426 | 78 | 165 | .473 | 73 | 90 | .811 | 21 | 33 | 54 | 36 | 13 | 6 | 24 | 233 | 4.5 | 3.0 | 19.4 |
| 87-88—Milwaukee | 5 | 173 | 24 | 50 | .480 | 26 | 27 | .963 | 6 | 13 | 19 | 26 | 3 | 1 | 11 | 75 | 3.8 | 5.2 | 15.0 |
| 88-89—Milwaukee | 9 | 184 | 19 | 48 | .396 | 15 | 16 | .938 | 8 | 18 | 26 | 13 | 5 | 2 | 11 | 55 | 2.9 | 1.4 | 6.1 |
| 90-91—Atlanta | 5 | 91 | 11 | 22 | .500 | 13 | 16 | .813 | 6 | 10 | 16 | 2 | 3 | 0 | 3 | 36 | 3.2 | 0.4 | 7.2 |
| Totals | 93 | 3226 | 491 | 1033 | .475 | 488 | 602 | .811 | 189 | 280 | 469 | 317 | 106 | 36 | 225 | 1487 | 5.0 | 3.4 | 16.0 |

Three-point field goals: 1981-82, 0-for-1. 1982-83, 0-for-1. 1983-84, 1-for-4 (.250). 1984-85, 4-for-10 (.400). 1985-86, 4-for-14 (.286). 1986-87, 4-for-14 (.286). 1987-88, 1-for-1. 1988-89, 2-for-7 (.286). 1990-91, 1-for-6 (.167). Totals, 17-for-58 (.293).
Personal fouls/disqualifications: 1979-80, 14/0. 1980-81, 24/0. 1981-82, 22/1. 1982-83, 25/1. 1983-84, 54/1. 1984-85, 26/0. 1985-86, 30/0. 1986-87, 43/0. 1987-88, 14/0. 1988-89, 17/0. 1990-91, 16/0. Totals, 285/3.

## NBA ALL-STAR GAME RECORD

| | | | | | | | REBOUNDS | | | | | | | | |
|---|---|---|---|---|---|---|---|---|---|---|---|---|---|---|---|
| Season Team | Min. | FGM | FGA | Pct. | FTM | FTA | Pct. | Off. | Def. | Tot. | Ast. | PF | Dq. | St. | Blk. | TO | Pts. |
| 1982—Milwaukee | 22 | 3 | 11 | .273 | 0 | 2 | .000 | 3 | 1 | 4 | 1 | 2 | 0 | 1 | 0 | 1 | 6 |
| 1983—Milwaukee | 23 | 8 | 14 | .571 | 4 | 5 | .800 | 3 | 2 | 5 | 4 | 1 | 0 | 6 | 1 | 1 | 20 |
| 1984—Milwaukee | 26 | 3 | 6 | .500 | 2 | 2 | 1.000 | 1 | 4 | 5 | 2 | 3 | 0 | 4 | 0 | 4 | 8 |
| 1985—Milwaukee | 22 | 1 | 5 | .200 | 6 | 6 | 1.000 | 2 | 3 | 5 | 4 | 1 | 0 | 0 | 0 | 2 | 8 |
| 1986—Milwaukee | 26 | 4 | 11 | .364 | 7 | 7 | 1.000 | 3 | 0 | 3 | 1 | 0 | 0 | 1 | 0 | 0 | 16 |
| Totals | 119 | 19 | 47 | .404 | 19 | 22 | .864 | 12 | 10 | 22 | 12 | 7 | 0 | 12 | 2 | 8 | 58 |

Three-point field goals: 1986, 1-for-1.

## HEAD COACHING RECORD

| | REGULAR SEASON | | | | PLAYOFFS | | |
|---|---|---|---|---|---|---|---|
| Season Team | W | L | Pct. | Finish | W | L | Pct. |
| 99-00—Arkansas-Little Rock | 4 | 23 | .148 | 9th/Sun Belt Conference | | | |

# MONROE, EARL                                        G

**PERSONAL:** Born November 21, 1944, in Philadelphia. ... 6-3/190 (1,90/86,2). ... Full name: Vernon Earl Monroe. ... Nickname: The Pearl.
**HIGH SCHOOL:** John Bartram (Philadelphia).
**COLLEGE:** Winston-Salem (N.C.) State.
**TRANSACTIONS:** Selected by Baltimore Bullets in first round (second pick overall) of 1967 NBA Draft. ... Traded by Bullets to New York Knicks for F Dave Stallworth, G Mike Riordan and cash (November 10, 1971).
**CAREER HONORS:** Elected to Naismith Memorial Basketball Hall of Fame (1990). ... One of the 50 Greatest Players in NBA History (1996).
**MISCELLANEOUS:** Member of NBA championship team (1973).

## COLLEGIATE RECORD

**NOTES:** The Sporting News All-America first team (1966). ... Holds NCAA Division II single-season record for most points—1329 (1967). ... Inducted into NAIA Basketball Hall of Fame (1975). ... NCAA College Division and NAIA Leading Scorer (1967). ... Outstanding Player in NCAA College Division Tournament (1967). ... Member of NCAA College Division tournament championship team (1967). ... Led NCAA Division II with 41.5 points per game (1967).

ALL-TIME GREAT PLAYERS

| Season Team | G | Min. | FGM | FGA | Pct. | FTM | FTA | Pct. | Reb. | Ast. | Pts. | RPG | APG | PPG |
|---|---|---|---|---|---|---|---|---|---|---|---|---|---|---|
| 63-64—Winst.-Salem State | 23 | ... | 71 | ... | ... | 21 | | | | ... | 163 | ... | ... | 7.1 |
| 64-65—Winst.-Salem State | 30 | ... | 286 | ... | ... | 125 | 176 | .710 | 211 | ... | 697 | 7.0 | ... | 23.2 |
| 65-66—Winst.-Salem State | 25 | ... | 292 | 519 | .563 | 162 | 187 | .866 | 167 | | 746 | 6.7 | ... | 29.8 |
| 66-67—Winst.-Salem State | 32 | ... | 509 | 839 | .607 | 311 | 391 | .795 | 218 | | 1329 | 6.8 | ... | 41.5 |
| Totals | 110 | ... | 1158 | | | 619 | | | | | 2935 | ... | ... | 26.7 |

## NBA REGULAR-SEASON RECORD

**HONORS:** NBA Rookie of the Year (1968). ... All-NBA first team (1969). ... NBA All-Rookie team (1968).

| Season Team | G | Min. | FGM | FGA | Pct. | FTM | FTA | Pct. | Reb. | Ast. | PF | Dq. | Pts. | RPG | APG | PPG |
|---|---|---|---|---|---|---|---|---|---|---|---|---|---|---|---|---|
| 67-68—Baltimore | 82 | 3012 | 742 | 1637 | .453 | 507 | 649 | .781 | 465 | 349 | 282 | 3 | 1991 | 5.7 | 4.3 | 24.3 |
| 68-69—Baltimore | 80 | 3075 | 809 | 1837 | .440 | 447 | 582 | .768 | 280 | 392 | 261 | 1 | 2065 | 3.5 | 4.9 | 25.8 |
| 69-70—Baltimore | 82 | 3051 | 695 | 1557 | .446 | 532 | 641 | .830 | 257 | 402 | 258 | 3 | 1922 | 3.1 | 4.9 | 23.4 |
| 70-71—Baltimore | 81 | 2843 | 663 | 1501 | .442 | 406 | 506 | .802 | 213 | 354 | 220 | 3 | 1732 | 2.6 | 4.4 | 21.4 |
| 71-72—Balt.-N.Y. | 63 | 1337 | 287 | 662 | .434 | 175 | 224 | .781 | 100 | 142 | 139 | 1 | 749 | 1.6 | 2.3 | 11.9 |
| 72-73—New York | 75 | 2370 | 496 | 1016 | .488 | 171 | 208 | .822 | 245 | 288 | 195 | 1 | 1163 | 3.3 | 3.8 | 15.5 |

| Season Team | G | Min. | FGM | FGA | Pct. | FTM | FTA | Pct. | Off. | Def. | Tot. | Ast. | St. | Blk. | TO | Pts. | RPG | APG | PPG |
|---|---|---|---|---|---|---|---|---|---|---|---|---|---|---|---|---|---|---|---|
| 73-74—New York | 41 | 1194 | 240 | 513 | .468 | 93 | 113 | .823 | 22 | 99 | 121 | 110 | 34 | 19 | ... | 573 | 3.0 | 2.7 | 14.0 |
| 74-75—New York | 78 | 2814 | 668 | 1462 | .457 | 297 | 359 | .827 | 56 | 271 | 327 | 270 | 108 | 29 | ... | 1633 | 4.2 | 3.5 | 20.9 |
| 75-76—New York | 76 | 2889 | 647 | 1354 | .478 | 280 | 356 | .787 | 48 | 225 | 273 | 304 | 111 | 22 | ... | 1574 | 3.6 | 4.0 | 20.7 |
| 76-77—N.Y. Knicks | 77 | 2656 | 613 | 1185 | .517 | 307 | 366 | .839 | 45 | 178 | 223 | 366 | 91 | 23 | ... | 1533 | 2.9 | 4.8 | 19.9 |
| 77-78—New York | 76 | 2369 | 556 | 1123 | .495 | 242 | 291 | .832 | 47 | 135 | 182 | 361 | 60 | 19 | 179 | 1354 | 2.4 | 4.8 | 17.8 |
| 78-79—New York | 64 | 1393 | 329 | 699 | .471 | 129 | 154 | .838 | 26 | 48 | 74 | 189 | 48 | 6 | 98 | 787 | 1.2 | 3.0 | 12.3 |
| 79-80—New York | 51 | 633 | 161 | 352 | .457 | 56 | 64 | .875 | 16 | 20 | 36 | 67 | 21 | 3 | 28 | 378 | 0.7 | 1.3 | 7.4 |
| Totals | 926 | 29636 | 6906 | 14898 | .464 | 3642 | 4513 | .807 | ... | ... | 2796 | 3594 | 473 | 121 | 305 | 17454 | 3.0 | 3.9 | 18.8 |

Personal fouls/disqualifications: 1973-74, 97/0. 1974-75, 200/0. 1975-76, 209/1. 1976-77, 197/0. 1977-78, 189/0. 1978-79, 123/0. 1979-80, 46/0. Totals, 2416/13.

## NBA PLAYOFF RECORD

| Season Team | G | Min. | FGM | FGA | Pct. | FTM | FTA | Pct. | Reb. | Ast. | PF | Dq. | Pts. | RPG | APG | PPG |
|---|---|---|---|---|---|---|---|---|---|---|---|---|---|---|---|---|
| 68-69—Baltimore | 4 | 171 | 44 | 114 | .386 | 25 | 31 | .806 | 21 | 16 | 10 | 0 | 113 | 5.3 | 4.0 | 28.3 |
| 69-70—Baltimore | 7 | 299 | 74 | 154 | .481 | 48 | 60 | .800 | 23 | 28 | 23 | 0 | 196 | 3.3 | 4.0 | 28.0 |
| 70-71—Baltimore | 18 | 671 | 145 | 356 | .407 | 107 | 135 | .793 | 64 | 74 | 56 | 0 | 397 | 3.6 | 4.1 | 22.1 |
| 71-72—New York | 16 | 429 | 76 | 185 | .411 | 45 | 57 | .789 | 45 | 47 | 41 | 0 | 197 | 2.8 | 2.9 | 12.3 |
| 72-73—New York | 16 | 504 | 111 | 211 | .526 | 36 | 48 | .750 | 51 | 51 | 39 | 0 | 258 | 3.2 | 3.2 | 16.1 |

| Season Team | G | Min. | FGM | FGA | Pct. | FTM | FTA | Pct. | Off. | Def. | Tot. | Ast. | St. | Blk. | TO | Pts. | RPG | APG | PPG |
|---|---|---|---|---|---|---|---|---|---|---|---|---|---|---|---|---|---|---|---|
| 73-74—New York | 12 | 407 | 81 | 165 | .491 | 47 | 55 | .855 | 8 | 40 | 48 | 25 | 8 | 9 | ... | 209 | 4.0 | 2.1 | 17.4 |
| 74-75—New York | 3 | 89 | 12 | 45 | .267 | 18 | 22 | .818 | 1 | 8 | 9 | 6 | 4 | 2 | ... | 42 | 3.0 | 2.0 | 14.0 |
| 77-78—New York | 6 | 145 | 24 | 62 | .387 | 11 | 18 | .611 | 1 | 4 | 5 | 17 | 6 | 0 | 6 | 59 | 0.8 | 2.8 | 9.8 |
| Totals | 82 | 2715 | 567 | 1292 | .439 | 337 | 426 | .791 | ... | ... | 266 | 264 | 18 | 11 | 6 | 1471 | 3.2 | 3.2 | 17.9 |

Personal fouls/disqualifications: 1973-74, 26/0. 1974-75, 6/0. 1977-78, 15/0. Totals, 216/0.

## NBA ALL-STAR GAME RECORD

| Season Team | Min. | FGM | FGA | Pct. | FTM | FTA | Pct. | Reb | Ast. | PF | Dq. | Pts. |
|---|---|---|---|---|---|---|---|---|---|---|---|---|
| 1969—Baltimore | 27 | 6 | 15 | .400 | 9 | 12 | .750 | 4 | 4 | 4 | 0 | 21 |
| 1971—Baltimore | 18 | 3 | 9 | .333 | 0 | 0 | ... | 5 | 2 | 3 | 0 | 6 |

| Season Team | Min. | FGM | FGA | Pct. | FTM | FTA | Pct. | Off. | Def. | Tot. | Ast. | PF | Dq. | St. | Blk. | TO | Pts. |
|---|---|---|---|---|---|---|---|---|---|---|---|---|---|---|---|---|---|
| 1975—New York | 25 | 3 | 8 | .375 | 3 | 5 | .600 | 0 | 3 | 3 | 2 | 2 | 0 | 1 | 0 | ... | 9 |
| 1977—N.Y. Knicks | 15 | 2 | 7 | .286 | 0 | 0 | ... | 0 | 0 | 0 | 3 | 1 | 0 | 0 | 0 | 0 | 4 |
| Totals | 85 | 14 | 39 | .359 | 12 | 17 | .706 | ... | ... | 12 | 11 | 10 | 0 | 1 | 0 | | 40 |

# MULLIN, CHRIS                                F

**PERSONAL:** Born July 30, 1963, in New York. ... 6-7/215. (2,01/97,5). ... Full Name: Christopher Paul Mullin.
**HIGH SCHOOL:** Power Memorial (New York), then Xaverian (Brooklyn, N.Y.).
**COLLEGE:** St. John's.
**TRANSACTIONS:** Selected by Golden State Warriors in first round (seventh pick overall) of 1985 NBA Draft. ... Traded by Warriors to Indiana Pacers for C Erick Dampier and F Duane Ferrell (August 12, 1997). ... Waived by Pacers (September 12, 2000). ... Signed as free agent by Warriors (September 28, 2000).
**CAREER NOTES:** Special assistant, Warriors (2002-April 22, 2004). ... Executive vice president of basketball operations, Warriors (April 22, 2004-present).
**MISCELLANEOUS:** Member of gold-medal-winning U.S. Olympic team (1984, 1992). ... Golden State Warriors franchise all-time steals leader with 1,376 (1985-86 through 1996-97 and 2000-01).

## COLLEGIATE RECORD

**NOTES:** Wooden Award winner (1985). ... The Sporting News All-America first team (1985). ... The Sporting News All-America second team (1984).

| Season Team | G | Min. | FGM | FGA | Pct. | FTM | FTA | Pct. | Reb. | Ast. | Pts. | RPG | APG | PPG |
|---|---|---|---|---|---|---|---|---|---|---|---|---|---|---|
| 81-82—St. John's | 30 | 1061 | 175 | 328 | .534 | 148 | 187 | .791 | 97 | 92 | 498 | 3.2 | 3.1 | 16.6 |
| 82-83—St. John's | 33 | 1210 | 228 | 395 | .577 | 173 | 197 | .878 | 123 | 101 | 629 | 3.7 | 3.1 | 19.1 |
| 83-84—St. John's | 27 | 1070 | 225 | 394 | .571 | 169 | 187 | .904 | 120 | 109 | 619 | 4.4 | 4.0 | 22.9 |
| 84-85—St. John's | 35 | 1327 | 251 | 482 | .521 | 192 | 233 | .824 | 169 | 151 | 694 | 4.8 | 4.3 | 19.8 |
| Totals | 125 | 4668 | 879 | 1599 | .550 | 682 | 804 | .848 | 509 | 453 | 2440 | 4.1 | 3.6 | 19.5 |

## NBA REGULAR-SEASON RECORD

**HONORS:** All-NBA first team (1992). ... All-NBA second team (1989, 1991). ... All-NBA third team (1990).

| Season Team | G | Min. | FGM | FGA | Pct. | FTM | FTA | Pct. | Off. | Def. | Tot. | Ast. | St. | Blk. | TO | Pts. | RPG | APG | PPG |
|---|---|---|---|---|---|---|---|---|---|---|---|---|---|---|---|---|---|---|---|
| 85-86—Golden State | 55 | 1391 | 287 | 620 | .463 | 189 | 211 | .896 | 42 | 73 | 115 | 105 | 70 | 23 | 75 | 768 | 2.1 | 1.9 | 14.0 |
| 86-87—Golden State | 82 | 2377 | 477 | 928 | .514 | 269 | 326 | .825 | 39 | 142 | 181 | 261 | 98 | 36 | 154 | 1242 | 2.2 | 3.2 | 15.1 |
| 87-88—Golden State | 60 | 2033 | 470 | 926 | .508 | 239 | 270 | .885 | 58 | 147 | 205 | 290 | 113 | 32 | 156 | 1213 | 3.4 | 4.8 | 20.2 |
| 88-89—Golden State | 82 | 3093 | 830 | 1630 | .509 | 493 | 553 | .892 | 152 | 331 | 483 | 415 | 176 | 39 | 296 | 2176 | 5.9 | 5.1 | 26.5 |
| 89-90—Golden State | 78 | 2830 | 682 | 1272 | .536 | 505 | 568 | .889 | 130 | 333 | 463 | 319 | 123 | 45 | 239 | 1956 | 5.9 | 4.1 | 25.1 |

| Season Team | G | Min. | FGM | FGA | Pct. | FTM | FTA | Pct. | Off. | Def. | Tot. | Ast. | St. | Blk. | TO | Pts. | RPG | APG | PPG |
|---|---|---|---|---|---|---|---|---|---|---|---|---|---|---|---|---|---|---|---|
| | | | | | | | | | REBOUNDS | | | | | | | | AVERAGES | | |
| 90-91—Golden State... | 82 | *3315 | 777 | 1449 | .536 | 513 | 580 | .884 | 141 | 302 | 443 | 329 | 173 | 63 | 245 | 2107 | 5.4 | 4.0 | 25.7 |
| 91-92—Golden State... | 81 | *3346 | 830 | 1584 | .524 | 350 | 420 | .833 | 127 | 323 | 450 | 286 | 173 | 62 | 202 | 2074 | 5.6 | 3.5 | 25.6 |
| 92-93—Golden State... | 46 | 1902 | 474 | 930 | .510 | 183 | 226 | .810 | 42 | 190 | 232 | 166 | 68 | 41 | 139 | 1191 | 5.0 | 3.6 | 25.9 |
| 93-94—Golden State... | 62 | 2324 | 410 | 869 | .472 | 165 | 219 | .753 | 64 | 281 | 345 | 315 | 107 | 53 | 178 | 1040 | 5.6 | 5.1 | 16.8 |
| 94-95—Golden State... | 25 | 890 | 170 | 348 | .489 | 94 | 107 | .879 | 25 | 90 | 115 | 125 | 38 | 19 | 93 | 476 | 4.6 | 5.0 | 19.0 |
| 95-96—Golden State... | 55 | 1617 | 269 | 539 | .499 | 137 | 160 | .856 | 44 | 115 | 159 | 194 | 75 | 32 | 122 | 734 | 2.9 | 3.5 | 13.3 |
| 96-97—Golden State... | 79 | 2733 | 438 | 792 | .553 | 184 | 213 | .864 | 75 | 242 | 317 | 322 | 130 | 33 | 192 | 1143 | 4.0 | 4.1 | 14.5 |
| 97-98—Indiana.......... | 82 | 2177 | 333 | 692 | .481 | 154 | 164 | *.939 | 38 | 211 | 249 | 186 | 95 | 39 | 117 | 927 | 3.0 | 2.3 | 11.3 |
| 98-99—Indiana.......... | 50 | 1179 | 177 | 371 | .477 | 80 | 92 | .870 | 25 | 135 | 160 | 81 | 47 | 13 | 60 | 507 | 3.2 | 1.6 | 10.1 |
| 99-00—Indiana.......... | 47 | 582 | 80 | 187 | .428 | 37 | 41 | .902 | 14 | 62 | 76 | 37 | 28 | 9 | 28 | 242 | 1.6 | 0.8 | 5.1 |
| 00-01—Golden State... | 20 | 374 | 36 | 106 | .340 | 24 | 28 | .857 | 10 | 31 | 41 | 19 | 16 | 10 | 19 | 115 | 2.1 | 1.0 | 5.8 |
| Totals ................. | 986 | 32163 | 6740 | 13243 | .509 | 3616 | 4178 | .865 | 1026 | 3008 | 4034 | 3450 | 1530 | 549 | 2315 | 17911 | 4.1 | 3.5 | 18.2 |

Three-point field goals: 1985-86, 5-for-27 (.185). 1986-87, 19-for-63 (.302). 1987-88, 34-for-97 (.351). 1988-89, 23-for-100 (.230). 1989-90, 87-for-234 (.372). 1990-91, 40-for-133 (.301). 1991-92, 64-for-175 (.366). 1992-93, 60-for-133 (.451). 1993-94, 55-for-151 (.364). 1994-95, 42-for-93 (.452). 1995-96, 59-for-150 (.393). 1996-97, 83-for-202 (.411). 1997-98, 107-for-243 (.440). 1998-99, 73-for-157 (.465). 1999-00, 45-for-110 (.409). 2000-01, 19-for-52 (.365). Totals, 815-for-2120 (.384).

Personal fouls/disqualifications: 1985-86, 130/1. 1986-87, 217/1. 1987-88, 136/3. 1988-89, 178/1. 1989-90, 142/1. 1990-91, 176/2. 1991-92, 171/1. 1992-93, 76/0. 1993-94, 114/0. 1994-95, 53/0. 1995-96, 127/0. 1996-97, 155/0. 1997-98, 186/0. 1998-99, 101/0. 1999-00, 60/0. 2000-01, 28/0. Totals, 2050/10.

## NBA PLAYOFF RECORD

| Season Team | G | Min. | FGM | FGA | Pct. | FTM | FTA | Pct. | Off. | Def. | Tot. | Ast. | St. | Blk. | TO | Pts. | RPG | APG | PPG |
|---|---|---|---|---|---|---|---|---|---|---|---|---|---|---|---|---|---|---|---|
| | | | | | | | | | REBOUNDS | | | | | | | | AVERAGES | | |
| 86-87—Golden State... | 10 | 262 | 49 | 98 | .500 | 12 | 16 | .750 | 2 | 13 | 15 | 23 | 9 | 2 | 16 | 113 | 1.5 | 2.3 | 11.3 |
| 88-89—Golden State... | 8 | 341 | 88 | 163 | .540 | 58 | 67 | .866 | 11 | 36 | 47 | 36 | 14 | 11 | 32 | 235 | 5.9 | 4.5 | 29.4 |
| 90-91—Golden State... | 8 | 366 | 69 | 131 | .527 | 43 | 50 | .860 | 9 | 49 | 58 | 23 | 15 | 12 | 25 | 190 | 7.3 | 2.9 | 23.8 |
| 91-92—Golden State... | 4 | 168 | 27 | 63 | .429 | 13 | 14 | .929 | 3 | 9 | 12 | 12 | 5 | 2 | 8 | 71 | 3.0 | 3.0 | 17.8 |
| 93-94—Golden State... | 3 | 135 | 30 | 51 | .588 | 10 | 11 | .909 | 4 | 10 | 14 | 11 | 0 | 5 | 7 | 76 | 4.7 | 3.7 | 25.3 |
| 97-98—Indiana.......... | 16 | 412 | 52 | 113 | .460 | 18 | 21 | .857 | 13 | 44 | 57 | 23 | 15 | 9 | 24 | 142 | 3.6 | 1.4 | 8.9 |
| 98-99—Indiana.......... | 13 | 283 | 41 | 100 | .410 | 20 | 23 | .870 | 2 | 18 | 20 | 15 | 10 | 3 | 20 | 124 | 1.5 | 1.2 | 9.5 |
| 99-00—Indiana.......... | 9 | 90 | 10 | 21 | .476 | 9 | 11 | .818 | 2 | 12 | 14 | 5 | 6 | 1 | 4 | 31 | 1.6 | 0.6 | 3.4 |
| Totals ................... | 71 | 2057 | 366 | 740 | .495 | 183 | 213 | .859 | 46 | 191 | 237 | 148 | 74 | 45 | 136 | 982 | 3.3 | 2.1 | 13.8 |

Three-point field goals: 1986-87, 3-for-4 (.750). 1988-89, 1-for-8 (.125). 1990-91, 9-for-13 (.692). 1991-92, 4-for-12 (.333). 1993-94, 6-for-12 (.500). 1997-98, 20-for-52 (.385). 1998-99, 22-for-55 (.400). 1999-00, 2-for-8 (.250). Totals, 67-for-164 (.409).

Personal fouls/disqualifications: 1986-87, 31/0. 1988-89, 19/0. 1990-91, 23/0. 1991-92, 8/0. 1993-94, 4/0. 1997-98, 32/0. 1998-99, 21/0. 1999-00, 7/0. Totals, 145/0.

## NBA ALL-STAR GAME RECORD

| Season Team | Min. | FGM | FGA | Pct. | FTM | FTA | Pct. | Off. | Def. | Tot. | Ast. | PF | Dq. | St. | Blk. | TO | Pts. |
|---|---|---|---|---|---|---|---|---|---|---|---|---|---|---|---|---|---|
| | | | | | | | | REBOUNDS | | | | | | | | | |
| 1989—Golden State ........ | 14 | 1 | 4 | .250 | 2 | 2 | 1.000 | 2 | 0 | 2 | 2 | 0 | 0 | 0 | 0 | 1 | 4 |
| 1990—Golden State ........ | 16 | 1 | 5 | .200 | 1 | 2 | .500 | 1 | 2 | 3 | 1 | 0 | 0 | 2 | 1 | 1 | 3 |
| 1991—Golden State ........ | 24 | 4 | 8 | .500 | 4 | 4 | 1.000 | 0 | 2 | 2 | 2 | 2 | 0 | 2 | 0 | 2 | 13 |
| 1992—Golden State ........ | 24 | 6 | 7 | .857 | 0 | 0 | ... | 0 | 1 | 1 | 3 | 0 | 0 | 0 | 0 | 1 | 13 |
| 1993—Golden State ........ | | | | | | | Selected, did not play—injured. | | | | | | | | | | |
| Totals .......................... | 78 | 12 | 24 | .500 | 7 | 8 | .875 | 3 | 5 | 8 | 8 | 2 | 0 | 4 | 1 | 5 | 33 |

Three-point field goals: 1991, 1-for-1. 1992, 1-for-1. Totals, 2-for-2 (1.000).

## MURPHY, CALVIN          G

**PERSONAL:** Born May 9, 1948, in Norwalk, Conn. ... 5-9/165 (1,76/74,8). ... Full name: Calvin Jerome Murphy.
**HIGH SCHOOL:** Norwalk (Conn.).
**COLLEGE:** Niagara.
**TRANSACTIONS:** Selected by San Diego Rockets in second round (18th pick overall) of 1970 NBA Draft. ... Rockets franchise moved from San Diego to Houston for 1971-72 season.
**CAREER NOTES:** Community services adviser, Houston Rockets (1989-90 to present).
**CAREER HONORS:** Elected to Naismith Memorial Basketball Hall of Fame (1993).
**MISCELLANEOUS:** Houston Rockets franchise all-time assists leader with 4,402 (1970-71 through 1982-83).

### COLLEGIATE RECORD

**NOTES:** The Sporting News All-America second team (1969, 1970).

| Season Team | G | Min. | FGM | FGA | Pct. | FTM | FTA | Pct. | Reb. | Ast. | Pts. | RPG | APG | PPG |
|---|---|---|---|---|---|---|---|---|---|---|---|---|---|---|
| | | | | | | | | | | | | AVERAGES | | |
| 66-67—Niagara‡...................... | 19 | ... | 364 | 719 | .506 | 201 | 239 | .841 | 102 | ... | 929 | 5.4 | ... | 48.9 |
| 67-68—Niagara.......... | 24 | ... | 337 | 772 | .437 | 242 | 288 | .840 | 118 | ... | 916 | 4.9 | ... | 38.2 |
| 68-69—Niagara.......... | 24 | ... | 294 | 700 | .420 | 190 | 230 | .826 | 87 | ... | 778 | 3.6 | ... | 32.4 |
| 69-70—Niagara.......... | 29 | ... | 316 | 692 | .457 | 222 | 252 | .881 | 103 | ... | 854 | 3.6 | ... | 29.4 |
| Varsity totals ....................... | 77 | ... | 947 | 2164 | .438 | 654 | 770 | .849 | 308 | ... | 2548 | 4.0 | ... | 33.1 |

### NBA REGULAR-SEASON RECORD

**RECORDS:** Holds single-season record for highest free-throw percentage—.958 (1981).
**HONORS:** NBA All-Rookie team (1971). ... J. Walter Kennedy Citizenship Award (1979).

| Season Team | G | Min. | FGM | FGA | Pct. | FTM | FTA | Pct. | Reb. | Ast. | PF | Dq. | Pts. | RPG | APG | PPG |
|---|---|---|---|---|---|---|---|---|---|---|---|---|---|---|---|---|
| | | | | | | | | | | | | | | AVERAGES | | |
| 70-71—San Diego.......................... | 82 | 2020 | 471 | 1029 | .458 | 356 | 434 | .820 | 245 | 329 | 263 | 4 | 1298 | 3.0 | 4.0 | 15.8 |
| 71-72—Houston.......................... | 82 | 2538 | 571 | 1255 | .455 | 349 | 392 | .890 | 258 | 393 | 298 | 6 | 1491 | 3.1 | 4.8 | 18.2 |
| 72-73—Houston.......................... | 77 | 1697 | 381 | 820 | .465 | 239 | 269 | .888 | 149 | 262 | 211 | 3 | 1001 | 1.9 | 3.4 | 13.0 |

ALL-TIME GREAT PLAYERS

| Season Team | G | Min. | FGM | FGA | Pct. | FTM | FTA | Pct. | REBOUNDS Off. | Def. | Tot. | Ast. | St. | Blk. | TO | Pts. | RPG | APG | PPG |
|---|---|---|---|---|---|---|---|---|---|---|---|---|---|---|---|---|---|---|---|
| 73-74—Houston | 81 | 2922 | 671 | 1285 | .522 | 310 | 357 | .868 | 51 | 137 | 188 | 603 | 157 | 4 | ... | 1652 | 2.3 | 7.4 | 20.4 |
| 74-75—Houston | 78 | 2513 | 557 | 1152 | .484 | 341 | 386 | .883 | 52 | 121 | 173 | 381 | 128 | 4 | ... | 1455 | 2.2 | 4.9 | 18.7 |
| 75-76—Houston | 82 | 2995 | 675 | 1369 | .493 | 372 | 410 | .907 | 52 | 157 | 209 | 596 | 151 | 6 | ... | 1722 | 2.5 | 7.3 | 21.0 |
| 76-77—Houston | 82 | 2764 | 596 | 1216 | .490 | 272 | 307 | .886 | 54 | 118 | 172 | 386 | 144 | 8 | ... | 1464 | 2.1 | 4.7 | 17.9 |
| 77-78—Houston | 76 | 2900 | 852 | *1737 | .491 | 245 | 267 | .918 | 57 | 107 | 164 | 259 | 112 | 3 | 173 | 1949 | 2.2 | 3.4 | 25.6 |
| 78-79—Houston | 82 | 2941 | 707 | 1424 | .496 | 246 | 265 | .928 | 78 | 95 | 173 | 351 | 117 | 6 | 187 | 1660 | 2.1 | 4.3 | 20.2 |
| 79-80—Houston | 76 | 2676 | 624 | 1267 | .493 | 271 | 302 | .897 | 68 | 82 | 150 | 299 | 143 | 9 | 162 | 1520 | 2.0 | 3.9 | 20.0 |
| 80-81—Houston | 76 | 2014 | 528 | 1074 | .492 | 206 | 215 | *.958 | 33 | 54 | 87 | 222 | 111 | 6 | 129 | 1266 | 1.1 | 2.9 | 16.7 |
| 81-82—Houston | 64 | 1204 | 277 | 648 | .427 | 100 | 110 | .909 | 20 | 41 | 61 | 163 | 43 | 1 | 82 | 655 | 1.0 | 2.5 | 10.2 |
| 82-83—Houston | 64 | 1423 | 337 | 754 | .447 | 138 | 150 | *.920 | 34 | 40 | 74 | 158 | 59 | 4 | 89 | 816 | 1.2 | 2.5 | 12.8 |
| **Totals** | 1002 | 30607 | 7247 | 15030 | .482 | 3445 | 3864 | .892 | ... | ... | 2103 | 4402 | 1165 | 51 | 822 | 17949 | 2.1 | 4.4 | 17.9 |

Three-point field goals: 1979-80, 1-for-25 (.040). 1980-81, 4-for-17 (.235). 1981-82, 1-for-16 (.063). 1982-83, 4-for-14 (.286). Totals, 10-for-72 (.139).
Personal fouls/disqualifications: 1973-74, 310/8. 1974-75, 281/8. 1975-76, 294/3. 1976-77, 281/6. 1977-78, 241/4. 1978-79, 288/5. 1979-80, 269/3. 1980-81, 209/0. 1981-82, 142/0. 1982-83, 163/3. Totals, 3250/53.

### NBA PLAYOFF RECORD

| Season Team | G | Min. | FGM | FGA | Pct. | FTM | FTA | Pct. | REBOUNDS Off. | Def. | Tot. | Ast. | St. | Blk. | TO | Pts. | RPG | APG | PPG |
|---|---|---|---|---|---|---|---|---|---|---|---|---|---|---|---|---|---|---|---|
| 74-75—Houston | 8 | 305 | 72 | 156 | .462 | 51 | 57 | .895 | 9 | 10 | 19 | 45 | 14 | 1 | ... | 195 | 2.4 | 5.6 | 24.4 |
| 76-77—Houston | 12 | 420 | 102 | 213 | .479 | 28 | 30 | .933 | 7 | 12 | 19 | 75 | 19 | 2 | ... | 232 | 1.6 | 6.3 | 19.3 |
| 78-79—Houston | 2 | 73 | 9 | 31 | .290 | 8 | 9 | .889 | 2 | 1 | 3 | 6 | 8 | 1 | 2 | 26 | 1.5 | 3.0 | 13.0 |
| 79-80—Houston | 7 | 265 | 58 | 108 | .537 | 13 | 13 | 1.000 | 4 | 6 | 10 | 26 | 11 | 0 | 16 | 131 | 1.4 | 3.7 | 18.7 |
| 80-81—Houston | 19 | 540 | 142 | 287 | .495 | 58 | 60 | .967 | 7 | 17 | 24 | 57 | 26 | 0 | 42 | 344 | 1.3 | 3.0 | 18.1 |
| 81-82—Houston | 3 | 57 | 5 | 22 | .227 | 7 | 8 | .875 | 2 | 1 | 3 | 4 | 1 | 0 | 4 | 17 | 1.0 | 1.3 | 5.7 |
| **Totals** | 51 | 1660 | 388 | 817 | .475 | 165 | 177 | .932 | 31 | 47 | 78 | 213 | 79 | 4 | 64 | 945 | 1.5 | 4.2 | 18.5 |

Three-point field goals: 1979-80, 2-for-4 (.500). 1980-81, 2-for-7 (.286). 1981-82, 0-for-3. Totals, 4-for-14 (.286).
Personal fouls/disqualifications: 1974-75, 36/2. 1976-77, 47/1. 1978-79, 9/0. 1979-80, 23/0. 1980-81, 69/0. 1981-82, 7/0. Totals, 197/4.

### NBA ALL-STAR GAME RECORD

| Season Team | Min. | FGM | FGA | Pct. | FTM | FTA | Pct. | REBOUNDS Off. | Def. | Tot. | Ast. | PF | Dq. | St. | Blk. | TO | Pts. |
|---|---|---|---|---|---|---|---|---|---|---|---|---|---|---|---|---|---|
| 1979—Houston | 15 | 3 | 5 | .600 | 0 | 0 | ... | 0 | 1 | 1 | 5 | 4 | 0 | 2 | 0 | 4 | 6 |

## NIXON, NORM                 G

**PERSONAL:** Born October 10, 1955, in Macon, Ga. ... 6-2/175 (1,88/79,4). ... Full name: Norman Ellard Nixon.
**HIGH SCHOOL:** Southwest (Macon, Ga.).
**COLLEGE:** Duquesne.
**TRANSACTIONS:** Selected by Los Angeles Lakers in first round (22nd pick overall) of 1977 NBA Draft. ... Traded by Lakers with G Eddie Jordan and 1986 and 1987 second-round draft choices to San Diego Clippers for C Swen Nater and draft rights to G Byron Scott (October 10, 1983). ... Played in Italy (1988-89).
**MISCELLANEOUS:** Member of NBA championship team (1980, 1982).

### COLLEGIATE RECORD

| Season Team | G | Min. | FGM | FGA | Pct. | FTM | FTA | Pct. | Reb. | Ast. | Pts. | RPG | APG | PPG |
|---|---|---|---|---|---|---|---|---|---|---|---|---|---|---|
| 73-74—Duquesne | 24 | ... | 113 | 257 | .440 | 31 | 45 | .689 | 99 | 144 | 257 | 4.1 | 6.0 | 10.7 |
| 74-75—Duquesne | 25 | ... | 147 | 282 | .521 | 69 | 92 | .750 | 88 | 105 | 363 | 3.5 | 4.2 | 14.5 |
| 75-76—Duquesne | 25 | ... | 214 | 434 | .493 | 96 | 127 | .756 | 105 | 150 | 524 | 4.2 | 6.0 | 21.0 |
| 76-77—Duquesne | 30 | 1106 | 279 | 539 | .518 | 103 | 138 | .746 | 119 | 178 | 661 | 4.0 | 5.9 | 22.0 |
| **Totals** | 104 | ... | 753 | 1512 | .498 | 299 | 402 | .744 | 411 | 577 | 1805 | 4.0 | 5.5 | 17.4 |

**HONORS:** NBA All-Rookie team (1978).

### NBA REGULAR-SEASON RECORD

| Season Team | G | Min. | FGM | FGA | Pct. | FTM | FTA | Pct. | REBOUNDS Off. | Def. | Tot. | Ast. | St. | Blk. | TO | Pts. | RPG | APG | PPG |
|---|---|---|---|---|---|---|---|---|---|---|---|---|---|---|---|---|---|---|---|
| 77-78—Los Angeles | 81 | 2779 | 496 | 998 | .497 | 115 | 161 | .714 | 41 | 198 | 239 | 553 | 138 | 7 | 251 | 1107 | 3.0 | 6.8 | 13.7 |
| 78-79—Los Angeles | 82 | 3145 | 623 | 1149 | .542 | 158 | 204 | .775 | 48 | 183 | 231 | 737 | 201 | 17 | 231 | 1404 | 2.8 | 9.0 | 17.1 |
| 79-80—Los Angeles | 82 | *3226 | 624 | 1209 | .516 | 197 | 253 | .779 | 52 | 177 | 229 | 642 | 147 | 14 | 288 | 1446 | 2.8 | 7.8 | 17.6 |
| 80-81—Los Angeles | 79 | 2962 | 576 | 1210 | .476 | 196 | 252 | .778 | 64 | 168 | 232 | 696 | 146 | 11 | 285 | 1350 | 2.9 | 8.8 | 17.1 |
| 81-82—Los Angeles | 82 | 3024 | 628 | 1274 | .493 | 181 | 224 | .808 | 38 | 138 | 176 | 652 | 132 | 7 | 237 | 1440 | 2.1 | 8.0 | 17.6 |
| 82-83—Los Angeles | 79 | 2711 | 533 | 1123 | .475 | 125 | 168 | .744 | 61 | 144 | 205 | 566 | 104 | 4 | 237 | 1191 | 2.6 | 7.2 | 15.1 |
| 83-84—San Diego | 82 | 3053 | 587 | 1270 | .462 | 206 | 271 | .760 | 56 | 147 | 203 | 914 | 94 | 4 | 257 | 1391 | 2.5 | 11.1 | 17.0 |
| 84-85—L.A. Clippers | 81 | 2894 | 596 | 1281 | .465 | 170 | 218 | .780 | 55 | 163 | 218 | 711 | 95 | 4 | 273 | 1395 | 2.7 | 8.8 | 17.2 |
| 85-86—L.A. Clippers | 67 | 2138 | 403 | 921 | .438 | 131 | 162 | .809 | 45 | 135 | 180 | 576 | 84 | 3 | 190 | 979 | 2.7 | 8.6 | 14.6 |
| 87-88—L.A. Clippers | | | | | | | | Did not play—Achilles' tendon injury. | | | | | | | | | | | |
| 88-89—L.A. Clippers | 53 | 1318 | 153 | 370 | .414 | 48 | 65 | .738 | 13 | 65 | 78 | 339 | 46 | 0 | 118 | 362 | 1.5 | 6.4 | 6.8 |
| **Totals** | 768 | 27250 | 5219 | 10805 | .483 | 1527 | 1978 | .772 | 473 | 1518 | 1991 | 6386 | 1187 | 71 | 2368 | 12065 | 2.6 | 8.3 | 15.7 |

Three-point field goals: 1979-80, 1-for-8 (.125). 1980-81, 2-for-12 (.167). 1981-82, 3-for-12 (.250). 1982-83, 0-for-13. 1983-84, 11-for-46 (.239). 1984-85, 33-for-99 (.333). 1985-86, 42-for-121 (.347). 1988-89, 8-for-29 (.276). Totals, 100-for-340 (.294).
Personal fouls/disqualifications: 1977-78, 259/3. 1978-79, 250/6. 1979-80, 241/1. 1980-81, 226/2. 1981-82, 264/3. 1982-83, 176/1. 1983-84, 180/1. 1984-85, 175/2. 1985-86, 143/0. 1988-89, 69/0. Totals, 1983/19.

### NBA PLAYOFF RECORD

| Season Team | G | Min. | FGM | FGA | Pct. | FTM | FTA | Pct. | REBOUNDS Off. | Def. | Tot. | Ast. | St. | Blk. | TO | Pts. | RPG | APG | PPG |
|---|---|---|---|---|---|---|---|---|---|---|---|---|---|---|---|---|---|---|---|
| 77-78—Los Angeles | 3 | 92 | 11 | 24 | .458 | 2 | 3 | .667 | 4 | 5 | 9 | 16 | 4 | 1 | 5 | 24 | 3.0 | 5.3 | 8.0 |
| 78-79—Los Angeles | 8 | 327 | 56 | 119 | .471 | 11 | 15 | .733 | 6 | 22 | 28 | 94 | 11 | 0 | 24 | 123 | 3.5 | 11.8 | 15.4 |
| 79-80—Los Angeles | 16 | 648 | 114 | 239 | .477 | 41 | 51 | .804 | 13 | 43 | 56 | 125 | 32 | 3 | 49 | 270 | 3.5 | 7.8 | 16.9 |
| 80-81—Los Angeles | 3 | 133 | 25 | 49 | .510 | 8 | 10 | .800 | 1 | 10 | 11 | 26 | 1 | 1 | 5 | 58 | 3.7 | 8.7 | 19.3 |
| 81-82—Los Angeles | 14 | 549 | 121 | 253 | .478 | 43 | 57 | .754 | 13 | 30 | 43 | 114 | 23 | 2 | 34 | 286 | 3.1 | 8.1 | 20.4 |
| 82-83—Los Angeles | 14 | 538 | 113 | 237 | .477 | 37 | 50 | .740 | 13 | 35 | 48 | 89 | 18 | 1 | 34 | 266 | 3.4 | 6.4 | 19.0 |
| **Totals** | 58 | 2287 | 440 | 921 | .478 | 142 | 186 | .763 | 50 | 145 | 195 | 464 | 89 | 8 | 151 | 1027 | 3.4 | 8.0 | 17.7 |

Three-point field goals: 1979-80, 1-for-5 (.200). 1981-82, 1-for-3 (.333). 1982-83, 3-for-7 (.429). Totals, 5-for-15 (.333).
Personal fouls/disqualifications: 1977-78, 13/0. 1978-79, 37/1. 1979-80, 59/0. 1980-81, 9/0. 1981-82, 43/0. 1982-83, 40/0. Totals, 201/1.

## NBA ALL-STAR GAME RECORD

| Season Team | Min. | FGM | FGA | Pct. | FTM | FTA | Pct. | REBOUNDS Off. | Def. | Tot. | Ast. | PF | Dq. | St. | Blk. | TO | Pts. |
|---|---|---|---|---|---|---|---|---|---|---|---|---|---|---|---|---|---|
| 1982—Los Angeles ......... | 19 | 7 | 14 | .500 | 0 | 0 | ... | 0 | 0 | 0 | 2 | 0 | 0 | 1 | 0 | 0 | 14 |
| 1985—L.A. Clippers ........ | 19 | 5 | 7 | .714 | 1 | 2 | .500 | 0 | 2 | 2 | 8 | 0 | 0 | 1 | 0 | 1 | 11 |
| 1987—L.A. Clippers ........ | | | | | | | Did not play—Achilles' tendon injury. | | | | | | | | | | |
| Totals ........................... | 38 | 12 | 21 | .571 | 1 | 2 | .500 | 0 | 2 | 2 | 10 | 0 | 0 | 2 | 0 | 1 | 25 |

## ITALIAN LEAGUE RECORD

| Season Team | G | Min. | FGM | FGA | Pct. | FTM | FTA | Pct. | Reb. | Ast. | Pts. | AVERAGES RPG | APG | PPG |
|---|---|---|---|---|---|---|---|---|---|---|---|---|---|---|
| 88-89—Scavolini Pesaro............ | 6 | 217 | 37 | 75 | .493 | 4 | 7 | .571 | 15 | 19 | 87 | 2.5 | 3.2 | 14.5 |

# OAKLEY, CHARLES                                    F

**PERSONAL:** Born December 18, 1963, in Cleveland. ... 6-9/245. (2,06/111,1).
**HIGH SCHOOL:** John Hay (Cleveland).
**COLLEGE:** Virginia Union.
**TRANSACTIONS/CAREER NOTES:** Selected by Cleveland Cavaliers in first round (ninth pick overall) of 1985 NBA Draft. ... Draft rights traded by Cavaliers with draft rights to G Calvin Duncan to Chicago Bulls for G Ennis Whatley and draft rights to F Keith Lee (June 18, 1985). ... Traded by Bulls with 1988 first- and third-round draft choices to New York Knicks for C Bill Cartwright and 1988 first- and third-round draft choices (June 27, 1988). ... Traded by Knicks with draft rights to F/C Sean Marks and cash to Toronto Raptors for F Marcus Camby (June 25, 1998). ... Traded by Raptors with 2002 second-round draft choice to Bulls for F/C Brian Skinner (July 18, 2001). ... Signed as free agent by Washington Wizards (October 12, 2002). ... Signed by Houston Rockets to first of two consecutive 10-day contracts (March 18, 2004).

## COLLEGIATE RECORD

**NOTES:** Led NCAA Division II with 17.3 rebounds per game (1985).

| Season Team | G | Min. | FGM | FGA | Pct. | FTM | FTA | Pct. | Reb. | Ast. | Pts. | AVERAGES RPG | APG | PPG |
|---|---|---|---|---|---|---|---|---|---|---|---|---|---|---|
| 81-82—Virginia Union ............... | 28 | ... | 169 | 274 | .617 | 106 | 174 | .609 | 349 | ... | 444 | 12.5 | 0.0 | 15.9 |
| 82-83—Virginia Union ............... | 28 | ... | 220 | 378 | .582 | 100 | 170 | .588 | 365 | 28 | 540 | 13.0 | 1.0 | 19.3 |
| 83-84—Virginia Union ............... | 30 | ... | 256 | 418 | .612 | 139 | 224 | .621 | 393 | ... | 651 | 13.1 | 0.0 | 21.7 |
| 84-85—Virginia Union ............... | 31 | ... | 283 | 453 | .625 | 178 | 266 | .669 | 535 | 66 | 744 | 17.3 | 2.1 | 24.0 |
| Totals ..................................... | 117 | ... | 928 | 1523 | .609 | 523 | 834 | .627 | 1642 | ... | 2379 | 14.0 | ... | 20.3 |

## NBA REGULAR-SEASON RECORD

**HONORS:** NBA All-Defensive first team (1994). ... NBA All-Defensive second team (1998). ... NBA All-Rookie team (1986).

| Season Team | G | Min. | FGM | FGA | Pct. | FTM | FTA | Pct. | REBOUNDS Off. | Def. | Tot. | Ast. | St. | Blk. | TO | Pts. | AVERAGES RPG | APG | PPG |
|---|---|---|---|---|---|---|---|---|---|---|---|---|---|---|---|---|---|---|---|
| 85-86—Chicago ......... | 77 | 1772 | 281 | 541 | .519 | 178 | 269 | .662 | 255 | 409 | 664 | 133 | 68 | 30 | 175 | 740 | 8.6 | 1.7 | 9.6 |
| 86-87—Chicago ......... | 82 | 2980 | 468 | 1052 | .445 | 245 | 357 | .686 | 299 | *775 | *1074 | 296 | 85 | 36 | 299 | 1192 | 13.1 | 3.6 | 14.5 |
| 87-88—Chicago ......... | 82 | 2816 | 375 | 776 | .483 | 261 | 359 | .727 | 326 | *740 | *1066 | 248 | 68 | 28 | 241 | 1014 | 13.0 | 3.0 | 12.4 |
| 88-89—New York ....... | 82 | 2604 | 426 | 835 | .510 | 197 | 255 | .773 | 343 | 518 | 861 | 187 | 104 | 14 | 248 | 1061 | 10.5 | 2.3 | 12.9 |
| 89-90—New York ....... | 61 | 2196 | 336 | 641 | .524 | 217 | 285 | .761 | 258 | 469 | 727 | 146 | 46 | 16 | 165 | 889 | 11.9 | 2.4 | 14.6 |
| 90-91—New York ....... | 76 | 2739 | 307 | 595 | .516 | 239 | 305 | .784 | 305 | 615 | 920 | 204 | 62 | 17 | 215 | 853 | 12.1 | 2.7 | 11.2 |
| 91-92—New York ....... | 82 | 2309 | 210 | 402 | .522 | 86 | 117 | .735 | 256 | 444 | 700 | 133 | 67 | 15 | 123 | 506 | 8.5 | 1.6 | 6.2 |
| 92-93—New York ....... | 82 | 2230 | 219 | 431 | .508 | 127 | 176 | .722 | 288 | 420 | 708 | 126 | 85 | 15 | 124 | 565 | 8.6 | 1.5 | 6.9 |
| 93-94—New York ....... | 82 | 2932 | 363 | 760 | .478 | 243 | 313 | .776 | 349 | 616 | 965 | 218 | 110 | 18 | 193 | 969 | 11.8 | 2.7 | 11.8 |
| 94-95—New York ....... | 50 | 1567 | 192 | 393 | .489 | 119 | 150 | .793 | 155 | 290 | 445 | 126 | 60 | 7 | 103 | 506 | 8.9 | 2.5 | 10.1 |
| 95-96—New York ....... | 53 | 1775 | 211 | 448 | .471 | 175 | 210 | .833 | 162 | 298 | 460 | 137 | 58 | 14 | 104 | 604 | 8.7 | 2.6 | 11.4 |
| 96-97—New York ....... | 80 | 2873 | 339 | 694 | .488 | 181 | 224 | .808 | 246 | 535 | 781 | 221 | 111 | 21 | 171 | 864 | 9.8 | 2.8 | 10.8 |
| 97-98—New York ....... | 79 | 2734 | 307 | 698 | .440 | 97 | 114 | .851 | 218 | 506 | 724 | 201 | 123 | 22 | 126 | 711 | 9.2 | 2.5 | 9.0 |
| 98-99—Toronto ......... | 50 | 1633 | 140 | 327 | .428 | 67 | 83 | .807 | 96 | 278 | 374 | 168 | 46 | 21 | 96 | 348 | 7.5 | 3.4 | 7.0 |
| 99-00—Toronto ......... | 80 | 2431 | 234 | 560 | .418 | 66 | 85 | .776 | 117 | 423 | 540 | 253 | 102 | 45 | 154 | 548 | 6.8 | 3.2 | 6.9 |
| 00-01—Toronto .......... | 78 | 2767 | 305 | 786 | .388 | 127 | 152 | .836 | 142 | 599 | 741 | 264 | 76 | 48 | 139 | 748 | 9.5 | 3.4 | 9.6 |
| 01-02—Chicago ......... | 57 | 1383 | 97 | 263 | .369 | 21 | 28 | .750 | 72 | 271 | 343 | 114 | 49 | 11 | 87 | 216 | 6.0 | 2.0 | 3.8 |
| 02-03—Washington ... | 42 | 514 | 23 | 55 | .418 | 28 | 34 | .824 | 37 | 70 | 107 | 40 | 13 | 6 | 21 | 74 | 2.5 | 1.0 | 1.8 |
| 03-04—Houston......... | 7 | 25 | 2 | 6 | .333 | 5 | 6 | .833 | 0 | 5 | 5 | 2 | 0 | 0 | 1 | 9 | 0.7 | 0.3 | 1.3 |
| Totals .................. | 1282 | 40280 | 4835 | 10263 | .471 | 2679 | 3522 | .761 | 3924 | 8281 | 12205 | 3217 | 1351 | 384 | 2785 | 12417 | 9.5 | 2.5 | 9.7 |

Three-point field goals: 1985-86, 0-for-3. 1986-87, 11-for-30 (.367). 1987-88, 3-for-12 (.250). 1988-89, 12-for-48 (.250). 1989-90, 0-for-3. 1990-91, 0-for-2. 1991-92, 0-for-3. 1992-93, 0-for-1. 1993-94, 0-for-3. 1994-95, 3-for-12 (.250). 1995-96, 7-for-26 (.269). 1996-97, 5-for-19 (.263). 1997-98, 0-for-6. 1998-99, 1-for-5 (.200). 1999-00, 14-for-41 (.341). 2000-01, 11-for-49 (.224). 2001-02, 1-for-6 (.167). Totals, 68-for-269 (.253).

Personal fouls/disqualifications: 1985-86, 250/9. 1986-87, 315/4. 1987-88, 272/2. 1988-89, 270/1. 1989-90, 220/3. 1990-91, 288/4. 1991-92, 258/2. 1992-93, 289/5. 1993-94, 293/4. 1994-95, 179/3. 1995-96, 169/2. 1996-97, 305/4. 1997-98, 280/4. 1998-99, 182/4. 1999-00, 294/6. 2000-01, 258/0. 2001-02, 175/2. 2002-03, 90/0. 2003-04, 8/0. Totals, 4421/63.

## NBA PLAYOFF RECORD

| Season Team | G | Min. | FGM | FGA | Pct. | FTM | FTA | Pct. | REBOUNDS Off. | Def. | Tot. | Ast. | St. | Blk. | TO | Pts. | AVERAGES RPG | APG | PPG |
|---|---|---|---|---|---|---|---|---|---|---|---|---|---|---|---|---|---|---|---|
| 85-86—Chicago ......... | 3 | 88 | 11 | 21 | .524 | 8 | 13 | .615 | 10 | 20 | 30 | 3 | 6 | 2 | 5 | 30 | 10.0 | 1.0 | 10.0 |
| 86-87—Chicago ......... | 3 | 129 | 19 | 50 | .380 | 20 | 24 | .833 | 17 | 29 | 46 | 6 | 4 | 1 | 8 | 60 | 15.3 | 2.0 | 20.0 |
| 87-88—Chicago ......... | 10 | 373 | 40 | 91 | .440 | 21 | 24 | .875 | 39 | 89 | 128 | 32 | 6 | 4 | 18 | 101 | 12.8 | 3.2 | 10.1 |
| 88-89—New York ....... | 9 | 299 | 35 | 73 | .479 | 16 | 24 | .667 | 43 | 58 | 101 | 11 | 12 | 1 | 22 | 87 | 11.2 | 1.2 | 9.7 |
| 89-90—New York ....... | 10 | 336 | 43 | 84 | .512 | 34 | 52 | .654 | 39 | 71 | 110 | 27 | 11 | 2 | 22 | 121 | 11.0 | 2.7 | 12.1 |
| 90-91—New York ....... | 3 | 100 | 10 | 21 | .476 | 3 | 6 | .500 | 15 | 16 | 31 | 3 | 2 | 1 | 7 | 23 | 10.3 | 1.0 | 7.7 |
| 91-92—New York ....... | 12 | 354 | 22 | 58 | .379 | 20 | 27 | .741 | 44 | 64 | 108 | 8 | 8 | 5 | 15 | 64 | 9.0 | 0.7 | 5.3 |
| 92-93—New York ....... | 15 | 507 | 63 | 131 | .481 | 40 | 55 | .727 | 71 | 94 | 165 | 17 | 16 | 2 | 36 | 166 | 11.0 | 1.1 | 11.1 |

| Season Team | G | Min. | FGM | FGA | Pct. | FTM | FTA | Pct. | REBOUNDS Off. | Def. | Tot. | Ast. | St. | Blk. | TO | Pts. | AVERAGES RPG | APG | PPG |
|---|---|---|---|---|---|---|---|---|---|---|---|---|---|---|---|---|---|---|---|
| 93-94—New York | 25 | 992 | 125 | 262 | .477 | 79 | 102 | .775 | 116 | 176 | 292 | 59 | 35 | 5 | 65 | 329 | 11.7 | 2.4 | 13.2 |
| 94-95—New York | 11 | 421 | 49 | 109 | .450 | 42 | 51 | .824 | 31 | 62 | 93 | 41 | 19 | 6 | 24 | 144 | 8.5 | 3.7 | 13.1 |
| 95-96—New York | 8 | 308 | 39 | 78 | .500 | 25 | 36 | .694 | 28 | 41 | 69 | 14 | 8 | 0 | 28 | 105 | 8.6 | 1.8 | 13.1 |
| 96-97—New York | 10 | 358 | 38 | 86 | .442 | 22 | 29 | .759 | 23 | 65 | 88 | 16 | 22 | 3 | 18 | 98 | 8.8 | 1.6 | 9.8 |
| 97-98—New York | 10 | 342 | 29 | 71 | .408 | 23 | 25 | .920 | 21 | 64 | 85 | 14 | 11 | 2 | 13 | 81 | 8.5 | 1.4 | 8.1 |
| 99-00—Toronto | 3 | 110 | 14 | 29 | .483 | 0 | 1 | .000 | 2 | 21 | 23 | 11 | 6 | 1 | 5 | 30 | 7.7 | 3.7 | 10.0 |
| 00-01—Toronto | 12 | 391 | 47 | 108 | .435 | 14 | 17 | .824 | 20 | 56 | 76 | 21 | 12 | 7 | 22 | 111 | 6.3 | 1.8 | 9.3 |
| Totals | 144 | 5108 | 584 | 1272 | .459 | 367 | 486 | .755 | 519 | 926 | 1445 | 283 | 178 | 42 | 308 | 1550 | 10.0 | 2.0 | 10.8 |

Three-point field goals: 1986-87, 2-for-4 (.500). 1987-88, 0-for-2. 1988-89, 1-for-2 (.500). 1989-90, 1-for-1. 1994-95, 4-for-10 (.400). 1995-96, 2-for-6 (.333). 1996-97, 0-for-1. 1999-00, 2-for-7 (.286). 2000-01, 3-for-8 (.375). Totals, 15-for-41 (.366).

Personal fouls/disqualifications: 1985-86, 13/0. 1986-87, 13/0. 1987-88, 33/0. 1988-89, 31/1. 1989-90, 33/1. 1990-91, 13/0. 1991-92, 36/0. 1992-93, 51/1. 1993-94, 87/1. 1994-95, 42/0. 1995-96, 33/1. 1996-97, 37/0. 1997-98, 38/1. 1999-00, 14/0. 2000-01, 29/0. Totals, 503/6.

### NBA ALL-STAR GAME RECORD

| Season Team | Min. | FGM | FGA | Pct. | FTM | FTA | Pct. | REBOUNDS Off. | Def. | Tot. | Ast. | PF | Dq. | St. | Blk. | TO | Pts. |
|---|---|---|---|---|---|---|---|---|---|---|---|---|---|---|---|---|---|
| 1994—New York | 11 | 1 | 3 | .333 | 0 | 0 | ... | 1 | 2 | 3 | 3 | 3 | 0 | 0 | 0 | 0 | 2 |

## OLAJUWON, HAKEEM   C

**PERSONAL:** Born January 21, 1963, in Lagos, Nigeria. ... 7-0/255. (2,13/115,7). ... Full Name: Hakeem Abdul Olajuwon. ... Known as Akeem Olajuwon until March 9, 1991. ... Nickname: The Dream. ... Name pronounced ah-KEEM a-lie-shoe-on.
**HIGH SCHOOL:** Muslim Teachers College (Lagos, Nigeria).
**COLLEGE:** Houston.
**TRANSACTIONS/CAREER NOTES:** Selected by Houston Rockets in first round (first pick overall) of 1984 NBA Draft. ... Traded by Rockets to Toronto Raptors for 2002 first-round draft choice and 2002 second-round draft choice (August 2, 2001).
**CAREER HONORS:** NBA 50th Anniversary All-Time Team (1996).
**MISCELLANEOUS:** Member of NBA championship team (1994, 1995). ... Member of gold-medal-winning U.S. Olympic team (1996). ... Houston Rockets franchise all-time leading scorer with 26,511 points, all-time leading rebounder with 13,382, all-time steals leader with 2,088 and all-time blocked shots leader with 3,740 (1984-85 through 2000-01).

### COLLEGIATE RECORD

**NOTES:** The Sporting News All-America first team (1984). ... NCAA Division I Tournament Most Outstanding Player (1983). ... Led NCAA Division I with .675 field goal percentage (1984). ... Led NCAA Division I with 13.5 rebounds per game (1984). ... Led NCAA Division I with 5.6 blocked shots per game (1984).

| Season Team | G | Min. | FGM | FGA | Pct. | FTM | FTA | Pct. | Reb. | Ast. | Pts. | AVERAGES RPG | APG | PPG |
|---|---|---|---|---|---|---|---|---|---|---|---|---|---|---|
| 80-81—Houston | | | | | | | Did not play. | | | | | | | |
| 81-82—Houston | 29 | 529 | 91 | 150 | .607 | 58 | 103 | .563 | 179 | 11 | 240 | 6.2 | 0.4 | 8.3 |
| 82-83—Houston | 34 | 932 | 192 | 314 | .611 | 88 | 148 | .595 | 388 | 29 | 472 | 11.4 | 0.9 | 13.9 |
| 83-84—Houston | 37 | 1260 | 249 | 369 | .675 | 122 | 232 | .526 | 500 | 48 | 620 | 13.5 | 1.3 | 16.8 |
| Totals | 100 | 2721 | 532 | 833 | .639 | 268 | 483 | .555 | 1067 | 88 | 1332 | 10.7 | 0.9 | 13.3 |

### NBA REGULAR-SEASON RECORD

**RECORDS:** Holds career record for most blocked shots—3,830.
**HONORS:** NBA Most Valuable Player (1994). ... NBA Defensive Player of the Year (1993, 1994). ... IBM Award, for all-around contributions to team's success (1993). ... All-NBA First Team (1987, 1988, 1989, 1993, 1994, 1997). ... All-NBA Second Team (1986, 1990, 1996). ... All-NBA Third Team (1991, 1995, 1999). ... NBA All-Defensive first team (1987, 1988, 1990, 1993, 1994). ... NBA All-Defensive second team (1985, 1991, 1996, 1997). ... NBA All-Rookie team (1985).
**NOTES:** Led NBA with 4.59 blocked shots per game (1990), 3.95 blocked shots per game (1991) and 4.17 blocked shots per game (1993). ... Led NBA with 344 personal fouls (1985).

| Season Team | G | Min. | FGM | FGA | Pct. | FTM | FTA | Pct. | REBOUNDS Off. | Def. | Tot. | Ast. | St. | Blk. | TO | Pts. | AVERAGES RPG | APG | PPG |
|---|---|---|---|---|---|---|---|---|---|---|---|---|---|---|---|---|---|---|---|
| 84-85—Houston | 82 | 2914 | 677 | 1258 | .538 | 338 | 551 | .613 | *440 | 534 | 974 | 111 | 99 | 220 | 234 | 1692 | 11.9 | 1.4 | 20.6 |
| 85-86—Houston | 68 | 2467 | 625 | 1188 | .526 | 347 | 538 | .645 | 333 | 448 | 781 | 137 | 134 | 231 | 195 | 1597 | 11.5 | 2.0 | 23.5 |
| 86-87—Houston | 75 | 2760 | 677 | 1332 | .508 | 400 | 570 | .702 | 315 | 543 | 858 | 220 | 140 | 254 | 228 | 1755 | 11.4 | 2.9 | 23.4 |
| 87-88—Houston | 79 | 2825 | 712 | 1385 | .514 | 381 | 548 | .695 | 302 | 657 | 959 | 163 | 162 | 214 | 243 | 1805 | 12.1 | 2.1 | 22.8 |
| 88-89—Houston | 82 | 3024 | 790 | 1556 | .508 | 454 | 652 | .696 | 338 | *767 | *1105 | 149 | 213 | 282 | 275 | 2034 | *13.5 | 1.8 | 24.8 |
| 89-90—Houston | 82 | 3124 | 806 | 1609 | .501 | 382 | 536 | .713 | 299 | *850 | *1149 | 234 | 174 | *376 | 316 | 1995 | *14.0 | 2.9 | 24.3 |
| 90-91—Houston | 56 | 2062 | 487 | 959 | .508 | 213 | 277 | .769 | 219 | 551 | 770 | 131 | 121 | 221 | 174 | 1187 | 13.8 | 2.3 | 21.2 |
| 91-92—Houston | 70 | 2636 | 591 | 1177 | .502 | 328 | 428 | .766 | 246 | 599 | 845 | 157 | 127 | 304 | 187 | 1510 | 12.1 | 2.2 | 21.6 |
| 92-93—Houston | 82 | 3242 | 848 | 1603 | .529 | 444 | 570 | .779 | 283 | 785 | 1068 | 291 | 150 | *342 | 262 | 2140 | 13.0 | 3.5 | 26.1 |
| 93-94—Houston | 80 | 3277 | 894 | *1694 | .528 | 388 | 542 | .716 | 229 | 726 | 955 | 287 | 128 | 297 | 271 | 2184 | 11.9 | 3.6 | 27.3 |
| 94-95—Houston | 72 | 2853 | 798 | 1545 | .517 | 406 | 537 | .756 | 172 | 603 | 775 | 255 | 133 | 242 | 237 | 2005 | 10.8 | 3.5 | 27.8 |
| 95-96—Houston | 72 | 2797 | 768 | 1494 | .514 | 397 | 548 | .724 | 176 | 608 | 784 | 257 | 113 | 207 | 247 | 1936 | 10.9 | 3.6 | 26.9 |
| 96-97—Houston | 78 | 2852 | 727 | 1426 | .510 | 351 | 446 | .787 | 173 | 543 | 716 | 236 | 117 | 173 | 281 | 1810 | 9.2 | 3.0 | 23.2 |
| 97-98—Houston | 47 | 1633 | 306 | 633 | .483 | 160 | 212 | .755 | 116 | 344 | 460 | 143 | 84 | 96 | 126 | 772 | 9.8 | 3.0 | 16.4 |
| 98-99—Houston | 50 | 1784 | 373 | 725 | .514 | 195 | 272 | .717 | 106 | 372 | 478 | 88 | 82 | 123 | 139 | 945 | 9.6 | 1.8 | 18.9 |
| 99-00—Houston | 44 | 1049 | 193 | 421 | .458 | 69 | 112 | .616 | 65 | 209 | 274 | 61 | 41 | 70 | 73 | 455 | 6.2 | 1.4 | 10.3 |
| 00-01—Houston | 58 | 1545 | 283 | 568 | .498 | 123 | 198 | .621 | 124 | 307 | 431 | 72 | 70 | 88 | 81 | 689 | 7.4 | 1.2 | 11.9 |
| 01-02—Toronto | 61 | 1378 | 194 | 418 | .464 | 47 | 84 | .560 | 98 | 268 | 366 | 66 | 74 | 90 | 98 | 435 | 6.0 | 1.1 | 7.1 |
| 02-03—Toronto | | | | | | | | Did not play—injured. | | | | | | | | | | | |
| Totals | 1238 | 44222 | 10749 | 20991 | .512 | 5423 | 7621 | .712 | 4034 | 9714 | 13748 | 3058 | 2162 | 3830 | 3667 | 26946 | 11.1 | 2.5 | 21.8 |

Three-point field goals: 1986-87, 1-for-5 (.200). 1987-88, 0-for-4. 1988-89, 0-for-10. 1989-90, 1-for-6 (.167). 1990-91, 0-for-4. 1991-92, 0-for-1. 1992-93, 0-for-8. 1993-94, 8-for-19 (.421). 1994-95, 3-for-16 (.188). 1995-96, 3-for-14 (.214). 1996-97, 5-for-16 (.313). 1997-98, 0-for-3. 1998-99, 4-for-13 (.308). 1999-00, 0-for-2. 2000-01, 0-for-1. 2001-02, 0-for-2. Totals, 25-for-124 (.202).

Personal fouls/disqualifications: 1984-85, 344/10. 1985-86, 271/9. 1986-87, 294/8. 1987-88, 324/7. 1988-89, 329/10. 1989-90, 314/6. 1990-91, 221/5. 1991-92, 263/7. 1992-93, 305/5. 1993-94, 289/4. 1994-95, 250/3. 1995-96, 242/0. 1996-97, 249/3. 1997-98, 152/0. 1998-99, 160/3. 1999-00, 88/0. 2000-01, 141/0. 2001-02, 147/0. Totals, 4383/80.

## NBA PLAYOFF RECORD

**NOTES:** NBA Finals Most Valuable Player (1994, 1995). ... Shares NBA Finals single-game record for most blocked shots—8 (June 5, 1986, vs. Boston). ... Shares single-game playoff record for most blocked shots—10 (April 29, 1990, vs. Los Angeles Lakers).

| Season Team | G | Min. | FGM | FGA | Pct. | FTM | FTA | Pct. | REBOUNDS Off. | Def. | Tot. | Ast. | St. | Blk. | TO | Pts. | AVERAGES RPG | APG | PPG |
|---|---|---|---|---|---|---|---|---|---|---|---|---|---|---|---|---|---|---|---|
| 84-85—Houston | 5 | 187 | 42 | 88 | .477 | 22 | 46 | .478 | 33 | 32 | 65 | 7 | 7 | 13 | 11 | 106 | 13.0 | 1.4 | 21.2 |
| 85-86—Houston | 20 | 766 | 205 | 387 | .530 | 127 | 199 | .638 | 101 | 135 | 236 | 39 | 40 | 69 | 43 | 537 | 11.8 | 2.0 | 26.9 |
| 86-87—Houston | 10 | 389 | 110 | 179 | .615 | 72 | 97 | .742 | 39 | 74 | 113 | 25 | 13 | 43 | 36 | 292 | 11.3 | 2.5 | 29.2 |
| 87-88—Houston | 4 | 162 | 56 | 98 | .571 | 38 | 43 | .884 | 20 | 47 | 67 | 7 | 9 | 11 | 9 | 150 | 16.8 | 1.8 | 37.5 |
| 88-89—Houston | 4 | 162 | 42 | 81 | .519 | 17 | 25 | .680 | 14 | 38 | 52 | 12 | 10 | 11 | 10 | 101 | 13.0 | 3.0 | 25.3 |
| 89-90—Houston | 4 | 161 | 31 | 70 | .443 | 12 | 17 | .706 | 15 | 31 | 46 | 8 | 10 | 23 | 11 | 74 | 11.5 | 2.0 | 18.5 |
| 90-91—Houston | 3 | 129 | 26 | 45 | .578 | 14 | 17 | .824 | 12 | 32 | 44 | 6 | 4 | 8 | 8 | 66 | 14.7 | 2.0 | 22.0 |
| 92-93—Houston | 12 | 518 | 123 | 238 | .517 | 62 | 75 | .827 | 52 | 116 | 168 | 57 | 21 | 59 | 45 | 308 | 14.0 | 4.8 | 25.7 |
| 93-94—Houston | 23 | 989 | 267 | 514 | .519 | 128 | 161 | .795 | 55 | 199 | 254 | 98 | 40 | 92 | 83 | 664 | 11.0 | 4.3 | 28.9 |
| 94-95—Houston | 22 | 929 | 306 | 576 | .531 | 111 | 163 | .681 | 44 | 183 | 227 | 98 | 26 | 62 | 69 | 725 | 10.3 | 4.5 | 33.0 |
| 95-96—Houston | 8 | 329 | 75 | 147 | .510 | 29 | 40 | .725 | 17 | 56 | 73 | 31 | 15 | 17 | 29 | 179 | 9.1 | 3.9 | 22.4 |
| 96-97—Houston | 16 | 629 | 147 | 249 | .590 | 76 | 104 | .731 | 46 | 128 | 174 | 54 | 33 | 41 | 46 | 370 | 10.9 | 3.4 | 23.1 |
| 97-98—Houston | 5 | 190 | 39 | 99 | .394 | 24 | 33 | .727 | 9 | 45 | 54 | 12 | 5 | 16 | 13 | 102 | 10.8 | 2.4 | 20.4 |
| 98-99—Houston | 4 | 123 | 23 | 54 | .426 | 7 | 8 | .875 | 5 | 24 | 29 | 2 | 5 | 3 | 5 | 53 | 7.3 | 0.5 | 13.3 |
| 01-02—Toronto | 5 | 86 | 12 | 22 | .545 | 4 | 6 | .667 | 9 | 10 | 19 | 2 | 7 | 4 | 6 | 28 | 3.8 | 0.4 | 5.6 |
| Totals | 145 | 5749 | 1504 | 2847 | .528 | 743 | 1034 | .719 | 471 | 1150 | 1621 | 458 | 245 | 472 | 424 | 3755 | 11.2 | 3.2 | 25.9 |

Three-point field goals: 1985-86, 0-for-1. 1986-87, 0-for-1. 1987-88, 0-for-1. 1990-91, 0-for-1. 1992-93, 0-for-1. 1993-94, 2-for-4 (.500). 1994-95, 2-for-4 (.500). 1995-96, 0-for-1. 1996-97, 0-for-3. 1997-98, 0-for-1. Totals, 4-for-18 (.222).

Personal fouls/disqualifications: 1984-85, 22/0. 1985-86, 87/3. 1986-87, 44/1. 1987-88, 14/0. 1988-89, 17/0. 1989-90, 19/0. 1990-91, 11/0. 1992-93, 37/0. 1993-94, 82/0. 1994-95, 95/0. 1995-96, 28/1. 1996-97, 61/0. 1997-98, 18/0. 2001-02, 9/0. Totals, 562/5.

## NBA ALL-STAR GAME RECORD

**NOTES:** Shares single-game records for most offensive rebounds—9 (1990); and most blocked shots in one half—4 (1994).

| Season Team | Min. | FGM | FGA | Pct. | FTM | FTA | Pct. | REBOUNDS Off. | Def. | Tot. | Ast. | PF | Dq. | St. | Blk. | TO | Pts. |
|---|---|---|---|---|---|---|---|---|---|---|---|---|---|---|---|---|---|
| 1985—Houston | 15 | 2 | 2 | 1.000 | 2 | 6 | .333 | 2 | 3 | 5 | 1 | 1 | 0 | 0 | 2 | 0 | 6 |
| 1986—Houston | 15 | 1 | 8 | .125 | 1 | 2 | .500 | 1 | 4 | 5 | 0 | 3 | 0 | 1 | 2 | 1 | 3 |
| 1987—Houston | 26 | 2 | 6 | .333 | 6 | 8 | .750 | 4 | 9 | 13 | 2 | 6 | 1 | 0 | 3 | 1 | 10 |
| 1988—Houston | 28 | 8 | 13 | .615 | 5 | 7 | .714 | 7 | 2 | 9 | 2 | 3 | 0 | 2 | 2 | 4 | 21 |
| 1989—Houston | 25 | 5 | 12 | .417 | 2 | 3 | .667 | 4 | 3 | 7 | 3 | 2 | 0 | 3 | 2 | 3 | 12 |
| 1990—Houston | 31 | 2 | 14 | .143 | 4 | 10 | .400 | 9 | 7 | 16 | 2 | 1 | 0 | 1 | 1 | 4 | 8 |
| 1992—Houston | 20 | 3 | 6 | .500 | 1 | 2 | .500 | 0 | 4 | 4 | 2 | 3 | 0 | 2 | 1 | 3 | 7 |
| 1993—Houston | 21 | 1 | 5 | .200 | 1 | 2 | .500 | 2 | 5 | 7 | 1 | 3 | 0 | 2 | 3 | 3 | 3 |
| 1994—Houston | 30 | 8 | 15 | .533 | 3 | 6 | .500 | 4 | 7 | 11 | 2 | 4 | 0 | 2 | 5 | 3 | 19 |
| 1995—Houston | 25 | 6 | 13 | .462 | 0 | 2 | .000 | 4 | 7 | 11 | 1 | 2 | 0 | 2 | 2 | 3 | 13 |
| 1996—Houston | 14 | 2 | 8 | .250 | 0 | 0 | ... | 1 | 2 | 3 | 0 | 2 | 0 | 0 | 0 | 0 | 4 |
| 1997—Houston | 20 | 5 | 8 | .625 | 1 | 2 | .500 | 0 | 3 | 3 | 1 | 1 | 0 | 0 | 1 | 1 | 11 |
| Totals | 270 | 45 | 110 | .409 | 26 | 50 | .520 | 38 | 56 | 94 | 17 | 31 | 1 | 15 | 23 | 26 | 117 |

Three-point field goals: 1995, 1-for-1. Totals, 1-for-1 (1.000).

# PARISH, ROBERT                    C

**PERSONAL:** Born August 30, 1953, in Shreveport, La. ... 7-1/244 (2,16/110,7). ... Full name: Robert Lee Parish. ... Second cousin of Larry Robinson, forward/guard with eight NBA teams (1990-91 through 2001-02). ... Nickname: Chief.

**HIGH SCHOOL:** Woodlawn (Shreveport, La.).

**COLLEGE:** Centenary (La.).

**TRANSACTIONS/CAREER NOTES:** Selected by Golden State Warriors in first round (eighth pick overall) of 1976 NBA Draft. ... Traded by Warriors with 1980 first-round draft choice to Boston Celtics for two 1980 first-round draft choices (June 9, 1980). ... Signed as unrestricted free agent by Charlotte Hornets (August 4, 1994). ... Signed as free agent by Chicago Bulls (September 25, 1996). ... Announced retirement (August 25, 1997).

**CAREER HONORS:** Elected to Naismith Memorial Basketball Hall of Fame (2003). ... One of the 50 Greatest Players in NBA History (1996).

**MISCELLANEOUS:** Member of NBA championship team (1981, 1984, 1986, 1997). ... Boston Celtics all-time blocked shots leader with 1,703 (1980-81 through 1993-94).

**CAREER NOTES:** Head coach, Maryland Mustangs (USBL).

## COLLEGIATE RECORD

**NOTES:** THE SPORTING NEWS All-America first team (1976).

| Season Team | G | Min. | FGM | FGA | Pct. | FTM | FTA | Pct. | Reb. | Ast. | Pts. | AVERAGES RPG | APG | PPG |
|---|---|---|---|---|---|---|---|---|---|---|---|---|---|---|
| 72-73—Centenary | 27 | 885 | 285 | 492 | .579 | 50 | 82 | .610 | 505 | 25 | 620 | 18.7 | 0.9 | 23.0 |
| 73-74—Centenary | 25 | 841 | 224 | 428 | .523 | 49 | 78 | .628 | 382 | 34 | 497 | 15.3 | 1.4 | 19.9 |
| 74-75—Centenary | 29 | 900 | 237 | 423 | .560 | 74 | 112 | .661 | 447 | 43 | 548 | 15.4 | 1.5 | 18.9 |
| 75-76—Centenary | 27 | 939 | 288 | 489 | .589 | 93 | 134 | .694 | 486 | 48 | 669 | 18.0 | 1.8 | 24.8 |
| Totals | 108 | 3565 | 1034 | 1832 | .564 | 266 | 406 | .655 | 1820 | 150 | 2334 | 16.9 | 1.4 | 21.6 |

## NBA REGULAR-SEASON RECORD

**RECORDS:** Holds career records for most seasons played—21; most games played—1,611; and most defensive rebounds—10,117.

**HONORS:** All-NBA second team (1982). ... All-NBA third team (1989).

| Season Team | G | Min. | FGM | FGA | Pct. | FTM | FTA | Pct. | REBOUNDS Off. | Def. | Tot. | Ast. | St. | Blk. | TO | Pts. | AVERAGES RPG | APG | PPG |
|---|---|---|---|---|---|---|---|---|---|---|---|---|---|---|---|---|---|---|---|
| 76-77—Golden State | 77 | 1384 | 288 | 573 | .503 | 121 | 171 | .708 | 201 | 342 | 543 | 74 | 55 | 94 | ... | 697 | 7.1 | 1.0 | 9.1 |
| 77-78—Golden State | 82 | 1969 | 430 | 911 | .472 | 165 | 264 | .625 | 211 | 469 | 680 | 95 | 79 | 123 | 201 | 1025 | 8.3 | 1.2 | 12.5 |
| 78-79—Golden State | 76 | 2411 | 554 | 1110 | .499 | 196 | 281 | .698 | 265 | 651 | 916 | 115 | 100 | 217 | 233 | 1304 | 12.1 | 1.5 | 17.2 |
| 79-80—Golden State | 72 | 2119 | 510 | 1006 | .507 | 203 | 284 | .715 | 247 | 536 | 783 | 122 | 58 | 115 | 225 | 1223 | 10.9 | 1.7 | 17.0 |
| 80-81—Boston | 82 | 2298 | 635 | 1166 | .545 | 282 | 397 | .710 | 245 | 532 | 777 | 144 | 81 | 214 | 191 | 1552 | 9.5 | 1.8 | 18.9 |
| 81-82—Boston | 80 | 2534 | 669 | 1235 | .542 | 252 | 355 | .710 | 288 | 578 | 866 | 140 | 68 | 192 | 221 | 1590 | 10.8 | 1.8 | 19.9 |

| Season Team | G | Min. | FGM | FGA | Pct. | FTM | FTA | Pct. | REBOUNDS Off. | Def. | Tot. | Ast. | St. | Blk. | TO | Pts. | AVERAGES RPG | APG | PPG |
|---|---|---|---|---|---|---|---|---|---|---|---|---|---|---|---|---|---|---|---|
| 82-83—Boston | 78 | 2459 | 619 | 1125 | .550 | 271 | 388 | .698 | 260 | 567 | 827 | 141 | 79 | 148 | 185 | 1509 | 10.6 | 1.8 | 19.3 |
| 83-84—Boston | 80 | 2867 | 623 | 1140 | .546 | 274 | 368 | .745 | 243 | 614 | 857 | 139 | 55 | 116 | 184 | 1520 | 10.7 | 1.7 | 19.0 |
| 84-85—Boston | 79 | 2850 | 551 | 1016 | .542 | 292 | 393 | .743 | 263 | 577 | 840 | 125 | 56 | 101 | 186 | 1394 | 10.6 | 1.6 | 17.6 |
| 85-86—Boston | 81 | 2567 | 530 | 966 | .549 | 245 | 335 | .731 | 246 | 524 | 770 | 145 | 65 | 116 | 187 | 1305 | 9.5 | 1.8 | 16.1 |
| 86-87—Boston | 80 | 2995 | 588 | 1057 | .556 | 227 | 309 | .735 | 254 | 597 | 851 | 173 | 64 | 144 | 191 | 1403 | 10.6 | 2.2 | 17.5 |
| 87-88—Boston | 74 | 2312 | 442 | 750 | .589 | 177 | 241 | .734 | 173 | 455 | 628 | 115 | 55 | 84 | 154 | 1061 | 8.5 | 1.6 | 14.3 |
| 88-89—Boston | 80 | 2840 | 596 | 1045 | .570 | 294 | 409 | .719 | 342 | 654 | 996 | 175 | 79 | 116 | 200 | 1486 | 12.5 | 2.2 | 18.6 |
| 89-90—Boston | 79 | 2396 | 505 | 871 | .580 | 233 | 312 | .747 | 259 | 537 | 796 | 103 | 38 | 69 | 169 | 1243 | 10.1 | 1.3 | 15.7 |
| 90-91—Boston | 81 | 2441 | 485 | 811 | .598 | 237 | 309 | .767 | 271 | 585 | 856 | 66 | 66 | 103 | 153 | 1207 | 10.6 | 0.8 | 14.9 |
| 91-92—Boston | 79 | 2285 | 468 | 874 | .535 | 179 | 232 | .772 | 219 | 486 | 705 | 70 | 58 | 97 | 131 | 1115 | 8.9 | 0.9 | 14.1 |
| 92-93—Boston | 79 | 2146 | 416 | 777 | .535 | 162 | 235 | .689 | 246 | 494 | 740 | 61 | 57 | 107 | 120 | 994 | 9.4 | 0.8 | 12.6 |
| 93-94—Boston | 74 | 1987 | 356 | 725 | .491 | 154 | 208 | .740 | 141 | 401 | 542 | 82 | 42 | 96 | 108 | 866 | 7.3 | 1.1 | 11.7 |
| 94-95—Charlotte | 81 | 1352 | 159 | 372 | .427 | 71 | 101 | .703 | 93 | 257 | 350 | 44 | 27 | 36 | 66 | 389 | 4.3 | 0.5 | 4.8 |
| 95-96—Charlotte | 74 | 1086 | 120 | 241 | .498 | 50 | 71 | .704 | 89 | 214 | 303 | 29 | 21 | 54 | 50 | 290 | 4.1 | 0.4 | 3.9 |
| 96-97—Chicago | 43 | 406 | 70 | 143 | .490 | 21 | 31 | .677 | 42 | 47 | 89 | 22 | 6 | 19 | 28 | 161 | 2.1 | 0.5 | 3.7 |
| Totals | 1611 | 45704 | 9614 | 17914 | .537 | 4106 | 5694 | .721 | 4598 | 10117 | 14715 | 2180 | 1219 | 2361 | 3183 | 23334 | 9.1 | 1.4 | 14.5 |

Three-point field goals: 1979-80, 0-for-1. 1980-81, 0-for-1. 1982-83, 0-for-1. 1986-87, 0-for-1. 1987-88, 0-for-1. 1990-91, 0-for-1. Totals, 0-for-6.

Personal fouls/disqualifications: 1976-77, 224/7. 1977-78, 291/10. 1978-79, 303/10. 1979-80, 248/6. 1980-81, 310/9. 1981-82, 267/5. 1982-83, 222/4. 1983-84, 266/7. 1984-85, 223/2. 1985-86, 215/3. 1986-87, 266/5. 1987-88, 195/5. 1988-89, 209/2. 1989-90, 189/2. 1990-91, 197/1. 1991-92, 172/2. 1992-93, 201/3. 1993-94, 190/3. 1994-95, 132/0. 1995-96, 80/0. 1996-97, 40/0. Totals, 4443/86.

## NBA PLAYOFF RECORD

**NOTES:** Holds career playoff record for most offensive rebounds—571.

| Season Team | G | Min. | FGM | FGA | Pct. | FTM | FTA | Pct. | REBOUNDS Off. | Def. | Tot. | Ast. | St. | Blk. | TO | Pts. | AVERAGES RPG | APG | PPG |
|---|---|---|---|---|---|---|---|---|---|---|---|---|---|---|---|---|---|---|---|
| 76-77—Golden State | 10 | 239 | 52 | 108 | .481 | 17 | 26 | .654 | 43 | 60 | 103 | 11 | 7 | 11 | ... | 121 | 10.3 | 1.1 | 12.1 |
| 80-81—Boston | 17 | 492 | 108 | 219 | .493 | 39 | 58 | .672 | 50 | 96 | 146 | 19 | 21 | 39 | 44 | 255 | 8.6 | 1.1 | 15.0 |
| 81-82—Boston | 12 | 426 | 102 | 209 | .488 | 51 | 75 | .680 | 43 | 92 | 135 | 18 | 5 | 48 | 39 | 255 | 11.3 | 1.5 | 21.3 |
| 82-83—Boston | 7 | 249 | 43 | 89 | .483 | 17 | 20 | .850 | 21 | 53 | 74 | 9 | 5 | 9 | 17 | 103 | 10.6 | 1.3 | 14.7 |
| 83-84—Boston | 23 | 869 | 139 | 291 | .478 | 64 | 99 | .646 | 76 | 172 | 248 | 27 | 23 | 41 | 45 | 342 | 10.8 | 1.2 | 14.9 |
| 84-85—Boston | 21 | 803 | 136 | 276 | .493 | 87 | 111 | .784 | 57 | 162 | 219 | 31 | 21 | 34 | 50 | 359 | 10.4 | 1.5 | 17.1 |
| 85-86—Boston | 18 | 591 | 106 | 225 | .471 | 58 | 89 | .652 | 52 | 106 | 158 | 25 | 9 | 30 | 44 | 270 | 8.8 | 1.4 | 15.0 |
| 86-87—Boston | 21 | 734 | 149 | 263 | .567 | 79 | 103 | .767 | 59 | 139 | 198 | 28 | 18 | 35 | 38 | 377 | 9.4 | 1.3 | 18.0 |
| 87-88—Boston | 17 | 626 | 100 | 188 | .532 | 50 | 61 | .820 | 51 | 117 | 168 | 21 | 11 | 19 | 38 | 250 | 9.9 | 1.2 | 14.7 |
| 88-89—Boston | 3 | 112 | 20 | 44 | .455 | 7 | 9 | .778 | 6 | 20 | 26 | 6 | 4 | 2 | 6 | 47 | 8.7 | 2.0 | 15.7 |
| 89-90—Boston | 5 | 170 | 31 | 54 | .574 | 17 | 18 | .944 | 23 | 27 | 50 | 13 | 5 | 7 | 12 | 79 | 10.0 | 2.6 | 15.8 |
| 90-91—Boston | 10 | 296 | 58 | 97 | .598 | 42 | 61 | .689 | 33 | 59 | 92 | 6 | 8 | 7 | 16 | 158 | 9.2 | 0.6 | 15.8 |
| 91-92—Boston | 10 | 335 | 50 | 101 | .495 | 20 | 28 | .714 | 38 | 59 | 97 | 14 | 7 | 15 | 9 | 120 | 9.7 | 1.4 | 12.0 |
| 92-93—Boston | 4 | 146 | 31 | 57 | .544 | 6 | 7 | .857 | 13 | 25 | 38 | 5 | 1 | 6 | 6 | 68 | 9.5 | 1.3 | 17.0 |
| 94-95—Charlotte | 4 | 71 | 6 | 11 | .545 | 2 | 5 | .400 | 4 | 5 | 9 | 1 | 0 | 3 | 1 | 14 | 2.3 | 0.3 | 3.5 |
| 96-97—Chicago | 2 | 18 | 1 | 7 | .143 | 0 | 0 | ... | 2 | 2 | 4 | 0 | 0 | 3 | 0 | 2 | 2.0 | 0.0 | 1.0 |
| Totals | 184 | 6177 | 1132 | 2239 | .506 | 556 | 770 | .722 | 571 | 1194 | 1765 | 234 | 145 | 309 | 365 | 2820 | 9.6 | 1.3 | 15.3 |

Three-point field goals: 1986-87, 0-for-1.

Personal fouls/disqualifications: 1976-77, 42/1. 1980-81, 74/2. 1981-82, 47/1. 1982-83, 18/0. 1983-84, 100/6. 1984-85, 68/0. 1985-86, 47/1. 1986-87, 79/4. 1987-88, 42/0. 1988-89, 5/0. 1989-90, 21/0. 1990-91, 34/1. 1991-92, 22/0. 1992-93, 14/0. 1994-95, 2/0. 1996-97, 2/0. Totals, 617/16.

## NBA ALL-STAR GAME RECORD

| Season Team | Min. | FGM | FGA | Pct. | FTM | FTA | Pct. | REBOUNDS Off. | Def. | Tot. | Ast. | PF | Dq. | St. | Blk. | TO | Pts. |
|---|---|---|---|---|---|---|---|---|---|---|---|---|---|---|---|---|---|
| 1981—Boston | 25 | 5 | 18 | .278 | 6 | 6 | 1.000 | 6 | 4 | 10 | 2 | 3 | 0 | 0 | 2 | 1 | 16 |
| 1982—Boston | 20 | 9 | 12 | .750 | 3 | 4 | .750 | 0 | 7 | 7 | 1 | 2 | 0 | 0 | 2 | 1 | 21 |
| 1983—Boston | 18 | 5 | 6 | .833 | 3 | 4 | .750 | 0 | 3 | 3 | 0 | 2 | 0 | 1 | 1 | 1 | 13 |
| 1984—Boston | 28 | 5 | 11 | .455 | 2 | 4 | .500 | 4 | 11 | 15 | 2 | 1 | 0 | 3 | 0 | 4 | 12 |
| 1985—Boston | 10 | 2 | 5 | .400 | 0 | 0 | ... | 3 | 3 | 6 | 1 | 0 | 0 | 0 | 0 | 0 | 4 |
| 1986—Boston | 7 | 0 | 0 | ... | 0 | 2 | .000 | 0 | 1 | 1 | 0 | 0 | 0 | 0 | 1 | 1 | 0 |
| 1987—Boston | 8 | 2 | 3 | .667 | 0 | 0 | ... | 0 | 3 | 3 | 0 | 1 | 0 | 0 | 1 | 0 | 4 |
| 1990—Boston | 21 | 7 | 11 | .636 | 0 | 1 | .000 | 2 | 2 | 4 | 2 | 4 | 0 | 0 | 1 | 1 | 14 |
| 1991—Boston | 5 | 1 | 2 | .500 | 0 | 0 | ... | 1 | 3 | 4 | 0 | 2 | 0 | 0 | 1 | 1 | 2 |
| Totals | 142 | 36 | 68 | .529 | 14 | 21 | .667 | 16 | 37 | 53 | 8 | 15 | 0 | 4 | 8 | 10 | 86 |

## USBL COACHING RECORD

**NOTES:** USBL Coach of the Year (2001).

| Season Team | REGULAR SEASON W | L | Pct. | Finish | PLAYOFFS W | L | Pct. |
|---|---|---|---|---|---|---|---|
| 00-01—Maryland | 19 | 11 | .633 | 1st | 0 | 1 | .000 |

**NOTES:**
2001—Lost to Dodge City in quarterfinals.

---

# PETTIT, BOB                    F/C

**PERSONAL:** Born December 12, 1932, in Baton Rouge, La. ... 6-9/215 (2,05/97,5). ... Full name: Robert Lee Pettit Jr.
**HIGH SCHOOL:** Baton Rouge (La.).
**COLLEGE:** Louisiana State.
**TRANSACTIONS:** Selected by Milwaukee Hawks in first round of 1954 NBA Draft. ... Hawks franchise moved from Milwaukee to St. Louis for 1955-56 season.

**CAREER HONORS:** Elected to Naismith Memorial Basketball Hall of Fame (1970). ... NBA 25th Anniversary All-Time Team (1970), 35th Anniversary All-Time Team (1980) and One of the 50 Greatest Players in NBA History (1996).

**MISCELLANEOUS:** Member of NBA championship team (1958). ... Atlanta Hawks franchise all-time leading rebounder with 12,851 (1954-55 through 1964-65).

## COLLEGIATE RECORD

| Season Team | G | Min. | FGM | FGA | Pct. | FTM | FTA | Pct. | Reb. | Ast. | Pts. | RPG | APG | PPG |
|---|---|---|---|---|---|---|---|---|---|---|---|---|---|---|
| 50-51—Louisiana State‡............ | 10 | ... | ... | ... | ... | ... | ... | ... | ... | ... | 270 | ... | ... | 27.0 |
| 51-52—Louisiana State.............. | 23 | ... | 237 | 549 | .432 | 115 | 192 | .599 | 315 | ... | 589 | 13.7 | ... | 25.6 |
| 52-53—Louisiana State.............. | 21 | ... | 193 | 394 | .490 | 133 | 215 | .619 | 263 | ... | 519 | 12.5 | ... | 24.7 |
| 53-54—Louisiana State.............. | 25 | ... | 281 | 573 | .490 | 223 | 308 | .724 | 432 | ... | 785 | 17.3 | ... | 31.4 |
| **Varsity totals** ........................ | 69 | ... | 711 | 1516 | .469 | 471 | 715 | .659 | 1010 | ... | 1893 | 14.6 | ... | 27.4 |

## NBA REGULAR-SEASON RECORD

**HONORS:** NBA Most Valuable Player (1956, 1959). ... NBA Rookie of the Year (1955). ... All-NBA first team (1955, 1956, 1957, 1958, 1959, 1960, 1961, 1962, 1963, 1964). ... All-NBA second team (1965).

| Season Team | G | Min. | FGM | FGA | Pct. | FTM | FTA | Pct. | Reb. | Ast. | PF | Dq. | Pts. | RPG | APG | PPG |
|---|---|---|---|---|---|---|---|---|---|---|---|---|---|---|---|---|
| 54-55—Milwaukee ......................... | 72 | 2659 | 520 | 1279 | .407 | 426 | 567 | .751 | 994 | 229 | 258 | 5 | 1466 | 13.8 | 3.2 | 20.4 |
| 55-56—St. Louis ......................... | 72 | 2794 | *646 | *1507 | .429 | *557 | *757 | .736 | *1164 | 189 | 202 | 1 | *1849 | 16.2 | 2.6 | *25.7 |
| 56-57—St. Louis ......................... | 71 | 2491 | *613 | *1477 | .415 | 529 | 684 | .773 | 1037 | 133 | 181 | 1 | 1755 | 14.6 | 1.9 | 24.7 |
| 57-58—St. Louis ......................... | 70 | 2528 | 581 | 1418 | .410 | 557 | 744 | .749 | 1216 | 157 | 222 | 6 | 1719 | 17.4 | 2.2 | 24.6 |
| 58-59—St. Louis ......................... | 72 | 2873 | *719 | 1640 | .438 | *667 | *879 | .759 | 1182 | 221 | 200 | 3 | *2105 | 16.4 | 3.1 | *29.2 |
| 59-60—St. Louis ......................... | 72 | 2896 | 669 | 1526 | .438 | 544 | 722 | .753 | 1221 | 257 | 204 | 0 | 1882 | 17.0 | 3.6 | 26.1 |
| 60-61—St. Louis ......................... | 76 | 3027 | 769 | 1720 | .447 | 582 | 804 | .724 | 1540 | 262 | 217 | 1 | 2120 | 20.3 | 3.4 | 27.9 |
| 61-62—St. Louis ......................... | 78 | 3282 | 867 | 1928 | .450 | 695 | 901 | .771 | 1457 | 289 | 296 | 4 | 2429 | 18.7 | 3.7 | 31.1 |
| 62-63—St. Louis ......................... | 79 | 3090 | 778 | 1746 | .446 | *685 | 885 | .774 | 1195 | 245 | 282 | 8 | 2241 | 15.1 | 3.1 | 28.4 |
| 63-64—St. Louis ......................... | 80 | 3296 | 791 | 1708 | .463 | 608 | 771 | .789 | 1224 | 259 | 300 | 3 | 2190 | 15.3 | 3.2 | 27.4 |
| 64-65—St. Louis ......................... | 50 | 1754 | 396 | 923 | .429 | 332 | 405 | .820 | 621 | 128 | 167 | 0 | 1124 | 12.4 | 2.6 | 22.5 |
| **Totals**.................... | 792 | 30690 | 7349 | 16872 | .436 | 6182 | 8119 | .761 | 12851 | 2369 | 2529 | 32 | 20880 | 16.2 | 3.0 | 26.4 |

## NBA PLAYOFF RECORD

**NOTES:** Holds NBA Finals single-game record for most free throws made—19 (April 9, 1958, vs. Boston). ... Shares NBA Finals record for most free throws attempted in one quarter—11 (April 9, 1958, vs. Boston).

| Season Team | G | Min. | FGM | FGA | Pct. | FTM | FTA | Pct. | Reb. | Ast. | PF | Dq. | Pts. | RPG | APG | PPG |
|---|---|---|---|---|---|---|---|---|---|---|---|---|---|---|---|---|
| 55-56—St. Louis ......................... | 8 | 274 | 47 | 128 | .367 | 59 | 70 | .843 | 84 | 18 | 20 | 0 | 153 | 10.5 | 2.3 | 19.1 |
| 56-57—St. Louis ......................... | 10 | 430 | 98 | 237 | .414 | 102 | 133 | .767 | 168 | 25 | 33 | 0 | 298 | 16.8 | 2.5 | 29.8 |
| 57-58—St. Louis ......................... | 11 | 430 | 90 | 230 | .391 | 86 | 118 | .729 | 181 | 20 | 31 | 0 | 266 | 16.5 | 1.8 | 24.2 |
| 58-59—St. Louis ......................... | 6 | 257 | 58 | 137 | .423 | 51 | 65 | .785 | 75 | 14 | 20 | 0 | 167 | 12.5 | 2.3 | 27.8 |
| 59-60—St. Louis ......................... | 14 | 576 | 129 | 292 | .442 | 107 | 142 | .754 | 221 | 52 | 43 | 1 | 365 | 15.8 | 3.7 | 26.1 |
| 60-61—St. Louis ......................... | 12 | 526 | 117 | 284 | .412 | 109 | 144 | .757 | 211 | 38 | 42 | 0 | 343 | 17.6 | 3.2 | 28.6 |
| 62-63—St. Louis ......................... | 11 | 463 | 119 | 259 | .459 | 112 | 144 | .778 | 166 | 33 | 34 | 0 | 350 | 15.1 | 3.0 | 31.8 |
| 63-64—St. Louis ......................... | 12 | 494 | 93 | 226 | .412 | 66 | 79 | .835 | 174 | 33 | 44 | 0 | 252 | 14.5 | 2.8 | 21.0 |
| 64-65—St. Louis ......................... | 4 | 95 | 15 | 41 | .366 | 16 | 20 | .800 | 24 | 8 | 10 | 0 | 46 | 6.0 | 2.0 | 11.5 |
| **Totals**.................... | 88 | 3545 | 766 | 1834 | .418 | 708 | 915 | .774 | 1304 | 241 | 277 | 1 | 2240 | 14.8 | 2.7 | 25.5 |

## NBA ALL-STAR GAME RECORD

**NOTES:** NBA All-Star Game Most Valuable Player (1956, 1958, 1962). ... NBA All-Star Game co-Most Valuable Player (1959). ... Holds single-game records for most rebounds—27; and most rebounds in one quarter—10 (1962). ... Shares single-game record for most rebounds in one half—16 (1962).

| Season Team | Min. | FGM | FGA | Pct. | FTM | FTA | Pct. | Reb | Ast. | PF | Dq. | Pts. |
|---|---|---|---|---|---|---|---|---|---|---|---|---|
| 1955—Milwaukee ...................... | 27 | 3 | 14 | .214 | 2 | 4 | .500 | 9 | 2 | 0 | 0 | 8 |
| 1956—St. Louis ...................... | 31 | 7 | 17 | .412 | 6 | 7 | .857 | 24 | 7 | 4 | 0 | 20 |
| 1957—St. Louis ...................... | 31 | 8 | 18 | .444 | 5 | 6 | .833 | 11 | 2 | 2 | 0 | 21 |
| 1958—St. Louis ...................... | 38 | 10 | 21 | .476 | 8 | 10 | .800 | 26 | 1 | 1 | 0 | 28 |
| 1959—St. Louis ...................... | 34 | 8 | 21 | .381 | 9 | 9 | 1.000 | 16 | 5 | 1 | 0 | 25 |
| 1960—St. Louis ...................... | 28 | 4 | 15 | .267 | 3 | 6 | .500 | 14 | 2 | 2 | 0 | 11 |
| 1961—St. Louis ...................... | 32 | 13 | 22 | .591 | 3 | 7 | .429 | 9 | 0 | 2 | 0 | 29 |
| 1962—St. Louis ...................... | 37 | 10 | 20 | .500 | 5 | 5 | 1.000 | 27 | 2 | 5 | 0 | 25 |
| 1963—St. Louis ...................... | 32 | 7 | 16 | .438 | 11 | 12 | .917 | 13 | 0 | 1 | 0 | 25 |
| 1964—St. Louis ...................... | 36 | 6 | 15 | .400 | 7 | 9 | .778 | 17 | 2 | 3 | 0 | 19 |
| 1965—St. Louis ...................... | 34 | 5 | 14 | .357 | 3 | 5 | .600 | 12 | 0 | 4 | 0 | 13 |
| **Totals** .................... | 360 | 81 | 193 | .420 | 62 | 80 | .775 | 178 | 23 | 25 | 0 | 224 |

## NBA COACHING RECORD

| | REGULAR SEASON | | | | PLAYOFFS | | |
|---|---|---|---|---|---|---|---|
| Season Team | W | L | Pct. | Finish | W | L | Pct. |
| 61-62—St. Louis............................................ | 4 | 2 | .667 | 4th/Western Division | — | — | — |

**NOTES:**

1962—Replaced Paul Seymour (5-9) and Andrew Levane (20-40) as St. Louis head coach (March), with record of 25-49.

## PIPPEN, SCOTTIE      F

**PERSONAL:** Born September 25, 1965, in Hamburg, Ark. ... 6-7/228. (2,01/103,4).
**HIGH SCHOOL:** Hamburg (Ark.).
**COLLEGE:** Central Arkansas.
**TRANSACTIONS/CAREER NOTES:** Selected by Seattle SuperSonics in first round (fifth pick overall) of 1987 NBA Draft. ... Draft rights traded by SuperSonics to Chicago Bulls for draft rights to F/C Olden Polynice, 1988 or 1989 second-round draft choice and option to exchange 1989 first-round draft choices (June 22, 1987). ... Traded by Bulls to Houston Rockets for F Roy Rogers

and 1999 or 2000 second-round draft choice (January 22, 1999). ... Traded by Rockets to Portland Trail Blazers for C Kelvin Cato, F Stacy Augmon, G/F Walt Williams, G Brian Shaw, G Ed Gray and F/C Carlos Rogers (October 2, 1999). ... Signed as free agent by Chicago Bulls (July 20, 2003).

**CAREER HONORS:** NBA 50th Anniversary All-Time Team (1996).

**MISCELLANEOUS:** Member of NBA championship team (1991, 1992, 1993, 1996, 1997, 1998). ... Member of gold-medal-winning U.S. Olympic teams (1992, 1996).

## COLLEGIATE RECORD

| Season Team | G | Min. | FGM | FGA | Pct. | FTM | FTA | Pct. | Reb. | Ast. | Pts. | AVERAGES RPG | APG | PPG |
|---|---|---|---|---|---|---|---|---|---|---|---|---|---|---|
| 83-84—Central Arkansas | 20 | ... | 36 | 79 | .456 | 13 | 19 | .684 | 59 | 14 | 85 | 3.0 | 0.7 | 4.3 |
| 84-85—Central Arkansas | 19 | ... | 141 | 250 | .564 | 69 | 102 | .676 | 175 | 30 | 351 | 9.2 | 1.6 | 18.5 |
| 85-86—Central Arkansas | 29 | ... | 229 | 412 | .556 | 116 | 169 | .686 | 266 | 102 | 574 | 9.2 | 3.5 | 19.8 |
| 86-87—Central Arkansas | 25 | ... | 231 | 390 | .592 | 105 | 146 | .719 | 249 | 107 | 590 | 10.0 | 4.3 | 23.6 |
| Totals | 93 | | 637 | 1131 | .563 | 303 | 436 | .695 | 749 | 253 | 1600 | 8.1 | 2.7 | 17.2 |

Three-point field goals: 1986-87, 23-for-40 (.575). .

## NBA REGULAR-SEASON RECORD

**HONORS:** All-NBA First Team (1994, 1995, 1996). ... All-NBA Second Team (1992, 1997). ... All-NBA Third Team (1993, 1998). ... NBA All-Defensive first team (1992, 1993, 1994, 1995, 1996, 1997, 1998, 1999). ... NBA All-Defensive second team (1991, 2000).

**NOTES:** Led NBA with 2.94 steals per game (1995).

| Season Team | G | Min. | FGM | FGA | Pct. | FTM | FTA | Pct. | REBOUNDS Off. | Def. | Tot. | Ast. | St. | Blk. | TO | Pts. | AVERAGES RPG | APG | PPG |
|---|---|---|---|---|---|---|---|---|---|---|---|---|---|---|---|---|---|---|---|
| 87-88—Chicago | 79 | 1650 | 261 | 564 | .463 | 99 | 172 | .576 | 115 | 183 | 298 | 169 | 91 | 52 | 131 | 625 | 3.8 | 2.1 | 7.9 |
| 88-89—Chicago | 73 | 2413 | 413 | 867 | .476 | 201 | 301 | .668 | 138 | 307 | 445 | 256 | 139 | 61 | 199 | 1048 | 6.1 | 3.5 | 14.4 |
| 89-90—Chicago | 82 | 3148 | 562 | 1150 | .489 | 199 | 295 | .675 | 150 | 397 | 547 | 444 | 211 | 101 | 278 | 1351 | 6.7 | 5.4 | 16.5 |
| 90-91—Chicago | 82 | 3014 | 600 | 1153 | .520 | 240 | 340 | .706 | 163 | 432 | 595 | 511 | 193 | 93 | 232 | 1461 | 7.3 | 6.2 | 17.8 |
| 91-92—Chicago | 82 | 3164 | 687 | 1359 | .506 | 330 | 434 | .760 | 185 | 445 | 630 | 572 | 155 | 93 | 253 | 1720 | 7.7 | 7.0 | 21.0 |
| 92-93—Chicago | 81 | 3123 | 628 | 1327 | .473 | 232 | 350 | .663 | 203 | 418 | 621 | 507 | 173 | 73 | 246 | 1510 | 7.7 | 6.3 | 18.6 |
| 93-94—Chicago | 72 | 2759 | 627 | 1278 | .491 | 270 | 409 | .660 | 173 | 456 | 629 | 403 | 211 | 58 | 232 | 1587 | 8.7 | 5.6 | 22.0 |
| 94-95—Chicago | 79 | 3014 | 634 | 1320 | .480 | 315 | 440 | .716 | 175 | 464 | 639 | 409 | *232 | 89 | 271 | 1692 | 8.1 | 5.2 | 21.4 |
| 95-96—Chicago | 77 | 2825 | 563 | 1216 | .463 | 220 | 324 | .679 | 152 | 344 | 496 | 452 | 133 | 57 | 207 | 1496 | 6.4 | 5.9 | 19.4 |
| 96-97—Chicago | 82 | 3095 | 648 | 1366 | .474 | 204 | 291 | .701 | 160 | 371 | 531 | 467 | 154 | 45 | 214 | 1656 | 6.5 | 5.7 | 20.2 |
| 97-98—Chicago | 44 | 1652 | 315 | 704 | .447 | 150 | 193 | .777 | 53 | 174 | 227 | 254 | 79 | 43 | 109 | 841 | 5.2 | 5.8 | 19.1 |
| 98-99—Houston | 50 | 2011 | 261 | 604 | .432 | 132 | 183 | .721 | 63 | 260 | 323 | 293 | 98 | 37 | 159 | 726 | 6.5 | 5.9 | 14.5 |
| 99-00—Portland | 82 | 2749 | 388 | 860 | .451 | 160 | 223 | .717 | 114 | 399 | 513 | 406 | 117 | 41 | 208 | 1022 | 6.3 | 5.0 | 12.5 |
| 00-01—Portland | 64 | 2133 | 269 | 596 | .451 | 119 | 161 | .739 | 70 | 263 | 333 | 294 | 94 | 35 | 154 | 721 | 5.2 | 4.6 | 11.3 |
| 01-02—Portland | 62 | 1996 | 246 | 597 | .411 | 113 | 146 | .774 | 77 | 244 | 321 | 363 | 101 | 35 | 171 | 659 | 5.2 | 5.9 | 10.6 |
| 02-03—Portland | 64 | 1911 | 265 | 597 | .444 | 121 | 148 | .818 | 57 | 221 | 278 | 285 | 105 | 25 | 164 | 689 | 4.3 | 4.5 | 10.8 |
| 03-04—Chicago | 23 | 412 | 53 | 140 | .379 | 17 | 27 | .630 | 20 | 48 | 68 | 50 | 21 | 9 | 29 | 136 | 3.0 | 2.2 | 5.9 |
| Totals | 1178 | 41069 | 7420 | 15700 | .473 | 3122 | 4437 | .704 | 2068 | 5426 | 7494 | 6135 | 2307 | 947 | 3257 | 18940 | 6.4 | 5.2 | 16.1 |

Three-point field goals: 1987-88, 4-for-23 (.174). 1988-89, 21-for-77 (.273). 1989-90, 28-for-112 (.250). 1990-91, 21-for-68 (.309). 1991-92, 16-for-80 (.200). 1992-93, 22-for-93 (.237). 1993-94, 63-for-197 (.320). 1994-95, 109-for-316 (.345). 1995-96, 150-for-401 (.374). 1996-97, 156-for-424 (.368). 1997-98, 61-for-192 (.318). 1998-99, 72-for-212 (.340). 1999-00, 86-for-263 (.327). 2000-01, 64-for-186 (.344). 2001-02, 54-for-177 (.305). 2002-03, 38-for-133 (.286). 2003-04, 13-for-48 (.271). Totals, 978-for-3002 (.326).

Personal fouls/disqualifications: 1987-88, 214/3. 1988-89, 261/8. 1989-90, 298/6. 1990-91, 270/3. 1991-92, 242/2. 1992-93, 219/3. 1993-94, 227/1. 1994-95, 238/4. 1995-96, 198/0. 1996-97, 213/2. 1997-98, 116/0. 1998-99, 118/0. 1999-00, 208/0. 2000-01, 158/2. 2001-02, 162/3. 2002-03, 149/0. 2003-04, 38/0. Totals, 3329/37.

## NBA PLAYOFF RECORD

**NOTES:** Holds NBA Finals career record for most three-point field goals attempted—117. ... Shares NBA Finals single-game record for most three-point field goals made in one game—7 (June 6, 1997, vs. Utah). ... Holds career playoff record for most three-point field goals attempted—640.

| Season Team | G | Min. | FGM | FGA | Pct. | FTM | FTA | Pct. | REBOUNDS Off. | Def. | Tot. | Ast. | St. | Blk. | TO | Pts. | AVERAGES RPG | APG | PPG |
|---|---|---|---|---|---|---|---|---|---|---|---|---|---|---|---|---|---|---|---|
| 87-88—Chicago | 10 | 294 | 46 | 99 | .465 | 5 | 7 | .714 | 24 | 28 | 52 | 24 | 8 | 8 | 26 | 100 | 5.2 | 2.4 | 10.0 |
| 88-89—Chicago | 17 | 619 | 84 | 182 | .462 | 32 | 50 | .640 | 34 | 95 | 129 | 67 | 23 | 16 | 41 | 222 | 7.6 | 3.9 | 13.1 |
| 89-90—Chicago | 15 | 612 | 104 | 210 | .495 | 71 | 100 | .710 | 33 | 75 | 108 | 83 | 31 | 19 | 49 | 289 | 7.2 | 5.5 | 19.3 |
| 90-91—Chicago | 17 | 704 | 142 | 282 | .504 | 80 | 101 | .792 | 37 | 114 | 151 | 99 | 42 | 19 | 55 | 368 | 8.9 | 5.8 | 21.6 |
| 91-92—Chicago | 22 | 899 | 152 | 325 | .468 | 118 | 155 | .761 | 59 | 134 | 193 | 147 | 41 | 25 | 70 | 428 | 8.8 | 6.7 | 19.5 |
| 92-93—Chicago | 19 | 789 | 152 | 327 | .465 | 74 | 116 | .638 | 37 | 95 | 132 | 107 | 41 | 13 | 71 | 381 | 6.9 | 5.6 | 20.1 |
| 93-94—Chicago | 10 | 384 | 85 | 196 | .434 | 46 | 52 | .885 | 17 | 66 | 83 | 46 | 24 | 7 | 37 | 228 | 8.3 | 4.6 | 22.8 |
| 94-95—Chicago | 10 | 396 | 58 | 131 | .443 | 48 | 71 | .676 | 24 | 62 | 86 | 58 | 14 | 10 | 27 | 178 | 8.6 | 5.8 | 17.8 |
| 95-96—Chicago | 18 | 742 | 112 | 287 | .390 | 51 | 80 | .638 | 62 | 91 | 153 | 107 | 47 | 16 | 41 | 305 | 8.5 | 5.9 | 16.9 |
| 96-97—Chicago | 19 | 753 | 129 | 309 | .417 | 68 | 86 | .791 | 36 | 93 | 129 | 72 | 28 | 18 | 55 | 365 | 6.8 | 3.8 | 19.2 |
| 97-98—Chicago | 21 | 836 | 122 | 294 | .415 | 91 | 134 | .679 | 49 | 101 | 150 | 110 | 45 | 20 | 51 | 353 | 7.1 | 5.2 | 16.8 |
| 98-99—Houston | 4 | 172 | 23 | 70 | .329 | 21 | 26 | .808 | 20 | 27 | 47 | 22 | 7 | 3 | 13 | 73 | 11.8 | 5.5 | 18.3 |
| 99-00—Portland | 16 | 614 | 83 | 198 | .419 | 52 | 70 | .743 | 22 | 92 | 114 | 69 | 32 | 7 | 37 | 239 | 7.1 | 4.3 | 14.9 |
| 00-01—Portland | 3 | 117 | 16 | 38 | .421 | 6 | 9 | .667 | 2 | 15 | 17 | 7 | 8 | 2 | 12 | 41 | 5.7 | 2.3 | 13.7 |
| 01-02—Portland | 3 | 99 | 18 | 39 | .462 | 7 | 8 | .875 | 8 | 20 | 28 | 17 | 4 | 2 | 10 | 49 | 9.3 | 5.7 | 16.3 |
| 02-03—Portland | 4 | 75 | 9 | 22 | .409 | 2 | 2 | 1.000 | 2 | 9 | 11 | 13 | 0 | 0 | 7 | 23 | 2.8 | 3.3 | 5.8 |
| Totals | 208 | 8105 | 1335 | 3009 | .444 | 772 | 1067 | .724 | 466 | 1117 | 1583 | 1048 | 395 | 185 | 602 | 3642 | 7.6 | 5.0 | 17.5 |

Three-point field goals: 1987-88, 3-for-6 (.500). 1988-89, 22-for-56 (.393). 1989-90, 10-for-31 (.323). 1990-91, 4-for-17 (.235). 1991-92, 6-for-24 (.250). 1992-93, 3-for-17 (.176). 1993-94, 12-for-45 (.267). 1994-95, 14-for-38 (.368). 1995-96, 30-for-105 (.286). 1996-97, 39-for-113 (.345). 1997-98, 18-for-79 (.228). 1998-99, 6-for-22 (.273). 1999-00, 21-for-70 (.300). 2000-01, 3-for-17 (.176). 2001-02, 6-for-11 (.545). 2002-03, 2-for-9 (.333). Totals, 200-for-660 (.303).

Personal fouls/disqualifications: 1987-88, 33/1. 1988-89, 63/2. 1989-90, 62/0. 1990-91, 58/1. 1991-92, 72/1. 1992-93, 62/0. 1993-94, 33/1. 1994-95, 40/1. 1995-96, 51/0. 1996-97, 49/0. 1997-98, 66/1. 1998-99, 12/0. 1999-00, 49/1. 2000-01, 14/1. 2001-02, 14/1. 2002-03, 8/0. Totals, 686/11.

## NBA ALL-STAR GAME RECORD

**NOTES:** NBA All-Star Game Most Valuable Player (1994). ... Holds career record for most three-point field goal attempts—22. ... Holds single-game record for most three-point field goal attempts in one half—7 (1994). ... Shares single-game record for most three-point field goal attempts—9 (1994).

| Season | Team | Min. | FGM | FGA | Pct. | FTM | FTA | Pct. | REBOUNDS Off. | Def. | Tot. | Ast. | PF | Dq. | St. | Blk. | TO | Pts. |
|---|---|---|---|---|---|---|---|---|---|---|---|---|---|---|---|---|---|---|
| 1990 | —Chicago | 12 | 2 | 4 | .500 | 0 | 0 | ... | 0 | 1 | 1 | 0 | 1 | 0 | 1 | 1 | 1 | 4 |
| 1992 | —Chicago | 21 | 6 | 13 | .462 | 2 | 3 | .667 | 4 | 0 | 4 | 1 | 0 | 0 | 2 | 1 | 1 | 14 |
| 1993 | —Chicago | 29 | 4 | 14 | .286 | 2 | 3 | .667 | 2 | 3 | 5 | 4 | 4 | 0 | 5 | 2 | 0 | 10 |
| 1994 | —Chicago | 31 | 9 | 15 | .600 | 6 | 10 | .600 | 0 | 11 | 11 | 2 | 2 | 0 | 4 | 1 | 2 | 29 |
| 1995 | —Chicago | 30 | 5 | 15 | .333 | 0 | 0 | ... | 0 | 7 | 7 | 3 | 1 | 0 | 2 | 1 | 4 | 12 |
| 1996 | —Chicago | 25 | 4 | 7 | .571 | 0 | 0 | ... | 2 | 6 | 8 | 5 | 0 | 0 | 3 | 0 | 6 | 8 |
| 1997 | —Chicago | 25 | 4 | 9 | .444 | 0 | 0 | ... | 0 | 3 | 3 | 2 | 0 | 0 | 0 | 0 | 2 | 8 |
| Totals | | 173 | 34 | 77 | .442 | 10 | 16 | .625 | 8 | 31 | 39 | 17 | 8 | 0 | 17 | 6 | 16 | 85 |

Three-point field goals: 1990, 0-for-1. 1993, 0-for-2. 1994, 5-for-9 (.556). 1995, 2-for-6 (.333). 1996, 0-for-1. 1997, 0-for-3. Totals, 7-for-22 (.318).

# POLLARD, JIM                    F

**PERSONAL:** Born July 9, 1922, in Oakland, Calif. ... Died January 22, 1993. ... 6-5/185 (1,96/83,9). ... Full name: James Clifford Pollard. ... Nickname: The Kangaroo Kid.
**HIGH SCHOOL:** Oakland Technical.
**COLLEGE:** Stanford.
**TRANSACTIONS:** Signed by Minneapolis Lakers of National Basketball League (1947). ... Lakers franchise transferred to Basketball Association of America for 1948-49 season.
**CAREER HONORS:** Elected to Naismith Memorial Basketball Hall of Fame (1977).
**MISCELLANEOUS:** Member of NBA championship team (1950, 1952, 1953, 1954). ... Member of BAA championship team (1949). ... Member of NBL championship team (1948).

## COLLEGIATE RECORD

**NOTES:** Member of NCAA Division I championship team (1942). ... In military service during 1942-43, 1943-44 and 1944-45 seasons; played with Alameda, Calif. Coast Guard team.

| Season Team | G | Min. | FGM | FGA | Pct. | FTM | FTA | Pct. | Reb. | Ast. | Pts. | RPG | APG | PPG |
|---|---|---|---|---|---|---|---|---|---|---|---|---|---|---|
| 40-41—Stanford‡ | | | | | | Freshman team statistics unavailable. | | | | | | | | |
| 41-42—Stanford | 23 | ... | 103 | ... | ... | 35 | 48 | .729 | ... | ... | 241 | ... | ... | 10.5 |
| Varsity totals | 23 | ... | 103 | ... | ... | 35 | 48 | .729 | ... | ... | 241 | ... | ... | 10.5 |

## AAU REGULAR-SEASON RECORD

| Season Team | G | Min. | FGM | FGA | Pct. | FTM | FTA | Pct. | Reb. | Ast. | Pts. | RPG | APG | PPG |
|---|---|---|---|---|---|---|---|---|---|---|---|---|---|---|
| 45-46—San Diego Dons | 15 | ... | 84 | ... | ... | 55 | ... | ... | ... | ... | *223 | ... | ... | 14.9 |
| 46-47—Oakland Bittners | 20 | ... | 113 | ... | ... | 53 | ... | ... | ... | ... | *279 | ... | ... | 14.0 |
| Totals | 35 | ... | 197 | ... | ... | 108 | ... | ... | ... | ... | 502 | ... | ... | 14.3 |

## NBL AND NBA REGULAR-SEASON RECORD

**HONORS:** All-NBL first team (1950). ... All-NBA second team (1952, 1954). ... All-BAA first team (1949).

| Season Team | G | Min. | FGM | FGA | Pct. | FTM | FTA | Pct. | Reb. | Ast. | PF | Dq. | Pts. | RPG | APG | PPG |
|---|---|---|---|---|---|---|---|---|---|---|---|---|---|---|---|---|
| 47-48—Minneapolis (NBL) | 59 | ... | 310 | ... | ... | 140 | 207 | .676 | ... | ... | 147 | ... | 760 | ... | ... | 12.9 |
| 48-49—Minneapolis (BAA) | 53 | ... | 314 | 792 | .396 | 156 | 227 | .687 | ... | 142 | 144 | ... | 784 | ... | 2.7 | 14.8 |
| 49-50—Minneapolis | 66 | ... | 394 | 1140 | .346 | 185 | 242 | .764 | ... | 252 | 143 | ... | 973 | ... | 3.8 | 14.7 |
| 50-51—Minneapolis | 54 | ... | 256 | 728 | .352 | 117 | 156 | .750 | 484 | 184 | 157 | 4 | 629 | 9.0 | 3.4 | 11.6 |
| 51-52—Minneapolis | 65 | 2545 | 411 | 1155 | .356 | 183 | 260 | .704 | 593 | 234 | 199 | 4 | 1005 | 9.1 | 3.6 | 15.5 |
| 52-53—Minneapolis | 66 | 2403 | 333 | 933 | .357 | 193 | 251 | .769 | 452 | 231 | 194 | 3 | 859 | 6.8 | 3.5 | 13.0 |
| 53-54—Minneapolis | 71 | 2483 | 326 | 882 | .370 | 179 | 230 | .778 | 500 | 214 | 161 | 0 | 831 | 7.0 | 3.0 | 11.7 |
| 54-55—Minneapolis | 63 | 1960 | 265 | 749 | .354 | 151 | 186 | .812 | 458 | 160 | 147 | 3 | 681 | 7.3 | 2.5 | 10.8 |
| Totals | 497 | ... | 2609 | ... | ... | 1304 | 1759 | .741 | ... | ... | 1292 | ... | 6522 | ... | ... | 13.1 |

## NBL AND NBA PLAYOFF RECORD

| Season Team | G | Min. | FGM | FGA | Pct. | FTM | FTA | Pct. | Reb. | Ast. | PF | Dq. | Pts. | RPG | APG | PPG |
|---|---|---|---|---|---|---|---|---|---|---|---|---|---|---|---|---|
| 47-48—Minn. (NBL) | 10 | ... | 48 | ... | ... | 27 | 41 | .659 | ... | ... | ... | ... | 123 | ... | ... | 12.3 |
| 48-49—Minneapolis (BAA) | 10 | ... | 43 | 147 | .293 | 44 | 62 | .710 | ... | 39 | 31 | ... | 130 | ... | 3.9 | 13.0 |
| 49-50—Minneapolis | 12 | ... | 50 | 175 | .286 | 44 | 62 | .710 | ... | 56 | 36 | ... | 144 | ... | 4.7 | 12.0 |
| 50-51—Minneapolis | 7 | ... | 35 | 108 | .324 | 25 | 30 | .833 | 62 | 27 | 27 | 1 | 95 | 8.9 | 3.9 | 13.6 |
| 51-52—Minneapolis | 11 | 469 | 70 | 173 | .405 | 37 | 50 | .740 | 71 | 33 | 34 | 1 | 177 | 6.5 | 3.0 | 16.1 |
| 52-53—Minneapolis | 12 | 455 | 62 | 167 | .371 | 48 | 62 | .774 | 86 | 49 | 37 | 2 | 172 | 7.2 | 4.1 | 14.3 |
| 53-54—Minneapolis | 13 | 543 | 56 | 155 | .361 | 48 | 60 | .800 | 110 | 41 | 27 | 0 | 160 | 8.5 | 3.2 | 12.3 |
| 54-55—Minneapolis | 7 | 257 | 33 | 104 | .317 | 33 | 46 | .717 | 78 | 14 | 13 | 0 | 99 | 11.1 | 2.0 | 14.1 |
| Totals | 82 | ... | 397 | ... | ... | 306 | 413 | .741 | ... | ... | ... | ... | 1100 | ... | ... | 13.4 |

## NBA ALL-STAR GAME RECORD

| Season Team | Min. | FGM | FGA | Pct. | FTM | FTA | Pct. | Reb | Ast. | PF | Dq. | Pts. |
|---|---|---|---|---|---|---|---|---|---|---|---|---|
| 1951—Minneapolis | ... | 2 | 11 | .182 | 0 | 0 | ... | 4 | 5 | 1 | 0 | 4 |
| 1952—Minneapolis | 29 | 2 | 17 | .118 | 0 | 0 | ... | 11 | 5 | 3 | 0 | 4 |
| 1954—Minneapolis | 41 | 10 | 22 | .455 | 3 | 5 | .600 | 3 | 3 | 3 | 0 | 23 |
| 1955—Minneapolis | 27 | 7 | 19 | .368 | 3 | 3 | 1.000 | 4 | 0 | 1 | 0 | 17 |
| Totals | ... | 21 | 69 | .304 | 6 | 8 | .750 | 22 | 13 | 8 | 0 | 48 |

## COLLEGIATE COACHING RECORD

| Season Team | W | L | Pct. |
|---|---|---|---|
| 55-56—LaSalle | 15 | 10 | .600 |
| 56-57—LaSalle | 17 | 9 | .654 |
| 57-58—LaSalle | 16 | 9 | .640 |
| Totals (3 years) | 48 | 28 | .632 |

## NBA COACHING RECORD

| Season Team | W | L | Pct. | Finish | W | L | Pct. |
|---|---|---|---|---|---|---|---|
| | | | | REGULAR SEASON | PLAYOFFS | | |
| 59-60—Minneapolis | 14 | 25 | .359 | 3rd/Western Division | 5 | 4 | .556 |
| 61-62—Chicago | 18 | 62 | .225 | 5th/Western Division | — | — | — |
| Totals (2 years) | 32 | 87 | .269 | Totals (1 year) | 5 | 4 | .556 |

## ABA COACHING RECORD

| Season Team | W | L | Pct. | Finish | W | L | Pct. |
|---|---|---|---|---|---|---|---|
| | | | | REGULAR SEASON | PLAYOFFS | | |
| 67-68—Minnesota | 50 | 28 | .641 | 2nd/Eastern Division | 4 | 6 | .400 |
| 68-69—Miami | 43 | 35 | .551 | 2nd/Eastern Division | 5 | 7 | .417 |
| 69-70—Miami | 5 | 15 | .250 | | — | — | — |
| Totals (3 years) | 98 | 78 | .557 | Totals (2 years) | 9 | 13 | .409 |

**NOTES:**

1960—Replaced John Castellani as Minneapolis head coach (January 2), with 11-25 record. Defeated Detroit, 2-0, in Western Division Semifinals; lost to St. Louis, 4-3, in Western Division Finals.

1968—Defeated Kentucky, 3-2, in Eastern Division Semifinals; lost to Pittsburgh, 4-1, in Eastern Division Finals. Minnesota Muskies franchise moved to Miami and renamed the Floridians for 1968-69 season.

1969—Defeated Minnesota, 4-3, in Eastern Division Semifinals; lost to Indiana, 4-1, in Eastern Division Finals. Replaced as Miami head coach by Hal Blitman (November).

## PORTER, TERRY        G

**PERSONAL:** Born April 8, 1963, in Milwaukee. ... 6-3/205. (1,91/93,0).
**HIGH SCHOOL:** South Division (Milwaukee).
**COLLEGE:** Wisconsin-Stevens Point.
**TRANSACTIONS:** Selected by Portland Trail Blazers in first round (24th pick overall) of 1985 NBA Draft. ... Signed as free agent by Minnesota Timberwolves (October 14, 1995). ... Signed as free agent by Miami Heat (January 22, 1999). ... Signed as free agent by San Antonio Spurs (August 5, 1999).
**CAREER NOTES:** Hired as assistant coach by Sacramento Kings (July 29, 2002).
**MISCELLANEOUS:** Portland Trail Blazers all-time assists leader with 5,319 (1985-86 through 1994-95).

### COLLEGIATE RECORD

| Season Team | G | Min. | FGM | FGA | Pct. | FTM | FTA | Pct. | Reb. | Ast. | Pts. | RPG | APG | PPG |
|---|---|---|---|---|---|---|---|---|---|---|---|---|---|---|
| 81-82—Wis.-Stevens Point........ | 25 | 273 | 21 | 57 | .368 | 9 | 13 | .692 | 13 | 21 | 51 | 0.5 | 0.8 | 2.0 |
| 82-83—Wis.-Stevens Point........ | 30 | 949 | 140 | 229 | .611 | 62 | 89 | .697 | 117 | 157 | 342 | 3.9 | 5.2 | 11.4 |
| 83-84—Wis.-Stevens Point........ | 32 | 1040 | 244 | 392 | .622 | 112 | 135 | .830 | 165 | 133 | 600 | 5.2 | 4.2 | 18.8 |
| 84-85—Wis.-Stevens Point........ | 30 | 1042 | 233 | 405 | .575 | 126 | 151 | .834 | 155 | 129 | 592 | 5.2 | 4.3 | 19.7 |
| Totals ...................................... | 117 | 3304 | 638 | 1083 | .589 | 309 | 388 | .796 | 450 | 440 | 1585 | 3.8 | 3.8 | 13.5 |

### NBA REGULAR-SEASON RECORD

**HONORS:** J. Walter Kennedy Citizenship Award (1993).

| Season Team | G | Min. | FGM | FGA | Pct. | FTM | FTA | Pct. | Off. | Def. | Tot. | Ast. | St. | Blk. | TO | Pts. | RPG | APG | PPG |
|---|---|---|---|---|---|---|---|---|---|---|---|---|---|---|---|---|---|---|---|
| 85-86—Portland.......... | 79 | 1214 | 212 | 447 | .474 | 125 | 155 | .806 | 35 | 82 | 117 | 198 | 81 | 1 | 106 | 562 | 1.5 | 2.5 | 7.1 |
| 86-87—Portland.......... | 80 | 2714 | 376 | 770 | .488 | 280 | 334 | .838 | 70 | 267 | 337 | 715 | 159 | 9 | 255 | 1045 | 4.2 | 8.9 | 13.1 |
| 87-88—Portland.......... | 82 | 2991 | 462 | 890 | .519 | 274 | 324 | .846 | 65 | 313 | 378 | 831 | 150 | 16 | 244 | 1222 | 4.6 | 10.1 | 14.9 |
| 88-89—Portland.......... | 81 | 3102 | 540 | 1146 | .471 | 272 | 324 | .840 | 85 | 282 | 367 | 770 | 146 | 8 | 248 | 1431 | 4.5 | 9.5 | 17.7 |
| 89-90—Portland.......... | 80 | 2781 | 448 | 969 | .462 | 421 | 472 | .892 | 59 | 213 | 272 | 726 | 151 | 4 | 245 | 1406 | 3.4 | 9.1 | 17.6 |
| 90-91—Portland.......... | 81 | 2665 | 486 | 944 | .515 | 279 | 339 | .823 | 52 | 230 | 282 | 649 | 158 | 12 | 189 | 1381 | 3.5 | 8.0 | 17.0 |
| 91-92—Portland.......... | 82 | 2784 | 521 | 1129 | .461 | 315 | 368 | .856 | 51 | 204 | 255 | 477 | 127 | 12 | 188 | 1485 | 3.1 | 5.8 | 18.1 |
| 92-93—Portland.......... | 81 | 2883 | 503 | 1108 | .454 | 327 | 388 | .843 | 58 | 258 | 316 | 419 | 101 | 10 | 199 | 1476 | 3.9 | 5.2 | 18.2 |
| 93-94—Portland.......... | 77 | 2074 | 348 | 836 | .416 | 204 | 234 | .872 | 45 | 170 | 215 | 401 | 79 | 18 | 166 | 1010 | 2.8 | 5.2 | 13.1 |
| 94-95—Portland.......... | 35 | 770 | 105 | 267 | .393 | 58 | 82 | .707 | 18 | 63 | 81 | 133 | 30 | 2 | 58 | 312 | 2.3 | 3.8 | 8.9 |
| 95-96—Minnesota....... | 82 | 2072 | 269 | 608 | .442 | 164 | 209 | .785 | 36 | 176 | 212 | 452 | 89 | 15 | 173 | 773 | 2.6 | 5.5 | 9.4 |
| 96-97—Minnesota....... | 82 | 1568 | 187 | 449 | .416 | 127 | 166 | .765 | 31 | 145 | 176 | 295 | 54 | 11 | 128 | 568 | 2.1 | 3.6 | 6.9 |
| 97-98—Minnesota....... | 82 | 1786 | 259 | 577 | .449 | 167 | 195 | .856 | 37 | 131 | 168 | 271 | 63 | 16 | 104 | 777 | 2.0 | 3.3 | 9.5 |
| 98-99—Miami ............ | 50 | 1365 | 172 | 370 | .465 | 123 | 148 | .831 | 13 | 127 | 140 | 146 | 48 | 11 | 74 | 525 | 2.8 | 2.9 | 10.5 |
| 99-00—San Antonio .... | 68 | 1613 | 207 | 463 | .447 | 137 | 170 | .806 | 24 | 167 | 191 | 221 | 50 | 9 | 100 | 641 | 2.8 | 3.3 | 9.4 |
| 00-01—San Antonio .... | 80 | 1678 | 197 | 440 | .448 | 92 | 116 | .793 | 24 | 177 | 201 | 251 | 52 | 11 | 104 | 573 | 2.5 | 3.1 | 7.2 |
| 01-02—San Antonio .... | 72 | 1294 | 136 | 321 | .424 | 68 | 83 | .819 | 12 | 152 | 164 | 205 | 45 | 16 | 85 | 399 | 2.3 | 2.8 | 5.5 |
| Totals .................. | 1274 | 35354 | 5428 | 11734 | .463 | 3433 | 4107 | .836 | 715 | 3157 | 3872 | 7160 | 1583 | 181 | 2666 | 15586 | 3.0 | 5.6 | 12.2 |

Three-point field goals: 1985-86, 13-for-42 (.310). 1986-87, 13-for-60 (.217). 1987-88, 24-for-69 (.348). 1988-89, 79-for-219 (.361). 1989-90, 89-for-238 (.374). 1990-91, 130-for-313 (.415). 1991-92, 128-for-324 (.395). 1992-93, 143-for-345 (.414). 1993-94, 110-for-282 (.390). 1994-95, 44-for-114 (.386). 1995-96, 71-for-226 (.314). 1996-97, 67-for-200 (.335). 1997-98, 92-for-233 (.395). 1998-99, 58-for-141 (.411). 1999-00, 90-for-207 (.435). 2000-01, 87-for-205 (.424). 2001-02, 59-for-142 (.415). Totals, 1297-for-3360 (.386).

Personal fouls/disqualifications: 1985-86, 136/0. 1986-87, 192/0. 1987-88, 204/1. 1988-89, 187/1. 1989-90, 150/0. 1990-91, 151/2. 1991-92, 155/1. 1992-93, 122/0. 1993-94, 132/0. 1994-95, 60/0. 1995-96, 154/0. 1996-97, 104/0. 1997-98, 103/0. 1998-99, 97/0. 1999-00, 79/0. 2000-01, 88/1. 2001-02, 89/0. Totals, 2203/6.

### NBA PLAYOFF RECORD

**NOTES:** Holds NBA Finals single-game record for most free throws made, none missed—15 (June 7, 1990, at Detroit, OT).

| Season Team | G | Min. | FGM | FGA | Pct. | FTM | FTA | Pct. | Off. | Def. | Tot. | Ast. | St. | Blk. | TO | Pts. | RPG | APG | PPG |
|---|---|---|---|---|---|---|---|---|---|---|---|---|---|---|---|---|---|---|---|
| 85-86—Portland.......... | 4 | 68 | 12 | 27 | .444 | 2 | 4 | .500 | 1 | 4 | 5 | 12 | 3 | 2 | 6 | 27 | 1.3 | 3.0 | 6.8 |
| 86-87—Portland.......... | 4 | 150 | 24 | 50 | .480 | 18 | 20 | .900 | 1 | 18 | 19 | 40 | 10 | 2 | 13 | 68 | 4.8 | 10.0 | 17.0 |
| 87-88—Portland.......... | 4 | 149 | 29 | 52 | .558 | 9 | 13 | .692 | 4 | 10 | 14 | 28 | 10 | 0 | 13 | 68 | 3.5 | 7.0 | 17.0 |
| 88-89—Portland.......... | 3 | 124 | 26 | 52 | .500 | 10 | 12 | .833 | 6 | 10 | 16 | 25 | 1 | 1 | 7 | 66 | 5.3 | 8.3 | 22.0 |
| 89-90—Portland.......... | 21 | 815 | 127 | 274 | .464 | 139 | 165 | .842 | 9 | 52 | 61 | 155 | 28 | 3 | 62 | 433 | 2.9 | 7.4 | 20.6 |
| 90-91—Portland.......... | 16 | 595 | 102 | 204 | .500 | 68 | 79 | .861 | 8 | 36 | 44 | 105 | 24 | 1 | 32 | 289 | 2.8 | 6.6 | 18.1 |
| 91-92—Portland.......... | 21 | 870 | 147 | 285 | .516 | 119 | 143 | .832 | 25 | 72 | 97 | 141 | 22 | 3 | 46 | 450 | 4.6 | 6.7 | 21.4 |
| 92-93—Portland.......... | 4 | 152 | 27 | 68 | .397 | 9 | 11 | .818 | 4 | 16 | 20 | 8 | 4 | 0 | 6 | 66 | 5.0 | 2.0 | 16.5 |
| 93-94—Portland.......... | 4 | 76 | 12 | 35 | .343 | 11 | 14 | .786 | 1 | 11 | 12 | 9 | 4 | 0 | 2 | 41 | 3.0 | 2.3 | 10.3 |
| 94-95—Portland.......... | 3 | 21 | 7 | 13 | .538 | 3 | 5 | .600 | 1 | 2 | 4 | 0 | 0 | 1 | 0 | 19 | 0.7 | 1.3 | 6.3 |
| 96-97—Minnesota...... | 3 | 46 | 5 | 13 | .385 | 3 | 4 | .750 | 1 | 2 | 3 | 9 | 2 | 2 | 2 | 16 | 1.0 | 3.0 | 5.3 |
| 97-98—Minnesota...... | 5 | 188 | 27 | 63 | .429 | 15 | 18 | .833 | 7 | 18 | 25 | 16 | 5 | 0 | 4 | 79 | 5.0 | 3.2 | 15.8 |
| 98-99—Miami .......... | 5 | 139 | 15 | 32 | .469 | 12 | 15 | .800 | 3 | 16 | 19 | 15 | 3 | 0 | 8 | 45 | 3.8 | 3.0 | 9.0 |
| 99-00—San Antonio ... | 4 | 89 | 8 | 31 | .258 | 0 | 0 | ... | 0 | 1 | 1 | 5 | 6 | 0 | 7 | 20 | 0.3 | 1.3 | 5.0 |
| 00-01—San Antonio ... | 13 | 326 | 39 | 86 | .453 | 17 | 22 | .773 | 1 | 23 | 24 | 44 | 11 | 0 | 22 | 108 | 1.8 | 3.4 | 8.3 |
| 01-02—San Antonio ... | 10 | 131 | 13 | 35 | .371 | 2 | 4 | .500 | 1 | 8 | 9 | 8 | 4 | 0 | 5 | 33 | 0.9 | 0.8 | 3.3 |
| Totals .................. | 124 | 3939 | 620 | 1320 | .470 | 437 | 529 | .826 | 73 | 298 | 371 | 624 | 137 | 14 | 236 | 1828 | 3.0 | 5.0 | 14.7 |

Three-point field goals: 1985-86, 1-for-6 (.167). 1986-87, 2-for-5 (.400). 1987-88, 1-for-3 (.333). 1988-89, 4-for-11 (.364). 1989-90, 40-for-102 (.392). 1990-91, 17-for-47 (.362). 1991-92, 37-for-78 (.474). 1992-93, 3-for-19 (.158). 1993-94, 6-for-14 (.429). 1994-95, 2-for-5 (.400). 1996-97, 3-for-9 (.333). 1997-98, 10-for-25 (.400). 1998-99, 3-for-12 (.250). 1999-00, 4-for-14 (.286). 2000-01, 13-for-39 (.333). 2001-02, 5-for-17 (.294). Totals, 151-for-406 (.372).

Personal fouls/disqualifications: 1985-86, 10/0. 1986-87, 14/0. 1987-88, 13/0. 1988-89, 8/0. 1989-90, 51/1. 1990-91, 32/0. 1991-92, 49/0. 1992-93, 10/0. 1993-94, 3/0. 1994-95, 6/0. 1996-97, 2/0. 1997-98, 10/0. 1998-99, 8/0. 1999-00, 4/0. 2000-01, 15/0. 2001-02, 10/0. Totals, 245/1.

## NBA ALL-STAR GAME RECORD

| Season Team | Min. | FGM | FGA | Pct. | FTM | FTA | Pct. | REBOUNDS Off. | Def. | Tot. | Ast. | PF | Dq. | St. | Blk. | TO | Pts. |
|---|---|---|---|---|---|---|---|---|---|---|---|---|---|---|---|---|---|
| 1991—Portland ............... | 15 | 2 | 6 | .333 | 0 | 0 | ... | 1 | 2 | 3 | 4 | 2 | 0 | 2 | 1 | 3 | 4 |
| 1993—Portland ............... | 19 | 3 | 8 | .375 | 0 | 0 | ... | 0 | 0 | 0 | 3 | 1 | 0 | 1 | 0 | 1 | 7 |
| Totals.......................... | 34 | 5 | 14 | .357 | 0 | 0 | ... | 1 | 2 | 3 | 7 | 3 | 0 | 3 | 1 | 4 | 11 |

Three-point field goals: 1991, 0-for-2. 1993, 1-for-5 (.200). Totals, 1-for-7 (.143).

## NBA COACHING RECORD

**BACKGROUND:** Assistant coach, Sacramento Kings (2002-03).

| | | REGULAR SEASON | | | | PLAYOFFS | | |
|---|---|---|---|---|---|---|---|---|
| Season Team | W | L | Pct. | Finish | | W | L | Pct. |
| 03-04—Milwaukee .................................................. | 41 | 41 | .500 | 4th/Central Division | | 1 | 4 | .200 |
| 04-05—Milwaukee .................................................. | 30 | 52 | .366 | 5th/Central Division | | — | — | — |
| Totals (2 years)................................................. | 71 | 93 | .433 | | Totals (1 year)........ | 5 | 4 | .556 |

**NOTES:**
2004—Lost to Detroit, 4-1, in Eastern Conference first round.

---

# PRICE, MARK                    G

**PERSONAL:** Born February 15, 1964, in Bartlesville, Okla. ... 6-0/180 (1,83/81,6). ... Full name: William Mark Price. ... Brother of Brent Price, guard with Sacramento Kings.
**HIGH SCHOOL:** Enid (Okla.).
**COLLEGE:** Georgia Tech.
**TRANSACTIONS/CAREER NOTES:** Selected by Dallas Mavericks in second round (25th pick overall) of 1986 NBA Draft. ... Draft rights traded by Mavericks to Cleveland Cavaliers for 1989 second-round draft choice and cash (June 17, 1986). ... Traded by Cavaliers to Washington Bullets for 1996 first-round draft choice (September 27, 1995). ... Signed as free agent by Golden State Warriors (July 21, 1996). ... Traded by Warriors to Orlando Magic for G Brian Shaw and F David Vaughn (October 28, 1997). ... Waived by Magic (June 30, 1998).
**MISCELLANEOUS:** Cleveland Cavaliers all-time assists leader with 4,206 and all-time steals leader with 734 (1986-87 through 1994-95).

## COLLEGIATE RECORD

| Season Team | G | Min. | FGM | FGA | Pct. | FTM | FTA | Pct. | Reb. | Ast. | Pts. | AVERAGES RPG | APG | PPG |
|---|---|---|---|---|---|---|---|---|---|---|---|---|---|---|
| 82-83—Georgia Tech ................ | 28 | 1020 | 201 | 462 | .435 | 93 | 106 | .877 | 105 | 91 | 568 | 3.8 | 3.3 | 20.3 |
| 83-84—Georgia Tech ................ | 29 | 1078 | 191 | 375 | .509 | 70 | 85 | .824 | 61 | 121 | 452 | 2.1 | 4.2 | 15.6 |
| 84-85—Georgia Tech ................ | 35 | 1302 | 223 | 462 | .483 | 137 | 163 | .840 | 71 | 150 | 583 | 2.0 | 4.3 | 16.7 |
| 85-86—Georgia Tech ................ | 34 | 1204 | 233 | 441 | .528 | 124 | 145 | .855 | 94 | 148 | 590 | 2.8 | 4.4 | 17.4 |
| Totals ............................ | 126 | 4604 | 848 | 1740 | .487 | 424 | 499 | .850 | 331 | 510 | 2193 | 2.6 | 4.0 | 17.4 |

Three-point field goals: 1982-83, 73-for-166 (.440).

## NBA REGULAR-SEASON RECORD

**RECORDS:** Holds career record for highest free throw percentage (minimum 1,200 made)—.904.
**HONORS:** Long Distance Shootout winner (1993, 1994). ... All-NBA first team (1993). ... All-NBA third team (1989, 1992, 1994).

| Season Team | G | Min. | FGM | FGA | Pct. | FTM | FTA | Pct. | REBOUNDS Off. | Def. | Tot. | Ast. | St. | Blk. | TO | Pts. | AVERAGES RPG | APG | PPG |
|---|---|---|---|---|---|---|---|---|---|---|---|---|---|---|---|---|---|---|---|
| 86-87—Cleveland ........ | 67 | 1217 | 173 | 424 | .408 | 95 | 114 | .833 | 33 | 84 | 117 | 202 | 43 | 4 | 105 | 464 | 1.7 | 3.0 | 6.9 |
| 87-88—Cleveland ........ | 80 | 2626 | 493 | 974 | .506 | 221 | 252 | .877 | 54 | 126 | 180 | 480 | 99 | 12 | 184 | 1279 | 2.3 | 6.0 | 16.0 |
| 88-89—Cleveland ........ | 75 | 2728 | 529 | 1006 | .526 | 263 | 292 | .901 | 48 | 178 | 226 | 631 | 115 | 7 | 212 | 1414 | 3.0 | 8.4 | 18.9 |
| 89-90—Cleveland ........ | 73 | 2706 | 489 | 1066 | .459 | 300 | 338 | .888 | 66 | 185 | 251 | 666 | 114 | 5 | 214 | 1430 | 3.4 | 9.1 | 19.6 |
| 90-91—Cleveland ........ | 16 | 571 | 97 | 195 | .497 | 59 | 62 | .952 | 8 | 37 | 45 | 166 | 42 | 2 | 56 | 271 | 2.8 | 10.4 | 16.9 |
| 91-92—Cleveland ........ | 72 | 2138 | 438 | 897 | .488 | 270 | 285 | *.947 | 38 | 135 | 173 | 535 | 94 | 12 | 159 | 1247 | 2.4 | 7.4 | 17.3 |
| 92-93—Cleveland ........ | 75 | 2380 | 477 | 986 | .484 | 289 | 305 | *.948 | 37 | 164 | 201 | 602 | 89 | 11 | 196 | 1365 | 2.7 | 8.0 | 18.2 |
| 93-94—Cleveland ........ | 76 | 2386 | 480 | 1005 | .478 | 238 | 268 | .888 | 39 | 189 | 228 | 589 | 103 | 11 | 189 | 1316 | 3.0 | 7.8 | 17.3 |
| 94-95—Cleveland ........ | 48 | 1375 | 253 | 612 | .413 | 148 | 162 | .914 | 25 | 87 | 112 | 335 | 35 | 4 | 142 | 757 | 2.3 | 7.0 | 15.8 |
| 95-96—Washington ...... | 7 | 127 | 18 | 60 | .300 | 10 | 10 | 1.000 | 1 | 6 | 7 | 18 | 6 | 0 | 12 | 56 | 1.0 | 2.6 | 8.0 |
| 96-97—Golden State ... | 70 | 1876 | 263 | 589 | .447 | 155 | 171 | *.906 | 36 | 143 | 179 | 342 | 67 | 3 | 161 | 793 | 2.6 | 4.9 | 11.3 |
| 97-98—Orlando ........... | 63 | 1430 | 229 | 531 | .431 | 87 | 103 | .845 | 24 | 105 | 129 | 297 | 53 | 5 | 162 | 597 | 2.0 | 4.7 | 9.5 |
| Totals .................. | 722 | 21560 | 3939 | 8345 | .472 | 2135 | 2362 | .904 | 409 | 1439 | 1848 | 4863 | 860 | 76 | 1790 | 10989 | 2.6 | 6.7 | 15.2 |

Three-point field goals: 1986-87, 23-for-70 (.329). 1987-88, 72-for-148 (.486). 1988-89, 93-for-211 (.441). 1989-90, 152-for-374 (.406). 1990-91, 18-for-53 (.340). 1991-92, 101-for-261 (.387). 1992-93, 122-for-293 (.416). 1993-94, 118-for-297 (.397). 1994-95, 103-for-253 (.407). 1995-96, 10-for-30 (.333). 1996-97, 112-for-283 (.396). 1997-98, 52-for-155 (.335). Totals, 976-for-2428 (.402).
Personal fouls/disqualifications: 1986-87, 75/1. 1987-88, 119/1. 1988-89, 98/0. 1989-90, 89/0. 1990-91, 23/0. 1991-92, 113/0. 1992-93, 105/0. 1993-94, 93/0. 1994-95, 50/0. 1995-96, 7/0. 1996-97, 100/0. 1997-98, 92/0. Totals, 964/2.

## NBA PLAYOFF RECORD

**NOTES:** Holds career playoff record for highest free throw percentage (minimum 100 made)—.944.

| Season Team | G | Min. | FGM | FGA | Pct. | FTM | FTA | Pct. | REBOUNDS Off. | Def. | Tot. | Ast. | St. | Blk. | TO | Pts. | AVERAGES RPG | APG | PPG |
|---|---|---|---|---|---|---|---|---|---|---|---|---|---|---|---|---|---|---|---|
| 87-88—Cleveland ........ | 5 | 205 | 38 | 67 | .567 | 24 | 25 | .960 | 3 | 15 | 18 | 38 | 3 | 0 | 8 | 105 | 3.6 | 7.6 | 21.0 |
| 88-89—Cleveland ........ | 4 | 158 | 22 | 57 | .386 | 14 | 15 | .933 | 4 | 9 | 13 | 22 | 3 | 0 | 19 | 64 | 3.3 | 5.5 | 16.0 |
| 89-90—Cleveland ........ | 5 | 192 | 32 | 61 | .525 | 30 | 30 | 1.000 | 0 | 14 | 14 | 44 | 9 | 1 | 15 | 100 | 2.8 | 8.8 | 20.0 |
| 91-92—Cleveland ........ | 17 | 603 | 118 | 238 | .496 | 66 | 73 | .904 | 10 | 32 | 42 | 128 | 24 | 4 | 56 | 327 | 2.5 | 7.5 | 19.2 |
| 92-93—Cleveland ........ | 9 | 288 | 43 | 97 | .443 | 23 | 24 | .958 | 1 | 18 | 19 | 55 | 15 | 0 | 33 | 117 | 2.1 | 6.1 | 13.0 |
| 93-94—Cleveland ........ | 3 | 102 | 15 | 43 | .349 | 13 | 14 | .929 | 1 | 5 | 6 | 14 | 4 | 0 | 9 | 45 | 2.0 | 4.7 | 15.0 |
| 94-95—Cleveland ........ | 4 | 143 | 12 | 40 | .300 | 32 | 33 | .970 | 2 | 10 | 12 | 26 | 6 | 0 | 18 | 60 | 3.0 | 6.5 | 15.0 |
| Totals .................. | 47 | 1691 | 280 | 603 | .464 | 202 | 214 | .944 | 21 | 103 | 124 | 327 | 64 | 5 | 158 | 818 | 2.6 | 7.0 | 17.4 |

Three-point field goals: 1987-88, 5-for-12 (.417). 1988-89, 6-for-16 (.375). 1989-90, 6-for-17 (.353). 1991-92, 25-for-69 (.362). 1992-93, 8-for-26 (.308). 1993-94, 2-for-9 (.222). 1994-95, 4-for-17 (.235). Totals, 56-for-166 (.337).
Personal fouls/disqualifications: 1987-88, 11/1. 1988-89, 3/0. 1989-90, 9/0. 1991-92, 34/0. 1992-93, 13/0. 1993-94, 6/0. 1994-95, 5/0. Totals, 81/1.

## NBA ALL-STAR GAME RECORD

| Season Team | Min. | FGM | FGA | Pct. | FTM | FTA | Pct. | REBOUNDS Off. | Def. | Tot. | Ast. | PF | Dq. | St. | Blk. | TO | Pts. |
|---|---|---|---|---|---|---|---|---|---|---|---|---|---|---|---|---|---|
| 1989—Cleveland ............. | 20 | 3 | 9 | .333 | 2 | 2 | 1.000 | 1 | 2 | 3 | 1 | 2 | 0 | 2 | 0 | 2 | 9 |
| 1992—Cleveland ............. | 15 | 1 | 5 | .200 | 4 | 4 | 1.000 | 0 | 0 | 0 | 3 | 1 | 0 | 1 | 0 | 3 | 6 |
| 1993—Cleveland ............. | 23 | 6 | 11 | .545 | 1 | 2 | .500 | 0 | 1 | 1 | 4 | 5 | 0 | 1 | 0 | 3 | 19 |
| 1994—Cleveland ............. | 22 | 8 | 10 | .800 | 2 | 2 | 1.000 | 0 | 2 | 2 | 5 | 1 | 0 | 1 | 0 | 0 | 20 |
| Totals.......................... | 80 | 18 | 35 | .514 | 9 | 10 | .900 | 1 | 5 | 6 | 13 | 9 | 0 | 5 | 1 | 8 | 54 |

Three-point field goals: 1989, 1-for-4 (.250). 1992, 0-for-3. 1993, 6-for-9 (.667). 1994, 2-for-3 (.667). Totals, 9-for-19 (.474).

ALL-TIME GREAT PLAYERS

# REED, WILLIS        C/F

**PERSONAL:** Born June 25, 1942, in Hico, La. ... 6-10/240 (2,08/108,4). ... Full name: Willis Reed Jr.
**HIGH SCHOOL:** West Side (Lillie, La.).
**COLLEGE:** Grambling State.
**TRANSACTIONS:** Selected by New York Knicks in second round (10th pick overall) of 1964 NBA Draft.
**CAREER HONORS:** Elected to Naismith Memorial Basketball Hall of Fame (1982). ... One of the 50 Greatest Players in NBA History (1996).
**CAREER NOTES:** General manager/vice president of basketball operations, New Jersey Nets (1988-89 to 1995-96). ... Senior vice president, Nets (1996-97 to 2003-04). ... Named vice president of basketball operations, New Orleans Hornets (June 29, 2004).
**MISCELLANEOUS:** Member of NBA championship team (1970, 1973).

## COLLEGIATE RECORD
**NOTES:** Member of NAIA championship team (1961). ... Elected to NAIA Basketball Hall of Fame (1970).

| | | | | | | | | | | | | AVERAGES | | |
|---|---|---|---|---|---|---|---|---|---|---|---|---|---|---|
| Season Team | G | Min. | FGM | FGA | Pct. | FTM | FTA | Pct. | Reb. | Ast. | Pts. | RPG | APG | PPG |
| 60-61—Grambling State | 35 | ... | 146 | 239 | .611 | 86 | 122 | .705 | 312 | ... | 378 | 8.9 | ... | 10.8 |
| 61-62—Grambling State | 26 | ... | 189 | 323 | .585 | 80 | 102 | .784 | 380 | ... | 458 | 14.6 | ... | 17.6 |
| 62-63—Grambling State | 33 | ... | 282 | 489 | .577 | 135 | 177 | .763 | 563 | ... | 699 | 17.1 | ... | 21.2 |
| 63-64—Grambling State | 28 | ... | 301 | 486 | .619 | 143 | 199 | .719 | 596 | ... | 745 | 21.3 | ... | 26.6 |
| Totals | 122 | ... | 918 | 1537 | .597 | 444 | 600 | .740 | 1851 | ... | 2280 | 15.2 | ... | 18.7 |

## NBA REGULAR-SEASON RECORD
**HONORS:** NBA Most Valuable Player (1970). ... NBA Rookie of the Year (1965). ... All-NBA first team (1970). ... All-NBA second team (1967, 1968, 1969, 1971). ... NBA All-Defensive first team (1970). ... NBA All-Rookie team (1965).

| | | | | | | | | | | | | | | AVERAGES | | |
|---|---|---|---|---|---|---|---|---|---|---|---|---|---|---|---|---|
| Season Team | G | Min. | FGM | FGA | Pct. | FTM | FTA | Pct. | Reb. | Ast. | PF | Dq. | Pts. | RPG | APG | PPG |
| 64-65—New York | 80 | 3042 | 629 | 1457 | .432 | 302 | 407 | .742 | 1175 | 133 | 339 | 14 | 1560 | 14.7 | 1.7 | 19.5 |
| 65-66—New York | 76 | 2537 | 438 | 1009 | .434 | 302 | 399 | .757 | 883 | 91 | 323 | 13 | 1178 | 11.6 | 1.2 | 15.5 |
| 66-67—New York | 78 | 2824 | 635 | 1298 | .489 | 358 | 487 | .735 | 1136 | 126 | 293 | 9 | 1628 | 14.6 | 1.6 | 20.9 |
| 67-68—New York | 81 | 2879 | 659 | 1346 | .490 | 367 | 509 | .721 | 1073 | 159 | 343 | 12 | 1685 | 13.2 | 2.0 | 20.8 |
| 68-69—New York | 82 | 3108 | 704 | 1351 | .521 | 325 | 435 | .747 | 1191 | 190 | 314 | 7 | 1733 | 14.5 | 2.3 | 21.1 |
| 69-70—New York | 81 | 3089 | 702 | 1385 | .507 | 351 | 464 | .756 | 1126 | 161 | 287 | 2 | 1755 | 13.9 | 2.0 | 21.7 |
| 70-71—New York | 73 | 2855 | 614 | 1330 | .462 | 299 | 381 | .785 | 1003 | 148 | 228 | 1 | 1527 | 13.7 | 2.0 | 20.9 |
| 71-72—New York | 11 | 363 | 60 | 137 | .438 | 27 | 39 | .692 | 96 | 22 | 30 | 0 | 147 | 8.7 | 2.0 | 13.4 |
| 72-73—New York | 69 | 1876 | 334 | 705 | .474 | 92 | 124 | .742 | 590 | 126 | 205 | 0 | 760 | 8.6 | 1.8 | 11.0 |

| | | | | | | | | | REBOUNDS | | | | | | | | AVERAGES | | |
|---|---|---|---|---|---|---|---|---|---|---|---|---|---|---|---|---|---|---|---|
| Season Team | G | Min. | FGM | FGA | Pct. | FTM | FTA | Pct. | Off. | Def. | Tot. | Ast. | St. | Blk. | TO | Pts. | RPG | APG | PPG |
| 73-74—New York | 19 | 500 | 84 | 184 | .457 | 42 | 53 | .792 | 47 | 94 | 141 | 30 | 12 | 21 | ... | 210 | 7.4 | 1.6 | 11.1 |
| Totals | 650 | 23073 | 4859 | 10202 | .476 | 2465 | 3298 | .747 | ... | ... | 8414 | 1186 | 12 | 21 | ... | 12183 | 12.9 | 1.8 | 18.7 |

Personal fouls/disqualifications: 1973-74, 49/0.

## NBA PLAYOFF RECORD
**NOTES:** NBA Finals Most Valuable Player (1970, 1973).

| | | | | | | | | | | | | | | AVERAGES | | |
|---|---|---|---|---|---|---|---|---|---|---|---|---|---|---|---|---|
| Season Team | G | Min. | FGM | FGA | Pct. | FTM | FTA | Pct. | Reb. | Ast. | PF | Dq. | Pts. | RPG | APG | PPG |
| 66-67—New York | 4 | 148 | 43 | 80 | .538 | 24 | 25 | .960 | 55 | 7 | 19 | 1 | 110 | 13.8 | 1.8 | 27.5 |
| 67-68—New York | 6 | 210 | 53 | 98 | .541 | 22 | 30 | .733 | 62 | 11 | 24 | 1 | 128 | 10.3 | 1.8 | 21.3 |
| 68-69—New York | 10 | 429 | 101 | 198 | .510 | 55 | 70 | .786 | 141 | 19 | 40 | 1 | 257 | 14.1 | 1.9 | 25.7 |
| 69-70—New York | 18 | 732 | 178 | 378 | .471 | 70 | 95 | .737 | 248 | 51 | 60 | 0 | 426 | 13.8 | 2.8 | 23.7 |
| 70-71—New York | 12 | 504 | 81 | 196 | .413 | 26 | 39 | .667 | 144 | 27 | 41 | 0 | 188 | 12.0 | 2.3 | 15.7 |
| 72-73—New York | 17 | 486 | 97 | 208 | .466 | 18 | 21 | .857 | 129 | 30 | 65 | 1 | 212 | 7.6 | 1.8 | 12.5 |

| | | | | | | | | | REBOUNDS | | | | | | | | AVERAGES | | |
|---|---|---|---|---|---|---|---|---|---|---|---|---|---|---|---|---|---|---|---|
| Season Team | G | Min. | FGM | FGA | Pct. | FTM | FTA | Pct. | Off. | Def. | Tot. | Ast. | St. | Blk. | TO | Pts. | RPG | APG | PPG |
| 73-74—New York | 11 | 132 | 17 | 45 | .378 | 3 | 5 | .600 | 4 | 18 | 22 | 4 | 2 | 0 | ... | 37 | 2.0 | 0.4 | 3.4 |
| Totals | 78 | 2641 | 570 | 1203 | .474 | 218 | 285 | .765 | ... | 4 | 801 | 149 | 2 | 0 | ... | 1358 | 10.3 | 1.9 | 17.4 |

Personal fouls/disqualifications: 1973-74, 26/0.

## NBA ALL-STAR GAME RECORD
**NOTES:** NBA All-Star Game Most Valuable Player (1970).

| Season Team | Min. | FGM | FGA | Pct. | FTM | FTA | Pct. | Reb | Ast. | PF | Dq. | Pts. |
|---|---|---|---|---|---|---|---|---|---|---|---|---|
| 1965—New York | 25 | 3 | 11 | .273 | 1 | 2 | .500 | 5 | 1 | 2 | 0 | 7 |
| 1966—New York | 23 | 7 | 11 | .636 | 2 | 2 | 1.000 | 8 | 1 | 3 | 0 | 16 |
| 1967—New York | 17 | 2 | 6 | .333 | 0 | 0 | ... | 9 | 1 | 0 | 0 | 4 |
| 1968—New York | 25 | 7 | 14 | .500 | 2 | 3 | .667 | 8 | 1 | 4 | 0 | 16 |
| 1969—New York | 14 | 5 | 8 | .625 | 0 | 0 | ... | 4 | 2 | 2 | 0 | 10 |
| 1970—New York | 30 | 9 | 18 | .500 | 3 | 3 | 1.000 | 11 | 0 | 6 | 1 | 21 |
| 1971—New York | 27 | 5 | 16 | .313 | 4 | 6 | .667 | 13 | 1 | 3 | 0 | 14 |
| Totals | 161 | 38 | 84 | .452 | 12 | 16 | .750 | 58 | 7 | 20 | 1 | 88 |

## HEAD COACHING RECORD
**BACKGROUND:** Volunteer assistant, St. John's University (1980-81). ... Assistant coach, Atlanta Hawks (1985-86 and 1986-87). ... Assistant coach, Sacramento Kings (1987-88).

### NBA COACHING RECORD

| | REGULAR SEASON | | | | PLAYOFFS | | |
|---|---|---|---|---|---|---|---|
| Season Team | W | L | Pct. | Finish | W | L | Pct. |
| 77-78—New York | 43 | 39 | .524 | 2nd/Atlantic Division | 2 | 4 | .333 |
| 78-79—New York | 6 | 8 | .429 | | — | — | — |
| 87-88—New Jersey | 7 | 21 | .250 | 5th/Atlantic Division | — | — | — |
| 88-89—New Jersey | 26 | 56 | .317 | 5th/Atlantic Division | — | — | — |
| Totals (4 years) | 82 | 124 | .398 | Totals (1 year) | 2 | 4 | .333 |

### COLLEGIATE COACHING RECORD

| Season Team | W | L | Pct. | Finish |
|---|---|---|---|---|
| 81-82—Creighton | 7 | 20 | .259 | 8th/Missouri Valley Conference |
| 82-83—Creighton | 8 | 19 | .296 | 10th/Missouri Valley Conference |
| 83-84—Creighton | 17 | 14 | .548 | 4th/Missouri Valley Conference |
| 84-85—Creighton | 20 | 11 | .645 | 4th/Missouri Valley Conference |
| Totals (4 years) | 52 | 64 | .448 | |

**NOTES:**
1978—Defeated Cleveland, 2-0, in Eastern Conference First Round; lost to Philadelphia, 4-0, in Eastern Conference Semifinals. Replaced as New York head coach by Red Holzman (November).
1984—Lost to Nebraska, 56-54, in NIT first round.
1988—Replaced interim head coach Bob MacKinnon as New Jersey head coach (February 29), with record of 12-42.

## RICE, GLEN                               F

**PERSONAL:** Born May 28, 1967, in Flint, Mich. ... 6-8/220. (2,03/99,8). ... Full Name: Glen Anthony Rice.
**HIGH SCHOOL:** Northwestern Community (Flint, Mich.).
**COLLEGE:** Michigan.
**TRANSACTIONS/CAREER NOTES:** Selected by Miami Heat in first round (fourth pick overall) of 1989 NBA Draft. ... Traded by Heat with G Khalid Reeves, C Matt Geiger and 1996 first-round draft choice to Charlotte Hornets for C Alonzo Mourning, C LeRon Ellis and G Pete Myers (November 3, 1995). ... Traded by Hornets with F/C J.R. Reid and G B.J. Armstrong to Los Angeles Lakers for G Eddie Jones and F/C Elden Campbell (March 10, 1999). ... Traded by Lakers to New York Knicks as part of four-team trade in which Knicks acquired C Luc Longley, F/C Travis Knight, G Vernon Maxwell, C Vladimir Stepania, F Lazaro Borrell, two 2001 first-round draft choices and two 2001 second-round draft choices, Seattle SuperSonics acquired C Patrick Ewing, Phoenix Suns acquired C Chris Dudley and 2001 first-round draft choice and Lakers acquired F Horace Grant, C Greg Foster, F Chuck Person and G Emanual Davis (September 20, 2000). ... Traded by Knicks to Houston Rockets as part of three-team trade in which Knicks acquired F Shandon Anderson from Rockets and G Howard Eisley from Mavericks, Mavericks acquired G Muggsy Bogues from Knicks and Rockets acquired draft rights to G Kyle Hill from Mavericks (August 10, 2001). ... Traded by Rockets with first-round draft choice and additional draft consideration to Utah Jazz for C John Amaechi, 2004 second-round draft choice and conditional second-round draft choice (September 30, 2003). ... Signed as free agent by Los Angeles Clippers (October 10, 2003). ... Waived by Clippers (January 16, 2004).
**MISCELLANEOUS:** Member of NBA championship team (2000). ... Miami Heat all-time leading scorer with 9,248 points (1989-90 through 1994-95).

### COLLEGIATE RECORD

**NOTES:** Member of NCAA Division I championship team (1989). ... THE SPORTING NEWS All-America second team (1989). ... NCAA Division I Tournament Most Outstanding Player (1989).

| Season Team | G | Min. | FGM | FGA | Pct. | FTM | FTA | Pct. | Reb. | Ast. | Pts. | RPG | APG | PPG |
|---|---|---|---|---|---|---|---|---|---|---|---|---|---|---|
| 85-86—Michigan | 32 | 520 | 105 | 191 | .550 | 15 | 25 | .600 | 97 | 21 | 225 | 3.0 | 0.7 | 7.0 |
| 86-87—Michigan | 32 | 1056 | 226 | 402 | .562 | 85 | 108 | .787 | 294 | 76 | 540 | 9.2 | 2.4 | 16.9 |
| 87-88—Michigan | 33 | 1155 | 308 | 539 | .571 | 79 | 98 | .806 | 236 | 92 | 728 | 7.2 | 2.8 | 22.1 |
| 88-89—Michigan | 37 | 1258 | 363 | 629 | .577 | 124 | 149 | .832 | 232 | 85 | 949 | 6.3 | 2.3 | 25.6 |
| Totals | 134 | 3989 | 1002 | 1761 | .569 | 303 | 380 | .797 | 859 | 274 | 2442 | 6.4 | 2.0 | 18.2 |

Three-point field goals: 1986-87, 3-for-12 (.250). 1987-88, 33-for-77 (.429). 1988-89, 99-for-192 (.516). Totals, 135-for-281 (.480).

### NBA REGULAR-SEASON RECORD

**HONORS:** Long Distance Shootout winner (1995). ... All-NBA Second Team (1997). ... All-NBA Third Team (1998). ... NBA All-Rookie second team (1990).
**NOTES:** Led NBA with .470 three-point field goal percentage (1997).

| Season Team | G | Min. | FGM | FGA | Pct. | FTM | FTA | Pct. | Off. | Def. | Tot. | Ast. | St. | Blk. | TO | Pts. | RPG | APG | PPG |
|---|---|---|---|---|---|---|---|---|---|---|---|---|---|---|---|---|---|---|---|
| 89-90—Miami | 77 | 2311 | 470 | 1071 | .439 | 91 | 124 | .734 | 100 | 252 | 352 | 138 | 67 | 27 | 113 | 1048 | 4.6 | 1.8 | 13.6 |
| 90-91—Miami | 77 | 2646 | 550 | 1193 | .461 | 171 | 209 | .818 | 85 | 296 | 381 | 189 | 101 | 26 | 166 | 1342 | 4.9 | 2.5 | 17.4 |
| 91-92—Miami | 79 | 3007 | 672 | 1432 | .469 | 266 | 318 | .836 | 84 | 310 | 394 | 184 | 90 | 35 | 145 | 1765 | 5.0 | 2.3 | 22.3 |
| 92-93—Miami | 82 | 3082 | 582 | 1324 | .440 | 242 | 295 | .820 | 92 | 332 | 424 | 180 | 92 | 25 | 157 | 1554 | 5.2 | 2.2 | 19.0 |
| 93-94—Miami | 81 | 2999 | 663 | 1421 | .467 | 250 | 284 | .880 | 76 | 358 | 434 | 184 | 110 | 32 | 130 | 1708 | 5.4 | 2.3 | 21.1 |
| 94-95—Miami | 82 | 3014 | 667 | 1403 | .475 | 312 | 365 | .855 | 99 | 279 | 378 | 192 | 112 | 14 | 153 | 1831 | 4.6 | 2.3 | 22.3 |
| 95-96—Charlotte | 79 | 3142 | 610 | 1296 | .471 | 319 | 381 | .837 | 86 | 292 | 378 | 232 | 91 | 19 | 163 | 1710 | 4.8 | 2.9 | 21.6 |
| 96-97—Charlotte | 79 | *3362 | 722 | 1513 | .477 | 464 | 535 | .867 | 67 | 251 | 318 | 160 | 72 | 26 | 177 | 2115 | 4.0 | 2.0 | 26.8 |
| 97-98—Charlotte | 82 | 3295 | 634 | 1386 | .457 | 428 | 504 | .849 | 89 | 264 | 353 | 182 | 77 | 22 | 182 | 1826 | 4.3 | 2.2 | 22.3 |
| 98-99—L.A. Lakers | 27 | 985 | 171 | 396 | .432 | 77 | 90 | .856 | 9 | 90 | 99 | 71 | 17 | 6 | 45 | 472 | 3.7 | 2.6 | 17.5 |
| 99-00—L.A. Lakers | 80 | 2530 | 421 | 980 | .430 | 346 | 396 | .874 | 56 | 271 | 327 | 176 | 47 | 12 | 114 | 1272 | 4.1 | 2.2 | 15.9 |
| 00-01—New York | 75 | 2212 | 331 | 752 | .440 | 155 | 182 | .852 | 61 | 246 | 307 | 89 | 41 | 13 | 96 | 899 | 4.1 | 1.2 | 12.0 |
| 01-02—Houston | 20 | 606 | 65 | 167 | .389 | 24 | 30 | .800 | 5 | 42 | 47 | 31 | 12 | 3 | 24 | 172 | 2.4 | 1.6 | 8.6 |
| 02-03—Houston | 62 | 1532 | 196 | 457 | .429 | 63 | 83 | .759 | 28 | 126 | 154 | 65 | 23 | 5 | 55 | 556 | 2.5 | 1.0 | 9.0 |
| 03-04—L.A. Clippers | 18 | 262 | 22 | 76 | .289 | 17 | 17 | 1.000 | 9 | 32 | 41 | 24 | 6 | 0 | 13 | 66 | 2.3 | 1.3 | 3.7 |
| Totals | 1000 | 34985 | 6776 | 14867 | .456 | 3225 | 3813 | .846 | 946 | 3441 | 4387 | 2097 | 958 | 265 | 1733 | 18336 | 4.4 | 2.1 | 18.3 |

Three-point field goals: 1989-90, 17-for-69 (.246). 1990-91, 71-for-184 (.386). 1991-92, 155-for-395 (.391). 1992-93, 148-for-386 (.383). 1993-94, 132-for-346 (.382). 1994-95, 185-for-451 (.410). 1995-96, 171-for-403 (.424). 1996-97, 207-for-440 (.470). 1997-98, 130-for-300 (.433). 1998-99, 53-for-135 (.393). 1999-00, 84-for-229 (.367). 2000-01, 82-for-211 (.389). 2001-02, 18-for-64 (.281). 2002-03, 101-for-254 (.398). 2003-04, 5-for-28 (.179). Totals, 1559-for-3896 (.400).
Personal fouls/disqualifications: 1989-90, 198/1. 1990-91, 216/0. 1991-92, 170/0. 1992-93, 201/0. 1993-94, 186/0. 1994-95, 203/1. 1995-96, 217/1. 1996-97, 190/0. 1997-98, 200/0. 1998-99, 67/1. 1999-00, 179/0. 2000-01, 179/1. 2001-02, 34/0. 2002-03, 99/0. 2003-04, 22/0. Totals, 2361/5.

### NBA PLAYOFF RECORD

| Season Team | G | Min. | FGM | FGA | Pct. | FTM | FTA | Pct. | Off. | Def. | Tot. | Ast. | St. | Blk. | TO | Pts. | RPG | APG | PPG |
|---|---|---|---|---|---|---|---|---|---|---|---|---|---|---|---|---|---|---|---|
| 91-92—Miami | 3 | 119 | 24 | 64 | .375 | 6 | 7 | .857 | 3 | 7 | 10 | 5 | 2 | 0 | 6 | 57 | 3.3 | 1.7 | 19.0 |
| 93-94—Miami | 5 | 195 | 26 | 68 | .382 | 6 | 8 | .750 | 6 | 30 | 36 | 10 | 11 | 2 | 14 | 65 | 7.2 | 2.0 | 13.0 |
| 96-97—Charlotte | 3 | 137 | 28 | 57 | .491 | 21 | 23 | .913 | 1 | 10 | 11 | 11 | 4 | 1 | 4 | 83 | 3.7 | 3.7 | 27.7 |
| 97-98—Charlotte | 9 | 369 | 82 | 173 | .474 | 30 | 36 | .833 | 11 | 40 | 51 | 13 | 5 | 3 | 13 | 205 | 5.7 | 1.4 | 22.8 |
| 98-99—L.A. Lakers | 7 | 307 | 45 | 101 | .446 | 28 | 29 | .966 | 4 | 23 | 27 | 11 | 5 | 1 | 9 | 128 | 3.9 | 1.6 | 18.3 |
| 99-00—L.A. Lakers | 23 | 766 | 93 | 228 | .408 | 71 | 89 | .798 | 10 | 82 | 92 | 48 | 15 | 4 | 36 | 285 | 4.0 | 2.1 | 12.4 |
| 00-01—New York | 5 | 144 | 24 | 52 | .462 | 7 | 8 | .875 | 3 | 19 | 22 | 3 | 3 | 1 | 7 | 61 | 4.4 | 0.6 | 12.2 |
| Totals | 55 | 2037 | 322 | 743 | .433 | 169 | 200 | .845 | 38 | 211 | 249 | 101 | 45 | 12 | 89 | 884 | 4.5 | 1.8 | 16.1 |

Three-point field goals: 1991-92, 3-for-12 (.250). 1993-94, 7-for-23 (.304). 1996-97, 6-for-16 (.375). 1997-98, 11-for-36 (.306). 1998-99, 10-for-28 (.357). 1999-00, 28-for-67 (.418). 2000-01, 6-for-14 (.429). Totals, 71-for-196 (.362).

Personal fouls/disqualifications: 1991-92, 7/0. 1993-94, 14/0. 1996-97, 11/0. 1997-98, 26/0. 1998-99, 15/0. 1999-00, 50/0. 2000-01, 10/0. Totals, 133/0.

## NBA ALL-STAR GAME RECORD

**NOTES:** NBA All-Star Game Most Valuable Player (1997). … Holds single-game records for most points in one half—24; most points in one quarter—20; most field-goal attempts in one half—17; and most three-point field goals made in one quarter—4 (1997). … Shares single-game record for most field goals made in one quarter—8 (1997).

| Season Team | Min. | FGM | FGA | Pct. | FTM | FTA | Pct. | REBOUNDS Off. | Def. | Tot. | Ast. | PF | Dq. | St. | Blk. | TO | Pts. |
|---|---|---|---|---|---|---|---|---|---|---|---|---|---|---|---|---|---|
| 1996—Charlotte .............. | 15 | 1 | 5 | .200 | 4 | 4 | 1.000 | 0 | 0 | 0 | 2 | 2 | 0 | 0 | 0 | 2 | 7 |
| 1997—Charlotte .............. | 25 | 10 | 24 | .417 | 2 | 2 | 1.000 | 1 | 1 | 2 | 1 | 2 | 0 | 2 | 0 | 1 | 26 |
| 1998—Charlotte .............. | 16 | 6 | 14 | .429 | 0 | 0 | ... | 1 | 0 | 1 | 0 | 0 | 0 | 0 | 0 | 1 | 16 |
| **Totals** .............. | 56 | 17 | 43 | .395 | 6 | 6 | 1.000 | 2 | 1 | 3 | 3 | 4 | 0 | 2 | 0 | 4 | 49 |

Three-point field goals: 1996, 1-for-2 (.500). 1997, 4-for-7 (.571). 1998, 4-for-6 (.667). Totals, 9-for-15 (.600).

# RICHMOND, MITCH      G

**PERSONAL:** Born June 30, 1965, in Fort Lauderdale. … 6-5/220. (1,96/99,8). … Full Name: Mitchell James Richmond.
**HIGH SCHOOL:** Boyd Anderson (Fort Lauderdale).
**JUNIOR COLLEGE:** Moberly (Mo.) Area Junior College.
**COLLEGE:** Kansas State.
**TRANSACTIONS/CAREER NOTES:** Selected by Golden State Warriors in first round (fifth pick overall) of 1988 NBA Draft. … Traded by Warriors with C Les Jepsen to Sacramento Kings for F/G Billy Owens (November 1, 1991). … Traded by Kings with F Otis Thorpe to Washington Wizards for F Chris Webber (May 14, 1998). … Waived by Wizards (July 2, 2001). … Signed as free agent by Los Angeles Lakers (July 20, 2001).
**MISCELLANEOUS:** Member of NBA championship team (2002). … Member of bronze-medal-winning U.S. Olympic team (1988) and gold-medal-winning U.S. Olympic team (1996).

## COLLEGIATE RECORD

**NOTES:** THE SPORTING NEWS All-America second team (1988).

| Season Team | G | Min. | FGM | FGA | Pct. | FTM | FTA | Pct. | Reb. | Ast. | Pts. | AVERAGES RPG | APG | PPG |
|---|---|---|---|---|---|---|---|---|---|---|---|---|---|---|
| 84-85—Moberly Area J.C........... | 40 | ... | 180 | 375 | .480 | 55 | 85 | .647 | 185 | 98 | 415 | 4.6 | 2.5 | 10.4 |
| 85-86—Moberly Area J.C........... | 38 | ... | 242 | 506 | .478 | 124 | 180 | .689 | 251 | 99 | 608 | 6.6 | 2.6 | 16.0 |
| 86-87—Kansas State ................ | 30 | 964 | 201 | 450 | .447 | 118 | 155 | .761 | 170 | 80 | 559 | 5.7 | 2.7 | 18.6 |
| 87-88—Kansas State ................ | 34 | 1200 | 268 | 521 | .514 | 186 | 240 | .775 | 213 | 125 | 768 | 6.3 | 3.7 | 22.6 |
| **Junior College Totals**............. | 78 | ... | 422 | 881 | .479 | 179 | 265 | .675 | 436 | 197 | 1023 | 5.6 | 2.5 | 13.1 |
| **4-Year-College Totals** ............ | 64 | 2164 | 469 | 971 | .483 | 304 | 395 | .770 | 383 | 205 | 1327 | 6.0 | 3.2 | 20.7 |

Three-point field goals: 1986-87, 39-for-108 (.361). 1987-88, 46-for-98 (.469). Totals, 85-for-206 (.413).

## NBA REGULAR-SEASON RECORD

**HONORS:** NBA Rookie of the Year (1989). … All-NBA Second Team (1994, 1995, 1997). … All-NBA Third Team (1996, 1998). … NBA All-Rookie first team (1989).

| Season Team | G | Min. | FGM | FGA | Pct. | FTM | FTA | Pct. | REBOUNDS Off. | Def. | Tot. | Ast. | St. | Blk. | TO | Pts. | AVERAGES RPG | APG | PPG |
|---|---|---|---|---|---|---|---|---|---|---|---|---|---|---|---|---|---|---|---|
| 88-89—Golden State ... | 79 | 2717 | 649 | 1386 | .468 | 410 | 506 | .810 | 158 | 310 | 468 | 334 | 82 | 13 | 269 | 1741 | 5.9 | 4.2 | 22.0 |
| 89-90—Golden State ... | 78 | 2799 | 640 | 1287 | .497 | 406 | 469 | .866 | 98 | 262 | 360 | 223 | 98 | 24 | 201 | 1720 | 4.6 | 2.9 | 22.1 |
| 90-91—Golden State ... | 77 | 3027 | 703 | 1424 | .494 | 394 | 465 | .847 | 147 | 305 | 452 | 238 | 126 | 34 | 230 | 1840 | 5.9 | 3.1 | 23.9 |
| 91-92—Sacramento .... | 80 | 3095 | 685 | 1465 | .468 | 330 | 406 | .813 | 62 | 257 | 319 | 411 | 92 | 34 | 247 | 1803 | 4.0 | 5.1 | 22.5 |
| 92-93—Sacramento .... | 45 | 1728 | 371 | 782 | .474 | 197 | 233 | .845 | 18 | 136 | 154 | 221 | 53 | 9 | 130 | 987 | 3.4 | 4.9 | 21.9 |
| 93-94—Sacramento .... | 78 | 2897 | 635 | 1428 | .445 | 426 | 511 | .834 | 70 | 216 | 286 | 313 | 103 | 17 | 216 | 1823 | 3.7 | 4.0 | 23.4 |
| 94-95—Sacramento .... | 82 | 3172 | 668 | 1497 | .446 | 375 | 445 | .843 | 69 | 288 | 357 | 311 | 91 | 29 | 234 | 1867 | 4.4 | 3.8 | 22.8 |
| 95-96—Sacramento .... | 81 | 2946 | 611 | 1368 | .447 | 425 | 491 | .866 | 54 | 215 | 269 | 255 | 125 | 19 | 220 | 1872 | 3.3 | 3.1 | 23.1 |
| 96-97—Sacramento .... | 81 | 3125 | 717 | 1578 | .454 | 457 | 531 | .861 | 59 | 260 | 319 | 338 | 118 | 24 | 237 | 2095 | 3.9 | 4.2 | 25.9 |
| 97-98—Sacramento .... | 70 | 2569 | 543 | 1220 | .445 | 407 | 471 | .864 | 50 | 179 | 229 | 279 | 88 | 15 | 181 | 1623 | 3.3 | 4.0 | 23.2 |
| 98-99—Washington .... | 50 | 1912 | 331 | 803 | .412 | 251 | 293 | .857 | 30 | 142 | 172 | 122 | 64 | 10 | 136 | 983 | 3.4 | 2.4 | 19.7 |
| 99-00—Washington .... | 74 | 2397 | 447 | 1049 | .426 | 298 | 340 | .876 | 37 | 176 | 213 | 185 | 110 | 13 | 154 | 1285 | 2.9 | 2.5 | 17.4 |
| 00-01—Washington .... | 37 | 1216 | 205 | 504 | .407 | 143 | 160 | .894 | 15 | 94 | 109 | 111 | 43 | 7 | 84 | 598 | 2.9 | 3.0 | 16.2 |
| 01-02—L.A. Lakers ..... | 64 | 709 | 100 | 247 | .405 | 42 | 44 | .955 | 14 | 80 | 94 | 57 | 18 | 6 | 40 | 260 | 1.5 | 0.9 | 4.1 |
| **Totals** ................... | 976 | 34309 | 7305 | 16038 | .455 | 4561 | 5365 | .850 | 881 | 2920 | 3801 | 3398 | 1211 | 254 | 2579 | 20497 | 3.9 | 3.5 | 21.0 |

Three-point field goals: 1988-89, 33-for-90 (.367). 1989-90, 34-for-95 (.358). 1990-91, 40-for-115 (.348). 1991-92, 103-for-268 (.384). 1992-93, 48-for-130 (.369). 1993-94, 127-for-312 (.407). 1994-95, 156-for-424 (.368). 1995-96, 225-for-515 (.437). 1996-97, 204-for-477 (.428). 1997-98, 130-for-334 (.389). 1998-99, 70-for-221 (.317). 1999-00, 93-for-241 (.386). 2000-01, 45-for-133 (.338). 2001-02, 18-for-62 (.290). Totals, 1326-for-3417 (.388).

Personal fouls/disqualifications: 1988-89, 223/5. 1989-90, 210/3. 1990-91, 207/0. 1991-92, 231/1. 1992-93, 137/3. 1993-94, 211/3. 1994-95, 227/2. 1995-96, 233/6. 1996-97, 211/1. 1997-98, 154/0. 1998-99, 121/1. 1999-00, 191/2. 2000-01, 86/0. 2001-02, 61/0. Totals, 2503/27.

## NBA PLAYOFF RECORD

| Season Team | G | Min. | FGM | FGA | Pct. | FTM | FTA | Pct. | REBOUNDS Off. | Def. | Tot. | Ast. | St. | Blk. | TO | Pts. | AVERAGES RPG | APG | PPG |
|---|---|---|---|---|---|---|---|---|---|---|---|---|---|---|---|---|---|---|---|
| 88-89—Golden State ... | 8 | 314 | 62 | 135 | .459 | 34 | 38 | .895 | 10 | 48 | 58 | 35 | 14 | 1 | 24 | 161 | 7.3 | 4.4 | 20.1 |
| 90-91—Golden State ... | 9 | 372 | 85 | 169 | .503 | 23 | 24 | .958 | 10 | 37 | 47 | 22 | 5 | 6 | 17 | 201 | 5.2 | 2.4 | 22.3 |
| 95-96—Sacramento .... | 4 | 146 | 24 | 54 | .444 | 28 | 35 | .800 | 3 | 14 | 17 | 12 | 3 | 0 | 15 | 84 | 4.3 | 3.0 | 21.0 |
| 01-02—L.A. Lakers ..... | 2 | 4 | 1 | 1 | 1.000 | 1 | 2 | .500 | 0 | 1 | 1 | 0 | 0 | 0 | 1 | 3 | 0.5 | 0.0 | 1.5 |
| **Totals** ................... | 23 | 836 | 172 | 359 | .479 | 86 | 99 | .869 | 23 | 100 | 123 | 69 | 22 | 7 | 57 | 449 | 5.3 | 3.0 | 19.5 |

Three-point field goals: 1988-89, 3-for-16 (.188). 1990-91, 8-for-24 (.333). 1995-96, 8-for-23 (.348). Totals, 19-for-63 (.302).

Personal fouls/disqualifications: 1988-89, 25/0. 1990-91, 28/1. 1995-96, 11/0. Totals, 64/1.

## NBA ALL-STAR GAME RECORD

**NOTES:** NBA All-Star Game Most Valuable Player (1995).

| Season Team | Min. | FGM | FGA | Pct. | FTM | FTA | Pct. | REBOUNDS Off. | Def. | Tot. | Ast. | PF | Dq. | St. | Blk. | TO | Pts. |
|---|---|---|---|---|---|---|---|---|---|---|---|---|---|---|---|---|---|
| 1993—Sacramento.......... | | | | | | | Selected, did not play—injured. | | | | | | | | | | |
| 1994—Sacramento.......... | 24 | 5 | 16 | .313 | 0 | 0 | ... | 0 | 2 | 2 | 3 | 0 | 0 | 0 | 0 | 0 | 10 |
| 1995—Sacramento.......... | 22 | 10 | 13 | .769 | 0 | 0 | ... | 3 | 1 | 4 | 2 | 0 | 0 | 0 | 0 | 0 | 23 |
| 1996—Sacramento.......... | 25 | 3 | 10 | .300 | 1 | 2 | .500 | 0 | 2 | 2 | 2 | 0 | 0 | 1 | 0 | 2 | 7 |
| 1997—Sacramento.......... | 22 | 3 | 7 | .429 | 0 | 0 | ... | 1 | 2 | 3 | 4 | 1 | 0 | 0 | 0 | 1 | 9 |
| 1998—Sacramento.......... | 17 | 4 | 11 | .364 | 0 | 0 | ... | 0 | 1 | 1 | 2 | 0 | ... | 0 | 0 | 0 | 8 |
| **Totals**.......................... | 110 | 25 | 57 | .439 | 1 | 2 | .500 | 4 | 8 | 12 | 13 | 1 | 0 | 1 | 0 | 3 | 57 |

Three-point field goals: 1995, 3-for-3. 1996, 0-for-3. 1997, 3-for-4 (.750). 1998, 0-for-2. Totals, 6-for-12 (.500).

# ROBERTSON, OSCAR      G

**PERSONAL:** Born November 24, 1938, in Charlotte, Tenn. ... 6-5/220 (1,96/99,8). ... Full name: Oscar Palmer Robertson. ... Nickname: Big O.
**HIGH SCHOOL:** Crispus Attucks (Indianapolis).
**COLLEGE:** Cincinnati.
**TRANSACTIONS:** Selected by Cincinnati Royals in 1960 NBA Draft (territorial pick). ... Traded by Royals to Milwaukee Bucks for G Flynn Robinson and F Charlie Paulk (April 21, 1970).
**CAREER HONORS:** Elected to Naismith Memorial Basketball Hall of Fame (1980). ... NBA 35th Anniversary All-Time Team (1980) and One of the 50 Greatest Players in NBA History (1996).
**MISCELLANEOUS:** Member of NBA championship team (1971). ... Member of gold-medal-winning U.S. Olympic team (1960). ... Sacramento Kings franchise all-time leading scorer with 22,009 points and all-time assists leader with 7,731 (1960-61 through 1969-70).

### COLLEGIATE RECORD

**NOTES:** The Sporting News College Player of the Year (1958, 1959, 1960). ... The Sporting News All-America first team (1958, 1959, 1960). ... Led NCAA Division I with 35.1 points per game (1958), 32.6 points per game (1959) and 33.7 points per game (1960).

| Season Team | G | Min. | FGM | FGA | Pct. | FTM | FTA | Pct. | Reb. | Ast. | Pts. | AVERAGES RPG | APG | PPG |
|---|---|---|---|---|---|---|---|---|---|---|---|---|---|---|
| 56-57—Cincinnati‡ .................... | 13 | ... | 151 | ... | ... | 127 | 178 | .713 | ... | ... | 429 | ... | ... | 33.0 |
| 57-58—Cincinnati ...................... | 28 | 1085 | 352 | 617 | .571 | 280 | 355 | .789 | 425 | ... | 984 | 15.2 | ... | 35.1 |
| 58-59—Cincinnati ...................... | 30 | 1172 | 331 | 650 | .509 | 316 | 398 | .794 | 489 | 206 | 978 | 16.3 | 6.9 | 32.6 |
| 59-60—Cincinnati ...................... | 30 | 1155 | 369 | 701 | .526 | 273 | 361 | .756 | 424 | 219 | 1011 | 14.1 | 7.3 | 33.7 |
| **Varsity totals** ........................ | 88 | 3412 | 1052 | 1968 | .535 | 869 | 1114 | .780 | 1338 | ... | 2973 | 15.2 | ... | 33.8 |

### NBA REGULAR-SEASON RECORD

**RECORDS:** Shares single-game record for most free throws attempted in one quarter—16 (December 27, 1964, vs. Baltimore).
**HONORS:** NBA Most Valuable Player (1964). ... NBA Rookie of the Year (1961). ... All-NBA first team (1961, 1962, 1963, 1964, 1965, 1966, 1967, 1968, 1969). ... All-NBA second team (1970, 1971).

| Season Team | G | Min. | FGM | FGA | Pct. | FTM | FTA | Pct. | Reb. | Ast. | PF | Dq. | Pts. | AVERAGES RPG | APG | PPG |
|---|---|---|---|---|---|---|---|---|---|---|---|---|---|---|---|---|
| 60-61—Cincinnati.......................... | 71 | 3012 | 756 | 1600 | .473 | 653 | 794 | .822 | 716 | *690 | 219 | 3 | 2165 | 10.1 | *9.7 | 30.5 |
| 61-62—Cincinnati.......................... | 79 | 3503 | 866 | 1810 | .478 | 700 | 872 | .803 | 985 | *899 | 258 | 1 | 2432 | 12.5 | *11.4 | 30.8 |
| 62-63—Cincinnati.......................... | 80 | 3521 | 825 | 1593 | .518 | 614 | 758 | .810 | 835 | 758 | 293 | 1 | 2264 | 10.4 | 9.5 | 28.3 |
| 63-64—Cincinnati.......................... | 79 | 3559 | 840 | 1740 | .483 | *800 | 938 | *.853 | 783 | *868 | 280 | 3 | 2480 | 9.9 | *11.0 | 31.4 |
| 64-65—Cincinnati.......................... | 75 | 3421 | 807 | 1681 | .480 | *665 | 793 | .839 | 674 | *861 | 205 | 2 | 2279 | 9.0 | *11.5 | 30.4 |
| 65-66—Cincinnati.......................... | 76 | 3493 | 818 | 1723 | .475 | 742 | 881 | .842 | 586 | *847 | 227 | 1 | 2378 | 7.7 | *11.1 | 31.3 |
| 66-67—Cincinnati.......................... | 79 | 3468 | 838 | 1699 | .493 | 736 | 843 | .873 | 486 | 845 | 226 | 2 | 2412 | 6.2 | *10.7 | 30.5 |
| 67-68—Cincinnati.......................... | 65 | 2765 | 660 | 1321 | .500 | *576 | 660 | *.873 | 391 | 633 | 199 | 2 | 1896 | 6.0 | *9.7 | *29.2 |
| 68-69—Cincinnati.......................... | 79 | 3461 | 656 | 1351 | .486 | *643 | 767 | .838 | 502 | *772 | 231 | 2 | 1955 | 6.4 | *9.8 | 24.7 |
| 69-70—Cincinnati.......................... | 69 | 2865 | 647 | 1267 | .511 | 454 | 561 | .809 | 422 | 558 | 175 | 1 | 1748 | 6.1 | 8.1 | 25.3 |
| 70-71—Milwaukee ........................ | 81 | 3194 | 592 | 1193 | .496 | 385 | 453 | .850 | 462 | 668 | 203 | 0 | 1569 | 5.7 | 8.2 | 19.4 |
| 71-72—Milwaukee ........................ | 64 | 2390 | 419 | 887 | .472 | 276 | 330 | .836 | 323 | 491 | 116 | 0 | 1114 | 5.0 | 7.7 | 17.4 |
| 72-73—Milwaukee ........................ | 73 | 2737 | 446 | 983 | .454 | 238 | 281 | .847 | 360 | 551 | 167 | 0 | 1130 | 4.9 | 7.5 | 15.5 |

| Season Team | G | Min. | FGM | FGA | Pct. | FTM | FTA | Pct. | REBOUNDS Off. | Def. | Tot. | Ast. | St. | Blk. | TO | Pts. | AVERAGES RPG | APG | PPG |
|---|---|---|---|---|---|---|---|---|---|---|---|---|---|---|---|---|---|---|---|
| 73-74—Milwaukee ...... | 70 | 2477 | 338 | 772 | .438 | 212 | 254 | .835 | 71 | 208 | 279 | 446 | 77 | 4 | ... | 888 | 4.0 | 6.4 | 12.7 |
| **Totals** ................... | 1040 | 43866 | 9508 | 19620 | .485 | 7694 | 9185 | .838 | ... | ... | 7804 | 9887 | 77 | 4 | ... | 26710 | 7.5 | 9.5 | 25.7 |

Personal fouls/disqualifications: 1973-74, 132/0.

### NBA PLAYOFF RECORD

| Season Team | G | Min. | FGM | FGA | Pct. | FTM | FTA | Pct. | Reb. | Ast. | PF | Dq. | Pts. | AVERAGES RPG | APG | PPG |
|---|---|---|---|---|---|---|---|---|---|---|---|---|---|---|---|---|
| 61-62—Cincinnati.......................... | 4 | 185 | 42 | 81 | .519 | 31 | 39 | .795 | 44 | 44 | 18 | 1 | 115 | 11.0 | 11.0 | 28.8 |
| 62-63—Cincinnati.......................... | 12 | 570 | 124 | 264 | .470 | 133 | 154 | .864 | 156 | 108 | 41 | 0 | 381 | 13.0 | 9.0 | 31.8 |
| 63-64—Cincinnati.......................... | 10 | 471 | 92 | 202 | .455 | 109 | 127 | .858 | 89 | 84 | 30 | 0 | 293 | 8.9 | 8.4 | 29.3 |
| 64-65—Cincinnati.......................... | 4 | 195 | 38 | 89 | .427 | 36 | 39 | .923 | 19 | 48 | 14 | 0 | 112 | 4.8 | 12.0 | 28.0 |
| 65-66—Cincinnati.......................... | 5 | 224 | 49 | 120 | .408 | 61 | 68 | .897 | 38 | 39 | 20 | 1 | 159 | 7.6 | 7.8 | 31.8 |
| 66-67—Cincinnati.......................... | 4 | 183 | 33 | 64 | .516 | 33 | 37 | .892 | 16 | 45 | 9 | 0 | 99 | 4.0 | 11.3 | 24.8 |
| 70-71—Milwaukee ........................ | 14 | 520 | 102 | 210 | .486 | 52 | 69 | .754 | 70 | 124 | 39 | 0 | 256 | 5.0 | 8.9 | 18.3 |
| 71-72—Milwaukee ........................ | 11 | 380 | 57 | 140 | .407 | 30 | 36 | .833 | 64 | 83 | 29 | 0 | 144 | 5.8 | 7.5 | 13.1 |
| 72-73—Milwaukee ........................ | 6 | 256 | 48 | 96 | .500 | 31 | 34 | .912 | 28 | 45 | 21 | 1 | 127 | 4.7 | 7.5 | 21.2 |

| Season Team | G | Min. | FGM | FGA | Pct. | FTM | FTA | Pct. | REBOUNDS Off. | Def. | Tot. | Ast. | St. | Blk. | TO | Pts. | AVERAGES RPG | APG | PPG |
|---|---|---|---|---|---|---|---|---|---|---|---|---|---|---|---|---|---|---|---|
| 73-74—Milwaukee ...... | 16 | 689 | 90 | 200 | .450 | 44 | 52 | .846 | 15 | 39 | 54 | 149 | 15 | 4 | ... | 224 | 3.4 | 9.3 | 14.0 |
| **Totals** ................... | 86 | 3673 | 675 | 1466 | .460 | 560 | 655 | .855 | ... | ... | 578 | 769 | 15 | 4 | ... | 1910 | 6.7 | 8.9 | 22.2 |

Personal fouls/disqualifications: 1973-74, 46/0.

### NBA ALL-STAR GAME RECORD

**NOTES:** NBA All-Star Game Most Valuable Player (1961, 1964, 1969). ... Shares career record for most free throws attempted—98. ... Shares single-game record for most free throws made—12 (1965).

| Season Team | Min. | FGM | FGA | Pct. | FTM | FTA | Pct. | Reb. | Ast. | PF | Dq. | Pts. |
|---|---|---|---|---|---|---|---|---|---|---|---|---|
| 1961—Cincinnati | 34 | 8 | 13 | .615 | 7 | 9 | .778 | 9 | 14 | 5 | 0 | 23 |
| 1962—Cincinnati | 37 | 9 | 20 | .450 | 8 | 14 | .571 | 7 | 13 | 3 | 0 | 26 |
| 1963—Cincinnati | 37 | 9 | 15 | .600 | 3 | 4 | .750 | 3 | 6 | 5 | 0 | 21 |
| 1964—Cincinnati | 42 | 10 | 23 | .435 | 6 | 10 | .600 | 14 | 8 | 4 | 0 | 26 |
| 1965—Cincinnati | 40 | 8 | 18 | .444 | 12 | 13 | .923 | 6 | 8 | 5 | 0 | 28 |
| 1966—Cincinnati | 25 | 6 | 12 | .500 | 5 | 6 | .833 | 10 | 8 | 0 | 0 | 17 |
| 1967—Cincinnati | 34 | 9 | 20 | .450 | 8 | 10 | .800 | 2 | 5 | 4 | 0 | 26 |
| 1968—Cincinnati | 22 | 7 | 9 | .778 | 4 | 7 | .571 | 1 | 5 | 2 | 0 | 18 |
| 1969—Cincinnati | 32 | 8 | 16 | .500 | 8 | 8 | 1.000 | 6 | 5 | 3 | 0 | 24 |
| 1970—Cincinnati | 29 | 9 | 11 | .818 | 3 | 4 | .750 | 6 | 4 | 3 | 0 | 21 |
| 1971—Milwaukee | 24 | 2 | 6 | .333 | 1 | 3 | .333 | 2 | 2 | 3 | 0 | 5 |
| 1972—Milwaukee | 24 | 3 | 9 | .333 | 5 | 10 | .500 | 3 | 3 | 4 | 0 | 11 |
| Totals | 380 | 88 | 172 | .512 | 70 | 98 | .714 | 69 | 81 | 41 | 0 | 246 |

## ROBINSON, DAVID — C

**PERSONAL:** Born August 6, 1965, in Key West, Fla. ... 7-1/250. (2,16/113,4). ... Full Name: David Maurice Robinson. ... Nickname: The Admiral.
**HIGH SCHOOL:** Osbourn Park (Manassas, Va.).
**COLLEGE:** Navy.
**TRANSACTIONS/CAREER NOTES:** Selected by San Antonio Spurs in first round (first pick overall) of 1987 NBA Draft.
**CAREER HONORS:** NBA 50th Anniversary All-Time Team (1996).
**MISCELLANEOUS:** Member of NBA championship team (1999, 2003). ... Member of bronze-medal-winning U.S. Olympic team (1988) and gold-medal-winning U.S. Olympic teams (1992, 1996). ... Member of gold-medal winning U.S. World Championship team (1986). ... San Antonio Spurs all-time points leader with 20,790, all-time rebound leader with 10,497, all-time steals leader with 1,388 and all-time blocked shots leader with 2,954 (1989-90 through 2002-03).

### COLLEGIATE RECORD

**NOTES:** The Sporting News College Player of the Year (1987). ... Naismith Award winner (1987). ... Wooden Award winner (1987). ... The Sporting News All-America first team (1986, 1987). ... Holds NCAA Division I single-season records for most blocked shots—207 (1986). ... Shares NCAA Division I single-game record for most blocked shots—14 (January 4, 1986, vs. UNC Wilmington). ... Led NCAA Division I with 13.0 rebounds per game (1986). ... Led NCAA Division I with 5.91 blocked shots per game (1986) and 4.50 blocked shots per game (1987).

| | | | | | | | | | | | AVERAGES | | |
|---|---|---|---|---|---|---|---|---|---|---|---|---|---|
| Season Team | G | Min. | FGM | FGA | Pct. | FTM | FTA | Pct. | Reb. | Ast. | Pts. | RPG | APG | PPG |
| 83-84—Navy | 28 | 372 | 86 | 138 | .623 | 42 | 73 | .575 | 111 | 6 | 214 | 4.0 | 0.2 | 7.6 |
| 84-85—Navy | 32 | 1075 | 302 | 469 | .644 | 152 | 243 | .626 | 370 | 19 | 756 | 11.6 | 0.6 | 23.6 |
| 85-86—Navy | 35 | 1187 | 294 | 484 | .607 | 208 | 331 | .628 | 455 | 24 | 796 | 13.0 | 0.7 | 22.7 |
| 86-87—Navy | 32 | 1107 | 350 | 592 | .591 | 202 | 317 | .637 | 378 | 33 | 903 | 11.8 | 1.0 | 28.2 |
| Totals | 127 | 3741 | 1032 | 1683 | .613 | 604 | 964 | .627 | 1314 | 82 | 2669 | 10.3 | 0.6 | 21.0 |

Three-point field goals: 1986-87, 1-for-1.

### NBA REGULAR-SEASON RECORD

**HONORS:** NBA Most Valuable Player (1995). ... NBA Defensive Player of the Year (1992). ... NBA Rookie of the Year (1990). ... IBM Award, for all-around contributions to team's success (1990, 1991, 1994, 1995, 1996). ... NBA Sportsmanship Award (2001). ... All-NBA first team (1991, 1992, 1995, 1996). ... All-NBA second team (1994, 1998). ... All-NBA third team (1990, 1993, 2000, 2001). ... NBA All-Defensive first team (1991, 1992, 1995, 1996). ... NBA All-Defensive second team (1990, 1993, 1994, 1998). ... NBA All-Rookie first team (1990). ... J. Walter Kennedy Citizenship Award (2003).
**NOTES:** Led NBA with 4.49 blocked shots per game (1992).

| | | | | | | | | | REBOUNDS | | | | | | | | AVERAGES | | |
|---|---|---|---|---|---|---|---|---|---|---|---|---|---|---|---|---|---|---|---|
| Season Team | G | Min. | FGM | FGA | Pct. | FTM | FTA | Pct. | Off. | Def. | Tot. | Ast. | St. | Blk. | TO | Pts. | RPG | APG | PPG |
| 87-88—San Antonio | | | | | | Did not play—in military service. | | | | | | | | | | | | | |
| 88-89—San Antonio | | | | | | Did not play—in military service. | | | | | | | | | | | | | |
| 89-90—San Antonio | 82 | 3002 | 690 | 1300 | .531 | 613 | 837 | .732 | 303 | 680 | 983 | 164 | 138 | 319 | 257 | 1993 | 12.0 | 2.0 | 24.3 |
| 90-91—San Antonio | 82 | 3095 | 754 | 1366 | .552 | 592 | 777 | .762 | 335 | 728 | *1063 | 208 | 127 | *320 | 270 | 2101 | *13.0 | 2.5 | 25.6 |
| 91-92—San Antonio | 68 | 2564 | 592 | 1074 | .551 | 393 | 561 | .701 | 261 | 568 | 829 | 181 | 158 | *305 | 182 | 1578 | 12.2 | 2.7 | 23.2 |
| 92-93—San Antonio | 82 | 3211 | 676 | 1348 | .501 | 561 | 766 | .732 | 229 | 727 | 956 | 301 | 127 | 264 | 241 | 1916 | 11.7 | 3.7 | 23.4 |
| 93-94—San Antonio | 80 | 3241 | 840 | 1658 | .507 | *693 | *925 | .749 | 241 | 614 | 855 | 381 | 139 | 265 | 253 | *2383 | 10.7 | 4.8 | *29.8 |
| 94-95—San Antonio | 81 | 3074 | 788 | 1487 | .530 | *656 | 847 | .774 | 234 | 643 | 877 | 236 | 134 | 262 | 233 | 2238 | 10.8 | 2.9 | 27.6 |
| 95-96—San Antonio | 82 | 3019 | 711 | 1378 | .516 | *626 | *823 | .761 | 319 | *681 | *1000 | 247 | 111 | 271 | 190 | 2051 | 12.2 | 3.0 | 25.0 |
| 96-97—San Antonio | 6 | 147 | 36 | 72 | .500 | 34 | 52 | .654 | 19 | 32 | 51 | 8 | 6 | 6 | 8 | 106 | 8.5 | 1.3 | 17.7 |
| 97-98—San Antonio | 73 | 2457 | 544 | 1065 | .511 | 485 | 660 | .735 | 239 | 536 | 775 | 199 | 64 | 192 | 202 | 1574 | 10.6 | 2.7 | 21.6 |
| 98-99—San Antonio | 49 | 1554 | 268 | 527 | .509 | 239 | 363 | .658 | 148 | 344 | 492 | 103 | 69 | 119 | 108 | 775 | 10.0 | 2.1 | 15.8 |
| 99-00—San Antonio | 80 | 2557 | 528 | 1031 | .512 | 371 | 511 | .726 | 193 | 577 | 770 | 142 | 97 | 183 | 164 | 1420 | 9.6 | 1.8 | 17.8 |
| 00-01—San Antonio | 80 | 2371 | 400 | 823 | .486 | 351 | 470 | .747 | 208 | 483 | 691 | 116 | 80 | 197 | 122 | 1151 | 8.6 | 1.5 | 14.4 |
| 01-02—San Antonio | 78 | 2303 | 341 | 672 | .507 | 269 | 395 | .681 | 191 | 456 | 647 | 94 | 86 | 140 | 104 | 951 | 8.3 | 1.2 | 12.2 |
| 02-03—San Antonio | 64 | 1676 | 197 | 420 | .469 | 152 | 214 | .710 | 163 | 345 | 508 | 61 | 52 | 111 | 83 | 546 | 7.9 | 1.0 | 8.5 |
| Totals | 987 | 34271 | 7365 | 14221 | .518 | 6035 | 8201 | .736 | 3083 | 7414 | 10497 | 2441 | 1388 | 2954 | 2417 | 20790 | 10.6 | 2.5 | 21.1 |

Three-point field goals: 1989-90, 0-for-2. 1990-91, 1-for-7 (.143). 1991-92, 1-for-8 (.125). 1992-93, 3-for-17 (.176). 1993-94, 10-for-29 (.345). 1994-95, 6-for-20 (.300). 1995-96, 3-for-9 (.333). 1997-98, 1-for-4 (.250). 1998-99, 0-for-1. 1999-00, 0-for-2. 2000-01, 0-for-1. Totals, 25-for-100 (.250).
Personal fouls/disqualifications: 1989-90, 259/3. 1990-91, 264/5. 1991-92, 219/2. 1992-93, 239/5. 1993-94, 228/3. 1994-95, 230/2. 1995-96, 262/1. 1996-97, 9/0. 1997-98, 204/2. 1998-99, 143/0. 1999-00, 247/1. 2000-01, 212/1. 2001-02, 193/3. 2002-03, 126/1. Totals, 2835/29.

### NBA PLAYOFF RECORD

| | | | | | | | | | REBOUNDS | | | | | | | | AVERAGES | | |
|---|---|---|---|---|---|---|---|---|---|---|---|---|---|---|---|---|---|---|---|
| Season Team | G | Min. | FGM | FGA | Pct. | FTM | FTA | Pct. | Off. | Def. | Tot. | Ast. | St. | Blk. | TO | Pts. | RPG | APG | PPG |
| 89-90—San Antonio | 10 | 375 | 89 | 167 | .533 | 65 | 96 | .677 | 36 | 84 | 120 | 23 | 11 | 40 | 24 | 243 | 12.0 | 2.3 | 24.3 |
| 90-91—San Antonio | 4 | 166 | 35 | 51 | .686 | 33 | 38 | .868 | 11 | 43 | 54 | 8 | 6 | 15 | 15 | 103 | 13.5 | 2.0 | 25.8 |

| Season Team | G | Min. | FGM | FGA | Pct. | FTM | FTA | Pct. | Off. | Def. | Tot. | Ast. | St. | Blk. | TO | Pts. | RPG | APG | PPG |
|---|---|---|---|---|---|---|---|---|---|---|---|---|---|---|---|---|---|---|---|
| | | | | | | | | | REBOUNDS | | | | | | | | AVERAGES | | |
| 92-93—San Antonio.... | 10 | 421 | 79 | 170 | .465 | 73 | 110 | .664 | 29 | 97 | 126 | 40 | 10 | 36 | 25 | 231 | 12.6 | 4.0 | 23.1 |
| 93-94—San Antonio.... | 4 | 146 | 30 | 73 | .411 | 20 | 27 | .741 | 13 | 27 | 40 | 14 | 3 | 10 | 9 | 80 | 10.0 | 3.5 | 20.0 |
| 94-95—San Antonio.... | 15 | 623 | 129 | 289 | .446 | 121 | 149 | .812 | 57 | 125 | 182 | 47 | 22 | 39 | 56 | 380 | 12.1 | 3.1 | 25.3 |
| 95-96—San Antonio.... | 10 | 353 | 83 | 161 | .516 | 70 | 105 | .667 | 37 | 64 | 101 | 24 | 15 | 25 | 24 | 236 | 10.1 | 2.4 | 23.6 |
| 97-98—San Antonio.... | 9 | 353 | 57 | 134 | .425 | 61 | 96 | .635 | 41 | 86 | 127 | 23 | 11 | 30 | 25 | 175 | 14.1 | 2.6 | 19.4 |
| 98-99—San Antonio.... | 17 | 600 | 87 | 180 | .483 | 91 | 126 | .722 | 36 | 132 | 168 | 43 | 28 | 40 | 40 | 265 | 9.9 | 2.5 | 15.6 |
| 99-00—San Antonio.... | 4 | 155 | 31 | 83 | .373 | 32 | 42 | .762 | 17 | 38 | 55 | 10 | 7 | 12 | 8 | 94 | 13.8 | 2.5 | 23.5 |
| 00-01—San Antonio.... | 13 | 409 | 75 | 159 | .472 | 66 | 95 | .695 | 39 | 114 | 153 | 22 | 17 | 31 | 28 | 216 | 11.8 | 1.7 | 16.6 |
| 01-02—San Antonio.... | 4 | 81 | 9 | 19 | .474 | 0 | 4 | .000 | 6 | 17 | 23 | 5 | 3 | 3 | 2 | 18 | 5.8 | 1.3 | 4.5 |
| 02-03—San Antonio.... | 23 | 539 | 64 | 118 | .542 | 52 | 78 | .667 | 45 | 107 | 152 | 21 | 18 | 31 | 24 | 180 | 6.6 | 0.9 | 7.8 |
| Totals ................... | 123 | 4221 | 768 | 1604 | .479 | 684 | 966 | .708 | 367 | 934 | 1301 | 280 | 151 | 312 | 280 | 2221 | 10.6 | 2.3 | 18.1 |

Three-point field goals: 1990-91, 0-for-1. 1992-93, 0-for-1. 1993-94, 0-for-1. 1994-95, 1-for-5 (.200). 1999-00, 0-for-1. 2000-01, 0-for-1. Totals, 1-for-10 (.100).

Personal fouls/disqualifications: 1989-90, 35/1. 1990-91, 11/0. 1992-93, 39/0. 1993-94, 14/0. 1994-95, 63/1. 1995-96, 38/2. 1997-98, 28/1. 1998-99, 61/1. 1999-00, 15/0. 2000-01, 42/0. 2001-02, 14/0. 2002-03, 63/3. Totals, 423/9.

## NBA ALL-STAR GAME RECORD

| Season Team | Min. | FGM | FGA | Pct. | FTM | FTA | Pct. | Off. | Def. | Tot. | Ast. | PF | Dq. | St. | Blk. | TO | Pts. |
|---|---|---|---|---|---|---|---|---|---|---|---|---|---|---|---|---|---|
| | | | | | | | | REBOUNDS | | | | | | | | | |
| 1990—San Antonio ......... | 25 | 7 | 12 | .583 | 1 | 2 | .500 | 2 | 8 | 10 | 1 | 1 | 0 | 2 | 1 | 1 | 15 |
| 1991—San Antonio ......... | 18 | 6 | 13 | .462 | 4 | 5 | .800 | 3 | 3 | 6 | 0 | 5 | 0 | 2 | 3 | 2 | 16 |
| 1992—San Antonio ......... | 18 | 7 | 9 | .778 | 5 | 8 | .625 | 1 | 4 | 5 | 2 | 3 | 0 | 3 | 1 | 0 | 19 |
| 1993—San Antonio ......... | 26 | 7 | 10 | .700 | 7 | 12 | .583 | 2 | 8 | 10 | 1 | 4 | 0 | 0 | 1 | 1 | 21 |
| 1994—San Antonio ......... | 21 | 6 | 13 | .462 | 7 | 10 | .700 | 3 | 2 | 5 | 0 | 2 | 0 | 2 | 1 | 1 | 19 |
| 1995—San Antonio ......... | 14 | 3 | 5 | .600 | 4 | 6 | .667 | 0 | 3 | 3 | 2 | 2 | 0 | 2 | 1 | 1 | 10 |
| 1996—San Antonio ......... | 23 | 8 | 13 | .615 | 2 | 2 | 1.000 | 6 | 5 | 11 | 2 | 4 | 0 | 2 | 2 | 1 | 18 |
| 1998—San Antonio ......... | 22 | 3 | 4 | .750 | 9 | 10 | .900 | 2 | 4 | 6 | 0 | 1 | ... | 2 | 2 | 2 | 15 |
| 2000—San Antonio ......... | 7 | 0 | 1 | .000 | 0 | 0 | ... | 1 | 1 | 2 | 0 | 1 | 0 | 0 | 0 | 1 | 0 |
| 2001—San Antonio ......... | 10 | 3 | 5 | .600 | 2 | 4 | .500 | 2 | 2 | 4 | 0 | 3 | 0 | 0 | 0 | 1 | 8 |
| Totals ............................ | 184 | 50 | 85 | .588 | 41 | 59 | .695 | 22 | 40 | 62 | 8 | 26 | 0 | 13 | 13 | 11 | 141 |

## RODGERS, GUY                                    G

**PERSONAL:** Born September 1, 1935, in Philadelphia. ... Died February 19, 2001. ... 6-0/185 (1,83/83,9). ... Full name: Guy William Rodgers Jr.
**HIGH SCHOOL:** Northeast (Philadelphia).
**COLLEGE:** Temple.
**TRANSACTIONS:** Selected by Philadelphia Warriors in 1958 NBA Draft (territorial pick). ... Warriors franchise moved from Philadelphia to San Francisco for 1962-63 season. ... Traded by Warriors to Chicago Bulls for draft choice, cash and two players to be named later (September 7, 1966); G Jim King and G Jeff Mullins sent to Warriors to complete deal. ... Traded by Bulls to Cincinnati Royals for G Flynn Robinson, cash and two future draft choices (October 20, 1967). ... Selected by Milwaukee Bucks from Royals in NBA Expansion Draft (May 6, 1968).
**MISCELLANEOUS:** Golden State Warriors franchise all-time assists leader with 4,855 (1958-59 through 1965-66).

### COLLEGIATE RECORD

NOTES: The Sporting News All-America first team (1958).

| Season Team | G | Min. | FGM | FGA | Pct. | FTM | FTA | Pct. | Reb. | Ast. | Pts. | RPG | APG | PPG |
|---|---|---|---|---|---|---|---|---|---|---|---|---|---|---|
| | | | | | | | | | | | | AVERAGES | | |
| 54-55—Temple‡......................... | 15 | ... | ... | ... | ... | ... | ... | ... | ... | ... | 278 | ... | ... | 18.5 |
| 55-56—Temple......................... | 31 | ... | 243 | 552 | .440 | 87 | 155 | .561 | 186 | ... | 573 | 6.0 | ... | 18.5 |
| 56-57—Temple......................... | 29 | ... | 216 | 565 | .382 | 159 | 224 | .710 | 202 | ... | 591 | 7.0 | ... | 20.4 |
| 57-58—Temple......................... | 30 | ... | 249 | 564 | .441 | 105 | 171 | .614 | 199 | ... | 603 | 6.6 | ... | 20.1 |
| Varsity totals ........................ | 90 | ... | 708 | 1681 | .421 | 351 | 550 | .638 | 587 | ... | 1767 | 6.5 | ... | 19.6 |

### NBA REGULAR-SEASON RECORD

| Season Team | G | Min. | FGM | FGA | Pct. | FTM | FTA | Pct. | Reb. | Ast. | PF | Dq. | Pts. | RPG | APG | PPG |
|---|---|---|---|---|---|---|---|---|---|---|---|---|---|---|---|---|
| | | | | | | | | | | | | | | AVERAGES | | |
| 58-59—Philadelphia ...................... | 45 | 1565 | 211 | 535 | .394 | 61 | 112 | .545 | 281 | 261 | 132 | 1 | 483 | 6.2 | 5.8 | 10.7 |
| 59-60—Philadelphia ...................... | 68 | 2483 | 338 | 870 | .389 | 111 | 181 | .613 | 391 | 482 | 196 | 3 | 787 | 5.8 | 7.1 | 11.6 |
| 60-61—Philadelphia ...................... | 78 | 2905 | 397 | 1029 | .386 | 206 | 300 | .687 | 509 | 677 | 262 | 3 | 1000 | 6.5 | 8.7 | 12.8 |
| 61-62—Philadelphia ...................... | 80 | 2650 | 267 | 749 | .356 | 121 | 182 | .665 | 348 | 643 | 312 | 12 | 655 | 4.4 | 8.0 | 8.2 |
| 62-63—San Francisco ................... | 79 | 3249 | 445 | 1150 | .387 | 208 | 286 | .727 | 394 | *825 | 296 | 7 | 1098 | 5.0 | *10.4 | 13.9 |
| 63-64—San Francisco ................... | 79 | 2695 | 337 | 923 | .365 | 198 | 280 | .707 | 328 | 556 | 245 | 4 | 872 | 4.2 | 7.0 | 11.0 |
| 64-65—San Francisco ................... | 79 | 2699 | 465 | 1225 | .380 | 223 | 325 | .686 | 323 | 565 | 256 | 4 | 1153 | 4.1 | 7.2 | 14.6 |
| 65-66—San Francisco ................... | 79 | 2902 | 586 | 1571 | .373 | 296 | 407 | .727 | 421 | 846 | 241 | 6 | 1468 | 5.3 | 10.7 | 18.6 |
| 66-67—Chicago .......................... | 81 | 3063 | 538 | 1377 | .391 | 383 | 475 | .806 | 346 | *908 | 243 | 1 | 1459 | 4.3 | *11.2 | 18.0 |
| 67-68—Chicago-Cincinnati.............. | 79 | 1546 | 148 | 426 | .347 | 107 | 133 | .805 | 150 | 380 | 167 | 1 | 403 | 1.9 | 4.8 | 5.1 |
| 68-69—Milwaukee ........................ | 81 | 2157 | 325 | 862 | .377 | 184 | 232 | .793 | 226 | 561 | 207 | 2 | 834 | 2.8 | 6.9 | 10.3 |
| 69-70—Milwaukee ........................ | 64 | 749 | 68 | 191 | .356 | 67 | 90 | .744 | 74 | 213 | 73 | 1 | 203 | 1.2 | 3.3 | 3.2 |
| Totals.................................. | 892 | 28663 | 4125 | 10908 | .378 | 2165 | 3003 | .721 | 3791 | 6917 | 2630 | 45 | 10415 | 4.3 | 7.8 | 11.7 |

### NBA PLAYOFF RECORD

| Season Team | G | Min. | FGM | FGA | Pct. | FTM | FTA | Pct. | Reb. | Ast. | PF | Dq. | Pts. | RPG | APG | PPG |
|---|---|---|---|---|---|---|---|---|---|---|---|---|---|---|---|---|
| | | | | | | | | | | | | | | AVERAGES | | |
| 59-60—Philadelphia ...................... | 9 | 370 | 49 | 136 | .360 | 20 | 36 | .556 | 77 | 54 | 39 | 3 | 118 | 8.6 | 6.0 | 13.1 |
| 60-61—Philadelphia ...................... | 3 | 121 | 21 | 57 | .368 | 11 | 20 | .550 | 21 | 15 | 16 | 2 | 53 | 7.0 | 5.0 | 17.7 |
| 61-62—Philadelphia ...................... | 13 | 482 | 52 | 145 | .359 | 35 | 55 | .636 | 7 | 88 | 57 | 3 | 139 | 0.5 | 6.8 | 10.7 |
| 63-64—San Fran. ....................... | 12 | 419 | 57 | 173 | .329 | 33 | 47 | .702 | 58 | 90 | 46 | 1 | 147 | 4.8 | 7.5 | 12.3 |
| 66-67—Chicago .......................... | 3 | 97 | 15 | 40 | .375 | 4 | 5 | .800 | 6 | 18 | 11 | 0 | 34 | 2.0 | 6.0 | 11.3 |
| 69-70—Milwaukee ........................ | 7 | 68 | 4 | 14 | .286 | 9 | 12 | .750 | 4 | 21 | 7 | 0 | 17 | 0.6 | 3.0 | 2.4 |
| Totals.................................. | 47 | 1557 | 198 | 565 | .350 | 112 | 175 | .640 | 173 | 286 | 176 | 9 | 508 | 3.7 | 6.1 | 10.8 |

ALL-TIME GREAT PLAYERS

| Season Team | Min. | FGM | FGA | Pct. | FTM | FTA | Pct. | Reb. | Ast. | PF | Dq. | Pts. |
|---|---|---|---|---|---|---|---|---|---|---|---|---|
| 1963—San Francisco | 17 | 3 | 6 | .500 | 1 | 2 | .500 | 2 | 4 | 2 | 0 | 7 |
| 1964—San Francisco | 22 | 3 | 6 | .500 | 0 | 0 | ... | 2 | 2 | 4 | 0 | 6 |
| 1966—San Francisco | 34 | 4 | 11 | .364 | 0 | 0 | ... | 7 | 11 | 4 | 0 | 8 |
| 1967—Chicago | 28 | 0 | 4 | .000 | 1 | 1 | 1.000 | 2 | 8 | 3 | 0 | 1 |
| **Totals** | 101 | 10 | 27 | .370 | 2 | 3 | .667 | 13 | 25 | 13 | 0 | 22 |

## RODMAN, DENNIS                     F

**PERSONAL:** Born May 13, 1961, in Trenton, N.J. ... 6-7/228. (2.01 m/103 kg). ... Full Name: Dennis Keith Rodman. ... Nickname: Worm.

**HIGH SCHOOL:** South Oak Cliff (Dallas), did not play basketball.

**JUNIOR COLLEGE:** Cooke County (Texas) Junior College.

**COLLEGE:** Southeastern Oklahoma State.

**TRANSACTIONS/CAREER NOTES:** Selected by Detroit Pistons in second round (27th pick overall) of 1986 NBA Draft. ... Traded by Pistons to San Antonio Spurs for F Sean Elliott and F David Wood (October 1, 1993). ... Traded by Spurs to Chicago Bulls for C Will Perdue (October 2, 1995). ... Signed as free agent by Los Angeles Lakers (February 23, 1999). ... Waived by Lakers (April 16, 1999). ... Signed as free agent by Dallas Mavericks (February 3, 2000). ... Waived by Mavericks (March 8, 2000).

**MISCELLANEOUS:** Member of NBA championship team (1989, 1990, 1996, 1997, 1998).

### COLLEGIATE RECORD

**NOTES:** Led NAIA with 15.9 rebounds per game (1985) and 17.8 rebounds per game (1986).

| Season Team | G | Min. | FGM | FGA | Pct. | FTM | FTA | Pct. | Reb. | Ast. | Pts. | RPG | APG | PPG |
|---|---|---|---|---|---|---|---|---|---|---|---|---|---|---|
| 82-83—Cooke County J.C. | 16 | ... | 114 | 185 | .616 | 53 | 91 | .582 | 212 | ... | 281 | 13.3 | 0.5 | 17.6 |
| 83-84—SE Oklahoma State | 30 | ... | 303 | 490 | .618 | 173 | 264 | .655 | 392 | 23 | 779 | 13.1 | 0.8 | 26.0 |
| 84-85—SE Oklahoma State | 32 | ... | 353 | 545 | .648 | 151 | 267 | .566 | 510 | 12 | 857 | 15.9 | 0.4 | 26.8 |
| 85-86—SE Oklahoma State | 34 | ... | 332 | 515 | .645 | 165 | 252 | .655 | 605 | 26 | 829 | 17.8 | 0.8 | 24.4 |
| **Junior College Totals** | 16 | ... | 114 | 185 | .616 | 53 | 91 | .582 | 212 | ... | 281 | 13.3 | 0.5 | 17.6 |
| **4-Year-College Totals** | 96 | ... | 988 | 1550 | .637 | 489 | 783 | .625 | 1507 | 61 | 2465 | 15.7 | 0.6 | 25.7 |

### NBA REGULAR-SEASON RECORD

**RECORDS:** Holds career records for most consecutive seasons leading league in rebounds—7; and most seasons leading league in defensive rebounds—3.

**HONORS:** NBA Defensive Player of the Year (1990, 1991). ... IBM Award, for all-around contributions to team's success (1992). ... All-NBA third team (1992, 1995). ... NBA All-Defensive first team (1989, 1990, 1991, 1992, 1993, 1995, 1996). ... NBA All-Defensive second team (1994).

| Season Team | G | Min. | FGM | FGA | Pct. | FTM | FTA | Pct. | Off. | Def. | Tot. | Ast. | St. | Blk. | TO | Pts. | RPG | APG | PPG |
|---|---|---|---|---|---|---|---|---|---|---|---|---|---|---|---|---|---|---|---|
| 86-87—Detroit | 77 | 1155 | 213 | 391 | .545 | 74 | 126 | .587 | 163 | 169 | 332 | 56 | 38 | 48 | 93 | 500 | 4.3 | 0.7 | 6.5 |
| 87-88—Detroit | 82 | 2147 | 398 | 709 | .561 | 152 | 284 | .535 | 318 | 397 | 715 | 110 | 75 | 45 | 156 | 953 | 8.7 | 1.3 | 11.6 |
| 88-89—Detroit | 82 | 2208 | 316 | 531 | *.595 | 97 | 155 | .626 | 327 | 445 | 772 | 99 | 55 | 76 | 126 | 735 | 9.4 | 1.2 | 9.0 |
| 89-90—Detroit | 82 | 2377 | 288 | 496 | .581 | 142 | 217 | .654 | 336 | 456 | 792 | 72 | 52 | 60 | 90 | 719 | 9.7 | 0.9 | 8.8 |
| 90-91—Detroit | 82 | 2747 | 276 | 560 | .493 | 111 | 176 | .631 | *361 | 665 | 1026 | 85 | 65 | 55 | 94 | 669 | 12.5 | 1.0 | 8.2 |
| 91-92—Detroit | 82 | 3301 | 342 | 635 | .539 | 84 | 140 | .600 | *523 | *1007 | *1530 | 191 | 68 | 70 | 140 | 800 | *18.7 | 2.3 | 9.8 |
| 92-93—Detroit | 62 | 2410 | 183 | 429 | .427 | 87 | 163 | .534 | *367 | 765 | *1132 | 102 | 48 | 45 | 103 | 468 | *18.3 | 1.6 | 7.5 |
| 93-94—San Antonio | 79 | 2989 | 156 | 292 | .534 | 53 | 102 | .520 | *453 | *914 | *1367 | 184 | 52 | 32 | 138 | 370 | *17.3 | 2.3 | 4.7 |
| 94-95—San Antonio | 49 | 1568 | 137 | 240 | .571 | 75 | 111 | .676 | 274 | 549 | 823 | 97 | 31 | 23 | 98 | 349 | *16.8 | 2.0 | 7.1 |
| 95-96—Chicago | 64 | 2088 | 146 | 304 | .480 | 56 | 106 | .528 | *356 | 596 | 952 | 160 | 36 | 27 | 138 | 351 | *14.9 | 2.5 | 5.5 |
| 96-97—Chicago | 55 | 1947 | 128 | 286 | .448 | 50 | 88 | .568 | *320 | 563 | 883 | 170 | 32 | 19 | 111 | 311 | *16.1 | 3.1 | 5.7 |
| 97-98—Chicago | 80 | 2856 | 155 | 360 | .431 | 61 | 111 | .550 | 421 | *780 | *1201 | 230 | 47 | 18 | 147 | 375 | *15.0 | 2.9 | 4.7 |
| 98-99—L.A. Lakers | 23 | 657 | 16 | 46 | .348 | 17 | 39 | .436 | 62 | 196 | 258 | 30 | 10 | 12 | 31 | 49 | 11.2 | 1.3 | 2.1 |
| 99-00—Dallas | 12 | 389 | 12 | 31 | .387 | 10 | 14 | .714 | 48 | 123 | 171 | 14 | 2 | 1 | 19 | 34 | 14.3 | 1.2 | 2.8 |
| **Totals** | 911 | 28839 | 2766 | 5310 | .521 | 1069 | 1832 | .584 | 4329 | 7625 | 11954 | 1600 | 611 | 531 | 1484 | 6683 | 13.1 | 1.8 | 7.3 |

Three-point field goals: 1986-87, 0-for-1. 1987-88, 5-for-17 (.294). 1988-89, 6-for-26 (.231). 1989-90, 1-for-9 (.111). 1990-91, 6-for-30 (.200). 1991-92, 32-for-101 (.317). 1992-93, 15-for-73 (.205). 1993-94, 5-for-24 (.208). 1994-95, 0-for-2. 1995-96, 3-for-27 (.111). 1996-97, 5-for-19 (.263). 1997-98, 4-for-23 (.174). 1998-99, 0-for-1. 1999-00, 0-for-1. Totals, 82-for-354 (.232).

Personal fouls/disqualifications: 1986-87, 166/1. 1987-88, 273/5. 1988-89, 292/4. 1989-90, 276/2. 1990-91, 281/7. 1991-92, 248/0. 1992-93, 201/0. 1993-94, 229/0. 1994-95, 159/1. 1995-96, 196/1. 1996-97, 172/1. 1997-98, 71/0. 1999-00, 41/2. Totals, 2843/26.

### NBA PLAYOFF RECORD

**NOTES:** Shares NBA Finals single-game record for most offensive rebounds—11 (June 7, 1996, vs. Seattle; and June 16, 1996, vs. Seattle).

| Season Team | G | Min. | FGM | FGA | Pct. | FTM | FTA | Pct. | Off. | Def. | Tot. | Ast. | St. | Blk. | TO | Pts. | RPG | APG | PPG |
|---|---|---|---|---|---|---|---|---|---|---|---|---|---|---|---|---|---|---|---|
| 86-87—Detroit | 15 | 245 | 40 | 74 | .541 | 18 | 32 | .563 | 32 | 39 | 71 | 3 | 6 | 17 | 17 | 98 | 4.7 | 0.2 | 6.5 |
| 87-88—Detroit | 23 | 474 | 71 | 136 | .522 | 22 | 54 | .407 | 51 | 85 | 136 | 21 | 14 | 14 | 31 | 164 | 5.9 | 0.9 | 7.1 |
| 88-89—Detroit | 17 | 409 | 37 | 70 | .529 | 24 | 35 | .686 | 56 | 114 | 170 | 16 | 6 | 12 | 24 | 98 | 10.0 | 0.9 | 5.8 |
| 89-90—Detroit | 19 | 560 | 54 | 95 | .568 | 18 | 35 | .514 | 55 | 106 | 161 | 17 | 9 | 13 | 31 | 126 | 8.5 | 0.9 | 6.6 |
| 90-91—Detroit | 15 | 495 | 41 | 91 | .451 | 10 | 24 | .417 | 67 | 110 | 177 | 14 | 11 | 10 | 13 | 94 | 11.8 | 0.9 | 6.3 |
| 91-92—Detroit | 5 | 156 | 16 | 27 | .593 | 4 | 8 | .500 | 16 | 35 | 51 | 9 | 4 | 2 | 7 | 36 | 10.2 | 1.8 | 7.2 |
| 93-94—San Antonio | 3 | 114 | 12 | 24 | .500 | 1 | 6 | .167 | 24 | 24 | 48 | 2 | 6 | 4 | 6 | 25 | 16.0 | 0.7 | 8.3 |
| 94-95—San Antonio | 14 | 459 | 52 | 96 | .542 | 20 | 35 | .571 | 69 | 138 | 207 | 18 | 12 | 0 | 25 | 124 | 14.8 | 1.3 | 8.9 |
| 95-96—Chicago | 18 | 620 | 50 | 103 | .485 | 35 | 59 | .593 | 98 | 149 | 247 | 37 | 14 | 8 | 41 | 135 | 13.7 | 2.1 | 7.5 |
| 96-97—Chicago | 19 | 535 | 30 | 81 | .370 | 15 | 26 | .577 | 59 | 101 | 160 | 27 | 10 | 4 | 28 | 79 | 8.4 | 1.4 | 4.2 |
| 97-98—Chicago | 21 | 722 | 39 | 105 | .371 | 23 | 38 | .605 | 99 | 149 | 248 | 41 | 14 | 13 | 35 | 102 | 11.8 | 2.0 | 4.9 |
| **Totals** | 169 | 4789 | 442 | 902 | .490 | 190 | 352 | .540 | 625 | 1050 | 1676 | 205 | 106 | 97 | 258 | 1081 | 9.9 | 1.2 | 6.4 |

Three-point field goals: 1987-88, 0-for-2. 1988-89, 0-for-4. 1990-91, 2-for-9 (.222). 1991-92, 0-for-2. 1993-94, 0-for-5. 1994-95, 0-for-5. 1996-97, 4-for-16 (.250). 1997-98, 1-for-4 (.250). Totals, 7-for-47 (.149).

Personal fouls/disqualifications: 1987-88, 87/1. 1988-89, 58/0. 1990-91, 55/1. 1991-92, 17/0. 1993-94, 14/0. 1994-95, 51/1. 1996-97, 74/3. 1997-98, 88/4. Totals, 630/12.

## NBA ALL-STAR GAME RECORD

| Season Team | Min. | FGM | FGA | Pct. | FTM | FTA | Pct. | REBOUNDS Off. | Def. | Tot. | Ast. | PF | Dq. | St. | Blk. | TO | Pts. |
|---|---|---|---|---|---|---|---|---|---|---|---|---|---|---|---|---|---|
| 1990—Detroit | 11 | 2 | 4 | .500 | 0 | 0 | ... | 3 | 1 | 4 | 1 | 1 | 0 | 0 | 1 | 2 | 4 |
| 1992—Detroit | 25 | 2 | 7 | .286 | 0 | 0 | ... | 7 | 6 | 13 | 0 | 1 | 0 | 1 | 0 | 2 | 4 |
| Totals | 36 | 4 | 11 | .364 | 0 | 0 | ... | 10 | 7 | 17 | 1 | 2 | 0 | 1 | 1 | 4 | 8 |

# RUSSELL, BILL — C

**PERSONAL:** Born February 12, 1934, in Monroe, La. ... 6-10/220 (2,08/99,8). ... Full name: William Felton Russell.
**HIGH SCHOOL:** McClymonds (Oakland, Calif.).
**COLLEGE:** San Francisco.
**TRANSACTIONS:** Selected by St. Louis Hawks in first round (third pick overall) of 1956 NBA Draft. ... Draft rights traded by Hawks to Boston Celtics for F/C Ed Macauley and draft rights to F Cliff Hagan (April 29, 1956).
**CAREER HONORS:** Elected to Naismith Memorial Basketball Hall of Fame (1975). ... Declared Greatest Player in the History of the NBA by Professional Basketball Writers' Association of America (1980). ... NBA 25th Anniversary All-Time Team (1970), 35th Anniversary All-Time Team (1980) and One of the 50 Greatest Players in NBA History (1996).
**CAREER NOTES:** Consultant, Boston Celtics (1999-2000-present).
**MISCELLANEOUS:** Member of NBA championship team (1957, 1959, 1960, 1961, 1962, 1963, 1964, 1965, 1966, 1968, 1969). ... Member of gold-medal-winning U.S. Olympic team (1956). ... Boston Celtics all-time leading rebounder with 21,620 (1956-57 through 1968-69).

## COLLEGIATE RECORD

**NOTES:** NCAA Tournament Most Outstanding Player (1955). ... Member of NCAA championship team (1955, 1956).

| Season Team | G | Min. | FGM | FGA | Pct. | FTM | FTA | Pct. | Reb. | Ast. | Pts. | AVERAGES RPG | APG | PPG |
|---|---|---|---|---|---|---|---|---|---|---|---|---|---|---|
| 52-53—San Francisco‡ | 23 | ... | ... | ... | ... | ... | ... | ... | ... | ... | 461 | ... | ... | 20.0 |
| 53-54—San Francisco | 21 | ... | 150 | 309 | .485 | 117 | 212 | .552 | 403 | ... | 417 | 19.2 | ... | 19.9 |
| 54-55—San Francisco | 29 | ... | 229 | 423 | .541 | 164 | 278 | .590 | 594 | ... | 622 | 20.5 | ... | 21.4 |
| 55-56—San Francisco | 29 | ... | 246 | 480 | .513 | 105 | 212 | .495 | 609 | ... | 597 | 21.0 | ... | 20.6 |
| Varsity totals | 79 | ... | 625 | 1212 | .516 | 386 | 702 | .550 | 1606 | ... | 1636 | 20.3 | ... | 20.7 |

## NBA REGULAR-SEASON RECORD

**RECORDS:** Holds single-game record for most rebounds in one half—32 (November 16, 1957, vs. Philadelphia).
**HONORS:** NBA Most Valuable Player (1958, 1961, 1962, 1963, 1965). ... All-NBA first team (1959, 1963, 1965). ... All-NBA second team (1958, 1960, 1961, 1962, 1964, 1966, 1967, 1968). ... NBA All-Defensive first team (1969).

| Season Team | G | Min. | FGM | FGA | Pct. | FTM | FTA | Pct. | Reb. | Ast. | PF | Dq. | Pts. | AVERAGES RPG | APG | PPG |
|---|---|---|---|---|---|---|---|---|---|---|---|---|---|---|---|---|
| 56-57—Boston | 48 | 1695 | 277 | 649 | .427 | 152 | 309 | .492 | 943 | 88 | 143 | 2 | 706 | *19.6 | 1.8 | 14.7 |
| 57-58—Boston | 69 | 2640 | 456 | 1032 | .442 | 230 | 443 | .519 | *1564 | 202 | 181 | 2 | 1142 | *22.7 | 2.9 | 16.6 |
| 58-59—Boston | 70 | *2979 | 456 | 997 | .457 | 256 | 428 | .598 | *1612 | 222 | 161 | 3 | 1168 | *23.0 | 3.2 | 16.7 |
| 59-60—Boston | 74 | 3146 | 555 | 1189 | .467 | 240 | 392 | .612 | 1778 | 277 | 210 | 0 | 1350 | 24.0 | 3.7 | 18.2 |
| 60-61—Boston | 78 | 3458 | 532 | 1250 | .426 | 258 | 469 | .550 | 1868 | 268 | 155 | 0 | 1322 | 23.9 | 3.4 | 16.9 |
| 61-62—Boston | 76 | 3433 | 575 | 1258 | .457 | 286 | 481 | .595 | 1790 | 341 | 207 | 3 | 1436 | 23.6 | 4.5 | 18.9 |
| 62-63—Boston | 78 | 3500 | 511 | 1182 | .432 | 287 | 517 | .555 | 1843 | 348 | 189 | 1 | 1309 | 23.6 | 4.5 | 16.8 |
| 63-64—Boston | 78 | 3482 | 466 | 1077 | .433 | 236 | 429 | .550 | *1930 | 370 | 190 | 0 | 1168 | *24.7 | 4.7 | 15.0 |
| 64-65—Boston | 78 | *3466 | 429 | 980 | .438 | 244 | 426 | .573 | *1878 | 410 | 204 | 1 | 1102 | *24.1 | 5.3 | 14.1 |
| 65-66—Boston | 78 | 3386 | 391 | 943 | .415 | 223 | 405 | .551 | 1779 | 371 | 221 | 4 | 1005 | 22.8 | 4.8 | 12.9 |
| 66-67—Boston | 81 | 3297 | 395 | 870 | .454 | 285 | 467 | .610 | 1700 | 472 | 258 | 4 | 1075 | 21.0 | 5.8 | 13.3 |
| 67-68—Boston | 78 | 2953 | 365 | 858 | .425 | 247 | 460 | .537 | 1451 | 357 | 242 | 2 | 977 | 18.6 | 4.6 | 12.5 |
| 68-69—Boston | 77 | 3291 | 279 | 645 | .433 | 204 | 388 | .526 | 1484 | 374 | 231 | 2 | 762 | 19.3 | 4.9 | 9.9 |
| Totals | 963 | 40726 | 5687 | 12930 | .440 | 3148 | 5614 | .561 | 21620 | 4100 | 2592 | 24 | 14522 | 22.5 | 4.3 | 15.1 |

## NBA PLAYOFF RECORD

**NOTES:** Holds career playoff record for most rebounds—4,104. ... Holds NBA Finals records for highest rebounds-per-game average—29.5 (1959); and highest rebounds-per-game average by a rookie—22.9 (1957). ... Shares NBA Finals single-game records for most rebounds—40 (March 29, 1960, vs. St. Louis and April 18, 1962, vs. Los Angeles); most rebounds by a rookie—32 (April 13, 1957, vs. St. Louis); and most rebounds in one quarter—19 (April 18, 1962, vs. Los Angeles).

| Season Team | G | Min. | FGM | FGA | Pct. | FTM | FTA | Pct. | Reb. | Ast. | PF | Dq. | Pts. | AVERAGES RPG | APG | PPG |
|---|---|---|---|---|---|---|---|---|---|---|---|---|---|---|---|---|
| 56-57—Boston | 10 | 409 | 54 | 148 | .365 | 31 | 61 | .508 | 244 | 32 | 41 | 1 | 139 | 24.4 | 3.2 | 13.9 |
| 57-58—Boston | 9 | 355 | 48 | 133 | .361 | 40 | 66 | .606 | 221 | 24 | 24 | 0 | 136 | 24.6 | 2.7 | 15.1 |
| 58-59—Boston | 11 | 496 | 65 | 159 | .409 | 41 | 67 | .612 | 305 | 40 | 28 | 1 | 171 | 27.7 | 3.6 | 15.5 |
| 59-60—Boston | 13 | 572 | 94 | 206 | .456 | 53 | 75 | .707 | 336 | 38 | 38 | 1 | 241 | 25.8 | 2.9 | 18.5 |
| 60-61—Boston | 10 | 462 | 73 | 171 | .427 | 45 | 86 | .523 | 299 | 48 | 24 | 0 | 191 | 29.9 | 4.8 | 19.1 |
| 61-62—Boston | 14 | 672 | 116 | 253 | .459 | 82 | 113 | .726 | 370 | 70 | 49 | 0 | 314 | 26.4 | 5.0 | 22.4 |
| 62-63—Boston | 13 | 617 | 96 | 212 | .453 | 72 | 109 | .661 | 326 | 66 | 36 | 0 | 264 | 25.1 | 5.1 | 20.3 |
| 63-64—Boston | 10 | 451 | 47 | 132 | .356 | 37 | 67 | .552 | 272 | 44 | 33 | 0 | 131 | 27.2 | 4.4 | 13.1 |
| 64-65—Boston | 12 | 561 | 79 | 150 | .527 | 40 | 76 | .526 | 302 | 76 | 43 | 2 | 198 | 25.2 | 6.3 | 16.5 |
| 65-66—Boston | 17 | 814 | 124 | 261 | .475 | 76 | 123 | .618 | 428 | 85 | 60 | 0 | 324 | 25.2 | 5.0 | 19.1 |
| 66-67—Boston | 9 | 390 | 31 | 86 | .360 | 33 | 52 | .635 | 198 | 50 | 32 | 1 | 95 | 22.0 | 5.6 | 10.6 |
| 67-68—Boston | 19 | 869 | 99 | 242 | .409 | 76 | 130 | .585 | 434 | 99 | 73 | 1 | 274 | 22.8 | 5.2 | 14.4 |
| 68-69—Boston | 18 | 829 | 77 | 182 | .423 | 41 | 81 | .506 | 369 | 98 | 65 | 1 | 195 | 20.5 | 5.4 | 10.8 |
| Totals | 165 | 7497 | 1003 | 2335 | .430 | 667 | 1106 | .603 | 4104 | 770 | 546 | 8 | 2673 | 24.9 | 4.7 | 16.2 |

## NBA ALL-STAR GAME RECORD

**NOTES:** NBA All-Star Game Most Valuable Player (1963).

| Season Team | Min. | FGM | FGA | Pct. | FTM | FTA | Pct. | Reb. | Ast. | PF | Dq. | Pts. |
|---|---|---|---|---|---|---|---|---|---|---|---|---|
| 1958—Boston | 26 | 5 | 12 | .417 | 1 | 3 | .333 | 11 | 2 | 5 | 0 | 11 |
| 1959—Boston | 27 | 3 | 10 | .300 | 1 | 1 | 1.000 | 9 | 1 | 4 | 0 | 7 |
| 1960—Boston | 27 | 3 | 7 | .429 | 0 | 2 | .000 | 8 | 3 | 1 | 0 | 6 |
| 1961—Boston | 28 | 9 | 15 | .600 | 6 | 8 | .750 | 11 | 1 | 2 | 0 | 24 |
| 1962—Boston | 27 | 5 | 12 | .417 | 2 | 3 | .667 | 12 | 2 | 2 | 0 | 12 |

| Season Team | Min. | FGM | FGA | Pct. | FTM | FTA | Pct. | Reb. | Ast. | PF | Dq. | Pts. |
|---|---|---|---|---|---|---|---|---|---|---|---|---|
| 1963—Boston | 37 | 8 | 14 | .571 | 3 | 4 | .750 | 24 | 5 | 3 | 0 | 19 |
| 1964—Boston | 42 | 6 | 13 | .462 | 1 | 2 | .500 | 21 | 2 | 4 | 0 | 13 |
| 1965—Boston | 33 | 7 | 12 | .583 | 3 | 9 | .333 | 13 | 5 | 6 | 1 | 17 |
| 1966—Boston | 23 | 1 | 6 | .167 | 0 | 0 | ... | 10 | 2 | 2 | 0 | 2 |
| 1967—Boston | 22 | 1 | 2 | .500 | 0 | 0 | ... | 5 | 5 | 2 | 0 | 2 |
| 1968—Boston | 23 | 2 | 4 | .500 | 0 | 0 | ... | 9 | 8 | 5 | 0 | 4 |
| 1969—Boston | 28 | 1 | 4 | .250 | 1 | 2 | .500 | 6 | 3 | 1 | 0 | 3 |
| Totals | 343 | 51 | 111 | .459 | 18 | 34 | .529 | 139 | 39 | 37 | 1 | 120 |

## NBA COACHING RECORD

**BACKGROUND:** Player/head coach, Boston Celtics (1966-67 through 1968-69). ... Head coach/general manager, Seattle Supersonics (1973-74 through 1976-77).

| Season Team | REGULAR SEASON | | | | PLAYOFFS | | |
|---|---|---|---|---|---|---|---|
| | W | L | Pct. | Finish | W | L | Pct. |
| 66-67—Boston | 60 | 21 | .741 | 2nd/Eastern Division | 4 | 5 | .444 |
| 67-68—Boston | 54 | 28 | .659 | 2nd/Eastern Division | 12 | 7 | .632 |

| Season Team | REGULAR SEASON | | | | PLAYOFFS | | |
|---|---|---|---|---|---|---|---|
| | W | L | Pct. | Finish | W | L | Pct. |
| 68-69—Boston | 48 | 34 | .585 | 4th/Eastern Division | 12 | 6 | .667 |
| 73-74—Seattle | 36 | 46 | .439 | 3rd/Pacific Division | — | — | — |
| 74-75—Seattle | 43 | 39 | .524 | 2nd/Pacific Division | 4 | 5 | .444 |
| 75-76—Seattle | 43 | 39 | .524 | 2nd/Pacific Division | 2 | 4 | .333 |
| 76-77—Seattle | 40 | 42 | .488 | 4th/Pacific Division | — | — | — |
| 87-88—Sacramento | 17 | 41 | .293 | | | | |
| Totals (8 years) | 341 | 290 | .540 | Totals (5 years) | 34 | 27 | .557 |

**NOTES:**

1967—Defeated New York, 3-1, in Eastern Division Semifinals; lost to Philadelphia, 4-1, in Eastern Division Finals.

1968—Defeated Detroit, 4-2, in Eastern Division Semifinals; defeated Philadelphia, 4-3, in Eastern Division Finals; defeated Los Angeles, 4-2, in NBA Finals.

1969—Defeated Philadelphia, 4-1, in Eastern Division Semifinals; defeated New York, 4-2, in Eastern Division Finals; defeated Los Angeles, 4-3, in NBA Finals.

1975—Defeated Detroit, 2-1, in Western Conference First Round; lost to Golden State, 4-2, in Western Conference Semifinals.

1976—Lost to Phoenix in Western Conference Semifinals.

1988—Replaced as Sacramento head coach by Jerry Reynolds (March 7).

# SCHAYES, DOLPH      F/C

**PERSONAL:** Born May 19, 1928, in New York. ... 6-8/220 (2,03/99,8). ... Full name: Adolph Schayes. ... Father of Dan Schayes, center with seven NBA teams (1981-82 through 1998-99).

**HIGH SCHOOL:** DeWitt Clinton (Bronx, N.Y.).

**COLLEGE:** New York University.

**TRANSACTIONS:** Selected by Tri-Cities Hawks in 1948 National Basketball League Draft. ... NBL draft rights obtained from Hawks by Syracuse Nationals (1948). ... Nationals franchise became part of NBA for 1949-50 season. ... Nationals franchise moved from Syracuse to Philadelphia and renamed 76ers for 1963-64 season.

**CAREER HONORS:** Elected to Naismith Memorial Basketball Hall of Fame (1973). ... NBA 25th Anniversary All-Time Team (1970) and One of the 50 Greatest Players in NBA History (1996)

**MISCELLANEOUS:** Member of NBA championship team (1955). ... Philadelphia 76ers franchise all-time leading rebounder with 11,256 (1948-49 through 1963-64).

### COLLEGIATE RECORD

| Season Team | G | Min. | FGM | FGA | Pct. | FTM | FTA | Pct. | Reb. | Ast. | Pts. | AVERAGES | | |
|---|---|---|---|---|---|---|---|---|---|---|---|---|---|---|
| | | | | | | | | | | | | RPG | APG | PPG |
| 44-45—New York U. | 11 | ... | 46 | ... | ... | 23 | ... | ... | ... | ... | 115 | ... | ... | 10.5 |
| 45-46—New York U. | 22 | ... | 54 | ... | ... | 41 | ... | ... | ... | ... | 149 | ... | ... | 6.8 |
| 46-47—New York U. | 21 | ... | 66 | ... | ... | 63 | ... | ... | ... | ... | 195 | ... | ... | 9.3 |
| 47-48—New York U. | 26 | ... | 124 | ... | ... | 108 | ... | ... | ... | ... | 356 | ... | ... | 13.7 |
| Totals | 80 | ... | 290 | ... | ... | 235 | ... | ... | ... | ... | 815 | ... | ... | 10.2 |

### NBL AND NBA REGULAR-SEASON RECORD

**HONORS:** All-NBA first team (1952, 1953, 1954, 1955, 1957, 1958). ... All-NBA second team (1950, 1951, 1956, 1959, 1960, 1961). ... NBL Rookie of the Year (1949).

| Season Team | G | Min. | FGM | FGA | Pct. | FTM | FTA | Pct. | Reb. | Ast. | PF | Dq. | Pts. | AVERAGES | | |
|---|---|---|---|---|---|---|---|---|---|---|---|---|---|---|---|---|
| | | | | | | | | | | | | | | RPG | APG | PPG |
| 48-49—Syr. (NBL) | 63 | ... | 271 | ... | ... | 267 | 370 | .722 | ... | ... | 232 | ... | 809 | ... | ... | 12.8 |
| 49-50—Syracuse | 64 | ... | 348 | 903 | .385 | 376 | 486 | .774 | ... | 259 | 225 | ... | 1072 | ... | 4.0 | 16.8 |
| 50-51—Syracuse | 66 | ... | 332 | 930 | .357 | 457 | 608 | .752 | *1080 | 251 | 271 | 9 | 1121 | *16.4 | 3.8 | 17.0 |
| 51-52—Syracuse | 63 | 2004 | 263 | 740 | .355 | 342 | 424 | .807 | 773 | 182 | 213 | 5 | 868 | 12.3 | 2.9 | 13.8 |
| 52-53—Syracuse | 71 | 2668 | 375 | 1002 | .374 | 512 | 619 | .827 | 920 | 227 | 271 | 9 | 1262 | 13.0 | 3.2 | 17.8 |
| 53-54—Syracuse | 72 | 2655 | 370 | 973 | .380 | 488 | 590 | .827 | 870 | 214 | 232 | 4 | 1228 | 12.1 | 3.0 | 17.1 |
| 54-55—Syracuse | 72 | 2526 | 422 | 1103 | .383 | 489 | 587 | .833 | 887 | 213 | 247 | 6 | 1333 | 12.3 | 3.0 | 18.5 |
| 55-56—Syracuse | 72 | 2517 | 465 | 1202 | .387 | 542 | 632 | .858 | 891 | 200 | 251 | 9 | 1472 | 12.4 | 2.8 | 20.4 |
| 56-57—Syracuse | 72 | *2851 | 496 | 1308 | .379 | *625 | 691 | .904 | 1008 | 229 | 219 | 5 | 1617 | 14.0 | 3.2 | 22.5 |
| 57-58—Syracuse | 72 | *2918 | 581 | 1458 | .399 | 629 | 696 | *.904 | 1022 | 224 | 244 | 6 | 1791 | 14.2 | 3.1 | 24.9 |
| 58-59—Syracuse | 72 | 2645 | 504 | 1304 | .387 | 526 | 609 | .864 | 962 | 178 | 280 | 9 | 1534 | 13.4 | 2.5 | 21.3 |
| 59-60—Syracuse | 75 | 2741 | 578 | 1440 | .401 | 533 | 597 | *.893 | 959 | 256 | 263 | 10 | 1689 | 12.8 | 3.4 | 22.5 |
| 60-61—Syracuse | 79 | 3007 | 594 | 1595 | .372 | *680 | 783 | .868 | 960 | 296 | 296 | 9 | 1868 | 12.2 | 3.7 | 23.6 |
| 61-62—Syracuse | 56 | 1480 | 268 | 751 | .357 | 286 | 319 | *.897 | 439 | 120 | 167 | 4 | 822 | 7.8 | 2.1 | 14.7 |
| 62-63—Syracuse | 66 | 1438 | 223 | 575 | .388 | 181 | 206 | .879 | 375 | 175 | 177 | 2 | 627 | 5.7 | 2.7 | 9.5 |
| 63-64—Philadelphia | 24 | 350 | 44 | 143 | .308 | 46 | 57 | .807 | 110 | 48 | 76 | 3 | 134 | 4.6 | 2.0 | 5.6 |
| Totals | 1059 | ... | 6134 | ... | ... | 6979 | 8274 | .843 | ... | ... | 3664 | ... | 19247 | ... | ... | 18.2 |

## NBL AND NBA PLAYOFF RECORD

| Season Team | G | Min. | FGM | FGA | Pct. | FTM | FTA | Pct. | Reb. | Ast. | PF | Dq. | Pts. | AVERAGES RPG | APG | PPG |
|---|---|---|---|---|---|---|---|---|---|---|---|---|---|---|---|---|
| 48-49—Syr. (NBL) | 6 | ... | 27 | ... | ... | 32 | 42 | .762 | ... | ... | 26 | ... | 86 | ... | ... | 14.3 |
| 49-50—Syracuse | 11 | ... | 57 | 148 | .385 | 74 | 101 | .733 | ... | 28 | 43 | ... | 188 | ... | 2.5 | 17.1 |
| 50-51—Syracuse | 7 | ... | 47 | 105 | .448 | 49 | 64 | .766 | 102 | 20 | 28 | 2 | 143 | 14.6 | 2.9 | 20.4 |
| 51-52—Syracuse | 7 | 248 | 41 | 91 | .451 | 60 | 78 | .769 | 90 | 15 | 34 | 2 | 142 | 12.9 | 2.1 | 20.3 |
| 52-53—Syracuse | 2 | 58 | 4 | 16 | .250 | 10 | 13 | .769 | 17 | 1 | 7 | 0 | 18 | 8.5 | 0.5 | 9.0 |
| 53-54—Syracuse | 13 | 374 | 64 | 140 | .457 | 80 | 108 | .741 | 136 | 24 | 40 | 1 | 208 | 10.5 | 1.8 | 16.0 |
| 54-55—Syracuse | 11 | 363 | 60 | 167 | .359 | 89 | 106 | .840 | 141 | 40 | 48 | 3 | 209 | 12.8 | 3.6 | 19.0 |
| 55-56—Syracuse | 8 | 310 | 52 | 142 | .366 | 73 | 83 | .880 | 111 | 27 | 27 | 0 | 177 | 13.9 | 3.4 | 22.1 |
| 56-57—Syracuse | 5 | 215 | 29 | 95 | .305 | 49 | 55 | .891 | 90 | 14 | 18 | 0 | 107 | 18.0 | 2.8 | 21.4 |
| 57-58—Syracuse | 3 | 131 | 25 | 64 | .391 | 30 | 36 | .833 | 45 | 6 | 10 | 0 | 80 | 15.0 | 2.0 | 26.7 |
| 58-59—Syracuse | 9 | 351 | 78 | 195 | .400 | 98 | 107 | .916 | 117 | 41 | 36 | 0 | 254 | 13.0 | 4.6 | 28.2 |
| 59-60—Syracuse | 3 | 126 | 30 | 66 | .455 | 28 | 30 | .933 | 48 | 8 | 10 | 0 | 88 | 16.0 | 2.7 | 29.3 |
| 60-61—Syracuse | 8 | 308 | 51 | 152 | .336 | 63 | 70 | .900 | 91 | 21 | 32 | 2 | 165 | 11.4 | 2.6 | 20.6 |
| 61-62—Syracuse | 5 | 95 | 24 | 66 | .364 | 9 | 13 | .692 | 35 | 5 | 21 | 0 | 57 | 7.0 | 1.0 | 11.4 |
| 62-63—Syracuse | 5 | 108 | 20 | 44 | .455 | 11 | 12 | .917 | 28 | 7 | 17 | 0 | 51 | 5.6 | 1.4 | 10.2 |
| Totals | 103 | ... | 609 | ... | ... | 755 | 918 | .822 | ... | ... | 397 | ... | 1973 | ... | ... | 19.2 |

## NBA ALL-STAR GAME RECORD

| Season Team | Min. | FGM | FGA | Pct. | FTM | FTA | Pct. | Reb | Ast. | PF | Dq. | Pts. |
|---|---|---|---|---|---|---|---|---|---|---|---|---|
| 1951—Syracuse | ... | 7 | 10 | .700 | 1 | 2 | .500 | 14 | 3 | 1 | 0 | 15 |
| 1952—Syracuse | | | | Selected, did not play—injured. | | | | | | | | |
| 1953—Syracuse | 26 | 2 | 7 | .286 | 4 | 4 | 1.000 | 13 | 3 | 3 | 0 | 8 |
| 1954—Syracuse | 24 | 1 | 3 | .333 | 4 | 6 | .667 | 12 | 1 | 1 | 0 | 6 |
| 1955—Syracuse | 29 | 6 | 12 | .500 | 3 | 3 | 1.000 | 13 | 1 | 4 | 0 | 15 |
| 1956—Syracuse | 25 | 4 | 8 | .500 | 6 | 10 | .600 | 4 | 2 | 2 | 0 | 14 |
| 1957—Syracuse | 25 | 4 | 6 | .667 | 1 | 1 | 1.000 | 10 | 1 | 1 | 0 | 9 |
| 1958—Syracuse | 39 | 6 | 15 | .400 | 6 | 6 | 1.000 | 9 | 2 | 4 | 0 | 18 |
| 1959—Syracuse | 22 | 3 | 14 | .214 | 7 | 8 | .875 | 13 | 1 | 6 | 1 | 13 |
| 1960—Syracuse | 27 | 8 | 19 | .421 | 3 | 3 | 1.000 | 10 | 0 | 3 | 0 | 19 |
| 1961—Syracuse | 27 | 7 | 15 | .467 | 7 | 7 | 1.000 | 6 | 3 | 4 | 0 | 21 |
| 1962—Syracuse | 4 | 0 | 0 | ... | 0 | 0 | ... | 1 | 0 | 3 | 0 | 0 |
| Totals | ... | 48 | 109 | .440 | 42 | 50 | .840 | 105 | 17 | 32 | 1 | 138 |

## NBA COACHING RECORD

**BACKGROUND:** Player/head coach, Philadelphia 76ers (1963-64).
**HONORS:** NBA Coach of the Year (1966).

| Season Team | REGULAR SEASON W | L | Pct. | Finish | PLAYOFFS W | L | Pct. |
|---|---|---|---|---|---|---|---|
| 63-64—Philadelphia | 34 | 46 | .425 | 3rd/Eastern Division | 2 | 3 | .400 |
| 64-65—Philadelphia | 40 | 40 | .500 | 3rd/Eastern Division | 6 | 5 | .545 |
| 65-66—Philadelphia | 55 | 25 | .688 | 1st/Eastern Division | 1 | 4 | .200 |
| 70-71—Buffalo | 22 | 60 | .268 | 4th/Atlantic Division | — | — | — |
| 71-72—Buffalo | 0 | 1 | .000 | | — | — | — |
| Totals (5 years) | 151 | 172 | .467 | Totals (3 years) | 9 | 12 | .429 |

**NOTES:**
1964—Lost to Cincinnati in Eastern Division Semifinals.
1965—Defeated Cincinnati, 3-1, in Eastern Division Semifinals; lost to Boston, 4-3, in Eastern Division Finals.
1966—Lost to Boston in Eastern Division Finals.
1971—Replaced as Buffalo head coach by John McCarthy (October).

# SHARMAN, BILL                    G

**PERSONAL:** Born May 25, 1926, in Abilene, Texas. ... 6-1/190 (1,85/86). ... Full name: William Walton Sharman.
**HIGH SCHOOL:** Narbonne (Lomita, Calif.), then Porterville (Calif.).
**COLLEGE:** Southern California.
**TRANSACTIONS:** Selected by Washington Capitols in second round of 1950 NBA Draft. ... Selected by Fort Wayne Pistons in 1951 NBA Dispersal Draft of Capitols franchise (did not report to Fort Wayne). ... Traded by Pistons with F Bob Brannum to Boston Celtics for NBA rights to C Charlie Share (1951). ... Signed as player/head coach by Los Angeles Jets of American Basketball League (1961).
**CAREER HONORS:** Elected to Naismith Memorial Basketball Hall of Fame as a player (1976) and a head coach (2004). ... NBA 25th Anniversary All-Time Team (1970) and One of the 50 Greatest Players in NBA History (1996).
**CAREER NOTES:** General manager, Los Angeles Lakers (1975-76 through 1981-82). ... President, Lakers (1982-83 through 1989-90). ... Consultant, Lakers (1990-91 to present).
**MISCELLANEOUS:** Member of NBA championship team (1957, 1959, 1960, 1961).

## COLLEGIATE RECORD

**NOTES:** THE SPORTING NEWS All-America first team (1950). ... THE SPORTING NEWS All-America third team (1949). ... In military service during 1944-45 and 1945-46 seasons.

| Season Team | G | Min. | FGM | FGA | Pct. | FTM | FTA | Pct. | Reb. | Ast. | Pts. | AVERAGES RPG | APG | PPG |
|---|---|---|---|---|---|---|---|---|---|---|---|---|---|---|
| 46-47—Southern Cal | 10 | ... | 16 | ... | ... | 9 | 12 | .750 | ... | ... | 41 | ... | ... | 4.1 |
| 47-48—Southern Cal | 24 | ... | 100 | ... | ... | 38 | 44 | .864 | ... | ... | 238 | ... | ... | 9.9 |
| 48-49—Southern Cal | 24 | ... | 142 | ... | ... | 98 | 125 | .784 | ... | ... | 382 | ... | ... | 15.9 |
| 49-50—Southern Cal | 24 | ... | 171 | 421 | .406 | 104 | 129 | .806 | ... | ... | 446 | ... | ... | 18.6 |
| Totals | 82 | ... | 429 | ... | ... | 249 | 310 | .803 | ... | ... | 1107 | ... | ... | 13.5 |

## NBA REGULAR-SEASON RECORD

**HONORS:** All-NBA first team (1956, 1957, 1958, 1959). ... All-NBA second team (1953, 1955, 1960).

| Season Team | G | Min. | FGM | FGA | Pct. | FTM | FTA | Pct. | Reb. | Ast. | PF | Dq. | Pts. | AVERAGES | | |
|---|---|---|---|---|---|---|---|---|---|---|---|---|---|---|---|---|
| | | | | | | | | | | | | | | RPG | APG | PPG |
| 50-51—Washington | 31 | ... | 141 | 361 | .391 | 96 | 108 | .889 | 96 | 39 | 86 | 3 | 378 | 3.1 | 1.3 | 12.2 |
| 51-52—Boston | 63 | 1389 | 244 | 628 | .389 | 183 | 213 | .859 | 221 | 151 | 181 | 3 | 671 | 3.5 | 2.4 | 10.7 |
| 52-53—Boston | 71 | 2333 | 403 | 925 | .436 | 341 | 401 | *.850 | 288 | 191 | 240 | 7 | 1147 | 4.1 | 2.7 | 16.2 |
| 53-54—Boston | 72 | 2467 | 412 | 915 | .450 | 331 | 392 | *.844 | 255 | 229 | 211 | 4 | 1155 | 3.5 | 3.2 | 16.0 |
| 54-55—Boston | 68 | 2453 | 453 | 1062 | .427 | 347 | 387 | *.897 | 302 | 280 | 212 | 2 | 1253 | 4.4 | 4.1 | 18.4 |
| 55-56—Boston | 72 | 2698 | 538 | 1229 | .438 | 358 | 413 | *.867 | 259 | 339 | 197 | 1 | 1434 | 3.6 | 4.7 | 19.9 |
| 56-57—Boston | 67 | 2403 | 516 | 1241 | .416 | 381 | 421 | *.905 | 286 | 236 | 188 | 1 | 1413 | 4.3 | 3.5 | 21.1 |
| 57-58—Boston | 63 | 2214 | 550 | 1297 | .424 | 302 | 338 | .894 | 295 | 167 | 156 | 3 | 1402 | 4.7 | 2.7 | 22.3 |
| 58-59—Boston | 72 | 2382 | 562 | 1377 | .408 | 342 | 367 | *.932 | 292 | 179 | 173 | 1 | 1466 | 4.1 | 2.5 | 20.4 |
| 59-60—Boston | 71 | 1916 | 559 | 1225 | .456 | 252 | 291 | .866 | 262 | 144 | 154 | 2 | 1370 | 3.7 | 2.0 | 19.3 |
| 60-61—Boston | 61 | 1538 | 383 | 908 | .422 | 210 | 228 | *.921 | 223 | 146 | 127 | 0 | 976 | 3.7 | 2.4 | 16.0 |
| Totals | 711 | ... | 4761 | 11168 | .426 | 3143 | 3559 | .883 | 2779 | 2101 | 1925 | 27 | 12665 | 3.9 | 3.0 | 17.8 |

## NBA PLAYOFF RECORD

| Season Team | G | Min. | FGM | FGA | Pct. | FTM | FTA | Pct. | Reb. | Ast. | PF | Dq. | Pts. | AVERAGES | | |
|---|---|---|---|---|---|---|---|---|---|---|---|---|---|---|---|---|
| | | | | | | | | | | | | | | RPG | APG | PPG |
| 51-52—Boston | 1 | 27 | 7 | 12 | .583 | 1 | 1 | 1.000 | 3 | 7 | 4 | 0 | 15 | 3.0 | 7.0 | 15.0 |
| 52-53—Boston | 6 | 201 | 20 | 60 | .333 | 30 | 32 | .938 | 15 | 15 | 26 | 1 | 70 | 2.5 | 2.5 | 11.7 |
| 53-54—Boston | 6 | 206 | 35 | 81 | .432 | 43 | 50 | .860 | 25 | 10 | 29 | 2 | 113 | 4.2 | 1.7 | 18.8 |
| 54-55—Boston | 7 | 290 | 55 | 110 | .500 | 35 | 38 | .921 | 38 | 38 | 24 | 1 | 145 | 5.4 | 5.4 | 20.7 |
| 55-56—Boston | 3 | 119 | 18 | 46 | .391 | 16 | 17 | .941 | 7 | 12 | 7 | 0 | 52 | 2.3 | 4.0 | 17.3 |
| 56-57—Boston | 10 | 377 | 75 | 197 | .381 | 61 | 64 | .953 | 35 | 29 | 23 | 1 | 211 | 3.5 | 2.9 | 21.1 |
| 57-58—Boston | 11 | 406 | 90 | 221 | .407 | 52 | 56 | .929 | 54 | 25 | 28 | 0 | 232 | 4.9 | 2.3 | 21.1 |
| 58-59—Boston | 11 | 322 | 82 | 193 | .425 | 57 | 59 | .966 | 36 | 28 | 35 | 0 | 221 | 3.3 | 2.5 | 20.1 |
| 59-60—Boston | 13 | 364 | 88 | 209 | .421 | 43 | 53 | .811 | 45 | 20 | 22 | 1 | 219 | 3.5 | 1.5 | 16.8 |
| 60-61—Boston | 10 | 261 | 68 | 133 | .511 | 32 | 36 | .889 | 27 | 17 | 22 | 0 | 168 | 2.7 | 1.7 | 16.8 |
| Totals | 78 | 2573 | 538 | 1262 | .426 | 370 | 406 | .911 | 285 | 201 | 220 | 6 | 1446 | 3.7 | 2.6 | 18.5 |

## NBA ALL-STAR GAME RECORD

**NOTES:** NBA All-Star Game Most Valuable Player (1955). ... Holds single-game record for most field goals attempted in one quarter—12 (1960).

| Season Team | Min. | FGM | FGA | Pct. | FTM | FTA | Pct. | Reb | Ast. | PF | Dq. | Pts. |
|---|---|---|---|---|---|---|---|---|---|---|---|---|
| 1953—Boston | 26 | 5 | 8 | .625 | 1 | 1 | 1.000 | 4 | 0 | 2 | 0 | 11 |
| 1954—Boston | 30 | 6 | 9 | .667 | 2 | 4 | .500 | 2 | 3 | 3 | 0 | 14 |
| 1955—Boston | 18 | 5 | 10 | .500 | 5 | 5 | 1.000 | 4 | 2 | 4 | 0 | 15 |
| 1956—Boston | 22 | 2 | 8 | .250 | 3 | 5 | .600 | 3 | 1 | 2 | 1 | 7 |
| 1957—Boston | 23 | 5 | 17 | .294 | 2 | 2 | 1.000 | 6 | 5 | 1 | 0 | 12 |
| 1958—Boston | 25 | 6 | 19 | .316 | 3 | 3 | 1.000 | 4 | 3 | 2 | 0 | 15 |
| 1959—Boston | 24 | 3 | 12 | .250 | 5 | 6 | .833 | 2 | 0 | 1 | 0 | 11 |
| 1960—Boston | 26 | 8 | 21 | .381 | 1 | 1 | 1.000 | 6 | 2 | 1 | 0 | 17 |
| Totals | 194 | 40 | 104 | .385 | 22 | 27 | .815 | 31 | 16 | 16 | 1 | 102 |

## ABL REGULAR-SEASON RECORD

| Season Team | G | Min. | FGM | FGA | Pct. | FTM | FTA | Pct. | Reb. | Ast. | Pts. | AVERAGES | | |
|---|---|---|---|---|---|---|---|---|---|---|---|---|---|---|
| | | | | | | | | | | | | RPG | APG | PPG |
| 61-62—Los Angeles | 19 | 346 | 35 | 80 | .438 | 37 | 34 | 1.088 | 43 | 37 | 107 | 2.3 | 1.9 | 5.6 |

## HEAD COACHING RECORD

**BACKGROUND:** Player/head coach, Los Angeles Jets of American Basketball League (1961-62). ... Assistant coach, New Orleans Jazz (1974-75 and 1975-76).

**HONORS:** NBA Coach of the Year (1972). ... ABA co-Coach of the Year (1970).

## COLLEGIATE COACHING RECORD

| Season Team | W | L | Pct. | Finish |
|---|---|---|---|---|
| 62-63—Cal State-Los Angeles | 10 | 12 | .455 | 4th/California Collegiate Athletic Association |
| 63-64—Cal State-Los Angeles | 17 | 8 | .680 | 2nd/California Collegiate Athletic Association |
| Totals (2 years) | 27 | 20 | .574 | |

## ABL COACHING RECORD

| Season Team | REGULAR SEASON | | | | PLAYOFFS | | |
|---|---|---|---|---|---|---|---|
| | W | L | Pct. | Finish | W | L | Pct. |
| 61-62—Los Angeles-Cleveland | 43 | 26 | .623 | | 5 | 2 | .714 |

## NBA COACHING RECORD

| Season Team | REGULAR SEASON | | | | PLAYOFFS | | |
|---|---|---|---|---|---|---|---|
| | W | L | Pct. | Finish | W | L | Pct. |
| 66-67—San Francisco | 44 | 37 | .543 | 1st/Western Division | 9 | 6 | .600 |
| 67-68—San Francisco | 43 | 39 | .524 | 3rd/Western Division | 4 | 6 | .400 |
| 71-72—Los Angeles | 69 | 13 | .841 | 1st/Pacific Division | 12 | 3 | .800 |
| 72-73—Los Angeles | 60 | 22 | .732 | 1st/Pacific Division | 9 | 8 | .529 |
| 73-74—Los Angeles | 47 | 35 | .573 | 1st/Pacific Division | 1 | 4 | .200 |
| 74-75—Los Angeles | 30 | 52 | .366 | 5th/Pacific Division | — | — | — |
| 75-76—Los Angeles | 40 | 42 | .488 | 4th/Pacific Division | — | — | — |
| Totals (7 years) | 333 | 240 | .581 | | Totals (5 years) 35 | 27 | .565 |

## ABA COACHING RECORD

| Season Team | REGULAR SEASON | | | | PLAYOFFS | | |
|---|---|---|---|---|---|---|---|
| | W | L | Pct. | Finish | W | L | Pct. |
| 68-69—Los Angeles | 33 | 45 | .423 | 5th/Western Division | — | — | — |
| 69-70—Los Angeles | 43 | 41 | .512 | 4th/Western Division | 10 | 7 | .588 |
| 70-71—Utah | 57 | 27 | .679 | 2nd/Western Division | 12 | 6 | .667 |
| Totals (3 years) | 133 | 113 | .541 | | Totals (2 years) 22 | 13 | .629 |

**NOTES:**
1962—Los Angeles Jets had 24-15 record when they folded after first half of season (January 10); Sharman then replaced John McLendon, who resigned as Cleveland Pipers head coach (January 28), and guided Pipers to ABL Championship.
1967—Defeated Los Angeles, 3-0, in Western Division Semifinals; defeated St. Louis, 4-2, in Western Division Finals; lost to Philadelphia, 4-2, in World Championship Series.
1968—Defeated St. Louis, 4-2, in Western Division Semifinals; lost to Los Angeles, 4-0, in Western Division Finals.
1970—Defeated Dallas, 4-2, in Western Division Semifinals; defeated Denver, 4-1, in Western Division Finals; lost to Indiana, 4-2, in ABA Finals.
1971—Defeated Texas, 4-0, in Western Division Semifinals; defeated Indiana, 4-3, in Western Division Finals; defeated Kentucky, 4-3, in ABA Finals.
1972—Defeated Chicago, 4-0, in Western Conference Semifinals; defeated Milwaukee, 4-2, in Western Conference Finals; defeated New York, 4-1, in World Championship Series.
1973—Defeated Chicago, 4-3, in Western Conference Semifinals; defeated Golden State, 4-1, in Western Conference Finals; lost to New York, 4-1, in World Championship Series.
1974—Lost to Milwaukee in Western Conference First Round.

### RECORD AS BASEBALL PLAYER

| Year  Team (League) | Pos. | G | AB | R | H | 2B | 3B | HR | RBI | Avg. | BB | SO | SB | PO | A | E | Avg. |
|---|---|---|---|---|---|---|---|---|---|---|---|---|---|---|---|---|---|
| 1950—Elmira (Eastern)......... | OF | 10 | 38 | 5 | 11 | 2 | 0 | 1 | 11 | .289 | 0 | 5 | 0 | 17 | 0 | 1 | .944 |
| —Pueblo (Western) ...... | OF | 111 | 427 | 65 | 123 | 22 | 8 | 11 | 70 | .288 | 42 | 47 | 11 | 214 | 16 | 10 | .958 |
| 1951—Fort Worth (Texas)...... | OF | 157 | 570 | 84 | 163 | 18 | 5 | 8 | 53 | .286 | 57 | 44 | 23 | 254 | 11 | 2 | .993 |
| 1952—St. Paul (A.A.)............ | OF | 137 | 411 | 63 | 121 | 16 | 4 | 16 | 77 | .294 | 29 | 32 | 2 | 215 | 15 | 3 | .987 |
| 1953—Mobile (South.) ......... | OF | 90 | 228 | 21 | 48 | 8 | 1 | 5 | 17 | .211 | 30 | 26 | 0 | 136 | 6 | 2 | .986 |
| 1954— | | | | | | | | Out of organized baseball. | | | | | | | | | |
| 1955—St. Paul (A.A.)............ | OF-3B | 133 | 424 | 59 | 124 | 15 | 0 | 11 | 58 | .292 | 34 | 33 | 3 | 183 | 100 | 11 | .963 |

# SIKMA, JACK                    C/F

**PERSONAL:** Born November 14, 1955, in Kankakee, Ill. ... 7-0/250 (2,13/113,4). ... Full name: Jack Wayne Sikma.
**HIGH SCHOOL:** St. Anne (Ill.).
**COLLEGE:** Illinois Wesleyan.
**TRANSACTIONS:** Selected by Seattle SuperSonics in first round (eighth pick overall) of 1977 NBA Draft. ... Traded by SuperSonics with 1987 and 1989 second-round draft choices to Milwaukee Bucks for C Alton Lister and 1987 and 1989 first-round draft choices (July 1, 1986).
**MISCELLANEOUS:** Member of NBA championship team (1979). ... Seattle SuperSonics all-time leading rebounder with 7,729 (1977-78 through 1985-86).

### COLLEGIATE RECORD

| Season Team | G | Min. | FGM | FGA | Pct. | FTM | FTA | Pct. | Reb. | Ast. | Pts. | RPG | APG | PPG |
|---|---|---|---|---|---|---|---|---|---|---|---|---|---|---|
| 73-74—Illinois Wesleyan ............ | 21 | ... | 148 | 306 | .484 | 28 | 37 | .757 | 223 | ... | 324 | 10.6 | ... | 15.4 |
| 74-75—Illinois Wesleyan ............ | 30 | ... | 265 | 537 | .493 | 80 | 112 | .714 | 415 | ... | 610 | 13.8 | ... | 20.3 |
| 75-76—Illinois Wesleyan .......... | 25 | ... | 204 | 385 | .530 | 93 | 126 | .738 | 290 | ... | 501 | 11.6 | ... | 20.0 |
| 76-77—Illinois Wesleyan ........... | 31 | ... | 302 | 324 | .932 | 189 | 235 | .804 | 477 | ... | 837 | 15.4 | ... | 27.0 |
| Totals ..................................... | 107 | ... | 919 | 1552 | .592 | 390 | 510 | .765 | 1405 | ... | 2272 | 13.1 | ... | 21.2 |

### NBA REGULAR-SEASON RECORD

**HONORS:** NBA All-Defensive second team (1982). ... NBA All-Rookie team (1978).
**NOTES:** Tied for NBA lead with 11 disqualifications (1988).

| Season Team | G | Min. | FGM | FGA | Pct. | FTM | FTA | Pct. | Off. | Def. | Tot. | Ast. | St. | Blk. | TO | Pts. | RPG | APG | PPG |
|---|---|---|---|---|---|---|---|---|---|---|---|---|---|---|---|---|---|---|---|
| 77-78—Seattle ............ | 82 | 2238 | 342 | 752 | .455 | 192 | 247 | .777 | 196 | 482 | 678 | 134 | 68 | 40 | 186 | 876 | 8.3 | 1.6 | 10.7 |
| 78-79—Seattle ............ | 82 | 2958 | 476 | 1034 | .460 | 329 | 404 | .814 | 232 | 781 | 1013 | 261 | 82 | 67 | 253 | 1281 | 12.4 | 3.2 | 15.6 |
| 79-80—Seattle ............ | 82 | 2793 | 470 | 989 | .475 | 235 | 292 | .805 | 198 | 710 | 908 | 279 | 68 | 77 | 202 | 1175 | 11.1 | 3.4 | 14.3 |
| 80-81—Seattle ............ | 82 | 2920 | 595 | 1311 | .454 | 340 | 413 | .823 | 184 | 668 | 852 | 248 | 78 | 93 | 201 | 1530 | 10.4 | 3.0 | 18.7 |
| 81-82—Seattle ............ | 82 | 3049 | 581 | 1212 | .479 | 447 | 523 | .855 | 223 | *815 | 1038 | 277 | 102 | 107 | 213 | 1611 | 12.7 | 3.4 | 19.6 |
| 82-83—Seattle ............ | 75 | 2564 | 484 | 1043 | .464 | 400 | 478 | .837 | 213 | 645 | 858 | 233 | 87 | 65 | 190 | 1368 | 11.4 | 3.1 | 18.2 |
| 83-84—Seattle ............ | 82 | 2993 | 576 | 1155 | .499 | 411 | 480 | .856 | 225 | *686 | 911 | 327 | 95 | 92 | 236 | 1563 | 11.1 | 4.0 | 19.1 |
| 84-85—Seattle ............ | 68 | 2402 | 461 | 943 | .489 | 335 | 393 | .852 | 164 | 559 | 723 | 285 | 83 | 91 | 160 | 1259 | 10.6 | 4.2 | 18.5 |
| 85-86—Seattle ............ | 80 | 2790 | 508 | 1100 | .462 | 355 | 411 | .864 | 146 | 602 | 748 | 301 | 92 | 73 | 214 | 1371 | 9.4 | 3.8 | 17.1 |
| 86-87—Milwaukee ...... | 82 | 2536 | 390 | 842 | .463 | 265 | 313 | .847 | 208 | 614 | 822 | 203 | 88 | 90 | 160 | 1045 | 10.0 | 2.5 | 12.7 |
| 87-88—Milwaukee ...... | 82 | 2923 | 514 | 1058 | .486 | 321 | 348 | *.922 | 195 | 514 | 709 | 279 | 93 | 80 | 157 | 1352 | 8.6 | 3.4 | 16.5 |
| 88-89—Milwaukee ...... | 80 | 2587 | 360 | 835 | .431 | 266 | 294 | .905 | 141 | 482 | 623 | 289 | 85 | 61 | 145 | 1068 | 7.8 | 3.6 | 13.4 |
| 89-90—Milwaukee ...... | 71 | 2250 | 344 | 827 | .416 | 230 | 260 | .885 | 109 | 383 | 492 | 229 | 76 | 48 | 139 | 986 | 6.9 | 3.2 | 13.9 |
| 90-91—Milwaukee ...... | 77 | 1940 | 295 | 691 | .427 | 166 | 197 | .843 | 108 | 333 | 441 | 143 | 65 | 64 | 130 | 802 | 5.7 | 1.9 | 10.4 |
| Totals ................... | 1107 | 36943 | 6396 | 13792 | .464 | 4292 | 5053 | .849 | 2542 | 8274 | 10816 | 3488 | 1162 | 1048 | 2586 | 17287 | 9.8 | 3.2 | 15.6 |

Three-point field goals: 1979-80, 0-for-1. 1980-81, 0-for-5. 1981-82, 2-for-13 (.154). 1982-83, 0-for-8. 1983-84, 0-for-2. 1984-85, 2-for-10 (.200). 1985-86, 0-for-13. 1986-87, 0-for-2. 1987-88, 3-for-14 (.214). 1988-89, 82-for-216 (.380). 1989-90, 68-for-199 (.342). 1990-91, 46-for-135 (.341). Totals, 203-for-618 (.328).

Personal fouls/disqualifications: 1977-78, 300/6. 1978-79, 295/4. 1979-80, 232/5. 1980-81, 282/5. 1981-82, 268/5. 1982-83, 263/4. 1983-84, 301/6. 1984-85, 239/1. 1985-86, 293/4. 1986-87, 328/14. 1987-88, 316/11. 1988-89, 300/6. 1989-90, 244/5. 1990-91, 218/4. Totals, 3879/80.

### NBA PLAYOFF RECORD

| Season Team | G | Min. | FGM | FGA | Pct. | FTM | FTA | Pct. | Off. | Def. | Tot. | Ast. | St. | Blk. | TO | Pts. | RPG | APG | PPG |
|---|---|---|---|---|---|---|---|---|---|---|---|---|---|---|---|---|---|---|---|
| 77-78—Seattle ............ | 22 | 701 | 115 | 247 | .466 | 71 | 91 | .780 | 50 | 128 | 178 | 27 | 18 | 11 | 35 | 301 | 8.1 | 1.2 | 13.7 |
| 78-79—Seattle ............ | 17 | 655 | 102 | 224 | .455 | 48 | 61 | .787 | 39 | 160 | 199 | 43 | 16 | 24 | 40 | 252 | 11.7 | 2.5 | 14.8 |
| 79-80—Seattle ............ | 15 | 534 | 65 | 163 | .399 | 46 | 54 | .852 | 30 | 96 | 126 | 55 | 17 | 5 | 35 | 176 | 8.4 | 3.7 | 11.7 |

| Season Team | G | Min. | FGM | FGA | Pct. | FTM | FTA | Pct. | REBOUNDS | | | Ast. | St. | Blk. | TO | Pts. | AVERAGES | | |
|---|---|---|---|---|---|---|---|---|---|---|---|---|---|---|---|---|---|---|---|
| | | | | | | | | | Off. | Def. | Tot. | | | | | | RPG | APG | PPG |
| 81-82—Seattle | 8 | 315 | 57 | 128 | .445 | 50 | 58 | .862 | 21 | 76 | 97 | 24 | 9 | 8 | 16 | 164 | 12.1 | 3.0 | 20.5 |
| 82-83—Seattle | 2 | 75 | 11 | 31 | .355 | 8 | 12 | .667 | 6 | 20 | 26 | 11 | 2 | 2 | 5 | 30 | 13.0 | 5.5 | 15.0 |
| 83-84—Seattle | 5 | 193 | 49 | 98 | .500 | 12 | 14 | .857 | 11 | 40 | 51 | 5 | 3 | 7 | 9 | 110 | 10.2 | 1.0 | 22.0 |
| 86-87—Milwaukee | 12 | 426 | 73 | 150 | .487 | 48 | 49 | .980 | 33 | 97 | 130 | 23 | 15 | 10 | 18 | 194 | 10.8 | 1.9 | 16.2 |
| 87-88—Milwaukee | 5 | 190 | 35 | 76 | .461 | 25 | 30 | .833 | 24 | 38 | 62 | 13 | 2 | 4 | 15 | 95 | 12.4 | 2.6 | 19.0 |
| 88-89—Milwaukee | 9 | 301 | 37 | 94 | .394 | 23 | 28 | .821 | 9 | 41 | 50 | 30 | 8 | 4 | 21 | 105 | 5.6 | 3.3 | 11.7 |
| 89-90—Milwaukee | 4 | 117 | 6 | 23 | .261 | 6 | 8 | .750 | 0 | 14 | 14 | 7 | 2 | 4 | 12 | 20 | 3.5 | 1.8 | 5.0 |
| 90-91—Milwaukee | 3 | 51 | 6 | 15 | .400 | 1 | 2 | .500 | 3 | 9 | 12 | 6 | 5 | 1 | 31 | 14 | 4.0 | 2.0 | 4.7 |
| Totals | 102 | 3558 | 556 | 1249 | .445 | 338 | 407 | .830 | 226 | 719 | 945 | 244 | 97 | 80 | 237 | 1461 | 9.3 | 2.4 | 14.3 |

Three-point field goals: 1979-80, 0-for-2. 1982-83, 0-for-1. 1983-84, 0-for-1. 1986-87, 0-for-1. 1987-88, 0-for-3. 1988-89, 8-for-28 (.286). 1989-90, 2-for-7 (.286). 1990-91, 1-for-2 (.500). Totals, 11-for-45 (.244).

Personal fouls/disqualifications: 1977-78, 101/7. 1978-79, 70/2. 1979-80, 55/1. 1981-82, 34/1. 1982-83, 7/0. 1983-84, 22/1. 1986-87, 56/3. 1987-88, 23/0. 1988-89, 41/2. 1989-90, 19/0. 1990-91, 4/0. Totals, 432/17.

## NBA ALL-STAR GAME RECORD

| Season Team | Min. | FGM | FGA | Pct. | FTM | FTA | Pct. | REBOUNDS | | | Ast. | PF | Dq. | St. | Blk. | TO | Pts. |
|---|---|---|---|---|---|---|---|---|---|---|---|---|---|---|---|---|---|
| | | | | | | | | Off. | Def. | Tot. | | | | | | | |
| 1979—Seattle | 18 | 4 | 5 | .800 | 0 | 0 | ... | 1 | 3 | 4 | 0 | 1 | 0 | 0 | 0 | 0 | 8 |
| 1980—Seattle | 28 | 4 | 10 | .400 | 0 | 0 | ... | 2 | 6 | 8 | 4 | 5 | 0 | 2 | 3 | 3 | 8 |
| 1981—Seattle | 21 | 2 | 5 | .400 | 2 | 2 | 1.000 | 1 | 3 | 4 | 4 | 5 | 0 | 1 | 1 | 1 | 6 |
| 1982—Seattle | 21 | 5 | 11 | .455 | 0 | 0 | ... | 2 | 7 | 9 | 1 | 2 | 0 | 2 | 1 | 1 | 10 |
| 1983—Seattle | 17 | 4 | 6 | .667 | 0 | 0 | ... | 1 | 2 | 3 | 1 | 2 | 0 | 1 | 1 | 1 | 5 |
| 1984—Seattle | 30 | 5 | 12 | .417 | 5 | 6 | .833 | 5 | 7 | 12 | 1 | 4 | 0 | 3 | 0 | 0 | 15 |
| 1985—Seattle | 12 | 0 | 2 | .000 | 0 | 0 | ... | 0 | 2 | 2 | 0 | 1 | 0 | 0 | 1 | 1 | 0 |
| Totals | 147 | 24 | 51 | .471 | 7 | 8 | .875 | 12 | 30 | 42 | 11 | 20 | 0 | 9 | 7 | 7 | 52 |

Three-point field goals: 1980, 0-for-1. 1981, 0-for-1. Totals, 0-for-2.

# SILAS, PAUL                          F/C

**PERSONAL:** Born July 12, 1943, in Prescott, Ark. ... 6-7/230. (2,00/104,3). ... Full name: Paul Theron Silas.

**HIGH SCHOOL:** McClymonds (Oakland, Calif.).

**COLLEGE:** Creighton.

**TRANSACTIONS:** Selected by St. Louis Hawks in second round (12th pick overall) of 1964 NBA Draft. ... Played in Eastern Basketball League with Wilkes-Barre Barons (1965-66). ... Hawks franchise moved from St. Louis to Atlanta for 1968-69 season. ... Traded by Hawks to Phoenix Suns for F Gary Gregor (May 8, 1969). ... Traded by Suns to Boston Celtics (September 19, 1972) to complete deal in which Suns acquired draft rights to G Charlie Scott (March 14, 1972). ... Traded by Celtics to Denver Nuggets in three-way deal, in which F Curtis Rowe was traded by Detroit Pistons to Celtics, and G Ralph Simpson was traded by Nuggets to Pistons (October 20, 1976). ... Traded by Nuggets with F Willie Wise and C Marvin Webster to Seattle SuperSonics for C Tom Burleson, G/F Bob Wilkerson and 1977 second-round draft choice (May 24, 1977). ... Signed as veteran free agent by San Diego Clippers (May 21, 1980); SuperSonics received 1985 second-round draft choice as compensation.

**MISCELLANEOUS:** Member of NBA championship team (1974, 1976, 1979).

## COLLEGIATE RECORD

**NOTES:** Led NCAA Division I with 20.6 rebounds per game (1963). ... Holds NCAA record for most rebounds in three-year career—1,751.

| Season Team | G | Min. | FGM | FGA | Pct. | FTM | FTA | Pct. | Reb. | Ast. | Pts. | AVERAGES | | |
|---|---|---|---|---|---|---|---|---|---|---|---|---|---|---|
| | | | | | | | | | | | | RPG | APG | PPG |
| 60-61—Creighton‡ | 21 | ... | 225 | ... | ... | 96 | 119 | .807 | 568 | ... | 546 | 27.0 | ... | 26.0 |
| 61-62—Creighton | 25 | ... | 213 | 524 | .406 | 125 | 215 | .581 | 563 | ... | 551 | 22.5 | ... | 22.0 |
| 62-63—Creighton | 27 | ... | 220 | 531 | .414 | 133 | 228 | .583 | 557 | ... | 573 | 20.6 | ... | 21.2 |
| 63-64—Creighton | 29 | ... | 210 | 529 | .397 | 117 | 194 | .603 | 631 | ... | 537 | 21.8 | ... | 18.5 |
| Varsity totals | 81 | ... | 643 | 1584 | .406 | 375 | 637 | .589 | 1751 | ... | 1661 | 21.6 | ... | 20.5 |

## NBA REGULAR-SEASON RECORD

**HONORS:** NBA All-Defensive first team (1975, 1976). ... NBA All-Defensive second team (1971, 1972, 1973).

| Season Team | G | Min. | FGM | FGA | Pct. | FTM | FTA | Pct. | Reb. | Ast. | PF | Dq. | Pts. | AVERAGES | | |
|---|---|---|---|---|---|---|---|---|---|---|---|---|---|---|---|---|
| | | | | | | | | | | | | | | RPG | APG | PPG |
| 64-65—St. Louis | 79 | 1243 | 140 | 375 | .373 | 83 | 164 | .506 | 576 | 48 | 161 | 1 | 363 | 7.3 | 0.6 | 4.6 |
| 65-66—St. Louis | 46 | 586 | 70 | 173 | .405 | 35 | 61 | .574 | 236 | 22 | 72 | 0 | 175 | 5.1 | 0.5 | 3.8 |
| 66-67—St. Louis | 77 | 1570 | 207 | 482 | .429 | 113 | 213 | .531 | 669 | 74 | 208 | 4 | 527 | 8.7 | 1.0 | 6.8 |
| 67-68—St. Louis | 82 | 2652 | 399 | 871 | .458 | 299 | 424 | .705 | 958 | 162 | 243 | 4 | 1097 | 11.7 | 2.0 | 13.4 |
| 68-69—Atlanta | 79 | 1853 | 241 | 575 | .419 | 204 | 333 | .613 | 745 | 140 | 166 | 0 | 686 | 9.4 | 1.8 | 8.7 |
| 69-70—Phoenix | 78 | 2836 | 373 | 804 | .464 | 250 | 412 | .607 | 916 | 214 | 266 | 5 | 996 | 11.7 | 2.7 | 12.8 |
| 70-71—Phoenix | 81 | 2944 | 338 | 789 | .428 | 285 | 416 | .685 | 1015 | 247 | 227 | 3 | 961 | 12.5 | 3.0 | 11.9 |
| 71-72—Phoenix | 80 | 3082 | 485 | 1031 | .470 | 433 | 560 | .773 | 955 | 343 | 201 | 2 | 1403 | 11.9 | 4.3 | 17.5 |
| 72-73—Boston | 80 | 2618 | 400 | 851 | .470 | 266 | 380 | .700 | 1039 | 251 | 197 | 1 | 1066 | 13.0 | 3.1 | 13.3 |

| Season Team | G | Min. | FGM | FGA | Pct. | FTM | FTA | Pct. | REBOUNDS | | | Ast. | St. | Blk. | TO | Pts. | AVERAGES | | |
|---|---|---|---|---|---|---|---|---|---|---|---|---|---|---|---|---|---|---|---|---|
| | | | | | | | | | Off. | Def. | Tot. | | | | | | RPG | APG | PPG |
| 73-74—Boston | 82 | 2599 | 340 | 772 | .440 | 264 | 337 | .783 | 334 | 581 | 915 | 186 | 63 | 20 | ... | 944 | 11.2 | 2.3 | 11.5 |
| 74-75—Boston | 82 | 2661 | 312 | 749 | .417 | 244 | 344 | .709 | 348 | 677 | 1025 | 224 | 60 | 22 | ... | 868 | 12.5 | 2.7 | 10.6 |
| 75-76—Boston | 81 | 2662 | 315 | 740 | .426 | 236 | 333 | .709 | *365 | 660 | 1025 | 203 | 56 | 33 | ... | 866 | 12.7 | 2.5 | 10.7 |
| 76-77—Denver | 81 | 1959 | 206 | 572 | .360 | 170 | 255 | .667 | 236 | 370 | 606 | 132 | 58 | 23 | ... | 582 | 7.5 | 1.6 | 7.2 |
| 77-78—Seattle | 82 | 2172 | 184 | 464 | .397 | 109 | 186 | .586 | 289 | 377 | 666 | 145 | 65 | 16 | 152 | 477 | 8.1 | 1.8 | 5.8 |
| 78-79—Seattle | 82 | 1957 | 170 | 402 | .423 | 116 | 194 | .598 | 259 | 316 | 575 | 115 | 31 | 19 | 98 | 456 | 7.0 | 1.4 | 5.6 |
| 79-80—Seattle | 82 | 1595 | 113 | 299 | .378 | 89 | 136 | .654 | 204 | 232 | 436 | 66 | 25 | 5 | 83 | 315 | 5.3 | 0.8 | 3.8 |
| Totals | 1254 | 34989 | 4293 | 9949 | .432 | 3196 | 4748 | .673 | ... | ... | 12357 | 2572 | 358 | 138 | 333 | 11782 | 9.9 | 2.1 | 9.4 |

Personal fouls/disqualifications: 1973-74, 246/3. 1974-75, 229/3. 1975-76, 227/4. 1976-77, 183/0. 1977-78, 182/0. 1978-79, 177/3. 1979-80, 120/0. Totals, 3105/32.

## NBA PLAYOFF RECORD

| Season Team | G | Min. | FGM | FGA | Pct. | FTM | FTA | Pct. | Reb. | Ast. | PF | Dq. | Pts. | RPG | APG | PPG |
|---|---|---|---|---|---|---|---|---|---|---|---|---|---|---|---|---|
| 64-65—St. Louis | 4 | 42 | 4 | 10 | .400 | 3 | 4 | .750 | 18 | 1 | 6 | 0 | 11 | 4.5 | 0.3 | 2.8 |
| 65-66—St. Louis | 7 | 80 | 5 | 18 | .278 | 8 | 11 | .727 | 34 | 2 | 11 | 0 | 18 | 4.9 | 0.3 | 2.6 |
| 66-67—St. Louis | 8 | 122 | 9 | 36 | .250 | 11 | 18 | .611 | 52 | 6 | 17 | 0 | 29 | 6.5 | 0.8 | 3.6 |
| 67-68—St. Louis | 6 | 178 | 22 | 51 | .431 | 27 | 38 | .711 | 57 | 21 | 17 | 0 | 71 | 9.5 | 3.5 | 11.8 |
| 68-69—Atlanta | 11 | 258 | 21 | 58 | .362 | 19 | 37 | .514 | 92 | 21 | 32 | 0 | 61 | 8.4 | 1.9 | 5.5 |
| 69-70—Phoenix | 7 | 286 | 46 | 109 | .422 | 21 | 32 | .656 | 111 | 30 | 29 | 1 | 113 | 15.9 | 4.3 | 16.1 |
| 72-73—Boston | 13 | 512 | 47 | 120 | .392 | 31 | 50 | .620 | 196 | 39 | 39 | 0 | 125 | 15.1 | 3.0 | 9.6 |

| Season Team | G | Min. | FGM | FGA | Pct. | FTM | FTA | Pct. | Off. | Def. | Tot. | Ast. | St. | Blk. | TO | Pts. | RPG | APG | PPG |
|---|---|---|---|---|---|---|---|---|---|---|---|---|---|---|---|---|---|---|---|
| 73-74—Boston | 18 | 574 | 50 | 126 | .397 | 44 | 53 | .830 | 53 | 138 | 191 | 47 | 13 | 9 | ... | 144 | 10.6 | 2.6 | 8.0 |
| 74-75—Boston | 11 | 405 | 42 | 92 | .457 | 16 | 25 | .640 | 46 | 84 | 130 | 40 | 12 | 2 | ... | 100 | 11.8 | 3.6 | 9.1 |
| 75-76—Boston | 18 | 741 | 69 | 154 | .448 | 56 | 69 | .812 | 78 | 168 | 246 | 42 | 24 | 6 | ... | 194 | 13.7 | 2.3 | 10.8 |
| 76-77—Denver | 6 | 141 | 14 | 33 | .424 | 13 | 24 | .542 | 16 | 24 | 40 | 16 | 2 | 4 | ... | 41 | 6.7 | 2.7 | 6.8 |
| 77-78—Seattle | 22 | 605 | 33 | 94 | .351 | 41 | 60 | .683 | 73 | 114 | 187 | 36 | 12 | 6 | 28 | 107 | 8.5 | 1.6 | 4.9 |
| 78-79—Seattle | 17 | 418 | 21 | 54 | .389 | 31 | 46 | .674 | 40 | 58 | 98 | 19 | 9 | 5 | 34 | 73 | 5.8 | 1.1 | 4.3 |
| 79-80—Seattle | 15 | 257 | 13 | 43 | .302 | 11 | 13 | .846 | 33 | 42 | 75 | 15 | 9 | 2 | 9 | 37 | 5.0 | 1.0 | 2.5 |
| Totals | 163 | 4619 | 396 | 998 | .397 | 332 | 480 | .692 | ... | ... | 1527 | 335 | 81 | 34 | 71 | 1124 | 9.4 | 2.1 | 6.9 |

Personal fouls/disqualifications: 1973-74, 51/2. 1974-75, 45/1. 1975-76, 67/1. 1976-77, 23/1. 1977-78, 59/0. 1978-79, 44/1. 1979-80, 29/0. Totals, 469/7.

## NBA ALL-STAR GAME RECORD

| Season Team | Min. | FGM | FGA | Pct. | FTM | FTA | Pct. | Reb | Ast. | PF | Dq. | Pts. |
|---|---|---|---|---|---|---|---|---|---|---|---|---|
| 1972—Phoenix | 15 | 0 | 6 | .000 | 2 | 3 | .667 | 9 | 1 | 1 | 0 | 2 |

| Season Team | Min. | FGM | FGA | Pct. | FTM | FTA | Pct. | Off. | Def. | Tot. | Ast. | PF | Dq. | St. | Blk. | TO | Pts. |
|---|---|---|---|---|---|---|---|---|---|---|---|---|---|---|---|---|---|
| 1975—Boston | 15 | 2 | 4 | .500 | 2 | 2 | 1.000 | 0 | 2 | 2 | 2 | 2 | 0 | 4 | 0 | ... | 6 |
| Totals | 30 | 2 | 10 | .200 | 4 | 5 | .800 | ... | ... | 11 | 3 | 3 | 0 | 4 | 0 | ... | 8 |

## EBL REGULAR-SEASON RECORD

| Season Team | G | Min. | FGM | FGA | Pct. | FTM | FTA | Pct. | Reb. | Ast. | PF | Dq. | Pts. | RPG | APG | PPG |
|---|---|---|---|---|---|---|---|---|---|---|---|---|---|---|---|---|
| 65-66—Wil.-Barre | 5 | ... | 25 | ... | ... | 13 | 21 | .619 | 85 | 9 | ... | ... | 63 | 17.0 | 1.8 | 12.6 |

## NBA COACHING RECORD

**BACKGROUND:** Assistant coach, New Jersey Nets (1988-89 and 1992-93 through 1994-95). ... Assistant coach, New York Knicks (1989-90 through 1991-92). ... Assistant coach, Phoenix Suns (1995-96 and 1996-97). ... Assistant coach, Charlotte Hornets (1997-98 through March 7, 1999).

| Season Team | W | L | Pct. | Finish | W | L | Pct. |
|---|---|---|---|---|---|---|---|
| 80-81—San Diego | 36 | 46 | .439 | 5th/Pacific Division | — | — | — |
| 81-82—San Diego | 17 | 65 | .207 | 6th/Pacific Division | — | — | — |
| 82-83—San Diego | 25 | 57 | .305 | 6th/Pacific Division | — | — | — |
| 98-99—Charlotte | 22 | 13 | .629 | 5th/Central Division | — | — | — |
| 99-00—Charlotte | 49 | 33 | .598 | 2nd/Central Division | 1 | 3 | .250 |
| 00-01—Charlotte | 46 | 36 | .561 | 3rd/Central Division | 6 | 4 | .600 |
| 01-02—Charlotte | 44 | 38 | .537 | 2nd/Central Division | 4 | 5 | .444 |
| 02-03—New Orleans | 47 | 35 | .573 | 3rd/Central Division | 2 | 4 | .333 |
| 03-04—Cleveland | 35 | 47 | .427 | 5th/Central Division | — | — | — |
| Totals (9 years) | 321 | 370 | .465 | Totals (4 years) | 13 | 16 | .448 |

**NOTES:**

1999—Replaced Dave Cowens as head coach (March 7), with record of 4-11 and club in seventh place.

2000—Lost to Philadelphia in Eastern Conference first round.

2001—Defeated Miami, 3-0, in Eastern Conference first round; lost to Milwaukee, 4-3, in Eastern Conference finals.

2002—Defeated Orlando, 3-1, in Eastern Conference first round, lost to New Jersey, 4-1, in Eastern Conference semifinals.

2003—Lost to Philadelphia, 4-2, in Eastern Conference first round.

# STOCKTON, JOHN G

**PERSONAL:** Born March 26, 1962, in Spokane, Wash. ... 6-1/175. (1,85/79,4). ... Full Name: John Houston Stockton.

**HIGH SCHOOL:** Gonzaga Prep School (Spokane, Wash.).

**COLLEGE:** Gonzaga.

**TRANSACTIONS/CAREER NOTES:** Selected by Utah Jazz in first round (16th pick overall) of 1984 NBA Draft. ... Announced retirement (May 2, 2003).

**CAREER HONORS:** NBA 50th Anniversary All-Time Team (1996).

**MISCELLANEOUS:** Member of gold-medal-winning U.S. Olympic teams (1992, 1996). ... Utah Jazz franchise all-time assists leader with 15,806 and all-time steals leader with 3,265 (1984-85 through 2002-03).

## COLLEGIATE RECORD

| Season Team | G | Min. | FGM | FGA | Pct. | FTM | FTA | Pct. | Reb. | Ast. | Pts. | RPG | APG | PPG |
|---|---|---|---|---|---|---|---|---|---|---|---|---|---|---|
| 80-81—Gonzaga | 25 | 235 | 26 | 45 | .578 | 26 | 35 | .743 | 11 | 34 | 78 | 0.4 | 1.4 | 3.1 |
| 81-82—Gonzaga | 27 | 1054 | 117 | 203 | .576 | 69 | 102 | .676 | 67 | 135 | 303 | 2.5 | 5.0 | 11.2 |
| 82-83—Gonzaga | 27 | 1036 | 142 | 274 | .518 | 91 | 115 | .791 | 87 | 184 | 375 | 3.2 | 6.8 | 13.9 |
| 83-84—Gonzaga | 28 | 1053 | 229 | 397 | .577 | 126 | 182 | .692 | 66 | 201 | 584 | 2.4 | 7.2 | 20.9 |
| Totals | 107 | 3378 | 514 | 919 | .559 | 312 | 434 | .719 | 231 | 554 | 1340 | 2.2 | 5.2 | 12.5 |

## NBA REGULAR-SEASON RECORD

**RECORDS:** Holds career records for most seasons leading league in assists—9; most consecutive seasons leading league in assists—9 (1987-88 through 1995-96); most assists—15,806; and most steals—3,265. ... Holds single-season records for most assists—1,164

(1991); and highest assists-per-game average (minimum 70 games)—14.5 (1990).

**HONORS:** All-NBA First Team (1994, 1995). ... All-NBA Second Team (1988, 1989, 1990, 1992, 1993, 1996). ... All-NBA Third Team (1991, 1997, 1999). ... NBA All-Defensive second team (1989, 1991, 1992, 1995, 1997).

**NOTES:** Led NBA with 3.21 steals per game (1989) and 2.98 steals per game (1992).

| Season Team | G | Min. | FGM | FGA | Pct. | FTM | FTA | Pct. | REBOUNDS Off. | Def. | Tot. | Ast. | St. | Blk. | TO | Pts. | AVERAGES RPG | APG | PPG |
|---|---|---|---|---|---|---|---|---|---|---|---|---|---|---|---|---|---|---|---|
| 84-85—Utah | 82 | 1490 | 157 | 333 | .471 | 142 | 193 | .736 | 26 | 79 | 105 | 415 | 109 | 11 | 150 | 458 | 1.3 | 5.1 | 5.6 |
| 85-86—Utah | 82 | 1935 | 228 | 466 | .489 | 172 | 205 | .839 | 33 | 146 | 179 | 610 | 157 | 10 | 168 | 630 | 2.2 | 7.4 | 7.7 |
| 86-87—Utah | 82 | 1858 | 231 | 463 | .499 | 179 | 229 | .782 | 32 | 119 | 151 | 670 | 177 | 14 | 164 | 648 | 1.8 | 8.2 | 7.9 |
| 87-88—Utah | 82 | 2842 | 454 | 791 | .574 | 272 | 324 | .840 | 54 | 183 | 237 | *1128 | 242 | 16 | 262 | 1204 | 2.9 | *13.8 | 14.7 |
| 88-89—Utah | 82 | 3171 | 497 | 923 | .538 | 390 | 452 | .863 | 83 | 165 | 248 | *1118 | *263 | 14 | 308 | 1400 | 3.0 | *13.6 | 17.1 |
| 89-90—Utah | 78 | 2915 | 472 | 918 | .514 | 354 | 432 | .819 | 57 | 149 | 206 | *1134 | 207 | 18 | 272 | 1345 | 2.6 | *14.5 | 17.2 |
| 90-91—Utah | 82 | 3103 | 496 | 978 | .507 | 363 | 434 | .836 | 46 | 191 | 237 | *1164 | 234 | 16 | 298 | 1413 | 2.9 | *14.2 | 17.2 |
| 91-92—Utah | 82 | 3002 | 453 | 939 | .482 | 308 | 366 | .842 | 68 | 202 | 270 | *1126 | *244 | 22 | *286 | 1297 | 3.3 | *13.7 | 15.8 |
| 92-93—Utah | 82 | 2863 | 437 | 899 | .486 | 293 | 367 | .798 | 64 | 173 | 237 | *987 | 199 | 21 | 266 | 1239 | 2.9 | *12.0 | 15.1 |
| 93-94—Utah | 82 | 2969 | 458 | 868 | .528 | 272 | 338 | .805 | 72 | 186 | 258 | *1031 | 199 | 22 | 266 | 1236 | 3.1 | *12.6 | 15.1 |
| 94-95—Utah | 82 | 2867 | 429 | 791 | .542 | 246 | 306 | .804 | 57 | 194 | 251 | *1011 | 194 | 22 | 267 | 1206 | 3.1 | *12.3 | 14.7 |
| 95-96—Utah | 82 | 2915 | 440 | 818 | .538 | 234 | 282 | .830 | 54 | 172 | 226 | *916 | 140 | 15 | 246 | 1209 | 2.8 | *11.2 | 14.7 |
| 96-97—Utah | 82 | 2896 | 416 | 759 | .548 | 275 | 325 | .846 | 45 | 183 | 228 | 860 | 166 | 15 | 248 | 1183 | 2.8 | 10.5 | 14.4 |
| 97-98—Utah | 64 | 1858 | 270 | 511 | .528 | 191 | 231 | .827 | 35 | 131 | 166 | 543 | 89 | 10 | 161 | 770 | 2.6 | 8.5 | 12.0 |
| 98-99—Utah | 50 | 1410 | 200 | 410 | .488 | 137 | 169 | .811 | 31 | 115 | 146 | 374 | 81 | 13 | 110 | 553 | 2.9 | 7.5 | 11.1 |
| 99-00—Utah | 82 | 2432 | 363 | 725 | .501 | 221 | 257 | .860 | 45 | 170 | 215 | 703 | 143 | 15 | 179 | 990 | 2.6 | 8.6 | 12.1 |
| 00-01—Utah | 82 | 2397 | 328 | 651 | .504 | 227 | 278 | .817 | 54 | 173 | 227 | 713 | 132 | 21 | 203 | 944 | 2.8 | 8.7 | 11.5 |
| 01-02—Utah | 82 | 2566 | 401 | 775 | .517 | 275 | 321 | .857 | 59 | 204 | 263 | 674 | 152 | 24 | 208 | 1102 | 3.2 | 8.2 | 13.4 |
| 02-03—Utah | 82 | 2275 | 309 | 640 | .483 | 237 | 287 | .826 | 51 | 150 | 201 | 629 | 137 | 16 | 182 | 884 | 2.5 | 7.7 | 10.8 |
| **Totals** | 1504 | 47764 | 7039 | 13658 | .515 | 4788 | 5796 | .826 | 966 | 3085 | 4051 | 15806 | 3265 | 315 | 4244 | 19711 | 2.7 | 10.5 | 13.1 |

Three-point field goals: 1984-85, 2-for-11 (.182). 1985-86, 2-for-15 (.133). 1986-87, 7-for-38 (.184). 1987-88, 24-for-67 (.358). 1988-89, 16-for-66 (.242). 1989-90, 47-for-113 (.416). 1990-91, 58-for-168 (.345). 1991-92, 83-for-204 (.407). 1992-93, 72-for-187 (.385). 1993-94, 48-for-149 (.322). 1994-95, 102-for-227 (.449). 1995-96, 95-for-225 (.422). 1996-97, 76-for-180 (.422). 1997-98, 39-for-91 (.429). 1998-99, 16-for-50 (.320). 1999-00, 43-for-121 (.355). 2000-01, 61-for-132 (.462). 2001-02, 25-for-78 (.321). 2002-03, 29-for-80 (.363). Totals, 845-for-2202 (.384).

Personal fouls/disqualifications: 1984-85, 203/3. 1985-86, 227/2. 1986-87, 224/1. 1987-88, 247/5. 1988-89, 241/3. 1989-90, 233/3. 1990-91, 233/1. 1991-92, 234/3. 1992-93, 224/2. 1993-94, 236/3. 1994-95, 215/3. 1995-96, 207/1. 1996-97, 194/2. 1997-98, 138/0. 1998-99, 107/0. 1999-00, 192/0. 2000-01, 194/1. 2001-02, 209/1. 2002-03, 184/1. Totals, 3942/35.

## NBA PLAYOFF RECORD

**NOTES:** Shares NBA Finals single-game record for most assists in one quarter—8 (June 10, 1998, at Chicago). ... Holds single-game playoff record for most assists in one quarter—11 (May 5, 1994, vs. San Antonio). ... Shares single-game playoff record for most assists—24 (May 17, 1988, vs. Los Angeles Lakers).

| Season Team | G | Min. | FGM | FGA | Pct. | FTM | FTA | Pct. | REBOUNDS Off. | Def. | Tot. | Ast. | St. | Blk. | TO | Pts. | AVERAGES RPG | APG | PPG |
|---|---|---|---|---|---|---|---|---|---|---|---|---|---|---|---|---|---|---|---|
| 84-85—Utah | 10 | 186 | 21 | 45 | .467 | 26 | 35 | .743 | 7 | 21 | 28 | 43 | 11 | 2 | 16 | 68 | 2.8 | 4.3 | 6.8 |
| 85-86—Utah | 4 | 73 | 9 | 17 | .529 | 8 | 9 | .889 | 3 | 3 | 6 | 14 | 5 | 0 | 4 | 27 | 1.5 | 3.5 | 6.8 |
| 86-87—Utah | 5 | 157 | 18 | 29 | .621 | 10 | 13 | .769 | 2 | 9 | 11 | 40 | 15 | 1 | 11 | 50 | 2.2 | 8.0 | 10.0 |
| 87-88—Utah | 11 | 478 | 68 | 134 | .507 | 75 | 91 | .824 | 14 | 31 | 45 | 163 | 37 | 3 | 48 | 215 | 4.1 | 14.8 | 19.5 |
| 88-89—Utah | 3 | 139 | 30 | 59 | .508 | 19 | 21 | .905 | 2 | 8 | 10 | 41 | 11 | 5 | 11 | 82 | 3.3 | 13.7 | 27.3 |
| 89-90—Utah | 5 | 194 | 29 | 69 | .420 | 16 | 20 | .800 | 4 | 12 | 16 | 75 | 6 | 0 | 14 | 75 | 3.2 | 15.0 | 15.0 |
| 90-91—Utah | 9 | 373 | 58 | 108 | .537 | 37 | 44 | .841 | 10 | 32 | 42 | 124 | 20 | 2 | 32 | 164 | 4.7 | 13.8 | 18.2 |
| 91-92—Utah | 16 | 623 | 77 | 182 | .423 | 65 | 78 | .833 | 10 | 37 | 47 | 217 | 34 | 5 | 58 | 237 | 2.9 | 13.6 | 14.8 |
| 92-93—Utah | 5 | 193 | 23 | 51 | .451 | 15 | 18 | .833 | 5 | 7 | 12 | 55 | 12 | 0 | 15 | 66 | 2.4 | 11.0 | 13.2 |
| 93-94—Utah | 16 | 597 | 88 | 193 | .456 | 51 | 63 | .810 | 14 | 38 | 52 | 157 | 27 | 8 | 40 | 231 | 3.3 | 9.8 | 14.4 |
| 94-95—Utah | 5 | 193 | 34 | 74 | .459 | 13 | 17 | .765 | 6 | 11 | 17 | 51 | 7 | 1 | 14 | 89 | 3.4 | 10.2 | 17.8 |
| 95-96—Utah | 18 | 679 | 70 | 157 | .446 | 48 | 59 | .814 | 14 | 44 | 58 | 195 | 29 | 7 | 58 | 199 | 3.2 | 10.8 | 11.1 |
| 96-97—Utah | 20 | 739 | 113 | 217 | .521 | 77 | 90 | .856 | 18 | 60 | 78 | 191 | 33 | 5 | 62 | 322 | 3.9 | 9.6 | 16.1 |
| 97-98—Utah | 20 | 596 | 81 | 164 | .494 | 51 | 71 | .718 | 16 | 44 | 60 | 155 | 31 | 3 | 48 | 222 | 3.0 | 7.8 | 11.1 |
| 98-99—Utah | 11 | 352 | 42 | 105 | .400 | 34 | 46 | .739 | 11 | 25 | 36 | 92 | 18 | 1 | 31 | 122 | 3.3 | 8.4 | 11.1 |
| 99-00—Utah | 10 | 350 | 41 | 89 | .461 | 23 | 30 | .767 | 7 | 23 | 30 | 103 | 13 | 2 | 26 | 112 | 3.0 | 10.3 | 11.2 |
| 00-01—Utah | 5 | 186 | 17 | 37 | .459 | 15 | 21 | .714 | 11 | 17 | 28 | 57 | 10 | 3 | 7 | 49 | 5.6 | 11.4 | 9.8 |
| 01-02—Utah | 4 | 141 | 18 | 40 | .450 | 12 | 13 | .923 | 3 | 13 | 16 | 44 | 11 | 1 | 8 | 50 | 4.0 | 10.0 | 12.5 |
| 02-03—Utah | 5 | 149 | 18 | 39 | .462 | 20 | 20 | 1.000 | 5 | 11 | 16 | 26 | 8 | 1 | 14 | 56 | 3.2 | 5.2 | 11.2 |
| **Totals** | 182 | 6398 | 855 | 1809 | .473 | 615 | 759 | .810 | 162 | 446 | 608 | 1839 | 338 | 50 | 517 | 2436 | 3.3 | 10.1 | 13.4 |

Three-point field goals: 1984-85, 0-for-2. 1985-86, 1-for-1. 1986-87, 4-for-5 (.800). 1987-88, 4-for-14 (.286). 1988-89, 3-for-4 (.750). 1989-90, 1-for-13 (.077). 1990-91, 11-for-27 (.407). 1991-92, 18-for-58 (.310). 1992-93, 5-for-13 (.385). 1993-94, 4-for-24 (.167). 1994-95, 8-for-20 (.400). 1995-96, 11-for-38 (.289). 1996-97, 19-for-50 (.380). 1997-98, 9-for-26 (.346). 1998-99, 4-for-12 (.333). 1999-00, 7-for-18 (.389). 2000-01, 0-for-8. 2001-02, 2-for-7 (.286). 2002-03, 0-for-1. Totals, 111-for-341 (.326).

Personal fouls/disqualifications: 1984-85, 30/0. 1985-86, 10/0. 1986-87, 18/0. 1987-88, 36/0. 1988-89, 15/0. 1989-90, 20/0. 1990-91, 33/0. 1991-92, 38/0. 1992-93, 16/0. 1993-94, 44/0. 1994-95, 13/0. 1995-96, 50/0. 1996-97, 52/0. 1997-98, 54/0. 1998-99, 32/0. 1999-00, 30/0. 2000-01, 19/0. 2001-02, 16/1. 2002-03, 13/0. Totals, 539/1.

## NBA ALL-STAR GAME RECORD

**NOTES:** NBA All-Star Game Co-Most Valuable Player (1993). ... Holds single-game record for most assists in one quarter—9 (1989).

| Season Team | Min. | FGM | FGA | Pct. | FTM | FTA | Pct. | REBOUNDS Off. | Def. | Tot. | Ast. | PF | Dq. | St. | Blk. | TO | Pts. |
|---|---|---|---|---|---|---|---|---|---|---|---|---|---|---|---|---|---|
| 1989—Utah | 32 | 5 | 6 | .833 | 0 | 0 | ... | 0 | 2 | 2 | 17 | 4 | 0 | 5 | 0 | 12 | 11 |
| 1990—Utah | 15 | 1 | 4 | .250 | 0 | 0 | ... | 0 | 0 | 0 | 6 | 1 | 0 | 1 | 1 | 3 | 2 |
| 1991—Utah | 12 | 1 | 6 | .167 | 2 | 4 | .500 | 0 | 1 | 1 | 2 | 2 | 0 | 0 | 0 | 0 | 4 |
| 1992—Utah | 18 | 5 | 8 | .625 | 0 | 0 | ... | 0 | 1 | 1 | 5 | 2 | 0 | 3 | 0 | 3 | 12 |
| 1993—Utah | 31 | 3 | 6 | .500 | 2 | 2 | 1.000 | 0 | 6 | 6 | 15 | 3 | 0 | 2 | 0 | 5 | 9 |
| 1994—Utah | 26 | 6 | 10 | .600 | 0 | 0 | ... | 1 | 4 | 5 | 10 | 2 | 0 | 1 | 0 | 4 | 13 |
| 1995—Utah | 14 | 2 | 6 | .333 | 0 | 0 | ... | 0 | 1 | 1 | 6 | 0 | 0 | 2 | 0 | 0 | 4 |
| 1996—Utah | 18 | 2 | 9 | .222 | 0 | 0 | ... | 0 | 1 | 1 | 3 | 2 | 0 | 0 | 0 | 1 | 4 |
| 1997—Utah | 20 | 5 | 6 | .833 | 0 | 0 | ... | 0 | 1 | 1 | 5 | 2 | 0 | 1 | 0 | 1 | 12 |
| 2000—Utah | 11 | 5 | 5 | 1.000 | 0 | 0 | ... | 0 | 0 | 0 | 2 | 2 | 0 | 1 | 0 | 0 | 10 |
| **Totals** | 197 | 35 | 66 | .530 | 4 | 6 | .667 | 2 | 15 | 17 | 71 | 20 | 0 | 16 | 1 | 29 | 81 |

Three-point field goals: 1989, 1-for-1. 1990, 0-for-1. 1992, 2-for-3 (.667). 1993, 1-for-2 (.500). 1994, 1-for-1. 1995, 0-for-3. 1996, 0-for-7. 1997, 2-for-2. Totals, 7-for-20 (.350).

## THEUS, REGGIE     G

**PERSONAL:** Born October 13, 1957, in Inglewood, Calif. ... 6-7/213 (2,00/96,6). ... Full name: Reggie Wayne Theus. ... Name pronounced THEE-us.
**HIGH SCHOOL:** Inglewood (Calif.).
**COLLEGE:** UNLV.
**TRANSACTIONS:** Selected after junior season by Chicago Bulls in first round (ninth pick overall) of 1978 NBA Draft. ... Traded by Bulls to Kansas City Kings for C Steve Johnson, 1984 second-round draft choice and two 1985 second-round draft choices (February 15, 1984). ... Kings franchise moved from Kansas City to Sacramento for 1985-86 season. ... Traded by Kings with 1988 third-round draft choice and future considerations to Atlanta Hawks for G/F Randy Wittman and 1988 first-round draft choice (June 27, 1988). ... Selected by Orlando Magic from Hawks in NBA Expansion Draft (June 15, 1989). ... Traded by Magic to New Jersey Nets for 1993 and 1995 second-round draft choices (June 25, 1990). ... Waived by Nets (August 15, 1991). ... Played in Italy (1991-92).
**CAREER NOTES:** Broadcaster, Turner Sports (1994-2000).

### COLLEGIATE RECORD

| Season Team | G | Min. | FGM | FGA | Pct. | FTM | FTA | Pct. | Reb. | Ast. | Pts. | RPG | APG | PPG |
|---|---|---|---|---|---|---|---|---|---|---|---|---|---|---|
| 75-76—UNLV | 31 | 496 | 68 | 163 | .417 | 48 | 60 | .800 | 53 | 139 | 184 | 1.7 | 4.5 | 5.9 |
| 76-77—UNLV | 32 | 814 | 178 | 358 | .497 | 108 | 132 | .818 | 145 | 136 | 464 | 4.5 | 4.3 | 14.5 |
| 77-78—UNLV | 28 | 990 | 181 | 389 | .465 | 167 | 207 | .807 | 191 | 126 | 529 | 6.8 | 4.5 | 18.9 |
| Totals | 91 | 2300 | 427 | 910 | .469 | 323 | 399 | .810 | 389 | 401 | 1177 | 4.3 | 4.4 | 12.9 |

### NBA REGULAR-SEASON RECORD

**HONORS:** NBA All-Rookie team (1979).

| Season Team | G | Min. | FGM | FGA | Pct. | FTM | FTA | Pct. | Off. | Def. | Tot. | Ast. | St. | Blk. | TO | Pts. | RPG | APG | PPG |
|---|---|---|---|---|---|---|---|---|---|---|---|---|---|---|---|---|---|---|---|
| 78-79—Chicago | 82 | 2753 | 537 | 1119 | .480 | 264 | 347 | .761 | 92 | 136 | 228 | 429 | 93 | 18 | 303 | 1338 | 2.8 | 5.2 | 16.3 |
| 79-80—Chicago | 82 | 3029 | 566 | 1172 | .483 | 500 | 597 | .838 | 143 | 186 | 329 | 515 | 114 | 20 | 348 | 1660 | 4.0 | 6.3 | 20.2 |
| 80-81—Chicago | 82 | 2820 | 543 | 1097 | .495 | 445 | 550 | .809 | 124 | 163 | 287 | 426 | 122 | 20 | 259 | 1549 | 3.5 | 5.2 | 18.9 |
| 81-82—Chicago | 82 | 2838 | 560 | 1194 | .469 | 363 | 449 | .808 | 115 | 197 | 312 | 476 | 87 | 16 | 277 | 1508 | 3.8 | 5.8 | 18.4 |
| 82-83—Chicago | 82 | 2856 | 749 | 1567 | .478 | 434 | 542 | .801 | 91 | 209 | 300 | 484 | 143 | 17 | 321 | 1953 | 3.7 | 5.9 | 23.8 |
| 83-84—Chi.-K.C. | 61 | 1498 | 262 | 625 | .419 | 214 | 281 | .762 | 50 | 79 | 129 | 352 | 50 | 12 | 156 | 745 | 2.1 | 5.8 | 12.2 |
| 84-85—Kansas City | 82 | 2543 | 501 | 1029 | .487 | 384 | 387 | .863 | 106 | 164 | 270 | 656 | 95 | 18 | 307 | 1341 | 3.3 | 8.0 | 16.4 |
| 85-86—Sacramento | 82 | 2919 | 546 | 1137 | .480 | 405 | 490 | .827 | 73 | 231 | 304 | 788 | 112 | 20 | 327 | 1503 | 3.7 | 9.6 | 18.3 |
| 86-87—Sacramento | 79 | 2872 | 577 | 1223 | .472 | 429 | 495 | .867 | 86 | 180 | 266 | 692 | 78 | 16 | 289 | 1600 | 3.4 | 8.8 | 20.3 |
| 87-88—Sacramento | 73 | 2653 | 619 | 1318 | .470 | 320 | 385 | .831 | 72 | 160 | 232 | 463 | 59 | 16 | 234 | 1574 | 3.2 | 6.3 | 21.6 |
| 88-89—Atlanta | 82 | 2517 | 497 | 1067 | .466 | 285 | 335 | .851 | 86 | 156 | 242 | 387 | 108 | 16 | 194 | 1296 | 3.0 | 4.7 | 15.8 |
| 89-90—Orlando | 76 | 2350 | 517 | 1178 | .439 | 378 | 443 | .853 | 75 | 146 | 221 | 407 | 60 | 12 | 226 | 1428 | 2.9 | 5.4 | 18.9 |
| 90-91—New Jersey | 81 | 2955 | 583 | 1247 | .468 | 292 | 343 | .851 | 69 | 160 | 229 | 378 | 85 | 35 | 252 | 1510 | 2.8 | 4.7 | 18.6 |
| Totals | 1026 | 34603 | 7057 | 14973 | .471 | 4663 | 5644 | .826 | 1182 | 2167 | 3349 | 6453 | 1206 | 236 | 3493 | 19015 | 3.3 | 6.3 | 18.5 |

Three-point field goals: 1979-80, 28-for-105 (.267). 1980-81, 18-for-90 (.200). 1981-82, 25-for-100 (.250). 1982-83, 21-for-91 (.231). 1983-84, 7-for-42 (.167). 1984-85, 5-for-38 (.132). 1985-86, 6-for-35 (.171). 1986-87, 17-for-78 (.218). 1987-88, 16-for-59 (.271). 1988-89, 17-for-58 (.293). 1989-90, 26-for-105 (.248). 1990-91, 52-for-144 (.361). Totals, 238-for-945 (.252).

Personal fouls/disqualifications: 1978-79, 270/2. 1979-80, 264/4. 1980-81, 258/1. 1981-82, 243/1. 1982-83, 281/6. 1983-84, 171/3. 1984-85, 250/0. 1985-86, 231/3. 1986-87, 208/3. 1987-88, 173/0. 1988-89, 236/0. 1989-90, 194/1. 1990-91, 231/0. Totals, 3008/24.

### NBA PLAYOFF RECORD

| Season Team | G | Min. | FGM | FGA | Pct. | FTM | FTA | Pct. | Off. | Def. | Tot. | Ast. | St. | Blk. | TO | Pts. | RPG | APG | PPG |
|---|---|---|---|---|---|---|---|---|---|---|---|---|---|---|---|---|---|---|---|
| 80-81—Chicago | 6 | 232 | 40 | 90 | .444 | 37 | 43 | .860 | 7 | 14 | 21 | 38 | 9 | 0 | 15 | 119 | 3.5 | 6.3 | 19.8 |
| 83-84—Kansas City | 3 | 81 | 17 | 43 | .395 | 9 | 10 | .900 | 4 | 7 | 11 | 16 | 5 | 0 | 9 | 43 | 3.7 | 5.3 | 14.3 |
| 85-86—Sacramento | 3 | 102 | 18 | 46 | .391 | 9 | 12 | .750 | 3 | 5 | 8 | 19 | 3 | 2 | 14 | 45 | 2.7 | 6.3 | 15.0 |
| 88-89—Atlanta | 5 | 127 | 14 | 38 | .368 | 9 | 12 | .750 | 3 | 4 | 7 | 24 | 1 | 0 | 10 | 37 | 1.4 | 4.8 | 7.4 |
| Totals | 17 | 542 | 89 | 217 | .410 | 64 | 77 | .831 | 17 | 30 | 47 | 97 | 18 | 2 | 48 | 244 | 2.8 | 5.7 | 14.4 |

Three-point field goals: 1980-81, 2-for-9 (.222). 1983-84, 0-for-3. 1985-86, 0-for-1. 1988-89, 0-for-2. Totals, 2-for-15 (.133).
Personal fouls/disqualifications: 1980-81, 22/0. 1983-84, 9/0. 1985-86, 9/0. 1988-89, 18/1. Totals, 58/1.

### NBA ALL-STAR GAME RECORD

| Season Team | Min. | FGM | FGA | Pct. | FTM | FTA | Pct. | Off. | Def. | Tot. | Ast. | PF | Dq. | St. | Blk. | TO | Pts. |
|---|---|---|---|---|---|---|---|---|---|---|---|---|---|---|---|---|---|
| 1981—Chicago | 19 | 4 | 7 | .571 | 0 | 0 | ... | 0 | 1 | 1 | 3 | 0 | 0 | 2 | 0 | 4 | 8 |
| 1983—Chicago | 8 | 0 | 5 | .000 | 0 | 0 | ... | 1 | 0 | 1 | 1 | 1 | 0 | 0 | 0 | 0 | 0 |
| Totals | 27 | 4 | 12 | .333 | 0 | 0 | ... | 1 | 1 | 2 | 4 | 1 | 0 | 2 | 0 | 4 | 8 |

### ITALIAN LEAGUE RECORD

| Season Team | G | Min. | FGM | FGA | Pct. | FTM | FTA | Pct. | Reb. | Ast. | Pts. | RPG | APG | PPG |
|---|---|---|---|---|---|---|---|---|---|---|---|---|---|---|
| 91-92—Ranger Varese | 30 | 1151 | 268 | 572 | .469 | 288 | 340 | .847 | 118 | 161 | 878 | 3.9 | 5.4 | 29.3 |

### HEAD COACHING RECORD

**BACKGROUND:** Assistant coach, University of Louisville (2003-05). ... Head coach, New Mexico State University (2005-present).

## THOMAS, ISIAH     G

**PERSONAL:** Born April 30, 1961, in Chicago. ... 6-1/182. (1,85/82,6). ... Full name: Isiah Lord Thomas III.
**HIGH SCHOOL:** St. Joseph's (Westchester, Ill.).
**COLLEGE:** Indiana.
**TRANSACTIONS:** Selected after sophomore season by Detroit Pistons in first round (second pick overall) of 1981 NBA

Draft. ... Announced retirement (May 11, 1994).

**CAREER NOTES:** Vice president, (May 24, 1994-Nov. 20, 1997) and part owner, Toronto Raptors. ... Broadcaster, NBC Sports (Nov. 25, 1997-June 2000). ... Majority owner, Continental Basketball Association (1999-2000). ... President, New York Knicks (December 22, 2003-present).

**CAREER HONORS:** One of the 50 Greatest Players in NBA History (1996).

**MISCELLANEOUS:** Member of NBA championship team (1989, 1990). ... Member of U.S. Olympic team (1980). ... Member of gold-medal-winning U.S. World Championship team (1994). ... Detroit Pistons franchise all-time leading scorer with 18,822 points, all-time assists leader with 9,061 and all-time steals leader with 1,861 (1981-82 through 1993-94). ... Elected to Naismith Memorial Basketball Hall of Fame (2000).

## COLLEGIATE RECORD

**NOTES:** Member of NCAA Division I championship team (1981). ... NCAA Division I Tournament Most Outstanding Player (1981). ... THE SPORTING NEWS All-America first team (1981).

| Season Team | G | Min. | FGM | FGA | Pct. | FTM | FTA | Pct. | Reb. | Ast. | Pts. | RPG | APG | PPG |
|---|---|---|---|---|---|---|---|---|---|---|---|---|---|---|
| 79-80—Indiana | 29 | 986 | 154 | 302 | .510 | 115 | 149 | .772 | 116 | 159 | 423 | 4.0 | 5.5 | 14.6 |
| 80-81—Indiana | 34 | 1190 | 212 | 383 | .554 | 121 | 163 | .742 | 105 | 197 | 545 | 3.1 | 5.8 | 16.0 |
| Totals | 63 | 2176 | 366 | 685 | .534 | 236 | 312 | .756 | 221 | 356 | 968 | 3.5 | 5.7 | 15.4 |

## NBA REGULAR-SEASON RECORD

**HONORS:** All-NBA first team (1984, 1985, 1986). ... All-NBA second team (1983, 1987). ... NBA All-Rookie team (1982). ... J. Walter Kennedy Citizenship Award (1987).

| Season Team | G | Min. | FGM | FGA | Pct. | FTM | FTA | Pct. | Off. | Def. | Tot. | Ast. | St. | Blk. | TO | Pts. | RPG | APG | PPG |
|---|---|---|---|---|---|---|---|---|---|---|---|---|---|---|---|---|---|---|---|
| 81-82—Detroit | 72 | 2433 | 453 | 1068 | .424 | 302 | 429 | .704 | 57 | 152 | 209 | 565 | 150 | 17 | †299 | 1225 | 2.9 | 7.8 | 17.0 |
| 82-83—Detroit | 81 | *3093 | 725 | 1537 | .472 | 368 | 518 | .710 | 105 | 223 | 328 | 634 | 199 | 29 | *326 | 1854 | 4.0 | 7.8 | 22.9 |
| 83-84—Detroit | 82 | 3007 | 669 | 1448 | .462 | 388 | 529 | .733 | 103 | 224 | 327 | †914 | 204 | 33 | 307 | 1748 | 4.0 | 11.1 | 21.3 |
| 84-85—Detroit | 81 | 3089 | 646 | 1410 | .458 | 399 | 493 | .809 | 114 | 247 | 361 | *1123 | 187 | 25 | 302 | 1720 | 4.5 | *13.9 | 21.2 |
| 85-86—Detroit | 77 | 2790 | 609 | 1248 | .488 | 365 | 462 | .790 | 83 | 194 | 277 | 830 | 171 | 20 | 289 | 1609 | 3.6 | 10.8 | 20.9 |
| 86-87—Detroit | 81 | 3013 | 626 | 1353 | .463 | 400 | 521 | .768 | 82 | 237 | 319 | 813 | 153 | 20 | 343 | 1671 | 3.9 | 10.0 | 20.6 |
| 87-88—Detroit | 81 | 2927 | 621 | 1341 | .463 | 305 | 394 | .774 | 64 | 214 | 278 | 678 | 141 | 17 | 273 | 1577 | 3.4 | 8.4 | 19.5 |
| 88-89—Detroit | 80 | 2924 | 569 | 1227 | .464 | 287 | 351 | .818 | 49 | 224 | 273 | 663 | 133 | 20 | 298 | 1458 | 3.4 | 8.3 | 18.2 |
| 89-90—Detroit | 81 | 2993 | 579 | 1322 | .438 | 292 | 377 | .775 | 74 | 234 | 308 | 765 | 139 | 19 | *322 | 1492 | 3.8 | 9.4 | 18.4 |
| 90-91—Detroit | 48 | 1657 | 289 | 665 | .435 | 179 | 229 | .782 | 35 | 125 | 160 | 446 | 75 | 10 | 185 | 776 | 3.3 | 9.3 | 16.2 |
| 91-92—Detroit | 78 | 2918 | 564 | 1264 | .446 | 292 | 378 | .772 | 68 | 179 | 247 | 560 | 118 | 15 | 252 | 1445 | 3.2 | 7.2 | 18.5 |
| 92-93—Detroit | 79 | 2922 | 526 | 1258 | .418 | 278 | 377 | .737 | 71 | 161 | 232 | 671 | 123 | 18 | 284 | 1391 | 2.9 | 8.5 | 17.6 |
| 93-94—Detroit | 58 | 1750 | 318 | 763 | .417 | 181 | 258 | .702 | 46 | 113 | 159 | 399 | 68 | 6 | 202 | 856 | 2.7 | 6.9 | 14.8 |
| Totals | 979 | 35516 | 7194 | 15904 | .452 | 4036 | 5316 | .759 | 951 | 2527 | 3478 | 9061 | 1861 | 249 | 3682 | 18822 | 3.6 | 9.3 | 19.2 |

Three-point field goals: 1981-82, 17-for-59 (.288). 1982-83, 36-for-125 (.288). 1983-84, 22-for-65 (.338). 1984-85, 29-for-113 (.257). 1985-86, 26-for-84 (.310). 1986-87, 19-for-98 (.194). 1987-88, 30-for-97 (.309). 1988-89, 33-for-121 (.273). 1989-90, 42-for-136 (.309). 1990-91, 19-for-65 (.292). 1991-92, 25-for-86 (.291). 1992-93, 61-for-198 (.308). 1993-94, 39-for-126 (.310). Totals, 398-for-1373 (.290).

Personal fouls/disqualifications: 1981-82, 253/2. 1982-83, 318/8. 1983-84, 324/8. 1984-85, 288/8. 1985-86, 245/9. 1986-87, 251/5. 1987-88, 217/0. 1988-89, 209/0. 1989-90, 206/0. 1990-91, 118/4. 1991-92, 194/2. 1992-93, 222/2. 1993-94, 126/0. Totals, 2971/48.

## NBA PLAYOFF RECORD

**NOTES:** NBA Finals Most Valuable Player (1990). ... Holds NBA Finals single-game records for most points in one quarter—25 (June 19, 1988, vs. Los Angeles Lakers); and most field goals in one quarter—11 (June 19, 1988, vs. Los Angeles Lakers). ... Shares NBA Finals single-game record for most field goals in one half—14 (June 19, 1988, vs. Los Angeles Lakers).

| Season Team | G | Min. | FGM | FGA | Pct. | FTM | FTA | Pct. | Off. | Def. | Tot. | Ast. | St. | Blk. | TO | Pts. | RPG | APG | PPG |
|---|---|---|---|---|---|---|---|---|---|---|---|---|---|---|---|---|---|---|---|
| 83-84—Detroit | 5 | 198 | 39 | 83 | .470 | 27 | 35 | .771 | 7 | 12 | 19 | 55 | 13 | 6 | 23 | 107 | 3.8 | 11.0 | 21.4 |
| 84-85—Detroit | 9 | 355 | 83 | 166 | .500 | 47 | 62 | .758 | 11 | 36 | 47 | 101 | 19 | 4 | 30 | 219 | 5.2 | 11.2 | 24.3 |
| 85-86—Detroit | 4 | 163 | 41 | 91 | .451 | 24 | 36 | .667 | 8 | 14 | 22 | 48 | 9 | 3 | 17 | 106 | 5.5 | 12.0 | 26.5 |
| 86-87—Detroit | 15 | 562 | 134 | 297 | .451 | 83 | 110 | .755 | 21 | 46 | 67 | 130 | 39 | 4 | 42 | 361 | 4.5 | 8.7 | 24.1 |
| 87-88—Detroit | 23 | 911 | 183 | 419 | .437 | 125 | 151 | .828 | 26 | 81 | 107 | 201 | 66 | 8 | 85 | 504 | 4.7 | 8.7 | 21.9 |
| 88-89—Detroit | 17 | 633 | 115 | 279 | .412 | 71 | 96 | .740 | 24 | 49 | 73 | 141 | 27 | 4 | 43 | 309 | 4.3 | 8.3 | 18.2 |
| 89-90—Detroit | 20 | 758 | 148 | 320 | .463 | 81 | 102 | .794 | 21 | 88 | 109 | 163 | 43 | 7 | 72 | 409 | 5.5 | 8.2 | 20.5 |
| 90-91—Detroit | 13 | 436 | 60 | 149 | .403 | 50 | 69 | .725 | 13 | 41 | 54 | 111 | 13 | 2 | 41 | 176 | 4.2 | 8.5 | 13.5 |
| 91-92—Detroit | 5 | 200 | 22 | 65 | .338 | 22 | 28 | .786 | 3 | 23 | 26 | 37 | 5 | 0 | 16 | 70 | 5.2 | 7.4 | 14.0 |
| Totals | 111 | 4216 | 825 | 1869 | .441 | 530 | 689 | .769 | 134 | 390 | 524 | 987 | 234 | 38 | 369 | 2261 | 4.7 | 8.9 | 20.4 |

Three-point field goals: 1983-84, 2-for-6 (.333). 1984-85, 6-for-15 (.400). 1985-86, 0-for-5. 1986-87, 10-for-33 (.303). 1987-88, 13-for-44 (.295). 1988-89, 8-for-30 (.267). 1989-90, 32-for-68 (.471). 1990-91, 6-for-22 (.273). 1991-92, 4-for-11 (.364). Totals, 81-for-234 (.346).

Personal fouls/disqualifications: 1983-84, 22/1. 1984-85, 30/2. 1985-86, 17/0. 1986-87, 51/1. 1987-88, 71/2. 1988-89, 39/0. 1989-90, 65/1. 1990-91, 41/1. 1991-92, 18/0. Totals, 363/8.

## NBA ALL-STAR GAME RECORD

**NOTES:** NBA All-Star Game Most Valuable Player (1984, 1986).

| Season Team | Min. | FGM | FGA | Pct. | FTM | FTA | Pct. | Off. | Def. | Tot. | Ast. | PF | Dq. | St. | Blk. | TO | Pts. |
|---|---|---|---|---|---|---|---|---|---|---|---|---|---|---|---|---|---|
| 1982—Detroit | 17 | 5 | 7 | .714 | 2 | 4 | .500 | 1 | 0 | 1 | 4 | 1 | 0 | 3 | 0 | 1 | 12 |
| 1983—Detroit | 29 | 9 | 14 | .643 | 1 | 1 | 1.000 | 3 | 1 | 4 | 7 | 0 | 0 | 4 | 0 | 5 | 19 |
| 1984—Detroit | 39 | 9 | 17 | .529 | 3 | 3 | 1.000 | 3 | 2 | 5 | 15 | 4 | 0 | 4 | 0 | 6 | 21 |
| 1985—Detroit | 25 | 9 | 14 | .643 | 1 | 1 | 1.000 | 1 | 1 | 2 | 5 | 2 | 0 | 2 | 0 | 1 | 22 |
| 1986—Detroit | 36 | 11 | 19 | .579 | 8 | 9 | .889 | 0 | 1 | 1 | 10 | 2 | 0 | 5 | 0 | 5 | 30 |
| 1987—Detroit | 24 | 4 | 6 | .667 | 8 | 9 | .889 | 2 | 1 | 3 | 9 | 1 | 0 | 0 | 0 | 6 | 16 |
| 1988—Detroit | 28 | 4 | 10 | .400 | 0 | 0 | ... | 1 | 1 | 2 | 15 | 1 | 0 | 1 | 0 | 6 | 8 |
| 1989—Detroit | 33 | 7 | 13 | .538 | 4 | 6 | .667 | 1 | 1 | 2 | 14 | 2 | 0 | 4 | 0 | 6 | 19 |
| 1990—Detroit | 27 | 7 | 12 | .583 | 0 | 0 | ... | 1 | 3 | 4 | 9 | 0 | 0 | 3 | 0 | 1 | 15 |
| 1991—Detroit | | | | | | | Selected, did not play—injured. | | | | | | | | | | |
| 1992—Detroit | 28 | 7 | 14 | .500 | 0 | 0 | ... | 0 | 1 | 1 | 5 | 0 | 0 | 3 | 0 | 3 | 15 |
| 1993—Detroit | 32 | 4 | 7 | .571 | 0 | 2 | .000 | 0 | 2 | 2 | 4 | 2 | 0 | 2 | 0 | 2 | 8 |
| Totals | 318 | 76 | 133 | .571 | 27 | 35 | .771 | 13 | 14 | 27 | 97 | 17 | 0 | 31 | 0 | 41 | 185 |

Three-point field goals: 1984, 0-for-2. 1985, 3-for-4 (.750). 1986, 0-for-1. 1989, 1-for-3 (.333). 1990, 1-for-1. 1992, 1-for-3 (.333). 1993, 0-for-1. Totals, 6-for-15 (.400).

## NBA COACHING RECORD

| Season Team | REGULAR SEASON | | | | PLAYOFFS | | |
|---|---|---|---|---|---|---|---|
| | W | L | Pct. | Finish | W | L | Pct. |
| 00-01—Indiana | 41 | 41 | .500 | 4th/Central Division | 1 | 3 | .250 |
| 01-02—Indiana | 42 | 40 | .512 | T3rd/Central Division | 2 | 3 | .400 |
| 02-03—Indiana | 48 | 34 | .585 | 2nd/Central Division | 2 | 4 | .333 |
| Totals (3 years) | 131 | 115 | .533 | Totals (3 years) | 5 | 10 | .333 |

**NOTES:**
2001—Lost to Philadelphia, 3-1, in Eastern Conference first round.
2002—Lost to New Jersey, 3-2, in Eastern Conference first round.
2003—Lost to Boston, 4-2, in Eastern Conference first round.

# THORPE, OTIS — F/C

**PERSONAL:** Born August 5, 1962, in Boynton Beach, Fla. ... 6-10/248. (2,08/112,5). ... Full Name: Otis Henry Thorpe.
**HIGH SCHOOL:** Lake Worth (Fla.) Community.
**COLLEGE:** Providence.
**TRANSACTIONS/CAREER NOTES:** Selected by Kansas City Kings in first round (ninth pick overall) of 1984 NBA Draft. ... Kings franchise moved from Kansas City to Sacramento for 1985-86 season. ... Traded by Kings to Houston Rockets for F/G Rodney McCray and F/C Jim Petersen (October 11, 1988). ... Traded by Rockets with rights to F Marcelo Nicola and 1995 first-round draft choice to Portland Trail Blazers for G Clyde Drexler and F Tracy Murray (February 14, 1995). ... Traded by Trail Blazers to Detroit Pistons for F Bill Curley and draft rights to G Randolph Childress (September 20, 1995). ... Traded by Pistons to Vancouver Grizzlies for first-round draft choice between 1998 and 2003 (August 7, 1997). ... Traded by Grizzlies with G Chris Robinson to Sacramento Kings for G Bobby Hurley and F Michael Smith (February 18, 1998). ... Traded by Kings with G Mitch Richmond to Washington Wizards for F Chris Webber (May 14, 1998). ... Signed as free agent by Miami Heat (August 4, 1999). ... Traded by Heat with F P.J. Brown, F Jamal Mashburn, F Tim James and G/F Rodney Buford to Charlotte Hornets for G Eddie Jones, F Anthony Mason, G Ricky Davis and G/F Dale Ellis (August 1, 2000).
**MISCELLANEOUS:** Member of NBA championship team (1994).

## COLLEGIATE RECORD

| Season Team | G | Min. | FGM | FGA | Pct. | FTM | FTA | Pct. | Reb. | Ast. | Pts. | AVERAGES | | |
|---|---|---|---|---|---|---|---|---|---|---|---|---|---|---|
| | | | | | | | | | | | | RPG | APG | PPG |
| 80-81—Providence | 26 | 668 | 100 | 194 | .515 | 50 | 76 | .658 | 137 | 11 | 250 | 5.3 | 0.4 | 9.6 |
| 81-82—Providence | 27 | 942 | 153 | 283 | .541 | 74 | 115 | .643 | 216 | 36 | 380 | 8.0 | 1.3 | 14.1 |
| 82-83—Providence | 31 | 1041 | 204 | 321 | .636 | 91 | 138 | .659 | 249 | 24 | 499 | 8.0 | 0.8 | 16.1 |
| 83-84—Providence | 29 | 1051 | 167 | 288 | .580 | 162 | 248 | .653 | 300 | 36 | 496 | 10.3 | 1.2 | 17.1 |
| Totals | 113 | 3702 | 624 | 1086 | .575 | 377 | 577 | .653 | 902 | 107 | 1625 | 8.0 | 0.9 | 14.4 |

## NBA REGULAR-SEASON RECORD

**NOTES:** Tied for NBA lead with 300 personal fouls (1996) and nine disqualifications (1999).

| Season Team | G | Min. | FGM | FGA | Pct. | FTM | FTA | Pct. | REBOUNDS | | | Ast. | St. | Blk. | TO | Pts. | AVERAGES | | |
|---|---|---|---|---|---|---|---|---|---|---|---|---|---|---|---|---|---|---|---|
| | | | | | | | | | Off. | Def. | Tot. | | | | | | RPG | APG | PPG |
| 84-85—Kansas City | 82 | 1918 | 411 | 685 | .600 | 230 | 371 | .620 | 187 | 369 | 556 | 111 | 34 | 37 | 187 | 1052 | 6.8 | 1.4 | 12.8 |
| 85-86—Sacramento | 75 | 1675 | 289 | 492 | .587 | 164 | 248 | .661 | 137 | 283 | 420 | 84 | 35 | 34 | | 742 | 5.6 | 1.1 | 9.9 |
| 86-87—Sacramento | 82 | 2956 | 567 | 1050 | .540 | 413 | 543 | .761 | 259 | 560 | 819 | 201 | 46 | 60 | 189 | 1547 | 10.0 | 2.5 | 18.9 |
| 87-88—Sacramento | 82 | 3072 | 622 | 1226 | .507 | 460 | 609 | .755 | 279 | 558 | 837 | 266 | 62 | 56 | 228 | 1704 | 10.2 | 3.2 | 20.8 |
| 88-89—Houston | 82 | 3135 | 521 | 961 | .542 | 328 | 450 | .729 | 272 | 515 | 787 | 202 | 82 | 37 | 225 | 1370 | 9.6 | 2.5 | 16.7 |
| 89-90—Houston | 82 | 2947 | 547 | 998 | .548 | 307 | 446 | .688 | 258 | 476 | 734 | 261 | 66 | 24 | 229 | 1401 | 9.0 | 3.2 | 17.1 |
| 90-91—Houston | 82 | 3039 | 549 | 988 | .556 | 304 | 480 | .696 | 287 | 559 | 846 | 197 | 73 | 20 | 217 | 1435 | 10.3 | 2.4 | 17.5 |
| 91-92—Houston | 82 | 3056 | 558 | 943 | .592 | 304 | 463 | .657 | 285 | 577 | 862 | 250 | 52 | 37 | 237 | 1420 | 10.5 | 3.0 | 17.3 |
| 92-93—Houston | 72 | 2357 | 385 | 690 | .558 | 153 | 256 | .598 | 219 | 370 | 589 | 181 | 43 | 19 | 151 | 923 | 8.2 | 2.5 | 12.8 |
| 93-94—Houston | 82 | 2909 | 449 | 801 | .561 | 251 | 382 | .657 | 271 | 599 | 870 | 189 | 66 | 28 | 185 | 1149 | 10.6 | 2.3 | 14.0 |
| 94-95—Hou.-Port. | 70 | 2096 | 385 | 681 | .565 | 167 | 281 | .594 | 202 | 356 | 558 | 112 | 41 | 28 | 132 | 937 | 8.0 | 1.6 | 13.4 |
| 95-96—Detroit | 82 | 2841 | 452 | 853 | .530 | 257 | 362 | .710 | 211 | 477 | 688 | 158 | 53 | 39 | 195 | 1161 | 8.4 | 1.9 | 14.2 |
| 96-97—Detroit | 79 | 2661 | 419 | 787 | .532 | 198 | 303 | .653 | 226 | 396 | 622 | 133 | 59 | 17 | 145 | 1036 | 7.9 | 1.7 | 13.1 |
| 97-98—Van.-Sac. | 74 | 2197 | 294 | 624 | .471 | 164 | 240 | .683 | 151 | 386 | 537 | 222 | 48 | 30 | 152 | 752 | 7.3 | 3.0 | 10.2 |
| 98-99—Washington | 49 | 1539 | 240 | 440 | .545 | 74 | 106 | .698 | 96 | 238 | 334 | 101 | 42 | 19 | 88 | 554 | 6.8 | 2.1 | 11.3 |
| 99-00—Miami | 51 | 777 | 125 | 243 | .514 | 29 | 48 | .604 | 56 | 110 | 166 | 33 | 26 | 9 | 59 | 279 | 3.3 | 0.6 | 5.5 |
| 00-01—Charlotte | 49 | 647 | 59 | 131 | .450 | 20 | 24 | .833 | 50 | 95 | 145 | 29 | 12 | 7 | 32 | 138 | 3.0 | 0.6 | 2.8 |
| Totals | 1257 | 39822 | 6872 | 12593 | .546 | 3853 | 5612 | .687 | 3446 | 6924 | 10370 | 2730 | 840 | 501 | 2774 | 17600 | 8.2 | 2.2 | 14.0 |

Three-point field goals: 1984-85, 0-for-2. 1986-87, 0-for-3. 1987-88, 0-for-6. 1988-89, 0-for-2. 1989-90, 0-for-10. 1990-91, 3-for-7 (.429). 1991-92, 0-for-7. 1992-93, 0-for-3. 1993-94, 0-for-2. 1994-95, 0-for-7. 1995-96, 0-for-4. 1996-97, 0-for-2. 1997-98, 0-for-5. 1998-99, 0-for-2. 1999-00, 0-for-1. Totals, 3-for-64 (.047).
Personal fouls/disqualifications: 1984-85, 256/2. 1985-86, 233/3. 1986-87, 292/11. 1987-88, 264/3. 1988-89, 259/6. 1989-90, 270/5. 1990-91, 278/10. 1991-92, 307/7. 1992-93, 234/3. 1993-94, 253/1. 1994-95, 224/3. 1995-96, 300/7. 1996-97, 298/7. 1997-98, 238/4. 1998-99, 196/9. 1999-00, 136/4. 2000-01, 108/0. Totals, 4146/85.

## NBA PLAYOFF RECORD

| Season Team | G | Min. | FGM | FGA | Pct. | FTM | FTA | Pct. | REBOUNDS | | | Ast. | St. | Blk. | TO | Pts. | AVERAGES | | |
|---|---|---|---|---|---|---|---|---|---|---|---|---|---|---|---|---|---|---|---|
| | | | | | | | | | Off. | Def. | Tot. | | | | | | RPG | APG | PPG |
| 85-86—Sacramento | 3 | 35 | 3 | 13 | .231 | 6 | 13 | .462 | 8 | 4 | 12 | 0 | 0 | 1 | 1 | 12 | 4.0 | 0.0 | 4.0 |
| 88-89—Houston | 4 | 152 | 24 | 37 | .649 | 16 | 21 | .762 | 6 | 14 | 20 | 12 | 5 | 1 | 15 | 64 | 5.0 | 3.0 | 16.0 |
| 89-90—Houston | 4 | 164 | 27 | 45 | .600 | 26 | 38 | .684 | 14 | 19 | 33 | 7 | 5 | 0 | 9 | 80 | 8.3 | 1.8 | 20.0 |
| 90-91—Houston | 3 | 116 | 22 | 38 | .579 | 3 | 6 | .500 | 7 | 18 | 25 | 8 | 2 | 0 | 6 | 47 | 8.3 | 2.7 | 15.7 |
| 92-93—Houston | 12 | 419 | 73 | 115 | .635 | 28 | 43 | .651 | 36 | 67 | 103 | 31 | 6 | 1 | 17 | 174 | 8.6 | 2.6 | 14.5 |
| 93-94—Houston | 23 | 854 | 111 | 194 | .572 | 38 | 67 | .567 | 68 | 160 | 228 | 54 | 13 | 10 | 37 | 261 | 9.9 | 2.3 | 11.3 |
| 94-95—Portland | 3 | 66 | 12 | 21 | .571 | 7 | 10 | .700 | 5 | 8 | 13 | 2 | 0 | 0 | 3 | 31 | 4.3 | 0.7 | 10.3 |
| 95-96—Detroit | 3 | 101 | 13 | 24 | .542 | 9 | 12 | .750 | 14 | 21 | 35 | 7 | 0 | 0 | 7 | 35 | 11.7 | 2.3 | 11.7 |
| 96-97—Detroit | 5 | 152 | 21 | 41 | .512 | 7 | 9 | .778 | 12 | 20 | 32 | 4 | 2 | 0 | 9 | 49 | 6.4 | 0.8 | 9.8 |
| 99-00—Miami | 10 | 136 | 13 | 27 | .481 | 7 | 14 | .500 | 6 | 23 | 29 | 3 | 0 | 2 | 11 | 33 | 2.9 | 0.3 | 3.3 |
| 00-01—Charlotte | 8 | 57 | 2 | 9 | .222 | 0 | 0 | ... | 6 | 11 | 17 | 0 | 0 | 0 | 2 | 4 | 2.1 | 0.0 | 0.5 |
| Totals | 78 | 2252 | 321 | 564 | .569 | 147 | 233 | .631 | 182 | 365 | 547 | 128 | 33 | 15 | 117 | 790 | 7.0 | 1.6 | 10.1 |

Three-point field goals: 1993-94, 1-for-2 (.500). 1999-00, 0-for-1. Totals, 1-for-3 (.333).
Personal fouls/disqualifications: 1985-86, 4/0. 1988-89, 17/1. 1989-90, 12/0. 1990-91, 8/0. 1992-93, 35/0. 1993-94, 86/2. 1994-95, 12/1. 1995-96, 9/0. 1996-97, 21/0. 1999-00, 29/0. 2000-01, 8/0. Totals, 241/4.

## NBA ALL-STAR GAME RECORD

| Season Team | Min. | FGM | FGA | Pct. | FTM | FTA | Pct. | REBOUNDS | | | Ast. | PF | Dq. | St. | Blk. | TO | Pts. |
|---|---|---|---|---|---|---|---|---|---|---|---|---|---|---|---|---|---|---|
| | | | | | | | | Off. | Def. | Tot. | | | | | | | |
| 1992—Houston | 4 | 1 | 1 | 1.000 | 0 | 0 | ... | 0 | 0 | 0 | 0 | 0 | 0 | 0 | 0 | 0 | 2 |

# THURMOND, NATE C/F

**PERSONAL:** Born July 25, 1941, in Akron, Ohio. ... 6-11/235 (2,10/106,6). ... Full name: Nathaniel Thurmond.
**HIGH SCHOOL:** Central Hower (Akron, Ohio).
**COLLEGE:** Bowling Green State.
**TRANSACTIONS:** Selected by San Francisco Warriors in first round of 1963 NBA Draft. ... Warriors franchise renamed Golden State Warriors for 1971-72 season. ... Traded by Warriors to Chicago Bulls for C Clifford Ray, cash and 1975 first-round draft choice (September 3, 1974). ... Traded by Bulls with F Rowland Garrett to Cleveland Cavaliers for C/F Steve Patterson and F Eric Fernsten (November 27, 1975).
**CAREER HONORS:** Elected to Naismith Memorial Basketball Hall of Fame (1985). ... One of the 50 Greatest Players in NBA History (1996).
**CAREER NOTES:** Community Relations Director, Golden State Warriors (1981-82 through 1994-95) ... Community Relations Ambassador, Warriors (1995-96-present).
**MISCELLANEOUS:** Golden State Warriors franchise all-time leading rebounder with 12,771 (1963-64 through 1973-74).

## COLLEGIATE RECORD

**NOTES:** THE SPORTING NEWS All-America first team (1963).

| Season Team | G | Min. | FGM | FGA | Pct. | FTM | FTA | Pct. | Reb. | Ast. | Pts. | RPG | APG | PPG |
|---|---|---|---|---|---|---|---|---|---|---|---|---|---|---|
| 59-60—Bowling Green‡ | 17 | ... | ... | ... | ... | ... | ... | ... | 208 | ... | 225 | 12.2 | ... | 13.2 |
| 60-61—Bowling Green | 24 | ... | 170 | 427 | .398 | 87 | 129 | .674 | 449 | ... | 427 | 18.7 | ... | 17.8 |
| 61-62—Bowling Green | 25 | ... | 163 | 358 | .455 | 67 | 113 | .593 | 394 | ... | 393 | 15.8 | ... | 15.7 |
| 62-63—Bowling Green | 27 | ... | 206 | 466 | .442 | 124 | 197 | .629 | 452 | ... | 536 | 16.7 | ... | 19.9 |
| **Varsity totals** | 76 | ... | 539 | 1251 | .431 | 278 | 439 | .633 | 1295 | ... | 1356 | 17.0 | ... | 17.8 |

## NBA REGULAR-SEASON RECORD

**RECORDS:** Holds single-game record for most rebounds in one quarter—18 (February 28, 1965, vs. Baltimore).
**HONORS:** NBA All-Defensive first team (1969, 1971). ... NBA All-Defensive second team (1972, 1973, 1974). ... NBA All-Rookie team (1964).

| Season Team | G | Min. | FGM | FGA | Pct. | FTM | FTA | Pct. | Reb. | Ast. | PF | Dq. | Pts. | RPG | APG | PPG |
|---|---|---|---|---|---|---|---|---|---|---|---|---|---|---|---|---|
| 63-64—San Francisco | 76 | 1966 | 219 | 554 | .395 | 95 | 173 | .549 | 790 | 86 | 184 | 2 | 533 | 10.4 | 1.1 | 7.0 |
| 64-65—San Francisco | 77 | 3173 | 519 | 1240 | .419 | 235 | 357 | .658 | 1395 | 157 | 232 | 3 | 1273 | 18.1 | 2.0 | 16.5 |
| 65-66—San Francisco | 73 | 2891 | 454 | 1119 | .406 | 280 | 428 | .654 | 1312 | 111 | 223 | 7 | 1188 | 18.0 | 1.5 | 16.3 |
| 66-67—San Francisco | 65 | 2755 | 467 | 1068 | .437 | 280 | 445 | .629 | 1382 | 166 | 183 | 3 | 1214 | 21.3 | 2.6 | 18.7 |
| 67-68—San Francisco | 51 | 2222 | 382 | 929 | .411 | 282 | 438 | .644 | 1121 | 215 | 137 | 1 | 1046 | 22.0 | 4.2 | 20.5 |
| 68-69—San Francisco | 71 | 3208 | 571 | 1394 | .410 | 382 | 621 | .615 | 1402 | 253 | 171 | 0 | 1524 | 19.7 | 3.6 | 21.5 |
| 69-70—San Francisco | 43 | 1919 | 341 | 824 | .414 | 261 | 346 | .754 | 762 | 150 | 110 | 1 | 943 | 17.7 | 3.5 | 21.9 |
| 70-71—San Francisco | 82 | 3351 | 623 | 1401 | .445 | 395 | 541 | .730 | 1128 | 257 | 192 | 1 | 1641 | 13.8 | 3.1 | 20.0 |
| 71-72—Golden State | 78 | 3362 | 628 | 1454 | .432 | 417 | 561 | .743 | 1252 | 230 | 214 | 1 | 1673 | 16.1 | 2.9 | 21.4 |
| 72-73—Golden State | 79 | 3419 | 517 | 1159 | .446 | 315 | 439 | .718 | 1349 | 280 | 240 | 2 | 1349 | 17.1 | 3.5 | 17.1 |

| Season Team | G | Min. | FGM | FGA | Pct. | FTM | FTA | Pct. | Off. | Def. | Tot. | Ast. | St. | Blk. | TO | Pts. | RPG | APG | PPG |
|---|---|---|---|---|---|---|---|---|---|---|---|---|---|---|---|---|---|---|---|
| 73-74—Golden State | 62 | 2463 | 308 | 694 | .444 | 191 | 287 | .666 | 249 | 629 | 878 | 165 | 41 | 179 | ... | 807 | 14.2 | 2.7 | 13.0 |
| 74-75—Chicago | 80 | 2756 | 250 | 686 | .364 | 132 | 224 | .589 | 259 | 645 | 904 | 328 | 46 | 195 | ... | 632 | 11.3 | 4.1 | 7.9 |
| 75-76—Chi.-Clev. | 78 | 1393 | 142 | 337 | .421 | 62 | 123 | .504 | 115 | 300 | 415 | 94 | 22 | 98 | ... | 346 | 5.3 | 1.2 | 4.4 |
| 76-77—Cleveland | 49 | 997 | 100 | 246 | .407 | 68 | 106 | .642 | 121 | 253 | 374 | 83 | 16 | 81 | ... | 268 | 7.6 | 1.7 | 5.5 |
| **Totals** | 964 | 35875 | 5521 | 13105 | .421 | 3395 | 5089 | .667 | ... | ... | 14464 | 2575 | 125 | 553 | ... | 14437 | 15.0 | 2.7 | 15.0 |

Personal fouls/disqualifications: 1973-74, 179/4. 1974-75, 271/6. 1975-76, 160/1. 1976-77, 128/2. Totals, 2624/34.

## NBA PLAYOFF RECORD

| Season Team | G | Min. | FGM | FGA | Pct. | FTM | FTA | Pct. | Reb. | Ast. | PF | Dq. | Pts. | RPG | APG | PPG |
|---|---|---|---|---|---|---|---|---|---|---|---|---|---|---|---|---|
| 63-64—San Francisco | 12 | 410 | 42 | 98 | .429 | 36 | 53 | .679 | 148 | 12 | 46 | 0 | 120 | 12.3 | 1.0 | 10.0 |
| 66-67—San Francisco | 15 | 690 | 93 | 215 | .433 | 52 | 91 | .571 | 346 | 47 | 52 | 1 | 238 | 23.1 | 3.1 | 15.9 |
| 68-69—San Francisco | 6 | 263 | 40 | 102 | .392 | 20 | 34 | .588 | 117 | 28 | 18 | 0 | 100 | 19.5 | 4.7 | 16.7 |
| 70-71—San Francisco | 5 | 192 | 36 | 97 | .371 | 16 | 20 | .800 | 51 | 15 | 20 | 0 | 88 | 10.2 | 3.0 | 17.6 |
| 71-72—Golden State | 5 | 230 | 53 | 122 | .434 | 21 | 28 | .750 | 89 | 26 | 12 | 0 | 127 | 17.8 | 5.2 | 25.4 |
| 72-73—Golden State | 11 | 460 | 64 | 161 | .398 | 32 | 40 | .800 | 145 | 40 | 30 | 1 | 160 | 13.2 | 3.6 | 14.5 |

| Season Team | G | Min. | FGM | FGA | Pct. | FTM | FTA | Pct. | Off. | Def. | Tot. | Ast. | St. | Blk. | TO | Pts. | RPG | APG | PPG |
|---|---|---|---|---|---|---|---|---|---|---|---|---|---|---|---|---|---|---|---|
| 74-75—Chicago | 13 | 254 | 14 | 38 | .368 | 18 | 37 | .486 | 24 | 63 | 87 | 31 | 5 | 21 | ... | 46 | 6.7 | 2.4 | 3.5 |
| 75-76—Cleveland | 13 | 375 | 37 | 79 | .468 | 13 | 32 | .406 | 38 | 79 | 117 | 28 | 6 | 29 | ... | 87 | 9.0 | 2.2 | 6.7 |
| 76-77—Cleveland | 1 | 1 | 0 | 0 | ... | 0 | 0 | ... | 0 | 1 | 1 | 0 | 0 | 1 | ... | 0 | 1.0 | 0.0 | 0.0 |
| **Totals** | 81 | 2875 | 379 | 912 | .416 | 208 | 335 | .621 | ... | ... | 1101 | 227 | 11 | 51 | ... | 966 | 13.6 | 2.8 | 11.9 |

Personal fouls/disqualifications: 1974-75, 36/0. 1975-76, 52/2. Totals, 266/4.

## NBA ALL-STAR GAME RECORD

| Season Team | Min. | FGM | FGA | Pct. | FTM | FTA | Pct. | Reb | Ast. | PF | Dq. | Pts. |
|---|---|---|---|---|---|---|---|---|---|---|---|---|
| 1965—San Francisco | 10 | 0 | 2 | .000 | 0 | 0 | ... | 3 | 0 | 1 | 0 | 0 |
| 1966—San Francisco | 33 | 3 | 16 | .188 | 1 | 3 | .333 | 16 | 1 | 1 | 0 | 7 |
| 1967—San Francisco | 42 | 7 | 16 | .438 | 2 | 4 | .500 | 18 | 0 | 1 | 0 | 16 |
| 1968—San Francisco | | | | | Selected, did not play—injured. | | | | | | | |
| 1970—San Francisco | | | | | Selected, did not play—injured. | | | | | | | |
| 1973—Golden State | 14 | 2 | 5 | .400 | 0 | 0 | ... | 4 | 1 | 2 | 0 | 4 |
| 1974—Golden State | 5 | 2 | 4 | .500 | 0 | 1 | .000 | 1 | 2 | 3 | 0 | 0 | ... | 4 |
| **Totals** | 104 | 14 | 43 | .326 | 3 | 8 | .375 | ... | ... | 44 | 2 | 5 | 0 | ... | 31 |

# TWYMAN, JACK F/G

**PERSONAL:** Born May 11, 1934, in Pittsburgh. ... 6-6/210 (1,98/95,3). ... Full name: John Kennedy Twyman.
**HIGH SCHOOL:** Pittsburgh Central Catholic.
**COLLEGE:** Cincinnati.
**TRANSACTIONS:** Selected by Rochester Royals in second round (10th pick overall) of 1955 NBA Draft. ... Royals franchise moved from Rochester to Cincinnati for 1957-58 season.
**CAREER HONORS:** Elected to Naismith Memorial Basketball Hall of Fame (1983).

## COLLEGIATE RECORD

| Season Team | G | Min. | FGM | FGA | Pct. | FTM | FTA | Pct. | Reb. | Ast. | Pts. | AVERAGES RPG | APG | PPG |
|---|---|---|---|---|---|---|---|---|---|---|---|---|---|---|
| 51-52—Cincinnati | 16 | ... | 27 | 83 | .325 | 13 | 27 | .481 | 55 | ... | 67 | 3.4 | ... | 4.2 |
| 52-53—Cincinnati | 24 | 716 | 136 | 323 | .421 | 89 | 143 | .622 | 362 | ... | 361 | 15.1 | ... | 15.0 |
| 53-54—Cincinnati | 21 | 777 | 174 | 443 | .393 | 110 | 145 | .759 | 347 | ... | 458 | 16.5 | ... | 21.8 |
| 54-55—Cincinnati | 29 | 1097 | 285 | 628 | .454 | 142 | 192 | .740 | 478 | ... | 712 | 16.5 | ... | 24.6 |
| Totals | 90 | ... | 622 | 1477 | .421 | 354 | 507 | .698 | 1242 | ... | 1598 | 13.8 | ... | 17.8 |

## NBA REGULAR-SEASON RECORD

HONORS: All-NBA second team (1960, 1962).

| Season Team | G | Min. | FGM | FGA | Pct. | FTM | FTA | Pct. | Reb. | Ast. | PF | Dq. | Pts. | AVERAGES RPG | APG | PPG |
|---|---|---|---|---|---|---|---|---|---|---|---|---|---|---|---|---|
| 55-56—Rochester | 72 | 2186 | 417 | 987 | .423 | 204 | 298 | .685 | 466 | 171 | 239 | 4 | 1038 | 6.5 | 2.4 | 14.4 |
| 56-57—Rochester | 72 | 2338 | 449 | 1023 | .439 | 276 | 363 | .760 | 354 | 123 | 251 | 4 | 1174 | 4.9 | 1.7 | 16.3 |
| 57-58—Cincinnati | 72 | 2178 | 465 | 1028 | *.452 | 307 | 396 | .775 | 464 | 110 | 224 | 3 | 1237 | 6.4 | 1.5 | 17.2 |
| 58-59—Cincinnati | 72 | 2713 | 710 | *1691 | .420 | 437 | 558 | .783 | 653 | 209 | 277 | 6 | 1857 | 9.1 | 2.9 | 25.8 |
| 59-60—Cincinnati | 75 | 3023 | 870 | 2063 | .422 | *598 | 762 | .785 | 664 | 260 | 275 | 10 | 2338 | 8.9 | 3.5 | 31.2 |
| 60-61—Cincinnati | 79 | 2920 | 796 | 1632 | .488 | 405 | 554 | .731 | 672 | 225 | 279 | 5 | 1997 | 8.5 | 2.8 | 25.3 |
| 61-62—Cincinnati | 80 | 2991 | 739 | 1542 | .479 | 353 | 435 | .812 | 638 | 215 | 323 | 5 | 1831 | 8.0 | 2.7 | 22.9 |
| 62-63—Cincinnati | 80 | 2623 | 641 | 1335 | .480 | 304 | 375 | .811 | 598 | 214 | 286 | 7 | 1586 | 7.5 | 2.7 | 19.8 |
| 63-64—Cincinnati | 68 | 1996 | 447 | 993 | .450 | 189 | 228 | .829 | 364 | 137 | 267 | 7 | 1083 | 5.4 | 2.0 | 15.9 |
| 64-65—Cincinnati | 80 | 2236 | 479 | 1081 | .443 | 198 | 239 | .828 | 383 | 137 | 239 | 4 | 1156 | 4.8 | 1.7 | 14.5 |
| 65-66—Cincinnati | 73 | 943 | 224 | 498 | .450 | 95 | 117 | .812 | 168 | 60 | 122 | 1 | 543 | 2.3 | 0.8 | 7.4 |
| Totals | 823 | 26147 | 6237 | 13873 | .450 | 3366 | 4325 | .778 | 5424 | 1861 | 2782 | 56 | 15840 | 6.6 | 2.3 | 19.2 |

## NBA PLAYOFF RECORD

| Season Team | G | Min. | FGM | FGA | Pct. | FTM | FTA | Pct. | Reb. | Ast. | PF | Dq. | Pts. | AVERAGES RPG | APG | PPG |
|---|---|---|---|---|---|---|---|---|---|---|---|---|---|---|---|---|
| 57-58—Cincinnati | 2 | 74 | 15 | 45 | .333 | 7 | 12 | .583 | 22 | 1 | 6 | 0 | 37 | 11.0 | 0.5 | 18.5 |
| 61-62—Cincinnati‡ | 4 | 149 | 34 | 78 | .436 | 8 | 8 | 1.000 | 29 | 12 | 18 | 0 | 76 | 7.3 | 3.0 | 19.0 |
| 62-63—Cincinnati | 12 | 410 | 92 | 205 | .449 | 65 | 77 | .844 | 98 | 30 | 47 | 1 | 249 | 8.2 | 2.5 | 20.8 |
| 63-64—Cincinnati | 10 | 354 | 83 | 176 | .472 | 29 | 49 | .592 | 87 | 16 | 41 | 1 | 205 | 8.7 | 1.6 | 20.5 |
| 64-65—Cincinnati | 4 | 97 | 19 | 48 | .396 | 11 | 11 | 1.000 | 17 | 3 | 16 | 0 | 49 | 4.3 | 0.8 | 12.3 |
| 65-66—Cincinnati | 2 | 11 | 2 | 4 | .500 | 1 | 2 | .500 | 2 | 0 | 3 | 0 | 5 | 1.0 | 0.0 | 2.5 |
| Totals | 34 | 1095 | 245 | 556 | .441 | 121 | 159 | .761 | 255 | 62 | 131 | 2 | 621 | 7.5 | 1.8 | 18.3 |

## NBA ALL-STAR GAME RECORD

| Season Team | Min. | FGM | FGA | Pct. | FTM | FTA | Pct. | Reb | Ast. | PF | Dq. | Pts. |
|---|---|---|---|---|---|---|---|---|---|---|---|---|
| 1957—Rochester | 17 | 1 | 8 | .125 | 1 | 3 | .333 | 0 | 1 | 1 | 0 | 3 |
| 1958—Cincinnati | 25 | 8 | 13 | .615 | 2 | 2 | 1.000 | 3 | 0 | 3 | 0 | 18 |
| 1959—Cincinnati | 23 | 8 | 12 | .667 | 2 | 4 | .500 | 8 | 3 | 4 | 0 | 18 |
| 1960—Cincinnati | 28 | 11 | 17 | .647 | 5 | 8 | .625 | 5 | 1 | 4 | 0 | 27 |
| 1962—Cincinnati | 8 | 4 | 6 | .667 | 3 | 3 | 1.000 | 1 | 2 | 0 | 0 | 11 |
| 1963—Cincinnati | 16 | 6 | 12 | .500 | 0 | 0 | ... | 4 | 1 | 2 | 0 | 12 |
| Totals | 117 | 38 | 68 | .559 | 13 | 20 | .650 | 21 | 8 | 14 | 0 | 89 |

# UNSELD, WES — C/F

**PERSONAL:** Born March 14, 1946, in Louisville, Ky. ... 6-7/245 (2,00/111,1). ... Full name: Westley Sissel Unseld.
**HIGH SCHOOL:** Seneca (Louisville, Ky.).
**COLLEGE:** Louisville.
**TRANSACTIONS:** Selected by Baltimore Bullets in first round (second pick overall) of 1968 NBA Draft. ... Bullets franchise moved from Baltimore to Washington and renamed Capital Bullets for 1973-74 season. ... Bullets franchise renamed Washington Bullets for 1974-75 season.
**CAREER HONORS:** Elected to Naismith Memorial Basketball Hall of Fame (1988). ... One of the 50 Greatest Players in NBA History (1996).
**MISCELLANEOUS:** Member of NBA championship team (1978). ... Washington Wizards franchise all-time leading rebounder with 13,769 and all-time assists leader with 3,822 (1968-69 through 1980-81).
**CAREER NOTES:** Vice president, Washington Bullets (1981-82 to 1995-96). ... Executive vice president/general manager, Washington Bullets (1996-97 season to present). ... Bullets franchise renamed Washington Wizards for 1997-98 season.

## COLLEGIATE RECORD

NOTES: THE SPORTING NEWS All-America second team (1967, 1968).

| Season Team | G | Min. | FGM | FGA | Pct. | FTM | FTA | Pct. | Reb. | Ast. | Pts. | AVERAGES RPG | APG | PPG |
|---|---|---|---|---|---|---|---|---|---|---|---|---|---|---|
| 64-65—Louisville‡ | 14 | ... | 214 | 312 | .686 | 73 | 124 | .589 | 331 | ... | 501 | 23.6 | ... | 35.8 |
| 65-66—Louisville | 26 | ... | 195 | 374 | .521 | 128 | 202 | .634 | 505 | ... | 518 | 19.4 | ... | 19.9 |
| 66-67—Louisville | 28 | ... | 201 | 374 | .537 | 121 | 177 | .684 | 533 | ... | 523 | 19.0 | ... | 18.7 |
| 67-68—Louisville | 28 | ... | 234 | 382 | .613 | 177 | 275 | .644 | 513 | ... | 645 | 18.3 | ... | 23.0 |
| Varsity totals | 82 | ... | 630 | 1130 | .558 | 426 | 654 | .651 | 1551 | ... | 1686 | 18.9 | ... | 20.6 |

## NBA REGULAR-SEASON RECORD

HONORS: NBA Most Valuable Player (1969). ... NBA Rookie of the Year (1969). ... All-NBA first team (1969). ... NBA All-Rookie team (1969). ... J. Walter Kennedy Citizenship Award (1975).
NOTES: Led NBA with .561 field goal percentage (1976).

| Season Team | G | Min. | FGM | FGA | Pct. | FTM | FTA | Pct. | Reb. | Ast. | PF | Dq. | Pts. | AVERAGES RPG | APG | PPG |
|---|---|---|---|---|---|---|---|---|---|---|---|---|---|---|---|---|
| 68-69—Baltimore | 82 | 2970 | 427 | 897 | .476 | 277 | 458 | .605 | 1491 | 213 | 276 | 4 | 1131 | 18.2 | 2.6 | 13.8 |
| 69-70—Baltimore | 82 | 3234 | 526 | 1015 | .518 | 273 | 428 | .638 | 1370 | 291 | 250 | 2 | 1325 | 16.7 | 3.5 | 16.2 |
| 70-71—Baltimore | 74 | 2904 | 424 | 846 | .501 | 199 | 303 | .657 | 1253 | 293 | 235 | 2 | 1047 | 16.9 | 4.0 | 14.1 |
| 71-72—Baltimore | 76 | 3171 | 409 | 822 | .498 | 171 | 272 | .629 | 1336 | 278 | 218 | 1 | 989 | 17.6 | 3.7 | 13.0 |
| 72-73—Baltimore | 79 | 3085 | 421 | 854 | .493 | 149 | 212 | .703 | 1260 | 347 | 168 | 0 | 991 | 15.9 | 4.4 | 12.5 |

| Season Team | G | Min. | FGM | FGA | Pct. | FTM | FTA | Pct. | REBOUNDS Off. | Def. | Tot. | Ast. | St. | Blk. | TO | Pts. | AVERAGES RPG | APG | PPG |
|---|---|---|---|---|---|---|---|---|---|---|---|---|---|---|---|---|---|---|---|
| 73-74—Capital ............ | 56 | 1727 | 146 | 333 | .438 | 36 | 55 | .655 | 152 | 365 | 517 | 159 | 56 | 16 | ... | 328 | 9.2 | 2.8 | 5.9 |
| 74-75—Washington .... | 73 | 2904 | 273 | 544 | .502 | 126 | 184 | .685 | 318 | 759 | 1077 | 297 | 115 | 68 | ... | 672 | *14.8 | 4.1 | 9.2 |
| 75-76—Washington .... | 78 | 2922 | 318 | 567 | *.561 | 114 | 195 | .585 | 271 | 765 | 1036 | 404 | 84 | 59 | ... | 750 | 13.3 | 5.2 | 9.6 |
| 76-77—Washington .... | 82 | 2860 | 270 | 551 | .490 | 100 | 166 | .602 | 243 | 634 | 877 | 363 | 87 | 45 | ... | 640 | 10.7 | 4.4 | 7.8 |
| 77-78—Washington .... | 80 | 2644 | 257 | 491 | .523 | 93 | 173 | .538 | 286 | 669 | 955 | 326 | 98 | 45 | 173 | 607 | 11.9 | 4.1 | 7.6 |
| 78-79—Washington .... | 77 | 2406 | 346 | 600 | .577 | 151 | 235 | .643 | 274 | 556 | 830 | 315 | 71 | 37 | 156 | 843 | 10.8 | 4.1 | 10.9 |
| 79-80—Washington .... | 82 | 2973 | 327 | 637 | .513 | 139 | 209 | .665 | 334 | 760 | 1094 | 366 | 65 | 61 | 153 | 794 | 13.3 | 4.5 | 9.7 |
| 80-81—Washington .... | 63 | 2032 | 225 | 429 | .524 | 55 | 86 | .640 | 207 | 466 | 673 | 170 | 52 | 36 | 97 | 507 | 10.7 | 2.7 | 8.0 |
| Totals ................... | 984 | 35832 | 4369 | 8586 | .509 | 1883 | 2976 | .633 | ... | | 13769 | 3822 | 628 | 367 | 579 | 10624 | 14.0 | 3.9 | 10.8 |

Three-point field goals: 1979-80, 1-for-2 (.500). 1980-81, 2-for-4 (.500). Totals, 3-for-6 (.500).

Personal fouls/disqualifications: 1973-74, 121/1. 1974-75, 180/1. 1975-76, 203/3. 1976-77, 253/5. 1977-78, 234/2. 1978-79, 204/2. 1979-80, 249/5. 1980-81, 171/1. Totals, 2762/29.

## NBA PLAYOFF RECORD

**NOTES:** NBA Finals Most Valuable Player (1978).

| Season Team | G | Min. | FGM | FGA | Pct. | FTM | FTA | Pct. | Reb. | Ast. | PF | Dq. | Pts. | AVERAGES RPG | APG | PPG |
|---|---|---|---|---|---|---|---|---|---|---|---|---|---|---|---|---|
| 68-69—Baltimore .......................... | 4 | 165 | 30 | 57 | .526 | 15 | 19 | .789 | 74 | 5 | 14 | 0 | 75 | 18.5 | 1.3 | 18.8 |
| 69-70—Baltimore .......................... | 7 | 289 | 29 | 70 | .414 | 15 | 19 | .789 | 165 | 24 | 25 | 1 | 73 | 23.6 | 3.4 | 10.4 |
| 70-71—Baltimore .......................... | 18 | 759 | 96 | 208 | .462 | 46 | 81 | .568 | 339 | 69 | 60 | 0 | 238 | 18.8 | 3.8 | 13.2 |
| 71-72—Baltimore .......................... | 6 | 266 | 32 | 65 | .492 | 10 | 19 | .526 | 75 | 25 | 22 | 0 | 74 | 12.5 | 4.2 | 12.3 |
| 72-73—Baltimore .......................... | 5 | 201 | 20 | 48 | .417 | 9 | 19 | .474 | 76 | 17 | 12 | 0 | 49 | 15.2 | 3.4 | 9.8 |

| Season Team | G | Min. | FGM | FGA | Pct. | FTM | FTA | Pct. | REBOUNDS Off. | Def. | Tot. | Ast. | St. | Blk. | TO | Pts. | AVERAGES RPG | APG | PPG |
|---|---|---|---|---|---|---|---|---|---|---|---|---|---|---|---|---|---|---|---|
| 73-74—Capital ............ | 7 | 297 | 31 | 63 | .492 | 9 | 15 | .600 | 22 | 63 | 85 | 27 | 4 | 1 | ... | 71 | 12.1 | 3.9 | 10.1 |
| 74-75—Washington .... | 17 | 734 | 71 | 130 | .546 | 40 | 61 | .656 | 65 | 211 | 276 | 64 | 15 | 20 | ... | 182 | 16.2 | 3.8 | 10.7 |
| 75-76—Washington .... | 7 | 310 | 18 | 39 | .462 | 13 | 24 | .542 | 26 | 59 | 85 | 28 | 6 | 4 | ... | 49 | 12.1 | 4.0 | 7.0 |
| 76-77—Washington .... | 9 | 368 | 30 | 54 | .556 | 7 | 12 | .583 | 24 | 81 | 105 | 44 | 8 | 6 | ... | 67 | 11.7 | 4.9 | 7.4 |
| 77-78—Washington .... | 18 | 677 | 71 | 134 | .530 | 27 | 46 | .587 | 72 | 144 | 216 | 79 | 17 | 7 | 36 | 169 | 12.0 | 4.4 | 9.4 |
| 78-79—Washington .... | 19 | 736 | 78 | 158 | .494 | 39 | 64 | .609 | 90 | 163 | 253 | 64 | 17 | 14 | 30 | 195 | 13.3 | 3.4 | 10.3 |
| 79-80—Washington .... | 2 | 87 | 7 | 14 | .500 | 4 | 6 | .667 | 7 | 21 | 28 | 7 | 0 | 3 | 3 | 18 | 14.0 | 3.5 | 9.0 |
| Totals ................... | 119 | 4889 | 513 | 1040 | .493 | 234 | 385 | .608 | ... | | 1777 | 453 | 67 | 55 | 69 | 1260 | 14.9 | 3.8 | 10.6 |

Three-point field goals: 1979-80, 0-for-1.

Personal fouls/disqualifications: 1973-74, 15/0. 1974-75, 39/0. 1975-76, 19/0. 1976-77, 32/0. 1977-78, 62/2. 1978-79, 66/2. 1979-80, 5/0. Totals, 371/5.

## NBA ALL-STAR GAME RECORD

| Season Team | Min. | FGM | FGA | Pct. | FTM | FTA | Pct. | Reb | Ast. | PF | Dq. | Pts. |
|---|---|---|---|---|---|---|---|---|---|---|---|---|
| 1969—Baltimore ..................... | 14 | 5 | 7 | .714 | 1 | 3 | .333 | 8 | 1 | 3 | 0 | 11 |
| 1971—Baltimore ..................... | 21 | 4 | 9 | .444 | 0 | 0 | ... | 10 | 2 | 2 | 0 | 8 |
| 1972—Baltimore‡ .................... | 16 | 1 | 5 | .200 | 0 | 0 | ... | 7 | 1 | 3 | 0 | 2 |
| 1973—Baltimore ..................... | 11 | 2 | 4 | .500 | 0 | 0 | ... | 5 | 1 | 0 | 0 | 4 |

| Season Team | Min. | FGM | FGA | Pct. | FTM | FTA | Pct. | REBOUNDS Off. | Def. | Tot. | Ast. | PF | Dq. | St. | Blk. | TO | Pts. |
|---|---|---|---|---|---|---|---|---|---|---|---|---|---|---|---|---|---|
| 1975—Washington.......... | 15 | 2 | 3 | .667 | 2 | 2 | 1.000 | 2 | 4 | 6 | 1 | 2 | 0 | 2 | 0 | ... | 6 |
| Totals.......................... | 77 | 14 | 28 | .500 | 3 | 5 | .600 | ... | | 36 | 6 | 10 | 0 | 2 | 0 | ... | 31 |

## NBA COACHING RECORD

**BACKGROUND:** Assistant coach, Bullets (1987-January 3, 1988).

| Season Team | REGULAR SEASON W | L | Pct. | Finish | PLAYOFFS W | L | Pct. |
|---|---|---|---|---|---|---|---|
| 87-88—Washington .............................. | 30 | 25 | .545 | T2nd/Atlantic Division | 2 | 3 | .400 |
| 88-89—Washington .............................. | 40 | 42 | .488 | 4th/Atlantic Division | — | — | — |
| 89-90—Washington .............................. | 31 | 51 | .378 | 4th/Atlantic Division | — | — | — |
| 90-91—Washington .............................. | 30 | 52 | .366 | 4th/Atlantic Division | — | — | — |
| 91-92—Washington .............................. | 25 | 57 | .305 | 6th/Atlantic Division | — | — | — |
| 92-93—Washington .............................. | 22 | 60 | .268 | 7th/Atlantic Division | — | — | — |
| 93-94—Washington .............................. | 24 | 58 | .293 | 7th/Atlantic Division | — | — | — |
| Totals (7 years)................................ | 202 | 345 | .369 | Totals (1 year)......... | 2 | 3 | .400 |

**NOTES:**

1988—Replaced Kevin Loughery as Washington head coach (January 3), with record of 8-19. Lost to Detroit in Eastern Conference First Round.

# WALKER, CHET — F/G

**PERSONAL:** Born February 22, 1940, in Benton Harbor, Mich. ... 6-7/220 (2,00/99,8). ... Full name: Chester Walker. ... Nickname: The Jet.

**HIGH SCHOOL:** Benton Harbor (Mich.).

**COLLEGE:** Bradley.

**TRANSACTIONS:** Selected by Syracuse Nationals in second round (14th pick overall) of 1962 NBA Draft. ... Nationals franchise moved from Syracuse to Philadelphia and renamed 76ers for 1963-64 season. ... Traded by 76ers with F Shaler Halimon to Chicago Bulls for F Jim Washington and player to be named later (September 2, 1969).

**MISCELLANEOUS:** Member of NBA championship team (1967).

## COLLEGIATE RECORD

**NOTES:** THE SPORTING NEWS All-America first team (1962). ... THE SPORTING NEWS All-America second team (1961).

| Season Team | G | Min. | FGM | FGA | Pct. | FTM | FTA | Pct. | Reb. | Ast. | Pts. | AVERAGES RPG | APG | PPG |
|---|---|---|---|---|---|---|---|---|---|---|---|---|---|---|
| 58-59—Bradley‡ ......................... | 15 | ... | 146 | 264 | .553 | 56 | 93 | .602 | 246 | ... | 348 | 16.4 | ... | 23.2 |
| 59-60—Bradley ......................... | 29 | ... | 244 | 436 | .560 | 144 | 234 | .615 | 388 | ... | 632 | 13.4 | ... | 21.8 |
| 60-61—Bradley ......................... | 26 | ... | 238 | 423 | .563 | 180 | 250 | .720 | 327 | ... | 656 | 12.6 | ... | 25.2 |
| 61-62—Bradley ......................... | 26 | ... | 268 | 500 | .536 | 151 | 236 | .640 | 321 | ... | 687 | 12.3 | ... | 26.4 |
| Varsity totals ......................... | 81 | ... | 750 | 1359 | .552 | 475 | 720 | .660 | 1036 | ... | 1975 | 12.8 | ... | 24.4 |

**HONORS:** NBA All-Rookie team (1963).

## NBA REGULAR-SEASON RECORD

| | | | | | | | | | | | | | | AVERAGES | | |
|---|---|---|---|---|---|---|---|---|---|---|---|---|---|---|---|---|
| Season Team | G | Min. | FGM | FGA | Pct. | FTM | FTA | Pct. | Reb. | Ast. | PF | Dq. | Pts. | RPG | APG | PPG |
| 62-63—Syracuse | 78 | 1992 | 352 | 751 | .469 | 253 | 362 | .699 | 561 | 83 | 220 | 3 | 957 | 7.2 | 1.1 | 12.3 |
| 63-64—Philadelphia | 76 | 2775 | 492 | 1118 | .440 | 330 | 464 | .711 | 784 | 124 | 232 | 3 | 1314 | 10.3 | 1.6 | 17.3 |
| 64-65—Philadelphia | 79 | 2187 | 377 | 936 | .403 | 288 | 388 | .742 | 528 | 132 | 200 | 2 | 1042 | 6.7 | 1.7 | 13.2 |
| 65-66—Philadelphia | 80 | 2603 | 443 | 982 | .451 | 335 | 468 | .716 | 636 | 201 | 238 | 3 | 1221 | 8.0 | 2.5 | 15.3 |
| 66-67—Philadelphia | 81 | 2691 | 561 | 1150 | .488 | 445 | 581 | .766 | 660 | 188 | 232 | 4 | 1567 | 8.1 | 2.3 | 19.3 |
| 67-68—Philadelphia | 82 | 2623 | 539 | 1172 | .460 | 387 | 533 | .726 | 607 | 157 | 252 | 3 | 1465 | 7.4 | 1.9 | 17.9 |
| 68-69—Philadelphia | 82 | 2753 | 554 | 1145 | .484 | 369 | 459 | .804 | 640 | 144 | 244 | 0 | 1477 | 7.8 | 1.8 | 18.0 |
| 69-70—Chicago | 78 | 2726 | 596 | 1249 | .477 | 483 | 568 | .850 | 604 | 192 | 203 | 1 | 1675 | 7.7 | 2.5 | 21.5 |
| 70-71—Chicago | 81 | 2927 | 650 | 1398 | .465 | 480 | 559 | *.859 | 588 | 179 | 187 | 2 | 1780 | 7.3 | 2.2 | 22.0 |
| 71-72—Chicago | 78 | 2588 | 619 | 1225 | .505 | 481 | 568 | .847 | 473 | 178 | 171 | 0 | 1719 | 6.1 | 2.3 | 22.0 |
| 72-73—Chicago | 79 | 2455 | 597 | 1248 | .478 | 376 | 452 | .832 | 395 | 179 | 166 | 1 | 1570 | 5.0 | 2.3 | 19.9 |

| | | | | | | | | | REBOUNDS | | | | | | AVERAGES | | |
|---|---|---|---|---|---|---|---|---|---|---|---|---|---|---|---|---|---|
| Season Team | G | Min. | FGM | FGA | Pct. | FTM | FTA | Pct. | Off. | Def. | Tot. | Ast. | St. | Blk. | TO | Pts. | RPG | APG | PPG |
| 73-74—Chicago | 82 | 2661 | 572 | 1178 | .486 | 439 | 502 | .875 | 131 | 275 | 406 | 200 | 68 | 4 | ... | 1583 | 5.0 | 2.4 | 19.3 |
| 74-75—Chicago | 76 | 2452 | 524 | 1076 | .487 | 413 | 480 | .860 | 114 | 318 | 432 | 169 | 49 | 6 | ... | 1461 | 5.7 | 2.2 | 19.2 |
| Totals | 1032 | 33433 | 6876 | 14628 | .470 | 5079 | 6384 | .796 | ... | ... | 7314 | 2126 | 117 | 10 | ... | 18831 | 7.1 | 2.1 | 18.2 |

Personal fouls/disqualifications: 1973-74, 201/1. 1974-75, 181/0. Totals, 2727/23.

## NBA PLAYOFF RECORD

| | | | | | | | | | | | | | | AVERAGES | | |
|---|---|---|---|---|---|---|---|---|---|---|---|---|---|---|---|---|
| Season Team | G | Min. | FGM | FGA | Pct. | FTM | FTA | Pct. | Reb. | Ast. | PF | Dq. | Pts. | RPG | APG | PPG |
| 62-63—Syracuse | 5 | 130 | 27 | 53 | .509 | 22 | 30 | .733 | 47 | 9 | 8 | 0 | 76 | 9.4 | 1.8 | 15.2 |
| 63-64—Philadelphia | 5 | 190 | 30 | 77 | .390 | 34 | 46 | .739 | 52 | 13 | 15 | 0 | 94 | 10.4 | 2.6 | 18.8 |
| 64-65—Philadelphia | 11 | 469 | 83 | 173 | .480 | 57 | 75 | .760 | 79 | 18 | 38 | 0 | 223 | 7.2 | 1.6 | 20.3 |
| 65-66—Philadelphia | 5 | 181 | 24 | 64 | .375 | 25 | 31 | .806 | 37 | 15 | 18 | 0 | 73 | 7.4 | 3.0 | 14.6 |
| 66-67—Philadelphia | 15 | 551 | 115 | 246 | .467 | 96 | 119 | .807 | 114 | 32 | 44 | 0 | 326 | 7.6 | 2.1 | 21.7 |
| 67-68—Philadelphia | 13 | 485 | 86 | 210 | .410 | 76 | 112 | .679 | 96 | 24 | 44 | 1 | 248 | 7.4 | 1.8 | 19.1 |
| 68-69—Philadelphia | 4 | 109 | 23 | 43 | .535 | 8 | 12 | .667 | 23 | 8 | 5 | 0 | 54 | 5.8 | 2.0 | 13.5 |
| 69-70—Chicago | 5 | 178 | 35 | 83 | .422 | 27 | 33 | .818 | 42 | 11 | 14 | 0 | 97 | 8.4 | 2.2 | 19.4 |
| 70-71—Chicago | 7 | 234 | 44 | 100 | .440 | 17 | 24 | .708 | 50 | 22 | 20 | 0 | 105 | 7.1 | 3.1 | 15.0 |
| 71-72—Chicago | 4 | 97 | 16 | 38 | .421 | 13 | 16 | .813 | 14 | 4 | 7 | 0 | 45 | 3.5 | 1.0 | 11.3 |
| 72-73—Chicago | 7 | 229 | 42 | 121 | .347 | 33 | 37 | .892 | 62 | 14 | 15 | 0 | 117 | 8.9 | 2.0 | 16.7 |

| | | | | | | | | | REBOUNDS | | | | | | AVERAGES | | |
|---|---|---|---|---|---|---|---|---|---|---|---|---|---|---|---|---|---|
| Season Team | G | Min. | FGM | FGA | Pct. | FTM | FTA | Pct. | Off. | Def. | Tot. | Ast. | St. | Blk. | TO | Pts. | RPG | APG | PPG |
| 73-74—Chicago | 11 | 403 | 81 | 159 | .509 | 68 | 79 | .861 | 26 | 35 | 61 | 18 | 10 | 1 | ... | 230 | 5.5 | 1.6 | 20.9 |
| 74-75—Chicago | 13 | 432 | 81 | 164 | .494 | 66 | 75 | .880 | 10 | 50 | 60 | 24 | 13 | 1 | ... | 228 | 4.6 | 1.8 | 17.5 |
| Totals | 105 | 3688 | 687 | 1531 | .449 | 542 | 689 | .787 | ... | ... | 737 | 212 | 23 | 2 | ... | 1916 | 7.0 | 2.0 | 18.2 |

Personal fouls/disqualifications: 1973-74, 26/0. 1974-75, 32/2. Totals, 286/3.

## NBA ALL-STAR GAME RECORD

| Season Team | Min. | FGM | FGA | Pct. | FTM | FTA | Pct. | Reb | Ast. | PF | Dq. | Pts. |
|---|---|---|---|---|---|---|---|---|---|---|---|---|
| 1964—Philadelphia | 12 | 2 | 5 | .400 | 0 | 0 | ... | 0 | 0 | 1 | 0 | 4 |
| 1966—Philadelphia | 25 | 3 | 10 | .300 | 2 | 3 | .667 | 6 | 4 | 2 | 0 | 8 |
| 1967—Philadelphia | 22 | 6 | 9 | .667 | 3 | 4 | .750 | 4 | 1 | 2 | 0 | 15 |
| 1970—Chicago | 17 | 1 | 3 | .333 | 2 | 2 | 1.000 | 2 | 1 | 2 | 0 | 4 |
| 1971—Chicago | 19 | 3 | 9 | .333 | 4 | 5 | .800 | 3 | 1 | 1 | 0 | 10 |
| 1973—Chicago | 16 | 1 | 5 | .200 | 2 | 2 | 1.000 | 1 | 0 | 2 | 0 | 4 |

| | | | | | | | | REBOUNDS | | | | | | | |
|---|---|---|---|---|---|---|---|---|---|---|---|---|---|---|---|
| Season Team | Min. | FGM | FGA | Pct. | FTM | FTA | Pct. | Off. | Def. | Tot. | Ast. | PF | Dq. | St. | Blk. | TO | Pts. |
| 1974—Chicago | 14 | 4 | 5 | .800 | 4 | 4 | 1.000 | 0 | 2 | 2 | 1 | 1 | 0 | 0 | 0 | ... | 12 |
| Totals | 125 | 20 | 46 | .435 | 17 | 20 | .850 | ... | ... | 18 | 8 | 11 | 0 | 0 | 0 | ... | 57 |

# WALTON, BILL          C

**PERSONAL:** Born November 5, 1952, in La Mesa, Calif. ... 6-11/235 (2,10/106,6). ... Full name: William Theodore Walton III. ... Brother of Bruce Walton, offensive lineman with Dallas Cowboys (1973-75).

**HIGH SCHOOL:** Helix (La Mesa, Calif.).

**COLLEGE:** UCLA.

**TRANSACTIONS:** Selected by Portland Trail Blazers in first round (first pick overall) of 1974 NBA Draft. ... Signed as veteran free agent by San Diego Clippers (May 13, 1979); Trail Blazers received C Kevin Kunnert, F Kermit Washington, 1980 first-round draft choice and cash as compensation (September 18, 1979). ... Clippers franchise moved from San Diego to Los Angeles for 1984-85 season. ... Traded by Clippers to Boston Celtics for F Cedric Maxwell, 1986 first-round draft choice and cash (September 6, 1985).

**CAREER HONORS:** Elected to Naismith Memorial Basketball Hall of Fame (1993). ... One of the 50 Greatest Players in NBA History (1996).

**CAREER NOTES:** Broadcaster, NBC Sports (1992-2002). ... Analyst, ABC/ESPN (2002-03 – present).

**MISCELLANEOUS:** Member of NBA championship team (1977, 1986).

## COLLEGIATE RECORD

**NOTES:** THE SPORTING NEWS College Player of the Year (1972, 1973, 1974). ... Naismith Award winner (1972, 1973, 1974). ... THE SPORTING NEWS All-America first team (1972, 1973, 1974). ... NCAA Division I Tournament Most Outstanding Player (1972, 1973). ... Member of NCAA Division I championship team (1972, 1973). ... Holds NCAA Tournament career record for highest field goal percentage (minimum of 60 made)—68.6 percent, 109-of-159 (1972 through 1974). ... Holds NCAA Tournament single-season record for highest field goal percentage (minimum of 40 made)—76.3 percent, 45-of-59 (1973).

| | | | | | | | | | | | | AVERAGES | | |
|---|---|---|---|---|---|---|---|---|---|---|---|---|---|---|
| Season Team | G | Min. | FGM | FGA | Pct. | FTM | FTA | Pct. | Reb. | Ast. | Pts. | RPG | APG | PPG |
| 70-71—UCLA‡ | 20 | ... | 155 | 266 | .583 | 52 | 82 | .634 | 321 | 74 | 362 | 16.1 | 3.7 | 18.1 |
| 71-72—UCLA | 30 | ... | 238 | 372 | .640 | 157 | 223 | .704 | 466 | ... | 633 | 15.5 | ... | 21.1 |
| 72-73—UCLA | 30 | ... | 277 | 426 | .650 | 58 | 102 | .569 | 506 | 168 | 612 | 16.9 | 5.6 | 20.4 |
| 73-74—UCLA | 27 | ... | 232 | 349 | .665 | 58 | 100 | .580 | 398 | 148 | 522 | 14.7 | 5.5 | 19.3 |
| Varsity totals | 87 | ... | 747 | 1147 | .651 | 273 | 425 | .642 | 1370 | ... | 1767 | 15.7 | ... | 20.3 |

## NBA REGULAR-SEASON RECORD

**HONORS:** NBA Most Valuable Player (1978). ... NBA Sixth Man Award (1986). ... All-NBA first team (1978). ... All-NBA second team (1977). ... NBA All-Defensive first team (1977, 1978).
**NOTES:** Led NBA with 3.25 blocked shots per game (1977).

| | | | | | | | | | REBOUNDS | | | | | | | | AVERAGES | | |
|---|---|---|---|---|---|---|---|---|---|---|---|---|---|---|---|---|---|---|---|
| Season Team | G | Min. | FGM | FGA | Pct. | FTM | FTA | Pct. | Off. | Def. | Tot. | Ast. | St. | Blk. | TO | Pts. | RPG | APG | PPG |
| 74-75—Portland | 35 | 1153 | 177 | 345 | .513 | 94 | 137 | .686 | 92 | 349 | 441 | 167 | 29 | 94 | ... | 448 | 12.6 | 4.8 | 12.8 |
| 75-76—Portland | 51 | 1687 | 345 | 732 | .471 | 133 | 228 | .583 | 132 | 549 | 681 | 220 | 49 | 82 | ... | 823 | 13.4 | 4.3 | 16.1 |
| 76-77—Portland | 65 | 2264 | 491 | 930 | .528 | 228 | 327 | .697 | 211 | 723 | 934 | 245 | 66 | 211 | ... | 1210 | *14.4 | 3.8 | 18.6 |
| 77-78—Portland | 58 | 1929 | 460 | 882 | .522 | 177 | 246 | .720 | 118 | 648 | 766 | 291 | 60 | 146 | 206 | 1097 | 13.2 | 5.0 | 18.9 |
| 78-79—Portland | | | | | | | | | Did not play—injured. | | | | | | | | | | |
| 79-80—San Diego | 14 | 337 | 81 | 161 | .503 | 32 | 54 | .593 | 28 | 98 | 126 | 34 | 8 | 38 | 37 | 194 | 9.0 | 2.4 | 13.9 |
| 80-81—San Diego | | | | | | | | | Did not play—injured. | | | | | | | | | | |
| 81-82—San Diego | | | | | | | | | Did not play—injured. | | | | | | | | | | |
| 82-83—San Diego | 33 | 1099 | 200 | 379 | .528 | 65 | 117 | .556 | 75 | 248 | 323 | 120 | 34 | 119 | 105 | 465 | 9.8 | 3.6 | 14.1 |
| 83-84—San Diego | 55 | 1476 | 288 | 518 | .556 | 92 | 154 | .597 | 132 | 345 | 477 | 183 | 45 | 88 | 177 | 668 | 8.7 | 3.3 | 12.1 |
| 84-85—L.A. Clippers | 67 | 1647 | 269 | 516 | .521 | 138 | 203 | .680 | 168 | 432 | 600 | 156 | 50 | 140 | 174 | 676 | 9.0 | 2.3 | 10.1 |
| 85-86—Boston | 80 | 1546 | 231 | 411 | .562 | 144 | 202 | .713 | 136 | 408 | 544 | 165 | 38 | 106 | 151 | 606 | 6.8 | 2.1 | 7.6 |
| 86-87—Boston | 10 | 112 | 10 | 26 | .385 | 8 | 15 | .533 | 11 | 20 | 31 | 9 | 1 | 10 | 15 | 28 | 3.1 | 0.9 | 2.8 |
| 87-88—Boston | | | | | | | | | Did not play—injured. | | | | | | | | | | |
| **Totals** | 468 | 13250 | 2552 | 4900 | .521 | 1111 | 1683 | .660 | 1103 | 3820 | 4923 | 1590 | 380 | 1034 | 865 | 6215 | 10.5 | 3.4 | 13.3 |

Three-point field goals: 1983-84, 0-for-2. 1984-85, 0-for-2. Totals, 0-for-4.
Personal fouls/disqualifications: 1974-75, 115/4. 1975-76, 144/3. 1976-77, 174/5. 1977-78, 145/3. 1979-80, 37/0. 1982-83, 113/0. 1983-84, 153/1. 1984-85, 184/0. 1985-86, 210/1. 1986-87, 23/0. Totals, 1298/17.

## NBA PLAYOFF RECORD

**NOTES:** NBA Finals Most Valuable Player (1977). ... Holds NBA Finals single-game record for most defensive rebounds—20 (June 3, 1977, vs. Philadelphia; and June 5, 1977, vs. Philadelphia). ... Shares NBA Finals single-game record for most blocked shots—8 (June 5, 1977, vs. Philadelphia). ... Shares single-game NBA playoff record for most defensive rebounds—20 (June 3, 1977, vs. Philadelphia; and June 5, 1977, vs. Philadelphia).

| | | | | | | | | | REBOUNDS | | | | | | | | AVERAGES | | |
|---|---|---|---|---|---|---|---|---|---|---|---|---|---|---|---|---|---|---|---|
| Season Team | G | Min. | FGM | FGA | Pct. | FTM | FTA | Pct. | Off. | Def. | Tot. | Ast. | St. | Blk. | TO | Pts. | RPG | APG | PPG |
| 76-77—Portland | 19 | 755 | 153 | 302 | .507 | 39 | 57 | .684 | 56 | 232 | 288 | 104 | 20 | 64 | ... | 345 | 15.2 | 5.5 | 18.2 |
| 77-78—Portland | 2 | 49 | 11 | 18 | .611 | 5 | 7 | .714 | 5 | 17 | 22 | 4 | 3 | 3 | 6 | 27 | 11.0 | 2.0 | 13.5 |
| 85-86—Boston | 16 | 291 | 54 | 93 | .581 | 19 | 23 | .826 | 25 | 78 | 103 | 27 | 6 | 12 | 22 | 127 | 6.4 | 1.7 | 7.9 |
| 86-87—Boston | 12 | 102 | 12 | 25 | .480 | 5 | 14 | .357 | 9 | 22 | 31 | 10 | 3 | 4 | 8 | 29 | 2.6 | 0.8 | 2.4 |
| **Totals** | 49 | 1197 | 230 | 438 | .525 | 68 | 101 | .673 | 95 | 349 | 444 | 145 | 32 | 83 | 36 | 528 | 9.1 | 3.0 | 10.8 |

Three-point field goals: 1985-86, 0-for-1.
Personal fouls/disqualifications: 1976-77, 80/3. 1977-78, 1/0. 1985-86, 45/1. 1986-87, 23/0. Totals, 149/4.

## NBA ALL-STAR GAME RECORD

| | | | | | | | | REBOUNDS | | | | | | | | |
|---|---|---|---|---|---|---|---|---|---|---|---|---|---|---|---|---|
| Season Team | Min. | FGM | FGA | Pct. | FTM | FTA | Pct. | Off. | Def. | Tot. | Ast. | PF | Dq. | St. | Blk. | TO | Pts. |
| 1977—Portland | | | | | | | | Selected, did not play—injured. | | | | | | | | | |
| 1978—Portland | 31 | 6 | 14 | .429 | 3 | 3 | 1.000 | 2 | 8 | 10 | 2 | 3 | 0 | 3 | 2 | 4 | 15 |
| **Totals** | 31 | 6 | 14 | .429 | 3 | 3 | 1.000 | 2 | 8 | 10 | 2 | 3 | 0 | 3 | 2 | 4 | 15 |

# WEST, JERRY          G

**PERSONAL:** Born May 28, 1938, in Chelyan, W.Va. ... 6-2/185 (1,88/83,9). ... Full name: Jerry Alan West.
**HIGH SCHOOL:** East Bank (W.Va.).
**COLLEGE:** West Virginia.
**TRANSACTIONS:** Selected by Minneapolis Lakers in first round (second pick overall) of 1960 NBA Draft. ... Lakers franchise moved from Minneapolis to Los Angeles for 1960-61 season.
**CAREER HONORS:** Elected to Naismith Memorial Basketball Hall of Fame (1980). ... NBA 35th Anniversary All-Time Team (1980) and One of the 50 Greatest Players in NBA History (1996).
**CAREER NOTES:** Consultant, Los Angeles Lakers (1979-80 through 1981-82). ... General manager, Lakers (1982-83 through 1993-94). ... Executive vice president, basketball operations, Lakers (1994-95 to 1999-2000). ... President of basketball operations, Memphis Grizzlies (2002-present).
**MISCELLANEOUS:** Member of NBA championship team (1972). ... Member of gold-medal-winning U.S. Olympic team (1960). ... Los Angeles Lakers franchise all-time leading scorer with 25,192 points (1960-61 through 1973-74).

## COLLEGIATE RECORD

**NOTES:** THE SPORTING NEWS All-America first team (1959, 1960). ... NCAA Tournament Most Outstanding Player (1959).

| | | | | | | | | | | | AVERAGES | | |
|---|---|---|---|---|---|---|---|---|---|---|---|---|---|
| Season Team | G | Min. | FGM | FGA | Pct. | FTM | FTA | Pct. | Reb. | Ast. | Pts. | RPG | APG | PPG |
| 56-57—West Virginia‡ | 17 | ... | 114 | ... | ... | 104 | ... | ... | ... | ... | 332 | ... | ... | 19.5 |
| 57-58—West Virginia | 28 | 799 | 178 | 359 | .496 | 142 | 194 | .732 | 311 | 41 | 498 | 11.1 | 1.5 | 17.8 |
| 58-59—West Virginia | 34 | 1210 | 340 | 656 | .518 | 223 | 320 | .697 | 419 | 86 | 903 | 12.3 | 2.5 | 26.6 |
| 59-60—West Virginia | 31 | 1129 | 325 | 645 | .504 | 258 | 337 | .766 | 510 | 134 | 908 | 16.5 | 4.3 | 29.3 |
| **Varsity totals** | 93 | 3138 | 843 | 1660 | .508 | 623 | 851 | .732 | 1240 | 261 | 2309 | 13.3 | 2.8 | 24.8 |

## NBA REGULAR-SEASON RECORD

**RECORDS:** Holds single-season record for most free throws made—840 (1966).
**HONORS:** All-NBA first team (1962, 1963, 1964, 1965, 1966, 1967, 1970, 1971, 1972, 1973). ... All-NBA second team (1968, 1969). ... NBA All-Defensive first team (1970, 1971, 1972, 1973). ... NBA All-Defensive second team (1969).

| | | | | | | | | | | | | | | AVERAGES | | |
|---|---|---|---|---|---|---|---|---|---|---|---|---|---|---|---|---|
| Season Team | G | Min. | FGM | FGA | Pct. | FTM | FTA | Pct. | Reb. | Ast. | PF | Dq. | Pts. | RPG | APG | PPG |
| 60-61—Los Angeles | 79 | 2797 | 529 | 1264 | .419 | 331 | 497 | .666 | 611 | 333 | 213 | 1 | 1389 | 7.7 | 4.2 | 17.6 |
| 61-62—Los Angeles | 75 | 3087 | 799 | 1795 | .445 | 712 | 926 | .769 | 591 | 402 | 173 | 4 | 2310 | 7.9 | 5.4 | 30.8 |
| 62-63—Los Angeles | 55 | 2163 | 559 | 1213 | .461 | 371 | 477 | .777 | 384 | 307 | 150 | 1 | 1489 | 7.0 | 5.6 | 27.1 |
| 63-64—Los Angeles | 72 | 2906 | 740 | 1529 | .484 | 584 | 702 | .832 | 443 | 403 | 200 | 2 | 2064 | 6.2 | 5.6 | 28.7 |
| 64-65—Los Angeles | 74 | 3066 | 822 | 1655 | .497 | 648 | 789 | .821 | 447 | 364 | 221 | 2 | 2292 | 6.0 | 4.9 | 31.0 |
| 65-66—Los Angeles | 79 | 3218 | 818 | 1731 | .473 | *840 | *977 | .860 | 562 | 480 | 243 | 1 | 2476 | 7.1 | 6.1 | 31.3 |
| 66-67—Los Angeles | 66 | 2670 | 645 | 1389 | .464 | 602 | 686 | .878 | 392 | 447 | 160 | 1 | 1892 | 5.9 | 6.8 | 28.7 |
| 67-68—Los Angeles | 51 | 1919 | 476 | 926 | .514 | 391 | 482 | .811 | 294 | 310 | 152 | 1 | 1343 | 5.8 | 6.1 | 26.3 |

*ALL-TIME GREAT PLAYERS* (vertical side text)

| Season Team | G | Min. | FGM | FGA | Pct. | FTM | FTA | Pct. | Reb. | Ast. | PF | Dq. | Pts. | RPG | APG | PPG |
|---|---|---|---|---|---|---|---|---|---|---|---|---|---|---|---|---|
| 68-69—Los Angeles | 61 | 2394 | 545 | 1156 | .471 | 490 | 597 | .821 | 262 | 423 | 156 | 1 | 1580 | 4.3 | 6.9 | 25.9 |
| 69-70—Los Angeles | 74 | 3106 | 831 | 1673 | .497 | *647 | *785 | .824 | 338 | 554 | 160 | 3 | 2309 | 4.6 | 7.5 | *31.2 |
| 70-71—Los Angeles | 69 | 2845 | 667 | 1351 | .494 | 525 | 631 | .832 | 320 | 655 | 180 | 0 | 1859 | 4.6 | 9.5 | 26.9 |
| 71-72—Los Angeles | 77 | 2973 | 735 | 1540 | .477 | 515 | 633 | .814 | 327 | 747 | 209 | 0 | 1985 | 4.2 | *9.7 | 25.8 |
| 72-73—Los Angeles | 69 | 2460 | 618 | 1291 | .479 | 339 | 421 | .805 | 289 | 607 | 138 | 0 | 1575 | 4.2 | 8.8 | 22.8 |

| Season Team | G | Min. | FGM | FGA | Pct. | FTM | FTA | Pct. | REBOUNDS Off. | Def. | Tot. | Ast. | St. | Blk. | TO | Pts. | AVERAGES RPG | APG | PPG |
|---|---|---|---|---|---|---|---|---|---|---|---|---|---|---|---|---|---|---|---|
| 73-74—Los Angeles | 31 | 967 | 232 | 519 | .447 | 165 | 198 | .833 | 30 | 86 | 116 | 206 | 81 | 23 | ... | 629 | 3.7 | 6.6 | 20.3 |
| Totals | 932 | 36571 | 9016 | 19032 | .474 | 7160 | 8801 | .814 | ... | ... | 5376 | 6238 | 81 | 23 | ... | 25192 | 5.8 | 6.7 | 27.0 |

Personal fouls/disqualifications: 1973-74, 80/0.

### NBA PLAYOFF RECORD

**NOTES:** NBA Finals Most Valuable Player (1969). ... Holds single-series playoff record for highest points-per-game average—46.3 (1965).

| Season Team | G | Min. | FGM | FGA | Pct. | FTM | FTA | Pct. | Reb. | Ast. | PF | Dq. | Pts. | RPG | APG | PPG |
|---|---|---|---|---|---|---|---|---|---|---|---|---|---|---|---|---|---|
| 60-61—Los Angeles | 12 | 461 | 99 | 202 | .490 | 77 | 106 | .726 | 104 | 63 | 39 | 0 | 275 | 8.7 | 5.3 | 22.9 |
| 61-62—Los Angeles | 13 | 557 | 144 | 310 | .465 | 121 | 150 | .807 | 88 | 57 | 38 | 0 | 409 | 6.8 | 4.4 | 31.5 |
| 62-63—Los Angeles | 13 | 538 | 144 | 286 | .504 | 74 | 100 | .740 | 106 | 61 | 34 | 0 | 362 | 8.2 | 4.7 | 27.8 |
| 63-64—Los Angeles | 5 | 206 | 57 | 115 | .496 | 42 | 53 | .792 | 36 | 17 | 20 | 0 | 156 | 7.2 | 3.4 | 31.2 |
| 64-65—Los Angeles | 11 | 470 | 155 | 351 | .442 | 137 | 154 | .890 | 63 | 58 | 37 | 0 | 447 | 5.7 | 5.3 | 40.6 |
| 65-66—Los Angeles | 14 | 619 | 185 | 357 | .518 | 109 | 125 | .872 | 88 | 79 | 40 | 0 | 479 | 6.3 | 5.6 | 34.2 |
| 66-67—Los Angeles | 1 | 1 | 0 | 0 | ... | 0 | 0 | ... | 1 | 0 | 0 | 0 | 0 | 1.0 | 0.0 | 0.0 |
| 67-68—Los Angeles | 15 | 622 | 165 | 313 | .527 | 132 | 169 | .781 | 81 | 82 | 47 | 0 | 462 | 5.4 | 5.5 | 30.8 |
| 68-69—Los Angeles | 18 | 757 | 196 | 423 | .463 | 164 | 204 | .804 | 71 | 135 | 52 | 1 | 556 | 3.9 | 7.5 | 30.9 |
| 69-70—Los Angeles | 18 | 830 | 196 | 418 | .469 | 170 | 212 | .802 | 66 | 151 | 55 | 1 | 562 | 3.7 | 8.4 | 31.2 |
| 71-72—Los Angeles | 15 | 608 | 128 | 340 | .376 | 88 | 106 | .830 | 73 | 134 | 39 | 0 | 344 | 4.9 | 8.9 | 22.9 |
| 72-73—Los Angeles | 17 | 638 | 151 | 336 | .449 | 99 | 127 | .780 | 76 | 132 | 49 | 1 | 401 | 4.5 | 7.8 | 23.6 |

| Season Team | G | Min. | FGM | FGA | Pct. | FTM | FTA | Pct. | REBOUNDS Off. | Def. | Tot. | Ast. | St. | Blk. | TO | Pts. | AVERAGES RPG | APG | PPG |
|---|---|---|---|---|---|---|---|---|---|---|---|---|---|---|---|---|---|---|---|
| 73-74—Los Angeles | 1 | 14 | 2 | 9 | .222 | 0 | 0 | ... | 0 | 2 | 2 | 1 | 0 | 0 | ... | 4 | 2.0 | 1.0 | 4.0 |
| Totals | 153 | 6321 | 1622 | 3460 | .469 | 1213 | 1506 | .805 | ... | ... | 855 | 970 | 0 | 0 | ... | 4457 | 5.6 | 6.3 | 29.1 |

Personal fouls/disqualifications: 1973-74, 1/0.

### NBA ALL-STAR GAME RECORD

**NOTES:** NBA All-Star Game Most Valuable Player (1972).

| Season Team | Min. | FGM | FGA | Pct. | FTM | FTA | Pct. | Reb | Ast. | PF | Dq. | Pts. |
|---|---|---|---|---|---|---|---|---|---|---|---|---|
| 1961—Los Angeles | 25 | 2 | 8 | .250 | 5 | 6 | .833 | 2 | 4 | 3 | 0 | 9 |
| 1962—Los Angeles | 31 | 7 | 14 | .500 | 4 | 6 | .667 | 3 | 1 | 2 | 0 | 18 |
| 1963—Los Angeles | 32 | 5 | 15 | .333 | 3 | 4 | .750 | 7 | 5 | 1 | 0 | 13 |
| 1964—Los Angeles | 42 | 8 | 20 | .400 | 1 | 1 | 1.000 | 4 | 5 | 3 | 0 | 17 |
| 1965—Los Angeles | 40 | 8 | 16 | .500 | 4 | 6 | .667 | 5 | 6 | 2 | 0 | 20 |
| 1966—Los Angeles | 11 | 1 | 5 | .200 | 2 | 2 | 1.000 | 1 | 0 | 2 | 0 | 4 |
| 1967—Los Angeles | 30 | 6 | 11 | .545 | 4 | 4 | 1.000 | 3 | 6 | 3 | 0 | 16 |
| 1968—Los Angeles | 32 | 7 | 17 | .412 | 3 | 4 | .750 | 6 | 6 | 4 | 0 | 17 |
| 1969—Los Angeles | | | | | Selected, did not play—injured. | | | | | | | |
| 1970—Los Angeles | 31 | 7 | 12 | .583 | 8 | 12 | .667 | 5 | 5 | 3 | 0 | 22 |
| 1971—Los Angeles | 20 | 2 | 4 | .500 | 1 | 3 | .333 | 1 | 9 | 1 | 0 | 5 |
| 1972—Los Angeles | 27 | 6 | 9 | .667 | 1 | 2 | .500 | 6 | 5 | 2 | 0 | 13 |
| 1973—Los Angeles | 20 | 3 | 6 | .500 | 0 | 0 | ... | 4 | 3 | 2 | 0 | 6 |
| 1974—Los Angeles | | | | | Selected, did not play—injured. | | | | | | | |
| Totals | 341 | 62 | 137 | .453 | 36 | 50 | .720 | 47 | 55 | 28 | 0 | 160 |

### NBA COACHING RECORD

| | | REGULAR SEASON | | | | | PLAYOFFS | | |
|---|---|---|---|---|---|---|---|---|---|
| Season Team | W | L | Pct. | Finish | | W | L | Pct. |
| 76-77—Los Angeles | 53 | 29 | .646 | 1st/Pacific Division | | 4 | 7 | .364 |
| 77-78—Los Angeles | 45 | 37 | .549 | 4th/Pacific Division | | 1 | 2 | .333 |
| 78-79—Los Angeles | 47 | 35 | .573 | 3rd/Pacific Division | | 3 | 5 | .375 |
| Totals (3 years) | 145 | 101 | .589 | | Totals (3 years) | 8 | 14 | .364 |

**NOTES:**
1977—Defeated Golden State, 4-3, in Western Conference Semifinals; lost to Portland, 4-0, in Western Conference Finals.
1978—Lost to Seattle in Western Conference First Round.
1979—Defeated Denver, 2-1, in Western Conference First Round; lost to Seattle, 4-1, in Western Conference Semifinals.

## WESTPHAL, PAUL                    G

**PERSONAL:** Born November 30, 1950, in Torrance, Calif. ... 6-4/195 (1,93/88,4). ... Full name: Paul Douglas Westphal.
**HIGH SCHOOL:** Aviation (Redondo Beach, Calif.).
**COLLEGE:** Southern California.
**TRANSACTIONS:** Selected by Boston Celtics in first round (10th pick overall) of 1972 NBA Draft. ... Traded by Celtics with 1975 and 1976 second-round draft choices to Phoenix Suns for G Charlie Scott (May 23, 1975). ... Traded by Suns to Seattle SuperSonics for G Dennis Johnson (June 4, 1980). ... Signed as veteran free agent by New York Knicks (March 12, 1982). ... Waived by Knicks (June 20, 1983). ... Signed by Suns (September 27, 1983). ... Waived by Suns (October 12, 1984).
**MISCELLANEOUS:** Member of NBA championship team (1974).

### COLLEGIATE RECORD

**NOTES:** The Sporting News All-America second team (1972).

| Season Team | G | Min. | FGM | FGA | Pct. | FTM | FTA | Pct. | Reb. | Ast. | Pts. | AVERAGES RPG | APG | PPG |
|---|---|---|---|---|---|---|---|---|---|---|---|---|---|---|
| 68-69—Southern Cal‡ | 19 | ... | 134 | 262 | .511 | 87 | 119 | .731 | 106 | ... | 355 | 5.6 | ... | 18.7 |
| 69-70—Southern Cal | 26 | ... | 147 | 277 | .531 | 84 | 110 | .764 | 68 | 45 | 378 | 2.6 | 1.7 | 14.5 |
| 70-71—Southern Cal | 26 | ... | 157 | 328 | .479 | 109 | 150 | .727 | 84 | 84 | 423 | 3.2 | 3.2 | 16.3 |
| 71-72—Southern Cal | 14 | ... | 106 | 219 | .484 | 72 | 95 | .758 | 74 | 71 | 284 | 5.3 | 5.1 | 20.3 |
| Varsity totals | 66 | ... | 410 | 824 | .498 | 265 | 355 | .746 | 226 | 200 | 1085 | 3.4 | 3.0 | 16.4 |

## NBA REGULAR-SEASON RECORD

**HONORS:** NBA Comeback Player of the Year (1983). ... All-NBA first team (1977, 1979, 1980). ... All-NBA second team (1978).

| Season Team | G | Min. | FGM | FGA | Pct. | FTM | FTA | Pct. | Off. | Def. | Tot. | Ast. | St. | Blk. | TO | Pts. | RPG | APG | PPG |
|---|---|---|---|---|---|---|---|---|---|---|---|---|---|---|---|---|---|---|---|
| | | | | | | | | | REBOUNDS | | | | | | | | AVERAGES | | |
| 72-73—Boston | 60 | 482 | 89 | 212 | .420 | 67 | 86 | .779 | ... | ... | 67 | 69 | ... | ... | ... | 245 | 1.1 | 1.2 | 4.1 |
| 73-74—Boston | 82 | 1165 | 238 | 475 | .501 | 112 | 153 | .732 | 49 | 94 | 143 | 171 | 39 | 34 | ... | 588 | 1.7 | 2.1 | 7.2 |
| 74-75—Boston | 82 | 1581 | 342 | 670 | .510 | 119 | 156 | .763 | 44 | 119 | 163 | 235 | 78 | 33 | ... | 803 | 2.0 | 2.9 | 9.8 |
| 75-76—Phoenix | 82 | 2960 | 657 | 1329 | .494 | 365 | 440 | .830 | 74 | 185 | 259 | 440 | 210 | 38 | ... | 1679 | 3.2 | 5.4 | 20.5 |
| 76-77—Phoenix | 81 | 2600 | 682 | 1317 | .518 | 362 | 439 | .825 | 57 | 133 | 190 | 459 | 134 | 21 | ... | 1726 | 2.3 | 5.7 | 21.3 |
| 77-78—Phoenix | 80 | 2481 | 809 | 1568 | .516 | 396 | 487 | .813 | 41 | 123 | 164 | 437 | 138 | 31 | 280 | 2014 | 2.1 | 5.5 | 25.2 |
| 78-79—Phoenix | 81 | 2641 | 801 | 1496 | .535 | 339 | 405 | .837 | 35 | 124 | 159 | 529 | 111 | 26 | 232 | 1941 | 2.0 | 6.5 | 24.0 |
| 79-80—Phoenix | 82 | 2665 | 692 | 1317 | .525 | 382 | 443 | .862 | 46 | 141 | 187 | 416 | 119 | 35 | 207 | 1792 | 2.3 | 5.1 | 21.9 |
| 80-81—Seattle | 36 | 1078 | 221 | 500 | .442 | 153 | 184 | .832 | 11 | 57 | 68 | 148 | 46 | 14 | 78 | 601 | 1.9 | 4.1 | 16.7 |
| 81-82—New York | 18 | 451 | 86 | 194 | .443 | 36 | 47 | .766 | 9 | 13 | 22 | 100 | 19 | 8 | 47 | 210 | 1.2 | 5.6 | 11.7 |
| 82-83—New York | 80 | 1978 | 318 | 693 | .459 | 148 | 184 | .804 | 19 | 96 | 115 | 439 | 87 | 16 | 196 | 798 | 1.4 | 5.5 | 10.0 |
| 83-84—Phoenix | 59 | 865 | 144 | 313 | .460 | 117 | 142 | .824 | 8 | 35 | 43 | 148 | 41 | 6 | 77 | 412 | 0.7 | 2.5 | 7.0 |
| **Totals** | 823 | 20947 | 5079 | 10084 | .504 | 2596 | 3166 | .820 | ... | ... | 1580 | 3591 | 1022 | 262 | 1117 | 12809 | 1.9 | 4.4 | 15.6 |

Three-point field goals: 1979-80, 26-for-93 (.280). 1980-81, 6-for-25 (.240). 1981-82, 2-for-8 (.250). 1982-83, 14-for-48 (.292). 1983-84, 7-for-26 (.269). Totals, 55-for-200 (.275).

Personal fouls/disqualifications: 1972-73, 88/0. 1973-74, 173/1. 1974-75, 192/0. 1975-76, 218/3. 1976-77, 171/1. 1977-78, 162/0. 1978-79, 159/1. 1979-80, 162/0. 1980-81, 70/0. 1981-82, 61/1. 1982-83, 180/1. 1983-84, 69/0. Totals, 1705/8.

## NBA PLAYOFF RECORD

| Season Team | G | Min. | FGM | FGA | Pct. | FTM | FTA | Pct. | Off. | Def. | Tot. | Ast. | St. | Blk. | TO | Pts. | RPG | APG | PPG |
|---|---|---|---|---|---|---|---|---|---|---|---|---|---|---|---|---|---|---|---|
| | | | | | | | | | REBOUNDS | | | | | | | | AVERAGES | | |
| 72-73—Boston | 11 | 109 | 19 | 39 | .487 | 5 | 7 | .714 | ... | ... | 7 | 9 | ... | ... | ... | 43 | 0.6 | 0.8 | 3.9 |
| 73-74—Boston | 18 | 241 | 46 | 100 | .460 | 11 | 15 | .733 | 6 | 15 | 21 | 31 | 8 | 2 | ... | 103 | 1.2 | 1.7 | 5.7 |
| 74-75—Boston | 11 | 183 | 38 | 81 | .469 | 12 | 18 | .667 | 5 | 8 | 13 | 32 | 6 | 2 | ... | 88 | 1.2 | 2.9 | 8.0 |
| 75-76—Phoenix | 19 | 685 | 165 | 323 | .511 | 71 | 93 | .763 | 14 | 33 | 47 | 96 | 34 | 9 | ... | 401 | 2.5 | 5.1 | 21.1 |
| 77-78—Phoenix | 2 | 66 | 22 | 47 | .468 | 8 | 9 | .889 | 3 | 3 | 6 | 19 | 1 | 0 | 5 | 52 | 3.0 | 9.5 | 26.0 |
| 78-79—Phoenix | 15 | 534 | 142 | 287 | .495 | 52 | 66 | .788 | 7 | 26 | 33 | 64 | 15 | 5 | 38 | 336 | 2.2 | 4.3 | 22.4 |
| 79-80—Phoenix | 8 | 253 | 69 | 142 | .486 | 28 | 32 | .875 | 2 | 8 | 10 | 31 | 11 | 3 | 13 | 167 | 1.3 | 3.9 | 20.9 |
| 82-83—New York | 6 | 156 | 22 | 50 | .440 | 10 | 13 | .769 | 0 | 8 | 8 | 34 | 2 | 2 | 9 | 57 | 1.3 | 5.7 | 9.5 |
| 83-84—Phoenix | 17 | 222 | 30 | 80 | .375 | 28 | 32 | .875 | 3 | 5 | 8 | 37 | 12 | 0 | 24 | 90 | 0.5 | 2.2 | 5.3 |
| **Totals** | 107 | 2449 | 553 | 1149 | .481 | 225 | 285 | .789 | ... | ... | 153 | 353 | 89 | 23 | 89 | 1337 | 1.4 | 3.3 | 12.5 |

Three-point field goals: 1979-80, 1-for-12 (.083). 1982-83, 3-for-8 (.375). 1983-84, 2-for-9 (.222). Totals, 6-for-29 (.207).

Personal fouls/disqualifications: 1972-73, 24/1. 1973-74, 37/0. 1974-75, 21/0. 1975-76, 61/1. 1977-78, 4/0. 1978-79, 38/0. 1979-80, 20/0. 1982-83, 13/0. 1983-84, 23/0. Totals, 241/2.

## NBA ALL-STAR GAME RECORD

| Season Team | Min. | FGM | FGA | Pct. | FTM | FTA | Pct. | Off. | Def. | Tot. | Ast. | PF | Dq. | St. | Blk. | TO | Pts. |
|---|---|---|---|---|---|---|---|---|---|---|---|---|---|---|---|---|---|
| | | | | | | | | REBOUNDS | | | | | | | | | |
| 1977—Phoenix | 31 | 10 | 16 | .625 | 0 | 0 | | 0 | 1 | 1 | 6 | 2 | 0 | 3 | 2 | ... | 20 |
| 1978—Phoenix | 24 | 9 | 14 | .643 | 2 | 5 | .400 | 0 | 0 | 0 | 5 | 4 | 0 | 1 | 1 | 3 | 20 |
| 1979—Phoenix | 21 | 8 | 12 | .667 | 1 | 2 | .500 | 0 | 1 | 1 | 5 | 0 | 0 | 0 | 1 | 1 | 17 |
| 1980—Phoenix | 27 | 8 | 14 | .571 | 5 | 6 | .833 | 1 | 0 | 1 | 5 | 5 | 0 | 2 | 1 | 3 | 21 |
| 1981—Seattle | 25 | 8 | 12 | .667 | 3 | 3 | 1.000 | 2 | 2 | 4 | 3 | 3 | 0 | 0 | 1 | 4 | 19 |
| **Totals** | 128 | 43 | 68 | .632 | 11 | 16 | .688 | 3 | 4 | 7 | 24 | 14 | 0 | 6 | 5 | 11 | 97 |

Three-point field goals: 1980, 0-for-2.

## HEAD COACHING RECORD

**BACKGROUND:** Assistant coach, Phoenix Suns (1988-89 through 1991-92).

### COLLEGIATE COACHING RECORD

| | REGULAR SEASON | | | |
|---|---|---|---|---|
| Season Team | W | L | Pct. | Finish |
| 85-86—S'western Baptist Bible Coll. | 21 | 9 | .700 | |
| 86-87—Grand Canyon College (Ariz.) | 26 | 12 | .684 | NAIA Independent |
| 87-88—Grand Canyon College (Ariz.) | 37 | 6 | .860 | NAIA Independent |
| 01-02—Pepperdine | 22 | 9 | .710 | T1st/West Coast Conference |
| 02-03—Pepperdine | 15 | 13 | .536 | 4th/West Coast Conference |
| 03-04—Pepperdine | 15 | 16 | .484 | T2nd/West Coast Conference |
| 04-05—Pepperdine | 17 | 14 | .548 | T5th/West Coast Conference |
| **Totals (7 years)** | 131 | 70 | .652 | |

### NBA COACHING RECORD

| | REGULAR SEASON | | | | PLAYOFFS | | |
|---|---|---|---|---|---|---|---|
| Season Team | W | L | Pct. | Finish | W | L | Pct. |
| 92-93—Phoenix | 62 | 20 | .756 | 1st/Pacific Division | 13 | 11 | .542 |
| 93-94—Phoenix | 56 | 26 | .683 | 2nd/Pacific Division | 6 | 4 | .600 |
| 94-95—Phoenix | 59 | 23 | .720 | 1st/Pacific Division | 6 | 4 | .600 |
| 95-96—Phoenix | 14 | 19 | .424 | | — | — | — |
| 98-99—Seattle | 25 | 25 | .500 | 5th/Pacific Division | — | — | — |
| 99-00—Seattle | 45 | 37 | .549 | 4th/Pacific Division | 2 | 3 | .400 |
| 00-01—Seattle | 6 | 9 | .400 | | — | — | — |
| **Totals (7 years)** | 273 | 168 | .619 | **Totals (4 years)** | 27 | 22 | .551 |

**NOTES:**

1987—Defeated Fort Lewis College (Colo.), 94-87, in NAIA District 7 first round; lost to Western State College (Colo.), 74-69, in NAIA District 7 championship.

1988—Defeated Southern Colorado, 68-62, in NAIA District 7 first round; defeated Colorado School of Mines, 113-79, in District 7 championship; defeated Hastings College (Neb.), 103-75, in NAIA Tournament first round; defeated Fort Hays State (Kan.), 101-95, in second round; defeated College of Idaho, 99-96 (OT), in third round; defeated Waynesburg State (Pa.), 108-106, in fourth round; defeated Auburn-Montgomery (Ala.), 88-86 (OT), in NAIA championship game.

1993—Defeated Los Angeles Lakers, 3-2, in Western Conference first round; defeated San Antonio, 4-2, in Western Conference semifinals; defeated Seattle, 4-3, in Western Conference finals; lost to Chicago, 4-2, in NBA Finals.

1994—Defeated Golden State, 3-0, in Western Conference first round; lost to Houston, 4-3, in Western Conference semifinals.

1995—Defeated Portland, 3-0, in Western Conference first round; lost to Houston, 4-3, in Western Conference semifinals.

1996—Replaced as Phoenix head coach by Cotton Fitzsimmons (January 16), with club in fifth place.

2000—Lost to Utah in Western Conference first round. Replaced as Seattle head coach by Nate McMillan (November 27) with club in fifth place.

2002—Lost to Wake Forest, 83-74, in NCAA Tournament first round.

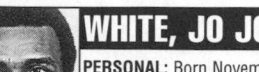

# WHITE, JO JO      G

**PERSONAL:** Born November 16, 1946, in St. Louis. ... 6-3/190 (1,90/86,2). ... Full name: Joseph Henry White.
**HIGH SCHOOL:** Vashon (St. Louis), then McKinley (St. Louis).
**COLLEGE:** Kansas.
**TRANSACTIONS:** Selected by Boston Celtics in first round (ninth pick overall) of 1969 NBA Draft. ... Traded by Celtics to Golden State Warriors for 1979 first-round draft choice (January 30, 1979). ... Contract sold by Warriors to Kansas City Kings (September 10, 1980). ... Played in Continental Basketball Association with Topeka Sizzlers (1987-88).
**CAREER NOTES:** Director of special projects, Boston Celtics (2000-present).
**MISCELLANEOUS:** Member of NBA championship team (1974, 1976). ... Member of gold-medal-winning U.S. Olympic team (1968).

### COLLEGIATE RECORD

**NOTES:** The Sporting News All-America first team (1968, 1969).

| Season Team | G | Min. | FGM | FGA | Pct. | FTM | FTA | Pct. | Reb. | Ast. | Pts. | RPG | APG | PPG |
|---|---|---|---|---|---|---|---|---|---|---|---|---|---|---|
| 64-65—Kansas‡ | 2 | ... | 11 | 34 | .324 | 11 | 15 | .733 | 25 | ... | 33 | 12.5 | ... | 16.5 |
| 65-66—Kansas | 6 | ... | 35 | 88 | .398 | 18 | 27 | .667 | 32 | ... | 88 | 5.3 | ... | 14.7 |
| 65-66—Kansas | 9 | ... | 44 | 112 | .393 | 14 | 26 | .538 | 68 | ... | 102 | 7.6 | ... | 11.3 |
| 66-67—Kansas | 27 | ... | 170 | 416 | .409 | 59 | 72 | .819 | 150 | ... | 399 | 5.6 | ... | 14.8 |
| 67-68—Kansas | 30 | ... | 188 | 462 | .407 | 83 | 115 | .722 | 107 | ... | 459 | 3.6 | ... | 15.3 |
| 68-69—Kansas | 18 | ... | 134 | 286 | .469 | 58 | 79 | .734 | 84 | ... | 326 | 4.7 | ... | 18.1 |
| **Varsity totals** | 84 | ... | 536 | 1276 | .420 | 214 | 292 | .733 | 409 | ... | 1286 | 4.9 | ... | 15.3 |

### NBA REGULAR-SEASON RECORD

**HONORS:** All-NBA second team (1975, 1977). ... NBA All-Rookie team (1970).

| | | | | | | | | | | | | | AVERAGES | | |
|---|---|---|---|---|---|---|---|---|---|---|---|---|---|---|---|
| Season Team | G | Min. | FGM | FGA | Pct. | FTM | FTA | Pct. | Reb. | Ast. | PF | Dq. | Pts. | RPG | APG | PPG |
| 69-70—Boston | 60 | 1328 | 309 | 684 | .452 | 111 | 135 | .822 | 169 | 145 | 132 | 1 | 729 | 2.8 | 2.4 | 12.2 |
| 70-71—Boston | 75 | 2787 | 693 | 1494 | .464 | 215 | 269 | .799 | 376 | 361 | 255 | 5 | 1601 | 5.0 | 4.8 | 21.3 |
| 71-72—Boston | 79 | 3261 | 770 | 1788 | .431 | 285 | 343 | .831 | 446 | 416 | 227 | 1 | 1825 | 5.6 | 5.3 | 23.1 |
| 72-73—Boston | 82 | 3250 | 717 | 1665 | .431 | 178 | 228 | .781 | 414 | 498 | 185 | 2 | 1612 | 5.0 | 6.1 | 19.7 |

| | | | | | | | | | REBOUNDS | | | | | | | AVERAGES | | |
|---|---|---|---|---|---|---|---|---|---|---|---|---|---|---|---|---|---|---|
| Season Team | G | Min. | FGM | FGA | Pct. | FTM | FTA | Pct. | Off. | Def. | Tot. | Ast. | St. | Blk. | TO | Pts. | RPG | APG | PPG |
| 73-74—Boston | 82 | 3238 | 649 | 1445 | .449 | 190 | 227 | .837 | 100 | 251 | 351 | 448 | 105 | 25 | ... | 1488 | 4.3 | 5.5 | 18.1 |
| 74-75—Boston | 82 | 3220 | 658 | 1440 | .457 | 186 | 223 | .834 | 84 | 227 | 311 | 458 | 128 | 17 | ... | 1502 | 3.8 | 5.6 | 18.3 |
| 75-76—Boston | 82 | 3257 | 670 | 1492 | .449 | 212 | 253 | .838 | 61 | 252 | 313 | 445 | 107 | 20 | ... | 1552 | 3.8 | 5.4 | 18.9 |
| 76-77—Boston | 82 | 3333 | 638 | 1488 | .429 | 333 | 383 | .869 | 87 | 296 | 383 | 492 | 118 | 22 | ... | 1609 | 4.7 | 6.0 | 19.6 |
| 77-78—Boston | 46 | 1641 | 289 | 690 | .419 | 103 | 120 | .858 | 53 | 127 | 180 | 209 | 49 | 7 | 117 | 681 | 3.9 | 4.5 | 14.8 |
| 78-79—Boston-G.S. | 76 | 2338 | 404 | 910 | .444 | 139 | 158 | .880 | 42 | 158 | 200 | 347 | 80 | 7 | 212 | 947 | 2.6 | 4.6 | 12.5 |
| 79-80—Golden State | 78 | 2052 | 336 | 706 | .476 | 97 | 114 | .851 | 42 | 139 | 181 | 239 | 88 | 13 | 157 | 770 | 2.3 | 3.1 | 9.9 |
| 80-81—Kansas City | 13 | 236 | 36 | 82 | .439 | 11 | 18 | .611 | 3 | 18 | 21 | 37 | 11 | 1 | 18 | 83 | 1.6 | 2.8 | 6.4 |
| **Totals** | 837 | 29941 | 6169 | 13884 | .444 | 2060 | 2471 | .834 | ... | ... | 3345 | 4095 | 686 | 112 | 504 | 14399 | 4.0 | 4.9 | 17.2 |

Three-point field goals: 1979-80, 1-for-6 (.167).
Personal fouls/disqualifications: 1973-74, 185/1. 1974-75, 207/1. 1975-76, 183/2. 1976-77, 193/5. 1977-78, 109/2. 1978-79, 173/1. 1979-80, 186/0. 1980-81, 21/0. Totals, 2056/21.

### NBA PLAYOFF RECORD

**NOTES:** NBA Finals Most Valuable Player (1976).

| | | | | | | | | | | | | | AVERAGES | | |
|---|---|---|---|---|---|---|---|---|---|---|---|---|---|---|---|---|
| Season Team | G | Min. | FGM | FGA | Pct. | FTM | FTA | Pct. | Reb. | Ast. | PF | Dq. | Pts. | RPG | APG | PPG |
| 71-72—Boston | 11 | 432 | 109 | 220 | .495 | 40 | 48 | .833 | 59 | 58 | 31 | 0 | 258 | 5.4 | 5.3 | 23.5 |
| 72-73—Boston | 13 | 583 | 135 | 300 | .450 | 49 | 54 | .907 | 64 | 83 | 44 | 2 | 319 | 4.9 | 6.4 | 24.5 |

| | | | | | | | | | REBOUNDS | | | | | | | AVERAGES | | |
|---|---|---|---|---|---|---|---|---|---|---|---|---|---|---|---|---|---|---|
| Season Team | G | Min. | FGM | FGA | Pct. | FTM | FTA | Pct. | Off. | Def. | Tot. | Ast. | St. | Blk. | TO | Pts. | RPG | APG | PPG |
| 73-74—Boston | 18 | 765 | 132 | 310 | .426 | 34 | 46 | .739 | 17 | 58 | 75 | 98 | 15 | 2 | ... | 298 | 4.2 | 5.4 | 16.6 |
| 74-75—Boston | 11 | 462 | 100 | 227 | .441 | 27 | 33 | .818 | 18 | 32 | 50 | 63 | 11 | 4 | ... | 227 | 4.5 | 5.7 | 20.6 |
| 75-76—Boston | 18 | 791 | 165 | 371 | .445 | 78 | 95 | .821 | 12 | 59 | 71 | 98 | 23 | 1 | ... | 408 | 3.9 | 5.4 | 22.7 |
| 76-77—Boston | 9 | 395 | 91 | 201 | .453 | 28 | 33 | .848 | 10 | 29 | 39 | 52 | 14 | 0 | ... | 210 | 4.3 | 5.8 | 23.3 |
| **Totals** | 80 | 3428 | 732 | 1629 | .449 | 256 | 309 | .828 | ... | ... | 358 | 452 | 63 | 7 | ... | 1720 | 4.5 | 5.7 | 21.5 |

Personal fouls/disqualifications: 1973-74, 56/1. 1974-75, 32/0. 1975-76, 51/0. 1976-77, 27/0. Totals, 241/3.

### NBA ALL-STAR GAME RECORD

| Season Team | Min. | FGM | FGA | Pct. | FTM | FTA | Pct. | Reb | Ast. | PF | Dq. | Pts. |
|---|---|---|---|---|---|---|---|---|---|---|---|---|
| 1971—Boston | 22 | 5 | 10 | .500 | 0 | 0 | ... | 9 | 2 | 2 | 0 | 10 |
| 1972—Boston | 18 | 6 | 15 | .400 | 0 | 2 | .000 | 4 | 3 | 1 | 0 | 12 |
| 1973—Boston | 18 | 3 | 7 | .429 | 0 | 0 | ... | 5 | 5 | 0 | 0 | 6 |
| 1974—Boston | 22 | 6 | 12 | .500 | 1 | 3 | .333 | 2 | 4 | 6 | 4 | 1 | 0 | 2 | 1 | 13 |
| 1975—Boston | 13 | 1 | 2 | .500 | 5 | 6 | .833 | 1 | 4 | 1 | 0 | 7 |
| 1976—Boston | 16 | 3 | 7 | .429 | 0 | 0 | ... | 1 | 1 | 0 | 0 | 6 |
| 1977—Boston | 15 | 5 | 7 | .714 | 0 | 0 | ... | 2 | 0 | 1 | 0 | 10 |
| **Totals** | 124 | 29 | 60 | .483 | 6 | 11 | .545 | ... | 27 | 21 | 6 | 0 | 4 | 1 | 64 |

### CBA REGULAR-SEASON RECORD

| | | | | | | | | | | | | AVERAGES | | |
|---|---|---|---|---|---|---|---|---|---|---|---|---|---|---|
| Season Team | G | Min. | FGM | FGA | Pct. | FTM | FTA | Pct. | Reb. | Ast. | Pts. | RPG | APG | PPG |
| 87-88—Topeka | 5 | 122 | 12 | 30 | .400 | 4 | 6 | .667 | 6 | 21 | 28 | 1.2 | 4.2 | 5.6 |

Three-point field goals: 1987-88, 0-for-3.

# WILKENS, LENNY      G

See All-Time Great Coaches, page 485.

# WILKINS, DOMINIQUE      F/G

**PERSONAL:** Born January 12, 1960, in Paris. ... 6-8/224 (2,03/101,6). ... Full name: Jacques Dominique Wilkins. ... Brother of Gerald Wilkins, guard/forward with New York Knicks (1985-86 through 1991-92), Cleveland Cavaliers (1992-93 through 1994-95), Vancouver Grizzlies (1995-96) and Orlando Magic (1996-97 through 1998-99).
**HIGH SCHOOL:** Washington (N.C.).
**COLLEGE:** Georgia.
**TRANSACTIONS:** Selected after junior season by Utah Jazz in first round (third pick overall) of 1982 NBA Draft. ... Draft

rights traded by Jazz to Atlanta Hawks for F John Drew, G Freeman Williams and cash (September 2, 1982). ... Traded by Hawks with 1994 conditional first-round draft choice to Los Angeles Clippers for F Danny Manning (February 24, 1994). ... Signed as unrestricted free agent by Boston Celtics (July 25, 1994). ... Played in Greece (1995-96). ... Signed as free agent by San Antonio Spurs (October 4, 1996). ... Played in Italy (1997-98). ... Signed as free agent by Orlando Magic (February 5, 1999). ... Waived by Magic (June 14, 1999).

**CAREER NOTES:** Special assistant to executive vice president, Atlanta Hawks (2001-02-present).

**MISCELLANEOUS:** Atlanta Hawks franchise all-time leading scorer with 23,292 points (1982-83 through 1993-94).

## COLLEGIATE RECORD

**NOTES:** THE SPORTING NEWS All-America second team (1981, 1982).

| Season Team | G | Min. | FGM | FGA | Pct. | FTM | FTA | Pct. | Reb. | Ast. | Pts. | RPG | APG | PPG |
|---|---|---|---|---|---|---|---|---|---|---|---|---|---|---|
| 79-80—Georgia | 16 | 508 | 135 | 257 | .525 | 27 | 37 | .730 | 104 | 23 | 297 | 6.5 | 1.4 | 18.6 |
| 80-81—Georgia | 31 | 1157 | 310 | 582 | .533 | 112 | 149 | .752 | 234 | 52 | 732 | 7.5 | 1.7 | 23.6 |
| 81-82—Georgia | 31 | 1083 | 278 | 526 | .529 | 103 | 160 | .644 | 250 | 41 | 659 | 8.1 | 1.3 | 21.3 |
| Totals | 78 | 2748 | 723 | 1365 | .530 | 242 | 346 | .699 | 588 | 116 | 1688 | 7.5 | 1.5 | 21.6 |

## NBA REGULAR-SEASON RECORD

**RECORDS:** Holds single-game record for most free throws made without a miss—23 (December 8, 1992, vs. Chicago).

**HONORS:** Slam Dunk championship winner (1985, 1990). ... All-NBA first team (1986). ... All-NBA second team (1987, 1988, 1991, 1993). ... All-NBA third team (1989, 1994). ... NBA All-Rookie team (1983).

| Season Team | G | Min. | FGM | FGA | Pct. | FTM | FTA | Pct. | Off. | Def. | Tot. | Ast. | St. | Blk. | TO | Pts. | RPG | APG | PPG |
|---|---|---|---|---|---|---|---|---|---|---|---|---|---|---|---|---|---|---|---|
| 82-83—Atlanta | 82 | 2697 | 601 | 1220 | .493 | 230 | 337 | .682 | 226 | 252 | 478 | 129 | 84 | 63 | 180 | 1434 | 5.8 | 1.6 | 17.5 |
| 83-84—Atlanta | 81 | 2961 | 684 | 1429 | .479 | 382 | 496 | .770 | 254 | 328 | 582 | 126 | 117 | 87 | 215 | 1750 | 7.2 | 1.6 | 21.6 |
| 84-85—Atlanta | 81 | 3023 | 853 | *1891 | .451 | 486 | 603 | .806 | 226 | 331 | 557 | 200 | 135 | 54 | 225 | 2217 | 6.9 | 2.5 | 27.4 |
| 85-86—Atlanta | 78 | 3049 | 888 | *1897 | .468 | 577 | 705 | .818 | 261 | 357 | 618 | 206 | 138 | 49 | 251 | 2366 | 7.9 | 2.6 | *30.3 |
| 86-87—Atlanta | 79 | 2969 | 828 | 1787 | .463 | 607 | 742 | .818 | 210 | 284 | 494 | 261 | 117 | 51 | 215 | 2294 | 6.3 | 3.3 | 29.0 |
| 87-88—Atlanta | 78 | 2948 | 909 | 1957 | .464 | 541 | 655 | .826 | 211 | 291 | 502 | 224 | 103 | 47 | 218 | 2397 | 6.4 | 2.9 | 30.7 |
| 88-89—Atlanta | 80 | 2997 | 814 | 1756 | .464 | 442 | 524 | .844 | 256 | 297 | 553 | 211 | 117 | 52 | 181 | 2099 | 6.9 | 2.6 | 26.2 |
| 89-90—Atlanta | 80 | 2888 | 810 | 1672 | .484 | 459 | 569 | .807 | 217 | 304 | 521 | 200 | 126 | 47 | 174 | 2138 | 6.5 | 2.5 | 26.7 |
| 90-91—Atlanta | 81 | 3078 | 770 | 1640 | .470 | 476 | 574 | .829 | 261 | 471 | 732 | 265 | 123 | 65 | 201 | 2101 | 9.0 | 3.3 | 25.9 |
| 91-92—Atlanta | 42 | 1601 | 424 | 914 | .464 | 294 | 352 | .835 | 103 | 192 | 295 | 158 | 52 | 24 | 122 | 1179 | 7.0 | 3.8 | 28.1 |
| 92-93—Atlanta | 71 | 2647 | 741 | 1584 | .468 | 519 | 627 | .828 | 187 | 295 | 482 | 227 | 70 | 27 | 184 | 2121 | 6.8 | 3.2 | 29.9 |
| 93-94—Atl.-L.A.C. | 74 | 2635 | 698 | 1588 | .440 | 442 | 522 | .847 | 182 | 299 | 481 | 169 | 92 | 30 | 172 | 1923 | 6.5 | 2.3 | 26.0 |
| 94-95—Boston | 77 | 2423 | 496 | 1169 | .424 | 266 | 340 | .782 | 157 | 244 | 401 | 166 | 61 | 14 | 173 | 1370 | 5.2 | 2.2 | 17.8 |
| 96-97—San Antonio | 63 | 1945 | 397 | 953 | .417 | 281 | 350 | .803 | 169 | 233 | 402 | 119 | 39 | 31 | 135 | 1145 | 6.4 | 1.9 | 18.2 |
| 98-99—Orlando | 27 | 252 | 50 | 132 | .379 | 29 | 42 | .690 | 30 | 41 | 71 | 16 | 4 | 1 | 23 | 134 | 2.6 | 0.6 | 5.0 |
| Totals | 1074 | 38113 | 9963 | 21589 | .461 | 6031 | 7438 | .811 | 2950 | 4219 | 7169 | 2677 | 1378 | 642 | 2669 | 26668 | 6.7 | 2.5 | 24.8 |

Three-point field goals: 1982-83, 2-for-11 (.182). 1983-84, 25-for-81 (.309). 1984-85, 25-for-81 (.309). 1985-86, 13-for-70 (.186). 1986-87, 31-for-106 (.292). 1987-88, 38-for-129 (.295). 1988-89, 29-for-105 (.276). 1989-90, 59-for-183 (.322). 1990-91, 85-for-249 (.341). 1991-92, 37-for-128 (.289). 1992-93, 120-for-316 (.380). 1993-94, 85-for-295 (.288). 1994-95, 112-for-289 (.388). 1996-97, 70-for-239 (.293). 1998-99, 5-for-19 (.263). Totals, 711-for-2231 (.319).

Personal fouls/disqualifications: 1982-83, 210/1. 1983-84, 197/1. 1984-85, 170/0. 1985-86, 170/0. 1986-87, 149/0. 1987-88, 162/0. 1988-89, 138/0. 1989-90, 141/0. 1990-91, 156/0. 1991-92, 77/0. 1992-93, 116/0. 1993-94, 126/0. 1994-95, 130/0. 1996-97, 100/0. 1998-99, 19/0. Totals, 2061/2.

## NBA PLAYOFF RECORD

| Season Team | G | Min. | FGM | FGA | Pct. | FTM | FTA | Pct. | Off. | Def. | Tot. | Ast. | St. | Blk. | TO | Pts. | RPG | APG | PPG |
|---|---|---|---|---|---|---|---|---|---|---|---|---|---|---|---|---|---|---|---|
| 82-83—Atlanta | 3 | 109 | 17 | 42 | .405 | 12 | 14 | .857 | 8 | 7 | 15 | 1 | 2 | 1 | 10 | 47 | 5.0 | 0.3 | 15.7 |
| 83-84—Atlanta | 5 | 197 | 35 | 84 | .417 | 26 | 31 | .839 | 21 | 20 | 41 | 11 | 12 | 1 | 15 | 96 | 8.2 | 2.2 | 19.2 |
| 85-86—Atlanta | 9 | 360 | 94 | 217 | .433 | 68 | 79 | .861 | 20 | 34 | 54 | 25 | 9 | 2 | 30 | 257 | 6.0 | 2.8 | 28.6 |
| 86-87—Atlanta | 9 | 360 | 86 | 210 | .410 | 66 | 74 | .892 | 27 | 43 | 70 | 25 | 16 | 8 | 26 | 241 | 7.8 | 2.8 | 26.8 |
| 87-88—Atlanta | 12 | 473 | 137 | 300 | .457 | 96 | 125 | .768 | 37 | 40 | 77 | 34 | 16 | 6 | 30 | 374 | 6.4 | 2.8 | 31.2 |
| 88-89—Atlanta | 5 | 212 | 52 | 116 | .448 | 27 | 38 | .711 | 10 | 17 | 27 | 17 | 4 | 8 | 12 | 136 | 5.4 | 3.4 | 27.2 |
| 90-91—Atlanta | 5 | 195 | 35 | 94 | .372 | 32 | 35 | .914 | 6 | 26 | 32 | 13 | 9 | 5 | 11 | 104 | 6.4 | 2.6 | 20.8 |
| 92-93—Atlanta | 3 | 113 | 32 | 75 | .427 | 23 | 30 | .767 | 12 | 4 | 16 | 9 | 3 | 1 | 10 | 90 | 5.3 | 3.0 | 30.0 |
| 94-95—Boston | 4 | 150 | 26 | 61 | .426 | 16 | 18 | .889 | 17 | 26 | 43 | 8 | 2 | 3 | 9 | 76 | 10.8 | 2.0 | 19.0 |
| 98-99—Orlando | 1 | 3 | 1 | 2 | .500 | 0 | 0 | ... | 0 | 0 | 0 | 0 | 0 | 0 | 0 | 2 | 0.0 | 0.0 | 2.0 |
| Totals | 56 | 2172 | 515 | 1201 | .429 | 366 | 444 | .824 | 158 | 217 | 375 | 143 | 73 | 35 | 153 | 1423 | 6.7 | 2.6 | 25.4 |

Three-point field goals: 1982-83, 1-for-1. 1983-84, 0-for-1. 1985-86, 1-for-5 (.200). 1986-87, 3-for-10 (.300). 1987-88, 4-for-18 (.222). 1988-89, 5-for-17 (.294). 1990-91, 2-for-15 (.133). 1992-93, 3-for-12 (.250). 1994-95, 8-for-17 (.471). Totals, 27-for-96 (.281).

Personal fouls/disqualifications: 1982-83, 9/0. 1983-84, 13/0. 1985-86, 24/0. 1986-87, 25/0. 1987-88, 24/0. 1988-89, 5/0. 1990-91, 8/0. 1992-93, 8/0. 1994-95, 7/0. Totals, 123/0.

## NBA ALL-STAR GAME RECORD

| Season Team | Min. | FGM | FGA | Pct. | FTM | FTA | Pct. | Off. | Def. | Tot. | Ast. | PF | Dq. | St. | Blk. | TO | Pts. |
|---|---|---|---|---|---|---|---|---|---|---|---|---|---|---|---|---|---|
| 1986—Atlanta | 17 | 6 | 15 | .400 | 1 | 2 | .500 | 2 | 1 | 3 | 2 | 2 | 0 | 0 | 1 | 1 | 13 |
| 1987—Atlanta | 24 | 3 | 9 | .333 | 4 | 7 | .571 | 3 | 2 | 5 | 1 | 2 | 0 | 0 | 1 | 2 | 10 |
| 1988—Atlanta | 30 | 12 | 22 | .545 | 5 | 6 | .833 | 1 | 4 | 5 | 0 | 3 | 0 | 0 | 1 | 0 | 29 |
| 1989—Atlanta | 15 | 3 | 8 | .375 | 3 | 3 | 1.000 | 1 | 1 | 2 | 0 | 0 | 0 | 3 | 0 | 2 | 9 |
| 1990—Atlanta | 16 | 5 | 10 | .500 | 2 | 2 | 1.000 | 0 | 0 | 0 | 4 | 1 | 0 | 1 | 0 | 0 | 13 |
| 1991—Atlanta | 22 | 3 | 11 | .273 | 6 | 8 | .750 | 0 | 3 | 3 | 4 | 2 | 0 | 1 | 1 | 2 | 12 |
| 1992—Atlanta | | | | | | | Selected, did not play—injured. | | | | | | | | | | |
| 1993—Atlanta | 18 | 2 | 11 | .182 | 4 | 4 | 1.000 | 4 | 3 | 7 | 0 | 2 | 0 | 1 | 0 | 1 | 9 |
| 1994—Atlanta | 17 | 4 | 9 | .444 | 3 | 6 | .500 | 2 | 0 | 2 | 4 | 1 | 0 | 0 | 0 | 0 | 11 |
| Totals | 159 | 38 | 95 | .400 | 28 | 38 | .737 | 16 | 11 | 27 | 15 | 13 | 0 | 6 | 4 | 8 | 106 |

Three-point field goals: 1990, 1-for-1. 1991, 0-for-2. 1993, 1-for-3 (.333). 1994, 0-for-2. Totals, 2-for-8 (.250).

## GREEK LEAGUE RECORD

| Season Team | G | Min. | FGM | FGA | Pct. | FTM | FTA | Pct. | Reb. | Ast. | Pts. | RPG | APG | PPG |
|---|---|---|---|---|---|---|---|---|---|---|---|---|---|---|
| 95-96—Panathinaikos | 14 | ... | ... | ... | ... | ... | ... | ... | 95 | 19 | 292 | 6.8 | 1.4 | 20.9 |

## ITALIAN LEAGUE RECORD

| Season Team | G | Min. | FGM | FGA | Pct. | FTM | FTA | Pct. | Reb. | Ast. | Pts. | RPG | APG | PPG |
|---|---|---|---|---|---|---|---|---|---|---|---|---|---|---|
| 97-98—Teamsystem Bologna | 23 | 775 | 159 | 322 | .494 | 111 | 134 | .828 | 158 | 40 | 450 | 6.9 | 1.7 | 19.6 |

# WILLIAMS, BUCK     F

**PERSONAL:** Born March 8, 1960, in Rocky Mount, N.C. ... 6-8/225 (2,03/102,1). ... Full name: Charles Linwood Williams.
**HIGH SCHOOL:** Rocky Mount (N.C.).
**COLLEGE:** Maryland.
**TRANSACTIONS/CAREER NOTES:** Selected after junior season by New Jersey Nets in first round (third pick overall) of 1981 NBA Draft. ... Traded by Nets to Portland Trail Blazers for C Sam Bowie and 1989 first-round draft choice (June 24, 1989). ... Rights renounced by Trail Blazers (July 23, 1996). ... Signed as free agent by New York Knicks (July 26, 1996). ... Announced retirement (January 27, 1999).
**MISCELLANEOUS:** Member of U.S. Olympic team (1980). ... New Jersey Nets franchise all-time leading scorer with 10,440 points and all-time leading rebounder with 7,576 (1981-82 through 1988-89).

## COLLEGIATE RECORD

| Season Team | G | Min. | FGM | FGA | Pct. | FTM | FTA | Pct. | Reb. | Ast. | Pts. | AVERAGES RPG | APG | PPG |
|---|---|---|---|---|---|---|---|---|---|---|---|---|---|---|
| 78-79—Maryland | 30 | 906 | 120 | 206 | .583 | 60 | 109 | .550 | 323 | 18 | 300 | 10.8 | 0.6 | 10.0 |
| 79-80—Maryland | 24 | 872 | 143 | 236 | .606 | 85 | 128 | .664 | 242 | 27 | 371 | 10.1 | 1.1 | 15.5 |
| 80-81—Maryland | 31 | 1080 | 183 | 283 | .647 | 116 | 182 | .637 | 363 | 31 | 482 | 11.7 | 1.0 | 15.5 |
| Totals | 85 | 2858 | 446 | 725 | .615 | 261 | 419 | .623 | 928 | 76 | 1153 | 10.9 | 0.9 | 13.6 |

## NBA REGULAR-SEASON RECORD

**HONORS:** NBA Rookie of the Year (1982). ... All-NBA second team (1983). ... NBA All-Defensive first team (1990, 1991). ... NBA All-Defensive second team (1988, 1992). ... NBA All-Rookie team (1982).

| Season Team | G | Min. | FGM | FGA | Pct. | FTM | FTA | Pct. | REBOUNDS Off. | Def. | Tot. | Ast. | St. | Blk. | TO | Pts. | AVERAGES RPG | APG | PPG |
|---|---|---|---|---|---|---|---|---|---|---|---|---|---|---|---|---|---|---|---|
| 81-82—New Jersey | 82 | 2825 | 513 | 881 | .582 | 242 | 388 | .624 | 347 | 658 | 1005 | 107 | 84 | 84 | 235 | 1268 | 12.3 | 1.3 | 15.5 |
| 82-83—New Jersey | 82 | 2961 | 536 | 912 | .588 | 324 | 523 | .620 | 365 | 662 | 1027 | 125 | 91 | 110 | 246 | 1396 | 12.5 | 1.5 | 17.0 |
| 83-84—New Jersey | 81 | 3003 | 495 | 926 | .535 | 284 | 498 | .570 | *355 | 645 | 1000 | 130 | 81 | 125 | 237 | 1274 | 12.3 | 1.6 | 15.7 |
| 84-85—New Jersey | 82 | *3182 | 577 | 1089 | .530 | 336 | 538 | .625 | 323 | 682 | 1005 | 167 | 63 | 110 | 238 | 1491 | 12.3 | 2.0 | 18.2 |
| 85-86—New Jersey | 82 | 3070 | 500 | 956 | .523 | 301 | 445 | .676 | 329 | 657 | 986 | 131 | 73 | 96 | 244 | 1301 | 12.0 | 1.6 | 15.9 |
| 86-87—New Jersey | 82 | 2976 | 521 | 936 | .557 | 430 | 588 | .731 | 322 | 701 | 1023 | 129 | 78 | 91 | 280 | 1472 | 12.5 | 1.6 | 18.0 |
| 87-88—New Jersey | 70 | 2637 | 466 | 832 | .560 | 346 | 518 | .668 | 298 | 536 | 834 | 109 | 68 | 44 | 189 | 1279 | 11.9 | 1.6 | 18.3 |
| 88-89—New Jersey | 74 | 2446 | 373 | 702 | .531 | 213 | 320 | .666 | 249 | 447 | 696 | 78 | 61 | 36 | 142 | 959 | 9.4 | 1.1 | 13.0 |
| 89-90—Portland | 82 | 2801 | 413 | 754 | .548 | 288 | 408 | .706 | 250 | 550 | 800 | 116 | 69 | 39 | 168 | 1114 | 9.8 | 1.4 | 13.6 |
| 90-91—Portland | 80 | 2582 | 358 | 595 | *.602 | 217 | 308 | .705 | 227 | 524 | 751 | 97 | 47 | 47 | 137 | 933 | 9.4 | 1.2 | 11.7 |
| 91-92—Portland | 80 | 2519 | 340 | 563 | *.604 | 221 | 293 | .754 | 260 | 444 | 704 | 108 | 62 | 41 | 130 | 901 | 8.8 | 1.4 | 11.3 |
| 92-93—Portland | 82 | 2498 | 270 | 528 | .511 | 138 | 214 | .645 | 232 | 458 | 690 | 75 | 81 | 61 | 101 | 678 | 8.4 | 0.9 | 8.3 |
| 93-94—Portland | 81 | 2636 | 291 | 524 | .555 | 201 | 296 | .679 | 315 | 528 | 843 | 80 | 58 | 47 | 111 | 783 | 10.4 | 1.0 | 9.7 |
| 94-95—Portland | 82 | 2422 | 309 | 604 | .512 | 138 | 205 | .673 | 251 | 418 | 669 | 78 | 67 | 69 | 119 | 757 | 8.2 | 1.0 | 9.2 |
| 95-96—Portland | 70 | 1672 | 192 | 384 | .500 | 125 | 187 | .668 | 159 | 245 | 404 | 42 | 40 | 47 | 90 | 511 | 5.8 | 0.6 | 7.3 |
| 96-97—New York | 74 | 1496 | 175 | 326 | .537 | 115 | 179 | .642 | 166 | 231 | 397 | 53 | 40 | 38 | 79 | 465 | 5.4 | 0.7 | 6.3 |
| 97-98—New York | 41 | 738 | 75 | 149 | .503 | 52 | 71 | .732 | 78 | 105 | 183 | 21 | 17 | 15 | 38 | 202 | 4.5 | 0.5 | 4.9 |
| Totals | 1307 | 42464 | 6404 | 11661 | .549 | 3971 | 5979 | .664 | 4526 | 8491 | 13017 | 1646 | 1080 | 1100 | 2784 | 16784 | 10.0 | 1.3 | 12.8 |

Three-point field goals: 1981-82, 0-for-1. 1982-83, 0-for-4. 1983-84, 0-for-4. 1984-85, 1-for-4 (.250). 1985-86, 0-for-2. 1986-87, 0-for-1. 1987-88, 1-for-1. 1988-89, 0-for-3. 1989-90, 0-for-1. 1991-92, 0-for-1. 1992-93, 0-for-1. 1993-94, 0-for-1. 1994-95, 1-for-2 (.500). 1995-96, 2-for-3 (.667). 1996-97, 0-for-1. Totals, 5-for-30 (.167).
Personal fouls/disqualifications: 1981-82, 285/5. 1982-83, 270/4. 1983-84, 298/3. 1984-85, 293/7. 1985-86, 294/9. 1986-87, 315/8. 1987-88, 266/5. 1988-89, 223/0. 1989-90, 285/4. 1990-91, 247/2. 1991-92, 244/4. 1992-93, 270/0. 1993-94, 239/1. 1994-95, 254/2. 1995-96, 187/1. 1996-97, 204/2. 1997-98, 93/1. Totals, 4267/58.

## NBA PLAYOFF RECORD

| Season Team | G | Min. | FGM | FGA | Pct. | FTM | FTA | Pct. | REBOUNDS Off. | Def. | Tot. | Ast. | St. | Blk. | TO | Pts. | AVERAGES RPG | APG | PPG |
|---|---|---|---|---|---|---|---|---|---|---|---|---|---|---|---|---|---|---|---|
| 81-82—New Jersey | 2 | 79 | 14 | 26 | .538 | 7 | 15 | .467 | 11 | 10 | 21 | 3 | 1 | 2 | 4 | 35 | 10.5 | 1.5 | 17.5 |
| 82-83—New Jersey | 2 | 85 | 11 | 22 | .500 | 16 | 20 | .800 | 9 | 14 | 23 | 4 | 2 | 2 | 5 | 38 | 11.5 | 2.0 | 19.0 |
| 83-84—New Jersey | 11 | 473 | 63 | 130 | .485 | 45 | 81 | .556 | 57 | 98 | 155 | 16 | 15 | 17 | 29 | 171 | 14.1 | 1.5 | 15.5 |
| 84-85—New Jersey | 3 | 123 | 26 | 40 | .650 | 22 | 30 | .733 | 14 | 18 | 32 | 1 | 3 | 5 | 6 | 74 | 10.7 | 0.3 | 24.7 |
| 85-86—New Jersey | 3 | 126 | 21 | 29 | .724 | 20 | 26 | .769 | 12 | 19 | 31 | 2 | 6 | 1 | 6 | 62 | 10.3 | 0.7 | 20.7 |
| 89-90—Portland | 21 | 776 | 101 | 199 | .508 | 71 | 105 | .676 | 67 | 126 | 193 | 39 | 13 | 6 | 41 | 273 | 9.2 | 1.9 | 13.0 |
| 90-91—Portland | 16 | 572 | 65 | 130 | .500 | 35 | 58 | .603 | 53 | 90 | 143 | 14 | 10 | 4 | 24 | 165 | 8.9 | 0.9 | 10.3 |
| 91-92—Portland | 21 | 758 | 66 | 130 | .508 | 69 | 91 | .758 | 61 | 118 | 179 | 22 | 27 | 17 | 45 | 201 | 8.5 | 1.0 | 9.6 |
| 92-93—Portland | 4 | 119 | 11 | 23 | .478 | 13 | 19 | .684 | 12 | 17 | 29 | 1 | 1 | 3 | 6 | 35 | 7.3 | 0.3 | 8.8 |
| 93-94—Portland | 4 | 125 | 19 | 28 | .679 | 13 | 15 | .867 | 14 | 21 | 35 | 2 | 4 | 2 | 8 | 51 | 8.8 | 0.5 | 12.8 |
| 94-95—Portland | 3 | 103 | 9 | 15 | .600 | 7 | 11 | .636 | 8 | 11 | 19 | 1 | 4 | 2 | 4 | 25 | 6.3 | 0.3 | 8.3 |
| 95-96—Portland | 5 | 133 | 9 | 23 | .391 | 5 | 7 | .714 | 13 | 12 | 25 | 1 | 1 | 4 | 5 | 24 | 5.0 | 0.2 | 4.8 |
| 96-97—New York | 10 | 193 | 17 | 35 | .486 | 9 | 17 | .529 | 13 | 27 | 40 | 6 | 3 | 4 | 4 | 43 | 4.0 | 0.6 | 4.3 |
| 97-98—New York | 3 | 45 | 4 | 9 | .444 | 6 | 8 | .750 | 7 | 9 | 16 | 1 | 0 | 1 | 3 | 14 | 5.3 | 0.3 | 4.7 |
| Totals | 108 | 3710 | 436 | 839 | .520 | 338 | 503 | .672 | 351 | 590 | 941 | 113 | 90 | 70 | 190 | 1211 | 8.7 | 1.0 | 11.2 |

Three-point field goals: 1995-96, 1-for-2 (.500).
Personal fouls/disqualifications: 1981-82, 7/0. 1982-83, 12/2. 1983-84, 44/2. 1984-85, 12/0. 1985-86, 15/1. 1989-90, 74/1. 1990-91, 55/1. 1991-92, 73/1. 1992-93, 12/1. 1993-94, 11/0. 1994-95, 14/1. 1995-96, 18/0. 1996-97, 34/0. 1997-98, 5/0. Totals, 386/10.

## NBA ALL-STAR GAME RECORD

| Season Team | Min. | FGM | FGA | Pct. | FTM | FTA | Pct. | REBOUNDS Off. | Def. | Tot. | Ast. | PF | Dq. | St. | Blk. | TO | Pts. |
|---|---|---|---|---|---|---|---|---|---|---|---|---|---|---|---|---|---|
| 1982—New Jersey | 22 | 2 | 7 | .286 | 0 | 2 | .000 | 1 | 9 | 10 | 1 | 3 | 0 | 2 | 3 | 4 |
| 1983—New Jersey | 19 | 3 | 4 | .750 | 2 | 4 | .500 | 3 | 4 | 7 | 1 | 0 | 0 | 1 | 0 | 0 | 8 |
| 1986—New Jersey | 20 | 5 | 8 | .625 | 3 | 5 | .600 | 3 | 4 | 7 | 4 | 0 | 0 | 0 | 0 | 1 | 13 |
| Totals | 61 | 10 | 19 | .526 | 5 | 11 | .455 | 7 | 17 | 24 | 6 | 3 | 0 | 1 | 2 | 4 | 25 |

# WORTHY, JAMES     F

**PERSONAL:** Born February 27, 1961, in Gastonia, N.C. ... 6-9/225 (2,05/102,1). ... Full name: James Ager Worthy.
**HIGH SCHOOL:** Ashbrook (Gastonia, N.C.).
**COLLEGE:** North Carolina.
**TRANSACTIONS:** Selected after junior season by Los Angeles Lakers in first round (first pick overall) of 1982 NBA Draft. ... Announced retirement (November 10, 1994).
**CAREER HONORS:** Elected to Naismith Memorial Basketball Hall of Fame (2003). ... One of the 50 Greatest Players in NBA History (1996).
**MISCELLANEOUS:** Member of NBA championship team (1985, 1987, 1988).

## COLLEGIATE RECORD

**NOTES:** Member of NCAA Division I championship team (1982). ... NCAA Division I Tournament Most Outstanding Player (1982). ... THE SPORTING NEWS All-America first team (1982).

| Season Team | G | Min. | FGM | FGA | Pct. | FTM | FTA | Pct. | Reb. | Ast. | Pts. | RPG | APG | PPG |
|---|---|---|---|---|---|---|---|---|---|---|---|---|---|---|
| 79-80—North Carolina | 14 | 396 | 74 | 126 | .587 | 27 | 45 | .600 | 104 | 26 | 175 | 7.4 | 1.9 | 12.5 |
| 80-81—North Carolina | 36 | 1214 | 208 | 416 | .500 | 96 | 150 | .640 | 301 | 100 | 512 | 8.4 | 2.8 | 14.2 |
| 81-82—North Carolina | 34 | 1178 | 203 | 354 | .573 | 126 | 187 | .674 | 215 | 82 | 532 | 6.3 | 2.4 | 15.6 |
| Totals | 84 | 2788 | 485 | 896 | .541 | 249 | 382 | .652 | 620 | 208 | 1219 | 7.4 | 2.5 | 14.5 |

### NBA REGULAR-SEASON RECORD

HONORS: All-NBA third team (1990, 1991). ... NBA All-Rookie team (1983).

| Season Team | G | Min. | FGM | FGA | Pct. | FTM | FTA | Pct. | REBOUNDS | | | Ast. | St. | Blk. | TO | Pts. | AVERAGES | | |
|---|---|---|---|---|---|---|---|---|---|---|---|---|---|---|---|---|---|---|---|
| | | | | | | | | | Off. | Def. | Tot. | | | | | | RPG | APG | PPG |
| 82-83—Los Angeles | 77 | 1970 | 447 | 772 | .579 | 138 | 221 | .624 | 157 | 242 | 399 | 132 | 91 | 64 | 178 | 1033 | 5.2 | 1.7 | 13.4 |
| 83-84—Los Angeles | 82 | 2415 | 495 | 890 | .556 | 195 | 257 | .759 | 157 | 358 | 515 | 207 | 77 | 70 | 181 | 1185 | 6.3 | 2.5 | 14.5 |
| 84-85—L.A. Lakers | 80 | 2696 | 610 | 1066 | .572 | 190 | 245 | .776 | 169 | 342 | 511 | 201 | 87 | 67 | 198 | 1410 | 6.4 | 2.5 | 17.6 |
| 85-86—L.A. Lakers | 75 | 2454 | 629 | 1086 | .579 | 242 | 314 | .771 | 136 | 251 | 387 | 201 | 82 | 77 | 149 | 1500 | 5.2 | 2.7 | 20.0 |
| 86-87—L.A. Lakers | 82 | 2819 | 651 | 1207 | .539 | 292 | 389 | .751 | 158 | 308 | 466 | 226 | 108 | 83 | 168 | 1594 | 5.7 | 2.8 | 19.4 |
| 87-88—L.A. Lakers | 75 | 2655 | 617 | 1161 | .531 | 242 | 304 | .796 | 129 | 245 | 374 | 289 | 72 | 55 | 155 | 1478 | 5.0 | 3.9 | 19.7 |
| 88-89—L.A. Lakers | 81 | 2960 | 702 | 1282 | .548 | 251 | 321 | .782 | 169 | 320 | 489 | 288 | 108 | 56 | 182 | 1657 | 6.0 | 3.6 | 20.5 |
| 89-90—L.A. Lakers | 80 | 2960 | 711 | 1298 | .548 | 248 | 317 | .782 | 160 | 318 | 478 | 288 | 99 | 49 | 160 | 1685 | 6.0 | 3.6 | 21.1 |
| 90-91—L.A. Lakers | 78 | 3008 | 716 | 1455 | .492 | 212 | 266 | .797 | 107 | 249 | 356 | 275 | 104 | 35 | 127 | 1670 | 4.6 | 3.5 | 21.4 |
| 91-92—L.A. Lakers | 54 | 2108 | 450 | 1007 | .447 | 166 | 204 | .814 | 98 | 207 | 305 | 252 | 76 | 23 | 127 | 1075 | 5.6 | 4.7 | 19.9 |
| 92-93—L.A. Lakers | 80 | 2359 | 510 | 1142 | .447 | 171 | 211 | .810 | 73 | 174 | 247 | 278 | 92 | 27 | 137 | 1221 | 3.0 | 3.4 | 14.9 |
| 93-94—L.A. Lakers | 80 | 1597 | 340 | 838 | .406 | 100 | 135 | .741 | 48 | 133 | 181 | 154 | 45 | 18 | 97 | 812 | 2.3 | 1.9 | 10.2 |
| Totals | 926 | 30001 | 6878 | 13204 | .521 | 2447 | 3184 | .769 | 1561 | 3147 | 4708 | 2791 | 1041 | 624 | 1859 | 16320 | 5.1 | 3.0 | 17.6 |

Three-point field goals: 1982-83, 1-for-4 (.250). 1983-84, 0-for-6. 1984-85, 0-for-7. 1985-86, 0-for-13. 1986-87, 0-for-13. 1987-88, 2-for-16 (.125). 1988-89, 2-for-23 (.087). 1989-90, 15-for-49 (.306). 1990-91, 26-for-90 (.289). 1991-92, 9-for-43 (.209). 1992-93, 30-for-111 (.270). 1993-94, 32-for-111 (.288). Totals, 117-for-486 (.241).

Personal fouls/disqualifications: 1982-83, 221/2. 1983-84, 244/5. 1984-85, 196/0. 1985-86, 195/0. 1986-87, 206/0. 1987-88, 175/1. 1988-89, 175/0. 1989-90, 190/0. 1990-91, 117/0. 1991-92, 89/0. 1992-93, 87/0. 1993-94, 80/0. Totals, 1975/8.

### NBA PLAYOFF RECORD

NOTES: NBA Finals Most Valuable Player (1988).

| Season Team | G | Min. | FGM | FGA | Pct. | FTM | FTA | Pct. | REBOUNDS | | | Ast. | St. | Blk. | TO | Pts. | AVERAGES | | |
|---|---|---|---|---|---|---|---|---|---|---|---|---|---|---|---|---|---|---|---|
| | | | | | | | | | Off. | Def. | Tot. | | | | | | RPG | APG | PPG |
| 83-84—Los Angeles | 21 | 708 | 164 | 274 | .599 | 42 | 69 | .609 | 36 | 69 | 105 | 56 | 27 | 11 | 39 | 371 | 5.0 | 2.7 | 17.7 |
| 84-85—L.A. Lakers | 19 | 626 | 166 | 267 | .622 | 75 | 111 | .676 | 35 | 61 | 96 | 41 | 17 | 13 | 26 | 408 | 5.1 | 2.2 | 21.5 |
| 85-86—L.A. Lakers | 14 | 539 | 121 | 217 | .558 | 32 | 47 | .681 | 22 | 43 | 65 | 45 | 16 | 10 | 36 | 274 | 4.6 | 3.2 | 19.6 |
| 86-87—L.A. Lakers | 18 | 681 | 176 | 298 | .591 | 73 | 97 | .753 | 31 | 70 | 101 | 63 | 28 | 22 | 40 | 425 | 5.6 | 3.5 | 23.6 |
| 87-88—L.A. Lakers | 24 | 896 | 204 | 390 | .523 | 97 | 128 | .758 | 53 | 86 | 139 | 106 | 33 | 19 | 55 | 506 | 5.8 | 4.4 | 21.1 |
| 88-89—L.A. Lakers | 15 | 600 | 153 | 270 | .567 | 63 | 80 | .788 | 37 | 64 | 101 | 42 | 18 | 16 | 33 | 372 | 6.7 | 2.8 | 24.8 |
| 89-90—L.A. Lakers | 9 | 366 | 90 | 181 | .497 | 36 | 43 | .837 | 11 | 39 | 50 | 27 | 14 | 3 | 22 | 218 | 5.6 | 3.0 | 24.2 |
| 90-91—L.A. Lakers | 18 | 733 | 161 | 346 | .465 | 53 | 72 | .736 | 25 | 48 | 73 | 70 | 19 | 2 | 40 | 379 | 4.1 | 3.9 | 21.1 |
| 92-93—L.A. Lakers | 5 | 148 | 32 | 86 | .372 | 3 | 5 | .600 | 7 | 10 | 17 | 13 | 5 | 0 | 7 | 69 | 3.4 | 2.6 | 13.8 |
| Totals | 143 | 5297 | 1267 | 2329 | .544 | 474 | 652 | .727 | 257 | 490 | 747 | 463 | 177 | 96 | 298 | 3022 | 5.2 | 3.2 | 21.1 |

Three-point field goals: 1983-84, 1-for-2 (.500). 1984-85, 1-for-2 (.500). 1985-86, 0-for-4. 1986-87, 0-for-2. 1987-88, 1-for-9 (.111). 1988-89, 3-for-5 (.375). 1989-90, 2-for-8 (.250). 1990-91, 4-for-24 (.167). 1992-93, 2-for-8 (.250). Totals, 14-for-67 (.209).

Personal fouls/disqualifications: 1983-84, 57/0. 1984-85, 53/1. 1985-86, 43/0. 1986-87, 42/1. 1987-88, 58/0. 1988-89, 36/0. 1989-90, 18/0. 1990-91, 34/0. 1992-93, 11/0. Totals, 352/2.

### NBA ALL-STAR GAME RECORD

| Season Team | Min. | FGM | FGA | Pct. | FTM | FTA | Pct. | REBOUNDS | | | Ast. | PF | Dq. | St. | Blk. | TO | Pts. |
|---|---|---|---|---|---|---|---|---|---|---|---|---|---|---|---|---|---|
| | | | | | | | | Off. | Def. | Tot. | | | | | | | |
| 1986—L.A. Lakers | 28 | 10 | 19 | .526 | 0 | 0 | ... | 2 | 1 | 3 | 2 | 3 | 0 | 0 | 2 | 1 | 20 |
| 1987—L.A. Lakers | 29 | 10 | 14 | .714 | 2 | 2 | 1.000 | 6 | 2 | 8 | 3 | 3 | 0 | 1 | 0 | 2 | 22 |
| 1988—L.A. Lakers | 13 | 2 | 8 | .250 | 0 | 1 | .000 | 1 | 2 | 3 | 1 | 1 | 0 | 0 | 1 | 0 | 4 |
| 1989—L.A. Lakers | 18 | 4 | 7 | .571 | 0 | 0 | ... | 0 | 2 | 2 | 2 | 0 | 0 | 2 | 0 | 0 | 8 |
| 1990—L.A. Lakers | 19 | 1 | 11 | .091 | 0 | 0 | ... | 3 | 1 | 4 | 0 | 1 | 0 | 1 | 0 | 1 | 2 |
| 1991—L.A. Lakers | 21 | 3 | 11 | .273 | 3 | 4 | .750 | 0 | 2 | 2 | 0 | 2 | 0 | 0 | 1 | 0 | 9 |
| 1992—L.A. Lakers | 14 | 4 | 7 | .571 | 1 | 2 | .500 | 0 | 4 | 4 | 1 | 0 | 0 | 1 | 0 | 0 | 9 |
| Totals | 142 | 34 | 77 | .442 | 6 | 9 | .667 | 12 | 14 | 26 | 9 | 10 | 0 | 7 | 4 | 4 | 74 |

Three-point field goals: 1986, 0-for-2. 1989, 0-for-1. Totals, 0-for-3.

## YARDLEY, GEORGE     F

PERSONAL: Born November 23, 1928, in Hollywood, Calif. ... 6-5/195 (1,96/88,4). ... Full name: George Harry Yardley III.
HIGH SCHOOL: Newport Harbor (Calif.).
COLLEGE: Stanford.
TRANSACTIONS: Selected by Fort Wayne Pistons in first round of 1950 NBA Draft. ... Played with the San Francisco Stewart Chevrolets in the National Industrial Basketball League, an Amateur Athletic Union League, during 1950-51 season (finished third in the league in scoring with a 13.1 point average on 104 field goals and 53 free throws for 261 points in 20 games). ... In military service during 1951-52 and 1952-53 seasons. ... Signed by Pistons (1953). ... Pistons franchise moved from Fort Wayne to Detroit for 1957-58 season. ... Traded by Pistons to Syracuse Nationals for F/G Ed Conlin (February 13, 1959). ... Played in American Basketball League with Los Angeles Jets (1961-62).
CAREER HONORS: Elected to Naismith Memorial Basketball Hall of Fame (1996).

### COLLEGIATE RECORD

| Season Team | G | Min. | FGM | FGA | Pct. | FTM | FTA | Pct. | Reb. | Ast. | Pts. | RPG | APG | PPG |
|---|---|---|---|---|---|---|---|---|---|---|---|---|---|---|
| 46-47—Stanford‡ | | | | | Freshman team statistics unavailable. | | | | | | | | | |
| 47-48—Stanford | 18 | ... | 22 | ... | ... | 8 | 20 | .400 | ... | ... | 52 | ... | ... | 2.9 |
| 48-49—Stanford | 28 | ... | 126 | 377 | .334 | 93 | 131 | .710 | ... | ... | 345 | ... | ... | 12.3 |
| 49-50—Stanford | 25 | ... | 164 | 452 | .363 | 95 | 130 | .731 | ... | ... | 423 | ... | ... | 16.9 |
| Varsity totals | 71 | ... | 312 | ... | ... | 196 | 281 | .698 | ... | ... | 820 | ... | ... | 11.5 |

### NBA REGULAR-SEASON RECORD

HONORS: All-NBA first team (1958). ... All-NBA second team (1957).

| Season Team | G | Min. | FGM | FGA | Pct. | FTM | FTA | Pct. | Reb. | Ast. | PF | Dq. | Pts. | RPG | APG | PPG |
|---|---|---|---|---|---|---|---|---|---|---|---|---|---|---|---|---|
| 53-54—Fort Wayne | 63 | 1489 | 209 | 492 | .425 | 146 | 205 | .712 | 407 | 99 | 166 | 3 | 564 | 6.5 | 1.6 | 9.0 |
| 54-55—Fort Wayne | 60 | 2150 | 363 | 869 | .418 | 310 | 416 | .745 | 594 | 126 | 205 | 7 | 1036 | 9.9 | 2.1 | 17.3 |
| 55-56—Fort Wayne | 71 | 2353 | 434 | 1067 | .407 | 365 | 492 | .742 | 686 | 159 | 212 | 2 | 1233 | 9.7 | 2.2 | 17.4 |

| Season Team | G | Min. | FGM | FGA | Pct. | FTM | FTA | Pct. | Reb. | Ast. | PF | Dq. | Pts. | RPG | APG | PPG |
|---|---|---|---|---|---|---|---|---|---|---|---|---|---|---|---|---|
| 56-57—Fort Wayne | 72 | 2691 | 522 | 1273 | .410 | 503 | 639 | .787 | 755 | 147 | 231 | 2 | 1547 | 10.5 | 2.0 | 21.5 |
| 57-58—Detroit | 72 | 2843 | 673 | *1624 | .414 | *655 | *808 | .811 | 768 | 97 | 226 | 3 | *2001 | 10.7 | 1.3 | *27.8 |
| 58-59—Det.-Syr. | 61 | 1839 | 446 | 1042 | .428 | 317 | 407 | .779 | 431 | 65 | 159 | 2 | 1209 | 7.1 | 1.1 | 19.8 |
| 59-60—Syracuse | 73 | 2402 | 546 | 1205 | .453 | 381 | 467 | .816 | 579 | 122 | 227 | 3 | 1473 | 7.9 | 1.7 | 20.2 |
| Totals | 472 | 15767 | 3193 | 7572 | .422 | 2677 | 3434 | .780 | 4220 | 815 | 1426 | 22 | 9063 | 8.9 | 1.7 | 19.2 |

### NBA PLAYOFF RECORD

| Season Team | G | Min. | FGM | FGA | Pct. | FTM | FTA | Pct. | Reb. | Ast. | PF | Dq. | Pts. | RPG | APG | PPG |
|---|---|---|---|---|---|---|---|---|---|---|---|---|---|---|---|---|
| 53-54—Fort Wayne | 4 | 107 | 16 | 33 | .485 | 10 | 12 | .833 | 24 | 3 | 10 | 0 | 42 | 6.0 | 0.8 | 10.5 |
| 54-55—Fort Wayne | 11 | 420 | 57 | 143 | .399 | 60 | 79 | .760 | 99 | 36 | 37 | 2 | 174 | 9.0 | 3.3 | 15.8 |
| 55-56—Fort Wayne | 10 | 406 | 77 | 183 | .421 | 76 | 98 | .776 | 139 | 26 | 25 | 0 | 230 | 13.9 | 2.6 | 23.0 |
| 56-57—Fort Wayne | 2 | 85 | 24 | 53 | .453 | 9 | 11 | .818 | 19 | 8 | 7 | 0 | 57 | 9.5 | 4.0 | 28.5 |
| 57-58—Detroit | 7 | 254 | 52 | 127 | .409 | 60 | 67 | .896 | 72 | 17 | 26 | 0 | 164 | 10.3 | 2.4 | 23.4 |
| 58-59—Syracuse | 9 | 333 | 83 | 189 | .439 | 60 | 70 | .857 | 87 | 21 | 29 | 0 | 226 | 9.7 | 2.3 | 25.1 |
| 59-60—Syracuse | 3 | 88 | 15 | 39 | .385 | 10 | 12 | .833 | 17 | 1 | 9 | 0 | 40 | 5.7 | 0.3 | 13.3 |
| Totals | 46 | 1693 | 324 | 767 | .422 | 285 | 349 | .817 | 457 | 112 | 143 | 2 | 933 | 9.9 | 2.4 | 20.3 |

### NBA ALL-STAR GAME RECORD

| Season Team | Min. | FGM | FGA | Pct. | FTM | FTA | Pct. | Reb | Ast. | PF | Dq. | Pts. |
|---|---|---|---|---|---|---|---|---|---|---|---|---|
| 1955—Fort Wayne | 22 | 4 | 11 | .364 | 3 | 4 | .750 | 4 | 2 | 2 | 0 | 11 |
| 1956—Fort Wayne | 19 | 3 | 7 | .429 | 2 | 3 | .667 | 6 | 1 | 1 | 0 | 8 |
| 1957—Fort Wayne | 25 | 4 | 10 | .400 | 1 | 1 | 1.000 | 9 | 0 | 2 | 0 | 9 |
| 1958—Detroit | 32 | 8 | 15 | .533 | 3 | 5 | .600 | 9 | 1 | 1 | 0 | 19 |
| 1959—Detroit | 17 | 2 | 8 | .250 | 2 | 2 | 1.000 | 4 | 0 | 3 | 0 | 6 |
| 1960—Syracuse | 16 | 5 | 9 | .556 | 1 | 2 | .500 | 3 | 0 | 4 | 0 | 11 |
| Totals | 131 | 26 | 60 | .433 | 12 | 17 | .706 | 35 | 4 | 13 | 0 | 64 |

### ABL REGULAR-SEASON RECORD

| Season Team | G | Min. | FGM | FGA | Pct. | FTM | FTA | Pct. | Reb. | Ast. | Pts. | RPG | APG | PPG |
|---|---|---|---|---|---|---|---|---|---|---|---|---|---|---|
| 61-62—Los Angeles | 25 | 948 | 159 | 378 | .421 | 148 | 122 | 1.213 | 172 | 65 | 482 | 6.9 | 2.6 | 19.3 |

## ZASLOFSKY, MAX          G/F

**PERSONAL:** Born December 7, 1925, in Brooklyn, N.Y. ... Died October 15, 1985. ... 6-2/170 (1,88/77,1). ... Full name: Max Zaslofsky.
**HIGH SCHOOL:** Thomas Jefferson (Brooklyn, N.Y.).
**COLLEGE:** St. John's.
**TRANSACTIONS:** Signed after freshman season as free agent by Chicago Stags of Basketball Association of America (1946). ... Name drawn out of hat by New York Knicks in dispersal of Stags franchise (1950). ... Traded by Knicks to Baltimore Bullets for G/F Jim Baechtold (1953). ... Traded by Bullets to Milwaukee Hawks (November 1953). ... Traded by Hawks to Fort Wayne Pistons (December 1953).

**NOTES:** In military service (1944-45 season).

### COLLEGIATE RECORD

| Season Team | G | Min. | FGM | FGA | Pct. | FTM | FTA | Pct. | Reb. | Ast. | Pts. | RPG | APG | PPG |
|---|---|---|---|---|---|---|---|---|---|---|---|---|---|---|
| 45-46—St. John's | 18 | ... | 59 | ... | ... | 22 | 38 | .579 | ... | ... | 140 | ... | ... | 7.8 |

**HONORS:** All-NBA first team (1950). ... All-BAA first team (1947, 1948, 1949).

### NBA REGULAR-SEASON RECORD

| Season Team | G | Min. | FGM | FGA | Pct. | FTM | FTA | Pct. | Reb. | Ast. | PF | Dq. | Pts. | RPG | APG | PPG |
|---|---|---|---|---|---|---|---|---|---|---|---|---|---|---|---|---|
| 46-47—Chicago (BAA) | 61 | ... | 336 | 1020 | .329 | 205 | 278 | .737 | ... | 40 | 121 | ... | 877 | ... | 0.7 | 14.4 |
| 47-48—Chicago (BAA) | 48 | ... | *373 | 1156 | .323 | 261 | 333 | .784 | ... | 29 | 125 | ... | *1007 | ... | 0.6 | *21.0 |
| 48-49—Chicago (BAA) | 58 | ... | 425 | 1216 | .350 | 347 | 413 | .840 | ... | 149 | 156 | ... | 1197 | ... | 2.6 | 20.6 |
| 49-50—Chicago | 68 | ... | 397 | 1132 | .351 | 321 | 381 | *.843 | ... | 155 | 185 | ... | 1115 | ... | 2.3 | 16.4 |
| 50-51—New York | 66 | ... | 302 | 853 | .354 | 231 | 298 | .775 | 228 | 136 | 150 | 3 | 835 | 3.5 | 2.1 | 12.7 |
| 51-52—New York | 66 | ... | 322 | 958 | .336 | 287 | 380 | .755 | 194 | 156 | 183 | 5 | 931 | 2.9 | 2.4 | 14.1 |
| 52-53—New York | 29 | ... | 123 | 320 | .384 | 98 | 142 | .690 | 75 | 55 | 81 | 1 | 344 | 2.6 | 1.9 | 11.9 |
| 53-54—Bal-Mil-FW | 65 | ... | 278 | 756 | .368 | 255 | 357 | .714 | 160 | 154 | 142 | 1 | 811 | 2.5 | 2.4 | 12.5 |
| 54-55—Fort Wayne | 70 | ... | 269 | 821 | .328 | 247 | 352 | .702 | 191 | 203 | 130 | 0 | 785 | 2.7 | 2.9 | 11.2 |
| 55-56—Fort Wayne | 9 | ... | 29 | 81 | .358 | 30 | 35 | .857 | 16 | 16 | 18 | 1 | 88 | 1.8 | 1.8 | 9.8 |
| Totals | 540 | ... | 2854 | 8313 | .343 | 2282 | 2969 | .769 | ... | 1093 | 1291 | ... | 7990 | ... | 2.0 | 14.8 |

### NBA PLAYOFF RECORD

| Season Team | G | Min. | FGM | FGA | Pct. | FTM | FTA | Pct. | Reb. | Ast. | PF | Dq. | Pts. | RPG | APG | PPG |
|---|---|---|---|---|---|---|---|---|---|---|---|---|---|---|---|---|
| 46-47—Chicago (BAA) | 11 | ... | 60 | 199 | .302 | 29 | 44 | .659 | ... | 4 | 26 | ... | 149 | ... | 0.4 | 13.5 |
| 47-48—Chicago (BAA) | 5 | ... | 30 | 88 | .341 | 37 | 47 | .787 | ... | 0 | 17 | ... | 97 | ... | 0.0 | 19.4 |
| 48-49—Chicago (BAA) | 2 | ... | 15 | 49 | .306 | 14 | 18 | .778 | ... | 6 | 3 | 0 | 44 | ... | 3.0 | 22.0 |
| 49-50—Chicago | 2 | ... | 15 | 32 | .469 | 15 | 18 | .833 | ... | 6 | 7 | ... | 45 | ... | 3.0 | 22.5 |
| 50-51—New York | 14 | ... | 88 | 217 | .406 | 74 | 100 | .740 | 58 | 38 | 43 | ... | 250 | 4.1 | 2.7 | 17.9 |
| 51-52—New York | 14 | ... | 69 | 185 | .373 | 89 | 110 | .809 | 44 | 23 | 51 | ... | 227 | 3.1 | 1.6 | 16.2 |
| 53-54—Fort Wayne | 4 | ... | 11 | 36 | .306 | 13 | 15 | .867 | 3 | 6 | 7 | ... | 35 | 0.8 | 1.5 | 8.8 |
| 54-55—Fort Wayne | 11 | ... | 18 | 44 | .409 | 16 | 20 | .800 | 16 | 18 | 20 | ... | 52 | 1.5 | 1.6 | 4.7 |
| Totals | 63 | ... | 306 | 850 | .360 | 287 | 372 | .772 | ... | 101 | 174 | ... | 899 | ... | 1.6 | 14.3 |

### NBA ALL-STAR GAME RECORD

| Season Team | Min. | FGM | FGA | Pct. | FTM | FTA | Pct. | Reb | Ast. | PF | Dq. | Pts. |
|---|---|---|---|---|---|---|---|---|---|---|---|---|
| 1952—New York | ... | 3 | 7 | .429 | 5 | 5 | 1.000 | 4 | 2 | 0 | 0 | 11 |

### ABA COACHING RECORD

| Season Team | REGULAR SEASON W | L | Pct. | Finish | PLAYOFFS W | L | Pct. |
|---|---|---|---|---|---|---|---|
| 67-68—New Jersey | 36 | 42 | .462 | T4th/Eastern Division | — | — | — |
| 67-68—New York | 17 | 61 | .218 | 5th/Eastern Division | — | — | — |
| Totals (2 years) | 53 | 103 | .340 | | — | — | — |

## ATTLES, AL

**PERSONAL:** Born November 7, 1936, in Newark, N.J. ... 6-0/185 (1,83/83,9). ... Full name: Alvin A. Attles.
**HIGH SCHOOL:** Weequahic (Newark, N.J.).
**COLLEGE:** North Carolina A&T.
**TRANSACTIONS:** Selected by Philadelphia Warriors in fifth round (39th pick overall) of 1960 NBA Draft. ... Warriors franchise moved from Philadelphia to San Francisco for 1962-63 season.
**CAREER NOTES:** Vice president/assistant general manager, Golden State Warriors (1987-88 to present).

### COLLEGIATE RECORD

| | | | | | | | | | | | | AVERAGES | | |
|---|---|---|---|---|---|---|---|---|---|---|---|---|---|---|
| Season Team | G | Min. | FGM | FGA | Pct. | FTM | FTA | Pct. | Reb. | Ast. | Pts. | RPG | APG | PPG |
| 56-57—North Carolina A&T....... | | | | | | Statistics unavailable. | | | | | | | | |
| 57-58—North Carolina A&T....... | | | | | | Statistics unavailable. | | | | | | | | |
| 58-59—North Carolina A&T....... | 29 | ... | 105 | 225 | .467 | 56 | 91 | .615 | ... | ... | 266 | ... | ... | 9.2 |
| 59-60—North Carolina A&T....... | 24 | ... | 190 | 301 | .631 | 47 | 71 | .662 | 80 | ... | 427 | 3.3 | ... | 17.8 |
| Totals ..................................... | 53 | ... | 295 | 526 | .561 | 103 | 162 | .636 | ... | ... | .693 | ... | ... | 13.1 |

### NBA REGULAR-SEASON RECORD

| | | | | | | | | | | | | | | AVERAGES | | |
|---|---|---|---|---|---|---|---|---|---|---|---|---|---|---|---|---|
| Season Team | G | Min. | FGM | FGA | Pct. | FTM | FTA | Pct. | Reb. | Ast. | PF | Dq. | Pts. | RPG | APG | PPG |
| 60-61—Philadelphia ..................... | 77 | 1544 | 222 | 543 | .409 | 97 | 162 | .599 | 214 | 174 | 235 | 5 | 541 | 2.8 | 2.3 | 7.0 |
| 61-62—Philadelphia ..................... | 75 | 2468 | 343 | 724 | .474 | 158 | 267 | .592 | 355 | 333 | 279 | 8 | 844 | 4.7 | 4.4 | 11.3 |
| 62-63—San Francisco. .................... | 71 | 1876 | 301 | 630 | .478 | 133 | 206 | .646 | 205 | 184 | 253 | 7 | 735 | 2.9 | 2.6 | 10.4 |
| 63-64—San Francisco. .................... | 70 | 1883 | 289 | 640 | .452 | 185 | 275 | .673 | 236 | 197 | 249 | 4 | 763 | 3.4 | 2.8 | 10.9 |
| 64-65—San Francisco. .................... | 73 | 1733 | 254 | 662 | .384 | 171 | 274 | .624 | 239 | 205 | 242 | 7 | 679 | 3.3 | 2.8 | 9.3 |
| 65-66—San Francisco. .................... | 79 | 2053 | 364 | 724 | .503 | 154 | 252 | .611 | 322 | 225 | 265 | 7 | 882 | 4.1 | 2.8 | 11.2 |
| 66-67—San Francisco. .................... | 70 | 1764 | 212 | 467 | .454 | 88 | 151 | .583 | 321 | 269 | 265 | 13 | 512 | 4.6 | 3.8 | 7.3 |
| 67-68—San Francisco. .................... | 67 | 1992 | 252 | 540 | .467 | 150 | 216 | .694 | 276 | 390 | 284 | 9 | 654 | 4.1 | 5.8 | 9.8 |
| 68-69—San Francisco. .................... | 51 | 1516 | 162 | 359 | .451 | 95 | 149 | .638 | 181 | 306 | 183 | 3 | 419 | 3.5 | 6.0 | 8.2 |
| 69-70—San Francisco. .................... | 45 | 676 | 78 | 202 | .386 | 75 | 113 | .664 | 74 | 142 | 103 | 0 | 231 | 1.6 | 3.2 | 5.1 |
| 70-71—San Francisco. .................... | 34 | 321 | 22 | 54 | .407 | 24 | 41 | .585 | 40 | 58 | 59 | 2 | 68 | 1.2 | 1.7 | 2.0 |
| Totals........................................ | 712 | 17826 | 2499 | 5545 | .451 | 1330 | 2106 | .632 | 2463 | 2483 | 2417 | 65 | 6328 | 3.5 | 3.5 | 8.9 |

### NBA PLAYOFF RECORD

| Season Team | G | Min. | FGM | FGA | Pct. | FTM | FTA | Pct. | Reb. | Ast. | PF | Dq. | Pts. | RPG | APG | PPG |
|---|---|---|---|---|---|---|---|---|---|---|---|---|---|---|---|---|
| 60-61—Philadelphia ..................... | 3 | 110 | 12 | 26 | .462 | 5 | 14 | .357 | 12 | 9 | 14 | 0 | 29 | 4.0 | 3.0 | 9.7 |
| 61-62—Philadelphia ..................... | 12 | 338 | 28 | 76 | .368 | 17 | 31 | .548 | 55 | 27 | 54 | 4 | 73 | 4.6 | 2.3 | 6.1 |
| 63-64—San Francisco. .................... | 12 | 386 | 58 | 144 | .403 | 30 | 56 | .536 | 37 | 30 | 54 | 5 | 146 | 3.1 | 2.5 | 12.2 |
| 66-67—San Francisco. .................... | 15 | 237 | 20 | 46 | .435 | 6 | 16 | .375 | 62 | 38 | 45 | 1 | 46 | 4.1 | 2.5 | 3.1 |
| 67-68—San Francisco. .................... | 10 | 277 | 25 | 62 | .403 | 23 | 30 | .767 | 53 | 70 | 49 | 2 | 73 | 5.3 | 7.0 | 7.3 |
| 68-69—San Francisco. .................... | 6 | 109 | 7 | 21 | .333 | 1 | 4 | .250 | 18 | 21 | 17 | 0 | 15 | 3.0 | 3.5 | 2.5 |
| 70-71—San Francisco. .................... | 4 | 47 | 4 | 7 | .571 | 4 | 7 | .571 | 8 | 11 | 13 | 0 | 12 | 2.0 | 2.8 | 3.0 |
| Totals........................................ | 62 | 1504 | 154 | 382 | .403 | 86 | 158 | .544 | 245 | 206 | 246 | 12 | 394 | 4.0 | 3.3 | 6.4 |

### HEAD COACHING RECORD
**BACKGROUND:** Assistant coach, Warriors (February 13, 1995-remainder of season).

### NBA COACHING RECORD

| | REGULAR SEASON | | | | PLAYOFFS | | |
|---|---|---|---|---|---|---|---|
| Season Team | W | L | Pct. | Finish | W | L | Pct. |
| 69-70—San Francisco ............................... | 8 | 22 | .267 | 6th/Western Division | — | — | — |
| 70-71—San Francisco ............................... | 41 | 41 | .500 | 2nd/Pacific Division | 1 | 4 | .200 |
| 71-72—Golden State ............................... | 51 | 31 | .622 | 2nd/Pacific Division | 1 | 4 | .200 |
| 72-73—Golden State ............................... | 47 | 35 | .573 | 2nd/Pacific Division | 5 | 6 | .455 |
| 73-74—Golden State ............................... | 44 | 38 | .537 | 2nd/Pacific Division | — | — | — |
| 74-75—Golden State ............................... | 48 | 34 | .585 | 1st/Pacific Division | 12 | 5 | .706 |
| 75-76—Golden State ............................... | 59 | 23 | .720 | 1st/Pacific Division | 7 | 6 | .538 |
| 76-77—Golden State ............................... | 46 | 36 | .561 | 3rd/Pacific Division | 5 | 5 | .500 |
| 77-78—Golden State ............................... | 43 | 39 | .524 | 5th/Pacific Division | — | — | — |
| 78-79—Golden State ............................... | 38 | 44 | .463 | 6th/Pacific Division | — | — | — |
| 79-80—Golden State ............................... | 18 | 43 | .295 | 6th/Pacific Division | — | — | — |
| 80-81—Golden State ............................... | 39 | 43 | .476 | 4th/Pacific Division | — | — | — |
| 81-82—Golden State ............................... | 45 | 37 | .549 | 4th/Pacific Division | — | — | — |
| 82-83—Golden State ............................... | 30 | 52 | .366 | 5th/Pacific Division | — | — | — |
| Totals (14 years)................................... | 557 | 518 | .518 | Totals (6 years) | 31 | 30 | .508 |

**NOTES:**
1970—Replaced George Lee as San Francisco head coach with record of 22-30.
1971—Lost to Milwaukee in Western Conference Semifinals.
1972—Lost to Milwaukee in Western Conference Semifinals.

1973—Defeated Milwaukee, 4-2, in Western Conference Semifinals; lost to Los Angeles, 4-1, in Western Conference Finals.
1975—Defeated Seattle, 4-2, in Western Conference Semifinals; defeated Chicago, 4-3, in Western Conference Finals; defeated Washington, 4-0, in NBA Finals.
1976—Defeated Detroit, 4-2, in Western Conference Semifinals; lost to Phoenix, 4-3, in Western Conference Finals.
1977—Defeated Detroit, 2-1, in Western Conference First Round; lost to Los Angeles, 4-3, in Western Conference Semifinals.
1980—Missed final 21 games of season due to injury; replaced by assistant coach John Bach (6-15) for remainder of season.

# AUERBACH, RED

**PERSONAL:** Born September 20, 1917, in Brooklyn, N.Y. ... 5-10/170 (1,78/77,1). ... Full name: Arnold Jacob Auerbach. ... Name pronounced HOUR-back.
**HIGH SCHOOL:** Eastern District (Brooklyn, N.Y.).
**JUNIOR COLLEGE:** Seth Low Junior College (N.Y.).
**COLLEGE:** George Washington.
**CAREER NOTES:** Vice president, Boston Celtics (1950-51 through 1963-64). ... Vice president and general manager, Celtics (1964-65). ... Executive vice president and general manager, Celtics (1965-66 through 1969-70). ... President and general manager, Celtics (1970-71 through 1983-84). ... President, Celtics (1984-85 through 1996-97, 2001-02-present). .. Vice chairman of the board, Celtics (1997-98 to present).
**CAREER HONORS:** Elected to Naismith Memorial Basketball Hall of Fame (1968). ... One of the Top 10 Coaches in NBA History (1996).

### COLLEGIATE RECORD

| Season Team | G | Min. | FGM | FGA | Pct. | FTM | FTA | Pct. | Reb. | Ast. | Pts. | RPG | APG | PPG |
|---|---|---|---|---|---|---|---|---|---|---|---|---|---|---|
| 36-37—Seth Low J.C. | | | | | | Statistics unavailable. | | | | | | | | |
| 37-38—George Washington | 17 | ... | 22 | ... | ... | 8 | 12 | .667 | ... | ... | 52 | ... | ... | 3.1 |
| 38-39—George Washington | 20 | ... | 54 | ... | ... | 12 | 19 | .632 | ... | ... | 120 | ... | ... | 6.0 |
| 39-40—George Washington | 19 | ... | 69 | ... | ... | 24 | 39 | .615 | ... | ... | 162 | ... | ... | 8.5 |
| 4-year-college totals | 56 | ... | 145 | ... | ... | 44 | 70 | .629 | ... | ... | 334 | ... | ... | 6.0 |

### HEAD COACHING RECORD

**BACKGROUND:** Head coach, St. Alban's Prep (Washington, D.C.). ... Head coach, Roosevelt High School (Washington, D.C.). ... Assistant coach, Duke University (1949-50).
**HONORS:** NBA Coach of the Year (1965). ... NBA 25th Anniversary All-Time team coach (1970). ... NBA Executive of the Year (1980). ... Selected as the "Greatest Coach in the History of the NBA" by the Professional Basketball Writers' Association of America (1980).

### NBA COACHING RECORD

| Season Team | REGULAR SEASON | | | | PLAYOFFS | | |
|---|---|---|---|---|---|---|---|
| | W | L | Pct. | Finish | W | L | Pct. |
| 46-47—Washington (BAA) | 49 | 11 | .817 | 1st/Eastern Division | 2 | 4 | .333 |
| 47-48—Washington (BAA) | 28 | 20 | .583 | T2nd/Western Division | 0 | 1 | .000 |
| 48-49—Washington (BAA) | 38 | 22 | .633 | 1st/Eastern Division | 6 | 5 | .545 |
| 49-50—Tri-Cities | 28 | 29 | .491 | 3rd/Western Division | 1 | 2 | .333 |
| 50-51—Boston | 39 | 30 | .565 | 2nd/Eastern Division | 0 | 2 | .000 |
| 51-52—Boston | 39 | 27 | .591 | 2nd/Eastern Division | 1 | 2 | .333 |
| 52-53—Boston | 46 | 25 | .648 | 3rd/Eastern Division | 3 | 3 | .500 |
| 53-54—Boston | 42 | 30 | .583 | T2nd/Eastern Division | 2 | 4 | .333 |
| 54-55—Boston | 36 | 36 | .500 | 3rd/Eastern Division | 3 | 4 | .429 |
| 55-56—Boston | 39 | 33 | .542 | 2nd/Eastern Division | 1 | 2 | .333 |
| 56-57—Boston | 44 | 28 | .611 | 1st/Eastern Division | 7 | 3 | .700 |
| 57-58—Boston | 49 | 23 | .681 | 1st/Eastern Division | 6 | 5 | .545 |
| 58-59—Boston | 52 | 20 | .722 | 1st/Eastern Division | 8 | 3 | .727 |
| 59-60—Boston | 59 | 16 | .787 | 1st/Eastern Division | 8 | 5 | .615 |
| 60-61—Boston | 57 | 22 | .722 | 1st/Eastern Division | 8 | 2 | .800 |
| 61-62—Boston | 60 | 20 | .750 | 1st/Eastern Division | 8 | 6 | .571 |
| 62-63—Boston | 58 | 22 | .725 | 1st/Eastern Division | 8 | 5 | .615 |
| 63-64—Boston | 59 | 21 | .738 | 1st/Eastern Division | 8 | 2 | .800 |
| 64-65—Boston | 62 | 18 | .775 | 1st/Eastern Division | 8 | 4 | .667 |
| 65-66—Boston | 54 | 26 | .675 | 2nd/Eastern Division | 11 | 6 | .647 |
| Totals (20 years) | 938 | 479 | .662 | Totals (20 years) | 99 | 70 | .586 |

**NOTES:**
1947—Lost to Chicago in BAA Semifinals.
1948—Lost to Chicago, 74-70, in Western Division tiebreaker.
1949—Defeated Philadelphia, 2-0, in Eastern Division Semifinals; defeated New York, 2-1, in Eastern Division Finals; lost to Minneapolis, 4-2, in NBA Finals. Replaced Roger Potter as Tri-Cities head coach with record of 1-6.
1950—Lost to Anderson in Western Division Semifinals.
1951—Lost to New York in Eastern Division Semifinals.
1952—Lost to New York in Eastern Division Semifinals.
1953—Defeated Syracuse, 2-0, in Eastern Division Semifinals; lost to New York, 3-1, in Eastern Division Finals.
1954—Defeated New York, 93-71; lost to Syracuse, 96-95 (OT); defeated New York, 79-78; lost to Syracuse, 98-85, in Eastern Division round robin; lost to Syracuse, 2-0, in Eastern Division Finals.

1955—Defeated New York, 2-1, in Eastern Division Semifinals; lost to Syracuse, 3-1, in Eastern Division Finals.
1956—Lost to Syracuse in Eastern Division Semifinals.
1957—Defeated Syracuse, 3-0, in Eastern Division Finals; defeated St. Louis, 4-3, in NBA Finals.
1958—Defeated Philadelphia, 4-1, in Eastern Division Finals; lost to St. Louis, 4-2, in NBA Finals.
1959—Defeated Syracuse, 4-3, in Eastern Division Finals; defeated Minneapolis, 4-0, in NBA Finals.
1960—Defeated Philadelphia, 4-2, in Eastern Division Finals; defeated St. Louis, 4-3, in NBA Finals.
1961—Defeated Syracuse, 4-1, in Eastern Division Finals; defeated St. Louis, 4-1, in NBA Finals.
1962—Defeated Philadelphia, 4-3, in Eastern Division Finals; defeated Los Angeles, 4-3, in NBA Finals.
1963—Defeated Cincinnati, 4-3, in Eastern Division Finals; defeated Los Angeles, 4-2, in NBA Finals.
1964—Defeated Cincinnati, 4-1, in Eastern Division Finals; defeated San Francisco, 4-1, in NBA Finals.
1965—Defeated Philadelphia, 4-3, in Eastern Division Finals; defeated Los Angeles, 4-1, in NBA Finals.
1966—Defeated Cincinnati, 3-2 in Eastern Division Semifinals; defeated Philadelphia, 4-1, in Eastern Division Finals; defeated Los Angeles, 4-3, in NBA Finals.

# BROWN, HUBIE

**PERSONAL:** Born September 25, 1933, in Elizabeth, N.J. ... 6-0/160. (1,83/72,6). ... Full Name: Hubert Jude Brown.
**HIGH SCHOOL:** St. Mary's (Elizabeth, N.J.).
**COLLEGE:** Niagara.
**TRANSACTIONS/CAREER NOTES:** Played with Rochester in Eastern Basketball League (1958-59).

### COLLEGIATE RECORD

| Season Team | G | Min. | FGM | FGA | Pct. | FTM | FTA | Pct. | Reb. | Ast. | Pts. | RPG | APG | PPG |
|---|---|---|---|---|---|---|---|---|---|---|---|---|---|---|
| 51-52—Niagara | 8 | ... | 3 | ... | ... | 4 | 5 | .800 | ... | ... | 10 | ... | ... | 1.3 |
| 52-53—Niagara | 21 | ... | 15 | ... | ... | 15 | ... | ... | ... | ... | 45 | ... | ... | 2.1 |
| 53-54—Niagara | 30 | ... | 24 | ... | ... | 27 | ... | ... | ... | ... | 75 | ... | ... | 3.5 |
| 54-55—Niagara | 23 | ... | 63 | ... | ... | 66 | ... | ... | ... | ... | 192 | ... | ... | 8.3 |
| Totals | 82 | ... | 105 | ... | ... | 112 | ... | ... | ... | ... | 322 | ... | ... | 3.9 |

### EBL REGULAR-SEASON RECORD

| Season Team | G | Min. | FGM | FGA | Pct. | FTM | FTA | Pct. | Off. | Def. | Tot. | Ast. | St. | Blk. | TO | Pts. | RPG | APG | PPG |
|---|---|---|---|---|---|---|---|---|---|---|---|---|---|---|---|---|---|---|---|
| 58-59—Rochester | 8 | ... | 49 | ... | ... | 12 | ... | ... | ... | ... | ... | ... | ... | ... | ... | 110 | ... | ... | 13.8 |

### HEAD COACHING RECORD

**BACKGROUND:** Assistant coach, William & Mary (1967-68). ... Assistant coach, Duke University (1968-69 through 1971-72). ... Assistant coach, Milwaukee Bucks (1972-73 through 1973-74).
**HONORS:** Coach of ABA championship team (1974-75). ... NBA Coach of the Year (1978, 2004).

### ABA COACHING RECORD

| | REGULAR SEASON | | | | PLAYOFFS | | |
|---|---|---|---|---|---|---|---|
| Season Team | W | L | Pct. | Finish | W | L | Pct. |
| 74-75—Kentucky | 58 | 26 | .690 | T1st/Eastern Division | 12 | 3 | .800 |
| 75-76—Kentucky | 46 | 38 | .548 | 4th/Eastern Division | 5 | 5 | .500 |
| Totals (2 years) | 104 | 64 | .619 | Totals (2 years) | 17 | 8 | .680 |

### NBA COACHING RECORD

| | REGULAR SEASON | | | | PLAYOFFS | | |
|---|---|---|---|---|---|---|---|
| Season Team | W | L | Pct. | Finish | W | L | Pct. |
| 76-77—Atlanta | 31 | 51 | .378 | 6th/Central Division | — | — | — |
| 77-78—Atlanta | 41 | 41 | .500 | 4th/Central Division | 0 | 2 | .000 |
| 78-79—Atlanta | 46 | 36 | .561 | 3rd/Central Division | 5 | 4 | .556 |
| 79-80—Atlanta | 50 | 32 | .610 | 1st/Central Division | 1 | 4 | .200 |
| 80-81—Atlanta | 31 | 48 | .392 | 4th/Atlantic Division | — | — | — |
| 82-83—New York | 44 | 38 | .537 | 4th/Atlantic Division | 2 | 4 | .333 |
| 83-84—New York | 47 | 35 | .573 | 3rd/Atlantic Division | 6 | 6 | .500 |
| 84-85—New York | 24 | 58 | .293 | 5th/Atlantic Division | — | — | — |
| 85-86—New York | 23 | 59 | .280 | 5th/Atlantic Division | — | — | — |
| 86-87—New York | 4 | 12 | .250 | | — | — | — |
| 02-03—Memphis | 28 | 46 | .378 | 6th/Midwest Division | — | — | — |
| 03-04—Memphis | 50 | 32 | .610 | 4th/Midwest Division | 0 | 4 | .000 |
| 04-05—Memphis | 5 | 7 | .417 | | | | |
| Totals (13 years) | 424 | 495 | .461 | Totals (6 years) | 14 | 24 | .368 |

**NOTES:**
1975—Defeated Memphis, 4-1, in Eastern Division semifinals; defeated St. Louis, 4-1, in Eastern Division finals; defeated Indiana, 4-1, in ABA Championship Series.
1976—Defeated Indiana, 2-1, in first round; lost to Denver, 4-3, in Eastern Division semifinals.
1978—Lost to Washington, 2-0, in Eastern Conference first round.
1979—Defeated Houston, 2-0, in Eastern Conference first round; lost to Washington, 4-3, in Eastern Conference semifinals.
1980—Lost to Philadelphia, 4-1, in Eastern Conference semifinals.
1983—Defeated New Jersey, 2-0, in Eastern Conference first round; lost to Philadelphia, 4-0, in Eastern Conference semifinals.
1984—Defeated Detroit, 3-2, in Eastern Conference first round; lost to Boston, 4-3, in Eastern Conference semifinals.
1986—Replaced by Bob Hill as New York head coach (December 1).
2002—Replaced Sidney Lowe as Memphis head coach (November 12) with record of 0-8 and club in seventh place.
2004—Stepped down as Memphis head coach (November 25); replaced by Mike Fratello with team in fourth place.

# COSTELLO, LARRY

**PERSONAL:** Born July 2, 1931, in Minoa, N.Y. ... Died December 11, 2001. ... 6-1/188 (1,85/85,3). ... Full name: Lawrence Ronald Costello.
**HIGH SCHOOL:** Minoa (N.Y.).
**COLLEGE:** Niagara.
**TRANSACTIONS:** Selected by Philadelphia Warriors in second round of 1954 NBA Draft. ... Sold by Warriors to Syracuse Nationals (October 10, 1957). ... Nationals franchise moved from Syracuse to Philadelphia and renamed 76ers for 1963-64 season. ... Played in Eastern Basketball League with Wilkes-Barre Barons (1965-66). ... Drafted by Milwaukee Bucks from 76ers in NBA Expansion Draft (May 6, 1968).
**MISCELLANEOUS:** Member of NBA championship team (1967).

## COLLEGIATE RECORD

| Season Team | G | Min. | FGM | FGA | Pct. | FTM | FTA | Pct. | Reb. | Ast. | Pts. | AVERAGES RPG | APG | PPG |
|---|---|---|---|---|---|---|---|---|---|---|---|---|---|---|
| 50-51—Niagara‡ | | | | | | Freshman team statistics unavailable. | | | | | | | | |
| 51-52—Niagara | 28 | ... | 131 | ... | ... | 58 | 87 | .667 | ... | ... | 320 | ... | ... | 11.4 |
| 52-53—Niagara | 28 | ... | 185 | ... | ... | 140 | 194 | .722 | ... | ... | 510 | ... | ... | 18.2 |
| 53-54—Niagara | 29 | ... | 160 | ... | ... | 125 | 152 | .822 | ... | ... | 445 | ... | ... | 15.3 |
| Varsity totals | 85 | ... | 476 | ... | ... | 323 | 433 | .746 | ... | ... | 1275 | ... | ... | 15.0 |

## NBA REGULAR-SEASON RECORD

**HONORS:** All-NBA second team (1961).

| Season Team | G | Min. | FGM | FGA | Pct. | FTM | FTA | Pct. | Reb. | Ast. | PF | Dq. | Pts. | AVERAGES RPG | APG | PPG |
|---|---|---|---|---|---|---|---|---|---|---|---|---|---|---|---|---|
| 54-55—Philadelphia | 19 | 463 | 46 | 139 | .331 | 26 | 32 | .813 | 49 | 78 | 37 | 0 | 118 | 2.6 | 4.1 | 6.2 |
| 55-56—Philadelphia | | | | | | Did not play—in military service. | | | | | | | | | | |
| 56-57—Philadelphia | 72 | 2111 | 186 | 497 | .374 | 175 | 222 | .788 | 323 | 236 | 182 | 2 | 547 | 4.5 | 3.3 | 7.6 |
| 57-58—Syracuse | 72 | 2746 | 378 | 888 | .426 | 320 | 378 | .847 | 378 | 317 | 246 | 3 | 1076 | 5.3 | 4.4 | 14.9 |
| 58-59—Syracuse | 70 | 2750 | 414 | 948 | .437 | 280 | 349 | .802 | 365 | 379 | 263 | 7 | 1108 | 5.2 | 5.4 | 15.8 |
| 59-60—Syracuse | 71 | 2469 | 372 | 822 | .453 | 249 | 289 | .862 | 388 | 449 | 234 | 4 | 993 | 5.5 | 6.3 | 14.0 |
| 60-61—Syracuse | 75 | 2167 | 407 | 844 | .482 | 270 | 338 | .799 | 292 | 413 | 286 | 9 | 1084 | 3.9 | 5.5 | 14.5 |
| 61-62—Syracuse | 63 | 1854 | 310 | 726 | .427 | 247 | 295 | .837 | 245 | 359 | 220 | 5 | 867 | 3.9 | 5.7 | 13.8 |
| 62-63—Syracuse | 78 | 2066 | 285 | 660 | .432 | 288 | 327 | *.881 | 237 | 334 | 263 | 4 | 858 | 3.0 | 4.3 | 11.0 |
| 63-64—Philadelphia | 45 | 1137 | 191 | 408 | .468 | 147 | 170 | .865 | 105 | 167 | 150 | 3 | 529 | 2.3 | 3.7 | 11.8 |
| 64-65—Philadelphia | 64 | 1967 | 309 | 695 | .445 | 243 | 277 | *.877 | 169 | 275 | 242 | 10 | 861 | 2.6 | 4.3 | 13.5 |
| 66-67—Philadelphia | 49 | 976 | 130 | 293 | .444 | 120 | 133 | .902 | 103 | 140 | 141 | 2 | 380 | 2.1 | 2.9 | 7.8 |
| 67-68—Philadelphia | 28 | 492 | 67 | 148 | .453 | 67 | 81 | .827 | 51 | 68 | 62 | 0 | 201 | 1.8 | 2.4 | 7.2 |
| Totals | 706 | 21198 | 3095 | 7068 | .438 | 2432 | 2891 | .841 | 2705 | 3215 | 2326 | 49 | 8622 | 3.8 | 4.6 | 12.2 |

## NBA PLAYOFF RECORD

| Season Team | G | Min. | FGM | FGA | Pct. | FTM | FTA | Pct. | Reb. | Ast. | PF | Dq. | Pts. | AVERAGES RPG | APG | PPG |
|---|---|---|---|---|---|---|---|---|---|---|---|---|---|---|---|---|
| 56-57—Philadelphia | 2 | 16 | 3 | 8 | .375 | 0 | 1 | .000 | 5 | 2 | 3 | 0 | 6 | 2.5 | 1.0 | 3.0 |
| 57-58—Syracuse | 3 | 134 | 10 | 34 | .294 | 14 | 14 | 1.000 | 25 | 12 | 6 | 0 | 34 | 8.3 | 4.0 | 11.3 |
| 58-59—Syracuse | 9 | 361 | 54 | 121 | .446 | 51 | 61 | .836 | 53 | 54 | 40 | 2 | 159 | 5.9 | 6.0 | 17.7 |
| 59-60—Syracuse | 3 | 122 | 20 | 47 | .426 | 10 | 12 | .833 | 14 | 20 | 15 | 1 | 50 | 4.7 | 6.7 | 16.7 |
| 60-61—Syracuse | 8 | 269 | 42 | 103 | .408 | 47 | 55 | .855 | 35 | 52 | 39 | 3 | 131 | 4.4 | 6.5 | 16.4 |
| 61-62—Syracuse | 5 | 167 | 22 | 51 | .431 | 29 | 33 | .879 | 16 | 28 | 21 | 0 | 73 | 3.2 | 5.6 | 14.6 |
| 62-63—Syracuse | 5 | 134 | 16 | 37 | .432 | 19 | 23 | .826 | 4 | 23 | 27 | 2 | 51 | 0.8 | 4.6 | 10.2 |
| 63-64—Philadelphia | 5 | 36 | 3 | 14 | .214 | 10 | 10 | 1.000 | 3 | 4 | 14 | 1 | 16 | 0.6 | 0.8 | 3.2 |
| 64-65—Philadelphia | 10 | 207 | 22 | 53 | .415 | 11 | 16 | .688 | 12 | 20 | 43 | 2 | 55 | 1.2 | 2.0 | 5.5 |
| 66-67—Philadelphia | 2 | 25 | 6 | 8 | .750 | 5 | 5 | 1.000 | 4 | 3 | 2 | 0 | 17 | 2.0 | 1.5 | 8.5 |
| Totals | 52 | 1471 | 198 | 476 | .416 | 196 | 230 | .852 | 171 | 218 | 210 | 11 | 592 | 3.3 | 4.2 | 11.4 |

## NBA ALL-STAR GAME RECORD

| Season Team | Min. | FGM | FGA | Pct. | FTM | FTA | Pct. | Reb. | Ast. | PF | Dq. | Pts. |
|---|---|---|---|---|---|---|---|---|---|---|---|---|
| 1958—Syracuse | 17 | 0 | 6 | .000 | 1 | 1 | 1.000 | 1 | 4 | 2 | 0 | 1 |
| 1959—Syracuse | 18 | 3 | 8 | .375 | 1 | 1 | 1.000 | 3 | 3 | 1 | 0 | 7 |
| 1960—Syracuse | 20 | 5 | 9 | .556 | 0 | 0 | ... | 4 | 2 | 1 | 0 | 10 |
| 1961—Syracuse | 5 | 1 | 2 | .500 | 0 | 0 | ... | 0 | 0 | 2 | 0 | 2 |
| 1962—Syracuse | | | | | Selected, did not play—injured. | | | | | | | |
| 1965—Philadelphia | 11 | 2 | 7 | .286 | 0 | 0 | ... | 1 | 2 | 2 | 0 | 4 |
| Totals | 71 | 11 | 32 | .344 | 2 | 2 | 1.000 | 9 | 11 | 8 | 0 | 24 |

## EBL REGULAR-SEASON RECORD

| Season Team | G | Min. | FGM | FGA | Pct. | FTM | FTA | Pct. | Reb. | Ast. | PF | Dq. | Pts. | AVERAGES RPG | APG | PPG |
|---|---|---|---|---|---|---|---|---|---|---|---|---|---|---|---|---|
| 65-66—Wilkes-Barre | 12 | ... | 54 | ... | ... | 53 | 59 | .898 | 22 | 83 | ... | . | 167 | 1.8 | 6.9 | 13.9 |

## HEAD COACHING RECORD

**BACKGROUND:** Head coach, Minoa High School, N.Y. (1965-66). ... Head coach, Milwaukee Does of Women's Professional Basketball League (1979-80).

## NBA COACHING RECORD

| Season Team | REGULAR SEASON W | L | Pct. | Finish | PLAYOFFS W | L | Pct. |
|---|---|---|---|---|---|---|---|
| 68-69—Milwaukee | 27 | 55 | .329 | 7th/Eastern Division | — | — | — |
| 69-70—Milwaukee | 56 | 26 | .683 | 2nd/Eastern Division | 5 | 5 | .500 |
| 70-71—Milwaukee | 66 | 16 | .805 | 1st/Midwest Division | 12 | 2 | .857 |
| 71-72—Milwaukee | 63 | 19 | .768 | 1st/Midwest Division | 6 | 5 | .545 |
| 72-73—Milwaukee | 60 | 22 | .732 | 1st/Midwest Division | 2 | 4 | .333 |
| 73-74—Milwaukee | 59 | 23 | .720 | 1st/Midwest Division | 11 | 5 | .688 |
| 74-75—Milwaukee | 38 | 44 | .463 | 4th/Midwest Division | — | — | — |
| 75-76—Milwaukee | 38 | 44 | .463 | 1st/Midwest Division | 1 | 2 | .333 |
| 76-77—Milwaukee | 3 | 15 | .167 | | — | — | — |
| 78-79—Chicago | 20 | 36 | .357 | | — | — | — |
| **Totals (10 years)** | 430 | 300 | .589 | **Totals (6 years)** | 37 | 23 | .617 |

### COLLEGIATE COACHING RECORD

| Season Team | W | L | Pct. | Finish |
|---|---|---|---|---|
| 80-81—Utica | 13 | 12 | .520 | Independent |
| 81-82—Utica | 4 | 22 | .154 | Independent |
| 82-83—Utica | 11 | 15 | .423 | Independent |
| 83-84—Utica | 11 | 15 | .423 | Independent |
| 84-85—Utica | 15 | 12 | .556 | Independent |
| 85-86—Utica | 13 | 14 | .481 | Independent |
| 86-87—Utica | 10 | 16 | .385 | Independent |
| **Totals (7 years)** | 77 | 106 | .421 | |

**NOTE:**
1970—Defeated Philadelphia, 4-1, in Eastern Division Semifinals; lost to New York, 4-1, in Eastern Division Finals.
1971—Defeated San Francisco, 4-1, in Western Conference Semifinals; defeated Los Angeles, 4-1, in Western Conference Finals; defeated Baltimore, 4-0, in NBA Finals.
1972—Defeated Golden State, 4-1, in Western Conference Semifinals; lost to Los Angeles, 4-2, in Western Conference Finals.
1973—Lost to Golden State in Western Conference Semifinals.
1974—Defeated Los Angeles, 4-1, in Western Conference Semifinals; defeated Chicago, 4-0, in Western Conference Finals; lost to Boston, 4-3, in NBA Finals.
1976—Lost to Detroit in Western Conference First Round. Resigned as Milwaukee head coach and replaced by Don Nelson (November 22).
1979—Replaced as Chicago head coach by Scotty Robertson (February 16).

# CUNNINGHAM, BILLY

**PERSONAL:** Born June 3, 1943, in Brooklyn, N.Y. ... 6-7/210 (2,00/95,3). ... Full name: William John Cunningham.
**HIGH SCHOOL:** Erasmus Hall (Brooklyn, N.Y.).
**COLLEGE:** North Carolina.
**TRANSACTIONS:** Selected by Philadelphia 76ers in first round of 1965 NBA Draft. ... Signed as free agent by Carolina Cougars of American Basketball Association (August 1969). ... Signed as free agent by 76ers (1969). ... Suspended by NBA (1972). ... Restored by NBA (1974). ... Returned to 76ers (1974).
**CAREER HONORS:** Elected to Naismith Memorial Basketball Hall of Fame (1986). ... One of the 50 Greatest Players in NBA History (1996).
**CAREER NOTES:** Part owner, Miami Heat (1987-88 to 1994-95).
**MISCELLANEOUS:** Member of NBA championship team (1967).

### COLLEGIATE RECORD

**NOTES:** THE SPORTING NEWS All-America second team (1965).

| Season Team | G | Min. | FGM | FGA | Pct. | FTM | FTA | Pct. | Reb. | Ast. | Pts. | AVERAGES RPG | APG | PPG |
|---|---|---|---|---|---|---|---|---|---|---|---|---|---|---|
| 61-62—North Carolina‡ | 10 | ... | 81 | 162 | .500 | 45 | 78 | .577 | 127 | ... | 207 | 12.7 | ... | 20.7 |
| 62-63—North Carolina | 21 | ... | 186 | 380 | .489 | 105 | 170 | .618 | 339 | ... | 477 | 16.1 | ... | 22.7 |
| 63-64—North Carolina | 24 | ... | 233 | 526 | .443 | 157 | 249 | .631 | 339 | ... | 623 | 15.8 | ... | 26.0 |
| 64-65—North Carolina | 24 | ... | 237 | 481 | .493 | 135 | 213 | .634 | 344 | ... | 609 | 14.3 | ... | 25.4 |
| **Varsity totals** | 69 | ... | 656 | 1387 | .473 | 397 | 632 | .628 | 1062 | ... | 1709 | 15.4 | ... | 24.8 |

### NBA REGULAR-SEASON RECORD

**HONORS:** All-NBA first team (1969, 1970, 1971). ... All-NBA second team (1972). ... NBA All-Rookie team (1966).

| Season Team | G | Min. | FGM | FGA | Pct. | FTM | FTA | Pct. | Reb. | Ast. | PF | Dq. | Pts. | AVERAGES RPG | APG | PPG |
|---|---|---|---|---|---|---|---|---|---|---|---|---|---|---|---|---|
| 65-66—Philadelphia | 80 | 2134 | 431 | 1011 | .426 | 281 | 443 | .634 | 599 | 207 | 301 | 12 | 1143 | 7.5 | 2.6 | 14.3 |
| 66-67—Philadelphia | 81 | 2168 | 556 | 1211 | .459 | 383 | 558 | .686 | 589 | 205 | 260 | 2 | 1495 | 7.3 | 2.5 | 18.5 |
| 67-68—Philadelphia | 74 | 2076 | 516 | 1178 | .438 | 368 | 509 | .723 | 562 | 187 | 260 | 3 | 1400 | 7.6 | 2.5 | 18.9 |
| 68-69—Philadelphia | 82 | 3345 | 739 | 1736 | .426 | 556 | 754 | .737 | 1050 | 287 | *329 | 10 | 2034 | 12.8 | 3.5 | 24.8 |
| 69-70—Philadelphia | 81 | 3194 | 802 | 1710 | .469 | 510 | 700 | .729 | 1101 | 352 | 331 | 15 | 2114 | 13.6 | 4.3 | 26.1 |
| 70-71—Philadelphia | 81 | 3090 | 702 | 1519 | .462 | 455 | 620 | .734 | 946 | 395 | 328 | 5 | 1859 | 11.7 | 4.9 | 23.0 |
| 71-72—Philadelphia | 75 | 2900 | 658 | 1428 | .461 | 428 | 601 | .712 | 918 | 445 | 295 | 12 | 1744 | 12.2 | 5.9 | 23.3 |

| Season Team | G | Min. | FGM | FGA | Pct. | FTM | FTA | Pct. | REBOUNDS Off. | Def. | Tot. | Ast. | Stl. | Blk. | TO | Pts. | AVERAGES RPG | APG | PPG |
|---|---|---|---|---|---|---|---|---|---|---|---|---|---|---|---|---|---|---|---|
| 74-75—Philadelphia | 80 | 2859 | 609 | 1423 | .428 | 345 | 444 | .777 | 130 | 596 | 726 | 442 | 91 | 35 | ... | 1563 | 9.1 | 5.5 | 19.5 |
| 75-76—Philadelphia | 20 | 640 | 103 | 251 | .410 | 68 | 88 | .773 | 29 | 118 | 147 | 107 | 24 | 10 | ... | 274 | 7.4 | 5.4 | 13.7 |
| **Totals** | 654 | 22406 | 5116 | 11467 | .446 | 3394 | 4717 | .720 | ... | ... | 6638 | 2625 | 115 | 45 | ... | 13626 | 10.1 | 4.0 | 20.8 |

Personal fouls/disqualifications: 1974-75. 270/4. 1975-76, 57/1. Totals, 2431/64.

## NBA PLAYOFF RECORD

| Season Team | G | Min. | FGM | FGA | Pct. | FTM | FTA | Pct. | Reb. | Ast. | PF | Dq. | Pts. | RPG | APG | PPG |
|---|---|---|---|---|---|---|---|---|---|---|---|---|---|---|---|---|
| | | | | | | | | | | | | | | AVERAGES | | |
| 65-66—Philadelphia | 4 | 69 | 5 | 31 | .161 | 11 | 13 | .846 | 18 | 10 | 11 | 0 | 21 | 4.5 | 2.5 | 5.3 |
| 66-67—Philadelphia | 15 | 339 | 83 | 221 | .376 | 59 | 90 | .656 | 93 | 33 | 53 | 1 | 225 | 6.2 | 2.2 | 15.0 |
| 67-68—Philadelphia | 3 | 86 | 24 | 43 | .558 | 14 | 17 | .824 | 22 | 10 | 16 | 1 | 62 | 7.3 | 3.3 | 20.7 |
| 68-69—Philadelphia | 5 | 217 | 49 | 117 | .419 | 24 | 38 | .632 | 63 | 12 | 24 | 1 | 122 | 12.6 | 2.4 | 24.4 |
| 69-70—Philadelphia | 5 | 205 | 61 | 123 | .496 | 24 | 36 | .667 | 52 | 20 | 19 | 0 | 146 | 10.4 | 4.0 | 29.2 |
| 70-71—Philadelphia | 7 | 301 | 67 | 142 | .472 | 47 | 67 | .701 | 108 | 40 | 28 | 0 | 181 | 15.4 | 5.7 | 25.9 |
| Totals | 39 | 1217 | 289 | 677 | .427 | 179 | 261 | .686 | 356 | 125 | 151 | 3 | 757 | 9.1 | 3.2 | 19.4 |

## NBA ALL-STAR GAME RECORD

| Season Team | Min. | FGM | FGA | Pct. | FTM | FTA | Pct. | Reb. | Ast. | PF | Dq. | Pts. |
|---|---|---|---|---|---|---|---|---|---|---|---|---|
| 1969—Philadelphia | 22 | 5 | 10 | .500 | 0 | 0 | ... | 5 | 1 | 3 | 0 | 10 |
| 1970—Philadelphia | 28 | 7 | 13 | .538 | 5 | 5 | 1.000 | 4 | 2 | 3 | 0 | 19 |
| 1971—Philadelphia | 19 | 2 | 8 | .250 | 1 | 2 | .500 | 4 | 3 | 1 | 0 | 5 |
| 1972—Philadelphia | 24 | 4 | 13 | .308 | 6 | 8 | .750 | 10 | 3 | 4 | 0 | 14 |
| Totals | 93 | 18 | 44 | .409 | 12 | 15 | .800 | 23 | 9 | 11 | 0 | 48 |

## ABA REGULAR-SEASON RECORD

**NOTES:** ABA Most Valuable Player (1973). ... ABA All-Star first team (1973).

| Season Team | G | Min. | 2-POINT | | | 3-POINT | | | FTM | FTA | Pct. | Reb. | Ast. | Pts. | AVERAGES | | |
|---|---|---|---|---|---|---|---|---|---|---|---|---|---|---|---|---|---|
| | | | FGM | FGA | Pct. | FGM | FGA | Pct. | | | | | | | RPG | APG | PPG |
| 72-73—Carolina | 84 | 3248 | 757 | 1534 | .493 | 14 | 49 | .286 | 472 | 598 | .789 | 1012 | 530 | 2028 | 12.0 | 6.3 | 24.1 |
| 73-74—Carolina | 32 | 1190 | 252 | 529 | .476 | 1 | 8 | .125 | 149 | 187 | .797 | 331 | 150 | 656 | 10.3 | 4.7 | 20.5 |
| Totals | 116 | 4438 | 1009 | 2063 | .489 | 15 | 57 | .263 | 621 | 785 | .791 | 1343 | 680 | 2684 | 11.6 | 5.9 | 23.1 |

## ABA PLAYOFF RECORD

| Season Team | G | Min. | 2-POINT | | | 3-POINT | | | FTM | FTA | Pct. | Reb. | Ast. | Pts. | AVERAGES | | |
|---|---|---|---|---|---|---|---|---|---|---|---|---|---|---|---|---|---|
| | | | FGM | FGA | Pct. | FGM | FGA | Pct. | | | | | | | RPG | APG | PPG |
| 72-73—Carolina | 12 | 472 | 111 | 219 | .507 | 1 | 4 | .250 | 57 | 83 | .687 | 142 | 61 | 282 | 11.8 | 5.1 | 23.5 |
| 73-74—Carolina | 3 | 61 | 9 | 29 | .310 | 0 | 2 | .000 | 4 | 5 | .800 | 16 | 6 | 22 | 5.3 | 2.0 | 7.3 |
| Totals | 15 | 533 | 120 | 248 | .484 | 1 | 6 | .167 | 61 | 88 | .693 | 158 | 67 | 304 | 10.5 | 4.5 | 20.3 |

## ABA ALL-STAR GAME RECORD

| Season Team | Min. | 2-POINT | | | 3-POINT | | | FTM | FTA | Pct. | Reb. | Ast. | Pts. |
|---|---|---|---|---|---|---|---|---|---|---|---|---|---|
| | | FGM | FGA | Pct. | FGM | FGA | Pct. | | | | | | |
| 1973—Carolina | 20 | 9 | 11 | .818 | 0 | 1 | .000 | 0 | 0 | ... | 6 | 4 | 18 |

## COMBINED ABA AND NBA REGULAR-SEASON RECORDS

| | G | Min. | FGM | FGA | Pct. | FTM | FTA | Pct. | REBOUNDS | | | Ast. | Stl. | Blk. | TO | Pts. | AVERAGES | | |
|---|---|---|---|---|---|---|---|---|---|---|---|---|---|---|---|---|---|---|---|
| | | | | | | | | | Off. | Def. | Tot. | | | | | | RPG | APG | PPG |
| Totals | 770 | 26844 | 6140 | 13587 | .452 | 4015 | 5502 | .730 | ... | ... | 7981 | 3305 | ... | ... | ... | 16310 | 10.4 | 4.3 | 21.2 |

Three-point field goals: 15-for-57 (.263).
Personal fouls: 2845.

## NBA COACHING RECORD

| Season Team | REGULAR SEASON | | | | PLAYOFFS | | |
|---|---|---|---|---|---|---|---|
| | W | L | Pct. | Finish | W | L | Pct. |
| 77-78—Philadelphia | 53 | 23 | .697 | 1st/Atlantic Division | 6 | 4 | .600 |
| 78-79—Philadelphia | 47 | 35 | .573 | 2nd/Atlantic Division | 5 | 4 | .556 |
| 79-80—Philadelphia | 59 | 23 | .720 | 2nd/Atlantic Division | 12 | 6 | .667 |
| 80-81—Philadelphia | 62 | 20 | .756 | T1st/Atlantic Division | 9 | 7 | .563 |
| 81-82—Philadelphia | 58 | 24 | .707 | 2nd/Atlantic Division | 12 | 9 | .571 |
| 82-83—Philadelphia | 65 | 17 | .793 | 1st/Atlantic Division | 12 | 1 | .923 |
| 83-84—Philadelphia | 52 | 30 | .634 | 2nd/Atlantic Division | 2 | 3 | .400 |
| 84-85—Philadelphia | 58 | 24 | .707 | 2nd/Atlantic Division | 8 | 5 | .615 |
| Totals (8 years) | 454 | 196 | .698 | Totals (8 years) | 66 | 39 | .629 |

**NOTES:**

1977—Replaced Gene Shue as Philadelphia head coach (November 4), with record of 2-4.

1978—Defeated New York, 4-0, in Eastern Conference Semifinals; lost to Washington, 4-2, in Eastern Conference Finals.

1979—Defeated New Jersey, 2-0, in Eastern Conference First Round; lost to San Antonio, 4-3, in Eastern Conference Semifinals.

1980—Defeated Washington, 2-0, in Eastern Conference First Round; defeated Atlanta, 4-1, in Eastern Conference Semifinals; defeated Boston, 4-1, in Eastern Conference Finals; lost to Los Angeles, 4-2, in NBA Finals.

1981—Defeated Indiana, 2-0, in Eastern Conference First Round; defeated Milwaukee, 4-3, in Eastern Conference Semifinals; lost to Boston, 4-3, in Eastern Conference Finals.

1982—Defeated Atlanta, 2-0, in Eastern Conference First Round; defeated Milwaukee, 4-2, in Eastern Conference Semifinals; defeated Boston, 4-3, in Eastern Conference Finals; lost to Los Angeles, 4-2, in NBA Finals.

1983—Defeated New York, 4-0, in Eastern Conference Semifinals; defeated Milwaukee, 4-1, in Eastern Conference Finals; defeated Los Angeles, 4-0, in NBA Finals.

1984—Lost to New Jersey in Eastern Conference First Round.

1985—Defeated Washington, 3-1, in Eastern Conference First Round; defeated Milwaukee, 4-0, in Eastern Conference Semifinals; lost to Boston, 4-1, in Eastern Conference Finals.

# DALY, CHUCK

**PERSONAL:** Born July 20, 1930, in St. Mary's, Pa. ... 6-2/180 (1,88/81,6). ... Full name: Charles Jerome Daly.
**HIGH SCHOOL:** Kane Area (Pa.).
**COLLEGE:** St. Bonaventure, then Bloomsburg (Pa.) State.
**CAREER NOTES:** Broadcaster, 76ers (1982-83). ... Broadcaster, Turner Sports (1994-95 through 1996-97). ... Special consultant to the president, Vancouver Grizzlies (May 10, 2000-present). ... Vancouver franchise moved to Memphis for 2001-02 season.
**MISCELLANEOUS:** Head coach, gold-medal-winning U.S. Olympic team (1992).
**CAREER HONORS:** Elected to Naismith Memorial Basketball Hall of Fame (1994). ... One of the Top 10 Coaches in NBA History (1996).

## COLLEGIATE RECORD

| Season Team | G | Min. | FGM | FGA | Pct. | FTM | FTA | Pct. | Reb. | Ast. | Pts. | RPG | APG | PPG |
|---|---|---|---|---|---|---|---|---|---|---|---|---|---|---|
| 48-49—St. Bonaventure‡ | | | | | | Freshman team statistics unavailable. | | | | | | | | |
| 49-50—Bloomsburg State | | | | | | Did not play—transfer student. | | | | | | | | |
| 50-51—Bloomsburg State | 16 | ... | ... | ... | ... | ... | ... | ... | ... | ... | 215 | ... | ... | 13.4 |
| 51-52—Bloomsburg State | 16 | ... | ... | ... | ... | ... | ... | ... | ... | ... | 203 | ... | ... | 12.7 |
| **Varsity totals** | 32 | ... | ... | ... | ... | ... | ... | ... | ... | ... | 418 | ... | ... | 13.1 |

## HEAD COACHING RECORD

**BACKGROUND:** Head coach, Punxsutawney High School, Pa (1955-56 through 1962-63; record: 111-70, .613). ... Assistant coach, Duke University (1963-64 through 1968-69). ... Assistant coach, Philadelphia 76ers (1978-December 4, 1981).

### COLLEGIATE COACHING RECORD

| Season Team | W | L | Pct. | Finish |
|---|---|---|---|---|
| 69-70—Boston College | 11 | 13 | .458 | Independent |
| 70-71—Boston College | 15 | 11 | .577 | Independent |
| 71-72—Pennsylvania | 25 | 3 | .893 | 1st/Ivy League |
| 72-73—Pennsylvania | 21 | 7 | .750 | 1st/Ivy League |
| 73-74—Pennsylvania | 21 | 6 | .778 | 1st/Ivy League |
| 74-75—Pennsylvania | 23 | 5 | .821 | 1st/Ivy League |
| 75-76—Pennsylvania | 17 | 9 | .654 | 2nd/Ivy League |
| 76-77—Pennsylvania | 18 | 8 | .692 | 2nd/Ivy League |
| **Totals (8 years)** | 151 | 62 | .709 | |

### NBA COACHING RECORD

| Season Team | REGULAR SEASON | | | | PLAYOFFS | | |
|---|---|---|---|---|---|---|---|
| | W | L | Pct. | Finish | W | L | Pct. |
| 81-82—Cleveland | 9 | 32 | .220 | | — | — | — |
| 83-84—Detroit | 49 | 33 | .598 | 2nd/Central Division | 2 | 3 | .400 |
| 84-85—Detroit | 46 | 36 | .561 | 2nd/Central Division | 5 | 4 | .556 |
| 85-86—Detroit | 46 | 36 | .561 | 3rd/Central Division | 1 | 3 | .250 |
| 86-87—Detroit | 52 | 30 | .634 | 2nd/Central Division | 10 | 5 | .667 |
| 87-88—Detroit | 54 | 28 | .659 | 1st/Central Division | 14 | 9 | .609 |
| 88-89—Detroit | 63 | 19 | .768 | 1st/Central Division | 15 | 2 | .882 |
| 89-90—Detroit | 59 | 23 | .720 | 1st/Central Division | 15 | 5 | .750 |
| 90-91—Detroit | 50 | 32 | .610 | 2nd/Central Division | 7 | 8 | .467 |
| 91-92—Detroit | 48 | 34 | .585 | 3rd/Central Division | 2 | 3 | .400 |
| 92-93—New Jersey | 43 | 39 | .524 | 3rd/Atlantic Division | 2 | 3 | .400 |
| 93-94—New Jersey | 45 | 37 | .549 | 3rd/Atlantic Division | 1 | 3 | .250 |
| 97-98—Orlando | 41 | 41 | .500 | 5th/Atlantic Division | — | — | — |
| 98-99—Orlando | 33 | 17 | .660 | T1st/Atlantic Division | 1 | 3 | .250 |
| **Totals (14 years)** | 638 | 437 | .593 | **Totals (12 years)** | 75 | 51 | .595 |

### OLYMPIC RECORD

| Season Team | W | L | Pct. | Finish |
|---|---|---|---|---|
| 1992—Team USA | 8 | 0 | 1.000 | Gold medal |

**NOTES:**
1972—Defeated Providence, 76-60, in NCAA Tournament first round; defeated Villanova, 78-67, in second round; lost to North Carolina, 73-59, in regional final.
1973—Defeated St. John's, 62-61, in NCAA Tournament first round; lost to Providence, 87-65, in second round; lost to Syracuse, 69-68, in regional consolation game.
1974—Lost to Providence, 84-69, in NCAA Tournament first round.
1975—Lost to Kansas State, 69-62, in NCAA Tournament first round.
1981—Replaced Don Delaney (4-13) and Bob Kloppenburg (0-1) as Cleveland head coach (December 4), with record of 4-14.
1982—Replaced as Cleveland head coach by Bill Musselman (February), with record of 13-46.
1984—Lost to New York in Eastern Conference First Round.
1985—Defeated New Jersey, 3-0, in Eastern Conference First Round; lost to Boston, 4-2, in Eastern Conference Semifinals.
1986—Lost to Atlanta in Eastern Conference First Round.
1987—Defeated Washington, 3-0, in Eastern Conference First Round; defeated Atlanta, 4-1, in Eastern Conference Semifinals; lost to Boston, 4-3, in Eastern Conference Finals.
1988—Defeated Washington, 3-2, in Eastern Conference First Round; defeated Chicago, 4-1, in Eastern Conference Semifinals; defeated Boston, 4-2, in Eastern Conference Finals; lost to Los Angeles Lakers, 4-3, in NBA Finals.
1989—Defeated Boston, 3-0, in Eastern Conference First Round; defeated Milwaukee, 4-0, in Eastern Conference Semifinals; defeated Chicago, 4-2, in Eastern Conference Finals; defeated Los Angeles Lakers, 4-0, in NBA Finals.

1990—Defeated Indiana, 3-0, in Eastern Conference First Round; defeated New York, 4-1, in Eastern Conference Semifinals; defeated Chicago, 4-3, in Eastern Conference Finals; defeated Portland, 4-1, in NBA Finals.
1991—Defeated Atlanta, 3-2, in Eastern Conference First Round; defeated Boston, 4-2, in Eastern Conference Semifinals; lost to Chicago, 4-0, in Eastern Conference Finals.
1992—Lost to New York in Eastern Conference First Round.
Team USA defeated Angola, 116-48; Croatia, 103-70; Germany, 111-68; Brazil, 127-83; and Spain, 122-81, in preliminary round. Defeated Puerto Rico, 115-77, in medal round quarterfinals; defeated Lithuania, 127-76, in semifinals; defeated Croatia, 117-85, in gold-medal game.
1993—Lost to Cleveland in Eastern Conference First Round.
1994—Lost to New York in Eastern Conference First Round.
1999—Lost to Philadelphia in Eastern Conference First Round.

## FITCH, BILL

**PERSONAL:** Born May 19, 1934, in Davenport, Iowa. ... 6-2/205 (1,88/93,0). ... Full name: Billy Charles Fitch.
**HIGH SCHOOL:** Cedar Rapids (Iowa).
**COLLEGE:** Coe College (Iowa).
**CAREER HONORS:** One of the Top 10 Coaches in NBA History (1996).

### COLLEGIATE RECORD

| Season Team | G | Min. | FGM | FGA | Pct. | FTM | FTA | Pct. | Reb. | Ast. | Pts. | RPG | APG | PPG |
|---|---|---|---|---|---|---|---|---|---|---|---|---|---|---|
| 50-51—Coe College | | | | | | Freshman team statistics unavailable. | | | | | | | | |
| 51-52—Coe College | 20 | ... | 63 | ... | ... | 50 | ... | ... | ... | ... | 176 | ... | ... | 8.8 |
| 52-53—Coe College | 19 | ... | 83 | ... | ... | 72 | ... | ... | ... | ... | 238 | ... | ... | 12.5 |
| 53-54—Coe College | 22 | ... | 123 | ... | ... | 92 | ... | ... | ... | ... | 338 | ... | ... | 15.4 |
| Totals | 61 | ... | 269 | ... | ... | 214 | ... | ... | ... | ... | 752 | ... | ... | 12.3 |

### HEAD COACHING RECORD

**BACKGROUND:** Head baseball coach and assistant basketball coach, Creighton University (1956-57 and 1957-58).
**HONORS:** NBA Coach of the Year (1976, 1980).

### COLLEGIATE COACHING RECORD

| Season Team | W | L | Pct. | Finish |
|---|---|---|---|---|
| 58-59—Coe College | 11 | 9 | .550 | 6th/Midwest Collegiate Athletic Conference |
| 59-60—Coe College | 12 | 9 | .571 | T5th/Midwest Collegiate Athletic Conference |
| 60-61—Coe College | 10 | 12 | .455 | T4th/Midwest Collegiate Athletic Conference |
| 61-62—Coe College | 11 | 10 | .524 | T6th/Midwest Collegiate Athletic Conference |
| 62-63—North Dakota | 14 | 13 | .519 | 3rd/North Central Intercollegiate Athletic Conference |
| 63-64—North Dakota | 10 | 16 | .385 | T3rd/North Central Intercollegiate Athletic Conference |
| 64-65—North Dakota | 26 | 5 | .839 | 1st/North Central Intercollegiate Athletic Conference |
| 65-66—North Dakota | 24 | 5 | .828 | 1st/North Central Intercollegiate Athletic Conference |
| 66-67—North Dakota | 20 | 6 | .769 | 1st/North Central Intercollegiate Athletic Conference |
| 67-68—Bowling Green | 18 | 7 | .720 | 1st/Mid-American Conference |
| 68-69—Minnesota | 12 | 12 | .500 | T5th/Big Ten Conference |
| 69-70—Minnesota | 13 | 11 | .542 | 5th/Big Ten Conference |
| Totals (12 years) | 181 | 115 | .611 | |

### NBA COACHING RECORD

| Season Team | REGULAR SEASON W | L | Pct. | Finish | PLAYOFFS W | L | Pct. |
|---|---|---|---|---|---|---|---|
| 70-71—Cleveland | 15 | 67 | .183 | 4th/Central Division | — | — | — |
| 71-72—Cleveland | 23 | 59 | .280 | 4th/Central Division | — | — | — |
| 72-73—Cleveland | 32 | 50 | .390 | 4th/Central Division | — | — | — |
| 73-74—Cleveland | 29 | 53 | .354 | 4th/Central Division | — | — | — |
| 74-75—Cleveland | 40 | 42 | .488 | 3rd/Central Division | — | — | — |
| 75-76—Cleveland | 49 | 33 | .598 | 1st/Central Division | 6 | 7 | .462 |
| 76-77—Cleveland | 43 | 39 | .524 | 4th/Central Division | 1 | 2 | .538 |
| 77-78—Cleveland | 43 | 39 | .524 | 3rd/Central Division | 0 | 2 | .000 |
| 78-79—Cleveland | 30 | 52 | .366 | T4th/Central Division | — | — | — |
| 79-80—Boston | 61 | 21 | .744 | 1st/Atlantic Division | 5 | 4 | .556 |
| 80-81—Boston | 62 | 20 | .756 | T1st/Atlantic Division | 12 | 5 | .706 |
| 81-82—Boston | 63 | 19 | .768 | 1st/Atlantic Division | 7 | 5 | .583 |
| 82-83—Boston | 56 | 26 | .683 | 2nd/Atlantic Division | 2 | 5 | .286 |
| 83-84—Houston | 29 | 53 | .354 | 6th/Midwest Division | — | — | — |
| 84-85—Houston | 48 | 34 | .585 | 2nd/Midwest Division | 2 | 3 | .400 |
| 85-86—Houston | 51 | 31 | .622 | 1st/Midwest Division | 13 | 7 | .650 |
| 86-87—Houston | 42 | 40 | .512 | 3rd/Midwest Division | 5 | 5 | .500 |
| 87-88—Houston | 46 | 36 | .561 | 4th/Midwest Division | 1 | 3 | .250 |
| 89-90—New Jersey | 17 | 65 | .207 | 6th/Atlantic Division | — | — | — |
| 90-91—New Jersey | 26 | 56 | .317 | 5th/Atlantic Division | — | — | — |
| 91-92—New Jersey | 40 | 42 | .489 | 3rd/Atlantic Division | 1 | 3 | .250 |

| Season Team | REGULAR SEASON | | | | | | PLAYOFFS | | |
|---|---|---|---|---|---|---|---|---|---|
| | W | L | Pct. | Finish | | | W | L | Pct. |
| 94-95—L.A. Clippers | 17 | 65 | .207 | 7th/Pacific Division | | | — | — | — |
| 95-96—L.A. Clippers | 29 | 53 | .354 | 7th/Pacific Division | | | — | — | — |
| 96-97—L.A. Clippers | 36 | 46 | .439 | 5th/Pacific Division | | | 0 | 3 | .000 |
| 97-98—L.A. Clippers | 17 | 65 | .207 | 7th/Pacific Division | | | — | — | — |
| **Totals (25 years)** | **944** | **1106** | **.460** | | **Totals (13 years)** | | **55** | **54** | **.505** |

**NOTES:**

1965—Defeated Minnesota-Duluth, 67-57, in College Division Tournament first round; defeated Moorhead (Minn.) State in second round; defeated Seattle Pacific, 97-83, in national quarterfinals; lost to Southern Illinois, 97-64, in national semifinals; defeated St. Michael's (Vt.), 94-86, in national third-place game.

1966—Defeated Northern Colorado, 84-71, in College Division Tournament regional semifinals; defeated Valparaiso, 112-82, in regional finals; defeated Abilene Christian, 63-62, in national quarterfinals; lost to Southern Illinois, 69-61, in national semifinals; lost to Akron, 76-71, in national third-place game.

1967—Lost to Louisiana Tech, 86-77, in College Division Tournament regional semifinals; defeated Parsons (Ia.), 107-56, in regional third-place game.

1968—Lost to Marquette, 72-71, in NCAA Tournament first round.

1976—Defeated Washington, 4-3, in Eastern Conference Semifinals; lost to Boston, 4-2, in Eastern Conference Finals.

1977—Lost to Washington in Eastern Conference First Round.

1978—Lost to New York in Eastern Conference First Round.

1980—Defeated Houston, 4-0, in Eastern Conference Semifinals; lost to Philadelphia, 4-1, in Eastern Conference Finals.

1981—Defeated Chicago, 4-0, in Eastern Conference Semifinals; defeated Philadelphia, 4-3, in Eastern Conference Finals; defeated Houston, 4-2, in NBA Finals.

1982—Defeated Washington, 4-1, in Eastern Conference Semifinals; lost to Philadelphia, 4-3, in Eastern Conference Finals.

1983—Defeated Atlanta, 2-1, in Eastern Conference First Round; lost to Milwaukee, 4-0, in Eastern Conference Semifinals.

1985—Lost to Utah in Western Conference First Round.

1986—Defeated Sacramento, 3-0, in Western Conference First Round; defeated Denver, 4-2, in Western Conference Semifinals; defeated Los Angeles Lakers, 4-1, in Western Conference Finals; lost to Boston, 4-2, in NBA Finals.

1987—Defeated Portland, 3-1, in Western Conference First Round; lost to Seattle, 4-2, in Western Conference Semifinals.

1988—Lost to Dallas in Western Conference First Round.

1992—Lost to Cleveland in Eastern Conference First Round.

1997—Lost to Utah in Western Conference First Round.

## FITZSIMMONS, COTTON

**PERSONAL:** Born October 7, 1931, in Hannibal, Mo. ... Died July 24, 2004. ... 5-7/160 (1,70/72,6). ... Full name: Lowell Fitzsimmons.

**HIGH SCHOOL:** Bowling Green (Mo.).

**COLLEGE:** Hannibal (Mo.)-LaGrange, then Midwestern State (Texas).

**CAREER NOTES:** Director of player personnel, Golden State Warriors (1976-77). ... Director of player personnel, Phoenix Suns (1987-88). ... Head coach/director of player personnel, Suns (1988-89 through 1991-92). ... Senior executive vice president, Suns (1992-93 through January 16, 1996 and November 15, 1996 through present).

### COLLEGIATE RECORD

| Season Team | G | Min. | FGM | FGA | Pct. | FTM | FTA | Pct. | Reb. | Ast. | Pts. | AVERAGES | | |
|---|---|---|---|---|---|---|---|---|---|---|---|---|---|---|
| | | | | | | | | | | | | RPG | APG | PPG |
| 52-53—Hann.-LaGrange‡ | 33 | ... | ... | ... | ... | ... | ... | ... | ... | ... | 838 | ... | ... | 25.4 |
| 53-54—Midwestern State | 27 | ... | 53 | 161 | .329 | 128 | 173 | .740 | ... | ... | 234 | ... | ... | 8.7 |
| 54-55—Midwestern State | 27 | ... | 118 | 258 | .457 | 162 | 210 | .771 | ... | ... | 398 | ... | ... | 14.7 |
| 55-56—Midwestern State | 28 | ... | 148 | 319 | .464 | 164 | 223 | .735 | ... | ... | 460 | ... | ... | 16.4 |
| **Varsity totals** | **82** | ... | **319** | **738** | **.432** | **454** | **606** | **.749** | ... | ... | **1092** | ... | ... | **13.3** |

### HEAD COACHING RECORD

**BACKGROUND:** Assistant coach, Kansas State University (1967-68).

**HONORS:** NBA Coach of the Year (1979, 1989).

### COLLEGE COACHING RECORD

| Season Team | W | L | Pct. | Finish |
|---|---|---|---|---|
| 58-59—Moberly J.C. (Mo.) | 16 | 15 | .516 | |
| 59-60—Moberly J.C. (Mo.) | 19 | 8 | .704 | |
| 60-61—Moberly J.C. (Mo.) | 26 | 5 | .839 | |
| 61-62—Moberly J.C. (Mo.) | 26 | 9 | .743 | |
| 62-63—Moberly J.C. (Mo.) | 26 | 6 | .813 | |
| 63-64—Moberly J.C. (Mo.) | 24 | 5 | .828 | |
| 64-65—Moberly J.C. (Mo.) | 25 | 5 | .833 | |
| 65-66—Moberly J.C. (Mo.) | 29 | 5 | .853 | |
| 66-67—Moberly J.C. (Mo.) | 31 | 2 | .939 | |
| 68-69—Kansas State | 14 | 12 | .538 | T2nd/Big Eight Conference |
| 69-70—Kansas State | 20 | 8 | .714 | 1st/Big Eight Conference |
| **Junior college totals (9 years)** | **222** | **60** | **.787** | |
| **4-year college totals (2 years)** | **34** | **20** | **.630** | |

## NBA COACHING RECORD

| Season Team | W | L | Pct. | Finish | W | L | Pct. |
|---|---|---|---|---|---|---|---|
| | | REGULAR SEASON | | | | PLAYOFFS | |
| 70-71—Phoenix | 48 | 34 | .585 | 3rd/Midwest Division | — | — | — |
| 71-72—Phoenix | 49 | 33 | .598 | 3rd/Midwest Division | — | — | — |
| 72-73—Atlanta | 46 | 36 | .561 | 2nd/Central Division | 2 | 4 | .333 |
| 73-74—Atlanta | 35 | 47 | .427 | 2nd/Central Division | — | — | — |
| 74-75—Atlanta | 31 | 51 | .378 | 4th/Central Division | — | — | — |
| 75-76—Atlanta | 28 | 46 | .378 | | — | — | — |
| 77-78—Buffalo | 27 | 55 | .329 | 4th/Atlantic Division | — | — | — |
| 78-79—Kansas City | 48 | 34 | .585 | 1st/Midwest Division | 1 | 4 | .200 |
| 79-80—Kansas City | 47 | 35 | .573 | 2nd/Midwest Division | 1 | 2 | .333 |
| 80-81—Kansas City | 40 | 42 | .488 | T2nd/Midwest Division | 7 | 8 | .467 |
| 81-82—Kansas City | 30 | 52 | .366 | 4th/Midwest Division | — | — | — |
| 82-83—Kansas City | 45 | 37 | .549 | T2nd/Midwest Division | — | — | — |
| 83-84—Kansas City | 38 | 44 | .463 | T3rd/Midwest Division | 0 | 3 | .000 |
| 84-85—San Antonio | 41 | 41 | .500 | T4th/Midwest Division | 2 | 3 | .400 |
| 85-86—San Antonio | 35 | 47 | .427 | 6th/Midwest Division | 0 | 3 | .000 |
| 88-89—Phoenix | 55 | 27 | .671 | 2nd/Pacific Division | 7 | 5 | .583 |
| 89-90—Phoenix | 54 | 28 | .659 | 3rd/Pacific Division | 9 | 7 | .563 |
| 90-91—Phoenix | 55 | 27 | .671 | 3rd/Pacific Division | 1 | 3 | .250 |
| 91-92—Phoenix | 53 | 29 | .646 | 3rd/Pacific Division | 4 | 4 | .500 |
| 95-96—Phoenix | 27 | 22 | .551 | 4th/Pacific Division | 1 | 3 | .250 |
| 96-97—Phoenix | 0 | 8 | .000 | | — | — | — |
| Totals (21 years) | 832 | 775 | .518 | Totals (12 years) | 35 | 49 | .417 |

**NOTES:**

1966—Won National Junior College Athletic Association national tournament.

1967—Won National Junior College Athletic Association national tournament.

1970—Lost to New Mexico, 70-66, in NCAA Tournament regional semifinal.

1973—Lost to Boston in Eastern Conference Semifinals.

1976—Replaced as Atlanta head coach by Gene Tormohlen (March) with club in fifth place.

1979—Lost to Phoenix in Western Conference Semifinals.

1980—Lost to Phoenix in Western Conference First Round.

1981—Defeated Portland, 2-1, in Western Conference First Round; defeated Phoenix, 4-3, in Western Conference Semifinals; lost to Houston, 4-1, in Western Conference Finals.

1984—Lost to Los Angeles Lakers in Western Conference First Round.

1985—Lost to Denver in Western Conference First Round.

1986—Lost to Los Angeles Lakers in Western Conference First Round.

1989—Defeated Denver, 3-0, in Western Conference First Round; defeated Golden State, 4-1, in Western Conference Semifinals; lost to Los Angeles Lakers, 4-0, in Western Conference Finals.

1990—Defeated Utah, 3-2, in Western Conference First Round; defeated Los Angeles Lakers, 4-1, in Western Conference Semifinals; lost to Portland, 4-2, in Western Conference Finals.

1991—Lost to Utah in Western Conference First Round.

1992—Defeated San Antonio, 3-0, in Western Conference First Round; lost to Portland, 4-1, in Western Conference Semifinals.

1996—Replaced Paul Westphal as Phoenix head coach (January 16) with record of 14-19 and club in sixth place. Lost to San Antonio in Western Conference First Round. Replaced as Phoenix head coach by Danny Ainge with record of 0-8 and club in seventh place (November 15).

# FRATELLO, MIKE

See Head Coaches, page 299.

# HANNUM, ALEX

**PERSONAL:** Born July 19, 1923, in Los Angeles. ... Died January 18, 2002. ... 6-7/225 (2,00/102,1). ... Full name: Alexander Murray Hannum.

**HIGH SCHOOL:** Hamilton (Los Angeles).

**COLLEGE:** Southern California.

**TRANSACTIONS:** Played for Los Angeles Shamrocks, an Amateur Athletic Union team and averaged 9.8 points per game (1945-46). ... Signed by Oshkosh All-Stars of National Basketball League (1948). ... Sold by Oshkosh of NBL to Syracuse Nationals of NBA (1949). ... Traded by Nationals with Fred Scolari to Baltimore Bullets for Red Rocha (1951). ... Sold by Bullets to Rochester Royals during 1951-52 season. ... Sold by Royals to Milwaukee Hawks (1954). ... Hawks franchise moved from Milwaukee to St. Louis for 1955-56 season. ... Released by Hawks (1956). ... Signed by Fort Wayne Pistons (1956). ... Released by Pistons (December 12, 1956). ... Signed by Hawks (December 17, 1956).

**CAREER HONORS:** Elected to Naismith Memorial Basketball Hall of Fame (1998).

## COLLEGIATE RECORD

**NOTES:** In military service (1943-44 through 1945-46).

| Season Team | G | Min. | FGM | FGA | Pct. | FTM | FTA | Pct. | Reb. | Ast. | Pts. | AVERAGES RPG | APG | PPG |
|---|---|---|---|---|---|---|---|---|---|---|---|---|---|---|
| 41-42—Southern California‡ ..... | | | | | | Freshman team statistics unavailable. | | | | | | | | |
| 42-43—Southern California ....... | 15 | ... | 23 | ... | ... | 9 | 20 | .450 | ... | ... | 55 | ... | ... | 3.7 |
| 46-47—Southern California ....... | 24 | ... | ... | ... | ... | ... | ... | ... | ... | ... | 251 | ... | ... | 10.5 |
| 47-48—Southern California ....... | 23 | ... | 108 | ... | ... | ... | ... | ... | ... | ... | 263 | ... | ... | 11.4 |
| Varsity totals.......................... | 62 | ... | | | | | | | | | 569 | ... | ... | 9.2 |

## NBL AND NBA REGULAR-SEASON RECORD

| Season Team | G | Min. | FGM | FGA | Pct. | FTM | FTA | Pct. | Reb. | Ast. | PF | Dq. | Pts. | AVERAGES RPG | APG | PPG |
|---|---|---|---|---|---|---|---|---|---|---|---|---|---|---|---|---|
| 48-49—Oshkosh (NBL) ................. | 62 | ... | 126 | ... | ... | 113 | 191 | .592 | ... | ... | 188 | ... | 365 | ... | ... | 5.9 |
| 49-50—Syracuse ........................ | 64 | ... | 177 | 488 | .363 | 128 | 186 | .688 | ... | 129 | 264 | ... | 482 | ... | 2.0 | 7.5 |
| 50-51—Syracuse ........................ | 63 | ... | 182 | 494 | .368 | 107 | 197 | .543 | 301 | 119 | 271 | 16 | 471 | 4.8 | 1.9 | 7.5 |
| 51-52—Balt.-Roch. .................... | 66 | 1508 | 170 | 462 | .368 | 98 | 138 | .710 | 336 | 133 | 271 | 16 | 438 | 5.1 | 2.0 | 6.6 |
| 52-53—Rochester ...................... | 68 | 1288 | 129 | 360 | .358 | 88 | 133 | .662 | 279 | 81 | 258 | 18 | 346 | 4.1 | 1.2 | 5.1 |
| 53-54—Rochester ...................... | 72 | 1707 | 175 | 503 | .348 | 102 | 164 | .622 | 350 | 105 | 279 | 11 | 452 | 4.9 | 1.5 | 6.3 |
| 54-55—Milwaukee ...................... | 53 | 1088 | 126 | 358 | .352 | 61 | 107 | .570 | 245 | 105 | 206 | 9 | 313 | 4.6 | 2.0 | 5.9 |
| 55-56—St. Louis ....................... | 71 | 1480 | 146 | 453 | .322 | 93 | 154 | .604 | 344 | 157 | 271 | 10 | 385 | 4.8 | 2.2 | 5.4 |
| 56-57—Fort Wayne-St. Louis........ | 59 | 642 | 77 | 223 | .345 | 37 | 56 | .661 | 158 | 28 | 135 | 2 | 191 | 2.7 | 0.5 | 3.2 |
| Totals............................ | 578 | ... | 1308 | ... | ... | 827 | 1326 | .624 | ... | ... | 2143 | ... | 3443 | ... | ... | 6.0 |

## NBL AND NBA PLAYOFF RECORD

| Season Team | G | Min. | FGM | FGA | Pct. | FTM | FTA | Pct. | Reb. | Ast. | PF | Dq. | Pts. | AVERAGES RPG | APG | PPG |
|---|---|---|---|---|---|---|---|---|---|---|---|---|---|---|---|---|
| 48-49—Oshkosh (NBL) ................. | 7 | ... | 12 | ... | ... | 16 | 26 | .615 | ... | ... | ... | ... | 40 | ... | ... | 5.7 |
| 49-50—Syracuse ........................ | 11 | ... | 38 | 86 | .442 | 17 | 34 | .500 | ... | 10 | 50 | ... | 93 | ... | 0.9 | 8.5 |
| 50-51—Syracuse ........................ | 7 | ... | 17 | 39 | .436 | 8 | 10 | .800 | 47 | 17 | 37 | 3 | 42 | 6.7 | 2.4 | 6.0 |
| 51-52—Rochester ...................... | 6 | 146 | 16 | 42 | .381 | 8 | 13 | .615 | 26 | 8 | 30 | 3 | 40 | 4.3 | 1.3 | 6.7 |
| 52-53—Rochester ...................... | 3 | 52 | 4 | 10 | .400 | 3 | 8 | .375 | 4 | 2 | 16 | 1 | 11 | 1.3 | 0.7 | 3.7 |
| 53-54—Rochester ...................... | 6 | 107 | 12 | 29 | .414 | 15 | 24 | .625 | 22 | 5 | 28 | 3 | 39 | 3.7 | 0.8 | 6.5 |
| 55-56—St. Louis ....................... | 8 | 159 | 21 | 66 | .318 | 19 | 35 | .543 | 29 | 10 | 36 | 3 | 61 | 3.6 | 1.3 | 7.6 |
| 56-57—St. Louis ....................... | 2 | 6 | 0 | 2 | .000 | 0 | 0 | ... | 0 | 0 | 2 | 0 | 0 | 0.0 | 0.0 | 0.0 |
| Totals............................ | 50 | ... | 120 | ... | ... | 86 | 150 | .573 | ... | ... | ... | ... | 326 | ... | ... | 6.5 |

## HEAD COACHING RECORD

**HONORS:** NBA Coach of the Year (1964). ... ABA Coach of the Year (1969).

### NBA COACHING RECORD

| Season Team | REGULAR SEASON W | L | Pct. | Finish | PLAYOFFS W | L | Pct. |
|---|---|---|---|---|---|---|---|
| 56-57—St. Louis................................. | 15 | 16 | .484 | T1st/Western Division | 8 | 4 | .667 |
| 57-58—St. Louis................................. | 41 | 31 | .569 | 1st/Western Division | 8 | 3 | .727 |
| 60-61—Syracuse ............................... | 38 | 41 | .481 | 3rd/Eastern Division | 4 | 4 | .500 |
| 61-62—Syracuse ............................... | 41 | 39 | .513 | 3rd/Eastern Division | 2 | 3 | .400 |
| 62-63—Syracuse ............................... | 48 | 32 | .600 | 2nd/Eastern Division | 2 | 3 | .400 |
| 63-64—San Francisco ....................... | 48 | 32 | .600 | 1st/Western Division | 5 | 7 | .417 |
| 64-65—San Francisco ....................... | 17 | 63 | .215 | 5th/Western Division | — | — | — |
| 65-66—San Francisco ....................... | 35 | 45 | .438 | 4th/Western Division | — | — | — |
| 66-67—Philadelphia............................ | 68 | 13 | .840 | 1st/Eastern Division | 11 | 4 | .733 |
| 67-68—Philadelphia............................ | 62 | 20 | .756 | 1st/Eastern Division | 7 | 6 | .538 |
| 69-70—San Diego .............................. | 18 | 38 | .321 | 7th/Western Division | — | — | — |
| 70-71—San Diego .............................. | 40 | 42 | .488 | 3rd/Pacific Division | — | — | — |
| Totals (12 years)........................... | 471 | 412 | .533 | Totals (8 years) | 47 | 34 | .580 |

### NIBL COACHING RECORD

| Season Team | REGULAR SEASON W | L | Pct. | Finish |
|---|---|---|---|---|
| 58-59—Wichita.................................. | 19 | 11 | .633 | 2nd |
| 59-60—Wichita.................................. | 22 | 10 | .688 | 2nd |
| Totals (2 years)............................. | 41 | 21 | .661 | |

### ABA COACHING RECORD

| Season Team | REGULAR SEASON W | L | Pct. | Finish | PLAYOFFS W | L | Pct. |
|---|---|---|---|---|---|---|---|
| 68-69—Oakland ................................. | 60 | 18 | .769 | 1st/Western Division | 12 | 4 | .750 |
| 71-72—Denver................................... | 34 | 50 | .405 | 4th/Western Division | 3 | 4 | .429 |
| 72-73—Denver................................... | 47 | 37 | .560 | 3rd/Western Division | 1 | 4 | .200 |
| 73-74—Denver................................... | 37 | 47 | .440 | T4th/Western Division | — | — | — |
| Totals (4 years)............................. | 178 | 152 | .539 | Totals (3 years) | 16 | 12 | .571 |

**NOTES:**
1957—Replaced Red Holzman (14-19) and Slater Martin (5-3) as St. Louis head coach (January), with record of 19-22. Defeated Fort Wayne, 115-103, and Minneapolis, 114-111, in Western Division tiebreakers; defeated Minneapolis, 3-0, in Western Division Finals; lost to Boston, 4-3, in NBA Finals.
1958—Defeated Detroit, 4-1, in Western Division Finals; defeated Boston, 4-2, in NBA Finals.
1961—Defeated Philadelphia, 3-0, in Eastern Division Semifinals; lost to Boston, 4-1, in Eastern Division Finals.
1962—Lost to Philadelphia in Eastern Division Semifinals.
1963—Lost to Cincinnati in Eastern Division Semifinals.
1964—Defeated St. Louis, 4-3, in Western Division Finals; lost to Boston, 4-1, in NBA Finals.

1967—Defeated Cincinnati, 3-1, in Eastern Division Semifinals; defeated Boston, 4-1, in Eastern Division Finals; defeated San Francisco, 4-2, in NBA Finals.

1968—Defeated New York, 4-2, in Eastern Division Semifinals; lost to Boston, 4-3, in Eastern Division Finals.

1969—Defeated Denver, 4-3, in Western Division Semifinals; defeated New Orleans, 4-0, in Western Division Finals; defeated Indiana, 4-1, in ABA Finals. Replaced Jack McMahon as San Diego head coach (December), with record of 9-17.

1972—Lost to Indiana in Western Division Semifinals.

1973—Lost to Indiana in Western Division Semifinals.

# HARRIS, DEL

**PERSONAL:** Born June 18, 1937, in Plainfield, Ind. ... 6-4/205 (1,93/93,0). ... Full name: Delmer W. Harris.
**HIGH SCHOOL:** Plainfield (Ind.).
**COLLEGE:** Milligan College (Tenn.).
**CAREER NOTES:** Vice president, Bucks (1987 through 1992). ... Consultant, Sacramento Kings (1993-94).

## COLLEGIATE RECORD

**NOTES:** Field goal attempts for five games and rebounds for 13 games are unavailable.

| Season Team | G | Min. | FGM | FGA | Pct. | FTM | FTA | Pct. | Reb. | Ast. | Pts. | RPG | APG | PPG |
|---|---|---|---|---|---|---|---|---|---|---|---|---|---|---|
| 55-56—Milligan College | 24 | ... | 101 | 232 | .435 | 89 | 126 | .706 | 122 | ... | 291 | 5.1 | ... | 12.1 |
| 56-57—Milligan College | 24 | ... | 162 | 375 | .432 | 141 | 197 | .716 | 165 | ... | 465 | 6.9 | ... | 19.4 |
| 57-58—Milligan College | 22 | ... | 167 | 378 | .442 | 119 | 149 | .799 | 240 | ... | 453 | 10.9 | ... | 20.6 |
| 58-59—Milligan College | 21 | ... | 136 | 306 | .444 | 158 | 202 | .782 | 338 | ... | 430 | 16.1 | ... | 20.5 |
| Totals | 91 | ... | 566 | 1291 | .438 | 507 | 674 | .752 | 865 | ... | 1639 | 9.5 | ... | 18.0 |

## HEAD COACHING RECORD

**BACKGROUND:** Head coach, Superior League, Puerto Rico (1969 through 1975). ... Assistant coach, Utah Stars of ABA (1975-76). ... Assistant coach, Houston Rockets (1976-77 through 1978-79). ... Scout, Milwaukee Bucks (1983 through 1986). ... Assistant coach, Bucks (1986-87). ... Assistant coach, Dallas Mavericks (2000-present).

**HONORS:** NBA Coach of the Year (1995).

### COLLEGIATE COACHING RECORD

| Season Team | W | L | Pct. | Finish |
|---|---|---|---|---|
| 65-66—Earlham College | 14 | 8 | .636 | Hoosier Collegiate Conference |
| 66-67—Earlham College | 15 | 9 | .625 | 4th/Hoosier Collegiate Conference |
| 67-68—Earlham College | 25 | 3 | .893 | 1st/Hoosier Collegiate Conference |
| 68-69—Earlham College | 18 | 8 | .692 | 2nd/Hoosier Collegiate Conference |
| 69-70—Earlham College | 22 | 8 | .733 | 1st/Hoosier Collegiate Conference |
| 70-71—Earlham College | 24 | 5 | .828 | 1st/Hoosier Collegiate Conference |
| 71-72—Earlham College | 21 | 9 | .700 | 1st/Hoosier Collegiate Conference |
| 72-73—Earlham College | 17 | 11 | .607 | 3rd/Hoosier Collegiate Conference |
| 73-74—Earlham College | 19 | 9 | .679 | 3rd/Hoosier Collegiate Conference |
| Totals (9 years) | 175 | 70 | .714 | |

### NBA COACHING RECORD

| | REGULAR SEASON | | | | PLAYOFFS | | |
|---|---|---|---|---|---|---|---|
| Season Team | W | L | Pct. | Finish | W | L | Pct. |
| 79-80—Houston | 41 | 41 | .500 | T2nd/Central Division | 2 | 5 | .286 |
| 80-81—Houston | 40 | 42 | .488 | T2nd/Midwest Division | 12 | 9 | .571 |
| 81-82—Houston | 46 | 36 | .561 | T2nd/Midwest Division | 1 | 2 | .333 |
| 82-83—Houston | 14 | 68 | .171 | 6th/Midwest Division | — | — | — |
| 87-88—Milwaukee | 42 | 40 | .512 | T4th/Central Division | 2 | 3 | .400 |
| 88-89—Milwaukee | 49 | 33 | .598 | 4th/Central Division | 3 | 6 | .333 |
| 89-90—Milwaukee | 44 | 38 | .537 | 3rd/Central Division | 1 | 3 | .250 |
| 90-91—Milwaukee | 48 | 34 | .585 | 3rd/Central Division | 0 | 3 | .000 |
| 91-92—Milwaukee | 8 | 9 | .471 | | — | — | — |
| 94-95—L.A. Lakers | 48 | 34 | .585 | 3rd/Pacific Division | 5 | 5 | .500 |
| 95-96—L.A. Lakers | 53 | 29 | .646 | 2nd/Pacific Division | 1 | 3 | .250 |
| 96-97—L.A. Lakers | 56 | 26 | .683 | 2nd/Pacific Division | 4 | 5 | .444 |
| 97-98—L.A. Lakers | 61 | 21 | .744 | T1st/Pacific Division | 7 | 6 | .538 |
| 98-99—L.A. Lakers | 6 | 6 | .500 | | | | |
| Totals (14 years) | 556 | 457 | .549 | Totals (11 years) | 38 | 50 | .432 |

**NOTES:**

1968—Posted 1-1 record in NAIA District Tournament.

1969—Posted 0-1 record in NAIA District Tournament.

1970—Posted 1-1 record in NAIA District Tournament.

1971—Posted 2-0 record in NAIA District Tournament; posted 1-1 record in NAIA National Tournament.

1972—Posted 1-1 record in NAIA District Tournament.

1973—Posted 2-1 record in NAIA District Tournament.

1980—Defeated San Antonio, 2-1, in Eastern Conference First Round; lost to Boston, 4-0, in Eastern Conference Semifinals.

1981—Defeated Los Angeles Lakers, 2-1, in Western Conference First Round; defeated San Antonio, 4-3, in Western Conference Semifinals; defeated Kansas City, 4-1, in Western Conference Finals; lost to Boston, 4-2, in NBA Finals.

1982—Lost to Seattle in Western Conference First Round.

1988—Lost to Atlanta in Eastern Conference First Round.

1989—Defeated Atlanta, 3-2, in Eastern Conference First Round; lost to Detroit, 4-0, in Eastern Conference Semifinals.

1990—Lost to Chicago in Eastern Conference First Round.

1991—Lost to Philadelphia in Eastern Conference First Round. Resigned as Milwaukee head coach (December 4) to concentrate on duties as team's head of basketball operations.

1995—Defeated Seattle, 3-1, in Western Conference First Round; lost to San Antonio, 4-2, in Western Conference Semifinals.

1996—Lost to Houston in Western Conference First Round.

1997—Defeated Portland, 3-1, in Western Conference First Round; lost to Utah, 4-1, in Western Conference Semifinals.

1998—Defeated Portland, 3-1, in Western Conference First Round; defeated Seattle, 4-1, in Western Conference Semifinals; lost to Utah, 4-0, in Western Conference Finals.

1999—Replaced as head coach on an interim basis by Kurt Rambis (February 24) with club in fourth place.

# HEINSOHN, TOM

**PERSONAL:** Born August 26, 1934, in Jersey City, N.J. ... 6-7/218 (2,00/98,9). ... Full name: Thomas William Heinsohn.
**HIGH SCHOOL:** St. Michael's (Union City, N.J.).
**COLLEGE:** Holy Cross.
**TRANSACTIONS:** Selected by Boston Celtics in 1956 NBA Draft (territorial pick).
**CAREER HONORS:** Elected to Naismith Memorial Basketball Hall of Fame (1986).
**MISCELLANEOUS:** Member of NBA championship team (1957, 1959, 1960, 1961, 1962, 1963, 1964, 1965).

### COLLEGIATE RECORD

| Season Team | G | Min. | FGM | FGA | Pct. | FTM | FTA | Pct. | Reb. | Ast. | Pts. | RPG | APG | PPG |
|---|---|---|---|---|---|---|---|---|---|---|---|---|---|---|
| 52-53—Holy Cross‡ | 15 | ... | 97 | ... | ... | 70 | ... | ... | ... | ... | 264 | ... | ... | 17.6 |
| 53-54—Holy Cross | 28 | ... | 175 | 364 | .481 | 94 | 142 | .662 | 300 | ... | 444 | 10.7 | ... | 15.9 |
| 54-55—Holy Cross | 26 | ... | 232 | 499 | .465 | 141 | 215 | .656 | 385 | ... | 605 | 14.8 | ... | 23.3 |
| 55-56—Holy Cross | 27 | ... | 254 | 630 | .403 | 232 | 304 | .763 | 569 | ... | 740 | 21.1 | ... | 27.4 |
| **Varsity totals** | 81 | ... | 661 | 1493 | .443 | 467 | 661 | .707 | 1254 | ... | 1789 | 15.5 | ... | 22.1 |

### NBA REGULAR-SEASON RECORD

**HONORS:** NBA Rookie of the Year (1957). ... All-NBA second team (1961, 1962, 1963, 1964).

| Season Team | G | Min. | FGM | FGA | Pct. | FTM | FTA | Pct. | Reb. | Ast. | PF | Dq. | Pts. | RPG | APG | PPG |
|---|---|---|---|---|---|---|---|---|---|---|---|---|---|---|---|---|
| 56-57—Boston | 72 | 2150 | 446 | 1123 | .397 | 271 | 343 | .790 | 705 | 117 | 304 | 12 | 1163 | 9.8 | 1.6 | 16.2 |
| 57-58—Boston | 69 | 2206 | 468 | 1226 | .382 | 294 | 394 | .746 | 705 | 125 | 274 | 6 | 1230 | 10.2 | 1.8 | 17.8 |
| 58-59—Boston | 66 | 2089 | 465 | 1192 | .390 | 312 | 391 | .798 | 638 | 164 | 271 | 11 | 1242 | 9.7 | 2.5 | 18.8 |
| 59-60—Boston | 75 | 2420 | 673 | 1590 | .423 | 283 | 386 | .733 | 794 | 171 | 275 | 8 | 1629 | 10.6 | 2.3 | 21.7 |
| 60-61—Boston | 74 | 2256 | 627 | 1566 | .400 | 325 | 424 | .767 | 732 | 141 | 260 | 7 | 1579 | 9.9 | 1.9 | 21.3 |
| 61-62—Boston | 79 | 2383 | 692 | 1613 | .429 | 358 | 437 | .819 | 747 | 165 | 280 | 2 | 1742 | 9.5 | 2.1 | 22.1 |
| 62-63—Boston | 76 | 2004 | 550 | 1300 | .423 | 340 | 407 | .835 | 569 | 95 | 270 | 4 | 1440 | 7.5 | 1.3 | 18.9 |
| 63-64—Boston | 76 | 2040 | 487 | 1223 | .398 | 283 | 342 | .827 | 460 | 183 | 268 | 3 | 1257 | 6.1 | 2.4 | 16.5 |
| 64-65—Boston | 67 | 1706 | 365 | 954 | .383 | 182 | 229 | .795 | 399 | 157 | 252 | 5 | 912 | 6.0 | 2.3 | 13.6 |
| **Totals** | 654 | 19254 | 4773 | 11787 | .405 | 2648 | 3353 | .790 | 5749 | 1318 | 2454 | 58 | 12194 | 8.8 | 2.0 | 18.6 |

### NBA PLAYOFF RECORD

| Season Team | G | Min. | FGM | FGA | Pct. | FTM | FTA | Pct. | Reb. | Ast. | PF | Dq. | Pts. | RPG | APG | PPG |
|---|---|---|---|---|---|---|---|---|---|---|---|---|---|---|---|---|
| 56-57—Boston | 10 | 370 | 90 | 231 | .390 | 49 | 69 | .710 | 117 | 20 | 40 | 1 | 229 | 11.7 | 2.0 | 22.9 |
| 57-58—Boston | 11 | 349 | 68 | 194 | .351 | 56 | 72 | .778 | 119 | 18 | 52 | 3 | 192 | 10.8 | 1.6 | 17.5 |
| 58-59—Boston | 11 | 348 | 91 | 220 | .414 | 37 | 56 | .661 | 98 | 32 | 41 | 0 | 219 | 8.9 | 2.9 | 19.9 |
| 59-60—Boston | 13 | 423 | 112 | 267 | .419 | 60 | 80 | .750 | 126 | 27 | 53 | 2 | 284 | 9.7 | 2.1 | 21.8 |
| 60-61—Boston | 10 | 291 | 82 | 201 | .408 | 33 | 43 | .767 | 99 | 20 | 36 | 1 | 197 | 9.9 | 2.0 | 19.7 |
| 61-62—Boston | 14 | 445 | 116 | 291 | .399 | 58 | 76 | .763 | 115 | 34 | 58 | 4 | 290 | 8.2 | 2.4 | 20.7 |
| 62-63—Boston | 13 | 413 | 123 | 270 | .456 | 75 | 98 | .765 | 116 | 15 | 55 | 2 | 321 | 8.9 | 1.2 | 24.7 |
| 63-64—Boston | 10 | 308 | 70 | 180 | .389 | 34 | 42 | .810 | 80 | 26 | 36 | 0 | 174 | 8.0 | 2.6 | 17.4 |
| 64-65—Boston | 12 | 276 | 66 | 181 | .365 | 20 | 32 | .625 | 84 | 23 | 46 | 1 | 152 | 7.0 | 1.9 | 12.7 |
| **Totals** | 104 | 3223 | 818 | 2035 | .402 | 422 | 568 | .743 | 954 | 215 | 417 | 14 | 2058 | 9.2 | 2.1 | 19.8 |

### NBA ALL-STAR GAME RECORD

| Season Team | Min. | FGM | FGA | Pct. | FTM | FTA | Pct. | Reb. | Ast. | PF | Dq. | Pts. |
|---|---|---|---|---|---|---|---|---|---|---|---|---|
| 1957—Boston | 23 | 5 | 17 | .294 | 2 | 2 | 1.000 | 7 | 0 | 3 | 0 | 12 |
| 1961—Boston | 19 | 2 | 16 | .125 | 0 | 0 | ... | 6 | 1 | 4 | 0 | 4 |
| 1962—Boston | 13 | 4 | 11 | .364 | 2 | 2 | 1.000 | 2 | 1 | 4 | 0 | 10 |
| 1963—Boston | 21 | 6 | 11 | .545 | 3 | 4 | .750 | 2 | 1 | 4 | 0 | 15 |
| 1964—Boston | 21 | 5 | 12 | .417 | 0 | 0 | ... | 3 | 0 | 5 | 0 | 10 |
| 1965—Boston | | | | | Selected, did not play—injured. | | | | | | | |
| **Totals** | 97 | 22 | 67 | .328 | 7 | 8 | .875 | 20 | 3 | 20 | 0 | 51 |

### HEAD COACHING RECORD

**NOTES:** NBA Coach of the Year (1973).

### NBA COACHING RECORD

| Season Team | REGULAR SEASON | | | | PLAYOFFS | | |
|---|---|---|---|---|---|---|---|
| | W | L | Pct. | Finish | W | L | Pct. |
| 69-70—Boston | 34 | 48 | .415 | 6th/Eastern Division | — | — | — |
| 70-71—Boston | 44 | 38 | .537 | 3rd/Atlantic Division | — | — | — |

| Season Team | W | L | Pct. | Finish | W | L | Pct. |
|---|---|---|---|---|---|---|---|
| | **REGULAR SEASON** | | | | **PLAYOFFS** | | |
| 71-72—Boston | 56 | 26 | .683 | 1st/Atlantic Division | 5 | 6 | .455 |
| 72-73—Boston | 68 | 14 | .829 | 1st/Atlantic Division | 7 | 6 | .538 |
| 73-74—Boston | 56 | 26 | .683 | 1st/Atlantic Division | 12 | 6 | .667 |
| 74-75—Boston | 60 | 22 | .732 | 1st/Atlantic Division | 6 | 5 | .545 |
| 75-76—Boston | 54 | 28 | .659 | 1st/Atlantic Division | 12 | 6 | .667 |
| 76-77—Boston | 44 | 38 | .537 | 2nd/Atlantic Division | 5 | 4 | .556 |
| 77-78—Boston | 11 | 23 | .324 | | — | — | — |
| **Totals (9 years)** | **427** | **263** | **.619** | **Totals (6 years)** | **47** | **33** | **.588** |

**NOTES:**

1972—Defeated Atlanta, 4-2, in Eastern Conference Semifinals; lost to New York, 4-1, in Eastern Conference Finals.

1973—Defeated Atlanta, 4-2, in Eastern Conference Semifinals; lost to New York, 4-3, in Eastern Conference Finals.

1974—Defeated Buffalo, 4-2, in Eastern Conference Semifinals; defeated New York, 4-1, in Eastern Conference Finals; defeated Milwaukee, 4-3, in NBA Finals.

1975—Defeated Houston, 4-1, in Eastern Conference Semifinals; lost to Washington, 4-2, in Eastern Conference Finals.

1976—Defeated Buffalo, 4-2, in Eastern Conference Semifinals; defeated Cleveland, 4-2, in Eastern Conference Finals; defeated Phoenix, 4-2, in NBA Finals.

1977—Defeated San Antonio, 2-0, in Eastern Conference First Round; lost to Philadelphia, 4-3, in Eastern Conference Semifinals.

1978—Replaced as Boston head coach by Tom Sanders with club in third place (January 3).

# HOLZMAN, RED

**PERSONAL:** Born August 10, 1920, in Brooklyn, N.Y. ... Died November 13, 1998. ... 5-10/175 (1,78/79,4). ... Full name: William Holzman.

**HIGH SCHOOL:** Franklin K. Lane (Brooklyn, N.Y.).

**COLLEGE:** Baltimore, then City College of New York.

**TRANSACTIONS:** Played in New York State League with Albany (1941-42). ... In military service during 1942-43, 1943-44 and 1944-45 seasons; played at Norfolk, Va., Naval Training Station and scored 305 points in 1942-43 and 258 points in 1943-44. ... Signed by Rochester Royals of National Basketball League (1945). ... Played in American Basketball League with New York (1945-46). ... Royals franchise transferred to Basketball Association of America for 1948-49 season. ... Royals franchise became part of NBA for 1949-50 season. ... Acquired from Royals by Milwaukee Hawks (1953).

**CAREER NOTES:** Basketball consultant, New York Knicks (1991 to 1998).

**CAREER HONORS:** Elected to Naismith Memorial Basketball Hall of Fame (1986). ... One of the Top 10 Coaches in NBA History (1996).

**MISCELLANEOUS:** Member of NBL championship team (1946). ... Member of NBA championship team (1951).

## COLLEGIATE RECORD

| Season Team | G | Min. | FGM | FGA | Pct. | FTM | FTA | Pct. | Reb. | Ast. | Pts. | RPG | APG | PPG |
|---|---|---|---|---|---|---|---|---|---|---|---|---|---|---|
| | | | | | | | | | | | | **AVERAGES** | | |
| 38-39—Baltimore | | | | | | Statistics unavailable. | | | | | | | | |
| 39-40—City College. (N.Y.) | | | | | | Did not play—transfer student. | | | | | | | | |
| 40-41—City College. (N.Y.) | 21 | ... | 96 | ... | ... | 37 | ... | ... | ... | ... | 229 | ... | ... | 10.9 |
| 41-42—City College. (N.Y.) | 18 | ... | 87 | ... | ... | 51 | ... | ... | ... | ... | 225 | ... | ... | 12.5 |
| **Totals** | **39** | ... | **183** | ... | ... | **88** | ... | ... | ... | ... | **454** | ... | ... | **11.6** |

## ABL REGULAR-SEASON RECORD

| Season Team | G | Min. | FGM | FGA | Pct. | FTM | FTA | Pct. | Reb. | Ast. | Pts. | RPG | APG | PPG |
|---|---|---|---|---|---|---|---|---|---|---|---|---|---|---|
| | | | | | | | | | | | | **AVERAGES** | | |
| 45-46—New York | 4 | ... | 18 | ... | ... | 12 | ... | ... | ... | ... | 48 | ... | ... | 12.0 |

## NBL AND NBA REGULAR-SEASON RECORD

**HONORS:** All-NBL first team (1946, 1948). ... All-NBL second team (1947).

| Season Team | G | Min. | FGM | FGA | Pct. | FTM | FTA | Pct. | Reb. | Ast. | PF | Dq. | Pts. | RPG | APG | PPG |
|---|---|---|---|---|---|---|---|---|---|---|---|---|---|---|---|---|
| | | | | | | | | | | | | | | **AVERAGES** | | |
| 45-46—Rochester (NBL) | 34 | ... | 144 | ... | ... | 77 | 115 | .670 | ... | ... | 54 | ... | 365 | ... | ... | 10.7 |
| 46-47—Rochester (NBL) | 44 | ... | 227 | ... | ... | 74 | 139 | .532 | ... | ... | 68 | ... | 528 | ... | ... | 12.0 |
| 47-48—Rochester (NBL) | 60 | ... | 246 | ... | ... | 117 | 182 | .643 | ... | ... | 58 | ... | 609 | ... | ... | 10.2 |
| 48-49—Rochester (BAA) | 60 | ... | 225 | 691 | .326 | 96 | 157 | .611 | ... | 149 | 93 | ... | 546 | ... | 2.5 | 9.1 |
| 49-50—Rochester | 68 | ... | 206 | 625 | .330 | 144 | 210 | .686 | ... | 200 | 67 | ... | 556 | ... | 2.9 | 8.2 |
| 50-51—Rochester | 68 | ... | 183 | 561 | .326 | 130 | 179 | .726 | 152 | 147 | 94 | 0 | 496 | 2.2 | 2.2 | 7.3 |
| 51-52—Rochester | 65 | 1065 | 104 | 372 | .280 | 61 | 85 | .718 | 106 | 115 | 95 | 1 | 269 | 1.6 | 1.8 | 4.1 |
| 52-53—Rochester | 46 | 392 | 38 | 149 | .255 | 27 | 38 | .711 | 40 | 35 | 56 | 2 | 103 | 0.9 | 0.8 | 2.2 |
| 53-54—Milwaukee | 51 | 649 | 74 | 224 | .330 | 48 | 73 | .658 | 46 | 75 | 73 | 1 | 196 | 0.9 | 1.5 | 3.8 |
| **Totals** | **496** | ... | **1447** | ... | ... | **774** | **1178** | **.657** | ... | ... | **658** | ... | **3668** | ... | ... | **7.4** |

## NBL AND NBA PLAYOFF RECORD

| Season Team | G | Min. | FGM | FGA | Pct. | FTM | FTA | Pct. | Reb. | Ast. | PF | Dq. | Pts. | RPG | APG | PPG |
|---|---|---|---|---|---|---|---|---|---|---|---|---|---|---|---|---|
| | | | | | | | | | | | | | | **AVERAGES** | | |
| 45-46—Rochester (NBL) | 7 | ... | 30 | ... | ... | 21 | 31 | .677 | ... | ... | 10 | ... | 81 | ... | ... | 11.6 |
| 46-47—Rochester (NBL) | 11 | ... | 42 | ... | ... | 22 | 29 | .759 | ... | ... | 22 | ... | 106 | ... | ... | 9.6 |
| 47-48—Rochester (NBL) | 10 | ... | 35 | ... | ... | 10 | 15 | .667 | ... | ... | 6 | ... | 80 | ... | ... | 8.0 |

| Season Team | G | Min. | FGM | FGA | Pct. | FTM | FTA | Pct. | Reb. | Ast. | PF | Dq. | Pts. | AVERAGES RPG | APG | PPG |
|---|---|---|---|---|---|---|---|---|---|---|---|---|---|---|---|---|
| 48-49—Rochester (BAA) | 4 | ... | 18 | 40 | .450 | 5 | 6 | .833 | ... | 13 | 3 | ... | 41 | ... | 3.3 | 10.3 |
| 49-50—Rochester | 2 | ... | 3 | 9 | .333 | 1 | 2 | .500 | ... | 0 | 3 | ... | 7 | ... | 0.0 | 3.5 |
| 50-51—Rochester | 14 | ... | 31 | 76 | .408 | 23 | 34 | .676 | 19 | 20 | 14 | 0 | 85 | 1.4 | 1.4 | 6.1 |
| 51-52—Rochester | 6 | 65 | 3 | 15 | .200 | 1 | 6 | .167 | 6 | 2 | 3 | 0 | 7 | 1.0 | 0.3 | 1.2 |
| 52-53—Rochester | 2 | 14 | 1 | 5 | .200 | 1 | 4 | .250 | 1 | 1 | 4 | 0 | 3 | 0.5 | 0.5 | 1.5 |
| Totals | 56 | ... | 163 | ... | ... | 84 | 127 | .661 | ... | ... | 65 | ... | 410 | ... | ... | 7.3 |

### HEAD COACHING RECORD

**BACKGROUND:** Chief scout, New York Knicks (1959-60 through 1966-67).
**HONORS:** NBA Coach of the Year (1970).

### NBA COACHING RECORD

| Season Team | REGULAR SEASON W | L | Pct. | Finish | PLAYOFFS W | L | Pct. |
|---|---|---|---|---|---|---|---|
| 53-54—Milwaukee | 10 | 16 | .385 | 4th/Western Division | — | — | — |
| 54-55—Milwaukee | 26 | 46 | .361 | 4th/Western Division | — | — | — |
| 55-56—St. Louis | 33 | 39 | .458 | T2nd/Western Division | 4 | 5 | .444 |
| 56-57—St. Louis | 14 | 19 | .424 | | — | — | — |
| 67-68—New York | 28 | 17 | .622 | 3rd/Eastern Division | 2 | 4 | .333 |
| 68-69—New York | 54 | 28 | .659 | 3rd/Eastern Division | 6 | 4 | .600 |
| 69-70—New York | 60 | 22 | .732 | 1st/Eastern Division | 12 | 7 | .632 |
| 70-71—New York | 52 | 30 | .634 | 1st/Atlantic Division | 7 | 5 | .583 |
| 71-72—New York | 48 | 34 | .585 | 2nd/Atlantic Division | 9 | 7 | .563 |
| 72-73—New York | 57 | 25 | .695 | 2nd/Atlantic Division | 12 | 5 | .706 |
| 73-74—New York | 49 | 33 | .598 | 2nd/Atlantic Division | 5 | 7 | .417 |
| 74-75—New York | 40 | 42 | .488 | 3rd/Atlantic Division | 1 | 2 | .333 |
| 75-76—New York | 38 | 44 | .463 | 4th/Atlantic Division | — | — | — |
| 76-77—New York | 40 | 42 | .488 | 3rd/Atlantic Division | — | — | — |
| 78-79—New York | 25 | 43 | .368 | 4th/Atlantic Division | — | — | — |
| 79-80—New York | 39 | 43 | .476 | T3rd/Atlantic Division | — | — | — |
| 80-81—New York | 50 | 32 | .610 | 3rd/Atlantic Division | 0 | 2 | .000 |
| 81-82—New York | 33 | 49 | .402 | 5th/Atlantic Division | — | — | — |
| Totals (18 years) | 696 | 604 | .535 | Totals (10 years) | 58 | 48 | .547 |

**NOTES:**
1954—Replaced Fuzzy Levane as Milwaukee head coach with record of 11-35.
1955—Milwaukee franchise transferred to St. Louis.
1956—Lost to Minneapolis, 103-97, in Western Division 2nd place game; defeated Minneapolis, 2-1, in Western Division Semifinals; lost to Fort Wayne, 3-2, in Western Division Finals.
1957—Replaced as St. Louis head coach by Slater Martin (January).
1967—Replaced Dick McGuire as New York head coach (December), with record of 15-22 and in fifth place.
1968—Lost to Philadelphia in Eastern Division Semifinals.
1969—Defeated Baltimore, 4-0, in Eastern Division Semifinals; lost to Boston, 4-2, in Eastern Division Finals.
1970—Defeated Baltimore, 4-3, in Eastern Division Semifinals; defeated Milwaukee, 4-1, in Eastern Division Finals; defeated Los Angeles, 4-3, in NBA Finals.
1971—Defeated Atlanta, 4-1, in Eastern Conference Semifinals; lost to Baltimore, 4-3, in Eastern Conference Finals.
1972—Defeated Baltimore, 4-2, in Eastern Conference Semifinals; defeated Boston, 4-1, in Eastern Conference Finals; lost to Los Angeles, 4-1, in NBA Finals.
1973—Defeated Baltimore, 4-1, in Eastern Conference Semifinals; defeated Boston, 4-3, in Eastern Conference Finals; defeated Los Angeles, 4-1, in NBA Finals.
1974—Defeated Capital, 4-3, in Eastern Conference Semifinals; lost to Boston, 4-1, in Eastern Conference Finals.
1975—Lost to Houston in Eastern Conference First Round.
1978—Replaced Willis Reed as New York head coach (November) with record of 6-8.
1981—Lost to Chicago in Eastern Conference First Round.

## JACKSON, PHIL

See Head Coaches, page 300.

## JONES, K.C.

**PERSONAL:** Born May 25, 1932, in Taylor, Texas. ... 6-1/200 (1,85/90,7).
**HIGH SCHOOL:** Commerce (San Francisco).
**COLLEGE:** San Francisco.
**TRANSACTIONS:** Selected by Boston Celtics in second round of 1956 NBA Draft. ... In military service (1956-57 and 1957-58); played at Fort Leonard Wood, Mo.; named to Amateur Athletic Union All-America team as a member of 1957-58 Fort Leonard Wood team. ... Played in Eastern Basketball League with Hartford Capitols (1967-68).
**CAREER HONORS:** Elected to Naismith Memorial Basketball Hall of Fame (1989).
**MISCELLANEOUS:** Member of NBA championship team (1959, 1960, 1961, 1962, 1963, 1964, 1965, 1966). ... Selected by Los Angeles Rams in 30th round of 1955 National Football League Draft. ... Member of gold-medal-winning U.S. Olympic team (1956).

### COLLEGIATE RECORD

**NOTES:** Underwent appendectomy after one game of the 1953-54 season and was granted an extra year of eligibility by the University of San Francisco; however, he was ineligible for the 1955-56 NCAA Tournament because he was playing his fifth season of college basketball. ... Member of NCAA championship team (1955).

| Season Team | G | Min. | FGM | FGA | Pct. | FTM | FTA | Pct. | Reb. | Ast. | Pts. | RPG | APG | PPG |
|---|---|---|---|---|---|---|---|---|---|---|---|---|---|---|
| 51-52—San Francisco‡............... | 24 | ... | 44 | 128 | .344 | 46 | 64 | .719 | ... | ... | 134 | ... | ... | 5.6 |
| 52-53—San Francisco............... | 23 | ... | 63 | 159 | .396 | 81 | 149 | .544 | ... | ... | 207 | ... | ... | 9.0 |
| 53-54—San Francisco............... | 1 | ... | 3 | 12 | .250 | 2 | 2 | 1.000 | 3 | ... | 8 | 3.0 | ... | 8.0 |
| 54-55—San Francisco............... | 29 | ... | 105 | 293 | .358 | 97 | 144 | .674 | 148 | ... | 307 | 5.1 | ... | 10.6 |
| 55-56—San Francisco............... | 25 | ... | 76 | 208 | .365 | 93 | 142 | .655 | 130 | ... | 245 | 5.2 | ... | 9.8 |
| Totals .................. | 78 | ... | 247 | 672 | .368 | 273 | 437 | .625 | ... | ... | 767 | ... | ... | 9.8 |

## NBA REGULAR-SEASON RECORD

| Season Team | G | Min. | FGM | FGA | Pct. | FTM | FTA | Pct. | Reb. | Ast. | PF | Dq. | Pts. | RPG | APG | PPG |
|---|---|---|---|---|---|---|---|---|---|---|---|---|---|---|---|---|
| 58-59—Boston.............. | 49 | 609 | 65 | 192 | .339 | 41 | 68 | .603 | 127 | 70 | 58 | 0 | 171 | 2.6 | 1.4 | 3.5 |
| 59-60—Boston.............. | 74 | 1274 | 169 | 414 | .408 | 128 | 170 | .753 | 199 | 189 | 109 | 1 | 466 | 2.7 | 2.6 | 6.3 |
| 60-61—Boston.............. | 78 | 1607 | 203 | 601 | .338 | 186 | 320 | .581 | 279 | 253 | 200 | 3 | 592 | 3.6 | 3.2 | 7.6 |
| 61-62—Boston.............. | 79 | 2023 | 289 | 707 | .409 | 145 | 231 | .628 | 291 | 339 | 204 | 2 | 723 | 3.7 | 4.3 | 9.2 |
| 62-63—Boston.............. | 79 | 1945 | 230 | 591 | .389 | 112 | 177 | .633 | 263 | 317 | 221 | 3 | 572 | 3.3 | 4.0 | 7.2 |
| 63-64—Boston.............. | 80 | 2424 | 283 | 722 | .392 | 88 | 168 | .524 | 372 | 407 | 253 | 0 | 654 | 4.7 | 5.1 | 8.2 |
| 64-65—Boston.............. | 78 | 2434 | 253 | 639 | .396 | 143 | 227 | .630 | 318 | 437 | 263 | 5 | 649 | 4.1 | 5.6 | 8.3 |
| 65-66—Boston.............. | 80 | 2710 | 240 | 619 | .388 | 209 | 303 | .690 | 304 | 503 | 243 | 4 | 689 | 3.8 | 6.3 | 8.6 |
| 66-67—Boston.............. | 78 | 2446 | 182 | 459 | .397 | 119 | 189 | .630 | 239 | 389 | 273 | 7 | 483 | 3.1 | 5.0 | 6.2 |
| Totals.................. | 675 | 17472 | 1914 | 4944 | .387 | 1171 | 1853 | .632 | 2392 | 2904 | 1824 | 25 | 4999 | 3.5 | 4.3 | 7.4 |

## NBA PLAYOFF RECORD

| Season Team | G | Min. | FGM | FGA | Pct. | FTM | FTA | Pct. | Reb. | Ast. | PF | Dq. | Pts. | RPG | APG | PPG |
|---|---|---|---|---|---|---|---|---|---|---|---|---|---|---|---|---|
| 58-59—Boston.............. | 8 | 75 | 5 | 20 | .250 | 5 | 5 | 1.000 | 12 | 10 | 8 | 0 | 15 | 1.5 | 1.3 | 1.9 |
| 59-60—Boston.............. | 13 | 232 | 27 | 80 | .338 | 17 | 22 | .773 | 45 | 14 | 28 | 0 | 71 | 3.5 | 1.1 | 5.5 |
| 60-61—Boston.............. | 9 | 103 | 9 | 30 | .300 | 7 | 14 | .500 | 19 | 15 | 17 | 0 | 25 | 2.1 | 1.7 | 2.8 |
| 61-62—Boston.............. | 14 | 329 | 44 | 102 | .431 | 38 | 53 | .717 | 56 | 55 | 50 | 1 | 126 | 4.0 | 3.9 | 9.0 |
| 62-63—Boston.............. | 13 | 250 | 19 | 64 | .297 | 21 | 30 | .700 | 36 | 37 | 42 | 1 | 59 | 2.8 | 2.8 | 4.5 |
| 63-64—Boston.............. | 10 | 312 | 25 | 72 | .347 | 13 | 25 | .520 | 37 | 68 | 40 | 0 | 63 | 3.7 | 6.8 | 6.3 |
| 64-65—Boston.............. | 12 | 396 | 43 | 104 | .413 | 35 | 45 | .778 | 39 | 74 | 49 | 1 | 121 | 3.3 | 6.2 | 10.1 |
| 65-66—Boston.............. | 17 | 543 | 45 | 109 | .413 | 39 | 57 | .684 | 52 | 75 | 65 | 0 | 129 | 3.1 | 4.4 | 7.6 |
| 66-67—Boston.............. | 9 | 254 | 24 | 75 | .320 | 11 | 18 | .611 | 24 | 48 | 36 | 1 | 59 | 2.7 | 5.3 | 6.6 |
| Totals.................. | 105 | 2494 | 241 | 656 | .367 | 186 | 269 | .691 | 320 | 396 | 335 | 4 | 668 | 3.0 | 3.8 | 6.4 |

## EBL REGULAR-SEASON RECORD

| Season Team | G | Min. | FGM | FGA | Pct. | FTM | FTA | Pct. | Reb. | Ast. | PF | Dq. | Pts. | RPG | APG | PPG |
|---|---|---|---|---|---|---|---|---|---|---|---|---|---|---|---|---|
| 67-68—Hartford............................ | 6 | ... | 15 | ... | ... | 9 | 18 | .500 | 24 | 41 | ... | ... | 39 | 4.0 | 6.8 | 6.5 |

## HEAD COACHING RECORD

**BACKGROUND:** Assistant coach, Harvard University (1970-71). ... Assistant coach, Los Angeles Lakers (1971-72). ... Assistant coach, Milwaukee Bucks (1976-77). ... Assistant coach, Boston Celtics (1978-79 through 1982-83 and 1996-97). ... Vice president/basketball operations, Celtics (1988-89). ... Assistant coach, Seattle SuperSonics (1989-90). ... Assistant coach, Detroit Pistons (1994-95). ... Assistant coach, Celtics (1996-97).

## COLLEGIATE COACHING RECORD

| Season Team | W | L | Pct. |
|---|---|---|---|
| 67-68—Brandeis........................... | 11 | 10 | .524 |
| 68-69—Brandeis........................... | 12 | 9 | .571 |
| 69-70—Brandeis........................... | 11 | 13 | .458 |
| Totals (3 years)........................... | 34 | 32 | .515 |

## ABA COACHING RECORD

| Season Team | REGULAR SEASON | | | | PLAYOFFS | | |
|---|---|---|---|---|---|---|---|
| | W | L | Pct. | Finish | W | L | Pct. |
| 72-73—San Diego ................................ | 30 | 54 | .357 | 4th/Western Division | 0 | 4 | .000 |

## ABL COACHING RECORD

| Season Team | REGULAR SEASON | | | | PLAYOFFS | | |
|---|---|---|---|---|---|---|---|
| | W | L | Pct. | Finish | W | L | Pct. |
| 97-98—New England ................................ | 24 | 20 | .545 | 2nd/Eastern Conference | 0 | 2 | .000 |
| 98-99—New England ................................ | 3 | 10 | .231 | | — | — | — |
| Totals (2 years)................................ | 27 | 30 | .474 | | | | |

## NBA COACHING RECORD

| Season Team | REGULAR SEASON | | | | PLAYOFFS | | |
|---|---|---|---|---|---|---|---|
| | W | L | Pct. | Finish | W | L | Pct. |
| 73-74—Capital ........................... | 47 | 35 | .573 | 1st/Central Division | 3 | 4 | .429 |
| 74-75—Washington ........................... | 60 | 22 | .732 | 1st/Central Division | 8 | 9 | .471 |
| 75-76—Washington ........................... | 48 | 34 | .585 | 2nd/Central Division | 3 | 4 | .429 |
| 83-84—Boston ........................... | 62 | 20 | .756 | 1st/Atlantic Division | 15 | 8 | .652 |
| 84-85—Boston ........................... | 63 | 19 | .768 | 1st/Atlantic Division | 13 | 8 | .619 |
| 85-86—Boston ........................... | 67 | 15 | .817 | 1st/Atlantic Division | 15 | 3 | .833 |
| 86-87—Boston ........................... | 59 | 23 | .720 | 1st/Atlantic Division | 13 | 10 | .565 |
| 87-88—Boston ........................... | 57 | 25 | .695 | 1st/Atlantic Division | 9 | 8 | .529 |
| 90-91—Seattle ........................... | 41 | 41 | .500 | 5th/Pacific Division | 2 | 3 | .400 |
| 91-92—Seattle ........................... | 18 | 18 | .500 | | — | — | — |
| Totals (10 years)........................... | 522 | 252 | .674 | Totals (9 years) | 81 | 57 | .587 |

**NOTES:**

1973—Lost to Utah in Western Division Semifinals.

1974—Lost to New York in Eastern Conference Semifinals.

1975—Defeated Buffalo, 4-3, in Eastern Conference Semifinals; defeated Boston, 4-2, in Eastern Conference Finals; lost to Golden State, 4-0, in NBA Finals.

1976—Lost to Cleveland in Eastern Conference Semifinals.

1984—Defeated Washington, 3-1, in Eastern Conference First Round; defeated New York, 4-3, in Eastern Conference Semifinals; defeated Milwaukee, 4-1, in Eastern Conference Finals; defeated Los Angeles, 4-3, in NBA Finals.

1985—Defeated Cleveland, 3-1, in Eastern Conference First Round; defeated Detroit, 4-2, in Eastern Conference Semifinals; defeated Philadelphia, 4-1, in Eastern Conference Finals; lost to Los Angeles Lakers, 4-2, in NBA Finals.

1986—Defeated Chicago, 3-0, in Eastern Conference First Round; defeated Atlanta, 4-1, in Eastern Conference Semifinals; defeated Milwaukee, 4-0, in Eastern Conference Finals; defeated Houston, 4-2, in NBA Finals.

1987—Defeated Chicago, 3-0, in Eastern Conference First Round; defeated Milwaukee, 4-3, in Eastern Conference Semifinals; defeated Detroit, 4-3, in Eastern Conference Finals; lost to Los Angeles Lakers, 4-2, in NBA Finals.

1988—Defeated New York, 3-1, in Eastern Conference First Round; defeated Atlanta, 4-3, in Eastern Conference Semifinals; lost to Detroit, 4-2, in Eastern Conference Finals.

1991—Lost to Portland in Western Conference First Round.

1992—Replaced as Seattle head coach by interim coach Bob Kloppenburg with club in sixth place (January 15).

# KARL, GEORGE

See Head Coaches, page 304.

# KUNDLA, JOHN

**PERSONAL:** Born July 3, 1916, in Star Junction, Pa. ... 6-2/180 (1,88/81,6). ... Full name: John Albert Kundla.
**HIGH SCHOOL:** Central (Minneapolis).
**COLLEGE:** Minnesota.
**CAREER HONORS:** Elected to Naismith Memorial Basketball Hall of Fame (1995). ... One of the Top 10 Coaches in NBA History (1996).

## COLLEGIATE RECORD

| Season Team | G | Min. | FGM | FGA | Pct. | FTM | FTA | Pct. | Reb. | Ast. | Pts. | RPG | APG | PPG |
|---|---|---|---|---|---|---|---|---|---|---|---|---|---|---|
| 35-36—Minnesota‡ ................ | | | | | | Freshman team statistics unavailable. | | | | | | | | |
| 36-37—Minnesota ................ | 15 | ... | 53 | ... | ... | 34 | 53 | .642 | ... | ... | 140 | ... | ... | 9.3 |
| 37-38—Minnesota ................ | 20 | ... | 62 | ... | ... | 41 | 77 | .532 | ... | ... | 165 | ... | ... | 8.3 |
| 38-39—Minnesota ................ | 17 | ... | 71 | ... | ... | 40 | 63 | .635 | ... | ... | 182 | ... | ... | 10.7 |
| Varsity totals.................. | 52 | ... | 186 | ... | ... | 115 | 193 | .596 | ... | ... | 487 | ... | ... | 9.4 |

## HEAD COACHING RECORD

**BACKGROUND:** Head coach, De La Salle High School (Minn.).

### COLLEGIATE COACHING RECORD

| Season Team | W | L | Pct. | Finish |
|---|---|---|---|---|
| 46-47—St. Thomas (Minn.)................................ | 11 | 11 | .500 | |
| 59-60—Minnesota ................................ | 12 | 12 | .500 | T3rd/Big Ten Conference |
| 60-61—Minnesota ................................ | 10 | 13 | .435 | T4th/Big Ten Conference |
| 61-62—Minnesota ................................ | 10 | 14 | .417 | 7th/Big Ten Conference |
| 62-63—Minnesota ................................ | 12 | 12 | .500 | T4th/Big Ten Conference |
| 63-64—Minnesota ................................ | 17 | 7 | .708 | 3rd/Big Ten Conference |
| 64-65—Minnesota ................................ | 19 | 5 | .792 | 2nd/Big Ten Conference |
| 65-66—Minnesota ................................ | 14 | 10 | .583 | T5th/Big Ten Conference |
| 66-67—Minnesota ................................ | 9 | 15 | .375 | 9th/Big Ten Conference |
| 67-68—Minnesota ................................ | 7 | 17 | .292 | T9th/Big Ten Conference |
| Totals (10 years).................. | 121 | 116 | .511 | |

### NBL COACHING RECORD

| Season Team | REGULAR SEASON | | | | PLAYOFFS | | |
|---|---|---|---|---|---|---|---|
| | W | L | Pct. | Finish | W | L | Pct. |
| 47-48—Minneapolis................ | 43 | 17 | .717 | 1st/Western Division | 8 | 2 | .800 |

### NBA COACHING RECORD

| Season Team | REGULAR SEASON | | | | PLAYOFFS | | |
|---|---|---|---|---|---|---|---|
| | W | L | Pct. | Finish | W | L | Pct. |
| 48-49—Minneapolis................ | 44 | 16 | .733 | 2nd/Western Division | 8 | 2 | .800 |
| 49-50—Minneapolis................ | 51 | 17 | .750 | T1st/Central Division | 10 | 2 | .833 |
| 50-51—Minneapolis................ | 44 | 24 | .647 | 1st/Western Division | 3 | 4 | .429 |
| 51-52—Minneapolis................ | 40 | 26 | .606 | 2nd/Western Division | 9 | 4 | .692 |
| 52-53—Minneapolis................ | 48 | 22 | .686 | 1st/Western Division | 9 | 3 | .750 |
| 53-54—Minneapolis................ | 46 | 26 | .639 | 1st/Western Division | 9 | 4 | .692 |
| 54-55—Minneapolis................ | 40 | 32 | .556 | 2nd/Western Division | 3 | 4 | .429 |

| Season Team | W | L | Pct. | Finish | W | L | Pct. |
|---|---|---|---|---|---|---|---|
| | | | **REGULAR SEASON** | | | **PLAYOFFS** | |
| 55-56—Minneapolis | 33 | 39 | .458 | T2nd/Western Division | 1 | 2 | .333 |
| 56-57—Minneapolis | 34 | 38 | .472 | T1st/Western Division | 2 | 3 | .400 |
| 57-58—Minneapolis | 10 | 23 | .303 | 4th/Western Division | — | — | — |
| 58-59—Minneapolis | 33 | 39 | .458 | 2nd/Western Division | 6 | 7 | .462 |
| **Totals (11 years)** | 423 | 302 | .583 | **Totals (10 years)** | 60 | 35 | .632 |

**NOTES:**

1948—Defeated Oshkosh, 3-1, in NBL playoffs; defeated Tri-Cities, 2-0, in NBL semifinals; defeated Rochester, 3-1, in NBL championship series.

1949—Defeated Chicago, 2-0, in Western Division Semifinals; defeated Rochester, 2-0, in Western Division Finals; defeated Washington, 4-2, in NBA Finals.

1950—Defeated Rochester, 78-76, in Central Division first-place game; defeated Chicago, 2-0, in Central Division Semifinals; defeated Fort Wayne, 2-0, in Central Division Finals; defeated Anderson, 2-0, in NBA Semifinals; defeated Syracuse, 4-2, in NBA Finals.

1951—Defeated Indianapolis, 2-1, in Western Division Semifinals; lost to Rochester, 3-1, in Western Division Finals.

1952—Defeated Indianapolis, 2-0, in Western Division Semifinals; defeated Rochester, 3-1, in Western Division Finals; defeated New York, 4-3, in NBA Finals.

1953—Defeated Indianapolis, 2-0, in Western Division Semifinals; defeated Fort Wayne, 3-2, in Western Division Finals; defeated New York, 4-1, in NBA Finals.

1954—Defeated Rochester, 109-88; Fort Wayne, 90-85; and Fort Wayne, 78-73, in Western Division round robin; defeated Rochester, 2-1, in Western Division Semifinals; defeated Syracuse, 4-3, in NBA Finals.

1955—Defeated Rochester, 2-1, in Western Division Semifinals; lost to Fort Wayne, 3-1, in Western Division Finals.

1956—Defeated St. Louis, 103-97, in Western Division second-place game; lost to St. Louis, 2-1, in Western Division Semifinals.

1957—Lost to St. Louis, 114-111, in Western Division tiebreaker; defeated Fort Wayne, 2-0, in Western Division Semifinals; lost to St. Louis, 3-0, in Western Division Finals.

1958—Replaced George Mikan as Minneapolis head coach (January 14), with record of 9-30 and in fourth place.

1959—Defeated Detroit, 2-1, in Western Division Semifinals; defeated St. Louis, 4-2, in Western Division Finals; lost to Boston, 4-0, in NBA Finals.

## LAPCHICK, JOE

**PERSONAL:** Born April 12, 1900, in Yonkers, N.Y. ... Died August 10, 1970. ... 6-5/185 (1,96/83,9). ... Full name: Joseph Bohomiel Lapchick.

**TRANSACTIONS:** Played with independent teams, including the Original Celtics (1917 through 1920, 1924 through 1926, 1932 through 1936).

**CAREER HONORS:** Elected to Naismith Memorial Basketball Hall of Fame (1966).

**MISCELLANEOUS:** Did not play high school or college basketball.

### PRO RECORD

| Season Team | League | G | FGM | FTM | Pts. | Avg. |
|---|---|---|---|---|---|---|
| 20-21—Holyoke | IL | 11 | 14 | 40 | 68 | 6.2 |
| Schenectady | NYSL | 5 | 2 | 10 | 14 | 2.8 |
| 21-22—Schenectady-Troy | NYSL | 32 | 12 | 95 | 119 | 3.7 |
| Brooklyn | MBL | 10 | 6 | 20 | 32 | 3.2 |
| Holyoke | IL | 16 | 13 | 40 | 66 | 4.1 |
| 22-23—Brooklyn | MBL | 33 | 34 | 109 | 177 | 5.4 |
| Troy | NYSL | 24 | 13 | 59 | 85 | 3.5 |
| Holyoke | IL | | | Statistics unavailable. | | |
| 26-27—Brooklyn | ABL | 32 | 35 | 131 | 201 | 6.3 |
| New York | NBL | 17 | 20 | 66 | 106 | 6.2 |
| 27-28—New York | ABL | 47 | 103 | 110 | 316 | 6.7 |
| 28-29—Cleveland | ABL | 39 | 51 | 86 | 188 | 4.8 |
| 29-30—Cleveland | ABL | 52 | 47 | 92 | 186 | 3.6 |
| 30-31—Cleveland-Toledo | ABL | 30 | 22 | 49 | 93 | 3.1 |
| 32-33—Yonkers | MBL | 1 | 0 | 0 | 0 | 0.0 |
| 33-34—Plymouth | PSL | 1 | 1 | 3 | 5 | 5.0 |
| **ABL pro totals** | | 200 | 258 | 468 | 984 | 4.9 |
| **MBL pro totals** | | 44 | 40 | 129 | 209 | 4.8 |

### COLLEGIATE COACHING RECORD

| Season Team | W | L | Pct. | Finish |
|---|---|---|---|---|
| 36-37—St. John's | 12 | 7 | .632 | Independent |
| 37-38—St. John's | 15 | 4 | .789 | Independent |
| 38-39—St. John's | 18 | 4 | .818 | Independent |
| 39-40—St. John's | 15 | 5 | .750 | Independent |
| 40-41—St. John's | 11 | 6 | .647 | Independent |
| 41-42—St. John's | 16 | 5 | .762 | Independent |
| 42-43—St. John's | 21 | 3 | .875 | Independent |
| 43-44—St. John's | 18 | 5 | .783 | Independent |
| 44-45—St. John's | 21 | 3 | .875 | Independent |
| 45-46—St. John's | 17 | 6 | .739 | Independent |
| 46-47—St. John's | 16 | 7 | .696 | Independent |
| 56-57—St. John's | 14 | 9 | .609 | Independent |

ALL-TIME GREAT COACHES

| Season Team | W | L | Pct. | Finish |
|---|---|---|---|---|
| 57-58—St. John's | 18 | 8 | .692 | Independent |
| 58-59—St. John's | 20 | 6 | .769 | Independent |
| 59-60—St. John's | 17 | 8 | .680 | Independent |
| 60-61—St. John's | 20 | 5 | .800 | Independent |
| 61-62—St. John's | 21 | 5 | .808 | Independent |
| 62-63—St. John's | 9 | 15 | .375 | Independent |
| 63-64—St. John's | 14 | 11 | .560 | Independent |
| 64-65—St. John's | 21 | 8 | .724 | Independent |
| Totals (20 years) | 334 | 130 | .720 | |

## ABL COACHING RECORD

| Season Team | REGULAR SEASON | | | | PLAYOFFS | | |
|---|---|---|---|---|---|---|---|
| | W | L | Pct. | Finish | W | L | Pct. |
| 61-62—Cleveland | 6 | 6 | .500 | | — | — | — |

## NBA COACHING RECORD

| Season Team | REGULAR SEASON | | | | PLAYOFFS | | |
|---|---|---|---|---|---|---|---|
| | W | L | Pct. | Finish | W | L | Pct. |
| 47-48—New York (BAA) | 26 | 22 | .542 | 2nd/Eastern Division | 1 | 2 | .333 |
| 48-49—New York (BAA) | 32 | 28 | .533 | 2nd/Eastern Division | 3 | 3 | .500 |
| 49-50—New York | 40 | 28 | .588 | 2nd/Eastern Division | 3 | 2 | .600 |
| 50-51—New York | 36 | 30 | .545 | 3rd/Eastern Division | 8 | 6 | .571 |
| 51-52—New York | 37 | 29 | .561 | 3rd/Eastern Division | 8 | 6 | .571 |
| 52-53—New York | 47 | 23 | .671 | 1st/Midwest Division | 6 | 5 | .545 |
| 53-54—New York | 44 | 28 | .611 | 1st/Eastern Division | 0 | 4 | .000 |
| 54-55—New York | 38 | 34 | .528 | 2nd/Eastern Division | 1 | 2 | .333 |
| 55-56—New York | 26 | 25 | .510 | | — | — | — |
| Totals (9 years) | 326 | 247 | .569 | Totals (8 years) | 30 | 30 | .500 |

**NOTES:**

1939—Defeated Roanoke, 71-47, in NIT quarterfinals; lost to Loyola, 51-46, in semifinals; lost to Bradley, 40-35, in third-place game.

1940—Lost to Duquesne, 38-31, in NIT quarterfinals.

1943—Defeated Rice, 51-49, in NIT quarterfinals; defeated Fordham, 69-43, in semifinals; defeated Toledo, 48-27, in finals.

1944—Defeated Bowling Green, 44-40, in NIT quarterfinals; defeated Kentucky, 48-45, in semifinals; defeated DePaul, 47-39, in finals.

1945—Defeated Muhlenberg, 34-33, in NIT quarterfinals; lost to Bowling Green, 57-44, in semifinals; lost to Rhode Island, 64-57, in third-place game.

1946—Lost to West Virginia, 70-58, in NIT quarterfinals.

1947—Lost to North Carolina State, 61-55, in NIT quarterfinals.

1948—Lost to Baltimore in quarterfinals.

1949—Defeated Baltimore, 2-1, in Eastern Division Semifinals; lost to Washington, 2-1, in Eastern Division Finals.

1950—Defeated Washington, 2-0, in Eastern Division Semifinals; lost to Syracuse, 2-1, in Eastern Division Finals.

1951—Defeated Boston, 2-0, in Eastern Division Semifinals; defeated Syracuse, 3-2, in Eastern Division Finals; lost to Rochester, 4-3, in NBA Finals.

1952—Defeated Boston, 2-1, in Eastern Division Semifinals; defeated Syracuse, 3-1, in Eastern Division Finals; lost to Minneapolis, 4-3, in NBA Finals.

1953—Defeated Baltimore, 2-0, in Eastern Division Semifinals; defeated Boston, 3-1, in Eastern Division Finals; lost to Minneapolis, 4-1, in NBA Finals.

1954—Lost to Boston, 93-71; Syracuse, 75-68; Boston, 79-78; and Syracuse, 103-99, in Eastern Division round robin.

1955—Lost to Boston in Eastern Division Semifinals.

1956—Resigned as New York head coach.

1958—Defeated Butler, 76-69, in NIT first round; defeated Utah, 71-70, in quarterfinals; lost to Dayton, 80-56, in semifinals; lost to St. Bonaventure, 84-69, in third-place game.

1959—Defeated Villanova, 75-67, in NIT first round; defeated St. Bonaventure, 82-74, in quarterfinals; defeated Providence, 76-55, in semifinals; defeated Bradley, 76-71 (OT), in finals.

1960—Lost to St. Bonaventure, 106-71, in NIT quarterfinals.

1961—Lost to Wake Forest, 97-74, in NCAA Tournament first round.

1962—Defeated Holy Cross, 80-74, in NIT quarterfinals; defeated Duquesne, 76-65, in semifinals; lost to Dayton, 73-67, in finals.

1965—Defeated Boston College, 114-92, in NIT first round; defeated New Mexico, 61-54, in quarterfinals; defeated Army, 67-60, in semifinals; defeated Villanova, 55-51, in finals.

## LOUGHERY, KEVIN

**PERSONAL:** Born March 28, 1940, in Brooklyn, N.Y. ... 6-3/190 (1,90/86,2). ... Full name: Kevin Michael Loughery.
**HIGH SCHOOL:** Cardinal Hayes (Bronx, N.Y.).
**COLLEGE:** Boston College, then St. John's.
**TRANSACTIONS:** Selected by Detroit Pistons in second round (13th pick overall) of 1962 NBA Draft. ... Traded by Pistons to Baltimore Bullets for Larry Staverman (October 28, 1963). ... Traded by Bullets with Fred Carter to Philadelphia 76ers for Archie Clark and future draft choice (October 18, 1971).
**CAREER NOTES:** Broadcaster (1988-89 and 1989-90). ... Scout, Miami Heat (1988-89 and 1989-90). ... Vice president/director of player personnel, Heat (February 1995 to 1995-96) ... Vice president/consultant, Heat (1996-97).

## COLLEGIATE RECORD

| Season Team | G | Min. | FGM | FGA | Pct. | FTM | FTA | Pct. | Reb. | Ast. | Pts. | RPG | APG | PPG |
|---|---|---|---|---|---|---|---|---|---|---|---|---|---|---|
| 57-58—Boston College‡ | 19 | ... | 133 | ... | ... | 55 | ... | ... | ... | ... | 321 | ... | ... | 16.9 |
| 58-59—Boston College | 19 | ... | 128 | ... | ... | 65 | ... | ... | ... | ... | 321 | ... | ... | 16.9 |
| 59-60—St. John's | | | | | Did not play—transfer student. | | | | | | | | | |
| 60-61—St. John's | 25 | ... | 106 | 252 | .421 | 54 | 77 | .701 | 116 | ... | 266 | 4.6 | ... | 10.6 |
| 61-62—St. John's | 26 | ... | 169 | 378 | .447 | 65 | 76 | .855 | 151 | ... | 403 | 5.8 | ... | 15.5 |
| **Varsity totals** | 70 | ... | 403 | | | 184 | ... | ... | | ... | 990 | ... | ... | 14.1 |

## NBA REGULAR-SEASON RECORD

| Season Team | G | Min. | FGM | FGA | Pct. | FTM | FTA | Pct. | Reb. | Ast. | PF | Dq. | Pts. | RPG | APG | PPG |
|---|---|---|---|---|---|---|---|---|---|---|---|---|---|---|---|---|
| 62-63—Detroit | 57 | 845 | 146 | 397 | .368 | 71 | 100 | .710 | 109 | 104 | 135 | 1 | 363 | 1.9 | 1.8 | 6.4 |
| 63-64—Det.-Balt. | 66 | 1459 | 236 | 631 | .374 | 126 | 177 | .712 | 138 | 182 | 175 | 2 | 598 | 2.1 | 2.8 | 9.1 |
| 64-65—Baltimore | 80 | 2417 | 406 | 957 | .424 | 212 | 281 | .754 | 235 | 296 | 320 | 13 | 1024 | 2.9 | 3.7 | 12.8 |
| 65-66—Baltimore | 74 | 2455 | 526 | 1264 | .416 | 297 | 358 | .830 | 227 | 356 | 273 | 8 | 1349 | 3.1 | 4.8 | 18.2 |
| 66-67—Baltimore | 76 | 2577 | 520 | 1306 | .398 | 340 | 412 | .825 | 349 | 288 | 294 | 10 | 1380 | 4.6 | 3.8 | 18.2 |
| 67-68—Baltimore | 77 | 2297 | 458 | 1127 | .406 | 305 | 392 | .778 | 247 | 256 | 301 | 13 | 1221 | 3.2 | 3.3 | 15.9 |
| 68-69—Baltimore | 80 | 3135 | 717 | 1636 | .438 | 372 | 463 | .803 | 266 | 384 | 299 | 3 | 1806 | 3.3 | 4.8 | 22.6 |
| 69-70—Baltimore | 55 | 2037 | 477 | 1082 | .441 | 253 | 298 | .849 | 168 | 292 | 183 | 3 | 1207 | 3.1 | 5.3 | 21.9 |
| 70-71—Baltimore | 82 | 2260 | 481 | 1193 | .403 | 275 | 331 | .831 | 219 | 301 | 246 | 2 | 1237 | 2.7 | 3.7 | 15.1 |
| 71-72—Balt.-Phil. | 76 | 1771 | 341 | 809 | .422 | 263 | 320 | .822 | 183 | 196 | 213 | 3 | 945 | 2.4 | 2.6 | 12.4 |
| 72-73—Philadelphia | 32 | 955 | 169 | 427 | .396 | 107 | 130 | .823 | 113 | 148 | 104 | 0 | 445 | 3.5 | 4.6 | 13.9 |
| **Totals** | 755 | 22208 | 4477 | 10829 | .413 | 2621 | 3262 | .803 | 2254 | 2803 | 2543 | 58 | 11575 | 3.0 | 3.7 | 15.3 |

## NBA PLAYOFF RECORD

| Season Team | G | Min. | FGM | FGA | Pct. | FTM | FTA | Pct. | Reb. | Ast. | PF | Dq. | Pts. | RPG | APG | PPG |
|---|---|---|---|---|---|---|---|---|---|---|---|---|---|---|---|---|
| 62-63—Detroit | 2 | 26 | 1 | 10 | .100 | 1 | 1 | 1.000 | 0 | 4 | 3 | 0 | 3 | 0.0 | 0.0 | 1.5 |
| 64-65—Baltimore | 10 | 297 | 53 | 137 | .387 | 34 | 38 | .895 | 34 | 30 | 36 | 0 | 140 | 3.4 | 3.0 | 14.0 |
| 65-66—Baltimore | 3 | 27 | 3 | 7 | .429 | 3 | 6 | .500 | 1 | 1 | 4 | 0 | 9 | 0.3 | 0.3 | 3.0 |
| 68-69—Baltimore | 4 | 173 | 29 | 79 | .367 | 23 | 35 | .657 | 18 | 21 | 16 | 0 | 81 | 4.5 | 5.3 | 20.3 |
| 69-70—Baltimore | 7 | 153 | 26 | 77 | .338 | 15 | 21 | .714 | 16 | 8 | 24 | 0 | 67 | 2.3 | 1.1 | 9.6 |
| 70-71—Baltimore | 17 | 500 | 84 | 212 | .396 | 64 | 85 | .753 | 38 | 52 | 57 | 2 | 232 | 2.2 | 3.1 | 13.6 |
| **Totals** | 43 | 1176 | 196 | 522 | .375 | 140 | 186 | .753 | 107 | 116 | 140 | 2 | 532 | 2.5 | 2.7 | 12.4 |

## HEAD COACHING RECORD

**BACKGROUND:** Player/head coach, Philadelphia 76ers (February 1973-remainder of 1972-73 season). ... Assistant coach, Atlanta Hawks (1990-91).

## NBA COACHING RECORD

| | REGULAR SEASON | | | | PLAYOFFS | | |
|---|---|---|---|---|---|---|---|
| Season Team | W | L | Pct. | Finish | W | L | Pct. |
| 72-73—Philadelphia | 5 | 26 | .161 | 4th/Atlantic Division | — | — | — |
| 76-77—New York Nets | 22 | 60 | .268 | 5th/Atlantic Division | — | — | — |
| 77-78—New Jersey | 24 | 58 | .293 | 5th/Atlantic Division | — | — | — |
| 78-79—New Jersey | 37 | 45 | .451 | 3rd/Atlantic Division | 0 | 2 | .000 |
| 79-80—New Jersey | 34 | 48 | .415 | 5th/Atlantic Division | — | — | — |
| 80-81—New Jersey | 12 | 23 | .343 | | — | — | — |
| 81-82—Atlanta | 42 | 40 | .512 | 2nd/Central Division | 0 | 2 | .000 |
| 82-83—Atlanta | 43 | 39 | .524 | 2nd/Central Division | 1 | 2 | .333 |
| 83-84—Chicago | 27 | 55 | .329 | 5th/Central Division | — | — | — |
| 84-85—Chicago | 38 | 44 | .463 | 3rd/Central Division | 1 | 3 | .250 |
| 85-86—Washington | 7 | 6 | .538 | T3rd/Atlantic Division | 2 | 3 | .400 |
| 86-87—Washington | 42 | 40 | .512 | 3rd/Atlantic Division | 0 | 3 | .000 |
| 87-88—Washington | 8 | 19 | .296 | | — | — | — |
| 91-92—Miami | 38 | 44 | .463 | 4th/Atlantic Division | 0 | 3 | .000 |
| 92-93—Miami | 36 | 46 | .439 | 5th/Atlantic Division | — | — | — |
| 93-94—Miami | 42 | 40 | .512 | 4th/Atlantic Division | 2 | 3 | .400 |
| 94-95—Miami | 17 | 29 | .370 | 5th/Atlantic Division | — | — | — |
| **Totals (17 years)** | 474 | 662 | .417 | **Totals (8 years)** | 6 | 21 | .222 |

## ABA COACHING RECORD

| | REGULAR SEASON | | | | PLAYOFFS | | |
|---|---|---|---|---|---|---|---|
| Season Team | W | L | Pct. | Finish | W | L | Pct. |
| 73-74—New York Nets | 55 | 29 | .655 | 1st/Eastern Division | 12 | 2 | .857 |
| 74-75—New York Nets | 58 | 26 | .690 | T1st/Eastern Division | 1 | 4 | .200 |
| 75-76—New York Nets | 55 | 29 | .655 | 2nd | 8 | 5 | .615 |
| **Totals (3 years)** | 168 | 84 | .667 | **Totals (3 years)** | 21 | 11 | .656 |

## NOTES:

1973—Replaced Roy Rubin as Philadelphia head coach (February), with record of 4-47.
1974—Defeated Virginia, 4-1, in Eastern Division Semifinals; defeated Kentucky, 4-0, in Eastern Division Finals; defeated Utah, 4-1, in ABA Finals.
1975—Lost to St. Louis in Eastern Division Semifinals.
1976—Defeated San Antonio, 4-3, in semifinals; defeated Denver, 4-2, in ABA Finals.
1979—Lost to Philadelphia in Eastern Conference First Round.
1980—Resigned as New Jersey head coach (December); replaced by Bob MacKinnon with club in fifth place.
1982—Lost to Philadelphia in Eastern Conference First Round.

ALL-TIME GREAT COACHES

1983—Lost to Boston in Eastern Conference First Round.
1985—Lost to Milwaukee in Eastern Conference First Round.
1986—Replaced Gene Shue as Washington head coach (March 19), with record of 32-37. Lost to Philadelphia in Eastern Conference First Round.
1987—Lost to Detroit in Eastern Conference First Round.
1988—Replaced as Washington head coach by Wes Unseld (January 3) with club in fourth place.
1992—Lost to Chicago in Eastern Conference First Round.
1994—Lost to Atlanta in Eastern Conference First Round.
1995—Replaced as Miami head coach by Alvin Gentry (February 14) with club in fifth place.

# MacLEOD, JOHN

**PERSONAL:** Born October 3, 1937, in New Albany, Ind. ... 6-0/170 (1,83/77,1). ... Full name: John Matthew MacLeod.
**HIGH SCHOOL:** New Providence (Clarksville, Ind.).
**COLLEGE:** Bellarmine (Ky.).
**CAREER NOTES:** Head coach, Oklahoma (1967-68 through 1972-73). ... Head coach, Notre Dame (1991-92 to 1998-99).

## COLLEGIATE RECORD

| Season Team | G | Min. | FGM | FGA | Pct. | FTM | FTA | Pct. | Reb. | Ast. | Pts. | RPG | APG | PPG |
|---|---|---|---|---|---|---|---|---|---|---|---|---|---|---|
| 55-56—Bellarmine | | | | | | Freshman team statistics unavailable. | | | | | | | | |
| 56-57—Bellarmine | 10 | ... | 0 | ... | ... | 1 | ... | ... | ... | ... | 1 | ... | ... | 0.1 |
| 57-58—Bellarmine | 8 | ... | 2 | ... | ... | 3 | 10 | .300 | ... | ... | 7 | ... | ... | 0.9 |
| 58-59—Bellarmine | 5 | ... | 2 | ... | ... | 4 | ... | ... | ... | ... | 8 | ... | ... | 1.6 |
| **Totals** | 23 | ... | 4 | ... | ... | 8 | ... | ... | ... | ... | 16 | ... | ... | 0.7 |

## HEAD COACHING RECORD

**BACKGROUND:** Assistant coach, DeSales High School, Ky. (1959-60 through 1961-62). ... Head coach, Smithville High School, Ind. (1963-64 and 1964-65; record: 16-24). ... Assistant coach, Cathedral High School, Ind. (1965-66). ... Assistant coach, University of Oklahoma (1966-67).

### COLLEGIATE COACHING RECORD

| Season Team | W | L | Pct. | Finish |
|---|---|---|---|---|
| 67-68—Oklahoma | 13 | 13 | .500 | T3rd/Big Eight Conference |
| 68-69—Oklahoma | 7 | 19 | .269 | 8th/Big Eight Conference |
| 69-70—Oklahoma | 19 | 9 | .679 | 3rd/Big Eight Conference |
| 70-71—Oklahoma | 19 | 8 | .704 | 2nd/Big Eight Conference |
| 71-72—Oklahoma | 14 | 12 | .538 | 3rd/Big Eight Conference |
| 72-73—Oklahoma | 18 | 8 | .692 | 4th/Big Eight Conference |
| 91-92—Notre Dame | 18 | 15 | .545 | Independent |
| 92-93—Notre Dame | 9 | 18 | .333 | Independent |
| 93-94—Notre Dame | 12 | 17 | .414 | Independent |
| 94-95—Notre Dame | 15 | 12 | .555 | Independent |
| 95-96—Notre Dame | 9 | 18 | .333 | 13th/Big East Conference |
| 96-97—Notre Dame | 16 | 14 | .533 | T4th/Big East Six Division/Big East Conference |
| 97-98—Notre Dame | 13 | 14 | .481 | 5th/Big East Six Division/Big East Conference |
| 98-99—Notre Dame | 14 | 16 | .467 | 4th/Big East Six Division/Big East Conference |
| **Totals (14 years)** | 196 | 193 | .504 | |

## NBA COACHING RECORD

| | REGULAR SEASON | | | | PLAYOFFS | | |
|---|---|---|---|---|---|---|---|
| Season Team | W | L | Pct. | Finish | W | L | Pct. |
| 73-74—Phoenix | 30 | 52 | .396 | 4th/Pacific Division | — | — | — |
| 74-75—Phoenix | 32 | 50 | .390 | 4th/Pacific Division | — | — | — |
| 75-76—Phoenix | 42 | 40 | .512 | 3rd/Pacific Division | 10 | 9 | .526 |
| 76-77—Phoenix | 34 | 48 | .415 | 5th/Pacific Division | — | — | — |
| 77-78—Phoenix | 49 | 33 | .598 | 2nd/Pacific Division | 0 | 2 | .000 |
| 78-79—Phoenix | 50 | 32 | .610 | 2nd/Pacific Division | 9 | 6 | .600 |
| 79-80—Phoenix | 55 | 27 | .671 | 3rd/Pacific Division | 3 | 5 | .375 |
| 80-81—Phoenix | 57 | 25 | .695 | 1st/Pacific Division | 3 | 4 | .429 |
| 81-82—Phoenix | 46 | 36 | .561 | 3rd/Pacific Division | 2 | 5 | .286 |
| 82-83—Phoenix | 53 | 29 | .646 | 2nd/Pacific Division | 1 | 2 | .333 |
| 83-84—Phoenix | 41 | 41 | .500 | 4th/Pacific Division | 9 | 8 | .529 |
| 84-85—Phoenix | 36 | 46 | .439 | 3rd/Pacific Division | 0 | 3 | .000 |
| 85-86—Phoenix | 32 | 50 | .390 | T3rd/Pacific Division | — | — | — |
| 86-87—Phoenix | 22 | 34 | .393 | | — | — | — |
| 87-88—Dallas | 53 | 29 | .646 | 2nd/Midwest Division | 10 | 7 | .588 |
| 88-89—Dallas | 38 | 44 | .463 | 4th/Midwest Division | — | — | — |
| 89-90—Dallas | 5 | 6 | .455 | | — | — | — |
| 90-91—New York | 32 | 35 | .478 | 3rd/Atlantic Division | 0 | 3 | .000 |
| **Totals (18 years)** | 707 | 657 | .518 | **Totals (11 years)** | 47 | 54 | .465 |

**NOTES:**
1970—Defeated Louisville, 74-73, in NIT first round; lost to Louisiana State, 97-94, in quarterfinals.
1971—Lost to Hawaii, 87-86 (2 OT), in NIT first round.
1976—Defeated Seattle, 4-2, in Western Conference Semifinals; defeated Golden State, 4-3, in Western Conference Finals; lost to Boston, 4-2, in NBA Finals.

1978—Lost to Milwaukee in Western Conference First Round.

1979—Defeated Portland, 2-1, in Western Conference First Round; defeated Kansas City, 4-1, in Western Conference Semifinals; lost to Seattle, 4-3, in Western Conference Finals.

1980—Defeated Kansas City, 2-1, in Western Conference First Round; lost to Los Angeles Lakers, 4-1, in Western Conference Semifinals.

1981—Lost to Kansas City in Western Conference Semifinals.

1982—Defeated Denver, 2-1, in Western Conference Semifinals; lost to Los Angeles Lakers, 4-0, in Western Conference Finals.

1983—Lost to Denver in Western Conference First Round.

1984—Defeated Portland, 3-2, in Western Conference First Round; defeated Utah, 4-2, in Western Conference Semifinals; lost to Los Angeles Lakers, 4-2, in Western Conference Finals.

1985—Lost to Los Angeles Lakers in Western Conference First Round.

1987—Replaced as Phoenix head coach by Dick Van Arsdale (February 26).

1988—Defeated Houston, 3-1, in Western Conference First Round; defeated Denver, 4-2, in Western Conference Semifinals; lost to Los Angeles Lakers, 4-3, in Western Conference Finals.

1989—Replaced as Dallas head coach by Richie Adubato (November 29).

1990—Replaced Stu Jackson as New York head coach (December 3) with record of 7-8.

1991—Lost to Chicago in Eastern Conference First Round.

1992—Defeated Western Michigan, 63-56, in NIT first round; defeated Kansas State, 64-47, in second round; defeated Manhattan, 74-58, in quarterfinals; defeated Utah, 58-55, in semifinals; lost to Virginia, 81-76, in final.

1997—Defeated Oral Roberts, 74-58, in NIT first round; defeated TCU, 82-72, in NIT second round; lost to Michigan, 67-66, in NIT quarter finals.

## MOE, DOUG

**PERSONAL:** Born September 21, 1938, in Brooklyn, N.Y. ... 6-5/220 (1,96/99,8). ... Full name: Douglas Edwin Moe.

**HIGH SCHOOL:** Erasmus Hall (Brooklyn, N.Y.), then Bullis Prep School (Silver Springs, Md.).

**COLLEGE:** North Carolina, then Elon College (N.C.).

**TRANSACTIONS:** Selected by Chicago Packers in second round (22nd pick overall) of 1961 NBA Draft. ... Signed by Packers (1961). ... Packers later refused to honor contract when Moe was implicated in college point-shaving scandal; Moe was exonerated but did not play basketball from 1961-62 through 1964-65. ... Played with Padua, Italy (1965-66 and 1966-67). ... Signed by New Orleans Buccaneers of American Basketball Association (1967). ... Traded by Buccaneers with Larry Brown to Oakland Oaks for Steve Jones, Ron Franz and Barry Leibowitz (June 18, 1968). ... Traded by Oaks to Carolina Cougars in three-way deal in which Cougars sent Stew Johnson to Pittsburgh Pipers and Pipers sent Frank Card to Oaks (June 12, 1969). ... Traded by Cougars to Washington Capitols for Gary Bradds and Ira Harge (July 24, 1970). ... Capitols franchise moved from Washington to Virginia and renamed Squires for 1970-71 season.

### COLLEGIATE RECORD

**NOTES:** The Sporting News All-America second team (1959, 1961).

| Season Team | G | Min. | FGM | FGA | Pct. | FTM | FTA | Pct. | Reb. | Ast. | Pts. | RPG | APG | PPG |
|---|---|---|---|---|---|---|---|---|---|---|---|---|---|---|
| 57-58—North Carolina‡ | | | | | | Freshman team statistics unavailable. | | | | | | | | |
| 58-59—North Carolina | 25 | ... | 106 | 265 | .400 | 104 | 164 | .634 | 179 | 67 | 316 | 7.2 | 2.7 | 12.6 |
| 59-60—North Carolina | 12 | ... | 60 | 144 | .417 | 82 | 113 | .726 | 135 | ... | 202 | 11.3 | ... | 16.8 |
| 60-61—North Carolina | 23 | ... | 163 | 401 | .406 | 143 | 207 | .691 | 321 | ... | 469 | 14.0 | ... | 20.4 |
| Totals | 60 | ... | 329 | 810 | .406 | 329 | 484 | .680 | 635 | ... | 987 | 10.6 | ... | 16.5 |

### ABA REGULAR-SEASON RECORD

**NOTES:** Member of ABA championship team (1969). ... ABA All-Star first team (1968). ... ABA All-Star second team (1969).

| Season Team | G | Min. | 2-POINT | | | 3-POINT | | | FTM | FTA | Pct. | Reb. | Ast. | Pts. | AVERAGES | | |
|---|---|---|---|---|---|---|---|---|---|---|---|---|---|---|---|---|---|
| | | | FGM | FGA | Pct. | FGM | FGA | Pct. | | | | | | | RPG | APG | PPG |
| 67-68—New Orleans | 78 | 3113 | 662 | 1588 | .417 | 3 | 22 | .136 | 551 | 693 | .795 | 795 | 202 | 1884 | 10.2 | 2.6 | 24.2 |
| 68-69—Oakland | 75 | 2528 | 524 | 1213 | .432 | 5 | 14 | .357 | 360 | 444 | .811 | 614 | 151 | 1423 | 8.2 | 2.0 | 19.0 |
| 69-70—Carolina | 80 | 2671 | 527 | 1220 | .432 | 8 | 34 | .235 | 304 | 399 | .762 | 437 | 425 | 1382 | 5.5 | 5.3 | 17.3 |
| 70-71—Virginia | 78 | 2297 | 395 | 861 | .459 | 2 | 10 | .200 | 221 | 259 | .853 | 473 | 270 | 1017 | 6.1 | 3.5 | 13.0 |
| 71-72—Virginia | 67 | 1472 | 174 | 406 | .429 | 1 | 9 | .111 | 104 | 129 | .806 | 241 | 149 | 455 | 3.6 | 2.2 | 6.8 |
| Totals | 378 | 12081 | 2282 | 5288 | .432 | 19 | 89 | .213 | 1540 | 1924 | .800 | 2560 | 1197 | 6161 | 6.8 | 3.2 | 16.3 |

### ABA PLAYOFF RECORD

| Season Team | G | Min. | 2-POINT | | | 3-POINT | | | FTM | FTA | Pct. | Reb. | Ast. | Pts. | AVERAGES | | |
|---|---|---|---|---|---|---|---|---|---|---|---|---|---|---|---|---|---|
| | | | FGM | FGA | Pct. | FGM | FGA | Pct. | | | | | | | RPG | APG | PPG |
| 67-68—New Orleans | 17 | 715 | 140 | 335 | .418 | 4 | 11 | .364 | 107 | 149 | .718 | 169 | 40 | 399 | 9.9 | 2.4 | 23.5 |
| 68-69—Oakland | 16 | 593 | 115 | 280 | .411 | 0 | 4 | .000 | 87 | 111 | .784 | 124 | 31 | 317 | 7.8 | 1.9 | 19.8 |
| 69-70—Carolina | 4 | 168 | 25 | 72 | .347 | 0 | 4 | .000 | 12 | 16 | .750 | 26 | 25 | 62 | 6.5 | 6.3 | 15.5 |
| 70-71—Virginia | 12 | 421 | 89 | 174 | .511 | 1 | 3 | .333 | 31 | 41 | .756 | 57 | 37 | 212 | 4.8 | 3.1 | 17.7 |
| 71-72—Virginia | 11 | 245 | 37 | 84 | .440 | 0 | 1 | .000 | 22 | 25 | .880 | 43 | 27 | 96 | 3.9 | 2.5 | 8.7 |
| Totals | 60 | 2142 | 406 | 945 | .430 | 5 | 23 | .217 | 259 | 342 | .757 | 419 | 160 | 1086 | 7.0 | 2.7 | 18.1 |

### ABA ALL-STAR GAME RECORD

| Season Team | Min. | 2-POINT | | | 3-POINT | | | FTM | FTA | Pct. | Reb. | Ast. | Pts. |
|---|---|---|---|---|---|---|---|---|---|---|---|---|---|
| | | FGM | FGA | Pct. | FGM | FGA | Pct. | | | | | | |
| 1968—New Orleans | 29 | 7 | 12 | .583 | 0 | 1 | .000 | 3 | 5 | .600 | 7 | 5 | 17 |
| 1969—Oakland | 26 | 6 | 13 | .462 | 0 | 0 | ... | 5 | 8 | .625 | 6 | 6 | 17 |
| 1970—Carolina | 36 | 0 | 5 | .000 | 0 | 0 | ... | 2 | 3 | .667 | 8 | 6 | 2 |
| Totals | 91 | 13 | 30 | .433 | 0 | 1 | .000 | 10 | 16 | .625 | 21 | 17 | 36 |

## HEAD COACHING RECORD

**BACKGROUND:** Assistant coach, Elon College, N.C. (1963-64 and 1964-65). ... Assistant coach/director of player personnel, Carolina Cougars of ABA (1972-73 and 1973-74). ... Assistant coach/director of player personnel, Denver Nuggets of ABA (1974-75 and 1975-76). ... Assistant coach, Nuggets (1980).

**HONORS:** NBA Coach of the Year (1988).

### NBA COACHING RECORD

| Season Team | REGULAR SEASON | | | | PLAYOFFS | | |
|---|---|---|---|---|---|---|---|
| | W | L | Pct. | Finish | W | L | Pct. |
| 76-77—San Antonio | 44 | 38 | .537 | 3rd/Central Division | 0 | 2 | .000 |
| 77-78—San Antonio | 52 | 30 | .634 | 1st/Central Division | 2 | 4 | .333 |
| 78-79—San Antonio | 48 | 34 | .585 | 1st/Central Division | 7 | 7 | .500 |
| 79-80—San Antonio | 33 | 33 | .500 | | — | — | — |
| 80-81—Denver | 26 | 25 | .510 | 4th/Midwest Division | — | — | — |
| 81-82—Denver | 46 | 36 | .561 | T2nd/Midwest Division | 1 | 2 | .333 |
| 82-83—Denver | 45 | 37 | .549 | T2nd/Midwest Division | 3 | 5 | .375 |
| 83-84—Denver | 38 | 44 | .463 | T3rd/Midwest Division | 2 | 3 | .400 |
| 84-85—Denver | 52 | 30 | .634 | 1st/Midwest Division | 8 | 7 | .533 |
| 85-86—Denver | 47 | 35 | .573 | 2nd/Midwest Division | 5 | 5 | .500 |
| 86-87—Denver | 37 | 45 | .451 | 4th/Midwest Division | 0 | 3 | .000 |
| 87-88—Denver | 54 | 28 | .659 | 1st/Midwest Division | 5 | 6 | .455 |
| 88-89—Denver | 44 | 38 | .537 | 3rd/Midwest Division | 0 | 3 | .000 |
| 89-90—Denver | 43 | 39 | .524 | 4th/Midwest Division | 0 | 3 | .000 |
| 92-93—Philadelphia | 19 | 37 | .339 | | — | — | — |
| **Totals (15 years)** | **628** | **529** | **.543** | **Totals (12 years)** | **33** | **50** | **.398** |

**NOTES:**

1977—Lost to Boston in Eastern Conference First Round.

1978—Lost to Washington in Eastern Conference Semifinals.

1979—Defeated Philadelphia, 4-3, in Eastern Conference Semifinals; lost to Washington, 4-3, in Eastern Conference Finals.

1980—Replaced as San Antonio head coach by Bob Bass (March 1). Replaced Donnie Walsh as Denver head coach (December), with record of 11-20.

1982—Lost to Phoenix in Western Conference First Round.

1983—Defeated Phoenix, 2-1, in Western Conference First Round; lost to San Antonio, 4-1, in Western Conference Semifinals.

1984—Lost to Utah in Western Conference First Round.

1985—Defeated San Antonio, 3-2, in Western Conference First Round; defeated Utah, 4-1, in Western Conference Semifinals; lost to Los Angeles Lakers, 4-1, in Western Conference Finals.

1986—Defeated Portland, 3-1, in Western Conference First Round; lost to Houston, 4-2, in Western Conference Semifinals.

1987—Lost to Los Angeles Lakers in Western Conference First Round.

1988—Defeated Seattle, 3-2, in Western Conference First Round; lost to Dallas, 4-2, in Western Conference Semifinals.

1989—Lost to Phoenix in Western Conference First Round.

1990—Lost to San Antonio, 3-0, in Western Conference First Round.

1993—Replaced as Philadelphia head coach by Fred Carter (March 7) with club in sixth place.

## MOTTA, DICK

**PERSONAL:** Born September 3, 1931, in Midvale, Utah. ... 5-10/170 (1,78/77,1). ... Full name: John Richard Motta.
**HIGH SCHOOL:** Jordan (Utah); did not play varsity basketball.
**COLLEGE:** Utah State (did not play basketball).

### HEAD COACHING RECORD

**BACKGROUND:** Head coach, Grace Junior High School (1954-55). ... Head coach, Grace High School (1955-56 through 1959-60). ... Head coach, Weber Junior College (1960-61 and 1961-62). ... Broadcaster, Detroit Pistons (1988 through January 1990). ... Consultant, Dallas Mavericks (1990). ... Assistant coach, Denver Nuggets (July 19-November 26, 1996).

**HONORS:** NBA Coach of the Year (1971).

### COLLEGIATE COACHING RECORD

| Season Team | W | L | Pct. | Finish |
|---|---|---|---|---|
| 62-63—Weber State | 22 | 4 | .846 | Independent |
| 63-64—Weber State | 17 | 8 | .680 | 2nd/Big Sky Conference |
| 64-65—Weber State | 22 | 3 | .880 | 1st/Big Sky Conference |
| 65-66—Weber State | 20 | 5 | .765 | 2nd/Big Sky Conference |
| 66-67—Weber State | 18 | 7 | .720 | 3rd/Big Sky Conference |
| 67-68—Weber State | 21 | 6 | .778 | 1st/Big Sky Conference |
| **Totals (6 years)** | **120** | **33** | **.784** | |

### NBA COACHING RECORD

| Season Team | REGULAR SEASON | | | | PLAYOFFS | | |
|---|---|---|---|---|---|---|---|
| | W | L | Pct. | Finish | W | L | Pct. |
| 68-69—Chicago | 33 | 49 | .402 | 5th/Western Division | — | — | — |
| 69-70—Chicago | 39 | 43 | .476 | T3rd/Western Division | 1 | 4 | .250 |
| 70-71—Chicago | 51 | 31 | .622 | 2nd/Midwest Division | 3 | 4 | .429 |
| 71-72—Chicago | 57 | 25 | .695 | 2nd/Midwest Division | 0 | 4 | .000 |

| Season Team | REGULAR SEASON | | | | | PLAYOFFS | | |
|---|---|---|---|---|---|---|---|---|
| | W | L | Pct. | Finish | | W | L | Pct. |
| 72-73—Chicago | 51 | 31 | .622 | 2nd/Midwest Division | | 3 | 4 | .429 |
| 73-74—Chicago | 54 | 28 | .659 | 2nd/Midwest Division | | 4 | 7 | .364 |
| 74-75—Chicago | 47 | 35 | .573 | T1st/Midwest Division | | 7 | 6 | .538 |
| 75-76—Chicago | 24 | 58 | .293 | 4th/Midwest Division | | — | — | — |
| 76-77—Washington | 48 | 34 | .585 | 2nd/Central Division | | 4 | 5 | .444 |
| 77-78—Washington | 44 | 38 | .537 | 2nd/Central Division | | 14 | 7 | .666 |
| 78-79—Washington | 54 | 28 | .659 | 1st/Atlantic Division | | 9 | 10 | .474 |
| 79-80—Washington | 39 | 43 | .476 | 3rd/Atlantic Division | | 0 | 2 | .000 |
| 80-81—Dallas | 15 | 67 | .183 | 6th/Midwest Division | | — | — | — |
| 81-82—Dallas | 28 | 54 | .341 | 5th/Midwest Division | | — | — | — |
| 82-83—Dallas | 38 | 44 | .463 | 4th/Midwest Division | | — | — | — |
| 83-84—Dallas | 43 | 39 | .524 | 2nd/Midwest Division | | 4 | 6 | .400 |
| 84-85—Dallas | 44 | 38 | .537 | 3rd/Midwest Division | | 1 | 3 | .250 |
| 85-86—Dallas | 44 | 38 | .537 | 3rd/Midwest Division | | 5 | 5 | .500 |
| 86-87—Dallas | 55 | 27 | .671 | 1st/Midwest Division | | 1 | 3 | .250 |
| 89-90—Sacramento | 16 | 38 | .296 | 7th/Pacific Division | | — | — | — |
| 90-91—Sacramento | 25 | 57 | .305 | 7th/Pacific Division | | — | — | — |
| 91-92—Sacramento | 7 | 18 | .280 | | | — | — | — |
| 94-95—Dallas | 36 | 46 | .439 | 5th/Midwest Division | | — | — | — |
| 95-96—Dallas | 26 | 56 | .317 | T5th/Midwest Division | | — | — | — |
| 96-97—Denver | 17 | 52 | .246 | 5th/Midwest Division | | — | — | — |
| **Totals (25 years)** | **935** | **1017** | **.479** | **Totals (14 years)** | | **56** | **70** | **.444** |

**NOTES:**

1970—Lost to Atlanta in Western Division First Round.

1971—Lost to Los Angeles in Western Conference First Round.

1972—Lost to Los Angeles in Western Conference First Round.

1973—Lost to Los Angeles in Western Conference First Round.

1974—Defeated Detroit, 4-3, in Western Conference First Round; lost to Milwaukee, 4-0, in Western Conference Semifinals.

1975—Defeated Kansas City/Omaha, 4-2, in Western Conference First Round; lost to Golden State, 4-3, in Western Conference Semifinals.

1977—Defeated Cleveland, 2-1, in Eastern Conference First Round; lost to Houston, 4-2, in Eastern Conference Semifinals.

1978—Defeated Atlanta, 2-0, in Eastern Conference First Round; defeated San Antonio, 4-2, in Eastern Conference Semifinals; defeated Philadelphia, 4-2, in Eastern Conference Finals; defeated Seattle, 4-3, in NBA Finals.

1979—Defeated Atlanta, 4-3, in Eastern Conference Semifinals; defeated San Antonio, 4-3, in Eastern Conference Finals; lost to Seattle, 4-1, in NBA Finals.

1980—Lost to Philadelphia in Eastern Conference First Round.

1984—Defeated Seattle, 3-2, in Western Conference First Round; lost to Los Angeles Lakers, 4-1, in Western Conference Semifinals.

1985—Lost to Portland in Western Conference First Round.

1986—Defeated Utah, 3-1, in Western Conference First Round; lost to Los Angeles Lakers, 4-2, in Western Conference Semifinals.

1987—Lost to Seattle in Western Conference First Round.

1990—Replaced Jerry Reynolds as Sacramento head coach (January 4) with record of 7-21 and club in seventh place.

1991—Replaced as Sacramento head coach by Rex Hughes (December 24) with club in seventh place.

1996—Replaced Bernie Bickerstaff as Denver head coach (November 26) with record of 4-9 and club in fourth place.

# NELSON, DON

**PERSONAL:** Born May 15, 1940, in Muskegon, Mich. ... 6-6/210. (1,98/95,3). ... Full name: Don Arvid Nelson.
**HIGH SCHOOL:** Rock Island (Ill.).
**COLLEGE:** Iowa.
**TRANSACTIONS:** Selected by Chicago Zephyrs in third round (19th pick overall) of 1962 NBA Draft. ... Zephyrs franchise moved from Chicago to Baltimore and renamed Bullets for 1963-64 season. ... Contract sold by Bullets to Los Angeles Lakers (September 6, 1963). ... Waived by Lakers (October 21, 1965). ... Signed as free agent by Boston Celtics (October 28, 1965).
**MISCELLANEOUS:** Member of NBA championship team (1966, 1968, 1969, 1974, 1976). ... Head coach of gold-medal-winning 1994 USA Basketball World Championship Team.

### COLLEGIATE RECORD

| Season Team | G | Min. | FGM | FGA | Pct. | FTM | FTA | Pct. | Reb. | Ast. | Pts. | AVERAGES | | |
|---|---|---|---|---|---|---|---|---|---|---|---|---|---|---|
| | | | | | | | | | | | | RPG | APG | PPG |
| 58-59—Iowa‡ | | | | | Freshman team did not play intercollegiate schedule. | | | | | | | | | |
| 59-60—Iowa | 24 | ... | 140 | 320 | .438 | 100 | 155 | .645 | 241 | ... | 380 | 10.0 | ... | 15.8 |
| 60-61—Iowa | 24 | ... | 197 | 377 | .523 | 176 | 268 | .657 | 258 | ... | 570 | 10.8 | ... | 23.8 |
| 61-62—Iowa | 24 | ... | 193 | 348 | .555 | 186 | 264 | .705 | 285 | ... | 572 | 11.9 | ... | 23.8 |
| **Varsity totals** | **72** | **...** | **530** | **1045** | **.507** | **462** | **687** | **.672** | **784** | **...** | **1522** | **10.9** | **...** | **21.1** |

### NBA REGULAR-SEASON RECORD

| Season Team | G | Min. | FGM | FGA | Pct. | FTM | FTA | Pct. | Reb. | Ast. | PF | Dq. | Pts. | AVERAGES | | |
|---|---|---|---|---|---|---|---|---|---|---|---|---|---|---|---|---|
| | | | | | | | | | | | | | | RPG | APG | PPG |
| 62-63—Chicago | 62 | 1071 | 129 | 293 | .440 | 161 | 221 | .729 | 279 | 72 | 136 | 3 | 419 | 4.5 | 1.2 | 6.8 |
| 63-64—Los Angeles | 80 | 1406 | 135 | 323 | .418 | 149 | 201 | .741 | 323 | 76 | 181 | 1 | 419 | 4.0 | 1.0 | 5.2 |
| 64-65—Los Angeles | 39 | 238 | 36 | 85 | .424 | 20 | 26 | .769 | 73 | 24 | 40 | 1 | 92 | 1.9 | 0.6 | 2.4 |
| 65-66—Boston | 75 | 1765 | 271 | 618 | .439 | 223 | 326 | .684 | 403 | 79 | 187 | 1 | 765 | 5.4 | 1.1 | 10.2 |
| 66-67—Boston | 79 | 1202 | 227 | 509 | .446 | 141 | 190 | .742 | 295 | 65 | 143 | 0 | 595 | 3.7 | 0.8 | 7.5 |

| Season Team | G | Min. | FGM | FGA | Pct. | FTM | FTA | Pct. | Reb. | Ast. | PF | Dq. | Pts. | AVERAGES RPG | APG | PPG |
|---|---|---|---|---|---|---|---|---|---|---|---|---|---|---|---|---|
| 67-68 —Boston | 82 | 1498 | 312 | 632 | .494 | 195 | 268 | .728 | 431 | 103 | 178 | 1 | 819 | 5.3 | 1.3 | 10.0 |
| 68-69 —Boston | 82 | 1773 | 374 | 771 | .485 | 201 | 259 | .776 | 458 | 92 | 198 | 2 | 949 | 5.6 | 1.1 | 11.6 |
| 69-70 —Boston | 82 | 2224 | 461 | 920 | .501 | 337 | 435 | .775 | 601 | 148 | 238 | 3 | 1259 | 7.3 | 1.8 | 15.4 |
| 70-71 —Boston | 82 | 2254 | 412 | 881 | .468 | 317 | 426 | .744 | 565 | 153 | 232 | 2 | 1141 | 6.9 | 1.9 | 13.9 |
| 71-72 —Boston | 82 | 2086 | 389 | 811 | .480 | 356 | 452 | .788 | 453 | 192 | 220 | 3 | 1134 | 5.5 | 2.3 | 13.8 |
| 72-73 —Boston | 72 | 1425 | 309 | 649 | .476 | 159 | 188 | .846 | 315 | 102 | 155 | 1 | 777 | 4.4 | 1.4 | 10.8 |

| Season Team | G | Min. | FGM | FGA | Pct. | FTM | FTA | Pct. | REBOUNDS Off. | Def. | Tot. | Ast. | Stl. | Blk. | TO | Pts. | AVERAGES RPG | APG | PPG |
|---|---|---|---|---|---|---|---|---|---|---|---|---|---|---|---|---|---|---|---|
| 73-74—Boston | 82 | 1748 | 364 | 717 | .508 | 215 | 273 | .788 | 90 | 255 | 345 | 162 | 19 | 13 | ... | 943 | 4.2 | 2.0 | 11.5 |
| 74-75—Boston | 79 | 2052 | 423 | 785 | *.539 | 263 | 318 | .827 | 127 | 342 | 469 | 181 | 32 | 15 | ... | 1109 | 5.9 | 2.3 | 14.0 |
| 75-76—Boston | 75 | 943 | 175 | 379 | .462 | 127 | 161 | .789 | 56 | 126 | 182 | 77 | 14 | 7 | ... | 477 | 2.4 | 1.0 | 6.4 |
| Totals | 1053 | 21685 | 4017 | 8373 | .480 | 2864 | 3744 | .765 | ... | ... | 5192 | 1526 | 65 | 35 | ... | 10898 | 4.9 | 1.4 | 10.3 |

## NBA PLAYOFF RECORD

| Season Team | G | Min. | FGM | FGA | Pct. | FTM | FTA | Pct. | Reb. | Ast. | PF | Dq. | Pts. | AVERAGES RPG | APG | PPG |
|---|---|---|---|---|---|---|---|---|---|---|---|---|---|---|---|---|
| 63-64—Los Angeles | 5 | 56 | 7 | 13 | .538 | 3 | 3 | 1.000 | 13 | 2 | 11 | 1 | 17 | 2.6 | 0.4 | 3.4 |
| 64-65—Los Angeles | 11 | 212 | 24 | 53 | .453 | 19 | 25 | .760 | 59 | 19 | 31 | 0 | 67 | 5.4 | 1.7 | 6.1 |
| 65-66—Boston | 17 | 316 | 50 | 118 | .424 | 42 | 52 | .808 | 85 | 13 | 50 | 0 | 142 | 5.0 | 0.8 | 8.4 |
| 66-67—Boston | 9 | 142 | 27 | 59 | .458 | 10 | 17 | .588 | 42 | 9 | 12 | 0 | 64 | 4.7 | 1.0 | 7.1 |
| 67-68—Boston | 19 | 468 | 91 | 175 | .520 | 55 | 74 | .743 | 143 | 32 | 49 | 0 | 237 | 7.5 | 1.7 | 12.5 |
| 68-69—Boston | 18 | 348 | 87 | 168 | .518 | 50 | 60 | .833 | 83 | 21 | 51 | 0 | 224 | 4.6 | 1.2 | 12.4 |
| 71-72—Boston | 11 | 308 | 52 | 99 | .525 | 41 | 48 | .854 | 61 | 21 | 30 | 0 | 145 | 5.5 | 1.9 | 13.2 |
| 72-73—Boston | 13 | 303 | 47 | 101 | .465 | 49 | 56 | .875 | 38 | 15 | 29 | 0 | 143 | 2.9 | 1.2 | 11.0 |

| Season Team | G | Min. | FGM | FGA | Pct. | FTM | FTA | Pct. | REBOUNDS Off. | Def. | Tot. | Ast. | Stl. | Blk. | TO | Pts. | AVERAGES RPG | APG | PPG |
|---|---|---|---|---|---|---|---|---|---|---|---|---|---|---|---|---|---|---|---|
| 73-74—Boston | 18 | 467 | 82 | 164 | .500 | 41 | 53 | .774 | 25 | 72 | 97 | 35 | 8 | 3 | ... | 205 | 5.4 | 1.9 | 11.4 |
| 74-75—Boston | 11 | 274 | 66 | 117 | .564 | 37 | 41 | .902 | 18 | 27 | 45 | 26 | 2 | 2 | ... | 169 | 4.1 | 2.4 | 15.4 |
| 75-76—Boston | 18 | 315 | 52 | 108 | .481 | 60 | 69 | .870 | 17 | 36 | 53 | 17 | 3 | 2 | ... | 164 | 2.9 | 0.9 | 9.1 |
| Totals | 150 | 3209 | 585 | 1175 | .498 | 407 | 498 | .817 | ... | ... | 719 | 210 | 13 | 7 | ... | 1577 | 4.8 | 1.4 | 10.5 |

## HEAD COACHING RECORD

**BACKGROUND:** Assistant coach, Milwaukee Bucks (September 9-November 22, 1976). ... Head coach/director of player personnel, Bucks (November 22, 1976 through 1985). ... Head coach/vice president of basketball operations, Bucks (1985-May 27, 1987). ... Executive vice president, Golden State Warriors (1987-88). ... Head coach/general manager, Warriors (1988-89 to February 13, 1995). ... General manager, Dallas Mavericks (February 7, 1997 to present).

**HONORS:** NBA Coach of the Year (1983, 1985, 1992). ... One of the Top 10 Coaches in NBA History (1996).

## NBA COACHING RECORD

| Season Team | REGULAR SEASON W | L | Pct. | Finish | PLAYOFFS W | L | Pct. |
|---|---|---|---|---|---|---|---|
| 76-77—Milwaukee | 27 | 37 | .422 | 6th/Midwest Division | — | — | — |
| 77-78—Milwaukee | 44 | 38 | .537 | 2nd/Midwest Division | 5 | 4 | .556 |
| 78-79—Milwaukee | 38 | 44 | .463 | 4th/Midwest Division | — | — | — |
| 79-80—Milwaukee | 49 | 33 | .598 | 1st/Midwest Division | 3 | 4 | .429 |
| 80-81—Milwaukee | 60 | 22 | .732 | 1st/Central Division | 3 | 4 | .429 |
| 81-82—Milwaukee | 55 | 27 | .671 | 1st/Central Division | 2 | 4 | .333 |
| 82-83—Milwaukee | 51 | 31 | .622 | 1st/Central Division | 5 | 4 | .556 |
| 83-84—Milwaukee | 50 | 32 | .610 | 1st/Central Division | 8 | 8 | .500 |
| 84-85—Milwaukee | 59 | 23 | .720 | 1st/Central Division | 3 | 5 | .375 |
| 85-86—Milwaukee | 57 | 25 | .695 | 1st/Central Division | 7 | 7 | .500 |
| 86-87—Milwaukee | 50 | 32 | .610 | 3rd/Central Division | 6 | 6 | .500 |
| 88-89—Golden State | 43 | 39 | .524 | 4th/Pacific Division | 4 | 4 | .500 |
| 89-90—Golden State | 37 | 45 | .451 | 5th/Pacific Division | — | — | — |
| 90-91—Golden State | 44 | 38 | .537 | 4th/Pacific Division | 4 | 5 | .444 |
| 91-92—Golden State | 55 | 27 | .671 | 2nd/Pacific Division | 1 | 3 | .250 |
| 92-93—Golden State | 34 | 48 | .415 | 6th/Pacific Division | — | — | — |
| 93-94—Golden State | 50 | 32 | .610 | 3rd/Pacific Division | 0 | 3 | .000 |
| 94-95—Golden State | 14 | 31 | .311 | — | — | — | — |
| 95-96—New York | 34 | 25 | .576 | — | — | — | — |
| 97-98—Dallas | 16 | 50 | .242 | 5th/Midwest Division | — | — | — |
| 98-99—Dallas | 19 | 31 | .380 | 5th/Midwest Division | — | — | — |
| 99-00—Dallas | 40 | 42 | .488 | 4th/Midwest Division | — | — | — |
| 00-01—Dallas | 53 | 29 | .646 | T2nd/Midwest Division | 4 | 6 | .400 |
| 01-02—Dallas | 57 | 25 | .695 | 2nd/Midwest Division | 4 | 4 | .500 |
| 02-03—Dallas | 60 | 22 | .732 | 2nd/Midwest Division | 10 | 10 | .500 |
| 03-04—Dallas | 52 | 30 | .634 | 3rd/Midwest Division | 1 | 4 | .200 |
| 04-05—Dallas | 42 | 22 | .656 | | | | |
| Totals (27 years) | 1190 | 880 | .575 | | Totals (17 years) 70 | 85 | .452 |

## WORLD CHAMPIONSHIP COACHING RECORD

| Season Team | REGULAR SEASON W | L | Pct. | Finish |
|---|---|---|---|---|
| 1994—Team USA | 8 | 0 | 1.000 | Gold medal |

## NOTES:

1976—Replaced Larry Costello as Milwaukee head coach (November 22), with record of 3-15 and club in sixth place.

1978—Defeated Phoenix, 2-0, in Western Conference first round; lost to Denver, 4-3, in Western Conference semifinals.

1980—Lost to Seattle in Western Conference semifinals.

1981—Lost to Philadelphia in Eastern Conference semifinals.

1982—Lost to Philadelphia in Eastern Conference semifinals.

1983—Defeated Boston, 4-0, in Eastern Conference semifinals; lost to Philadelphia, 4-1, in Eastern Conference finals.

1984—Defeated Atlanta, 3-2, in Eastern Conference first round; defeated New Jersey, 4-2, in Eastern Conference semifinals; lost to Boston, 4-1, in Eastern Conference finals.

1985—Defeated Chicago, 3-1, in Eastern Conference first round; lost to Philadelphia, 4-0, in Eastern Conference semifinals.

1986—Defeated New Jersey, 3-0, in Eastern Conference first round; defeated Philadelphia, 4-3, in Eastern Conference semifinals; lost to Boston, 4-0, in Eastern Conference finals.

**ALL-TIME GREAT COACHES**

1987—Defeated Philadelphia, 3-2, in Eastern Conference first round; lost to Boston, 4-3, in Eastern Conference semifinals.
1989—Defeated Utah, 3-0, in Western Conference first round; lost to Phoenix, 4-1, in Western Conference semifinals.
1991—Defeated San Antonio, 3-1, in Western Conference first round; lost to Los Angeles Lakers, 4-1, in Western Conference semifinals.
1992—Lost to Seattle in Western Conference first round.
1994—Lost to Phoenix in Western Conference first round.
1995—Replaced as Golden State head coach by Bob Lanier (February 13) with club in sixth place.
1996—Replaced as New York head coach by Jeff Van Gundy (March 8) with club in second place.
1997—Replaced Jim Cleamons as Dallas head coach (December 4), with record of 4-12 and club in sixth place.
2001—Defeated Utah, 3-2, in Western Conference first round; lost to San Antonio, 4-1, in Western Conference semifinals.
2002—Defeated Minnesota, 3-0, in Western Conference first round; lost to Sacramento, 4-1, in Western Conference semifinals.
2003—Defeated Portland, 4-3, in Western Conference first round; defeated Sacramento, 4-3, in Western Conference semifinals; lost to San Antonio, 4-2, in Western Conference finals.
2004—Lost to Sacramento, 4-1, in Western Conference first round.
2005—Stepped down as Dallas head coach (March 19, 2005); replaced by Avery Johnson with team in second place.

# RAMSAY, JACK

**PERSONAL:** Born February 21, 1925, in Philadelphia. ... 6-1/180 (1,85/81,6). ... Full name: John T. Ramsay.
**HIGH SCHOOL:** Upper Darby Senior (Pa.).
**COLLEGE:** St. Joseph's, then Villanova, then Pennsylvania.
**TRANSACTIONS:** Played with San Diego Dons, an Amateur Athletic Union team (1945-46). ... Played in Eastern Basketball League with Harrisburg and Sunbury (1949-50 through 1954-55).
**CAREER NOTES:** Analyst, ESPN (January 1996-present).
**CAREER HONORS:** Elected to Naismith Memorial Basketball Hall of Fame (1992). ... One of the Top 10 Coaches in NBA History (1996).

## COLLEGIATE RECORD

| Season Team | G | Min. | FGM | FGA | Pct. | FTM | FTA | Pct. | Reb. | Ast. | Pts. | RPG | APG | PPG |
|---|---|---|---|---|---|---|---|---|---|---|---|---|---|---|
| 42-43—St. Joseph's‡............... | | | | | | Freshman team statistics unavailable. | | | | | | | | |
| 43-44........................... | | | | | | Did not play—in military service. | | | | | | | | |
| 44-45........................... | | | | | | Did not play—in military service. | | | | | | | | |
| 45-46........................... | | | | | | Did not play—in military service. | | | | | | | | |
| 46-47—St. Joseph's............... | 21 | ... | 72 | 214 | .336 | 20 | 32 | .625 | ... | ... | 164 | ... | ... | 7.8 |
| 47-48—St. Joseph's............... | 14 | ... | 60 | ... | ... | 38 | ... | ... | ... | ... | 158 | ... | ... | 11.3 |
| 48-49—St. Joseph's............... | 23 | ... | 75 | ... | ... | 52 | ... | ... | ... | ... | 202 | ... | ... | 8.8 |
| **Varsity totals**.................. | 58 | ... | 207 | ... | ... | 110 | ... | ... | ... | ... | 524 | ... | ... | 9.0 |

### EBL REGULAR-SEASON RECORD

| Season Team | G | Min. | FGM | FGA | Pct. | FTM | FTA | Pct. | Reb. | Ast. | PF | Dq. | Pts. | RPG | APG | PPG |
|---|---|---|---|---|---|---|---|---|---|---|---|---|---|---|---|---|
| 49-50—Harrisburg .............. | 25 | ... | 134 | ... | ... | 68 | ... | ... | ... | ... | ... | ... | 336 | ... | ... | 13.4 |
| 50-51—Harrisburg .............. | 20 | ... | 96 | ... | ... | 43 | ... | ... | ... | ... | ... | ... | 235 | ... | ... | 11.8 |
| 51-52—Sunbury ................ | 26 | ... | 159 | ... | ... | 86 | ... | ... | ... | ... | ... | ... | 404 | ... | ... | 15.5 |
| 52-53—Sunbury ................ | 21 | ... | 116 | ... | ... | 97 | ... | ... | ... | ... | ... | ... | 329 | ... | ... | 15.7 |
| 53-54—Sunbury ................ | 28 | ... | 112 | ... | ... | 101 | ... | ... | ... | ... | ... | ... | 325 | ... | ... | 11.6 |
| 54-55—Sunbury ................ | 30 | ... | 164 | ... | ... | 155 | ... | ... | ... | ... | ... | ... | 483 | ... | ... | 16.1 |
| **Totals**........................ | 130 | ... | 685 | ... | ... | 507 | ... | ... | ... | ... | ... | ... | 1877 | ... | ... | 14.4 |

## HEAD COACHING RECORD

**BACKGROUND:** Head coach, St. James High School (Pa.) and later head coach, Mount Pleasant High School, Del. (1949-1955). ... General manager, Philadelphia 76ers (1966-67 and 1967-68). ... Head coach/general manager, 76ers (1968-69 and 1969-70).

### COLLEGIATE COACHING RECORD

| Season Team | W | L | Pct. | Finish |
|---|---|---|---|---|
| 55-56—St. Joseph's ................... | 23 | 6 | .793 | Independent |
| 56-57—St. Joseph's ................... | 17 | 7 | .708 | Independent |
| 57-58—St. Joseph's ................... | 18 | 9 | .667 | 2nd/Middle Atlantic Conference |
| 58-59—St. Joseph's ................... | 22 | 5 | .815 | 1st/Middle Atlantic Conference |
| 59-60—St. Joseph's ................... | 20 | 7 | .741 | 1st/Middle Atlantic Conference |
| 60-61—St. Joseph's ................... | 25 | 5 | .833 | 1st/Middle Atlantic Conference |
| 61-62—St. Joseph's ................... | 18 | 10 | .643 | 1st/Middle Atlantic Conference |
| 62-63—St. Joseph's ................... | 23 | 5 | .821 | 1st/Middle Atlantic Conference |
| 63-64—St. Joseph's ................... | 18 | 10 | .643 | T2nd/Middle Atlantic Conference |
| 64-65—St. Joseph's ................... | 26 | 3 | .897 | 1st/Middle Atlantic Conference |
| 65-66—St. Joseph's ................... | 24 | 5 | .828 | 1st/Middle Atlantic Conference |
| **Totals (11 years)**..................... | 234 | 72 | .765 | |

### NBA COACHING RECORD

| | REGULAR SEASON | | | | PLAYOFFS | | |
|---|---|---|---|---|---|---|---|
| Season Team | W | L | Pct. | Finish | W | L | Pct. |
| 68-69—Philadelphia.............. | 55 | 27 | .671 | 2nd/Eastern Division | 1 | 4 | .200 |
| 69-70—Philadelphia.............. | 42 | 40 | .512 | 4th/Eastern Division | 1 | 4 | .200 |
| 70-71—Philadelphia.............. | 47 | 35 | .573 | 2nd/Atlantic Division | 3 | 4 | .429 |
| 71-72—Philadelphia.............. | 30 | 52 | .366 | 3rd/Atlantic Division | — | — | — |
| 72-73—Buffalo .................. | 21 | 61 | .256 | 3rd/Atlantic Division | — | — | — |
| 73-74—Buffalo .................. | 42 | 40 | .512 | 3rd/Atlantic Division | 2 | 4 | .333 |
| 74-75—Buffalo .................. | 49 | 33 | .598 | 2nd/Atlantic Division | 3 | 4 | .429 |
| 75-76—Buffalo .................. | 46 | 36 | .561 | T2nd/Atlantic Division | 4 | 5 | .444 |
| 76-77—Portland ................ | 49 | 33 | .598 | 2nd/Pacific Division | 14 | 5 | .737 |
| 77-78—Portland ................ | 58 | 24 | .707 | 1st/Pacific Division | 2 | 4 | .333 |
| 78-79—Portland ................ | 45 | 37 | .549 | 4th/Pacific Division | 1 | 2 | .333 |

| | | REGULAR SEASON | | | | | PLAYOFFS | |
|---|---|---|---|---|---|---|---|---|
| Season Team | W | L | Pct. | Finish | | W | L | Pct. |
| 79-80—Portland | 38 | 44 | .463 | 4th/Pacific Division | | 1 | 2 | .333 |
| 80-81—Portland | 45 | 37 | .549 | 3rd/Pacific Division | | 1 | 2 | .333 |
| 81-82—Portland | 42 | 40 | .512 | 5th/Pacific Division | | — | — | — |
| 82-83—Portland | 46 | 36 | .561 | 4th/Pacific Division | | 3 | 4 | .429 |
| 83-84—Portland | 48 | 34 | .585 | 2nd/Pacific Division | | 2 | 3 | .400 |
| 84-85—Portland | 42 | 40 | .512 | 2nd/Pacific Division | | 4 | 5 | .444 |
| 85-86—Portland | 40 | 42 | .488 | 2nd/Pacific Division | | 1 | 3 | .250 |
| 86-87—Indiana | 41 | 41 | .500 | 4th/Central Division | | 1 | 3 | .250 |
| 87-88—Indiana | 38 | 44 | .463 | 6th/Central Division | | — | — | — |
| 88-89—Indiana | 0 | 7 | .000 | | | — | — | — |
| **Totals (21 years)** | **864** | **783** | **.525** | **Totals (16 years)** | | **44** | **58** | **.431** |

**NOTES:**

1956—Defeated Seton Hall, 74-65, in NIT quarterfinals; lost to Louisville, 89-79, in semifinals; defeated St. Francis-New York, 93-82, in third-place game.

1958—Defeated St. Peter's, 83-72, in NIT first round; lost to St. Bonaventure, 79-75, in quarterfinals.

1959—Lost to West Virginia, 95-92, in NCAA Tournament first round; lost to Navy, 70-59, in regional consolation game.

1960—Lost to Duke, 58-56, in NCAA Tournament first round; lost to West Virginia, 106-100, in regional consolation game.

1961—Defeated Princeton, 72-67, in NCAA Tournament regional semifinal; defeated Wake Forest, 96-86, in regional final; lost to Ohio State, 95-69, in national semifinal; defeated Utah, 127-120 (4 OT), in consolation game.

1962—Lost to Wake Forest, 96-85 (OT), in NCAA Tournament regional semifinal; lost to New York University, 94-85, in regional consolation game.

1963—Defeated Princeton, 82-81, in NCAA Tournament first round; defeated West Virginia, 97-88, in regional semifinal; lost to Duke, 73-59, in regional final.

1964—Defeated Miami (Fla.), 86-76, in NIT first round; lost to Bradley, 83-81, in quarterfinals.

1965—Defeated Connecticut, 67-61, in NCAA Tournament first round; lost to Providence, 81-73 (OT), in regional semifinal; lost to North Carolina State, 103-81, in regional consolation game.

1966—Defeated Providence, 65-48, in NCAA Tournament first round; lost to Duke, 76-74, in regional semifinal; defeated Davidson, 92-76, in regional consolation game.

1969—Lost to Boston in Eastern Division Semifinals.

1970—Lost to Milwaukee in Eastern Division Semifinals.

1971—Lost to Baltimore in Eastern Conference Semifinals.

1974—Lost to Boston in Eastern Conference Semifinals.

1975—Lost to Washington in Eastern Conference Semifinals.

1976—Defeated Philadelphia, 2-1, in Eastern Conference First Round; lost to Boston, 4-2, in Eastern Conference Semifinals.

1977—Defeated Chicago, 2-1, in Western Conference First Round; defeated Denver, 4-2, in Western Conference Semifinals; defeated Los Angeles Lakers, 4-0, in Western Conference Finals; defeated Philadelphia, 4-2, in NBA Finals.

1978—Lost to Seattle in Western Conference Semifinals.

1979—Lost to Phoenix in Western Conference First Round.

1980—Lost to Seattle in Western Conference First Round.

1981—Lost to Kansas City in Western Conference First Round.

1983—Defeated Seattle, 2-0, in Western Conference First Round; lost to Los Angeles Lakers, 4-1, in Western Conference Semifinals.

1984—Lost to Phoenix in Western Conference First Round.

1985—Defeated Dallas, 3-1, in Western Conference First Round; lost to Los Angeles Lakers, 4-1, in Western Conference Semifinals.

1986—Lost to Denver in Western Conference First Round.

1987—Lost to Atlanta in Eastern Conference First Round.

1988—Resigned as Indiana head coach (November 17); replaced by Mel Daniels with club in sixth place.

## RILEY, PAT

**PERSONAL:** Born March 20, 1945, in Rome, N.Y. ... 6-4/205. (1,93/93,0). ... Full name: Patrick James Riley. ... Son of Leon Riley, outfielder/catcher with Philadelphia Phillies (1944) and minor league manager; and brother of Lee Riley, defensive back with Detroit Lions, Philadelphia Eagles and New York Giants (1955-1960) and New York Titans of American Football League (1961 and 1962).

**HIGH SCHOOL:** Linton (Schenectady, N.Y.).

**COLLEGE:** Kentucky.

**TRANSACTIONS/CAREER NOTES:** Selected by San Diego Rockets in first round (seventh pick overall) of 1967 NBA Draft. ... Selected by Portland Trail Blazers from Rockets in NBA expansion draft (May 11, 1970). ... Contract sold by Trail Blazers to Los Angeles Lakers (October 9, 1970). ... Traded by Lakers to Phoenix Suns for draft rights to G John Roche and 1976 second-round draft choice (November 3, 1975).

**CAREER NOTES:** Broadcaster, Los Angeles Lakers (1977-78 and 1978-79). ... Broadcaster, NBC Sports (1990-91). ... President, Miami Heat (1995-96 to present).

**MISCELLANEOUS:** Member of NBA championship team (1972). ... Selected by Dallas Cowboys in 11th round of 1967 NFL Draft.

### COLLEGIATE RECORD

| | | | | | | | | | | | | | AVERAGES | | |
|---|---|---|---|---|---|---|---|---|---|---|---|---|---|---|---|
| Season Team | G | Min. | FGM | FGA | Pct. | FTM | FTA | Pct. | Reb. | Ast. | Pts. | RPG | APG | PPG |
| 63-64—Kentucky‡ | 16 | ... | 120 | 259 | .463 | 93 | 146 | .637 | 235 | ... | 333 | 14.7 | ... | 20.8 |
| 64-65—Kentucky | 25 | 825 | 160 | 370 | .432 | 55 | 89 | .618 | 212 | 27 | 375 | 8.5 | 1.1 | 15.0 |
| 65-66—Kentucky | 29 | 1078 | 265 | 514 | .516 | 107 | 153 | .699 | 259 | 64 | 637 | 8.9 | 2.2 | 22.0 |
| 66-67—Kentucky | 26 | 953 | 165 | 373 | .442 | 122 | 156 | .782 | 201 | 68 | 452 | 7.7 | 2.6 | 17.4 |
| **Varsity totals** | **80** | **2856** | **590** | **1257** | **.469** | **284** | **398** | **.714** | **672** | **159** | **1464** | **8.4** | **2.0** | **18.3** |

## NBA REGULAR-SEASON RECORD

| Season Team | G | Min. | FGM | FGA | Pct. | FTM | FTA | Pct. | Reb. | Ast. | PF | Dq. | Pts. | RPG | APG | PPG |
|---|---|---|---|---|---|---|---|---|---|---|---|---|---|---|---|---|
| 67-68 —San Diego | 80 | 1263 | 250 | 660 | .379 | 128 | 202 | .634 | 177 | 138 | 205 | 1 | 628 | 2.2 | 1.7 | 7.9 |
| 68-69 —San Diego | 56 | 1027 | 202 | 498 | .406 | 90 | 134 | .672 | 112 | 136 | 146 | 1 | 494 | 2.0 | 2.4 | 8.8 |
| 69-70 —San Diego | 36 | 474 | 75 | 180 | .417 | 40 | 55 | .727 | 57 | 85 | 68 | 0 | 190 | 1.6 | 2.4 | 5.3 |
| 70-71 —Los Angeles | 54 | 506 | 105 | 254 | .413 | 56 | 87 | .644 | 54 | 72 | 84 | 0 | 266 | 1.0 | 1.3 | 4.9 |
| 71-72 —Los Angeles | 67 | 926 | 197 | 441 | .447 | 55 | 74 | .743 | 127 | 75 | 110 | 0 | 449 | 1.9 | 1.1 | 6.7 |
| 72-73 —Los Angeles | 55 | 801 | 167 | 390 | .428 | 65 | 82 | .793 | 65 | 81 | 126 | 0 | 399 | 1.2 | 1.5 | 7.3 |

| Season Team | G | Min. | FGM | FGA | Pct. | FTM | FTA | Pct. | Off. | Def. | Tot. | Ast. | St. | Blk. | TO | Pts. | RPG | APG | PPG |
|---|---|---|---|---|---|---|---|---|---|---|---|---|---|---|---|---|---|---|---|
| 73-74—Los Angeles .. | 72 | 1361 | 287 | 667 | .430 | 110 | 144 | .764 | 38 | 90 | 128 | 148 | 54 | 3 | ... | 684 | 1.8 | 2.1 | 9.5 |
| 74-75—Los Angeles .. | 46 | 1016 | 219 | 523 | .419 | 69 | 93 | .742 | 25 | 60 | 85 | 121 | 36 | 4 | ... | 507 | 1.8 | 2.6 | 11.0 |
| 75-76—L.A.-Phoenix. | 62 | 813 | 117 | 301 | .389 | 55 | 77 | .714 | 16 | 34 | 50 | 57 | 22 | 6 | ... | 289 | 0.8 | 0.9 | 4.7 |
| Totals | 528 | 8187 | 1619 | 3914 | .414 | 668 | 948 | .705 | ... | ... | 855 | 913 | 112 | 13 | ... | 3906 | 1.6 | 1.7 | 7.4 |

Personal fouls/disqualifications: 1973-74, 173/1. 1974-75, 128/0. 1975-76, 112/0. Totals, 1152/3.

## NBA PLAYOFF RECORD

| Season Team | G | Min. | FGM | FGA | Pct. | FTM | FTA | Pct. | Reb. | Ast. | PF | Dq. | Pts. | RPG | APG | PPG |
|---|---|---|---|---|---|---|---|---|---|---|---|---|---|---|---|---|
| 68-69 —San Diego | 5 | 76 | 16 | 37 | .432 | 5 | 6 | .833 | 11 | 2 | 13 | 0 | 37 | 2.2 | 0.4 | 7.4 |
| 70-71 —Los Angeles | 7 | 135 | 29 | 69 | .420 | 8 | 11 | .727 | 15 | 14 | 12 | 0 | 66 | 2.1 | 2.0 | 9.4 |
| 71-72 —Los Angeles | 15 | 244 | 33 | 99 | .333 | 12 | 16 | .750 | 29 | 14 | 37 | 0 | 78 | 1.9 | 0.9 | 5.2 |
| 72-73 —Los Angeles | 7 | 53 | 9 | 27 | .333 | 0 | 0 | ... | 5 | 7 | 10 | 0 | 18 | 0.7 | 1.0 | 2.6 |

| Season Team | G | Min. | FGM | FGA | Pct. | FTM | FTA | Pct. | Off. | Def. | Tot. | Ast. | St. | Blk. | TO | Pts. | RPG | APG | PPG |
|---|---|---|---|---|---|---|---|---|---|---|---|---|---|---|---|---|---|---|---|
| 73-74—Los Angeles .. | 5 | 106 | 18 | 50 | .360 | 3 | 4 | .750 | 3 | 3 | 6 | 10 | 4 | 0 | ... | 39 | 1.2 | 2.0 | 7.8 |
| 75-76—Phoenix | 5 | 27 | 6 | 15 | .400 | 1 | 1 | 1.000 | 0 | 0 | 0 | 5 | 0 | 0 | ... | 13 | 0.0 | 1.0 | 2.6 |
| Totals | 44 | 641 | 111 | 297 | .374 | 29 | 38 | .763 | ... | ... | 66 | 52 | 4 | 0 | ... | 251 | 1.5 | 1.2 | 5.7 |

Personal fouls/disqualifications: 1973-74, 11/0. 1975-76, 3/0. Totals, 86/0.

## HEAD COACHING RECORD

**BACKGROUND:** Assistant coach, Lakers (1979-80 to November 19, 1981).
**HONORS:** NBA Coach of the Year (1990, 1993 and 1997). ... One of the Top 10 Coaches in NBA History (1996).

## NBA COACHING RECORD

| | REGULAR SEASON | | | | PLAYOFFS | | |
|---|---|---|---|---|---|---|---|
| Season Team | W | L | Pct. | Finish | W | L | Pct. |
| 81-82 —Los Angeles | 50 | 21 | .704 | 1st/Pacific Division | 12 | 2 | .857 |
| 82-83 —Los Angeles | 58 | 24 | .707 | 1st/Pacific Division | 8 | 7 | .533 |
| 83-84 —Los Angeles | 54 | 28 | .659 | 1st/Pacific Division | 14 | 7 | .667 |
| 84-85 —Los Angeles Lakers | 62 | 20 | .756 | 1st/Pacific Division | 15 | 4 | .789 |
| 85-86 —Los Angeles Lakers | 62 | 20 | .756 | 1st/Pacific Division | 8 | 6 | 571 |
| 86-87 —Los Angeles Lakers | 65 | 17 | .793 | 1st/Pacific Division | 15 | 3 | .833 |
| 87-88 —Los Angeles Lakers | 62 | 20 | .756 | 1st/Pacific Division | 15 | 9 | .625 |
| 88-89 —Los Angeles Lakers | 57 | 25 | .695 | 1st/Pacific Division | 11 | 4 | .733 |
| 89-90 —Los Angeles Lakers | 63 | 19 | .768 | 1st/Pacific Division | 4 | 5 | .444 |
| 91-92 —New York | 51 | 31 | .622 | T1st/Atlantic Division | 6 | 6 | .500 |
| 92-93 —New York | 60 | 22 | .732 | 1st/Atlantic Division | 9 | 6 | .600 |
| 93-94 —New York | 57 | 25 | .695 | 1st/Atlantic Division | 14 | 11 | .560 |
| 94-95 —New York | 55 | 27 | .671 | 2nd/Atlantic Division | 6 | 5 | .545 |
| 95-96 —Miami | 42 | 40 | .512 | 3rd/Atlantic Division | 0 | 3 | .000 |
| 96-97 —Miami | 61 | 21 | .744 | 1st/Atlantic Division | 8 | 9 | .471 |
| 97-98 —Miami | 55 | 27 | .671 | 1st/Atlantic Division | 2 | 3 | .400 |
| 98-99 —Miami | 33 | 17 | .660 | T1st/Atlantic Division | 2 | 3 | .400 |
| 99-00 —Miami | 52 | 30 | .634 | 1st/Atlantic Division | 6 | 4 | .600 |
| 00-01 —Miami | 50 | 32 | .610 | 2nd/Atlantic Division | 0 | 3 | .000 |
| 01-02 —Miami | 36 | 46 | .439 | 6th/Atlantic Division | — | — | — |
| 02-03 —Miami | 25 | 57 | .305 | 7th/Atlantic Division | | | |
| Totals (21 years) | 1110 | 569 | .661 | Totals (19 years) | 155 | 100 | .608 |

**NOTES:**

1981—Replaced Paul Westhead as Los Angeles head coach (November 19), with record of 7-4 and club in second place.

1982—Defeated Phoenix, 4-0, in Western Conference semifinals; defeated San Antonio, 4-0, in Western Conference finals; defeated Philadelphia, 4-2, in NBA Finals.

1983—Defeated Portland, 4-1, in Western Conference semifinals; defeated San Antonio, 4-2, in Western Conference finals; lost to Philadelphia, 4-0, in NBA Finals.

1984—Defeated Kansas City, 3-0, in Western Conference first round; defeated Dallas, 4-1, in Western Conference semifinals; defeated Phoenix, 4-2, in Western Conference finals; lost to Boston, 4-3, in NBA Finals.

1985—Defeated Phoenix, 3-0, in Western Conference first round; defeated Portland, 4-1, in Western Conference semifinals; defeated Denver, 4-1, in Western Conference finals; defeated Boston, 4-2, in NBA Finals.

1986—Defeated San Antonio, 3-0, in Western Conference first round; defeated Dallas, 4-2, in Western Conference semifinals; lost to Houston, 4-1, in Western Conference finals.

1987—Defeated Denver, 3-0, in Western Conference first round; defeated Golden State, 4-1, in Western Conference semifinals; defeated Seattle, 4-0, in Western Conference finals; defeated Boston, 4-2, in NBA Finals.

1988—Defeated San Antonio, 3-0, in Western Conference first round; defeated Utah, 4-3, in Western Conference semifinals; defeated Dallas, 4-3, in Western Conference finals; defeated Detroit, 4-3, in NBA Finals.

1989—Defeated Portland, 3-0, in Western Conference first round; defeated Seattle, 4-0, in Western Conference semifinals; defeated Phoenix, 4-0, in Western Conference finals; lost to Detroit, 4-0, in NBA Finals.

ALL-TIME GREAT COACHES

1990—Defeated Houston, 3-1, in Western Conference first round; lost to Phoenix, 4-1, in Western Conference semifinals.

1992—Defeated Detroit, 3-2, in Eastern Conference first round; lost to Chicago, 4-3, in Eastern Conference semifinals.

1993—Defeated Indiana, 3-1, in Eastern Conference first round; defeated Charlotte, 4-1, in Eastern Conference semifinals; lost to Chicago, 4-2, in Eastern Conference finals.

1994—Defeated New Jersey, 3-1, in Eastern Conference first round; defeated Chicago, 4-3, in Eastern Conference semifinals; defeated Indiana, 4-3, in Eastern Conference finals; lost to Houston, 4-3, in NBA Finals.

1995—Defeated Cleveland, 3-1, in Eastern Conference first round; lost to Indiana, 4-3, in Eastern Conference semifinals.

1996—Lost to Chicago in Eastern Conference first round.

1997—Defeated Orlando, 3-2, in Eastern Conference first round; defeated New York, 4-3, in Eastern Conference semifinals; lost to Chicago, 4-1, in Eastern Conference finals.

1998—Lost to New York in Eastern Conference first round.

1999—Lost to New York in Eastern Conference first round.

2000—Defeated Detroit, 3-0, in Eastern Conference first round; lost to New York, 4-3, in Eastern Conference semifinals.

2001—Lost to Charlotte in Eastern Conference first round.

## SHUE, GENE

**PERSONAL:** Born December 18, 1931, in Baltimore. ... 6-2/175 (1,88/79,4).

**COLLEGE:** Maryland.

**TRANSACTIONS:** Selected by Philadelphia Warriors in first round (third pick overall) of 1954 NBA Draft. ... Contract sold by Warriors to New York Knicks (November 29, 1954). ... Traded by Knicks to Fort Wayne Pistons for rights to G Ron Sobieszcyk (April 30, 1956). ... Pistons moved from Fort Wayne to Detroit for 1957-58 season. ... Traded by Pistons to Knicks for C Darrall Imhoff and cash (August 29, 1962). ... Traded by Knicks with C Paul Hogue to Baltimore Bullets for G/F Bill McGill (October 30, 1963).

**CAREER NOTES:** General manager, Philadelphia 76ers (1990-91 and 1991-92). ... Director of player personnel, 76ers (1992-93 through 1996-97).

### COLLEGIATE RECORD

| Season Team | G | Min. | FGM | FGA | Pct. | FTM | FTA | Pct. | Reb. | Ast. | Pts. | RPG | APG | PPG |
|---|---|---|---|---|---|---|---|---|---|---|---|---|---|---|
| 50-51—Maryland‡ | 14 | ... | ... | ... | ... | ... | ... | ... | ... | ... | 181 | ... | ... | 12.9 |
| 51-52—Maryland | 22 | ... | 91 | 243 | .374 | 53 | 75 | .707 | ... | ... | 205 | ... | ... | 9.3 |
| 52-53—Maryland | 23 | ... | 176 | 375 | .469 | 156 | 223 | .700 | ... | ... | 508 | ... | ... | 22.1 |
| 53-54—Maryland | 30 | ... | 237 | 469 | .505 | 180 | 228 | .789 | ... | ... | 654 | ... | ... | 21.8 |
| Varsity totals | 75 | ... | 504 | 1087 | .464 | 389 | 526 | .740 | ... | ... | 1367 | ... | ... | 18.2 |

### NBA REGULAR-SEASON RECORD

**HONORS:** All-NBA first team (1960). ... All-NBA second team (1961).

| Season Team | G | Min. | FGM | FGA | Pct. | FTM | FTA | Pct. | Reb. | Ast. | PF | Dq. | Pts. | RPG | APG | PPG |
|---|---|---|---|---|---|---|---|---|---|---|---|---|---|---|---|---|
| 54-55—Phil.-N.Y. | 62 | 947 | 100 | 289 | .346 | 59 | 78 | .756 | 154 | 89 | 64 | 0 | 259 | 2.5 | 1.4 | 4.2 |
| 55-56—New York | 72 | 1750 | 240 | 625 | .384 | 181 | 237 | .764 | 212 | 179 | 111 | 0 | 661 | 2.9 | 2.5 | 9.2 |
| 56-57—Fort Wayne | 72 | 2470 | 273 | 710 | .385 | 241 | 316 | .763 | 421 | 238 | 137 | 0 | 787 | 5.8 | 3.3 | 10.9 |
| 57-58—Detroit | 63 | 2333 | 353 | 919 | .384 | 276 | 327 | .844 | 333 | 172 | 150 | 1 | 982 | 5.3 | 2.7 | 15.6 |
| 58-59—Detroit | 72 | 2745 | 464 | 1197 | .388 | 338 | 421 | .803 | 335 | 231 | 129 | 1 | 1266 | 4.7 | 3.2 | 17.6 |
| 59-60—Detroit | 75 | †3338 | 620 | 1501 | .413 | 472 | 541 | .872 | 409 | 295 | 146 | 2 | 1712 | 5.5 | 3.9 | 22.8 |
| 60-61—Detroit | 78 | 3361 | 650 | 1545 | .421 | 465 | 543 | .856 | 334 | 530 | 207 | 1 | 1765 | 4.3 | 6.8 | 22.6 |
| 61-62—Detroit | 80 | 3143 | 580 | 1422 | .408 | 362 | 447 | .810 | 372 | 465 | 192 | 1 | 1522 | 4.7 | 5.8 | 19.0 |
| 62-63—New York | 78 | 2288 | 354 | 894 | .396 | 208 | 302 | .689 | 191 | 259 | 171 | 0 | 916 | 2.4 | 3.3 | 11.7 |
| 63-64—Baltimore | 47 | 963 | 81 | 276 | .293 | 36 | 61 | .590 | 94 | 150 | 98 | 2 | 198 | 2.0 | 3.2 | 4.2 |
| Totals | 699 | 23338 | 3715 | 9378 | .396 | 2638 | 3273 | .806 | 2855 | 2608 | 1405 | 8 | 10068 | 4.1 | 3.7 | 14.4 |

### NBA PLAYOFF RECORD

| Season Team | G | Min. | FGM | FGA | Pct. | FTM | FTA | Pct. | Reb. | Ast. | PF | Dq. | Pts. | RPG | APG | PPG |
|---|---|---|---|---|---|---|---|---|---|---|---|---|---|---|---|---|
| 54-55—New York | 3 | 49 | 8 | 17 | .471 | 6 | 7 | .857 | 12 | 4 | 5 | 0 | 22 | 4.0 | 1.3 | 7.3 |
| 56-57—Fort Wayne | 2 | 79 | 14 | 27 | .519 | 4 | 4 | 1.000 | 7 | 8 | 3 | 0 | 32 | 3.5 | 4.0 | 16.0 |
| 57-58—Detroit | 7 | 281 | 45 | 123 | .366 | 40 | 43 | .930 | 46 | 33 | 15 | 0 | 130 | 6.6 | 4.7 | 18.6 |
| 58-59—Detroit | 3 | 118 | 28 | 60 | .467 | 27 | 33 | .818 | 14 | 10 | 7 | 0 | 83 | 4.7 | 3.3 | 27.7 |
| 59-60—Detroit | 2 | 89 | 15 | 38 | .395 | 18 | 20 | .900 | 12 | 6 | 5 | 0 | 48 | 6.0 | 3.0 | 24.0 |
| 60-61—Detroit | 5 | 186 | 35 | 72 | .486 | 23 | 29 | .793 | 12 | 22 | 11 | 0 | 93 | 2.4 | 4.4 | 18.6 |
| 61-62—Detroit | 10 | 369 | 62 | 151 | .411 | 37 | 48 | .771 | 30 | 49 | 29 | 0 | 161 | 3.0 | 4.9 | 16.1 |
| Totals | 32 | 1171 | 207 | 488 | .424 | 155 | 184 | .842 | 133 | 132 | 75 | 0 | 569 | 4.2 | 4.1 | 17.8 |

### NBA ALL-STAR GAME RECORD

| Season Team | Min. | FGM | FGA | Pct. | FTM | FTA | Pct. | Reb | Ast. | PF | Dq. | Pts. |
|---|---|---|---|---|---|---|---|---|---|---|---|---|
| 1958—Detroit | 25 | 8 | 11 | .727 | 2 | 3 | .667 | 2 | 0 | 3 | 0 | 18 |
| 1959—Detroit | 31 | 6 | 12 | .500 | 1 | 2 | .500 | 4 | 3 | 4 | 0 | 13 |
| 1960—Detroit | 34 | 6 | 13 | .462 | 1 | 2 | .500 | 6 | 6 | 0 | 0 | 13 |
| 1961—Detroit | 23 | 6 | 10 | .600 | 3 | 4 | .750 | 3 | 6 | 1 | 0 | 15 |
| 1962—Detroit | 17 | 3 | 6 | .500 | 1 | 1 | 1.000 | 5 | 4 | 3 | 0 | 7 |
| Totals | 130 | 29 | 52 | .558 | 8 | 12 | .667 | 20 | 19 | 11 | 0 | 66 |

### HEAD COACHING RECORD

**HONORS:** NBA Coach of the Year (1969, 1982).

## NBA COACHING RECORD

| Season Team | W | L | Pct. | Finish | W | L | Pct. |
|---|---|---|---|---|---|---|---|
| | | REGULAR SEASON | | | | PLAYOFFS | |
| 66-67—Baltimore | 16 | 40 | .286 | 5th/Eastern Division | — | — | — |
| 67-68—Baltimore | 36 | 46 | .439 | 6th/Eastern Division | — | — | — |
| 68-69—Baltimore | 57 | 25 | .695 | 1st/Eastern Division | 0 | 4 | .000 |
| 69-70—Baltimore | 50 | 32 | .610 | 3rd/Central Division | 3 | 4 | .429 |
| 70-71—Baltimore | 42 | 40 | .512 | 1st/Central Division | 8 | 10 | .444 |
| 71-72—Baltimore | 38 | 44 | .463 | 1st/Central Division | 2 | 4 | .333 |
| 72-73—Baltimore | 52 | 30 | .634 | 1st/Central Division | 1 | 4 | .200 |
| 73-74—Philadelphia | 25 | 57 | .305 | 4th/Atlantic Division | — | — | — |
| 74-75—Philadelphia | 34 | 48 | .415 | 4th/Atlantic Division | — | — | — |
| 75-76—Philadelphia | 46 | 36 | .561 | T2nd/Atlantic Division | 1 | 2 | .333 |
| 76-77—Philadelphia | 50 | 32 | .610 | 1st/Atlantic Division | 10 | 9 | .526 |
| 77-78—Philadelphia | 2 | 4 | .333 | | | | |
| 78-79—San Diego | 43 | 39 | .524 | 5th/Pacific Division | — | — | — |
| 79-80—San Diego | 35 | 47 | .427 | 5th/Pacific Division | — | — | — |
| 80-81—Washington | 39 | 43 | .476 | 4th/Atlantic Division | — | — | — |
| 81-82—Washington | 43 | 39 | .524 | 4th/Atlantic Division | 3 | 4 | .429 |
| 82-83—Washington | 42 | 40 | .512 | 5th/Atlantic Division | — | — | — |
| 83-84—Washington | 35 | 47 | .427 | 4th/Atlantic Division | 1 | 3 | .250 |
| 84-85—Washington | 40 | 42 | .488 | 4th/Atlantic Division | 1 | 3 | .250 |
| 85-86—Washington | 32 | 37 | .464 | | | | |
| 87-88—L.A. Clippers | 17 | 65 | .207 | 6th/Pacific Division | — | — | — |
| 88-89—L.A. Clippers | 10 | 28 | .263 | | | | |
| Totals (22 years) | 784 | 861 | .477 | Totals (10 years) | 30 | 47 | .390 |

### NOTES:
1966—Replaced Mike Farmer (1-8) and Buddy Jeannette (3-13) as Baltimore head coach (December) with record of 4-21.
1969—Lost to New York in Eastern Division Semifinals.
1970—Lost to New York in Eastern Division Semifinals.
1971—Defeated Philadelphia, 4-3, in Eastern Conference Semifinals; defeated New York, 4-3, in Eastern Conference Finals; lost to Milwaukee, 4-0, in NBA Finals.
1972—Lost to New York in Eastern Conference Semifinals.
1973—Lost to New York in Eastern Conference Semifinals.
1976—Lost to Buffalo in Eastern Conference First Round.
1977—Defeated Boston, 4-3, in Eastern Conference Semifinals; defeated Houston, 4-2, in Eastern Conference Finals; lost to Portland, 4-2, in NBA Finals. Replaced as Philadelphia head coach by Billy Cunningham (November 4).
1982—Defeated New Jersey, 2-0, in Eastern Conference First Round; lost to Boston, 4-1, in Eastern Conference Semifinals.
1984—Lost to Boston in Eastern Conference First Round.
1985—Lost to Philadelphia in Eastern Conference First Round.
1986—Replaced as Washington head coach by Kevin Loughery (March 19).
1989—Replaced as L.A. Clippers head coach by Don Casey (January 19).

## TOMJANOVICH, RUDY

**PERSONAL:** Born November 24, 1948, in Hamtramck, Mich. ... 6-8/220. (2,03/99,8). ... Full name: Rudolph Tomjanovich. ... Name pronounced Tom-JOHN-a-vitch.
**HIGH SCHOOL:** Hamtramck (Mich.).
**COLLEGE:** Michigan.
**TRANSACTIONS/CAREER NOTES:** Selected by San Diego Rockets in first round (second pick overall) of 1970 NBA Draft. ... Rockets franchise moved from San Diego to Houston for 1971-72 season.
**MISCELLANEOUS:** Head coach of bronze-medal-winning 1998 USA Basketball World Championship Team. ... Head coach of gold-medal-winning 2000 U.S. Olympic Team.

### COLLEGIATE RECORD

**NOTES:** The Sporting News All-America first team (1970). ... The Sporting News All-America second team (1969).

| Season Team | G | Min. | FGM | FGA | Pct. | FTM | FTA | Pct. | Reb. | Ast. | Pts. | RPG | APG | PPG |
|---|---|---|---|---|---|---|---|---|---|---|---|---|---|---|
| | | | | | | | | | | | | AVERAGES | | |
| 66-67—Michigan‡ | 3 | ... | 28 | ... | ... | 6 | 15 | .400 | ... | ... | 62 | ... | ... | 20.7 |
| 67-68—Michigan | 24 | ... | 210 | 446 | .471 | 49 | 78 | .628 | 323 | ... | 469 | 13.5 | ... | 19.5 |
| 68-69—Michigan | 24 | ... | 269 | 541 | .497 | 79 | 131 | .603 | 340 | ... | 617 | 14.2 | ... | 25.7 |
| 69-70—Michigan | 24 | ... | 286 | 604 | .474 | 150 | 200 | .750 | 376 | ... | 722 | 15.7 | ... | 30.1 |
| Varsity totals | 72 | ... | 765 | 1591 | .481 | 278 | 409 | .680 | 1039 | ... | 1808 | 14.4 | ... | 25.1 |

### NBA REGULAR-SEASON RECORD

| Season Team | G | Min. | FGM | FGA | Pct. | FTM | FTA | Pct. | Reb. | Ast. | PF | Dq. | Pts. | RPG | APG | PPG |
|---|---|---|---|---|---|---|---|---|---|---|---|---|---|---|---|---|
| | | | | | | | | | | | | | | AVERAGES | | |
| 70-71—San Diego | 77 | 1062 | 168 | 439 | .383 | 73 | 112 | .652 | 381 | 73 | 124 | 0 | 409 | 4.9 | 0.9 | 5.3 |
| 71-72—Houston | 78 | 2689 | 500 | 1010 | .495 | 172 | 238 | .723 | 923 | 117 | 193 | 2 | 1172 | 11.8 | 1.5 | 15.0 |
| 72-73—Houston | 81 | 2972 | 655 | 1371 | .478 | 250 | 335 | .746 | 938 | 178 | 225 | 1 | 1560 | 11.6 | 2.2 | 19.3 |

| Season Team | G | Min. | FGM | FGA | Pct. | FTM | FTA | Pct. | Off. | Def. | Tot. | Ast. | St. | Blk. | TO | Pts. | RPG | APG | PPG |
|---|---|---|---|---|---|---|---|---|---|---|---|---|---|---|---|---|---|---|---|
| | | | | | | | | | REBOUNDS | | | | | | | | AVERAGES | | |
| 73-74—Houston | 80 | 3227 | 788 | 1470 | .536 | 385 | 454 | .848 | 230 | 487 | 717 | 250 | 89 | 66 | ... | 1961 | 9.0 | 3.1 | 24.5 |
| 74-75—Houston | 81 | 3134 | 694 | 1323 | .525 | 289 | 366 | .790 | 184 | 429 | 613 | 236 | 76 | 24 | ... | 1677 | 7.6 | 2.9 | 20.7 |
| 75-76—Houston | 79 | 2912 | 622 | 1202 | .517 | 221 | 288 | .767 | 167 | 499 | 666 | 188 | 42 | 19 | ... | 1465 | 8.4 | 2.4 | 18.5 |
| 76-77—Houston | 81 | 3130 | 733 | 1437 | .510 | 287 | 342 | .839 | 172 | 512 | 684 | 172 | 57 | 27 | ... | 1753 | 8.4 | 2.1 | 21.6 |
| 77-78—Houston | 23 | 849 | 217 | 447 | .485 | 61 | 81 | .753 | 40 | 98 | 138 | 32 | 15 | 5 | 38 | 495 | 6.0 | 1.4 | 21.5 |
| 78-79—Houston | 74 | 2641 | 620 | 1200 | .517 | 168 | 221 | .760 | 170 | 402 | 572 | 137 | 44 | 18 | 138 | 1408 | 7.7 | 1.9 | 19.0 |
| 79-80—Houston | 62 | 1834 | 370 | 778 | .476 | 118 | 147 | .803 | 132 | 226 | 358 | 109 | 32 | 10 | 98 | 880 | 5.8 | 1.8 | 14.2 |
| 80-81—Houston | 52 | 1264 | 263 | 563 | .467 | 65 | 82 | .793 | 78 | 130 | 208 | 81 | 19 | 6 | 58 | 603 | 4.0 | 1.6 | 11.6 |
| Totals | 768 | 25714 | 5630 | 11240 | .501 | 2089 | 2666 | .784 | ... | ... | 6198 | 1573 | 374 | 175 | 332 | 13383 | 8.1 | 2.0 | 17.4 |

Three-point field goals: 1979-80, 22-for-79 (.278). 1980-81, 12-for-51 (.235). Totals, 34-for-130 (.262).
Personal fouls/disqualifications: 1973-74, 230/0. 1974-75, 230/1. 1975-76, 206/1. 1976-77, 198/1. 1977-78, 63/0. 1978-79, 186/0. 1979-80, 161/2. 1980-81, 121/0. Totals, 1937/8.

## NBA PLAYOFF RECORD

| Season Team | G | Min. | FGM | FGA | Pct. | FTM | FTA | Pct. | Off. | Def. | Tot. | Ast. | St. | Blk. | TO | Pts. | RPG | APG | PPG |
|---|---|---|---|---|---|---|---|---|---|---|---|---|---|---|---|---|---|---|---|
| | | | | | | | | | REBOUNDS | | | | | | | | AVERAGES | | |
| 74-75—Houston | 8 | 304 | 72 | 128 | .563 | 40 | 48 | .833 | 22 | 42 | 64 | 23 | 1 | 4 | ... | 184 | 8.0 | 2.9 | 23.0 |
| 76-77—Houston | 12 | 457 | 107 | 212 | .505 | 29 | 37 | .784 | 24 | 41 | 65 | 24 | 7 | 3 | ... | 243 | 5.4 | 2.0 | 20.3 |
| 78-79—Houston | 2 | 64 | 9 | 23 | .391 | 2 | 5 | .400 | 7 | 7 | 14 | 2 | 1 | 1 | 1 | 20 | 7.0 | 1.0 | 10.0 |
| 79-80—Houston | 7 | 185 | 24 | 64 | .375 | 9 | 13 | .692 | 12 | 28 | 40 | 10 | 2 | 0 | 14 | 58 | 5.7 | 1.4 | 8.3 |
| 80-81—Houston | 8 | 31 | 1 | 9 | .111 | 4 | 6 | .667 | 2 | 4 | 6 | 0 | 0 | 0 | 2 | 6 | 0.8 | 0.0 | 0.8 |
| Totals | 37 | 1041 | 213 | 436 | .489 | 84 | 109 | .771 | 67 | 122 | 189 | 59 | 11 | 8 | 17 | 511 | 5.1 | 1.6 | 13.8 |

Three-point field goals: 1979-80, 1-for-7 (.143). 1980-81, 0-for-3. Totals, 1-for-10 (.100).
Personal fouls/disqualifications: 1974-75, 17/0. 1976-77, 36/0. 1978-79, 1/0. 1979-80, 21/1. 1980-81, 3/0. Totals, 78/1.

## NBA ALL-STAR GAME RECORD

| Season Team | Min. | FGM | FGA | Pct. | FTM | FTA | Pct. | Off. | Def. | Tot. | Ast. | PF | Dq. | St. | Blk. | TO | Pts. |
|---|---|---|---|---|---|---|---|---|---|---|---|---|---|---|---|---|---|
| | | | | | | | | REBOUNDS | | | | | | | | | |
| 1974—Houston | 17 | 2 | 5 | .400 | 0 | 0 | ... | 2 | 3 | 5 | 0 | 1 | 0 | 0 | 0 | ... | 4 |
| 1975—Houston | 14 | 0 | 3 | .000 | 0 | 0 | ... | 1 | 2 | 3 | 0 | 3 | 0 | 0 | 0 | ... | 0 |
| 1976—Houston | 12 | 1 | 2 | .500 | 0 | 0 | ... | 1 | 2 | 3 | 0 | 2 | 0 | 0 | 0 | ... | 2 |
| 1977—Houston | 22 | 3 | 9 | .333 | 0 | 0 | ... | 2 | 8 | 10 | 1 | 1 | 0 | 1 | 1 | ... | 6 |
| 1979—Houston | 24 | 6 | 13 | .462 | 0 | 0 | ... | 4 | 2 | 6 | 1 | 2 | 0 | 0 | 0 | 0 | 12 |
| Totals | 89 | 12 | 32 | .375 | 0 | 0 | ... | 10 | 17 | 27 | 2 | 9 | 0 | 1 | 1 | 0 | 24 |

## HEAD COACHING RECORD

**BACKGROUND:** Scout, Houston Rockets (1981-82 and 1982-83). ... Assistant coach, Rockets (1983-84 to February 18, 1992).

## NBA COACHING RECORD

| Season Team | W | L | Pct. | Finish | W | L | Pct. |
|---|---|---|---|---|---|---|---|
| | REGULAR SEASON | | | | PLAYOFFS | | |
| 91-92—Houston | 16 | 14 | .533 | 3rd/Midwest Division | — | — | — |
| 92-93—Houston | 55 | 27 | .671 | 1st/Midwest Division | 6 | 6 | .500 |
| 93-94—Houston | 58 | 24 | .707 | 1st/Midwest Division | 15 | 8 | .652 |
| 94-95—Houston | 47 | 35 | .573 | 3rd/Midwest Division | 15 | 7 | .682 |
| 95-96—Houston | 48 | 34 | .585 | 2nd/Midwest Division | 3 | 5 | .375 |
| 96-97—Houston | 57 | 25 | .695 | 2nd/Midwest Division | 9 | 7 | .563 |
| 97-98—Houston | 41 | 41 | .500 | 4th/Midwest Division | 2 | 3 | .400 |
| 98-99—Houston | 31 | 19 | .620 | 3rd/Midwest Division | 1 | 3 | .250 |
| 99-00—Houston | 34 | 48 | .415 | 6th/Midwest Division | — | — | — |
| 00-01—Houston | 45 | 37 | .549 | 5th/Midwest Division | — | — | — |
| 01-02—Houston | 28 | 54 | .341 | 5th/Midwest Division | — | — | — |
| 02-03—Houston | 43 | 39 | .524 | 5th/Midwest Division | — | — | — |
| 04-05—Los Angeles Lakers | 24 | 19 | .558 | | | | |
| Totals (13 years) | 527 | 416 | .559 | | Totals (7 years) 51 | 39 | .567 |

## WORLD CHAMPIONSHIP RECORD

| Season Team | W | L | Pct. | Finish |
|---|---|---|---|---|
| | REGULAR SEASON | | | |
| 1998—Team USA | 7 | 2 | .778 | Bronze medal |

## OLYMPIC RECORD

| Season Team | W | L | Pct. | Finish |
|---|---|---|---|---|
| | REGULAR SEASON | | | |
| 2000—Team USA | 8 | 0 | 1.000 | Gold medal |

## NOTES:

1992—Replaced Don Chaney as Houston head coach (February 18), with record of 26-26 and club in third place.

1993—Defeated L.A. Clippers, 3-2, in Western Conference first round; lost to Seattle, 4-3, in Western Conference semifinals.

1994—Defeated Portland, 3-1, in Western Conference first round; defeated Phoenix, 4-3, in Western Conference semifinals; defeated Utah, 4-1, in Western Conference finals; defeated New York, 4-3, in NBA Finals.

1995—Defeated Utah, 3-2, in Western Conference first round, defeated Phoenix, 4-3, in Western Conference semifinals; defeated San Antonio, 4-2, in Western Conference finals; defeated Orlando, 4-0, in NBA Finals.

1996—Defeated Los Angeles Lakers, 3-1, in Western Conference first round; lost to Seattle, 4-0, in Western Conference semifinals.

1997—Defeated Minnesota, 3-0, in Western Conference first round; defeated Seattle, 4-3, in Western Conference semifinals; lost to Utah, 4-2, in Western Conference finals.

1998—Lost to Utah in Western Conference first round.

1999—Lost to Los Angeles Lakers in Western Conference first round.

2005—Stepped down as Los Angeles head coach (February 2); replaced by Frank Hamblen with team in third place.

# WILKENS, LENNY  G

**PERSONAL:** Born October 28, 1937, in Brooklyn, N.Y. ... 6-1/180 (1,85/81,6). ... Full name: Leonard Randolph Wilkens.

**HIGH SCHOOL:** Boys (Brooklyn, N.Y.).
**COLLEGE:** Providence.
**TRANSACTIONS/CAREER NOTES:** Selected by St. Louis Hawks in first round of 1960 NBA Draft. ... Hawks franchise moved from St. Louis to Atlanta for 1968-69 season. ... Traded by Hawks to Seattle SuperSonics for G Walt Hazzard (October 12, 1968). ... Player/head coach, SuperSonics (1969-70 through 1971-72). ... Traded by SuperSonics with F Barry Clemens to Cleveland Cavaliers for G Butch Beard (August 23, 1972). ... Playing rights transferred from Cavaliers to Portland Trail Blazers for cash (October 7, 1974).
**CAREER NOTES:** Director of player personnel, SuperSonics (May 13-November 1977). ... Vice president/general manager, SuperSonics (1985-86).
**CAREER HONORS:** Elected to Naismith Memorial Basketball Hall of Fame as player (1988) and head coach (1998). ... One of the 50 Greatest Players in NBA History (1996). ... One of the Top 10 Coaches in NBA History (1996).
**MISCELLANEOUS:** Head coach, 1996 gold medal-winning U.S. Olympic Team.

## COLLEGIATE RECORD

**NOTES:** THE SPORTING NEWS All-America second team (1960).

| Season Team | G | Min. | FGM | FGA | Pct. | FTM | FTA | Pct. | Reb. | Ast. | Pts. | RPG | APG | PPG |
|---|---|---|---|---|---|---|---|---|---|---|---|---|---|---|
| 56-57—Providence‡ | 23 | ... | ... | ... | ... | ... | ... | ... | ... | ... | 488 | ... | ... | 21.2 |
| 57-58—Providence | 24 | ... | 137 | 316 | .434 | 84 | 130 | .646 | 190 | ... | 358 | 7.9 | ... | 14.9 |
| 58-59—Providence | 27 | ... | 167 | 390 | .428 | 89 | 144 | .618 | 188 | ... | 423 | 7.0 | ... | 15.7 |
| 59-60—Providence | 29 | ... | 157 | 362 | .434 | 98 | 140 | .700 | 205 | ... | 412 | 7.1 | ... | 14.2 |
| **Varsity totals** | 80 | ... | 461 | 1068 | .432 | 271 | 414 | .655 | 583 | ... | 1193 | 7.3 | ... | 14.9 |

## NBA REGULAR-SEASON RECORD

| Season Team | G | Min. | FGM | FGA | Pct. | FTM | FTA | Pct. | Reb. | Ast. | PF | Dq. | Pts. | RPG | APG | PPG |
|---|---|---|---|---|---|---|---|---|---|---|---|---|---|---|---|---|
| 60-61—St. Louis | 75 | 1898 | 333 | 783 | .425 | 214 | 300 | .713 | 335 | 212 | 215 | 5 | 880 | 4.5 | 2.8 | 11.7 |
| 61-62—St. Louis | 20 | 870 | 140 | 364 | .385 | 84 | 110 | .764 | 131 | 116 | 63 | 0 | 364 | 6.6 | 5.8 | 18.2 |
| 62-63—St. Louis | 75 | 2569 | 333 | 834 | .399 | 222 | 319 | .696 | 403 | 381 | 256 | 6 | 888 | 5.4 | 5.1 | 11.8 |
| 63-64—St. Louis | 78 | 2526 | 334 | 808 | .413 | 270 | 365 | .740 | 335 | 359 | 287 | 7 | 938 | 4.3 | 4.6 | 12.0 |
| 64-65—St. Louis | 78 | 2854 | 434 | 1048 | .414 | 416 | 558 | .746 | 365 | 431 | 283 | 7 | 1284 | 4.7 | 5.5 | 16.5 |
| 65-66—St. Louis | 69 | 2692 | 411 | 954 | .431 | 422 | 532 | .793 | 322 | 429 | 248 | 4 | 1244 | 4.7 | 6.2 | 18.0 |
| 66-67—St. Louis | 78 | 2974 | 448 | 1036 | .432 | 459 | 583 | .787 | 412 | 442 | 280 | 6 | 1355 | 5.3 | 5.7 | 17.4 |
| 67-68—St. Louis | 82 | 3169 | 546 | 1246 | .438 | 546 | 711 | .768 | 438 | 679 | 255 | 3 | 1638 | 5.3 | 8.3 | 20.0 |
| 68-69—Seattle | 82 | 3463 | 644 | 1462 | .441 | 547 | 710 | .770 | 511 | 674 | 294 | 8 | 1835 | 6.2 | 8.2 | 22.4 |
| 69-70—Seattle | 75 | 2802 | 448 | 1066 | .420 | 438 | 556 | .788 | 378 | *683 | 212 | 5 | 1334 | 5.0 | 9.1 | 17.8 |
| 70-71—Seattle | 71 | 2641 | 471 | 1125 | .419 | 461 | 574 | .803 | 319 | 654 | 201 | 3 | 1403 | 4.5 | 9.2 | 19.8 |
| 71-72—Seattle | 80 | 2989 | 479 | 1027 | .466 | 480 | 620 | .774 | 338 | *766 | 209 | 4 | 1438 | 4.2 | 9.6 | 18.0 |
| 72-73—Cleveland | 75 | 2973 | 572 | 1275 | .449 | 394 | 476 | .828 | 346 | 628 | 221 | 2 | 1538 | 4.6 | 8.4 | 20.5 |

| Season Team | G | Min. | FGM | FGA | Pct. | FTM | FTA | Pct. | Off. | Def. | Tot. | Ast. | St. | Blk. | TO | Pts. | RPG | APG | PPG |
|---|---|---|---|---|---|---|---|---|---|---|---|---|---|---|---|---|---|---|---|
| 73-74—Cleveland | 74 | 2483 | 462 | 994 | .465 | 289 | 361 | .801 | 80 | 197 | 277 | 522 | 97 | 17 | ... | 1213 | 3.7 | 7.1 | 16.4 |
| 74-75—Portland | 65 | 1161 | 134 | 305 | .439 | 152 | 198 | .768 | 38 | 82 | 120 | 235 | 77 | 9 | ... | 420 | 1.8 | 3.6 | 6.5 |
| **Totals** | 1077 | 38064 | 6189 | 14327 | .432 | 5394 | 6973 | .774 | ... | ... | 5030 | 7211 | 174 | 26 | ... | 17772 | 4.7 | 6.7 | 16.5 |

Personal fouls/disqualifications: 1973-74, 165/2. 1974-75, 96/1. Totals, 3285/63.

## NBA PLAYOFF RECORD

| Season Team | G | Min. | FGM | FGA | Pct. | FTM | FTA | Pct. | Reb. | Ast. | PF | Dq. | Pts. | RPG | APG | PPG |
|---|---|---|---|---|---|---|---|---|---|---|---|---|---|---|---|---|
| 60-61—St. Louis | 12 | 437 | 63 | 166 | .380 | 44 | 58 | .759 | 72 | 42 | 51 | 4 | 170 | 6.0 | 3.5 | 14.2 |
| 62-63—St. Louis | 11 | 400 | 57 | 154 | .370 | 37 | 49 | .755 | 69 | 69 | 51 | 2 | 151 | 6.3 | 6.3 | 13.7 |
| 63-64—St. Louis | 12 | 413 | 64 | 143 | .448 | 44 | 58 | .759 | 60 | 64 | 42 | 0 | 172 | 5.0 | 5.3 | 14.3 |
| 64-65—St. Louis | 4 | 147 | 20 | 57 | .351 | 24 | 29 | .828 | 12 | 15 | 14 | 0 | 64 | 3.0 | 3.8 | 16.0 |
| 65-66—St. Louis | 10 | 391 | 57 | 143 | .399 | 57 | 83 | .687 | 54 | 70 | 43 | 0 | 171 | 5.4 | 7.0 | 17.1 |
| 66-67—St. Louis | 9 | 378 | 58 | 145 | .400 | 77 | 90 | .856 | 68 | 65 | 34 | 0 | 193 | 7.6 | 7.2 | 21.4 |
| 67-68—St. Louis | 6 | 237 | 40 | 91 | .440 | 30 | 40 | .750 | 38 | 47 | 23 | 1 | 110 | 6.3 | 7.8 | 18.3 |
| **Totals** | 64 | 2403 | 359 | 899 | .399 | 313 | 407 | .769 | 373 | 372 | 258 | 7 | 1031 | 5.8 | 5.8 | 16.1 |

## NBA ALL-STAR GAME RECORD

**NOTES:** NBA All-Star Game Most Valuable Player (1971).

| Season Team | Min. | FGM | FGA | Pct. | FTM | FTA | Pct. | Reb | Ast. | PF | Dq. | Pts. |
|---|---|---|---|---|---|---|---|---|---|---|---|---|
| 1963—St. Louis | 25 | 2 | 7 | .286 | 0 | 1 | .000 | 2 | 3 | 0 | 0 | 4 |
| 1964—St. Louis | 14 | 1 | 5 | .200 | 1 | 1 | 1.000 | 0 | 0 | 3 | 0 | 3 |
| 1965—St. Louis | 20 | 2 | 6 | .333 | 4 | 4 | 1.000 | 3 | 3 | 3 | 0 | 8 |
| 1967—St. Louis | 16 | 2 | 6 | .333 | 2 | 3 | .667 | 2 | 6 | 2 | 0 | 6 |
| 1968—St. Louis | 22 | 4 | 10 | .400 | 6 | 8 | .750 | 3 | 3 | 1 | 0 | 14 |
| 1969—Seattle | 24 | 3 | 15 | .200 | 4 | 5 | .800 | 7 | 5 | 3 | 0 | 10 |
| 1970—Seattle | 17 | 5 | 7 | .714 | 2 | 3 | .667 | 2 | 4 | 1 | 0 | 12 |
| 1971—Seattle | 20 | 8 | 11 | .727 | 5 | 5 | 1.000 | 1 | 1 | 1 | 0 | 21 |
| 1973—Cleveland | 24 | 3 | 8 | .375 | 1 | 2 | .500 | 2 | 1 | 1 | 0 | 7 |
| **Totals** | 182 | 30 | 75 | .400 | 25 | 32 | .781 | 22 | 26 | 15 | 0 | 85 |

## HEAD COACHING RECORD

**BACKGROUND:** Player/head coach, Seattle SuperSonics (1969-70 through 1971-72). ... Player/head coach, Portland Trail Blazers (1974-75). ... Head coach/director of player personnel, SuperSonics (November 1977 through 1984-85). ... Assistant coach, U.S. Olympic team (1992).

**HONORS:** NBA Coach of the Year (1994). ... One of the Top 10 Coaches in NBA History (1996).

**RECORDS:** Holds NBA career record for most wins—1,315.

## NBA COACHING RECORD

| Season  Team | REGULAR SEASON | | | | PLAYOFFS | | |
|---|---|---|---|---|---|---|---|
| | W | L | Pct. | Finish | W | L | Pct. |
| 69-70—Seattle | 36 | 46 | .439 | 5th/Western Division | — | — | — |
| 70-71—Seattle | 38 | 44 | .463 | 4th/Pacific Division | — | — | — |
| 71-72—Seattle | 47 | 35 | .573 | 3rd/Pacific Division | — | — | — |
| 74-75—Portland | 38 | 44 | .463 | 3rd/Pacific Division | — | — | — |
| 75-76—Portland | 37 | 45 | .451 | 5th/Pacific Division | — | — | — |
| 77-78—Seattle | 42 | 18 | .700 | 3rd/Pacific Division | 13 | 9 | .591 |
| 78-79—Seattle | 52 | 30 | .634 | 1st/Pacific Division | 12 | 5 | .706 |
| 79-80—Seattle | 56 | 26 | .683 | 2nd/Pacific Division | 7 | 8 | .467 |
| 80-81—Seattle | 34 | 48 | .415 | 6th/Pacific Division | — | — | — |
| 81-82—Seattle | 52 | 30 | .634 | 2nd/Pacific Division | 3 | 5 | .375 |
| 82-83—Seattle | 48 | 34 | .585 | 3rd/Pacific Division | 0 | 2 | .000 |
| 83-84—Seattle | 42 | 40 | .512 | 3rd/Pacific Division | 2 | 3 | .400 |
| 84-85—Seattle | 31 | 51 | .378 | 4th/Pacific Division | — | — | — |
| 86-87—Cleveland | 31 | 51 | .378 | 6th/Central Division | — | — | — |
| 87-88—Cleveland | 42 | 40 | .512 | T4th/Central Division | 2 | 3 | .400 |
| 88-89—Cleveland | 57 | 25 | .695 | 2nd/Central Division | 2 | 3 | .400 |
| 89-90—Cleveland | 42 | 40 | .512 | T4th/Central Division | 2 | 3 | .400 |
| 90-91—Cleveland | 33 | 49 | .402 | 6th/Central Division | — | — | — |
| 91-92—Cleveland | 57 | 25 | .695 | 2nd/Central Division | 9 | 8 | .529 |
| 92-93—Cleveland | 54 | 28 | .659 | 2nd/Central Division | 3 | 6 | .333 |
| 93-94—Atlanta | 57 | 25 | .695 | 1st/Central Division | 5 | 6 | .455 |
| 94-95—Atlanta | 42 | 40 | .512 | 5th/Central Division | 0 | 3 | .000 |
| 95-96—Atlanta | 46 | 36 | .561 | 4th/Central Division | 4 | 6 | .400 |
| 96-97—Atlanta | 56 | 26 | .683 | 2nd/Central Division | 4 | 6 | .400 |
| 97-98—Atlanta | 50 | 32 | .610 | 4th/Central Division | 1 | 3 | .250 |
| 98-99—Atlanta | 31 | 19 | .620 | 2nd/Central Division | 3 | 6 | .333 |
| 99-00—Atlanta | 28 | 54 | .341 | 7th/Central Division | — | — | — |
| 00-01—Toronto | 47 | 35 | .573 | 2nd/Central Division | 6 | 6 | .500 |
| 01-02—Toronto | 42 | 40 | .512 | T3rd/Central Division | 2 | 3 | .400 |
| 02-03—Toronto | 24 | 58 | .293 | 7th/Central Division | — | — | — |
| 03-04—New York | 23 | 19 | .548 | 3rd/Atlantic Division | 0 | 4 | .000 |
| 04-05—New York | 17 | 22 | .294 | | — | — | — |
| Totals (32 years) | 1332 | 1155 | .536 | Totals (20 years)..... | 80 | 98 | .450 |

## OLYMPIC RECORD

| Season  Team | REGULAR SEASON | | | | PLAYOFFS | | |
|---|---|---|---|---|---|---|---|
| | W | L | Pct. | Finish | W | L | Pct. |
| 1996—Team USA | 8 | 0 | 1.000 | Gold medal | — | — | — |

**NOTES:**

1977—Replaced Bob Hopkins as Seattle head coach (November), with record of 5-17.

1978—Defeated Los Angeles Lakers, 2-1, in Western Conference first round; defeated Portland, 4-2, in Western Conference semifinals; defeated Denver, 4-2, in Western Conference finals; lost to Washington, 4-3, in NBA Finals.

1979—Defeated Los Angeles Lakers, 4-1, in Western Conference semifinals; defeated Phoenix, 4-3, in Western Conference finals; defeated Washington, 4-1, in NBA Finals.

1980—Defeated Portland, 2-1, in Western Conference first round; defeated Milwaukee, 4-3, in Western Conference semifinals; lost to Los Angeles Lakers, 4-1, in Western Conference finals.

1982—Defeated Houston, 2-1, in Western Conference first round; lost to San Antonio, 4-1, in Western Conference semifinals.

1983—Lost to Portland in Western Conference first round.

1984—Lost to Dallas in Western Conference first round.

1988—Lost to Chicago in Eastern Conference first round.

1989—Lost to Chicago in Eastern Conference first round.

1990—Lost to Philadelphia in Eastern Conference first round.

1992—Defeated New Jersey, 3-1, in Eastern Conference first round; defeated Boston, 4-3, in Eastern Conference semifinals; lost to Chicago, 4-2, in Eastern Conference finals.

1993—Defeated New Jersey, 3-2, in Eastern Conference first round; lost to Chicago, 4-0, in Eastern Conference semifinals.

1994—Defeated Miami, 3-2, in Eastern Conference first round; lost to Indiana, 4-2, in Eastern Conference semifinals.

1995—Lost to Indiana in Eastern Conference first round.

1996—Defeated Indiana, 3-2, in Eastern Conference first round; lost to Orlando, 4-1, in Eastern Conference semifinals.
    Team USA defeated Argentina, 96-68; Angola, 87-54; Lithuania, 104-82; China, 133-70; and Croatia, 102-71, in preliminary round. Defeated Brazil, 98-75, in medal round quarterfinals; defeated Australia, 101-73, in semifinals; defeated Yugoslavia, 95-69, in gold-medal game.

1997—Defeated Detroit, 3-2, in Eastern Conference first round; lost to Chicago, 4-1, in Eastern Conference semifinals.

1998—Lost to Charlotte in Eastern Conference first round.

1999—Defeated Detroit, 3-2, in Eastern Conference first round; lost to New York, 4-0, in Eastern Conference semifinals.

2001—Defeated New York, 3-2, in Eastern Conference first round; lost to Philadelphia, 4-3, in Eastern Conference semifinals.

2002—Lost to Detroit, 3-2, in Eastern Conference first round.

2004—Replaced Don Chaney as New York head coach (January 14) with record of 15-24 and club in fifth place. Lost to New Jersey, 4-0, in Eastern Conference first round.

2005—Stepped down as New York head coach (January 22); replaced by Herb Williams with team in third place.

# 2004-05 STATISTICAL LEADERS

## SCORING
*(minimum 70 games or 1,400 points)*

|  | G | FGM | FTM | Pts. | Avg. |
|---|---|---|---|---|---|
| Iverson, Phi. | 75 | 771 | 656 | 2302 | 30.7 |
| Bryant, LA-L. | 66 | 573 | 542 | 1819 | 27.6 |
| James, Cle. | 80 | 795 | 477 | 2175 | 27.2 |
| Nowitzki, Dal. | 78 | 663 | 615 | 2032 | 26.1 |
| Stoudemire, Pho. | 80 | 747 | 583 | 2080 | 26.0 |
| McGrady, Hou. | 78 | 715 | 431 | 2003 | 25.7 |
| Arenas, Was. | 80 | 656 | 521 | 2038 | 25.5 |
| Carter, Tor.-N.J. | 77 | 696 | 367 | 1886 | 24.5 |
| Wade, Mia. | 77 | 630 | 581 | 1854 | 24.1 |
| Allen, Sea. | 78 | 640 | 378 | 1867 | 23.9 |
| Redd, Mil. | 75 | 625 | 369 | 1723 | 23.0 |
| O'Neal, Mia. | 73 | 658 | 353 | 1669 | 22.9 |
| Maggette, LA-C. | 66 | 425 | 563 | 1464 | 22.2 |
| Garnett, Min. | 82 | 683 | 445 | 1817 | 22.2 |
| Marbury, N.Y. | 82 | 604 | 458 | 1781 | 21.7 |
| Richardson, G.S. | 72 | 610 | 214 | 1559 | 21.7 |
| Pierce, Bos. | 82 | 556 | 549 | 1769 | 21.6 |
| Francis, Orl. | 78 | 563 | 499 | 1663 | 21.3 |
| Anthony, Den. | 75 | 530 | 456 | 1558 | 20.8 |
| Lewis, Sea. | 71 | 532 | 220 | 1457 | 20.5 |

## FIELD-GOAL PERCENTAGE
*(minimum 300 made)*

|  | FGM | FGA | Pct. |
|---|---|---|---|
| O'Neal, Mia. | 658 | 1095 | .601 |
| Stoudemire, Pho. | 747 | 1336 | .559 |
| Yao, Hou. | 538 | 975 | .552 |
| Haslem, Mia. | 346 | 641 | .540 |
| Curry, Chi. | 393 | 730 | .538 |
| Patterson, Por. | 319 | 601 | .531 |
| Blount, Bos. | 327 | 618 | .529 |
| Miller, Sac. | 319 | 609 | .524 |
| Boozer, Utah | 361 | 693 | .521 |
| Howard, Orl. | 352 | 677 | .520 |

## FREE THROW PERCENTAGE
*(minimum 125 made)*

|  | FTM | FTA | Pct. |
|---|---|---|---|
| Miller, Ind. | 250 | 268 | .933 |
| Boykins, Den. | 279 | 303 | .921 |
| Stojakovic, Sac. | 253 | 275 | .920 |
| Stoudamire, Por. | 182 | 199 | .915 |
| Billups, Det. | 343 | 382 | .898 |
| Nash, Pho. | 211 | 238 | .887 |
| Ridnour, Sea. | 159 | 180 | .883 |
| Allen, Sea. | 378 | 428 | .883 |
| Croshere, Ind. | 226 | 256 | .883 |
| Fortson, Sea. | 227 | 258 | .880 |

## ASSISTS
*(minimum 70 games or 400 assists)*

|  | G | No. | Avg. |
|---|---|---|---|
| Nash, Pho. | 75 | 861 | 11.5 |
| Knight, Cha. | 66 | 591 | 9.0 |
| Kidd, N.J. | 66 | 545 | 8.3 |
| Marbury, N.Y. | 82 | 668 | 8.1 |
| Iverson, Phi. | 75 | 596 | 7.9 |
| James, Cle. | 80 | 577 | 7.2 |
| Francis, Orl. | 78 | 547 | 7.0 |
| Miller, Den. | 82 | 569 | 6.9 |
| Bibby, Sac. | 80 | 541 | 6.8 |
| Wade, Mia. | 77 | 520 | 6.8 |
| Alston, Tor. | 80 | 514 | 6.4 |
| Hinrich, Chi. | 77 | 494 | 6.4 |
| Parker, S.A. | 80 | 491 | 6.1 |
| Payton, Bos.-Atl.-Bos. | 77 | 469 | 6.1 |
| Williams, Mil. | 80 | 484 | 6.1 |
| Ridnour, Sea. | 82 | 483 | 5.9 |
| Billups, Det. | 80 | 464 | 5.8 |
| McGrady, Hou. | 78 | 448 | 5.7 |
| Garnett, Min. | 82 | 466 | 5.7 |
| Stoudamire, Por. | 81 | 458 | 5.7 |

## REBOUNDS
*(minimum 70 games or 800 rebounds)*

|  | G | Off. | Def. | Tot. | Avg. |
|---|---|---|---|---|---|
| Garnett, Min. | 82 | 247 | 861 | 1108 | 13.5 |
| B. Wallace, Det. | 74 | 292 | 610 | 902 | 12.2 |
| Marion, Pho. | 81 | 235 | 680 | 915 | 11.3 |
| Okafor, Cha. | 73 | 275 | 520 | 795 | 10.9 |
| Murphy, G.S. | 70 | 251 | 505 | 756 | 10.8 |
| O'Neal, Mia. | 73 | 253 | 507 | 760 | 10.4 |
| K. Thomas, N.Y. | 80 | 170 | 661 | 831 | 10.4 |
| Howard, Orl. | 82 | 287 | 536 | 823 | 10.0 |
| Nowitzki, Dal. | 78 | 96 | 661 | 757 | 9.7 |
| Chandler, Chi. | 80 | 261 | 514 | 775 | 9.7 |
| Brand, LA-C. | 81 | 296 | 474 | 770 | 9.5 |
| Evans, Sea. | 79 | 254 | 482 | 736 | 9.3 |
| Gooden, Cle. | 82 | 207 | 546 | 753 | 9.2 |
| Haslem, Mia. | 80 | 239 | 487 | 726 | 9.1 |
| Walker, Atl.-Bos. | 77 | 182 | 513 | 695 | 9.0 |
| Brown, N.O. | 82 | 266 | 471 | 737 | 9.0 |
| Stoudemire, Pho. | 80 | 219 | 494 | 713 | 8.9 |
| Bosh, Tor. | 81 | 194 | 524 | 718 | 8.9 |
| Ilgauskas, Cle. | 78 | 299 | 373 | 672 | 8.6 |
| Yao, Hou. | 80 | 208 | 461 | 669 | 8.4 |

## STEALS
*(mimum 70 games or 125 steals)*

|  | G | No. | Avg. |
|---|---|---|---|
| Hughes, Was. | 61 | 176 | 2.89 |
| Iverson, Phi. | 75 | 180 | 2.40 |
| James, Cle. | 80 | 177 | 2.21 |
| Marion, Pho. | 81 | 163 | 2.01 |
| Knight, Cha. | 66 | 131 | 1.98 |
| Arenas, Was. | 80 | 139 | 1.74 |
| McGrady, Hou. | 78 | 135 | 1.73 |
| Iguodala, Phi. | 82 | 138 | 1.68 |
| Wallace, Cha. | 70 | 117 | 1.67 |
| Pierce, Bos. | 82 | 133 | 1.62 |

## BLOCKED SHOTS
*(minimum 70 games or 100 blocked shots)*

|  | G | No. | Avg. |
|---|---|---|---|
| Kirilenko, Utah | 41 | 136 | 3.32 |
| Camby, Den. | 66 | 199 | 3.02 |
| Duncan, S.A. | 66 | 174 | 2.64 |
| Ratliff, Por. | 63 | 158 | 2.51 |
| B. Wallace, Det. | 74 | 176 | 2.38 |
| O'Neal, Mia. | 73 | 171 | 2.34 |
| Przybilla, Por. | 76 | 163 | 2.14 |
| Ilgauskas, Cle. | 78 | 165 | 2.12 |
| Brand, LA-C. | 81 | 169 | 2.09 |
| Foyle, G.S. | 78 | 159 | 2.04 |

## 3-POINT FIELD GOALS
*(minimum 55 made)*

|  | FGM | FGA | Pct. |
|---|---|---|---|
| Hoiberg, Min. | 70 | 145 | .483 |
| Johnson, Pho. | 177 | 370 | .478 |
| Mobley, Orl.-Sac. | 150 | 342 | .439 |
| Miller, Mem. | 140 | 323 | .433 |
| D. Jones, Mia. | 225 | 521 | .432 |
| Nash, Pho. | 94 | 218 | .431 |
| Barry, Atl.-Hou. | 71 | 165 | .430 |
| Billups, Det. | 165 | 387 | .426 |
| Piatkowski, Chi. | 57 | 134 | .425 |
| Terry, Dal. | 103 | 245 | .420 |

# AWARD WINNERS

## MAJOR AWARDS

**NBA Most Valuable Player:**
Steve Nash, Phoenix

**NBA Red Auerbach Coach of the Year:**
Mike D'Antoni, Phoenix

**Got Milk? NBA Rookie of the Year:**
Emeka Okafor, Charlotte

**NBA Most Improved Player:**
Bobby Simmons, L.A. Clippers

**NBA Executive of the Year:**
Bryan Colangelo, Phoenix

**J. Walter Kennedy Citizenship Award:**
Eric Snow, Philadelphia

**NBA Sportsmanship Award:**
Grant Hill, Orlando

**NBA Defensive Player of the Year:**
Ben Wallace, Detroit

**NBA Sixth Man Award:**
Ben Gordon, Chicago

**NBA Finals Most Valuable Player:**
Tim Duncan, San Antonio

**All-Star Game Most Valuable Player:**
Allen Iverson, Philadelphia

## ALL-NBA TEAMS

### FIRST
Tim Duncan, San Antonio
Dirk Nowitzki, Dallas
Shaquille O'Neal, L.A. Lakers
Allen Iverson, Philadelphia
Steve Nash, Phoenix

### SECOND
LeBron James, Cleveland
Kevin Garnett, Minnesota
Amaré Stoudemire, Phoenix
Dwyane Wade, Miami
Ray Allen, Seattle

### THIRD
Tracy McGrady, Houston
Shawn Marion, Phoenix
Ben Wallace, Detroit
Kobe Bryant, L.A. Lakers
Gilbert Arenas, Washington

## GOT MILK? ALL-ROOKIE TEAMS

### FIRST
Emeka Okafor, Charlotte
Dwight Howard, Orlando
Ben Gordon, Chicago
Andre Iguodala, Philadelphia
Luol Deng, Chicago

### SECOND
Nenad Krstic, New Jersey
Josh Smith, Atlanta
Josh Childress, Atlanta
Jameer Nelson, Orlando
Al Jefferson, Boston

## ALL-DEFENSIVE TEAMS

### FIRST
Ben Wallace, Detroit
Kevin Garnett, Minnesota
Bruce Bowen, San Antonio
Tim Duncan, San Antonio
Larry Hughes, Washington

### SECOND
Tayshaun Prince, Detroit
Marcus Camby, Denver
Chauncey Billups, Detroit
Andrei Kirilenko, Utah
Jason Kidd, New Jersey
Dwyane Wade, Miami

## NBA PLAYERS OF THE WEEK

Nov. 2— Dwyane Wade, Miami (E)
Kevin Garnett, Minnesota (W)
Nov. 9— LeBron James, Cleveland (E)
Ray Allen, Seattle (W)
Nov. 15—Grant Hill, Orlando (E)
Amaré Stoudemire, Pho. (W)
Nov. 22—LeBron James, Cleveland (E)
Shawn Marion, Phoenix (W)
Nov. 29—Gilbert Arenas, Washington (E)
Dirk Nowitzki, Dallas (W)
Dec. 6— Richard Jefferson, N.J. (E)
Amaré Stoudemire, Pho. (W)
Dec. 13—Shaquille O'Neal, Miami (E)
Shawn Marion, Phoenix (W)
Dec. 20—Allen Iverson, Philadelphia (E)
Steve Nash, Phoenix (W)
Dec. 27—Stephon Marbury, N.Y. (E)
Pau Gasol, Memphis (W)
Jan. 3— Chris Bosh, Toronto (E)
Bruce Bowen, Dallas (W)
Jan. 10— Larry Hughes, Washington (E)
Tracy McGrady, Houston (W)
Jan. 17—LeBron James, Cleveland (E)
Jason Terry, Dallas (W)
Jan. 24—Vince Carter, New Jersey (E)
Brad Miller, Sacramento (W)
Jan. 31—Paul Pierce, Boston (E)
Tracy McGrady, Houston (W)
Feb. 7— Allen Iverson, Philadelphia (E)
Steve Nash, Phoenix (W)
Feb. 14—All-Star Week (no award)
Feb. 21—Jalen Rose, Toronto (E)
Mike Bibby, Sacramento (W)
Feb. 28—Allen Iverson, Philadelphia (E)
Marcus Camby, Denver (W)
Mar. 7—Paul Pierce, Boston (E)
Tracy McGrady, Houston (W)
Mar. 14—Chauncey Billups, Detroit (E)
J. Richardson, Golden State (W)
Mar. 21—Allen Iverson, Philadelphia (E)
Ray Allen, Seattle (W)
Mar. 28—Reggie Miller, Indiana (E)
Baron Davis, Golden State (W)
Apr. 4— Vince Carter, New Jersey (E)
Baron Davis, Golden State (W)
Apr. 11— Jason Kidd, New Jersey (E)
Tracy McGrady, Houston (W)

## NBA PLAYERS OF THE MONTH

Nov.—LeBron James, Cleveland (E)
Steve Nash, Phoenix (W)
Dec.—Dwyane Wade, Miami (E)
Dirk Nowitzki, Dallas (W)
Jan.—LeBron James, Cleveland (E)
Chris Webber, Sacramento (W)
Feb.—Vince Carter, New Jersey (E)
Dirk Nowitzki, Dallas (W)
Mar.—Shaquille O'Neal, Miami (E)
Kevin Garnett, Minnesota (W)
Apr.—Allen Iverson, Philadelphia (E)
Amaré Stoudemire, Phoenix (W)

## GOT MILK? ROOKIES OF THE MONTH

Nov.—Emeka Okafor, Charlotte (E)
Devin Harris, Dallas (W)
Dec.—Emeka Okafor, Charlotte (E)
Beno Udrih, San Antonio (W)
Jan.—Ben Gordon, Chicago (E)
J.R. Smith, New Orleans (W)
Feb.—Ben Gordon, Chicago (E)
J.R. Smith, New Orleans (W)
Mar.—Ben Gordon, Chicago (E)
J.R. Smith, New Orleans (W)
Apr.— Emeka Okafor, Charlotte (E)
Shaun Livingston, L.A. Clippers (W)

## NBA COACHES OF THE MONTH

Nov.—Johnny Davis, Orlando (E)
Nate McMillan, Seattle (W)
Dec.—Stan Van Gundy, Miami (E)
Mike D'Antoni, Phoenix (W)
Jan.—Scott Skiles, Chicago (E)
Mike Fratello, Memphis (W)
Feb.—Larry Brown, Detroit (E)
George Karl, Denver (W)
Mar.—Stan Van Gundy, Miami (E)
George Karl, Denver (W)
Apr.—Lawrence Frank, New Jersey (E)
Avery Johnson, Dallas (W)

## COMMUNITY ASSIST AWARD

Oct.—Damon Stoudamire, Portland
Nov.—Steven Hunter, Phoenix
Dec.—Shaquille O'Neal, Miami
Jan.—Marcus Camby, Denver
Feb.—Rasheed Wallace, Detroit
Mar.—Bruce Bowen, San Antonio
Apr.—Derek Fisher, L.A. Lakers
May—Jerome Williams, New York
Jun.—Chris Bosh, Toronto